Random House
Latin-American
Spanish Dictionary

Second Edition

David L. Gold
Doctor in Romance Philology
University of Barcelona

Revised and Updated by
Kathleen O'Connor
Associate Professor of Spanish
Houghton College

RANDOM HOUSE
NEW YORK

Random House Latin-American Spanish Dictionary, Second Edition

This book is available for special purchases in bulk by organizations and institutions, not for resale, at special discounts. Please direct your inquiries to the Random House Special Sales Department, toll-free 888-591-1200 or fax 212-572-4961.

Please address inquiries about electronic licensing of reference products, for use on a network or in software or on CD-ROM, to the Subsidiary Rights Department, Random House Reference & Information Publishing, fax 212-940-7370.

Library of Congress Cataloging-in-Publication Data
Gold, David L.
    Random House Latin-American Spanish dictionary second edition : Spanish-English. English-Spanish / David L. Gold.
        p.   cm.
    ISBN 0-375-40720-0 (hc).—ISBN 0-375-70736-0 (pbk.)
    1. Spanish language—Provincialisms—Latin America—Dictionaries.
    2. Spanish language—Dictionaries—English. 3. English language Dictionaries—Spanish. I. Title.
    PC4822.G65 1997
    463´.21—dc20   96-27274
                                                                    CIP

Visit the Random House Web site at www.randomhouse.com

Typeset by Random House Reference & Information Publishing and Seaside Press
Typeset and printed in the United States of America

Second Edition
0 9 8 7 6 5 4 3 2 1
November 1999

ISBN: 0-375-40720-0 (Hardcover)
SAP Network: 10040702

ISBN: 0-375-70736-0 (Paperback)
SAP Network: 10038439

New York   Toronto   London   Sydney   Auckland

Contents

Preface

New Second Edition

This is a revised Second Edition of *Random House Latin-American Spanish Dictionary*, first published in 1997. New to this edition are pronunciations for all Spanish and English main entries, using IPA (International Phonetic Alphabet) symbols. The IPA symbols are explained in the pronunciation key for English on page vii and for Spanish on page xiii. Also included in this dictionary are detailed guides to the pronunciation of both languages.

Selection of Vocabulary

This dictionary emphasizes Spanish of the Western Hemisphere, featuring words and meanings unique to Central America, South America, and the Caribbean. It also tries to convey some of the regional variation that may be found from country to country within these areas. It covers the distinctive dialects of countries such as Argentina, Uruguay, Mexico, Chile, Venezuela, Bolivia, Costa Rica, Cuba, the Dominican Republic, Guatemala, and Peru.

Hundreds of new words and meanings have been added to this edition. The aim of this dictionary is to cover as much current vocabulary as possible, as well as certain terms found in standard works of modern Spanish and English literature.

Spanish Spelling and Alphabetization

On January 1, 1959, the Spanish language academies changed certain spelling rules and on April 27, 1994, they eliminated **ch** and **ll** as separate letters of the alphabet. Thus, whereas words like **chico** and **chocolate** were formerly alphabetized under their own letter (**ch,** which came between **c** and **d**) and words like **llamar** and **llegar** were formerly alphabetized under their own letter (**ll,** which came between **l** and **m**), words containing **ch** or **ll,** in whatever part of the word they may appear, are now alphabetized as they would be in English (**chico** therefore now appears under **c** and **llegar** under **l**).

Regional Labels for Spanish

Regional variation in Spanish ranges from nonexistent to extreme. On one hand, the words for "flower" and "mother-in-law," for example, are everywhere **flor** and **suegra** respectively. On the other hand, the language has many words for "bus" and "ballpoint pen."

Regional labels are given in this dictionary when a less than universal usage is found in a certain region or country. Certain usages are labeled *Lat. Am.* or *West. Hem.* (if they are in general use throughout Latin America or the Western Hemisphere) and others are given more restricted labels, like *Argentina* and *Mexico* (if they appear to be limited to just certain countries).

A regional label should be interpreted as meaning that the usage so labeled is found in that particular place, but it may also be found elsewhere. For instance, the regional label *Mexico* means that the usage so labeled is found in Mexico, but further research would be necessary to determine whether the usage is present or absent in other countries.

Field Labels

Only essential field labels are given in this dictionary. For example, the label *medicine* or *pathology* is unnecessary at **flebitis** "phlebitis" (in the Spanish–English section) because both the Spanish and English words refer only to the medical condition so called in those languages.

In contrast to that entry, we do need a label at **foca** "seal" (in the Spanish–English section) because English **seal** has several meanings and only the zoological one is intended here. English speakers looking up **foca** thus need the label *zoology* (Spanish speakers need no label because they know that **foca** is the name of an animal).

Subentries

If a main entry head is repeated in a subentry in exactly the same form, it is abbreviated to its first letter (for instance, at **fin** in the Spanish–English section we find **a f. de,** which stands for **a fin de**). If the main entry head appears in any other form, the full form is given in the subentry (thus, at **fin,** the subentry head **a fines de** is spelled without abbreviation).

Irregular Spanish Verbs and the Direction "See..."

If a Spanish verb is irregular, it has been treated in one of two ways: either its principal parts are shown (see for example the end of the entry for **caber**) or you are referred to an analogous irregular verb for guidance (see for example the end of the entry for **comparecer,** where you are directed to **conocer**). Thus, since the irregular form **conozco** is shown at **conocer,** you may infer that **comparecer** has the irregular form **comparezco.**

If "See..." is all you find at an entry, you are being directed to a synonym. Thus, "**descompasarse** See **descomedirse**" means that the translations of **descomedirse** are those of **descompasarse** too.

Spanish Equivalents of "you"

Today's Spanish, when taken as a whole, has at least six equivalents of "you": **tú, vos, usted** (abbreviated to **Vd.**), and **su merced** (all of which are used in addressing one person); and **ustedes** (abbreviated to **Vds.**), **vosotros, vosotras,** and **sus mercedes** (all used in addressing more than one person).

When **you** occurs in this dictionary, usually only one of those words has been chosen to translate it, though three are never used here: **su merced** and **sus mercedes,** because they are now limited to only a small area of the Spanish-speaking world (the Cundinamarca Savanna, in Colombia) and even there they are now obsolescent; and **vos,** because the verb forms corresponding to this pronoun often vary from country to country.

The editors of this *Second Edition* of the *Random House Latin-American Spanish Dictionary* are always grateful to receive suggestions for new words to add to subsequent editions. Any suggestions or queries should be sent to:

Random House Reference & Information Publishing
201 East 50th Street
New York, NY 10022

Guía de Pronunciación del inglés
Pronunciation Key for English

Símbolos del AFI IPA Symbols	Ejemplos Examples
Vocales y Diptongos	
/æ/	*ingl.* hat; como la **a** de *esp.* paro, pero más cerrada
/ei/	*ingl.* stay; *esp.* reina
/ɛə/ [followed by /r/]	*ingl.* hair; *esp.* ver
/ɑ/	*ingl.* father; similar a las **as** de *esp.* casa, pero más larga
/ɛ/	*ingl.* bet; *esp.* entre
/i/	*ingl.* bee; como la **i** de *esp.* vida, pero más larga
/ɪə/ [followed by /r/]	*ingl.* hear; como la **i** de *esp.* venir, pero menos cerrada
/ɪ/	*ingl.* sit; como la **i** de *esp.* Chile, pero menos cerrada
/ai/	*ingl.* try; *esp.* hay
/ɒ/	*ingl.* hot; *esp.* poner
/ou/	*ingl.* boat; similar a la **o** de *esp.* saco, pero más cerrada
/ɔ/	*ingl.* saw; similar a la **o** de *esp.* corte, pero más cerrada
/ɔi/	*ingl.* toy; *esp.* hoy
/ʊ/	*ingl.* book; como la **u** de *esp.* insulto, pero menos cerrada
/u/	*ingl.* too; como la **u** de *esp.* luna, pero más larga
/au/	*ingl.* cow; *esp.* pausa
/ʌ/	*ingl.* up; entre la **o** de *esp.* borde y la **a** de *esp.* barro
/ɜ/ [followed by /r/]	*ingl.* burn; *fr.* fleur
/ə/	*ingl.* alone; *fr.* demain
/ᵊ/	*ingl.* fire (fiᵊr); *fr.* bastille

Símbolos del AFI IPA Symbols	Ejemplos Examples
Consonantes	
/b/	*ingl.* boy; como la b de *esp.* boca, pero más aspirada
/tʃ/	*ingl.* child; *esp.* mucho
/d/	*ingl.* dad; *esp.* dar
/f/	*ingl.* for; *esp.* fecha
/g/	*ingl.* give; *esp.* gato
/h/	*ingl.* happy; como la j de *esp.* jabón, pero más aspirada y menos aspera
/dʒ/	*ingl.* just; *it.* giorno
/k/	*ingl.* kick; similar a la k de *esp.* kilogramo, pero más aspirada
/l/	*ingl.* love; *esp.* libro
/m/	*ingl.* mother; *esp.* limbo
/n/	*ingl.* now; *esp.* noche
/ŋ/	*ingl.* sing; *esp.* blanco
/p/	*ingl.* pot; como las ps de *esp.* papa, pero más aspirada
/r/	*ingl.* read; como la r de *esp.* para, pero con la lengua elevada hacia el paladar, sin tocarlo
/s/	*ingl.* see; *esp.* hasta
/ʃ/	*ingl.* shop; *fr.* chercher
/t/	*ingl.* ten; similar a la t de *esp.* tomar, pero más aspirada
/θ/	*ingl.* thing; *esp.* (en España) cerdo, zapato
/ð/	*ingl.* father; *esp.* codo
/v/	*ingl.* victory; como la b de *esp.* haba, pero es labiodental en vez de bilabial
/w/	*ingl.* witch; como la u de *esp.* puesto, pero con labios más cerrados
/y/	*ingl.* yes; *esp.* yacer
/z/	*ingl.* zipper; fr. zéro
/ʒ/	*ingl.* pleasure; *fr.* jeune

Las consonantes /l̩/, /m̩/, y /n̩/ son similar a las l, m, y n del español, pero alargada y resonante.

Los sonidos del inglés americano

Vocales y diptongos

a   Cuando representa el sonido /æ/, se pronuncia más cerrada que la *a* de *paro* (por ejemplo: **act, at, bat, hat, marry**); también se encuentra este sonido en palabras deletreadas con: -ah- (d*ah*lia), -ai- (pl*ai*d), -al- (h*al*f), -au- (l*au*gh), -ua- (g*ua*rantee).

a   Cuando representa el sonido /ei/, se pronuncia más cerrada que la *e* de *hablé* y como si fuera seguido de *i* (por ejemplo: **age, gate, rate**); también se encuentra este sonido en palabras deletreadas con: -ai- (r*ai*n, *ai*r), -aigh- (str*aigh*t), -au- (g*au*ge), -ay- (s*ay*), -ea- (st*ea*k), -ei- (v*ei*l, w*ei*gh), -ey- (ob*ey*).

a /ɑ/   Equivale aproximadamente a la *a* de *sentado* y *bajo* (por ejemplo: **ah, father, part**); también se encuentra este sonido en palabras deletreadas con: -al- (c*al*m), -e(r)- (s*er*geant), -ea(r)- (h*ear*t), -ua- (g*ua*rd).

a /ə/   Equivale aproximadamente a la *e* de las palabras francesas *de* y *le* (por ejemplo: **alone, about**); también se encuentra este sonido en palabras deletreadas con: -e- (syst*e*m), -i- (eas*i*ly), -o- (gall*o*p), -u- (circ*u*s), -y- (mart*y*r).

e /ɛ/   Equivale aproximadamente a la *e* de *templo* y *perro* (por ejemplo: **edge, set, merry**); también se encuentra este sonido en palabras deletreadas con: a-, -a- (*a*ny, m*a*ny), -ai- (s*ai*d), -ay- (s*ay*s), -ea- (l*ea*ther), -ei- (h*ei*fer), -eo- (j*eo*pardy), -ie- (fr*ie*nd).

e /i/   Equivale aproximadamente a la *i* de *Chile* (por ejemplo: **be, equal, secret**); también se encuentra este sonido en palabras deletreadas con: ea- (*ea*ch, t*ea*), -ee- (f*ee*, k*ee*p), -ei- (rec*ei*ve), -eo- (p*eo*ple), -ey- (k*ey*), -ie- (f*ie*ld), -y (cit*y*).

i /ɪ/   Se pronuncia menos cerrada que la *i* de *Chile* (por ejemplo: **if, big, fit, mirror**); también se encuentra este sonido en palabras deletreadas con: e- (*E*ngland), -ee- (b*ee*n), -ei- (counterf*ei*t), -ia- (carr*ia*ge), -ie- (s*ie*ve), -o- (w*o*man), (b)u(s)- (b*u*siness), -y- (s*y*mpathetic).

i /ai/   Equivale aproximadamente a la *ai* de *aire*, *baile* (por ejemplo: **bite, ice, pirate**); también se encuentra este sonido en palabras deletreadas con: ais- (*ai*sle), -ei- (h*ei*ght, st*ei*n), -eye- (*eye*), -ie (p*ie*), -igh- (h*igh*), is- (*i*sland), -uy- (b*uy*), -y (cycl*e*, sk*y*), -ye (l*ye*).

o /ou/   Se pronuncia más cerrada que la *o* de *supo* (por ejemplo: **hope, go, oh, over**); también se encuentra este sonido en palabras deletreadas con: -au- (m*au*ve), -aux (f*aux* pas), -eau (b*eau*), -ew (s*ew*), -oa- (r*oa*d), -oe (t*oe*), -oo- (br*oo*ch), -ot (dep*o*t), -ou- (s*ou*l), -ow (fl*ow*), -owe- (*owe*).

o /ɔ/   Se pronuncia más cerrada que la *o* de *corre* (por ejemplo: **alcohol, order, raw**); también se encuentra este sonido en palabras deletreadas con: -a- (t*a*ll), -al- (w*al*k), au- (*au*thor, v*au*lt), -augh- (c*augh*t), -oa- (br*oa*d), -oo- (fl*oo*r), -ough- (s*ough*t).

oi /oi/   Equivale aproximadamente a la *oy* de *doy* (por ejemplo: **oil, joint, voice**); también se encuentra este sonido en palabras deletreadas con: -awy- (l*awy*er), -oy- (b*oy*).

oo /ʊ/   Se pronuncia menos cerrada que la *u* de *insulto* (por ejemplo: **book, foot**); también se encuentra este sonido en palabras deletreadas con: -o- (w*o*lf), -ou- (t*ou*r), -u- (p*u*ll).

oo /u/   Se pronuncia más largo que la *u* de *susto* (por ejemplo: **too, ooze, fool**); también se encuentra este sonido en palabras deletreadas con: -eu- (man*eu*ver), -ew (gr*ew*), -o (wh*o*), -o. . .e (m*o*ve), -oe (can*oe*), -ou- (tr*ou*pe), -u. . .e (r*u*le), -ue (fl*ue*), -ui- (s*ui*t).

ou /au/   Equivale aproximadamente a la *au* de *aurora* (por ejemplo: **loud, out**); también se encuentra este sonido en palabras deletreadas con -ow (br*ow*, c*ow*, pl*ow*).

u /yiu/   Equivale aproximadamente a la *iu* de *ciudad* (por ejemplo: **cue, use, utility**); también se encuentra este sonido en palabras deletreadas con: -eau- (b*eau*ty), -eu- (f*eu*d), -ew (f*ew*), (h)u- (h*u*man), (h)u. . .e (h*u*ge), -iew (v*iew*), you *(you)*, yu. . .e *(yule)*.

u /ʌ/   Es sonido intermedio entre la *o* de *borro* y la *a* de *barro*, algo parecido a la pronunciación de la *eu* francesa de *peur*; (por ejemplo: **up, sun, mud**); también se encuentra este sonido en palabras deletreadas con: o- (*o*ther), -o- (s*o*n), -oe- (d*oe*s), o. . .e (l*o*ve), -oo- (bl*oo*d), -ou- (tr*ou*ble).

Consonantes

b   Se pronuncia igual que la *p* española salvo que en la pronunciación de la *b* suenan las cuerdas vocales. La *b* inglesa es más fuerte (más aspirada) que la española. Se encuentra en palabras escritas con *b* (**bed, amber, rub**) y también en palabras deletreadas con -bb- (ho*bb*y).

c   Como la *c* española, lleva dos sonidos, /s/ y /k/. La /s/ se pronuncia igual que la *s* española y se encuentra en palabras deletreadas con ce- (**center**) y ci- (**city**). La /k/ es semejante a la *c* española cuando aparece delante de -a, -o, y -u *(católica, cómo, cuándo)* pero se pronuncia más fuerte (más aspirada). La /k/ se encuentra en palabras deletreadas con ca-, co-, y cu- (**cat, account, cut**).

ch   Equivale aproximadamente a la *ch* española (por ejemplo: **chief, beach**); también se encuentra en palabras deletreadas con: -tch- (ca*tch*, bu*tch*er), -te- (righ*te*ous), -ti- (ques*ti*on), -tu- (na*tu*ral). A veces equivale a la /ʃ/ de la palabra francesa *chèrie* (**chef**), o a la /k/ de *cómo* (**character**).

d   Equivale aproximadamente a la *d* de *onda* (por ejemplo: **do, odor, red**); también se encuentra en palabras deletreadas con -dd- (la*dd*er) y -de- (fa*de*). La *d* inglesa es siempre más fuerte (más aspirada) que la española y no se pronuncia nunca /dʒ/ como la *d* de *padre* o las *d*'s de *Madrid*.

f   Equivale aproximadamente a la *f* española (por ejemplo: **feed, safe**); también se encuentra en palabras deletreadas con -ff- (mu*ff*in) y -fe (li*fe*).

g   Equivale aproximadamente a la *g* de *globo* (por ejemplo: **give, fog**); también se encuentra en palabras deletreadas con -gg- (e*gg*), gh- (*gh*ost), y -gue (pla*gue*). La *g* cuando cae delante de -i y -e se pronuncia /dʒ/ (**George, gem, legitimate**). El sonido /dʒ/ es semejante a, pero más fuerte que, la *y* y la *ll* españolas de *yo* y *llevar*. Véase *j*.

h   Se pronuncia más aspirada pero menos áspera que la *j* española en *jabón* (por ejemplo: **hit, hope**); tambièn se encuentra en palabras deletreadas con wh- (*wh*o).

j   Equivale aproximadamente a la *y* de *yo* en su pronunciación enfática (p.ej. . . . *yo, y yo sólo soy el dueño aquí!*) o como la *y* de *cónyuge* en ciertas modalidades del español (por ejemplo: **just, joke**); también se encuentra en palabras deletreadas con: -dg- (ju*dg*e), -di- (sol*di*er), -ge (sa*ge*), -gg- (exa*gg*erate), gi- (*gi*n). La pronunciación de la *j* y de la *g* delante de -i y -e /dʒ/ es igual que la de la *ch* española, salvo que suenan las cuerdas vocales en la pronunciación del sonido /dʒ/.

k   (Por ejemplo: **keep, make, token**) equivale a la *qui*- y *que* españolas pero se pronuncia más fuerte (más aspirada). La *k* inglesa no se pronuncia cuando cae delante de una *n* (**knife, knight, knee**).

l   Se pronuncia aproximadamente como la *l* de *lago* (por ejemplo: **leap, sail**); también se encuentra en palabras deletreadas con -le (mi*le*) y -ll (ca*ll*).

m   Equivale aproximadamente a la *m* española (por ejemplo: **more, drum, him, summer**). Tengan cuidado de pronunciar la *m* al final de una palabra igual que se pronuncia en medio de la palabra y de no convertir el sonido en *n*.

n   Equivale aproximadamente a la *n* de *bueno* (por ejemplo: **now, sunny**); tambièn se encuentra en palabras deletreadas con gn- (*gn*at) y kn- (*kn*ife).

ng   (Por ejemplo: **sing, Washington**) equivale aproximadamente a la *n* de *blanco.*

p   (Por ejemplo: **pool, spool, supper, stop**) tras consonante equivale aproximadamente a la *p* española, pero lleva más aspiración. La *p* delante de una *s* (**psychologist, psyche**) no se pronuncia.

r   Se pronuncia con la punta de la lengua elevada hacia el paladar (sin tocarlo) y doblada para atrás (por ejemplo: **red, hurry, near**); también se encuentra en palabras deletreadas con: -re (pu*re*), rh- (*rh*ythm), y wr- (*wr*ong).

s   Equivale aproximadamente a la *s* de *salir,* pero algo más tensa y larga (por ejemplo: **see, kiss**).

sh   Equivale aproximadamente a la *ch* de las palabras francesas *changer* and *chapeau* (por ejemplo: **ship, wash**); también se encuentra en palabras deletreadas con: -ce- (o*ce*an), -ch- (ma*ch*ine), -ci- (spe*ci*al), s(u)- (*su*gar), -sci- (con*sci*ence), -si- (man*si*on), -ss- (ti*ss*ue, mi*ss*ion), -ti- (cap*ti*on).

t   (Por ejemplo: **team, ten, steam, bit**) tras consonante equivale aproximadamente a la *t* española salvo con más aspiración; también se encuentra en palabras deletreadas con: -bt (dou*bt*), -cht (ya*cht*), -ed (talk*ed*), -ght (bou*ght*), -te (bi*te*), th- (*th*yme), -tt- (bo*tt*om), tw- (*tw*o).

th   (Por ejemplo: **thin, ether, path**) equivale aproximadamente a la *z* española en el norte de España.

th   (Por ejemplo: **that, the, either, smooth**) equivale aproximadamente a la *d* de *adoptar.*

v   (Por ejemplo: **voice, river, live**) equivale aproximadamente a la *b* de *haba* pero es labiodental en vez de bilabial. La pronunciación de la *v* inglesa es igual que la de la *f,* salvo que suenan las cuerdas vocales en la pronunción de la *v.*

w   (Por ejemplo: **west, witch, away**) equivale aproximadamente a la *u* de *puesto.*

y (Por ejemplo: **yes, beyond**) equivale aproximadamente a la *i* de *bien;* también se encuentra en palabras deletreadas con -i- (on*i*on, un*i*on), -j- (hallelu*j*ah), y -ll- (torti*ll*a).

z Tiene dos sonidos: /z/ y /zh/. La /z/, la más común (por ejemplo: **zoo, lazy, zone**), equivale aproximadamente a la *s* de *isla* y *mismo* en ciertas modalidades del español, pero con más sonoridad. Este sonido se pronuncia igual que la *s* española, salvo que en la pronunciación de la /z/ suenan las cuerdas vocales. Se encuentra el sonido /z/ en algunas palabras deletreadas con: -s- (ha*s*), -se (ri*se*), x- (*x*ylophone), y -zz- (bu*zz*ard, fu*zz*). El sonido /zh/ que se encuentra en **azure** y **brazier** equivale aproximadamente a la *ll* del español de la gente mayor de la cuidad de Buenos Aires (o sea, como la *j* de la palabra francesa *bonjour*). El sonido /zh/ también se encuentra en ciertas palabras deletreadas con -ge (gara*ge*, mira*ge*), -si- (vi*si*on), y su- (plea*su*re).

Pronunciation Key for Spanish
Guía de Pronunciación del español

IPA Symbols Símbolos del AFI	Key Words Ejemplos	Approximate Equivalents
a	alba, banco, cera	father, depart
e	esto, del, parte, mesa	bet; like rain when e ends syllable and is not followed by r, rr, or t
i	ir, fino, adiós, muy	like beet, but shorter
o	oler, flor, grano	like vote, but shorter
u	un, luna, cuento, vergüenza, guarda	fool, group
b	bajo, ambiguo, vaca	by, abet
β	hablar, escribir, lavar	like vehicle, but with lips almost touching
d	dar, desde, andamio, dueña	deal, adept
ð	pedir, edredón, verdad	that, gather
f	fecha, afectar, golf	fan, after
g	gato, grave, gusto, largo, guerra	garden, ugly
h	gemelo, giro, junta, bajo	horse
k	cacao, claro, cura, cuenta, que, quinto	kind, actor
l	lado, lente, habla, papel	lot, altar
ʎ	(in Spain) llama, calle, olla	like million, but with tongue behind teeth
m	mal, amor	more, commit
n	nada, nuevo, mano, bien	not, enter
ɲ	ñapa, año	canyon, companion
ŋ	angosto, aunque	ring, anchor
p	peso, guapo	pill, applaud
r	real, faro, deber	like rice, but with single flap of tongue on roof of mouth
rr	perro, sierra	like rice, but with trill, or vibration of tongue, against upper teeth

IPA Symbols	Key Words	Approximate Equivalents
s	sala, espejo, mas; (in Latin America) cena, hacer, vez	say, clasp
θ	(in Spain) cena, hacer, cierto, cine, zarzuela, lazo, vez	thin, myth
t	tocar, estado, cenit	table, attract
y	ya, ayer; (in Latin America) llama, calle	you, voyage
tʃ	chica, mucho	chill, batch

Diphthongs

ai	baile, hay	high, rye
au	audacia, laudable	out, round
ei	veinte, seis, rey	ray
ie	miel, tambien	fiesta
oi	estoico, hoy	coin, loyal
ua	cuanto	quantity
ue	buena, suerte	sway, quaint

The Basics of Standard Spanish Pronunciation

Whereas the fit between English spelling and pronunciation has for centuries been less than ideal (think, for example, of the various pronunciations of -ough, as in **although, bough, cough,** and **slough**), the fit between today's Spanish spelling and pronunciation is quite good, thanks to the regulatory efforts of the Spanish academies.

The following instructions thus take spelling as their starting point. Pronunciation is described in two ways: with phonetic symbols (enclosed in slashes) and by way of approximate comparisons with English. A wavy line separates variants (like **esnob ~ snob**). A stress mark (') means that the syllable following it is stressed (as in /re'lo/). An asterisk indicates a nonexistent form (like English *llion). A right-facing "arrow" (>), or "greater than" sign, means "became in Spanish" (as in English **rum** and French **rhum** > **ron ~ romo**).

As may be expected of a language that has been used for many centuries, over a vast area, and by many diverse people, Spanish is now pronounced in various ways. Of the many current pronunciations, two are offered as most suitable for speakers of Spanish as a second language. The two standards are identical to a large extent, differing chiefly with respect to the pronunciation of **c** before **e; c** before **i; z** in any position; and, optionally, **ll, g,** and **j.**

To the extent that the two standards differ, features belonging to just one of them are labeled either *Standard 1* or *Standard 2* below.

Features labeled *Standard 1* are accepted as standard in Spain but not in the Western Hemisphere. Features labeled *Standard 2* are accepted as standard in the Western Hemisphere but not in Spain. If you speak Spanish mostly with Spaniards or mostly with people from the Western Hemisphere, your choice of standard will thus be straightforward. If you speak with people from both areas, you can either try to master both standards or, if you want to follow just one of them no matter to whom you speak, pick Standard 2.

a is pronounced /a/, which is similar to the second vowel of the English interjection **aha!** and the vowel of the English interjection **ah,** although much shorter in duration. See also "Diphthongs and Triphthongs" below.

b has three pronunciations. At the beginning of an utterance, after /m/ (whether represented by **m** or by **n**), or after /n/ (whether represented by **n** or by **m**), the letter **b** is pronounced /b/, which is similar to the pronunciation of the first consonant of English **beach, broth, pebble,** etc. For example, in the sentence **Bulgaria envió a ambos embajadores en un barco japonés,** each of the four instances of **b** (and the one instance of **v**) is pronounced in this way.

At the end of a word, more than one pronunciation of **b** may be heard. For example, **club** may be /klub/, /kluβ/, or /klu/. Its plural, **clubs,** may be /klups/, /klus/, and possibly /kluβs/, unless the plural **clubes** is used, whose universal pronunciation is /kluβɛs/ (see the next paragraph for interpreting /β/, and **e** for interpreting /ɛ/). All of the foregoing holds for compounds of **club,** like **aeroclub.** In **esnob ~ snob,** the final **b** is pronounced /b/.

In all other positions (for example, **hablas, hablar,** and **habré**), **b** is pronounced /β/, a sound absent in English, which is made by bringing the lips close together without letting them touch each other (as if you were blowing dust away or blowing out a match or candle), expelling air through the mouth, and vibrating the vocal cords. This sound is thus similar to /v/ (as in English **very** and **vowel**), except that the latter is made by making the lower lip touch the upper teeth. English-speakers should not mistake Spanish /β/ for English /v/.

It follows from the foregoing that if the position of **b** in the utterance changes, its pronunciation may change. For example, when the word **baba** is pronounced in isolation, the first **b** is rendered /b/ and the second one /β/, but in the phrase **la baba,** the first **b** is no longer at the beginning of an utterance (nor is it preceded by the sounds /m/ or /n/), hence the phrase is pronounced /laβaβa/.

These rules of pronunciation also hold true for the letter **v**, which is pronounced /b/ at the beginning of words, and /β/ in the middle. See also **v**.

c has several pronunciations. If it is followed by **e** or **i**, the letter **c** is pronounced /θ/ in Standard 1 and /s/ in Standard 2. The pronunciation of /θ/ in Spanish is similar to that of **th** in English **thatch, think,** etc., but made with somewhat more protrusion of the tongue. The sound /s/ is similar to the pronunciation of **s** in English **say, simple,** etc.

Although Standard 1 has /θ/ for **c** before **e** or **i**, people who use that pronunciation will not be put off if they hear you pronounce the **c** as /s/, because the latter is widespread (though not standard) in Spain. In the Western Hemisphere, **c** before **e** or **i** is always pronounced /s/ and never /θ/. Speakers of Western Hemispheric Spanish will react to /θ/ either as "the correct pronunciation" ("though we don't use it") or as a pretentious pronunciation (unless it comes from people to the manner born, i.e., many Spaniards). Thus, whereas it is desirable though not obligatory that you use Standard 1 in Spain, you would be well advised to use only Standard 2 in the Western Hemisphere, where /θ/ is bound to elicit a sharp reaction of one kind or another (as sharp as British **drawing pin, lorry,** or **trunk call** instead of **thumbtack, truck,** and **long-distance call** would probably elicit in the United States).

ch, wherever it is found, is always pronounced as /tʃ/, which is similar to the pronunciation of **ch** in English **church, child,** etc.

If **c** ends a syllable (for instance, **accionista, facsimíl,** and **técnico**), **c** is pronounced as /k/. Spanish /k/ is similar to the pronunciation of **c** in English **escape, scandal,** etc. To achieve a good rendition of Spanish /k/, hold your open palm in front of your mouth and pronounce first **cape** and **coop,** then **escape** and **scandal.** When pronouncing the first two words, you felt a noticeable puff of air on your palm, but in the last two words you felt almost no puff at all. A noticeable puff of air accompanying a speech sound is called *aspiration;* sounds pronounced with aspiration are *aspirated,* and those pronounced without it are *unaspirated.* Spanish /k/ (like Spanish /p/ and /t/) is always unaspirated, wherever it occurs. Thus, you should have no trouble with Spanish **escapar** and **escandalo** because here /k/ occurs after /s/, and as an English speaker you will automatically pronounce it as unaspirated, just as you would the **c** of the English cognates of those words: **escape** and **scandal.** It is in other positions that you have to be careful not to aspirate: **claro, crear,** etc. (contrast them with their English cognates, both of which have an aspirated /k/: **clear, create**).

See also **k, ll** (under **l**), **q, s,** and **z**.

d has several pronunciations. At the beginning of an utterance, after /n/, or after /l/, this letter is pronounced /d/, which is similar to the pronunciation of **d** in English **dear, dust,** etc., with this difference: in the production of Spanish /d/, the tongue touches the lower edge of the upper front incisors.

When between two vowels, when preceded by a vowel and followed by **r,** or when at the end of a word and not preceded by **r** (as in **pedir, Pedro,** and

libertad), the letter **d** is pronounced /ð/, which is similar to the pronunciation of **th** in English **that, there,** etc., but less interdental than English /ð/ (in the production of the Spanish sound, the tip of the tongue gently touches the lower edge of the upper incisors).

It follows from the foregoing that if the position of **d** in the utterance changes, its pronunciation may change. Contrast, for example, these three utterances: (1) **Dinamarca mandó embajadores a doce países,** (2) **En Dinamarca viven unos cuantos americanos,** and (3) **Iremos a Dinamarca.** In (1), the **d** of **Dinamarca** is pronounced /d/ because it comes at the beginning of an utterance; in (2) the same **d** is also pronounced /d/ because it comes after /n/; but in (3) the same **d** is pronounced /ð/ because none of the conditions for pronouncing it /d/ is met. Similarly, when the word **dedo** is pronounced in isolation, the first **d** is rendered /d/ (and the second one /ð/), but in the phrase **mi dedo,** the first **d** is no longer at the beginning of an utterance (nor is it preceded by /n/ or /l/); hence the phrase is pronounced /miðeðo/.

e has two pronunciations. The instruction given in some books that **e** is pronounced /e/ when stressed and /ɛ/ when unstressed does not hold true for today's Spanish and may never have been an accurate description of its pronunciation in any variety of the language.

Here are better guidelines for **e** (except when it is part of a diphthong or triphthong):

. If **e** is found in a syllable ending in a consonant (see "Syllabification" below), it is pronounced /ɛ/, which is similar to the pronunciation of **è** in French or to the vowel of **bet, let, met,** etc., as pronounced in Standard English, that is, with considerable lowering of the jaw, for example, **embaldosar, fresco, hablen,** and **mestizo.**

If **e** ends a syllable and the next one begins with **r, rr,** or **t,** it is pronounced /ɛ/, for instance, **pero, caballete** (the first **e**), **cerrar,** and **jinete.**

Otherwise, **e** is pronounced /e/, which is similar to the pronunciation of **é** in French, that is, the jaw is lowered only minimally (the closest English comes to having a sound like /e/ is the vowel of **ache, rake, stake,** etc.), for example, **caballete** (the second **e**), **hablé,** and **mesa.** In this dictionary, the sounds /e/ and /ɛ/ are both represented by /e/.

See also "Diphthongs and Triphthongs" below.

g has several pronunciations. At the beginning of an utterance and when followed by **a, o, u,** or a consonant letter except **n** (as in **gato, goma, gusto,** or **glaciar**), **g** is pronounced /g/, which is similar to the pronunciation of **g** in English **get, go, gumption,** etc.

At the beginning of a word and when followed by **n,** the letter **g** is silent (as in **gnomo**). That pronunciation is in fact so widespread and reputable that a **g**-less spelling is now acceptable and is in fact preferred in this dictionary (see "Miscellaneous" below).

When **g** occurs at the end of a syllable and is preceded by **n,** it is silent, as in **búmerang.** In older borrowings from other languages, that **g** was systematically or sometimes omitted, as in **sterling > esterlina, pudding > pudín.**

Before **e** or **i** (as in **gemir** and **gigante**), except if it comes at the end of a word, the letter **g** is pronounced /x/, which is absent in most varieties of current English. This sound is similar to the pronunciation of **ch** in German **Bach,** that of **ch** in Israeli Hebrew **zecher,** and that of **ch** in Scots English **loch, Lochaber,** etc. Press the back of the tongue against the soft palate, expel air (as if coughing), and do not vibrate the vocal chords. **g** before **e** or **i** can also be pronounced /h/, as in English **"house,"** which is common in Latin America and in southern Spain. In this dictionary, both /x/ and /h/ are represented by /h/.

If **g** ends a syllable that is not the last syllable of the word (as in **dogma** and the first syllable of **zigzag**), this letter is pronounced /g/. In such cases, the next syllable always begins with a consonant.

Otherwise, **g** is pronounced /ɣ/, a sound absent in English, which is made by bringing the back of the tongue close to the soft palate (without letting them touch), expelling air through the mouth, and vibrating the vocal chords. Examples are **hago** and **hígado**. In this dictionary, both sounds, /g/ and /ɣ/, are represented by /g/.

h is silent.

i is pronounced /i/, which is similar to the vowel of English **beet, feet, sheen,** etc., but shorter (for instance, **dicho, isla,** and **cursi**).

See also **y.**

j is almost always pronounced /x/, although a pronunciation as /h/ is also acceptable in parts of Latin America and southern Spain (see **g** for interpreting these symbols). A notable exception is **reloj,** which many speakers pronounce /re'lo/. That pronunciation of **reloj** is so widespread that **reló** is an alternate spelling of the singular form, but only in informal writing. In the plural, everyone pronounces /x/ or /h/ and therefore writes the **j: relojes.**

l when not doubled is pronounced /l/, which is formed by putting the tip of the tongue against the sockets of the upper incisors, the remainder of the tongue lying flat. Spanish /l/ thus does not have the hollow sound of English /l/, in whose formation the back of the tongue rises toward the palate.

ll has two pronunciations, /ʎ/ and /y/, which vary by region and class rather than by placement within a word. /ʎ/, a sound similar to the Italian **gli,** has no real equivalent in English, although the **lli** of **million** comes close. While /ʎ/ is held to be the "correct" pronunciation by Spanish radio and television guidelines, it is almost never used in Latin America, except among some academics and the very wealthy. In Spain it is only heard in the northern regions of Castile. Much more common, and almost universally accepted today, is the pronunciation /y/, which is similar to our **y** in **yes** or **yam.**

In the Southern Cone of Latin America, a third pronunciation, /ʒ/ (like the French **Geneviève**), is also used.

Traditionally, Spanish does not have /m/ at the end of a word when it is pronounced in isolation. However, a few words (all learned borrowings from other languages) end in **m** (for example, **álbum, factótum, ídem, médium, memorándum, ultimátum,** and **vademécum**), and that letter always appears in the Spanish names of many places outside Spanish-speaking areas, like **Bírmingham, Búckingham, Siam,** and **Vietnam.** Both /m/ and /n/ are heard in such words, depending on people's ability to pronounce /m/ at the end of a word (as more and more Spanish-speakers study other languages, they find it easier to produce that sound in that position) and their interest in maintaining the supposedly "correct" (i.e., non-Spanish) pronunciation of that letter.

n has several pronunciations. If immediately followed by a labial consonant (represented by **b, f, m, p,** or **v**) whether in the same word or in the next one, it is pronounced /m/ (as in the words **anfitrión, inmediato, anverso,** or the sentences **insiste en bucear, insiste en pelear,** and **en muchos casos hay más**). Since /m/ + /m/ is reduced to a single /m/, **en muchos casos** actually has just one /m/.

However, /m/ + /n/ (as in **insomne**) is not reduced.

Before /k/ or /g/ (as in **aunque** and **angosto**), **n** is pronounced /ŋ/, which is similar to the final consonant of **sing, long,** and **song** as pronounced in English.

In all other positions (as in **Anatolia, andan,** and **nombrar**), **n** is pronounced /n/, which is similar to the pronunciation of **n** in English **hand, near,** etc.

ñ is pronounced /ɲ/, which is similar to the pronunciation of **ny** in English **canyon** or **ni** in English **onion.**

o is pronounced similarly to the **o** in the English words **tote** and **gloat.** English speakers, however, must be careful not to end the pronunciation of this vowel with an "off-glide" (an "off-glide," in this case, would close the **o** into a **u** sound at the end of the vowel). Thus, the Spanish **no** and the English **no** are not exactly alike, as the Spanish ends in a pure /o/ sound, while the English "off-glides" into a /u/, producing /nou/.

p, where it is pronounced, stands for /p/, which is similar to the pronunciation of **p** in English **space, spare, spook,** etc., but different from that of **p** in English **pike, peak, poke,** etc., in that it is not aspirated (see **c** for definitions of aspirated and unaspirated sounds).

Spanish **ps** at the beginning of a word is pronounced /s/.

q is always followed by **ue** or **ui.** The sequence **que** is pronounced /ke/ and **qui** is pronounced /ki/ (for example, **quince**).

To represent the sound sequences /kue/ and /kui/, Spanish has **cue** and **cui** respectively (as in **cueva** and **cuidar**).

Because **q** is always followed by **u,** if Spanish-speakers borrow words containing just **q** from other languages, that letter is changed to **k.** Thus, the Spanish names of Iraq and Qatar, for example, are **Irak** and **Katar.**

r has two pronunciations. At the beginning of a word or when it comes after **l, n,** or **s** (for example, **reir, alrededor, enrojecer,** and **Israel**), this letter has the same pronunciation as **rr** (see below).

In all other positions, **r** is pronounced with one flip of the upper part of the tongue against the sockets of the upper incisors (for instance, **leer, para, pera, pero, tercero,** and **treinta**).

rr is pronounced with a trill (several flips) of the upper front part of the tongue against the sockets of the upper incisors (for instance, **parra, perra, perro,** and **sierra**). Thus, **para** and **parra** are different words, with different meanings. The same applies to **caro** and **carro, pera** and **perra, pero** and **perro, torero** and **torrero,** and other pairs of words.

s has several pronunciations. When it represents the plural ending of nouns recently borrowed from other languages, it is silent in certain words, like **cabarets, carnets, complots, conforts, superávits, tíckets, trusts, vermuts.**

Before the letters **b, v, d, g** (but only when the letter is not followed by **e** or **i**), **l, m, n,** or **r** (whether any of those eight letters appear in the same word as **s** or they appear in the next word), you have an alternative in both standards if **s** is not the last letter of the word: it may be pronounced /z/ (a sound similar to the pronunciation of **z** in English **zebra, zoo,** etc.) or /s/ (see **c** for interpreting that symbol): **esbelto, esdrújulo, esgrimir, isla, esmalte, Israel, los baúles, los varones, los dedos, los guantes, los lagos, los maestros, los nervios, los ratones,** etc. If **s** is the last letter, only /s/ is found (for instance, in the family name **Pons**).

If **s** is followed by **r** (whether in the same word or in the next one), besides the two pronunciations suggested above, /s/ or /z/, a third possibility is not to pronounce the **s** at all and, as compensation, trill the **r** more. The word **Israel** (and its derivatives) thus has three pronunciations: /isrrael/, /izrrael/, and /irrrael/.

Otherwise, **s** is pronounced /s/ (as in **ese, especial, hablas, hasta, insistir, seco**).

If **s** is followed by **h,** the foregoing paragraph applies, except in the case of Spanish words recently borrowed from other languages or words modeled on such recently borrowed words, in which **sh** constitutes a unit, to be pronounced /ʃ/ (a sound similar to the pronunciation of **sh** in English **shall, sheet, should,** etc.). Thus, in **deshacer,** an old Spanish word not recently borrowed from another language, the instructions about **s** apply and the **h** is silent (hence the first two syllables of that word are /desa/), whereas in **riksha, sh** is pronounced /ʃ/.

See also **b, c, t, z,** and "Syllabification" below.

t is pronounced /t/, which is similar to the pronunciation of **t** in English **stoop, stake, steer,** etc., but different from that of **t** in English **take, teak, took,** etc., in that it is less aspirated (see **c**).

The Spanish /t/ is made by touching the tip of the tongue against the upper incisors (in contrast to English /t/, in whose production the tongue touches the gums). In two positions, **t** may not be pronounced as described above. First, before **l** or **m** in the same word (as in **atleta, aritmético,** and **ritmo**) you have an alternative: **t** may be pronounced as described or it may be pronounced /ð/ (see **d** for interpreting that symbol).

Second, the **t** at the end of a word may be silent. Probably many, most, or all Spanish-speakers pronounce it in **cenit, déficit, fagot, mamut, superavít,** and **el Tíbet ~ el Tibet,** whereas in other words the **t** is silent, for instance **cabaret, carnet, complot, tícket, trust,** and **vermut,** which are pronounced as if written *cabaré, *carné, *compló, *tique, *trus, and *vermú (the plurals are pronounced identically to their singulars). In still other words you have an alternative: **confort** is pronounced either /kom'for/ or /kom'fort/ (the plural **conforts** has both variants too).

u has two pronunciations. In the combinations **gue, gui, que,** and **qui,** the letter **u** is silent, for example, **guedeja** /geðeha/, **quedar** /keðar/, and **quien** /kien/ (see **q** and **e** on the pronunciation of those letters).

In all other cases, it is pronounced /u/, which is similar to the vowel sound of English **who** and **cool.** Thus, **puesto** and **seudonónimo,** for example, are pronounced /puesto/ and /seuðonónimo/.

v has two pronunciations. At the beginning of an utterance or after **n** (which in this position is pronounced /m/), the letter **v** is pronounced /b/, which is similar to the first consonant of English **beach, broth,** etc. In all other positions, this letter is pronounced /β/ (see **b** for interpreting that symbol). For example, in the sentence **¿Es verdad que en el anverso de la medalla se ve un pavo real?,** the second and sixth words have /b/ and the eleventh and thirteenth have /β/.

The instructions for pronouncing **b** and those for pronouncing **v** are identical (depending on the position of those letters in the utterance), as a consequence of which pairs of words like **baca** and **vaca** or **hube** and **uve** are homophones in today's Spanish and, as a further consequence of which, if you hear /b/ or /β/, you cannot tell whether it is to be represented by **b** or by **v** unless you know how to spell the word.

See also **b.**

w, which is found only in borrowings from Germanic languages and French, has several pronunciations. In several words, it is pronounced as if it were **b** or **v** and in such cases alternate spellings with **v** are found too: **wagneriano ~ vagneriano, Westfalia ~ Vestfalia.** The forms with **v** are preferable.

In at least a few words, **w** is pronounced /w/ (a sound similar to the first sound of English **win** and **won**), and for one of them an alternate spelling with **u** exists: **Malawi, Taiwán, Zimbabwe.**

In **whisky,** the letter combination **wh** is pronounced /w/ or /gw/.

x has several pronunciations. If **x** occurs before a consonant (as in **experiencia, extremidad,** and **mixto**), pronounce it /ks/. That pronunciation is probably the most frequent in words beginning with the prefix **ex-** followed by a consonant, for example **excelente,** widely pronounced /eksselente/ in Latin America, or / eksθelente/ in Castile.

If **x** occurs between vowels, you have an alternative in certain words (**examen** and **exiguo,** for example, may be pronounced with /ks/ or /gz/, but not in others (for instance, all Spanish-speakers, it seems, now pronounce **sexo** with /ks/).

At the end of a word, the pronunciation of **x** is in flux. In **ántrax, Benelux, dux, fénix, látex,** and **tórax,** /ks/ seems to be the most frequent if not universal pronunciation today, although /s/ is also heard.

At least some exceptions to those pronunciations are heard in words of Native American origin: for example, in **México** and **mexicano,** the **x** is now always pronounced /x/ (those are the spellings official and universal in Mexico; elsewhere, **Méjico** and **mejicano** are used); in **Xochimilco** (a Mexican place name), the **x** is always pronounced /s/.

Further exceptions are certain given and family names, which are found in two variants: one preserving a now archaic spelling with **x** (like **Xavier** and **Ximénez**) and the other spelled in modern fashion with **j** (**Javier** and **Jiménez**). Here, **x** is pronounced /h/, that is, just like **j.**

y has several pronunciations. In the word **y,** it is pronounced /i/ (see **i** for interpreting that symbol).

When it represents the first or last segment of a diphthong or triphthong (see "Diphthongs and Triphthongs" below), as in **ya, yegua, yunque, ley, rey, soy,** and **Paraguay,** the letter **y** is pronounced /y/ (see **ll** for interpreting that symbol).

In certain varieties of Spanish, **y** is pronounced with more occlusion, so that it has come to be close to /ʒ/ if not actually that sound (see **ll** for interpreting the latter symbol); and in still other varieties it is pronounced with so much occlusion that is has come to be close to /dʒ/ if not actually that (/dʒ/ is similar to the first consonant of English **Jacob, Jerusalem, Jew,** etc.)

Certain family names have two spelling variants, an archaic one with **y** and one spelled in modern fashion with **i** (like **Yglesias ~ Iglesias**). Here, **y** is pronounced /i/, that is, just like **i.**

z has several pronunciations. In Standard 1, you have an alternative: (1) In all positions, pronounce it /θ/ (see **c** for interpreting that symbol). Or, (2) Before the letters **b, v, d, g, l, m, n,** or **r** (whether in the same word or in the next one), pronounce it /ð/ (see **d** for interpreting that symbol), and in all other positions pronounce it /θ/.

In Standard 2, you have an alternative: (3) In all positions, pronounce it /s/ (see **c** for interpreting that symbol). Or, (4) Before the letters **b, v, d, g, l, m, n,** or **r** (whether in the same word or in the next one), pronounce it /z/, and in all other positions pronounce it /s/.

Diphthongs and Triphthongs

Spanish has fifteen diphthongs and eight triphthongs.
Eight of the diphthongs begin with a semivowel:

ia /ia/ is spelled **ya** at the beginning of a word, e.g., **desahuciar, yámbico.**
ua /ua/, e.g., **guardar.**
ie /ie/ is spelled **ye** at the beginning of a word, e.g., **agüero, bien, higiene, siete, yema.**
ue /ue/ is spelled **üe** after **g** that is not pronounced /h/, e.g., **huelga, hueste, huevo, vergüenza.**
io /io/ e.g., **biombo, piojo.** The spelling **io** at the beginning of a word is an imitation of Greek.
uo /uo/, e.g., **arduo.**
iu /iu/ is spelled **yu** at the beginning of a word, e.g., **yuca, yugo, triunfo.**
ui /ui/ (spelled **uy** in **muy**), e.g., **cuidar, muy.** For **uy** representing /uy/, see **uy** in the next section.

Take care to pronounce diphthongs beginning with a semivowel as diphthongs and not as two syllables. Thus, whereas English **barrio** has three syllables, Spanish **barrio** has two (**ba-rrio**), pronounced /barrio/.

Seven of the diphthongs end in a semivowel:

ai /ai/ is spelled **ay** at the end of most words; rarely, **ay** is found in the middle of a word, e.g., **aimará ~ aymará, hay, Raimundo, Seychelles.** If **ay** occurs before a vowel in the same word, it represents not a diphthong but /a/ + /y/, and each of those sounds belongs to a different syllable (thus, **aya** and **haya** for example are syllabified **a-ya** and **ha-ya**).

au /au/, e.g., **caudillo.**

ei is almost always pronounced /ey/ and is almost always spelled **ey** at the end of a word, e.g., **reina, rey.** A pronunciation exception is **reir,** which is pronounced as if it is spelled *reír. If **ey** occurs before a vowel in the same word, it represents not a diphthong but /e/ + /y/, and each of those sounds belongs to a different syllable (thus, **reyes** and **leyenda** for instance are syllabified **re-yes** and **le-yen-da**).

eu /eu/, e.g., **seudonónimo.**

oi is almost always pronounced /oi/ and is spelled **oy** at the end of a word, e.g., **hoy,** and in certain family names in other positions too (like **Goytisolo**). A pronunciation exception is **oir,** which is pronounced as if spelled *oír. If **oy** occurs before a vowel in the same word, it represents not a diphthong but /o/ + /y/ and each of those sounds belongs to a different syllable (thus, **Goya** is syllabified **Go-ya**).

uy, which always occurs at the end of a word, is almost always pronounced /ui/ (as in ¡**huy!, Jujuy**). The exception is **muy,** whose pronunciation is given in the previous section. If **uy** occurs before a vowel in the same word, it represents not a diphthong but /u/ + /y/ and each of those sounds belongs to a different syllable (thus, **cuyo** and **tuyas** are syllabified **cu-yo** and **tu-yas**).

The triphthongs are:
iai /iai/ e.g., **despreciáis.**
iau /iau/ e.g., **miau.**
iei /iei/ e.g., **despreciéis.**
uai /uai/ (spelled **uay** at the end of a word), e.g., **evaluáis, Uruguay.**
uau /uau/ e.g., **guau.**
uei /uei/ (spelled **uey** at the end of a word), e.g., **evaluéis, buey.**

List of Abbreviations Used in this Dictionary

a adjective
Abbr. abbreviation
acc accusative
adv adverb
Aer. aeronautics
Agr. agriculture
Anat. anatomy
Archit. architecture
Archeol. archeology
art. article
art art
Astron. astronomy
Astrol. astrology
Auto. automobiles
aux auxiliary
Biol. biology
Bot. botany
Cards. card games
Chem. chemistry
Com. commerce
Compar. comparative
condit conditional
conjunc conjunction
Cul. culinary
Dance. dancing
dat dative
dim diminutive
Eccl. ecclesiastical
Educ. education
Elec. electricity
Engin. engineering
Ent. entomology
esp. español, Spanish
Euph. euphemism
f feminine
Fig. figurative
Fig. Inf. used
  figuratively in
  informal speech
  or writing
fut future
gen generally; genitive

Geog. geography
Geol. geology
Geom. geometry
Gram. grammar
Gym. gymnastics
Herald. heraldry
Hist. history
Ichth. ichthyology
imperf imperfect
impers impersonal
indic indicative
indef art indefinite
  article
Inf. informal
infin infinitive
ing. inglés, English
insep inseparable
interj interjection,
  exclamation
interr interrogative
Ironic. ironical
irr irregular
Lat. Am. Latin America
Law. law
Ling. linguistics
Lit. literature
m masculine
Mas. masonry
Math. mathematics
Mech. mechanics
Med. medical
Metall. metallurgy
mf masculine or femi-
  nine
Mil. military
Mineral. mineralogy
Mus. music
Myth. mythology
n noun
Naut. nautical
Nav. naval
neut neuter

Obs obsolete
Opt. optics
Ornith. ornithology
part participle
Pers. personal; person
Pharm. pharmacy
Philos. philosophy
Phonet. phonetics
Photo. photography
Phys. physics
Physiol. physiology
pl plural
Poet. poetic
Polit. political
Polit. Econ. political
  economy
poss possessive
prep preposition
pres present
Print. printing
pron pronoun
Psychol. psychology
Radio. radio
Rail. railway
Sew. sewing
sing singular
Spirit. spiritualism
Sports. sports
subjunc subjunctive
Superl superlative
Surg. surgery
Surv. surveying
Tan. tanning
Theat. theater
Theol. theology
v aux auxiliary verb
vi intransitive verb
vr reflexive verb
vt transitive verb
West. Hem. Western
  Hemispheric Spanish
Zool. zoology

Spanish–English
Dictionary

A

a /a/ *f*, name of the letter A

a /a/ *prep* to; at; on; by; in, into; up to; according to; if, etc. 1. Denotes the direct complement of verb before objects representing specified persons or animals, personified nouns, pronouns referring to specific persons (**alguien, entrambos, cualquiera,** etc.), demonstrative or relative pronouns, collective nouns representing persons (**el público, la muchedumbre,** etc.), names of countries, cities, rivers, etc., except where these invariably take the def. art., e.g. *Dejé a Varsovia,* I left Warsaw, *but Dejé el Perú,* I left Peru. 2. Introduces indirect obj. when this is a noun governed by a verb implying motion, or an emphatic pers. pron., e.g. *Nos conviene a ti y a mí,* It suits both you and me. It is also used before indirect obj. to avoid ambiguity when there is both an indirect and direct obj. 3. Denotes the complement of verb when this is an infin., e.g. *Enseñó a pintar a María,* He taught Mary to paint. 4. Indicates direction or destination, e.g. *Vamos a Edimburgo,* We are going to Edinburgh. 5. Signifies location, or point of time when action takes place, e.g. *Vinieron a las doce.* They came at twelve o'clock. 6. Describes position of persons or things, e.g. *Se sentaron a la puerta,* They sat down at the door. *La casa queda a la derecha,* The house is on the right. 7. Denotes interval of time or place between one thing and another, e.g. *de tres a cinco de la tarde,* from three to five in the afternoon, *de calle a calle,* from street to street. 8. Expresses manner of action, e.g. *a la francesa,* in the French way, *bordado a mano,* embroidered by hand. 9. Indicates rate or price, e.g. *a cuatro pesetas la libra,* at four pesetas the lb. 10. Indicates difference or comparison, e.g. *Va mucho de querer a hacer,* There's a difference between wishing and doing. 11. Sometimes is synonymous with *hasta, según, hacia* and governs almost all parts of speech. Has many idiomatic uses. 12. Before infin. sometimes has conditional sense, e.g. *A haber sabido las noticias no lo hubiéramos hecho,* If we had heard the news we would not have done it. 13. Before infin. expresses "to be," e.g. *la nueva constitución a implementar en dos semanas...,* the new constitution to be implemented in two weeks.... 14. With certain nouns, adjectives, and infinitives forms adverbial phrases, e.g. *poco a poco,* little by little, *a veces,* sometimes, *a ciegas,* blindly, etc. *¡a ver!* let's see!; *Colombia* hello! (on telephone). **A + el** becomes **al,** e.g. *al rey,* to the king. **Al + infin.** means when or on, e.g. *al marcharme yo,* when I left (on my leaving); *Lat. Am.* **al año** a year later; *Lat. Am.* **a la semana** a week later; *Lat. Am.* **al mes** a month later

abacería /aβase'ria; aβaθe'ria/ *f*, grocery shop

abacero /aβa'sero; aβa'θero/ **(-ra)** *n* grocer

ábaco /aβako/ *m*, *Archit.* abacus; counting frame

abad /a'βað/ *m*, abbot

abajo /a'βaho/ *adv* under; underneath; below; down. Used immediately after noun in adverbial phrases, e.g. *cuesta a., escalera a.,* downhill, downstairs. *interj* Down with! e.g., *¡A. el rey!* Down with the king! *venirse a.,* to fall down; *Fig.* collapse

abalanzamiento /aβa,lansa'miento; aβa,lanθa'miento/ *m*, balancing; rushing upon; dashing

abalanzar /aβalan'sar; aβalan'θar/ *vt* to balance; impel violently; *vr* throw oneself upon; attack, rush upon; *(with prep a)* rush into, risk. **Se abalanzó hacia ellos,** He rushed toward them

abalear /aβale'ar/ *vt*, *Lat. Am.* to shoot at

abalorio /aβa'lorio/ *m*, glass bead; bead work

abanderado /aβande'raðo/ *m*, standardbearer; *Argentina* valedictorian

abanderizar /aβanderi'sar; aβanderi'θar/ *vt* to organize in groups; *vr* band together

abandonado /aβando'naðo/ *a* deserted; forlorn; helpless; indolent, careless; slovenly

abandonamiento /a,βandona'miento/ *m*, desertion; forlornness; helplessness; carelessness; slovenliness

abandonar /aβando'nar/ *vt* to forsake, desert; neglect; leave; give up; renounce; *vr* neglect oneself; grow discouraged; *(with prep a)* give oneself over to

abandono /aβan'dono/ *m*, abandonment; defenselessness; forlornness; dilapidation; renunciation; neglect; slovenliness; debauchery

abanicar /aβani'kar/ *vt* to fan

abanico /aβa'niko/ *m*, fan; anything fan-shaped; *Inf.* sword; railway signal; *Naut.* derrick. **en a.,** fan-shaped

abaniqueo /aβani'keo/ *m*, fanning; swinging; oscillation; gesticulation

abaratar /aβara'tar/ *vt* to lower the price; make less expensive; *vr* fall in price

abarca /a'βarka/ *f*, leather sandal, worn chiefly in the Basque provinces

abarcador /aβarka'ðor/ **(-ra)** *n* one who clasps or embraces; monopolist

abarcadura /aβarka'ðura/ *f*, **abarcamiento** /aβarka-'miento/ *m*, inclusion; scope

abarcar /aβar'kar/ *vt* to clasp, encircle; include, comprise; undertake, attempt; monopolize

abarquillar /aβarki'yar; aβarki'ʎar/ *vt* to shape into a roll; roll; curl

abarracar **(se)** *vi* and *vr Mil.* to go into barracks

abarrancadero /aβarranka'ðero/ *m*, rough road; ravine, precipice; *Fig.* difficult situation

abarrancar /aβarran'kar/ *vt* to ditch; make a ravine; *vr* fall into a pit; stick (in the mud, etc.); get into difficulties; *Naut.* run aground

abarrotería /aβarrote'ria/ *f*, *Mexico* grocery store, grocery, grocer's

abarrotero, -a /aβarro'tero/ *mf Lat. Am.* grocer

abarrotes /aβa'rrotes/ *m pl, Lat. Am.* groceries

abastar /aβas'tar/ see **abastecer**

abastecedor /aβastese'ðor; aβasteθe'ðor/ **(-ra)** *a* provisioning, supplying. *n* provider; purveyor, supplier; caterer

abastecer /aβaste'ser; aβaste'θer/ *vt irr* to supply, provide; purvey. See **conocer**

abastecimiento /aβastesi'miento; aβasteθi'miento/ *m*, providing; supply, provision; catering; supplies

abasto /a'βasto/ *m*, provisions, food; *Com.* supply. *adv* plentifully, abundantly

abate /a'βate/ *m*, abbé

abatido /aβa'tiðo/ *a* dejected, depressed; spiritless; discouraged; crushed, humbled; *Com.* depreciated

abatimiento /aβati'miento/ *m*, dejection, depression; humiliation; discouragement; falling; lowering; *(Aer. Naut.)* drift

abatir /aβa'tir/ *vt* to knock down; overthrow; demolish; lower, take down; droop; humiliate; discourage; *Naut.* dismantle; *vi (Aer. Naut.)* drift; *vr* be despondent, despair; humble oneself; swoop down (of birds). **a. el vuelo,** to fly down

ABC /aβe'se; aβe'θe/ *m*, ABCs (e.g. *el ABC de la física,* the ABC of physics)

abdicación /aβðika'sion; aβðika'θion/ *f*, abdication

abdicar /aβði'kar/ *vt* to abdicate; revoke, cancel; give up (rights, opinions)

abdomen /aβ'ðomen/ *m*, abdomen

abdominal /aβðomi'nal/ *a* abdominal

abecé /aβe'se; aβe'θe/ *m*, ABCs

abecedario /aβese'ðario; aβeθe'ðario/ *m*, ABCs, alphabet; reading book, primer

abedul /aβe'ðul/ *m*, birch tree; birch wood

abeja /a'βeha/ *f*, bee. **a. maestra,** queen bee. **a. o-brera,** worker

abejar /aβe'har/ *m*, beehive

abejero /aβe'hero/ **(-ra)** *n* beekeeper

abejón /aβe'hon/ *m*, drone; hornet

abejorro /aβe'horro/ *m*, bumblebee

aberración /aβerra'sion; aβerra'θion/ f, deviation; error, lapse; (*Astron. Phys. Biol.*) aberration

abertura /aβer'tura/ f, opening; aperture, gap, hole; fissure, cleft; mountain pass; naturalness, frankness

abeto /a'βeto/ m, fir tree

abierto /a'βierto/ a open, not enclosed; open, full-blown (flowers); frank, sincere. *adv* openly. *m*, open (tournament); *Colombia* clearing

abigarrado /aβiga'rraðo/ a variegated; varied; speckled

abigotado /aβigo'taðo/ a having a thick mustache

abintestato /aβintes'tato/ a *Law.* intestate

abismal /aβis'mal/ a abysmal

abismar /aβis'mar/ vt to plunge into an abyss; depress, sadden; vr despair; be plunged in thought; be amazed

abismo /a'βismo/ m, chasm, abyss, gulf; hell

abjuración /aβhura'sion; aβhura'θion/ f, abjuration

abjurar /aβhu'rar/ vt to forswear, retract

ablactar /aβlak'tar/ vt to wean

ablandamiento /aβlanda'miento/ m, softening; placating

ablandante /aβlan'dante/ a softening; placatory

ablandar /aβlan'dar/ vt to soften; appease, placate; loosen; relax; vi and vr be softened; be appeased; grow less stormy; (elements) decrease in force

ablandecer /aβlande'ser; aβlande'θer/ vt *irr* to soften. See **conocer**

ablución /aβlu'sion; aβlu'θion/ f, ablution

abnegación /aβnega'sion; aβnega'θion/ f, abnegation, self-sacrifice

abnegado /aβne'gaðo/ a self-sacrificing

abnegarse /aβne'garse/ vr *irr* to deprive oneself, sacrifice oneself. See **cegar**

abobado /aβo'βaðo/ a bewildered; foolish-looking, silly

abobar /aβo'βar/ vt to daze, bewilder; make stupid

abocado /aβo'kaðo/ a full-flavored, pleasant (of wine)

abocar /aβo'kar/ vt to seize with the mouth; bring nearer; transfer (contents of one jug to another); vr meet, assemble; vi *Naut.* enter (a channel, port, etc.).

abocarse (con...), to contact (...), get in touch (with...)

abocetado /aβose'taðo; aβoθe'taðo/ a *Art.* unfinished; sketchy

abochornado /aβotʃor'naðo/ a flushed (of the face); ashamed; embarrassed

abochornar /aβotʃor'nar/ vt to overheat, make flushed; shame; embarrass; vr (plants) dry up

abofetear /aβofete'ar/ vt to slap, hit; buffet

abogacía /aβoga'sia; aβoga'θia/ f, legal profession; practice of law; advocacy

abogaderas, abogaderías /aβoga'ðeras/ f pl *Lat. Am.* hair-splitting, specious arguments, legalistics

abogado /aβo'gaðo/ **(-da)** n lawyer

abogar /aβo'gar/ vi to defend at law; intercede for; advocate, champion

abolengo /aβo'leŋgo/ m, lineage, descent, family; inheritance

abolición /aβoli'sion; aβoli'θion/ f, abolition

abolir /aβo'lir/ vt to abolish; cancel; annul

abolladura /aβoya'ðura; aβoʎa'ðura/ f, bruise; dent; embossment

abollar /aβo'yar; aβo'ʎar/ vt to bruise; dent

abombado /aβom'baðo/ a convex; domed; *Mexico* tight (tipsy)

abombar /aβom'bar/ vt to make convex; *Inf.* deafen, bewilder; vr begin to putrefy; get intoxicated; *Mexico* become tight, get tight (tipsy)

abominable /aβomi'naβle/ a abominable

abominación /aβomina'sion; aβomina'θion/ f, abomination; loathing, detestation

abominar /aβomi'nar/ vt to abominate, loathe, detest

abonable /aβo'naβle/ a subscribable; payable

abonado /aβo'naðo/ **(-da)** a trustworthy, reliable; ready, prepared, inclined. n subscriber; season ticket holder (for concerts, etc.)

abonanzar /aβonan'sar; aβonan'θar/ vi *impers* to clear up, be fine (weather)

abonar /aβo'nar/ vt to guarantee; go surety for; improve, better; manure; ratify, confirm; pay; *Com.* place to the credit of; vr subscribe, become a subscriber; take out (season tickets, etc.)

abonaré /aβona're/ m, *Com.* due bill; promissory note, I.O.U.

abono /a'βono/ m, subscription; voucher; guarantee; manure. **a. verde,** leaf mold. **en a. de,** in payment of; in support of

aboquillado /aβoki'yaðo; aβoki'ʎaðo/ a tipped (of cigarettes)

abordar /aβor'ðar/ vt *Naut.* to board a ship; *Naut.* collide, run into; accost, tackle; undertake; vi *Naut.* put into port

aborigen /aβor'ihen/ a aboriginal

aborígenes /aβo'rihenes/ m pl, aborigines

aborrachado /aβorra'tʃaðo/ a bright red; highly colored; flushed

aborrascarse /aβorras'karse/ vr to grow stormy

aborrecedor /aβorrese'ðor; aβorreθe'ðor/ **(-ra)** a hateful. n hater, loather

aborrecer /aβorre'ser; aβorre'θer/ vt *irr* to hate, loathe; desert offspring (animals, birds). See **conocer**

aborrecible /aβorre'siβle; aβorre'θiβle/ a hateful, detestable

aborrecimiento /aβorresi'miento; aβorreθi'miento/ m, hate, detestation; dislike

abortar /aβor'tar/ vt to abort; foil (a plot); vi *Med.* miscarry; fail, go awry

abortivo /aβor'tiβo/ a abortive

aborto /a'βorto/ m, abortion; miscarriage; failure

abotagarse /aβota'garse/ vr to swell up, become bloated

abotonador /aβotona'ðor/ m, button-hook

abotonar /aβoto'nar/ vt to button; vi bud, sprout

abra /'aβra/ f, cove, small bay; narrow gorge; fissure, cleft; *Argentina* clearing (in a forest)

abrasador /aβrasa'ðor/ a burning, flaming

abrasamiento /aβrasa'miento/ m, burning; ardor, heat

abrasar /aβra'sar/ vt to burn; dry up, parch (plants); squander, waste; shame; vi burn; vr be very hot, glow; burn with passion

abrasión /aβra'sion/ f, abrasion

abrasivo /aβra'siβo/ a and m, abrasive

abrazadera /aβrasa'ðera; aβraθa'ðera/ f, clasp; clamp

abrazamiento /aβrasa'miento; aβraθa'miento/ m, embracing

abrazar /aβra'sar; aβra'θar/ vt to embrace, clasp in one's arms; follow, adopt; engage in; seize, take advantage of; comprise, include; surround; take in hand; clamp; clasp. **abrazarse a,** to clutch, hang on to

abrazo /a'βraso; a'βraθo/ m, embrace

abrelatas /aβre'latas/ m, can opener

abrevar /aβre'βar/ vt to water cattle; irrigate, water

abreviación /aβreβia'sion; aβreβia'θion/ f, abbreviation, shortening; summary; hastening

abreviador /aβreβia'ðor/ m, abridger; condenser

abreviar /aβre'βiar/ vt to abbreviate, shorten; hasten, accelerate; condense, abridge. **a. tiempo,** to save time. **Y para a....,** And, to make a long story short...

abreviatura /aβreβia'tura/ f, abbreviation, contraction; shorthand

abridor /aβri'ðor/ m, opener. **a. de guantes,** glovestretcher. **a. de láminas,** engraving needle. **a. de latas,** can opener

abridura /aβri'ðura/ f, (act of) opening (e.g. of a trunk)

abrigada /aβri'gaða/ f, **abrigadero** m, sheltered place

abrigar /aβri'gar/ vt to shelter, protect (against the cold, etc.); defend, help; hold (opinions); nurse (a hope, etc.); cover; vr take shelter; wrap oneself up

abrigo /a'βrigo/ m, shelter; defense; protection; help; sheltered place; wrap, coat; *Naut.* haven

abril /a'βril/ m, April; youth; pl *Poet.* years

abrillantar /aβriyan'tar; aβriʎan'tar/ vt polish, burnish; cause to shine

abrir /a'βrir/ vt to open; reveal; unlock; slide the bolt of; extend, spread out; cleave; engrave; clear (the way, etc.); begin; head, lead; separate; dig; inaugurate. *vi* unfold (flowers); expand; **en un abrir y cerrar de ojos,** in the twinkling of an eye, in the wink of an eye; *vr* open; expand; (*with con*) confide in. **a. el camino (a...),** to pave the way (for...).

abrirse camino, to make one's way; **abrirse paso a codazos,** to elbow one's way out, (or through)

abrochador /aβrotʃa'ðor/ *m,* button-hook

abrochar /aβro'tʃar/ *vt* to button; fasten, clasp; hook up (a dress, etc.); buckle; *Lat. Am.* **abrocharse (con...)** struggle (with...), wrestle (with...)

abrogar /aβro'gar/ *vt* to repeal, annul

abrojo /a'βroho/ *m,* thistle; *Bot.* caltrops; thorn, prickle; *pl* submerged rocks in sea

abroncar /aβron'kar/ *vt Inf.* to bore, annoy

abrumador /aβruma'ðor/ *a* burdensome, crushing, oppressive; troublesome, tiresome; exhausting

abrumar /aβru'mar/ *vt* to weigh down; overwhelm, oppress; weary, exhaust; *vr* grow misty

abrupto /a'βrupto/ *a* sudden, abrupt; rough, broken (ground); rugged

absceso /aβ'sseso/ *m,* abscess

absentismo /aβsen'tismo/ *m,* absenteeism

ábside /'aβsiðe/ *mf, Archit.* apse. *m, Astron.* apsis

absolución /aβsolu'sion; aβsolu'θion/ *f,* (*Eccl.* and *Law.*) absolution; remission, pardon

absoluta /aβso'luta/ *f, Mil.* discharge

absolutista /aβsolu'tista/ *mf* absolutist

absoluto /aβso'luto/ *a* absolute; categorical; *Inf.* despotic. **en a.,** absolutely

absolver /aβsol'βer/ *vt irr* to absolve; acquit (of a charge). *Law.* **a. de la instancia,** to dismiss the case. See **mover**

absorbente /aβsor'βente/ *a* and *m,* absorbent

absorber /aβsor'βer/ *vt* to absorb; consume, use up; attract, hold (the attention, etc.); imbibe

absorción /aβsor'sion; aβsor'θion/ *f,* absorption

absortar /aβsor'tar/ *vt* to amaze, dumbfound

absorto /aβ'sorto/ *a* amazed, astounded; abstracted, lost in thought

abstemio /aβs'temio/ *a* abstemious. *mf,* teetotaler

abstención /aβsten'sion; aβsten'θion/ *f,* abstention

abstenerse /aβste'nerse/ *vr irr* to refrain; abstain. See **tener**

abstinencia /aβsti'nensia; aβsti'nenθia/ *f,* abstinence; fasting

abstinente /aβsti'nente/ *a* abstinent; temperate

abstracción /aβstrak'sion; aβstrak'θion/ *f,* abstraction; preoccupation; absent-mindedness

abstracto /aβs'trakto/ *a* abstract. **en a.,** in the abstract

abstraer /aβstra'er/ *vt irr* to abstract; consider separately; *vi* (*with de*) do without, exclude; *vr* be preoccupied; let one's thoughts wander. See **traer**

abstraído /aβstra'iðo/ *a* retired, recluse; preoccupied; absent-minded

abstruso /aβ'struso/ *a* abstruse

absurdidad /aβsurði'ðað/ *f,* absurdity; folly, nonsense

absurdo /aβ'surðo/ *a* ridiculous, absurd. *m,* piece of folly, nonsense

abuchear /aβutʃe'ar/ *vt vi* to boo, hoot, jeer

abuela /a'βuela/ *f,* grandmother

abuelo /a'βuelo/ *m,* grandfather; *gen pl* ancestor; *pl* grandparents

abulia /a'βulia/ *f,* lack of will-power, abulia

abúlico /a'βuliko/ *a* abulic, lacking will-power

abultado /aβul'taðo/ *a* bulky, large; voluminous; exaggerated

abultamiento /aβulta'miento/ *m,* bulkiness; enlargement, increase; mound; exaggeration

abultar /aβul'tar/ *vt* to enlarge, increase; exaggerate; model in rough (sculpture); *vi* be bulky; be large

abundancia /aβun'dansia; aβun'danθia/ *f,* abundance, plenty

abundante /aβun'dante/ *a* abundant, plentiful; abounding (in)

abundar /aβun'dar/ *vi* to be plentiful, abound

aburrido /aβu'rriðo/ *a* (*with ser*) boring, tedious, dull; tired, weary; (*with estar*) bored

aburrimiento /aβurri'miento/ *m,* boredom, dullness; wearisomeness, tediousness

aburrir /aβu'rrir/ *vt* to bore; *Inf.* spend (time, money); (birds) desert the nest; *vr* grow bored; be weary

¡abusado! /aβu'saðo/ *Mexico* careful!, look out!, watch out!

abusar /aβu'sar/ *vi* to abuse; exceed one's rights, go too far; (*with de*) take advantage of

abusivo /aβu'siβo/ *a* abusive

abuso /a'βuso/ *m,* abuse. **a. de confianza,** abuse of trust

abyección /aβyek'sion; aβyek'θion/ *f,* degradation, misery; abjectness, servility

abyecto /aβ'yekto/ *a* abject, wretched; servile

acá /a'ka/ *adv* here; at this time, now. **desde ayer a.,** from yesterday until now. **por a.,** around here

acabable /aka'βaβle/ *a* terminable, finishable; achievable

acabado /aka'βaðo/ *a* complete; perfect; expert, consummate; old, worn out; ill, infirm. *m,* finish

acabamiento /akaβa'miento/ *m,* finishing, completion; end; death, decease

acabar /aka'βar/ *vt* to end, terminate; finish; complete, perfect; kill; (*with con*) destroy, finish off; suppress; squander; *vi* end; die; be destroyed; (*with de* + *infin*) to have just (e.g. *Acaba de salir,* He has just gone out); *vr* end, be exhausted, run out of (e.g. *Se le acabó el dinero,* His money ran out); fade, grow weak; be destroyed. **Se les acabaron las dudas,** Their doubts were cleared up. **a. de desconcertar,** to nonplus completely; **a. de decidirse,** to come to a decision; **a. de saber,** to finally learn

acacia /a'kasia; a'kaθia/ *f, Bot.* acacia

academia /aka'ðemia/ *f,* academy

académico /aka'ðemiko/ **(-ca)** *a* academic. *n* academician. **a. de la lengua,** member of the Royal Spanish Academy

acaecer /akae'ser; akae'θer/ *vi irr* to happen, occur. See **conocer**

acaecimiento /akaesi'miento; akaeθi'miento/ *m,* happening, occurrence, event

acalambrarse /akalam'brarse/ (muscle) to contract with cramps. **Estar acalambrado,** to have cramps

acalenturarse /akalentu'rarse/ *vr* to grow feverish

acallar /aka'yar; aka'ʎar/ *vt* to quieten, hush; soothe, appease

acalorado /akalo'raðo/ *a* hot; fervent; *Fig.* heated

acaloramiento /akalora'miento/ *m,* excitement, agitation, vehemence; ardor

acalorar /akalo'rar/ *vt* to warm; aid, encourage; excite, stimulate; stir, move (to enthusiasm); inflame, rouse; tire (by exercise); *vr* grow hot; become agitated or excited; become heated (arguments)

acamar /aka'mar/ *vt* to lay flat (plants by the wind); *vr* be flattened (plants); lie down (animals); go rotten (fruit)

acampar /akam'par/ *vi* and *vt* to encamp

acanalar /akana'lar/ *vt* to groove, striate, flute; corrugate; furrow, channel

acantilado /akanti'laðo/ *a* steep, precipitous; shelving (ocean-bed). *m,* cliff

acanto /a'kanto/ *m,* (*Archit. Bot.*) acanthus

acantonamiento /akantona'miento/ *m,* billeting; cantonment

acantonar /akanto'nar/ *vt* to billet or quarter troops

acaparador /akapara'ðor/ **(-ra)** *n* monopolist

acaparar /akapa'rar/ *vt Com.* to monopolize, corner; seize, take possession of

acápite /a'kapite/ *m, West. Hem.* new paragraph

acaracolado /akarako'laðo/ *a* spiral, winding, twisting

acardenalar /akarðena'lar/ *vt* to bruise; *vr* be bruised; be covered with livid marks

acarear /akare'ar/ *vt* to face; face up to, meet with courage

acariciador /akarisia'ðor/ akariθia'ðor/ **(-ra)** *a* caressing, loving. *n* fondler

acariciar /akari'siar; akari'θiar/ *vt* to caress; brush, touch lightly; cherish, treat affectionately; toy with (a suggestion)

acarraladura /akarra'ðura/ f, Lat. Am. run (in a stocking)

acarreador /akarrea'ðor/ (-ra) n carrier, carter

acarreamiento, acarreo /akarrea'miento, aka'reo/ m, cartage, carting; transport, carriage; occasioning

acarrear /akarre'ar/ vt to cart, transport; occasion, bring (gen. evil). **La guerra acarreó la carestía,** The war brought scarcity

acartonado /akarto'naðo/ a shriveled; shrunken; of cardboard; Fig. forced (dialogue)

acaso /a'kaso/ m, chance. adv by chance; perhaps, perchance. **por si a.,** in case (e.g. Por si a. venga, In case he comes)

acatable /aka'taβle/ a venerable, worthy

acatamiento /akata'miento/ m, respect; reverence; observance

acatar /aka'tar/ vt to treat with respect, honor, revere; observe

acatarrar /akata'rrar/ vt, Lat. Am. to annoy, bother, pester

acatarrarse /akata'rrarse/ vr to catch a cold; Argentina booze up, tank up

acaudalado /akauða'laðo/ a wealthy, well-to-do

acaudalar /akauða'lar/ vt to make money; hoard up wealth; acquire (learning, etc.)

acaudillar /akauði'yar; akauði'ʎar/ vt Mil. to command, lead; head (a party, etc.)

acceder /akse'ðer; akθe'ðer/ vi (with prep a) to concede, grant; accede to, agree to

accesibilidad /ak,sesiβili'ðað; ak,θesiβili'ðað/ f, accessibility; approachableness

accesible /akse'siβle; akθe'siβle/ a accessible; approachable

accesión /akse'sion; akθe'sion/ f, agreement, acquiescence; accession; accessory; feverish attack

acceso /ak'seso; ak'θeso/ m, access; paroxysm, outburst; Med. attack

accesorio /akse'sorio; akθe'sorio/ a accessory

accesorios /akse'sorios; akθe'sorios/ m pl, accessories; Theat. properties

accidentado /aksiðen'taðo; akθiðen'taðo/ a rough, uneven; stormy, troubled (life, etc.)

accidentar /aksiðen'tar; akθiðen'tar/ vt to cause (someone) an accident; vr to be the victim of an accident; be seized by a fit

accidente /aksi'ðente; akθi'ðente/ m, chance; accident, mishap; illness, indisposition; Med. fit; Gram. accidence; Mus. accidental. **a. del trabajo,** accident at work. **por a.,** by chance, accidentally

acción /ak'sion; ak'θion/ f, action; battle; skirmish; Mech. drive; Com. share; gesture; lawsuit; Lit. action (of play, etc.); Art. posture, pose. **a. de gracias,** thanksgiving; Com. **a. liberada,** paid-up share. **a. privilegiada,** preference share

accionar /aksio'nar; akθio'nar/ vi to gesture, gesticulate; Lat. Am. act, be active

accionista /aksio'nista; akθio'nista/ mf Com. shareholder

acechar /ase'tʃar; aθe'tʃar/ vt to spy upon, watch; lie in ambush for

acecho /a'setʃo; a'θetʃo/ m, spying upon, watch; waylaying, ambush. **al a.,** in ambush; on the watch

acechona /ase'tʃona; aθe'tʃona/ f, waylaying; ambush

acecinar /asesi'nar; aθeθi'nar/ vt to salt and dry (meat); vr (persons) wither, dry up

acedar /ase'ðar; aθe'ðar/ vt to make bitter, sour; embitter, displease; vr turn sour; wither (plants)

acefalía /asefa'lia; aθefa'lia/ f, acephalia, headlessness

acéfalo /a'sefalo; a'θefalo/ a acephalous

aceitar /asei'tar; aθei'tar/ vt to oil, lubricate; rub with oil

aceite /a'seite; a'θeite/ m, olive oil; oil. **a. de hígado de bacalao,** cod-liver oil. **a. de linaza,** linseed oil. **a. de ricino,** castor-oil. **a. de trementina,** oil of turpentine

aceitera /asei'tera; aθei'tera/ f, woman who sells oil; oil can; oil bottle; pl cruet

aceitero /asei'tero; aθei'tero/ m, oil seller. a oil

aceitoso /asei'toso; aθei'toso/ a oily

aceituna /asei'tuna; aθei'tuna/ f, Bot. olive

aceitunado /aseitu'naðo; aθeitu'naðo/ a olive-colored

aceitunero /aseitu'nero; aθeitu'nero/ (-ra) n olive picker; olive seller. m, warehouse for storing olives

aceituno /asei'tuno; aθei'tuno/ m, olive tree; a, Lat. Am. olive-colored

aceleración /aselera'sion; aθelera'θion/ f, speed, acceleration

aceleradamente /asele,raða'mente; aθele,raða'mente/ adv hastily, swiftly

acelerador /aselera'ðor; aθelera'ðor/ a accelerating. m, hastener; Auto. accelerator

acelerar /asele'rar; aθele'rar/ vt to speed up; accelerate

acémila /a'semila; a'θemila/ f, beast of burden, mule

acendrado /asen'draðo; aθen'draðo/ a pure, unblemished, spotless

acendrar /asen'drar; aθen'drar/ vt to refine (metals); purify, make spotless

acento /a'sento; a'θento/ m, accent; tone, inflection; Poet. voice, words. **a. agudo,** acute accent. **a. circunflejo,** circumflex accent. **a. grave,** grave accent. **a. ortográfico,** graphic accent, written accent. **a. tónico,** tonic accent

acentuación /asentua'sion; aθentua'θion/ f, accentuation, stress; emphasis

acentuar /asen'tuar; aθen'tuar/ vt to accent; stress, emphasize; vr become evident, become marked, be noticeable

aceña /a'seɲa; a'θeɲa/ f, water-mill; irrigation water-wheel; chain-well

acepción /asep'sion; aθep'θion/ f, meaning, significance, acceptation. **a. de personas,** partiality, preference

acepilladura /ase,piya'ðura; aθe,piʎa'ðura/ f, brushing; planing; wood-shaving

acepillar /asepi'yar; aθepi'ʎar/ vt to brush; plane; Inf. brush up, polish up

aceptabilidad /a,septaβili'ðað; a,θeptaβili'ðað/ f, acceptability

aceptable /asep'taβle; aθep'taβle/ a acceptable

aceptación /asepta'sion; aθepta'θion/ f, acceptance; popularity; approval

aceptador /asepta'ðor; aθepta'ðor/ (-ra) a accepting. n acceptor

aceptar /asep'tar; aθep'tar/ vt to accept; approve; accept a challenge; Com. honor

acequia /ase'kia; aθe'kia/ f, ditch, trench; irrigation channel

acera /a'sera; a'θera/ f, sidewalk, pavement. **a. del sol,** sunny side of the street

acerado /ase'raðo; aθe'raðo/ a steel; steel-like; strong, tough; mordant, incisive

acerar /ase'rar; aθe'rar/ vt to steel; treat (liquids) with steel; harden, make obdurate

acerbidad /aserβi'ðað; aθerβi'ðað/ f, bitterness, acerbity, sourness; harshness, cruelty

acerbo /a'serβo; a'θerβo/ a sour, tart, bitter; cruel, harsh

acerca de /a'serka de; a'θerka de/ adv about, concerning

acercamiento /aserka'miento; aθerka'miento/ m, approach

acercar /aser'kar; aθer'kar/ vt to bring nearer; vr be near at hand, draw near; (with prep a) approach

acerico /ase'riko; aθe'riko/ m, small cushion; pincushion

acero /a'sero; a'θero/ m, steel; blade, sword; pl bravery, spirit; Inf. good appetite. **a. inoxidable,** stainless steel

acérrimo /a'serrimo; a'θerrimo/ a sup extremely strong, mighty; most harsh; most resolute, unflinching; very strong (taste, smell)

acerrojar /aserro'har; aθerro'har/ vt to lock, padlock; bolt

acertado /aser'taðo; aθer'taðo/ a well-aimed; fitting, suitable; wise; successful

acertar /aser'tar; aθer'tar/ vt irr to hit the mark; find, come across; succeed (in), achieve; guess, find out; **No acertaba a explicármelo,** I couldn't quite understand it. **a. por chambra,** to make a lucky guess. vi be successful; thrive (of plants); (with prep a + infin) happen, occur, come to pass. Pres. Ind. **acierto, aciertas, acierta, aciertan.** Pres. Subjunc. **acierte, aciertes, acierte, acierten**

acertijo /aser'tiho; aθer'tiho/ m, riddle

acervo /a'serβo; a'θerβo/ m, pile, heap; Fig. storehouse, wealth (e.g. of words)

acetaminofén /aθetamino'fen/ m, acetaminophen

acetato /ase'tato; aθe'tato/ m, acetate

acetileno /aseti'leno; aθeti'leno/ m, acetylene

achacar /atʃa'kar/ vt to attribute, impute, assign.

achacable a, imputable to

achacoso /atʃa'koso/ a ailing, ill, sickly

achantarse /atʃan'tarse/ vr Inf. to hide from danger; put up with, bear

achaparrado /atʃapa'rraðo/ a stocky

achaque /a'tʃake/ m, ailment, illness (permanent); Inf. period, menstruation; pregnancy; matter, affair; pretext; failing, bad habit. **En a. de...,** Re..., concerning...

achatamiento /atʃata'miento/ m, flattening

achatar /atʃa'tar/ vt to flatten, make flat

achicado /atʃi'kaðo/ a childish

achicar /atʃi'kar/ vt to make smaller, diminish; drain, bail out; depreciate, belittle

achicarse /atʃi'karse/ Inf. to get smaller

achicharrar /atʃitʃa'rrar/ vt Cul. to overcook; overheat; annoy, importune

achicoria /atʃi'koria/ f, chicory

achique /a'tʃike/ m, bailing, draining

achispado /atʃis'paðo/ a Inf. tipsy

achubascarse /atʃuβas'karse/ vr to become overcast, grow stormy

achuchar /atʃu'tʃar/ vt Inf. to squeeze, hug; jostle, push against

achuchón /atʃu'tʃon/ m, Inf. shove, push; hug, squeeze

achulado /atʃu'laðo/ a Inf. brazen, tough

aciago /a'siago; a'θiago/ a unhappy, ill-omened; fateful

acíbar /a'siβar; a'θiβar/ m, aloe tree; bitter aloes; sorrow, bitterness

acibarar /asiβa'rar; aθiβa'rar/ vt to add bitter aloes to; embitter, sadden

acicalado /asika'laðo; aθika'laðo/ a polished; neat; well-groomed. m, polishing, burnishing (of weapons)

acicalador /asikala'ðor; aθikala'ðor/ **(-ra)** a polishing. n polisher. m, burnisher (machine)

acicalar /asika'lar; aθika'lar/ vt to burnish (weapons); adorn, deck; vr dress oneself with care

acicate /asi'kate; aθi'kate/ m, Moorish spur; incitement, stimulus

acicatear /asikate'ar; aθikate'ar/ vt to induce, spur on. **a. la curiosidad,** arouse curiosity

acidez /asi'ðes; aθi'ðeθ/ f, acidity, bitterness

acidia /a'siðia; a'θiðia/ f, indolence; sluggishness

ácido /'asiðo; 'aθiðo/ a acid; sour; harsh. m, acid. **a. fénico,** carbolic acid. **a. graso,** fatty acid

acidular /asiðu'lar; aθiðu'lar/ vt Chem. to acidulate

acídulo /a'siðulo; a'θiðulo/ a Chem. acidulous

acierto /a'sierto; a'θierto/ m, good hit, bull's-eye; success; achievement; cleverness; dexterity, skill; wisdom, sense; tact

acimut /asi'mut; aθi'mut/ m, Astron. azimuth

aclamación /aklama'sion; aklama'θion/ f, acclamation; shout of acclamation. **por a.,** unanimously

aclamador /aklama'ðor; aklama'ðor/ **(-ra)** a acclaiming. n applauder, acclaimer

aclamar /akla'mar/ vt to acclaim; applaud

aclaración /aklara'sion; aklara'θion/ f, explanation; elucidation

aclarado /akla'raðo/ m, rinse; rinsing

aclarador, aclaratorio /aklara'ðor, aklara'torio/ a explanatory

aclarar /akla'rar/ vt to clarify, purify; clear; rinse (clothes); explain; thin; vi clear; (sky) clear up; dawn

aclimatación /aklimata'sion; aklimata'θion/ f, acclimatization; Lat. Am. air-conditioning

aclimatar /aklima'tar/ vt to acclimatize

acné /ak'ne/ m, acne

acobardar /akoβar'ðar/ vt to intimidate, frighten

acocear /akose'ar; akoθe'ar/ vt to kick; Inf. insult, humiliate

acocharse /ako'tʃarse/ vr to squat, crouch

acocil /ako'sil; ako'θil/ m, Mexico freshwater shrimp

acodalar /akoða'lar/ vt to prop

acodiciar /akoði'siar; akoði'θiar/ vt to yearn for, covet, desire

acogedizo /akohe'ðiso; akohe'ðiθo/ a gathered haphazardly

acogedor /akohe'ðor/ **(-ra)** a welcoming, friendly; inviting (e.g. a chair or room); n protector

acoger /ako'her/ vt to receive, welcome, admit; protect, harbor; vr take refuge; (with prep a) make use of, resort to; **acogerse a sagrado,** seek sanctuary

acogida /ako'hiða/ f, reception, welcome; protection; shelter; meeting place; confluence (of waters). **tener buena a.,** to be well received

acogollar /akogo'yar; akogo'ʎar/ vt to protect, cover (plants); vi sprout, shoot

acogotar /akogo'tar/ vt to fell by a blow on the neck; Inf. knock out

acolada /ako'laða/ f, accolade

acolitar /akoli'tar/ vi to serve as an altar boy; serve as an altar girl

acólito /a'kolito/ m, acolyte

acomedido, -a /akome'ðiðo/ Lat. Am. helpful, obliging

acometedor /akomete'ðor/ **(-ra)** a capable, enterprising; aggressive. n aggressor, attacker

acometer /akome'ter/ vt to attack furiously; undertake; take in hand; overcome (of sleep, etc.)

acometida /akome'tiða/ f, **acometimiento** m, assault, onrush; undertaking

acometividad /akometiβi'ðað/ f, aggressiveness; Argentina touchiness

acomodable /akomo'ðaβle/ a easily arranged

acomodación /akomoða'sion; akomoða'θion/ f, adjustment; adaptation; accommodation

acomodadizo /akomoða'ðiso; akomoða'ðiθo/ a accommodating, easy-going

acomodado /akomo'ðaðo/ a suitable; convenient; wealthy, well-off; comfort-loving; moderate, low (of price)

acomodador /akomoða'ðor/ **(-ra)** n theater attendant, usher

acomodamiento /akomoða'miento/ m, agreement, transaction; accommodation

acomodar /akomo'ðar/ vt to arrange, adjust, accommodate; adapt; appoint; place; reconcile; employ, take on; equip, provide; lodge; vi suit, be convenient; vr compromise, agree

acomodaticio /akomoða'tisio; akomoða'tiθio/ a accommodating

acomodo /ako'moðo/ m, post, employment; arrangement; settlement

acompañamiento /akompaɲa'miento/ m, accompaniment; following; retinue; Mus. accompaniment; Theat. crowd, chorus

acompañanta /akompa'ɲanta/ f, chaperon; maid, servant

acompañante /akompa'ɲante/ m, Mus. accompanist

acompañar /akompa'ɲar/ vt to accompany; follow, escort; enclose (a letter, etc.); Mus. accompany

acompasado /akompa'saðo/ a rhythmic; deliberate, slow

acondicionado /akondisio'naðo; akondiθio'naðo/ a conditioned; (with bien or mal) in good or bad condition; of good or bad quality; good- or ill-natured. **reflejo acondicionado** Med. conditioned reflex

acondicionar /akondisio'nar; akondiθio'nar/ vt to prepare; mend, repair; vr condition oneself

acongojar /akongo'har/ vt to sadden, grieve; oppress

aconsejable /akonse'haβle/ *a* advisable

aconsejar /akonse'har/ *vt* to advise; *vr* (*with con*) consult, ask advice of

acontecedero /akontese'ðero; akonteθe'ðero/ *a* possible

acontecer /akonte'ser; akonte'θer/ *vi irr impers* to happen. See **conocer**

acontecimiento /akontesi'miento; akonteθi'miento/ *m*, event, occurrence

acopiar /ako'piar/ *vt* to collect, amass, gather

acopio /a'kopio/ *m*, collection, store; accumulation, gathering

acopladura /akopla'ðura/ *f*, **acoplamiento** *m*, (*Mech.*) joint; coupling; yoking; mating (of animals)

acoplar /ako'plar/ *vt* to join, couple; yoke; mate (animals); reconcile (opinions); *vr Inf.* fall in love

acoquinar /akoki'nar/ *vt Inf.* to intimidate, terrify

acorazado /akora'saðo; akora'θaðo/ *a* (*Nav. Mil.*) armored, iron-clad. *m*, iron-clad, battleship

acorcharse /akor'tʃarse/ *vr* to dry up, shrivel; go numb (limbs)

acordadamente /akor,ðaða'mente/ *adv* by common consent, unanimously; deliberately, after due thought

acordar /akor'ðar/ *vt irr* to decide unanimously; resolve; remind; tune; harmonize (colors); *vi* agree; *vr* remember; come to an agreement. **Si mal no me acuerdo,** If memory serves me well. *Pres. Ind.* **acuerdo, acuerdas, acuerda, acuerdan.** *Pres. Subjunc.* **acuerde, acuerdes, acuerde, acuerden**

acorde /a'korðe/ *a* agreed; in harmony; in agreement. *m, Mus.* chord; harmony

acordeón /akorðe'on/ *m*, accordion; (slang) crib sheet

acordonar /akorðo'nar/ *vt* to lace; cordon off, surround; mill (coins)

acornear /akorne'ar/ *vt* to butt, toss (bulls)

acorralado /akorra'laðo/ *a* at bay, intimidated

acorralamiento /akorrala'miento/ *m*, corralling, penning

acorralar /akorra'lar/ *vt* to corral, pen; confine; corner, silence (in argument); frighten; harass

acorrer /ako'rrer/ *vt* to aid, assist; *vi* run, hasten; *vr* take refuge

acortamiento /akorta'miento/ *m*, shortening

acortar /akor'tar/ *vt* to shorten; *vr* be speechless, be shy. **a. las velas,** to take in sail

acosador /akosa'ðor/ (**-ra**) *a* persecuting. *n* persecutor

acosamiento /akosa'miento/ *m*, persecution

acosar /ako'sar/ *vt* to persecute relentlessly; annoy, harass

acostado /ako'staðo/ *a* in bed; stretched out; *Herald.* couchant

acostar /ako'star/ *vt irr* to lay down, stretch out; put to bed; *vi* lean, tilt; *vr* lie down; go to bed; *Naut.* come alongside. See **contar**

acostumbrado /akostum'braðo/ *a* accustomed, usual

acostumbrar /akostum'brar/ *vt* to habituate, accustom; *vi* be in the habit of (e.g. *Acostumbramos ir a la playa en el verano,* We generally go to the seashore in summer); *vr* (*with prep a*) become used to

acotación /akota'sion; akota'θion/ *f*, noting; marginal note; stage direction; ordnance survey number

acotar /ako'tar/ *vt* to annotate; mark out boundaries; fix, establish; accept; *Inf.* choose; testify; fill in elevation figures (on a map); *vr* seek refuge

acotejar /akote'har/ *vt, Lat. Am.* to arrange, put in order

acre /'akre/ *a* bitter, sour; harsh; biting, mordant. *m*, acre (land measure)

acrecencia /akre'sensia; akre'θenθia/ *f*, **acrecentamiento** *m*, increase; addition

acrecentar /akresen'tar; akreθen'tar/ *vt irr* to increase; augment; promote, prefer. See **acertar**

acrecer /akre'ser; akre'θer/ *vt irr* to increase; augment. See **conocer**

acreción /akre'sion; akre'θion/ *f*, accretion

acreditado /akreði'taðo/ *a* accredited, well-reputed; respected

acreditar /akreði'tar/ *vt* to prove; verify; accredit;

recommend; sanction, authorize; vouch for, guarantee; *Com.* credit

acreedor /akree'ðor/ (**-ra**) *n* creditor; claimant. *a* deserving. **a. hipotecario,** mortgagee

acreencia /akre'ensia; akre'enθia/ *f*, debt; *Com.* claim

acribillar /akriβi'yar; akriβi'ʎar/ *vt* to riddle with holes; wound repeatedly; pelt; torment; *Inf.* pester, harass

acriminación /akrimina'sion; akrimina'θion/ *f*, accusation

acriminador /akrimina'ðor/ (**-ra**) *a* incriminating. *n* accuser

acriminar /akrimi'nar/ *vt* to accuse, charge

acrimonia /akri'monia/ *f*, acrimony

acriollarse /akrio'jarse; akrio'ʎarse/ *vr, Lat. Am.* to adopt local customs, go native

acrisolar /akriso'lar/ *vt* to refine, purify (metals); perfect; clarify, elucidate

acrobacia /akro'βasia; akro'βaθia/ *f*, acrobatics

acróbata /a'kroβata/ *mf* acrobat

acrobático /akro'βatiko/ *a* acrobatic

acromatópsico /akroma'topsiko/ *a* color-blind

acróstico /a'krostiko/ *a* and *m*, acrostic

acta /'akta/ *f*, minutes, record; certificate of election (as deputy to Cortes, etc.); *pl* deeds (of a martyr). **a. matrimonial,** marriage register

actitud /akti'tuð/ *f*, attitude

activar /akti'βar/ *vt* to stimulate, make active; accelerate, hasten

actividad /aktiβi'ðað/ *f*, activity; movement; bustle. **en a.,** in action; at work

activo /ak'tiβo/ *a* active. *m, Com.* assets

acto /'akto/ *m*, act, deed, action; act, law; act (of a play); public ceremony; *pl* minutes (of a meeting), proceedings (of a conference). **a. continuo** *or* **a. seguido,** immediately afterwards. **a. vandálico,** act of vandalism. **los Actos de los Apóstoles,** Acts of the Apostles. **en a.,** in the act (of doing). **en el a.,** in the act; immediately

actor /ak'tor/ *m*, actor; *Law.* plaintiff

actriz /ak'tris; ak'triθ/ *f*, actress

actuación /aktua'sion; aktua'θion/ *f*, operation, functioning; action; *pl* legal functions, judicial acts

actual /ak'tual/ *a* present; contemporary

actualidad /aktuali'ðað/ *f*, present, present time; topic of interest. **actualidades,** current events. **en la a.,** at the present time

actuar /ak'tuar/ *vt* to operate, set in motion; *vi* act; exercise legal functions

actuario /ak'tuario/ (**de seguros**) *m*, actuary

acuarela /akua'rela/ *f*, water-color painting

acuarelista /akuare'lista/ *mf* water-colorist

acuario /a'kuario/ *m*, aquarium; Aquarius

acuartelamiento /a,kuartela'miento/ *m*, billeting (of troops); billet, quarters

acuartelar /akuarte'lar/ *vt* to billet

acuático, acuátil /a'kuatiko, a'kuatil/ *a* aquatic

acuatinta /akua'tinta/ *f*, aquatint

acuatizar /akuati'sar; akuati'θar/ *vi, Lat. Am.* to land on water, touch down on water

acuchillado /akutʃi'yaðo; akutʃi'ʎaðo/ *a* taught by experience, schooled

acuchillar /akutʃi'yar; akutʃi'ʎar/ *vt* to hack, cut about; stab, put to the sword; slash (sleeves, etc.); *vr* fight with swords, daggers

acucia /a'kusia; a'kuθia/ *f*, fervor, zeal; yearning, longing

acuciar /aku'siar; aku'θiar/ *vt* to incite; goad; stimulate; encourage

acuciosidad /akusiosi'ðað; akuθiosi'ðað/ *f*, eagerness, fervor, zeal

acucioso /aku'sioso; aku'θioso/ *a* eager, fervent, keen, zealous

acuclillarse /akukli'yarse; akukli'ʎarse/ *vr* to squat, crouch

acudir /aku'ðir/ *vi* to go, repair (to); come; go or come to the aid of; attend, be present; **No me acude ningún ejemplo a la memoria,** No example comes to mind; resort (to), seek protection; reply, respond

acueducto /akueˈðukto/ *m*, aqueduct

acuerdo /aˈkuerðo/ *m*, motion, resolution; decision; harmony, agreement; opinion, belief; remembrance; report; meeting (of members of a tribunal); *Art.* harmony (of colors). **de a.**, in agreement, in conformity; unanimously; *Inf.* OK. **estar de a. (con)**, to agree (with). **estar de acuerdo en** (+ infin.), to agree to (+ infin.) **ponerse de a.**, to come to an understanding

acuilmarse /akuilˈmarse/ *vr Central America* to get depressed, get the blues

acuitar /akuiˈtar/ *vt* to distress, trouble; grieve

acumulación /akumulaˈsion; akumulaˈθion/ *f*, accumulation, collection

acumulador /akumulaˈðor/ **(-ra)** *a* accumulative. *m*, accumulator, car battery. *n* collector, accumulator

acumulamiento /akumulaˈmiento/ *m*, accumulation (act)

acumular /akumuˈlar/ *vt* to accumulate, amass, collect; accuse, charge with

acuñación /akuɲaˈsion; akuɲaˈθion/ *f*, minting, coining; wedging

acuñador /akuɲaˈðor/ **(-ra)** *n* coiner, stamper; wedge. *m*, coining machine

acuñar /akuˈɲar/ *vt* to mint, stamp, coin; wedge

acuoso /aˈkuoso/ *a* aqueous, watery

acurrucarse /akurruˈkarse/ *vr* to huddle; curl up; crouch

acusación /akusaˈsion; akusaˈθion/ *f*, accusation; *Law.* charge; *Law.* prosecution

acusado /akuˈsaðo/ **(-da)** *a* accused; prominent; well-defined. *n* accused; *Law.* defendant

acusador /akusaˈðor/ **(-ra)** *a* accusing. *n* accuser; *Law.* prosecutor

acusar /akuˈsar/ *vt* to accuse; blame; denounce; *Com.* acknowledge receipt; *Law.* prosecute; *Law.* charge. **acusarle a uno las cuarenta**, *inf* to give someone a piece of one's mind

acusatorio /akusaˈtorio/ *a* accusatory

acusón /akuˈson/ **(-ona)** *n Inf.* telltale, sneak, informer

acústica /aˈkustika/ *f*, acoustics

acústico /aˈkustiko/ *a* acoustic

adagio /aˈðahio/ *m*, adage; *Mus.* adagio

adalid /aðaˈlið/ *m*, chieftain; head, leader

adamado /aðaˈmaðo/ *a* refined; genteel; effeminate

adamantino /aðamanˈtino/ *a* adamantine

adaptabilidad /aðaptaβiliˈðað/ *f*, adaptability

adaptación /aðaptaˈsion; aðaptaˈθion/ *f*, adaptation

adaptar /aðapˈtar/ *vt* to adapt, make suitable; *vr* adapt oneself

adarme /aˈðarme/ *m*, tittle, jot. **por adarmes**, in bits and pieces, in drabs and driblets

adecentar /aðesenˈtar; aðeθenˈtar/ *vt* to tidy up; *vr* tidy oneself

adecuación /aðekuaˈsion; aðekuaˈθion/ *f*, adequacy; suitability

adecuado /aðeˈkuaðo/ *a* adequate; suitable

adecuar /aðeˈkuar/ *vt* to proportion, fit; *Fig.* tailor

adefesio /aðeˈfesio/ *m*, *Inf.* folly, absurdity (gen. *pl*); extravagant attire; guy, sight

adelantado /aðelanˈtaðo/ *a* precocious; forward, pert; fast (clocks); early (of fruit); excellent; capable, proficient. *m*, *Obs.* provincial governor *or* chief justice *or* captain-general (Spanish history). **por a.**, in advance

adelantamiento /aðelantaˈmiento/ *m*, promotion, furtherance; progress, advancement; betterment, improvement; *Obs.* office of **adelantado**; anticipation

adelantar /aðelanˈtar/ *vt* to advance, move on; hasten; forestall; overtake; move forward (the hands of clocks); improve, better; beat, excel; place in front; *vi* progress, advance; be fast (clocks); grow, develop; *vr* come forward

adelante /aðeˈlante/ *adv* on, forward; further on; straight ahead. **¡A.!** Onward!; Come in! **de hoy en a.**, henceforth, from today

adelanto /aðeˈlanto/ *m*, anticipation; progress; *Com.* payment in advance. **el a. de la hora,** moving the clock forward

adelgazamiento /aðel,gasaˈmiento; aðel,gaθaˈmiento/ *m*, loss of weight; slenderness; thinness

adelgazar /aðelgaˈsar; aðelgaˈθar/ *vt* to make slender *or* thin; *Fig.* split hairs; whittle, taper; *vi* grow slender *or* thin

ademán /aðeˈman/ *m*, posture, attitude; gesture; *pl* behavior, manners

además /aðeˈmas/ *adv* besides, in addition; moreover. **a. de**, as well as

adentro /aˈðentro/ *adv* inside, within

adentros /aˈðentros/ *m pl*, private thoughts (e.g. *Pensé para mis adentros*, I thought to myself). *Interj* **¡Adentro!** Come in!; Go in!

adepto /aˈðepto/ *a* affiliated; adept, proficient

aderezamiento /aðe,resaˈmiento; aðe,reθaˈmiento/ *m*, dressing; seasoning; embellishment

aderezar /aðereˈsar; aðereˈθar/ *vt* to deck, embellish; cook; *Cul.* season; *Cul.* dress; prepare; repair, mend; guide, direct; dress (cloth)

aderezo /aðeˈreso; aðeˈreθo/ *m*, dressing, adornment; beautifying; finery, ornament; preparation; seasoning; set of jewels; horse's trappings; gum starch (for dressing cloth); equipment

adeudar /aðeuˈðar/ *vt* to owe; be dutiable (goods); *Com.* debit; *vi* become related (by marriage); *vr* run into debt

adeudo /aˈðeuðo/ *m*, debt; customs duty; *Com.* debit

adherencia /aðeˈrensia; aðeˈrenθia/ *f*, adherence; adhesion

adherente /aðeˈrente/ *a* adhesive; connected, attached. *mf* adherent, follower; *m pl.* **adherentes,** accessories, requisites

adherirse /aðeˈrirse/ *vr irr* to adhere, stick; follow; believe (in). See **herir**

adhesión /aðeˈsion/ *f*, adhesion; adherence

adhesivo /aðeˈsiβo/ *a* adhesive

adición /aðiˈsion; aðiˈθion/ *f*, addition; *Argentina* check (in a restaurant)

adicional /aðisioˈnal; aðiθioˈnal/ *a* additional, extra

adicionar /aðisioˈnar; aðiθioˈnar/ *vt* to add up; add to

adicto /aˈðikto/ **(-ta)** *a* addicted. *n* addict; *Lat. Am.* (drug) addict

adiestrador /aðiestraˈðor/ **(-ra)** *n* trainer, coach; guide, teacher

adiestrar /aðiesˈtrar/ *vt* to train, coach; guide, teach; lead; *vr* practice, perfect oneself

adietar /aðieˈtar/ *vt Med.* to put on a diet

adifés /aðiˈfes/ *adv*, *Central America* deliberately, on purpose

adinerado /aðineˈraðo/ *a* wealthy, well-off, rich

adiós /aˈðios/ *interj* Good-bye! *m*, farewell

aditamento /aðitaˈmento/ *m*, addition, appendix

adive /aˈðiβe/ *m*, jackal

adivinación /aðiβinaˈsion; aðiβinaˈθion/ *f*, divination; guess

adivinanza /aðiβiˈnansa; aðiβiˈnanθa/ *f*, divination; riddle; puzzle. **adivinanzas,** guessing games. **no estar para jugar a las a.,** to be in no mood for guessing games

adivinar /aðiβiˈnar/ *vt* to prophesy, foretell; divine; guess; solve, guess (riddles, etc.)

adivino /aðiˈβino/ **(-na)** *n* soothsayer, prophet

adjetivo /aðheˈtiβo/ *a* adjectival. *m*, adjective

adjudicación /aðhuðikaˈsion; aðhuðikaˈθion/ *f*, adjudication, award

adjudicador /aðhuðikaˈðor/ **(-ra)** *n* adjudicator

adjudicar /aðhuðiˈkar/ *vt* to adjudge; award; *vr* appropriate

adjudicatario /aðhuðikaˈtario/ **(-ia)** *n* recipient (of a prize, etc.); grantee

adjuntar /aðhunˈtar/ *vt* to enclose (with a letter, etc.)

adjunto /aðˈhunto/ *a* attached; enclosed, accompanying; assistant, deputy; adjectival. *m*, addition, supplement; adjunct (professor)

administración /aðministraˈsion; aðministraˈθion/ *f*, administration; direction, control; administratorship

administrador /aðministraˈðor/ **(-ra)** *a* administrative. *n* administrator. **a. de correos,** postmaster

administrar /aðminis'trar/ *vt* to control, manage; provide, supply; administer. **administrarse el tiempo**, to budget one's time

administrativo /aðministra'tiβo/ *a* administrative, executive

admirable /aðmi'raβle/ *a* admirable

admirablemente /aðmi,raβle'mente/ *adv* admirably, excellently

admiración /aðmira'sion; aðmira'θion/ *f*, amazement; admiration; wonder; exclamation mark

admirador /aðmira'ðor/ **(-ra)** *a* admiring. *n* admirer

admirar /aðmi'rar/ *vt* to admire; surprise, amaze (e.g. *Me admira su acción*, His action surprises me); to see (e.g. *Desde la colina se pueden admirar varios edificios de la ciudad*, From the hill several buildings in the city can be seen); *vr* (*with de*) be surprised at or by

admisibilidad /aðmisiβili'ðað/ *f*, allowability, permissibility

admisible /aðmi'siβle/ *a* admissible; permissible

admisión /aðmi'sion/ *f*, admission; acceptance; allowance

admitir /aðmi'tir/ *vt* to admit; receive, accept; tolerate, brook; allow, permit

admonición /aðmoni'sion; aðmoni'θion/ *f*, admonition, warning; reprimand

adobar /aðo'βar/ *vt* to prepare; *Cul.* garnish; pickle (meat); cook; dress (hides)

adobe /a'ðoβe/ *m*, adobe, mudbrick

adobo /a'ðoβo/ *m*, repairing; dressing (for cloth, leather); *Cul.* savory sauce; pickling sauce; make-up, cosmetic

adocenado /aðose'naðo; aðoθe'naðo/ *a* ordinary; narrow-minded

adoctrinar /aðoktri'nar/ *vt* to instruct

adolecer /aðole'ser; aðole'θer/ *vi irr* to fall ill; (*with de*) suffer from (diseases, defects); *vr* be sorry for, regret. See **conocer**

adolescencia /aðoles'sensia; aðoles'θenθia/ *f*, adolescence

adolescente /aðoles'sente; aðoles'θente/ *a* and *mf* adolescent

adonde /a'ðonde/ *adv* (*interr* **a dónde**) where to, whither (e.g. *¿A dónde fuiste?* Where did you go to?)

adondequiera /a,ðonde'kiera/ *adv* wherever

adopción /aðop'sion; aðop'θion/ *f*, adoption

adoptador /aðopta'ðor/ **(-ra)** *a* adopting. *n* adopter

adoptar /aðop'tar/ *vt* to adopt (children); make one's own, embrace (opinions); take (decisions)

adoptivo /aðop'tiβo/ *a* adoptive

adoquín /aðo'kin/ *m*, cobble-stone; *Fig.* blockhead

adoquinado /aðoki'naðo/ *m*, cobbling, paving. *m*, cobbled pavement

adoquinar /aðoki'nar/ *vt* to pave with cobble-stones

adorable /aðo'raβle/ *a* adorable

adoración /aðora'sion; aðora'θion/ *f*, worship, adoration. **A. de los Reyes**, Adoration of the Magi; Epiphany

adorador /aðora'ðor/ **(-ra)** *a* adoring. *n* adorer

adorar /aðo'rar/ *vt* to adore; worship; (*with en*) dote on; *vi* pray

adormecedor /aðormese'ðor; aðormeθe'ðor/ *a* soporific, drowsy

adormecer /aðorme'ser; aðorme'θer/ *vt irr* to make drowsy, soothe, lull; hush to sleep; *vr* go to sleep (limbs); fall asleep; (*with en*) persist in. See **conocer**

adormecimiento /aðormesi'miento; aðormeθi'miento/ *m*, sleepiness; lulling asleep; numbness

adormitarse /aðormi'tarse/ *vr* to doze, take a nap, snooze

adornamiento /aðorna'miento/ *m*, adornment, decoration

adornar /aðor'nar/ *vt* to deck, beautify; decorate; trim, embellish; adorn (of virtues, etc.)

adorno /a'ðorno/ *m*, decoration, adornment; ornament; trimming. **de a.**, ornamental; flowering (shrubs)

adquiridor /aðkiri'ðor/ **(-ra)** *a* acquiring. *n* acquirer

adquirir /aðki'rir/ *vt irr* to acquire, get; achieve, obtain. *Pres. Ind.* **adquiero, adquieres, adquiere, ad-**

quieren. *Pres. Subjunc.* **adquiera, adquieras, adquiera, adquieran**

adquisición /aðkisi'sion; aðkisi'θion/ *f*, acquirement; acquisition. **poder de a.**, purchasing power

adquisidor /aðkisi'ðor/ **(-ra)** *a* acquiring. *n* acquirer, obtainer

adquisitivo /aðkisi'tiβo/ *a* acquisitive

adquisividad /aðkisiβi'ðað/ *f*, acquisitiveness

adrazo /a'ðraso; a'ðraθo/ *m*, salt-water still

adrede /a'ðreðe/ *adv* on purpose, intentionally

adrenalina /aðrena'lina/ *f*, adrenaline

adscribir /aðskri'βir/ *vt* to ascribe, attribute; appoint (to a post, etc.). See **escribir**

adscripción /aðskrip'sion; aðskrip'θion/ *f*, ascription, attribution; appointment

aduana /a'ðuana/ *f*, customs house, customs. **pasar por la a.**, to go through customs

aduanero /aðua'nero/ *a* customs. *m*, customs officer

aducir /aðu'sir; aðu'θir/ *vt irr* to adduce, allege, cite; add. See **conducir**

adueñarse /aðue'ɲarse/ **(de)** *vr* to appropriate, take possession (of)

adulación /aðula'sion; aðula'θion/ *f*, adulation, flattery

adulador /aðula'ðor/ **(-ra)** *a* fawning. *n* flatterer

adular /aðu'lar/ *vt* to flatter, fawn over, adulate

adulonería /aðulone'ria/ *f*, *Lat. Am.* flattery, fawning

adulteración /aðultera'sion; aðultera'θion/ *f*, adulteration; falsification

adulterador /aðultera'ðor/ **(-ra)** *a* adulterant. *n* adulterator; falsifier; coiner

adulterar /aðulte'rar/ *vi* to commit adultery; *vt* adulterate; falsify

adulterino /aðulte'rino/ *a* adulterous; false

adulterio /aðul'terio/ *m*, adultery

adúltero /a'ðultero/ **(-ra)** *a* adulterous; corrupt. *n* adulterer

adulto /a'ðulto/ **(-ta)** *a* and *n* adult

adunar /aðu'nar/ *vt* to join, unite; unify, combine

adusto /a'ðusto/ *a* extremely hot (of climate); grave, austere; standoffish, reserved

advenedizo /aðβene'ðiso; aðβene'ðiθo/ *a* foreign, unknown; upstart; newly rich. *m*, newcomer, social climber; *Lat. Am.* novice, tyro

advenimiento /aðβeni'miento/ *m*, advent, arrival; ascension (to the throne)

advenir /aðβe'nir/ *vi irr* to come, arrive; happen, befall. See **venir**

adventicio /aðβen'tisio; aðβen'tiθio/ *a* casual, accidental; *Bot.* adventitious

adverbio /að'βerβio/ *m*, adverb

adversario /aðβer'sario/ **(-ia)** *n* adversary, rival; opponent

adversidad /aðβersi'ðað/ *f*, adversity, misfortune, sorrow

adverso /að'βerso/ *a* unfavorable, contrary, adverse; opposite

advertencia /aðβer'tensia; aðβer'tenθia/ *f*, warning; introduction, preface; remark

advertido /aðβer'tiðo/ *a* capable, clever; experienced; expert

advertir /aðβer'tir/ *vt irr* to warn; advise; point out, indicate; inform; discover. See **sentir**

adyacencia /aðja'sensia; aðja'θenθia/ *f*, *Argentina* nearness, proximity

adyacente /aðya'sente; aðya'θente/ *a* adjacent, near-by, neighboring

aeración /aera'sion; aera'θion/ *f*, aeration

aéreo /'aereo/ *a* aerial; airborne; airy; air; aeronautic; unsubstantial, fantastic. **correo a.**, airmail. **linea aérea** airline

aerobismo /aero'βismo/ *m*, aerobics

aerodinámica /aeroði'namika/ *f*, aerodynamics

aeromozo, -a /aero'moso; aero'moθo/ *mf*, *Lat. Am.* flight attendant

aeronauta /aero'nauta/ *mf* aeronaut, balloonist

aeronáutica /aero'nautika/ *f*, aeronautics

aeronáutico /aero'nautiko/ *a* aeronautic

aeropuerto /aero'puerto/ *m*, airport

aeróstato /ae'rostato/ *m*, dirigible

afabilidad /afaβili'ðað/ *f*, affability, geniality, friendliness

afable /a'faβle/ *a* affable, genial, pleasant

afamado /afa'maðo/ *a* famous, well-known

afamar /afa'mar/ *vt* to make famous

afán /a'fan/ *m*, effort; manual labor; desire, anxiety. **a. de mando,** thirst for power

afanar /afa'nar/ *vt* to press, urge on; filch; *vr* toil, labor; (*with por*) work hard to, try to

afanoso /afa'noso/ *a* hard, laborious; hard-working, painstaking; eager, anxious

afasia /a'fasia/ *f*, *Med.* aphasia

afear /afe'ar/ *vt* to make ugly; distort, deform; blame; criticize

afección /afek'sion; afek'θion/ *f*, fondness, affection; complaint, ailment, trouble

afectación /afekta'sion; afekta'θion/ *f*, affectation

afectado /afek'taðo/ *a* affected

afectar /afek'tar/ *vt* to feign, assume; affect; move, touch; *Law.* encumber; *Lat. Am.* damage, hurt, injure

afectivo /afek'tiβo/ *a* affective

afecto /a'fekto/ *a* fond, affectionate; *Law.* encumbered; (*with prep a*) addicted to. *m*, emotion, sentiment; affection

afectuosidad /afektuosi'ðað/ *f*, affectionateness

afectuoso /afek'tuoso/ *a* affectionate, fond

afeitada /afei'taða/ *f*, shave, shaving

afeitadora /afeita'ðora/ *f*, razor

afeitar /afei'tar/ *vt* to shave; make up (one's face); adorn, beautify

afeite /a'feite/ *m*, cosmetic; make-up (for the complexion)

afelpado /afel'paðo/ *a* velvet-like, plushy

afeminación /afemina'sion; afemina'θion/ *f*, effeminacy; weakness, languor

afeminado /afemi'naðo/ *a* effeminate

afeminar /afemi'nar/ *vt* to make effeminate; *vr* grow effeminate

aferradamente /aferraða'mente/ *adv* tenaciously, persistently, obstinately

aferramiento /aferra'miento/ *m*, seizing, clutching; *Naut.* furling; *Naut.* grappling; mooring, anchoring; obstinacy

aferrar /afe'rrar/ *vt* to seize, clutch; *Naut.* take in, furl; *Naut.* grapple; *vi Naut.* anchor; *vr* (*with con, en, a*) persist in, insist on

afestonado /afesto'naðo/ *a* festooned

Afganistán /afganis'tan/ Afghanistan

afgano /af'gano/ (**-na**) *a* and *n* Afghan

afianzamiento /afiansa'miento; afianθa'miento/ *m*, fastening, fixing; propping; grasping; guarantee, security

afianzar /afian'sar/ afian'θar/ *vt* to fasten, fix; prop; consolidate (e.g. one's power); guarantee, be security for; grasp

afición /afi'sion; afi'θion/ *f*, propensity, inclination; fondness. **tomar a. (a),** to take a liking to

aficionado /afisio'naðo; afiθio'naðo/ (**-da**) *a* amateur. *n* amateur, fan, enthusiast. **ser a a.,** to be fond of, have a liking for

aficionar /afisio'nar; afiθio'nar/ *vt* to inspire liking or affection; *vr* (*with prep a*) take a liking to, grow fond of; become an enthusiast of

afijo /a'fiho/ *m*, *Gram.* affix

afiladera /afila'ðera/ *f*, whetstone, grindstone

afilado /afi'laðo/ *a* sharp, keen (of edges)

afilador /afila'ðor/ *m*, grinder (of scissors, etc.); razor strop

afilalápices /afila'lapises; afila'lapiθes/ *m*, pencil sharpener

afilar /afi'lar/ *vt* to sharpen; grind, whet; taper; *Lat. Am.* flatter; *Lat. Am.* court, woo; *vr* grow thin; taper

afiliación /afilia'sion; afilia'θion/ *f*, affiliation

afiliar /afi'liar/ *vt* (*with prep a*) to affiliate with; *vr* (*with prep a*) become affiliated with; join, become a member of

afiligranado /afiligra'naðo/ *a* filigree; delicate, fine; slender

afilón /afi'lon/ *m*, steel, knife sharpener; razor-strop

afín /a'fin/ *a* nearby, contiguous; similar, related. *mf* relative by marriage

afinador /afina'ðor/ *m*, tuning key; tuner (of pianos, etc.)

afinar /afi'nar/ *vt* to finish, perfect; *Fig.* polish, refine; tune (musical instruments); refine (metals); *vi* sing in tune; *vr* grow refined

afinidad /afini'ðað/ *f*, affinity, analogy; relationship (by marriage); *Chem.* affinity

afirmación /afirma'sion; afirma'θion/ *f*, affirmation, statement

afirmadamente /afir,maða'mente/ *adv* firmly

afirmar /afir'mar/ *vt* to make firm; fix, fasten; affirm; *vr* steady oneself; hold on to

afirmativa /afirma'tiβa/ *f*, affirmative

afirmativo /afirma'tiβo/ *a* affirmative

aflicción /aflik'sion; aflik'θion/ *f*, affliction, grief

aflictivo /aflik'tiβo/ *a* sorrowful, grievous

afligir /afli'hir/ *vt* to sadden; afflict, trouble; *vr* lament, mourn

aflojamiento /afloha'miento/ *m*, slackening; loosening; diminution

aflojar /aflo'har/ *vt* to slacken; loosen; *vi* relax, weaken; abate, diminish. **a. el paso,** to slow down

afluencia /a'fluensia; a'fluenθia/ *f*, crowd, concourse; eloquence, fluency

afluente /a'fluente/ *a* fluent, eloquent. *m*, tributary (river)

afluir /aflu'ir/ *vi irr* to crowd, swarm; flow (into). See **huir**

afonía /afo'nia/ *f*, *Med.* aphonia, loss of voice; hoarseness

afónico /a'foniko/ *a* hoarse

aforismo /afo'rismo/ *m*, aphorism

aforrador /aforra'ðor/ (**-ra**) *n* one who lines jackets, etc.

aforrar /afo'rrar/ *vt* to line (clothes, etc.); *vr* wrap oneself up; *Inf.* gormandize

afortunadamente /afortu,naða'mente/ *adv* luckily, fortunately

afortunado /afortu'naðo/ *a* lucky, fortunate; happy; stormy

afortunar /afortu'nar/ *vt* to bring luck to, make happy

afrancesado /afranse'saðo; afranθe'saðo/ (**-da**) *a* Francophile; Frenchified. *n* Francophile

afrancesamiento /afransesa'miento; afranθesa'miento/ *m*, adoption of the French way of life; servile imitation of everything French

afrancesar /afranse'sar; afranθe'sar/ *vt* to make French, gallicize; Frenchify; *vr* become a Francophile

afrenta /a'frenta/ *f*, insult, affront; disgrace

afrentar /afren'tar/ *vt* to insult; *vr* be ashamed

afrentoso /afren'toso/ *a* insulting, outrageous; disgraceful

África /'afrika/ Africa

africanismo /,afrikan'ismo/ *m*, Africanism

africano /afri'kano/ **-na** *a* and *n* African

afroamericano /afroameri'kano/ (**-na**) *a* and *n* African-American

afrodisíaco /afroði'siako/ *a* and *m*, aphrodisiac

afrontar /afron'tar/ *vt* to place opposite; confront; face (danger, etc.)

afuera /a'fuera/ *adv* outside, out

afueras /a'fueras/ *f pl*, suburbs, outskirts

afusilar /afusi'lar/ *vt*, *Lat. Am.* to shoot

agachada /aga't∫aða/ *f*, crouch, duck; jerk

agachar /aga't∫ar/ *vt Inf.* bend, bow; *vr Inf.* crouch down; lie low, hide

agalla /a'gaʎa/ *f*, *a* ga'ʎa/ *f*, oak-apple; tonsil (gen. *pl*); *Zool.* gill; *Inf.* gall, cheek

agalludo, -a /aga'juðo; aga'ʎuðo/ *a*, *Argentina* mean, stingy, tight; bold, daring

ágape /'agape/ *m*, agape; banquet, feast

Agar /a'gar/ Hagar

agárico /a'gariko/ *m*, *Bot.* agaric

agarrada /aga'rraða/ *f*, *Inf.* brawl, scuffle

agarradero /agarra'ðero/ *m*, handle; heft; *Inf.* influence, pull

agarrado /aga'rraðo/ *a Inf.* tight-fisted, mean

agarrar /aga'rrar/ vt to grip, grasp; seize, take; *Inf.* nab (jobs); vr grip, hold on

agarro /a'garro/ m, hold; grip, grasp

agarrotar /agarro'tar/ vt to garrotte; tighten (ropes, etc.); press, squeeze; vr (limbs) go numb

agasajar /agasa'har/ vt to indulge, spoil, pet; receive kindly; entertain; caress

agasajo /aga'saho/ m, indulgence, kindness; affability, geniality; entertainment; gift, offering

agauchado /agau'tʃaðo/ a gaucho-like

agazapar /agasa'par; agaθa'par/ vt *Inf.* to nab, catch; vr *Inf.* squat, crouch

agencia /a'hensia; a'henθia/ f, influence, agency

agenciar /ahen'siar; ahen'θiar/ vt to negotiate, arrange; procure, manage

agenda /a'henda/ f, notebook; agenda

agente /a'hente/ m, agent. **a. de bolsa** or **a. de cambio**, bill broker. **a. de negocios**, business agent. **a. de policía**, police officer. **a. fiscal**, revenue officer

agestado /ahes'taðo/ a used generally with advs. **bien** or **mal**, well or ill-featured

agigantado /ahigan'taðo/ a enormous, gigantic; outstanding, extraordinary

ágil /'ahil/ a agile, nimble; easy to use (e.g. un libro ágil, a book easy to use)

agilidad /ahili'ðað/ f, agility, nimbleness

agilizar /ahili'sar; ahili'θar/ vt to make agile, limber; refresh one's knowledge of (e.g. Quiero agilizar mi español, I want to refresh my knowledge of Spanish); to enable; vr limber up

agitación /ahita'sion; ahita'θion/ f, shaking; agitation, excitement

agitador /ahita'ðor/ (-ra) a stirring; agitating. n agitator. m, stirrer, stirring rod

agitar /ahi'tar/ vt to stir; shake; agitate, excite. **a. una cuestión**, raise a question; discuss a question

aglomeración /aglomera'sion; aglomera'θion/ f, agglomeration

aglomerar /aglome'rar/ vt to agglomerate, amass

aglutinación /aglutina'sion; aglutina'θion/ f, agglutination

aglutinar(se) /agluti'nar se/ vt and vr to stick, agglutinate

agnóstico /ag'nostiko/ (-ca) a and n agnostic

agobiar /ago'βiar/ vt to bow, bend down; *Fig.* weigh down, oppress; overwhelm; vr bend (beneath a weight)

agobio /a'goβio/ m, bowing, bending down; oppression, burden, weight

agolparse /agol'parse/ vr to rush, crowd, swarm

agonía /ago'nia/ f, agony, anguish

agonizante /agoni'sante; agoni'θante/ a dying

agonizar /agoni'sar; agoni'θar/ vt to attend a dying person; *Inf.* pester, annoy; vi be dying (gen. **estar agonizando**)

agorar /ago'rar/ vt to prophesy, foretell

agorero /ago'rero/ (-ra) a prophetic; ill-boding. n seer, augur

agostarse /agos'tarse/ vt and vr to dry up, shrivel

agosto /a'gosto/ m, August; harvest. *Inf.* hacer su a., to make hay while the sun shines

agotable /ago'taβle/ a exhaustible

agotado /ago'taðo/ a exhausted; out of print (of books)

agotador /agota'ðor/ a exhausting; exhaustive

agotamiento /a,gota'miento/ m, exhaustion

agotar /ago'tar/ vt to drain off (water); empty (a glass); exhaust; run through (money); study thoroughly, examine closely (a subject)

agraciado /agra'siaðo; agra'θiaðo/ a graceful; pretty

agraciar /agra'siar; agra'θiar/ vt to lend grace to; make pretty; favor

agradable /agra'ðaβle/ a agreeable, pleasant

agradar /agra'ðar/ vi to be pleasing, like, please (e.g. Me agrada su sinceridad, I like his sincerity)

agradecer /agraðe'ser; agraðe'θer/ vt irr to be grateful for; thank for; *Fig.* repay, requite. See **conocer**

agradecido /agraðe'siðo; agraðe'θiðo/ a grateful; thankful

agradecimiento /agraðesi'miento; agraðeθi'miento/ m, gratitude; thankfulness

agrado /a'graðo/ m, pleasure; desire; liking; amiability, affability

agrandar /agran'dar/ vt to enlarge

agrario /a'grario/ a agrarian

agrarismo /agra'rismo/ m, *Mexico* farmers' movement, peasant movement

agravación /agraβa'sion; agraβa'θion/ f, **agravamiento** m, aggravation, worsening

agravador /agraβa'ðor/ a aggravating; worsening; increasing

agravar /agra'βar/ vt to aggravate, increase; oppress (taxes, responsibilities); make worse; exaggerate; vr grow worse

agraviador /agraβia'ðor/ **-ra** a offensive. n offender

agraviar /agra'βiar/ vt to offend; wrong; vr take offense, be insulted

agravio /a'graβio/ m, offense, insult; wrong, injury

agraz /a'gras; a'graθ/ m, unripened grape; verjuice; *Fig.* bitterness

agredir /agre'ðir/ vt to attack; assault

agregación /agrega'sion; agrega'θion/ f, association, aggregation; total, collection, aggregate

agregado /agre'gaðo/ m, aggregate; assistant; attaché; *Lat. Am.* sharecropper

agregar /agre'gar/ vt to add; collect, amass; appoint (to a post). **agregarse a...**, to join... (e.g. an association)

agresión /agre'sion/ f, aggression

agresivo /agre'siβo/ a aggressive

agresor /agre'sor/ **(-ra)** a and n aggressor

agreste /a'greste/ a rural, rustic; wild; uncouth, rude

agriar /a'griar/ vt to make bitter or sour; exasperate, provoke

agrícola /a'grikola/ a agricultural; mf agriculturalist, farmer

agricultura /agrikul'tura/ f, agriculture

agridulce /agri'ðulse; agri'ðulθe/ a bitter-sweet

agrietarse /agrie'tarse/ vr to crack, split

agrimensor /agrimen'sor/ m, surveyor

agrimensura /agrimen'sura/ f, surveying

agrio /a'grio/ a bitter, sour; rough, uneven (ground); brittle; sharp (of color contrast); unsociable; disagreeable

agriparse /agri'parse/ vr to catch a cold, come down with a cold

agronomía /agrono'mia/ f, agronomy

agrónomo /a'gronomo/ a agronomic. m, agronomist

agrupación /agrupa'sion; agrupa'θion/ f, congregation, assembly; group; crowd; crowding, grouping

agrupar /agru'par/ vt to assemble, group; vr crowd, cluster

agrura /a'grura/ f, bitterness; sourness; asperity

agua /'agua/ f, water; rain; slope of a roof; pl shot or watered effect on silks, etc.; medicinal waters; waves; water (of precious stones). **a. abajo**, down-stream. **a. arriba**, upstream. **a. bendita**, holy water. **a. cruda**, hard water. **a. de colonia**, eau de Cologne. **a. dulce**, fresh water. **a. fresca**, cold water. **a. nieve**, sleet. **a. oxigenada**, hydrogen peroxide. *Fig. Inf.* estar con el **a. al cuello**, to be in low water. *Fig. Inf.* estar entre **dos aguas**, to be between two fires. *Naut.* hacer **a.**, to leak. **Todo eso es ya a. pasada**, That's all water under the bridge

aguacate /agua'kate/ m, avocado

aguacero /agua'sero; agua'θero/ m, heavy rainfall, shower

aguada /a'guaða/ f, water supply on board ship; flood (in mines); watering station; *Art.* water color

aguadero /agua'ðero/ m, (animals') watering place

aguado /a'guaðo/ a watery; abstemious; watered

aguador /agua'ðor/ **(-ra)** n water carrier, water seller; drawer (of water)

aguafiestas /,agua'fiestas/ mf *fig inf* wet blanket

aguafuerte /,agua'fuerte/ f, etching

aguaje /a'guahe/ m, tide, waves; sea current; water supply (on board ship); wake (of a ship)

aguamanil /aguama'nil/ m, washstand; pitcher, ewer

aguamanos /agua'manos/ *m*, water for washing hands; pitcher

aguamarina /aguama'rina/ *f*, aquamarine

aguamiel /agua'miel/ *f*, honey and water, hydromel

aguantable /aguan'taβle/ *a* tolerable, bearable

aguantar /aguan'tar/ *vt* to bear, tolerate, endure; restrain, resist, oppose; *vr* bear in silence, keep quiet

aguante /a'guante/ *m*, patience, endurance; resistance

aguar /a'guar/ *vt* to water down (wine, etc.); spoil (fun, etc.); *vr* be filled with water; be flooded; become watery or thin

aguardar /aguar'ðar/ *vt* to await; expect; allow time to (debtors)

aguardentería /aguar,ðente'ria/ *f*, liquor shop

aguardentoso /aguarðen'toso/ *a* spirituous, containing **aguardiente** hoarse, husky (of the voice)

aguardiente /aguar'ðiente/ *m*, liquor. **a. de caña,** rum

aguarrás /agua'rras/ *m*, oil of turpentine

aguatinta /agua'tinta/ *f*, aquatint

aguatocha /agua'totʃa/ *f*, pump (for water, etc.)

aguaturma /agua'turma/ *f*, Jerusalem artichoke

agudeza /agu'ðesa; agu'ðeθa/ *f*, sharpness; keenness; distinctness; alertness, cleverness; witty sally, repartee; wit; swiftness

agudo /a'guðo/ *a* sharp; alert, clever; (*Geom. Med.*) acute; fine, keen; rapid; high-pitched; strong (of scents, etc.)

agüero /a'guero/ *m*, omen, sign; prophecy, prediction

aguerrido /age'rriðo/ *a* veteran, war-hardened

aguerrir /age'rrir/ *vt defective* to harden to war; toughen

aguijada /agi'haða/ *f*, goad, spur

aguijar /agi'har/ *vt* to prick (with a goad); urge on, encourage (animals); incite, instigate; spur on; *vi* walk swiftly

aguijón /agi'hon/ *m*, goad; sting; thorn, prickle; spur; incitement, stimulus. **tener aguijones,** to be on pins and needles

aguijonazo /agiho'naso; agiho'naθo/ *m*, prick (with a goad)

águila /'agila/ *f*, eagle; master mind. **a. caudal** *or* **a. real,** royal eagle. **á. o sol,** *Mexico* heads or tails

aguileña /agi'leɲa/ *f*, *Bot.* columbine

aguileño /agi'leɲo/ *a* aquiline

aguilón /agi'lon/ *m*, *Archit.* gable; boom (of a crane)

aguinaldo /agi'naldo/ *m*, Christmas present; New Year's gift

aguja /a'guha/ *f*, needle; hand, pointer; hatpin; engraver's burin; switch; *Rail.* point; *Rail.* rail; obelisk; spire; bodkin; knitting needle; crochet hook; (compass) needle. *pl Bot.* plumelet. **a. capotera, a. de zurcir,** darning needle. **a. de marear** *Naut.,* binnacle; mariner's compass. **a. de media,** knitting needle. **a. espartera,** packing needle

agujerear /aguhere'ar/ *vt* to perforate, make holes in

agujero /agu'hero/ *m*, hole, aperture; needle maker or seller; needle case

agujeta /agu'heta/ *f*, lace (for shoes, etc.); *pl* muscular pains, aches; tip, gratuity

agusanarse /agusa'narse/ *vr* to become worm-infested

aguzadura /agusa'ðura; aguθa'ðura/ *f*, sharpening, grinding, whetting

aguzar /agu'sar; agu'θar/ *vt* to sharpen; grind, whet; stimulate, encourage; urge on, incite

ahechadura /aetʃa'ðura/ *f*, chaff (of grain)

ahembrado /aem'braðo/ *a* effeminate

aherrojar /aerro'har/ *vt* to put (a prisoner) in irons; oppress

aherrumbrar /aerrum'brar/ *vt* to give the color or taste of iron to; *vr* taste or look like iron; get rusty; rust

ahí /a'i/ *adv* there; over there. **de a.,** thus, so. **por a.,** somewhere about, near at hand.

ahidalgado /aiðal'gaðo/ *a* gentlemanly; noble, generous

ahijado /ai'haðo/ **(-da)** *n* godchild; protégé

ahijar /ai'har/ *vt* to adopt (children); mother (animals); attribute, impute; *vi* bring forth offspring; *Bot.* sprout. See **prohibir**

ahincado /ain'kaðo/ *a* earnest, eager

ahincar /ain'kar/ *vt* to urge, press; *vr* hurry, hasten. See **prohibir**

ahínco /a'inko/ *m*, earnestness, eagerness

ahitar /ai'tar/ *vt* to stuff with food; bore, disgust. See **prohibir**

ahíto /a'ito/ *a* full of food; *Fig.* fed up. *m*, indigestion

ahogado /ao'gaðo/ **(-da)** *a* drowned; suffocated; stuffy, unventilated; stifling. *n* drowned person; victim of suffocation

ahogamiento /aoga'miento/ *m*, drowning; suffocation

ahogar /ao'gar/ *vt* to drown; suffocate; put out (the fire); stifle (yawns, etc.); suppress, extinguish; tire; overwater (plants); *vr Naut.* sink, founder; drown; suffocate

ahogo /a'ogo/ *m*, anxiety, grief; difficulty in breathing, oppression; asthma; embarrassment; suffocation; straitened circumstances

ahondamiento /aonda'miento/ *m*, in-depth treatment (e.g. *el a. de un problema,* in-depth treatment of a problem)

ahondar /aon'dar/ *vt* to deepen; excavate, dig; go into thoroughly; go deep into, penetrate; *vr* (earth) subside

ahora /a'ora/ *adv* now; very soon; just now, a short time ago. *conjunc* whether; now. **a. bien,** well now, given that. **a. mismo,** immediately, at once. **por a.,** for the present

ahorcado /aor'kaðo/ **(-da)** *n* hanged man

ahorcar /aor'kar/ *vt* to execute by hanging, hang. *Inf.* **a. los hábitos,** to leave the priesthood, cease to be an ecclesiastic

ahorita /ao'rita/ *adv*, *Mexico* right away, right now; *elsewhere in Lat. Am.* in a little while

ahormar /aor'mar/ *vt* to adjust, shape; break in (new shoes); make (a person) see reason

ahorrar /ao'rrar/ *vt* to save, economize; avoid, eschew; *vr* avoid; remove clothing

ahorro /a'orro/ *m*, economy, thrift; *pl* savings

ahuchar /au'tʃar/ *vt* to hoard; expel, drive away

ahuciar /au'siar; au'θiar/ *vt* take possession of (a house)

ahuecar /aue'kar/ *vt* to hollow out; loosen; shake out; puff out, inflate; put on a solemn voice; hoe, dig; *Inf. vr* puff oneself out; put on airs

ahumada /au'maða/ *f*, smoke signal

ahumado /au'maðo/ *a* smoked; smoky

ahumar /au'mar/ *vt* to smoke (herrings, etc.); fill with smoke; *vi* smoke, burn; *vr* be full of smoke; taste smoked; *Inf.* get drunk. See **desahuciar**

ahusado /au'saðo/ *a* spindle-shaped

ahuyentar /auyen'tar/ *vt* to frighten off; drive away; dismiss, banish (anxiety, etc.); *vr* flee

airadamente /airaða'mente/ *adv* wrathfully, angrily

airado /ai'raðo/ *a* angry

airar /ai'rar/ *vt* to annoy, anger; *vr* grow annoyed

aire /'aire/ *m*, air; atmosphere (sometimes *pl*); breeze, wind; bearing, appearance; vanity; (horse's) gait; futility, frivolity; grace, charm; gracefulness; *Mus.* air; *Mus.* tempo. **a. popular,** popular tune. **al a. libre,** in the open air, outdoors. *Inf.* **beber los aires (por),** to yearn (for)

aireación /airea'sion; airea'θion/ *f*, airing; ventilation

airear /aire'ar/ *vt* to air; ventilate; aerate; *vr* take the air; catch a chill

airecito /aire'sito; aire'θito/ *m*, *Lat. Am.* breeze, gentle wind

airosidad /airosi'ðað/ *f*, gracefulness; jauntiness

airoso /ai'roso/ *a* airy, open; windy, breezy, fresh; graceful; handsome; jaunty; victorious, successful

aislacionamismo /aislasiona'mismo; aisla-θiona'mismo/ *m*, *Polit.* isolationism

aislacionista /aislasion'ista; aislaθion'ista/ *mf Polit.* isolationist

aislado /ais'laðo/ *a* isolated; remote; individual; single; *Elec.* insulated

aislador /aisla'ðor/ *m*, *Phys*. insulator
aislamiento /aisla'miento/ *m*, isolation; *Phys*. insulation
aislante /ais'lante/ *a* isolating; insulating
aislar /ais'lar/ *vt* to isolate; *Elec*. insulate; *vr* become a recluse; become isolated
¡ajá! /a'ha/ *interj Inf*. Aha! Good!
ajar /a'har/ *vt* to crease, crumple, spoil; humiliate; *vr* fade, wither (flowers)
ajedrecista /aheðre'sista; aheðre'θista/ *mf* chess player
ajedrez /ahe'ðres; ahe'ðreθ/ *m*, chess
ajenjo /a'henho/ *m*, *Bot*. wormwood; absinthe
ajeno /a'heno/ *a* alien; belonging to another; various, diverse; free, exempt; unsuitable; irrelevant
ajetrear /ahetre'ar/ *vt* to tire out, exhaust; *vr* be over-tired
ajetreo /ahe'treo/ *m*, exhaustion, fatigue
ají /a'hi/ *m*, *Lat. Am*. chili, red pepper; chili sauce; **estar hecho un ají** to be hopping mad, be fuming
ajo /'aho/ *m*, garlic; *Inf*. make up, paint; disreputable affair, shady business; curse, oath. *Inf*. **revolver el a.,** to stir up trouble
ajorca /a'horka/ *f*, bracelet; slave bangle
ajornalar /ahorna'lar/ *vt* to hire by the day
ajuar /ahu'ar/ *m*, trousseau; household equipment
ajustado /ahus'taðo/ *a* exact; tight-fitting; trim
ajustador /ahusta'ðor/ **(-ra)** *a* adjusting. *n* adjuster. *m*, tight-fitting jacket
ajustamiento /ahusta'miento/ *m*, adjustment; agreement
ajustar /ahus'tar/ *vt* to adjust; fit; arrange; make an agreement about; reconcile; settle (accounts); engage, employ; retain (a barrister); regulate; tune up (a motor); *vi* fit; *vr* adapt oneself. *Inf*. **a. cuentas viejas,** to settle old accounts
ajuste /a'huste/ *m*, fitting; adjustment; agreement; arrangement; *Print*. make-up; reconciliation; settlement; regulation; engagement, appointment
ajusticiado /ahusti'siaðo; ahusti'θiaðo/ **(-da)** *n* executed person
ajusticiar /ahusti'siar; ahusti'θiar/ *vt* to put to death
al /al/ (contraction of *a* + *el*). 1. *prep a* + *m. def. art.*, to the, e.g. *Han ido al mar,* They have gone to the sea. 2. *prep a* + *el* used as *dem. pron* to that, to the one, e.g. *Mi sombrero se parece mucho al que tiene Vd.,* My hat is very similar to the one you have. *al* + *infin.* means when, as, at the same time as, e.g. *Al llamar a la puerta la vi en el jardín,* As I was knocking at the door, I saw her in the garden
ala /'ala/ *f*, *Zool*. wing; row, line; brim (of a hat); eaves; (*Archit. Aer. Mil. Bot.*) wing; blade (of propeller); fin (of fish); *pl* courage. **a. del corazón,** *Anat*. auricle. **arrastrar el a.,** to woo, flirt with. *Fig*. **cortar** (*or* **quebrar) las alas (a),** to clip a person's wings
alabador /alaβa'ðor/ **(-ra)** *n* praiser, extoller
alabanza /ala'βansa; ala'βanθa/ *f*, praise; eulogy
alabar /ala'βar/ *vt* to praise; *vr* brag, boast
alabastrino /alaβas'trino/ *a* alabastrine, alabaster
alabastro /ala'βastro/ *m*, alabaster
alacena /ala'sena; ala'θena/ *f*, cupboard; recess; closet; safe (for food)
alacrán /ala'kran/ *m*, scorpion
alacre /a'lakre/ *a*, *Mexico* agile, nimble
alacridad /alakri'ðað/ *f*, alacrity, eagerness; *Mexico* agility, nimbleness
alado /a'laðo/ *a* winged; feathered; *Fig*. soaring
alambicado /alambi'kaðo/ *a* sparing, frugal; subtle; euphuistic
alambicar /alambi'kar/ *vt* to distill; examine carefully, scrutinize; make over-subtle or euphuistic (of style)
alambique /alam'bike/ *m*, still
alambrada /alam'braða/ *f*, *Mil*. wire-entanglement
alambrado /alam'braðo/ *m*, wire-netting; *Mil*. wire-entanglement; wire cover
alambrar /alam'brar/ *vt* to wire (fence)
alambre /a'lambre/ *m*, wire; sheep bells. **a. espinoso,** barbed wire

alambrera /alam'brera/ *f*, wire fence; wire-netting; wire cover
alambrista /alam'brista/ *mf* tight-rope walker; (Mexico) wetback
alameda /ala'meða/ *f*, poplar wood or grove; avenue of poplars
álamo /'alamo/ *m*, poplar. **a. temblón,** aspen tree
alano /a'lano/ *m*, mastiff
alarde /a'larðe/ *m*, *Mil*. parade; display, ostentation. **hacer a. de,** to brag about
alargamiento /alarga'miento/ *m*, lengthening; stretching
alargar /alar'gar/ *vt* to lengthen; prolong; pass, hand (things); pay out (ropes, etc.); increase; *vr* go away, depart; be wordy, spread oneself; lengthen
alarido /ala'riðo/ *m*, yell, shout; shriek, scream; howl; yelp; cry (of a seagull)
alarma /a'larma/ *f*, alarm. **a. aérea,** air-raid warning
alarmante /alar'mante/ *a* alarming
alarmar /alar'mar/ *vt* to give the alarm; frighten; *vr* be alarmed
alarmista /alar'mista/ *mf* alarmist
alazán /ala'san; ala'θan/ *a* sorrel-colored. *m*, sorrel horse
alazo /a'laso; a'laθo/ *m*, flap or stroke of the wings
alba /'alβa/ *f*, dawn; *Eccl*. alb, vestment. **al a.,** at dawn
albacea /alβa'sea; alβa'θea/ *mf* executor, executrix; testator
albanés /alβa'nes/ **(-esa)** *a* and *n* Albanian. *m*, Albanian language
albañil /alβa'ɲil/ *m*, mason, bricklayer
albañilería /alβaɲile'ria/ *f*, masonry; bricklaying
albarda /al'βarða/ *f*, pack-saddle; *Lat. Am*. saddle
albardilla /alβar'ðiya; alβar'ðiʎa/ *f*, small saddle; pad; small pillow; *Archit*. coping
albaricoque /alβari'koke/ *m*, apricot
albaricoquero /alβariko'kero/ *m*, apricot tree
albarrada /alβa'rraða/ *f*, stone wall; mud fence
albatros /alβa'tros/ *m*, albatross
albear /alβe'ar/ *vi* to become white, whiten
albedrío /alβe'ðrio/ *m*, free will; fancy, caprice
albéitar /al'βeitar/ *m*, veterinary surgeon; farrier
alberca /al'βerka/ *f*, reservoir, tank; vat; artificial lake; *Lat. Am*. (swimming) pool
albergar /alβer'gar/ *vt* to shelter; nourish, harbor; *vi* and *vr* take refuge or shelter; lodge
albergue /al'βerge/ *m*, shelter, refuge; den, lair; hospitality; lodging; asylum
albo /'alβo/ *a* pure white
albóndiga /al'βondiga/ *f*, meat ball, rissole
albor /al'βor/ *m*, whiteness; dawnlight, dawn. **a. de la vida,** life's dawning, childhood
alborada /alβo'raða/ *f*, dawn; reveille; *Mil*. dawn attack; *Mus*. aubade
alborear /alβore'ar/ *vi* to grow light, dawn
albornoz /alβor'nos; alβor'noθ/ *m*, burnouse
alborotado /alβoro'taðo/ *a* impulsive; turbulent; noisy; excitable
alborotar /alβoro'tar/ *vt* to disturb; *vi* make a noise; be gay; *vr* riot; grow rough (sea)
alboroto /alβo'roto/ *m*, noise; confusion; tumult; riot; rejoicing, gaiety
alborotos /alβo'rotos/ *mpl*, *Argentina, Central America, Peru* popcorn
alborozar /alβoro'sar; alβoro'θar/ *vt* to overjoy, gladden; *vr* rejoice, be glad
alborozo /alβo'roso; alβo'roθo/ *m*, gladness, rejoicing, joy
albricias /al'βrisias; al'βriθias/ *f pl*, reward for bringer of good tidings. *interj* **¡A.!** Joy! Congratulations!
álbum /'alβum/ *m*, album
albúmina /al'βumina/ *f*, albumin
albur /al'βur/ *m*, *Ichth*. dace; chance, risk. **al a. de,** at the risk of
alcachofa /alka'tʃofa/ *f*, artichoke
alcahuete /alka'uete/ *m*, procurer, go-between, pimp, pander; *Fig. Inf*. protector, screen; *Inf*. scandalmonger
alcahuetear /alkauete'ar/ *vt* to procure, act as a go-between for; *vi* be a pimp or a procuress

alcaide /al'kaiðe/ *m*, governor of a fortress *Obs.*; governor of a prison

alcalde /al'kalde/ (**-desa**) *n* mayor; magistrate. *Inf.* **tener el padre a.**, to have a friend at court

alcaldía /alkal'dia/ *f*, office or authority of an alcalde

álcali /'alkali/ *m*, *Chem.* alkali

alcalino /alka'lino/ *a* alkaline

alcance /al'kanse; al'kanθe/ *m*, reach, reaching, attainment; range (of firearms, etc.); scope; arm's length or reach; pursuit; stop press *or* extra edition (newspapers); *Com.* deficit; importance; *pl* talent; capacity. **al a. de la voz**, within call. **hombre de cortos alcances**, a limited, dull man. **poner al a. de**, to make available to; make intelligible to

alcancía /alkan'sia; alkan'θia/ *f*, money-box; coin bank, piggy bank

alcanfor /alkan'for/ *m*, camphor

alcantarilla /alkanta'riya; alkanta'riʎa/ *f*, little bridge; sewer; culvert; bed for electric cable

alcantarillado /alkantari'yaðo; alkantari'ʎaðo/ *m*, sewage system; main sewer

alcanzable /alkan'saβle; alkan'θaβle/ *a* obtainable; attainable

alcanzadizo /alkansa'ðiso; alkanθa'ðiθo/ *a* attainable, easily reached

alcanzar /alkan'sar; alkan'θar/ *vt* to overtake; reach; range (of guns, etc.); attain, achieve; understand; *Fig.* equal (in attainments); live at the same time as, be contemporaneous with; be capable of, be able; *vi* reach; share, participate in; be enough

alcaparra /alka'parra/ *f*, *Bot.* caper; caper bush

alcaucil /alkau'sil; alkau'θil/ *m*, (in most places) wild artichoke; (in some places) cultivated artichoke

alcazaba /alka'saβa; alka'θaβa/ *f*, fortress (within a walled town or city), casbah

alcázar /al'kasar; al'kaθar/ *m*, fortress; royal residence, castle; *Naut.* quarterdeck

alción /al'sion; al'θion/ *m*, *Ornith.* kingfisher

alcista /al'sista; al'θista/ *mf* speculator (on Stock Exchange)

alcoba /al'koβa/ *f*, bedroom; alcove, recess; Moorish flute

alcohol /al'kool/ *m*, alcohol; spirits of wine. **a. desnaturalizado**, industrial alcohol, methylated spirit. **a. metílico**, wood alcohol

alcohólico /alko'oliko/ *a* alcoholic

alcoholismo /alkool'ismo/ *m*, alcoholism

Alcorán /alko'ran/ *m*, Koran

alcornoque /alkor'noke/ *m*, cork tree; dolt

alcorzar /alkor'sar; alkor'θar/ *vt Cul.* to ice, cover with sugar; decorate; adorn

alcurnia /al'kurnia/ *f*, lineage, family, descent

alcuza /al'kusa; al'kuθa/ *f*, oil-bottle; oil-can; cruet

aldaba /al'daβa/ *f*, door knocker; bolt, latch; *pl* protectors, influential helpers. *Inf.* **tener buenas aldabas**, to have plenty of pull

aldabada /alda'βaða/ *f*, rap with the knocker; sudden shock

aldabeo /alda'βeo/ *m*, knocking

aldea /al'dea/ *f*, village

aldeano /alde'ano/ (**-na**) *a* village; country, ignorant. *n* villager; countryman, peasant

aldehído /alde'iðo/ *m*, *Chem.* aldehyde

aleación /alea'sion; alea'θion/ *f*, alloy

alear /ale'ar/ *vi* to flutter, beat the wings; flap one's arms; recuperate, grow well; *vt* alloy

aleatorio /alea'torio/ *a* accidental, fortuitous

aleccionamiento /aleksiona'miento; alekθiona'miento/ *m*, teaching, training, coaching

aleccionar /aleksio'nar; alekθio'nar/ *vt* to teach, train, coach

aledaño /ale'ðaɲo/ *a* adjoining; border. *m*, boundary, border

alegación /alega'sion; alega'θion/ *f*, allegation, statement

alegar /ale'gar/ *vt* to allege, state; cite; *vi Law.* bring forward, adduce

alegato /ale'gato/ *m*, *Law.* speech (for the prosecution or defense)

alegoría /alego'ria/ *f*, allegory

alegórico /ale'goriko/ *a* allegorical

alegorizar /alegori'sar; alegori'θar/ *vt* to interpret allegorically, treat as an allegory

alegrar /ale'grar/ *vt* to make happy, gladden, rejoice; adorn, beautify; stir (fires); *vr* be glad, rejoice; *Inf.* be merry (tipsy)

alegre /a'legre/ *a* joyful, glad; cheerful, gay; bright (colors, etc.); pretty, attractive; *Inf.* risqué; *Inf.* flirtatious, light

alegría /ale'gria/ *f*, joy, gladness; cheerfulness, gaiety; *pl* public rejoicings

alegrón /ale'gron/ *m*, sudden unexpected joy; *Inf.* flash of light. *a Inf.* flirtatious

alejamiento /aleha'miento/ *m*, placing at a distance, removal; withdrawal

Alejandría /alehan'dria/ Alexandria

alejar /ale'har/ *vt* to place at a distance, remove; withdraw; ward off (dangers, etc.); *vr* depart, go away; withdraw. **alejarse de**, to abandon (a belief, custom, superstition, etc.)

alelar /ale'lar/ *vt* to make silly or stupid

aleluya /ale'luya/ *mf*, alleluia. *m*, Eastertide. *f*, small Easter cake; *Inf.* daub, poor painting; *Inf.* doggerel; joy, rejoicing

alemán /ale'man/ (**-ana**) *a* and *n* German. *m*, German language.

Alemania /ale'mania/ Germany

alentada /alen'taða/ *f*, deep breath

alentado /alen'taðo/ *a* valiant, spirited; proud; *Argentina* strong, vigorous

alentador /alenta'ðor/ *a* encouraging, inspiring, stimulating

alentar /alen'tar/ *vi irr* to breathe; *vt* encourage, inspire; *vr* be encouraged. See **sentar**

alerce /a'lerse; a'lerθe/ *m*, larch tree and wood

alergia /a'ler'hia/ *f*, allergy

alergólogo /aler'gologo/ *m*, allergist

alero /a'lero/ *m*, projecting roof; splashboard (of carriages); eaves; gable end

alerón /ale'ron/ *m*, *Aer.* aileron

alerta /a'lerta/ *adv* watchfully. *interj* Take care! Look out! **estar ojo a.**, to be on the watch

alerto /a'lerto/ *a* watchful, alert

aleta /a'leta/ *f*, *dim* small wing; fin

aletargado /aletar'gaðo/ *a* lethargic; comatose

aletargamiento /aletarga'miento/ *m*, lethargy

aletargar /aletar'gar/ *vt* to cause lethargy; *vr* become lethargic

aletazo /ale'taso; ale'taθo/ *m*, flapping, beating (of wings); *Inf.* theft

aletear /alete'ar/ *vi* to flap the wings, flutter; move the arms up and down; become convalescent

aleteo /ale'teo/ *m*, fluttering, flapping of wings; beating, palpitation (of heart)

aleve /a'leβe/ *a* See **alevoso**

alevosía /aleβo'sia/ *f*, *Law.* malice; treachery

alevoso /ale'βoso/ *a Law.* malicious; treacherous

alfabético /alfa'βetiko/ *a* alphabetical

alfabetización /alfaβetisa'sion; alfaβetiθa'θion/ *f*, literacy work

alfabetizador /alfaβetisa'ðor; alfaβetiθa'ðor/ *m*, literacy worker

alfabeto /alfa'βeto/ *m*, alphabet. **a. manual**, sign language

alfalfa /al'falfa/ *f*, *Bot.* alfalfa, lucerne

alfandoque /alfan'doke/ *m*, *Lat. Am.* cheesecake; maraca

alfanje /al'fanhe/ *m* cutlass; *Mexico* machete

alfar /al'far/ *m*, potter's workshop; pottery, earthenware

alfarería /alfare'ria/ *f*, pottery making; potter's workshop; potter's craft

alfarero /alfa'rero/ *m*, potter

alfeñique /alfe'ɲike/ *m*, *Cul.* icing, sugarpaste; *Inf.* affectation

alférez /al'feres; al'fereθ/ *m*, *Mil.* ensign; second lieutenant; lieutenant. *Nav.* **a. de fragata**, sub-lieutenant. *Nav.* **a. de navío**, lieutenant

alfil /al'fil/ *m*, bishop (in chess)

alfiler /alfi'ler/ *m*, pin; brooch with a pin; tiepin; *pl* pin-money, dress-allowance; *Fig. Inf.* **no estar uno con sus alfileres,** to have a slate loose. *Inf.* **vestido de veinticinco alfileres,** dressed to the nines

alfiletero /alfile'tero/ *m,* needle-case

alfombra /al'fombra/ *f,* carpet; rug

alfombrado /alfom'braðo/ *m,* carpeting

alfombrar /alfom'brar/ *vt* to carpet

alfombrilla eléctrica /alfom'briya e'lektrika; alfom'briʎa e'lektrika/ *f,* electric pad or blanket

alfombrista /alfom'brista/ *m,* carpet merchant; layer of carpets

alforja /al'forha/ *f,* saddle-bag; *Mil.* knapsack

alforza /al'forsa; al'forθa/ *f, Sew.* tuck; *Inf.* scar

alforzar /alfor'sar; alfor'θar/ *vt Sew.* to tuck

alga /'alga/ *f,* alga, seaweed

algarabía /algara'βia/ *f,* Arabic; *Inf.* gibberish; din of voices, uproar

algarada /alga'raða/ *f,* troop of horse; uproar, hubbub; outcry

algarroba /alga'rroβa/ *f, Bot.* carob bean

algazara /alga'sara; alga'θara/ *f,* Moorish war cry; rejoicing, merriment; noise, clamor

álgebra /'alheβra/ *f,* algebra; art of bone setting

algebrista /alhe'βrista/ *mf* bonesetter; algebraist

álgido /'alhiðo/ *a* icy cold

algo /'algo/ *indef pron* some, something (e.g. *Se ve que hay a. que le molesta,* You can see that something is irritating him). *adv* somewhat, a bit. **en a.,** in some way

algodón /algo'ðon/ *m,* cotton plant; cotton flower; cotton fabric; candy floss (UK), cotton candy (USA). **a. en rama,** cotton-wool. **a. hidró-filo,** absorbent cotton wool. **a. pólvora,** nitrocellulose

algodonal /algoðo'nal/ *m,* cotton plantation

alguacil /algua'sil; algua'θil/ *m,* policeman, constable; *Obs.* city governor; short-legged spider

alguien /'algien/ *indef pron* someone, somebody, e.g. *Dime si viene a.,* Tell me if anyone comes

algún /al'gun/ *abb* of **alguno** bef. *m sing* noun, e.g. *a. libro*

alguno /al'guno/ *a* (*abb* **algún** bef. *m, sing*) some, any. *indef pron* someone, somebody; *pl* some, some people. **alguno que otro,** a few

alhaja /al'aha/ *f,* jewel; ornament; treasure, precious object; *Inf.* gem, excellent person (also ironic, e.g. *Es una a.,* He's a fine fellow)

alhajar /ala'har/ *vt* to adorn with jewels, bejewel; furnish, equip

alharaca /alar'aka/ *f,* vehemence, demonstration, fuss (gen. *pl*)

alheña /al'eɲa/ *f, Bot.* privet; henna

alhóndiga /al'ondiga/ *f,* corn exchange; public granary

aliado /a'liaðo/ **(-da)** *a* allied. *n* ally

alianza /a'liansa; a'lianθa/ *f,* alliance; pact, agreement; relationship (by marriage); sum total, whole (of factors, etc.); wedding-ring

aliarse /a'liarse/ *vr* to join together, become allies; be associated

alicaído /alika'iðo/ *a* drooping; *Inf.* weak, exhausted; discouraged, downhearted; come down in the world

alicates /ali'kates/ *m pl,* pincers, pliers

aliciente /ali'siente; ali'θiente/ *m,* attraction, inducement

alícuota /a'likuota/ *f, a* aliquot; proportional. **partes alícuotas,** aliquot parts

alienación /aliena'sion; aliena'θion/ *f,* alienation

alienado /alie'naðo/ *a* insane, mad

alienar /alie'nar/ *vt* See **enajenar**

alienista /alie'nista/ *mf Med.* alienist

aliento /a'liento/ *m,* breathing; breath; courage, spirit; encouragement. **el posterior a.,** one's last breath. **cobrar a.,** to regain one's breath; take heart. **de un a.,** in one breath; without stopping

alifafe /ali'fafe/ *m, Inf.* ailment; tumor on horse's hock

aligación /aliga'sion; aliga'θion/ *f,* binding together, alligation

aligeramiento /a‚lihera'miento/ *m,* lightening, reduction in weight

aligerar /alihe'rar/ *vt* to lighten, make less heavy; quicken, hasten; ease, alleviate; moderate; shorten, abbreviate

alimaña /ali'maɲa/ *f,* destructive animal, predator

alimentación /alimenta'sion; alimenta'θion/ *f,* nourishment; feeding

alimentar /alimen'tar/ *vt* to feed; nourish; encourage, foment; assist, aid; keep, support

alimenticio /alimen'tisio; alimen'tiθio/ *a* nourishing; feeding

alimento /ali'mento/ *m,* food, nourishment; stimulus, encouragement; *pl* alimony; allowance

alindar /alin'dar/ *vt* to mark the boundary of; beautify, adorn; *vi* border, be contiguous

alineación /alinea'sion; alinea'θion/ *f,* alignment

alinear /aline'ar/ *vt* to align, range in line; dress (troops); *vr* fall into line

aliñar /ali'ɲar/ *vt* to decorate, adorn; *Cul.* season; prepare; set (bones)

aliño /a'liɲo/ *m,* decoration, ornament; preparation; condiment, seasoning; setting (bones)

aliquebrado /alike'βraðo/ *a* broken-winged; *Inf.* down in the mouth

alisador /alisa'ðor/ **(-ra)** *a* smoothing; polishing. *n* polisher

alisar /ali'sar/ *vt* to smooth; polish; sleek; plane; comb lightly

alisios /a'lisios/ *m pl,* trade winds

aliso /a'liso/ *m,* alder tree and wood

alistador /alista'ðor/ *m,* enroller

alistamiento /alista'miento/ *m,* enlistment; conscription; enrolment

alistar /alis'tar/ *vt* to enroll, list; enlist; conscript; prepare, get ready; *vr* enroll; *Mil.* enlist; get ready

alitranca /ali'tranka/ *f, Chile, Peru* brake

aliviar /ali'βiar/ *vt* to lighten; alleviate, mitigate; relieve; ease; quicken (one's step); hasten, speed up; steal

alivio /a'liβio/ *m,* lightening; relief; alleviation; ease

aljaba /al'haβa/ *f,* quiver (for arrows); *Lat. Am.* fuchsia

aljibe /al'hiβe/ *m,* tank, cistern; watership or tanker

aljófar /al'hofar/ *m,* small irregular shaped pearl; dew-drop, raindrop, tear drop

aljofifa /alho'fifa/ *f,* floorcloth

allá /a'ya; a'ʎa/ *adv* there; to that place. **más a.,** farther on, beyond. Used in conjunction with phrases of time, indicates remoteness, e.g. *a. en tiempos de los Reyes Católicos,* long ago in the time of the Catholic Monarchs. *a. por 1900,* way back in 1900

allanamiento /ayana'miento; aʎana'miento/ *m,* leveling, flattening; condescension, affability; (police) raid, (police) search acceptance of a judicial finding

allanar /aya'nar; aʎa'nar/ *vt* to level, flatten; overcome (difficulties); soothe; break into (a house, etc.); give entrance to the police; *vr* collapse (buildings, etc.); abide by, adapt oneself (to); condescend, be affable. **a. el camino (a...),** to pave the way (for...)

allegado /aye'gaðo; aʎe'gaðo/ **(-da)** *a* near, allied; related. *n* follower, ally

allegar /aye'gar; aʎe'gar/ *vt* to gather, collect; draw nearer; *Agr.* reap; add; *vi* arrive

allende /a'yende; a'ʎende/ *adv* beyond; besides. **de a. el mar,** from beyond the sea

allí /a'yi; a'ʎi/ *adv* there; to that place, thereto; thereupon, then. **por a.,** through there; that way

alma /'alma/ *f,* soul; living person; essence, core; vivacity, animation; energy, vitality; spirit, ghost; core (of a rope). **a. de cántaro,** fool, ninny. **a. de Dios,** simple soul, kind person. **a. en pena,** soul in purgatory. **¡A. mía!** My darling! **con todo el a.,** with all my heart. **Lo siento en el a.,** I feel it deeply

almacén /alma'sen; alma'θen/ *m,* warehouse; store, shop

almacenaje /almase'nahe; almaθe'nahe/ *m,* act of storing, cost of storage

almacenar /almase'nar; almaθe'nar/ *vt* to store; put in store; hoard

almacenero /almase'nero; almaθe'nero/ *m,* warehouseman; storekeeper

almacenista /almase'nista; almaθe'nista/ *mf* owner of a store; assistant, salesman (saleswoman)

almáciga /al'masiga; al'maθiga/ *f*, mastic; tree plantation or nursery

almagre /al'magre/ *m*, *Mineral.* red ocher; stain, mark

almanaque /alma'nake/ *m*, calendar, almanac

almeja /al'meha/ *f*, *Ichth.* clam

almenara /alme'nara/ *f*, beacon fire

almendra /al'mendra/ *f*, almond; kernel; crystal drop (of chandeliers, etc.); cocoon; bean (of cocoa tree, etc.). **a. garapiñada,** sugar almond

almendro /al'mendro/ *m*, almond tree

almendruco /almen'druko/ *m*, green almond

almete /al'mete/ *m*, casque, helmet; helmeted soldier

almiar /al'miar/ *m*, haystack, hayrick

almíbar /al'miβar/ *m*, sugar syrup; nectar

almibarado /almiβa'raðo/ *a* syrupy; *Inf.* sugary

almibarar /almiβa'rar/ *vt* to coat with sugar; preserve (fruit) in syrup; flatter with sweet words

almidón /almi'ðon/ *m*, starch

almidonado /almiðo'naðo/ *a* starched; *Fig. Inf.* stiff, unbending; prim, starchy

almidonar /almiðo'nar/ *vt* to starch

alminar /almi'nar/ *m*, minaret (of mosque)

almirantazgo /almiran'tasgo; almiran'taθgo/ *m*, Admiralty; admiralship; Admiralty Court

almirante /almi'rante/ *m*, admiral

almizcle /al'miskle; al'miθkle/ *m*, musk

almizcleño /almis'kleɲo; almiθ'kleɲo/ *a* musk (of scents)

almizclero /almis'klero; almiθ'klero/ *a* musky. *m*, *Zool.* musk-deer

almocafre /almo'kafre/ *m*, *Agr.* hoe; trowel, dibble

almohada /almo'aða/ *f*, pillow; pillowcase; cushion. *Inf.* **aconsejarse** *or* **consultar con la a.,** to think over (a matter) carefully, sleep on it

almohadilla /almoa'ðiya; almoa'ðiʎa/ *f*, *dim* small cushion; lace or sewing cushion; pin cushion

almohadillado /almoaði'yaðo; almoaði'ʎaðo/ *a* cushioned; padded

almoneda /almo'neða/ *f*, auction; furniture sale

almonedear /almoneðe'ar/ *vt* to auction; sell off (furniture)

almorranas /almo'rranas/ *f pl,* hemorrhoids

almorzar /almor'sar; almor'θar/ *vi irr* to lunch; breakfast. See **forzar**

almuecín, almuédano /almue'sin, al'mueðano; almue'θin, al'mueðano/ *m*, muezzin

almuercería /almuerse'ria; almuerθe'ria/ *f*, *Mexico* lunch counter, luncheonette

almuerzo /al'muerso; al'muerθo/ *m*, luncheon; breakfast (not so usual)

alocado /alo'kaðo/ *a* feather-brained, reckless; crazy, wild

alocución /aloku'sion; aloku'θion/ *f*, allocution, address, harangue

áloe /'aloe/ *m*, *Bot.* aloe

alojado /alo'haðo/ **(-da)** *m*, billeted soldier. *n* lodger, guest

alojamiento /aloha'miento/ *m*, lodging; dwelling; *Mil.* billeting; *Naut.* steerage; camp, encampment

alojar /alo'har/ *vt* to lodge; billet, quarter (troops); insert, introduce; *vi* and *vr* lodge; live, dwell

alondra /a'londra/ *f*, *Ornith.* lark

alopatía /alopa'tia/ *f*, *Med.* allopathy

alpaca /al'paka/ *f*, alpaca (animal and fabric); nickel silver

alpargata /alpar'gata/ *f*, sandal with hemp sole

alpargatero /alparga'tero/ **(-ra)** *n* manufacturer or seller of alpargatas

Alpes, los /'alpes, los/ the Alps

alpestre /al'pestre/ *a* Alpine; rock (of plants); mountainous, lofty

alpinismo /alpi'nismo/ *m*, mountaineering

alpinista /alpi'nista/ *mf* mountaineer, climber

alpino /al'pino/ *a* Alpine

alpiste /al'piste/ *m*, bird seed

alquería /alke'ria/ *f*, farmstead

alquiladizo /alkila'ðiso; alkila'ðiθo/ *a* rentable, hirable

alquilador /alkila'ðor/ **(-ra)** *n* hirer

alquilamiento /alkila'miento/ *m*, See **alquiler**

alquilar /alki'lar/ *vt* to rent; hire out; hire; *vr* hire oneself out, serve on a wage basis

alquiler /alki'ler/ *m*, hiring out; renting; rental; hire; wages. **de a.,** for hire, on hire

alquimia /al'kimia/ *f*, alchemy

alquimista /alki'mista/ *mf* alchemist

alquitrán /alki'tran/ *m*, tar, pitch. **a. mineral, coal tar**

alquitranado /alkitra'naðo/ *a* tarred. *m*, *Naut.* tarpaulin

alrededor /alreðe'ðor/ *adv* around, about. **a. de,** around; approximately, about (e.g. *a. de cinco dólares*, about $5)

alrededores /alreðe'ðores/ *m pl,* environs, surrounding country

Alsacia /al'sasia; al'saθia/ Alsace

alsaciano /alsa'siano; alsa'θiano/ **(-na)** *a* and *n* Alsatian

alta /'alta/ *f*, certificate of discharge from hospital

altanería /altane'ria/ *f*, hawking; haughtiness, disdain; superciliousness

altanero /alta'nero/ *a* soaring, high-flying (of birds); supercilious; haughty, disdainful

altar /al'tar/ *m*, altar. **a. mayor,** high altar

altavoz /,alta'βos; ,alta'βoθ/ *m*, loudspeaker; megaphone

altearse /alte'arse/ *vr* to rise, grow steep (of land)

alterabilidad /alteraβili'ðað/ *f*, alterability, changeability

alteración /altera'sion; altera'θion/ *f*, alteration, change; debasement (of coinage); agitation

alterar /alte'rar/ *vt* to change, alter; debase (coinage); disturb, agitate; *vr* grow angry; become excited

altercación, /alterka'sion; alterka'θion/ *f*. **altercado** *m*, altercation, quarrel

altercar /alter'kar/ **(se)** *vi* and *vr* to quarrel, dispute, altercate

alternación /alterna'sion; alterna'θion/ *f*, alternation

alternado /alter'naðo/ *a* alternate

alternador /alterna'ðor/ *a* alternating. *m*, *Elec.* alternator

alternante /alter'nante/ *a* alternating

alternar /alter'nar/ *vt* to alternate; make one's debut as a **matador;** *vi* alternate; *(with con)* have dealings with, know

alternativa /alterna'tiβa/ *f*, alternative, option; service performed by turns; alternation

alternativo /alterna'tiβo/ *a* alternative

alterno /al'terno/ *a* alternative; *Bot.* alternate

alteza /al'tesa; al'teθa/ *f*, altitude, height; sublimity, perfection; **(A.)** Highness (title)

altibajo /alti'βaho/ *m*, embossed velvet; *pl Inf.* rough ground; *Inf.* vicissitudes of fortune

altillo /al'tiyo; al'tiʎo/ *m*, hillock; loft, garret, attic

altímetro /al'timetro/ *m*, *Aer.* altimeter

altiplanicie /altipla'nisie; altipla'niθie/ *f*, plateau; highland

altiplano /alti'plano/ *m* plateau; **el A.** the High Andes, the high Andean plateau

altisonante /altiso'nante/ *a* sonorous; sublime; high-flown, pompous

altitud /alti'tuð/ *f*, altitude, height

altivez /alti'βes; alti'βeθ/ *f*, arrogance, haughtiness

altivo /al'tiβo/ *a* arrogant, haughty

alto /'alto/ *a* high; tall; difficult, arduous; sublime; deep; most serious (of crimes, etc.); expensive (of price); small, early (hours). *m*, height; hill; story, floor; *Mil.* halt; red light (traffic light). *adv* up, above, on high; loudly. *interj* ¡**A.!** *Mil.* Halt! *Mil.* **A. Mando,** High Command. **las altas horas de la noche,** the wee (or early) hours. **en alta voz,** in a loud voice. **en alto,** on high; up above. **hacer alto,** to halt, stop

altozano /alto'sano; alto'θano/ *m*, mound, hillock; viewpoint, open space

altruismo /altru'ismo/ *m*, altruism

altruista /altru'ista/ *a* altruistic. *mf* altruist

altura /al'tura/ f, height; altitude; Geom. altitude or height; top, peak; sublimity; tallness

alucinación /alusina'sion; aluθina'θion/ f, **alucinamiento**, m, hallucination

alucinado /alusi'naðo; aluθi'naðo/ m, person suffering from hallucinations

alucinador /alusina'ðor; aluθina'ðor/ a hallucinatory, deceptive

alucinar /alusi'nar; aluθi'nar/ vt to dazzle, fascinate; deceive

alud /a'luð/ m, avalanche

aludir /alu'ðir/ vi to allude (to); refer (to), cite

alumbrado /alum'braðo/ m, lighting; pl illuminati

alumbramiento /alumbra'miento/ m, lighting, supply of light; childbirth

alumbrar /alum'brar/ vt to light, illuminate; give sight to the blind; instruct, teach; inflict (blows); hoe vine roots; vi give birth to a child; vr Inf. grow tipsy

alumbre /a'lumbre/ m, alum

aluminio /alu'minio/ m, aluminum

alumno /a'lumno/ (**-na**) n ward, adopted child; pupil. **a. externo**, day pupil. **a. interno**, boarder

alunizaje /aluni'sahe; aluni'θahe/ m, landing on the moon, moon-landing

alunizar /aluni'sar; aluni'θar/ vi to land on the moon

alusión /alu'sion/ f, allusion

alusivo /alu'siβo/ a allusive, suggestive; hinting

aluvial /alu'βial/ a alluvial

aluvión /alu'βion/ m, alluvium. **de a.**, alluvial

alverjana /alβer'hana/ f, Lat. Am. pea

alza /'alsa; 'alθa/ f, rise (of temperature, etc.); increase (in price); front sight (of guns)

alzacuello /alsa'kueyo; alθa'kueʎo/ m, high collar, clerical collar; neck stock

alzada /al'saða; al'θaða/ f, horse's stature; mountain pasture; Law. appeal

alzado /al'saðo; al'θaðo/ a fraudulent (of bankruptcy); fixed (of price); Mexico haughty, proud m, theft; Lat. Am. wild; insolent; rebellious; Archit. front elevation

alzamiento /alsa'miento; alθa'miento/ m, raising, lifting; higher bid (at auction); rising, rebellion; fraudulent bankruptcy

alzaprima /alsa'prima; alθa'prima/ f, lever; wedge; bridge (of string instruments)

alzar /al'sar; al'θar/ vt to raise; lift up; elevate (the Host); steal, remove; hide; gather in the harvest; build, construct; Naut. heave; vr rise (of temperature, mercury, price, etc.); make a fraudulent bankruptcy; Law. appeal; (with con) run off with, steal. Naut. **a. la vela**, to set sail

ama /'ama/ f, mistress of the house; owner; housekeeper; wet nurse. **a. de casa**, homemaker, housewife. **a. de leche**, foster-mother. **a. de llaves** or **a. de gobierno**, housekeeper. **a. seca**, children's nurse

amabilidad /amaβili'ðað/ f, lovableness; kindness; niceness, goodness, helpfulness

amable /a'maβle/ a lovable; kind; nice, good, helpful

amador /ama'ðor/ (**-ra**) a loving. n lover, admirer

amadrigar /amaðri'gar/ vt to welcome, receive well; vr go into a burrow or lair; go into seclusion

amaestrar /amaes'trar/ vt to train, instruct; tame; break in (horses)

amagar /ama'gar/ vt and vi to threaten; vt show signs of (diseases, etc.); vr Inf. hide

amago (contra...), /a'mago/ threat (to...), menace (to...)

amainar /amai'nar/ vt Naut. to take in the sails; vi drop (of the wind); vi and vt relax (efforts, etc.)

amaine /a'maine/ m, dropping, abatement (of the wind)

amalgama /amal'gama/ f, Chem. amalgam

amalgamación /amalgama'sion; amalgama'θion/ f, amalgamation

amalgamar /amalga'mar/ vt to amalgamate; vr be amalgamated

amamantamiento /amamanta'miento/ m, suckling, nursling

amamantar /amaman'tar/ vt to suckle

amancillar /amansi'yar; amanθi'ʎar/ vt to discredit, dishonor; tarnish; stain

amanecer /amane'ser; amane'θer/ vi irr to dawn; arrive or be somewhere or be doing, at dawn (e.g. Amanecimos en el barco, Dawn came while we were on the ship. Amanecimos escribiendo la carta, The day broke as we were writing the letter); appear at daybreak; begin to appear. m, dawn, daybreak. See **conocer**

amanerado /amane'raðo/ a mannered; affected

amaneramiento /amanera'miento/ m, manneredness; mannerism

amanerarse /amane'rarse/ vr to acquire mannerisms or tricks of style; become affected

amansador /amansa'ðor/ (**-ra**) a soothing, calming. n appeaser

amansar /aman'sar/ vt to tame; appease, moderate; soothe, pacify; break in (horses)

amante /a'mante/ a loving. mf lover

amanuense /ama'nuense/ mf amanuensis, secretary, clerk

amanzanar /amansa'nar; amanθa'nar/ to lay out the streets of

amañar /ama'ɲar/ vt to execute with skill; vr grow skillful

amaño /a'maɲo/ m, skill, dexterity; pl schemes, intrigues; tools, equipment

amapola /ama'pola/ f, poppy

amar /a'mar/ vt to love

amaranto /ama'ranto/ m, Bot. amaranth

amarar /ama'rar/ vi to alight on the water (of hydroplanes)

amarchantarse con /amartʃan'tarse kon/ vr, Lat. Am. deal regularly with, do business with

amargar /amar'gar/ vi to taste or be bitter; vt make bitter; embitter

amargo /a'margo/ a bitter; embittered; grievous. sad. m, bitterness; pl bitters

amargor /amar'gor/ m, **amargura,** f, bitter taste, bitterness; trouble, affliction, pain

amaricado /amari'kaðo/ a Inf. effeminate

amarillear /amariye'ar; amariʎe'ar/ vi to look yellow; turn yellow; tend to yellow

amarillento /amari'yento; amari'ʎento/ a yellowish, turning yellow

amarilleo /amari'yeo; amari'ʎeo/ m, yellowing

amarillez /amari'yes; amari'ʎeθ/ f, yellowness

amarillo /ama'riyo; ama'riʎo/ a and m, yellow

amarilloso /amari'joso; amari'ʎoso/ a, Lat. Am. yellowish, turning yellow

amarra /a'marra/ f, Naut. cable, thick rope

amarradero /amarra'ðero/ m, Naut. mooring berth; mooring-post; hitchingpost or ring

amarraje /ama'rrahe/ m, Naut. mooring charge

amarrar /ama'rrar/ vt to tie up, hitch; moor

amarre /a'marre/ m, mooring; hitching

amartelar /amarte'lar/ vt to make jealous; court, woo, make love to; vr be jealous; fall madly in love

amartillar /amarti'yar; amarti'ʎar/ vt to hammer, knock; cock (firearms)

amasadera /amasa'ðera/ f, kneading-trough

amasador /amasa'ðor/ (**-ra**) a kneading. n kneader

amasar /ama'sar/ vt to knead; massage; scheme, plot

amasia /a'masia/ f, concubine

amasiato /ama'siato/ m, concubinage

amasijo /ama'siho/ m, Cul. dough; kneading; portion of plaster or mortar; Inf. hotchpotch, mixture; scheme, plot

amatista /ama'tista/ f, amethyst

amazacotado /a,masako'taðo; a,maθako'taðo/ a heavy, dense; Fig. stodgy (of writings, etc.)

amazona /ama'sona; ama'θona/ f, Amazon; independent woman; woman rider; woman's riding habit

ambages /am'bahes/ m pl, maze, intricate paths; circumlocutions

ámbar /'ambar/ m, amber. **a. gris,** ambergris

ambarino /amba'rino/ a amber

Amberes /am'beres/ Antwerp

ambición /ambi'sion; ambi'θion/ f, ambition

ambicionar /ambisio'nar; ambiθio'nar/ *vt* to long for; desire eagerly; be ambitious to

ambicioso /ambi'sioso; ambi'θioso/ *a* ambitious; eager, desirous

ambidextro /ambi'ðekstro/ *a* ambidextrous

ambiente /am'biente/ *a* ambient, surrounding. *m,* air, atmosphere; environment

ambigú /ambi'gu/ *m,* cold buffet; buffet (in theaters, etc.)

ambigüedad /ambigue'ðað/ *f,* ambiguity

ambiguo /am'biguo/ *a* ambiguous

ámbito /'ambito/ *m,* precincts; boundary, limit; compass, scope

amblar /am'blar/ *vi* to pace (of a horse)

ambos, /'ambos,/ *a m pl,* **ambas** *a f pl,* both, e.g. *ambas casas,* both houses

ambulancia /ambu'lansia; ambu'lanθia/ *f,* ambulance. **a. de correos,** railway post office. **a. fija,** field-hospital

ambulante /ambu'lante/ *a* walking; traveling, wandering

amedrentar /ameðren'tar/ *vt* to frighten, scare; intimidate

ameliorar /amelio'rar/ *vt* to better, improve

amelonado /amelo'naðo/ *a* melon-shaped; *Inf.* madly in love

amén /a'men/ *m,* amen, so be it. **a. de,** besides, in addition to. *Inf.* **en un decir a.,** in a split second

amenaza /ame'nasa; ame'naθa/ *f,* threat

amenazador, **amenazante** /amenasa'ðor, amena'sante; amenaθa'ðor, amena'θante/ *a* menacing, threatening

amenazar /amena'sar; amena'θar/ *vt* to threaten; *vt* and *vi* presage, be pending

amenguamiento /amengua'miento/ *m,* lessening, diminution; discredit; loss of prestige

amenguar /amen'guar/ *vt* to lessen, decrease; dishonor, discredit

amenidad /ameni'ðað/ *f,* amenity; agreeableness

amenizar /ameni'sar; ameni'θar/ *vt* to make pleasant or attractive

ameno /a'meno/ *a* pleasant; entertaining; agreeable, delightful

América /a'merika/ America

América del Norte /a'merika del 'norte/ North America

América del Sur /a'merika del sur/ South America

americana /ameri'kana/ *f,* (man's) jacket

americanismo /amerika'nismo/ *m,* usage typical of Western-Hemisphere Spanish

americano /ameri'kano/ **(-na)** *a* Western Hemispheric; *mf* native of the Western Hemisphere; resident of the Western Hemisphere

ameritar /ameri'tar/ *vt WH* to deserve, merit

ametrallador /ametraya'ðor; ametraʎa'ðor/ *m,* machine-gunner

ametralladora /ametraya'ðora; ametraʎa'ðora/ *f,* machine-gun

amianto /a'mianto/ *m, Mineral.* amianthus, asbestos

amiba /a'miβa/ *f, Zool.* ameba

amicísimo /ami'sisimo; ami'θisimo/ *a sup.* **amigo,** most friendly

amiga /a'miga/ *f,* woman friend; mistress, lover; dame, schoolmistress; dame school

amigabilidad /amigaβili'ðað/ *f,* friendliness, amicability

amigable /ami'gaβle/ *a* friendly, amicable; harmonious; suitable

amígdala /a'migðala/ *f,* tonsil

amigdalitis /amigða'litis/ *f,* tonsillitis

amigo /a'migo/ **(-ga)** *a* friendly; fond, addicted. *n* friend. *m,* lover. *Inf.* **ser muy a. de,** to be very friendly with; be very keen on or fond of

amilanado /amila'naðo/ *a* cowed, spiritless

amilanar /amila'nar/ *vt* to terrify, intimidate; *vr* grow discouraged

aminorar /amino'rar/ *vt* to diminish, lessen

amistad /amis'tað/ *f,* friendship; liaison; favor; *pl* acquaintances, friends

amistar /amis'tar/ *vt* to introduce, make known to each other; bring about a reconciliation between or with

amistoso /amis'toso/ *a* friendly

amnesia /am'nesia/ *f,* amnesia

amnistía /amnis'tia/ *f,* amnesty

amnistiar /amnisti'ar/ *vt* to concede an amnesty, pardon

amo /'amo/ *m,* head of the house; master; owner; overlord; overseer. **a. de huéspedes,** keeper of a boarding house. **Nuestro A.** Our Lord. *Inf.* **ser el a. del cotarro,** to rule the roost

amoblado /amo'βlaðo/ *m, Central America, Mexico* furniture

amodorramiento /amoðorra'miento/ *m,* stupor, deep sleep

amodorrarse /amoðo'rrarse/ *vr* to fall into a stupor; fall into a heavy sleep

amoladera /amola'ðera/ *f,* whetstone

amolador /amola'ðor/ *m,* scissors grinder; knife grinder; sharpener

amoladura /amola'ðura/ *f,* grinding, whetting, sharpening

amolar /amo'lar/ *vt irr* to grind, sharpen; *Inf.* pester, annoy. See **colar**

amoldar /amol'dar/ *vt* to mold; adjust; *vr* adapt oneself

amonedar /amone'ðar/ *vt* to coin, mint

amonestación /amonesta'sion; amonesta'θion/ *f,* warning; advice. **correr las amonestaciones,** to publish banns of marriage

amonestador /amonesta'ðor/ **(-ra)** *a* warning, admonitory. *n* admonisher

amonestar /amones'tar/ *vt* to warn; advise; rebuke; *Eccl.* publish bans of marriage

amoníaco /amo'niako/ *m,* ammonia

amontillado /amonti'yaðo; amonti'ʎaðo/ *m,* kind of pale, dry sherry

amontonamiento /amontona'miento/ *m,* accumulation; gathering, collection; piling up, heaping

amontonar /amonto'nar/ *vt* to pile up, heap; gather; collect; accumulate; *vr Inf.* fly into a rage

amor /a'mor/ *m,* love; beloved; willingness, pleasure; *pl* love affairs; caresses. **a. propio,** self-esteem; vanity. *Inf.* **con mil amores,** with great pleasure. **por a. de,** for love of; for the sake of

amoral /amo'ral/ *a* amoral

amoratado /amora'taðo/ *a* livid, bluish

amorcillo /amor'siyo; amor'θiʎo/ *m, Dim.* little love; unimportant love affair; Cupid

amordazar /amorða'sar; amorða'θar/ *vt* to muzzle; gag; prevent speaking

amorfo /a'morfo/ *a* amorphous

amorío /amo'rio/ *m, Inf.* wooing, love making; *pl* love affairs

amoroso /amo'roso/ *a* loving; gentle; mild, balmy

amorrar /amo'rrar/ *vi Inf.* to hang one's head; sulk; be sullen

amortajar /amorta'har/ *vt* to wrap in a shroud; enshroud

amortiguador /amortigua'ðor/ *m, Mech.* shock absorber. *Auto.* **a. de los muelles,** shock-absorber

amortiguamiento /amortigua'miento/ *m,* softening, deadening; mitigation, lessening

amortiguar /amorti'guar/ *vt* to soften, deaden; absorb (shocks); moderate, mitigate; soften (colors)

amortización /amortisa'sion; amortiθa'θion/ *f,* amortization

amortizar /amorti'sar; amorti'θar/ *vt* to amortize; recover, redeem; suppress, abolish (posts)

amoscarse /amos'karse/ *vr Inf.* to be piqued or annoyed; become agitated

amostazar /amosta'sar; amosta'θar/ *vt Inf.* to annoy; *vi* become peeved

amotinador /amotina'ðor/ **(-ra)** *a* mutinous, rebellious. *n* rebel, mutineer; rioter

amotinar /amoti'nar/ *vt* to incite to rebellion; unbalance, unhinge (mind); *vr* rebel; riot; *Fig.* be unhinged

amovible /amo'βiβle/ *a* movable, removable; removable (of officials, etc.)

amovilidad /amoβili'ðað/ *f*, movability, removability; liability to discharge or dismissal
amparador /ampara'ðor/ **(-ra)** *a* protective; sheltering. *n* protector, defender, helper; shelterer
amparar /ampa'rar/ *vt* to protect, favor, help; shelter; *vr* take refuge, take shelter; defend oneself
amparo /am'paro/ *m*, shelter, refuge; protection, favor, help; defense
amper /am'per/ *m, Elec.* ampere
amperímetro /ampe'rimetro/ *m, Elec.* ammeter
amperio /am'perio/ *m, Elec.* ampere
ampliable /am'pliaβle/ *a* amplifiable
ampliación /amplia'sion; amplia'θion/ *f*, enlargement, increase, extension; *Photo.* enlargement
ampliador /amplia'ðor/ **(-ra)** *a* enlarging. *n* enlarger
ampliadora /amplia'ðora/ *f, Photo.* enlarger
ampliar /amp'liar/ *vt* to extend, enlarge, increase; *Photo.* enlarge
amplificación /amplifika'sion; amplifika'θion/ *f*, extension, amplification; *Photo.* enlargement
amplificar /amplifi'kar/ *vt* to enlarge; extend; increase; amplify, expatiate upon
amplio /'amplio/ *a* wide; extensive; roomy, ample; prolix
amplitud /ampli'tuð/ *f*, extension; width; spaciousness, amplitude
ampolla /am'poya; am'poʎa/ *f*, blister; ampoule; bubble; *Elec.* bulb
ampulosidad /ampulosi'ðað/ *f*, pomposity, redundancy (of style)
ampuloso /ampu'loso/ *a* pompous, high-flown (style)
amputación /amputa'sion; amputa'θion/ *f*, amputation
amputar /ampu'tar/ *vt* to amputate
amuchachado /amutʃa'tʃaðo/ *a* boyish
amueblar /amue'βlar/ *vt* to furnish; provide with furniture
amuinar /amui'nar/ *vt, Mexico* to anger, make angry
amuleto /amu'leto/ *m*, amulet, charm
amurallar /amura'yar; amura'ʎar/ *vt* to surround with a wall, wall
amurrarse /amu'rrarse/ *vr, Lat. Am.* get depressed, get the blues
amusgar /amus'gar/ *vt* and *vi* to flatten the ears (animals); *vt* screw up the eyes (to see better)
anacardo /ana'karðo/ *m*, cashew (nut)
anacoreta /anako'reta/ *mf* anchorite, hermit
anacreóntico /anakre'ontiko/ *a* Anacreontic
anacrónico /ana'kroniko/ *a* anachronous
anacronismo /anakro'nismo/ *m*, anachronism
ánade /'anaðe/ *mf* duck
anadear /anaðe'ar/ *vi* to waddle (like a duck)
anadeo /ana'ðeo/ *m*, waddle
anadino /ana'ðino/ **(-na)** *n* duckling
anadón /ana'ðon/ *m*, drake
anáfora /a'nafora/ *f*, anaphora
anafrodisíaco /anafroði'siako/ *a* anaphrodisiac
anagrama /ana'grama/ *m*, anagram
analectas /ana'lektas/ *f, pl* analects
anales /a'nales/ *m, pl* annals
analfabetismo /analfaβe'tismo/ *m*, illiteracy
analfabeto /analfa'βeto/ **(-ta)** *a* and *n* illiterate
analgesia /anal'hesia/ *f*, analgesia
analgésico /anal'hesiko/ *a* and *m, Med.* analgesic
análisis /a'nalisis/ *m*, analysis; *Gram.* parsing
analista /ana'lista/ *mf* analyst
analizar /anali'sar; anali'θar/ *vt* to analyse
analogía /analo'hia/ *f*, analogy
analógico, análogo /ana'lohiko, a'nalogo/ *a* analogous
ananás /ana'nas/ *m*, pineapple
anaquel /ana'kel/ *m*, shelf, ledge
anaranjado /anaran'haðo/ *a* and *m*, orange (color)
anarquía /anar'kia/ *f*, anarchy
anárquico /a'narkiko/ *a* anarchical
anarquismo /anar'kismo/ *m*, anarchism
anarquista /anar'kista/ *mf* anarchist
anatema /ana'tema/ *mf*. anathema
anatomía /anato'mia/ *f*, anatomy

anatómico /ana'tomiko/ *a* anatomical
anca /'anka/ *f*, croup, hindquarters of a horse
ancho /'antʃo/ *a* wide, broad. *m*, width, breadth. *Inf. a mis* (**tus, sus,** etc.) **anchas** *or* **anchos,** at my (your, his, etc.) ease, with complete freedom
anchoa /an'tʃoa/ *f*, anchovy
anchura /an'tʃura/ *f*, width, breadth; ease, freedom; extent
anchuroso /antʃu'roso/ *a* very wide; extensive; spacious
ancianidad /ansiani'ðað; anθiani'ðað/ *f*, old age; seniority; oldness
anciano /an'siano; an'θiano/ **(-na)** *a* old; ancient. *n* old person
ancla /'ankla/ *f*, anchor. **a. de la esperanza,** sheet anchor. **echar anclas,** to anchor
ancladero, anclaje /ankla'ðero, an'klahe/ *m*, anchorage
anclar /an'klar/ *vi* to anchor
ancón /an'kon/ *m*, cove, *Mexico* corner
áncora /'ankora/ *f*, anchor; refuge, haven
andada /an'daða/ *f*, wandering, roving; hard bread roll; pasture; *pl* trail, tracks. *Fig. Inf.* **volver a las andadas,** to return to one's old tricks
andaderas /anda'ðeras/ *f pl*, go-cart (for learning to walk)
andador /anda'ðor/ *a* walking; swift walking; wandering. *m*, walker; garden path; *pl* leading-strings, reins
andadura /anda'ðura/ *f*, walk, gait; pace, step
Andalucía /andalu'sia; andalu'θia/ Andalusia
andaluz /anda'lus; anda'luθ/ **(-za)** *a* and *n* Andalusian
andaluzada /andalu'saða; andalu'θaða/ *f, Inf.* exaggeration, tall story
andamio /an'damio/ *m*, scaffolding; stand, platform
andanada /anda'naða/ *f, Naut.* broadside; cheapest priced seat in a bullring; *Inf.* dressing-down, scolding
andante /an'dante/ *a* walking, strolling; errant (of knights). *a* and *m, Mus.* andante
andanza /an'dansa; an'danθa/ *f*, happening, occurrence; *pl* doings, deeds. **buena a.,** good fortune
andar /an'dar/ *vi irr* to walk; move; work, operate, run (machines, etc.); progress, get along (negotiations, etc.); be, feel; elapse (of time); be occupied; behave; (*with prep a*) administer (blows, etc.); (*with en*) upset, turn over (papers, etc.); ride in or on (cars, bicycles, etc.); be engaged in; (*with con*) use, handle; *vt* traverse. *m*, gait, walk. **a. por los cuarenta,** to be in one's forties. **a. con paños tibios,** not to be firm. **a. con pies de plomo,** to be extremely cautious. **a. tras,** to follow, go after; persecute; desire ardently (things). **andarse a la flor del berro,** to sow one's wild oats. *Fig. Inf.* **andarse por las ramas,** to beat about the bush. **¡Anda!** Get along with you!; Hurry up!; You don't say so! **¡Andando!** Let's get going!, Let's get a move on it! *Preterite* **anduve,** etc. *Imperf subjunc* **anduviese,** etc.
andariego /anda'riego/ **(-ga)** *a* swift walking; wandering, vagrant. *n* walker.
andarín (-ina) /anda'rin/ *n* good walker; professional walker
andas /'andas/ *f pl*, kind of stretcher; bier
andén /an'den/ *m*, railway platform; *Lat. Am.* sidewalk
andero /an'dero/ *m*, bearer (of a bier)
andinismo /andi'nismo/ *m, Lat. Am.* mountain climbing **andinista** *mf Lat. Am.* mountain climber
andino /an'dino/ *a* Andean
andorrano (-na) /ando'rrano/ *a* and *n* Andorran
andrajo /an'draho/ *m*, rag, wisp of cloth, tatter
andrajoso /andra'hoso/ *a* ragged, tattered
andurriales /andu'rriales/ *m pl*, byways, unfrequented paths; remote places
anécdota /a'nekðota/ *f*, anecdote
anecdótico /anek'ðotiko/ *a* anecdotal
anegación /anega'sion; anega'θion/ *f*, drowning, flooding, inundation
anegar /ane'gar/ *vt* to drown; inundate; shipwreck; *vr* drown; be flooded

anejo /a'neho/ *a* attached, annexed. *m*, annexed borough

anemia /a'nemia/ *f*, anemia

anémico /a'nemiko/ *a* anemic

anémona, anémone /a'nemona, a'nemone/ *f*, anemone.

anémona de mar, sea-anemone

anestesia /anes'tesia/ *f*, anesthesia

anestesiador (-ra) /anestesia'ðor/ *n* anesthetist

anestesiar /aneste'siar/ *vt* to anesthetize

anestésico /anes'tesiko/ *a* and *m*, anesthetic

aneurisma /aneu'risma/ *mf Med.* aneurism

anexar /anek'sar/ *vt* to annex

anexión /anek'sion/ *f*, annexation

anexo /a'nekso/ *a* attached, joined. *m*, annex

anfibio /an'fiβio/ *a* amphibious. *m*, amphibian

anfiteatro /anfite'atro/ *m*, amphitheater; operating theater; dissecting room; morgue; *Theat.* dress-circle

anfitrión /anfitri'on/ *m*, *Inf.* host, one who entertains guests

ánfora /'anfora/ *f*, amphora; *Lat. Am.* ballot box

angarillas /aŋga'riyas; aŋga'riʎas/ *f pl*, hand barrow; table cruet; yoke and panniers

ángel /'anhel/ *m*, angel; *Lat. Am.* (hand) microphone **á. de la guarda,** guardian angel. **estar con los ángeles,** to be in Heaven (euphem. for "to be dead")

angelical, angélico /anheli'kal, an'heliko/ *a* angelic; divine, excellent

angina /an'hina/ *f*, *Med.* angina, tonsillitis. **a. de pecho,** angina pectoris

anglicanismo /aŋglika'nismo/ *m*, Anglicanism

anglicano (-na) /aŋgli'kano/ *a* and *n* Anglican

anglicismo /aŋgli'sismo; aŋgli'θismo/ *m*, anglicism

anglo (-la) /'aŋglo/ *a* and *n* Angle. *a* Anglo-

anglófilo (-la) /aŋ'glofilo/ *n* Anglophile

anglosajón (-ona) /aŋglosa'hon/ *a* and *n* Anglo-Saxon. *m*, Anglo-Saxon language

angostar /aŋgos'tar/ *vi* and *vt* to narrow; tighten

angosto /aŋ'gosto/ *a* narrow; tight

angostura /aŋgos'tura/ *f*, narrowness; tightness; narrow pass; strait; *Fig.* tight corner, fix

anguila /aŋ'gila/ *f*, eel; *pl Naut.* slipway, slips

angula /aŋ'gula/ *f*, elver (young eel)

ángulo /'aŋgulo/ *m*, angle. **á. inferior izquierdo,** lower lefthand corner. **á. inferior derecho,** lower righthand corner. **á. superior izquierdo,** upper lefthand corner. **á. superior derecho,** upper righthand corner. **á. recto,** right angle

anguloso /aŋgu'loso/ *a* angulate; angular, gaunt; cornered

angustia /aŋ'gustia/ *f*, anguish, grief

angustiante /aŋgus'tiante/ *a* distressing

angustiar /aŋgus'tiar/ *vt* to grieve; afflict; *vr* be full of anguish

anhelación /anela'sion; anela'θion/ *f*, panting, hard breathing; yearning, longing

anhelar /ane'lar/ *vi* to pant, breathe with difficulty; *vi* and *vt* long for, yearn for, desire

anhélito /a'nelito/ *m*, pant, hard breathing

anhelo (de) /a'nelo/ *m*, longing (for), desire (for), yearning (for)

anheloso /ane'loso/ *a* difficult, labored (of breathing); anxious, longing

anidar /ani'ðar/ *vi* to nest (birds); swell; *vt* shelter, protect; *vr* nest; dwell; nestle

anilla /a'niya; a'niʎa/ *f*, curtain ring; *pl* gymnastic rings

anillo /a'niyo; a'niʎo/ *m*, finger ring; small ring; coil (of serpents and ropes). **a. de compromiso** *Mexico* engagement ring. *Inf.* **venir como a. al dedo,** to fit like a glove; come just at the right moment

ánima /'anima/ *f*, soul, spirit; soul in purgatory; bore (of firearms); *pl* prayer bell for the souls of the departed

animación /anima'sion; anima'θion/ *f*, liveliness, gaiety; animation, vivacity; bustle, movement

animal /ani'mal/ *m*, animal; *Inf.* dolt, brute. *a* animal; *Inf.* brutish, doltish

animalada /anima'laða/ *f*, *Inf.* stupidity, foolishness

animalidad /animali'ðað/ *f*, animalism

animar /ani'mar/ *vt* to animate; encourage, incite; invigorate, enliven; cheer up; make attractive, adorn; *vr* take heart; make up one's mind; cheer up

animismo /ani'mismo/ *m*, animism

ánimo /'animo/ *m*, soul, spirit; courage; endurance, fortitude; will, intention; mind

animosidad /animosi'ðað/ *f*, hatred, animosity, dislike

animoso /ani'moso/ *a* spirited, lively; valiant

aniñado /ani'paðo/ *a* childlike, childish

aniquilable /aniki'laβle/ *a* destructible

aniquilación /anikila'sion; anikila'θion/ *f*, destruction, annihilation; suppression; decay

aniquilador (-ra) /anikila'ðor/ *a* destructive, annihilating. *n* destroyer

aniquilamiento /anikila'miento/ *m*, See **aniquilación**

aniquilar /aniki'lar/ *vt* to annihilate, destroy completely; *vr* waste away, decay

anís /a'nis/ *m*, aniseed, anise; anisette (liqueur)

anisar /ani'sar/ *vt* to flavor with aniseed

anisete /ani'sete/ *m*, anisette

aniversario /aniβer'sario/ *a* annual. *m*, anniversary

Anjeo /an'heo/ Anjou

ano /'ano/ *m*, anus

anoche /a'notʃe/ *adv* last night

anochecer /anotʃe'ser; anotʃe'θer/ *vi irr* to grow night; become dark; be in a place *or* be doing something at nightfall (e.g. *Anochecimos en Lérida,* We were in Lerida at nightfall). *vr Poet.* be obscured or darkened. *m*, nightfall, dusk. See **conocer**

anochecida /anotʃe'siða; anotʃe'θiða/ *f*, dusk, late twilight

anodino /ano'ðino/ *a Med.* anodyne; ineffective, useless; inoffensive. *m*, anodyne

anomalía /anoma'lia/ *f*, anomaly, inconstancy, irregularity; *Astron.* anomaly

anómalo /a'nomalo/ *a* anomalous, abnormal, unusual

anonadación /anonaða'sion; anonaða'θion/, *f*, **anonadamiento** *m*, destruction, annihilation; despair, melancholy; suppression

anonadar /anona'ðar/ *vt* to destroy, annihilate; suppress; *Fig.* overwhelm, depress; humble

anónimo /a'nonimo/ *a* anonymous. *m*, anonymity; anonymous letter; unsigned literary work

anorexia /ano'reksia/ *f*, anorexia

anormal /anor'mal/ *a* abnormal; irregular, unusual. *mf* abnormal person

anormalidad /anormali'ðað/ *f*, abnormality; irregularity, inconsistency

anotación /anota'sion; anota'θion/ *f*, annotation; *Lat. Am.* score (in sports)

anotador (-ra) /anota'ðor/ *n* annotator

anotar /ano'tar/ *vt* to annotate; note down

anquilostoma /ankilos'toma/ *m*, *Med.* hookworm

ánsar /an'sar/ *m*, goose; drake

ansarino /ansa'rino/ *a* goose. *m*, gosling

anseático /anse'atiko/ *a* Hanseatic

ansia (de) /'ansia/ *f*, anxiety, trouble; grief; longing (for), yearning (for); greed

ansiar /an'siar/ *vt* to long for, yearn for; covet, desire

ansiedad /ansie'ðað/ *f*, anxiety, anguish, worry

ansión /an'sion/ *f*, intense desire

ansioso /an'sioso/ *a* anxious; grievous, painful; eager, desirous; greedy

anta /'anta/ *f*, *Zool.* elk; obelisk

antagónico /anta'goniko/ *a* antagonistic

antagonismo /antago'nismo/ *m*, antagonism

antagonista /antago'nista/ *mf* antagonist, adversary

antaño /an'tapo/ *adv* last year, yesteryear; long ago

antártico /an'tartiko/ *a* antarctic

ante /'ante/ *m*, *Zool.* elk; suede; buffalo

ante /'ante/ *prep* in the presence of, before; regarding, in the face of (e.g. *a. deber tan alto,* in the face of so noble a duty)

anteado /ante'aðo/ *a* beige, buff-colored, fawn

anteanoche /antea'notʃe/ *adv* the night before last

anteayer /antea'yer/ *adv* the day before yesterday

antebrazo /ante'βraso; ante'βraθo/ *m*, forearm

antecámara /ante'kamara/ *f*, antechamber

antecedente /antese'ðente; anteθe'ðente/ *m*, antecedent. **antecedentes** *m pl* background (of a case, situation, etc.)

antecedentemente /antese,ðente'mente; anteθe,ðente'mente/ *adv* previously

antecedente /antese'ðer; anteθe'ðer/ *vt* to precede

antecesor /antese'sor; anteθe'sor/ **(-ra)** *a* previous. *n* predecessor. *m*, forebear, ancestor

antecoger /anteko'her/ *vt* to carry in front, lead before; pick too soon

antecomedor /antekome'ðor/ *m*, breakfast nook, breakfast room

antedata /ante'ðata/ *f*, antedate

antedatar /anteða'tar/ *vt* to backdate

antedicho /ante'ðitʃo/ *a* aforementioned, aforesaid

antediluviano /anteðilu'βiano/ *a* antediluvian

antelación /antela'sion; antela'θion/ *f*, advance, anticipation

antellevar /anteje'βar; anteʎe'βar/ *vt*, *Mexico* to knock down, run over

antemano, de /ante'mano, de/ *adv* in advance, beforehand

antemeridiano /antemeri'ðiano/ *a* antemeridian, forenoon

antena /an'tena/ *f*, antenna; *Radio.* aerial

antenacido /antena'siðo; antena'θiðo/ *a* born prematurely

antenombre /ante'nombre/ *m*, title (placed before name)

anteojera /anteo'hera/ *f*, horse's blinker; eyeglass case

anteojo /ante'oho/ *m*, spy-glass, small telescope; *pl* horse's blinkers; eyeglasses, glasses; spectacles; goggles. **anteojos para el sol**, sunglasses

antepagar /antepa'gar/ *vt* to pay in advance

antepalco /ante'palko/ *m*, vestibule of a box in a theater

antepasado /antepa'saðo/ *a* previous, past. *m*, ancestor (gen. *pl*)

antepecho /ante'petʃo/ *m*, parapet; windowsill; railing, balustrade; front (of a theater box, etc.); *Naut.* bulwark

antepenúltimo /antepe'nultimo/ *a* antepenultimate, third to last

anteponer /antepo'ner/ *vt irr* to place before; prefer, favor. See **poner**

anteproyecto /antepro'yekto/ *m*, first sketch, preliminary work or plan

antepuerta /ante'puerta/ *f*, door-curtain, portiere; *Mil.* anteport

anterior /ante'rior/ *a* previous, former; anterior; aforementioned, preceding

anteriormente /anterior'mente/ *adv* beforehand, previously

antes /'antes/ *adv* before; rather, on the contrary; previously. **a. bien**, rather, sooner. **a. con a.** *or* **cuanto a.**, *or* **lo a. posible**, as soon as possible

antesala /ante'sala/ *f*, antechamber

antevíspera /ante'βispera/ *f*, two days previously

antiaéreo /anti'aereo/ *a* antiaircraft. *m pl.* **(cañones) antiaéreos**, A.A. guns

anticiclón /antisi'klon; antiθi'klon/ *m*, anticyclone

anticipación /antisipa'sion; antiθipa'θion/ *f*, anticipation; advance. **con a.**, ahead of time

anticipada /antisi'paða; antiθi'paða/ *f*, foul thrust (in fencing, etc.)

anticipadamente /antisi,paða'mente; antiθi,paða'mente/ *adv* in advance; prematurely

anticipado /antisi'paðo; antiθi'paðo/ *a* in advance; premature

anticipador /antisipa'ðor; antiθipa'ðor/ *a* anticipatory

anticipar /antisi'par; antiθi'par/ *vt* to anticipate; foresee; forestall; advance (money); lend; *vr* happen before time; (*with prep a*) act in advance of, anticipate; get ahead of oneself

anticipo /anti'sipo; anti'θipo/ *m*, anticipation, advance; advance payment; sum of money lent

anticlerical /antikleri'kal/ *a* anticlerical

anticlímax /anti'klimaks/ *m*, anticlimax

anticonstitucional /antikonstitusio'nal; antikonstituθio'nal/ *a* unconstitutional

anticuado /anti'kuaðo/ *a* antiquated, ancient

anticuario /anti'kuario/ *m*, antiquarian, antique dealer

antídoto /an'tiðoto/ *m*, antidote

antiesclavista /antieskla'βista/ *a* antislavery. *mf* antislavist

antiespasmódico /antiespas'moðiko/ *a* and *m*, *Med.* antispasmodic

antiestético /anties'tetiko/ *a* unesthetic

antietimológico /antietimo'lohiko/ *a* non-etymological, unetymological

antifaz /anti'fas; anti'faθ/ *m*, mask; face-covering

antiflogístico /antiflo'histiko/ *a* and *m*, *Med.* antiphlogistic

antigramatical /antigramati'kal/ *a* ungrammatical

antigualla /anti'guaya; anti'guaʎa/ *f*, antique; ancient custom; anything out-of-date

antiguamente /antigua'mente/ *adv* in time past, formerly

antiguamiento /antigua'miento/ *m*, seniority

antigüedad /antigue'ðað/ *f*, antiquity; ancients; length of service, seniority (in employment); *pl* antiquities

antiguo /an'tiguo/ *a* ancient, very old; antique; senior (in an employment); former. *m*, senior member (of a community, etc.). *m pl*, ancients. **A. Testamento**, Old Testament. **de a.**, from ancient times. **en lo antiguo**, in ancient times; in former times, in days of yore

antillano /anti'yano; anti'ʎano/ **(-na)** *a* and *n* of or from the Antilles

Antillas, las /an'tiyas, las; an'tiʎas, las/ the Antilles

antílope /an'tilope/ *m*, antelope

antimacasar /antimaka'sar/ *m*, antimacassar

antimilitarismo /antimilita'rismo/ *m*, antimilitarism

antimilitarista /antimilita'rista/ *a* antimilitaristic

antimonárquico /antimo'narkiko/ *a* antimonarchical

antimonio /anti'monio/ *m*, *Metall.* antimony

antipalúdico /antipa'luðiko/ *a* antimalarial

antipara /anti'para/ *f*, screen, shield

antiparras /anti'parras/ *f pl*, *Inf.* spectacles, eyeglasses, glasses

antipatía /antipa'tia/ *f*, antipathy

antipático /anti'patiko/ *a* disagreeable; unattractive

antipatriótico /antipa'triotiko/ *a* unpatriotic

antipoda /an'tipoða/ *a* and *m*, or *f*, antipode

antiquísimo /anti'kisimo/ *a sup*, **antiguo**, most ancient

antisemita /antise'mita/ *a* anti-Semitic. *mf* anti-Semite

antisemitismo /antisemi'tismo/ *m*, anti-Semitism

antiséptico /anti'septiko/ *a* and *m*, antiseptic

antisifilítico /antisifi'litiko/ *a Med.* anti-syphilitic

antisocial /antiso'sial; antiso'θial/ *a* antisocial

antítesis /an'titesis/ *f*, antithesis

antitético /anti'tetiko/ *a* antithetical, contrasted

antófago /an'tofago/ *a* anthophagous, flower-eating

antojadizo /antoha'ðiso; antoha'ðiθo/ *a* capricious, fanciful, whimsical

antojarse /anto'harse/ *vr* to have a fancy for, want (e.g. *Se me antoja marcharme al campo*, I have a yen to go to the country); suspect, imagine

antojito /anto'hito/ *m*, *Mexico* typical Mexican dish (of food)

antojo /an'toho/ *m*, caprice, fancy, whim; desire, will; *pl* birthmark

antología /antolo'hia/ *f*, anthology

antólogo /an'tologo/ *m*, anthologist

antonomasia /antono'masia/ *f*, antonomasia. **por a.**, by analogy, by transference

antorcha /an'tortʃa/ *f*, torch, flambeau

antracita /antra'sita; antra'θita/ *f*, anthracite

ántrax /'antraks/ *m*, *Med.* anthrax

antro /'antro/ *m*, cave, cavern; *Anat.* antrum

antropofagia /antropo'fahia/ *f*, cannibalism, anthropophagy

antropófago /antro'pofago/ **(-ga)** *a* cannibalistic. *n* cannibal

antropología /antropolo'hia/ *f,* anthropology
antropológico /antropo'lohiko/ *a* anthropological
antropólogo /antro'pologo/ *m,* anthropologist
antropometría /antropome'tria/ *f,* anthropometry
antropomorfo /antropo'morfo/ *a* anthropomorphous
antroposofía /antroposo'fia/ *f,* anthroposophy
antruejo /antru'eho/ *m,* three days of carnival before Lent
anual /a'nual/ *a* yearly, annual
anualidad /anuali'ðað/ *f,* annuity
anuario /a'nuario/ *m,* directory, yearbook, handbook
anubarrado /anuβa'rraðo/ *a* covered with clouds, cloudy
anublado /anu'βlaðo/ *a* lowering, overcast; clouded
anublar /anu'βlar/ *vt* to cloud; darken, obscure; blight (plants); *vr* cloud over; become blighted or mildewed
anudar /anu'ðar/ *vt* to knot; tie, fasten; join; continue; **a. amistad de,** to strike up a friendship with. **a. la corbata,** to put on one's tie, tie one's tie; *vr* grow stunted
anulable /anu'laβle/ *a* annulable, voidable
anulación /anula'sion; anula'θion/ *f,* annulment, abrogation
anular /anu'lar/ *a* annular, ring-shaped. *vt* to annul, cancel; *Math.* cancel out
anuloso /anu'loso/ *a* annulate, formed of rings
anunciación /anunsia'sion; anunθia'θion/ *f, Eccl.* Annunciation; announcement
anunciador /anunsia'ðor; anunθia'ðor/ **(-ra),** *n* **anunciante** *mf* announcer; advertiser
anunciar /anun'siar; anun'θiar/ *vt* to announce; publish, proclaim; advertise; foretell, presage. **Anuncian lluvia,** The forecast calls for rain
anuncio /a'nunsio; a'nunθio/ *m,* announcement; publication, proclamation; advertisement; T.V. commercial; presage, omen. **a. luminoso,** sky-sign
anverso /am'berso/ *m,* obverse, face
anzuelo /an'suelo; an'θuelo/ *m,* fish-hook; *Cul.* fritter; *Inf.* attraction, inducement
añadido /aɲa'ðiðo/ *m,* hair-switch; make-weight
añadidura /aɲaði'ðura/ *f,* addition; make-weight, extra
añadir /aɲa'ðir/ *vt* to add; increase
añagaza /aɲa'gasa; aɲa'gaθa/ *f,* decoy bird; enticement, lure
añejo /a'ɲeho/ *a* very old
añicos /a'ɲikos/ *m pl,* fragments, small pieces. **hacer a.,** to break into fragments
añil /a'ɲil/ *m,* indigo; indigo blue
año /'aɲo/ *m,* year; *pl* birthday. **a. bisiesto,** leap-year. **a. económico,** fiscal year. **A. Nuevo,** New Year. **tener (siete) años,** to be (seven) years old. **los Años Bobos,** the period from 1874 to 1898 in Spain
añoranza /aɲo'ransa; aɲo'ranθa/ *f,* homesickness, loneliness; nostalgia
añorar /aɲo'rar/ *vi* to be homesick or lonely
añoso /a'ɲoso/ *a* very old, full of years
añublo /a'ɲuβlo/ *m,* mildew
aojamiento /aoha'miento/ *m,* evil eye, wicked spell
aojar /ao'har/ *vt* to bewitch, place under a spell; spoil, frustrate
aojo /a'oho/ *m,* evil eye; magic spell
aorta /a'orta/ *f, Anat.* aorta
aovillarse /aoβi'yarse; aoβi'ʎarse/ *vr* to roll oneself into a ball; curl up
apabullante /apaβu'yante; apaβu'ʎante/ *a* crushing, flattening
apacentadero /apasenta'ðero; apaθenta'ðero/ *m,* grazing land, pasture
apacentamiento /apasenta'miento; apaθenta'miento/ *m,* pasturage; grazing
apacentar /apasen'tar; apaθen'tar/ *vt irr* to put out to grass; teach, instruct; satisfy (one's desires); *vr* graze (cattle). See **acertar**
apachurrar /apatʃu'rrar/ *vt, Mexico* to press (button, etc.)
apacibilidad /apasiβili'ðað; apaθiβili'ðað/ *f,* agreeableness; mildness; peaceableness

apacible /apa'siβle; apa'θiβle/ *a* agreeable; mild; peaceable; calm, peaceful
apaciguamiento /a,pasigua'miento; a,paθigua'miento/ *m,* appeasement, soothing, pacification
apaciguar /apasi'guar; apaθi'guar/ *vt* to appease, pacify; calm
apadrinar /apaðri'nar/ *vt* to act as godfather to; be best man to (at a wedding); act as a second for (in a duel); sponsor; favor
apagable /apa'gaβle/ *a* extinguishable
apagado /apa'gaðo/ *a* timid, nervous; pale (of colors); dull, lusterless
apagador /apaga'ðor/ *a* quenching. *n* extinguisher. *m,* candle-snuffer; damper (of a piano)
apagaincendios /a,pagain'sendios; a,pagain'θendios/ *m,* ship's fire-extinguisher
apagamiento /apaga'miento/ *m,* quenching, extinguishment
apagar /apa'gar/ *vt* to extinguish, put out; *Fig.* quench, moderate; slake (lime); *Art.* tone down (colors); shut off (engines)
apagarrisas /apaga'rrisas/ *mf* crapehanger, killjoy, wet blanket
apagavelas /apaga'βelas/ *m,* candle-snuffer
apalabrar /apala'βrar/ *vt* to make an appointment with; discuss, consider
apaleamiento /apalea'miento/ *m,* beating, thrashing
apalear /apale'ar/ *vt* to beat, thrash; knock down with a stick
apandillarse /apandi'yarse; apandi'ʎarse/ *vr* to form a gang or group
apañar /apa'ɲar/ *vt* to take away, remove; seize; steal; dress, get ready; *Inf.* wrap up; patch, repair; *vr Inf.* grow skillful
apaño /a'paɲo/ *m,* dexterity, skill; craft, guile
aparador /apara'ðor/ *m,* sideboard; workshop; *Eccl.* credence (table); *Mexico* (shop) window
aparato /apa'rato/ *m,* apparatus; equipment, utensils; pomp, ostentation; symptoms; sign, circumstance, token. **a. digestivo,** digestive system; digestive tract. **a. fonador,** speech apparatus
aparatoso /apara'toso/ *a* showy, ostentatious. **incendio. a.,** conflagration, large fire
aparear /apare'ar/ *vt* to match, make equal; pair; mate (animals); *vr* form up in pairs
aparecer /apare'ser; apare'θer/ **(se)** *vi* and *vr irr* to appear; seem; be. See **conocer**
aparecido /apare'siðo; apare'θiðo/ *m,* apparition, specter
aparejador /apareha'ðor/ *m,* overseer, foreman; *Naut.* rigger
aparejar /apare'har/ *vt* to prepare, make ready; saddle (horses); prime, size; rig (a ship)
aparejo /apa'reho/ *m,* preparation, arrangement; harness, trappings; *Naut.* rig; *Naut.* gear; priming, sizing; *Mech.* tackle; *pl* equipment
aparentar /aparen'tar/ *vt* to pretend, simulate
aparente /apa'rente/ *a* seeming, apparent; obvious, visible; suitable, proper
aparición /apari'sion; apari'θion/ *f,* appearance, arrival; apparition, phantom
apariencia /apa'riensia; apa'rienθia/ *f,* appearance, looks, probability, likelihood; outward semblance; *pl Theat.* scenery
apartadamente /apartaða'mente/ *adv* apart, in private; secretly
apartadero /aparta'ðero/ *m,* passing place for cars; railway siding; grass verge. **a. ferroviario,** railway marshaling yard
apartado /apar'taðo/ *a* distant, far off; secluded; different. *m,* post-office box; secluded room; smelting house; sorting of cattle; selection of bulls for a bullfight
apartamento /aparta'mento/ *m Lat. Am.* (*except Argentina*) apartment
apartamiento /aparta'miento/ *m,* separation; withdrawal, retiral; seclusion; apartment, flat; *Law.* withdrawal of an action
apartar /apar'tar/ *vt* to separate; remove (e.g. an obstacle), take away; *Rail.* shunt; dissuade; sort; *vr* ob-

tain a divorce; *Law.* withdraw an action. **apartarse de la tradición,** to depart from tradition

aparte /a'parte/ *adv* aside, on one side; separately; *Theat.* aside; besides; beyond. *m, Theat.* aside; paragraph; space between words. **¡Aparte!** Move to one side!

apartidario /aparti'ðario/ *a* non-partisan

apasionado /apasio'naðo/ **(-da)** *a* impassioned; fervent, devoted; passionate; enthusiastic. *n* admirer, lover; enthusiast

apasionamiento /apasiona'miento/ *m,* passion

apasionar /apasio'nar/ *vt* to arouse to passion; pain; *vr* (*with por*) grow passionately fond of; become enthusiastic for

apatía /apa'tia/ *f,* apathy

apático /a'patiko/ *a* apathetic

apeadero /apea'ðero/ *m,* mounting-block; halt, stopping place; wayside railway station; pied-à-terre, occasional dwelling

apear /ape'ar/ *vt* to dismount; hobble (horse); survey, map out; fell a tree; *Fig.* overcome (difficulties); *Inf.* dissuade; prop; remove, bring down; scotch (a wheel); *vr* dismount; alight, step off

apechugar /apetʃu'gar/ *vi* to push with the breast; *Inf.* put up with reluctantly

apedazar /apeða'sar; apeða'θar/ *vt* to tear; break; mend, repair

apedrear /apeðre'ar/ *vt* to stone; stone to death; *vi impers* hail; *vr* be damaged by hail (crops)

apegarse /ape'garse/ *vr* to grow fond (of), become attached (to)

apego /a'pego/ *m,* fondness, inclination; affection, attachment

apelación /apela'sion; apela'θion/ *f, Law.* appeal; *Inf.* doctor's consultation

apelante /ape'lante/ *a* and *mf Law.* appellant

apelar /ape'lar/ *vi Law.* to appeal; (*with prep a*) have recourse to; *vi* be of the same color (horses)

apellidar /apeyi'ðar; apeʎi'ðar/ *vt* to name, call; acclaim; call to arms; *vr* be named

apellido /ape'yiðo; ape'ʎiðo/ *m,* surname; nickname; call to arms; clamor; name

apenar /ape'nar/ *vt* to grieve, afflict; cause sorrow

apenarse /ape'narse/ *vr Lat. Am.* to be ashamed

apenas /a'penas/ *adv* scarcely; immediately, as soon as; with trouble or difficulty

apéndice /a'pendise; a'pendiθe/ *m,* appendix, supplement; *Anat.* appendix

apendicitis /apendi'sitis; apendi'θitis/ *f,* appendicitis

Apeninos, los /ape'ninos, los/ the Apennines

apeo /a'peo/ *m,* survey; scaffolding; prop, support

apercibimiento /apersiβi'miento; aperθiβi'miento/ *m,* preparation; provision; warning; *Law.* summons

apercibir /apersi'βir; aperθi'βir/ *vt* to prepare, furnish; warn; *Law.* summon

apergaminarse /apergami'narse/ *vr Inf.* to shrivel, dry up (with old age, etc.)

aperitivo /aperi'tiβo/ *a* aperitive. *m,* aperient; appetizer

apertura /aper'tura/ *f,* opening; inauguration; reading (of a will)

apesadumbrar /apesaðum'brar/ *vt* to sadden, afflict, grieve

apestar /apes'tar/ *vt* to infect with the plague; catch the plague; *Fig.* corrupt; *Inf.* pester, annoy; *vi* stink

apestoso /apes'toso/ *a* stinking, putrid

apetecer /apete'ser; apete'θer/ *vt irr* to want, desire; attract. See **conocer**

apetecible /apete'siβle; apete'θiβle/ *a* attractive, desirable

apetencia /ape'tensia; ape'tenθia/ *f,* appetite; desire

apetito /ape'tito/ *m,* appetite

apetitoso /apeti'toso/ *a* appetizing; tasty, savory; attractive

apiadarse /apia'ðarse/ *vr* (*with de*) to have compassion on, be sorry for

ápice /'apise; 'apiθe/ *m,* apex; tip, point; peak, summit, top; orthographic accent; iota, tittle; crux (of a problem)

apicultor /apikul'tor/ **(-ra)** *n* apiarist, beekeeper

apicultura /apikul'tura/ *f,* apiculture, beekeeping

apilar /api'lar/ *vt* to pile, heap

apimplado, -a /apim'plaðo/ *a, Lat. Am.* boozed up, drunk

apiñado /api'ɲaðo/ *a* crowded, serried

apiñamiento /apiɲa'miento/ *m,* crowding; congestion

apiñar /api'ɲar/ *vt* to group together, crowd; *vr* crowd

apio /'apio/ *m,* celery

apisonadora /apisona'ðora/ *f,* steam-roller; roller

apisonar /apiso'nar/ *vt* to roll, stamp, flatten, ram down; tamp, pack down (e.g. tobacco in a pipe)

apizarrado /apisa'rraðo; apiθa'rraðo/ *a* slate-colored

aplacable /apla'kaβle/ *a* appeasable, placable

aplacamiento /aplaka'miento/ *m,* appeasement

aplacar /apla'kar/ *vt* to appease, calm; moderate, mitigate

aplacible /apla'siβle; apla'θiβle/ *a* agreeable, pleasant

aplanacalles /aplana'kajes; aplana'kaʎes/ *mf, Lat. Am.* idler, lay about, lazybones

aplanar /apla'nar/ *vt* to flatten, level; roll (pastry); *Inf.* dumbfound, overwhelm; *vr* collapse (buildings); lose heart

aplastar /aplas'tar/ *vt* to flatten, squash, crush; *Inf.* squash flat, floor

aplaudir /aplau'ðir/ *vt* to applaud, clap; praise, commend, approve

aplauso /a'plauso/ *m,* applause; clapping, plaudit; approbation, commendation

aplazamiento /aplasa'miento; aplaθa'miento/ *m,* postponement; appointment, summons

aplazar /apla'sar; apla'θar/ *vt* to summon, arrange a meeting; postpone; adjourn

aplicabilidad /aplikaβili'ðað/ *f,* applicability

aplicable /apli'kaβle/ *a* applicable

aplicación /aplika'sion; aplika'θion/ *f,* application; diligence, assiduity; appliqué, ornamentation

aplicado /apli'kaðo/ *a* diligent, hardworking; appliqué

aplicar /apli'kar/ *vt* to apply; impute; intend, destine (for processions); *Law.* adjudge; *vr* engage in; apply oneself. **a. el oído,** to listen intently. **a. sanciones,** *Polit.* to impose sanctions

aplomado /aplo'maðo/ *a* self-possessed, dignified; leaden, lead-colored

aplomar /aplo'mar/ *vt* and *vi* to plumb, test with a plumb-line; *vr* collapse, fall down

aplomo /a'plomo/ *m,* self-possession, dignity; sang-froid

apocado /apo'kaðo/ *a* spiritless, timid; base, mean

Apocalipsis /apoka'lipsis/ *m,* Apocalypse

apocalíptico /apoka'liptiko/ *a* apocalyptic

apocamiento /apoka'miento/ *m,* timidity, pusillanimity; depression, discouragement; shyness; baseness, meanness

apocar /apo'kar/ *vt* to diminish, reduce; humiliate, scorn

apócrifo /a'pokrifo/ *a* fictitious, false; apocryphal. **Apócrifos,** Apocrypha

apodar /apo'ðar/ *vt* to nickname

apoderado /apoðe'raðo/ *a* authorized. *m,* attorney; deputy; proxy

apoderar /apoðe'rar/ *vt* to authorize; grant powers of attorney to; *vr* (*with de*) seize, take possession of

apodo /a'poðo/ *m,* nickname

apogeo /apo'heo/ *m, Astron.* apogee; *Fig.* zenith, peak (of fame, etc.)

apolillar /apoli'yar; apoli'ʎar/ *vt* to eat clothes (moths); *vr* be moth-eaten

apologista /apolo'hista/ *mf* apologist

apólogo /a'pologo/ *m,* apologue, moral fable

apoltronarse /apoltro'narse/ *vr* to grow idle

apoplejía /apople'hia/ *f,* apoplexy

aporrear /aporre'ar/ *vt* to beat, cudgel; *vr* work hard, slog away

aportación /aporta'sion; aporta'θion/ *f,* contribution; occasionwhich

aportar /apor'tar/ *vt* to cause, occasion; contribute; *vi Naut.* reach port; **El buque aportó a Nueva York,**

The ship reached New York, The ship sailed into New York harbor; arrive at an unexpected place

aposentador /aposenta'ðor/ *m*, usher; *Mil.* billeting officer

aposentar /aposen'tar/ *vt* to lodge, give hospitality to; *vr* lodge, settle down

aposento /apo'sento/ *m*, room; suite, apartments; lodging, accommodation; *Theat.* box

aposición /aposi'sion; aposi'θion/ *f*, *Gram.* apposition

apósito /a'posito/ *m*, poultice, external application; (medical) dressing

apostadero /aposta'ðero/ *m*, *Naut.* naval station; placing or stationing (of soldiers)

apostar /apos'tar/ *vt irr* to bet; station (soldiers); *vi* compete, rival. See **contar**

apostasía /aposta'sia/ *f*, apostasy

apóstata /a'postata/ *mf* apostate

apostilla /apos'tiya; apos'tiʎa/ *f*, marginal note, gloss

apóstol /a'postol/ *m*, apostle

apostólico /apos'toliko/ *a* apostolic

apóstrofe /a'postrofe/ *m*, or *f*, apostrophe, hortatory exclamation

apóstrofo /a'postrofo/ *m*, *Gram.* apostrophe

apostura /apos'tura/ *f*, neatness, spruceness

apotegma /apo'tegma/ *m*, apothegm, maxim

apoteosis /apote'osis/ *f*, apotheosis

apoyar /apo'yar/ *vt* (*with en*) to lean against; rest upon; *vt* uphold, favor; confirm, bear out; droop the head (horses); second (a motion); *vi* (*with en*) rest on; lean against; *vr* (*with en*) rest on; lean against; **apoyarse de codos,** to lean on one's elbows; be upheld by; *Fig.* be founded on; *Fig.* depend on, lean on

apoyo /a'poyo/ *m*, support, prop; windowsill; sill; assistance; backing, support

apreciable /apresia'βle; apreθia'βle/ *a* appreciable; estimable; important

apreciación /apresia'sion; apreθia'θion/ *f*, appreciation; valuation, estimate

apreciador /apresia'ðor; apreθia'ðor/ **(-ra)** *a* appreciatory. *n* appraiser

apreciar /apre'siar; apre'θiar/ *vt* to estimate (values); appreciate; like, esteem, have a regard for

apreciativo /apresia'tiβo; apreθia'tiβo/ *a* appreciative

aprecio /a'presio; a'preθio/ *m*, valuation; appreciation, regard

aprehender /apreen'der/ *vt* to apprehend, catch; seize (contraband); understand, grasp

aprehensión /apreen'sion/ *f*, seizure, apprehension

apremiador, apremiante /apremia'ðor, apre'miante/ *a* urgent, pressing

apremiar /apre'miar/ *vt* to hurry; urge, press; force, oblige; burden, oppress (with taxes)

apremio /a'premio/ *m*, insistence, pressure; compulsion; demand note

aprendedor /aprende'ðor/ **(-ra)** *n* learner

aprender /apren'der/ *vt* to learn. **a. de memoria,** to learn by heart

aprendiz /apren'dis; apren'diθ/ **(-za)** *n* apprentice

aprendizaje /aprendi'sahe; aprendi'θahe/ *m*, apprenticeship. **hacer el a.,** to serve an apprenticeship

aprensión /apren'sion/ *f*, capture; fear, apprehension; suspicion, fancy; prejudice, scruple

aprensivo /apren'siβo/ *a* apprehensive, nervous, fearful

apresar /apre'sar/ *vt* to nab, catch; capture (a ship); imprison; fetter

aprestar /apres'tar/ *vt* to prepare, arrange; dress (fabrics)

apresto /a'presto/ *m*, preparation, arrangement; dressing (for cloth)

apresurar /apresu'rar/ *vt* to quicken; *vr* hasten, be quick

apretado /apre'taðo/ *a* difficult, dangerous; tight; crabbed (of handwriting); clustered (e.g. *casas apretadas alrededor de la sinagoga,* houses clustered around the synagogue). *Inf.* mean, close-fisted. *m*, small close handwriting

apretadura /apreta'ðura/ *f*, tightening, compression

apretar /apre'tar/ *vt irr* to tighten; compress; urge on, press; harass, vex; trouble, worry; speed up; squeeze; press (bells, gun triggers, etc.); *vi* increase, grow worse (storms, heat, etc.); pinch, hurt (shoes). **a. los pasos,** to quicken one's pace. *Inf.* **a. a correr,** to take to one's heels. **¡Aprieta!** *Inf.* Nonsense! It can't be! See **acertar**

apretón /apre'ton/ *m*, squeeze, grip, pressure; *Inf.* sprint, spurt; *Inf.* fix, pickle. **a. de manos,** handshake

apretujamiento /apretuha'miento/ *m*, squeezing together

apretujar /apretu'har/ *vt Inf.* to squeeze, hug

aprieto /a'prieto/ *m*, crowd, crush; urgency; *Inf.* jam, trouble, fix

aprisa /a'prisa/ *adv* quickly, in a hurry

aprisco /a'prisko/ *m*, cattle-shed; sheepfold

aprisionar /aprisio'nar/ *vt* to imprison; bind, fetter; tie

aprobación /aproβa'sion; aproβa'θion/ *f*, approbation, approval, commendation; ratification (of a bill); pass (in an examination)

aprobado /apro'βaðo/ *m*, pass certificate (in examinations)

aprobar /apro'βar/ *vt irr* to approve; pass (in an examination). See **contar**

aprontar /apron'tar/ *vt*, *Lat. Am.* to pay in advance, prepay

apropiación /apropia'sion; apropia'θion/ *f*, appropriation; application; adaptation

apropiado /apro'piaðo/ *a* appropriate, suitable, proper

apropiar /apro'piar/ *vt* to appropriate; adapt, fit; *vr* appropriate, take possession

aprovechable /aproβe'tʃaβle/ *a* usable, available

aprovechado /aproβe'tʃaðo/ *a* advantageous; assiduous, conscientious; capable; thrifty

aprovechador /aproβetʃa'ðor/ *a* self-seeking

aprovechamiento /aproβetʃa'miento/ *m*, utilization, employment; exploitation; profitable use

aprovechar /aproβe'tʃar/ *vi* to be advantageous or useful; be beneficial; make progress (in studies, etc.); *vt* use; profit by; *vr* take advantage of, make use of. **¡Que aproveche!** May it do you good! (said to anyone eating)

aprovisionar /aproβi'sionar/ *vt* to provision, supply

aproximación /aproksima'sion; aproksima'θion/ *f*, approximation; consolation prize (in a lottery)

aproximadamente /aproksimaða'mente/ *adv* approximately; nearly, almost

aproximar /aproksi'mar/ *vt* to bring or draw nearer; *vr* approach; be almost, be approximately; draw closer

aptitud /apti'tuð/ *f*, aptitude, ability; fitness; propensity

apto /'apto/ *a* suitable, fitting; competent. **no apta para menores,** not suitable for children (of films, etc.)

apuesta /a'puesta/ *f*, bet, wager; competition

apuestas benéficas de fútbol /a'puestas be'nefikas de 'futβol/ football pools

apuesto /a'puesto/ *a* elegant; handsome, well set-up

apuntación /apunta'sion; apunta'θion/ *f*, noting down; note; *Mus.* notation

apuntador /apunta'ðor/ **(-ra)** *n* note-taker; observer. *m*, *Theat.* prompter; *Theat.* stage-manager

apuntalar /apunta'lar/ *vt* to prop, prop up, underpin, bolster

apuntamiento /apunta'miento/ *m*, summary; *Law.* indictment, minute

apuntar /apun'tar/ *vt* to aim (a gun, etc.); point to, indicate; note down; mark; sketch; sharpen; bet (at cards); fasten temporarily; *Inf.* mend; *Theat.* prompt; suggest, hint (e.g. *La fecha está apuntada en varios manuscritos,* The date is hinted at in various manuscripts); *vi* begin to appear. *Inf.* **a. y no dar,** to promise and do nothing

apunte /a'punte/ *m*, abstract; note; annotation; sketch; *Theat.* prompt *or* prompter *or* prompt book *or* cue; stake in a card game

apuñalado /apuɲa'laðo/ *a* dagger-shaped

apuñalar /apuɲa'lar/ *vt* to stab, attack with a dagger

apurado /apu'raðo/ *a* poor, needy; dangerous; difficult; accurate, exact; hurried

apurar /apu'rar/ *vt* to purify; drain; exhaust; finish, conclude; examine closely, scrutinize (e.g. *apurar una materia,* to exhaust a subject, examine a subject thoroughly); irritate, make impatient; urge on, hasten; *vr* be anxious, fret; *Lat. Am.* hurry, hurry up

apuro /a'puro/ *m,* difficulty, fix; poverty, want; anxiety, worry. **pasar apuros,** to have a hard time

aquejar /ake'har/ *vt* to afflict; weary, beset, harass; *vr* complain

aquel, /a'kel,/ *a m* **aquella,** *a f* **aquellos,** *a m pl* **aquellas** *a f pl,* that, those; that or those over there (farther off than **ese**)

aquel /a'kel,/ *m,* charm, attraction, it

aquél, aquélla, aquéllos, aquéllas /a'kel,/ *dem pron m, f, sing.* and *pl.,* that, the one, those, those ones; the former. e.g. *La casa que ve usted a lo lejos aquélla es la vivienda de mi tío,* The house that you see in the distance, that is my uncle's dwelling. *Éste no me gusta pero aquél sí,* I do not like the latter, but I like the former

aquelarre /ake'larre/ *m,* witches' sabbath

aquello /a'keyo; a'keʎo/ *dem pron neut* that; the fact; the matter, the affair, the former (remark, idea, etc.). e.g. *Todo a. por fin acabó,* All that came to an end at last. *a. de,* the fact that

aquí /a'ki/ *adv* here. **de a.,** hence the fact that. **¡He a.!** Behold!

aquietar /akie'tar/ *vt* to calm, soothe

aquilatar /akila'tar/ *vt* to assay; scrutinize; examine, weigh up (persons)

aquistar /akis'tar/ *vt* to attain, acquire

ara /'ara/ *f,* altar; **en aras de,** in honor of; for the sake of

árabe /'araβe/ *a* Arab, Arabic. *mf* Arab. *m,* Arabic (language)

arabesco /ara'βesko/ *a* Arabic. *m, Art.* arabesque

Arabia Saudita /a'raβia sau'ðita/ Saudi Arabia

arábigo /a'raβigo/ *a* Arabic. *m,* Arabic (language)

arácnido /a'rakniðo/ *m, Zool.* arachnid

arado /a'raðo/ *m,* plow

arador /ara'ðor/ *a* plowing. *m,* plowman. **a. de la sarna,** *Ent.* scabies mite

aragonés /arago'nes/ **(-esa)** *a* and *n* Aragonese

araguato /ara'guato/ *m, Lat. Am.* howler monkey

arahuaco /ara'uako/ *a* and *n* Arawak, Arawakian

arancel /aran'sel; aran'θel/ *m,* tariff, duty, tax

arancelar /aranse'lar; aranθe'lar/ to charge tuition for (e.g. *a. la universidad,* charge tuition for college studies)

arancelario /aranse'lario; aranθe'lario/ *a* tariff, tax; customs

arándano /a'randano/ *m, Bot.* bilberry

arandela /aran'dela/ *f,* candle-dripper; *Mech.* washer; wall candelabrum

araña /a'raɲa/ *f,* spider; chandelier; *Inf.* whore

arañacielos /a,raɲa'sielos; a,raɲa'θielos/ *m,* skyscraper

arañar /ara'ɲar/ *vt* to scratch; *Inf.* scrape together, hoard

arañazo /ara'ɲaso; ara'ɲaθo/ *m,* scratch

arar /a'rar/ *vt* to plow. **a. en el mar,** to labor in vain

arbitrador /arβitra'ðor/ **(-ra)** *n* arbitrator

arbitraje /arβi'trahe/ *m,* arbitration; decision; arbitrage

arbitrar /arβi'trar/ *vt* to judge freely; *Law.* arbitrate, mediate; devise; invent; marshal (money, resources, etc.); draft (a law) *vr* make shift, contrive

arbitrariedad /arβitrarie'ðað/ *f,* arbitrariness

arbitrario /arβi'trario/ *a* arbitral, mediatory; arbitrary, capricious

arbitrio /ar'βitrio/ *m,* free will; arbitration; means, way; discretion; arbitrament, judgment; *pl* rates, municipal taxes

árbitro /'arβitro/ **(-ra)** *a* arbitrary. *n* arbiter. *m, Sports.* umpire; referee

árbol /'arβol/ *m,* tree; *Mech.* shaft; *Naut.* mast; axis of a winding stair. **a. de amor** *or* **a. de Judas,** Judas tree. **a. de la ciencia (del bien y del mal),** Tree of

Knowledge (of good and evil). **a. de levas,** *Mech.* camshaft. **a. del pan,** breadfruit tree. *Naut.* **a. mayor,** mainmast. **a. motor** *Mech.,* drivingshaft

arbolado /arβo'laðo/ *a* tree-covered, wooded. *m,* copse, woodland

arboladura /arβola'ðura/ *f, Naut.* masts and spars

arbolar /arβo'lar/ *vt* to hoist (flags); *Naut.* fit with masts; place upright; *vr* rear, prance (horses)

arboleda /arβo'leða/ *f,* copse, grove, spinney

arbotante /arβo'tante/ *m,* flying buttress

arbusto /ar'βusto/ *m,* shrub, woody plant

arca /'arka/ *f,* chest; money-box, coffer; ark; *pl* (treasury) vaults. **a. caudal,** strong box. **a. de agua,** water-tower. **a. de la alianza.** *or* **a. del testamento,** Ark of the Covenant (Bible). **a. de Noé,** Noah's Ark; lumber box

arcabucero /arkaβu'sero; arkaβu'θero/ *m,* arquebusier; maker of arquebuses

arcabuz /arka'βus; arka'βuθ/ *m,* arquebus

arcada /ar'kaða/ *f,* arcade; series of arches; *pl* sickness, nausea

árcade /'ar'kaðe/ *a* and *mf* Arcadian

arcaico /ar'kaiko/ *a* archaic

arcaísmo /arka'ismo/ *m,* archaism

arcángel /ar'kanhel/ *m,* archangel

arcano /ar'kano/ *a* secret. *m,* mystery, arcanum

arce /'arse; 'arθe/ *m, Bot.* maple tree

archifeliz /artʃife'lis; artʃife'liθ/ *a* extremely happy, in bliss

archimillonario /artʃimiyo'nario; artʃimiʎo'nario/ **(-ia)** *a* and *n* multimillionaire

archipiélago /artʃi'pielago/ *m,* archipelago

Archipiélago de Colón /artʃi'pielago de ko'lon/ *m,* Galapagos Islands

archivar /artʃi'βar/ *vt* to place in an archive; file (papers)

archivero /artʃi'βero/ *m,* archivist, keeper of the archives; librarian; registrar; (Mexico) file cabinet, filing cabinet

archivista /artʃi'βista/ *mf* archivist; file clerk, filing clerk

archivo /ar'tʃiβo/ *m,* archives, file

arcilla /ar'siya; ar'θiʎa/ *f,* clay

arcilloso /arsi'yoso; arθi'ʎoso/ *a* clayey, like or full of clay

arcipreste /arsi'preste; arθi'preste/ *m,* archpriest

arco /'arko/ *m, Geom.* arc; *Mil.* bow; bow (of a stringed instrument); hoop (of casks, etc.); *Archit.* arch; *Lat. Am.* goal (in sports). **a. del cielo** *or* **a. de San Martín** *or* **a. iris,** rainbow. **a. voltaico,** electric arc. *Mus.* **para a.,** for strings

arder /ar'ðer/ *vt* to burn; shine, gleam; *Fig.* burn (with passion, etc.); *vt* to set alight, burn

ardid /ar'ðið/ *a* crafty. *m,* trick, stratagem

ardiente /ar'ðiente/ *a* burning; ardent, passionate; vehement; enthusiastic; flame-colored; fiery-red

ardilla /ar'ðiya; ar'ðiʎa/ *f,* squirrel; *Lat. Am.* wheeler-dealer

ardite /ar'ðite/ *m,* ancient Spanish coin of little value; *Fig.* farthing, fig, straw. **no valer un a.,** to be not worth a straw

ardor /ar'ðor/ *m,* great heat; zeal, earnestness; passion, ardor; courage

ardoroso /arðo'roso/ *a* ardorous

arduo /'arðuo/ *a* arduous

área /'area/ *f,* area; small plot of ground; common threshing floor; arc (surface measure)

arena /a'rena/ *f,* sand; arena; grit, gravel. **a. movediza,** quicksand

arenal /are'nal/ *m,* quicksand; sand pit; sandy place

arenero /are'nero/ **(-ra)** *n* sand merchant. *m,* sandbox (carried by railway engines)

arenga /a'renga/ *f,* harangue, discourse *Argentina* argument, fight, quarrel

arenilla /are'niya; are'niʎa/ *f,* sand (for drying writing)

arenisca /are'niska/ *f,* sandstone

arenisco /are'nisko/ *a* sandy

arenque /a'renke/ *m,* herring

arete /a'rete/ *m,* earring

argamasa /arga'masa/ *f*, mortar

argayo /ar'gayo/ *m*, landslide; (Asturias) **a. de nieve,** avalanche

Árgel /'arhel/ Algiers

Argelia /ar'helia/ Algeria

argelino /arhe'lino/ **(-na)** *a* and *n* Algerian

argentado /arhen'taðo/ *a* silvered; silvery

argénteo /ar'henteo/ *a* silver; silvery

argentífero /arhen'tifero/ *a* silver-yielding

Argentina /arhen'tina/ Argentina

argentino /arhen'tino/ **(-na)** *a* silvery. *a* and *n* Argentinian. *m*, Argentinian gold coin

argento /ar'hento/ *m*, silver. *a.* **vivo,** mercury

argolla /ar'goya; ar'goʎa/ *f*, thick metal ring (for hitching, etc.); croquet (game); stocks, pillory; hoop, iron arch; *Lat. Am.* wedding ring

argonauta /argo'nauta/ *m*, *Myth.* Argonaut; *Zool.* paper nautilus, argonaut

argucia /ar'gusia; ar'guθia/ *f*, sophism, quibble; subtlety

argüir /ar'guir/ *vt irr* to deduce, imply; prove; reveal, manifest; accuse; *vi* argue, debate; dispute, oppose. See **huir**

argumentador /argumenta'ðor/ **(-ra)** *a* argumentative. *n* arguer

argumentar /argumen'tar/ *vi* to argue; dispute; oppose

argumento /argu'mento/ *m*, contention, case; theme (of a book, etc.); argument, discussion

aridez /ari'ðes; ari'ðeθ/ *f*, aridity, dryness; drought; sterility, barrenness; dullness, lack of interest

árido /'ariðo/ *a* dry, arid; sterile, barren; uninteresting, dull

ariete /a'riete/ *m*, *Mil.* battering ram

arisco /a'risko/ *a* unsociable, surly; wild, shy (animals)

arista /a'rista/ *f*, *Bot.* arista, awn, beard; pebble; edge, side

aristocracia /aristo'krasia; aristo'kraθia/ *f*, aristocracy

aristócrata /aris'tokrata/ *mf* aristocrat

aristocrático /aristo'kratiko/ *a* aristocratic

aristotélico /aristo'teliko/ *a* Aristotelian

aritmética /arit'metika/ *f*, arithmetic

aritmético /arit'metiko/ **(-ca)** *a* arithmetical. *n* arithmetician

arlequín /arle'kin/ *m*, harlequin; *Inf.* fool, buffoon; Neapolitan ice-cream

arma /'arma/ *f*, weapon; *Mil.* arm, branch; bull's horn; *pl* troops, army; means, way; arms, coat of arms. **a. arrojadiza,** missile. **a. blanca,** steel weapon. **a. de fuego,** fire-arm. **¡Armas al hombro!** Shoulder Arms! **armas portátiles,** small arms. *Inf.* **de armas tomar,** belligerent; resolute. **pasar por las armas,** *Mil.* to shoot. **presentar las armas,** *Mil.* to present arms. **ser a. de dos filos,** *Fig.* to cut both ways

armada /ar'maða/ *f*, navy, armada; fleet, squadron; *Argentina* lasso

armadía /arma'ðia/ *f*, raft, pontoon

armador /arma'ðor/ **(-ra)** *n* supplier, outfitter. *m*, shipowner; pirate, privateer; jacket; assembler, fitter

armadura /arma'ðura/ *f*, armature, armor; frame, framework; skeleton (of a building); skeleton (of vertebrates); *Phys.* armature; plate armor (of persons)

armamento /arma'mento/ *m*, *Mil.* armament; arms, military equipment

armar /ar'mar/ *vt* to arm; *Mech.* mount; man (guns); put together, assemble; roll (a cigarette); reinforce (concrete); *Inf.* arrange, prepare; *Inf.* occasion (quarrels); *Inf.* outfit; *Naut.* equip; commission (a ship); *vr* prepare oneself, arm oneself. **a. caballero,** to knight. **a. los remos,** to ship the oars. *Inf.* **armarla,** to cause a row or quarrel

armario /ar'mario/ *m*, cupboard; wardrobe. **a. de luna,** wardrobe with a mirror

armatoste /arma'toste/ *m*, unwieldy piece of furniture; *Fig. Inf.* dead weight, clumsy person; snare

armazón /arma'son; arma'θon/ *f*, frame, framework; ship's hulk. *m*, *Anat.* skeleton

armenio /ar'menio/ **(-ia)** *a* and *n* Armenian. *m*, Armenian language

armería /arme'ria/ *f*, armory; heraldry; gunsmith's craft or shop

armero /ar'mero/ *m*, gunsmith, armorer; stand for weapons

armiño /ar'miɲo/ *m*, ermine

armisticio /armis'tisio; armis'tiθio/ *m*, armistice

armón de artillería /ar'mon de artiye'ria; ar'mon de artiʎe'ria/ *m*, gun-carriage

armonía /armo'nia/ *f*, harmony; friendship, concord; *Mus.* harmony

armónica /ar'monika/ **(de boca)** *f*, mouth-organ

armónico /ar'moniko/ *a* harmonious. *a* and *m*, *Mus.* harmonic

armonio /ar'monio/ *m*, harmonium

armonioso /armo'nioso/ *a* harmonious

armonización /armonisa'sion; armoniθa'θion/ *f*, *Mus.* harmonization

armonizar /armoni'sar; armoni'θar/ *vt* to bring into harmony; *Mus.* harmonize

arnero /ar'nero/ *m*, *Lat. Am.* sieve

arnés /ar'nes/ *m*, armor; harness; *pl* horse trappings; *Inf.* equipment, tools

aro /'aro/ *m*, hoop; rim (of wheel, etc.); napkin-ring; croquet hoop; *Bot.* wild arum; child's hoop; *Lat. Am.* earring **a. de empaquetadura,** *Mech.* gasket

aroma /a'roma/ *m*, aroma, fragrance; balsam; sweet-smelling herb

aromático /aro'matiko/ *a* aromatic

arpa /'arpa/ *f*, harp. **a. eolia,** Eolian harp

arpar /ar'par/ *vt* to scratch, claw; tear, rend

arpegio /ar'pehio/ *m*, *Mus.* arpeggio

arpía /ar'pia/ *f*, harpy

arpicordio /arpi'korðio/ *m*, harpsichord

arpista /ar'pista/ *mf* harpist, harp player

arpón /ar'pon/ *m*, harpoon

arponear /arpone'ar/ *vt* to harpoon

arponero /arpo'nero/ *m*, harpooner; harpoon maker

arquear /arke'ar/ *vt* to arch; bend; beat (wool); gauge (ship's capacity); *vi* retch

arqueo /ar'keo/ *m*, arching; bending, curving; *Naut.* tonnage; gauging (of ship's capacity); *Com.* examination of deposits and contents of safe

arqueología /arkeolo'hia/ *f*, archeology

arqueológico /arkeo'lohiko/ *a* archeological

arqueólogo /arke'ologo/ *m*, archeologist

arquero /ar'kero/ *m*, *Com.* cashier, treasurer; *Mil.* archer

arquitecto /arki'tekto/ *m*, architect. **a. de jardines,** landscape gardener

arquitectura /arkitek'tura/ *f*, architecture

arquitrabe /arki'traβe/ *m*, architrave

arrabal /arra'βal/ *m*, suburb, district; *pl* outskirts

arracada /arra'kaða/ *f*, pendant-earring

arracimarse /arrasi'marse; arraθi'marse/ *vr* to cluster; group

arraigadamente /arrai,gaða'mente/ *adv* deeply, firmly

arraigado /arrai'gaðo/ *a* deep-rooted; firm; convinced

arraigar /arrai'gar/ *vi* to take root; *vi* and *vr* *Fig.* become established, take hold; *vr* settle; take up residence

arraigo /a'rraigo/ *m*, rooting; settlement, establishment; landed property

arrancaclavos /a,rranka'klaβos/ *m*, nail-puller

arrancadero /a,rranka'ðero/ *m*, *Sports.* starting-point

arrancar /arran'kar/ *vt* to uproot; pull out; wrench; tear off; extirpate; obtain by threats; clear one's throat; *vt* and *Naut.* put on speed; *vi* start (a car); *Inf.* leave, quit; derive, originate **¡Arrancan!** And they're off! (races)

arrancarse /arran'karse/ *vr*, *Lat. Am.* to kick the bucket, pop off

arranque /a'rranke/ *m*, uprooting; extirpation; wrenching, pulling, seizing; stimulus (of passion); sudden impulse; *Mech.* start; *Mech.* starter. **a. automático,** self-starter

arras /'arras/ *f pl*, dowry; coins given by bridegroom to his bride; earnest money, token

arrasamiento /arrasa'miento/ *m*, demolition, destruction; leveling

arrasar /arra'sar/ *vt* to demolish, destroy; level; fill to the brim; *vi* and *vr* clear up (sky). **ojos arrasados de lágrimas,** eyes brimming with tears

arrastrado /arras'traðo/ *a Inf.* poverty-stricken, wretched; *Inf.* knavish; unhappy, unfortunate

arrastrar /arras'trar/ *vt* to drag; trail; convince; haul; *vi* trail along or touch the ground; trump (at cards); *vr* crawl, creep; shuffle along; humble oneself

arrastre /a'rrastre/ *m*, dragging, trailing; haulage; trumping (at cards); *Central America, Mexico* clout, pull

¡arre! /'arre/ *interj* Gee up! Get along!

arrear /arre'ar/ *vt* to spur on, whip up (horses, etc.). *interj Inf.* **¡Arrea!** Hurry up! Get on!

arrebañar /arreβa'ɲar/ *vt* to pick clean, clear; eat or drink up

arrebatado /arreβa'taðo/ *a* precipitate, headlong; rash; flushed, red

arrebatador /arreβata'ðor/ *a* overwhelming; violent; bewitching, captivating; delightful

arrebatamiento /arreβata'miento/ *m*, abduction; seizure; fury; ecstasy

arrebatar /arreβa'tar/ *vt* to abduct, carry off; seize, grab; attract, charm; grip (the attention); *vr* be overcome with rage

arrebatiña /arreβa'tiɲa/ *f*, grab; scuffle, scrimmage

arrebato /arre'βato/ *m*, fit (gen. of anger); ecstasy, rapture

arrebozar /arreβo'sar; arreβo'θar/ *vt* to muffle; envelop

arrebujarse /arreβu'harse/ *vr* to huddle; wrap oneself up

arrechucho /arre'tʃutʃo/ *m*, *Inf.* fit of rage; sudden slight ailment

arreciar /arre'siar; arre'θiar/ *vi* to increase in intensity; *vr* grow strong

arrecife /arre'sife; arre'θife/ *m*, reef (in the sea); stone-paved road

arredrar /arre'ðrar/ *vt* to separate, remove; force back, repel; terrify

arregazar /arrega'sar; arrega'θar/ **(se)** *vt* and *vr* to tuck up one's skirts

arreglado /arre'glaðo/ *a* regular; regulated; ordered; methodical

arreglar /arre'glar/ *vt* to regulate; arrange; adjust, put right; tidy; make up (the face); *vr* (*with prep a*) conform to; (*with con*) reach an agreement with. **Me voy a a.,** I am going to make myself presentable. *Inf.* **arreglárselas,** to shift for oneself

arreglo /a'rreglo/ *m*, arrangement; rule; regulation; method, order; agreement; adjustment; compromise

arrellanarse /arreya'narse; arreʎa'narse/ *vr* to settle comfortably in one's chair; be happy in one's work

arremangar /arremaŋ'gar/ *vt* to roll up (sleeves, trousers, etc.); *vr Inf.* make a decision

arremango /arre'maŋgo/ *m*, rolling or tucking up (of sleeve, etc.)

arremetedor /arremete'ðor/ **(-ra)** *n* attacker, assailant

arremeter /arreme'ter/ *vt* to attack, assail; *vi* launch oneself (at); *Fig.* spoil the view, shock the eye

arremetida /arreme'tiða/ *f*, attack, assault

arremolinarse /arremoli'narse/ *vr* to crowd, cluster, group

arrendador /arrenda'ðor/ **(-ra)** *n* landlord; renter; hirer; tenant

arrendamiento /arrenda'miento/ *m*, renting; hiring; rental; agreement, lease

arrendar /arren'dar/ *vt irr* to let, lease; hire; rent (as a tenant); train (horses); tie up (horses); restrain; mimic, imitate. See **recomendar**

arrendatario /arrenda'tario/ **(-ia)** *a* rent, lease. *n* tenant; lessee; hirer. **a. de contribuciones,** tax farmer

arreo /a'rreo/ *m*, ornament; apparel; *pl* horse trappings; appurtenances, equipment

¡Arrepa! /a'rrepa/ But look!, Hold on!, Hold your horses!, Not so fast!

arrepentimiento /arrepenti'miento/ *m*, repentance

arrepentirse /arrepen'tirse/ *vr irr* to repent, to change one's mind. See **sentir**

arrestado /arres'taðo/ *a* courageous, audacious, bold

arrestar /arres'tar/ *vt* to arrest, detain; *vr* be bold, dare

arresto /a'rresto/ *m*, arrest; detention; imprisonment; audacity, boldness

arriada /a'rriaða/ *f*, lowering (of a boat); taking in (of sail)

arriar /a'rriar/ *vt Naut.* to strike (colors); take in (sail); pay out (ropes, etc.); lower (boats); flood, inundate

arriate /a'rriate/ *m*, garden border; avenue, walk; trellis (for plants)

arriba /a'rriβa/ *adv* up, above; overhead; upstairs; earlier, before; upwards (with prices). *interj* **¡A.!** Up with!; Long live! **de a. abajo,** from head to foot, from one end to the other; completely, wholly

arribada /arri'βaða/ *f*, *Naut.* arrival. **de a.,** emergency (port)

arribar /arri'βar/ *vi Naut.* to arrive; put into an emergency port; reach, arrive at; *Inf.* convalesce; attain; *Naut.* drift

arribista /arri'βista/ *mf* social climber

arriero /a'rriero/ *m*, farrier; muleteer

arriesgado /arries'gaðo/ *a* dangerous, risky; rash, daring

arriesgar /arries'gar/ *vt* to risk; *vr* run into danger; dare, risk

arrimado /arri'maðo/ *m*, *Mexico* parasite

arrimar /arri'mar/ *vt* to bring or draw near; abandon (professions, etc.); lay aside, discard; *Inf.* administer (blows); *Naut.* stow (cargo); *vr* (*with prep a*) lean against, rest on; join, go with; seek the protection of. **Cada cual se arrima a su cada cual,** Birds of a feather flock together

arrimo /a'rrimo/ *m*, bringing or placing near; leaning or resting against; abandonment, giving up; protection; staff, support

arrinconado /arrinko'naðo/ *a* remote, secluded; forgotten, neglected

arrinconar /arrinko'nar/ *vt* to discard, lay aside; corner, besiege; set aside, dismiss; forsake; *vr* go into retirement, withdraw

arriscado /arris'kaðo/ *a* craggy, rugged; bold, resolute; sprightly, handsome

arriscarse /arris'karse/ *vr Lat. Am.* to dress to kill, dress to the nines

arro, arro, arro /'arro, 'arro, 'arro/ purrrr (echoic of a cat's purr)

arrobamiento /arroβa'miento/ *m*, ecstasy, rapture; trance

arrobar /arro'βar/ *vt* to charm, entrance; *vr* be enraptured; be in ecstasy

arrodillar /arroði'yar; arroði'ʎar/ *vt* to cause to kneel down; *vi* and *vr* kneel down

arrogancia /arro'gansia; arro'ganθia/ *f*, arrogance; courage; majesty, pride

arrogante /arro'gante/ *a* arrogant, haughty; courageous; proud, majestic

arrogar /arro'gar/ *vt* to adopt (as a son); *vr* usurp, appropriate

arrojadizo /arroha'ðiso; arroha'ðiθo/ *a* easily cast or hurled; projectile

arrojado /arro'haðo/ *a* bold, determined; rash

arrojar /arro'har/ *vt* to throw, hurl, cast; shed (light, etc.; e.g. *La cuenta arroja un total de cien dólares,* The bill shows a total of a hundred dollars); *Com.* show (a balance, etc.); put out (sprouts); dismiss, send away; *vr* cast oneself; (*with prep a*) hurl oneself against or upon; undertake, venture upon. **a. de sí (a),** to get rid of, dismiss

arrojo /a'rroho/ *m*, daring, intrepidity; boldness

arrollar /arro'yar; arro'ʎar/ *vt* to roll; make into a roll, roll up; defeat (the enemy); silence, confound; rock to sleep; bear along, carry off

arromar /arro'mar/ *vt* to blunt; flatten

arropar /arro'par/ *vt* to wrap up, cover

arrostrar /arros'trar/ *vt* to confront, defy, face up to; *vr* fight hand to hand. **a. las consecuencias,** *Fig.* to face the music

arroyada /arro'yaða/ *f*, gorge, gully; course, channel; flood

arroyo /a'rroyo/ *m*, stream, brook; street gutter; road, street; *Fig.* flood, plenty

arroz /a'rros; a'rroθ/ *m*, rice

arrozal /arro'sal; arro'θal/ *m*, rice field

arruga /a'rruga/ *f*, wrinkle; fold, pleat; crease

arrugamiento /arruga'miento/ *m*, wrinkling; fold, pleating; crumpling, creasing; corrugation

arrugar /arru'gar/ *vt* to wrinkle; pleat; corrugate; crumple, crease. **a. el ceño**, to knit one's brow, scowl

arruinamiento /arruina'miento/ *m*, ruin, decay, decline

arruinar /arrui'nar/ *vt* to ruin; destroy, damage severely

arrullar /arru'yar; arru'ʎar/ *vt* to bill and coo (doves); lull to sleep; *Inf.* whisper sweet words to, make love to

arrullo /a'rruyo; a'rruʎo/ *m*, cooing of doves; lullaby

arrumaco /arru'mako/ *m*, *Inf.* embrace, caress (gen. *pl*); ornament in bad taste

arrumaje /arru'mahe/ *m*, *Naut.* stowage; clouds on the horizon

arrurruz /arru'rrus; arru'rruθ/ *m*, arrowroot

arsenal /arse'nal/ *m*, dockyard; arsenal; *Fig.* store (of information, etc.)

arsénico /ar'seniko/ *m*, arsenic

arte /'arte/ *mf*, art; skill; ability, talent; guile, craftiness. **las bellas artes**, fine arts. *Inf.* **no tener a. ni parte en**, to have nothing to do with, have no part in

artefacto /arte'fakto/ *m*, machine, mechanism, apparatus; device, appliance. **a. atómico**, atomic bomb

arteria /ar'teria/ *f*, *Med.* artery; main line (of communication)

artería /ar'teria/ *f*, craftiness, guile

arterial /arte'rial/ *a* arterial

artesa /ar'tesa/ *f*, wooden trough; kneading bowl

artesano /arte'sano/ *n* (**-na**) artisan; mechanic

artesiano /arte'siano/ *a* artesian

artesón /arte'son/ *m*, bucket, pail; *Archit.* curved ceiling-panel; paneled ceiling

artesonado /arteso'naðo/ *a Archit.* paneled (ceiling). *m*, paneled ceiling

ártico /'artiko/ *a* Arctic

articulación /artikula'sion; artikula'θion/ *f*, joint, articulation; jointing; enunciation, pronunciation

articular /artiku'lar/ *vt* to joint, articulate; enunciate, pronounce clearly

articulista /artiku'lista/ *mf* article writer

artículo /ar'tikulo/ *m*, finger knuckle; heading; article; *Anat.* joint; *Gram.* article; *pl* goods, things. **a. de fondo**, leading article (in a newspaper). **a. de primera necesidad**, prime necessity, essential

artífice /ar'tifise; ar'tifiθe/ *mf* craftsman, artificer; author, creator; forger

artificial /artifi'sial; artifi'θial/ *a* artificial

artificio /arti'fiçio; arti'fiθio/ *m*, skill, art; appliance, contraption, mechanism; trick, cunning device; guile, craftiness

artificioso /artifi'sioso; artifi'θioso/ *a* skilful; artificial; crafty, cunning

artillería /artiye'ria; artiʎe'ria/ *f*, artillery. **a. de costa**, coastal guns. **a. ligera, a. montada, a. rodada** *or* **a. volante**, field artillery

artillero /arti'yero; arti'ʎero/ *m*, gunner

artimaña /arti'maɲa/ *f*, trick, ruse, stratagem

artista /ar'tista/ *mf* artist; performer

artístico /ar'tistiko/ *a* artistic

artrítico /ar'tritiko/ *a Med.* arthritic

artritis /ar'tritis/ *f*, *Med.* arthritis

arveja /ar'βeha/ *f*, *Bot.* vetch; *Lat. Am.* pea

arzobispo /arso'βispo; arθo'βispo/ *m*, archbishop

as /as/ *m*, Roman copper coin; ace (*Aer.* cards, etc.)

asa /'asa/ *f*, handle; pretext, excuse

asadero /asa'ðero/ *m*, *Mexico* cottage cheese

asado /a'saðo/ *m*, *Cul.* roast

asador /asa'ðor/ *m*, *Cul.* roasting-spit; roaster

asadura /asa'ðura/ *f*, *Cul.* chitterlings; offal

asalariar /asala'riar/ *vt* to fix a salary for

asaltador /asalta'ðor/ (**-ra**) *a* attacking. *n* assailant, attacker

asaltar /asal'tar/ *vt* to storm, besiege; assault, attack; occur to (ideas); come on suddenly (illness)

asalto /a'salto/ *m*, storming, besieging; assault, attack; bout (in fencing, boxing, wrestling); round (in a fight)

asamblea /asam'βlea/ *f*, congregation, assembly; meeting; legislative assembly; *Mil.* assembly (bugle call)

asambleísta /asamble'ista/ *mf* member of an assembly

asar /a'sar/ *vt Cul.* to roast; grill; *vr* be burning-hot; *Fig.* burn (with enthusiasm)

asaz /a'sas; a'saθ/ *adv* sufficiently, enough; very; in abundance. *a* sufficient; many

asbesto /as'βesto/ *m*, asbestos

ascalonia /aska'lonia/ *f*, *Bot.* shallot

ascendencia /assen'densia; asθen'denθia/ *f*, lineage, ancestry, origin

ascendente /assen'dente; asθen'dente/ *a* ascending

ascender /assen'der; asθen'der/ *vi irr* to ascend, climb; be promoted; (*with prep a*) amount to (bills, etc.); *vt* promote. See **entender**

ascendiente /assen'diente; asθen'diente/ *mf* ancestor, forbear. *m*, influence, ascendancy

ascensión /assen'sion; asθen'sion/ *f*, ascension; promotion; *Astron.* exaltation

ascenso /as'senso; as'θenso/ *m*, ascent; promotion, preferment

ascensor /assen'sor; asθen'sor/ *m*, lift, elevator

ascensorista /assenso'rista; asθenso'rista/ *mf* elevator operator

asceta /as'seta; as'θeta/ *mf* ascetic

ascético /as'setiko; as'θetiko/ *a* ascetic

ascetismo /asse'tismo; asθe'tismo/ *m*, asceticism

asco /'asko/ *m*, nausea; repugnance, loathing; revolting thing. *Inf.* **Me da a.**, it sickens me

ascua /'askua/ *f*, live coal, ember. **estar como una a. de oro**, to be as bright as a new pin. **estar en ascuas**, *Fig.* to be on pins

aseado /ase'aðo/ *a* clean, tidy

asear /ase'ar/ *vt* to tidy, make neat; clean up; decorate, adorn

asechanza /ase'tʃansa; ase'tʃanθa/ *f*, ambush; trick, snare, stratagem

asechar /ase'tʃar/ *vt* to ambush, waylay; *Fig.* lay snares for

asediador /aseðia'ðor/ (**-ra**) *n* besieger

asediar /ase'ðiar/ *vt* to besiege; pester, importune

asedio /a'seðio/ *m*, siege; importunity

asegurado /asegu'raðo/ (**-da**) *a* insured. *n* insured person

asegurador /asegura'ðor/ (**-ra**) *a* insuring. *n* insurer

asegurar /asegu'rar/ *vt* to fasten, make secure; pinion, grip; reassure, soothe; assert, state; *Com.* insure; guarantee; ensure, secure; *vr Com.* insure oneself; (*with de*) make sure of

asemejar /aseme'har/ *vt* to imitate, copy; make similar to; *vr* (*with prep a*) be like, be similar to

asenderear /asendere'ar/ *vt* to make a pathway through; persecute, harass

asenso /a'senso/ *m*, assent. **dar a.**, to believe, give credence (to)

asentaderas /asenta'ðeras/ *f pl*, *Inf.* buttocks, seat

asentado /asen'taðo/ *a* prudent, circumspect; permanent, stable

asentamiento /asenta'miento/ *m*, seating; settlement, residence; prudence, judgment

asentar /asen'tar/ *vt irr* to seat; place; fasten, fix; found; plant (flags); pitch (a tent); establish, make firm; smooth; hone (razors); estimate, budget, arrange, set forth; note down; affirm, believe; *Com.* enter (in an account); *vi* fit (clothes); *vr* seat oneself; alight (birds); settle (liquids); *Archit.* settle, subside; to be located (e.g. *El edificio se asienta en una esquina,* The building is located on a corner). **a. la mano en**, to strike hard. See **acertar**

asentimiento /asenti'miento/ *m*, assent; consent, approval

asentir /asen'tir/ *vi irr* to assent, agree; (*with en*) consent to. See **sentir**

aseñorado /aseɲo'raðo/ *a* refined, gentlemanly; lady-like; presumptuous

aseo /a'seo/ *m*, cleanliness, neatness

asepsia /a'sepsia/ *f*, asepsis

asequible /ase'kiβle/ *a* attainable; obtainable

aserción /aser'sion; aser'θion/ *f*, assertion

aserradero /aser'raðero/ *m*, sawmill; saw-pit

aserrador /aserra'ðor/ (**-ra**) *n* sawyer

aserrar /ase'rrar/ *vt irr* to saw. See **acertar**

aserrín /ase'rrin/ *m*, sawdust

aserruchar /aserru'tʃar/ *vt*, *Lat. Am.* to saw

asertivo /aser'tiβo/ *a* assertive

aserto /a'serto/ *m*, assertion

asesinar /asesi'nar/ *vt* to assassinate, murder

asesinato /asesi'nato/ *m*, assassination, murder

asesino /ase'sino/ *mf* assassin, murderer; murderess

asesor /ase'sor/ (**-ra**) *n* assessor

asesorar /aseso'rar/ *vt* to give advice; *vr* take legal advice; seek advice

asestar /ases'tar/ *vt* to aim (firearms); fire; deal (a blow)

aseveración /aseβera'sion; aseβera'θion/ *f*, assertion, statement

aseveradamente /aseβeraða'mente/ *adv* affirmatively

aseverar /aseβe'rar/ *vt* to affirm, assert

asfaltado /asfal'taðo/ *m*, asphalting; asphalt pavement

asfaltar /asfal'tar/ *vt* to asphalt

asfalto /as'falto/ *m*, asphalt

asfixia /as'fiksia/ *f*, *Med.* asphyxia

asfixiante /asfik'siante/ *a* asphyxiating

asfixiar /asfik'siar/ *vt* to asphyxiate

así /a'si/ *adv* thus, so, in this way; like this (e.g. *en días a.*, on days like this); even if; so that, therefore. **a. a.**, so-so. **a. como**, as well as; as soon as. **a. las cosas**, that being the case, **a. que**, as soon as, immediately; consequently, thus

asiático /a'siatiko/ (**-ca**) *a* and *n* Asiatic

asidero /asi'ðero/ *m*, hold, grasp; handle, haft; pretext, excuse

asido a /a'siðo a/ wedded to (e.g. a belief)

asiduo /a'siðuo/ *a* assiduous

asiento /a'siento/ *m*, seat; place, position; site; base (of a vase, etc.); lees, sediment; indigestion; *Archit.* subsidence, settling; treaty, pact; contract; note, reminder; *Com.* entry; permanence, stability; prudence; bit (of a bridle); *pl* buttocks, seat. **estar de a.**, to be established (in a place)

asignación /asigna'sion; asigna'θion/ *f*, assignation; appropriation (of money); salary; portion, share

asignar /asig'nar/ *vt* to assign; apportion; destine, intend; appoint

asignatario, -a /asigna'tario/ *mf Lat. Am.* heir, heiress, legatee

asignatura /asigna'tura/ *f*, subject (of study in schools, etc.)

asilar /asi'lar/ *vt* to give shelter to, receive; put into an institution

asilo /a'silo/ *m*, shelter, refuge; sanctuary, asylum; *Fig.* protection, defense; home, institution

asimetría /asime'tria/ *f*, asymmetry

asimétrico /asi'metriko/ *a* asymmetrical

asimiento /asi'miento/ *m*, hold, grasp; attachment, affection

asimilación /asimila'sion; asimila'θion/ *f*, assimilation

asimilar /asimi'lar/ *vt* to compare, liken; (*Bot. Zool. Gram.*) assimilate; *vi* resemble, be like; *Fig.* assimilate, digest (ideas)

asimismo /asi'mismo/ *adv* similarly, likewise

asir /a'sir/ *vt irr* to grasp, take hold of; seize; *vi* take root (plants); *vr* (*with de*) lay hold of; take advantage of; make an excuse to. *Pres. Ind.* **asgo, ases,** etc. *Pres. Subjunc.* **asga,** etc.

asirio /a'sirio/ (**-ia**) *a* and *n* Assyrian. *m*, Assyrian language

asistencia /asisten'sia; asis'tenθia/ *f*, presence, attendance; minimal attendance required (e.g. *Los alumnos*

tienen que completar una a., Pupils must attend a certain number of classes) assistance, help; service, attendance; medical treatment; remuneration; *pl* allowance. **a. pública**, Public Assistance. **a. social**, social work

asistenta /asis'tenta/ *f*, daily maid; waiting-maid

asistente /asis'tente/ *m*, assistant; *Mil.* orderly

asistir /asis'tir/ *vt* to accompany; assist, help; attend, treat; (*with de*) act as; *vi* (*with prep a*) be present at, attend; follow suit (in cards)

asma /'asma/ *f*, asthma

asmático /as'matiko/ (**-ca**) *a* asthmatic. *n* asthma sufferer

asnal /as'nal/ *a* asinine; brutish, stupid

asno /'asno/ *m*, ass

asociación /asosia'sion; asoθia'θion/ *f*, association; company, partnership; society, fellowship

asociado /aso'siaðo; aso'θiaðo/ (**-da**) *n* associate; member; partner

asociar /aso'siar; aso'θiar/ *vt* to associate; *vr* associate oneself; join together; form a partnership

asolar /aso'lar/ *vt irr* to destroy, devastate, lay flat; *vr* wither; settle (liquids). See **contar**

asoldar /asol'dar/ *vt irr* to employ, engage, hire. See **contar**

asolear /asole'ar/ *vt* to expose to the sun; *vr* sun oneself; become sunburnt

asomada /aso'maða/ *f*, brief appearance; vantage point

asomar /aso'mar/ *vt* to show, allow to appear, put forth; *vi* begin to show; *vr* show oneself, appear; *Inf.* be flushed (with wine); (*with prep a, por*) look out of. **asomarse a la ventana,** to show oneself at, or look out of, the window

asombrar /asom'βrar/ *vt* to shade, shadow; darken (a color); terrify; amaze

asombro /a'sombro/ *m*, fright, terror; amazement; wonder, marvel

asombroso /asom'βroso/ *a* amazing; marvelous, wonderful

asonancia /aso'nansia; aso'nanθia/ *f*, assonance; congruity, harmony

asordar /asor'ðar/ *vt* to deafen

asorocharse /asoro'tʃarse/ *vr*, *Peru* to come down with altitude sickness, get altitude sickness

aspa /'aspa/ *f*, cross; sail of a windmill

aspaviento /aspa'βiento/ *m*, exaggerated display of emotion; gesture (of horror, etc.); **hacer aspavientos,** to make a fuss

aspecto /as'pekto/ *m*, look, appearance; aspect, outlook

aspereza /aspe'resa; aspe'reθa/ *f*, roughness, harshness; ruggedness, rockiness; severity, asperity

áspero /'aspero/ *a* rough, harsh; uneven, rocky; jarring, grating; hard, severe

aspersión /asper'sion/ *f*, *Eccl.* aspersion; sprinkling

áspid /'aspið/ *m*, asp, viper

aspiración /aspira'sion; aspira'θion/ *f*, breath; breathing; aspiration, desire; *Mus.* pause

aspirador /aspira'ðor/ (**de polvo**) *m*, vacuum cleaner

aspirante /aspi'rante/ *m*, aspirant, novice; office-seeker; applicant

aspirar /aspi'rar/ *vt* to breathe in, inhale; *Gram.* aspirate; (*with prep a*) aspire to, desire

aspirina /aspi'rina/ *f*, aspirin

asquear /aske'ar/ *vi* and *vt* to hate, loathe

asquerosidad /askerosi'ðað/ *f*, filthiness, loathsomeness; vileness, hatefulness

asqueroso /aske'roso/ *a* nauseating; loathsome, revolting; vile, hateful

asta /'asta/ *f*, lance, spear, pike; horn (of bull); antler; flagstaff; shaft. **a media a.,** at half-mast

asterisco /aste'risko/ *m*, asterisk

astigmático /astig'matiko/ *a* astigmatic

astigmatismo /astigma'tismo/ *m*, astigmatism

astil /as'til/ *m*, handle, pole, shaft; bar of a balance; beam feather

astilla /as'tiya; as'tiʎa/ *f*, splinter

astillar /asti'yar; asti'ʎar/ *vt* to splinter, chip

astillero /asti'yero; asti'ʎero/ *m*, shipyard; rack for lances and pikes

astilloso /asti'yoso; asti'ʎoso/ *a* splintery, fragile

astracán /astra'kan/ *m*, astrakhan

astringente /astrin'hente/ *a* astringent

astringir /astrin'hir/ *vt* to tighten up; compress; constrain

astro /'astro/ *m*, heavenly body

astrolatría /astrola'tria/ *f*, astrolatry, star worship

astrología /astrolo'hia/ *f*, astrology

astrológico /astro'lohiko/ *a* astrological

astrólogo /as'trologo/ (**-ga**) *n* astrologist

astronauta /astro'nauta/ *m*, astronaut

astronomía /astrono'mia/ *f*, astronomy

astronómico /astro'nomiko/ *a* astronomical

astrónomo /as'tronomo/ *m*, astronomer

astucia /as'tusia; as'tuθia/ *f*, astuteness, guile, craftiness

asturiano /astu'riano/ (**-na**) *a* and *n* Asturian

astuto /as'tuto/ *a* guileful, crafty, astute

asueto /a'sueto/ *m*, day's holiday

asumir /asu'mir/ *vt* to assume; adopt, appropriate

asunción /asun'sion; asun'θion/ *f*, assumption. **La Asunción,** the Feast of the Assumption

asunto /a'sunto/ *m*, matter, theme, subject; business, affair

asustadizo /asusta'ðiso; asusta'ðiθo/ *a* timid, nervous, easily frightened

asustar /asus'tar/ *vt* to frighten; **que asusta,** terribly (e.g. *Es de una ñoñería que asusta,* It's a terribly timid thing to do) *vr* be frightened

atablar /ata'βlar/ *vt* to roll, flatten (earth)

atacado /ata'kaðo/ *a Inf.* hesitant; mean, stingy

atacador /ataka'ðor/ (**-ra**) *a* attacking. *n* aggressor, attacker

atacar /ata'kar/ *vt* to attack; fasten, button; fit (clothes); ram (guns); *Fig.* press hard, corner (persons). **a. a los nervios,** to jar on the nerves

ataché /ata'tʃe/ *m. Central America* (paper) clip

atadero /ata'ðero/ *m*, rope, tie, cord; hook, ring, etc. (for hitching); hindrance, impediment; hitching or fastening point

atado /a'taðo/ *m*, bundle, roll

atadura /ata'ðura/ *f*, tying, stringing, fastening, tie; knot; connection

atajar /ata'har/ *vi* to take a short cut; *vt* intercept, cut off; screen off, divide; impede, stop; interrupt (people); **atajarle la palabra a uno,** to cut somebody off, interrupt *vr* be overcome (by fear, shame, etc.)

atajo /a'taho/ *m*, short cut, quick way; cutting, abbreviation; division. *Inf.* **echar por el a.,** to go to the root of (a matter)

atalaya /ata'laya/ *f*, look out, watch tower; observation point. *m*, lookout

atalayar /atala'yar/ *vt* to scan, watch; spy upon

atalón /ata'lon/ *m*, atoll, coral island

atañadero /ataɲa'ðero/ *n:* **en lo atañadero a** with regard to, with respect to

atañer /ata'ɲer/ *vi impers* to concern, affect; belong, pertain

ataque /a'take/ *m*, (*Mil. Med.*) attack; quarrel, fight

atar /a'tar/ *vt* to tie; fasten; lace; stop, paralyse; *vr* get in a fix; confine oneself. **a. cabos,** to put two and two together

atardecer /atarðe'ser; atarðe'θer/ *vi irr impers* to grow dusk. See **conocer**

atardecer /atarðe'ser; atarðe'θer/ *m*, dusk, evening

atarear /atare'ar/ *vt* to set to work, assign work to; *vr* work hard

atarugar /ataru'gar/ *vt* to wedge; stop up; plug; block; *Inf.* silence, shut up; stuff, cram; *vr Fig. Inf.* lose one's head

atasajar /atasa'har/ *vt* to cut up, jerk (beef, etc.)

atascadero /ataska'ðero/ *m*, deep rut, boggy place; impediment, obstacle

atascar /atas'kar/ *vt* to plug; block up; stop (a leak); hinder, obstruct; *vr* stick in the mud; be held up or delayed; *Inf.* get stuck in a speech

atasco /a'tasko/ *m*, obstruction, block

ataúd /ata'uð/ *m*, coffin

ataviar /ata'βiar/ *vt* to deck, apparel, adorn

atavío /ata'βio/ *m*, get-up, dress, apparel; *pl* ornaments

atavismo /ata'βismo/ *m*, atavism

ate /'ate/ *m*, *Mexico* kind of Turkish delight

ateísmo /ate'ismo/ *m*, atheism

atejonarse /ateho'narse/ *vr Mexico* to hide

atelaje /ate'lahe/ *m*, team, yoke (of horses); trappings, harness; *Inf.* trousseau

atemperación /atempera'sion; atempera'θion/ *f*, moderation, mitigation; tempering

atemperar /atempe'rar/ *vt* to moderate, mitigate; adapt, adjust; temper, cool. **atemperarse a la realidad,** to adjust to reality

Atenas /a'tenas/ Athens

atenazar /atena'sar; atena'θar/ *vt* to grip, grasp; torture

atención /aten'sion; aten'θion/ *f*, attention; solicitude, kindness; courtesy, civility; *pl* business affairs. *interj* **¡A.!** Take care! Look out!; *Mil.* Attention! **en a.** (**a**), taking into consideration. **estar en a.,** (patient) to be under treatment

atender /aten'der/ *vt irr* to await, expect; take care of, look after; *vi* (*with prep a*) attend to, listen to; *vi* remember. See **entender**

ateneo /ate'neo/ *m*, atheneum. *a* Athenian

atenerse /ate'nerse/ *vr irr* (*with prep a*) to abide by; resort to, rely on. See **tener**

ateniense /ate'niense/ *a* and *mf* Athenian

atentado /aten'taðo/ *a* prudent, sensible; secret, silent. *m*, infringement, violation; attempt (on a person's life); crime

atentar /aten'tar/ *vt irr* to do illegally; attempt a crime; *vr* proceed cautiously; restrain oneself. See **acertar**

atento /a'tento/ *a* attentive; courteous, civil. *adv* taking into consideration. **su atenta** (**atta**), *Com.* your favor

atenuación /atenua'sion; atenua'θion/ *f*, attenuation, diminution

atenuante /ate'nuante/ *a* attenuating; extenuating (of circumstances)

atenuar /ate'nuar/ *vt* to attenuate, diminish; extenuate

ateo /a'teo/ (**-ea**) *a* atheistic. *n* atheist

aterirse /ate'rirse/ *vr defective* to grow stiff with cold

aterrador /aterra'ðor/ *a* terrifying, dreadful

aterraje /ate'rrahe/ *m*, (*Aer., Naut.*) landing

aterramiento /aterra'miento/ *m*, horror, terror; terrorization; *Naut.* landing; ruin, demolition

aterrar /ate'rrar/ *vt irr* to demolish; discourage; cover with earth; *vi* land; *vr Naut.* draw near to land. See **acertar**

aterrizaje /aterri'sahe; aterri'θahe/ *m*, *Aer.* landing. **a. forzoso,** forced landing. **campo de a.,** landing field

aterrizar /aterri'sar; aterri'θar/ *vi Aer.* to land, touch down

aterrorizar /aterrori'sar; aterrori'θar/ *vt* to terrify; terrorize

atesar /ate'sar/ *vt Lat. Am.* to tighten (up)

atesorar /ateso'rar/ *vt* to hoard, treasure up

atestación /atesta'sion; atesta'θion/ *f*, attestation, affidavit

atestar /ates'tar/ *vt irr* to stuff, cram; insert, pack; *Inf.* stuff with food; crowd, fill with people; attest, testify. See **acertar**

atestiguación /atestigua'sion; atestigua'θion/ *f*, deposition, testimony

atestiguar /atesti'guar/ *vt* to testify, attest

atetar /ate'tar/ *vt* to suckle; *vi* suck

atezado /ate'saðo; ate'θaðo/ *a* bronzed, sunburnt; black

ático /'atiko/ *a* Attic; *m*, penthouse

atiesar /atie'sar/ *vt* to stiffen

atildar /atil'dar/ *vt* to place a tilde over; blame, criticize; decorate, ornament

atimia /a'timia/ *f*, loss of status

atinado /ati'naðo/ *a* pertinent, relevant

atinar /ati'nar/ *vi* to find by touch; discover by chance; guess; hit the mark

atinente a... /ati'nente a / concerning...

atingencia /atiŋ'gensia; atiŋ'genθia/ f, Lat. Am. connection, relationship

atingir /atiŋ'gir/ vt, Lat. Am. to concern, relate to

atisbadura /atisβa'ðura/ f, watching, spying, prying

atisbar /atis'βar/ vt to spy upon, watch

atisbo /a'tisβo/ m, prying, watching; suspicion, hint

atisbón /atis'βon/ a penetrating (mind, vision)

atizador /atisa'ðor; atiθa'ðor/ m, poker (for the fire)

atizar /ati'sar; ati'θar/ vt to poke (the fire); dowse, snuff; trim (lamps); excite, rouse; Inf. slap, wallop

atlántico /at'lantiko/ a Atlantic. m, Atlantic Ocean

atleta /at'leta/ m, athlete

atlético /at'letiko/ a athletic

atletismo /atle'tismo/ m, athletics

atmósfera /at'mosfera/ f, atmosphere

atmosférico /atmos'feriko/ a atmospheric

atolladero /atoya'ðero; atoʎa'ðero/ m, rut; mud; bog

atolón /ato'lon/ m, atoll, coral island

atolondrado /atolon'draðo/ a scatter-brained, flighty

atolondramiento /atolondra'miento/ m, rashness, recklessness; bewilderment

atolondrar /atolon'drar/ vt to bewilder, confuse

atómico /a'tomiko/ a atomic

átomo /a'tomo/ m, atom; speck, particle

atónito /a'tonito/ a amazed, astounded

atontar /aton'tar/ vt to confuse, daze; make stupid; stun

atormentador /atormenta'ðor/ (-ra) a torturing. n tormentor; torturer

atormentar /atormen'tar/ vt to torment; torture; grieve, harass

atorrante /ato'rrante/ a and mf (Argentina) good-for-nothing

atracadero /atraka'ðero/ m, jetty, landingstage

atracar /atra'kar/ vt Inf. to stuff with food; Naut. tie up, moor; hold up, rob; vi Naut. moor, stop; vr Inf. guzzle, gorge

atracción /atrak'sion; atrak'θion/ f, attraction

atraco /a'trako/ (a) m, hold up (of), ambush (of)

atracón /atra'kon/ m, Inf. gorge, fill; surfeit. **darse atracones de,** to gorge oneself on

atractivo /atrak'tiβo/ a attractive. m, attraction, charm

atractriz /atrak'tris; atrak'triθ/ a attracting; f, force of attraction; (fig.) lure

atraer /atra'er/ vt irr to attract; charm, enchant. See **traer**

atragantarse /atragan'tarse/ vr to choke; Inf. be at a loss, dry up (in conversation)

atraíble /atra'iβle/ a attractable, able to be attracted

atrancar /atran'kar/ vt to bar the door; obstruct; block; hinder; vi Inf. stride; skip (in reading)

atrapar /atra'par/ vt Inf. grab, seize, catch; net, obtain; deceive

atrás /a'tras/ adv behind, back; past; previously. **¡A.!** Back! **años a.,** years ago

atrasado /atra'saðo/ a slow (of clocks); backward; old-fashioned; hard-up, poor. **a. mental,** retarded person

atrasar /atra'sar/ vt to delay, retard; fix a later date than the true one; put back (clocks). vi be slow (clocks); vr be late; be left behind

atraso /a'traso/ m, delay; backwardness, dullness; slowness (clocks); lateness; pl arrears. **El reloj lleva cinco minutos de a.,** The watch is five minutes slow

atravesado /atraβe'saðo/ a slightly squint-eyed; mongrel, crossbreed; half-caste; ill-intentioned

atravesar /atraβe'sar/ vt irr to lay across, put athwart; cross, traverse; pierce; obstruct; Naut. lie to; vr be among, mingle (with); interrupt; interfere, take part; quarrel; occur, arise. See **confesar**

atrayente /atra'yente/ a attractive

atreverse /atre'βerse/ vr to dare, risk, venture; be overbold or insolent

atrevido /atre'βiðo/ a bold, audacious; hazardous, dangerous; brazen, impudent

atribución /atriβu'sion; atriβu'θion/ f, attribution; perquisite, attribute

atribuible /atri'βuiβle/ a attributable

atribuir /atri'βuir/ vt irr to impute, attribute; assign, turn over to; vr take upon oneself, assume. See **huir**

atributo /atri'βuto/ m, attribute, quality

atril /a'tril/ m, lectern, reading desk; music stand

atrincherar /atrintʃe'rar/ vt to protect with entrenchments; vr entrench oneself

atrio /'atrio/ m, atrium; hall, vestibule; Archit. parvis

atrocidad /atrosi'ðað; atroθi'ðað/ f, atrocity, cruelty; Inf. terrific amount; enormity, crime

atrofia /a'trofia/ f, atrophy

atrofiarse /atro'fiarse/ vr to atrophy

atrojarse /atro'harse/ vr Mexico to be stumped, be stuck (for an answer)

atronado /atro'naðo/ a harebrained, foolish

atronar /atro'nar/ vt irr to deafen, stun with noise; confuse, daze. See **tronar**

atropelladamente /atropeyaða'mente; atropeʎaða'mente/ adv in disorder, helter-skelter

atropellado /atrope'yaðo; atrope'ʎaðo/ a rash, foolhardy

atropellar /atrope'yar; atrope'ʎar/ vt to trample upon; thrust out of the way; knock down; run over (with a vehicle), crash; disregard, violate (feelings); insult, abuse; transgress; do hastily; vr act rashly

atropello /atro'peyo; atro'peʎo/ m, trampling; road accident; knocking over; upsetting; violation; outrage

atroz /a'ntros; a'troθ/ a atrocious, savage; monstrous, outrageous; Inf. terrific, enormous

atufar /atu'far/ vt to irritate, vex; vr grow irritated; turn sour (wine, etc.)

atún /a'tun/ m, tuna fish, tuna

aturdido /atur'ðiðo/ a reckless, scatterbrained, silly; thoughtless; stunned

aturdimiento /aturði'miento/ m, daze; confusion, bewilderment

aturdir /atur'ðir/ vt to daze; confuse, bewilder; amaze; stun

atusar /atu'sar/ vt to trim (hair, beard); Agr. prune; smooth down (hair); vr dress over-carefully

audacia /au'ðasia; au'ðaθia/ f, audacity

audaz /au'ðas; au'ðaθ/ a audacious, daring

audibilidad /auðiβili'ðað/ f, audibility

audición /auði'sion; auði'θion/ f, audition

audiencia /au'ðiensia; au'ðienθia/ f, audience, hearing; Law. audience; audience chamber

audífono /au'ðifono/ m, hearing aid

audioteca /auðio'teka/ f, audio library

auditor /auði'tor/ m, magistrate, judge

auditorio /auði'torio/ a auditory. m, audience

auge /'auhe/ m, Fig. zenith, height; Astron. apogee

augusto /au'gusto/ a august, awesome

aula /'aula/ f, lecture or class room; Poet. palace

aullar /au'yar; au'ʎar/ vi to howl; bay

aullido /au'yiðo; au'ʎiðo/ m, howl; baying

aumentar /aumen'tar/ (se) vt vi vr to increase, augment

aumentativo /aumenta'tiβo/ a Gram. augmentative

aumento /au'mento/ m, increase; progress; enlargement; Mexico postscript **ir en a.,** to increase; advance, progress; prosper

aun /a'un/ adv even. **A. los que viven lejos han de oíros,** Even those who live far must hear you. **a. así** or **a. siendo así,** even so. **a. ayer,** only yesterday. **a. cuando,** even if. **más a.,** even more. **ni a. si,** not even if.

aún /a'un/ adv still, yet. **A. no te creen** or **No te creen a.,** They still don't believe you **¿A. se lo darás?** or **¿Se lo darás a.?** Will you still give it to her?

aunque /'aunke/ conjunc although, even if, even though. It takes the Indicative referring to statement of fact and Subjunctive referring to a hypothesis, e.g. A. vino, no lo hizo, Although he came, he did not do it. A. él cantase yo no iría allí, Even though he sang (were to sing), I should not go there

aura /'aura/ f, zephyr, gentle breeze; popularity, approbation; aura. **a. epiléptica,** Med. epileptic aura

áureo /'aureo/ a gold, gilt; golden

auricular /auriku'lar/ a auricular. m, little finger; receiver, ear-piece (of a telephone); earphone (radio)

aurífero /au'rifero/ a gold-yielding, auriferous

auriga /au'riga/ m, charioteer

aurora /au'rora/ f, dawn; genesis, beginnings. **a. boreal,** aurora borealis, Northern Lights

auscultación /auskulta'sion; auskulta'θion/ f, Med. auscultation

auscultar /auskul'tar/ vt Med. to auscultate

ausencia /au'sensia; au'senθia/ f, absence. **en ausencia de,** in the absence of

ausentar /ausen'tar/ vt to send away; vr absent oneself

ausente /au'sente/ a absent. mf absent person

auspicio /aus'pisio; aus'piθio/ m, augury, prediction; favor, patronage; pl auspices

austeridad /austeri'ðað/ f, austerity; mortification of the flesh

austero /aus'tero/ a austere, ascetic; severe, harsh; honest, upright

austral /aus'tral/ a southerly, austral

australiano /austra'liano/ **(-na)** a and n Australian

austríaco /aus'triako/ **(-ca)** a and n Austrian

austrófilo /aus'trofilo/ a and n Austrophile

autenticación /autentika'sion; autentika'θion/ f, authentication

autenticar /autenti'kar/ vt to authenticate, attest; prove genuine

autenticidad /autentisi'ðað; autentiθi'ðað/ f, authenticity

auténtico /au'tentiko/ a authentic

autero, -a /au'tero/ mf, Lat. Am. car thief

auto /'auto/ m, Law. sentence, decision; Theat. one-act allegory (gen. religious); pl proceedings. **a. de fe,** auto-da-fé. **a. de reconocimiento,** search-warrant. **a. sacramental,** one-act religious drama on theme of mystery of the Eucharist. **hacer a. de fe de,** to burn at the stake

autobiografía /autoβiogra'fia/ f, autobiography

autobús /auto'βus/ m, motor bus, bus

autocitarse /autosi'tarse; autoθi'tarse/ vr to quote from one's own works

autoclave /auto'klaβe/ m, pressure cooker

autocracia /auto'krasia; auto'kraθia/ f, autocracy

autócrata /au'tokrata/ mf autocrat

autocrático /auto'kratiko/ a autocratic

autocrueldad /autokruel'dað/ f, self-inflicted pain

autodescubrimiento /autoðeskuβri'miento/ m, self-discovery

autodidacto /autoði'ðakto/ a autodidactic; self-educated, self-taught

autódromo /au'toðromo/ m, speedway

autógeno /au'toheno/ a autogenous, self-generating

autogiro /auto'hiro/ m, Aer. autogyro

autografía /autogra'fia/ f, autography

autográfico /auto'grafiko/ a autographic, in lithographic reproduction

autógrafo /au'tografo/ a autographical. m, autograph

autoinducción /autoinduk'sion; autoinduk'θion/ f, self-induction

autómata /au'tomata/ m, automaton

automático /auto'matiko/ a automatic. m, Sew. press stud

automatismo /automa'tismo/ m, automatism

automejoramiento /autome,hora'miento/ m, self-improvement

automóvil /auto'moβil/ m, automobile, motor car. a automatic

automovilismo /automoβi'lismo/ m, motoring

automovilista /automoβi'lista/ mf motorist

autonombrarse /autonom'βrarse/ vr to call oneself, go by the name of

autonomía /autono'mia/ f, autonomy

autónomo /au'tonomo/ a autonomous

autopista /auto'pista/ f, motor road

autopsia /au'topsia/ f, Med. autopsy, post-mortem

autor /au'tor/ **(-ra)** n agent, originator; author; inventor; Law. perpetrator

autoridad /autori'ðað/ f, authority; pomp, show

autoritario /autori'tario/ a authoritarian; authoritative

autorización /autorisa'sion; autoriθa'θion/ f, authorization

autorizado /autori'saðo; autori'θaðo/ a approved, authorized, responsible

autorizar /autori'sar; autori'θar/ vt to authorize; Law. attest, testify; cite, prove by reference; approve; exalt

autorretratarse /autorretra'tarse/ vr to have one's portrait painted, sit for one's portrait

autorretrato /autorre'trato/ m, self-portrait

autostopista /autosto'pista/ mf hitchhiker

autosugestión /autosuhes'tion/ f, autosuggestion

auxiliador /auksilia'ðor/ **(-ra)** a assistant; helpful. n helper, assistant

auxiliar /auksi'liar/ vt to help, aid; attend (the dying). m, Educ. lecturer. a assisting

auxiliaría /auksilia'ria/ f, Educ. lectureship

auxilio /auk'silio/ m, help, aid, assistance

aval /a'βal/ m, Com. endorsement; voucher

avalar /aβa'lar/ vt to enhance. **avalado por la tradición,** hallowed by tradition

avalentado /aβalen'taðo/ a boastful, bragging

avalorar /aβalo'rar/ vt to value, estimate; put spirit into, encourage

avance /a'βanse; a'βanθe/ m, advance; advance payment; balance sheet; attack

avanzada /aβan'saða; aβan'θaða/ f, Mil. advance guard

avanzado /aβan'saðo; aβan'θaðo/ a advanced, progressive

avanzar /aβan'sar; aβan'θar/ vt to advance; promote; vi advance; attack; grow late (time)

avanzo /a'βanso; a'βanθo/ m, balance sheet; price estimate

avaricia /aβa'risia; aβa'riθia/ f, greed, avarice

avaricioso, avariento /aβari'sioso, aβa'riento; aβari'θioso, aβa'riento/ a avaricious, greedy

avaro /a'βaro/ **(-ra)** a miserly; greedy. n miser

avasallador /aβasaʎa'ðor; aβasaʎa'ðor/ a dominating; Fig. overwhelming; enslaving

avasallar /aβasa'ʎar; aβasa'ʎar/ vt to subdue, dominate; vr become a vassal; surrender, yield

ave /'aβe/ f, bird. **a. de paso,** migratory bird; Fig. bird of passage. **a. de rapiña,** bird of prey. **a. fría,** Ornith. plover. **ave cantora,** songbird

avecinarse /aβesi'narse; aβeθi'narse/ vr to be approaching (e.g. el año que avecina, the coming year)

avellana /aβe'yana; aβe'ʎana/ f, hazel nut

avellano /aβe'yano; aβe'ʎano/ m, Bot. hazel

avemaría /aβema'ria/ f, Hail Mary (prayer); Angelus; rosary bead. Inf. **en un a.,** in a split second

avena /a'βena/ f, oats; Poet. oaten pipe. **a. loca,** wild oats

avenal /aβe'nal/ m, oatfield

avenar /aβe'nar/ vt to drain (land); drain off (liquids)

avenencia /aβe'nensia; aβe'nenθia/ f, agreement, arrangement; transaction; conformity, harmony

avenida /aβe'niða/ f, flood, spate; avenue; abundance; way, approach (to a place)

avenido /aβe'niðo/ a (with bien or mal) well or ill-suited

avenidor /aβeni'ðor/ **(-ra)** n arbitrator, mediator

avenir /aβe'nir/ vt to reconcile; vi happen (used in infinitive and third singular and plural); vr be reconciled; agree; compromise, give way; harmonize (things); (with con) get on with, agree with. See **venir**

aventador /aβenta'ðor/ m, Agr. winnower; pitchfork

aventajado /aβenta'haðo/ a outstanding, talented; advantageous. m, Mil. private who enjoys extra pay

aventajar /aβenta'har/ vt to improve, better; promote, prefer; excel; vr (with prep a) surpass, excel. **Te aventajo en diez años,** I'm ten years older than you

aventamiento /aβenta'miento/ m, winnowing

aventar /aβen'tar/ vt irr to fan; air, ventilate; winnow; Inf. drive away, expel; vr be inflated; Inf. flee; smell (bad meat). See **sentar**

aventón /aβen'ton/ m, Mexico hitch, lift, ride

aventura /aβen'tura/ f, adventure; chance, luck; risk, danger

aventurar /aβentu'rar/ *vt* to risk, hazard

aventurero /aβentu'rero/ *a* adventurous; unscrupulous, intriguing; undisciplined (of troops). *n* adventurer

avergonzar /aβergon'sar; aβergon'θar/ *vt irr* to shame; make shy, abash; *vr* be ashamed; be shy or sheepish. *Pres. Ind.* **avergüenzo, avergüenzas, avergüenza, avergüenzan.** *Pres. Subjunc.* **avergüence, avergüences, avergüence, avergüencen**

avería /aβe'ria/ *f*, aviary; damage (to merchandise); loss, harm; *Elec.* fault; breakdown. **a. gruesa,** general average (marine insurance)

averiarse /aβe'riarse/ *vr* to be damaged; deteriorate; break down

averiguable /aβeri'guaβle/ *a* examinable, investigable; discoverable

averiguación /aβerigua'sion; aβerigua'θion/ *f*, inquiry, investigation; discovery

averiguar /aβeri'guar/ *vt* to investigate, inquire into; discover, ascertain. **¡averígüelo Vargas!** Beats me!, Search me!

averigüetas /aβeri'guetas/ *mf*, *Lat. Am.* snoopers, nosy parker

averío /aβe'rio/ *m*, flock of birds

aversión /aβer'sion/ *f*, aversion, repugnance

avestruz /aβes'trus; aβes'truθ/ *m*, ostrich

avetado /aβe'taðo/ *a* veined, mottled, streaked

avezar /aβe'sar; aβe'θar/ *vt* to accustom; *vr* grow accustomed (to)

aviación /aβia'sion; aβia'θion/ *f*, aviation

aviador /aβia'ðor/ *m*, aviator

aviar /a'βiar/ *vt* to outfit, equip; prepare, make ready; *Inf.* speed up; caulk (ship). *Fig. Inf.* **estar aviado,** to be in a mess

avidez /aβi'ðes; aβi'ðeθ/ *f*, avidity, greed; longing, desire

ávido /'aβiðo/ *a* avid, greedy

avieso /a'βieso/ *a* twisted, crooked; ill-natured; sinister; *m Colombia* abortion

avillanado /aβiya'naðo; aβiʎa'naðo/ *a* countrified; gross, vulgar; boorish

avío /a'βio/ *m*, preparation, provision; picnic lunch; money advanced (to miners or laborers); *pl Inf.* equipment, tools. **avíos de pesca,** fishing tackle

avión /a'βion/ *m*, airplane; *Ornith.* martin or swift. **a. de bombardeo,** bomber. **a. de caza,** fighter plane. **a. de combate nocturno,** night fighter. **a. de hostigamiento,** interceptor. **a. de reacción,** jet airplane. **a. de transporte,** *Aer.* transport. **a. en picado,** divebomber. **a. taxi,** air taxi. **por a.,** by airmail **«Avión»** "Airmail"

avioneta /aβio'neta/ *f*, light airplane, small airplane

avisado /aβi'saðo/ *a* shrewd, sensible. **mal a.,** ill-advised, imprudent

avisar /aβi'sar/ *vt* to inform, acquaint; warn; advise

aviso /a'βiso/ *m*, notice, announcement; warning; advice; care, caution; attention; shrewdness, prudence. **estar sobre a.,** to be on call; be on the alert

avispa /a'βispa/ *f*, wasp

avispado /aβis'paðo/ *a Inf.* smart, clever, quick; wide-awake

avispar /aβis'par/ *vt* to goad, prick; *Inf.* rouse, incite; *vr* be uneasy, fret

avispero /aβis'pero/ *m*, wasp's nest; swarm of wasps; *Fig. Inf.* hornet's nest

avispón /aβis'pon/ *m*, hornet

avistamiento /aβista'miento/ *m*, sighting, spotting (e.g. of a ship)

avistar /aβis'tar/ *vt* to descry, sight, spot; *vr* **avistarse con,** to interview

avituallar /aβitua'yar; aβitua'ʎar/ *vt* to victual, supply with food

avivar /aβi'βar/ *vt* to enliven; stimulate, encourage; stir (fire); trim (wicks); brighten (colors); inflame; vivify, invigorate; *vi* revive, recover

avizor /aβi'sor; aβi'θor/ *m*, watcher, spy. *a* watchful, vigilant

avizorar /aβiso'rar; aβiθo'rar/ *vt* to watch, spy upon

avutarda /aβu'tarða/ *f*, bustard

axila /ak'sila/ *f*, *Bot.* axil; *Anat.* axilla, armpit

axioma /ak'sioma/ *m*, axiom

axiomático /aksio'matiko/ *a* axiomatic

¡ay! /ai/ *interj* Alas! Woe is me! *m*, complaint, sigh

ayer /a'yer/ *adv* yesterday; a short while ago; in the past. *m*, past

ayllu /'aiju; 'aiʎu/ *m*, *Peru* Native American commune

ayo /'ayo/ *mf*, tutor

ayote /a'yote/ *m*, *Mexico, Central America* pumpkin

ayuda /a'yuða/ *f*, help, assistance; enema; clyster; watch dog. *m*, **a. de cámara,** valet

ayudador /ayuða'ðor/ **(-ra)** *a* helping, assisting. *n* helper

ayudante /ayu'ðante/ *m*, assistant; teaching assistant; *Mil.* adjutant. **a. a cátedra,** *Educ.* assistant lecturer. **a. de plaza,** post adjutant

ayudar /ayu'ðar/ *vt* to assist; help, aid; *vr* make an effort; avail oneself of another's help

ayunador /ayuna'ðor/ **(-ra)** *a* fasting. *n* faster; abstainer

ayunar /ayu'nar/ *vi* to fast

ayuno /a'yuno/ *m*, fast. *a* fasting; ignorant, unaware. **en a.** or **en ayunas,** before breakfast, fasting; *Inf.* ignorant, unaware

ayuntamiento /ayunta'miento/ *m*, meeting, assembly; municipal government; town hall; sexual union

azabache /asa'βatʃe; aθa'βatʃe/ *m*, *Mineral.* jet

azada /a'saða; a'θaða/ *f*, *Agr.* spade; hoe

azadón /asa'ðon; aθa'ðon/ *m. Agr.* hoe

azafata /asa'fata; aθa'fata/ *f*, queen's waiting-maid *Obs.*; flight attendant

azafate /asa'fate; aθa'fate/ *m*, flat basket; small tray

azafrán /asa'fran; aθa'fran/ *m*, *Bot.* saffron; crocus

azafranado /asafra'naðo; aθafra'naðo/ *a* saffron-colored

azahar /a'saar; a'θaar/ *m*, flower of orange, lemon or sweet lime tree

azar /a'sar; a'θar/ *m*, chance, hazard; unexpected misfortune; losing card or throw of dice

azararse /asa'rarse; aθa'rarse/ *vr* to go wrong, fail (negotiations, etc.); grow nervous; become confused; blush

azaroso /asa'roso; aθa'roso/ *a* unlucky, ill-omened; hazardous

ázimo /'asimo; 'aθimo/ *a* unleavened (bread)

ázoe /'asoe; 'aθoe/ *m*, nitrogen

azogar /aso'gar; aθo'gar/ *vt* to silver (mirrors, etc.); slake lime; *vr* suffer from mercury poisoning; *Inf.* grow uneasy, be agitated

azogue /a'soge; a'θoge/ *m*, *Mineral.* mercury, quicksilver; market-place

azolve /a'solβe; a'θolβe/ *m*, silt

azoramiento /asora'miento; aθora'miento/ *m*, alarm, terror; confusion, stupefaction; incitement

azorar /aso'rar; aθo'rar/ *vt* to alarm, terrify; confuse, stun, dumbfound; excite, stimulate; encourage

azotacalles /asota'kayes; aθota'kaʎes/ *mf Inf.* idler, street loafer

azotaina /aso'taina; aθo'taina/ *f*, *Inf.* whipping, spanking

azotamiento /asota'miento; aθota'miento/ *m*, flogging, beating, whipping

azotar /aso'tar; aθo'tar/ *vt* to whip, beat, flog; scourge, ravage; knock against or strike repeatedly

azotazo /aso'taso; aθo'taθo/ *m*, spank

azote /a'sote; a'θote/ *m*, whip; scourge; lash, blow with a whip; spank, slap; misfortune, disaster. *Inf.* **azotes y galeras,** monotonous diet

azotea /aso'tea; aθo'tea/ *f*, flat terrace roof

azotera /aso'tera; aθo'tera/ *f*, *Lat. Am.* beating, thrashing

azozador /asosa'ðor; aθoθa'ðor/ *party whip, whip*

azteca /as'teka; aθ'teka/ *a* and *mf* Aztec

azúcar /a'sukar; a'θukar/ *m*, sugar. **a. blanco** or **a. de flor,** white sugar. **a. de pilón,** loaf sugar. **a. moreno,** brown sugar. **a. quebrado,** brown sugar. **a. y canela,** sorrel gray (of horses)

azucarado /asuka'raðo; aθuka'raðo/ *a* sugary; sugared, sugar-coated; *Inf.* honeyed, flattering

azucarar /asuka'rar; aθuka'rar/ *vt* to coat with sugar;

sweeten; *Inf.* soften, mitigate; *vr* crystallize; go sugary (jam)

azucarera /asuka'rera; aθuka'rera/ *f*, sugar-basin

azucarero /asuka'rero; aθuka'rero/ *a* sugar-producing (e.g. province)

azucarillo /asuka'riyo; aθuka'riʎo/ *m*, *Cul.* bar made of white of egg and sugar for sweetening water

azucena /asu'sena; aθu'θena/ *f*, white lily. **a. de agua,** water-lily

azuela /a'suela; a'θuela/ *f*, adze

azufre /a'sufre; a'θufre/ *m*, sulphur

azul /a'sul; a'θul/ *a* and *m*, blue. **a. celeste,** sky blue, azure. **a. de mar** *or* **a. marino,** navy blue. **a. de ultramar,** ultramarine. **a. turquí,** indigo

azulado /asu'laðo; aθu'laðo/ *a* bluish, blue

azulear /asule'ar; aθule'ar/ *vi* to look bluish, have a blue tint

azulejo /asu'leho; aθu'leho/ *m*, ornamental glazed tile

azurumbado /asurum'βaðo; aθurum'βaðo/ *m*, *Central America* dumb, silly, stupid; boozed up, drunk

azuzar /asu'sar; aθu'θar/ *vt* to set on (dogs); irritate, provoke; incite, urge

B

baba /'baβa/ *f*, saliva; secretion (of snails, etc.); viscous fluid (of plants). *Inf.* **caérsele (a uno) la b.,** to ooze satisfaction; be dumbfounded

babador, babero /baβa'ðor, ba'βero/ *m*, bib, feeder

babear /baβe'ar/ *vi* to dribble, slaver; *Fig. Inf.* slobber over, be sloppy

babel /ba'βel/ *m*, babel

babélico /ba'βeliko/ *a* Babelian, Babel-like; confused; unintelligible

Babia, estar en /'baβia, es'tar en/ to be daydreaming

babieca /ba'βieka/ *mf Inf.* stupid person. **Babieca** *f*, the Cid's horse

Babilonia /baβi'lonia/ Babylon

babilónico /baβi'loniko/ *a* Babylonian

bable /'baβle/ *m*, Asturian (language)

babor /ba'βor/ *m*, *Naut.* larboard, port

babosa /ba'βosa/ *f*, slug; young onion

baboso /ba'βoso/ *a* slavering; *Fig. Inf.* "sloppy"; *Inf.* incompetent, useless; *Lat. Am.* dumb, stupid

babucha /ba'βutʃa/ *f*, heelless slipper, babouche

babuino /ba'βuino/ *m*, *Zool.* baboon

baca /'baka/ *f*, luggage carrier (on roof of bus, etc.)

bacalao /baka'lao/ *m*, codfish

bacanales /baka'nales/ *f pl*, Bacchanalia

bacante /ba'kante/ *f*, Bacchante

bacará /baka'ra/ *m*, baccarat (card game)

baceta /ba'seta; ba'θeta/ *f*, pool (in card games)

bache /'batʃe/ *m*, rut (in road); pothole

bacheo /ba'tʃeo/ *m*, repairing of streets

bachiller /batʃi'yer; batʃi'ʎer/ *mf* high-school graduate *m*, *Inf.* babbler. *f*. **bachillera,** *Inf.* blue-stocking; garrulous woman

bachillerarse /batʃiye'rarse; batʃiʎe'rarse/ *vr* to graduate as a bachelor

bachillerato /batʃiye'rato; batʃiʎe'rato/ *m*, baccalaureate, bachelor's degree

bacho /'batʃo/ *m*, *Peru* fib, tall tale

bacía /ba'sia; ba'θia/ *f*, bowl; barber's circular shaving-dish; barber's trade sign

bacilar /basi'lar; baθi'lar/ *a* bacillary

bacilo /ba'silo; ba'θilo/ *m*, bacillus

bacterial, bacteriano /bakte'rial, bakte'riano/ *a* bacterial

bactericida /bakteri'siða; bakteri'θiða/ *m*, bactericide

bacteriología /bakteriolo'hia/ *f*, bacteriology

bacteriológico /bakterio'lohiko/ *a* bacteriological

bacteriólogo /bakte'riologo/ *m*, bacteriologist

báculo /'bakulo/ *m*, staff; walking-stick; *Fig.* support. **b. episcopal,** bishop's crozier

badajo /ba'ðaho/ *m*, clapper (of a bell); chatterbox, gossip

badana /ba'ðana/ *f*, cured sheepskin, chamois leather, sawhleather; sweat band; *Inf.* **zurrar (a uno) la b.,** to take the hide off; insult

badén /ba'ðen/ *m*, channel made by rain, furrow; conduit

badulaque /baðu'lake/ *m*, *Inf.* good-for-nothing

bagaje /ba'gahe/ *m*, *Mil.* baggage; beast of burden, transport animal; luggage

bagatela /baga'tela/ *f*, trifle, oddment, bagatelle

bagazo /ba'gaso; ba'gaθo/ *m*, oilcake, bagasse

bagual /ba'gual/ *a* *WH* untamed, wild; doltish, dull. *m*, untamed horse, wild horse

bahía /ba'ia/ *f*, bay, harbor

bailable /bai'laβle/ *a* dance (of music). *m*, *Theat.* dance number

bailador /baila'ðor/ **(-ra)** *n* dancer

bailar /bai'lar/ *vi* to dance; spin around. **b. al son que le toca,** to adapt oneself to circumstances

bailarín /baila'rin/ *a* dancing. *m*, professional dancer. **b. de cuerda, bailarín de la cuerda floja,** tightrope dancer

bailarina /baila'rina/ *f*, ballerina

baile /'baile/ *m*, dance; ball; ballet. **b. de máscaras, b. de trajes,** fancy-dress ball. **b. de San Vito,** St. Vitus' dance. **b. ruso,** ballet

bailotear /bailote'ar/ *vi* to jig about; dance

baja /'baha/ *f*, drop, diminution; fall (in price, etc.); *Mil.* casualty; discharge. *Inf.* **darse de b.,** to leave an employment

bajada /ba'haða/ *f*, descent, fall; slope, incline; hollow, depression. **b. de aguas,** roof gutter

bajalato /baha'lato/ *m*, pashalik

bajamar /baha'mar/ *f*, low tide

bajamente /baha'mente/ *adv* basely, abjectly

bajar /ba'har/ *vi* to descend; go down; get off; drop; fall, decrease; *vt* lower, take down, bring down; let down; dismount, alight; bend, droop; drop; reduce (price); *Fig.* lower (voices); humiliate, humble; download. **b. a tierra,** to step ashore; **b. la cabeza ante,** to submit to (e.g. a judgment) *vr* alight, dismount; humble oneself

bajel /ba'hel/ *m*, *Naut.* galley, ship

bajeza /ba'hesa; ba'heθa/ *f*, base action; meanness; *Fig.* humble estate, lowliness. **b. de ánimo,** timorousness

bajío /ba'hio/ *m*, *Naut.* shallows, shoal; depression, hollow

bajista /ba'hista/ *mf* speculator, bear (Stock Exchange)

bajo /'baho/ *a* low; short, not tall; downcast; under; subordinate; pale (of colors); humble (origin); base; coarse, vulgar; cheap (price); low (sounds). *m*, depth; shoal, sand bank; *Mus.* bass; *pl* petticoats, skirts; horses' hoofs. *adv* beneath, below. *prep* under, beneath. **b. juramento,** upon oath. **bajo relieve,** bas relief. **en voz baja,** in a low voice. **planta baja,** ground floor. **por lo b.,** in a whisper; in secret, on the sly

bajolatino /bahola'tino/ *a* Low Latin

bajón /ba'hon/ *m*, *Mus.* bassoon; bassoon player; *Fig. Inf.* downfall

bajonista /baho'nista/ *mf* bassoon player

bala /'bala/ *f*, bullet, ball; bale. **b. fría,** spent bullet. **b. luminosa,** tracer bullet. **b. perdida,** stray bullet. *Inf.* **como una b.,** like a shot

balacear /balase'ar; balaθe'ar/ *vt*, *Central America, Mexico* to shoot (at)

balada /ba'laða/ *f*, ballad, song

baladí /bala'ði/ *a* worthless, insignificant

baladro /ba'laðro/ *m*, yell, outcry, shout

baladrón /bala'ðron/ *a* braggart

baladronada /balaðro'naða/ *f*, bravado, bragging

balagar /bala'gar/ *m*, straw rick

balance /ba'lanse; ba'lanθe/ *m*, balance; swinging, oscillation; rolling, rocking (of a ship, etc.); doubt, insecurity, *Com*. balance; *Com*. balance sheet **b. de situación** *Lat. Am*. balance sheet

balancear /balanse'ar; balanθe'ar/ *vi* to swing; oscillate; vacillate, hesitate; *vt* balance; *vr* balance oneself; rock or swing oneself

balanceo /balan'seo; balan'θeo/ *m*, balancing; rocking; swinging; rolling (of a ship, etc.)

balancín /balan'sin; balan'θin/ *m*, swing-bar; whipple-tree; balance beam; tight-rope dancer's pole; minting-mill; yoke (for carrying pails); *pl Naut*. lifts

balandra /ba'landra/ *f*, *Naut*. sloop, cutter

balanza /ba'lansa; ba'lanθa/ *f*, balance; scale; judgment; comparison. **b. de comercio**, balance of trade. **en balanzas**, in doubt or danger, in the balance

balar /ba'lar/ *vi* to bleat (sheep)

balasto /ba'lasto/ *m*, *Rail*. ballast

balaustrada /balaus'traða/ *f*, balustrade

balaustre /bala'ustre/ *m*, baluster

balazo /ba'laso; ba'laθo/ *m*, shot; bullet wound

balbuceo /balβu'seo; balβu'θeo/ *m*, stammering; babbling; lisping; **balbuceos** *Fig*. beginnings, early stages (e.g. *los b. de la literatura yídica*, the beginnings of Yiddish literature)

balbuciente /balβu'siente; balβu'θiente/ *a* stammering; babbling; lisping

balbucir /balβu'sir; balβu'θir/ *vi irr defective* to stammer; lisp; babble; read hesitantly. See **lucir**

Balcanes, los /bal'kanes, los/ the Balkans

balcón /bal'kon/ *m*, balcony

baldaquín /balda'kin/ *m*, canopy, baldachin

baldar /bal'dar/ *vt* to cripple; impede, obstruct

balde /'balde/ *m*, bucket

balde /'balde/ **(en)** *adv* in vain. **de b.**, gratis, free of charge

baldear /balde'ar/ *vt Naut*. to wash the decks

baldío /bal'dio/ *a* untilled; fallow; useless, worthless; vagrant

baldón /bal'don/ *m*, insult; dishonor

baldonar /baldo'nar/ *vt* to insult

baldosa /bal'dosa/ *f*, paving stone; tile

baldrufa /bal'drufa/ *f*, top, spinning top

balduque /bal'duke/ *m*, red tape

Baleares, las Islas /bale'ares, las 'islas/ the Balearic Islands

baleárico /bale'ariko/ *a* Balearic

balido /ba'liðo/ *m*, bleat, bleating

balística /ba'listika/ *f*, ballistics

baliza /ba'lisa; ba'liθa/ *f*, *Naut*. buoy, beacon

balizamiento /balisa'miento; baliθa'miento/ *m*, marking with beacons, marking with buoys; traffic signs and signals

ballena /ba'yena; ba'ʎena/ *f*, whale; whalebone

ballenero /baye'nero; baʎe'nero/ *a* whaling. *m*, whaler

ballesta /ba'yesta; ba'ʎesta/ *f*, crossbow; spring (of carriages)

ballestería /bayeste'ria; baʎeste'ria/ *f*, archery; crossbowmen

ballestero /bayes'tero; baʎes'tero/ *m*, archer; crossbowman; crossbow maker

balneario /balne'ario/ *a* pertaining to public baths; bathing; holiday; spa. *m*, watering place, spa

balompié /balom'pie/ *m*, football (game)

balón /ba'lon/ *m*, large ball; football; *Chem*. balloon; bundle; bale. **b. de ensayo**, *Fig*. feeler

baloncesto /balon'sesto; balon'θesto/ *m*, *Sports*. basketball

balota /ba'lota/ *f*, ballot

balotaje /balo'tahe/ *m*, balloting; run-off election

balotar /balo'tar/ *vi* to ballot

balsa /'balsa/ *f*, pond; raft

balsamera /balsa'ðera/ *f*, ferry

bálsamo /'balsamo/ *m*, balm

balsero /bal'sero/ *m*, ferryman; rafter (person fleeing a country by raft, rowboat, etc.)

báltico /'baltiko/ *a* Baltic. **el Mar Báltico** the Baltic Sea

baluarte /ba'luarte/ *m*, bulwark; bastion; protection, defense

bamboleante /bambole'ante/ *a* swaying, swinging; *Fig*. tottering (e.g. empire)

bambolearse /bambole'arse/ *vr* to sway; swing; totter; be shaky; stagger

bamboleo /bambo'leo/ *m*, rocking; swinging; tottering; staggering; reeling

bambolla /bam'βoya; bam'βoʎa/ *f*, *Inf*. ostentation, swank

bambú /bam'βu/ *m*, bamboo

banal /ba'nal/ *a* banal, commonplace

banana /ba'nana/ *f*, banana

banasta /ba'nasta/ *f*, big basket

banastero /banas'tero/ **(-ra)** *n* basket maker or dealer

banca /'banka/ *f*, bench; card game; stall; *Com*. banking

bancada /ban'kaða/ *f*, rowing seat

bancal /ban'kal/ *m*, oblong garden plot; terrace

bancario /ban'kario/ *a* banking, bank, banker

bancarrota /banka'rrota/ *f*, bankruptcy. **hacer b.**, to go bankrupt

banco /'banko/ *m*, form, bench; rowing seat; settle; seat; bench; *Com*. bank; *Naut*. bar, shoal; school (of fish). **b. azul**, government benches in Spanish Parliament. **b. de arena**, sand-bank. **b. de descuento**, discount bank. **b. de emisión, banco emisor**, bank of issue. **b. de hielo**, iceberg. **b. de nivel**, benchmark

banda /'banda/ *f*, wide ribbon; sash; ribbon, insignia; strip; border; party, group; gang; flock (of birds); zone, belt; side (of ship); *Mus*. band; cushion (billiards); *Herald*. bar, bend. **b. elástica**, rubber band. *Naut*. **dar a la b.**, to lie along

bandada /ban'daða/ *f*, flock (of birds)

bandeja /ban'deha/ *f*, tray, salver

bandera /ban'dera/ *f*, banner, flag; colors, standard. **b. de popa**, ensign. **jurar la b.**, *(Mil. Nav.)* to take the oath of allegiance

banderilla /bande'riya; bande'riʎa/ *f*, banderilla (bullfighting)

banderillear /banderiye'ar; banderiʎe'ar/ *vt* to put banderillas on bulls

banderillero /banderi'yero; banderi'ʎero/ *m*, man who puts banderillas on bulls

banderín /bande'rin/ *m*, *dim* small flag; recruiting post

banderizo /bande'riso; bande'riθo/ *a* factious; vehement, excitable

banderola /bande'rola/ *f*, banderole, pennon; bannerole

bandido /ban'diðo/ **(-da)** *a* and *n* outlaw, fugitive. *m*, bandit; highwayman; rogue, desperado

bando /'bando/ *m*, proclamation, order; faction, group, party

bandola /ban'dola/ *f*, *Mus*. pandora, pandore

bandolerismo /bandole'rismo/ *m*, brigandage

bandolero /bando'lero/ *m*, robber, footpad, brigand

bandolín /bando'lin/ *m*, mandolin

bandurria /ban'durria/ *f*, *Mus*. mandolin

banjo /'banho/ *m*, banjo

banquero /ban'kero/ *m*, banker

banqueta /ban'keta/ *f*, three-legged stool; seat; footstool; *Mexico* sidewalk

banquete /ban'kete/ *m*, banquet, feast

banquetear /bankete'ar/ *vt* and *vi* to banquet

banqueteo /banke'teo/ *m*, banqueting, feasting

bañadera /baɲa'ðera/ *f*, *Argentina* bathtub

bañado /ba'ɲaðo/ *m*, chamber pot; *WH* marshy land, marsh; **bañados** *pl* marsh

bañador /baɲa'ðor/ **(-ra)** *a* bathing. *n* bather. *m*, bathing dress; bath, vat

bañar /ba'ɲar/ *vt* to bathe; coat, cover; dip; lave, wash; *Fig*. bathe (of sunlight, etc.). *vr* take a bath; bathe

bañera /ba'ɲera/ *f*, bath attendant; bathtub

bañista /ba'ɲista/ *mf* bather; one who takes spa waters

baño /'baɲo/ *m*, bathing; bath; bathroom; bathtub; bagnio, Turkish prison; covering, coat; *pl* mineral baths, spa. **b. de China** *Argentina* shower bath, shower **b. de mar,** sea bath. **b. de María,** double saucepan. **b. de sol,** sunbath. **casa de baños,** public baths. **cuarto de b.,** bathroom

bao /'bao/ *m, Naut.* beam

baptisterio /baptis'terio/ *m,* baptistery; *Eccl.* font

baquelita /bake'lita/ *f,* bakelite

baqueta /ba'keta/ *f,* ramrod; *pl* drumsticks; *Mil.* gauntlet

bar /bar/ *m,* bar; café

barahúnda /bara'unda/ *f,* See **baraúnda**

baraja /ba'raha/ *f,* pack (of cards); game of cards

barajar /bara'har/ *vt* to shuffle (cards); jumble, mix; *vi* quarrel

baranda /ba'randa/ *f,* handrail, banister; cushion (of billiard table)

barandilla /baran'diya; baran'diʎa/ *f, dim* railing

barata /ba'rata/ *f, Mexico* bargain sale, sale

baratija /bara'tiha/ *f,* (gen. *pl*) trifle, oddment

baratillo /bara'tiyo; bara'tiʎo/ *m,* second-hand article, frippery; second-hand shop or stall; bargain counter

barato /ba'rato/ *a* cheap. *m,* bargain sale. *adv* cheaply

baratura /bara'tura/ *f,* cheapness

baraúnda /bara'unda/ *f,* uproar, confusion

barba /'barβa/ *f,* chin; beard; whiskers; fin; barb (of a feather); *m,* actor who plays old men. *f pl,* fibers of plants. **b. bien poblada,** a thick beard. **barbas de ballena,** whalebone. *Fig. Inf.* **echar a las barbas,** to throw in a person's face. **en la barba, en las barbas,** to ones face (e.g. *Me lo dijeron en las barbas.* They told me so to my face). **hacer la b.,** to shave; *Inf.* annoy

barbacoa /barβa'koa/ *f, West Hem.* barbecue; trellis (for climbing plants)

barbado /bar'βaðo/ *a* bearded. *m,* shoot; sucker; transplanted plant

barbárico /bar'βariko/ *a* barbarian; barbaric

barbaridad /barβari'ðað/ *f,* barbarity; blunder; atrocity; outrage; *Inf.* huge amount. **¡Qué b.!** How awful! You don't say so!

barbarie /bar'βarie/ *f,* barbarism; barbarity, cruelty

barbarismo /barβa'rismo/ *m,* barbarism; cruelty; barbarians

bárbaro /'barβaro/ **(-ra)** *a* and *n* barbarian. *a* fierce; headstrong; uncivilized. **como un b.,** like crazy (e.g. *estudiar como un b.,* to study like crazy)

barbechar /barβe'tʃar/ *vt* to plow; leave fallow

barbecho /bar'βetʃo/ *m, Agr.* fallow; first plowing

barbería /barβe'ria/ *f,* barber shop

barbero /bar'βero/ *m,* barber; *Guatemala, Mexico* flatterer

barbihecho /bar'βietʃo/ *a* fresh-shaved

barbilampiño /barβilam'piɲo/ *a* smooth-faced, beardless, clean-shaven

barbilindo /barβi'lindo/ *a* dandified, dappy; *m,* dandy

barbilla /bar'βiya; bar'βiʎa/ *f,* point of the chin; chin. **acariciar la b. (de),** to chuck under the chin

barbiquejo /barβi'keho/ *m, Naut.* bobstay; hat-guard

barbudo /bar'βuðo/ *a* heavily bearded

barbulla /bar'βuya; bar'βuʎa/ *f, Inf.* babble, chatter; murmur of voices

barca /'barka/ *f,* small boat, bark; barge. **b. de pasaje,** ferryboat. **b. plantaminas** minelayer

barcada /bar'kaða/ *f,* boat-load; ferry crossing

barcaza /bar'kasa; bar'kaθa/ *f, Naut.* lighter; barge. **b. de desembarco,** landingcraft

barcelonés /barselo'nes; barθelo'nes/ **(-esa)** *a* and *n* of or from Barcelona

barcino /bar'sino; bar'θino/ *a* ruddy (of animals); fawn and white; *Inf.* turncoat (of politicians)

barco /'barko/ *m,* boat; ship; hollow, rut. **b. barredero,** trawler. **b. siembraminas,** minelayer

barda /'barða/ *f,* horse armor; thatch; shingle; (Mexico) cement fence, cement wall

bardal /bar'ðal/ *m,* thatched wall; mud wall

bardar /bar'ðar/ *vt* to thatch

bardo /'barðo/ *m,* poet, bard

bario /'bario/ *m,* barium

barítono /ba'ritono/ *m,* baritone

barloventear /barloβente'ar/ *vi Naut.* to tack; ply to windward; *Inf.* wander about

barlovento /barlo'βento/ *m, Naut.* windward

barnacla /bar'nakla/ *m,* barnacle

barniz /bar'nis; bar'niθ/ *m,* varnish; glaze; smattering, veneer

barnizar /barni'sar; barni'θar/ *vt* to varnish; glaze

barométrico /baro'metriko/ *a* barometric

barómetro /ba'rometro/ *m,* barometer

barón /ba'ron/ *m,* baron

baronesa /baro'nesa/ *f,* baroness

barquero /bar'kero/ *m,* boatman; bargee; *Ent.* water-boatman

barquillero /barki'yero; barki'ʎero/ *m,* seller of wafers; waffle-iron

barquillo /bar'kiyo; bar'kiʎo/ *m,* wafer, cornet

barquín /bar'kin/ *m,* furnace bellows

barra /'barra/ *f,* bar; ingot; railing (in courtroom); sandbank; fault (in cloth); lever, crossbar; (in cricket) bail; *Mus.* bar. **b. de jabón de afeitar,** shaving-soap. **a barras derechas,** without deceit

barrabasada /barraβa'saða/ *f, Inf.* wilfulness, escapade

barraca /ba'rraka/ *f,* cabin, hut; stall; sideshow; *Lat. Am.* barracks. **b. de tiro,** shooting gallery

barracón /barra'kon/ *m,* side-show; stall

barragana /barra'gana/ *f,* concubine, mistress

barranca /ba'rranka/ *f,* **barranco** *m,* furrow, channel, rut; gorge; difficulty, fix

barrancoso /barran'koso/ *a* rutty, uneven

barredor /barre'ðor/ **(-ra)** *n* sweeper

barredura /barre'ðura/ *f,* sweeping; *pl* sweepings; rubbish

barrena /ba'rrena/ *f,* borer, gimlet, drill, auger. *Aer.* **b. de cola,** tail-spin

barrenar /barre'nar/ *vt* to drill, bore; blast (in quarries)

barrendero /barren'dero/ **(-ra)** *n* sweeper, scavenger

barrenero /barre'nero/ *m,* driller; blaster

barreno /ba'rreno/ *m,* blast hole; bore, drill; vanity; *Lat. Am.* mania, pet peeve

barreño /ba'rreno/ *m,* earthenware bowl (for dish washing, etc.)

barrer /ba'rrer/ *vt* to sweep; *Fig.* clear, make a clean sweep

barrera /ba'rrera/ *f,* barrier; barricade; *Fig.* obstacle. **b. de golpe,** automatic gate (at level crossings, etc.). **b. de minas,** minefield

barriada /barria'ða/ *f,* district; quarter (of a city); *Peru* slum, shanty town

barrica /ba'rrika/ *f,* cask; barrel

barricada /barri'kaða/ *f,* barricade

barriga /ba'rriga/ *f, Inf.* belly

barrigón, barrigudo /barri'gon, barri'guðo/ *a* potbellied

barril /ba'rril/ *m,* barrel; cask; water-butt

barrilero /barri'lero/ *m,* cooper

barrio /'barrio/ *m,* district, quarter; suburb. **barrios bajos,** slums, back streets. **el otro b.,** the other world, Eternity

barrizal /barri'sal; barri'θal/ *m,* muddy place; claypit

barro /'barro/ *m,* mud; clay; earthenware drinking vessel; *Inf.* money

barroco /ba'rroko/ *a* baroque

barroso /ba'rroso/ *a* muddy; pimpled; mud-colored

barrote /ba'rrote/ *m,* thick iron bar; stave, bond

barruntar /barrun'tar/ *vt* to conjecture; suspect

barrunto /ba'rrunto/ *m,* conjecture; indication, sign

bártulos /'bartulos/ *m pl,* household goods; *Fig.* means, wherewithal

barullo /ba'ruyo; ba'ruʎo/ *m, Inf.* confusion, disorder; mob

basa /'basa/ *f,* base; *Archit.* pedestal; foundation, basis

basalto /ba'salto/ *m,* basalt

basar /ba'sar/ *vt* to base, place on a base; *Fig.* found, base; *vr* (*with en*) rely upon, base oneself on

basca /'baska/ *f,* (gen. *pl*) nausea; retching; wave of anger

báscula /'baskula/ f, weighing-machine, platform-scale; weigh-bridge

base /'base/ f, base; (*Chem. Geom. Mil.*) base; basis; *Archit.* pedestal; *Mus.* root. **sin b.,** baseless

básico /'basiko/ a basic

Basilea /basi'lea/ Basel, Basle

basílica /ba'silika/ f, palace; church, basilica

basquear /baske'ar/ vi to retch; feel squeamish

bastante /bas'tante/ a sufficient, enough. *adv* sufficiently; enough; fairly; a good deal; somewhat. **Hace b. calor,** It is quite hot. **Tengo b.,** I have enough. **Tenemos b. tiempo,** We have sufficient time

bastar /bas'tar/ vi to suffice. **¡Basta!** Enough! No more! Stop! **¡Basta de...!** Enough of...! **Basta decir que...,** Suffice it to say that...

bastardía /bastar'ðia/ f, bastardy, illegitimacy; baseness, meanness

bastardilla /bastar'ðiya; bastar'ðiʎa/ f, *Print.* italics

bastardo /bas'tarðo/ **(-da)** a bastard; spurious. n bastard

bastear /baste'ar/ vt *Sew.* to baste

bastidor /basti'ðor/ m, embroidery frame; *Art.* stretcher (for canvas); *Theat.* wing; *Mech.* underframe; chassis, carriage; frame (of a window). *Fig.* **entre bastidores,** behind the scenes

bastilla /bas'tiya; bas'tiʎa/ f, *Sew.* hem; bastille

bastimentar /bastimen'tar/ vt to provision; supply

bastimento /basti'mento/ m, supplies; provisioning

bastión /bas'tion/ m, bastion

basto /'basto/ m, pack-saddle; ace of clubs; clubs (cards). a rude; tough; *Fig.* unpolished, rough

bastón /bas'ton/ m, cane, walking-stick; rod (of office); truncheon. **b. de junquillo,** Malacca cane. **empuñar el b.,** to take control, take over. **meter el b.,** to mediate

bastonear /bastone'ar/ vt to cane; stir with a stick

basura /ba'sura/ f, rubbish, refuse; dung; sweepings

basural /basu'ral/ m, *Lat. Am.* garbage dump

basurero /basu'rero/ m, garbage collector; dunghill, garbage dump; kitchen middens; trash bin

bata /'bata/ f, dressing-gown; smoking-jacket; old-fashioned dress; overall, smock

batacazo /bata'kaso; bata'kaθo/ m, bump, noise of a fall; *Polit.* dark horse

batahola /bata'ola/ f, *Inf.* hurly-burly, hubbub

batalla /ba'taya; ba'taʎa/ f, battle; *Fig.* struggle, conflict; tournament; *Art.* battle-piece. **b. campal,** pitched battle

batallador /bataya'ðor; bataʎa'ðor/ a fighting, warlike

batallar /bata'yar; bata'ʎar/ vi to battle, fight; dispute, argue; hesitate

batallón /bata'yon; bata'ʎon/ m, battalion

batata /ba'tata/ f, sweet potato, yam

batayola /bata'yola/ f, *Naut.* rail

batea /ba'tea/ f, wooden tray; punt

bateador, -a /batea'ðor/ mf, *Lat. Am.* batter (baseball)

batear /bate'ar/ vt, *Lat. Am.* to bat

batería /bate'ria/ f, (*Mil. Elec. Naut.*) battery. **b. de cocina,** kitchen utensils. **b. de pilas secas,** dry battery. **b. de teatro,** stage lights. **b. eléctrica,** electric battery

baticola /bati'kola/ f, crupper

batida /ba'tiða/ f, game drive; attack; *Metall.* beating

batido /ba'tiðo/ a beaten (of metals); shot (of silk); trodden, worn (roads, etc.). m, *Cul.* batter; hunting party

batidor /bati'ðor/ m, beater; scout; outrider; hair comb; *Cul.* whisk. **b. de oro** (or **de plata),** gold (or silver) beater

batiente /ba'tiente/ m, jamb (of door, etc.); damper (piano); leaf (of door); place where sea beats against cliffs, etc.

batihoja /bati'oha/ m, gold beater; metal worker

batimiento /bati'miento/ m, beating

batín /ba'tin/ m, smoking-jacket; man's dressing-gown

batintín /batin'tin/ m, Chinese gong

batir /ba'tir/ vt to beat, slap; demolish; dismantle,

take down (stall, etc.); hammer, flatten; batter; *Fig.* beat (of sun, etc.); stir; pound; churn; comb (hair); vanquish, defeat; coin; reconnoiter, beat; throw down or drop; vr fight; swoop (birds of prey). **b. palmas,** to clap, applaud

batista /ba'tista/ f, cambric, batiste

baturrillo /batu'rriyo; batu'rriʎo/ m, hodgepodge (gen. food); *Inf.* farrago, medley

batuta /ba'tuta/ f, baton, conductor's wand. **llevar la b.,** *Inf.* boss the show, call the music, be in charge, to rule the roost

baúl /ba'ul/ m, trunk; *Inf.* belly; *Lat. Am. also* trunk (of a car) **b. escaparate** or **b. mundo,** wardrobe trunk

bauprés /bau'pres/ m, *Naut.* bowsprit

bausán /bau'san/ (-ana) n guy, strawman; puppet; fool, idiot; lazybones

bautismo /bau'tismo/ m, baptism

bautista /bau'tista/ m, baptizer, baptist. **San Juan B.,** St. John the Baptist

bautisterio /bautis'terio/ m, baptistery

bautizar /bauti'sar; bauti'θar/ vt to baptize, christen; *Inf.* nickname; *Inf.* water (wine); accidentally shower with water

bautizo /bau'tiso; bau'tiθo/ m, baptism; christening party

baya /'baia/ f, berry

bayeta /ba'yeta/ f, baize; flannel

bayo /'bayo/ **(-ya)** a bay (of horses)

Bayona /ba'yona/ Bayonne

bayoneta /bayo'neta/ f, bayonet. **b. calada,** fixed bayonet

bayonetazo /bayone'taso; bayone'taθo/ m, bayonet thrust

baza /'basa; 'baθa/ f, tricks taken (playing cards). *Fig. Inf.* **meter b.,** to stick one's oar in

bazar /ba'sar; ba'θar/ m, bazaar; shop, store; department store

bazo /'baso; 'baθo/ m, *Anat.* spleen. a yellow-brown

bazucar, bazuquear /basu'kar, basuke'ar; baθu'kar, baθuke'ar/ vt to shake or stir (liquids)

bazuqueo /basu'keo; baθu'keo/ m, shaking or stirring of liquids

be /be/ f, letter B. m, baa

beata /be'ata/ f, devout woman; *Inf.* pious hypocrite, prude; Sister of Mercy; over-religious woman

beatería /beate'ria/ f, sanctimoniousness; bigotry

beatificación /beatifika'sion; beatifika'θion/ f, beatification

beatificar /beatifi'kar/ vt to make happy; sanctify; beatify

beatífico /bea'tifiko/ a beatific

beatitud /beati'tuð/ f, blessedness, beatitude; happiness

beato /be'ato/ **(-ta)** a happy; blessed, beatified; devout; prudish. n devout person; over-pious person

beba /'beβa/ f, *Argentina* baby (girl)

bebé /be'βe/ m, baby

bebedero /beβe'ðero/ a drinkable. m, drinking trough or place

bebedizo /beβe'ðiso; beβe'ðiθo/ a drinkable. m, draught of medicine; love-potion; poisonous drink

bebedor /beβe'ðor/ **(-ra)** a drinkable. n drinker; toper

beber /be'βer/ vt to drink; absorb; vi toast, drink to the health (of); tipple. m, drinking; drink

bebida /be'βiða/ f, drink; beverage; alcoholic liquor

beca /'beka/ f, academic scarf or sash; scholarship, exhibition

becado, becario /be'kaðo, be'kario/ m, exhibitioner; scholarship holder

becerra /be'serra; be'θerra/ f, calf; *Bot.* snapdragon

becerro /be'serro; be'θerro/ m, bullock; bull calf; calf-skin. **b. marino,** *Zool.* seal

Beda el Venerable /'beða el bene'raβle/ the Venerable Bede

bedel /be'ðel/ m, beadle; servitor; university porter

beduino /be'ðuino/ **(-na)** a and n Bedouin. m, savage, bloodthirsty man

befar /be'far/ vt to mock, ridicule

befo /'befo/ *a* thick-lipped; knock-kneed. *m*, animal's lip

begonia /be'gonia/ *f*, *Bot.* begonia

bejín /be'hin/ *m*, *Bot.* puff-ball; spoiled child

bejuco /be'huko/ *m*, rattan

beldad /bel'dað/ *f*, beauty; belle

beldar /bel'dar/ *vt* *Agr.* to winnow

Belén /be'len/ Bethlehem

belén /be'len/ *m*, nativity, manager; *Inf.* bedlam; *Inf.* gossip

belfo /'belfo/ *a* thick-lipped

belga /'belga/ *a* and *mf* Belgian

Bélgica /'belhika/ Belgium

bélgico /'belhiko/ *a* Belgian

Belgrado /bel'graðo/ Belgrade

Belice /be'lise; be'liθe/ Belize

belicista /beli'sista; beli'θista/ *adj* war, militaristic; *mf* warmonger

bélico /'beliko/ *a* warlike, military

belicoso /beli'koso/ *a* bellicose, aggressive; warlike

beligerancia /belihe'ransia; belihe'ranθia/ *f*, belligerency

beligerante /belihe'rante/ *a* and *mf* belligerent

belitre /be'litre/ *a* *Inf.* knavish, cunning

bellaco /be'yako; be'ʎako/ (-ca) *a* artful, cunning. *n* knave; *Lat. Am.* untamed horse

belladona /beya'ðona; beʎa'ðona/ *f*, belladonna

bellaquería /beyake'ria; beʎake'ria/ *f*, roguery, knavery, cunning

bellasombra /beya'sombra; beʎa'sombra/ *f*, umbra tree

belleza /be'yesa; be'ʎeθa/ *f*, beauty, loveliness

bello /'beyo; 'beʎo/ *a* beautiful

bellota /be'yota; be'ʎota/ *f*, acorn; carnation bud; ornamental button, knob

bemol /be'mol/ *a* and *m*, *Mus.* flat. *Inf.* **tener bemoles,** to be thorny, be difficult

bencina /ben'sina; ben'θina/ *f*, benzine; gasoline, gas

bendecir /bende'sir; bende'θir/ *vt irr* to praise, extol; bless; dedicate, consecrate. See **decir**

bendición /bendi'sion; bendi'θion/ *f*, benediction; blessing; consecration; *pl* marriage ceremony. **b. de la mesa,** grace before meals

bendito /ben'dito/ *a* holy, blessed; fortunate; simple. **ser un b.,** to be a simpleton; be a good soul. ¡Benditos los ojos que te ven! It's so nice to see you!

benedictino /beneðik'tino/ (-na) *a* and *n* Benedictine. *m*, Benedictine liqueur

beneficencia /benefi'sensia; benefi'θenθia/ *f*, beneficence; charitable institutions

beneficiación /benefisia'sion; benefiθia'θion/ *f*, benefaction

beneficiado /benefi'siaðo; benefi'θiaðo/ (-da) *n* beneficiary. *m*, incumbent of a benefice

beneficiador /benefisia'ðor; benefiθia'ðor/ (-ra) *n* benefactor

beneficiar /benefi'siar; benefi'θiar/ *vt* to benefit; improve; cultivate (land); exploit (mine); purchase (directorship, etc.); sell at a loss (bonds, etc.)

beneficiario /benefi'siario; benefi'θiario/ (-ia) *n* beneficiary

beneficiencia /benefi'siensia; benefi'θienθia/ *f*, beneficence, charity

beneficio /bene'fisio; bene'fiθio/ *m*, benefit; profit; cultivation (land, etc.); working (mine); *Eccl.* benefice; *Theat.* benefit

beneficioso /benefi'sioso; benefi'θioso/ *a* beneficial; useful

benéfico /be'nefiko/ *a* beneficent; kind, helpful; charitable

benemérito /bene'merito/ *a* benemeritus, worthy, meritorious

beneplácito /bene'plasito; bene'plaθito/ *m*, approbation; consent

benevolencia /beneβo'lensia; beneβo'lenθia/ *f*, benevolence, goodwill

benévolo /be'neβolo/ *a* benevolent, kind

Bengala /beŋ'gala/ Bengal

bengalí /beŋga'li/ *a* and *mf* Bengali

benignidad /benigni'ðað/ *f*, kindness; mildness (of the weather, etc.)

benigno /be'nigno/ *a* kind; benign; mild; balmy

beodo /be'oðo/ (-da) *a* drunk, intoxicated. *n* drunkard

berbén /ber'βen/ *m*, *Mexico* scurvy

Berbería /berβe'ria/ Barbary

bereber /bere'βer/ *a* and *mf* Berber

berenjena /beren'hena/ *f*, eggplant

bergante /ber'gante/ *m*, rascal, rogue

berilo /be'rilo/ *m*, beryl

Berlín /ber'lin/ Berlin

berlinés /ber'lines/ (-esa) *a* and *n* of or from Berlin

bermejear /bermehe'ar/ *vi* to be or look reddish

bermejo /ber'meho/ *a* reddish; red; redgold; carroty (of hair)

bermellón /berme'yon; berme'ʎon/ *m*, vermilion

bernardina /bernar'ðina/ *f*, lie; boast; gibberish

bernardo /ber'narðo/ (-da) *a* and *n* *Eccl.* Bernardine (Order of St. Bernard)

berquelio /ber'kelio/ *m*, berkelium

berrear /berre'ar/ *vi* to low, bellow; yell, squall; shriek; *vr* reveal, confess

berrido /be'rriðo/ *m*, lowing, bellowing; *Inf.* yell

berrinche /be'rrintfe/ *m*, *Inf.* tantrum, fit, fit of sulks

berro /'berro/ *m*, watercress

berroqueña /berro'keɲa/ *f*, granite

berza /'bersa; 'berθa/ *f*, cabbage

besamanos /besa'manos/ *m*, ceremony of kissing royal hand, levee; kissing fingers (in salute)

besar /be'sar/ *vt* to kiss; *Inf.* brush against, touch (of things); *vr* kiss one another; *Inf.* bang into, knock against one another

beso /'beso/ *m*, kiss; knock, collision

bestia /'bestia/ *f*, quadruped (especially horses or mules); beast. *mf* *Inf.* nasty piece of work. **b. de carga,** beast of burden. **como una b.,** like a dog (e.g. *Trabaja como una b.* I work like a dog)

bestial /bes'tial/ *a* bestial; brutal; beastly

bestialidad /bestiali'ðað/ *f*, brutality; bestiality; beastliness

bestialismo /bestia'lismo/ *m*, bestiality (sexual orientation)

besuquear /besuke'ar/ *vt* *Inf.* to cover with kisses; *vr* *Inf.* spoon, make love

besuqueo /besu'keo/ *m*, *Inf.* kissing and spooning

betabel /beta'βel/ *m*, *Mexico* beetroot

bético /'betiko/ *a* Andalusian

betún /be'tun/ *m*, bitumen; shoe blacking; kind of cement. **b. de Judea** *or* **b. judaico,** asphalt

bezo /'beso; 'beθo/ *m*, blubber lip; proud flesh (of a wound)

bezudo /be'suðo; be'θuðo/ *a* thick-lipped

biberón /biβe'ron/ *m*, feeding bottle

Biblia /'biβlia/ *f*, Bible

bíblico /'biβliko/ *a* biblical

bibliófilo /biβli'ofilo/ *m*, bibliophile

bibliografía /biβliogra'fia/ *f*, bibliography

bibliográfico /biβlio'grafiko/ *a* bibliographical

biblioteca /biβlio'teka/ *f*, library; book series. **b. por subscripción,** circulating library

bibliotecario /biβliote'kario/ (-ia) *n* librarian

biblotecnia, biblotecología, biblioteconomía /biβlio'teknia, biβlioteko'lohia, biβliotekono'mia/ *f*, library science

bicarbonato /bikarβo'nato/ *m*, bicarbonate

bíceps /'biseps; 'biθeps/ *m*, biceps

bicherío /bitfe'rio/ *m*, *Lat. Am.* bugs, insects

bicho /'bitfo/ *m*, any small animal or reptile; quadruped; fighting bull; scarecrow, sight. **b. viviente,** *Inf.* living soul. **mal b.,** rogue

bicicleta /bisi'kleta; biθi'kleta/ *f*, bicycle, bike. **ir** (*or* **andar** *or* **montar**) **en b.,** to bicycle, bike, go by bicycle, go by bike

bicoca /bi'koka/ *f*, *Inf.* trifle, bagatelle

bicolor /biko'lor/ *a* bicolored

bidé /bi'ðe/ *m*, bidet

biela /'biela/ *f*, axle-tree; connecting-rod; big-end

bielda /'bielda/ *f*, pitchfork; *Agr.* winnowing

bien /bien/ *m*, ideal goodness, perfection; benefit, advantage; welfare; *pl* property, wealth. *adv* well; willingly; happily; perfectly; easily; enough, sufficient; all right! very well! **b. que**, although. **b. de equipo**, capital good. **bienes muebles**, movables, goods and chattels. **bienes raíces**, real estate. **el B. y el Mal**, Good and Evil. **¡Está b.!** All right! **no b.**, scarcely, as soon as. **si b.**, although, even if. **¿Y b.?** And so what? Well, then; What next?

bienal /bie'nal/ *a* biennial

bienamado /biena'maðo/ *a* dearly beloved

bienandante /bienan'dante/ *a* prosperous; happy

bienandanza /bienan'dansa; bienan'danθa/ *f*, happiness, welfare; prosperity

bienaventurado /bienaβentu'raðo/ *a* blessed, holy; happy; *Inf.* over-simple, innocent, foolish

bienaventuranza /bienaβentu'ransa; bienaβentu'ranθa/ *f*, blessedness

bienestar /bienes'tar/ *m*, wellbeing; ease; comfort

bienhablado /biena'βlaðo/ *a* well-spoken; civil, polite

bienhadado /biena'ðaðo/ *a* fortunate, happy

bienhechor /biene'tʃor/ **(-ra)** *a* kind, helpful. *n* benefactor

bienintencionado /bienintensio'naðo; bieninten-θio'naðo/ *a* well-meaning

bienio /'bienio/ *m*, biennium, space of two years, period of two years

bienquisto /bien'kisto/ *a* respected; generally esteemed

bienvenida /biembe'niða/ *f*, safe or happy arrival; welcome. **dar la b.**, to welcome

bienvivir /biembi'βir/ *vi* to live comfortably; live decently or uprightly

bies /bies/ *m*, bias, cross; slant

bife /'bife/ *m Argentina* beefsteak, steak

biftec /bif'tek/ *m*, beefsteak, steak

bifurcación /bifurka'sion; bifurka'θion/ *f*, bifurcation; fork, branch, junction

bifurcarse /bifur'karse/ *vr* to fork, branch

bigamia /bi'gamia/ *f*, bigamy

bígamo /'bigamo/ **(-ma)** *a* bigamous. *n* bigamist

bigornia /bi'gornia/ *f*, anvil

bigote /bi'gote/ *m*, mustache; *pl* whiskers

bigotudo /bigo'tuðo/ *a* moustached, whiskered

bikini /bi'kini/ *m*, bikini

bilateral /bilate'ral/ *a* bilateral

bilingüe /bi'liŋgue/ *a* bilingual

bilioso /bi'lioso/ *a* bilious

bilis /'bilis/ *f*, bile

billar /bi'yar; bi'ʎar/ *m*, billiards; billiard table

billete /bi'yete; bi'ʎete/ *m*, note, short letter; ticket; banknote. **b. circular**, excursion ticket. **b. de abono**, season ticket. **b. de andén**, platform ticket. **b. de banco**, banknote. **b. de favor**, free ticket. **b. de ida y vuelta**, round trip ticket. **b. entero**, full fare. **b. kilométrico**, tourist ticket. **b. sencillo**, one-way. **medio b.**, half-fare

billón /bi'yon; bi'ʎon/ *m*, billion

bimestral /bimes'tral/ *a* bimonthly

bimestre /bi'mestre/ *a* bimonthly. *m*, two months' duration; money paid or received at two-monthly intervals

bimotor /bimo'tor/ *a* two-motor. *m*, twin-engined aircraft

binario /bi'nario/ *a* binary

bincha /'bintʃa/ *f, Lat. Am.* hairband

binóculo /bi'nokulo/ *m*, opera glasses

biodedegradable /βioðeðgradaβle/ *a* biodegradable

biodegradable /bioðegra'ðaβle/ *a* biodegradable

biodiversidad /bioðiβersiðað/ *f*, biodiversity

biofísica /bio'fisika/ *f*, biophysics

biografía /biogra'fia/ *f*, biography

biográfico /bio'grafiko/ *a* biographical

biógrafo /'biografo/ **(-fa)** *n* biographer; (Chile) movie theater (e.g. *¡Vamos al biógrafo!* Let's go to the movies!)

biología /biolo'hia/ *f*, biology

biológico /bio'lohiko/ *a* biological

biólogo /bi'ologo/ *m*, biologist

biombo /'biombo/ *m*, screen

bioquímica /bio'kimika/ *f*, biochemistry

bioquímico /bio'kimiko/ *m*, biochemist

bipartido /bipar'tiðo/ *a* bipartite

bípedo /'bipeðo/ *a* and *m*, biped

biplano /bi'plano/ *m*, biplane

biplaza /biplasa; bi'plaθa/ *a* two-seater

birla /'birla/ *f*, skittle

birlar /bir'lar/ *vt* to bowl from where the bowl stopped; *Inf.* knock down; snatch away; *Inf.* rob

birlocha /bir'lotʃa/ *f*, child's kite

Birmania /bir'mania/ Burma

birmano /bir'mano/ **(-na)** *a* and *n* Burmese

birreta /bi'rreta/ *f*, biretta

birrete /bi'rrete/ *m*, biretta; university cap; cap

bis /bis/ *adv* twice; repeat; encore. *a* duplicate; **B** (in addresses, e.g., *Calle de Alcalá 18bis*, 18b Alcalá St.)

bisabuela /bisa'βuela/ *f*, great-grandmother

bisabuelo /bisa'βuelo/ *m*, great-grandfather

bisagra /bi'sagra/ *f*, hinge; shoemaker's polisher

bisbís /bis'βis/ *m*, game of chance

bisbisar /bisβi'sar/ *vt Inf.* to mutter; whisper

bisbiseo /bisβi'seo/ *m*, *Inf.* muttering; murmuring; whispering

bisecar /bise'kar/ *vt* to bisect

bisección /bisek'sion; bisek'θion/ *f*, *Geom.* bisection

bisectriz /bisek'tris; bisek'triθ/ *f*, bisector

bisel /bi'sel/ *m*, bevel, chamfer

bisiesto /bi'siesto/ *a* leap and *m*, leap (year)

bisílabo /bi'silaβo/ *a* two-syllabled

bismuto /bis'muto/ *m*, bismuth

bisnieto /bis'nieto/ **(-ta)** *n* great-grandchild

bisonte /bi'sonte/ *m*, bison

bisoño /bi'soɲo/ **(-ña)** *a* inexperienced, raw. *n* recruit; *Inf.* greenhorn

bistec /bis'tek/ *m*, beef steak

bisturí /bistu'ri/ *m*, surgical knife

bisunto /bi'sunto/ *a* grubby, greasy

bisutería /bisute'ria/ *f*, imitation jewelry

bituminoso /bitumi'noso/ *a* bituminous

bivalvo /bi'βalβo/ *a* bivalve

Bizancio /bi'sansio; bi'θanθio/ Byzantium

bizantinismo /bisanti'nismo; biθanti'nismo/ *m*, Byzantinism

bizarría /bisa'rria; biθa'rria/ *f*, handsomeness; dash; verve; gallantry, courage; magnificence; liberality; whim, caprice

bizarro /bi'sarro; bi'θarro/ *a* handsome; dashing; gallant, courageous; liberal; splendid, magnificent

bizcaitarrismo /biskaita'rrismo; biθkaita'rrismo/ *m*, doctrine of Basque autonomy; Basque autonomy movement

bizco /'bisko; 'biθko/ *a* squint-eyed, cross-eyed

bizcocho /bis'kotʃo; biθ'kotʃo/ *m*, biscuit; sponge-cake; bisque

bizma /'bisma; 'biθma/ *f*, poultice. **poner bizmas**, to poultice

biznieto /bis'nieto; biθ'nieto/ *n* See **bisnieto**

blanca /'blanka/ *f*, old Spanish coin; *Inf.* penny; *Mus.* minim. **sin b.**, penniless

blanco /'blanko/ *a* white; fair-skinned; blank, vacant; *Inf.* cowardly. *m*, target; blank left in writing; white person; interval. **b. de España**, whiting. **b. de la uña**, half-moon of the nail. **dar en el b.**, to hit the mark. **en b.**, blank, unused; *Inf.* in vain; uncomprehendingly; (of nights) sleepless

blancor, /blan'kor,/ *m*. **blancura** *f*, whiteness; fairness (of skin)

blandear /blande'ar/ *vt* to moderate, soothe; brandish; *vi Fig.* give way, yield

blandir /blan'dir/ *vt* to brandish, wield, flourish

blando /'blando/ *a* soft; mild (weather); delicate; kind; peaceable; delicate, effeminate; *Inf.* cowardly

blandón /blan'don/ *m*, wax taper

blandura /blan'dura/ *f*, softness; poultice; blandishment, compliment; mildness (of weather); gentleness, affability; luxury

blanquear /blanke'ar/ *vt* to bleach; whitewash; whiten; *vi* appear white; show white

blanquecino /blanke'sino; blanke'θino/ *a* whitish

blanqueo /blan'keo/ *m*, whitening; whitewashing; bleaching

blanquillo /blan'kijo; blan'kiʎo/ *m*, *Central America, Mexico* egg; *Chile, Peru,* white peach

blanquizal /blanki'sal; blanki'θal/ *m*, pipe-clay

blasfemador /blasfema'ðor/ **(-ra)** *a* blaspheming. *n* blasphemer

blasfemar /blasfe'mar/ *vi* to blaspheme; curse, swear

blasfemia /blas'femia/ *f*, blasphemy; insult

blasfemo /blas'femo/ **(-ma)** *n* blasphemer. *a* blasphemous

blasón /bla'son/ *m*, heraldry; escutcheon; glory, honor. **una familia con antiguos blasones,** a family of ancient lineage

blasonar /blaso'nar/ *vt* to blazon; *vi* boast, brag, blazon abroad

bledo /'bleðo/ *m*, blade, leaf. **no importar un b.,** not to matter a straw

blenda /'blenda/ *f*, *Mineral.* blende

blindado /blin'daðo/ *a Nav.* armored, ironclad

blindaje /blin'dahe/ *m*, *Nav.* armor-plating; *Mil.* blindage

blindar /blin'dar/ *vt* to plate with armor, to case with steel

blofista /blo'fista/ *mf, Lat. Am.* bluffer

blonda /'blonda/ *f*, blonde (of lace)

blondo /'blondo/ *a* fair, blond, flaxen-haired

bloque /'bloke/ *m*, block, slab

bloquear /bloke'ar/ *vt* to blockade; besiege. **¡No me bloquees!** Don't cut me off!

bloqueo /blo'keo/ *m*, blockade; siege; blocking; freezing (of assets). **violar el b.,** to run the blockade

blusa /'blusa/ *f*, blouse

boa /'boa/ *f*, boa, large snake. *m*, boa (fur)

boato /bo'ato/ *m*, outward show, ostentation

bobería /boβe'ria/ *f*, foolishness, stupidity

bóbilis, bóbilis /'boβilis, 'boβilis/ **(de)** *adv Inf.* free of charge; without effort

bobina /bo'βina/ *f*, bobbin, spool, reel; *Elec.* coil; spool (of fishing rod)

bobo /'boβo/ **(-ba)** *a* stupid, idiotic; simple, innocent. *n* fool. *m*, clown, jester

boca /'boka/ *f*, mouth; pincers (of crustaceans); entrance or exit; mouth (of a river), gulf, inlet; orifice, opening; muzzle (of guns); cutting edge (of tools); taste (of wine, etc.). **b. abajo,** face down, prone. **b. arriba,** on one's back, face up, supine. **b. del estómago,** pit of the stomach. **b. rasgada,** large mouth. **a b.,** verbally. **a b. de jarro,** point-blank. **a pedir de b.,** just as one would wish. **de b.,** by word of mouth. *Inf.* **sin decir esta b. es mía,** without a word, in silence

bocacalle /boka'kaye; boka'kaʎe/ *f*, entrance (to a street); street junction

bocadillo /boka'ðiyo; boka'ðiʎo/ *m*, narrow ribbon; sandwich

bocado /bo'kaðo/ *m*, mouthful. **b. de reyes,** delicacy, exquisite dish (of food); snack; bite; (horse's) bit; bridle; *pl* preserved fruit cut up

bocamanga /boka'maŋga/ *f*, wrist (of sleeve)

bocana /bo'kana/ *f*, *Lat. Am.* estuary

bocanada /boka'naða/ *f*, mouthful (of liquid); cloud (of smoke). **b. de aire,** gust of wind

boceto /bo'seto; bo'θeto/ *m*, sketch; outline; roughcast model

bocha /'botʃa/ *f*, *Sports.* bowl; *pl* bowls

bochorno /bo'tʃorno/ *m*, sultry weather; heat, stuffiness; blush, hot flush; shame

bochornoso /botʃor'noso/ *a* sultry; shameful

bocina /bo'sina; bo'θina/ *f*, trumpet; megaphone; foghorn; hooter; *Auto.* horn; horn (of gramophone); *Astron.* Ursa Minor

bocio /'bosio; 'boθio/ *m*, *Med.* goiter

bocoy /bo'koi/ *m*, hogshead; large cask

boda /'boða/ *f*, wedding, marriage. **bodas de oro,** fiftieth (golden) anniversary. **bodas de plata,** silver wedding anniversary

bodega /bo'ðega/ *f*, wine-cellar; storeroom; stock-

room; granary; *Puerto Rico* grocery store; *Naut.* hold (of ship)

bodegón /boðe'gon/ *m*, eating-house; tavern; *Art.* still-life; genre picture

bofes /'bofes/ *m pl*, lungs, lights. *Inf.* **echar los b.,** to work oneself to death

bofetada /bofe'taða/ *f.* **bofetón** *m*, blow, slap; box on the ear

boga /'boga/ *f*, rowing; fashion, vogue; *Mech.* bogie. *mf* oarsman, rower. **estar en b.,** to be fashionable

bogador /boga'ðor/ **(-ra)** *n* rower, oarsman

bogar /bo'gar/ *vi* to row

bogavante /boga'βante/ *m*, lobster

bogotano /bogo'tano/ **(-na)** *a* and *n* of or from Bogotá

bohemio /bo'emio/ **(-ia)** *a* and *n* gipsy; bohemian; Bohemian. *m*, archer's short cloak

bohío /bo'io/ *m*, *Lat. Am.* hut

boicot, boicoteo /boi'kot, boiko'teo/ *m*, boycott

boicotear /boikote'ar/ *vt* to boycott

boina /'boina/ *f*, Basque cap; beret

bola /'bola/ *f*, globe; ball; *Sports.* bowl; *Archit.* balloon; *Inf.* trick, lie; (Cuba) rumor; *Mexico* shoeshine, shine. **b. de nieves,** snowball. *Inf.* **dejar rodar la b.,** to let things slide

bolardo /bo'larðo/ *m*, bollard

bolchevismo /boltʃe'βismo/ *m*, Bolshevism

bolea /bo'lea/ *f*, (tennis) volley; throw

bolera /bo'lera/ *f*, bowling alley

bolero /bo'lero/ *m*, bolero; dancer; *Inf.* top hat; *Mexico* bootblack

boleta /bo'leta/ *f*, admission ticket; billet ticket; warrant, voucher; summons, ticket, traffic ticket

boletería /bolete'ria/ *f. Lat. Am.* ticket office, box office

boletín /bole'tin/ *m*, bulletin; admission ticket; pay warrant; *Com.* price list; learned periodical. **b. de noticias,** news bulletin. **b. meteorológico,** weather report

boleto /bo'leto/ *m. Lat. Am.* ticket

boliche /bo'litʃe/ *m*, jack (in bowls); cup-and-ball toy; small oven (for charcoal); dragnet; *Mexico* bowling **juego de b.,** bowls

bólido /'boliðo/ *m*, *Astron.* bolide, meteor

bolígrafo /bo'ligrafo/ *m*, ballpoint pen

bolillo /bo'liyo; bo'liʎo/ *m*, bobbin (lace making); *Mexico* roll (food)

bolina /bo'lina/ *f*, *Naut.* bowline; *Naut.* sounder; *Inf.* uproar, tumult

bolita /bo'lita/ *f*, pellet

Bolivia /βo'liβia/ Bolivia

boliviano /boli'βiano/ **(-na)** *a* and *n* Bolivian. *m*, silver coin

bollo /'boyo; 'boʎo/ *m*, bread roll; bun; bulge, bruise (in metal); *Med.* lump

bollón /bo'yon; bo'ʎon/ *m*, round-headed or brassheaded nail; *Bot.* bud (especially vines)

bolo /'bolo/ *m*, skittle, ninepin; pillow (for lace making); Cuban coin; *Med.* large pill; *Fig. Inf.* blockhead; *pl* skittles (game of)

bolsa /'bolsa/ *f*, purse; bag; footmuff; fold, pucker; pouch; exchange, stock exchange, capital, money; prize money; *Med.* sac; *Mineral.* pocket. **b. de estudio,** scholarship grant. **b. de trabajo,** labor exchange. **b. de valores,** stock exchange. **bajar** (*or* **subir**) **la b.,** to fall (or rise) (of stock exchange quotations). **jugar a la b.,** to speculate on the stock exchange

bolsillo /bol'siyo; bol'siʎo/ *m*, pocket; purse; money

bolsista /bol'sista/ *mf* stock-broker; speculator (on the stock exchange)

bomba /'bomba/ *f*, *Mech.* pump; pumping engine; bomb; *Mil.* shell; lamp globe; *Inf.* improvised verses; *Inf.* drinking bout. **¡B.!** Listen! Here goes! **b. de incendios,** fire-engine. **b. marina,** waterspout. **b. de mecha atrasada,** time bomb. **b. volante,** flying-bomb. **a prueba de b.,** bombproof. **arrojar bombas,** to bomb. *Inf.* **caer como una b.,** to be a bombshell

bombachos /bom'βatʃos/ *a* baggy, loose-fitting; *m pl*, plus fours

bombardear /bombarðe'ar/ *vt* to bombard; bomb; shell

bombardeo /bombar'ðeo/ *m*, bombardment, bombing; shelling

bombardero /bombar'ðero/ *m*, gunner, bombardier; *Aer.* bomber. **b. pesado**, *Aer.* heavy bomber. **Servicio de b.**, Bomber Command

bombástico /bom'βastiko/ *a* bombastic, high sounding

bombazo /bom'βaso/ bom'βaθo/ *m*, bombshell; bomb crater; noise of an exploding bomb

bombear /bombe'ar/ *vt* to pump; bombard, shell; praise

bombero /bom'βero/ *m*, worker of a pressure pump; fireman; mortar, howitzer

bombilla /bom'βiya/ bom'βiʎa/ *f*, *Naut.* lantern; (*Elec. Phys.*) bulb; small pump; straw for drinking maté *West Hem.*

bombillo /bom'βiyo/ bom'βiʎo/ *m*, w.c. siphon; handpump

bombo /'bombo/ *m*, big drum or player of it; *Naut.* barge, ferry; ballot box; exaggerated praise

bombón /bom'βon/ *m*, bonbon, sweet

bombonera /bombo'nera/ *f*, box for toffee, etc.

bonachón /bona'tʃon/ *a* *Inf.* genial, good-natured

bonaerense /bonae'rense/ *a* and *mf* of or from the Province of Buenos Aires

Bonaira /bo'naira/ Bonaire

bonancible /bonan'siβle/ bonan'θiβle/ *a* calm (of weather, sea)

bonanza /bo'nansa/ bo'nanθa/ *f*, fair weather; prosperity

bondad /bon'dað/ *f*, goodness; kindness, helpfulness. **Tenga la b. de...**, Be good enough to..., Please...

bondadoso /bonda'ðoso/ *a* good, kind

bonete /bo'nete/ *m*, academic cap; *Zool.* reticulum (ruminants); *Eccl.* biretta. **gran b.**, important person. *Inf.* **a tente b.**, insistently

bonetero /bone'tero/ (**-ra**) *n* seller or maker of caps and birettas

boniato /bo'niato/ *m*, *Lat. Am.* sweet potato, yam

bonificación /bonifika'sion/ bonifika'θion/ *f*, bonus; allowance, discount

bonito /bo'nito/ *a* pretty; graceful; (ironical) fine. *m*, *Ichth.* tuna, bonito

bono /'bono/ *m*, voucher; *Com.* bond, certificate. **b. postal**, postal money order. **bono del gobierno**, government bond

boñiga /bo'ɲiga/ *f*, cow-dung, animal manure

boqueada /boke'aða/ *f*, gasp, opening of the mouth. **dar las boqueadas, estar en las últimas boqueadas**, to be at the last gasp

boquear /boke'ar/ *vi* to gasp; be dying; *Inf.* be at last gasp (of things); *vt* say, utter

boquera /bo'kera/ *f*, sluice (in irrigation canal)

boquerón /boke'ron/ *m*, large opening; *Ichth.* anchovy (fish); whitebait

boquete /bo'kete/ *m*, narrow entrance, aperture; gap, breach; hole

boquiabierto /bokia'βierto/ *a* open-mouthed; amazed

boquiancho /bo'kiantʃo/ *a* wide-mouthed

boquiasombrado /bokiasom'βraðo/ *a* gaping

boquilla /bo'kiya/ bo'kiʎa/ *f*, *dim* small mouth; mouthpiece (of wind instruments, etc.); cigar- or cigarette-holder; gas-burner; nozzle; tip (of cigarettes)

boquirroto /boki'rroto/ *a* *Inf.* loquacious, indiscreet

borbollar /borβo'yar/ borβo'ʎar/ *vi* to bubble, foam, froth

borbollón, borbotón /borβo'yon/, borβo'ton/ borβo'ʎon, borβo'ton/ *m*, gushing, bubbling, welling up. **a borbollones**, in a torrent; hastily, impetuously

borbotar /borβo'tar/ *vi* to gush out, well up

borda /'borða/ *f*, hut, cabin; *Naut.* gunwale

bordado /bor'ðaðo/ *m*, embroidery

bordador /borða'ðor/ (**-ra**) *n* embroiderer

bordar /bor'ðar/ *vt* to embroider; *Fig.* perform perfectly

borde /'borðe/ *m*, edge; fringe; verge; rim; mount (of a picture); brim (of a hat); side (of ship). *a* wild

(of plants); illegitimate. **estar lleno hasta los bordes**, to be full to the brim

bordear /borðe'ar/ *vt* to border, trim with a bordear; line (a street, e.g. *Diez mil personas bordearon las calles durante el desfile*, Ten thousand people lined the streets during the parade)

bordillo /bor'ðiyo/ bor'ðiʎo/ *m*, curbstone, curb.

bordo /'borðo/ *m*, side (of ships); border, edge. **a b.**, on board

bordón /bor'ðon/ *m*, pilgrim's staff; monotonous repetition; refrain; *Mus.* bass string; *Fig.* guide, stay

borgoña /bor'goɲa/ *m*, Burgundy wine

borgoñón /borgo'ɲon/ (**-ona**) *a* and *n* Burgundian

bórico /'boriko/ *a* boric

boricua /bori'kua/ *a*, **borinqueño, -a** *a*, *mf* Puerto Rican

borla /'borla/ *f*, tassel; puff (for powder). *Fig.* **tomar la b.**, to take one's doctorate, graduate

bornear /borne'ar/ *vt* to bend, twist; *Archit.* hoist into position; *vr* warp (wood)

borra /'borra/ *f*, yearling ewe; thickest wool; wadstuffing; lees, sediment; fluff, dust; *Inf.* trash. **b. de algodón**, cotton-waste

borrachera /borra'tʃera/ *f*, drunkenness; orgy, carousal; *Inf.* blunder

borrachín /borra'tʃin/ (**-ina**) *n* tippler, toper

borrachito /borra'tʃito/ *a* high (on liquor), tipsy

borracho /bo'rratʃo/ (**de**) *a* drunk (on), intoxicated (with); *Inf.* blind (with rage, etc.). *n* tippler, drunkard

borrador /borra'ðor/ *m*, rough draft. **en borrador**, in the works (e.g. *Tiene dos ensayos en borrador*, She has two essays in the works). **estar en borrador**, to be in the works

borradura /borra'ðura/ *f*, erasure

borrajear /borrahe'ar/ *vt* to scribble

borrar /bo'rrar/ *vt* to erase; cross out; blot out; *Fig.* obliterate

borrasca /bo'rraska/ *f*, storm, tempest; peril, danger; *Inf.* orgy

borrascosidad /borraskosi'ðað/ *f*, storminess

borrascoso /borras'koso/ *a* stormy; disordered, turbulent

borrego /bo'rrego/ (**-ga**) *n* lamb; *Inf.* nincompoop, simpleton; *m pl*, fleecy clouds; white horses (waves)

borrico /bo'rriko/ (**-ca**) *a* donkey; fool. *m*, sawinghorse

borrón /bo'rron/ *m*, blot; rough draft; defect; *Fig.* stigma

borroso /bo'rroso/ *a* blurred, indistinct; full of dregs, muddy

boscaje /bos'kahe/ *m*, grove, group of trees, thicket

Bósforo, el /'bosforo, el/ the Bosporus

bosque /'boske/ *m*, wood, forest

bosquejar /boske'har/ *vt* *Art.* to sketch; sketch out, draft; model in rough (sculpture); outline

bosquejo /bos'keho/ *m*, outline, sketch; rough plan or idea; unfinished work. **en bosquejo**, grosso modo

bostar /bos'tar/ *m*, ox barn

bostezar /boste'sar/ boste'θar/ *vi* to yawn

bostezo /bos'teso/ bos'teθo/ *m*, yawning; yawn

bota /'bota/ *f*, small wineskin; barrel, butt; boot. **b. de montar**, riding boot. **botas de campaña**, topboots. **botas de vadear**, waders

botada, botadura /bo'taða, bota'ðura/ *f*, launching (of a ship)

botador /bota'ðor/ *m*, thrower; boating-pole; nailpuller

botafuego /bota'fuego/ *m*, *Mil.* linstock; *Inf.* quicktempered, irascible person

botalón /bota'lon/ *m*, *Naut.* boom. **b. de foque**, jibboom

botana /bo'tana/ *f*, *Lat. Am.* bite (to eat), snack

botánica /bo'tanika/ *f*, botany

botánico /bo'taniko/ (**-ca**) *a* botanical. *n* botanist

botar /bo'tar/ *vt* to fling; launch (boat); *Lat. Am.* to discard, throw away, throw out *Naut.* shift the helm; *vi* jump; bounce, rebound; rear, prance (horses)

botarate /bota'rate/ *m*, *Inf.* madcap, devil-may-care

botarel, botarete /bota'rel, bota'rete/ *m*, *arch* abutment, buttress, flying buttress

botarga /bo'targa/ *f*, motley; harlequin
bote /'bote/ *m*, thrust (with lance, etc.); rearing (of horse); rebound; *Aer.* bump; open boat; small bottle, jar. **b. salvavidas,** lifeboat. *Inf.* **de b. en b.,** chockful
botella /bo'teʎa/ *f*, bottle; bottleful; flask
botica /bo'tika/ *f*, chemist's shop; medicines, remedies; physic; store, shop; medicine chest
boticario /boti'kario/ *m*, apothecary, chemist
botija /bo'tiha/ *f*, earthen jug; *Slang.* chunky person
botijo /bo'tiho/ *m*, earthenware jar with spout and handle
botillería /botiye'ria/ botiʎe'ria/ *f*, ice-cream bar
botín /bo'tin/ *m*, gaiter; buskin; booty
botiquín /boti'kin/ *m*, first-aid kit; medicine chest
botón /bo'ton/ *m*, bud; button; knob, handle; switch (electric); press button (bell); *Bot.* center; button (on a foil); *Mech.* stud
botonero /boto'nero/ **(-ra)** *n* button maker or seller
bóveda /b'oβeða/ *f*, *Archit.* vault, arch; crypt; cavern. **b. celeste,** sky
boxeador /boksea'ðor/ *m*, boxer
boxear /bokse'ar/ *vi Sports.* to box
boxeo /bok'seo/ *m*, *Sports.* boxing
boya /'boya/ *f*, *Naut.* buoy; float
boyante /bo'yante/ *a* floating; light, buoyant; prosperous
boyar /bo'yar/ *vi Naut.* to float
boyero /bo'yero/ *m*, cowherd
boza /'bosa; 'boθa/ *f*, painter (of a boat)
bozal /bo'sal; bo'θal/ *m*, muzzle; nosebag; harness bells. *mf Inf.* greenhorn; *a* wild, untamed (horses)
bozo /'boso; 'boθo/ *m*, down which precedes beard; muzzle; headstall; lips, snout
bracero /bra'sero; bra'θero/ *m*, one who offers his arm (to a lady); day laborer; strong man. **de b.,** arm-in-arm
bracete /bra'sete; bra'θete/ *m*, small arm. **de b.,** arm-in-arm
bracmán /brak'man/ *m*, Brahmin
braga /'braga/ *f*, (gen. *pl*) breeches; knickerbockers; hoist or pulley rope
bragazas /bra'gasas; bra'gaθas/ *m*, *Inf.* weak-willed, fellow, soft specimen
braguero /bra'gero/ *m*, *Med.* truss
bragueta /bra'geta/ *f*, fly (of trousers)
brahmanismo /brama'nismo/ *m*, Brahmanism
bramante /bra'mante/ *a* roaring. *m*, twine, packthread
bramar /bra'mar/ *vi* to roar; rage; *Fig.* howl (of the wind, etc.)
bramido /bra'miðo/ *m*, bellowing; roaring; yell of rage; *Fig.* howling (wind, sea, etc.)
brancada /bran'kaða/ *f*, drag net
branquia /'brankia/ *f*, (gen. *pl*) *Ichth.* gill
branquial /bran'kial/ *a* branchiate
braquicefalia /bra,kise'falia; bra,kiθe'falia/ *f*, brachycephaly
braquiotomía /brakioto'mia/ *f*, *Surg.* brachiotomy, amputation of the arms
brasa /'brasa/ *f*, live coal. **estar como en brasas,** to be like a cat on hot bricks
brasero /bra'sero/ *m*, brazier; *Mexico* fireplace
Brasil /bra'sil/ Brazil
brasileño /brasi'leɲo/ **(-ña)** *a* and *n* Brazilian
bravata /bra'βata/ *f*, bravado; threat
braveza /bra'βesa; bra'βeθa/ *f*, ferocity, savageness; valor; violence, fury (of elements)
bravío /bra'βio/ *a* savage, untamed; wild (plants); uncultured
bravo /'braβo/ *a* valiant; surly, rude; independent, strong-minded, good, excellent; savage (animals); stormy (sea); rough, rugged; violent, angry; *Inf.* sumptuous, magnificent.
bravura /bra'βura/ *f*, ferocity (animals); courage (persons); boastful threat
braza /'brasa; 'braθa/ *f*, *Naut.* fathom; stroke (in swimming)
brazado /bra'saðo; bra'θaðo/ *m*, armful
brazal /bra'sal; bra'θal/ *m*, armlet, brassard

brazalete /brasa'lete; braθa'lete/ *m*, bracelet; brassard
brazo /'braso; 'braθo/ *m*, arm; upper arm; front paw; *Mech.* arm; branch (of chandelier, etc.); bough; arm (of chair); power, courage; *pl* protectors; workmen, hands. **b. de mar,** firth, arm of the sea. **a b. partido,** in unarmed fight, man to man. **con los brazos abiertos,** welcomingly; willingly, gladly. **dar los brazos** **(a),** to embrace. *Inf.* **hecho un b. de mar,** dressed up to the nines
brea /'brea/ *f*, pitch, tar; sacking, canvas
brebaje /bre'βahe/ *m*, beverage; unpleasant drink; *Naut.* draft (of beer, grog, etc.)
brecha /'bretʃa/ *f*, *Mil.* breach; opening; *Fig.* impression (on mind). **morir en la b.,** to fight to the last ditch; die in harness
brécol /'brekol/ *m*, *Bot.* broccoli
brega /'breγa/ *f*, fight; quarrel; disappointment, trick. **andar a la b.,** to work hard. **dar b.,** to play a trick
bregar /bre'γar/ *vi* to fight; work hard; *Fig.* struggle; **bregarse con,** to tackle (a problem)
breña /'breɲa/ *f*, rough ground, bramble patch
breñal /bre'ɲal/ *m*, scrub, brushwood
breñoso /bre'ɲoso/ *a* rugged, rocky
Bretaña /bre'taɲa/ Brittany
brete /'brete/ *m*, fetters, shackles; *Fig.* fix, squeeze, tight spot, tight squeeze (e.g. *Estoy en un brete.* I'm in a tight spot)
bretón /bre'ton/ **(-ona)** *a* and *n* Breton. *m*, Breton (language)
breva /'breβa/ *f*, early fig; early acorn; *Fig.* advantage, "plum''; *Inf.* peach (girl); *Inf.* windfall, piece of luck; Havana cigar
breve /'breβe/ *a* brief; concise. *m*, papal brief. *f*, *Mus.* breve. **en b.,** shortly, concisely; in a short while, soon
brevedad /breβe'ðað/ *f*, brevity **a la mayor b.,** *Lat. Am.* as soon as possible
breviario /bre'βiario/ *m*, breviary
brezal /bre'sal; bre'θal/ *m*, heath, moor
brezo /'breso; 'breθo/ *m*, *Bot.* heath
bribón /bri'βon/ **(-ona)** *n* rogue, ruffian. *a* knavish, dishonest; lazy
bribonada /briβo'naða/ *f*, knavery, mischievous trick
bribonear /briβone'ar/ *vi* to idle; play tricks, be a rogue
bribonería /briβone'ria/ *f*, rascality, vagrant life
brida /'briða/ *f*, bridle
brigada /bri'gaða/ *f*, *Mil.* brigade; *Naut.* division of fleet; beasts of burden. **b. millonaria,** (Castroist Cuba) team of thirty sugarcane cutters who cut a million or more arrobas in one harvest
brillante /bri'yante; bri'ʎante/ *a* sparkling, brilliant; *Fig.* outstanding. *m*, diamond
brillantez /briyan'tes; briʎan'teθ/ *f*, brightness, luster; fame; *Fig.* brilliance
brillantina /briyan'tina; briʎan'tina/ *f*, brilliantine
brillar /bri'yar; bri'ʎar/ *vi* to shine, sparkle, gleam, glisten; *Fig.* be brilliant or outstanding
brillo /'briyo; 'briʎo/ *m*, brilliancy, brightness, shine; fame, glory; distinction, brilliance, splendor
brincar /brin'kar/ *vi* to spring, leap, skip, frisk; *Fig. Inf.* skip, omit; *Inf.* grow angry; *vt* jump a child up and down
brinco /'brinko/ *m*, leap, spring; skip, frolicking
brindar /brin'dar/ *vi* to invite, provoke (of things); (with *prep a* or *por*) drink the health of, toast; *vt* and *vi* give, present; offer; *vr* offer one's services
brindis /'brindis/ *m*, toast (drink)
brío /'brio/ *m*, vigor; spirit, courage; gusto, verve
brioso /'brioso/ *a* vigorous, enterprising; spirited, courageous; dashing, lively
briqueta /bri'keta/ *f*, briquette
brisa /'brisa/ *f*, breeze; grape pressings
británico /bri'taniko/ *a* British
brizna /'brisna; 'briθna/ *f*, shred, paring; blade (grass); filament, fiber; string (of bean-pod, etc.); splinter, chip
briznar /bris'nar; briθ'nar/ *vi*, *Lat. Am.* to drizzle

broca /'broka/ *f*, reel; tack (shoemaker's); *Mech.* drill, bit

brocado /bro'kaðo/ *m*, brocade. *a* brocade or embroidered like brocade

brocal /bro'kal/ *m*, puteal (of a well); mouthpiece (of wineskin); metal ring (of sword-sheath)

brocamantón /brokaman'ton/ *m*, large jeweled brooch

brocatel /broka'tel/ *m*, imitation brocade

brocha /'brotʃa/ *f*, brush. **b. de afeitar,** shaving brush. **de b. gorda,** crudely painted. **pintor de b. gorda,** decorator

brochada /bro'tʃaða/ *f*, stroke (of the brush)

brochado /bro'tʃaðo/ *a* brocaded, embossed

brochadura /brotʃa'ðura/ *f*, fastening, set of hooks and eyes

broche /'brotʃe/ *m*, clasp, fastening; brooch; hooks and eyes; *Lat. Am.* (paper) clip

brochón /bro'tʃon/ *m*, whitewash brush

broma /'broma/ *f*, merriment; joke, jest; ship-worm. **b. literaria,** literary hoax

bromear /brome'ar/ **(se)** *vi* and *vr* to joke, make fun

bromista /bro'mista/ *a* joking, jesting; mischievous. *mf* genial person; prankster, tease

bromo /'bromo/ *m*, bromine

bronca /'bronka/ *f*, *Inf.* shindy

bronce /'bronse; 'bronθe/ *m*, bronze; brass; *Poet.* gun, bell, trumpet; bronze statue; sunburn

bronceado /bronse'aðo; bronθe'aðo/ *a* bronzed; sunburned. *m*, sunburn

broncear /bronse'ar; bronθe'ar/ *vt* to bronze; sunburn

bronco /'bronko/ *a* rough, coarse; brittle; (of metals); harsh (voice, musical instruments); rigid, stiff; surly

bronconeumonía /ˌbronkoneumo'nia/ *f*, bronchopneumonia

bronquial /bron'kial/ *a* bronchial

bronquio /'bronkio/ *m*, (gen. *pl*) bronchi

bronquitis /bron'kitis/ *f*, bronchitis

broquel /bro'kel/ *m*, shield; *Fig.* protection

broquelero /broke'lero/ *m*, shield maker; quarrelsome man

broqueta /bro'keta/ *f*, skewer

brotadura /brota'ðura/ *f*, budding

brotar /bro'tar/ *vi* to germinate, sprout; gush forth (water); issue forth, burst out; *Fig.* appear (of rash); *Fig.* begin to appear; *vt* to bring forth; produce (of earth)

brote /'brote/ *m*, bud, sprout; *Fig.* germ, genesis; iota, jot, atom

broza /'brosa; 'broθa/ *f*, garden rubbish; debris; thicket

bruces /'bruses; 'bruθes/ **(a** or **de)** *adv* face downwards. **caer de b.,** to fall flat. Also with other verbs: *dar, echarse,* etc.

bruja /'bruha/ *f*, witch; owl; *Inf.* hag

brujear /bruhe'ar/ *vi* to practice witchcraft

brujería /bruhe'ria/ *f*, witchcraft

brujo /'bruho/ *m*, magician, wizard

brújula /'bruhula/ *f*, magnetic needle; compass; mariner's compass. **b. de bolsillo,** pocket compass. **b. giroscópica,** gyrocompass

bruma /'bruma/ *f*, haze; sea-mist

brumoso /bru'moso/ *a* misty, hazy

bruno /'bruno/ *a* dark brown

bruñido /bru'ɲiðo/ *m*, polishing; burnish

bruñidor /bruɲi'ðor/ **(-ra)** *a* polishing. *n* burnisher. *m*, polisher (instrument)

bruñir /bru'ɲir/ *vt* to polish, burnish; *Inf.* apply make up

brusco /'brusko/ *a* brusque, rude; blunt; sudden, unexpected; sharp (of bends)

Bruselas /bru'selas/ Brussels

bruselense /bruse'lense/ *a* and *mf* of or from Brussels

brusquedad /bruske'ðað/ *f*, brusquerie, rudeness; bluntness; suddenness, unexpectedness; sharpness (of a bend)

brutal /bru'tal/ *a* brutal

brutalidad /brutali'ðað/ *f*, brutality; *Fig.* brutishness; viciousness

bruto /'bruto/ *a* stupid, unreasonable; vicious; unpolished, rough. *m*, animal (gen. quadruped). **en b.,** in the rough; *Com.* in bulk. **diamante en b.,** an uncut diamond

bruza /'brusa; 'bruθa/ *f*, strong brush; scrubbing brush

Bs. As. /ˌbuenos 'aires/ abbrev. of Buenos Aires

bu /bu/ *m*, *Inf.* bogey man

buba /'buβa/ *f*, pustule; *pl* buboes

bubónico /bu'βoniko/ *a* bubonic

bucal /bu'kal/ *a* buccal

bucanero /buka'nero/ *m*, buccaneer

búcaro /'bukaro/ *m*, arsenican clay; jar made of arsenican clay

buceador /busea'ðor; buθea'ðor/ *m*, diver

bucear /buse'ar; buθe'ar/ *vi* to dive, work as a diver; swim under water; *Fig.* investigate

bucéfalo /bu'sefalo; bu'θefalo/ *m*, bucephalus; *Inf.* fool, blockhead

buceo /bu'seo; bu'θeo/ *m*, diving; dive; *Fig.* investigation

buchaca /bu'tʃaka/ *f*, *Lat. Am.* saddlebag; billiard pocket

buche /'butʃe/ *m*, craw or crop; mouthful; wrinkle, pleat; *Inf.* stomach, belly. *Fig. Inf.* inmost heart

bucle /'bukle/ *m*, ringlet, curl

bucólico /bu'koliko/ *a* bucolic

budín /bu'ðin/ *m*, pudding

budismo /bu'ðismo/ *m*, Buddhism

budista /bu'ðista/ *a* and *mf* Buddhist

buen /buen/ *a abb* of **bueno,** good. Used before *m*, singular nouns and infinitives used as nouns, e.g. *un b. libro,* a good book. *el b. cantar,* good singing

buenamente /buena'mente/ *adv* easily; comfortably, conveniently; willingly

buenaventura /buenaβen'tura/ *f*, good luck; fortune told from hand

bueno /'bueno/ (see **buen**) *a* good; kind; useful; convenient; pleasant; healthy; large (drink, etc.); simple, innocent; suitable; sufficient; opportune. **¡B.!** Good!; Enough!; *Mexico* Hello! (on telephone); All right! **a buenas,** willingly. **de buenas a primeras,** at first sight, from the beginning. **hacer b.,** to prove, justify (a claim)

buey /buei/ *m*, ox. **b. suelto,** *Inf.* freelance; bachelor

búfalo /'bufalo/ **(-la)** *n* buffalo

bufanda /bu'fanda/ *f*, scarf

bufar /bu'far/ *vi* to bellow; snort; *Inf.* snort with rage

bufete /bu'fete/ *m*, desk, writing table; lawyer's office or practice; sideboard

bufido /bu'fiðo/ *m*, snort; bellow

bufo /'bufo/ *a* comic. *m*, clown, buffoon

bufón /bu'fon/ *m*, buffoon, clown; jester. *a* comical, clownish

bufonada /bufo'naða/ *f*, buffoonery, clowning; raillery, taunt

bufonear /bufone'ar/ **(se)** *vr* and *vi* to joke, jest, parody

bufonería. /bufone'ria/ See **bufonada**

buhardilla /buar'ðiya; buar'ðiʎa/ *f*, garret; skylight

búho /'buo/ *m*, owl; *Inf.* hermit, unsociable person

buhonería /buone'ria/ *f*, peddling; hawking; peddler's wares

buhonero /buo'nero/ *m*, pedler

buido /'buiðo/ *a* sharp-pointed; sharp

buitre /'buitre/ *m*, vulture

bujía /bu'hia/ *f*, candle; candlestick; *Elec.* candlepower; *Auto.* sparking plug

bula /'bula/ *f*, (Papal) bull

bulbo /'bulβo/ *m*, *Bot.* bulb. **b. dentario,** pulp (of teeth)

bulboso /bul'βoso/ *a* bulbous

bulevar /bule'βar/ *m*, boulevard, promenade

bulimia /bu'limia/ *f*, bulimia

bulla /'buya/ *f*, noise; bustle; confusion; fuss. *Inf.* **meter a b.,** to throw into great confusion

bullebulle /buye'βuye; buʎe'βuʎe/ *mf* busybody; madcap

bullente /bu'yente; bu'ʎente/ *adj* boiling, bubbling; frothy (beer); swarming, teeming. **b. de sol,** drenched in sunlight, sun-drenched
bullicio /bu'yisio; bu'ʎiθio/ *m,* noise, bustle; rioting; uproar
bullicioso /buyi'sioso; buʎi'θioso/ *a* noisy, merry, boisterous; rebellious; lively, restless
bullir /bu'yir; bu'ʎir/ *vi* to boil; foam, bubble; *Fig.* seethe; *Fig.* swarm (insects); bustle; *vt* move, stir; *vr* stir, give signs of life
bulto /'bulto/ *m,* bulk, mass, size; form of person, etc., seen indistinctly; swelling; bust, statue; bundle, package, piece of luggage; pillowcase. *Fig. Inf.* **poner de b.,** to put clearly, emphasize. **ser de b.,** to be obvious
bumerang /bume'raŋ/ *m,* boomerang
buñolería /buɲole'ria/ *f,* bun or waffle shop
buñuelo /bu'ɲuelo/ *m,* bun; waffle, fritter; *Fig.* botch
buque /'buke/ *m,* ship, vessel; capacity of ship; ship's hull. **b. barreminas,** minesweeper. **b. de guerra,** battleship, man-of-war. **b. de vapor,** steamer. **b. de vela,** sailing ship. **b. escuela,** trainingship. **b. mercante,** merchant vessel. **b. submarino,** submarine. **b. transbordador,** train-ferry
burbuja /bur'βuha/ *f,* bubble
burbujear /burβuhe'ar/ *vi* to bubble
burdel /bur'ðel/ *m,* brothel; *Inf.* untidy, noisy place. *a* lascivious
burdo /'burðo/ *a* coarse, tough
burgalés /burga'les/ **(-esa)** *a* and *n* of or from Burgos
burgo /'burgo/ *m,* borough, burgh
burgomaestre /burgoma'estre/ *m,* burgomaster
burgués /bur'ges/ **(-esa)** *a* and *n* bourgeois
burguesía /burge'sia/ *f,* bourgeoisie
buriel /bu'riel/ *a* dark red
buril /bu'ril/ *m,* burin, engraver's tool
burla /'burla/ *f,* mockery; joke, jest; trick. **b. burlando,** without effort; negligently. **de burlas,** in fun. **entre burlas y veras,** half-jokingly
burlador /burla'ðor/ *a* mocking. *m,* libertine, rake; deceiver
burlar /bur'lar/ *vt* to play a trick on; deceive; disappoint; *vr* and *vi* (*with de*) make fun of, laugh at, ridicule
burlesco /bur'lesko/ *a* jocular, comic, burlesque

burlón /bur'lon/ **(-ona)** *a* joking; mocking, scoffing. *n* joker; scoffer
buró /bu'ro/ *m,* bureau, writing-desk; *Mexico* night table
burocracia /buro'krasia; buro'kraθia/ *f,* bureaucracy
burócrata /bu'rokrata/ *mf* bureaucrat
burocrático /buro'kratiko/ *a* bureaucratic
burocratismo /burokra'tismo/ *m,* bureaucracy, red tape
burra /'burra/ *f,* she-ass; foolish, unteachable woman; painstaking, patient woman
burrajo /bu'rraho/ *m,* dry stable dung used as fuel
burro /'burro/ *m,* ass, donkey; sawing-horse; card game
bursátil /bur'satil/ *a Com.* relating to the stock exchange; financial
busca /'buska/ *f,* search; hunting party; research; pursuit
buscado /bus'kaðo/ *adj* deliberate, intentional (negligence, etc.)
buscador /buska'ðor/ **(-ra)** *n* searcher; investigator. *m,* finder (of a camera, etc.)
buscapié /buska'pie/ *m,* hint or suggestion; *Fig.* feeler
buscapiés /buska'pies/ *m,* squib, cracker, firecracker
buscapleitos /buska'pleitos/ *mf Lat. Am.* troublemaker
buscar /bus'kar/ *vt* to search, look for; pursue. **ir a b.,** to go to look for, go and get; bring, fetch
buscarruidos /buska'rruiðos/ *mf Inf.* quarrel maker
buscavidas /buska'βiðas/ *mf Inf.* busybody; *Inf.* gogetter
buscón /bus'kon/ **(-ona)** *n* searcher; pickpocket, thief, swindler, rogue
buscona /bus'kona/ *f,* prostitute
busilis /bu'silis/ *m, Inf.* knotty problem, snag; **ahí está el b.,** there's the rub; core, main point
búsqueda /'buskeða/ **(de)** *f,* search (for)
busto /'busto/ *m, Art.* bust, head and shoulders
butaca /bu'taka/ *f,* armchair; *Theat.* orchestra stall; seat (in movies, etc.); *Lat. Am.* stool
butifarra /bu'tifarra/ *f,* sausage made principally in Catalonia and the Balearic Islands; *Inf.* badly fitting stocking
buzo /'buso; 'buθo/ *m,* diver
buzón /bu'son; bu'θon/ *m,* mailbox; letter-box; canal, channel; sluice

---

C

C. /k/ abbrev. of ciudadano
¡ca! /ka/ *interj* Fancy! Oh no!
cabal /ka'βal/ *a* just, exact; perfect; complete; faultless. *interj* Exactly! **por sus cabales,** according to plan; perfectly
cábala /'kaβala/ *f,* cabala; divination; *Inf.* intrigue. **hacer cábalas,** to venture a guess
cabalgada /kaβal'gaða/ *f,* cavalcade; foray, raid
cabalgador /kaβalga'ðor/ **(-ra)** *n* rider, horseman
cabalgadura /kaβalga'ðura/ *f,* riding horse; beast of burden
cabalgar /kaβal'gar/ *vi* to ride a horse; ride in procession
cabalístico /kaβa'listiko/ *a* cabalistic; mysterious
caballa /ka'βaya; ka'βaʎa/ *f,* mackerel
caballada /kaβa'yaða; kaβa'ʎaða/ *f,* pack of horses; stud (of horses)
caballeresco /kaβaye'resko; kaβaʎe'resko/ *a* gentlemanly; knightly; chivalrous
caballería /kaβaye'ria; kaβaʎe'ria/ *f,* riding animal; cavalry; knightly deed or quest; any of Spanish Military Orders; knight-errantry; knighthood; chivalry; share of the spoils of war; horsemanship. **c. andante,** knight-errantry. **c. ligera,** *Mil.* light horse. **c. mayor,** horses, mares, mules. **c. menor,** asses, donkeys
caballeriza /kaβaye'risa; kaβaʎe'riθa/ *f,* stable; stud of horses; staff of a stable
caballerizo /kaβaye'riso; kaβaʎe'riθo/ *m,* head sta-

ble-groom. **c. mayor del rey,** Master of the King's Horse
caballero /kaβa'yero; kaβa'ʎero/ *m,* gentleman; cavalier; knight. **c. andante,** knight-errant. *Inf.* **c. de industria,** adventurer, sharper. **el C. de la Mancha,** Knight of La Mancha. **el C. Sin Miedo y Sin Tacha,** the Seigneur de Bayart. **c. del hábito,** knight of one of the Spanish Military Orders. **c. novel,** untried knight. **armar c.,** to dub a knight
caballerosidad /kaβayerosi'ðað; kaβaʎerosi'ðað/ *f,* gentlemanliness; nobility; generosity; chivalry
caballeroso /kaβaye'roso; kaβaʎe'roso/ *a* gentlemanly; noble; generous; chivalrous
caballete /kaβa'yete; kaβa'ʎete/ *m,* ridge (of a roof); *Mil.* wooden horse; brake (for flax and hemp); *Agr.* furrow; easel; sawing-frame; trestle; bridge (of the nose)
caballito /kaβa'yito; kaβa'ʎito/ *m, dim* little horse; *pl* merry-go-round; automatic horse gambling game; circus equestrian act. **c. del diablo,** dragonfly
caballo /ka'βayo; ka'βaʎo/ *m,* horse; (chess) knight; (Spanish cards) queen; sawing-frame; *pl* cavalry. **c. balancín,** rocking horse. **c. de batalla,** war-horse; *Fig.* hobby-horse; forte; crux. **c. de cartón,** hobbyhorse; rocking horse. **c. de carrera,** racehorse. **c. de tiro,** draft-horse. **c. de vapor,** horsepower. **c. marino,** sea-horse. **a c.,** on horseback. **A c. regalado no le mires el diente,** Never look a gift horse in the mouth. **caer bien a c.,** to have a good seat (on a horse). **ser**

un c. loco en una cacharrería, to be like a bull in a china shop
cabaña /ka'βaɲa/ *f*, hut, cabin, cottage; flock (of sheep); drove (of mules); *Argentina* cattle ranch; *Art.* pastoral scene; balk (billiards)
cabaret /kaβa'ret/ *m*, cabaret, nightclub
cabaretero /kaβare'tero/ *m*, nightclub owner
cabeceada /kaβese'aða; kaβeθe'aða/ *f, Lat. Am.* nod (of the head)
cabecear /kaβese'ar; kaβeθe'ar/ *vi* to nod; shake the head in disapproval; move the head from side to side; toss the head (horses); (*Aer. Naut.*) pitch; sway (of a carriage); lean; *vt* refoot (socks); head (wine)
cabeceo /kaβe'seo; kaβe'θeo/ *m*, nod, shake (of head); (*Naut. Aer.*) pitching; lurching (of a carriage, etc.); bight (of river)
cabecera /kaβe'sera; kaβe'θera/ *f*, top, upper portion, head; seat of honor; bed-head; river source; capital (country or county); illustrated chapter heading; pillow; inscription, heading
cabecilla /kaβe'siya; kaβe'θiʎa/ *dim f*, small head. *mf Inf.* hothead. *m*, rebel leader
cabellera /kaβe'yera; kaβe'ʎera/ *f*, head of long hair; hair-switch; tail (of comet)
cabello /ka'βeyo; ka'βeʎo/ *m*, hair; head of hair; silk (of maize). *Fig. Inf.* asirse de un c., to clutch at a straw
cabelludo /kaβe'yuðo; kaβe'ʎuðo/ *a* hairy; *Bot.* fibrous
caber /ka'βer/ *vi irr* to be room for, contain; fit into, go into (e.g. *No cabemos todos en este coche*, There isn't room for all of us in this car)); happen, befall, have (e.g. *No les cupo tal suerte*, They did not have such luck–Such luck did not befall them); be possible (e.g. *Todo cabe en Dios*, All things are possible with God). **No cabe más,** There's no room for anything else; *Fig.* That's the limit. *Fig.* **no c. en sí,** to be beyond oneself (with joy, pride, etc.). **No cabe duda de que,** There's no doubt that. *Pres. Ind.* **quepo, cabes, etc.** *Fut.* **cabré, etc.** *Condit.* **cabría, etc.** *Preterite* **cupe, cupiste, etc.** *Pres. Subjunc.* **quepa, quepas, etc.** *Imperf. Subjunc.* **cupiese, etc.**
cabestrar /kaβes'trar/ *vt* to halter
cabestrillo /kaβes'triyo; kaβes'triʎo/ *m*, sling; thin chain (for ornament). **en c.,** in a sling (e.g. *Tenía el brazo en c.*, His arm was in a sling)
cabestro /ka'βestro/ *m*, halter; sling; leading ox
cabeza /ka'βesa; ka'βeθa/ *f*, head; top, upper end; nail-head; brain; mind; judgment; self-control; edge (of book); peak, summit; source, origin; individual, person; head of cattle; capital city. *m*, leader, chief, head. *Mech.* **c. de biela,** big-end. *Inf.* **c. de chorlito,** scatterbrain (person). **c. de hierro,** blockhead. *Mil.* **c. de puente,** bridgehead. **c. de partido,** principal town of a region. **c. de turco,** scapegoat. **irse la c. (a al-guien),** to feel giddy. *Fig. Inf.* **meter a uno en la c.,** to put into someone's head. *Inf.* **quebrarse la c.,** to rack one's brains. *Inf.* **quitar a uno de la c. (una cosa),** to dissuade; get an idea out of someone's head
cabezada /kaβe'saða; kaβe'θaða/ *f*, blow with or on the head; nod; headshake; headstall; *Naut.* pitching. **dar cabezadas,** to nod, go to sleep
cabezal /kaβe'sal; kaβe'θal/ *m*, small head pillow; *Surg.* pad; bolster; narrow mattress; *Mech.* head
cabezo /ka'βeso; ka'βeθo/ *m*, summit (of mountain); hill; *Naut.* reef
cabezón /kaβe'son; kaβe'θon/ *m*, tax-register; collarband; head-opening (of a garment)
cabezudo /kaβe'suðo; kaβe'θuðo/ *a* large-headed; *Inf.* obstinate; *Inf.* heady (of wine). *m*, carnival grotesque
cabida /ka'βiða/ *f*, space, capacity; extent, area
cabildear /kaβilde'ar/ *vi* to canvass votes, lobby
cabildo /ka'βildo/ *m*, *Eccl.* chapter; municipal council; meeting, or meeting place of council. **c. abierto,** town meeting
cabina /ka'βina/ *f*, cabin. **c. telefónica** phone booth
cabinero, -a /kaβi'nero/ *mf, Lat. Am.* flight attendant
cabizbajo /kaβis'βaho; kaβiθ'βaho/ *a* crestfallen; pensive, melancholy
cable /'kaβle/ *m*, cable; string (of bridge); cable's

length; **c. aéreo,** overhead cable. **c. alimentario,** feed line. **c. eléctrico,** electric cable
cabo /'kaβo/ *m*, end, extremity; stump, stub; handle, shaft, leader; *Geog.* cape; end, conclusion; *Naut.* rope; ply (of wool, etc.); *Mil.* corporal; *pl* accessories (clothes); horse's tail and mane. **c. de maestranza,** foreman. **c. de mar,** naval quartermaster. **c. furriel,** *Mil.* quartermaster. **al c.,** in the end. **llevar a c.,** to finish
Cabo de Hornos /'kaβo de 'ornos/ Cape Horn
cabotaje /kaβo'tahe/ *m*, *Naut.* coasting trade
cabra /'kaβra/ *f*, nanny-goat; goat. **c. montesa,** wild goat
cabrerizo /kaβre'riso; kaβre'riθo/ **(-za)** *a* goatish. *m*, goatherd
cabrero /ka'βrero/ **(-ra)** *m*, goatherd; *a Argentina* bad-tempered, cantankerous
cabria /'kaβria/ *f*, winch, hoist
cabrilla /ka'βriya; ka'βriʎa/ *f*, saw-horse; *pl Astron.* Pleiades; burn marks on legs from sitting too near fire; white crests (of waves)
cabrillear /kaβriye'ar; kaβriʎe'ar/ *vi* to foam, froth (the sea)
cabrío /ka'βrio/ *a* goatish. *m*, herd of goats. **macho c.,** male goat, he-goat
cabriola /ka'βriola/ *f*, fouetté (in dancing); spin in the air (acrobats); curvet (horses); caper
cabriolar /kaβrio'lar/ *vi* to curvet; caper, skip
cabriolé /kaβrio'le/ *m*, cabriolet; short cape with or without sleeves
cabritilla /kaβri'tiya; kaβri'tiʎa/ *f*, dressed kid; lambskin, etc.
cabrito /ka'βrito/ *m*, *Zool.* kid; *pl* toasted maize, popcorn
cabrón /ka'βron/ *m*, billy goat, buck, he-goat; *Inf.* complaisant husband, cuckold; *Chile* owner or operator of a brothel; *vulgar, Mexico* bastard
cabrona /ka'βrona/ *f*, *Chile* bawd
cabruno /ka'βruno/ *a* goatish
cabujón /kaβu'hon/ *m*, *Mineral.* uncut gem; unpolished ruby; *pl* vignettes
cacahual /kaka'ual/ *m*, cacao plantation
cacahuete /kaka'uete/ *m*, *Bot.* peanut, monkey nut
cacao /ka'kao/ *m*, *Bot.* cacao tree; cacaonut
cacarear /kakare'ar/ *vi* to crow, cackle; *vt Inf.* boast
cacareo /kaka'reo/ *m*, crowing, cackling; *Inf.* boast
cacatúa /kaka'tua/ *f*, cockatoo
cacera /ka'sera; ka'θera/ *f*, irrigation channel
cacería /kase'ria; kaθe'ria/ *f*, hunting party; hunting bag, booty; *Art.* hunting scene
cacerola /kase'rola; kaθe'rola/ *f*, stew-pot, casserole
cachalote /katʃa'lote/ *m*, sperm whale
cachano /ka'tʃano/ *m*, Old Nick
cachar /ka'tʃar/ *vt* to break in fragments; split (wood)
cacharrería /katʃarre'ria/ *f*, crockery store
cacharro /ka'tʃarro/ *m*, coarse earthenware vessel; *Inf.* decrepit, worthless object
cachazudo /katʃa'suðo; katʃa'θuðo/ *a* phlegmatic, slow
cachear /katʃe'ar/ *vt* to search (a person) for weapons
Cachemira /katʃe'mira/ Kashmir
cachemira /katʃe'mira/ *f*, cashmere
cacheo /ka'tʃeo/ *m*, search (of persons) for weapons
cachetada /katʃe'taða/ *f, Lat. Am.* slap (in the face)
cachete /ka'tʃete/ *m*, blow on the head or face with one's fist; cheek (especially fat one)
cachetero /katʃe'tero/ *m*, dagger
cachetina /katʃe'tina/ *f*, hand-to-hand fight
cachimba /ka'tʃimba/ *f, Lat. Am.* pipe (for smoking)
cachiporra /katʃi'porra/ *f*, club, bludgeon
cachivache /katʃi'βatʃe/ *m*, *Inf.* (gen. *pl*) trash; pots, pans, utensils
cacho /'katʃo/ *m*, small slice (gen. of bread or fruit)
cachón /ka'tʃon/ *m*, breaker, wave; small waterfall
cachorro /ka'tʃorro/ **(-rra)** *n* puppy; cub. *m*, small pistol
cacillo /ka'siyo; ka'θiʎo/ *m*, ladle; basting spoon
cacique /ka'sike; ka'θike/ *m*, Indian chief, cacique; *Inf.* political "boss"

caciquismo /kasi'kismo; kaθi'kismo/ *m*, political "bossism"

caco /'kako/ *m*, pickpocket, thief; *Inf.* poltroon

cacofonía /kakofo'nia/ *f*, cacophony

cacografía /kakogra'fia/ *f*, cacography

cacto /'kakto/ *m*, cactus

cacumen /ka'kumen/ *m*, *Inf.* brains, acumen

cada /'kaða/ *a* every, each. **c. cual,** each. **c. que,** whenever; every time that. **c. y cuando que,** whenever

cadalso /ka'ðalso/ *m*, scaffold; platform, stand

cadáver /ka'ðaβer/ *m*, corpse

cadavérico /kaða'βeriko/ *a* cadaverous, ghastly

cadena /ka'ðena/ *f*, chain; link, tie; *Fig.* bond; *Fig.* sequence (of events); *Law.* imprisonment; *Archit.* buttress; grand chain (dancing); **c. de montañas,** range of mountains. **c. perpetua,** life imprisonment

cadencia /ka'ðensia; ka'ðenθia/ *f*, cadence; rhythm; *Mus.* measure, time; *Mus.* cadenza

cadencioso /kaðen'sioso; kaðen'θioso/ *a* rhythmic

cadente /ka'ðente/ *a* falling, declining; decaying, dying; rhythmic

cadera /ka'ðera/ *f*, hip; flank

cadete /ka'ðete/ *m*, *Mil.* cadet

cadi /'kaði/ *mf* caddy

Cádiz /'kaðis; 'kaðiθ/ Cadiz

caducar /kaðu'kar/ *vi* to become senile; become invalid, be annulled; expire, lapse; *Fig.* be worn out

caduceo /kaðu'seo; kaðu'θeo/ *m*, Mercury's wand

caducidad /kaðusi'ðað; kaðuθi'ðað/ *f*, decrepitude; lapse, expiration

caduco /ka'ðuko/ *a* senile; decrepit; perishable; lapsed; obsolete

caduquez /kaðu'kes; kaðu'keθ/ *f*, senility

caedizo /kae'ðiso; kae'ðiθo/ *a* ready to fall; timid, cowardly, weak

caer /ka'er/ *vi irr* to fall, drop; drop out or off; suit, fit, become; fail; fade (colors); *Fig.* drop (voice); (*with sobre*) attack, fall upon; (*with en*) fall in or on to; decay, collapse; understand; (*with preps. a, hacia*) *Fig.* look on to, face; (*with por, en*) *Fig.* fall on, occur on; *vr Aer.* crash; fly off (buttons, etc.). **c. de cabeza,** to fall head foremost. **c. en conflicto (con),** to come into conflict (with) **c. en las manos de uno,** to come into somebody's possession (come to be owned by somebody). **c. en gracia,** to make a good impression, arouse affection. **caerse de suyo,** to be self-evident. **c. por tierra,** (plan, etc.) to fall through. **Cayó enfermo,** He was taken ill. **cayendo y levantado,** dying. **Se me cayó,** It dropped (I dropped it). *Pres. Ind.* **caigo, caes, etc.** *Pres. Part.* **cayendo.** *Preterite* **cayó cayeron.** *Pres. Subjunc.* **caiga, etc.**

café /ka'fe/ *m*, coffee (tree, berry, drink); café, coffee-house. **c. con leche,** café au lait. **c. negro** *Lat. Am.* (*except Columbia*) black coffee. **c. solo** *Spain* black coffee. **c. tinto** *Colombia* black coffee

cafeína /kafe'ina/ *f*, caffeine

cafetal /kafe'tal/ *m*, coffee plantation

cafetera /kafe'tera/ *f*, coffeepot; *Peru* cab, taxi

cafeto /ka'feto/ *m*, coffee tree

cafiche /ka'fitʃe/ *m*, *Argentina, Chile* pimp

caficultor /kafikul'tor/ *m*, coffee-grower

caficultura /kafikul'tura/ *f*, coffee-growing

cafúa /ka'fua/ *f*, *Argentina* clink, slammer

cagadas /ka'gaðas/ *f pl*, droppings, dung

cagar /ka'gar/ (**se**) *vi vt vr* to evacuate (bowels); *vt Inf.* spoil, make a botch of

cagarruta /kaga'rruta/ *f*, dung of sheep, deer, rabbits, etc.

caída /ka'iða/ *f*, falling; fall; ruin; failure; close (of day); *Fig.* falling off; hanging (curtains, etc.); diminution; incline; *pl* coarse wool; *Inf.* repartee. **a la c. de la tarde,** at the end of the afternoon. **a la c. del sol,** at sunset

caído /ka'iðo/ (**-da**) *a* debilitated, languid; lapsed; (of a shoulder) sloping. **los caídos,** the fallen, the dead (in war, etc.)

caimán /kai'man/ *m*, alligator; *Inf.* shark, astute person

caite /'kaite/ *m*, *Central America* sandal

caja /'kaha/ *f*, box; safe, cash box; coffin; (of a vehicle) body; *Mus.* drum; case (of piano, watch, etc.); cavity; well (of a stair); *Com.* cash; cash-desk; cashier's office; *Bot.* sheath. **c. de ahorros,** savings bank. **c. de caudales,** strong-box. *Print.* **c. de imprenta,** type case. **c. de música,** musical box. **c. de reclutamiento,** recruiting office. **c. de velocidades,** gearbox. **c. registradora,** cash register. **c. torácica,** rib cage, thoracic cage

cajero /ka'hero/ (**-ra**) *m*, boxmaker; *n Com.* cashier; peddler. **c. automática,** automatic-teller machine, ATM, cash machine

cajetilla /kahe'tiya; kahe'tiʎa/ *f*, packet (cigarettes, etc.)

cajón /ka'hon/ *m*, chest, locker, case; drawer. **c. de municiones,** ammunition-box

cajonera /kaho'nera/ *f*, *Eccl.* chest of drawers in sacristy; *Agr.* frame

cal /kal/ *f*, lime. **c. muerta,** slaked lime. **c. viva,** quicklime. *Fig. Inf.* **de c. y canto,** tough, strong

cala /'kala/ *f*, sample slice (of fruit); *Naut.* hold; *Surg.* probe; cove, small bay; *Bot.* iris

calabacera /kalaβa'sera; kalaβa'θera/ *f*, *Bot.* pumpkin or gourd plant

calabacín /kalaβa'sin; kalaβa'θin/ *m*, kind of vegetable marrow; *Inf.* dolt

calabaza /kala'βasa; kala'βaθa/ *f*, *Bot.* pumpkin (plant and fruit); gourd; *Inf.* dolt. **dar calabazas,** to refuse (suitor); flunk (an examinee). *Inf.* **llevar calabazas,** to get the sack; be jilted

calabobos /kala'βoβos/ *m*, *Inf.* drizzle

calabocero /kalaβo'sero; kalaβo'θero/ *m*, jailer

calabozo /kala'βoso; kala'βoθo/ *m*, dungeon; prison cell; pruning knife

calada /ka'laða/ *f*, soaking, wetting through; flight of bird of prey; swoop. **dar una c.,** *Fig. Inf.* to dress down

calado /ka'laðo/ *a* soaked, wet through. *m, Sew.* open-work; fretwork; *Naut.* draft of a ship; water level; *pl* lace. **c. hasta los huesos,** soaked to the skin; madly in love

calador /kala'ðor/ *m*, one who does open or fretwork; caulking iron; borer; *Surg.* probe

calafate /kala'fate/ *m*, caulker

calafatear /kalafate'ar/ *vt Naut.* to caulk

calamaco /kala'mako/ *m*, *Mexico* kidney bean

calamar /kala'mar/ *m*, *Zool.* squid, calamary

calambre /ka'lambre/ *m*, cramp. **c. del escribiente,** writer's cramp

calamidad /kalami'ðað/ *f*, misfortune, calamity

calamina /kala'mina/ *f*, *Mineral.* calamine

calamitoso /kalami'toso/ *a* calamitous; unfortunate, unhappy

cálamo /'kalamo/ *m*, ancient flute; stalk (of grass); *Poet.* pen

calamocano /kalamo'kano/ *a* maudlin, tipsy

calandria /ka'landria/ *f*, *Ornith.* calender, lark; *Mech.* calender; treadmill. *mf Inf.* malingerer

calaña /ka'laɲa/ *f*, sample; model; pattern; kind, quality; temperament; cheap fan

calar /ka'lar/ *vt* to permeate, soak through; pierce; do openwork (in cloth, paper, metal); cut a sample slice from fruit; pull (hat, etc.) well down on head; put down (an eyeshade or visor); fix (bayonets, etc.); *Inf.* understand (persons); *Inf.* guess, realize; *Naut.* let down; *vi Naut.* draw (water); *vr* be drenched, wet through; swoop (birds of prey); *Inf.* sneak in. *a* calcareous

calar /ka'lar/ *m*, limestone deposit or region

calatear /kalate'ar/ *vt*, *Peru* to undress

calato, -a /ka'lato/ *a*, *Peru* naked, nude; broke, penniless

calavera /kala'βera/ *f*, skull. *m*, dare-devil, madcap; roué; *Mexico* taillight

calaverada /kalaβe'raða/ *f*, *Inf.* dare-devilment, foolishness; escapade

calcañar /kalka'ɲar/ *m*, heel (of foot)

calcar /kal'kar/ *vt* to trace (drawing); press with foot; copy servilely, imitate

calcáreo /kal'kareo/ *a* calcareous

calce /'kalse; 'kalθe/ *m*, rim of a wheel; wedge; tire
calcés /kal'ses; kal'θes/ *m*, *Naut.* masthead
calceta /kal'seta; kal'θeta/ *f*, stocking; fetter. *Inf.* **hacer c.**, to knit
calcetería /kalsete'ria; kalθete'ria/ *f*, hosiery shop; hosiery trade
calcetero /kalse'tero; kalθe'tero/ **(-ra)** *n* hosier; hose maker or darner
calcetín /kalse'tin; kalθe'tin/ *m*, sock
calcificación /kalsifika'sion; kalθifika'θion/ *f*, *Med.* calcification
calcinación /kalsina'sion; kalθina'θion/ *f*, calcination
calcinar /kalsi'nar; kalθi'nar/ *vt* to calcine
calcio /'kalsio; 'kalθio/ *m*, calcium
calco /'kalko/ *m*, tracing (drawing)
calcografía /kalkogra'fia/ *f*, chalcography
calcografiar /kalkogra'fiar/ *vt* to transfer; make chalcographies of
calcomanía /kalkoma'nia/ *f*, transfer
calculación /kalkula'sion; kalkula'θion/ *f*, calculation
calculado /kalku'laðo/ *a* calculated
calculador /kalkula'ðor/ *a* calculating. *m*, calculating machine, calculator
calcular /kalku'lar/ *vt* to calculate
cálculo /'kalkulo/ *m*, calculation; *Math.* estimate; investigation; conjecture; *Math. Med.* calculus. **c. hepático,** *Med.* gallstone
calda /'kalda/ *f*, heating; *pl* hot mineral baths
caldear /kalde'ar/ *vt* to heat
caldeo /kal'deo/ *m*, heating
caldera /kal'dera/ *f*, cauldron; cauldron full; *West. Hem.* teapot; *Engin.* boiler. **c. de vapor,** steam-boiler
calderería /kaldere'ria/ *f*, coppersmith's trade and shop
calderero /kalde'rero/ *m*, boiler maker; coppersmith; tinker
calderilla /kalde'riya; kalde'riʎa/ *f*, holy water stoup; any copper coin
caldero /kal'dero/ *m*, small cauldron; casserole; kettle
calderón /kalde'ron/ *m*, large cauldron; *Mus.* rest; *Mus.* trill; pause
caldo /'kaldo/ *m*, broth; salad dressing; *pl Agr.* oil, wine, vegetable juices
calefacción /kalefak'sion; kalefak'θion/ *f*, heating. **c. central,** central heating
calendario /kalen'dario/ *m*, calendar. **c. deportivo,** fixture card. **c. gregoriano,** Gregorian calendar
calendas /ka'lendas/ *f pl*, calends. **en las c. griegas,** at the Greek calends
caléndula /ka'lendula/ *f*, marigold
calentador /kalenta'ðor/ *a* heating, warming. *m*, heater; warming-pan
calentamiento /kalenta'miento/ *m*, heating, warming
calentar /kalen'tar/ *vt irr* to heat, warm; rev-up (an engine); hasten; *Inf.* spank; *vr* warm oneself; be in heat (animals); grow excited. See **acertar**
calentura /kalen'tura/ *f*, fever
calenturiento /kalentu'riento/ *a* feverish
calera /ka'lera/ *f*, lime-pit; lime-kiln; fishing smack
calesa /ka'lesa/ *f*, calash, calèche, chaise (two-wheeled carriage)
calesita /kale'sita/ *f*, *Lat. Am.* merry-go-round
caleta /ka'leta/ *f*, cove, creek
caletre /ka'letre/ *m*, *Inf.* discernment, head, sense
calibrar /kali'βrar/ *vt* to calibrate; gauge
calibre /ka'liβre/ *m*, *Mech.* gauge; bore, caliber; diameter (tubes, pipes, etc.)
calidad /kali'ðað/ *f*, quality; role; character, temperament; condition, requisite; importance, gravity; personal particulars; nobility; *pl* qualities of the mind. **c. originaria,** rank and birth. **c. de oficio,** justification for action. **en c. de,** in the capacity of
cálido /'kaliðo/ *a* warm, hot; warming, heating; vehement, ardent; *Art.* warm
calidoscopio /kaliðos'kopio/ *m*, kaleidoscope
calientalibros /kalienta'liβros/ *mf*, bookworm (person)
calientapiés /kalienta'pies/ *m*, footwarmer

calientaplatos /kalienta'platos/ *m*, hot plate, plate-warmer
caliente /ka'liente/ *a* warm, hot; excited; *Art.* warm
calientito /kalien'tito/ *a* piping hot
califa /ka'lifa/ *m*, caliph
calificable /kalifi'kaβle/ *a* classifiable; qualifiable
calificación /kalifika'sion; kalifika'θion/ *f*, classification; qualification; judgment; grade, place (examinations)
calificar /kalifi'kar/ *vt* to class; grade (exams); authorize; judge (qualities); *Fig.* ennoble; *vr* prove noble descent
calificativo /kalifika'tiβo/ *a* *Gram.* qualifying. *m*, epithet
californio /kali'fornio/ **(-ia)** *a* and *n* Californian
caliginoso /kalihi'noso/ *a* murky, dark
caligrafía /kaligra'fia/ *f*, calligraphy
calígrafo /ka'ligrafo/ *m*, calligraphist
calistenia /kalis'tenia/ *f*, callisthenics
cáliz /'kalis; 'kaliθ/ *m*, chalice; *Poet.* cup; *Bot.* calyx
caliza /ka'lisa; ka'liθa/ *f*, limestone
calizo /ka'liso; ka'liθo/ *a* calcareous
callado /ka'yaðo; ka'ʎaðo/ *a* silent; reserved; secret
callar /ka'yar; ka'ʎar/ **(se)** *vi* and *vr* to say nothing, keep silent; stop speaking; stop making any sound (persons, animals, things); *vt* conceal, keep secret; omit, leave out; *Inf. interj* ¡**Calle!** You don't say so! **Quien calla otorga,** Silence gives consent
calle /'kaye; 'kaʎe/ *f*, street. **c. de un sentido, c. de una corrida** *Mexico* one-way street. **c. de una sola mano** *Argentina* one-way street *Inf.* **abrir c.,** to clear the way. *Inf.* **dejar en la c.,** to leave destitute. *Inf.* **echar a la c.,** put out of the house, to throw out of the house; make known, publish. **ponerse en la c.,** to go out
calleja, callejuela /ka'yeha, kaye'huela; ka'ʎeha, kaʎe'huela/ *f*, small street, alley, side street
callejear /kayehe'ar; kaʎehe'ar/ *vi* to walk the streets, wander about the streets, loaf around the streets
callejero /kaye'hero; kaʎe'hero/ *a* fond of gadding. *m*, street directory
callejón /kaye'hon; kaʎe'hon/ *m*, alley, lane. **c. sin salida,** cul-de-sac; *Fig.* impasse
callicida /kayi'siða; kaʎi'θiða/ *m*, corn cure
callista /ka'yista; ka'ʎista/ *mf* chiropodist
callo /'kayo; 'kaʎo/ *m*, corn, callosity; *Med.* callus; *pl* tripe
calloso /ka'yoso; ka'ʎoso/ *a* callous, horny
calma /'kalma/ *f*, calm, airlessness; serenity, composure; quiet, tranquillity, peace. **c. chicha,** dead calm. **en c.,** at peace; tranquil; calm (of the sea)
calmante /kal'mante/ *a* calming, soothing. *Med. a* and *m*, sedative, tranquilizer
calmar /kal'mar/ *vt* to soothe, calm; moderate, mitigate; pacify; quench (thirst); *vi* grow calm; moderate; be becalmed
calmoso /kal'moso/ *a* calm, tranquil; *Inf.* sluggish, lazy; imperturbable
calor /ka'lor/ *m*, heat; ardor, vehemence; cordiality; *Fig.* heat (of battle); excitement
caloría /kalo'ria/ *f*, *Phys.* calorie
calórico /ka'loriko/ *a* *Phys.* caloric, thermic
calorífero /kalo'rifero/ *a* heat-giving. *m*, heater, radiator
calumnia /ka'lumnia/ *f*, calumny; *Law.* slander
calumniador /kalumnia'ðor/ **(-ra)** *a* slandering. *n* calumniator, slanderer
calumniar /kalumni'ar/ *vt* to calumniate; *Law.* slander
calumnioso /kalum'nioso/ *a* calumnious, slanderous
caluroso /kalu'roso/ *a* hot, warm; cordial, friendly; enthusiastic; ardent, impassioned; excited
calva /'kalβa/ *f*, bald patch on head; worn place (cloth, etc.); bare spot, clearing (trees, etc.)
Calvario /kal'βario/ *m*, Calvary; *Inf.* series of disasters; *Inf.* debts
calvero /kal'βero/ *m*, clearing (in a wood); chalk or marl pit
calvicie /kal'βisie; kal'βiθie/ *f*, baldness

calvo /'kalβo/ *a* bald; bare, barren (land); worn (cloth, etc.)

calza /'kalsa; 'kalθa/ *f*, breeches (gen. *pl*); wedge; *Inf.* stocking. *Inf.* **tomar calzas,** to beat it

calzada /kal'saδa; kal'θaδa/ *f*, roadway. **c. romana,** Roman road

calzado /kal'saδo; kal'θaδo/ *m*, footwear, shoes

calzador /kalsa'δor; kalθa'δor/ *m*, shoehorn

calzadura /kalsa'δura; kalθa'δura/ *f*, wedging (of a wheel); act of putting on shoes; felloe of a wheel

calzar /kal'sar; kal'θar/ *vt* to put on shoes; wear (spurs, gloves, etc.); wedge, block (wheel); scotch (a wheel). *Fig. Inf.* **c. el coturno,** don the buskin; write in the sublime style; write a tragedy, write tragedies.

calzarse a una persona, to have a person in one's pocket

calzón /kal'son; kal'θon/ *m*, long underwear, *Lat. Am.* panties. *Fig. Inf.* **ponerse los calzones,** (of a woman) to wear the pants

calzonazos /kalso'nasos; kalθo'naθos/ *m*, *Inf.* weak-willed, easily led fellow

calzoncillos /kalson'siyos; kalθon'θiʎos/ *m pl*, drawers, pants

calzoneras /kalso'neras; kalθo'neras/ *fpl*, *Mexico* pants buttoned down the sides

cama /'kama/ *f*, bed; bedstead; bedhanging; lair, form; floor (of a cart); check (of bridle) (gen. *pl*). **c. de campaña,** camp bed. **c. de matrimonio,** double bed. **c. de monja,** single bed. **c. de operaciones,** operating table. **c. turca,** settee-bed. **guardar c.,** to stay in bed

camada /ka'maδa/ *f*, brood, litter; *Inf.* gang

camafeo /kama'feo/ *m*, cameo

camaleón /kamale'on/ *m*, chameleon; *Inf.* changeable person

cámara /'kamara/ *f*, chamber; hall; house (of deputies); granary; *Naut.* state room; chamber (firearms, mines); *Phys.* camera; human excrement; *Auto.* inner tube. **c. acorazada,** strong-room. **c. alta,** Upper House, **c. baja** *or* **c. de los comunes,** lower house, house of commons. **c. de comercio,** chamber of commerce. **c. oscura,** (optics) dark room

camarada /kama'raδa/ *mf* pal, companion, comrade

camaradería /kamaraδe'ria/ *f*, comradeship, companionship

camarera /kama'rera/ *f*, waitress; chambermaid; stewardess

camarero /kama'rero/ *m*, waiter; papal chamberlain; chamberlain; steward; valet. **c. mayor,** lord chamberlain

camarilla /kama'riya; kama'riʎa/ *f*, palace or other clique, coterie; *Inf.* back-scratch

camarín /kama'rin/ *m*, *Theat.* dressing-room; closet; boudoir; cage (of a lift); niche

camarón /kama'ron/ *m*, prawn, shrimp; tip, reward

camarote /kama'rote/ *m*, cabin; berth

cambalache /kamβa'latʃe/ *m*, *Lat. Am.* secondhand shop; exchange

cambalachear /kambalatʃe'ar/ *vt Inf.* to barter

cámbaro /'kambaro/ *m*, sea-crab

cambiable /kam'βiaβle/ *a* exchangeable; changeable

cambiante /kam'βiante/ *a* exchanging; changing. *m*, sheen, luster (gen. *pl*); money changer

cambiar /kam'βiar/ *vt* to exchange; convert. *vt* and *vi* change, alter; *vi* and *vr* to veer (wind). **c. de aguas,** *Poet.* to move (change one's residence). **c. de aire,** get a change of scenery. **c. de frente,** to face about; *Fig.* change front

cambio /'kambio/ *m*, exchange; change; *Com.* rate of exchange; money change; *Com.* premium on bills of exchange. **a c. de, en c. de,** in exchange for; instead of. **en c.,** instead, on the other hand. **c. de velocidad,** *Auto.* gear-changing. **letra de c.,** bill of exchange. **libre c.,** free trade

cambista /kam'βista/ *mf* money changer. *m*, banker

cambullón /kambu'jon; kambu'ʎon/ *m*, *Lat. Am.* swindle

cambur /kam'βur/ *m*, *Venezuela* banana

camelar /kame'lar/ *vt Inf.* to woo; seduce

camelia /ka'melia/ *f*, camelia. **c. japonesa,** japonica

camellero /kame'yero; kame'ʎero/ *m*, camel keeper or driver

camello /ka'meyo; ka'meʎo/ *m*, camel. **c. pardal,** giraffe

camellón /kame'yon; kame'ʎon/ *m*, furrow; drinking trough; *Mexico* island, traffic island, median strip

camelo /ka'melo/ *m*, *Inf.* eyewash

camilla /ka'miya; ka'miʎa/ *f*, couch; small round skirted table with brazier underneath; stretcher, litter

camillero /kami'yero; kami'ʎero/ *m*, *Mil.* stretcher-bearer

caminador /kamina'δor/ *a* in the habit of walking a great deal

caminante /kami'nante/ *mf* walker, traveler

caminar /kami'nar/ *vi* to travel; walk; *Fig.* move on, go (inanimate things). *Fig. Inf.* **c. derecho,** to walk uprightly

caminata /kami'nata/ *f*, long, tiring walk; excursion

caminejo /kami'neho/ *m*, worn path

camino /ka'mino/ *m*, road; route; journey; way, means; **c. de hierro,** railway. **c. de mesa,** table-runner. **c. de sirga,** towpath. **c. real,** highway, main road. **de c.,** on the way, in passing. **ponerse en c.,** to set out

camión /ka'mion/ *m*, truck. **c. de volteo, c. volquete** dump truck; *Mexico* bus; truck

camionera /kamio'nera/ *f*, *Mexico* bus station

camioneta /kamio'neta/ *f*, light truck, pick-up truck; *WH* station wagon

camisa /ka'misa/ *f*, shirt, stiff shirt; thin skin (of fruit); sloughed skin of snakes; coat (of whitewash, etc.); *Mech.* jacket; mantle (gas). **c. de fuerza,** strait-jacket. **dejar sin c.,** *Inf.* to leave penniless

camisería /kamise'ria/ *f*, shirt shop or factory

camisero /kami'sero/ *(-ra)* *n* shirt maker or seller

camiseta /kami'seta/ *f*, undershirt, T-shirt. **c. de fútbol,** soccer player's jersey

camisola /kami'sola/ *f*, stiff shirt; ruffled shirt

camisón /kami'son/ *m*, large wide shirt; night shirt

camomila /kamo'mila/ *f*, chamomile

camorra /ka'morra/ *f*, *Inf.* brawl, shindy. **armar c.,** to start a row

camote /ka'mote/ *m*, *Lat. Am.* sweet potato

campal /kam'pal/ *a* field, country

campamento /kampa'mento/ *m*, camping; *Mil.* encampment; camp; jamboree

campana /kam'pana/ *f*, bell; anything bell-shaped; church, parish. **c. de chimenea,** mantelpiece. **c. de hogar,** hood, shutter (of a fireplace)

campanada /kampa'naδa/ *f*, peal of a bell; scandal

campanario /kampa'nario/ *m*, belfry, bell tower

campanear /kampane'ar/ *vi* to ring bells frequently

campaneo /kampa'neo/ *m*, bell-ringing; chime

campanero /kampa'nero/ *m*, bell-founder; bell ringer

campanil /kampa'nil/ *m*, small belfry, campanile

campanilla /kampa'niya; kampa'niʎa/ *f*, hand-bell; bubble; any bell-shaped flower

campante /kam'pante/ *a* outstanding; *Inf.* proud, satisfied

campanudo /kampa'nuδo/ *a* bell-shaped; sonorous (of words); pompous (of speech)

campaña /kam'paɲa/ *f*, level country; campaign. *Naut.* voyage, cruise. **correr la c.,** to reconnoiter. **la C. del Desierto,** the War against the Gauchos (in Argentina)

campar /kam'par/ *vi* to camp. *Inf.* **c. por sus respetos,** to stand on one's own feet

campeador /kampea'δor/ *a* mighty in battle

campear /kampe'ar/ *vi* to go out to graze; grow green (crops); excel; *Mil.* be engaged in a campaign, reconnoiter

campechano /kampe'tʃano/ *a* *Inf.* hearty; frank; cheerful; generous

campeche /kam'petʃe/ *m*, *Bot.* logwood

campeón /kampe'on/ *m*, champion; advocate, defender

campeonato /kampeo'nato/ *m*, championship

campesinado /kampesi'naδo/ *m*, peasantry

campesino /kampe'sino/ *(-na)* *a* rural, rustic. *n* country dweller

campestre /kam'pestre/ *a* rural

campiña /kam'piɲa/ *f*, expanse of cultivated land; countryside, landscape

campo /'kampo/ *m*, country (as opposed to urban areas); field; *Fig.* sphere, province; (*Phys. Herald. Mil.*) field; *Art.* ground; *Mil.* camp, army; plain ground (of silks, etc.). **«C. Abierto»**, "Miscellaneous" (e.g. as the title of a section in a book catalog). **c. de aterrizaje,** *Aer.* landing-field. **c. de batalla,** battlefield. **c. de concentración,** concentration camp. **c. de experimentación,** testing ground. **c. de golf,** golf course. **c. de prisioneros** *Mil.* prison camp. **c. de tiro,** rifle-range. **c. santo,** graveyard. **c. visual,** field of vision. **a c. abierto,** in the open air. **a c. travieso,** cross-country

camuflaje /kamu'flahe/ *m*, camouflage

camuflar /kamu'flar/ *vt* to camouflage

can /kan/ *m*, dog; trigger; *Archit.* modillion; *Astron.* Dog Star

cana /'kana/ *f*, gray hair

Canadá /kana'ða/ Canada

canadiense /kana'ðiense/ *a* and *mf* Canadian

canal /ka'nal/ *m*, canal. *mf*, *Geol.* subterranean waterway; channel; *Anat.* canal, duct; defile, narrow valley; gutter; drinking trough; animal carcass. **abrir en c.,** to open up, split open

canalera /kana'lera/ *f*, roof gutter

canaleta /kana'leta/ *f*, (wooden) trough; gutter (on roof)

canalete /kana'lete/ *m*, paddle

canalización /kanalisa'sion; kanaliθa'θion/ *f*, canalization; *Elec.* main, mains; piping, tubing

canalizar /kanali'sar; kanali'θar/ *vt* to make canals or channels; regulate waters of rivers, etc.; canalize

canalla /ka'naya; ka'naʎa/ *f*, *Inf.* mob, rabble. *m*, *Inf.* scoundrel

canallesco /kana'yesko; kana'ʎesko/ *a* scoundrelly, knavish; despicable

canalón /kana'lon/ *m*, gutter, spout; shovel hat; pantile

canana /ka'nana/ *f*, cartridge belt

canapé /kana'pe/ *m*, sofa

canario /ka'nario/ **(-ia)** *m*, canary. *a* and *n* pertaining to or native of the Canary Islands.

canasta /ka'nasta/ *f*, hamper, basket; card game

canastilla /kanas'tiya; kanas'tiʎa/ *f*, small basket; layette

canastillo /kanas'tiyo; kanas'tiʎo/ *m*, basket-work tray

cáncamo /'kankamo/ *m*, ring-bolt

cancamusa /kanka'musa/ *f*, *Inf.* trick, deception

cancel /kan'sel; kan'θel/ *m*, draftscreen; *Eccl.* screen

cancela /kan'sela; kan'θela/ *f*, wrought-iron door

cancelación /kansela'sion; kanθela'θion/ *f*, cancellation; expunging

cancelar /kanse'lar; kanθe'lar/ *vt* to cancel; expunge, annul; abolish, blot out; pay off, clear (a mortgage)

cancelaría /kanse'laria; kanθe'laria/ *f*, papal chancery

cancelario /kanse'lario; kanθe'lario/ *m*, chancellor (universities)

cáncer /'kanser; 'kanθer/ *m*, cancer

cancerar /kanse'rar; kanθe'rar/ *vt* to consume; weaken; mortify; *vr* suffer from cancer; become cancerous

cancerbero /kanser'βero; kanθer'βero/ *m*, *Myth.* Cerberus; *Fig.* unbribable guard

canceroso /kanse'roso; kanθe'roso/ *a* cancerous

cancha /'kantʃa/ *f*, *Sports.* fronton; (tennis) court; cockpit; yard; hippodrome; widest part of a river; road; toasted maize. **estar en su cancha** *Argentina, Chile* to be in one's element. **tener cancha** *Argentina* to be experienced; *Venezuela* have charisma, charm, allure

canciller /kansi'yer; kanθi'ʎer/ *m*, chancellor; foreign minister; assistant vice-consul

cancillería /kansiye'ria; kanθiʎe'ria/ *f*, chancellorship; chancellery; foreign ministry

canción /kan'sion; kan'θion/ *f*, song; lyric poem; musical accompaniment; old name for any poetical

composition. **volver a la misma c.,** *Fig.* to be always harping on the same theme

cancionero /kansio'nero; kanθio'nero/ *m*, collection of songs and verses; songbook

cancionista /kansio'nista; kanθio'nista/ *mf* singer; song writer

candado /kan'daðo/ *m*, padlock; earring

candeal /kande'al/ *a* white (of bread)

candela /kan'dela/ *f*, candle; horse-chestnut flower; candlestick; *Inf.* fire. **en c.,** *Naut.* vertical (of masts, etc.)

candelabro /kande'laβro/ *m*, candelabrum

candelero /kande'lero/ *m*, candlestick; lamp; candle maker or seller; *Naut.* stanchion

candente /kan'dente/ *a* candescent, red-hot

candidatear /kandiðate'ar/ *vi* to run (for office)

candidato /kandi'ðato/ **(-ta)** *n* candidate

candidatura /kandiða'tura/ *f*, candidature

candidez /kandi'ðes; kandi'ðeθ/ *f*, simplicity, ingenuousness; candidness

cándido /'kandiðo/ *a* white; simple, ingenuous; candid, frank

candil /kan'dil/ *m*, oil lamp; Greek lamp; tips of stag's horns; *Inf.* cock of a hat

candileja /kandi'leha/ *f*, oil reservoir of lamp; *pl* footlights, floats

candor /kan'dor/ *m*, extreme whiteness; sincerity, candor; simplicity, innocence

candoroso /kando'roso/ *a* candid, open; simple, honest

canela /ka'nela/ *f*, *Bot.* cinnamon; *Fig.* anything exquisitely perfect

canelo /ka'nelo/ *m*, cinnamon tree. *a* cinnamon-colored

cangilón /kanhi'lon/ *m*, pitcher, jar; bucket (for water); dredging bucket

cangreja /kaŋ'greha/ *f*, *Naut.* gaffsail. **c. de mesana,** *Naut.* jigger

cangrejo /kaŋ'greho/ *m*, crab. **c. de mar,** sea-crab. **c. ermitaño,** hermit crab

canguro /kaŋ'guro/ *m*, kangaroo

caníbal /ka'niβal/ *a* and *mf* cannibal

canibalismo /kaniβa'lismo/ *m*, cannibalism

canica /ka'nika/ *f*, marble (for playing with)

canícula /ka'nikula/ *f*, dog days; *Astron.* Dog star

caniculares /kaniku'lares/ *m pl* dog days

canijo /ka'niho/ *a* *Inf.* delicate, sickly; anemic, stunted

canilla /ka'niya; ka'niʎa/ *f*, long bone of leg or arm; any principal bones in bird's wing; tap, faucet; spool, reel; fault (in cloth)

canillera /kani'jera; kani'ʎera/ *f*, *Lat. Am.* cowardice; fear

canillito, -a /kani'jito; kani'ʎito/ *mf*, *Lat. Am.* newsboy, newsgirl

canino /ka'nino/ *a* canine

canje /'kanhe/ *m*, (diplomacy, mil., com.) exchange, substitution. **c. de prisioneros,** exchange of prisoners

canjear /kanhe'ar/ *vt* to exchange

cano /'kano/ *a* white-haired, hoary; ancient; *Poet.* white

canoa /ka'noa/ *f*, canoe; launch. **c. automóvil,** motor launch

canódromo /ka'noðromo/ *m*, dog-race track

canoero /kano'ero/ **(-ra)** *n* canoeist

canon /'kanon/ *m*, rule; (*Eccl. Print.*) canon; catalog; part of the Mass; *Mus.* canon, catch; tax. *pl* canon law

canónico /ka'noniko/ *a* canonic, canonical

canónigo /ka'nonigo/ *m*, canon; prebendary

canonización /kanonisa'sion; kanoniθa'θion/ *f*, canonization

canonizar /kanoni'sar; kanoni'θar/ *vt* to canonize; extol, exalt; approve, acclaim

canonjía /kanon'hia/ *f*, canonry, canonship; *Inf.* sinecure

canoso /ka'noso/ *a* white-haired, hoary

cansado /kan'saðo/ **(-da)** *a* tired; weary; exhausted; decadent; tiresome; *Inf.* fed up. *n* bore, tedious person

cansancio /kan'sansio; kan'sanθio/ *m*, fatigue, weariness

cansar /kan'sar/ *vt* to tire, weary; *Agr.* exhaust soil; bore; badger, annoy; *vr* be tired; grow weary

cansino /kan'sino/ *a* worn-out (of horses, etc.)

cantable /kan'taβle/ *a* singable; *Mus.* cantabile

cantábrico /kan'taβriko/ **(-ca)** *a* and *n* Cantabrian

cantante /kan'tante/ *a* singing. *mf* professional singer

cantar /kan'tar/ *vi* to sing; twitter, chirp; extol; *Inf.* squeak, creak; *Fig.* call (cards); *Inf.* squeal, confess. *m*, song. **C. de los Cantares,** Song of Songs. **cantarlas claras,** to call a spade a spade

cántara /'kantara/ *f*, pitcher, jug

cantárida /kan'tariða/ *f*, Spanish fly

cántaro /'kantaro/ *m*, pitcher, jug; jugful; varying wine measure; ballot box; tax on spirits and oil. **llover a cántaros,** to rain heavily; pour

cantata /kan'tata/ *f*, cantata

cantatriz /kanta'tris; kanta'triθ/ *f*, singer, prima donna

cante /'kante/ *m*, song; singing

cantera /kan'tera/ *f*, *Mineral.* quarry; capacity, talent

cantería /kante'ria/ *f*, stone-cutting; quarrying; building made of hewn stone

cantero /kan'tero/ *m*, stone-cutter; quarryman

cántico /'kantiko/ *m*, *Eccl.* canticle; *Poet.* poem

cantidad /kanti'ðað/ *f*, quantity; large part; portion; sum of money; quantity (prosody). **c. llovida,** rainfall

cantiga /kan'tiga/ *or* **cántiga** *f*, old poetic form designed to be sung

cantil /kan'til/ *m*, cliff; steep rock

cantimplora /kantim'plora/ *f*, water cooler; canteen (of water); siphon

cantina /kan'tina/ *f*, wine cellar; canteen; refreshment room

cantinero /kanti'nero/ *m*, sutler; owner of a canteen

canto /'kanto/ *m*, singing; song; canto; epic or other poem; end, rim, edge; non-cutting edge (knives, swords); pebble, stone; angle (of a building). *Mus.* **c. llano,** plain-song. **al c. del gallo,** at cockcrow. **de c.,** on edge

cantón /kan'ton/ *m*, province, region; corner (of a street); cantonment; *Herald.* canton, quartering

cantonera /kanto'nera/ *f*, corner-piece (books, furniture, etc., as ornament); angle-iron; bracket, small shelf

cantor /kan'tor/ **(-ra)** *a* singing. *n* singer; song-bird

cantuja /kan'tuha/ *f*, *Peru* underworld slang

canturía /kantu'ria/ *f*, singing exercise; vocal music; monotonous song; droning; *Mus.* execution, technique

canturreo, /kantu'rreo,/ *m*, **canturria** *f*, humming; droning

canturriar /kantu'rriar/ *vi Inf.* to hum, sing under one's breath

caña /'kaɲa/ *f*, stalk; reed; bone of arm or leg; leg (of a trouser, stocking, boot, etc.); marrow; *Bot.* cane; tumbler, glass; wine measure; gallery (of mine); *pl* mock joust on horseback using **cañas** as spears. **c. de azúcar,** sugar-cane. **c. de pescar,** fishing rod. **c. del timón,** tiller *Naut.*

cañada /ka'ɲaða/ *f*, glen, gulch, gully, hollow, ravine, vale, cattle path; *West Hem.* brook, cattle track

cañal /ka'ɲal/ *m*, cane-break; weir (for fish)

cañamazo /kaɲa'maso; kaɲa'maθo/ *m*, hempen canvas; embroidery canvas; embroidered canvas

cañamelar /kaɲame'lar/ *m*, sugar-cane plantation

cáñamo /'kaɲamo/ *m*, hemp; *Lat. Am.* marijuana

cañar /ka'ɲar/ *m*, canebrake; growth of reeds; fishgarth made of reeds

cañavalera /kaɲaβa'lera/ *f*, canefield

cañaveral /kaɲaβe'ral/ *m*, cane-brake; *West Hem.* bamboo field

cañazo /ka'ɲaso; ka'ɲaθo/ *m*, blow with a cane

cañería /kaɲe'ria/ *f*, conduit; pipe; piping

cañero /ka'ɲero/ *m*, pipe layer

caño /'kaɲo/ *m*, pipe, tube, sewer; organ pipe; jet (of water); mine gallery

cañón /ka'ɲon/ *m*, pipe, cylindrical tube; flue; quill (of birds); cannon; soft down; *Archit.* shaft (of column); stack (of a chimney). **c. antiaéreo,** A.A. gun. **c. antitanque,** anti-tank gun. **c. de escalera,** well of a staircase; *Slang.* terrific-looking, absolutely gorgeous (e.g. mujer cañón)

cañonazo /kaɲo'naso; kaɲo'naθo/ *m*, cannon shot; roar of a cannon

cañoneo /kaɲo'neo/ *m*, cannonade; bombardment

cañonería /kaɲone'ria/ *f*, *Mil.* group of cannon; *Mus.* set of organ pipes

cañonero /kaɲo'nero/ *m*, gunboat

cañuto /ka'ɲuto/ *m*, *Bot.* internode; small pipe or tube; *Inf.* tale-bearer

caoba /ka'oβa/ *f*, *Bot.* mahogany

caos /'kaos/ *m*, chaos; confusion

caótico /ka'otiko/ *a* chaotic

capa /'kapa/ *f*, cloak; cape; *Eccl.* cope; coating; layer; cover; coat (animals); *Fig.* cloak, disguise; *Geol.* stratum. **la c. del cielo,** the canopy of heaven. *Fig. Inf.* **echar la c. al toro,** to throw one's cap over the windmill. *Naut.* **estarse** (*or* **ponerse) a la c.,** to lie to

capacete /kapa'sete; kapa'θete/ *m*, helmet

capacha /ka'patʃa/ *f* basket; *Argentina, Chile* clink, jug (jail)

capacidad /kapasi'ðað; kapaθi'ðað/ *f*, capacity; extension, space; mental capacity, talent; opportunity; means; *Law.* capacity. **c. de compra,** buying power, purchasing power. **c. de producción,** output

capacitación /kapasita'sion; kapaθita'θion/ *f*, qualification, (act of) qualifying; (act of) training

capacitar /kapasi'tar; kapaθi'tar/ *vt* to capacitate, qualify, enable

capadura /kapa'ðura/ *f*, castration

capar /ka'par/ *vt* to castrate, geld; *Inf.* diminish, reduce

caparazón /kapara'son; kapara'θon/ *m*, caparison, horse blanket; waterproof cover; hood (of carriages); nosebag; shell (insects, crustaceans)

capataz /kapa'tas; kapa'taθ/ *m*, foreman; steward; overseer

capaz /ka'pas; ka'paθ/ *a* capacious; large, spacious; capable, competent; *Law.* able

capcioso /kap'sioso; kap'θioso/ *a* deceitful, artful; captious, carping

capear /kape'ar/ *vt* to steal a cape; play the bull with a cape (bullfighting); *Inf.* put off with excuses, deceive; *Naut.* lie to

capellán /kape'yan; kape'ʎan/ *m*, chaplain; any ecclesiastic

capelo /ka'pelo/ *m*, cardinal's hat; cardinalate

capeo /ka'peo/ *m*, playing the bull with a cape (bullfighting)

caperuza /kape'rusa; kape'ruθa/ *f*, hood, pointed cap; *Archit.* coping-stone

capigorrón /kapigo'rron/ *a Inf.* loafing. *m*, loafer, idler

capilar /kapi'lar/ *a* capillary

capilaridad /kapilari'ðað/ *f*, capillarity

capilla /ka'piya; ka'piʎa/ *f*, cowl, hood; chapel; *Eccl.* chapter; *Eccl.* choir. **c. ardiente,** chapelle ardente. **estar en c.,** to await execution (criminals); *Inf.* be in suspense, await anxiously

capillero /kapi'yero; kapi'ʎero/ *m*, sexton; churchwarden

capillo /ka'piyo; ka'piʎo/ *m*, baby's bonnet; cocoon of silkworm; flowerbud

capirotazo /kapiro'taso; kapiro'taθo/ *m*, box on the ear; fillip

capirote /kapi'rote/ *m*, academic hood and cap; hood (falconry); tall pointed cap. **ser tonto de c.,** *Inf.* to be a complete fool

capitación /kapita'sion; kapita'θion/ *f*, poll-tax, capitation

capital /kapi'tal/ *a* relating to the head; capital (sins, etc.); main, principal. *m*, capital, patrimony; *Com.* capital stock. *f*, capital (city). **c. pagado,** paid-in capital stock

capitalino, -a /kapita'lino/ *Lat. Am. a* of the capital; *n* native of the capital; resident of the capital

capitalismo /kapita'lismo/ *m*, capitalism

capitalista /kapita'lista/ *a* capitalistic. *mf* capitalist

capitalización /kapitalisa'sion; kapitaliθa'θion/ *f*, capitalization

capitalizar /kapitali'sar; kapitali'θar/ *vt* to capitalize

capitán /kapi'tan/ *m*, captain, skipper; chief, leader; ringleader. *Aer*. **c. de aviación**, group captain. **c. de fragata**, *Nav*. commander. **c. de puerto**, harbor master. **c. general de ejército**, field-marshal

capitana /kapi'tana/ *f*, admiral's ship; *Inf*. captain's wife

capitanear /kapitane'ar/ *vt* to captain, command; *Fig*. guide, lead

capitanía /kapita'nia/ *f*, captaincy; captainship

capitolio /kapi'tolio/ *m*, dignified building; *Archit*. acropolis; Capitol

capitulación /kapitula'sion; kapitula'θion/ *f*, agreement, pact; capitulation; *pl* marriage articles

capitular /kapitu'lar/ *a* capitulary, belonging to a Chapter. *m*, capitular, member of a Chapter. *vi* to make an agreement; capitulate; sing prayers; arrange order

capítulo /ka'pitulo/ *m*, *Eccl*. Chapter; meeting of town council, etc.; chapter (of book); item (in a budget); determination, decision

capó /ka'po/ *m*, *Auto*. hood

capón /ka'pon/ *a* castrated; gelded. *m*, capon; bundle of firewood or vines

caponera /kapo'nera/ *f*, coop for fattening capons; *Inf*. jail; *Inf*. place where one lives well free of charge

capota /ka'pota/ *f*, *Bot*. head of teasel; bonnet; hood (of vehicles)

capote /ka'pote/ *m*, short, brightly colored cape (used by bullfighters); cape coat; (cards) slam; *Inf*. scowl

capricho /ka'pritʃo/ *m*, caprice, fancy; strong desire

caprichoso /kapri'tʃoso/ *a* capricious; whimsical

caprichudo /kapri'tʃuðo/ *a* headstrong; capricious

cápsula /'kapsula/ *f*, cartridge-case; bottlecap; (*Bot*. *Med*. *Chem*. *Zool*.) capsule

captar /kap'tar/ *vt* gain, attract (goodwill, attention, etc.); *Mech*. collect; monitor (foreign broadcasts)

captor /kap'tor/ *m*, capturer

captura /kap'tura/ *f*, *Law*. capture; seizing, arrest

capturar /kaptu'rar/ *vt* to capture; arrest, apprehend

capucha /ka'putʃa/ *f*, hood; cowl; *Print*. circumflex accent

capuchina /kapu'tʃina/ *f*, Capuchin nun; *Bot*. nasturtium; table-lamp with an extinguisher

capucho /ka'putʃo/ *m*, cowl

capullo /ka'puyo; ka'puʎo/ *m*, cocoon; flower bud; acorn cup; *Anat*. prepuce

caqui /'kaki/ *m*, khaki; khaki color

cara /'kara/ *f*, face; likeness, aspect; façade, front; surface; side (of metal, etc.); mien. **c. a c.**, face to face; frankly; openly. *Inf*. **c. de juez**, severe face. *Inf*. **c. de pascua**, smiling face. *Inf*. **c. de vinagre**, sour face. **c. o cruz**, heads or tails. **c. o sello** *Argentina*, *Chile*, heads or tails **de c.**, opposite. **hacer a dos caras**, to be deceitful; be two-faced. **hacer c. (a)**, to stand up to

caraba /ka'raβa/ *f*, *Slang*. 25-centimo coin

cárabe /'karaβe/ *m*, amber

carabina /kara'βina/ *f*, carbine; rifle

carabinazo /karaβi'naso; karaβi'naθo/ *m*, report of a carbine

carabinero /karaβi'nero/ *m*, carabineer; customs' guard, revenue guard; customs officer, customs official

caracol /kara'kol/ *m*, snail; snail's shell; cure; *Zool*. cochlea; winding stair. **c. marino**, periwinkle. **¡Caracoles!** Fancy!

caracola /kara'kola/ *f*, conch shell used as a horn

caracolear /karakole'ar/ *vi* to prance from side to side (horses)

carácter /ka'rakter/ *m*, sign, mark; character, writing (gen. *pl*); style of writing; brand (animals); nature, temperament; character, individuality, strong-mindedness, energy, firmness; condition, state, capacity. **comedia de c.**, psychological play. **en su c. de**, as in one's capacity as. **caracteres de imprenta**, printing types

característica /karakte'ristika/ *f*, quality, characteristic; *Math*. characteristic; actress who plays the part of an old woman

característico /karakte'ristiko/ *a* characteristic, distinctive. *m*, actor who plays roles of old men

caracterización /karakterisa'sion; karakteriθa'θion/ *f*, characterization; *Theat*. make-up

caracterizar /karakteri'sar; karakteri'θar/ *vt* to characterize; confer an office, honor, dignity, on; *Theat*. create a character; *vr Theat*. to make up, dress as, a character

caraíta /kara'ita/ *a* and *mf* Karaite

¡caramba! /ka'ramba/ *interj* gosh!; blast!

carámbano /ka'rambano/ *m*, icicle

carambola /karam'βola/ *f*, cannon (billiards); *Inf*. double effect; *Inf*. trick, deception

caramelo /kara'melo/ *m*, caramel; toffee

caramillo /kara'miyo; kara'miʎo/ *m*, flageolet; small flute, pipe; gossip, intrigue

carancho /ka'rantʃo/ *m*, *Argentina* vulture; *Peru* owl

carantamaula /karanta'maula/ *f*, *Inf*. hideous mask; ugly person

carapacho /kara'patʃo/ *m*, carapace, shell

carátula /ka'ratula/ *f*, mask; *Fig*. dramatic art, the theater

caravana /kara'βana/ *f*, caravan, group of traders, pilgrims, etc. (especially in East); *Inf*. crowd of excursionists, picnickers, etc.

¡caray! /ka'rai/ *interj* blast!; gosh!

carbólico /kar'βoliko/ *a* carbolic

carbón /kar'βon/ *m*, coal; charcoal; black chalk, crayon. **c. bituminoso**, soft coal. **c. de coque**, coke. **c. de leña**, charcoal. **c. mineral**, coal, anthracite. **mina de c.**, coal-mine

carbonada /karβo'naða/ *f*, *Lat. Am.* meat stew

carboncillo /karβon'siyo; karβon'θiʎo/ *m*, charcoal crayon

carbonear /karβone'ar/ *vt* to turn into charcoal; *Naut*. coal

carboneo /karβo'neo/ *m*, coaling

carbonera /karβo'nera/ *f*, coal-cellar, coal-house, etc.; coal-scuttle; woman who sells charcoal or coal; charcoal burner

carbonería /karβone'ria/ *f*, coal or charcoal merchant's office

carbonero /karβo'nero/ *a* relating to coal or charcoal. *m*, collier; charcoal maker; coal merchant; *Naut*. coal-ship

carbónico /kar'βoniko/ *a* *Chem*. carbonic

carbonífero /karβo'nifero/ *a* carboniferous

carbonizar /karβoni'sar; karβoni'θar/ *vt* to carbonize

carbono /kar'βono/ *m*, *Chem*. carbon

carbunco /kar'βunko/ *m*, *Med*. carbuncle

carbúnculo /kar'βunkulo/ *m*, carbuncle, ruby

carburador /karβura'ðor/ *m*, carburetor

carcaj /kar'kah/ *m*, quiver (for arrows); *Mexico* rifle case

carcajada /karka'haða/ *f*, burst of laughter, guffaw. **reírse a carcajadas**, to roar with laughter

carcajearse /karkahe'arse/ *vi* to guffaw

carcamal /karka'mal/ *m*, *Inf*. dotard

cárcel /'karsel; 'karθel/ *f*, prison, jail

carcelario /karse'lario; karθe'lario/ *a* prison, jail

carcelero /karse'lero; karθe'lero/ **(-ra)** *a* jail. *n* jailer

cárcola /'karkola/ *f*, treadle (of a loom)

carcoma /kar'koma/ *f*, wood-worm; dry rot; *Fig*. gnawing care; spendthrift

carcomer /karko'mer/ *vt* to gnaw wood (worms); *Fig*. undermine (health, etc.); *vr* be worm-eaten

carda /'karða/ *f*, card, carding; teasel head; card brush; *Inf*. reprimand

cardador /karða'ðor/ **(-ra)** *n* carder, comber

cardadura /karða'ðura/ *f*, carding; carding frame

cardar /kar'ðar/ *vt* to card, tease; brush up (felt, etc.)

cardenal /karðe'nal/ *m*, cardinal; cardinal bird; bruise

cardenalato /karðena'lato/ *m*, cardinalate, cardinalship

cardenillo /karðe'niyo; karðe'niʎo/ *m*, verdigris; *Art*. verditer

cárdeno /'karðeno/ *a* livid

cardíaco /kar'ðiako/ *a* Med. cardiac

cardinal /karði'nal/ *a* principal; cardinal (point); *Gram.* cardinal (number)

cardiógrafo /kar'ðiografo/ *m*, Med. cardiograph

cardiograma /karðio'grama/ *m*, Med. cardiogram

cardo /'karðo/ *m*, Bot. thistle

carear /kare'ar/ *vt* to confront; compare; *vi* turn towards, face; *vr* meet; come together

carecer /kare'ser; kare'θer/ *vi irr* to be short; lack, need (e.g. *Carece de las condiciones necesarias,* It lacks the necessary conditions). See **conocer**

carencia /ka'rensia; ka'renθia/ *f*, shortage, lack

carestía /kares'tia/ *f*, shortage, scarcity; famine; dearness, high price

careta /ka'reta/ *f*, mask; beekeeper's veil; fencing mask. *Fig.* **quitar la c.** (**a**), to unmask

carey /ka'rei/ *m*, Zool. shell turtle; tortoise-shell

carga /'karga/ *f*, loading; *Elec.* charging, charge; load; burden, weight; cargo; explosive charge; *Fig.* imposition; tax; duty, obligation. *Naut.* **c. de profundidad,** depth charge

cargadero /karga'ðero/ *m*, place where goods are loaded or unloaded

cargado /kar'gaðo/ *a* loaded; heavy, sultry; strong (tea, coffee). **c. de cadenas,** (prisoner, etc.) in chains. **c. de espaldas,** round-shouldered

cargador /karga'ðor/ *m*, loader; porter; dockhand; pitchfork; rammer; *Mech.* stoker; *Elec.* charger

cargamento /karga'mento/ *m*, Naut. cargo, freight, shipload

cargar /kar'gar/ *vt* to load; charge (guns, etc.); stoke; overburden; tax, impose; blame for, charge with; *Inf.* annoy, bore; *Argentina Inf.* to kid, tease; *Com.* charge, book; *Mil.* attack; (football) tackle; *vi* tip, slope; (*with con*) carry away; be loaded with (fruit); assume responsibility; (*with sobre*) importune, urge; lean against; *vr* turn (head, etc.); lower, grow darker (sky); (*with de*) be abundant (in or with); load oneself with

cargazón /karga'son; karga'θon/ *f*, cargo; loading; heaviness; darkness (of the sky)

cargo /'kargo/ *m*, loading; load, weight; post, office; duty, obligation; management, charge; care; *Com.* debit; accusation. *Com.* **el c. y la data,** debit and credit. **hacerse c. de,** to take charge of; understand; consider carefully. **ser en c.** (**a**), to be debtor (to)

cargosear /kargose'ar/ *vt*, *Lat. Am.* to annoy, pester

cargoso, -a /kar'goso/ *a*, *Lat. Am.* annoying, pestering

cariacontecido /kariakonte'siðo; kariakonte'θiðo/ *a* crestfallen, disappointed; glum

cariancho /kari'antʃo/ *a Inf.* broadfaced

cariarse /ka'riarse/ *vr* to become carious

caribe /ka'riβe/ *a* Caribbean. *mf* cannibal, savage

caricatura /karika'tura/ *f*, caricature

caricaturista /karikatu'rista/ *mf* caricaturist

caricaturizar /karikaturi'sar; karikaturi'θar/ *vt* to caricature

caricia /ka'risia; ka'riθia/ *f*, caress

caridad /kari'ðað/ *f*, charity; charitableness; alms

caries /'karies/ *f*, caries, tooth decay

carilargo /kari'largo/ *a Inf.* long-faced

carilla /ka'riya; ka'riʎa/ *f*, *dim* small face; mask; page (of a book)

carilleno /kari'yeno; kari'ʎeno/ *a Inf.* plump-faced, round-faced

carillón /kari'yon; kari'ʎon/ *m*, peal (of bells)

cariño /ka'riɲo/ *m*, affection; love; caress affectionately (gen. *pl*); fondness, inclination. **con c.,** affectionately

cariñoso /kari'ɲoso/ *a* affectionate; loving; kind

carioca /ka'rioka/ *a* of Rio de Janeiro; *n* native of Rio de Janeiro; resident of Rio de Janeiro

carirredondo /karirre'ðondo/ *a Inf.* roundfaced

carismático /karis'matiko/ *a* charismatic

caritativo /karita'tiβo/ *a* charitable

cariz /ka'ris; ka'riθ/ *m*, appearance of the sky; look, face; aspect; *Inf.* outlook (for a business deal, etc.)

carlista /kar'lista/ *a* and *mf* Carlist

carmelita /karme'lita/ *a* and *mf* Carmelite

carmen /'karmen/ *m*, country house and garden (Granada); song; poem

carmesí /karme'si/ *a* crimson. *m*, crimson color; cramoisy

carmín /kar'min/ *m*, red, carmine color; red wild rose-tree and flower

carnada /kar'naða/ *f*, bait

carnaje /kar'nahe/ *m*, salted meat

carnal /kar'nal/ *a* carnal; lascivious; materialistic, worldly; related by blood

carnalidad /karnali'ðað/ *f*, carnality

carnaval /karna'βal/ *m*, carnival. **martes de c.,** Shrove Tuesday

carnavalesco /karnaβa'lesko/ *a* carnival

carne /'karne/ *f*, flesh; meat; pulpy part of fruit; carnality, *c.* **concentrada,** meat extract. **c. congelada,** frozen meat. **c. de gallina** *Fig.* gooseflesh. **c. de membrillo,** quince cheese or conserve. **c. y hueso,** *Fig.* flesh and blood. *Inf.* **cobrar carnes,** to put on weight. **poner toda la c. en el asador,** *Inf.* to put all one's eggs in one basket

carné de conductor /'karne de konduk'tor/ *Argentina* driver's license

carnerada /karne'raða/ *f*, flock of sheep

carnerero /karne'rero/ (**-ra**) *n* shepherd

carnero /kar'nero/ *m*, sheep; mutton; mortuary; charnel-house; family burial vault. **c. marino,** Zool. seal

carnestolendas /karnesto'lendas/ *f pl* three days of carnival before Ash Wednesday

carnet /kar'net/ *m*, notebook, diary; identity card; membership card, pass. **c. de chófer,** driver's license

carnicería /karniθe'ria; karniθe'ria/ *f*, butcher's shop; carnage, slaughter

carnicero /karni'sero; karni'θero/ *a* carnivorous; inhuman, cruel. *m*, butcher

carnívoro /kar'niβoro/ *a* carnivorous. *m*, carnivore

carnosidad /karnosi'ðað/ *f*, proud flesh; local fat; fatness

carnoso /kar'noso/ *a* meaty; fleshy; full of marrow; *Bot.* pulpy, juicy

caro /'karo/ *a* beloved; expensive; dear. *adv* expensively; dear

carolingio /karo'linhio/ (**-ia**) *a* and *n* Carolingian

carótida /ka'rotiða/ *f*, carotid artery

carpa /'karpa/ *f*, Ichth. carp. **c. dorada,** goldfish; *Lat. Am.* tent; awning

carpanta /kar'panta/ *f*, *Inf.* violent hunger; *Mexico* gang

Cárpatos, los Montes /'karpatos, los 'montes/ the Carpathian Mountains

carpeta /kar'peta/ *f*, table or chest cover, doily; writing case; portfolio; docket, letter file

carpetazo, dar /karpe'taso, dar; karpe'taθo, dar/ *vt* to shelve (a project, etc.)

carpintear /karpinte'ar/ *vi* to carpenter

carpintería /karpinte'ria/ *f*, carpenter's shop; carpentry

carpinteril /karpinte'ril/ *a* carpentering

carpintero /karpin'tero/ *m*, carpenter, joiner; *Theat.* scene-shifter. **c. de carretas,** wheelwright. **c. de ribera,** shipwright

carraca /ka'rraka/ *f*, rattle; ratchet-drill

Carrapempe /karra'pempe/ *m*, Old Nick

carrascal /karras'kal/ *m*, field of pinoaks

carraspear /karraspe'ar/ *vi* to clear one's throat; cough

carraspera /karras'pera/ *f*, *Inf.* hoarseness

carrera /ka'rrera/ *f*, run; race; racing; racecourse; *Astron.* course; high road; route; *Mas.* layer, course; line, row; *Fig.* run (in stockings, etc.); course; duration (of life); career, profession; *Mexico* major (academic); conduct; girders. **c. de fondo,** long-distance race. **c. de relevos, c. de equipos,** relay race. **a c. abierta, a c. tendida,** at full speed

carrerista /karre'rista/ *mf* racing enthusiast; professional racer

carreta /ka'rreta/ *f*, long, narrow two-wheeled cart; wagon; tumbril

carretada /karre'taða/ *f*, cart-load; *Inf.* great deal, mass

carretaje /karre'tahe/ *m*, cartage; carriage, transport

carrete /ka'rrete/ *m*, spool, reel, bobbin; fishing reel; *Elec.* coil; *Photo.* film spool

carretear /karrete'ar/ *vt* to cart; drive a cart

carretera /karre'tera/ *f*, high road; highway

carretería /karre'ria/ *f*, number of carts; carting trade; cartwright's yard

carretero /karre'tero/ *m*, cartwright; carter, driver

carretilla /karre'tiya; karre'tiʎa/ *f*, wheelbarrow; hand cart; railway truck; squib. **de c.,** *Inf.* mechanically, without thought; (*with saber, repetir,* etc.) by rote

carretón /karre'ton/ *m*, truck, trolley; hand cart

carril /ka'rril/ *m*, wheel mark; furrow, rut; cart road, narrow road; rail (railways, etc.)

carrillera /karri'yera; karri'ʎera/ *f*, jaw (of some animals); chin strap; *pl* bonnet strings, etc.

carrillo /ka'rriyo; ka'rriʎo/ *m*, cheek; jowl

carriola /ka'rriola/ *f*, truckle bed; curricle

carro /'karro/ *m*, cart; cartload; car, chariot; carriage (of a typewriter, etc.); chassis; *Astron.* Plow, Great Bear; *Lat. Am.* automobile, auto, car; *Mil.* **c. blindado,** armored car. *Mil.* **c. de asalto,** tank. **c. de mudanzas,** moving van. **c. de regar,** watercart

carrocería /karrose'ria; karroθe'ria/ *f*, place where carriages are made, sold, repaired; *Auto.* coachwork, body shop

carrocha /ka'rrotʃa/ *f*, eggs (of insects)

carrochar /karro'tʃar/ *vi* to lay eggs (insects)

carromato /karro'mato/ *m*, road wagon; covered wagon

carroña /ka'rroɲa/ *f*, putrid flesh, carrion

carroza /ka'rrosa; ka'rroθa/ *f*, elegant coach; state coach; carriage; float (for tableaux, etc.); *Naut.* awning

carruaje /ka'rruahe/ *m*, carriage; any vehicle

carta /'karta/ *f*, letter; charter; royal order; playing card; chart, map. **c. certificada,** registered letter. **c. de amparo,** safe-conduct. **c. de crédito,** *Com.* letter of credit. **c. de marear,** sea chart. **c. de naturaleza,** naturalization papers. **c. de pésame,** letter of condolence. **c. de venta,** *Com.* bill of sale. **c. ejecutoria de hidalguía,** letters patent of nobility. **carta-poder,** letter of proxy, proxy. **cartas rusas,** (game of) consequences. **poner las cartas boca arriba,** *Fig.* to lay one's cards on the table

cartabón /karta'βon/ *m*, set-square; shoemaker's slide; quadrant

cartaginés /kartahi'nes/ (**-esa**) *a* and *n* Carthaginian

Cartago /'kartago/ Carthage

cartapacio /karta'pasio; karta'paθio/ *m*, note-book; schoolbag, satchel; file, batch of papers

cartear /karte'ar/ *vi Cards.* to play low; *vr* to correspond by letter

cartel /kar'tel/ *m*, placard, poster; cartel; pasquinade, lampoon. **fijar carteles,** to placard

cartela /kar'tela/ *f*, tablet (for writing); slip of paper, etc.); *Archit.* console, bracket

cartelera /karte'lera/ *f*, billboard

cartelero /karte'lero/ *m*, billpaster, billsticker

carteo /kar'teo/ *m*, correspondence (by letter)

cartera /kar'tera/ *f*, pocketbook; wallet; dispatch-case; portfolio; notebook; pocket flap; office of a cabinet minister; *Com.* shares

cartería /karte'ria/ *f*, sorting room (in a post-office)

carterista /karte'rista/ *mf* pickpocket

cartero /kar'tero/ (**-ra**) *n* mail carrier

cartesiano /karte'siano/ (**-na**) *a* and *n* Cartesian

Cartesio /kar'tesio/ Descartes

carteta /kar'teta/ *f*, lansquenet (card game)

cartilaginoso /kartilahi'noso/ *a* cartilaginous

cartílago /kar'tilago/ *m*, cartilage

cartilla /kar'tiya; kar'tiʎa/ *f*, first reading book; primer; certificate of ordination; note-book; liturgical calendar. **c. de racionamiento,** ration book

cartografía /kartogra'fia/ *f*, cartography

cartógrafo /kar'tografo/ *m*, map maker

cartón /kar'ton/ *m*, pasteboard, cardboard; *Archit.* bracket; *Art.* cartoon, design

cartucho /kar'tutʃo/ *m*, cartridge; paper cone

cartuja /kar'tuha/ *f*, Carthusian Order or monastery

cartujano /kartu'hano/ *a* Carthusian

cartujo /kar'tuho/ *m*, Carthusian monk; *Inf.* taciturn, reserved man

cartulina /kartu'lina/ *f*, Bristol board, oaktag, pasteboard, card

carúncula /ka'runkula/ *f*, caruncle, comb of cock, etc.

casa /'kasa/ *f*, house; home; household; residence, dwelling; family house; *Com.* firm. **c. consistorial,** town hall. **c. cuna,** crèche. **c. de campo,** countryhouse. **c. de empeño,** pawnshop. **c. de huéspedes,** boarding house, lodging-house. **c. de los sustos,** haunted house (at amusement park). **c. de moneda,** mint. **c. de socorro,** First Aid Post. **c. de vecindad,** tenement. **c. mala,** house of ill repute. **c. solar** *or* **c. solariega,** family seat. **en c.,** at home (also sport usage). **poner c.,** to set up house

casaca /ka'saka/ *f*, dress coat. **volver la c.,** to become a turncoat, change one's allegiance

casación /kasa'sion; kasa'θion/ *f*, *Law.* cassation

casadero /kasa'ðero/ *a* marriageable

casadoro /kasa'ðoro/ *m*, Costa Rica bus

casamiento /kasa'miento/ *m*, marriage; wedding

casar /ka'sar/ *vt* to marry (of a priest); *Law.* repeal; *Inf.* marry off; join; match, harmonize; *vi* and *vr* (*with con*) to get married

casar /ka'sar/ *m*, group of houses

casca /'kaska/ *f*, grape skin; tan (bark); shell, peel, rind

cascabel /kaska'βel/ *m*, small bell (for harness, etc.). **serpiente de c.,** rattlesnake. *Inf.* **ser un c.,** to be feather-brained

cascabeleo /kaska'βeleo/ *m*, jingling of bells

cascabillo /kaska'βiyo; kaska'βiʎo/ *m*, husk (of cereals)

cascada /kas'kaða/ *f*, cascade; waterfall

cascadura /kaska'ðura/ *f*, cracking, crack

cascajo /kas'kaho/ *m*, gravel, shingle; *Inf.* broken, old things, junk; nuts

cascanueces /kaska'nueses; kaska'nueθes/ *m*, nutcrackers

cascar /kas'kar/ *vt* to crack, split, break; *Inf.* beat; *Fig. Inf.* break down (of health); *vi Inf.* talk, chatter

cáscara /'kaskara/ *f*, shell; peel, rind; bark. *Med.* **c. sagrada,** cascara

cascarón /kaska'ron/ *m*, eggshell; *Archit.* vault

cascarrabias /kaska'rrabias/ *mf Inf.* spitfire

cascarriento, -a /kaska'rriento/ *Argentina* filthy; greasy

casco /'kasko/ *m*, cranium; broken fragment of china, glass, etc.; crown of hat; helmet; tree of saddle; bottle; tank; pipe; barrel; *Naut.* hull; hoof; quarter (of fruit); *pl Inf.* head. **c. colonial,** sun-helmet. **c. respiratorio,** smoke-helmet

cascote /kas'kote/ *m*, rubble, ruins

caseoso /kase'oso/ *a* cheesy

caserío /kase'rio/ *m*, group of houses; country house

casero /ka'sero/ *a* home made; home bred; familiar; informa; *Inf.* domesticated, home-loving; domestic. *m*, landlord; caretaker; tenant

caserón /kase'ron/ *m*, large tumbledown house, mansion, hall

caseta /ka'seta/ *f*, hut; cottage; booth, stall. **c. de baños,** bathing van

casi /'kasi/ *adv* almost, nearly. **c. c.,** very nearly

casilla /ka'siya; ka'siʎa/ *f*, hut; cabin; lodge; ticket office; pigeon-hole; *Argentina, Chile* post-office box *Aer.* **c. del piloto,** cockpit

casillero /kasi'yero; kasi'ʎero/ *m*, file cabinet, filing cabinet; locker (as in a locker room); set of pigeon-holes; *Sports.* scoreboard; *Rail.* crossing guard

casino /ka'sino/ *m*, casino; club

caso /'kaso/ *m*, happening, event; chance, hazard; occasion, opportunity; case, matter; (*Med. Gram.*) case. **en el c. de,** in a position to (e.g. *No estamos en el c. de pagar tanto dinero.* We are in no position to pay so much money). **en tal c.,** in such a case. **en**

todo c., in any case. **no hacer c. de,** to take no notice of. **venir al c.**, to be opportune

caspa /'kaspa/ *f*, dandruff; scab

¡cáspita! /'kaspita/ *interj* Amazing! Wonderful!

casquete /kas'kete/ *m*, helmet; skullcap; half wig

casquijo /kas'kiho/ *m*, gravel

casquillo /kas'kiyo; kas'kiʎo/ *m*, tip, cap, ferrule; socket; arrow-head; metal cartridge-case

casquivano /kaski'βano/ *a Inf.* giddy, feather-brained

casta /'kasta/ *f*, race; caste; breed (animals); kind, species, quality. **de buena c.**, pedigree (e.g. *perros de buena c.*, pedigree dogs)

castaña /kas'taɲa/ *f, Bot.* chestnut; knot, bun (of hair)

castañar /kasta'ɲar/ *m*, chestnut plantation or grove

castañetear /kastaɲete'ar/ *vi* to play the castanets; snap one's fingers; chatter (of teeth); knock together (of knees)

castaño /kas'taɲo/ *a* chestnut-colored. *m*, chestnut tree; chestnut wood. **c. de Indias,** horse-chestnut tree

castañuela /kasta'ɲuela/ *f*, castanet. **tocar las castañuelas,** to play the castanets

castellán /kaste'yan; kaste'ʎan/ *m*, castellan

castellano /kaste'yano; kaste'ʎano/ **(-na)** *n* Castilian; Spaniard. *m*, Spanish (language); castellan. *a* Castilian; Spanish

casticismo /kasti'sismo; kasti'θismo/ *m*, purity (of language); Spanish spirit; traditionalism

castidad /kasti'ðað/ *f*, chastity

castigador /kastiga'ðor/ *a* punishing. *m*, punisher; *Inf.* lady-killer

castigadora /kastiga'ðora/ *f, Inf.* man-hunter

castigar /kasti'gar/ *vt* to punish; chastise; chasten, advise; pain, grieve; correct, edit; decrease (expenses); *Com.* allow a discount

castigo /kas'tigo/ *m*, punishment; emendation, correction

Castilla /kas'tiya; kas'tiʎa/ Castile

castillo /kas'tiyo; kas'tiʎo/ *m*, castle; howdah. **c. de naipes,** house of cards. **c. de proa,** *Naut.* forecastle. **c. fuerte,** fortified castle. *Inf.* **hacer castillos en el aire,** to build castles in the air or in Spain

castizo /kas'tiso; kas'tiθo/ *a* pure-blooded; prolific; pure (of language); typically Spanish; traditional

casto /'kasto/ *a* chaste; pure, unsullied

castor /kas'tor/ *m, Zool.* beaver (animal and fur); soft, woollen cloth

castración /kastra'sion; kastra'θion/ *f*, castration, gelding

castrado /kas'traðo/ *a* castrated. *m, Inf.* eunuch

castrador /kastra'ðor/ *m*, castrator, gelder

castrapo /kas'trapo/ *m*, mixed Spanish and Galician spoken in Galicia, Spain

castrar /kas'trar/ *vt* to castrate, geld; prune; remove honeycomb from hives; weaken

castrense /kas'trense/ *a* military

castrista /kas'trista/ *v* and *mf* Castroite

casual /ka'sual/ *a* accidental, casual

casualidad /kasuali'ðað/ *f*, chance, coincidence. **por c.**, by chance. **ser mucha c. que...**, to be too much of a coincidence that...

casucha /ka'sutʃa/ *f, Inf.* tumbledown hut

casuista /ka'suista/ *a* casuistic. *mf* casuist

casuística /ka'suistika/ *f*, casuistry

casulla /ka'suya; ka'suʎa/ *f*, chasuble

cata /'kata/ *f*, tasting; taste, sample; *Lat. Am.* parrot

catabolismo /kataβo'lismo/ *m*, catabolism

cataclismo /kata'klismo/ *m*, cataclysm

catacumbas /kata'kumbas/ *f pl*, catacombs

catador /kata'ðor/ *m*, taster, sampler

catadura /kata'ðura/ *f*, tasting; look, countenance (gen. qualified)

catafalco /kata'falko/ *m*, catafalque

catalán /kata'lan/ **(-ana)** *a* and *n* Catalan, Catalonian. *m*, Catalan (language)

catalejo /kata'leho/ *m*, telescope

cataléptico /kata'leptiko/ *a* cataleptic

catálisis /ka'talisis/ *f, Chem.* catalysis

catalítico /kata'litiko/ *a* catalytic

catalogar /katalo'gar/ *vt* to catalog, list

catálogo /ka'talogo/ *m*, catalog, list

Cataluña /kata'luɲa/ Catalonia

cataplasma /kata'plasma/ *f*, cataplasm

catapulta /kata'pulta/ *f*, catapult

catar /ka'tar/ *vt* to taste, sample; see, examine; inspect; regard

catarata /kata'rata/ *f*, cataract, waterfall; *Med.* cataract (of the eyes)

catarral /kata'rral/ *a* catarrhal

catarro /ka'tarro/ *m*, catarrh; common cold

catástrofe /ka'tastrofe/ *f, Lit.* tragic climax; catastrophe

catastrófico /katas'trofiko/ *a* catastrophic

catavino /kata'βino/ *m*, taster (cup)

catavinos /kata'βinos/ *mf*, professional wine taster; *Inf.* tippler, tavern haunter

cate /'kate/ *m, slang* flunk (failure in a course at school)

catecismo /kate'sismo; kate'θismo/ *m*, catechism

catecúmeno /kate'kumeno/ **(-na)** *n* catechumen

cátedra /'kateðra/ *f*, university chair; chair in a Spanish **instituto**; professorship; university lecture room; subject taught by professor; reading desk, lectern; *Eccl.* throne; *Eccl.* see. **c. del espíritu santo,** pulpit. **c. de San Pedro,** Holy See

catedral /kate'ðral/ *f*, and *a* cathedral

catedrático /kate'ðratiko/ **(-ca)** *n* professor

categoría /katego'ria/ *f, Philos.* category; class, rank

categórico /kate'goriko/ *a* categorical, downright

cateo /ka'teo/ *m, West Hem.* sampling; prospecting; house search (by the police)

catequismo /kate'kismo/ *m*, catechism; question and answer method of teaching

catequista /kate'kista/ *mf* catechist

catequizar /kateki'sar; kateki'θar/ *vt* to catechize; persuade, induce

caterva /ka'terβa/ *f*, crowd, throng; jumble, collection

catéter /ka'teter/ *m, Surg.* probe; catheter

catoche /ka'totʃe/ *m, Lat. Am.* bad temper

catódico /ka'toðiko/ *a Elec.* cathodic

cátodo /'katoðo/ *m*, cathode

catolicidad /katolisi'ðað; katoliθi'ðað/ *f*, catholicity; catholic world

catolicismo /katoli'sismo; katoli'θismo/ *m*, Catholicism

católico /ka'toliko/ **(-ca)** *a* universal, catholic; infallible. *a* and *n* Catholic (by religion)

catorce /ka'torse; ka'torθe/ *a* fourteen; fourteenth. *m*, number fourteen; fourteenth (of days of month)

catorzavo /kator'saβo; kator'θaβo/ *a* fourteenth

catre /'katre/ *m*, camp-bed; truckle-bed; cot

Cáucaso, el /'kaukaso, el/ the Caucasus

cauce /'kause; 'kauθe/ *m*, river or stream bed; ditch, irrigation canal

cauchal /kau'tʃal/ *m*, rubber plantation

cauchera /kau'tʃera/ *f*, rubber tree

cauchero /kau'tʃero/ *m*, rubber planter; rubber-plantation worker

caucho /'kautʃo/ *m*, caoutchouc; rubber; *Lat. Am.* tire

caución /kau'sion; kau'θion/ *f*, caution, precaution; surety; security

caucional /kausio'nal; kauθio'nal/ *a* See **libertad**

caudal /kau'ðal/ *m*, wealth, capital; flow, volume (of water); plenty, abundance (e.g. *un c. de conocimientos,* a wealth of knowledge)

caudaloso /kauða'loso/ *a* carrying much water; wealthy; abundant

caudillo /kau'ðiyo; kau'ðiʎo/ *m*, head, leader; chieftain. **el C.**, (title of Francisco Franco)

causa /'kausa/ *f*, cause; reason, motive; lawsuit; *Law.* trial. **c. final,** *Philos.* final cause. **c. pública,** public welfare. **ser c. bastante para...**, to be reason enough to...

causador /kausa'ðor/ **(-ra)** *a* motivating. *n* occasioner, originator

causalidad /kausali'ðað/ *f*, causality

causante /kau'sante/ *a* causative, causing. *m, Law.* principal; *Mexico* taxpayer

causar /kau'sar/ *vt* to cause; occasion

causticidad /kausisti'ðað; kaustiθi'ðað/ *f*, causticity; mordacity

cáustico /'kaustiko/ *a* burning, caustic; scathing; mordant; *Surg.* caustic

cautela /kau'tela/ *f*, caution; astuteness, cunning

cauteloso /kaute'loso/ *a* cautious; cunning

cauterio /kau'terio/ *m*, cautery

cauterización /kauterisa'sion; kauteriθa'θion/ *f*, cauterization

cauterizar /kauteri'sar; kauteri'θar/ *vt* to cauterize

cautivar /kauti'βar/ *vt* to capture; captivate, charm; attract; *vi* become a prisoner

cautiverio /kauti'βerio/ *m*, captivity

cautivo /kau'tiβo/ **(-va)** *a* and *n* captive

cauto /'kauto/ *a* cautious; prudent; sly

cava /'kaβa/ *f*, digging (especially vines); wine cellar in royal palaces

cavador /kaβa'ðor/ **(-ra)** *n* digger, hoer

cavadura /kaβa'ðura/ *f*, digging, hoeing; sinking (wells)

cavar /ka'βar/ *vt* to dig, hoe; sink (wells); *vi* hollow; *Fig.* go deeply into a thing

caverna /ka'βerna/ *f*, cavern, cave; *Med.* cavity (generally in the lung)

cavernícola /kaβer'nikola/ *a* cave. **hombre c.**, caveman

cavernoso /kaβer'noso/ *a* cavernous; caverned; *Fig.* hollow (cough, etc.); deaf

cavidad /kaβi'ðað/ *f*, cavity; sinus; cell

cavilación /kaβila'sion; kaβila'θion/ *f*, caviling

cavilar /kaβi'lar/ *vt* to cavil; criticize

caviloso /kaβi'loso/ *a* captious

caz /kas; kaθ/ *m*, channel, canal; head-race, flume

caza /'kasa; 'kaθa/ *f*, hunting; hunt, chase; game. *m*, *Aer.* fighter. *Aer.* **c. lanzacohetes**, rocket-launching aircraft. **c. nocturno**, night fighter. *Naut.* **dar c.**, to pursue

cazaautógrafos /,kasaau'tografos; ,kaθaau'tografos/ *mf*, autograph hunter

cazabombardero /,kasaβombar'ðero; ,kaθaβombar'ðero/ *m*, *Aer.* fighter bomber

cazadero /kasa'ðero; kaθa'ðero/ *m*, hunting ground

cazador /kasa'ðor; kaθa'ðor/ *a* hunting. *m*, *Mil.* chasseur; huntsman

cazadora /kasa'ðora; kaθa'ðora/ *f*, huntress; jacket; forage cap

cazadotes /kasa'ðotes; kaθa'ðotes/ *m*, dowry hunter

cazafortunas /kasafor'tunas; kaθafor'tunas/ *mf* fortune hunter

cazar /ka'sar; ka'θar/ *vt* to hunt, chase; *Fig. Inf.* run to earth; *Fig. Inf.* catch out; *Inf.* overcome by flattery

cazasubmarino /kasasuβma'rino; kaθasuβma'rino/ *m*, submarine chaser

cazatorpedero /kasatorpe'ðero; kaθatorpe'ðero/ *m*, *Naut.* torpedo-boat destroyer

cazo /'kaso; 'kaθo/ *m*, ladle; dipper

cazolada /kaso'laða; kaθo'laða/ *f*, panful

cazoleta /kaso'leta; kaθo'leta/ *f*, small pan; bowl (of pipe, etc.); sword guard; boss of a shield; pan (of a firelock)

cazuela /ka'suela; ka'θuela/ *f*, earthenware cooking dish; stew-pot; part of theater formerly reserved for women; *Theat.* gallery

cazumbrón /kasum'βron; kaθum'βron/ *m*, cooper

cazurro /ka'surro; ka'θurro/ *a* *Inf.* unsociable; surly, boorish

c.c.p. /sese'pe; θeθe'pe/ abbrev. of **con copia para**

ce /se; θe/ *f*, name of the letter C. *interj* Look! Chist! **ce por be**, in detail

cebada /se'βaða; θe'βaða/ *f*, barley (plant and grain). **c. perlada**, pearl barley

cebadal /seβa'ðal; θeβa'ðal/ *m*, barley field

cebadera /seβa'ðera; θeβa'ðera/ *f*, nose-bag; barley bin

cebadero /seβa'ðero; θeβa'ðero/ *m*, barley dealer

cebado /se'βaðo; θe'βaðo/ *a* on the prowl; having tasted human flesh (animal)

cebar /se'βar; θe'βar/ *vt* to feed or fatten (animals); fuel, feed (furnace, etc.); prime, charge (fire-arms, etc.); start up (machines); bait (fish hook); stimulate (passion, etc.); *vi* stick in, penetrate (nails, screws, etc.); *vr* put one's mind to; grow angry. **cebarse en vanas esperanzas**, to nurture vain hopes

cebiche /θe'bit$\int$e/ *m*, dish of marinated raw fish

cebo /'seβo; 'θeβo/ *m*, fodder; detonator; encouragement, food; bait

cebolla /se'βoya; θe'βoΛa/ *f*, onion; onion bulb; any bulbous stem; oil bulb (of lamp). **c. escalonia**, shallot

cebollana /seβo'yana; θeβo'Λana/ *f*, chive

cebollero /seβo'yero; θeβo'Λero/ **(-ra)** *n* onion seller

cebolleta /seβo'yeta; θeβo'Λeta/ *f*, leek; young onion

cebollino /seβo'yino; θeβo'Λino/ *m*, onion seed; onion bed; chive

cebra /'seβra; 'θeβra/ *f*, zebra

ceca /'seka; 'θeka/ *f*, mint (for coining money); name of mosque in Cordova. **de C. en Meca**, from pillar to post, hither and thither

cecear /sese'ar; θeθe'ar/ *vi* to lisp

ceceo /se'seo; θe'θeo/ *m*, lisping, Spanish pronunciation of s as T

ceceoso /sese'oso; θeθe'oso/ *a* lisping

cecial /se'sial; θe'θial/ *m*, dried fish

cecina /se'sina; θe'θina/ *f*, dried salt meat

cedazo /se'ðaso; θe'ðaθo/ *m*, sieve, strainer

ceder /se'ðer; θe'ðer/ *vt* to cede, give up; transfer; *vi* give in, yield; diminish, decrease (fever, storm, etc.); fail, end; happen, turn out; sag, give, stretch. **No c. la fama a**, to be no less famous than. **ceda el paso**, yield right of way

cedro /'seðro; 'θeðro/ *m*, cedar tree; cedar wood. **c. dulce**, red cedar

cédula /'seðula; 'θeðula/ *f*, document, certificate, card. *Eccl.* **c. de comunión**, Communion card. **c. personal**, identity card. **c. real**, royal letters patent

céfiro /'sefiro; 'θefiro/ *m*, west wind; *Poet.* zephyr

cegajoso /sega'hoso; θega'hoso/ *a* blear-eyed

cegar /se'gar; θe'gar/ *vi irr* to become blind; *vt* to put out the eyes; *Fig.* blind; wall up, close up, stop up; infatuate. *Pres. Ind.* **ciego, ciegas, ciega, ciegan**. *Pres. Subjunc.* **ciegue, ciegues, ciegue, cieguen**

cegato /se'gato; θe'gato/ *a* *Inf.* short-sighted

ceguedad, ceguera /sege'ðað, se'gera; θege'ðað, θe'gera/ *f*, blindness; delusion; ignorance

Ceilán /sei'lan; θei'lan/ Ceylon

ceja /'seha; 'θeha/ *f*, eyebrow; cloud cap; mountain peak; *Mus.* bridge (of stringed instruments). *Fig.* **quemarse las cejas**, to burn the midnight oil

cejar /se'har; θe'har/ *vi* to go backwards; give way, hesitate

cejijunto /sehi'hunto; θehi'hunto/ *a* having eyebrows that almost meet, beetle-browed

cejo /'seho; 'θeho/ *m*, river mist

cejudo /se'huðo; θe'huðo/ *a* having long thick eyebrows

celada /se'laða; θe'laða/ *f*, helmet; ambush; fraud, trick

celador /sela'ðor; θela'ðor/ **(-ra)** *a* watchful, zealous. *n* supervisor; caretaker; guard (at a museum, etc.)

celaje /se'lahe; θe'lahe/ *m*, sky with scudding clouds (gen. *pl*); skylight, window; promising sign, presage

celar /se'lar; θe'lar/ *vt* to be zealous in discharge of duties; spy upon; watch; oversee, superintend; conceal; engrave

celda /'selda; 'θelda/ *f*, cell

celdilla /sel'diya; θel'diΛa/ *f*, cell (bees, wasps, etc.); (*Zool. Bot.*) cell; *Bot.* capsule

celebérrimo, /sele'βerrimo,; θele'βerrimo/ *a* *sup* **célebre** most celebrated

celebración /seleβra'sion; θeleβra'θion/ *f*, celebration; applause

celebrador /seleβra'ðor; θeleβra'ðor/ **(-ra)** *n* celebrator; applauder

celebrante /sele'βrante; θele'βrante/ *a* celebrating. *m*, *Eccl.* celebrant

celebrar /sele'βrar; θele'βrar/ *vt* to celebrate; applaud; praise; venerate; hold, conduct; **c. que** + *subj*, to be happy that, be glad that. *vt* and *vi* *Eccl.* officiate; *vr* take place

célebre /'seleβre; 'θeleβre/ *a* famous

celebridad /seleβri'ðað; θeleβri'ðað/ f, fame, celebrity; magnificence, show, pomp

celeridad /seleri'ðað; θeleri'ðað/ f, celerity

celeste /se'leste; θe'leste/ a celestial, heavenly

celestial /seles'tial; θeles'tial/ a celestial, heavenly; perfect, delightful; Inf. foolish (ironical)

celestina /seles'tina; θeles'tina/ f, procuress (allusion to Tragicomedia de Calixto y Melibea); Inf. matchmaker

celibato /seli'βato; θeli'βato/ m, celibacy; Inf. bachelor

célibe /'seliβe; 'θeliβe/ a celibate, unmarried. mf unmarried person

celo /'selo; 'θelo/ m, enthusiasm, ardor; religious zeal; devotion; jealousy; heat, rut; pl jealousy, suspicion. **dar celos (a),** to make jealous

celosía /selo'sia; θelo'sia/ f, lattice; Venetian blind

celoso /se'loso; θe'loso/ a zealous; jealous; suspicious

célula /'selula; 'θelula/ f, cell

celular /selu'lar; θelu'lar/ a cellular

celuloide /selu'loiðe; θelu'loiðe/ f, celluloid

celulosa /selu'losa; θelu'losa/ f, cellulose

celuloso /selu'loso; θelu'loso/ a cellular

cementación /sementa'sion; θementa'θion/ f, cementation

cementar /semen'tar; θemen'tar/ vt to cement

cementerio /semen'terio; θemen'terio/ m, cemetery

cemento /se'mento; θe'mento/ m, cement

cena /'sena; 'θena/ f, evening meal; supper. **La Última Cena,** Last Supper

cenacho /se'natʃo; θe'natʃo/ m, marketing bag

cenáculo /se'nakulo; θe'nakulo/ m, cenacle

cenador /sena'ðor; θena'ðor/ m, diner out; arbor, pergola

cenagal /sena'gal; θena'gal/ m, quagmire; Fig. impasse

cenagoso /sena'goso; θena'goso/ a miry, muddy

cenar /se'nar; θe'nar/ vi to dine, sup; vt eat for evening meal, sup off

cenceño /sen'seɲo; θen'θeɲo/ a slim, thin

cencerrada /sense'rraða; θenθe'rraða/ f, noisy mock serenade given to widows or widowers on the first night of their new marriage

cencerrear /senserre'ar; θenθerre'ar/ vi to jingle; Inf. play out of tune; bang in the wind, rattle; squeak

cencerreo /sense'rreo; θenθe'rreo/ m, jingling; jangle; rattling; squeaking

cencerro /sen'serro; θen'θerro/ m, cow-bell

cendal /sen'dal; θen'dal/ m, gauze; Eccl. stole; barbs of a feather

cenefa /se'nefa; θe'nefa/ f, border; valance; flounce; edging

cenicero /seni'sero; θeni'θero/ m, ash-pan; ash-pit; ash-tray

ceniciento /seni'siento; θeni'θiento/ a ash colored, ashen. **la Cenicienta,** Cinderella

cenit /'senit; 'θenit/ m, Astron. zenith; Fig. peak, summit

ceniza /se'nisa; θe'niθa/ f, ash, cinders

cenotafio /seno'tafio; θeno'tafio/ m, cenotaph

cenote /se'note; θe'note/ m, Central America, Mexico cenote (deep natural well or sinkhole)

censo /'senso; 'θenso/ m, census; agreement for settlement of an annuity; annual ground rent; leasehold

censor /sen'sor; θen'sor/ m, censor; censorious person; Educ. proctor

censual /sen'sual; θen'sual/ a pertaining to census, annuity, rents

censualista /sensua'lista; θensua'lista/ mf annuitant

censura /sen'sura; θen'sura/ f, censorship; criticism; blame, reproach; scandal, gossip; Psychol. censorship

censurable /sensu'raβle; θensu'raβle/ a reprehensible; censorable

censurar /sensu'rar; θensu'rar/ vt to judge; censure; criticize

centauro /sen'tauro; θen'tauro/ m, Myth. centaur

centavo /sen'taβo; θen'taβo/ m, hundredth part; cent; Lat. Am. centavo

centella /sen'teya; θen'teʎa/ f, lightning; spark; flash; Fig. spark (of anger, affection, etc.)

centellador /senteya'ðor; θenteʎa'ðor/ a flashing

centellear /senteye'ar; θenteʎe'ar/ vi to flash; twinkle; sparkle

centelleo /sente'yeo; θente'ʎeo/ m, scintillation; sparkle; flash

centén /sen'ten; θen'ten/ m, Spanish gold coin once worth 100 reals and later 25 pesetas

centena /sen'tena; θen'tena/ f, hundred

centenal, centenar /sente'nal, sente'nar; θente'nal, θente'nar/ m, hundred; centenary; rye field. **a centenares,** by the hundred, in crowds

centenario /sente'nario; θente'nario/ **(-ia)** a centenary. n centenarian. m, centenary

centeno /sen'teno; θen'teno/ m, Bot. rye

centésimo /sen'tesimo; θen'tesimo/ a and m, hundredth

centígrado /sen'tigraðo; θen'tigraðo/ a centigrade

centigramo /senti'gramo; θenti'gramo/ m, centigram

centilitro /senti'litro; θenti'litro/ m, centiliter

centímetro /senti'metro; θenti'metro/ m, centimeter. **c. cúbico,** cubic centimeter, milliliter

céntimo /'sentimo; 'θentimo/ a hundredth. m, centime (coin)

centinela /senti'nela; θenti'nela/ mf Mil. sentry, sentinel; person on watch. **estar de c.,** to be on sentry duty; be on guard

centolla /sen'toya; θen'toʎa/ f, marine crab

centón /sen'ton; θen'ton/ m, patchwork quilt

central /sen'tral; θen'tral/ a central; centric. f, head office; central depot; mother house. **c. de fuerza,** power-house. **c. telefónica,** telephone exchange

centralilla, centralita /sentra'liya, sentra'lita; θentra'liʎa, θentra'lita/ f, local exchange; private exchange

centralismo /sentra'lismo; θentra'lismo/ m, centralism

centralización /sentralisa'sion; θentraliθa'θion/ f, centralization

centralizador /sentralisa'ðor; θentraliθa'ðor/ a centralizing

centralizar /sentrali'sar; θentrali'θar/ vt to centralize

centrar /sen'trar; θen'trar/ vt to center

céntrico /'sentriko; 'θentriko/ a central, centric; centrally located; downtown

centrífugo /sen'trifugo; θen'trifugo/ a centrifugal

centrípeto /sen'tripeto; θen'tripeto/ a centripetal

centro /'sentro; 'θentro/ m, center; headquarters, meeting place, club; center, hub; middle; core (of a rope); Fig. focus. Phys. **c. de gravedad,** center of gravity. **c. de mesa,** table center-piece. Anat. **centro nervioso,** nerve center

Centroamérica /sentroa'merika; θentroa'merika/ f. Central America

centroamericano /sentroameri'kano; θentroameri'kano/ **(-na)** a and n Central American

céntuplo /'sentuplo; 'θentuplo/ a centuple

centuria /sen'turia; θen'turia/ f, century

ceñidamente /seɲiða'mente; θeɲiða'mente/ tightly (e.g. un argumento c. organizado, a tightly organized plot)

ceñido /se'ɲiðo; θe'ɲiðo/ a thrifty; wasp-waisted, slender waisted; fitting (of garments)

ceñidor /seɲi'ðor; θeɲi'ðor/ m, girdle, belt

ceñir /se'ɲir; θe'ɲir/ vt irr to girdle; surround; shorten, abbreviate; vr be moderate (speech, expenditure, etc.); conform, confine oneself (to). **ceñirse a las reglas,** to abide by the rules. Pres. Ind. **ciño, ciñes, ciñen.** Pres. Part. **ciñendo.** Preterite **ciñó, ciñeron.** Pres. Subjunc. **ciña, etc.** Imperf. Subjunc. **ciñese, etc.**

ceño /'seɲo; 'θeɲo/ m, band, hoop; frown; Fig. dark outlook

ceñudo /se'ɲuðo; θe'ɲuðo/ a frowning

cepa /'sepa; 'θepa/ f, stump; vine-stock; root (tails, antlers, etc.); Fig. origin, trunk (of a family); Biol. strain. **de la más pura c.,** of the best quality

cepillar /sepi'yar; θepi'ʎar/ *vt* to brush; plane; smooth

cepillo /se'piyo; θe'piʎo/ *m*, brush; plane; poor-box, offertory-box. **c. para los dientes,** toothbrush. **c. para ropa,** clothes-brush. **c. para el suelo,** scrubbing-brush. **c. para las uñas,** nail-brush

cepo /'sepo; 'θepo/ *m*, bough; wooden stocks; snare; trap; poor-box; collecting-box

cera /'sera; 'θera/ *f*, beeswax; wax; wax candles, etc., used at a function. *Inf.* **ser como una c.,** to be like wax (in the hands of)

cerador /sera'ðor; θera'ðor/ *m*, floor waxer (person)

ceradora /sera'ðora; θera'ðora/ *f*, floor waxer (machine)

cerámica /se'ramika; θe'ramika/ *f*, ceramics; ceramic art, pottery

cerámico /se'ramiko; θe'ramiko/ *a* ceramic

cerbatana /serβa'tana; θerβa'tana/ *f*, blow-pipe, pop-gun; pea-shooter; ear-trumpet

cerca /'serka; 'θerka/ *f*, fence, wall

cerca /'serka; 'θerka/ *adv* near. **c. de,** near to; almost, nearly (e.g. *c. de las once,* nearly eleven o'clock)

cercado /ser'kaðo; θer'kaðo/ *m*, enclosure, fenced in place; fence

cercanía /serka'nia; θerka'nia/ *f*, nearness, proximity; (*gen. pl*) outskirts, surroundings

cercano /ser'kano; θer'kano/ *a* near, neighboring; impending, early

cercar /ser'kar; θer'kar/ *vt* to enclose; build a wall or fence round; to lay siege to; crowd round; *Mil.* surround

cercenamiento /sersena'miento; θerθena'miento/ **(a)** *m*, curtailment (of)

cercenar /serse'nar; θerθe'nar/ *vt* to lop off the ends, clip; curtail, diminish; abridge; whittle

cerciorar /sersio'rar; θerθio'rar/ *vt* to assure, confirm; *vr* make sure

cerco /'serko; 'θerko/ *m*, ring, hoop; fence; siege; small conversational circle; spin, circling; halo (sun, moon); frame; sash (of a window). **poner c. (a),** to lay siege to, blockade

cerda /'serða; 'θerða/ *f*, sow; bristle

Cerdeña /ser'ðeɲa; θer'ðeɲa/ Sardinia

cerdo /'serðo; 'θerðo/ *m*, pig, hog

cerdoso /ser'ðoso; θer'ðoso/ *a* bristly

cereal /sere'al; θere'al/ *a* and *m*, cereal

cerebelo /sere'βelo; θere'βelo/ *m*, *Anat.* cerebellum

cerebral /sere'βral; θere'βral/ *a* cerebral

cerebro /se'reβro; θe're'βro/ *m*, cerebrum; brain; intelligence

cerebro-espinal /se'reβro-espi'nal; θe'reβro-espi'nal/ *a* cerebrospinal

ceremonia /sere'monia; θere'monia/ *f*, ceremony; function, display; formality. **de c.,** ceremonial; formally. **por c.,** for politeness' sake

ceremonial /seremo'nial; θeremo'nial/ *a* ceremonial. *m*, ceremony; rite; protocol (rules of behavior)

ceremonioso /seremo'nioso; θeremo'nioso/ *a* ceremonious; formal, over-courteous

cerero /se'rero; θe'rero/ *m*, wax-chandler

cereza /se'resa; θe'reθa/ *f*, cherry

cerezal /sere'sal; θere'θal/ *m*, cherry orchard

cerezo /se'reso; θe'reθo/ *m*, cherry tree; cherry wood

cerilla /se'riya; θe'riʎa/ *f*, wax taper; match; ear wax

cerillo /se'rijo; θe'riʎo/ *m*, *Mexico* matchstick

cerner /ser'ner; θer'ner/ *vt irr* to sieve; watch, observe; *Fig.* sift, clarify; *vi* bolt (of plants); drizzle; *vr* waddle; hover; threaten (of evil, etc.). *Pres. Ind.* **cierno, ciernes, cierne, ciernen.** *Pres. Subjunc.* **cierna, ciernas, cierna, ciernan**

cernícalo /ser'nikalo; θer'nikalo/ *m*, *Ornith.* kestrel; *Inf.* lout

cernidillo /serni'ðiyo; θerni'ðiʎo/ *m*, drizzle; teetering walk

cernido /ser'niðo; θer'niðo/ *m*, sifting, sieving; sifted flour

cerniduras /serni'ðuras; θerni'ðuras/ *f pl*, siftings

cero /'sero; 'θero/ *m*, *Math.* zero; naught; (tennis) love. *Fig. Inf.* **ser un c.,** to be a mere cipher

cerote /se'rote; θe'rote/ *m*, cobbler's wax. *Inf.* fear

cerquillo /ser'kiyo; θer'kiʎo/ *m*, tonsure; welt (of a shoe); *Lat. Am.* fringe

cerquita /ser'kita; θer'kita/ *adv* very near, hard by

cerradero /serra'ðero,; θerra'ðero/ *m*, **cerradera** *f*, bolt staple; catch of a lock; clasp or strings of a purse

cerradizo /serra'ðiso; θerra'ðiðo/ *a* closable, lockable

cerrado /se'rraðo; θe'rraðo/ *a* closed; compact; incomprehensible, obscure; overcast, cloudy; *Inf.* taciturn; secretive. *m*, enclosure

cerradura /serra'ðura; θerra'ðura/ *f*, fastening; lock; closing, locking

cerraja /se'rraha; θe'rraha/ *f*, lock (of a door); bolt

cerrajería /serrahe'ria; θerrahe'ria/ *f*, locksmith's craft; locksmith's workshop or shop

cerrajero /serra'hero; θerra'hero/ *m*, locksmith

cerramiento /serra'miento; θerra'miento/ *m*, closing, locking up; fence; enclosure, shooting preserve; partition wall

cerrar /se'rrar; θe'rrar/ *vt irr* to close; lock, fasten, bolt; shut up; *Mech.* shut off, turn off; fold up; block or stop up; seal (letters, etc.); close down; terminate; obstruct; (*with con*) attack; *vi* close; close in (of night, etc.); *vr* heal up (wounds); close (flowers); *Radio.* close down; crowd together; *Fig.* stand firm. *Inf.* **cerrarse la espuela,** to take a nightcap, have a last drink. **c. la marcha,** to bring up the rear. **al c. la edición,** stop press. See **acertar**

cerrazón /serra'son; θerra'θon/ *f*, dark, overcast sky heralding a storm

cerril /se'rril; θe'rril/ *a* rough, rocky; wild, untamed (cattle, horses); *inf* boorish

cerro /'serro; 'θerro/ *m*, neck of an animal; spine, backbone; hill. *Fig.* **irse por los cerros de Úbeda,** to go off the track, indulge in irrelevancies

cerrojo /se'rroho; θe'rroho/ *m*, bolt (of a door, etc.); lock (of a door, gun, etc.)

certamen /ser'tamen; θer'tamen/ *m*, contest; competition; match

certero /ser'tero; θer'tero/ *a* well-aimed; sure, well-timed; knowledgeable, sure

certeza, certidumbre /ser'tesa, serti'ðumbre; θer'teθa, θerti'ðumbre/ *f*, certitude, assurance

certificación /sertifika'sion; θertifika'θion/ *f*, certification; certificate; affidavit

certificado /sertifi'kaðo; θertifi'kaðo/ *a* certified; registered. *m*, registered letter; certificate

certificar /sertifi'kar; θertifi'kar/ *vt* to certify; register (letter, etc.)

certificatorio /sertifika'torio; θertifika'torio/ *a* certifying or serving to certify

certísimo /ser'tisimo; θer'tisimo/ *a* learned form of the superlative of **cierto** (see **certísimo**)

certitud /serti'tuð; θerti'tuð/ *f*, certitude

cervantino /serβan'tino; θerβan'tino/ *a* Cervantine

cervecería /serβese'ria; θerβese'ria/ *f*, brewery; ale-house

cervecero /serβe'sero; θerβe'θero/ **(-ra)** *n* brewer; beer seller

cerveza /ser'βesa; θer'βeθa/ *f*, beer, ale. **c. negra,** stout

cerviz /ser'βis; θer'βiθ/ *f*, cervix, nape (of neck). **doblar** (*or* **bajar**) **la c.,** to humble oneself

cesación /sesa'sion; θesa'θion/ *f*, cessation, stopping

cesante /se'sante; θe'sante/ *a* dismissed; pensioned off. **declarar c. (a),** to dismiss (a person from a post). **estar c.,** to be out of a job

cesantía /sesan'tia; θesan'tia/ *f*, status of dismissed or retired official; retirement pension

cesar /se'sar; θe'sar/ *vi* to cease, stop, end; leave an employment; desist; retire

cesáreo /se'sareo; θe'sareo/ *a* Cesarean; imperial

cese /'sese; 'θese/ *m*, stopping of payment for an employment

cesión /se'sion; θe'sion/ *f*, cession; transfer; resignation; *Law.* release

cesionario /sesio'nario; θesio'nario/ **(-ia)** *n* cessionary, transferee

césped /'sespeð; 'θespeð/ *m*, grass, sward; sod, lawn

cesta /'sesta; 'θesta/ *f*, basket, hamper; *Sports.* racket; cradle (for a wine bottle)

cestada /ses'taða; θes'taða/ f, basketful
cestería /seste'ria; θeste'ria/ f, basketmaking, basketweaving; basket factory; basket shop; basketwork
cestero /ses'tero; θes'tero/ **(-ra)** n basket maker or seller
cesto /'sesto; 'θesto/ m, basket, hamper, skip
cesura /se'sura; θe'sura/ f, cesura
cetorrino /seto'rrino; θeto'rrino/ m, basking shark
cetrería /setre'ria; θetre'ria/ f, falconry
cetrino /se'trino; θe'trino/ a greenish-yellow; sallow; citrine; melancholy; reserved, aloof
cetro /'setro; 'θetro/ m, scepter; verge; reign
chabacanería /tʃaβakane'ria/ f, bad taste; vulgarity
chabacano /tʃaβa'kano/ a vulgar, common; rude, uncouth
chacal /tʃa'kal/ m, Zool. jackal
cháchara /'tʃatʃara/ f, Inf. empty chatter; verbiage
chacharear /tʃatʃare'ar/ vi to chatter; gabble, cackle
chacharero /tʃatʃa'rero/ a Inf. chattering; talkative
chacolotear /tʃakolote'ar/ vi to clatter, clink (loose horseshoe)
chacota /tʃa'kota/ f, merriment, mirth
chacotear /tʃakote'ar/ vi Inf. to be merry, have fun
chacotón /tʃako'ton/ a of a boisterous humor
chacra /'tʃakra/ f, Lat. Am. small farm, small holding
chafado /tʃa'faðo/ a taken aback; disappointed
chafallar /tʃafa'yar; tʃafa'ʎar/ vt Inf. to mend carelessly, botch
chafandín /tʃafan'din/ m, vain fool
chafar /tʃa'far/ vt to flatten; crumple, crease (clothes); Inf. heckle
chafarrinar /tʃafarri'nar/ vt to stain, mark, blot
chaflán /tʃa'flan/ m, bevel edge, chamfer
chagrén /tʃa'gren/ m, shagreen leather
chagüe /'tʃage/ m, Central America bog, marsh, swamp
chal /tʃal/ m, shawl
chalán /tʃa'lan/ m, horse-dealer
chalana /tʃa'lana/ f, Naut. wherry, lighter
chalanear /tʃalane'ar/ vt to bargain; indulge in sharp practice
chalar /tʃa'lar/ vt to drive mad; enamor
chaleco /tʃa'leko/ m, waistcoat; cardigan
chalequear /tʃaleke'ar/ vt, Mexico to pilfer, swipe
chalina /tʃa'lina/ f, flowing scarf, artist's bow
Chalo /'tʃalo/ pet form of the male given name Carlos "Charles', hence = English Chuck; Bud, Mac (in direct address to a male whose name one does not know)
chalote /tʃa'lote/ m, shallot
chalupa /tʃa'lupa/ f, shallop; launch; canoe; long boat, ship's boat
chamar /tʃa'mar/ vt Inf. to palm off, barter
chamarasca /tʃama'raska/ f, brushwood, tinder
chamarilero /tʃamari'lero/ **(-ra)** n secondhand dealer
chamarreta /tʃama'rreta/ f, sheepskin jacket; Mexico jacket
chambergo /tʃam'βergo/ a pertaining to the Chambergo regiment. m, broad-brimmed hat
chambón /tʃam'βon/ a Inf. awkward, clumsy; lucky
chambonada /tʃambo'naða/ f, Inf. blunder; fluke, chance
chambra /'tʃambra/ f, dressing-jacket, peignoir, negligee
chamicera /tʃami'sera; tʃami'θera/ f, piece of scorched earth (woodland, etc.)
chamorro /tʃa'morro/ a close-cropped, shorn (hair), crew-cut
champán /tʃam'pan/ m, champagne. **c. obrero,** humorous cider
champaña /tʃam'paɲa/ m, champagne
champar /tʃam'par/ vt Inf. to cast in a person's face, remind
champú /tʃam'pu/ m, shampoo
chamuscar /tʃamus'kar/ vt to scorch; singe
chamusquina /tʃamus'kina/ f, scorching; singeing; Inf. brawl
chanada /tʃa'naða/ f, Inf. trick, mischievous act
chancaca /tʃan'kaka/ f, Lat. Am. syrup cake

chancada /tʃan'kaða/ f, Lat. Am. dirty trick
chancearse /tʃanse'arse; tʃanθe'arse/ vr to joke
chancero /tʃan'sero; tʃan'θero/ a joking, facetious
chancho, -a /'tʃantʃo/ mf, Lat. Am. pig
chanchollada /tʃantʃo'yaða; tʃantʃo'ʎaða/ f, dirty trick, foul play, trick
chanchullo /tʃan'tʃuyo; tʃan'tʃuʎo/ m, Inf. fraud
chanciller /tʃansi'yer; tʃanθi'ʎer/ m, chancellor
chancillería /tʃansiye'ria; tʃanθiʎe'ria/ f, chancery
chancla /'tʃankla/ f, down at heel shoe; heelless slipper
chancleta /tʃan'kleta/ f, heelless slipper, babouche. mf Inf. ninny
chanclo /'tʃanklo/ m, overshoe; Wellington
chanfaina /tʃan'faina/ f, Cul. savory fricassee
chanflón /tʃan'flon/ a tough, coarse; ungainly
changador /tʃanga'ðor/ m, Argentina porter
chantaje /tʃan'tahe/ m, blackmail
chantajista /tʃanta'hista/ mf blackmailer
chantar /tʃan'tar/ vt to put on, clothe; Inf. tell plainly. Inf. **c. sus verdades,** to tell hometruths
chanza /'tʃansa; 'tʃanθa/ f, joke, jest
chanzoneta /tʃanso'neta; tʃanθo'neta/ f, canzonetta; Inf. joke
¡chao! /'tʃao/ Argentina, Chile bye!
chapa /'tʃapa/ f, plate, sheet; veneer; clasp; Inf. prudence, common sense; rouge. **c. de hierro,** sheetiron. **c. de identidad,** number plate
chapado a la antigua /tʃa'paðo a la an'tigua/ a old-fashioned
chapalear /tʃapale'ar/ vi to dabble in water; splash; clatter (of a horseshoe)
chapaleo /tʃapa'leo/ m, dabbling, paddling; splash; clattering, clink (of a horseshoe)
chapaleteo /tʃapale'teo/ m, lapping of water; splashing (of rain)
chaparrear /tʃaparre'ar/ vi to pour with rain
chaparrón /tʃapa'rron/ m, heavy shower of rain, downpour
chapear /tʃape'ar/ vt to veneer; vi clatter (loose horseshoe)
chaperón /tʃape'ron/ m, hood
chapeta /tʃa'peta/ f, dim clasp; red flush or spot on cheek
chapetón /tʃape'ton/ **(-ona)** n West Hem. recently arrived European, especially Spaniard
chapín /tʃa'pin/ m, cork-soled leather overshoe (for women) Obs.
chapino /tʃa'pino/ a and m, Mexico contemptuous Guatemalan
chapodar /tʃapo'ðar/ vt to prune, lop off branches; cut down, reduce
chapotear /tʃapote'ar/ vt to sponge, moisten, damp; vt paddle, splash; dabble or trail the hands (in water)
chapoteo /tʃapo'teo/ m, moistening, sponging; paddling, splashing; dabbling
chapucear /tʃapuse'ar; tʃapuθe'ar/ vt to botch, do badly; bungle
chapuceramente /tʃapusera'mente; tʃapuθera'mente/ adv awkwardly. **hablar el japonés c.,** to speak broken Japanese
chapucería /tʃapuse'ria; tʃapuθe'ria/ f, roughness, poor workmanship; botch
chapucero /tʃapu'sero; tʃapu'θero/ a rough, badly finished; bungling, clumsy, awkward
chapurrado /tʃapu'rraðo/ a broken (e.g. hablar un italiano c., to speak broken Italian)
chapurrar, chapurrear /tʃapu'rrar, tʃapurre'ar/ vt to speak badly (a language); jabber; Inf. mix (drinks)
chapuz /tʃa'pus; tʃa'puθ/ m, ducking, submerging; plunge; unimportant job; clumsiness
chapuzar /tʃapu'sar; tʃapu'θar/ vt to duck, submerge; plunge
chaqué /tʃa'ke/ m, morning coat; morning suit
chaqueta /tʃa'keta/ f, jacket; Mech. casing
chaquete /tʃa'kete/ m, backgammon
chaquetilla /tʃake'tiya; tʃake'tiʎa/ f, short jacket; coatee; blazer
chaquetón /tʃake'ton/ m, short coat. **c. de piloto,** Aer. pea-jacket

charabán /tʃara'βan/ m, charabanc

charada /tʃa'raða/ f, charade

charamusca /tʃara'muska/ f, Lat. Am. firewood, kindling

charanguero /tʃaraŋ'guero/ a rough, badly finished; clumsy. m, Andalusian boat

charca /'tʃarka/ f, pond, pool; reservoir

charco /'tʃarko/ m, puddle; Inf. sea

charla /'tʃarla/ f, Inf. chatter; conversation; talk, informal lecture

charlar /'tʃarlar/ vi Inf. to prattle, chatter; chat, converse; give a talk (on)

charlatán /tʃarla'tan/ (-ana) a loquacious, garrulous; indiscreet; fraudulent, false. n charlatan; chatterer

charlatanería /tʃarlatane'ria/ f, loquacity, garrulity; quackery

charlatanismo /tʃarlata'nismo/ m, charlatanism, quackery

charnela /tʃar'nela/ f, hinge; hinged joint

charol /tʃa'rol/ m, varnish; patent leather

charolar /tʃaro'lar/ vt to varnish

charolista /tʃaro'lista/ mf, varnisher

charpa /'tʃarpa/ f, pistol-belt; sling

charrán /tʃa'rran/ (-ana) n rogue, trickster

charranada /tʃarra'naða/ f, roguery, knavery

charrería /tʃarre'ria/ f, tawdriness; gaudiness

charretera /tʃarre'tera/ f, Mil. epaulet; garter

charro /'tʃarro/ a churlish, coarse; flashy, tawdry

chasca /'tʃaska/ f, brushwood, firewood

chascar /tʃas'kar/ vi to creak, crack; clack (the tongue); swallow

chascarrillo /tʃaska'rriyo; tʃaska'rriʎo/ m, Inf. amusing anecdote, good story

chasco /'tʃasko/ m, trick, practical joke; disappointment. **llevarse un c.,** to meet with a disappointment

chasis /'tʃasis/ m, Auto. chassis; Photo. plate-holder; Mech. underframe

chasquear /tʃaske'ar/ vt to play a trick on; wag (one's tongue); crack (a whip, one's knuckles); break a promise, disappoint; vi creak, crack; meet with a disappointment

chasquido /tʃas'kiðo/ m, crack (of whip); creaking (of wood); click (of the tongue)

chatarra /tʃa'tarra/ f, scrap iron; junk

chato /'tʃato/ a flat-nosed; flat

chauvinismo /tʃauβi'nismo/ m, chauvinism

chaval /tʃa'βal/ a Inf. young. m, lad

chaveta /tʃa'βeta/ f, Mech. bolt, pin, peg, cotter, key

checo /'tʃeko/ (-ca) a and n Czech. Czech (language)

Chejov /tʃe'hoβ/ Chekhov

chelín /tʃe'lin/ m, shilling

Chengis-Jan /tʃenhis-'han/ Genghis Khan

chepa /'tʃepa/ f, Inf. hunch (back); hump

cheque /'tʃeke/ m, check. **c. cruzado,** crossed check

chica /'tʃika/ f, girl; Inf. dear

chicana /tʃi'kana/ f, chicanery

chicano /tʃi'kano/ (-na) a and n Chicano, American of Mexican ancestry

chicha /'tʃitʃa/ f, Lat. Am. corn liquor

chícharo /'tʃitʃaro/ m, pea

chicharrón /tʃitʃa'rron/ m, Cul. crackling; burnt meat; Inf. sunburned person

chichón /tʃi'tʃon/ m, bruise, bump

chichonera /tʃitʃo'nera/ f, child's protective hat (something like a straw crash-helmet)

chicle /'tʃikle/ m, chewing gum

chiclero /tʃi'klero/ m, chicle-gatherer

chico /'tʃiko/ a little, small; young. m, little boy; youth; Inf. old boy, dear. **Es un buen c.,** He's a good fellow

chicoleo /tʃiko'leo/ m, Inf. compliment

chicote /tʃi'kote/ mf sturdy child. m, Inf. cigar; Lat. Am. whip

chifla /'tʃifla/ f, whistling, whistle; tanner's paring knife

chiflado /tʃi'flaðo/ a Inf. cracked, daft; crack-brained

chifladura /tʃifla'ðura/ f, whistling; Inf. whim, mania, hobby

chiflar /tʃi'flar/ vi to whistle; vt to make fun of, hiss;

pare or scrape leather; Inf. swill, tipple; vr Inf. have a slate loose; be slightly mad; Inf. lose one's head over, adore

chifle /'tʃifle/ m, whistle, whistling; decoy call (birds)

chiflón /tʃi'flon/ m, Lat. Am. draft (of air)

chile /'tʃile/ m, Bot. red pepper, chilli

chileno /tʃi'leno/ (-na) a and n Chilean

chilla /'tʃija; 'tʃiʎa/ f, Argentina fox

chillador /tʃiya'ðor; tʃiʎa'ðor/ a screaming, shrieking

chillar /tʃi'yar; tʃi'ʎar/ vi to scream, shriek; creak; squeak; jabber (monkeys, etc.); Art. be strident (of colors)

chillería /tʃiye'ria; tʃiʎe'ria/ f, shrieking, screaming

chillido /tʃi'yiðo; tʃi'ʎiðo/ m, scream, shriek; squeak (of mice, etc.); jabber (of monkeys, etc.)

chillón /tʃi'yon; tʃi'ʎon/ a Inf. screaming, yelling; strident, piercing; crude, loud (colors)

chimenea /tʃime'nea/ f, chimney; funnel; fireplace; kitchen range

chimpancé /tʃimpan'se; tʃimpan'θe/ m, chimpanzee

china /'tʃina/ f, pebble; porcelain, china; Chinese silk

chinche /'tʃintʃe/ f, bedbug; thumbtack, drawing-pin. mf Inf. bore

chinchona /tʃin'tʃona/ f, quinine

chinchorrería /tʃintʃorre'ria/ f, Inf. impertinence, tediousness; gossip

chinela /tʃi'nela/ f, mule, slipper; overshoe, patten Obs.

chinero /tʃi'nero/ m, china cupboard

chinesco /tʃi'nesko/ a Chinese. **a la chinesca,** in Chinese fashion

chingana /tʃiŋ'gana/ f, Lat. Am. bar

chino /'tʃino/ (-na) a and n Chinese. m, Chinese (language)

Chipre /'tʃipre/ Cyprus

chiquero /tʃi'kero/ m, pigsty; stable for bulls

chiquillada /tʃiki'yaða; tʃiki'ʎaða/ f, childishness, puerility

chiquillería /tʃikiye'ria; tʃikiʎe'ria/ f, Inf. crowd of children

chiquillo /tʃi'kiyo; tʃi'kiʎo/ (-lla) n small boy

chiquito /tʃi'kito/ (-ta) a dim chico, tiny, very small. n little one, small boy

chiripa /tʃi'ripa/ f, (billiards) fluke; Inf. happy coincidence, stroke of luck; lucky guess

chirivía /tʃiri'βia/ f, Bot. parsnip; Ornith. wagtail

chirlar /tʃir'lar/ vi Inf. to gabble, talk loudly

chirlo /'tʃirlo/ m, knife wound, saber cut; knife scar

chirona /tʃi'rona/ f, Inf. jail

chirriador /tʃirria'ðor/ a sizzling, crackling; creaking, squeaking

chirriar /tʃi'rriar/ vi to sizzle, crackle; creak, squeak; squawk; Inf. croak, sing out of tune

chirrido /tʃi'rriðo/ m, squawk; croaking; noise of grasshoppers; squeaking; creaking, creak

¡chis! /tʃis/ interj Shh! Silence!

chisme /'tʃisme/ m, gossip, tale; Inf. small household utensil, trifle

chismear /tʃisme'ar/ vt to tell tales, gossip

chismero /tʃis'mero/ (-ra), **chismoso** (-sa) a gossiping, talebearing. n gossip, tale bearer

chispa /'tʃispa/ f, spark; ember; Elec. spark; tiny diamond; small particle; wit; quickwittedness; Inf. drunkenness. **c. del encendido,** ignition spark

chispazo /tʃis'paso; tʃis'paθo/ m, flying out of a spark, sparking; damage done by spark; Inf. gossip, rumor

chispeante /tʃispe'ante/ a sparking; sparkling; Fig. scintillating (with wit etc.)

chispear /tʃispe'ar/ vi to throw out sparks, spark; sparkle, gleam; Fig. scintillate; drizzle gently

chisporrotear /tʃisporrote'ar/ vi Inf. to sputter; fizz

chisposo /tʃis'poso/ a sputtering, throwing out sparks

chistar /tʃis'tar/ vi to speak, break silence (gen. used negatively)

chiste /'tʃiste/ m, witticism, bon mot; amusing incident; joke

chistera /tʃis'tera/ f, creel (for fish); Inf. top-hat, tile

chistoso /tʃis'toso/ a joking; amusing, funny

chiticallando /tʃitika'yando; tʃitika'ʎando/ adv quietly, stealthily; Inf. on the quiet, in secret

¡chito! ¡chitón! /'tʃito tʃi'ton/ interj Hush! Sh!

chiva /'tʃiβa/ f, Colombia, Panama bus; Venezuela beard, goatee; **chivas** f, Venezuela hand-me-downs

chivo /'tʃiβo/ n Zool. kid. **c. expiatorio**, scapegoat

chocante /tʃo'kante/ a colliding; provoking; shocking; surprising

chocar /tʃo'kar/ vi to collide; strike (against); run into; fight, clash; vt clink (glasses); provoke, annoy; surprise, shock. **¡Choca cinco!** Clasp five!, Gimme five!, Put it there!, Give some skin! (invitation to shake hands)

chocarrería /tʃokarre'ria/ f, coarse joke

chochear /tʃotʃe'ar/ vi to be senile; Fig. Inf. dote (on)

chocho /'tʃotʃo/ a senile; Fig. Inf. doting

choco /'tʃoko/ m, small hump, hunchback

chocolate /tʃoko'late/ m, chocolate; drinking chocolate. **c. a la española**, thick chocolate. **c. a la francesa**, French drinking chocolate

chocolatería /tʃokolate'ria/ f, chocolate factory or shop

chocolatero /tʃokola'tero/ **(-ra)** a fond of chocolate. n chocolate maker or seller

chófer /'tʃofer/ m, chauffeur; driver

chompa /'tʃompa/ f, Lat. Am. jumper, pullover

chonta /'tʃonta/ f, Lat. Am. palm tree

chopera /tʃo'pera/ f, grove or plantation of black poplar trees

chopo /'tʃopo/ m, Bot. black poplar; Inf. gun

choque /'tʃoke/ m, collision; shock; jar; Med. concussion; fight; clink (of glasses); clash; Mil. skirmish

choricera /tʃori'sera; tʃori'θera/ f, sausage-making machine

choricero /tʃori'sero; tʃori'θero/ **(-ra)** n sausage maker

chorizo /tʃo'riso; tʃo'riθo/ m, kind of pork sausage; counterweight

chorrear /tʃorre'ar/ vi to spout, jet; drip; Fig. Inf. trickle, arrive slowly

chorreo /tʃo'rreo/ m, drip, dripping; spouting, gushing

chorrera /tʃo'rrera/ f, spout; drip; jabot, lace front

chorro /'tʃorro/ m, jet; stream (of water, etc.); Fig. shower. **a chorros**, in a stream; in abundance, plentifully

chova /'tʃoβa/ f, rook; carrion crow; jackdaw

choza /'tʃosa; 'tʃoθa/ f, hut, cabin; cottage

chubasco /tʃu'βasko/ m, squall, downpour; storm; transitory misfortune

chuchería /tʃutʃe'ria/ f, gewgaw, trinket; savory titbit; snaring, trapping

chucruta /tʃu'kruta/ f, sauerkraut

chueca /'tʃueka/ f, round head of a bone; small ball; game like shinty; Inf. practical joke

chueco /'tʃueko/ a Mexico bent, crooked, twisted

chufa /'tʃufa/ f, Bot. chufa; Inf. joke, trick

chufería /tʃufe'ria/ f, place where drink made of **chufas** is sold

chufla /'tʃufla/ f, flippant remark

chufleta /tʃu'fleta/ f, Inf. joke; taunt

chulada /tʃu'laða/ f, mean trick, base action; drollery

chulería /tʃule'ria/ f, drollness; attractive personality

chuleta /tʃu'leta/ f, Cul. cutlet, chop; mutton-chop; Inf. slap

chulo /'tʃulo/ a droll, amusing; attractive. m, slaughterhouse worker; bullfighter's assistant; pimp; rogue

chumbera /tʃum'βera/ f, prickly pear; Indian fig

chupada /tʃu'paða/ f, sucking; suck; suction

chupado de cara, c. de mofletes /mof'letes; tʃu'paðo de 'kara/ a lantern-jawed

chupador /tʃupa'ðor/ a sucking. m, baby's comforter or dummy

chupar /tʃu'par/ vt to suck; absorb (of plants); Fig. Inf. drain, rob; vr grow thin. **chuparse los dedos**, Inf. to lick one's lips; be delighted

chupatintas /tʃupa'tintas/ mf, Inf. scrivener, clerk (scornful)

churdón /tʃur'ðon/ m, raspberry cane; raspberry; raspberry vinegar

churrería /tʃurre'ria/ f, place where **churros** are made or sold

churrero /tʃu'rrero/ **(-ra)** n maker or seller of **churros**

churrigueresco /tʃurrige'resko/ a Churrigueresque

churro /'tʃurro/ a coarse (of wool). m, Cul. a kind of fritter eaten with chocolate, coffee, etc.

churumbela /tʃurum'βela/ f, Mus. pipe; reed for drinking mate West Hem.

chusco /'tʃusko/ a droll, witty, amusing

chusma /'tʃusma/ f, galley hands, crew; rabble, mob

chutar /tʃu'tar/ vt Sports. to shoot (a goal)

chuzo /'tʃuso; 'tʃuθo/ m, Mil. pike

chuzón /tʃu'son; tʃu'θon/ a wily, suspicious, cunning

cianuro /sia'nuro; θia'nuro/ m, cyanide

ciar /siar; θiar/ vi to go backwards; Naut. row backwards; Fig. make no headway (negotiations)

ciática /'siatika; 'θiatika/ f, sciatica

ciático /'siatiko; 'θiatiko/ a sciatic

ciberespacio /θiβeres'paθio/ m, cyberspace

cicatería /sikate'ria; θikate'ria/ f, niggardliness, avarice

cicatero /sika'tero; θika'tero/ a avaricious, niggardly, mean

cicatriz /sika'tris; θika'triθ/ f, cicatrice; Fig. scar, mark, impression

cicatrizar /sikatri'sar; θikatri'θar/ vt to cicatrize, heal; vr scar over

cíclico /'sikliko; 'θikliko/ a cyclic, cyclical

ciclismo /si'klismo; θi'klismo/ m, bicycling

ciclista /si'klista; θi'klista/ mf cyclist

ciclo /'siklo; 'θiklo/ m, cycle (of time). **c. artúrico, c. de Artús,** Arthurian Cycle. **c. de conferencias,** series of lectures

ciclón /si'klon; θi'klon/ m, cyclone

ciclópeo /si'klopeo; θi'klopeo/ a cyclopean

cicuta /si'kuta; θi'kuta/ f, hemlock

cid /siδ; θiδ/ m, great warrior, chief. **el Cid,** national hero of Spanish wars against the Moors

cidra /'siδra; 'θiδra/ f, citron

cidro /'siðro; 'θiðro/ m, citron tree

ciego /'siego; 'θiego/ a blind; dazed, blinded; choked up. m, blind man; Anat. cæcum. **a ciegas,** blindly, heedlessly

cielo /'sielo; 'θielo/ m, sky, firmament; atmosphere; climate; paradise; Providence; bliss, glory; roof, canopy; Inf. darling. **a c. abierto,** in the open air. **parecer una c.,** to be heavenly

ciempiés /siem'pies; θiem'pies/ m, centipede

cien /sien; θien/ a abb. **ciento,** hundred. Used always before substantives (e.g. c. hombres, 100 men)

ciénaga /'sienaga; 'θienaga/ f, swamp; morass

ciencia /'siensia; 'θienθia/ f, science; knowledge; erudition, ability. **ciencias naturales,** natural science. **a c. cierta,** for certain, without doubt (gen. with saber)

cienmilésimo /siemi'lesimo; θiemi'lesimo/ a hundred-thousandth

cieno /'sieno; 'θieno/ m, slime, mud; silt

científico /sien'tifiko; θien'tifiko/ a scientific. m, scientist

ciento /'siento; 'θiento/ (cf. **cien**) a hundred; hundredth. m, hundred. **por c.,** per cent.

cierne, en /'sierne, en; 'θierne, en/ in flower; Fig. in the early stages, in embryo

cierre /'sierre; 'θierre/ m, closing, shutting; closing time of shops, etc.; fastening; fastener; clasp (of a necklace, handbag, etc.). **c. cremallera,** zip fastener. **c. metálico,** doorshutter

ciertamente /sierta'mente; θierta'mente/ adv certainly; undoubtedly; indeed

ciertísimo /sier'tisimo; θier'tisimo/ a everyday form of the superlative of **cierto** (see **certisimo**)

cierto /'sierto; 'θierto/ a certain, sure; true; particular (e.g. c. hombre, a certain man (note no def. art.)). **un c. sabor,** a special flavor. **una cosa cierta,** something certain. **no, por c.,** no, certainly not. **por c.,** truly, indeed

cierva /'sierβa; 'θierβa/ f, hind

ciervo /'sierβo; 'θierβo/ m, stag. **c. volante,** stag-beetle

cierzo /'sierso; 'θierθo/ m, northerly wind

cifra /'sifra; 'θifra/ *f*, number; figure; sum total; cipher, code; monogram; abbreviation

cifrar /si'frar; θi'frar/ *vt* to write in cipher; summarize, abridge; (*with en*) be dependent on; depend on

cigarra /si'garra; θi'garra/ *f*, *Ent.* cicada, harvest fly

cigarral /siga'rral; θiga'rral/ *m*, (Toledo) country-house and orchard

cigarrera /siga'rrera; θiga'rrera/ *f*, woman who makes or sells cigars; cigar-cabinet; cigar-case

cigarrería /sigarre'ria; θigarre'ria/ *f*, *Lat. Am.* tobacco shop

cigarrillo /siga'rriyo; θiga'rriʎo/ *m*, cigarette

cigarro /si'garro; θi'garro/ *m*, cigar; *Lat. Am.* cigarette

cigüeña /si'gueɲa; θi'gueɲa/ *f*, *Ornith.* stork; *Mech.* crank

ciliar /si'liar; θi'liar/ *a* ciliary

cilicio /si'lisio; θi'liθio/ *m*, hairshirt

cilindrar /silin'drar; θilin'drar/ *vt* to roll; calendar; bore

cilindrero /silin'drero; θilin'drero/ *m*, organ grinder

cilíndrico /si'lindriko; θi'lindriko/ *a* cylindrical

cilindro /si'lindro; θi'lindro/ *m*, cylinder; roller

cima /'sima; 'θima/ *f*, summit; top of trees; apex; *Archit.* coping; head (thistle, etc.); *Fig.* aim, goal, end

cimbalero /simba'lero; θimba'lero/ (**-ra**) *n* cymbalist

címbalo /'simbalo; 'θimbalo/ *m*, cymbal

cimborrio /sim'βorrio; θim'βorrio/ *m*, *Archit.* cupola; cimborium

cimbrar, cimbrear /sim'βrar, simbre'ar; θim'βrar, θimbre'ar/ *vt* to bend; brandish; *vr* sway (in walking)

cimbreño /sim'βreɲo; θim'βreɲo/ *a* graceful, lithe, willowy

cimbreo /sim'βreo; θim'βreo/ *m*, swaying, bending

cimbrón /sim'βron; θim'βron/ *m*, *Lat. Am.* vibration

cimentar /simen'tar; θimen'tar/ *vt irr* to lay foundations; refine (gold, metals, etc.); found; *Fig.* ground (in virtue, etc.). See **acertar**

cimera /si'mera; θi'mera/ *f*, crest of helmet

cimiento /si'miento; θi'miento/ *m*, foundation (of a building); bottom; groundwork; origin, base. **abrir los cimientos,** to lay the foundations

cimitarra /simi'tarra; θimi'tarra/ *f*, scimitar

cinabrio /si'naβrio; θi'naβrio/ *m*, cinnabar; vermilion

cinc /sink; θink/ *m*, zinc

cincel /sin'sel; θin'θel/ *m*, chisel; burin, engraver

cincelador /sinsela'ðor; θinθela'ðor/ (**-ra**) *n* engraver; chiseler

cincelar /sinse'lar; θinθe'lar/ *vt* to chisel; carve; engrave

cincha /'sintʃa; 'θintʃa/ *f*, girth of a saddle

cinchar /sin'tʃar; θin'tʃar/ *vt* to tighten the saddle girths

cincho /'sintʃo; 'θintʃo/ *m*, belt, girdle; iron hoop

cinco /'sinko; 'θinko/ *a* and *m*, five; fifth. **a las c.,** at five o'clock

cincuenta /sin'kuenta; θin'kuenta/ *a* and *m*, fifty; fiftieth

cincuentavo /sinkuen'taβo; θinkuen'taβo/ *a* fiftieth

cincuentenario /sinkuente'nario; θinkuente'nario/ *m*, fiftieth anniversary

cincuentón /sinkuen'ton; θinkuen'ton/ (**-ona**) *a* and *n* fifty years old (person)

cine, cinema /'sine, si'nema; 'θine, θi'nema/ *m*, cinema, movies. **c. sonoro,** sound film

cinemática /sine'matika; θine'matika/ *f*, *Phys.* kinematics

cinematografía /sinematogra'fia; θinematogra'fia/ *f*, cinematography

cinematografiar /sinematogra'fiar; θinematogra'fiar/ *vt* to film

cinematográfico /sinemato'grafiko; θinemato'grafiko/ *a* cinematographic

cinematógrafo /sinema'tografo; θinema'tografo/ *m*, motion-picture camera; cinema

cínico /'siniko; 'θiniko/ *a* cynical; impudent; untidy. *m*, cynic

cinismo /si'nismo; θi'nismo/ *m*, cynicism

cinta /'sinta; 'θinta/ *f*, ribbon; tape; strip; film (cinematograph). **c. métrica,** tape-measure

cintillo /sin'tiyo; θin'tiʎo/ *m*, hatband; small ring set with gems

cinto /'sinto; 'θinto/ *m*, belt, girdle. **c. de pistolas,** pistol-belt

cintoteca /sinto'teka; θinto'teka/ *f*, tape library

cintura /sin'tura; θin'tura/ *f*, waist; belt, girdle

cinturón /sintu'ron; θintu'ron/ *m*, large waist; belt girdle; sword-belt; that which encircles or surrounds. **c. de seguridad,** seat belt

ciprés /si'pres; θi'pres/ *m*, *Bot.* cypress tree or wood

cipresal /sipre'sal; θipre'sal/ *m*, cypress grove

cipresino /sipre'sino; θipre'sino/ *a* cypress; cypress-like

circasiano /sirka'siano; θirka'siano/ (**-na**) *a* and *n* Circassian

circo /'sirko; 'θirko/ *m*, circus; amphitheater

circón /sir'kon; θir'kon/ *m*, zircon

circuir /sir'kuir; θir'kuir/ *vt. irr* to surround, encircle. See **huir**

circuito /sir'kuito; θir'kuito/ *m*, periphery; contour; (*Elec. Phys.*) circuit. **corto c.,** short circuit

circulación /sirkula'sion; θirkula'θion/ *f*, circulation; traffic. **c. de la sangre,** circulation of the blood. **calle de gran c.,** busy street

circular /sirku'lar; θirku'lar/ *a* circular. *f*, circular. *vt* to pass round; *vi* circle; circulate; move in a circle; move about; run, travel (traffic)

circulatorio /sirkula'torio; θirkula'torio/ *a* circulatory

círculo /'sirkulo; 'θirkulo/ *m*, circle; circumference; circuit; casino, social club

circuncidar /sirkunsi'ðar; θirkunθi'ðar/ *vt* to circumcise; modify, reduce

circuncisión /sirkunsi'sion; θirkunθi'sion/ *f*, circumcision

circunciso /sirkun'siso; θirkun'θiso/ *a* circumcised

circundar /sirkun'dar; θirkun'dar/ *vt* to surround

circunferencia /sirkunfe'rensia; θirkunfe'renθia/ *f*, circumference

circunflejo /sirkun'fleho; θirkun'fleho/ *a* circumflex. **acento c.,** circumflex accent

circunlocución /sirkunloku'sion; θirkunloku'θion/ *f*, circumlocution

circunnavegación /sirkunnaβega'sion; θirkunnaβega'θion/ *f*, circumnavigation

circunnavegar /sirkunnaβe'gar; θirkunnaβe'gar/ *vt* to circumnavigate

circunscribir /sirkunskri'βir; θirkunskri'βir/ *vt* to circumscribe. *Past Part.* **circunscrito**

circunscripción /sirkunskrip'sion; θirkunskrip'θion/ *f*, circumscription

circunspección /sirkunspek'sion; θirkunspek'θion/ *f*, circumspection; seriousness, dignity

circunspecto /sirkuns'pekto; θirkuns'pekto/ *a* circumspect; serious, dignified

circunstancia /sirkuns'tansia; θirkuns'tanθia/ *f*, circumstance; incident, detail; condition. **c. agravante,** aggravating circumstance. **c. atenuante,** extenuating circumstance. **bajo las circunstancias,** under the circumstances. **de circunstancias,** occasional (e.g. *poesías de circunstancias,* occasional verse). **estar al nivel de las circunstancias,** to rise to the occasion

circunstanciado /sirkunstan'siaðo; θirkunstan'θiaðo/ *a* circumstantiated, detailed

circunstancial /sirkunstan'sial; θirkunstan'θial/ *a* circumstantial; occasional (e.g. *poesías circunstanciales,* occasional verse)

circunstante /sirkuns'tante; θirkuns'tante/ *a* surrounding; present. *mf* person present, bystander

circunvecino /sirkumbe'sino; θirkumbe'θino/ *a* adjacent, neighboring

circunvolución /sirkumbolu'sion; θirkumbolu'θion/ *f*, circumvolution

cirial /si'rial; θi'rial/ *m*, processional candlestick

cirio /'sirio; 'θirio/ *m*, wax candle

cirro /'sirro; 'θirro/ *m*, *Med.* scirrhus; *Bot.* tendril; *Zool.* cirrus

cirrosis /si'rrosis; θi'rrosis/ *f*, cirrhosis

cirroso /si'rroso; θi'rroso/ a Med. scirrhous; (Zool. Bot.) cirrose

ciruela /si'ruela; θi'ruela/ f, plum; prune. **c. claudia, c. veidal,** greengage. **c. damascena,** damson

ciruelo /si'ruelo; θi'ruelo/ m, plum tree

cirugía /siru'hia; θiru'hia/ f, surgery

cirujano /siru'hano; θiru'hano/ m, surgeon

cisco /'sisko; 'θisko/ m, coal dust, slack coal; Inf. hubbub, quarrel

cisma /'sisma; 'θisma/ m, or f, schism; disagreement, discord. **el C. de Occidente,** the Western Schism

cismático /sis'matiko; θis'matiko/ a schismatic; discordant, inharmonious

cisne /'sisne; 'θisne/ m, swan

cisterciense /sister'siense; θister'θiense/ a Cistercian

cisterna /sis'terna; θis'terna/ f, water-tank, cistern

cístico /'sistiko; 'θistiko/ a cystic

cistitis /sis'titis; θis'titis/ f, cystitis

cita /'sita; 'θita/ f, appointment; quotation, citation

citable /si'taβle; θi'taβle/ a quotable

citación /sita'sion; θita'θion/ f, quotation; Law. summons

citar /si'tar; θi'tar/ vt to make an appointment; cite, quote; Law. summon. **c. en comparecencia,** to summon to appear in court

cítara /'sitara; 'θitara/ f, Mus. zither

citatorio /sita'torio; θita'torio/ m, summons

citerior /site'rior; θite'rior/ a hither, nearer

citrato /si'trato; θi'trato/ m, Chem. citrate

cítrico /'sitriko; 'θitriko/ a citric

ciudad /siu'ðað; θiu'ðað/ f, city; municipal body. **la c. señorial,** the Aristocratic City (Ponce, Puerto Rico)

ciudadanía /siuðaða'nia; θiuðaða'nia/ f, citizenship

ciudadano /siuða'ðano; θiuða'ðano/ **(-na)** a city; civic, born in or belonging to a city. n citizen; burgess; bourgeois. **c. de honor,** freeman (of a city)

ciudadela /siuða'ðela; θiuða'ðela/ f, citadel

cívico /'siβiko; 'θiβiko/ a civic; patriotic; Lat. Am. police officer

civicultura /siβikul'tura; θiβikul'tura/ f, raising of civets

civil /si'βil; θi'βil/ a civil; civilian; polite

civilidad /siβili'ðað; θiβili'ðað/ f, politeness, civility

civilización /siβilisa'sion; θiβiliθa'θion/ f, civilization

civilizador /siβilisa'ðor; θiβiliθa'ðor/ a civilizing

civilizar /siβili'sar; θiβili'θar/ vt to civilize; educate; vr grow civilized; be educated

civismo /si'βismo; θi'βismo/ m, civism; patriotism; civics

cizalla /si'saya; θi'θaλa/ f, shears, shearing machine; metal filings

cizaña /si'saɲa; θi'θaɲa/ f, Bot. darnel, weed, tare; vice, evil, dissension, discord (gen. with meter and sembrar)

clac /klak/ m, opera-hat; tricorne

clamar /kla'mar/ vi to cry out; Fig. demand (of inanimate things); vociferate; speak solemnly

clamor /kla'mor/ m, outcry, shouting; shriek, complaint; knell, tolling of bells

clamorear /klamore'ar/ vt to implore, clamor (for); vi toll (of bells)

clamoroso /klamo'roso/ a noisy, clamorous

clandestino /klandes'tino/ a clandestine, secret

clangor /klaŋ'gor/ m, Poet. blare, bray (of trumpet)

claqué /kla'ke/ m, tap-dance

clara /'klara/ f, white of egg; bald patch (in fur); Inf. fair interval on a rainy day

claraboya /klara'βoya/ f, skylight; Archit. clerestory

claramente /klara'mente/ adv clearly, evidently

clarear /klare'ar/ vt to clear; give light to; vi to dawn; grow light; vr be transparent; Inf. reveal secrets unwittingly

clarete /kla'rete/ a, claret (wine); claret color. a claret; claret-colored

claridad /klari'ðað/ f, clearness; transparency; lightness, brightness; distinctness; clarity; good reputation, renown; plain truth, home truth (gen. pl)

clarificación /klarifika'sion; klarifika'θion/ f, clarification; purifying, refining

clarificar /klarifi'kar/ vt to illuminate; clarify, purify; refine (sugar, etc.)

clarín /kla'rin/ m, bugle; clarion; organ stop; bugler

clarinete /klari'nete/ m, clarinet; clarinet player

clarión /kla'rion/ m, white chalk, crayon

clarividencia /klariβi'ðensia; klariβi'ðenθia/ f, perspicuity, clear-sightedness, clairvoyance

clarividente /klariβi'ðente/ a perspicacious, clear-sighted, clairvoyant

claro /'klaro/ a clear; light, bright; distinct; pure, clean; transparent, translucent; light (of colors); easily understood; evident, obvious; frank; cloudless; shrewd, quick-thinking; famous. m, skylight; space between words; break in a speech; space in procession, etc.; Art. (gen. pl) high lights. interj ¡C.! or ¡C. está! Of course! **a las claras,** openly, frankly

claroscuro /klaros'kuro/ m, chiaroscuro; monochrome

clase /'klase/ f, class, group; kind, sort, quality; class (school, university); lecture room; lecture, lesson; order, family. **c. dirigente,** ruling class. **c. media,** middle class. **c. social,** social class

clasicismo /klasi'sismo; klasi'θismo/ m, classicism

clasicista /klasi'sista; klasi'θista/ a and mf classicist

clásico /'klasiko/ a classic; notable; classical. m, classic

clasificación /klasifika'sion; klasifika'θion/ f, classification

clasificador /klasifika'ðor; **(-ra)** n classifier. **c. de billetes,** ticket-punch

clasificar /klasifi'kar/ vt to classify, arrange. **c. correspondencia,** to file letters

claudicación /klauðika'sion; klauðika'θion/ f, limping; negligence; hesitancy, weakness; backing down

claudicar /klauði'kar/ vi to limp; be negligent; hesitate, give way

claustral /klaus'tral/ a cloistral

claustro /'klaustro/ m, cloister; council, faculty, senate (of university); monastic rule

claustrofobia /klaustro'foβia/ f, claustrophobia

cláusula /'klausula/ f, clause. **c. de negación implícita,** contrary-to-fact clause. **c. principal,** main clause. **c. subordinada,** dependent clause, subordinate clause. **c. substantiva,** noun clause

clausura /klau'sura/ f, sanctum of convent; claustration; solemn ending ceremony of tribunal, etc. **la vida de c.,** monastic or conventual life

clava /'klaβa/ f, club, truncheon; Naut. scupper

clavadizo /klaβa'ðiso; klaβa'ðiθo/ a nail-studded (doors, etc.)

clavar /kla'βar/ vt to nail; fasten with nails; pierce, prick; set gems (jeweler); spike (cannon, gum); Fig. fix (eyes, attention, etc.); Inf. cheat

clave /'klaβe/ m, clavichord. f, code, key; Mus. clef; Archit. keystone; plug (telephones); **c. (de),** key to. Mus. **c. de sol,** treble clef

clavel /kla'βel/ m, Bot. carnation plant and flower

clavelito /klaβe'lito/ m, Bot. pink plant and flower

clavero /kla'βero/ **(-ra)** n keeper of the keys. m, clove tree

clavetear /klaβete'ar/ vt to stud with nails; Fig. round off (business affairs)

clavicordio /klaβi'korðio/ m, clavichord

clavícula /kla'βikula/ f, clavicle

clavija /kla'βiha/ f, peg, pin; plug; peg of stringed instrument; axle-pin

clavo /'klaβo/ m, nail, spike, peg; corn (on foot); anguish. **c. de especia,** clove. **c. de herradura,** hob-nail

claymore /klai'more/ f, claymore

clemátide /kle'matiðe/ f, Bot. clematis

clemencia /kle'mensia; kle'menθia/ f, mildness; clemency; mercy

clemente /kle'mente/ a mild; clement; merciful

cleptomanía /kleptoma'nia/ f, kleptomania

cleptómano /klep'tomano/ **(-na)** a and n kleptomaniac

clerecía /klere'sia; klere'θia/ f, clergy

clerical /kleri'kal/ a belonging to the clergy; clerical

clericalismo /klerika'lismo/ m, clericalism

clerigalla /kleri'gaya; kleri'gaʌa/ f, (contemptuous) dog-collar men
clérigo /'klerigo/ m, cleric, clergyman; clerk (in Middle Ages)
clero /'klero/ m, clergy
cliente /'kliente/ mf client, customer; protégé, ward
clientela /klien'tela/ f, patronage, protection; clientele
clima /'klima/ m, climate, clime
climatérico /klima'teriko/ a climacteric
climático /kli'matiko/ a climatic
climatología /klimatolo'hia/ f, climatology
clímax /'klimaks/ m, climax
clínica /'klinika/ f, clinic, nursing home; department of medicine or surgery
clínico /'kliniko/ a clinical
clíper /'kliper/ m, (Aer. and Naut.) clipper
clisar /kli'sar/ vt Print. to cast from a mold, stereotype
clisé /kli'se/ m, Print. stereotype plate
cloaca /klo'aka/ f, sewer, drain; Zool. cloaca
cloquear /kloke'ar/ vi to go broody (hen); cluck
cloqueo /klo'keo/ m, cluck, clucking
cloquera /klo'kera/ f, broodiness (hens)
clorato /klo'rato/ m, chlorate
clorhídrico /klor'iðriko/ a hydrochloric
cloro /'kloro/ m, chlorine
clorofila /kloro'fila/ f, chlorophyll
cloroformizar /kloroformi'sar; kloroformi'θar/ vt to chloroform
cloroformo /kloro'formo/ m, chloroform
clorosis /klo'rosis/ f, chlorosis
cloruro /klo'ruro/ m, chloride
club /kluβ/ m, club
clueca /'klueka/ f, broody hen
clueco /'klueko/ a broody (hens); Inf. doddering
coacción /koak'sion; koak'θion/ f, coercion
coactivo /koak'tiβo/ a coercive
coadjutor /koaðhu'tor/ m, co-worker, assistant
coadunar /koaðu'nar/ vt to join or mingle together
coadyuvar /koaðyu'βar/ vt to assist
coagulación /koagula'sion; koagula'θion/ f, coagulation
coagular /koagu'lar/ vt to coagulate; clot; curdle
coágulo /ko'agulo/ m, clot; coagulation; congealed blood
coalición /koali'sion; koali'θion/ f, coalition
coartada /koar'taða/ f, alibi. **probar la c.,** to prove an alibi
coartar /koar'tar/ vt to limit, restrict
coautor /koau'tor/ **(-ra)** n co-author
cobalto /ko'βalto/ m, cobalt
cobarde /ko'βarðe/ a cowardly; irresolute. m, coward
cobardía /koβar'ðia/ f, cowardice
cobayo /ko'βayo/ m, guinea-pig
cobertera /koβer'tera/ f, lid, cover
cobertizo /koβer'tiso; koβer'tiθo/ m, overhanging roof; shack, shed, hut. **c. de aeroplanos,** Aer. hangar
cobertura /koβer'tura/ f, covering; coverlet; wrapping
cobija /ko'βiha/ f, imbrex tile; cover; Lat. Am. blanket
cobijar /koβi'har/ vt to cover; shelter
cobra /'koβra/ f, Zool. cobra; rope or thong for yoking oxen; retrieval (of game)
cobradero /koβra'ðero/ a that which can be collected, recoverable
cobrador /koβra'ðor/ m, collector, receiver. a collecting. **c. de tranvía,** tram conductor
cobranza /ko'βransa; ko'βranθa/ f, receiving, collecting; collection of fruit or money
cobrar /ko'βrar/ vt to collect (what is owed); charge; earn; regain, recover; feel, experience (emotions); wind, pull in (ropes, etc.); gain, acquire; retrieve (game); vr recuperate. **c. ánimo,** to take courage. **c. cariño (a),** to grow fond of. **c. fuerzas,** to gather strength. **c. importancia,** to gain importance. **¿Cuánto cobra Vd.?** How much do you charge?; How much do you earn?
cobre /'koβre/ m, Mineral. copper; copper kitchen utensils; pl Mus. brass; Lat. Am. (copper) cent, centavo

cobrizo /ko'βriso; ko'βriθo/ a containing copper; copper-colored
cocacolismo /kokako'lismo/ n Inf. economic dependence on the United States and adoption of its pop culture
cocacolonización /kokakolonisa'sion; kokakoloniθa'θion/ f, economic domination by the United States and introduction of its pop culture
cocacolonizar /kokakoloni'sar; kokakoloni'θar/ vt (United States) to gain economic control of... and introduce into its pop culture
cocaína /koka'ina/ f, cocaine
cocción /kok'sion; kok'θion/ f, coction
coceador /kosea'ðor; koθea'ðor/ a inclined to kick; kicking (animals)
coceadura /kosea'ðura; koθea'ðura/ f, kicking
cocear /kose'ar; koθe'ar/ vi to kick; Inf. kick against, oppose
cocedero /kose'ðero; koθe'ðero/ a easily cooked
cocer /ko'ser; ko'θer/ vt. irr to boil; cook; bake (bricks, etc.); digest; Surg. suppurate; vi boil (of a liquid); ferment; vr suffer pain or inconvenience over a long period. Pres. Ind. **cuezo, cueces, cuece, cuecen.** Pres. Subjunc. **cueza, cuezas, cueza, cuezan**
cochayuyo /kotʃa'yujo/ m, Lat. Am. edible seaweed
coche /'kotʃe/ m, carriage, car. **c. camas,** sleeping car. **c. -camioneta,** station wagon. **c. cerrado,** Auto. sedan. **c. de muchos caballos,** high-powered car. **c. de plaza,** hackney-carriage. **c. fúnebre,** hearse. **c. -línea,** intercity bus. f, Ecuador puddle
cochera /ko'tʃera/ f, coach house; tramway depot
cochero /ko'tʃero/ m, coachman; driver. a easily cooked
¡cochi! /'kotʃi/ (call to pigs)
cochina /ko'tʃina/ f, sow
cochinería /kotʃine'ria/ f, Inf. filthiness; mean trick
cochinilla /kotʃi'niya; kotʃi'niʌa/ f, wood louse; cochineal insect; cochineal
cochinillo /kotʃi'niyo; kotʃi'niʌo/ m, sucking-pig. **c. de Indias,** guinea-pig
cochino /ko'tʃino/ m, pig; Inf. filthy person. a filthy
cocido /ko'siðo; ko'θiðo/ a boiled, cooked, baked. m, dish of stewed meat, pork, chicken, with peas, etc.
cociente /ko'siente; ko'θiente/ m, quotient
cocimiento /kosi'miento; koθi'miento/ m, cooking; decoction
cocina /ko'sina; ko'θina/ f, kitchen; pottage; broth; cookery. **c. de campaña,** field-kitchen. **c. económica,** cooking range
cocinar /kosi'nar; koθi'nar/ vt to cook; vi Inf. meddle, interfere
cocinería /kosine'ria; koθine'ria/ f, Naut. galley
cocinero /kosi'nero; koθi'nero/ **(-ra)** n cook, chef
cocinilla /kosi'niya; koθi'niʌa/ f, spirit-stove
coco /'koko/ m, Bot. coconut tree and fruit; coconut shell; grub, maggot; bogeyman; hobgoblin; Inf. grimace. Inf. **ser un c.,** to be hideously ugly
cocodrilo /koko'ðrilo/ m, crocodile
cócora /'kokora/ mf Inf. bore, nosy Parker
cocotal /koko'tal/ m, grove of coconut palms
cocotero /koko'tero/ m, coconut palm
coctel /kok'tel/ m, cocktail
cocuyo /ko'kuyo/ m, firefly
codal /ko'ðal/ a cubital. m, shoot of a vine; prop, strut; frame of a hand-saw
codazo /ko'ðaso; ko'ðaθo/ m, blow or nudge of the elbow. **dar codazos,** to elbow, shoulder out of the way
codear /koðe'ar/ vi to jostle; elbow, nudge; vr be on terms of equality with
codeína /koðe'ina/ f, codeine
codelincuente /koðelin'kuente/ mf partner in crime, accomplice
codera /ko'ðera/ f, elbow rash; elbow-piece or patch
codeso /ko'ðeso/ m, laburnum
códice /'koðise; 'koðiθe/ m, codex
codicia /ko'ðisia; ko'ðiθia/ f, covetousness; greed
codiciar /koðisi'ar; koðiθi'ar/ vt to covet

codicilo /koði'silo; koði'θilo/ *m*, codicil
codicioso /koðisi'oso; koðiθi'oso/ **(-sa)** *a* covetous; *Inf.* hardworking. *n* covetous person
codificación /koðifika'sion; koðifika'θion/ *f*, codification
codificar /koðifi'kar/ *vt* to codify, compile
código /'koðigo/ *m*, code of laws. **c. de barras,** bar code. **c. civil,** civil laws. **c. de la circulación, c. de la vía pública,** highway code, traffic code. *Naut.* **c. de señales,** signal code. **c. penal,** criminal laws. **c. postal,** zip code
codillo /ko'ðiyo; ko'ðiʎo/ *m*, knee (of quadrupeds); shaft (of branch); bend (pipe, tube); stirrup
codo /'koðo/ *m*, elbow; angle, bend (pipe, tube); cubit. *Inf.* **hablar por los codos,** to chatter
codorniz /koðor'nis; koðor'niθ/ *f*, *Ornith.* quail
coeducación /koeðuka'sion; koeðuka'θion/ *f*, coeducation
coeficiente /koefi'siente; koefi'θiente/ *m*, coefficient
coercer /koer'ser; koer'θer/ *vt* to restrain, coerce
coerción /koer'sion; koer'θion/ *f*, *Law.* coercion
coercitivo /koersi'tiβo; koerθi'tiβo/ *a* coercive
coetáneo /koe'taneo/ **(-ea)** *a* contemporaneous. *n* contemporary
coevo /ko'eβo/ *a* coeval
coexistencia /koeksis'tensia; koeksis'tenθia/ *f*, co-existence
coexistir /koeksis'tir/ *vi* to co-exist
cofia /'kofia/ *f*, hairnet; coif
cofín /ko'fin/ *m*, basket
cofradía /kofra'ðia/ *f*, confraternity, brotherhood or sisterhood **c. de gastronomía,** eating club (US), dining society (UK)
cofre /'kofre/ *m*, trunk, chest (for clothes); coffer
cogedor /kohe'ðor/ *m*, collector, gatherer; dustpan; coal-shovel
coger /ko'her/ *vt* to seize, hold; catch; take, collect, gather; have room for; take up or occupy space; find; catch in the act; attack, surprise; reach; **c. un berrinche,** have a fit, have a tantrum. *vi* have room, fit
cogida /ko'hiða/ *f*, gathering, picking; *Inf.* fruit harvest; toss (bullfighting)
cogido /ko'hiðo/ *m*, pleat, fold; crease. **estar c. de tiempo** to be pressed for time.
cogitabundo /kohita'βundo/ *a* very pensive
cognación /kogna'sion; kogna'θion/ *f*, cognation; kinship
cognoscitivo /kognossi'tiβo; kognosθi'tiβo/ *a* cognitive. **las ciencias cognoscitivas,** cognitive science
cogollo /ko'goyo; ko'goʎo/ *m*, heart (of lettuce, etc.); shoot; topmost branches of pine tree
cogote /ko'gote/ *m*, nape (of neck)
cogulla /ko'guya; ko'guʎa/ *f*, monk's habit
cohabitación /koaβita'sion; koaβita'θion/ *f*, cohabitation
cohabitar /koaβi'tar/ *vi* to cohabit
cohechador /koetʃa'ðor/ **(-ra)** *a* bribing. *n* briber
cohechar /koe'tʃar/ *vt* to bribe, corrupt, suborn
cohecho /ko'etʃo/ *m*, bribing; bribe
coherencia /koe'rensia; koe'renθia/ *f*, coherence, connection
coherente /koe'rente/ *a* coherent
cohesión /koe'sion/ *f*, cohesion
cohesivo /koe'siβo/ *a* cohesive
cohete /ko'ete/ *m*, rocket
cohetero /koe'tero/ *f*, firework manufacturer
cohibir /koi'βir/ *vt* to restrain; repress. See **prohibir.**
cohombrillo /koom'briyo; koom'briʎo/ *m*, *dim* gherkin
cohombro /ko'ombro/ *m*, cucumber
cohonestar /koones'tar/ *vt* *Fig.* to gloss over, cover up; make appear decent (actions, etc.)
cohorte /ko'orte/ *f*, cohort
coima /'koima/ *f*, *Lat. Am.* bribe
coincidencia /koinsi'ðensia; koinθi'ðenθia/ *f*, coincidence
coincidir /koinsi'ðir; koinθi'ðir/ *vt* to coincide; (two or more people) be in the same place at the same time. **c. con que...** to agree that...
coito /'koito/ *m*, coitus

cojear /kohe'ar/ *vi* to limp; wobble, be unsteady (of furniture); *Fig. Inf.* go wrong or astray; *Inf.* suffer from (vice, bad habit)
cojera /ko'hera/ *f*, lameness, limp
cojijoso /kohi'hoso/ *a* peevish
cojín /ko'hin/ *m*, cushion; pad; pillow (for lace-making)
cojinete /kohi'nete/ *m*, small cushion; *Mech.* bearing. **c. de bolas,** ball-bearing
cojo /'koho/ *a* lame; unsteady, wobbly (of furniture, etc.)
col /kol/ *f*, cabbage. **c. de Bruselas,** Brussels sprouts
cola /'kola/ *f*, tail; train (of gown); shank (of a button); queue; tailpiece (of a violin, etc.); appendage; glue. **c. de milano,** dovetail. **c. de pescado,** isinglass. **formar c.,** to line up, queue up
colaboración /kolaβora'sion; kolaβora'θion/ *f*, collaboration. **en c.,** joint (e.g. *obra en colaboración,* joint work)
colaboracionista /kolaβorasio'nista; kolaβoraθio'nista/ *mf* collaborationist
colaborador /kolaβora'ðor/ **(-ra)** *n* collaborator
colaborar /kolaβo'rar/ *vt* to collaborate
colación /kola'sion; kola'θion/ *f*, conferment of a degree; collation (of texts); light repast; cold supper; area of a parish
colada /ko'laða/ *f*, wash; bleaching; mountain path; *Metall.* casting; *Inf.* trusty sword (allusion to name of one of the Cid's swords)
coladero /kola'ðero/ *m*, colander, sieve, strainer; narrow path
colador /kola'ðor/ *m*, colander
coladura /kola'ðura/ *f*, straining, filtration; *Inf.* untruth; *Inf.* howler, mistake
colapso /ko'lapso/ *m*, *Med.* prostration, collapse
colar /ko'lar/ *vt irr* to filter, strain; bleach; *Metall.* cast; *vi* go through a narrow place; *Inf.* drink wine; *vr* thread one's way; *Inf.* enter by stealth, steal in; *Inf.* tell untruths. *Pres. Ind.* **cuelo, cuelas, cuela, cuelan.** *Pres. Subjunc.* **cuele, cueles, cuele, cuelen**
colateral /kolate'ral/ *a* collateral
colcha /'koltʃa/ *f*, bedspread, counterpane, quilt
colchadura /koltʃa'ðura/ *f*, quilting
colchero /kol'tʃero/ *m*, quilt maker
colchón /kol'tʃon/ *m*, mattress. **c. de muelles,** spring-mattress. **c. de viento,** air-bed
colchoneta /koltʃo'neta/ *f*, pad, thin mattress
coleada /kole'aða/ *f*, wag of the tail
colear /kole'ar/ *vi* to wag the tail
colección /kolek'sion; kolek'θion/ *f*, collection
coleccionador /koleksiona'ðor; kolekθiona'ðor/ **(-ra)** *n* collector
coleccionar /koleksio'nar; kolekθio'nar/ *vt* to collect
coleccionista /koleksio'nista; kolekθio'nista/ *mf* collector
colecta /ko'lekta/ *f*, assessment; collection (of donations); *Eccl.* collect; voluntary offering
colectivero /kolekti'βero/ *m*, bus driver
colectividad /kolektiβi'ðað/ *f*, collectivity; body of people
colectivismo /kolekti'βismo/ *m*, collectivism
colectivista /kolekti'βista/ *a* collectivist
colectivo /kolek'tiβo/ *a* collective; *Argentina* (local) bus
colector /kolek'tor/ *m*, gatherer; collector; tax-collector; water-pipe; water-conduit; *Elec.* commutator, collector
colega /ko'lega/ *m*, colleague
colegiado /kole'hiaðo/ *a* collegiate
colegial /kole'hial/ **(-la)** *a* college, collegiate. *n* student; pupil; *Fig. Inf.* novice.
colegiarse /kole'hiarse/ *vr* to meet as an association (professional, etc.)
colegiata /kole'hiata/ *f*, college church
colegiatura /kolehia'tura/ *f*, scholarship, fellowship (money granted a student); tuition (fee paid by a student), tuition fee, tuition fees
colegio /ko'lehio/ *m*, college; school; academy; association (professional); council, convocation; college or school buildings. **c. de abogados,** bar association.

c. de cardenales, College of Cardinals. **c. electoral,** polling-booth. **c. militar,** military academy

colegir /kole'hir/ *vt irr* to collect, gather; deduce, infer. See **elegir**

cólera /'kolera/ *f,* bile, anger. *m,* cholera. **montar en c.,** to fly into a rage

colérico /ko'leriko/ *a* angry; choleric; suffering from cholera

colesterina /koleste'rina/ *f, Chem.* cholesterol

coleta /ko'leta/ *f,* pigtail; queue; *Inf.* postscript

coletazo /kole'taso; kole'taθo/ *m,* blow with one's tail, lash with one's tail; lash of a dying fish; *Fig.* last hurrah

coleto /ko'leto/ *m,* leather jerkin; *Inf.* body of a man

colgadero /kolga'ðero/ *a* able to be hung up. *m,* coat-hanger, hook

colgadizo /kolga'ðiso; kolga'ðiθo/ *a* hanging. *m,* overhanging roof

colgadura /kolga'ðura/ *f,* hangings, drapery, tapestries. **c. de cama,** bedhangings

colgajo /kol'gaho/ *m,* tatter; bunch (of grapes, etc.); *Surg.* skin lap

colgar /kol'gar/ *vt irr* to hang up; decorate with hangings; *Inf.* hang, kill; *vi* hang, be suspended; *Fig.* be dependent. See **contar**

colibrí /koli'βri/ *m,* hummingbird

cólico /'koliko/ *m,* colic

colicuar /koli'kuar/ *vt* to dissolve

coliflor /koli'flor/ *f,* cauliflower

coligarse /koli'garse/ *vr* to confederate, unite

colilla /ko'liya; ko'liʎa/ *f,* stub (of a cigar or cigarette)

colina /ko'lina/ *f,* hill; cabbage seed; *Chem.* choline

colindante /kolin'dante/ *a* adjacent, contiguous

coliseo /koli'seo/ *m,* coliseum; theater

colisión /koli'sion/ *f,* collision; abrasion, bruise; *Fig.* clash (of ideas)

colitis /ko'litis/ *f,* colitis

collado /ko'yaðo; ko'ʎaðo/ *m,* hill, hillock

collar /ko'yar; ko'ʎar/ *m,* necklace; chain of office or honor; collar (dogs, etc.)

collera /ko'yera; ko'ʎera/ *f,* horse collar; *Chile* cuff link

collerón /koje'ron; koʎe'ron/ *m,* horse collar

colmado /kol'maðo/ *a* abundant. *m,* provision shop

colmar /kol'mar/ *vt* to fill to overflowing; bestow generously, heap upon

colmena /kol'mena/ *f,* beehive

colmenero /kolme'nero/ **(-ra)** *n* beekeeper

colmillo /kol'miyo; kol'miʎo/ *m,* canine tooth; tusk; fang

colmilludo /kolmi'yuðo; kolmi'ʎuðo/ *a* having large canine teeth; tusked; fanged; sagacious

colmo /'kolmo/ *m,* overflow; highest point; completion, limit, end. **ser el c.,** *Inf.* to be the last straw. **el c. de los colmos,** the absolute limit

colocación /koloka'sion; koloka'θion/ *f,* placing, putting; situation, place; employment; *Sports.* placing; order, arrangement; *Ling.* collocation

colocar /kolo'kar/ *vt* to place, put, arrange; place in employment. **c. bajo banderas,** to draft (into the armed forces). *vr* place oneself

colocho /ko'lotʃo/ *m, Guatemala* (naturally) curly hair

colofón /kolo'fon/ *m, Print.* colophon

colofonia /kolo'fonia/ *f,* solid resin (for bows of stringed instruments, etc.)

colombiano /kolom'biano/ **(-na)** *a* and *n* Colombian

colombina /kolom'bina/ *f,* columbine

colombofilia /kolombo'filia/ *f,* pigeon fancying

colonia /ko'lonia/ *f,* colony; plantation

coloniaje /kolo'niahe/ *m, Lat. Am.* colonial period; colonial government

colonial /kolo'nial/ *a* colonial

colonización /koloniza'sion; koloniθa'θion/ *f,* colonization

colonizador /koloniza'ðor; koloniθa'ðor/ **(-ra)** *a* colonizing. *n* colonizer

colonizar /koloni'sar; koloni'θar/ *vt* to colonize; settle

colono /ko'lono/ *m,* settler, colonist; farmer

coloquio /ko'lokio/ *m,* colloquy, conversation, talk; colloquium

color /ko'lor/ *m,* color; dye; paint; rouge; coloring; pretext, excuse; character, individuality; *pl* natural colors. **c. estable, c. sólido,** fast color. **mudar de c.,** to change color. **de c.,** of color (people). **so c.,** under the pretext. **ver las cosas c. de rosa,** to see things through rose-colored glasses

colorado /kolo'raðo/ *a* colored. *West Hem.* red, reddish; *Inf.* blue, obscene; specious

colorante /kolo'rante/ *a* coloring. *m,* dyestuff; coloring (substance)

colorar /kolo'rar/ *vt* to color; dye

colorear /kolore'ar/ *vt* to color; pretext; *Fig.* whitewash, excuse; *vi* show color; be reddish; grow red, ripe (tomatoes, cherries, etc.)

colorero /kolo'rero/ *m,* dyer

colorete /kolo'rete/ *m,* rouge

colorido /kolo'riðo/ *m,* coloring, color

colorín /kolo'rin/ *m,* goldfinch; bright color

colosal /kolo'sal/ *a* colossal, enormous; extraordinary, excellent

coloso /ko'loso/ *m,* colossus; *Fig.* outstanding person or thing, giant; **el C. del Norte, el Gran C. del Norte,** (contemptuous epithet for the United States of America)

columbino /kolum'bino/ *a* pertaining to a dove; dovelike; candid, innocent; purply-red

columbrar /kolum'brar/ *vt* to discern in the distance, glimpse; conjecture, guess

columna /ko'lumna/ *f, Mil. Archit. Print.* column; *Fig.* protection, shelter; *Naut.* stanchion. **c. cerrada,** *Mil. etc.* mass formation. **c. de los suspiros,** agony column (in a newspaper)

columnata /kolum'nata/ *f,* colonnade

columpiar /kolum'piar/ *vt* to swing; dangle (one's feet); *vr Inf.* sway in walking; swing

columpio /ko'lumpio/ *m,* swing

colusión /kolu'sion/ *f,* collusion

colusorio /kolu'sorio/ *a* collusive

coma /'koma/ *f, Gram.* comma. *m, Med.* coma

comadre /ko'maðre/ *f,* best female friend, midwife; *Inf.* procuress, go-between; *Inf.* pal, gossip

comadrear /komaðre'ar/ *vi Inf.* to gossip

comadreja /koma'ðreha/ *f, Zool.* weasel

comadrón /koma'ðron/ *m,* accoucheur

comadrona /koma'ðrona/ *f,* midwife

comandancia /koman'dansia; koman'danθia/ *f, Mil.* command; commandant's H.Q.

comandante /koman'dante/ *m,* commandant; commander; major; squadron-leader. *a Mil.* commanding. **c. en jefe,** commanding officer

comandar /koman'dar/ *vt Mil.* to command

comandita /koman'dita/ *f, Com.* sleeping partnership; private company

comando /ko'mando/ *m, Mil.* commando

comarca /ko'marka/ *f,* district, region

comatoso /koma'toso/ *a* comatose

comba /'komba/ *f,* bend, warping; jump rope, skipping-rope; camber (of road)

combadura /komba'ðura/ *f,* curvature; warping; camber (of a road)

combar /kom'bar/ *vt* to bend; twist; warp; camber

combate /kom'bate/ *m,* fight, combat; mental strife; contradiction, opposition. **c. judicial,** trial by combat. **dejar fuera de c.,** (a) (boxing) to knock out

combatiente /komba'tiente/ *m,* combatant, soldier

combatir /komba'tir/ *vi* to fight; *vt* attack; struggle against (winds, water, etc.); contradict, oppose; *Fig.* disturb, trouble (emotions)

combi /'kombi/ *f, Mexico* minibus

combinación /kombina'sion; kombina'θion/ *f,* combination; list of words beginning with same letter; project; concurrence; underskirt, petticoat. **estar en c. (con),** to be in cahoots (with), connive (with)

combinar /kombi'nar/ *vt* to combine; (*Mil. Nav.*) join forces; arrange, plan; *Chem.* combine; **combinar para + inf.** (two or more people) to make arrangements to + inf.

combustible /kombus'tiβle/ *a* combustible. *m,* fuel

combustión /kombus'tion/ *f*, combustion. **c. activa,** rapid combustion. **c. espontánea,** spontaneous combustion

comedero /kome'ðero/ *a* edible. *m*, feeding-trough; dining-room

comedia /ko'meðia/ *f*, comedy; play; theater; comic incident; *Fig.* play-acting, theatricalism. **c. alta,** art theater. **c. de costumbres,** comedy of manners. **c. de enredo,** play with very involved plot. *Inf.* **hacer la c.,** to play-act, pretend

comedianta /kome'ðianta/ *f*, actress

comediante /kome'ðiante/ *m*, actor; *Inf.* dissembler.

comedido /kome'ðiðo/ *a* courteous; prudent; moderate

comedimiento /komeðimiento/ *m*, courtesy; moderation; prudence

comedir /kome'ðir/ *vt irr* to prepare, premeditate; *vr* restrain oneself, be moderate; offer one's services. See **pedir**

comedor /kome'ðor/ *a* voracious. *m*, dining-room

comendador /komenda'ðor/ *m*, knight commander

comendatorio /komenda'torio/ *a* commendatory (of letters)

comensal /komen'sal/ *mf* table companion

comentador /komenta'ðor/ **(-ra)** *n* commentator

comentar /komen'tar/ *vt* explain (document); *Inf.* comment

comentario /komen'tario/ **(a)** *m*, commentary (on)

comentarista /komenta'rista/ *mf* commentator

comento /ko'mento/ *m*, comment; commentary

comenzante /komen'sante; komen'θante/ *mf* beginner, novice. *a* initial

comenzar /komen'sar; komen'θar/ *vt vi irr* to begin, commence. See **empezar**

comer /ko'mer/ *m*, eating; food. *vi* to eat; feed; dine. *vt* eat; *Inf.* enjoy an income; waste (patrimony); consume, exhaust; fade (of colors); *vr* be troubled, uneasy, remorseful. **ser de buen c.,** to have a good appetite; taste good. **tener que c.,** to be obliged to eat; have to eat; have enough to eat

comerciable /komer'siaβle; komer'θiaβle/ *a* marketable; sociable, pleasant (of persons)

comercial /komer'sial; komer'θial/ *a* commercial

comerciante /komer'siante; komer'θiante/ *a* trading. *mf* merchant, trader

comerciar /komer'siar; komer'θiar/ *vt* to trade; have dealings (with)

comercio /ko'mersio; ko'merθio/ *m*, trade, commerce; intercourse, traffic; illicit sexual intercourse; shop, store; tradesmen; commercial quarter of town

comestible /komes'tiβle/ *a* edible, eatable. *m*, (gen. *pl*) provisions

cometa /ko'meta/ *m*, *Astron.* comet. *f*, kite (toy). **c. celular,** box-kite

cometedor /komete'ðor/ **(-ra)** *n* perpetrator

cometer /kome'ter/ *vt* to entrust, hand over to; commit (crime, sins, etc.); *Com.* order

cometido /kome'tiðo/ *m*, charge, commission; moral obligation; function

comezón /kome'son; kome'θon/ *f*, itching, irritation; hankering, longing

cómico /'komiko/ *a* comic; funny, comical. *m*, actor; comedian. **c. de la legua,** strolling player

comida /ko'miða/ *f*, food; meal; dinner; eating. **c. corrida** *Mexico* table d'hôte **c. de gala,** state banquet. **c. de prueba,** *Med.* test meal

comienzo /ko'mienso; ko'mienθo/ *m*, beginning, origin

comillas /ko'miyas; ko'miʎas/ *f pl*, *Gram.* inverted commas, quotation marks. **entre c.,** in quotes

comilón /komi'lon/ **(-ona)** *a Inf.* gluttonous. *n* glutton

comino /ko'mino/ *m*, *Bot.* cumin. **no valer un c.,** to be not worth a jot

comisar /komi'sar/ *vt* to confiscate, sequestrate

comisaría /komisa'ria/ *f*, commissaryship; commissariat. **c. de policía,** police station

comisario /komi'sario/ *m*, deputy, agent; commissary, head of police; commissioner; *Argentina,*

purser. **alto c.,** high commissioner. **c. propietario,** stockholders' representative

comisión /komi'sion/ *f*, perpetration, committal; commission; committee; *Com.* commission

comisionado /komisio'naðo/ **(-da)** *a* commissioned. *m*, commissary

comisionar /komisio'nar/ *vt* to commission

comisionista /komisio'nista/ *mf Com.* commission agent

comiso /ko'miso/ *m*, *Law.* confiscation, sequestration; contraband

comité /komi'te/ *m*, committee

comitiva /komi'tiβa/ *f*, retinue, following

como /'komo/ *adv* like, as; in the same way; thus, accordingly; in the capacity of; so that; since. *conjunc* if (*followed by subjunc.*); because. **c. no,** unless. ¿Cómo? How? In what way? Why? Pardon? What did you say? *interj* **¡Cómo!** What! You don't say! **¡Cómo no!** Why not! Of course! Surely! **¿Cómo que...?** What do you mean that...?

cómo /'komo/ *m*, the wherefore. **no saber el porqué ni el c.,** not to know the why or wherefore

cómoda /'komoða/ *f*, chest of drawers

comodidad /komoði'ðað/ *f*, comfort; convenience; advantage; utility, interest

comodín /komo'ðin/ *m*, (in cards) joker

cómodo /'komoðo/ *a* comfortable; convenient; opportune

comodón /komo'ðon/ *a Inf.* comfort-loving; easygoing; egoistical

comodoro /komo'ðoro/ *m*, *Naut.* commodore

comoquiera que /komo'kiera ke/ *adv* by any means that, anyway; whereas, given that

compacto /kom'pakto/ *a* compact, dense; close (type)

compadecer /kompaðe'ser; kompaðe'θer/ *vt irr* to pity; *vr* (*with de*) sympathize with; pity; harmonize, agree with. See **conocer**

compadre /kom'paðre/ *m*, best friend, *Inf.* pal; *Argentina* bully

compaginación /kompahina'sion; kompahina'θion/ *f*, joining, fixing; *Print.* making-up

compaginar /kompahi'nar/ *vt* to fit together; join, put in order; harmonize, square (e.g. *compaginé una cuenta con la otra,* I squared one account with the other); *Print.* make up

compañero /kompa'ɲero/ **(-ra)** *n* companion, comrade; fellow-member; partner (games); *Fig.* pair, fellow, mate (things). **c. de armas,** brother-in-arms, companion-at-arms. **c. de cabina,** boothmate. **c. de exilio,** companion in exile, fellow exile. **c. de generación,** contemporary, person of the same generation. **c. de viaje,** traveling companion; *Polit.* fellow traveler (communist sympathizer)

compañía /kompa'ɲia/ *f*, company; society, association; theatrical company; (*Com. Mil.*) company. **C. de Jesús,** Society of Jesus. **c. de la zarza,** guild of guards and woodcutters for autos de fe. **c. de navegación,** shipping company. **c. por acciones,** joint stock company

comparable /kompa'raβle/ *a* comparable

comparación /kompara'sion; kompara'θion/ *f*, comparison

comparar /kompa'rar/ *vt* to compare; collate

comparativo /kompara'tiβo/ *a* comparative

comparecencia /kompare'sensia; kompare'θenθia/ *f*, (gen. *Law.*) appearance

comparecer /kompare'ser; kompare'θer/ *vi irr Law.* to appear (before tribunal, etc.); present oneself. See **conocer**

comparendo /kompa'rendo/ *m*, *Law.* summons

comparsa /kom'parsa/ *f*, retinue; *Theat.* chorus; troop of carnival revelers dressed alike. *mf Theat.* supernumerary actor

comparte /kom'parte/ *mf Law.* partner; accomplice

compartimiento /komparti'miento/ *m*, share, division; railway carriage. *Naut.* **c. estanco,** compartment

compartir /kompar'tir/ *vt* to share, share out, divide; participate

compás /kom'pas/ *m*, compasses; callipers; size; compass, time; range of voice; (*Naut. Mineral.*) compass; *Mus.* time, rhythm, bar, marking time. **c. de mar,** mariner's compass. **c. de puntas,** dividers, callipers. **fuera de c.,** *Mus.* out of time; out of joint (of the times). *Mus.* **llevar el c.,** to beat time

compasar /kompa'sar/ *vt* to measure with compasses; arrange or apportion accurately; *Mus.* put into bars

compasillo /kompa'siyo; kompa'siʎo/ *m*, *Mus.* $\frac{4}{4}$ measure

compasivo /kompa'siβo/ *a* compassionate; tenderhearted

compatibilidad /kompatiβili'ðað/ *f*, compatibility

compatible /kompa'tiβle/ *a* compatible

compatriota /kompa'triota/ *mf* compatriot

compeler /kompe'ler/ *vt* to compel, force

compendiar /kompen'diar/ *vt* to abridge, summarize

compendio /kom'pendio/ *m*, compendium. **en c.,** briefly

compendioso /kompen'dioso/ *a* summary, condensed; compendious

compenetración /kompenetra'sion; kompenetra'θion/ *f*, co-penetration; intermingling

compenetrado /kompene'traðo/ **(de)** *a* thoroughly convinced (of)

compenetrarse /kompene'trarse/ *vr* to co-penetrate; intermingle

compensación /kompensa'sion; kompensa'θion/ *f*, compensating; compensation

compensar /kompen'sar/ *vt* to equalize, counterbalance; compensate

compensatorio /kompensa'torio/ *a* compensatory; equalizing

competencia /kompe'tensia; kompe'tenθia/ *f*, competition, contest; rivalry; competence; aptitude; *Law.* jurisdiction

competente /kompe'tente/ *a* adequate, opportune; rightful, correct; apt, suitable; learned, competent

competer /kompe'ter/ *vi irr* to belong to; devolve on; concern. See **pedir**

competición /kompeti'sion; kompeti'θion/ *f*, competition

competidor /kompeti'ðor/ **(-ra)** *n* competitor

competir /kompe'tir/ *vi irr* to compete, contest; be equal (to), vie (with). See **pedir**

compilación /kompila'sion; kompila'θion/ *f*, compilation

compilador /kompila'ðor/ **(-ra)** *n* compiler. *a* compiling

compilar /kompi'lar/ *vt* to compile

compinche /kom'pintʃe/ *mf Inf.* pal, chum

complacencia /kompla'sensia; kompla'θenθia/ *f*, satisfaction, pleasure

complacer /kompla'ser; kompla'θer/ *vt irr* to oblige, humor; *vr* (*with en*) be pleased or satisfied with; delight in, like to. See **nacer**

complaciente /kompla'siente; kompla'θiente/ *a* pleasing; obliging, helpful

complejidad /komplehi'ðað/ *f*, complexity

complejo /kom'pleho/ *a* complex; intricate. *m*, complex. **c. de inferioridad,** inferiority complex

complementario /komplemen'tario/ *a* complementary

complemento /komple'mento/ *m*, complement (all meanings)

completar /komple'tar/ *vt* to complete; perfect

completo /kom'pleto/ *a* full; finished; perfect

complexión /komplek'sion/ *f*, physical constitution

complexo /kom'plekso/ *a* complex; intricate

complicación /komplika'sion; komplika'θion/ *f*, complication

complicar /kompli'kar/ *vt* to complicate; muddle, confuse; *vr* be complicated; be muddled or confused

cómplice /'komplise; 'kompliθe/ *mf* accomplice

complicidad /komplisi'ðað; kompliθi'ðað/ *f*, complicity

complot /kom'plot/ *m*, *Inf.* conspiracy, plot, intrigue

complutense /komplu'tense/ *a* native of, or belonging to, Alcalá de Henares

componedor /kompone'ðor/ **(-ra)** *n* repairer; arbitrator; bone-setter; *Mus.* writer, author, compiler; *Print.* compositor

componenda /kompo'nenda/ *f*, mending, repair; *Inf.* settlement; compromise, arbitration; *Inf.* shady business

componente /kompo'nente/ *a* and *m*, component

componer /kompo'ner/ *vt irr* to construct, form; *Mech.* resolve; compose, create; *Print.* compose; prepare, concoct, mend, repair; settle (differences); remedy; trim; correct, adjust; *Lit. Mus.* compose; add up to, amount to; *vi* write (verses); *Mus.* compose; *vr* dress oneself up. **c. el semblante,** to compose one's features; *Inf.* **componérselas,** to fix matters, use one's wits. See **poner**

componible /kompo'niβle/ *a* reparable, mendable; able to be arranged or adjusted

comportamiento /komporta'miento/ *m*, conduct; deportment

comportar /kompor'tar/ *vt* to tolerate; *vr* behave, comport oneself

composición /komposi'sion; komposi'θion/ *f*, composition; repair; arrangement; *Print.* composition; *Gram.* compound; *Chem.* constitution; *Mech.* resolution

compositor /komposi'tor/ **(-ra)** *n Mus.* composer; *Print.* compositor

Compostela /kompos'tela/ Compostella

compostura /kompos'tura/ *f*, composition, structure; repair; neatness (of person); adulteration; arrangement, agreement; discretion, modesty

compota /kom'pota/ *f*, fruit preserve, compote; thick sauce

compotera /kompo'tera/ *f*, jam or preserve dish

compra /'kompra/ *f*, buying; marketing, shopping; purchase. **estar de compras,** *Euph.* to be in the family way. **ir de compras,** to go shopping

comprable /kom'praβle/ *a* purchasable

comprador /kompra'ðor/ **(-ra)** *n* purchasing. *n* purchaser; buyer; shopper

comprar /kom'prar/ *vt* to buy

comprender /kompren'der/ *vt* to encircle, surround; include, comprise, contain; understand

comprensible /kompren'siβle/ *a* comprehensible

comprensión /kompren'sion; kompren'θion/ *f*, comprehension, understanding

comprensivo /kompren'siβo/ *a* understanding; comprehensive

compresa /kom'presa/ *f*, *Med.* compress, swab; pack (for the face, etc.)

compresión /kompre'sion; kompre'θion/ *f*, compression; squeeze

compresivo /kompre'siβo/ *a* compressive

compresor /kompre'sor/ *m*, compressor; *Auto. Aer.* supercharger

comprimido /kompri'miðo/ *m*, tablet, pill

comprimir /kompri'mir/ *vt* to compress; squeeze; restrain; *vr* restrain oneself

comprobación /komproβa'sion; komproβa'θion/ *f*, verification; checking; proof

comprobante /kompro'βante/ *a* verifying; confirmatory

comprobar /kompro'βar/ *vt irr* to verify, check; confirm, prove. See **probar**

comprobatorio /komproβa'torio/ *a* confirmatory; verifying; testing

comprometedor /kompromete'ðor/ *a Inf.* compromising; jeopardizing

comprometer /komprome'ter/ *vt* to submit to arbitration; compromise; imperil, jeopardize; *vr* pledge oneself; *Inf.* compromise oneself

comprometido /komprome'tiðo/ *a* awkward, embarrassing; (e.g. literature of a writer) committed, engagé

compromiso /kompro'miso/ *m*, commitment, compromise, agreement, arbitration, obligation; appointment, engagement; jeopardy; difficulty

compuerta /kom'puerta/ *f*, half-door, wicket, hatch; floodgate, sluice. **c. flotante,** floating dam

compuesto /kom'puesto/ *a* and *past part* made-up, built-up; composite; circumspect; *Bot. Gram.* compound. *m*, composite; preparation, compound

compulsar /kompul'sar/ *vt* to collate; *Law.* make a transcript of

compulsivo /kompul'siβo/ *a* compelling

compunción /kompun'sion; kompun'θion/ f, compunction

compungir /kompun'hir/ vt to cause remorse or pity; vr repent; sympathize with, pity

computable /kompu'taβle/ a computable

computación /komputa'sion; komputa'θion/ f, **cómputo** m, calculation, computation

computador /komputa'ðor/ (**-ra**) n computer

computar /kompu'tar/ vt to compute

cómputo /'komputo/ m, computation; estimate

comulgar /komul'gar/ vt to administer Holy Communion; vi receive Holy Communion

comulgatorio /komulga'torio/ m, communion rail, altar rail

común /ko'mun/ a general, customary, ordinary; public, communal; universal, common; vulgar, low. m, community, population; water-closet. **en c.**, in common; generally. **por lo c.**, generally. **sentido c.**, common sense

comuna /ko'muna/ f, Lat. Am. district

comunal /komu'nal/ a communal; common. m, commonalty

comunero /komu'nero/ a popular, affable, democratic. m, joint owner; commoner; Hist. commune

comunicable /komuni'kaβle/ a communicable; communicative, sociable

comunicación /komunika'sion; komunika'θion/ f, communication; (telephone) call, message; letter (to the press); Mil. communiqué; pl lines of communication, transport

comunicado /komuni'kaðo/ m, official communication, communiqué; letter (to the press)

comunicante /komuni'kante/ a communicating

comunicar /komuni'kar/ vt to communicate; transmit; impart, share; vr **comunicarse con**, (door) to open onto (e.g. Esta puerta se comunica con el jardín. This door opens onto the garden); communicate, converse, correspond with each other

comunicativo /komunika'tiβo/ a communicative; talkative, not reserved

comunidad /komuni'ðað/ f, the common people; community; generality, majority; pl Hist. Commune

comunión /komu'nion/ f, communion; intercourse, fellowship; Eccl. Communion

comunismo /komu'nismo/ m, communism

comunista /komu'nista/ a and mf communist

comúnmente /komu'mente/ adv commonly, generally; frequently

con /kon/ prep with; by means of; in the company of; towards, to; although (followed by infin.), but generally translated by an inflected verb, e.g. C. ser almirante, no le gusta el mar, Although he is an admiral, he doesn't like the sea); by (followed by infin. and generally translated by a gerund, e.g. c. hacer todo esto, by doing all this). **c. bien**, safe and sound, safely (e.g. Llegamos con bien. We arrived safely.) **c. cuentagotas**, sparingly; stingily. **c. que**, so, then. **c. tal que**, provided that, on condition that. **c. todo**, nevertheless. **¿Con...?** Is this...? (on the telephone, e.g. ¿Con el Sr. Piñangos? Is this Mr. Piñangos?)

conato /ko'nato/ m, effort, endeavor; tendency; Law. attempted crime

concatenación /konkatena'sion; konkatena'θion/ f, concatenation

concavidad /konkaβi'ðað/ f, concavity; hollow

cóncavo /'konkaβo/ a concave. m, concavity; hollow

concebible /konse'βiβle; konθe'βiβle/ a conceivable

concebimiento /konseβi'miento; konθeβi'miento/ m, See **concepción**

concebir /konse'βir; konθe'βir/ vi irr to become pregnant; conceive, imagine; understand; vt conceive, acquire (affection, etc.). See **pedir**

concedente /konse'ðente; konθe'ðente/ a conceding

conceder /konse'ðer; konθe'ðer/ vt to confer, grant; concede; agree to

concejal /konse'hal; konθe'hal/ m, councillor; alderman

concejil /konse'hil; konθe'hil/ a pertaining to a municipal council; public

concejo /kon'seho; kon'θeho/ m, town council; town hall; council meeting

concentración /konsentra'sion; konθentra'θion/ f, concentration

concentrado /konsen'traðo; konθen'traðo/ a concentrated; (of persons) reserved

concentrar /konsen'trar; konθen'trar/ vt to concentrate

concéntrico /kon'sentriko; kon'θentriko/ a concentric

concepción /konsep'sion; konθep'θion/ f, conception; idea, concept; Eccl. Immaculate Conception

conceptismo /konsep'tismo; konθep'tismo/ m, Lit. Conceptism

concepto /kon'septo; kon'θepto/ m, idea, concept; epigram; opinion. **en mi c.**, in my opinion; judgment. **por c. de**, in payment of

conceptuar /konsep'tuar; konθep'tuar/ vt to judge, take to be; believe; imagine

conceptuoso /konsep'tuoso; konθep'tuoso/ a witty, ingenious

concernencia /konser'nensia; konθer'nenθia/ f, respect, relation

concerniente /konser'niente; konθer'niente/ a concerning

concernir /konser'nir; konθer'nir/ vi irr defective to concern. See **discernir**

concertadamente /konsertaða'mente; konθertaða'mente/ adv methodically, orderly; by arrangement, or agreement

concertar /konser'tar; konθer'tar/ vt irr to arrange, settle, adjust; bargain; conclude (business deal); harmonize; compare, correlate; tune instruments; vi reach an agreement. See **acertar**

concertina /konser'tina; konθer'tina/ f, concertina

concertista /konser'tista; konθer'tista/ mf Mus. performer, soloist; Mus. manager. **c. de piano**, concert pianist

concesión /konse'sion; konθe'sion/ f, conceding, grant; concession; lease

concesionario /konsesio'nario; konθesio'nario/ m, Law. concessionaire, leaseholder

concha /'kontʃa/ f, shell; turtle-shell; prompter's box; cove, creek; anything shell-shaped. Fig. **meterse en su c.**, to retire into one's shell. Inf. **tener más conchas que un galápago**, to be very cunning

conchado /kon'tʃaðo/ a scaly, having a shell

concho /'kontʃo/ m, Lat. Am. dregs, sediment

conciencia /kon'siensia; kon'θienθia/ f, consciousness; conscience; conscientiousness. **c. doble**, dual personality. **ancho de c.**, broad-minded. **a c.**, conscientiously

concienzudo /konsien'suðo; konθien'θuðo/ a of a delicate conscience, scrupulous; conscientious

concierto /kon'sierto; kon'θierto/ m, methodical arrangement; agreement; Mus. concert; Mus. concerto. **de c.**, by common consent

conciliable /konsi'liaβle; konθi'liaβle/ a reconcilable, compatible

conciliábulo /konsi'liaβulo; konθi'liaβulo/ m, conclave, private meeting; secret meeting

conciliación /konsilia'sion; konθilia'θion/ f, conciliation; similarity, affinity; protection, favor

conciliador /konsilia'ðor; konθilia'ðor/ a conciliatory

conciliar /konsi'liar; konθi'liar/ vt, councilor. vt to conciliate; Fig. reconcile (opposing theories, etc.). **c. el sueño**, to induce sleep, woo sleep. vr win liking (or sometimes dislike)

concilio /kon'silio; kon'θilio/ m, council; Eccl. assembly; conciliary decree; findings of council

concisión /konsi'sion; konθi'sion/ f, conciseness, brevity

conciso /kon'siso; kon'θiso/ a concise

concitar /konsi'tar; konθi'tar/ vt to stir up, foment

conciudadano /konsiuða'ðano; konθiuða'ðano/ (**-na**) n fellow citizen; fellow countryman

cónclave /'konklaβe/ m, conclave; meeting

concluir /kon'kluir/ vt irr to conclude, finish; come to a conclusion, decide; infer, deduce; convince by reasoning; Law. close legal proceedings; vr expire, terminate. **c. con**, to put an end to. See **huir**

conclusión /konklu'sion/ f, finish, end; decision;

close, denouement; theory, proposition (gen. *pl*); deduction, inference; *Law*. close. **en c.,** in conclusion

conclusivo /konklu'siβo/ *a* final; conclusive

concluyente /konklu'yente/ *a* concluding; convincing; conclusive

concomer /konko'mer/ *vi Inf.* to give a shrug, shrug one's shoulders; fidget with an itch. **c. de placer,** to itch with pleasure

concomitancia /konkomi'tansia; konkomi'tanθia/ *f,* concomitance

concomitante /konkomi'tante/ *a* and *m,* concomitant

concordable /konkor'ðaβle/ *a* conformable, agreeable

concordador /konkorða'ðor/ **(-ra)** *a* peacemaking. *n* peacemaker

concordancia /konkor'ðansia; konkor'ðanθia/ *f,* harmony, agreement; (*Mus. Gram.*) concord; *pl* concordance

concordar /konkor'ðar/ *vt irr* to bring to agreement; *vi* agree. See **acordar**

concordato /konkor'ðato/ *m,* concordat

concorde /kon'korðe/ *a* agreeing; harmonious

concordia /kon'korðia/ *f,* concord, agreement, harmony; written agreement

concreción /konkre'sion; konkre'θion/ *f,* concretion

concretar /konkre'tar/ *vt* to combine, bring together; make concise; resume; *vr Fig.* confine oneself (to a subject) to hammer out, work out (an agreement)

concreto /kon'kreto/ *a* concrete, real, not abstract. **en c.,** in definite terms; finally, to sum up

concubina /konku'βina/ *f,* concubine, mistress

concubinato /konkuβi'nato/ *m,* concubinage

conculcación /konkulka'sion; konkulka'θion/ *f,* trampling, treading; violation

conculcador /konkulka'ðor/ *m,* violator

conculcar /konkul'kar/ *vt* to trample under foot, tread on; break, violate

concupiscencia /konkupis'sensia; konkupis'θenθia/ *f,* concupiscence, lust; greed

concupiscente /konkupis'sente; konkupis'θente/ *a* concupiscent, lustful; greedy

concurrencia /konku'rrensia; konku'rrenθia/ *f,* assembly; coincidence; attendance; help, influence

concurrido /konku'rriðo/ *a* crowded; busy; frequented

concurrir /konku'rrir/ *vi* to coincide; contribute; meet together; agree, be of same opinion; compete (in an examination, etc.)

concurso /kon'kurso/ *m,* crowd, concourse; conjunction, coincidence; help; competition; (tennis) tournament; competitive examination; invitation to offer tenders. **c. de acreedores,** creditors' meeting. **c. interno,** competitive examination for a position open to staff members only

concusión /konku'sion/ *f,* concussion; shock; extortion

condado /kon'daðo/ *m,* earldom; county

condal /kon'dal/ *a* of an earl, earl's; of a count, count's; of Barcelona

conde /'konde/ *m,* earl; king of the gypsies

condecir /konde'sir; konde'θir/ **(con)** *vi* to agree (with)

condecoración /kondekora'sion; kondekora'θion/ *f,* conferment of an honor, decoration; medal

condecorar /kondeko'rar/ *vt* to confer a decoration or medal

condena /kon'dena/ *f, Law.* sentence; punishment; penalty

condenable /konde'naβle/ *a* culpable, guilty; worthy of damnation

condenado /konde'naðo/ **(-da)** *a* damned; wicked, harmful. *n Law.* convicted criminal

condenador /kondena'ðor/ *a* condemning; incriminating; blaming

condenar /konde'nar/ *vt Law.* to pronounce sentence (on), convict; condemn; disapprove; wall or block or close up. **c. a galeras,** to condemn to the gallies. *vr* blame oneself; be eternally damned

condenatorio /kondena'torio/ *a* condemnatory; incriminating

condensación /kondensa'sion; kondensa'θion/ *f,* condensation

condensador /kondensa'ðor/ *a* condensing. *m,* (*Elec. Mech. Chem.*) condenser

condensante /konden'sante/ *a* condensing

condensar /konden'sar/ *vt* to condense; thicken; abridge

condesa /kon'desa/ *f,* countess

condescendencia /kondessen'densia; kondessen'denθia/ *f,* affability, graciousness

condescender /kondessen'der; kondesθen'der/ *vi irr* to be obliging, helpful, agreeable. See **entender**

condescendiente /kondessen'diente; kondesθen'diente/ *a* affable, gracious

condestable /kondes'taβle/ *m, Hist.* constable, commander-in-chief

condición /kondi'sion; kondi'θion/ *f,* condition; quality; temperament, character; (social) position; rank, family; nobility, circumstance; stipulation, condition, requirement. **estar en condiciones de,** to be in a position to. **no estar en condiciones de,** to be in no condition to

condicional /kondisio'nal; kondiθio'nal/ *a* conditional

condicionar /kondisio'nar; kondiθio'nar/ *vi* to come to an agreement, arrange; *vt* impose conditions

condigno /kon'digno/ *a* condign

condimentación /kondimenta'sion; kondimenta'θion/ *f, Cul.* seasoning

condimentar /kondimen'tar/ *vt* to flavor, season (food)

condimento /kondi'mento/ *m,* condiment, flavoring

condiscípulo /kondis'sipulo; kondis'θipulo/ *m,* schoolfellow

condolencia /kondo'lensia; kondo'lenθia/ *f,* compassion; condolence

condolerse /kondo'lerse/ *vr* (*with de*) to sympathize with, be sorry for. See **doler**

condominio /kondo'minio/ *m,* condominium

condón /kon'don/ *m,* condom

condonar /kondo'nar/ *vt* to condone

conducción /konduk'sion; konduk'θion/ *f.* **conducencia,** *f,* transport, conveyance, carriage; guiding; direction, management; *Phys.* conduction; *Mech.* control-gear. *Auto.* **c. a izquierda,** left-hand drive

conducente /kondu'sente; kondu'θente/ *a* conducting, conducive

conducir /kondu'sir; kondu'θir/ *vt irr* to transport, convey, carry; *Phys.* conduct; guide, lead; manage, direct; *Auto.* drive; conduce; *vi* be suitable; *vr* behave, conduct oneself. *Pres. Ind.* **conduzco, conduces, etc.** *Preterite* **conduje, condujiste, etc.** *Pres. Subjunc.* **conduzca, conduzcas, etc.** *Imperf. Subjunc.* **condujese, etc.**

conducta /kon'dukta/ *f,* transport, conveyance; management, conduct, direction; behavior

conductibilidad /konduktiβili'ðað/ *f, Phys.* conductivity

conductivo /konduk'tiβo/ *a* conductive

conducto /kon'dukto/ *m,* pipe, conduit, drain, duct; *Fig.* channel, means; *Anat.* tube

conductor /konduk'tor/ **(-ra)** *n* guide; leader; driver (vehicles); *m, Phys.* conductor. **c. de caballos,** teamster. **c. de entrada,** *Radio.* lead-in. **c. del calor,** heat-conductor. **c. eléctrico,** electric wire or cable

conección /konek'sion; konek'θion/ *f,* connection; *Elec.* switching on, connection; joint; joining; *pl* friends, connections; *Elec.* wiring

conectar /konek'tar/ *vt Elec.* to connect, switch on; couple; attach, join

conectivo /konek'tiβo/ *a* connective; (*Elec. Mech.*) connecting

conejera /kone'hera/ *f,* rabbit-warren; *Inf.* low dive or haunt

conejillo de Indias /kone'hiyo de 'indias; kone'hiλo de 'indias/ *m,* guineapig

conejo /ko'neho/ *m,* rabbit

conejuna /kone'huna/ *f,* rabbit fur, cony

conejuno /kone'huno/ *a* rabbit, rabbit-like

conexo /ko'nekso/ *a* connected

confabulación /konfaβula'sion; konfaβula'θion/ *f*, confabulation, conspiracy

confabular /konfaβu'lar/ *vi* to confer; *vr* scheme, plot

confalón /konfa'lon/ *m*, standard, banner

confección /konfek'sion; konfek'θion/ *f*, making; confection; making-up; concoction, remedy; ready-made garment

confeccionador /konfeksiona'ðor; konfekθiona'ðor/ **(-ra)** *n* maker (of clothes, etc.)

confeccionar /konfeksio'nar; konfekθio'nar/ *vt* to make; prepare; make up (pharmaceuticals)

confederación /konfeðera'sion; konfeðera'θion/ *f*, alliance, pact; confederacy, federation

confederarse /konfeðe'rarse/ *vr* to confederate, be allied

conferencia /konfe'rensia; konfe'renθia/ *f*, conference, meeting; lecture; (telephone) long-distance call

conferenciante /konferen'siante; konferen'θiante/ *mf* lecturer

conferenciar /konferen'siar; konferen'θiar/ *vi* to confer

conferencista /konferen'sista; konferen'θista/ *mf*, *Lat. Am.* lecturer

conferir /konfe'rir/ *vt irr* to grant, concede; consider, discuss; compare, correlate. See **herir**

confesable /konfe'saβle/ *a* acknowledgeable, avowable

confesar /konfe'sar/ *vt irr* to avow, declare; acknowledge, admit; *Eccl.* hear confession; *vr Eccl.* confess. *Pres. Ind.* **confieso, confiesas, confiesa, confiesan**. *Pres. Subjunc.* **confiese, confieses, confiese, confiesen**

confesión /konfe'sion/ *f*, confession

confesional /konfesio'nal/ *a* confessional

confesionario, confesonario, confesorio /konfesio'nario, konfeso'nario, konfe'sorio/ *m*, *Eccl.* confessional

confeso /kon'feso/ *a* confessed; converted (of Jews). *m*, *Eccl.* lay brother

confesor /konfe'sor/ *m*, confessor

confeti /kon'feti/ *m*, confetti

confianza /kon'fiansa; kon'fianθa/ *f*, confidence, trust; assurance, courage; over-confidence, conceit; intimacy; familiarity. **de c.,** reliable (e.g. *persona de c.*, reliable person); informal (e.g. *reunión de c.*, informal meeting). **en c.,** in confidence, confidentially

confianzudo /konfian'suðo; konfian'θuðo/ *a Inf.* overconfident

confiar /kon'fiar/ *vi* (*with en*) to trust in, hope; *vt* (*with prep a* or *en*) entrust, commit to the care of; confide in

confidencia /konfi'ðensia; konfi'ðenθia/ *f*, trust; confidence; confidential information

confidencial /konfiðen'sial; konfiðen'θial/ *a* confidential

confidente /konfi'ðente/ **(-ta)** *a* trustworthy, true. *m*, seat for two. *n* confidant(e); spy

configuración /konfigura'sion; konfigura'θion/ *f*, configuration, form, lie

configurar /konfigu'rar/ *vt* to shape

confín /kon'fin/ *m*, boundary, frontier; limit. *a* boundary

confinado /konfi'naðo/ *a* banished. *m*, *Law.* prisoner

confinar /konfi'nar/ *vi* (*with con*) to be bounded by, contiguous to; *vt* banish; place in confinement

confirmación /konfirma'sion; konfirma'θion/ *f*, corroboration; *Eccl.* confirmation

confirmar /konfir'mar/ *vt* to corroborate; uphold; *Eccl.* confirm

confiscación /konfiska'sion; konfiska'θion/ *f*, confiscation

confiscar /konfis'kar/ *vt* to confiscate

confitar /konfi'tar/ *vt* to candy, crystallize or preserve (fruit, etc.); *Fig.* sweeten

confite /kon'fite/ *m*, bonbon, sugared almond, etc.

confitería /konfite'ria/ *f*, confectionery

confitero /konfi'tero/ **(-ra)** *n* confectioner

confitura /konfi'tura/ *f*, preserve, jam

conflagración /konflagra'sion; konflagra'θion/ *f*, conflagration, blaze; uprising, rebellion

conflicto /kon'flikto/ *m*, strife, struggle; spiritual conflict; *Fig.* difficult situation

confluencia /kon'fluensia; kon'fluenθia/ *f*, confluence; crowd

confluir /kon'fluir/ *vi irr* to meet, flow together (rivers); run together (roads); crowd. See **huir**

conformación /konforma'sion; konforma'θion/ *f*, conformation; make-up, structure (e.g. of an organization)

conformar /konfor'mar/ *vt* to fit, adjust; *vr* agree, be of the same opinion; submit, comply; to make up (e.g. *los grupos sociales que conforman este país*, the social groups who make up this country)

conforme /kon'forme/ *a* similar, alike; consistent; in agreement; long-suffering, resigned. *adv* according (to), in proportion (to)

conformidad /konformi'ðað/ *f*, conformity; similarity; resignation; agreement, harmony; proportion, symmetry. **de c.,** by common consent. **en c.,** according to

confort /kon'fort/ *m*, comfort

confortante /konfor'tante/ *a* comforting; consoling; strengthening (of beverages)

confortar /konfor'tar/ *vt* to comfort, reassure; encourage; console

confortativo /konforta'tiβo/ *a* comforting; comfortable; strengthening, warming (of beverages); encouraging, cheering

confrontación /konfronta'sion; konfronta'θion/ *f*, confrontment; comparison (of texts, etc.)

confrontar /konfron'tar/ *vt* to bring face to face; compare, correlate; *vi* face; (*with con*) be contiguous to, border on

confucianismo /konfusia'nismo; konfuθia'nismo/ *m*, Confucianism

confundible /konfun'diβle/ *a* mistakable, liable to be confused

confundimiento /konfundi'miento/ *m*, confounding; mistaking; confusion

confundir /konfun'dir/ *vt* to mix, confuse; jumble together; mistake; *Fig.* confound (in argument); humble; bewilder, perplex; *vr* be mixed together; mistake, confuse; be ashamed; be bewildered

confusión /konfu'sion/ *f*, confusion; perplexity; shame; jumble

confuso /kon'fuso/ *a* mixed, upset; jumbled; obscure; indistinct; blurred; bewildered

confutación /konfuta'sion; konfuta'θion/ *f*, confutation

confutar /konfu'tar/ *vt* to confute

conga /'koŋga/ *f*, conga (dance; drum)

congelación /konhela'sion; konhela'θion/ *f*, freezing; congealment. **punto de c.,** freezing point

congelar /konhe'lar/ *vt* to congeal; freeze

congeniar /konhe'niar/ *vi* to be congenial

congénito /kon'henito/ *a* congenital

congestión /konhes'tion/ *f*, *Med.* congestion

congestionar /konhestio'nar/ *vt* to congest; *vr Med.* be overcharged (with blood)

conglomeración /koŋglomera'sion; koŋglomera'θion/ *f*, conglomeration

conglomerar /koŋglome'rar/ *vt* to conglomerate

congoja /koŋ'goha/ *f*, anguish, anxiety, grief

congraciarse /koŋgra'siarse; koŋgra'θiarse/ (*con*), *vr* to ingratiate oneself (with), get into the good graces (of)

congratulación /koŋgratula'sion; koŋgratula'θion/ *f*, congratulation

congratular /koŋgratu'lar/ *vt* to congratulate; *vr* congratulate oneself

congratulatorio /koŋgratula'torio/ *a* congratulatory

congregación /koŋgrega'sion; koŋgrega'θion/ *f*, gathering, meeting, congregation; brotherhood, guild

congregar /koŋgre'gar/ **(se)** *vt* and *vr* to meet, assemble

congresista /koŋgre'sista/ *mf* member of a congress

congreso /koŋ'greso/ *m*, congress; conference, meeting; sexual intercourse

congrio /'koŋgrio/ *m*, conger eel

congruencia /koŋ'gruensia; koŋ'gruenθia/ *f*, suitability, convenience; *Math.* congruence
congruente /koŋ'gruente/ *a* convenient, opportune; *Math.* congruent
cónico /'koniko/ *a* conical, tapering *Math.* conic
conífera /ko'nifera/ *f*, conifer
conífero /ko'nifero/ *a* coniferous
conjetura /konhe'tura/ *f*, conjecture
conjetural /konhetu'ral/ *a* conjectural
conjeturar /konhetu'rar/ *vt* to conjecture, surmise
conjugación /konhuga'sion; konhuga'θion/ *f*, conjugation
conjugar /konhu'gar/ *vt* to conjugate
conjunción /konhun'sion; konhun'θion/ *f*, connection, union association; (*Astron. Gram.*) conjunction
conjuntivitis /konhunti'βitis/ *f*, conjunctivitis
conjunto /kon'hunto/ *a* united, associated adjoining; mingled, mixed (with) bound, affiliated. *m*, whole; combo, ensemble (of musicians). **c. habitacional,** housing complex, housing project
conjura, conjuración /kon'hura, konhura'sion; kon'hura, konhura'θion/ *f*, conspiracy, plot
conjurador /konhura'ðor/ **(-ra)** *n* conspirator, plotter; exorcist
conjurar /konhu'rar/ *vi* to conspire, plot *vt* swear, take an oath; exorcise; implore, beg; ward off (danger)
conjuro /kon'huro/ *m*, plot, conspiracy, spell, incantation; entreaty
conllevar /konye'βar/ konʎe'βar/ *vt* to share (troubles) bear, put up with; endure
conmemoración /komemora'sion; komemora'θion/ *f*, commemoration
conmemorar /komemo'rar/ *vt* to commemorate
conmemorativo /komemora'tiβo/ *a* commemorative
conmensurable /komensu'raβle/ *a* commensurable
conmigo /ko'migo/ *pers. pron* 1st pers. sing. *mf* with myself, with me
conminar /komi'nar/ *vt* to threaten
conminatorio /komina'torio/ *a* threatening
conmiseración /komisera'sion; komisera'θion/ *f*, commiseration, compassion, pity
conmoción /komo'sion; komo'θion/ *f*, disturbance (mind or body); upheaval, commotion. **c. eléctrica,** electric shock
conmovedor /komoβe'ðor/ *a* moving, pitiful; stirring, thrilling
conmover /komo'βer/ *vt irr* to perturb, stir; move to pity. **c. los cimientos de,** to shake the foundations of; *vr* be emotionally moved. See **mover**
conmutable /komu'taβle/ *a* commutable
conmutación /komuta'sion; komuta'θion/ *f*, commutation
conmutador /komuta'ðor/ *m*, *Elec.* commutator; change-over switch
conmutar /komu'tar/ *vt* to commute; *Elec.* switch, convert
conmutatriz /komuta'tris; komuta'triθ/ *f*, *Elec.* converter
connato /kon'nato/ *a* contemporary
connatural /konnatu'ral/ *a* innate, inborn
connaturalizar /konnaturali'sar; konnaturali'θar/ *vt* to connaturalize
connaturalizarse /konnaturali'sarse; konnaturali'θarse/ **(con)** *vr* to become accustomed (to), become acclimated (to)
connivencia /konni'βensia; konni'βenθia/ *f*, connivance
connotación /konnota'sion; konnota'θion/ *f*, connotation
connotado, -a /konno'taðo/ *a*, *Lat. Am.* well-known
connotar /konno'tar/ *vt* to connote
cono /'kono/ *m*, (*Geom. Bot.*) cone. **el C. Sur,** the Southern Cone
conocedor /konose'ðor/ kono'θe'ðor/ **(-ra)** *n* one who knows; connoisseur; expert
conocer /kono'ser; kono'θer/ *vt irr* to know; understand; observe, perceive; meet, be acquainted (with); conjecture; confess, acknowledge; know carnally; *vr* know oneself; know one another. **conocerle a uno la**

voz, to recognize somebody's voice (e.g. *Le conozco la voz.* I recognize her by her voice.) **conocerle a uno en su manera de andar,** to recognize somebody by his gait, recognize somebody by his walk. *Pres. Indic.* **conozco, conoces, etc.** *Pres. Subjunc.* **conozca, etc.**
conocido /kono'siðo; kono'θiðo/ **(-da)** *a* illustrious, distinguished. *n* acquaintance
conocimiento /konosi'miento; konoθi'miento/ *m*, knowledge; understanding; intelligence; acquaintance (*not* friend); consciousness; *Com.* bill of lading; *pl* knowledge, learning
conque /'konke/ *conjunc* so, so that (e.g. *¿C. Juan se va?* So John's going away?)
conquista /kon'kista/ *f*, conquest
conquistador /konkista'ðor/ **(-ra)** *a* conquering. *n* conqueror
conquistar /konkis'tar/ *vt* to conquer; *Fig.* captivate, win
consabido /konsa'βiðo/ *a* aforesaid, beforementioned
consagración /konsagra'sion; konsagra'θion/ *f*, consecration; dedication
consagrar /konsa'grar/ *vt* to consecrate; dedicate, devote; deify; *vr* (*with prep a*) dedicate oneself to, engage in
consanguíneo /konsaŋ'guineo/ *a* consanguineous
consciente /kons'siente; kons'θiente/ *a* conscious; aware; sane. *m*, *Psychol.* conscious
conscripción /konskrip'sion; konskrip'θion/ *f*, conscription
conscripto /kons'kripto/ *m*, conscript
consecución /konseku'sion; konseku'θion/ *f*, obtainment; attainment
consecuencia /konse'kuensia; konse'kuenθia/ *f*, consequence, outcome; logical consequence, conclusion; importance; consistence (of people)
consecuente /konse'kuente/ *a* consequent, resultant; consistent. **c. consigo mismo,** self-consistent *m*, consequence; *Math.* consequent
consecutivo /konseku'tiβo/ *a* consecutive, successive
conseguir /konse'gir/ *vt irr* to obtain, achieve. See **seguir**
conseja /kon'seha/ *f*, story, fairy-tale; old wives' tale
consejero /konse'hero/ **(-ra)** *n* adviser; member of council. *m*. **c. de estado,** counselor of state
consejo /kon'seho/ *m*, advice; council, commission, board; council chamber or building. **c. de administración,** board of directors. **c. de guerra,** council of war. **c. del reino,** council of the realm. **c. privado,** privy council
consenso /kon'senso/ *m*, consensus of opinion, unanimity
consentido /konsen'tiðo/ *a* complaisant (of husband); spoiled, over-indulged
consentimiento /konsenti'miento/ *m*, consent; assent
consentir /konsen'tir/ *vt irr* to permit, allow; believe; tolerate, put up with; over-indulge, spoil; *vr* crack, give way (furniture, etc.). **c. en,** to consent to; to agree to. See **sentir**
conserje /kon'serhe/ *m*, concierge, porter; warden or keeper (of castle, etc.)
conserjería /konserhe'ria/ *f*, conciergerie, porter's lodge; warden's dwelling (in castles, etc.)
conserva /kon'serβa/ *f*, jam; preserve; pickles; *Naut.* convoy. **en c.,** preserved, tinned
conservación /konserβa'sion; konserβa'θion/ *f*, upkeep; preservation, maintenance; *Cul.* preserving; conservation. **c. refrigerada,** cold storage
conservador /konserβa'ðor/ **(-ra)** *a* keeping, preserving. *a* and *n* preserver; *Polit.* conservative; traditionalist. *m*, curator
conservadurismo /konserβaðu'rismo/ *m*, conservatism
conservar /konser'βar/ *vt* to keep, maintain, preserve; keep up (custom, etc.); guard; *Cul.* preserve. **c. en buen estado,** to keep in repair
conservatorio /konserβa'torio/ *m*, conservatoire; academy; *Lat. Am.* greenhouse. **c. de música,** academy of music, conservatoire
considerable /konsiðe'raβle/ *a* considerable; worthy

of consideration, powerful; numerous; large; important

consideración /konsiðera'sion; konsiðera'θion/ *f*, consideration, attention; reflection, thought; civility; importance. **en c. de,** considering

considerado /konsiðe'raðo/ *a* considerate; prudent; distinguished; important

considerar /konsiðe'rar/ *vt* to consider, reflect upon; treat with consideration (persons); judge, estimate, feel (e.g. *Considero que...* I feel that...)

consigna /kon'signa/ *f, Mil.* watchword; left luggage office

consignador /konsigna'ðor/ **(-ra)** *n Com.* consigner, sender

consignar /konsig'nar/ *vt* to assign, lay aside; deposit; *Com.* consign; entrust, commit; put in writing; *Law.* deposit in trust; book (a suspect)

consignatario /konsigna'tario/ *m, Law.* trustee; mortgagee; *Com.* consignee. **c. de buques,** shipping agent

consigo /kon'sigo/ *pers. pron* 3rd sing. and pl. *mf* with himself, herself, oneself, yourself, yourselves, themselves

consiguiente /konsi'giente/ *a* consequent, resulting. *m*, consequence. **por c.,** in consequence

consistencia /konsis'tensia; konsis'tenθia/ *f*, solidity; consistence, density; consistency, congruity, relevance

consistente /konsis'tente/ *a* of a certain consistency; solid

consistir /konsis'tir/ *vi* (*with en*) to consist in; be comprised of; be the result of

consistorio /konsis'torio/ *m*, consistory; municipal council (in some Spanish towns); town hall

consola /kon'sola/ *f*, console table; piertable; *Mech.* bracket

cónsola /kon'sola/ *f*, radio cabinet

consolación /konsola'sion; konsola'θion/ *f*, consolation

consolador /konsola'ðor/ **(-ra)** *n* comforter, consoler

consolar /konso'lar/ *vt irr* to comfort, console. **consolarse de + inf.,** to console oneself for + *pp.* See **contar**

consolidación /konsoliða'sion; konsoliða'θion/ *f*, consolidation; stiffening

consolidar /konsoli'ðar/ *vt* to consolidate; strengthen; combine, unite; *vr Law.* unite

consomé /konso'me/ *m*, consommé

consonancia /konso'nansia; konso'nanθianb/ *f*, harmony; agreement

consonante /konso'nante/ *a* consonant, consistent. *m*, rhyme. *f, Gram.* consonant

consonantísmo /konsonan'tismo/ *m*, consonantism, consonant system

consorcio /kon'sorsio; kon'sorθio/ *m*, partnership; trust; intimacy, common life; consortium

consorte /kon'sorte/ *mf* consort; companion, associate, partner; spouse

conspicuo /kons'pikuo/ *a* outstanding, distinguished; conspicuous

conspiración /konspira'sion; konspira'θion/ *f*, conspiracy

conspirador /konspira'ðor/ **(-ra)** *n* conspirator

conspirar /konspi'rar/ *vi* to conspire; plot, scheme; tend, combine

constancia /kons'tansia; kons'tanθia/ *f*, constancy, steadfastness; stability, steadiness; transcript (of grades); *Lat. Am. law* deposition. **c. de estudios,** transcript (of grades)

constante /kons'tante/ *a* constant; durable; *Mech.* steady, non-oscillating. *m*, constant

Constantinopla /konstanti'nopla/ Constantinople

Constanza /kons'tansa; kons'tanθa/ Constance (female given name and lake)

constar /kons'tar/ *vi* to be evident, be clear; (*with de*) be composed of, consist of, comprise

constelación /konstela'sion; konstela'θion/ *f*, *Astron.* constellation; climate

consternación /konsterna'sion; konsterna'θion/ *f*, dismay, alarm

consternarse /konster'narse/ *vr* to be dismayed or alarmed

constipado /konsti'paðo/ *m, Med.* cold; chill

constiparse /konsti'parse/ *vr* to catch a cold or chill

constitución /konstitu'sion; konstitu'θion/ *f*, constitution; composition, make-up (e.g. *la c. del suelo,* the make-up of the soil)

constitucional /konstitusio'nal; konstituθio'nal/ *a* constitutional

constituir /konsti'tuir/ *vt irr* to constitute, form; found, establish; (*with en*) appoint, nominate; *Fig.* place in (a difficult situation, etc.); *vr* (*with en* or *por*) be appointed or authorized; be under (an obligation). See **huir**

constituyente, constitutivo /konstitu'yente, konstitu'tiβo/ *a* and *m*, constituent

constreñir /konstre'nir/ *vt irr* to constrain, oblige; constrict; constipate. See **ceñir**

constricción /konstrik'sion; konstrik'θion/ *f*, constriction; contraction, shrinkage

construcción /konstruk'sion; konstruk'θion/ *f*, construction; art or process of construction; fabric, structure; *Gram.* construction; building, erection. **c. de caminos,** road making. **c. naval,** shipbuilding

constructor /konstruk'tor/ **(-ra)** *a* building, constructive. *n* builder; constructor

construir /kons'truir/ *vt irr* to construct; build, make; *Gram.* construct. See **huir**

consuelo /kon'suelo/ *m*, consolation; comfort, solace; joy, delight

cónsul /'konsul/ *m*, consul

consulado /konsu'laðo/ *m*, consulate. **c. general,** consulate general

consulta /kon'sulta/ *f*, deliberation, consideration; advice; reference; conference, consultation

consultar /konsul'tar/ *vt* to discuss, consider; seek advice, consult. **consultarlo con la almohada,** *Fig.* to sleep on it, think it over, mull it over

consultor /konsul'tor/ **(-ra)** *a* consultative, advisory; consulting. *n* consultant; adviser. **c. externo,** outside consultant

consultorio /konsul'torio/ *m, Med.* consulting rooms; surgery; technical information bureau

consumación /konsuma'sion; konsuma'θion/ *f*, consummation; completion, attainment; extinction, end

consumado /konsu'maðo/ *a* consummate; *Inf.* thorough, perfect

consumar /konsu'mar/ *vt* to consummate; complete, accomplish, perfect

consumido /konsu'miðo/ *a Inf.* emaciated, wasted away; timid, spiritless

consumidor /konsumi'ðor/ **(-ra)** *a* consuming. *n* consumer, user

consumir /konsu'mir/ *vt* to destroy; consume, use; waste away, wear away; *Eccl.* take communion; *Inf.* grieve; *vr* be destroyed; *Inf.* be consumed with grief

consumo /kon'sumo/ *m*, consumption; demand. **c. de combustible,** fuel consumption

contabilidad /kontaβili'ðað/ *f*, bookkeeping; accounts; accounting

contable /kon'taβle/ *m*, bookkeeper

contacto /kon'takto/ *m*, contact (also *Elec. Mil.*). **en c.,** in common (e.g. *Los dos libros tienen mucho en c.* The two books have much in common.)

contado /kon'taðo/ *a* few; infrequent; rare. **al c.,** *Com.* cash down. **por de c.,** presumably; of course, naturally

contador /konta'ðor/ *m*, a counting. *m*, accountant; *Law.* auditor; counter (in banks); *Elec.* meter, counter; *Naut.* purser. **c. oficial,** *Argentina* certified public accountant. **c. público titulado,** certified public accountant

contaduría /kontaðu'ria/ *f*, accountancy; counting house; accountant's office; auditorship; *Theat.* boxoffice; *Naut.* purser's office

contagiar /konta'hiar/ *vt* to infect; corrupt, pervert; *vr* (*with con, de* or *por*) be infected by or through

contagio /kon'tahio/ *m*, infection; contagious disease; *Fig.* contagion, perversion, corruption

contagioso /konta'hioso/ *a* infectious; *Fig.* catching, contagious

contaminación /kontamina'sion; kontamina'θion/ *f*, contamination, pollution
contaminar /kontami'nar/ *vt* to pollute, contaminate; infect; *Fig.* corrupt
contante /kon'tante/ *a* ready (of money)
contar /kon'tar/ *vt irr* to count; recount, tell; place to account; include, count among; *vi* calculate, compute. **contarle a uno las cuarenta,** *inf* to give someone a piece of one's mind. **c. con,** to rely upon; reckon upon. *Pres. Ind.* **cuento, cuentas, cuenta, cuentan.** *Pres. Subjunc.* **cuente, cuentes, cuente, cuenten**
contemplación /kontempla'sion; kontempla'θion/ *f*, meditation, contemplation; consideration
contemplar /kontem'plar/ *vt* to consider, reflect upon; look at, contemplate; indulge, please
contemplativo /kontempla'tiβo/ *a Eccl.* contemplative; reflective, thoughtful; kind, indulgent
contemporáneo /kontempo'raneo/ **(de)** *a* contemporaneous (to *or* with) *n* contemporary
contemporizar /kontempori'sar; kontempori'θar/ *vi* to temporize, gain time
contencioso /konten'sioso; konten'θioso/ *a* contentious, argumentative; *Law.* litigious
contender /konten'der/ *vi irr* to contain; restrain, hold back; comprise; *vr* control oneself. See **entender**
contendiente /konten'diente/ *mf* contestant
contener /konte'ner/ *vt irr* to contain; include; comprise; hold back; restrain; check, repress; hold down, subdue; suppress, put down; *vr* contain oneself; keep one's temper; keep quiet; refrain. See **tener**
contenido /konte'niðo/ *m*, contents. *a* contained; *Fig.* restrained; reserved (of persons)
contentamiento /kontenta'miento/ *m*, contentment
contentar /konten'tar/ *vt* to satisfy, please; *Com.* endorse; *vr* be pleased or satisfied
contento /kon'tento/ *a* happy; content; satisfied; pleased. *m*, pleasure; contentment. **no caber de c.,** to be overjoyed
contestación /kontesta'sion; kontesta'θion/ *f*, reply, answer; discussion, argument, dispute
contestar /kontes'tar/ *vt* to reply, answer; confirm, attest; *vi* accord, harmonize
contexto /kon'teksto/ *m*, context
contextura /konteks'tura/ *f*, structure; context; physique, frame
contienda /kon'tienda/ *f*, struggle, fight; quarrel, dispute; discussion
contigo /kon'tigo/ *pers. pron* 2nd sing. *mf* with thee, with you
contigüidad /kontigui'ðað/ *f*, proximity, nearness
contiguo /kon'tiguo/ *a* adjacent, near, contiguous
continencia /konti'nensia; konti'nenθia/ *f*, moderation, self-restraint; continence; chastity; containing
continental /konti'nental/ *a* continental. *m*, express messenger service; *Puerto Rico* person from the mainland United States
continente /konti'nente/ *a* continent. *m*, container; demeanor, bearing; *Geog.* continent; mainland
contingencia /kontin'hensia; kontin'henθia/ *f*, contingency; risk, danger
contingente /kontin'hente/ *a* incidental; fortuitous; dependent; *m*, *Mil.* taskforce, contingent
continuación /kontinua'sion; kontinua'θion/ *f*, continuation; prolongation; sequel (of a story, etc.)
continuador /kontinua'ðor/ **(-ra)** *n* continuer
continuar /konti'nuar/ *vt* to continue; *vi* continue; last, remain, go on; *vr* be prolonged
continuidad /kontinui'ðað/ *f*, continuity
continuo /kon'tinuo/ *a* continuous, steady, uninterrupted; persevering, tenacious; persistent, lasting, unremitting. *m*, a united whole. **de c.,** continuously
contonearse /kontone'arse/ *vr* to swing the hips (in walking); strut
contorno /kon'torno/ *m*, contour, outline; (gen. *pl*) environs, surrounding district
contorsión /kontor'sion/ *f*, contortion
contorsionista /kontorsio'nista/ *mf* contortionist
contra /'kontra/ *prep* against, counter, athwart; opposed to, hostile to; in front of, opposite; towards. *m*,

opposite view or opinion. *f, Inf.* difficulty, trouble. **c. la corriente,** upstream. **el pro y el c.,** the pros and cons. **en c.,** in opposition, against
contraalmirante /kontraalmi'rante/ *m*, rear admiral
contraataque /kontraa'take/ *m*, counterattack
contraaviso /kontraa'βiso/ *m*, countermand
contrabajo /kontra'βaho/ *m*, doublebass; player of this instrument; deep bass voice
contrabalancear /kontraβalanse'ar; kontraβalanθe'ar/ *vt* to counterbalance; *Fig.* compensate
contrabandista /kontraβan'dista/ *a* smuggling. *mf* smuggler
contrabando /kontra'βando/ *m*, contraband; smuggling
contracción /kontrak'sion; kontrak'θion/ *f*, contraction; shrinkage; abridgment; abbreviation
contracubierta /kontraku'βierta/ *f*, book jacket, jacket
contradanza /kontra'ðansa; kontra'ðanθa/ *f*, square dance
contradecir /kontraðe'sir; kontraðe'θir/ *vt irr* to contradict; *vr* contradict oneself. See **decir**
contradicción /kontraðik'sion; kontraðik'θion/ *f*, contradiction
contradictorio /kontraðik'torio/ *a* contradictory
contraer /kontra'er/ *vt irr* to shrink, reduce in size, shorten; abridge; contract (matrimony, obligations); *Fig.* acquire (diseases, habits); *vr* shorten, contract, shrink. See **traer**
contrafuerte /kontra'fuerte/ *m*, buttress, counterfort, abutment; *Geog.* spur
contrahacer /kontraa'ser; kontraa'θer/ *vt irr* to forge, counterfeit; mimic; imitate. See **hacer**
contrahecho /kontra'etʃo/ *a* deformed
contralor /kontra'lor/ *m*, comptroller
contraloría /kontralo'ria/ *f*, comptrollership, office of comptroller (position); comptroller's office (place)
contralto /kon'tralto/ *m*, contralto (voice)
contraluz /kontra'lus; kontra'luθ/ *f*, counterlight
contramaestre /kontrama'estre/ *m*, *Naut.* boatswain; overseer, superintendent, foreman
contramarcha /kontra'martʃa/ *f*, retrogression; *Mil.* countermarch
contramedida /kontrame'ðiða/ *f*, counter-measure
contraorden /kontra'orðen/ *f*, countermand
contrapedalear /kontrapeðale'ar/ *vi* to backpedal
contrapelo /kontra'pelo/ *a adv* the wrong way of the hair, against the grain; *Inf.* reluctantly, distastefully
contrapeso /kontra'peso/ *m*, counterpoise, counterweight; balancing-pole (acrobats); *Fig.* counterbalance; makeweight
contraponer /kontrapo'ner/ *vt irr* to compare; place opposite; oppose. See **poner**
contraproducente /kontraproðu'sente; kontraproðu'θente/ *a* counteractive, counterproductive, unproductive, self-deceiving; self-defeating
contrapuesto /kontra'puesto/ *a* opposing, divergent
contrapunto /kontra'punto/ *m*, counterpoint
contrariar /kontra'riar/ *vt* to counter, oppose; impede; vex, annoy
contrariedad /kontrarie'ðað/ *f*, contrariety, opposition; obstacle; setback, annoyance; vexation, trouble
contrario /kon'trario/ **(-ia)** *a* opposite; hostile, opposed; harmful; adverse, contrary. *n* adversary; opponent. *m*, obstacle. *f*. **contraria,** contrary, opposite. **al contrario,** on the contrary. **llevar la contraria (a),** to oppose; contradict
contrarreforma /kontrarre'forma/ *f*, counter-Reformation
contrasentido /kontrasen'tiðo/ *m*, wrong sense, opposite sense (of words); contradiction of initial premise; self-contradiction; nonsense
contraseña /kontra'seɲa/ *f*, countersign; *Mil.* password
contrastar /kontras'tar/ *vt* to contrast; oppose, resist; check (weights and measures); assay; *Mech.* calibrate, gauge; *vi* contrast
contraste /kon'traste/ *m*, contrast; opposition, difference; weights and measures inspector; dispute, clash. **en c. a,** in contrast to

contrata /kon'trata/ f, See **contrato**

contratación /kontrata'sion; kontrata'θion/ f, hiring; *Com.* transaction; commerce, trade

contratapa /kontra'tapa/ f, back cover (of a periodical, etc.)

contratar /kontra'tar/ vt to contract, enter into an agreement; make a bargain (with), deal (with); hire, contract

contratiempo /kontra'tiempo/ m, mishap, accident

contratista /kontra'tista/ mf contractor

contrato /kon'trato/ m, contract. **contrato de arrendamiento,** lease

contratorpedero /kontratorpe'ðero/ m, torpedoboat destroyer

contravención /kontraβen'sion; kontraβen'θion/ f, contravention; violation. **en c. a,** in violation of

contraveneno /kontraβe'neno/ m, *Med.* antidote; remedy, precaution

contravenir /kontraβe'nir/ vt irr to infringe, contravene. See **venir**

contraventana /kontraβen'tana/ f, shutter (for windows)

contravidriera /kontraβið'riera/ f, storm window

contrayente /kontra'yente/ a contracting. mf contracting party (used of matrimony)

contribución /kontriβu'sion; kontriβu'θion/ f, contribution; tax. **c. sobre la propiedad,** property tax

contribuir /kontri'βuir/ vt irr to pay (taxes); contribute. See **huir**

contribuyente /kontriβu'yente/ a contributing; contributory. mf contributor; taxpayer

contrición /kontri'sion; kontri'θion/ f, contrition

contrincante /kontrin'kante/ m, competitor, candidate (public examinations); rival, opponent

contrito /kon'trito/ a contrite

control /kon'trol/ m, control; checking. **c. de precios,** price control

controlar /kontro'lar/ vt to control

controversia /kontro'βersia/ f, controversy

controvertir /kontroβer'tir/ vi and vt irr to dispute, argue against, deny. See **sentir**

contumacia /kontu'masia; kontu'maθia/ f, obstinacy; *Law.* contumacy

contumaz /kontu'mas; kontu'maθ/ a stubborn; impenitent; *Law.* contumacious; *Med.* obstinate, resistant (to cure)

contumelia /kontu'melia/ f, contumely

conturbar /kontur'βar/ vt to perturb, make anxious, disturb; vr be perturbed

contuso /kon'tuso/ a contused, bruised

convalecencia /kombale'sensia; kombale'θenθia/ f, convalescence; convalescent home

convalecer /kombale'ser; kombale'θer/ vi irr to convalesce, get better; *Fig.* recover, regain (influence, etc.). See **conocer**

convaleciente /kombale'siente; kombale'θiente/ a and mf convalescent

convalidar /kombali'ðar/ vt to ratify, confirm

convecino /kombe'sino; kombe'θino/ a nearby; neighboring

convencedor /kombense'ðor; kombenθe'ðor/ a convincing

convencer /komben'ser; komben'θer/ vt to convince; prove beyond doubt, demonstrate to (persons); be convincing (e.g. *No convence,* It's not convincing; He's not convincing.) vr be convinced

convencimiento /kombensi'miento; kombenθi'miento/ m, conviction, belief, assurance

convención /komben'sion; komben'θion/ f, pact, formal agreement; harmony, conformity; convention

convencional /kombensio'nal; kombenθio'nal/ a conventional (all meanings)

convencionalismo /kombensiona'lismo; kombenθiona'lismo/ m, conventionality

convenido /kombe'niðo/ a agreed

conveniencia /kombe'niensia; kombe'nienθia/ f, conformity, harmony, adjustment; experience, suitability, convenience; advantage; agreement, pact; post as domestic; ease, comfort; pl income; social conventions

conveniente /kombe'niente/ a convenient, opportune; suitable, fitting; profitable; useful; decorous. **tener por c. + inf,** to think it fitting to + *Inf.*, find it appropriate to + *Inf.*

convenio /kom'benio/ m, pact, treaty; *Com.* agreement, contract

convenir /kombe'nir/ vi irr to agree; assemble, congregate; belong; be suitable; vr agree; suit oneself. **No me conviene salir esta tarde,** It does not suit me to go out this afternoon. **Me convendría pasar un mes allí,** It would be a good idea (or a wise thing) for me to spend a month there. See **venir**

conventillo /komben'tijo; komben'tiʎo/ m, *Lat. Am.* tenement

convento /kom'bento/ m, convent; monastery; religious community

conventual /komben'tual/ a conventual; monastic. m, *Eccl.* conventual

convergencia /komber'hensia; komber'henθia/ f, convergence

convergir /komber'hir/ vi to converge; *Fig.* coincide (views, etc.)

conversación /kombersa'sion; kombersa'θion/ f, conversation; intercourse, company; *Law.* criminal conversation

conversar /komber'sar/ vi to converse; chat; live with others; know socially

conversión /komber'sion/ f, conversion; change, transformation; *Com.* conversion; *Mil.* wheel; wheeling

converso /kom'berso/ **(-sa)** n convert (especially a Jew forced to convert during Spanish Inquisition)

convertible /komber'tiβle/ a convertible

convertir /komber'tir/ vt irr to change, transform; convert; reform; vr to become; be transformed; be converted; be reformed. See **sentir**

convexo /kom'bekso/ a convex

convicción /kombik'sion; kombik'θion/ f, conviction; certitude; *Law.* conviction

convicto /kom'bikto/ **(-ta)** a and n *Law.* convict

convidado /kombi'ðaðo/ **(-da)** n guest

convidar /kombi'ðar/ vt to invite (persons); encourage, provoke; entice, attract; vr invite oneself; offer one's services

convincente /kombin'sente; kombin'θente/ a convincing

convite /kom'bite/ m, invitation; banquet; party

convivencia /kombi'βensia; kombi'βenθia/ f, coexistence, common life, life together. **c. pacífica,** peaceful coexistence

convivial /kombi'βial/ a convivial

convivir /kombi'βir/ vi to live together, live under the same roof

convocación /komboka'sion; komboka'θion/ f, convocation

convocar /kombo'kar/ vt to convene, convoke

convoy /kom'boi/ m, convoy; escort; following; cruet-stand

convoyar /kombo'yar/ vt to convoy, escort

convulsión /kombul'sion/ f, convulsion

convulsivo /kombul'siβo/ a convulsive

conyugal /konyu'gal/ a conjugal

cónyuge /'konyuhe/ mf husband or (and) wife (used gen. in pl)

coñac /ko'ɲak/ m, brandy

coñete /ko'ɲete/ a, *Chile, Peru* mean, stingy

cooperación /koopera'sion; koopera'θion/ f, cooperation

cooperador /koopera'ðor/ **(-ra)** a cooperative. n cooperator, collaborator

cooperar /koope'rar/ vt to cooperate

cooperativa /koopera'tiβa/ f, cooperative society

cooperativo /koopera'tiβo/ a cooperative

coordenada /koorðe'naða/ f, coordinate

coordinación /koorðina'sion; koorðina'θion/ f, coordination

coordinar /koorði'nar/ vt to coordinate, classify

copa /'kopa/ f, wineglass, goblet; glassful; top branches (of trees); crown (of hat); *Cards.* heart; gill (liquid measure); *Inf.* drink, glass; *pl Cards.* hearts (in Spanish pack, goblets)

copal /ko'pal/ *m*, *Central America, Mexico* resin

copartícipe /kopar'tisipe; kopar'tiθipe/ *mf* co-partner, partaker, participant

copec /'kopek/ *m*, kopeck

Copenhague /kope'nage/ Copenhagen

copernicano /koperni'kano/ *a* Copernican

copero /ko'pero/ *m*, cupbearer; sideboard; cocktail cabinet

copete /ko'pete/ *m*, lock, tress (hair); tuft, crest; forelock (horses); head, top (ice-cream, drinks); *Inf.* **de alto c.**, aristocratic; socially prominent

copetudo, -a /kope'tuðo/ *a*, *Lat. Am.* tufted, crested; haughty, stuck-up

copia /'kopia/ *f*, abundance, plenty; copy, reproduction; transcript; imitation

copiador /kopia'ðor/ **(-ra)** *a* copying. *n* copier; transcriber. *m*, copybook

copiar /ko'piar/ *vt* to copy

copioso /ko'pioso/ *a* abundant, plentiful

copla /'kopla/ *f*, couplet; popular four-line poem; couple, pair; *pl Inf.* verses

coplero /kop'lero/ **(-ra)** *n* balladmonger; poetaster

copo /'kopo/ *m*, cop (of a spindle); snowflake, ball (of cotton)

copón /ko'pon/ *m*, large goblet; *Eccl.* ciborium, chalice

coprófago /ko'profago/ *a* coprophagous

copropietario /kopropie'tario/ **(-ia)** *n* coproprietor, coowner

copto /'kopto/ **(-ta)** *n* Copt

cópula /'kopula/ *f*, connection; coupling; joining; copulation

copular /kopu'lar/ *vi* to copulate

coque /'koke/ *m*, coke

coqueluche /koke'lutʃe/ *f*, whooping cough

coqueta /ko'keta/ *f*, coquette, flirt

coquetear /kokete'ar/ *vi* to flirt

coqueteo /koke'teo/ *m*, coquetry; flirtation

coquetería /kokete'ria/ *f*, coquetry

coquetón /koke'ton/ *a* coquettish

coraje /ko'rahe/ *m*, courage, valor; anger; *Mexico Inf.* fury. **¡Qué c.!** What nerve!

coral /ko'ral/ *m*, coral. *f*, coral snake. *m*, *Bot.* coral tree; *pl* coral beads

coral /ko'ral/ *a* choral

coralina /kora'lina/ *f*, coral (polyp)

coraza /ko'rasa; ko'raθa/ *f*, cuirass; shell (of tortoise); armor-plate, armor (ships, etc.)

corazón /kora'son; kora'θon/ *m*, heart; courage, spirit; love, tenderness; goodwill, benevolence; core (of a fruit); *Fig.* pith. **de c.**, sincerely. **tener el c. en la mano,** to wear one's heart on one's sleeve

corazonada /koraso'naða; koraθo'naða/ *f*, feeling, instinct; presentiment, apprehension

corbata /kor'βata/ *f*, necktie; scarf; ribbon (insignia)

corbatería /korβate'ria/ *f*, necktie shop

corbatero /korβa'tero/ *m*, necktie maker; necktie dealer; tie rack

Córcega /'korsega; 'korθega/ Corsica

corchea /kor'tʃea/ *f*, *Mus.* quaver

corchete /kor'tʃete/ *m*, *Sew.* hook and eye; hook

corcho /'kortʃo/ *m*, *Bot.* cork, cork bark; stopper, cork; cork mat; bee hive

corcova /kor'koβa/ *f*, hump, abnormal protuberance

corcovado /korko'βaðo/ **(-da)** *a* hunchbacked, crooked. *n* hunchback

corcovear /korko'βear/ *vi* to curvet, caper

cordaje /kor'ðahe/ *m*, *Naut.* cordage, tackling, rope

cordel /kor'ðel/ *m*, cord; *Naut.* line. **a c.**, in a straight line

cordelería /korðele'ria/ *f*, rope making; ropeyard; cordage

cordelero /korðe'lero/ **(-ra)** *n* rope maker

cordera /kor'ðera/ *f*, ewe lamb; sweet, gentle woman

corderillano, -a /korðeri'jano; korðeri'ʎano/ *a*, *Argentina, Chile* Andean

cordero /kor'ðero/ *m*, lamb; dressed lambskin; peaceable, mild man; Jesus (gen. **Divino C.**)

cordial /kor'ðial/ *a* warming, invigorating; affectionate, loving, friendly. *m*, *Med.* cordial

cordialidad /korðiali'ðað/ *f*, cordiality, friendliness

cordillera /korði'jera; korði'ʎera/ *f*, mountain range

Córdoba /'korðoβa/ Cordova

cordobán /korðo'βan/ *m*, cured goatskin; Cordovan leather, Spanish leather

cordobés /korðo'βes/ **(-esa)** *a* and *n* Cordovan

cordón /kor'ðon/ *m*, cord; cordon; *Eccl.* rope girdle; *Archit.* string-course

cordoncillo /korðon'siyo; korðon'θiʎo/ *m*, rib (in cloth); ridge, milling (of coins); *Sew.* piping

cordura /kor'ðura/ *f*, good sense, prudence

Corea /ko'rea/ Korea

coreografía /koreogra'fia/ *f*, choreography; art of dancing

coreográfico /koreo'grafiko/ *a* choreographic

coreógrafo /kore'ografo/ *m*, choreographer

corintio /ko'rintio/ **(-ia)** *a* and *n* Corinthian

Corinto /ko'rinto/ Corinth

corista /ko'rista/ *m*, *Eccl.* chorister. *mf Theat.* member of the chorus

cornada /kor'naða/ *f*, horn thrust or wound (bulls, etc.)

cornamenta /korna'menta/ *f*, horns (bulls, deer, etc.)

córnea /'kornea/ *f*, cornea

corneja /kor'neha/ *f*, carrion or black crow

córneo /'korneo/ *a* horny, corneous

corneta /kor'neta/ *f*, *Mus.* bugle; *Mus.* cornet; swineherd's horn; *Mil.* pennon. *m*, bugler; *Mil.* cornet. **c. de monte,** hunting horn

cornetín /korne'tin/ *m*, *dim* **corneta,** *Mus.* cornet; cornet player

cornezuelo /korne'suelo; korne'θuelo/ *m*, *dim* little horn; *Med.* ergot; *Bot.* variety of olive

cornisa /kor'nisa/ *f*, cornice

cornucopia /kornu'kopia/ *f*, cornucopia, horn of plenty; sconce; mirror

cornudo /kor'nuðo/ *a* horned. *m*, cuckold. **el C.,** the Devil

coro /'koro/ *m*, choir; chorus; *Archit.* choir. **hacer c. (a),** to listen to; support. **saber de c.,** to know by heart

corolario /koro'lario/ *m*, corollary

corona /ko'rona/ *f*, garland, wreath; halo; (*Astron. Archit.*) corona; crown (of tooth); crown (of head); tonsure; crown (coin); royal power; kingdom; triumph; reward; summit, height, peak; circlet (for candles)

coronación /korona'sion; korona'θion/ *f*, coronation; coping stone

coronamiento /korona'miento/ *m*, coronation; coping stone; *Fig.* crowning touch; *Naut.* taffrail

coronar /koro'nar/ *vt* to crown; crown (in checkers); complete, round off; *vr* be crowned; crown oneself; be tipped or capped

coronel /koro'nel/ *m*, colonel

coronela /koro'nela/ *f*, *Inf.* colonel's wife

coronelía /korone'lia/ *f*, colonelcy

coronilla /koro'niya; koro'niʎa/ *f*, *dim* small crown; crown of head; *Fig. Inf.* **estar hasta la c.,** to be fed up

coroza /ko'rosa; ko'roθa/ *f*, dunce's cap

corpiño /kor'piɲo/ *m*, bodice

corporación /korpora'sion; korpora'θion/ *f*, corporation, body, association

corporal /korpo'ral/ *a* and *m*, *Eccl.* corporal

corporativo /korpora'tiβo/ *a* corporate, corporative

corpóreo /kor'poreo/ *a* corporeal

corporizar /korpori'sar; korpori'θar/ *vt* to embody

corpulento /korpu'lento/ *a* corpulent, stout

Corpus /'korpus/ *m*, Corpus Christi

corpúsculo /kor'puskulo/ *m*, corpuscle

corral /ko'rral/ *m*, yard; pen, enclosure, corral; oldtime theater. **c. de madera,** timber yard. *Inf.* **hacer corrales,** to play truant

correa /ko'rrea/ *f*, leather strap or thong; flexibility; *Mech.* belt, band

corrección /korrek'sion; korrek'θion/ *f*, correction;

correctness; punishment; emendation. **c. de pruebas,** proofreading, proofing, reading proof

correcional /korre'sional; korre'θional/ *a* correctional. *m,* reformatory

correcto /ko'rrekto/ *a* correct; well-bred; unexceptionable, irreproachable; regular (of features)

corredera /korre'ðera/ *f,* link (engines); *Mech.* slide; *Naut.* log; racecourse; *Inf.* procuress

corredizo /korre'ðiso; korre'ðiθo/ *a* easy to untie; running (of knots); sliding

corredor /korre'ðor/ **(-ra)** *n* runner. *m, Com.* broker; corridor; *Inf.* meddler; *Inf.* procurer, pimp. *a* running. **c. de bolsa,** stockbroker

corregible /korre'hiβle/ *a* corrigible

corregidor /korrehi'ðor/ *m,* Spanish magistrate; *Obs.* mayor

corregidora /korrehi'ðora/ *f,* wife of corregidor; mayoress

corregir /korre'hir/ *vt irr* to correct; scold, punish; moderate, counteract; *Mech.* adjust; *vr* mend one's ways. **c. pruebas,** to read proof. *Pres. Ind.* **corrijo, corriges, corrige, corrigen.** *Pres. Part.* **corrigiendo.** *Pres. Subjunc.* **corrija, corrijas, etc.** *Imperf. Subjunc.* **corrigiese, etc.**

correligionario /korrelihio'nario/ **(-ia)** *n* coreligionist; fellow-supporter or believer

correlón, -ona /korre'lon/ *a Mexico, Venezuela* cowardly

correntada /korren'taða/ *f, Argentina* rapids

correo /ko'rreo/ *m,* courier; mail; post-office; letters. **c. aéreo,** air-mail. **c. certificado,** registered mail. **c. de voz,** voice mail. **c. electrónico,** e-mail, electronic mail. **a vuelta de c.,** by return of mail. **tren c.,** mail train

correr /ko'rrer/ *vi* to run; race; sail, steam; flow; blow; flood; extend, stretch; pass (of time); fall due (salary, etc.); be current or general; (*with con*) be in charge of or responsible for; *vt* run (a horse); fasten, slide (bolts, etc.); draw (curtains); undergo, suffer; sell, auction; *Inf.* steal; *Fig.* embarrass; spread (a rumor, etc.); catch, make (bus, train, etc.); *vr* slide, glide, slip; run (of colors); *Inf.* spread oneself, talk too much. **c. cañas,** to participate in a mock joust using reeds as spears

correría /korre'ria/ *f,* raid, foray; excursion, trip

correspondencia /korrespon'densia; korrespon'denθia/ *f,* relationship, connection; intercourse, communication; correspondence, letters; equivalence, exact translation

corresponder /korrespon'der/ *vi* to requite, repay; be grateful; belong to, concern; devolve upon, fall to; suit, harmonize (with); fit; *vr* correspond by letters; like or love each other

correspondiente /korrespon'diente/ *a* suitable; proportionate; corresponding. *mf* correspondent

corresponsal /korrespon'sal/ *mf* correspondent (especially professional); *Com.* agent

corretear /korrete'ar/ *vi* to wander about the streets; gad

correveidile /korreβei'ðile/ *mf Inf.* tale-bearer, gossip

corrida /ko'rriða/ *f,* race, run; *Aer.* taxying; bull fight (abb. for **c. de toros**)

corrido /ko'rriðo/ *a* extra, over (of weight); embarrassed; experienced

corriente /ko'rriente/ *a* current, present; well-known; usual, customary; fluent (style); ordinary, average; easy. *f,* flow, stream; *Fig.* course (of events, etc.); *Elec.* current. *adv* quite, exactly. *Elec.* **c. alterna,** alternating current. **c. continua,** direct current. **c. de aire,** draft. **cuenta c.,** savings account. **estar al c.,** to be informed (of something)

Corriente del Golfo /ko'rriente del 'golfo/ Gulf Stream

corrillo /ko'rriyo; ko'rriʎo/ *m,* knot, group, huddle (of people)

corro /'korro/ *m,* circle, group; ring (for children's games)

corroboración /korroβora'sion; korroβora'θion/ *f,* corroboration, confirmation

corroborar /korroβo'rar/ *vt* to fortify; corroborate, support

corroer /korro'er/ *vt irr* to corrode, waste away; *Fig.* gnaw. See **roer**

corromper /korrom'per/ *vt* to rot; mar; spoil, ruin; seduce; corrupt (texts); bribe; *Fig.* contaminate, corrupt; *vi* stink; *vr* putrefy, not; be spoiled; *Fig.* be corrupted

corrosión /korro'sion/ *f,* corrosion

corrosivo /korro'siβo/ *a* corrosive

corrugación /korruga'sion; korruga'θion/ *f,* corrugation, wrinkling

corrupción /korrup'sion; korrup'θion/ *f,* rot, putrefaction; corruption, depravity; decay; stink; bribery; falsification (of texts); corruption (of language, etc.)

corrupto /ko'rrupto/ *a* corrupt

corruptor /korrup'tor/ **(-ra)** *n* corrupter

corsario /kor'sario/ *m,* pirate; privateer

corsé /kor'se/ *m,* corset

corsetería /korsete'ria/ *f,* corset shop or manufactory

corso /'korso/ **(-sa)** *a* and *n* Corsican

corta /'korta/ *f,* felling, cutting

cortacircuitos /kortasir'kuitos; kortaθir'kuitos/ *m, Elec.* circuit breaker, cut-out; disconnecting switch

cortado /kor'taðo/ *a* fitting, proportioned; disjointed (style); confused, shamefaced

cortador /korta'ðor/ *m,* cutter; cutter-out (dresses, etc.); butcher

cortadura /korta'ðura/ *f,* cut, wound; cutting (from periodicals); defile; *pl* clippings, cuttings

cortafrío /korta'frio/ *m,* cold chisel; hammer-head chisel

cortalápices /korta'lapises; korta'lapiθes/ *m,* pencil sharpener

cortante /kor'tante/ *a* cutting; sharp; piercing (of wind, etc.); trenchant; *m, Argentina* scissors *pl.*

cortapapel /kortapa'pel/ *m,* paper-knife

cortapisa /korta'pisa/ *f,* condition, stipulation

cortaplumas /korta'plumas/ *m,* penknife

cortapuros /korta'puros/ *m,* cigar cutter

cortar /kor'tar/ *vt* to cut; cut out (dresses, etc.); switch off, shut off (water, electricity, etc.); cleave, divide; cut (cards); pierce (wind, etc.); interrupt, impede; omit, cut; *Fig.* interrupt (conversation); decide, determine; *vr* be confused or shamefaced; curdle, turn sour (e.g. *Se cortó la leche,* The milk turned sour); split, fray; chap. **Se cortó el pelo,** She cut her hair

cortavidrios /korta'βiðrios/ *m,* diamond, glasscutter

cortaviento /korta'βiento/ *m,* windscreen

corte /'korte/ *m,* court (royal); retinue; yard; *pl* Spanish parliament. *m,* cutting, cut; blade, cutting edge; cutting out, dressmaking; length, material required for garment, shoes, etc.; cut, fit; style; book edge; *Archit.* section; means, expedient; counting of money (in a till). **c. de caja,** counting of money (in a till). **c. trasversal,** side view

cortedad /korte'ðað/ *f,* shortness, brevity; smallness; stupidity, dullness; timidity, shyness. **c. de fuerzas,** lack of strength

cortejar /korte'har/ *vt* to accompany, escort; woo, court

cortejo /kor'teho/ *m,* courtship, wooing; suite, accompaniment; gift, present; homage, attention; *Inf.* lover, beau

cortés /kor'tes/ *a* polite, attentive, courteous, civil

cortesana /korte'sana/ *f,* courtesan

cortesano /korte'sano/ *a* court; courtly. *m,* courtier

cortesía /korte'sia/ *f,* politeness, courtesy; attentiveness; civility; gift, present; favor. **c. internacional,** courtesy of nations. **c. de boca mucho vale y poco cuesta.** Courtesy is worth much and costs little

corteza /kor'tesa; kor'teθa/ *f, Bot.* bark; *Anat.* cortex; skin, peel, crust; aspect, appearance; roughness. **c. terrestre,** Earth's crust, crust of the Earth. **de c.,** superficial (e.g. explanation)

cortijo /kor'tiho/ *m,* farmhouse and land

cortina /kor'tina/ *f,* curtain; *Fig.* veil; *Inf.* heel taps; *Mil.* curtain, screen. **c. de fuego de artillería,** antiaircraft barrage. **c. de globos de intercepción,** balloon barrage. **c. de humo,** smoke screen. **c. metálica,** metal shutter

cortinaje /korti'nahe/ *m*, curtains, hangings

corto /'korto/ *a* short, brief; timid, bashful; concise; defective; stupid, dull; tongue-tied, inarticulate. **c. circuito,** *Elec.* short-circuit. **c. de alcances,** dull-witted. **c. de vista,** short-sighted

coruscar /korus'kar/ *vi* to glitter, shine

corvadura /korβa'ðura/ *f*, bend; curvature

corveta /kor'βeta/ *f*, curvet, prancing; *a*, *Central America* bow-legged

corvetear /korβete'ar/ *vi* to curvet

corzo /'korso; 'korθo/ *m*, roe-deer, fallow-deer

cosa /'kosa/ *f*, thing. **cualquier c.,** anything. **c. rara,** strange to relate; an extraordinary thing. **como si tal c.,** as though nothing had happened. *Inf.* **poquita c.,** a person of no account

cosaco /ko'sako/ **(-ca)** *a* and *n* Cossack

coscorrón /kosko'rron/ *m*, blow on the head, cuff

cosecha /ko'setʃa/ *f*, harvest; harvest time; reaping, gathering, lifting; yield, produce; crop, shower (of honors, etc.). **c. de vino,** vintage

cosechar /kose'tʃar/ *vi* and *vt* to harvest, reap

coseno /ko'seno/ *m*, cosine

coser /ko'ser/ *vt* to sew, stitch; join, unite; press together (lips, etc.). **c. a puñaladas,** to stab repeatedly

Cosme /'kosme/ Cosmo

cosmético /kos'metiko/ *a* and *m*, cosmetic

cósmico /'kosmiko/ *a* cosmic

cosmografía /kosmogra'fia/ *f*, cosmography

cosmógrafo /kos'mografo/ *m*, cosmographer

cosmonave /kosmo'naβe/ *f*, spaceship

cosmopolita /kosmopo'lita/ *a* and *mf* cosmopolitan

cosmopolitismo /kosmopoli'tismo/ *m*, cosmopolitanism

cosmos /'kosmos/ *m*, cosmos

cospel /kos'pel/ *m*, blank (from which to stamp coins); to ken; subway to ken

cosquillas /kos'kiyas; kos'kiʎas/ *f pl*, tickling. **hacer c. (a),** to tickle. **¿tienes c.?** Are you ticklish?

cosquillear /koskiye'ar; koskiʎe'ar/ *vt* to tickle

cosquilleo /koski'yeo; koski'ʎeo/ *m*, tickle, tickling

cosquilloso /koski'yoso; koski'ʎoso/ *a* ticklish; hypersensitive, touchy

costa /'kosta/ *f*, cost; expense; coast; *pl Law.* costs. **a c. de,** by dint of; at the cost of. **a toda c.,** at all costs

Costa del Oro, la /'kosta del 'oro, la/ the Gold Coast

Costa de Marfil /'kosta de mar'fil/ Ivory Coast

costado /kos'taðo/ *m*, *Anat.* side; *Mil.* flank; side; *pl* line of descent, genealogy. *Naut.* **dar el c.,** to be broadside on

costal /kos'tal/ *m*, sack, bag

costanero /kosta'nero/ *a* sloping; coast, coastal

costar /kos'tar/ *vi irr* to cost; cause. See **contar**

costarricense /kostarri'sense; kostarri'θense/ *a* and *n* Costa Rican

coste /'koste/ *m*, cost, price

costear /koste'ar/ *vt* to pay for, defray the expense of; *Naut.* coast; *Argentina* pasture; *vr* pay (for itself)

costilla /kos'tiya; kos'tiʎa/ *f*, (*Anat. Aer. Naut. Archit.*) rib; *Fig. Inf.* better half, wife; *pl Inf.* back, behind

costillaje, costillar /kosti'yahe, kosti'yar; kosti'ʎahe, kosti'ʎar/ *m*, *Anat.* ribs; *Naut.* ship's frame

costoso /kos'toso/ *a* expensive, costly; valuable; dear, costly, difficult

costra /'kostra/ *f*, crust; scab; rind (of cheese)

costumbre /kos'tumbre/ *f*, habit; custom

costumbrista /kostum'brista/ *mf* writer on everyday life and customs. *a* (of literary work) dealing with life and customs

costura /kos'tura/ *f*, sewing; seam; needlework; joint; riveting

costurar, costurear /kostu'rar/ *vi*, *Lat. Am.* to sew

costurera /kostu'rera/ *f*, seamstress

costurero /kostu'rero/ *m*, work-box, sewing bag

cota /'kota/ *f*, *Surv.* elevation, height; coat (of mail); quota. **c. de malla,** chain-mail

cotangente /kotan'hente/ *f*, cotangent

cotejar /kote'har/ *vt* to compare; collate

cotejo /ko'teho/ *m*, comparison; collation

cótel /'kotel/ *m*, cocktail, drink

cotelera /kote'lera/ *f*, cocktail shaker

cotidiano /koti'ðiano/ *a* daily

cotizable /koti'saβle; koti'θaβle/ *a* valued at; (of prices, shares) quoted

cotización /kotisa'sion; kotiθa'θion/ *f*, *Com.* quotation; *Com.* rate. **boletín de c.,** price list (of shares, etc.)

cotizar /koti'sar; koti'θar/ *vt Com.* to quote (prices, rates)

coto /'koto/ *m*, enclosed ground; boundary stone; preserve, covert; hand's breadth; end, stop, limit. **c. de caza,** game preserve

cotorra /ko'torra/ *f*, small green parrot; magpie; *Inf.* chatterbox

cotufa /ko'tufa/ *f*, earthnut; titbit; *Inf.* **pedir cotufas en el golfo,** to ask for the moon; **cotufas** *f pl Venezuela* popcorn

coyote /ko'yote/ *m*, coyote, prairie wolf; *Mexico* fixer (anyone who can pull strings to cut red tape or achieve something illegally); smuggler (of goods or people)

coyuntura /koyun'tura/ *f*, *Anat.* joint; juncture, occasion

coz /kos; koθ/ *f*, kick, recoil (of gun); butt (of a rifle); *Inf.* slap in the face, unprovoked rudeness. **dar coces,** to kick

craneal /krane'al/ *a* cranial

cranearse /krane'arse/ *vr*, *Chile* to burn the midnight oil

cráneo /'kraneo/ *m*, cranium, skull

crápula /'krapula/ *f*, drunkenness; depravity, immorality, debauchery

craquear /krake'ar/ *vt* to crack (petroleum)

crasitud /krasi'tuð/ *f*, greasiness; fatness; crassness

craso /'kraso/ *a* fat, greasy; thick; unpardonable, crass (often with *ignorancia*). *m*, fatness; ignorance

creación /krea'sion; krea'θion/ *f*, creation; universe; world; foundation, establishment; appointment (dignitaries)

creador /krea'ðor/ **(-ra)** *n* creator, originator. *m*, God. *a* creative

crear /kre'ar/ *vt* to create; found, institute, establish; make, appoint

crecer /kre'ser; kre'θer/ *vi irr* to grow; grow up; increase in size; grow longer; wax (moon); come in (of the tide); increase in value (money); *vr* become more sure of oneself; swell with pride; grow in authority. See **nacer**

creces /'kreses; 'kreθes/ *f pl*, increase, interest. **con c.,** fully, amply. **pagar con c.,** *Fig.* to pay with interest

crecida /kre'siða; kre'θiða/ *f*, swollen river or stream; food; rising (of the tide)

crecido /kre'siðo; kre'θiðo/ *a* grown up; considerable; abundant, plentiful; large; full; serious, important

crecidos /kre'siðos; kre'θiðos/ *m pl*, widening stitches (knitting)

creciente /kre'siente; kre'θiente/ *a* growing; rising (of the tide); crescent (moon). *m*, *Herald.* crescent. *f*, rising of the tide; crescent moon

crecimiento /kresi'miento; kreθi'miento/ *m*, growing; growth, development; increase (in value, money); waxing (of moon)

credenciales /kreðen'siales; kreðen'θiales/ *f pl*, credentials

credibilidad /kreðiβili'ðað/ *f*, credibility

crédito /'kreðito/ *m*, belief, credence; assent, acquiescence; reputation, name; favor, popularity, acceptance; *Com.* credit; *Com.* letter of credit. **créditos activos,** assets. **créditos pasivos,** liabilities. **a c.,** on credit

credo /'kreðo/ *m*, creed. *Inf.* **en un c.,** in a jiffy

credulidad /kreðuli'ðað/ *f*, credulity

crédulo /'kreðulo/ *a* credulous

creencia /kre'ensia; kre'enθia/ *f*, belief; religion, sect, faith

creer /kre'er/ *vt irr* to believe; think, consider, opine; think likely or probable. **¡Ya lo creo!** I should just think so! Rather! **creerse la divina garza,** *Mexico* to think one is God's gift to the world. **creerse descender del sobaco de Jesucristo,** to think one is

God's gift to the world. *Pres. Part.* **creyendo.** *Preterite* **creyó, creyeron.** *Imperf. Subjunc.* **creyese, etc.**

creíble /kre'iβle/ *a* credible

creído, -a /kre'iðo/ *a, Lat. Am.* credulous, trusting

crema /'krema/ *f,* cream (off milk); custard mold, cream, shape; face cream; cold cream; elect, flower (of society, etc.)

cremación /krema'sion; krema'θion/ *f,* cremation; burning, incineration

cremallera /krema'yera; krema'ʎera/ *f, Mech.* rack, ratch; zipper. **colgar la c.,** to give a house-warming

crematístico /krema'tistiko/ *a* economic, financial

crematorio /krema'torio/ *m,* crematorium. *a* burning; cremating

cremor /kre'mor/ *m, Chem.* cream of tartar

cremoso /kre'moso/ *a* creamy

crencha /'krentʃa/ *f,* parting (of the hair); each side of parting

crepitación /krepita'sion; krepita'θion/ *f,* crackling, sputtering; hissing; roar (of a fire); *Med.* crepitation

crepitar /krepi'tar/ *vi* to crackle; sputter; hiss; roar (of a fire); *Med.* crepitate

crepuscular /krepusku'lar/ *a* twilight

crepúsculo /kre'puskulo/ *m,* twilight, half light

cresa /'kresa/ *f,* maggot; cheese-mite; fly's egg

Creso /'kreso/ Croesus

crespo /'krespo/ *a* curly, frizzy (hair); rough (of animal's fur); curled (leaves); artificial, involved (style)

crespón /kres'pon/ *m,* crape

cresta /'kresta/ *f,* comb (of cock, etc.); tuft, topknot (birds); plume; summit, top (of mountains); crest (of a wave); *Herald.* crest

Creta /'kreta/ Crete

creta /'kreta/ *f,* chalk

cretense /kre'tense/ *a* Cretan

cretinismo /kreti'nismo/ *m,* cretinism

cretino /kre'tino/ **(-na)** *a* and *n* cretin

creyente /kre'yente/ *a* believing; religious. *mf* believer

cría /'kria/ *f,* rearing; bringing up; nursing; suckling; breeding; brood; litter

criadero /kria'ðero/ *m, Mineral.* vein, deposit; tree nursery, plantation; breeding farm or place. *a* prolific

criado /kri'aðo/ **(-da)** *n* servant. *a* bred, brought up (used with *bien* or *mal,* well or badly brought up)

criador /kria'ðor/ **(-ra)** *n* breeder, keeper, raiser. *a* creating; rearing; creative; fertile, rich

criandera /krian'dera/ *f. Lat. Am.* nursemaid, wet nurse

crianza /kri'ansa; kri'anθa/ *f,* feeding, suckling; lactation; manners. **buena** (or **mala**) **c.,** good (or bad) breeding or upbringing

criar /kri'ar/ *vt* to create; procreate; rear, educate, bring up; feed, nurse, suckle; raise (birds, animals); inspire, give rise to. **Me crié raquítico,** I grew up delicate

criatura /kria'tura/ *f,* being, creature; man, human being; infant; small child; fetus; *Fig.* puppet, tool

criba /'kriβa/ *f,* sieve, cribble

cribar /kri'βar/ *vt* to sieve; riddle (earth, etc.)

crimen /'krimen/ *m,* crime. **c. pasional,** crime of passion

criminal /krimi'nal/ *a* and *m,* criminal

criminalidad /kriminali'ðað/ *f,* guilt; crime ratio; delinquency

criminalista /krimina'lista/ *mf* criminal lawyer; criminologist

criminología /kriminolo'hia/ *f,* criminology

crin /krin/ *f,* horsehair; (gen. *pl*) mane

crinolina /krino'lina/ *f,* crinoline

crío /'krio/ *m, Inf.* kid, brat

criollo /'krioyo; 'krioʎo/ **(-lla)** *n* creole, descendant of Europeans born in colonial Spanish America. *a* creole

cripta /'kripta/ *f,* crypt

criptografía /kriptogra'fia/ *f,* cryptography

criquet /kri'ket/ *m, Sports.* cricket

crisantemo /krisan'temo/ *m,* chrysanthemum

crisis /'krisis/ *f,* crisis. **c. de desarrollo,** growing pains. **c. de vivienda,** housing shortage

crisma /'krisma/ *m,* or *f,* chrism

crisol /kri'sol/ *m,* crucible; melting pot

crispado /kris'paðo/ *a* stiffened

crispar /kris'par/ *vt* to cause to contract or twitch; *vr* twitch. *Inf.* **Se me crispan los nervios,** My nerves are all on edge

cristal /kris'tal/ *m,* crystal; glass; windowpane; mirror; water. **c. tallado,** cut glass

cristalería /kristale'ria/ *f,* glassware; glass manufacture; glass panes; glass and china shop

cristalino /krista'lino/ *a* crystalline. *m,* lens (of the eye)

cristalización /kristalisa'sion; kristaliθa'θion/ *f,* crystallization

cristalizar /kristali'sar; kristali'θar/ *vi* to crystallize; *Fig.* take shape; *vt* cause to crystallize

cristalografía /kristalogra'fia/ *f,* crystallography

cristiandad /kristian'daδ/ *f,* Christendom

cristianismo /kristia'nismo/ *m,* Christianity; Christendom

cristianizar /kristiani'sar; kristiani'θar/ *vt* to convert to Christianity, christianize

cristiano /kris'tiano/ **(-na)** *a* and *n* Christian. *a Inf.* watered (of wine). *m, Inf.* Spanish (contrasted with other languages); *Inf.* soul, person

cristino /kris'tino/ **(-na)** *a* and *n* supporting, or follower of, Queen Regent Maria Cristina during Carlist wars

Cristo /'kristo/ *m,* Christ; **cristo,** crucifix. *Inf.* **donde C. dio las tres voces,** in the middle of nowhere

cristus /'kristus/ *m,* Christ-cross; alphabet. **no saber el c.,** to be extremely ignorant

criterio /kri'terio/ *m,* criterion, standard; judgment, discernment; opinion. **a c. de,** in the opinion of. **según mi c.,** in my opinion

crítica /'kritika/ **(a)** *f,* criticism (of)

criticar /kriti'kar/ *vt* to criticize; censure, find fault with, blame

crítico /'kritiko/ *a* critical; censorious; dangerous, difficult; *Med.* critical. *m,* critic; fault-finder

criticón /kriti'kon/ **(-ona)** *a* censorious, hyper-critical. *n* fault-finder

Croacia /kro'asia; kro'aθia/ Croatia

croar /kro'ar/ *vi* (frog) to croak

croata /kro'ata/ *a* and *mf* Croatian

croché /kro'tʃe/ *m,* crochet work

crol /krol/ *m,* crawl (swimming)

cromado /kro'maðo/ *a* chromium-plated

cromático /kro'matiko/ *a* chromatic

crómico /'kromiko/ *a* chromic

cromo /'kromo/ *m,* chrome; chromium; chromolithograph

crónica /'kronika/ *f,* chronicle; diary of events

crónico /'kroniko/ *a* chronic; inveterate

cronista /kro'nista/ *mf* chronicler

cronología /kronolo'hia/ *f,* chronology

cronológico /krono'lohiko/ *a* chronological

cronómetro /kro'nometro/ *m,* stop-watch

croqueta /kro'keta/ *f,* croquette

croquis /'krokis/ *m,* sketch, outline, drawing. **c. de nivel,** (optical) foresight

crótalo /'krotalo/ *m,* rattlesnake; snapper (kind of castanet)

cruce /'kruse; 'kruθe/ *m,* crossing; point of intersection; crossroads

crucero /kru'sero; kru'θero/ *m, Eccl.* cross-bearer; crossroads; *Archit.* transept; *Astron.* Cross; *Naut.* cruiser

crucificar /krusifi'kar; kruθifi'kar/ *vt* to crucify; *Fig. Inf.* torment, torture

crucifijo /krusi'fiho; kruθi'fiho/ *m,* crucifix

crucifixión /krusifik'sion; kruθifik'sion/ *f,* crucifixion

crucigrama /krusi'grama; kruθi'grama/ *m,* crossword puzzle

cruda /'kruða/ *f, Mexico* hangover

crudelísimo /kruðe'lisimo/ *a sup* **cruel,** most cruel, exceedingly cruel

crudeza /kru'ðesa; kru'ðeθa/ *f,* rawness, uncookedness; unripeness; rawness (silk, etc.); crudeness; harshness; *Inf.* boasting

crudo /'kruðo/ *a* uncooked, raw; green, unripe; indigestible; raw, natural, unbleached; harsh, cruel; cold, raw; *Inf.* boastful. **crudos de petróleo,** *m pl* crude oil

crueldad /kruel'dað/ *f,* cruelty; harshness

cruento /'kruento/ *a* bloody

crujía /kru'hia/ *f,* passage, corridor; *Naut.* midship gangway

crujidero /kruhi'ðero/ *a* crackling; creaking; crispy; clattering; rustling; chattering

crujido /kru'hiðo/ *m,* creak, crack, crackling, rustle

crujir /kru'hir/ *vi* to creak, crackle, rustle

crup /krup/ *m,* croup

crupié /kru'pie/ *m,* croupier

crustáceo /krus'taseo; krus'taθeo/ *a* and *m,* crustacean

cruz /krus; kruθ/ *f,* cross; tails (of coin); withers (of animals); insignia, decoration; affliction, trouble; *Astron.* Southern Cross; *Print.* dagger, obelisk, obelus. **c. doble,** diesis, double dagger. **c. de mayo,** May cross. **c. gamada,** swastika. *Inf.* **¡C. y raya!** An end to this! **en c.,** in the shape of a cross. *Inf.* **hacerse cruces,** to be left speechless, be dumbfounded

cruza /'krusa; 'kruθa/ *f, Lat. Am.* intersection

cruzada /kru'saða; kru'θaða/ *f,* crusade; crossroads; campaign

cruzado /kru'saðo; kru'θaðo/ *a* cross; double-breasted (of coats). *m,* crusader; member of military order

cruzamiento /krusa'miento; kruθa'miento/ *m,* crossing; intersection

cruzar /kru'sar; kru'θar/ *vt* to cross; intersect; interbreed; bestow a cross upon; *Naut.* cruise; *Chile, Peru* quarrel with; *vr* take part in a crusade; cross one another; coincide; *Geom.* intersect

cu /ku/ *f,* name of the letter Q

cuaco /'kuako/ *m, Lat. Am.* horse

cuacuac /kua'kuak/ *m,* quack (of a duck)

cuaderna /kua'ðerna/ *f, Naut.* ship's frame, timber; double fours (backgammon)

cuaderno /kua'ðerno/ *m,* notebook, jotter, account book; *Inf.* card pack. *Naut.* **c. de bitácora,** logbook

cuadra /'kuaðra/ *f,* stable; ward, dormitory; hall, large room; quarter of a mile; *Lat. Am.* block (of houses)

cuadrado /kua'ðraðo/ *a* square; perfect, exact. *m,* square; *(Mil. Math.)* square; window-frame; clock (of a stocking)

cuadragésima /kuaðra'hesima/ *f,* Quadragesima

cuadragésimo /kuaðra'hesimo/ *a* fortieth

cuadrángulo /kua'ðrangulo/ *m,* quadrangle

cuadrante /kua'ðrante/ *m,* quadrant; dial, face

cuadrar /kua'ðrar/ *vt (Math.)* to square; make square; *vi* correspond, tally; fit, be appropriate. *vr Mil.* stand at attention; *Fig. Inf.* dig one's heels in

cuadrática /kua'ðratika/ *f,* quadratic equation

cuadrático /kua'ðratiko/ *a* quadratic

cuadratura /kuaðra'tura/ *f,* squareness; *(Math. Astron.)* quadrature

cuadrienio /kua'ðrienio/ *m,* space of four years

cuadriga /kua'ðriga/ *f,* quadriga

cuadrilátero /kuaðri'latero/ *m,* quadrilateral; boxing ring. *a* quadrilateral

cuadrilla /kua'ðriya; kua'ðriλa/ *f,* gang; company, band, group; police patrol; quadrille (dance); matadors and their assistants (at a bull fight). **c. carrillana,** track gang

cuadrilongo /kuaðri'longo/ *a* and *m,* oblong

cuadrimotor /kuaðrimo'tor/ *a Aer.* four-engined

cuadrivio /kua'ðriβio/ *m,* quadrivium

cuadro /'kuaðro/ *m,* square; picture-frame; frame (of bicycle); flowerbed; *Theat.* tableau, scene; spectacle, sight; board (of instruments); description (in novel, etc.); *Mil.* command, officers; square (of troops). **c. de distribución,** *Elec.* main switchboard. **c. enrejado,** play pen. **cuadro de costumbres,** word-picture of everyday life and customs. **cuadro vivo,** tableau vivant. **a cuadros,** checked, in squares

cuadrúpedo /kua'ðrupeðo/ **(-da)** *a* and *n* quadruped

cuadruple /kua'ðruple/ *a* quadruple

cuadruplicar /kuaðrupli'kar/ *vt* to quadruple

cuajada /kua'haða/ *f,* curd (of milk)

cuajar /kua'har/ *m,* maw (of a ruminant)

cuajar /kua'har/ *vt* to coagulate; curdle; *vi Inf.* achieve, get away with; *vr* be coagulated or curdled; *Inf.* be packed or chock full; get stuck (e.g. a piece of food in one's throat)

cuajarón /kuaha'ron/ *m,* clot (of blood, etc.)

cuajo /'kuaho/ *m,* rennet; coagulation; curdling; *Anat.* abomasum

cual /kual/ *rel. pron* sing. *mf* and *neut* pl **cuales,** which; who; such as (e.g. *Le detuvieron sucesos cuales suelen ocurrir,* He was detained by events such as usually happen). **a c. mas,** vying (with) (e.g. *Los dos canónigos a c. más grueso,* The two canons each fatter (vying in fatness) than the other). **c.** is used with *def. art* **el (la, lo, los, las) cual(es),** who; which, when the antecedent is a noun (e.g. *Juan saltó en el barco, el c. zarpó en seguida,* John jumped into the boat which sailed at once). **por lo c.,** for which reason. *adv* like (gen. literary or poet.). **¿cuál?** *interr. pron* (no article) which? what? e.g. *Aquí tienes dos cuadros, ¿cuál de ellos te gusta?* Here are two pictures, which one do you like? Also expresses an implicit question, e.g. *No sé cuál te guste,* I don't know which you will like. **¡cuál!** *adv interj* how! **c.... c.** *indef pron* some... some

cualesquier /kuales'kier/ *a pl* of **cualquier**

cualesquiera /kuales'kiera/ *a pl* of **cualquiera**

cualidad /kuali'ðað/ *f,* quality; characteristic; talent

cualitativo /kualita'tiβo/ *a* qualitative

cualquier /kual'kier/ *abb* of **cualquiera,** any; *pl* **cualesquier.** Only used as abb. *before* noun

cualquiera /kual'kiera/ *a mf* any, e.g. *una canción c.,* any song. *pron* anybody, each, anyone whatsoever, whoever (e.g. *¡C. diría que no te gusta!* Anyone would say you don't like it!) *Inf.* **un c.,** a nobody

cuán /ku'an/ *adv* how (e.g. *¡C. bello es!* How beautiful it is). Used only before *a* or *adv.* Abbr. of **cuánto**

cuando /'kuando/ *adv* when; if. *interr* **¿cuándo?** *conjunc* although; since; sometimes; *prep* during (e.g. *c. la guerra,* during the war) **c. más,** at most, at best. **c. menos,** at the least. **c. no,** if not (e.g. *Es agnóstica cuando no atea,* She's an agnostic, if not an atheist) **de c. en c.,** from time to time

cuandoquiera /kuando'kiera/ *adv* whenever

cuanta, teoría de la /'kuanta, teo'ria de la/ *f,* quantum theory

cuantía /kuan'tia/ *f,* quantity, amount; importance, rank, distinction

cuantiar /kuan'tiar/ *vt* to value, estimate; tax

cuantidad /kuanti'ðað/ *f,* quantity

cuantioso /kuan'tioso/ *a* large, considerable; numerous; plentiful, abundant

cuantitativo /kuantita'tiβo/ *a* quantitative

cuanto /'kuanto/ *a* as much as, all the; *pl* as many as, all the (e.g. *Te daré cuantas muñecas veas allí,* I'll give you all the dolls you see there). *a.* correlative the... the, as... as (e.g. *C. más tanto, mejor,* The more the better). **cuánto,** *a* and *pron interr* and *interj* how much; *pl* how many (e.g. *¡Cuánto tiempo sin verla!* How long without seeing her!) *pron neut* **cuanto,** as much as, all that (e.g. *Te daré c. quieras,* I shall give you all that you wish). *adv* **cuanto,** as soon as. **c. antes,** as soon as possible. **c. a** or **en c. a,** concerning. *adv* and *conjunc* **c. más,** and the more (e.g. *Se lo diré c. más que tenía esa intención,* I shall tell him all the more because I meant to do so). *adv* **en c.,** as soon as, immediately (e.g. *Lo haré en c. venga,* I shall do it immediately he comes). **en c. a,** with regard to. **por c.,** inasmuch, for this reason. *adv interj* **¿cuánto?** How much? How long? *adv interj* How! How much! (e.g. *¡Cuánto me gustaría ir!* How much I should like to go!)

cuaquerismo /kuake'rismo/ *m,* Quakerism

cuáquero /'kuakero/ **(-ra)** *n* Quaker

cuarenta /kua'renta/ *a,* forty; fortieth. **esas son otras cuarenta** *Argentina, Peru* that's a different story, that's a horse of another color

cuarentena /kuaren'tena/ *f,* fortieth; period of forty days, months or years; Lent; quarantine

cuarentón /kuaren'ton/ **(-ona)** *n* person forty years old

cuaresma /kua'resma/ *f*, Lent

cuaresmal /kuares'mal/ *a* Lenten

cuarta /'kuarta/ *f*, quarter, fourth; hand's breadth; *Mus.* fourth; *Astron.* quadrant

cuarteadura /kuartea'ðura/ *f*, crack

cuartear /kuarte'ar/ *vt* to quarter, divide into quarters; cut or divide into pieces

cuartel /kuar'tel/ *m*, barracks; *Naut.* hatch; quarter, fourth; *Herald.* quarter; district, ward; flowerbed; *Inf.* house, accommodation; *Mil.* quarter, mercy; *Mil.* billet, station. *Mil.* **c. general,** general headquarters

cuartelada /kuarte'laða/ *f*, *Naut.* quarter; military rebellion, military uprising, mutiny

cuartelazo /kuarte'laso; kuarte'laθo/ *m*, military rebellion, military uprising, mutiny

cuarteta /kuar'teta/ *f*, quatrain

cuarteto /kuar'teto/ *m*, *Mus.* quartet; *Poet.* quatrain

cuartilla /kuar'tiya; kuar'tiʎa/ *f*, sheet of paper; liquid measure; quarter of an arroba; pastern (horses)

cuarto /'kuarto/ *m*, room; quarter, fourth; point (of compass); watch (on battleships); *Astron.* quarter, phase; portion, quarter; joint (of meat); *pl* quarters (of animals); *Inf.* penny, farthing. *a* quarter, fourth. **c. creciente,** first phase (of moon). **c. de hora,** quarter of an hour. **c. doble** *Mexico* double room. **c. sencillo** *Mexico* single room. **en c.,** *Print.* in quarto. *Inf.* **no tener un c.,** to be broke

cuarzo /'kuarso; 'kuarθo/ *m*, quartz

cuasidelito /kuasiðe'lito/ *m*, *Law.* technical offense

cuasimodo /kuasi'moðo/ *m*, *Eccl.* Low Sunday, Quasimodo

cuatrillón /kuatri'yon; kuatri'ʎon/ *m*, quadrillion

cuatrimestre /kuatri'mestre/ *a* of four months' duration. *m*, space of four months

cuatrimotor /kuatrimo'tor/ *m*, *Aer.* four-engine airplane

cuatrisílabo /kuatri'silaβo/ *a* quadrisyllabic

cuatro /'kuatro/ *a* four; fourth. *m*, figure four; fourth (of days of months); playing-card with four spots; *Mus.* quartet. **el c. de mayo,** the fourth of May. **Son las c.,** It is four o'clock

cuatrocientos /kuatro'sientos; kuatro'θientos/ *a* four hundred; four hundredth.

cuba /'kuβa/ *f*, barrel, cask; tub, vat; *Inf.* pot-bellied person; *Inf.* drunkard, toper

Cuba /'kuβa/ Cuba

cubano /ku'βano/ **(-na)** *a* and *n* Cuban

cubería /kuβe'ria/ *f*, cooperage

cubeta /ku'βeta/ *f*, *dim* keg, small cask; bucket; pail; *Photo.* developing dish

cubicar /kuβi'kar/ *vt* *Math.* to cube; *Geom.* measure the volume of

cúbico /'kuβiko/ *a* cubic

cubículo /ku'βikulo/ *m*, cubicle

cubierta /ku'βierta/ *f*, cover; envelope; casing; deck (of ship); tire cover; book-jacket; pretext, excuse. **c. de escotilla,** *Naut.* companion-hatch. **c. de paseo,** promenade deck

cubierto /ku'βierto/ *m*, cover, place at table; course (of a meal); table d'hôte, complete meal; roof. **un c. de doscientas pesetas,** a two hundred peseta meal

cubil /ku'βil/ *m*, lair, den (of animals)

cubilete /kuβi'lete/ *m*, *Cul.* mold; dice box; conjurer's cup

cubismo /ku'βismo/ *m*, cubism

cubista /ku'βista/ *mf* cubist. *a* cubistic

cubo /'kuβo/ *m*, bucket, pail; *Mech.* socket; *Math.* cube; hub (of a wheel); mill-pond

cubrecama /kuβre'kama/ *m*, bedspread

cubrimiento /kuβri'miento/ *m*, covering

cubrir /ku'βrir/ *vt* to cover; *Mil.* defend; spread over; extend over; conceal, hide; *Com.* cover; dissemble; *Archit.* roof; *vr* cover one's head; pay, meet (debts, etc.); cover or protect oneself (by insurance, etc.). *Past Part.* **cubierto**

cucaña /ku'kaɲa/ *f*, greasy pole; *Inf.* snip, cinch, bargain

cucaracha /kuka'ratʃa/ *f*, cockroach

cuchara /ku'tʃara/ *f*, spoon; ladle; *Naut.* boat scoop; scoop, dipper. *Fig.* **meter c.,** to stick one's oar in

cucharada /kutʃa'raða/ *f*, spoonful; ladleful

cucharita /kutʃa'rita/ *f*, *Lat. Am.* teaspoonful

cuchí /'kutʃi/ *m*, *Peru* hog

cúchi /'kutʃi/ *a* *inf* *Venezuela* cute, sweet

cuchicheador /kutʃitʃea'ðor/ **(-ra)** *n* whisperer

cuchichear /kutʃitʃe'ar/ *vi* to whisper

cuchicheo /kutʃi'tʃeo/ *m*, whisper; whispering; murmur

cuchillada /kutʃi'yaða; kutʃi'ʎaða/ *f*, knife thrust or wound; *pl* (in sleeves, etc.) slashes; fight, blows

cuchillero /kutʃi'yero; kutʃi'ʎero/ *m*, cutler

cuchillo /ku'tʃiyo; ku'tʃiʎo/ *m*, knife; *Sew.* gore, gusset (gen. *pl*); authority, power; anything triangular in shape. **pasar a c.,** to put to the sword

cuclillas, en /ku'kliyas, en; ku'kliʎas, en/ *adv* in a squatting position

cuclillo /ku'kliyo; ku'kliʎo/ *m*, *Ornith.* cuckoo; *Inf.* cuckold

cuco /'kuko/ *a* *Inf.* pretty, cute; crafty, smart

Cucufo /ku'kufo/ *m*, the Devil

cuculla /ku'kuya; ku'kuʎa/ *f*, cowl, hood

cucurucho /kuku'rutʃo/ *m*, paper cornet

cueca /'kueka/ *f*, *Chile* cueca (Chilean dance)

cuello /'kueyo; 'kueʎo/ *m*, *Anat.* neck; neck (of bottle, etc.); *Sew.* neck; collar; necklet (of fur, etc.)

cuenca /'kuenka/ *f*, socket (of eye); *Geog.* catchment-basin; gorge, deep valley. **c. de un río,** river-basin

cuenta /'kuenta/ *f*, count, counting; calculation; account; bead; charge, responsibility; reckoning; explanation, reason; *Com.* bill. **c. a cero, c. a la inversa, c. atrás,** countdown. **c. corriente,** savings, day-to-day account. **cuentas alegres, cuentas galanas,** *inf* idle dreams, illusions. **c. pendiente,** outstanding account. *Inf.* **caer en la c.,** to tumble to. **darse c. de,** to realize. **llevar la c.,** to reckon, keep account. **sin c.,** countless. **tener en c.,** to bear in mind

cuentacorrentista /kuentakorren'tista/ *mf* one who has a bank account

cuentagotas /kuenta'gotas/ *m*, dropper, dropping tube

cuentakilómetros /kuentaki'lometros/ *m*, speedometer

cuentapasos /kuenta'pasos/ *m*, pedometer

cuentista /kuen'tista/ *mf* storyteller; *Inf.* gossip

cuento /'kuento/ *m*, story, tale; narrative; calculation; *Inf.* gossip, fairytale; *Math.* million. **c. de viejas,** old wives' tale. *Fig.* **dejarse de cuentos,** to go straight to the point. *Inf.* **Va de c.,** It is told, they say

cuerda /'kuerða/ *f*, rope; cord; string; *Geom.* chord; *Mus.* string; catgut; chain (of clock); *Mus.* chord; vocal range. **dar c.** (a), to wind up (a watch); lead on, make talk. **de cuerdas cruzadas,** overstrung (of a piano)

cuerdo /'kuerðo/ *a* sane; prudent; levelheaded

cuerno /'kuerno/ *m*, *Anat.* horn; feeler, antenna; *Mus.* horn; horn (of the moon). **c. de abundancia,** horn of plenty. *Inf.* **poner en los cuernos de la luna,** to praise to the skies

cuero /'kuero/ *m*, hide, pelt; leather. **c. charolado,** patent leather. **en cueros,** stark naked

cuerpo /'kuerpo/ *m*, *Anat.* body or trunk; flesh (as opposed to spirit); bodice; volume, book; main portion; collection; size, volume; physical appearance; corpse; group, assembly; corporation, association; *Geom.* solid; *Chem.* element; thickness, density; *Mil.* corps. **c. de bomberos,** fire brigade. **c. de guardia,** guardhouse. **c. de la vida,** staff of life; *Inf.* **dar con el c. en tierra,** to fall flat. **de c. entero,** *Art.* full-length (portrait). **en c.,** without a coat, lightly clad. **un c. a c.,** a clinch (in wrestling)

cuervo /'kuerβo/ *m*, raven; crow

cuesco /'kuesko/ *m*, stone, seed, pip

cuesta /'kuesta/ *f*, slope, rise, gradient. **c. abajo (arriba),** down (up) hill. **a cuestas,** on one's back; having the responsibility of

cuestión /kues'tion/ *f*, problem, question; quarrel, disagreement; affair, matter; torture

cuestionable /kuestio'naβle/ *a* doubtful, questionable

cuestionar /kuestio'nar/ *vt* to discuss, debate

cuestionario /kuestio'nario/ *m*, questionnaire

cueva /'kueβa/ *f*, cave, cavern; basement, cellar. *Fig.*
c. de ladrones, den of thieves
cuévano /'kueβano/ *m*, hamper, basket
cui /kui/ *m*, *Lat. Am.* guinea pig
cuico, -a /'kuiko/ *mf*, *Argentina, Chile* foreigner, outsider; *Mexico, informal* cop (police officer)
cuidado /kui'ðaðo/ *m*, carefulness, pains; attention; charge, care, responsibility; anxiety, fear. *interj* **¡C.!** Careful! Look out! **Me tiene sin c. su opinión,** I am not interested in his (your) opinion. *Inf.* **estar al c. de,** to be under the direction of. **estar de c.,** to be dangerously ill
cuidadoso /kuiða'ðoso/ **(de)** *a* careful (about *or* with); anxious (about); concerned (with); watchful; conscientious
cuidar /kui'ðar/ *vt* to care for; tend; take care of, look after; mind, be careful of; *vr* look after oneself
cuita /'kuita/ *f*, misfortune, anxiety, trouble
cuitado /kui'taðo/ *a* unfortunate, worried; timid, bashful, humble
cuitla /'kuitla/ *f*, *Mexico* poultry manure
culata /ku'lata/ *f*, *Anat.* haunch; butt (of fire-arms); back, rear; *Auto.* sump. **salir por la c.,** to backfire
culebra /ku'leβra/ *f*, snake; *Inf.* trick, joke; *Inf.* sudden uproar. **hacer c.,** to stagger along
culebrear /kuleβre'ar/ *vi* to wriggle; grovel; meander, wind
culí /ku'li/ *m*, coolie
culinario /kuli'nario/ *a* culinary
culminación /kulmina'sion; kulmina'θion/ *f*, culmination, peak; *Astron.* zenith
culminante /kulmi'nante/ *a* culminating; *Fig.* outstanding
culminar /kulmi'nar/ *vi* to culminate (in)
culo /'kulo/ *m*, buttocks, seat; rump; anus; base, bottom. **c. de lámpara,** *Archit.* pendant; *Print.* tail-piece
culpa /'kulpa/ *f*, fault; blame. **echar la c.** (a), to blame. **por c. de,** through the fault of. **tener la c.,** to be to blame
culpabilidad /kulpaβili'ðað/ *f*, guilt
culpable /kul'paβle/ *a* culpable
culpado /kul'paðo/ **(-da)** *n* culprit
culpar /kul'par/ *vt* to blame, accuse; criticize, censure
cultígeno /kul'tiheno/ *m*, cultigen
cultismo /kul'tismo/ *m*, cultism (Gongorism); learned form, learnedism, learned word
cultivación /kultiβa'sion; kultiβa'θion/ *f*, cultivation; culture
cultivador /kultiβa'ðor/ **(-ra)** *n* cultivator; planter
cultivar /kulti'βar/ *vt* to cultivate; develop; exercise, practice (professions); culture (bacteriology)
cultivo /kul'tiβo/ *m*, cultivation; farming; culture (bacteriological)
culto /'kulto/ *a* cultivated; educated; cultured; elegant, artificial (style). *m*, worship; cult; religion; creed; homage; religious service (Protestant)
cultura /kul'tura/ *f*, cultivation; culture. **de c. universitaria,** college-educated
cultural /kultu'ral/ *a* cultural
cumbre /'kumbre/ *f*, peak, crest, summit; *Fig.* zenith, acme
cumpleaños /kumple'aɲos/ *m*, birthday
cumplidamente /kumpliða'mente/ *adv* fully, completely
cumplido /kum'pliðo/ *a* complete; thorough; long; plentiful; courteous, punctilious; fulfilled. *m*, courtesy, attention; formality. **gastar cumplidos,** to stand on ceremony; be formal
cumplimentar /kumplimen'tar/ *vt* to congratulate; perform, carry out
cumplimentero /kumplimen'tero/ *a* over-complimentary; *Inf.* gushing
cumplimiento /kumpli'miento/ *m*, fulfillment, performance; courtesy, formality; completion; complement
cumplir /kum'plir/ *vt* to perform, carry into effect; reach (of age); keep (promises). **c. su palabra,** to keep one's word; *vi* perform a duty; expire, fall due; serve the required term of military service; be neces-

sary, behove; *vr* be fulfilled, come true. **por c.,** as a matter of form
cumulativo /kumula'tiβo/ *a* cumulative
cúmulo /'kumulo/ *m*, heap, pile; great many, host, mass, myriad; (cloud) cumulus, thunderhead
cuna /'kuna/ *f*, cradle; foundling hospital; birthplace; origin, genesis; *pl* cat's cradle (game)
cundir /kun'dir/ *vi* to extend, spread (gen. liquids); be diffused (news); expand, grow
cuneco, -a /ku'neko/ *mf* *Venezuela* baby of the family
cuneiforme /kunei'forme/ *a* wedge-shaped, cuneiform
cunero /ku'nero/ **(-ra)** *n* foundling, orphan
cuña /'kuɲa/ *f*, wedge; *Mech.* quoin. *Mil.* **practicar una c.,** to make a wedge
cuñada /ku'ɲaða/ *f*, sister-in-law
cuñado /ku'ɲaðo/ *m*, brother-in-law
cuño /'kuɲo/ *m*, die, stamp; *Fig.* impression; mark on silver, hallmark. **de viejo c.,** old-guard (e.g. socialites)
cuota /'kuota/ *f*, quota; share; subscription; fee
cupé /ku'pe/ *m*, coupé
Cupido /ku'piðo/ *m*, Cupid; philanderer
cuplé /ku'ple/ *m*, couplet; song
cupo /'kupo/ *m*, quota; share; tax rate; *Mil.* contingent
cupón /ku'pon/ *m*, coupon
cúpula /'kupula/ *f*, *Archit.* dome, cupola; *Bot.* cup
cuquería /kuke'ria/ *f*, craftiness, smartness; cuteness, prettiness
cura /'kura/ *m*, parish priest; *Inf.* Roman Catholic priest. *f*, cure (e.g. *La enfermedad tiene c.,* The illness can be cured); healing; remedy. **c. de almas,** cure of souls. **primera c.,** first aid. *inf* **c. de misa y olla,** ignorant priest
curación /kura'sion; kura'θion/ *f*, cure, remedy; healing
curador /kura'ðor/ **(-ra)** *n* curer, salter. *m*, (*Scots Law.*) curator. *a* curing; healing
curaduría /kuraðu'ria/ *f*, *Law.* guardianship
curanderismo /kurande'rismo/ *m*, quackery, charlatanism; quack medicine
curandero /kuran'dero/ **(-ra)** *n* quack doctor; charlatan
curar /ku'rar/ *vi* to heal, cure; (*with de*) take care of; care about, mind; *vt* cure, salt; treat medically (bandage, give medicines, etc.); cure (leather); bleach (cloth); season (timber); *Fig.* remedy (an evil)
curasao /kura'sao/ *m*, curaçao (drink)
curativo /kura'tiβo/ *a* curative
curato /ku'rato/ *m*, *Eccl.* parish, cure
Curazao /kura'sao; kura'θao/ Curaçao
cúrcuma /'kurkuma/ *f*, turmeric
cureña /ku'reɲa/ *f*, gun-carriage
curia /'kuria/ *f*, *Law.* bar; tribunal; *Eccl.* curia; care, attention
curiana /ku'riana/ *f*, cockroach
curiche /ku'ritʃe/ *m*, swamp
curiosear /kuriose'ar/ *vi* to pry; be curious (about); meddle; be a busybody
curiosidad /kuriosi'ðað/ *f*, curiosity; inquisitiveness, meddlesomeness; neatness; carefulness, conscientiousness; curio
curioso /ku'rioso/ *a* curious; inquisitive; interesting; odd; neat, clean; conscientious, careful
Curita /ku'rita/ *f*, *trademark* Band-Aid
cursado /kur'saðo/ *a* experienced, versed
cursante /kur'sante/ *m*, student
cursar /kur'sar/ *vt* to frequent, visit; do repeatedly; study, attend classes, take courses (e.g. *¿En qué escuela cursan?* At what school are you studying?); expedite (public admin.)
cursi /'kursi/ *a* *Inf.* vulgar, in bad taste; loud, crude
cursilería /kursile'ria/ *f*, *Inf.* vulgarity, bad taste
cursillo /kur'siʎo/ *m*, minicourse, short course; short series of lectures
cursiva /kur'siβa/ *f*, italics. **en c.,** in italics, italicized
cursivo /kur'siβo/ *a* cursive
curso /'kurso/ *m*, course, direction; duration, passage

(time); progress; route; course of study; academic year; succession, series; *Com.* tender

curtido /kur'tiðo/ *m*, tanning; leather; tanned leather (gen. *pl*)

curtidor /kurti'ðor/ *m*, tanner

curtiduría /kurtiðu'ria/ *f*, tannery

curtimiento /kurti'miento/ *m*, tanning; effect of weather on the complexion; toughening-up; hardening

curtir /kur'tir/ *vt* to tan; *Fig.* bronze (complexions); make hardy, harden up; *vr* be weatherbeaten; be hardy. *Inf.* **estar curtido en,** to be experienced in; be expert at

curul /ku'rul/ *a* **curule** *m*, seat (in parliament)

curva /'kurβa/ *f*, curve; bend. *Surv.* **c. de nivel,** contour line

curvatura, curvidad /kurβa'tura, kurβi'ðað/ *f*, curvature

curvo /'kurβo/ *a* curved; bent. *m*, curve

cusma /'kusma/ *f*, *Lat. Am.* sleeveless shirt, tunic

cúspide /'kuspiðe/ *f*, peak, summit; (*Geom. Archit.*) cusp

custodia /kus'toðia/ *f*, custody; guardianship, care; *Eccl.* monstrance; custodian, keeper; guardian; guard

custodiar /kusto'ðiar/ *vt* to watch, guard; look after, care for; *Naut.* convoy

custodio /kus'toðio/ *a* guardian; guarding; custodial. *m*, custodian; guard. **angel c.,** guardian angel

cutama /ku'tama/ *f*, *Argentina* blanket; *Chile* bag, sack

cutáneo /ku'taneo/ *a* cutaneous, skin

cúter /'kuter/ *m*, *Naut.* cutter

cutícula /ku'tikula/ *f*, cuticle

cutis /'kutis/ *m*, complexion; skin (sometimes *f*)

cuyo /'kuyo/ (**cuya, cuyos, cuyas**) *rel pron poss* whose, of which (e.g. *el viejo cuya barba era más blanca que la nieve,* the old man whose beard was whiter than snow). *interr* **¿Cúyo?** Whose? (e.g. *¿Cúyos son estos lápices?* Whose pencils are these?) (gen. **de quién** or **de quiénes** is used rather than **cúyo**). *m*, beau, lover

D

dable /'daβle/ *a* practicable, possible

daca /'daka/ Give me!

dactilografía /daktilogra'fia/ *f*, typewriting

dactilógrafo /dakti'lografo/ **(-fa)** *n* typist

dactilología /daktilolo'hia/ *f*, dactylology

dadista /da'ðista/ *mf*, *Mexico* gambler

dádiva /'daðiβa/ *f*, gift, present

dadivoso /daði'βoso/ *a* generous, liberal

dado /'daðo/ *m*, die; *Archit.* dado. *conjunc* **d. que,** given that, supposing that. **cargar los dados,** to load the dice

dador /da'ðor/ **(-ra)** *n* giver, donor. *m*, *Com.* bearer; *Com.* drawer (of a bill of exchange)

daga /'daga/ *f*, dagger

daguerrotipo /dagerro'tipo/ *m*, daguerreotype

daifa /'daifa/ *f*, concubine

¡dale! /'dale/ *interj* Stop! No more about...!

dalia /'dalia/ *f*, *Bot.* dahlia

dallar /da'yar; da'ʎar/ *vt* to scythe (grass)

dalle /'daye; 'daʎe/ *m*, scythe

dálmata /'dalmata/ *a* and *mf* Dalmatian

daltoniano /dalto'niano/ *a* color-blind

daltonismo /dalto'nismo/ *m*, color-blindness

dama /'dama/ *f*, lady; noblewoman; lady-in-waiting; lady-love; mistress, concubine; queen (chess); king (checkers); *Theat.* **d. primera,** leading lady

damajuana /dama'huana/ *f*, demijohn

damas /'damas/ *f pl*, checkers (game)

damasceno /damas'seno; damas'θeno/ **(-na)** *a* and *n* Damascene

Damasco /da'masko/ Damascus

damasco /da'masko/ *m*, damask

damasquino /damas'kino/ *a* damascened (swords, etc.)

damería /dame'ria/ *f*, prudery, affectation

damisela /dami'sela/ *f*, damsel; *Inf.* woman of the town

damnificar /damnifi'kar/ *vt* to injure

dandi /'dandi/ *m*, dandy

dandismo /dan'dismo/ *m*, dandyism

danés /da'nes/ **(-esa)** *a* Danish. *n* Dane. *m*, Danish (language)

danta /'danta/ *f*, *Zool.* tapir

dantesco /dan'tesko/ *a* Dantesque

danubiano /da'nuβiano/ *a* Danubian

Danubio, el /da'nuβio/ the Danube

danza /'dansa; 'danθa/ *f*, dance; set (of dancers); *Fig. Inf.* dirty business. **d. de arcos,** dance of the arches. **d. de cintas,** maypole dance. **d. de monos,** amusing spectacle

danzador /dansa'ðor; danθa'ðor/ **(-ra)** *n* dancer; *a* dancing

danzante /dan'sante; dan'θante/ **(-ta)** *n* dancer; *Fig. Inf.* live wire; *Inf.* busybody

danzar /dan'sar; dan'θar/ *vt* and *vi* to dance; *vi* jump up and down, rattle; *Inf.* interfere, meddle

danzarín /dansa'rin; danθa'rin/ **(-ina)** *n* good dancer; *Inf.* meddler; *Inf.* playboy

danzón /dan'son; dan'θon/ *m*, Cuban dance

dañable /da'ɲaβle/ *a* harmful; worthy of condemnation

dañado /da'ɲaðo/ *a* evil, perverse; damned; spoiled, damaged

dañador /daɲa'ðor/ **(-ra)** *a* harmful. *n* injurer, offender

dañar /da'ɲar/ *vt* to hurt, harm; damage, spoil; *vr* spoil, deteriorate

dañino /da'ɲino/ *a* destructive (often of animals); hurtful, harmful. **animales dañinos,** vermin, pests

daño /'daɲo/ *m*, hurt; damage; loss. *Law.* **daños y perjuicios,** damages. **hacerse d.,** to hurt oneself

dañoso /da'ɲoso/ *a* hurtful, harmful

dar /dar/ *vt irr* to give; hand over; concede, grant; produce, yield; cause, create; sacrifice; propose, put forward; take (a walk); believe, consider; deliver (blows, etc.); administer (medicine); provide with; apply, coat with; occasion, perform (plays); propose (a toast); give forth, emit; set (norms), render (thanks, etc.); hold (banquets, etc.); proffer, hold out; *vi* to strike (clocks); (*with prep a*) overlook, look on to (e.g. *Su ventana da a la calle,* His window looks on to the street); (*with con*) find, meet (things, persons); (*with el*) fall on, fall down (e.g. *Dio de cabeza,* He fell head first. *Dio de espaldas,* He fell on his back); (*with en*) fall into, incur; insist on or persist in (doing something); acquire the habit of (e.g. *Dieron en no venir a vernos,* They took to not coming to see us); solve, guess (riddles, etc.); strike, wound, hurt (e.g. *La bala le dio en el brazo,* The bullet struck him in the arm); (*with por*) decide on (e.g. *Di por no hacerlo,* I decided not to do it). *vr* to yield, give in; (*with prep a*) engage in, devote oneself to; (*with por*) think or consider oneself (e.g. *Me di por muerto,* I gave myself up for dead). **d. alas a,** to propagate, spread (a belief). **darse a la vela,** to set sail. **darse cuenta de,** to realize. **darse la mano,** to shake hands. **darse por buenos,** to make up a quarrel, be friends. **darse prisa,** to hurry up, make haste. **darse uno a conocer,** to make oneself known. **darse uno por entendido,** to show that one understands; be grateful. **No se me da un bledo,** I couldn't care less. **d. abajo,** to fall down. **d. bien por mal,** to return good for evil. **d. a conocer,** to make known. **d. a entender,** to suggest, hint. **d. a luz,** to give birth; publish, issue. **d. cuenta de,** to give an account of. **d. de baja,** *Mil.* to muster out, discharge. **d. de comer,** to feed. **d. de sí,** to stretch, expand; produce, yield; give of itself (oneself, himself, themselves) (either in good or bad sense). **d. diente con diente,** to chatter (of teeth), shiver. **d. el pésame,** to tender condolences. **d. en cara,** *Fig. Inf.* to throw in one's face. **d. en el clavo,** *Fig.* to hit the mark. **d. en qué pensar,** to make suspicious, cause to think. **d. fe,** to certify, attest. **d. fiado,** to give on credit. **d. fianza,** to give security. **d. fin a,** to finish. **d. licencia,** to permit, allow. **d. los buenos días,** to wish good day or good morning. **d. mal,** to have bad luck at cards. **d. parte de,** to announce; issue a communiqué about (e.g. *Dieron parte de la pérdida del buque,* They announced the loss of the ship). **d. prestado,** to lend. **d. qué decir,** to cause a scandal. **d. qué hacer,** to cause trouble. **d. razón de,** to give an account of. **d. sobre uno,** to assault a person. **d. un abrazo,** to embrace. **d. voces,** to shriek; call out. *Inf.* **Donde las dan las toman,** It's only tit-for-tat. *Inf.* **No me da la real gana,** I darn well don't want to. *Pres. Ind.* **doy, das,** etc. *Preterite* **di, diste, etc.** *Pres. Subjunc.* **dé, etc.** *Imperf. Subjunc.* **diese, etc.**

Dardanelos, los /darða'nelos, los/ the Dardanelles

dardo /'darðo/ *m,* (*Mil. Sports.*) dart; *Ichth.* dace; lampoon

dares y tomares /dares i tomares/ *m, pl* give and take; *Inf.* back-chat. Generally used with *andar, haber* or *tener*

dársena /'darsena/ *f, Naut.* dock

darviniano /darβi'niano/ *a* Darwinian

darvinismo /darβi'nismo/ *m,* Darwinism

darvinista /darβi'nista/ *mf* Darwinian

data /'data/ *f,* date (calendar); *Com.* credit

datar /'datar/ *vt* to date; *vi* (*with de*) date from; *vr Com.* credit

dátil /'datil/ *m, Bot.* date

datilado /dati'aðo/ *a* date-like or date-colored

datilera /dati'era/ *f, Bot.* date-palm

dativo /da'tiβo/ *m, Gram.* dative

dato /'dato/ *m,* datum; basis, fact

davídico /da'βiðiko/ *a* Davidic

de /de/ *f,* name of letter D. *prep* of (possessive) (e.g. *Este cuadro es de Vd.,* This picture is yours); from (place and time) (e.g. *Vengo de Madrid,* I come from Madrid. *de vez en cuando,* from time to time); with, of, from, as the result of (e.g. *Lloraban de miedo,* They were crying with fright. *Murió de un ataque del corazón,* He died from a heart attack); for, to (e.g. *Es hora de marchar,* It is time to leave); with (of characteristics) (e.g. *el señor de los lentes,* the gentleman with the eyeglasses. *el cuarto de la alfombra azul,* the room with the blue carpet); when, as (e.g. *De niños nos gustaban los juguetes,* When we were children we liked toys); by (e.g. *Es un ensayo del mismo autor,* It is an essay by the same author. *Fue amado de todos,* He was loved by all. *Es hidalgo de nacimiento,* He is a gentleman by birth). Indicates the material of which a thing is made (e.g. *La mesa es de mármol,* The table is marble). Indicates contents of a thing (e.g. *un vaso de leche,* a glass of milk). Shows manner in which an action is performed (e.g. *Lo hizo de prisa,* He did it hurriedly). Shows the use to which an article is put (e.g. *una mesa de escribir,* a writing-table. *una máquina de coser,* a sewing-machine. *un caballo de batalla,* a war-horse). Sometimes used for emphasis (e.g. *El tonto de tu secretario,* That fool of a secretary of yours). Used by Spanish married women before husband's family name (e.g. *Señora Martínez de Cabra,* Mrs. Cabra (née Martínez)). Used after many adverbs (generally of time or place) to form prepositional phrases (e.g. *detrás de,* behind. *enfrente de,* opposite to; in front of. *de acá para allá,* here and there. *de allí a poco,* shortly afterward. *de allí a pocos días,* a few days later. *de bamba,* by chance. *de cabo a rabo,* from cover to cover. *además de,* besides, etc.). Used at beginning of various adverbial phrases (e.g. *de noche,* at night. *de día,* by day. *de antemano,* previously, *la persona de mi derecha* the person at my right, etc.). Used partitively before nouns, pronouns, adjectives (e.g. *Estas historias tienen algo de verdad,* These stories have some truth in them. *¿Qué hay de nuevo?* What's the news?) Forms many compound words (e.g. *deponer, denegar,* etc.). With **"uno"**

means "at" (e.g. *Lo cogió de un salto,* He caught it at one bound). **de a** is used before expressions of price, weight, etc. (e.g. *un libro de a cinco pesetas,* a five-peseta book)

dea /dea/ *f, Poet.* goddess

deán /de'an/ *m,* dean

debajo /de'βaho/ *adv* underneath; below

debate /de'βate/ *m,* discussion, debate; dispute

debatible /deβa'tiβle/ *a* debatable

debatir /deβa'tir/ *vt* to discuss, debate, argue

debe /'deβe/ *m, Com.* debtor

debelación /deβela'sion; deβela'θion/ *f,* conquest

debelador /deβela'ðor/ **(-ra)** *a* conquering. *n* conqueror

debelar /deβe'lar/ *vt* to conquer, overthrow

deber /de'βer/ *vt* to owe (e.g. *Le debo mil pesetas,* I owe him one thousand pesetas). Used as auxiliary verb followed by infinitive, ought to, be obliged to (e.g. *Debía haberlo hecho,* I ought to have done it. *Deberá hacerlo,* He will have to do it); be destined to (e.g. *La princesa que más tarde debió ser reina,* The princess who later was destined to be queen); be essential, must (e.g. *La cuestión debe ser resuelta,* The question must be settled); (*with de + infin.*) be probable (indicates supposition) (e.g. *Debe de tener cincuenta años,* He is probably about fifty. *Debía de sufrir del corazón,* He probably suffered from heart trouble); (preceded by a negative *with de + infin.*) be impossible (e.g. *No debe de ser verdad,* It can't be true)

deber /de'βer/ *m,* duty, obligation; debt. **hacer su d.,** to do one's duty

debidamente /deβiða'mente/ *adv* justly, rightly; duly

debido /de'βiðo/ *a* correct, due. **d. a,** owing to, because of

débil /'deβil/ *a* weak; *Fig.* spineless; frail

debilidad /deβili'ðað/ *f,* weakness; feebleness

debilitación /deβilitasion; deβilita'θion/ *f,* debilitation

debilitante /deβili'tante/ *a* weakening

debilitar /deβili'tar/ *vt* to weaken; *vr* become weak

débito /'deβito/ *m,* debit, debt; duty

debutar /deβu'tar/ *vi* to appear for the first time, make one's début

década /'dekaða/ *f,* decade

decadencia /dekaðensia; deka'ðenθia/ *f,* decadence, decline

decadente /deka'ðente/ *a* decadent, decaying

decaer /deka'er/ *vi irr* to fail (persons); decay, decline. See **caer**

decagramo /deka'gramo/ *m,* decagram

decaimiento /dekai'miento/ *m,* decadence; *Med.* prostration

decalaje /deka'lahe/ *m, Aer.* stagger

decalitro /deka'litro/ *m,* decaliter

decálogo /de'kalogo/ *m,* decalogue, the Ten Commandments

decámetro /de'kametro/ *m,* decameter

decampar /dekam'par/ *vi Mil.* to decamp

decanato /dekan'ato/ *m,* deanery; *Educ.* dean's rooms

decano /de'kano/ *m,* senior member; *Educ.* dean

decantación /dekantasion; dekanta'θion/ *f,* decantation

decantar /dekan'tar/ *vt* to decant (wines); praise

decapitación /dekapitasion; dekapita'θion/ *f,* decapitation

decapitar /dekapi'tar/ *vt* to decapitate, behead

decena /de'sena; de'θena/ *f,* ten; *Mus.* tenth

decenal /de'senal; de'θenal/ *a* decennial

decenario /dese'nario; deθe'nario/ *m,* decade

decencia /de'sensia; de'θenθia/ *f,* propriety, decency; decorum, modesty

decenio /de'senio; de'θenio/ *m,* decade

deceno /de'seno; de'θeno/ *a* a tenth

decentar /desen'tar; deθen'tar/ *vt irr* to begin, cut (loaves, etc.); *Fig.* undermine (health, etc.); *vr* suffer from bedsores. See **acertar**

decente /de'sente; de'θente/ *a* decent, honest; respectable; suitable; tidy

decepción /desep'sion; deθep'θion/ *f*, disillusionment, disappointment

dechado /de'tʃaðo/ *m*, model, ideal; *Sew.* sampler; exemplar, ideal

decible /de'siβle; de'θiβle/ *a* expressible

decidero /de'siðero; de'θiðero/ *a* that which can be safely said

decidido /desi'ðiðo; deθi'ðiðo/ *a* decided; resolute, determined

decidir /desi'ðir; deθi'ðir/ *vt* to resolve, decide; *vr* make up one's mind

decidor /desi'ðor; deθi'ðor/ **(-ra)** *a* talkative, fluent, eloquent. *n* good talker

decigramo /desi'gramo; deθi'gramo/ *m*, decigram

décima /'desima; 'deθima/ *f*, tenth; ten-line stanza of eight-syllable verse

decimal /desi'mal; deθi'mal/ *a* decimal; pertaining to tithes. **sistema d.**, metric system

decímetro /de'simetro; de'θimetro/ *m*, decimeter

décimo /'desimo; 'deθimo/ *a* tenth. *m*, tenth part; tenth of a lottery ticket

decimoctavo /desimok'taβo; deθimok'taβo/ *a* eighteenth

decimocuarto /desimo'kuarto; deθimo'kuarto/ *a* fourteenth

decimonono /desimo'nono; deθimo'nono/ *a* nineteenth

decimoquinto /desimo'kinto; deθimo'kinto/ *a* fifteenth

decimoséptimo /desimo'septimo; deθimo'septimo/ *a* and *m*, seventeenth

decimosexto /desimo'seksto; deθimo'seksto/ *a* sixteenth

decimotercio /desimoter'sio; deθimoter'θio/ *a* thirteenth

decir /de'sir; de'θir/ *vt irr* to say; name; indicate, show; tell. **d. bien**, to speak truth; speak the truth; be eloquent. **d. entre** (*or* **para**) **sí,** to say to oneself. *Inf.* **d. nones,** to refuse. **¿Cómo se dice... en español?** How do you say... in Spanish? **¡Diga!** Hello! (telephone). *Inf.* **el que dirán**, public opinion (what will people say!). **Es d.,** That is to say. **Se dice,** It is said, people say. *Pres. Ind.* **digo, dices, etc.** *Pres. Part.* **diciendo.** *Past Part.* **dicho.** *Fut.* **diré, etc.** *Condit.* **diría, etc.** *Preterite* **dije, etc.** *Pres. Subjunc.* **diga, etc.** *Imperf. Subjunc.* **dijese, etc.**

decir /de'sir; de'θir/ *m*, saying, saw; maxim, witticism (often *pl.*)

decisión /desi'sion; deθi'sion/ *f*, decision, resolution; *Law.* judgment; firmness, strength (of character)

decisivo /desi'siβo; deθi'siβo/ *a* decisive

declamación /deklama'sion; deklama'θion/ *f*, declamation, oration; *Theat.* delivery; recitation

declamador /deklama'ðor/ **(-ra)** *a* declamatory. *n* reciter; orator

declamar /dekla'mar/ *vi* to make a speech, declaim; recite

declamatorio /deklama'torio/ *a* declamatory, rhetorical

declaración /deklara'sion; deklara'θion/ *f*, declaration; exposition, explanation; confession; statement; *Law.* deposition. **d. jurada,** affidavit, sworn statement

declaradamente /deklaraða'mente/ *adv* avowedly

declarante /dekla'rante/ *a* declaring. *mf Law.* deponent

declarar /dekla'rar/ *vt* to declare; make clear, explain; *Law.* find; *vi Law.* give evidence; *vr* avow, confess (one's sentiments, etc.); show, reveal itself

declarativo, declaratorio /deklara'tiβo, deklara'torio/ *a* explanatory, declarative

declinación /deklina'sion; deklina'θion/ *f*, fall, descent; decadence, decay; *Astron.* declination; *Gram.* declension. *Inf.* **no saber las declinaciones,** not to know one's ABC, be very ignorant

declinante /dekli'nante/ *a* declining; sloping

declinar /dekli'nar/ *vi* to slope; diminish, fall; decline, deteriorate; *Fig.* near the end; *vt Gram.* decline

declive, ** /de'kliβe,/ *m*. **declividad *f*, slope, incline; gradient

decocción /dekok'sion; dekok'θion/ *f*, decoction

decoloración /dekolora'sion; dekolora'θion/ *f*, decoloration; decolorization

decomisar /dekomi'sar/ *vt* to confiscate, seize

decoración /dekora'sion; dekora'θion/ *f*, decoration; ornament, embellishment; *Theat.* scenery

decorado /deko'raðo/ *m*, *Theat.* scenery, décor

decorador /dekora'ðor/ *m*, decorator

decorar /deko'rar/ *vt* to adorn, ornament; *Poet.* decorate, honor

decorativo /dekora'tiβo/ *a* decorative

decoro /de'koro/ *m*, respect, reverence; prudence, circumspection; decorum, propriety; integrity, decency; *Archit.* decoration

decoroso /deko'roso/ *a* decorous, honorable, decent

decrecer /dekre'ser; dekre'θer/ *vi irr* to decrease, grow less. See **conocer**

decreciente /dekre'siente; dekre'θiente/ *a* decreasing

decrepitación /dekrepita'sion; dekrepita'θion/ *f*, *Chem.* decrepitation, crackling

decrepitar /dekrepi'tar/ *vi Chem.* to decrepitate, crackle

decrépito /de'krepito/ *a* decrepit

decrepitud /dekrepi'tuð/ *f*, decrepitude

decretar /dekre'tar/ *vt* to decree, decide; *Law.* give a judgment (in a suit)

decreto /de'kreto/ *m*, decree, order; judicial decree

decuplar, decuplicar /dekup'lar, dekupli'kar/ *vt* to multiply by ten

décuplo /'dekuplo/ *a* tenfold

decurso /de'kurso/ *m*, course, lapse (of time)

dedada /de'ðaða/ *f*, thimbleful, finger; pinch

dedal /de'ðal/ *m*, thimble; finger-stall

dédalo /'deðalo/ *m*, labyrinth

dedeo /de'ðeo/ *m*, *Mus.* touch

dedicación /deðika'sion; deðika'θion/ *f*, dedication (all meanings)

dedicar /deði'kar/ *vt* to dedicate; devote; consecrate; *vr* (*with prep a*) dedicate oneself to, engage in

dedicatoria /deðika'toria/ *f*, dedication (of a book, etc.)

dedicatorio /deðika'torio/ *a* dedicatory

dedil /de'ðil/ *m*, finger-stall

dedillo, saber al /de'ðiyo, saβer al; de'ðiʎo, saβer al/ *Fig.* to have at one's fingertips, know perfectly

dedo /'deðo/ *m*, finger; toe; finger's breadth. **d. anular,** third (ring) finger. **d. de en medio or del corazón,** middle finger. **d. índice,** forefinger. **d. meñique,** little finger. **d. pulgar,** thumb or big toe. *Fig. Inf.* **a dos dedos de,** within an inch of. *Fig. Inf.* **chuparse los dedos,** to smack one's lips over. *Inf.* **estar unidos como los dedos de la mano,** to be as thick as thieves

deducción /deðuk'sion; deðuk'θion/ *f*, inference, deduction; derivation; (*Mus. Math.*) progression

deduciente /deðu'siente; deðu'θiente/ *a* deductive

deducir /deðu'sir; deðu'θir/ *vt irr* to deduce, infer; deduct, subtract; *Law.* plead, allege in pleading. See **conducir**

deductivo /deðuk'tiβo/ *a* deductive

defecación /defeka'sion; defeka'θion/ *f*, purification; defecation

defecar /defe'kar/ *vt* to clarify, purify; defecate

defección /defek'sion; defek'θion/ *f*, defection

defectible /defek'tiβle/ *a* defective; imperfect

defecto /de'fekto/ *m*, defect, fault; imperfection

defectuoso /defek'tuoso/ *a* imperfect, defective

defender /defen'der/ *vt irr* to defend, protect; maintain, uphold; forbid; hinder; *vr* defend oneself. See **entender**

defendible /defen'diβle/ *a* defensible

defensa /de'fensa/ *f*, defense; protection; (hockey) pad; *Law.* defense; *Sports.* back; *pl Mil.* defenses; *Naut.* fenders. **d. química,** chemical warfare. *Mil.* **defensas costeras,** coastal defenses

defensiva /defen'siβa/ *f*, defensive

defensivo /defen'siβo/ *a* defensive. *m*, safeguard

defensor /defen'sor/ **(-ra)** *n* defender. *m*, *Law.* counsel for the defense

deferencia /defe'rensia; defe'renθia/ *f*, deference

deferente /defe'rente/ *a* deferential

deferir /defe'rir/ *vi irr* to defer, yield; *vt* delegate. *Pres. Ind.* **defiero, defieres, defiere, defieren.** *Pres. Part.* **defiriendo.** *Preterite* **defirió, defirieron.** *Pres. Subjunc.* **defiera, etc.** *Imperf. Subjunc.* **defiriese, etc.**

deficiencia /defi'siensia; defi'θienθia/ *f*, defect, deficiency

deficiente /defi'siente; defi'θiente/ *a* faulty, deficient

déficit /'defisit; 'defiθit/ *m*, deficit

definible /defi'niβle/ *a* definable

definición /defini'sion; defini'θion/ *f*, definition; decision

definido /defi'niðo/ *a* definite

definir /defi'nir/ *vt* to define; decide

definitivo /defini'tiβo/ *a* definitive. **en definitiva,** definitely; in short

deflagración /deflagra'sion; deflagra'θion/ *f*, sudden blaze, deflagration

deflagrador /deflagra'ðor/ *m*, *Elec.* deflagrator

deflagrar /defla'grar/ *vi* to go up in flames

deformación /deforma'sion; deforma'θion/ *f*, deformation; *Radio.* distortion

deformado /defor'maðo/ *a* deformed; misshapen

deformador /deforma'ðor/ **(-ra)** *a* disfiguring, deforming. *n* disfigurer

deformar /defor'mar/ *vt* to deform; *vr* become deformed or misshapen

deformidad /deformi'ðað/ *f*, deformity; gross error; vice, lapse

defraudación /defrauða'sion; defrauða'θion/ *f*, defrauding; deceit

defraudador /defrauða'ðor/ **(-ra)** *n* defrauder

defraudar /defrau'ðar/ *vt* to defraud; usurp; frustrate, disappoint; impede

defuera /de'fuera/ *adv* outwardly, externally

defunción /defun'sion; defun'θion/ *f*, decease, death

degeneración /dehenera'sion; dehenera'θion/ *f*, degeneration. **d. grasienta,** fatty degeneration

degenerado /dehene'raðo/ **(-da)** *a* and *n* degenerate

degenerar /dehene'rar/ *vi* to degenerate

deglución /deglu'sion; deglu'θion/ *f*, swallowing, deglutition

deglutir /deglu'tir/ *vi* and *vt* to swallow

degollación /degoya'sion; degoʎa'θion/ *f*, decollation, throat slitting

degolladero /degoya'ðero; degoʎa'ðero/ *m*, slaughterhouse; execution block

degollador /degoya'ðor; degoʎa'ðor/ *m*, executioner

degolladura /degoya'ðura; degoʎa'ðura/ *f*, slitting of the throat

degollar /dego'yar; dego'ʎar/ *vt irr* to behead; slit the throat; *Fig.* destroy; (*Fig. Theat.*) murder; *Inf.* annoy, bore. *Pres. Ind.* **degüello, degüellas, degüella, degüellan.** *Pres. Subjunc.* **degüelle, degüelles, degüelle, degüellen**

degollina /dego'yina; dego'ʎina/ *f*, *Inf.* massacre

degradación /degraða'sion; degraða'θion/ *f*, degradation; humiliation, debasement; *Art.* gradation, shading (colors, light)

degradante /degra'ðante/ *a* degrading, humiliating

degradar /degra'ðar/ *vt* to degrade; humiliate; *Art.* grade, blend; *vr* degrade oneself

degüello /de'gueyo; de'gueʎo/ *m*, decollation; havoc, destruction; haft (of swords, etc.)

degustación /degusta'sion; degusta'θion/ *f*, act of tasting or sampling

dehesa /de'esa/ *f*, pasture, meadow

deicida /dei'siða; dei'θiða/ *mf* deicide (person)

deicidio /dei'siðio; dei'θiðio/ *m*, deicide (act)

deidad /dei'ðað/ *f*, divinity; deity, idol

deificación /deifika'sion; deifika'θion/ *f*, deification

deificar /deifi'kar/ *vt* to deify; overpraise

deífico /de'ifiko/ *a* deific, divine

deísmo /de'ismo/ *m*, Deism

deísta /de'ista/ *mf* deist. *a* deistic

dejación /deha'sion; deha'θion/ *f*, relinquishment, abandonment

dejadez /deha'ðes; deha'ðeθ/ *f*, slovenliness; neglect; laziness; carelessness

dejado /de'haðo/ *a* lazy; neglectful; slovenly; discouraged, depressed

dejamiento /deha'miento/ *m*, relinquishment; negligence; lowness of spirits; indifference

dejar /de'har/ *vt* to leave; omit, forget, allow, permit (e.g. *Déjame salir,* Let me go out); yield, produce, entrust, leave in charge; believe, consider; intend, appoint; cease, stop; forsake, desert; renounce, relinquish; bequeath; give away; *vr* neglect oneself; engage (in); lay oneself open to, allow oneself; abandon oneself (to), fling oneself (into); *Fig.* be depressed or languid; (*with de* + *infin.*) cease to (e.g. *Se dejó de hacerlo,* He stopped doing it); *vi* (*with de* + *adjective*) be none the less, be rather (e.g. *No deja de ser sorprendente,* It isn't any the less surprising). **d. aparte,** to omit, leave out. **d. atrás,** to overtake; *Fig.* leave behind, beat. **d. caer,** to let fall. **dejarse caer,** to let oneself fall; *Fig. Inf.* to let fall, utter; appear suddenly. **dejarse vencer,** to give way, allow oneself to be persuaded

dejo /'deho/ *m*, relinquishment; end; accent (of foreign languages); savor, after-taste; negligence; *Fig.* touch, flavor

del /del/ contraction of **de + el,** (*def. art. m.*) of the (e.g. *del perro,* of the dog)

delación /dela'sion; dela'θion/ *f*, accusation, denunciation

delantal /delan'tal/ *m*, apron

delante /de'lante/ *adv* before, in front, in the presence (of)

delantera /delan'tera/ *f*, front, front portion; *Theat.* orchestra stall, front seat; front (of garment). **tomar la d.,** to take the lead; *Inf.* steal a march on

delantero /delan'tero/ *a* fore, front. *m*, postilion; *Sports.* forward. **d. centro,** *Sports.* centerforward

delatable /dela'taβle/ *a* impeachable; blameworthy

delatar /dela'tar/ *vt* to inform against, accuse; impeach

delator /dela'tor/ **(-ra)** *a* denunciatory, accusing. *n* denouncer, informer

delectación /delekta'sion; delekta'θion/ *f*, delectation, pleasure

delegación /delega'sion; delega'θion/ *f*, delegation; proxy

delegado /dele'gaðo/ **(-da)** *n* delegate; proxy

delegar /dele'gar/ *vt* to delegate

deleitable /delei'taβle/ *a* delightful

deleitar /delei'tar/ *vt* to delight, charm, please; *vr* delight (in)

deleite /de'leite/ *m*, delight; pleasure

deleitoso /delei'toso/ *a* delightful, pleasant

deletéreo /dele'tereo/ *a* deleterious; poisonous

deletrear /deletre'ar/ *vi* to spell; *Fig.* decipher

deletreo /dele'treo/ *m*, spelling; *Fig.* decipherment

deleznable /deles'naβle; deleθ'naβle/ *a* fragile, brittle; slippery; brief, fugitive, transitory

délfico /'delfiko/ *a* Delphic

delfín /del'fin/ *m*, (*Ichth. Astron.*) dolphin; dauphin

delfina /del'fina/ *f*, dauphiness

Delfos /'delfos/ Delphi

delgadez /delga'ðes; delga'ðeθ/ *f*, thinness; slenderness, leanness

delgado /del'gaðo/ *a* slim; thin; scanty; poor (of land); sharp, perspicacious

delgaducho /delga'ðutʃo/ *a* slenderish, somewhat thin

deliberación /deliβera'sion; deliβera'θion/ *f*, deliberation; consideration; discussion

deliberadamente /deliβeraða'mente/ *adv* deliberately

deliberante /deliβe'rante/ *a* deliberative, considering

deliberar /deliβe'rar/ *vi* to deliberate, consider; *vt* decide after reflection; discuss

delicadez /delika'ðes; delika'ðeθ/ *f*, weakness; delicacy; hypersensitiveness; amiability

delicadeza /delika'ðesa; delika'ðeθa/ *f*, delicacy; fastidiousness; refinement, subtlety; sensitiveness; consideration, tact; scrupulosity

delicado /deli'kaðo/ *a* courteous; tactful; fastidious; weak, delicate; fragile, perishable; delicious, tasty;

exquisite; difficult, embarrassing; refined, discriminating, sensitive; scrupulous; subtle; hypersensitive, suspicious. **d. de salud,** in poor health

delicia /deli'sia; deli'θia/ f, pleasure, delight; sensual pleasure

delicioso /deli'sioso; deli'θioso/ a delightful, agreeable, pleasant

delimitar /delimi'tar/ vt to delimit

delincuencia /delin'kuensia; delin'kuenθia/ f, delinquency, default

delincuente /delin'kuente/ a and mf delinquent, in default

delineación /delinea'sion; delinea'θion/ f, delineation; diagram, design, plan

delineador /delinea'ðor/ (-ra), n delineante m, draftsman, designer

delineamiento /delinea'miento/ m, delineation

delinear /deline'ar/ vt to delineate; sketch; describe

delinquimiento /delinki'miento/ m, delinquency; crime

delinquir /delin'kir/ vi irr to commit a crime. *Pres. Ind.* **delinco.** *Pres. Subjunc.* **delinca**

deliquio /deli'kio/ m, faint, swoon

delirante /deli'rante/ a delirious

delirar /deli'rar/ vi to be delirious; act or speak foolishly

delirio /de'lirio/ m, delirium; frenzy; foolishness, nonsense. **d. de grandezas,** illusions of grandeur

delito /de'lito/ m, delict, offense against the law, crime

delta /'delta/ f, fourth letter of Greek alphabet. m, delta (of a river)

delusorio /delu'sorio/ a deceptive

demacración /demakrasion; demakra'θion/ f, emaciation

demacrado /dema'kraðo/ a emaciated

demacrarse /dema'krarse/ vr to become emaciated

demagogia /dema'gohia/ f, demagogy

demagógico /dema'gohiko/ a demagogic

demagogo /dema'gogo/ (-ga) n demagogue

demanda /de'manda/ f, petition, request; collecting (for charity); collecting box; want ad; question; search; undertaking; *Com.* order or demand; *Law.* claim

demandadero /demanda'ðero/ (-ra) n convent or prison messenger; errandboy

demandado /deman'daðo/ (-da) n *Law.* defendant; *Law.* respondent

demandante /deman'dante/ mf *Law.* plaintiff

demandar /deman'dar/ vt to ask, request; desire, yearn for; question; *Law.* claim

demarcación /demarka'sion; demarka'θion/ f, demarcation, limit

demarcar /demar'kar/ vt to fix boundaries, demarcate

demás /de'mas/ a other. adv besides. **lo d.,** the rest. **los (las) d.,** the others. **por d.,** useless; superfluous. **por lo d.,** otherwise; for the rest

demasía /dema'sia/ f, excess; daring; insolence; guilt, crime. **en d.,** excessively

demasiado /dema'siaðo/ a too; too many; too much. adv excessively

demencia /de'mensia; de'menθia/ f, madness, insanity

demencial /demen'sial; demen'θial/ a insane

dementar /demen'tar/ vt to render insane; vr become insane

demente /de'mente/ a insane, mad. mf lunatic

demérito /de'merito/ m, demerit, fault

demeritorio /demeri'torio/ a undeserving, without merit

demisión /demi'sion/ f, submission, acquiescence

democracia /demo'krasia; demo'kraθia/ f, democracy

demócrata /de'mokrata/ mf democrat

democrático /demo'kratiko/ a democratic

democratizar /demokrati'sar; demokrati'θar/ vt to make democratic

demoledor /demole'ðor/ (-ra) a demolition. n demolisher

demoler /demo'ler/ vt irr to demolish, destroy, dismantle. See **moler**

demolición /demoli'sion; demoli'θion/ f, demolition, destruction, dismantling

demoníaco /demo'niako/ a devilish; possessed by a demon

demonio /de'monio/ m, devil; evil spirit. *interj* **¡Demonios!** Deuce take it! *Inf.* **tener el d. en el cuerpo,** to be always on the move, be very energetic

demontre /de'montre/ m, *Inf.* devil

demora /de'mora/ f, delay; *Naut.* bearing; *Com.* demurrage

demorar /demo'rar/ vt to delay; vi stay, remain, tarry; *Naut.* bear

demorón, -ona /demo'ron/ a, *Lat. Am.* slow

demostrable /demos'traβle/ a demonstrable

demostración /demostra'sion; demostra'θion/ f, demonstration; proof

demostrador /demostra'ðor/ (-ra) a demonstrating. n demonstrator

demostrar /demos'trar/ vt irr to demonstrate, explain; prove; teach. See **mostrar**

demostrativo /demostra'tiβo/ a demonstrative. *Gram.* **pronombre d.,** demonstrative pronoun

demudación /demuða'sion; demuða'θion/ f, change; alteration

demudar /demu'ðar/ vt to change, vary; alter, transform; vr change suddenly (color, facial expression, etc.); grow angry

denario /de'nario/ a denary. m, denarius

denegación /denega'sion; denega'θion/ f, denial; refusal

denegar /dene'gar/ vt irr to deny, refuse. See **acertar**

dengoso /den'goso/ a fastidious, finicky

dengue /'dengue/ m, affectation, faddiness, fastidiousness

denigrable /deni'graβle/ a odious

denigración /denigra'sion; denigra'θion/ f, slander, defamation (of character)

denigrante /deni'grante/ a slanderous

denigrar /deni'grar/ vt to slander; insult

denodado /deno'ðaðo/ a valiant, daring

denominación /denomina'sion; denomina'θion/ f, denomination

denominador /denomina'ðor/ a denominating m, *Math.* denominator

denominar /denomi'nar/ vt to name, designate

denostada /denos'taða/ f, insult

denostar /denos'tar/ vt irr to revile, insult. See **acordar**

denotar /deno'tar/ vt to denote, indicate

densidad /densi'ðað/ f, density; closeness, denseness; *Phys.* specific gravity; obscurity

denso /'denso/ a compact, close; thick, dense; crowded; dark, confused

dentado /den'taðo/ a toothed; pronged; dentate

dentadura /denta'ðura/ f, set of teeth (real or false). **d. de rumiante,** teeth like an ox. **d. postiza,** false teeth

dental /den'tal/ a dental

dentar /den'tar/ vt irr to provide with teeth, prongs, etc.; vi cut teeth. See **sentar**

dentellada /dente'yaða; dente'ʎaða/ f, gnashing or chattering of teeth; bite; toothmark

dentellar /dente'yar; dente'ʎar/ vt to chatter, grind, gnash (teeth)

dentellear /denteye'ar; denteʎe'ar/ vt to bite, sink the teeth into

dentera /den'tera/ f, (dar) to set one's teeth on edge; *Fig. Inf.* make one's mouth water

dentición /denti'sion; denti'θion/ f, teething, dentition

dentífrico /den'tifriko/ m, toothpaste

dentista /den'tista/ mf dentist

dentro /'dentro/ adv within, inside. **d. de poco,** soon, shortly. **por d.,** from the inside; on the inside

dentudo /den'tuðo/ a having large teeth

denudación /denuða'sion; denuða'θion/ f, denudation; *Geol.* erosion

denudar /denu'ðar/ vt to denude

denuedo /de'nueðo/ *m,* courage, daring

denuesto /de'nuesto/ *m,* insult

denuncia /de'nunsia; de'nunθia/ *f,* denunciation, accusation

denunciante /denun'siante; denun'θiante/ *a* accusing. *mf Law.* denouncer

denunciar /denun'siar; denun'θiar/ *vt* to give notice, inform; herald, presage; declare, proclaim; denounce; *Law.* accuse

denunciatorio /denunsia'torio; denunθia'torio/ *a* denunciatory

deparar /depa'rar/ *vt* to furnish, offer, present

departamental /departamen'tal/ *a* departmental

departamento /departa'mento/ *m,* department; compartment (railway); branch, section; *Argentina* apartment. **d. de lactantes,** nursery (in a hospital)

departir /depar'tir/ *vi* to converse

depauperación /depaupera'sion; depaupera'θion/ *f,* impoverishment; *Med.* emaciation

depauperar /depaupe'rar/ *vt* to impoverish; *vr Med.* grow weak, become emaciated

dependencia /depen'densia; depen'denθia/ *f,* dependence; subordination; dependency; *Com.* branch; firm, agency; business affair; kinship or affinity; *pl Archit.* offices; *Com.* staff; accessories

depender /depen'der/ *vi* (*with de*) to be subordinate to; depend on; be dependent on, need

dependiente /depen'diente/ (**-ta**) *a* and *n* dependent, subordinate. *m,* employee; shop assistant

depilar /depi'lar/ *vt* to pluck, wax; *vr* to shave, wax (legs, etc.)

depilatorio /depila'torio/ *m,* depilatory

deplorar /deplo'rar/ *vt* to deplore, lament

deponente /depo'nente/ *a* deposing; affirming. *mf* deponent. *Gram.* **verbo d.,** deponent verb

deponer /depo'ner/ *vt irr* to lay aside; depose, oust; affirm, testify; remove, take from its place; *Law.* depose; *Central America, Mexico* throw up, vomit. See **poner**

deportación /deporta'sion; deporta'θion/ *f,* deportation

deportar /depor'tar/ *vt* to exile; deport

deporte /de'porte/ *m,* sport; *pl* games. **d. de vela,** sailing; boating

deportismo /depor'tismo/ *m,* sport

deportista /depor'tista/ *a* sporting. *mf* sportsman (sportswoman)

deportivo /depor'tiβo/ *a* sporting

deposición /deposi'sion; deposi'θion/ *f,* affirmation, statement; *Law.* deposition; degradation, removal (from office, etc.)

depositador /deposita'ðor/ (**-ra**) *a* depositing. *n* depositor

depositar /deposi'tar/ *vt* to deposit; place in safety; entrust; lay aside, put away; *vr Chem.* settle

depositaría /deposita'ria/ *f,* depository; trusteeship; accounts office

depositario /deposi'tario/ (**-ia**) *a* pertaining to a depository. *n* depositary, trustee

depósito /de'posito/ *m,* deposit; depository; *Com.* depot, warehouse; *Chem.* deposit, sediment; tank, reservoir; *Mil.* depot. **d. de bencina, d. de gasolina,** gas tank; service station. **d. de municiones,** munitions dump. *Com.* **en d.,** in bond. **Queda hecho el d. que marca la ley,** Copyright reserved

depravación /depraβa'sion; depraβa'θion/ *f,* depravity

depravar /depra'βar/ *vt* to deprave, corrupt; *vr* become depraved

deprecación /depreka'sion; depreka'θion/ *f,* supplication, petition; deprecation

deprecar /depre'kar/ *vt* to supplicate, petition; deprecate

depreciación /depresia'sion; depreθia'θion/ *f,* depreciation, fall in value

depreciar /depre'siar; depre'θiar/ *vt* to depreciate, reduce the value (of)

depredación /depreða'sion; depreða'θion/ *f,* depredation, robbery

depredar /depre'ðar/ *vt* to pillage

depresión /depre'sion/ *f,* depression. **d. nerviosa,** nervous breakdown

depresivo /depre'siβo/ *a* depressive; humiliating

deprimir /depri'mir/ *vt* to depress, compress, press down; depreciate, belittle; *vr* be compressed

depuración /depura'sion; depura'θion/ *f,* cleansing, purification; *Polit.* purge

depurar /depu'rar/ *vt* to cleanse, purify; *Polit.* purge

derecha /de'retʃa/ *f,* right hand; *Polit.* (gen. *pl*) Right. *Mil.* **¡D.!** Right Turn! **a la d.,** on the right

derechamente /deretʃa'mente/ *adv* straight, directly; prudently, justly; openly, frankly

derechera /dere'tʃera/ *f,* direct road

derechista /dere'tʃista/ *mf Polit.* rightist

derecho /de'retʃo/ *a* straight; upright; right (not left); just, reasonable; *Sports.* forehand. *adv* straightaway. *m,* right; law; just claim; privilege; justice, reason; exemption; right side (cloth, etc.); *pl* dues, taxes; fees. **d. a la vía,** right of way. **d. de apelación,** right to appeal. **d. de visita,** (international law) right of search. **derechos de aduana,** customhouse duties. **derechos de entrada,** import duties. **según d.,** according to law. **usar de su d.,** to exercise one's right

derechura /dere'tʃura/ *f,* directness, straightness; uprightness; *Lat. Am.* good luck

deriva /de'riβa/ *f,* (*Naut. Aer.*) drift, leeway. **d. continental,** continental drift

derivación /deriβa'sion; deriβa'θion/ *f,* origin, derivation; inference, consequence; *Gram.* derivation

derivar /deri'βar/ *vi* to originate; *Naut.* drift; *vt* conduct, lead; *Gram.* derive; *Elec.* tap

dermatología /dermatolo'hia/ *f,* dermatology

dermatólogo /derma'tologo/ *m,* dermatologist

derogación /deroga'sion; deroga'θion/ *f,* repeal, annulment; deterioration

derogar /dero'gar/ *vt* to annul, repeal; destroy, suppress

derogatorio /deroga'torio/ *a Law.* repealing

derrama /de'rrama/ *f,* apportionment of tax

derramado /derra'maðo/ *a* extravagant, wasteful

derramamiento /derrama'miento/ *m,* pouring out; spilling; scattering

derramar /derra'mar/ *vt* to pour out; spill; shed (blood); scatter; apportion (taxes); publish abroad, spread; *vr* be scattered; overflow

derrame /de'rrame/ *m,* spilling; leakage; overflow; scattering; slope

derredor /derre'ðor/ *m,* circumference. **al** (*or* **en**) **d.,** round about

derrelicto /derre'likto/ *a* abandoned; derelict. *m, Naut.* derelict

derrengado /derren'gaðo/ *a* crooked; crippled

derretimiento /derreti'miento/ *m,* melting; thaw; liquefaction; *Inf.* burning passion

derretir /derre'tir/ *vt irr* to melt, liquefy; waste, dissipate; *vr* be very much in love; *Inf.* be susceptible (to love); *Inf.* long, be impatient. See **pedir**

derribar /derri'βar/ *vt* to demolish; knock down; fell; throw down; *Aer.* shoot down; throw (in wrestling); *Fig.* overthrow; demolish, explode (a myth); control (emotions); *vr* fall down; prostrate oneself; throw oneself down. **d. el chapeo,** *humorous* to doff one's hat

derribo /de'rriβo/ *m,* demolition; debris, rubble; throw (in wrestling)

derrocadero /derroka'ðero/ *m,* rocky precipice

derrocar /derro'kar/ *vt* to throw down from a rock; demolish (buildings); overthrow, oust

derrochador /derrotʃa'ðor/ (**-ra**) *a* wasteful, extravagant. *n* spendthrift

derrochar /derro'tʃar/ *vt* to waste, squander

derroche /de'rrotʃe/ *m,* squandering

derrota /de'rrota/ *f,* road; route, path; *Naut.* course; *Mil.* defeat

derrotar /derro'tar/ *vt* to defeat; overthrow (government); destroy, harm; *Mil.* defeat; *vr Naut.* drift, lose course; be a failure

derrotero /derro'tero/ *m, Naut.* course; *Naut.* ship's itinerary; number of sea charts; means to an end, course of action

derrotismo /derro'tismo/ *m*, defeatism

derrotista /derro'tista/ *mf* defeatist

derruir /de'rruir/ *vt irr* to demolish (a building). See **huir**

derrumbadero /derrumba'ðero/ *m*, precipice; risk, danger

derrumbamiento /derrumba'miento/ *m*, landslide; collapse, downfall

derrumbar /derrum'bar/ *vt* to precipitate; *vr* throw oneself down, collapse, tumble down (buildings, etc.)

derrumbe /de'rrumbe/ *m*, collapse; subsidence

derviche /der'βitʃe/ *m*, dervish

desabarrancar /desaβarran'kar/ *vt* to pull out of a ditch or rut; extricate (from a difficulty)

desabillé /desaβi'ye; desaβi'ʎe/ *m*, deshabille

desabor /desa'βor/ *m*, insipidity

desabotonar /desaβoto'nar/ *vt* to unbutton; *vi* open (flowers)

desabrido /desa'βriðo/ *a* insipid, poor-tasting; inclement (weather); disagreeable; unsociable; homely, plain (woman)

desabrigar /desaβri'gar/ *vt* to uncover; leave without shelter

desabrigo /desa'βrigo/ *m*, want of clothing or shelter; poverty, destitution

desabrimiento /desaβri'miento/ *m*, insipidity; harshness, disagreeableness; melancholy, depression

desabrir /desa'βrir/ *vt* to give a bad taste (to food); annoy, trouble

desabrochar /desaβro'tʃar/ *vt* to unbutton, untie; open; *vr Inf.* confide, open up

desacatar /desaka'tar/ *vt* to behave disrespectfully (towards); disobey; lack reverence

desacato /desa'kato/ *m*, irreverence; disrespect

desacertado /desaser'taðo; desaθer'taðo/ *a* wrong, erroneous; imprudent

desacertar /desaser'tar; desaθer'tar/ *vi irr* to be wrong; act imprudently. See **acertar**

desacierto /desa'sierto; desa'θierto/ *m*, mistake, miscalculation, blunder

desacomodado /desakomo'ðaðo/ *a* lacking means of subsistence; poor; unemployed (servants); troublesome

desacomodar /desakomo'ðar/ *vt* to incommode, make uncomfortable, inconvenience; dismiss, discharge

desaconsejado /desakonse'haðo/ *a* ill-advised

desaconsejar /desakonse'har/ *vt* to advise against, dissuade

desacoplar /desakop'lar/ *vt* to disconnect

desacordar /desakor'ðar/ *vt irr Mus.* to put out of tune; *vr* (*with de*) forget. See **acordar**

desacorde /desa'korðe/ *a* discordant, inharmonious; *Mus.* out of tune

desacostumbrado /desakostum'braðo/ *a* unaccustomed; unusual

desacostumbrar /desakostum'brar/ *vt* to break of a habit

desacotar /desako'tar/ *vt* to remove (fences); refuse, deny; *vi* withdraw (from agreement, etc.)

desacreditar /desakreði'tar/ *vt* to discredit

desacuerdo /desa'kuerðo/ *m*, disagreement, discord; mistake; forgetfulness; swoon, loss of consciousness

desadeudar /desaðeu'ðar/ *vt* to free from debt

desadornar /desaðor'nar/ *vt* to denude of ornaments

desadorno /desa'ðorno/ *m*, lack of ornaments; bareness

desafecto /desa'fekto/ *a* disaffected; hostile. *m*, disaffection

desaferrar /desafe'rrar/ *vt irr* to untie, unfasten; *Fig.* wean from; *Naut.* weigh anchor. See **acertar**

desafiador /desafia'ðor/ (**-ra**) *a* challenging. *n* challenger. *m*, duelist

desafiar /desa'fiar/ *vt* to challenge; compete with; oppose; *Mexico* fight

desafinar /desafi'nar/ *vi Mus.* to go out of tune; *Fig. Inf.* speak out of turn

desafío /desa'fio/ *m*, challenge; competition; duel

desaforado /desafo'raðo/ *a* lawless; outrageous; enormous

desaforar /desafo'rar/ *vt* to infringe (laws, etc.); *vr* be disorderly

desaforrar /desafo'rrar/ *vt* to remove the lining of or from

desafortunado /desafortu'naðo/ *a* unfortunate

desafuero /desa'fuero/ *m*, act of injustice; outrage, excess

desagarrar /desaga'rrar/ *vt Inf.* to release, loosen; unhook

desagraciado /desagra'siaðo; desagra'θiaðo/ *a* ugly, unsightly

desagraciar /desagra'siar; desagra'θiar/ *vt* to disfigure, make ugly

desagradable /desagra'ðaβle/ *a* disagreeable; unpleasant

desagradar /desagra'ðar/ *vi* to be disagreeable, displease (e.g. *Me desagrada su voz,* I find his voice unpleasant)

desagradecer /desagraðe'ser; desagraðe'θer/ *vt irr* to be ungrateful (for). See **conocer**

desagradecido /desagraðe'siðo; desagraðe'θiðo/ *a* ungrateful

desagradecimiento /desagraðesimiento; desagraðeθi'miento/ *m*, ingratitude

desagrado /desa'graðo/ *m*, displeasure, dislike, dissatisfaction

desagraviar /desagra'βiar/ *vt* to make amends, apologize; indemnify

desagravio /desa'graβio/ *m*, satisfaction, reparation; compensation

desagregar /desagre'gar/ (**se**) *vt* and *vr* to separate

desaguadero /desagua'ðero/ *m*, drain, waste pipe

desaguar /desa'guar/ *vt* to drain off; dissipate; *vi* flow (into sea, etc.)

desagüe /de'sague/ *m*, drainage; outlet, drain; catchment

desaguisado /desagi'saðo/ *a* outrageous, lawless. *m*, offense, insult

desahogado /desao'gaðo/ *a* brazen, insolent; clear, unencumbered; in comfortable circumstances

desahogar /desao'gar/ *vt* to ease, relieve; *vr* unburden oneself; recover (from illness, heat, etc.); get out of debt; speak one's mind

desahogo /desa'ogo/ *m*, relief, alleviation; ease; comfort, convenience; freedom, frankness; unburdening (of one's mind). *Inf.* **vivir con d.,** to be comfortably off

desahuciar /desau'siar; desau'θiar/ *vt* to banish all hope; give up, despair of the life of; put out (tenants); *Chile* dismiss

desahucio /desa'usio; desa'uθio/ *m*, ejection, dispossession (of tenants); *Chile* dismissal

desahumar /desau'mar/ *vt* to clear of smoke

desairado /desai'raðo/ *a* unattractive, graceless, ugly; unsuccessful, crestfallen; slighted

desairar /desai'rar/ *vt* to disdain, slight, disregard; underrate (things)

desaire /des'aire/ *m*, gracelessness, ugliness; insult, slight

desalabanza /desala'βansa; desala'βanθa/ *f*, disparagement; criticism

desalabar /desala'βar/ *vt* to censure, disparage

desalación /desala'sion; desala'θion/ *f*, desalinization

desalado /desa'laðo/ *a* anxious, precipitate, hasty

desalar /desa'lar/ *vt* to remove the salt from; take off wings; *vr* walk or run at great speed; long for, yearn

desalentar /desalen'tar/ *vt irr* to make breathing difficult (work, fatigue); discourage; *vr* be depressed or sad. See **sentar**

desaliento /desa'liento/ *m*, depression, discouragement, dismay

desalinear /desaline'ar/ *vt* to throw out of the straight

desaliñado /desali'ɲaðo/ *a* slovenly; slipshod

desaliñar /desali'ɲar/ *vt* to disarrange, make untidy, crumple

desaliño /desa'liɲo/ *m*, untidiness, slovenliness; negligence, carelessness

desalmado /desal'maðo/ *a* soulless, conscienceless; cruel

desalmamiento /desalma'miento/ *m*, inhumanity, consciencelessness; cruelty

desalmidonar /desalmiðo'nar/ *vt* to remove starch from

desalojamiento /desaloha'miento/ *m*, dislodgement, ejection

desalojar /desalo'har/ *vt* to dislodge, remove, eject; *vi* move out, remove

desalquilado /desalki'laðo/ *a* untenanted, vacant

desalquilar /desalki'lar/ *vt* to leave, or cause to leave, rented premises

desalterar /desalte'rar/ *vt* to soothe, calm

desamar /desa'mar/ *vt* to cease to love; hate

desamarrar /desama'rrar/ *vt* to untie; separate; *Naut.* unmoor

desamor /desa'mor/ *m*, indifference; lack of sentiment or affection; hatred

desamotinarse /desamoti'narse/ *vr* to cease from rebellion; submit

desamparar /desampa'rar/ *vt* to abandon, forsake; leave (a place)

desamparo /desam'paro/ *m*, desertion; need

desamueblado /desamue'βlaðo/ *a* unfurnished

desamueblar /desamue'βlar/ *vt* to empty of furniture

desandar lo andado /desan'dar lo an'daðo/ *vt irr* to retrace one's steps. See **andar**

desangrar /desaŋ'grar/ *vt Med.* to bleed; drain (lake, etc.); impoverish, bleed; *vr* lose much blood

desangre /de'saŋgre/ *m*, *Lat. Am.* bleeding, loss of blood

desanidar /desani'ðar/ *vi* to leave the nest; *vt* eject, expel

desanimado /desani'maðo/ *a* downhearted; (of places) dull, quiet

desanimar /desani'mar/ *vt* to discourage, depress

desanublar /desanu'βlar,/ *vt* **desanublarse** *vr* to clear up (weather)

desanudar /desanu'ðar/ *vt* to untie; disentangle

desaojar /desao'har/ *vt* to cure of the evil eye

desapacibilidad /desapasiβili'ðað; desapaθiβili'ðað/ *f*, disagreeableness, unpleasantness

desapacible /desapa'siβle; desapa'θiβle/ *a* disagreeable; unpleasant; unsociable

desaparecer /desapare'ser; desapare'θer/ *vt irr* to disappear; *vi* and *vr* disappear. **hacer d.,** to cause to disappear. See **conocer**

desaparecido /desapare'siðo; desapare'θiðo/ *a* late (deceased); *Mil.* missing

desaparejar /desapare'har/ *vt* to unharness

desaparición /desapari'sion; desapari'θion/ *f*, disappearance

desapegar /desape'gar/ *vt* to unstick, undo; *vr* be indifferent, cast off a love or affection

desapego /desa'pego/ *m*, lack of affection or interest, coolness

desapercibido /desapersi'βiðo; desaperθi'βiðo/ *a* unnoticed; unprovided, unprepared

desapestar /desapes'tar/ *vt* to disinfect

desapiadado /desapia'ðaðo/ *a* merciless

desaplicación /desaplika'sion; desaplika'θion/ *f*, laziness, lack of application; carelessness, negligence

desaplicado /desapli'kaðo/ *a* lazy; careless

desapoderado /desapoðe'raðo/ *a* precipitate, uncontrolled; furious, violent

desapoderar /desapoðe'rar/ *vt* to dispossess, rob; remove from office

desapolillar /desapoli'yar; desapoli'ʎar/ *vt* to free from moths; *vr Inf.* take an airing

desaposentar /desaposen'tar/ *vt* to evict; drive away

desapreciar /desapre'siar; desapre'θiar/ *vt* to scorn

desaprensivo /desapren'siβo/ *a* unscrupulous

desapretar /desapre'tar/ **(se)** *vt* and *vr irr* to slacken. See **acertar**

desaprisionar /desaprisio'nar/ *vt* to release from prison

desaprobación /desaproβa'sion; desaproβa'θion/ *f*, disapproval

desaprobar /desapro'βar/ *vt irr* to disapprove; disagree with. See **probar**

desapropiamiento /desapropia'miento/ *m*, renunciation or transfer of property

desapropiarse /desapropi'arse/ *vr* to renounce or transfer (property)

desaprovechado /desaproβe'tʃaðo/ *a* unprofitable; backward; unintelligent

desaprovechar /desaproβe'tʃar/ *vt* to take no advantage of, waste; *vi Fig.* lose ground, lose what one has gained

desapuntar /desapun'tar/ *vt* to unstitch; lose one's aim

desarbolar /desarβo'lar/ *vt Naut.* to unmast

desarenar /desare'nar/ *vt* to clear of sand

desarmador /desarma'ðor/ *m*, *Mexico* screwdriver

desarmar /desar'mar/ *vt* to disarm; dismantle, dismount; appease

desarme /de'sarme/ *m*, disarming; disarmament

desarraigar /desarrai'gar/ *vt* to pull up by root (plants); extirpate, suppress; eradicate (opinion, etc.); exile

desarraigo /desa'rraigo/ *m*, uprooting; extirpation; eradication; exile

desarrebujar /desarreβu'har/ *vt* to disentangle, uncover; explain

desarreglado /desarre'glaðo/ *a* disarranged; untidy; intemperate, immoderate

desarreglar /desarre'glar/ *vt* to disarrange

desarreglo /desa'rreglo/ *m*, disorder; disarrangement; irregularity

desarrendar /desarren'dar/ *vt irr* to unbridle a horse; end a tenancy or lease. See **recomendar**

desarrollar /desarro'yar; desarro'ʎar/ *vt* to unroll; increase, develop, grow, unfold; explain (theory); *vr* develop, grow

desarrollo /des'arroyo; desa'rroʎo/ *m*, unrolling; development, growth; explanation

desarropar /desarro'par/ *vt* to uncover, remove the covers, etc. from

desarrugar /desarru'gar/ *vt* to take out wrinkles or creases

desarticulación /desartikula'sion; desartikula'θion/ *f*, disarticulation

desarticular /desartiku'lar/ *vt* to disarticulate; *Mech.* disconnect

desaseado /desase'aðo/ *a* dirty; unkempt, slovenly

desaseo /desa'seo/ *m*, dirtiness; slovenliness

desasimiento /desasi'miento/ *m*, loosening; liberality; disinterestedness, indifference, coldness

desasir /desa'sir/ *vt irr* to loosen, undo. *vr* disengage oneself. See **asir**

desasosegar /desasose'gar/ *vt irr* to disturb, make anxious. See **cegar**

desasosiego /desaso'siego/ *m*, uneasiness, disquiet

desastre /de'sastre/ *m*, disaster, calamity

desastroso /desas'troso/ *a* unfortunate, calamitous

desatacar /desata'kar/ *vt* to unfasten, undo, unbutton

desatadura /desata'ðura/ *f*, untying

desatar /desa'tar/ *vt* to untie; melt, dissolve; elucidate, explain; *vr* loosen the tongue; lose self control; lose all reserve; unbosom oneself

desatascar /desatas'kar/ *vt* to pull out of the mud; free from obstruction; extricate from difficulties

desataviar /desata'βiar/ *vt* to strip of ornaments

desatavío /desata'βio/ *m*, carelessness in dress, slovenliness

desatención /desaten'sion; desaten'θion/ *f*, inattention, abstraction; incivility

desatender /desaten'der/ *vt* to pay no attention to; disregard, ignore. See **entender**

desatentado /desaten'taðo/ *a* imprudent, ill-advised; excessive, immoderate

desatento /desa'tento/ *a* inattentive, abstracted; discourteous

desatinado /desati'naðo/ *a* foolish, imprudent, wild

desatinar /desati'nar/ *vt* to bewilder; *vi* behave foolishly; lose one's bearings

desatino /desa'tino/ *m*, folly, foolishness, imprudence, rashness; blunder, faux pas, mistake

desatracar /desatra'kar/ *vi Naut.* to push off

desatrancar /desatran'kar/ vt to unbar the door; remove obstacles

desaturdir /desatur'ðir/ vt to rouse (from torpor, etc.)

desautorizar /desautori'sar; desautori'θar/ vt to remove from authority; discredit

desavenencia /desaβe'nensia; desaβe'nenθia/ f, disharmony, disagreement

desavenido /desaβe'niðo/ a disagreeing, discordant

desavenir /desaβe'nir/ vt irr to upset. See **venir**

desaventajado /desaβenta'haðo/ a disadvantageous; unfavorable, inferior

desaviar /desa'βiar/ vt to lead astray; deprive of a necessity; vr lose one's way

desavisado /desaβi'saðo/ a unaware, unprepared

desavisar /desaβi'sar/ vt to take back one's previous advice

desayunador /desayuna'ðor/ m, breakfast nook

desayunarse /desayu'narse/ vr to have breakfast, eat breakfast

desayuno /desa'yuno/ m, breakfast

desazón /desa'son; desa'θon/ f, insipidity, lack of flavor; poorness (soil); anxiety, trouble; vexation

desazonar /desaso'nar; desaθo'nar/ vt to make insipid; make anxious, worry; vex; vr feel out of sorts

desbancar /desβan'kar/ vt to break the bank (gambling); supplant

desbandada /desβan'daða/ f, dispersal, rout. **a la d.,** in confusion or disorder

desbandarse /desβan'darse/ vr to disband, retreat in disorder; Mil. desert

desbaratado /desβara'taðo/ a Inf. corrupt, vicious

desbaratar /desβara'tar/ vt to spoil, destroy; dissipate, waste; foil, thwart (a plot); Mil. rout; vi talk foolishly; vr go too far, behave badly

desbarbado /desβar'βaðo/ a beardless

desbastar /desβas'tar/ vt to plane, dress; polish, refine, civilize

desbocado /desβo'kaðo/ a (of tools) blunt; runaway (of a horse); Inf. foul-tongued; Lat. Am. overflowing (its banks)

desbocar /desβo'kar/ vt to break the spout or neck (of jars, etc.); vi run (into) (of streets, etc.); vr bolt (horses); curse, swear

desboquillar /desβoki'yar; desβoki'ʎar/ vt to remove or break a stem or mouthpiece

desbordamiento /desβorða'miento/ m, overflowing, flood

desbordarse /desβor'ðarse/ vr to overflow; lose self-control. **d. en alabanzas para,** to heap praise on

desbravar /desβra'βar/ vt to break in (horses, etc.); vi grow less savage; lose force, decrease

desbrozar /desβro'sar; desβro'θar/ vt to free of rubbish, clear up

descabalgadura /deskaβalga'ðura/ f, alighting (from horses, etc.)

descabalgar /deskaβal'gar/ vi to alight (from horse); vt dismantle (gun)

descabellado /deskaβe'yaðo; deskaβe'ʎaðo/ a disheveled; ridiculous, foolish

descabellar /deskaβe'yar; deskaβe'ʎar/ vt to disarrange, ruffle (hair)

descabezado /deskaβe'saðo; deskaβe'θaðo/ a headless; rash, impetuous

descabezar /deskaβe'sar; deskaβe'θar/ vt to behead; cut the top off (trees, etc.); Fig. Inf. break the back of (work); vi abut, join; vr (with con or en) rack one's brains about

descacharrado, -a /deskatʃa'rraðo/ a, Central America dirty, filthy, slovenly

descafeinado /deskafei'naðo/ a decaffeinated

descalabazarse /deskalaβa'sarse; deskalaβa'θarse/ vr Inf. to rack one's brains

descalabradura /deskalaβra'ðura/ f, head wound or scar

descalabrar /deskala'βrar/ vt to wound in the head; wound; harm

descalabro /deska'laβro/ m, misfortune, mishap

descalzar /deskal'sar; deskal'θar/ vt to remove the shoes and stockings; undermine; vr remove one's shoes and stockings; lose a shoe (horses)

descalzo /des'kalso; des'kalθo/ a barefoot

descaminar /deskami'nar/ vt to lead astray; pervert, corrupt

descamisado /deskami'saðo/ **(-da)** a Inf. shirtless; ragged, poor. n Inf. down and out, outcast; vagabond

descansadero /deskansa'ðero/ m, resting place

descansado /deskan'saðo/ a rested, refreshed; tranquil

descansar /deskan'sar/ vi to rest, repose oneself; have relief (from anxiety, etc.); sleep; Agr. lie fallow; sleep in death; (with en) trust, have confidence in; (with sobre) lean on or upon; vt (with sobre) rest (a thing) on another. **¡Que en paz descanse!** May he rest in peace!

descanso /des'kanso/ m, rest, repose; relief (from care); landing of stairs; Mech. bench, support; Mil. stand easy

descarado /deska'raðo/ a impudent, brazen

descararse /deska'rarse/ vr to behave impudently

descarbonizar /deskarβoni'sar; deskarβoni'θar/ vt to decarbonize

descarga /des'karga/ f, unloading; Naut. discharge of cargo; Elec. discharge; Mil. volley. **d. cerrada,** dense volley, fusillade

descargadero /deskarga'ðero/ m, wharf

descargador /deskarga'ðor/ m, unloader, docker; Elec. discharger

descargar /deskar'gar/ vt to unload; Mil. fire; unload (fire-arms); Elec. discharge; rain (blows) upon; Fig. free, exonerate; download; vi disembogue (of rivers); burst (clouds); vr relinquish (employment); shirk responsibility; Law. clear oneself

descargo /des'kargo/ m, unloading; Com. acquittance; Law. answer to an impeachment

descargue /des'karge/ m, unloading

descarnado /deskar'naðo/ a fleshless; scraggy; spare, lean

descarnador /deskarna'ðor/ m, dental scraper; tanner's scraper

descarnar /deskar'nar/ vt to scrape off flesh; corrode; inspire indifference to earthly things

descaro /des'karo/ m, impudence

descarriar /deska'rriar/ vt to lead astray; vr be lost, be separated (from others); Fig. go astray

descarrilamiento /deskarrila'miento/ m, derailment

descarrilar /deskarri'lar/ vi to run off the track, be derailed

descarrío /deska'rrio/ m, losing one's way

descartar /deskar'tar/ vt to put aside; vr discard (cards); shirk, make excuses

descarte /des'karte/ m, discard (cards); excuse, pretext

descascarar /deskaska'rar/ vt to peel; shell; vr peel off

descendencia /dessen'densia; desθen'denθia/ f, descendants, offspring; lineage, descent

descender /dessen'der; desθen'der/ vi irr to descend; flow (liquids); (with de) descend from, derive from; vt lower, let down. See **entender**

descendiente /dessen'diente; desθen'diente/ mf descendant, offspring. a descending

descendimiento /dessendi'miento; desθendi'miento/ m, descent

descenso /des'senso; des'θenso/ m, descent; lowering, letting down; degradation

descentralizar /dessentrali'sar; desθentrali'θar/ vt to decentralize

desceñir /desse'ɲir; desθe'ɲir/ **(se)** vt and vr irr to ungird, remove a girdle, etc. See **ceñir**

descepar /desse'par; desθe'par/ vt to tear up by the roots; Fig. extirpate

descercado /desser'kaðo; desθer'kaðo/ a unfenced, open

descercar /desser'kar; desθer'kar/ vt to pull down a wall or fence; Mil. raise a siege

descerrajar /desserra'har; desθerra'har/ vt to remove the locks (of doors, etc.)

descifrable /dessi'fraβle; desθi'fraβle/ a decipherable

descifrador /dessifra'ðor; desθifra'ðor/ m, decipherer, decoder

descifrar /dessi'frar; desθi'frar/ *vt* to decipher; decode

descinchar /dessin'tʃar; desθin'tʃar/ *vt* to loosen or remove girths (of horse)

desclavar /deskla'βar/ *vt* to remove nails; unnail, unfasten

descoagular /deskoagu'lar/ *vt* to liquefy, dissolve, melt

descobijar /deskoβi'har/ *vt* to uncover; undress

descocado /desko'kaðo/ *a Inf.* brazen, saucy

descoco /des'koko/ *m, Inf.* impudence

descogollar /deskogo'yar; deskogo'ʎar/ *vt* to prune a tree of shoots; remove hearts (of lettuces, etc.)

descolar /desko'lar/ *vt irr* to cut off or dock an animal's tail; *Mexico* slight, snub. See **colar**

descolgar /deskol'gar/ *vt irr* to unhang; lower; *vr* lower oneself (by rope, etc.); come down, descend; *Inf.* come out (with), utter. See **volcar**

descollar /desko'yar; desko'ʎar/ *vi irr* to excel, be outstanding. See **degollar**

descoloramiento /deskolora'miento/ *m,* discoloration

descolorar /deskolo'rar/ *vt* to discolor; *vr* be discolored

descolorido /deskolo'riðo/ *a* discolored; pale-colored; pallid

descomedido /deskome'ðiðo/ *a* excessive, disproportionate; rude

descomedimiento /deskomeði'miento/ *m,* disrespect, lack of moderation, rudeness

descomedirse /deskome'ðirse/ *vr irr* to be disrespectful or rude. See **pedir**

descompasarse /deskompa'sarse/ *vr* See **descomedirse**

descomponer /deskompo'ner/ *vt irr* to disorder, disarrange; *Chem.* decompose; unsettle; *vr* go out of order; rot, putrefy; be ailing; lose one's temper. See **poner**

descomposición /deskomposi'sion; deskomposi'θion/ *f,* disorder, confusion; discomposure; *Chem.* decomposition; putrefaction

descompostura /deskompos'tura/ *f,* decomposition; slovenliness, dirtiness, untidiness; impudence, rudeness

descompuesto /deskom'puesto/ *a* rude, impudent; *Lat. Am.* tipsy; *Venezuela* ill, sick

descomunal /deskomu'nal/ *a* enormous, extraordinary

desconcertar /deskonser'tar; deskonθer'tar/ *vt irr* to disorder, disarrange; dislocate (bones); disconcert, embarrass; *vr* disagree; be impudent. See **acertar**

desconcharse /deskon'tʃarse/ *vr* to flake off, peel

desconcierto /deskon'sierto; deskon'θierto/ *m,* disorder, disarrangement; dislocation; embarrassment; disagreement; impudence

desconectar /deskonek'tar/ *vt* to disconnect; switch off

desconfianza /deskon'fiansa; deskon'fianθa/ *f,* lack of confidence

desconfiar /deskon'fiar/ *vi* to lack confidence, mistrust

desconformidad /deskonformi'ðað/ *f,* See **disconformidad**

desconformismo /deskonfor'mismo/ *m,* nonconformism

desconocer /deskono'ser; deskono'θer/ *vt irr* to forget; be unaware of; deny, disown; pretend ignorance; not to understand (persons, etc.). See **conocer**

desconocido /deskonos'iðo; deskono'θiðo/ **(-da)** *a* unknown; ungrateful. *n* stranger; ingrate

desconocimiento /deskonosi'miento; deskonoθi'miento/ *m,* unawareness; ignorance; ingratitude

desconsiderado /deskonsiðe'raðo/ *a* inconsiderate; discourteous; rash

desconsolación /deskonsola'sion; deskonsola'θion/ *f,* affliction, trouble

desconsolar /deskonso'lar/ *vt irr* to afflict, make disconsolate; *vr* grieve, despair. See **colar**

desconsuelo /deskon'suelo/ *m,* anguish, affliction, despair

descontar /deskon'tar/ *vt irr Com.* to make a discount; ignore, discount; take for granted, leave aside. See **contar**

descontentadizo /deskontenta'ðiso; deskontenta'ðiθo/ *a* discontented, difficult to please; fastidious, finicky

descontentar /deskonten'tar/ *vt* to displease; *vr* be dissatisfied

descontento /deskon'tento/ *m,* discontent, dissatisfaction

descontextualizar /deskontekstuali'sar; deskontekstuali'θar/ *vt* to take out of context

descontrolarse /deskontro'larse/ *vr* to lose control, lose control of oneself.

desconveniencia /deskombe'niensia; deskombe'nienθia/ *f,* inconvenience, unsuitability, disagreement

desconvenir /deskombe'nir/ *vi irr* to disagree; be unsuitable, unsightly or odd (things). See **venir**

descorazonamiento /deskorasona'miento; deskoraθona'miento/ *m,* depression, despair

descorazonar /deskoraso'nar; deskoraθo'nar/ *vt* to tear out the heart; depress, discourage

descorchar /deskor'tʃar/ *vt* to take the cork from cork tree; draw a cork (bottles); force, break into (safes)

descorrer /desko'rrer/ *vt* to re-run (race, etc.); draw back (curtains, etc.); *vi* run, flow (liquids)

descorrimiento /deskorri'miento/ *m,* overflow (liquids)

descortés /deskor'tes/ *a* impolite

descortesía /deskorte'sia/ *f,* impoliteness, discourtesy

descortezadura /deskortesa'ðura; deskorteθa'ðura/ *f,* peeling (of bark)

descortezar /deskorte'sar; deskorte'θar/ *vt* to decorticate; remove crust (bread, etc.); polish, civilize

descoser /desko'ser/ *vt Sew.* to unpick; *vr* be unpicked; be indiscreet or tactless

descosido /desko'siðo/ *a* tactless, talkative; *Fig.* disjointed; desultory; unsewn. *m, Sew.* rent, hole

descoyuntamiento /deskoyunta'miento/ *m,* dislocation (bones); irritation, bore; ache, pain

descoyuntar /deskoyun'tar/ *vt* to dislocate (bones); bore, annoy; *vr* be dislocated

descrédito /des'kreðito/ *m,* fall in value (things); discredit (persons)

descreer /deskre'er/ *vt irr* to disbelieve; depreciate; disparage (persons). See **creer**

descreído /deskre'iðo/ **(-da)** *a* unbelieving. *n* unbeliever; infidel

descremar /deskre'mar/ *vt, Lat. Am.* to skim (milk)

describir /deskri'βir/ *vt* to describe; outline, sketch. *Past Part.* **descrito**

descripción /deskrip'sion; deskrip'θion/ *f,* description; *Law.* inventory

descriptible /deskrip'tiβle/ *a* describable

descriptivo /deskrip'tiβo/ *a* descriptive

descuajar /deskua'har/ *vt* to liquefy; *Inf.* discourage; *Agr.* pull up by the root

descuartizar /deskuarti'sar; deskuarti'θar/ *vt* to quarter; joint (meat); *Inf.* carve, cut into pieces, break up

descubierto /desku'βierto/ *a* bareheaded; exposed. *m,* deficit. **al d.,** openly; in the open, without shelter. **girar en d.,** to overdraw (a bank account)

descubridero /deskuβri'ðero/ *m,* viewpoint, lookout

descubridor /deskuβri'ðor/ **(-ra)** *n* discoverer; inventor; explorer. *m, Mil.* scout

descubrimiento /deskuβri'miento/ *m,* find; discovery; revelation; newly discovered territory

descubrir /desku'βrir/ *vt* to reveal; show; discover; learn; unveil (memorials, etc.); *vr* remove one's hat; show oneself, reveal one's whereabouts. *Past Part.* **descubierto**

descuello /des'kueyo; des'kueʎo/ *m,* extra height; *Fig.* pre-eminence; arrogance

descuento /des'kuento/ *m,* reduction; *Com.* rebate, discount

descuidado /deskui'ðaðo/ *a* negligent; careless; untidy; unprepared

descuidar /deskui'ðar/ *vt* to relieve (of responsibility, etc.); distract, occupy (attention, etc.); *vi and vr* be careless; *vr* (*with de or en*) neglect

descuido /des'kuiðo/ *m*, carelessness, negligence; oversight, mistake; incivility; forgetfulness; shameful act

desde /'desðe/ *prep* since, from (time or space); after (e.g. *d. hoy,* from today). **d. la ventana,** from the window. **d. allá,** from the other world. **d. aquella época,** since that time

desdecir /desðe'sir; desðe'θir/ *vi irr* (*with de*) to degenerate, be less good than; be discordant, clash; be unworthy of; *vr* unsay one's words, retract. See **decir**

desdén /des'ðen/ *m*, indifference, coldness; disdain, scorn

desdentado /desðen'taðo/ *a* toothless; *Zool.* edentate

desdentar /desðen'tar/ *vt* to remove teeth

desdeñar /desðe'ɲar/ *vt* to scorn; *vr* (*with de*) dislike, be reluctant

desdeñoso /desðe'ɲoso/ *a* disdainful, scornful

desdibujado /desðiβu'haðo/ *a* badly drawn; blurred, confused

desdicha /des'ðitʃa/ *f*, misfortune; extreme poverty, misery. **por d.,** unfortunately

desdichado /desði'tʃaðo/ *a* unfortunate; *Inf.* timid, weak-kneed

desdicharse /desði'tʃarse/ *vr* to bewail one's fate

desdinerarse una fortuna /desðine'rarse 'una for'tuna/ *vr* to spend a fortune

desdoblar /desðo'βlar/ *vt* to unfold

desdorar /desðo'rar/ *vt* to remove the gilt; *Fig.* tarnish, sully

desdoro /des'ðoro/ *m*, discredit, dishonor

deseable /dese'aβle/ *a* desirable

desear /dese'ar/ *vt* to desire; yearn or long for

desecar /dese'kar/ *vt* to dry; *vr* be desiccated

desechar /dese'tʃar/ *vt* to reject, refuse; scorn; cast out, expel; put away (thoughts, etc.); cast off (old clothes); turn (key); give up

desecho /de'setʃo/ *m*, residue, rest, remains; cast-off; scorn; *Lat. Am.* shortcut

desegregación /desegrega'θion/ *f*, desegregation

desembalar /desemba'lar/ *vt* to unpack

desembanastar /desembana'star/ *vt* to take out of a basket; *Inf.* unsheath (sword); *vr* break loose (animals); *Inf.* get out, alight

desembarazar /desembara'sar; desembara'θar/ *vt* to clear of obstruction; disembarrass, free; vacate; *vr Fig.* rid oneself of obstacles

desembarazo /desemba'raso; desemba'raθo/ *m*, freedom, insouciance, naturalness

desembarcadero /desembarka'ðero/ *m*, landing-stage

desembarcar /desembar'kar/ *vt* to unload; *vi* disembark; alight from vehicle

desembarco /desem'barko/ *m*, disembarkation, landing; staircase landing

desembargar /desembar'gar/ *vt* to free of obstacles or impediments; *Law.* remove an embargo

desembargo /desem'bargo/ *m*, *Law.* removal of an embargo

desembarque /desem'barke/ *m*, disembarkation, landing

desembarrancar /desembarran'kar/ *vt* and *vi Naut.* to refloat

desembaular /desembau'lar/ *vt* to unpack from a trunk; disinter, empty; *Inf.* unbosom oneself

desembocadero /desemboka'ðero/ *m*, exit, way out; mouth (rivers, etc.)

desembocadura /desemboka'ðura/ *f*, mouth (rivers, etc.); street opening

desembocar /desembo'kar/ *vi* (*with en*) to lead to, end in; flow into (rivers)

desembolsar /desembol'sar/ *vt* to take out of a purse; pay, spend

desembolso /desem'bolso/ *m*, disbursement; expenditure

desemboscarse /desembos'karse/ *vr* to get out of the wood; extricate oneself from an ambush

desembozar /desembo'sar; desembo'θar/ *vt* to unmuffle

desembragar /desembra'gar/ *vt Mech.* to disengage (the clutch, etc.)

desembravecer /desembraβe'ser; desembraβe'θer/ *vt irr* to tame, domesticate. See **conocer**

desembriagar /desembria'gar/ **(se)** *vt* and *vr* to sober up (after a drinking bout)

desembrollar /desembro'yar; desembro'ʎar/ *vt Inf.* to disentangle, unravel

desemejanza /deseme'hansa; deseme'hanθa/ *f*, unlikeness

desemejar /deseme'har/ *vi* to be unlike; *vt* disfigure, deform

desempacar /desempa'kar/ *vt* to unpack

desempapelar /desempape'lar/ *vt* to unwrap, remove the paper from; remove wallpaper

desempaquetar /desempake'tar/ *vt* to unpack

desemparejar /desempare'har/ *vt* to split (a pair); make unequal

desemparentado /desemparen'taðo/ *a* without relatives

desempedrar /desempe'ðrar/ *vt irr* to take up the flags (of a pavement). See **acertar**

desempeñar /desempe'ɲar/ *vt* to redeem (pledges); free from debt; fulfill (obligations, etc.); take out of pawn; hold, fill (an office); extricate (from difficulties, etc.); perform, carry out; *Theat.* act

desempeño /desempe'ɲo/ *m*, redemption of a pledge; fulfillment (of an obligation, etc.); performance, accomplishment; *Theat.* acting of a part

desempolvar /desempol'βar/ *vt* to free from dust, dust

desenamorar /desenamo'rar/ *vt* to kill the affection of; *vr* fall out of love

desencadenar /desenkaðe'nar/ *vt* to unchain, unfetter; *Fig.* unleash, let loose; *vr Fig.* break loose

desencajamiento /desenkaha'miento/ *m*, disjointedness, dislocation; ricketiness, broken-down appearance

desencajar /desenka'har/ *vt* to disconnect, disjoint; dislocate; *vr* be out of joint; be contorted (of the face); be tired looking

desencaje /desen'kahe/ *m*, See **desencajamiento**

desencantar /desenkan'tar/ *vt* to disenchant

desencanto /desen'kanto/ *m*, disenchantment; disillusionment

desencerrar /desense'rrar; desenθe'rrar/ *vt irr* to set at liberty; unlock; disclose, reveal. See **acertar**

desenchufar /desentʃu'far/ *vt* to disconnect, unplug (electric plugs, etc.)

desenclavijar /desenklaβi'har/ *vt* to remove the pegs or pins; disconnect, disjoint

desencoger /desenko'her/ *vt* to unfold, spread out; *vr* grow bold

desencolerizar /desenkoleri'sar; desenkoleri'θar/ *vt* to placate; *vr* lose one's anger, grow calm

desenconar /desenko'nar/ *vt* to reduce (inflammation); appease (anger, etc.); *vr* become calm

desencono /desen'kono/ *m*, reduction of inflammation; appeasement (of anger, etc.)

desencordelar /desenkorðe'lar/ *vt* to untie the ropes (of), unstring

desencorvar /desenkor'βar/ *vt* to straighten (curves, etc.)

desenfadado /desenfa'ðaðo/ *a* expeditious; natural, at ease; gay; forward, bold; wide, spacious

desenfadar /desenfa'ðar/ *vt* to appease, make anger disappear

desenfado /desen'faðo/ *m*, freedom; ease; unconcern, frankness

desenfrailar /desenfrai'lar/ *vi* to leave the cloister, become secularized; *Inf.* emancipate oneself

desenfrenar /desenfre'nar/ *vt* to unbridle (horses); *vr* give rein to one's passions, etc.; break loose (storms, etc.)

desenfreno /desen'freno/ *m*, license, lasciviousness; complete freedom from restraint

desengalanar /deseŋgala'nar/ *vt* to strip of ornaments

desenganchar /deseŋgan'tʃar/ *vt* to unhook; uncouple; unfasten; unharness

desengañador /deseŋgaɲa'ðor/ *a* undeceiving

desengañar /deseŋga'ɲar/ *vt* to undeceive, disillusion

desengaño /deseŋ'gaɲo/ *m*, undeceiving, disabuse; disillusionment

desengarzar /deseŋgar'sar; deseŋgar'θar/ *vt* to loosen from its setting; unlink, unhook, unclasp

desengastar /deseŋgas'tar/ *vt* to remove from its setting (jewelry, etc.)

desengrasar /deseŋgra'sar/ *vt* to remove the grease from, clean; *vi Inf.* grow thin

desenlace /desen'lase; desen'laθe/ *m*, loosening, untying; *Lit.* denouement, climax (of play, etc.)

desenlatar /desenla'tar/ *vt*, *Lat. Am.* to open (canned food)

desenlazar /desenla'sar; desenla'θar/ *vt* to untie, unloose; *Lit.* unravel (a plot)

desenlosar /desenlo'sar/ *vt* to remove flagstones

desenmarañar /desemara'ɲar/ *vt* to disentangle; *Fig.* straighten out

desenmascarar /desemaska'rar/ *vt* to remove the mask from; *Fig.* unmask

desenmudecer /desemuðe'ser; desemuðe'θer/ *vi irr* to be freed of a speech impediment; break silence, speak. See **conocer**

desenojar /deseno'har/ *vt* to soothe, appease; *vr* distract oneself, amuse oneself

desenojo /dese'noho/ *m*, relenting, abatement of anger

desenredar /desenre'ðar/ *vt* to disentangle; *Fig.* set right; straighten out; *vr* extricate oneself, get out of a difficulty

desenredo /desen'reðo/ *m*, disentanglement; *Lit.* climax

desenroscar /desenros'kar/ *vt Lat. Am.* to unscrew

desentablar /desenta'βlar/ *vt* to tear up planks or boards; disorder, disrupt

desentenderse /desenten'derse/ *vr irr* (*with de*) to pretend to be ignorant of; take no part in. See **entender**

desenterrador /desenterra'ðor/ *m*, disinterrer, unearther

desenterramiento /desenterra'miento/ *m*, disinterment; *Fig.* unearthing, recollection

desenterrar /desente'rrar/ *vt irr* to unbury, disinter; rummage out; *Fig.* unearth, bring up, recall. See **acertar**

desentoldar /desentol'dar/ *vt* to take away an awning; *Fig.* strip of ornament

desentonar /desento'nar/ *vt* to humiliate; *vi Mus.* be out of tune; speak rudely; *vr* be inharmonious; raise the voice (anger, etc.), behave badly

desentono /desen'tono/ *m*, bad behavior, rudeness; *Mus.* discord; grating quality or harshness (of voice)

desentorpecer /desentorpe'ser; desentorpe'θer/ *vt irr* to restore feeling to (numbed limbs); free from torpor; *vr* become bright and intelligent. See **conocer**

desentramparse /desentram'parse/ *vr Inf.* free oneself from debt

desentrañar /desentra'ɲar/ *vt* to disembowel; *Fig.* unravel, penetrate; *vr* give away one's all

desentumecer /desentume'ser; desentume'θer/ *vt irr* to free from numbness (limbs); *vr* be restored to feeling (numb limbs). See **conocer**

desenvainar /desembai'nar/ *vt* to unsheath; *Inf.* reveal, bring into the open

desenvoltura /desembol'tura/ *f*, naturalness, ease, freedom; eloquence, facility (of speech); effrontery, audacity, shamelessness (especially in women)

desenvolver /desembol'βer/ *vt irr* to unroll; unfold; *Fig.* unravel, explain; *Fig.* develop, work out (theories, etc.); *vr* unroll; unfold; lose one's timidity, blossom out; be over-bold; extricate oneself (from a difficulty). See **resolver**

desenvuelto /desem'buelto/ *a* natural, easy; impudent, bold

deseo /de'seo/ *m*, desire, will, wish

deseoso /dese'oso/ *a* desirous, wishful

desequilibrar /desekili'βrar/ (**se**) *vt* and *vr* to unbalance

desequilibrio /deseki'liβrio/ *m*, lack of balance; confusion, disorder; mental instability

deserción /deser'sion; deser'θion/ *f*, *Mil.* desertion.
d. estudiantil, school dropout

desertar /deser'tar/ *vt Mil.* to desert; *Inf.* quit

desertor /deser'tor/ *m*, *Mil.* deserter; *Inf.* quitter

deservicio /deserβisio; deser'βiθio/ *m*, disservice

desesperación /desespera'sion; desespera'θion/ *f*, desperation, despair; frenzy, violence

desesperado /desespe'raðo/ *a* desperate, hopeless; frenzied

desesperanza /desespe'ransa; desespe'ranθa/ *f*, despair; hopelessness

desesperanzar /desesperan'sar; desesperan'θar/ *vt* to render hopeless; *vr* despair, lose hope

desesperar /desespe'rar/ *vt* to make hopeless; *Inf.* annoy, make furious; *vr* lose hope, despair; be frenzied

desestañar /desesta'ɲar/ *vt* to unsolder

desestimación /desestima'sion; desestima'θion/ *f*, disrespect, lack of esteem; rejection

desestimar /desesti'mar/ *vt* to scorn; reject

desfachatado /desfatʃa'taðo/ *a Inf.* impudent, brazen

desfachatez /desfatʃa'tes; desfatʃa'teθ/ *f*, *Inf.* effrontery, cheek

desfalcador /desfalka'ðor/ (**-ra**) *a* embezzling. *n* embezzler

desfalcar /desfal'kar/ *vt* to remove a part of; embezzle

desfalco /des'falko/ *m*, diminution, reduction; embezzlement

desfallecer /desfaye'ser; desfaʎe'θer/ *vt irr* to weaken; *vi* grow weak; faint, swoon. See **conocer**

desfallecimiento /desfayesi'miento/ *m*, weakness, languor; depression, discouragement; faint, swoon

desfavorable /desfaβo'raβle/ *a* unfavorable; hostile, contrary

desfavorecer /desfaβore'ser; desfaβore'θer/ *vt irr* to withdraw one's favor, scorn; disfavor; oppose. See **conocer**

desfiguración /desfigura'sion; desfigura'θion/ *f*, deformation; disfigurement

desfigurar /desfigu'rar/ *vt* to deform, misshape; disfigure; *Fig.* disguise, mask; obscure, darken; distort, misrepresent; *vr* be disfigured (by rage, etc.)

desfijar /desfi'har/ *vt* to unfix, pull off, remove

desfiladero /desfila'ðero/ *m*, defile, gully

desfilar /desfi'lar/ *vi* to walk in file; *Inf.* file out; *Mil.* file or march past

desfile /des'file/ *m*, *Mil.* march past; parade; walk past; procession

desflecarse /desfle'karse/ (**en**) *vr* to disintegrate (into)

desfloración /desflora'sion; desflora'θion/ *f*, defloration

desflorar /desflo'rar/ *vt* to tarnish, stain; deflower, violate; *Fig.* touch upon, deal lightly with

desfortalecer /desfortale'ser; desfortale'θer/ *vt irr Mil.* to dismantle a fortress. See **conocer**

desfruncir /desfrun'sir; desfrun'θir/ *vt* to unfold, shake out

desgaire /des'gaire/ *m*, untidiness, slovenliness; affectation of carelessness (in dress); scornful gesture.
al d., with an affectation of carelessness, negligently

desgajar /desga'har/ *vt* to tear off a tree branch; break; *vr* break off; dissociate oneself (from)

desgalgar /desgal'gar/ *vt* to throw headlong

desgana /des'gana/ *f*, lack of appetite; lack of interest, indifference; reluctance

desganar /desga'nar/ *vt* to dissuade; *vr* lose one's appetite; become bored or indifferent, lose interest

desgarbado /desgar'βaðo/ *a* slovenly, slatternly; gawky, graceless

desgarrado /desga'rraðo/ *a* dissolute, vicious; impudent, brazen

desgarrador /desgarra'ðor/ *a* tearing; heart-rending

desgarrar /desga'rrar/ *vt* to tear; *vr* leave, tear oneself away

desgarro /des'garro/ *m*, tearing; rent, breach; boastfulness, impudence, effrontery; *Lat. Am.* phlegm

desgastar /desgas'tar/ *vt* to corrode, wear away; spoil, corrupt; *vr* lose one's vigor, grow weak; wear away

desgaste /des'gaste/ *m*, attrition; wearing down or away; corrosion; wear and tear

desgobernado /desgoβer'naðo/ *a* uncontrolled (of persons)

desgobernar /desgoβer'nar/ *vt irr* to upset or rise against the government; dislocate (bones); *Naut.* neglect the tiller; *vr* affect exaggerated movements in dancing. See **recomendar**

desgobierno /desgo'βierno/ *m*, misgovernment; mismanagement; maladministration; disorder, tumult

desgomar /desgo'mar/ *vt* to ungum (fabrics)

desgorrarse /desgo'rrarse/ *vr* to doff one's cap, doff one's hat

desgoznar /desgos'nar; desgoθ'nar/ *vt* to unhinge; *vr Fig.* lose one's self-control

desgracia /des'grasia; des'graθia/ *f*, misfortune, adversity; mishap, piece of bad luck; disgrace, disfavor; disagreeableness, brusqueness; ungraciousness. **por d.,** unhappily, unfortunately

desgraciado /desgra'siaðo; desgra'θiaðo/ *a* unfortunate, unhappy; unlucky; dull, boring; disagreeable

desgraciar /desgra'siar; desgra'θiar/ *vt* to displease; spoil the development (of), destroy; maim; *vr* fall out of friendship; be out of favor; turn out badly, fail; be destroyed or spoiled; be maimed

desgranar /desgra'nar/ *vt Agr.* to thresh, flail; *vr* break (string of beads, etc.)

desgrasante /desgra'sante/ *m*, grease remover

desgreñar /desgre'ɲar/ *vt* to dishevel the hair; *vr Inf.* pull each other's hair, come to blows

desguarnecer /desguarne'ser; desguarne'θer/ *vt irr* to strip of trimming; *Mil.* demilitarize; *Mil.* disarm; dismantle; unharness. See **conocer**

desguazar /desgua'sar; desgua'θar/ *vt* to break up (ships)

deshabitado /desaβi'taðo/ *a* uninhabited, empty

deshabitar /desaβi'tar/ *vt* to desert, quit, leave (a place)

deshabituar /desaβi'tuar/ *vt* to disaccustom; *vr* lose the habit, become unaccustomed

deshacer /desa'ser; desa'θer/ *vt irr* to undo; destroy; *Mil.* rout, defeat; take to pieces; melt; pulp (paper); untie (knots, etc.); open (parcels); diminish, decrease; break in pieces, smash; *Fig.* obstruct, spoil; *vr* be wasted or spoiled; be full of anxiety; vanish; try or work very hard; injure oneself; be emaciated, grow extremely thin; (*with de*) part with. **d. agravios,** to right wrongs. See **hacer**

desharrapado /desarra'paðo/ *a* tattered, shabby

deshebillar /deseβi'yar; deseβi'ʎar/ *vt* to unbuckle

deshebrar /dese'βrar/ *vt* to unravel; shred

deshecha /des'etʃa/ *f*, pretense, evasion; courteous farewell; obligatory departure

deshechizar /desetʃi'sar; desetʃi'θar/ *vt* to disenchant

deshecho /des'etʃo/ *a* torn; undone; (of storms) violent

deshelar /dese'lar/ *vt irr* to thaw, melt. See **acertar**

desherbar /deser'βar/ *vt irr* to pull up weeds. See **acertar**

desheredar /desere'ðar/ *vt* disinherit; *vr Fig.* lower oneself

desherrar /dese'rrar/ *vt irr* to unfetter, unchain; strike off horseshoes; *vr* lose a shoe (horses). See **acertar**

desherrumbrar /deserrum'brar/ *vt* to remove the rust from; clean off rust from

deshidratación /desiðrata'sion; desiðrata'θion/ *f*, dehydration

deshidratar /desiðra'tar/ *vt* to dehydrate

deshielo /des'ielo/ *m*, thaw, thawing out

deshilado /desi'laðo/ *a* in single file. *m*, *Sew.* drawnthread work (gen. *pl*). **a la deshilada,** *Mil.* in file formation; secretly

deshiladura /desila'ðura/ *f*, unraveling

deshilar /desi'lar/ *vt* to unravel; *Sew.* draw threads; *Cul.* shred, grate

deshilvanado /desilβa'naðo/ *a Fig.* disjointed, disconnected

deshilvanar /desilβa'nar/ *vt Sew.* to remove the tacking threads

deshincar /desin'kar/ *vt* to pull out, remove, draw out

deshinchar /desin'tʃar/ *vt* to remove a swelling; deflate; lessen the anger of; *vr* decrease, subside (swellings); deflate; *Inf.* grow humble

deshojar /deso'har/ *vt* to strip the leaves from, strip the petals from; *Lat. Am.* husk (corn); peel (fruit)

deshollejar /desoye'har; desoʎe'har/ *vt* to skin, peel (fruit); shell (peas, etc.)

deshollinador /desoyina'ðor; desoʎina'ðor/ *m*, chimney-sweep; wall-brush; chemical chimney cleaner

deshollinar /desoyi'nar; desoʎi'nar/ *vt* to sweep chimneys; clean down walls; *Inf.* examine closely

deshonestidad /desonesti'ðað/ *f*, immodesty, shamelessness; indecency

deshonesto /deso'nesto/ *a* shameless, immodest; dissolute, vicious; indecent

deshonor /deso'nor/ *m*, dishonor; disgrace, insult

deshonra /de'sonra/ *f*, dishonor

deshonrabuenos /desonra'βuenos/ *mf Inf.* slanderer; degenerate

deshonrador /desonra'ðor/ **(-ra)** *a* dishonorable. *n* dishonorer

deshonrar /deson'rar/ *vt* to dishonor; insult; seduce (women)

deshonroso /deson'roso/ *a* dishonorable, insulting, indecent

deshora /de'sora/ *f*, inconvenient time. **a d.,** *or* **a deshoras,** at an inconvenient time, unseasonably; extempore

deshuesar /desue'sar/ *vt* to bone, remove the bone (from meat); stone (fruit)

deshumedecer /desumeðe'ser; desumeðe'θer/ *vt irr* to dry; *vr* become dry. See **conocer**

desidia /de'siðia/ *f*, negligence; laziness

desidioso /desi'ðioso/ *a* negligent; lazy

desierto /de'sierto/ *a* deserted, uninhabited, solitary. *m*, desert; wilderness

designación /designa'sion; designa'θion/ *f*, designation; appointment

designar /desig'nar/ *vt* to plan, intend; designate; appoint

designio /de'signio/ *m*, intention, idea

desigual /desi'gual/ *a* unequal; uneven (ground); rough; arduous, difficult; changeable

desigualar /desigua'lar/ *vt* to make unequal; *vr* prosper

desigualdad /desigual'dað/ *f*, inequality, unevenness, rockiness; *Fig.* changeability; variability

desilusión /desilu'sion/ *f*, disillusionment; disappointment

desilusionar /desilusio'nar/ *vt* to disillusion; *vr* become disillusioned; be undeceived

desinclinar /desinkli'nar/ *vt* to dissuade

desinfectante /desinfek'tante/ *a* and *m*, disinfectant

desinfectar /desinfek'tar/ *vt* to disinfect

desinflar /desin'flar/ *vt* to deflate

desinterés /desinte'res/ *m*, disinterestedness

desinteresado /desintere'saðo/ *a* disinterested; generous

desinteresarse /desintere'sarse/ *vr* to lose interest, grow indifferent

desistencia, /desis'tensia,; desis'tenθia,/ *f*, **desistimiento** *m*, desistance, ceasing

desistir /desis'tir/ *vi* to desist; cease; *Law.* renounce

desjuntamiento /deshunta'miento/ *m*, separation; division

desjuntar /deshun'tar/ **(se)** *vt* and *vr* to separate; divide

deslavado /desla'βaðo/ *a* brazen, impudent

deslavar /desla'βar/ *vt* to wash superficially; spoil by washing, take away the body of (cloth, etc.)

desleal /desle'al/ *a* disloyal, treacherous

deslealtad /desleal'tað/ *f*, disloyalty

desleír /desle'ir/ *vt irr* to dissolve; dilute. See **reír**

deslenguado /desleŋ'guaðo/ *a* shameless, foulmouthed

deslenguar /desleŋ'guar/ *vt* to remove the tongue; *vr Inf.* be insolent

desliar /des'liar/ *vt* to untie, undo, unloose

desligadura /desliga'ðura/ *f*, untying, loosening

desligar /desli'gar/ *vt* to unfasten, unbind; *Fig.* solve, unravel; relieve of an obligation; *Mus.* play staccato; *vr* come unfastened, grow loose. **desligarse de,** to weasel out of, wiggle out of (a promise)

deslindador /deslinda'ðor/ *m*, one who fixes boundaries or limits

deslindar /deslin'dar/ *vt* to fix the boundaries (of); limit, circumscribe

deslinde /des'linde/ *m*, demarcation, boundary

desliz /des'lis; des'liθ/ *m*, slipping, slip, slide; skid; indiscretion, slip; peccadillo, trifling fault

deslizadero /deslisa'ðero; desliθa'ðero/ *m*, slippery place; chute

deslizadizo /deslisa'ðiso; desliθa'ðiθo/ *a* slippery

deslizar /desli'sar; desli'θar/ *vt* to slip, slide; skid; *vr* commit an indiscretion; speak or act unwisely; escape, slip away; slip; skid

deslucido /des'lusiðo; des'luθiðo/ *a* fruitless, vain; stupid, clumsy, awkward; discolored; tarnished, dull; unsuccessful

deslucimiento /deslusi'miento; desluθi'miento/ *m*, clumsiness, gracelessness; failure, lack of success

deslucir /deslu'sir; deslu'θir/ *vt irr* to fade; discolor, stain; tarnish; spoil; sully the reputation of; *vr* do a thing badly, fail at. See **lucir**

deslumbrador /deslumbra'ðor/ *a* dazzling

deslumbramiento /deslumbra'miento/ *m*, brilliant light, glare, dazzle; bewilderment, confusion

deslumbrar /deslumb'rar/ *vt* to dazzle; confuse, bewilder; *Fig.* daze (with magnificence)

deslustrar /deslus'trar/ *vt* to dull, dim, tarnish; frost (glass); discredit, sully (reputation)

deslustre /des'lustre/ *m*, dullness, tarnish; frosting (of glass); disgrace, stigma

deslustroso /deslus'troso/ *a* ugly, unsuitable, unbecoming

desmadejar /desmaðe'har/ *vt* to debilitate, enervate

desmalezar /desmale'sar; desmale'θar/ *vt*, *Lat. Am.* to clear the underbrush from; weed

desmán /des'man/ *m*, outrageous behavior; disaster, misfortune

desmandado /desman'daðo/ *a* disobedient

desmandar /desman'dar/ *vt* to cancel, revoke (orders); withdraw (an offer). *vr* behave badly; stray

desmantelado /desmante'laðo/ *a* dismantled, dilapidated

desmantelamiento /desmantela'miento/ *m*, dismantling; dilapidation

desmantelar /desmante'lar/ *vt* to dismantle; abandon, forsake

desmaña /des'maɲa/ *f*, lack of dexterity, clumsiness, awkwardness

desmañado /desma'ɲaðo/ *a* clumsy, awkward, unhandy

desmayado /desma'yaðo/ *a* pale, faint (of colors); weak (of a voice)

desmayar /desma'yar/ *vt* to cause to faint; *vi* grow discouraged, lose heart; *vr* swoon, faint

desmayo /des'mayo/ *m*, depression, discouragement; faint, swoon

desmedido /desme'ðiðo/ *a* disproportionate; excessive

desmedirse /desme'ðirse/ *vr* to misbehave, go too far

desmedrado /desme'ðraðo/ *a* thin, emaciated; deteriorated, spoiled

desmedrar /desme'ðrar/ *vt* to spoil, ruin; *vi* deteriorate; decline

desmedro /des''meðro/ *m*, impairment; decline, deterioration. **en d. de,** to the detriment of

desmejora /desme'hora/ *f*, deterioration

desmejorar /desmeho'rar/ *vt* to spoil, impair, cause to deteriorate; *vr* deteriorate; *vi* and *vr* decline in health; lose one's beauty

desmelenar /desmele'nar/ *vt* to ruffle or dishevel the hair

desmembración /desmembrasion; desmembra'θion/ *f*, dismemberment

desmembrar /desmem'brar/ *vt* to dismember; separate, divide

desmemoriarse /desmemo'riarse/ *vr* to forget, lose one's memory

desmenguar /desmeŋ'guar/ *vt* to reduce, decrease; *Fig.* diminish

desmentida /desmen'tiða/ *f*, action of giving the lie to

desmentir /desmen'tir/ *vt irr* to give the lie to; contradict, deny; lower oneself; behave unworthily; *vi* deviate (from right direction, etc.). See **sentir**

desmenuzar /desmenu'sar; desmenu'θar/ *vt* to crumble, break into small pieces; *Fig.* examine in detail; *vr* be broken up

desmeollar /desmeo'yar; desmeo'ʎar/ *vt* to remove the marrow of

desmerecedor /desmerese'ðor; desmereθe'ðor/ *a* unworthy

desmerecer /desmere'ser; desmere'θer/ *vt irr* to become undeserving of; *vi* deteriorate; be inferior to. See **conocer**

desmesura /desme'sura/ *f*, insolence; disproportion; excess

desmesurado /desmesu'raðo/ *a* disproportionate; excessive, enormous; insolent, uncivil

desmesurar /desmesu'rar/ *vt* to disarrange, disorder; *vr* be insolent

desmigajar /desmiga'har/ **(se)** *vt* and *vr* to crumble

desmigar /desmi'gar/ *vt Cul.* to make breadcrumbs

desmilitarizar /desmilitari'sar; desmilitari'θar/ *vt* to demilitarize

desmochar /desmo'tʃar/ *vt* to lop off the top; pollard (trees)

desmonetización /desmonetisa'sion; desmonetiθa'θion/ *f*, demonetization; conversion of coin into bullion

desmonetizar /desmoneti'sar; desmoneti'θar/ *vt* to convert money into bullion; demonetize; *vr* depreciate (shares, etc.)

desmontable /desmon'taβle/ *a* movable; sectional

desmontadura /desmonta'ðura/ *f*, clearing; deforestation; leveling; demounting, dismounting

desmontar /desmon'tar/ *vt* to clear wholly or partly of trees or shrubs; clear up (rubbish); level (ground); dismantle; dismount; uncock (firearms); *vi* and *vr* dismount (from horse, etc.)

desmonte /des'monte/ *m*, clearing of trees and shrubs; clearing, cleared ground; timber remaining

desmoralización /desmoralisa'sion; desmoraliθa'θion/ *f*, demoralization, corruption

desmoralizador /desmoralisa'ðor; desmoraliθa'ðor/ *a* demoralizing

desmoralizar /desmorali'sar; desmorali'θar/ *vt* to demoralize, corrupt

desmoronamiento /desmorona'miento/ *m*, crumbling; decay, ruin

desmoronar /desmoro'nar/ *vt* to destroy, decay; crumble; *vr* crumble away, fall into ruin; decline, decay; wane, fade (power, etc.)

desmovilización /desmoβilisa'sion; desmoβiliθa'θion/ *f*, demobilization

desmovilizar /desmoβili'sar; desmoβili'θar/ *vt* to demobilize

desnacificación /desnasifika'sion; desnaθifika'θion/ *f*, denazification

desnatar /desna'tar/ *vt* to skim; *Fig.* take the cream or best

desnaturalización /desnaturalisa'sion; desnaturaliθa'θion/ *f*, denaturalization

desnaturalizar /desnaturali'sar; desnaturali'θar/ *vt* to denaturalize; exile; deform, disfigure, pervert; *vr* give up one's country

desnivel /desni'βel/ *m*, unevenness; slope, drop

desnivelar /desniβe'lar/ **(se)** *vi* and *vr* to become uneven

desnudar /desnu'ðar/ *vt* to undress; *Fig.* despoil, strip, denude; *vr* undress oneself; deprive oneself

desnudez /desnu'ðes; desnu'ðeθ/ *f,* nudity; nakedness; bareness; plainness

desnudo /des'nuðo/ *a* nude; ill-clad; bare, naked; clear, patent; *Fig.* destitute (of grace, etc.). *m, Art.* nude

desnutrición /desnutri'sion; desnutri'θion/ *f,* malnutrition

desobedecer /desoβeðe'ser; desoβeðe'θer/ *vt irr* to disobey. See **conocer**

desobediencia /desoβeðien'sia; desoβeðien'θia/ *f,* disobedience

desobediente /desoβe'ðiente/ *a* disobedient

desobligar /desoβli'gar/ *vt* to free from obligation; offend, hurt

desocupación /desokupa'sion; desokupa'θion/ *f,* lack of occupation; leisure

desocupado /desoku'paðo/ *a* idle; vacant, unoccupied

desocupar /desoku'par/ *vt* to empty; vacate; *vr* give up an employment or occupation

desodorante /desoðo'rante/ *a* and *m,* deodorant

desoir /deso'ir/ *vt irr* to pay no attention, pretend not to hear. See **oir**

desolación /desola'sion; desola'θion/ *f,* destruction, desolation; affliction

desolador /desola'ðor/ *a* desolate; grievous

desolar /deso'lar/ *vt irr* to lay waste, destroy; *vr* grieve, be disconsolate. See **contar**

desoldar /desol'dar/ *vt* to unsolder; *vr* become unsoldered

desolladero /desoya'ðero; desoʎa'ðero/ *m,* slaughterhouse

desollado /deso'yaðo; deso'ʎaðo/ *a Inf.* impertinent, barefaced. *m,* carcass

desolladura /desoya'ðura; desoʎa'ðura/ *f,* flaying, skinning; *Inf.* slander

desollar /deso'yar; deso'ʎar/ *vt irr* to flay, skin; harm, discredit. **d. vivo,** *Inf.* to extort an exorbitant price; slander. See **contar**

desopinado /desopi'naðo/ *a* discredited

desopinar /desopi'nar/ *vt* to discredit, defame

desorden /de'sorðen/ *m,* disorder, disarray; confusion; excess

desordenado /desorðe'naðo/ *a* disordered; vicious; licentious

desordenar /desorðe'nar/ *vt* to disorder; confuse; *vr* go beyond the just limits; behave badly; be impertinent

desorganización /desorganisa'sion; desorganiθa'θion/ *f,* disorganization

desorganizador /desorganisa'ðor; desorganiθa'ðor/ *a* disorganizing

desorganizar /desorgani'sar; desorgani'θar/ *vt* to disorganize; disband

desorientación /desorienta'sion; desorienta'θion/ *f,* disorientation, loss of bearings; lack of method, confusion

desorientar /desorien'tar/ *vt* to disorient; perplex, confuse; *vr* lose one's way; be disoriented

desovar /deso'βar/ *vi* to spawn

desove /de'soβe/ *m,* spawning; spawning season

desovillar /desoβi'yar; desoβi'ʎar/ *vt* to unwind; uncoil; unravel; explain, clarify

despabiladeras /despaβila'ðeras/ *f pl,* snuffers

despabilado /despaβi'laðo/ *a* alert, wide-awake; watchful, vigilant

despabiladura /despaβila'ðura/ *f,* snuff of a candle; lamp, etc.

despabilar /despaβi'lar/ *vt* to snuff (a candle); trim (lamps); hasten, expedite; finish quickly; steal, rob; *Fig.* quicken (intelligence, etc.); *Inf.* kill; *vr* rouse oneself, wake up

despachador /despatʃa'ðor/ **(-ra)** *n* dispatcher, sender

despachar /despa'tʃar/ *vt* to expedite; dispatch, conclude; forward, send; attend to correspondence; sell; dismiss; *Inf.* serve in a shop; *Inf.* kill; *vi* hasten; carry letters to be signed (in offices, etc.); *vr* get rid of

despachero, -a /despa'tʃero/ *mf Chile* shopkeeper, storekeeper

despacho /despa'tʃo/ *m,* transaction, execution; study; office, room; department; booking-office; dispatch, shipment; expedient; commission, warrant; dispatch (diplomatic); telegram; telephone message. **d. particular,** private office

despachurrar /despa'tʃurrar/ *vt Inf.* to crush, squash; recount in a muddled fashion; *Fig.* squash flat, confound

despacio /des'pasio; des'paθio/ *adv* slowly, little by little; deliberately, leisurely. *interj* Careful! Gently now!

despacito /despa'sito; despa'θito/ *adv Inf.* very slowly

despalmador /despalma'ðor/ *m,* dockyard

despampanar /despampa'nar/ *vt Agr.* to prune vines; *Inf.* amaze, stun, astound; *vi Inf.* relieve one's feelings; *vr Inf.* receive a serious injury (through falling)

desparpajar /desparpa'har/ *vt* to spoil; *vi Inf.* chatter

desparpajo /despar'paho/ *m, Inf.* loquaciousness, pertness; disorder, muddle

desparramar /desparra'mar/ *vt* to disperse, scatter; squander, waste (money, etc.); *vr* amuse oneself; be dissipated

despavorido /despaβo'riðo/ *a* terrified, panicstricken

despechar /despe'tʃar/ *vt* to anger; make despair; *Inf.* wean; *vr* be angry; be in despair

despecho /des'petʃo/ *m,* rancor, malice; despair. **a d. de,** in spite of

despechugar /despetʃu'gar/ *vt* to cut off the breast (fowls); *vr Inf.* show the bosom

despectivo /despek'tiβo/ *a* contemptuous, depreciatory

despedazar /despeða'sar; despeða'θar/ *vt* to cut or break into pieces; *Fig.* break (heart, etc.)

despedida /despe'ðiða/ *f,* dismissal, discharge; seeing off (a visitor, etc.); farewell, good-by

despedir /despe'ðir/ *vt irr* to throw out, emit, cast up; dismiss, discharge; see off (on a journey or after a visit); banish (from the mind); get rid of; *vr* say good-by; leave (employment). See **pedir**

despedregar /despeðre'gar/ *vt* to clear of stones

despegadamente /despegaða'mente/ *adv* uninterestedly, unconcernedly, indifferently

despegado /despe'gaðo/ *a Inf.* indifferent, unconcerned, cold

despegar /despe'gar/ *vt* to unstick; unglue; separate, detach; *vr* become estranged; come apart or unstuck; *vi Aer.* take off. **sin d. los labios,** without saying a word

despegue /des'pege/ *m, Aer.* take-off

despeinar /despei'nar/ *vt* to disarrange the hair; undo the coiffure

despejado /despe'haðo/ *a* lively, sprightly; logical, clear-cut; cloudless; spacious, unobstructed, clear, clear skies (in weather reports)

despejar /despe'har/ *vt* to clear, free of obstacles; **d. el camino de,** to clear the way for; *Fig.* elucidate, solve; *Math.* find the value of; *vr* smarten up, grow gay; amuse oneself; clear up (weather, sky, etc.); improve (a patient)

despejo /des'peho/ *m,* freeing of obstacles; smartness, gaiety; grace, elegance; perkiness; clearsightedness, intelligence

despellejar /despe'yehar; despe'ʎehar/ *vt* to flay, skin; slander

despeluzar /despelu'sar; despelu'θar/ *vt* to disorder the hair; cause the hair to stand on end; horrify; *vr* stand on end (hair); be horrified or terrified

despeluznante /despelus'nante; despeluθ'nante/ *a* hair-raising, terrifying

despendedor /despende'ðor/ **(-ra)** *n* spendthrift, waster

despender /despen'der/ *vt* to spend; waste

despensa /des'pensa/ *f,* larder, pantry; store (of food); *Naut.* steward's room; stewardship

despensero /despen'sero/ **(-ra)** *n* steward; caterer; victualler; *Naut.* steward

despeñadero /despeɲa'ðero/ *m*, precipice, crag; dangerous undertaking, risk. *a* steep, precipitous
despeñar /despe'ɲar/ *vt* to precipitate, fling down from a height, hurl down; *vr* fling oneself headlong; throw oneself into (vices, etc.)
despeño /des'peɲo/ *m*, precipitation; headlong fall; *Fig.* collapse, ruin
despepitar /despepi'tar/ *vt* to remove seeds or pips; *vr* vociferate; act wildly; *Inf.* desire, long (for)
desperdiciador /desperði'siaðor; desperði'θiaðor/ **(-ra)** *a* squandering, wasting. *n* squanderer
desperdiciar /desperði'siar; desperði'θiar/ *vt* to squander; *Fig.* misspend, waste
desperdicio /desper'ðisio; desper'ðiθio/ *m*, waste; remains, leftovers (gen. *pl*)
desperdigar /desperði'gar/ *vt* to separate, sever; scatter
desperecerse /despere'serse; despere'θerse/ *vr irr* to crave, yearn (for). See **conocer**
desperezarse /despere'sarse; despere'θarse/ *vr* to stretch oneself
desperfecto /desper'fekto/ *m*, imperfection, flaw; slight deterioration
despernado /desper'naðo/ *a* weary, footsore
despertador /desperta'ðor/ **(-ra)** *a* awakening. *n* awakener. *m*, alarm clock; incentive, stimulus
despertar /desper'tar/ *vt irr* to awaken; bring to mind, recall; incite, stimulate; *vi* waken; *Fig.* wake up, become more intelligent. See **acertar**
despiadado /despia'ðaðo/ *a* cruel, merciless
despicar /despi'kar/ *vt* to satisfy, content; *vr* revenge oneself
despierto /des'pierto/ *a* wide-awake, clever
despilfarrado /despilfa'rraðo/ *a* ragged, shabby; wasteful; spendthrift
despilfarrar /despilfa'rrar/ *vt* to squander, waste
despilfarro /despil'farro/ *m*, slovenliness; waste, extravagance; mismanagement, poor administration
despintar /despin'tar/ *vt* to paint out; wash off the paint; efface, blot out; disfigure, deform; *vi* be unlike or unworthy (of); *vr* fade (colors); forget
despiojar /despio'har/ *vt* to remove lice, delouse; *Inf.* rescue from misery
despique /des'pike/ *m*, vengeance, revenge
despistar /despis'tar/ *vt* to throw off the scent; mislead
desplacer /despla'ser; despla'θer/ *vt irr* to displease. *m*, disgust, displeasure, sorrow. See **placer**
desplantar /desplan'tar/ **(se)** *vt* and *vr* to deviate from the vertical
desplazamiento /desplasa'miento; desplaθa'miento/ *m*, *Naut.* displacement
desplegadura /desplega'ðura/ *f*, unfolding
desplegar /desple'gar/ *vt irr* to unfold; spread open; *Fig.* reveal, disclose, explain; evince, display; *Mil.* deploy troops; *vr* unfold, open (flowers, etc.); *Mil.* deploy. See **cegar**
despliegue /des'pliege/ *m*, unfolding; spreading out; evincing, demonstration; *Mil.* deployment
desplomar /desplo'mar/ *vt* to put out of the straight, cause to lean (walls, buildings); *vr* lean, tilt (buildings); topple, fall down (walls, etc.); collapse (people); be ruined
desplome /des'plome/ *m*, collapse
desplomo /des'plomo/ *m*, tilt, cant, deviation from vertical
desplumar /desplu'mar/ *vt* to remove feathers, pluck; rob, despoil
despoblación /despoβla'sion; despoβla'θion/ *f*, depopulation. **d. forestal,** deforestation
despoblado /despo'βlaðo/ *m*, wilderness; deserted place
despoblar /despo'βlar/ *vt* to depopulate; despoil, rob; *vr* become depopulated
despojador /despoha'ðor/ **(-ra)** *a* robbing, despoiling. *n* despoiler
despojar /despo'har/ *vt* to plunder, despoil; dispossess; *vr* (*with de*) remove (garments, etc.); relinquish, give up
despojo /des'poho/ *m*, pillaging, spoliation; booty,

plunder; butcher's offal; *pl* remains, leavings; debris, rubble; corpse
despolvorear /despolβore'ar/ *vt* to remove dust; *Fig.* shake off
desposado /despo'saðo/ *a* recently married; fettered, handcuffed. **los desposados,** the newlyweds
desposar /despo'sar/ *vt* to perform the marriage ceremony; *vr* become betrothed; marry
desposeer /despose'er/ *vt* to dispossess; *vr* renounce one's possessions. See **creer**
desposeimiento /desposei'miento/ *m*, dispossession
desposorio /despo'sorio/ *m*, betrothal, promise of marriage; (gen. *pl*) wedding, marriage
déspota /'despota/ *m*, despot, tyrant
despótico /des'potiko/ *a* tyrannical
despotismo /despo'tismo/ *m*, despotism
despotricarse /despotri'karse/ *vr* to rave (against), rail (against)
despreciable /despre'siaβle; despre'θiaβle/ *a* worthless, contemptible
despreciar /despre'siar; despre'θiar/ *vt* to scorn, despise; *vr* despise oneself
despreciativo /despresia'tiβo; despreθia'tiβo/ *a* contemptuous, scornful
desprecio /des'presio; des'preθio/ *m*, contempt, scorn
desprender /despren'der/ *vt* to loosen, remove, unfix; give off (gases, etc.); *vr* work loose, give way; deduce, infer; give away, deprive oneself (of)
desprendido /despren'diðo/ *a* disinterested; generous
desprendimiento /desprendi'miento/ *m*, loosening, removal, separation; emission; indifference, lack of interest; generosity; impartiality
despreocupación /despreokupa'sion; despreokupa'θion/ *f*, fair mindedness, impartiality; lack of interest
despreocupado /despreoku'paðo/ *a* unprejudiced, broadminded; indifferent, uninterested
despreocuparse /despreoku'parse/ *vr* to shake off prejudice; (*with de*) pay no attention to; set aside
desprestigiar /despresti'hiar/ *vt* to discredit; *vr* lose prestige; lose caste
desprestigio /despres'tihio/ *m*, loss of prestige, discredit
desprevenido /despreβe'niðo/ *a* unprepared, improvident
desproporción /despropor'sion; despropor'θion/ *f*, disproportion
desproporcionado /desproporsio'naðo; desproporθio'naðo/ *a* disproportionate; out of proportion
despropósito /despro'posito/ *m*, nonsense, absurdity
desproveer /desproβe'er/ *vt irr* to deprive of necessities. See **creer**
despueble /des'pueβle/ *m*, depopulation
después /des'pues/ *adv* afterwards, after, next (of time and place)
despuntar /despun'tar/ *vt* to blunt the point; *Naut.* double, sail round; *vi* show green, sprout; appear (the dawn); grow clever; *Fig.* stand out, excel
desquiciamiento /deskisia'miento; deskiθia'miento/ *m*, unhinging; disconnecting; *Fig.* upsetting, throwing out of gear; downfall, fall from favor
desquiciar /deski'siar; deski'θiar/ *vt* to unhinge; disconnect; *Fig.* throw out of gear, upset; banish from favor; *vr* become unhinged; *Fig.* be disordered; upset
desquitar /deski'tar/ **(se)** *vt* and *vr* to retrieve a loss; take revenge, retaliate
desquite /des'kite/ *m*, compensation; revenge
desrielar /desrie'lar/ *vt*, *Lat. Am.* to derail
destacamento /destaka'mento/ *m*, *Mil.* detachment
destacar /desta'kar/ *vt Mil.* to detach; *vr* excel; be prominent; be conspicuous; *Art.* stand out
destajador /destaha'ðor/ *m*, smith's hammer
destajar /desta'har/ *vt* to cut (cards); set forth conditions, stipulate, contract; *Lat. Am.* cut up
destajista /desta'hista/ *mf* pieceworker; jobber (worker)
destajo /des'taho/ *m*, piecework; job. **a d.,** quickly

and diligently. *Inf.* **hablar a d.**, to chatter, talk too much

destapar /desta'par/ *vt* to remove the cover or lid; reveal, uncover; *vr* be uncovered; reveal oneself. **no destaparse,** to keep quiet, be mum

destartalado /destarta'laðo/ *a* tumble-down, rickety; poverty-stricken

destechado /deste'tʃaðo/ *a* roofless

destejar /deste'har/ *vt* to remove tiles or slates; leave unprotected

destejer /deste'her/ *vt* to unweave, unravel; *Fig.* undo, spoil

destello /deste'yo; des'teʎo/ *m*, gleam, sparkle, brilliance; flash, beam, ray; *Fig.* gleam (of talent)

destemplado /destem'plaðo/ *a* out of tune; inharmonious; intemperate; *Art.* inharmonious; *Inf.* out of sorts, indisposed

destemplanza /destem'plansa; destem'planθa/ *f*, inclemency, rigor (weather); intemperance, excess, abuse; *Inf.* indisposition; lack of moderation (actions, speech)

destemplar /destem'plar/ *vt* to disturb, upset, alter; *Mus.* put out of tune; put to confusion; *vr* be unwell; *Fig.* go too far, behave badly; lose temper (metals)

destemple /des'temple/ *m*, *Mus.* being out of tune; *Med.* indisposition; uncertainty (weather); lack of temper (metals); disturbance, disorder; intemperance, excess, confusion

desternillarse de risa /desterni'yarse de 'rrisa; desterni'ʎarse de 'rrisa/ to shake with laughter

desterrado /deste'rraðo/ **(-da)** *a* exiled. *n* exile

desterrar /deste'rrar/ *vt irr* to exile; shake off the soil; *Fig.* discard, lay aside; extirpate (an error). See **recomendar**

destetar /deste'tar/ *vt* to wean

destete /des'tete/ *m*, weaning

destiempo, a /des'tiempo, a/ *adv* untimely, inopportunely

destierro /des'tierro/ *m*, banishment, exile; place of exile; remote place

destilación /destila'sion; destila'θion/ *f*, distillation

destilador /destila'ðor/ **(-ra)** *n* distiller. *m*, still

destilar /desti'lar/ *vt* to distill; filter; *vi* to drip

destilatorio /destila'torio/ *a* distilling. *m*, distillery; still

destilería /destile'ria/ *f*, distillery

destinar /desti'nar/ *vt* to destine; appoint; assign

destino /des'tino/ *m*, fate, destiny; post, appointment; destination. **con d. a,** going to, bound for

destitución /destitu'sion; destitu'θion/ *f*, destitution; discharge, dismissal

destituir /destitu'ir/ *vt irr* (*with de*) to dismiss or discharge from (employment); deprive of. See **huir**

destorcer /destor'ser; destor'θer/ *vt irr* to untwist; straighten out; *vr Naut.* drift. See **torcer**

destornillado /destorni'yaðo; destorni'ʎaðo/ *a* reckless; *Fig. Inf.* with a screw loose

destornillador /destorni'yaðor; destorni'ʎaðor/ *m*, screwdriver

destornillamiento /destorniya'miento; destorniʎa'miento/ *m*, unscrewing

destornillar /destorni'yar; destorni'ʎar/ *vt* to unscrew; *vr* act rashly

destrenzar /destren'sar; destren'θar/ *vt* to unbraid. **destrenzarse las cintas,** to unlace one's shoes

destreza /des'tresa; des'treθa/ *f*, dexterity; agility

destrón /des'tron/ *m*, blind person's guide

destronamiento /destrona'miento/ *m*, dethronement

destronar /destro'nar/ *vt* to dethrone, depose; oust

destroncamiento /destronka'miento/ *m*, detruncation

destroncar /destron'kar/ *vt* to lop, detruncate (trees); dislocate, disjoint; mutilate; *Fig.* ruin, seriously harm; tire out; *Lat. Am.* uproot *vr* be exhausted or tired

destrozar /destro'sar; destro'θar/ *vt* to destroy; break in pieces, shatter; *Mil.* wipe out, annihilate; squander, dissipate

destrozo /des'troso; des'troθo/ *m*, destruction, ruin; shattering; *Mil.* rout; dissipation, waste

destrozón /destro'son; destro'θon/ *a* hard on wearing apparel, shoes, etc.

destrucción /destruk'sion; destruk'θion/ *f*, destruction; ruin, irreparable loss

destructible /destruk'tiβle/ *a* destructible

destructivo /destruk'tiβo/ *a* destructive

destructor /destruk'tor/ **(-ra)** *a* destructive. *n* destroyer. *m, Nav.* destroyer

destruible /destrui'βle/ *a* destructible

destruir /destruir/ *vt irr* to destroy, ruin, annihilate; frustrate, blast, disappoint; deprive of means of subsistence; squander, waste; *vr Math.* cancel. See **huir**

desuello /desue'yo; desue'ʎo/ *m*, flaying, skinning; forwardness, impertinence; extortion, fleecing. *Fig. Inf.* **¡Es un d.!** It's highway robbery!

desunión /desu'nion/ *f*, disunion, separation; *Fig.* discord, disharmony

desunir /desu'nir/ *vt* to disunite, separate; *Fig.* cause discord or disharmony

desusarse /desu'sarse/ *vr* to fall into disuse, become obsolete

desuso /de'suso/ *m*, disuse

desvaído /desβa'iðo/ *a* gaunt, lanky; pale, faded, dull (of colors)

desvainar /desβai'nar/ *vt* to shell (peas, beans)

desvalido /des'βaliðo/ *a* unprotected, helpless

desvalijar /desβali'har/ *vt* to rifle (a suitcase, etc.); swindle

desvalimiento /desβali'miento/ *m*, defenselessness, lack of protection; lack of favor; desertion, abandonment

desvalorización /desβalorisa'sion; desβaloriθa'θion/ *f*, devaluation

desván /des'βan/ *m*, garret

desvanecer /desβane'ser; desβane'θer/ *vt irr* to cause to disappear; disintegrate; make vain; remove; *vr* evaporate; faint, swoon; grow vain or conceited. See **conocer**

desvanecimiento /desβanesimiento; desβaneθi'miento/ *m*, faintness, loss of consciousness; vanity, conceit

desvarar /desβa'rar/ *vt* to slip, slide; *Naut.* refloat

desvariar /desβa'riar/ *vi* to be delirious; rave, talk wildly

desvarío /desβa'rio/ *m*, foolish action, absurdity; delirium; monstrosity; whim, caprice

desvedar /desβe'ðar/ *vt* to raise a ban or prohibition

desvelar /desβe'lar/ *vt* to keep awake; *vr* be sleepless; (*with por*) take great care over

desvelo /des'βelo/ *m*, sleeplessness, vigil; care, attention, vigilance; anxiety. **con d.,** watchfully

desvencijar /desβensi'har; desβenθi'har/ *vt* to loosen, disconnect, disjoint; *vr* work loose, become disjointed

desventaja /desβen'taha/ *f*, disadvantage. **estar en d.,** to be at a disadvantage

desventajoso /desβenta'hoso/ *a* disadvantageous

desventura /desβen'tura/ *f*, misfortune

desventurado /desβentu'raðo/ *a* unfortunate; timid, faint-hearted; miserly

desvergonzado /desβergonsaðo; desβergon'θaðo/ *a* shameless, brazen, impudent

desvergonzarse /desβergon'sarse; desβergon'θarse/ *vr irr* to be brazen, be impudent. See **avergonzar**

desvergüenza /desβer'guensa; desβer'guenθa/ *f*, insolence; shamelessness

desvestir /desβes'tir/ **(se)** *vt* and *vr irr* to undress. See **pedir**

desviación /desβia'sion; desβia'θion/ *f*, deviation, deflection

desviadero /desβia'ðero/ *m*, diversion; *Rail.* siding

desviar /des'βiar/ *vt* to divert, deflect; dissuade

desvío /des'βio/ *m*, deviation; indifference, coldness; repugnance

desvirgar /desβir'gar/ *vt* to deflower

desvirtuar /desβir'tuar/ *vt* to decrease in strength or merit

desvivirse /desβi'βirse/ *vr* (*with por*) to adore, love dearly, yearn for, be dying to; do one's best to

please, (e.g. *Juan se desvive por servirme,* John does his best to help me)
detallar /deta'yar; deta'ʎar/ *vt* to tell in detail; relate
detalle /de'taye; de'taʎe/ *m,* retail account; detail, particular; *Com.* itemized bill
detallismo /deta'yismo; deta'ʎismo/ *m,* meticulous attention to details
detective /de'tektiβe/ *mf* detective
detector /detek'tor/ *m,* detector; *Radio.* catwhisker
detención /deten'sion; deten'θion/ *f,* stop, halt; delay; prolixity; arrest, detention. **con d.,** carefully, meticulously
detener /dete'ner/ *vt irr* to detain, stop; arrest; retain, keep; *vr* go slowly; tarry; halt, stop; *(with en)* pause over, stop at. See **tener**
detenido /dete'niðo/ *a* timid, irresolute; miserable, mean
deterioración /deteriora'sion; deteriora'θion/ *f,* deterioration
deteriorar /deterio'rar/ **(se)** *vt* and *vr* to deteriorate
determinación /determina'sion; determina'θion/ *f,* determination; daring; decision
determinado /determi'naðo/ *a* resolute, determined
determinar /determi'nar/ *vt* to determine, limit; discern, distinguish; specify, appoint; decide, resolve; *Law.* define, judge; *vr* make up one's mind
determinativo /determina'tiβo/ *a* determining
determinismo /determi'nismo/ *m,* determinism
determinista /determi'nista/ *mf* determinist. *a* deterministic
detersorio /deter'sorio/ *a* and *m,* detergent
detestable /detes'taβle/ *a* detestable
detestación /detesta'sion; detesta'θion/ *f,* detestation
detestar /detes'tar/ *vt* to abominate, detest
detonación /detona'sion; detona'θion/ *f,* detonation
detonador /detona'ðor/ *m,* detonator
detonar /deto'nar/ *vi* to detonate
detractor /detrak'tor/ **(-ra)** *a* slandering *n* detractor, slanderer
detraer /detra'er/ *vt irr* to detract, take away; separate; slander. See **traer**
detrás /de'tras/ *adv* behind, after (place). **por d.,** in the rear; *Fig.* behind one's back
detrimento /detri'mento/ *m,* detriment; moral harm. **en d. de,** to the detriment of
deuda /'deuða/ *f,* debt; fault, offense; sin. **d. exterior,** foreign debt. **estar en d. con,** to be indebted to. **Perdónanos nuestras deudas,** Forgive us our trespasses
deudo /'deuðo/ *m,* relative, kinsman; kinship, relationship
deudor /deu'ðor/ **(-ra)** *a* indebted. *n* debtor. **d. hipotecario,** mortgagor
devanadera /deβana'ðera/ *f,* bobbin, reel, spool; winder (machine)
devanador /deβana'ðor/ **(-ra)** *n* winder (person). *m,* spool, bobbin
devanar /deβa'nar/ *vt* to reel, wind. *Inf.* **devanarse los sesos,** to rack one's brains
devanear /deβane'ar/ *vi* to rave, talk nonsense
devaneo /deβa'neo/ *m,* delirium; foolishness, nonsense; dissipation; love affair
devastación /deβasta'sion; deβasta'θion/ *f,* devastation
devastar /deβas'tar/ *vt* to devastate, lay waste; *Fig.* destroy, ruin
develador /deβela'ðor/ *m,* betrayer
devengar /deβeŋ'gar/ *vt* to have a right to, earn (salary, interest, etc.)
devoción /deβo'sion; deβo'θion/ *f,* piety; affection, love; pious custom; prayer
devocionario /deβosio'nario; deβoθio'nario/ *m,* prayer book
devolución /deβolu'sion; deβolu'θion/ *f,* restitution; return; its devolution
devolutivo /deβolu'tiβo/ *a Law.* returnable
devolver /deβol'βer/ *vt irr* to restore to original state; return, give back; repay; **devolverse** *vr Lat. Am.* to come back, go back, return. See **resolver**

devorador /deβora'ðor/ **(-ra)** *a* devouring. *n* devourer
devorar /deβo'rar/ *vt* to devour; destroy, consume
devoto /de'βoto/ **(-ta)** *a* devout, pious; devoted, fond. *n* devotee. *m,* object of devotion
día /dia/ *m,* day; daylight; *pl* name or saint's day; birthday (e.g. *Hoy son los días de María,* This is Mary's saint's day (or birthday)). **d. de Año Nuevo,** New Year's Day. **d. de asueto,** day off. **d. de ayuno** or **de vigilia,** fast day. **d. del cura,** *humorous* wedding day. **d. del juicio,** Day of Judgment. **d. de los difuntos,** All Souls' Day. **d. de recibo,** at home day. **d. de Reyes,** Epiphany (when Spanish children receive their Christmas presents). **d. de trabajo** or **d. laborable,** working day. **d. por medio,** every other day. **días caniculares,** dog days. **d. por d.,** day by day. **al d.,** up to date; per day. **al otro d.,** next day. **¡Buenos días!** Good morning! Good day! **de d.,** by day. **de d. en d.,** from day to day. **de un d. a otro,** any time now, very soon. **el d. de mañana,** tomorrow, the near future. **un d. sí y otro no,** every other day. **vivir al d.,** to live up to one's income
diabético /dia'βetiko/ *a* diabetic
diablillo /dia'βliyo; dia'βliʎo/ *m, dim* devilkin; imp; *Inf.* madcap
diablo /'diaβlo/ *m,* devil; Satan; *Fig.* fiend. *Inf.* **d. cojuelo,** mischievous devil; *Fig. Inf.* imp. *Inf.* **Anda el d. suelto,** The Devil's abroad, there's trouble. *Inf.* **tener el d. en el cuerpo,** to be as clever as the Devil; be mischievous
diablura /dia'βlura/ *f,* mischief, prank; devilry
diabólico /dia'βoliko/ *a* diabolical, devilish; *Inf.* fiendish, iniquitous
diaconisa /dia'konisa/ *f,* deaconess
diácono /'diakono/ *m,* deacon
diadema /dia'ðema/ *f,* diadem; crown; tiara
diafanidad /diafani'ðað/ *f,* transparency
diáfano /'diafano/ *a* transparent, diaphanous
diafragma /dia'fragma/ *m, Anat. Mech.* diaphragm; sound-box (of a phonograph)
diagnosticar /diagnosti'kar/ *vt Med.* to diagnose
diagnóstico /diag'nostiko/ *a* diagnostic. *m,* diagnosis. **d. precoz,** early diagnosis
diagonal /diago'nal/ *a* diagonal; oblique
diagrama /dia'grama/ *m,* diagram
diagramación /diagrama'sion; diagrama'θion/ *f,* layout (of a publication)
dialectal /dialek'tal/ *a* dialect
dialéctica /dia'lektika/ *f,* dialectic. **La d. de Hegel,** Hegelian dialectic
dialéctico /dia'lektiko/ *a* dialectic. *m,* logician
dialecto /dia'lekto/ *m,* dialect
dialogar /dialo'gar/ *vi* to hold dialogue, converse; *vt* write dialogue
diálogo /'dialogo/ *m,* dialogue
diamante /dia'mante/ *m,* diamond; miner's lamp; glass-cutting diamond. **d. bruto,** rough diamond
diamantífero /diaman'tifero/ *a* diamond-bearing
diamantino /diaman'tino/ *a* diamantine; *Poet.* adamant
diamantista /diaman'tista/ *mf* diamond-cutter; diamond merchant
diámetro /'diametro/ *m,* diameter
diana /'diana/ *f, Mil.* reveille; bull's-eye (of a target); the moon
¡diantre! /'diantre/ *interj Inf.* the deuce!
diapasón /diapa'son/ *m, Mus.* tuning fork; diapason; neck (of violins, etc.). **d. normal,** tuning fork. **d. vocal,** pitch-pipe
diapositiva /diaposi'tiβa/ *f, Photo.* diapositive; (lantern) slide
diario /'diario/ *a* daily. *m,* diary; daily paper; daily expenses. **d. de navegación,** ship's log. **d. de viaje,** travel diary, trip journal
diarismo /dia'rismo/ *m, Lat. Am.* journalism
diarista /dia'rista/ *mf* journalist, diarist
diarrea /dia'rrea/ *f,* diarrhea
diatónico /dia'toniko/ *a Mus.* diatonic
diatriba /dia'triβa/ *f,* diatribe
diávolo /'diaβolo/ *m,* diabolo (game)

dibujante /diβu'hante/ *m*, sketcher; draftsman; designer

dibujar /diβu'har/ *vt Art.* to draw; describe, depict; *vr* appear, be revealed; be outlined, stand out

dibujo /di'βuho/ *m*, drawing; sketch, design, pattern; depiction, description. **d. a la pluma,** pen-and-ink drawing. **d. a pulso,** freehand drawing. **d. del natural,** drawing from life

dicción /dik'sion; dik'θion/ *f*, word; diction, language, style

diccionario /diksio'nario; dikθio'nario/ *m*, dictionary

díceres /'diseres; 'diθeres/ *m pl West Hem.* news

dicha /'ditʃa/ *f*, happiness; good fortune. **por d.,** by chance; fortunately

dicharacho /ditʃa'ratʃo/ *m*, *Inf.* vulgar expression, slangy expression

dicho /'ditʃo/ *m*, saying, phrase, expression; witty remark; *Law.* declaration; *Inf.* insult. *a* said, aforementioned. *past part* **decir,** "said." **D. y hecho,** No sooner said than done. **Del d.** al hecho hay muy gran **trecho,** There's many a slip 'twixt the cup and the lip. **Lo d. d.,** The agreement stands

dichoso /di'tʃoso/ *a* happy; lucky; *Inf.* blessed, wretched, darn

diciembre /di'siembre; di'θiembre/ *m*, December

dictado /dik'taðo/ *m*, title of honor; dictation; *pl* promptings (of heart, etc.). **escribir al d.,** to write to dictation

dictador /dikta'ðor/ *m*, dictator

dictadura /dikta'ðura/ *f*, dictatorship

dictamen /dik'tamen/ *m*, judgment, opinion

dictaminar /diktami'nar/ *vi* to give judgment or opinion

dictar /dik'tar/ *vt* to dictate; suggest, inspire; *Lat. Am.* give (a lecture). **dictar fallo,** to hand down a decision, render judgment

dictatorial, dictatorio /diktato'rial, dikta'torio/ *a* dictatorial

dicterio /dik'terio/ *m*, taunt, insult

didáctica /di'ðaktika/ *f*, didactics

didáctico /di'ðaktiko/ *a* didactic

diecinuevavo /diesinue'βeaβo; dieθinue'βeaβo/ *a* and *m*, nineteenth

diecinueve /diesi'nueβe; dieθi'nueβe/ *a* and *m*, nineteen

dieciochavo /diesio'tʃaβo; dieθio'tʃaβo/ *a* and *m*, eighteenth

dieciocheno /diesio'tʃeno; dieθio'tʃeno/ *a* See **décimoctavo**

dieciocho /die'siotʃo; die'θiotʃo/ *a* and *m*, eighteen

dieciséis /diesi'seis; dieθi'seis/ *a* and *m*, sixteen

dieciseisavo /diesisei'saβo; dieθisei'saβo/ *a* and *m*, sixteenth

dieciseiseno /diesisei'seno; dieθisei'seno/ *a* See **décimosexto**

diecisiete /diesi'siete; dieθi'siete/ *a* and *m*, seventeen

diecisieteavo /diesisiete'aβo; dieθisiete'aβo/ *a* and *m*, seventeenth

diente /diente/ *m*, tooth; tooth (of saw, etc.); tusk; cog (of wheel); prong (of fork); tongue (of a buckle). **d. de leche,** milk-tooth. *Bot.* **d. de león,** dandelion. **d. de perro,** *Sew.* feather-stitch. *Inf.* **dar d. con d.,** to chatter (teeth). *Fig. Inf.* **enseñar** (*or* **mostrar**) **los dientes,** to show one's teeth; threaten. *Inf.* **estar a d.,** to be famished. **hablar entre dientes,** to mutter; fume, grumble. *Inf.* **tener buen d.,** to have a good appetite. **traer a uno entre dientes,** to loathe someone; speak scandal of

diestra /'diestra/ *f*, right hand; protection

diestro /'diestro/ *a* right (hand); skillful, dextrous; shrewd; astute, cunning; favorable, happy. *m*, expert fencer; bullfighter; halter; bridle

dieta /'dieta/ *f*, *Med.* diet; *Inf.* fast, abstinence; legislative assembly; travel allowance (gen. *pl*); day's journey of ten leagues; daily fee (gen. *pl*)

dietario /die'tario/ *m*, household accounts' book

dietética /die'tetika/ *f*, dietetics

dietético /die'tetiko/ *a* dietetic

dietista /die'tista/ *mf* dietician

diez /dies; dieθ/ *a* ten; tenth. *m*, ten; decade of rosary

diezmar /dies'mar; dieθ'mar/ *vt* to tithe; decimate; punish every tenth person

diezmero /dies'mero; dieθ'mero/ (**-ra**) *n* tax-gatherer

diezmesino /diesme'sino; dieθme'sino/ *a* ten months old

diezmillo /dies'mijo; dieθ'miʎo/ *m*, *Mexico* sirloin

diezmo /'diesmo; 'dieθmo/ *m*, ten per cent tax; tithe

difamación /difama'sion; difama'θion/ *f*, defamation, libel

difamador /difama'ðor/ (**-ra**) *a* libeling. *n* libeler

difamar /difa'mar/ *vt* to libel; denigrate

difamatorio /difama'torio/ *a* libelous, defamatory

diferencia /dife'rensia; dife'renθia/ *f*, unlikeness, dissimilarity; *Math.* difference; dissension, disagreement. **a d. de,** unlike; in contrast to

diferenciación /diferensia'sion; diferenθia'θion/ *f*, differentiation. **d. del trabajo,** division of labor

diferencial /diferen'sial; diferen'θial/ *a* differential

diferenciar /diferen'siar; diferen'θiar/ *vt* to differentiate; change the function (of); *vi* dissent, disagree; *vr* be different, differ; distinguish oneself

diferente /dife'rente/ *a* different, various

diferir /dife'rir/ *vt irr* to delay, retard; postpone; suspend, interrupt; *vi* be different. See **discernir**

difícil /di'fisil; di'fiθil/ *a* difficult

dificultad /difikul'taô/ *f*, difficulty; impediment, obstacle; objection

dificultar /difikul'tar/ *vt* to raise difficulties; put obstacles in the way; *vi* think difficult (of achievements)

dificultoso /difikul'toso/ *a* difficult; *Inf.* ugly (face, figure, etc.)

difidencia /difi'ðensia; difi'ðenθia/ *f*, mistrust; lack of faith, doubt

difidente /difi'ðente/ *a* mistrustful

difracción /difrak'sion; difrak'θion/ *f*, diffraction

difractar /difrak'tar/ *vt* to diffract

difteria /dif'teria/ *f*, diphtheria

difundir /difun'dir/ *vt* to diffuse (fluids); spread, publish, divulge; *Radio.* broadcast

difunto /di'funto/ (**-ta**) *a* and *n* deceased. *m*, corpse

difusión /difu'sion/ *f*, diffusion; prolixity; *Radio.* broadcasting

difusivo /difu'siβo/ *a* diffusive

difuso /di'fuso/ *a* widespread, diffuse; prolix, wordy

digerible /dihe'riβle/ *a* digestible

digerir /dihe'rir/ *vt irr* to digest; bear patiently; consider carefully; *Chem.* digest. See **sentir**

digestible /dihes'tiβle/ *a* easily digested

digestivo /dihes'tiβo/ *a* digestive

digesto /di'hesto/ *m*, *Law.* digest

digitación /dihita'sion; dihita'θion/ *f*, *Mus.* fingering

digital /dihi'tal/ *a* digital. *f*, *Bot.* foxglove, digitalis

dígito /'dihito/ *a* digital. *m*, (*Astron. Math.*) digit

dignación /digna'sion; digna'θion/ *f*, condescension

dignarse /dig'narse/ *vr* to deign, condescend

dignatario /digna'tario/ *m*, dignitary

dignidad /digni'ðaô/ *f*, dignity, stateliness; serenity, loftiness; high office or rank; high repute, honor; *Eccl.* dignitary

dignificar /dignifi'kar/ *vt* to dignify

digno /'digno/ *a* worthy, deserving; upright, honorable; fitting, suitable, appropriate

digresión /digre'sion/ *f*, digression

dije /'dihe/ *m*, charm; trinket; any small piece of jewelry; *Inf.* person of excellent qualities, jewel

dilacerar /dilase'rar; dilaθe'rar/ *vt* to lacerate, tear flesh; *Fig.* discredit

dilación /dila'sion; dila'θion/ *f*, delay

dilapidación /dilapi'ðasion; dilapiða'θion/ *f*, waste, dissipation, squandering

dilapidar /dilapi'ðar/ *vt* to waste, squander

dilatación /dilata'sion; dilata'θion/ *f*, expansion; enlargement, widening; prolongation; *Surg.* dilatation; respite (in trouble)

dilatador /dilata'ðor/ *a* dilating. *m*, *Surg.* dilater

dilatar /dila'tar/ *vt* to dilate, enlarge; expand; delay, postpone; spread, publish abroad; prolong; *vr* expand; be prolix, spread oneself; *Lat. Am.* to be slow, take a long time

dilatorio /dila'torio/ *a* procrastinating, dilatory

dilección /dilek'sion; dilek'θion/ *f,* affection, love

dilema /di'lema/ *m,* dilemma

diletantismo /diletan'tismo/ *m,* dilettantism

diligencia /dili'hensia; dili'henθia/ *f,* care, conscientiousness, industry; haste, briskness; diligence (coach); *Inf.* business, occupation. **hacer diligencias,** to run errands. **hacer sus diligencias,** to try one's best

diligenciar /dilihen'siar; dilihen'θiar/ *vt* to set on foot, put into motion

diligente /dili'hente/ *a* diligent, conscientious, industrious; speedy, prompt

dilucidación /dilusiδa'sion; diluθiδa'θion/ *f,* elucidation, clarification

dilucidar /dilusi'δar; diluθi'δar/ *vt* to elucidate, clarify

dilución /dilu'sion; diluθ'θion/ *f,* dilution

diluir /di'luir/ *vt irr* to dilute. See **huir**

diluviar /dilu'βiar/ *vi* to teem with rain

diluvio /di'luβio/ *m,* flood, inundation; *Inf.* very heavy rain, deluge; overabundance

dimanación /dimana'sion; dimana'θion/ *f,* emanation, source

dimanar /dima'nar/ *vi* (*with de*) to rise in (rivers); proceed from, originate in

dimensión /dimen'sion/ *f,* dimension; size, extent

dimes y diretes /'dimes i di'retes/ *m pl, Inf.* chat

diminutivo /diminu'tiβo/ *a* diminutive; diminishing; *Gram.* diminutive

diminuto /dimi'nuto/ *a* defective, incomplete; minute, very small

dimisión /dimi'sion/ *f,* resignation (of office, etc.)

dimisorias /dimi'sorias/ *f pl, Eccl.* letter dimissory. *Inf.* **dar d. a uno,** to give a person his marching orders, dismiss

dimitente /dimi'tente/ *a* resigning; retiring. *mf* resigner (of a post)

dimitir /dimi'tir/ *vt* to resign (office, post, etc.)

Dinamarca /dina'marka/ Denmark

dinamarqués /dinamar'kes/ **(-esa)** *a* Danish. *n* Dane

dinámica /di'namika/ *f,* dynamics

dinámico /di'namiko/ *a* dynamic

dinamita /dina'mita/ *f,* dynamite

dinamo /'dinamo/ *f,* dynamo

dinasta /di'nasta/ *mf* dynast

dinastía /dinas'tia/ *f,* dynasty

dinástico /di'nastiko/ *a* dynastic

dineral /dine'ral/ *m,* large amount of money, fortune

dinero /di'nero/ *m,* money; Peruvian coin; wealth, fortune; currency. **d. contante, d. junto,** ready cash, **Poderoso caballero es Don D.,** Money talks

dinosauro /dino'sauro/ *m,* dinosaur

dintel /'dintel/ *m,* lintel; *Lat. Am.* threshold

diocesano /diose'sano/ *a* diocesan

diócesis /'diosesis; 'dioθesis/ *f,* diocese

Dios /dios/ *m,* God; deity. **¡D. le guarde!** God keep you! **¡D. lo quiera!** God grant it! **D. mediante,** God willing (D.V.). **¡D. mío!** Good gracious! **De menos nos hizo D.,** Nothing is impossible, Never say die. **¡No lo quiera D.!** God forbid! **¡Plegue a D.!** Please God! **¡Por D.!** For goodness sake! Heavens! **¡Válgame D.!** Bless me! **¡Vaya Vd. con D.!** Goodbye! Off with you! Depart! **¡Vive D.!** By God!

diosa /'diosa/ *f,* goddess

diploma /di'ploma/ *m,* license, bull; diploma. **d. de suficiencia,** general diploma

diplomacia /diplo'masia; diplo'maθia/ *f,* diplomacy; tactfulness; *Inf.* astuteness

diplomarse /diplo'marse/ *vr, Lat. Am.* to get one's degree, receive one's degree

diplomático /diplo'matiko/ *a* diplomatic; tactful; *Inf.* astute. *m,* diplomat. **cuerpo d.,** diplomatic corps

dipsomanía /dipsoma'nia/ *f,* dipsomania

diptongo /dip'toŋgo/ *m,* diphthong

diputación /diputa'sion; diputa'θion/ *f,* deputation; mission

diputado /dipu'taδo/ **(-da)** *n* deputy, delegate. **d. a**

Cortes, member of the Spanish Parliament, congressman

diputar /dipu'tar/ *vt* to appoint, depute; delegate; empower

dique /'dike/ *m,* dike; dam; dry dock; *Fig.* bulwark, check; **d. flotante,** floating dock

dirección /direk'sion; direk'θion/ *f,* direction; management, control, guidance; directorate; instruction; information; order, wish, command; editorial board; directorship, managership; (postal) address; managerial office. **d. cablegráfica,** cable address. **d. particular,** home address

directiva /direk'tiβa/ *f,* board, governing body

directivo /direk'tiβo/ *a* directive, control, ling, guiding, managing

directo /di'rekto/ *a* direct; straight

director /direk'tor/ **(-ra)** *a* directing, controlling. *n* director; manager; principal, head (schools, etc.); editor. **d. del ceremonial,** chief of protocol. **d. de escena,** stagemanager. **d. espiritual,** *Eccl.* father confessor. **d. gerente,** managing director

directorio /direk'torio/ *a* directory, advising. *m,* directory; directorate, board of directors

dirigible /diri'hiβle/ *m,* airship

dirigir /diri'hir/ *vt* to direct; regulate; govern; supervise; guide; *Mus.* conduct; address (an envelope, etc.); keep (a shop, etc.); edit; put (a question); point (a gun); cast (a glance); *vr* go; plan one's way. **d. la palabra** (a), to speak to, address. **d. la vista a,** to look towards, look in the direction of, turn towards, turn in the direction of. **dirigirse a,** to go towards; make one's way to; address (someone)

dirimir /diri'mir/ *vt* to annul, make void; break, dissolve; settle (disputes, etc.)

discernimiento /disserni'miento; disθerni'miento/ *m,* discernment; judgment; discrimination

discernir /disser'nir; disθer'nir/ *vt irr* to discern, distinguish. *Pres. Ind.* **discierno, disciernes, discierne, disciernen.** *Pres. Subjunc.* **discierna, disciernas, discierna, disciernan**

disciplina /dissi'plina; disθi'plina/ *f,* discipline; system, philosophy, education; submission, obedience; subject (arts or science); *pl* scourge

disciplinante /dissipli'nante; disθipli'nante/ *a* disciplinary. *m,* scourge

disciplinar /dissipli'nar; disθipli'nar/ *vt* to train; educate; scourge, beat; discipline; *vr* scourge oneself

disciplinario /dissipli'nario; disθipli'nario/ *a* disciplinary

discipulado /dissipu'laδo; disθipu'laδo/ *m,* pupilship, studentship; education, teaching; discipleship; body of pupils (of a school, etc.)

discípulo /dis'sipulo; dis'θipulo/ **(-la)** *n* pupil, student; disciple, follower

disco /'disko/ *m,* discus; disk; phonograph record; *Astron.* disk. **d. compacto,** compact disc. **d. de señales,** railway signal. **d. giratorio,** turntable (of a phonograph)

discóbolo /dis'koβolo/ *m,* discus thrower

díscolo /'diskolo/ *a* willful, unmanageable

disconformidad /diskonformi'δaδ/ *f,* disagreement; disconformity

discontinuo /diskon'tinuo/ *a* intermittent, discontinuous

discordancia /diskor'δansia; diskor'δanθia/ *f,* discord, disagreement

discordar /diskor'δar/ *vi* to be discordant; disagree; *Mus.* be out of tune

discorde /dis'korδe/ *a* discordant; *Mus.* dissonant

discordia /dis'korδia/ *f,* discord, disagreement

discreción /diskre'sion; diskre'θion/ *f,* discretion; circumspection; prudence, good sense; shrewdness; pithy or clever saying. **a d.,** at discretion; at will; voluntarily. *Mil.* **darse** (*or* **entregarse**) **a d.,** to surrender unconditionally

discrecional /diskresio'nal; diskreθio'nal/ *a* optional, voluntary

discrepancia /diskre'pansia; diskre'panθia/ *f,* discrepancy; disagreement

discrepar /diskre'par/ *vi* to be discrepant; differ; disagree

discreto /dis'kreto/ *a* discreet; ingenious, witty

disculpa /dis'kulpa/ *f*, excuse

disculpabilidad /diskulpaβili'ðað/ *f*, pardonableness

disculpable /diskul'paβle/ *a* excusable

disculpar /diskul'par/ *vt* to excuse; forgive, pardon; *vr* apologize; excuse oneself

discurrir /disku'rrir/ *vi* to wander, roam; flow, run (rivers, etc.); (*with en*) consider, think about; (*with sobre*) discourse on; *vt* invent; conjecture

discursivo /diskur'siβo/ *a* discursive; thoughtful, reflective

discurso /dis'kurso/ *m*, reasoning power; oration, discourse; consideration, reflection; speech, conversation; dissertation. **d. aceptatorio,** acceptance speech

discusión /disku'sion/ *f*, discussion

discutible /disku'tiβle/ *a* debatable; disputable

discutir /disku'tir/ *vt* to discuss, debate, consider

disecar /dise'kar/ *vt Anat.* to dissect; stuff animals; mount plants

disección /disek'sion; disek'θion/ *f*, dissection

disector /disek'tor/ *m*, dissector, anatomist

diseminación /disemina'sion; disemina'θion/ *f*, dissemination

diseminar /disemi'nar/ *vt* to disseminate; spread

disensión /disen'sion/ *f*, dissension

disentería /disente'ria/ *f*, dysentery

disentimiento /disenti'miento/ *m*, dissent

disentir /disen'tir/ *vi irr* to dissent; disagree. See **sentir**

diseñador /diseɲa'ðor/ *m*, delineator, drawer

diseñar /dise'ɲar/ *vt* to outline, sketch

diseño /di'seɲo/ *m*, outline, sketch; plan; description

disertación /diserta'sion; diserta'θion/ *f*, dissertation

disertar /diser'tar/ *vi* (*with sobre*) to discourse on, discuss, treat of

diserto /di'serto/ *a* eloquent

disfavor /disfa'βor/ *m*, disfavor, discourtesy, slight

disforme /dis'forme/ *a* deformed; ugly; enormous

disfraz /dis'fras; dis'fraθ/ *m*, disguise; mask; fancy dress; pretense

disfrazar /disfra'sar; disfra'θar/ *vt* to disguise; dissemble, misrepresent; *vr* disguise oneself; wear fancy dress

disfrutar /disfru'tar/ *vt* to enjoy (health, comfort, friendship, etc.); reap the benefit of; *vi* take pleasure in, enjoy

disfrute /dis'frute/ *m*, enjoyment, use, benefit

disgregación /disgrega'sion; disgrega'θion/ *f*, separation, disjunction

disgregar /disgre'gar/ *vt* to separate, disjoin

disgustado /disgus'taðo/ *a* annoyed; discontented, dissatisfied; melancholy, depressed

disgustar /disgus'tar/ *vt* to displease, dissatisfy; annoy; *Fig.* depress, vr quarrel, fall out. **Me disgusta la idea de marcharme,** I don't like the idea of going away

disgusto /dis'gusto/ *m*, displeasure, dissatisfaction; discontent; annoyance; affliction, sorrow, trouble; quarrel; boredom; repugnance

disidente /disi'ðente/ *a* dissenting. *mf* dissenter, nonconformist

disidir /disi'ðir/ *vi* to dissent

disímil /di'simil/ *a* dissimilar, different, unlike

disimulación /disimula'sion; disimula'θion/ *f*, dissimulation, pretense

disimulado /disimu'laðo/ *a* feigned, pretended

disimular /disimu'lar/ *vt* to dissemble; pretend, feign; put up with, tolerate; misrepresent, misinterpret

disimulo /di'simulo/ *m*, pretense, dissimulation; tolerance, patience

disipación /disipa'sion; disipa'θion/ *f*, dispersion; dissipation, frivolity; immorality

disipado /disi'paðo/ *a* spendthrift; dissipated, frivolous

disipar /disi'par/ *vt* to disperse; squander; *vr* evaporate; vanish, fade, disappear

dislate /di'slate/ *m*, absurdity, nonsense

dislexia /dis'leksia/ *f*, dyslexia.

dislocación /disloka'sion; disloka'θion/ *f*, dislocation

dislocar /dislo'kar/ *vt* to dislocate; *vr* dislocate; sprain

disminución /disminu'sion; disminu'θion/ *f*, diminution. **ir** (**una cosa**) **en d.,** to diminish, decrease; taper, grow to a point

disminuido físico /dismi'nuiðo 'fisiko/ *m*, physically impaired person, physically handicapped person

disminuir /dismi'nuir/ *vt* and *vi irr* to diminish, decrease. See **huir**

disociación /disosia'sion; disoθia'θion/ *f*, dissociation. **d. nuclear,** nuclear fission

disociar /diso'siar; diso'θiar/ *vt* to dissociate, separate; *Chem.* dissociate

disoluble /diso'luβle/ *a* dissoluble

disolución /disolu'sion; disolu'θion/ *f*, dissolution; immorality, laxity; disintegration; loosening, relaxation

disolutivo /disolu'tiβo/ *a* dissolvent, solvent

disoluto /diso'luto/ *a* dissolute, vicious

disolvente /disol'βente/ *m*, dissolvent, solvent

disolver /disol'βer/ *vt irr* to loosen, undo; *Chem.* dissolve; separate, disintegrate; annul. See **resolver**

disonancia /diso'nansia; diso'nanθia/ *f*, dissonance; disagreement; *Mus.* dissonant

disonante /diso'nante/ *a* dissonant; discordant, inharmonious

disonar /diso'nar/ *vi irr* to be inharmonious; disagree. See **sonar**

dísono /di'sono/ *a* dissonant

dispar /dis'par/ *a* unequal; unlike, different

disparadero /dispara'ðero/ *m*, trigger of a firearm

disparador /dispara'ðor/ *m*, shooter, firer; trigger (of firearms); ratchet (of watch); *a, Mexico* lavish

disparar /dispa'rar/ *vt* to shoot, fire; throw or discharge with violence; *vr* run precipitately; rush (towards); bolt (horses); race (of a machine); explode, go off; *Inf.* go too far, misbehave; *Mexico* spend lavishly

disparatado /dispara'taðo/ *a* foolish; absurd, unreasonable

disparatar /dispara'tar/ *vi* to act or speak foolishly

disparate /dispa'rate/ *m*, foolishness, nonsense

disparidad /dispari'ðað/ *f*, disparity, dissimilarity

disparo /dis'paro/ *m*, shooting; explosion; racing (of an engine); discharge; foolishness

dispendio /dis'pendio/ *m*, squandering, extravagance

dispendioso /dispen'dioso/ *a* costly, expensive

dispensa /dis'pensa/ *f*, dispensation; privilege

dispensable /dispen'saβle/ *a* dispensable; excusable

dispensación /dispensa'sion; dispensa'θion/ *f*, dispensation; exemption

dispensar /dispen'sar/ *vt* to grant, concede, distribute; exempt; excuse, forgive

dispensario /dispen'sario/ *m*, dispensary

dispepsia /dis'pepsia/ *f*, dyspepsia

dispéptico /dis'peptiko/ (**-ca**) *a* and *n* dyspeptic

dispersar /disper'sar/ *vt* to disperse, scatter, separate; *Mil.* rout

dispersión /disper'sion/ *f*, dispersion

disperso /dis'perso/ *a* dispersed, scattered; *Mil.* separated from regiment

displicencia /displi'sensia; displi'θenθia/ *f*, disagreeableness, coldness; hesitation, lack of enthusiasm

displicente /displi'sente; displi'θente/ *a* unpleasant, disagreeable; difficult, peevish

disponer /dispo'ner/ *vt irr* to arrange, dispose; direct, order; decide; prepare, get ready; *vi* (*with de*) dispose of, make free with; possess; have at one's disposal; *vr* prepare oneself to die; make one's will; get ready. See **poner**

disponible /dispo'niβle/ *a* disposable; available

disposición /disposi'sion; disposi'θion/ *f*, arrangement; order, instruction; decision; preparation; aptitude, talent; disposal; condition of health; temperament; grace of bearing; promptitude, competence; measure, step, preliminary; *Archit.* plan; proviso, stipulation; symmetry. **A la d. de Vd,** I (we, he, it, etc.) am at your disposal. **hallarse en d. de hacer una cosa,** to be ready to do something. **última d.,** last will and testament

dispositivo /disposi'tiβo/ a directory, advisory
dispuesto /dis'puesto/ a ready, prepared; handsome, gallant; clever, wide-awake. **bien d.**, well-disposed; well, healthy. **mal d.**, ill-disposed; disinclined; out of sorts, indisposed
disputa /dis'puta/ f, dispute. **sin d.**, undoubtedly
disputar /dispu'tar/ vt to argue, debate; dispute, question; Fig. fight for
disquisición /diskisi'sion; diskisi'θion/ f, disquisition
distancia /dis'tansia; dis'tanθia/ f, distance; interval of time; difference, dissimilarity; unfriendliness, coolness
distanciar /distan'siar; distan'θiar/ vt to separate, place farther apart
distante /dis'tante/ a separated; distant; far off
distar /dis'tar/ vi to be distant (time and place); be different, unlike
distender /disten'der/ **(se)** vt and vr Med. to distend, swell
distinción /distin'sion; distin'θion/ f, distinction, differentiation; difference, individuality; privilege, honor; clarity, order; distinction (of bearing or mind). **a d. de,** unlike, different from
distinguible /distiŋ'guiβle/ a distinguishable
distinguido /distiŋ'guiðo/ a distinguished, illustrious
distinguir /distiŋ'guir/ vt to distinguish, discern; differentiate; characterize; esteem, honor, respect; discriminate; see with difficulty; make out; vr be different; excel, distinguish oneself
distintivo /distin'tiβo/ a distinguishing; distinctive. m, distinguishing mark
distinto /dis'tinto/ a different; distinct; clear
distracción /distrak'sion; distrak'θion/ f, distraction; abstraction, heedlessness, absentmindedness; pleasure, amusement; licentiousness
distraer /distra'er/ vt irr to lead astray; distract (attention); influence for bad; amuse. vr be absentminded; amuse oneself. See **traer**
distraído /distra'iðo/ a abstracted, absentminded; inattentive; licentious Lat. Am. slovenly
distribución /distriβu'sion; distriβu'θion/ f, distribution; (gen. pl) share
distribuidor /distriβui'ðor/ **(-ra)** a distributing. n distributor
distribuir /distri'βuir/ vt irr to distribute; share out, divide. See **huir**
distributivo /distriβu'tiβo/ a distributive
distrito /dis'trito/ m, district
disturbio /dis'turβio/ m, disturbance
disuadir /disua'ðir/ vt to dissuade
disuasión /disua'sion/ f, dissuasion
disuasivo /disua'siβo/ a dissuasive
disyunción /disyun'sion; disyun'θion/ f, disjunction
dita /'dita/ f, Lat. Am. debt
ditirambo /diti'rambo/ m, dithyramb; excessive praise
diurético /diu'retiko/ a diuretic
diurno /'diurno/ a diurnal
diva /'diβa/ f, prima donna; woman singer
divagación /diβaga'sion; diβaga'θion/ f, wandering, roaming; digression
divagar /diβa'gar/ vi to wander, roam; digress
diván /di'βan/ m, divan (Turkish supreme council); divan, sofa; collection of Arabic, Persian or Turkish poems
divergencia /diβer'hensia; diβer'henθia/ f, divergence; disagreement
divergente /diβer'hente/ a divergent; conflicting, dissentient
divergir /diβer'hir/ vi to diverge; dissent
diversidad /diβersi'ðað/ f, diversity, unlikeness, difference; variety
diversificar /diβersifi'kar/ vt to differentiate; vary
diversión /diβer'sion/ f, pastime, amusement; Mil. diversion
diverso /di'βerso/ a diverse, unlike; pl various, many
divertido /diβer'tiðo/ a amusing, funny, entertaining
divertir /diβer'tir/ vt irr to lead astray, turn aside; entertain; Mil. create a diversion. vr amuse oneself. See **sentir**

dividendo /diβi'ðendo/ m, dividend. Com. **d. activo,** dividend
dividir /diβi'ðir/ vt to divide; distribute; stir up discord; vr (with de) part company with, leave
divieso /di'βieso/ m, Med. boil
divinamente /diβina'mente/ adv divinely; excellently, admirably, perfectly
divinidad /diβini'ðað/ f, divinity, Godhead; person or thing of great beauty
divino /di'βino/ a divine; excellent, admirable, superb
divisa /di'βisa/ f, badge, emblem; Herald. motto
divisar /diβi'sar/ vt to glimpse, descry
divisibilidad /diβisiβili'ðað/ f, divisibility
divisible /diβi'siβle/ a divisible
división /diβi'sion/ f, division, partition; discord; (Math. Mil.) division; hyphen; apportionment; district, ward
divisor /diβi'sor/ **(-ra)** a dividing, separating. m, Math. divisor. n divider, separator
divisoria /diβi'soria/ f, dividing line
divisorio /diβi'sorio/ a dividing
divorciar /diβor'siar; diβor'θiar/ vt to divorce; separate; vr be divorced, be separated
divorcio /di'βorsio; di'βorθio/ m, divorce
divulgación /diβulga'sion; diβulga'θion/ f, spreading, publication, propagation
divulgar /diβul'gar/ **(se)** vt and vr to spread abroad, publish
DNA DNA, m
do /do/ m, Mus. doh, C. Poet. where
dobladillo /doβla'ðiyo; doβla'ðiʎo/ m, Sew. hem; turn-up (of a trouser)
doblado /do'βlaðo/ a stocky, thickset, sturdy; rocky, rough, uneven; dissembling. m, garret
dobladura /doβla'ðura/ f, fold, crease; crease mark
doblamiento /doβla'miento/ m, doubling; folding
doblar /do'βlar/ vt to double, multiply by two; fold, double; bend; persuade, induce; Naut. double, sail round; turn, walk round; vi Eccl. ring the passing bell; Theat. double a role; vr fold, double; bend; bow; stoop; allow oneself to be persuaded
doble /'doβle/ a double, twofold; duplicate; insincere, false; thick (cloth); Bot. double (flowers); hardy, robust; m, fold, crease; Eccl. passing-bell; Spanish dance step. adv double, twice. Eccl. **rito d.,** full rites
doblegar /doβle'gar/ vt to fold; bend; brandish; dissuade in favor of another proposition; vr submit, give way, acquiesce
doblete /do'βlete/ a of medium thickness. m, imitation jewel
doblez /do'βles; do'βleθ/ m, fold, crease; fold mark. mf, double dealing, treachery
doblilla /do'βliya; do'βliʎa/ f, twenty-real coin
doblón /do'βlon/ m, doubloon
doce /'dose; 'doθe/ a twelve. m, twelve; twelfth (of the month). **las d.,** twelve o'clock
docena /do'sena; do'θena/ f, dozen. **la d. del fraile,** baker's dozen
docente /do'sente; do'θente/ a teaching
dócil /'dosil; 'doθil/ a docile; obedient; flexible, easily worked (metals, etc.)
docilidad /dosili'ðað; doθili'ðað/ f, docility; obedience; flexibility
docto /'dokto/ a learned, erudite
doctor /dok'tor/ **(-ra)** n doctor; physician; teacher. f, Inf. blue-stocking
doctorado /dokto'raðo/ m, doctorate
doctorarse /dokto'rarse/ vr to get one's doctorate
doctrina /dok'trina/ f, doctrine; instruction, teaching; theory, conception; Eccl. sermon
doctrinar /doktri'nar/ vt to teach, instruct
documentación /dokumenta'sion; dokumenta'θion/ f, documentation; collection of documents, papers
documental /dokumen'tal/ a documental. m, documentary film
documentar /dokumen'tar/ vt to document
Dodecaneso, el /doðeka'neso, el/ the Dodecanese

dogal /do'gal/ *m*, halter; noose; slipknot. *Fig.* **estar con el d.** **a la garganta,** to be in a fix

dogma /'dogma/ *m*, dogma

dogmático /dog'matiko/ *a* dogmatic

dogmatizar /dogmati'sar; dogmati'θar/ *vt* to teach heretical doctrines; dogmatize

dólar /'dolar/ *m*, dollar

dolencia /do'lensia; do'lenθia/ *f*, ailment; pain; ache

doler /do'ler/ *vi irr* to be in pain; be reluctant; *vr* be sorry, regretful; grieve; sympathize, be compassionate; complain. *Pres. Ind.* **duelo, dueles, duele, duelen.** *Pres. Subjunc.* **duela, duelas, duela, duelan**

doliente /do'liente/ *a* suffering; ill; afflicted, sad. *mf* sufferer, ill person. *m*, chief mourner

dolo /'dolo/ *m*, fraud; deception; deceit; *Law.* premeditation

dolor /do'lor/ *m*, pain, ache; mental suffering. **d. sordo,** dull pain

dolorido /dolo'riðo/ *a* painful; afflicted, sad

doloroso /dolo'roso/ *a* sad, regrettable; mournful, sorrowful; pitiful; painful

doloso /do'loso/ *a* deceitful, fraudulent

domable /do'maβle/ *a* tamable; controllable

domador /doma'ðor/ **(-ra)** *n* subduer, controller; wild animal tamer; horsebreaker

domadura /doma'ðura/ *f*, taming, breaking in; controlling (emotions)

domar /do'mar/ *vt* to tame, break in; control, repress (emotions)

domesticable /domesti'kaβle/ *a* tamable; domesticable

domesticar /domesti'kar/ *vt* to tame; domesticate; *vr* grow tame; become domesticated

domesticidad /domestisi'ðað; domestiθi'ðað/ *f*, domesticity

doméstico /do'mestiko/ **(-ca)** *a* domestic, domesticated; tame. *n* domestic worker

domiciliar /domisi'liar; domiθi'liar/ *vt* to domicile; *vr* become domiciled, settle down; *Mexico* address (a piece of mail)

domiciliario /domisi'liario; domiθi'liario/ *a* domiciliary

domicilio /domi'silio; domi'θilio/ *m*, domicile; house

dominación /domina'sion; domina'θion/ *f*, domination; power, authority; command (of a military position, etc.); *Mil.* high ground; *pl* dominions, angels

dominador /domina'ðor/ *a* dominating; overbearing

dominante /domi'nante/ *a* dominating; overbearing, domineering; dominant. *f*, *Mus.* dominant

dominar /domi'nar/ *vt* to dominate; repress, subdue; *Fig.* master (branch of knowledge); *vi* stand out; *vr* control oneself

dómine /'domine/ *m*, *Inf.* teacher; pedant, know-all

domingo /do'miŋgo/ *m*, Sunday. **d. de Cuasimodo,** Low Sunday. **d. de Pentecostés,** Pentecost Sunday. **d. de Ramos,** Palm Sunday. **d. de Resurrección,** Easter Sunday

dominguero /domiŋ'guero/ *a* *Inf.* Sunday; special, excursion (trains)

dominicano /domini'kano/ **(-na)** *a* and *n* Dominican; native of Santo Domingo

dominio /do'minio/ *m*, authority, power; rule, sovereignty; dominion (country); domain

dominó /domi'no/ *m*, domino; game of dominoes

don /don/ *m*, gift; quality, characteristic; talent. **d. de gentes,** the human touch; charm

don /don/ *m*, title of respect equivalent to English Mr. or Esquire. Used only before given name and *not* before a family name, e.g. *don Juan Martínez,* or *don Juan*

donación /dona'sion; dona'θion/ *f*, donation, gift, grant

donador /dona'ðor/ **(-ra)** *a* donating. *n* donor

donaire /do'naire/ *m*, discretion, wit; witticism; gracefulness, elegance

donar /do'nar/ *vt* to bestow, give; transfer; grant

donatario /dona'tario/ *m*, recipient, grantee

doncel /don'sel/ *m*, squire, youth not yet armed; knight; male virgin; king's page

doncella /don'seya; don'θeʎa/ *f*, virgin, maid; maidservant; lady's maid

donde /'donde/ *adv* where, wherein. Sometimes used as relative pronoun "in which" (e.g. *La casa d. estaba,* The house in which I was); *Lat. Am.* at the house of, at...'s; to the house of, to...'s (e.g. *Mi tía está donde mis abuelos* My aunt is at my grandparents' *Mi tío no fue donde mis primos* My uncle did not go to my cousins') *interrog* **¿dónde? ¿A dónde va Vd.?** Where are you going to? **¿De dónde viene Vd.?** Where do you come from? **¿Por dónde se va a Madrid?** Which is the way to Madrid?

dondequiera /donde'kiera/ *adv* wherever, anywhere, everywhere

donoso /do'noso/ *a* witty; graceful

donostiarra /donos'tiarra/ *a* and *mf* of or from San Sebastian (N. Spain)

donosura /dono'sura/ *f*, wit; grace; dash, verve

doña /'doɲa/ *f*, feminine equivalent of **don** (e.g. *D. Catalina Palacios*)

dorado /do'raðo/ *a* golden, gilded; fortunate, happy. *m*, gilding

dorador /dora'ðor/ *m*, gilder

doradura /dora'ðura/ *f*, gilding

dorar /do'rar/ *vt* to gild; make golden; *Fig.* gild the pill; *Cul.* toast lightly; *vr* become golden

dormidero /dormi'ðero/ *a* soporiferous, narcotic; *m*, *Lat. Am.* roost (of chickens)

dormilón /dormi'lon/ **(-ona)** *a* *Inf.* sleepy. *n* sleepyhead

dormir /dor'mir/ *vi irr* to sleep; spend the night; *Fig.* grow calm; sleep (tops); (*with sobre*) sleep on, consider; *vt* put to sleep; *vr* to go to sleep; go slow and, neglect; be dormant; go numb (limbs). **d. como un lirón,** to sleep like a top. *Inf.* **d. la mona,** to sleep oneself sober. **entre duerme y vela,** half-awake. *Pres. Ind.* **duermo, duermes, duerme, duermen.** *Pres. Part.* **durmiendo.** *Preterite* **durmió, durmieron.** *Pres. Subjunc.* **duerma, duermas, duerma, duerman**

dormitar /dormi'tar/ *vi* to doze

dormitivo /dormi'tiβo/ *a* and *m*, sedative

dormitorio /dormi'torio/ *m*, dormitory; bedroom

dorso /'dorso/ *m*, back; dorsum

dos /dos/ *a* two. *m*, two; second (of the month). **las d.,** two o'clock. **de d. en d.,** two against two. **de d. en d.,** two by two. *Inf.* **en un d. por tres,** in a twinkling

doscientos /dos'sientos; dos'θientos/ *a* and *m*, two hundred; two hundredth

dosel /do'sel/ *m*, canopy; dais

dosis /'dosis/ *f*, dose; quantity

dotación /dota'sion; dota'θion/ *f*, endowment; *Naut.* crew; staff, workers; equipment

dotar /do'tar/ *vt* to give as dowry; endow, found; *Fig.* endow (with talents, etc.); equip; apportion (salary)

dote /'dote/ *mf*, dowry. *f*, (gen. *pl*) gifts, talents. **dotes de mando,** capacity for leadership

dracma /'drakma/ *f*, drachma; dram

draga /'draga/ *f*, dredger

dragado /dra'gaðo/ *m*, dredging

dragaminas /draga'minas/ *m*, *Nav.* minesweeper

dragar /dra'gar/ *vt* to dredge

dragón /dra'gon/ *m*, dragon; *Bot.* snapdragon; *Mil.* dragoon; *Zool.* dragon, giant lizard; *Astron.* Draco

dragona /dra'gona/ *f*, female dragon; *Mil.* shoulderstrap

dragonear /dragone'ar/ *vi*, *Lat. Am.* to boast, brag

drama /'drama/ *m*, play; drama. **d. lírico,** opera

dramática /dra'matika/ *f*, dramatic art

dramático /dra'matiko/ *a* dramatic; vivid, unexpected, moving

dramaturgo /drama'turgo/ *m*, dramatist, playwright

drenaje /dre'nahe/ *m*, drainage (of land and wounds)

dril /dril/ *m*, drill, cotton cloth

droga /'droga/ *f*, drug; falsehood, deception; nuisance

droguería /droge'ria/ *f*, chemist's shop; drug trade

droguero /dro'gero/ **(-ra)** *n* chemist, druggist

dromedario /drome'ðario/ *m*, *Zool.* dromedary

druida /'druiða/ *m*, Druid

dualidad /duali'ðað/ *f*, duality
ducado /du'kaðo/ *m*, dukedom; duchy; ducat
ducentésimo /dusen'tesimo; duθen'tesimo/ *a* two hundredth
ducha /'dutʃa/ *f*, shower-bath; douche; stripe in cloth; furrow
ducho /'dutʃo/ *a* experienced, skillful
ductilidad /duktili'ðað/ *f*, ductility; adaptability
duda /'duða/ *f*, doubt, hesitation; problem. **sin d.,** doubtless
dudable /du'ðaβle/ *a* doubtful
dudar /du'ðar/ *vi* to be in doubt; *vt* doubt, disbelieve
dudoso /du'ðoso/ *a* doubtful; uncertain, not probable
duela /'duela/ *f*, hoop, stave
duelista /due'lista/ *mf* dueler; duelist
duelo /'duelo/ *m*, sorrow, grief; mourning; mourners; duel; (gen. *pl*) troubles, trials. **duelos y quebrantos,** *Cul.* fried offal. **sin d.,** in abundance
duende /'duende/ *m*, imp, elf, sprite, ghost
dueña /'dueɲa/ *f*, owner, proprietress, mistress; duenna; married lady *Obs.*
dueño /'dueɲo/ *m*, owner, proprietor; master (of servants). **d. de sí mismo,** self-controlled
Duero, el /'duero, el/ the Douro
duetista /due'tista/ *mf* duetist
dula /'dula/ *f*, common pasture ground or herds
dulce /dulse; 'dulθe/ *a* sweet; fresh, pure; fresh, not salty; fragrant; melodious; pleasant, agreeable; tender, gentle; soft (metals). *m*, sweetmeat, bonbon. **d. de almíbar,** preserved fruit.
dulcedumbre /dulse'ðumbre; dulθe'ðumbre/ *f*, sweetness; softness
dulcémele /dulse'mele; dulθe'mele/ *m*, dulcimer
dulcera /dul'sera; dul'θera/ *f*, preserve dish, fruit dish
dulcería /dulse'ria; dulθe'ria/ *f*, See **confitería**

dulcificar /dulsifi'kar; dulθifi'kar/ *vt* to make sweet; alleviate, sweeten
dulcinea /dul'sinea; dul'θinea/ *f*, *Inf.* sweetheart; ideal
dulzaina /dul'saina; dul'θaina/ *f*, *Mus.* flageolet
dulzura /dul'sura; dul'θura/ *f*, sweetness; gentleness; pleasure; meekness; agreeableness
duna /'duna/ *f*, (gen. *pl*) sand dune
Dunquerque /dun'kerke/ Dunkirk
dúo /'duo/ *m*, *Mus.* duet
duodécimo /duoðesimo; duo'ðeθimo/ *a* twelfth
duodeno /duo'ðeno/ *a* twelfth. *m*, *Anat.* duodenum
duplicación /duplika'sion; duplika'θion/ *f*, duplication
duplicado /dupli'kaðo/ *m*, duplicate
duplicar /dupli'kar/ *vt* to duplicate; double
duplicidad /duplisi'ðað; dupliθi'ðað/ *f*, duplicity; falseness
duplo /'duplo/ *a*, double
duque /'duke/ *m*, duke
duquesa /du'kesa/ *f*, duchess
duración /dura'sion; dura'θion/ *f*, duration; durability
duradero /dura'ðero/ *a* lasting; durable
durante /du'rante/ *adv* during
durar /du'rar/ *vi* to continue; endure, last
dureza /du'resa; du'reθa/ *f*, hardness; *Med.* callosity; severity, harshness
durmiente /dur'miente/ *a* sleeping. *mf* sleeper; *m*, *Archit.* dormant
duro /'duro/ *a* hard; firm, unyielding; vigorous, robust; severe, inclement; exacting, cruel; *Mus.* metallic, harsh; *Art.* crude, too sharply defined; miserly, avaricious; obstinate; self-opinionated; unbearable, intolerable; merciless, hard; harsh (style). *m*, Spanish coin worth five pesetas

E

e /e/ *f*, letter E. *conjunc* used instead of *y* (and) before words beginning with *i* or *hi*, provided this last is not followed by a diphthong (e.g. *e invierno, e hijos, but y hierro*)
¡ea! /'ea/ *interj* Well!; Come on!; Let's see! (often used with **pues**)
ebanista /eβa'nista/ *mf* cabinetmaker
ebanistería /eβaniste'ria/ *f*, cabinetmaker's shop; cabinetmaking or work
ébano /'eβano/ *m*, ebony
ebonita /eβo'nita/ *f*, ebonite, vulcanite
ebrio /'eβrio/ *a* intoxicated, inebriated
ebullición /eβuyi'sion; eβuʎi'θion/ *f*, boiling, ebullition
ebúrneo /e'βurneo/ *a* eburnine, ivory-like
echada /e'tʃaða/ *f*, throw, cast; pitch; fling; length of a man
echador /etʃa'ðor/ (**-ra**) *n* thrower. *m*, *Inf.* chucker-out
echadura /etʃa'ðura/ *f*, sitting on eggs to hatch them; (gen. *pl*) gleanings
echamiento /etʃa'miento/ *m*, throw, fling; throwing, casting; expulsion; rejection
echar /e'tʃar/ *vt* to throw, fling; eject, drive away; cast out, expel; put forth, sprout; emit, give forth; cut (teeth); dismiss, discharge; couple (animals); pour (liquids); place, apply; put into, fill; turn (keys, locks); impute; attribute; impose (penalty, taxes, etc.); play (game); try one's luck; distribute; publish, make known; perform (plays); (*with por*) go in direction of; (*with prep a* + *infin.*) begin to (**e. a andar,** to begin to walk); *vr* throw oneself down, lie down; sit on eggs (birds); abate, calm (wind); apply oneself, concentrate on; rush (towards), fling oneself (upon). **e. abajo,** to overthrow; demolish. **e. aceite al fuego,** to add fuel to the flames. **e. a perder,** to spoil, deteriorate. *Naut.* **e. a pique,** to sink. **e. a vuelo,** to ring (bells). **e. carnes,** to put on weight, grow fat. **e. cuentas,** to reckon up. **e. de menos,** to miss; mourn

absence of. **e. de ver,** to notice. *Fig.* **e. en cara,** to throw in one's face, reproach. **echarla de majo,** to play the gallant. **e. las cartas al correo,** to post the letters. **e. las cartas,** to tell fortunes. **e. el pie atrás,** *Fig.* to climb down; *Fig.* back out. **e. raíces,** to take root; **e. las bases de, e. los cimientos de,** to lay the foundation of, lay the foundation for. *Fig.* become established. **e. rayos por la boca,** to fly into a rage. **e. suertes,** to draw lots. **echarlo todo a rodar,** to spoil everything. **e. una mano,** to lend a hand. **echar un volado** *Mexico* to toss a coin
echazón /etʃa'son; etʃa'θon/ *f*, throw, cast; jetsam
eclecticismo /eklekti'sismo; eklekti'θismo/ *m*, eclecticism
ecléctico /e'klektiko/ (**-ca**) *a* and *n* eclectic
eclipsar /eklip'sar/ *vt* *Astron.* to eclipse; surpass, outvie; *vr* *Astron.* be in eclipse; disappear
eclipse /e'klipse/ *m*, *Astron.* eclipse; retirement, withdrawal
eco /'eko/ *m*, echo; verse-echo; muffled sound; slavish imitation or imitator
ecología /ekolo'hia/ *f*, ecology
economato /ekono'mato/ *m*, trusteeship; cooperative store
econometría /ekonome'tria/ *f*, econometrics
economía /ekono'mia/ *f*, economy, thrift; structure, organization; poverty, shortage; saving (of time, labor, etc.); *pl* savings. **e. dirigida,** planned economy. **e. doméstica,** domestic economy. **e. política,** political economy
económico /eko'nomiko/ *a* economic; thrifty; avaricious; cheap
economista /ekono'mista/ *mf* economist
economizar /ekonomi'sar; ekonomi'θar/ *vt* to economize; save
ecónomo /e'konomo/ *m*, trustee, guardian
ecosistema /ekosis'tema/ *m*, ecosystem

ecuación /ekua'sion; ekua'θion/ f, (Math. and Astron.) equation

e. personal, personal equation

ecuador /ekua'ðor/ m, equator

ecuánime /ekua'nime/ a calm, unruffled; impartial

ecuanimidad /ekuanimi'ðað/ f, calmness, serenity; impartiality

ecuatorial /ekuato'rial/ a equatorial

ecuatoriano /ekuato'riano/ **(-na)** a and n Ecuadorian

ecuestre /e'kuestre/ a equestrian

ecuménico /eku'meniko/ a ecumenical

eczema /'eksema; 'ekθema/ m, eczema

edad /e'ðað/ f, age; epoch; period. **e. de piedra,** Stone Age. **e. media,** Middle Ages. **de cierta e.,** middle-aged. **ser mayor de e.,** to have attained one's majority. **ser menor de e.,** to be a minor

edecán /eðe'kan/ m, aide-de-camp

edema /e'ðema/ m, edema

Edén /e'ðen/ m, Eden; Fig. paradise

edición /eði'sion; eði'θion/ f, edition. **e. diamante,** miniature edition. **e. príncipe,** first edition

edicto /e'ðikto/ m, edict, decree; public notice

edificación /eðifika'sion; eðifika'θion/ f, building, construction; edification

edificador /eðifika'ðor/ **(-ra)** a uplifting, edifying; building. n builder

edificante /eðifi'kante/ a building, constructing; edifying

edificar /eðifi'kar/ vt to build, construct; edify

edificio /eði'fisio; eði'fiθio/ m, building, structure

Edimburgo /eðim'burgo/ Edinburgh

editar /eði'tar/ vt (of a publisher) to publish; edit

editor /eði'tor/ **(-ra)** n publisher; editor

editorial /eðito'rial/ a publishing; editorial. m, editorial, leading article

edredón /eðre'ðon/ m, down of an eiderduck; eiderdown, quilt

eduardiano /eðuar'ðiano/ **(-na)** a and n Edwardian

educable /eðu'kaβle/ a educable

educación /eðuka'sion; eðuka'θion/ f, upbringing; education; good breeding, good manners

educado /eðu'kaðo/ a educated. **ser mal e.,** to be badly brought up; be ill-mannered or impolite

educador /eðuka'ðor/ **(-ra)** a educating. n educator

educando /eðu'kando/ **(-da)** n pupil

educar /eðu'kar/ vt to educate; bring up, train, teach, develop

educativo /eðuka'tiβo/ a educational, educative

educción /eðuk'sion; eðuk'θion/ f, eduction; inference, deduction

educir /eðu'sir; eðu'θir/ vt irr to educe; infer, deduce. See **conducir**

efe /'efe/ f, name of letter F

efectismo /efek'tismo/ m, sensationalism; striving after effect

efectista /efek'tista/ a (Art. Lit.) striking, sensational

efectivo /efek'tiβo/ a effective; real. m, cash. **hacer e.,** to put into effect

efecto /e'fekto/ m, effect, result; purpose, intent; impression; pl assets; goods, chattels. **efectos de escritorio,** stationery. **efectos públicos,** public securities. **en e.,** in fact, actually. **llevar a e.,** to put into effect; make effective

efectuación /efektua'sion; efektua'θion/ f, accomplishment, execution

efectuar /efek'tuar/ vt to accomplish, effect; make (a payment); vr be effected; happen, take place

eferente /efe'rente/ a efferent

efervescencia /eferβes'sensia; eferβes'θenθia/ f, effervescence; excitement, enthusiasm

efervescente /eferβes'sente; eferβes'θente/ a effervescent

Éfeso /e'feso/ Ephesus

eficacia /efi'kasia; efi'kaθia/ f, efficacy; effectiveness

eficaz /efi'kas; efi'kaθ/ a efficacious; effective

eficiencia /efi'siensia; efi'θienθia/ f, efficiency

eficiente /efi'siente; efi'θiente/ a efficient, effective

efigie /e'fihie/ f, effigy; image, representation, symbol

efímero /e'fimero/ a ephemeral; brief

eflorescencia /eflores'sensia; eflores'θenθia/ f, Chem. efflorescence

efluvio /e'fluβio/ m, effluvium; exhalation

efugio /e'fuhio/ m, subterfuge, evasion

efusión /efu'sion/ f, effusion; Fig. spate (of words, etc.)

efusivo /efu'siβo/ a effusive, expansive

Egeo, Mar /e'heo, mar/ Aegean Sea

égida /'ehiða/ f, shield; egis, protection

egipcíaco /ehip'siako; ehip'θiako/ **(-ca), egipcio (-ia)** a and n Egyptian

Egipto /e'hipto/ Egypt

egiptólogo /ehip'tologo/ **(-ga)** n Egyptologist

egoísmo /ego'ismo/ m, egoism, selfishness

egoísta /ego'ista/ a egoistic. mf egoist, selfish person

egolatría /egola'tria/ f, self-love

egotismo /ego'tismo/ m, egotism

egotista /ego'tista/ a egotistical. mf egotist

egregio /e'grehio/ a distinguished, celebrated

egresado /egre'saðo/ a, graduate (of a certain school)

egresar (de...) /egre'sar/ vi, Lat. Am. to go out (of...), leave (...); be graduated (from...)

egreso /e'greso/ m, Lat. Am. departure, leaving; graduation

eje /'ehe/ m, axis; axle-tree; shaft; pivot, fundamental idea. **e. trasero,** rear-axle. Mexico **ejes viales,** main highways

ejecución /eheku'sion; eheku'θion/ f, accomplishment, performance; execution; technique; death penalty

ejecutable /eheku'taβle/ a feasible, practicable

ejecutante /eheku'tante/ mf Mus. executant, performer

ejecutar /eheku'tar/ vt to discharge, perform; put to death; (Art. Mus.) execute; serve (a warrant, etc.); Law. seize (property)

ejecutivo /eheku'tiβo/ a executive; urgent

ejecutor /eheku'tor/ m, executor

ejecutoria /eheku'toria/ f, letters patent of nobility; Law. judgment, sentence

ejemplar /ehem'plar/ a exemplary. m, copy, specimen; precedent; example; warning

ejemplificar /ehemplifi'kar/ vi to exemplify

ejemplo /e'hemplo/ m, example, precedent; illustration, instance; specimen. **dar e.,** to set an example. **por e.,** for example

ejercer /eher'ser; eher'θer/ vt to practice (a profession); perform, fulfill; exercise, use

ejercicio /eher'sisio; eher'θiθio/ m, exercise; practice; performance; exertion, effort; Mil. exercises (gen. pl). **ejercicios espirituales,** spiritual exercises. **ejercicios físicos,** physical training

ejercitar /ehersi'tar; eherθi'tar/ vt to exercise; train, teach; vr exercise; practice

ejército /e'hersito; e'herθito/ m, army

ejote /e'hote/ m, Central America, Mexico string bean

el /el/ def art. m, sing the

él /el/ pers pron sing m, he; it (f. **ella.** neut **ello**) (e.g. Lo hizo él, He did it). Also used with prep. (e.g. Lo hicimos por él, We did it for him)

elaboración /elaβora'sion; elaβora'θion/ f, elaboration, working out

elaborado /elaβo'raðo/ a elaborate

elaborar /elaβo'rar/ vt to elaborate; produce, work out

elasticidad /elastisi'ðað; elastiθi'ðað/ f, elasticity; adaptability

elástico /e'lastiko/ a elastic; adaptable. m, elastic tape; elastic material

ele /'ele/ f, name of letter L

elección /elek'sion; elek'θion/ f, choice; election; selection; discrimination

electivo /elek'tiβo/ a elective

elector /elek'tor/ **(-ra)** n elector, voter. m, German prince Obs.

electorado /elekto'raðo/ m, electorate

electoral /elekto'ral/ a electoral

electricidad /elektrisi'ðað; elektriθi'ðað/ f, electricity

electricista /elektri'sista; elektri'θista/ mf electrician

eléctrico /e'lektriko/ *a* electric; electrical
electrificación /elektrifika'sion; elektrifika'θion/ *f*, electrification
electrificar /elektrifi'kar/ *vt* to electrify
electrizar /elektri'sar; elektri'θar/ *vt* to electrify; startle; *vr* be electrified
electrocución /elektroku'sion; elektroku'θion/ *f*, electrocution
electrocutar /elektroku'tar/ *vt* to electrocute
electrodo /elek'troðo/ *m*, electrode
electroimán /elektroi'man/ *m*, electromagnet
electrólisis /elek'trolisis/ *f*, electrolysis
electrolizar /elektroli'sar; elektroli'θar/ *vt* to electrolyze
electromagnético /elektromag'netiko/ *a* electromagnetic
electromotriz /elektro'motris; elektro'motriθ/ *a* electromotive. **fuerza e.**, electromotive force
electrón /elek'tron/ *m*, electron
electroquímica /elektro'kimika/ *f*, electrochemistry
electroscopio /elektro'skopio/ *m*, electroscope
electrotecnia /elektro'teknia/ *f*, electrical engineering
electroterapia /elektrote'rapia/ *f*, *Med.* electrotherapy
elefante /ele'fante/ **(-ta)** *n* elephant
elefantíasis /elefan'tiasis/ *f*, elephantiasis
elefantino /elefan'tino/ *a* elephantine
elegancia /ele'gansia; ele'ganθia/ *f*, elegance, grace; fashionableness; *Lit.* beauty of style
elegante /ele'gante/ *a* elegant; graceful, lovely; fashionable, stylish
elegantoso, -a /elegan'toso/ *a*, *Lat. Am.* = **elegante**
elegía /ele'hia/ *f*, elegy
elegíaco /ele'hiako/ *a* elegiac
elegibilidad /elehiβili'ðað/ *f*, eligibility
elegible /ele'hiβle/ *a* eligible
elegir /ele'hir/ *vt irr* to select, prefer; elect. *Pres. Ind.* **elijo, eliges, elige, elegimos, elegís, eligen.** *Pres. Part.* **eligiendo.** *Preterite* **eligió, eligieron.** *Pres. Subjunc.* **elija, etc.**
elemental /elemen'tal/ *a* elemental; fundamental; elementary
elemento /ele'mento/ *m*, element; component, constituent; *Elec.* element; *pl* rudiments. *Mil.* **elementos de choque**, shock troops
elenco /e'lenko/ *m*, *Lat. Am.* cast (of characters)
elevación /eleβa'sion; eleβa'θion/ *f*, lifting, raising; height, high ground; elevation; altitude; *Fig.* eminence; elevation, advancement; ecstasy; raising (of the voice)
elevado /ele'βaðo/ *a* sublime, lofty
elevar /ele'βar/ *vt* to raise, lift; *Fig.* exalt; *vr* be in ecstasy, be transported. **elevarse de categoría**, to rise in status
elfo /'elfo/ *m*, elf
elidir /eli'ðir/ *vt* (phonetics) to elide
eliminación /elimina'sion; elimina'θion/ *f*, elimination
eliminador /elimina'ðor/ *a* eliminatory. *m*, eliminator
eliminar /elimi'nar/ *vt* to eliminate
elíptico /e'liptiko/ *a* elliptic
elíseo /e'liseo/ *m*, Elysium. *a* Elysian. **campos elíseos**, Elysian fields
ella /'eya; 'eʎa/ *pers. pron 3rd sing. f* she; it. See **él**
elle /'eye; 'eʎe/ *f*, name of letter LL
ello /'eyo; 'eʎo/ *pers. pron 3rd sing. neut* that, the fact, it. **Ello es que...**, The fact is that... **No tengo tiempo para ello**, I have no time for that
ellos, ellas /'eyos, 'eyas; 'eʎos, 'eʎas/ *pers. pron 3rd pl. m* and *f*, they. See **él**
elocución /eloku'sion; eloku'θion/ *f*, elocution; style of speech
elocuencia /elo'kuensia; elo'kuenθia/ *f*, eloquence
elocuente /elo'kuente/ *a* eloquent
elogiador /elohia'ðor/ **(-ra)** *a* eulogistic. *n* eulogist
elogiar /elo'hiar/ *vt* to eulogize, praise
elogio /e'lohio/ *m*, eulogy, praise. **«Elogio de la Locura»**, "In Praise of Folly"
elote /e'lote/ *m*, *Central America, Mexico* ear of corn
elucidación /elusiða'sion; eluθiða'θion/ *f*, elucidation, explanation
elucidar /elusi'ðar; eluθi'ðar/ *vt* to elucidate, clarify

eludible /elu'ðiβle/ *a* escapable, avoidable
eludir /elu'ðir/ *vt* to elude, avoid
elusivo, -a /elu'siβo/ *a*, *Lat. Am.* evasive, tricky
emaciación /emasia'sion; emaθia'θion/ *f*, emaciation
emanación /emana'sion; emana'θion/ *f*, emanation; effluvium
emanar /ema'nar/ *vi* to emanate (from), originate (in)
emancipación /emansipa'sion; emanθipa'θion/ *f*, emancipation; enfranchisement
emancipador /emansipa'ðor; emanθipa'ðor/ **(-ra)** *a* emancipatory. *n* emancipator
emancipar /emansi'par; emanθi'par/ *vt* to emancipate, free; enfranchise; *vr* emancipate oneself; become independent; free oneself
emascular /emasku'lar/ *vt* to emasculate
embadurnar /embaður'nar/ *vt* to smear, smudge, daub
embajada /emba'haða/ *f*, embassy; ambassadorship; embassy building; *Fig.* message
embajador /embaha'ðor/ *m*, ambassador; emissary
embajadora /embaha'ðora/ *f*, wife of ambassador; woman ambassador
embalador /embala'ðor/ *m*, packer
embalaje /emba'lahe/ *m*, packing; bale; wrapper; packing charge
embalar /emba'lar/ *vt* to pack
embaldosado /embaldo'saðo/ *m*, tiled pavement or floor
embaldosar /embaldo'sar/ *vt* to tile, pave with tiles
embalsamador /embalsama'ðor/ *a* embalming. *m*, embalmer
embalsamar /embalsa'mar/ *vt* to embalm; perfume
embalse /em'balse/ *m*, dam; damming, impounding (of water)
embanastar /embanas'tar/ *vt* to place in a basket; crowd, squeeze
embarazada /embara'saða; embara'θaða/ *a f*, pregnant
embarazar /embara'sar; embara'θar/ *vt* to impede, hinder, embarrass; *vr* be hindered or embarrassed; be pregnant
embarazo /emba'raso; emba'raθo/ *m*, difficulty, impediment; pregnancy; timidity, embarrassment
embarazoso /emba'rasoso; emba'raθoso/ *a* embarrassing; inconvenient; difficult, troublesome
embarcación /embarka'sion; embarka'θion/ *f*, ship, vessel; embarkation
embarcadero /embarka'ðero/ *m*, wharf, dock; quay; pier; jetty
embarcador /embarka'ðor/ *m*, shipper
embarcar /embar'kar/ *vt* to embark, ship; board (boat, train, etc.); *vr* embark; board
embarco /em'barko/ *m*, embarking, embarkation
embargar /embar'gar/ *vt* to obstruct, impede; *Law.* seize; suspend, paralyse
embargo /em'bargo/ *m*, *Law.* seizure; embargo. **sin e.**, nevertheless, however
embarque /em'barke/ *m*, loading, embarkation (goods)
embarrancar /embarran'kar/ *vi Naut.* to run aground; *vr Naut.* be stuck on a reef or in the mud
embarrilar /embarri'lar/ *vt* to barrel
embarullar /embaru'yar; embaru'ʎar/ *vt Inf.* to mix up, muddle; do hastily and badly
embastar /embas'tar/ *vt Sew.* to baste; tack
embaste /em'baste/ *m*, *Sew.* basting; tacking stitch
embate /em'bate/ *m*, beating of the waves; sudden attack; unexpected misfortune
embaucamiento /embauka'miento/ *m*, trick, deception
embaucar /embau'kar/ *vt* to deceive, hoodwink
embaular /embau'lar/ *vt* to pack in a trunk; *Inf.* stuff with food
embazar /emba'sar; emba'θar/ *vt* to dye brown; hinder; amaze; *vr* be amazed; be tired or bored; be satiated
embebecer /embeβe'ser; embeβe'θer/ *vt irr* to entertain, amuse; engross, fascinate; *vr* be dumbfounded. See **conocer**

embebecimiento /embeβesi'miento; embeβeθi'miento/ *m*, astonishment; absorption, engrossment

embeber /embe'βer/ *vt* to absorb; contain; shrink, contract; saturate; insert, introduce; incorporate; *vi* shrink; *vr* be amazed; master or absorb (a subject).

embedido en sus pensamientos, absorbed in thought

embelecar /embele'kar/ *vt* to dupe, deceive, trick

embeleco /embe'leko/ *m*, deception, fraud

embelesar /embele'sar/ *vt* to astonish; fascinate, enchant; *vr* be astonished or fascinated

embeleso /embe'leso/ *m*, astonishment; fascination; charm

embellecer /embeye'ser; embeʎe'θer/ *vt irr* to embellish; *vr* beautify oneself. See **conocer**

embellecimiento /embeyesi'miento; embeʎeθi'miento/ *m*, beautifying, embellishment

emberizo /embe'riso; embe'riθo/ *m*, Ornith. yellowhammer

embermejecer /embermehe'ser; embermehe'θer/ *vt irr* to dye red; shame, make blush; *vi* turn red or reddish; *vr* blush. See **conocer**

embestida /embes'tiða/ *f*, assault, attack, onrush; *Inf.* importunity

embestir /embes'tir/ *vt irr* to rush upon, assault; *Inf.* importune, be a nuisance to; *vi Fig. Inf.* clash, be inharmonious. See **pedir**

emblema /em'blema/ *m*, emblem; symbol; badge

emblemático /emble'matiko/ *a* emblematic; symbolical

embobamiento /emboβa'miento/ *m*, stupefaction, amazement

embobar /embo'βar/ *vt* to entertain, fascinate; *vr* be dumbfounded

embobecer /emboβe'ser; emboβe'θer/ *vt irr* to make stupid. See **conocer**

embobecimiento /emboβesi'miento; emboβeθi'miento/ *m*, stupefaction

embocadero /emboka'ðero/ *m*, narrow entrance, bottleneck; mouth of a channel

embocadura /emboka'ðura/ *f*, entrance by a narrow passage; *Mus.* mouthpiece; flavor (of wine); estuary, mouth of a river; *Theat.* proscenium

embocar /embo'kar/ *vt* to put in the mouth; go through a narrow passage; deceive; *Inf.* devour, wolf; initiate a business deal

embolador, -a /emβola'ðor/ *mf*, *Lat. Am.* bootblack

embolia /em'bolia/ *f*, embolism

émbolo /'embolo/ *m*, Mech. piston, plunger

embolsar /embol'sar/ *vt* to place money in a purse; collect (a debt, etc.)

emborrachar /emborra'tʃar/ *vt* to intoxicate; daze, stupefy; *vr* become intoxicated; run (of dyes)

emborrascarse /emborras'karse/ *vr* to be furious; become stormy (weather); *Fig.* go downhill (business concern)

emborronar /emborro'nar/ *vt* to blot; scribble, write hastily

emboscada /embos'kaða/ *f*, ambuscade, ambush; intrigue, spying

emboscar /embos'kar/ *vt Mil.* to set an ambush; *vr* lie in ambush

embosquecer /emboske'ser; emboske'θer/ *vi irr* to become wooded. See **conocer**

embotar /embo'tar/ *vt* to blunt (cutting edge); *vi Fig.* weaken; *vr* become blunt

embotellado /embote'yaðo; embote'ʎaðo/ *m*, bottling; *Fig.* bottleneck

embotellador /embote'yaðor; embote'ʎaðor/ **(-ra)** *a* bottler. *f*. **embotelladora,** bottling outfit

embotellar /embote'yar; embote'ʎar/ *vt* to bottle; bottle up, prevent from escaping

embotijar /emboti'har/ *vt* to put into jars; *vr Inf.* be enraged

embozar /embo'sar; embo'θar/ *vt Fig.* to cloak, dissemble; muffle; *vr* muffle oneself up

embozo /em'boso; em'boθo/ *m*, anything used to cover or muffle the face; pretense, pretext; facings (gen. *pl*); yashmak

embragar /embra'gar/ *vt* to sling, lift; *Mech.* let in the clutch

embrague /em'brage/ *m*, hoisting, slinging; *Mech.* clutch

embravecer /embraβe'ser; embraβe'θer/ *vt irr* to infuriate; *vr* be enraged; be boisterous (sea). See **conocer**

embravecimiento /embraβesi'miento; embraβeθi'miento/ *m*, fury, rage

embrazadura /embrasa'ðura; embraθa'ðura/ *f*, grasping, clasping; handle, clasp

embreadura /embrea'ðura/ *f*, tarring

embrear /embre'ar/ *vt* to tar, paint with pitch

embriagador /embriaga'ðor/ *a* intoxicating

embriagar /embria'gar/ *vt* to intoxicate; enrapture; *vr* become inebriated

embriaguez /embria'ges; embria'geθ/ *f*, intoxication, inebriation; rapture

embriología /embriolo'hia/ *f*, embryology

embrión /em'brion/ *m*, embryo; germ, rough idea

embrionario /embrio'nario/ *a* embryonic

embrollar /embro'yar; embro'ʎar/ *vt* to entangle; embroil

embrollo /em'broyo; em'broʎo/ *m*, tangle; falsehood; difficult situation

embromar /embro'mar/ *vt* to tease, chaff; trick, deceive; waste the time of; annoy; harm

embrujar /embru'har/ *vt* to bewitch

embrutecer /embrute'ser; embrute'θer/ *vt irr* to make brutish or stupid; *vr* become brutish. See **conocer**

embudo /em'buðo/ *m*, *Chem.* funnel

embullo /em'βujo; em'βuʎo/ *m*, *Central America* noise; excitement; revelry

embuste /em'buste/ *m*, lie, fraud; *pl* trinkets

embustero /embus'tero/ **(-ra)** *a* deceitful, knavish. *n* liar, cheat, trickster

embutido /embu'tiðo/ *m*, inlaid work; *Cul.* sausage

embutir /embu'tir/ *vt* to inlay; stuff full, cram; *vt* and *vr Inf.* stuff with food

eme /'eme/ *f*, name of letter M

emergencia /emer'hensia; emer'henθia/ *f*, emergence; accident, emergency

emergente /emer'hente/ *a* emergent

emerger /emer'her/ *vi* to emerge; have its source (rivers, etc.)

emérito /e'merito/ *a* emeritus

emético /e'metiko/ *a* and *m*, emetic

emigración /emigra'sion; emigra'θion/ *f*, emigration; migration; number of emigrants

emigrado /emi'graðo/ *m*, emigrant, emigré

emigrante /emi'grante/ *a* and *mf* emigrant

emigrar /emi'grar/ *vi* to emigrate; migrate

emigratorio /emigra'torio/ *a* emigration

eminencia /emi'nensia; emi'nenθia/ *f*, highland; importance, prominence; outstanding personality, genius; title given to cardinals

eminente /emi'nente/ *a* high, elevated; prominent, illustrious

emirato /emi'rato/ *m*, emirate

emisario /emi'sario/ **(-ia)** *n* emissary

emisión /emi'sion/ *f*, emission; *Radio.* broadcast; *Com.* issue (bonds, etc.); floating (of a loan)

emisor /emi'sor/ *m*, *Elec.* transmitter.

emisora /emi'sora/ *f*, *Radio.* broadcasting station

emitir /emi'tir/ *vt* to emit; *Radio.* broadcast; *Com.* issue (bonds, paper money, etc.); utter, give voice to

emoción /emo'sion; emo'θion/ *f*, emotion

emocional /emo'sional; emo'θional/ *a* emotional; emotive

emocionante /emosio'nante; emoθio'nante/ *a* moving, causing emotion; thrilling

emocionar /emosio'nar; emoθio'nar/ *vt* to cause emotion, move; *vr* be stirred by emotion; be thrilled

emoliente /emo'liente/ *a* and *m*, emollient

emolumento /emolu'mento/ *m*, emolument (gen. *pl*)

empachado /empa'tʃaðo/ *a* awkward, clumsy

empachar /empa'tʃar/ *vt* to hinder, impede; disguise, dissemble; *vr* overeat, stuff; be bashful

empacho /em'patʃo/ *m*, bashfulness, timidity; embarrassment, impediment; indigestion, satiety

empadronamiento /empaðrona'miento/ *m*, census

empadronar /empaðro'nar/ *vt* to take the census

empalagar /empala'gar/ *vt* to cloy (of food); tire, annoy

empalagoso /empala'goso/ *a* sickly, oversweet; cloying; *Fig.* sugary, honeyed

empalar /empa'lar/ *vt* to impale

empalizada /empali'saða; empali'θaða/ *f*, stockade, fencing

empalmar /empal'mar/ *vt* to dovetail; splice (ropes); clamp; *Fig.* combine (plans, actions, etc.); *vi* join (railroad lines); couple (railroad trains); *vr* palm (as in conjuring)

empalme /em'palme/ *m*, connection; splicing; *Fig.* combination (of plans, etc.); railroad junction; continuation; palming, secreting

empanada /empa'naða/ *f*, savory turnover or pie; secret negotiations, intrigue

empanar /empa'nar/ *vt* to bread; *Cul.* cover with breadcrumbs; *Agr.* sow grain

empantanar /empanta'nar/ *vt* to turn into marsh; embog; delay, embarrass

empañar /empa'ɲar/ *vt* to swaddle; tarnish, dim; blur; *Fig.* sully (fame, etc.)

empapar /empa'par/ *vt* to saturate; absorb; impregnate; *vr* be saturated; absorb; *Fig.* be imbued

empapelado /empape'laðo/ *m*, paperhanging; wallpaper

empapelador /empapela'ðor/ *m*, paperhanger

empapelar /empape'lar/ *vt* to wrap in paper; paper (a room, etc.)

empaque /em'pake/ *m*, packing; paneling; *Inf.* mien, air; pomposity

empaquetador /empaketa'ðor/ **(-ra)** *n* packer

empaquetar /empake'tar/ *vt* to pack; make up parcels or packages; overcrowd

emparedado /empare'ðaðo/ **(-da)** *a* cloistered, reclusive. *n* recluse. *m*, *Cul.* sandwich

emparedar /empare'ðar/ *vt* to shut up, immure; *vr* become a recluse

emparejar /empare'har/ *vt* to pair, match; equalize, make level; *vi* come abreast (of); be equal

emparentar /emparen'tar/ *vi irr* to become related by marriage. See **acertar**

emparrado /empa'rraðo/ *m*, vine arbor; vine prop; pergola

empastadura /empasta'ðura/ *f*, filling (of teeth)

empastar /empas'tar/ *vt* to cover with glue or paste; bind in boards (books); fill (teeth). **empastado en tela,** clothbound

empaste /em'paste/ *m*, pasting; gluing; filling (teeth)

empatar /empa'tar/ *vt* to equal, tie with

empate /em'pate/ *m*, tie, draw; dead heat

empavonarse /empaβo'narse/ *vr*, *Central America* to dress to the nines

empecatado /empeka'taðo/ *a* willful; evil-minded, wicked; incorrigible, impenitent; extremely unlucky

empecer /empe'ser; empe'θer/ *vt irr* to harm, damage; *vi* hinder. See **conocer**

empecinado, -a /empesi'naðo; empeθi'naðo/ *a*, *Lat. Am.* pigheaded, stubborn

empedernido /empeðer'niðo/ *a* stony-hearted, cruel

empedrado /empe'ðraðo/ *a* dappled (horses); *Fig.* flecked (with clouds). *m*, paving; pavement

empedrar /empe'ðrar/ *vt irr* to pave with stones. See **acertar**

empegar /empe'gar/ *vt* to coat with pitch; mark with pitch (sheep)

empeine /em'peine/ *m*, groin; instep

empellar /empe'ʎar/ *vt* to push, jostle

empellón /empe'ʎon; empe'ʎon/ *m*, hard push. *Inf.* **a empellones,** by pushing and shoving

empeñado /empe'ɲaðo/ *a* violent, heated (of disputes)

empeñar /empe'ɲar/ *vt* to pledge, leave as surety; pawn; oblige, compel; appoint as mediator; *vr* bind oneself; be under an obligation; (*with en*) insist on;

persist in; *vr* intercede; mediate; *Mil.* begin (a battle).

empeñado en, determined to, intent on

empeño /em'peɲo/ *m*, pledge, surety; obligation, engagement; fervent desire; purpose, intention; determination, resolve; guarantor; *Inf.* influence, favor

empeoramiento /empeora'miento/ *m*, worsening; deterioration

empeorar /empeo'rar/ *vt* to make worse; *vi* and *vr* deteriorate, grow worse

empequeñecer /empekeɲe'ser; empekeɲe'θer/ *vt irr* to diminish, lessen; make smaller; belittle. See **conocer**

emperador /empera'ðor/ *m*, emperor

emperatriz /empera'tris; empera'triθ/ *f*, empress

emperezar /empere'sar; empere'θar/ *vt* to obstruct, hinder; *vr* be lazy

empernar /emper'nar/ *vt* to peg, bolt

empero /em'pero/ *conjunc* but; nevertheless

empezar /empe'sar; empe'θar/ *vt irr* to begin, commence; initiate; *vi* begin. *Pres. Ind.* **empiezo, empiezas, empieza, empiezan.** *Preterite* **empecé, empezaste, etc.** *Pres. Subjunc.* **empiece, empieces, empiece, empecemos, empecéis, empiecen**

empicotar /empiko'tar/ *vt* to pillory

empiezo /em'pieso; em'pieθo/ *m*, *Lat. Am.* beginning

empilonar /empilo'nar/ *vt*, *Lat. Am.* to pile up

empinado /empi'naðo/ *a* steep; lofty; arrogant; exalted

empinar /empi'nar/ *vt* to raise; tip, tilt (drinking vessels); *vr* stand on tiptoe; rear, prance; tower, rise; *Aer.* zoom, climb steeply. *Inf.* **e. el codo,** to lift the elbow, tipple

empingorotado /empiŋgoro'taðo/ *a* important, prominent; *Inf.* stuck-up

empírico /em'piriko/ **(-ca)** *a* empiric. *n* quack, charlatan

empizarrado /empisa'rraðo; empiθa'rraðo/ *m*, slate roof

empizarrar /empisa'rrar; empiθa'rrar/ *vt* to roof with slate

emplastar /emplas'tar/ *vt Med.* to apply plasters; make up; paint; *Inf.* hinder, obstruct; *vr* be smeared

emplasto /em'plasto/ *m*, *Med.* plaster; poultice; *Inf.* put-up job, fraud

emplazamiento /emplasa'miento; emplaθa'miento/ *m*, placing, location; site; *Law.* summons; *Naut.* berth

emplazar /empla'sar; empla'θar/ *vt* to convene, arrange a meeting; *Law.* summon

empleado /emple'aðo/ **(-da)** *n* employee; clerk. **e. público,** civil servant

emplear /emple'ar/ *vt* to employ; lay out, invest (money); use; *vr* be employed or occupied

empleo /em'pleo/ *m*, employment; investment; laying out (of money); occupation; post, office

emplomar /emplo'mar/ *vt* to lead, solder or cover with lead; affix lead seals on or to; weight (a stick, etc.); *Argentina* fill (a tooth)

emplumar /emplu'mar/ *vt* to feather; decorate with feathers; tar and feather

emplumecer /emplume'ser; emplume'θer/ *vi irr* to fledge, grow feathers. See **conocer**

empobrecer /empoβre'ser; empoβre'θer/ *vt irr* to impoverish; *vi* and *vr* become poor; decay. See **conocer**

empobrecimiento /empoβresi'miento; empoβreθi'miento/ *m*, impoverishment

empollar /empo'ʎar/ *vt* to hatch; *vi* produce a brood (of bees); *Inf.* brood on, consider; *Inf.* grind, cram, swot (of students)

empollón /empo'ʎon; empo'ʎon/ **(-ona)** *n Inf.* plodder, grind, swot

empolvar /empol'βar/ *vt* to cover with dust; powder

emponzoñar /emponso'ɲar; emponθo'ɲar/ *vt* to poison; pervert, corrupt

emporio /em'porio/ *m*, emporium

empotrar /empo'trar/ *vt* to embed, implant; fix down

emprendedor /emprende'ðor/ *a* capable, efficient, enterprising

emprender /empren'der/ vt to undertake; (with prep a or con) Inf. accost, tackle, buttonhole

empresa /em'presa/ f, undertaking, task; motto, device; intention, design; management, firm; enterprise, deal

empresarial /empresa'rial/ a entrepreneurial

empresario /empre'sario/ m, contractor; theatrical manager

empréstito /em'prestito/ m, loan

empujar /empu'har/ vt to push; Fig. exert pressure, influence

empuje /em'puhe/ m, push; Archit. pressure; energy; power, influence

empujón /empu'hon/ m, violent thrust or push. Inf. a empujones, by pushing and shoving; intermittently

empuñar /empu'ɲar/ vt to grasp; grip; clutch

empurrarse /empu'rrarse/ vr, Central America to get angry

emu /'emu/ m, emu

emulación /emula'sion; emula'θion/ f, emulation, competition, rivalry

emulador /emula'ðor/ a emulative

emular /emu'lar/ vt to emulate, rival, compete with

émulo /'emulo/ (-la) a emulative, rival. n competitor, rival

emulsión /emul'sion/ f, emulsion

en /en/ prep in; into; on, upon; at; by. **en Madrid,** in Madrid. **en junio,** in June. **Se echó en un sillón,** He threw himself into an armchair. **Se transformó en mariposa,** It turned into a butterfly. **Hay un libro en la mesa,** There is a book on the table. **María está en casa,** Mary is at home. **en un precio muy alto,** at a very high price. **El número de candidatos ha disminuido en un treinta por ciento,** The number of candidates has decreased by thirty percent. **En** appears in a number of adverbial phrases, e.g. en particular, in particular, en secreto, in secret, en seguida, immediately. When it is used with a gerund, it means after, as soon as, when, e.g. En llegando a la puerta llamó, When he arrived at the door, he knocked. En todas partes se cuecen habas, That happens everywhere; It happens in the best of families

enaceitar /enasei'tar; enaθei'tar/ vt, Argentina to oil

enagua /e'nagua/ f, slip, crinoline, petticoat

enajenación /enahena'sion; enahena'θion/ f, transference, alienation (property); abstraction, absentmindedness. **e. mental,** lunacy

enajenar /enahe'nar/ vt to transfer (property)

enaltecer /enalte'ser; enalte'θer/ vt irr to elevate, raise; exalt. See conocer

enamoradizo /enamora'ðiso; enamora'ðiθo/ a susceptible, easily enamored; fickle

enamorado /enamo'raðo/ a in love, lovesick; easily enamored

enamorar /enamo'rar/ vt to arouse love in; court, make love to; vr fall in love; (with de) become fond of (things)

enano /e'nano/ (-na) a dwarf, dwarfed. n dwarf

enarbolar /enarβo'lar/ vt to hoist (flags); vr prance (horses); become angry

enardecer /enarðe'ser; enarðe'θer/ vt irr to kindle, stimulate (passion, quarrel, etc.); vr be afire (with passion); Med. be inflamed. See conocer

encabestrar /enkaβe'strar/ vt to halter; lead, dominate

encabestrarse /enkaβes'trarse/ vr, Lat. Am. to dig one's heels in

encabezamiento /enkaβesa'miento; enkaβeθa'miento/ m, census taking; tax register; tax assessment; heading, inscription, running head

encabezar /enkaβe'sar; enkaβe'θar/ vt to take the census of; put on the tax register; open a subscription list; put a heading or title to; lead, head; vr compound, settle by agreement (taxes, etc.)

encadenamiento /enkaðena'miento/ m, fettering, chaining; connection, link, relation

encadenar /enkaðe'nar/ vt to chain, fetter; Fig. link up, connect; Fig. paralyze. **encadenar el interés de,** to capture the interest of

encajar /enka'har/ vt to insert, fit one thing inside another; force in; fit tightly; Inf. be opportune, fit in

(often with bien); vr squeeze or crowd in; Inf. butt in, interfere

encaje /en'kahe/ m, fitting, insertion; socket, groove; joining; lace; inlay, mosaic

encajero, -a /enka'hero/ mf, lace maker; lace seller

encaladura /enkala'ðura/ f, whitewashing

encalar /enka'lar/ vt to whitewash

encalladero /enkaya'ðero; enkaʎa'ðero/ m, Naut. sandbank, reef, shoal

encallar /enka'yar; enka'ʎar/ vi Naut. to run aground; Fig. be held up (negotiations, etc.)

encalmado /enkal'maðo/ a calm; Com. dull

encalmarse /enkal'marse/ vr to become calm (wind, weather)

encalvecer /enkalβe'ser; enkalβe'θer/ vi irr to grow bald. See conocer

encamado /enka'maðo/ a bedridden, confined to one's bed; m, person confined to his bed

encamarse /enka'marse/ vr to go to bed (gen. illness); be laid flat (grain, etc.); crouch

encaminadura /enkamina'ðura/ f, **encaminamiento** m, directing, forwarding, routing

encaminar /enkami'nar/ vt to guide; direct; regulate; manage; promote, advance; vr (with prep a) make for, go in the direction of

encandecer /enkande'ser; enkande'θer/ vt irr to make incandescent. See conocer

encandilar /enkandi'lar/ vt to dazzle; mislead; Inf. poke (the fire); vr be bloodshot (eyes)

encanecer /enkane'ser; enkane'θer/ vi irr to grow gray- or white-haired; grow mold; grow old. See conocer

encanijar /enkani'har/ vt to make weak, sickly (gen. of babies); vr be delicate or ailing

encantado /enkan'taðo/ a Inf. daydreaming, abstracted; haunted; rambling (of houses)

encantador /enkanta'ðor/ a captivating, bewitching, delightful. m, sorcerer, magician. **e. de serpientes,** snake charmer

encantamiento /enkanta'miento/ m, enchantment, spell, charm

encantar /enkan'tar/ vt to enchant, weave a spell; delight, captivate, charm

encañada /enka'naða/ f, gorge, ravine

encañado /enka'ɲaðo/ m, trellis; pipeline

encañar /enka'ɲar/ vt to run water through a pipe; stake plants; wind thread on a spool

encañonar /enkaɲo'nar/ vt to run into pipes; pleat, fold

encapotarse /enkapo'tarse/ vr to muffle oneself in a cloak; scowl; be overcast; lower (sky)

encapricharse /enkapri'tʃarse/ vr to take a fancy (to); insist on having one's own way, be stubborn

encaramar /enkara'mar/ vt to raise, lift; climb; praise, extol. **e. al poder,** to put in power (e.g. a dictator). **encaramarse por,** to climb up

encarar /enka'rar/ vt to place face to face; aim (at); vt and vr face; come face to face

encarcelación /enkarsela'sion; enkarθela'θion/ f, incarceration

encarcelar /enkarse'lar; enkarθe'lar/ vt to imprison; jail; clamp

encarecer /enkare'ser; enkare'θer/ vt irr to raise the price; overpraise, exaggerate; recommend strongly; vi and vr increase in price. See conocer

encarecimiento /enkaresi'miento; enkareθi'miento/ m, increase (in price); enhancement; exaggeration. **con e.,** insistently, earnestly

encargado /enkar'gaðo/ m, person in charge; manager; agent, representative. **e. de negocios,** chargé d'affaires

encargar /enkar'gar/ vt to enjoin; commission; recommend; advise; Com. order

encargo /en'kargo/ m, charge, commission; order; office, employ; responsibility

encariñarse /enkari'ɲarse/ vi (con), vi to become fond (of)

encarnación /enkarna'sion; enkarna'θion/ f, incarnation

encarnadino /enkarna'ðino/ a incarnadine

encarnado /enkar'naðo/ *a* incarnate; flesh-colored; red

encarnar /enkar'nar/ *vi* to incarnate; pierce the flesh; *Fig.* leave a strong impression; *vt* symbolize, personify; *vr* mingle, blend

encarnizado /enkarni'saðo; enkarni'θaðo/ *a* bloodshot (eyes); flesh-colored; bloody, cruel (gen. of battles)

encarnizamiento /enkarnisa'miento; enkarniθa'miento/ *m*, cruelty, fury

encarnizar /enkarni'sar; enkarni'θar/ *vt* to infuriate; *vr* devour flesh (animals); persecute, ill-treat. *vr* **e. se con,** to attack viciously

encaro /en'karo/ *m*, stare, gaze; aim

encarrilar /enkarri'lar/ *vt* to set on the track or rails (vehicles); *Fig.* put right, set on the right track

encartamiento /enkarta'miento/ *m*, proscription; charter

encartar /enkar'tar/ *vt* to proscribe, outlaw; place on the tax register; *Law.* summon, cite

encartonar /enkarto'nar/ *vt* to cover with cardboard; bind in boards (books)

encasar /enka'sar/ *vt Surg.* to set (a bone)

encasillado /enkasi'yaðo; enkasi'ʎaðo/ *m*, set of pigeonholes

encasillar /enkasi'yar; enkasi'ʎar/ *vt* to pigeonhole; file, classify

encasquetar /enkaske'tar/ **(se)** *vt* and *vr* to pull a hat well down on the head; *vr* get a fixed idea

encasquillador, -a /enkaskija'ðor; enkaskiʎa'ðor/ *mf*, *Lat. Am.* blacksmith

encastillar /enkasti'yar; enkasti'ʎar/ *vt* to fortify with castles; *vr* retire to a castle; be headstrong, obstinate

encauzamiento /enkausa'miento; enkauθa'miento/ *m*, channeling; *Fig.* direction

encauzar /enkau'sar; enkau'θar/ *vt* to channel; *Fig.* direct, guide

encefalitis /ensefa'litis; enθefa'litis/ *f*, encephalitis. **e. letárgica,** encephalitis lethargica, sleeping sickness.

enceguedor *a* blinding, dazzling

encéfalo /en'sefalo; en'θefalo/ *m*, *Anat.* brain

encenagarse /ensena'garse; enθena'garse/ *vr* to wallow in mire; muddy oneself; take to vice

encendedor /ensende'ðor; enθende'ðor/ *a* lighting. *m*, lighter. **e. de bolsillo,** pocket lighter

encender /ensen'der; enθen'der/ *vt irr* to light; switch on; set fire to, kindle; arouse (emotions); inflame, incite; *vr* blush. See **entender**

encendido /ensen'diðo; enθen'diðo/ *a* high-colored; inflamed; ardent. *m*, *Auto.* ignition

encerado /ense'raðo; enθe'raðo/ *a* wax-colored. *m*, oilskin; sticking plaster; blackboard; tarpaulin

enceramiento /ensera'miento; enθera'miento/ *m*, waxing

encerar /ense'rar; enθe'rar/ *vt* to wax, varnish with wax; stain with wax; inspissate (lime)

encercar /enser'kar; enθer'kar/ *vt*, *Lat. Am.* to encircle

encerotar /ensero'tar; enθero'tar/ *vt* to wax (thread)

encerrar /ense'rrar; enθe'rrar/ *vt irr* to shut up, imprison; include, contain; *vr* go into seclusion. See **acertar**

encerrona /ense'rrona; enθe'rrona/ *f*, *Inf.* voluntary retreat; *Fig. Inf.* tight corner

encespedar /ensespe'ðar; enθespe'ðar/ *vt* to cover with sod

enchilada /entʃi'laða/ *f*, *Mexico* rolled-up tortilla filled with meat or cheese and covered with sauce or cream

enchufar /entʃu'far/ *vt* to connect tubes; *Fig.* combine (jobs, etc.); *Elec.* plug, connect

enchufe /en'tʃufe/ *m*, joint, fitting together (of tubes); *Elec.* wall socket, plug; part-time post; *Inf.* cushy job. **e. de reducción,** *Elec.* adapter

encía /en'sia; en'θia/ *f*, gum (of the mouth)

encíclica /en'siklika; en'θiklika/ *f*, encyclical

enciclopedia /ensiklo'peðia; enθiklo'peðia/ *f*, encyclopedia

enciclopédico /ensiklo'peðiko; enθiklo'peðiko/ *a* encyclopedic

encierro /en'sierro; en'θierro/ *m*, act of closing or shutting up; prison; retreat, confinement

encima /en'sima; en'θima/ *adv* over; above; at the top; besides; (*with de*) on, on top of. **por e. de esto,** over and above this, besides this

encinta /en'sinta; en'θinta/ *a f*, pregnant

encintar /ensin'tar; enθin'tar/ *vt* to decorate with ribbons

enclavar /enkla'βar/ *vt* to nail; pierce; embed; *Inf.* deceive

enclenque /en'klenke/ *a* ailing, weak; puny, anemic

enclocar /enklo'kar/ *vi irr* to begin to brood (hens). See **contar**

encobar /enko'βar/ *vi* to hatch eggs

encoger /enko'her/ *vt* to shrink, contract, recoil; discourage; *vi* shrink (wood, cloth, etc.); *vr* shrink from, recoil; be discouraged; be timid or bashful

encogimiento /enkohi'miento/ *m*, shrinkage; contraction; depression, discouragement; timidity; bashfulness

encoladura /enkola'ðura/ *f*. **encolamiento** *m*, gluing; sizing

encolerizar /enkoleri'sar; enkoleri'θar/ *vt* to anger; *vr* be angry

encomendar /enkomen'dar/ *vt irr* to charge with, entrust; recommend, commend; *vr* (*with prep a*) put one's trust in; send greetings to. See **acertar**

encomiar /enko'miar/ *vt* to eulogize, praise

encomienda /enko'mienda/ *f*, commission, charge; knight commandership; insignia of knight commander; land in Indian residents formerly granted in America to *conquistadores;* recommendation, commendation; protection, defense; *pl* greetings, compliments, messages

encomio /en'komio/ *m*, eulogy; strong recommendation

enconar /enko'nar/ *vt* to irritate, exasperate; *vr Med.* be inflamed; be exasperated; (*with en*) burden one's conscience with

encono /en'kono/ *m*, rancor, resentment, ill will

encontrado /enkon'traðo/ *a* facing, opposite, in front; hostile, inimical, opposed (to)

encontrar /enkon'trar/ *vt irr* to meet; find; *vi* meet; encounter unexpectedly; (*with con*) run into, collide with; *vr* be antagonistic; find; feel, be; differ, disagree (opinions); (*with con*) meet, come across. **e. eco,** to strike a responsive chord. **encontrarse con el cura de su pueblo,** to find someone who knows all about, meet someone who knows all about. **¿Cómo se encuentra Vd?** How are you? *Pres. Ind.* **encuentro, etc.** *Pres. Subjunc.* **encuentre, etc.**

encontrón /enkon'tron/ *m*, collision, violent impact

encopetado /enkope'taðo/ *a* conceited, proud; of noble descent; prominent, important

encorajar /enkora'har/ *vt* to encourage, inspire, hearten; *vr* be angry

encordelar /enkorðe'lar/ *vt* to cord, rope

encorsetar /enkorse'tar/ *vt* to correct

encorvadura /enkorβa'ðura/ *f*, bending, curving

encorvar /enkor'βar/ *vt* to bend, curve; *vr* have a leaning toward, favor

encostrar /enkos'trar/ *vt* to cover with a crust; *vr* form a crust

encrespador /enkrespa'ðor/ *m*, curling irons

encrespar /enkres'par/ *vt* to curl (hair); enrage; *vr* be curly (hair); stand on end (hair, feathers, from fright); be angry; grow rough (sea); become complicated, entangled

encrestado /enkres'taðo/ *a* crested; haughty, arrogant

encrestarse /enkres'tarse/ *vr* to stiffen the comb or crest (birds)

encrucijada /enkrusi'haða; enkruθi'haða/ *f*, crossroad, intersection; ambush

encrudecer /enkruðe'ser; enkruðe'θer/ *vt irr* to make raw-looking; annoy; *vr* be annoyed. See **conocer**

encuadernación /enkuaðerna'sion; enkuaðerna'θion/ *f*, bookbinding; binding (of a book); bookbinder's workshop. **e. en tela,** cloth binding

encuadernador /enkuaðerna'ðor/ **(-ra)** *n* bookbinder

encuadernar /enkuaðer'nar/ *vt* to bind (a book)

encuadrar /enkuaðˈrar/ *vt* to frame; fit one thing into another, insert; limit; *Mil.* enlist

encubar /enkuˈβar/ *vt* to put into casks (wine, etc.)

encubiertamente /enkuβiertaˈmente/ *adv* secretly; deceitfully

encubierto /enkuˈβierto/ *a* concealed; secret

encubridor /enkuβriˈðor/ **(-ra)** *a* concealing, hiding. *n* hider; harborer; accomplice; receiver (of stolen goods); *Law.* accessory after the fact

encubrimiento /enkuβriˈmiento/ *m*, hiding, concealment; *Law.* accessory before (after) the fact; receiving (of stolen goods)

encubrir /enkuˈβrir/ *vt* to conceal; receive (stolen goods); *Law.* prosecute as an accessory. *Past Part.* **encubierto**

encuentro /enˈkuentro/ *m*, collision; meeting, encounter; opposition, hostility; *Mil.* fight, skirmish; *Archit.* angle. **ir al e. de,** to go in search of. **salir al e. (de),** to go to meet; resist

encuerado, -a /enkueˈraðo/ *a*, *Lat. Am.* naked, nude, in the buff

encuesta /enˈkuesta/ *f*, survey, investigation, inquiry

encumbrado /enkumˈbraðo/ *a* elevated, high

encumbramiento /enkumbraˈmiento/ *m*, act of elevating; height; aggrandizement; advancement

encumbrar /enkumˈbrar/ *vt* to raise, elevate; exalt; promote; ascend, climb to the top; *vr* be proud; be lofty, tower

encurtido /enkurˈtiðo/ *m*, pickle

encurtir /enkurˈtir/ *vt* to pickle

ende /ˈende/ *adv Obs.* there. **por e.,** therefore

endeble /enˈdeβle/ *a* weak, frail

endeblez /endeˈβles; endeˈβleθ/ *f*, weakness

endémico /enˈdemiko/ *a Med.* endemic

endemoniado /endemoˈniaðo/ *a* devil-possessed; *Inf.* fiendish, malevolent

endemoniar /endemoˈniar/ *vt* to possess with a devil; *Inf.* enrage

endentar /endenˈtar/ *vt irr Mech.* to cut the cogs (of a wheel); engage, interlock (gears, wheels, etc.). See **regimentar**

endentecer /endenteˈser; endenteˈθer/ *vi irr* to cut teeth. See **conocer**

enderezamiento /enderesaˈmiento; endereθaˈmiento/ *m*, straightening; directing; guiding; putting right, correction

enderezar /endereˈsar; endereˈθar/ *vt* to straighten; direct, guide; put right, correct; *vi* take the right road; *vr* straighten oneself; prepare to

endeudarse /endeuˈðarse/ *vr* to contract debts; be under an obligation

endiablado /endiaˈβlaðo/ *a* ugly, monstrous; *Inf.* fiendish

endiosar /endioˈsar/ *vt* to deify; *vr* be puffed up with pride; be abstracted or lost in ecstasy

enditarse /endiˈtarse/ *vr*, *Lat. Am.* to go into debt

endocrino /enˈdokrino/ *a* endocrine

endocrinología /endokrinoloˈhia/ *f*, endocrinology

endomingarse /endomiŋˈgarse/ *vr* to put on one's Sunday best

endosante /endoˈsante/ *m*, endorser

endosar /endoˈsar/ *vt Com.* to endorse; transfer, pass on

endoso /enˈdoso/ *m*, *Com.* endorsement

endrogarse /endroˈgarse/ *vr*, *Mexico* = **enditarse**

endulzar /endulˈsar; endulˈθar/ *vt* to sweeten; soften, mitigate

endurecer /endureˈser; endureˈθcr/ *vt irr* to harden; toughen, inure; make severe or cruel; *vr* grow hard; become hardened or robust; be harsh or cruel. **endurecerse al trabajo,** to become hardened to work. See **conocer**

endurecimiento /enduresiˈmiento; endureθiˈmiento/ *m*, hardness; obstinacy, tenacity

ene /ˈene/ *f*, name of letter N

enemiga /eneˈmiɣa/ *f*, hostility, enmity

enemigo /eneˈmigo/ **(-ga)** *a* hostile. *n* enemy; antagonist. *m*, devil

enemistad /enemisˈtað/ *f*, enmity, hostility

enemistar /enemisˈtar/ *vt* to make enemies of; *vr*

(*with con*) become an enemy of; cease to be friendly with

energético, -a /enerˈhetiko/ *a*, *Lat. Am.* = **enérgico**

energía /enerˈhia/ *f*, energy, vigor

enérgico /eˈnerhiko/ *a* energetic, vigorous

energúmeno /enerˈgumeno/ **(-na)** *n* energumen

enero /eˈnero/ *m*, January

enervación /enerβaˈsion; enerβaˈθion/ *f*, enervation

enervar /enerˈβar/ *vt* to enervate, weaken; *Fig.* take the force out of (reasons, etc.)

enfadar /enfaˈðar/ *vt* to make angry; *vr* become angry; *Lat. Am.* to get bored

enfado /enˈfaðo/ *m*, anger; annoyance; trouble, toil

enfadoso /enfaˈðoso/ *a* vexatious; troublesome, wearisome

enfaldada /enfalˈdaða/ *f*, skirtful

enfaldar /enfalˈdar/ *vt* to tuck up the skirts; lop off lower branches (of trees)

enfangarse /enfaŋˈgarse/ *vr* to cover oneself with mud; *Inf.* dirty one's hands, sully one's reputation; wallow in vice

énfasis /ˈenfasis/ *m*, or *f*, emphasis

enfático /enˈfatiko/ *a* emphatic

enfermar /enferˈmar/ *vi* to fall ill; *vt* cause illness; *Fig.* weaken. **Enfermó del corazón,** He fell ill with heart trouble.

enfermedad /enfermeˈðað/ *f*, illness; *Fig.* malady, distemper. **e. del sueño,** sleeping sickness

enfermería /enfermeˈria/ *f*, infirmary; hospital; first-aid station

enfermero, -a /enferˈmero/ *mf* nurse

enfermizo /enferˈmiso; enferˈmiθo/ *a* ailing, delicate; unhealthy, unwholesome

enfermo /enˈfermo/ **(-ma)** *a* ill; *Fig.* corrupt, diseased; delicate, sickly. *n* patient. **e. venéreo,** person with a venereal disease

enfilar /enfiˈlar/ *vt* to place in line; string; *Mil.* enfilade

enflaquecer /enflakeˈser; enflakeˈθer/ *vt irr* to make thin; weaken, enervate; *vi* grow thin; lose heart. See **conocer**

enflaquecimiento /enflakesiˈmiento; enflakeθiˈmiento/ *m*, loss of flesh; discouragement

enfocar /enfoˈkar/ *vt* to focus; envisage

enfoque /enˈfoke/ *m*, focus

enfoscado /enfosˈkaðo/ *a* ill-humored; immersed in business matters

enfrascar /enfrasˈkar/ *vt* to bottle; *vr* (*with en*) plunge into, entangle oneself in (undergrowth, etc.); become engrossed or absorbed in

enfrenar /enfreˈnar/ *vt* to bridle; curb (a horse); restrain, repress; check

enfrente /enˈfrente/ *adv* in front, opposite, facing; in opposition

enfriadero /enfriaˈðero/ *m*, cooling place, cold cellar, root cellar

enfriamiento /enfriaˈmiento/ *m*, cooling

enfriar /enˈfriar/ *vt* to cool; *Fig.* chill, make indifferent; *vr* grow cold; *Fig.* grow stormy (weather)

enfurecer /enfureˈser; enfureˈθer/ *vt irr* to enrage. See **conocer**

enfurecimiento /enfuresiˈmiento; enfureθiˈmiento/ *m*, fury

enfurruñarse /enfurruˈɲarse/ *vr Inf.* to fume, be angry; be disgruntled

engalanar /eŋgalaˈnar/ *vt* to decorate, embellish. **engalanado como nunca,** dressed to the nines, dressed to kill

enganchar /eŋganˈtʃar/ *vt* to hook; couple, connect; hitch, harness, yoke; *Inf.* seduce, hook; *Mil.* bribe into army; *vr* be hooked or caught on a hook; *Mil.* enlist

enganche /eŋˈgantʃe/ *m*, hooking; coupling (of railroad trains, etc.); connection; yoke, harness; hook; *Inf.* enticement; *Mil.* enlistment; *Mexico* down payment

engañadizo /eŋgaɲaˈðiso; eŋgaɲaˈðiθo/ *a* easily deceived, simple

engañador /eŋgaɲaˈðor/ **(-ra)** *a* deceiving; deceptive. *n* deceiver, impostor

engañar /eŋga'ɲar/ *vt* to deceive; defraud, cheat; beguile, while away; hoax, humbug; *vr* be mistaken; deceive oneself. **e. como a un chino**, *Inf.* to pull the wool over a person's eyes. **Las apariencias engañan,** Appearances are deceptive

engañifa /eŋga'nhook;ifa/ *f, Inf.* swindle, fraud

engaño /eŋ'gaɲo/ *m*, deceit; deception, illusion; fraud; falsehood

engañoso /eŋga'ɲoso/ *a* deceitful, false; fraudulent; deceptive, misleading

engarabatar /eŋgaraβa'tar/ *vt Inf.* to hook; *vr* become hooked, curved, crooked

engaratusar /eŋgaratu'sar/ *vt, inf, Lat. Am.* = **engatusar**

engarce /eŋgarse; eŋ'garθe/ *m*, hooking; coupling; setting (of jewels)

engarzar /eŋgar'sar; eŋgar'θar/ *vt* to link, couple, enchain; hook; curl; set (jewels)

engastar /eŋgas'tar/ *vt* to set (jewels)

engaste /eŋ'gaste/ *m*, setting (of jewels)

engatusar /eŋgatu'sar/ *vt Inf.* to wheedle, coax, flatter

engendrador /enhendra'ðor/ **(-ra)** *a* engendering; original. *n* begetter

engendrar /enhen'drar/ *vt* to procreate; engender, produce, cause

engendro /en'hendro/ *m*, fetus; abnormal embryo; literary monstrosity

engestarse /eŋges'tarse/ *vr, Mexico* to make a wry face

englobar /eŋglo'βar/ *vt* to include, comprise, embrace

engolfarse /eŋgol'farse/ *vr* to sail out to sea; (*with en*) *Fig.* be absorbed in

engomar /eŋgo'mar/ *vt* to gum

engordar /eŋgor'ðar/ *vt* to fatten; *vi* grow fat; *Inf.* prosper, grow rich

engorde /eŋ'gorðe/ *m*, fattening (of stock)

engorrar /eŋgo'rrar/ *vt, Lat. Am.* to annoy, needle

engorro /eŋ'gorro/ *m*, impediment, obstacle, difficulty

engorroso /eŋgo'rroso/ *a* difficult, troublesome

engranaje /eŋgra'nahe/ *m, Mech.* gearing; gear; *Fig.* connection, link

engrandecer /eŋgrande'ser; eŋgrande'θer/ *vt irr* to enlarge; augment; eulogize; promote, exalt. See **conocer**

engrandecimiento /eŋgrandesi'miento; eŋgrandeθi'miento/ *m*, enlargement; increase; exaggeration, eulogization; advancement, promotion

engrasador /eŋgrasa'ðor/ *m*, greaser, lubricator; oiler

engrasar /eŋgra'sar/ *vt* to grease; lubricate, oil; manure; stain with grease

engreimiento /eŋgrei'miento/ *m*, conceit, vanity

engreír /eŋgre'ir/ *vt irr* to make conceited; *vr* become vain or conceited. See **reír**

engrescar /eŋgres'kar/ **(se)** *vt* and *vr* to start a quarrel

engrosar /eŋgro'sar/ *vt irr* to fatten, thicken; *Fig.* increase, swell; manure; *vi* put on weight, grow fat. See **contar**

engrudar /eŋgru'ðar/ *vt* to paste, glue

engrudo /eŋ'gruðo/ *m*, paste, glue

enguijarrado /eŋguiha'rraðo/ *a* pebbled. *m*, pebbled path

engullir /eŋgu'yir; eŋgu'ʎir/ *vt* to gobble, swallow

enhebrar /ene'βrar/ *vt* to thread (needles); string

enhestar /enes'tar/ *vt irr* to erect; set upright; *vr* rise; rear up; straighten oneself up. See **acertar**

enhiesto /en'iesto/ *a* upright, erect

enhorabuena /enora'βuena/ *f*, congratulation. *adv* well and good. **dar la e.,** to congratulate

enhoramala /enora'mala/ *adv* in an evil hour. *Inf.* **¡Vete e.!** Go to the devil!

enhorquetado /enorke'taðo/ *a* in the saddle

enigma /e'nigma/ *m*, enigma

enigmático /enig'matiko/ *a* enigmatical

enjabonar /enhaβo'nar/ *vt* to soap; *Inf.* soap down, flatter

enjaezar /enhae'sar; enhae'θar/ *vt* to harness (a horse)

enjalbegar /enhalβe'gar/ *vt* to whitewash

enjambrar /enhamb'rar/ *vt* to hive bees; *vi* multiply, increase

enjambre /en'hambre/ *m*, swarm (of bees); crowd

enjaretado /enhare'taðo/ *m*, latticework

enjaular /enhau'lar/ *vt* to cage; *Inf.* jail

enjoyar /enho'yar/ *vt* to adorn with jewels; beautify; set with precious stones

enjuagadura /enhuaga'ðura/ *f*, rinsing (the mouth); rinse water; mouthwash

enjuagar /enhua'gar/ *vt* to rinse; *vr* rinse the mouth

enjuague /en'huage/ *m*, rinse; rinsing; mouthwash; tooth mug; scheme, plan

enjugar /enhu'gar/ *vt* to dry; cancel, write off; wipe, mop (perspiration, tears, etc.); *vr* grow lean

enjuiciar /enhui'siar; enhui'θiar/ *vt* to submit a matter to arbitration; *Law.* prosecute; *Law.* render judgment; *Law.* adjudicate (a case)

enjundia /en'hundia/ *f*, animal fat or grease; *Fig.* substance, meat; strength, vigor; constitution, temperament

enjuto /en'huto/ *a* dry; lean. *m pl*, brushwood; *Cul.* canapés, savories

enlace /en'lase; en'laθe/ *m*, connection; link; tie; *Chem.* bond; alliance, relationship; marriage, *Phonet.* linking

enladrillado /enlaðri'yaðo; enlaðri'ʎaðo/ *m*, brick floor or pavement

enlardar /enlar'ðar/ *vt Cul.* to baste

enlazar /enla'sar; enla'θar/ *vt* to tie, bind; join, link; lasso; *vr* marry; be allied, related. **e. con,** to connect with (of trains); link up with

enlentecerse /enlente'serse; enlente'θerse/ *vr* to decelerate, go slow, slow down

enlodar /enlo'ðar/ *vt* to muddy; *Fig.* smirch, sully

enloquecer /enloke'ser; enloke'θer/ *vt irr* to drive insane; *vi* go mad. See **conocer**

enlosado /enlo'saðo/ *m*, tile floor

enlosar /enlo'sar/ *vt* to pave with flags

enlozar /enlo'sar; enlo'θar/ *vt, Lat. Am.* to enamel, glaze

enlucir /enlu'sir; enlu'θir/ *vt irr* to plaster (walls); polish (metals). See **lucir**

enlutar /enlu'tar/ *vt* to put in mourning, drape with crepe; darken, obscure; sadden; *vr* go into mourning; become dark

enmaderar /enmaðe'rar/ *vt* to panel in wood, board up

enmarañar /emara'ɲar/ *vt* to tangle, disorder (hair, etc.); complicate, confuse; *vr* be tangled; be sprinkled with clouds

enmaridar /emari'ðar/ *vi* to become a wife

enmarillecerse /emariye'serse; emariʎe'θerse/ *vr irr* to grow yellow. See **conocer**

enmascarar /emaska'rar/ *vt* to mask; disguise, dissemble; *vr* be masked

enmasillar /emasi'yar; emasi'ʎar/ *vt* to putty

enmendar /emen'dar/ *vt irr* to correct, improve; reform; compensate, indemnify; *Law.* repeal; *vr* be improved or corrected; mend one's ways. See **acertar**

enmienda /e'mienda/ *f*, correction; reform; indemnity; compensation; amendment; *pl Agr.* fertilizers

enmohecer /emoe'ser; emoe'θer/ *vt irr* to rust; *vr* become moldy. See **conocer**

enmudecer /emuðe'ser; emuðe'θer/ *vt irr* to silence; *vi* become dumb; be silent. See **conocer**

enmugrecer /emugre'ser; emugre'θer/ *vt irr* to cover with grime; *vr* be grimy, dirty. See **conocer**

enmugrentar /emugren'tar/ *vt, Chile* = **enmugrecer**

ennegrecer /ennegre'ser; ennegre'θer/ *vt irr* to dye black; make black; *vr* become black; become dark or cloudy. See **conocer**

ennoblecer /ennoβle'ser; ennoβle'θer/ *vt irr* to ennoble; enrich, embellish; adorn, befit. See **conocer**

ennoblecimiento /ennoβlesi'miento; ennoβleθi'miento/ *m*, ennoblement; enrichment

enojadizo /enoha'ðiso; enoha'ðiθo/ *a* irritable, peevish

enojar /eno'har/ *vt* to anger; annoy, irritate; *vr* be angry; rage, be rough (wind, sea)

enojo /e'noho/ *m*, anger; resentment; vexations, troubles, trials (gen. *pl*). **con gran e. de,** much to the annoyance of

enojoso /eno'hoso/ *a* annoying; troublesome, tiresome

enorgullecer /enorguye'ser; enorguʎe'θer/ *vt irr* to make proud; *vr* be proud. See **conocer**

enorme /e'norme/ *a* enormous, huge; monstrous, heinous

enormidad /enormi'ðað/ *f*, hugeness; enormity; wickedness

enramar /enra'mar/ *vt* to intertwine branches; embower; *vi* branch (trees)

enrarecer /enrare'ser; enrare'θer/ *vt irr* to rarefy; *vr* become rarefied; grow rare. See **conocer**

enrarecimiento /enraresi'miento; enrareθi'miento/ *m*, rarefaction

enredadera /enreða'ðera/ *f*, convolvulus. *a f*, climbing, twining (plant)

enredador /enreða'ðor/ **(-ra)** *a* mischievous, willful; intriguing, scheming; *Inf.* gossiping, meddlesome. *n* intriguer; *Inf.* meddler

enredar /enre'ðar/ *vt* to catch in a net; put down nets or snares; entangle; sow discord; compromise, involve (in difficulties); *vi* be mischievous; *vr* be entangled; be involved (in difficulties)

enredo /en'reðo/ *m*, tangle; mischief, prank; intrigue, malicious falsehood; difficult situation; plot

enredoso /enre'ðoso/ *a* tangled; fraught with difficulties

enrejado /enre'haðo/ *m*, railing, paling; trellis or latticework; *Sew.* openwork

enrejar /enre'har/ *vt* to fence with a railing; cover with grating

enriquecer /enrike'ser; enrike'θer/ *vt irr* to enrich; exalt, aggrandize; *vi* grow rich; prosper, flourish. See **conocer**

enriscado /enris'kaðo/ *a* craggy, rocky

enristrar /enris''trar/ *vt* to couch (a lance); string (onions, etc.); *Fig.* surmount (difficulties); go straight to (a place)

enrojecer /enrohe'ser; enrohe'θer/ *vt irr* to redden; make blush; *vr* grow red; blush. See **conocer**

enroscar /enros'kar/ *vt* to twist, twine; *vr* turn (screw); twist; coil

ensaimada /ensai'maða/ *f*, Spanish pastry cake

ensalada /ensa'laða/ *f*, salad; hodgepodge

ensaladera /ensala'ðera/ *f*, salad bowl

ensalmar /ensal'mar/ *vt Surg.* to set (bones); cure by spells

ensalmo /en'salmo/ *m*, spell, charm. **por e.,** as if by magic, rapidly

ensalzar /ensal'sar; ensal'θar/ *vt* to exalt, promote; praise

ensamblador /ensambla'ðor/ *m*, joiner, assembler

ensambladura /ensambla'ðura/ *f*, assemblage, joinery; joining; dovetailing

ensamblar /ensam'blar/ *vt* to assemble; join, dovetail, mortise

ensanchador, -a /ensantʃa'ðor/ *mf*, glove stretcher

ensanchar /ensan'tʃar/ *vt* to widen, enlarge, extend; *Sew.* let out, stretch; *vr* put on airs

ensanche /en'santʃe/ *m*, dilatation, widening; stretch; extension; *Sew.* turnings, letting out; (city) extension

ensangrentar /ensaŋgren'tar/ *vt irr* to stain with blood; *vr* be bloodstained; be overhasty. See **regimentar**

ensañar /ensa'ɲar/ *vt* to irritate, infuriate; *vr* be merciless (with vanquished)

ensartar /ensar'tar/ *vt* to string (beads); thread (needles); spit, pierce; tell a string (of falsehoods)

ensayar /ensa'yar/ *vt* to try out; *Chem.* test; *Theat.* rehearse; assay

ensayista /ensa'yista/ *mf* essayist

ensayo /ensa'yo/ *m*, test, trial; *Lit.* essay; assay; experiment; rehearsal. **e. general,** dress rehearsal

ensenada /ense'naða/ *f*, cove, inlet

enseñanza /ense'ɲansa; ense'ɲanθa/ *f*, teaching; education; example, experience. **e. primaria,** elementary education. **e. secundaria,** secondary education. **e. superior,** higher education

enseñar /ense'ɲar/ *vt* to teach, instruct; train; point out; exhibit, show; *vr* become accustomed. **e. la oreja,** *Fig.* to show the cloven hoof

enseñorearse /enseɲore'arse/ *vr* to take possession (of)

enseres /en'seres/ *m pl*, household goods; utensils; equipment

ensilladero /ensiya'ðero; ensiʎa'ðero/ *m*, paddock

ensillar /ensi'yar; ensi'ʎar/ *vt* to saddle

ensimismarse /ensimis'marse/ *vr* to be lost in thought; *Lat. Am.* to become conceited, become self-absorbed

ensoberbecer /ensoβerβe'ser; ensoβerβe'θer/ *vt irr* to make haughty; *vr* become arrogant; grow rough (sea). See **conocer**

ensordecedor /ensorðese'ðor; ensorðeθe'ðor/ *a* deafening

ensordecer /ensorðe'ser; ensorðe'θer/ *vt irr* to deafen; *vi* become deaf; keep silent, refuse to reply. See **conocer**

ensuciar /ensu'siar; ensu'θiar/ *vt* to soil, dirty; *Fig.* sully; *vr* be dirty; *Inf.* accept bribes

ensueño /en'sueɲo/ *m*, dream; illusion, fancy

entabicar /entaβi'kar/ *vt, Lat. Am.* to partition off

entablado /enta'βlaðo/ *m*, stage, dais; wooden floor; planking

entablar /enta'βlar/ *vt* to plank, floor with boards; board up; *Surg.* splint; undertake, initiate (negotiations, etc.); begin (conversations, etc.); *vr* settle (winds). **e. acción judicial,** to take legal action

entalegar /entale'gar/ *vt* to put into sacks or bags; hoard (money)

entalladura /entaya'ðura; entaʎa'ðura/ *f*, carving; sculpture; mortise, notch

entallar /enta'yar; enta'ʎar/ *vt* to carve; sculpture; engrave; notch, groove; tap (trees); fit (well or ill) at the waist

entallecer /entaye'ser; entaʎe'θer/ *vi irr* to sprout (plants). See **conocer**

entapizar /entapi'sar; entapi'θar/ *vt* to hang with tapestry; upholster; *Fig.* cover, carpet

entarimado /entari'maðo/ *m*, wooden floor; dais

ente /'ente/ *m*, entity, being; *Inf.* object, individual

entechar /ente'tʃar/ *vt, Lat. Am.* to roof, to put a roof on

enteco /en'teko/ *a* sickly, ailing, delicate

entendederas /entende'ðeras/ *f pl, Inf.* understanding

entendedor /entende'ðor/ **(-ra)** *a* understanding, comprehending. *n* one who understands. **A buen e. pocas palabras,** A word to the wise is sufficient

entender /enten'der/ *vt irr* to comprehend, understand; know; deduce, infer; intend; believe; (*with de*) be familiar with or knowledgeable about; (*with en*) have as a profession or trade; be engaged in; have authority (for behavior); understand each other; have an amatory understanding; be meant, signify; (*with con*) have an understanding with. **a mi e.,** in my opinion, as I see it. *Pres. Ind.* **entiendo, entiendes, entiende, entienden.** *Pres. Subjunc.* **entienda, entiendas, entienda, entiendan**

entendido /enten'diðo/ *a* learned, knowledgeable

entendimiento /entendi'miento/ *m*, understanding; mind, reason, intelligence

enteramente /entera'mente/ *adv* completely, entirely, wholly

enterar /ente'rar/ *vt* to inform, advise

entereza /enteresa; ente'reθa/ *f*, entirety; completeness; impartiality, integrity; fortitude, constancy; strictness, rigor

enternecer /enterne'ser; enterne'θer/ *vt irr* to soften, make tender; move to pity; *vr* be touched by compassion. See **conocer**

enternecimiento /enternesi'miento; enterneθi'miento/ *m*, compassion, pity; tenderness

entero /en'tero/ *a* entire; whole; robust, healthy; upright, just; constant, loyal; pure; *Inf.* strong, tough (cloth); *Math.* integral; *Lat. Am.* payment

enterrador /enterra'ðor/ *m*, gravedigger

enterrar /ente'rrar/ *vt irr* to inter; outlive; bury, forget. See **acertar**

entibiar /enti'βiar/ *vt* to make lukewarm; *Fig.* cool, temper

entidad /enti'ðað/ *f*, entity; value, importance

entierro /en'tierro/ *m*, interment, burial; grave; funeral; buried treasure

entoldar /entol'dar/ *vt* to cover with an awning; hang with tapestry, etc., drape; cover (sky, clouds)

entomología /entomolo'hia/ *f*, entomology

entomológico /entomo'lohiko/ *a* entomological

entomólogo /ento'mologo/ *m*, entomologist

entonación /entona'sion; entona'θion/ *f*, intonation; modulation (voice); conceit

entonado /ento'naðo/ *a*, haughty, conceited

entonar /ento'nar/ *vt* to modulate (voice); intone; blow (organ bellows); lead (song); *Med.* tone up; *Art.* harmonize; *vr* become conceited; *Com.* improve, harden (stock, etc.)

entonces /entonses; en'tonθes/ *adv* then, at that time; in that case, that being so

entonelar /entone'lar/ *vt* to put in barrels or casks

entontecer /entonteser; entonte'θer/ *vt irr* to make stupid or foolish; *vr* become stupid. See **conocer**

entornar /entor'nar/ *vt* to leave ajar; half-close; upset, turn upside down

entorpecer /entorpe'ser; entorpe'θer/ *vt irr* to numb, make torpid; confuse, daze; obstruct, delay; *vr* go numb; be confused. See **conocer**

entorpecimiento /entorpesi'miento; entorpeθi'miento/ *m*, numbness, torpidity; stupidity, dullness; delay, obstruction

entrada /en'traða/ *f*, entrance; door, gate; admission; *Cul.* entree; admission ticket; *Theat.* house; takings, gate; *Mil.* entry; beginnings (of month, etc.); intimacy; right of entry. **entradas y salidas,** comings and goings; collusion; *Com.* ingoing and outgoing

entrampar /entram'par/ *vt* to trap (animals); swindle; *Fig. Inf.* entangle (business affairs); *Inf.* load with debts; *vr* be bogged down; *Inf.* be in debt

entrante /en'trante/ *a* incoming, entrant; next, coming (month)

entraña /en'traɲa/ *f*, entrail; *pl* heart; *Fig.* center, core; humaneness; temperament. *Inf.* **no tener entrañas,** to be heartless, be without feeling

entrañable /entra'ɲaβle/ *a* intimate; dearly loved

entrar /en'trar/ *vi* (*with en*) to enter, go into, come in; flow into; *Fig.* have access to; join, become a member; *Fig.* be taken by (fever, panic, etc.); *Mil.* enter; be an ingredient of; (*with por, en*) penetrate, pierce; (*with de*) embrace (professions, etc.); (*with prep a* + *infin*) begin to; (*with en* + *noun*) begin to be (e.g. *e. en calor,* begin to be hot) or begin to take part in (e.g. *e. en lucha,* begin to fight); *vt* introduce, make enter; *Mil.* (*with en*) occupy; *vr* (*with en*) squeeze in. **e. en apetito,** to work up an appetite, get an appetite. *Inf.* **no e. ni salir en,** to take no part in. *Inf.* **No me entra,** I don't understand it

entre /'entre/ *prep* between; among; to. **e. joyas,** among jewels. **E. las dos se escribió la carta,** Between them, they wrote the letter. **Dije e. mí,** I said to myself. **los días de e. semana,** weekdays. **e. tanto,** in the meanwhile.

entreabrir /entrea'βrir/ *vt* to leave ajar; half-open. *Past Part.* **entreabierto**

entreacto /entre'akto/ *m*, interval, entr'acte; small cigar

entrecano /entre'kano/ *a* going gray, grayish (hair)

entrecejo /entre'seho; entre'θeho/ *m*, space between the eyebrows; frown

entrecerrar /entrese'rrar; entreθe'rrar/ *vt, Lat. Am* to close halfway; half-close; leave ajar

entrecoger /entreko'her/ *vt* to intercept, catch; constrain, compel

entrecortado /entrekor'taðo/ *a* intermittent (sounds); faltering, broken (voice)

entrecubiertas /entreku'βiertas/ *f pl, Naut.* between decks

entredicho /entre'ðitʃo/ *m*, prohibition; *Eccl.* interdiction

entredós /en'treðos/ *m, Sew.* insertion

entrefino /entre'fino/ *a* middling, fairly fine

entrega /en'trega/ *f*, handing over; delivery; *Lit.* part, serial; installment. **por entregas,** as a serial, serial (of stories)

entregar /entre'gar/ *vt* to hand over; deliver; surrender; *vr* give oneself up; surrender; submit; (*with prep a*) engage in, be absorbed in; (*with prep a* or *en*) give oneself over to (vice, etc.)

entreguista /entre'gista/ *mf* defeatist

entrelazar /entrela'sar; entrela'θar/ *vt* to interlace, intertwine; interweave

entrelistado /entrelis'taðo/ *a* striped

entrelucir /entrelu'sir; entrelu'θir/ *vi irr* to show through, be glimpsed. See **lucir**

entremedias /entre'meðias/ *adv* in between, halfway; in the meantime

entremés /entre'mes/ *m*, hors d'oeuvres (gen. *pl*); interlude, one-act farce

entremeter /entreme'ter/ *vt* to place between or among; *vr* intrude; meddle, pry

entremetido /entreme'tiðo/ **(-da)** *a* meddlesome. *n* busybody, meddler

entremetimiento /entremeti'miento/ *m*, meddlesomeness

entremezclar /entremes'klar; entremeθ'klar/ *vt* to intermingle

entrenador /entrena'ðor/ **(-ra)** *n* trainer; *Sports.* coach

entrenamiento /entrena'miento/ *m*, training, exercise

entrenar /entre'nar/ **(se)** *vt* and *vr* to train; exercise; *Sports.* coach

entreoír /entreo'ir/ *vt* to overhear; hear imperfectly

entrepaño /entre'paɲo/ *m, Archit.* panel; pier (between windows, etc.)

entrepiernas /entre'piernas/ *f pl*, crotch

entresacar /entresa'kar/ *vt* to choose or pick out; thin out (plants); thin (hair)

entresuelo /entre'suelo/ *m*, mezzanine, entresol; ground floor

entresueño /entre'sueɲo/ *m*, daydream

entretallar /entreta'yar; entreta'ʎar/ *vt* to carve in bas-relief; engrave; *Sew.* do openwork; intercept; *vr* connect, dovetail

entretejer /entrete'her/ *vt* to interweave; interlace; *Lit.* insert

entretela /entre'tela/ *f, Sew.* interlining

entretener /entrete'ner/ *vt irr* to keep waiting; make more bearable; amuse, entertain; delay, postpone; maintain, upkeep; *vr* amuse oneself. See **tener**

entretenido /entrete'niðo/ *a* amusing, entertaining

entretenimiento /entreteni'miento/ *m*, amusement; pastime, diversion; upkeep, maintenance

entretiempo /entre'tiempo/ *m*, between seasons, spring or autumn

entreventana /entreβen'tana/ *f*, space between windows

entreverado /entreβe'raðo/ *a* variegated; streaky (of bacon)

entreverar /entreβe'rar/ *vt* to intermingle

entrevista /entre'βista/ *f*, meeting, interview

entristecer /entriste'ser; entriste'θer/ *vt irr* to sadden; *vr* grieve. See **conocer**

entristecimiento /entristesi'miento; entristeθi'miento/ *m*, sadness

entrometer /entrome'ter/ *vt* See **entremeter**

entromparse /entrom'parse/ *vt, Lat. Am.* to get angry

entronar /entro'nar/ *vt* See **entronizar**

entroncar /entron'kar/ *vt* to prove descent; *vi* be related, or become related (by marriage)

entronerar /entrone'rar/ *vt* to pocket (in billiards)

entronizar /entroni'sar; entroni'θar/ *vt* to enthrone; exalt

entronque /entron'ke/ *m*, blood relationship, cognation; junction

entrucharse /entru'tʃarse/ *vr, Mexico* to meddle into other people's business

entumecer /entume'ser; entume'θer/ *vt irr* to numb; *vr* go numb; swell, rise (sea, etc.). See **conocer**

enturbiar /entur'βiar/ *vt* to make turbid or cloudy; confuse, disorder; *vr* become turbid; be in disorder

entusiasmar /entusias'mar/ *vt* to inspire enthusiasm; *vr* be enthusiastic

entusiasmo /entu'siasmo/ *m*, enthusiasm

entusiasta /entu'siasta/ *a* enthusiastic. *mf* enthusiast

enumeración /enumera'sion; enumera'θion/ *f*, enumeration

enumerar /enume'rar/ *vt* to enumerate

enunciación /enunsia'sion; enunθia'θion/ *f*, statement, declaration, enunciation

enunciar /enun'siar; enun'θiar/ *vt* to state clearly, enunciate

envainar /embai'nar/ *vt* to sheathe

envalentonamiento /embalentona'miento/ *m*, boldness; braggadocio, bravado

envalentonar /embalento'nar/ *vt* to make bold (gen. in a bad sense); *vr* strut, brag; take courage

envanecer /embane'ser; embane'θer/ *vt irr* to make vain or conceited; *vr* be vain; be conceited

envanecimiento /embanesi'miento; embaneθi-miento/ *m*, conceit, vanity

envasador /embasa'ðor/ **(-ra)** *n* packer. *m*, funnel

envasar /emba'sar/ *vt* to bottle; barrel; sack (grain, etc.); pack in any container; pierce (with sword)

envase /em'base/ *m*, bottling; filling; container; packing

envejecer /embehe'ser; embehe'θer/ *vt irr* to make old, wear out; *vi* grow old. See **conocer**

envenenador /embenena'ðor/ **(-ra)** *n* poisoner

envenenamiento /embenena'miento/ *m*, poisoning

envenenar /embene'nar/ *vt* to poison; corrupt, pervert; put a malicious interpretation on; embitter; *vr* take poison

envergadura /emberga'ðura/ *f*, wingspan

envés /em'bes/ *m*, wrong side of anything; *Inf.* back. **al e.,** wrong side out

enviado /em'biaðo/ *m*, messenger; envoy. **e. extraordinario,** special envoy

enviar /em'biar/ *vt* to send, dispatch

enviciar /embi'siar; embi'θiar/ *vt* to corrupt, make vicious; *vr* (*with con, en*) take to (drink, etc.)

envidia /em'biðia/ *f*, envy; emulation; desire (to possess)

envidiable /embi'ðiaβle/ *a* enviable

envidiar /embi'ðiar/ *vt* to envy, grudge; emulate

envidioso /embi'ðioso/ *a* envious

envilecer /embile'ser; embile'θer/ *vt irr* to debase; *vr* degrade oneself. See **conocer**

envinarse /embi'narse/ *vr, Mexico* to get drunk (on wine)

envío /em'bio/ *m*, *Com.* remittance; consignment, shipment. **fecha de e.,** date sent

envite /em'bite/ *m*, stake (at cards); offer; push, shove

enviudar /embiu'ðar/ *vi* to become a widow or widower

envoltorio /embol'torio/ *m*, bundle

envoltura /embol'tura/ *f*, swaddling clothes; covering; wrapping

envolver /embol'βer/ *vt irr* to enfold; envelop; wrap up, parcel; *Fig.* contain, enshrine; swaddle, swathe; roll into a ball; confound (in argument); *Mil.* outflank; implicate (person). See **mover**

enyesado /enye'saðo/ *m*, plastering; stucco

enyesar /enye'sar/ *vt* to plaster; *Surg.* apply a plaster bandage

enzarzar /ensar'sar; enθar'θar/ *vt* to fill or cover with brambles; *vr* be caught on brambles; set one person against another; get in difficulties; quarrel

eñe /'eɲe/ *f*, name of the letter Ñ

eón /e'on/ *m*, eon

eperlano /eper'lano/ *m*, smelt

épica /'epika/ *f*, epic

épico /'epiko/ *a* epic

epicúreo /epi'kureo/ **(-ea)** *a* epicurean; sensual, voluptuous. *n* epicure

epidemia /epi'ðemia/ *f*, epidemic

epidémico /epi'ðemiko/ *a* epidemic

epifanía /epifa'nia/ *f*, Epiphany, Twelfth Night

epiglotis /epi'glotis/ *f*, epiglottis

epígrafe /epi'grafe/ *m*, epigraph, inscription; title, motto

epigrafía /epigra'fia/ *f*, epigraphy

epigrama /epi'grama/ *m*, inscription; epigram

epigramático /epigra'matiko/ **(-ca)** *a* epigrammatic. *n* epigrammatist

epilepsia /epi'lepsia/ *f*, epilepsy

epiléptico /epi'leptiko/ **(-ca)** *a* and *n* epileptic

epilogar /epilo'gar/ *vt* to summarize, recapitulate

epílogo /e'pilogo/ *m*, recapitulation; summary, digest; epilogue

episcopado /episko'paðo/ *m*, episcopate; bishopric

episodio /epi'soðio/ *m*, episode; digression

epistolar /episto'lar/ *a* epistolary

epitafio /epi'tafio/ *m*, epitaph

epíteto /e'piteto/ *m*, epithet

epítome /e'pitome/ *m*, epitome; summary, abstract

época /'epoka/ *f*, epoch, period; space of time. **é. de celo,** mating season. **é. de lluvias,** rainy season. **é. de secas,** dry season. **en aquella é.,** at that time

épodo /'epoðo/ *m*, *Poet.* epode

epopeya /epo'peya/ *f*, epic poem; *Fig.* epic

equidad /eki'ðað/ *f*, fairness; reasonableness; equity

equidistancia /ekiðis'tansia; ekiðis'tanθia/ *f*, equidistance

equidistante /ekiðis'tante/ *a* equidistant

equilibrar /ekili'βrar/ *vt* to balance; *Fig.* maintain in equilibrium, counterbalance

equilibrio /eki'liβrio/ *m*, equilibrium; equanimity; *Fig.* balance

equilibrista /ekili'βrista/ *mf* equilibrist, tightrope walker

equino /e'kino/ *a* equine. *m*, *Archit.* echinus; sea urchin

equinoccio /ekinoksio; eki'nokθio/ *m*, equinox

equipaje /eki'pahe/ *m*, luggage, baggage; *Naut.* crew

equipar /eki'par/ *vt* to equip, furnish

equipo /e'kipo/ *m*, outfitting, furnishing; equipment; team; trousseau

equis /'ekis/ *f*, name of the letter X

equitación /ekita'sion; ekita'θion/ *f*, horsemanship, riding

equitativo /ekita'tiβo/ *a* equitable, just, fair

equivalencia /ekiβalensia; ekiβa'lenθia/ *f*, equivalence, equality

equivalente /ekiβa'lente/ *a* equivalent

equivaler /ekiβa'ler/ *vi irr* to be equivalent; *Geom.* be equal. See **valer**

equivocación /ekiβoka'sion; ekiβoka'θion/ *f*, error, mistake

equivocadamente /ekiβokaða'mente/ *adv* mistakenly, by mistake

equivocar /ekiβo''kar/ *vt* to mistake; *vr* be mistaken or make a mistake. **equivocarse de medio a medio,** to be off by a long shot

equívoco /e'kiβoko/ *a* equivocal, ambiguous. *m*, equivocation

era /'era/ *f*, era; threshing floor; vegetable or flower bed

erario /e'rario/ *m*, public treasury, exchequer

erección /erek'sion; erek'θion/ *f*, raising; erection, elevation; foundation, institution

eremita /ere'mita/ *mf* hermit

erguir /er'gir/ *vt irr* to raise; straighten; lift up; *vr* straighten up; tower; grow proud. *Pres. Ind.* **irgo** (or **yergo**), **irgues, irguen.** *Pres. Part.* **irguiendo.** *Preterite* **irguió, irguieron.** *Pres. Subjunc.* **irga or yerga, etc.**

erial /e'rial/ *m*, uncultivated land

erigir /eri'hir/ *vt* to found, establish; promote, exalt. **erigirse contra,** to rise up against

erisipela /erisi'pela/ *f*, erysipelas

erizado /eri'saðo; eri'θaðo/ *a* standing on end (of hair); prickly, covered with bristles or quills. **e. de**

espinas, bristling with thorns; covered with bristles or quills

erizar /eri'sar; eri'θar/ *vt* to set on end (hair); beset with difficulties; *vr* stand on end, bristle (hair, quills, etc.)

erizo /e'riso; e'riθo/ *m,* hedgehog; husk (of some fruits); *Inf.* touch-me-not, unsociable person; *Mech.* sprocket wheel. **e. de mar,** sea urchin

ermita /er'mita/ *f,* hermitage

ermitaño /ermi'taɲo/ *m,* hermit

erogación /eroga'sion; eroga'θion/ *f, Lat. Am.* expenditure

erosión /ero'sion/ *f,* erosion

erótico /e'rotiko/ *a* erotic

errabundo /erra'βundo/ *a* wandering, errant, vagrant

erradamente /erraða'mente/ *adv* erroneously

erradicable /erraði'kaβle/ *a* eradicable

erradicación /erraðika'sion; erraðika'θion/ *f,* eradication

erradicar /erraði'kar/ *vt* to eradicate

errante /e'rrante/ *a* wandering; erring; errant

errar /e'rrar/ *vi irr* to err, fail; rove, roam; wander (attention, etc.); *vr* be mistaken. *Auto.* **e. el encendido,** to misfire. *Pres. Ind.* **yerro, yerras, yerra, yerran.** *Pres. Subjunc.* **yerre, yerres, yerre, yerren**

errata /e'rrata/ *f,* misprint

errático /e'rratiko/ *a* wandering, vagrant; *Med.* erratic

erre /'erre/ *f,* name of the letter R

erróneo /e'rroneo/ *a* erroneous, mistaken

error /e'rror/ *m,* error. **error de más,** an overestimate. **error de menos,** an underestimate

eructar /eruk'tar/ *vi* to eructate, belch

eructo /e'rukto/ *m,* eructation, belching

erudición /eruði'sion; eruði'θion/ *f,* erudition

erudito /eru'ðito/ *a* learned, erudite. *m,* scholar. **e. a la violeta,** pseudo-learned

erupción /erup'sion; erup'θion/ *f, Med.* rash; eruption

eruptivo /erup'tiβo/ *a* eruptive

es /es/ *irr 3rd pers. sing Pres. Ind.* of ser, is

esa /'esa/ *f, dem a* that. **ésa,** *f, dem. pron* that one; the former; the town in which you are (e.g. *Iré a é. mañana,* I shall come to your town tomorrow). Used generally in letters. See **ése**

esbeltez /esβel'tes; esβel'teθ/ *f,* slenderness

esbelto /es'βelto/ *a* tall and slim and graceful, willowy

esbozar /esβo'sar; esβo'θar/ *vt* to sketch, outline

esbozo /es'βoso; es'βoθo/ *m,* sketch; outline, rough plan, first draft

escabechar /eskaβe'tʃar/ *vt* to pickle; dye (the hair, etc.); *Inf.* kill in anger; *Inf.* fail (an examination)

escabeche /eska'βetʃe/ *m, Cul.* pickle; hair dye

escabechina /eskaβe'tʃina/ *f, Inf.* heavy failure (in an examination)

escabel /eska'βel/ *m,* footstool; small backless chair; *Fig.* steppingstone

escabioso /eska'βioso/ *a* scabby, scabious

escabro /es'kaβro/ *m,* scab, mange

escabroso /eska'βroso/ *a* rough; rocky; uneven; rude, unpolished, uncivil; risqué, improper

escabullirse /eskaβu'yirse; eskaβu'ʎirse/ *vr irr* to escape; run away; slip out unnoticed. See **mullir**

escafandra /eska'fandra/ *f,* diving suit, diving outfit

escala /es'kala/ *f,* ladder; (*Mus. Math.*) scale; dial (of machines); proportion, ratio; stage, stopping place; measuring rule; *Naut.* port of call. **e. de toldilla,** companion ladder. *Mus.* **e. mayor,** major scale. **e. menor,** minor scale. *Naut.* **hacer e. en un puerto,** to call at a port

escalada /eska'laða/ *f,* escalade

escalafón /eskala'fon/ *m,* salary scale; roll, list

escalamiento /eskala'miento/ *m,* scaling, climbing; storming

escalar /eska'lar/ *vt* to scale; climb, ascend; storm, assail, enter or leave violently

escaldadura /eskalda'ðura/ *f,* scalding; scald

escaldar /eskal'dar/ *vt* to scald; make red-hot; *vr* scald or burn oneself. **Gato escaldado del agua fría huye,** Once bitten, twice shy

escalera /eska'lera/ *f,* staircase; stair. **e. abajo,** below stairs. **e. de caracol,** spiral staircase. **e. de mano,** ladder. **e. de tijera,** stepladder. **e. móvil,** escalator

escalfar /eskal'far/ *vt* to poach (eggs); burn (bread)

escalinata /eskali'nata/ *f,* outside staircase or flight of steps, perron

escalofrío /eskalo'frio/ *m,* (gen. *pl*) shiver, shudder

escalón /eska'lon/ *m,* step, stair; rung (of a ladder); *Fig.* steppingstone; grade, rank. **en escalones,** in steps

escalpar /eskal'par/ *vt* to scalp

escalpelo /eskal'pelo/ *m,* scalpel

escama /es'kama/ *f, Zool.* scale; anything scale-shaped; flake; suspicion, resentment

escamar /eska'mar/ *vt* to scale (fish); make suspicious. *vr Inf.* be suspicious or disillusioned

escamondar /eskamon'dar/ *vt Agr.* to prune

escamoso /eska'moso/ *a* scaly

escamotear /eskamote'ar/ *vt* to make disappear; palm (in conjuring); steal

escamoteo /eskamo'teo/ *m,* disappearance; stealing

escampada /eskam'paða/ *f, Inf.* clear interval on a rainy day

escampar /eskam'par/ *vi* to cease raining; clear up (of the weather, sky); stop (work, etc.)

escamujar /eskamu'har/ *vt Agr.* to cut out superfluous wood (of trees, etc.)

escanciar /eskan'siar; eskan'θiar/ *vt* to pour out wine; *vi* drink wine

escandalizar /eskandali'sar; eskandali'θar/ *vt* to shock, scandalize; disturb with noise; *vr* be vexed or irritated

escandallo /eskan'dayo; eskan'daʎo/ *m, Naut.* deep-sea lead; random test

escándalo /es'kandalo/ *m,* scandal; commotion, uproar; bad example; viciousness; astonishment

escandaloso /eskanda'loso/ *a* disgraceful, scandalous; turbulent

Escandinavia /eskandi'naβia/ Scandinavia

escandinavo /eskandi'naβo/ **(-va)** *a* and *n* Scandinavian

escantillón /eskanti'yon; eskanti'ʎon/ *m,* template, pattern; rule

escaño /es'kaɲo/ *m,* bench with a back

escapada /eska'paða/ *f,* escape; escapade

escapar /eska'par/ *vi* to spur on (a horse); *vi* escape; flee; avoid, evade; *vr* escape; leak (gas, etc.). **Se me escapó su nombre,** His name escaped me. **e. por un pelo,** to have a narrow escape

escaparate /eskapa'rate/ *m,* showcase, cabinet; shop window

escapatoria /eskapa'toria/ *f,* escape, flight; *Inf.* way out, loophole

escape /es'kape/ *m,* flight; evasion; escape (gas, etc.); *Auto.* exhaust. **a e.,** at full speed

escápula /es'kapula/ *f,* scapula

escaque /es'kake/ *m,* square (chessboard or checkerboard); *pl* chess

escaqueado /eskake'aðo/ *a* checked, worked in squares

escara /es'kara/ *f,* scar

escarabajo /eskara'βaho/ *m,* beetle, scarab; *Fig. Inf.* dwarf; *pl Inf.* scrawl

escaramuza /eskara'musa; eskara'muθa/ *f,* skirmish

escaramuzar /eskaramu'sar; eskaramu'θar/ *vi* to skirmish

escarapela /eskara'pela/ *f,* cockade, rosette; brawl

escarbadientes /eskarβa'ðientes/ *m,* toothpick

escarbar /eskar'βar/ *vt* to scratch, scrabble (fowls); root, dig; rake out (the fire); inquire into

escarcha /es'kartʃa/ *f,* frost

escarchar /eskar'tʃar/ *vt Cul.* to frost, ice; spread with frosting; *vi* freeze lightly

escarda /es'karða/ *f,* weeding; *Fig.* weeding out

escardador /eskarða'ðor/ **(-ra)** *n* weeder

escardar /eskar'ðar/ *vt* to weed; *Fig.* separate good from bad

escarificación /eskarifika'sion; eskarifika'θion/ *f,* scarification

escarlata /eskar'lata/ *f,* scarlet; scarlet cloth

escarlatina /eskarla'tina/ *f*, scarlet fever, scarlatina

escarmentar /eskarmen'tar/ *vt irr* to reprehend or punish severely; *vi* learn from experience, be warned. See **acertar**

escarmiento /eskar'miento/ *m*, disillusionment, experience; warning; punishment, fine

escarnecedor /eskarneseðor; eskarneθe'ðor/ **(-ra)** *a* mocking. *n* mocker

escarnecer /eskarne'ser; eskarne'θer/ *vt irr* to mock. See **conocer**

escarnio /es'karnio/ *m*, gibe, jeer, *Poet.* scornful poem

escarola /eska'rola/ *f*, endive; frilled ruff

escarpa /es'karpa/ *f*, steep slope, declivity; escarpment; *Mexico* pavement

escarpado /eskar'paðo/ *a* steep, precipitous

escarpín /eskar'pin/ *m*, pump, slipper

escasear /eskase'ar/ *vt* to dole out, give grudgingly; save, husband; *vi* be scarce or short; grow less

escasez /eska'ses; eska'seθ/ *f*, meanness, frugality; want; shortage, scarcity

escaso /es'kaso/ *a* scarce; short; bare; parsimonious

escatimar /eskati'mar/ *vt* to cut down, curtail

escatimoso /eskati'moso/ *a* malicious, guileful

escayola /eska'yola/ *f*, plaster of Paris

escena /es'sena; es'θena/ *f*, *Theat.* stage; scene; scenery; theater, drama; spectacle, sight; episode, incident. **director de e.**, producer. **poner en e.**, *Theat.* to produce

escenario /esse'nario; esθe'nario/ *m*, *Theat.* stage; scenario

escénico /es'seniko; es'θeniko/ *a* scenic

escenografía /essenogra'fia; esθenogra'fia/ *f*, scenography

escenógrafo /esse'nografo; esθe'nografo/ **(-fa)** *n* scenographer, scene painter

escepticismo /essepti'sismo; esθepti'θismo/ *m*, scepticism

escéptico /es'septiko; es'θeptiko/ **(-ca)** *a* sceptical. *n* sceptic

escindir /essin'dir; esθin'dir/ *vt* to split

escisión /essi'sion; esθi'sion/ *f*, cleavage, split; splitting; schism; disagreement

esclarecer /esklare'ser; esklare'θer/ *vt irr* to illuminate; ennoble, make illustrious; *Fig.* enlighten; elucidate; *vi* dawn. See **conocer**

esclarecido /esklare'siðo; esklare'θiðo/ *a* distinguished, illustrious

esclavina /eskla'βina/ *f*, short cape

esclavitud /esklaβi'tuð/ *f*, slavery

esclavizar /esklaβi'sar; esklaβi'θar/ *vt* to enslave

esclavo /es'klaβo/ **(-va)** *n* slave. *a* enslaved. *f*, slave bracelet; ID bracelet

esclerosis /eskle'rosis/ *f*, sclerosis

esclerótica /eskle'rotika/ *f*, sclerotic

esclusa /es'klusa/ *f*, lock; sluice gate; weir

esclusero, -a /esklu'sero/ *mf*, lock keeper

escoba /es'koβa/ *f*, broom, brush; *Bot.* yellow broom

escobada /esko'βaða/ *f*, sweep, stroke (of a broom)

escobar /esko'βar/ *vt* to sweep with a broom

escobazo /esko'βaso; esko'βaθo/ *m*, brush with a broom

escobero, -a /esko'βero/ brush maker; brush seller

escobilla /esko'βiya; esko'βiʎa/ *f*, brush

escocer /esko'ser; esko'θer/ *vi irr* to smart; *Fig.* sear; *vr* hurt, smart; be chafed. See **mover**

escocés /esko'ses; esko'θes/ **(-esa)** *a* Scots, Scottish. *n* Scot

Escocia /eskosia; es'koθia/ Scotland

escoda /es'koða/ *f*, claw hammer

escofina /esko'fina/ *f*, rasp, file

escoger /esko'her/ *vt* to choose, select

escogido /esko'hiðo/ *a* choice, select

escolar /esko'lar/ *a* school; pupil. *m*, pupil

escolasticismo /eskolasti'sismo; eskolasti'θismo/ *m*, scholasticism

escolástico /esko'lastiko/ *a* scholastic

escoleta /esko'leta/ *f*, *Mexico* amateur band

escollera /esko'yera; esko'ʎera/ *f*, breakwater, sea wall, jetty

escollo /es'koyo; es'koʎo/ *m*, reef; danger, risk; difficulty, obstacle

escolopendra /eskolo'pendra/ *f*, centipede; hart's-tongue fern

escolta /es'kolta/ *f*, escort, guard

escoltar /eskol'tar/ *vt* to escort; guard, conduct

escombrar /eskom'brar/ *vt* to remove obstacles, free of rubbish; *Fig.* clean up

escombro /es'kombro/ *m*, debris, rubble, rubbish; mackerel

esconder /eskon'der/ *vt* to hide, conceal; *Fig.* contain, embrace; *vr* hide

escondidas, a /eskon'diðas, a/ *adv* secretly

escondite, escondrijo /eskon'dite, eskon'driho/ *m*, hiding place. **jugar al escondite**, to play hide-and-seek

escopeta /esko'peta/ *f*, shotgun. **e. de aire comprimido**, air gun, popgun. **e. de pistón**, repercussion gun. **e. de viento**, air gun

escopetazo /eskope'taso; eskope'taθo/ *m*, gunshot; gunshot wound; *Fig.* bombshell

escopetear /eskopete'ar/ *vt* to shoot repeatedly

escopetero /eskope'tero/ *m*, musketeer; gunsmith; man with a gun

escoplear /eskople'ar/ *vt* to notch; chisel; gouge

escoplo /es'koplo/ *m*, chisel

escorbuto /eskor'βuto/ *m*, scurvy

escoria /es'koria/ *f*, dross, slag; scoria, volcanic ash; *Fig.* dregs

escorial /esko'rial/ *m*, slag heap

escorpión /eskor'pion/ *m*, scorpion; Scorpio

escorzo /es'korso; es'korθo/ *m*, *Art.* foreshortening

escotado /eskota'ðo/ *a* low-cut (of dresses)

escotadura /eskota'ðura/ *a* low neck (of a dress); piece cut out of something; *Theat.* large trapdoor; recess

escotar /esko'tar/ *vt* to cut low in the neck (of dresses); pay one's share (of expenses)

escote /es'kote/ *m*, low neck (of a dress); shortness (of sleeves); share (of expenses); lace yoke

escotilla /esko'tiya; esko'tiʎa/ *f*, *Naut.* hatch

escozor /esko'sor; esko'θor/ *m*, smart, pricking pain; irritation, prickle; heartache

escriba /es'kriβa/ *m*, (*Jewish hist.*) scribe

escribanía /eskriβa'nia/ *f*, secretaryship; notaryship; bureau, office; writing case; inkstand

escribano /eskri'βano/ *m*, notary public; secretary

escribiente /eskri'βiente/ *mf* clerk

escribir /eskri'βir/ *vt* to write; *vr* enlist; enroll; correspond by writing. *Past Part.* **escrito**

escrito /es'krito/ *m*, writing, manuscript; literary or scientific work; *Law.* writ. **por e.**, in writing

escritor /eskri'tor/ **(-ra)** *n* writer, author

escritorio /eskri'torio/ *m*, desk; *Lat. Am.* office

escritura /eskri'tura/ *f*, writing; handwriting; *Law.* deed; literary work. **Sagrada E.**, Holy Scripture

escrófula /es'krofula/ *f*, scrofula

escrofuloso /eskrofu'loso/ *a* scrofulous

escroto /es'kroto/ *m*, scrotum

escrúpulo /es'krupulo/ *m*, scruple, qualm; conscientiousness; scruple (pharmacy)

escrupulosidad /eskrupulosi'ðað/ *f*, conscientiousness, scrupulousness

escrupuloso /eskrupu'loso/ *a* scrupulous; exact, accurate

escrutador /eskruta'ðor/ **(-ra)** *n* scrutinizer. *a* examining, inspecting

escrutar /eskru'tar/ *vt* to scrutinize, examine; count (votes)

escrutinio /eskru'tinio/ *m*, scrutiny, examination; count (votes)

escuadra /es'kuaðra/ *f*, carpenter's square; architect's square; *Nav.* fleet; *Aer.* squadron; *Mil.* squad. **e. de agrimensor,** *Surv.* cross-staff

escuadrar /eskuaðrar/ *vt* (and *Mas.*) to square

escuadrilla /eskuað'riya; eskuað'riʎa/ *f*, squadron (airplanes, small ships)

escuadrón /eskuað'ron/ *m*, squadron

escualidez /eskuali'ðes; eskuali'ðeθ/ *f*, squalor, sordidness

escuálido /es'kualiðo/ a filthy, squalid; sordid; thin
escucha /es'kutʃa/ f, listening; peephole; *Mil.* sentinel
escuchar /esku'tʃar/ vt to listen; attend to, heed; vr like the sound of one's own voice
escudar /esku'ðar/ vt to shield, protect
escudero /esku'ðero/ m, squire, page; gentleman; shield maker
escudete /esku'ðete/ m, escutcheon; shield; gusset; white water lily
escudilla /esku'ðiya; esku'ðiʎa/ f, bowl
escudo /es'kuðo/ m, shield; escudo; escutcheon; protection, defense; ward (of a keyhole)
escudriñador /eskuðriɲa'ðor/ (-ra) a searching; curious, prying. n scrutinizer; pryer
escudriñar /eskuðri'ɲar/ vt to scrutinize; scan; investigate; pry into
escuela /es'kuela/ f, school; school building; style; (*Lit.* and *Art.*) school. **e. de artes y oficios,** industrial school. **e. industrial,** technical school. **e. normal,** normal school
escuelante /eskue'lante/ m, *Mexico* schoolmaster
escueto /es'kueto/ a dry, bare, unadorned; simple, exact; unencumbered
escuincle /es'kuinkle/ mf, *Mexico* child
esculpir /eskul'pir/ vt to sculpture; engrave
escultor /eskul'tor/ (-ra) n sculptor
escultórico /eskul'toriko/ a sculptural
escultura /eskul'tura/ f, sculpture; carving; modeling
escupidera /eskupi'ðera/ f, spittoon
escupir /esku'pir/ vi to expectorate; vt *Fig.* spit out; cast away, throw out
escurreplatos /eskurre'platos/ m, dishrack, draining rack
escurrido /esku'rriðo/ a narrow-hipped; skintight (of skirts)
escurridor /eskurri'ðor/ m, colander, sieve; dishrack; drainingboard
escurriduras /eskurri'ðuras/ f pl, lees, dregs
escurrir /esku'rrir/ vt to drain to the dregs; wring, press out, drain; vi trickle, drip; slip, slide; vr slip away, edge away; escape, slip out; skid
esdrújulo /esðru'hulo/ a *Gram.* of words where the stress falls on the antepenultimate syllable
ese /'ese/ f, name of letter S; S-shaped link (in a chain). *Inf.* **andar haciendo eses,** to reel about drunkenly
ese /'ese/ m, dem a (f, **esa,** pl **esos, esas**) that; those. **ése,** m, dem pron (f, **ésa.** neut **eso.** pl **ésos, ésas**) that one; the former (e.g. *Me gusta éste, pero ése no me gusta,* I like this one, but I do not like that one)
esencia /e'sensia; e'senθia/ f, essence, nature, character; extract; *Chem.* essence
esencial /esen'sial; esen'θial/ a essential
esfera /es'fera/ f, *Geom.* sphere, globe, ball; sky; rank; face, dial; province, scope
esférico /es'feriko/ a spherical
esfinge /es'finhe/ f, sphinx
esforzado /esfor'saðo; esfor'θaðo/ a valiant, courageous; spirited
esforzador /esforsa'ðor; esforθa'ðor/ a encouraging
esforzar /esfor'sar; esfor'θar/ vt irr to encourage; invigorate; vr make an effort. See **contar**
esfuerzo /es'fuerso; es'fuerθo/ m, effort; courage; spirit; vigor; exertion, strain; *Mech.* stress. **sin e.,** effortless
esfumar /esfu'mar/ vt *Art.* shade; *Art.* stump; dim; vr disappear
esfumino /esfu'mino/ m, *Art.* stump
esgrima /es'grima/ f, (art of) fencing
esgrimidor /esgrimi'ðor/ m, fencer, swordsman
esgrimir /esgri'mir/ vt to fence; fend off
esguince /es'ginse; es'ginθe/ m, dodging, twist; expression or gesture of repugnance; *Med.* sprain
eslabón /esla'βon/ m, link (in a chain); steel for producing fire. **e. perdido,** *Fig.* missing link
eslabonar /eslaβo'nar/ vt to link; connect, unite
eslavo /es'laβo/ (-va) a Slavic. n Slav
eslora /es'lora/ f, *Naut.* length (of a ship)
eslovaco /eslo'βako/ (-ca) a Slovakian. n Slovak

esmaltador /esmalta'ðor/ (-ra) n enameler
esmaltar /esmal'tar/ vt to enamel; decorate, adorn
esmalte /es'malte/ m, enamel; enamelwork; smalt; brilliance
esmerado /esme'raðo/ a careful, painstaking
esmeralda /esme'ralda/ f, emerald
esmerar /esme'rar/ vt to polish; vr (*with en*) take great pains with (or to)
esmeril /es'meril/ m, emery
esmerilar /esmeri'lar/ vt to polish with emery
esmero /es'mero/ m, great care, conscientiousness
esmoladera /esmola'ðera/ f, grindstone
esnob /es'noβ/ a snobbish. mf snob
eso /'eso/ neut dem pron that; the fact that; that idea, affair, etc.; about (of time) (e.g. *Vendrá a las nueve,* He will come about nine o'clock). **Eso** refers to an abstraction, never to one definite object. **No me gusta e.,** I don't like that kind of thing. **e. es,** that's it. **por e.,** therefore, for that reason
esófago /e'sofago/ m, esophagus
esotérico /eso'teriko/ a esoteric
espaciar /espa'siar; espa'θiar/ vt to space; *Print.* lead; vr spread oneself, enlarge (upon)
espacio /es'pasio; es'paθio/ m, space; capacity; interval, duration; slowness; *Print.* lead
espaciosidad /espasiosi'ðað; espaθiosi'ðað/ f, spaciousness; capacity
espada /es'paða/ f, sword; matador; swordsman; (cards) spade. **entre la e. y la pared,** *Fig.* between a rock and a hard place; between undesirable alternatives.
espadachín /espaða'tʃin/ m, good swordsman; bully, quarrelsome fellow
espadaña /espa'ðaɲa/ f, open belfry; gladiolus
espadería /espaðe'ria/ f, sword cutler's workshop or shop
espadero /espa'ðero/ m, sword cutler
espadín /espa'ðin/ m, small dress sword
espalda /es'palda/ f, *Anat.* back (often pl); pl rear, back portion; *Mil.* rear guard. **de espaldas,** with one's (its, his, etc.) back turned; on one's (its, etc.) back
espaldar /espal'dar/ m, backpiece of a cuirass; back (of chair); garden trellis, espalier
espaldarazo /espalda'raso; espalda'raθo/ m, accolade
espaldera /espal'dera/ f, espalier, trellis
espantadizo /espanta'ðiso; espanta'ðiθo/ a easily frightened
espantapájaros /espanta'paharos/ m, scarecrow
espantar /espan'tar/ vt to frighten, terrify; chase off; vr be amazed; be scared
espanto /es'panto/ m, terror, panic; dismay; amazement; threat
espantoso /espan'toso/ a horrible, terrifying, awesome; amazing
España /es'paɲa/ Spain
español /espa'ɲol/ (-la) a Spanish. n Spaniard. m, Spanish (language). **a la española,** in Spanish fashion
españolía /espaɲo'lia/ f, Spanish colony, Spanish community (outside Spain)
españolismo /espaɲo'lismo/ m, love of things Spanish; Hispanicism
españolizar /espaɲoli'sar; espaɲoli'θar/ vt to hispanize; vr adopt Spanish customs
esparadrapo /espara'ðrapo/ m, court plaster
esparavel /espara'βel/ m, casting net
esparcimiento /esparsi'miento; esparθi'miento/ m, scattering; naturalness, frankness; geniality
esparcir /espar'sir; espar'θir/ vt to scatter, sprinkle; disperse; spread, publish abroad; entertain; vr be scattered; amuse oneself
espárrago /es'parrago/ m, asparagus
esparraguera /esparra'gera/ f, asparagus plant; asparagus bed; asparagus dish
Esparta /es'parta/ Sparta
espartano /espar'tano/ (-na) a and n Spartan
espartería /esparte'ria/ f, esparto industry, esparto shop
esparto /es'parto/ m, esparto grass
espasmo /es'pasmo/ m, spasm

espasmódico /espas'moðiko/ a spasmodic

espátula /es'patula/ f, spatula; palette knife

especia /es'pesia; es'peθia/ f, spice. **nuez de e.**, nutmeg

especial /espe'sial; espe'θial/ a special; particular

especialidad /espesiali'ðað; espeθiali'ðað/ f, specialty; branch (of learning)

especialista /espesia'lista; espeθia'lista/ mf specialist

especialización /espesialisa'sion; espeθialiθa'θion/ f, specialization

especializarse /espesiali'sarse; espeθiali'θarse/ vr to specialize

especie /es'pesie; es'peθie/ f, class, kind; species; affair, matter, case; idea, image; news; pretext, appearance

especiería /espesie'ria; espeθie'ria/ f, spice trade; spice shop

especiero /espe'siero; espe'θiero/ (**-ra**) n spice merchant; spice rack

especificación /espesifika'sion; espeθifika'θion/ f, specification. **e. normalizada,** standard specification

especificar /espesifi'kar; espeθifi'kar/ vt to specify, particularize

específico /espe'sifiko; espe'θifiko/ a and m, specific patent medicine

espécimen /es'pesimen; es'peθimen/ m, specimen, sample

especioso /espe'sioso; espe'θioso/ a lovely, perfect; specious

espectacular /espektaku'lar/ a spectacular

espectáculo /espek'takulo/ m, spectacle, sight; show, display

espectador /espekta'ðor/ (**-ra**) n spectator

espectral /espek'tral/ a spectral; faint, dim

espectro /es'pektro/ m, phantom, specter; Phys. spectrum

especulación /espekula'sion; espekula'θion/ f, conjecture; Com. speculation

especulador /espekula'ðor/ (**-ra**) n speculator

especular /espeku'lar/ vt to examine, look at; (with en) reflect on, consider; vi Com. speculate

especulativo /espekula'tiβo/ a speculative; thoughtful, meditative

espejería /espehe'ria/ f, mirror shop or factory

espejero /espe'hero/ m, mirror manufacturer or seller

espejismo /espe'hismo/ m, mirage; illusion

espejo /es'peho/ m, mirror; Fig. model. **e. de cuerpo entero,** full-length mirror. **e. retrovisor,** rearview mirror

espejuelo /espe'huelo/ m, small mirror; Mineral. selenite; Mineral. sheet of talc; pl lenses, eyeglasses

espeluznante /espelus'nante; espeluθ'nante/ a hairraising

espeluznar /espelus'nar; espeluθ'nar/ vt to dishevel, untidy (hair, etc.); vr stand on end (hair)

espera /es'pera/ f, waiting; expectation; Law. adjournment; caution, restraint; Law. respite

esperantista /esperan'tista/ mf Esperantist

esperanto /espe'ranto/ m, Esperanto

esperanza /espe'ransa; espe'ranθa/ f, hope

esperanzar /esperan'sar; esperan'θar/ vt to inspire hope in

esperar /espe'rar/ vt to hope; expect; await; (with en) have faith in. **e. sentado,** Fig. Inf. to whistle for

esperma /es'perma/ f, sperm, semen. **e. de ballena,** spermaceti

esperpento /esper'pento/ m, Inf. scarecrow, grotesque; folly, madness; fantastic dramatic composition

espesar /espe'sar/ vt to thicken; make closer; tighten (fabrics); vr thicken; grow denser or thicker

espeso /es'peso/ a thick; dense; greasy, dirty

espesor /espe'sor/ m, thickness; density

espesura /espe'sura/ f, thickness; density; thicket; filth

espetar /espe'tar/ vt Cul. to spit, skewer; pierce; Inf. utter, give; vr be stiff or affected; Inf. push oneself in, intrude

espetera /espe'tera/ f, kitchen or pot rack

espetón /espe'ton/ m, Cul. spit; poker; large pin

espía /es'pia/ mf spy. f, Naut. warp

espiar /es'piar/ vt to spy upon, watch; vi Naut. warp

espiche /es'pitʃe/ m, sharp-pointed weapon or instrument; spit, spike

espiga /es'piga/ f, Bot. spike, ear; sprig; peg; tang, shank (of sword); tenon, dowel; Naut. masthead; Herald. garb

espigador /espiga'ðor/ (**-ra**) n gleaner

espigar /espi'gar/ vt to glean; tenon; vi Bot. begin to show the ear or spike; vr Bot. bolt; shoot up, grow (persons)

espigón /espi'gon/ m, sting; sharp point; breakwater; bearded spike (corn, etc.)

espigueo /espi'geo/ m, gleaning

espiguero /espi'gero/ m, Mexico granary

espín /es'pin/ m, porcupine

espina /es'pina/ f, thorn; prickle; splinter; fish bone; Anat. spine; suspicion, doubt

espinaca /espi'naka/ f, spinach

espinal /espi'nal/ a spinal

espinar /espi'nar/ m, thorn brake; Fig. awkward position. vt to prick, wound, hurt

espinazo /espi'naso; espi'naθo/ m, backbone

espinilla /espi'niya; espi'niʎa/ f, shinbone; blackhead

espinoso /espi'noso/ a thorny; difficult, intricate

espión /es'pion/ m, See **espía**

espionaje /espio'nahe/ m, espionage; spying

espira /es'pira/ f, (Geom. Archit.) helix; turn, twist (of winding stairs); whorl (of a shell)

espiración /espira'sion; espira'θion/ f, expiration; respiration

espiral /espi'ral/ a spiral. f, Geom. spiral; spiral watchspring

espirar /espi'rar/ vt to exhale, breathe out; inspire; encourage; vi breathe; breathe out; Poet. blow (wind)

espiritisimo /espiri'tisimo/ m, spiritualism

espiritista /espiri'tista/ a spiritualist. mf spiritualist

espiritoso /espiri'toso/ a lively, active, spirited; spirituous

espíritu /es'piritu/ m, spirit; apparition, specter; soul; intelligence, mind; mood, temper, outlook; underlying principle, spirit; devil (gen. pl) vigor, ardor, vivacity; Chem. essence; Chem. spirits; turn of mind. **E. Santo,** Holy Spirit

espiritual /espiri'tual/ a spiritual

espiritualidad /espirituali'ðað/ f, spirituality

espiritualismo /espiritua'lismo/ m, Philos. spiritualism

espita /es'pita/ f, spigot, tap; Inf. tippler

esplender /esplen'der/ vi Poet. to shine

esplendidez /esplendiðes; esplendi'ðeθ/ f, liberality, abundance; splendor, pomp

espléndido /es'plendiðo/ a magnificent; liberal; resplendent (gen. pl)

esplendor /esplen'dor/ m, splendor, brilliance; distinction, nobility

esplendoroso /esplendo'roso/ a splendid, brilliant, radiant

espliego /es'pliego/ m, lavender

esplín /es'plin/ m, spleen, melancholy

espolada /espo'laða/ f, prick with the spur

espolear /espole'ar/ vt to prick with the spur; encourage, stimulate

espoleta /espo'leta/ f, fuse (of explosives); breastbone (of fowls); wishbone. **e. de tiempo, e. graduada,** time fuse. **e. de seguridad,** safety fuse

espolón /espo'lon/ m, spur (of a bird or mountain range); Naut. ram; breakwater; buttress; Naut. fender

espolvorear /espolβore'ar/ vt to sprinkle with powder

esponja /es'ponha/ f, sponge

esponjadura /esponha'ðura/ f, sponging

esponjar /espon'har/ vt to make spongy; sponge; vr swell with pride; Inf. bloom with health

esponjera /espon'hera/ f, sponge holder

esponjosidad /esponhosi'ðað/ f, sponginess

esponjoso /espon'hoso/ a spongy, porous

esponsales /espon'sales/ m pl, betrothal; marriage contract

espontaneidad /espontanei'ðað/ f, spontaneity
espontáneo /espon'taneo/ a spontaneous
espora /es'pora/ f, spore
esporádico /espo'raðiko/ a sporadic
esportillo /espor'tiyo; espor'tiʎo/ m, bass, frail
esposa /es'posa/ f, wife; pl handcuffs
esposo /es'poso/ m, husband; pl husband and wife
espuela /es'puela/ f, spur; stimulus; (Ornith. Bot.) spur. **e. de caballero,** larkspur
espuelar /espue'lar/ vt, Lat. Am. to spur, spur on
espulgar /espul'gar/ vt to delouse; examine carefully
espuma /es'puma/ f, froth, foam; Cul. scum; Fig. the best of anything, flower; Inf. **crecer como la e.,** to flourish like weeds
espumadera /espuma'ðera/ f, skimming ladle
espumajear /espumahe'ar/ vi to foam at the mouth
espumajoso /espuma'hoso/ a frothy, foaming
espumar /espu'mar/ vt to skim (soup, etc.); vi foam; increase rapidly
espumilla /espu'mija; espu'miʎa/ f, Lat. Am. meringue
espumoso /espu'moso/ a frothy, foaming
espurio /es'purio/ a bastard; spurious
esputo /es'puto/ m, sputum
esqueje /es'kehe/ m, Agr. cutting
esquela /es'kela/ f, note; (printed) card
esqueleto /eske'leto/ m, skeleton; Mexico, blank, form (to be filled out) Inf. skinny person; framework
esquema /es'kema/ f, diagram, layout sketch; scheme, plan. **e. de una máquina,** drawing of a machine
esquemático /eske'matiko/ a schematic; diagrammatic
esquematizar /eskemati'sar; eskemati'θar/ vt to plan, outline
esquí /es'ki/ m, ski, snowshoe
esquiador, -a /eskia'ðor/ mf, skier
esquiar /es'kiar/ vi to ski
esquila /es'kila/ f, cattle bell; small bell, hand bell; sheep shearing; (Ichth. Bot.) squill
esquilador /eskila'ðor/ a shearing. m, sheep shearer
esquiladora /eskila'ðora/ f, shearing machine
esquilar /eski'lar/ vt to shear, clip (sheep, etc.)
esquileo /eski'leo/ m, shearing; shearing time or place
esquilmar /eskil'mar/ vt to harvest; impoverish
esquilmo /es'kilmo/ m, harvest
esquimal /eski'mal/ a and mf Eskimo
esquina /es'kina/ f, corner; Lat. Am. corner shop; village shop
esquinado /eski'naðo/ a having corners; Fig. difficult to approach (people)
esquirol /eski'rol/ m, Inf. strikebreaker, blackleg
esquisto /es'kisto/ m, Mineral. slate; shale
esquivada /eski'βaða/ f, Lat. Am. evasion
esquivar /eski'βar/ vt to avoid; vr slip away, disappear; excuse oneself
esquivez /eski'βes; eski'βeθ/ f, unsociableness; unfriendliness, aloofness
esquivo /es'kiβo/ a unsociable, elusive, aloof
estabilidad /estaβili'ðað/ f, stability; fastness (of colors)
estabilizar /estaβili'sar; estaβili'θar/ vt to stabilize
estable /es'taβle/ a stable; fast (of colors)
establecer /estaβle'ser; estaβle'θer/ vt irr to establish, found, institute; decree; vr take up residence; open (a business firm). See **conocer**
establecimiento /estaβlesi'miento; estaβleθi'miento/ m, law, statute; foundation, institution; establishment
establo /es'taβlo/ m, stable
estaca /es'taka/ f, stake, pole; Agr. cutting; cudgel
estacada /esta'kaða/ f, fence; Mil. palisade; place fixed for a duel
estacar /esta'kar/ vt to stake; fence; tie to a stake; vr Fig. be as still as a post
estación /esta'sion; esta'θion/ f, position, situation; season; station (railroad, etc.); depot; time, period; stop, halt; building, headquarters; Bot. habitat; (Surv. Geom. Eccl.) station

estacional /estasio'nal; estaθio'nal/ a seasonal; Astron. stationary
estacionamiento /estasiona'miento; estaθiona'miento/ m, stationing; Auto. parking
estacionar /estasio'nar; estaθio'nar/ vt to station, place; Auto. park (a car); vr remain stationary; place oneself
estacionario /estasio'nario; estaθio'nario/ a motionless; Astron. stationary. m, stationer
estacionómetro /estasio'nometro; estaθio'nometro/ m, Mexico parking meter
estada /es'taða/ f, sojourn
estadía /esta'ðia/ f, stay, sojourn; Art. sitting (of a model)
estadio /es'taðio/ m, racetrack; stadium; furlong
estadista /esta'ðista/ mf. statistician; statesman, stateswoman
estadística /esta'ðistika/ f, statistics
estadístico /esta'ðistiko/ a statistical
estadizo /esta'ðiso; esta'ðiθo/ a stagnant
estado /es'taðo/ m, state; condition; rank, position; Polit. state; profession; status; Com. statement. **e. de guerra,** state of war; martial law. **e. mayor central,** (Nav. Mil.) general staff. **e. tapón,** Polit. buffer state. **tomar e.,** to marry; Eccl. profess; be ordained a priest
Estados Unidos de América /es'taðos u'niðos de a'merika/ United States of America
estadounidense /estaðouni'ðense/ a United States
estafa /es'tafa/ f, swindle
estafador /estafa'ðor/ (-ra) n swindler
estafar /esta'far/ vt to swindle
estafeta /esta'feta/ f, courier, messenger; branch post office; diplomatic pouch
estagnación /estagna'sion; estagna'θion/ f, stagnation
estalactita /estalak'tita/ f, stalactite
estalagmita /estalag'mita/ f, stalagmite
estallar /esta'yar; esta'ʎar/ vi to explode; burst; Fig. break out
estallido /esta'yiðo; esta'ʎiðo/ m, explosion, report; crash, crack; Fig. outbreak; Auto. **e. de un neumático,** blowout (of a tire)
estambre /es'tambre/ m, woolen yarn, worsted; stamen
estameña /esta'meɲa/ f, serge
estampa /es'tampa/ f, illustration, picture; print; aspect; printing press; track, step; Metall. boss, stud
estampación /estampa'sion; estampa'θion/ f, stamping; printing; imprinting. **e. en seco,** tooling (of a book)
estampado /estam'paðo/ a printed (of textiles). m, textile printing; printed fabric
estampar /estam'par/ vt to print, stamp; leave the print (of); bestow, imprint. **e. en relieve,** to emboss. **e. en seco,** to tool (a book)
estampería /estampe'ria/ f, print or picture shop; trade in prints
estampero /estam'pero/ m, print dealer, picture dealer
estampido /estam'piðo/ m, report, bang, detonation; crash
estampilla /estam'piya; estam'piʎa/ f, rubber stamp; seal; Lat. Am (except Mexico), (postage) stamp
estampillar /estampi'yar; estampi'ʎar/ vt to stamp, imprint
estancación /estanka'sion; estanka'θion/ f, stagnation
estancado /estan'kaðo/ a stagnant; blocked, held up
estancar /estan'kar/ vt to check, stem; set up a monopoly; Fig. hold up (negotiations, etc.); vr be stagnant
estancia /es'tansia; es'tanθia/ f, stay, residence; dwelling; lounge, livingroom; stanza; West Hem. farm; ranch
estanciero /estan'siero; estan'θiero/ m, West Hem. farmer; rancher
estanco /es'tanko/ a Naut. watertight. m, monopoly; shop selling government monopoly goods; archive
estandarte /estan'darte/ m, standard, flag. **e. real,** royal standard

estanque /es'tanke/ *m*, tank; pool; reservoir

estanquero /estan'kero/ **(-ra)** *n* seller of government monopoly goods (tobacco, matches, etc.)

estante /es'tante/ *a* present; extant; permanent. *m*, shelf; bookcase; bin (for wine)

estantería /estante'ria/ *f*, shelving; shelves, bookcase

estantigua /estan'tigua/ *f*, hobgoblin, specter; *Fig. Inf.* scarecrow

estañador /estaɲa'ðor/ *m*, tinsmith

estañar /esta'ɲar/ *vt* to tin; solder

estaño /es'taɲo/ *m*, tin

estaquilla /esta'kiya; esta'kiʎa/ *f*, peg, cleat

estar /es'tar/ *vi irr* to be. Indicates: 1. Position or place (e.g. *Está a la puerta,* He is at the door). 2. State (e.g. *Las flores están marchitas,* The flowers are faded). 3. Used to form the continuous or progressive tense (e.g. **Siempre está (estaba) escribiendo,** He is (was) always writing). 4. In contrast to verb *ser,* indicates impermanency (e.g. *Está enfermo,* He is ill). 5. **Estar** forms an apparent passive where no action is implied (e.g. *El cuadro está pintado al óleo,* The picture is painted in oils). 6. Used in some impersonal expressions (e.g. *¡Bien está!* All right! *¡Claro está!* Of course! etc.). **e. de,** to be in, or on, or acting as (e.g. *e. de prisa,* to be in a hurry. *e. de capitán,* to be acting as a captain). **e. para,** to be on the point of; to be nearly; to be in the mood for. **e. para llover,** to be on the point of raining. **e. por,** to remain to be done; have a mind to (e.g. *La historia está por escribir,* The story remains to be written). **e. a mano (con...)** *Lat. Am.* to be even (with...), be quits (with...) **e. bien,** to be well (healthy). *Mech.* **e. bajo presión,** to have the steam up. *Polit.* **e. en el poder,** to be in office. **e. en una cuenca,** *Dominican Republic* to be broke. *¿A cómo* (*or* A **cuántos**) **estamos? ¿En qué día estamos?** What is the date? *Pres. Ind.* **estoy, estás, está, estamos, estáis, están.** *Preterite* **estuve, etc.** *Pres. Subjunc.* **esté, estés, esté, estén.** *Imperf. Subjunc.* **estuviese, etc.**

estarcir /estar'sir; estar'θir/ *vt* to stencil

estatal /esta'tal/ *a* state

estática /es'tatika/ *f*, *Mech.* statics

estático /es'tatiko/ *a* static

estatizar /estati'sar; estati'θar/ *vt*, *Lat. Am.* to nationalize

estatua /es'tatua/ *f*, statue

estatuaria /esta'tuaria/ *f*, statuary

estatuir /esta'tuir/ *vt irr* to establish, order. See **huir**

estatura /esta'tura/ *f*, stature, height (of persons)

estatuto /esta'tuto/ *m*, statute, law

estay /es'tai/ *m*, *Naut.* stay. **e. mayor,** *Naut.* mainstay

este /'este/ *m*, east

este /'este/ *m*, *dem a* this (*f*, **esta,** *pl* **estos, estas,** these). **éste,** *m*, *dem pron* this one; the latter. (*f*, **ésta,** *neut* **esto,** *pl* **éstos, éstas,** these ones; the latter) (e.g. *Aquel cuadro no es tan hermoso como éste,* That picture is not as beautiful as this one)

este /'este/ *interj* uh, um

estela /es'tela/ *f*, wake, track (of a ship)

estenografía /estenogra'fia/ *f*, shorthand

estenordeste /estenor'ðeste/ *m*, east-northeast

estentóreo /esten'toreo/ *a* stentorian

estepa /es'tepa/ *f*, steppe, arid plain

estera /es'tera/ *f*, matting

esterar /este'rar/ *vt* to cover with matting; *vi Inf.* muffle oneself up

estercoladura /esterkola'ðura/ *f*, manuring

estercolar /esterko'lar/ *vt* to manure

estercolero /esterko'lero/ *m*, manure pile; driver of a dung cart

estereoscopio /estereo'skopio/ *m*, stereoscope

esterería /estere'ria/ *f*, matting factory, matting shop

esterero /este'rero/ **(-ra)** *n* matting maker, matting seller

estéril /es'teril/ *a* sterile, barren; unfruitful, unproductive

esterilidad /esterili'ðað/ *f*, sterility; barrenness, unfruitfulness

esterilización /esterilisa'sion; esteriliθa'θion/ *f*, sterilization

esterilizador /esterilisa'ðor; esteriliθa'ðor/ *a* sterilizing. *m*, sterilizer

esterilizar /esterili'sar; esterili'θar/ *vt* to make barren; *Med.* sterilize

esterilla /este'riya; este'riʎa/ *f*, mat, matting

esterlina /ester'lina/ *a f*, sterling. **libra e.,** pound sterling

esternón /ester'non/ *m*, sternum

estero /es'tero/ *m*, salt marsh

estertor /ester'tor/ *m*, stertorous breathing, rattle

estesudeste /estesu'ðeste/ *m*, east-southeast

estética /es'tetika/ *f*, aesthetics. *a* aesthete

estético /es'tetiko/ *a* aesthetic. *m*, aesthete

estetoscopio /esteto'skopio/ *m*, stethoscope

esteva /es'teβa/ *f*, plow handle

estevado /este'βaðo/ *a* bandy-legged

estiaje /es'tiahe/ *m*, low water level (of rivers)

estibador /estiβa'ðor/ *m*, stevedore, dock worker

estibar /esti'βar/ *vt Naut.* to stow

estiércol /es'tierkol/ *m*, dung; manure

estigio /es'tihio/ *a* Stygian; (*Fig. Poet.*) infernal

estigma /es'tigma/ *m*, stigma

estigmatizar /estigmati'sar; estigmati'θar/ *vt* to brand; stigmatize; insult

estilar /esti'lar/ *vi* to be accustomed; *vt* draw up (document)

estilete /esti'lete/ *m*, stiletto, dagger; needle, hand, pointer; *Med.* stylet

estilista /esti'lista/ *mf* stylist

estilística /esti'listika/ *f*, stylism, stylistics

estilizar /estili'sar; estili'θar/ *vt* to stylize

estilo /es'tilo/ *m*, (*Art. Archit. Lit.*) style, writing instrument; gnomon, pointer; manner, way; *Bot.* style. **por el e.,** in some such way, like that

estilográfico /estilo'grafiko/ *a* stylographic. **pluma estilográfica,** fountain pen

estima /es'tima/ *f*, appreciation, esteem, consideration

estimable /esti'maβle/ *a* estimable

estimación /estima'sion; estima'θion/ *f*, valuation, estimate; regard, esteem. **e. prudente,** conservative estimate

estimado /esti'maðo/ **(-da)** *a* esteemed, respected. (correspondence) **estimados señores,** Dear Sirs/ Madams

estimar /esti'mar/ *vt* to value, estimate; esteem, judge

estimulante /estimu'lante/ *m*, *Med.* stimulant. *a* stimulating

estimular /estimu'lar/ *vt* to stimulate, excite; goad on, encourage, incite

estímulo /es'timulo/ *m*, stimulus; incitement, encouragement

estío /es'tio/ *m*, summer

estipendiar /estipen'diar/ *vt* to pay a stipend to

estipendiario /estipen'diario/ *m*, stipendiary

estipendio /esti'pendio/ *m*, stipend, pay, remuneration

estipulación /estipula'sion; estipula'θion/ *f*, stipulation; *Law.* clause, condition

estipular /estipu'lar/ *vt* to stipulate; arrange terms; *Law.* covenant

estirado /esti'raðo/ *a* stretched out; tight, stiff; wiredrawn (metals); stiff, pompous; parsimonious

estirador /estira'ðor/ *m*, wire drawer

estirar /esti'rar/ *vt* to stretch; iron roughly (clothes); *Metall.* wire-draw; dole out (money); *Fig.* stretch, go beyond the permissible; *vr* stretch oneself

estirpe /es'tirpe/ *f*, race, stock, lineage

estival /esti'βal/ *a* summer

esto /'esto/ *dem pron neut* this, this matter, this idea, etc. Always refers to abstractions, never to a definite object. **e. de,** the matter of. **e. es,** that's it; namely. **por e.,** for this reason. **a todo e.,** meanwhile

estocada /esto'kaða/ *f*, sword thrust

Estocolmo /esto'kolmo/ Stockholm

estofa /es'tofa/ *f*, *Sew.* quilting; kind, quality

estofado /esto'faðo/ *m*, stew. *a Sew.* quilted; stewed

estofar /esto'far/ *vt Sew.* to quilt; make a stew
estoicismo /estoi'sismo; estoi'θismo/ *m*, stoicism
estoico /es'toiko/ **(-ca)** *n* stoic. *a* stoical
estolidez /estoli'ðes; estoli'ðeθ/ *f*, idiocy
estólido /es'toliðo/ **(-da)** *a* idiotic. *n* idiot
estomacal /estoma'kal/ *a* stomach
estómago /es'tomago/ *m*, stomach
estomático /esto'matiko/ *a* pertaining to the mouth, oral
estomatitis /estoma'titis/ *f*, stomatitis
estonio /es'tonio/ **(-ia)** *a* and *n* Estonian. *m*, Estonian (language)
estopa /es'topa/ *f*, tow; oakum
estopilla /esto'piya; esto'piʎa/ *f*, batiste, lawn; calico, cotton cloth
estopín /esto'pin/ *m*, *Mil.* quick march
estoque /es'toke/ *m*, rapier; narrow sword
estoquear /estoke'ar/ *vt* to wound or kill with a rapier
estoqueo /esto''keo/ *m*, swordplay
estorbador /estorβa'ðor/ **(-ra)** *a* obstructive. *n* obstructer
estorbar /estor'βar/ *vt* to obstruct, impede; hinder
estorbo /es'torβo/ *m*, obstruction; hindrance, nuisance
estornino /estor'nino/ *m*, starling
estornudar /estornu'ðar/ *vi* to sneeze
estornudo /estor'nuðo/ *m*, sneezing; sneeze
estrabismo /estra'βismo/ *m*, *Med.* strabismus, squint, cast
estrada /es'traða/ *f*, road, highway
estrado /es'traðo/ *m*, dais
estrafalario /estrafa'lario/ *a Inf.* slovenly, untidy; *Inf.* eccentric, odd
estragar /estra'gar/ *vt* to corrupt, spoil, vitiate; ruin, destroy
estrago /es'trago/ *m*, devastation, destruction, ruin, havoc
estrambólico, -a /estram'βoliko/ *Lat. Am.* = **estrambótico**
estrambote /estram'bote/ *m*, refrain
estrambótico /estram'botiko/ *a Inf.* eccentric, odd, outlandish
estrangul /estraŋ'gul/ *m*, *Mus.* mouthpiece
estrangulación /estraŋgula'sion; estraŋgula'θion/ *f*, strangulation; *Auto.* throttling
estrangulador /estraŋgula'ðor/ **(-ra)** *a* strangling. *n* strangler. *m*, *Auto.* throttle
estrangular /estraŋgu'lar/ *vt* to strangle
estraperlista /estraper'lista/ *mf* black marketeer
estraperlo /estra'perlo/ *m*, black market
estratagema /estrata'hema/ *f*, stratagem, trick
estrategia /estra'tehia/ *f*, strategy
estratégico /estra'tehiko/ *a* strategic
estratego /estra'tego/ *m*, strategist
estratificación /estratifika'sion; estratifika'θion/ *f*, stratification
estrato /es'trato/ *m*, *Geol.* stratum
estratosfera /estratos'fera/ *f*, stratosphere
estraza /es'trasa; es'traθa/ *f*, rag. **papel de e.,** brown paper
estrechar /estre'tʃar/ *vt* to make narrower, tighten; hold tightly, clasp; compel, oblige; *vr* tighten oneself up; reduce one's expenses; *Fig.* tighten the bonds (of friendship, etc.). **e. la mano,** to shake hands
estrechez /estre'tʃes; estre'tʃeθ/ *f*, narrowness; tightness; scantiness; poverty, want. **e. de miras,** narrow-mindedness
estrecho /es'tretʃo/ *a* narrow; tight; intimate, close; austere, rigid; meanspirited. *m*, *Geog.* strait
estregadera /estrega'ðera/ *f*, shoe scraper; scourer
estregar /estre'gar/ *vt irr* to rub, scour, scrub, scrape, scratch. See **cegar**
estrella /es'treya; es'treʎa/ *f*, star; fortune, fate; anything star-shaped; *Fig.* star. **e. de la pantalla,** movie star. **e. de mar,** starfish. **e. de rabo,** comet. **e. fugaz,** shooting star. **tener e.,** to be born under a lucky star
estrellado /estre'yaðo; estre'ʎaðo/ *a* star-shaped; full of stars, starry; shattered, broken; fried (eggs)

estrellamar /estreya'mar; estreʎa'mar/ *f*, starfish
estrellar /estre'yar; estre'ʎar/ *vt Inf.* to shatter, break into fragments; fry (eggs); *vr* be starry or sprinkled with stars; be dashed against; fail in, come up against
estrellón /estre'yon; estre'ʎon/ *m*, large, artificial star (painted or otherwise); star-like firework; *Lat. Am.* crash
estremecer /estreme'ser; estreme'θer/ *vt irr* to cause to tremble; perturb; *vr* shudder, tremble. See **conocer**
estremecimiento /estremesi'miento; estreme-θi'miento/ *m*, shudder, trembling; agitation
estrenar /estre'nar/ *vt* to use or do for the first time; inaugurate; give the first performance of (plays, etc.); *vr* do for the first time; *Com.* make the first sale of the day
estreno /es'treno/ *m*, commencement, inauguration; first appearance; *Theat.* first performance, opening night, premiere
estrenque /es'trenke/ *m*, strong esparto rope
estrenuo /es'trenuo/ *a* strong, energetic, agile
estreñimiento /estreɲi'miento/ *m*, constipation
estreñir /estre'ɲir/ *vt* to constipate
estrépito /es'trepito/ *m*, clamor, din, great noise; fuss, show
estrepitoso /estrepi'toso/ *a* noisy, clamorous
estreptomicina /estreptomi'sina; estreptomi'θina/ *f*, streptomycin
estría /es'tria/ *f*, *Archit.* fluting, stria
estribadero /estriβa'ðero/ *m*, prop, support, strut
estribar /estri'βar/ *vi* (*with en*) to lean on, rest on, be supported by; *Fig.* be based on
estribillo /estri'βiyo; estri'βiʎo/ *m*, refrain
estribo /es'triβo/ *m*, stirrup; footboard, step, running board (of vehicles); *Archit.* buttress or pier; *Fig.* stay, support; *Anat.* stapes; *Mech.* stirrup piece. **perder los estribos,** to lose patience, forget oneself
estribor /estri'βor/ *m*, starboard
estricnina /estrik'nina/ *f*, strychnine
estricto /es'trikto/ *a* strict, exact; unbending, severe
estridente /estri'ðente/ *a* strident, shrill
estridor /estri'ðor/ *m*, strident or harsh sound; screech; creak
estro /'estro/ *m*, inspiration
estrofa /es'trofa/ *f*, strophe; verse, stanza
estropajo /estro'paho/ *m*, scourer, dishcloth; worthless person or thing
estropajoso /estropa'hoso/ *a Inf.* indistinct, stammering; dirty and ragged; tough (meat, etc.)
estropear /estrope'ar/ *vt* to spoil, damage; ruin, undo; spoil (plans, effects, etc.); ill-treat, maim; *vr* hurt oneself, be maimed; spoil, deteriorate
estropicio /estro'pisio; estro'piθio/ *m*, *Inf.* crash (of china, etc.)
estructura /estruk'tura/ *f*, structure; *Fig.* construction
estructural /estruktu'ral/ *a* structural
estruendo /es'truendo/ *m*, din, clatter; clamor, noise; ostentation
estruendoso /estruen'doso/ *a* noisy
estrujar /estru'har/ *vt* to squeeze, crush (fruit); hold tightly, press, squeeze, bruise; *Fig. Inf.* squeeze dry
estrujón /estru'hon/ *m*, squeeze, pressure; final pressing (grapes)
estuario /es'tuario/ *m*, estuary
estucado /estu'kaðo/ *m*, stucco
estucar /estu'kar/ *vt* to stucco
estuche /es'tutʃe/ *m*, case, casket, box; cover; sheath
estuco /es'tuko/ *m*, stucco; plaster
estudiantado /estuðian'taðo/ *m*, *Lat. Am.* student body, students
estudiante /estu'ðiante/ *mf* student
estudiantil /estuðian'til/ *a Inf.* student
estudiantina /estuðian'tina/ *f*, strolling band of students playing and singing, generally in aid of charity
estudiantino /estuðian'tino/ *a Inf.* student
estudiantón /estuðian'ton/ *m*, *Inf.* grind
estudiar /estu'ðiar/ *vt* to study. **e. de,** study to be a (e.g. **e.** *de rabino,* study to be a rabbi); learn; *Art.* copy
estudio /es'tuðio/ *m*, study; sketch; disquisition, dis-

sertation; studio; diligence; *Art.* study; reading room, den

estudiosidad /estuðiosi'ðað/ *f,* studiousness

estudioso /estu'ðioso/ *a* studious

estufa /es'tufa/ *f,* heating stove; hothouse; hot room (in bathhouses); drying chamber; *Elec.* heater

estufador /estufa'ðor/ *m,* stewpot or casserole

estufista /estu'fista/ *mf* stove maker or repairer, stove seller

estulto /es'tulto/ *a* foolish

estupefacción /estupefak'sion; estupefak'θion/ *f,* stupefaction

estupefacto /estupe'fakto/ *a* stupefied, stunned, amazed

estupendo /estu'pendo/ *a* wonderful, marvelous

estupidez /estupi'ðes; estupi'ðeθ/ *f,* stupidity

estúpido /es'tupiðo/ *a* stupid

estupor /estu'por/ *m, Med.* stupor; astonishment

estupro /es'tupro/ *m, Law.* rape

estuque /es'tuke/ *m,* stucco

estuquería /estuke'ria/ *f,* stuccowork

esturión /estu'rion/ *m,* sturgeon

esvástica /es'βastika/ *f,* swastika

etapa /e'tapa/ *f, Mil.* field ration; *Mil.* halt, camp; stage, juncture. **a pequeñas etapas,** by easy stages (of a journey)

etcétera /et'setera; et'θetera/ et cetera, and so on

éter /'eter/ *m,* ether; *Poet.* sky

etéreo /e'tereo/ *a* etheric; ethereal

eterizar /eteri'sar; eteri'θar/ *vt* to etherize

eternidad /eterni'ðað/ *f,* eternity

eternizar /eterni'sar; eterni'θar/ *vt* to drag out, prolong; eternize, perpetuate

eterno /e'terno/ *a* eternal, everlasting; lasting, enduring

ética /'etika/ *f,* ethics

ético /'etiko/ *a* ethical. *m,* moralist

etimología /etimolo'hia/ *f,* etymology

etimológico /etimo'lohiko/ *a* etymological

etimologista /etimolo'hista/ *mf* etymologist

etimólogo /eti'mologo/ *m,* etymologist

etiología /etiolo'hia/ *f,* etiology

etíope /e'tiope/, **etiope** *a* and *mf* Ethiopian

Etiopía /etio'pia/ Ethiopia

etiqueta /eti'keta/ *f,* etiquette; label

etiquetero /etike'tero/ *a* ceremonious, stiff; prim

étnico /'etniko/ *a* ethnic; heathen

etnografía /etnogra'fia/ *f,* ethnography

etnográfico /etno'grafiko/ *a* ethnographic

etnología /etnolo'hia/ *f,* ethnology

etnólogo /et'nologo/ *m,* ethnologist

etrusco /e'trusko/ **(-ca)** *a* and *n* Etruscan

eubolia /eu'βolia/ *f,* discretion in speech

eucalipto /euka'lipto/ *m,* eucalyptus

Eucaristía /eukaris'tia/ *f,* Eucharist

euclídeo /eu'kliðeo/ *a* Euclidean

eufemismo /eufe'mismo/ *m,* euphemism

eufonía /eufo'nia/ *f,* euphony

eufónico /eu'foniko/ *a* euphonious

euforia /eu'foria/ *f,* resistance to disease; buoyancy, well-being

eufuismo /eu'fuismo/ *m,* euphuism

eugenesia /euhe'nesia/ *f,* eugenics

eugenésico /euhe'nesiko/ *a* eugenic

eunuco /eu'nuko/ *m,* eunuch

euritmia /eu'ritmia/ *f,* eurythmics

eurítmico /eu'ritmiko/ *a* eurythmic

euro /'euro/ *m, Poet.* east wind

Europa /eu'ropa/ Europe

europeizar /europei'sar; europei'θar/ *vt* to Europeanize

europeo /euro'peo/ **(-ea)** *a* and *n* European

éuscaro /'euskaro/ *a* Basque. *m,* Basque (language)

eutanasia /euta'nasia/ *f,* euthanasia

evacuación /eβakua'sion; eβakua'θion/ *f,* evacuation

evacuar /eβa'kuar/ *vt* to vacate; evacuate, empty; finish, conclude (a business deal, etc.)

evadir /eβa'ðir/ *vt* to avoid, elude; *vr* escape; elope

evaluación /eβalua'sion; eβalua'θion/ *f,* valuation; estimation

evaluar /eβa'luar/ *vt* to evaluate, estimate; gauge; value

evangélico /eβan'heliko/ **(-ca)** *a* and *n* evangelical

evangelio /eβan'helio/ *m,* Gospel; Christianity; *Inf.* indisputable truth

evangelista /eβanhe'lista/ *m,* evangelist

evangelizar /eβanheli'sar; eβanheli'θar/ *vt* to evangelize

evaporación /eβapora'sion; eβapora'θion/ *f,* evaporation

evaporar /eβapo'rar/ **(se)** *vt* and *vr* to evaporate; disappear, vanish

evasión, evasiva /eβa'sion, eβa'siβa/ *f,* subterfuge, evasion; flight, escape

evasivo /eβa'siβo/ *a* evasive

evento /e'βento/ *m,* happening, event; contingency

eventual /eβen'tual/ *a* possible, fortuitous; accidental (expenses); extra (emoluments)

eventualidad /eβentuali'ðað/ *f,* eventuality

evicción /eβik'sion; eβik'θion/ *f, Law.* eviction

evidencia /eβi'ðensia; eβi'ðenθia/ *f,* proof, evidence. **ponerse en e.,** to put oneself forward

evidenciar /eβiðen'siar; eβiðen'θiar/ *vt* to show, make obvious

evidente /eβi'ðente/ *a* obvious, evident

evitable /eβi'taβle/ *a* avoidable

evitación /eβita'sion; eβita'θion/ *f,* avoidance

evitar /eβi'tar/ *vt* to avoid; shun, eschew

evocación /eβoka'sion; eβoka'θion/ *f,* evocation

evocador /eβoka'ðor/ *a* evocative

evocar /eβo'kar/ *vt* to evoke

evolución /eβolu'sion; eβolu'θion/ *f,* evolution; development; (*Mil. Nav.*) maneuver; change; *Geom.* involution

evolucionar /eβolusio'nar; eβoluθio'nar/ *vi* to evolve; (*Nav. Mil.*) maneuver; change, alter

evolucionismo /eβolusio'nismo; eβoluθio'nismo/ *m,* evolutionism

evolutivo /eβolu'tiβo/ *a* evolutional

ex /eks/ *prefix* out of; from; formerly

exacción /eksak'sion; eksak'θion/ *f,* exaction; tax

exacerbación /eksaserβa'sion; eksaθerβa'θion/ *f,* exacerbation

exacerbar /eksaser'βar; eksaθer'βar/ *vt* to exasperate; exacerbate

exactitud /eksakti'tuð/ *f,* exactitude; correctness; punctuality

exacto /ek'sakto/ *a* exact; correct; punctual

exactor /eksak'tor/ *m,* tax collector; tyrant, oppressor

exageración /eksahera'sion; eksahera'θion/ *f,* exaggeration

exagerador /eksahera'ðor/ **(-ra)** *a* given to exaggerating. *n* exaggerater

exagerar /eksahe'rar/ *vt* to exaggerate

exaltación /eksalta'sion; eksalta'θion/ *f,* exaltation

exaltar /eksal'tar/ *vt* to exalt, elevate; extol; *vr* grow excited or agitated

exalumna /eksa'lumna/ *f, Lat. Am.* alumna, graduate

exalumno /eksa'lumno/ *m, Lat. Am.* alumnus, graduate

examen /ek'samen/ *m,* inquiry; investigation; research; examination; *Geol.* survey. **e. parcial,** quiz (at school)

examinador /eksamina'ðor/ **(-ra)** *n* examiner

examinando /eksami'nando/ **(-da)** *n* candidate, examinee

examinar /eksami'nar/ *vt* to inquire into; investigate; inspect; examine; *vr* take an examination

exangüe /ek'saŋgue/ *a* bloodless, pale; exhausted, weak; dead

exánime /eksa'nime/ *a* lifeless; spiritless, weak

exasperación /eksaspera'sion; eksaspera'θion/ *f,* exasperation

exasperador, exasperante /eksaspera'ðor, eksaspe'rante/ *a* exasperating

exasperar /eksaspe'rar/ *vt* to exasperate; irritate, annoy

excarcelar /ekskarse'lar; ekskarθe'lar/ vt to release from jail

excavación /ekskaβa'sion; ekskaβa'θion/ f, excavation

excavador /ekskaβa'ðor/ (-ra) n excavator. f, Mech. excavator

excavar /ekska'βar/ vt to hollow; excavate; Agr. hoe (roots of plants)

excedente /eksse'ðente; eksθe'ðente/ a exceeding; excessive; surplus

exceder /eksse'ðer; eksθe'ðer/ vt to exceed; vr forget oneself, go too far

excelencia /eksse'lensia; eksθe'lenθia/ f, excellence, superiority; Excellency (title)

excelente /eksse'lente; eksθe'lente/ a excellent; Inf. first-rate

excelso /eks'selso; eks'θelso/ a lofty, high; eminent, mighty; sublime

excentricidad /ekssentrisi'ðað; eksθentriθi'ðað/ f, eccentricity

excéntrico /eks'sentriko; ek'θentriko/ a unconventional; erratic; Geom. eccentric

excepción /ekssep''sion; eksθep'θion/ f, exception

excepcional /ekssepsio'nal; eksθepθio'nal/ a exceptional

exceptuar /ekssep'tuar; eksθep'tuar/ vt to except

excerpta, excerta /eks'serpta, eks'serta; eks'θerpta, eks'θerta/ f, excerpt, extract

excesivo /eksse'siβo; eksθe'siβo/ a excessive

exceso /eks'seso; eks'θeso/ m, excess; Com. surplus; pl crimes, excesses. **e. de peso** or **e. de equipaje**, excess baggage

excisión /ekssi'sion; eksθi'sion/ f, excision

excitabilidad /ekssitaβili'ðað; eksθitaβili'ðað/ f, excitability

excitable /ekssi'taβle; eksθi'taβle/ a excitable, highstrung

excitación /ekssita'sion; eksθita'θion/ f, excitation; excitement

excitador /ekssita'ðor; eksθita'ðor/ a exciting, stimulating. m, Phys. exciter

excitar /ekssi'tar; eksθi'tar/ vt to excite, stimulate, provoke; Elec. energize; vr become agitated or excited

exclamación /eksklama'sion; eksklama'θion/ f, exclamation, interjection

exclamar /ekskla'mar/ vi to exclaim

excluir /eksk'luir/ vt irr to exclude, keep out; reject, bar. See **huir**

exclusiva /eksklu'siβa/ f, exclusion; special privilege, sole right

exclusive /eksklu'siβe/ adv exclusively; excluded

exclusivismo /eksklusi'βismo/ m, exclusivism

exclusivista /eksklusi'βista/ a exclusive. mf exclusivist

exclusivo /eksklu'siβo/ a exclusive

excomulgado /ekskomul'gaðo/ (-da) a and n Eccl. excommunicate; Inf. wicked (person)

excomulgar /ekskomul'gar/ vt to excommunicate

excomunión /ekskomu'nion/ f, excommunication

excoriar /eksko'riar/ vt to flay, excoriate; vr graze oneself

excrecencia /ekskre'sensia; ekskre'θenθia/ f, excrescence

excreción /ekskre'sion; ekskre'θion/ f, excretion

excremento /ekskre'mento/ m, excrement

excretar /ekskre'tar/ vi to excrete

excretorio /ekskre'torio/ a excretory

exculpación /ekskulpa'sion; ekskulpa'θion/ f, exoneration

exculpar /ekskul'par/ (se) vt and vr to exonerate

excursión /ekskur'sion/ f, excursion, outing, trip; Mil. incursion

excursionarse /ekskursio'narse/ vr, Lat. Am. to go on a trip, go on an outing, go on an excursion

excursionismo /ekskursio'nismo/ m, sightseeing; hiking

excursionista /ekskursio'nista/ mf excursionist; hiker

excusa /eks'kusa/ f, excuse

excusado /eksku'saðo/ a excused; exempt; unnecessary, superfluous; reserved, private. m, lavatory, toilet

excusar /eksku'sar/ vt to excuse; avoid, ward off, prevent; exempt; vr excuse oneself

execración /eksekra'sion; eksekra'θion/ f, execration

execrar /ekse'krar/ vt to execrate; denounce; loathe

exención /eksen'sion; eksen'θion/ f, exemption

exentar /eksen'tar/ vt to exempt

exento /ek'sento/ a exempt; free, liberated; open (of buildings, etc.)

exequias /ekse'kias/ f pl, funeral, obsequies

exfoliar /eksfo'liar/ vt to strip off; vr flake off

exhalación /eksala'sion; eksala'θion/ f, exhalation; shooting star; lightning; emanation, effluvium

exhalar /eksa'lar/ vt to exhale, give off; Fig. give vent to

exhibición /eksiβi'sion; eksiβi'θion/ f, exhibition

exhibicionismo /eksiβisio'nismo; eksiβiθio'nismo/ m, exhibitionism

exhibicionista /eksiβisio'nista; eksiβiθio'nista/ mf exhibitionist

exhibir /eksi'βir/ vt to exhibit, show

exhortación /eksorta'sion; eksorta'θion/ f, exhortation

exhortar /eksor'tar/ vt to exhort

exhumación /eksuma'sion; eksuma'θion/ f, exhumation

exhumar /eksu'mar/ vt to exhume, disinter

exigencia /eksi'hensia; eksi'henθia/ f, exigency; demand

exigente /eksi'hente/ a exigent

exigir /eksi'hir/ vt to exact, collect; need, require; demand

exigüidad /eksigui'ðað/ f, exiguousness

exiguo /ek'siguo/ a exiguous, meager

eximio /ek'simio/ a most excellent; illustrious

eximir /eksi'mir/ vt to exempt

existencia /eksis'tensia; eksis'tenθia/ f, existence; pl Com. stock on hand

existir /eksis'tir/ vi to exist, be; live

éxito /'eksito/ m, success; result, conclusion

exitoso, -a /eksi'toso/ a, Lat. Am. successful

exliado, -a /eks'liaðo/ Lat. Am. a exiled, in exile; mf exile

éxodo /'eksoðo/ m, exodus, emigration. **Éxodo,** Exodus. **é. rural,** rural depopulation

exoneración /eksonera'sion; eksonera'θion/ f, exoneration

exonerar /eksone'rar/ vt to exonerate; discharge (from employment)

exorbitancia /eksorβi'tansia; eksorβi'tanθia/ f, exorbitance

exorbitante /eksorβi'tante/ a exorbitant, excessive

exorcismo /eksor'sismo; eksor'θismo/ m, exorcism

exorcista /eksor'sista; eksor'θista/ m, exorcist

exorcizar /eksorsi'sar; eksorθi'θar/ vt to exorcize

exordio /ek'sorðio/ m, exordium, introduction

exornar /eksor'nar/ vt to adorn; embellish (Lit. style)

exótico /ek'sotiko/ a exotic, rare

expandir /ekspan'dir/ vt to expand

expansión /ekspan'sion/ f, expansion; recreation, hobby

expansivo /ekspan'siβo/ a expansive; communicative, frank

expatriación /ekspatria'sion; ekspatria'θion/ f, expatriation

expatriarse /ekspa'triarse/ vr to emigrate, leave one's country

expectante /ekspek'tante/ a expectant

expectativa /ekspekta'tiβa/ f, expectancy; expectation

expectoración /ekspektora'sion; ekspektora'θion/ f, expectoration

expectorar /ekspekto'rar/ vt to expectorate

expedición /ekspeði'sion; ekspeði'θion/ f, expedition; speed, promptness; Eccl. bull, dispensation; excursion; forwarding, dispatch

expediente /ekspe'ðiente/ m, Law. proceedings; file of documents; expedient, device, means; expedition, promptness; motive, reason; provision

expedir /ekspe'ðir/ vt irr to expedite; forward, send,

ship; issue, make out (checks, receipts, etc.); draw up (documents); dispatch, deal with. See **pedir**

expedito /ekspe'ðito/ *a* expeditious, speedy

expeler /ekspe'ler/ *vt* to expel, discharge, emit

expendedor /ekspende'ðor/ **(-ra)** *a* spending. *n* spender; agent; retailer; seller; *Law*. **e. de moneda falsa,** distributor of counterfeit money

expendeduría /ekspendeðou'ria/ *f,* shop where government monopoly goods are sold (tobacco, stamps, etc.)

expender /ekspen'der/ *vt* to spend (money); *Com*. retail; *Com*. sell on commission; *Law*. distribute counterfeit money

expendio /eks'pendio/ *m, Lat. Am*. tobacco shop

expensas /ek'spensas/ *f pl,* costs, charges

experiencia /ekspe'riensia; ekspe'rienθia/ *f,* experience; practice, experiment

experimentación /eksperimenta'sion; eksperimenta'θion/ *f,* experiencing

experimentar /eksperimen'tar/ *vt* to test, try; experience; feel

experimento /eksperi'mento/ *m,* experiment

experto /ek'sperto/ **(-ta)** *a* practiced, expert. *n* expert

expiación /ekspia'sion; ekspia'θion/ *f,* expiation

expiar /eks'piar/ *vt* to expiate, atone for; pay the penalty of; *Fig*. purify

expiatorio /ekspia'torio/ *a* expiatory

expiración /ekspira'sion; ekspira'θion/ *f,* expiration

expirar /ekspi'rar/ *vi* to die; *Fig*. expire; die down; exhale, expire

explanación /eksplana'sion; eksplana'θion/ *f,* leveling; explanation, elucidation

explanada /ekspla'naða/ *f,* esplanade; *Mil*. glacis

explanar /ekspla'nar/ *vt* to level; explain

explayar /ekspla'yar/ *vt* to extend, enlarge; *vr* spread oneself, enlarge (upon); enjoy an outing; confide (in)

explicación /eksplika'sion; eksplika'θion/ *f,* explanation; elucidation

explicar /ekspli'kar/ *vt* to explain; expound; interpret, elucidate; *vr* explain oneself

explicativo /eksplika'tiβo/ *a* explanatory

explícito /eks'plisito; eks'pliθito/ *a* explicit, clear

exploración /eksplora'sion; eksplora'θion/ *f,* exploration

explorador /eksplora'ðor/ *a* exploring. *m,* explorer; prospector; boy scout; *Mil*. scout

explorar /eksplo'rar/ *vt* to explore; investigate; *Med*. probe

exploratorio /eksplora'torio/ *a* exploratory

explosión /eksplo'sion/ *f,* explosion; outburst, outbreak. **hacer falsas explosiones,** *Mech*. to misfire

explosivo /eksplo'siβo/ *a* and *m,* explosive. **e. violento,** high explosive

explotación /eksplota'sion; eksplota'θion/ *f,* development, exploitation

explotar /eksplo'tar/ *vt* to work (mines); *Fig*. exploit

expoliación /ekspolia'sion; ekspolia'θion/ *f,* spoliation

expoliar /ekspo'liar/ *vt* to despoil

exponente /ekspo'nente/ *a* and *mf* exponent. *m, Math*. index

exponer /ekspo'ner/ *vt irr* to show, expose; expound; interpret; risk, jeopardize; abandon (child). See **poner**

exportación /eksporta'sion; eksporta'θion/ *f,* exportation; export

exportador /eksporta'ðor/ **(-ra)** *a* export. *n* exporter

exportar /ekspor'tar/ *vt* to export

exposición /eksposi'sion; eksposi'θion/ *f,* exposition, demonstration; petition; exhibition; *Lit*. exposition; *Photo*. exposure; orientation, position

expósito /eks'posito/ **(-ta)** *a* and *n* foundling

expositor /eksposi'tor/ **(-ra)** *a* and *n* exponent. *n* exhibitor

expremijo /ekspre'miho/ *m,* cheese vat

exprés /eks'pres/ *a* express. *m,* messenger or delivery service; express train; transport office

expresar /ekspre'sar/ *vt* to express (all meanings)

expresión /ekspre'sion/ *f,* statement, utterance;

phrase, wording; expression; presentation; manifestation; gift, present; squeezing; pressing (of fruits, etc.)

expresivo /ekspre'siβo/ *a* expressive; affectionate

expreso /eks'preso/ *a* express; clear, obvious. *m,* courier, messenger

exprimelimones /eksprimeli'mones/ *m,* **exprimidera,** *f,* lemon squeezer

exprimidor de la ropa /eksprimi'ðor de la 'rropa/ *m,* wringer, mangle

exprimir /ekspri'mir/ *vt* to squeeze, press (fruit); press, hold tightly; express, utter

expropiación /ekspropia'sion; ekspropia'θion/ *f,* expropriation

expropiar /ekspro'piar/ *vt* to expropriate; commandeer

expugnar /ekspug'nar/ *vt Mil*. to take by storm

expulsar /ekspul'sar/ *vt* to expel, eject, dismiss

expulsión /ekspul'sion/ *f,* expulsion

expurgar /ekspur'gar/ *vt* to cleanse, purify; expurgate

expurgatorio /ekspurga'torio/ *a* expurgatory. *m, Eccl*. index

exquisitez /ekskisi'tes; ekskisi'teθ/ *f,* exquisiteness

exquisito /eks'kisito/ *a* exquisite, choice; delicate, delicious

extasiarse /eksta'siarse/ *vr* to fall into ecstasy; marvel (at), delight (in)

éxtasis /'ekstasis/ *m,* ecstasy; rapture

extático /eks'tatiko/ *a* ecstatic

extemporáneo /ekstempo'raneo/ *a* untimely; inopportune, inconvenient

extender /eksten'der/ *vt irr* to spread; reach, extend; elongate; enlarge; amplify; unfold, open out, stretch; draw up (documents); make out (checks, etc.); *vr* stretch out; lie down; spread, be generalized; extend; last (of time); record; stretch, open out. **extenderse en,** to expatiate on. See **entender**

extensión /eksten'sion/ *f,* extension; expanse; length; extent; duration; extension (logic)

extensivo /eksten'siβo/ *a* extensive, spacious; extensible

extenso /eks'tenso/ *a* extensive, vast

extensor /eksten'sor/ *a* extensor. *m,* chest expander

extenuación /ekstenua'sion; ekstenua'θion/ *f,* emaciation, weakness; extenuation

extenuar /ekste'nuar/ *vt* to exhaust, weaken; *vr* become weak

exterior /ekste'rior/ *a* external; foreign (trade, etc.). *m,* outside, exterior; outward appearance

exterioridad /eksteriori'ðað/ *f,* outward appearance; outside, externality; *pl* ceremonies, forms; ostentation

exteriorizar /eksteriori'sar; eksteriori'θar/ *vt* to exteriorize, reveal

exterminador /ekstermina'ðor/ **(-ra)** *a* exterminating. *n* exterminator

exterminar /ekstermi'nar/ *vt* to exterminate; devastate

exterminio /ekster'minio/ *m,* extermination; devastation

externado /ekster'naðo/ *m,* day school

externarse /ekster'narse/ *vr* to stand out

externo /eks'terno/ **(-na)** *a* external. *n* day

extinción /ekstin'sion; ekstin'θion/ *f,* extinction; extinguishment; abolition, cancellation

extinguir /ekstin'guir/ *vt* to extinguish; destroy

extintor /ekstin'tor/ *m,* fire extinguisher

extirpación /ekstirpa'sion; ekstirpa'θion/ *f,* extirpation

extirpador /ekstirpa'ðor/ **(-ra)** *a* extirpating. *n* extirpator

extirpar /ekstir'par/ *vt* to extirpate; *Fig*. eradicate

extorsión /ekstor'sion/ *f,* extortion

extorsionar /ekstorsio'nar/ *vt* to extort

extra /'ekstra/ *prefix* outside, without, beyond. *prep* besides. *a* extremely, most. *m, Inf*. extra

extracción /ekstrak'sion; ekstrak'θion/ *f,* extraction; drawing (lottery); origin, lineage; exportation

extractar /ekstrak'tar/ *vt* to abstract, summarize

extracto /eks'trakto/ *m,* abstract, summary; *Chem*. extract

extractor /ekstrak'tor/ *a* extracting. *m,* extractor

extradición /ekstraði'sion; ekstraði'θion/ *f*, extradition

extraer /ekstra'er/ *vt irr* to extract; draw out; export; *Chem.* extract. See **traer**

extranjero /ekstran'hero/ **(-ra)** *a* alien, foreign. *n* foreigner. *m*, abroad, foreign country

extrañar /ekstra'ɲar/ *vt* to exile; alienate, estrange; wonder at; miss, feel the loss of; *vr* be exiled; be estranged; be amazed (by); refuse (to do a thing)

extrañeza /ekstra'ɲesa; ekstra'ɲeθa/ *f*, strangeness; estrangement; surprise

extraño /eks'traɲo/ *a* strange, unusual; foreign, extraneous

extraoficial /ekstraofi'sial; ekstraofi'θial/ *a* unofficial

extraordinario /ekstraorði'nario/ *a* extraordinary; special. *m*, *Cul.* extra course

extraterrenal /ekstraterre'nal/ **extraterreno** *a*, *Lat. Am.* extraterrestrial, unearthly

extraterritorialidad /ekstraterritoriali'ðað/ *f*, exterritoriality

extravagancia /ekstraβa'gansia; ekstraβa'ganθia/ *f*, eccentricity; queerness; folly

extravagante /ekstraβa'gante/ *a* eccentric; queer, strange; absurd

extravertido /ekstraβer'tiðo/ *m*, extrovert

extraviar /ekstra'βiar/ *vt* to mislead; mislay; *vr* lose one's way; be lost (of things); *Fig.* go astray

extravío /ekstra'βio/ *m*, deviation, divergence; error; aberration, lapse

extremado /ekstre'maðo/ *a* extreme

extremar /ekstre'mar/ *vt* to take to extremes; *vr* do one's best

extremaunción /ekstremaun'sion; ekstremaun'θion/ *f*, extreme unction

extremidad /ekstremi'ðað/ *f*, end; extremity; remotest part; edge; limit; *pl* extremities

extremista /ekstre'mista/ *a* and *mf* extremist

extremo /eks'tremo/ *a* last, ultimate; extreme; furthest; great, exceptional; utmost. *m*, end, extreme; highest degree; extreme care; *pl* excessive emotional display

extremoso /ekstre'moso/ *a* immoderate, exaggerated; very affectionate

extrínseco /ekstrin'seko/ *a* extrinsic

exuberancia /eksuβeransia; eksuβe'ranθia/ *f*, abundance; exuberance

exuberante /eksuβe'rante/ *a* abundant, copious; exuberant

exudar /eksu'ðar/ *vi* and *vt* to exude

exultación /eksulta'sion; eksulta'θion/ *f*, exultation; rejoicing

exultante /eksul'tante/ *a* exultant

exultar /eksul'tar/ *vi* to exult

eyaculación /eyakula'sion; eyakula'θion/ *f*, *Med.* ejaculation

eyacular /eyaku'lar/ *vt Med.* to ejaculate

F

fa /fa/ *m*, *Mus.* fa, F

fabada /fa'βaða/ *f*, dish of broad beans with pork, sausage or bacon

fábrica /'faβrika/ *f*, manufacture; making; factory, works; fabric, structure, building; creation; invention. **f. de papel,** paper mill. **marca de f.,** trademark

fabricación /faβrika'sion; faβrika'θion/ *f*, make; making; construction. **f. en serie,** mass production

fabricador /faβrika'ðor/ **(-ra)** *a* creative, inventive. *n* fabricator; maker

fabricante /faβri'kante/ *a* manufacturing. *m*, manufacturer; maker

fabricar /faβri'kar/ *vt* to manufacture; make; construct, build; devise; invent, create

fabril /fa'βril/ *a* manufacturing

fabriquero /faβri'kero/ *m*, manufacturer; churchwarden; charcoal burner

fábula /'faβula/ *f*, rumor, gossip; fiction; fable; story, plot; mythology; myth; laughingstock; falsehood.

fabulista /faβu'lista/ *mf* fabulist; mythologist

fabulosidad /faβulosi'ðað/ *f*, fabulousness

fabuloso /faβu'loso/ *a* fabulous; fictitious; incredible, amazing

faca /'faka/ *f*, jackknife

facción /fak'sion; fak'θion/ *f*, rebellion; faction, party, band; feature (of the face) (gen. *pl*); military exploit; any routine military duty

faccionario /faksio'nario; fakθio'nario/ *a* factional

faccioso /fak'sioso; fak'θioso/ **(-sa)** *a* factional; factious, seditious. *n* rebel

faceta /fa'seta; fa'θeta/ *f*, facet (gems); aspect, view

facha /'fatʃa/ *f*, *Inf.* countenance, look, face; guy, scarecrow. *Naut.* **ponerse en f.,** to lie to

fachada /fa'tʃaða/ *f*, facade, front (of a building, ship, etc.); *Inf.* build, presence (of a person); frontispiece (of a book)

fachenda /fa'tʃenda/ *f*, *Inf.* boastfulness, vanity

fachinal /fatʃi'nal/ *m*, *Argentina* swamp

fachoso, -a /fa'tʃoso/ *a*, *Lat. Am.* elegant, smart

facial /fa'sial; fa'θial/ *a* facial; intuitive

fácil /'fasil; 'faθil/ *a* easy; probable; easily led; docile; of easy virtue (women). *adv* easy

facilidad /fasili'ðað; faθili'ðað/ *f*, easiness; facility; aptitude; ready compliance; opportunity

facilitar /fasili'tar; faθili'tar/ *vt* to facilitate; expedite; provide, deliver

facineroso /fasine'roso; faθine'roso/ *a* criminal, delinquent. *m*, criminal; villain

facistol /fasis'tol; faθis'tol/ *m*, *Eccl.* lectern; chorister's stand

facsímile /fak'simile/ *m*, facsimile

factibilidad /faktiβili'ðað/ *f*, feasibility, practicability

factible /fak'tiβle/ *a* feasible, practicable

facticio /fak'tisio; fak'tiθio/ *a* factitious, artificial

factor /fak'tor/ *m*, *Com.* factor, agent; *Math.* factor; element; consideration

factoría /fakto'ria/ *f*, agency; factorage; factory; merchants' trading post, especially in a foreign country

factótum /fak'totum/ *m*, *Inf.* factotum, handyman; *Inf.* busybody; confidential agent or deputy

factura /fak'tura/ *f*, *Com.* invoice, bill, account; *Art.* execution; workmanship; making

facturar /faktu'rar/ *vt Com.* to invoice; register (luggage on a railroad)

facultad /fakulta'ð/ *f*, faculty; mental or physical aptitude, capability; authority, right; science, art; *Educ.* faculty; license

facultar /fakul'tar/ *vt* to authorize, permit

facultativo /fakulta'tiβo/ *a* belonging to a faculty; optional, permissive. *m*, physician

facundia /fa'kundia/ *f*, eloquence

facundo /fa'kundo/ *a* eloquent

faena /fa'ena/ *f*, manual labor; mental work; business affairs (gen. *pl*)

faetón /fae'ton/ *m*, phaeton

fagocito /fago'sito; fago'θito/ *m*, phagocyte

fagot /fa'got/ *m*, bassoon

fagotista /fago'tista/ *mf* bassoon player

faisán /fai'san/ **(-ana)** *Ornith.* cock (hen) pheasant

faisanera /faisa'nera/ *f*, pheasantry

faja /'faha/ *f*, belt; sash, scarf; corset, girdle; *Geog.* zone; newspaper wrapper; *Archit.* fascia; swathing band

fajar /fa'har/ *vt* to swathe; swaddle (a child)

fajero /fa'hero/ *m*, swaddling band

fajín /fa'hin/ *m*, ceremonial ribbon or sash worn by generals, etc.

fajina /fa'hina/ *f*, stack; brushwood; (*fort.*) fascine; *Mexico* lunch

fajo /'faho/ *m*, bundle, sheaf; *pl* swaddling clothes

falacia /fa'lasia; fa'laθia/ *f*, fraud, deceit; deceitfulness; fallacy

falange /fa'lanhe/ *f*, *Mil*. phalanx; *Anat*. phalange; (*Spanish Pol*.) Falange

falangista /falan'hista/ *a* and *mf* Falangist

falaz /fa'las; fa'laθ/ *a* deceitful; fallacious

falda /'falda/ *f*, skirt; lap, flap, panel (of a dress); slope (of a hill); the lap; loin (of beef, etc.); brim of a hat; *pl Inf*. petticoats, women. **f. escocesa,** kilt. **f.- pantalón,** divided skirt, culottes.

faldellín /falde'yin; falde'ʎin/ *m*, skirt; underskirt

faldero /fal'dero/ *a* lap (dog); fond of the company of women

faldillas /fal'diyas; fal'diʎas/ *f pl*, coattails

faldistorio /faldis'torio/ *m*, faldstool

faldón /fal'don/ *m*, long, flowing skirt; shirttail; coattail

falibilidad /faliβili'ðað/ *f*, fallibility

falible /fa'liβle/ *a* fallible

falla /faya; 'faʎa/ *f*, deficiency, defect; failure; *Geol*. displacement; bonfire (Valencia); *Mineral*. slide

fallar /fa'yar; fa'ʎar/ *vt Law*. to pass sentence; *vi* be deficient

fallecer /faye'ser; faʎe'θer/ *vi irr* to die; fail. See **conocer**

fallecimiento /fayesi'miento; faʎeθi'miento/ *m*, death, decease

fallido /fa'yiðo; fa'ʎiðo/ *a* frustrated; bankrupt

fallo /'fayo; 'faʎo/ *m*, *Law*. verdict; judgment

falsario /fal'sario/ *a* falsifying, forging, counterfeiting; deceiving, lying. *m*, falsifier, forger, counterfeiter

falseamiento /falsea'miento/ *m*, falsifying; forging

falsear /false'ar/ *vt* to falsify; forge; counterfeit; penetrate; *vi* weaken; *Mus*. be out of tune (strings)

falsedad /false'ðað/ *f*, falseness; falsehood

falsete /fal'sete/ *m*, spigot; *Mus*. falsetto voice

falsificación /falsifika'sion; falsifika'θion/ *f*, falsification; forgery

falsificador /falsifika'ðor/ *a* falsifying; forging. *m*, falsifier; forger

falsificar /falsifi'kar/ *vt* to forge, counterfeit; falsify

falso /'falso/ *a* false; forged, counterfeit; treacherous, untrue, deceitful; incorrect; sham; vicious (horses). **de f.,** falsely; deceitfully

falta /'falta/ *f*, lack, shortage; defect; mistake; *Sports*. fault; shortcoming; nonappearance, absence; deficiency in legal weight of coin; *Law*. offense. **f. de éxito,** failure. **hacer f.,** to be necessary. **sin f.,** without fail

faltar /fal'tar/ *vi* to be lacking; fail, die; fall short; be absent from an appointment; not to fulfill one's obligations. **hacer f.,** to be necessary, need. **f. a,** to be unfaithful to, break (e.g. *Faltó a su palabra,* He broke his promise). **Me hace falta dinero,** I need money. *Inf*. **¡No faltaba más!** I should think not!; That's the limit!

falto /'falto/ *a* lacking, wanting; defective; wretched, mean, timid. **f. de personal,** short-handed

faltriquera /faltri'kera/ *f*, pocket; hip pocket

falúa /fa'lua/ *f*, *Naut*. tender; longboat

falucho /fa'lutʃo/ *m*, felucca

fama /'fama/ *f*, rumor, report; reputation; fame

famélico /fa'meliko/ *a* ravenous

familia /fa'milia/ *f*, family; household; kindred. **ser de f.,** to run in the family

familiar /fami'liar/ *a* family; familiar; well known; unceremonious; plain, simple; colloquial (language). *m*, *Eccl*. familiar; servant; intimate friend; familiar spirit

familiaridad /familiari'ðað/ *f*, familiarity

familiarizar /familiari'sar; familiari'θar/ *vt* to familiarize; *vr* become familiar; accustom oneself

familiarmente /familiar'mente/ *adv* familiarly

famoso /fa'moso/ *a* famous; notorious; *Inf*. excellent, perfect; *Inf*. conspicuous

fámula /'famula/ *f*, *Inf*. female servant

fámulo /'famulo/ *m*, servant of a college; *Inf*. servant

fanal /fa'nal/ *m*, lantern (of a lighthouse); *Naut*. poop lantern; lantern; lamp glass

fanático /fa'natiko/ **(-ca)** *a* fanatical. *n* fanatic; *Inf*. fan, enthusiast

fanatismo /fana'tismo/ *m*, fanaticism

fanatizar /fanati'sar; fanati'θar/ *vt* to make fanatical; turn into a fanatic

fandango /fan'dango/ *m*, lively Andalusian dance; *Lat. Am*. rowdy party

fanega /fa'nega/ *f*, grain measure about the weight of 1.60 bushel; land measure (about 1½ acres)

fanfarrón /fanfa'rron/ **(-ona)** *a Inf*. boastful; swaggering. *n* swashbuckler; boaster

fanfarronear /fanfarrone'ar/ *vi* to swagger; brag

fanfarronería /fanfarrone'ria/ *f*, bragging

fango /'fango/ *m*, mud, mire; degradation

fangoso /faŋ'goso/ *a* muddy, miry

fantasear /fantase'ar/ *vi* to let one's fancy roam; boast

fantasía /fanta'sia/ *f*, fancy, imagination; fantasy; caprice; fiction; *Inf*. presumption; *Mus*. fantasia

fantasma /fan'tasma/ *m*, ghost, phantom; vision; image, impression; presumptuous person. *f*, *Inf*. scarecrow; apparition

fantasmagoría /fantasmago'ria/ *f*, phantasmagoria

fantasmagórico /fantasma'goriko/ *a* phantasmagoric

fantástico /fan'tastiko/ *a* fanciful, imaginary; fantastic, imaginative; presumptuous, conceited

fantoche /fan'totʃe/ *m*, puppet; *Inf*. yes-man, mediocrity

faquín /fa'kin/ *m*, porter, carrier

faquir /fa'kir/ *m*, fakir

farabute /fara'βute/ *mf*, *Argentina* rogue

faradio /fa'raðio/ *m*, farad

faralá /fara'la/ *m*, flounce, frill

faramallear /faramaje'ar; faramaʎe'ar/ *vi*, *Lat. Am*. to boast, brag

farándula /fa'randula/ *f*, profession of low comedian; troupe of strolling players; cunning trick

farandulero /farandu'lero/ *m*, actor, strolling player. *a Inf*. plausible

faraón /fara'on/ *m*, pharaoh; faro (card game)

fardel /far'ðel/ *m*, bag, knapsack; bundle

fardo /far'ðo/ *m*, bundle, bale, package

farfulla /far'fuya; far'fuʎa/ *f*, *Inf*. mumbling; gibbering. *mf Inf*. mumbler

farfullar /farfu'yar; farfu'ʎar/ *vt Inf*. to mumble; gibber; *Inf*. act in haste

faringe /fa'rinhe/ *f*, pharynx

faríngeo /fa'rinheo/ *a* pharyngeal

faringitis /farin'hitis/ *f*, pharyngitis

farmacéutico /farma'seutiko; farma'θeutiko/ *a* pharmaceutical. *m*, pharmacist

farmacia /far'masia; far'maθia/ *f*, pharmacy

farmacología /farmakolo'hia/ *f*, pharmacology

farmacólogo /farma'kologo/ *m*, pharmacologist

faro /'faro/ *m*, lighthouse; beacon, guide; *Auto*. headlight

farol /fa'rol/ *m*, lantern, lamp; streetlamp; cresset

farola /fa'rola/ *f*, lamppost (generally with several branches); lantern

farolero /faro'lero/ *m*, lantern maker; lamplighter; lamp tender. *a Inf*. swaggering, braggart

fárrago /'farrago/ *m*, hodgepodge

farruto, -a /fa'rruto/ *a*, *Lat. Am*. sickly, weak

farsa /'farsa/ *f*, old name for a play; farce; theatrical company; poor, badly constructed play; sham, trick, deception

farsante /far'sante/ *m*, comedian; *Obs*. actor; *Fig. Inf*. humbug

fascinación /fassina'sion; fasθina'θion/ *f*, evil eye; enchantment, fascination

fascinador /fassina'ðor; fasθina'ðor/ **(-ra)** *a* bewitching; fascinating. *n* charmer

fascinante /fassi'nante; fasθi'nante/ *a* fascinating

fascinar /fassi'nar; fasθi'nar/ *vt* to bewitch, place under a spell; deceive, impose upon; attract, fascinate

fascismo /fas'sismo; fas'θismo/ *m*, fascism

fascista /fas'sista; fas'θista/ *a* and *mf* fascist

fase /'fase/ *f*, phase; aspect

fastidiar /fasti'ðiar/ *vt* to disgust, bore; annoy; *vr* be bored

fastidio /fasti'ðio/ *m*, sickness, squeamishness; annoyance, boredom, dislike, repugnance

fastidioso /fasti'ðioso/ a disgusting, sickening; annoying; boring, tiresome

fastuoso /fas'tuoso/ a ostentatious; pompous

fatal /fa'tal/ a fatal, mortal; predetermined, inevitable; ill-fated, unhappy, disastrous; evil

fatalidad /fatali'ðað/ f, fatality; inevitability; disaster, ill-fatedness

fatalismo /fata'lismo/ m, fatalism

fatalista /fata'lista/ a fatalistic. mf fatalist

fatalmente /fatal'mente/ adv inevitably, unavoidably; unhappily, unfortunately; extremely badly

fatídico /fa'tiðiko/ a prophetic (gen. of evil)

fatiga /fa'tiga/ f, fatigue; toil; difficult breathing; hardship, troubles (gen. pl.)

fatigar /fati'gar/ vt to tire; annoy; vr be tired

fatigoso /fati'goso/ a tired; tiring; tiresome, annoying

fatuidad /fatui'ðað/ f, fatuousness, inanity, foolishness; conceit; priggishness

fatuo /fa'tuo/ a fatuous, foolish; conceited; priggish. m, self-satisfied fool. **fuego f.,** will-o'-the-wisp

fauces /'fauses; 'fauθes/ f pl, snout, jaws (animal)

faul /faul/ m, Lat. Am. foul

faulear /faule'ar/ vt, Lat. Am. to foul

fauna /'fauna/ f, fauna

fauno /'fauno/ m, faun

fausto /'fausto/ a, pomp, magnificence, ostentation. a fortunate, happy

favonio /fa'βonio/ m, Poet. zephyr, westerly wind

favor /fa'βor/ m, aid, protection, support; favor, honor, service; love favor, sign of favor. **a f. de,** in favor of; on behalf of

favorable /faβo'raβle/ a kind, helpful; favorable

favorecedor /faβorese'ðor; faβoreθe'ðor/ **(-ra)** a favoring, helping. n helper; protector

favorecer /faβore'ser; faβore'θer/ vt irr to aid, protect, support; favor; do a service, grant a favor. See **conocer**

favoritismo /faβori'tismo/ m, favoritism

favorito /faβo'rito/ **(-ta)** a and n favorite

fax /faks/ m, fax

fayenza /fa'yensa; fa'yenθa/ f, faience

faz /fas; faθ/ f, face; external surface of a thing, side; frontage

fe /fe/ f, faith; confidence, trust, good opinion; belief; solemn promise; assertion; certificate, attestation; faithfulness. **f. de erratas,** Print. errata. **dar f.,** Law. to testify. **de buena f.,** in good faith. **en f.,** in proof

fealdad /feal'dað/ f, ugliness; base action

febo /'feβo/ m, Phoebus; Poet. sun

febrero /fe'βrero/ m, February

febril /fe'βril/ a feverish; ardent, violent; passionate

fecha /'fetʃa/ f, date. **a la f.,** at present, now. **hasta la f.,** up to the present (day)

fechar /fe'tʃar/ vt to date, write the date

feculento /feku'lento/ a starchy; dreggy

fecundación /fekunda'sion; fekunda'θion/ f, fecundation

fecundar /fekun'dar/ vt to fertilize; fecundate

fecundidad /fekundi'ðað/ f, fecundity; fertility, fruitfulness

fecundizar /fekundi'sar; fekundi'θar/ vt to fertilize; make fruitful

fecundo /fe'kundo/ a fertile, fecund, prolific; abundant

federación /feðera'sion; feðera'θion/ f, federation, league

federal /feðe'ral/ a federal. mf federalist

federalismo /feðera'lismo/ m, federalism

federalista /feðera'lista/ a federal, federalist. mf federalist

federativo /feðera'tiβo/ a federative

fehaciente /fea'siente; fea'θiente/ a Law. authentic, attested

felicidad /felisi'ðað; feliθi'ðað/ f, happiness; contentment, satisfaction; good fortune

felicitación /felisita'sion; feliθita'θion/ f, congratulation

felicitar /felisi'tar; feliθi'tar/ vt to congratulate; wish well; vr congratulate oneself

feligrés /feli'gres/ **(-esa)** n parishioner

feligresía /feligre'sia/ f, parish

felino /fe'lino/ a and m, feline

feliz /fe'lis; fe'liθ/ a happy; fortunate; skillful, felicitous (of phrases, etc.)

felón /fe'lon/ **(-ona)** n felon

felonía /felo'nia/ f, felony

felpa /'felpa/ f, plush; Inf. drubbing, beating

felpilla /fel'piya; fel'piʎa/ f, chenille

felpudo /fel'puðo/ a plush

femenino /feme'nino/ a feminine; female; Fig. weak

fementido /femen'tiðo/ a sly, false, treacherous, unfaithful

feminismo /femi'nismo/ m, feminism

feminista /femi'nista/ a feminist. mf feminist

fémur /'femur/ m, femur, thigh bone

fenecer /fene'ser; fene'θer/ vt irr to conclude, finish; vi die; be ended. See **conocer**

fenecimiento /fenesi'miento; feneθi'miento/ m, end; death

fenicio /fe'nisio; fe'niθio/ **(-ia)** a and n Phoenician

fénico /'feniko/ a phenic, carbolic

fénix /'feniks/ f, phoenix

fenomenal /fenome'nal/ a phenomenal; Inf. terrific

fenómeno /fe'nomeno/ m, phenomenon; Inf. something of great size

feo /'feo/ a ugly; alarming, horrid; evil. m, Inf. slight, insult

feraz /'feras; 'feraθ/ a fruitful, fertile

féretro /'feretro/ m, coffin; bier

feria /'feria/ f, fair, market; workday; holiday; rest

feriar /fe'riar/ vt to buy at a fair; bargain. vi cease work, take a vacation. **día feriado,** holiday

fermentación /fermenta'sion; fermenta'θion/ f, fermentation

fermentar /fermen'tar/ vi to ferment; be agitated; vt cause to ferment

fermento /fer'mento/ m, ferment; leaven; Chem. enzyme

ferocidad /ferosi'ðað; feroθi'ðað/ f, ferocity, cruelty

feroz /fe'ros; fe'roθ/ a ferocious, cruel; Lat. Am. ugly

férreo /'ferreo/ a ferrous; hard, tenacious. **línea férrea,** railroad

ferrería /ferre'ria/ f, ironworks

ferretería /ferrete'ria/ f, ironworks; ironmonger's shop; ironware, hardware

férrico /'ferriko/ a ferric

ferrífero /fe'rrifero/ a iron-bearing

ferrocarril /ferroka'rril/ m, railroad, railway; railroad train. **f. de cremallera,** rack railroad. **f. funicular,** funicular railway

ferroso /fe'rroso/ a ferrous

ferroviario /ferro'βiario/ a railroad, railway. m, railroad employee

fértil /'fertil/ a fertile; fruitful, productive

fertilidad /fertili'ðað/ f, fertility

fertilización /fertilisa'sion; fertiliθa'θion/ f, fertilization

fertilizar /fertili'sar; fertili'θar/ vt to fertilize, make fruitful

férula /'ferula/ f, ferule; Surg. splint; Fig. yoke, rule

fervor /fer'βor/ m, intense heat; fervor, devotion; zeal

fervoroso /ferβo'roso/ a fervent, zealous, devoted

festejar /feste'har/ vt to feast, entertain; woo; celebrate; vr amuse oneself; Mexico to thrash

festejo /fes'teho/ m, feast, entertainment; courtship, wooing; pl public celebrations

festín /fes'tin/ m, private dinner or party; sumptuous banquet

festival /festi'βal/ m, musical festival; festival

festividad /festiβi'ðað/ f, festivity; Eccl. celebration, solemnity; witticism

festivo /fes'tiβo/ a joking, witty; happy, gay; solemn, worthy of celebration. **día f.,** holiday

festón /fes'ton/ m, garland, wreath; festoon; border; scalloped edging

festonear /festone'ar/ *vt* to garland, festoon; border
fetal /fe'tal/ *a* fetal
fetiche /fe'titʃe/ *m*, fetish
fetichismo /feti'tʃismo/ *m*, fetishism
fetidez /feti'ðes; feti'ðeθ/ *f*, fetidness, fetor, stink
fétido /'fetiðo/ *a* stinking, fetid
feto /'feto/ *m*, fetus
feudal /feu'ðal/ *a* feudal; despotic
feudalismo /feuða'lismo/ *m*, feudalism
fez /fes; feθ/ *m*, fez
fiado, al /'fiaðo, al/ *adv* on credit. **en f.**, on bail
fiador /fia'ðor/ **(-ra)** *n* guarantor; bail. *m*, fastener, loop (of a coat, clock, etc.); safety catch, bolt. **salir f.**, to be surety (for); post bail
fiambre /'fiambre/ *m*, cold meat, cold dish; *Inf.* stale, out-of-date news, etc.; *Inf.* corpse
fiambrera /fiam'brera/ *f*, lunchbox, lunchpail
fiambrería /fiamβre'ria/ *f* delicatessen
fianza /'fiansa; 'fianθa/ *f*, guarantee, bail; surety; security. *Law.* **dar f.**, to guarantee; post bail
fiar /fi'ar/ *vt* to go surety for, post bail; sell on credit; trust; confide; *vr* (*with de*) confide in; trust
fibra /'fiβra/ *f*, fiber; filament; energy, strength; *Mineral.* vein; grain (of wood)
fibroso /fi'βroso/ *a* fibrous; fibroid
ficción /fik'sion; fik'θion/ *f*, falsehood; invention; fiction, imaginative creation; pretense
ficha /'fitʃa/ *f*, chip, counter; domino; index card, filing card. **f. antropométrica,** personal particulars card
fichar /fi'tʃar/ *vt* to record personal particulars on a filing card; file, index
fichero /fi'tʃero/ *m*, filing cabinet; card catalog
fichú /fi'tʃu/ *m*, fichu, scarf
ficticio /fik'tisio; fik'tiθio/ *a* fictitious
fidedigno /fiðe'ðigno/ *a* trustworthy, bona fide
fidelidad /fiðeli'ðað/ *f*, fidelity, honesty; loyalty; punctiliousness
fideos /fi'ðeos/ *m pl*, vermicelli. *m*, *Inf.* scraggy person
fiduciario /fiðu'siario; fiðu'θiario/ *a Law.* fiduciary. *m*, *Law.* trustee
fiebre /'fieβre/ *f*, fever; great agitation, excitement. **f. de oro,** gold fever. **f. palúdica,** malarial fever. **f. puerperal,** puerperal fever. **f. tifoidea,** typhoid fever
fiel /fiel/ *a* faithful, loyal; true, exact. *m*, axis; pointer (of a scale or balance)
fieltro /'fieltro/ *m*, felt
fiera /'fiera/ *f*, wild beast; cruel person
fiereza /fie'resa; fie'reθa/ *f*, savageness, wildness; cruelty, fierceness; deformity
fiero /'fiero/ *a* wild, savage; ugly; huge, enormous; horrible, alarming; haughty
fiesta /'fiesta/ *f*, merriment, gaiety; entertainment; feast, *Inf.* joke; festivity, celebration; public holiday; caress, cajolery (gen. *pl*); *pl* holidays. **f. fija** *Eccl.* immovable feast. *Inf.* **estar de f.,** to be making merry. **hacer f.,** to take a holiday. *Inf.* **Se acabó la f.,** It's all over and done with
fifiriche /fifi'ritʃe/ *a*, *Central America, Mexico* sickly, weak
figón /fi'gon/ *m*, eating house, diner
figulino /figu'lino/ *a* fictile, made of terra cotta
figura /fi'gura/ *f*, shape, form; face; *Art.* image, figure; *Law.* form; court card; *Mus.* note; *Theat.* character, role; (*Geom. Gram. Dance.*) figure. **f. de nieve,** snowman. **f. de proa,** figurehead. *Fig.* **f. decorativa,** figurehead. *Fig.* **hacer f.,** to cut a figure
figurado /fi'guraðo/ *a* figurative; rhetorical
figurar /figu'rar/ *vt* to shape, mold; simulate, pretend; represent; *vi* be numbered among; cut a figure; *vr* imagine
figurilla /figu'riya; figu'riʎa/ *mf Inf.* ridiculous, dwarfish figure. *f*, *Art.* statuette
figurín /figu'rin/ *m*, fashion plate or model
figuroso, -a /figu'roso/ *a*, *Lat. Am.* flashy, loud, showy
fijación /fiha'sion; fiha'θion/ *f*, fixing; nailing; sticking, posting; attention, fixity; *Chem.* fixation; firmness, stability

fijador /fiha'ðor/ *m*, (*Med. Photo.*) fixative; setting lotion; *Art.* varnish. *a* fixing
fijamente /fiha'mente/ *adv* firmly; attentively
fijar /fi'har/ *vt* to fix; glue, stick; nail; make firm; settle, appoint (a date); fix, concentrate (attention, gaze); (*Photo. Med.*) fix; *vr* decide; notice (e.g. *No me había fijado,* I hadn't noticed). **f. anuncios,** to post bills
fijeza /fi'hesa; fi'heθa/ *f*, fixedness; firmness, stability; constancy, steadfastness
fijo /'fiho/ *a* firm; fixed; stable; steadfast; permanent; exact. **de f.,** certainly, without doubt
fila /'fila/ *f*, line, row; *Mil.* rank; antipathy, hatred. **en f.,** in a line
filacteria /filak'teria/ *f*, phylactery
filamento /fila'mento/ *m*, filament
filantropía /filantro'pia/ *f*, philanthropy
filantrópico /filan'tropiko/ *a* philanthropic
filántropo /fi'lantropo/ *m*, philanthropist
filarmónico /filar'moniko/ *a* philharmonic
filatelia /fila'telia/ *f*, philately, stamp collecting
filatélico /fila'teliko/ *a* philatelic
filatelista /filate'lista/ *mf* philatelist, stamp collector
filete /fi'lete/ *m*, *Archit.* filet; *Cul.* small spit; filet (of meat or fish); thread of a screw; *Sew.* hem
filiación /filia'sion; filia'θion/ *f*, filiation; affiliation, relationship; *Mil.* regimental register
filial /fi'lial/ *a* filial; affiliated
filibustero /filiβus'tero/ *m*, filibuster
filiforme /fili'forme/ *a* filamentous
filigrana /fili'grana/ *f*, filigree; watermark (of paper); *Fig.* delicate creation
filípica /fi'lipika/ *f*, philippic
Filipinas, las /fili'pinas, las/ the Philippines
filipino /fili'pino/ **(-na)** *a* and *n* Philippine
filisteo /filis'teo/ **(-ea)** *a* and *n* philistine
filmar /fil''mar/ *vt* to film
filo /'filo/ *m*, cutting edge; dividing line
filología /filolo'hia/ *f*, philology
filológico /filo'lohiko/ *a* philological
filólogo /fi'lologo/ *m*, philologist
filomela /filo'mela/ *f*, *Poet.* nightingale
filón /fi'lon/ *m*, *Mineral.* vein, lode; *Fig.* gold mine
filoso, -a /fi'loso/ *a*, *Lat. Am.* sharp
filosofar /filoso'far/ *vi* to philosophize
filosofía /filoso'fia/ *f*, philosophy. **f. moral,** moral philosophy. **f. natural,** natural philosophy
filosófico /filo'sofiko/ *a* philosophic
filósofo /fi'losofo/ *m*, philosopher. *a* philosophic
filoxera /filo'ksera/ *f*, phylloxera
filtración /filtra'sion; filtra'θion/ *f*, filtration
filtrar /fil'trar/ *vt* to filter; *vi* filter through, percolate; *vr Fig.* disappear (of money, etc.)
filtro /'filtro/ *m*, filter, strainer; love potion, philter
filudo, -a /fi'luðo/ *a*, *Lat. Am.* = **filoso**
fin /fin/ *m*, finish, end, conclusion; purpose, goal, aim; limit, extent. **a f. de,** in order to, so that. **a fines de,** toward the end of (with months, years, etc.) (e.g. *a fines de octubre,* toward the end of October). **en f.,** at last; in fine; well then! **por f.,** finally
finado /fi'naðo/ **(-da)** *n* deceased, dead person
final /fi'nal/ *a* final. *m*, end, finish; *Sports.* final (gen. *pl*)
finalidad /finali'ðað/ *f*, finality; purpose
finalista /fina'lista/ *mf Sports.* finalist
finalizar /finali'sar; finali'θar/ *vt* to conclude, finish; *vi* be finished; close (stock exchange)
finalmente /final'mente/ *adv* finally
financiar /finan'siar; finan'θiar/ *vt* to finance
financiero /finan'siero; finan'θiero/ *a* financial. *m*, financier
finanzas /fi'nansas; fi'nanθas/ *f pl*, finance
finar /fi'nar/ *vi* to die; *vr* desire, long for a thing
finca /'finka/ *f*, land, real estate; house property, country house, ranch
fineza /fi'nesa; fi'neθa/ *f*, fineness; excellence; goodness; kindness, expression of affection; good turn, friendly act; gift; beauty, delicacy

fingido /fin'hiðo/ *a* pretended; assumed; feigned; sham

fingimiento /finhi'miento/ *m*, pretense; affectation, assumption

fingir /fin'hir/ *vt* to pretend, feign; imagine

finiquitar /finiki'tar/ *vt* to close and pay up an account; *Inf.* end

finiquito /fini'kito/ *m*, closing of an account; final receipt, quittance; quietus

finito /fi'nito/ *a* finite

finlandés /finlan'des/ **(-esa)** *a* Finnish. *n* Finn. *m*, Finnish (language)

fino /'fino/ *a* fine; excellent, good; slim, slender, thin; delicate, subtle; dainty (of people); cultured, polished; constant, loving; sagacious, shrewd; *Mineral.* refined

finta /'finta/ *f*, feint (in fencing); menace, threat

finura /fi'nura/ *f*, fineness; excellence; delicacy; courtesy

fiordo /'fiorðo/ *m*, fjord

firma /'firma/ *f*, signature; act of signing; *Com.* firm name, firm

firmamento /firma'mento/ *m*, firmament

firmante /fir'mante/ *a* signing. *mf* signatory

firmar /fir'mar/ *vt* to sign

firme /'firme/ *a* firm; hard; steady, solid; constant, resolute, loyal. *m*, foundation, base. *Mil.* **¡Firmes!** Attention! **batir de f.,** to strike hard

firmeza /fir'mesa; fir'meθa/ *f*, stability, firmness; constancy, resoluteness, loyalty

fiscal /fis'kal/ *a* fiscal. *m*, attorney general; public prosecutor; meddler. **f. de quiebras,** official receiver

fiscalizar /fiskali'sar; fiskali'θar/ *vt* to prosecute; pry into; meddle with; censure, criticize

fisco /'fisko/ *m*, national treasury, exchequer, revenue

fisgar /fis'gar/ *vt* to harpoon; pry; *vi* mock, make fun of

fisgón /fis'gon/ **(-ona)** *a* prying; mocking. *n* pryer; mocker; eavesdropper

fisgoneo /fisgo'neo/ *m*, prying; eavesdropping

física /'fisika/ *f*, physics

físico /'fisiko/ *a* physical. *m*, physicist; physician; physique

fisiología /fisiolo'hia/ *f*, physiology

fisiológico /fisio'lohiko/ *a* physiological

fisiólogo /fisi'ologo/ *m*, physiologist

fisioterapia /fisiote'rapia/ *f*, physiotherapy

fisonomía /fisono'mia/ *f*, physiognomy

fistol /fis'tol/ *m*, *Mexico* tie pin; crafty person, sly person

fístula /'fistula/ *f*, pipe, conduit; *Mus.* pipe; *Surg.* fistula

fisura /fi'sura/ *f*, fissure

flaccidez /flaksi'ðes; flakθi'ðeθ/ *f*, flabbiness

fláccido /'flaksiðo; 'flakθiðo/ *a* flaccid, soft, flabby

flaco /'flako/ *a* thin; weak, feeble; *Fig.* weak-minded; dispirited. *m*, failing, weakness. *Inf.* **hacer un f. servicio,** to do an ill turn. **estar f. de memoria,** to have a weak memory

flagelación /flahela'sion; flahela'θion/ *f*, flagellation

flagelante /flahe'lante/ *m*, flagellant

flagelar /flahe'lar/ *vt* to scourge; *Fig.* lash

flagelo /fla'helo/ *m*, whip, scourge

flagrante /fla'grante/ *a* *Poet.* refulgent; present; actual. **en f.,** in the very act, flagrante delicto

flagrar /fla'grar/ *vi* *Poet.* to blaze, be refulgent

flamante /fla'mante/ *a* resplendent; brand-new; fresh, spick-and-span

flamenco /fla'menko/ **(-ca)** *m*, *Ornith.* flamingo. *a* and *n* Flemish. *a* Andalusian; gypsy; buxom, fresh

flan /flan/ *m*, baked custard, creme caramel. **estar como un f.,** to shake like a leaf, be nervous

flanco /'flanko/ *m*, side; *Mil.* flank

flanquear /flanke'ar/ *vt* *Mil.* to flank

flanqueo /flan'keo/ *m*, *Mil.* outflanking

flaquear /flake'ar/ *vi* to grow weak; weaken; totter (buildings, etc.); be disheartened, flag

flaqueza /fla'kesa; fla'keθa/ *f*, weakness; thinness; faintness, feebleness; frailty, fault; loss of zeal

flato /'flato/ *m*, flatulence, gas

flatulento /flatu'lento/ *a* flatulent, gassy

flauta /'flauta/ *f*, flute

flautín /flau'tin/ *m*, piccolo

flautista /flau'tista/ *mf* flutist

flebitis /fle'βitis/ *f*, phlebitis

flecha /'fletʃa/ *f*, arrow, dart

flechar /fle'tʃar/ *vt* to shoot an arrow or dart; wound or kill with arrows; *Inf.* inspire love; *vi* bend a bow to shoot

flechazo /fle'tʃaso; fle'tʃaθo/ *m*, wound with an arrow; *Inf.* love at first sight

flechero /fle'tʃero/ *m*, archer; arrow maker

fleco /'fleko/ *m*, fringe; fringe (of hair)

fleje /'flehe/ *m*, iron hoop (for barrels, etc.)

flema /'flema/ *f*, phlegm; sluggishness

flemático /fle'matiko/ *a* phlegmatic; sluggish

flemón /fle'mon/ *m*, gumboil; abscess

flequetero, -a /fleke'tero/ *a*, *Lat. Am.* dishonest, tricky

flequillo /fle'kiyo; fle'kiʎo/ *m*, fringe (of hair)

fletamento /fleta'mento/ *m*, chartering (a ship)

fletar /fle'tar/ *vt* to charter a ship; embark merchandise or people

flete /'flete/ *m*, freightage; cargo, freight

flexibilidad /fleksiβili'ðað/ *f*, flexibility; suppleness, adaptability

flexible /fle'ksiβle/ *a* pliant, supple; flexible, adaptable. *m*, *Elec.* flex

flirtear /flirte'ar/ *vi* to flirt

flirteo /flir'teo/ *m*, flirtation

flojedad /flohe'ðað/ *f*, flabbiness; weakness, feebleness; laziness, negligence

flojo /'floho/ *a* flabby; slack, loose; weak, feeble; lazy, slothful; poor (of a literary work, etc.)

floqueado /floke'aðo/ *a* fringed

flor /flor/ *f*, flower; best (of anything); bloom (on fruit); virginity; grain (of leather); compliment (gen. *pl*); menstruation (gen. *pl*). **f. de especia,** mace. **f. de la edad,** prime, youth. **f. del cuclillo,** mayflower. **f. del estudiante,** French marigold. **flores de mano,** artificial flowers. **flores de oblón,** hops. **a f. de,** on the surface of, level with. **andarse en flores,** *Fig.* to beat around the bush. **echar flores,** to pay compliments. **en f.,** in bloom

flora /'flora/ *f*, flora

floral /flo'ral/ *a* floral. **juegos florales,** poetry contest

florear /flore'ar/ *vt* to adorn with flowers; *vi* execute a flourish on the guitar

florecer /flore'ser; flore'θer/ *vi* *irr* to flower, bloom; flourish, prosper; *vr* grow mold (of cheese, etc.). See **conocer**

floreciente /flore'siente; flore'θiente/ *a* flowering; prosperous

florecimiento /floresi'miento; floreθi'miento/ *m*, flowering; prosperity

floreo /flo'reo/ *m*, witty conversation; flourish (on the guitar or in fencing)

florero /flo'rero/ *m*, vase; flower pot; *Art.* flower piece

florescencia /flores'sensia; flores'θenθia/ *f*, flowering; flowering season, florescence

floresta /flo'resta/ *f*, grove, wooded park, woodland; *Fig.* collector of beautiful things; anthology

florete /flo'rete/ *m*, fencing foil

floricultor /florikul'tor/ **(-ra)** *n* floriculturist

floricultura /florikul'tura/ *f*, floriculture

floridamente /floriða'mente/ *adv* elegantly, with a flourish

florido /flo'riðo/ *a* flowery; best, most select; florid, ornate

florilegio /flori'lehio/ *m*, anthology, collection

florín /flo'rin/ *m*, florin

florista /flo'rista/ *mf* artificial-flower maker; florist; flower seller

florón /flo'ron/ *m*, large flower; *Archit.* fleuron; honorable deed

flota /'flota/ *f*, fleet of merchant ships. **f. aérea,** air force

flotación /flota'sion; flota'θion/ *f*, floating. *Naut.* **línea de f.,** water line

flotador /flota'ðor/ a floating. m, float
flotamiento /flota'miento/ m, floating
flotante /flo'tante/ a floating
flotar /flo'tar/ vi to float on water or in air
flote /'flote/ m, floating. **a f.,** afloat; independent, solvent
flotilla /flo'tiya; flo'tiʎa/ f, flotilla; fleet of small ships. **f. aérea,** air fleet
fluctuación /fluktua'sion; fluktua'θion/ f, fluctuation; hesitation, vacillation
fluctuante /fluk'tuante/ a fluctuating
fluctuar /fluktu'ar/ vi to fluctuate; be in danger (things); vacillate, hesitate; undulate; oscillate
fluidez /flui'ðes; flui'ðeθ/ f, fluidity
flúido /'fluiðo/ a fluid; fluent. m, fluid; Elec. current
fluir /flu'ir/ vi irr to flow. See **huir**
flujo /'fluho/ m, flow, flux; rising tide. **f. de sangre,** hemorrhage
fluminense /flumi'nense/ formal a of Rio de Janeiro; mf native of Rio de Janeiro; resident of Rio de Janeiro
fluorescencia /fluores'sensia; fluores'θenθia/ f, fluorescence
fluorescente /fluores'sente; fluores'θente/ a fluorescent
flus /flus/ m, Colombia, Venezuela suit (of clothes)
fluvial /flu'βial/ a fluvial
flux /fluks/ m, flush (in cards)
foca /'foka/ f, Zool. seal
focal /fo'kal/ a focal
foco /'foko/ m, focus; center; origin; source; Theat. spotlight; core (of an abscess)
fofo /'fofo/ a spongy, soft; flabby
fogata /fo'gata/ f, bonfire
fogón /fo'gon/ m, fire, cooking area, kitchen range, kitchen stove; furnace of a steamboiler; vent of a firearm
fogonazo /fogo'naso; fogo'naθo/ m, powder flash
fogonero /fogo'nero/ m, stoker
fogosidad /fogosi'ðað/ f, enthusiasm; vehemence; ardor
fogoso /fo'goso/ a ardent; vehement; enthusiastic
folclórico /fol'kloriko/ a pertaining to folklore
folclorista /folklo'rista/ mf folklorist
folículo /fo'likulo/ m, follicle
folio /'folio/ m, leaf of a book or manuscript, folio. **en f.,** in folio
follaje /fo'yahe; fo'ʎahe/ m, foliage; leafy ornamentation; crude, unnecessary decoration; verbosity
folletín /foye'tin; foʎe'tin/ m, feuilleton, literary article; serial story; Inf. dime novel, potboiler
folletinista /foyeti'nista; foʎeti'nista/ mf pamphleteer
folleto /fo'yeto; fo'ʎeto/ m, pamphlet, leaflet
follisca /fo'jiska; fo'ʎiska/ f, Lat. Am. brawl
follón /fo'yon; fo'ʎon/ a lazy; caddish; craven
fomentación /fomenta'sion; fomenta'θion/ f, Med. fomentation, poultice
fomentador /fomenta'ðor/ a fomenting. m, fomenter
fomentar /fomen'tar/ vt to warm, foment; incite, instigate; Med. apply poultices
fomento /fo'mento/ m, heat, shelter; fuel; protection, encouragement; Med. fomentation
fonda /'fonda/ f, inn; restaurant
fondeadero /fondea'ðero/ m, anchorage, anchoring ground
fondear /fonde'ar/ vt Naut. to sound; search a ship; examine carefully; vi Naut. anchor; vr, Lat. Am. get rich
fondillos /fon'diyos; fon'diʎos/ m pl, seat (of the trousers)
fondista /fon'dista/ mf owner of an inn or restaurant
fondo /'fondo/ m, bottom (of a well, etc.); bed (of the sea, etc.); depth; rear, portion at the back; ground (of fabrics); background; Com. capital; Com. stock; Fig. fund (of humor, etc.); character, nature; temperament; Fig. substance, core, essence; Naut. bottom; pl Com. resources, funds. **f. de amortización,** sinking fund. **f. doble** or **f. secreto,** false bottom. **f. muerto, f. perdido** or **f. vitalicio,** life annuity. Com. **fondos inactivos,** idle capital. **a fondo,** com-

pletely, thoroughly. **artículo de f.,** editorial, lead article. Sports. **carrera de f.,** long-distance race. Naut. **irse a f.,** to sink, founder
fonética /fo'netika/ f, phonetics
fonético /fo'netiko/ a phonetic
fonetista /fone'tista/ mf phonetician
fonógrafo /fo'nografo/ m, phonograph
fonología /fonolo'hia/ f, phonology
fonológico /fono'lohiko/ a phonological
fontanar /fonta'nar/ m, spring, stream
fontanería /fontane'ria/ f, pipe laying, plumbing
fontanero /fonta'nero/ m, pipe layer; plumber
forajido /fora'hiðo/ **(-da)** a fugitive, outlawed. n robber, fugitive
foramen /fora'men/ m, Lat. Am. hole
forastero /foras'tero/ **(-ra)** a strange, foreign; alien, exotic. n stranger
forcejear /forsehe'ar; forθehe'ar/ vi to struggle; try, strive; oppose, contradict
forcejo /for'seho; for'θeho/ m, struggle; endeavor; opposition, hostility
fórceps /'forseps; 'forθeps/ m pl, forceps
forense /fo'rense/ a forensic
forillo /fo'riyo; fo'riʎo/ m, Theat. backdrop
forja /'forha/ f, forge
forjador /forha'ðor/ m, smith, ironworker
forjar /for'har/ vt to forge; fabricate; create; counterfeit
forma /'forma/ f, shape, form; arrangement; method; style; manifestation, expression; formula, formulary; ceremonial; Print. form; manner; means, way; mold, matrix; style of handwriting. Law. **en debida f.,** in due form
formación /forma''sion; forma'θion/ f, formation; form, contour, shape; (Mil. Geol.) formation. **f. del censo,** census taking
formador /forma'ðor/ a forming, shaping
formal /for'mal/ a apparent, formal; serious, punctilious, steady; truthful, reliable; sedate; orderly, regular, methodical
formaldehído /formalde'iðo/ m, formaldehyde
formalidad /formali'ðað/ f, orderliness, propriety; formality; requirement, requisite; ceremony; seriousness, sedateness; punctiliousness
formalismo /forma'lismo/ m, formalism; bureaucracy, red tape
formalizar /formali'sar; formali'θar/ vt to put into final form; legalize; formulate, enunciate; vr take seriously (a joke)
formar /for'mar/ vt to shape; form; educate, mold; Mil. form. **formarle causa a uno,** to bring charges against someone. vr develop, grow; Mexico get in line
formativo /forma'tiβo/ a formative
formato /for'mato/ m, Print. format; Chem. formate
formidable /formi'ðaβle/ a formidable, awe-inspiring; huge, enormous
fórmula /'formula/ f, formula; prescription; mode of expression. (Math. Chem.) **f. clásica,** standard formula
formular /formu'lar/ vt to formulate; prescribe
formulario /formu'lario/ m, Law. formulary; handbook; Lat. Am. form
formulismo /formu'lismo/ m, formulism; bureaucracy, red tape
fornicación /fornika'sion; fornika'θion/ f, fornication
fornicador /fornika'ðor/ **(-ra)** a and n fornicator
fornicar /forni'kar/ vi to fornicate
fornido /for'niðo/ a stalwart, muscular, strong
foro /'foro/ m, forum; law courts; law, bar, legal profession; Theat. back scenery; leasehold
forraje /fo'rrahe/ m, forage, fodder; foraging
forrajeador /forrahea'ðor/ m, forager
forrajear /forrahe'ar/ vt to gather forage, go foraging
forrar /fo'rrar/ vt Sew. to line; cover, encase, make a cover for
forro /'forro/ m, lining, inner covering; cover (of a book); Argentina condom; Lat. Am. fraud, swindle
fortalecedor /fortalese'ðor; fortaleθe'ðor/ a fortifying
fortalecer /fortale'ser; fortale'θer/ vt irr to fortify. See **conocer**

fortaleza /forta'lesa; forta'leθa/ *f*, vigor; fortitude; fortress; natural defense; *Lat. Am.* stench, stink. *Aer.*

f. volante, flying fortress
fortificable /fortifi'kaβle/ *a* fortifiable
fortificación /fortifika'sion; fortifika'θion/ *f*, fortification
fortificador /fortifika'ðor/ *a* fortifying
fortificar /fortifi'kar/ *vt* to fortify
fortísimo /for'tisimo/ *a sup* **fuerte** extremely strong
fortuito /for'tuito/ *a* fortuitous, chance
fortuna /for'tuna/ *f*, fate, destiny; fortune, capital, estate; tempest. **por f., probar f.,** fortunately. **probar f.,** to try one's luck
forzado /for'saðo; for'θaðo/ *a* forced, obliged. *m*, convict condemned to the galleys
forzador /forsa'ðor; forθa'ðor/ *m*, violator, seducer
forzar /for'sar; for'θar/ *vt irr* to force, break open; take by force; rape, ravish; oblige, compel. *Pres. Ind.* **fuerzo, fuerzas, fuerza, fuerzan.** *Preterite* **forcé, forzaste, etc.** *Pres. Subjunc.* **fuerce, fuerces, fuerce, forcemos, forcéis, fuercen**
forzoso /for'soso; for'θoso/ *a* obligatory, unavoidable, necessary
forzudo /for'suðo; for'θuðo/ *a* brawny, stalwart
fosa /'fosa/ *f*, grave; socket (of a joint). **f. común,** potter's field
fosar /fo'sar/ *vt* to undermine; dig a trench around
fosfato /fos'fato/ *m*, phosphate
fosforecer /fosfore'ser; fosfore'θer/ *vi irr* to phosphoresce. See **conocer**
fosforera /fosfo'rera/ *f*, matchbox
fosforero /fosfo'rero/ **(-ra)** *n* match seller
fosforescente /fosfores'sente; fosfores'θente/ *a* phosphorescent
fósforo /'fosforo/ *m*, phosphorus; match; morning star
fósil /'fosil/ *a* and *m*, fossil; *Inf.* antique
foso /'foso/ *m*, hole, hollow, pit; trench; pit (in garages); *Theat.* room under the stage.
foto /'foto/ *f*, snapshot, photo
fotocopia /foto'kopia/ *f*, photocopy
fotogénico /foto'heniko/ *a* photogenic
fotograbado /fotogra'βaðo/ *m*, photogravure
fotografía /fotogra'fia/ *f*, photography; photograph
fotografiar /fotogra'fiar/ *vt* to photograph
fotográfico /foto'grafiko/ *a* photographic
fotógrafo /fo'tografo/ *m*, photographer
fotograma /foto'grama/ *m*, (cinema) shot
fotoquímica /foto'kimika/ *f*, photochemistry
fotostato /foto'stato/ *m*, photostat
frac /frak/ *m*, tail coat
fracasar /fraka'sar/ *vi* to break, crumble, be shattered; collapse (of plans, etc.); fail; be disappointed, frustrate
fracaso /fra'kaso/ *m*, shattering; collapse (of plans, etc.); disaster; failure, disappointment, downfall, frustration
fracción /frak'sion; frak'θion/ *f*, division into parts; fraction. **f. impropia,** *Math.* improper fraction
fractura /frak'tura/ *f*, fracture. **f. conminuta,** compound fracture
fracturar /fraktu'rar/ *vt* to fracture
fragancia /fra'gansia; fra'ganθia/ *f*, fragrance, perfume; renown, good name
fragante /fra'gante/ *a* fragrant; perfumed; flagrant
fragata /fra'gata/ *f*, frigate
frágil /'frahil/ *a* fragile, brittle; perishable, frail; weak, sinful
fragilidad /frahili'ðað/ *f*, fragility; frailty, sinfulness
fragmentario /fragmen'tario/ *a* fragmentary
fragmento /frag'mento/ *m*, fragment
fragor /fra'gor/ *m*, noise, crash
fragosidad /fragosi'ðað/ *f*, roughness, rockiness, unevenness
fragoso /fra'goso/ *a* craggy, rocky; rough; noisy, clamorous
fragua /'fragua/ *f*, forge
fraguar /fra'guar/ *vt* to forge, work; plot, scheme; *vi* set (concrete, etc.)

fraile /'fraile/ *m*, friar, monk. *Inf.* **f. de misa y olla,** ignorant friar
frailesco /frai'lesko/ *a* *Inf.* pertaining to friars, friarlike
frambuesa /fram'buesa/ *f*, raspberry
francachela /franka'tʃela/ *f*, *Inf.* binge
francés /fran'ses; fran'θes/ **(-esa)** *a* French. *n* Frenchman (-woman). *m*, French (language). **a la francesa,** in French fashion
francesilla /franse'siya; franθe'siʎa/ *f*, *Cul.* French roll
Francia /'fransia; 'franθia/ France
francmasón /frankma'son/ **(-ona)** *n* Freemason
francmasonería /frankmasone'ria/ *f*, freemasonry
franco /'franko/ *a* generous, liberal; exempt; sincere, genuine, frank; duty-free; Frank; Franco (in compound words). *m*, franc (coin). **f. de porte,** post-free; prepaid
francotirador /frankotira'ðor/ *m*, sharpshooter, franc tireur
franela /fra'nela/ *f*, flannel; *Lat. Am.* undershirt; T-shirt
frangir /fran'hir/ *vt* to divide, quarter
frangollar /fraŋgo'yar; fraŋgo'ʎar/ *vt* to scamp, skimp (work); botch, bungle
franja /'franha/ *f*, fringe; border, trimming; stripe. *Radio.* **f. undosa,** wave band
franjar /fran'har/ *vt* *Sew.* to fringe, trim
franqueadora /frankea'ðora/ *f*, postage meter
franquear /franke'ar/ *vt* to exempt; make free, make a gift of; clear the way; stamp, prepay; free (slaves); *vr* fall in easily with others' plans; make confidences
franqueo /fran'keo/ *m*, exemption; bestowal, making free; postage, stamping; enfranchisement (of slaves)
franqueza /fran'kesa; fran'keθa/ *f*, exemption, freedom; generosity, liberality; sincerity, frankness
franquicia /fran'kisia; fran'kiθia/ *f*, exemption from excise duties
franquista /fran'kista/ *mf* Franquist, supporter of Franco
frasco /'frasko/ *m*, bottle, flask; powder flask or horn. **f. cuentagotas,** drop bottle
frase /'frase/ *f*, sentence; phrase; epigram; idiom, style. **f. hecha,** cliché
frasear /frase'ar/ *vt* to phrase
fraseología /fraseolo'hia/ *f*, phraseology; wording
fratás /fra'tas/ *m*, plastering trowel
fraternal /frater'nal/ *a* brotherly
fraternidad /fraterni'ðað/ *f*, fraternity, brotherhood
fraternizar /fraterni'sar; fraterni'θar/ *vi* to fraternize
fraterno /fra'terno/ *a* fraternal
fratricida /fratri'siða; fratri'θiða/ *a* fratricidal. *mf* fratricide
fratricidio /fratri'siðio; fratri'θiðio/ *m*, fratricide (act)
fraude /'frauðe/ *m*, fraud, deception
fraudulento /frauðu'lento/ *a* fraudulent
fray /frai/ *m*, abb **fraile.** Always followed by a proper name (e.g. *F. Bartolomé,* Friar Bartholomew)
frazada /fra'saða; fra'θaða/ *f*, blanket
frecuencia /fre'kuensia; fre'kuenθia/ *f*, frequency. **f. radioeléctrica,** radiofrequency
frecuentación /frekuenta'sion; frekuenta'θion/ *f*, frequenting, visiting
frecuentador /frekuenta'ðor/ **(-ra)** *n* frequenter
frecuentar /frekuen'tar/ *vt* to frequent
frecuente /fre'kuente/ *a* frequent
fregada /fre'gaða/ *f*, *Lat. Am.* bother, hassle, nuisance
fregadero /frega'ðero/ *m*, kitchen sink
fregado /fre'gaðo/ *m*, scrubbing; rubbing; scouring; washing; *Inf.* murky business
fregador /frega'ðor/ *m*, kitchen sink; scrub brush; dishcloth. **f. mecánico de platos,** dishwasher
fregandera /fregan'dera/ *f*, *Mexico* charwoman, cleaning woman
fregar /fre'gar/ *vt irr* to rub; scour; wash (dishes). See **cegar**
fregona /fre'gona/ *f*, kitchen maid
fregotear /fregote'ar/ *vt* *Inf.* to clean or scour inefficiently

freiduría /freiðu'ria/ *f*, fried-fish shop

freír /fre'ir/ *vt irr Cul.* to fry. See **reír**

frenar /fre'nar/ *vt* to restrain, hold back; bridle, check; *Mech.* brake

frenesí /frene'si/ *m*, madness, frenzy; vehemence, exaltation

frenético /fre'netiko/ *a* mad, frenzied; vehement, exalted

freno /'freno/ *m*, bridle; *Mech.* brake; restraint, check. **f. de pedal,** foot brake. **f. neumático,** vacuum brake, pneumatic brake

frente /'frente/ *f*, brow, forehead; front portion; countenance; head; heading; beginning (of a letter, etc.). *m*, *Mil.* front. *mf* facade; front; obverse (of coins). *adv* in front, opposite. **f. a f.,** face to face. **con la f. levantada,** with head held high; proudly; insolently. **de f.,** abreast

freo /'freo/ *m*, strait, narrow channel

fresa /'fresa/ *f*, strawberry plant and fruit (especially small or wild varieties); *Mech.* milling cutter, miller

fresadora /fresa'ðora/ *f*, milling machine

fresal /fre'sal/ *m*, strawberry bed

fresca /'freska/ *f*, cool air; fresh air; *Inf.* home truth

fresco /'fresko/ *a* cool; fresh, new; recent; buxom, fresh-colored; calm, serene; *Inf.* impudent, cheeky, bold; thin (cloths). *m*, coolness; fresh air; *Art.* fresco. **al f.,** in the open air. **hacer f.,** to be cool or fresh

frescote /fres'kote/ *a Inf.* ruddy and corpulent

frescura /fres'kura/ *f*, coolness; freshness; pleasant verdure and fertility; *Inf.* cheek, nerve; piece of insolence; unconcern, indifference; calmness, serenity

fresero /fre'sero/ **(-ra)** *n* strawberry seller

fresno /'fresno/ *m*, *Bot.* ash

fresón /fre'son/ *m*, strawberry (large, cultivated varieties)

fresquera /fres'kera/ *f*, meat locker; cool place

fresquería /freske'ria/ *f*, *Mexico* refreshment stand

fresquista /fres'kista/ *mf* fresco painter

friable /'friaβle/ *a* brittle; friable, powdery

frialdad /frial'dað/ *f*, coldness, chilliness; *Med.* frigidity; indifference, lack of interest; foolishness; negligence

fríamente /fria'mente/ *adv* coldly; coolly, with indifference; dully, flatly

fricción /frik'sion; frik'θion/ *f*, friction

friccionar /friksio'nar; frikθio'nar/ *vt* to rub; give a massage

friega /'friega/ *f*, friction, massage

frigidez /frihi'ðes; frihi'ðeθ/ *f*, See **frialdad**

frígido /'frihiðo/ *a* frigid

frigio /'frihio/ *a* and *n* Phrygian

frigorífico /frigo'rifiko/ *a* refrigerative. *m*, refrigerator, cold-storage locker

frijol /fri'hol/ *m*, bean; *Bot.* kidney bean. **frijoles refritos con queso,** *Mexico* refried beans with cheese

frío /'frio/ *a* cold; *Med.* frigid; indifferent, uninterested; dull, uninteresting; inefficient. *m*, coldness, chill; cold

friolera /frio'lera/ *f*, bagatelle, trifle, mere nothing

friolero /frio'lero/ *a* sensitive to cold

frisa /'frisa/ *f*, frieze cloth

frisar /fri'sar/ *vt* to frizz, curl (cloth); scrub, rub; *vi* approach, be nearly (e.g. *Frisa en los setenta años,* He's nearly seventy)

friso /'friso/ *m*, frieze; dado, border

fritada /fri'taða/ *f*, *Cul.* fry, fried food

frito /'frito/ *a* fried

fritura /fri'tura/ *f*, frying; fried food

frivolidad /friβoli'ðað/ *f*, frivolity

frivolité /friβoli'te/ *m*, *Sew.* tatting

frívolo /'friβolo/ *a* frivolous, superficial; futile, unconvincing

fronda /'fronda/ *f*, *Bot.* leaf; frond (of ferns); *pl* foliage

frondoso /fron'doso/ *a* leafy

frontera /fron'tera/ *f*, frontier; facade

fronterizo /fronte'riso; fronte'riθo/ *a* frontier; facing, opposite

frontero /fron'tero/ *a* facing, opposite. *m*, (*Obs. Mil.*) frontier commander

frontispicio /frontis'pisio; frontis'piθio/ *m*, frontispiece; facade; *Fig. Inf.* face, dial

frontón /fron'ton/ *m*, pelota court; jai alai court; *Archit.* pediment; *Mexico* jai alai

frotamiento, frote /frota'miento, 'frote/ *m*, rubbing, friction

frotar /fro'tar/ *vt* to rub

frotis /'frotis/ *m*, *Med.* smear

fructífero /fruk'tifero/ *a* fruitful, fructiferous

fructuoso /fruk'tuoso/ *a* fruitful, fertile; useful

frufrú /fru'fru/ *m*, rustle (of silk, etc.)

frugal /fru'gal/ *a* frugal; saving, economical

frugalidad /frugali'ðað/ *f*, frugality, abstemiousness, moderation

fruición /frui'sion; frui'θion/ *f*, enjoyment; fruition; satisfaction

fruir /fruir/ *vi irr* to enjoy what one has long desired. See **huir**

frunce /'frunse; 'frunθe/ *m*, *Sew.* shirring; gather; ruffling; tuck; pucker; wrinkle

fruncimiento /frunsi'miento; frunθi'miento/ *m*, wrinkling; puckering; *Sew.* shirring

fruncir /frun'sir; frun'θir/ *vt* to frown; purse (the lips); pucker; *Sew.* shirr, pleat, gather; reduce in size; conceal the truth; *vr* pretend to be prudish. **f. el ceño,** to knit one's brow, scowl

fruslería /frusle'ria/ *f*, trifle, nothing

frustración /frustra'sion; frustra'θion/ *f*, frustration

frustrar /frus'trar/ *vt* to disappoint; frustrate, thwart

fruta /'fruta/ *f*, fruit; *Inf.* consequence, result. **f. bomba,** *Cuba* papaya **f. de hueso,** stone fruit. *Cul.* **f. de sartén,** fritter

frutal /fru'tal/ *a* fruit-bearing. *m*, fruit tree

frutar /fru'tar/ *vi* to bear fruit

frutería /frute'ria/ *f*, fruit

frutero /fru'tero/ **(-ra)** *a* fruit. *n* fruit seller. *m*, fruit dish; *Art.* painting of fruit; basket of imitation fruit

frútice /'frutise; 'frutiθe/ *m*, bush, shrub

fruticultura /frutikul'tura/ *f*, fruit farming

fruto /'fruto/ *m*, fruit; product, result; profit, proceeds; *Agr.* grain

fu /fu/ spitting (of cats). *interj* expression of scorn. *Inf.* **ni f. ni fa,** neither one thing nor the other

fucsia /'fuksia/ *f*, fuchsia

fuego /'fuego/ *m*, fire; conflagration; firing (of firearms); beacon; hearth, home; rash; ardor; heat (of an argument, etc.); *interj* **¡F.!** *Mil.* Fire! **fuegos artificiales,** fireworks. **a sangre y f.,** by fire and sword. *Mil.* **hacer f.,** to fire (a weapon). **pegar f.,** to set on fire

fuelle /'fueye; 'fueʎe/ *m*, bellows; bag (of a bagpipe); *Sew.* pucker, wrinkle; hood (of a carriage, etc.); wind cloud; *Inf.* talebearer. **f. de pie,** foot pump

fuente /'fuente/ *f*, stream, spring; fountain; meat dish; genesis, origin; source, headwaters; tap

fuera /'fuera/ *adv* outside, out. *interj* get out! **f. de,** besides, in addition to. **f. de alcance,** out of reach. **f. de sí,** beside oneself (with rage, etc.). **de f.,** from the outside. **por f.,** on the outside, externally

fuereño, -a /fue'reɲo/ *mf*, *Mexico* foreigner

fuero /'fuero/ *m*, municipal charter; jurisdiction; compilation of laws; legal right or privilege; *pl Inf.* arrogance. **los fueros de León,** the laws of León

fuerte /'fuerte/ *a* strong, resistant; robust; spirited, vigorous; hard (of diamonds, etc.); rough, uneven; impregnable; terrible, tremendous; overweight (of coins); active; efficacious, effective; expert, knowledgeable; *Gram.* strong; intense; loud; tough. *m*, fort; talent, strong point; *Mus.* forte. *adv* strongly; excessively. **tener genio f.,** to be quick-tempered

fuerza /'fuersa; 'fuerθa/ *f*, strength; power, might; force; efficacy; fortress; *Sew.* stiffening; *Mech.* power; violence; toughness, durability, solidity; potency; authority; courage; vigor; *pl Fig. Inf.* livewires, influential people. **a f. de,** by means of, by dint of. **a la f.,** forcibly. **en f. de,** because of, on account of. **por f. mayor,** by main force. **ser f.,** to be necessary

fuga /'fuga/ *f*, flight, escape, running away; leak (gas, etc.); elopement; *Mus.* fugue; ardor; strength. **f. de cerebros,** brain drain

fugarse /fu'garse/ *vr* to run away; elope; escape
fugaz /fu'gas; fu'gaθ/ *a* fugitive; fleeting, brief
fugitivo /fuhi'tiβo/ (**-va**) *a* fugitive; runaway, escaping; transient. *n* fugitive
fulano /fu'lano/ (**-na**) *n* so-and-so, such a person **f., zutano, y mengano,** *Inf.* Tom, Dick, and Harry
fulcro /'fulkro/ *m*, fulcrum
fulgente, fúlgido /ful'hente, 'fulhiðo/ *a* brilliant, shining
fulgor /ful'gor/ *m*, brilliance, brightness
fulgurar /fulgu'rar/ *vi* to shine, be resplendent, scintillate; flare
fulguroso /fulgu'roso/ *a* shining, sparkling
fullería /fuye'ria; fuʎe'ria/ *f*, cheating at play; craftiness, low guile
fullero /fu'yero; fu'ʎero/ (**-ra**) *a* cheating; crafty, astute. *n* cheat, cardsharper
fulminante /fulmi'nante/ *a Med.* fulminant; fulminating; thundering. *m*, percussion cap
fulminar /fulmi'nar/ *vt* to fulminate (all meanings)
fulminato /fulmi'nato/ *m*, *Chem.* fulminate
fulmíneo, fulminoso /ful'mineo, fulmi'noso/ *a* fulminous, pertaining to lightning
fumadero /fuma'ðero/ *m*, smoking room
fumador /fuma'ðor/ (**-ra**) *a* smoking. *n* smoker. «**No fumadores**», "Nonsmoking" (area)
fumar /fu'mar/ *vi* to smoke; *vr Inf.* dissipate, waste
fumarola /fuma'rola/ *f*, fumarole
fumigación /fumiga'sion; fumiga'θion/ *f*, fumigation
fumigador /fumiga'ðor/ (**-ra**) *n* fumigator
fumigar /fumi'gar/ *vt* to fumigate
fumigatorio /fumiga'torio/ *a* fumigatory. *m*, perfume burner
fumista /fu'mista/ *mf* stove maker; stove dealer; *Argentina* joker, tease
fumistería /fumiste'ria/ *f*, stove factory or store
funámbulo /fu'nambulo/ *n* tightrope walker, acrobat
función /fun'sion; fun'θion/ *f*, function; working, operation; *Theat.* performance; activity, duty; ceremony; celebration; *Math.* function; *Mil.* battle
funcional /funsio'nal; funθio'nal/ *a* functional
funcionamiento /funsiona'miento; funθiona'miento/ *m*, functioning
funcionar /funsio'nar; funθio'nar/ *vi* to function, work. «**No funciona**», "Out of order"
funcionario /funsio'nario; funθio'nario/ *m*, functionary, official; civil servant
funda /'funda/ *f*, case, cover, sheath; hold-all. **f. de almohada,** pillowcase
fundación /funda'sion; funda'θion/ *f*, foundation
fundadamente /fundaða'mente/ *adv* with reason, on good evidence
fundador /funda'ðor/ (**-ra**) *n* founder, creator; originator
fundamental /funda'mental/ *a* fundamental
fundamento /funda'mento/ *m*, *Mas.* foundation; basis; basic principle, reason; origin, root
fundar /fun'dar/ *vt* to build, erect; base; found, institute; create, establish; *vr* (*with en*) found, base upon. **f. una compañía,** *Com.* to float a company
fundición /fundi'sion; fundi'θion/ *f*, foundry; smelting, founding, casting; cast iron; *Print.* font
fundido fotográfico /fun'diðo foto'grafiko/ *m*, composite photograph

fundidor /fundi'ðor/ *m*, founder, smelter.
fundir /fun'dir/ *vt* to melt; found, smelt; cast (metals); *vr* join together, unite; *Elec.* blow (fuses)
fúnebre /'funeβre/ *a* funeral; dismal, lugubrious, mournful
funerala, /fune'rala,/ (**a la**) *adv Mil.* with reversed arms
funerales /fune'rales/ *m pl*, funeral; *Eccl.* memorial masses
funeraria /fune'raria/ *f*, funeral home, undertaker
funéreo /fu'nereo/ *a* funereal, mournful
funestidad /funesti'ðað/ *f*, *Mexico* calamity, catastrophe
funesto /fu'nesto/ *a* unlucky, unfortunate; mournful, melancholy, sad
fungoso /fuŋ'goso/ *a* spongy, fungous
funicular /funiku'lar/ *a* funicular. *n* cable car
furgón /fur'gon/ *m*, wagon; van; guard's van, baggage car, luggage cart. **f. postal,** mail truck
furia /'furia/ *f*, *Myth.* fury; rage, wrath; fit of madness; raging, violence (of the elements); speed, haste
furibundo /furi'βundo/ *a* frantic, furious; raging
fúrico /'furiko/ *a* stark raving mad
furioso /fu'rioso/ *a* furious, enraged; mad, insane; violent, terrible; enormous, excessive
furor /fu'ror/ *m*, fury, rage; poetic frenzy; violence; furor
furtivo /fur'tiβo/ *a* furtive; covert, clandestine; pirate (editions)
fusa /'fusa/ *f*, demisemiquaver
fusco /'fusko/ *a* dark
fuselado /fuse'laðo/ *a* streamlined
fuselaje /fuse'lahe/ *m*, fuselage
fusible /fu'siβle/ *a* fusible. *m*, *Elec.* fuse; fuse wire
fusil /fu'sil/ *m*, rifle
fusilamiento /fusila'miento/ *m*, execution by shooting
fusilar /fusi'lar/ *vt* to execute by shooting; *Inf.* plagiarize
fusilazo /fusi'laso; fusi'laθo/ *m*, rifle shot
fusión /fu'sion/ *f*, melting, liquefying; fusion, blending; mixture, union; *Com.* merger, amalgamation
fusionar /fusio'nar/ *vt* to blend, fuse, merge; *vr Com.* combine, form a merger
fusta /'fusta/ *f*, brushwood; whip
fustán /fus'tan/ *m Lat. Am.* skirt
fuste /'fuste/ *m*, wood, timber; *Poet.* saddle; *Fig.* core, essence; importance, substance; shaft of a lance; *Archit.* shaft. **hombre de buen f.,** a man with a good (physical) constitution
fustigar /fusti'gar/ *vt* to whip, lash; rebuke harshly
fútbol /'futβol/ *m*, football; soccer
futbolista /futβo'lista/ *mf* football player; soccer player
fútil /'futil/ *a* futile, ineffectual, worthless
futilidad /futili'ðað/ *f*, futility, worthlessness
futura /fu'tura/ *f*, *Law.* reversion (of offices); *Inf.* fiancée
futurismo /futu'rismo/ *m*, futurism
futurista /futu'rista/ *mf* futurist
futurístico /futu'ristiko/ *a* futuristic
futuro /fu'turo/ (**-ra**) *a* future. *m*, future. *n Inf.* betrothed

G

gabacho /ga'βatʃo/ (**-cha**) *a* and *n* (*inf* scornful) Frenchman
gabán /ga'βan/ *m*, overcoat; cloak
gabardina /gaβar'ðina/ *f*, gabardine; weatherproof coat
gabarra /ga'βarra/ *f*, *Naut.* lighter, gabbard, barge
gabarro /ga'βarro/ *m*, flaw (in cloth); knot (in stone); snag, drawback; slip, error (in accounts)
gabela /ga'βela/ *f*, duty, tax; imposition; burden
gabinete /gaβi'nete/ *m*, study, library; sitting room;

den; *Polit.* cabinet; collection, museum, gallery; laboratory; boudoir; studio; display cabinet. **g. de lectura,** reading room
gablete /ga'βlete/ *m*, *Archit.* gable
gaceta /ga'seta; ga'θeta/ *f*, bulletin, review, record; newspaper; gazette (official Spanish government organ); *Inf.* newshound
gacetero /gase'tero; gaθe'tero/ (**-ra**) *n* newsdealer. *m*, news reporter
gacetilla /gase'tiya; gaθe'tiʎa/ *f*, news in brief, mis-

cellany column, society news; gossip column; *Inf.* newshound

gacetillero /gaseti'yero; gaθeti'ʎero/ *m,* paragrapher, penny-a-liner; reporter

gacha /'gatʃa/ *f,* unglazed crock; *pl* pap; porridge

gaché /ga'tʃe/ *m,* (among the Romany) Andalusian; *Inf.* fellow

gacho /'gatʃo/ *a* drooping, bent downward; slouch (hat); (of ears) lop; *Mexico* unpleasant

gachón /ga'tʃon/ *a Inf.* attractive, charming

gaélico /ga'eliko/ *a* and *m,* Gaelic

gafar /ga'far/ *vt* to claw; seize with a hook, hook; mend with a bracket (pottery)

gafas /'gafas/ *f pl,* eyeglasses; goggles; spectacle earhooks; grapplehooks

gafete /ga'fete/ *m,* hook and eye; clasp

gaita /'gaita/ *f,* bagpipe; hand organ; kind of clarinet; *Inf.* neck. **g. gallega,** bagpipe

gaitería /gaite'ria/ *f,* crude, gaudy garment or ornament

gaitero /gai'tero/ *a Inf.* overmerry; loud, crude. *m,* piper

gajes /'gahes/ *m pl,* salary; emoluments; perquisites

gajo /'gaho/ *m,* branch, bough (gen. cut); little cluster (of grapes); bunch (of fruit); quarter (of oranges, etc.); prong (of forks, etc.)

gala /'gala/ *f,* evening or full dress; grace, wit; flower, cream, best; gala; *pl* finery; trappings; wedding presents. **de g.,** full dress. **hacer g. de,** to glory in, boast of

galactita /galak'tita/ *f,* fuller's earth

galaico /ga'laiko/ *a* See **gallego**

galán /ga'lan/ *m,* handsome, well-made man; lover, wooer, gallant; *Theat.* leading man or one of leading male roles

galancete /galan'sete; galan'θete/ *m,* handsome little man; *Theat.* male juvenile lead

galano /ga'lano/ *a* smart, well-dressed; agreeable, pleasing; beautiful; ornamented; *Fig.* elegant (speech, style, etc.)

galante /ga'lante/ *a* gallant, courtly, attentive; flirtatious (of women); licentious

galanteador /galantea'ðor/ *a* flirtatious. *m,* philanderer; wooer

galantear /galante'ar/ *vt* to court; flirt with; make love to; *Fig.* procure assiduously

galanteo /galan'teo/ *m,* courtship; flirtation; love-making; wooing

galantería /galante'ria/ *f,* courtesy; attention; compliment; elegance, grace; gallantry; generosity, liberality

galanura /gala'nura/ *f,* showiness, gorgeousness; elegance, grace; prettiness

galápago /ga'lapago/ *m,* freshwater tortoise; cleat

galardón /galar'ðon/ *m,* reward, recompense, prize

galardonar /galarðo'nar/ *vt* to reward, recompense

galbana /gal'βana/ *f,* laziness, inertia

galbanoso /galβa'noso/ *a Inf.* slothful

galdrufa /gal'drufa/ *f,* top, spinning top

galera /ga'lera/ *f,* van, wagon, cart; *Naut.* galley; prison for women; *Print.* galley; *Central America, Mexico* shed. **echar a galeras,** to condemn to the galleys

galerada /gale'raða/ *f,* galley proof

galería /gale'ria/ *f,* gallery; corridor, passage; collection of paintings; *Mineral.* gallery, drift; *Theat.* gallery

galerna /ga'lerna/ *f,* tempestuous northwest wind (gen. on Spanish north coast)

Gales /'gales/ Wales

galés /'gales/ **(-esa)** *a* Welsh. *n* Welshman. *m,* Welsh (language)

galga /'galga/ *f,* boulder, rolling stone; female greyhound

galgo /'galgo/ *m,* greyhound. **g. ruso,** borzoi

Galia /'galia/ Gaul

gálibo /'galiβo/ *m, Naut.* mold; elegance

galicado /gali'kaðo/ *a* gallicized

galicismo /gali'sismo; gali'θismo/ *m,* gallicism

gálico /'galiko/ *m,* syphilis. *a* gallic

Galilea /gali'lea/ Galilee

galileo /gali'leo/ **(-ea)** *a* and *n* Galilean

galimatías /galima'tias/ *m, Inf.* gibberish, nonsense

gallardear /gayarðe'ar; gaʎarðe'ar/ *vi* to behave with ease and grace

gallardete /gayar'ðete; gaʎar'ðete/ *m,* pennant; bunting

gallardía /gayar'ðia; gaʎar'ðia/ *f,* grace, dignity; spirit, dash; courage; liveliness

gallardo /ga'yarðo; ga'ʎarðo/ *a* handsome, upstanding; gallant; spirited; fine, noble; lively

gallear /gaye'ar; gaʎe'ar/ *vi Inf.* to put on airs; be a bully; shout, bawl (with anger, etc.); *Fig. Inf.* stand out

gallego /ga'yego; ga'ʎego/ **(-ga)** *a* and *n* Galician. *m,* Galician (language)

galleta /ga'yeta; ga'ʎeta/ *f,* biscuit; cookie; cracker; *Inf.* slap; anthracite, lump coal; small jar or vessel

gallina /ga'yina; ga'ʎina/ *f,* hen. *mf Inf.* coward. **g. ciega,** blindman's buff. *Inf.* **acostarse con las gallinas,** to go to bed early

gallinaza /gayi'nasa; gaʎi'naθa/ *f,* hen dung

gallinero /gayi'nero; gaʎi'nero/ **(-ra)** *n* poultry dealer. *m,* henhouse; brood of hens; *Theat.* gallery; babel, noisy place

gallito /ga'yito; ga'ʎito/ *m,* small cock; cock of the walk; bully

gallo /'gayo; ga'ʎo/ *m, Ornith.* cock; *Inf.* false note (in singing); *Inf.* boss, chief. **g. de viento,** weathercock. *Inf.* **alzar el g.,** to put on airs, boast. **Cada g. canta en su muladar,** Every man is boss in his own house. *Inf.* **Otro g. nos cantara,** Our lot (or fate) would have been very different

gallofero /gayo'fero; gaʎo'fero/ **(-ra)** *a* mendicant, vagabond. *n* beggar

galocha /ga'lotʃa/ *f,* patten, clog; cap with earflaps

galón /ga'lon/ *m,* galloon, braid; *Mil.* stripe; gallon (measure)

galoneadura /galonea'ðura/ *f,* braiding, trimming

galonear /galone'ar/ *vt* to trim with braid

galopante /galo'pante/ *a* galloping (of consumption, etc.)

galopar /galo'par/ *vi* to gallop; *Mech.* wobble

galope /ga'lope/ *m,* gallop. **a** or **de g.,** at the gallop; on the run, quickly. **andar a g. corto,** to canter

galopillo /galo'piyo; galo'piʎo/ *m,* scullion

galopín /galo'pin/ *m,* ragamuffin, urchin; rogue, knave; *Inf.* clever rogue; *Naut.* cabin boy

galvanización /galβanisa'sion; galβaniθa'θion/ *f,* galvanization

galvanizar /galβani'sar; galβani'θar/ *vt Elec.* to galvanize; electroplate; *Fig.* shock into life

gama /'gama/ *f, Mus.* scale; gamut, range; doe

gamba /'gamba/ *f,* prawn

gambado /gam'βaðo/ *a Lat. Am.* knock-kneed

gambito /gam'bito/ *m,* gambit (in chess)

gamella /ga'meya; ga'meʎa/ *f,* trough (for washing, feeding animals, etc.)

gamo /'gamo/ *m,* buck (of the fallow deer)

gamuza /ga'musa; ga'muθa/ *f,* chamois; chamois leather

gana /'gana/ *f,* appetite; wish, desire. **de buena g.,** willingly. **de mala g.,** reluctantly. **tener ganas (de),** to wish, desire, want. **no tener g.,** to have no appetite, not be hungry. **No me da la g.,** I don't want (to), I won't

ganable /ga'naβle/ *a* attainable; earnable

ganadería /ganaðe'ria/ *f,* livestock; strain (of cattle); cattle raising; stock farm; cattle dealing

ganadero /gana'ðero/ *m,* cattle raiser or dealer; herdsman

ganado /ga'naðo/ *m,* livestock, herd; flock; hive (of bees); *Inf.* mob. **g. mayor,** cattle, mules, horses. **g. menor,** sheep, goats, etc. **g. moreno,** hogs, swine. **g. vacuno,** cattle

ganador /gana'ðor/ **(-ra)** *a* winning. *n* winner

ganancia /ga'nansia; ga'nanθia/ *f,* winning; gain, profit

ganancial, ganancioso /ganan'sial, ganan'sioso; ganan'θial, ganan'θioso/ *a* gainful, profitable; lucrative

ganapán /gana'pan/ *m,* laborer; porter; *Inf.* boor

ganar /ga'nar/ *vt* to gain; win; conquer; arrive at; earn; surpass, beat; achieve; acquire; *vi* prosper

ganchero /gan'tʃero/ *m*, lumberjack

ganchillo /gan'tʃiʝo; gan'tʃiʎo/ *m*, crochet hook; crochet. **hacer g.,** to crochet

gancho /'gantʃo/ *m*, hook; stump (of a branch); shepherd's crook; crochet hook; *Inf.* trickster, pimp; *Inf.* scribble

ganchoso /gan'tʃoso/ *a* hooked; bent; curved

gandujar /gandu'har/ *vt Sew.* to pleat, tuck, shirr

gandul /gan'dul/ **(-la)** *a Inf.* lazy. *n* lazybones, loafer

gandulería /gandule'ria/ *f*, loafing, idleness

ganga /'gaŋga/ *f, Mineral.* gangue, matrix; bargain, cinch

ganglio /'gaŋglio/ *m*, ganglion

gangoso /gaŋ'goso/ *a* nasal; with a twang (of speech)

gangrena /gaŋ'grena/ *f*, gangrene

gangrenarse /gaŋgre'narse/ *vr* to become gangrenous, mortify

gangrenoso /gaŋgre'noso/ *a* gangrenous

ganguear /gaŋgue'ar/ *vi* to speak nasally, or with a twang

ganoso /ga'noso/ *a* wishful, desirous, anxious

gansada /gan'saða/ *f, Inf.* impertinence, foolishness

ganso /'ganso/ **(-sa)** *n* goose, gander; slow-moving person; yokel, bumpkin

ganuar /ga'nuar/ *vi Lat. Am.* to drizzle

ganzúa /gan'sua; gan'θua/ *f*, skeleton key; *Inf.* picklock, burglar; *Inf.* pumper, inquisitive person

gañán /ga'ɲan/ *m*, farm worker; day laborer; brawny fellow

gañido /ga'ɲiðo/ *m*, yowl, yelp, howl

gañir /ga'ɲir/ *vi irr* to yowl, yelp, howl (of dogs, etc.); crow, croak; *Inf.* talk hoarsely. See **mullir**

garabatear /garaβate'ar/ *vi* to hook, catch with hooks; scribble; *Fig. Inf.* beat around the bush

garabateo /garaβa'teo/ *m*, hooking; scribbling

garabato /gara'βato/ *m*, hook; *Agr.* weed clearer; scrawl, scribble; *Inf.* charm, sex appeal; pothook; boat hook; *pl* gestures, movements (with the hands)

garaje /ga'rahe/ *m*, garage

garambaina /garam'baina/ *f*, tawdry finery; gaudiness; *pl Inf.* grimaces of affectation; *Inf.* scribble, scrawl

garante /ga'rante/ *mf* guarantor; reference (person). *a* responsible, guaranteeing

garantía /garan'tia/ *f*, guarantee; security, pledge; *Law.* warranty

garantir /garan'tir/ *vt* to guarantee; warrant, vouch for

garañón /gara'ɲon/ *m Lat. Am.* stallion

garapiñar /garapi'ɲar/ *vt* to ice, freeze (drinks, syrups, etc.); *Cul.* candy, coat with sugar

garbanzo /gar'βanso; gar'βanθo/ *m*, chickpea. **g. negro,** *Fig.* black sheep

garbillar /garβi'yar; garβi'ʎar/ *vt Agr.* to sift; *Mineral.* riddle

garbo /'garβo/ *m*, jaunty air; grace, elegance; frankness; generosity, liberality

garboso /gar'βoso/ *a* attractive; handsome, sprightly, gay; graceful; munificent

garduña /gar'ðuɲa/ *f*, weasel; marten

garduño /gar'ðuɲo/ **(-ña)** *n Inf.* sneak thief

garete /ga'rete/ (**ir** or **irse al**) *Naut.* to be adrift

garfa /'garfa/ *f*, claw (of a bird or animal)

garfear /garfe'ar/ *vi* to catch with a hook, hook

garfio /'garfio/ *m*, grappling iron, hook, drag hook, cramp; gaff

gargajear /gargahe'ar/ *vi* to expectorate

gargajo /gar'gaho/ *m*, phlegm

garganta /gar'ganta/ *f*, throat; gullet; instep; defile; neck, shaft, narrowest part

gargantear /gargante'ar/ *vi* to warble, trill

gárgara /'gargara/ *f*, gargling (gen. *pl*). **hacer gárgaras,** to gargle

gargarismo /garga'rismo/ *m*, gargling; gargle

gárgol /'gargol/ *a* rotten (eggs). *m*, groove, mortise

gárgola /'gargola/ *f, Archit.* gargoyle; linseed

garguero /gar'gero/ *m*, windpipe; esophagus

garita /ga'rita/ *f*, sentry box; porter's lodge; hut; cabin. **g. de señales,** (railroad) signal box

garitero /gari'tero/ *m*, gambling house keeper; gambler

garito /ga'rito/ *m*, gambling house; profits of a gambling house

garra /'garra/ *f*, paw with claws; talon; hand; *Mech.* clamp, claw. *Fig.* **caer en las garras de,** to fall into the clutches (of)

garrafa /ga'rrafa/ *f*, decanter, carafe; carboy

garrapata /garra'pata/ *f, Ent.* tick

garrapatear /garrapate'ar/ *vi* to scribble

garrapaticida /garrapati'siða; garrapati'θiða/ *m, Lat. Am.* insecticide

garrapato /garra'pato/ *m*, scribble, scrawl

garrido /ga'rriðo/ *a* handsome; gallant; elegant; graceful

garroba /ga'rroβa/ *f*, carob bean

garrocha /ga'rrotʃa/ *f*, goad. **salto a la g.,** pole jumping

garrotazo /garro'taso; garro'taθo/ *m*, blow with a truncheon or cudgel. **dar garrotazos de ciego,** to lay about one

garrote /ga'rrote/ *m*, truncheon, club; *Med.* tourniquet; garrote. **dar g. (a),** to strangle

garrotillo /garro'tiyo; garro'tiʎo/ *m*, croup

garrucha /ga'rrutʃa/ *f*, pulley; *Mech.* gin block

garrulidad /garruli'ðað/ *f*, garrulity, loquaciousness

gárrulo /'garrulo/ *a* twittering, chirping (birds); garrulous; murmuring, babbling (wind, water, etc.)

garza /'garsa; 'garθa/ *f*, heron

garzo /'garso; 'garθo/ *a* blue (gen. of eyes)

gas /gas/ *m*, gas; fumes. **g. asfixiante,** poison gas. **cámara de g.,** gasbag, gas chamber

gasa /'gasa/ *f*, gauze. **tira de g.,** black mourning band

gasconada /gasko'naða/ *f*, bravado, gasconade

gaseosa /gase'osa/ *f*, aerated water

gaseoso /gase'oso/ *a* gaseous

gasista /ga'sista/ *mf* gas fitter; gasman

gasolina /gaso'lina/ *f*, gasoline, petrol

gasómetro /ga'sometro/ *m*, gas meter; gasometer

gastado /gas'taðo/ *a* worn; worn-out; exhausted

gastador /gasta'ðor/ **(-ra)** *a* extravagant, wasteful. *n* spendthrift. *m, Mil.* sapper; convict condemned to hard labor

gastar /gas'tar/ *vt* to spend (money); wear out; exhaust; ruin, destroy; display or have habitually; possess, use, wear; *vr* wear out; run down (of a battery)

gasto /'gasto/ *m*, spending; expenditure; consumption (of gas, etc.); expense, cost, charge; wear (and tear). **g. suplementario,** extra charge

gástrico /'gastriko/ *a* gastric

gastritis /gas'tritis/ *f*, gastritis

gastronomía /gastrono'mia/ *f*, gastronomy

gastronómico /gastro'nomiko/ *a* gastronomic

gastrónomo /gas'tronomo/ **(-ma)** *n* gastronome

gata /'gata/ *f*, she-cat; wreath of mist; *Inf.* Madrilenian woman. **a gatas,** on all fours

gatada /ga'taða/ *f, Inf.* sly trick

gatear /gate'ar/ *vi* to climb like a cat; *Inf.* crawl on all fours; *vt Inf.* scratch (of a cat); steal, pinch

gatillo /ga'tiyo; ga'tiʎo/ *m, dim* small cat; dental forceps; trigger (of gun); *Inf.* juvenile petty thief

gato /'gato/ *m*, cat; tomcat; moneybag or its contents; *Mech.* jack; mousetrap; *Inf.* cat burglar, sneak thief; *Inf.* Madrilenian; clamp. **g. atigrado,** tiger cat. **g. de algalia,** civet cat. **g. de Angora,** Persian cat. **g. montés,** wildcat. **g. romano,** tabby cat. **dar g. por liebre,** to serve cat for hare, to deceive; misrepresent. *Inf.* **Hay g. encerrado,** There's more to this than meets the eye

gatuno /ga'tuno/ *a* feline

gaucho /'gautʃo/ **(-cha)** *n* gaucho; cowboy, rider

gaveta /ga'βeta/ *f*, drawer (of a desk)

gavia /'gaβia/ *f*, main topsail; *pl* topsails; crow's-nest

gavilán /gaβi'lan/ *m*, sparrow hawk; thistle flower; *Lat. Am.* ingrown toenail

gavilla /ga'βiya; ga'βiʎa/ *f*, sheaf (of corn, etc.); gang, rabble

gaviota /ga'βiota/ f, seagull

gavota /ga'βota/ f, gavotte

gayo /'gayo/ a gay, happy; showy, attractive. **gaya ciencia,** minstrelsy, art of poetry

gazapera /gasa'pera; gaθa'pera/ f, rabbit warren; Inf. thieves' den; Inf. brawl

gazapo /ga'sapo; ga'θapo/ m, young rabbit; Inf. cunning fellow; fib, lie; slip, blunder

gazmoñería /gasmoɲe'ria; gaθmoɲe'ria/ f, prudery, priggish affectation

gazmoño /gas'moɲo; gaθ'moɲo/ a hypocritical, prudish, priggish

gaznápiro /gas'napiro; gaθ'napiro/ (**-ra**) n ninny, simpleton

gaznate /gas'nate; gaθ'nate/ m, windpipe

gazpacho /gas'patʃo; gaθ'patʃo/ m, cold soup containing tomatoes, onions, vinegar, oil, etc.

ge /he/ f, name of the letter G

gehena /he'ena/ m, gehenna, hell

géiser /'heiser/ m, geyser

gelatina /hela'tina/ f, gelatin. **g. incendiaria,** napalm. **g. seca,** cooking gelatin

gelatinoso /helati'noso/ a gelatinous

gélido /'heliðo/ a Poet. icy; very cold

gema /'hema/ f, gem; Bot. bud

gemelo /he'melo/ (**-la**) a and n twin. m pl, field or opera glasses, binoculars; cuff links; Astron. Gemini

gemido /he'miðo/ m, groan, lament, moan

gemidor /hemi'ðor/ a groaning, moaning; wailing (of the wind, etc.)

gemir /he'mir/ vi irr to moan, groan, lament; Fig. wail, howl. See **pedir**

gene /'hene/ m, gene

genealogía /henealo'hia/ f, genealogy

genealógico /henea'lohiko/ a genealogical

genealogista /henealo'hista/ mf genealogist

generación /henera'sion; henera'θion/ f, generation, reproduction; species; generation

generador /henera'ðor/ a generative. m, Mech. generator

general /hene'ral/ a general; universal; widespread; common, usual. m, (Mil. Eccl.) general. **g. de división,** Mil. major general. **en** or **por lo g.,** generally

generalato /henera'lato/ m, generalship

generalidad /henerali'ðað/ f, majority, bulk; generality

generalísimo /henera'lisimo/ m, generalissimo, commander in chief

generalización /heneralisa'sion; heneraliθa'θion/ f, generalization

generalizar /henerali'sar; henerali'θar/ vt to generalize; vr become widespread or general

generar /hene'rar/ vt to generate

genérico /he'neriko/ a generic

género /'henero/ m, kind; class; way, mode; Com. goods; species, genus; Gram. gender; cloth, material. **g. chico,** short theatrical pieces (gen. one act). **g. humano,** humankind

generosidad /henerosi'ðað/ f, hereditary nobility; generosity, magnanimity; liberality, munificence; courage

generoso /hene'roso/ a noble (by birth); magnanimous; generous (of wine); munificent; courageous; excellent

genésico /he'nesiko/ a genetic

génesis /'henesis/ m, **Génesis,** Genesis. f, beginning, origin

genial /he'nial/ a of genius; highly talented; brilliant; characteristic, individual; pleasant; cheerful

genialidad /heniali'ðað/ f, genius; talent; brilliance; eccentricity, oddity

genio /'henio/ m, nature, individuality, temperament; temper; character; talent; genius; genie, spirit. **corto de g.,** unintelligent. **mal g.,** bad temper

genital /heni'tal/ a genital. m, testicle (gen. pl)

genitivo /heni'tiβo/ a reproductive, generative. m, Gram. genitive

Génova /'henoβa/ Genoa

gente /'hente/ f, people, a crowd; nation; army; Inf. family; followers, adherents. **g. baja,** rabble. **g. de bien,** honest folk; respectable people. **g. de paz,** friends (reply to sentinel's challenge). **g. fina,** nice, cultured people. **g. menuda,** children, small fry

gentecilla /hente'siya; hente'θiʎa/ f, dim Inf. rabble; contemptible people

gentil /hen'til/ a pagan, idolatrous; spirited, dashing, handsome; notable, extraordinary; graceful, charming

gentileza /henti'lesa; henti'leθa/ f, grace; elegance; beauty; verve, sprightliness; courtesy; show, ostentation

gentilhombre /hentil'ombre/ m, gentleman; handsome man; kind sir! **gentileshombres de cámara,** gentlemen-in-waiting

gentilicio /henti'lisio; henti'liθio/ a national; family

gentílico /hen'tiliko/ a pagan, idolatrous

gentilidad /hentili'ðað/ f, idolatry, paganism; heathendom

gentío /hen'tio/ m, crowd, throng

gentualla, gentuza /hen'tuaya, hen'tusa; hen'tuaʎa, hen'tuθa/ f, canaille, rabble

genuflexión /henuflek'sion/ f, genuflection

genuino /he'nuino/ a pure; authentic, genuine; Colombia great, wonderful

geodesia /heo'ðesia/ f, geodesy

geodésico /heo'ðesiko/ a geodesic

geografía /heogra'fia/ f, geography

geográfico /heo'grafiko/ a geographical

geógrafo /he'ografo/ m, geographer

geología /heolo'hia/ f, geology

geológico /heo'lohiko/ a geological

geólogo /he'ologo/ m, geologist

geometría /heome'tria/ f, geometry. **g. del espacio,** solid geometry

geométrico /heo'metriko/ a geometrical

geranio /he'ranio/ m, geranium

gerencia /he'rensia; he'renθia/ f, Com. managership; manager's office; management

gerente /he'rente/ m, Com. manager

germanía /herma'nia/ f, thieves' slang; association of thieves; sixteenth-century political brotherhood

germánico /her'maniko/ a germanic

germanófilo /herma'nofilo/ (**-la**) a and n germanophile

germen /'hermen/ m, germ, sprout; Bot. embryo; genesis, origin

germinación /hermina'sion; hermina'θion/ f, germination

germinar /hermi'nar/ vi to germinate, sprout; develop, grow

germinativo /hermina'tiβo/ a germinative

gerundio /he'rundio/ m, Gram. gerund; Inf. pompous ass; Inf. tub-thumper

gesta /'hesta/ f, heroic deed. **cantar de g.,** epic or heroic poem

gestación /hesta'sion; hesta'θion/ f, gestation

gestear /heste'ar/ vi to gesture, grimace

gesticulación /hestikula'sion; hestikula'θion/ f, gesticulation; grimace

gesticular /hestiku'lar/ vi to grimace, gesticulate. a gesticulatory

gestión /hes'tion/ f, negotiation; management, conduct; effort, exertion; measure

gestionar /hestio'nar/ vt to negotiate, conduct; undertake; take steps to attain

gesto /'hesto/ m, gesture; facial expression; grimace; face, visage

gestor /hes'tor/ (**-ra**) n manager; partner; promoter. a managing

Getsemaní /hetsema'ni/ Gethsemane

giba /'hiβa/ f, hump, hunchback; Inf. nuisance, inconvenience

gibón /hi'βon/ m, gibbon

giboso /hi'βoso/ a hunchbacked

gibraltareño /hiβralta'reɲo/ a Gibraltarian

giganta /hi'ganta/ f, giantess

gigante /hi'gante/ a gigantic. m, giant.

gigantesco /higan'tesko/ a giant, gigantic; Fig. outstanding

gigantez /higan'tes; higan'teθ/ f, gigantic size

gigantón /higan'ton/ **(-ona)** n enormous giant; carnival grotesque

gimnasia /him'nasia/ f, gymnastics

gimnasio /him'nasio/ m, gymnasium; school, academy

gimnasta /him'nasta/ mf gymnast

gimnástico /him'nastiko/ a gymnastic

gimotear /himote'ar/ vi Inf. to whine (often used scornfully)

gimoteo /himo'teo/ m, Inf. whining, whimpering

ginebra /hi'neβra/ f, gin (drink); confusion; babble, din

ginebrés /hine'βres/ **(-esa), ginebrino (-na)** a and n Genevan

gineceo /hine'seo/ hine'θeo/ m, (Bot. and in ancient Greece) gynaecium

ginecología /hinekolo'hia/ f, gynecology

ginecológico /hineko'lohiko/ a gynecological

ginecólogo /hine'kologo/ **(-ga)** n gynecologist

girado /hi'raðo/ m, Com. drawee

girador /hira'ðor/ m, Com. drawer

giralda /hi'ralda/ f, weathercock in the shape of a person or animal; tower at Seville

girar /hi'rar/ vi to revolve; deal (with), concern; turn, branch (streets, etc.); Com. trade; Mech. turn on, revolve; vt and vi Com. draw, cash. **g. en descubierto,** Com. to overdraw

girasol /hira'sol/ m, sunflower

giratorio /hira'torio/ a revolving, gyrating; swiveling

giro /'hiro/ m, revolution, turn; revolving; trend; course (of affairs); style, turn (of phrase); threat; knife gang; Com. draft, drawing; Com. line of business, specialty. **g. postal,** postal order

giroscopio /hiro'skopio/ m, gyroscope

gis /his/ m Lat. Am. chalk; Mexico also pulque

gitanería /hitane'ria/ f, cajolery, wheedling; gypsies; gypsy saying or action

gitanesco /hita'nesko/ a gypsy, gypsy-like

gitano /hi'tano/ **(-na)** a gypsy; gypsy-like; seductive, attractive; sly. n gypsy

glaciar /gla'siar/ gla'θiar/ m, glacier

gladiador /glaðia'ðor/ m, gladiator

glanco /'glanko/ a Lat. Am. light green

glándula /'glandula/ f, gland

glicerina /glise'rina/ gliθe'rina/ f, glycerin, glycerol

globo /'gloβo/ m, Geom. sphere; globe, world; globe (Elec. Gas.); balloon. **g. aerostático,** air balloon. **g. terrestre,** world; geographical globe

globular /gloβu'lar/ a globular

glóbulo /'gloβulo/ m, globule.

globuloso /gloβu'loso/ a globulous

gloria /'gloria/ f, heavenly bliss; fame, glory; delight, pleasure; magnificence, splendor; Art. apotheosis, glory. m, Eccl. doxology

gloriar /glo'riar/ vt to praise; vr (with de or en) boast about; be proud of, rejoice in

glorieta /glo'rieta/ f, bower, arbor; open space in a garden; street square, traffic circle

glorificación /glorifika'sion/ glorifika'θion/ f, glorification

glorificador /glorifika'ðor/ a glorifying

glorificar /glorifi'kar/ vt to exalt, raise up; glorify, extol; vr (with de or en) be proud of; glory in; boast of

glorioso /glo'rioso/ a glorious; Eccl. blessed; boastful, bragging

glosa /'glosa/ f, gloss; explanation, note

glosador /glosa'ðor/ **(-ra)** n glossator; commentator. a explanatory

glosar /glo'sar/ vt Lit. to gloss

glosario /glo'sario/ m, glossary

glosopeda /gloso'peða/ f, foot-and-mouth disease

glotón /glo'ton/ **(-ona)** a greedy, gluttonous. n glutton

glotonería /glotone'ria/ f, gluttony, greed

glucosa /glu'kosa/ f, glucose

glúteo /'gluteo/ a gluteal

glutinoso /gluti'noso/ a glutinous

gn- /gn-/ For words so beginning, see spellings without **g.**

gobernación /goβerna'sion/ goβerna'θion/ f, government; governor's office or building; ministry of the interior, home office (abb. for **ministerio de G.**)

gobernador /goβerna'ðor/ **(-ra)** a governing, n governor

gobernalle /goβer'naye/ goβer'naʎe/ m, helm

gobernante /goβer'nante/ a governing. m, Inf. self-appointed director or manager

gobernar /goβer'nar/ vt irr to govern, rule; lead, conduct; manage; steer; control; vi govern; Naut. obey the tiller. See **recomendar**

gobierno /go'βierno/ m, government (all meanings); Naut. helm; control (of machines, business, etc.)

goce /'gose/ 'goθe/ m, enjoyment; possession

godo /'goðo/ **(da)** a Gothic; aristocratic, noble. n Goth; aristocrat

gol /gol/ m, Sports. goal

gola /'gola/ f, throat; gullet; gorget; tucker, bib

goleta /go'leta/ f, schooner

golf /golf/ m, golf. **palo de g.,** golf club

golfear /golfe'ar/ vi to loaf

golfería /golfe'ria/ f, loafing; vagabondage; loafers

golfo /'golfo/ **(-fa)** m, Geog. gulf; sea, ocean. n ragamuffin, urchin. m, Inf. loafer; lounge lizard, wastrel

golilla /go'liya/ go'liʎa/ f, ruff; Lat. Am. scarf; m, Inf. magistrate

gollería /goye'ria/ goʎe'ria/ f, dainty, tidbit; Inf. affectation, persnicketiness

gollete /go'yete/ go'ʎete/ m, gullet; neck (of a bottle, etc.); Mech. nozzle

golondrina /golon'drina/ f, Ornith. swallow; Chile moving van. **g. de mar,** tern

golosina /golo'sina/ f, tidbit, delicacy; desire, caprice; pleasant useless thing

goloso /go'loso/ a fond of sweet things; greedy, desirous; appetizing

golpe /'golpe/ m, blow, knock; pull (at the oars); ring (of a bell); Mech. stroke; crowd; fall (of rain, etc.); mass, torrent; misfortune; shock, collision; spring lock; beating (of the heart); flap (of a pocket); Sew. passementerie; surprise; point, wit; bet. **g. de estado,** coup d'état. **g. de fortuna,** stroke of fortune. **g. de mano,** rising, insurrection. **g. en vago,** blow in the air; disappointment. **g. franco,** Sports. free kick. **de g.,** suddenly; quickly

golpeadura /golpea'ðura/ f. **golpeo** m, knocking, striking; beating, throbbing

golpear /golpe'ar/ vt and vi to knock, strike; beat, throb

goma /'goma/ f, gum, rubber; India rubber; rubber band, eraser

gomería /gome'ria/ f, tire store

gomero /go'mero/ a gum; rubber. m, West Hem. rubber planter

gomoso /go'moso/ a gummy; gum

gónada /'gonaða/ f, gonad

góndola /'gondola/ f, gondola

gondolero /gondo'lero/ m, gondolier

gongorino /goŋgo'rino/ a gongoristic, euphuistic

gonorrea /gono'rrea/ f, gonorrhea

gordo /'gorðo/ a fat, stout; greasy, oily; thick (thread, etc.). m, animal fat, suet. Inf. **ganar el g.,** to win first prize (in a lottery, etc.)

gordura /gor'ðura/ f, grease, fat; stoutness, corpulence

gorgojo /gor'goho/ m, weevil; Fig. dwarf

gorgoritear /gorgorite'ar/ vi Inf. to trill, quaver

gorgorito /gorgo'rito/ m, Inf. quaver, tremolo, trill (gen. pl)

gorgoteo /gorgo'teo/ m, gurgle

gorjear /gorhe'ar/ vi to trill, warble; twitter; vr crow (of a baby)

gorjeo /gor'heo/ m, trill, shake; warbling, twitter; crowing, lisping (of a child)

gorra /'gorra/ f, cap; bonnet; Mil. busby; hunting cap. **vivir de g.,** Inf. to sponge

gorrión /go'rrion/ m, sparrow

gorrista /go'rrista/ mf Inf. parasite; sponger

gorro /'gorro/ m, cap; bonnet

gorrón /go'rron/ m, smooth, round pebble; Mech. pivot, gudgeon; sponger, waster. a parasitical

gota /'gota/ *f*, drop (of liquid); gout

gotear /gote'ar/ *vi* to drop, trickle, drip; leak; drizzle; give or receive in driblets

goteo /go'teo/ *m*, trickling, dripping

gotera /go'tera/ *f*, dripping; trickle; leak; leakage; valance

gotero /go'tero/ *m Lat. Am.* (medicine) dropper

gótico /'gotiko/ *a* Gothic; noble, illustrious

gotoso /go'toso/ **(-sa)** *a* gouty. *n* sufferer from gout

gozar /go'sar; go'θar/ *vt* to enjoy, have; take pleasure (in), delight (in); know carnally; *vi* (*with de*) enjoy; have, possess

gozne /'gosne; 'goθne/ *m*, hinge

gozo /'goso; 'goθo/ *m*, enjoyment, possession; gladness, joy; *pl* couplets in honor of the Virgin Mary or a saint. *Inf.* **¡Mi g. en el pozo!** I'm sunk! All is lost!

gozoso /go'soso; go'θoso/ *a* glad, happy. *adv* gladly; with pleasure

grabado /gra'βaðo/ *m*, engraver's art; engraving; illustration, picture. **g. al agua fuerte,** etching. **g. al agua tinta,** aquatint

grabador /graβa'ðor/ **(-ra)** *n* engraver

grabadura /graβa'ðura/ *f*, act of engraving

grabar /gra'βar/ *vt* to engrave; *Fig.* leave a deep impression

gracejo /gra'seho; gra'θeho/ *m*, humor, wit; cheerfulness

gracia /'grasia; 'graθia/ *f*, grace; attraction, grace; favor; kindness; jest, witticism; pardon, mercy; pleasant manner; obligingness, willingness; *pl* thanks, thank you. **gracias a,** thanks to. **¡Gracias a Dios!** Thank God! Thank goodness! **las Gracias,** the Three Graces

grácil /'grasil; 'graθil/ *a* slender; small

graciosidad /grasiosi'ðað; graθiosi'ðað/ *f*, beauty, perfection, grace

gracioso /gra'sioso; gra'θioso/ **(-sa)** *a* attractive, graceful, elegant; witty, humorous; free, gratis. *n Theat.* comic role; *m, Theat.* fool

grada /'graða/ *f*, step, stair; gradin, seat; stand, gallery; *Agr.* harrow; *Naut.* runway; *pl* perron, flight of stairs

gradación /graða'sion; graða'θion/ *f*, gradation; climax

gradería /graðe'ria/ *f*, flight of steps

grado /'graðo/ *m*, step, stair; degree (of relationship); university degree; grade, class (in schools); (*Fig. Geom. Phys.*) degree; will, desire. **de buen g.,** willingly. **en sumo g.,** in the highest degree

graduación /graðua'sion; graðua'θion/ *f*, graduation; *Mil.* rank; rating (of a ship's company). **g. de oficial,** *Mil.* commission

graduado /gra'ðuaðo/ *a* graded; *Mil.* brevet. *m*, graduate

gradual /gra'ðual/ *a* gradual

graduar /gra'ðuar/ *vt* to classify; *Mil.* grade; confer a degree on; measure; test; *Com.* standardize; *Mech.* calibrate; *vr* graduate, receive a degree. **g. la vista,** to test the eyes. **graduarse de oficial,** *Mil.* to get one's commission

gráfica /'grafika/ *f*, graph

gráfico /'grafiko/ *a* graphic; vivid

grafito /gra'fito/ *m*, graphite

grafología /grafolo'hia/ *f*, graphology

grajear /grahe'ar/ *vi* to caw; gurgle, burble (of infants)

grajo /'graho/ *m, Ornith.* rook

grama /'grama/ *f Dominican Republic, Venezuela* grass, lawn

gramática /gra'matika/ *f*, grammar. *Inf.* **g. parda,** horse sense

gramático /gra'matiko/ *a* grammatical. *m*, grammarian

gramo /'gramo/ *m*, gram

gran /gran/ *a abb* See **grande.** Used before a singular noun. big; great; grand

grana /'grana/ *f*, grain, seed; seed time; cochineal; kermes; red

granada /gra'naða/ *f, Mil.* grenade; shell; pomegranate

granadero /grana'ðero/ *m*, grenadier; *Inf.* very tall person; *Lat. Am.* riot policeman

granadilla /grana'ðiya; grana'ðiʎa/ *f*, passionflower

granadina /grana'ðina/ *f*, grenadine

granar /gra'nar/ *vi Agr.* to seed; run to seed

granate /gra'nate/ *m*, garnet; dark red

Gran Bretaña /gran bre'taɲa/ Great Britain

grande /'grande/ *a* big, large; great, illustrious; grand. *m*, great man; grandee. **en g.,** in a large size; as a whole; in style, lavishly

grandeza /gran'desa; gran'deθa/ *f*, largeness; greatness, magnificence; grandeeship; vastness, magnitude

grandilocuencia /grandilo'kuensia; grandilo'kuenθia/ *f*, grandiloquence

grandílocuo /gran'dilokuo/ *a* grandiloquent

grandiosidad /grandiosi'ðað/ *f*, grandeur, greatness

grandioso /gran'dioso/ *a* grandiose, magnificent

grandor /gran'dor/ *m*, size

granear /grane'ar/ *vt Agr.* to sow; grain (of leather)

granero /gra'nero/ *m*, granary; grain-producing country

granito /gra'nito/ *m, dim* small grain; granite; small pimple

granizar /grani'sar; grani'θar/ *vi* to hail, sleet; *vi* and *vt Fig.* shower down, deluge

granizo /gra'niso; gra'niθo/ *m*, hail, sleet; hailstorm; *Fig.* shower, deluge

granja /'granha/ *f*, farm; farmhouse; dairy farm, dairy

granjear /granhe'ar/ *vt* to trade, profit, earn; obtain, acquire; *vr* gain, win

granjería /granhe'ria/ *f*, farming; agricultural profits; earnings, profits

granjero /gran'hero/ **(-ra)** *n* farmer

grano /'grano/ *m, Agr.* grain; seed; bean (coffee, etc.); particle; markings, grain (of wood, etc.); pimple; grain (measure). *Fig. Inf.* **ir al g.,** to go to the root of the matter; come to the point

granuja /gra'nuha/ *f*, grape pit. *m, Inf.* urchin, scamp; knave, rogue

granujiento /granu'hiento/ *a* pimply

gránulo /'granulo/ *m*, granule

granuloso /granu'loso/ *a* granulous

grapa /'grapa/ *f*, cramp, dowel, clamp; block hook; *Elec.* cleat; staple

grasa /'grasa/ *f*, fat; grease; oil; dripping, suet

grasiento /gra'siento/ *a* greasy; grubby, dirty

gratificación /gratifika'sion; gratifika'θion/ *f*, monetary reward; fee, remuneration; gratuity

gratificar /gratifi'kar/ *vt* to recompense; please, gratify

gratis /'gratis/ *a* and *adv* gratis

gratitud /grati'tuð/ *f*, gratitude

grato /'grato/ *a* pleasing, agreeable; free, gratuitous; *Lat. Am.* appreciative, grateful

gratuito /gra'tuito/ *a* gratuitous, free; baseless, unfounded

grava /'graβa/ *f*, gravel; stone chip, pebble; metal (of a road)

gravamen /gra'βamen/ *m*, obligation; burden; tax

gravar /gra'βar/ *vt* to burden, weigh upon; tax

grave /'graβe/ *a* heavy; important, momentous; grave; dignified, serious; sedate; tiresome; low-pitched, low; *Gram.* grave accent

gravedad /graβe'ðað/ *f, Phys.* gravity

gravitación /graβita'sion; graβita'θion/ *f, Phys.* gravitation; seriousness; weightiness; importance; enormity, gravity

gravitar /graβi'tar/ *vi* to gravitate; lean or rest (upon)

gravoso /gra'βoso/ *a* grievous, oppressive; onerous; costly

graznar /gras'nar; graθ'nar/ *vi* to caw; cackle; quack; croak; sing stridently, screech

graznido /gras'niðo; graθ'niðo/ *m*, caw; cackle; croaking; quack; screech

Grecia /'gresia; 'greθia/ Greece

greco /'greko/ **(-ca)** *a* and *n* Greek

gregario /gre'gario/ *a* gregarious

gregoriano /grego'riano/ *a* Gregorian

gregüescos /gre'gueskos/ *m pl*, wide breeches (sixteenth and seventeenth centuries)

gremial /gre'mial/ *a* pertaining to a guild, union, or association. *m*, member of a guild, union, or association

gremio /'gremio/ *m*, guild, corporation, union; society, association; (univ.) general council

greña /'greɲa/ *f*, tangled lock (of hair) (gen. *pl*); tangle, confused mass

gresca /'greska/ *f*, uproar, tumult; fight, row

grey /grei/ *f*, flock, drove, herd; *Eccl.* flock, company; people, nation

griego /'griego/ **(-ga)** *a* and *n* Greek. *m*, Greek (language); *Inf.* gibberish

grieta /'grieta/ *f*, fissure; crevice; chink; split; flaw; vein (in stone, etc.); *Mech.* leak

grietado /grie'taðo/ *a* fissured; cracked

grifo /'grifo/ *m*, griffin; tap; cock

grillo /'griyo; 'griʎo/ *m*, cricket; *Bot.* shoot; *pl* fetters, irons, chains; *Fig.* shackles

grima /'grima/ *f*, revulsion, horror

gringo /'gringo/ **(-ga)** *n Inf.* foreigner (scornful)

gripe /'gripe/ *f*, influenza; grippe

gris /gris/ *a* and *m*, gray

grisú /gri'su/ *m*, firedamp

gritador /grita'ðor/ **(-ra)** *a* shouting. *n* shouter

gritar /gri'tar/ *vi* to shout, yell, scream; howl down; hoot

gritería /grite'ria/ *f*, shouting, yelling, clamor

grito /'grito/ *m*, shout, yell, shriek, scream. *Inf.* **poner el g. en el cielo,** to cry to high heaven, complain. **el Grito de Dolores** the Proclamation of Mexican Independence (1810)

groenlandés /groenlan'des/ **(-esa)** *a* Greenland. *n* Greenlander

Groenlandia /groen'landia/ Greenland

grosella /gro'seya/ *f*, currant. **g. blanca,** gooseberry

grosería /grose'ria/ *f*, crudeness, insult; rudeness; roughness (of workmanship); ignorance; rusticity

grosero /gro'sero/ *a* coarse; rough; thick; unpolished, rude

grotesco /gro'tesko/ *a* grotesque, absurd

grúa /'grua/ *f*, *Mech.* crane, hoist, derrick. **g. de pescante,** jib crane. **g. móvil,** traveling crane

gruesa /'gruesa/ *f*, twelve dozen, gross

grueso /'grueso/ *a* stout, corpulent; large. *m*, bulk, body; major portion, majority; thick stroke (of a letter); thickness, density. **en g.,** in bulk

grulla /'gruya; 'gruʎa/ *f*, *Ornith.* crane

grumete /gru'mete/ *m*, ship's boy, cabin boy

grumo /'grumo/ *m*, clot; heart (of vegetables); bunch, cluster; bud

gruñido /gru'ɲiðo/ *m*, grunt; growl

gruñidor /gruɲi'ðor/ *a* grunting; growling

gruñir /gru'ɲir/ *vi* to grunt; growl; grumble; squeak, creak (doors, etc.). *Pres. Part.* **gruñendo.** *Pres. Ind.* **gruño, gruñes, etc.**

grupa /'grupa/ *f*, croup (of a horse); pillion (of a motorcycle)

grupera /gru'pera/ *f*, pillion (of a horse, etc.)

grupo /'grupo/ *m*, knot, cluster; band, group; *Art.* group; *Mech.* set

gruta /'gruta/ *f*, cavern, grotto

guacamayo /guaka'mayo/ *m*, macaw

guadamecí /guaðame'si; guaðame'θi/ *m*, embossed decorated leather

guadaña /gua'ðaɲa/ *f*, scythe

guagua /'guagua/, *f Caribbean* bus

gualdo /'gualdo/ *a* yellow, golden

gualdrapa /gual'drapa/ *f*, saddlecloth, trappings; *Inf.* tatter, rag

guante /'guante/ *m*, glove. **g. con puño,** gauntlet glove. **g. de boxeo,** boxing glove. **g. de cabritilla,** kid glove. **arrojar el g.,** to throw down the gauntlet; challenge, defy

guantelete /guante'lete/ *m*, gauntlet

guantería /guante'ria/ *f*, glove trade, shop, or factory

guantero /guan'tero/ **(-ra)** *n* glove maker or seller, glover

guapear /guape'ar/ *vi Inf.* to make the best of a bad job; *Inf.* pride oneself on being well dressed

guapeza /gua'pesa; gua'peθa/ *f*, prettiness; *Inf.* resolution, courage; *Inf.* smartness or showiness of dress; boastful act or behavior

guapo /'guapo/ *a* pretty; handsome; *Inf.* daring, enterprising; *Inf.* smart, well-dressed, foppish; *Inf.* handsome; *Dominican Republic* angry, mad. *m*, braggart, brawler; beau, lover; *Inf.* fine fellow, son of a gun

guaracha /gua'ratʃa/ *f*, *Cuba, Puerto Rico* guaracha (vigorous dance in triple meter; music for this dance)

guarda /'guarða/ *mf* keeper, guard. *f*, guarding, keeping, custodianship, preservation; guardianship; observance, fulfillment; flyleaf, end page (books); warder (of locks or keys); *Mech.* guard; guard (of a fan)

guardabarrera /guarðaβa'rrera/ *mf* gatekeeper at a level crossing (railroad)

guardabarro /guarða'βarro/ *m*, mudguard

guardabosque /guarða'βoske/ *mf* gamekeeper

guardabrisa /guarða'βrisa/ *m*, *Auto.* windshield; glass candle shield

guardacostas /guarða'kostas/ *m*, coast guard; *Naut.* revenue cutter

guardafrenos /guarða'frenos/ *m*, brakeman (railroad)

guardalmacén /guarðalma'sen; guarðalma'θen/ *mf* storekeeper

guardameta /guarða'meta/ *mf* goalkeeper

guardamuebles /guarða'mueβles/ *m*, furniture warehouse

guardapelo /guarða'pelo/ *m*, locket

guardapolvo /guarða'polβo/ *m*, dustcover; light overcoat; inner case of a pocket watch

guardar /guar'ðar/ *vt* to keep; preserve, retain; maintain, observe; save, put aside, lay away; defend, protect; guard; *vr* (*with de*) avoid, guard against. **g. compás con,** to be in tune with. **guardarse mucho,** to think twice before. **g. silencio,** to keep silent. **¡Guarda!** Take care! **¡Guárdate del agua mansa!** Still waters run deep!

guardarropa /guarða'rropa/ *m*, cloakroom. *mf* cloakroom attendant; keeper of the wardrobe. *m*, wardrobe, clothes closet

guardarropía /guarðarro'pia/ *f*, theatrical wardrobe

guardavía /guarða'βia/ *m*, signalman (railroad)

guardería /guarðe'ria/ *f*, day nursery, day-care center

guardia /'guarðia/ *f*, guard, escort; protection; (*Mil. Naut.*) watch; regiment, body (of troops); guard (fencing). *m*, guardsman; policeman. **g. de asalto,** armed police. **g. de corps,** royal bodyguard. **g. civil,** civil guard. **g. marina,** midshipman. **g. municipal,** city police. *Mil.* **montar la g.,** to mount guard

guardián /guar'ðian/ **(-ana)** *n* keeper; custodian; warden. *m*, watchman; jailer

guardilla /guar'ðiya; guar'ðiʎa/ *f*, attic, garret

guarecer /guare'ser; guare'θer/ *vt irr* to shelter, protect, aid; preserve, keep; cure; *vr* take shelter. See **conocer**

guarida /gua'riða/ *f*, lair, den; refuge, shelter; haunt, resort

guarismo /gua'rismo/ *m*, *Math.* figure; number, numeral

guarnecer /guarne'ser; guarne'θer/ *vt irr* to decorate, adorn; *Sew.* trim, face, border; *Mil.* garrison; *Mas.* plaster. See **conocer**

guarnecido /guarne'siðo; guarne'θiðo/ *m*, *Mas.* plastering

guarnición /guarni'sion; guarni'θion/ *f*, *Sew.* trimming, ornament, border, fringe; *Mech.* packing; *Mil.* garrison; setting (of jewels); guard (of a sword, etc.); *pl* harness; fittings

guarnir /guar'nir/ *vt Naut.* to reeve

guasa /'guasa/ *f*, *Inf.* dullness, boringness; joke. **de g.,** jokingly

guasón /gua'son/ *a Inf.* dull, tedious; humorous, jocose

guatemalteco /guatemal'teko/ **(-ca)** *a* and *n* Guatemalan

guau /guau/ *m*, bowwow, bark of a dog

guayaba /gua'yaβa/ f, guava; guava jelly; *Lat. Am.*
also hoax
Guayana /gua'yana/ Guiana
gubernamental /guβernamen'tal/ a governmental
gubernativo /guβerna'tiβo/ a governmental; administrative
gubia /'guβia/ f, chisel; gouge
guedeja /ge'ðeha/ f, long tress or lock of hair; forelock; lion's mane
Guernesey /gerne'sei/ Guernsey
guerra /'gerra/ f, war; struggle, fight; *Fig.* hostility.
Inf. **dar g.,** to give trouble, annoy. **en g. con,** at war with. **la g. de Cuba,** the Spanish-American War
guerrear /gerre'ar/ *vi* to make war, fight; oppose
guerrero /ge'rrero/ **(-ra)** a war, martial; warrior; *Inf.* troublesome, annoying. *n* fighter. *m*, warrior, soldier
guerrillear /gerriye'ar; gerriʎe'ar/ *vi* to wage guerrilla warfare; fight as a guerrilla
guerrillero /gerri'yero; gerri'ʎero/ *m*, guerrilla fighter
guía /'gia/ *mf* guide, conductor; adviser, director. *f*, guide, aid; guidebook; *Mech.* guide, slide; directory; signpost. **g. de ferrocarriles,** train schedule, railroad timetable. **g. de teléfonos,** telephone directory
guiar /giar/ *vt* to guide; lead, conduct; *Mech.* work, control; *Auto.* drive; pilot; teach, direct, govern
guija /'giha/ f, pebble
guijarro /gi'harro/ *m*, smooth, round pebble; boulder; cobblestone
guijarroso /giha'rroso/ a pebbly, cobbled
guijo /'giho/ *m*, gravel; granite chips; pebble
guillotina /giyo'tina; giʎo'tina/ f, guillotine; papercutting machine
guillotinar /giyoti'nar; giʎoti'nar/ *vt* to guillotine, decapitate
guinda /'ginda/ f, mazard cherry; *Naut.* height of masts
guinea /gi'nea/ f, guinea
guinga /'ginga/ f, gingham
guiñada /gi'ɲaða/ f, wink; blink; *Naut.* yaw
guiñapo /gi'ɲapo/ *m*, rag, tatter; sloven, ragamuffin

guiñar /gi'ɲar/ *vt* to wink; blink; *Naut.* yaw; *vr* wink at each other
guiño /'giɲo/ *m*, wink
guión /gi'on/ *m*, royal standard; banner; summary; leader of a dance; *Gram.* hyphen; subtitle (in films). **g. mayor,** *Gram.* dash
guirigay /giri'gai/ *m*, *Inf.* gibberish; uproar, babble
guirnalda /gir'nalda/ f, garland, wreath
guisa /'gisa/ f, way, manner; will, desire. **a g. de,** in the manner or fashion of
guisado /gi'saðo/ *m*, *Cul.* stew; cooked dish
guisante /gi'sante/ *m*, *Agr.* pea; pea plant. **g. de olor,** sweetpea
guisar /gi'sar/ *vt* to cook; stew; *Cul.* prepare, dress; adjust, arrange
guiso /'giso/ *m*, cooked dish
güisquisoda /giski'soða/ f *Spain* highball
guitarra /gi'tarra/ f, guitar
guitarrista /gita'rrista/ *mf* guitar player
guito /'gito/ a vicious (horses, mules)
gula /'gula/ f, greed, gluttony
gusaniento /gusa'niento/ a worm-eaten; maggoty
gusano /gu'sano/ *m*, worm; caterpillar; maggot; meek, downtrodden person. **g. de seda,** silkworm
gusanoso /gusa'noso/ a wormy
gustar /gus'tar/ *vt* to taste, savor; try; *vi* be pleasing, give pleasure; like. **Me gusta el libro,** I like the book. **La película no me gustó,** I didn't like the film. **g. de,** to like, is used only when a person is the subject
gusto /'gusto/ *m*, taste; flavor, savor; pleasure, delight; will, desire; discrimination, taste, style, fashion; manner; whim, caprice. **a g.,** to taste; according to taste. **con mucho g.,** with great pleasure. **dar g.,** to please. **de buen g.,** in good taste. **mucho g. en conocerlo (-la),** pleased to meet you
gustoso /gus'toso/ a savory, palatable; willingly, with pleasure; pleasant, agreeable
gutapercha /guta'pertʃa/ f, guttapercha
gutural /gutu'ral/ a guttural

H

haba /'aβa/ f, broad bean; bean (coffee, cocoa, etc.). **h. de las Indias,** sweetpea. **Esas son habas contadas,** That's a certainty
Habana, la /a'βana, la/ Havana
habanero /aβa'nero/ **(-ra), habano (-na)** a and *n* Havanese, from Havana. *m*. **habano,** Havana cigar
haber /a'βer/ *m*, estate, property (gen. *pl*); income; *Com.* credit balance. **h. monedado,** specie
haber /a'βer/ *vt irr* to be there (*3rd pers. sing*), have in compound tenses, catch, lay hands on (e.g. *El reo fue habido,* The criminal was caught). *v aux* (e.g. *Hemos escrito la carta,* We have written the letter). *v impers* to happen, take place; be. *3rd pers. sing Pres. Ind.* **ha** is replaced by **hay,** meaning there is or there are (e.g. *No hay naranjas en las tiendas,* There are no oranges in the shops). In certain weather expressions, **hay** means it is (e.g. *Hay luna,* It is moonlight). Used of expressions of time, **haber** means to elapse and **ha** (*3rd pers. sing Pres. Ind.*) has adverbial force of "ago" (e.g. *muchos días ha,* many days ago). **h. de,** to be necessary (less strong than **h. que**) (e.g. *Hemos de verle mañana,* We must see him tomorrow. *He de hacer el papel de Manolo,* I am to play the part of Manolo). **h. que,** to be unavoidable, be essential. With this construction the form **hay** is used (e.g. *Hay que darse prisa,* We (or one) must hurry. **No hay que enojarse,** There's no need to get annoyed). **no h., más que pedir,** to leave nothing to be desired. **no h. tal,** to be no such thing. *Inf.* **habérselas con,** to quarrel or fall out with. **Hubo una vez...,** Once upon a time... **¡No hay de qué!,** Don't mention it!; Not at all!; You're welcome! **No hay para que...,** There's no point in.... **poco tiempo ha,** a little while ago. **¿Qué hay?** What's the matter?; What's new? **¿Qué hay de nuevo?** What's new? *Pres. Ind.* **he, has, ha, hemos,**

habéis, han. *Fut.* **habré, etc.** *Condit.* **habría, etc.** *Preterite* **hube, hubiste, hubo, hubimos, hubisteis, hubieron.** *Pres. Subjunc.* **haya, etc.** *Imperf. Subjunc.* **hubiese, etc.**
habichuela /aβi'tʃuela/ f, kidney bean
hábil /'aβil/ a clever; skillful; able; lawful
habilidad /aβili'ðað/ f, ability; skill; accomplishment; craftsmanship, workmanship
habilidoso /aβili'ðoso/ a accomplished; able; skillful
habilitación /aβilita'sion; aβilita'θion/ f, habilitation; paymastership; equipment; furnishing
habilitado /aβili'taðo/ *m*, paymaster
habilitar /aβili'tar/ *vt* to qualify; equip; furnish; habilitate; enable; *Com.* capitalize
habitabilidad /aβitaβili'ðað/ f, habitability
habitable /aβi'taβle/ a habitable
habitación /aβita'sion; aβita'θion/ f, habitation, dwelling; room in a house; residence; (*Bot. Zool.*) habitat; caretaking
habitante /aβi'tante/ *m*, inhabitant
habitar /aβi'tar/ *vt* to inhabit, reside in
hábito /'aβito/ *m*, attire; *Eccl.* habit; use, custom; skill, facility; *pl* vestments; gown, robe. **tomar el h.,** to become a monk or nun
habitual /aβi'tual/ a habitual, usual
habituar /aβi'tuar/ *vt* to accustom; *vr* accustom oneself; grow used (to)
habitud /aβi'tuð/ f, habit, custom; connection, relationship
habla /'aβla/ f, speech; language; dialect; discourse. **al h.,** within speaking distance. **de h. hispana,** Spanish-speaking
hablado /a'βlaðo/ a spoken. **bien h.,** well-spoken; courteous. **mal h.,** ill-spoken; rude

hablador /aβla'ðor/ **(-ra)** *a* talkative; gossipy; *Mexico also* boastful. *n* chatterbox; gossip

habladuría /aβlaðu'ria/ *f*, gossip; impertinent chatter

hablanchín /aβlan'tʃin/ *a Inf.* chattering, gossiping

hablar /a'βlar/ *vi* to speak; converse; express oneself; arrange; (*with de*) speak about, discuss; gossip about, criticize; (*with por*) intercede on behalf of; *vt* speak (a language); say, speak; *vr* speak to one another. **no hablarse,** to not be on speaking terms. **h. a gritos,** to shout. **h. alto,** to speak loudly or in strong terms. **h. bien** (*or* **mal**), to be well- (or ill-) spoken; be polite (or rude). **h. claro,** to speak frankly. **h. consigo** *or* **h. entre sí,** to talk to oneself. *Inf.* **h. cristiano, h. en cristiano,** to speak clearly or intelligibly; speak frankly. **hablarlo todo,** to talk too much. **h. por h.,** to talk for talking's sake. *Inf.* **h. por los codos,** to chatter. **h. sin ton ni son,** to speak foolishly

hablilla /a'βliya; a'βliʎa/ *f*, rumor, tittletattle, gossip

hacecillo /ase'siyo; aθe'θiʎo/ *m*, small sheaf; small bundle; *Bot.* fascicle; beam (of light)

hacedero /ase'ðero; aθe'ðero/ *a* feasible, practicable

hacedor /ase'ðor; aθe'ðor/ *m*, maker; steward, manager; Creator

hacendado /asen'daðo; aθen'daðo/ **(-da)** *a* landed. *n* landowner; *West. Hem.* cattle rancher

hacendista /asen'dista; aθen'dista/ *mf* political economist

hacendoso /asen'doso; aθen'doso/ *a* diligent, hardworking

hacer /a'ser; a'θer/ *vt irr* to make; fashion, form, construct; do, perform; cause, effect; arrange, put right; contain; accustom, harden; pack (luggage); imagine, invent, create; improve, perfect; compel, oblige; deliver (speeches); compose; earn; *Math.* add up to; suppose, imagine (e.g. *Sus padres hacían a María en casa,* Her parents imagined that Mary was at home); put into practice, execute; play the part of or act like (e.g. *h. el gracioso,* to play the buffoon); shed, cast (e.g. *El roble hace sombra,* The oak casts a shadow); assemble, convoke (meetings, gatherings); give off, produce (e.g. *La chimenea hace humo,* The chimney is smoking); perform (plays); (*with el, la, lo,* and *some nouns*) pretend to be (e.g. *Se hizo el desconocido,* He pretended to be ignorant). (**h.** followed by infin. is sometimes translated by a past participle in English (e.g. *Lo hice h.,* I had it done).) *vi* to matter, be important, signify (e.g. *Su llegada no hace nada al caso,* His arrival makes no difference to the case. *Se me hace muy poco...,* It matters to me very little...); be fitting or suitable; concern, be pertinent; match, go with; agree, be in harmony; (*with de*) act as, discharge duties of temporarily (e.g. *h. de camarero,* to be a temporary waiter); (*with por*) try, to attempt to (e.g. *Haremos por decírselo,* We shall try to tell him). *vi impers* Used in expressions concerning: 1. the weather. 2. lapse of time. English uses the verb "to be" in both cases, e.g.: 1. *hace buen* (or *mal*) **tiempo,** it is fine (or bad) weather. **hace mucho frío,** it is very cold. **hace sol,** it is sunny. **hace viento,** it is windy. **¿Qué tiempo hace?** What is the weather like? 2. **hace** + an expression of time is followed by **que** introducing a clause (e.g. *Hace dos horas que llegamos,* We arrived two hours ago) or **hace** + an expression of time may be followed by **desde** + a noun (e.g. *Hace dos años desde aquel día,* It is two years since that day) When an action or state that has begun in the past is still continuing in the present, the Spanish verb is in the Pres. Ind., whereas the English verb is in the Perfect (e.g. *Hace un mes que la veo todos los días,* I have been seeing her every day for a month). This rule holds good with other tenses. English Pluperfect, Future Perfect, Conditional Perfect become in Spanish Imperfect, Future, Conditional, respectively. *Naut.* **h. agua,** to leak. **h. aguas,** to pass water, urinate. **h. alarde de,** to boast of. **h. América,** to strike it rich. **h. el amor a,** to make love to, court, woo. **h. autoridad,** to be authoritative. **h. a todo,** to have many uses; be adaptable. **h. bancarrota,** to go bankrupt. **h. un berrinche, hacerse un berrinche,** to have a fit, have a tantrum. *Fig. Inf.* **h. buena,** to justify. **h. calceta,** to knit. **h. cara** *or* **frente a,** to face; resist. **h. caso,** to take notice, mind (e.g. *¡No hagas*

caso! Never mind!). **h. causas,** to bring charges, institute proceedings. **h. cuentas,** to reckon up. **h. daño,** to harm. *Inf.* **h. de las suyas,** to behave in his usual manner or play one of his usual tricks. **h. diligencias por,** to endeavor to. **h. fiesta,** to take a holiday. **h. fuerza,** to struggle. **h. fuerza a,** *Fig.* to do violence to (e.g. *Hizo fuerza a sus creencias,* He did violence to his beliefs). **h. h.,** to cause to be made (e.g. *He hecho hacer un vestido,* I have had a dress made). **h. juego,** to make a set, match (e.g. *El sombrero hace juego con el traje,* The hat goes with the dress). **h. la corte (a),** to court, woo. *Fig. Inf.* **h. la vista gorda,** to turn a blind eye. **h. la vida del claustro,** to lead a cloistered existence. **h. mal,** to do wrong; be harmful (food, etc.). **h. pedazos,** to break. **h. pinos** (or **pinitos**) to totter; toddle; stagger. *Aer.* **h. rizos,** to loop the loop. **h. saber,** to make known; notify. **h. seguir,** to forward (letters). **h. señas,** to make signs (wave, beckon, etc.). *Inf.* **h. una que sea sonada,** to cause a big scandal. **¡Hágame el favor!** Please! *Pres. Ind.* **hago, haces,** etc. *Fut.* **haré,** etc. *Condit.* **haría,** etc. *Imperat.* **haz, haga, hagamos, haced, hagan.** *Preterite* **hice, hiciste, hizo, hicimos, hicisteis, hicieron.** *Pres. Subjunc.* **haga,** etc. *Imperf. Subjunc.* **hiciese, etc.**

hacerse /a'serse; a'θerse/ *vr irr* to become (e.g. *Se ha hecho muy importante,* It (or he) has become very important); grow up (e.g. *Miguel se ha hecho hombre,* Michael has grown up (become a man)); develop, mature; pass oneself off as, pretend to be; (*with prep a*) become accustomed to or used to (e.g. *Me haré a este clima,* I shall grow used to this climate); withdraw or retire to (of places); (*with de or con*) provide oneself with. **h. a la vela,** to set sail. **h. a (uno),** to seem (e.g. *Eso que me cuentas se me hace increíble,* What you tell me seems incredible). *Inf.* **h. chiquito,** to be modest. **h. tarde,** to grow late; *Fig.* be too late. See **hacer**

hacha /'atʃa/ *f*, large candle; torch; ax. **h. pequeña,** hatchet

hachazo /a'tʃaso; a'tʃaθo/ *m*, stroke of an ax

hache /'atʃe/ *f*, name of the letter H

hachero /a'tʃero/ *m*, candlestick; woodcutter; axman

hacho /'atʃo/ *m*, torch; beacon

hacia /'asia; 'aθia/ *prep* toward, near, about. **h. adelante,** forward, onward

hacienda /a'sienda; a'θienda/ *f*, country estate, land; property; *pl* domestic tasks; cattle. **h. pública,** public funds. **ministerio de h.,** national treasury, exchequer

hacina /a'sina; a'θina/ *f*, *Agr.* stack; heap, pile

hacinamiento /asina'miento; aθina'miento/ *m*, stacking, piling; accumulation

hacinar /asi'nar; aθi'nar/ *vt Agr.* to stack sheaves; accumulate, amass; pile up, heap

hada /'aða/ *f*, fairy

hado /'aðo/ *m*, fate; destiny

hagiografía /ahiogra'fia/ *f*, hagiography

hagiógrafo /a'hiografo/ *m*, hagiographer

Haití /ai'ti/ Haiti

haitiano /ai'tiano/ **(-na)** *a* and *n* Haitian

halagar /ala'gar/ *vt* to caress; flatter; coax; please, delight

halago /a'lago/ *m*, flattery; coaxing; caress; source of pleasure, delight

halagüeño /ala'gueɲo/ *a* flattering; pleasing; caressing; hopeful, promising

halar /a'lar/ *vt Naut.* to haul, tow

halcón /al'kon/ *m*, falcon

halconero /alko'nero/ *m*, hawker, hunter

hálito /'alito/ *m*, breath; vapor; *Poet.* breeze

hallado /a'yaðo; a'ʎaðo/ *a* and *Past Part.* found, met. **bien h.,** welcome; happy, contented. **mal h.,** unwelcome; uneasy, discontented

hallador /aya'ðor; aʎa'ðor/ **(-ra)** *n* finder

hallar /a'yar; a'ʎar/ *vt* to find; meet; observe; discover; find out; *vr* be present; be, find oneself

hallazgo /a'yasgo; a'ʎaθgo/ *m*, finding; thing found; finder's reward

halo /'alo/ *m*, halo

halterofilia /altero'filia/ *f*, weightlifting

hamaca /a'maka/ *f*, hammock

hambre /'ambre/ f, hunger; famine; desire, yearning. **tener h.**, to be hungry

hambriento /am'briento/ a hungry; famished; Fig. starved (of affection, etc.)

hamburguesa /ambur'gesa/ f, hamburger

hamo /'amo/ m, fishhook

hampa /'ampa/ f, rogue's life; gang of rogues; underworld, slum

hangar /aŋ'gar/ m, hangar

haragán /ara'gan/ (**-ana**) a lazy, idle. n idler, lazybones

harapiento /ara'piento/ a ragged

harapo /a'rapo/ m, tatter, rag

haraposo /ara'poso/ a ragged

harén /a'ren/ m, harem

harina /a'rina/ f, flour; powder; farina. Inf. **ser h. de otro costal**, to be a horse of another color

harinero /ari'nero/ a relating to flour. m, flour merchant; flour bin

harinoso /ari'noso/ a floury, mealy; farinaceous

harmónica /ar'monika/ f, (Phys. Math.) harmonic

harmonizar /armoni'sar; armoni'θar/ vt to arrange (music)

harnear /arne'ar/ vt Lat. Am. to sieve, sift

harnero /ar'nero/ m, sieve

harón /a'ron/ a slothful, slow; lazy, idle

harpillera /arpi'yera; arpi'ʎera/ f, sackcloth, sacking

hartar /ar'tar/ vt to satiate; tire, annoy; satisfy the appetite; shower (with blows, etc.)

hartazgo /ar'tasgo; ar'taθgo/ m, satiety

harto /'arto/ a satiated; tired (of), adv enough

hartón /ar'ton/ a Central America, Mexico gluttonous

hartura /ar'tura/ f, satiety; abundance

hasta /'asta/ prep until; as far as; down or up to. conjunc also, even. **h. la vista**, See you! Ciaio! Au revoir! **h. mañana**, until tomorrow

hastial /as'tial/ m, gable, end wall; boor, lout

hastío /as'tio/ m, loathing; distaste; nausea

hato /'ato/ m, bundle of personal clothing; herd of cattle; gang (of suspicious characters); crowd, mob; Inf. group, party. Inf. **liar el h.**, to pack up

Hawai /'awai/ Hawaii

hay /ai/ there is; there are. See **haber**

haya /'aya/ f, beech tree; beechwood

hayal /a'yal/ m, wood of beech trees, beech plantation

hayuco /a'yuko/ m, beech mast

haz /as; aθ/ m, bundle, sheaf; Mil. file; pl fasces. f, visage; surface, face. **h. de la tierra**, face of the earth. **h. de luz**, beam of light. Fig. **ser de dos haces**, to be two-faced

haz /as; aθ/ 2nd pers Imperat **hacer**

hazaña /a'saɲa; a'θaɲa/ f, exploit, prowess

hazañoso /asa'ɲoso; aθa'ɲoso/ a heroic, dauntless, courageous

hazmerreír /asmerre'ir; aθmerre'ir/ m, Inf. laughingstock

he /e/ interj and adv Behold! **¡Heme aquí!** Here I am. **he aquí**, here is...

hebilla /e'βiya; e'βiʎa/ f, buckle, clasp

hebra /'eβra/ f, thread; fiber; flesh; Mineral. vein, streak; filament (textiles); grain (of wood); pl Poet. hair. Inf. **pegar la h.**, to start a conversation

hebraísmo /eβra'ismo/ m, Hebraism

hebraísta /eβra'ista/ m, Hebraist

hebreo /e'βreo/ (**-ea**) a Hebraic, Jewish. n Jew. m, Hebrew (language)

hecatombe /eka'tombe/ f, hecatomb; slaughter, massacre

hechicería /etʃise'ria; etʃiθe'ria/ f, sorcery; spell, enchantment

hechicero /etʃi'sero; etʃi'θero/ a bewitching; magic; charming, attractive

hechizar /etʃi'sar; etʃi'θar/ vt to bewitch; charm, attract, delight

hechizo /e'tʃiso; e'tʃiθo/ m, magic spell; fascination; charm; delight, pleasure; a Lat. Am. homemade, produced locally, locally produced

hecho /'etʃo/ a developed, mature; accustomed, used; perfected, finished; ready-made. **h. una furia**, like a

fury, very angry. **bien h.**, well-made, well-proportioned; well or rightly done

hecho /'etʃo/ m, deed, action; fact; happening, event. **los Hechos de los Apóstoles**, the Acts of the Apostles

hechura /e'tʃura/ f, making, make; creation; form; figure, statue; Lit. composition; build (of body); Fig. puppet, creature; pl price paid for work done. **de h. sastre**, a tailor-made

hectárea /ekta'rea/ f, hectare

hectógrafo /ek'tografo/ m, hectograph

hectogramo /ekto'gramo/ m, hectogram

hectolitro /ekto'litro/ m, hectoliter

hectovatio /ekto'βatio/ m, hectowatt

heder /e'ðer/ vi irr to stink; be intolerable. See **entender**

hediondez /eðion'des; eðion'deθ/ f, stink, stench

hediondo /e'ðiondo/ a stinking; intolerable, pestilential; obscene

hedonismo /eðo'nismo/ m, hedonism

hedonista /eðo'nista/ mf hedonist

hegeliano /ehe'liano/ a Hegelian

hegemonía /ehemo'nia/ f, hegemony

helada /e'laða/ f, frost. **h. blanca**, hoarfrost

heladera /ela'ðera/ f, refrigerator

helado /e'laðo/ a frozen; ice-cold; astounded, disdainful. m, iced drink; sherbet, ice cream

helamiento /ela'miento/ m, icing; freezing

helar /e'lar/ vt irr to freeze; ice, chill; astound; discourage; vr become iced; freeze; become ice-cold. v impers to freeze. See **acertar**

helecho /e'letʃo/ m, fern

helénico /e'leniko/ a Hellenic

helenismo /ele'nismo/ m, Hellenism

helenista /ele'nista/ mf Hellenist

helenizar /eleni'sar; eleni'θar/ vt to Hellenize

hélice /'elise; 'eliθe/ f, spiral, helical line; screw, propeller; Geom. helix; Astron. Ursa Major

helicóptero /eli'koptero/ m, Aer. helicopter

helio /'elio/ m, helium

heliógrafo /e'liografo/ m, heliograph

helioscopio /elio'skopio/ m, helioscope

helióstato /e'liostato/ m, heliostat

helioterapia /eliote'rapia/ f, heliotherapy

heliotropismo /eliotro'pismo/ m, heliotropism

heliotropo /elio'tropo/ m, heliotrope; agate

helvecio /el'βesio; el'βeθio/ (**-ia**) a and n Helvetian

hembra /'embra/ f, female; Inf. woman; nut of a screw; eye of a hook. Inf. **una real h.**, a fine figure of a woman

hemiciclo /emi'siklo; emi'θiklo/ m, hemicycle; floor (of a legislative building)

hemisférico /emis'feriko/ a hemispherical

hemisferio /emis'ferio/ m, hemisphere

hemofilia /emo'filia/ f, hemophilia.

hemoglobina /emoglo'βina/ f, hemoglobin

hemorragia /emo'rrahia/ f, hemorrhage

hemorroides /emo'rroiðes/ f, hemorrhoids

henchido /en'tʃiðo/ a swollen

henchimiento /entʃi'miento/ m, swelling; inflation; filling

henchir /en'tʃir/ vt irr to fill; stuff; swell. Pres. Ind. **hincho, hinches, hinche, hinchen.** Pres. Part. **hinchiendo.** Pres. Subjunc. **hincha, etc.** Imperf. Subjunc. **hinchiese, etc.** Imperat. **hinche, hincha, hinchamos, henchid, hinchan**

hendedura /ende'ðura/ f, fissure; rift

hender /en'der/ vt irr to split, crack; Fig. cleave (air, water, etc.); make one's way through. See **entender**

hendidura /endi'ðura/ f, split, fissure, crack, chink

hendija /en'diha/ f, Lat. Am. crack, crevice

henil /e'nil/ m, hayloft

heno /'eno/ m, hay

hepático /e'patiko/ a hepatic

heráldica /e'raldika/ f, heraldry

heráldico /e'raldiko/ a heraldic

heraldo /e'raldo/ m, herald; harbinger

herbaje /er'βahe/ m, herbage; pasture; grass; thick woolen cloth

herbario /er'βario/ *m*, herbalist; botanist; herbarium.
a herbal
herbívoro /er'βiβoro/ *a* herbivorous
herbolaria /erβo'laria/ *f*, herbal
hercúleo /er'kuleo/ *a* herculean
heredad /ere'ðað/ *f*, landed property; country estate
heredar /ere'ðar/ *vt* to inherit; make a deed of gift to; inherit characteristics, etc.; take as heir
heredera /ere'ðera/ *f*, heiress
heredero /ere'ðero/ *m*, heir; inheritor. **h. aparente,** heir apparent. **presunto h.,** heir presumptive
hereditario /ereði'tario/ *a* hereditary
hereje /e'rehe/ *mf* heretic
herejía /ere'hia/ *f*, heresy
herencia /e'rensia; e'renθia/ *f*, inheritance; heredity; heritage
heresiarca /ere'siarka/ *mf* heresiarch
herético /e'retiko/ *a* heretical
herida /e'riða/ *f*, wound; insult; anguish. **h. contusa,** contusion. **h. penetrante,** deep wound
herir /e'rir/ *vt irr* to wound; strike, harm; *Fig.* pierce (of sun's rays); *Fig.* pluck (strings of a musical instrument); impress (the senses); affect (the emotions); offend (gen. of words). *Pres. Part.* **hiriendo.** *Pres. Ind.* **hiero, hieres, hiere, hieren.** *Preterite* **hirió, hirieron.** *Pres. Subjunc.* **hiera, hieras, hiera, hiramos, hiráis, hieran.** *Imperf. Subjunc.* **hiriese, etc.**
hermafrodita /ermafro'ðita/ *a* and *mf* hermaphrodite
hermafroditismo /ermafroði'tismo/ *m*, hermaphroditism
hermana /er'mana/ *f*, sister; twin, pair (of things). **h. de leche,** foster sister. **h. política,** sister-in-law
hermanar /erma'nar/ *vt* to join; mate; harmonize; *Chile* to pair (like socks); *vt* and *vr* be the spiritual brother of, be compatible
hermanastra /erma'nastra/ *f*, stepsister, half-sister
hermanastro /erma'nastro/ *m*, stepbrother, half-brother
hermandad /erman'dað/ *f*, brotherhood; friendship; intimacy; relationship (of one thing to another); confraternity. **Santa H.,** Spanish rural police force instituted in the fifteenth century
hermano /er'mano/ *m*, brother; pair, twin (of things); *Eccl.* brother. **h. de raza,** member of the same race. **h. político,** brother-in-law
hermético /er'metiko/ *a* hermetic
hermosear /ermose'ar/ *vt* to embellish, beautify, adorn
hermoso /er'moso/ *a* beautiful; shapely; handsome; fine, wonderful (weather, view, etc.)
hermosura /ermo'sura/ *f*, beauty; pleasantness, attractiveness, perfection of form; belle
hernia /'ernia/ *f*, hernia
héroe /'eroe/ *m*, hero
heroicidad /eroisi'ðað; eroiθi'ðað/ *f*, heroism
heroico /e'roiko/ *a* heroic
heroína /ero'ina/ *f*, heroine
heroísmo /ero'ismo/ *m*, heroism
herpes /'erpes/ *m pl*, or *f pl*, herpes
herrada /e'rraða/ *f*, pail
herradero /erra'ðero/ *m*, branding of livestock
herrador /erra'ðor/ *m*, blacksmith
herradura /erra'ðura/ *f*, horseshoe
herraje /e'rrahe/ *m*, ironwork; *Lat. Am.* horseshoe
herramienta /erra'mienta/ *f*, tool; set of tools
herrar /e'rrar/ *vt irr* to shoe horses; brand (cattle); decorate with iron. See **acertar**
herrería /erre'ria/ *f*, forge; ironworks; blacksmith's shop; clamor, tumult, confusion
herrero /e'rrero/ *m*, smith
herrete /e'rrete/ *m*, ferrule, tag
herrumbre /e'rrumbre/ *f*, rust
herrumbroso /errum'broso/ *a* rusty
hervidero /erβi'ðero/ *m*, boiling, bubbling; *Fig.* ebullition; swarm, crowd
hervir /er'βir/ *vi irr* to boil; foam and froth (sea); seethe (emotions); surge (crowds); (*with en*) abound in, swarm with. See **sentir**
hervor /er'βor/ *m*, boiling; ebullition, vigor, zest; seething, agitation

hesitación /esita'sion; esita'θion/ *f*, hesitation, doubt, uncertainty
hesitar /esi'tar/ *vi* to hesitate, vacillate
heterodina /etero'ðina/ *a f*, *Radio.* heterodyne
heterodoxia /etero'ðoksia/ *f*, heterodoxy
heterodoxo /etero'ðokso/ *a* heterodox
heterogeneidad /eterohenei'ðað/ *f*, heterogeneity
heterogéneo /etero'heneo/ *a* heterogeneous
heterosexual /eterosek'sual/ *mf* and *a* heterosexual
hético /'etiko/ *a* hectic, consumptive
hexagonal /eksago'nal/ *a* hexagonal
hexágono /e'ksagono/ *m*, hexagon
hexámetro /e'ksametro/ *m*, hexameter
hez /es; eθ/ *f*, (gen. *pl* **heces**) lees, dregs
hiato /'iato/ *m*, hiatus
hibernal /iβer'nal/ *a* wintry
hibernés /iβer'nes/ *a* Hibernian
hibisco /i'βisko/ *m*, hibiscus
hibridación /iβriða'sion; iβriða'θion/ *f*, hybridization
hibridismo /iβri'ðismo/ *m*, hybridism
híbrido /'iβriðo/ *a* and *m*, hybrid
hidalgo /i'ðalgo/ **(-ga)** *n* noble, aristocrat. *a* noble; illustrious; generous
hidalguía /iðal'gia/ *f*, nobility; generosity, nobility of spirit
hidra /'iðra/ *f*, *Zool.* hydra; poisonous snake; *Astron.* Hydra
hidratar /iðra'tar/ *vt Chem.* to hydrate
hidrato /i'ðrato/ *m*, hydrate. **h. de carbono,** carbohydrate
hidráulica /i'ðraulika/ *f*, hydraulics
hidráulico /i'ðrauliko/ *a* hydraulic
hidroavión /iðroa'βion/ *m*, flying boat
hidrocarburo /iðrokar'βuro/ *m*, hydrocarbon
hidrocéfalo /iðro'sefalo; iðro'θefalo/ *a* hydrocephalic
hidrodinámica /iðroði'namika/ *f*, hydrodynamics
hidroeléctrico /iðroe'lektriko/ *a* hydroelectric
hidrofobia /iðro'foβia/ *f*, hydrophobia; rabies
hidrógeno /i'ðroheno/ *m*, hydrogen
hidrografía /iðrogra'fia/ *f*, hydrography
hidrología /iðrolo'hia/ *f*, hydrology
hidropesía /iðrope'sia/ *f*, dropsy
hidrópico /i'ðropiko/ *a* dropsical
hidroplano /iðro'plano/ *m*, seaplane
hidroquinona /iðroki'nona/ *f*, hydroquinone
hidroscopio /iðro'skopio/ *m*, hydroscope
hidrostática /iðro'statika/ *f*, hydrostatics
hidroterapia /iðrote'rapia/ *f*, hydrotherapy
hiedra /'ieðra/ *f*, ivy
hiel /iel/ *f*, gall, bile, bitterness, affliction; *pl* troubles
hielo /'ielo/ *m*, ice, frost; freezing, icing; stupefaction; indifference, coldness. *Inf.* **estar hecho un h.,** to be as cold as ice
hiena /'iena/ *f*, hyena
hierático /ie'ratiko/ *a* hieratical
hierba /'ierβa/ *f*, grass; small plant; herb. **h. cana,** groundsel. **mala h.,** weed
hierbabuena /ierβa'βuena/ *f*, *Bot.* mint
hierra /'ierra/ *f*, branding time
hierro /'ierro/ *m*, iron; brand with hot iron; iron or steel head of a lance, etc.; instrument or shape made of iron; weapon of war. *pl* fetters. **h. colado,** cast iron. **h. dulce,** wrought iron. **h. en planchas,** sheet iron. **h. viejo,** scrap iron
hígado /'igaðo/ *m*, liver; courage; *Central America, Mexico also* nuisance
higiene /i'hiene/ *f*, hygiene; cleanliness, neatness. **h. privada,** personal hygiene. **h. pública,** public health
higiénico /i'hieniko/ *a* hygienic
higo /'igo/ *m*, fig. **h. chumbo,** prickly pear
higrómetro /i'grometro/ *m*, hygrometer
higuera /i'gera/ *f*, fig tree
hija /'iha/ *f*, daughter; native of a place; offspring
hijastro /i'hastro/ **(-ra)** *n* stepchild
hijo /'iho/ *m*, son; child; native of a place; offspring; shoot, sprout; *pl* descendants. **h. de la cuna,** foundling. **h. de leche,** foster child. **h. natural,** natural child. **h. político,** son-in-law
hijuela /i'huela/ *f*, little daughter; small mattress;

small drain; side road; accessory, subordinate thing; piece of material for widening a garment; *Law.* part of an inheritance; *Lat. Am.* rural property

hila /'ila/ *f,* row, line; gut; *Surg.* lint (gen. *pl*)

hilacha /i'latʃa/ *f,* thread raveled from cloth; fiber, filament. **h. de vidrio,** spun glass

hilado /i'laðo/ *m,* spinning; thread, yarn

hilandería /ilande'ria/ *f,* spinning; spinning mill; mill. **h. de algodón,** cotton mill

hilandero /ilan'dero/ **(-ra)** *n* spinner

hilar /i'lar/ *vt* to spin; reason, infer, discourse

hilaridad /ilari'ðað/ *f,* hilarity; quiet happiness

hilaza /i'lasa; i'laθa/ *f,* yarn

hilera /i'lera/ *f,* line, file, row; fine yarn; *Mil.* file, rank; *Metall.* wire drawer; *Mas.* course (of bricks)

hilo /'ilo/ *m,* thread; linen; wire; mesh (spiders, silkworm's web, etc.); edge (of a blade); thin stream (of liquid); thread (of discourse)

hilván /il'βan/ *m, Sew.* basting; tack

hilvanar /ilβa'nar/ *vt Sew.* to baste

himen /'imen/ *m,* hymen

himeneo /ime'neo/ *m,* marriage, wedding

himnario /im'nario/ *m,* hymnal

himno /'imno/ *m,* hymn

hin /in/ *m,* whinny, neigh

hincapié /inka'pie/ *m,* foothold. **hacer h.,** to insist, make a stand

hincar /in'kar/ *vt* to thrust in; drive in, sink; *vr* kneel. **h. el diente,** to bite. **h. la uña,** to scratch. **hincarse de rodillas,** to kneel down

hinchado /in'tʃaðo/ *a* puffed up, vain; pompous, high-flown, redundant (style)

hinchar /in'tʃar/ *vt* to inflate; puff out (the chest); swell (of a river, etc.); exaggerate (events); *vr* swell; grow vain, be puffed up

hinchazón /intʃa'son; intʃa'θon/ *f,* swelling; vanity, presumption; pomposity, euphuism (style)

hiniesta /i'niesta/ *f,* Spanish broom

hinojo /i'noho/ *m, Bot.* fennel; knee. **de hinojos,** on bended knee

hipar /i'par/ *vi* to hiccup; pant (of dogs); be overanxious; be overtired; sob, cry

hipérbole /i'perβole/ *f,* hyperbole

hiperbólico /iper'βoliko/ *a* hyperbolical

hipercrítico /iper'kritiko/ *m,* hypercritic. *a* hypercritical

hipertensión /iperten'θion/ *f,* hypertension

hipertrofiarse /ipertro'fiarse/ *vr* to hypertrophy

hípico /'ipiko/ *a* equine

hipnosis /ip'nosis/ *f,* hypnosis

hipnótico /ip'notiko/ *a* hypnotic. *m,* hypnotic drug

hipnotismo /ipno'tismo/ *m,* hypnotism

hipnotización /ipnotisa'sion; ipnotiθa'θion/ *f,* hypnotization

hipnotizar /ipnoti'sar; ipnoti'θar/ *vt* to hypnotize

hipo /'ipo/ *m,* hiccup; sob; longing, desire; dislike, disgust

hipocondría /ipokon'dria/ *f,* hypochondria

hipocondríaco /ipokon'driako/ **(-ca)** *a* hypochondriacal. *n* hypochondriac

hipocrático /ipo'kratiko/ *a* Hippocratic

hipocresía /ipokre'sia/ *f,* hypocrisy

hipócrita /i'pokrita/ *a* hypocritical. *mf* hypocrite

hipodérmico /ipo'ðermiko/ *a* hypodermic

hipódromo /i'poðromo/ *m,* hippodrome, racetrack

hipopótamo /ipo'potamo/ *m,* hippopotamus

hipostático /ipo'statiko/ *a* hypostatic

hipoteca /ipo'teka/ *f,* mortgage

hipotecable /ipote'kaβle/ *a* mortgageable

hipotecar /ipote'kar/ *vt* to mortgage

hipotecario /ipote'kario/ *a* belonging to a mortgage

hipotenusa /ipote'nusa/ *f,* hypotenuse

hipótesis /i'potesis/ *f,* hypothesis

hipotético /ipo'tetiko/ *a* hypothetical

hirsuto /ir'suto/ *a* hirsute, hairy

hirviente /ir'βiente/ *a* boiling

hisca /'iska/ *f,* birdlime

hisopear /isope'ar/ *vt Eccl.* to sprinkle, asperse

hisopo /i'sopo/ *m, Bot.* hyssop; *Eccl.* hyssop, sprinkler; *Lat. Am. also* (paint)brush

hispánico /is'paniko/ *a* Spanish

hispanismo /ispa'nismo/ *m,* Hispanism

hispanista /ispa'nista/ *mf* Hispanist

hispano /is'pano/ *a* Hispanic, Spanish American.

hispanoamericano /ispanoameri'kano/ **(-na)** *a* and *n* Spanish-American, Hispano-American

histeria /is'teria/ *f,* hysteria

histérico /is'teriko/ *a* hysterical; hysteric

histerismo /iste'rismo/ *m, Med.* hysteria

histología /istolo'hia/ *f,* histology

histólogo /is'tologo/ *m,* histologist

historia /is'toria/ *f,* history; narrative, story; tale; *Inf.* gossip (gen. *pl*); *Art.* historical piece. **h. natural,** natural history. **h. sagrada,** biblical history. *Fig.* **dejarse de historias,** to stop beating around the bush

historiador /istoria'ðor/ **(-ra)** *n* historian

historiar /isto'riar/ *vt* to narrate, relate; record, chronicle

histórico /is'toriko/ *a* historical; historic

historieta /isto'rieta/ *f,* short story; anecdote

historiografía /istoriogra'fia/ *f,* historiography

historiógrafo /isto'riografo/ *m,* historiographer

histriónico /ist'rioniko/ *a* histrionic

hitlerismo /itle'rismo/ *m,* Hitlerism

hito /'ito/ *m,* milestone; boundary mark; *Fig.* mark, target. **de h. en h.,** from head to foot

hocico /o'siko; o'θiko/ *m,* snout; *Inf.* face, mug; *Inf.* angry gesture; *Naut.* prow. **meter el h.,** to stick one's nose into other people's business

hogaño /o'gaɲo/ *adv Inf.* during this year; at the present time

hogar /o'gar/ *m,* hearth, fireplace; home, house; family life; firebox (of a locomotive)

hoguera /o'gera/ *f,* bonfire

hoja /'oha/ *f, Bot.* leaf; petal; sheet (metal, paper, etc.); page (of book); blade (sharp instruments); leaf (door, window); sword. **h. de cálculo,** spreadsheet. **h. de servicios,** service or professional record. **h. de tocino,** side of bacon. **h. extraordinaria,** extra, special edition (of a newspaper). **h. volante,** handbill, supplement. **volver la h.,** to turn over (pages); change one's opinion; turn the conversation

hojalata /oha'lata/ *f,* tin plate

hojalatería /ohalate'ria/ *f,* tinware; tin shop

hojalatero /ohala'tero/ *m,* tinsmith

hojalda, hojalde /o'halda, o'halde/ *m* = **hojaldre**

hojaldre /o'haldre/ *m,* or *f,* puff pastry

hojarasca /oha'raska/ *f,* withered leaves; excessive foliage; rubbish, trash

hojear /ohe'ar/ *vt* to turn the leaves of a book; skip, skim, read quickly; *vi* exfoliate

hojuela /o'huela/ *f, dim* little leaf; *Bot.* leaflet; pancake

¡hola! /'ola/ *interj* Hi! Hello!

Holanda /o'landa/ Holland

holandés /olan'des/ **(-esa)** *a* and *n* Dutchman (-woman) *m,* Dutch (language)

holgado /ol'gaðo/ *a* leisured, free; loose, wide; comfortable; well-off, rich

holganza /ol'gansa; ol'ganθa/ *f,* repose, leisure, ease; idleness; pleasure

holgar /ol'gar/ *vi irr* to rest; be idle; be glad; be unused or unnecessary (things). *vr* enjoy oneself, amuse oneself; be glad. See **contar**

holgazán /olga'san; olga'θan/ **(-ana)** *a* idle. *n* idler

holgazanear /olgasane'ar; olgaθane'ar/ *vi* to idle

holgazanería /olgasane'ria; olgaθane'ria/ *f,* idleness, sloth

holgorio /ol'gorio/ *m,* rejoicing, festivity, merriment

holgura /ol'gura/ *f,* enjoyment, merrymaking; width; comfort, ease; *Mech.* free play

hollar /o'ʎar; o'ʎar/ *vt irr* to trample under foot; humiliate. See **degollar**

hollejo /o'ʎeho; o'ʎeho/ *m,* peel, thin skin (of fruit); *Agr.* chaff

hollín /o'ʎin; o'ʎin/ *m,* soot

holocausto /olo'kausto/ *m,* holocaust. **el H.** the Holocaust

hológrafo /o'lografo/ *m*, holograph

hombradía /ombra'ðia/ *f*, manliness; courage

hombre /'ombre/ *m*, man; adult; omber (cards). *interj* ¡**h.**! *Inf.* Old fellow! You don't say so! ¡**h. al agua!** Man overboard! **h. de bien,** honest, honorable man. **h. de estado,** statesman. **h. de muchos oficios,** jack-of-all-trades. **h. de negocios,** businessman; man of affairs. **h. de pro,** worthy man; famous man. **ser muy h.,** to be a real man, be very manly

hombrera /om'brera/ *f*, epaulette; shoulderpad

hombro /'ombro/ *m*, shoulder. **echar al h.,** to shoulder; undertake, take the responsibility of. **encogerse de hombros,** to shrug one's shoulders; be indifferent or uninterested

hombruno /om'bruno/ *a Inf.* mannish (of a woman)

homenaje /ome'nahe/ *m*, allegiance; homage; veneration, respect

homeópata /ome'opata/ *a* homeopathic. *mf* homeopath

homeopatía /omeopa'tia/ *f*, homeopathy

homérico /o'meriko/ *a* Homeric

homicida /omi'siða; omi'θiða/ *a* murderous, homicidal. *mf* murderer (-ess)

homicidio /omi'siðio; omi'θiðio/ *m*, homicide (act)

homilía /omi'lia/ *f*, homily

homogeneidad /omohenei'ðað/ *f*, homogeneity

homogéneo /omo'heneo/ *a* homogeneous

homónimo /o'monimo/ *a* homonymous. *m*, homonym

homosexual /omose'ksual/ *a* and *mf* homosexual

honda /'onda/ *f*, sling, catapult, slingshot

hondear /onde'ar/ *vt Naut.* to sound, plumb; *Naut.* unload; *Lat. Am.* to hit with a slingshot

hondo /'ondo/ *a* deep; low; *Fig.* profound; deep, intense (emotion). *m*, depth

hondón /on'don/ *m*, depth, recess

hondonada /ondo'naða/ *f*, hollow; glen; valley

hondura /on'dura/ *f*, depth

Honduras /on'duras/ Honduras

hondureño /ondu'repo/ (-ña) *a* and *n* Honduran

honestidad /onesti'ðað/ *f*, honorableness; virtue; respectability; modesty; courtesy

honesto /o'nesto/ *a* honorable, virtuous; modest; honest, just

hongo /'oŋgo/ *m*, fungus; toadstool; bowler hat

honor /o'nor/ *m*, honor; fame; reputation (women); modesty (women); praise; *pl* rank, position; honors

honorable /ono'raβle/ *a* honorable

honorario /ono'rario/ *a* honorary. *m*, honorarium, fee

honorífico /ono'rifiko/ *a* honorary; honorable

honra /'onra/ *f*, self-respect, honor, personal dignity; reputation; chastity and modesty (women); *pl* obsequies

honradez /onra'ðes; onra'ðeθ/ *f*, honesty; honorableness, integrity; respectability

honrado /on'raðo/ *a* honest; honorable

honrar /on'rar/ *vt* to respect; honor; *vr* to be honored

honroso /on'roso/ *a* honor-giving, honorable

¡**hopa!** /'opa/ *interj Argentina* cut it out!, stop it!

hora /'ora/ *f*, hour; opportune moment; *pl* book of hours. **horas hábiles,** working hours. **horas muertas,** wee hours; wasted time. **a la h.,** on time. **a última h.,** at the last minute. **dar la h.,** to strike the hour. **decir la h.,** tell time. **por h.,** per hour. **¿Qué h. es?** What time is it?

horadar /ora'ðar/ *vt* to bore, pierce

horario /o'rario/ *a* hourly. *m*, timetable; hour hand of a clock; watch

horca /'orka/ *f*, gallows; *Agr.* pitchfork; fork; prop for trees

horcajadas /orka'haðas/ (**a**) *adv* astride

horcajadura /orkaha'ðura/ *f*, crotch

horchata /or'tʃata/ *f*, drink made of chufas or crushed almonds

horda /'orða/ *f*, horde

horizontal /orison'tal; oriθon'tal/ *a* horizontal

horizonte /ori'sonte; ori'θonte/ *m*, horizon. **nuevos horizontes,** new opportunities

horma /'orma/ *f*, mold; cobbler's last; stone wall.

Fig. Inf. **hallar la h. de su zapato,** to find what suits one; meet one's match

hormiga /or'miga/ *f*, ant

hormigón /ormi'gon/ *m*, concrete. **h. armado,** reinforced concrete

hormiguear /ormige'ar/ *vi* to itch; crowd, swarm

hormiguero /ormi'gero/ *m*, anthill; crowd, swarm

hormona /or'mona/ *f*, hormone

hornero /or'nero/ (-ra) *n* baker

horno /'orno/ *m*, oven; furnace; kiln; bakery. **h. alfarero,** firing oven (for pottery). **h. de cocina,** kitchen stove. **h. de cuba,** blast furnace. **h. de ladrillo,** brick kiln. **alto h.,** iron-smelting furnace

horóscopo /o'roskopo/ *m*, horoscope

horquilla /or'kiya; or'kiʎa/ *f*, forked stick; hairpin; hatpin; *Agr.* fork; hook. **viraje en h.,** hairpin turn

horrendo /o'rrendo/ *a* horrible, frightful

hórreo /'orreo/ *m*, granary, barn

horribilidad /orriβili'ðað/ *f*, horribleness

horribilísimo /orriβi'lisimo/ *a sup* most horrible, exceedingly horrible

horrible /o'rriβle/ *a* horrible

horrífico /o'rrifiko/ *a* horrific

horripilante /orripi'lante/ *a* hair-raising, horrifying

horrísono /o'rrisono/ *a Poet.* horrid-sounding, terrifying

horror /o'rror/ *m*, horror; horribleness; atrocity, enormity

horrorizar /orrori'sar; orrori'θar/ *vt* to horrify; *vr* be horrified, be terrified

horroroso /orro'roso/ *a* dreadful, horrible; horrid; *Inf.* hideous, most ugly

hortaliza /orta'lisa; orta'liθa/ *f*, green vegetable, garden produce

hortelano /orte'lano/ *m*, market gardener

hortensia /or'tensia/ *f*, hydrangea

horticultura /ortikul'tura/ *f*, horticulture

horticultural /ortikultu'ral/ *a* horticultural

hosanna /o'sanna/ *m*, hosanna

hosco /'osko/ *a* dark brown; unsociable, sullen; crabbed

hospedaje /ospe'ðahe/ *m*, lodging; board, payment

hospedar /ospe'ðar/ *vt* to lodge, receive as a guest; *vr* and *vi* lodge, stay

hospedería /ospeðe'ria/ *f*, hostelry, inn; lodging

hospedero /ospe'ðero/ (-ra) *n* innkeeper

hospicio /os'pisio; os'piθio/ *m*, hospice; almshouse, workhouse; lodging; orphanage

hospital /ospi'tal/ *m*, hospital; hospice. **h. de sangre,** field hospital

hospitalario /ospita'lario/ *a* hospitable

hospitalidad /ospitali'ðað/ *f*, hospitality; hospitableness; hospital

hostelero /oste'lero/ (-ra) *n* innkeeper

hostería /oste'ria/ *f*, hostelry; inn

hostia /'ostia/ *f*, *Eccl.* wafer, Host

hostigamiento /ostiga'miento/ *m*, harassment. **h. sexual,** sexual harassment

hostigar /osti'gar/ *vt* to chastise; harass, tease, annoy

hostil /'ostil/ *a* hostile

hostilidad /ostili'ðað/ *f*, hostility

hostilizar /ostili'sar; ostili'θar/ *vt* to commit hostile acts against; antagonize

hotel /'otel/ *m*, hotel; villa

hotelero /ote'lero/ (-ra) *n* hotelkeeper

hoy /oi/ *adv* today; at present. **h. día** or **h. en día,** today. **h. por h.,** day by day; at the present time. **de h. en adelante,** from today forward

hoya /'oya/ *f*, hole; grave; valley, glen; bed (of a river)

hoyo /'oyo/ *m*, hole; pockmark; grave; hollow

hoyuelo /o'yuelo/ *m*, *dim* little hole; dimple

hoz /os; oθ/ *f*, sickle; defile

hozar /o'sar; o'θar/ *vt* to root (pigs, etc.)

hucha /'utʃa/ *f*, large chest; strongbox; savings

hueco /'ueko/ *a* empty; hollow; vain; hollow (sound); pompous (style); spongy, soft; inflated. *m*, hollow; interval of time or place; *Inf.* vacancy; gap in a wall, etc.

huelga /'uelga/ *f*, strike; leisure; lying fallow; merry-making. **h. de brazos caídos,** sit-down strike. **h. patronal,** lockout strike

huelguista /uel'gista/ *mf* striker

huella /'ueya; 'ueʎa/ *f*, footprint, track; footstep; tread (of stairs); *Print.* impression; vestige, trace. **h. digital,** fingerprint

huérfano /'uerfano/ **(-na)** *n* orphan. *a* unprotected, uncared for

huero /'uero/ *a* addled; empty, hollow

huerta /'uerta/ *f*, vegetable garden; orchard; irrigation land

huerto /'uerto/ *m*, orchard; vegetable garden

hueso /'ueso/ *m*, bone; stone (of fruit); kernel, core; drudgery; cheap, useless thing of poor quality. *Inf.* **no dejar un h. sano,** to tear (a person) to pieces. **tener los huesos molidos,** to be tired out; be bruised

huésped /'uespeð/ **(-da)** *n* guest; host; innkeeper

hueste /'ueste/ *f*, (gen. *pl*) army on the march, host; party, supporters

huesudo /ue'suðo/ *a* bony

hueva /'ueβa/ *f*, fish roe

huevera /ue'βera/ *f*, egg seller; eggcup

huevo /'ueβo/ *m*, egg. **h. duro,** hard-boiled egg. **h. estrellado,** fried egg. **h. pasado por agua,** soft-boiled egg. **huevos revueltos,** scrambled eggs

hugonote /ugo'note/ **(-ta)** *a* and *n* Huguenot

huida /'uiða/ *f*, flight, escape; bolting (of a horse); outlet

huir /uir/ *vi irr* to flee; fly (of time); elope; run away, bolt; (*with de*) avoid. *Pres. Part.* **huyendo.** *Pres. Ind.* **huyo, huyes, huyen.** *Preterite* **huyó, huyeron.** *Pres. Subjunc.* **huya,** etc. *Imperf. Subjunc.* **huyese, etc.**

hule /'ule/ *m*, oilcloth; rubber; *Central America, Mexico* rubber tree

hulla /'uya; 'uʎa/ *f*, coal mine, coal, soft coal

hullera /u'yera; u'ʎera/ *f*, colliery, coal mine

humanidad /umani'ðað/ *f*, humanity; human nature; human weakness; compassion; affability; *Inf.* stoutness; *pl* study of humanities

humanismo /uma'nismo/ *m*, humanism

humanista /uma'nista/ *mf* humanist. *a* humanistic

humanitario /umani'tario/ *a* humanitarian

humanizar /umani'sar; umani'θar/ *vt* to humanize

humano /u'mano/ *a* human; understanding, sympathetic. *m*, human being

humareda /uma'reða/ *f*, cloud of smoke

humeante /ume'ante/ *a* smoking; smoky

humear /ume'ar/ *vi* to give forth smoke; give oneself airs; *Lat. Am.* fumigate; beat, thrash

humedad /ume'ðað/ *f*, humidity; dampness; moisture

humedecer /umeðe'ser; umeðe'θer/ *vt irr* to moisten, wet, damp; *vr* grow moist. See **conocer**

húmedo /'umeðo/ *a* humid; damp; wet

humildad /umil'dað/ *f*, humility; lowliness; humbleness

humilde /u'milde/ *a* meek; lowly; humble

humillación /umiya'sion; umiʎa'θion/ *f*, humiliation

humillante /umi'yante; umi'ʎante/ *a* humiliating; debasing; mortifying

humillar /umi'yar; umi'ʎar/ *vt* to humble; humiliate; *vr* humble oneself

humo /'umo/ *m*, smoke; vapor, fume; vanity, airs

humor /u'mor/ *m*, *Med.* humor; temperament, disposition; mood. **de buen h.,** good-tempered. **de mal h.,** ill-tempered

humorada /umo'raða/ *f*, humorous saying, extravagance, witticism

humorismo /umo'rismo/ *m*, humor, comic sense; humorousness

humorista /umo'rista/ *mf* humorist

humorístico /umo'ristiko/ *a* humorous

humoso /u'moso/ *a* smoky, reeky

hundible /un'diβle/ *a* sinkable

hundido /un'diðo/ *a* sunken (of cheeks, etc.); hollow, deep-set (of eyes)

hundimiento /undi'miento/ *m*, sinking; collapse; subsidence (of earth)

hundir /un'dir/ *vt* to sink; oppress; confound; destroy, ruin; *vr* collapse (building); sink; *Fig. Inf.* disappear

húngaro /'ungaro/ **(-ra)** *a* and *n* Hungarian. *m*, Hungarian (language)

Hungría /uŋ'gria/ Hungary

huracán /ura'kan/ *m*, hurricane

huraña /ura'ɲia/ *f*, shyness, unsociableness; diffidence; wildness (of animals, etc.)

huraño /u'raɲo/ *a* shy, unsociable; diffident; wild (of animals, etc.)

hurgar /ur'gar/ *vt* to stir; poke, rake; touch; rouse, incite. *vr* pick one's nose

hurgón /ur'gon/ *m*, fire rake, poker; *Inf.* sword

hurgonada /urgo'naða/ *f*, raking (of the fire, etc.)

hurguete /ur'gete/ *mf*, *Argentina* busybody, nosy parker

hurón /u'ron/ **(-ona)** *n* ferret. *a* shy, unsociable

¡hurra! /'urra/ *interj* Hurrah!

hurtadillas /urta'ðiyas; urta'ðiʎas/ **(a)** *adv* by stealth, secretly, sneakily

hurtar /ur'tar/ *vt* to steal; encroach (sea, river); plagiarize; *vr* hide oneself

hurto /'urto/ *m*, theft. **coger con el h. en las manos,** *Fig.* to catch red-handed

husmear /usme'ar/ *vt* to sniff out; *Inf.* pry; *vi* smell bad (of meat)

huso /'uso/ *m*, spindle; bobbin

¡huy! /'ui/ *interj* (denoting pain or surprise) Oh!

I

ibérico /i'βeriko/ *a* Iberian

ibero /i'βero/ **(-ra)** *a* and *n* Iberian

íbice /'iβise; 'iβiθe/ *m*, ibex

icnografía /iknogra'fia/ *f*, ichnography

icnográfico /ikno'grafiko/ *a* ichnographical

icono /i'kono/ *m*, icon

iconoclasta /ikono'klasta/ *a* iconoclastic. *mf* iconoclast

iconografía /ikonogra'fia/ *f*, iconography

ictericia /ikte'risia; ikte'riθia/ *f*, jaundice

ida /'iða/ *f*, setting out, departure, going; impetuous action; precipitancy; track, trail (of animals). **de i. y vuelta,** round trip (of tickets)

idea /i'ðea/ *f*, idea. *Inf.* **¡Qué ideas tienes!** What (odd) ideas you have!

ideal /i'ðeal/ *a* ideal; perfect. *m*, model; ideal

idealidad /ideali'ðað/ *f*, ideality

idealismo /iðea'lismo/ *m*, idealism

idealista /iðea'lista/ *a* idealistic. *mf* idealist

idealización /iðealisa'sion; iðealiθa'θion/ *f*, idealization

idealizar /iðeali'sar; iðeali'θar/ *vt* to idealize

idear /iðe'ar/ *vt* to imagine; devise; plan; design; draft, draw up

ideático, -a /iðe'atiko/ *a*, *Lat. Am.* eccentric

ídem /'iðem/ *adv* idem

idéntico /i'ðentiko/ *a* identical

identidad /iðenti'ðað/ *f*, identity

identificable /iðentifi'kaβle/ *a* identifiable

identificación /iðentifika'sion; iðentifika'θion/ *f*, identification

identificar /iðentifi'kar/ *vt* to identify; recognize; *vr* (*with con*) identify oneself with

ideografía /iðeogra'fia/ *f*, ideography

ideograma /iðeo'grama/ *m*, ideogram

ideología /iðeolo'hia/ *f*, ideology. **i. racista,** racial ideology

ideológico /iðeo'lohiko/ *a* ideological

ideólogo /iðe'ologo/ **(-ga)** *n* ideologist; dreamer, planner

idílico /i'ðiliko/ *a* idyllic

idilio /i'ðilio/ *m*, idyll

idioma /i'ðioma/ *m*, language, tongue

idiomático /iðio'matiko/ *a* idiomatic

idiosincrasia /iðiosin'krasia/ *f*, idiosyncrasy

idiosincrásico /iðiosin'krasiko/ *a* idiosyncratic

idiota /i'ðiota/ *a* idiot; idiotic. *mf* idiot

idiotez /iðio'tes; iðio'teθ/ *f*, idiocy

idólatra /iðo'latra/ *a* idolatrous; adoring. *mf* idolater, heathen

idolatrar /iðola'trar/ *vt* to idolize; worship, love excessively

idolatría /iðola'tria/ *f*, idolatry; adoration, idolization

ídolo /'iðolo/ *m*, idol

idoneidad /iðonei'ðað/ *f*, fitness, suitability; competence; capacity

idóneo /i'ðoneo/ *a* suitable; competent, fit

idus /i'ðus/ *m pl*, ides

iglesia /i'glesia/ *f*, church. **i. colegial,** collegiate church. **cumplir con la i.,** to discharge one's religious duties. **llevar a una mujer a la i.,** to lead a woman to the altar

ígneo /'igneo/ *a* igneous

ignición /igni'sion; igni'θion/ *f*, ignition

ignominia /igno'minia/ *f*, ignominy, disgrace

ignominioso /ignomi'nioso/ *a* ignominious

ignorancia /igno'ransia; igno'ranθia/ *f*, ignorance. **pretender i.,** to plead ignorance

ignorante /igno'rante/ *a* ignorant; unaware, uninformed. *mf* ignoramus

ignorar /igno'rar/ *vt* to be unaware of, not to know

ignoto /ig'noto/ *a* unknown, undiscovered

igual /i'gual/ *a* equal; level; even, smooth; very similar; alike; uniform; proportionate; unchanging; constant; indifferent; same. *mf* equal. *m*, Math. equal sign. **al i.,** equally. **sin i.,** peerless, without equal. **Me es completamente i.,** It's all the same to me

iguala /i'guala/ *f*, equalizing; leveling; agreement, arrangement; cash adjustment

igualación /iguala'sion; iguala'θion/ *f*, equalization; leveling; arrangement, agreement; matching; Math. equation

igualador /iguala'ðor/ *a* equalizing; leveling

igualar /igua'lar/ *vt* to equalize, make equal; match; pair; level, flatten; smooth; adjust; arrange, agree upon; weigh, consider; Math. equate; *vi* be equal

igualdad /igual'dað/ *f*, equality; uniformity, harmony; evenness; smoothness; identity, sameness. **i. de ánimo,** equability, equanimity

igualitario /iguali'tario/ *a* equalizing; egalitarian

igualmente /igual'mente/ *adv* equally; the same, likewise

ijada /i'haða/ *f*, side, flank; pain in the side

ijadear /ihaðe'ar/ *vi* to pant

ijar /i'har/ *m*, See **ijada**

ilación /ila'sion; ila'θion/ *f*, connection, reference

ilegal /ile'gal/ *a* illegal

ilegalidad /ilegali'ðað/ *f*, illegality

ilegible /ile'hiβle/ *a* illegible, unreadable

ilegitimidad /ilehitimi'ðað/ *f*, illegitimacy

ilegítimo /ile'hitimo/ *a* illegitimate; false

ileso /i'leso/ *a* unharmed, unhurt

iletrado /ile'traðo/ *a* unlettered, uncultured

Ilíada /i'liaða/ *f*, Iliad

iliberal /iliβe'ral/ *a* illiberal; narrow-minded

iliberalidad /iliβerali'ðað/ *f*, illiberality; narrow-mindedness

ilícito /i'lisito; i'liθito/ *a* illicit

ilicitud /ilisi'tuð; iliθi'tuð/ *f*, illicitness

ilimitado /ilimi'taðo/ *a* unlimited, boundless

iliterato /ilite'rato/ *a* illiterate, uncultured

ilógico /i'lohiko/ *a* illogical

iluminación /ilumina'sion; ilumina'θion/ *f*, illumination; lighting. **i. intensiva,** floodlighting

iluminador /ilumina'ðor/ **(-ra)** *a* lighting; illuminating. *n* Art. illuminator

iluminar /ilumi'nar/ *vt* to illuminate; light; Art. illuminate; enlighten; *vr. Lat. Am.* get drunk

iluminativo /ilumina'tiβo/ *a* illuminating

ilusión /ilu'sion/ *f*, illusion; illusoriness; hope; dream

ilusionarse /ilusio'narse/ *vr* to harbor illusions

ilusivo /ilu'siβo/ *a* deceptive, illusive

iluso /i'luso/ *a* deceived, deluded; dreamy; visionary

ilusorio /ilu'sorio/ *a* illusory; deceptive; null

ilustración /ilustra'sion; ilustra'θion/ *f*, illustration, picture; enlightenment; explanation; illustrated newspaper or magazine; erudition, knowledge; example, illustration. **La Ilustración,** the Age of Enlightenment

ilustrado /ilu'straðo/ *a* erudite, learned; knowledgeable, well-informed

ilustrador /ilustra'ðor/ **(-ra)** *a* illustrative. *n* illustrator

ilustrar /ilus'trar/ *vt* to explain, illustrate; enlighten, instruct; illustrate (books); make illustrious; inspire with divine light

ilustrativo /ilustra'tiβo/ *a* illustrative

ilustre /i'lustre/ *a* illustrious, distinguished

ilustrísimo /ilus'trisimo/ *a sup* most illustrious (title of bishops, etc.)

imagen /i'mahen/ *f*, image; effigy, statue; idea; metaphor, simile. **i. nítida,** sharp image

imaginable /imahi'naβle/ *a* imaginable

imaginación /imahina'sion; imahina'θion/ *f*, imagination

imaginar /imahi'nar/ *vi* to imagine; *vt* suppose, conjecture; discover, invent; imagine. **¡Imagínese!** Just imagine!

imaginario /imahi'nario/ *a* imaginary

imaginativa /imahina'tiβa/ *f*, imagination; common sense

imaginativo /imahina'tiβo/ *a* imaginative

imaginería /imahine'ria/ *f*, imagery

imán /i'man/ *m*, magnet; attraction, charm; imam

imanación /imana'sion; imana'θion/ *f*, magnetization

imanar /ima'nar/ *vt* to magnetize

imbécil /im'besil; im'beθil/ *a* imbecile; stupid, idiotic. *mf* imbecile

imbecilidad /imbesili'ðað; imbeθili'ðað/ *f*, imbecility; folly, stupidity

imberbe /im'berβe/ *a* beardless. *Inf.* **joven i.,** stripling

imbibición /imbiβi'sion; imbiβi'θion/ *f*, imbibing, absorption

imborrable /imbo'rraβle/ *a* ineffaceable

imbuir /im'buir/ *vt irr* to imbue. See **huir**

imitable /imi'taβle/ *a* imitable

imitación /imita'sion; imita'θion/ *f*, imitation; reproduction, copy

imitado /imi'taðo/ *a* imitation; imitated

imitador /imita'ðor/ **(-ra)** *a* imitation; imitative. *n* imitator

imitar /imi'tar/ *vt* to imitate; counterfeit

imitativo /imita'tiβo/ *a* imitative

impacción /impak'sion; impak'θion/ *f*, impact

impaciencia /impa'siensia; impa'θienθia/ *f*, impatience

impacientar /impasien'tar; impaθien'tar/ *vt* to make impatient, annoy; *vr* grow impatient

impaciente /impa'siente; impa'θiente/ *a* impatient

impacto /im'pakto/ *m*, impact. **i. de lleno,** direct hit

impago, -a /im'pago/ *a Lat. Am.* remaining to be paid, still to be paid, unpaid; *m* non-payment

impalpabilidad /impalpaβili'ðað/ *f*, impalpability

impalpable /impal'paβle/ *a* impalpable

impar /im'par/ *a* odd; unpaired; single, uneven. **número impar,** odd number

imparcial /impar'sial; impar'θial/ *a* impartial

imparcialidad /imparsiali'ðað; imparθiali'ðað/ *f*, impartiality

imparisilábico /imparisi'laβiko/ *a* imparisyllabic

impartible /impar'tiβle/ *a* indivisible

impasibilidad /impasiβili'ðað/ *f*, impassivity, indifference

impasible /impa'siβle/ *a* impassive

impavidez /impaβi'ðes; impaβi'ðeθ/ *f* dauntlessness;

serenity in the face of danger; *Lat. Am.* cheek, cheekiness, effrontery

impávido /im'paβiðo/ *a* dauntless; calm, composed, imperturbable; *Lat. Am.* cheeky, fresh

impecabilidad /impekaβili'ðað/ *f*, impeccability, perfection

impecable /impe'kaβle/ *a* impeccable, perfect

impedido /impe'ðiðo/ *a* disabled

impedimento /impeði'mento/ *m*, obstacle; hindrance; *Law.* impediment

impedir /impe'ðir/ *vt irr* to impede; obstruct; prevent; thwart; disable; delay; *Poet.* amaze. See **pedir**

impeler /impe'ler/ *vt* to push; incite; drive; urge

impender /impen'der/ *vt* to spend money

impenetrabilidad /impenetraβili'ðað/ *f*, impenetrability; imperviousness; obscurity, difficulty

impenetrable /impene'traβle/ *a* impenetrable, dense; impervious; *Fig.* unfathomable; obscure

impenitencia /impeni'tensia; impeni'tenθia/ *f*, impenitence

impenitente /impeni'tente/ *a* impenitent

impensado /impen'saðo/ *a* unexpected, unforeseen

imperante /impe'rante/ *a* ruling, dominant

imperar /impe'rar/ *vi* to rule; command

imperativo /impera'tiβo/ *a* commanding. *a* and *m*, *Gram.* imperative

imperatorio /impera'torio/ *a* imperial, imperatorial

imperceptible /impersep'tiβle; imperθep'tiβle/ *a* imperceptible

imperdible /imper'ðiβle/ *m*, safety pin

imperdonable /imperðo'naβle/ *a* unpardonable, inexcusable

imperecedero /imperese'ðero; impereθe'ðero/ *a* undying, eternal, everlasting

imperfección /imperfek'sion; imperfek'θion/ *f*, imperfection, inadequacy; fault, blemish; weakness

imperfecto /imper'fekto/ *a* imperfect; inadequate; faulty. *a* and *m*, *Gram.* imperfect

imperial /impe'rial/ *a* imperial. *f*, upper deck of a bus or streetcar

imperialismo /imperia'lismo/ *m*, imperialism

imperialista /imperia'lista/ *a* imperialistic. *mf* imperialist

impericia /impe'risia; impe'riθia/ *f*, inexpertness; unskillfulness, unhandiness

imperio /im'perio/ *m*, empire; rule, reign; command; sway; imperial dignity; arrogance, haughtiness. *Fig. Inf.* **valer un i.,** to be priceless

imperioso /impe'rioso/ *a* imperious

imperito /impe'rito/ *a* inexpert; clumsy, unskilled

impermeabilidad /impermeaβili''ðað/ *f*, watertightness; imperviousness; impermeability

impermeabilizar /impermeaβili'sar; impermeaβili'θar/ *vt* to waterproof

impermeable /imper'meaβle/ *a* watertight, impermeable; impervious. *m*, raincoat, mackintosh

impertérrito /imper'territo/ *a* unafraid, dauntless

impertinencia /impertinen'sia; impertinen'θia/ *f*, impertinence, insolence; peevishness; fancy, whim; overexactness, meticulousness; interference, intrusion

impertinente /imperti'nente/ *a* impertinent; irrelevant; inopportune; officious, interfering

imperturbabilidad /imperturβaβili'ðað/ *f*, imperturbability

imperturbable /impertur'βaβle/ *a* calm, imperturbable

impetrar /impe'trar/ *vt* to obtain by entreaty; implore

ímpetu /'impetu/ *m*, impetus, momentum; speed, swiftness; violence

impetuosidad /impetuosi'ðað/ *f*, impetuosity

impetuoso /impe'tuoso/ *a* impetuous; precipitate

impiedad /impie'ðað/ *f*, cruelty, harshness; irreligion

impío /im'pio/ *a* impious, wicked; irreverent, irreligious

implacabilidad /implakaβili'ðað/ *f*, implacability, relentlessness

implacable /impla'kaβle/ *a* implacable

implantación /implanta'sion; implanta'θion/ *f*, inculcation, implantation

implantar /implan'tar/ *vt* to inculcate, implant (ideas, etc.)

implicación /implika'sion; implika'θion/ *f*, implication; contradiction (in terms); complicity

implicar /impli'kar/ *vt* to implicate; imply, infer; involve, entangle; *vi* imply contradiction (gen. with negatives)

implicatorio /implika'torio/ *a* contradictory; implicated (in crime)

implícito /im'plisito; im'pliθito/ *a* implicit; implied

implorante /implo'rante/ *a* imploring

implorar /implo'rar/ *vt* to implore, entreat

implume /im'plume/ *a* without feathers, unfeathered

impolítico /impo'litiko/ *a* impolitic; unwise, inexpedient; tactless

imponderabilidad /imponderaβili'ðað/ *f*, imponderability

imponderable /imponde'raβle/ *a* imponderable, immeasurable; most excellent

imponencia /impo'nensia; impo'nenθia/ *f. Lat. Am.* impressiveness

imponente /impo'nente/ *a* imposing, impressive; awe-inspiring

imponer /impo'ner/ *vt irr* to exact, impressive; impose; malign, accuse falsely; instruct, acquaint; *Fig.* impress (with respect, etc.); invest or deposit (money); *Print.* impose; give, bestow (a name). *vr* assert oneself. See **poner**

imponible /impo'niβle/ *a* taxable; ratable

impopular /impopu'lar/ *a* unpopular

impopularidad /impopulari'ðað/ *f*, unpopularity

importable /impor'taβle/ *a* importable

importación /importa'sion; importa'θion/ *f, Com.* importation; import

importador /importa'ðor/ **(-ra)** *a* import, importing. *n* importer

importancia /impor'tansia; impor'tanθia/ *f*, importance; magnitude

importante /impor'tante/ *a* important

importar /impor'tar/ *vi* to matter; be important; concern, interest; *vt* amount to; import; include, comprise. **¡No importa!** It doesn't matter! Never mind!

importe /im'porte/ *m*, amount; value, cost. **i. bruto,** gross or total amount. **i. líquido** *or* **neto,** net amount

importunación /importuna'sion; importuna'θion/ *f*, importuning; importunity

importunadamente /importunaða'mente/ *adv* importunately

importunar /importu'nar/ *vt* to importune, pester

importunidad /importuni'ðað/ *(also* **importunación)** *f*, importunity

importuno /impor'tuno/ *a* importunate, inopportune, ill-timed; persistent; tedious

imposibilidad /imposiβili'ðað/ *f*, impossibility

imposibilitado /imposiβili'taðo/ *a* disabled, crippled; incapable, unable

imposibilitar /imposiβili'tar/ *vt* to disable; render unable; make impossible

imposible /impo'siβle/ *a* impossible

imposición /imposi'sion; imposi'θion/ *f*, imposition; exaction; tax, duty, tribute; *Print.* makeup **i. de manos,** *Eccl.* laying on of hands

impostor /impos'tor/ **(-ra)** *n* impostor

impostura /impos'tura/ *f*, swindle, imposture; aspersion, slur, imputation

impotable /impo'taβle/ *a* undrinkable

impotencia /impo'tensia; impo'tenθia/ *f*, impotence

impotente /impo'tente/ *a* impotent; powerless

impracticabilidad /impraktikaβili'ðað/ *f*, impracticability; impassability (of roads, etc.)

impracticable /imprakti'kaβle/ *a* impracticable; impossible; impassable (roads, etc.)

imprecación /impreka'sion; impreka'θion/ *f*, imprecation; curse, malediction

imprecar /impre'kar/ *vt* to imprecate, curse

impregnación /impregna'sion; impregna'θion/ *f*, impregnation, permeation, saturation

impregnar /impreg'nar/ *vt* impregnate; to permeate; *vr* become impregnated

impremeditado /impremeði'taðo/ *a* unpremeditated

imprenta /im'prenta/ f, printing; printing house or office; print; letterpress

impreparación /imprepara'sion; imprepara'θion/ f, unpreparedness

imprescindible /impressin'diβle; impresθin'diβle/ a indispensable, essential

impresión /impre'sion/ f, printing; impression; effect; influence; imprint, stamp; Print. impression; print. **impresión digital,** fingerprint

impresionable /impresio'naβle/ a impressionable, susceptible

impresionante /impresio'nante/ a imposing; moving, affecting

impresionar /impresio'nar/ vt to impress; affect; fix in the mind; Fig. move deeply, stir; (Radio. cinema) record

impresionismo /impresio'nismo/ m, impressionism

impresionista /impresio'nista/ mf impressionist. a impressionistic

impreso /im'preso/ m, (gen. pl) printed matter

impresor /impre'sor/ m, printer

imprevisión /impreβi'sion/ f, lack of foresight; improvidence

imprevisto /impre'βisto/ a unforeseen, unexpected, sudden

imprevistos /impre'βistos/ m pl, incidental expenses

imprimación /imprima'sion; imprima'θion/ f, priming (of paint, etc.)

imprimar /impri'mar/ vt to prime (of paint)

imprimir /impri'mir/ vt to print; stamp; impress upon (the mind)

improbabilidad /improβaβili'ðað/ f, improbability

improbable /impro'βaβle/ a improbable

improbo /im'proβo/ a vicious, corrupt, dishonest; hard, arduous

improductivo /improðuk'tiβo/ a unproductive; unprofitable; fruitless

impronta /im'pronta/ f, Art. cast, mold

impronunciable /impronun'siaβle; impronun'θiaβle/ a unpronounceable; ineffable

improperio /impro'perio/ m, insult, affront

impropiedad /impropie'ðað/ f, inappropriateness; unsuitableness; impropriety

impropio /im'propio/ a unsuitable; inappropriate; inadequate; improper

improporcionado /improporsio'naðo; improporθio'naðo/ a disproportionate, out of proportion

impróvido /im'proβiðo/ a improvident, heedless

improvisación /improβisa'sion; improβisa'θion/ f, improvisation

improvisador /improβisa'ðor/ (-ra) n improviser

improvisamente /improβisa'mente/ adv unexpectedly, suddenly

improvisar /improβi'sar/ vt to improvise

improviso, improvisto /impro'βiso, impro'βisto/ a unexpected, unforeseen. **al** (or **de**) **improviso,** unexpectedly

imprudencia /impru'ðensia; impru'ðenθia/ f, imprudence, rashness, indiscretion

imprudente /impru'ðente/ a imprudent, unwise, rash

impúbero /im'puβero/ a below the age of puberty

impudencia /impu'ðensia; impu'ðenθia/ f, impudence, impertinence

impudente /impu'ðente/ a brazen, impudent

impudicia /impu'ðisia; impu'ðiθia/ f, immodesty, brazenness

impúdico /im'puðiko/ a immodest, brazen

impuesto /im'puesto/ m, tax; duty. **i. de utilidades,** income tax. **i. sucesorio,** inheritance tax

impugnable /impug'naβle/ a impugnable, refutable

impugnación /impugna'sion; impugna'θion/ f, refutation; contradiction

impugnar /impug'nar/ vt to refute, contradict; oppose; criticize

impulsar /impul'sar/ vt to impel; prompt, cause; drive, operate, propel

impulsión /impul'sion/ f, impulse; impetus; Mech. operation, driving; propulsion

impulsivo /impul'siβo/ a impulsive; irreflexive, precipitate

impulso /im'pulso/ m, stimulus, incitement; impulse, desire; Mech. drive, impulse

impulsor /impul'sor/ (-ra) a driving, impelling. n driver, operator

impune /im'pune/ a unpunished

impunemente /impune'mente/ adv with impunity

impunidad /impuni'ðað/ f, impunity

impureza /impu'resa; impu'reθa/ f, impurity; lack of chastity; obscenity, indecency

impurificar /impurifi'kar/ vt to defile; make impure; adulterate

impuro /im'puro/ a impure; adulterated; polluted; immoral, unchaste

imputable /impu'taβle/ a imputable

imputación /imputa'sion; imputa'θion/ f, imputation

imputador /imputa'ðor/ (-ra) n imputer, attributer

imputar /impu'tar/ vt to impute; attribute

inacabable /inaka'βaβle/ a endless, interminable, ceaseless; wearisome

inaccesibilidad /inaksesiβili'ðað; inakθesiβili'ðað/ f, inaccessibility

inaccesible /inakse'siβle; inakθe'siβle/ a inaccessible; incomprehensible

inacción /inak'sion; inak'θion/ f, inaction

inaceptable /inasep'taβle; inaθep'taβle/ a unacceptable

inactividad /inaktiβi'ðað/ f, inactivity; quiescence; idleness

inactivo /inak'tiβo/ a inactive; idle; unemployed; Naut. laid-up

inadaptable /inaðap'taβle/ a inadaptable

inadecuado /inaðe'kuaðo/ a inadequate, insufficient

inadmisible /inaðmi'siβle/ a inadmissible

inadvertencia /inaðβer'tensia; inaðβer'tenθia/ f, inadvertence; oversight, mistake, slip

inadvertido /inaðβer'tiðo/ a unnoticed; inattentive; inadvertent, unintentional; negligent

inafectado /inafek'taðo/ a unaffected, natural

inagotable /inago'taβle/ a inexhaustible, unfailing; abundant

inaguantable /inaguan'taβle/ a unbearable, intolerable

inajenable /inahe'naβle/ a inalienable

inalámbrica /ina'lambrika/ f, radio station

inalienable /inalie'naβle/ a inalienable

inalterable /inalte'raβle/ a unalterable

inamovibilidad /inamoβiβili'ðað/ f, immovability

inamovible /inamo'βiβle/ a immovable

inanición /inani'sion; inani'θion/ f, inanition

inanimado /inani'maðo/ a inanimate

inapagable /inapa'gaβle/ a inextinguishable

inapelable /inape'laβle/ a unappealable; irremediable, inevitable

inapetencia /inape'tensia; inape'tenθia/ f, lack of appetite

inaplazable /inapla'saβle; inapla'θaβle/ a undeferable, unable to be postponed

inaplicable /inapli'kaβle/ a inapplicable

inaplicación /inaplika'sion; inaplika'θion/ f, laziness, inattention, negligence

inaplicado /inapli'kaðo/ a lazy; inattentive; careless

inapreciable /inapre'siaβle; inapre'θiaβle/ a inappreciable; invaluable

inarmónico /inar'moniko/ a unharmonious, discordant

inarticulado /inartiku'laðo/ a inarticulate

inasequible /inase'kiβle/ a unattainable; out of reach

inaudible /inau'ðiβle/ a inaudible

inaudito /inau'ðito/ a unheard of, unprecedented; extraordinary, strange

inauguración /inaugura'sion; inaugura'θion/ f, inauguration; induction; inception, commencement

inaugural /inaugu'ral/ a inaugural

inaugurar /inaugu'rar/ vt to inaugurate; induct

inaveriguable /inaβeri'guaβle/ a unascertainable

inca /'inka/ mf Inca

incaico /in'kaiko/ *a* Incan

incalculable /inkalku'laβle/ *a* incalculable; innumerable

incalificable /inkalifi'kaβle/ *a* indescribable, unclassable; vile

incandescencia /inkandes'sensia; inkandes'θenθia/ *f*, incandescence, white heat

incandescente /inkandes'sente; inkandes'θente/ *a* incandescent

incansable /inkan'saβle/ *a* indefatigable; unflagging; unwearying

incapacidad /inkapasi'ðað; inkapaθi'ðað/ *f*, incapacity; incompetence

incapacitar /inkapasi'tar; inkapaθi'tar/ *vt* to incapacitate; disable

incapaz /inka'pas; inka'paθ/ *a* incapable, incompetent; inefficient

incasable /inka'saβle/ *a* unmarriageable; antimarriage

incásico, -a /in'kasiko/ *a, Lat. Am.* Inca

incautarse /inkau'tarse/ *vr* to seize, take possession (of)

incauto /in'kauto/ *a* incautious; unwary

incendiar /insen'diar; inθen'diar/ *vt* to set on fire, set alight

incendiario /insen'diario; inθen'diario/ **(-ia)** *a* and *n* incendiary

incendiarismo /insendia'rismo; inθendia'rismo/ *m*, incendiarism

incendio /in'sendio; in'θendio/ *m*, conflagration, fire; consuming passion

incensar /insen'sar; inθen'sar/ *vt irr Eccl.* to cense, incense; flatter. See **acertar**

incensario /insen'sario; inθen'sario/ *m*, incense burner, incensory

incentivo /insen'tiβo; inθen'tiβo/ *m*, incentive; encouragement

incertidumbre /inserti'ðumbre; inθerti'ðumbre/ *f*, uncertainty, incertitude

incesable, incesante /inse'saβle, inse'sante; inθe'saβle, inθe'sante/ *a* incessant, continuous

incesto /in'sesto; in'θesto/ *m*, incest

incestuoso /inses'tuoso; inθes'tuoso/ *a* incestuous

incidencia /insi'ðensia; inθi'ðenθia/ *f*, incidence

incidente /insi'ðente; inθi'ðente/ *a* incidental. *m*, incident, event, occurrence

incidir /insi'ðir; inθi'ðir/ *vi* (*with en*) to incur, fall into (e.g. *Incidió en el pecado,* He fell into sin)

incienso /in'sienso; in'θienso/ *m*, incense; flattery

incierto /in'sierto; in'θierto/ *a* untrue, false; uncertain; unknown

incineración /insinera'sion; inθinera'θion/ *f*, incineration

incinerador /insinera'ðor; inθinera'ðor/ *m*, incinerator

incinerar /insine'rar; inθine'rar/ *vt* incinerate, reduce to ashes

incipiente /insi'piente; inθi'piente/ *a* incipient

incircunciso /insirkun'siso; inθirkun'θiso/ *a* uncircumcised

incisión /insi'sion; inθi'sion/ *f*, incision

incisivo /insi'siβo; inθi'siβo/ *a* sharp, keen; incisive, sarcastic, caustic

inciso /in'siso; in'θiso/ *m*, clause; comma

incitación /insita'sion; inθita'θion/ *f*, incitement; *Fig.* spur, stimulus

incitar /insi'tar; inθi'tar/ *vt* to incite; stimulate, encourage

incivil /insi'βil; inθi'βil/ *a* rude, discourteous, uncivil

incivilidad /insiβili'ðað; inθiβili'ðað/ *f*, rudeness, incivility

inclasificable /inklasifi'kaβle/ *a* unclassifiable

inclemencia /inkle'mensia; inkle'menθia/ *f*, harshness, severity; inclemency (of the weather). **a la i.,** at the mercy of the elements

inclemente /inkle'mente/ *a* inclement

inclinación /inklina'sion; inklina'θion/ *f*, inclination; slope; slant; tendency, propensity; predilection, fondness; bow (in greeting); *Geom.* inclination

inclinar /inkli'nar/ *vt* to incline, tilt, slant; bow; bend; influence; persuade; *vi* resemble; *vr* lean;

stoop; tilt; tend, incline (to), view favorably (e.g. *Me inclino a creerlo,* I am inclined to believe it)

ínclito /in'klito/ *a* famous, celebrated

incluir /in'kluir/ *vt irr* to comprise, embrace, contain; include, take into account. See **huir**

inclusa /in'klusa/ *f*, children's home

inclusión /inklu'sion/ *f*, inclusion; relationship, intercourse, friendship

inclusive /inklu'siβe/ *adv* including

inclusivo /inklu'siβo/ *a* inclusive

incluso /in'kluso/ *adv* including, inclusive. *prep* even

incoar /inko'ar/ *vt* to begin (especially lawsuits)

incobrable /inko'βraβle/ *a* irrecoverable; irredeemable

incógnita /in'kognita/ *f*, *Math.* X; unknown quantity; secret motive; unknown lady

incógnito /in'kognito/ *a* unknown. *m*, incognito, assumed name, disguise

incoherencia /inkoe'rensia; inkoe'renθia/ *f*, incoherence

incoherente /inkoe'rente/ *a* incoherent, disconnected, illogical

íncola /'inkola/ *mf* resident, dweller, inhabitant

incoloro /inko'loro/ *a* colorless, uncolored

incólume /in'kolume/ *a* unharmed, unscathed; untouched, undamaged

incombustibilidad /inkombustiβili'ðað/ *f*, incombustibility

incommensurabilidad /inkommensuraβili'ðað/ *f*, incommensurability

incommutable /inkommu'taβle/ *a* unalterable, immutable, unchangeable

incomodar /inkomo'ðar/ *vt* to disturb, incommode, inconvenience; annoy; *vr* disturb oneself, put oneself out; grow angry. **¡No se incomode!** Please don't move!; Please don't be angry!

incomodidad /inkomoði'ðað/ *f*, discomfort; inconvenience; trouble, upset; annoyance

incómodo /in'komoðo/ *a* uncomfortable; inconvenient; troublesome, tiresome; *Argentina, Chile* fed up *m*, discomfort; inconvenience

incomparable /inkompa'raβle/ *a* incomparable

incompartible /inkompar'tiβle/ *a* indivisible

incompasivo /inkompa'siβo/ *a* unsympathetic, hard

incompatibilidad /inkompatiβili'ðað/ *f*, incompatibility

incompetencia /inkompe'tensia; inkompe'tenθia/ *f*, incompetence

incompetente /inkompe'tente/ *a* incompetent

incomplejo, incomplexo /inkom'pleho, inkom'plekso/ *a* noncomplex, simple

incompleto /inkom'pleto/ *a* incomplete

incomponible /inkompo'niβle/ *a* unrepairable, unmendable

incomprensibilidad /inkomprensiβili'ðað/ *f*, incomprehensibility

incomprensible /inkompren'siβle/ *a* incomprehensible

incomprensión /inkompren'sion/ *f*, incomprehension

incomunicado /inkomuni'kaðo/ *a* in solitary confinement (of a prisoner)

incomunicar /inkomuni'kar/ *vt* to sentence to solitary confinement; isolate, deprive of means of communication; *vr* become a recluse

inconcebible /inkonseβiβle; inkonθe'βiβle/ *a* inconceivable

inconciliable /inkonsi'liaβle; inkonθi'liaβle/ *a* irreconcilable

incondicional /inkondisio'nal; inkondiθio'nal/ *a* unconditional; *Lat. Am.* fawning, servile

inconexión /inkone'ksion/ *f*, disconnectedness

inconexo /inko'nekso/ *a* unconnected; incoherent

inconfeso /inkon'feso/ *a* unconfessed

incongruencia /inkoŋgru'ensia; inkoŋgru'enθia/ *f*, incongruity

incongruente /inkoŋgru'ente/ *a* incongruous, inappropriate

inconmovible /inkomo'βiβle/ *a* immovable; unflinching, unshakable

inconquistable /inkonkis'taβle/ a unconquerable; *Fig.* resolute, inflexible

inconsciencia /inkonssiensia; inkon's0ien0ia/ f, unconsciousness; subconscious

inconsciente /inkons'siente; inkon's0iente/ a unconscious, involuntary; subconscious

inconsecuencia /inkonse'kuensia; inkonse'kuen0ia/ f, inconsequence; inconsistency

inconsecuente /inkonse'kuente/ a inconsequential; inconsistent

inconsideración /inkonsiðera'sion; inkonsiðera'0ion/ f, thoughtlessness

inconsiderado /inkonsiðe'raðo/ a thoughtless; heedless, selfish

inconsiguiente /inkonsi'giente/ a illogical, inconsistent

inconsistencia /inkonsis'tensia; inkonsis'ten0ia/ f, inconsistency

inconsistente /inkonsis'tente/ a inconsistent

inconsolable /inkonso'laβle/ a inconsolable

inconstancia /inkons'tansia; inkons'tan0ia/ f, inconstancy, infidelity

inconstante /inkons'tante/ a inconstant, fickle

inconstitucional /inkonstitusio'nal; inkonstitu-0io'nal/ a unconstitutional

incontaminado /inkontami'naðo/ a uncontaminated

incontestable /inkontes'taβle/ a undeniable, unquestionable

incontinencia /inkonti'nensia; inkonti'nen0ia/ f, incontinence

incontinente /inkonti'nente/ a incontinent

incontrastable /inkontras'taβle/ a insuperable, invincible; undeniable, unanswerable; *Fig.* unshakable, inconvincible

incontrovertible /inkontroβer'tiβle/ a undeniable, incontrovertible

inconvencible /inkomben'siβle; inkomben'0iβle/ a inconvincible

inconveniencia /inkombe'niensia; inkombe'nien0ia/ f, discomfort; inconvenience; unsuitability

inconveniente /inkombe'niente/ a awkward, inconvenient; uncomfortable; inappropriate. *m*, inconvenience; obstacle, impediment; disadvantage

inconvertible /inkomber'tiβle/ a inconvertible

incorporación /inkorpora'sion; inkorpora'0ion/ f, incorporation

incorporar /inkorpo'rar/ vt to incorporate; cause to sit up, lift up; vr sit up, raise oneself; become a member, join (associations); be incorporated; blend, mix

incorporeidad /inkorporei'ðað/ f, incorporeity

incorpóreo /inkor'poreo/ a incorporeal; immaterial

incorrección /inkorrek'sion; inkorrek'0ion/ f, incorrectness; indecorum, impropriety

incorrecto /inko'rrekto/ a incorrect; indecorous, unbecoming, improper

incorregible /inkorre'hiβle/ a incorrigible

incorrupción /inkorrup'sion; inkorrup'0ion/ f, incorruption; purity; integrity; wholesomeness

incorrupto /inko'rrupto/ a incorrupt; pure; chaste

incredibilidad /inkreðiβili'ðað/ f, incredibility

incredulidad /inkreðuli'ðað/ f, incredulity, scepticism

incrédulo /in'kreðulo/ (**-la**) a incredulous; atheistic. *n* atheist; unbeliever, sceptic

increíble /inkre'iβle/ a incredible; marvelous, extraordinary

incremento /inkre'mento/ *m*, increment, increase

increpación /inkrepa'sion; inkrepa'0ion/ f, scolding, harsh rebuke

increpar /inkre'par/ vt to scold, rebuke harshly

incriminante /inkrimi'nante/ a incriminating

incriminar /inkrimi'nar/ vt to incriminate, accuse; exaggerate (a charge, etc.)

incruento /inkru'ento/ a bloodless, unstained with blood

incrustación /inkrusta'sion; inkrusta'0ion/ f, incrustation; *Art.* inlay

incubación /inkuβa'sion; inkuβa'0ion/ f, hatching; *Med.* incubation

incubadora /inkuβa'ðora/ f, incubator (for chickens)

incubar /inku'βar/ vi to sit on eggs (of hens); vt hatch; *Med.* incubate

inculcación /inkulka'sion; inkulka'0ion/ f, inculcation, instillment

inculcar /inkul'kar/ vt to press one thing against another; instill, inculcate; vr grow more fixed in one's views

inculpable /inkul'paβle/ a blameless, innocent

inculpar /inkul'par/ vt to blame; accuse

incultivable /inkulti'βaβle/ a uncultivatable; untillable

inculto /in'kulto/ a uncultivated, untilled; uncultured; uncivilized

incultura /inkul'tura/ f, lack of cultivation; lack of culture

incumbencia /inkumbensia; inkum'ben0ia/ f, obligation, moral responsibility, duty

incumbir /inkum'bir/ vi to be incumbent on; concern

incumplimiento /inkumpli'miento/ *m*, nonfulfilment

incurable /inku'raβle/ a incurable; inveterate, hopeless

incuria /in'kuria/ f, negligence, carelessness

incurioso /inku'rioso/ a incurious

incurrir /inku'rrir/ vi (*with en*) to fall into (error, etc.); incur (dislike, etc.)

incursión /inkur'sion/ f, incursion; inroad

indagación /indaga'sion; indaga'0ion/ f, investigation, inquiry

indagador /indaga'ðor/ (**-ra**) a investigating, inquiring. *n* investigator

indagar /inda'gar/ vt to investigate, examine; inquire. **i. precios,** to inquire about prices

indebido /inde'βiðo/ a undue, immoderate improper; illegal, illicit

indecencia /inde'sensia; inde'0en0ia/ f, indecency; obscenity; impropriety

indecente /inde'sente; inde'0ente/ a indecent; obscene; improper

indecible /inde'siβle; inde'0iβle/ a unutterable, ineffable, unspeakable

indeciso /inde'siso; inde'0iso/ a undecided; hesitant, irresolute; vague; noncommittal

indeclinable /indekli'naβle/ a obligatory; unavoidable; *Gram.* indeclinable, uninflected

indecoro /inde'koro/ *m*, impropriety, indecorum

indecoroso /indeko'roso/ a indecorous, unbecoming; base, mean

indefectible /indefek'tiβle/ a unfailing; perfect

indefectiblemente /indefektiβle'mente/ adv invariably

indefendible /indefen'diβle/ a indefensible

indefenso /inde'fenso/ a unprotected, defenseless

indefinible /indefi'niβle/ a indefinable, vague; indescribable

indefinido /indefi'niðo/ a indefinite, vague; undefined; *Gram.* indefinite

indeleble /inde'leβle/ a indelible

indeliberado /indeliβe'raðo/ a unpremeditated; unconsidered

indemne /in'demne/ a unharmed, undamaged

indemnidad /indemni'ðað/ f, indemnity

indemnización /indemnisa'sion; indemni0a'0ion/ f, compensation, indemnification; indemnity

indemnizar /indemni'sar; indemni'0ar/ vt to indemnify, compensate

indemostrable /indemo'straβle/ a indemonstrable, incapable of demonstration

independencia /indepen'densia; indepen'den0ia/ f, independence

independiente /indepen'diente/ a independent; self-contained

indescifrable /indessi'fraβle; indes0i'fraβle/ a undecipherable; illegible

indestructible /indestruk'tiβle/ a indestructible

indeterminado /indetermi'naðo/ a indeterminate; vague, doubtful, uncertain; hesitant, irresolute; *Math.* indeterminate

indiano /in'diano/ (**-na**) a and *n* Indian; East Indian; West Indian. *m*, nouveau riche, one who returns rich from the Western Hemisphere

indicación /indika'sion; indika'θion/ f, indication; sign, evidence; intimation, hint

indicador /indika'ðor/ a indicative. m, indicator. **i. del nivel de gasolina,** gas gauge

indicar /indi'kar/ vt to indicate; show; point out; simply, suggest; intimate

indicativo /indika'tiβo/ a indicative. a and m, Gram. indicative

índice /'indise; 'indiθe/ m, index; indication, sign; library catalog; catalog room; hand (of a clock); pointer, needle (of instruments); gnomon (of a sundial); Math. index; forefinger. **I. expurgatorio,** the Index

indicio /in'disio; in'diθio/ m, indication; sign; evidence. **indicios vehementes,** circumstantial evidence

indiferencia /indife'rensia; indife'renθia/ f, indifference

indiferente /indife'rente/ a indifferent

indígena /in'dihena/ a native, indigenous. mf native

indigencia /indi'hensia; indi'henθia/ f, destitution, indigence; impecuniosity

indigenismo /indihe'nismo/ m, Lat. Am. Native American movement, indigenous peoples

indigente /indi'hente/ a destitute, indigent; impecunious

indigestión /indihes'tion/ f, indigestion

indigesto /indi'hesto/ a indigestible; Lit. muddled, confused; unsociable, brusque

indignación /indigna'sion; indigna'θion/ f, indignation, anger

indignado /indig'naðo/ a indignant

indignar /indig'nar/ vt to anger, make indignant; vr grow angry

indignidad /indigni'ðað/ f, unworthiness; indignity; personal affront

indigno /in'digno/ a unworthy; base, despicable

índigo /'indigo/ m, indigo

indio /'indio/ **(-ia)** a Indian; blue. n Indian. m, indium

indirecta /indi'rekta/ f, hint, covert suggestion, innuendo. Inf. **i. del padre Cobos,** strong hint

indirecto /indi'rekto/ a indirect

indisciplina /indissi'plina; indisθi'plina/ f, indiscipline

indisciplinado /indissipli'naðo; indisθipli'naðo/ a undisciplined

indiscreción /indiskre'sion; indiskre'θion/ f, indiscretion

indiscreto /indis'kreto/ a indiscreet

indiscutible /indisku'tiβle/ a unquestionable, undeniable

indisoluble /indiso'luβle/ a indissoluble

indispensable /indispen'saβle/ a indispensable

indisponer /indispo'ner/ vt irr to make unfit or incapable; indispose, make ill; (with con or contra) set against, make trouble with; vr be indisposed; (with con or contra) quarrel with. See **poner**

indisposición /indisposi'sion; indisposi'θion/ f, reluctance, disinclination; indisposition, brief illness

indistinguible /indistiŋ'guiβle/ a undistinguishable

indistinto /indis'tinto/ a indistinct; indeterminate; vague

individual /indiβi'ðual/ a individual; peculiar, characteristic. m, (tennis) single

individualidad /indiβiðuali'ðað/ f, individuality

individualismo /indiβiðua'lismo/ m, individualism

individualista /indiβiðua'lista/ a individualistic. mf individualist

individuo /indi'βiðuo/ **(-ua)** a individual; indivisible. m, individual; member, associate; Inf. self. n Inf. person

indivisibilidad /indiβisiβili'ðað/ f, indivisibility

indivisible /indiβi'siβle/ a indivisible

indiviso /indi'βiso/ a undivided

indochino /indo'tʃino/ **(-na)** a and n Indochinese

indócil /in'dosil; in'doθil/ a unmanageable; disobedient; brittle, unpliable (of metals)

indocilidad /indosili'ðað; indoθili'ðað/ f, indocility; disobedience; brittleness (of metals)

indoeuropeo /indoeuro'peo/ a Indo-European

indoísmo /indo'ismo/ m, Hinduism

índole /'indole/ f, temperament, nature; kind, sort

indolencia /indo'lensia; indo'lenθia/ f, idleness, indolence

indolente /indo'lente/ a nonpainful; indifferent, insensible; idle, indolent

indoloro /indo'loro/ a painless

indomable /indo'maβle/ a untamable; invincible; indomitable; ungovernable, unmanageable

indomado /indo'maðo/ a untamed

indómito /in'domito/ a untamed; untamable; unmanageable, unruly; indomitable

indonesio /indo'nesio/ **(-ia)** a and n Indonesian

indostanés /indosta'nes/ a Hindustani

indostani /indos'tani/ m, Hindustani (language)

indubitable /induβi'taβle/ a unquestionable

inducción /induk'sion; induk'θion/ f, persuasion; Phys. induction

inducir /indu'sir; indu'θir/ vt irr to persuade, prevail upon; induce; infer, conclude. See **conducir**

inductivo, inductor /induk'tiβo, induk'tor/ a inductive

indudable /indu'ðaβle/ a indubitable

indulgencia /indul'hensia; indul'henθia/ f, overkindness, tenderness; Eccl. indulgence

indulgente /indul'hente/ a indulgent, tender; tolerant

indultar /indul'tar/ vt to pardon; exempt

indulto /in'dulto/ m, amnesty; exemption; forgiveness; Eccl. indult

indumentaria /indumen'taria/ f, clothing; outfit (of clothes)

industria /in'dustria/ f, assiduity, industriousness; pains, effort, ingenuity; industry. **i. pesada,** heavy industry. **i. cárnica,** meat industry. **i. extractivos,** mining industry

industrial /indus'trial/ a industrial. m, industrialist

industrialismo /industria'lismo/ m, industrialism

industrialización /industrialisa'sion; industriali'θa'θion/ f, industrialization

industriar /indus'triar/ vt to teach, train; vr find a way, manage, succeed in

industrioso /indus'trioso/ a industrious; diligent, assiduous

inédito /i'neðito/ a unpublished; unedited

inefable /ine'faβle/ a ineffable

ineficacia /inefi'kasia; inefi'kaθia/ f, inefficiency; ineffectiveness

ineficaz /inefi'kas; inefi'kaθ/ a ineffective; inefficient

ineludible /inelu'ðiβle/ a unavoidable

ineptitud /inepti'tuð/ f, ineptitude

inepto /i'nepto/ a inept, incompetent; unfit, unsuitable

inequívoco /ine'kiβoko/ a unequivocal

inercia /i'nersia; i'nerθia/ f, inertia

inerme /i'nerme/ a defenseless, unprotected; (Bot. Zool.) unarmed

inerte /i'nerte/ a inert

inescrutable /ineskru'taβle/ a inscrutable, unfathomable

inesperado /inespe'raðo/ a unexpected, sudden

inestabilidad /inestaβili'ðað/ f, instability, unsteadiness, shakiness, unreliability, inconstancy

inestable /ines'taβle/ a unstable

inestimable /inesti'maβle/ a inestimable

inevitable /ineβi'taβle/ a inevitable

inexactitud /ineksakti'tuð/ f, inexactitude, inaccuracy; error, mistake

inexacto /ine'ksakto/ a inexact, inaccurate; erroneous

inexcusable /ineksku'saβle/ a inexcusable, unforgivable; indispensable

inexhausto /ineks'austo/ a inexhaustible

inexistente /ineksis'tente/ a nonexistent

inexorable /inekso'raβle/ a inexorable

inexperiencia /inekspe'riensia; inekspe'rienθia/ f, inexperience

inexperto /ineks'perto/ a inexperienced; inexpert

inexplicable /inekspli'kaβle/ a inexplicable

inexplorado /ineksplo'raðo/ a unexplored

inexplosible /ineksplo'siβle/ *a* inexplosive
inexpresivo /inekspre'siβo/ *a* inexpressive; reticent
inexpugnable /inekspug'naβle/ *a* impregnable; *Fig.* unshakable, firm; obstinate
inextinguible /inekstiŋ'guiβle/ *a* inextinguishable; everlasting, perpetual
infalibilidad /infaliβili'ðað/ *f*, infallibility
infalible /infa'liβle/ *a* infallible
infamación /infama'sion; infama'θion/ *f*, defamation
infamador /infama'ðor/ **(-ra)** *a* slandering. *n* slanderer
infamar /infa'mar/ *vt* to defame, slander
infame /in'fame/ *a* infamous, vile
infamia /in'famia/ *f*, infamy; baseness, vileness
infancia /in'fansia; in'fanθia/ *f*, infancy; babyhood; childhood
infanta /in'fanta/ *f*, female child under seven years; infanta, any Spanish royal princess; wife of a Spanish royal prince
infantado /infan'taðo/ *m*, land belonging to an *infante* or *infanta*
infante /in'fante/ *m*, male child under seven years; infante, any Spanish royal prince except an heir-apparent; infantryman. **i. de coro,** choir boy
infantería /infante'ria/ *f*, infantry. **i. de marina,** Marine Corps
infanticida /infanti'siða; infanti'θiða/ *a* infanticidal. *mf* infanticide (person)
infanticidio /infanti'siðio; infanti'θiðio/ *m*, infanticide (act)
infantil /infan'til/ *a* infantile, babyish; innocent, candid
infatigable /infati'gaβle/ *a* unwearying, indefatigable
infatuación /infatua'sion; infatua'θion/ *f*, infatuation
infatuar /infa'tuar/ *vt* to infatuate; *vr* become infatuated
infausto /in'fausto/ *a* unlucky, unfortunate
infección /infek'sion; infek'θion/ *f*, infection
infeccioso /infek'sioso; infek'θioso/ *a* infectious
infectar /infek'tar/ *vt* to infect; corrupt, pervert; *vr* become infected; be corrupted
infecto /in'fekto/ *a* infected; corrupt, perverted; tainted
infecundidad /infekundi'ðað/ *f*, sterility
infecundo /infe'kundo/ *a* sterile, barren
infelice /infe'lise; infe'liθe/ *a Poet.* unhappy, unfortunate
infelicidad /infelisi'ðað; infeliθi'ðað/ *f*, unhappiness
infeliz /infe'lis; infe'liθ/ *a* unhappy; unfortunate; *Inf.* simple, good-hearted
inferencia /infe'rensia; infe'renθia/ *f*, inference, connection
inferior /infe'rior/ *a* inferior; lower; second-rate; subordinate. *mf* inferior, subordinate
inferioridad /inferiori'ðað/ *f*, inferiority
inferir /infe'rir/ *vt irr* to infer, deduce; involve, imply; occasion; inflict. See **sentir**
infernáculo /infer'nakulo/ *m*, hopscotch
infernal /infer'nal/ *a* infernal; devilish, fiendish; wicked, inhuman; *Inf.* confounded
inferno /in'ferno/ *a Poet.* infernal
infértil /in'fertil/ *a* infertile
infestación /infesta'sion; infesta'θion/ *f*, infestation
infestar /infes'tar/ *vt* to infest, swarm in; infect; injure, damage
infesto /in'festo/ *a Poet.* harmful, dangerous
inficionar /infisio'nar; infiθio'nar/ *vt* to infect; pervert, corrupt
infidelidad /infiðeli'ðað/ *f*, faithlessness, infidelity; disbelief in Christian religion; unbelievers, infidels
infidelísimo /infiðe'lisimo/, *a sup* **infiel** most disloyal; most incorrect; most incredulous, faithless
infidencia /infi'ðensia; infi'ðenθia/ *f*, disloyalty, faithlessness
infiel /in'fiel/ *a* unfaithful, disloyal; inaccurate, incorrect; infidel, unbelieving. *mf* infidel, nonbeliever
infierno /in'fierno/ *m*, hell; hades (gen. *pl*); *Fig. Inf.* inferno. **en el quinto i.,** very far off, at the end of the

world. **en los quintos infiernos,** at the end of nowhere
infiltración /infiltra'sion; infiltra'θion/ *f*, infiltration; inculcation, implantation
infiltrar /infil'trar/ *vt* to infiltrate; imbue, inculcate
ínfimo /'infimo/ *a* lowest; meanest, vilest, most base; cheapest, poorest (in quality)
infinidad /infini'ðað/ *f*, infinity; infinitude; great number
infinitivo /infini'tiβo/ *a* and *m*, *Gram.* infinitive
infinito /infi'nito/ *a* infinite; endless; boundless; countless. *m*, *Math.* infinite. *adv* excessively, immensely
infinitud /infini'tuð/ *f*, See **infinidad**
inflación /infla'sion; infla'θion/ *f*, inflation; distension; pride, vanity
inflacionismo /inflasio'nismo; inflaθio'nismo/ *m*, inflationism
inflacionista /inflasio'nista; inflaθio'nista/ *mf* inflationist
inflador /infla'ðor/ *m*. *Lat. Am.* bicycle pump
inflamabilidad /inflamaβili'ðað/ *f*, inflammability
inflamable /infla'maβle/ *a* inflammable
inflamación /inflama'sion; inflama'θion/ *f*, inflammation; *Engin.* ignition
inflamador /inflama'ðor/ *a* inflammatory
inflamar /infla'mar/ *vt* to set on fire; *Fig.* inflame, excite; *vr* take fire; *Med.* become inflamed; grow hot or excited
inflamatorio /inflama'torio/ *a Med.* inflammatory
inflar /in'flar/ *vt* to inflate; blow up, distend; throw out (one's chest); exaggerate; make haughty or vain; *vr* be swollen or inflated; be puffed up with pride
inflexibilidad /infleksiβili'ðað/ *f*, inflexibility; rigidity; immovability, constancy
inflexible /infle'ksiβle/ *a* inflexible
inflexión /infle'ksion/ *f*, bending, flexion; diffraction (optics); inflection
infligir /infli'hir/ *vt* to impose, inflict (penalties)
influencia /influ'ensia; influ'enθia/ *f*, influence; power, authority; *Elec.* charge
influir /in'fluir/ *vt irr* to influence; affect; (*with en*) cooperate in, assist with. See **huir**
influjo /in'fluho/ *m*, influence; flux, inflow of the tide
influyente /influ'yente/ *a* influential
información /informa'sion; informa'θion/ *f*, information; legal inquiry; report; research, investigation
informador /informa'ðor/ **(-ra)** *a* informing, acquainting. *n* informant
informal /infor'mal/ *a* informal, irregular; unreliable (of persons); unconventional
informalidad /informali'ðað/ *f*, irregularity; unconventionality; unreliability
informante /infor'mante/ *mf* informant
informar /infor'mar/ *vt* to inform, acquaint with; *vi Law.* plead; *vr* (*with de, en, or sobre*) find out about, investigate
informática /infor'matika/ *f*, computer science; information sciences
informativo /informa'tiβo/ *a* informative
informe /in'forme/ *a* formless, shapeless. *m*, report, statement; information; *Law.* plea; *pl* data, particulars; references
infortificable /infortifi'kaβle/ *a* unfortifiable
infortuna /infor'tuna/ *f*, *Astrol.* evil influence
infortunado /infortu'naðo/ *a* unfortunate
infortunio /infor'tunio/ *m*, misfortune; unhappiness, adversity; mischance, ill luck
infracción /infrak'sion; infrak'θion/ *f*, transgression, infringement
infracto /in'frakto/ *a* imperturbable
infractor /infrak'tor/ **(-ra)** *a* infringing. *n* transgressor, infringer
infrangible /infran'hiβle/ *a* unbreakable
infranqueable /infranke'aβle/ *a* insuperable, unsurmountable
infrarrojo /infra'rroho/ *a* infrared
infrascrito /infras'krito/ *a* undersigned; undermentioned

infrecuente /infre'kuente/ *a* infrequent

infringir /infrin'hir/ *vt* to infringe, transgress, break

infructífero /infruk'tifero/ *a* unfruitful; worthless, useless

infructuosidad /infruktuosi'ðað/ *f*, unfruitfulness; worthlessness, uselessness

infructuoso /infruk'tuoso/ *a* fruitless; useless, worthless

infumable /infu'maβle/ *a* unsmokable (of tobacco)

infundado /infun'daðo/ *a* unfounded, groundless

infundio /in'fundio/ *m*, *Inf.* nonsense, untruth

infundir /infun'dir/ *vt* to infuse, imbue with

infusión /infu'sion/ *f*, infusion

ingeniar /inhe'niar/ *vt* to devise, concoct, plan; *vr* contrive, find a way, manage

ingeniería /inhenie'ria/ *f*, engineering

ingeniero /inhe'niero/ *m*, engineer. **i. agrónomo,** agricultural engineer. **i. de caminos, canales y puertos,** civil engineer. **i. radiotelegrafista,** radio engineer. **cuerpo de ingenieros,** royal engineers

ingenio /in'henio/ *m*, mind; inventive capacity; imaginative talent; man of genius; talent, cleverness; ingeniousness; machine; guillotine (bookbinding)

ingeniosidad /inheniosi'ðað/ *f*, ingeniousness; witticism, clever remark

ingenioso /inhe'nioso/ *a* talented, clever; ingenious

ingénito /in'henito/ *a* unengendered, unconceived; innate, inborn

ingente /in'hente/ *a* huge, enormous

ingenuidad /inhenui'ðað/ *f*, ingenuousness, naiveté

ingenuo /in'henuo/ *a* ingenuous, naive, artless, unaffected

Inglaterra /iŋgla'terra/ England

ingle /'iŋgle/ *f*, groin

inglés /iŋ'gles/ **(-esa)** *a* English; British. *n* Englishman; Briton. *m*, English (language); *Inf.* creditor. **a la inglesa,** in English fashion. **marcharse a la inglesa,** *Inf.* to take French leave

inglesismo /iŋgle'sismo/ *m*, Anglicism

ingobernable /iŋgoβer'naβle/ *a* ungovernable, unruly

ingratitud /iŋgrati'tuð/ *f*, ingratitude

ingrato /iŋ'grato/ *a* ungrateful; irksome, thankless; disagreeable

ingrávido /iŋ'graβiðo/ *a* light weight

ingrediente /iŋgre'ðiente/ *m*, ingredient; *Argentina* appetizer

ingresar /iŋgre'sar/ *vi* to return, come in (money); (*with en*) join, become a member of, enter

ingreso /iŋ'greso/ *m*, joining, entering, admission; *Com.* money received; opening, commencement; *pl* earnings, takings, revenue

ingurgitación /iŋgurhita'sion; iŋgurhita'θion/ *f*, *Med.* ingurgitation

inhábil /in'aβil/ *a* unskillful; unpracticed; incompetent, unfit; unsuitable, ill-chosen

inhabilidad /inaβili'ðað/ *f*, unskillfulness; incompetence; unsuitability; inability

inhabilitación /inaβilita'sion; inaβilita'θion/ *f*, incapacitation; disqualification; disablement

inhabilitar /inaβili'tar/ *vt* to make ineligible; disqualify; incapacitate, make unfit; *vr* become ineligible; be incapacitated

inhabitable /inaβi'taβle/ *a* uninhabitable

inhabitado /inaβi'taðo/ *a* uninhabited, deserted

inhalación /inala'sion; inala'θion/ *f*, inhalation

inhalador /inala'ðor/ *m*, *Med.* inhaler

inhalar /ina'lar/ *vt* to inhale

inhallable /ina'ʝaβle; ina'ʎaβle/ *a* nowhere to be found, unfindable

inheredhitable /inereði'taβle/ *a* uninheritable

inherencia /ine'rensia; ine'renθia/ *f*, inherency

inherente /ine'rente/ *a* inherent, innate

inhestar /ines'tar/ *vt irr* to raise, lift up; erect. See **acertar**

inhibición /iniβi'sion; iniβi'θion/ *f*, inhibition

inhibir /ini'βir/ *vt Law.* to inhibit; *vr* inhibit or restrain oneself. See **prohibir**

inhibitorio /iniβi'torio/ *a Law.* inhibitory

inhonesto /ino'nesto/ *a* indecent, obscene; immodest

inhospedable, inhospitalario /inospe'ðaβle, inospita'lario/ *a* inhospitable; bleak, uninviting; exposed

inhospitalidad /inospitali'ðað/ *f*, inhospitality

inhumación /inuma'sion; inuma'θion/ *f*, inhumation, burial

inhumadora /inuma'ðora/ *f*, crematory

inhumanidad /inumani'ðað/ *f*, inhumanity; brutality

inhumano /inu'mano/ *a* inhuman; brutal, barbarous

inhumar /inu'mar/ *vt* to bury, inter

iniciación /inisia'sion; iniθia'θion/ *f*, initiation

iniciador /inisia'ðor; iniθia'ðor/ **(-ra)** *a* initiating; *n* initiator

inicial /ini'sial; ini'θial/ *a* and *f*, initial

iniciar /ini'siar; ini'θiar/ *vt* to initiate; admit, introduce; originate; *vr* be initiated; *Eccl.* take minor or first orders

iniciativa /inisia'tiβa; iniθia'tiβa/ *f*, initiative

inicuo /ini'kuo/ *a* iniquitous, most unjust, wicked

inimaginable /inimahi'naβle/ *a* inconceivable

inimicísimo /inimi'sisimo; inimi'θisimo/ *a sup* **enemigo** most hostile

inimitable /inimi'taβle/ *a* inimitable

ininteligible /ininteli'hiβle/ *a* unintelligible

iniquidad /iniki'ðað/ *f*, iniquity, wickedness

injerir /inhe'rir/ *vt irr* to insert, place within, introduce; interpolate; *vr* meddle. See **sentir**

injertar /inher'tar/ *vt Agr.* to graft

injerto /in'herto/ *m*, *Agr.* graft; grafting; grafted plant, briar, or tree

injuria /in'huria/ *f*, insult; slander; outrage; wrong, injustice; harm, damage

injuriador /inhuria'ðor/ **(-ra)** *a* insulting. *n* offender, persecutor

injuriar /inhu'riar/ *vt* to insult; slander; outrage; wrong, persecute; harm, damage

injurioso /inhu'rioso/ *a* insulting; slanderous; offensive, abusive; harmful

injusticia /inhus'tisia; inhus'tiθia/ *f*, injustice; lack of justice; unjust action

injustificable /inhustifi'kaβle/ *a* unjustifiable

injustificado /inhustifi'kaðo/ *a* unjustified

injusto /in'husto/ *a* unjust; unrighteous

inllevable /inʝe'βaβle; inʎe'βaβle/ *a* unbearable, intolerable

inmaculado /imaku'laðo/ *a* immaculate, pure

inmaturo /ima'turo/ *a* immature; unripe

inmanejable /imane'haβle/ *a* unmanageable; uncontrollable

inmanencia /ima'nensia; ima'nenθia/ *f*, immanence

inmanente /ima'nente/ *a* immanent

inmarcesible, inmarchitable /imarsesiβle; imartʃitaβle; imarθe'siβle, imartʃi'taβle/ *a* unfading, imperishable

inmaterial /imate'rial/ *a* incorporeal; immaterial

inmaterialidad /imateriali'ðað/ *f*, incorporeity; immateriality

inmediación /imeðia'sion; imeðia'θion/ *f*, nearness, proximity; contact; *pl* outskirts, neighborhood, environs

inmediatamente /imeðiata'mente/ *adv* near; immediately, at once

inmediato /ime'ðiato/ *a* adjoining, close, nearby; immediate, prompt

inmejorable /imeho'raβle/ *a* unsurpassable, unbeatable

inmemorable, inmemorial /imemo'raβle, imemo'rial/ *a* immemorial

inmensidad /imensi'ðað/ *f*, vastness, huge extent; infinity; infinite space; immensity; huge number

inmenso /i'menso/ *a* vast; infinite; immense; innumerable

inmensurable /imensu'raβle/ *a* immeasurable, incalculable

inmerecido /imere'siðo; imere'θiðo/ *a* undeserved, unmerited

inmérito /i'merito/ *a* wrongful, unjust

inmeritorio /imeri'torio/ *a* unmeritorious, unpraiseworthy

inmersión /imer'sion/ *f*, immersion; dip

inmigración /imigra'sion; imigra'θion/ *f*, immigration

inmigrante /imi'grante/ *a* and *mf* immigrant

inmigrar /imi'grar/ *vi* to immigrate

inminencia /imi'nensia; imi'nenθia/ *f*, imminence

inminente /imi'nente/ *a* imminent

inmiscuir /imis'kuir/ *vt* to mix; *vr* meddle. May be conjugated regularly or like **huir**

inmisión /imi'sion/ *f*, inspiration

inmobiliario /imoβi'liario/ *a* concerning real estate

inmoble /i'moβle/ *a* immovable; motionless, immobile, stationary; *Fig.* unshakable, unflinching

inmoderación /imoðera'sion; imoðera'θion/ *f*, immoderateness, excess

inmoderado /imoðe'raðo/ *a* immoderate; unrestrained, excessive

inmodestia /imo'ðestia/ *f*, immodesty

inmodesto /imo'ðesto/ *a* immodest

inmolación /imola'sion; imola'θion/ *f*, immolation

inmolador /imola'ðor/ **(-ra)** *a* sacrificing. *n* immolator

inmolar /imo'lar/ *vt* to immolate; *Fig.* sacrifice, give up; *vr Fig.* sacrifice oneself

inmoral /imo'ral/ *a* immoral

inmoralidad /imorali'ðað/ *f*, immorality

inmortal /imor'tal/ *a* immortal

inmortalidad /imortali'ðað/ *f*, immortality

inmortalizar /imortali'sar; imortali'θar/ *vt* to immortalize

inmotivado /imoti'βaðo/ *a* unfounded, without reason

inmoto /i'moto/ *a* motionless, stationary

inmóvil /i'moβil/ *a* immovable, fixed; motionless; steadfast, constant

inmovilidad /imoβili'ðað/ *f*, immovability; immobility; constancy, steadfastness

inmovilizar /imoβili'sar; imoβili'θar/ *vt* to immobilize

inmueble /i'mueβle/ *m, Law.* immovable estate

inmundicia /imun'disia; imun'diθia/ *f*, filth, nastiness; dirt; rubbish, refuse; obscenity, indecency

inmundo /i'mundo/ *a* dirty, filthy; obscene, indecent; unclean

inmune /i'mune/ *a* exempt; *Med.* immune

inmunidad /imuni'ðað/ *f*, exemption; immunity

inmunizar /imuni'sar; imuni'θar/ *vt* to immunize

inmutabilidad /imutaβili'ðað/ *f*, immutability, changelessness; imperturbability

inmutable /imu'taβle/ *a* immutable, unchangeable; imperturbable

inmutación /imuta'sion; imuta'θion/ *f*, change, alteration, difference

inmutar /imu'tar/ *vt* to change, alter, vary; *vr* change one's expression (through fear, etc.)

innato /in'nato/ *a* innate; inherent; instinctive, inborn

innatural /innatu'ral/ *a* unnatural

innavegable /innaβe'gaβle/ *a* unnavigable; unseaworthy (of ships)

innecesario /innese'sario; inneθe'sario/ *a* unnecessary

innegable /inne'gaβle/ *a* undeniable; indisputable, irrefutable

innoble /in'noβle/ *a* plebeian; ignoble

innocuo /inno'kuo/ *a* harmless, innocuous

innovación /innoβa'sion; innoβa'θion/ *f*, innovation

innovador /innoβa'ðor/ **(-ra)** *a* innovative. *n* innovator

innovar /inno'βar/ *vt* to innovate, introduce innovations

innumerabilidad /innumeraβili'ðað/ *f*, countless number, multitude

innumerable /innume'raβle/ *a* innumerable, countless

innúmero /in'numero/ *a* countless, innumerable

inobediencia /inoβe'ðiensia; inoβe'ðienθia/ *f*, disobedience

inobediente /inoβe'ðiente/ *a* disobedient

inobjetable /inoβhe'taβle/ *a, Lat. Am.* unobjectionable

inobservable /inoβser'βaβle/ *a* unobservable

inobservancia /inoβser'βansia; inoβser'βanθia/ *f*, inobservance

inobservante /inoβser'βante/ *a* unobservant

inocencia /ino'sensia; ino'θenθia/ *f*, innocence; simplicity, candor; harmlessness

inocentada /inosen'taða; inoθen'taða/ *f, Inf.* naive remark or action; fool's trap; practical joke

inocente /ino'sente; ino'θente/ *a* innocent; candid, simple; harmless; easily deceived

inocentón /inosen'ton; inoθen'ton/ *a Inf.* extremely credulous and easily taken in

inocuidad /inokui'ðað/ *f*, innocuousness

inoculación /inokula'sion; inokula'θion/ *f*, inoculation

inoculador /inokula'ðor/ *m*, inoculator

inocular /inoku'lar/ *vt* to inoculate; pervert, corrupt; contaminate

inodoro /ino'ðoro/ *a* odorless. *m*, toilet, lavatory

inofensivo /inofen'siβo/ *a* inoffensive, harmless

inolvidable /inolβi'ðaβle/ *a* unforgettable

inoperable /inope'raβle/ *a* inoperable

inopia /i'nopia/ *f*, poverty; scarcity. *Inf.* **estar en la i.**, to be without a clue (about)

inopinable /inopi'naβle/ *a* indisputable, unquestionable

inopinado /inopi'naðo/ *a* unexpected, sudden

inoportunidad /inoportuni'ðað/ *f*, inopportuneness, unseasonableness; unsuitability

inoportuno /inopor'tuno/ *a* inopportune, untimely

inordenado /inorðe'naðo/ *a* inordinate, immoderate, excessive

inorgánico /inor'ganiko/ *a* inorganic

inoxidable /inoksi'ðaβle/ *a* rustless

inquebrantable /inkeβran'taβle/ *a* unbreakable; final, irrevocable

inquietador /inkieta'ðor/ **(-ra)** *a* disturbing. *n* disturber

inquietar /inkie'tar/ *vt* to disturb; trouble, make anxious, worry; *vr* be disquieted, worry

inquieto /in'kieto/ *a* restless; unquiet; fidgety; disturbed, anxious, worried, uneasy

inquietud /inkie'tuð/ *f*, restlessness; uneasiness; worry; trouble, care, anxiety

inquilinato /inkili'nato/ *m*, tenancy; rent; *Law.* lease; (rental) rates

inquilino /inki'lino/ **(-na)** *n* tenant; lessee; *Chile* tenant farmer

inquina /in'kina/ *f*, dislike, grudge

inquinar /inki'nar/ *vt* to contaminate, corrupt, infect

inquiridor /inkiri'ðor/ **(-ra)** *a* inquiring, examining. *n* investigator

inquirir /inki'rir/ *vt irr* to inquire; examine, look into. See **adquirir**

inquisición /inkisi'sion; inkisi'θion/ *f*, inquiry, investigation; *Eccl.* Inquisition

inquisidor /inkisi'ðor/ **(-ra)** *a* inquiring, investigating. *n* investigator. *m, Eccl.* inquisitor; judge

inquisitorial /inkisito'rial/ *a* inquisitorial

insaciabilidad /insasiaβili'ðað; insaθiaβili'ðað/ *f*, insatiability

insaciable /insa'siaβle; insa'θiaβle/ *a* insatiable

insalubre /insa'luβre/ *a* unhealthy

insanable /insa'naβle/ *a* incurable

insania /in'sania/ *f*, insanity

insano /in'sano/ *a* insane, mad

inscribir /inskri'βir/ *vt* to inscribe; record; enter (a name on a list, etc.), register, enroll; engrave; *Geom.* inscribe. *Past Part.* **inscrito**

inscripción /inskrip'sion; inskrip'θion/ *f*, inscription; record, enrollment; registration; government bond

insecable /inse'kaβle/ *a* undryable, undrying

insecticida /insekti'siða; insekti'θiða/ *a* insecticide

insecto /in'sekto/ *m*, insect

inseguridad /inseguri'ðað/ *f*, insecurity

inseguro /inse'guro/ *a* insecure; unsafe; uncertain

insensatez /insensa'tes; insensa'teθ/ *f*, folly, foolishness

insensato /insen'sato/ *a* foolish, stupid, mad

insensibilidad /insensiβili'ðað/ *f*, insensibility; imperception; callousness, hard-heartedness

insensibilizar /insensiβili'sar; insensiβili'θar/ *vt* to make insensible (to sensations)

insensible /insen'siβle/ *a* insensible; imperceptive, insensitive; unconscious, senseless; imperceptible, inappreciable; callous

inseparabilidad /inseparaβili'ðað/ *f*, inseparability

inseparable /insepa'raβle/ *a* inseparable

insepulto /inse'pulto/ *a* unburied (of the dead)

inserción /inser'sion; inser'θion/ *f*, insertion; interpolation; grafting

insertar /inser'tar/ *vt* to insert; introduce; interpolate; *vr* (*Bot. Zool.*) become attached

inservible /inser'βiβle/ *a* useless; unfit; unsuitable

insidia /in'siðia/ *f*, insidiousness; snare, ambush

insidiador /insiðia'ðor/ **(-ra)** *a* ensnaring. *n* schemer, ambusher

insidiar /insi'ðiar/ *vt* to waylay, ambush; set a trap for; scheme against

insidioso /insi'ðioso/ *a* insidious; treacherous; scheming, guileful

insigne /in'signe/ *a* illustrious, famous; distinguished

insignia /in'signia/ *f*, symbol; badge; token; banner, standard; *Naut.* pennant; *pl* insignia

insignificancia /insignifi'kansia; insignifi'kanθia/ *f*, meaninglessness; unimportance, triviality; insignificance, insufficiency

insignificante /insignifi'kante/ *a* meaningless; unimportant; insignificant, small

insinuación /insinua'sion; insinua'θion/ *f*, insinuation; hint; implication; suggestion

insinuador /insinua'ðor/ *a* insinuating; suggestive, implicative

insinuar /insi'nuar/ *vt* to insinuate; suggest, hint; *vr* ingratiate oneself; creep in

insinuativo /insinua'tiβo/ *a* insinuative

insipidez /insipi'ðes; insipi'ðeθ/ *f*, tastelessness, insipidity; *Fig.* dullness

insípido /in'sipiðo/ *a* tasteless, insipid; dull, uninteresting, boring

insistencia /insis'tensia; insis'tenθia/ *f*, insistence

insistente /insis'tente/ *a* insistent

insistir /insis'tir/ *vi* (*with en or sobre*) to lay stress upon, insist on; persist in

ínsito /'insito/ *a* inherent, innate

insociabilidad /insosiaβili'ðað; insoθiaβili'ðað/ *f*, unsociability

insociable /inso'siaβle; inso'θiaβle/ *a* unsociable

insolación /insola'sion; insola'θion/ *f*, insolation, exposure to the sun; sunstroke

insolar /inso'lar/ *vt* to expose to the sun's rays; *vr* contract sunstroke

insoldable /insol'daβle/ *a* unsolderable, unable to be soldered

insolencia /inso'lensia; inso'lenθia/ *f*, insolence; impudence, impertinence

insolentarse /insolen'tarse/ *vr* to grow insolent; be impudent

insolente /inso'lente/ *a* insolent; impudent, impertinent

insólito /in'solito/ *a* unaccustomed; infrequent; unusual; unexpected

insolubilidad /insoluβili'ðað/ *f*, insolubility

insoluble /inso'luβle/ *a* insoluble

insoluto /inso'luto/ *a* unpaid, outstanding

insolvencia /insol'βensia; insol'βenθia/ *f*, insolvency

insolvente /insol'βente/ *a* insolvent

insomne /in'somne/ *a* sleepless

insomnio /in'somnio/ *m*, insomnia

insondable /inson'daβle/ *a* unfathomable, bottomless; inscrutable, secret

insoportable /insopor'taβle/ *a* intolerable, unbearable

insostenible /insoste'niβle/ *a* indefensible; arbitrary, baseless

inspección /inspek'sion; inspek'θion/ *f*, inspection; supervision; examination; inspectorship; inspector's office

inspeccionar /inspeksio'nar; inspekθio'nar/ *vt* to inspect; survey, examine. **i. una casa,** to view a house

inspector /inspek'tor/ **(-ra)** *a* inspecting, examining. *n* supervisor. *m*, inspector; surveyor

inspiración /inspira'sion; inspira'θion/ *f*, inspiration; inhalation

inspirador /inspira'ðor/ **(-ra)** *a* inspiring. *n* inspirer

inspirar /inspi'rar/ *vt* to breathe in, inhale; blow (of the wind); inspire; *vr* be inspired; (*with en*) find inspiration in, imitate

instalación /instala'sion; instala'θion/ *f*, plant, apparatus; erection, fitting; induction; installment, settling in

instalador /instala'ðor/ **(-ra)** *n* fitter; one who installs (electricity, etc.)

instalar /insta'lar/ *vt* to appoint, induct; erect (a plant, etc.); install, put in; lay on; *Elec.* wire; *vr* install oneself, settle down

instancia /ins'tansia; ins'tanθia/ *f*, instance; argument; suggestion; supplication; request; formal petition. **de primera i.,** in the first instance, firstly

instantánea /instan'tanea/ *f*, *Photo.* snapshot

instantáneo /instan'taneo/ *a* instantaneous

instante /ins'tante/ *a* urgent. *m*, second; instant, moment. **a cada i.,** every minute; frequently. **al i.,** at once, immediately. **por instantes,** continually; immediately

instar /ins'tar/ *vt* to press; persuade; insist upon; *vi* be urgent, press

instauración /instaura'sion; instaura'θion/ *f*, restoration; renewal; renovation; *Lat. Am.* establishment

instaurador /instaura'ðor/ **(-ra)** *a* renovating, renewing. *n* restorer, renovator

instaurar /instau'rar/ *vt* to restore; repair; renovate, renew; *Lat. Am.* establish, set up

instaurativo /instaura'tiβo/ *a* restorative

instigación /instiga'sion; instiga'θion/ *f*, instigation, incitement

instigador /instiga'ðor/ **(-ra)** *n* instigator

instigar /insti'gar/ *vt* to instigate, incite; induce

instilación /instila'sion; instila'θion/ *f*, instillment, pouring drop by drop; inculcation, implantation

instilar /insti'lar/ *vt* *Chem.* instill; implant, inculcate

instintivo /instin'tiβo/ *a* instinctive

instinto /ins'tinto/ *m*, instinct. **por i.,** by instinct, naturally

institución /institu'sion; institu'θion/ *f*, setting up, establishment; institution; teaching, instruction; *pl* institutes, digest

institucional /institusio'nal; instituθio'nal/ *a* institutional

instituir /insti'tuir/ *vt irr* to found, establish; institute; instruct, teach. See **huir**

instituto /insti'tuto/ *m*, institute; secondary school. **i. de belleza,** beauty parlor, beauty salon

institutor /institu'tor/ *m*, founder, instituter; tutor

institutriz /institu'tris; institu'triθ/ *f*, governess

instrucción /instruk'sion; instruk'θion/ *f*, teaching, instruction; knowledge, learning; education; *pl* orders; rules; instructions. **i. primaria,** primary education. **i. pública,** public education

instructivo /instruk'tiβo/ *a* instructive

instructor /instruk'tor/ **(-ra)** *a* instructive. *n* instructor

instruido /ins'truiðo/ *a* cultured; well-educated; knowledgeable

instruir /ins'truir/ *vt irr* to teach, instruct; train; inform, acquaint with; *Law.* formulate. See **huir**

instrumentación /instrumenta'sion; instrumenta'θion/ *f*, *Mus.* instrumentation

instrumentista /instrumen'tista/ *mf Mus.* instrumentalist; instrument maker

instrumento /instru'mento/ *m*, tool, implement; machine, apparatus; *Mus.* instrument; means, medium; legal document. **i. de cuerda,** string instrument. **i. de percusión,** percussion instrument. **i. de viento,** wind instrument

insuave /in'suaβe/ *a* unpleasant (to the senses); rough

insubordinación /insuβorðina'sion; insuβorðina'θion/ *f*, insubordination, rebellion

insubordinado /insuβorði'naðo/ *a* insubordinate, unruly

insubordinar /insuβorði'nar/ *vt* to rouse to rebellion; *vr* become insubordinate, rebel

insubsistencia /insuβsis'tensia; insuβsis'tenθia/ f, instability

insubsistente /insuβsis'tente/ a unstable; groundless, unfounded

insubstancial /insuβstan'sial; insuβstan'θial/ a insubstantial, unreal, illusory; pointless, worthless, superficial

insubstancialidad /insuβstansiali'ðað; insuβstanθiali'ðað/ f, superficiality, worthlessness

insuficiencia /insufi'siensia; insufi'θienθia/ f, insufficiency, shortage; incompetence, inefficiency

insuficiente /insufi'siente; insufi'θiente/ a insufficient, scarce, inadequate

insufrible /insu'friβle/ a insufferable, unbearable, intolerable

insular /insu'lar/ a insular

insulina /insu'lina/ f, insulin

insulsez /insul'ses; insul'seθ/ f, insipidity, tastelessness; dullness; tediousness

insulso /in'sulso/ a insipid, tasteless; tedious; dull

insultador /insulta'ðor/ (**-ra**) a insulting. n insulter

insultante /insul'tante/ a insulting

insultar /insul'tar/ vt to insult; call names; vr take offense

insulto /in'sulto/ m, insult; sudden attack; sudden illness, fit; Argentina fit of fainting; Mexico indigestion

insumable /insu'maβle/ a incalculable; excessive, exorbitant

insumergible /insumer'hiβle/ a unsinkable

insumiso /insu'miso/ a rebellious

insuperable /insupe'raβle/ a insuperable

insurgente /insur'hente/ a insurgent, rebellious. m, rebel

insurrección /insurrek'sion; insurrek'θion/ f, insurrection

insurreccionar /insurreksio'nar; insurrekθio'nar/ vt to incite to rebellion; vr rise in rebellion

insurrecto /insu'rrekto/ (**-ta**) n rebel

insustancial /insustan'sial; insustan'θial/ a See **insubstancial**

insustituible /insusti'tuiβle/ a indispensable

intachable /inta'tʃaβle/ a irreproachable; impeccable, perfect

intacto /in'takto/ a untouched; intact, uninjured; whole, entire; complete; pure

intangibilidad /intanhiβili'ðað/ f, intangibility

intangible /intan'hiβle/ a intangible

integración /integra'sion; integra'θion/ f, integration

integrar /inte'grar/ vt to integrate; Com. repay

integridad /integri'ðað/ f, wholeness; completeness; integrity, probity, honesty; virginity

íntegro /'integro/ a integral, whole; upright, honest

integumento /integu'mento/ m, integument; pretense, simulation

intelectiva /intelek'tiβa/ f, understanding

intelecto /inte'lekto/ m, intellect

intelectual /intelek'tual/ a intellectual

intelectualidad /intelektuali'ðað/ f, understanding, intellectuality; intelligentsia

inteligencia /inteli'hensia; inteli'henθia/ f, intelligence; intellect; mental alertness; mind; meaning, sense; experience, skill; understanding, secret agreement; information, knowledge; Intelligence, Secret Service

inteligente /inteli'hente/ a intelligent; clever; skillful; capable, competent

inteligible /inteli'hiβle/ a intelligible; understandable; able to be heard

intemperancia /intempe'ransia; intempe'ranθia/ f, intemperance, lack of moderation

intemperante /intempe'rante/ a intemperate

intemperie /intem'perie/ f, stormy weather. **a la i.,** at the mercy of the elements; in the open air

intempestivo /intempes'tiβo/ a inopportune, ill-timed

intención /inten'sion; inten'θion/ f, intention; determination, purpose; viciousness (of animals); caution. Inf. **con segunda i.,** with a double meaning, slyly

intencionado /intensio'naðo; intenθio'naðo/ a intentioned, disposed

intencional /intensio'nal; intenθio'nal/ a intentional, designed, premeditated

intendencia /inten'densia; inten'denθia/ f, management; supervision; administration; Polit. intendancy; Argentina mayoralty. Mil. **cuerpo de i.,** quartermaster corps, army supply corps

intendente /inten'dente/ m, director; manager; Polit. intendant; Argentina mayor. **i. de ejército,** quartermaster general

intensar /inten'sar/ vt to intensify

intensidad /intensi'ðað/ f, intensity; ardor; vehemence

intensificar /intensifi'kar/ vt to intensify

intensivo /inten'siβo/ a intensive

intenso /in'tenso/ a intense; ardent; fervent; vehement

intentar /inten'tar/ vt to intend, mean; propose; try, endeavor; initiate. **i. fortuna,** to try one's luck

intento /in'tento/ m, intention, determination; purpose. **de i.,** on purpose; knowingly

intentona /inten'tona/ f, Inf. foolhardy attempt

interacción /interak'sion; interak'θion/ f, interaction; reciprocal effect; Chem. reaction

intercalación /interkala'sion; interkala'θion/ f, interpolation; insertion

intercalar /interka'lar/ vt to intercalate; interpolate, include, insert

intercambiable /interkam'biaβle/ a interchangeable

intercambio /inter'kambio/ m, interchange

interceder /interse'ðer; interθe'ðer/ vi to intercede, plead for

interceptación /intersepta'sion; interθepta'θion/ f, interception

interceptar /intersep'tar; interθep'tar/ vt to intercept; interrupt; hinder

intercesión /interse'sion; interθe'sion/ f, intercession

intercesor /interse'sor; interθe'sor/ (**-ra**) a interceding. n intercessor

intercutáneo /interku'taneo/ a intercutaneous

interdecir /inter'ðesir; inter'ðeθir/ vt irr to forbid, prohibit. See **decir**

interdicción /interðik'sion; interðik'θion/ f, interdiction, prohibition

interdicto /inter'ðikto/ m, interdict

interés /inte'res/ m, interest; yield, profit; advantage; Com. interest; inclination, fondness; attraction, fascination; pl money matters. **i. compuesto,** compound interest. **intereses creados,** bonds of interest; vested interests

interesado /intere'saðo/ (**-da**) a involved, concerned; biased; selfish. n Law. interested party

interesante /intere'sante/ a interesting

interesar /intere'sar/ (**se**) vi and vr to be interested; vt Com. invest; interest

interfecto /inter'fekto/ (**-ta**) n Law. victim (of murder)

interferencia /interfe'rensia; interfe'renθia/ f, Phys. interference

interfoliar /interfo'liar/ vt to interleave (of books)

ínterin /'interin/ m, interim. adv meanwhile, in the meantime

interinamente /interina'mente/ adv in the interim; provisionally

interinar /interi'nar/ vt to discharge (duties) provisionally, act temporarily as

interino /inte'rino/ a acting, provisional, temporary

interior /inte'rior/ a interior; inner; inside; indoor; inland; internal, domestic (policies, etc.); inward, spiritual. m, interior, inside; mind, soul; pl entrails

interiorizar /interiori'sar; interiori'θar/ vt, Lat. Am. to investigate closely, look into, scrutinize

interjección /interhek'sion; interhek'θion/ f, Gram. interjection, exclamation

interlinear /interline'ar/ vt to write between the lines; Print. lead

interlocución /interloku'sion; interloku'θion/ f, dialogue, conversation

interlocutorio /interloku'torio/ a Law. interlocutory

intérlope /in'terlope/ mf interloper

interludio /inter'luðio/ m, interlude

intermediario /interme'ðiario/ **(-ia)** *a* and *n* intermediary. *m, Com.* middleman

intermedio /inter'meðio/ *a* intermediate. *m,* interim; *Theat.* interval. **por i. de,** through, by the mediation of

intermisión /intermi'sion/ *f,* intermission, interval

intermitencia /intermi'tensia; intermi'tenθia/ *f,* intermittence

intermitente /intermi'tente/ *a* intermittent

intermitir /intermi'tir/ *vt* to interrupt, suspend, discontinue

internación /interna'sion; interna'θion/ *f,* going inside; penetration; taking into

internacional /internasio'nal; internaθio'nal/ *a* international

internacionalismo /internasiona'lismo; internaθiona'lismo/ *m,* internationalism

internacionalista /internasiona'lista; internaθiona'lista/ *mf* internationalist

internacionalización /internasionalisa'sion; internaθionaliθa'θion/ *f,* internationalization

internado /inter'naðo/ *m,* boarding school

internamiento /interna'miento/ *m,* internment

internar /inter'nar/ *vt* to take or send inland; *vi* penetrate; *vr* (*with en*) go into the interior of (a country); get into the confidence of; study deeply (a subject)

Internet /inter'net/ *m,* the Internet

interno /in'terno/ **(-na)** *a* interior; internal; inner; inside; boarding (student). *n* boarding school student; *Med.* intern

internuncio /inter'nunsio; inter'nunθio/ *m, Eccl.* internuncio; interlocutor; representative

interoceánico /interose'aniko; interoθe'aniko/ *a* interoceanic

interpaginar /interpahi'nar/ *vt* to interleave (of books)

interpelación /interpela'sion; interpela'θion/ *f, Law.* interpellation; appeal

interpelar /interpe'lar/ *vt Law.* to interpellate; appeal to, ask protection from

interpolación /interpola'sion; interpola'θion/ *f,* interpolation, insertion; interruption

interpolador /interpola'ðor/ **(-ra)** *n* interpolator; interrupter

interpolar /interpo'lar/ *vt* to interpolate; interject

interponer /interpo'ner/ *vt irr* to interpose, insert, intervene; designate as an arbitrator; *vr* intervene. See **poner**

interposición /interposi'sion; interposi'θion/ *f,* interposition; intervention; mediation, arbitration

interpresa /inter'presa/ *f, Mil.* surprise attack

interpretación /interpreta'sion; interpreta'θion/ *f,* interpretation; translation

interpretador /interpreta'ðor/ **(-ra)** *a* interpretative. *n* interpreter

interpretar /interpre'tar/ *vt* to interpret; translate; attribute; expound, explain. **i. mal,** to misconstrue; translate wrongly

intérprete /in'terprete/ *mf* interpreter

interregno /inte'rregno/ *m,* interregnum; *Lat. Am.* interim. **i. parlamentario,** parliamentary recess

interrogación /interroga'sion; interroga'θion/ *f,* interrogation, question; *Gram.* question mark

interrogador /interroga'ðor/ **(-ra)** *n* questioner

interrogante /interro'gante/ *a* interrogating. *m, Print.* question mark

interrogar /interro'gar/ *vt* to interrogate, question

interrogativo /interroga'tiβo/ *a* interrogative

interrogatorio /interroga'torio/ *m,* interrogatory

interrumpir /interrum'pir/ *vt* to interrupt; hinder, obstruct; *Elec.* break contact

interrupción /interrup'sion; interrup'θion/ *f,* interruption; stoppage (of work); *Elec.* break

interruptor /interrup'tor/ **(-ra)** *a* interrupting. *n* interrupter. *m, Elec.* switch, interruptor. **i. de dos direcciones,** *Elec.* two-way switch

intersticio /inter'stisio; inter'stiθio/ *m,* interstice, crack, crevice; interval, intervening space

intervalo /inter'βalo/ *m,* interval

intervención /interβen'sion; interβen'θion/ *f,* intervention; mediation, intercession; auditing (of accounts)

intervenir /interβe'nir/ *vi irr* to take part (in); intervene, interfere; arbitrate, mediate; happen, occur; *vt Com.* audit. See **venir**

interventor /interβen'tor/ **(-ra)** *a* intervening. *n* one who intervenes. *m,* auditor; inspector

intervocálico /interβo'kaliko/ *a* intervocalic

intestado /intes'taðo/ **(-da)** *a* and *n Law.* intestate

intestino /intes'tino/ *a* intestinal. *m,* intestine

íntima, intimación /'intima, intima'sion; 'intima, intima'θion/ *f,* intimation, notification

intimar /inti'mar/ *vt* to intimate; inform, notify; *vr* penetrate; *vr* and *vi* become intimate or friendly

intimidación /intimiða'sion; intimiða'θion/ *f,* intimidation, terrorization

intimidad /intimi'ðað/ *f,* intimacy

intimidar /intimi'ðar/ *vt* to intimidate, terrorize, cow

íntimo /'intimo/ *a* intimate; deep-seated, inward; private, personal

intitular /intitu'lar/ *vt* to give a title to, entitle, call; *vr* call oneself

intolerable /intole'raβle/ *a* intolerable; unbearable

intolerancia /intole'ransia; intole'ranθia/ *f,* narrow-mindedness, intolerance, bigotry

intolerante /intole'rante/ *a* narrow-minded, illiberal; *Med.* intolerant

intonso /in'tonso/ *a* long-haired, unshorn; boorish, ignorant

intoxicación /intoksika'sion; intoksika'θion/ *f,* poisoning

intoxicar /intoksi'kar/ *vt* to poison

intraducible /intraðu'siβle; intraðu'θiβle/ *a* untranslatable

intramuros /intra'muros/ *adv* within the town walls, within the city

intranquilidad /intrankili'ðað/ *f,* disquiet, restlessness; anxiety

intranquilizador /intrankilisa'ðor; intrankiliθa'ðor/ *a* disquieting, perturbing

intranquilizar /intrankili'sar; intrankili'θar/ *vt* to disquiet, make uneasy, worry

intranquilo /intran'kilo/ *a* uneasy, anxious

intransferible /intransfe'riβle/ *a* untransferable, not transferable

intransigencia /intransi'hensia; intransi'henθia/ *f,* intolerance, intransigence

intransigente /intransi'hente/ *a* intolerant, intransigent

intransitable /intransi'taβle/ *a* impassable; unsurmountable

intransitivo /intransi'tiβo/ *a* intransitive

intrascendente /intrassen'dente; intrasθen'dente/ *a, Lat. Am.* unimportant

intratable /intra'taβle/ *a* intractable; impassable; rough; unsociable, difficult

intrauterino /intraute'rino/ *a* intrauterine. **dispositivo i.,** intrauterine device

intravenoso /intraβe'noso/ *a* intravenous

intrepidez /intrepi'ðes; intrepi'ðeθ/ *f,* intrepidity, dauntlessness, gallantry

intrépido /in'trepiðo/ *a* intrepid, dauntless, gallant

intriga /in'triga/ *f,* scheme, intrigue; entanglement; *Lit.* plot

intrigante /intri'gante/ *mf* intriguer, schemer

intrigar /intri'gar/ *vi* to intrigue, scheme, plot; **intrigarse** *Lat. Am.* to be intrigued, be puzzled

intrincación /intrinka'sion; intrinka'θion/ *f,* intricacy

intrincado /intrin'kaðo/ *a* intricate

intrincar /intrin'kar/ *vt* to complicate; obscure, confuse

intríngulis /in'triŋgulis/ *m, Inf.* ulterior motive

intrínseco /in'trinseko/ *a* intrinsic, inherent; essential

introducción /introðuk'sion; introðuk'θion/ *f,* introduction

introducir /introðu'sir; introðu'θir/ *vt irr* to introduce; insert; fit in; drive in; present, introduce; bring into use; cause, occasion; show in, bring in; *vr* interfere, meddle; enter. See **conducir**

introductor /introðuk'tor/ **(-ra)** n introducer
introito /introito/ m, preamble, introduction; *Eccl.* introit; (*Theat. Obs.*) prologue
intromisión /intromi'sion/ f, intromission; interference; *Geol.* intrusion
introspección /introspek'sion; introspek'θion/ f, introspection
introverso /intro'βerso/ a introvert
intruso /in'truso/ **(-sa)** a intruding, intrusive. n intruder
intuición /intui'sion; intui'θion/ f, intuition
intuir /in'tuir/ vt irr to know by intuition. See **huir**
intuitivo /intui'tiβo/ a intuitive
intuito /in'tuito/ m, glance, look, view
inulto /i'nulto/ a *Poet.* unavenged, unpunished
inundación /inunda'sion; inunda'θion/ f, flood; flooding; excess, superabundance
inundar /inun'dar/ vt to flood; swamp; *Fig.* inundate, overwhelm
inurbanidad /inurβani'ðað/ f, discourtesy, impoliteness
inurbano /inur'βano/ a discourteous, uncivil, impolite
inusitado /inusi'taðo/ a unusual, unaccustomed; rare
inútil /i'nutil/ a useless
inutilidad /inutili'ðað/ f, uselessness
inutilizar /inutili'sar; inutili'θar/ vt to render useless; disable, incapacitate; spoil, damage
invadeable /imbaðe'aβle/ a impassable, unfordable
invadir /imba'ðir/ vt to invade
invaginación /imbahina'sion; imbahina'θion/ f, invagination
invalidación /imbaiiða'sion; imbaliða'θion/ f, invalidation
invalidar /imbali'ðar/ vt to invalidate
invalidez /imbali'ðes; imbali'ðeθ/ f, invalidity; disablement; infirmity
inválido /im'baliðo/ **(-da)** a weak, infirm; invalid, null; disabled. n invalid; disabled soldier
invariable /imba'riaβle/ a invariable
invariación /imbaria'sion; imbaria'θion/ f, invariableness
invariante /imba'riante/ m, invariant
invasión /imba'sion/ f, invasion, encroachment, incursion
invasor /imba'sor/ **(-ra)** a invading; *Med.* attacking. n invader
invectiva /imbek'tiβa/ f, invective
invencibilidad /imbensiβili'ðað; imbenθiβili'ðað/ f, invincibility
invencible /imben'siβle; imben'θiβle/ a invincible
invención /imben'sion; imben'θion/ f, invention, discovery; deception, fabrication, lie; creative imagination; finding (e.g. *i. de la Santa Cruz*, Invention of the Holy Cross)
invencionero /imbensio'nero; imbenθio'nero/ **(-ra)** n inventor; schemer, deceiver
invendible /imben'diβle/ a unsalable
inventar /imben'tar/ vt to invent; create; imagine; concoct, fabricate (lies, etc.)
inventariar /imbenta'riar/ vt to make an inventory of; *Com.* take stock of
inventario /imben'tario/ m, inventory; *Com.* stock taking
inventiva /imben'tiβa/ f, inventiveness, ingenuity; creativeness
inventivo /imben'tiβo/ a inventive
invento /im'bento/ m, See **invención**
inventor /imben'tor/ **(-ra)** n inventor, discoverer; liar, storyteller
inverecundia /imbere'kundia/ f, impertinence, impudence
inverecundo /imbere'kundo/ a shameless, brazen
inverisímil /imberi'simil/ a See **inverosímil**
invernáculo /imber'nakulo/ m, greenhouse; conservatory
invernada /imber'naða/ f, winter season; hibernation; *Lat. Am.* winter pasture
invernadero /imberna'ðero/ m, winter quarters; greenhouse

invernal /imber'nal/ a wintry; winter
invernar /imber'nar/ vi irr to winter; hibernate; be wintertime. See **acertar**
invernizo /imber'niso; imber'niθo/ a wintry, winter
inverosímil /imbero'simil/ a unlikely, improbable
inverosimilitud /imberosimili'tuð/ f, improbability
inversamente /imbersa'mente/ adv inversely
inverso /im'berso/ a inverse; inverted
inversor, -a /im'bersor/ mf, *Lat. Am.* investor
invertebrado /imberte'βraðo/ a and m, invertebrate
invertir /imber'tir/ vt irr to invert, transpose; reverse; *Com.* invest; spend (time). See **sentir**
investidura /imbesti'ðura/ f, investiture
investigación /imbestiga'sion; imbestiga'θion/ f, investigation, examination; research; inquiry
investigador /imbestiga'ðor/ **(-ra)** a investigating. n investigator; researcher
investigar /imbesti'gar/ vt to investigate, examine; research on
investir /imbes'tir/ vt irr to confer upon, decorate with; invest, appoint. See **pedir**
inveterado /imbete'raðo/ a inveterate
inviable /im'biaβle/ a unfeasible
invicto /im'bikto/ a invincible; unconquered
invierno /im'bierno/ m, winter; rainy season
inviolabilidad /imbiolaβili'ðað/ f, inviolability. **i. parlamentaria,** parliamentary immunity
inviolable /imbio'laβle/ a inviolable; infallible
inviolado /imbio'laðo/ a inviolate
invisibilidad /imbisiβili'ðað/ f, invisibility
invisible /imbi'siβle/ a invisible; m, *Argentina* hairpin; *Mexico* hairnet
invitación /imbita'sion; imbita'θion/ f, invitation
invitado /imbi'taðo/ **(-da)** n guest
invitar /imbi'tar/ vt to invite; urge, request; allure, attract
invocación /imboka'sion; imboka'θion/ f, invocation
invocador /imboka'ðor/ **(-ra)** n invoker
invocar /imbo'kar/ vt to invoke
involuntariedad /imboluntarie'ðað/ f, involuntariness
involuntario /imbolun'tario/ a involuntary
invulnerabilidad /imbulneraβili'ðað/ f, invulnerability
invulnerable /imbulne'raβle/ a invulnerable
inyección /inyek'sion; inyek'θion/ f, injection
inyectado /inyek'taðo/ a bloodshot (of eyes)
inyectar /inyek'tar/ vt to inject
ipecacuana /ipeka'kuana/ f, ipecac
iperita /i'perita/ f, mustard gas
ir /ir/ vi irr to go; suit, be becoming, fit (e.g. *El vestido no te va bien,* The dress doesn't suit you); extend; lead, go in the direction of (e.g. *Este camino va a Lérida,* This road leads to Lerida); get along, do, proceed, be (e.g. *¿Cómo te va estos días?* How are you getting along these days?); come (e.g. *Ahora voy,* I'm coming now); bet (e.g. *Van cinco pesetas que no lo hace,* I bet five pesetas he doesn't do it); be different, be changed (e.g. *¡Qué diferencia va entre esto y aquello!* What a difference there is between this and that!); *Math.* carry (e.g. *siete y van cuatro,* seven, and four to carry); *Math.* leave (e.g. *De quince a seis van nueve,* Six from fifteen leaves nine). With a gerund, **ir** indicates the continuance of the action, or may mean to become or to grow (e.g. *Iremos andando hacia el mar,* We will go on walking toward the sea, or *Entre tanto iba amaneciendo,* In the meanwhile it was growing light). With a past participle, **ir** means "to be' (e.g. *Voy encantado de lo que he visto,* I am delighted with what I have seen). With *prep a + infin,* **ir** expresses the periphrastic future, and means to prepare (to do) or to intend (to do) or to be on the point of doing (e.g. *Van a cantar la canción que te gusta,* They are going (or preparing) to sing the song you like). With *prep a + noun,* **ir** indicates destination (e.g. *Voy al cine,* I'm going to the cinema. *¿A dónde vamos?* Where are we going to?). **ir** + *con* means to go in the company of, or to do a thing in a certain manner (e.g. *Hemos de ir con cuidado,* We must go carefully). **ir** + *en* means to concern, interest (e.g.

¿Qué le va a él en este asunto? What has this affair to do with him?). **ir** + *por* means to follow the career of, become (e.g. *Juan va por abogado,* John is going to be a lawyer). It also means to go and bring, or to go for (e.g. *Iré por agua,* I shall go and bring (or for) water). *vr* to go away, leave, depart; die; leak (of liquids); evaporate; overbalance, slip (e.g. *Se le fueron los pies,* He slipped (and lost his balance)); be worn out, grow old, deteriorate; be incontinent; *Fig. Inf.* **irsele a uno una cosa,** not to notice or not to understand a thing. *Naut.* **irse a pique,** to founder, sink. **Se le fueron los ojos tras María,** He couldn't keep his eyes off Mary. **i. a caballo,** to ride, go on horseback. **i. adelante,** to go on ahead, lead; *Fig. Inf.* forge ahead, go ahead. **i. al cuartel,** to go into the army. **i. a una,** to cooperate in. **i. bien** *Fig. Inf.* to go on well; be well. **i. de brazo,** to walk arm in arm. **i. de compras,** to go shopping. **i. de juerga** *Inf.* to go on a binge. **i. de bicicleta** *or* **en coche,** to go by bicycle or to ride (in a car or carriage). **i. por,** to do things in order, take one thing at a time. *Fig. Inf.* **i. tirando,** to carry on, manage. **¿Cómo le va?** How are things with you? How are you getting along? *Inf.* **no irle ni venirle a uno nada en un asunto,** to be not in the least concerned in (an affair). **¡Qué va!** Rubbish! Nothing of the sort! **¿Quién va?** *Mil.* Who goes there? **Vamos,** Let's go (also used as an exclamation: Good gracious! You don't say so! Well!) **Vamos a ver...,** Let's see.... **¡Vaya!** What a...!; Come now! Never mind! **¡Vaya a paseo!** *or* **¡Vaya con su música a otra parte!** Take yourself off! Get out! **¡Vaya con Dios!** God keep you! Good-bye! *Pres. Ind.* **voy, vas, va, vamos, váis, van.** *Pres. Part.* **yendo.** *Preterite* **fui, fuiste, fue, fuimos, fuisteis, fueron.** *Imperf.* **iba,** etc. *Pres. Subjunc.* **vaya,** etc. *Imperf. Subjunc.* **fuese,** etc. *Imperat.* **vé**

ira /'ira/ *f,* wrath, anger; vengeance; raging, fury (of elements); *pl* cruelties, acts of vengeance

iracundia /ira'kundia/ *f,* irascibility, irritability; anger

iracundo /ira'kundo/ *a* irascible, irritable, choleric; angry; raging, tempestuous

iranio /i'ranio/ **(-ia)** *a* and *n* Iranian

irascibilidad /irassiβili'ðað; irasθiβili'ðað/ *f,* irascibility; petulance

iridiscencia /iriðis'sensia; iriðis'θenθia/ *f,* iridescence

iridiscente /iriðis'sente; iriðis'θente/ *a* iridescent

iris /'iris/ *m,* rainbow; *Anat.* iris (of the eye)

irisación /irisa'sion; irisa'θion/ *f,* irisation

irisar /iri'sar/ *vi* to be iridescent

Irlanda /ir'landa/ Ireland

irlandés /irlan'des/ **(-esa)** *a* and *n* Irishman (woman)

ironía /iro'nia/ *f,* irony

irónico /i'roniko/ *a* ironical

iroqués /iro'kes/ **(-esa)** *a* and *n* Iroquois

irracional /irrasio'nal; irraθio'nal/ *a* irrational; illogical, unreasonable; *Math.* irrational, absurd

irracionalidad /irrasionali'ðað; irraθionali'ðað/ *f,* irrationality, unreasonableness

irradiación /irraðia'sion; irraðia'θion/ *f,* radiation, irradiation

irradiar /irra'ðiar/ *vt* to radiate, irradiate

irrazonable /irraso'naβle; irraθo'naβle/ *a* unreasonable

irreal /irre'al/ *a* unreal

irrealidad /irreali'ðað/ *f,* unreality

irrealizable /irreali'saβle; irreali'θaβle/ *a* unachievable, unattainable

irrebatible /irreβa'tiβle/ *a* irrefutable, evident

irreconciliable /irrekonsi'liaβle; irrekonθi'liaβle/ *a* irreconcilable, intransigent

irrecuperable /irrekupe'raβle/ *a* irretrievable

irredimible /irreði'miβle/ *a* irredeemable

irreemplazable /irreempla'saβle; irreempla'θaβle/ *a* irreplaceable

irreflexión /irreflek'sion/ *f,* thoughtlessness; impetuosity

irreflexivo /irreflek'siβo/ *a* thoughtless; rash, impetuous

irreformable /irrefor'maβle/ *a* unreformable

irrefragable /irrefra'gaβle/ *a* indisputable, unquestionable

irrefrenable /irrefre'naβle/ *a* unmanageable, uncontrollable

irrefutable /irrefu'taβle/ *a* irrefutable

irregular /irregu'lar/ *a* irregular; infrequent, rare

irregularidad /irregulari'ðað/ *f,* irregularity; abnormality; *Inf.* moral lapse

irreligión /irreli'hion/ *f,* irreligion

irreligiosidad /irrelihiosi'ðað/ *f,* impiety, godlessness

irreligioso /irreli'hioso/ *a* irreligious, impious

irremediable /irreme'ðiaβle/ *a* irremediable

irremediablemente /irremeðiaβle'mente/ *adv* unavoidably; hopelessly

irremisible /irremi'siβle/ *a* unpardonable, inexcusable

irremunerado /irremune'raðo/ *a* unremunerated, gratuitous

irreparable /irrepa'raβle/ *a* irreparable

irreprensible /irrepren'siβle/ *a* blameless, unexceptionable

irreprochable /irrepro'tʃaβle/ *a* irreproachable

irresistible /irresis'tiβle/ *a* irresistible; ravishing

irresolución /irresolu'sion; irresolu'θion/ *f,* vacillation, indecision

irresoluto /irreso'luto/ *a* hesitant, irresolute

irrespetuoso /irrespe'tuoso/ *a* disrespectful

irresponsabilidad /irresponsaβili'ðað/ *f,* irresponsibility

irresponsable /irrespon'saβle/ *a* irresponsible

irreverencia /irreβe'rensia; irreβe'renθia/ *f,* irreverence

irreverente /irreβe'rente/ *a* irreverent

irrevocabilidad /irreβokaβili'ðað/ *f,* irrevocability, finality

irrevocable /irreβo'kaβle/ *a* irrevocable

irrigación /irriga'sion; irriga'θion/ *f,* irrigation

irrigador /irriga'ðor/ *m,* spray, sprinkler; *Med.* syringe, spray

irrigar /irri'gar/ *vt* (*Med. Agr.*) to irrigate

irrisible /irri'siβle/ *a* ridiculous, laughable, absurd

irrisión /irri'sion/ *f,* derision; laughingstock

irrisorio /irri'sorio/ *a* ridiculous; derisive

irritabilidad /irritaβili'ðað/ *f,* irritability, petulance, irascibility

irritable /irri'taβle/ *a* irritable

irritación /irrita'sion; irrita'θion/ *f,* irritation; petulance, exasperation

irritador /irrita'ðor/ *a* irritating; exasperating. *m,* irritant

irritante /irri'tante/ *a* irritating; exasperating

irritar /irri'tar/ *vt* to exasperate, annoy; provoke, inflame; (*Med. Law.*) irritate

írrito /'irrito/ *a Law.* null, void

irrogar /irro'gar/ *vt* to occasion (damage, harm)

irrompible /irrom'piβle/ *a* unbreakable

irrumpir /irrum'pir/ *vi* to enter violently, break in

irrupción /irrup'sion; irrup'θion/ *f,* irruption, incursion, invasion

irruptor /irrup'tor/ *a* invading, attacking

isabelino /isaβe'lino/ *a* Isabelline (pertaining to Spanish Queen Isabella II (reigned 1830–68)); bay (of horses)

isla /'isla/ *f,* island; block (of houses)

islámico /is'lamiko/ *a* Islamic

islamismo /isla'mismo/ *m,* Islam

islamita /isla'mita/ *a* and *mf* Muslim

islandés /islan'des/ **(-esa), islándico (-ca)** *a* Icelandic. *n* Icelander. *m,* Icelandic (language)

Islandia /is'landia/ Iceland

isleño /is'leɲo/ **(-ña)** *a* island. *n* islander; native of the Canary Islands

isleta /is'leta/ *f,* islet

islote /is'lote/ *m,* small island, islet

isoca /i'soka/ *f, Argentina* caterpillar

isométrico /iso'metriko/ *a* isometric

isomorfo /iso'morfo/ *a* isomorphic

isotermo /iso'termo/ *a* isothermal

isótope, isótopo /i'sotope, i'sotopo/ *m,* isotope

israelita /israe'lita/ *mf* Israelite. *a* Israeli

istmeño /ist'meɲo/ **(-ña)** *n* native of an isthmus

ístmico /'istmiko/ *a* isthmian

istmo /'istmo/ *m*, isthmus
Istmo de Suez, el /'istmo de 'sues, el; 'istmo de 'sueθ, el/ the Suez Canal
Italia /i'talia/ Italy
italianismo /italia'nismo/ *m*, Italianism
italianizar /italiani'sar; italiani'θar/ *vt* to italianize
italiano /ita'liano/ **(-na)** *a* and *n* Italian. *m*, Italian (language)
itálico /i'taliko/ *a* italic
iteración /itera'sion; itera'θion/ *f*, iteration, repetition

iterar /ite'rar/ *vt* to repeat, reiterate
iterativo /itera'tiβo/ *a* iterative, repetitive
itinerario /itine'rario/ *a* and *m*, itinerary
izar /i'sar; i'θar/ *vt Naut.* to hoist
izote /i'sote; i'θote/ *m*, yucca
izquierda /is'kierða; iθ'kierða/ *f*, left, left-hand side; *Polit.* left. **¡I.!** *Mil.* Left face! **a la i.**, on the left
izquierdo /is'kierðo; iθ'kierðo/ *a* left, left-hand; left-handed; bent, twisted, crooked

JK

¡ja, ja, ja! /ha, ha, ha/ *interj* Ha! ha! ha!
jaba /'haβa/ *f*, *Lat. Am.* basket; *Mexico* crate
jabalí /haβa'li/ *m*, wild boar
jabalina /haβa'lina/ *f*, sow of wild boar; javelin
jabato /ha'βato/ *m*, young wild boar
jabón /ha'βon/ *m*, soap. **j. blando**, soft soap. **j. de olor** *or* **j. de tocador**, toilet soap. **j. de sastre**, French chalk, steatite
jabonadura /haβona'ðura/ *f*, soaping; *pl* soapsuds, lather
jabonar /haβo'nar/ *vt* to soap; wash, put on soap; *Inf.* dress down, scold
jaboncillo /haβon'siyo; haβon'θiλo/ *m*, toilet soap; steatite
jabonera /haβo'nera/ *f*, soapdish or box; soapwort
jabonería /haβone'ria/ *f*, soap factory or shop
jabonoso /haβo'noso/ *a* soapy
jaca /'haka/ *f*, pony; filly
jacal /ha'kal/ *m*, *Mexico* hut, shack
jácara /'hakara/ *f*, gay, roguish ballad; song and dance
jácena /'hasena; 'haθena/ *f*, *Archit.* beam, girder
jacinto /ha'sinto; ha'θinto/ *m*, hyacinth; jacinth. **j. de ceilán**, zircon. **j. occidental**, topaz. **j. oriental**, ruby
jaco /'hako/ *m*, short coat of mail; hack, jade
jactancia /hak'tansia; hak'tanθia/ *f*, bragging, boasting
jactancioso /haktan'sioso; haktan'θioso/ **(-sa)** *a* boastful. *n* braggart
jactarse /hak'tarse/ *vr* to brag, boast
jaculatoria /hakula'toria/ *f*, ejaculatory prayer
jade /'haðe/ *m*, *Mineral.* jade
jadeante /haðe'ante/ *a* panting
jadear /haðe'ar/ *vi* to pant
jadeo /ha'ðeo/ *m*, pant; panting; hard breathing
jaez /ha'es; ha'eθ/ *m*, harness (gen. *pl*); kind, sort; *pl* trappings
jaguar /ha'guar/ *m*, jaguar
jaiba /'haiβa/ *f*, *Lat. Am.* crab
jáibol /'haiβol/ *m*, *Lat. Am.* highball
jáilaif /'hailaif/ *m*, *Lat. Am.* high life
jalbegar /halβe'gar/ *vt* to whitewash; make up the face
jalbegue /hal'βege/ *m*, whitewash
jalde /'halde/ *a* bright yellow
jalea /ha'lea/ *f*, jelly. **j. de membrillo**, quince jelly
jalear /hale'ar/ *vt* to encourage, urge on (by shouts, etc.)
jaleo /ha'leo/ *m*, act of encouraging dancers by clapping, shouting, etc.; Andalusian song and dance, *Inf.* uproar
jalón /ha'lon/ *m*, surveying rod
jamaicano /hamai'kano/ **(-na)** *a* and *n* Jamaican
jamás /ha'mas/ *adv* never. **nunca j.**, never. **por siempre j.**, for always, forever
jamba /'hamba/ *f*, jamb (of a door or window)
jambarse /ham'βarse/ *vr*, *Lat. Am.* to overeat
jamelgo /ha'melgo/ *m*, sorry nag, miserable hack
jamón /ha'mon/ *m*, ham
jamona /ha'mona/ *f*, *Inf.* plumpish middle-aged woman
jansenista /hanse'nista/ *mf* and *a* Jansenist
Japón /ha'pon/ Japan

japonés /hapo'nes/ **(-esa)** *a* and *n* Japanese. *m*, Japanese (language)
jaque /'hake/ *m*, check (in chess); braggart. **j. mate**, checkmate. **en j.**, at bay
jaquear /hake'ar/ *vt* to check (in chess); *Mil.* harass the enemy
jaqueca /ha'keka/ *f*, migraine, sick headache. *Inf.* **dar una j.**, to annoy
jarabe /ha'raβe/ *m*, syrup, cough medicine. **j. tapatío**, Mexican hat dance
jarana /ha'rana/ *f*, roundhouse; *Inf.* revelry; fight, roughhouse; trick, deception
jarcia /'harsia; 'harθia/ *f*, equipment; *Naut.* tackle, rigging (gen. *pl*); fishing tackle; *Inf.* heap, mixture, medley
jardín /har'ðin/ *m*, garden
jardinar /harði'nar/ *vt* to landscape
jardinera /harði'nera/ *f*, plant stand, jardiniere; open streetcar
jardinería /harðine'ria/ *f*, gardening
jardinero /harði'nero/ **(-ra)** *n* gardener
jareta /ha'reta/ *f*, *Sew.* running hem; *Naut.* netting
jarra /'harra/ *f*, jar, jug. **en jarras**, arms akimbo
jarrero /ha'rrero/ *m*, jug seller or manufacturer
jarrete /ha'rrete/ *m*, calf (of the leg)
jarretera /harre'tera/ *f*, garter
jarro /'harro/ *m*, pitcher; jug; jar; vase
jarrón /ha'rron/ *m*, garden urn; vase
jaspe /'haspe/ *m*, jasper
jaspeado /haspe'aðo/ *a* marbled, mottled; dappled; frosted (of glass)
jauja /'hauha/ *f*, *Fig.* paradise, land of milk and honey
jaula /'haula/ *f*, cage; crate; miner's cage
jauría /hau'ria/ *f*, pack of hounds
jazmín /has'min; haθ'min/ *m*, jasmine. **j. amarillo**, yellow jasmine. **j. de la India**, gardenia
jefa /'hefa/ *f*, forewoman; manager; leader, head
jefatura /hefa'tura/ *f*, chieftainship; managership; leadership. **j. de policía**, police station or headquarters
jefe /'hefe/ *m*, chief; head, leader; manager; *Mil.* commanding officer. *Mil.* **j. de estado mayor**, chief of staff. **j. del tren**, railroad guard
jengibre /hen'hiβre/ *m*, ginger
jeque /'heke/ *m*, sheik
jerarca /he'rarka/ *m*, hierarch
jerarquía /herar'kia/ *f*, hierarchy
jerárquico /he'rarkiko/ *a* hierarchical
jerez /he'res; he'reθ/ *m*, sherry
jerga /'herga/ *f*, thick frieze cloth; jargon
jergón /her'gon/ *m*, straw or hay mattress; pallet; misfit (garments); *Inf.* fat, lazy person
Jericó /heri'ko/ Jericho
jerigonza /heri'gonsa; heri'gonθa/ *f*, jargon; gibberish
jeringa /he'riŋga/ *f*, syringe
jeringar /heriŋ'gar/ *vt* to inject; syringe; *Inf.* annoy
jeringuilla /heriŋ'guiya; heriŋ'guiλa/ *f*, small syringe; mock orange
jeroglífico /hero'glifiko/ *a* hieroglyphic. *m*, hieroglyph
jersey /her'sei/ *m*, jersey, sweater
Jerusalén /herusa'len/ Jerusalem

·

jesuita /he'suita/ *m*, Jesuit
Jesús /he'sus/ *m*, Jesus. *interj* Goodness!; Bless you! (said to someone after sneezing). **¡ay J.!** Alas! *Inf.* **en un decir J.**, in a trice
jeta /'heta/ *f*, hog's snout; blubber lip; *Inf.* face, mug
jibia /'hiβia/ *f*, cuttlefish
jícama /'hikama/ *f*, *Central America* sweet turnip
jícara /'hikara/ *f*, small cup
jicote /hi'kote/ *m*, *Lat. Am.* wasp
jifa /'hifa/ *f*, meat offal
jifia /'hifia/ *f*, swordfish
jinete /hi'nete/ *m*, horseman, rider; horse soldier, cavalryman
jip /hip/ *m*, jeep
jipijapa /hipi'hapa/ *f*, very fine straw. **sombrero de j.**, panama hat
jira /'hira/ *f*, strip of cloth; picnic; tour
jirafa /hi'rafa/ *f*, giraffe
jirón /hi'ron/ *m*, rag; piece of a dress, etc.; portion of a whole
jitomate, /hito'mate/ *m*, *Mexico* tomato. See **tomate**
jiujitsu /hiu'hitsu/ *m*, jujitsu
jocosidad /hokosi'ðað/ *f*, pleasantry, jocularity; joke
jocoso /ho'koso/ *a* waggish; jocose, joyous
jocundidad /hokundi'ðað/ *f*, jocundity
jocundo /ho'kundo/ *a* jocund
jofaina /ho'faina/ *f*, washbowl
jónico /'honiko/ **(-ca)** *a* Ionic. *n* Ionian. *m*, (metrics) Ionic foot
jonrón /hon'ron/ *m*, home run
Jordán /hor'ðan/ Jordan (river)
jornada /hor'naða/ *f*, day's journey; journey, trip; *Mil.* expedition; duration of a working day; opportunity; span of life; act of a drama. **a grandes jornadas,** by forced marches, rapidly
jornal /hor'nal/ *m*, day's wages or labor
jornalear /hornale'ar/ *vi* to work by the day
jornalero /horna'lero/ **(-ra)** *n* day laborer; wage earner
joroba /ho'roβa/ *f*, hump; *Inf.* impertinence, nuisance
jorobado /horo'βaðo/ **(-da)** *a* humpbacked. *n* hunchback
jota /'hota/ *f*, name of letter J; popular Spanish dance; jot, tittle (always used negatively). **no saber j.,** to be completely ignorant
joven /'hoβen/ *a* young. *mf* young man or woman
jovenzuelo /hoβen'suelo; hoβen'θuelo/ **(-la)** *n* youngster, boy
jovialidad /hoβiali'ðað/ *f*, joviality, cheerfulness
joya /'hoia/ *f*, jewel; present; *Archit.* astragal; *Fig.* a jewel of a person
joyería /hoie'ria/ *f*, jeweler's shop or workshop
joyero /ho'icro/ *m*, jeweler; jewel box
juanete /hua'nete/ *m*, bunion; prominent cheekbone; *Naut.* topgallant sail
juanetudo /huane'tuðo/ *a* having bunions; with prominent cheekbones
jubilación /huβila'sion; huβila'θion/ *f*, retirement; pensioning off; pension
jubilado /huβi'laðo/ *a* retired
jubilar /huβi'lar/ *vt* to pension off; excuse from certain duties; *Inf.* put aside as useless (things); *vr* rejoice; retire or be pensioned off
jubileo /huβi'leo/ *m*, jubilee
júbilo /'huβilo/ *m*, rejoicing, merriment. **j. de vivir,** joie de vivre
jubiloso /huβi'loso/ *a* jubilant, happy
jubón /hu'βon/ *m*, doublet; bodice
judaico /hu'ðaiko/ *a* Judaic
judaísmo /huða'ismo/ *m*, Judaism
judas /'huðas/ *m*, Judas; traitor
judería /huðe'ria/ *f*, Jewry
judesmo /hu'ðesmo/ *m*, Judezmo (Sephardic Spanish, Romance language of Jews)
judía /hu'ðia/ *f*, Jewish woman; Jewish quarter, Jewish neighborhood; haricot bean. **judías verdes,** string beans
judicatura /huðika'tura/ *f*, judicature; judgeship; judiciary

judío /hu'ðio/ **(-ía)** *a* Jewish. *n* Jew. **j. errante,** wandering Jew
juego /'huego/ *m*, play, sport; gambling; hand (of cards); set; suite; *Mech.* play, working. **j. de café,** coffee set. **j. de los cientos,** piquet. **j. de manos,** sleight of hand, conjuring. **j. de naipes,** game of cards. **j. limpio,** fair play. **j. sencillo,** single (at tennis). **j. sucio,** foul play. **juegos florales,** floral games, poetry contest. **juegos malabares,** juggling. **Juegos Olímpicos,** the Olympics. **en j.,** in operation; at stake. **entrar en j.,** to come into play. **hacer j.,** to match. **hacer juegos malabares,** to juggle
juerga /'huerga/ *f*, *Inf.* spree, binge. **ir de j.,** *Inf.* to go on a binge
jueves /'hueβes/ *m*, Thursday. **¡No es cosa del otro j.!** *Inf.* It's no great shakes! It's nothing to write home about!
juez /hues; hueθ/ *m*, judge. **j. arbitrador,** arbitrator; referee. **j. municipal,** magistrate
jugada /hu'gaða/ *f*, play; playing; move, throw; *Fig.* bad turn
jugador /huga'ðor/ **(-ra)** *a* gambling; playing. *n* gambler; player. **j. de manos,** conjurer
jugar /hu'gar/ *vi irr* to play; frolic; take part in a game; gamble; make a move (in a game); *Mech.* work; handle (a weapon); *Com.* intervene; *vt* play (a match); bet; handle (a weapon); risk. **j. el lance,** *Fig.* to play one's cards well. **j. limpio,** to play fair; *Fig. Inf.* be straightforward. **j. sucio,** to play foul. **jugarse el todo por el todo,** to stake everything. *Pres. Ind.* **juego, juegas, juega, juegan.** *Pres. Subjunc.* **juegue, juegues, juegue, jueguen**
jugarreta /huga'rreta/ *f*, *Inf.* bad play; dirty trick
juglar /hug'lar/ *m*, entertainer; buffoon, juggler; minstrel
juglaresco /hugla'resko/ *a* pertaining to minstrels
jugo /'hugo/ *m*, sap; juice; *Fig.* essence. **j. de muñeca,** elbow grease
jugosidad /hugosi'ðað/ *f*, juiciness, succulence; *Fig.* pithiness
jugoso /hu'goso/ *a* juicy, succulent; *Fig.* pithy
juguete /hu'gete/ *m*, toy; plaything; *Fig.* puppet
juguetear /hugete'ar/ *vi* to frolic, gambol
jugueteo /huge'teo/ *m*, gamboling; play, dalliance
juguetería /hugete'ria/ *f*, toy trade; toy shop
juguetón /huge'ton/ *a* playful
juicio /'huisio; 'hui θio/ *m*, judgment; wisdom, prudence; sanity, right mind; opinion; horoscope. **j. final,** Last Judgment. **j. sano,** right mind. **asentar el j.,** to settle down, become sensible. **estar fuera de j.,** to be insane. **pedir en j.,** to sue at law
juicioso /hui'sioso; hui'θioso/ *a* judicious; prudent
julepear /hulepe'ar/ *vt*, *Lat. Am.* to get scared, be terrified
julio /'hulio/ *m*, July; *Elec.* joule
jumento /hu'mento/ *m*, ass; beast of burden
juncal /hun'kal/ *a* reedy; rushy; *Inf.* slim, lissome
juncar /hun'kar/ *m*, reedy ground
junco /'hunko/ *m*, *Bot.* rush, reed; *Naut.* junk
junio /'hunio/ *m*, June
junquillo /hun'kiyo; hun'kiλo/ *m*, jonquil; *Archit.* reed molding
junta /'hunta/ *f*, joint; assembly; council; committee; union, association; session, sitting; entirety, whole; board, management; junta. **j. de comercio,** board of trade. **j. directiva,** managerial board
juntamente /hunta'mente/ *adv* jointly; simultaneously
juntar /hun'tar/ *vt* to join, unite (*with prep a or con*); couple; assemble; amass; leave ajar (door); *vr* (*with con*) frequent company of; meet; copulate
junto /'hunto/ *a* united, together. *adv* (*with prep a*) near; *adv* together, simultaneously. **en j.,** altogether, in all
juntura /hun'tura/ *f*, joining; joint; seam; juncture
jura /'hura/ *f*, solemn oath; swearing
jurado /hu'raðo/ *m*, jury; jury
juramentar /huramen'tar/ *vt* to swear in; *vr* take an oath

juramento /hura'mento/ *m*, oath; curse, imprecation. **j. falso**, perjury, **prestar j.**, to take an oath

jurar /hu'rar/ *vt* to swear an oath; swear allegiance; *vi* curse, be profane

jurídico /hu'riðiko/ *a* juridical, legal

jurisconsulto /huriskon'sulto/ *m*, jurisconsult

jurisdicción /hurisðik'sion; hurisðik'θion/ *f*, *Law.* jurisdiction; boundary; authority

jurisprudencia /hurispru'ðensia; hurispru'ðenθia/ *f*, jurisprudence

jurista /hu'rista/ *mf* jurist

justa /'husta/ *f*, joust; tournament; contest

justar /hus'tar/ *vi* to joust

justicia /hus'tisia; hus'tiθia/ *f*, justice; equity, right; penalty, punishment; righteousness; court of justice; *Inf.* death penalty, execution. **administrar j.**, to dispense justice

justiciero /husti'siero; husti'θiero/ *a* just

justificable /hustifi'kaβle/ *a* justifiable

justificación /hustifika'sion; hustifika'θion/ *f*, justification, impartiality, fairness; convincing proof

justificar /hustifi'kar/ *vt* to justify, vindicate; adjust, regulate; prove innocent; *vr* justify oneself; prove one's innocence

justipreciar /hustipre'siar; hustipre'θiar/ *vt* to appraise, value

justiprecio /husti'presio; husti'preθio/ *m*, appraisement, valuation

justo /'husto/ *a* just; righteous, virtuous; exact, accurate; tight-fitting, close. *adv* justly; exactly; tightly

juvenil /huβe'nil/ *a* young

juventud /huβen'tuð/ *f*, youthfulness, youth; younger generation

juzgado /hus'gaðo; huθ'gaðo/ *m*, court of law; jurisdiction; judgeship

juzgar /hus'gar; huθ'gar/ *vt* to judge, pass sentence on; decide, consider

ka /ka/ *f*, name of the letter K

káiser /'kaiser/ *m*, kaiser

kan /kan/ *m*, khan

kantiano /kan'tiano/ *a* Kantian

Kenia /'kenia/ Kenya

kermese /ker'mese/ *f*, kermis, festival

kerosén /kero'sen/ *m*, kerosene

kilo /'kilo/ *prefix* meaning a thousand. *m*, *abb* kilogram

kilociclo /kilo'siklo; kilo'θiklo/ *m*, *Elec.* kilocycle

kilogramo /kilo'gramo/ *m*, kilogram (2.17 lb.)

kilolitro /kilo'litro/ *m*, kiloliter

kilometraje /kilome'trahe/ *m*, number of kilometers; mileage

kilométrico /kilo'metriko/ *a* kilometric. **billete k.**, tourist ticket

kilómetro /ki'lometro/ *m*, kilometer (about $\frac{5}{8}$ mile)

kilovatio /kilo'βatio/ *m*, *Elec.* kilowatt

kiosco /'kiosko/ *m*, kiosk

klaxon /klak'son/ *m*, *Mexico* horn

L

la /la/ *def art. f*, *sing* the (e.g. *la mesa*, the table). **la** is replaced by el *m*, *sing* before feminine nouns beginning with stressed *a* or *ha* (e.g. *el hambre*, hunger). **la** is sometimes used before names of famous women (e.g. *la Juana de Arco, la Melba* (Joan of Arc, Melba)) and is generally not translated. *pers pron acc f sing* her; it (e.g. *La veo venir*, I see her coming). *dem. pron* followed by *de*, or by *que* introducing relative clause, that of, that which, the one that, she who (e.g. *La casa está lejos de la en que escribo*, The house is far from the one in which I write). **la de** is used familiarly for Mrs. (e.g. *la de Jiménez*, Mrs. Jimenez). **la** means some, any, one, as substitution for noun already given (e.g. *Su hija lo haría si la tuviera*, Her daughter would do it if she had one)

lábaro /'laβaro/ *m*, labarum, standard

laberíntico /laβe'rintiko/ *a* labyrinthine

laberinto /laβe'rinto/ *m*, labyrinth; *Fig.* tangle, complication; *Anat.* labyrinth of the ear

labia /'laβia/ *f*, *Inf.* blarney, gab

labial /la'βial/ *a* labial

labihendido /laβien'diðo/ *a* harelipped

labio /'laβio/ *m*, lip; rim, edge. *N.* leporino, harelip. **cerrar los labios**, to close one's lips; keep silent

labor /la'βor/ *f*, work, toil; sewing; needlework; husbandry, farming; silkworm egg; *Mineral.* working; trimming; plowing, harrowing; *Central America* small farm

laborable /laβo'raβle/ *a* workable; cultivable, tillable. **día l.**, workday

laborar /laβo'rar/ *vt* to work; till; plow; construct; *vi* scheme, plot, plan; *Central America* work

laboratorio /laβora'torio/ *m*, laboratory

laborear /laβore'ar/ *vt* to work; till, cultivate; *Naut.* reeve

laboreo /laβo'reo/ *m*, tilling, cultivation; working, development (of mines, etc.)

laboriosidad /laβoriosi'ðað/ *f*, laboriousness, diligence

laborioso /laβo'rioso/ *a* industrious, diligent; laborious, tedious, hard

laborista /laβo'rista/ *a* and *mf* belonging to the Labor Party

labra /'laβra/ *f*, stonecutting; carving or working (metal, stone, or wood)

labrada /la'βraða/ *f*, fallow land ready for sowing

labradero /laβra'ðero/ *a* workable; cultivable, tillable

labrado /la'βraðo/ *a* and *past part* worked; fashioned; carved; embroidered; figured, patterned. *m*, (gen. *pl*) cultivated ground

labrador /laβra'ðor/ *m*, laborer, worker; farmer; peasant

labradora /laβra'ðora/ *f*, peasant girl; farm girl

labradoresco, labradoril /laβraðo'resko, laβraðo'ril/ *a* rustic, peasant, farming

labrandera /laβran'dera/ *f*, seamstress

labrantío /labran'βtio/ *a* tillable, cultivable. *m*, farming

labranza /la'βransa; la'βranθa/ *f*, tillage, cultivation; farm; farmland; farming; employment, work

labrar /la'βrar/ *vt* to work, do; carve; fashion, construct, make; *Agr.* cultivate, till; plow; embroider; sew; bring about, cause; *vi Fig.* impress deeply, leave a strong impression

labriego /la'βriego/ **(-ga)** *n* agricultural laborer; peasant

laca /'laka/ *f*, lac; lacquer, varnish; *Art.* lake (pigment)

lacayo /la'kaio/ *m*, groom; lackey, footman

lacear /lase'ar; laθe'ar/ *vt Sew.* to trim with bows; tie, lace; snare, trap; *Lat. Am.* lasso

laceración /lasera'sion; laθera'θion/ *f*, laceration

lacerado /lase'raðo; laθe'raðo/ *a* unhappy, unfortunate; leprous

lacerar /lase'rar; laθe'rar/ *vt* to lacerate, mangle, tear; distress, wound the feelings of

lacería /lase'ria; laθe'ria/ *f*, poverty, misery; toil, drudgery; trouble, affliction

lacero /la'sero; la'θero/ *m*, cowboy, one who uses a lasso; poacher

lacio /'lasio; 'laθio/ *a* drooping, limp; withered, faded; straight (hair)

lacónico /la'koniko/ *a* laconic; concise; Laconian

lacra /'lakra/ *f*, aftereffect, trace (of illness); vice; fault; *Lat. Am.* sore, ulcer

lacrar /la'krar/ *vt* to impair the health; infect with an illness; injure, prejudice (the interests, etc.); seal with sealing wax

lacre /'lakre/ *m*, sealing wax. *a* red

lacrimoso /lakri'moso/ *a* tearful, lachrymose

lactancia /lak'tansia; lak'tanθia/ *f*, lactation

lactar /lak'tar/ vt to suckle; feed with milk; vi take or drink milk

lácteo /'lakteo/ a lacteal; milky

ladear /laðe'ar/ vt to incline; tilt; turn aside, twist; skirt, pass close to; reach by a roundabout way, go indirectly to; vr tilt; be in favor of, incline to; be equal to

ladeo /la'ðeo/ m, tilt; sloping; turning aside

ladera /la'ðera/ f, slope, incline; hillside

ladería /laðe'ria/ f, terrace on a hillside

ladero /la'ðero/ a lateral; Argentina helper

ladilla /la'ðiya; la'ðiʎa/ f, crab louse

ladino /la'ðino/ a eloquent; versatile linguistically; wily, crafty; m, Ladino (variety of Judezmo)

lado /'laðo/ m, side; edge, margin; slope, declivity; faction, party; side, flank; face (of a coin); Fig. aspect, view; line of descent; means, way; favor, protection; pl helpers, protectors; advisers. **al l.,** near at hand. Inf. **dar de l. (a),** to cool off, fall out with. **dejar a un l. (una cosa),** to omit, pass over (a thing). **mirar de l.** or **de medio l.,** to look upon with disapproval; steal a look at

ladrar /la'ðrar/ vi to bark; Inf. threaten without hurting

ladrido /la'ðriðo/ m, bark, barking; slander, gossip

ladrillado /laðri'yaðo; laðri'ʎaðo/ m, brick floor or pavement

ladrillar /laðri'yar; laðri'ʎar/ vt to floor or pave with bricks. m, brickyard; brickkiln

ladrillo /la'ðriyo; la'ðriʎo/ m, brick

ladrón /la'ðron/ **(-ona)** a robbing, thieving. n thief, robber; burglar. m. **l. de corazones,** ladykiller

ladronera /laðro'nera/ f, thieves' den; thieving, pilfering; strongbox

lagar /la'gar/ m, wine or olive press

lagarta /la'garta/ f, female lizard; Inf. she-serpent, cunning female

lagartera /lagar'tera/ f, lizard hole

lagartija /lagar'tiha/ f, wall lizard, small lizard

lagarto /la'garto/ m, lizard; Inf. sly, artful person, fox; Inf. insignia of Spanish Military Order of Santiago

lago /'lago/ m, lake

lagotear /lagote'ar/ vi Inf. to wheedle, play up to

lagotería /lagote'ria/ f, wheedling, coaxing, flattery

lágrima /'lagrima/ f, tear; drop (of liquid); exudation, oozing (from trees)

lagrimal /lagri'mal/ a lachrymal

lagrimear /lagrime'ar/ vi to shed tears

lagrimeo /lagri'meo/ m, weeping, crying; watering of the eyes

lagrimoso /lagri'moso/ a tearful; watery (of eyes); sad, tragic

laguna /la'guna/ f, small lake, lagoon; lacuna; gap, hiatus

lagunoso /lagu'noso/ a boggy, marshy

laicismo /lai'sismo; lai'θismo/ m, secularism, laity

laico /'laiko/ a lay, secular

laja /'laha/ f, Lat. Am. flagstone, slab

lama /'lama/ f, ooze, slime. m, lama, Buddhist priest

lambioche /lam'βiotʃe/ a, Mexico cringing, fawning

lameculos /lame'kulos/ mf Inf. toady

lamedura /lame'ðura/ f, licking; lapping

lamentable /lamen'taβle/ a lamentable

lamentación /lamenta'sion; lamenta'θion/ f, lamentation; lament

lamentador /lamenta'ðor/ **(-ra)** a lamenting, wailing. n wailer, mourner

lamentar /lamen'tar/ vt to mourn, lament; vr to bemoan, bewail

lamento /la'mento/ m, lament

lamentoso /lamen'toso/ a lamenting, afflicted; lamentable

lamer /la'mer/ vt to lick; pass the tongue over; touch lightly; lap

lámina /'lamina/ f, sheet (of metal); lamina; engraving; illustration, picture; engraving plate

laminación /lamina'sion; lamina'θion/ f, lamination, rolling (of metals)

laminado /lami'naðo/ a laminate; rolled (metals). m, rolling (of metals)

laminador /lamina'ðor/ m, rolling mill (for metals)

laminar /lami'nar/ a laminate; laminated. vt to roll (metals); laminate; lick

lampa /'lampa/ f, Chile, Peru hoe

lámpara /'lampara/ f, lamp; radiance, light, luminous body; grease spot. **l. de los mineros** or **l. de seguridad,** safety lamp. **l. de soldar,** blowpipe. **l. termiónica,** Radio. thermionic valve. **atizar la l.,** to trim the lamp; Inf. refill drinking glasses

lamparería /lampare'ria/ f, lamp factory; lamp shop

lamparero /lampa'rero/ **(-ra),** n **lamparista** mf lamplighter; lamp maker or seller

lamparilla /lampa'riya; lampa'riʎa/ f, night-light; Bot. aspen; small lamp

lamparón /lampa'ron/ m, scrofula; king's evil; tumor (disease of horses)

lampazo /lam'paso; lam'paθo/ m, Lat. Am. (floor) mop

lampiño /lam'piɲo/ a beardless, clean-shaven; smooth-faced; Inf. nonhirsute

lampista /lam'pista/ mf See **lamparero**

lamprea /lam'prea/ f, lamprey

lana /'lana/ f, wool; fleece; woolen garments or cloth; woolen trade (gen. pl)

lanar /la'nar/ a wool; wool-bearing. **ganado l.,** sheep

lance /'lanse; 'lanθe/ m, throw, cast; casting a fishing line; catch of fish; crisis, difficult moment; Lit. episode; quarrel; move (in a game). Fig. **l. apretado,** difficult position, tight corner. **l. de fortuna,** chance, fate. **l. de honor,** affair of honor; duel

lancear /lanse'ar; lanθe'ar/ vt to wound with a lance; lance

lancero /lan'sero; lan'θero/ m, Mil. lancer; pl lancers (dance and music)

lanceta /lan'seta; lan'θeta/ f, lancet; Lat. Am. goad

lancha /'lantʃa/ f, Naut. launch; lighter; ship's boat; small boat; flagstone. **l. bombardera** or **l. cañonera,** gunboat. **l. de salvamento,** ship's lifeboat. **l. escampavía,** patrol boat

lancinar /lansi'nar; lanθi'nar/ vt Med. to lance

landa /'landa/ f, lande

landó /lan'do/ m, landau

lanero /la'nero/ a woolen. m, wool merchant; wool warehouse

langosta /laŋ'gosta/ f, locust; lobster. **l. migratoria,** locust

langostín /laŋgos'tin/ m, crayfish

languidecer /laŋgwiðe'ser; laŋgwiðe'θer/ vi irr to languish, pine. See **conocer**

languidez /laŋgwi'ðes; laŋgwi'ðeθ/ f, lassitude, inertia; languor

lánguido /'laŋgwiðo/ a listless, weak, languid; half-hearted; languishing, languorous

lanolina /lano'lina/ f, lanolin

lanosidad /lanosi'ðað/ f, woolliness; down (on leaves, etc.)

lanoso, lanudo /la'noso, la'nuðo/ a woolly

lanza /'lansa; 'lanθa/ f, lance, spear; lancer; nozzle (of a hosepipe). **correr lanzas,** to joust (in a tournament). **estar con la l. en ristre,** to have the lance in rest; be prepared or ready. Inf. **ser una l.,** to be very clever

lanzabombas /lansa'βombas; lanθa'βombas/ m, (Aer. Nav.) bomb release

lanzada /lan'saða; lan'θaða/ f, lance or spear thrust

lanzadera /lansa'ðera; lanθa'ðera/ f, weaver's shuttle; sewing machine shuttle. Inf. **parecer una l.,** to be constantly on the go

lanzador /lansa'ðor; lanθa'ðor/ **(-ra)** m, batsman. n thrower, caster, tosser

lanzallamas /lansa'yamas; lanθa'ʎamas/ m, flamethrower

lanzamiento /lansa'miento; lanθa'miento/ m, throwing; cast, throw; Law. dispossession; Naut. launching

lanzaminas /lansa'minas; lanθa'minas/ m, minelayer

lanzar /lan'sar; lan'θar/ vt to throw, cast, hurl; Naut. launch; vomit; Law. dispossess; Agr. take root; vr hurl oneself, rush; take (to), embark (upon)

lanzatorpedos /lansator'peðos; lanθator'peðos/ (tubo) *m*, torpedo tube

lañar /la'ɲar/ *vt* to clamp; clean fish (for salting)

lapa /'lapa/ *f*, barnacle, limpet; *Mexico* scrounger

lapicera /lapi'sera; lapi'θera/ *f*, *Argentina* ballpoint (pen)

lapicero /lapi'sero; lapi'θero/ *m*, pencil holder, pencil case; mechanical pencil

lápida /'lapiða/ *f*, memorial tablet; gravestone

lapidar /lapi'ðar/ *vt* to stone, lapidate; throw stones at

lapidario /lapi'ðario/ *a* lapidary

lapislázuli /lapis'lasuli; lapis'laθuli/ *m*, lapis lazuli

lápiz /'lapis; 'lapiθ/ *m*, graphite; pencil; crayon. **l. para los labios,** lipstick

lapizar /lapi'sar; lapi'θar/ *m*, graphite mine. *vt* to pencil

lapón /la'pon/ (**-ona**) *a* Lappish. *n* Laplander. *m*, Sami (language)

lapso /'lapso/ *m*, lapse, period, passage; slip, error, failure

laquear /lake'ar/ *vt* to lacquer, paint

lardear /larðe'ar/ *vt Cul.* to baste

lardo /'larðo/ *m*, lard; animal fat

lardoso /lar'ðoso/ *a* greasy; fat; oily

larga /'larga/ *f*, longest billiard cue; delay (gen. *pl*). **a la l.,** in the long run

largamente /larga'mente/ *adv* fully, at length; generously; widely, extensively; comfortably

largar /lar'gar/ *vt* to slacken, loosen; *Naut.* unfurl; set at liberty; *Fig. Inf.* let fly (oaths, etc.); administer (blows, etc.); *vr Inf.* quit, leave (in a hurry or secretly); *Naut.* set sail

largo /'largo/ *a* long; generous, liberal; abundant, plentiful; protracted; prolonged; expeditious; *pl* many long (e.g. *por largos años*, for many long years). *m*, *Mus.* largo; length. *Inf.* **¡L. de aquí!** Get out! **a la larga,** in length; eventually, finally; slowly; with many digressions. **a lo l.,** lengthwise; along the length (of); in the distance, far off; along, the length (of). *Fig.* **ponerse de l.,** to make one's debut in society; come of age

largor /lar'gor/ *m*, length, **largura** *f*, length

largucho, -a /lar'gutʃo/ *a*, *Lat. Am.* lanky

largueza /lar'gesa; lar'geθa/ *f*, length; generosity, munificence

largura /lar'gura/ *f*, length

laringe /la'rinhe/ *f*, larynx

laríngeo /la'rinheo/ *a* laryngeal

laringitis /larin'hitis/ *f*, laryngitis

larva /'larβa/ *f*, larva; worm, grub; specter, phantom

las /las/ *def art. f pl*, of **la** the. *pers pron acc f pl*, of **la**, them

lascivia /las'siβia; las'θiβia/ *f*, lasciviousness

lascivo /las'siβo; las'θiβo/ *a* lascivious, lewd; wanton

lasitud /lasi'tuð/ *f*, lassitude, weariness, exhaustion

laso /'laso/ *a* weary, exhausted; weak; untwisted (of silk, etc.)

lástima /'lastima/ *f*, compassion, pity; pitiful sight; complaint, lamentation. **dar l.,** to cause pity. **Es l.,** It's a pity. **tener l. (a** *or* **de)** to be sorry for (persons)

lastimador /lastima'ðor/ *a* harmful, injurious; painful

lastimadura /lastima'ðura/ *f*, *Lat. Am.* injury, wound

lastimar /lasti'mar/ *vt* to hurt, harm, injure; pity; *Fig.* wound, distress; *vr* (*with de*) be sorry for or about; complain, lament

lastimero /lasti'mero/ *a* pitiful; mournful; injurious, harmful

lastimoso /lasti'moso/ *a* pitiful, heartbreaking; mournful

lastrar /las'trar/ *vt* to ballast

lastre /'lastre/ *m*, ballast; good sense, prudence

lata /'lata/ *f*, can; tin plate; can of food. **en l.,** canned, tinned (of food). *Inf.* **Es una l.,** It's a bore, It's an awful nuisance

latamente /lata'mente/ *adv* extensively, at length; broadly

latente /la'tente/ *a* latent

lateral /late'ral/ *a* lateral

látex /'lateks/ *m*, latex

latido /la'tiðo/ *m*, yelp, bark; beat; throb; palpitation

latifundios /lati'fundios/ *m pl*, latifundia (large agricultural estates)

latigazo /lati'gaso; lati'gaθo/ *m*, lash; crack of a whip; sudden blow of fate; *Inf.* draft (of wine, etc.); harsh scolding; *Naut.* jerk or flapping (of sails)

látigo /'latigo/ *m*, whip, lash; cinch, girth of a saddle

latín /la'tin/ *m*, Latin. **bajo l.,** low Latin. *Inf.* **saber l.,** to know the score; be smart

latinajo /lati'naho/ *m*, *Inf.* bad Latin

latinismo /lati'nismo/ *m*, Latinism

latinista /lati'nista/ *mf* Latinist

latinizar /latini'sar; latini'θar/ *vt* to latinize; *vi Inf.* use Latin phrases

latino /la'tino/ (**-na**) *a* and *n* Latin; Latin-American

latinoamericano /latinoameri'kano/ (**-na**) *a* and *n* Latin-American

latir /la'tir/ *vi* to yelp, howl; bark; throb, palpitate, beat **me late que...** *Mexico*, I have a hunch that...

latitud /lati'tuð/ *f*, latitude; area, extent; breadth

latitudinario /lati,tuði'nario/ *a* latitudinarian

lato /'lato/ *a* extensive; large; broad (of word meanings)

latón /la'ton/ *m*, brass

latonería /latone'ria/ *f*, brassworks; brass shop

latoso /la'toso/ *a* boring, troublesome, annoying

latrocinio /latro'sinio; latro'θinio/ *m*, larceny

latvio /'latβio/ (**-ia**) *a* and *n* Latvian

laúd /la'uð/ *m*, lute

laudable /lau'ðaβle/ *a* praiseworthy, laudable

laudatorio /lauða'torio/ *a* laudatory

laurear /laure'ar/ *vt* to crown with laurel; honor, reward

laurel /lau'rel/ *m*, bay tree. **l. cerezo,** laurel. **l. rosa,** rosebay, oleander

láureo /'laureo/ *a* laurel

lauréola /lau'reola/ *f*, laurel wreath

lauro /'lauro/ *m*, bay tree; glory, triumph

lava /'laβa/ *f*, lava

lavable /la'βaβle/ *a* washable

lavabo /la'βaβo/ *m*, sink, washbasin; cloakroom, lavatory

lavada /la'βaða/ *f*, load of wash, load

lavadedos /laβa'ðeðos/ *m*, fingerbowl

lavadero /laβa'ðero/ *m*, washing place; laundry

lavado /la'βaðo/ *m*, washing; cleaning; wash. **l. al seco,** dry cleaning

lavadura /laβa'ðura/ *f*, washing

lavamanos /laβa'manos/ *m*, sink; lavatory

lavamiento /laβa'miento/ *m*, washing, cleansing, ablution

lavanda /la'βanda/ *f*, lavender

lavandera /laβan'dera/ *f*, laundrywoman; washerwoman

lavandería /laβande'ria/ *f*, laundry

lavandero /laβan'dero/ *m*, laundry; laundryman

lavaplatos /laβa'platos/ *m*, dishwasher; *Chile, Mexico* (kitchen) sink

lavar /la'βar/ *vt* to wash; *Fig.* wipe out, purify; paint in watercolors. **l. al seco,** to dry-clean

lavativa /laβa'tiβa/ *f*, enema; syringe, clyster; *Inf.* nuisance, bore

lavatorio /laβa'torio/ *m*, washing, lavation; *Eccl.* lavabo; lavatory, washing place; *Eccl.* maundy

lavazas /la'βasas; la'βaθas/ *f pl*, dirty soapy water

laxante /lak'sante/ *a* and *m*, laxative

laxar /lak'sar/ *vt* to loosen, relax; soften

laxitud /laksi'tuð/ *f*, laxity

laxo /'lakso/ *a* lax; slack

laya /'laia/ *f*, *Agr.* spade; kind, sort, class

layar /la'iar/ *vt Agr.* to fork

lazar /la'sar; la'θar/ *vt* to lasso

lazareto /lasa'reto; laθa'reto/ *m*, leper hospital; quarantine hospital

lazarillo /lasa'riyo; laθa'riʎo/ *m*, boy who guides a blind person

lázaro /'lasaro; 'laθaro/ *m*, beggar. **Lázaro,** Lazarus

lazo /'laso; 'laθo/ *m*, bow; knot of ribbons; tie; ornamental tree; figure (in dancing); lasso; rope, bond;

lace (of a shoe); *Fig.* trap, snare; bond, obligation; slipknot. **l. corredizo,** running knot. *Fig. Inf.* **armar l.,** to set a trap. *Inf.* **caer en el l.,** to fall into the trap, be deceived

le /le/ *pers pron dat m,* or *f, 3rd pers sing* to him, to her, to it, to you (e.g. *María le dio el perro,* Mary gave him (her, you) the dog). Clarity may require the addition of **a él, a ella, a usted** (e.g. *Le dio el perro a ella,* etc.). *pers pron acc m, 3rd pers sing* him (e.g. *Le mandé a casa,* I sent him home)

leal /le'al/ *a* loyal; faithful (animals)

lealtad /leal'taδ/ *f,* loyalty; faithfulness; sincerity, truth

lebrel /le'βrel/ *m,* greyhound

lección /lek'sion; lek'θion/ *f,* reading; lesson; oral test; warning, example. **l. práctica,** object lesson. **dar l.,** to give a lesson. **tomar la l.,** to hear a lesson

leccionista /leksio'nista; lekθio'nista/ *mf* private teacher, coach, tutor

lechas /'letʃas/ *f pl,* soft roe; milt

leche /'letʃe/ *f,* milk; milky fluid of some plants and seeds; *Lat. Am.* good luck. *Inf.* **estar con la l. en los labios,** to be young and inexperienced

lechera /le'tʃera/ *f,* milkmaid; milk can or jug; *Lat. Am.* cow

lechería /letʃe'ria/ *f,* dairy; dairy shop; *Lat. Am.* meanness

lechero /le'tʃero/ **(-ra)** *a* dairy, milk; milky; milch, milk-giving. *n* milk seller. **industria lechera,** dairy farming

lecho /'letʃo/ *m,* bed; couch; animal's bed, litter; riverbed; bottom of the sea; layer; *Geol.* stratum

lechón /le'tʃon/ *m,* suckling pig; hog; *Inf.* slovenly man

lechosa /le'tʃosa/ *f, Dominican Republic, Venezuela,* papaya

lechoso /le'tʃoso/ *a* milky

lechudo, -a /le'tʃuδo/ *a, Lat. Am.* lucky

lechuga /le'tʃuga/ *f,* lettuce; frill, flounce. *Inf.* **como una l.,** as fresh as a daisy

lechuguero /letʃu'gero/ **(-ra)** *n* lettuce seller

lechuguilla /letʃu'giya; letʃu'giλa/ *f,* ruff; ruche

lechuguina /letʃu'gina/ *f, Inf.* affected, overdressed young woman

lechuguino /letʃu'gino/ *m,* lettuce plant; *Inf.* young blood, gallant; *Inf.* foppish young man

lechuza /le'tʃusa; le'tʃuθa/ *f,* barn owl

lector /lek'tor/ **(-ra)** *n* reader; lecturer

lectura /lek'tura/ *f,* reading; lecture; culture, knowledge

ledo /'leδo/ *a* happy, content

leer /le'er/ *vt irr* to read; explain, interpret; teach; take part in an oral test. See **creer**

lega /'lega/ *f, Eccl.* lay sister

legación /lega'sion; lega'θion/ *f, Eccl.* legateship; legation

legado /le'gaδo/ *m,* legacy; legate

legajo /le'gaho/ *m,* bundle, docket; file

legal /le'gal/ *a* legal; legitimate; upright, trustworthy

legalidad /legali'δaδ/ *f,* legality

legalización /legalisa'sion; legaliθa'θion/ *f,* legalization

legalizar /legali'sar; legali'θar/ *vt* to legalize

legamente /lega'mente/ *adv* ignorantly, stupidly

légamo /'legamo/ *m,* mud, slime

legamoso /lega'moso/ *a* slimy

legañoso /lega'ɲoso/ *a* bleary-eyed

legar /le'gar/ *vt* to bequeath; send as a legate

legatario /lega'tario/ **(-ia)** *n* legatee, one to whom a legacy is bequeathed

legendario /lehen'dario/ *a* legendary

legibilidad /lehiβili'δaδ/ *f,* legibility

legible /le'hiβle/ *a* legible

legión /le'hion/ *f,* legion

legionario /lehio'nario/ *a* and *m,* legionary

legislación /lehisla'sion; lehisla'θion/ *f,* legislation

legislador /lehisla'δor/ **(-ra)** *a* legislative. *n* legislator

legislar /lehis'lar/ *vi* to legislate

legislativo /lehisla'tiβo/ *a* legislative

legislatura /lehisla'tura/ *f,* legislature

legista /le'hista/ *mf* jurist; student of law

legítima /le'hitima/ *f,* portion of a married man's estate that cannot be willed away from his wife and children

legitimación /lehitima'sion; lehitima'θion/ *f,* legitimation

legitimar /lehiti'mar/ *vt* to legitimize

legitimidad /lehitimi'δaδ/ *f,* legitimacy

legítimo /le'hitimo/ *a* legitimate; real, true

lego /'lego/ *a* lay, secular. *m,* layman

legua /'legua/ *f,* league (approximately 5.573 meters). **a la l., de cien leguas, desde media l.,** from afar

legumbre /le'gumbre/ *f,* pulse; vegetable

leída /le'iδa/ *f, Lat. Am.* reading. **de una leída** in one reading, at one go

leído /le'iδo/ *a* well-read

leila /'leila/ *f,* nocturnal Moorish merrymaking or dance

lejanía /leha'nia/ *f,* distance

lejano /le'hano/ *a* distant, remote, far off

lejía /le'hia/ *f,* lye; bleaching solution; *Inf.* dressing-down, scolding

lejos /'lehos/ *adv* far off, far, distant. *m,* perspective, view from afar; *Art.* background. **a lo l.,** far off, in the distance. **de** or **desde l.,** from afar, from a distance

lelo /'lelo/ *a* stupid; fatuous, inane

lema /'lema/ *m,* chapter heading; argument, summary; motto; theme, subject

lémur /'lemur/ *m,* lemur

lencería /lense'ria; lenθe'ria/ *f,* linen goods; linen merchant's shop; linen closet

lencero /len'sero; len'θero/ *m,* linen merchant

lene /'lene/ *a* smooth, soft; kind, sweet, gentle; lightweight

lengua /'lengua/ *f, Anat.* tongue; mother tongue, language; clapper of a bell; information. *mf* spokes. **l. de escorpión** or **mala l.,** scandalmonger, backbiter. **l. de fuego,** *Eccl.* tongue of fire, flame. **l. del agua,** waterline, tidemark. **l. de oc,** langue d'oc. **l. de oil,** langue d'oïl. **l. de tierra,** neck of land, promontory. **l. viva,** modern language. *Inf.* **andar en lenguas,** to be rumored, be famous. *Inf.* **hacerse lenguas de,** to praise to the skies. *Inf.* **irse (a uno) la l.,** to be indiscreet, talk too much. **poner l.** or **lenguas en,** to gossip about. *Inf.* **tener mucha l.,** to be very talkative. **tomar l.** or **lenguas,** to find out about, inform oneself on

lenguado /leŋ'guaδo/ *m, Ichth.* sole

lenguaje /leŋ'guahe/ *m,* language; style; speech, idiom. **l. vulgar,** common speech

lengüeta /leŋ'gueta/ *f, dim* little tongue; *Mus.* tongue (of wind instruments); barb (of an arrow); needle (of a balance)

lengüeterías /leŋguete'rias/ *Lat. Am.* gossip

lenidad /leni'δaδ/ *f,* lenience, indulgence, mercy

lenitivo /leni'tiβo/ *a* lenitive; soothing. *m, Med.* lenitive; *Fig.* balm (of sorrow, etc.)

lente /'lente/ *m,* lens; *pl* eyeglasses. **l. de aumento,** magnifying glass. **l. de contacto,** contact lens

lenteja /len'teha/ *f,* lentil; lentil plant

lentejuela /lente'huela/ *f,* sequin

lentitud /lenti'tuδ/ *f,* lentitude; slowness, deliberation

lento /'lento/ *a* slow, deliberate; sluggish, heavy; *Med.* glutinous, adhesive

leña /'leɲa/ *f,* firewood; *Inf.* beating, birching. *Fig.* **echar l. al fuego,** to add fuel to the flame. *Fig.* **llevar l. al monte,** to carry coals to Newcastle

leñador /leɲa'δor/ **(-ra)** *n* woodcutter; firewood dealer

leñera /le'ɲera/ *f,* woodpile; woodshed

leño /'leɲo/ *m,* wooden log; wood, timber; *Poet.* ship; *Inf.* blockhead

leñoso /le'ɲoso/ *a* woody, ligneous

león /le'on/ *m,* lion. *Astron.* Leo; valiant man; *Lat. Am.* puma. **l. marino,** sea lion

leona /le'ona/ *f,* lioness; *Chile* confusion, mixup

leonera /leo'nera/ *f,* lion cage; lion's den; *Inf.* gambling den; *Inf.* lumber room; *Mexico* whore house

leonero /leo'nero/ **(-ra)** n lionkeeper; Inf. keeper of a gambling house

leopardo /leo'parðo/ m, leopard

leperada /lepe'raða/ f, Central America, Mexico coarse remark

lepra /'lepra/ f, leprosy

leproso /le'proso/ a leprous

lerdo /'lerðo/ a slow, lumbering (gen. horses); stupid, slow-witted, dull

les /les/ pers pron dat 3rd pers pl mf, to them (e.g. Les dimos las flores, We gave them flowers. Les hablé del asunto, I spoke to them about the matter)

lesbio /'lesβio/ **(-ia)** a and n lesbian

lesión /le'sion/ f, lesion, wound; Fig. injury

lesionar /lesio'nar/ vt to wound; Fig. injure

lesna /'lesna/ f, awl

leso /'leso/ a wounded, hurt; offensive, injurious; Fig. unbalanced, perturbed (of the mind); Lat. Am. dumb, stupid. **crimen de lesa majestad,** crime of lèse-majesté

letal /le'tal/ a lethal; deadly

letanía /leta'nia/ f, Eccl. litany

letargia /le'tarhia/ f, Med. lethargy

letárgico /le'tarhiko/ a lethargic

letargo /le'targo/ m, lethargy; indifference, apathy

letra /'letra/ f, letter (of alphabet); Print. type; penmanship, hand; Fig. letter, literal meaning; words (of a song); inscription; Com. bill, draft; cunning, shrewdness; pl learning, knowledge. **l. abierta,** Com. open credit. **l. de cambio,** Com. bill of exchange. **l. gótica,** Gothic characters. **l. itálica,** italics. **l. mayúscula,** capital letter. **l. paladial,** palatal. **facultad de letras,** faculty of arts. **La l. con sangre entra,** Learning is acquired with pain. **primeras letras,** early education, first letters

letrado /le'traðo/ a learned, educated; Inf. presumptuous; pedantic. m, lawyer

letrero /le'trero/ m, label; inscription; poster, bill; sign, indicator. **l. luminoso,** illuminated sign

letrilla /le'triya; le'triʎa/ f, short poem, often set to music

letrina /le'trina/ f, latrine

leva /'leβa/ f, Naut. weighing anchor; Mil. levy, forced enrollment; tappet; Mech. lever; Mech. cam; Inf. irse a l. y a monte, to flee, beat it, quit

levadizo /leβa'ðiso; leβa'ðiθo/ a able to be raised or lowered (bridges). **puente l.,** drawbridge

levadura /leβa'ðura/ f, leaven, yeast; rising (of bread)

levantada /leβan'taða/ f, act of rising from bed

levantamiento /leβanta'miento/ m, raising, lifting; rebellion, revolt; ennoblement, elevation; settlement of accounts

levantar /leβan'tar/ vt to raise, lift; pick up; build, construct; cancel; remove; encourage, rouse; recruit, enlist; cut (cards); leave, abandon; survey; disturb (game); produce, raise (a swelling); found, institute; increase (prices); raise (the voice); Fig. ennoble, elevate; cause, occasion; libel, accuse falsely; vr rise; get up; stand up; stand out, be prominent; rebel; leave one's bed after an illness. **l. bandera,** to rebel. **l. el campo,** to break camp. **levantarse del izquierdo,** Inf. to get out of bed on the wrong side

levante /le'βante/ m, east; Levant; east wind

levar /le'βar/ vt Naut. to weigh anchor; vr set sail

leve /'leβe/ a light (in weight); unimportant, trifling

levedad /leβe'ðað/ f, lightness (in weight); unimportance, levity, flippancy

leviatán /leβia'tan/ m, leviathan

levita /le'βita/ m, Levite; deacon. f, frock coat

levitación /leβita'sion; leβita'θion/ f, levitation

levítico /le'βitiko/ a Levitical. m, **Levítico,** Leviticus

levitón /leβi'ton/ m, frock coat

léxico /'leksiko/ m, lexicon

lexicografía /leksikogra'fia/ f, lexicography

lexicógrafo /leksi'kografo/ m, lexicographer

lexicólogo /leksi'kologo/ m, lexicologist

ley /lei/ f, law; precept; regulation, rule; doctrine; loyalty, faithfulness; affection, love; legal standard (weights, measures, quality); ratio of gold or silver in coins, jewelry; statute, ordinance; pl the Law. **l. de préstamo y arriendo,** Lend-Lease Act. **ley suntuaria,** sumptuary law. Inf. **a la l.,** with care and decorum. **a l. de caballero,** on the word of a gentleman. **de buena l.,** a excellent; adv genuinely; in good faith. **de mala l.,** a disreputable, base; adv in bad faith

leyenda /le'ienda/ f, legend; inscription; story, tale

leyente /le'iente/ a reading. mf reader

lezna /'lesna; 'leθna/ f, awl

lía /'lia/ f, plaited esparto rope; pl lees, dregs

liar /li'ar/ vt to fasten or tie up; wrap up, parcel; roll (a cigarette); Inf. entangle, embroil; vr take a lover, enter on a liaison. Inf. **liarlas,** to quit, sneak off; Inf. kick the bucket, die

libación /liβa'sion; liβa'θion/ f, libation

Líbano, el /'liβano, el/ Lebanon

libar /li'βar/ vt to suck; perform a libation; sip, taste; sacrifice

libelista /liβe'lista/ mf libeler

libelo /li'βelo/ m, libel; Law. petition

libélula /li'βelula/ f, dragonfly

liberación /liβera'sion; liβera'θion/ f, liberation, freeing; receipt, quittance; Law. reconveyance (of mortgages)

liberador /liβera'ðor/ **(-ra)** a liberating, freeing. n liberator

liberal /liβe'ral/ a generous, openhanded; liberal, tolerant; learned (of professions). a and mf Polit. liberal

liberalidad /liβerali'ðað/ f, generosity, magnanimity

liberalismo /liβera'lismo/ m, liberalism

liberalizar /liβerali'sar; liβerali'θar/ vt to liberalize, make liberal

liberar /liβe'rar/ vt to liberate

libérrimo /li'βerrimo/ a sup extremely free, most free

libertad /liβer'tað/ f, liberty, freedom; independence; privilege, right (gen. pl); exemption; licentiousness; forwardness, familiarity; naturalness, ease of manner; facility, capacity; immunity. **l. caucional,** freedom on bail, release on bail. **l. de cultos,** freedom of worship; religious toleration. **l. vigilada,** Law. probation. **poner en l.,** to set at liberty; (with de) Fig. free from

libertador /liβerta'ðor/ **(-ra)** a liberating, freeing. n liberator, deliverer

libertar /liβer'tar/ vt to liberate, free; save, deliver; exempt

libertario /liβer'tario/ **(-ia)** a anarchistic. n anarchist

libertinaje /liβerti'nahe/ m, libertinage, licentiousness

libertino /liβer'tino/ **(-na)** a debauched, licentious. m, libertine. n child of a freed slave

liberto /li'βerto/ **(-ta)** n freed slave, freedman

Libia /'liβia/ Libya

libídine /li'βiðine/ f, lust

libidinoso /liβiði'noso/ a libidinous, lustful

libio /'liβio/ **(-ia)** a and n Libyan

libra /'liβra/ f, pound (measure, coinage); Astron. Libra. **l. esterlina,** pound sterling. **l. medicinal,** pound troy

libración /liβra'sion; liβra'θion/ f, oscillation; Astron. libration

librador /liβra'ðor/ **(-ra)** a freeing, liberating. n deliverer, liberator. m, Com. drawer (of bill of exchange, etc.)

libramiento /liβra'miento/ m, liberation, deliverance; Com. delivery; order of payment

libranza /li'βransa; li'βranθa/ f, Com. draft. **l. de correos, l. postal** Lat. Am. (postal) money order

librar /li'βrar/ vt to liberate, free; protect (from misfortune); Com. draw (a draft); Com. deliver; place confidence in; issue, enact; vi bring forth children; vr (with de) escape from; get rid of

libre /'liβre/ a free; at liberty, disengaged; unhampered, untrammeled; independent; bold, brazen; dissolute, vicious; exempt; vacant, unoccupied; unmarried; clear, free; mutinous, rebellious; isolated, remote; innocent; unharmed; Mexico, Venezuela taxi. **l. cambio,** free trade

librea /li'βrea/ f, livery

librecambio /liβre'kambio/ m, tree trade

librecambista /liβrekam'βista/ a free trade. mf free trader
librepensador /liβrepensa'ðor/ (-ra) a freethinking. n freethinker
librepensamiento /liβrepensa'miento/ m, free thought
librera /li'βrera/ f, Lat. Am. bookcase
librería /liβre'ria/ f, bookshop; book trade, bookselling; bookcase
librero /li'βrero/ m, bookseller; Lat. Am. bookcase. **l. anticuario,** antiquarian bookseller; rare-book dealer
libreta /li'βreta/ f, Cul. 1-lb. loaf; notebook; passbook, bankbook
libretista /liβre'tista/ mf librettist
libreto /li'βreto/ m, libretto
librillo /li'βriyo; li'βriʎo/ m, dim small book; book of cigarette papers; tub, pail; Zool. omasum
libro /'liβro/ m, book; Mus. libretto; Zool. omasum. **l. copiador,** Com. letter book. **l. de actas,** minute book. **l. de caja,** Com. cash book. **l. de cheques,** checkbook. **l. de facturas,** Com. invoice book. **l. de reclamaciones,** complaint book. **l. de texto,** textbook. **l. diario,** Com. daybook. **l. mayor,** ledger. **l. talonario,** receipt book. Fig. Inf. **hacer l. nuevo,** to turn over a new leaf; introduce innovations
licencia /li'sensia; li'θenθia/ f, permission, license; licentiousness; boldness, insolence; Educ. bachelor's degree, licentiate. **l. absoluta,** Mil. discharge. **l. de manejar** Lat. Am. driver's license
licenciado /lisen'siaðo; liθen'θiaðo/ (-da) a pedantic; free, exempt; licensed. n Educ. bachelor; licentiate. m, discharged soldier
licenciar /lisen'siar; liθen'θiar/ vt to allow, permit; license; dismiss, discharge; confer degree of bachelor or licentiate; Mil. discharge; vr become licentious; receive bachelor's degree or licentiate
licenciatura /lisensia'tura; liθenθia'tura/ f, degree of licentiate or bachelor; graduation as such; licentiate course of study
licencioso /lisen'sioso; liθen'θioso/ a licentious, dissolute
liceo /li'seo; li'θeo/ m, lyceum; Lat. Am. secondary school, high school
licitación /lisita'sion; liθita'θion/ f, bidding (at auction)
licitador /lisita'ðor; liθita'ðor/ m, bidder (at auction); Lat. Am. auctioneer
licitar /lisi'tar; liθi'tar/ vt to bid for (at auction)
lícito /'lisito; 'liθito/ a permissible, lawful
licor /li'kor/ m, liquor, alcoholic drink; liquid
licorera /liko'rera/ f, liqueur set; decanter
licuadora /likua'ðora/ f, blender
licuar /li'kuar/ vt to liquefy
lid /liδ/ f, combat, fight; dispute, controversy. **en buena l.,** in fair fight; by fair means
líder /'liðer/ m, leader; chief
lidia /'liðia/ f, fighting; bullfight
lidiador /liðia'ðor/ (-ra) n combatant, fighter
lidiar /li'ðiar/ vi to fight; Fig. struggle; (with contra or con) oppose, fight against; vt fight (a bull). **¡Cuánto tienen que l. con...!** Fig. What a struggle they have with...!
liebre /'lieβre/ f, hare
liendre /'liendre/ f, nit
lienza /liensa; 'lienθa/ f, narrow strip (of cloth)
lienzo /'lienso; 'lienθo/ m, linen; cotton; cambric; hemp cloth; Art. canvas
liga /'liga/ f, garter; bandage; birdlime; mixture, blend; Metall. alloy; alliance, coalition; league (football, etc.)
ligación /liga'sion; liga'θion/ f, tying; binding; union
ligado /li'gaðo/ m, Mus. legato; Mus. tie
ligadura /liga'ðura/ f, bond, tie; binding, fastening; Fig. shackle, link; (Surg. Mus.) ligature; Naut. lashing
ligamento /liga'mento/ m, tie, bond; mixture; Anat. ligament
ligar /li'gar/ vt to tie, bind; Metall. alloy; join, connect; render impotent by sorcery; Mus. slur (notes); vr ally, join together; Fig. bind oneself. **l. cabos,** to put two and two together

ligazón /liga'son; liga'θon/ f, fastening; union; bond
ligereza /lihe'resa; lihe're θa/ f, lightness (of weight); swiftness, nimbleness, fickleness; tactless remark, indiscretion
ligero /li'hero/ a light (in weight); swift, nimble; light (sleep); unimportant, insignificant; easily digested (food); thin (fabrics, etc.); fickle, changeable. **l. de cascos,** frivolous, gay. **a la ligera,** lightly; quickly; without fuss. **de l.,** impetuously, thoughtlessly; easily, with ease
lignito /lig'nito/ m, lignite
lija /'liha/ f, dogfish; sandpaper
lijar /li'har/ vt to sandpaper
lila /'lila/ f, lilac bush and flower; lilac color. a Inf. foolish, vain
lima /'lima/ f, sweet lime, citron fruit; lime tree; file (tool); filing, polishing. **Lima,** Lima
limadura /lima'ðura/ f, filing; polishing; pl filings
limar /li'mar/ vt to file, smooth with a file; Fig. touch up, polish
limazo /li'maso; li'maθo/ m, slime, viscosity (especially of snails, etc.)
limbo /'limbo/ m, limbo; edge, hem; (Astron. Bot.) limb; limb (of a quadrant, etc.). Inf. **estar en el l.,** to be bewildered or abstracted
limen /'limen/ m, Poet. threshold; Psychol. limen
limeño /li'meɲo/ (-ña) a and n native of or belonging to Lima (Peru)
limero /li'mero/ (-ra) n seller of sweet limes. m, sweet lime tree (citron)
limitación /limita'sion; limita'θion/ f, limitation; limit, extent, bound; district, area
limitado /limi'taðo/ a dull-witted, limited
limitar /limi'tar/ vt to limit; curb, restrict; bound
límite /'limite/ m, limit, extent; boundary, border; end, confine
limítrofe /li'mitrofe/ a bordering, contiguous
limo /'limo/ m, mud, mire, slime; Lat. Am. lime tree
limón /li'mon/ m, lemon; lemon tree
limonada /limo'naða/ f, lemonade. **l. seca,** lemonade powder
limonar /limo'nar/ m, lemon grove
limonero /limo'nero/ (-ra) n lemon seller. m, lemon tree
limosna /li'mosna/ f, alms
limosnear /limosne'ar/ vi to beg, ask alms
limosnero, -a /limos'nero/ a charitable, generous. a charitable, generous. mf almoner; Lat. Am. beggar
limoso /li'moso/ a slimy, muddy
limpiabarros /limpia'βarros/ m, shoe scraper
limpiabotas /limpia'βotas/ m, bootblack (person)
limpiachimeneas /limpiatʃime'neas/ m, chimney-sweep
limpiador /limpia'ðor/ (-ra) a cleaning. n cleaner
limpiadura /limpia'ðura/ f, cleaning; pl rubbish
limpiamanos /limpia'manos/ m, Central America, Mexico towel
limpiamente /limpia'mente/ adv cleanly; dexterously, neatly; sincerely, candidly; generously, charitably
limpiametales /limpiame'tales/ m, metal polish
limpiaparabrisas /limpiapara'βrisas/ m, windshield wiper
limpiapipas /limpia'pipas/ m, pipe cleaner
limpiar /lim'piar/ vt to clean; Fig. cleanse, clear; empty, free (from); Agr. thin out; Inf. steal, pinch; Inf. win (gambling); vr clean oneself
limpidez /limpi'ðes; limpi'ðeθ/ f, Poet. limpidity
límpido /'limpiðo/ a Poet. limpid
limpieza /lim'piesa; lim'pieθa/ f, cleanliness; purity; chastity; purity; altruism; uprightness, integrity; neatness, tidiness; dexterity, skill, precision; fair play
limpio /'limpio/ a clean; pure, unalloyed, unmixed; neat, tidy; pure-blooded; unharmed, free. **en l.,** in substance; as a fair copy; clearly; Com. net
linaje /li'nahe/ m, lineage, family; offspring; kind; sort, quality
linajudo /lina'huðo/ (-da) a highborn. n noble, aristocrat; one who alleges his noble descent
linaza /li'nasa; li'naθa/ f, linseed

lince /'linse; 'linθe/ *m*, lynx; *Mexico* wild cat; *fig.* fox, crafty person

linchamiento /lintʃa'miento/ *m*, lynching

linchar /lin'tʃar/ *vt* to lynch

lindar /lin'dar/ *vi* to run together, be contiguous

linde /'linde/ *mf* limit, extent; boundary

lindero /lin'dero/ *a* bordering, contiguous. *m*, boundary. *Inf.* con **linderos y arrabales**, with many digressions

lindeza /lin'desa; lin'deθa/ *f*, beauty, loveliness; witticism; *pl* (*inf ironical*) insults

lindo /'lindo/ *a* lovely, beautiful; perfect, exquisite

línea /'linea/ *f*, line; kind, class; ancestry, lineage; limit, extent; *Mil.* file; equator. **l. aérea**, airline. **l. de abajo**, the bottom line. *Naut.* **l. de flotación**, waterline. **l. de toque**, touchline (in soccer). **l. recta**, direct line (of descent)

lineal /line'al/ *a* lineal; *computers* on-line

lineamento /linea'mento/ *m*, lineament

linear /line'ar/ *a* linear. *vt* to line, mark with lines; *Art.* sketch

linfa /'linfa/ *f*, *Med.* lymph; vaccine; *Poet.* water

linfático /lin'fatiko/ *a* lymphatic

lingote /liŋ'gote/ *m*, ingot; bar (of iron). **l. de fundición**, pig iron

lingüista /liŋ'guista/ *mf* linguist

lingüística /liŋ'guistika/ *f*, linguistics

lingüístico /liŋ'guistiko/ *a* linguistic

linimento /lini'mento/ *m*, liniment

lino /'lino/ *m*, *Bot.* flax; linen; *Poet.* ship's sail, canvas

linóleo /li'noleo/ *m*, linoleum

linotipia /lino'tipia/ *f*, linotype

linterna /lin'terna/ *f*, lantern; lighthouse; lamp. **l. sorda**, dark lantern

lío /'lio/ *m*, bundle; *Inf.* muddle, imbroglio; *Inf.* liaison, amour. *Inf.* **armar un l.**, to make a muddle, cause trouble. *Inf.* **hacerse un l.**, to get in a fix; get in a muddle

liposucción /liposuk'θion/ *f*, liposuction

liquen /'liken/ *m*, lichen

liquidable /liki'ðaβle/ *a* liquefiable

liquidación /likiða'sion; likiða'θion/ *f*, liquefaction; *Com.* clearance, sale; *Com.* settlement

liquidar /liki'ðar/ *vt* to liquefy; *Com.* settle; *Com.* liquidate; finish; *vr* liquefy; *Inf.* kill

liquidez /liki'ðes; liki'ðeθ/ *f*, liquidness

líquido /'likiðo/ *a* liquid; *Com.* net. *m*, liquid; *Com.* net profit

lira /'lira/ *f*, *Mus.* lyre; *Astron.* Lyra; lira (coin)

lírica /'lirika/ *f*, lyrical verse, lyric

lírico /'liriko/ *a* lyrical

lirio /'lirio/ *m*, lily. **l. cárdeno**, yellow flag (iris). **l. de los valles**, lily of the valley

lirismo /li'rismo/ *m*, lyricism

lirón /li'ron/ *m*, *Zool.* dormouse; *Inf.* sleepyhead

Lisboa /lis'βoa/ Lisbon

lisiado /li'siaðo/ *a* lame, crippled

lisiar /li'siar/ *vt* to cripple, lame; *vr* be disabled; be lame

liso /'liso/ *a* smooth; sleek; unadorned, plain; unicolored

lisonja /li'sonha/ *f*, flattery, adulation

lisonjear /lisonhe'ar/ *vt* to flatter; fawn upon; *Fig.* delight (the ear). **lisonjearse de...,** to flatter oneself on...

lisonjero /lison'hero/ **(-ra)** *a* flattering; sweet, pleasant (sounds). *n* flatterer

lista /'lista/ *f*, strip of cloth; streak; rib; stripe; catalog, list. **l. de correos**, general delivery, poste restante. **l. de platos**, bill of fare; *Mexico* **l. de raya** payroll. **pasar l.,** to call the roll; check the list

listado /lis'taðo/ *a* streaked; striped; ribbed. *m*, list, listing; printout

listo /'listo/ *a* clever; expeditious, diligent; ready, prepared

listón /lis'ton/ *m*, ribbon; strip (of wood)

lisura /li'sura/ *f*, smoothness; sleekness; flatness; sincerity

lisurero, -a, /lisu'rero/ *a*, *Peru* cheeky, impudent

litera /li'tera/ *f*, litter; *Naut.* berth

literal /lite'ral/ *a* literal

literario /lite'rario/ *a* literary

literatear /literate'ar/ *vi* to write on literary subjects

literato /lite'rato/ **(-ta)** *a* literary. *n* writer, litterateur. **los literatos,** the literati

literatura /litera'tura/ *f*, literature

litigación /litiga'sion; litiga'θion/ *f*, litigation

litigante /liti'gante/ *mf* litigant

litigar /liti'gar/ *vt* to litigate; *vi* dispute, argue

litigio /li'tihio/ *m*, lawsuit; dispute, argument

litigioso /liti'hioso/ *a* litigious; quarrelsome, disputatious

litisexpensas /litiseks'pensas/ *f pl*, *Law.* costs of a suit; legal expenses

litografía /litogra'fia/ *f*, lithography

litografiar /litogra'fiar/ *vt* to lithograph

litoral /lito'ral/ *a* and *m*, littoral

litro /'litro/ *m*, liter; *Chile* coarse woolen cloth

Lituania /li'tuania/ Lithuania

liturgia /li'turhia/ *f*, liturgy

litúrgico /li'turhiko/ *a* liturgical

liviandad /liβian'da ð/ *f*, lightness (of weight); fickleness; unimportance; frivolity; lewdness; act of folly, indiscretion

liviano /li'βiano/ *a* light weight; fickle; unimportant, trifling, frivolous; lascivious

lividez /liβi'ðes; liβi'ðeθ/ *f*, lividness

lívido /'liβiðo/ *a* livid; *Lat. Am.* pale, pallid

liza /'lisa; 'liθa/ *f*, list (at a tournament); arena

llaga /'yaga; 'ʎaga/ *f*, ulcer; sore; grief, affliction; *Fig.* thorn in the flesh

llagar /ya'gar; ʎa'gar/ *vt* to ulcerate; make or produce sores; *Fig.* wound; *vr* be covered with sores

llama /'yama; 'ʎama/ *f*, flame; ardor, vehemence; marsh; *Zool.* llama

llamada /ya'maða; ʎa'maða/ *f*, call; *Mil.* call-to-arms, call. **l. molestosa,** annoyance call, nuisance call

llamado /ya'maðo; ʎa'maðo/ *a* called; so-called

llamador /yama'ðor; ʎama'ðor/ **(-ra)** *n* caller. *m*, door knocker; doorbell

llamamiento /yama'miento; ʎama'miento/ *m*, calling; call; divine summons, inspiration; invocation, appeal; summons, convocation

llamar /ya'mar; ʎa'mar/ *vt* to call; invoke, call upon; summon, convoke; name; attract; *vi* knock (at a door); ring (a bell); *vr* be named, be called; *Naut.* veer (wind). **Se llama Pedro,** His name is Peter

llamarada /yama'raða; ʎama'raða/ *f*, flame, flash; blaze, flare (of anger, etc.)

llamativo /yama'tiβo; ʎama'tiβo/ *a* striking, showy; provocative

llamear /yame'ar; ʎame'ar/ *vi* to throw out flames, blaze

llampo /'yampo; 'ʎampo/ *m*, *Lat. Am.* ore

llana /'yana; 'ʎana/ *f*, mason's trowel; plain; surface of a page

llanada /ya'naða; ʎa'naða/ *f*, plain

llanamente /yana'mente; ʎana'mente/ *adv* frankly, plainly; naturally, simply; candidly, sincerely

llanero /ya'nero; ʎa'nero/ **(-ra)** *n* plain dweller

llaneza /ya'nesa; ʎa'neθa/ *f*, naturalness; candor; familiarity; simplicity (of style)

llano /'yano; 'ʎano/ *a* flat, level; smooth, even; shallow (of receptacles); unaffected, homely, natural; plain (of dresses); manifest, evident; easy; straightforward, candid; informal; simple (of style). *m*, plain; level stretch of ground

llanta /'yanta; 'ʎanta/ *f*, *Auto.* tire; rim, felloe. **l. de refacción,** *Mexico* spare tire. **l. de rueda,** wheel, rim

llanto /'yanto; 'ʎanto/ *m*, weeping, flood of tears

llanura /ya'nura; ʎa'nura/ *f*, smoothness, evenness, levelness; plain

llave /'yaβe; 'ʎaβe/ **(de)** *f*, key (to); spigot (of), faucet (of), tap (of); spanner, wrench; *Elec.* switch; clock winder; *Mus.* key, clef; *Archit.* keystone; *Print.* brace; *Mech.* wrench; lock (of a gun); tuning key; piston (of musical instruments); lock (in wrestling); *Fig.* key (of a problem or a study). **l. de transmisión,** sender (telegraphy). **l. inglesa,** monkey-wrench, spanner. **l. maestra,** master key, skeleton key. **echar la l.,** to lock. **torcer la l.,** to turn the key

llavero /ya'βero; ʎa'βero/ **(-ra)** *n* keeper of the keys. *m,* key ring. **l. de cárcel,** turnkey

llavín /ya'βin; ʎa'βin/ *m,* yale key, latchkey

llegada /ye'gaða; ʎe'gaða/ *f,* arrival, advent

llegar /ye'gar; ʎe'gar/ *vi* to arrive; last, endure; reach; achieve a purpose; be sufficient, suffice; amount (to), make; *vt* bring near, draw near; gather; *vr* come near, approach; adhere. **l. a ser,** to become. **l. a un punto muerto,** to reach a deadlock. **l. hasta...,** to stretch as far as...

llena /'yena; 'ʎena/ *f,* spate, overflow

llenar /ye'nar; ʎe'nar/ *vt* to fill; occupy (a post); satisfy, please; fulfill; satiate; pervade; fill up (a form); *vi* be full (of the moon); *vr Inf.* stuff, overeat; *Fig. Inf.* be fed-up

lleno /'yeno; 'ʎeno/ *a* full; replete; abundant; complete. *m,* full moon; *Theat.* full house; *Inf.* glut, abundance; perfection. **de l., de l. en l.,** entirely, completely

llenura /ye'nura; ʎe'nura/ *f,* abundance, plenty

lleva, llevada /'yeβa, ye'βaða; 'ʎeβa, ʎe'βaða/ *f,* carrying, bearing

llevadero /yeβa'ðero; ʎeβa'ðero/ *a* tolerable, bearable

llevar /ye'βar; ʎe'βar/ *vt* to carry, transport; charge (a price); yield, produce; carry off, take away; endure, bear; persuade; guide, take; direct; wear (clothes); carry (a handbag, etc.); introduce, present; gain, achieve; manage (a horse); pass, spend (of time); (*with past part*) have (e.g. *Llevo escrita la carta,* I have written the letter); *Math.* carry; (*with prep. a*) surpass, excel. **l. a cabo,** to accomplish. **l. a cuestas,** to carry on one's back; support. **l. la correspondencia,** to look after the correspondence. **l. la delantera,** to take the lead. **l. luto,** to be in mourning. **1. por delante** *Argentina, Chile* to run over (e.g., a pedesrian) **llevarse bien,** to get on well, agree

llorar /yo'rar; ʎo'rar/ *vi* to weep, cry; drip; water (eyes); *vt* lament, mourn; bewail one's troubles

lloriquear /yorike'ar; ʎorike'ar/ *vi* to whine, snivel

lloriqueo /yori'keo; ʎori'keo/ *m,* whining, sniveling

lloro /'yoro; 'ʎoro/ *m,* weeping, crying; flood of tears

llorón /yo'ron; ʎo'ron/ *a* weeping; sniveling, whining. *m,* long plume. **niño llorón,** crybaby

lloroso /yo'roso; ʎo'roso/ *a* tearful; grievous, sad; sorrowful

llovedizo /yoβe'ðiso; ʎoβe'ðiθo/ *a* leaky; rainy

llover /yo'βer; ʎo'βer/ *vi impers irr* to rain; come in abundance (of troubles, etc.); *vr* leak (roofs, etc.). **l. a cántaros,** to rain in torrents, rain cats and dogs. **l. sobre mojado,** to add insult to injury. **como llovido,** unexpectedly. See **mover**

llovida /jo'βiða; ʎo'βiða/ *f, Lat. Am.* rain, shower

llovido /yo'βiðo; ʎo'βiðo/ *m,* stowaway

llovizna /yo'βisna; ʎo'βiθna/ *f,* drizzle, fine rain

llovizna /yoβis'nar; ʎoβiθ'nar/ *vi* to drizzle

lluvia /'yuβia; 'ʎuβia/ *f,* rain; rainwater; *Fig.* shower; rose (of watering can) *Chile, Nicaragua* shower bath, shower

lluvioso /yu'βioso; ʎu'βioso/ *a* rainy, showery

lo /lo/ *def art. neut* the thing, part, fact, what, that which. Used before adjectives, past participles, sometimes before nouns and adverbs (e.g. *Lo barato es caro,* Cheap things are dear (in the long run).) **Lo mío es mío, pero lo tuyo es de ambos,** What's mine is mine, but what is yours belongs to both of us. **Juan siente mucho lo ocurrido,** John is very sorry for what has happened. **a lo lejos,** (in the distance). **lo... que,** how (e.g. *No sabes lo bueno que es,* You don't know how good he is). *pers pron acc m,* or *neut* him, it; that, it (e.g. *Lo harán mañana,* They will do it tomorrow). Means some, any, one, as substitute for noun already mentioned (e.g. *Carecemos de azúcar; no lo hay,* We are short of sugar; there isn't any). **Lo cortés no quita lo valiente,** One can be courteous and still insistent

loa /'loa/ *f,* praise, eulogy; *Theat.* prologue; short dramatic piece; *Obs.*; dramatic eulogy

loable /lo'aβle/ *a* praiseworthy

loar /lo'ar/ *vt* to praise; commend

lobero /lo'βero/ *a* wolf; wolfish

lobo /'loβo/ **(-ba)** *n* wolf. *m,* (*Bot. Anat.*) lobe; *Inf.* drinking fit. **l. marino,** *Zool.* seal. *Inf.* **pillar un l.,** to get drunk

lóbrego /'loβrego/ *a* murky, dark; dismal; mournful, lugubrious

lobreguez /loβre'ges; loβre'geθ/ *f,* obscurity, gloom, darkness

lóbulo /'loβulo/ *m,* lobe

locación /loka'sion; loka'θion/ *f, Law.* lease; agreement, contract

local /lo'kal/ *a* local. *m,* premises; place, spot, scene

localidad /lokali'ðað/ *f,* location; locality; place, spot; seat (in theaters, etc.)

localización /lokalisa'sion; lokaliθa'θion/ *f,* localization, placing; place

localizar /lokali'sar; lokali'θar/ *vt* to localize

locamente /loka'mente/ *adv* insanely, madly; extraordinarily, extremely

loción /lo'sion; lo'θion/ *f,* lotion

loco /'loko/ **(-ca)** *a* insane, mad; rash, foolish, crazy; excessive, enormous; amazing; extraordinary; infatuated. *n* lunatic; rash person. *Fig. Inf.* **Es un l. de atar,** He's completely crazy! **Ellos están locos conmigo,** They're crazy about me

locomoción /lokomo'sion; lokomo'θion/ *f,* locomotion

locomotor /lokomo'tor/ *a* locomotive

locomotora /lokomo'tora/ *f,* locomotive

locomóvil /loko'moβil/ *a* and *f,* locomotive

locro /'lokro/ *m, Lat. Am.* meat-and-vegetable stew

locuacidad /lokuasi'ðað; lokuaθi'ðað/ *f,* loquacity

locuaz /lo'kuas; lo'kuaθ/ *a* loquacious

locución /loku'sion; loku'θion/ *f,* style of speech; phrase, idiom; *Gram.* locution

locuelo /lo'kuelo/ **(-la)** *n* madcap

locura /lo'kura/ *f,* insanity, lunacy; madness, fury; folly, foolishness

locutor /loku'tor/ **(-ra)** *n* (radio) announcer; commentator

locutorio /loku'torio/ *m,* locutory; phone booth

lodazal, lodazar /loða'sal, loða'sar; loða'θal, loða'θar/ *m,* muddy place; quagmire

lodo /'loðo/ *m,* mud

lodoso /lo'ðoso/ *a* muddy

logarítmico /loga'ritmiko/ *a* logarithmic

logaritmo /loga'ritmo/ *m,* logarithm

logia /'lohia/ *f,* (Freemason's) lodge

lógica /'lohika/ *f,* logic. *Inf.* **l. parda,** common sense

lógico /'lohiko/ **(-ca)** *a* logical. *n* logician

logística /lo'histika/ *f,* logistics

lograr /lo'grar/ *vt* to achieve, attain, obtain; enjoy; (*with infin*) succeed in; *vr* succeed in, achieve; reach perfection

lograr /logre'ar/ *vi* to borrow or lend at interest

logrero /lo'grero/ **(-ra)** *n* moneylender; monopolist, profiteer

logro /'logro/ *m,* achievement, attainment; profit, gain; usury, money-lending

loma /'loma/ *f,* knoll, hill

lombarda /lom'βarða/ *f,* red cabbage

lombardo /lom'βarðo/ *m,* mortgage bank

lombriciento, -a /lomβri'siento; lomβri'θiento/ *a, Lat. Am.* having worms, suffering from worms

lombriz /lom'βris; lom'βriθ/ *f,* earthworm, common worm. **l. intestinal,** intestinal worm. **l. solitaria,** tapeworm

lomo /'lomo/ *m,* loin, back of a book; ridge between furrows; *pl* ribs; loins

lona /'lona/ *f,* canvas, sailcloth

lonchería /lontʃe'ria/ *f, Lat. Am.* luncheonette, lunch counter, snack bar

Londres /'londres/ London

longaniza /loŋga'nisa; loŋga'niθa/ *f, Cul.* pork sausage

longevidad /lonheβi'ðað/ *f,* longevity

longevo /lon'heβo/ *a* long-lived

longísimo /lon'hisimo/ *a sup* **luengo** exceedingly long

longitud /lonhi'tuð/ f, length; longitude. **l. de onda,** *Radio.* wavelength
lonja /'lonha/ f, slice, rasher; *Com.* exchange; market; grocery store; woolen warehouse
lonjista /lon'hista/ mf provision merchant, grocer
lontananza /lonta'nansa; lonta'nanθa/ f, distance (also *Art.*). **en l.,** in the distance, far off
loor /lo'or/ m, praise
loquear /loke'ar/ vi to play the fool; romp
loro /'loro/ m, *Ornith.* parrot
los /los/ def art. m pl, the (e.g. *l. sombreros,* the hats). *pers. pron acc 3rd pers m pl,* them. **Tus cigarrillos no están sobre la mesa; los tengo en mi bolsillo,** Your cigarettes are not on the table; I have them in my pocket. Means some, any, ones, as substitution for noun already stated (e.g. *Los cigarros están en la caja si los hay,* The cigars are in the box, if there are any). Used demonstratively followed by *de* or *que* introducing relative clause, those of; those which, those who; the ones that (who) (e.g. *Estaba leyendo algunos libros de los que tienes en tu cuarto,* I was reading some books from among those which you have in your room)
losa /'losa/ f, flagstone; slab; tombstone
lote /'lote/ m, lot, portion, share
lotería /lote'ria/ f, lottery; lotto (game); lottery office
lotero /lo'tero/ **(-ra)** n seller of lottery tickets
loto /'loto/ m, lotus; lotus flower or fruit
loza /'losa; 'loθa/ f, porcelain, china
lozanía /losa'nia; loθa'nia/ f, luxuriance (of vegetation); vigor, lustiness; arrogance
lozano /lo'sano; lo'θano/ a luxuriant, exuberant; vigorous, lusty; arrogant
lubricación /luβrika'sion; luβrika'θion/ f, lubrication
lubricante /luβri'kante/ a lubricant
lubricar /luβri'kar/ vt to lubricate
lúbrico /'luβriko/ a slippery, smooth; lascivious, lustful
lucera /lu'sera; lu'θera/ f, skylight
lucerna /lu'serna; lu'θerna/ f, large chandelier; skylight
lucero /lu'sero; lu'θero/ m, evening star; any bright star; white star (on a horse's head); brilliance, radiance; pl *Poet.* eyes, orbs. **l. del alba,** morning star
lucha /'lutʃa/ f, fight; struggle; wrestling match; argument, disagreement. **l. grecorromana,** wrestling. **l. igualada,** close fight. **l. libre,** catch-as-catch-can
luchador /lutʃa'ðor/ **(-ra)** n fighter; struggler
luchar /lu'tʃar/ vi to fight hand to hand; wrestle; fight; struggle; argue
lucidez /lusi'ðes; luθi'ðeθ/ f, brilliance, shine; lucidity, clarity
lucido /lu'siðo; lu'θiðo/ a splendid, brilliant; sumptuous; fine, elegant
lúcido /lu'siðo; lu'θiðo/ a *Poet.* brilliant; lucid; clear
luciente /lu'siente; lu'θiente/ a bright, shining
luciérnaga /lu'siernaga; lu'θiernaga/ f, firefly, glowworm
lucimiento /lusi'miento; luθi'miento/ m, brilliance, luster; success, triumph; elegance; display, ostentation
lucir /lu'sir; lu'θir/ vi irr to shine, scintillate; excel, outshine; be successful; vt illuminate; display, show off; show; vr dress elegantly; be successful; excel, be brilliant. *Pres. Ind.* **luzco, luces,** etc. *Pres. Subjunc.* **luzca,** etc.
lucrativo /lukra'tiβo/ a lucrative
lucro /'lukro/ m, gain, profit
lucroso /lu'kroso/ a profitable
luctuoso /luk'tuoso/ a lugubrious, mournful
lucubración /lukuβra'sion; lukuβra'θion/ f, lucubration
ludibrio /lu'ðiβrio/ m, mockery, ridicule
luego /'luego/ adv immediately; afterward, later; then; soon, presently. *conjunc* therefore. **l. que,** as soon as. **desde l.,** at once; of course, naturally; in the first place. **hasta l.,** see you later, good-by for the present

lueguito /lue'gito/ adv *Lat. Am.* at once, right away, right now; *Central America, Chile, Mexico* near, nearby
luengo /'luengo/ a long
lugar /lu'gar/ m, place; spot; village, town, city; region, locality; office, post; passage, text; opportunity, occasion; cause, motive; place on a list; room, space; seat. **l. común,** commonplace. **en l. de,** instead of. **en primer l.,** firstly, in the first place. **hacer l.,** to make room, make way. *Law.* **No ha l.,** The petition is refused. **tener l.,** to take place; have the time or opportunity (to)
lugarejo /luga'reho/ m, hamlet
lugareño /luga'reno/ **(-ña)** a peasant, regional. n villager, peasant
lugarteniente /lugarte'niente/ m, lieutenant; substitute, deputy
lúgubre /'luguβre/ a lugubrious, dismal, mournful
luis /'luis/ m, louis (French coin)
lujo /'luho/ m, luxury; abundance, profusion. **artículos de l.,** luxury goods
lujoso /lu'hoso/ a luxurious; abundant, profuse
lujuria /lu'huria/ f, lasciviousness; excess, intemperance
lujuriante /luhu'riante/ a luxuriant, abundant, profuse
lujurioso /luhu'rioso/ a lascivious, voluptuous
lumbago /lum'βago/ m, lumbago
lumbre /'lumbre/ f, fire; light; splendor, luster; transom window, opening, skylight; pl tinderbox
lumbrera /lum'βrera/ f, luminary; skylight; dormer window; eminent authority; *Mexico* box (in a theater or bullring)
luminar /lumi'nar/ m, luminary (also *Fig.*)
luminaria /lumi'naria/ f, illumination; fairy lamp, small light; lamp burning before the Sacrament in Catholic churches
luminosidad /luminosi'ðað/ f, luminosity
luminoso /lumi'noso/ a luminous; bright
luna /'luna/ f, moon; mirror; satellite; sheet of plate glass. **l. creciente,** new or rising moon. **l. de miel,** honeymoon. **l. llena,** full moon. **l. menguante,** waning moon. **media l.,** crescent moon
lunado /lu'naðo/ a half-moon, crescent
lunar /lu'nar/ m, beauty spot; *Fig.* stain, blot (on reputation, etc.); blemish, slight imperfection. a lunar
lunático /lu'natiko/ **(-ca)** a and n lunatic
lunes /'lunes/ m, Monday
luneta /lu'neta/ f, lens (of eyeglasses); *Theat.* orchestra stall; *Archit. Mil.*) lunette
lupa /'lupa/ f, magnifying glass
lupanar /lupa'nar/ m, brothel
lúpulo /'lupulo/ m, *Bot.* hop
luso /'luso/ **(-sa)** n Portuguese
lustrador /lustra'ðor/ m, polisher; *Lat. Am.* bootblack. **l. de piso,** floor polisher
lustrar /lus'trar/ vt to lustrate, purify; polish, burnish; roam, journey
lustre /'lustre/ m, polish, sheen, gloss; glory, luster
lustro /'lustro/ m, lustrum, period of five years; chandelier
lustroso /lus'troso/ a shining, glossy; brilliant; glorious, noble
luterano /lute'rano/ **(-na)** a and n Lutheran
luto /'luto/ m, mourning; grief, affliction; pl mourning draperies. **estar de l.,** to be in mourning
luxación /luksa'sion; luksa'θion/ f, *Surg.* luxation, dislocation
luz /lus; luθ/ f, light; glow; brightness, brilliance; information, news; *Fig.* luminary; day, daylight; pl culture, learning; windows. **luces de estacionamiento,** parking lights. **a buena l.,** in a good light; in a favorable light; after due consideration. **a primera l.,** at dawn. **dar a l.,** to publish (a book); bring forth (children); reveal. **entre dos luces,** in the dawn light; in the twilight; *Inf.* tipsy. **media l.,** half-light, twilight

M

maca /'maka/ *f*, bruise or blemish on fruit; defect, flaw; *Inf.* fraud, swindle

macabro /ma'kaβro/ *a* macabre

macagua /ma'kagua/ *f*, *Ornith.* macaw

macanudo /maka'nuðo/ *a* (*Inf. West Hem.*) extraordinary; enormous; robust; fine, excellent

macarrones /maka'rrones/ *m pl*, macaroni; *Naut.* stanchions

macarrónico /maka'rroniko/ *a* macaronic, recondite, stylized

macarse /ma'karse/ *vr* to go bad, rot (fruit)

maceración /masera'sion; maθera'θion/ *f*, maceration; steeping, soaking; mortification of the flesh

macerar /mase'rar; maθe'rar/ *vt* to macerate; steep, soak; mortify

macero /ma'sero; ma'θero/ *m*, mace bearer

maceta /ma'seta; ma'θeta/ *f*, *dim* small vase; handle, haft (of tools); stonecutter's hammer; flowerpot; *Lat. Am.* bouquet, bunch (of flowers)

macetero /mase'tero; maθe'tero/ *m*, flowerpot stand; *Lat. Am.* flowerpot

machaca /ma'tʃaka/ *f*, pestle; pulverizer. *mf Inf.* bore, tedious person

machacador /matʃaka'ðor/ **(-ra)** *a* crushing, pounding. *n* beater, crusher, pounder

machacar /matʃa'kar/ *vt* to crush, pound; *vi* importune; harp on a subject

machacón /matʃa'kon/ *a* tiresome, prolix

machado /ma'tʃaðo/ *m*, hatchet, ax

machete /ma'tʃete/ *m* machete

machetero /matʃe'tero/ *m*, one who cuts sugarcane with a machete

machihembrar /matʃiem'βrar/ *vt* to dovetail

machina /ma'tʃina/ *f*, derrick, crane; pile driver

macho /'matʃo/ *m*, male; male animal (he-goat, stallion, etc.); male plant; hook (of hook and eye); screw; *Metall.* core; tap (tool); *Inf.* dunderhead, fool; *Archit.* buttress. *a* male; stupid, ignorant; vigorous, strong. **m. cabrío,** he-goat

machucadura /matʃuka'ðura/ *f*, **machucamiento** *m*, pounding, crushing; bruising

machucar /matʃu'kar/ *vt* to crush, pound; bruise

machucho /ma'tʃutʃo/ *a* prudent, sensible; adult, mature

macicez /masi'ses; maθi'θeθ/ *f*, solidity; massiveness; thickness

macilento /masi'lento; maθi'lento/ *a* thin, lean, emaciated

macillo /ma'siyo; ma'θiʎo/ *m*, *dim* small mace; hammer (of a piano)

macis /'masis; 'maθis/ *f*, *Cul.* mace

macizar /masi'sar; maθi'θar/ *vt* to block up, fill up

macizo /ma'siso; ma'θiθo/ *a* massive; compact, solid; *Fig.* well-founded, unassailable; thick; strong. *m*, solidity, compactness; bulk, volume; flowerbed; solid tire

macrocosmo /makro'kosmo/ *m*, macrocosm

macuco, -a /ma'kuko/ *a*, *Lat. Am.* crafty, cunning, sly

mácula /'makula/ *f*, stain, spot; *Fig.* blot, blemish; *Inf.* trick, deception; *Astron.* macula

macuquero /maku'kero/ *m*, unauthorized worker of abandoned mines

madeja /ma'ðeha/ *f*, lock of hair; *Inf.* dummy, useless person

madera /ma'ðera/ *f*, wood; timber; *Inf.* kind, sort; *Mus.* wind instruments. **m. contrachapada,** plywood. **m. de construcción,** timber. **maderas de sierra,** lumber wood. *Inf.* **ser de mala m.,** to be a ne'er-do-well

maderada /maðe'raða/ *f*, lumber wood

maderaje /maðe'rahe/ *m*, woodwork, timber work

maderero /maðe'rero/ *m*, timber merchant; lumberjack; carpenter

madería /maðe'ria/ *f*, timber yard

madero /ma'ðero/ *m*, wooden beam; log, piece of lumber; ship, vessel; *Inf.* blockhead or insensible person

madrastra /ma'ðrastra/ *f*, stepmother

madraza /ma'ðrasa; ma'ðraθa/ *f*, *Inf.* overindulgent mother

madre /'maðre/ *f*, mother; matron; cause, genesis; *Inf.* dame, mother; riverbed; dam; womb; main sewer; chief irrigation channel. **m. de familia,** mother; housewife. **m. de leche,** wet nurse. **m. política,** mother-in-law; stepmother. *Inf.* **sacar de m.** (a), to provoke, irritate (a person)

madreperla /maðre'perla/ *f*, mother-of-pearl

madreselva /maðre'selβa/ *f*, honeysuckle

madrigado /maðri'gaðo/ *a* twice-married (women); *Inf.* experienced, wide-awake

madrigal /maðri'gal/ *m*, madrigal

madriguera /maðri'gera/ *f*, rabbit warren; burrow, den, hole, lair; haunt of thieves, etc.

madrina /ma'ðrina/ *f*, godmother; matron of honor or bridesmaid; sponsor; patroness; prop; stanchion

madroncillo /maðron'siyo; maðron'θiʎo/ *m*, strawberry

madroño /ma'ðroɲo/ *m*, strawberry tree; tuft, spot; tassel

madrugada /maðru'gaða/ *f*, dawn, daybreak; early rising. **de m.,** at dawn

madrugador /maðruga'ðor/ **(-ra)** *a* early rising. *n* early riser

madrugar /maðru'gar/ *vi* to get up early; gain time; anticipate, be beforehand

maduración /maðura'sion; maðura'θion/ *f*, ripening; mellowing; preparation; ripeness; maturity

madurador /maðura'ðor/ *a* ripening; maturing

maduramente /maðura'mente/ *adv* maturely; sensibly

madurar /maðu'rar/ *vt* to ripen; mature; think out; *vi* ripen; grow mature, learn wisdom

madurez /maðu'res; maðu'reθ/ *f*, ripeness; maturity; mellowness; wisdom

maduro /ma'ðuro/ *a* ripe; mature; mellow; adult; wise

maestra /ma'estra/ *f*, schoolmistress; teacher, instructor; queen bee; guide, model

maestral /maes'tral/ *a* referring to the grand master of one of the Spanish military orders; teaching, pedagogic. *m*, mistral (wind); cell of a queen bee

maestranza /maes'transa; maes'tranθa/ *f*, *Lat. Am.* machine shop

maestrear /maestre'ar/ *vt* to direct, control, manage; prune vines; *vi Inf.* bully, domineer

maestría /maes'tria/ *f*, mastery, skill; *Educ.* master's degree

maestril /maes'tril/ *m*, queen cell (of bees)

maestro /ma'estro/ *a* masterly; excellent; chief, main; midship. *m*, master, expert; teacher; instructor; master craftsman; *Educ.* master; *Mus.* composer; *Naut.* mainmast. **m. de armas,** fencing master. **m. de capilla,** *Eccl.* choirmaster. **m. de obras,** building contractor; master builder. **El ejercicio hace m.,** Practice makes perfect

Magallanes, Estrecho de /maga'yanes, es'tretʃo de; maga'ʎanes, es'tretʃo de/ Straits of Magellan

magdalena /magða'lena/ *f*, madeleine (cake); magdalen, penitent. *Inf.* **estar hecha una M.,** to be inconsolable

magia /'mahia/ *f*, magic

mágica /'mahika/ *f*, magic; enchantress, sorceress

mágico /'mahiko/ *a* magic; marvelous, wonderful. *m*, magician; enchanter, wizard

magín /ma'hin/ *m*, *Inf.* imagination; head, mind

magisterio /mahis'terio/ *m*, teaching profession; teaching diploma; teaching post; pedantry, pompousness. **ejercer su m. en,** to be employed as a teacher in

magistrado /mahis'traðo/ *m*, magistrate; magistracy

magistral /mahis'tral/ a magistral; authoritative, magisterial; pedantic, pompous

magistratura /mahistra'tura/ f, magistracy

magnanimidad /magnanimi'ðað/ f, magnanimity; generosity, liberality

magnánimo /mag'nanimo/ a magnanimous, generous, noble

magnate /mag'nate/ m, magnate

magnavoz /magna'βos; magna'βoθ/ m, Mexico loudspeaker

magnesia /mag'nesia/ f, magnesia

magnesio /mag'nesio/ m, magnesium

magnético /mag'netiko/ a magnetic

magnetizar /magneti'sar; magneti'θar/ vt to magnetize; mesmerize

magneto /mag'neto/ m, magneto

magnificar /magnifi'kar/ vt to magnify, enlarge; praise, extol

magnificencia /magnifi'sensia; magnifi'θenθia/ f, magnificence, pomp, splendor

magnífico /mag'nifiko/ a magnificent; splendid, wonderful, fine; excellent

magnitud /magni'tuð/ f, magnitude; quantity; importance

magno /'magno/ a great; famous. **Alejandro M.,** Alexander the Great

magnolia /mag'nolia/ f, magnolia

mago /'mago/ m, magician; pl magi

magra /'magra/ f, rasher (of bacon, ham)

magrez, magrura /ma'gres, ma'grura; ma'greθ, ma'grura/ f, leanness; scragginess

magro /'magro/ a lean; scraggy. m, Inf. lean pork

magulladura /maguya'ðura; maguʎa'ðura/ f, **magullamiento** m, bruising; bruise, contusion

magullar /magu'yar; magu'ʎar/ vt to bruise

magullón /magu'jon; magu'ʎon/ m, Lat. Am. bruise

mahometano /maome'tano/ **(-na)** a and n Muslim

mahonesa /mao'nesa/ f, mayonnaise

maíz /ma'is; ma'iθ/ m, corn

maizal /mai'sal; mai'θal/ m, cornfield

maja /'maha/ f, belle

majada /ma'haða/ f, sheepfold; dung

majaderear /mahaðere'ar/ vt, Lat. Am. to nag, pester

majadería /mahaðe'ria/ f, impertinence, insolence

majadero /maha'ðero/ a persistent, tedious. m, bobbin (for lace making); pestle. n fool, bore

majador /maha'ðor/ m, pestle

majar /ma'har/ vt to pound, crush; Inf. importune, annoy

majestad /mahes'tað/ f, majesty (title); dignity; stateliness

majestuosidad /mahestuosi'ðað/ f, majesty; dignity

majestuoso /mahes'tuoso/ a majestic; stately; dignified

majo /'maho/ a arrogant, aggressive; gaudily attired, smart; dashing, handsome; attractive, pretty; elegant, well-dressed. m, beau, gallant, man about town

majuelo /ma'huelo/ m, new vine; species of white hawthorn

mal /mal/ a abb **malo.** Used only before m sing nouns (e.g. un m. cuarto de hora, a bad quarter of an hour). m, evil; damage; harm; misfortune; illness, disease; trouble (e.g. El m. es, The trouble is). **el bien y el m.,** good and evil. **m. de altura,** air sickness. **m. de ojo,** evil eye. **m. de piedra,** lithiasis, stone. **m. francés,** syphilis. **el m. menor,** the lesser of two evils. interj **¡M. haya!** A curse upon! **echar a m.,** to scorn (things); waste, squander. **llevar a m. (una cosa),** to take (a thing) badly, complain. **No hay m. que por bien no venga,** It's an ill wind that blows no one any good, Every cloud has a silver lining. **parar en m.,** to come to a bad end

mal /mal/ adv badly; unfavorably; wrongly; wickedly; with difficulty; scarcely, barely. **m. que bien,** willingly or unwillingly; rightly or wrongly. **de m. en peor,** from bad to worse

mala /'mala/ f, mail, post. **m. real,** royal mail

malabarista /malaβa'rista/ mf juggler

malaconsejado /malakonse'haðo/ a ill-advised; imprudent

malacostumbrado /malakostum'βraðo/ a badly trained, spoiled; having bad habits

Málaga /'malaga/ Malaga

malandante /malan'dante/ a evildoing; unfortunate, miserable; poor

malandanza /malan'dansa; malan'danθa/ f, evildoing; misfortune, misery; poverty

malandrín /malan'drin/ a wicked, ill-disposed. m, scoundrel, miscreant

malanga /ma'laŋga/ f, Central America kind of tuber resembling a sweet potato

malaquita /mala'kita/ f, malachite

malaria /ma'laria/ f, malaria

malaventura /malaβen'tura/ f, misfortune, adversity, bad luck

malaventurado /malaβentu'raðo/ a unfortunate, unlucky

malayo /ma'laio/ **(-ya)** a Malay. n Malayan

malbaratador /malβarata'ðor/ **(-ra)** a wasteful, spendthrift. n squanderer, spendthrift

malbaratar /malβara'tar/ vt to squander, waste; sell at a loss

malcasado /malka'saðo/ a adulterous, unfaithful, unhappily married

malcasar /malka'sar/ **(se)** vt and vr to marry badly

malcomido /malko'miðo/ a underfed

malcontento /malkon'tento/ **(-ta)** a dissatisfied, discontented; rebellious. n malcontent, rebel

malcriado /mal'kriaðo/ a badly brought up; ill-bred; spoiled, peevish

maldad /mal'dað/ f, badness; depravity, wickedness

maldecidor /maldesi'ðor; maldeθi'ðor/ **(-ra)** a slanderous. n scandalmonger, slanderer

maldecir /malde'sir; malde'θir/ vt irr to curse; vt and vi slander, backbite. See **decir**

maldiciente /maldi'siente; maldi'θiente/ a defamatory, slanderous; cursing, reviling. m, slanderer; curser

maldición /maldi'sion; maldi'θion/ f, malediction; curse, imprecation

maldispuesto /maldis'puesto/ a indisposed, ill; reluctant

maldita /mal'dita/ f, Inf. tongue. Inf. **soltar la m.,** to say too much, go too far

maldito /mal'dito/ a accursed; wicked; damned; poor (of quality); Inf. not a...

maleabilidad /maleaβili'ðað/ f, malleability, flexibility

maleable /male'aβle/ a malleable, flexible

maleante /male'ante/ a rascally, villainous. mf evildoer

malecón /male'kon/ m, breakwater, wharf, seafront

maledicencia /maleði'sensia; maleði'θenθia/ f, slander, abuse, backbiting; cursing

maleficencia /malefi'sensia; malefi'θenθia/ f, wrongdoing

maleficio /male'fisio; male'fiθio/ m, (magic) curse; spell; charm

maléfico /ma'lefiko/ a malefic, harmful. m, sorcerer

malestar /males'tar/ m, indisposition, slight illness; discomfort

maleta /ma'leta/ f, suitcase, valise, grip; m, Inf. clumsy matador; duffer (at games, etc.). **hacer la m.,** to pack a suitcase; Inf. prepare for a journey, get ready to leave

maletero /male'tero/ m, seller or maker of traveling bags; porter

maletín /male'tin/ m, small suitcase or valise

malevolencia /maleβo'lensia; maleβo'lenθia/ f, malevolence, hatred, malice

malévolo /ma'leβolo/ a malevolent, malicious

maleza /ma'lesa; ma'leθa/ f, weeds; undergrowth; thicket

malgastador /malgasta'ðor/ **(-ra)** a thriftless, wasteful. n squanderer

malgastar /malgas'tar/ vt to waste (time); squander, throw away (money)

malhablado /mala'βlaðo/ a foul-tongued, indecent

malhadado /mala'ðaðo/ a ill-fated, unhappy

malhecho /mal'etʃo/ a deformed, twisted (persons). m, evil deed, wrongdoing

malhechor /male'tʃor/ **(-ra)** n malefactor; evildoer

malhumorado /malumo'raðo/ a ill-humored, bad-tempered

malicia /ma'lisia; ma'liθia/ f, wickedness, evil; malice, maliciousness; acuteness, subtlety, shrewdness; craftiness, guile; Inf. suspicion

maliciar /mali'siar; mali'θiar/ vt to suspect; spoil, damage; hurt, harm

malicioso /mali'sioso; mali'θioso/ a malicious; vindictive; wicked; shrewd, clever; Inf. suspicious; artful

malignidad /maligni'ðað/ f, malignancy, spite, ill will

maligno /ma'ligno/ a malignant, spiteful; wicked; Med. malignant

malintencionado /malintensio'naðo; malinten-θio'naðo/ a ill-intentioned, badly disposed

malla /'maya; 'maʎa/ f, mesh (of a net); coat of mail; pl Theat. tights. **m. de alambre,** wire netting. **cota de m.,** coat of mail

Mallorca /ma'yorka; ma'ʎorka/ Majorca

malmandado /malman'daðo/ a disobedient; reluctant, unwilling

malmaridada /malmari'ðaða/ f, adultress, faithless wife

malo /'malo/ a bad; wicked; evil; injurious; harmful; illicit; licentious; ill; difficult; troublesome, annoying; Inf. mischievous; knavish; rotten, decaying. interj **¡M.!** That's bad!; You shouldn't have done that!; That's a bad sign! **de malas,** unluckily, unhappily. **el M.,** the Evil One, the Devil. **estar m.,** to be ill. **Lo m. es,** The trouble is, The worst of it is. **por malas o por buenas,** willy-nilly, willingly or unwillingly. **ser m.,** to be wicked; be evil; behave badly (children)

malograr /malo'grar/ vt to lose (time); waste, throw away (opportunities); vr fall through, fail; wither, fade; die early, come to an untimely end

malogro /ma'logro/ m, loss, waste (time, opportunity); frustration; decline, fading; untimely death

malparar /malpa'rar/ vt to ill-treat; damage. **quedar malparado,** to get the worst of

malparir /malpa'rir/ vt Med. to miscarry

malparto /mal'parto/ m, miscarriage; abortion

malquerencia /malke'rensia; malke'renθia/ f, ill will, aversion, dislike

malquistar /malkis'tar/ vt to stir up trouble; make unpopular; estrange; vr make oneself disliked

malquisto /mal'kisto/ a unpopular, disliked

malsano /mal'sano/ a unhealthy

malta /'malta/ m, malt. **Malta,** Malta

malteada /malte'aða/ f, malted beverage

maltés /mal'tes/ **(-esa)** a and n Maltese

maltraer /maltra'er/ vt irr to ill-treat; insult. See **traer**

maltraído, -a /maltra'iðo/ a, Lat. Am. shabby

maltratamiento /maltrata'miento/ m, abuse, ill usage; damage, deterioration

maltratar /maltra'tar/ vt to ill-treat; abuse, insult; misuse, spoil, damage

maltrato /mal'trato/ m, maltreatment; misuse

maltrecho /mal'tretʃo/ a ill-treated, bruised; abused, insulted; damaged

maltusiano /maltu'siano/ a Malthusian

Malucas, las /ma'lukas, las/ the Moluccas

malucho /ma'lutʃo/ a Inf. off-color, below par, not well

malva /'malβa/ f, mallow. **m. real, m. rosa,** or **m. loca,** hollyhock. **ser como una m.,** Fig. Inf. to be a clinging vine

malvado /mal'βaðo/ a evil, malevolent, fiendish. n villain, fiend

malvasía /malβa'sia/ f, Bot. malvasia; malmsey (wine)

malvavisco /malβa'βisko/ m, Bot. marshmallow

malvender /malβen'der/ vt to sell at a loss

malversación /malβersa'sion; malβersa'θion/ f, malversation, maladministration; misappropriation (of funds)

malversador /malβersa'ðor/ **(-ra)** n bad or corrupt administrator

malversar /malβer'sar/ vt to misappropriate (funds)

Malvinas, las /mal'βinas/ fpl the Falkland Islands

mama /'mama/ f, Inf. breast; udder

mamá /'mama/ f, mama, mother

mamado, -a /ma'maðo/ a, Lat. Am. drunk, tipsy

mamar /ma'mar/ vt to suck (the breast); Inf. wolf, swallow; learn from an early age; enjoy, obtain unfairly; vr get drunk

mamario /ma'mario/ a mammary

mamarracho /mama'rratʃo/ m, Inf. scarecrow, dummy; anything grotesque looking

mameluco /mame'luko/ m, mameluke; Inf. ninny, fool

mamífero /ma'mifero/ a mammalian. m, mammal

mamotreto /mamo'treto/ m, notebook, memorandum; Inf. large book or bulky file of papers

mampara /mam'para/ f, folding screen; screen; partition

mamparo /mam'paro/ m, bulkhead

mampostería /mamposte'ria/ f, masonry, stonemasonry

mampostero /mampos'tero/ m, stonemason

maná /ma'na/ m, manna

manada /ma'naða/ f, handful; herd, flock; group, drove, crowd

manadero /mana'ðero/ m, herdsman, drover; spring, stream

manantial /manan'tial/ m, fountain, source, spring; head (of a river)

manar /ma'nar/ vi to flow, stream; be plentiful

manatí /mana'ti/ m, sea cow, manatee

mancar /man'kar/ vt to injure, maim; vi grow calm (elements)

manceba /man'seβa; man'θeβa/ f, concubine

mancebía /manse'βia; manθe'βia/ f, brothel; youth, young days

mancebo /man'seβo; man'θeβo/ m, youth, stripling; bachelor; shop assistant

mancha /'mantʃa/ f, spot, smear, stain; blotch; plot of ground; patch of vegetation; stigma, disgrace

manchar /man'tʃar/ vt to stain; smear; spot; speckle; disgrace; tarnish

manchuriano /mantʃu'riano/ **(-na)** a and n Manchurian

mancilla /man'siya; man'θiʎa/ f, stain; slur

mancillar /mansi'yar; manθi'ʎar/ vt to stain; Fig. smirch

manco /'manko/ **(-ca)** a maimed, disabled; one-handed; one-armed; armless; handless; incomplete, faulty. n disabled person. **El Manco de Lepanto,** Cervantes

mancomunidad /mankomuni'ðað/ f, association, society; community, union; commonwealth; regional legislative assembly

mancorna /man'korna/ f, Colombia cuff link **mancuerna, mancuernilla** f, Central America cuff link

manda /'manda/ f, offer, suggestion, proposition; legacy

mandadero /manda'ðero/ **(-ra)** n convent or prison messenger; errand boy (girl)

mandado /man'daðo/ m, order, command; errand

mandamiento /manda'miento/ m, order, command; Eccl. commandment; Law. writ; pl Inf. one's five fingers. **los diez mandamientos,** The Ten Commandments

mandar /man'dar/ vt to order, command; bequeath, will; send; control, drive; promise, offer; order (e.g. Mandó hacerse un traje, He ordered a suit to be made); vr walk unaided (convalescents, etc.); lead into one another (rooms, etc.); **¿Quién manda aquí?** Who is in charge here? **¡Mande!** Mexico Yes! (response to a call)

mandarín /manda'rin/ m, mandarin; Inf. bureaucrat; Lat. Am. bossy person, domineering person

mandarina /manda'rina/ f, (classical Chinese); mandarin orange

mandato /man'dato/ m, mandate; command; Eccl.

maundy. *Polit.* mandate. **cuarto m.,** fourth term (of President, Governor, etc.)

mandíbula /man'diβula/ *f,* jaw; jawbone, mandible

mandil /man'dil/ *m,* long leather apron; apron; Freemason's apron; close-meshed fishing net; *Lat. Am.* (horse) blanket

mandilón /mandi'lon/ *m, Inf.* coward, nincompoop

mandioca /man'dioka/ *f,* manioc, cassava; tapioca

mando /'mando/ *m,* authority, power; (*Mil. Nav.*) command; *Engin.* regulation; controls (of a machine, etc.). **m. a distancia,** remote control. *Aer.* **m. de dos pilotos,** dual-controlled. **mandos gemelos,** dual control. **al m. de,** under the command of; under the direction of

mandolín /mando'lin/ *m.* **mandolina** *f,* mandolin

mandón /man'don/ *a* domineering, bossy

mandril /man'dril/ *m, Mech.* mandrel, chuck; *Zool.* mandrill

manear /mane'ar/ *vt* to hobble (a horse); manage, control

manecilla /mane'siya; mane'θiʎa/ *f, dim* little hand; hand of a clock; *Print.* fist

manejable /mane'haβle/ *a* manageable, controllable

manejar /mane'har/ *vt* to handle; use, wield; control; manage, direct; ride (horses); *vr* manage to move around (after an accident, illness)

manejo /ma'neho/ *m,* handling; use, wielding; control; management, direction; horsemanship; intrigue

maneota /mane'ota/ *f,* hobble, shackle

manera /ma'nera/ *f,* manner, way, means; behavior, style (gen. *pl*); class (of people); *Art.* style, manner. **a la m. de,** like, in the style of. **de esa m.,** in that way; according to that, in that case. **de m. que,** so that. **en gran m.,** to a great extent. **sobre m.,** exceedingly

manga /'maŋga/ *f,* sleeve; bag; grip; handle; pipe (of a hose); strainer; waterspout; body of troops; beam, breadth of a ship; *pl* profits. **m. de viento,** whirlwind. **echar de m. a,** to make use of a person. *Inf.* **estar de m.,** to be in league. **tener m. ancha,** to be broad-minded. *Fig. Inf.* **traer (una cosa) en la m.,** to have (something) up one's sleeve. **de m. corta,** short-sleeved. **de m. larga,** long-sleeved

mangana /maŋ'gana/ *f,* lasso

manganilla /maŋga'niya; maŋga'niʎa/ *f,* sleight of hand; hoax, trick

mangle /'maŋgle/ *m,* mangrove tree

mango /'maŋgo/ *m,* handle, haft, stock; mango. **m. de cuchillo,** knife handle

mangonear /maŋgone'ar/ *vi Inf.* to loaf, roam about; interfere, meddle

mangonero /maŋgo'nero/ *a Inf.* meddlesome

mangosta /maŋ'gosta/ *f,* mongoose

mangote /maŋ'gote/ *m, Inf.* long, wide sleeve; black oversleeve

manguera /maŋ'guera/ *f,* hose; sleeve, tube; airshaft; waterspout

manguero /maŋ'guero/ *m,* fireman; hoseman

manguito /maŋ'guito/ *m,* muff; black oversleeve; wristlet, cuff; *Mech.* bush, sleeve

manía /ma'nia/ *f,* mania, obsession; whim, fancy

maniabierto, -a /mania'βierto/ *a, Lat. Am.* generous, giving, open-handed

maníaco /ma'niako/ **(-ca)** *a* maniacal; capricious, extravagant. *n* maniac

maniatar /mania'tar/ *vt* to handcuff; hobble (a cow, etc.)

maniático /ma'niatiko/ **(-ca)** *a* maniacal; capricious; faddy, fussy. *n* crank

manicomio /mani'komio/ *m,* insane asylum, mental hospital

manicura /mani'kura/ *f,* manicure

manicuro /mani'kuro/ **(-ra)** *n* manicurist

manida /ma'niða/ *f,* lair, den; dwelling, habitation

manifestación /manifesta'sion; manifesta'θion/ *f,* declaration, statement; exhibition; demonstration; *Eccl.* exposition (of the Blessed Sacrament)

manifestante /manifes'tante/ *mf* demonstrator

manifestar /manifes'tar/ *vt irr* to declare, make known; state; exhibit, show; *Eccl.* to expose (the Blessed Sacrament). See **acertar**

manifiesto /mani'fiesto/ *a* obvious, evident. *m,* manifesto; *Naut.* manifest; *Eccl.* exposition of the Blessed Sacrament. **poner de m.,** to show; make public; reveal

manigua /ma'nigua/ *f,* thicket, *Cuba* jungle

manija /ma'niha/ *f,* handle, stock, haft; hand lever; clamp; tether (for horses, etc.)

manileño /mani'leɲo/ *a* and *n* Manilan

manilla /ma'niya; ma'niʎa/ *f,* bracelet; handcuff, manacle

maniobra /ma'nioβra/ *f,* operation, process; *Mil.* maneuver; intrigue; tackle, gear; handling, management; *Naut.* working of a ship; *pl* shunting (trains)

maniobrar /manio'βrar/ *vi Mil.* to maneuver; *Naut.* handle, work (ships)

manipulación /manipula'sion; manipula'θion/ *f,* handling; manipulation; control, management

manipulador /manipula'ðor/ *a* manipulative. *m,* sending key (telegraphy)

manipular /manipu'lar/ *vt* to handle; manipulate; manage, direct

maniquete /mani'kete/ *m,* black lace mitten

maniquí /mani'ki/ *m,* mannequin; dummy; *Inf.* puppet, weak person

manirroto /mani'rroto/ **(-ta)** *a* wasteful, extravagant. *n* spendthrift

manivela /mani'βela/ *f, Mech.* crank, lever; *Lat. Am.* handle

manjar /man'har/ *m,* dish, food; pastime, recreation, pleasure. **m. blanco,** blancmange; *Lat. Am.* fudge

mano /'mano/ *f,* hand; coat, coating; quire (of paper); front paw (animals); elephant's trunk; side, hand; hand (of a clock); game (of cards, etc.); lead (at cards); way, means; ability; power; protection, favor; compassion; aid, help; scolding; *Mus.* scale; pestle; workers. *Inf.* editing, correction of a literary work (gen. by a person more skilled than the author). **m. de mortero,** pestle. **m. de obra,** (manual) labor. **manos muertas,** *Law.* mortmain. **m. sobre m.,** with folded hands; lazily, indolently. **a la m.,** at hand, nearby; within one's grasp. **a manos llenas,** in abundance, abundantly. **bajo m.,** in an underhand manner, secretly. **buenas manos,** cleverness, ability; dexterity. **de primera m.,** first-hand, new. **estar dejado de la m. de Dios,** to be very unlucky; be very foolish. **poner la m. en,** to ill-treat; slap, buffet. **Si a m. viene...,** If by chance... **tender la m.,** to put out one's hand, shake hands. **traer entre manos,** to have on hand, be engaged in

manojo /ma'noho/ *m,* bunch, handful. **a manojos,** in handfuls; plentifully, in abundance

manolo /ma'nolo/ **(-la)** *n* inhabitant of low quarters of Madrid noted for pride, gaiety, quarrelsomeness, and wit

manoseado /manose'aðo/ *a* hackneyed

manosear /manose'ar/ *vt* to handle; paw, touch repeatedly; finger

manoseo /mano'seo/ *m,* handling; fingering; *Inf.* pawing, feeling

manotada /mano'taða/ *f,* slap, cuff

manotear /manote'ar/ *vt* to slap, cuff; *vi* gesticulate, gesture with the hands

manoteo /mano'teo/ *m,* gesticulation with the hands

manquedad /manke'ðað/ *f,* disablement of hand or arm; lack of one of these; defect; incompleteness

mansalva /man'salβa/ **(a)** *adv* without danger

mansedumbre /manse'ðumbre/ *f,* meekness; kindness; gentleness

mansión /man'sion/ *f,* stay, visit; dwelling, abode; mansion

manso /'manso/ *a* soft, gentle; meek, mild; tame; peaceable, amiable; calm

manta /'manta/ *f,* blanket; horse blanket; traveling rug; *Inf.* hiding, thrashing. **m. de viaje,** traveling rug. *Inf.* **a m. de Dios,** in abundance. **dar una m.,** to toss in a blanket. *Fig. Inf.* **tirar de la m.,** to let the cat out of the bag

manteamiento /mantea'miento/ *m,* tossing in a blanket

mantear /mante'ar/ *vt* to toss in a blanket

manteca /man'teka/ *f*, lard; cooking fat; grease; *Argentina* butter. **como m.**, as mild as milk, as soft as butter

mantecada /mante'kaða/ *f*, buttered toast

mantecado /mante'kaðo/ *m*, French ice cream

mantecoso /mante'koso/ *a* greasy

mantel /man'tel/ *m*, tablecloth; altar cloth

mantelería /mantele'ria/ *f*, table linen

mantelete /mante'lete/ *m*, (*Eccl. Mil.*) mantlet

mantener /mante'ner/ *vt irr* to maintain; keep, feed; support; continue, persevere with; uphold, affirm; keep up; *vr* support oneself; remain in a place; (*with en*) continue to uphold (views, etc.), persevere in. **mantenerse firme,** *Fig.* to stand one's ground. See **tener**

mantenimiento /manteni'miento/ *m*, maintenance; support; sustenance, nourishment; affirmation; upkeep; livelihood

manteo /man'teo/ *m*, tossing in a blanket; long cloak

mantequera /mante'kera/ *f*, churn; dairymaid; butter dish

mantequero /mante'kero/ *m*, dairyman; butter dish

mantequilla /mante'kiya; mante'kiʎa/ *f*, butter

mantero /man'tero/ *m*, blanket seller or maker

mantilla /man'tiya; man'tiʎa/ *f*, mantilla; saddlecloth. *pl* baby's long clothes. **estar en mantillas,** to be in swaddling clothes; *Fig.* be in early infancy

manto /'manto/ *m*, cloak; cover, disguise; *Zool.* mantle; *Mineral.* layer

mantón /man'ton/ *m*, shawl. **m. de Manila,** Manila shawl

mantuano /man'tuano/ **(-na)** *a* and *n* Mantuan

manuable /ma'nuaβle/ *a* easy to handle or use, handy

manual /ma'nual/ *a* manual; handy, easy to use; docile, peaceable. *m*, manual, textbook; *Eccl.* book of ritual; notebook

manubrio /ma'nuβrio/ *m*, handle, crank; *Lat. Am.* handlebars

manuela /ma'nuela/ *f*, open carriage (Madrid)

manufactura /manufak'tura/ *f*, manufacture; manufactured article; factory

manufacturar /manufaktu'rar/ *vt* to manufacture

manufacturero /manufaktu'rero/ *a* manufacturing

manuscrito /manus'krito/ *a* and *m*, manuscript

manutención /manuten'sion; manuten'θion/ *f*, maintenance; upkeep; protection

manzana /man'sana; man'θana/ *f*, apple; block (of houses); city square; Adam's apple; *Argentina* 2.5 acres; *Central America* 1.75 acres

manzanal /mansa'nal; manθa'nal/ *m*, apple orchard; apple tree

manzanar /mansa'nar; manθa'nar/ *m*, apple orchard

manzanilla /mansa'niya; manθa'niʎa/ *f*, white sherry wine; *Bot.* chamomile; chamomile tea; knob, ball (on furniture); pad (on an animal's foot)

manzano /man'sano; man'θano/ *m*, apple tree

maña /'maɲa/ *f*, skill, dexterity; craftiness, guile; vice, bad habit (gen. *pl*). **darse m. para,** to contrive to

mañana /ma'ɲana/ *f*, morning; tomorrow. *m*, future, tomorrow. *adv* tomorrow; in time to come; soon. **¡M.!** Tomorrow! Another day! Not now! (generally to beggars). **de m.**, early in the morning. **muy de m.**, very early in the morning. **pasado m.**, the day after tomorrow

mañanica /maɲa'nika/ *f*, early morning

mañear /maɲe'ar/ *vt* to arrange cleverly; *vi* behave shrewdly

mañero /ma'ɲero/ *a* shrewd, clever; easily worked; handy

mañoso /ma'ɲoso/ *a* clever, skillful; crafty; vicious, with bad habits

mañuela /ma'ɲuela/ *f*, low guile

mapa /'mapa/ *m*, map; card. **m. en relieve,** relief map. **m. del estado mayor,** ordnance map. *Inf.* **no estar en el m.**, to be off the map; be most unusual (of things)

mapache /ma'patʃe/ *m*, raccoon

maqueta /ma'keta/ *f*, (*Art. Archit.*) model

maquiavélico /makia'βeliko/ *a* Machiavellian

maquiladora /makila'ðora/ *f*, maquiladora (factory run by a U.S. company in Mexico to take advantage of cheap labor and lax regulation)

maquillaje /maki'yahe; maki'ʎahe/ *m*, makeup, cosmetics; making up (of the face)

maquillar /maki'yar; maki'ʎar/ **(se)** *vt* and *vr* to make up (the face, etc.)

máquina /'makina/ *f*, machine, mechanism; engine; apparatus; plan, scheme; machine, puppet; *Inf.* mansion, palace; plenty; locomotive; fantasy, product of the imagination. **m. fax,** fax machine. **m. de vapor,** steam engine. **m. de arrastre,** traction engine; tractor. **m. de coser,** sewing machine. **m. de escribir,** typewriter. **m. fotográfica,** camera. **m. de impresionar,** movie camera. **m. de imprimir,** printing machine. **m. herramienta,** machine tool. **m. neumática,** air pump

maquinación /makina'sion; makina'θion/ *f*, intrigue, machination

maquinador /makina'ðor/ **(-ra)** *n* intriguer, schemer

maquinal /maki'nal/ *a* mechanical

maquinar /maki'nar/ *vt* to intrigue, scheme, plot

maquinaria /maki'naria/ *f*, machinery; applied mechanics; mechanism

maquinista /maki'nista/ *mf* driver, enginer; mechanic; machinist; locomotive driver

mar /mar/ *mf* sea; great many, abundance. **m. bonanza** *or* **m. en calma,** calm sea. **m. de fondo** *or* **m. de leva,** swell. **alta m.**, high seas. **a mares,** plentifully. **arar en el m.**, to labor in vain. *Naut.* **hacerse a la m.**, to put out to sea. **la m. de historias,** a great number of stories

maraña /ma'raɲa/ *f*, undergrowth; tangle; *Fig.* difficult position; intrigue; silk waste

marasmo /ma'rasmo/ *m*, *Med.* marasmus, atrophy; inactivity, paralysis

maravilla /mara'βiya; mara'βiʎa/ *f*, marvel, wonder; admiration; amazement; marigold. **a m.**, wonderfully. **a las mil maravillas,** to perfection, excellently. **por m.**, by chance; occasionally

maravillar /maraβi'yar; maraβi'ʎar/ *vt* to amaze, cause admiration; *vr* (*with de*) marvel at, admire; be amazed by

maravilloso /maraβi'yoso; maraβi'ʎoso/ *a* marvelous, wonderful

marbete /mar'βete/ *m*, label, tag; edge, border

marca /'marka/ *f*, mark, sign; brand; frontier zone, border country; standard, norm (of size); make, brand; measuring rule; *Sports.* record. **m. de fábrica,** brand, trademark. **m. de ley,** hallmark. **m. registrada,** registered name. **de m.**, excellent, of excellent quality

marcado /mar'kaðo/ *a* marked; pronounced; strong (of accents)

marcador /marka'ðor/ *a* marking. *m*, marker; scoreboard; bookmark

marcar /mar'kar/ *vt* to mark; brand; embroider initials on linen; tell the time (watches); show the amount (cash register, etc.); dial (telephone); *Sports.* score (a goal); notice, observe; set aside, earmark; *vr* *Naut.* check the course. **m. el compás** to beat time

marcha /'martʃa/ *f*, departure; running, working; *Mil.* march; speed (of trains, ships, etc.); *Mus.* march; progress, course (of events). **m. atrás,** backing, reversing. **m. de ensayo,** trial run. **m. forzada,** *Mil.* forced march. **a largas marchas,** with all speed. **a toda m.**, at top speed; full speed ahead; by forced marches; *Mil.* **batir la m.**, to strike up a march. **en m.**, underway; working; in operation

marchamero /martʃa'mero/ *m*, customs official who checks and marks goods

marchamo /mar'tʃamo/ *m*, customs mark on checked goods

marchante, -a /mar'tʃante/ *mf Lat. Am.* client, customer; dealer, merchant; peddler

marchar /mar'tʃar/ *vi* to run; work; function; go; leave, depart; progress, proceed; *Mil.* march; go (clocks); *vr* leave, go away

marchitable /martʃi'taβle/ *a* perishable, fragile

marchitar /mart∫i'tar/ vt to wither, fade; blight, spoil; weaken; vr wither; be blighted

marchito /mar't∫ito/ a withered; faded; blighted, frustrated

marcial /mar'sial; mar'θial/ a martial; courageous, militant

marcialidad /marsiali'ðað; marθiali'ðað/ f, war-like spirit, militancy

marciano /mar'siano; mar'θiano/ a Martian

marco /'marko/ m, mark (German coin); boundary mark; frame (of a picture, etc.). **m. de ventana,** window frame

Mar de las Indias /'mar de las 'indias/ Indian Ocean

Mar del Norte /'mar del 'norte/ North Sea

marea /ma'rea/ f, tide; strand, water's edge; light breeze; drizzle; dew; street dirt. **m. creciente,** flood tide. **m. menguante,** ebb tide. **m. muerta,** neap tide

mareaje /ma'reahe/ m, seamanship; ship's course

marear /mare'ar/ vt to navigate; sell; sell publicly; Inf. annoy; vr be seasick; feel faint; feel giddy; be damaged at sea (goods)

marejada /mare'haða/ f, surge, swell; high sea; tidal wave; commotion, uproar

mareo /ma'reo/ m, seasickness; nausea, dizziness; Inf. irritation, tediousness

mareta /ma'reta/ f, movement of the waves; sound, noise (of a crowd)

marfil /mar'fil/ m, ivory

marfileño /marfi'leɲo/ a ivory; ivory-like

marfuz /mar'fus; mar'fuθ/ a spurned, rejected; deceitful

marga /'marga/ f, loam, marl

margarina /marga'rina/ f, margarine

margarita /marga'rita/ f, pearl; marguerite, oxeye daisy; daisy; periwinkle

margen /'marhen/ mf edge, fringe, border, verge; margin (of a book); opportunity; marginal note. **dar m. para,** to provide an opportunity for; give rise to

marginal /marhi'nal/ a marginal

margoso /mar'goso/ a loamy, marly

marica /ma'rika/ f, magpie. m, (offensive) homosexual; milksop

maricón /mari'kon/ m, (offensive) homosexual

maridable /mari'ðaβle/ a marital, matrimonial

maridaje /mari'ðahe/ m, conjugal union and harmony; intimate relationship (between things)

maridar /mari'ðar/ vi to get married; mate, live as husband and wife; vt unite, link, join together

marido /ma'riðo/ m, husband

marihuana /mari'uana/ f, marijuana

marimacho /mari'mat∫o/ m, Inf. mannish woman

marina /ma'rina/ f, coast, seashore; Art. seascape; seamanship; navy, fleet. **m. de guerra,** navy. **m. mercante,** merchant navy

marinera /mari'nera/ f, sailor's blouse

marinería /marine'ria/ f, profession of a sailor; seamanship; crew of a ship; sailors (as a class)

marinero /mari'nero/ m, sailor, seaman. **m. de agua dulce,** freshwater sailor (a novice). **m. práctico,** able seaman. **a la marinera,** in a seaman-like fashion

marinesco /mari'nesko/ a seamanly

marino /ma'rino/ a marine, sea; seafaring; shipping. m, sailor, mariner

marioneta /mario'neta/ f, marionette, puppet

mariposa /mari'posa/ f, butterfly; night-light

mariposear /maripose'ar/ vi to flutter, flit, fly about; flirt; be fickle; follow about, dance attendance on

mariquita /mari'kita/ f, Ent. ladybird; parakeet.

marisabidilla /marisaβi'ðiya; marisaβi'ðiλa/ f, Inf. blue-stocking, know-it-all

mariscal /maris'kal/ m, Mil. marshal; field marshal; blacksmith

marisco /ma'risko/ m, shellfish

marisma /ma'risma/ f, bog, morass, swamp

marital /mari'tal/ a marital

marítimo /ma'ritimo/ a maritime, sea

marjal /mar'hal/ m, marshland, fen

marmita /mar'mita/ f, stewpot; copper, boiler; Mexico kettle

marmitón /marmi'ton/ m, kitchen boy, scullion

mármol /'marmol/ m, marble; work executed in marble

marmolería /marmole'ria/ f, marble works; work executed in marble

marmolista /marmo'lista/ mf marble cutter; dealer in marble

marmóreo /mar'moreo/ a marble; Poet. marmoreal

marmota /mar'mota/ f, Zool. marmot; sleepyhead, dormouse

Mar Muerto /mar 'muerto/ Dead Sea

maroma /ma'roma/ f, rope, hawser; Lat. Am. tightrope

maromero, -a /maro'mero/ mf, Lat. Am. acrobat, tightrope walker; opportunist

marquesina /marke'sina/ f, marquee

marquetería /markete'ria/ f, marquetry

marrana /ma'rrana/ f, sow; Inf. slattern, slut

marrano /ma'rrano/ m, pig, hog; Marrano

marras /'marras/ (de) adv long ago, in the dim past

marrasquino /marras'kino/ m, maraschino liqueur

marro /'marro/ m, tick, tag (game)

marrón /ma'rron/ a maroon; brown. m, brown color; maroon color; quoit

marroquí /marro'ki/ a and mf Moroccan. m, Morocco leather

marroquín /marro'kin/ **(-ina), marrueco (-ca)** a and n Moroccan

Marruecos /ma'rruekos/ Morocco

marrullería /marruye'ria; marruλe'ria/ f, flattery, cajolery

marrullero /marru'yero; marru'λero/ **(-ra)** a wheedling, flattering. n wheedler, cajoler

marsopa /mar'sopa/ f, porpoise

marta /'marta/ f, sable; marten

martajar /marta'har/ vt, Lat. Am. to grind, pound

Marte /'marte/ m, Mars

martes /'martes/ m, Tuesday. **m. de carnaval,** mardi gras

martillar /marti'yar; marti'λar/ vt to hammer; oppress

martillazo /marti'yaso; marti'λaθo/ m, hammer blow

martilleo /marti'yeo; marti'λeo/ m, hammering; noise of the hammer; clink, clatter

martillero, -a /marti'jero; marti'λero/ mf, Lat. Am. auctioneer

martillo /mar'tiyo; mar'tiλo/ m, hammer; oppressor, tyrant; auction rooms. **a m.,** by hammering. **de m.,** wrought (of metals)

martinete /marti'nete/ m, hammer (of a pianoforte); pile driver; drop hammer. **m. de báscula,** tilt hammer

Martinica /marti'nika/ Martinique

martín pescador /mar'tin peska'ðor/ m, kingfisher

mártir /'martir/ mf martyr

martirio /mar'tirio/ m, martyrdom

martirizar /martiri'sar; martiri'θar/ vt to martyr; torture, torment, martyrize; tease, annoy

marxismo /mark'sismo/ m, Marxism

marzo /'marso; 'marθo/ m, March

mas /mas/ conjunc but; yet

más /mas/ adv comp more; in addition, besides; rather, preferably. Math. plus. **el (la,** etc.) **más,** adv sup the most, etc. **m. bien,** more; rather; preferably. **m. que,** only; but; more than; although, even if. **a lo m.,** at the most; at the worst. **a m.,** besides, in addition. **de m.,** superfluous, unnecessary, unwanted. **m... m. que,** only. **por m. que,** however; even if. **sin m. ni m.,** without further ado. **M. vale un mal arreglo que un buen pleito,** A bad peace is better than a good war

masa /'masa/ f, mass; dough; whole, aggregate; majority (of people); mortar. **en la m. de la sangre,** Fig. in the blood, in a person's nature

masada /ma'saða/ f, farmhouse and stock

masadero /masa'ðero/ m, farmer; farm laborer

masaje /ma'sahe/ m, massage

masajista /masa'hista/ mf masseur; masseuse

masato /ma'sato/ m, Lat. Am. drink made from bananas, fermented corn, yucca, etc.

mascadura /maska'ðura/ f, chewing

mayor

mascar /mas'kar/ *vt* to chew; masticate; *Inf.* mumble, mutter

máscara /'maskara/ *f*, mask; fancy dress; pretext, excuse. *mf* masquerader, reveler; *pl* masquerade. **m. para gases,** gas mask

mascarada /maska'raða/ *f*, masquerade; company of revelers

mascarero /maska'rero/ **(-ra)** *n* theatrical costumer, fancy-dress dealer

mascarilla /maska'riya; maska'riʎa/ *f*, death mask

mascarón /maska'ron/ *m*, large mask; *Archit.* gargoyle. **m. de proa,** *Naut.* figurehead

mascota /mas'kota/ *f*, mascot

masculinidad /maskulini'ðað/ *f*, masculinity

masculino /masku'lino/ *a* masculine; male; manly, vigorous

mascullar /masku'yar; masku'ʎar/ *vt Inf.* to chew; mutter, mumble

masera /ma'sera/ *f*, kneading bowl; cloth for covering dough

masilla /ma'siya; ma'siʎa/ *f*, mastic, putty

masón /ma'son/ **(-ona)** *n* Freemason

masonería /masone'ria/ *f*, freemasonry

masónico /ma'soniko/ *a* masonic

masoquismo /maso'kismo/ *m*, masochism

mastelero /maste'lero/ *m*, *Naut.* topmast

masticación /mastika'sion; mastika'θion/ *f*, mastication

masticar /masti'kar/ *vt* to masticate, eat; *Inf.* chew upon, consider

masticatorio /mastika'torio/ *a* masticatory

mástil /'mastil/ *m*, *Naut.* mast; upright, stanchion; pole (of a tent); stem, trunk; neck (of a guitar, etc.)

mastín /mas'tin/ *m*, mastiff

mastodonte /masto'ðonte/ *m*, mastodon

mastoides /mastoi'ðes/ *a* mastoid

mastuerzo /mas'tuerso; mas'tuerθo/ *m*, watercress; fool, blockhead

masturbación /masturβa'sion; masturβa'θion/ *f*, masturbation

masturbarse /mastur'βarse/ *vr* to masturbate

mata /'mata/ *f*, plant, shrub; stalk, sprig; grove, copse. **m. de pelo,** mat of hair

matacandelas /matakan'delas/ *m*, candle snuffer

matachín /mata'tʃin/ *m*, mummer; butcher; *Inf.* swashbuckler

matadero /mata'ðero/ *m*, slaughterhouse, abattoir; *Lat. Am.* brothel

matadura /mata'ðura/ *f*, sore (on animals)

matafuego /mata'fuego/ *m*, fire extinguisher; fireman

matalotaje /matalo'tahe/ *m*, ship's supplies, stores; *Inf.* hodgepodge

matamoros /mata'moros/ *a* swashbuckling, swaggering

matamoscas /mata'moskas/ *m*, fly swatter

matanza /ma'tansa; ma'tanθa/ *f*, killing, massacre, slaughter; butchery (animals); *Inf.* persistence, determination

matar /ma'tar/ *vt* to kill; quench (thirst); put out (fire, light); slake (lime); tarnish (metal); bevel (corners, etc.); pester, importune; suppress; compel; *Art.* tone down; *vr* kill oneself; be disappointed, grieve; overwork. **estar a m.,** to be at daggers drawn. **matarse por,** to try hard to; work hard for

matasanos /mata'sanos/ *m*, *Inf.* quack (doctor); bad doctor

matasellos /mata'seyos; mata'seʎos/ *m*, cancellation, postmark

mate /'mate/ *a* matte, unpolished, dull. *m*, checkmate (chess); maté, Paraguayan tea; gourd; vessel made from gourd, coconut, etc., traditional tea of Argentina and the Andes drunk from a gourd

matemáticas /mate'matikas/ *f pl*, mathematics. **m. prácticas,** applied mathematics. **m. teóricas,** pure mathematics

matemático /mate'matiko/ *a* mathematical; exact. *m*, mathematician

materia /ma'teria/ *f*, matter; theme, subject matter; subject (of study); matter, stuff, substance; pus, matter; question, subject; reason, occasion. **m. colorante,** dye. **materias plásticas,** plastics. **materias primas,** raw materials. **en m. de,** concerning; in the matter of

material /mate'rial/ *a* material; dull, stupid, limited. *m*, material; ingredient; plant, factory; equipment. **m. móvil ferroviario,** rolling stock (railroads)

materialidad /materiali'ðað/ *f*, materiality; external appearance (of things)

materialismo /materia'lismo/ *m*, materialism

materialista /materia'lista/ *a* materialistic. *mf* materialist; *Mexico* truckdriver

materializar /materiali'sar; materiali'θar/ *vt* to materialize; *vr* materialize; grow materialistic, grow less spiritual

maternidad /materni'ðað/ *f*, maternity, motherhood

materno /ma'terno/ *a* maternal

matiz /ma'tis; ma'tiθ/ *m*, combination of colors; tone, hue; shade (of meaning, etc.)

matizar /mati'sar; mati'θar/ *vt* to combine, harmonize (colors); tint, shade; tinge (words, etc.)

matojo /ma'toho/ *m*, shrub, bush

matorral /mato'rral/ *m*, thicket, bush, undergrowth

matraca /ma'traka/ *f*, rattle; *Inf.* scolding, dressing-down; insistence, importunity

matraquear /matrake'ar/ *vi* to make a noise with a rattle; *Inf.* scold

matriarcado /matriar'kaðo/ *m*, matriarchy

matrícula /ma'trikula/ *f*, list, register; matriculation; registration number (of a car, etc.). **m. de buques,** maritime register. **m. de mar,** mariner's register; maritime register

matriculación /matrikula'sion; matrikula'θion/ *f*, matriculation; registration

matricular /matriku'lar/ *vt* to matriculate; enroll; *Naut.* register; *vr* matriculate; enroll, register

matrimonial /matrimo'nial/ *a* matrimonial

matrimonio /matri'monio/ *m*, marriage, matrimony; married couple. **m. a yuras,** secret marriage. **m. de la mano izquierda** *or* **m. morganático,** morganatic marriage. **contraer m.,** to get married

matritense /matri'tense/ *a* and *mf* Madrilenian

matriz /ma'tris; ma'triθ/ *f*, uterus, womb; matrix, mold; *Mineral.* matrix; nut, female screw

matrona /ma'trona/ *f*, married woman; matron; midwife; female customs officer

matusalén /matusa'len/ *m*, Methuselah, very old man

matute /ma'tute/ *m*, smuggling; contraband; gambling den

matutero /matu'tero/ **(-ra)** *n* smuggler, contrabandist

matutino /matu'tino/ *a* matutinal, morning

maula /'maula/ *f*, trash; remnant; deception, fraud, trick. *mf Inf.* good-for-nothing; lazybones. *Inf* **ser buena m.,** to be a trickster or a fraud

maulería /maule'ria/ *f*, remnant stall; trickery

maullar /mau'yar; mau'ʎar/ *vi* to meow, mew (cats)

maullido /mau'yiðo; mau'ʎiðo/ *m*, meow, cry of the cat

Mauricio, Isla de /mau'risio, 'isla de; mau'riθio, 'isla de/ Mauritius

mauritano /mauri'tano/ **(-na)** *a* and *n* Mauritian

mausoleo /mauso'leo/ *m*, mausoleum

maxilar /maksi'lar/ *a* maxillary. *m*, jaw

máxima /'maksima/ *f*, maxim, rule, precept, principle

máxime /'maksime/ *adv* principally, chiefly

máximo /'maksimo/ *a sup* **grande** greatest, maximum, top. *m*, maximum

maya /'maya/ *f*, common daisy; May queen

mayal /ma'yal/ *m*, flail

mayo /'mayo/ *m*, May; maypole; bouquet, wreath of flowers; *pl* festivities on eve of May Day

mayólica /ma'yolika/ *f*, majolica

mayonesa /mayo'nesa/ *f*, mayonnaise

mayor /ma'yor/ *a comp* **grande** bigger; greater; elder; main, principal; older; high (mass, etc.); *Mus.* major. *mf* major (of full age). *a sup* **grande. el, la, lo mayor, los (las) mayores,** the biggest, greatest; eldest; chief, principal. **por m.,** in short, briefly; *Com.*

wholesale. *m*, head, director; chief clerk; *Mil.* major; *pl* ancestors

mayoral /mayo'ral/ *m*, head shepherd; coachman, driver; foreman, overseer, supervisor, steward

mayorazgo /mayo'rasgo; mayo'raθgo/ *m*, *Law.* entail; entailed estate; heir (to an entail); eldest son; right of primogeniture

mayordoma /mayor'ðoma/ *f*, steward's wife; housekeeper; stewardess

mayordomo /mayor'ðomo/ *m*, steward, superintendent; butler; major-domo, royal chief steward

mayoreo /mayo'reo/ *m*, *Lat. Am.* wholesale

mayoría /mayo'ria/ *f*, majority

mayorista /mayo'rista/ *mf*, wholesaler

mayormente /mayor'mente/ *adv* chiefly; especially

mayúscula /ma'yuskula/ *f*, capital letter, upper-case letter

mayúsculo /ma'yuskulo/ *a* large; capital (letters).

letra mayúscula, capital letter, upper-case letter

maza /'masa; 'maθa/ *f*, mallet; club, bludgeon; mace; bass drum stick; pile driver; bone, stick, etc., tied to dog's tail in carnival; *Inf.* pedant, bore; important person, authority; *Lat. Am.* hub (of a wheel). **m. de polo,** polo mallet

mazacote /masa'kote; maθa'kote/ *m*, concrete; roughhewn work of art; *Inf.* stodgy overcooked dish; bore, tedious person

mazamorra /masa'morra; maθa'morra/ *f*, dish made of cornmeal; biscuit crumbs; broken fragments, remains

mazapán /masa'pan; maθa'pan/ *m*, marzipan

mazmorra /mas'morra; maθ'morra/ *f*, dungeon

mazo /'maso; 'maθo/ *m*, mallet; bundle, bunch; importunate person; clapper (of a bell); *Argentina*, deck (of cards)

mazonería /masone'ria; maθone'ria/ *f*, stonemasonry

mazonero /maso'nero; maθo'nero/ *m*, stonemason

mazorca /ma'sorka; ma'θorka/ *f*, spindleful; spike, ear (of corn); cocoa berry; camarilla, group

mazurca /ma'surka; ma'θurka/ *f*, mazurka

me /me/ *pers pron acc* or *dat 1st sing mf* me; to me

meandro /me'andro/ *m*, meandering, twisting, winding; wandering

meato /me'ato/ *m*, meatus

mecánica /me'kanika/ *f*, mechanics; mechanism, machinery; *Inf.* worthless thing; mean action

mecánico /me'kaniko/ *a* mechanical; power-operated; base, ill-bred. *m*, engineer; mechanic

mecanismo /meka'nismo/ *m*, mechanism; works, machinery

mecanizar /mekani'sar; mekani'θar/ *vt* to mechanize

mecanografía /mekanogra'fia/ *f*, typewriting

mecanografiar /mekanografi'ar/ *vt* to typewrite, type

mecanográfico /mekano'grafiko/ *a* typewriting, typing; typewritten, typed

mecanografista /mekanogra'fista/ *mf* **mecanógrafo (-fa)** *n* typist

mecate /me'kate/ *m*, *Lat. Am.* twine; coarse person

mecedor /mese'ðor; meθe'ðor/ *a* rocking, swaying. *m*, swing; *Lat. Am.* rocking chair

mecedora /mese'ðora; meθe'ðora/ *f*, rocking chair

mecenas /me'senas; me'θenas/ *m*, Maecenas, patron

mecer /me'ser; me'θer/ *vt* to stir, mix; shake; rock; swing

mecha /'metʃa/ *f*, wick; bit, drill; fuse (of explosives); match (for cannon, etc.); fat bacon (for basting); lock of hair; skein, twist; *Lat. Am.* fright, scare

mechar /me'tʃar/ *vt Cul.* to baste, lard

mechero /me'tʃero/ *m*, gas burner; pocket lighter; socket of a candlestick

mechón /me'tʃon/ *m*, tuft, skein, bundle; lock of hair; wisp

medalla /me'ðaya; me'ðaʎa/ *f*, medal; medallion; plaque, round panel; *Inf.* piece of eight (coin)

medallón /me'ðayon; meða'ʎon/ *m*, large medal; medallion; locket

media /'meðia/ *f*, stocking

mediación /meðia'sion; meðia'θion/ *f*, mediation, arbitration; intercession

mediado /me'ðiaðo/ *a* half-full. **a mediados (del mes,** etc.), toward the middle (of the month, etc.)

mediador /meðia'ðor/ **(-ra)** *n* mediator, arbitrator; intercessor

medianamente /meðiana'mente/ *adv* moderately; passably, fairly well

medianero /meðia'nero/ **(-ra)** *a* middle; intervening, intermediate; mediatory. *n* mediator. *m*, owner of a semidetached house or of one in a row

medianía /meðia'nia/ *f*, average; medium, mediocrity; moderate wealth or means

mediano /me'ðiano/ *a* medium, average; moderate; *Inf.* middling, passable, fair

medianoche /meðia'notʃe/ *f*, midnight

mediante /me'ðiante/ *a* mediatory. *adv* by means of, by, through

mediar /me'ðiar/ *vi* to reach the middle; get halfway; elapse half a given time; intercede, mediate; arbitrate; be in between or in the middle; intervene, take part

medicación /meðika'sion; meðika'θion/ *f*, medication

medicamento /meðika'mento/ *m*, medicine, remedy

medicar /meði'kar/ *vt* to medicate

medicastro /meði'kastro/ *m*, unskilled physician; quack, charlatan

medicina /meði'sina; meði'θina/ *f*, medicine

medicinar /meðisi'nar; meðiθi'nar/ *vt* to attend; treat (patients)

medición /meði'sion; meði'θion/ *f*, measuring; measurements; survey (land); scansion

médico /'meðiko/ **(-ca)** *a* medical. *n* doctor of medicine. **m. de cabecera,** family doctor. **m. general,** general practitioner

medida /me'ðiða/ *f*, measurement; measuring stick; measure, precaution (gen. with *tomar, adoptar*, etc.); gauge; judgment; wisdom; meter; standard. **a m. que,** while, at the same time as. **tomar las medidas (a),** *Fig.* to take a person's measure, sum him up. **tomar sus medidas,** to take his (their) measurements; take the necessary measures. **un traje hecho a m.,** a suit made to measure

medidor /meði'ðor/ *m Lat. Am.* gauge, meter. **m. de agua** water meter. **m. de gas** gas meter

medio /'meðio/ *a* half; middle; intermediate; half-way. *m*, half; middle; *Art.* medium; spiritualist medium; proceeding, measure, precaution; environment, medium; middle way, mean; *Sports.* halfback. **m. galope,** canter. **m. tiempo,** part-time (job), *Sports.* halftime. **a medias,** by halves; half, partly. **de por m.,** by halves; in between; in the way. **estar de por m.,** to be in the way; take part in. *Inf.* **quitar de en m.,** to get rid of. *Inf.* **quitarse de en m.,** to go away, remove oneself

mediocre /me'ðiokre/ *a* mediocre

mediodía /meðio'ðia/ *m*, noon, meridian; south

medioeval /meðioe'βal/ *a* medieval

mediquillo /meði'kiyo; meði'kiʎo/ *m*, *Inf.* quack; medicine man (in the Philippines)

medir /me'ðir/ *vt irr* to measure; (metrics) scan; survey (land); compare; *vr* measure one's words; act with restraint. See **pedir**

meditabundo /meðita'βundo/ *a* pensive, meditative, thoughtful

meditación /meðita'sion; meðita'θion/ *f*, meditation, consideration, reflection

meditador /meðita'ðor/ *a* meditative, thoughtful

meditar /meði'tar/ *vt* to meditate, consider, muse

meditativo /meðita'tiβo/ *a* meditative

mediterráneo /meðite'rraneo/ *a* mediterranean; inland, landlocked

médium /'meðium/ *m*, *Spirit.* medium

medra /'meðra/ *f*, progress; improvement, betterment; growth; prosperity

medrar /me'ðrar/ *vi* to flourish, grow; become prosperous or improve one's position

medro /'meðro/ *m*, improvement, progress. See **medra**

medroso /me'ðroso/ *a* timid, frightened; frightful, horrible

médula /'meðula/ *f*, marrow; *Bot.* pith; *Fig.* essence, core

medusa /me'ðusa/ f, jellyfish

mefistofélico /mefisto'feliko/ a Mephistophelian

mefítico /me'fitiko/ a noxious, mephitic, poisonous

megáfono /me'gafono/ m, megaphone

megalómano /mega'lomano/ **(-na)** n megalomaniac

mejicano /mehi'kano/ **(-na)** a and n Mexican

Méjico /'mehiko/ Mexico

mejilla /me'hiya; me'hiλa/ f, Anat. cheek

mejillón /mehi'yon; mehi'λon/ m, sea mussel

mejor /me'hor/ a comp **bueno** better. adv better; rather; sooner; preferably. a sup **bueno. el, la, lo mejor; los, las mejores,** the best; most preferable. **m. que m.,** better and better. Inf. **a lo m.,** probably, in all probability. **tanto m.,** so much the better

mejora /me'hora/ f, improvement; bettering; progress; higher bid (at auctions)

mejorable /meho'raβle/ a improvable

mejoramiento /mehora'miento/ m, betterment, improvement

mejorar /meho'rar/ vt to improve; better; outbid; vi grow better (in health); improve (weather); make progress; rally (of markets). **Mejorando lo presente,** Present company excepted

mejoría /meho'ria/ f, improvement, progress; betterment; superiority; advantage, profit

mejunje /me'hunhe/ m, Inf. brew, potion, cure-all, stuff; Lat. Am. mess

melado /me'laðo/ a honey-colored. m, cane syrup

melancolía /melanko'lia/ f, melancholia; sadness, depression, melancholy

melancólico /melan'koliko/ a melancholy, sad; depressing

melaza /me'lasa; me'laθa/ f, molasses

melena /me'lena/ f, long side whiskers; loose, flowing hair (in women); overlong hair (in men); lion's mane. Inf. **andar a la m.,** to start a fight or quarrel. Inf. **traer a la m.,** to drag by the hair, force

melifluo /me'lifluo/ a mellifluous, sweet-voiced; honeyed

melindre /me'lindre/ m, honey fritter; affectation, scruple, fastidiousness; narrow ribbon

melindroso /melin'droso/ a overfastidious, affected, prudish

mella /'meya; 'meλa/ f, nick, notch; dent; gap; harm, damage (to reputation, etc.). **hacer m.,** Fig. to make an impression (on the mind); Mil. breach, drive a wedge

mellar /me'yar; me'λar/ vt to nick, notch; dent; damage

mellizo /me'yiso; me'λiθo/ **(-za)** a and n twin (fraternal)

melocotón /meloko'ton/ m, peach; peach tree

melocotonero /melokoto'nero/ m, peach tree

melodía /melo'ðia/ f, melody, tune; melodiousness

melódico /me'loðiko/ a melodic, melodious

melodioso /melo'ðioso/ a melodious, tuneful, sweet-sounding

melodrama /melo'ðrama/ m, melodrama

melodramático /meloðra'matiko/ a melodramatic

melón /me'lon/ m, melon

melosidad /melosi'ðað/ f, sweetness

meloso /me'loso/ a honeyed; sweet; gentle; mellifluous

membrana /mem'brana/ f, membrane

membrete /mem'brete/ m, note, memorandum; note or card of invitation; superscription, heading; address (of person)

membrillo /mem'briyo; mem'briλo/ m, quince tree; quince; quince jelly

membrudo /mem'bruðo/ a brawny, strong, muscular

memo /'memo/ a silly, stupid

memorable /memo'raβle/ a memorable

memorándum /memo'randum/ m, notebook, jotter; memorandum

memorar /memo'rar/ **(se)** vt and vr to remember, recall

memoria /me'moria/ f, memory; remembrance, recollection; monument; memorial; report; essay, article; codicil; memorandum; record, chronicle; pl regards, compliments; greetings; memoirs; memo-

randa. Inf. **m. de grillo,** poor memory. **de m.,** by heart. **flaco de m.,** forgetful. **hacer m.,** to remember

memorial /memo'rial/ m, notebook; memorial, petition

memorioso /memo'rioso/ a mindful, unforgetful

mena /'mena/ f, Mineral. ore

menaje /me'nahe/ m, household or school equipment or furniture

mención /men'sion; men'θion/ f, mention. **m. honorífica,** honorable mention. **hacer m. de,** to mention

mencionar /mensio'nar; menθio'nar/ vt to mention

mendacidad /mendasi'ðað; mendaθi'ðað/ f, mendacity, untruthfulness

mendaz /men'das; men'daθ/ a mendacious, untruthful

mendicante /mendi'kante/ a begging; Eccl. mendicant. mf beggar

mendicidad /mendisi'ð; mendiθi'ðað/ f, mendicancy, begging

mendigar /mendi'gar/ vt to beg for alms; entreat, supplicate

mendigo /men'digo/ **(-ga)** n beggar

mendoso /men'doso/ a mendacious, untruthful; mistaken

mendrugo /men'drugo/ m, crust of bread

menear /mene'ar/ vt to sway, move; wag; shake; manage, control, direct; vr Inf. get a move on; sway, move; wriggle

meneo /me'neo/ m, swaying movement; wagging; shaking; wriggling; management, direction; Aer. bump; Inf. spanking

menester /menes'ter/ m, lack, shortage; necessity; occupation, employment; pl physical necessities; Inf. tools, implements, equipment. **haber m.,** to need, require. **ser m.,** to be necessary or requisite

menesteroso /meneste'roso/ a indigent, poverty-stricken, needy

menestra /me'nestra/ f, vegetable soup; dried vegetable (gen. pl)

mengano /meŋ'gano/ **(-na)** n so-and-so (used instead of the name of the person)

mengua /'meŋgua/ f, decrease; lack, shortage; waning (of the moon, etc.); dishonor, disgrace; poverty

menguado /meŋ'guaðo/ **(-da)** a timid, cowardly; silly, stupid; mean, avaricious. n coward; fool; skinflint. m, narrowing stitch when knitting socks

menguante /meŋ'guante/ a ebb; waning; decreasing. f, ebb tide; decadence, decline. **m. de la luna,** waning of the moon

menguar /meŋ'guar/ vi to decrease; decline, decay; wane; ebb; narrow (socks); vt diminish; disgrace, discredit

menina /me'nina/ f, child attendant (on Spanish royalty)

menino /me'nino/ m, Spanish royal page; little dandy

menjurje /men'hurhe/ m, See **mejunje**

menopausia /meno'pausia/ f, menopause

menor /me'nor/ a comp less, smaller; younger, minor; Mus. minor. m, minor. f, (logic) minor. a sup **el, la, lo m.; los, las menores,** the least; smallest; youngest. **m. de edad,** minor (in age). **por m.,** at retail; in detail

menoría /meno'ria/ f, subordination, dependence; inferiority; minority (underage); childhood, youth

menorista /meno'rista/ Lat. Am., a retail; mf retailer

menos /'menos/ adv less; minus; least; except. **m. de** or **m. que,** less than. **al m., por lo m.,** at least. **a m. que,** unless. **De m. nos hizo Dios,** Never say die, Nothing is impossible. **poco más o m.,** more or less, about

menoscabar /menoska'βar/ vt to lessen, diminish, decrease; deteriorate, impair; disgrace, discredit

menoscabo /menos'kaβo/ m, decrease, diminishment; harm, damage, loss

menospreciable /menospre'siaβle; menospre'θiaβle/ a despicable, contemptible

menospreciador /menospresia'ðor; menospreθia'ðor/ **(-ra)** a scornful. n scorner, despiser

menospreciar /menospre'siar; menospre'θiar/ *vt* to despise, scorn; underestimate, have a poor opinion of

menospreciativo /menospresia'tiβo; menospre-θia'tiβo/ *a* scornful, slighting, derisive

menosprecio /menos'presio; menos'preθio/ *m*, scorn, derision; underestimation

mensaje /men'sahe/ *m*, message; official communication

mensajería /mensahe'ria/ *f*, carrier service; steamship line

mensajero /mensa'hero/ **(-ra)** *n* messenger; errand boy

menso, -a /'menso/ *a*, *Mexico* dumb, silly, stupid

menstruación /menstrua'sion; menstrua'θion/ *f*, menstruation

menstruar /menstru'ar/ *vi* to menstruate

mensual /men'sual/ *a* monthly

mensualidad /mensuali'ðað/ *f*, monthly salary, monthly payment

mensurable /mensu'raβle/ *a* measurable

mensurar /mensu'rar/ *vt* to measure

menta /'menta/ *f*, menthe, mint; peppermint

mentado /men'taðo/ *a* celebrated, distinguished, famous

mental /men'tal/ *a* mental

mentalidad /mentali'ðað/ *f*, mentality

mentalmente /mental'mente/ *adv* mentally

mentar /men'tar/ *vt irr* to mention. See **sentar**

mentas /'mentas/ *fpl*, *Argentina* reputation, gossip

mente /'mente/ *f*, mind; intelligence, understanding; will, intention

mentecatería /mentekate'ria/ *f*, folly, stupidity

mentecato /mente'kato/ **(-ta)** *a* foolish, silly; feebleminded, simple. *n* fool, idiot

mentir /men'tir/ *vi irr* to lie, be untruthful; deceive, mislead; falsify; *Poet.* belie; disagree, be incompatible; *vt* break a promise, disappoint. **m. como un bellaco,** to lie like a trooper. See **sentir**

mentira /men'tira/ *f*, lie, falsehood; error (in writing); *Inf.* white spot (on a fingernail); cracking (of fingerjoints). **m. oficiosa,** white lie. **Parece m.,** It seems incredible

mentiroso /menti'roso/ *a* lying, false; full of errors (literary works); deceptive

mentís /men'tis/ *m*, giving the lie (literally, you lie); proof, demonstration (of error)

mentol /'mentol/ *m*, menthol

mentón /men'ton/ *m*, chin

menú /me'nu/ *m*, menu

menudamente /menuða'mente/ *adv* minutely; in detail, circumstantially

menudear /menuðe'ar/ *vt* to do frequently; do repeatedly; *vi* happen frequently; describe in detail; *Com.* sell by retail

menudencia /menu'ðensia; menu'ðenθia/ *f*, minuteness, smallness; exactness, care, accuracy; trifle, worthless object; small matter; *pl* offal; pork sausages

menudeo /menu'ðeo/ *m*, repetition; description in detail; *Com.* retail. **al m.,** at retail

menudillos /menu'ðiyos; menu'ðiʎos/ *m pl*, giblets; offal

menudo /menu'ðo/ *a* minute, tiny; despicable; thin; small; vulgar; meticulous, exact; small (money). *m*, small coal; *m pl*, offal, entrails; small change (money). **a m.,** often, frequently. **por m.,** in detail, carefully; *Com.* in small lots

meñique /me'ɲike/ *a Inf.* very small. *m*, little finger (in full, **dedo m.**)

meollo /me'oyo; me'oʎo/ *m*, brain; *Anat.* marrow; *Fig.* essence, core, substance; understanding; *Inf.* no **tener m. (una cosa),** to be worthless, unsubstantial (things)

me palpita que... /me pal'pita ke / *Argentina*, I have a hunch that...

mequetrefe /meke'trefe/ *m*, *Inf.* coxcomb, whippersnapper

meramente /mera'mente/ *adv* solely, simply, merely

mercachifle /merkat'ʃifle/ *m*, peddler; small merchant

mercadear /merkaðe'ar/ *vi* to trade, traffic

mercadeo /merka'ðeo/ *m*, marketing (study of markets)

mercader /merka'ðer/ *m*, dealer, merchant, trader. **m. de grueso,** wholesaler

mercadería /merkaðe'ria/ *f*, See **mercancía**

mercado /mer'kaðo/ *m*, market; marketplace

mercancía /merkan'sia; merkan'θia/ *f*, goods, merchandise; commerce, trade, traffic

mercante /mer'kante/ *a* trading; commercial. *m*, merchant, dealer, trader

mercantil /merkan'til/ *a* mercantile, commercial

merced /mer'seð; mer'θeð/ *f*, salary, remuneration; favor, benefit, kindness; will, desire, pleasure; mercy, grace; courtesy title given to untitled person (e.g. *vuestra m.,* your honor. Has now become *usted* and is universally used). **m. a,** thanks to. **estar uno a m. de,** to live at someone else's expense, be dependent on

mercenario /merse'nario; merθe'nario/ **(-ia)** *n Eccl.* member of the Order of la Merced. *m*, *Mil.* mercenary; day laborer. *a* mercenary

mercería /merse'ria; merθe'ria/ *f*, haberdashery, mercery

mercerizar /merseri'sar; merθeri'θar/ *vt* to mercerize

mercero /mer'sero; mer'θero/ *m*, haberdasher, mercer

mercurio /mer'kurio/ *m*, mercury, quicksilver; *Astron.* Mercury

merecedor /merese'ðor; mereθe'ðor/ *a* deserving, worthy

merecer /mere'ser; mere'θer/ *vt irr* to deserve, be worthy of; attain, achieve; be worth; *vi* deserve, be deserving. **m. bien de,** to deserve well of; have a claim on the gratitude of. See **conocer**

merecido /mere'siðo; mere'θiðo/ *m*, due reward

merecimiento /meresi'miento; mereθi'miento/ *m*, desert; merit

merendar /meren'dar/ *vi irr* to have lunch; pry into another's affairs; *vt* have (a certain food) for lunch. *Inf.* **merendarse (una cosa),** to obtain (a thing), have it in one's pocket. See **recomendar**

merendero /meren'dero/ *m*, lunchroom; tearoom

merengue /me'rengue/ *m*, *Cul.* meringue. **el Merengue,** Latin dance and music originating in the Dominican Republic

meridiana /meri'ðiana/ *f*, daybed, chaise longue; siesta

meridiano /meri'ðiano/ *a* meridian. *m*, meridian. **a la meridiana,** at noon

meridional /meriðio'nal/ *a* meridional, southern

merienda /me'rienda/ *f*, tea, snack; lunch; *Inf.* hunchback. *Inf.* **juntar meriendas,** to join forces, combine interests

merino /me'rino/ *a* merino. *m*, merino wool; shepherd of merino sheep

mérito /'merito/ *m*, merit; desert; worth, excellence. **de m.,** excellent, notable. **hacer m. de,** to mention

meritorio /meri'torio/ *a* meritorious. *m*, unpaid worker, learner

merluza /mer'lusa; mer'luθa/ *f*, hake; *Inf.* drinking bout. *Inf.* **pescar una m.,** to get drunk

merma /'merma/ *f*, decrease, drop; loss, waste, reduction; leakage

mermar /mer'mar/ *vi* to diminish, waste away, decrease; evaporate; leak; *vt* filch, pilfer; reduce, decrease

mermelada /merme'laða/ *f*, preserve; jam; marmalade

mero /'mero/ *a* mere; simple; plain

merodeador /meroðea'ðor/ *a* marauding. *m*, marauder, raider

merodear /meroðe'ar/ *vi* to maraud, raid; *Mexico* make money illegally

merodeo /mero'ðeo/ *m*, raiding, marauding

mes /'mes/ *m*, month; menses, menstruation

mesa /'mesa/ *f*, table; board, directorate; meseta, tableland; staircase landing; flat (of a sword, etc.); game of billiards. **m. de batalla,** post office sorting table. **m. de caballete,** trestle table. **m. de noche,**

bedside table. **m. de tenis,** *Mexico* tennis court. **m. de tijeras,** folding table. **m. giratoria,** turntable. **alzar** (*or* **levantar**) **la m.,** to clear the table. **cubrir** (*or* **poner**) **la m.,** to set the table

mesada /me'saða/ *f,* monthly wages, monthly payment

mesadura /mesa'ðura/ *f,* tearing of the hair or beard

mesarse /me'sarse/ *vr* to tear one's hair or beard

mesenterio /mesen'terio/ *m,* mesentery

mesera /me'sera/ *f Mexico* waitress

mesero /me'sero/ *m Mexico* waiter

meseta /me'seta/ *f,* staircase landing; plateau, tableland

mesiánico /me'sianiko/ *a* Messianic

Mesías /me'sias/ *m,* Messiah

mesilla /me'siya; me'siʎa/ *f,* small table; laughing admonition; landing (of a stair)

mesnada /mes'naða/ *f,* association, company, society

mesocracia /meso'krasia; meso'kraθia/ *f,* mesocracy; middle class, bourgeoisie

mesón /me'son/ *m,* inn, tavern

mesonero /meso'nero/ **(-ra)** *n* innkeeper; *Venezuela* waiter, waitress

mesta /'mesta/ *f,* ancient order of sheep farmers; *pl* confluence, meeting (of rivers)

mester /'mester/ *m,* craft, occupation. **m. de clerecía,** learned poetic meter of the Spanish Middle Ages. **m. de juglaría,** popular poetry and troubadour songs

mestizo /mes'tiso; mes'tiθo/ *a* half-breed; crossbreed, *Lat. Am.* of mixed Castilian and Native American ancestry

mesura /me'sura/ *f,* sedateness; dignity; courtesy; moderation

mesurado /mesu'raðo/ *a* sedate; dignified; moderate, restrained, temperate

meta /'meta/ *f,* goalpost *Fig.* aim, end; goal; goalkeeper

metabolismo /metaβo'lismo/ *m,* metabolism

metáfora /me'tafora/ *f,* metaphor

metafórico /meta'foriko/ *a* metaphorical

metal /me'tal/ *m,* metal; brass; timbre of the voice; state, condition; quality, substance; *Herald.* gold or silver; *Mus.* brass (instruments)

metalario /meta'lario/ *m,* metalworker

metálico /me'taliko/ *a* metallic. *m,* metalworker; coin, specie; bullion

metalistería /metaliste'ria/ *f,* metalwork

metalizar /metali'sar; metali'θar/ *vt* to metallize, make metallic; *vr* become metallized; grow greedy for money

metalurgia /metalur'hia/ *f,* metallurgy

metalúrgico /meta'lurhiko/ *a* metallurgical. *m,* metallurgist

metamorfosis /metamor'fosis/ *f,* metamorphosis

metano /me'tano/ *m,* methane

metate /me'tate/ *m, Central America, Mexico* flat stone for grinding and pounding

metátesis /me'tatesis/ *f,* metathesis

metedor /mete'ðor/ **(-ra)** *n* placer, inserter; smuggler, contrabandist

metellón, -ona /mete'jon; mete'ʎon/ *a, Mexico* meddling, meddlesome

metempsicosis /metempsi'kosis/ *f,* metempsychosis

metemuertos /mete'muertos/ *Inf.* meddler, Nosy Parker

meteórico /mete'oriko/ *a* meteoric

meteorito /meteo'rito/ *m,* meteorite

meteoro /mete'oro/ *m,* meteor

meteorología /meteorolo'hia/ *f,* meteorology

meteorológico /meteoro'lohiko/ *a* meteorological

meteorologista /meteorolo'hista/ *mf* meteorologist; weather forecaster

meter /me'ter/ *vt* to place; put; introduce, insert; stake (gambling); smuggle; cause, occasion; place close together; persuade to take part in; *Sew.* take in fullness; deceive, humbug; cram in, pack tightly; *Naut.* take in sail; *vr* interfere, butt in; meddle (with); take up, follow (occupations); be overfamiliar; disembogue, empty itself (rivers, etc.); attack with the sword; (*with prep a*) follow (occupations); become,

turn (e.g. *meterse a predicar,* to turn preacher); (*with con*) pick a quarrel with. **meterse en precisiones,** to go into details. *Inf.* **meterse en todo,** to be very meddlesome

metesillas y sacamuertos /mete'siyas i saka'muertos; mete'siʎas i saka'muertos/ *m,* scene shifter, stagehand

metiche /me'titʃe/ *a, Mexico* = **metellón**

meticulosidad /metikulosi'ðað/ *f,* meticulosity; timorousness

meticuloso /metiku'loso/ *a* meticulous, fussy; timid, nervous

metido /me'tiðo/ *a* tight; crowded; crabbed (of handwriting). *m, Sew.* material for letting out (seams). **m. en años,** quite old (person)

metílico /me'tiliko/ *a* methylic

metimiento /meti'miento/ *m,* insertion, introduction; influence, sway

metódico /me'toðiko/ *a* methodical

método /'metoðo/ *m,* method

metodología /metoðolo'hia/ *f,* methodology

metralla /me'traya; me'traʎa/ *f, Mil.* grapeshot, shrapnel

métrica /'metrika/ *f,* metrics

métrico /'metriko/ *a* metric; metrical

metro /'metro/ *m,* (verse) meter; meter (measurement); subway, underground railway

metrónomo /me'tronomo/ *m,* metronome

metrópoli /me'tropoli/ *f,* metropolis, capital; see of a metropolitan bishop; mother country

metropolitano /metropoli'tano/ *a* metropolitan. *m,* metropolitan bishop

mexicano /meksi'kano/ *Lat. Am.* = **mejicano**

México /'mehiko/ *Lat. Am.* = **Méjico**

mezcla /'meskla; 'meθkla/ *f,* mixture; blend, combination; mixed cloth, tweed; mortar

mezclar /mes'klar; meθ'klar/ *vt* to mix, blend, combine; *vr* mix, mingle; take part; interfere, meddle; intermarry

mezcolanza /mesko'lansa; meθko'lanθa/ *f, Inf.* hodgepodge

mezquindad /meskin'dað; meθkin'dað/ *f,* poverty; indigence; miserliness; paltriness; meanness, poorness

mezquino /mes'kino; meθ'kino/ *a* needy, impoverished; miserly, stingy; small, diminutive; unhappy; mean, paltry

mezquita /mes'kita; meθ'kita/ *f,* mosque

mi /'mi/ *poss pron* my. *m, Mus.* mi, E

mí /'mi/ *pers pron acc gen dat 1st pers sing* me. Used only after prepositions (e.g. *Lo hicieron por mí,* They did it for me)

miaja /'miaha/ *f,* See **migaja**

miasma /'miasma/ *m,* miasma

miasmático /mias'matiko/ *a* miasmatic, malarious

miau /'miau/ *m,* meow

mica /'mika/ *f, Mineral.* mica; coquette, flirt

micho /'mitʃo/ *m Inf.* puss, pussycat

micología /mikolo'hia/ *f,* mycology

micra /'mikra/ *f,* micron, thousandth part of a millimeter

micro /'mikro/ *m, Chile, Peru* (large, express) bus; *elsewhere in Lat. Am.* minibus

microbiano /mikro'βiano/ *a* microbial, microbic

microbio /mi'kroβio/ *m,* microbe

microbiología /mikroβiolo'hia/ *f,* microbiology

microbrigada /mikroβri'gaða/ *f,* team of volunteer workers (in Castroist Cuba)

microchip /mikro'tʃip/ *m,* microchip

microcosmo /mikro'kosmo/ *m,* microcosm

micrófono /mi'krofono/ *m,* microphone

microonda /mikro'onda/ *f,* microwave

microscópico /mikros'kopiko/ *a* microscopic

microscopio /mikros'kopio/ *m,* microscope

miedo /'mieðo/ *m,* fear, apprehension, terror. **m. al público,** stagefright. **tener m.,** to be afraid

miedoso /mie'ðoso/ *a Inf.* fearful, nervous

miel /miel/ *f,* honey. **m. de caña,** sugarcane syrup. *Inf.* **quedarse a media m.,** to see one's pleasure snatched away. *Inf.* **ser de mieles,** to be most pleasant or agreeable

mielitis /mie'litis/ *f,* myelitis

miembro /mi'embro/ *m, Anat.* limb; penis; member, associate; part, portion, section; *Math.* member

miente /mi'ente/ *f,* thought, imagination, mind. **parar** *or* **poner mientes en,** to consider, think about. **venírsele a las mientes,** to occur to one's mind

mientras /'mientras/ *adv* while. **m. más...,** the more.... **m. que,** while (e.g. *m. que esperaba en el jardín,* while he was waiting in the garden). **m. tanto,** in the meanwhile

miércoles /'mierkoles/ *m,* Wednesday. **m. de ceniza,** Ash Wednesday

mies /'mies/ *f,* cereal plant, grain; harvest time; *pl* grain fields

miga /'miga/ *f,* breadcrumb; crumb; *Inf.* essence, core; substance; bit, scrap; *pl* fried breadcrumbs. *Inf.* **hacer buenas** (*or* **malas**) **migas,** to get on well (*or* badly) together

migaja /mi'gaha/ *f,* breadcrumb; bit, scrap; trifle, mere nothing; *pl* crumbs (from the table); remains, remnants

migajón /miga'hon/ *m,* crumb (of a loaf): *Fig. Inf.* essence, substance, core

migración /migra'sion; migra'θion/ *f,* migration; emigration

migraña /mi'graɲa/ *f,* migraine

migratorio /migra'torio/ *a* migratory

mijo /'miho/ *m,* millet; maize

mil /mil/ *a* thousand; thousandth; many, large number. *m,* thousand; thousandth. *Inf.* **Son las m. y quinientas,** It's extremely late (of the hour)

miladi /mi'laði/ *f,* my lady

milagrero /mila'grero/ *a Inf.* miraculous

milagro /mi'lagro/ *m,* miracle; marvel, wonder. **¡M.!** Amazing! Just fancy!

milagroso /mila'groso/ *a* miraculous; marvelous, wonderful

mildeu /'mildeu/ *m,* mildew

milenario /mile'nario/ *a* millenary; millennial. *m,* millenary; millennium

milésimo /mi'lesimo/ *a* thousandth

milicia /mi'lisia; mi'liθia/ *f,* militia; military; art of war; military profession

miliciano /mili'siano; mili'θiano/ *a* military. *m,* militiaman

milico /mi'liko/ *m, Lat. Am.,* derogatory soldier

miligramo /mili'gramo/ *m,* milligram

mililitro /mili'litro/ *m,* milliliter

milímetro /mi'limetro/ *m,* millimeter

militante /mili'tante/ *a* militant

militar /mili'tar/ *a* military. *m,* soldier. *vi* to fight in the army; struggle (for a cause); *Fig.* militate (e.g. *Las circunstancias militan en favor de* (*or contra*) **sus ideas,** Circumstances militate against his ideas)

militarismo /milita'rismo/ *m,* militarism

militarista /milita'rista/ *a* militaristic. *mf* militarist

militarizar /militari'sar; militari'θar/ *vt* to militarize; make war-like

milla /'miya; 'miʎa/ *f,* mile

millar /mi'yar; mi'ʎar/ *m,* thousand; vast number (gen. *pl*)

millón /mi'yon; mi'ʎon/ *m,* million

millonario /miyo'nario; miʎo'nario/ (**-ia**) *a* and *n* millionaire

millonésimo /miyo'nesimo; miʎo'nesimo/ *a* millionth

milmillonésimo /milmiyo'nesimo; milmiʎo'nesimo/ *a* billionth

milpa /'milpa/ *f, Central America, Mexico* corn field

milpero, -a /mil'pero/ *mf, Lat. Am.* corn grower

mimar /mi'mar/ *vt* to spoil, overindulge; caress, fondle

mimbre /'mimbre/ *mf* osier; willow tree. *m,* wicker

mimbrear /mimbre'ar/ *vi* to sway, bend

mimbrera /mim'brera/ *f,* osier; osier bed; willow

mímica /'mimika/ *f,* mimicry; mime

mímico /'mimiko/ *a* mimic

mimo /'mimo/ *m,* mimic, buffoon; mime; caress, expression of affection, tenderness; overindulgence

mimoso /mi'moso/ *a* affectionate, demonstrative

mina /'mina/ *f,* mine; excavation, mining; underground passage; lead (in a pencil); (*Mil. Nav.*) mine; *Fig.* gold mine. *Mil.* **m. terrestre,** landmine

minador /mina'ðor/ *m,* excavator; *Nav.* minelayer; *Mil.* sapper

minar /mi'nar/ *vt* to excavate, mine; *Fig.* undermine; (*Mil. Nav.*) mine; work hard for

minarete /mina'rete/ *m,* minaret

mineraje /mine'rahe/ *m,* exploitation of a mine, mining; mineral products

mineral /mine'ral/ *a* and *m,* mineral

mineralogía /mineralo'hia/ *f,* mineralogy

mineralógico /minera'lohiko/ *a* mineralogical

mineralogista /mineralo'hista/ *mf* mineralogist

minería /mine'ria/ *f,* mining, mineworking; mineworkers

minero /mi'nero/ *a* mining. *m,* miner, mineworker; source, origin

minga /'miŋga/ *f, Lat. Am.* voluntary communal labor

miniar /mini'ar/ *vt Art.* to illuminate

miniatura /minia'tura/ *f,* miniature

miniaturista /miniatu'rista/ *mf* miniaturist

mínima /'minima/ *f, Mus.* minim; very small thing or portion

mínimo /'minimo/ *a sup* **pequeño** smallest; minimum; meticulous, precise. *m,* minimum; (meteorological) trough

ministerial /ministe'rial/ *a* ministerial

ministerio /minis'terio/ *m,* office, post; *Polit.* cabinet; ministry; government office; government department.

ministrar /minis'trar/ *vt* and *vi* to fill; administer (an office); *vt* minister to; give, provide

ministro /mi'nistro/ *m,* instrument, agency; minister of state, cabinet minister; clergyman, minister; minister plenipotentiary; policeman. **m. de estado,** secretary of state. **m. de gobernación,** secretary of the interior. **m. de hacienda,** treasurer. **m. de relaciones extranjeras,** foreign secretary. **primer m.** prime minister

minoración /minora'sion; minora'θion/ *f,* reduction, decrease

minorar /mino'rar/ *vt* to diminish, decrease

minoría /mino'ria/ *f,* minority, smaller number; minority (of age)

minoridad /minori'ðað/ *f,* minority (of age)

minorista /mino'rista/ *mf, Lat. Am.* retailer

minucia /minu'sia; minu'θia/ *f,* smallness; morsel, mite; *pl* details, trifles, minutiae

minucioso /minu'sioso; minu'θioso/ *a* meticulous, precise, minute

minúsculo /mi'nuskulo/ *a* minute, very small

minuta /mi'nuta/ *f,* memorandum, minute; note; list, catalogue

minutero /minu'tero/ *m,* minute hand (of a clock)

minuto /mi'nuto/ *a* minute, very small. *m,* minute

mío /'mio/ *m.* **mía,** *f,* (*m pl.* **míos,** *f pl.* **mías**) *poss pron* mine (e.g. *Las flores son mías,* The flowers are mine). **Mi** is used before nouns, *not* **mío.** Also used with article (e.g. *Este sombrero no es el mío,* This hat is not mine (my one)). **de mío,** by myself, without help. *Inf.* **¡Esta es la mía!** This is my chance!

miope /mi'ope/ *a* myopic. *mf* myopic person

miopía /mio'pia/ *f,* shortsightedness

miosota /mio'sota/ *f,* myosotis, forget-me-not

mira /'mira/ *f,* sight (optical instruments, guns); intention, design; *Mil.* watchtower; care, precaution. **andar, estar** *or* **quedar a la m.,** to be vigilant, be on the lookout

mirada /mi'raða/ *f,* look; gaze. **lanzar miradas de carnero degollado** (**a**), to cast sheep's eyes at

miradero /mira'ðero/ *m,* object of attention, cynosure; observation post, lookout

mirador /mira'ðor/ (**-ra**) *n* spectator. *m, Archit.* oriel; enclosed balcony; observatory

miramiento /mira'miento/ *m,* observation, gazing;

scruple, consideration; precaution, care; thoughtfulness

mirar /mi'rar/ *vt* to look at, gaze at; observe, behold; watch; consider, look after; value, appreciate; concern; believe, think; (*with prep a*) overlook, look on to; face; (*with por*) care for, protect; look after, consider. **m. contra el gobierno,** *Inf.* to be squint-eyed. **m. de hito en hito,** to look over, stare at. **mirarse en** (**una cosa**), to consider (a matter) carefully

miríada /mi'riaða/ *f,* myriad, huge number

mirilla /mi'riya; mi'riʎa/ *f,* peephole

miriñaque /miri'ɲake/ *m,* trinket, ornament; crinoline

mirlarse /mir'larse/ *vr Inf.* to give oneself airs

mirlo /'mirlo/ *m,* blackbird; *Inf.* pompous air

mirón /mi'ron/ *a* inquisitive, curious

mirra /'mirra/ *f,* myrrh

mirto /'mirto/ *m,* myrtle

misa /'misa/ *f,* (*Eccl. Mus.*) mass. **m. de difuntos,** requiem mass. **m. del gallo,** midnight mass. **m. mayor,** high mass. **m. rezada,** low mass. **como en m.,** in profound silence. **oír m.,** to attend mass

misal /mi'sal/ *m,* missal

misantropía /misantro'pia/ *f,* misanthropy

misantrópico /misan'tropiko/ *a* misanthropic

misántropo /mi'santropo/ *m,* misanthrope

miscelánea /misse'lanea; misθe'lanea/ *f,* medley, assortment, miscellany

misceláneo /misse'laneo; misθe'laneo/ *a* assorted, miscellaneous, mixed

miscible /mis'siβle; mis'θiβle/ *a* mixable

miserable /mise'raβle/ *a* miserable, unhappy; timid, pusillanimous; miserly, mean; despicable

miseria /mi'seria/ *f,* misery; poverty, destitution; avarice, miserliness; *Inf.* poor thing, trifle

misericordia /miseri'korðia/ *f,* mercy, compassion

misericordioso /miserikor'ðioso/ *a* merciful, compassionate

mísero /'misero/ *a Inf.* fond of churchgoing

misérrimo /mi'serrimo/ *a superl.* most miserable

misión /mi'sion/ *f,* mission; vocation; commission, duty, errand

misionar /misio'nar/ *vi* to missionize, act as a missionary; *Eccl.* conduct a mission

misionero /misio'nero/ *m,* missioner; missionary

Misisipí, el /misi'sipi, el/ the Mississippi

misiva /mi'siβa/ *f,* missive

mismo /'mismo/ *a* same; similar; self (e.g. *ellos mismos,* they themselves); very, same (e.g. *Ahora m. voy,* I'm going this very minute). **Me da lo m.,** It makes no difference to me. **por lo m.,** for that self-same reason

misógamo /mi'sogamo/ (**-ma**) *n* misogamist

misógino /mi'sohino/ *m,* misogynist

misterio /mis'terio/ *m,* mystery

misterioso /miste'rioso/ *a* mysterious

mística /'mistika/ *f,* misticismo *m,* mysticism

místico /'mistiko/ *a* mystic

mistificación /mistifika'sion; mistifika'θion/ *f,* mystification; mystery; deception

mistificar /mistifi'kar/ *vt* to mystify; deceive

Misuri, el /mi'suri, el/ the Missouri

mitad /mi'tað/ *f,* half; middle, center. *Fig. Inf.* **cara m.,** better half. *Inf.* **mentir por la m. de la barba,** to lie barefacedly

mítico /'mitiko/ *a* mythical

mitigación /mitiga'sion; mitiga'θion/ *f,* mitigation

mitigador /mitiga'ðor/ (**-ra**) *a* mitigatory. *n* mitigator

mitigar /miti'gar/ *vt* to mitigate, moderate, alleviate; appease

mitin /'mitin/ *m,* mass meeting

mito /'mito/ *m,* myth

mitología /mitolo'hia/ *f,* mythology

mitológico /mito'lohiko/ *a* mythological

mitologista, mitólogo /mitolo'hista, mi'tologo/ *m,* mythologist

mitón /mi'ton/ *m,* mitten

mitra /'mitra/ *f,* miter; bishopric; archbishopric

mitrado /mi'traðo/ *a* mitred

mixto /'miksto/ *a* mixed, blended; hybrid; composite; mongrel. *m,* mixed train (carrying freight and passengers); sulphur match

mixtura /miks'tura/ *f,* mixture, blend; compound; mixture (medicine)

¡miz, miz! /mis, mis; miθ, miθ/ puss, puss!

mobiliario /moβi'liario/ *a* movable (goods). *m,* furniture

moblaje /mo'βlahe/ *m,* household goods and furniture

mocasín /moka'sin/ *m,* moccasin

mocedad /mose'ðað; moθe'ðað/ *f,* youth, adolescence; mischief, prank. *Fig. Inf.* **correr sus mocedades,** to sow one's wild oats

mochila /mo'tʃila/ *f,* knapsack; nosebag; military rations for a march

mocho /'motʃo/ *a* blunted, topless, lopped; *Inf.* shorn, cropped. *m,* butt, butt end

mochuelo /mo'tʃuelo/ *m,* owl; *Inf.* difficult job

moción /mo'sion; mo'θion/ *f,* motion, movement; impulse, tendency; divine inspiration; motion (of a debate)

moco /'moko/ *m,* mucus; candle drips; snuff of a candle. *Inf.* **caérsele el m.,** to be very simple, be easily deceived

mocoso /mo'koso/ (**-sa**) *a* running of the nose, sniffling; unimportant, insignificant. *n* coxcomb, stripling; *Lat. Am.* child

moda /'moða/ *f,* fashion. **estar** *or* **ser de m.,** to be fashionable, be in fashion. **la última m.,** the latest fashion

modales /mo'ðales/ *m pl,* manners, behavior

modalidad /moðali'ðað/ *f,* form, nature; *Mus.* modality

modelado /moðe'laðo/ *m, Art.* modeling

modelar /moðe'lar/ *vt Art.* to model; *vr* model oneself (on), copy

modelo /mo'ðelo/ *m,* example, pattern; model. *mf Art.* life model

módem /'moðem/ *m,* modem

moderación /moðera'sion; moðera'θion/ *f,* moderation; restraint, temperance, equability

moderado /moðe'raðo/ *a* moderate; restrained, temperate

moderador /moðera'ðor/ (**-ra**) *a* moderating. *n* moderator

moderantismo /moðeran'tismo/ *m,* moderate opinion; moderate political party

moderar /moðe'rar/ *vt* to moderate; temper, restrain; *vr* regain one's self-control; behave with moderation

modernidad /moðerni'ðað/ *f,* modernity

modernismo /moðer'nismo/ *m,* modernism

modernista /moðer'nista/ *a* modernistic; modern. *mf* modernist

modernización /moðernisa'sion; moðerniθa'θion/ *f,* modernization

modernizar /moðerni'sar; moðerni'θar/ *vt* to modernize

moderno /mo'ðerno/ *a* modern. *m,* modern. **a la moderna,** in modern fashion

modestia /mo'ðestia/ *f,* modesty

modesto /mo'ðesto/ *a* modest

módico /'moðiko/ *a* moderate (of prices, etc.)

modificable /moðifi'kaβle/ *a* modifiable

modificación /moðifika'sion; moðifi'kaθion/ *f,* modification

modificador, modificante /moðifi'kaðor, moðifi'kante/ *a* modifying, moderating

modificar /moðifi'kar/ *vt* to modify; moderate

modismo /mo'ðismo/ *m,* idiom, idiomatic expression

modista /mo'ðista/ *mf* dressmaker; couturier; milliner

modo /'moðo/ *m,* mode, method, style; manner, way; moderation, restraint; civility, politeness (often *pl*); *Mus.* mode; *Gram.* mood. **m. de ser,** nature, temperament. **de m. que,** so that. **de ningún m.,** not at all, by no means. **de todos modos,** in any case

modorra /mo'ðorra/ *f,* deep sleep, stupor

modorro /mo'ðorro/ *a* drowsy, heavy

modoso /mo'ðoso/ *a* demure; well-behaved

modulación /moðula'sion; moðula'θion/ f, modulation

modulador /moðula'ðor/ **(-ra)** a modulative. n modulator, m, Mus. modulator

modular /moðu'lar/ vt and vi to modulate

mofa /'mofa/ f, mockery, ridicule, jeering

mofador /mofa'ðor/ **(-ra)** a jeering. n scoffer, mocker

mofarse /mo'farse/ vr (with de) to make fun of, jeer at

mofeta /mo'feta/ f, noxious gas; damp (gas); Zool. skunk

moflete /mo'flete/ m, Inf. plump cheek

mofletudo /mofle'tuðo/ a plump-cheeked

mogol /'mogol/ **(-la)** a and n Mongolian.

mogote /mo'gote/ m, hill; pyre, stack

mohín /mo'in/ m, grimace

mohína /mo'ina/ f, grudge, rancor; sullenness; sulkiness

mohíno /mo'ino/ a depressed, gloomy; sulky; black or black-nosed (of animals)

moho /'moo/ m, mold, fungoid growth; moldiness; moss. Inf. **no criar m.,** to be always on the move

mohoso /mo'oso/ a mossy; moldy

mojada /mo'haða/ f, wetting; Inf. stab; sop of bread

mojador /moha'ðor/ **(-ra)** n wetter. m, stamp moistener

mojar /mo'har/ vt to wet; moisten; Inf. stab, wound with a dagger; vi take part in; meddle, interfere; vr get wet

mojicón /mohi'kon/ m, kind of spongecake; Inf. slap in the face

mojiganga /mohi'ganga/ f, masquerade, mummer's show; farce; funny sight, figure of fun

mojigatería /mohigate'ria/ f, hypocrisy; sanctimoniousness; prudery

mojigato /mohi'gato/ **(-ta)** a hypocritical; sanctimonious; prudish. n hypocrite; bigot; prude

mojón /mo'hon/ m, boundary marker; milestone; heap. **m. kilométrico,** milestone

molar /mo'lar/ a molar

molde /'molde/ m, mold, matrix; Fig. model, pattern. **de m.,** printed; suitably, conveniently; perfectly. **letra de m.,** printed letters, print

moldeador /moldea'ðor/ **(-ra)** n molder

moldear /molde'ar/ vt to mold, cast

moldura /mol'dura/ f, molding

moldurar /moldu'rar/ vt to mold

mole /'mole/ f mass, bulk

molécula /mo'lekula/ f, molecule

molecular /moleku'lar/ a molecular

mole de guajolote /'mole de guaho'lote/ m, Mexico turkey served with a heavy dark sauce made of different kinds of chiles, spices, etc.

moler /mo'ler/ vt irr to grind, crush; tire, exhaust; illtreat; pester, annoy. **m. a palos,** to beat black and blue. Pres. Ind. **muelo, mueles, muele, muelen.** Pres. Subjunc. **muela, muelas, muela, muelan**

molestar /moles'tar/ vt to bother, annoy

molestia /mo'lestia/ f, inconvenience, trouble; annoyance; discomfort, pain; bore, nuisance. **Es una m.,** It's a nuisance

molesto /mo'lesto/ a inconvenient, troublesome; annoying; painful; uncomfortable; boring, tedious

molestoso, -a /moles'toso/ a, Lat. Am. annoying, bothersome

moletón /mole'ton/ m, flannelet

molicie /mo'lisie; mo'liθie/ f, softness, smoothness; effeminacy, weakness

molienda /mo'lienda/ f, milling; grinding; mill; portion ground at one time; Inf. exhaustion, fatigue; Inf. nuisance

molificar /molifi'kar/ vt to mollify, appease

molimiento /moli'miento/ m, milling; grinding; exhaustion, fatigue

molinera /moli'nera/ f, (woman) miller; miller's wife

molinero /moli'nero/ a mill. m, miller

molinillo /moli'niyo; moli'niʎo/ m, hand mill, small grinder; mincing machine; beater. **m. de café,** coffee mill

molino /mo'lino/ m, mill; harum-scarum, rowdy;

bore, tedious person; Inf. mouth. **m. de rueda de escalones,** treadmill. **m. de viento,** windmill

molleja /mo'yeha; mo'ʎeha/ f, gizzard

mollera /mo'yera; mo'ʎera/ f, crown of the head; brains, sense. Inf. **ser duro de m.,** to be obstinate; be stupid

molusco /mo'lusko/ m, mollusk

momentáneo /momen'taneo/ a momentary, brief; instantaneous, immediate

momento /mo'mento/ m, moment, minute; importance; Mech. moment. **al m.,** immediately. **a cada m.,** all the time; frequently. **por momentos,** continually; intermittently

momería /mome'ria/ f, mummery

momero /mo'mero/ **(-ra)** n mummer

momia /'momia/ f, mummy

momificación /momifika'sion; momifika'θion/ f, mummification

momificar /momifi'kar/ vt to mummify; vr become mummified

mona /'mona/ f, female monkey; Inf. imitator; drinking bout; drunk. Inf. **Aunque la m. se vista de seda, m. se queda,** Breeding will tell. Inf. **ser la última m.,** to be of no account, be unimportant

monacillo /mona'siyo; mona'θiʎo/ m, Eccl. acolyte

monada /mo'naða/ f, mischievous prank; affected gesture or grimace; small, pretty thing; childish cleverness; flattery; rash act; pl monkey shines

monaguillo /mona'giyo; mona'giʎo/ m, Eccl. acolyte

monarca /mo'narka/ mf monarch

monarquía /monar'kia/ f, monarchy

monárquico /mo'narkiko/ **(-ca)** a monarchic. n monarchist

monarquismo /monar'kismo/ m, monarchism

monasterio /mona'sterio/ m, monastery; convent

monástico /mo'nastiko/ a monastic

monda /'monda/ f, skinning, peeling; Agr. pruning; cleansing; Lat. Am. thrashing

mondadientes /monda'ðientes/ m, toothpick

mondar /mon'dar/ vt to skin, peel; Agr. prune; cut the hair; cleanse; free of rubbish; Inf. deprive of possessions; Lat. Am. to beat, beat up, thrash vr pick one's teeth

mondo /'mondo/ a simple, plain; bare; unadulterated, pure

mondongo /mon'dongo/ m, Lat. Am. tripe

moneda /mo'neða/ f, coin, piece of money; coinage; Inf. wealth; cash. **m. corriente,** currency. **m. metálica,** specie. **m. nacional,** national currency. **pagar en buena m.,** to give entire satisfaction. **pagar en la misma m.,** to pay back in the same coin, return like for like. Inf. **ser m. corriente,** to be usual or very frequent

monedero /mone'ðero/ m, coiner, mint; handbag; purse

monería /mone'ria/ f, mischievous trick; unimportant trifle; pretty thing; childish cleverness, pretty ways

monetario /mone'tario/ a monetary. m, collection of coins and medals

monetización /monetisa'sion; monetiθa'θion/ f, monetization

monigote /moni'gote/ m, Inf. boor; grotesque, puppet

monitor /moni'tor/ m, monitor

monitorio /moni'torio/ a monitory

monja /'monha/ f, nun; pl sparks

monje /'monhe/ m, monk

monjil /mon'hil/ a nun-like. m, nun's habit

mono /'mono/ a Inf. pretty, attractive; amusing, funny. m, monkey; person given to grimacing; rash youth; coverall. Inf. **estar de monos,** to be on bad terms

monocromo /mono'kromo/ a monochrome; monochromatic

monóculo /mo'nokulo/ m, monocle

monogamia /mono'gamia/ f, monogamy

monógamo /mo'nogamo/ a monogamous. n monogamist

monografía /monogra'fia/ f, monograph

monograma /mono'grama/ m, monogram

monolítico /mono'litiko/ *a* monolithic

monolito /mono'lito/ *m*, monolith

monólogo /mo'nologo/ *m*, monologue

monomanía /monoma'nia/ *f*, monomania, obsession

monomaníaco /monoma'niako/ **(-ca)** *n* monomaniac

monopatín /monopa'tin/ *m*, scooter

monoplano /mono'plano/ *m*, monoplane

monopolio /mono'polio/ *m*, monopoly

monopolista /monopo'lista/ *mf* monopolist

monopolizar /monopoli'sar; monopoli'θar/ *vt* to monopolize

monoteísmo /monote'ismo/ *m*, monotheism

monoteísta /monote'ista/ *mf* monotheist

monotipia /mono'tipia/ *f*, monotype

monotonía /monoto'nia/ *f*, monotony; monotone

monótono /mo'notono/ *a* monotonous

monroísmo /monro'ismo/ *m*, Monroe doctrine

monseñor /monse'ɲor/ *m*, monsignor

monserga /mon'serga/ *f*, *Inf.* rigmarole; jargon

monstruo /'monstruo/ *m*, monster; freak, monstrosity; cruel person; hideous person or thing

monstruosidad /monstruosi'ðað/ *f*, monstrousness, monstrosity

monstruoso /mon'struoso/ *a* monstrous, abnormal; enormous; extraordinary; atrocious, outrageous

monta /'monta/ *f*, mounting a horse; total; *Mil.* mounting signal; breeding station (horses)

montacargas /monta'kargas/ *m*, hoist, lift; freight elevator

montador /monta'ðor/ *m*, mounter; mounting block

montadura /monta'ðura/ *f*, mounting; mount, setting (of jewels)

montaje /mon'tahe/ *m*, assembling, setting up (machines); presentation (of a book); (cinema) montage

montano /mon'tano/ *a* hilly, mountainous

montante /mon'tante/ *a*, upright, stanchion; tent pole

montaña /mon'taɲa/ *f*, mountain; mountainous country. **montañas rusas,** roller coaster (at an amusement park)

montañés /monta'ɲes/ **(-esa)** *a* mountain. *n* mountain dweller; native of Santander

montañoso /monta'ɲoso/ *a* mountainous; hilly

montar /mon'tar/ *vi* to ascend, climb up, get on top; mount (a horse); ride (a horse); be important; *vt* get on top of; ride (a horse); total, amount to; set up (apparatus, machinery); *Naut.* sail around, double; set, mount (gems); cock (firearms); fine for trespassing; wind (a clock); command (a ship); *Naut.* carry, be fitted with (guns, etc.). **m. a horcajadas en,** to mount astride; straddle. **montarse en cólera,** to fly into a rage

montaraz /monta'ras; monta'raθ/ *a* mountaindwelling; wild, savage; rude, uncivilized, uncouth. *m*, gamekeeper; forester

monte /'monte/ *m*, mount, hill; woodland; obstacle, impediment. **m. de piedad,** pawnshop. **m. pío,** savings fund

montepío /monte'pio/ *m*, *Lat. Am.* pawnshop

montera /mon'tera/ *f*, cap; glass roof

montería /monte'ria/ *f*, hunt, chase; art of hunting

montero /mon'tero/ **(-ra)** *n* hunter, huntsman

montés /mon'tes/ *a* wild, savage, untamed

montevideano /monteβiðe'ano/ **(-na)** *a* and *n* Montevidean

montículo /mon'tikulo/ *m*, mound, hill

montón /mon'ton/ *m*, heap, pile; *Inf.* abundance, lot, bunch. *Inf.* **a, de** *or* **en m.,** all jumbled up together. **a montones,** in abundance

montonero, -a /monto'nero/ *mf* domineering, overbearing

montuoso /mon'tuoso/ *a* mountainous

montura /mon'tura/ *f*, riding animal, mount; horse trappings; setting up, mounting (artillery, etc.)

monumento /monu'mento/ *m*, monument; document, record; tomb

monzón /mon'son; mon'θon/ *mf*, monsoon

moña /'moɲa/ *f*, doll; dressmaker's model; bow for the hair; bullfighter's black bow; baby's bonnet; *Inf.* drinking bout

moño /'moɲo/ *m*, bun, chignon; topknot (birds); bunch of ribbons; *pl* tawdry trimmings

moquete /mo'kete/ *m*, slap in the face

moquillo /mo'kiyo; mo'kiʎo/ *m*, distemper (of animals)

mora /'mora/ *f*, blackberry; mulberry; bramble; Moorish girl, Moorish woman

morada /mo'raða/ *f*, dwelling, abode; sojourn, stay

morado /mo'raðo/ *a* purple

morador /mora'ðor/ **(-ra)** *n* dweller; sojourner

moral /mo'ral/ *a* moral, ethical. *f*, morality, ethics; morale. *m*, blackberry bush

moraleja /mora'leha/ *f*, moral, lesson

moralidad /morali'ðað/ *f*, morality

moralista /mora'lista/ *mf* moralist

moralización /moralisa'sion; moraliθa'θion/ *f*, moralization

moralizador /moralisa'ðor; moraliθa'ðor/ **(-ra)** *a* moralizing. *n* moralizer

moralizar /morali'sar; morali'θar/ *vt* to reform, correct; *vi* moralize

moratoria /mora'toria/ *f*, moratorium

morbidez /mor'βiðes; mor'βiðeθ/ *f*, *Art.* morbidezza; softness

mórbido /'morβiðo/ *a* morbid, diseased; *Art.* delicate (of flesh tones); soft

morbo /'morβo/ *m*, illness. **m. gálico,** syphilis

morboso /mor'βoso/ *a* ill; morbid, unhealthy

morcilla /mor'siya; mor'θiʎa/ *f*, *Cul.* black pudding; *(Inf. Theat.)* gag

morcillero /morsi'yero; morθi'ʎero/ **(-ra)** *n* seller of black puddings; *(Inf. Theat.)* actor who gags

mordacidad /morðasi'ðað; morðaθi'ðað/ *f*, corrosiveness; mordacity, sarcasm; *Cul.* piquancy

mordaz /mor'ðas; mor'ðaθ/ *a* corrosive; sarcastic, caustic, mordant; *Cul.* piquant

mordaza /mor'ðasa; mor'ðaθa/ *f*, gag

mordedor /morðe'ðor/ *a* biting; scandalmongering

mordedura /morðe'ðura/ *f*, bite, biting

mordelón, -ona /morðe'lon/ *mf*, *Central America, Mexico* given to taking bribes

morder /mor'ðer/ *vt irr* to bite; nibble, nip; seize, grasp; corrode, eat away; slander; etch. *Pres. Ind.* **muerdo, muerdes, muerde, muerden.** *Pres. Subjunc.* **muerda, muerdas, muerda, muerdan**

mordida /mor'ðiða/ *f*, *Lat. Am.* bite; *Central America, Mexico also* bribe

mordiente /mor'ðiente/ *m*, fixative (for dyeing); mordant. *a* mordant (of acid)

mordiscar /morðis'kar/ *vt* to nibble, bite gently; bite

mordisco /mor'ðisko/ *m*, nibble; nibbling; bite; biting; piece bitten off

morena /mo'rena/ *f*, moraine

moreno /mo'reno/ **(-na)** *a* dark brown; swarthy complexioned; dark (of people). *n Inf.* (ethnic) black, mulatto

morera /mo'rera/ *f*, mulberry bush

morería /more'ria/ *f*, Moorish quarter

morfina /mor'fina/ *f*, morphine

morfinómano /morfi'nomano/ **(-na)** *n* morphine addict

morfológico /morfo'lohiko/ *a* morphological

morganático /morga'natiko/ *a* morganatic

moribundo /mori'βundo/ **(-da)** *a* moribund, dying. *n* dying person

morillo /mo'riyo; mo'riʎo/ *m*, andiron, fire-dog

morir /mo'rir/ *vi irr* to die; fade, wither; decline, decay; disappear (years for); long (to); go out (lights, fire); *vr* die; go numb (limbs); *(with por)* adore, be mad about. *Inf.* **m. vestido,** to die a violent death. **¡Muera!** Down with! *Past Part.* **muerto.** For other tenses see **dormir**

morisco /mo'risko/ **(-ca)** *a* Moorish. *n* Morisco, Moor converted to Christianity

mormón /mor'mon/ **(-ona)** *n* Mormon

mormonismo /mormo'nismo/ *m*, Mormonism

moro /'moro/ **(-ra)** *a* Moorish. *n* Moor; Mohammedan. *Inf.* **haber moros y cristianos,** to be the deuce of a row

moronga /mo'roŋga/ f, Central America, Mexico blood sausage

morosidad /morosi'ðað/ f, slowness, delay; sluggishness, sloth

moroso /mo'roso/ a slow, dilatory; sluggish, lazy

morra /'morra/ f, crown of the head

morral /mo'rral/ m, nose-bag; knapsack; game-bag; Inf. lout

morriña /mo'rriɲa/ f, cattle plague, murrain; Inf. depression, blues; homesickness

morro /'morro/ m, anything round; hummock, hillock; round pebble; headland, cliff

morrón /mo'rron/ m, Lat. Am. hot red pepper

morsa /'morsa/ f, walrus

mortaja /mor'taha/ f, shroud, winding sheet

mortal /mor'tal/ a mortal; fatal, deadly; on the point of death; great, tremendous; certain, sure. mf mortal

mortalidad /mortali'ðað/ f, humanity, human race; mortality, death-rate

mortandad /mortan'dað/ f, mortality, number of deaths

mortecino /morte'sino/ a, morte'θino/ a dead from natural causes (animals); weak; fading; dull, dead (of eyes); flickering; on the point of death or extinction

mortero /mor'tero/ m, mortar (for building); Mil. mortar; pounding mortar

mortífero /mor'tifero/ a deadly, mortal

mortificación /mortifika'sion; mortifika'θion/ f, Med. gangrene; humiliation, wounding; mortification (of the flesh)

mortificar /mortifi'kar/ vt Med. to mortify; humiliate, wound, hurt; mortify (the flesh); vr become gangrenous

mortuorio /mor'tuorio/ a mortuary. m, funeral, obsequies

mosaico /mo'saiko/ a and m, mosaic

mosca /'moska/ f, fly; Inf. nuisance; bore, pest; cash; pl sparks. Inf. m. muerta, underhanded person. Inf. papar moscas, to gape, be dumbfounded. Inf. soltar la m., to give or spend money unwillingly

moscardón /moskar'ðon/ m, gadfly

moscatel /moska'tel/ a muscatel. m, muscatel (grapes and wine); Inf. pest, tedious person

Moscú /mos'ku/ Moscow

mosquear /moske'ar/ vt to drive off flies; reply crossly; whip; vr be exasperated; brush aside obstacles

mosquero /mos'kero/ m, flypaper

mosquete /mos'kete/ m, musket

mosquetería /moskete'ria/ f, musketry; (Obs. Theat.) male members of the audience who stood at the back of the pit

mosquetero /moske'tero/ m, musketeer; (Spanish theater of the sixteenth and seventeenth centuries) male member of the audience who stood at the back of the pit

mosquitero /moski'tero/ m, mosquito net

mosquito /mos'kito/ m, mosquito; midge, gnat; Inf. tippler, drunkard

mostacera /mosta'sera; mosta'θera/ f, mustard pot

mostacho /mos'tatʃo/ m, mustache, whiskers; Inf. smudge on the face

mostaza /mos'tasa; mos'taθa/ f, mustard plant or seed; Cul. mustard

mostela /mos'tela/ f, sheaf (of corn, etc.)

mosto /'mosto/ m, must, unfermented wine

mostrador /mostra'ðor/ (-ra) n one who shows, exhibitor. m, shop counter; face of a watch

mostrar /mos'trar/ vt irr to show; indicate, point out; demonstrate, prove; manifest, reveal; vr show oneself, be (e.g. Se mostró bondadoso, He showed himself to be kind). Pres. Ind. muestro, muestras, muestra, muestran. Pres. Subjunc. muestre, muestres, muestre, muestren

mostrenco /mos'trenko/ a Inf. stray, vagrant, homeless; Inf. dull, ignorant; Inf. fat, heavy

mota /'mota/ f, fault in cloth; mote, defect, fault; mound, hill; thread of cotton, speck of dust, etc.; fleck (of the sun, etc.); spot

mote /'mote/ m, maxim, saying; motto, device; catchword, slogan; nickname; Lat. Am. boiled corn

motear /mote'ar/ vt to speckle, dot, variegate, spot

motejar /mote'har/ vt to nickname, call names, dub

motete /mo'tete/ m, motet

motín /mo'tin/ m, mutiny; riot

motivar /moti'βar/ vt to motivate, cause; explain one's reasons

motivo /mo'tiβo/ a motive. m, cause, motive; Mus. motif. con m. de, on account of, because of. de m. propio, of one's own free will

motocicleta /motosi'kleta; motoθi'kleta/ f, motorcycle

motociclista /motosi'klista; motoθi'klista/ mf motorcyclist

motor /mo'tor/ (-ra) a motive, driving. m, motor, engine. n (person) mover, motive force. m. de combustión interna, internal combustion engine. m. de retroacción, jet engine

motorista /moto'rista/ mf motorist, driver

movedizo /moβe'ðiso; moβe'ðiθo/ a movable; insecure, unsteady; shaky; changeable, vacillating

mover /mo'βer/ vt irr to move; operate, drive; sway; wag; persuade, induce; excite; move (to pity, etc.); (with prep a) cause; vi sprout (plants); vr move. Pres. Ind. muevo, mueves, mueve, mueven. Pres. Subjunc. mueva, muevas, mueva, muevan

movible /mo'βiβle/ a movable; insecure, shaky. m, motive, cause, incentive

movilidad /moβili'ðað/ f, mobility; changeableness, inconstancy

movilización /moβilisa'sion; moβiliθa'θion/ f, mobilization

movilizar /moβili'sar; moβili'θar/ vt to mobilize

movimiento /moβi'miento/ m, movement; perturbation, excitement; Mus. movement; Lit. fire, spirit; Mech. motion, movement. Mil. m. envolvente, encircling movement

moza /'mosa; 'moθa/ f, maid; girl; waitress. m. de partido, party girl, prostitute. buena m., fine, upstanding young woman

mozalbete /mosal'βete; moθal'βete/ m, lad, stripling, boy

mozo /'moso; 'moθo/ a young, unmarried. m, boy, youth; bachelor; waiter; porter. m. de cordel or m. de esquina, street porter, message boy. m. de estación, railroad porter. buen m., fine, upstanding young man, Lat. Am. handsome

muaré /mua're/ m, moiré silk

mucama /mu'kama/ f, Argentina chambermaid

muceta /mu'seta; mu'θeta/ f, Educ. hood, short cape (of a graduate's gown)

muchacha /mu'tʃatʃa/ f, girl, lass; female servant

muchachada /mutʃa'tʃaða/ f, childish prank

muchachez /mutʃa'tʃes; mutʃa'tʃeθ/ f, boyhood; girlhood

muchachil /mutʃa'tʃil/ a boyish; girlish

muchacho /mu'tʃatʃo/ m, boy, youth; male servant

muchedumbre /mutʃe'ðumbre/ f, abundance, plenty; crowd, multitude; mass, mob

muchísimo /mu'tʃisimo/ a sup very much. adv very great deal, very much

mucho /'mutʃo/ a much; plenty of; very; long (time); pl many, numerous. adv a great deal; much; very much; yes, certainly; frequently, often; very (e.g. Me alegro m., I am very glad); to a great extent; long (time). con m., by far, easily. ni con m., nor anything like it, very far from it. ni m. menos, and much less. por m. que, however much

mucílago /mu'silago; mu'θilago/ m, mucilage, gum

mucosa /mu'kosa/ f, mucous membrane

mucoso /mu'koso/ a mucous

muda /'muða/ f, change, transformation; change of clothes; molting season; molt, sloughing of skin (snakes, etc.); change of voice (in boys)

mudable /mu'ðaβle/ a changeable, inconstant

mudanza /mu'ðansa; mu'ðanθa/ f, move (household); furniture removal; step, figure (in dancing); changeability, inconstancy

mudar /mu'ðar/ vt to change; alter, transform;

exchange; remove; dismiss (from employment); molt; slough the skin (snakes, etc.); change the voice (boys); *vr* alter one's behavior; change one's clothes; change one's residence, move; change one's expression; *Inf.* go away, depart

mudéjar /mu'ðehar/ *m*, *Archit.* style containing Moorish and Christian elements. *mf* Moor who remained in Spain under Christian rule

mudez /mu'ðes; mu'ðeθ/ *f*, dumbness; silence, muteness

mudo /'muðo/ *a* dumb; silent, mute, quiet

mueblaje /mue'βlahe/ *m*, household goods and furniture

mueble /'mueβle/ *m*, piece of furniture; furnishing

mueblería /mueβle'ria/ *f*, furniture store or factory

mueblista /mue'βlista/ *mf* furniture maker; furniture dealer

mueca /'mueka/ *f*, grimace

muela /'muela/ *f*, grindstone; molar (tooth); millstone; flat-topped hill. **m. del juicio,** wisdom tooth. **dolor de muelas,** toothache

muellaje /mue'yahe; mue'ʎahe/ *m*, wharfage, dock dues

muelle /'mueye; 'mueʎe/ *a* soft, smooth; voluptuous, sensuous; luxurious. *m*, spring (of a watch, etc.); wharf, quay; freight platform (railroad). **m. real,** mainspring (of a watch). **m. del volante,** hairspring.

muérdago /'muerðago/ *m*, mistletoe

muermo /'muermo/ *m*, boredom, apathy

muerte /'muerte/ *f*, death; destruction, annihilation; end, decline. *Inf.* **una m. chiquita,** a nervous shudder. **a m.,** to the death, with no quarter. **de m.,** implacably, inexorably (of hatred); very seriously (of being ill). **dar m.** (**a**), to kill. **estar a la m.,** to be on the point of death. **a cada m. de un obispo,** once in a blue moon

muerto /'muerto/ **(-ta)** *a* dead; slaked (lime); *Mech.* neutral; faded, dull (colors); languid, indifferent. **m.** is used in familiar speech as *past part* **matar** (e.g. *Le ha muerto,* He has killed him). *n* corpse. *Inf.* **desenterrar los muertos,** to speak ill of the dead. *Inf.* **echarle a uno el m.,** to pass the buck. *Inf.* **estar m. por,** to be dying, yearning for. **ser el m.,** to be dummy (at cards)

muesca /'mueska/ *f*, notch, mortise, groove

muestra /'muestra/ *f*, shop sign; sample, specimen; pattern, model; demeanor; watch or clock face; sign, indication; poster, placard; *Mil.* muster roll. **hacer m.,** to show

muestrario /mues'trario/ *m*, sample book, collection of samples

mufla /'mufla/ *f*, muffler (of a furnace)

mugido /mu'hiðo/ *m*, mooing or lowing (of cattle)

mugir /mu'hir/ *vi* to low or moo (cattle); bellow, shout; rage (elements)

mugre /'mugre/ *f*, grease, grime, dirt

mugriento /mu'griento/ *a* grimy, greasy

muguete /mu'gete/ *m*, lily of the valley

mujer /mu'her/ *f*, woman; wife. **m. de la vida airada** *or* **m. del partido** *or* **m. pública,** prostitute. **m. de la luna,** man in the moon. **m. de su casa,** good housewife. **tomar m.,** to take a wife

mujerero, -a /muhe'rero/ *a*, *Lat. Am.* fond of women

mujeriego /muhe'riego/ *a* (of men) womanizing, dissolute, given to philandering. **cabalgar a mujeriegas,** to ride sidesaddle

mujeril /muhe'ril/ *a* womanly, feminine

mula /'mula/ *f*, female mule; mule (heelless slipper); *Colombia* dope smuggler; *Mexico* junk, trash. *Inf.* **Se me fue la m.,** My tongue ran away with me

muladar /mula'ðar/ *m*, refuse heap, junkpile, dunghill

mular /mu'lar/ *a* mule; mulish

mulatero /mula'tero/ *m*, mule hirer; muleteer

mulato /mu'lato/ **(-ta)** *a* and *n* mulatto

muleta /mu'leta/ *f*, crutch; bullfighter's red flag; support, prop

mullir /mu'yir; mu'ʎir/ *vt irr* to make soft, shake out (wool, down, etc.); *Fig.* prepare the way; *Agr.* hoe the roots (of vines, etc.). *Pres. Part.* **mullendo.** *Preterite* **mulló, mulleron.** *Imperf. Subjunc.* **mullese, etc.**

mulo /'mulo/ *m*, mule

multa /'multa/ *f*, fine

multar /mul'tar/ *vt* to impose a fine on

multicolor /multiko'lor/ *a* multicolored

multiforme /multi'forme/ *a* multiform

multilátero /multi'latero/ *a* multilateral

multimillonario /multimiyo'nario; multimiʎo'nario/ **(-ia)** *a* and *n* multimillionaire

multiplicación /multiplika'sion; multiplika'θion/ *f*, multiplication

multiplicador /multiplika'ðor/ **(-ra)** *n* multiplier. *m*, *Math.* multiplier

multiplicando /multipli'kando/ *m*, multiplicand

multiplicar /multipli'kar/ **(se)** *vt* and *vr* to multiply; reproduce

multiplicidad /multiplisi'ðað; multipliθi'ðað/ *f*, multiplicity

múltiplo /'multiplo/ *m*, *Math.* multiple

multisecular /multiseku'lar/ *a* age-old, many centuries old

multitud /multi'tuð/ *f*, multitude, great number; crowd; rabble, masses, mob

mundanal, mundano /munda'nal, mun'dano/ *a* worldly, mundane

mundial /mun'dial/ *a* world, worldwide

mundo /'mundo/ *m*, world, universe; human race; earth; human society; world (of letters, science, etc.); secular life; *Eccl.* vanities of the flesh; geographical globe. **echar al m.,** to give birth to; produce, bring forth. **el Nuevo M.,** the New World, America. *Inf.* **medio m.,** half the earth, a great crowd. *Inf.* **ponerse el m. por montera,** to treat the world as one's oyster. **ser hombre/mujer del m.,** to be a man/woman of the world. *Inf.* **tener m.** *or* **mucho m.,** to be very experienced, know the world. **todo el m.,** everyone. **venir al m.,** to be born. **ver m.,** to travel, see the world

mundología /mundolo'hia/ *f*, worldliness, experience of the world

munición /muni'sion; muni'θion/ *f*, *Mil.* munition; small shot. *Mil.* **m. de boca,** fodder and food supplies

municionero /munisio'nero; muniθio'nero/ **(-ra)** *n* purveyor, supplier

municipal /munisi'pal/ *a* municipal. *m*, policeman

municipalidad /munisipali'ðað; muniθipali'ðað/ *f*, municipality

municipio /muni'sipio; muni'θipio/ *m*, municipality, town council

munificencia /munifi'sensia; munifi'θenθia/ *f*, munificence, generosity

munífico /mu'nifiko/ *a* munificent, generous

muñeca /mu'ɲeka/ *f*, *Anat.* wrist; doll; puppet; dressmaker's dummy; polishing pad; mannequin; boundary marker; *Inf.* flighty young woman

muñeco /mu'ɲeko/ *m*, boy doll; puppet; *Inf.* playboy

muñir /mu'ɲir/ *vt irr* to summon, convoke; arrange, dispose. See **mullir**

muñón /mu'ɲon/ *m*, *Surg.* stump of an amputated limb; *Mech.* gudgeon

mural /mu'ral/ *a* mural

muralla /mu'raya; mu'raʎa/ *f*, town wall; rampart, fortification

murar /mu'rar/ *vt* to surround with a wall, wall in

murciélago /mur'sielago; mur'θielago/ *m*, *Zool.* bat

murga /'murga/ *f*, band of street musicians

murmullo /mur'muyo; mur'muʎo/ *m*, whisper; whispering; rustling; purling, lapping, splashing; mumbling, muttering

murmuración /murmura'sion; murmura'θion/ *f*, slander, backbiting, gossip

murmurador /murmura'ðor/ **(-ra)** *a* gossiping, slanderous. *n* gossip, backbiter

murmurar /murmu'rar/ *vi* to rustle (leaves, etc.); purl, lap, splash (water); whisper; mumble, mutter; *vi* and *vt Inf.* slander, backbite

murmurio /mur'murio/ *m*, rustling; lapping (of water); whispering; murmur; *Inf.* slander

muro /'muro/ *m*, wall; defensive wall, rampart

musaraña /musa'raɲa/ *f*, *Zool.* shrew; any small

animal; *Inf.* ridiculous effigy, guy. *Inf.* **mirar a las musarañas,** to be absent-minded

muscular /musku'lar/ *a* muscular

musculatura /muskula'tura/ *f,* musculature

músculo /'muskulo/ *m,* muscle; strength; brawn

musculoso /musku'loso/ *a* muscular; strong, brawny

muselina /muse'lina/ *f,* muslin

museo /mu'seo/ *m,* museum. **m. de pintura,** art gallery, picture gallery

musgo /'musɡo/ *m,* moss

musgoso /mus'ɡoso/ *a* mossy, moss-grown

música /'musika/ *f,* music; melody, harmony; musical performance; musical composition; group of musicians; sheet music. *Inf.* **m. celestial,** vain words, moonshine. *Inf.* **m. ratonera,** badly played music. *Inf.* **¡Vaya con su m. a otra parte!** Get out! Go to hell!

musical /musi'kal/ *a* musical

músico /'musiko/ **(-ca)** *a* music. *n* musician. **m. ambulante,** strolling musician. **m. mayor,** bandleader

musitar /musi'tar/ *vi* to mutter, mumble

muslo /'muslo/ *m,* thigh

mustango /mus'taŋɡo/ *m, Lat. Am.* mustang

mustio /'mustio/ *a* sad, disheartened, depressed; faded, withered; *Mexico* hypocritical

musulmán /musul'man/ **(-ana)** *a* and *n* Muslim

mutabilidad /mutaβili'ðað/ *f,* mutability, changeability

mutación /muta'sion; muta'θion/ *f,* change, mutation; sudden change in the weather; *Theat.* change of scene

mutilación /mutila'sion; mutila'θion/ *f,* mutilation; damage; defacement

mutilar /muti'lar/ *vt* to mutilate; spoil, deface, damage; cut short; reduce

mutis /'mutis/ *m, Theat.* exit. **hacer m.** *Theat.* to exit; keep quiet, say nothing

mutismo /mu'tismo/ *m,* mutism, dumbness; silence, speechlessness

mutualidad /mutuali'ðað/ `f,` reciprocity, mutuality, interdependence; principle of mutual aid; mutual aid society

mutualismo /mutua'lismo/ *m,* mutualism, organized mutual aid

mutualista /mutua'lista/ *mf* member of a mutual aid society

mutuante /mu'tuante/ *mf Com.* lender

mutuo /'mutuo/ *a* reciprocal, mutual, interdependent

muy /'mui/ *adv* very; very much; much. Used to form absolute superlative (e.g. *m. rápidamente,* very quickly). Can modify adjectives, nouns used adjectivally, adverbs, participles (e.g. *María es m. mujer,* Mary is very much a woman (very womanly)). **m. temprano,** very early. **M. señor mío,** Dear Sir (in letters)

— N Ñ —

naba /'naβa/ *f,* Swedish turnip

nabar /na'βar/ *m,* turnip field

nabo /'naβo/ *m,* turnip; turnip root; any root stem; *Naut.* mast; stock (of a horse's tail)

nácar /'nakar/ *m,* mother-of-pearl

nacarado, nacáreo /naka'raðo, na'kareo/ *a* nacreous, mother-of-pearl

nacer /na'ser; na'θer/ *vi irr* to be born; rise (rivers, etc.); sprout; grow (plumage, fur, leaves, etc.); descend (lineage); appear (stars, etc.); originate; *Fig.* issue forth; appear suddenly; (*with prep a* or *para*) be destined for, have a natural leaning toward. **n. con pajitas de oro en la cuna,** to be born with a silver spoon in one's mouth. *vr* grow; sprout; *Sew.* split at the seams. *Pres. Ind.* **nazco, naces, etc.** *Pres. Subjunc.* **nazca, etc.**

nacido /na'siðo; na'θiðo/ *a* and *past part* born; suitable, fit. *m,* (gen. *pl*) the living and the dead. **bien n.,** noble, well-born; well-bred. **mal n.,** base-born; ill-bred

naciente /na'siente; na'θiente/ *a* growing; nascent. *m,* east

nacimiento /nasi'miento; naθi'miento/ *m,* birth; source (of rivers, etc.); birthplace; origin; lineage; *Astron.* rising; nativity crib, manger. **de n.,** from birth; by birth; born

nación /na'sion; na'θion/ *f,* nation; country; *Inf.* birth

nacional /nasio'nal; naθio'nal/ *a* national; native. *mf* citizen, national

nacionalidad /nasionali'ðað; naθionali'ðað/ *f,* nationality

nacionalismo /nasiona'lismo; naθiona'lismo/ *m,* nationalism

nacionalista /nasiona'lista; naθiona'lista/ *a* and *mf* nationalist

nacionalización /nasionalisa'sion; naθionaliθa'θion/ *f,* naturalization; nationalization; acclimatization

nacionalizar /nasionali'sar; naθionali'θar/ *vt* to naturalize; nationalize

nacionalsindicalismo /nasio͵nalsindika'lismo; naθio͵nalsindika'lismo/ *m,* national syndicalism

nacionalsocialismo /nasio͵nalsosia'lismo; naθio͵nalsosia'lismo/ *m,* national socialism, nazism

nada /'naða/ *f,* void, nothingness. *pron indef* nothing. *adv* by no means. **casi n.,** very little, practically noth-

ing. **¡De n.!** Not at all! Don't mention it! You're welcome! **No vale para n.,** He (it, she) is of no use

nadaderas /naða'ðeras/ *f pl,* water wings (for swimming)

nadador /naða'ðor/ **(-ra)** *n* swimmer. *a* swimming

nadar /na'ðar/ *vi* to swim; float; have an abundance (of); *Inf.* be too large (of garments, etc.). **n. y guardar la ropa,** *Fig.* to sit on the fence

nadería /naðe'ria/ *f,* trifle

nadie /'naðie/ *pron indef* no one. *m, Fig.* a nobody

nadir /na'ðir/ *m,* nadir

nado /'naðo/ *a* by swimming; afloat

nafta /'nafta/ *f,* naphtha; *Argentina* gas, gasoline

naftalina /nafta'lina/ *f,* naphthalene

naipe /'naipe/ *m,* playing card; pack of cards

naire /'naire/ *m,* elephant keeper or trainer

nalga /'nalɡa/ *f,* (gen. *pl*) buttock(s)

nana /'nana/ *f, Inf.* grandma; lullaby; *Mexico* wet nurse; nurserymaid

nao /'nao/ *f,* ship

napoleónico /napole'oniko/ *a* Napoleonic

Nápoles /'napoles/ Naples

napolitano /napoli'tano/ **(-na)** *a* and *n* Neapolitan

naranja /na'ranha/ *f,* orange. **n. dulce,** blood orange. **n. mandarina,** tangerine. *Inf.* **media n.,** better half

naranjada /naran'haða/ *f,* orangeade

naranjal /naran'hal/ *m,* orange grove

naranjero /naran'hero/ **(-ra)** *n* orange seller

naranjo /na'ranho/ *m,* orange tree; *Inf.* lout, blockhead

narciso /nar'siso; nar'θiso/ *m,* narcissus; dandy, fop. **n. trompón,** daffodil

narcótico /nar'kotiko/ *a* and *m,* narcotic

narcotizar /narkoti'sar; narkoti'θar/ *vt* to narcotize

narcotraficante /narkotrafi'kante/ *mf* drug dealer

nardo /'narðo/ *m,* tuberose, spikenard, nard

nariguado /nari'ɡuðo/ *a* large-nosed; nose-shaped

nariz /na'ris; na'riθ/ *f,* nose; nostril; snout; nozzle; sense of smell; bouquet (of wine). **n. perfilada,** well-shaped nose. **n. respingona,** snub nose. *Inf.* **meter las narices,** to meddle, interfere

narración /narra'sion; narra'θion/ *f,* narration, account

narrador /narra'ðor/ **(-ra)** *a* narrative. *n* narrator

narrar /na'rrar/ *vt* to narrate, tell, relate

narrativa /narra'tiβa/ f, narrative; account; narrative skill

narrativo, narratorio /narra'tiβo, narra'torio/ a narrative

nata /'nata/ f, cream; *Fig.* the flower, elite; *pl* whipped cream with sugar

natación /nata'sion; nata'θion/ f, swimming. **n. a la marinera,** trudgen stroke

natal /na'tal/ a natal; native. *m,* birth; birthday

natalicio /nata'lisio; nata'liθio/ a natal. *a* and *m,* birthday

natalidad /natali'ðað/ f, birth rate

natatorio /nata'torio/ a swimming. *m,* swimming pool

natillas /na'tiyas; na'tiʎas/ f pl, custard

natividad /natiβi'ðað/ f, nativity; birth; Christmas

nativo /na'tiβo/ a indigenous; native; innate

nato /'nato/ a born; inherent; ex officio

natura /na'tura/ f, nature; *Mus.* major scale

natural /natu'ral/ a natural; native; indigenous; spontaneous; sincere, candid; physical; usual, ordinary; *Mus.* natural; unadulterated, pure; *Herald.* proper. *mf* native, citizen. *m,* temperament; disposition; instinct (of animals); natural inclination. **al n.,** naturally, without art. **del n.,** *Art.* from life

naturaleza /natura'lesa; natura'leθa/ f, nature; character; disposition; instinct; temperament; nationality, origin; naturalization; kind, class; constitution, physique. **n. humana,** humankind. **n. muerta,** *Art.* still life

naturalidad /naturali'ðað/ f, naturalness; nationality

naturalista /natura'lista/ mf naturalist

naturalización /naturalisa'sion; naturaliθa'θion/ f, naturalization; acclimatization

naturalizar /naturali'sar; naturali'θar/ vt to naturalize; acclimatize; vr become naturalized; become acclimatized

naturalmente /natural'mente/ adv naturally; of course

naturismo /natu'rismo/ m, nature cure

naufragar /naufra'gar/ vi to be shipwrecked; fail, be unsuccessful

naufragio /nau'frahio/ m, shipwreck; disaster, loss

náufrago /'naufrago/ **(-ga)** n shipwrecked person. *m,* shark

náusea /'nausea/ f, nausea (pl more usual); repugnance

nauseabundo, nauseoso /nausea'βundo, nause'oso/ a nauseous; nauseating, repugnant

nauta /'nauta/ mf mariner

náutica /'nautika/ f, navigation; yachting; seamanship

náutico /'nautiko/ a nautical

navaja /na'βaha/ f, razor; clasp knife; boar tusk; sting; *Inf.* slanderous tongue. **n. de afeitar,** (shaving) razor

navajada /naβa'haða/ f, slash with a razor

navajero /naβa'hero/ m, razor case

naval /na'βal/ a naval

Navarra /na'βarra/ Navarre

navarro /na'βarro/ **(-ra)** a and n Navarrese

nave /'naβe/ f, ship; *Archit.* nave. **n. aérea,** airship. *Archit.* **n. lateral,** aisle. **n. principal,** *Archit.* nave

navegable /naβe'gaβle/ a navigable

navegación /naβega'sion; naβega'θion/ f, navigation; sea voyage

navegante /naβe'gante/ a voyaging; navigating. *m,* navigator

navegar /naβe'gar/ vi to navigate; sail; fly

navidad /naβi'ðað/ f, nativity; Christmas; pl Christmastime

naviero /na'βiero/ a shipping. *m,* ship owner

navío /na'βio/ m, warship; ship. **n. de transporte,** transport. **n. de tres puentes,** three-decker

náyade /'naiaðe/ f, naiad, water nymph

nazareno /nasa'reno; naθa'reno/ **(-na)** a and n Nazarene; Christian

Nazaret /nasa'ret; naθa'ret/ Nazareth

nazismo /na'sismo; na'θismo/ m, nazism

neblina /ne'βlina/ f, fog; mist

nebulosidad /neβulosi'ðað/ f, nebulousness; cloudiness

nebuloso /neβu'loso/ a foggy; misty; cloudy; somber, melancholy; confused, nebulous

necedad /nese'ðað; neθe'ðað/ f, silliness, foolishness

necesario /nese'sario; neθe'sario/ a necessary; unavoidable

neceser /nese'ser; neθe'ser/ m, dressing case. *Sew.* **n. de costura,** workbox

necesidad /nesesi'ðað; neθesi'ðað/ f, necessity; poverty, want; shortage, need; emergency. **de n.,** necessarily

necesitado /nesesi'taðo; neθesi'taðo/ **(-da)** a needy, poor. *n* poor person

necesitar /nesesi'tar; neθesi'tar/ vt to necessitate; compel, oblige; vi be necessary, need

necio /'nesio; 'neθio/ a stupid; senseless; unreasonable, foolish

necrología /nekrolo'hia/ f, necrology, obituary

necromancia /nekroman'sia; nekroman'θia/ f, necromancy

neerlandés /neerlan'des/ a Dutch

nefando /ne'fando/ a iniquitous

nefario /ne'fario/ a nefarious

nefasto /ne'fasto/ a disastrous, ill-omened

nefrítico /ne'fritiko/ a nephritic

nefritis /ne'fritis/ f, nephritis

negable /ne'gaβle/ a deniable

negación /nega'sion; nega'θion/ f, negation; privation; negative; nay; *Gram.* negative particle; *Law.* traverse

negado /ne'gaðo/ a inept, unfitted; stupid

negar /ne'gar/ vt irr to deny; refuse; prohibit; disclaim; dissemble; disown; *Law.* traverse; vr refuse, avoid; decline (to receive visitors). See **acertar**

negativa /nega'tiβa/ f, denial; refusal; *Photo.* negative

negativo /nega'tiβo/ a negative

negligencia /negli'hensia; negli'henθia/ f, negligence; omission; carelessness; forgetfulness

negligente /negli'hente/ a negligent; careless; neglectful

negociable /nego'siaβle; nego'θiaβle/ a negotiable

negociación /negosia'sion; negoθia'θion/ f, negotiation; business affair, deal

negociado /nego'siaðo; nego'θiaðo/ m, department, section (of a ministry, etc.); business; *Chile* shop, store; *elsewhere in Lat. Am.* shady deal

negociante /nego'siante; nego'θiante/ m, businessman. a negotiating; trading

negociar /nego'siar; nego'θiar/ vi to trade, traffic; negotiate

negocio /ne'gosio; ne'goθio/ m, occupation; trade; business; employment; transaction; *Argentina* shop, store; pl business affairs. **hombre de negocios,** busi nessman

negra /'negra/ f, black girl, black woman; *Inf.* honey, *West Hem.* sweetheart

negrecer /negre'ser; negre'θer/ vi irr to become black. See **conocer**

negro /'negro/ a black; dark; *Herald.* sable. *m,* black; black (color). **n. de humo,** lampblack

negrura /ne'grura/ f, blackness

negruzco /ne'grusko; ne'gruθko/ a blackish

neme /'neme/ m, *Colombia* asphalt

nemotécnica /nemo'teknika/ f, mnemonics

nene /'nene/ **(-na)** n *Inf.* baby; darling

nenúfar /ne'nufar/ m, white water lily

neo /'neo/ m, neon

neófito /ne'ofito/ **(-ta)** n neophyte

neologismo /neolo'hismo/ m, neologism

neoyorquino /neoior'kino/ **(-na)** a New York. *n* New Yorker

nepotismo /nepo'tismo/ m, nepotism

Neptuno /nep'tuno/ m, *Astron.* Neptune; *Poet.* sea

nervio /'nerβio/ m, nerve; sinew; *Bot.* vein; vigor; *Mus.* string. **n. ciático,** sciatic nerve

nervioso /ner'βioso/ a nervous; overwrought, agitated; vigorous; neural; sinewy; jerky (of style, etc.)

nervosidad /nerβosi'ðað/ f, nervousness; nervosity;

flexibility (metals); jerkiness (of style, etc.); force, efficacy

nervudo /ner'βuðo/ *a* strong-nerved, vigorous

nesga /'nesga/ *f, Sew.* gore

neto /'neto/ *a* neat; clean; pure; *Com.* net. *m, Archit.* dado

neumático /neu'matiko/ *a* pneumatic. *m*, rubber tire

neumococo /neumo'koko/ *m*, pneumococcus

neurálgico /neu'ralhiko/ *a* neuralgic

neurastenia /neuras'tenia/ *f*, neurasthenia

neurasténico /neuras'teniko/ **(-ca)** *a* and *n* neurasthenic

neurología /neurolo'hia/ *f*, neurology

neurólogo /neu'rologo/ *m*, neurologist

neurosis /neu'rosis/ *f*, neurosis. **n. de guerra,** war neurosis; shell shock

neurótico /neu'rotiko/ **(-ca)** *a* and *n* neurotic

neutral /neu'tral/ *a* neutral; indifferent

neutralidad /neutrali'ðað/ *f*, neutrality; impartiality, indifference

neutralizar /neutrali'sar; neutrali'θar/ *vt* to neutralize; counteract, mitigate

neutro /'neutro/ *a* neuter; *Chem.* neutral; *Mech.* neuter; sexless

nevada /ne'βaða/ *f*, snowfall

nevado /ne'βaðo/ *m, Lat. Am.* snow-capped mountain

nevar /ne'βar/ *vi irr impers* to snow. *Pres. Ind.* **nieva.** *Pres. Subjunc.* **nieve**

nevazón /neβa'son; neβa'θon/ *f, Lat. Am.* blizzard, snowstorm

nevera /ne'βera/ *f*, refrigerator; icehouse

nevero /ne'βero/ *m*, ice-cream man; iceman

nevisca /ne'βiska/ *f*, light snowfall

nevoso /ne'βoso/ *a* snowy

nexo /'nekso/ *m*, nexus; connection, union

ni /ni/ *conjunc* neither, nor. **ni bien ni mal,** neither good nor bad. **ni siquiera,** not even. **¡Ni crea!, ¡Ni creas!** Nonsense!

niara /'niara/ *f*, haystack, rick

nicaragüeño /nikara'gueɲo/ **(-ña)** *a* and *n* Nicaraguan

nicho /'nitʃo/ *m*, niche; recess (in a wall)

nicotina /niko'tina/ *f*, nicotine

nidada /ni'ðaða/ *f*, nest full of eggs; brood, clutch

nidal /ni'ðal/ *m*, nest; nest egg; haunt; cause, foundation

nido /'niðo/ *m*, nest; den; hole; dwelling; haunt. **n. de ametralladoras,** *Mil.* pillbox

niebla /'nieβla/ *f*, fog; mist; cloud; mildew; haze

nieto /'nieto/ **(-ta)** *n* grandchild; descendant

nieve /'nieβe/ *f*, snow; whiteness. **deportes de n.,** winter sports

nigromancia /nigro'mansia; nigro'manθia/ *f*, necromancy

nigromante /nigro'mante/ *m*, necromancer

nihilismo /nii'lismo/ *m*, nihilism

nihilista /nii'lista/ *mf* nihilist

Nilo, el /'nilo, el/ the Nile

nimbo /'nimbo/ *m*, halo, nimbus

nimiedad /nimie'ðað/ *f*, prolixity; *Inf.* fussiness; fastidiousness, delicacy

nimio /'nimio/ *a* prolix; *Inf.* fussy; fastidious; *Inf.* parsimonious

ninfa /'ninfa/ *f*, nymph; *Ent.* chrysalis

ningún /niŋ'gun/ *a abb* of **ninguno.** Used before *m, sing* nouns only. **De n. modo,** In no way! Certainly not!

niña /'niɲa/ *f*, girl. **n. del ojo,** pupil (of the eye). **n. de los ojos,** apple of one's eye, darling

niñada /ni'ɲaða/ *f*, childishness, foolish act

niñera /ni'ɲera/ *f*, nursemaid

niñería /niɲe'ria/ *f*, childish act; trifle; childishness, folly

niñez /ni'ɲes; ni'ɲeθ/ *f*, childhood; beginning, early days; *Fig.* cradle

niño /'niɲo/ **(-ña)** *a* childish; young; inexperienced; imprudent. *n* child; young or inexperienced person. **n. de la doctrina,** charity child. **n. terrible,** enfant terrible. **desde n.,** from childhood

nipón /ni'pon/ **(-ona)** *a* and *n* Japanese

níquel /'nikel/ *m, Chem.* nickel

niquelar /nike'lar/ *vt* to chrome-plate

niquelera /nike'lera/ *f, Colombia* purse, change purse

nirvana /nir'βana/ *m*, nirvana

níspero /'nispero/ *m*, medlar tree; medlar

níspola /'nispola/ *f*, medlar

nitidez /niti'ðes; niti'ðeθ/ *f*, brightness, neatness, cleanliness

nítido /'nitiðo/ *a* bright, neat, clean (often *poet.*)

nitrato /ni'trato/ *m*, nitrate

nítrico /'nitriko/ *a* nitric

nitrógeno /ni'troheno/ *m*, nitrogen

nivel /ni'βel/ *m*, level; levelness. **n. de albañil,** plummet. **n. de burbuja,** spirit level. **a n.,** on the level. **estar al n. de las circunstancias,** to rise to the occasion; save the day

nivelación /niβela'sion; niβela'θion/ *f*, leveling

nivelador /niβela'ðor/ **(-ra)** *a* leveling. *n* leveler

nivelar /niβe'lar/ *vt* to level; *Fig.* make equal

níveo /'niβeo/ *a* snowy; snow-white

no /no/ *adv* no; not. **no bien,** no sooner. **no sea que,** unless. **no tal,** no such thing

noble /'noβle/ *a* noble, illustrious; generous; outstanding, excellent; aristocratic. *mf* nobleman (-woman)

nobleza /no'βlesa; no'βleθa/ *f*, nobility

noche /'notʃe/ *f*, night; darkness; confusion, obscurity. *Inf.* **n. toledana,** restless night. **¡Buenas noches!** Good night! **de n.,** by night. **esta n.,** tonight

nochebuena /notʃe'βuena/ *f*, Christmas Eve

nochebueno /notʃe'βueno/ *m*, yule log; Christmas cake

nocherniego /notʃer'niego/ *a* night, nocturnal

nochote /no'tʃote/ *m, Mexico* cactus beer

noción /no'sion; no'θion/ *f*, notion, idea; *pl* elementary knowledge

nocividad /nosiβi'ðað; noθiβi'ðað/ *f*, noxiousness

nocivo /no'siβo; no'θiβo/ *a* noxious

nocturno /nok'turno/ *a* nocturnal; melancholy. *m, Mus.* nocturne

nodriza /no'ðrisa; no'ðriθa/ *f*, wet nurse

nogal /no'gal/ *m*, walnut tree; walnut wood

nómada /'nomaða/ *a* nomadic

nomadismo /noma'ðismo/ *m*, nomadism

nombradía /nomˈβraðia/ *f*, renown

nombramiento /nombra'miento/ *m*, naming; appointment; nomination

nombrar /nom'βrar/ *vt* to name; nominate; appoint; mention (in dispatches, etc.)

nombre /'nombre/ *m*, name; title; reputation; proxy; *Gram.* noun; *Mil.* password. **n. de pila,** Christian name. **por n.,** called; by name. **Su n. anda puesto en el cuerno de la Luna,** He (she) is praised to the skies

nomenclatura /nomenkla'tura/ *f*, nomenclature

nómina /'nomina/ *f*, list, register; payroll; amulet

nominación /nomina'sion; nomina'θion/ *f*, nomination, appointment

nominador /nomina'ðor/ **(-ra)** *a* nominating. *n* nominator

nominal /nomi'nal/ *a* nominal

nominalismo /nomina'lismo/ *m*, nominalism

nominalista /nomina'lista/ *mf* nominalistic. *mf* nominalist

nomo /'nomo/ *m*, gnome

non /non/ *a* odd (of numbers)

nonada /no'naða/ *f*, nothing, practically nothing

nonagenario /nonahe'nario/ **(-ia)** *a* and *n* nonagenarian

nonagésimo /nona'hesimo/ *a* ninetieth

nones /'nones/ *m, pl* certainly not, definitely not, nope

nopal /no'pal/ *m*, nopal, prickly pear tree

noque /'noke/ *m*, tanner's vat

noquear /noke'ar/ *vt (Box.)* to knock out, K.O.

norabuena /nora'βuena/ *f*, congratulation

nordeste /nor'ðeste/ *m*, northeast

nórdico /'norðiko/ **(-ca)** *a* and *n* Nordic

noria /'noria/ *f*, water well; chain pump; *Inf.* hard, monotonous work

norma /'norma/ *f*, square (used by builders, etc.); *Fig.* norm, standard, model

normal /nor'mal/ *a* normal, usual; standard, average. *f*, normal school, teacher's college (also **escuela n.**)

normalidad /normali'ðað/ *f*, normality

normalista /norma'lista/ *mf* student at a teacher's college

normalización /normalisa'sion; normaliθa'θion/ *f*, normalization; standardization

normalizar /normali'sar; normali'θar/ *vt* to make normal; standardize

Normandía /norman'dia/ Normandy

normando /nor'mando/ **(-da)** *a* Norman. *n* Northman; Norman

nornordeste /nornor'ðeste/ *m*, northnortheast

nornorueste /norno'rueste/ *m*, northnorthwest

noroeste /noro'este/ *m*, northwest

norte /'norte/ *m*, north pole; north; north wind; polestar; *Fig.* guide

norteamericano /norteameri'kano/ **(-na)** *a* and *n* North American; (*U.S.A.*) American

norteño /nor'teɲo/ *a* northerly, northern

Noruega /no'ruega/ Norway

noruego /no'ruego/ **(-ga)** *a* and *n* Norwegian. *m*, Norwegian (language)

nos /nos/ *pers pron pl mf acc* and *dat* (direct and indirect object) of **nosotros**, us; to us (e.g. *Nos lo dio*, He gave it to us)

nosotros, nosotras /no'sotros, no'sotras/ *pers pron pl mf* we; us. Also used with preposition (e.g. *Lo hicieron por nosotros*, They did it for us)

nostalgia /nos'talhia/ *f*, nostalgia

nostálgico /nos'talhiko/ *a* nostalgic; melancholy; homesick

nóstico /'nostiko/ **(-ca)** *a* and *n* gnostic

nota /'nota/ *f*, mark, sign; annotation, comment; *Mus.* note; memorandum; *Com.* bill, account; criticism, imputation; mark (in exams); repute, renown; note (diplomatic)

notabilidad /notaβili'ðað/ *f*, notability

notable /no'taβle/ *a* notable, remarkable; outstanding, prominent; with distinction (examination mark). *m pl*, notabilities

notación /nota'sion; nota'θion/ *f*, (*Mus. Math.*) notation; annotation

notar /no'tar/ *vt* to mark, indicate; observe, notice; note down; annotate; dictate, read out; criticize, reproach; discredit

notaría /nota'ria/ *f*, profession of a notary; notary's office

notarial /nota'rial/ *a* notarial

notario /no'tario/ *m*, notary public

noticia /no'tisia; no'tiθia/ *f*, rudiment, elementary knowledge; information; news (gen. *pl*); *pl* knowledge. **atrasado de noticias,** *Fig.* behind the times

noticiar /noti'siar; noti'θiar/ *vt* to inform, give notice

noticiario /noti'siario; noti'θiario/ *m*, news bulletin, newsreel.

noticiero /noti'siero; noti'θiero/ *m*, newspaper

noticioso /noti'sioso; noti'θioso/ *a* informed; learned; newsy

notificación /notifika'sion; notifika'θion/ *f*, *Law.* notification. **n. de reclutamiento,** draft notice

notificar /notifi'kar/ *vt* to notify officially; inform; warn

noto /'noto/ *a* known. *m*, south wind

notoriedad /notorie'ðað/ *f*, notoriety, publicity; flagrancy; fame, renown

notorio /no'torio/ *a* well-known; notorious, obvious; flagrant

novatada /noβa'taða/ *f*, *Inf.* practical joke, hazing (of a freshman); blunder

novato /no'βato/ **(-ta)** *a* new, inexperienced. *n* novice, beginner

novecientos /noβe'sientos; noβe'θientos/ *a* and *m*, nine hundred

novedad /noβe'ðað/ *f*, newness, novelty; change, alteration; latest news; surprise; *pl* novelties. **sin n.,** no change; all well (or as usual); safely, without incident

novel /no'βel/ *a* new; inexperienced

novela /no'βela/ *f*, novel; tale; falsehood. **n. caballista,** western, cowboy story. **n. por entregas,** serial (story)

novelero /noβe'lero/ **(-ra)** *a* fond of novelty and change; fond of novels; fickle. *n* newshound, gossip

novelesco /noβe'lesko/ *a* novelistic; imaginary

novelista /noβe'lista/ *mf* novelist

novelística /noβe'listika/ *f*, art of novel writing

novena /no'βena/ *f*, *Eccl.* novena, religious services spread over nine days

noveno /no'βeno/ *a* and *m*, ninth

noventa /no'βenta/ *a* and *m*, ninety; ninetieth

novia /'noβia/ *f*, bride; fiancée

noviar con /no'βiar kon/ *vi*, *Argentina* to court, woo

noviazgo /no'βiasgo; no'βiaθgo/ *m*, engagement, betrothal

noviciado /noβi'siaðo; noβi'θiaðo/ *m*, novitiate; training, apprenticeship

novicio /no'βisio; no'βiθio/ **(-ia)** *n* *Eccl.* novice; beginner, apprentice; unassuming person

noviembre /no'βiembre/ *m*, November

novillada /noβi'yaða; noβi'ʎaða/ *f*, herd of young bulls; bullock baiting

novillo /no'βiyo; no'βiʎo/ *m*, bullock. **hacer novillos,** to play truant

novilunio /noβi'lunio/ *m*, new moon

novio /'noβio/ *m*, bridegroom; fiancé; novice, beginner

novísimo /no'βisimo/ *a sup* **nuevo** newest; latest, most recent

nubada /nu'βaða/ *f*, cloudburst, rainstorm; abundance, plenty

nubarrón /nuβa'rron/ *m*, dense, lowering cloud, storm cloud

nube /'nuβe/ *f*, cloud; *Fig.* screen, impediment. **n. de verano,** summer cloud; passing annoyance

nublado /nu'βlaðo/ *a* cloudy; overcast. *m*, storm cloud; menace, threat; multitude, crowd

nublarse /nu'βlarse/ *vr* to cloud over

nubloso /nu'βloso/ *a* cloudy; unfortunate, unhappy

nuca /'nuka/ *f*, nape

núcleo /'nukleo/ *m*, kernel; stone, pip (of fruit); nucleus; *Fig.* core, essence

nudillo /nu'ðiyo; nu'ðiʎo/ *m*, knuckle; *Mas.* plug

nudo /'nuðo/ *m*, knot; (*Bot. Med.*) node; joint; *Naut.* knot; *Fig.* bond, tie; *Fig.* crux, knotty point. **n. al revés,** granny knot. **n. de comunicaciones,** communication center. **n. de marino,** reef knot. **n. de tejedor,** sheet bend (knot). **n. en la garganta,** *Fig.* lump in the throat (from emotion)

nudoso /nu'ðoso/ *a* knotted, knotty; gnarled

nuera /'nuera/ *f*, daughter-in-law

nuestro, nuestra /'nuestro, 'nuestra/ *poss pron 1st pers pl mf* our; ours. **los nuestros,** our friends, supporters, party, profession, etc.

nueva /'nueβa/ *f*, news

nuevamente /nueβa'mente/ *adv* again

Nueva Orleans /'nueβa orle'ans/ New Orleans

Nueva York /'nueβa york/ New York

Nueva Zelanda, Nueva Zelandia /'nueβa se'landa, se'landia; 'nueβa θe'landa, θe'landia/ New Zealand

nueve /'nueβe/ *a* nine; ninth. *m*, number nine; ninth (of the month) (e.g. *el nueve de marzo*, March 9th). **a las nueve,** at nine o'clock

nuevo /'nueβo/ *a* new; fresh; newly arrived; inexperienced; unused; scarcely worn. **de n.,** again. **¿Qué hay de n.?** What's the news? What's new?

Nuevo México /'nueβo 'meksiko/ *m* New Mexico

nuez /nues; nueθ/ *f*, walnut; *Anat.* Adam's apple. **n. moscada,** nutmeg

nulidad /nuli'ðað/ *f*, nullity; incompetence, ineptitude; worthlessness

nulo /'nulo/ *a* null, void; incapable; worthless

numen /'numen/ *m*, divinity; inspiration

numeración /numera'sion; numera'θion/ *f*, calculation; numbering

numerador /numera'ðor/ *m*, numerator

numerar /nume'rar/ *vt* to number; enumerate; calculate

numerario /nume'rario/ *a* numerary. *m*, cash

numérico /nu'meriko/ *a* numerical

número /'numero/ *m*, number; figure; numeral; size (of gloves, etc.); quantity; issue, copy; rhythm; *Gram.* number; item (of a program); *pl Eccl.* Numbers. **n. del distrito postal**, ZIP code. **n. quebrado**, *Math.* fraction. **sin n.**, numberless

numeroso /nume'roso/ *a* numerous; harmonious

numismática /numis'matika/ *f*, numismatics

nunca /'nunka/ *adv* never. **n. jamás**, nevermore. **N. digas «De esta agua no beberé!»** Never say "Never!"

nuncio /'nunsio/ 'nunθio/ *m*, messenger; papal nuncio; *Fig.* harbinger

nupcial /nup'sial; nup'θial/ *a* nuptial

nupcialidad /nupsiali'ðað; nupθiali'ðað/ *f*, marriage rate

nupcias /'nupsias; 'nupθias/ *f pl*, nuptials, marriage

nutria /'nutria/ *f*, otter, nutria

nutrición /nutri'sion; nutri'θion/ *f*, nourishment; nutrition

nutrido /nu'triðo/ *a* abundant; numerous

nutrimento /nutri'mento/ *m*, nutriment; nourishment; nutrition; *Fig.* food, encouragement

nutrir /nu'trir/ *vt* to nourish; encourage; *Fig.* fill

nutritivo /nutri'tiβo/ *a* nourishing, nutritive

ñácara /'ɲakara/ *f*, *Central America* sore, ulcer

ñaña /'ɲaɲa/ *f*, *Lat. Am.* wet nurse; nursemaid; elder sister

ñaques /'ɲakes/ *m pl*, odds and ends, rubbish

ñiquiñaque /ɲiki'ɲake/ *m*, *Inf.* good-for-nothing, wastrel; *Inf.* trash

ñoco, -a /'ɲoko/ *a*, *Lat. Am.* one-handed; missing a finger

ñoñería /ɲoɲe'ria/ *f*, *Inf.* drivel; folly, stupidity. **Déjate de ñoñerías,** *Inf.* Stop being a crybaby

ñoño /'ɲoɲo/ **(-ña)** *a* *Inf.* sentimental; foolish, idiotic. *n* fool.

O

o /o/ *f*, letter O. *conjunc* or, either. **o** becomes **u** before words beginning with **o** or **ho** (e.g. *gloria u honor*)

oasis /o'asis/ *m*, oasis; *Fig.* refuge, haven

obcecación /oβseka'sion; oβθeka'θion/ *f*, blindness; obstinacy; obsession

obcecar /oβse'kar; oβθe'kar/ *vt* to blind; obsess; *Fig.* dazzle; darken

obduración /oβðura'sion; oβðura'θion/ *f*, obstinacy, stubbornness, obduracy

obedecer /oβeðe'ser; oβeðe'θer/ *vt irr* to obey; *Fig.* respond; bend, yield (metals, etc.); *vi* result (from), arise (from). See **conocer**

obedecimiento /oβeðesi'miento; oβeðeθi'miento/ *m*, **obediencia** *f*, obedience

obediente /oβe'ðiente/ *a* obedient; docile

obelisco /oβe'lisko/ *m*, obelisk

obertura /oβer'tura/ *f*, *Mus.* overture

obesidad /oβesi'ðað/ *f*, obesity

obeso /o'βeso/ *a* obese

óbice /'oβise; 'oβiθe/ *m*, obstacle, impediment

obispado /oβis'paðo/ *m*, bishopric

obispo /o'βispo/ *m*, bishop. **o. sufragáneo**, suffragan bishop

óbito /'oβito/ *m*, death, demise

obituario /oβi'tuario/ *m*, obituary; obituary column

objeción /oβhe'sion; oβhe'θion/ *f*, objection

objetar /oβhe'tar/ *vt* to object to, oppose

objetivar /oβheti'βar/ *vt* to view objectively

objetividad /oβhetiβi'ðað/ *f*, objectivity

objetivo /oβhe'tiβo/ *a* objective. *m*, *Opt.* eyepiece; object finder; aim, goal

objeto /oβ'heto/ *m*, object; subject, theme; purpose; aim, goal. **sin o.**, without object; aimlessly

oblicuidad /oβlikui'ðað/ *f*, obliqueness

oblicuo /o'βlikuo/ *a* slanting, oblique

obligación /oβliga'sion; oβliga'θion/ *f*, obligation; *Com.* bond; *Com.* debenture; *pl* responsibilities; *Com.* liabilities

obligacionista /oβligasio'nista; oβligaθio'nista/ *mf* *Com.* bond holder, debenture holder

obligado /oβli'gaðo/ *m*, contractor (to a borough, etc.); *Mus.* obbligato

obligar /oβli'gar/ *vt* to compel, oblige, constrain; lay under an obligation; *Law.* mortgage; *vr* bind oneself, promise

obligatorio /oβliga'torio/ *a* obligatory

oblongo /o'βloŋgo/ *a* oblong

oboe /o'βoe/ *m*, oboe; oboe player, oboist

óbolo /'oβolo/ *m*, obol, ancient Greek coin

obra /'oβra/ *f*, work; anything made; literary, artistic, scientific production; structure, construction; repair, alteration (to buildings, etc.); means, influence, power; labor, or time spent; action, behavior. **o. de**

caridad, charitable act. **o. maestra,** masterpiece. **obras públicas,** public works. **poner por o.,** to put into effect; to set to work on. **o. de,** about, approximately

obrar /o'βrar/ *vt* to work; make, do; execute, perform; affect; construct, build; *vi* be, exist (things); act, behave. **o. mal,** to behave badly, do wrong

obrero /o'βrero/ **(-ra)** *a* working. *n* worker; *pl* workers

obscenidad /oβsseni'ðað; oβsθeni'ðað/ *f*, obscenity

obsceno /oβs'seno; oβs'θeno/ *a* obscene

obsequiar /oβse'kiar/ *vt* to entertain, be attentive (to); give presents (to); court, make love to. **Me obsequia con un reloj,** He is presenting me with a watch

obsequio /oβ'sekio/ *m*, attention; gift; deference. **en o. de,** as a tribute to

obsequioso /oβse'kioso/ *a* obliging, courteous, attentive

observable /oβser'βaβle/ *a* observable

observación /oβserβa'sion; oβserβa'θion/ *f*, observation; remark

observador /oβserβa'ðor/ **(-ra)** *a* observing. *n* observer

observancia /oβser'βansia; oβser'βanθia/ *f*, observance; respect, reverence

observar /oβser'βar/ *vt* to notice; inspect, examine; fulfill; remark; watch, spy upon; *Astron.* observe

observatorio /oβserβa'torio/ *m*, observatory

obsesión /oβse'sion/ *f*, obsession

obsesionar /oβsesio'nar/ *vt* to obsess

obseso /oβ'seso/ *a* obsessed

obsidiana /oβsi'ðiana/ *f*, obsidian

obsolecer /oβsole'ser; oβsole'θer/ *vi* to obsolesce, become obsolete

obsoleto /oβso'leto/ *a* obsolete

obstáculo /oβs'takulo/ *m*, impediment; obstacle

obstante, no /oβs'tante, no/ *adv* in spite of; nevertheless

obstar /oβs'tar/ *vi* to impede, hinder

obstetra /oβs'tetra/ *mf* obstetrician

obstetricia /oβste'trisia; oβste'triθia/ *f*, obstetrics

obstinación /oβstina'sion; oβstina'θion/ *f*, obstinacy

obstinado /oβsti'naðo/ *a* obstinate, stubborn

obstinarse /oβsti'narse/ *vr* (*with en*) to persist in, insist on, be stubborn about

obstinaz /oβsti'nas; oβsti'naθ/ *a* obstinate

obstrucción /oβstruk'sion; oβstruk'θion/ *f*, obstruction

obstruccionar /oβstruksio'nar; oβstrukθio'nar/ *vt*, *Lat. Am.* to obstruct, stonewall

obstruccionismo /oβstruksio'nismo; oβstrukθio'nismo/ *m*, obstructionism, stonewalling

obstruccionista /oβstruksio'nista; oβstrukθio'nista/ *mf* obstructionist

obstruir /oβs'truir/ *vt irr* to obstruct; block; hinder; *vr* become choked or stopped up (pipes, etc.). See **huir**

obtención /oβten'sion; oβten'θion/ *f*, obtainment; attainment, realization

obtener /oβte'ner/ *vt irr* to obtain; attain; maintain; preserve. See **tener**

obturador /oβtura'ðor/ *m*, stopper; shutter (of a camera)

obturar /oβtu'rar/ *vt* to stopper, plug; block, obstruct

obtuso /oβ'tuso/ *a* blunt, dull; (*Geom. and Fig.*) obtuse

obús /o'βus/ *m*, howitzer; *Mil.* shell

obviar /oβ'βiar/ *vt* to obviate

obvio /'oββio/ *a* obvious, evident, apparent

oca /'oka/ *f*, goose

ocasión /oka'sion/ *f*, occasion; opportunity; motive, cause; danger, risk; *Inf.* **asir la o. por la melena**, to take time by the forelock. **de o.**, second-hand

ocasional /okasio'nal/ *a* chance, fortuitous; occasional

ocasionar /okasio'nar/ *vt* to cause, occasion; excite, provoke; risk, endanger

ocaso /o'kaso/ *m*, sunset; west; dusk; decadence, decline

occidental /oksiðen'tal; okθiðen'tal/ *a* Western

occidente /oksi'ðente; okθi'ðente/ *m*, West, Occident

occiso /ok'siso; ok'θiso/ *a* murdered; killed

oceánico /ose'aniko; oθe'aniko/ *a* oceanic

océano /o'seano; o'θeano/ *m*, ocean; immensity, abundance

oceanografía /oseanogra'fia; oθeanogra'fia/ *f*, oceanography

ocelote /ose'lote; oθe'lote/ *m*, ocelot

ochava /o'tʃaβa/ *f*, eighth; *Eccl.* octave

ochavo /o'tʃaβo/ *m*, *Obs.* small Spanish copper coin

ochenta /o'tʃenta/ *a* and *m*, eighty; eightieth

ochentón /otʃen'ton/ **(-ona)** *n* octogenarian

ocho /'otʃo/ *a* eight; eighth. *m*, figure eight; playing card with eight pips; eight; eighth day (of the month). **las o.**, eight o'clock

ochocientos /otʃo'sientos; otʃo'θientos/ *a* and *m*, eight hundred; eight-hundredth

ocio /'osio; 'oθio/ *m*, leisure, idleness; *pl* pastimes; leisure time

ociosidad /osiosi'ðað; oθiosi'ðað/ *f*, idleness, laziness; leisure

ocioso /o'sioso; o'θioso/ **(-sa)** *a* idle; useless, worthless; unprofitable, fruitless. *n* idle fellow

ocozoal /okoso'al; okoθo'al/ *m*, *Mexico* rattlesnake

ocre /'okre/ *m*, ocher

octágono /ok'tagono/ *m*, octagon

octava /ok'taβa/ *f*, octave

octaviano /okta'βiano/ *a* Octavian

octavo /ok'taβo/ *a* eighth. *m*, eighth. **en o.**, in octavo

octeto /ok'teto/ *m*, octet; byte

octogenario /oktohe'nario/ **(-ia)** *a* and *n* octogenarian

octogésimo /okto'hesimo/ *a* eightieth

octubre /ok'tuβre/ *m*, October

óctuple /'oktuple/ *a* octuple, eightfold

ocular /oku'lar/ *a* ocular. *m*, eyepiece

oculista /oku'lista/ *mf* oculist

ocultación /okulta'sion; okulta'θion/ *f*, hiding, concealment

ocultamente /okulta'mente/ *adv* secretly

ocultar /okul'tar/ *vt* to hide, conceal; disguise; keep secret

ocultismo /okul'tismo/ *m*, occultism

oculto /o'kulto/ *a* hidden; secret; occult. **en o.**, secretly, quietly

ocupación /okupa'sion; okupa'θion/ *f*, occupancy; occupation, pursuit; employment, office, trade

ocupado /oku'paðo/ *a* occupied; busy

ocupante /oku'pante/ *m*, occupant

ocupar /oku'par/ *vt* to take possession of; obtain or hold (job); occupy, fill; inhabit; employ; hinder, em-

barrass; hold the attention (of); *vr* (*with en*) be engaged in, be occupied with; (*with con*) concentrate on (a business affair, etc.)

ocurrencia /oku'rrensia; oku'rrenθia/ *f*, occurrence, incident; bright idea; witty remark

ocurrir /oku'rrir/ *vi* to anticipate; happen, take place; occur, strike (ideas)

oda /'oða/ *f*, ode

odalisca /oða'liska/ *f*, odalisque

odiar /o'ðiar/ *vt* to hate; *Chile* annoy, irk

odio /'oðio/ *m*, hatred; malevolence

odioso /o'ðioso/ *a* hateful, odious; *Argentina, Chile, Peru* annoying, irksome

odisea /oði'sea/ *f*, odyssey

odontología /oðontolo'hia/ *f*, odontology

odontólogo /oðon'tologo/ *m*, odontologist

odorífero /oðo'rifero/ *a* odoriferous, fragrant

odre /'oðre/ *m*, goatskin, wineskin; *Inf.* wine bibber

oesnorueste /oesno'rueste/ *m*, westnorthwest

oessudueste /oessu'ðueste/ *m*, westsouthwest

oeste /o'este/ *m*, west

ofender /ofen'der/ *vt* to ill-treat, hurt; offend, insult; anger, annoy; *vr* be offended

ofendido /ofen'diðo/ *a* offended; resentful

ofensa /o'fensa/ *f*, injury, harm; offense, crime

ofensiva /ofen'siβa/ *f*, *Mil.* offensive. **tomar la o.**, to take the offensive

ofensivo /ofen'siβo/ *a* offensive

ofensor /ofen'sor/ **(-ra)** *n* offender

oferta /o'ferta/ *f*, offer; gift; proposal; *Com.* tender. **o. y demanda**, supply and demand

oficial /ofi'sial; ofi'θial/ *a* official. *m*, official; officer; clerk; executioner; worker

oficiala /ofi'siala; ofi'θiala/ *f*, trained female worker

oficialidad /ofisiali'ðað; ofiθiali'ðað/ *f*, officialdom; officers

oficiar /ofi'siar; ofi'θiar/ *vt Eccl.* to celebrate or serve (mass); communicate officially, inform; *Inf.* (*with de*) act as

oficina /ofi'sina; ofi'θina/ *f*, workshop; office; pharmaceutical laboratory; *pl* cellars, basement (of a house)

oficinesco /ofisi'nesko; ofiθi'nesko/ *a* bureaucratic, red-tape

oficinista /ofisi'nista; ofiθi'nista/ *mf* clerk, office employee, office worker

oficio /o'fisio; o'fiθio/ *m*, occupation, employment; office, function, capacity; craft; operation; trade, business; official communication; office, bureau; *Eccl.* office. **Santo O.**, Holy Office. *Fig.* **buenos oficios**, good offices

oficiosidad /ofisiosi'ðað; ofiθiosi'ðað/ *f*, diligence, conscientiousness; helpfulness, friendliness; officiousness

oficioso /ofi'sioso; ofi'θioso/ *a* conscientious; helpful, useful; officious; meddlesome; unofficial, informal

ofrecer /ofre'ser; ofre'θer/ *vt irr* to offer; present; exhibit; consecrate, dedicate; *vr* occur, suggest itself; volunteer. **¿Qué se le ofrece?** What do you require? What would you like? See **conocer**

ofrecimiento /ofresi'miento; ofreθi'miento/ *m*, offer, offering

ofrenda /o'frenda/ *f*, *Eccl.* offering; gift, present

oftalmología /oftalmolo'hia/ *f*, ophthalmology

oftalmólogo /oftal'mologo/ *m*, oculist, ophthalmologist

ofuscación /ofuska'sion; ofuska'θion/ *f*. **ofuscamiento** *m*, obfuscation, dazzle, dimness of sight; mental confusion, bewilderment

ofuscar /ofus'kar/ *vt* to dazzle, daze; dim, obfuscate; confuse, bewilder

ogro /'ogro/ *m*, ogre

ohmio /'omio/ *m*, ohm

oídas, de /o'iðas, de/ *adv* by hearsay

oído /o'iðo/ *m*, sense of hearing; ear. **de o.**, by ear. **decir al o.**, to whisper in a person's ear. *Mus.* **duro de o.**, hard of hearing; having a bad ear (for music). **estar sordo de un o.**, to be deaf in one ear

oidor /oi'ðor/ *m*, hearer; judge, *Obs.* magistrate

oir /o'ir/ *vt irr* to hear; give ear to, listen; understand. *Pres. Part.* **oyendo.** *Pres. Ind.* **oigo, oyes, oye, oyen.** *Preterite* **oyó, oyeron.** *Pres. Subjunc.* **oiga, etc.** *Imperf. Subjunc.* **oyese, etc.**

oíslo /o'islo/ *mf Inf.* better half

ojal /o'hal/ *m,* buttonhole; slit, hole

¡ojalá! /oha'la/ *interj* If only that were so! God grant! **O. que venga,** I hope he comes (with *subjunc.*)

ojeada /ohe'aða/ *f,* glance

ojear /ohe'ar/ *vt* to look at, stare at; bewitch; scare, startle

ojera /o'hera/ *f,* dark shadow (under the eye); eye bath

ojeriza /ohe'risa; ohe'riθa/ *f,* ill-will, spite

ojeroso /ohe'roso/ *a* having dark shadows under the eyes, wan, haggard

ojete /o'hete/ *m,* eyelet

ojinegro /ohi'negro/ *a* black-eyed

ojiva /o'hiβa/ *f,* ogive

ojo /'oho/ *m,* eye; hole; slit; socket; keyhole; eye (of a needle); span (of a bridge); core (of a corn); attention, care; mesh; spring, stream; well (of a staircase); *pl* darling. **¡Ojo!** Take care! **o. avizor,** sharp watch; lynx eye. **Ojos que no ven, corazón que no siente,** Out of sight, out of mind. **o. saltón,** prominent, bulging eye. **o. vivo,** bright eye. **a o. de buen cubero,** at a guess. **a ojos vistas,** visibly; patently

ojota /o'hota/ *f, Chile,* sandal

ola /'ola/ *f,* billow; wave (atmospheric)

ole /'ole/ *m,* Andalusian dance

¡olé! /'ole/ *interj* Bravo!

oleada /ole'aða/ *f,* big wave, breaker; swell (of the sea); *Fig.* surge (of a crowd)

oleaginoso /oleahi'noso/ *a* oleaginous

oleaje /ole'ahe/ *m,* swell, surge, billowing

olear /ole'ar/ *vt* to administer extreme unction

óleo /'oleo/ *m,* oil; *Eccl.* holy oil (gen. *pl*). **al ó.,** in oils

oleoducto /oleo'ðukto/ *m,* oil pipeline

oler /o'ler/ *vt irr* to smell; guess, discover; pry, smell out; *vi* smell; (*with prep a*) smell of; smack of, be reminiscent of. *Pres. Ind.* **huelo, hueles, huele, huelen.** *Pres. Subjunc.* **huela, huelas, huela, huelan**

olfatear /olfate'ar/ *vt* to sniff, snuff, smell; *Inf.* pry into

olfativo, olfatorio /olfa'tiβo, olfa'torio/ *a* olfactory

olfato /ol'fato/ *m,* sense of smell; shrewdness

olfatorio /olfa'torio/ *a* olfactory

oliente /o'liente/ (**mal**) *a* evil-smelling

oligárquico /oli'garkiko/ *a* oligarchic

olímpico /o'limpiko/ *a* Olympic; Olympian

olisco, -a /o'lisko/ *a, Lat. Am.* spoiled, tainted (meat)

oliva /o'liβa/ *f,* olive tree; olive; barn owl; peace

olivar /oli'βar/ *m,* olive grove

olivo /o'liβo/ *m,* olive tree

olla /'oya/ *f,* stew pot; Spanish stew; whirlpool. **o. podrida,** rich Spanish stew containing bacon, fowl, meat, vegetables, ham, etc. **las ollas de Egipto,** the fleshpots of Egypt

olmeda /ol'meða/ *f,* **olmedo** *m,* elm grove

olmo /'olmo/ *m,* elm tree

olor /o'lor/ *m,* odor, scent, smell; hope, promise; suspicion, hint; reputation. **o. de santidad,** odor of sanctity

oloroso /olo'roso/ *a* fragrant, perfumed

olvidadizo /olβiða'ðiso; olβiða'ðiθo/ *a* forgetful

olvidar /olβi'ðar/ (**se**) *vt* and *vr* to forget; neglect, desert. **Se me olvidó el libro,** I forgot the book. **Me olvidé de lo pasado,** I forgot the past

olvido /ol'βiðo/ *m,* forgetfulness; indifference, neglect; oblivion

ombligo /om'βligo/ *m,* navel; *Fig.* core, center

ominoso /omi'noso/ *a* ominous

omisión /omi'sion/ *f,* omission; carelessness, negligence; neglect

omiso /o'miso/ *a* omitted; remiss; careless. **hacer caso o. de,** to set aside, ignore

omitir /omi'tir/ *vt* to omit

ómnibus /'omniβus/ *m,* bus

omnímodo /om'nimoðo/ *a* all-embracing

omnipotencia /omnipo'tensia; omnipo'tenθia/ *f,* omnipotence

omnipotente /omnipo'tente/ *a* omnipotent, all-powerful

omnisciencia /omnis'siensia; omnis'θienθia/ *f,* omniscience

omniscio /om'nissio; om'nisθio/ *a* omniscient

omnívoro /om'niβoro/ *a* omnivorous

omoplato /omo'plato/ *m,* scapula, shoulder blade

once /'onse; 'onθe/ *a* eleven; eleventh. *m,* eleven; eleventh (of the month). **las o.,** eleven o'clock

onceno /on'seno; on'θeno/ *a* eleventh

onda /'onda/ *f,* wave; *Fig.* flicker (of flames); *Sew.* scallop; *Phys.* wave; ripple; (in hair). *Radio.* **o. corta,** short wave. **o. etérea,** ether wave. **o. sonora,** sound wave

ondeado /onde'aðo/ *a* undulating; wavy; scalloped

ondeante /onde'ante/ *a* waving; flowing

ondear /onde'ar/ *vi* to wave; ripple; undulate; roll (of the sea); float, flutter, stream; *Sew.* scallop; *vr* swing, sway

ondeo /on'deo/ *m,* waving; undulation

ondulación /ondula'sion; ondula'θion/ *f,* undulation; wave; wriggling; twisting. **o. permanente,** permanent wave, perm

ondulado /ondu'laðo/ *a* wavy; undulating; scalloped

ondular /ondu'lar/ *vi* to writhe, squirm, wriggle; twist; coil; *vt* wave (in hair)

oneroso /one'roso/ *a* onerous, heavy; troublesome

ónice /'onise; 'oniθe/ *m,* onyx

onomástico /ono'mastiko/ *a* onomastic. **día o.,** saint's day

onomatopeya /onomato'peia/ *f,* onomatopoeia

onza /'onsa; 'onθa/ *f,* ounce. **por onzas,** by ounces; sparingly

onzavo /on'saβo; on'θaβo/ *a* and *m,* eleventh

opacidad /opasi'ðað; opaθi'ðað/ *f,* opacity; obscurity; gloom

opaco /o'pako/ *a* opaque; dark; gloomy, sad

opalino /opa'lino/ *a* opaline

ópalo /'opalo/ *m,* opal

opción /op'sion; op'θion/ *f,* option; choice, selection; *Law.* option

ópera /'opera/ *f,* opera

operación /opera'sion; opera'θion/ *f,* operation; execution, performance; *Com.* transaction

operar /ope'rar/ *vt Surg.* to operate; *vi* act, have an effect; operate, control; *Com.* transact

operario /ope'rario/ (**-ia**) *n* worker, hand; operator; mechanic

opereta /ope'reta/ *f,* operetta, light opera

opinar /opi'nar/ *vi* to have or form an opinion, think; judge, consider

opinión /opi'nion/ *f,* opinion, view; reputation

opio /'opio/ *m,* opium. **fumadero de o.,** opium den

opíparo /o'piparo/ *a* magnificent, sumptuous (banquets, etc.)

oponer /opo'ner/ *vt irr* to oppose; resist, withstand; protest against; *vr* oppose; be contrary or hostile (to); face, be opposite; object (to), set oneself against; compete (in public exams.). See **poner**

oporto /o'porto/ *m,* port (wine)

oportunidad /oportuni'ðað/ *f,* opportunity, occasion

oportunismo /oportu'nismo/ *m,* opportunism

oportunista /oportu'nista/ *a* and *mf* opportunist

oportuno /opor'tuno/ *a* opportune, timely

oposición /oposi'sion; oposi'θion/ *f,* opposition; resistance; antagonism; public competitive exam for a post; (*Astron. Polit.*) opposition

opositor /oposi'tor/ (**-ra**) *n* opponent; competitor

opresión /opre'sion/ *f,* oppression; hardship; pressure. **o. de pecho,** difficulty in breathing

opresor /opre'sor/ (**-ra**) *a* oppressive. *n* oppressor

oprimir /opri'mir/ *vt* to oppress; treat harshly; press, crush; choke

oprobio /o'proβio/ *m,* opprobrium

optar /op'tar/ *vt* to take possession of; (*with por*) choose

óptica /'optika/ *f, Phys.* optics; peepshow

óptico /'optiko/ *a* optic, optical. *m,* optician

optimismo /opti'mismo/ *m,* optimism

optimista /opti'mista/ *mf* optimist. *a* optimistic

óptimo /'optimo/ *a sup* **bueno** best, optimal, optimum

opugnar /opug'nar/ *vt* to resist violently; *Mil.* assault, attack; impugn, challenge

opulencia /opu'lensia; opu'lenθia/ *f,* opulence, riches; excess, superabundance

opulento /opu'lento/ *a* opulent, rich

opúsculo /o'puskulo/ *m,* monograph, opuscule

oquedad /oke'ðað/ *f,* hollow, cavity; superficiality, banality

ora /'ora/ *adv* now

oración /ora'sion; ora'θion/ *f,* oration, speech; prayer; *Gram.* sentence

oráculo /o'rakulo/ *m,* oracle

orador /ora'ðor/ **(-ra)** *n* orator; speech maker. *m,* preacher

oral /o'ral/ *a* oral; verbal; buccal

orangután /oraŋgu'tan/ *m,* orangutan

orar /o'rar/ *vi* to harangue, make an oration; pray; *vt* request, beg

orate /o'rate/ *mf* lunatic

oratoria /ora'toria/ *f,* oratory, eloquence

oratorio /ora'torio/ *a* oratorical. *m,* oratory, chapel; *Mus.* oratorio

orbe /'orβe/ *m,* sphere; orb; world

órbita /'orβita/ *f, Astron.* orbit; *Fig.* sphere; *Anat.* orbit, eye socket

ordalía /orða'lia/ *f,* (medieval hist.) ordeal

orden /'orðen/ *mf* order, mode of arrangement; succession, sequence; group; system; orderliness, neatness; coherence, plan; *Eccl.* order, brotherhood; (*Zool. Bot.*) group, class; *Archit.* order; *Math.* degree. *f,* precept, command; *Com.* order; *pl Eccl.* ordination. (*Mil. Naut.*) **o. de batalla,** battle array. **o. de caballería,** order of knighthood. **o. del día,** order of the day. *Eccl.* **dar órdenes,** to ordain. **en o.,** in order; with regard (to). **por su o.,** in its turn; successively

ordenación /orðena'sion; orðena'θion/ *f,* order, orderly arrangement, disposition; ordinance, precept; *Eccl.* ordination

ordenador /orðena'ðor/ *m Spain* computer

ordenamiento /orðena'miento/ *m,* ordaining; ordinance; edict

ordenancista /orðenan'sista; orðenan'θista/ *mf Mil.* martinet; disciplinarian

ordenanza /orðe'nansa; orðe'nanθa/ *f,* order, method; command, instruction; ordinance, regulation (gen. *pl*). *m, Mil.* orderly

ordenar /orðe'nar/ *vt* to put in order, arrange; command, give instructions to; decree; direct, regulate; *Eccl.* ordain; *vr* (*with de*) *Eccl.* be ordained as

ordeñadero /orðeɲa'ðero/ *m,* milk pail

ordeñar /orðe'ɲar/ *vt* to milk

ordinal /orði'nal/ *a* ordinal. *m,* ordinal number

ordinariez /orðina'ries; orðina'rieθ/ *f,* rudeness, uncouthness; vulgarity

ordinario /orði'nario/ *a* ordinary, usual; vulgar, coarse, uncultured; rude; commonplace, average, mediocre. *m, Eccl.* ordinary; carrier; courier. **de o.,** usually, ordinarily

orear /ore'ar/ *vt* to ventilate; *vr* dry; air; take the air

orégano /o'regano/ *m,* wild marjoram

oreja /o'reha/ *f,* external ear; lug; tab, flap; tongue (of a shoe). *Inf.* **con las orejas caídas,** down in the mouth, depressed

orejera /ore'hera/ *f,* earflap; mold board (of a plow)

orejudo /ore'huðo/ *a* large- or long-eared

oreo /o'reo/ *m,* zephyr; ventilation; airing

orfanato /orfa'nato/ *m,* orphanage, orphan asylum

orfandad /orfan'dað/ *f,* orphanhood; defenselessness, lack of protection

orfebre /or'feβre/ *mf* gold- or silversmith

orfebrería /orfeβre'ria/ *f,* gold- or silverwork

orfeón /orfe'on/ *m,* choral society

organdí /organ'di/ *m,* organdy

orgánico /or'ganiko/ *a* organic; harmonious; *Fig.* organized

organillero /organi'yero; organi'ʎero/ **(-ra)** *n* organ grinder

organillo /orga'niyo; orga'niʎo/ *m,* barrel organ

organismo /orga'nismo/ *m,* organism; organization; association

organista /orga'nista/ *mf* organist

organización /organisa'sion; organiθa'θion/ *f,* organization; order, arrangement

organizador /organisa'ðor; organiθa'ðor/ **(-ra)** *a* organizing. *n* organizer

organizar /organi'sar; organi'θar/ *vt* to organize; regulate; constitute

órgano /'organo/ *m, Mus.* organ; (*Anat. Bot.*) organ; means, agency. **o. de manubrio,** barrel organ

orgasmo /or'gasmo/ *m,* orgasm

orgía /or'hia/ *f,* orgy

orgullo /or'guyo; or'guʎo/ *m,* pride; arrogance

orgulloso /orgu'yoso; orgu'ʎoso/ *a* proud; haughty

orientación /orienta'sion; orienta'θion/ *f,* orientation; exposure, prospect; bearings

oriental /orien'tal/ *a* Oriental, Eastern. *mf* Oriental; *Argentina* Uruguayan

orientalismo /orienta'lismo/ *m,* Orientalism

orientalista /orienta'lista/ *mf* Orientalist

orientar /orien'tar/ *vt* to orientate; *vr* find one's bearings; familiarize oneself (with)

oriente /o'riente/ *m,* Orient, the East; luster (of pearls); youth, childhood; origin, source

orificio /ori'fisio; ori'fiθio/ *m,* orifice; hole

oriflama /ori'flama/ *f,* oriflamme; standard, flag

origen /o'rihen/ *m,* origin, source, root; stock, extraction; reason, genesis. **dar o. a,** to give rise to. **país de o.,** native land

original /orihi'nal/ *a* original; earliest, primitive; new, first-hand; novel, fresh; inventive, creative; eccentric; quaint. *m,* original manuscript; original; sitter (for portraits); eccentric

originalidad /orihinali'ðað/ *f,* originality

originar /orihi'nar/ *vt* to cause, originate; invent; *vr* spring from, originate (in)

originario /orihi'nario/ *a* original, primary; primitive; native (of)

orilla /o'riya; o'riʎa/ *f,* limit, edge; hem, border; selvage; shore, margin; bank (of a river, etc.); sidewalk; brink, edge. **a la o.,** on the brink; nearly

orillar /ori'yar; ori'ʎar/ *vt* to settle, arrange, conclude; *vi* reach the shore or bank; *Sew.* leave a hem; *Sew.* border; leave a selvage on cloth

orillo /o'riyo; o'riʎo/ *m,* selvage (of cloth)

orín /o'rin/ *m,* rust; *pl* urine

orinal /ori'nal/ *m,* chamber pot, urinal

orinar /ori'nar/ *vi* to urinate

oriundo /o'riundo/ *a* native (of); derived (from)

orla /'orla/ *f,* border, fringe; selvage (of cloth, garments); ornamental border (on diplomas, etc.)

orlar /or'lar/ *vt* to border; edge, trim

ornamentación /ornamenta'sion; ornamenta'θion/ *f,* ornamentation

ornamental /ornamen'tal/ *a* ornamental

ornamentar /ornamen'tar/ *vt* to ornament; embellish

ornamento /orna'mento/ *m,* ornament; decoration; gift, virtue, talent; *pl Eccl.* vestments

ornar /or'nar/ *vt* to ornament, adorn, embellish

ornato /or'nato/ *m,* decoration, ornament

ornitología /ornitolo'hia/ *f,* ornithology

ornitológico /ornito'lohiko/ *a* ornithological

ornitólogo /orni'tologo/ *m,* ornithologist

oro /'oro/ *m,* gold; gold coins or jewelry; *Fig.* riches; *pl* diamonds (cards). **o. batido,** gold leaf. **o. en polvo,** gold dust. *Fig.* **como un o.,** shining with cleanliness. **el as de oros,** the ace of diamonds

orondo /o'rondo/ *a* hollow; *Inf.* pompous; *Inf.* swollen, spongy

oropel /oro'pel/ *m,* brass foil; showy, cheap thing; trinket; tinsel

orquesta /or'kesta/ *f,* orchestra

orquestación /orkesta'sion; orkesta'θion/ *f,* orchestration

orquestal /orkes'tal/ *a* orchestral

orquestar /orkes'tar/ *vt* to orchestrate

orquídea /or'kiðea/ f, orchid
ortega /or'tega/ f, Ornith. grouse
ortiga /or'tiga/ f, Bot. nettle
orto /'orto/ m, rising (of sun, stars)
ortodoxia /orto'ðoksia/ f, orthodoxy
ortodoxo /orto'ðokso/ a orthodox
ortografía /ortogra'fia/ f, orthography
ortográfico /orto'grafiko/ a orthographical
ortopedia /orto'peðia/ f, orthopedics
ortopédico /orto'peðiko/ **(-ca)** a orthopedic. n orthopedist
ortopedista /ortope'ðista/ mf orthopedist
oruga /o'ruga/ f, caterpillar
orzuelo /or'suelo; or'θuelo/ m, Med. sty; trap (for wild animals)
os /os/ pers pron 2nd pl mf dat and acc of **vos** and **vosotros** you, to you
osa /'osa/ f, she-bear; Astron. **O. mayor,** Big Bear; **O. menor,** Little Bear
osadía /osa'ðia/ f, boldness, audacity
osado /o'saðo/ a daring, bold
osamenta /osa'menta/ f, skeleton; bones (of a skeleton)
osar /o'sar/ vi to dare; risk, venture
osario /o'sario/ m, charnel house, ossuary
oscilación /ossila'sion; osθila'θion/ f, oscillation
oscilante /ossi'lante; osθi'lante/ a oscillating
oscilar /ossi'lar; osθi'lar/ vi to oscillate, sway; hesitate, vacillate
ósculo /'oskulo/ m, kiss, osculation
oscurantismo /oskuran'tismo/ m, obscurantism
oscurantista /oskuran'tista/ a and mf obscurantist
oscurear /oskure'ar/ Mexico = **oscurecer**
oscurecer /oskure'ser; oskure'θer/ vt irr to darken; Fig. tarnish, dim, sully; confuse, bewilder; express obscurely; Art. shade; vi grow dark; vr cloud over (sky); Inf. disappear (things, gen. by theft). See **conocer**
oscuridad /oskuri'ðað/ f, darkness; gloom, blackness; humbleness, obscurity, abstruseness
oscuro /os'kuro/ a dark; humble, unknown; abstruse, involved; obscure; uncertain, dangerous. **a oscuras,** in the dark; ignorant
óseo /'oseo/ a osseous
osera /o'sera/ f, bear's den
osezno /o'sesno; o'seθno/ m, bear cub
osificación /osifika'sion; osifika'θion/ f, ossification
osificarse /osifi'karse/ vr to ossify
ósmosis /'osmosis/ f, osmosis
oso /'oso/ m, bear. **o. blanco,** polar bear
ostensible /osten'siβle/ a ostensible; obvious

ostensión /osten'sion/ f, show, display, manifestation
ostensivo /osten'siβo/ a ostensive
ostentación /ostenta'sion; ostenta'θion/ f, manifestation; ostentation
ostentar /osten'tar/ vt to exhibit, show; boast, show off
ostentoso /osten'toso/ a magnificent, showy, ostentatious
osteópata /oste'opata/ mf osteopath
osteopatía /osteopa'tia/ f, osteopathy
ostión /os'tion/, m, Mexico oyster
ostra /'ostra/ f, oyster. **vivero de ostras,** oyster bed
ostracismo /ostra'sismo; ostra'θismo/ m, ostracism
otear /ote'ar/ vt to observe; look on at
otero /o'tero/ m, hill, height, eminence
otología /otolo'hia/ f, otology
otólogo /o'tologo/ m, otologist
otomana /oto'mana/ f, ottoman, couch
otomano /oto'mano/ a Ottoman
otoñal /oto'ɲal/ a autumnal, autumn, fall
otoño /o'toɲo/ m, autumn, fall
otorgamiento /otorga'miento/ m, granting; consent, approval; license, award
otorgar /otor'gar/ vt to grant; concede, approve; Law. grant, stipulate, execute
otro /'otro/ **(-ra)** a other, another. n another one
otrosí /otro'si/ adv besides, moreover
ovación /oβa'sion; oβa'θion/ f, ovation, triumph; applause
ovacionar /oβasio'nar; oβaθio'nar/ vt to applaud
oval /o'βal/ a oval
óvalo /'oβalo/ m, oval
ovario /o'βario/ m, ovary
oveja /o'βeha/ f, ewe
overol /oβe'rol/ m Lat. Am. overalls
ovillar /oβi'yar; oβi'ʎar/ vi to wind thread into a ball; vr curl up; huddle
ovillo /o'βiyo; o'βiʎo/ m, ball, bobbin (of thread); tangled heap (of things)
ovíparo /o'βiparo/ a oviparous
OVNI /'oβni/ m, UFO
ovulación /oβula'sion; oβula'θion/ f, ovulation
óvulo /'oβulo/ m, ovule
oxidación /oksiða'sion; oksiða'θion/ f, oxidation
oxidar /oksi'ðar/ vt oxidize; vr become oxidized
óxido /'oksiðo/ m, oxide. **ó. de carbono,** carbon monoxide. **ó. de cinc,** zinc oxide
oxígeno /ok'siheno/ m, oxygen
oyente /o'iente/ mf hearer; pl audience
ozono /o'sono; o'θono/ m, ozone

P

pabellón /paβe'yon; paβe'ʎon/ m, pavilion; colors, flag; bell tent. **p. británico,** Union Jack. **p. de reposo,** rest home. **en p.,** stacked (of arms)
pábulo /'paβulo/ m, food; Fig. pabulum
pacedero /pase'ðero; paθe'ðero/ a Agr. grazing, meadow
pacer /pa'ser; pa'θer/ vi irr Agr. to graze; vt nibble away; eat away. See **nacer**
paciencia /pa'siensia; pa'θienθia/ f, patience
paciente /pa'siente; pa'θiente/ a patient; long-suffering; complacent. mf Med. patient
pacienzudo /pasien'suðo; paθien'θuðo/ a extremely patient or long-suffering
pacificación /pasifika'sion; paθifika'θion/ f, pacification; serenity, peace of mind
pacificador /pasifika'ðor; paθifika'ðor/ **(-ra)** a peace making; pacifying. n peace maker
pacificar /pasifi'kar; paθifi'kar/ vt to pacify; vi make peace; vr grow quiet, become calm (sea, etc.)
pacífico /pa'sifiko; pa'θifiko/ a pacific, meek, mild; peace-loving, peaceful. **el Océano P.,** the Pacific Ocean

pacifismo /pasi'fismo; paθi'fismo/ m, pacifism
pacifista /pasi'fista; paθi'fista/ a and mf pacifist
pacotilla /pako'tiya; pako'tiʎa/ f, goods. Inf. **hacer su p.,** to make one's packet or fortune. **ser de p.,** to be poor stuff; be jerry-built (of houses)
pactar /pak'tar/ vt to stipulate, arrange; contract
pacto /'pakto/ m, agreement, contract; pact
padecer /paðe'ser; paðe'θer/ vt irr to suffer; feel keenly; experience, undergo; tolerate. **p. desnudez,** to go unclothed. **p. hambre,** to go hungry. See **conocer**
padecimiento /paðesi'miento; paðeθi'miento/ m, suffering
padrastro /pa'ðrastro/ m, stepfather; cruel father; Fig. impediment, obstacle; hangnail
padrazo /pa'ðraso; pa'ðraθo/ m, Inf. indulgent father
padre /'paðre/ m, father; stallion; head (of the family, etc.); Eccl. father; genesis, source; author, creator; pl parents; ancestors. **p. adoptivo,** foster father. **p. de familia,** paterfamilias. **P. Eterno,** Eternal Father. **p. nuestro,** Lord's Prayer. **P. Santo,** Holy Father, the Pope

padrear /paðre'ar/ *vi* to take after one's father; *Zool.* reproduce, breed

padrejón /paðre'hon/ *m, Argentina* stallion

padrino /pa'ðrino/ *m,* godfather; sponsor; second (in duels, etc.); patron; best man

padrón /pa'ðron/ *m,* census; pattern, model; memorial stone

paella /pa'eya; pa'eʎa/ *f, Cul.* savory rice dish of shellfish, chicken, and meat

paga /'paga/ *f,* payment; amends, restitution; pay; payment of fine; reciprocity (in love, etc.)

pagadero /paga'ðero/ *a* payable. *m,* date and place when payment is due

pagador /paga'ðor/ **(-ra)** *n* payer. *m,* teller; wages clerk; paymaster

pagaduría /pagaðu'ria/ *f,* pay office

paganismo /paga'nismo/ *m,* paganism; heathenism

pagano /pa'gano/ **(-na)** *a* and *n* pagan; heathen

pagar /pa'gar/ *vt* to pay; make restitution, expiate; return, requite (love, etc.); *vr (with de)* become fond of; be proud of. **p. adelantado,** to prepay. *Com.* **p. al contado,** to pay cash. **p. la casa,** to pay the rent (for one's residence)

pagaré /paga're/ *m, Com.* promissory note, I.O.U.

página /'pahina/ *f,* page (of a book); episode

paginación /pahina'sion; pahina'θion/ *f,* pagination

paginar /pahi'nar/ *vt* to paginate

pago /'pago/ *m,* payment; recompense, reward; region of vineyards, olive groves, etc.; *Argentina* area, region

paguro /pa'guro/ *m,* hermit crab

pailebote /paile'βote/ *m,* schooner

país /pa'is/ *m,* country, nation; region; *Art.* landscape. **del p.,** typical of the country of origin (gen. of food)

paisaje /pai'sahe/ *m,* countryside; landscape, scenery

paisajista, paisista /paisa'hista, pai'sista/ *mf* landscape painter

paisano /pai'sano/ **(-na)** *n* compatriot; peasant; civilian

Países Bajos, los /pa'ises 'bahos, los/ the Low Countries, the Netherlands

paja /'paha/ *f,* straw; chaff; trash; *Fig.* padding. **ver la p. en el ojo del vecino y no la viga en el nuestro,** to see the mote in our neighbor's eye and not the beam in our own

pajar /pa'har/ *m,* barn

pájara /'pahara/ *f,* hen (bird); kite (toy); *Inf.* jay; prostitute. **p. pinta,** game of forfeits

pajarear /pahare'ar/ *vt* to snare birds; loaf, idle about

pajarera /paha'rera/ *f,* aviary

pajarero /paha'rero/ *m,* bird catcher or seller. *a Inf.* frivolous, giddy; *Inf.* gaudy (colors); *Lat. Am.* skittish (horse)

pajarita /paha'rita/ *f,* bow tie

pájaro /'paharo/ *m,* bird. **p. bobo,** penguin. **p. carpintero,** woodpecker. *Fig. Inf.* **p. gordo,** big gun. **p. mosca,** hummingbird

pajarota /paha'rota/ *f, Inf.* canard, false report

paje /'pahe/ *m,* page; *Naut.* cabin boy

pajera /pa'hera/ *f,* hayloft

pajizo /pa'hiso; pa'hiθo/ *a* made of straw; covered or thatched with straw; strawcolored

pala /'pala/ *f,* paddle; blade (of an oar); shovel; spade; baker's peel (long-handled shovel); cutting edge of a spade, hoe, etc.; *Sports.* racket; vamp; upper (of a shoe); pelota or jai alai racket; tanner's knife; *Inf.* guile, cunning; cleverness, dexterity. **p. de hélice,** propeller blade. **p. para pescado,** fish server. *Inf.* **corta p.,** ignoramus; blockhead

palabra /pa'laβra/ *f,* word; power of speech; eloquence; offer, promise; *pl* magic formula, spell. **p. de clave,** code word. **p. de matrimonio,** promise of marriage. **p. de rey,** inviolable promise. **palabras cruzadas,** crossword puzzle. **bajo p. de,** under promise of. **cuatro palabras,** a few words; short conversation. **de p.,** verbally, by word of mouth. **dirigir la p. a,** to address, speak to. **faltar a su p.,** to break one's promise. **llevar la p.,** to be spokesperson. **medias palabras,** half-words; hint, insinuation. **su p. empeñada,** one's solemn word. **tener la p.,** to have the right to speak (in meetings, etc.) (e.g. *El señor Martínez tiene la p.,* Mr. Martinez has the floor)

palabrería /palaβre'ria/ *f,* verbosity, wordiness

palabrota /pala'βrota/ *f, Inf.* coarse language; long word

palaciego /pala'siego; pala'θiego/ **(-ga)** *a* pertaining to palaces; *Fig.* courtesan. *n* courtier

palacio /pa'lasio; pa'laθio/ *m,* palace; mansion

palada /pa'laða/ *f,* shovelful, spadeful; oar stroke

paladar /pala'ðar/ *m, Anat.* palate; taste; discernment, sensibility

paladear /palaðe'ar/ *vt* to taste with pleasure, savor; enjoy, relish

paladín /pala'ðin/ *m,* paladin

paladino /pala'ðino/ *a* public, clear, open

palafrén /pala'fren/ *m,* palfrey

palafrenero /palafre'nero/ *m,* groom; stablehand

palanca /pa'lanka/ *f, Mech.* lever; handle; bar; (high) diving board. **p. de arranque,** starting gear. **p. de cambio de velocidad,** gear-changing lever. **p. de mando,** control stick

palangana /palaŋ'gana/ *f,* washbasin

palanganear /palaŋgane'ar/ *vi, Lat. Am.* to show off

palanganero /palaŋga'nero/ *m,* washstand

palanqueta /palan'keta/ *f, dim* small lever; jimmy

palastro /pa'lastro/ *m,* sheet iron or steel

palatinado /palati'naðo/ *m,* Palatinate

palatino /pala'tino/ *a* palatine

palatizar /palati'sar; palati'θar/ *vt* to palatilize

palazón /pala'son; pala'θon/ *f,* woodwork

palco /'palko/ *m, Theat.* box; stand, raised platform, enclosure. **p. de platea,** orchestra

palenque /pa'lenke/ *m,* enclosure; stand; platform; palisade

paleografía /paleogra'fia/ *f,* paleography

paleógrafo /pale'ografo/ *m,* paleographer

paleolítico /paleo'litiko/ *a* paleolithic

paleología /paleolo'hia/ *f,* paleology

paleontología /paleontolo'hia/ *f,* paleontology

palestra /pa'lestra/ *f,* tilt yard

paleta /pa'leta/ *f, dim* little shovel; trowel; *Art.* palette; fireplace shovel; mason's trowel; *Anat.* shoulder blade; blade (of a propeller, ventilator, etc.); *Chem.* spatula

paliacate /palia'kate/ *m, Mexico* kerchief

paliación /palia'sion; palia'θion/ *f,* palliation; excuse

paliar /pa'liar/ *vt* to dissemble, excuse; palliate, mitigate

paliativo /palia'tiβo/ *a* palliative; extenuating

palidecer /paliðe'ser; paliðe'θer/ *vi irr* to turn pale. See **conocer**

palidez /pali'ðes; pali'ðeθ/ *f,* pallor, paleness

pálido /'paliðo/ *a* pale, pallid

paliducho /pali'ðutʃo/ *a* somewhat pale, palish; sallow

palillo /pa'liyo; pa'liʎo/ *m, dim* small stick; toothpick; bobbin (for lacemaking); drumstick; chopstick; *Fig.* chatter; *pl* castanets

palimpsesto /palimp'sesto/ *m,* palimpsest

palinodia /pali'noðia/ *f, lit* palinode. **cantar la p.,** to eat one's words, recant

palio /'palio/ *m,* Greek mantle; cape; *Eccl.* pallium; canopy, awning

palique /pa'like/ *m, Inf.* chat. **estar de p.,** to be having a chat

paliquear /palike'ar/ *vi* to chat

paliza /pa'lisa; pa'liθa/ *f,* caning, beating

palizada /pali'saða; pali'θaða/ *f,* paling, fence; palisade, stockade. **p. de tablas,** hoarding

palma /'palma/ *f,* palm tree; palm leaf; date palm; palm (of the hand); hand; triumph. **llevarse la p.,** to bear away the palm; take the cake

palmada /pal'maða/ *f,* slap; *pl* hand-clapping

palmado /pal'maðo/ *a* web (of feet); palmy

palmar /pal'mar/ *a* palmaceous; palmar; clear, obvious. *m,* palm grove

palmatoria /palma'toria/ *f,* ferule, ruler; candlestick

palmear /palme'ar/ *vi* to clap hands

palmera /pal'mera/ *f,* palm tree

palmeta /pal'meta/ *f*, ferrule, ruler
palmetazo /palme'taso; palme'taθo/ *m*, slap on the hand with a ruler; *Fig.* slap in the face
palmo /'palmo/ *m*, span; hand's breadth. **p. a p.**, inch by inch, piecemeal
palmotear /palmote'ar/ *vt* to applaud; clap
palo /'palo/ *m*, stick; rod; pole; timber, wood; wooden log; *Naut.* mast; blow with a stick; execution by hanging; suit (of playing cards); fruit stalk; *Herald.* pale. **p. de Campeche**, logwood. **p. de hule**, rubber tree. **p. de rosa**, tulipwood. *Naut.* **p. mayor**, mainmast. *Naut.* **a p. seco**, under bare poles. **de tal p.**, **tal astilla**, a chip off the old block; like father like son. **estar del mismo p.**, to be of the same mind, agree
paloma /pa'loma/ *f*, dove; pigeon; gentle person; *pl Naut.* white horses. **p. buchona**, pouter pigeon. **p. mensajera**, carrier pigeon. **p. torcaz**, wood pigeon
palomar /palo'mar/ *m*, dovecote; pigeon loft
palomero /palo'mero/ **(-ra)** *n* pigeon fancier; pigeon dealer
palomino /palo'mino/ *m*, young pigeon
palomo /pa'lomo/ *m*, male pigeon; wood pigeon
palotes /pa'lotes/ *m pl*, drumsticks; pothooks (in writing)
palpabilidad /palpaβili'ðað/ *f*, palpability
palpable /pal'paβle/ *a* palpable, tangible
palpación /palpa'sion; palpa'θion/ *f*, *Med.* palpation
palpar /pal'par/ *vt* to palpate, examine by touch; grope, walk by touch; *Fig.* see clearly
palpitación /palpita'sion; palpita'θion/ *f*, beating (of a heart); *Med.* palpitation; convulsive movement
palpitante /palpi'tante/ *a* palpitating; quivering; beating; (of a question) burning
palpitar /palpi'tar/ *vi* to beat (heart); throb, palpitate; shudder, move convulsively; *Fig.* manifest itself (passions, etc.)
palpo /'palpo/ *m*, palp, feeler
palta /'palta/ *f*, *Lat. Am.* avocado (pear)
palúdico /pa'luðiko/ *a* marshy, swampy; malarial
paludismo /palu'ðismo/ *m*, malaria; paludism
palurdo /pa'lurðo/ **(-da)** *a Inf.* gross, rude, boorish. *n* boor
palustre /pa'lustre/ *m*, mason's trowel. *a* marshy, swampy
pamela /pa'mela/ *f*, wide-brimmed straw sailor (woman's hat)
pamema /pa'mema/ *f*, *Inf.* unimportant trifle; *Inf.* caress
pampa /'pampa/ *f*, pampa, treeless plain
pamplina /pam'plina/ *f*, *Inf.* nonsense, rubbish
pan /pan/ *m*, bread; loaf; *Cul.* piecrust; *Fig.* food; wheat; gold leaf; *pl* cereals. **p. ázimo**, unleavened bread. **p. de oro**, gold leaf. **llamar al p. p. y al vino vino**, to call a spade a spade. **venderse como p. bendito**, to sell like hot cakes
pana /'pana/ *f*, velveteen, velour; *mf*, *Lat. Am. Inf.* pal
panacea /pana'sea; pana'θea/ *f*, panacea; cure-all
panadería /panaðe'ria/ *f*, bakery trade or shop; bakery
panadero /pana'ðero/ **(-ra)** *n* baker. *m pl*, Spanish dance
panadizo /pana'ðiso; pana'ðiθo/ *m*, *Med.* whitlow; *Inf.* ailing person, crock
panal /pa'nal/ *m*, honeycomb; wasp's nest
Panamá /pana'ma/ Panama
panamá /pana'ma/ *m*, *Lat. Am.* Panama hat
panameño /pana'meɲo/ **(-ña)** *a* and *n* Panamanian
panamericanismo /panamerika'nismo/ *m*, pan-Americanism
panarra /pa'narra/ *m*, *Inf.* simpleton
páncreas /'pankreas/ *m*, pancreas
pancreático /pankre'atiko/ *a* pancreatic
panda /'panda/ *f*, gallery of a cloister. *mf Zool.* panda
pandémico /pan'demiko/ *a* pandemic
pandemonio /pande'monio/ *m*, pandemonium
pandereta /pande'reta/ *f*, tambourine
pandero /pan'dero/ *m*, tambourine; *Inf.* windbag

pandilla /pan'diya; pan'diʎa/ *f*, league, group; gang (of burglars, etc.); party, crowd, band
pane /'pane/ *f*, breakdown
panecillo /pane'siyo; pane'θiʎo/ *m*, *dim* roll (of bread)
panegírico /pane'hiriko/ *a* and *m*, panegyric
panel /pa'nel/ *m*, panel
panetela /pane'tela/ *f*, panada
pánfilo /'panfilo/ **(-la)** *a* sluggish, phlegmatic, slow-moving. *n* sluggard
panfleto /pan'fleto/ *m*, pamphlet
paniaguado /pania'guaðo/ *m*, servant; favorite, protégé
pánico /'paniko/ *a* and *m*, panic
panoja /pa'noha/ *f*, *Bot.* panicle; *Bot.* ear, beard, awn
panoli /pa'noli/ *a Inf.* doltish, stupid
panorama /pano'rama/ *m*, panorama; view
panorámico /pano'ramiko/ *a* panoramic
pantalla /pan'taya; pan'taʎa/ *f*, lampshade; face screen; movie screen; shade, reflector
pantalón /panta'lon/ *m*, pant, trouser (gen. *pl*); knickers. **p. de corte**, striped trousers. **pantalones bombachos**, plus fours
pantano /pan'tano/ *m*, marsh, swamp; impediment; artificial pool
pantanoso /panta'noso/ *a* marshy, swampy; *Fig.* awkward, full of pitfalls
panteísmo /pante'ismo/ *m*, pantheism
panteón /pante'on/ *m*, pantheon; *Mexico* cemetery
pantera /pan'tera/ *f*, panther; *Venezuela* jaguar, ocelot
pantomima /panto'mima/ *f*, pantomime; mime
pantorrilla /panto'rriya; panto'rriʎa/ *f*, calf (of the leg)
pantuflo /pan'tuflo/ *m*, house slipper
panza /'pansa; 'panθa/ *f*, paunch, stomach; belly (of jugs, etc.). *Inf.* **un cielo de p. de burra**, a dark gray sky. **p. mojada** *Mexico* wetback
panzudo /pan'suðo; pan'θuðo/ *a* paunchy
pañal /pa'ɲal/ *m*, diaper; shirttail; *pl* long clothes, swaddling clothes; infancy
pañería /paɲe'ria/ *f*, drapery stores; drapery
pañero /pa'ɲero/ **(-ra)** *f* draper
paño /'paɲo/ *m*, woolen material; cloth, fabric; drapery, hanging; tapestry; linen, bandage; tarnish or other mark; *Naut.* canvas; *Sew.* breadth, width (of cloth); panel (in a dress); floor cloth, duster; livid mark on the face; *pl* garments. **p. de lágrimas**, consoler, sympathizer. **p. mortuorio**, pall (on a coffin). **paños menores**, underwear. **p. verde**, gambling table. al **p.**, *Theat.* from the wings, from without. *Inf.* **poner el p. al púlpito**, to hold forth, spread oneself
pañoleta /paɲo'leta/ *f*, kerchief, triangular scarf; fichu
pañuelo /pa'ɲuelo/ *m*, kerchief; handkerchief
papa /'papa/ *m*, pope; *Inf.* papa, daddy. *f*, *Inf.* potato; stupid rumor; nonsense; *pl* pap; *Cul.* sop; food
papá /pa'pa/ *m*, *Inf.* papa, daddy
papada /pa'paða/ *f*, double chin; dewlap
papado /pa'paðo/ *m*, papacy
papagayo /papa'gaio/ *m*, parrot
papal /pa'pal/ *m*, *Lat. Am.* potato field
papamoscas /papa'moskas/ *m*, *Ornith.* flycatcher; *Inf.* simpleton
papanatas /papa'natas/ *m*, *Inf.* simpleton
papar /pa'par/ *vt* to sip, take soft food; *Inf.* eat; neglect, be careless about
paparrucha /papa'rrutʃa/ *f*, *Inf.* stupid rumor; nonsense
papel /pa'pel/ *m*, paper; document; manuscript; *Theat.* role, part; pamphlet; sheet of paper; paper, monograph, essay; guise, role; *Theat.* character. **p. carbón**, carbon paper. **p. celofán**, cellophane. **p. cuadriculado**, graph paper, cartridge paper. **p. de calcar**, carbon paper; tracing paper. **p. de escribir**, writing paper. **p. de estaño**, tinfoil. **p. de estraza**, brown paper. **p. de fumar**, cigarette paper. **p. de lija**, emery- or sandpaper. **p. de paja de arroz**, rice paper. **p. de seda**, tissue paper. **p. de tornasol**, litmus paper. **p. del estado**, government bonds. **p.**

higiénico, toilet paper. **p. moneda,** paper money. **p. pintado,** wallpaper. **p. secante,** blotting paper. **p. sellado,** official stamped paper. **hacer buen (mal) p.,** to do well (badly). **hacer el p. (de),** *Theat.* to act the part (of). feign, pretend; **desempeñar el p.,** to play a part or role

papelear /papele'ar/ *vi* to turn over papers, search among them; *Inf.* cut a dash

papeleo /pape'leo/ *m,* bureaucracy, red tape

papelera /pape'lera/ *f,* mass of papers; desk (for keeping papers)

papelería /papele'ria/ *f,* heap of papers; stationer's shop; stationery

papelero /pape'lero/ **(-ra)** *a* paper, stationery. *n* paper maker; stationer

papeleta /pape'leta/ *f,* slip or scrap of paper

papelista /pape'lista/ *mf* paper maker; stationer; paperhanger

papelucho /pape'lutʃo/ *m,* old or dirty piece of paper; trash, worthless writing; *Inf.* rag (newspaper)

papera /pa'pera/ *f,* mumps

papilla /pa'piya; pa'piʎa/ *f,* pap; guile, wiliness

papillote /papi'yote; papi'ʎote/ *m,* curl-paper

papiro /pa'piro/ *m,* papyrus

papo /'papo/ *m,* dewlap; gizzard (of a bird); goiter. **p. de cardo,** thistledown

paquebote /pake'βote/ *m, Naut.* packet; mail boat; liner

paquete /pa'kete/ *m,* packet; parcel, package

paquidermo /paki'ðermo/ *m,* pachyderm

par /par/ *a* equal; alike; corresponding. *m,* pair, couple; team (of oxen, mules); peer (title); rafter (of a roof); *Mech.* torque, couple; *Elec.* cell. *f,* par. **a la p.,** jointly; simultaneously; *Com.* at par. **a pares,** two by two. **de p. en p.,** wide-open (doors, etc.). **sin p.,** peerless, excellent

para /'para/ *prep* in order to; for; to; for the sake of (e.g. *Lo hice p. ella,* I did it for her sake); enough to (gen. with *bastante,* etc.); in the direction of, toward; about, on the point of (e.g. *Está p. salir,* He is about to go out). Expresses: 1. *Purpose* (e.g. *La educan p. bailarina,* They are bringing her up to be a dancer. *Lo dije p. ver lo que harías,* I said it to (in order to) see what you would do) 2. *Destination* (e.g. *Salió p. Londres,* He left for London) 3. *Use* (e.g. *seda p. medias,* silk for stockings. *un vaso p. flores,* a vase for flowers)

parábola /pa'raβola/ *f,* parable; *Geom.* parabola

parabrisas /para'βrisas/ *m,* windshield

paracaídas /paraka'iðas/ *m,* parachute

paracaidista /parakai'ðista/ *mf* parachutist

parachoques /para'tʃokes/ *m, Auto.* bumper; buffer (railroad)

parada /pa'raða/ *f,* stopping, halting; stop; stoppage, suspension; halt; *Mil.* review; interval, pause; cattle stall; dam; gambling stakes; parry (in fencing); relay (of horses). **p. de coches,** taxi rank. **p. de tranvía,** streetcar stop. **p. discrecional,** request stop (buses, etc.)

paradear /paraðe'ar/ **(con...)** *vi, Argentina* to brag (about...)

paradero /para'ðero/ *m,* railroad station; stopping place; end, conclusion; whereabouts

paradisíaco /paraði'siako/ *a* paradisaical

parado /pa'raðo/ *a* still; indolent, lazy; unoccupied, leisured; silent, reticent; timid; unemployed

paradoja /para'ðoha/ *f,* paradox

paradójico /para'ðohiko/ *a* paradoxical

parador /para'ðor/ *m,* inn, tavern, hostelry

parafina /para'fina/ *f,* paraffin

parafrasear /parafrase'ar/ *vt* to paraphrase

paráfrasis /pa'rafrasis/ *f,* paraphrase

paraguas /pa'raguas/ *m,* umbrella

paraguayo /para'guayo/ **(-ya)** *a* and *n* Paraguayan

paragüería /parague'ria/ *f,* umbrella shop

paragüero /para'guero/ **(-ra)** *n* umbrella maker; umbrella seller. *m,* umbrella stand

paraíso /para'iso/ *m,* paradise; garden of Eden; heaven; (*Inf. Theat.*) gallery, gods

paraje /pa'rahe/ *m,* place, locality, spot; state, condition

paralela /para'lela/ *f, Mil.* parallel; *pl* parallel bars (for gymnastic exercises)

paralelismo /parale'lismo/ *m,* parallelism

paralelo /para'lelo/ *a* parallel; analogous; similar. *m,* parallel, similarity; *Geog.* parallel

parálisis /pa'ralisis/ *f,* paralysis

paralítico /para'litiko/ **(-ca)** *a* and *n* paralytic

paralización /paralisa'sion; paraliθa'θion/ *f,* paralysis; cessation; *Com.* dullness, quietness

paralizar /parali'sar; parali'θar/ *vt* to paralyze; stop

paramento /para'mento/ *m,* ornament; trappings (of a horse); face (of a wall); facing (of a building). **paramentos sacerdotales,** liturgical vestments or ornaments

páramo /'paramo/ *m,* paramo, treeless plain; desert, wilderness

parangón /paraŋ'gon/ *m,* comparison; similarity

parangonar /paraŋgo'nar/ *vt* to compare

paraninfo /para'ninfo/ *m, Archit.* paranymph, university hall; best man (weddings); messenger of good

paranoico /para'noiko/ *m,* paranoiac

parapetarse /parape'tarse/ *vr* to shelter behind a parapet; take refuge behind

parapeto /para'peto/ *m,* parapet

parapoco /para'poko/ *mf Inf.* ninny, numskull

parar /pa'rar/ *vi* to stop, halt; end, finish; lodge; come into the hands of; *vt* stop; detain; prepare; bet, stake; point (hunting dogs); parry (fencing); *vr* halt; be interrupted; *Lat. Am.* to get up, stand up. **p. mientes en,** to notice; consider. **sin p.,** immediately, at once; without stopping

pararrayos /para'rraios/ *m,* lightning conductor

parasitario, parasítico /parasi'tario, para'sitiko/ *a* parasitic

parásito /pa'rasito/ *m,* parasite; *Fig.* sponger; *pl Radio.* interference. *a* parasitic

parasitología /parasitolo'hia/ *f,* parasitology

parasol /para'sol/ *m,* sunshade; *Bot.* umbel

paratifoidea /paratifoi'ðea/ *f,* paratyphoid

parca /'parka/ *f,* Fate; *Poet.* death. **las Parcas,** the Three Fates

parcela /par'sela; par'θela/ *f,* plot, parcel (of land); atom, particle

parchar /par'tʃar/ *vt, Lat. Am.* to mend, patch, patch up

parche /'partʃe/ *m, Med.* plaster; *Auto.* patch; drum; drumhead, parchment of drum; patch, mend

parcial /par'sial; par'θial/ *a* partial, incomplete; biased, prejudiced; factional, party; participatory

parcialidad /parsiali'ðað; parθiali'ðað/ *f,* partiality, bias, prejudice; party, faction, group; intimacy, friendship

parco /'parko/ *a* scarce, scanty; temperate, moderate; frugal

parcómetro /par'kometro/ *m Lat. Am.* (except *Argentina and Mexico*) parking meter

pardo /'parðo/ *a* brown; gray, drab, dun-colored; cloudy, dark; husky (voices). *m,* leopard

pardusco /par'ðusko/ *a* grayish; fawn-colored

parear /pare'ar/ *vt* to pair, match; put in pairs; compare

parecer /pare'ser; pare'θer/ *vi irr* to appear; look, seem; turn up (be found). *impers* believe, think (e.g. *me parece,* it seems to me, I think, my opinion is); *vr* look alike, resemble one another. See **conocer**

parecer /pare'ser; pare'θer/ *m,* opinion, belief; appearance, looks

parecido /pare'siðo; pare'θiðo/ *a* (*with bien or mal*) good- or bad-looking. *m,* resemblance

pared /pa'reð/ *f,* wall; partition wall; side, face. **p. maestra,** main wall. **p. medianera,** party wall. **Las paredes oyen,** The walls have ears. *Inf.* **pegado a la p.,** confused, taken aback

pareja /pa'reha/ *f,* pair; dance partner; couple. **p. desparejada,** mismatched pair. **parejas mixtas,** mixed doubles (in tennis). **correr parejas** or **correr a las parejas,** to be equal; go together; happen simultaneously; be on a par

parejo /pa'reho/ *a* equal; similar; smooth, flat; even, regular

parentela /paren'tela/ *f*, relatives, kindred; parentage

parentesco /paren'tesko/ *m*, kinship; relationship; affinity; *Inf.* connection, link

paréntesis /pa'rentesis/ *m*, parenthesis; digression. **entre p.**, incidentally

paresa /pa'resa/ *f*, peeress

paria /'paria/ *mf* pariah; outcast

parida /pa'riða/ *a f*, newly delivered of a child

paridad /pari'ðað/ *f*, parity; analogy, similarity

pariente /pa'riente/ **(-ta)** *n* relative, relation; *Inf.* husband (wife)

parihuela /pari'uela/ *f*, wheelbarrow; stretcher

parir /pa'rir/ *vt* to give birth to; *Fig.* bring forth; reveal, publish; *vi* lay eggs

París /pa'ris/ Paris

parisiense /pari'siense/ *a* and *mf* Parisian

parla /'parla/ *f*, speech; loquaciousness, eloquence; verbiage

parlamentar /parlamen'tar/ *vi* to converse; discuss (contracts, etc.); *Mil.* parley

parlamentario /parlamen'tario/ *a* parliamentarian. *m*, member of parliament

parlamentarismo /parlamenta'rismo/ *m*, parliamentarianism

parlamento /parla'mento/ *m*, legislative assembly; parliament; discourse, speech; *Theat.* long speech; *Mil.* parley

parlanchín /parlan'tʃin/ *a Inf.* talkative, chattering, loquacious

parlar /par'lar/ *vt* and *vi* to speak freely or easily; chatter; reveal, speak indiscreetly; babble (of streams, etc.)

parlero /par'lero/ *a* talkative; gossiping, indiscreet; talking (birds); *Fig.* expressive (eyes, etc.); prattling, babbling (brook, etc.)

parlotear /parlote'ar/ *vi Inf.* to chatter, gossip

parloteo /parlo'teo/ *m*, chattering, gossip

parnaso /par'naso/ *m*, Parnassus; anthology of verse

paro /'paro/ *m*, *Inf.* work stoppage; lockout; *Ornith.* tit. **p. forzoso**, unemployment

parodia /pa'roðia/ *f*, parody

parodiar /paro'ðiar/ *vt* to parody

parodista /paro'ðista/ *mf* parodist

parótida /pa'rotiða/ *f*, parotid gland; parotitis, mumps

parotiditis /paroti'ðitis/ *f*, parotitis, mumps

paroxismo /parok'sismo/ *m*, *Med.* paroxysm; frenzy, ecstasy, fit

parpadear /parpaðe'ar/ *vi* to blink

parpadeo /parpa'ðeo/ *m*, blinking

párpado /'parpaðo/ *m*, eyelid

parque /'parke/ *m*, park; depot, park; paddock, pen. **p. de atracciones**, pleasure ground. **p. de** (*or* **para**) **automóviles**, car park, parking lot

parquear /parke'ar/ *vt*, *vi*, *Lat. Am.* to park

parquedad /parke'ðað/ *f*, scarcity; moderation, temperance; parsimony, frugality

parquímetro /par'kimetro/ *m Spain, Venezuela* parking meter

parra /'parra/ *f*, vine. **hoja de p.**, *Fig.* fig leaf

párrafo /'parrafo/ *m*, paragraph; *Gram.* paragraph sign. **p. aparte**, new paragraph. **echar un p.**, to chat, gossip

parranda /pa'rranda/ *f*, *Inf.* binge; strolling band of musicians. **ir de p.**, to go on a binge

parricida /parri'siða; parri'θiða/ *mf* parricide (person)

parricidio /parri'siðio; parri'θiðio/ *m*, parricide (act)

parrilla /pa'rriya; pa'rriʎa/ *f*, *Cul.* griller, broiler; grill; gridiron; *Engin.* grate. *Cul.* **a la p.**, grilled

párroco /'parroko/ *m*, parish priest; parson

parroquia /pa'rrokia/ *f*, parish church; parish; clergy of a parish; clientele, customers

parroquial /parro'kial/ *a* parochial

parroquiano /parro'kiano/ **(-na)** *a* parochial. *n* parishioner; client, customer

parsimonia /parsi'monia/ *f*, frugality, thrift; prudence, moderation

parsimonioso /parsimo'nioso/ *a* parsimonious

parte /'parte/ *f*, part; share; place; portion; side, faction; *Law.* party; *Theat.* part, role. *m*, communication, message; telegraph or telephone message; (*Mil. Nav.*) communiqué. *f pl*, parts, talents. **p. actora**, *Law.* prosecution. **p. de la oración**, part of speech. **partes litigantes**, *Law.* contending parties. **dar p.**, to notify; (*Mil. Naut.*) report; give a share (in a transaction). **de algún tiempo a esta p.**, for some time past. **de p. de**, in the name of, from. **en p.**, partly. **por todas partes**, on all sides, everywhere. **ser p. a** *or* **ser p. para que**, to contribute to. **tener de su p.** (a), to count on the favor of. **la quinta p.**, one-fifth, etc.

partear /parte'ar/ *vt* to assist in childbirth

partera /par'tera/ *f*, midwife

partero /par'tero/ *m*, accoucheur

partición /parti'sion; parti'θion/ *f*, partition, distribution; (*Aer. Naut.*) accommodation

participación /partisipa'sion; partiθipa'θion/ *f*, participation; notice, warning; announcement (of an engagement, etc.); *Com.* share

participante /partisi'pante; partiθi'pante/ *a* and *mf* participant

participar /partisi'par; partiθi'par/ *vi* to participate, take part (in), share; *vt* inform; announce (an engagement, etc.)

partícipe /par'tisipe; par'tiθipe/ *a* sharing. *mf* participant

participio /parti'sipio; parti'θipio/ *m*, participle

partícula /par'tikula/ *f*, particle, grain; *Gram.* particle

particular /partiku'lar/ *a* private; peculiar; special, particular; unusual; individual. *mf* private individual. *m*, matter, subject. **en p.**, especially; privately

particularidad /partikulari'ðað/ *f*, individuality; specialty; rareness, unusualness; detail, circumstance; intimacy, friendship

particularizar /partikulari'sar; partikulari'θar/ *vt* to detail, particularize; single out, choose; *vr* (*with en*) be characterized by

partida /par'tiða/ *f*, departure; entry, record (of birth, etc.); certificate (of marriage, etc.); *Com.* item; *Com.* lot, allowance; *Mil.* guerrilla; armed band; expedition, excursion; game (of cards, etc.); rubber (at bridge, etc.); *Inf.* conduct, behavior; place, locality; death. *Com.* **p. doble**, double entry. **punto de p.**, point of departure. **Las siete Partidas**, code of Spanish laws compiled by Alfonso X (1252–84)

partidario /parti'ðario/ **(-ia)** *a* partisan. *n* adherent, disciple. *m*, partisan, guerrilla

partidarismo /partiða'rismo/ *m*, partisanship

partido /par'tiðo/ *m*, party, group, faction; profit; *Sports.* match; team; agreement, pact. **p. conservador**, *Polit.* conservative party. **p. obrero** *or* **p. laborista**, *Polit.* labor party. **buen p.**, *Fig.* good match, catch. **sacar p. de**, to take advantage of, make the most of. **tomar p.**, to enlist; join; become a supporter (of)

partidor /parti'ðor/ *m*, divider, apportioner; cleaver, chopper; hewer

partir /par'tir/ *vt* to divide; split; crack, break; separate; *Math.* divide; *vi* go, depart; start (from). **p. como el rayo**, be off like a flash. *vr* disagree, become divided; leave, depart

partitura /parti'tura/ *f*, *Mus.* score

parto /'parto/ *m*, parturition, birth; newborn child; *Fig.* creation, offspring; important event

parturienta /partu'rienta/ *a f*, parturient

parva /'parβa/ *f*, light breakfast; threshed or unthreshed grain; heap, mass

parvedad /parβe'ðað/ *f*, smallness; scarcity; light breakfast (taken on fast days)

parvo /'parβo/ *a* little, small

párvulo /'parβulo/ **(-la)** *n* child. *a* small; innocent, simple; lowly, humble

pasa /'pasa/ *f*, raisin; *Naut.* channel; passage, flight (of birds). **p. de Corinto**, currant

pasacalle /pasa'kaye; pasa'kaʎe/ *m*, *Mus.* lively march

pasada /pa'saða/ *f*, passing, passage; money sufficient to live on; passage, corridor. **dar p.**, to let pass, put up with. *Inf.* **mala p.**, bad turn, dirty trick

pasadera /pasa'ðera/ *f*, steppingstone

pasadero /pasa'ðero/ a passable, traversable; fair (health); tolerable, passable. m, steppingstone

pasadizo /pasa'ðiso; pasa'ðiθo/ m, narrow corridor or passage; alley, narrow street; Naut. alleyway

pasado /pa'saðo/ m, past; pl ancestors. **Lo p., p.,** What's past is past. **p. de moda,** out of fashion, unfashionable

pasador /pasa'ðor/ m, bolt, fastener; Mech. pin, coupler; pin (of brooches, etc.); colander; Naut. marlin spike; shirt stud

pasajaretas /pasaha'retas/ m, bodkin

pasaje /pa'sahe/ m, passing; passage; fare; passage money; Naut. complement of passengers; channel, strait; (Mus. Lit.) passage; Mus. modulation, transition (of voice); voyage; passage; covered way; road; Lat. Am. dead-end street

pasajero /pasa'hero/ (-ra) a crowded public (thoroughfare); transitory, fugitive; passing; temporary. n passenger

pasamanería /pasamane'ria/ f, passementerie work, industry or shop

pasamano /pasa'mano/ m, passementerie; banister, handrail; Naut. gangway

pasante /pa'sante/ a Herald. passant. m, student teacher; articled clerk; apprentice; student. **p. de pluma,** law clerk

pasaporte /pasa'porte/ m, passport; license, permission. **dar el p. (a),** Inf. to give the sack (to)

pasar /pa'sar/ vt to pass; carry, transport; cross over; send; go beyond, overstep; run through, pierce; upset; overtake; transfer; suffer, undergo; sieve; study; dry (grapes, etc.); smuggle; surpass; omit; swallow (food); approve; dissemble; transform; spend (time); vi pass; be transferred; be infectious; have enough to live on; cease; last; die; pass away; pass (at cards); be transformed; be current (money); be salable (goods); (with prep a + infin) begin to; (with por) pass as; have a reputation as; visit; (with sin) do without. impers happen, occur. vr end; go over to another party; forget; go stale or bad; Fig. go too far, overstep the mark; permeate. **p. contrato,** to draw up a contract; sign a contract. **p. la voz,** to pass the word along. **p. por alto (de),** to omit, overlook. **p. de largo,** to go by without stopping. **pasarse de listo,** to be too clever. **¡No pases cuidado!** Don't worry!

pasarela /pasa'rela/ f, gangplank

pasatiempo /pasa'tiempo/ m, pastime, hobby, amusement

pasavante /pasa'βante/ m, Naut. safe conduct; navicert

pascua /'paskua/ f, Passover; Easter; Christmas; Twelfth Night; Pentecost; pl twelve days of Christmas. **P. florida,** Easter Sunday. **dar las pascuas,** to wish a merry Christmas. **¡Felices pascuas!** Merry Christmas!

pascual /pas'kual/ a paschal

pase /'pase/ m, pass (with the hands and in football, etc.); safe conduct; free pass; thrust (in fencing)

paseante /pase'ante/ mf stroller, promenader, passerby

pasear /pase'ar/ vt to take a walk; parade up and down, display; vi take a walk; go for a drive; go for a ride (on horseback, etc.); stroll up and down; vr touch upon lightly, pass over; loaf, be idle; drift; float

paseo /pa'seo/ m, walk, stroll; drive; outing, expedition; promenade; boulevard. **p. a caballo,** ride on horseback

pasiega /pa'siega/ f, wet nurse

pasillo /pa'siyo; pa'siʎo/ m, gallery; corridor; lobby; railway corridor; Sew. basting stitch

pasión /pa'sion/ f, suffering; passivity; passion; desire; Eccl. passion. **con p.,** passionately

pasionaria /pasio'naria/ f, passionflower

pasividad /pasiβi'ðað/ f, passivity

pasivo /pa'siβo/ a passive; inactive; Com. sleeping (partner); Gram. passive. m, Com. liabilities

pasmar /pas'mar/ vt to freeze to death (plants); dumbfound, amaze, stun; chill; vr be stunned or amazed

pasmo /'pasmo/ m, amazement, astonishment; wonder, marvel; Med. tetanus, lockjaw

pasmoso /pas'moso/ a astounding, amazing; wonderful

paso /'paso/ a dried (of fruit)

paso /'paso/ m, step; pace; passage, passing; way; footstep; progress, advancement; passage (in a book); Sew. tacking stitch; occurrence, event; Theat. short play; gait, walk; strait, channel; migratory flight (birds); Mech. pitch; event or scene from the Passion; armed combat; death; Lat. Am. ford. pl measures, steps. adv softly, in a low voice; gently. **p. a nivel,** level crossing. **p. a p.,** step by step. **p. doble,** quick march; Spanish dance. **p. volante,** (gymnastics) giant stride. **a cada p.,** at every step; often. **al p.,** without stopping; on the way, in passing. **ceder el p.,** to allow to pass. **de p.,** in passing; incidentally. **llevar el p.,** to keep in step. **marcar el p.,** to mark time. **salir al p. (a),** to waylay, confront; oppose. **seguir los pasos (a),** to follow; spy upon

paspa /'paspa/ f, Peru chapped skin

paspadura /paspa'ðura/ f, Argentina = **paspa**

pasparse /pas'parse/ vr, Lat. Am. to chap, crack

pasquín /pas'kin/ m, **pasquinada** f, pasquinade, lampoon

pasta /'pasta/ f, Cul. dough; paste; pastry; piecrust; batter; Cul. noodle paste; paper pulp; board (bookbinding). **ser de buena p.,** to be good-natured

pastar /pas'tar/ vt to take to pasture; vi graze, pasture

pastel /pas'tel/ m, cake; Art. pastel; pie; Inf. plot, secret understanding; cheating (at cards); Print. pie; Inf. fat, stocky person

pastelear /pastele'ar/ vi Inf. to indulge in shady business (especially in politics)

pastelería /pastele'ria/ f, cake bakery; cake shop; confectioner's art; confectionery

pastelero /paste'lero/ (-ra) n confectioner, pastry cook; Fig. Inf. spineless person, jellyfish

pastelillo /paste'liyo; paste'liʎo/ m, Cul. turnover

pastelón /paste'lon/ m, meat or game pie

pasteurización /pasteurisa'sion; pasteuriθa'θion/ f, pasteurization

pasteurizar /pasteuri'sar; pasteuri'θar/ vt to pasteurize

pastilla /pas'tiya; pas'tiʎa/ f, tablet; cake; lozenge; pastille, drop; tread (of a tire)

pasto /'pasto/ m, grazing land, pasture; fodder; Fig. fuel, food; spiritual food. **a p.,** in plenty, abundantly. **de p.,** of daily use

pastor /pas'tor/ (-ra) n shepherd. m, Eccl. pastor

pastoral /pasto'ral/ a rustic, country; Eccl. pastoral, f, pastoral poem; Eccl. pastoral letter

pastorear /pastore'ar/ vt to graze, put to grass; Eccl. have charge of souls

pastorela /pasto'rela/ f, pastoral

pastoreo /pasto'reo/ m, pasturage, grazing

pastoril /pasto'ril/ a shepherd, pastoral

pastoso /pas'toso/ a doughy; mealy; pasty; mellow

pata /'pata/ f, paw and leg (animals); foot (of table, etc.); duck; Inf. leg. **p. de gallo,** blunder; crow's-foot, wrinkle. **meter la p.,** to interfere, put one's foot in one's mouth. Inf. **tener mala p.,** to be unlucky

patada /pa'taða/ f, kick, stamp; Inf. step, pace

patagón /pata'gon/ (-ona) a and n Patagonian

patalear /patale'ar/ vi to stamp (with the feet)

pataleo /pata'leo/ m, kicking; stamping

pataleta /pata'leta/ f, Inf. convulsion; feigned hysterics

patán /pa'tan/ m, Inf. yokel; boor, churl

patanería /patane'ria/ f, Inf. boorishness, churlishness

patarata /pata'rata/ f, trash, useless thing; extravagant courtesy

patata /pa'tata/ f, potato

patatal, patatar /pata'tal, pata'tar/ m, potato patch

patatús /pata'tus/ m, Inf. petty worry; mishap; Med. stroke, fit

patear /pate'ar/ vt Inf. to stamp on; Fig. walk on, treat badly; *vi Inf.* stamp the feet; be furiously angry; (*golf*) putt

patena /pa'tena/ *f*, engraved medal worn by country women; *Eccl.* paten

patentar /paten'tar/ *vt* to issue a patent; take out a patent, patent

patente /pa'tente/ *a* obvious, patent; *f*, patent; warrant, commission; letters patent. **p. de invención,** patent. **p. de sanidad,** clean bill of health

patentizar /patenti'sar; patenti'θar/ *vt* to make evident

paternidad /paterni'ðað/ *f*, paternity

paterno /pa'terno/ *a* paternal

patético /pa'tetiko/ *a* pitiable; pathetic, moving

patiabierto /patia'βierto/ *a Inf.* knock-kneed

patibulario /patiβu'lario/ *a* heartrending, harrowing

patíbulo /pa'tiβulo/ *m*, scaffold

paticojo /pati'koho/ *a Inf.* lame; wobbly; unsteady

patilla /pa'tiya; pa'tiʎa/ *f*, side whisker (gen. *pl*); *pl* old Nick, the Devil

patín /pa'tin/ *m*, skate; runner (of a sled); (*Aer.* and of vehicles) skid; *Mech.* shoe. **p. del diablo,** scooter. **p. de ruedas,** roller skate

patinador /patina'ðor/ **(-ra)** *n* skater

patinaje /pati'nahe/ *m*, skating; skidding (of planes and vehicles)

patinar /pati'nar/ *vi* to skate; slip, lose one's footing; skid (vehicles and planes)

patinazo /pati'naso; pati'naθo/ *m*, skid (of a vehicle)

patinete /pati'nete/ *m*, child's scooter

patio /'patio/ *m*, courtyard; *Theat.* pit; *Mexico* shunting yard

patitieso /pati'tieso/ *a Inf.* paralyzed in the hands or feet; open-mouthed, amazed; stiff, unbending, proud

patituerto /pati'tuerto/ *a* crooked-legged; pigeon-toed; *Inf.* lopsided

patizambo /pati'sambo; pati'θambo/ *a* knock-kneed

pato /'pato/ *m*, duck; *Inf.* **pagar el p.,** to be a scapegoat

patógeno /pa'toheno/ *a* pathogenic

patojo /pa'toho/ *a* waddling

patología /patolo'hia/ *f*, pathology

patológico /pato'lohiko/ *a* pathological

patólogo /pa'tologo/ *m*, pathologist

patoso /pa'toso/ *a Fig.* heavy, pedestrian, tedious

patraña /pa'traɲa/ *f*, nonsense, rubbish, fairy tale

patria /'patria/ *f*, motherland, native country; native place. **p. chica,** native region

patriarca /pa'triarka/ *m*, patriarch

patriarcado /patriar'kaðo/ *m*, patriarchy

patriarcal /patriar'kal/ *a* patriarchal

patricio /pa'trisio; pa'triθio/ **(-ia)** *a* and *n* patrician

patrimonio /patri'monio/ *m*, patrimony

patriota /pa'triota/ *mf* patriot

patriótico /pa'triotiko/ *a* patriotic

patriotismo /patrio'tismo/ *m*, patriotism

patrocinar /patrosi'nar; patroθi'nar/ *vt* to protect, defend; favor, sponsor; patronize

patrocinio /patro'sinio; patro'θinio/ *m*, protection, defense; sponsorship; patronage

patrón /pa'tron/ **(-ona)** *n* patron, sponsor; patron saint; landlord; employer. *m*, coxswain; *Naut.* master, skipper; pattern, model; standard. **p. de oro,** gold standard

patronato /patro'nato/ *m*, patronage, protection; employers' association; charitable foundation. **p. de turismo,** tourist bureau

patronímico /patro'nimiko/ *a* and *m*, patronymic

patrono /pa'trono/ **(-na)** *n* protector; sponsor; patron; patron saint; employer

patrulla /pa'truya; pa'truʎa/ *f*, *Mil.* patrol; group, band

patrullar /patru'yar; patru'ʎar/ *vi Mil.* patrol; march about

patudo /pa'tuðo/ *a Inf.* large-footed

paulatinamente /paulatina'mente/ *adv* slowly, by degrees

pauperismo /paupe'rismo/ *m*, destitution, pauperism

pausa /'pausa/ *f*, pause, interruption; delay; *Mus.* rest; *Mus.* pause. **a pausas,** intermittently

pausado /pau'saðo/ *a* deliberate, slow. *adv* slowly, deliberately

pausar /pau'sar/ *vi* to pause

pauta /'pauta/ *f*, standard, norm, design; *Fig.* guide, model

pava /'paβa/ *f*, *Argentina* kettle; *Venezuela* broad-brimmed straw hat, *inf* bad luck

pavada /pa'βaða/ *f*, flock of turkeys

pavana /pa'βana/ *f*, pavane, stately dance

pavero /pa'βero/ **(-ra)** *a* vain; strutting. *n* turkey keeper or vendor. *m*, broad-brimmed Andalusian hat; *mf*, *Chile*, *Peru* practical joker

pavimentación /paβimenta'sion; paβimenta'θion/ *f*, paving, flagging

pavimento /paβi'mento/ *m*, pavement

pavo /'paβo/ **(-va)** *n Ornith.* turkey. **p. real,** peacock. *Inf.* **pelar la pava,** to serenade, court

pavón /pa'βon/ *m*, *Ornith.* peacock; peacock butterfly; preservative paint (for steel, etc.); gunmetal

pavonear /paβone'ar/ *vi* to strut, peacock (also *vr*); *Inf.* hoodwink, dazzle

pavor /pa'βor/ *m*, terror, panic

pavoroso /paβo'roso/ *a* fearful, awesome, dreadful

payador /paya'ðor/ *m*, *Argentina*, *Chile* gaucho minstrel

payasada /paia'saða/ *f*, clowning, practical joke; clown's patter

payasear /payase'ar/ *vi*, *Lat. Am.* to clown around

payaso /pa'iaso/ *m*, clown

paz /pas; paθ/ *f*, peace; harmony, concord; peaceableness. **¡P. sea en esta casa!** Peace be upon this house! (salutation). **estar en p.,** to be at peace; be quits, be even. **poner** (*or* **meter) p.,** to make peace (between dissentients). **venir de p.,** to come with peaceful intentions

pazguato /pas'guato; paθ'guato/ **(-ta)** *n* simpleton, *Inf.* dope

pe /pe/ *f*, name of the letter P. *Inf.* **de pe a pa,** from A to Z, from beginning to end

peaje /pe'ahe/ *m*, toll (on bridges, roads, etc.)

peatón /pea'ton/ *m*, pedestrian; walker; country postman

pebete /pe'βete/ *m*, joss stick; fuse; *Inf.* stench

peca /'peka/ *f*, mole, freckle

pecado /pe'kaðo/ *m*, sin; fault; excess; defect; *Inf.* the Devil. **p. capital,** mortal sin

pecador /peka'ðor/ *a* sinful. *m*, sinner. **¡P. de mí!** Poor me!

pecadora /peka'ðora/ *f*, sinner; *Inf.* prostitute

pecaminoso /pekami'noso/ *a* sinful

pecar /pe'kar/ *vi* to sin; trespass, transgress; (*with de*) be too... (e.g. *El libro peca de largo,* The book is too long)

peceño /pe'seɲo; pe'θeɲo/ *a* pitch-black (horses, etc.); tasting of pitch

pecera /pe'sera; pe'θera/ *f*, goldfish bowl; aquarium

pechera /pe'tʃera/ *f*, shirt front; chest protector; bib, tucker; shirt frill; *Inf.* bosom

pecho /'petʃo/ *m*, *Anat.* chest; breast; bosom; mind, conscience; courage, endurance; *Mus.* quality (of voice); incline, slope. **p. arriba,** uphill. **abrir su p. a** (*or* **con**), to unbosom oneself to. **dar el p. (a),** to suckle. **de pechos,** leaning on. **echar el p. al agua,** *Fig.* to embark courageously upon. **tomar a pechos** (**una cosa**), to take (a thing) very seriously; take to heart

pechuga /pe'tʃuga/ *f*, breast (of a bird); *Inf.* breast, bosom; slope, incline

pécora /'pekora/ *f*, sheep, head of sheep; wily woman, serpent

pecoso /pe'koso/ *a* freckled; spotted (with warts)

pecuario /pe'kuario/ *a Agr.* stock; cattle

peculiar /peku'liar/ *a* peculiar, individual

peculiaridad /pekuliari'ðað/ *f*, peculiarity

peculio /pe'kulio/ *m*, private money or property

pecunia /pe'kunia/ *f*, *Inf.* cash

pedagogía /peðago'hia/ *f*, education, pedagogy

pedagogo /peða'gogo/ *m*, schoolmaster; educationalist; *Fig.* mentor

pedal /pe'ðal/ *m*, *Mech.* treadle, lever, *Mus.* pedal;

Mus. sustained harmony. *Auto.* **p. de embrague,** clutch pedal

pedalear /peðale'ar/ *vi* to pedal

pedante /pe'ðante/ *a* pedantic. *mf* pedant

pedantería /peðante'ria/ *f,* pedantry

pedazo /pe'ðaso; pe'ðaθo/ *m,* bit, piece; lump; fragment, portion. *Inf.* **p. del alma, p. del corazón, p. de las entrañas,** loved one, dear one. **a pedazos** *or* **en pedazos,** in pieces, in bits. **hacer pedazos,** to break into fragments

pedernal /peðer'nal/ *m,* flint; anything very hard

pedestal /peðes'tal/ *m,* pedestal; base; stand; *Fig.* foundation

pedestre /pe'ðestre/ *a* pedestrian; dull, uninspired

pediatra /pe'ðiatra/ *mf* pediatrician

pedicuro /peði'kuro/ *m,* chiropodist

pedido /pe'ðiðo/ *m, Com.* order; request, petition

pedigüeño /peði'gueɲo/ *a* importunate, insistent

pedimento /peði'mento/ *m,* petition, demand; *Law.* claim; *Law.* motion

pedir /pe'ðir/ *vt irr* to ask, request; *Com.* order; demand; necessitate; desire; ask in marriage. **p. aventón** *Mexico* to hitch a ride **p. en juicio,** *Law.* to bring an action against. *Inf.* **pedírselo** (a uno) **el cuerpo,** to desire (something) ardently. **a p. de boca,** according to one's wish. *Pres. Part.* **pidiendo.** *Pres. Ind.* **pido, pides, pide, piden.** *Preterite* **pidió, pidieron.** *Pres. Subjunc.* **pida, etc.** *Imperf. Subjunc.* **pidiese, etc.**

pedo /'peðo/ *m,* fart

pedómetro /pe'ðometro/ *m,* pedometer

pedrada /pe'ðraða/ *f,* casting a stone; blow with a stone; innuendo

pedrea /pe'ðrea/ *f,* stone throwing; fight with stones; shower of hailstones

pedregal /peðre'gal/ *m,* stony ground, rocky ground

pedregoso /peðre'goso/ *a* stony

pedrera /pe'ðrera/ *f,* stone quarry

pedrería /peðre'ria/ *f,* precious stones

pedrisco /pe'ðrisko/ *m,* hailstone; shower of stones; pile of stones

pedrusco /pe'ðrusko/ *m, Inf.* rough, unpolished stone

pega /'pega/ *f,* sticking; cementing; joining; pitch; varnish; *Inf.* joke; beating; *Ornith.* magpie

pegadizo /pega'ðiso; pega'ðiθo/ *a* sticky, gummy, adhesive; detachable, removable; *Fig.* clinging, importunate (of people)

pegado /pe'gaðo/ *m,* sticking plaster; patch

pegajoso /pega'hoso/ *a* sticky, gluey; viscid; contagious, catching; *Inf.* oily, unctuous; *Fig. Inf.* cadging, sponging

pegar /pe'gar/ *vt* to stick; cement; join, fasten; press (against); infect with (diseases); hit, strike; give (a shout, jump, etc.); patch; *vi* spread, catch (fire, etc.); *Fig.* make an impression, have influence; be opportune; *vr Cul.* stick, burn; meddle; become enthusiastic about; take root in the mind. **p. un tiro (a),** to shoot

pegote /pe'gote/ *m,* sticking plaster; *Fig. Inf.* sponger; *Inf.* patch

peinado /pei'naðo/ *m,* hairdressing or style; headdress. *a Inf.* effeminate, overelegant (men); overcareful (style). **un p. al agua,** a finger wave

peinador /peina'ðor/ **(-ra)** *m,* peignoir, dressing gown; *Lat. Am.* dressing table. *n* hairdresser

peinadura /peina'ðura/ *f,* brushing or combing of hair; *pl* hair combings

peinar /pei'nar/ *vt* to comb, dress the hair; card (wool); cut away (rock)

peine /'peine/ *m,* comb; *Mech.* hackle, reed; instep; *Inf.* crafty person

peinería /peine'ria/ *f,* comb factory or shop

peinero /pei'nero/ *m,* comb manufacturer or seller

peineta /pei'neta/ *f,* high comb (for mantillas, etc.)

peladilla /pela'ðiya; pela'ðiʎa/ *f,* sugared almond; smooth, small pebble

pelado /pe'laðo/ *a* plucked; bare, unadorned; needy, poor; hairless; skinned; peeled; without shell; treeless

peladura /pela'ðura/ *f,* peeling; shelling; skinning; plucking (feathers)

pelafustán /pelafus'tan/ *m, Inf.* good-for-nothing, scamp

pelagatos /pela'gatos/ *m, Inf.* miserable wretch

pelágico /pe'lahiko/ *a* pelagian, oceanic

pelagra /pe'lagra/ *f,* pellagra

pelaje /pe'lahe/ *m,* fur, wool

pelamesa /pela'mesa/ *f,* brawl, fight; lock, tuft (of hair)

pelapatatas /pelapa'tatas/ *m,* potato peeler

pelar /pe'lar/ *vt* to tear out or cut the hair; pluck; skin; peel; shell; rob, fleece; *vr* lose one's hair

peldaño /pel'daɲo/ *m,* step, stair, tread, rung

pelea /pe'lea/ *f,* battle; quarrel, dispute; fight (among animals); effort, exertion; *Fig.* struggle

peleador /pelea'ðor/ *a* fighting; quarrelsome, aggressive

pelear /pele'ar/ *vi* to fight; quarrel; struggle, strive. **p. como perro y gato,** to fight like cat and mouse. *vr* come to blows; fall out, become enemies

pelechar /pele'tʃar/ *vi* to get a new coat (of animals); grow new feathers (of birds); *Inf.* prosper, flourish; grow well

pelele /pe'lele/ *m,* effigy; *Inf.* nincompoop

peletería /pelete'ria/ *f,* furrier; fur shop

peletero /pele'tero/ *m,* furrier; skinner

peliagudo /pelia'guðo/ *a* long-haired (animals); *Inf.* complicated, difficult; wily, downy

pelícano /pe'likano/ *m,* pelican

pelicorto /peli'korto/ *a* short-haired

película /pe'likula/ *f,* film. **p. fotográfica,** roll of film. **p. sonora,** sound film

peligrar /peli'grar/ *vi* to be in danger

peligro /pe'ligro/ *m,* danger, peril. **correr p.** *or* **estar en p.,** to be in danger

peligroso /peli'groso/ *a* dangerous, perilous, risky

pelilargo /peli'largo/ *a* long-haired

pelirrojo /peli'rroho/ *a* red-haired

pelleja /pe'yeha; pe'ʎeha/ *f,* hide, skin (of animals); sheepskin

pellejo /pe'yeho; pe'ʎeho/ *m,* hide; pelt; skin; wineskin; *Inf.* drunkard; peel, skin (of fruit)

pelliza /pe'yisa; pe'ʎiθa/ *f,* fur or fur-trimmed coat

pellizcar /peyis'kar; peʎiθ'kar/ *vt* to pinch, tweak, nip; pilfer

pellizco /pe'yisko; pe'ʎiθko/ *m,* pinch, nip, tweak; pilfering, pinching; bit, pinch

pelmazo /pel'maso; pel'maθo/ *m,* squashed mass; *Inf.* idler, sluggard; *Inf.* bore

pelo /'pelo/ *m,* hair; down (on birds and fruit); fiber, filament; hair trigger (firearms); hairspring (watches); kiss (in billiards); nap (of cloth), grain (of wood); flaw (in gems); raw silk. **p. chino,** *Mexico* (naturally) curly hair **p. de camello,** camel's hair. **a p.,** in the nude; without a hat; opportunely. **en p.,** bareback (of horses). **hacerse el p.,** to do one's hair; have one's hair cut. *Inf.* **no tener p. de tonto,** to be smart, clever. *Inf.* **no tener pelos en la lengua,** to be outspoken. *Inf.* **tomar el p. (a),** to pull a person's leg. **venir a p.,** to be apposite; come opportunely

pelón /pe'lon/ *a* hairless; *Fig. Inf.* broke, fleeced

pelonería /pelone'ria/ *f, Inf.* poverty, misery

pelota /pe'lota/ *f,* ball; ball game. **p. base,** baseball. **p. vasca,** pelota. **en p.,** stark naked

pelotari /pelo'tari/ *m,* professional pelota player

pelotazo /pelo'taso; pelo'taθo/ *m,* knock or blow with a ball

pelotear /pelote'ar/ *vt* to audit accounts; *vi* play ball; throw, cast; quarrel; argue

pelotera /pelo'tera/ *f, Inf.* brawl

pelotón /pelo'ton/ *m,* big ball; lump of hair; crowd, multitude; *Mil.* platoon. **p. de ejecución,** firing squad

peltre /'peltre/ *m,* pewter

peluca /pe'luka/ *f,* wig; periwig; *Inf.* scolding

peludo /pe'luðo/ *a* hairy. *m,* long-haired rug

peluquería /peluke'ria/ *f,* hairdressing establishment; hairdressing trade

peluquero /pelu'kero/ **(-ra)** *n* hairdresser; barber

peluquín /pelu'kin/ *m,* small wig

pelusa /pe'lusa/ *f,* down, soft hair; fluff, nap

pena /'pena/ *f,* punishment, penalty; grief; pain,

suffering; difficulty, trouble; mourning veil; hardship; anxiety; embarrassment; tail feather. **p. capital** *or* **p. de la vida,** capital punishment. **a duras penas,** with great difficulty. **so p. de,** under penalty of. **valer** (*or* **merecer**) **la p.,** to be worth while

penable /pe'naβle/ *a* punishable

penacho /pe'natʃo/ *m,* topknot, crest (of birds); plume, panache; *Inf.* pride, arrogance

penado /pe'naðo/ **(-da)** *a* difficult, laborious; painful, troubled, afflicted. *n* convict

penal /pe'nal/ *a* penal; punitive

penalidad /penali'ðað/ *f,* trouble, labor, difficulty; *Law.* penalty

penar /pe'nar/ *vt* to penalize; punish; *vi* suffer; undergo purgatorial pains; *vr* suffer anguish. **p. por,** to long for

penca /'penka/ *f, Bot.* fleshy leaf; lash, strap, cat-o'-nine-tails

penco /'penko/ *m, Inf.* wretched nag

pendejo /pen'deho/ *m,* pubic hair; *Inf.* coward; jerk

pendencia /pen'densia; pen'denθia/ *f,* fight; quarrel

pendenciar /penden'siar; penden'θiar/ *vi* to fight; quarrel

pendenciero /penden'siero; penden'θiero/ *a* quarrelsome, aggressive

pender /pen'der/ *vi* to hang; depend; be pending

pendiente /pen'diente/ *a* pending; hanging; *Com.* outstanding. *m,* earring; pendant. *f,* slope, incline; gradient

péndola /'pendola/ *f,* feather, plume; quill pen; pendulum (of a clock)

pendolista /pendo'lista/ *mf* calligrapher

pendón /pen'don/ *m,* pennon, banner; *Bot.* shoot; *Inf.* lanky, slatternly woman; *pl* reins

péndulo /'pendulo/ *a* pendulous, hanging. *m,* pendulum

pene /'pene/ *m,* penis

peneque /pe'neke/ *m, Mexico* roll of maize dough filled with cheese

penetrabilidad /penetraβili'ðað/ *f,* penetrability

penetración /penetra'sion; penetra'θion/ *f,* penetration; understanding, perspicuity; sagacity, shrewdness

penetrador /penetra'ðor/ *a* penetrating, perspicacious; sagacious, acute

penetrante /pene'trante/ *a* penetrating; deep; piercing (of sounds); acute, shrewd

penetrar /pene'trar/ *vt* to penetrate; permeate; master, comprehend; (*with en*) enter

penetrativo /penetra'tiβo/ *a* piercing

penicilina /penisi'lina; peniθi'lina/ *f,* penicillin

península /pe'ninsula/ *f,* peninsula. **la P.** the Iberian Peninsula

Península Ibérica, la /pe'ninsula i'βerika, la/ the Iberian Peninsula

penique /pe'nike/ *m,* penny

penitencia /peni'tensia; peni'tenθia/ *f,* penitence, repentance; penance

penitencial /peniten'sial; peniten'θial/ *a* penitential

penitenciaría /penitensia'ria; penitenθia'ria/ *f,* penitentiary

penitente /peni'tente/ *a* penitent, repentant. *mf* penitent

penoso /pe'noso/ *a* laborious, difficult; grievous; painful; troublesome; *Inf.* foppish; *Lat. Am.* shy, timid

pensado /pen'saðo/ *a* premeditated, deliberate. **de p.,** intentionally. **mal p.,** malicious, evil-minded

pensador /pensa'ðor/ *a* thinking; pensive. *m,* thinker

pensamiento /pensa'miento/ *m,* mind; thought; idea; suspicion, doubt; heartsease pansy; maxim; intention, project

pensar /pen'sar/ *vt irr* to think; purpose, intend; (*with en, sobre*) reflect upon; think about; *vt* feed (animals). **p. entre sí, p. para consigo** *or* **p. para sí,** to think to oneself. See **acertar**

pensativo /pensa'tiβo/ *a* reflective, pensive

pensil /pen'sil/ *a* hanging. *m,* hanging garden; delightful garden

pensión /pen'sion/ *f,* pension, allowance; boarding

house, private hotel; scholarship grant; cost of board; trouble, drudgery

pensionado /pensio'naðo/ **(-da)** *a* pensioned; retired. *n* scholarship holder. *m,* boarding school

pensionar /pensio'nar/ *vt* to pension, grant a pension to; charge a pension on

pensionista /pensio'nista/ *mf* pensioner; boarder

pentágono /pen'tagono/ *m,* pentagon. *a* pentagonal

pentámetro /pen'tametro/ *m,* pentameter

Pentateuco /penta'teuko/ *m,* Pentateuch

Pentecostés /pentekos'tes/ *m,* Pentecost, Whitsuntide

penúltimo /pe'nultimo/ *a* next to the last, penultimate

penuria /pe'nuria/ *f,* scarcity; want, penury

peña /'peɲa/ *f,* crag, rock; boulder; group of friends; club. **ser una p.,** to be stony-hearted

peñasco /pe'ɲasko/ *m,* craggy peak

peñascoso /peɲas'koso/ *a* craggy, rocky

peñón /pe'ɲon/ *m,* rock; cliff; peak

peón /pe'on/ *m,* pedestrian; laborer; *South America* farmhand; top (toy); piece (chess, checkers); *Mech.* axle; infantryman. **p. caminero,** road mender. **p. de ajedrez,** pawn (in chess)

peonada /peo'naða/ *f,* day's manual labor; gang of laborers

peonar /peo'nar/ *vi, Argentina* to do manual labor

peonía /peo'nia/ *f,* peony

peonza /pe'onsa; pe'onθa/ *f,* top; teetotum

peor /pe'or/ *a comp* **malo** worse. *adv comp* **mal,** worse. *a sup* **el (la, lo)** peor; los **(las)** peores, the worst. **p. que p.,** worse and worse. **tanto p.,** so much the worse

pepino /pe'pino/ *m,* cucumber plant; cucumber; *Fig.* pin, straw

pepita /pe'pita/ *f, Mineral.* nugget; pip, seed (of fruit)

péptico /'peptiko/ *a* peptic

pequeñez /peke'ɲes; peke'ɲeθ/ *f,* littleness, smallness; pettiness; childhood; infancy; trifle, insignificant thing; meanness, baseness

pequeño /pe'keɲo/ *a* little, small; petty; very young; short, brief; humble, lowly

pequero, -a /pe'kero/ *mf, Argentina* cardsharp

pera /'pera/ *f,* pear; goatee; *Fig.* plum, sinecure

peral /pe'ral/ *m,* pear tree; pearwood

perca /'perka/ *f, Ichth.* perch

percal /per'kal/ *m,* percale, calico

percalina /perka'lina/ *f,* percaline, binding cloth

percance /per'kanse; per'kanθe/ *m,* perquisite, attribute (gen. *pl*); disaster, mischance

percebe /per'seβe; per'θeβe/ *m,* (gen. *pl*) goose barnacle

percentaje /persen'tahe; perθen'tahe/ *m,* percentage

percepción /persep'sion; perθep'θion/ *f,* perception; idea, conception

perceptible /persep'tiβle; perθep'tiβle/ *a* perceptible

perceptivo /persep'tiβo; perθep'tiβo/ *a* perceptive

perceptor /persep'tor; perθep'tor/ **(-ra)** *a* perceptive. *n* observer

percha /'pertʃa/ *f,* stake, pole; coat hanger; perch (for birds); rack (for hay); hall stand, coat and hat stand, coatrack

perchero /per'tʃero/ *m,* hall stand; clothes rack; row of perches (for fowl, etc.)

percibir /persi'βir; perθi'βir/ *vt* to collect, draw, receive; perceive; understand, grasp

percibo /per'siβo; per'θiβo/ *m,* perceiving; collecting, drawing, receiving

percolador /perkola'ðor/ *m,* percolator (coffee)

percusión /perku'sion/ *f,* percussion; shock, vibration

percusor /perku'sor/ *m,* hammer (of a firearm)

percutir /perku'tir/ *vt* to percuss, strike

perdedor /perðe'ðor/ **(-ra)** *a* losing. *n* loser

perder /per'ðer/ *vt* to lose; throw away; squander; spoil, destroy; *vi* fade (of colors); *vr* lose one's way, be lost; be confused or perplexed; be shipwrecked; take to vice, become dissolute; be spoiled or destroyed; disappear; love madly. **p. la chaveta (por),** to go out of one's head (for), be wild (about). **p. la**

ocasión, to let the chance slip. **p. los estribos,** to lose patience. **p. terreno,** to lose ground. **perderse de vista,** to be lost to sight. **echarse a p.,** to spoil, be damaged. See **entender**

perdición /perði'sion; perði'θion/ *f,* loss; perdition, ruin; damnation; depravity, viciousness

pérdida /'perðiða/ *f,* loss; waste. **p. cuantiosa,** heavy losses

perdidamente /perðiða'mente/ *adv* ardently, desperately; uselessly

perdigón /perði'gon/ *m,* young partridge; decoy partridge; hailstone, pellet, shot

perdigonada /perðigo'naða/ *f,* volley of hailstone; hailstone wound

perdiguero /perði'gero/ **(-ra)** *n* game dealer; setter, retriever

perdiz /per'ðis; per'ðiθ/ *f,* partridge

perdón /per'ðon/ *m,* pardon, forgiveness; remission. **con p.,** with your permission; excuse me

perdonable /perðo'naβle/ *a* pardonable, excusable

perdonar /perðo'nar/ *vt* to pardon, forgive; remit, excuse; exempt; waste, lose; give up (a privilege)

perdonavidas /perðona'βiðas/ *m, Inf.* bully, braggart

perdulario /perðu'lario/ *a* careless, negligent; slovenly; vicious, depraved

perdurable /perðu'raβle/ *a* perpetual, everlasting; enduring, lasting

perdurar /perðu'rar/ *vi* to last, endure

perecedero /perese'ðero; pereθe'ðero/ *a* brief, fugitive, transient; perishable. *m, Inf.* poverty, want

perecer /pere'ser; pere'θer/ *vi irr* to end, finish; perish, die; suffer (damage, grief, etc.); be destitute; *vr* (*with por*) long for, crave; desire ardently. See **conocer**

peregrinación /peregrina'sion; peregrina'θion/ *f,* journey, peregrination; pilgrimage

peregrinamente /peregrina'mente/ *adv* rarely, not often; beautifully, perfectly

peregrinar /peregri'nar/ *vi* to journey, travel; make a pilgrimage

peregrino /pere'grino/ **(-na)** *a* and *n* pilgrim. *a* migratory (birds); rare, unusual; extraordinary, strange; beautiful, perfect

perejil /pere'hil/ *m,* parsley; *Inf.* ornament or apparel (gen. *pl*); *pl* honors, titles

perengano /pereŋ'gano/ **(-na)** *n* so-and-so, such a one

perenne /pe'renne/ *a* incessant, constant; *Bot.* perennial

perennidad /perenni'ðað/ *f,* perpetuity

perentoriedad /perentorie'ðað/ *f,* peremptoriness; urgency

perentorio /peren'torio/ *a* peremptory; conclusive, decisive; urgent, pressing

pereza /pe'resa; pe'reθa/ *f,* laziness; languor, inertia; slowness, deliberateness

perezoso /pere'soso; pere'θoso/ *a* lazy; languid; slothful; slow, deliberate. *m, Zool.* sloth

perfección /perfek'sion; perfek'θion/ *f,* perfection; perfecting, perfect thing, virtue, grace

perfeccionamiento /perfeksiona'miento; perfekθiona'miento/ *m,* perfecting; progress, improvement

perfeccionar /perfeksio'nar; perfekθio'nar/ *vt* to perfect; complete

perfectamente /perfekta'mente/ *adv* perfectly; quite, entirely

perfecto /per'fekto/ *a* perfect; excellent, very good; complete; whole; *Gram.* perfect

perfidia /per'fiðia/ *f,* perfidy, treachery

pérfido /'perfiðo/ *a* perfidious, treacherous

perfil /per'fil/ *m,* ornament, decoration; outline, contour; profile; section (of metal); fine stroke (of letters); *pl* finishing touches; politeness, attention, courtesy. **de p.,** in profile; sideways

perfilado /perfi'laðo/ *a* long, elongated (of faces, etc.)

perfilar /perfi'lar/ *vt* to draw in profile; outline; *vr* place oneself sideways, show one's profile; *Inf.* dress up, titivate

perforación /perfora'sion; perfora'θion/ *f,* perforation, boring; hole

perforador /perfora'ðor/ *a* perforating, boring. *m, Mech.* drill

perforar /perfo'rar/ *vt* to perforate, pierce; bore, drill, make a hole in

perfumador /perfuma'ðor/ **(-ra)** *a* perfuming. *n* perfumer. *m,* perfume burner

perfumar /perfu'mar/ *vt* to perfume; *vi* give off perfume

perfume /per'fume/ *m,* perfume; scent, fragrance

perfumería /perfume'ria/ *f,* scent factory; perfumery; perfume shop

perfumista /perfu'mista/ *mf* perfumer

perfunctorio /perfunk'torio/ *a* perfunctory

pergamino /perga'mino/ *m,* parchment, vellum; document; diploma; *pl* aristocratic descent

pericardio /peri'karðio/ *m,* pericardium

pericia /pe'risia; pe'riθia/ *f,* expertness; skilled workmanship

pericial /peri'sial; peri'θial/ *a* expert, skillful

perico /pe'riko/ *m,* parakeet; giant asparagus

periferia /peri'feria/ *f,* periphery

periférico /peri'feriko/ *a* peripheral

perifollos /peri'foyos; peri'foʎos/ *m pl, Inf.* frills, flounces, finery

perifrástico /peri'frastiko/ *a* periphrastic

perilla /pe'riya; pe'riʎa/ *f,* pear-shaped ornament; goatee; imperial. **p. de la oreja,** lobe of the ear. **venir de p.,** to be most opportune

perillán /peri'yan; peri'ʎan/ *m, Inf.* rascal, rogue

perímetro /pe'rimetro/ *m,* perimeter; precincts

perínclito /pe'rinklito/ *a* distinguished, illustrious; heroic

perineo /peri'neo/ *m,* perineum

perinola /peri'nola/ *f,* top, teetotum

periodicidad /perioðisi'ðað; perioðiθi'ðað/ *f,* periodicity

periódico /pe'rioðiko/ *a* periodic. *m,* newspaper; periodical publication

periodicucho /perioði'kutʃo/ *m,* rag (bad newspaper)

periodismo /perio'ðismo/ *m,* journalism

periodista /perio'ðista/ *mf* journalist

periodístico /perio'ðistiko/ *a* journalistic

período /pe'rioðo/ *m,* period; *Phys.* cycle; menstruation period; *Gram.* clause; age, era

periostio /pe'riostio/ *m,* periosteum

peripatético /peripa'tetiko/ *a* peripatetic

peripecia /peri'pesia; peri'peθia/ *f,* sudden change of fortune, vicissitude

peripuesto /peri'puesto/ *a Inf.* overelegant, spruce, too well-dressed; smart

periquete /peri'kete/ *m, Inf.* jiffy, trice

periquito /peri'kito/ *m,* parakeet; budgerigar

periscopio /peris'kopio/ *m,* periscope

perito /pe'rito/ **(-ta)** *a* expert; skillful, experienced. *n* expert

peritoneo /perito'neo/ *m,* peritoneum

perjudicador /perhuðika'ðor/ **(-ra)** *a* injurious, prejudicial. *n* injurer

perjudicar /perhuði'kar/ *vt* to harm, damage, injure; prejudice

perjudicial /perhuði'sial; perhuði'θial/ *a* injurious, noxious, harmful; prejudicial

perjuicio /per'huisio; per'huiθio/ *m,* injury, damage; harm; *Law.* prejudice

perjurador /perhura'ðor/ **(-ra)** *n* perjurer

perjurar /perhu'rar/ *vi* to perjure oneself, commit perjury; swear, curse

perjurio /per'hurio/ *m,* perjury

perjuro /per'huro/ **(-ra)** *a* perjured, forsworn. *n* perjurer

perla /'perla/ *f,* pearl; *Archit.* bead; *Fig.* treasure, jewel, dear. **de perlas,** excellent; exactly right

perlero /per'lero/ *a* pearl

perlesía /perle'sia/ *f,* paralysis; palsy

perlino /per'lino/ *a* pearly, pearl-colored

permanecer /permane'ser; permane'θer/ *vi irr* to stay, remain. **p. en posición de firme,** to stand at attention. See **conocer**

permanencia /perma'nensia; perma'nenθia/ f, stay, sojourn; permanence

permanente /perma'nente/ a permanent; lasting, enduring

permeabilidad /permeaβili'ðað/ f, permeability

permisible /permi'siβle/ a permissible, allowable

permisivo /permi'siβo/ a permissive

permiso /per'miso/ m, permission, leave; permit; (*Mil.* etc.) pass. **¡Con p.!** Excuse me!; Allow me!

permitir /permi'tir/ vt to permit, allow

permuta /per'muta/ f, exchange

permutación /permuta'sion; permuta'θion/ f, permutation, interchange

permutar /permu'tar/ vt to exchange

pernear /perne'ar/ vi to kick; *Inf.* bustle; fret, be impatient

pernetas, en /per'netas, en/ adv barelegged

perniciosidad /pernisiosi'ðað; perniθiosi'ðað/ f, perniciousness

pernicioso /perni'sioso; perni'θioso/ a pernicious

pernil /per'nil/ m, *Anat.* hock; ham; leg of pork; leg (of trousers)

pernio /'pernio/ m, hinge (of doors, windows)

perniquebrar /pernike'βrar/ vt irr to break the legs of. See **quebrar**

perno /'perno/ m, bolt, pin, spike

pernoctar /pernok'tar/ vi to spend the night (away from home)

pero /'pero/ conjunc but. m, *Inf.* defect; difficulty, snag

perogrullada /perogru'yaða; perogru'ʎaða/ f, *Inf.* truism

perol /pe'rol/ m, *Cul.* pan

peroné /pero'ne/ m, fibula

peronista /pero'nista/ a, mf Peronist

peroración /perora'sion; perora'θion/ f, peroration

perorar /pero'rar/ vi to make a speech; *Inf.* speak pompously; ask insistently

peróxido /pe'roksiðo/ m, peroxide

perpendicular /perpendiku'lar/ a perpendicular. f, perpendicular

perpetración /perpetra'sion; perpetra'θion/ f, perpetration

perpetrar /perpe'trar/ vt to perpetrate

perpetua /per'petua/ f, *Bot.* immortelle, everlasting

perpetuación /perpetua'sion; perpetua'θion/ f, perpetuation

perpetuar /perpe'tuar/ vt to perpetuate; vr last, endure

perpetuidad /perpetui'ðað/ f, perpetuity

perpetuo /per'petuo/ a everlasting; lifelong

perplejidad /perplehi'ðað/ f, perplexity, bewilderment, doubt

perplejo /per'pleho/ a perplexed, bewildered, doubtful

perquirir /perki'rir/ vt irr to search carefully. See **adquirir**

perra /'perra/ f, bitch; *Inf.* sot, drunkard; tantrums. **p. chica,** five-cent coin. **p. gorda,** ten-cent coin

perrada /pe'rraða/ f, pack of dogs; *Inf.* dirty trick

perramus /pe'rramus/ m, *Argentina* raincoat

perrengue /pe'rreŋgue/ m, *Inf.* short-tempered person

perrera /pe'rrera/ f, dog kennel; useless toil; *Inf.* tantrums

perrería /perre'ria/ f, pack of dogs; *Inf.* dirty trick; fit of anger

perrero /pe'rrero/ m, dog fancier; kennel worker

perro /'perro/ m, dog. **p. caliente** hot dog. **p. danés,** Great Dane. **p. de aguas,** poodle; spaniel. **p. de casta,** thoroughbred dog. **p. de lanas** poodle. **p. de muestra,** pointer. **p. de presa,** bulldog. **p. de San Bernardo,** St. Bernard (dog). **p. de Terranova,** Newfoundland (dog). **p. del hortelano,** dog in the manger. **p. dogo** bulldog. **p. esquimal** husky. **p. faldero,** lap dog. **p. lobo,** wolfhound. **p. pachón,** dachshund. **p. pastor alemán** or **p. policía,** German shepherd. **p. pequinés,** Pekingese. **p. perdiguero,** retriever. **p. pomerano,** spitz, Pomeranian (dog). **p. sabueso español,** spaniel. **p. zorrero,** foxhound. *Inf.* **A p. viejo**

no hay tus tus, You can't fool an old dog. **vivir como perros y gatos,** *Inf.* to live like cat and dog

persa /'persa/ a and mf Persian. m, Persian (language)

persecución /perseku'sion; perseku'θion/ f, pursuit; persecution; annoyance, importuning

perseguidor /persegi'ðor/ (**-ra**) a pursuing; tormenting. n pursuer; tormentor, persecutor

perseguimiento /persegi'miento/ m, pursuit

perseguir /perse'gir/ vi irr to pursue; persecute; torment; importune. See **seguir**

perseverancia /perseβe'ransia; perseβe'ranθia/ f, perseverance

perseverante /perseβe'rante/ a persevering; constant

perseverar /perseβe'rar/ vi to persevere; last, endure

persiana /per'siana/ f, Venetian blind; flowered silk material

pérsico /'persiko/ a Persian. m, peach tree; peach

persignar /persig'nar/ vt to sign; make the sign of the cross over; vr cross oneself

persistencia /persis'tensia; persis'tenθia/ f, persistence

persistente /persis'tente/ a persistent

persistir /persis'tir/ vi to persist

persona /per'sona/ f, person; personage; character (in a play, etc.); (*Gram. Eccl.*) person. **de p. a p.,** in private, face to face

personaje /perso'nahe/ m, important person, personage; character (in a play, etc.)

personal /perso'nal/ a personal. m, staff, personnel

personalidad /personali'ðað/ f, personality

personalismo /persona'lismo/ m, personality; personal question

personalizar /personali'sar; personali'θar/ vt to become personal, be offensive

personalmente /personal'mente/ adv personally

personarse /perso'narse/ vr to present oneself, call, appear

personificación /personifika'sion; personifika'θion/ f, personification

personificar /personifi'kar/ vt to personify

perspectiva /perspek'tiβa/ f, perspective; view; outlook; aspect, appearance. **p. aérea,** bird's-eye view

perspicacia /perspi'kasia; perspi'kaθia/ f, perspicacity, shrewdness

perspicaz /perspi'kas; perspi'kaθ/ a perspicacious, clear-sighted

perspicuidad /perspikui'ðað/ f, perspicuity

perspicuo /pers'pikuo/ a lucid, clear

persuadir /persua'ðir/ vt to persuade

persuasible /persua'siβle/ a persuadable

persuasión /persua'sion/ f, persuasion; belief, conviction, opinion

persuasiva /persua'siβa/ f, persuasiveness

persuasivo /persua'siβo/ a persuasive

pertenecer /pertene'ser; pertene'θer/ vi irr to belong; relate, concern. See **conocer**

perteneciente /pertene'siente; pertene'θiente/ a belonging (to), pertaining (to)

pertenencia /perte'nensia; perte'nenθia/ f, ownership, proprietorship; property, accessory

pértiga /'pertiga/ f, long rod; pole. **salto de p.,** pole vaulting

pertinacia /perti'nasia; perti'naθia/ f, pertinacity, doggedness

pertinaz /perti'nas; perti'naθ/ a pertinacious, stubborn, dogged

pertinencia /perti'nensia; perti'nenθia/ f, relevance, appropriateness

pertinente /perti'nente/ a relevant, apposite; appropriate

pertrechar /pertre'tʃar/ vt to supply, equip; prepare, make ready

pertrechos /per'tretʃos/ m pl, *Mil.* armaments, stores; equipment, appliances

perturbación /perturβa'sion; perturβa'θion/ f, disturbance; agitation

perturbador /perturβa'ðor/ (**-ra**) a disturbing. n disturber; heckler

perturbar /pertur'βar/ vt to disturb; agitate

Perú /pe'ru/ *m* Peru. **la República del P.**, Peru
peruano /pe'ruano/ **(-na)** *a* and *n* Peruvian
perversidad /perβersi'ðað/ *f*, wickedness, depravity
perversión /perβer'sion/ *f*, perversion; wickedness, evil
perversivo /perβer'siβo/ *a* perversive
perverso /per'βerso/ *a* wicked, iniquitous, depraved
pervertir /perβer'tir/ *vt irr* to pervert, corrupt; distort. See **sentir**
pesa /'pesa/ *f*, weight; clock weight; gymnast's weight. **pesas y medidas,** weights and measures
pesacartas /pesa'kartas/ *m*, letter scale, letter balance
pesada /pe'saða/ *f*, weighing
pesadez /pesa'ðes; pesa'ðeθ/ *f*, heaviness; obesity; tediousness, tiresomeness; slowness; fatigue
pesadilla /pesa'ðiya; pesa'ðiʎa/ *f*, nightmare
pesado /pe'saðo/ *a* heavy; obese; deep (of sleep); oppressive (of weather); slow; unwieldy; tedious; impertinent; dull, boring; offensive
pesadumbre /pesa'ðumbre/ *f*, heaviness; grief, sorrow; trouble, anxiety
pésame /'pesame/ *m*, expression of condolence. **dar el p.**, to present one's condolences
pesantez /pesan'tes; pesan'teθ/ *f*, weight, heaviness; seriousness, gravity
pesar /pe'sar/ *m*, grief, sorrow; remorse. **a p. de,** in spite of
pesar /pe'sar/ *vi* to weigh; be heavy; be important; grieve, cause regret (e.g. *Me pesa mucho,* I am very sorry); influence, affect; *vt* weigh; consider. **Mal que me (te,** etc.) **pese...,** Much as I regret...
pesaroso /pesa'roso/ *a* regretful, remorseful; sorrowful
pesca /'peska/ *f*, fishery; angling; fishing; catch of fish. **p. a la rastra,** trawling. **p. deportiva** sport fishing. **p. mayor,** deep-sea fishing
pescadería /peskaðe'ria/ *f*, fishery; fish store; fish market
pescadilla /peska'ðiya; peska'ðiʎa/ *f, Ichth.* whiting
pescado /pes'kaðo/ *m*, fish (out of the water), cooked fish; salt cod
pescador /peska'ðor/ **(-ra)** *n* fisherman; angler
pescante /pes'kante/ *m*, driving seat; coach box; jib (of a crane)
pescar /pes'kar/ *vt* to fish; *Inf.* catch in the act; acquire. **p. a la rastra,** to trawl
pescozón /pesko'son; pesko'θon/ *m*, slap on the neck or head
pescuezo /pes'kueso; pes'kueθo/ *m*, neck; throat; haughtiness, arrogance. **torcer el p.,** to wring the neck (of chickens, etc.)
pesebre /pe'seβre/ *m*, manger, stable; feeding trough
pesero /pe'sero/ *m, Mexico* jitney, jitney taxi
pésimamente /'pesimamente/ *adv* extremely badly
pesimismo /pesi'mismo/ *m*, pessimism
pesimista /pesi'mista/ *a* pessimistic. *mf* pessimist
pésimo /'pesimo/ *a sup* **malo** extremely bad
peso /'peso/ *m*, weighing; weight; heaviness; gravity; importance; influence; load; peso (money); scale, balance. **p. bruto,** gross weight. **p. de joyería,** troy weight. **p. específico,** *Phys.* specific gravity. **p. pluma,** (*Box.*) featherweight
pespunte /pes'punte/ *m*, backstitch
pesquera /pes'kera/ *f*, fishing ground, fishery
pesquería /peske'ria/ *f*, fishing, angling; fisherman's trade; fishing ground, fishery
pesquero /pes'kero/ *a* fishing (of boats, etc.)
pesquisa /pes'kisa/ *f*, investigation, examination; search
pesquisar /peski'sar/ *vt* to investigate, look into; search
pestaña /pes'taɲa/ *f*, eyelash; *Sew.* edging, fringe; ear, lug; *Naut.* fluke
pestañear /pestaɲe'ar/ *vi* to wink; blink; flutter one's eyelashes
pestañeo /pesta'ɲeo/ *m*, winking; blinking
peste /'peste/ *f*, plague, pestilence; nauseous smell; epidemic; pest; vice; *Chile* smallpox; *pl* oaths, curses. **p. bubónica,** bubonic plague. **p. roja** syphilis. **p. de las abejas,** foul brood. **echar pestes,** to swear; fume

pestífero /pes'tifero/ *a* noxious
pestilencia /pesti'lensia; pesti'lenθia/ *f*, plague, pestilence
pestilente /pesti'lente/ *a* pestilential
pestillo /pes'tiyo; pes'tiʎo/ *m*, latch; lock bolt. **p. de golpe,** safety latch
petaca /pe'taka/ *f*, cigarette or cigar case; tobacco pouch; *Mexico* suitcase.
pétalo /'petalo/ *m*, petal
petardista /petar'ðista/ *mf* swindler, impostor
petardo /pe'tarðo/ *m*, detonator; torpedo; firecracker; fraud
petición /peti'sion; peti'θion/ *f*, petition, request
peticionar /petisio'nar; petiθio'nar/ *vt, Lat. Am.* to petition
peticionario /petisio'nario; petiθio'nario/ **(-ia)** *n* petitioner. *a* petitionary
petimetra /peti'metra/ *f*, stylish and affected young woman
petimetre /peti'metre/ *m*, fop
petirrojo /peti'rroho/ *m*, robin
petitorio /peti'torio/ *a* petitionary. *m, Inf.* importunity
peto /'peto/ *m*, breastplate; front (of a shirt); bib
pétreo /'petreo/ *a* petrous
petrificación /petrifika'sion; petrifika'θion/ *f*, petrifaction
petrificar /petrifi'kar/ *vt* to petrify; *vr* become petrified
petrografía /petrogra'fia/ *f*, petrology
petróleo /pe'troleo/ *m*, petroleum; oil, mineral oil. **p. bruto,** crude oil. **p. de lámpara,** kerosene
petrolero /petro'lero/ **(-ra)** *a* oil, petroleum. *n* petroleum seller; incendiarist. *m*, oil tanker
petrolífero /petro'lifero/ *a* oil-bearing
petulancia /petu'lansia; petu'lanθia/ *f*, insolence; vanity
petulante /petu'lante/ *a* insolent; vain
pez /pes; peθ/ *m*, fish; *pl* Pisces. *f, Chem.* pitch. **p. sierra,** swordfish
pezón /pe'son; pe'θon/ *m, Bot.* stalk; nipple; axle pivot; point (of land, etc.)
pezuña /pe'suɲa; pe'θuɲa/ *f*, cloven hoof (of cows, pigs, etc.)
piada /'piaða/ *f*, chirping, twittering
piadoso /pia'ðoso/ *a* compassionate; kind, pitiful; pious, religious
piafar /pia'far/ *vi* to stamp, paw the ground (horses)
pianista /pia'nista/ *mf* piano maker; piano dealer; pianist
piano /'piano/ *m*, pianoforte. **p. de cola,** grand piano. **p. de media cola,** baby grand. **p. vertical,** upright piano
piante /'piante/ *a* chirping, twittering
piar /piar/ *vi* to chirp, twitter
piara /'piara/ *f*, herd of swine; pack (of horses, etc.)
pibe, -a /'piβe/ *mf, Argentina* kid, child
pica /'pika/ *f, Mil.* pike; bullfighter's goad; pike soldier; stonecutter's hammer. **a p. seca,** in vain. **pasar por las picas,** to suffer hardship. **poner una p. en Flandes,** to triumph over great difficulties
picacho /pi'katʃo/ *m*, peak, summit
picada /pi'kaða/ *f*, prick; bite; peck; *Aer.* dive
picadero /pika'ðero/ *m*, riding school; paddock (of a racetrack)
picado /pi'kaðo/ *a Sew.* pinked. *m, Cul.* hash
picador /pika'ðor/ *m*, horse trainer; meat chopper; horseman armed with a goad (bullfights)
picadura /pika'ðura/ *f*, puncture; prick; sting; *Sew.* pinking; peck (of birds); cut tobacco; black tobacco; beginning of caries in teeth
picajoso /pika'hoso/ *a* hypersensitive, touchy, peevish
picamaderos /pikama'ðeros/ *m*, woodpecker
picanear /pikane'ar/ *vt, Lat. Am.* to goad on, spur on
picante /pi'kante/ *a* piquant; mordant; hot, highly seasoned. *m*, mordancy; pungency
picantería /pikante'ria/ *f, Lat. Am.* restaurant specializing in spicy foods

picapleitos /pika'pleitos/ *m, Inf.* shady lawyer, *Inf.* ambulance chaser

picaporte /pika'porte/ *m,* latch, door catch; door knocker

picar /pi'kar/ *vt* to prick; sting; peck; bite; chop fine; mince; nibble (of fishing); irritate (the skin); *Sew.* pink; burn (the tongue); eat (grapes); goad; spur; stipple (walls); stimulate, encourage; split, cleave; *Mil.* harass; vex; *Mus.* play staccato; *vi* burn (of the sun); smart (of cuts, etc.); eat sparingly; *Auto.* knock; (*with en*) knock at (doors, etc.); *vr* be moth-eaten; go rotten (fruit, etc.); grow choppy (of the sea); be piqued; boast

picardear /pikar'ðe'ar/ *vi* to play the rogue; behave mischievously

picardía /pikar'ðia/ *f,* knavery, roguery; mischievousness; practical joke; wantonness

picaresco /pika'resko/ *a* roguish, picaresque, knavish

pícaro /'pikaro/ **(-ra)** *a* knavish; base, vile; astute; mischievous. *n* rogue

picatoste /pika'toste/ *m,* kind of fritter

picaza /pi'kasa; pi'kaθa/ *f,* magpie

picazo /pi'kaso; pi'kaθo/ *m,* blow with a pike or anything pointed; peck, tap with a beak (of birds); sting

picazón /pika'son; pika'θon/ *f,* itch, irritation; annoyance

pícea /'pisea; 'piθea/ *f, Bot.* spruce

píceo /'piseo; 'piθeo/ *a* piscine, fish-like

pichincha /pi'tʃintʃa/ *f, Argentina* bargain

pichón /pi'tʃon/ **(-ona)** *m,* male pigeon. *n Inf.* darling

pico /'piko/ *m,* beak (of birds); peak; woodpecker; odd amount (e.g. *treinta y p.,* thirty-odd); sharp point; spout (of a jug, etc.); *Inf.* mouth; blarney, gab. **p. de cigüeña,** crane's-bill. **p. de oro,** silver-tongued orator

picor /pi'kor/ *m,* burning sensation in the mouth; smarting; itching, irritation

picoso /pi'koso/ *a* pitted, marked by smallpox; *Mexico* hot, spicy (food)

picota /pi'kota/ *f,* pillory; peak; spire

picotazo /piko'taso; piko'taθo/ *m,* peck; dab; sting, bite

picotear /pikote'ar/ *vt* to peck (of a bird); *vi* toss the head (of horses); *Inf.* chatter senselessly; *vr Inf.* slang each other

picotero /piko'tero/ *a Inf.* chattering, talkative; indiscreet

pictórico /pik'toriko/ *a* pictorial

picudo /pi'kuðo/ *a* pointed, peaked; having a spout; *Inf.* chattering; *Mexico* clever, crafty, sly

pie /pie/ *m,* foot; stand, support; stem (of a glass, etc.); standard (of a lamp); *Bot.* trunk, stem; sapling; lees, sediment; *Theat.* cue; foot (measure); custom; (metrics) foot; motive, cause; pretext; (metrics) meter. **p. de cabra,** crowbar. **p. de imprenta,** printer's mark, printer's imprint. **p. de piña,** clubfoot. **p. de rey,** calliper. **p. palmado,** webfoot. **al p. de la letra,** punctiliously. *Inf.* **andar con pies de plomo,** to walk warily. **a p.,** on foot. **a p. firme,** without budging; steadfastly. *Inf.* **buscar tres pies al gato,** to look for something that isn't there; twist a person's words. **de a p.,** on foot. **en p. de guerra,** on a wartime footing. *Inf.* **poner pies en polvorosa,** to quit

piedad /pie'ðað/ *f,* piety; pity, compassion; *Art.* pietà

piedra /'pieðra/ *f,* stone; tablet; *Med.* gravel. **p. de amolar,** whetstone, grindstone. **p. angular,** cornerstone (also *Fig.*). **p. caliza,** limestone. **p. clave,** keystone. **p. de construcción,** building stone; child's block. **p. de toque,** touchstone, test. **p. filosofal,** philosopher's stone. **p. fundamental,** foundation stone. **p. miliaria,** milestone. **p. mortuoria,** tombstone. *Fig. Inf.* **no dejar p. sin remover,** to leave no stone unturned. **no dejar p. sobre p.,** to demolish, destroy completely

piel /piel/ *f,* skin; fur; hide; leather; peel (of some fruits); rind (of bacon). **p. de gallina,** *Fig.* goose flesh. **p. de rata,** horse blanket. **p. de Rusia,** Russian leather.

piélago /'pielago/ *m,* high seas; sea, ocean; glut, superabundance

pienso /'pienso/ *m, Agr.* fodder

pierna /'pierna/ *f, Anat.* leg; *Mech.* shank; leg of a compass. *Inf.* **a p. suelta,** at one's ease. **en piernas,** barelegged

pietista /pie'tista/ *a* pietistic. *mf* pietist

pieza /'piesa; 'pieθa/ *f,* portion; piece; component part; room; *Theat.* play; roll (of cloth); piece (in chess, etc.); coin; piece (of music). **p. de recambio** *or* **p. de repuesto,** spare part. **p. de recibo,** reception room. *Inf.* **quedarse en una p.,** to be struck dumb

pífano /'pifano/ *m,* fife; fife player, fifer

pigmentación /pigmenta'sion; pigmenta'θion/ *f,* pigmentation

pigmento /pig'mento/ *m,* pigment

pignoración /pignora'sion; pignora'θion/ *f,* hypothecation; pawning; mortgage

pignorar /pigno'rar/ *vt* to hypothecate; pawn; mortgage

pigre /'pigre/ *a* lazy; negligent, careless

pigricia /pi'grisia; pi'griθia/ *f,* laziness; negligence *Chile, Peru* trifle

pijama /pi'hama/ *m,* pajamas

pila /'pila/ *f,* trough, basin; heap, pile; *Elec.* battery; *Eccl.* parish; pier, pile; *Phys.* cell. **p. atómica,** atomic pile. **p. bautismal,** *Eccl.* font

pilar /pi'lar/ *m,* fountain basin; milestone; pillar

pilastra /pi'lastra/ *f,* pier, pile; pilaster

pilche /'piltʃe/ *m, Lat. Am.* calabash, gourd

píldora /'pilðora/ *f, Med.* pill; *Inf.* disagreeable news

pileta /pi'leta/ **(de natación)** *f, Argentina,* (swimming) pool

pillador /piya'ðor; piʎa'ðor/ **(-ra)** *a* pillaging, plundering. *n* plunderer

pillaje /pi'yahe; pi'ʎahe/ *m,* pillaging, looting; robbery, theft

pillar /pi'yar; pi'ʎar/ *vt* to pillage; steal, rob; seize, snatch; *Inf.* surprise, find out (in a lie, etc.). **pillarse el dedo,** to get one's finger caught (in a door, etc.)

pillastre /pi'yastre; pi'ʎastre/ *m, Inf.* rogue, ragamuffin

pillería /piye'ria; piʎe'ria/ *f, Inf.* gang of rogues; *Inf.* rogue's trick

pillo /'piyo; 'piʎo/ *m,* rogue, knave

pilón /pi'lon/ *m,* fountain basin; pestle; loaf sugar; pylon; *Mexico, Venezuela* gratuity, tip

pilongo /pi'loŋgo/ *a* thin, lean

píloro /'piloro/ *m,* pylorus

pilotaje /pilo'tahe/ *m,* pilotage; piling, pilework. **examen de p.,** flying test

pilotar /pilo'tar/ *vt* to pilot

pilote /pi'lote/ *m, Engin.* pile

pilotear /pilote'ar/ *vt* to pilot

piloto /pi'loto/ *m,* pilot; mate (in merchant ships). **p. de pruebas,** test pilot

pilsen /'pilsen/ *m, Chile* beer

pimentero /pimen'tero/ *m,* pepper plant; pepper shaker

pimentón /pimen'ton/ *m,* red pepper, cayenne

pimienta /pi'mienta/ *f,* pepper. **p. húngara,** paprika. *Inf.* **ser como una p.,** to be sharp as a needle

pimiento /pi'miento/ *m,* pimento; capsicum; red pepper; pepper plant. **p. de cornetilla,** chili pepper

pimpollo /pim'poyo; pim'poʎo/ *m,* sapling; sprout, shoot; rosebud

pina /'pina/ *f,* conical stone; felloe (of a wheel)

pinacoteca /pinako'teka/ *f,* art gallery, picture gallery

pináculo /pi'nakulo/ *m,* pinnacle, summit; climax, culmination; *Archit.* finial

pinar /pi'nar/ *m,* pinewood

pincel /pin'sel; pin'θel/ *m,* paintbrush; artist, painter; painting technique. **p. para las cejas,** eyebrow pencil

pincelada /pinse'laða; pinθe'laða/ *f,* brushstroke. **dar la última p.,** to add the finishing touch

pincelero /pinse'lero; pinθe'lero/ **(-ra)** *n* seller or maker of paintbrushes; brush box

pinchadura /pintʃa'ðura/ *f,* prick, puncture, piercing; sting; nipping, biting

pinchar /pin'tʃar/ *vt* to prick; puncture; pierce; sting; nip, bite. **no p. ni cortar,** to be ineffective (of persons)

pinchazo /pin'tʃaso; pin'tʃaθo/ *m*, prick; puncture; sting; incitement

pinche /'pintʃe/ *m*, scullion, kitchen boy; *Argentina* minor office clerk; *a, Mexico* damn

pineda /pi'neða/ *f*, pinewood

pingajo /piŋ'gaho/ *m*, *Inf.* tatter, rag

pingajoso /piŋga'hoso/ *a Inf.* tattered, ragged

pingo /'piŋgo/ *m*, *Inf.* tatter, rag; *pl Inf.* cheap clothes

pingüe /'piŋgue/ *a* fat, greasy; fertile, rich

pingüino /piŋ'guino/ *m*, penguin

pino /'pino/ *a* steep. *m*, *Bot.* pine, deal; *Poet.* ship. **p. de tea,** pitch pine. **p. silvestre,** red fir

pinta /'pinta/ *f*, spot; marking; mark; fleck; look, appearance; pint (measure); drop, drip; spot ball (in billiards)

pintamonas /pinta'monas/ *mf Inf.* dauber

pintar /pin'tar/ *vt* to paint; describe, picture; exaggerate; *vi* show, manifest itself; *vr* make up (one's face). *Inf.* **pintarse solo para,** to be very good at, excel at

pintiparado /pintipa'raðo/ *a* most similar, very alike; fitting, apposite

pintiparar /pintipa'rar/ *vt Inf.* to compare

pintor /pin'tor/ **(-ra)** *n* painter, artist. **p. callejero,** sidewalk artist, pavement artist. **p. de brocha gorda,** house painter

pintoresco /pinto'resko/ *a* picturesque, quaint, pretty

pintorrear /pintorre'ar/ *vt Inf.* to daub, paint badly

pintura /pin'tura/ *f*, painting; paint, pigment; picture, painting; description. **p. a la aguada,** watercolor painting. **p. al fresco,** fresco. **p. al látex,** latex paint. **p. al óleo,** oil painting. **p. al pastel,** pastel drawing

pinturería /pinture'ria/ *f*, paint store

pinturero /pintu'rero/ *a Inf.* affected, conceited; dandified, overdressed

pinza /'pinsa; 'pinθa/ *f*, clamp. **p. de la ropa,** clothes peg

pinzas /'pinsas; 'pinθas/ *f pl*, pincers; pliers; tweezers; forceps. **p. hemostáticas,** arterial forceps

piña /'piɲa/ *f*, pineapple; cluster, knot (of people, etc.); pinecone

piñón /pi'ɲon/ *m*, pine nut; *Mech.* pinion, chain wheel

pío /'pio/ *a* pious; compassionate; good; piebald. *m*, chirping, cheep; *Inf.* longing

piocha /'piotʃa/ *f*, *Lat. Am.* pickax

piojo /'pioho/ *m*, louse

piojoso /pio'hoso/ *a* lousy; avaricious, stingy

piola /'piola/ *f*, *Lat. Am.* cord, string; rope; tether

pionero /pio'nero/ *m*, pioneer

piorrea /pio'rrea/ *f*, pyorrhea

pipa /'pipa/ *f*, barrel, cask; tobacco pipe; pip (of fruits)

pipar /pi'par/ *vi* to smoke a pipe

pipeta /pi'peta/ *f*, pipette

pipiar /pi'piar/ *vi* to chirp, twitter

pique /'pike/ *m*, pique, resentment. **a p. de,** on the verge of, about to. **echar a p.,** *Naut.* to sink; destroy. **irse a p.,** to sink, founder

piqueta /pi'keta/ *f*, pick, mattock; mason's hammer

piquete /pi'kete/ *m*, puncture, small wound; *Mil.* picket; pole, stake; small hole (in garments); picket (in strikes)

pira /'pira/ *f*, funeral pyre; bonfire

piragua /pi'ragua/ *f*, piragua, canoe

pirámide /pi'ramiðe/ *f*, pyramid

piraña /pi'raɲa/ *f* piranha

pirarse /pi'rarse/ *vr Inf.* to slip away

pirata /pi'rata/ *a* piratical *mf* pirate; savage, cruel person

piratear /pirate'ar/ *vi* to play the pirate

piratería /pirate'ria/ *f*, piracy; plunder, robbery

pirático /pi'ratiko/ *a* piratical

pirca /'pirka/ *f*, *Lat. Am.* dry-stone wall

pirenaico, pirineo /pire'naiko, piri'neo/ *a* Pyrenean

pirético /pi'retiko/ *a* pyretic

piriforme /piri'forme/ *a* pear-shaped

Pirineos, los /piri'neos, los/ the Pyrenees

piropear /pirope'ar/ *vt Inf.* to pay compliments to

piropo /pi'ropo/ *m*, carbuncle; *Inf.* catcall, street comments, compliment. **echar piropos,** to pay compliments

pirotécnico /piro'tekniko/ *a* pyrotechnical. *m*, pyrotechnist

pirrarse /pi'rrarse/ *vr Inf.* to desire ardently

pírrico /'pirriko/ *a* Pyrrhic

pirueta /pi'rueta/ *f*, pirouette, twirl

pisada /pi'saða/ *f*, treading, stepping; footprint, footstep; stepping on a person's foot. **seguir las pisadas de alguien,** *Fig.* to follow in someone's footsteps, imitate someone

pisano /pi'sano/ **(-na)** *a* and *n* Pisan

pisapapeles /pisapa'peles/ *m*, paperweight

pisar /pi'sar/ *vt* to tread upon; trample upon; crush; *Mus.* press (strings); trespass upon; *vr*, *Argentina* to be mistaken

pisaverde /pisa'βerðe/ *m*, *Inf.* fop, dandy

piscicultura /pissikul'tura; pisθikul'tura/ *f*, pisciculture, fish farming

piscina /pis'sina; pis'θina/ *f*, fishpond; swimming pool; *Eccl.* piscina

piscolabis /pisko'laβis/ *m*, *Inf.* snack, light meal

piso /'piso/ *m*, treading, trampling; story, floor; flooring; apartment. **p. bajo,** ground floor

pisón /pi'son/ *m*, rammer, ram

pisotear /pisote'ar/ *vt* to trample; crush under foot; tread on; step on; humiliate, treat inconsiderately

pisoteo /piso'teo/ *m*, trampling under foot; treading

pista /'pista/ *f*, track, trail (of animals); circus ring; racetrack, racecourse. **p. de patinar,** skating rink. **p. de vuelo,** *Aer.* landing field. *Inf.* **seguir la p. a,** to spy upon

pistacho /pis'tatʃo/ *m*, pistachio

pistar /pis'tar/ *v* to pestle, pound

pistero /pis'tero/ *m*, feeding cup

pistilo /pis'tilo/ *m*, pistil

pisto, /'pisto/ *m*, *Central America*, *Slang.* dough (money)

pistola /pis'tola/ *f*, pistol. **p. ametralladora,** machine gun.

pistolera /pisto'lera/ *f*, holster; pistol case

pistolero /pisto'lero/ *m*, gangster

pistoletazo /pistole'taso; pistole'taθo/ *m*, pistol shot; pistol wound

pistón /pis'ton/ *m*, *Mus.* piston; *Mil.* percussion cap; *Mech.* piston

pitada /pi'taða/ *f*, blast on a whistle, whistling; impertinence

pitagórico /pita'goriko/ **(-ca)** *a* and *n* Pythagorean

pitanza /pi'tansa; pi'tanθa/ *f*, alms, charity; *Inf.* daily food; pittance, scanty remuneration

pitar /pi'tar/ *vi* to play the whistle; *vt* pay (debts); smoke; give alms to

pitido /pi'tiðo/ *m*, blast on a whistle; whistling (of birds)

pitillera /piti'yera; piti'ʎera/ *f*, cigarette case; female cigarette maker

pito /'pito/ *m*, whistle; *Mus.* fife. *Inf.* **Cuando pitos flautas, cuando flautas pitos,** It's always the unexpected that happens. *Inf.* **no valer un p.,** to be not worth a straw

pitoflero /pito'flero/ **(-ra)** *n* mediocre performer (gen. on a wind instrument); *Inf.* talebearer, gossip

pitón /pi'ton/ *m*, *Zool.* python; nascent horn (of goats, etc.); spout; protuberance; *Bot.* sprout

pitonisa /pito'nisa/ *f*, *Myth.* pythoness; witch, enchantress

pitorrearse /pitorre'arse/ *vr* to ridicule, mock

pituitario /pitui'tario/ *a* pituitary

pituso /pi'tuso/ *a* small and amusing (of children)

pivote /pi'βote/ *m*, pivot, swivel, gudgeon

piyama /pi'yama/ *m*, pajamas

pizarra /pi'sarra; pi'θarra/ *f*, slate; blackboard

pizarral /pisa'rral; piθa'rral/ *m*. **pizarrería** *f*, slate quarry

pizarrín /pisa'rrin; piθa'rrin/ *m*, slate pencil

pizca /'piska; 'piθka/ *f*, *Inf.* atom, speck, crumb; jot, whit. **¡Ni p.!** Not a scrap!

pizpireta /pispi'reta; piθpi'reta/ *a f, Inf.* coquettish; smart; dressed up

placa /'plaka/ *f,* plate, disk; *Art.* plaque; *Photo.* plate; star (insignia). **p. recordatorio,** commemorative plaque

placabilidad /plakaβili'ðað/ *f,* placability, appeasability

pláceme /'plaseme; 'plaθeme/ *m,* congratulation

placentero /plasen'tero; plaθen'tero/ *a* agreeable, pleasant

placer /pla'ser; pla'θer/ *vt irr* to please, give pleasure to, gratify. *m, Naut.* reef, sandbank; pleasure; wish, desire; permission, consent; entertainment, diversion. **a p.,** at one's convenience; at leisure. *Pres. Ind.* **plazco, places,** etc. *Preterite* **plugo,** *Pres. Subjunc.* **plazca,** etc. *Imperf. Subjunc.* **pluguiese,** etc.

placibilidad /plasiβili'ðað; plaθiβili'ðað/ *f,* agreeableness, pleasantness

placible /pla'siβle; pla'θiβle/ *a* agreeable, pleasant

placidez /plasi'ðes; plaθi'ðeθ/ *f,* placidity, calmness, serenity

plácido /'plasiðo; 'plaθiðo/ *a* placid, calm, serene

placiente /pla'siente; pla'θiente/ *a* pleasing, attractive

plácito /'plasito; 'plaθito/ *m,* decision, judgment, opinion

plafón /pla'fon/ *m,* ceiling light; *Archit.* panel

plaga /'plaga/ *f,* plague; disaster, calamity; epidemic; glut; pest; grief

plagar /pla'gar/ *vt (with de)* to infect with; *vr (with de)* be covered with; be overrun by; be infested with

plagiar /pla'hiar/ *vt* to plagiarize, copy; kidnap, hold for ransom

plagiario /pla'hiario/ **(-ia)** *n* plagiarist; *Lat. Am.* kidnapper

plagio /'plahio/ *m,* plagiary; kidnapping

plan /plan/ *m,* plan; scheme; plane. **p. quinquenal,** five-year plan

plana /'plana/ *f,* sheet, page; mason's trowel; plain. **p. mayor,** *(Mil. Nav.)* staff

planadora /plana'ðora/ *f,* steamroller

plancha /'plantʃa/ *f,* sheet, slab, plate; iron; horizontal suspension (in gymnastics); *Naut.* gangway, gangplank; *Inf.* howler

planchado /plan'tʃaðo/ *m,* ironing; ironing to be done or already finished

planchador /plantʃa'ðor/ **(-ra)** *n* ironer

planchar /plan'tʃar/ *vt* to iron, press with an iron

planchear /plantʃe'ar/ *vt* to plate (with metal)

planeador /planea'ðor/ *m, Aer.* glider

planear /plane'ar/ *vt* to plan out; make plans for; *vi Aer.* glide

planeo /pla'neo/ *m, Aer.* glide

planeta /pla'neta/ *m,* planet

planetario /plane'tario/ *a* planetary. *m,* planetarium

planicie /pla'nisie; pla'niθie/ *f,* levelness, evenness; plain

planilla /pla'nija; pla'niʎa/ *f, Lat. Am.* application, application form, blank; payroll; list; ballot

plano /'plano/ *a* flat, level; plane. *m, Geom.* plane; plan, map; *Aer.* aileron, wing

planta /'planta/ *f, Bot.* plant; sole (of the foot); plantation; layout, plan; position of the feet (in dancing, fencing); scheme, project. **p. baja,** ground floor. **p. vivaz,** perennial plant. *Inf.* **buena p.,** good appearance

plantación /planta'sion; planta'θion/ *f,* planting; plantation, nursery

plantador /planta'ðor/ **(-ra)** *n* planter. *m, Agr.* dibble. *f.* **plantadora,** mechanical planter

plantar /plan'tar/ *vt* to plant; erect; place; found, set up; pose (a problem); raise (a question, etc.); *Inf.* leave in the lurch; *vr* take up one's position; jib (of horses); oppose

planteamiento /plantea'miento/ *m,* execution; putting into practice; planning; statement (of problems)

plantel /plan'tel/ *m,* nursery garden; training school, nursery

plantilla /plan'tiya; plan'tiʎa/ *f,* young plant; insole (of shoes); *Mech.* template, jig

plantío /plan'tio/ *m,* plantation, afforestation; planting. *a* planted or ready for planting (ground)

plantón /plan'ton/ *m,* plant or sapling ready for transplanting; *Bot.* cutting; doorkeeper, porter. **dar un p. (a),** to keep (a person) waiting a long time

plañidero /plaɲi'ðero/ *a* mournful, piteous, anguished

plañido /pla'niðo/ *m,* lament, weeping, wailing

plañir /pla'ɲir/ *vi* and *vt irr* to lament, wail, weep. See **tañer**

plasma /'plasma/ *m,* plasma

plasmar /plas'mar/ *vt* to mold, throw (pottery)

plástica /'plastika/ *f,* art of clay modeling; plastic

plástico /'plastiko/ *a* plastic; flexible, malleable, soft

plata /'plata/ *f,* silver; silver (coins); *Lat. Am.,* money; white. **p. labrada,** silverware

plataforma /plata'forma/ *f,* platform; running board (of a train); *Rail.* turntable

platal /pla'tal/ *m, Lat. Am.* wealth

plátano /'platano/ *m,* banana tree, banana; plantain; plane tree

platea /pla'tea/ *f, Theat.* pit. **butaca de p.,** pit stall

plateado /plate'aðo/ *a* silvered; silver-plated; silvery

plateador /platea'ðor/ *m,* plater

platear /plate'ar/ *vt* to electroplate, silver

platería /plate'ria/ *f,* silversmith's art or trade; silversmith's shop or workshop

platero /pla'tero/ *m,* silversmith; jeweler

plática /'platika/ *f,* conversation; exhortation, sermon; address, discourse

platicar /plati'kar/ *vt* and *vi* to converse (about)

platija /pla'tiha/ *f,* plaice

platillo /pla'tiyo; pla'tiʎo/ *m,* saucer; kitty (in card games); pan (of a scale); *pl* cymbals

platinado /plati'naðo/ *m,* plating

platino /pla'tino/ *m,* platinum

platívolo /pla'tiβolo/ *m,* flying saucer

plato /'plato/ *m,* plate; dish; *Cul.* course, dish; pan (of a scale). **p. sopero,** soup plate. **p. trinchero,** meat dish. *Inf.* **comer en un mismo p.,** to be on intimate terms. **nada entre dos platos,** much ado about nothing

platónico /pla'toniko/ *a* Platonic

platonismo /plato'nismo/ *m,* Platonism

platudo, -a /pla'tuðo/ *mf,* rich, wealthy, well-heeled

plausible /plau'siβle/ *a* plausible, reasonable; commendable

playa /'plaia/ *f,* beach, seashore, strand

plaza /'plasa; 'plaθa/ *f,* square (in a town, etc.); marketplace; fortified town; space; duration; employment, post.; *Com.* market. **p. de armas,** garrison town; military camp. **p. de toros,** bullring. **p. fuerte,** strong place, fortress. **sentar p.,** to enlist in the army

plazo /'plaso; 'plaθo/ *m,* term, duration; expiration of term, date of payment; installment. **a plazos,** *Com.* by installments, on the installment system

plazoleta /plaso'leta; plaθo'leta/ *f,* small square (in gardens, etc.)

pleamar /plea'mar/ *f, Naut.* high water

plebe /'pleβe/ *f,* common people; rabble, mob

plebeyo /ple'βeio/ **(-ya)** *a* plebeian. *n* commoner, plebeian

plebiscito /pleβis'sito; pleβis'θito/ *m,* plebiscite

plectro /'plektro/ *m,* plectrum, pick (musical instruments)

plegable /ple'gaβle/ *a* foldable

plegadera /plega'ðera/ *f,* folder; folding knife; paper folder

plegadizo /plega'ðiso; plega'ðiθo/ *a* folding; collapsible; jointed

plegado /ple'gaðo/ *m,* pleating; folding

plegador /plega'ðor/ *a* folding. *m,* folding machine

plegadura /plega'ðura/ *f,* folding, doubling; fold, pleat

plegar /ple'gar/ *vt irr* to fold; pleat; *Sew.* gather; *vr* submit, give in. See **acertar**

plegaria /ple'garia/ *f,* fervent prayer

pleitear /pleite'ar/ *vt* to go to court about; indulge in litigation

pleitista /plei'tista/ *a* quarrelsome, litigious

pleito /'pleito/ *m*, action, lawsuit; dispute, quarrel; litigation. **p. de familia**, family squabble. **ver el p.**, *Law.* to try a case

plenamente /plena'mente/ *adv* fully, entirely

plenario /ple'nario/ *a* full, complete; *Law.* plenary

plenilunio /pleni'lunio/ *m*, full moon

plenipotencia /plenipo'tensia; plenipo'tenθia/ *f*, full powers (diplomatic, etc.)

plenipotenciario /plenipoten'siario; plenipoten'θiario/ *a* and *m*, plenipotentiary

plenitud /pleni'tuð/ *f*, fullness, completeness; plenitude, abundance

pleno /'pleno/ *a* full. *m*, general meeting

pleonasmo /pleo'nasmo/ *m*, *Gram.* pleonasm

pleonástico /pleo'nastiko/ *a* pleonastic

pleuresía /pleure'sia/ *f*, pleurisy

plexo /'plekso/ *m*, plexus

pliego /'pliego/ *m*, sheet (of paper); letter, packet of papers

pliegue /'pliege/ *m*, fold, pleat; *Sew.* gather

plinto /'plinto/ *m*, *Archit.* plinth (of a column); baseboard

plisar /pli'sar/ *vt* to pleat; fold

plomada /plo'maða/ *f*, plummet; sounding lead; plumb, lead

plomería /plome'ria/ *f*, plumbing; plumbing business; lead roofing

plomero /plo'mero/ *m*, plumber

plomizo /plo'miso; plo'miθo/ *a* lead-like; lead-colored, gray

plomo /'plomo/ *m*, lead (metal); plummet; bullet; *Inf.* bore, tedious person

pluma /'pluma/ *f*, feather; pen; plumage; quill; penmanship; writer; writing profession. **p. estilográfica**, fountain pen. **a vuela p.**, as the pen writes, written in a hurry

plumado /plu'maðo/ *a* feathered

pluma fuente /'pluma 'fuente/ *f*, *Lat. Am.* fountain pen

plumaje /plu'mahe/ *m*, plumage, feathers; plume

plúmbeo /'plumbeo/ *a* plumbeous, leaden

plúmeo /'plumeo/ *a* feathered, plumed

plumero /plu'mero/ *m*, feather duster; plume, feather; plumage

plumón /plu'mon/ *m*, down; feather bed; *Lat. Am.* felt-tipped pen

plumoso /plu'moso/ *a* feathered

plural /plu'ral/ *a* and *m*, plural

pluralidad /plurali'ðað/ *f*, plurality; multitude, number

pluralizar /plurali'sar; plurali'θar/ *vt* to pluralize

plurilingüe /pluri'liŋgue/ *a* multilingual

pluscuamperfecto /pluskuamper'fekto/ *m*, pluperfect

plusmarquista /plusmar'kista/ *mf* *Sports.* record-holder

plutocracia /pluto'krasia; pluto'kraθia/ *f*, plutocracy

plutócrata /plu'tokrata/ *mf* plutocrat

plutocrático /pluto'kratiko/ *a* plutocratic

pluviómetro /plu'βiometro/ *m*, rain gauge

poblacho /po'βlatʃo/ *m*, miserable town or village

población /poβla'sion; poβla'θion/ *f*, peopling; population; town

poblado /po'βlaðo/ *m*, inhabited place; town; village

poblador /poβla'ðor/ **(-ra)** *a* populating. *n* colonist, settler

poblar /po'βlar/ *vt irr* to colonize; people, populate; breed fast; stock, supply; *vr* put forth leaves (of trees). See **contar**

pobre /'poβre/ *a* poor; indigent, needy; mediocre; unfortunate; humble, meek. *mf* beggar, pauper, needy person. *Inf.* **ser p. de solemnidad**, to be down and out

pobrero /po'βrero/ *m*, *Eccl.* distributor of alms

pobretería /poβrete'ria/ *f*, poverty; needy people

pobretón /poβre'ton/ *a* extremely needy

pobreza /po'βresa; po'βreθa/ *f*, poverty, need; shortage; timidity; *Mineral.* baseness; poorness (of soil, etc.)

pocero /po'sero; po'θero/ *m*, well digger

pocilga /po'silga; po'θilga/ *f*, pigsty; *Inf.* filthy place

poción /po'sion; po'θion/ *f*, potion, drink; mixture, dose

poco /'poko/ *a* little, scanty; *pl* few. *m*, small amount, a little. *adv* little; shortly, in a little while. **p. a p.**, by degrees, little by little; slowly. **p. más o menos**, more or less, approximately. **por p.**, almost, nearly (always used with the present tense, e.g. *Por p. me caigo*, I almost fell). **tener en p.** (a), to have a poor opinion of; undervalue

poda /'poða/ *f*, *Agr.* pruning; pruning season

podadera /poða'ðera/ *f*, pruning knife

podar /po'ðar/ *vt Agr.* to prune, trim

poder /po'ðer/ *m*, power; authority, jurisdiction; *Law.* power of attorney; strength; ability; proxy; efficacy; possession; *pl* authority; power of attorney. **los poderes constituidos**, the established authorities; the powers that be. **p. de adquisición**, purchasing power. **casarse por poderes**, to be married by proxy

poder /po'ðer/ *vt irr* to be able to (e.g. *Podemos comprar estas naranjas*, We can (are able to) buy these oranges). **Dice que la calamidad podía haberse evitado**, He says that the disaster could have been averted). **p.** also expresses possibility (e.g. *Pueden haber ido a la ciudad*, They may have gone to the city. *¡Qué distinta pudo haber sido su vida!* How different his life might have been!). *impers* be possible. **a más no p.**, of necessity, without being able to help it; to the utmost. **no p. con**, to be unable to control or manage. **no p. hacer más**, to have no alternative, have to; be unable to do more. **no p. menos de**, to be obliged to, have no alternative but. **no p. contener su emoción**, to be overcome with emotion. **no p. ver a**, to hate (persons). *impers* **Puede que venga esta tarde**, He may come (perhaps he will come) this afternoon. *Pres. Part.* **pudiendo**. *Pres. Ind.* **puedo, puedes, puede, pueden**. *Fut.* **podré**, etc. *Condit.* **podría**, etc. *Preterite* **pude, pudiste**, etc. *Pres. Subjunc.* **pueda, puedas, pueda, puedan**. *Imperf. Subjunc.* **pudiese**, etc.

poderío /poðe'rio/ *m*, power, authority; sway, rule; dominion; wealth

poderoso /poðe'roso/ *a* powerful; opulent; effective, efficacious; mighty, magnificent

podredumbre /poðre'ðumbre/ *f*, decay; pus; *Fig.* canker, anguish

podredura, podrición /poðre'ðura, poðri'sion; poðre'ðura, poðri'θion/ *f*, putrefaction; decay

podrido /po'ðriðo/ *a* rotten; putrid; corrupt; decayed

podrir /po'ðrir/ *vt* See **pudrir**

poema /po'ema/ *m*, poem. **p. sinfónico**, tone poem

poesía /poe'sia/ *f*, poetry, verse; lyric, poem

poeta /po'eta/ *m*, poet

poetastro /poe'tastro/ *m*, poetaster

poética /po'etika/ *f*, poetics

poético /po'etiko/ *a* poetical

poetisa /poe'tisa/ *f*, poetess

poetizar /poeti'sar; poeti'θar/ *vi* to write verses; *vt* poeticize

polaco /po'lako/ **(-ca)** *a* Polish. *n* Pole. *m*, Polish (language)

polainas /po'lainas/ *f pl*, leggings, puttees, gaiters

polar /po'lar/ *a* polar

polaridad /polari'ðað/ *f*, polarity; polarization

polarización /polarisa'sion; polariθa'θion/ *f*, polarization

polarizar /polari'sar; polari'θar/ *vt* to polarize

polca /'polka/ *f*, polka

polea /po'lea/ *f*, pulley; *Naut.* block

polémica /po'lemika/ *f*, polemic, controversy, dispute

polémico /po'lemiko/ *a* polemical

polemista /pole'mista/ *mf* disputant, controversialist

polen /'polen/ *m*, pollen

polichinela /politʃi'nela/ *m*, Punchinello

policía /poli'sia; poli'θia/ *f*, police; government, polity, administration; civility, courtesy; cleanliness, tidiness. *m*, policeman. **p. urbana**, city police

policíaco /poli'siako; poli'θiako/ *a* police; detective

policial /poli'sial; poli'θial/ *a* police; *m*, *Lat. Am.* police officer

policromo /poli'kromo/ *a* polychrome

poliedro /po'lieðro/ *m*, polyhedron
polifacético /polifa'setiko; polifa'θetiko/ *a* many-sided
polifonía /polifo'nia/ *f*, polyphony
polifónico /poli'foniko/ *a* polyphonic
poligamia /poli'gamia/ *f*, polygamy
polígamo /po'ligamo/ **(-ma)** *a* polygamous. *n* polygamist
poliglota /poli'gloto/ **(-ta)** *n* polyglot. *f*, polyglot Bible
polígono /po'ligono/ *a* polygonal. *m*, polygon
polilla /po'liya; po'liʎa/ *f*, moth; moth grub; destroyer, ravager
polimorfismo /polimor'fismo/ *m*, *Chem.* polymorphism
polimorfo /poli'morfo/ *a* polymorphous
Polinesia /poli'nesia/ Polynesia
polinesio /poli'nesio/ *a* and *n* Polynesian
polinización /polinisa'sion; poliniθa'θion/ *f*, pollination
poliomielitis /poliomie'litis/ *f*, poliomyelitis, polio
pólipo /'polipo/ *m*, *Zool.* polyp; octopus; *Med.* polyp
polisílabo /poli'silaβo/ *a* polysyllabic. *m*, polysyllable
polista /po'lista/ *mf* polo player
politécnico /poli'tekniko/ *a* polytechnic
politeísmo /polite'ismo/ *m*, polytheism
politeísta /polite'ista/ *a* polytheistic. *mf* polytheist
política /po'litika/ *f*, politics; civility, courtesy; diplomacy; tact; policy
politicastro /politi'kastro/ *m*, corrupt politician
político /po'litiko/ *a* political; civil, courteous; in-law, by marriage (relationships). *m*, politician
politiquear /politike'ar/ *vi Inf.* to dabble in politics, talk politics
politizarse /politi'sarse; politi'θarse/ *vr* to enter the political arena
póliza /'polisa; 'poliθa/ *f*, *Com.* policy; *Com.* draft; share certificate; revenue stamp; admission ticket; lampoon. **p. a prima fija,** fixed-premium policy. **p. de seguros,** insurance policy. **p. dotal,** endowment policy
polizón /poli'son; poli'θon/ *m*, loafer, tramp; stowaway; bustle (of a dress)
polla /'poya; 'poʎa/ *f*, pullet; *Inf.* flapper, young woman
pollada /po'yaða; po'ʎaða/ *f*, brood, hatch (especially of chickens)
pollastro /po'yastro; po'ʎastro/ **(-ra)** *n* pullet.
pollera /po'yera; po'ʎera/ *f*, female poultry breeder or seller; chicken coop; go-cart; *Argentina, Chile* skirt
pollería /poye'ria; poʎe'ria/ *f*, poultry market or shop
pollero /po'yero; po'ʎero/ *m*, poultry breeder; poulterer. *m*, hen coop; *Lat. Am.* gambler
pollino /po'yino; po'ʎino/ **(-na)** *n* young ass; donkey
pollo /'poyo; 'poʎo/ *m*, chicken; *Inf.* youth, stripling; *Fig. Inf.* downy bird. *Inf.* **pera,** young blood, lad. **sacar pollos,** to hatch chickens
polo /'polo/ *m*, pole (all meanings); *Fig.* support; popular Andalusian song; *Sports.* polo. **de p. a p.,** from pole to pole
polonés /polo'nes/ **(-esa)** *a* Polish. *n* Pole
Polonia /po'lonia/ Poland
poltrón /pol'tron/ *a* lazy, idle
poltronear /poltrone'ar/ *vi* to loaf about
poltronería /poltrone'ria/ *f*, idleness, laziness
polución /polu'sion; polu'θion/ *f*, *Med.* ejaculation
polvareda /polβa'reða/ *f*, dust cloud; storm, agitation
polvera /pol'βera/ *f*, powder bowl; powder puff; powder compact
polvillo /pol'βiyo; pol'βiʎo/ *m*, *Lat. Am.* blight
polvo /'polβo/ *m*, dust; powder; pinch (of snuff, etc.); *pl* face or dusting powder. **Se hizo como por polvos de la madre celestina,** It was done as if by magic. *Inf.* **limpio de p. y paja,** gratis, for nothing; net (of profit)
pólvora /'polβora/ *f*, gunpowder; bad temper. **p. de algodón,** guncotton.
polvorear /polβore'ar/ *vt* to powder, dust with powder

polvoriento /polβo'riento/ *a* dusty; powdery, covered with powder
polvorín /polβo'rin/ *m*, very fine powder; powder magazine; powder flask
polvoroso /polβo'roso/ *a* dusty; covered with powder
pomada /po'maða/ *f*, pomade; salve, ointment
pomar /po'mar/ *m*, orchard (especially an apple orchard)
pómez /'pomes; 'pomeθ/ *f*, pumice stone (**piedra p.**)
pomo /'pomo/ *m*, *Bot.* pome; pomander; nosegay; pommel, hilt (of a sword); handle; rose (of watering can)
pomología /pomolo'hia/ *f*, pomology, art of fruit growing
pompa /'pompa/ *f*, pomp, splendor; ceremonial procession; air bubble; peacock's outspread tail; *Naut.* pump; billowing of clothes in the wind
Pompeya /pom'peia/ Pompeii
pomposidad /pomposi'ðað/ *f*, pomposity
pomposo /pom'poso/ *a* stately, ostentatious, magnificent; inflated, pompous; florid, bombastic
pómulo /'pomulo/ *m*, cheekbone
ponchada /pon'tʃaða/ *f Lat. Am.* great deal, large amount
ponche /'pontʃe/ *m*, punch, toddy
ponchera /pon'tʃera/ *f*, punch bowl
poncho /'pontʃo/ *a* lazy, negligent. *m*, military cloak; poncho, cape
ponderación /pondera'sion; pondera'θion/ *f*, weighing; reflection, consideration; exaggeration
ponderador /pondera'ðor/ *a* reflective, deliberate; exaggerated
ponderar /ponde'rar/ *vt* to weigh; consider, ponder; exaggerate; overpraise
ponderosidad /ponderosi'ðað/ *f*, heaviness; ponderousness, dullness
ponderoso /ponde'roso/ *a* heavy; ponderous; circumspect
ponedero /pone'ðero/ *a* egg-laying (of hens). *m*, nest
ponencia /po'nensia/ *f*, office, clause, section; office of referee or arbitrator; report, referendum, conference
poner /po'ner/ *vt irr* to place, put; arrange; set (the table); bet, stake; appoint (to an office); call, name; lay (eggs); set down (in writing); calculate, count; suppose; leave to a person's judgment; risk; contribute; prepare; need, take; cause, inspire (emotions); make, cause; adapt; add; cause to become (angry, etc.); insult; praise; (*with prep a + infin*) begin to. **p. a contribución,** to lay under contribution, turn to account, utilize. **ponerle el cascabel al gato** *or* **el collar al gato,** to bell the cat. **p. los cuernos (a),** to cuckold. **p. al corriente,** to bring up to date, inform. **p. a prueba,** to test. **p. casa,** to set up house. *Inf.* **p. colorado a,** to make blush. **p. coto a,** to put a stop to, check. **p. en comparación,** to compare. **p. conato en,** to put a great deal of effort into. **p. en cotejo,** to collate. **p. en limpio,** to make a fair copy (of). **p. en marcha,** to start, set in motion. **p. en práctica,** to put into effect. **p. por caso,** to take as an example (e.g. *Pongamos por caso...* For example,...). **p. por encima (de),** to prefer. *vr* to place oneself; become; put on (garments, etc.); dirty or stain oneself; set (of the sun, stars); oppose; deck oneself, dress oneself up; arrive; (*with prep a + infin*) begin to. **ponerse al corriente,** to bring oneself up to date. **ponerse al día,** to update. **ponerse bien,** to improve; get better (in health). **ponerse colorado,** to blush, flush. **p. una base racional a la fe,** to give faith a rational foundation. **p. los cimientos de,** lay the foundation of, lay the foundations for. **p. una conferencia,** to make a long-distance call. *Pres. Ind.* **pongo, pones, etc.** *Fut.* **pondré, etc.** *Condit.* **pondría, etc.** *Imperat.* **pon.** *Past Part.* **puesto.** *Preterite* **puse, pusiste, etc.** *Pres. Subjunc.* **ponga, etc.** *Imperf. Subjunc.* **pusiese, etc.**
pongo /'poŋgo/ *m Bolivia, Peru* Native American serf
pongueaje /poŋgue'ahe/ *m* **Bolivia, Peru** Native American serfdom
ponientada /ponien'taða/ *f*, steady west wind
poniente /po'niente/ *m*, west; west wind

pontazgo /pon'tasgo; pon'taθgo/ *m*, bridge toll

pontear /ponte'ar/ *vt* to bridge; make bridges

pontificado /pontifi'kaðo/ *m*, pontificate, papacy

pontífice /pon'tifise; pon'tifiθe/ *m*, pontifex; pope, pontiff; archbishop; bishop

pontón /pon'ton/ *m*, *Mil.* pontoon; hulk used as a prison, hospital, store, etc.; wooden bridge

pontonero /ponto'nero/ *m*, pontonier, military engineer

ponzoña /pon'soɲa; pon'θoɲa/ *f*, poison, venom

ponzoñoso /ponso'ɲoso; ponθo'ɲoso/ *a* poisonous, venomous; noxious; harmful

popa /'popa/ *f*, *Naut.* stern, poop. **en p.**, abaft, astern, aft

popelina /pope'lina/ *f*, poplin

popote /po'pote/ *m*, *Mexico* (drinking) straw

populachería /populatʃe'ria/ *f*, cheap popularity with the rabble

populachero /popula'tʃero/ *a* mob, vulgar

populacho /popu'latʃo/ *m*, mob, rabble

popular /popu'lar/ *a* popular

popularidad /populari'ðað/ *f*, popularity

popularizar /populari'sar; populari'θar/ *vt* to popularize; *vr* grow popular

populoso /popu'loso/ *a* populous, crowded

popurrí /popu'rri/ *m*, *Cul.* stew; potpourri; miscellany

poquedad /poke'ðað/ *f*, paucity, scarcity; timidity, cowardice; trifle, mere nothing

poquísimo /po'kisimo/ *a sup poco* very little

poquito /po'kito/ *m*, very little

por /por/ *prep* for; by; through, along; during; because, as (e.g. *Lo desecharon p. viejo,* They threw it away because it was old); however (e.g. *p. bonito que sea,* however pretty it is); during; in order to (e.g. *Lo hice p. no ofenderla,* I did it in order not to offend her); toward, in favor of, for; for the sake of; on account of, by reason of (e.g. *No pudo venir p. estar enfermo,* He could not come on account of his illness); via, by (e.g. *p. correo aéreo,* by airmail); as for (e.g. *P. mí, lo rechazo,* As for me, I refuse it. *p. mi cuenta,* to my way of thinking; on my own); in exchange for (e.g. *Me vendió dos libros p. seis dólares,* He sold me two books for six dollars); in the name of; as a substitute for, instead of (e.g. *Hace mi trabajo p. mí,* He is doing my work for me); per. **Por** has several uses: 1. Introduces the agent after a passive (e.g. *La novela fue escrita p. él,* The novel was written by him). 2. Expresses movement through, along or about (e.g. *Andaban p. la calle,* They were walking along (or down) the street). 3. Denotes time at or during which an action occurs (e.g. *Ocurrió p. entonces un acontecimiento de importancia,* About that time an important event occurred). 4. Expresses rate or proportion (e.g. *seis por ciento,* six percent). 5. With certain verbs, means "to be" and expresses vague futurity (e.g. *El libro queda p. escribir,* The book remains to be written). **p. cortesía,** by courtesy, out of politeness. **p. cortesía de,** by courtesy of. **p. escrito,** in writing. **p. fas or p. nefas,** by fair means or foul; at any cost. **p. mucho que,** however great, however much; in spite of, notwithstanding. **¿P. qué?** Why? **p. si acaso,** in case, if by chance. **estar p.,** to be about to; be inclined to. **P. un clavo se pierde la herradura,** For want of a nail, the shoe was lost.

porcelana /porse'lana; porθe'lana/ *f*, porcelain, china; chinaware

porcentaje /porsen'tahe; porθen'tahe/ *m*, percentage

porche /'portʃe/ *m*, porch, portico

porcino /por'sino; por'θino/ *a* porcine. *m*, young pig; bruise

porción /por'sion; por'θion/ *f*, portion; *Com.* share; *Inf.* crowd; allowance, pittance

porcionista /porsio'nista; porθio'nista/ *mf* shareholder; sharer; boarding school student

pordiosear /porðiose'ar/ *vi* to ask alms, beg

pordioseo /porðio'seo/ *m*, asking alms, begging

pordiosero /porðio'sero/ **(-ra)** *a* begging. *n* beggar

porfía /por'fia/ *f*, obstinacy; importunity; tenacity. **a p.,** in competition

porfiadamente /porfiaða'mente/ *adv* obstinately

porfiado /por'fiaðo/ *a* obstinate, obdurate, persistent

porfiar /por'fiar/ *vi* to be obstinate, insist; persist

pórfido /'porfiðo/ *m*, porphyry

pormenor /porme'nor/ *m*, particular, detail (gen. *pl*); secondary matter

pormenorizar /pormenori'sar; pormenori'θar/ *vt* to describe in detail

pornografía /pornogra'fia/ *f*, pornography

pornográfico /porno'grafiko/ *a* pornographic, obscene

poro /'poro/ *m*, pore; *Lat. Am. also* leek

porongo /po'roŋgo/ *m*, *Lat. Am.* calabash, gourd

porosidad /porosi'ðað/ *f*, porosity, permeability

poroso /po'roso/ *a* porous, leaky

poroto /po'roto/ *m*, *Lat. Am.* bean; *Chile* child, kid

porque /'porke/ *conjunc* because, for; in order that

porqué /'porke/ *m*, reason, wherefore, why; *Inf.* money. **el cómo y el p.,** the why and the wherefore

porquería /porke'ria/ *f*, *Inf.* filth, nastiness; dirty trick; rudeness, gross act; trifle, thing of no account

porquerizo, porquero /porke'riso; por'kero; porke'riθo, por'kero/ *m*, swineherd

porra /'porra/ *f*, club, bludgeon; last player (in children's games); *Inf.* vanity, boastfulness; bore, tedious person

porrada /po'rraða/ *f*, blow with a club; buffet, knock, fall; *Inf.* folly; glut, abundance

porrazo /po'rraso; po'rraθo/ *m*, blow with a club; buffet, knock, fall

porrear /porre'ar/ *vi Inf.* to insist, harp on

porrería /porre'ria/ *f*, *Inf.* folly; obduracy, persistence

porreta /po'rreta/ *f*, green leaves of leeks, onions, and cereals. *Inf.* **en p.,** stark-naked

porrino /po'rrino/ *m*, seed of a leek; young leek plant

porrón /po'rron/ *m*, winebottle with a spout; earthenware jug

porsiacaso /porsia'kaso/ *m*, *Argentina, Venezuela* knapsack

portaaviones /portaa'βiones/ *m*, aircraft carrier

portachuelo /porta'tʃuelo/ *m*, defile, narrow mountain pass

portada /por'taða/ *f*, front, facade; frontispiece; title page; portal, doorway

portado /por'taðo/ (**bien** *or* **mal**) *a* well- or illdressed or behaved

portador /porta'ðor/ **(-ra)** *n* carrier. *m*, *Com.* bearer; *Mech.* carrier

portaestandarte /ˌportaestan'darte/ *m*, standardbearer

portafolio /porta'folio/ *m*, portfolio; *Lat. Am. also* briefcase

portafusil /porta'fusil/ *m*, rifle sling

portal /por'tal/ *m*, entrance, porch; portico; city gate

portalámpara /porta'lampara/ *f*, lamp holder; *Elec.* socket

portalibros /porta'liβros/ *m*, bookstrap

portalón /porta'lon/ *m*, gangway

portamanteo /portaman'teo/ *m*, traveling bag

portamonedas /portamo'neðas/ *m*, pocketbook; handbag, purse

portanuevas /porta'nueβas/ *mf* bringer of news, newsmonger

portaobjetos /portaoβ'hetos/ *m*, stage (of a microscope)

portaplumas /porta'plumas/ *m*, pen holder

portar /por'tar/ *vt* to retrieve (of dogs); carry (arms); *vr* behave (well or badly); bear oneself, act; be well, or ill (in health)

portátil /por'tatil/ *a* portable

portavoz /porta'βos; porta'βoθ/ *m*, megaphone; spokesman, mouthpiece

portazgo /por'tasgo; por'taθgo/ *m*, toll; tollbooth

portazguero /portas'gero; portaθ'gero/ *m*, toll collector

portazo /por'taso; por'taθo/ *m*, bang of the door; slamming the door in a person's face

porte /'porte/ *m*, transport; *Com.* carriage; postage; freight, transport cost; porterage; behavior, conduct;

bearing, looks; capacity, volume; size, dimension; nobility (of descent); *Naut.* tonnage. **p. pagado,** charges prepaid

porteador /portea'ðor/ *m,* carrier; porter; carter

portear /porte'ar/ *vt* to carry, transport; *vr* migrate (of birds)

portento /por'tento/ *m,* marvel, prodigy, portent

portentoso /porten'toso/ *a* marvelous, portentous

porteño, -a /por'teɲo/ *a* of Buenos Aires; native of Buenos Aires; resident of Buenos Aires

porteo /por'teo/ *m,* porterage, cartage

portería /porte'ria/ *f,* porter's lodge; porter's employment; *Sports.* goal

portero /por'tero/ **(-ra)** *n* doorman, doorkeeper; porter; concierge; janitor; *Sports.* goalkeeper. **p. eléctrico,** door buzzer

portezuela /porte'suela/ porte'θuela/ *f, dim* small door; carriage door; pocket flap

pórtico /'portiko/ *m,* portico, piazza; porch; vestibule, hall

portillo /por'tiyo/ por'tiʎo/ *m,* breach, opening; defile, narrow pass; *Fig.* loophole

portón /por'ton/ *m,* hall door, inner door; *Chile* back door

portorriqueño /portorri'keɲo/ **(-ña)** *a* and *n* Puerto Rican

portuario /por'tuario/ *a* dock, port

Portugal /portu'gal/ Portugal

portugués /portu'ges/ **(-esa)** *a* and *n* Portuguese. *m,* Portuguese (language)

portuguesada /portuge'saða/ *f,* exaggeration

porvenir /porβe'nir/ *m,* future time

¡porvida! /por'βiða/ *interj* By the saints! By the Almighty!

pos /pos/ *prefix* after; behind. Also *adv* **en p.,** with the same meanings

posa /'posa/ *f,* tolling bell; *pl* buttocks

posada /po'saða/ *f,* dwelling; inn, tavern; lodging; hospitality

posaderas /posa'ðeras/ *f pl,* buttocks

posadero /posa'ðero/ **(-ra)** *n* innkeeper; boarding-house keeper

posar /po'sar/ *vi* to lodge, live; rest; alight, perch; *vt* set down (a burden); *vr* settle (liquids); (*with en or sobre*) perch upon

posdata /pos'ðata/ *f,* P.S., postscript

pose /'pose/ *f, Photo.* time exposure; *Inf.* pose

poseedor /posee'ðor/ **(-ra)** *n* possessor, holder

poseer /pose'er/ *vt irr* to own, possess; know (a language, etc.); *vr* restrain oneself. **estar poseído por,** to be possessed by (passion, etc.); be thoroughly convinced of. See **creer**

posesión /pose'sion/ *f,* ownership, occupancy; possession; property, territory (often *pl*)

posesionarse /posesio'narse/ *vr* to take possession; lay hold (of)

poseso /po'seso/ *a* possessed of an evil spirit

posesor /pose'sor/ **(-ra)** *n* owner, possessor

posfecha /pos'fetʃa/ *f,* postdate

posguerra /pos'gerra/ *f,* postwar period

posibilidad /posiβili'ðað/ *f,* possibility; probability; opportunity, means, chance; *pl* property, wealth

posibilitar /posiβili'tar/ *vt* to make possible, facilitate

posible /po'siβle/ *a* possible. *m pl,* property, personal wealth. **hacer lo p.** *or* **hacer todo lo p.,** to do everything possible; do one's best

posición /posi'sion/ posi'θion/ *f,* placing; position; situation; status

positivamente /positiβa'mente/ *adv* positively, definitely

positivismo /positi'βismo/ *m,* positivism

positivista /positi'βista/ *a* positivistic. *mf* positivist

positivo /posi'tiβo/ *a* positive; certain, definite; (*Math. Elec.*) plus; true, real

pósito /'posito/ *m,* public granary; cooperative association

posma /'posma/ *f, Inf.* sluggishness, sloth

poso /'poso/ *m,* sediment; lees, dregs; repose, quietness

posponer /pospo'ner/ *vt irr* (*with prep a*) to place after; make subordinate to; value less than. See **poner**

posta /'posta/ *f,* post horse; stage, post; stake (cards)

postal /pos'tal/ *a* postal. *f,* postcard, postal card

poste /'poste/ *m,* post, stake

postema /pos'tema/ *f,* tumor, abscess; bore, tedious person

postergación /posterga'sion/ posterga'θion/ *f,* delay; delaying; relegation; disregard of seniority (in promotion)

postergar /poster'gar/ *vt* to delay; disregard a senior claim to promotion

posteridad /posteri'ðað/ *f,* descendants; posterity

posterior /poste'rior/ *a* back, rear; hind; subsequent

posteriormente /posterior'mente/ *adv* later, subsequently

postigo /pos'tigo/ *m,* secret door; grating, hatch; postern; shutter (of a window)

postillón /posti'yon/ posti'ʎon/ *m,* postilion

postizo /pos'tiso/ pos'tiθo/ *a* false, artificial, not natural. *m,* switch of false hair

postor /pos'tor/ *m,* bidder (at an auction)

postración /postra'sion/ postra'θion/ *f,* prostration; exhaustion; depression, distress

postrar /pos'trar/ *vt* to cast down, demolish; prostrate, exhaust; *vr* kneel down; be prostrated or exhausted

postre /'postre/ *a* last (in order). *m, Cul.* dessert. **a la p.,** at last, finally

postrero /pos'trero/ *a* last (in order); rearmost, hindmost

postrimeramente /postrimera'mente/ *adv* lastly, finally

postrimería /postrime'ria/ *f, Eccl.* last period of life

postulación /postula'sion/ postula'θion/ *f,* entreaty, request

postulado /postu'laðo/ *m,* assumption; supposition; working hypothesis; *Geom.* postulate

postulante /postu'lante/ **(-ta)** *n Eccl.* postulant, applicant, candidate

postular /postu'lar/ *vt* to postulate; *Lat. Am.* nominate

póstumo /'postumo/ *a* posthumous

postura /pos'tura/ *f,* posture, bearing; laying (of an egg); bid (at an auction); position; agreement, pact; bet, stake; planting; transplanted tree. **p. de vida,** way of life

potable /po'taβle/ *a* drinkable. **agua p.,** drinking water

potación /pota'sion/ pota'θion/ *f,* potation, drink

potaje /po'tahe/ *m,* stew, potage; dried vegetables; mixed drink; hotchpotch

potasa /po'tasa/ *f,* potash

potasio /po'tasio/ *m,* potassium

pote /'pote/ *m,* pot; jar; flowerpot; *Cul.* cauldron; *Cul.* stew

potencia /po'tensia/ po'tenθia/ *f,* power; potency; *Mech.* performance, capacity; strength, force; *Math.* power; rule, dominion

potencial /poten'sial/ poten'θial/ *a* potential

potentado /poten'taðo/ *m,* potentate

potente /po'tente/ *a* potent; powerful; *Inf.* enormous

potestad /potes'tað/ *f,* authority, power; podesta, Italian magistrate; potentate; *Math.* power; *pl* angelic powers

potestativo /potesta'tiβo/ *a Law.* facultative

potingue /po'tinge/ *m, Inf.* brew; mixture; lotion; medicine; filthy place, pigsty

poto /'poto/ *m, Lat. Am.* calabash, gourd; backside

potra /'potra/ *f,* filly

potrear /potre'ar/ *vt Inf.* to tease, annoy

potro /'potro/ *m,* colt, foal; rack (for torture); vaulting horse. **p. mesteño,** mustang

poyo /'poio/ *m,* stone seat

pozal /po'sal/ po'θal/ *m,* pail, bucket

pozo /'poso/ po'θo/ *m,* well; shaft (in a mine). *Auto.* **p. colector,** crankcase

pozole, /po'sole/ po'θole/ *m, Mexico* stew of pork, corn, chile, etc.

práctica /'praktika/ f, practice; custom, habit; method; exercise
practicabilidad /praktikaβili'ðað/ f, feasibility
practicable /prakti'kaβle/ a feasible, practicable
prácticamente /'praktikamente/ adv practically, in practice
practicante /prakti'kante/ m, medical practitioner; medical student; Med. intern; first-aid practitioner
practicar /prakti'kar/ vt to execute, perform; practice; make
práctico /'praktiko/ a practical; experienced, expert; workable. m, Naut. pilot
pradeño /pra'ðeɲo/ a meadow, prairie
pradera /pra'ðera/ f, meadow, field; lawn
pradería /praðe'ria/ f, meadowland, prairie
prado /'praðo/ m, meadow; grassland; field; lawn; walk (in cities)
Praga /'praga/ Prague
pragmatista /pragma'tista/ a pragmatic. mf pragmatist
pravedad /praβe'ðað/ f, wickedness, immorality, depravity
pravo /'praβo/ a wicked, immoral, depraved
pre /pre/ m, Mil. daily pay. prep insep pre-
preámbulo /pre'ambulo/ m, preamble, preface; importunate digression
prebenda /pre'βenda/ f, Eccl. prebend, benefice; Inf. sinecure
preboste /pre'βoste/ m, provost
precario /pre'kario/ a precarious, uncertain, insecure
precaución /prekau'sion; prekau'θion/ f, precaution, safeguard
precaucionarse /prekausio'narse; prekauθio'narse/ vr to take precautions, safeguard oneself
precautelar /prekaute'lar/ vt to forewarn; take precautions
precaver /preka'βer/ vt to prevent, avoid; vr (with de or contra) guard against
precavido /preka'βiðo/ a cautious, forewarned
precedencia /prese'ðensia; preθe'ðenθia/ f, priority, precedence; superiority; preference, precedence
precedente /prese'ðente; preθe'ðente/ a preceding. m, antecedent; precedent
preceder /prese'ðer; preθe'ðer/ vt to precede; have precedence over, be superior to
preceptivo /presep'tiβo; preθep'tiβo/ a preceptive; didactic
precepto /pre'septo; pre'θepto/ m, precept; order, injunction; rule, commandment. de p., obligatory
preceptor /presep'tor; preθep'tor/ (-ra) n teacher, instructor, tutor, preceptor
preces /'preses; 'preθes/ f pl, Eccl. prayers; entreaties
preciado /pre'siaðo; pre'θiaðo/ a excellent, esteemed, precious; boastful
preciar /pre'siar; pre'θiar/ vt to esteem, value; valuate, price; vr boast
precintar /presin'tar; preθin'tar/ vt to seal; rope, string, tie up
precinto /pre'sinto; pre'θinto/ m, sealing; roping, tying up; strap
precio /'presio; 'preθio/ m, price, cost; recompense, reward; premium; rate; reputation, importance; esteem. p. de tasa, controlled price
preciosidad /presiosi'ðað; preθiosi'ðað/ f, preciousness; exquisiteness, fineness; richness; wittiness; Inf. loveliness, beauty; thing of beauty
precioso /pre'sioso; pre'θioso/ a precious; exquisite, fine, rare; rich; witty; Inf. lovely, delicious, attractive
preciosuna /presio'suna; preθio'suna/ f, Lat. Am. thing of beauty
precipicio /presi'pisio; preθi'piθio/ m, precipice; heavy fall; ruin, disaster
precipitación /presipita'sion; preθipita'θion/ f, precipitancy, haste; rashness; Chem. precipitation
precipitadamente /presipitaða'mente; preθipitaða'mente/ adv precipitately, in haste; rashly, foolishly
precipitado /presipi'taðo; preθipi'taðo/ a precipitate; rash, thoughtless. m, Chem. precipitate
precipitar /presipi'tar; preθipi'tar/ vt to precipitate,

hurl headlong; hasten; Chem. precipitate; vr hurl oneself headlong; hasten, rush
precipitoso /presipi'toso; preθipi'toso/ a precipitous; rash, heedless
precisamente /presisa'mente; preθisa'mente/ adv exactly, precisely, just; necessarily. **Y p. en aquel instante llegó,** And just at that moment he arrived
precisar /presi'sar; preθi'sar/ vt to fix, arrange; set forth, draw up, state; compel, force, oblige
precisión /presi'sion; preθi'sion/ f, accuracy, precision; necessity, conciseness, clarity; compulsion, obligation
preciso /pre'siso; pre'θiso/ a necessary, unavoidable; concise, clear; precise, exact
precitado /presi'taðo; preθi'taðo/ a aforementioned
preclaro /pre'klaro/ a illustrious, distinguished, celebrated
precocidad /prekosi'ðað; prekoθi'ðað/ f, precocity
precognición /prekogni'sion; prekogni'θion/ f, foreknowledge
precolombino, -a /prekolom'βino/ a pre-Columbian
preconcebido /prekonse'βiðo; prekonθe'βiðo/ a preconceived
preconcepto /prekon'septo; prekon'θepto/ m, preconceived idea, preconceived notion
preconizar /prekoni'sar; prekoni'θar/ vt to eulogize, praise publicly
preconocer /prekono'ser; prekono'θer/ vt irr to know beforehand; foresee. See **conocer**
precoz /pre'kos; pre'koθ/ a precocious
precursor /prekur'sor/ (-ra) a precursory; preceding, previous. n precursor
predecesor /preðese'sor; preðeθe'sor/ (-ra) n predecessor
predecir /preðe'sir; preðe'θir/ vt irr to foretell, prophesy. See **decir**
predestinación /preðestina'sion; preðestina'θion/ f, predestination
predestinado /preðesti'naðo/ (-da) a predestined; foreordained. n one of the predestined
predestinar /preðesti'nar/ vt to predestine, foreordain
predeterminar /preðetermi'nar/ vt to predetermine
prédica /'preðika/ f, inf (contemptuous) sermon
predicación /preðika'sion; preðika'θion/ f, preaching; homily, sermon
predicadera /preðika'ðera/ f, pulpit; pl Inf. talent for preaching
predicador /preðika'ðor/ (-ra) a preaching. n preacher
predicamento /preðika'mento/ m, predicament; reputation
predicar /preði'kar/ vt to publish; manifest; preach; vi overpraise; Inf. lecture, scold. **p. en el desierto,** to preach to the wind
predicción /preðik'sion; preðik'θion/ f, prediction, prophecy
predilección /preðilek'sion; preðilek'θion/ f, predilection, preference, partiality
predilecto /preði'lekto/ a favorite, preferred
predisponer /preðispo'ner/ vt irr to predispose. See **poner**
predisposición /preðisposi'sion; preðisposi'θion/ f, predisposition; tendency, prejudice
predominación /preðomina'sion; preðomina'θion/ f, predominance
predominante /preðomi'nante/ a predominant; prevailing
predominar /preðomi'nar/ vi and vt to predominate; prevail; tower above; overlook
predominio /preðo'minio/ m, predominance, ascendancy, preponderance
preeminencia /preemi'nensia; preemi'nenθia/ f, preeminence
preeminente /preemi'nente/ a preeminent
preexistencia /preeksis'tensia; preeksis'tenθia/ f, preexistence
preexistente /preeksis'tente/ a preexistent
preexistir /preeksis'tir/ vi to preexist, exist before
prefacio /pre'fasio; pre'faθio/ m, introduction, preface, prologue; Eccl. preface

prefecto /pre'fekto/ *m*, prefect

prefectura /prefek'tura/ *f*, prefecture

preferencia /prefe'rensia; prefe'renθia/ *f*, preference; superiority. **de p.**, preferred, favorite; preferably

preferente /prefe'rente/ *a* preferable; preferential; preferred (of stock)

preferible /prefe'riβle/ *a* preferable

preferir /prefe'rir/ *vt irr* to prefer; excel, exceed. *Pres. Part.* **prefiriendo.** *Pres. Ind.* **prefiero, prefieres, prefiere, preferimos, preferís, prefieren.** *Preterite* **prefirió, prefirieron.** *Pres. Subjunc.* **prefiera, prefieras, prefiera, prefiramos, prefiráis, prefieran.** *Imperf. Subjunc.* **prefiriese, etc.**

prefijar /prefi'har/ *vt* to prefix

prefijo /pre'fiho/ *m*, prefix

prefinir /prefi'nir/ *vt* to fix a time limit for

prefulgente /preful'hente/ *a* brilliant, shining, resplendent

pregón /pre'gon/ *m*, public proclamation; marriage banns

pregonar /prego'nar/ *vt* to proclaim publicly; cry one's wares; publish abroad; eulogize, praise; proscribe, outlaw. **p. a los cuatro vientos,** *Inf.* to shout from the rooftops

pregonería /pregone'ria/ *f*, office of the town crier

pregonero /prego'nero/ *m*, town crier; court crier

preguerra /pre'gerra/ *f*, prewar period

pregunta /pre'gunta/ *f*, question; *Com.* inquiry; questionnaire, interrogation. *Inf.* **andar** (*or* **estar**) **a la cuarta p.,** to be very hard up, be on the rocks. **hacer una p.,** to ask a question

preguntador /pregunta'ðor/ **(-ra)** *a* questioning; inquisitive. *n* questioner; inquisitive person

preguntar /pregun'tar/ *vt* to question, ask; (*with por*) inquire for; *vr* ask oneself, wonder

prehistoria /preis'toria/ *f*, prehistory

prehistórico /preis'toriko/ *a* prehistoric

prejuicio /pre'huisio; pre'huiθio/ *m*, prejudice

prejuzgar /prehus'gar; prehuθ'gar/ *vt* to prejudge, judge hastily

prelacía /prela'sia; prela'θia/ *f*, prelacy

prelación /prela'sion; prela'θion/ *f*, preference

prelado /pre'laðo/ *m*, prelate

preliminar /prelimi'nar/ *a* preliminary, prefatory. *m*, preliminary

preludiar /prelu'ðiar/ *vi* and *vt Mus.* to play a prelude (to); *vt* prepare, initiate

preludio /pre'luðio/ *m*, introduction, prologue; *Mus.* prelude; *Mus.* overture

prematuro /prema'turo/ *a* premature, untimely; unseasonable; immature, unripe

premeditación /premeðita'sion; premeðita'θion/ *f*, premeditation

premeditar /premeði'tar/ *vt* to premeditate, plan in advance

premiador /premia'ðor/ **(-ra)** *a* rewarding. *n* rewarder

premiar /pre'miar/ *vt* to reward, requite

premio /pre'mio/ *m*, prize; reward; premium; *Com.* interest. **p. en metálico,** cash prize. *Inf.* **p. gordo,** first prize (in a lottery)

premioso /pre'mioso/ *a* tight; troublesome, annoying; stern, strict; slow-moving; burdensome, hard; labored (of speech or style)

premisa /pre'misa/ *f*, premise; sign, indication

premonitorio /premoni'torio/ *a* premonitory

premura /pre'mura/ *f*, urgency, haste

prenda /'prenda/ *f*, pledge; token, sign; jewel; article of clothing; talent, gift; loved one; *pl* game of forfeits

prendador /prenda'ðor/ **(-ra)** *n* pledger

prendamiento /prenda'miento/ *m*, pawning

prendar /pren'dar/ *vt* to pawn; charm, delight; *vr* (*with de*) take a liking to

prender /pren'der/ *vt* to seize; arrest; capture, catch; turn on (lights, radio). *vi* take root (plants); catch fire; be infectious

prendería /prende'ria/ *f*, second-hand shop

prendero /pren'dero/ **(-ra)** *n* second-hand dealer

prendimiento /prendi'miento/ *m*, seizure, capture; arrest

prenombre /pre'nombre/ *m*, given name, praenomen

prensa /'prensa/ *f*, press; printing press; newspapers, the press. **dar a la p.,** to publish

prensado /pren'saðo/ *m*, **prensadura** *f*, pressing; flattening; squeezing

prensar /pren'sar/ *vt* to press; squeeze

prensil /pren'sil/ *a* prehensile

preñado /pre'ɲaðo/ *a* pregnant; bulging, sagging (walls, etc.); swollen. *m*, pregnancy

preñez /pre'ɲes; pre'ɲeθ/ *f*, pregnancy; suspense

preocupación /preokupa'sion; preokupa'θion/ *f*, anxiety, preoccupation; prejudice

preocupadamente /preokupaða'mente/ *adv* preoccupiedly, absentmindedly; with prejudice

preocupar /preoku'par/ *vt* to preoccupy; make anxious; bias, prejudice; *vr* be anxious; be prejudiced

preordinar /preorði'nar/ *vt Eccl.* to predestine

preparación /prepara'sion; prepara'θion/ *f*, preparation; treatment; compound, specific

preparado /prepa'raðo/ *a* ready, prepared. *m*, preparation, patent food, etc.

preparar /prepa'rar/ *vt* to prepare; *vr* prepare oneself; qualify

preparativo /prepara'tiβo/ *a* preparatory. *m*, preparation

preparatorio /prepara'torio/ *a* preparatory

preponderancia /preponde'ransia; preponde'ranθia/ *f*, preponderance

preponderante /preponde'rante/ *a* preponderant; dominant

preponderar /preponde'rar/ *vi* to preponderate; dominate; outweigh

preponer /prepo'ner/ *vt irr* to put before. See **poner**

preposición /preposi'sion; preposi'θion/ *f*, preposition

prepósito /pre'posito/ *m*, chairman, head, president; *Eccl.* provost

prepucio /pre'pusio; pre'puθio/ *m*, prepuce, foreskin

prerrogativa /prerroga'tiβa/ *f*, prerogative

presa /'presa/ *f*, hold, grasp; seizure, capture; booty; dam; lock (on rivers, canals); weir; ditch, trench; embankment; slice, bit. **hacer p.,** to seize; take advantage of (circumstances)

presagiar /presa'hiar/ *vt* to prophesy, presage, bode

presagio /pre'sahio/ *m*, presage, sign; presentiment, foreboding

présbita /'presβita/ *a* long-sighted, farsighted

presbiterado /presβite'raðo/ *m*, priesthood; holy orders

presbiteriano /presβite'riano/ **(-na)** *a* and *n* Presbyterian

presbítero /pres'βitero/ *m*, priest

presciencia /pres'siensia; pres'θienθia/ *f*, prescience, foresight

presciente /pres'siente; pres'θiente/ *a* prescient, farsighted

prescindible /pressin'diβle; presθin'diβle/ *a* nonessential, able to be dispensed with

prescindir /pressin'dir; presθin'dir/ *vi* (*with de*) to pass over, omit; do without. **Prescindiendo de esto...,** Leaving this aside....

prescribir /preskri'βir/ *vt* to prescribe, order

prescripción /preskrip'sion; preskrip'θion/ *f*, prescription

presea /pre'sea/ *f*, jewel, object of value

presencia /pre'sensia; pre'senθia/ *f*, presence, attendance; appearance, looks; ostentation. **p. de ánimo,** presence of mind

presenciar /presen'siar; presen'θiar/ *vt* to be present at; witness, behold

presentación /presenta'sion; presenta'θion/ *f*, presentation; introduction; *Lat. Am. also* petition

presentar /presen'tar/ *vt* to show; present, make a gift of; introduce (persons); *vr* occur; present oneself; offer one's services

presente /pre'sente/ *a* present. *m*, gift; present time. *Law.* **Por estas presentes...,** By these presents.... **tener p.,** to remember

presentimiento /presenti'miento/ *m*, presentiment, apprehension

presentir /presen'tir/ *vt irr* to have a presentiment of.
See **sentir**

preservación /preserβa'sion; preserβa'θion/ *f*, preservation, protection, saving

preservar /preser'βar/ *vt* to preserve, protect, save

preservativo /preserβa'tiβo/ *a* preservative. *m*, preservative, safeguard, protection

presidencia /presi'ðensia; presi'ðenθia/ *f*, presidency; chairmanship; presidential seat or residence

presidencial /presiðen'sial; presiðen'θial/ *a* presidential

presidenta /presi'ðenta/ *f*, female president; president's wife; chairwoman

presidente /presi'ðente/ *m*, president; chairman; head, director; presiding judge

presidiar /presi'ðiar/ *vt* to garrison

presidiario /presi'ðiario/ *m*, convict

presidio /pre'siðio/ *m*, garrison; garrison town; fortress; penitentiary; imprisonment; *Law*. hard labor; assistance, protection

presidir /presi'ðir/ *vt* to preside over; act as chairperson for; influence, determine

presilla /pre'siya; pre'siʎa/ *f*, loop, shank, noose; press stud; *Mexico* epaulet

presión /pre'sion/ *f*, pressure

preso /'preso/ **(-sa)** *n* prisoner, captive; convict

prestación /presta'sion; presta'θion/ *f*, lending, loan. **p. vecinal,** corvée

prestador /presta'ðor/ **(-ra)** *a* lending, loan. *n* lender

prestamente /presta'mente/ *adv* expeditiously, promptly

prestamista /presta'mista/ *mf* moneylender; pawnbroker

préstamo /'prestamo/ *m*, loan; lending. **casa de préstamos,** pawnshop

prestar /pres'tar/ *vt* to lend; assist; pay (attention); give; *Lat. Am.* to borrow; *vi* be useful; give, expand; *vr* be suitable; lend itself; offer oneself. **pedir/tomar prestado,** to borrow

prestatario /presta'tario/ **(-ia)** *n* money borrower, debtor

preste /'preste/ *m*, celebrant of high mass. **el p. Juan,** title of Prester John

presteza /pres'tesa; pres'teθa/ *f*, speed; promptness, dispatch

prestidigitación /prestiðihita'sion; prestiðihita'θion/ *f*, prestidigitation

prestidigitador /prestiðihita'ðor/ **(-ra)** *n* juggler, conjurer

prestigio /pres'tihio/ *m*, magic spell, sorcery; trick, illusion (of conjurers, etc.); influence, prestige

prestigioso /presti'hioso/ *a* illusory; influential

presto /'presto/ *a* quick, speedy; prompt, ready. *m*, pressure cooker. *adv* immediately; soon; quickly. **de p.,** speedily

presumido /presu'miðo/ *a* conceited, vain; presumptuous

presumir /presu'mir/ *vt* to suppose, presume; *vi* be conceited

presunción /presun'sion; presun'θion/ *f*, supposition, presumption; vanity, presumptuousness

presuntivo /presun'tiβo/ *a* presumptive

presuntuosidad /presuntuosi'ðað/ *f*, presumptuousness

presuntuoso /presun'tuoso/ *a* presumptuous, vain

presuponer /presupo'ner/ *vt irr* to presuppose, assume; budget, estimate. See **poner**

presuposición /presuposi'sion; presuposi'θion/ *f*, presupposition

presupuesto /presu'puesto/ *m*, motive, reason; supposition, assumption; estimate; *Com.* tender; national budget

presuroso /presu'roso/ *a* swift, speedy

pretencioso /preten'sioso; preten'θioso/ *a* pretentious, vain

pretender /preten'der/ *vt* to seek, solicit; claim; apply for; attempt, try; woo, court

pretendiente /preten'diente/ **(-ta)** *n* pretender; candidate; petitioner; suitor

pretensión /preten'sion/ *f*, pretension; claim; *pl* ambitions

pretérito /pre'terito/ *a* past. *m*, preterite

pretextar /preteks'tar/ *vt* to allege as a pretext or excuse

pretexto /pre'teksto/ *m*, pretext, excuse

prevalecer /preβale'ser; preβale'θer/ *vi irr* to prevail; be dominant; take root (plants). See **conocer**

prevaleciente /preβale'siente; preβale'θiente/ *a* prevailing; prevalent

prevaricador /preβarika'ðor/ **(-ra)** *n* prevaricator

prevaricar /preβari'kar/ *vi* to prevaricate

prevención /preβen'sion; preβen'θion/ *f*, prevention; precaution; prejudice; police station; *Mil.* guard room; foresight, prevision; preparation. **de p.,** as a precaution

prevenido /preβe'niðo/ *a* prepared; cautious, forewarned

prevenir /preβe'nir/ *vt irr* to prepare; prevent, avoid; warn; prejudice; occur, happen; *Fig.* overcome (obstacles); *vr* be ready; be forewarned. See **venir**

preventivo /preβen'tiβo/ *a* preventive

prever /pre'βer/ *vt irr* to foresee, forecast, anticipate. See **ver**

previamente /preβia'mente/ *adv* previously, in advance

previo /'preβio/ *a* previous, advance

previsión /preβi'sion/ *f*, forecast; foresight, prevision, prescience. **p. social,** social insurance

previsor /preβi'sor/ *a* farsighted, provident

prieto /'prieto/ *a* almost black, blackish; tight; mean, avaricious; *Lat. Am.* dark-skinned, swarthy

prima /'prima/ *f*, *Eccl.* prime; *Com.* premium; female cousin

primacía /prima'sia; prima'θia/ *f*, supremacy, preeminence; primacy; primateship

primada /pri'maða/ *f*, *Inf.* act of sponging on, taking advantage of

primado /pri'maðo/ *m*, primate; primateship

primario /pri'mario/ *a* primary. *m*, professor who gives the first lecture of the day

primavera /prima'βera/ *f*, springtime; primrose; figured silk material; beautifully colored thing; youth; prime

primaveral /primaβe'ral/ *a* spring, spring-like

primeramente /primera'mente/ *adv* first; in the first place

primerizo /prime'riso; prime'riθo/ **(-za)** *n* novice; beginner; apprentice; firstborn

primero /pri'mero/ *a* first; former; excellent, first-rate. *adv* first; in the first place. **primera enseñanza,** primary education. **primera materia,** raw material. **primer plano,** *Art.* foreground. **primera cura,** first aid. **de buenas a primeras,** all at once, suddenly

primicia /pri'misia; pri'miθia/ *f*, first fruits; offering of first fruits; *pl* first effects

primitivo /primi'tiβo/ *a* original, early; primitive

primo /'primo/ **(-ma)** *a* first; excellent, fine. *n* cousin; *Inf.* simpleton; *Inf.* pigeon, dupe. **p. carnal,** first cousin. *Inf.* **hacer el p.,** to be a dupe. *Inf.* **ser prima hermana de,** to be the twin of (of things)

primogénito /primo'henito/ **(-ta)** *a* and *n* firstborn

primogenitura /primoheni'tura/ *f*, primogeniture

primor /pri'mor/ *m*, exquisite care; beauty, loveliness; thing of beauty

primoroso /primo'roso/ *a* beautiful; exquisitely done; dexterous, skillful

princesa /prin'sesa; prin'θesa/ *f*, princess

principado /prinsi'paðo; prinθi'paðo/ *m*, principality; princedom; superiority, preeminence

principal /prinsi'pal; prinθi'pal/ *a* chief, principal; illustrious; fundamental, first. *m*, head, principal (of a firm); *Com.* capital, principal; first floor

principalmente /prinsipal'mente; prinθipal'mente/ *adv* principally, chiefly

príncipe /'prinsipe; 'prinθipe/ *m*, leader; prince. **p. de Asturias,** prince of Asturias. **p. de la sangre,** prince of the blood royal

principesco /prinsi'pesko; prinθi'pesko/ *a* princely

principiante /prinsi'piante; prinθi'piante/ **(-ta)** *n* beginner, novice; apprentice

principiar /prinsi'piar; prinθi'piar/ *vt* to begin, commence

principio /prin'sipio; prin'θipio/ *m*, beginning; principle; genesis, origin; rudiment; axiom; constituent. **al p.**, at first. **a principios**, at the beginning (of the month, year, etc.). **en p.**, in principle

pringar /priŋ'gar/ *vt Cul.* to soak in fat; stain with grease; *Inf.* wound; take part in a business deal; slander; *vr Inf.* appropriate, misuse (funds, etc.)

pringo /'priŋgo/ *m, Lat. Am.* drop (of a liquid)

pringoso /priŋ'goso/ *a* greasy

pringue /'priŋgue/ *mf*, animal fat, lard; grease spot

priora /'priora/ *f*, prioress

prioridad /priori'ðað/ *f*, priority

prisa /'prisa/ *f*, haste, speed; skirmish, foray. **a toda p.**, with all speed. **correr p.**, to be urgent. **dar p.**, to hasten, speed up. **darse** (*or* **estar de**) **p.**, to hurry

prisión /pri'sion/ *f*, prison, jail; seizure; captivity, imprisonment; *Fig.* bond; obstacle, shackle; *pl* fetters

prisma /'prisma/ *m*, prism

prismáticos /pris'matikos/ *m pl*, field glasses

prisonero /priso'nero/ **(-ra)** *n* prisoner; *Fig.* victim (of passion, etc.)

pristino /pris'tino/ *a* pristine

privación /priβa'sion; priβa'θion/ *f*, privation; lack, shortage; deprivation; degradation

privada /pri'βaða/ *f*, toilet, privy, water closet

privadamente /priβaða'mente/ *adv* privately; individually, separately

privado /pri'βaðo/ *a* private; individual, personal. *m*, favorite; confidant

privar /pri'βar/ *vt* to deprive; dismiss (from office); interdict, forbid; *vi* prevail, be in favor; *vr* swoon; deprive oneself

privilegiar /priβile'hiar/ *vt* to privilege; bestow a favor on

privilegio /priβi'lehio/ *m*, privilege; prerogative; concession; copyright; patent

pro /pro/ *mf* advantage, benefit. **el p. y el contra**, the pros and cons. **en p.**, in favor

proa /'proa/ *f*, prow, bow

probabilidad /proβaβili'ðað/ *f*, probability

probable /pro'βaβle/ *a* probable; likely; provable

probación /proβa'sion; proβa'θion/ *f*, proof, test; novitiate, probation

probado /pro'βaðo/ *a* tried, tested, proved

probar /pro'βar/ *vt irr* to prove; test; taste; try on (clothes); *vi* suit; (*with prep a* + *infin*) try to. **p. fortuna**, to try one's luck. *Pres. Ind.* **pruebo, pruebas, prueba, prueban**. *Pres. Subjunc.* **pruebe, pruebes, prueben**

probatorio /proβa'torio/ *a* probationary

probidad /proβi'ðað/ *f*, probity, trustworthiness, honesty

problema /pro'βlema/ *m*, problem

problemático /proβle'matiko/ *a* problematical, uncertain

probo /'proβo/ *a* honest, trustworthy

procacidad /prokasi'ðað; prokaθi'ðað/ *f*, insolence, pertness

procaz /pro'kas; pro'kaθ/ *a* insolent, pert, brazen

procedencia /prose'ðensia; proθe'ðenθia/ *f*, origin, source; parentage, descent; port of sailing or call

procedente /prose'ðente; proθe'ðente/ *a* arriving or coming from

proceder /prose'ðer; proθe'ðer/ *vi* to proceed; behave; originate, arise; continue, go on; act. *Law.* **p. contra**, to proceed against (a person)

procedimiento /proseði'miento; proθeði'miento/ *m*, proceeding, advancement; procedure; legal practice; process

proceloso /prose'loso; proθe'loso/ *a* tempestuous

prócer /'proser; 'proθer/ *a* exalted, eminent; lofty. *m*, exalted personage

procesado /prose'saðo; proθe'saðo/ **(-da)** *n* defendant

procesamiento /prosesa'miento; proθesa'miento/ *m*, suing, suit; indictment

procesar /prose'sar; proθe'sar/ *vt Law.* to proceed against, sue

procesión /prose'sion; proθe'sion/ *f*, proceeding, emanating; procession; *Inf.* train, string. **andar** (*or* **ir**) **por dentro la p.**, to feel keenly without betraying one's emotion

proceso /pro'seso; pro'θeso/ *m*, process; progress; advancement; lapse of time; lawsuit

proclama /pro'klama/ *f*, proclamation; announcement; publication of marriage banns

proclamación /proklama'sion; proklama'θion/ *f*, proclamation; acclaim, applause

proclamar /prokla'mar/ *vt* to proclaim; acclaim; publish abroad; reveal, show

proclividad /prokliβi'ðað/ *f*, proclivity, tendency

procomún /proko'mun/ *m*, social or public welfare

procreación /prokrea'sion; prokrea'θion/ *f*, procreation

procreador /prokrea'ðor/ **(-ra)** *a* procreative. *n* procreator

procrear /prokre'ar/ *vt* to procreate, beget, engender

procuración /prokura'sion; prokura'θion/ *f*, procurement; assiduity, care; *Law.* power of attorney; *Law.* attorneyship

procurador /prokura'ðor/ **(-ra)** *m*, proxy; *Law.* attorney; proctor. *n* procurer. **P. de la República**, Attorney General

procurar /proku'rar/ *vt* to try, attempt, procure, get; exercise the profession of a lawyer

prodigalidad /proðigali'ðað/ *f*, prodigality, lavishness; waste, extravagance

prodigar /proði'gar/ *vt* to waste, squander; lavish, bestow freely; *vr* make oneself cheap

prodigio /pro'ðihio/ *m*, marvel, wonder; prodigy; monster; miracle

prodigiosidad /proðihiosi'ðað/ *f*, prodigiousness

prodigioso /proði'hioso/ *a* wonderful; prodigious; monstrous; miraculous

pródigo /'proðigo/ **(-ga)** *a* wasteful, extravagant; lavish, generous. *n* spendthrift, wastrel, prodigal. **el hijo p.**, the prodigal son

producción /proðuk'sion; proðuk'θion/ *f*, production; output, yield; generation (of heat, etc.); crop

producir /proðu'sir; proðu'θir/ *vt irr* to produce; generate; yield, give; cause, occasion; publish; *vr* explain oneself; arise, appear, be produced. **p. efecto**, to have effect; take effect. See **conducir**

productividad /proðuktiβi'ðað/ *f*, productivity

productivo /proðuk'tiβo/ *a* productive; fertile; profitable

producto /pro'ðukto/ *m*, produce, product; profit; yield, gain; *Math.* product. *Chem.* **p. derivado**, by-product

productor /proðuk'tor/ **(-ra)** *a* productive. *n* producer

proemio /pro'emio/ *m*, prologue, preface, introduction

proeza /pro'esa; pro'eθa/ *f*, prowess, gallantry; skill; *Lat. Am.* boast

profanación /profana'sion; profana'θion/ *f*, profanation

profanador /profana'ðor/ **(-ra)** *n* profaner, transgressor

profanar /profa'nar/ *vt* to profane

profanidad /profani'ðað/ *f*, profanity

profano /pro'fano/ *a* profane; dissolute; pleasure-loving, worldly; immodest; lay, ignorant

profecía /profe'sia; profe'θia/ *f*, prophecy; *Eccl.* Book of the Prophets; opinion, view

proferir /profe'rir/ *vt irr* to utter, pronounce. See **herir**

profesar /profe'sar/ *vt* to exercise, practice (professions); *Eccl.* believe in; teach

profesión /profe'sion/ *f*, profession; trade, occupation; avowal, admission

profesional /profesio'nal/ *a* professional

profesionalismo /profesiona'lismo/ *m*, professionalism

profeso /pro'feso/ **(-sa)** *a Eccl.* professed. *n* professed monk

profesor /profe'sor/ **(-ra)** *n* teacher; professor

profesorado /profeso'raðo/ *m*, teaching staff; teaching profession; professorship; professorate
profeta /pro'feta/ *m*, prophet; seer
profético /pro'fetiko/ *a* prophetic
profetisa /profe'tisa/ *f*, prophetess
profetizar /profeti'sar; profeti'θar/ *vt* to prophesy; imagine, suppose
proficiente /profi'siente; profi'θiente/ *a* proficient
profiláctico /profi'laktiko/ *a* and *m*, prophylactic
prófugo /'profugo/ **(-ga)** *a* and *n* fugitive from justice. *m*, *Mil*. one who evades military service
profundamente /profunda'mente/ *adv* profoundly; acutely, deeply
profundidad /profundi'ðað/ *f*, depth; profundity, obscurity; *Geom.* depth; concavity; intensity (of feeling); vastness (of knowledge, etc.)
profundizar /profundi'sar; profundi'θar/ *vt* to deepen; hollow out; *Fig.* go into deeply, fathom
profundo /pro'fundo/ *a* deep; low; *Fig.* intense, acute; abstruse, profound; *Fig.* vast, extensive; high. *m*, depth, profundity; *Poet.* ocean, the deep; *Poet.* hell
profuso /pro'fuso/ *a* profuse, abundant; extravagant, wasteful
progenie /pro'henie/ *f*, descendants
prognosis /prog'nosis/ *f*, prognosis; forecast
programa /pro'grama/ *m*, program; edict, public notice; plan, scheme; *Educ.* calendar; syllabus; timetable
programador /programa'ðor/ **(-ra)** *n* (computer) programmer
progresar /progre'sar/ *vt* and *vi* to make progress; progress, advance
progresión /progre'sion/ *f*, progression; advancement, progress
progresista /progre'sista/ *a* *Polit.* progressive. *mf* progressive
progresivo /progre'siβo/ *a* progressive; advancing
progreso /pro'greso/ *m*, progress, advancement; growth; improvement, development
prohibente /proi'βente/ *a* prohibitory, prohibitive
prohibición /proiβi'sion; proiβi'θion/ *f*, forbidding, prohibition
prohibicionista /proiβisio'nista; proiβiθio'nista/ *mf* prohibitionist. *a* prohibitionist
prohibir /proi'βir/ *vt* to forbid, prohibit. «**Prohibido el paso,**» "No thoroughfare" *Pres. Indic.* **prohibo, prohíbes, prohíbe, prohíben.** *Pres. Subjunc.* **prohíba, prohíbas, prohíba, prohíban.**
prohibitivo, prohibitorio /proiβi'tiβo, proiβi'torio/ *a* prohibitive
prohijador /proiha'ðor/ **(-ra)** *n* adopter (of a child)
prohijamiento /proiha'miento/ *m*, child adoption; fathering (of a bill, etc.)
prohijar /proi'har/ *vt* to adopt (children, ideas); *Fig.* father. See **prohibir**
prohombre /pro'ombre/ *m*, master of a guild; respected, wellliked man
prójimo /'prohimo/ *m*, fellow man, brother, neighbor.
prole /'prole/ *f*, progeny, young offspring
proletariado /proleta'riaðo/ *m*, proletariat
proletario /prole'tario/ *a* poor; common, vulgar. *m*, plebeian; pauper; proletarian
prolífico /pro'lifiko/ *a* prolific; abundant, fertile
prolijidad /prolihi'ðað/ *f*, verbosity, prolixity; nicety, scruple; importunity, tediousness
prolijo /pro'liho/ *a* verbose, prolix; fussy, fastidious; tedious, importunate; *Argentina* indefatigable, untiring
prologar /prolo'gar/ *vt* to prologue; provide with a preface
prólogo /'prologo/ *m*, preface; prologue; introduction
prolongación /prolonga'sion; prolonga'θion/ *f*, lengthening; prolongation; protraction; extension
prolongado /prolon'gaðo/ *a* prolonged; oblong, long
prolongar /prolon'gar/ *vt* to lengthen; *Geom.* produce; prolong, spin out
promediar /prome'ðiar/ *vt* to distribute or divide into

two equal portions; average; *vi* arbitrate; place oneself between two people; reach half-time
promedio /pro'meðio/ *m*, average; middle, center
promesa /pro'mesa/ *f*, promise; augury, favorable sign
prometedor /promete'ðor/ **(-ra)** *a* promising. *n* promiser
prometer /prome'ter/ *vt* to promise; attest, certify; *vi* promise well, look hopeful; *vr* devote oneself to service of God; anticipate confidently, expect; become engaged (marriage). *Inf.* **prometérselas muy felices,** to have high hopes
prometido /prome'tiðo/ **(-da)** *n* betrothed. *m*, promise
prometimiento /prometi'miento/ *m*, promise; promising
prominencia /promi'nensia; promi'nenθia/ *f*, prominence, protuberance; eminence, hill
prominente /promi'nente/ *a* prominent, protuberant; eminent, elevated
promiscuar /promis'kuar/ *vi* to eat meat and fish on fast days
promiscuidad /promiskui'ðað/ *f*, promiscuity; ambiguity
promiscuo /pro'miskuo/ *a* indiscriminate, haphazard, promiscuous; ambiguous
promisión /promi'sion/ *f*, promise
promisorio /promi'sorio/ *a* promissory
promoción /promo'sion; promo'θion/ *f*, promotion; batch, class, year (of recruits, students, etc.)
promontorio /promon'torio/ *m*, headland; promontory; cumbersome object
promotor /promo'tor/ **(-ra)** *a* promotive. *n* promoter; supporter
promover /promo'βer/ *vt irr* to promote, further, advance; promote (a person). **p. un proceso (a),** to bring a suit (against). See **mover**
promulgación /promulga'sion; promulga'θion/ *f*, promulgation
promulgar /promul'gar/ *vt* to publish officially, proclaim; promulgate. *Law.* **p. sentencia,** to pass judgment
pronombre /pro'nombre/ *m*, pronoun
pronosticación /pronostika'sion; pronostika'θion/ *f*, prognostication; presage
pronosticar /pronosti'kar/ *vt* to prognosticate, forecast; presage
pronóstico /pro'nostiko/ *m*, omen, prediction; almanac; prognosis; sign, indication. **p. del tiempo,** weather forecast
prontitud /pronti'tuð/ *f*, quickness, promptness; quick wittedness; *Fig.* sharpness, liveliness; celerity, dispatch
pronto /'pronto/ *a* quick, speedy; prompt; ready, prepared. *m*, *Inf.* sudden decision. *adv* immediately; with all speed; soon. **de p.,** suddenly; without thinking. **por lo p.,** temporarily, provisionally
prontuario /pron'tuario/ *m*, compendium, handbook; summary
pronunciación /pronunsia'sion; pronunθia'θion/ *f*, pronunciation
pronunciamiento /pronunsia'miento; pronunθia'miento/ *m*, military uprising; political manifesto; *Law.* pronouncement of sentence
pronunciar /pronun'siar; pronun'θiar/ *vt* to pronounce, articulate; decide, determine; *Law.* pronounce judgment; give or make (a speech)
propagación /propaga'sion; propaga'θion/ *f*, propagation; dissemination; transmission
propagador /propaga'ðor/ *a* propagative. *m*, propagator
propaganda /propa'ganda/ *f*, propaganda organization; propaganda
propagandista /propagan'dista/ *mf* propagandist
propagar /propa'gar/ *vt* to reproduce; propagate, disseminate; *vr* reproduce, multiply; propagate, spread
propalar /propa'lar/ *vt* to disseminate, spread abroad
propasarse /propa'sarse/ *vr* to go too far, forget oneself; overstep one's authority

propender /propen'der/ *vi* to be inclined, have a leaning toward
propensión /propen'sion/ *f*, propensity, inclination; tendency
propenso /pro'penso/ *a* inclined, disposed; liable
propiamente /propia'mente/ *adv* properly, suitably
propiciación /propisia'sion; propiθia'θion/ *f*, propitiation
propiciador /propisia'ðor; propiθia'ðor/ **(-ra)** *a* propitiatory. *n* propitiator
propiciar /propi'siar; propi'θiar/ *vt* to propitiate, appease
propiciatorio /propisia'torio; propiθia'torio/ *a* propitiatory
propicio /pro'pisio; pro'piθio/ *a* propitious, auspicious; kind, favorable
propiedad /propie'ðað/ *f*, estate, property; ownership; landed property; attribute, quality, property; *Art.* resemblance, naturalness
propietario /propie'tario/ **(-ia)** *a* proprietary. *n* proprietor, owner
propina /pro'pina/ *f*, gratuity, tip. *Inf.* **de p.**, in addition, extra
propinar /propi'nar/ *vt* to treat to a drink; administer (medicine); *Inf.* give (slaps, etc.)
propincuidad /propinkui'ðað/ *f*, propinquity, proximity
propincuo /pro'pinkuo/ *a* near, contiguous, adjacent
propio /'propio/ *a* own, one's own; typical, characteristic; individual, peculiar; suitable, apt; natural, real; same. *m*, messenger; *pl* public lands
proponente /propo'nente/ *a* proposing. *m*, proposer; *Com.* tenderer
proponer /propo'ner/ *vt irr* to propose, suggest; make a proposition; propose (for a post, office, etc.); *Math.* state; *vr* intend, purpose. **proponerse para un empleo**, to apply for a post. See **poner**
proporción /propor'sion; propor'θion/ *f*, proportion; chance, opportunity; size; *Math.* proportion
proporcionado /proporsio'naðo; proporθio'naðo/ *a* fit, suitable; proportionate; symmetrical
proporcional /proporsio'nal; proporθio'nal/ *a* proportional
proporcionar /proporsio'nar; proporθio'nar/ *vt* to allot, proportion; supply, provide, give; adapt
proposición /proposi'sion; proposi'θion/ *f*, proposition; motion (in a debate)
propósito /pro'posito/ *m*, proposal; intention, aim; subject, question, matter. **a p.**, suitable, apropos; by the way, incidentally. **de p.**, with the intention, proposing. **fuera de p.**, irrelevant
propuesta /pro'puesta/ *f*, proposal, tender
propugnar /propug'nar/ *vt* to defend, protect
propulsar /propul'sar/ *vt* to repulse, throw back; propel, drive
propulsión /propul'sion/ *f*, repulse; propulsion
propulsor /propul'sor/ *a* driving, propelling. *m*, propeller
prorrata /pro'rrata/ *f*, quota, share, apportionment. **a p.**, in proportion
prorratear /prorrate'ar/ *vt* to apportion, distribute proportionately, prorate
prorrogación /prorroga'sion; prorroga'θion/ *f*, prorogation; adjournment; extension (of time); renewal (of a lease, etc.)
prorrogar /prorro'gar/ *vt* to extend, prolong; defer, suspend, prorogue; renew (leases, etc.)
prorrumpir /prorrum'pir/ *vt* (*with en*) to burst out; utter, give vent to, burst into
prosa /'prosa/ *f*, prose; prosaism, prosaic style; *Inf.* dull verbosity; monotony, tediousness; *Lat. Am.* pomposity
prosaico /pro'saiko/ *a* prosaic; prosy; monotonous, tedious; matter-of-fact
prosapia /pro'sapia/ *f*, family, lineage, descent
proscenio /pros'senio; pros'θenio/ *m*, proscenium
proscribir /proskri'βir/ *vt* to proscribe, outlaw; forbid, prohibit. *Past Part.* **proscrito**
proscripción /proskrip'sion; proskrip'θion/ *f*, proscription

proscrito /pros'krito/ **(-ta)** *n* outlaw, exile
prosecución /proseku'sion; proseku'θion/ *f*, prosecution, performance; pursuit
proseguir /prose'gir/ *vt irr* to continue, proceed with. See **pedir**
proselitismo /proseli'tismo/ *m*, proselytism
prosélito /pro'selito/ *m*, convert, proselyte
prosificar /prosifi'kar/ *vt* to turn verse into prose
prosista /pro'sista/ *mf* prose writer
prosodia /pro'soðia/ *f*, prosody
prospecto /pros'pekto/ *m*, prospectus
prosperar /prospe'rar/ *vt* to prosper; protect; *vi* flourish, prosper
prosperidad /prosperi'ðað/ *f*, prosperity; wealth; success
próspero /'prospero/ *a* favorable, propitious, fortunate; prosperous. **¡P. año nuevo!** Happy New Year!
próstata /'prostata/ *f*, prostate
prostitución /prostitu'sion; prostitu'θion/ *f*, prostitution
prostituir /prosti'tuir/ *vt irr* to prostitute; *vr* become a prostitute; sell oneself, debase oneself. See **huir**
prostituta /prosti'tuta/ *f*, prostitute
protagonista /protago'nista/ *mf* hero or heroine, principal character; leading figure, protagonist
protección /protek'sion; protek'θion/ *f*, protection, defense; favor, aid
proteccionismo /proteksio'nismo; protekθio'nismo/ *m*, protectionism
proteccionista /proteksio'nista; protekθio'nista/ *mf* protectionist
protector /protek'tor/ *a* protective. *m*, protector; guard
protectorado /protekto'raðo/ *m*, protectorate
protectriz /protek'tris; protek'triθ/ *f*, protectress
proteger /prote'her/ *vt* to protect, defend; favor, assist
protegido /prote'hiðo/ **(-da)** *n* protégé
proteico /pro'teiko/ *a* protean
proteína /prote'ina/ *f*, protein
protervia /pro'terβia/ *f*, depravity, perversity
protervo /pro'terβo/ *a* depraved, perverse
protesta /pro'testa/, **protestación** /pro'testa, protesta'sion; pro'testa, protesta'θion/ *f*, protest; protestation, declaration
protestante /protes'tante/ *a* and *mf* Protestant
protestantismo /protestan'tismo/ *m*, Protestantism
protestar /protes'tar/ *vt* to declare, attest; (*with contra*) protest against; (*with de*) affirm vigorously
protesto /pro'testo/ *m*, *Com.* protest; objection
protocolizar /protokoli'sar; protokoli'θar/ *vt* to protocol, draw up
protocolo /proto'kolo/ *m*, protocol
prototipo /proto'tipo/ *m*, model, prototype
protuberancia /protuβe'ransia; protuβe'ranθia/ *f*, protuberance, projection, swelling
provecho /pro'βetʃo/ *m*, gain, benefit; profit; advantage; progress, proficiency. **¡Buen p.!** Enjoy your food! Enjoy your meal! **ser de p.**, to be advantageous or useful
provechoso /proβe'tʃoso/ *a* beneficial; profitable; advantageous; useful
provecto /pro'βekto/ *a* ancient, venerable; mature, experienced
proveedor /proβee'ðor/ **(-ra)** *n* provider; purveyor, supplier
proveer /proβe'er/ *vt irr* to provide; furnish; supply; confer (an honor or office); transact, arrange. **p. de**, to furnish or supply with; fit with. See **creer**
provenir /proβe'nir/ *vi irr* (*with de*) to originate in, proceed from. See **venir**
provenzal /proβen'sal; proβen'θal/ *a* and *mf* Provençal. *m*, Provençal (language)
proverbio /pro'βerβio/ *m*, proverb; omen; *pl* Book of Proverbs
providencia /proβi'ðensia; proβi'ðenθia/ *f*, precaution, foresight; provision; furnishing; measure, preparation. **la Divina P.**, Providence
providencial /proβiðen'sial; proβiðen'θial/ *a* providential

próvido /'proβiðo/ *a* provident, thrifty, careful; kind, favorable

provincia /pro'βinsia; pro'βinθia/ *f*, province; *Fig.* sphere

provincial /proβin'sial; proβin'θial/ *a* provincial. *m*, *Eccl.* provincial

provincialismo /proβinsia'lismo; proβinθia'lismo/ *m*, provincialism

provinciano /proβin'siano; proβin'θiano/ **(-na)** *a* provincial. *n* provincial, rustic, countryman; native of Biscay

provisión /proβi'sion/ *f*, stock, store; provision; supply; food supply (gen. *pl*); catering; means, way

provisional /proβisio'nal/ *a* temporary, provisional

provisor /proβi'sor/ *m*, purveyor, supplier; *Eccl.* vicar general

provisorio, -a /proβi'sorio/ *a*, *Lat. Am.* = **provisional**

provocación /proβoka'sion; proβoka'θion/ *f*, provocation

provocador /proβoka'ðor/ **(-ra)** *a* provocative. *n* provoker; instigator

provocar /proβo'kar/ *vt* to provoke; incite; irritate; help, assist; *Inf.* vomit; *Lat. Am.* ¿te provoca ir al cine? Would you like to go to the movies?

provocativo /proβoka'tiβo/ *a* provocative

próximamente /'proksimamente/ *adv* proximately; soon; approximately

proximidad /proksimi'ðað/ *f*, nearness, proximity (in time or space)

próximo /'proksimo/ *a* near, neighboring; next; not distant (of time)

proyección /proiek'sion; proiek'θion/ *f*, projection (all meanings)

proyectante /proiek'tante/ *a* projecting, jutting

proyectar /proiek'tar/ *vt* to throw, cast; plan, contrive; design; project; *vr* jut out; be cast (a shadow, etc.)

proyectil /proyek'til/ *m*, projectile

proyectista /proiek'tista/ *mf* planner

proyecto /pro'iekto/ *a* placed in perspective. *m*, project, plan, scheme; planning; intention, idea

proyector /proiek'tor/ **(-ra)** *n* designer, planner. *m*, searchlight; spotlight; projector

prudencia /pru'ðensia; pru'ðenθia/ *f*, prudence, sagacity, caution; moderation

prudencial /pruðen'sial; pruðen'θial/ *a* prudent, discreet; safe

prudente /pru'ðente/ *a* prudent, cautious; provident

prueba /'prueβa/ *f*, proof; test; quiz (in school); testing; trial; fitting (of garments); sample; taste; *Law.* evidence; (*Photo. Print.*) proof. *Law.* **p. de indicios** *or* **p. indiciaria,** circumstantial evidence. *Photo.* **p. negativa,** negative. *Com.* **a p.,** on approval; on trial; up to standard, perfect. **a p. de,** proof against (water, etc.). **poner a p.,** to put to the test, try out

prurito /pru'rito/ *m*, pruritus; desire, longing

ps- /ps-/ For words too beginning (e.g. *psicología*, *psiquiatría*), see spellings without **p**

púa /'pua/ *f*, prong; tooth (of a comb); quill (of a porcupine); *Agr.* graft; plectrum (for playing the mandolin, etc.); anxiety, grief; pine needle; *Inf.* crafty person

púber /'puβer/ *a* pubescent

pubertad /puβer'tað/ *f*, puberty

púbico /'puβiko/ *a* pubic

publicación /puβlika'sion; puβlika'θion/ *f*, publication; announcement, proclamation; revelation; publishing of marriage banns

publicador /puβlika'ðor/ **(-ra)** *a* publishing. *n* publisher; announcer

publicar /puβli'kar/ *vt* to publish; reveal; announce, proclaim; publish (marriage banns)

publicidad /puβli'ðað; puβliθi'ðað/ *f*, publicity; advertising, propaganda

publicista /puβli'sista; puβli'θista/ *mf* publicist; publicity agent

público /'puβliko/ *a* well-known, universal; common, general; public. *m*, public; audience; gathering, attendance. **dar al p.** *or* **sacar al p.,** to publish

pucherazo /putʃe'raso; putʃe'raθo/ *m*, *Inf.* electoral fraud, vote-fixing

puchero /pu'tʃero/ *m*, *Cul.* kind of stew; stew pot; *Inf.* daily food; puckering of the face preceding tears

pudicia /pu'ðisia; pu'ðiθia/ *f*, modesty; bashfulness; chastity

púdico /'puðiko/ *a* modest; bashful; chaste

pudiente /pu'ðiente/ *a* rich, wealthy; powerful

pudín /pu'ðin/ *m*, pudding

pudor /pu'ðor/ *m*, modesty; bashfulness, shyness

pudoroso /puðo'roso/ *a* modest; shy

pudrir /pu'ðrir/ *vt* to rot, putrefy; irritate, worry, provoke; *vi* rot in the grave; *vr* rot; be consumed with anxiety

puebla /'pueβla/ *f*, town; population; gardener's seed setting

pueblada /pue'βlaða/ *f*, *Lat. Am.* riot; rebellion, revolt, uprising

pueblo /'pueβlo/ *m*, town; village, hamlet; people, population, inhabitants; common people; working classes; nation

puente /'puente/ *mf* bridge; *Mus.* bridge (of stringed instruments); *Naut.* bridge; crossbeam, transom. **p. colgante,** suspension bridge. **p. levadizo,** drawbridge. **hacer p. de plata (a),** to remove obstacles for, make plain sailing

puerco /'puerko/ *m*, pig; wild boar. *a* filthy; rough, rude; low, mean. **p. espín** *or* **p. espino,** porcupine. **p. marino,** dolphin. **p. montés** *or* **p. salvaje,** wild boar

puericultura /puerikul'tura/ *f*, child care

pueril /pue'ril/ *a* childish, puerile; foolish, silly; trivial

puerilidad /puerili'ðað/ *f*, puerility; foolishness; triviality

puerro /'puerro/ *m*, leek

puerta /'puerta/ *f*, door; gate; goal (football, soccer, hockey); means, way. **p. batiente,** swinging door. **p. caediza,** trapdoor. **p. corrediza,** sliding door. **p. de servicio,** tradesman's entrance. **p. falsa** *or* **p. secreta,** secret door; side door. **p. trasera,** back door. **a p. cerrada,** in camera; in secret. *Inf.* **dar con la p. en las narices (de),** to slam the door in a person's face; offend, insult. **llamar a la p.,** to knock at the door; be on the verge of happening. **tomar la p.,** to depart, go away

puerto /'puerto/ *m*, harbor; port; defile, narrow pass; refuge, haven. **p. fluvial,** river port. **p. franco,** free port. **tomar p.,** to put into port; take refuge

Puerto Rico /'puerto 'rriko/ Puerto Rico

puertorriqueño, -a /puertorri'keɲo/ *a* and *mf* Puerto Rican

pues /pues/ *conjunc* then; since, as; for, because; well. *adv* yes, certainly. *conjunc* **p. que,** since, as

puesta /'puesta/ *f*, *Astron.* setting, sinking; stake (in gambling). **p. al día,** aggiornamento, updating; modernization. **p. de largo,** coming of age; coming-out party. **p. del sol,** sunset

puesto /'puesto/ *m*, post, job; booth, stall; beat, pitch; place, position; state, condition; *Mil.* encampment, barracks; office, position. **p. de los testigos,** witness box. **p. de mando,** command, position of authority.

puesto /'puesto/ *a* (*with bien* or *mal*) well-or badly dressed. *conjunc* **p. que,** since, as; although

púgil /'puhil/ *mf* pugilist, boxer

pugilato /puhi'lato/ *m*, boxing; boxing match

pugilista /puhi'lista/ *mf* boxer

pugna /'pugna/ *f*, fight, struggle; rivalry, conflict

pugnante /pug'nante/ *a* hostile, conflicting, rival

pugnar /pug'nar/ *vi* to fight; quarrel; (*with con, contra*) struggle against, oppose; (*with por, para*) strive to

pugnaz /pug'nas; pug'naθ/ *a* pugnacious

puja /'puha/ *f*, outbidding (at an auction); higher bid; push, thrust

pujador /puha'ðor/ **(-ra)** *n* bidder or outbidder (at an auction)

pujante /pu'hante/ *a* strong, powerful, vigorous, pushy

pujanza /pu'hansa; pu'hanθa/ *f*, strength, vigor

pujar /pu'har/ *vt* to push on; bid or outbid (at an auction); *vi* stutter; hesitate, falter; *Inf.* show signs of weeping

pujo /'puho/ *m*, irresistible impulse; desire; will; purpose, intention

pulcritud /pulkri'tuð/ *f*, beauty, loveliness, delicacy; fastidiousness, subtlety

pulcro /'pulkro/ *a* beautiful, lovely; delicate, fine; fastidious, subtle

pulga /'pulga/ *f*, flea; small top (toy). **el juego de la p.**, tiddlywinks. *Inf.* **tener malas pulgas,** to be irritable. **mercado de p.,** flea market

pulgada /pul'gaða/ *f*, inch

pulgar /pul'gar/ *m*, thumb

pulgón /pul'gon/ *m*, aphid, greenfly

pulgoso /pul'goso/ *a* full of fleas

pulguiento /pul'giento/ *a*, *Lat. Am.* = **pulgoso**

pulidez /puli'ðes; puli'ðeθ/ *f*, elegance, fineness; polish, smoothness; neatness

pulido /pu'liðo/ *a* elegant, fine; polished, smooth; neat

pulidor /puli'ðor/ *m*, polisher (machine)

pulimentar /pulimen'tar/ *vt* to polish, burnish

pulir /pu'lir/ *vt* to polish, burnish; give the finishing touch to; beautify, decorate; *Fig.* polish up, civilize; *vr* beautify oneself; become polished and polite

pulla /'puya; 'puʎa/ *f*, lewd remark; strong hint; witty comment

pulmón /pul'mon/ *m*, lung

pulmonar /pulmo'nar/ *a* pulmonary

pulmonía /pulmo'nia/ *f*, pneumonia

pulpa /'pulpa/ *f*, fleshy part of fruit; *Anat.* pulp; wood pulp

pulpejo /pul'peho/ *m*, *Anat.* fleshy part, fat portion (of thumbs, etc.)

pulpería /pulpe'ria/ *f*, *West Hem.* grocery, grocery store, general store; bar, tavern

púlpito /'pulpito/ *m*, pulpit

pulpo /'pulpo/ *m*, octopus. *Inf.* **poner como un p.,** to beat to a pulp

pulposo /pul'poso/ *a* pulpy, pulpous

pulque /'pulke/ *m*, pulque (fermented maguey juice)

pulquérrimo /pul'kerrimo/ *a sup* **pulcro** most lovely, most exquisite

pulsación /pulsa'sion; pulsa'θion/ *f*, pulsation; throb, beat

pulsar /pul'sar/ *vt* to touch, feel; take the pulse of; *Fig.* explore (a possibility); *vi* beat (the heart, etc.)

pulsera /pul'sera/ *f*, bracelet; wrist bandage. **p. de pedida,** betrothal bracelet

pulso /'pulso/ *m*, pulse; steadiness of hand; tact, diplomacy, circumspection. **a p.,** freehand (drawing). **tomar a p. (una cosa),** to try a thing's weight. **tomar el p. (a),** to take a person's pulse

pulular /pulu'lar/ *vi* to pullulate, sprout; abound, be plentiful; swarm, teem; multiply (of insects)

pulverización /pulβerisa'sion; pulβeriθa'θion/ *f*, pulverization; atomization

pulverizador /pulβerisa'ðor; pulβeriθa'ðor/ *m*, atomizer, sprayer; scent spray

pulverizar /pulβeri'sar; pulβeri'θar/ *vt* to pulverize, grind, make into powder; atomize; spray

¡pum! /pum/ *interj* Bang! Thump!

pundonor /pundo'nor/ *m*, (**punto de honor**) point of honor, sense of honor

pundonoroso /pundono'roso/ *a* careful of one's honor; honorable, punctilious

pungir /pun'hir/ *vt* to prick, pierce; revive an old sorrow; *Fig.* wound, sting (passions)

punible /pu'niβle/ *a* punishable

punitivo /puni'tiβo/ *a* punitive, punitory

punta /'punta/ *f*, sharp end, point; butt (of a cigarette); end, point, tip; cape, headland; trace, touch, suspicion; nib (of a pen); pointing (pointer dogs); *Herald.* point; *pl* point lace. **p. de París,** wire nail. **p. seca,** drypoint, engraving needle. **cortar las puntas,** to trim one's hair. **sacar p.,** to sharpen; *Inf.* twist (a remark)

puntación /punta'sion; punta'θion/ *f*, dotting, placing dots over (letters)

puntada /pun'taða/ *f*, *Sew.* stitch; innuendo, hint

puntal /pun'tal/ *m*, *Naut.* draft, depth; stanchion, prop, brace, pile; *Fig.* basis, foundation; *Lat. Am.* bite (to eat), snack

puntapié /punta'pie/ *m*, kick

punteado /punte'aðo/ *m*, plucking the strings of a guitar, etc.; sewing

puntear /punte'ar/ *vt* to make dots; *Mus.* pluck the strings of; play the guitar; sew; *Art.* stipple; *vi Naut.* tack

puntera /pun'tera/ *f*, mend in the toe of a stocking; toe cap; new piece on the toe of shoe; *Inf.* kick

puntería /punte'ria/ *f*, aiming (of a firearm); aim, sight (of a firearm); marksmanship

puntero /pun'tero/ *a* of a good aim, having a straight eye. *m*, pointer, wand; stonecutter's chisel

puntiagudo /puntia'guðo/ *a* pointed, sharp-pointed

puntilla /pun'tiya; pun'tiʎa/ *f*, narrow lace edging; headless nail, wire nail; brad, tack. **de puntillas,** on tiptoe

puntilloso /punti'yoso; punti'ʎoso/ *a* punctilious; overfastidious, fussy

punto /'punto/ *m.;* dot; point; pen nib; gun sight; *Sew.* stitch; dropped stitch, hole; weaving stitch, mesh; *Gram.* full stop, period; hole (in belts for adjustment); place, spot; point, mark; subject matter; *Mech.* cog; degree, extent; taxi stand; instant; infinitesimal amount; opportunity, chance; vacation, recess; aim, goal; point of honor. **p. de congelación,** freezing point. **p. de ebullición,** boiling point. **p. de fuga,** vanishing point. **p. de fusión,** melting point. **p. de partida,** starting point. **p. de vista,** point of view. **p. final,** *Gram.* period, full stop. **p. interrogante,** question mark. **p. menos,** a little less. **p. y coma,** semicolon. **p. cardinal,** cardinal point. **p. suspensivo,** *Gram.* ellipsis point, suspension point, leader, dot. **a p.,** in readiness; immediately. **en p.,** sharp, prompt (e.g. *a las seis en p.,* at six o'clock sharp)

puntoso /pun'toso/ *a* many-pointed

puntuación /puntua'sion; puntua'θion/ *f*, punctuation; *Sports.* score

puntual /pun'tual/ *a* punctual; punctilious; certain, indubitable; suitable, convenient

puntualidad /puntuali'ðað/ *f*, punctuality; punctiliousness; certainty; exactitude, accuracy

puntualizar /puntuali'sar; puntuali'θar/ *vt* to describe in detail; give the finishing touch to, perfect; impress on the mind

puntualmente /puntual'mente/ *adv* punctually; carefully, diligently; exactly

puntuar /pun'tuar/ *vt* to punctuate

puntudo /pun'tuðo/ *a*, *Lat. Am.* = **puntiagudo**

punzada /pun'saða; pun'θaða/ *f*, prick, sting; puncture, piercing; sudden pain, twinge, stitch; *Fig.* anguish, pain

punzar /pun'sar; pun'θar/ *vt* to pierce, puncture; prick; punch, perforate; *vi* revive, make itself felt (pain or sorrow)

punzón /pun'son; pun'θon/ *m*, awl; punch; die; engraver's burin

puñado /pu'ɲaðo/ *m*, handful; a few, some, a small quantity. **a puñados,** in handfuls; liberally, lavishly

puñal /pu'ɲal/ *m*, dagger

puñalada /puɲa'laða/ *f*, dagger thrust; stab, wound; *Fig.* unexpected blow (of fate). **p. por la espalda,** stab in the back

puñetazo /puɲe'taso; puɲe'taθo/ *m*, blow with the fist

puño /'puɲo/ *m*, fist; handful; cuff (of a sleeve); wristband; handle, head, haft; hilt (of a sword); *pl Inf.* guts, courage. **p. de amura,** *Naut.* tack. **p. de un manillar,** handlebar grip. *Inf.* **meter en un p.,** to overawe. *Inf.* **ser como un p.,** to be tightfisted; be small (in stature)

pupila /pu'pila/ *f*, female child ward; *Anat.* pupil; *Inf.* cleverness, talent

pupilaje /pupi'lahe/ *m*, pupilage, minority; boarding house, guesthouse; boarding school; price of board residence; dependence; bondage

pupilo /pu'pilo/ **(-la)** *n* ward, minor; boarder; boarding school student; *Lat. Am.* prostitute, whore

pupitre /pu'pitre/ *m*, desk, school desk
puquío /pu'kio/ *m Lat. Am.* spring (of water)
puramente /pura'mente/ *adv* purely; simply, solely; *Law.* unconditionally, without reservation
puré /pu're/ *m*, purée, thick soup
pureza /pu'reθa/ *f*, purity; perfection, excellence; chastity; disinterestedness, genuineness; clearness
purga /'purga/ *f*, laxative, purge; waste product
purgación /purga'sion; purga'θion/ *f*, purging; menstruation; gonorrhea
purgante /pur'gante/ *a* purgative. *m*, purge, cathartic
purgar /pur'gar/ *vt* to cleanse, purify; expiate, atone for; (*Med. Law.*) purge; suffer purgatorial pains; clarify, refine; *vr* rid oneself, purge oneself
purgativo /purga'tiβo/ *a* purgative
purgatorio /purga'torio/ *m*, purgatory. *a* purgatorial
puridad /puri'ðað/ *f*, purity; secrecy, privacy. **en p.,** openly, without dissembling; secretly, in private
purificación /purifika'sion; purifika'θion/ *f*, purification; cleansing
purificador /purifika'ðor/ **(-ra)** *a* purifying; cleansing. *n* purifier; cleanser
purificar /purifi'kar/ *vt* to purify; cleanse; *vr* be purified
purificatorio /purifika'torio/ *a* purificatory
Purísima /pu'risima/ **(la)** *f*, the Most Blessed Virgin

purista /pu'rista/ *mf* purist
puritano /puri'tano/ **(-na)** *a* puritanical. *n* Puritan
puro /'puro/ *a* pure; undiluted; unalloyed; unmixed; disinterested, honest; virgin; absolute, sheer; mere, simple. *m*, cigar. **de p.,** by sheer..., by dint of
púrpura /'purpura/ *f*, purple; *Poet.* blood; purpura; *Herald.* purpure; purple (cloth); dignity of an emperor, cardinal, consul
purpurear /purpure'ar/ *vi* to look like purple; be tinged with purple
purpurina /purpu'rina/ *f Lat. Am.* metallic paint
purulencia /puru'lensia; puru'lenθia/ *f*, purulence
purulento /puru'lento/ *a* purulent
pus /pus/ *m*, pus, matter
pusilánime /pusi'lanime/ *a* pusillanimous, timid, cowardly
pústula /'pustula/ *f*, pustule
putativo /puta'tiβo/ *a* putative
puto, -a /'puto/ *mf* prostitute
putrefacción /putrefak'sion; putrefak'θion/ *f*, putrefaction; rottenness, putrescence
putrefacto /putre'fakto/ *a* rotten, decayed
pútrido /'putriðo/ *a* putrid, rotten
puya /'puya/ *f*, goad
puyar /pu'yar/ *vt Lat. Am.* to jab, prick, stick; *Fig.* needle
puyazo /pu'yaso; pu'yaθo/ *m*, prick with a goad

Q

que /ke/ *pron rel* all genders sing. and pl. who; which; that; whom; when (e.g. *Un poema en que habla de su juventud,* A poem in which he speaks of his youth. *El libro que tengo aquí,* The book (that) I have here. **No es oro todo lo que reluce,** All that glitters is not gold. **Un día que nos vimos,** One day when we met —*interr* **¿qué?** what? *interj* what a ------! what! how! (e.g. *¿Qué hay?* What's the matter? *¡Qué día más hermoso!* What a lovely day! *¿qué de...?* what's up with...? *¿qué tal?* How are you? *Inf. ¿Qué tal estás hoy?* How are you today? *¿qué tanto?* how much?) **¿a qué?** why? for what reason? (e.g. *¿A qué negarlo?* Why deny it?) —*conjunc* that (e.g. *Me dijo que vendría,* He said (that) he would come). Means "so that," 'that,' "for,' in commands (e.g. *Mandó que le trajesen el libro,* He ordered that they bring him the book (He ordered them to bring him the book)). Note that the translation of **que** is often omitted in English. In compound tenses where the participle is placed first, **que** means "when" (e.g. *llegado que hube,* when I had arrived). In comparisons, **que** means "than' (e.g. *más joven que yo,* younger than I). With subjunctives and expressing commands or wishes, **que** means "let' (e.g. *¡Que venga!* Let him come!) Preceding a subjunctive, **que** is generally translated by "to' (e.g. *Quiero, que venga or que llueva,* I want him to come *or* I want it to rain). Also means "may' (e.g. *¡Que lo pase bien!* May you enjoy yourself! (I hope you...)). **que le vaya bien,** May it go well with you (when saying goodbye). **es (era) que,** the fact is (was) that... **que... que,** whether... or...
quebrada /ke'βraða/ *f*, mountain gorge, ravine; *Com.* bankruptcy; *Lat. Am.* brook, stream
quebradizo /keβra'ðiso; keβra'ðiθo/ *a* brittle, fragile; ailing, infirm; delicate, frail
quebrado /ke'βraðo/ **(-da)** *m*, *Math.* fraction; *n Com.* bankrupt. *a* rough, uneven (ground); *Med.* ruptured; bankrupt; ailing, broken-down
quebradura /keβra'ðura/ *f*, snap, breaking; gap, crevice; hernia
quebraja /ke'βraha/ *f*, split, crack; flaw (in wood, metal, etc.)
quebrantahuesos /keβranta'uesos/ *m*, sea eagle, osprey; *Inf.* bore, tedious person
quebrantamiento /keβranta'miento/ *m*, crushing; splitting, cleaving; fracture, rupture; profanation, des-

ecration; burglary; violation, breaking; infringement; fatigue; *Law.* annulment; exhaustion
quebrantanueces /keβranta'nueθes; keβranta'nueθes/ *m*, nutcrackers
quebrantaolas /keβranta'olas/ *m*, breakwater
quebrantar /keβran'tar/ *vt* to break, shatter; crush, pound; transgress, infringe; break out, force; tone down, soften; moderate, lessen; bore, exhaust; move to pity; *Inf.* break in (horses); profane; overcome (difficulties); assuage, placate; *Law.* revoke (wills); *vr* be shaken or bruised, suffer from aftereffects
quebranto /ke'βranto/ *m*, breaking, shattering; crushing, pounding; infringement; breaking out (from prison); weakness, exhaustion; compassion, pity; loss, damage; pain, suffering
quebrar /ke'βrar/ *vt irr* to break, shatter; crush; impede, hinder; make pale (color, gen. of complexion); mitigate, moderate; bend, twist; overcome (difficulties); *vi* break off (a friendship); weaken, give way; go bankrupt; *vr Med.* suffer from hernia; be interrupted (of mountain ranges). **quebrarse los ojos,** to strain one's eyes. *Pres. Ind.* **quiebro, quiebras, quiebra, quiebran.** *Pres. Subjunc.* **quiebre, quiebres, quiebre, quiebren**
queda /'keða/ *f*, curfew; curfew bell
quedada /ke'ðaða/ *f*, stay, sojourn
quedar /ke'ðar/ *vi* to stay, sojourn; remain; be left over; (*with por + infin.*) remain to be (e.g. *Queda por escribir,* It remains to be written); (*with por*) be won by or be knocked down to; be, remain in a place; end, cease; (*with en*) reach an agreement (e.g. *Quedamos en no ir,* We have decided not to go). **q. en esta alternativa...,** to face this alternative:.... *vr* remain; abate (wind); grow calm (sea); (*with con*) keep, retain possession of. **q. bien o mal,** to behave well or badly, come off well or badly (in business affairs, etc.). **quedarse muerto,** to be astounded
quedo /'keðo/ *a* still, motionless; quiet, tranquil. *adv* in a low voice; quietly, noiselessly. **de q.,** slowly, gradually. *interj* **¡Q.!** Quiet!
quehacer /kea'ser; kea'θer/ *m*, odd job; task; business (gen. *pl*)
queja /'keha/ *f*, lamentation, grief; complaint, grudge; quarrel
quejarse /ke'harse/ *vr* to lament; complain, grumble; *Law.* lodge an accusation (against)
quejido /ke'hiðo/ *m*, complaint, moan
quejoso /ke'hoso/ *a* querulous, complaining

quejumbre /ke'humbre/ f, complaint, whine; querulousness

quejumbroso /kehum'βroso/ a complaining, grumbling

quelite /ke'lite/ m, Central America, Mexico vegetables

quema /'kema/ f, burn; burning; fire, conflagration

quemadero /kema'ðero/ a burnable. m, stake (for burning people)

quemado /ke'maðo/ m, burned patch of forest; Inf. anything burned or burning

quemador /kema'ðor/ **(-ra)** m, jet, burner. n incendiary

quemadura /kema'ðura/ f, burn; scald; burning

quemajoso /kema'hoso/ a smarting, burning, pricking

quemar /ke'mar/ vt to burn; dry up, parch; scorch; tan, bronze; scald; throw away, sell at a loss; vi burn, be excessively hot; vr be very hot; be dried up with the heat; burn with (passions); Inf. be near the attainment of a desired end. **quemarse las cejas,** to burn the midnight oil, study too hard

quemazón /kema'son; kema'θon/ f, burning; conflagration; intense heat; Inf. smarting; Inf. hurtful remark; Inf. vexation, soreness

quena /'kena/ f kind of Native American flute

querella /ke'reya; ke'reʎa/ f, complaint; quarrel, fight

querellarse /kere'yarse; kere'ʎarse/ vr to complain; lament, bemoan; Law. lodge an accusation; Law. contest a will

querelloso /kere'yoso; kere'ʎoso/ a complaining, grumbling, querulous

querencia /ke'rensia; ke'renθia/ f, love, affection; homing instinct; lair; natural inclination or desire

querer /ke'rer/ vt irr to desire, wish; want, will; attempt, endeavor; (with a) love. impers be on the point of. **q. decir,** to mean. **¿Qué quiere decir esto?** What does this mean? **sin q.,** unintentionally. See **entender**

querer /ke'rer/ m, affection, love

querido /ke'riðo/ **(-da)** n lover; beloved; darling. a dear

querub, querube /ke'ruβ, ke'ruβe/ Poet. **querubín** m, cherub

querúbico /ke'ruβiko/ a cherubic

quesadillas, /kesa'ðijas; kesa'ðiʎas/ fpl, Mexico maize dough with beans or cheese fried like a turnover

quesera /ke'sera/ f, dairymaid; dairy; cheese vat; cheese board; cheese dish

quesería /kese'ria/ f, dairy; cheese shop; season for making cheese

queso /'keso/ m, cheese. **q. rallado,** grated cheese

quetzal /ket'sal; ket'θal/ m, quetzal (monetary unit of Guatemala)

quevedos /ke'βeðos/ m pl, glasses, eyeglasses; pince-nez

¡quia! /kia/ interj Inf. You don't say so!

quianti /'kianti/ m, chianti

quicial /ki'sial; ki'θial/ m, doorjamb

quicio /'kisio; 'kiθio/ m, threshold; hinge; Mech. bushing. **fuera de q.,** out of order; unhinged. **sacar de q.,** to displace (things); annoy, irritate; drive crazy

quiebra /'kieβra/ f, breach, crack; rut, fissure; loss; bankruptcy

quiebro /'kieβro/ m, twisting of the body, dodging; Mus. trill

quien /kien/ rel pron mf pl **quienes.** interr **quién,** **quiénes** who; whom; he (she, etc.) who, anyone who, whoever; which; whichever (e.g. mis padres a quienes respeto, my parents whom I respect. Quien te quiere te hará llorar, Whoever (he, those, who) love(s) you will make you weep. **¿Quién está a la puerta?** Who is at the door? **¿De quién es?** Whose is it? To whom does it belong?). indef pron one (pl some)

quienquiera /kien'kiera/ indef pron mf pl **quienesquiera,** whosoever, whichever, whomsoever

quietador /kieta'ðor/ **(-ra)** a tranquilizing, soothing. n soother

quieto /'kieto/ a quiet, still; peaceful, tranquil; virtuous, respectable

quietud /kie'tuð/ f, stillness, repose; peacefulness; rest, quietness

quif /kif/ m, hashish, marijuana

quijada /ki'haða/ f, jawbone, jaw; Mech. jaw

quijo /'kiho/ m, ore (gold or silver)

quijotada /kiho'taða/ f, quixotic action, quixotism

quijote /ki'hote/ m, cuisse; thigh guard; quixotic person

quijotesco /kiho'tesko/ a quixotic

quilate /ki'late/ m, carat; degree of excellence (gen. pl). Inf. **por quilates,** in small bits, parsimoniously

quilla /'kiya; 'kiʎa/ f, Naut. keel; breastbone (of birds)

quillotrar /kiyo'trar; kiʎo'trar/ vt Inf. to encourage, incite; woo, make love to; consider; vr Inf. fall in love; dress up; whine, complain

quillotro /ki'yotro; ki'ʎotro/ m, Inf. incentive; indication, sign; love affair; puzzle, knotty point; compliment; dressing up

quimera /ki'mera/ f, chimera; fancy, vision; quarrel, dispute

quimérico /ki'meriko/ a chimerical, fanciful

quimerista /kime'rista/ mf dreamer, visionary; quarreler, disputant

química /'kimika/ f, chemistry

químico /'kimiko/ a chemical. m, chemist. **productos químicos,** chemicals

quimioterapia /kimiote'rapia/ f, chemotherapy

quimono /ki'mono/ m, kimono

quina /'kina/ f, cinchona; quinine; pl Arms of Portugal. Inf. **tragar q.,** to suffer in patience, put up with

quinario /ki'nario/ m, Argentina mud hut

quincalla /kin'kaya; kin'kaʎa/ f, cheap jewelery; fancy goods

quincallería /kinkaye'ria; kinkaʎe'ria/ f, cheap jewelry shop; hardware factory or industry; cheap jewelry; fancy goods

quince /'kinse; 'kinθe/ a and m, fifteen; fifteenth

quinceañero /kinsea'ɲero; kinθea'ɲero/ f, sweet sixteen party, sweet sixteen (in Spanish-speaking areas, held at age fifteen)

quincena /kin'sena; kin'θena/ f, fortnight, two weeks; bimonthly pay; Mus. fifteenth

quincenal /kinse'nal; kinθe'nal/ a fortnightly; lasting a fortnight, lasting two weeks

quinceno /kin'seno; kin'θeno/ a fifteenth

quincuagenario /kinkuahe'nario/ a quinquagenarian

quincuagésimo /kinkua'hesimo/ a fiftieth

quindécimo /kin'desimo; kin'deθimo/ a fifteenth

quinientos /ki'nientos/ a five hundred; five-hundredth. m, five hundred

quinina /ki'nina/ f, quinine

quinqué /kin'ke/ m, oil lamp, student's lamp, table lamp; perspicuity, talent

quinquenio /kin'kenio/ m, period of five years, lustrum

quinta /'kinta/ f, country house; Mus. fifth; conscripting men into army by drawing lots; Mil. draft

quintaesencia /kintae'sensia; kintae'senθia/ f, quintessence

quintal /kin'tal/ m, hundredweight

quintar /kin'tar/ vt to draw one out of every five; draw lots for conscription into the army; vi reach the fifth (day, etc., gen. of the moon)

quintería /kinte'ria/ f, farm

quintero /kin'tero/ m, farmer; farmworker

quinteto /kin'teto/ m, quintet

Quintín, San. armarse /kin'tin, san ar'marse/ (or **haber) la de San Q.** to quarrel, make trouble; be a row

quinto /'kinto/ a fifth. m, one-fifth; Mil. conscript; duty of twenty percent; Law. fifth part of an estate. **quinta columna,** fifth column. **quinta esencia,** quintessence

quintuplicar /kintupli'kar/ vt to quintuplicate

quíntuplo /'kintuplo/ a fivefold, quintuple

quiñón /ki'ɲon/ m, share of land owned jointly, share of the profits

quiosco /'kiosko/ m, kiosk, stand; pavilion, pagoda. **q. de música,** bandstand

quipo /'kipo/ *m* quipu (Native American rope writing in Peru)
quisquiriquí /kikiri'ki/ *m*, cock-a-doodle-doo; *Fig. Inf.* cock of the walk
quiromancia /kiro'mansia; kiro'manθia/ *f*, chiromancy, palmistry
quiromántico /kiro'mantiko/ **(-ca)** *n* chiromancer, palmist
quirúrgico /ki'rurhiko/ *a* surgical
quirurgo /ki'rurgo/ *m*, surgeon
quisicosa /kisi'kosa/ *f*, *Inf.* riddle, puzzle, enigma
quisquilla /kis'kiya; kis'kiʎa/ *f*, trifle, quibble, scruple; prawn, shrimp
quisquilloso /kiski'yoso; kiski'ʎoso/ *a* quibbling, overscrupulous, fastidious; hypersensitive; irascible, touchy
quistarse /kis'tarse/ *vr* to make oneself well-liked or loved
quiste /'kiste/ *m*, *Med.* cyst
quita /'kita/ *f*, *Law.* discharge (of part of a debt)
quitaesmalte /kitaes'malte/ *m*, nail polish remover (for fingernails)

quitamanchas /kita'mantʃas/ *mf*, dry cleaner, clothes cleaner
quitamotas /kita'motas/ *mf Inf.* flatterer, adulator
quitanieve /kita'nieβe/ *m*, snowplow
quitanza /ki'tansa; ki'tanθa/ *f*, quittance; quietus
quitapesares /kitape'sares/ *m*, *Inf.* consolation, solace, comfort
quitar /ki'tar/ *vt* to remove; take off or away; clear (the table); rob, steal; prevent, impede; parry (in fencing); separate; redeem (pledges); forbid; annul, repeal (laws, etc.); free from (obligations); *vr* shed, take off, remove; get rid of; leave, quit. **quitarse de encima (a),** to get rid of someone or something. **q. el polvo,** to dust. **de quita y pon,** detachable, removable; adjustable
quitasol /kita'sol/ *m*, parasol, sunshade
quitasueño /kita'sueɲo/ *m*, *Inf.* sleep banisher, anxiety
quite /'kite/ *m*, hindering, impeding; obstruction; parry (in fencing). **estar al q.,** to be ready to protect someone
quizá, quizás /ki'sa, ki'sas; ki'θa, ki'θas/ *adv* perhaps. **q. y sin q.,** without doubt, certainly

R

rabadán /rraβa'ðan/ *m*, head shepherd or herdsman
rabadilla /rraβa'ðiya; rraβa'ðiʎa/ *f*, rump, croup
rábano /'rraβano/ *m*, radish. **r. picante,** horseradish
rabel /rra'βel/ *m*, *Mus.* rebec; *Inf.* backside, seat
rabera /rra'βera/ *f*, tail-end; chaff, siftings
rabí /rra'βi/ *m*, rabbi
rabia /'rraβia/ *f*, rabies, hydrophobia; anger, fury. *Inf.* **tener r. (a),** to hate
rabiar /rra'βiar/ *vi* to suffer from hydrophobia; groan with pain; be furious; (*with por*) yearn for, desire. **a r.,** excessively
rabieta /rra'βieta/ *f*, *Inf.* tantrum
rabínico /rra'βiniko/ *a* rabbinical
rabinismo /rraβi'nismo/ *m*, rabbinism
rabino /rra'βino/ *m*, rabbi. **gran r.,** chief rabbi
rabioso /rra'βioso/ *a* rabid; furious, angry; vehement. **perro r.,** mad dog
rabo /'rraβo/ *m*, tail; *Bot.* stalk; *Inf.* train (of a dress); shank (of a button). **r. del ojo,** corner of the eye. *Fig. Inf.* **ir r. entre piernas,** to have one's tail between one's legs
rabón /rra'βon/ *a* tailless, docked; bobtailed
rabonear /rraβone'ar/ *vi*, *Lat. Am.* to play hookey
rabudo /rra'βuðo/ *a* big-tailed
racimo /rra'simo; rra'θimo/ *m*, bunch (of grapes or other fruits); cluster; raceme
raciocinar /rrasiosi'nar; rraθioθi'nar/ *vi* to reason
raciocinio /rrasio'sinio; rraθio'θinio/ *m*, reasoning; ratiocination; discourse, speech
ración /rra'sion; rra'θion/ *f*, ration; portion (in a restaurant); meal allowance; *Eccl.* prebendary. *Inf.* **r. de hambre,** starvation diet; pittance, starvation wages
racional /rrasio'nal; rraθio'nal/ *a* reasonable, logical; rational
racionalidad /rrasionali'ðað; rraθionali'ðað/ *f*, reasonableness; rationality
racionalismo /rrasiona'lismo; rraθiona'lismo/ *m*, rationalism
racionalista /rrasiona'lista; rraθiona'lista/ *a* and *mf* rationalist. *a* rationalistic
racionalización /rrasionalisa'sion; rraθionaliθa'θion/ *f*, rationalization
racionamiento /rrasiona'miento; rraθiona'miento/ *m*, rationing. *f.* **cartilla de r.,** ration book
racionar /rrasio'nar; rraθio'nar/ *vt* to ration
racismo /rra'θismo/ *m*, racism
rada /'rraða/ *f*, bay, cove; *Naut.* road, roadstead
radar /rra'ðar/ *m*, radar
radiación /rraðia'sion; rraðia'θion/ *f*, radiation; *Radio.* broadcasting
radiactividad /rraðiaktiβi'ðað/ *f*, radioactivity

radiactivo /rraðiak'tiβo/ *a* radioactive
radiador /rraðia'ðor/ *m*, radiator (for heating); *Auto.* radiator
radial /rra'ðial/ *a* radial
radiante /rra'ðiante/ *a Phys.* radiating; brilliant, shining; *Fig.* beaming (with satisfaction)
radiar /rra'ðiar/ *vi Phys.* to radiate; *vt* broadcast (by radio); *Lat. Am.* to cross off, delete, erase
radical /rraði'kal/ *a* radical; fundamental; *Polit.* radical. *m*, *Gram.* root; (*Math. Chem.*) radical. *mf Polit.* radical
radicalismo /rraðika'lismo/ *m*, radicalism
radicar /rraði'kar/ **(se)** *vi* and *vr* to take root. **r. una solicitud,** file an application, submit an application. *vi* be (in a place)
radio /'rraðio/ *m*, (*Geom. Anat.*) radius; radium. *f*, radio
radioaficionado /rraðioafisio'naðo; rraðioafiθio'naðo/ **(-da)** *n* radio amateur; *Inf.* ham, wireless fan or enthusiast
radioaudición /rraðioauði'sion; rraðioauði'θion/ *f*, radio broadcast
radiocomunicación /rraðiokomunika'sion; rraðiokomunika'θion/ *f*, radio transmission
radiodifundir /rraðioðifun'dir/ *vt Radio.* to broadcast
radiodifusión, radioemisión /rraðioðifu'sion, rraðioemi'sion/ *f*, *Radio.* broadcast; broadcasting
radiodifusora /rraðioðifu'sora/ *f*, *Lat. Am.* = **radioemisora**
radioemisora /rraðioemi'sora/ *f*, radio station; (radio) transmitter
radioescucha /rraðioes'kutʃa/ *mf* radio listener
radiofotografía /rraðiofotogra'fia/ *f*, radiophotography; x-ray photograph. **tomar una r. de,** to x-ray
radiofrecuencia /rraðiofre'kuensia; rraðiofre'kuenθia/ *f*, radiofrequency
radiografía /rraðiogra'fia/ *f*, radiography, x-ray
radiografiar /rraðiogra'fiar/ *vt* to x-ray, radiograph
radiografista /rraðiogra'fista/ *mf* radiographer
radiograma /rraðio'grama/ *m*, radiogram, cable
radiolocación /rraðioloka'sion; rraðioloka'θion/ *f*, radiolocation
radiología /rraðiolo'hia/ *f*, radiology
radiólogo /rra'ðiologo/ *mf* radiologist
radiometría /rraðiome'tria/ *f*, radiometry
radiómetro /rra'ðiometro/ *m*, radiometer
radiorreceptor /rraðiorresep'tor; rraðiorreθep'tor/ *m*, receiver, wireless set
radioscopia /rraðio'skopia/ *f*, radioscopy
radiotelefonía /rraðiotelefo'nia/ *f*, radiotelephony
radiotelegrafía /rraðiotelegra'fia/ *f*, radiotelegraphy

radiotelegráfico /rraðiotele'grafiko/ *a* radiotelegraphic, wireless

radiotelegrafista /rraðiotelegra'fista/ *mf* wireless operator

radiotelegrama /rraðiotele'grama/ *m*, radiogram, radiotelegram

radioterapia /rraðiote'rapia/ *f*, radiotherapy, radiotherapeutics

radiotransmisor /rraðiotransmi'sor/ *m*, (radio) transmitter

radioyente /rraðio'yente/ *mf* radio listener

raedera /rrae'ðera/ *f*, scraper

raedor /rrae'ðor/ *a* scraping; abrasive

raedura /rrae'ðura/ *f*, scraping; rubbing; fraying

raer /rra'er/ *vt irr* to scrape; abrade; fray; *Fig.* extirpate. See **caer**

ráfaga /'rrafaga/ *f*, gust or blast of wind; light cloud; flash (of light)

rafe /'rrafe/ *m*, eaves

rafia /'rrafia/ *f*, raffia

raicear /rraise'ar/ *vi*, *Lat. Am.* to take root

raído /'rraiðo/ *a* frayed, threadbare; brazen, barefaced

raíz /rra'is; rra'iθ/ *f*, root. **r. amarga,** horseradish. **r. cuadrada (cúbica),** square (cubed) root. **r. pivotante,** tap root. **r. fuerte,** *Mexico* horseradish **a r.,** close to the root, closely. **a r. de,** as a result of; after. **de r.,** from the root, entirely. **echar raíces,** to take root

raja /'rraha/ *f*, split, crack; chip, splinter (of wood); slice (of fruit, etc.)

rajadura /rraha'ðura/ *f*, splitting; crack, split, crevice; *Geol.* break

rajar /rra'har/ *vt* to crack, split; slice; *vi Inf.* boast; chatter; *vr* crack, split; *Inf.* take back one's words

ralea /rra'lea/ *f*, kind, quality; (*inf* scornful) race, lineage

ralear /rrale'ar/ *vi* to grow thin (cloth, etc.); behave true to type (gen. in a bad sense)

rallador /rraya'ðor; rraʎa'ðor/ *m*, *Cul.* grater

rallar /rra'yar; rra'ʎar/ *vt Cul.* to grate; *Inf.* bother, annoy

rallo /'rrayo; 'rraʎo/ *m*, *Cul.* grater; rasp

ralo /'rralo/ *a* sparse, thin

rama /'rrama/ *f*, bough, branch; *Fig.* branch (of family). *Fig. Inf.* **andarse por las ramas,** to beat around the bush. **en r.,** *Com.* raw; unbound (of books)

ramaje /rra'mahe/ *m*, thickness of branches, denseness of foliage

ramal /rra'mal/ *m*, strand (of rope); halter; branch line (of a railroad); fork (of a road, etc.); ramification, division

ramalazo /rrama'laso; rrama'laθo/ *m*, blow with a rope; mark left by this; bruise

rambla /'rrambla/ *f*, bed, channel, course; avenue, boulevard (in Catalonia)

ramera /rra'mera/ *f*, whore

ramificación /rramifika'sion; rramifika'θion/ *f*, ramification; *Anat.* bifurcation

ramificarse /rramifi'karse/ *vr* to branch, fork; *Fig.* spread

ramillete /rrami'yete; rrami'ʎete/ *m*, bouquet; table centerpiece; *Bot.* cluster

ramo /'rramo/ *m*, *Bot.* branch; twig, spray; bouquet, bunch; wreath; *Fig.* branch (of learning, etc.); *Com.* line (of business); *Fig.* touch, slight attack. **Domingo de Ramos,** Palm Sunday

ramoso /rra'moso/ *a* branchy, thick with branches

rampa /'rrampa/ *f*, gradient, incline; *Mil.* ramp; launching site

ramplón /rram'plon/ *a* stout, heavy (of shoes); coarse; vulgar; bombastic

rana /'rrana/ *f*, frog. **r. de San Antonio,** tree frog

ranchero /rran'tʃero/ *m*, *Mil.* cook; small farmer; *West Hem.* rancher

rancho /'rrantʃo/ *m*, mess, rations; settlement, camp; hut, cabin; *Inf.* group, huddle; *West Hem.* ranch; *Naut.* gang. **hacer r.,** *Inf.* to make room

rancidez /rransi'ðes; rranθi'ðeθ/ *f*, rancidness; staleness; rankness; antiquity

ranciedad /rransie'ðað; rranθie'ðað/ *f*, rancidness; antiquity, oldness; mustiness

rancio /'rransio; 'rranθio/ *a* rancid, rank; mellow (of wine); ancient; traditional; musty

rancotán /rranko'tan/ *adv*, *Lat. Am.* in cash

rango /'rrango/ *m*, grade, class; range; (*Mil. Nav.* and social) rank; file, line

ranura /rra'nura/ *f*, groove; rabbet; slot, notch

rapacidad /rrapasi'ðað; rrapaθi'ðað/ *f*, rapacity, avidity, greed

rapador /rrapa'ðor/ *a* scraping. *m*, *Inf.* barber

rapapolvo /rrapa'polβo/ *m*, *Inf.* severe scolding, dressing-down

rapar /rra'par/ **(se)** *vt* and *vr* to shave; *vt* crop, cut close (hair); *Inf.* steal, pinch

rapaz /rra'pas; rra'paθ/ *a* rapacious. *m*, young boy. **ave r.,** bird of prey

rapaza /rra'pasa; rra'paθa/ *f*, young girl

rape /'rrape/ *m*, *Inf.* hasty shave or haircut. **al r.,** close-cropped

rapidez /rrapi'ðes; rrapi'ðeθ/ *f*, speed, swiftness, rapidity

rápido /'rrapiðo/ *a* quick, swift; express (trains). *m*, torrent, rapid; express train

rapiña /rra'pina/ *f*, robbery, plundering, sacking

rapiñar /rrapi'nar/ *vt Inf.* to steal, pinch

raposa /rra'posa/ *f*, vixen, fox; *Inf.* wily person

raposear /rrapose'ar/ *vi* to behave like a fox

raposo /rra'poso/ *m*, (male) fox

rapsodia /rrap'soðia/ *f*, rhapsody

raptar /rrap'tar/ *vt* to abduct; rob

rapto /'rrapto/ *m*, abduction, rape; snatching, seizing; ecstasy, trance; *Med.* loss of consciousness

raptor /rrap'tor/ *m*, kidnapper, abductor

raquero /rra'kero/ *a* pirate. *m*, wrecker; pickpocket, dock rat

raqueta /rra'keta/ *f*, racket (tennis, badminton, squash rackets); croupier's rake. **r. de nieve,** snowshoe

raquianestesia /rrakianes'tesia/ *f*, spinal anesthesia

raquítico /rra'kitiko/ *a Med.* rachitic; small, minute; weak, feeble; rickety

raquitismo /rraki'tismo/ *m*, rickets

rarefacer /rrarefa'ser; rrarefa'θer/ **(se)** *vt* and *vr irr* to rarefy. See **satisfacer**

rareza /rra'resa; rra'reθa/ *f*, rareness, unusualness; eccentricity, whim; oddity, curio

raridad /rrari'ðað/ *f*, rarity; thinness; scarcity

raro /'rraro/ *a* rare, unusual, uncommon; notable, outstanding; odd, eccentric, queer; rarefied (gases, etc.). **rara vez,** seldom. **lo r. de,** the strange thing about (e.g. *Lo r. del caso es...,* the strange thing about the case is...)

ras /rras/ *m*, level. **a r.,** flush (with), nearly touching

rasa /'rrasa/ *f*, worn place in cloth; clearing, glade

rasar /rra'sar/ *vt* to level with a strickle; graze, brush, touch lightly; *vr* grow clear (of the sky, etc.)

rascacielos /rraska'sielos; rraska'θielos/ *m*, skyscraper

rascador /rraska'ðor/ *m*, scraper; ornamental hairpin

rascadura /rraska'ðura/ *f*, scraping; scratching

rascar /rras'kar/ *vt* to scratch; claw; scrape; twang (a guitar, etc.). *Inf.* **¡Que se rasque!** Let him put up with it! Let him lump it!

rascatripas /rraska'tripas/ *m*, *Inf.* caterwauler, squeaker (of violinists, etc.)

rascón /rras'kon/ *a* sour, tart

rasgado, -a /rras'gaðo/ *a*, *Lat. Am.* outspoken

rasgadura /rrasga'ðura/ *f*, tearing; tear, rip, rent

rasgar /rras'gar/ **(se)** *vt* and *vr* to tear, rip; *vt* strum the guitar

rasgo /'rrasgo/ *m*, flourish (of the pen); felicitous expression; characteristic, quality; *Lat. Am.* irrigation channel; *pl* features (of the face)

rasgón /rras'gon/ *m*, rip, tear

rasguear /rrasge'ar/ *vt* to strum, twang (the guitar); *vi* write with a flourish

rasgueo /rras'geo/ *m*, flourish (on a guitar); scratch (of a pen)

rasguñar /rrasgu'par/ *vt* to scratch, scrape; claw; *Art.* sketch

rasguño /rras'guɲo/ *m*, scratch; *Art.* sketch, outline

raso /'rraso/ *a* flat; free of obstacles; glossy; clear (sky, etc.); plain; undistinguished; backless (chairs). *m*, satin. **al r.**, in the open air

raspa /'rraspa/ *f*, *Bot.* beard (of cereals); fishbone; bunch of grapes; *Bot.* husk; scraper

raspador /rraspa'ðor/ *m*, eraser; scraper, rasp

raspadura /rraspa'ðura/ *f*, scraping; erasing; shavings, filings; *Lat. Am.* brown sugar

raspar /rras'par/ *vt* to scrape; erase; rob, steal; burn, bite (wine, etc.); *Lat. Am.* scold; *inf* to fail (student), fire (employee)

rastra /'rrastra/ *f*, trace, sign; sled; string of onions, etc.; anything dragging; *Agr.* harrow; *Agr.* rake. **a la r.**, dragging; reluctantly. **pescar a la r.**, to trawl

rastreador /rrastrea'ðor/ *m*, *Naut.* minesweeper. *a* dragging

rastrear /rrastre'ar/ *vt* to trace, trail; drag, trawl; surmise, conjecture, investigate; *vi Agr.* rake; fly low

rastreo /rras'treo/ *m*, dragging (of lakes, etc.)

rastrero /rras'trero/ *a* dragging, trailing; low-flying; servile, abject; *Bot.* creeping. *m*, slaughterhouse employee

rastrillador /rrastriya'ðor; rrastriʎa'ðor/ **(-ra)** *n* raker; hackler

rastrilladora /rrastriya'ðora; rrastriʎa'ðora/ *f*, mechanical harrow

rastrillaje /rrastri'yahe; rrastri'ʎahe/ *m*, raking

rastrillar /rrastri'yar; rrastri'ʎar/ *vt* to rake; dress, comb (flax)

rastrillo /rras'triyo; rras'triʎo/ *m*, *Agr.* rake; hackle; portcullis; *Agr.* rack

rastro /'rrastro/ *m*, *Agr.* rake; track, trail; wholesale meat market; slaughterhouse; trace, vestige; secondhand market (in Madrid)

rastrojo /rras'troho/ *m*, stubble; stubble field

rasura /rra'sura/ *f*, shaving

rasurar /rrasu'rar/ **(se)** *vt* and *vr* to shave

rata /'rrata/ *f*, rat. *m*, *Inf.* pickpocket. **r. almizclera**, muskrat. *Inf.* **más pobre que las ratas**, poorer than a church mouse

rataplán /rrata'plan/ *m*, beating of a drum

ratear /rrate'ar/ *vt* to rebate pro rata; apportion; thieve on a small scale, filch; *vi* crawl, creep

ratería /rrate'ria/ *f*, filching, petty theft, shoplifting, picking pockets; meanness, parsimony

ratero /rra'tero/ **(-ra)** *n* pilferer, petty thief, pickpocket, shoplifter

ratificación /rratifika'sion; rratifika'θion/ *f*, ratification

ratificador /rratifika'ðor/ **(-ra)** *n* ratifier

ratificar /rratifi'kar/ *vt* to ratify

ratificatorio /rratifika'torio/ *a* ratifying, confirmatory

rato /'rrato/ *m*, short interval of time, while. **buen (mal) r.**, pleasant (unpleasant) time. **r. perdido**, leisure moment. **a ratos**, sometimes, occasionally. **de r. en r.**, from time to time. **pasar el r.**, *Inf.* to while away the time

ratón /rra'ton/ **(-ona)** *n* mouse

ratonera /rrato'nera/ *f*, mousetrap; mousehole; mouse nest; *Lat. Am.* hovel. *Fig.* **caer en la r.**, to fall into a trap

ratonero, ratonesco, ratonil /rrato'nero, rrato'nesko, rrato'nil/ *a* mousy

rauco /'rrauko/ *a* *Poet.* hoarse

raudal /rrau'ðal/ *m*, torrent, cascade; *Fig.* flood, abundance

raudo /'rrauðo/ *a* swift, rapid

ravioles /rra'βioles/ *m pl*, ravioli

raya /'rraya/ *f*, stripe, streak; limit, end; part (of the hair); boundary; *Gram.* dash; score (some games). *m*, *Ichth.* ray. **pasar de r.**, to go too far; misbehave

rayadillo /rraya'ðiyo; rraya'ðiʎo/ *m*, striped cotton

rayano /rra'yano/ *a* neighboring; border; almost identical, very similar

rayar /rra'yar/ *vt* to draw lines; streak; stripe; cross out; underline; rifle (a gun); *vi* verge (on), border

(on); appear (of dawn, daylight); excel; be similar. **Raya en los catorce años**, He is about fourteen

rayo /'rrayo/ *m*, *Phys.* beam, ray; thunderbolt; flash of lightning; spoke; quick-witted person; capable, energetic person; sudden pain; disaster, catastrophe. **r. de sol**, sunbeam. **r. católico**, cathode ray. **r. x**, x-ray. *Fig.* **echar rayos**, to breathe forth fury

rayón /rra'yon/ *m*, rayon

raza /'rrasa; 'rraθa/ *f*, race; breed; lineage, family; kind, class; crack, crevice. **de r.**, purebred

razón /rra'son; rra'θon/ *f*, reason; reasoning; word, expression; speech, argument; motive, cause; order, method; justice, equity; right, authority; explanation; *Math.* ratio, proportion. **r. de estado**, raison d'état, reasons of state. *Com.* **r. social**, firm, trade name. **a r. de**, at a rate of. **dar la r. (a)**, to agree with. **estar puesto en r.**, to stand to reason. **tener r.**, to be right

razonable /rraso'naβle; rraθo'naβle/ *a* reasonable; moderate

razonador /rrasona'ðor; rraθona'ðor/ **(-ra)** *n* reasoner

razonamiento /rrasona'miento; rraθona'miento/ *m*, reasoning

razonar /rraso'nar; rraθo'nar/ *vi* to reason; speak; *vt* attest, confirm

razzia /'rrassia; 'rraθθia/ *f*, foray; pillaging, sacking; police raid

re /rre/ *m*, *Mus.* re, D

reabsorción /rreaβsor'sion; rreaβsor'θion/ *f*, reabsorption

reacción /rreak'sion; rreak'θion/ *f*, reaction. **r. de Bayardo**, quick reaction of someone always ready to help those in distress

reaccionar /rreaksio'nar; rreakθio'nar/ *vi* to react

reaccionario /rreaksio'nario; rreakθio'nario/ **(-ia)** *a* and *n* reactionary

reaccionarismo /rreaksiona'rismo; rreakθiona'rismo/ *m*, reactionism

reacio /rre'asio; rre'aθio/ *a* recalcitrant

reactivo /rreak'tiβo/ *m*, reagent. *a* reactive; reacting

readmisión /rreaðmi'sion/ *f*, readmission

readmitir /rreaðmi'tir/ *vt* to readmit

reajustar /rreahus'tar/ *vt* to readjust

real /rre'al/ *a* actual, real; kingly; royal; royalist; *Fig.* regal; *Inf.* fine, handsome. *m*, silver coin, real; *m pl*, encampment, camp. **alzar el r.**, *Mil.* to strike camp. **asentar el r.**, *Mil.* to encamp. **r. decreto**, royal decree. **sitio r.**, royal residence. **un r., sobre otro**, *Inf.* cash in hand

realce /rre'alse; rre'alθe/ *m*, raised or embossed work; renown, glory; *Art.* high light

realeza /rrea'lesa; rrea'leθa/ *f*, royalty, royal majesty

realidad /rreali'ðað/ *f*, reality; sincerity, truth. **en r.**, in fact, actually

realismo /rrea'lismo/ *m*, realism; regalism; royalism

realista /rrea'lista/ *a* realistic; royalist; *mf* realist; royalist; regalist

realizable /rreali'saβle; rreali'θaβle/ *a* realizable; practicable

realización /rrealisa'sion; rrealiθa'θion/ *f*, realization; performance, execution

realizar /rreali'sar; rreali'θar/ *vt* to perform, execute, carry out; *Com.* realize. **r. beneficio**, to make a profit

realmente /rreal'mente/ *adv* really, truly; actually

realzar /rreal'sar; rreal'θar/ *vt* to heighten, raise; emboss; exalt; enhance; *Art.* intensify (colors, etc.)

reanimar /rreani'mar/ *vt* to reanimate; revive, restore, resuscitate; encourage

reanudación /rreanuða'sion; rreanuða'θion/ *f*, resumption, renewal

reanudar /rreanu'ðar/ *vt* to resume, continue

reaparecer /rreapare'ser; rreapare'θer/ *vi irr* to reappear. See **conocer**

reaparición /rreapari'sion; rreapari'θion/ *f*, reappearance

rearmamento /rrearma'mento/ *m*, rearmament

rearmar /rrear'mar/ *vi* to rearm

reasegurador /rreasegura'ðor/ *m*, underwriter

reasegurar /rreasegu'rar/ *vt* to reinsure, underwrite

reaseguro /rrease'guro/ *m*, reinsurance, underwriting

reasunción /rreasun'sion; rreasun'θion/ *f*, reassumption; resumption

reata /rre'ata/ *f*, string of horses or mules. **de r.**, in single file; *Inf*. blindly, unquestioningly; *Inf*. at once

rebaja /rre'βaha/ *f*, diminution; *Com*. discount, rebate; remission

rebajar /rreβa'har/ *vt* to lower; curtail, lessen; remit; *Com*. reduce in price; *Mech*. file; *Elec*. step down; humble, humiliate; *vr* cringe, humble oneself

rebajo /rre'βaho/ *m*, reduction (in price, etc.); rabbet

rebanada /rreβa'naða/ *f*, slice, piece (of bread, etc.)

rebanar /rreβa'nar/ *vt* to cut into slices; split

rebaño /rre'βaɲo/ *m*, flock, drove, herd; *Eccl*. flock

rebasar /rreβa'sar/ *vt* to exceed, go beyond; *Mil*. bypass

rebate /rre'βate/ *m*, altercation, dispute, quarrel

rebatiña /rreβa'tiɲa/ *f*, grab; scrimmage. **andar a la r.**, to scuffle

rebatir /rreβa'tir/ *vt* to repulse, repel; fight again; fight hard; oppose, resist; *Com*. deduct; refuse, reject

rebato /rre'βato/ *m*, alarm, tocsin; *Mil*. surprise attack; panic, dismay

rebeca /rre'βeka/ *f*, cardigan, jersey

rebeco /rre'βeko/ *m*, *Zool*. chamois

rebelarse /rreβe'larse/ *vr* to mutiny, rebel; oppose, resist

rebelde /rre'βelde/ *a* mutinous, rebellious; wilful, disobedient; stubborn. *mf* rebel

rebeldía /rreβel'dia/ *f*, rebelliousness; willfulness; stubbornness; *Law*. nonappearance

rebelión /rreβe'lion/ *f*, insurrection, revolt

rebenque /rre'βenke/ *m*, *Lat. Am*. whip

rebién /rre'βien/ *adv* very well, extremely well

rebisabuelo /rreβisa'βuelo/ **(-la)** *n*. See **tatarabuelo**

reblandecer /rreβlande'ser; rreβlande'θer/ *vt irr* to soften; *vr* become soft. See **conocer**

reblandecimiento /rreβlandesi'miento; rreβlandeθi'miento/ *m*, softening; *Med*. flabbiness

reborde /rre'βorðe/ *m*, rim, edge; *Mech*. flange. **r. de acera,** curb

rebordear /rreβorðe'ar/ *vt* to flange

rebosar /rreβo'sar/ *vi* to overflow, run over; *Fig*. abound in; express one's feelings

rebotar /rreβo'tar/ *vi* to rebound; clinch (nails, etc.); refuse; *vr* change color; *Inf*. be vexed

rebote /rre'βote/ *m*, rebounding; rebound

rebotica /rreβo'tika/ *f*, back room of a pharmacy; back of a shop

rebozar /rreβo'sar; rreβo'θar/ *vt* to muffle up; coat with batter

rebozo /rre'βoso; rre'βoθo/ *m*, muffling up, hiding the face; head shawl; pretense, excuse. *Fig*. **sin r.,** openly

rebueno /rre'βueno/ *a Inf*. extremely good, fine

rebullicio /rreβu'yisio; rreβu'ʎiθio/ *m*, uproar, clamor

rebullir /rreβu'yir; rreβu'ʎir/ *vi* to stir, show signs of movement; *Fig*. swarm, seethe

rebusca /rre'βuska/ *f*, close search; gleaning; remains

rebuscado /rreβus'kaðo/ *a* affected, unnatural (of style)

rebuscar /rreβus'kar/ *vt* to search for; glean

rebuznar /rreβus'nar; rreβuθ'nar/ *vi* to bray

recadero /rreka'ðero/ **(-ra)** *n* messenger, errand boy

recado /rre'kaðo/ *m*, message; greeting, note; gift, present; daily marketing; outfit, implements; precaution, safeguard

recaer /rreka'er/ *vi irr* to fall again; *Med*. relapse; lapse, backslide; devolve, fall upon. See **caer**

recaída /rreka'iða/ *f*, falling again; *Med*. relapse; lapse

recalar /rreka'lar/ *vt* to impregnate; *Naut*. call at (a port), come within sight of land

recalcada /rrekal'kaða/ *f*, pressing down, squeezing; emphasis; *Naut*. list

recalcar /rrekal'kar/ *vt* to press down; squeeze; pack tight; stress, emphasize; *vi Naut*. list; *vr Inf*. say over and over, savor one's words

recalcitrante /rrekalsi'trante; rrekalθi'trante/ *a* obdurate, recalcitrant

recalentador /rrekalenta'ðor/ *m*, *Mech*. superheater

recalentar /rrekalen'tar/ *vt irr* to overheat; superheat; reheat. See **sentar**

recamado /rreka'maðo/ *m*, raised embroidery

recámara /rre'kamara/ *f*, dressing room; explosives chamber; breech of a gun; *Inf*. caution; *Mexico* room, bedroom

recamarera /rrekama'rera/ *f*, *Mexico* chambermaid

recambio /rre'kambio/ *m*, spare, spare part; *Com*. reexchange

recantación /rrekanta'sion; rrekanta'θion/ *f*, retraction, recantation

recapacitar /rrekapasi'tar; rrekapaθi'tar/ *vi* to search one's memory; think over

recapitulación /rrekapitula'sion; rrekapitula'θion/ *f*, summary, résumé

recapitular /rrekapitu'lar/ *vt* to recapitulate, summarize

recargar /rrekar'gar/ *vt* to recharge; load again; reaccuse; overcharge; overdress or overdecorate; *vr Med*. become more feverish. **r. acumuladores,** to recharge batteries

recargo /rre'kargo/ *m*, charge; new load; *Law*. new accusation; overcharge, extra cost; *Med*. temperature increase

recatado /rreka'taðo/ *a* prudent, discreet, circumspect; modest, shy

recatar /rreka'tar/ *vt* to hide, conceal; *vr* be prudent or cautious

recato /rre'kato/ *m*, caution, prudence; modesty, shyness, reserve

recauchutar /rrekautʃu'tar/ *vt* to retread (tires)

recaudación /rrekauða'sion; rrekauða'θion/ *f*, collecting; collection (of taxes, etc.); tax collector's office

recaudador /rrekauða'ðor/ *m*, tax collector

recaudar /rrekau'ðar/ *vt* to collect, recover (taxes, debts, etc.); deposit, place in custody

recaudo /rre'kauðo/ *m*, collecting; collection (of taxes, etc.); precaution, safeguard; *Law*. surety; *Lat. Am*. daily supply of vegetables

recelar /rrese'lar; rreθe'lar/ *vt* to suspect, fear, mistrust; *vr* (*with de*) be afraid or suspicious of

recelo /rre'selo; rre'θelo/ *m*, suspicion, mistrust, doubt, fear

receloso /rrese'loso; rreθe'loso/ *a* suspicious, distrustful, doubtful

recepción /rresep'sion; rreθep'θion/ *f*, receiving, reception; admission, acceptance; reception, party; *Law*. cross-examination

receptáculo /rresep'takulo; rreθep'takulo/ *m*, receptacle, container; *Fig*. refuge; *Bot*. receptacle

receptador /rresepta'ðor; rreθepta'ðor/ **(-ra)** *n* receiver (of stolen goods); accomplice

receptivo /rresep'tiβo; rreθep'tiβo/ *a* receptive

receptor /rresep'tor; rreθep'tor/ **(-ra)** *a* receiving. *n* recipient. *m*, *Elec*. receiver; wireless set. **r. de galena,** crystal set. **r. telefónico,** telephone receiver

receta /rre'seta; rre'θeta/ *f*, *Med*. prescription; *Cul*. recipe

recetar /rrese'tar; rreθe'tar/ *vt Med*. to prescribe; *Inf*. demand

rechapear /rretʃape'ar/ *vt* to replate

rechazar /rretʃa'sar; rretʃa'θar/ *vt* to repulse; resist; refuse; oppose, deny (the truth of); contradict

rechazo /rre'tʃaso; rre'tʃaθo/ *m*, recoil; rebound; refusal

rechinamiento, rechino /rretʃina'miento, rre'tʃino/ *m*, squeaking, creaking; gnashing (of teeth)

rechinar /rretʃi'nar/ *vi* to squeak, creak; gnash (teeth); chatter (teeth); do a bad grace

rechoncho /rre'tʃontʃo/ *a* squat, stocky, thickset

reciamente /rresia'mente; rreθia'mente/ *adv* hard; strongly, firmly, vigorously

recibí /rresi'βi; rreθi'βi/ *m*, *Com*. receipt

recibidor /rresiβi'ðor; rreθiβi'ðor/ **(-ra)** *a* receiving. *n* recipient. *m*, reception room

recibimiento /rresiβi'miento; rreθiβi'miento/ *m*, reception; welcome, greeting; reception room, waiting room; hall, vestibule

recibir /rresi'βir; rreθi'βir/ *vt* to obtain, receive; support, bear; suffer, experience (attack, injury); approve; accept, receive; entertain; stand up to (attack); *vr* (*with de*) graduate as, take office as

recibo /rre'siβo; rre'θiβo/ *m*, reception; *Com.* receipt; reception room, waiting room; hall, vestibule. *Com.* **acusar r.**, to acknowledge receipt

reciclar /rresi'klar; rreθi'klar/ *vt* recycle

recidiva /rresi'ðiβa; rreθi'ðiβa/ *f*, *Med.* relapse

recién /rre'sien; rre'θien/ *adv* recently, newly. Shortened form of **reciente** before a past participle (e.g. *r. llegado*, newly arrived)

reciente /rre'siente; rre'θiente/ *a* recent; new; fresh

recinto /rre'sinto; rre'θinto/ *m*, precinct; neighborhood; premises, place

recio /'rresio; 'rreθio/ *a* strong; robust; bulky, thick; rough, uncouth; grievous, hard; severe (weather); impetuous, precipitate

recipiente /rresi'piente; rreθi'piente/ *a* receiving. *m*, receptacle, container, vessel

reciprocar /rresipro'kar; rreθipro'kar/ *vt* to reciprocate

reciprocidad /rresiprosi'ðað; rreθiproθi'ðað/ *f*, reciprocity; reciprocation

recíproco /rre'siproko; rre'θiproko/ *a* reciprocal

recitación /rresita'sion; rreθita'θion/ *f*, recitation

recitado /rresi'taðo; rreθi'taðo/ *m*, recitative

recitador /rresita'ðor; rreθita'ðor/ (**-ra**) *n* elocutionist, reciter

recitar /rresi'tar; rreθi'tar/ *vt* to recite, declaim

reclamación /rreklama'sion; rreklama'θion/ *f*, reclamation; objection, opposition; *Com.* claim

reclamar /rrekla'mar/ *vi* to oppose, object to; *Poet.* resound; *vt* call repeatedly; *Com.* claim; decoy (birds)

reclamo /rre'klamo/ *m*, decoy bird; enticement, allurement; *Law.* reclamation; advertisement. **objeto de r.**, advertising sample. **venta de r.**, bargain sale

reclinación /rreklina'sion; rreklina'θion/ *f*, reclining; leaning

reclinatorio /rreklina'torio/ *m*, couch; prie-dieu

recluir /rre'kluir/ *vt irr* to immure, shut up; detain, arrest. See **huir**

reclusión /rreklu'sion/ *f*, confinement, seclusion; prison

recluso /rre'kluso/ (**-sa**) *n* recluse

recluta /rre'kluta/ *f*, recruiting. *mf Mil.* recruit

reclutador /rrekluta'ðor/ *m*, recruiting office

reclutamiento /rrekluta'miento/ *m*, recruiting

reclutar /rreklu'tar/ *vt* to enlist recruits, recruit; *Argentina* round up

recobrar /rreko'βrar/ *vt* to recover, regain; *vr* recuperate; regain consciousness

recobro /rre'koβro/ *m*, recovery; *Mech.* pick-up

recocer /rreko'ser; rreko'θer/ *vt irr* to reboil; recook; overboil; overcook; anneal (metals); *vr Fig.* be tormented (by emotion), be all burned up. See **cocer**

recodo /rre'koðo/ *m*, bend, turn, loop

recogedor /rrekohe'ðor/ *a* sheltering. *m*, *Agr.* gleaner

recoger /rreko'her/ *vt* to gather, pick; pick up; retake; collect (letters from a mailbox, etc.); amass; shrink, narrow; keep; hoard; shelter; reap, pick; *vr* withdraw, retire; go home; go to bed; retrench, economize; give oneself to meditation

recogida /rreko'hiða/ *f*, collection (of letters from a mailbox); withdrawal; retirement; harvest

recogido /rreko'hiðo/ *a* recluse; cloistered, confined

recogimiento /rrekohi'miento/ *m*, gathering, picking; collection, accumulation; seclusion; shelter; women's reformatory

recolección /rrekolek'sion; rrekolek'θion/ *f*, summary, résumé; harvest; collection (of taxes, etc.); *Eccl.* convent of a reformed order; mystic ecstasy

recoleto /rreko'leto/ *a Eccl.* reformed (of religious orders); recluse

recomendable /rrekomen'daβle/ *a* commendable, recommendable

recomendación /rrekomenda'sion; rrekomenda'θion/ *f*, recommendation (all meanings)

recomendar /rrekomen'dar/ *vt irr* to recommend (all meanings); entrust, commend. *Pres. Ind.* **recomiendo, recomiendas, recomienda, recomiendan.** *Pres. Sub-*

junc. **recomiende, recomiendes, recomiende, recomienden**

recompensa /rrekom'pensa/ *f*, compensation; recompense, reward

recompensar /rrekompen'sar/ *vt* to compensate; requite; reward, recompense

recomposición /rrekomposi'sion; rrekomposi'θion/ *f*, recomposition

recomprar /rrekom'prar/ *vt* to repurchase

reconcentrar /rrekonsen'trar; rrekonθen'trar/ *vt* to concentrate; dissemble; *vr* withdraw into oneself, meditate

reconciliable /rrekonsi'liaβle; rrekonθi'liaβle/ *a* reconcilable

reconciliación /rrekonsilia'sion; rrekonθilia'θion/ *f*, reconciliation

reconciliador /rrekonsilia'ðor; rrekonθilia'ðor/ (**-ra**) *a* reconciliatory. *n* reconciler

reconciliar /rrekonsi'liar; rrekonθi'liar/ *vt* to reconcile; *Eccl.* reconsecrate; *Eccl.* hear a short confession; *vr* become reconciled; *Eccl.* make an additional confession

recondicionar /rrekondisio'nar; rrekondiθio'nar/ *vt* to rebuild, overhaul, recondition

recóndito /rre'kondito/ *a* recondite

reconocer /rrekono'ser; rrekono'θer/ *vt irr* to examine, inspect; recognize; admit, acknowledge; own, confess; search; *Polit.* recognize; *Mil.* reconnoiter; (*with por*) adopt as (a son, etc.); recognize as; *vr* be seen, show; acknowledge, confess; know oneself. **Bien se reconoce que no está aquí,** It's easy to see he's not here. See **conocer**

reconocido /rrekono'siðo; rrekono'θiðo/ *a* grateful

reconocimiento /rrekonosi'miento; rrekonoθi'miento/ *m*, examination, inspection; recognition; acknowledgement, admission; search; *Mil.* reconnoitering; adoption; gratitude

reconquista /rrekon'kista/ *f*, reconquest

reconquistar /rrekonkis'tar/ *vt* to reconquer; *Fig.* recover, win back

reconstitución /rrekonstitu'sion; rrekonstitu'θion/ *f*, reconstitution

reconstituir /rrekonsti'tuir/ *vt irr* to reconstitute. See **huir**

reconstituyente /rrekonstitu'yente/ *m*, *Med.* tonic

reconstrucción /rrekonstruk'sion; rrekonstruk'θion/ *f*, reconstruction

reconstruir /rrekons'truir/ *vt irr* to reconstruct, rebuild; recreate. See **huir**

reconvención /rrekomben'sion; rrekomben'θion/ *f*, rebuke, reproof; recrimination; *Law.* countercharge

reconversión /rrekomber'sion/ *f*, reconversion

recopilación /rrekopila'sion; rrekopila'θion/ *f*, summary, compendium; collection (of writings); digest (of laws)

recopilador /rrekopila'ðor/ *m*, compiler

recopilar /rrekopi'lar/ *vt* to compile, collect

recordar /rrekor'ðar/ *vt irr* to cause to remember, remind; remember; *vi* remember; awake. See **acordar**

recordatorio /rrekorða'torio/ *m*, reminder. *a* commemorative (e.g. a plaque)

recorrer /rreko'rrer/ *vt* to travel over; pass through; wander around; examine, inspect; read hastily; overhaul, renovate

recorrido /rreko'rriðo/ *m*, journey, run; *Mech.* stroke; overhaul. **r. de despegue,** *Aer.* take-off run

recortado /rrekor'taðo/ *a Bot.* jagged, incised. *m*, paper cutout

recortar /rrekor'tar/ *vt* to clip, trim, pare; cut out; *Art.* outline; *vr* stand out (against), be outlined (against)

recorte /rre'korte/ *m*, clipping, paring; cutting; cutout; *Art.* outline; *pl* snippets, clippings. **r. de periódico,** newspaper cutting, newspaper clipping

recostar /rrekos'tar/ *vt* (*with en or contra*) to lean, rest against; *vr* (*with en or contra*) lean against, rest on; lean back; recline. See **contar**

recreación /rrekrea'sion; rrekrea'θion/ *f*, recreation, hobby

recrear /rrekre'ar/ *vt* to entertain; amuse; *vr* amuse oneself; delight (in), enjoy

recreo /rre'kreo/ *m*, recreation, hobby; playtime, recess (in schools); place of amusement. **salón de r.**, recreation room

recriminación /rrekrimina'sion; rrekrimina'θion/ *f*, recrimination

recriminador /rrekrimina'ðor/ *a* recriminatory

recriminar /rrekrimi'nar/ *vt* to recriminate

recrudecer /rrekruðe'ser; rrekruðe'θer/ **(se)** *vi* and *vr irr* to recur, return. See **conocer**

recrudescencia /rrekruðes'sensia; rrekruðes'θenθia/ *f*, recrudescence, recurrence

rectángulo /rrek'tangulo/ *m*, rectangle. *a* rectangular

rectificable /rrektifi'kaβle/ *a* rectifiable

rectificación /rrektifika'sion; rrektifika'θion/ *f*, rectification; *Mech.* grinding

rectificador /rrektifika'ðor/ *m*, rectifier

rectificar /rrektifi'kar/ *vt* to rectify; *Mech.* grind; *vr* mend one's ways; *Mil.* **r. el frente,** to straighten the line

rectilíneo /rrekti'lineo/ *a* rectilinear

rectitud /rrekti'tuð/ *f*, straightness; rectitude, integrity; exactness; righteousness

recto /'rrekto/ *a* straight; upright; erect; literal (meaning); just, fair; single-breasted (of coats); *m*, right angle; rectum

rector /rrek'tor/ **(-ra)** *n* director; principal, headmaster. *m*, *Eccl.* rector

rectorado /rrekto'raðo/ *m*, principalship, headmaster-(mistress-) ship, directorship; *Eccl.* rectorship

rectoría /rrekto'ria/ *f*, rectorate, rectorship

recua /'rrekua/ *f*, drove of beasts of burden; *Inf.* string or line (of things)

recubrir /rreku'βrir/ *vt* to re-cover; coat; plate. *Past Part.* **recubierto**

recuento /rre'kuento/ *m*, calculation; recount; inventory.

recuerdo /rre'kuerðo/ *m*, memory, remembrance; souvenir, memento; *pl* greetings, regards

reculada /rreku'laða/ *f*, drawing back; recoil

recular /rreku'lar/ *vi* to recoil, draw back; *Inf.* go back on, give up

recuperable /rrekupe'raβle/ *a* recoverable, recuperable

recuperación /rrekupera'sion; rrekupera'θion/ *f*, recovery, recuperation; *Chem.* recovery

recurrente /rreku'rrente/ *a* recurrent

recurrir /rreku'rrir/ *vi* to recur; *(with prep a)* have recourse to; appeal to

recurso /rre'kurso/ *m*, recourse, resort; choice, option; reversion; petition; *Law.* appeal; *pl* means of livelihood; *Fig.* way out, last hope

recusar /rreku'sar/ *vt* to refuse; challenge the authority (of), *Law.* recuse

red /rreð/ *f*, net; network; hairnet; railing, grating; *Fig.* snare; system (of communications, etc.); *Fig.* combination (of events, etc.); *Elec.* mains. **r. de arrastre,** trawl net. **Red Mundial,** World Wide Web. *Fig. Inf.* **caer en la r.,** to fall into the trap

redacción /rreðak'sion; rreðak'θion/ *f*, phrasing; editorial office; editing; editorial board

redactar /rreðak'tar/ *vt* to write, phrase; draw up; edit

redactor /rreðak'tor/ **(-ra)** *a* editorial. *n* editor

redada /rre'ðaða/ *f*, cast (of a fishing net); haul, catch

redecilla /rreðe'siya; rreðe'θiʎa/ *f*, *dim* small net; netting; hairnet

redención /rreðen'sion; rreðen'θion/ *f*, redemption; ransom; deliverance, salvation; redeeming, paying off (a mortgage, etc.)

redentor /rreðen'tor/ **(-ra)** *a* redeeming, redemptive. *n* redeemer

redificar /rreðifi'kar/ *vt* to rebuild

redifusión /rreðifu'sion/ *f*, *Radio.* relay

redil /rre'ðil/ *m*, sheepfold

redimible /rreði'miβle/ *a* redeemable

redimir /rreði'mir/ *vt* to ransom; redeem, buy back; pay off (a mortgage, etc.); deliver, free; *Eccl.* redeem

reditar /rreði'tar/ *vt* to reprint, reissue

rédito /'rreðito/ *m*, *Com.* income, revenue, interest, profit

redoblamiento /rreðoβla'miento/ *m*, redoubling; bending back (of nails, etc.); rolling (of a drum)

redoblar /rreðo'βlar/ *vt* to redouble; repeat; bend back (nails, etc.); *vi* roll (a drum)

redoble /rre'ðoβle/ *m*, doubling; redoubling; repetition; roll (of a drum)

redoma /rre'ðoma/ *f*, flask, vial

redomado /rreðo'maðo/ *a* astute, crafty, sly; complete, perfect

redonda /rre'ðonda/ *f*, district; pasture ground; *Naut.* square sail; *Mus.* semibreve. **a la r.,** around

redondear /rreðonde'ar/ *vt* to make round; round; free (from debt, etc.); *vr* acquire a fortune; clear oneself (of debts, etc.)

redondel /rreðon'del/ *m*, traffic circle, rotary, roundabout

redondez /rreðon'des; rreðon'deθ/ *f*, roundness

redondo /rre'ðondo/ *a* round; circular; unequivocal, plain. *m*, round, circle; *Inf.* cash. **suma redonda,** lump sum (cash)

reducción /rreðuk'sion; rreðuk'θion/ *f*, reduction; *Mil.* defeat, conquest; decrease; *Com.* rebate; *(Math. Chem.)* reduction

reducir /rreðu'sir; rreðu'θir/ *vt irr* to reduce; decrease, cut down; break up; *Art.* scale down; *Elec.* step down; subdue; *(Chem. Math. Surg.)* reduce; exchange; divide into small fragments; persuade; *vr* be obliged to, have to; live moderately. See **conducir**

redundancia /rreðun'dansia; rreðun'danθia/ *f*, redundance

redundante /rreðun'dante/ *a* redundant

redundar /rreðun'dar/ *vi* to overflow; be excessive or superfluous; *(with en)* redound to

reduplicación /rreðuplika'sion; rreðuplika'θion/ *f*, reduplication

reduplicar /rreðupli'kar/ *vt* to reduplicate, redouble

ree For words so beginning (e.g. *reeditar, reexaminación*), see spellings with one **e**

refacción /rrefak'sion; rrefak'θion/ *f*, refection, light meal; compensation, reparation. **«cerrado por r.,»** "closed for repairs"

refaccionar /rrefaksio'nar; rrefakθio'nar/ *vt*, *Lat. Am.* to fix, repair

refajo /rre'faho/ *m*, skirt, underskirt; *Colombia* mild drink consisting of champagne, soda and beer

refectorio /rrefek'torio/ *m*, refectory

referencia /rrefe'rensia; rrefe'renθia/ *f*, report, account; allusion; regard, relation; *Com.* reference (gen. *pl*); consideration

referente /rrefe'rente/ *a* concerning, related (to)

referir /rrefe'rir/ *vt irr* to narrate; describe; direct, guide; relate, refer, concern; *vr* allude (to); refer (to); concern. See **sentir**

refinación /rrefina'sion; rrefina'θion/ *f*, refining

refinado /rrefi'naðo/ *a* refined; polished, cultured; crafty

refinador /rrefina'ðor/ *m*, refiner

refinamiento /rrefina'miento/ *m*, refinement, subtlety, care

refinar /rrefi'nar/ *vt* to refine, purify; polish, perfect

refinería /rrefine'ria/ *f*, refinery

reflector /rreflek'tor/ *a* reflecting. *m*, reflector; searchlight; shade (for lamps, etc.)

reflejar /rrefle'har/ *vi Phys.* to reflect; *vt* consider; show, mirror; *vr Fig.* be reflected, be seen

reflejo /rre'fleho/ *m*, reflection; image; glare. *a* reflex; considered, judicious

reflexión /rreflek'sion; rreflek'θion/ *f*, *Phys.* reflection; consideration, thought

reflexionar /rrefleksio'nar/ *vt (with en or sobre)* to consider, reflect upon

reflexivo /rreflek'siβo/ *a Phys.* reflective; thoughtful

reflorecer /rreflore'ser; rreflore'θer/ *vi irr* to flower again; return to favor (ideas, etc.). See **conocer**

reflujo /rre'fluho/ *m*, reflux, refluence; ebb tide

refocilar /rrefosi'lar; rrefoθi'lar/ *vt* to warm up, brace up; give pleasure to; *vr* enjoy oneself

reforma /rre'forma/ *f*, reform; improvement; reformation; *Hist.* Reformation

reformación /rreforma'sion; rreforma'θion/ *f*, reform, improvement

reformador /rreforma'ðor/ **(-ra)** *a* reformatory, reforming. *n* reformer

reformar /rrefor'mar/ *vt* to remake; reshape; repair, mend, restore; improve, correct; *Eccl.* reform; reorganize; *vr* mend one's ways, improve; control oneself

reformatorio /rreforma'torio/ *m*, reformatory. *a* reforming, reformatory

reformista /rrefor'mista/ *mf* reformist, reformer. *a* reformatory

reforzador /rreforsa'ðor; rreforθa'ðor/ *m*, *Photo.* reinforcing bath; *Elec.* booster

reforzamiento /rreforsa'miento; rreforθa'miento/ *m*, stiffening, reinforcing

reforzar /rrefor'sar; rrefor'θar/ *vt irr* to reinforce, strengthen, stiffen; encourage, inspirit. See **forzar**

refractar /rrefrak'tar/ *vt* to refract

refractario /rrefrak'tario/ *a* stubborn; (*Phys. Chem.*) refractory; unmanageable, unruly; fireproof

refrán /rre'fran/ *m*, proverb

refranero /rrefra'nero/ *m*, collection of proverbs

refregamiento /rrefrega'miento/ *m*, rubbing; scrubbing, scouring

refregar /rrefre'gar/ *vt irr* to rub; scrub, scour; *Fig. Inf.* rub in, insist on. See **cegar**

refrenamiento /rrefrena'miento/ *m*, curbing; control, restraint

refrenar /rrefre'nar/ *vt* to curb, rein in (horses); control, restrain

refrendar /rrefren'dar/ *vt* to countersign, endorse, legalize

refrescante /rrefres'kante/ *a* refreshing, cooling

refrescar /rrefres'kar/ *vt* to cool, chill; repeat; *Fig.* brush up, revise; *vi* be rested or refreshed; grow cooler; take the air; freshen (wind); take a cool drink; *vr* grow cooler; take the air; take a cool drink

refresco /rre'fresko/ *m*, refreshment; cool drink; *Lat. Am.* soft drink, soda, pop

refresquería /rrefreske'ria/ *f*, *Lat. Am.* refreshment stand

refriega /rre'friega/ *f*, affray, scuffle, rough-and-tumble

refrigeración /rrefrihera'sion; rrefrihera'θion/ *f*, refrigeration

refrigerador /rrefrihera'ðor/ *m*, refrigerator

refrigerante /rrefrihe'rante/ *a* refrigerative; chilling; cooling. *m*, cooling chamber, cooler

refrigerar /rrefrihe'rar/ *vt* to chill; cool; freeze, refrigerate; refresh

refrigerio /rrefri'herio/ *m*, coolness; consolation; refreshment, food

refringente /rrefrin'hente/ *a Phys.* refringent

refuerzo /rre'fuerso; rre'fuerθo/ *m*, reinforcement, strengthening; aid, help

refugiado /rrefu'hiaðo/ **(-da)** *a* and *n* refugee

refugiar /rrefu'hiar/ *vt* to protect, shelter; *vr* take refuge

refugio /rre'fuhio/ *m*, refuge, shelter, protection; traffic island. **r. antiaéreo,** air raid shelter. **r. para peatones,** traffic island

refulgencia /rreful'hensia; rreful'henθia/ *f*, resplendence, splendor, brilliance

refulgente /rreful'hente/ *a* resplendent, refulgent, dazzling

refulgir /rreful'hir/ *vi* to shine, be dazzling

refundición /rrefundi'sion; rrefundi'θion/ *f*, recasting (of metals); adaptation; rehash, refurbishing

refundir /rrefun'dir/ *vt* to recast (metals); include, comprise; adapt; rehash, refurbish; *vi Fig.* promote, contribute to

refunfuñador /rrefunfuɲa'ðor/ *a* grumbling, fuming

refunfuñar /rrefunfu'ɲar/ *vi* to grumble, growl, fume

refunfuño /rrefun'fuɲo/ *m*, grumble, fuming; snort

refutable /rrefu'taβle/ *a* refutable

refutación /rrefuta'sion; rrefuta'θion/ *f*, refutation

refutar /rrefu'tar/ *vt* to refute

regadera /rrega'ðera/ *f*, watering can; irrigation canal; sprinkler; *Lat. Am.* shower bath, shower

regadío /rrega'ðio/ *m*, irrigated land; irrigation, watering. *a* irrigated

regajal, regajo /rrega'hal, rre'gaho/ *m*, pool, puddle; stream, brook

regalado /rrega'laðo/ *a* delicate, highly bred; luxurious, delightful

regalar /rrega'lar/ *vt* to make a gift of, give; caress, fondle; indulge, cherish; entertain, regale; *vr* live in luxury

regalía /rrega'lia/ *f*, royal privilege; right, exemption; perquisite, emolument

regaliz /rrega'lis; rrega'liθ/ *m*, **regaliza** *f*, licorice

regalo /rre'galo/ *m*, gift, present; satisfaction, pleasure; entertainment, regalement; luxury, comfort

regalón /rrega'lon/ *a Inf.* pampered

regalonear /rregalone'ar/ *vt*, *Lat. Am.* to pamper, spoil

regañadientes, a /rregaɲa'ðientes, a/ *adv* unwillingly, grumblingly

regañar /rrega'ɲar/ *vi* to snarl (dogs); crack (skin of fruits); grumble, mutter; *Inf.* quarrel; *vt Inf.* scold

regaño /rre'gaɲo/ *m*, angry look or gesture; *Inf.* scolding

regañón /rrega'ɲon/ **(-ona)** *a Inf.* grumbling, complaining; scolding. *n Inf.* grumbler

regar /rre'gar/ *vt irr* to water, sprinkle with water; flow through, irrigate; spray; *Fig.* shower (with), strew. See **cegar**

regata /rre'gata/ *f*, regatta; small irrigation channel (for gardens, etc.)

regate /rre'gate/ *m*, twist of the body, sidestep; dribbling; (in soccer); *Inf.* dodging, evasion

regatear /rregate'ar/ *vt* to haggle over, beat down (prices); resell, retail; dribble (a ball); *Fig. Inf.* dodge, avoid; *vi* bargain, haggle; *Naut.* take part in a regatta, race

regateo /rrega'teo/ *m*, haggling, bargaining

regatero /rrega'tero/ **(-ra)** *a* retail. *n* retailer

regatón /rrega'ton/ **(-ona)** *m*, ferrule, tip. *a* haggling, bargaining. *n* haggler; retailer

regatonear /rregatone'ar/ *vt* to resell at retail

regazo /rre'gaso; rre'gaθo/ *m*, lap, knees; *Fig.* heart, bosom

regeneración /rrehenera'sion; rrehenera'θion/ *f*, regeneration

regenerador /rrehenera'ðor/ **(-ra)** *n* regenerator. *a* regenerative, reforming

regenerar /rrehene'rar/ *vt* to regenerate, reform

regenta /rre'henta/ *f*, wife of the president of a court of session

regentar /rrehen'tar/ *vt* to fill temporarily (offices); rule, govern; manage, run (businesses)

regente /rre'hente/ *a* ruling. *mf* regent. *m*, president of a court of session; manager

regicidio /rrehi'siðio; rrehi'θiðio/ *m*, regicide (act)

regidor /rrehi'ðor/ *a* ruling, governing. *m*, magistrate, alderman

régimen /'rrehimen/ *m*, administration, management; regime; (*Med. Gram.*) regimen; *Mech.* rating

regimentación /rrehimenta'sion; rrehimenta'θion/ *f*, regimentation

regimentar /rrehimen'tar/ *vt irr* to form into regiments; regiment. *Pres. Ind.* **regimiento, regimientas, regimienta, regimientan.** *Pres. Subjunc.* **regimiente, regimientes, regimientéis, regimienten**

regimiento /rrehi'miento/ *m*, *Mil.* regiment; administration, rule; *Lat. Am.* crowd (of people)

regio /'rrehio/ *a* royal; magnificent, regal. **¡regio!** great!, wonderful!

región /rre'hion/ *f*, region, country; area, tract, space. **r. industrial,** industrial area

regionalismo /rrehiona'lismo/ *m*, regionalism

regionalista /rrehiona'lista/ *mf* regionalist. *a* regional

regir /rre'hir/ *vt irr* to govern, rule; administer, conduct; *Gram.* govern; *vi* be in force (laws, etc.); work, function; *Naut.* obey the helm. See **pedir**

registrador /rrehistra'ðor/ *a* recording. *m*, registrar, keeper of records; recorder. **caja (registradora)**, (cash) register

registrar /rrehis'trar/ *vt* to examine, inspect; search; copy, record; mark the place (in a book); observe, note; (of thermometers, etc.) record, show; look on to (houses, etc.); *vr* register (hotels, etc.)

registro /rre'histro/ *m*, search; registration, entry; record; recording; reading (of a thermometer, etc.); *Mech.* damper; registry; register (book); *Mus.* range, compass (voice); *Mus.* register (organ); (*Mech. Print.*) register; bookmark. **r. civil**, register of births, marriages, and deaths

regla /'rregla/ *f*, ruler, measuring stick; rule, principle, guide, precept; system, policy; *Med.* period; moderation; method, order. **r. de cálculo**, slide rule. **r. T**, T-square. **en r.**, in due form. **por r.**, general, generally, as a rule

reglamentación /rreglamenta'sion; rreglamenta'θion/ *f*, regulation; rules and regulations

reglamentar /rreglamen'tar/ *vt* to regulate

reglamento /rregla'mento/ *m*, bylaw; regulation, ordinance

reglar /rre'glar/ *vt* to rule (lines); regulate; govern; control; *vr* restrain oneself, mend one's ways

regocijar /rregosi'har; rregoθi'har/ *vt* to cheer, delight; *vr* enjoy oneself, rejoice

regocijo /rrego'siho; rrego'θiho/ *m*, happiness, joy; cheer, merriment

regordete /rregor'ðete/ *a Inf.* chubby

regresar /rregre'sar/ *vi* to return

regresión /rregre'sion/ *f*, return; retrogression; regression

regreso /rre'greso/ *m*, return

reguera /rre'gera/ *f*, irrigation channel, ditch

regulación /rregula'sion; rregula'θion/ *f*, regulation; *Mech.* control, timing

regulador /rregula'ðor/ *m*, *Mech.* governor, regulator. *a* regulating, controlling

regular /rregu'lar/ *vt* to adjust, regulate; *Mech.* govern. *a* methodical, ordered; moderate; average, medium; (*Eccl. Mil. Geom. Gram.*) regular; so-so, not bad; probable. **por lo r.**, generally

regularidad /rregulari'ðað/ *f*, regularity

regularización /rregularisa'sion; rregulariθa'θion/ *f*, regularization; regulation

regularizar /rregulari'sar; rregulari'θar/ *vt* to regularize; regulate

regurgitar /rregurhi'tar/ *vi* to regurgitate

rehabilitación /rreaβilita'sion; rreaβilita'θion/ *f*, rehabilitation

rehabilitar /rreaβili'tar/ *vt* to rehabilitate; *vr* rehabilitate oneself

rehacer /rrea'ser; rrea'θer/ *vt irr* to remake; repair, mend; *vr* recover one's strength; control one's emotions; *Mil.* rally. See **hacer**

rehén /rre'en/ *m*, hostage (gen. *pl*); *Mil.* pledge, security

rehenchir /rreen'tʃir/ *vt irr* to restuff; refill, recharge. See **henchir**

reherir /rree'rir/ *vt irr* to repulse. See **herir**

rehilar /rrei'lar/ *vt* to spin too much or twist the yarn; *vi* totter, stagger; whizz (arrows, etc.). See **prohibir**

rehuir /rre'uir/ *vt irr* to withdraw; avoid; reject. See **huir**

rehusar /rreu'sar/ *vt* to refuse, reject. See **desahuciar**

reimponer /rreimpo'ner/ *vt irr* to reimpose. See **poner**

reimportación /rreimporta'sion; rreimporta'θion/ *f*, reimportation

reimpresión /rreimpre'sion/ *f*, reprint

reimprimir /rreimpri'mir/ *vt* to reprint

reina /'rreina/ *f*, queen; queen (in chess); queen bee; peerless beauty, belle

reinado /rrei'naðo/ *m*, reign; heyday, fashion

reinante /rrei'nante/ *a* reigning; prevalent

reinar /rrei'nar/ *vi* to reign; influence; endure, prevail

reincidencia /rreinsi'ðensia; rreinθi'ðenθia/ *f*, relapse (into crime, etc.), recidivism

reincidente /rreinsi'ðente; rreinθi'ðente/ *mf* backslider

reincidir /rreinsi'ðir; rreinθi'ðir/ *vi* to relapse (into crime, etc.)

reincorporar /rreinkorpo'rar/ *vt* to reincorporate; *vr* join again, become a member again

reingresar /rreiŋgre'sar/ *vi* to reenter

reingreso /rreiŋ'greso/ *m*, reentry

reino /'rreino/ *m*, kingdom

reinstalación /rreinstala'sion; rreinstala'θion/ *f*, reinstatement

reinstalar /rreinsta'lar/ *vt* to reinstate; *vr* be reinstalled

reintegración /rreintegra'sion; rreintegra'θion/ *f*, reintegration

reintegrar /rreinte'grar/ *vt* to reintegrate; *vr* be reinstated, recuperate, recover

reir /rre'ir/ *vi irr* to laugh; sneer, jeer; *Fig.* smile (nature); *vt* laugh at; *vr Inf.* (*with de*) scorn. **reírse a carcajadas**, to shout with laughter. *Pres. Part.* **riendo**. *Pres. Ind.* **río, ríes, ríe, ríen**. *Preterite* **rió, rieron**. *Pres. Subjunc.* **ría, etc.** *Imperf. Subjunc.* **riese, etc.**

reiteración /rreitera'sion; rreitera'θion/ *f*, reiteration, repetition

reiteradamente /rreiteraða'mente/ *adv* repeatedly, reiteratively

reiterar /rreite'rar/ *vt* to reiterate, repeat

reivindicación /rreiβindika'sion; rreiβindika'θion/ *f*, *Law.* recovery

reivindicar /rreiβindi'kar/ *vt Law.* to recover

reja /'rreha/ *f*, colter, plowshare; plowing, tilling; grating, grille; *Lat. Am.* jail, prison

rejado /rre'haðo/ *m*, railing, grating

rejilla /rre'hiya; rre'hiʎa/ *f*, grating; grille, lattice; luggage rack (in a train); cane (for chairs, seats, etc.); wire mesh; small brazier; *Elec.* grid; *Mech.* grate

rejo /'rreho/ *m*, *Lat. Am.* whip

rejuntar /rrehun'tar/ *vt* to point (a wall)

rejuvenecer /rrehuβene'ser; rrehuβene'θer/ *vt irr* to rejuvenate; *Fig.* revive; bring up to date; *vi* and *vr* be rejuvenated, grow young again, rejuvenesce. See **conocer**

rejuvenecimiento /rrehuβenesi'miento; rrehuβeneθi'miento/ *m*, rejuvenation

relación /rrela'sion; rrela'θion/ *f*, relation; connection (of ideas); report, statement; narrative, account; *Math.* ratio; *Law.* brief; intercourse, association, dealings (gen. *pl*); list; analogy, relation. **tener relaciones con**, to have dealings with; be engaged or betrothed to; woo, court

relacionar /rrelasio'nar; rrelaθio'nar/ *vt* to recount, narrate, report; connect, relate; *vr* be connected

relajación /rrelaha'sion; rrelaha'θion/ *f*, relaxation; recreation; laxity, dissoluteness

relajar /rrela'har/ *vt* to relax; recreate, amuse; make less rigorous; *Law.* remit; *vr* become relaxed; be dissolute, lax, or vicious, *Dominican Republic* joke

relajo /rrela'ho/ *m*, relaxation; *Lat. Am.* joking

relamer /rrela'mer/ *vt* to lick again; *vr* lick one's lips; *Fig.* overpaint, make up too much; ooze satisfaction, brag

relamido /rrela'miðo/ *a* overdressed; affected

relámpago /rre'lampago/ *m*, lightning; flash, gleam; streak of lightning (of quick persons or things); flash of wit, witticism

relampaguear /rrelampage'ar/ *vi* to lighten (of lightning); flash, gleam

relapso /rre'lapso/ *a* relapsed, lapsed (into error, vice)

relatar /rrela'tar/ *vt* to relate, narrate, report, relay

relatividad /rrelatiβi'ðað/ *f*, relativeness; *Phys.* relativity

relativo /rrela'tiβo/ *a* relevant, pertinent; relative, comparative; *Gram.* relative

relato /rre'lato/ *m*, narration, account, report

relator /rrela'tor/ **(-ra)** *a* narrating. *n* narrator. *m*, *Law.* reporter

relavar /rrela'βar/ *vt* to rewash, wash again

relección /rrelek'sion; rrelek'θion/ *f*, reelection

releer /rrele'er/ *vt irr* to reread; revise. See **creer**

relegación /rrelega'sion; rrelega'θion/ *f*, relegation

relegar /rrele'gar/ *vt* to banish; relegate, set aside

relegir /rrele'hir/ *vt irr* to reelect. See **elegir**

relente /rre'lente/ *m*, night dew, dampness; *Inf.* cheek, impudence

relevación /rreleβa'sion; rreleβa'θion/ *f*, *Art.* relief; release; remission, exemption

relevar /rrele'βar/ *vt Art.* to work in relief; emboss; relieve, free; dismiss; excuse, pardon; aid, succor; *Fig.* aggrandize; *Mil.* relieve; *vi* carve in relief

relevo /rre'leβo/ *m*, relay; *Mil.* relief

relieve /rre'lieβe/ *m*, *Art.* relief; *pl* leftovers, remains (of food). **alto r.**, high relief. **bajo r.**, low relief

religar /rreli'gar/ *vt* to retie, fasten again; fasten more securely; solder

religión /rreli'hion/ *f*, religion; creed, faith, philosophy; devotion, religious practice. **r. reformada**, Protestantism. **entrar en r.**, *Eccl.* to profess

religiosidad /rrelihiosi'ðað/ *f*, religiosity; religiousness; conscientiousness, punctiliousness

religioso /rreli'hioso/ **(-sa)** *a* religious; punctilious, conscientious; moderate. *n* religious

relinchar /rrelin'tʃar/ *vi* to whinny, neigh

reliquia /rre'likia/ *f*, residue (gen. *pl*); *Eccl.* relic; vestige, remnant, memento; permanent disability or ailment

rellanar /rreʎa'nar/ *vt* to make level again; *vr* stretch oneself at full length

rellano /rre'ʎano/ *m*, landing (of a staircase); level stretch (of ground)

rellenar /rreʎe'nar/ *vt* to refill, replenish; fill up; *Mas.* plug, point; *Cul.* stuff; *Inf.* cram with food (gen. *vr*)

relleno /rre'ʎeno/ *m*, *Cul.* stuffing; replenishing; filling; *Fig.* padding (of speeches, etc.)

reloj /rre'loh/ *m*, clock; watch. **r. de arena**, hourglass. **r. de bolsillo**, watch. **r. de la muerte**, deathwatch beetle. **r. de péndulo**, grandfather clock. **r. de pulsera**, wristwatch. **r. de repetición**, repeater. **r. de sol** *or* **r. solar**, sundial

relojera /rrelo'hera/ *f*, clock stand; watch case

relojería /rrelohe'ria/ *f*, watch or clock making; jeweler, watch maker's shop

relojero /rrelo'hero/ **(-ra)** *n* watch maker, watch repairer

reluciente /rrelu'siente; rrelu'θiente/ *a* shining, sparkling; shiny

relucir /rrelu'sir; rrelu'θir/ *vi irr* to glitter, sparkle, gleam; *Fig.* shine, excel. See **lucir**

reluctante /rreluk'tante/ *a* unruly, refractory, disobedient

relumbrante /rrelum'βrante/ *a* resplendent, dazzling

relumbrar /rrelum'βrar/ *vi* to be resplendent, shine, glitter

remachar /rrema'tʃar/ *vt* to rivet; *Fig.* clinch

remache /rre'matʃe/ *m*, riveting; rivet

remaduro, -a /rrema'ðuro/ *a*, *Lat. Am.* overripe

remanente /rrema'nente/ *m*, remains, residue

remanso /rre'manso/ *m*, backwater; stagnant water; sloth, dilatoriness

remar /rre'mar/ *vi* to row, paddle, scull; toil, strive

rematadamente /rremataða'mente/ *adv* completely, entirely, absolutely

rematado /rrema'taðo/ *a* beyond hope, extremely ill; utterly lost; *Law.* convicted

rematar /rrema'tar/ *vt* to end, finish; finish off, kill; knock down at auction; *Sew.* finish; *vi* end; *vr* be ruined or spoiled

remate /rre'mate/ *m*, end, conclusion; extremity; *Archit.* coping; *Archit.* terminal; highest bid; auction. **de r.**, utterly hopeless

rematista /rrema'tista/ *mf*, *Lat. Am.* auctioneer

rembarcar /rrembar'kar/ *vt* to reembark, reship

rembolsable /rrembol'saβle/ *a* repayable

rembolsar /rrembol'sar/ *vt* to recover (money); refund, return (money)

rembolso /rrem'βolso/ *m*, repayment. **contra r.**, cash on delivery, C.O.D.

remedar /rreme'ðar/ *vt* to copy, imitate; mimic

remediador /rremeðia'ðor/ **(-ra)** *a* remedying. *n* benefactor, helper

remediar /rreme'ðiar/ *vt* to remedy; aid, help; save from danger; prevent (trouble)

remedio /rre'meðio/ *m*, remedy; emendation, correction; help; refuge, protection; *Med.* remedy. **No hay más r.**, There's nothing else to do, It's the only way open. **no tener más r.**, to be unable to help (doing something), be obliged to

remedo /rre'meðo/ *m*, imitation; poor copy

remembranza /rremem'βransa; rremem'βranθa/ *f*, remembrance, memory

rememorar /rrememo'rar/ *vt* to remember, recall to mind

remendar /rremen'dar/ *vt irr* to mend, patch; darn; repair; correct. See **recomendar**

remendón /rremen'don/ **(-ona)** *n* cobbler; mender of old clothes

remero /rre'mero/ **(-ra)** *n* oarsman, rower; sculler

remesa /rre'mesa/ *f*, remittance; consignment, shipment

remesar /rreme'sar/ **(se)** *vt* and *vr* to pluck out (hair); *vt Com.* remit; consign

remezón /rreme'son; rreme'θon/ *m*, *Lat. Am.* (earth) tremor

remiendo /rre'miendo/ *m*, *Sew.* patch; mend, darn; emendation; *Inf.* insignia of one of the Spanish military orders. **a remiendos**, *Inf.* piecemeal

remilgarse /rremil'garse/ *vr* to preen oneself, be overdressed

remilgo /rre'milgo/ *m*, affectation; mannerism; prudery, squeamishness

reminiscencia /rreminis'sensia; rreminis'θenθia/ *f*, reminiscence; memory, recollection

remirado /rremi'raðo/ *a* wary, cautious, prudent, circumspect

remirar /rremi'rar/ *vt* to revise, go over again; *vr* take great care over; behold with pleasure

remise /rre'mise/ *m*, *Argentina* limousine, hired taxi

remisión /rremi'sion/ *f*, sending; remission; pardon, forgiveness; foregoing, relinquishment; abatement, diminution; *Lit.* reference, allusion

remiso /rre'miso/ *a* timid, spiritless; languid, slow

remitente /rremi'tente/ *mf* sender. *a* sending

remitir /rremi'tir/ *vt* to remit, send; pardon, forgive; defer, postpone; abate, diminish; relinquish, forgo; *Lit.* refer; *vr* remit, submit, consult; refer (to), cite

remo /'rremo/ *m*, oar, scull, paddle; arm or leg (of men or animals, gen. *pl*); wing (gen. *pl*); hard, continuous toil; galleys. **al r.**, by dint of rowing; *Inf.* struggling with hardships

remojar /rremo'har/ *vt* to soak, steep; celebrate by drinking

remojo /rre'moho/ *m*, soaking, steeping

remolacha /rremo'latʃa/ *f*, beet

remolcador /rremolka'ðor/ *m*, *Naut.* tow, tugboat. *a Naut.* towing

remolcar /rremol'kar/ *vt* (*Naut. Auto.*) to tow; *Fig.* press into service, use

remoler /rremo'ler/ *vi*, *Lat. Am.* to live it up, live the life of Riley

remolinar /rremoli'nar/ *vi* to spin, whirl, eddy; *vr* throng, swarm

remolino /rremo'lino/ *m*, whirlwind; eddy, swirl; whirlpool; crowd, throng; swarm; disturbance, riot

remolonear /rremolone'ar/ *vi Inf.* to loiter, lag; avoid work; be lax or dilatory

remolque /rre'molke/ *m*, towage, towing; towline; barge; *Auto.* trailer. **a r.**, on tow

remonta /rre'monta/ *f*, resoling (of shoes); leather gusset (of riding breeches); *Mil.* remount

remontar /rremon'tar/ *vt* to scare off (game); *Mil.* supply with fresh horses; resole (shoes); *Fig.* rise to great heights (of oratory, etc.); *vr* soar (of birds); (*with prep a*) date from, go back to; originate in

remoquete /rremo'kete/ *m*, blow with the fist; witticism; *Inf.* flirtation; courtship

rémora /'rremora/ *f*, *Ichth.* remora; delay, hindrance

remorder /rremor'ðer/ *vt irr* to bite again or repeatedly; *Fig.* gnaw, nag, cause uneasiness or remorse; *vr* show one's feelings. See **morder**

remordimiento /rremorði'miento/ *m*, remorse

remoto /rre'moto/ *a* distant, remote; unlikely, improbable

remover /rremo'βer/ *vt irr* to remove, move; stir; turn over; dismiss, discharge. See **mover**

remozar /rremo'sar; rremo'θar/ *vt* to cause to appear young; freshen up, bring up to date; *vr* look young

remplazar /rrempla'sar; rrempla'θar/ *vt* to replace; exchange, substitute; succeed, take the place of

remplazo /rrem'plaso; rrem'plaθo/ *m*, replacement; exchange, substitute; successor; *Mil.* replacement

remuda /rre'muða/ *f*, replacement, exchange

remudar /rremu'ðar/ *vt* to replace

remuneración /rremunera'sion; rremunera'θion/ *f*, remuneration; reward

remunerador /rremunera'ðor/ **(-ra)** *a* remunerative, recompensing. *n* remunerator

remunerar /rremune'rar/ *vt* to recompense, reward

remusgar /rremus'gar/ *vi* to suspect, imagine

renacentista /rrenasen'tista; rrenaθen'tista/ *a* renaissance

renacimiento /rrenasi'miento; rrenaθi'miento/ *m*, rebirth; Renaissance

renacuajo /rrena'kuaho/ *m*, tadpole; *Mech.* frog; *Inf.* twerp

rencarcelar /rrenkarse'lar; rrenkarθe'lar/ *vt* to reimprison

rencarnación /rrenkarna'sion; rrenkarna'θion/ *f*, reincarnation

rencarnar /rrenkar'nar/ **(se)** *vi* and *vr* to be reincarnated

rencilla /rren'siya; rren'θiʎa/ *f*, grudge, grievance, resentment

rencilloso /rrensi'yoso; rrenθi'ʎoso/ *a* peevish, easily offended, touchy

rencor /rren'kor/ *m*, rancor, spite, old grudge. **guardar r.**, to hold a grudge

rencoroso /rrenko'roso/ *a* rancorous, malicious, spiteful

rencuadernar /rrenkuaðer'nar/ *vt* to rebind (books)

rencuentro /rren'kuentro/ *m*, collision; *Mil.* encounter, clash

rendición /rrendi'sion; rrendi'θion/ *f*, surrender; yield, profit

rendido /rren'diðo/ *a* submissive, obsequious

rendija /rren'diha/ *f*, crevice, cleft, crack, fissure

rendimiento /rrendi'miento/ *m*, weariness, fatigue; submissiveness, obsequiousness; yield, profit; *Mech.* efficiency

rendir /rren'dir/ *vt irr Mil.* to cause to surrender; defeat; overcome, conquer; give back, return; yield, provide; tire, exhaust; vomit; pay, render; *vr* be exhausted, be worn out; surrender. *Mil.* **r. el puesto,** to retire from or give up a post. See **pedir**

renegado /rrene'gaðo/ **(-da)** *n* renegade, apostate; turncoat; *Inf.* malignant person. *a* renegade

renegador /rrenega'ðor/ **(-ra)** *n* blasphemer; foulmouthed person

renegar /rrene'gar/ *vt irr* to deny, disown; loathe, hate; *vi* (*with de*) apostatize; blaspheme; *Inf.* curse. See **cegar**

renganchar /rreŋgan'tʃar/ **(se)** *vt* and *vr Mil.* to reenlist

renganche /rreŋ'gantʃe/ *m*, *Mil.* reenlistment

renglón /rreŋ'glon/ *m*, *Print.* line; *pl* writing, composition, line (of a poem)

renguear /rreŋgue'ar/ *vi*, *Lat. Am.* to limp

renguera /rreŋ'guera/ *f*, *Lat. Am.* limp

reniego /rre'niego/ *m*, blasphemy; *Inf.* foul language, cursing

renitencia /rreni'tensia; rreni'tenθia/ *f*, repugnance

renombrado /rrenom'βraðo/ *a* illustrious, famous

renombre /rre'nombre/ *m*, surname; renown, reputation, fame

renovable /rreno'βaβle/ *a* renewable, replaceable

renovación /rrenoβa'sion; rrenoβa'θion/ *f*, replacement; renewal; renovation; transformation, reform

renovador /rrenoβa'ðor/ **(-ra)** *n* reformer; renovator. *a* renovating; reforming

renovar /rreno'βar/ *vt irr* to renew; renovate; replace; exchange; reiterate, repeat. See **contar**

renta /'rrenta/ *f*, yield, profit; income; revenue; government securities; rent; tax

rentar /rren'tar/ *vt* to yield, produce an income

rentero /rren'tero/ **(-ra)** *n* tenant farmer. *m*, one who farms out land

rentista /rren'tista/ *mf* financier; bondholder; person who lives on a private income, rentier

rentístico /rren'tistiko/ *a* revenue, financial

renuente /rre'nuente/ *a* refractory, willful

renuevo /rre'nueβo/ *m*, *Bot.* shoot; renewal

renuncia, renunciación /rre'nunsia, rrenunsia'sion; rre'nunθia, rrenunθia'θion/ *f*, renunciation; resignation; abandonment, relinquishment

renunciar /rrenun'siar; rrenun'θiar/ *vt* to renounce; refuse; scorn; abandon, relinquish; resign; revoke (at cards). **r. a,** to give up

renuncio /rre'nunsio; rre'nunθio/ *m*, revoke (cards); *Inf.* falsehood

reñidamente /rreɲiða'mente/ *adv* strongly, stubbornly, fiercely

reñir /rre'ɲir/ *vi irr* to quarrel, dispute; fight; be on bad terms, fall out; *vt* scold; fight (battles, etc.). See **ceñir**

reo /'rreo/ *mf* criminal; offender, guilty party; *Law.* defendant

reojo /rre'oho/ *m*, **(mirar de)** to look out of the corner of the eye; *Fig.* look askance

reorganizador /rreorganisa'ðor; rreorganiθa'ðor/ **(-ra)** *a* reorganizing. *n* reorganizer

reóstato /rre'ostato/ *m*, rheostat

repantigarse /rrepanti'garse/ *vr* to stretch out one's legs, make oneself comfortable

reparable /rrepa'raβle/ *a* remediable, reparable; worthy of note

reparación /rrepara'sion; rrepara'θion/ *f*, repair, mending; reparation, satisfaction; indemnity, compensation

reparada /rrepa'raða/ *f*, shying (of horses)

reparador /rrepara'ðor/ *a* repairing, mending; faultfinding; restoring; satisfying, compensating

reparar /rrepa'rar/ *vt* to repair; restore; consider; correct, remedy; atone for, expiate; indemnify; hold up, detain; protect, guard; (*with en*) notice; *Lat. Am.* to ape, imitate, mimic; *vi* halt, be detained; *vr* control oneself

reparo /rre'paro/ *m*, repair; restoration; remedy; note, reflection; warning; doubt, scruple; guard, protection; parry (at fencing)

repartición /rreparti'sion; rreparti'θion/ *f*, distribution

repartidero /rreparti'ðero/ *a* distributable

repartidor /rreparti'ðor/ **(-ra)** *a* distributing. *n* distributor; tax assessor

repartimiento /rreparti'miento/ *m*, distribution, allotment; assessment

repartir /rrepar'tir/ *vt* to distribute; share out; allot; deal (cards); assess; *Com.* deliver

reparto /rre'parto/ *m*, distribution; assessment; delivery (of letters, etc.); *Theat.* cast; deal (at cards); *Lat. Am.* building site, construction site

repasador /rrepasa'ðor/ *m*, *Lat. Am.* dish cloth, dishrag

repasar /rrepa'sar/ *vt* to pass by again; peruse, reexamine; brush up, revise; skim, glance over; mend, repair (garments); edit, revise; hone

repaso /rre'paso/ *m*, second passage through; reexamination, perusal; revision, editing; brushing up, revision; repair, mending; *Inf.* dressing-down, scolding

repatriación /rrepatria'sion; rrepatria'θion/ *f*, repatriation

repatriado /rrepa'triaðo/ **(-da)** *a* repatriate

repatriar /rrepa'triar/ *vt* to repatriate; *vi* and *vr* return to one's own country

repecho /rre'petʃo/ *m*, steep slope. **a r.,** uphill

repelar /rrepe'lar/ *vt* to pull by the hair; put through its paces (of a horse); clip, cut; remove, diminish

repeler /rrepe'ler/ *vt* to repel, throw back; reject, refute

repelo /rre'pelo/ *m*, anything against the grain; *Inf.* skirmish; reluctance, repugnance

repente /rre'pente/ *m*, *Inf.* sudden or unexpected movement. **de r.**, suddenly

repentino /rrepen'tino/ *a* sudden, unexpected

repentizar /rrepenti'sar; rrepenti'θar/ *vi* *Mus.* to sight-read

repercusión /rreperku'sion/ *f*, repercussion; vibration

repercutir /rreperku'tir/ *vi* to recoil, rebound; *vr* reverberate; reecho; *Fig.* have repercussions; *vt* *Med.* repel

repertorio /rreper'torio/ *m*, repertory

~~repesar~~ /rrepe'sar/ *vt* to ~~reweigh, weigh again~~

repetición /rrepeti'sion; rrepeti'θion/ *f*, repetition; *Art.* replica, copy; repeater (in clocks); recital

repetidamente /rrepetiða'mente/ *adv* repeatedly

repetir /rrepe'tir/ *vt irr* to repeat, do over again; reiterate; *Art.* copy, make a replica of; recite. See **pedir**

repicar /rrepi'kar/ *vt* to chop, mince; peal (of bells); prick exam); *vr* pride oneself (on), boast

repique /rre'pike/ *m*, chopping, mincing; peal, pealing (of bells); disagreement, grievance

repisa /rre'pisa/ *f*, *Archit.* bracket; ledge; shelf. **r. de chimenea**, mantelpiece

replantar /rreplan'tar/ *vt* to replant; transplant

repleción /rreple'sion; rreple'θion/ *f*, repletion, satiety

replegar /rreple'gar/ *vt irr* to refold, fold many times; *vr* *Mil.* retreat in good order. See **cegar**

repleto /rre'pleto/ *a* replete

réplica /'rreplika/ *f*, reply, answer; replica

replicar /rrepli'kar/ *vi* to contradict, dispute; answer, reply. **¡No me repliques!** *Inf.* Don't answer back!

repliegue /rre'pliege/ *m*, double fold, crease; doubling, folding; *Mil.* withdrawal

repoblación /rrepoβla'sion; rrepoβla'θion/ *f*, repeopling, repopulation

repoblar /rrepo'βlar/ *vt* to repeople, repopulate

repollo /rre'poyo; rre'poʎo/ *m*, white cabbage; heart (of lettuce, etc.)

reponer /rrepo'ner/ *vt irr* to replace; reinstate; restore; reply; *vr* recover, regain (possessions); grow well again; grow calm. See **poner**

reportación /rreporta'sion; rreporta'θion/ *f*, serenity, moderation

reportaje /rrepor'tahe/ *m*, journalistic report

reportar /rrepor'tar/ *vt* to restrain, moderate; achieve, obtain; carry; bring; *vr* control oneself

reporte /rre'porte/ *m*, report, news; rumor

reporterismo /rreporte'rismo/ *m*, newspaper reporting

reportero /rrepor'tero/ **(-ra)** *a* news, report. *n* reporter

reposado /rrepo'saðo/ *a* quiet, peaceful, tranquil

reposar /rrepo'sar/ *vi* to rest, repose oneself; sleep, doze; lie in the grave; settle (liquids); rest (on)

reposición /rreposi'sion; rreposi'θion/ *f*, replacement; restoration; renewal; recovery (of health); *Theat.* revival

repositorio /rreposi'torio/ *m*, repository

reposo /rre'poso/ *m*, rest, repose; peace, tranquility; sleep

repostada /rrepos'taða/ *f*, *Lat. Am.* cheeky reply, saucy retort

repostería /rreposte'ria/ *f*, confectioner's shop; pantry; butler's pantry

repostero /rrepos'tero/ *m*, confectioner, pastry cook

repreguntar /rrepregun'tar/ *vt* to cross-examine

reprender /rrepren'der/ *vt* to scold, reprimand, rebuke

reprensible /rrepren'siβle/ *a* reprehensible, censurable

reprensión /rrepren'sion/ *f*, scolding, reprimand, rebuke

represa /rre'presa/ *f*, damming, holding back (water); dam, lock; restraining, controlling

represalia /rrepre'salia/ *f*, reprisal (gen. *pl*); retaliation

represar /rrepre'sar/ *vt* to dam, harness (water); *Naut.* retake, recapture; *Fig.* restrain, control

representación /rrepresenta'sion; rrepresenta'θion/ *f*, representation; *Theat.* performance; authority; dignity; *Com.* agency; portrait, image; depiction, expression; petition

representador /rrepresenta'ðor/ *a* representative

representante /rrepresen'tante/ *a* representative. *mf* representative; actor; performer

representar /rrepresen'tar/ *vt* to represent; *Theat.* perform; depict, express; describe, portray; *vr* imagine, picture to oneself

representativo /rrepresenta'tiβo/ *a* representative

represión /rrepre'sion/ *f*, repression; recapture

represivo /rrepre'siβo/ *a* repressive

reprimenda /rrepri'menda/ *f*, rebuke, reprimand

reprimir /rrepri'mir/ *vt* to repress, restrain, control; *vr* restrain oneself

reprobación /rreproβa'sion; rreproβa'θion/ *f*, censure; reprobation

reprobar /rrepro'βar/ *vt irr* to reprove; censure; fail (in an exam). See **probar**

réprobo /'rreproβo/ **(-ba)** *n* reprobate

reprochar /rrepro't ʃar/ *vt* to reproach

reproche /rre'protʃe/ *m*, reproaching; rebuke, reproach

reproducción /rreproðuk'sion; rreproðuk'θion/ *f*, reproduction. **r. a gran escala,** large-scale model

reproducir /rreproðu'sir; rreproðu'θir/ *vt irr* to reproduce. See **conducir**

reproductor /rreproðuk'tor/ **(-ra)** *a* reproductive. *n* breeding animal

reps /rreps/ *m*, rep (fabric)

reptil /rrep'til/ *a* reptilian; crawling. *m*, reptile

república /rre'puβlika/ *f*, republic; state, commonwealth. **la r. de las letras,** the republic of letters

República Dominicana /rre'puβlika domini'kana/ Dominican Republic

República Malgache /rre'puβlika mal'gatʃe/ Republic of Madagascar

republicanismo /rrepuβlika'nismo/ *m*, republicanism

republicano /rrepuβli'kano/ **(-na)** *a* and *n* republican

repudiación /rrepuðia'sion; rrepuðia'θion/ *f*, repudiation

repudiar /rrepu'ðiar/ *vt* to cast off (a wife); repudiate, renounce

repuesto /rre'puesto/ *a* retired, hidden. *m*, stock, provision; serving table; pantry; stake (at cards, etc.). **de r.,** spare, extra

repugnancia /rrepug'nansia; rrepug'nanθia/ *f*, inconsistency, contradiction; aversion, dislike; reluctance; repugnance

repugnante /rrepug'nante/ *a* repugnant, loathsome

repugnar /rrepug'nar/ *vt* to contradict, be inconsistent with; hate, be averse to (e.g. *La idea me repugna,* I hate the idea)

repujado /rrepu'haðo/ *m*, repoussé work

repujar /rrepu'har/ *vt* to work in repoussé

repulir /rrepu'lir/ *vt* to repolish, reburnish; *vt* and *vr* make up too much, overdress

repulsa /rre'pulsa/ *f*, snub, rebuff; rejection; repulse

repulsar /rrepul'sar/ *vt* to decline, reject, repulse; deny, refuse; rebuff

repulsión /rrepul'sion/ *f*, repulsion; rebuff; aversion, dislike

repulsivo /rrepul'siβo/ *a* repellent

repunta /rre'punta/ *f*, headland, cape; *Fig.* first sign; *Inf.* disgust; caprice; fight

reputación /rreputa'sion; rreputa'θion/ *f*, reputation

reputar /rrepu'tar/ *vt* to believe, consider (e.g. *Le reputo por honrado,* I believe him to be an honorable man); appreciate, esteem

requebrar /rreke'βrar/ *vt irr* to break into smaller pieces; make love to, woo; compliment, flatter. See **quebrar**

requemado /rreke'maðo/ *a* sunburned; brown

requemar /rreke'mar/ *vt* to burn again; overcook; dry up, parch (of plants, etc.); burn (the mouth) (of spicy foods, etc.); *vr* *Fig.* suffer inwardly

requerimiento /rrekeri'miento/ *m*, requirement, demand; *Law.* summons

requerir /rreke'rir/ *vt irr* to inform, notify; examine;

need, necessitate; require; summon; woo; persuade. See **sentir**

requesón /rreke'son/ *m*, cream cheese; curd

requetebién /rrekete'βien/ *adv Inf.* exceedingly well

requiebro /rre'kieβro/ *m*, compliment, expression of love; wooing, flirtation

requintar /rrekin'tar/ *vt*, *Lat. Am.* to tighten

requisa /rre'kisa/ *f*, inspection, visitation; *Mil.* requisitioning; *Lat. Am.* confiscation

requisar /rreki'sar/ *vt Mil.* to requisition

requisito /rreki'sito/ *m*, requisite

res /rres/ *f*, animal, beast; head of cattle. *Lat. Am.* **carne de r.**, steak

resabiar /rresa'βiar/ *vt* to make vicious, cause bad habits; *vr* contract bad habits or vices; be discontented; relish

resabio /rre'saβio/ *m*, disagreeable aftertaste; bad habit, vice

resaca /rre'saka/ *f*, surf, undertow, surge; *Com.* redraft

resacar /rresa'kar/ *vt* to distil

resalado /rresa'laðo/ *a Inf.* very witty; most attractive

resaltar /rresal'tar/ *vi* to rebound; project, jut out; grow loose, fall out; *Fig.* stand out, be prominent

resalto /rre'salto/ *m*, rebound; projection

resarcir /rresar'sir; rresar'θir/ *vt* to compensate, indemnify

resbaladizo /rresβala'ðiso; rresβala'ðiθo/ *a* slippery; difficult, delicate (of a situation)

resbalar /rresβa'lar/ *vi* to slip; slide; skid; err, fall into sin

resbalón /rresβa'lon/ *m*, slip; slide; skid; temptation, error

rescatador /rreskata'ðor/ **(-ra)** *n* ransomer; rescuer

rescatar /rreska'tar/ *vt* to ransom; redeem, buy back; barter; free, rescue; *Fig.* redeem (time, etc.)

rescate /rres'kate/ *m*, ransom; redemption; barter; amount of ransom

rescindir /rressin'dir; rresθin'dir/ *vt* to annul, repeal, rescind

rescoldo /rres'koldo/ *m*, ember, cinder; scruple, qualm, doubt

resentimiento /rresenti'miento/ *m*, deterioration, impairment; animosity, resentment

resentirse /rresen'tirse/ *vr irr* to deteriorate, be impaired; be hurt or offended. See **sentir**

reseña /rre'seɲa/ *f*, *Mil.* review; short description; review (of a book)

reseñar /rrese'ɲar/ *vt Mil.* to review; describe briefly, outline

reserva /rre'serβa/ *f*, store, stock; exception, qualification; reticence; restraint, moderation; (*Eccl. Law.*) reservation; (*Mil. Naut.*) reserve. **sin r.**, frankly, without reserve

reservación /rreserβa'sion; rreserβa'θion/ *f*, reservation; scruple

reservado /rreser'βaðo/ *a* reserved, reticent; prudent, moderate; kept, reserved. *m*, reserved compartment; private apartment, private garden, etc.

reservar /rreser'βar/ *vt* to keep, hold; postpone; reserve (rooms, etc.); exempt; keep secret; withhold (information); *Eccl.* reserve; *vr* await a better opportunity; be cautious

reservista /rreser'βista/ *a* (*Mil. Nav.*) reserved. *mf* reservist

resfriado /rres'friaðo/ *m*, *Med.* cold, chill

resfriar /rres'friar/ *vt* to chill; *Fig.* cool, moderate; *vi* grow cold; *vr* catch a cold; *Fig.* cool off (of love, etc.)

resguardar /rresguar'ðar/ *vt* to protect; shelter; *vr* take refuge; (*with de*) guard against; (*with con*) shelter by

resguardo /rres'guarðo/ *m*, protection, guard; *Com.* guarantee, security; *Com.* voucher; preservation; vigilance (to prevent smuggling, etc.); contraband guards

residencia /rresi'ðensia; rresi'ðenθia/ *f*, stay, residence; home, domicile; *Eccl.* residence

residencial /rresiðen'sial; rresiðen'θial/ *a* residential; resident, residentiary

residente /rresi'ðente/ *a* resident. *mf* inhabitant. *m*, resident, minister resident (diplomatic)

residir /rresi'ðir/ *vi* to live, inhabit; reside officially; be found, be, exist

residuo /rre'siðuo/ *m*, residue, remainder; *Math.* remainder; *Chem.* residue

resignación /rresigna'sion; rresigna'θion/ *f*, resignation; fortitude, submission

resignar /rresig'nar/ *vt* to resign, relinquish; *vr* submit, resign oneself

resina /rre'sina/ *f*, resin

resistencia /rresis'tensia; rresis'tenθia/ *f*, resistance, opposition; endurance; (*Phys. Mech. Psychol.*) resistance

resistente /rresis'tente/ *a* resistant; tough; hardy (of plants)

resistir /rresis'tir/ *vi* to resist, oppose; reject; *vt* endure, bear; resist; *vr* fight, resist

resollar /rreso'yar; rreso'ʎar/ *vi irr* to breathe; pant. See **degollar**

resolución /rresolu'sion; rresolu'θion/ *f*, decision; boldness, daring; determination, resolution; decree

resoluto /rreso'luto/ *a* resolute, bold; brief, concise; able, expert

resolver /rresol'βer/ *vt irr* to determine, decide; summarize; solve; dissolve; analyze; (*Phys. Med.*) resolve; *vr* decide, determine; be reduced to, become; *Med.* resolve. *Pres. Ind.* **resuelvo, resuelves, resuelve, resuelven.** *Past Part.* **resuelto.** *Pres. Subjunc.* **resuelva, resuelvas, resuelva, resuelvan**

resonancia /rreso'nansia; rreso'nanθia/ *f*, resonance, sonority, ring; fame, reputation

resonante /rreso'nante/ *a* resonant; resounding

resonar /rreso'nar/ *vi irr* to resound, echo. See **tronar**

resoplido, resoplo /rreso'pliðo, rre'soplo/ *m*, heavy breathing, pant, snort

resorber /rresor'βer/ *vt* to reabsorb

resorción /rresor'sion; rresor'θion/ *f*, reabsorption

resorte /rre'sorte/ *m*, *Mech.* spring; elasticity; *Fig.* means, instrument; *Lat. Am.* rubber band

respaldo /rres'paldo/ *m*, back (of chairs, etc.); reverse side (of a piece of paper), *Com.* endorsement

respectivo /rrespek'tiβo/ *a* respective

respecto /rres'pekto/ *m*, relation, regard, reference. **con r. a, or r. a,** with regard to, with respect to, concerning

respetabilidad /rrespetaβili'ðað/ *f*, respectability; worthiness

respetable /rrespe'taβle/ *a* worthy of respect; respectable; *Fig.* considerable, large

respetar /rrespe'tar/ *vt* to respect, revere

respeto /rres'peto/ *m*, respect, honor; consideration, reason. **de r.**, spare, extra; special, ceremonial

respetuoso /rrespe'tuoso/ *a* venerable, worthy of honor; respectful, courteous

respingar /rrespiŋ'gar/ *vi* to flinch, wince, kick; *Inf.* be uneven, rise (hem of garments); *Inf.* do (a thing) grumblingly

respingo /rres'piŋgo/ *m*, wincing; jerk, shake; *Inf.* gesture of reluctance or dislike

respiración /rrespira'sion; rrespira'θion/ *f*, breathing, respiration; ventilation

respiradero /rrespira'ðero/ *m*, ventilator; air hole, vent; rest, breathing space

respirador /rrespira'ðor/ *a* breathing; respiratory. *m*, respirator

respirar /rrespi'rar/ *vi* to breathe; exhale, give off; take courage; have a breathing space, rest; *Inf.* speak. **sin r.**, continuously, without stopping for breath

respiratorio /rrespira'torio/ *a* respiratory

respiro /rres'piro/ *m*, breathing; breathing space, respite

resplandecer /rresplande'ser; rresplande'θer/ *vi irr* to glitter, gleam; shine, excel. See **conocer**

resplandeciente /rresplande'siente; rresplande'θiente/ *a* glittering, resplendent, shining

resplandor /rresplan'dor/ *m*, radiance, brilliance; glitter, gleam; majesty, splendor

responder /rrespon'der/ *vt* to reply; satisfy, answer; *vi* reecho; requite, return; produce, provide; *Fig.* answer, have the desired effect; *Com.* (*with de*) answer for, guarantee; *Com.* correspond

respondón /rrespon'don/ *a Inf.* pert, impudent, cheeky, given to answering back

responsabilidad /rresponsaβili'ðað/ *f*, responsibility

responsable /rrespon'saβle/ *a* responsible

responso /rres'ponso/ *m*, *Eccl.* response, responsory

respuesta /rres'puesta/ *f*, answer, reply; response; refutation; repartee

resquebradura /rreskeβra'ðura/ *f*, fissure, crevice, crack

resquebrajarse /rreskeβra'harse/ *vr* to crack, split

resquemar /rreske'mar/ *vt* to bite, sting (of hot dishes)

resquicio /rres'kisio; rres'kiθio/ *m*, crack, chink, slit; opportunity; *Lat. Am.* sign, trace, vestige

resta /'rresta/ *f*, *Math.* subtraction; *Math.* remainder

restablecer /rrestaβle'ser; rrestaβle'θer/ *vt irr* to re-establish; restore; *vr* recover one's health; reestablish oneself. See **conocer**

restablecimiento /rrestaβlesi'miento; rrestaβleθi'miento/ *m*, reestablishment; restoration

restañar /rresta'ɲar/ *vt* to re-tin; staunch

restar /rres'tar/ *vt Math.* to subtract; deduct; return (a ball); *vi* remain. **No me resta más que decir adiós,** It only remains for me to say good-by

restauración /rrestaura'sion; rrestaura'θion/ *f*, restoration; renovation

restaurante /rrestau'rante/ *m*, restaurant

restaurantero /rrestauran'tero/ *m*, restaurant operator; restaurant owner; restaurateur

restaurar /rrestau'rar/ *vt* to recover, recuperate; renovate, repair; restore

restaurativo /rrestaura'tiβo/ *a* and *m*, restorative

restinga /rres'tiŋga/ *f*, sandbank, bar

restitución /rrestitu'sion; rrestitu'θion/ *f*, restitution

restituible /rresti'tuiβle/ *a* returnable, replaceable

restituir /rresti'tuir/ *vt irr* to return, give back; restore; reestablish; *vr* return to one's place of departure. See **huir**

resto /'rresto/ *m*, rest, balance; *Math.* remainder; *pl* remains

restorán /rresto'ran/ *m*, restaurant

restricción /rrestrik'sion; rrestrik'θion/ *f*, limitation, restriction

restrictivo /rrestrik'tiβo/ *a* restrictive; restraining

restringir /rrestriŋ'gir/ *vt* to limit, restrict; contract

resucitar /rresusi'tar; rresuθi'tar/ *vt* to raise from the dead; *Fig. Inf.* revive; *vi* resuscitate

resuello /rre'sueyo; rre'sueʎo/ *m*, breathing; panting, hard breathing

resuelto /rre'suelto/ *a* audacious, daring; resolute, capable

resulta /rre'sulta/ *f*, consequence, result; decision, resolution; vacant post. **de resultas de,** as the result of; in consequence of

resultado /rresul'taðo/ *m*, result, consequence, outcome

resultar /rresul'tar/ *vi* to result, follow; turn out, happen; result (in); *Inf.* turn out well. **El vestido no me resulta,** The dress isn't a success on me

resumen /rre'sumen/ *m*, summary. **en r.,** in short

resumir /rresu'mir/ *vt* to summarize, abridge; sum up, recapitulate; *vr* be contained, be included

resurgimiento /rresurhi'miento/ *m*, resurgence, revival

resurgir /rresur'hir/ *vi* to reappear, rise again, revive; resuscitate

resurrección /rresurrek'sion; rresurrek'θion/ *f*, resurrection

retablo /rre'taβlo/ *m*, *Archit.* altarpiece, retable; frieze; series of pictures

retador, -a /rreta'ðor/ *mf*, *Lat. Am.* challenger

retaguardia /rreta'guarðia/ *f*, rear guard. **a r.,** in the rear. **picar la r.,** to harass the rear guard

retajar /rreta'har/ *vt* to cut in the round; circumcise

retal /rre'tal/ *m*, clipping, filing, shaving; remnant

retama /rre'tama/ *f*, *Bot.* broom. **r. común** or **r. de olor,** Spanish broom. **r. de escobas,** common broom

retar /rre'tar/ *vt* to challenge; *Inf.* reproach, accuse

retardar /rretar'ðar/ *vt* to retard, delay

retardo /rre'tarðo/ *m*, delay, retardment

retazo /rre'taso; rre'taθo/ *m*, remnant, cutting; excerpt, fragment

retemblar /rretem'βlar/ *vi* to quiver, tremble constantly

retemplar /rretem'plar/ *vt*, *Lat. Am.* to cheer up

retén /rre'ten/ *m*, stock, reserve, provision; *Mil.* reserve

retención /rreten'sion; rreten'θion/ *f*, retention

retener /rrete'ner/ *vt irr* to keep, retain; recollect, remember; keep back; *Law.* detain; deduct. See **tener**

retenidamente /rreteniða'mente/ *adv* retentively

retentiva /rreten'tiβa/ *f*, retentiveness, memory

retentivo /rreten'tiβo/ *a* retentive

reticencia /rreti'sensia; rreti'θenθia/ *f*, reticence

reticente /rreti'sente; rreti'θente/ *a* reticent

retículo /rre'tikulo/ *m*, reticulum, network; *Phys.* reticle

retina /rre'tina/ *f*, retina

retintín /rretin'tin/ *m*, ringing; tinkling; *Inf.* sarcastic tone

retiñir /rreti'ɲir/ *vi* to tinkle, clink; jingle

retirada /rreti'raða/ *f*, withdrawal; retirement; seclusion, refuge; *Mil.* retreat

retirado /rreti'raðo/ *a* remote, secluded; *Mil.* retired

retirar /rreti'rar/ *vt* to withdraw; remove; repel; throw back; hide, put aside; *vr* withdraw; retire; *Mil.* retreat

retiro /rre'tiro/ *m*, withdrawal; removal; seclusion, privacy; *Mil.* retreat; retirement; *Eccl.* retreat. **dar el r. (a),** to place on the retired list

reto /'rreto/ *m*, challenge; threat

retocar /rreto'kar/ *vt* to touch again or repeatedly; *Photo.* retouch; restore (pictures); *Fig.* put the finishing touch to

retoñar /rreto'ɲar/ *vi* to sprout, shoot; *Fig.* revive, resuscitate

retoño /rre'toɲo/ *m*, sprout, shoot

retoque /rre'toke/ *m*, frequent touching; finishing touch; touch, slight attack

retorcer /rretor'ser; rretor'θer/ *vt irr* to twist; contort; confound with one's own argument; misconstrue, distort; *vr* contort; writhe. See **torcer**

retórica /rre'torika/ *f*, rhetoric; *pl Inf.* quibbling

retórico /rre'toriko/ **(-ca)** *a* rhetorical. *m* rhetorician

retornar /rretor'nar/ *vt* to return, give back; turn, twist; turn back; *vi* and *vr* return, go back

retorno /rre'torno/ *m*, return, going back; recompense, repayment; exchange; return journey

retorsión /rretor'sion/ *f*, twisting, writhing; *Fig.* misconstruction

retortijón /rretorti'hon/ *m*, twisting, curling. **r. de tripas,** stomachache

retozar /rreto'sar; rreto'θar/ *vi* to skip, frisk, frolic, gambol; romp; *Fig.* be aroused (passions)

retozón /rreto'son; rreto'θon/ *a* frolicsome

retracción /rretrak'sion; rretrak'θion/ *f*, drawing back, retraction

retractación /rretrakta'sion; rretrakta'θion/ *f*, retractation, recantation

retractar /rretrak'tar/ *vt* to retract, recant; withdraw

retráctil /rre'traktil/ *a* retractile

retraer /rretra'er/ *vt irr* to bring back again; dissuade; buy back, redeem; *vr* take refuge; retire; withdraw; go into seclusion. See **traer**

retraído /rre'traiðo/ *a* fugitive, refugee; retired, solitary; timid, nervous, unsociable

retraimiento /rretrai'miento/ *m*, withdrawal; seclusion, privacy; refuge, asylum, sanctuary; timidity, unsociability

retranca /rre'tranka/ *f*, *Lat. Am.* brake

retrancar /rretran'kar/ *vt*, *Lat. Am.* to brake

retrasar /rretra'sar/ *vt* to postpone, delay; turn back (the clock); *vi* be slow (of clocks); *vr* be behind time, be late; be backward (persons)

retraso /rre'traso/ *m*, lateness; delay, dilatoriness; loss of time (clocks); setting back (of the clock) (e.g. *El reloj lleva cinco minutos de r.,* The clock is five minutes slow)

retratar /rretra'tar/ *vt* to paint or draw the portrait of; portray, describe; photograph; copy, imitate

retratería /rretrate'ria/ *f*, *Lat. Am.* photographer's studio

retratista /rretra'tista/ *mf* portrait painter; photographer; portrayer

retrato /rre'trato/ *m*, portrait; portrayal; *Fig.* image, likeness

retrechería /rretretʃe'ria/ *f*, *Inf.* craftiness, evasiveness

retrete /rre'trete/ *m*, toilet

retribución /rretriβu'sion; rretriβu'θion/ *f*, recompense, reward

retribuir /rretri'βuir/ *vt irr* to recompense, reward. See **huir**

retroactivo /rretroak'tiβo/ *a* retroactive

retroceder /rretrose'ðer; rretroθe'ðer/ *vi* to withdraw, move back, draw back; recede

retroceso /rretro'seso; rretro'θeso/ *m*, retrocedence, withdrawal; *Med.* retrogression

retrogradación /rretrograða'sion; rretrograða'θion/ *f*, retrogression

retrógrado /rretro'graðo/ *a* retrogressive, retrograde; *Polit.* reactionary

retronar /rretro'nar/ *vi irr* to bang, thunder, resound with noise. See **tronar**

retrospectivo /rretrospek'tiβo/ *a* retrospective

retrotraer /rretrotra'er/ *vt irr* to antedate. See **traer**

retruécano /rre'truekano/ *m*, antithesis; play on words, pun

retumbante /rretum'βante/ *a* resounding; pompous, high-flown

retumbar /rretum'βar/ *vi* to resound, echo, reverberate; roll (of thunder); roar (of a cannon)

retumbo /rre'tumbo/ *m*, reverberation, echo; rumble; roll (of thunder); roar (of a cannon, etc.)

reuma /'rreuma/ *m*, rheumatism

reumático /rreu'matiko/ *a* rheumatic

reumatismo /rreuma'tismo/ *m*, rheumatism

reunión /rreu'nion/ *f*, reunion, union; meeting; assembly, gathering

reunir /rreu'nir/ *vt* to reunite; unite; join; gather, assemble; *vr* meet, assemble; unite

revacunación /rreβakuna'sion; rreβakuna'θion/ *f*, revaccination

revacunar /rreβaku'nar/ *vt* to revaccinate

revalidación /rreβaliðasion; rreβaliða'θion/ *f*, ratification, confirmation

revalidar /rreβali'ðar/ *vt* to ratify, confirm; *vr* pass a final examination

revejido /rreβe'hiðo/ *a* prematurely old

revelación /rreβela'sion; rreβela'θion/ *f*, revelation; *Photo.* developing

revelador /rreβela'ðor/ *a* revealing. *m*, *Photo.* developer

revelar /rreβe'lar/ *vt* to reveal; *Photo.* develop

revendedor /rreβende'ðor/ **(-ra)** *a* reselling, retail. *n* retailer

revender /rreβen'der/ *vt* to resell; retail (goods)

reventa /rre'βenta/ *f*, resale; retail

reventar /rreβen'tar/ *vi* irr to burst, explode; break in foam (waves); burst forth; *Fig.* burst (with impatience, etc.); *Inf.* explode (with anger, etc.); *vt* break, crush; *Fig.* wear out, exhaust; *Inf.* irritate, vex; *vr* burst; *Fig.* be exhausted. See **sentar**

reventón /rreβen'ton/ *a* bursting. *m*, explosion, bursting; steep hill; hole, fix, difficulty; uphill work, heavy toil

rever /rre'βer/ *vt* irr to look at again, revise; *Law.* retry. See **ver**

reverberación /rreβerβera'sion; rreβerβera'θion/ *f*, reflection (of light); reverberation, resounding

reverberar /rreβerβe'rar/ *vi* to reflect; resound, reverberate

reverbero /rreβer'βero/ *m*, reverberation; reflector; *Lat. Am.* small stove

reverdecer /rreβerðe'ser; rreβerðe'θer/ *vi irr* to grow green again; revive, acquire new vigor. See **conocer**

reverencia /rreβeren'sia; rreβeren'θia/ *f*, respect, veneration; bow; curtsy; *Eccl.* reverence (title)

reverencial /rreβeren'sial; rreβeren'θial/ *a* reverential, respectful

reverenciar /rreβeren'siar; rreβeren'θiar/ *vt* to revere; honor; respect

reverendo /rreβe'rendo/ *a* reverend; venerable; *Inf.* overprudent

reversión /rreβer'sion/ *f*, reversion

reverso /rre'βerso/ *m*, wrong side, back; reverse side (of coins)

reverter /rreβer'ter/ *vi irr* to overflow. See **entender**

revertir /rreβer'tir/ *vi* *Law.* to revert

revés /rre'βes/ *m*, wrong side, back, reverse; cuff, slap; backhand (in ballgames); check, setback, reverse; disaster, misfortune. **al r.**, on the contrary; wrong side out. **de r.**, from left to right, counterclockwise

revesado /rreβe'saðo/ *a* complicated, difficult; willful

revestimiento /rreβesti'miento/ *m*, *Mas.* lining, coating

revestir /rreβes'tir/ *vt irr* to dress; *Mas.* coat, line; *Fig.* cover, clothe; *vr* be dressed or dress oneself; *Fig.* be captivated (by an idea); become haughty or full of oneself; rise to the occasion, develop qualities necessary. See **pedir**

reviejo /rre'βieho/ *a* very old. *m*, dead branch (of trees)

revisar /rreβi'sar/ *vt* to revise; examine

revisión /rreβi'sion/ *f*, revision; reexamination; *Law.* retrial

revisor /rreβi'sor/ *a* revising, examining. *m*, reviser; ticket inspector

revista /rre'βista/ *f*, reexamination, revision; review, periodical; *Theat.* revue; reinspection; review (of a book, etc.); *Law.* new trial; *Mil.* review. **pasar r.,** to inspect; review

revivificación /rreβiβifika'sion; rreβiβifika'θion/ *f*, revivification

revivificar /rreβiβifi'kar/ *vt* to revivify, revive

revivir /rreβi'βir/ *vi* to resuscitate; revive

revocación /rreβoka'sion; rreβoka'θion/ *f*, revocation, cancellation, annulment

revocar /rreβo'kar/ *vt* to revoke, annul; dissuade; repel, throw back; wash (walls); *Law.* discharge

revolcadero /rreβolka'ðero/ *m*, bathing place (of animals)

revolcar /rreβol'kar/ *vt irr* to knock down, trample underfoot; lay flat (in an argument); *vr* wallow; dig one's heels in, be obstinate. See **volcar**

revolotear /rreβolote'ar/ *vi* to flutter, fly around; twirl; *vt* hurl, toss

revoltillo /rreβol'tiyo; rreβol'tiʎo/ *m*, jumble, hodgepodge; confusion, tangle; *Venezuela* scrambled eggs

revoltoso /rreβol'toso/ *a* rebellious; mischievous, willful; intricate

revoltura /rreβol'tura/ *f*, *Mexico* dish of eggs and vegetables

revolución /rreβolu'sion; rreβolu'θion/ *f*, turn, revolution; rebellion, uprising; revolution

revolucionar /rreβolusio'nar; rreβoluθio'nar/ *vt* to revolutionize

revolucionario /rreβolusio'nario; rreβoluθio'nario/ **(-ia)** *a* and *n* revolutionary

revolver /rreβol'βer/ *vt irr* to turn over; turn upside down; wrap up; revolve; stir; reflect upon; consider; upset, cause disharmony; search through, disorder (papers, etc.); *vr* move from side to side; change (in the weather). See **resolver**

revólver /rre'βolβer/ *m*, revolver

revoque /rre'βoke/ *m*, *Mas.* washing, whitewash; plastering

revuelco /rre'βuelko/ *m*, wallowing

revuelo /rre'βuelo/ *m*, second flight (of birds); irregular course of flight; disturbance, upset

revuelta /rre'βuelta/ *f*, second turn or revolution; revolt, rebellion; quarrel, fight; turning point; change of direction, turn; change (of opinions, posts, etc.)

revueltamente /rreβuelta'mente/ *adv* in confusion, higgledy-piggledy

revulsión /rreβul'sion/ *f*, revulsion

rexaminación /rreksamina'sion; rreksamina'θion/ *f*, reexamination

rexpedir /rrekspe'ðir/ *vt* to forward, send on

rey /rrei/ *m*, king (in cards, chess); queen bee; *Inf.* swineherd; *Fig.* king, chief. *Herald.* **r. de armas,** king-of-arms. **reyes magos,** magi. **día de Reyes,** Twelfth Night. **servir al r.,** to fight for the king

reyerta /rre'yerta/ *f*, quarrel, row, rumpus

reyezuelo /rreye'suelo; rreye'θuelo/ *m*, kinglet, petty king; golden-crested wren

rezagar /rresa'gar; rreθa'gar/ *vt* to leave behind; postpone, delay; *vr* lag behind, straggle

rezar /rre'sar; rre'θar/ *vt* to pray, say prayers; say mass; *Inf.* state, say; *vi* pray; *Inf.* fume, grumble. **El edicto reza así,** The edict runs like this, The edict reads like this

rezo /'rreso; 'rreθo/ *m*, prayer; devotions

rezongar /rreson'gar; rreθoŋ'gar/ *vi* to grouse, grumble

rezumar /rresu'mar; rreθu'mar/ **(se)** *vr* and *vi* to percolate, ooze through; *Inf.* leak out, be known

ría /'rria/ *f*, estuary, river mouth, firth

riachuelo /rria'tʃuelo/ *m*, rivulet, stream

riada /'rriaða/ *f*, flood. *Aer.* **r. de acero,** rain of flak

ribaldería /rriβalde'ria/ *f*, ribaldry

ribaldo /rri'βaldo/ *a* ribald. *m*, knave

ribazo /rri'βaso; rri'βaθo/ *m*, slope, incline

ribera /rri'βera/ *f*, bank, margin, shore, strand; *Lat. Am.* slum

ribereño /rriβe'reɲo/ **(-ña)** *a* and *n* riparian

ribero /rri'βero/ *m*, embankment, wall

ribete /rri'βete/ *m*, binding, border, trimming; stripe; increase, addition; dramatic touch, exaggeration; *pl* indications, signs

ribetear /rriβete'ar/ *vt Sew.* to bind, trim, edge

ricacho /rri'katʃo/ **(-cha)** *n Inf.* newly rich person, nouveau riche

ricahembra /rrika'embra/ *f*, lady; daughter or wife of a Spanish noble *Obs.*

ricamente /rrika'mente/ *adv* richly, opulently; beautifully, splendidly; luxuriously

ricino /rri'sino; rri'θino/ *m*, castor oil plant

rico /'rriko/ *a* wealthy, rich; abundant; magnificent, splendid; delicious. **r. como Creso,** rich as Croesus

ricohombre /rriko'ombre/ *m*, nobleman *Obs.*

ricura /rri'kura/ *f*, *Inf.* richness, wealth

ridiculez /rriðiku'les; rriðiku'leθ/ *f*, absurd action or remark; ridiculousness; affectation; folly

ridiculizar /rriðikuli'sar; rriðikuli'θar/ *vt* to ridicule, poke fun at

ridículo /rri'ðikulo/ *a* ridiculous, absurd; grotesque; preposterous, outrageous. *m*, reticule

riego /'rriego/ *m*, watering, spraying; irrigation

riel /'rriel/ *m*, ingot; rail (of a train or streetcar)

rielar /rrie'lar/ *vi* to glimmer, glisten; glitter; shimmer

rienda /'rrienda/ *f*, rein (gen. *pl*); restraint; *pl* administration, government. **a r. suelta,** swiftly; without restraint; *Fig.* with loose reins

riesgo /'rriesgo/ *m*, risk, danger

riesgoso, -a /rries'goso/ *a*, *Lat. Am.* dangerous, risky

rifa /'rrifa/ *f*, raffle; quarrel, disagreement

rifar /rri'far/ *vt* to raffle; *vi* quarrel, fall out

rifle /'rrifle/ *m*, rifle

rigidez /rrihi'ðes; rrihi'ðeθ/ *f*, stiffness; rigidity; harshness

rígido /'rrihiðo/ *a* stiff; rigid; inflexible; severe, harsh

rigor /rri'gor/ *m*, severity, sternness; rigor; hardness; inflexibility; *Med.* rigor. **en r.,** strictly speaking. **ser de r.,** to be essential, be indispensable

rigorista /rrigo'rista/ *mf* martinet

riguroso /rrigu'roso/ *a* rigorous; harsh, cruel; austere, rigid; strict, exact, scrupulous

rijoso /rri'hoso/ *a* quarrelsome; lascivious

rima /'rrima/ *f*, rhyme, rime; heap; *pl* lyrics

rimador /rrima'ðor/ **(-ra)** *a* rhyming, rimer. *n* rhymer, rimer

rimar /rri'mar/ *vi* to compose verses; *vi* and *vt* rhyme, rime

rimbombo /rrim'βombo/ *m*, reverberation (of a sound)

rimero /rri'mero/ *m*, heap, pile

Rin, el /rrin, el/ the Rhine

rincón /rrin'kon/ *m*, corner, angle; retreat, hiding place; *Inf.* home, nest, nook

rinconada /rrinko'naða/ *f*, corner, angle

rinconera /rrinko'nera/ *f*, corner cupboard; corner table

ringlera /rriŋ'glera/ *f*, file, line, row

ringlero /rriŋ'glero/ *m*, guiding line for writing

ringorrangos /rriŋgo'rraŋgos/ *m pl*, *Inf.* exaggerated flourishes in writing; *Inf.* unnecessary frills or ornaments

ringueletear /rriŋguelete'ar/ *vi*, *Lat. Am.* to wander through the streets

rinoceronte /rrinose'ronte; rrinoθe'ronte/ *m*, rhinoceros

riñón /rri'ɲon/ *m*, kidney; *Fig.* center, heart; *pl Anat.* back

río /'rrio/ *m*, river; *Fig.* stream, flood

rioja /'rrioha/ *m*, red wine from Rioja

rioplatense /rriopla'tense/ *a* of the River Plate area; *mf* native of the River Plate area; resident of the River Plate area

ripio /'rripio/ *m*, remains, rest; debris, rubbish; *Lit.* padding; verbiage, prolixity. **no perder r.,** to lose no occasion or opportunity

riqueza /rri'kesa; rri'keθa/ *f*, riches, wealth; abundance; richness, magnificence

risa /'rrisa/ *f*, laugh; laughter; cause of amusement, joke

risco /'rrisko/ *m*, crag

riscoso /rris'koso/ *a* craggy

risible /rri'siβle/ *a* laughable

risoles /rri'soles/ *m pl*, rissoles

risotada /rriso'taða/ *f*, loud laugh

ristra /'rristra/ *f*, string (of onions, etc.); file, line, row

risueño /rri'sueɲo/ *a* smiling; cheerful; pleasant, agreeable; favorable, hopeful

rítmico /'rritmiko/ *a* rhythmic

ritmo /'rritmo/ *m*, rhythm

rito /'rrito/ *m*, rite

ritualismo /rritua'lismo/ *m*, ritualism

ritualista /rritua'lista/ *mf* ritualist

rivalidad /rriβali'ðað/ *f*, rivalry, competition; hostility

rivalizar /rriβali'sar; rriβali'θar/ *vi* to compete, rival

rizado /rri'saðo; rri'θaðo/ *m*, curling; pleating, crimping; rippling, ruffling

rizar /rri'sar; rri'θar/ *vt* to curl (hair); ripple, ruffle (of water); pleat, crimp; *vr* be naturally wavy (of hair)

rizo /'rriso; 'rriθo/ *m*, curl, ringlet; cut velvet. *Aer.* **hacer el r.,** to loop the loop; *Naut.* to take in reefs

rizoso /rri'soso; rri'θoso/ *a* naturally curly or wavy (hair)

robador /rroβa'ðor/ **(-ra)** *a* robbing. *n* robber, thief. *m*, abductor

robar /rro'βar/ *vt* to rob; abduct; wash away, eat away (rivers, sea); remove honey from the hive; draw (in cards, dominoes); *Fig.* capture (love, etc.)

roblar /rro'βlar/ *vt* to reinforce, strengthen; clinch

roble /'rroβle/ *m*, oak tree; oak; *Fig.* bulwark, tower of strength

robledo /rro'βleðo/ *m*, oak grove

roblón /rro'βlon/ *m*, rivet

robo /'rroβo/ *m*, theft, robbery; booty

robustecer /rroβuste'ser; rroβuste'θer/ *vt irr* to strengthen. See **conocer**

robustez /rroβus'tes; rroβus'teθ/ *f*, strength, robustness

robusto /rro'βusto/ *a* vigorous, robust, hearty, strong

roca /'rroka/ *f*, rock; *Fig.* tower of strength

roce /'rrose; 'rroθe/ *m*, rubbing, brushing, touching, friction; social intercourse

rociada /rro'siaða; rro'θiaða/ *f*, dewing; sprinkling; dew-wet grass given as medicine to horses and mules; *Fig.* shower; general slander; harsh rebuke

rociar /rro'siar; rro'θiar/ *vi* to fall as dew; drizzle; *vt* sprinkle, spray; *Fig.* shower (with)

rocín /rro'sin; rro'θin/ *m*, sorry nag; hack; *Inf.* ignoramus, boor

rocinante /rrosi'nante; rroθi'nante/ *m*, poor nag (alluding to Don Quixote's horse)

rocío /'rrosio; 'rroθio/ *m*, dew; dewdrop; drizzle, light shower; *Fig.* sprinkling, spray

rocoso /rro'koso/ *a* rocky

rodaballo /rroða'βayo; rroða'βaʎo/ *m*, turbot; *Inf.* crafty man

rodada /rro'ðaða/ *f*, wheel mark or track

rodado /rro'ðaðo/ *a* dappled (of horses)

rodaje /rro'ðahe/ *m*, wheeling; shooting (of a film)

rodante /rro'ðante/ *a* rolling

rodar /rro'ðar/ *vi* to roll; revolve, turn; run on wheels; wander, roam; be moved about; be plentiful, abound; happen successively; (*with por*) fall down, roll down

rodear /rroðe'ar/ *vi* to walk around; go by a roundabout way; *Fig.* beat around the bush; *vt* encircle, surround; besiege; *West Hem.* round up (cattle)

rodela /rro'ðela/ *f*, round shield; buckler

rodeno /rro'ðeno/ *a* red (of rocks, earth, etc.)

rodeo /rro'ðeo/ *m*, encirclement; indirect and longer way; trick to evade pursuit; *West Hem.* rodeo, roundup; stockyard, cattle enclosure; *Fig.* beating around the bush; evasive reply

rodera /rro'ðera/ *f*, rail, track, line; cart rut or track

rodilla /rro'ðiya; rro'ðiʎa/ *f*, knee; floor cloth. **de rodillas,** on one's knees. **ponerse de rodillas,** *or* **hincar las rodillas,** to kneel down

rodillazo /rroði'yaso; rroði'ʎaθo/ *m*, push with the knee

rodillera /rroði'yera; rroði'ʎera/ *f*, kneecap, kneepad; mend at the knee of garments; bagginess of trouser knees

rodillo /rro'ðiyo; rro'ðiʎo/ *m*, roller; traction engine; *Print.* inking roller; garden roller. **r. de pastas,** *Cul.* rolling pin

rododendro /rroðo'ðendro/ *m*, rhododendron

rodrigón /rroðri'gon/ *m*, stake, prop (for plants); *Inf.* old retainer who serves as a ladies' escort

roedor /rroe'ðor/ *a* gnawing; *Fig.* nagging; biting. *a* and *m*, rodent

roedura /rroe'ðura/ *f*, biting, gnawing; corrosion

roer /rro'er/ *vt irr* to gnaw, nibble, eat; corrode, wear away; trouble, afflict. *Pres. Ind.* **roigo, roes, etc.** *Preterite* **royó, royeron.** *Imperf. Subjunc.* **royese, etc.**

rogación /rroga'sion; rroga'θion/ *f*, request, supplication, entreaty; *Eccl.* rogation

rogador /rroga'ðor/ **(-ra)** *a* requesting; beseeching. *n* suppliant

rogar /rro'gar/ *vt irr* to request; beseech, beg. See **contar**

rogativo /rroga'tiβo/ *a* supplicatory, petitioning

roído /rro'iðo/ *a* gnawed, eaten; *Inf.* miserable, stingy

rojal /rro'hal/ *a* red (of soil, etc.). *m*, red earth

rojear /rrohe'ar/ *vi* to appear red; be reddish

rojete /rro'hete/ *m*, rouge

rojez /rro'hes; rro'heθ/ *f*, redness

rojizo /rro'hiso; rro'hiθo/ *a* reddish

rojo /'rroho/ *a* red; fair; red-gold (of hair); *Polit.* radical, red

rol /rrol/ *m*, roll, list

roldana /rrol'dana/ *f*, pulley wheel

rollizo /rro'yiso; rro'ʎiθo/ *a* round; plump, sturdy. *m*, log

rollo /'rroyo; 'rroʎo/ *m*, roll; *Cul.* rolling pin; log; town cross or pillar; anything rolled (paper, etc.); twist (of tobacco)

Roma /'rroma/ Rome

romance /rro'manse; rro'manθe/ *a* and *m*, romance (language); *m*, Spanish; ballad; romance of chivalry; *pl Fig.* fairy tales, excuses. **en buen r.,** *Fig.* in plain words

romancear /rromanse'ar; rromanθe'ar/ *vt* to translate from Latin into the spoken language; translate into Spanish; paraphrase the Spanish to assist translation; *Lat. Am.* to flirt

romancero /rroman'sero; rroman'θero/ **(-ra)** *n* balladeer. *m*, collection of ballads

romancista /rroman'sista; rroman'θista/ *mf* romancist

románico /rro'maniko/ *a Archit.* Romanesque

romanista /rroma'nista/ *mf* expert in Roman law or Romance languages and literature

romanizar /rromani'sar; rromani'θar/ *vt* to romanize; *vr* become romanized

romano /rro'mano/ **(-na)** *a* and *n* Roman. **a la romana,** in the Roman way. **cabello a la romana,** *Inf.* bobbed hair

romanticismo /rromanti'sismo; rromanti'θismo/ *m*, romanticism

romántico /rro'mantiko/ **(-ca)** *a* romantic; emotional; fanciful. *n* romantic; romanticist

rombo /'rrombo/ *m*, rhombus

romería /rrome'ria/ *f*, pilgrimage; excursion, picnic (made on a saint's day)

romero /rro'mero/ **(-ra)** *m*, rosemary. *n* pilgrim

romo /'rromo/ *a* blunt, dull, unsharpened; flat (of noses); *m. Lat. Am.* rum

rompecabezas /rrompeka'βesas; rrompeka'βeθas/ *m*, bludgeon; knuckleduster; *Inf.* teaser, puzzle, riddle; jigsaw puzzle

rompeimágenes /rrompei'mahenes/ *mf* iconoclast

rompeolas /rrompe'olas/ *m*, jetty, breakwater

romper /rrom'per/ *vt* to break; shatter, break into fragments; spoil, ruin; break up, plow; *Fig.* cut, divide (of water, etc.); *Fig.* end, break; interrupt; infringe, break; *vi* break; break (of waves); sprout, flower; (*with prep a*) begin to. **Rompió a hablar,** He broke into speech. *Past Part.* **roto**

rompiente /rrom'piente/ *a* breaking. *m*, reef, shoal

rompimiento /rrompi'miento/ *m*, break, rupture; crack, split; breakage; infringement; plowing up; *Fig.* dividing (water, etc.); spoiling, ruining; opening (of buds, etc.)

ron /rron/ *m*, rum

roncar /rron'kar/ *vi* to snore; *Fig.* roar, howl (of the sea, wind, etc.); *Inf.* brag

roncear /rronθe'ar; rronθe'ar/ *vi* to be dilatory or unwilling; *Inf.* flatter, cajole; *Naut.* lag behind, sail slowly

roncero /rron'sero; rron'θero/ *a* dilatory, slow; grumbling, complaining; cajoling, flattering; *Lat. Am.* sly

roncha /'rrontʃa/ *f*, wheal; bruise, bump; *Inf.* money lost through trickery; thin, round slice

ronco /'rronko/ *a* hoarse, husky

ronda /'rronda/ *f*, round, beat, patrol; serenading party; *Inf.* round (of drinks)

rondador /rronda'ðor/ *m*, watchman; roundsman; serenader; night wanderer

rondalla /rron'daya; rron'daʎa/ *f*, tale, fairy tale

rondar /rron'dar/ *vi* to patrol; police; walk the streets by night; serenade; *vt* haunt; hover about; *Inf.* overcome (of sleep, etc.)

ronquear /rronke'ar/ *vi* to be hoarse

ronquera /rron'kera/ *f*, hoarseness

ronquido /rron'kiðo/ *m*, snore; hoarse sound

ronronear /rronrrone'ar/ *vi* to purr (of cats)

ronzal /rron'sal; rron'θal/ *m*, halter

ronzar /rron'sar; rron'θar/ *vt* to munch, crack with the teeth

roña /'rroɲa/ *f*, mange (in sheep); grime, filth; mold; moral corruption; *Inf.* stinginess; *Inf.* trick, deception

roñería /rroɲe'ria/ *f*, *Inf.* meanness, stinginess

roñoso /rro'ɲoso/ *a* scabby; filthy; rusty; *Inf.* mean, stingy

ropa /'rropa/ *f*, fabric, material, stuff; clothes, wearing apparel; garment, outfit; robe (of office). **r. blanca,** underclothes; (domestic) linen. **r. hecha,** ready-made clothing. **r. talar,** long gown; cassock

ropaje /rro'pahe/ *m*, clothes, garments; vestments; drapery; *Fig.* form, outline

ropavejería /rropaβehe'ria/ *f*, old-clothes shop

ropavejero /rropaβe'hero/ **(-ra)** *n* old-clothes dealer

ropería /rrope'ria/ *f*, clothier's shop or trade; wardrobe; cloakroom

ropero /rro'pero/ **(-ra)** *n* clothier; keeper of the wardrobe. *m*, wardrobe; charitable organization

ropilla /rro'piya; rro'piʎa/ *f*, doublet

ropón /rro'pon/ *m*, a loose-fitting gown generally worn over clothes

roque /'rroke/ *m*, rook (in chess)
roqueño /rro'keɲo/ *a* rocky; hard as rock
roquete /rro'kete/ *m*, *Eccl.* rochet; barb of a lance
rorro /'rrorro/ *m*, *Inf.* infant, baby
rosa /'rrosa/ *f*, rose; anything rose-shaped; artificial rose; red spot on the body; *Archit.* rose window; *pl* rosettes. *m*, rose color. **r. de los vientos**, mariner's compass. **r. laurel**, oleander
rosado /rro'saðo/ *a* rose-colored; rose; rosé (wines)
rosal /rro'sal/ *m*, rose tree. **r. de tallo**, standard rose tree
rosaleda, rosalera /rrosa'leða, rrosa'lera/ *f*, rose garden
rosario /rro'sario/ *m*, rosary; *Fig.* string; chain pump; *Inf.* backbone
rosbif /rros'βif/ *m*, roast beef
rosca /'rroska/ *f*, screw and nut; *Cul.* twist (of bread or cake); spiral
roscado /rros'kaðo/ *a* twisted, spiral
rosear /rrose'ar/ *vi* to turn to rose, become rose-colored
róseo /'rroseo/ *a* rose-colored
roseta /rro'seta/ *f*, *dim* small rose; rosette; rose of a watering can; rosette copper; *pl* toasted maize. **r. de fiebre**, rush of fever
rosetón /rrose'ton/ *m*, large rosette; *Archit.* rose window
rosicler /rrosi'kler/ *m*, rose-pink (first flush of dawn)
rosillo /rro'siyo/ *a* light red; roan (of horses)
rosmaro /rros'maro/ *m*, manatee, sea cow
roso /'rroso/ *a* bald, worn; red
rosquete /rros'kete/ *m*, *Lat. Am.* bun
rosquilla /rros'kiya; rros'kiʎa/ *f*, ring-shaped cake
rosquillero /rroski'yero; rroski'ʎero/ **(-ra)** *n* seller of rosquillas
rostrituerto /rrostri'tuerto/ *a* *Inf.* wry-faced (from sadness or anger)
rostro /'rrostro/ *m*, face, visage. **conocer de r.**, to know by sight. **dar en r.**, *Fig.* to throw in one's face
rota /'rrota/ *f*, *Mil.* defeat; *Eccl.* Rota; *Bot.* rattan
rotación /rrota'sion; rrota'θion/ *f*, rotation. **r. de cultivos**, rotation of crops
rotativa /rrota'tiβa/ *f*, rotary printing press
rotativo /rrota'tiβo/ *a* rotary
rotatorio /rrota'torio/ *a* rotatory
rotisería /rrotise'ria/ *f*, *Lat. Am.* steakhouse; grill-room
roto /'rroto/ *a* broken, torn; shabby, ragged; vicious, debauched
rotograbado /rrotogra'βaðo/ *m*, rotogravure
rotonda /rro'tonda/ *f*, rotunda
rótula /'rrotula/ *f*, rotula, patella
rotular /rrotu'lar/ *vt* to label; give a title or heading to
rótulo /'rrotulo/ *m*, title; poster, placard; label
rotundamente /rrotunda'mente/ *adv* tersely, roundly, plainly
rotundidad /rrotundi'ðað/ *f*, rotundity; roundness; finality (of words, etc.)
rotundo /rro'tundo/ *a* round; rotund; sonorous; final, plain (of words, etc.)
rotura /rro'tura/ *f*, breaking, shattering; plowing up; breakage; rupture
roturar /rrotu'rar/ *vt Agr.* to break up, plow up
roya /'rroya/ *f*, rust, mildew; tobacco
roza /'rrosa; 'rroθa/ *f*, *Agr.* clearing (of weeds, etc.); ground ready for sowing. **de r. abierta**, open cast (of mining)
rozador /rrosa'ðor; rroθa'ðor/ *m*, *Lat. Am.* machete
rozadura /rrosa'ðura; rroθa'ðura/ *f*, rubbing, friction; abrasion, chafing
rozagante /rrosa'gante; rroθa'gante/ *a* long and elaborate (dresses); upstanding; handsome; strapping, fine
rozamiento /rrosa'miento; rroθa'miento/ *m*, grazing, brushing, rubbing; discord, disharmony, disagreement; *Mech.* friction
rozar /rro'sar; rro'θar/ *vt Agr.* to clear of weeds; crop, nibble; scrape; brush against, touch; *vi* brush,

rub, touch; *vr* have dealings with, know; stammer; be like, resemble
rúa /'rrua/ *f*, village street; highway
ruar /rru'ar/ *vi* to walk or ride through the streets; parade through the streets flirting with the ladies
rubeola /rruβe'ola/ *f*, rubella
rubí /rru'βi/ *m*, ruby; jewel (of a watch)
rubia /'rruβia/ *f*, *Bot.* madder; blonde (girl, woman)
rubicundez /rruβikun'des; rruβikun'deθ/ *f*, rubicundity, ruddiness, redness
rubicundo /rruβi'kundo/ *a* red-gold; ruddy-complexioned; reddish
rubio /'rruβio/ *a* red-gold, gold; fair, blond
rubor /rru'βor/ *m*, blush, flush; bashfulness
ruborizarse /rruβori'sarse; rruβori'θarse/ *vr* to blush; be shamefaced
ruboroso /rruβo'roso/ *a* shamefaced; blushing
rúbrica /'rruβrika/ *f*, rubric; personal mark, flourish added to one's signature
rubricar /rruβri'kar/ *vt* to sign and seal; sign with an X or other symbol; sign with a flourish
rubro /'rruβro/ *a* red
rucio /'rrusio; 'rruθio/ *a* fawn, light-gray (of animals); *Inf.* going gray, gray-haired
rudamente /rruða'mente/ *adv* rudely, abruptly, churlishly; roughly
rudeza /rru'ðesa; rru'ðeθa/ *f*, roughness; rudeness, uncouthness; stupidity
rudimentario /rruðimen'tario/ *a* rudimentary
rudimento /rruði'mento/ *m*, embryo; *pl* rudiments
rudo /'rruðo/ *a* rough; unfinished; uncouth, boorish, rude; stupid
rueca /'rrueka/ *f*, distaff (in spinning); spinning wheel; curve, twist
rueda /'rrueða/ *f*, wheel; group, circle; spread of a peacock's tail; roller, castor; round piece or slice; turn, chance; succession (of events); wheel (used for torture). **r. libre**, freewheeling. *Inf.* **hacer la r. (a)**, to flatter, make a fuss of
ruedero /rrue'ðero/ *m*, wheelwright
ruedo /'rrueðo/ *m*, turning, rotation; circumference; lined hem of a cassock; circuit
ruego /'rruego/ *m*, request, entreaty
rufián /rru'fian/ *m*, ruffian; pimp
rufo /'rrufo/ *a* fair; red-haired; curly-haired
rugido /rru'hiðo/ *m*, roaring, roar; creaking; gnashing; rumbling
rugir /rru'hir/ *vi* to roar; squeak, creak; gnash (the teeth)
ruibarbo /rrui'βarβo/ *m*, rhubarb
ruido /'rruiðo/ *m*, noise, din; disturbance; rumor. **hacer** (*or* **meter**) **r.**, to cause a sensation. *Inf.* **ser más el r. que las nueces**, to be much ado about nothing
ruidoso /rrui'ðoso/ *a* noisy; notable
ruin /rru'in/ *a* base, vile; despicable; mean; puny
ruina /'rruina/ *f*, ruin, downfall; financial ruin; fall, decline; *pl* ruins
ruinar /rrui'nar/ *vt* to ruin
ruindad /rruin'dað/ *f*, baseness; meanness; pettiness, unworthiness; mean trick, despicable action
ruinoso /rrui'noso/ *a* half-ruined; ruinous; useless, worthless
ruiseñor /rruise'ɲor/ *m*, nightingale
ruleta /rru'leta/ *f*, roulette
rumano /rru'mano/ **(-na)** *a* and *n* Romanian. *m*, Romanian (language)
rumba /'rrumβa/ *f* rumba; *Lat. Am.* party (celebration)
rumbo /'rrumbo/ *m*, *Naut.* course, way, route; direction; *Inf.* swank; *Lat. Am.* party (celebration) **con r. a**, headed for, in the direction of. **hacer r. a**, to sail for; make for
rumboso /rrum'βoso/ *a Inf.* pompous, dignified; open-handed, generous
rumia /'rrumia/ *f*, rumination; cud
rumiante /rru'miante/ *a* and *mf Zool.* ruminant. *a Inf.* reflective, meditative
rumiar /rru'miar/ *vt Zool.* to ruminate; *Inf.* reflect upon, chew on; *Inf.* fume, rage

rumor /rru'mor/ *m*, noise; rumor; murmur, babble; dull sound

rúnico /'rruniko/ *a* runic

runrunearse /rrunrune'arse/ *v impers* to be rumored

rupia /'rrupia/ *f*, rupee

ruptura /rrup'tura/ *f*, *Fig*. rupture; *Surg*. hernia

rural /rru'ral/ *a* rustic, rural

ruralmente /rrural'mente/ *adv* rurally

Rusia /'rrusia/ Russia

rusificar /rrusifi'kar/ *vt* to russianize

ruso /'rruso/ **(-sa)** *a* and *n* Russian. *m*, Russian (language)

rusticación /rrustika'sion; rrustika'θion/ *f*, rustication

rusticar /rrusti'kar/ *vi* to rusticate

rusticidad /rrustisi'ðað; rrustiθi'ðað/ *f*, rusticity; boorishness, coarseness

rústico /'rrustiko/ *a* rustic, country; boorish, uncouth. *m*, countryman; yokel; peasant. **en rústica,** in paper covers (of books)

ruta /'rruta/ *f*, route; *Fig*. way. **r. de evitación,** by-pass, detour

ruteno /rru'teno/ **(-na)** *a* and *n* Ruthenian. *m*, Ruthenian (language)

rutilante /rruti'lante/ *a Poet*. sparkling, glowing

rutilar /rruti'lar/ *vi Poet*. to gleam, sparkle

rutina /rru'tina/ *f*, routine

rutinario /rruti'nario/ *a* routine

rutinero /rruti'nero/ **(-ra)** *a* routinistic. *n* routinist

S

sábado /'saβaðo/ *m*, Saturday; Jewish sabbath. **s. de gloria,** Easter Saturday

sábalo /'saβalo/ *m*, *Ichth*. shad

sabana /sa'βana/ *f*, savannah

sábana /sa'βana/ *f*, bed sheet; altar cloth. *Inf*. **pegársele (a uno) las sábanas,** to be tied to the bed, get up late

sabandija /saβan'diha/ *f*, any unpleasant insect or reptile; *Fig*. vermin

sabanero /saβa'nero/ **(-ra)** *n* savannah dweller. *a* savannah

sabanilla /saβa'niya; saβa'niʎa/ *f*, small piece of linen (kerchief, towel, etc.); altar cloth

sabañón /saβa'ɲon/ *m*, chilblain

sabatario /saβa'tario/ *a* sabbatarian

sabático /sa'βatiko/ *a* sabbatical

sabatino /saβa'tino/ *a* Saturday, Sabbath

sabedor /saβe'ðor/ *a* aware; knowledgeable, knowing

sabelotodo /saβelo'toðo/ *mf Inf*. know-it-all

saber /sa'βer/ *m*, learning; wisdom

saber /sa'βer/ *vt irr* to know; be able to, know how; *vi* know; be shrewd, be well aware of; *(with prep a)* taste of; be like or similar to. **s. al dedillo,** *Fig*. to have at one's fingertips. **a s.,** viz., namely. **no s. dónde meterse,** to be overcome by shame; have the jitters. **No sé cuántos,** I don't know how many. **No sé quién,** I don't know who (which person). **No sé qué,** I don't know what. **un no sé qué,** a certain something; a touch (of). **¡Quién sabe!** Who knows!; Time will tell. *Pres. Ind.* **sé, sabes,** etc. *Fut.* **sabré,** etc. *Condit.* **sabría,** etc. *Preterite* **supe,** etc. *Pres. Subjunc.* **sepa,** etc. *Imperf. Subjunc.* **supiese,** etc.

sabiamente /saβia'mente/ *adv* wisely, prudently

sabidillo /saβi'ðiyo; saβi'ðiʎo/ **(-lla)** *a* and *n Inf*. know-it-all

sabiduría /saβiðu'ria/ *f*, prudence, wisdom; erudition; learning; knowledge, awareness. **Libro de la S. de Salomón,** Book of Wisdom

sabiendas, a /sa'βiendas, a/ *adv* knowingly, consciously

sabihondo /sa'βiondo/ **(-da)** *n Inf*. know-it-all

sabio /'saβio/ **(-ia)** *a* wise; learned, erudite; prudent, sagacious; knowing (of animals); performing (of animals). *n* wise person; scholar, erudite person

sablazo /sa'βlaso; sa'βlaθo/ *m*, saber thrust or wound; *Inf*. sponging, taking advantage of. **dar un s. (a),** *Inf*. to sponge on; touch for money

sable /'saβle/ *m*, saber; *Herald*. sable; *Inf*. talent for sponging on people. *a Herald*. sable

sablear /saβle'ar/ *vi Inf*. to touch for invitations, loans, etc.; cadge

sablista /sa'βlista/ *mf Inf*. sponger, cadger

saboneta /saβo'neta/ *f*, hunting case watch, hunter

sabor /sa'βor/ *m*, taste, flavor; impression, effect. **a s.,** to taste; at pleasure

saboreamiento /saβorea'miento/ *m*, savoring; relishing, enjoyment

saborear /saβore'ar/ *vt* to flavor, season; relish, savor; appreciate, enjoy; *vr* relish, savor; enjoy

saboreo /saβo'reo/ *m*, tasting; savoring; relishing

sabotaje /saβo'tahe/ *m*, sabotage

saboteador /saβotea'ðor/ *m*, saboteur

Saboya /sa'βoya/ Savoy

saboyano /saβo'yano/ **(-na)** *a* and *n* Savoyard

sabroso /sa'βroso/ *a* tasty, savory, well-seasoned; delightful, delicious; *Inf*. piquant, racy; *Lat. Am*. garrulous, talkative

sabueso /sa'βueso/ *m*, cocker spaniel. **s. de artois,** hound

sabuloso /saβu'loso/ *a* sandy

saburra /sa'βurra/ *f*, fur (on the tongue)

saca /'saka/ *f*, drawing out, removing; export, transport, shipping; removal, extraction; legal copy (of a document). **estar de s.,** to be on sale; *Inf*. be marriageable (of women)

sacabocados /sakaβo'kaðos/ *m*, punch (tool); *Inf*. cinch, easy matter

sacabotas /saka'βotas/ *m*, bootjack

sacabrocas /saka'βrokas/ *m*, tack puller

sacabuche /saka'βutʃe/ *m*, *Mus*. sackbut; sackbut player; *Inf*. insignificant little man; *Naut*. hand pump

sacacorchos /saka'kortʃos/ *m*, corkscrew

sacacuartos /saka'kuartos/ *m*, *Inf*. catchpenny

sacada /sa'kaða/ *f*, territory cut off from a province

sacadineros /sakaði'neros/ *m*, *Inf*. catchpenny

sacamanchas /saka'mantʃas/ *mf*. See **quitamanchas**

sacamantas /saka'mantas/ *m*, *Inf*. tax collector

sacamiento /saka'miento/ *m*, removing, taking out

sacamuelas /saka'muelas/ *m*, *Inf*. dentist; charlatan, quack; *Inf*. windbag

sacapotras /saka'potras/ *m*, *Inf*. unskilled surgeon

sacar /sa'kar/ *vt* to draw out; extract; pull out; take out; remove; dispossess, turn out; free from, relieve; examine, investigate; extort (the truth); extract (sugar, etc.); win (prizes, games); copy; discover, find out; elect by ballot; obtain, achieve; exclude; show, exhibit; quote, mention; produce, invent; manufacture; note down; put forth; unsheath (swords); bowl (in cricket); serve (in tennis). **s. a bailar,** to invite to dance. **s. a luz,** to publish, print; reveal, bring out. **s. a paseo,** to take for a walk. **s. de pila,** to be a godfather or godmother to. **s. en claro** *or* **s. en limpio,** to copy; conclude, infer, gather. **sacarse en conclusión que...,** the conclusion is that...

sacarificar /sakarifi'kar/ *vt* to saccharify

sacarina /saka'rina/ *f*, saccharin

sacasillas /saka'siyas; saka'siʎas/ *mf*, *Inf*. *Theat*. stagehand

sacerdocio /saser'ðosio; saθer'ðoθio/ *m*, priesthood

sacerdotal /saser'ðotal; saθerðo'tal/ *a* priestly

sacerdote /saser'ðote; saθer'ðote/ *m*, priest

sacerdotisa /saserðo'tisa; saθerðo'tisa/ *f*, priestess. **sumo s.,** high priestess

sachar /sa'tʃar/ *vt* to weed

sacho /'satʃo/ *m*, weeder

saciable /sa'siaβle; sa'θiaβle/ *a* satiable

saciar /sa'siar; sa'θiar/ *vt* to satisfy; satiate; *vr* be satiated

saciedad /sasie'ðað; saθie'ðað/ *f*, satiety, surfeit

saco /'sako/ *m*, sack, handbag; bag; sackful; sack coat; *Biol.* sac; *Mil.* sack, plundering. **s. de noche,** dressing case, weekend case. *Inf.* **no echar en s. roto,** not to forget, to remember

sacramentalmente /sakramental'mente/ *adv* sacramentally; in confession

sacramentar /sakramen'tar/ *vt* to consecrate; administer the Blessed Sacrament; hide, conceal

sacramentario /sakramen'tario/ **(-ia)** *n* sacramentalist; sacramentarian

sacramento /sakra'mento/ *m*, sacrament; *Eccl.* Host; *Eccl.* mystery. **s. del altar,** Eucharist. **con todos los sacramentos,** with all the sacraments; done in order, complete with all formalities. **recibir los sacramentos,** to receive the last sacraments

sacratísimo /sakra'tisimo/ *a* most sacred

sacrificadero /sakrifika'ðero/ *m*, place of sacrifice

sacrificador /sakrifika'ðor/ **(-ra)** *a* sacrificing. *n* sacrificer

sacrificar /sakrifi'kar/ *vt* to sacrifice; slaughter; *vr* consecrate oneself to God; sacrifice oneself; devote or dedicate oneself (to)

sacrificio /sakri'fisio; sakri'fiθio/ *m*, sacrifice; offering, dedication; surrendering, forgoing; compliance; submission. **s. del altar,** sacrifice of the mass

sacrilegio /sakri'lehio/ *m*, sacrilege

sacrílego /sa'krilego/ *a* sacrilegious

sacristán /sakris'tan/ *m*, sacristan; sexton; hoop (for dresses). *Inf.* **s. de amén,** yes-man. *Inf.* **ser gran s.,** to be very crafty

sacristana /sakris'tana/ *f*, wife of a sacristan or sexton; nun in charge of a convent sacristy

sacristanía /sakrista'nia/ *f*, office of a sacristan or sexton

sacristía /sakris'tia/ *f*, sacristy; vestry; office of a sacristan or sexton

sacro /'sakro/ *a* sacred; *Anat.* sacral

sacrosanto /sakro'santo/ *a* sacrosanct

sacudida /saku'ðiða/ *f*, shake, shaking; jerk, jar, jolt; twitch, pull; *Aer.* bump

sacudido /saku'ðiðo/ *a* unsociable; difficult, wayward; determined, bold

sacudidor /sakuði'ðor/ **(-ra)** *a* shaking; jerking. *n* shaker. *m*, carpet beater; duster

sacudidura /sakuði'ðura/ *f*, shaking (especially to remove dust); jerking

sacudimiento /sakuði'miento/ *m*, shake, shaking; jerk; twitch, pull; jolt

sacudir /saku'ðir/ *vt* to shake; flap, wave; jerk, twitch; beat, bang; shake off; *vr* shake off, avoid

sadismo /sa'ðismo/ *m*, sadism

sadista /sa'ðista/ *mf* sadist

sadístico /sa'ðistiko/ *a* sadistic

saduceo /saðu'seo; saðu'θeo/ **(-ea)** *a* Sadducean. *n* Sadducee

saeta /sa'eta/ *f*, arrow, dart; clock hand, watch hand; magnetic needle; short sung expression of religious ecstasy; *Astron.* Sagitta

saetada /sae'taða/ *f*, **saetazo** *m*, arrow wound

saetera /sae'tera/ *f*, loophole; small window

saetero /sae'tero/ *a* arrow, arrow-like. *m*, archer, bowman

safado, -a /sa'faðo/ *a*, *Lat. Am.* cheeky, impudent, saucy

saga /'saga/ *f*, saga

sagacidad /sagasi'ðað; sagaθi'ðað/ *f*, sagacity

sagaz /sa'gas; sa'gaθ/ *a* sagacious, shrewd; farseeing; quick on the scent (dogs)

sagital /sahi'tal/ *a* arrow-shaped

sagitario /sahi'tario/ *m*, archer; *Astron.* Sagittarius

sagrado /sa'graðo/ *a* sacred; holy; sacrosanct, venerable; accursed, detestable. *m*, sanctuary, refuge; haven

sagrario /sa'grario/ *m*, sanctuary; sacrarium

sagú /sa'gu/ *m*, sago

Sáhara, el /'saara, el/ the Sahara

sahornarse /saor'narse/ *vr* to chafe, grow sore

sahorno /sa'orno/ *m*, chafing, abrasion

sahumado /sau'maðo/ *a* improved, rendered more excellent; perfumed; fumigated

sahumador /sauma'ðor/ *m*, perfumer; fumigating vessel

sahumar /sau'mar/ *vt* to perfume; fumigate. See **desahuciar**

sahumerio /sau'merio/ *m*, perfuming; fumigation; fume, smoke

saín /sa'in/ *m*, fat, grease; sardine oil (for lamps); grease spot (on clothes)

sainar /sai'nar/ *vt* to fatten up (animals)

sainete /sai'nete/ *m*, *Cul.* sauce; *Theat.* one-act parody or burlesque; farce; delicacy, tidbit; delicate taste (of food)

sainetero /saine'tero/ *m*, writer of sainetes

sainetesco /saine'tesko/ *a* pertaining to sainetes; burlesque, satirical

sajar /sa'har/ *vt* *Surg.* to scarify

sajón /sa'hon/ **(-ona)** *a* and *n* Saxon

Sajonia /sa'honia/ Saxony

sal /sal/ *f*, salt; wit; grace, gracefulness. **s. de cocina,** common kitchen salt. **s. de la Higuera,** Epsom salts. **s. gema,** rock salt. **s. marina,** sea salt. **sales inglesas,** smelling salts. *Inf.* **estar hecho de s.,** to be full of wit. *Inf.* **hacerse s. y agua,** to melt away, disappear (of riches, etc.)

sala /'sala/ *f*, drawing room; large room, hall; *Law.* courtroom; *Law.* bench; **s. de apelación,** court of appeal. **s. de hospital,** hospital ward. **s. de justicia,** court of justice. **s. de lectura,** reading room. *Law.* **guardar s.,** to respect the court

salacidad /salasi'ðað; salaθi'ðað/ *f*, lewdness, salaciousness

saladero /sala'ðero/ *m*, salting or curing place; *West Hem.* meat packing factory

saladillo /sala'ðiyo; sala'ðiʎo/ *m*, salt pork

salado /sa'laðo/ *a* salty, briny; brackish; witty; attractive, amusing

salador /sala'ðor/ **(-ra)** *a* salting, curing. *n* salter, curer. *m*, curing place

saladura /sala'ðura/ *f*, salting, curing

salamandra /sala'mandra/ *f*, salamander; fire sprite

salar /sa'lar/ *vt* to salt; season with salt; oversalt; cure, pickle (meat, etc.); *m*, *Lat. Am.* salt marsh

salario /sa'lario/ *m*, salary

salaz /sa'las; sa'laθ/ *a* lewd, lecherous

salazón /sala'son; sala'θon/ *f*, salting, curing; salt meat or fish trade

salazonero /salaso'nero; salaθo'nero/ *a* salting, curing

salchicha /sal'tʃitʃa/ *f*, sausage

salchichería /saltʃitʃe'ria/ *f*, sausage shop

salchichero /saltʃi'tʃero/ **(-ra)** *n* sausage maker, sausage seller

salchichón /saltʃi'tʃon/ *m*, *Cul.* salami, kind of sausage

saldar /sal'dar/ *vt* *Com.* to settle, pay in full; sell out cheap; balance

saldista /sal'dista/ *mf* remnant buyer

saldo /'saldo/ *m*, *Com.* balance; closing of an account; bargain sale. **s. acreedor,** credit balance. **s. deudor,** debit balance. **s. líquido,** net balance

salero /sa'lero/ *m*, saltshaker, saltcellar; salt storage warehouse; *Inf.* wit

saleta /sa'leta/ *f*, *dim* small hall; royal antechamber; court of appeal

salida /sa'liða/ *f*, going out; leaving; departure; sailing; exit, way out; projection, protrusion; *Fig.* escape, way out; outcome, result; witty remark; *Mil.* sally; *Com.* outlay, expense; *Com.* opening, sale, salability; environs, outskirts; *Argentina* bathrobe **s. de dólares,** dollar drain. **s. de tono,** *Inf.* an impertinent remark. **dar s.,** *Com.* to enter on the credit side

salidero /sali'ðero/ *a* fond of going out; *m*, exit, way out

salidizo /sali'ðiso; sali'ðiθo/ *m*, *Archit.* projection. *a* projecting

saliente /sa'liente/ *a* outgoing; salient, projecting. *m*, east; projection; salient. **s. continental,** continental shelf

salina /sa'lina/ *f*, salt mine; saltworks

salinero /sali'nero/ *m*, salt merchant; salter; salt worker

salino /sa'lino/ *a* saline. *m*, *Med.* saline

salir /salir/ *vi irr* to go out; depart, leave; succeed in getting out; escape; appear (of the sun, etc.); sprout, show green; fade, come out (of stains); project, stand out; grow, develop; turn out, result; happen, take place; cost; sail; end (of seasons, time); lead off, start (some games); be published (books); do (well or badly), succeed or fail; appear, show oneself; be drawn, win (lottery tickets); balance, come out right (accounts); be elected; become; give up (posts); lead to (of streets, etc.); *Naut.* overtake; (*with prep a*) guarantee, be surety for; resemble, be like; (*with con*) utter, come out with; commit, do inopportunely; succeed in, achieve (e.g. *Salió con la suya*, He got his own way). **¿Cómo salieron las cosas?**, How did it (things) turn out? (*with de*) originate in; break away from (traditions, conventions); get rid of; (*with por*) stand up for, protect; go surety for, guarantee. *vr* leak; boil over; overflow; (*with con*) achieve, get; (*with de*) *Fig.* break away from. *Theat.* **s. a la escena**, to enter, come on to the stage. **Salió a su papá**, He's just like his father. **s. de**, to recover from (an illness). **no acabar de s. de**, to not be completely recovered from. **s. del apuro**, to get out of trouble. **s. de estampía**, to stampede (of animals). **s. pitando**, *Inf.* to get out in a hurry. **Esta idea no salió de Juan**, This wasn't John's idea. **salga lo que saliere**, *Inf.* come what may.... *Pres. Ind.* **salgo, sales**, etc. *Fut.* **saldré**, etc. *Condit.* **saldría**, etc. *Pres. Subjunc.* **salga**, etc.

salitral /sali'tral/ *a* nitrous. *m*, saltpeter bed

salitre /sa'litre/ *m*, saltpeter

salitrería /salitre'ria/ *f*, saltpeter works

salitrero /sali'trero/ *n* saltpeter worker or dealer

saliva /sa'liβa/ *f*, saliva. *Inf.* **tragar s.**, to put up with; be unable to speak through emotion

salivación /saliβa'sion; saliβa'θion/ *f*, salivation

salival /sali'βal/ *a* salivary

salivar /sali'βar/ *vi* to salivate; spit

sallar /sa'yar; sa'ʎar/ *vt* to weed

salmantino /salman'tino/ **(-na)** *a* and *n* Salamanca

salmear /salme'ar/ *vi* to intone psalms

salmista /sal'mista/ *mf* psalmist; psalmodist, psalm chanter

salmo /'salmo/ *m*, psalm

salmodia /sal'moðia/ *f*, psalmody; *Inf.* drone; psalter

salmodiar /salmo'ðiar/ *vi* to chant psalms; *vt* drone

salmón /sal'mon/ *m*, salmon

salmonado /salmo'naðo/ *a* salmon-like

salmonera /salmo'nera/ *f*, salmon net

salmonete /salmo'nete/ *m*, red mullet

salmuera /sal'muera/ *f*, brine

salobre /sa'loβre/ *a* salt, salty; brackish

salobridad /saloβri'ðað/ *f*, saltiness

salomar /salo'mar/ *vi Naut.* to sing chanteys

salón /sa'lon/ *m*, drawing room; large room or hall; reception room; salon, reception, social gathering. **s. de muestras**, showroom

saloncillo /salon'siyo; salon'θiʎo/ *m*, *dim* small room; *Theat.* greenroom; rest room

salpicadura /salpika'ðura/ *f*, sprinkling, spattering, splashing

salpicar /salpi'kar/ *vt* to sprinkle, scatter; bespatter; splash

salpicón /salpi'kon/ *m*, *Cul.* kind of salmagundi; *Inf.* hodgepodge; spattering

salpimentar /salpimen'tar/ *vt irr* to season with pepper and salt; sprinkle; *Fig.* leaven, enliven (a speech, etc.). See **regimentar**

salpresar /salpre'sar/ *vt* to preserve in salt, salt

salpullido /salpu'yiðo; salpu'ʎiðo/ *m*, rash, skin eruption

salsa /'salsa/ *f*, sauce; gravy. **s. mahonesa** or **s. mayonesa**, mayonnaise sauce. **s. mayordoma**, sauce maître d'hôtel

salsera /sal'sera/ *f*, sauce boat, gravy boat

saltabanco /salta'βanko/ *m*, mountebank; street entertainer, juggler

saltabarrancos /saltaβa'rrankos/ *mf Inf.* madcap, harum-scarum

saltable /sal'taβle/ *a* jumpable

saltadero /salta'ðero/ *m*, jumping ground; fountain, jet

saltador /salta'ðor/ **(-ra)** *a* jumping. *n* jumper; acrobat. *m*, jump rope, skip rope

saltamontes /salta'montes/ *m*, grasshopper

saltaojos /salta'ohos/ *m*, peony

saltaparedes /saltapa'reðes/ *mf Inf.* madcap, romp

saltar /sal'tar/ *vi* to jump, leap, spring; prance; frisk; gambol; rebound; fly up; burst, break asunder; pop (of corks); fly off, come off (buttons, etc.); gush out, shoot up (liquids); break apart, be shattered; be obvious, stand out; come to mind, suggest itself; show anger; *Fig.* let slip, come out with (remarks); *vt* leap or jump over; poke out (eyes); cover (the female); omit, pass over; blow up, explode. **s. a la cuerda**, to jump rope, play with a skip rope. **s. a la vista**, to be obvious, leap to the eye. **s. diciendo**, *Inf.* to come out with, say

saltarín /salta'rin/ **(-ina)** *a* jumping, frolicking, dancing. *n* dancer

saltatriz /salta'tris; salta'triθ/ *f*, ballet dancer, female acrobat

saltatumbas /salta'tumbas/ *m*, (*inf* contemptuous) cleric who makes his living off funerals

salteador /saltea'ðor/ *m*, highwayman

salteamiento /saltea'miento/ *m*, highway robbery, holdup; assault, attack

saltear /salte'ar/ *vt* to hold up and rob; assault, attack; jump from one thing to another, do intermittently; forestall; surprise, amaze

salterio /sal'terio/ *m*, psaltery

saltimbanco, saltimbanqui /saltim'βanko, saltim-'βanki/ *m*, *Inf.* See **saltabanco**

salto /'salto/ *m*, jump, leap, bound; leapfrog (game); precipice, ravine; waterfall; assault; important promotion; omission (of words). **s. de agua**, waterfall. **s. de cama**, peignoir, bathrobe. **s. de campana**, overturning. *Inf.* **s. de mal año**, sudden improvement in circumstances. **s. de mata**, flight, escape. **s. mortal**, leap of death; somersault. **s. de pie**, spillway. **dar un s.**, to leap. **en un s.**, at one jump; swiftly

saltón /sal'ton/ *a* jumping, leaping; prominent (teeth, eyes). *m*, grasshopper

salubérrimo /salu'βerrimo/ *a sup* **salubre** most healthy

salubre /sa'luβre/ *a* salubrious, healthful

salubridad /saluβri'ðað/ *f*, healthfulness

salud /sa'luð/ *f*, health; salvation; welfare, well-being; *Eccl.* state of grace; *pl* civilities, greetings. **¡S. y pesetas!** Here's to your good health and prosperity! (on drinking). **gastar s.**, to enjoy good health. *Inf.* **vender** (or **verter**) **s.**, to look full of health

saludable /salu'ðaβle/ *a* healthy, wholesome

saludador /saluða'ðor/ **(-ra)** *a* greeting, saluting. *n* greeter. *m*, charlatan, quack

saludar /salu'ðar/ *vt* to greet, salute; hail (as king, etc.); send greetings to; bow; *Mil.* fire a salute

saludo /sa'luðo/ *m*, greeting, salutation; bow; (*Mil. Nav.*) salute

salutación /saluta'sion; saluta'θion/ *f*, greeting, salutation; Ave Maria

salutífero /salu'tifero/ *a* salubrious

salva /'salβa/ *f*, salutation, greeting; (*Mil. Nav.*) salvo, volley; salute (of guns); salver; ordeal (to establish innocence); solemn assurance, oath; sampling, tasting (of food, drink). **s. de veintiún cañonazos**, twenty-one-gun salute

salvación /salβa'sion; salβa'θion/ *f*, liberation, deliverance; salvation

salvado /sal'βaðo/ *m*, bran

salvador /salβa'ðor/ **(-ra)** *a* saving, redeeming. *n* deliverer. *m*, redeemer

salvadoreño /salβaðore'ɲo/ **(-ña)** *a* and *n* Salvadorean

salvaguardia /salβa'ɣuarðia/ *m*, guard, watch. *f*, safeguard; protection, defense; safe conduct, passport

salvajada /salβa'haða/ *f*, savagery, brutal action

salvaje /sal'βahe/ a wild (plants, animals); rough, uncultivated; uncultured, uncivilized. mf savage

salvajismo /salβa'hismo/ m, savagery

salvamano, a /salβa'mano, a/ adv safely

salvamente /salβa'mente/ adv safely, securely

salvamento /salβa'mento/ m, salvation; deliverance, security, safety; place of safety; salvage

salvante /sal'βante/ adv Inf. except, save

salvar /sal'βar/ vt to save; Eccl. redeem; avoid (difficulty, danger); exclude, except; leap, jump; pass over, clear; Law. prove innocent; Naut. salve. **s. la diferencia,** to bridge the gap. vi taste, sample (food, drink); vr be saved from danger; Eccl. be redeemed

salvavidas /salβa'βiðas/ m, life belt; safety belt; life preserver; traffic island

¡**salve!** /'salβe/ interj Poet. hail! ¡**S. María!,** Hail Mary. ¡**S. Regina!,** Salve Regina

salvedad /salβe'ðað/ f, qualification, reservation

salvia /'salβia/ f, Bot. sage

salvilla /sal'βiya/ f, salver

salvo /'salβo/ a safe, unharmed; excepting, omitting. adv except. **a s.,** safely, without harm. **a su s.,** to his (her, their) satisfaction; at his (her, etc.) pleasure. **dejar a s.,** to exclude, leave aside. **en s.,** in safety

salvoconducto /salβokon'dukto/ m, safe conduct, pass

samarita /sama'rita/ a and mf **samaritano (-na)** a and n Samaritan

samba /'samβa/ f samba

sambenito /sambe'nito/ m, penitent's gown (Inquisition); disgrace, dishonor

sambubia /sam'βuβia/ f, Mexico pineapple drink

Samotracia /samo'trasia; samo'traθia/ Samothrace

samotracio /samo'trasio; samo'traθio/ **(-ia)** a and n Samothracian

samoyedo /samo'yeðo/ **(-da)** n Samoyed

san /san/ a abb of **santo.** Used before masculine singular names of saints except **Santos Tomás** (or **Tomé**), **Domingo, Toribio**

sanable /sa'naβle/ a curable

sanador /sana'ðor/ **(-ra)** a healing, curing. n healer

sanalotodo /sanalo'toðo/ m, Inf. cure-all, universal remedy

sanar /sa'nar/ vt to cure, heal; vi recover, get well; heal

sanatorio /sana'torio/ m, sanatorium; convalescent home

sanción /san'sion; san'θion/ f, authorization, consent; sanction; penalty

sancionable /sansio'naβle; sanθio'naβle/ a sanctionable

sancionar /sansio'nar; sanθio'nar/ vt to authorize, approve; sanction

sancochar /sanko'tʃar/ vt Cul. to parboil, half-cook

sancocho /san'kotʃo/ m, parboiled meat

sandalia /san'dalia/ f, sandal

sándalo /'sandalo/ m, sandalwood

sandez /san'des; san'deθ/ f, foolishness, stupidity; folly

sandía /san'dia/ f, watermelon

sandio /'sandio/ a foolish, inane

sandunga /san'duŋga/ f, Inf. attractiveness, winsomeness, grace; Lat. Am. carousing

sandunguero /sanduŋ'guero/ a Inf. attractive, appealing, winsome

saneado /sane'aðo/ a unencumbered, nontaxable, free

saneamiento /sanea'miento/ m, guarantee, security; indemnity; stabilization (of currency); drainage

sanear /sane'ar/ vt Com. to guarantee, secure; indemnify; stabilize (currency); drain (land, etc.)

Sanedrín /sane'ðrin/ m, Sanhedrin

sangradera /saŋgra'ðera/ f, lancet; channel, sluice; drain

sangrador /saŋgra'ðor/ m, phlebotomist; outlet, drainage

sangradura /saŋgra'ðura/ f, inner bend of the arm; Surg. bleeding; draining off

sangrar /saŋ'grar/ vt Surg. to bleed; drain off; Inf. extort money, bleed; Print. indent; draw off resin (from

pines, etc.); vi bleed; vr bleed; have oneself bled; run (of colors)

sangre /'saŋgre/ f, blood; lineage, family. **s. fría,** sang-froid. **a s. fría,** in cold blood, premeditated. **a s. y fuego,** by fire and sword, without quarter. Inf. **bullir la s.,** to have youthful blood in one's veins. **llevar en la s.,** Fig. to be in the blood. **subírsele la s. a la cabeza,** to grow excited. Fig. Inf. **tener s. de horchata,** to have milk and water in one's veins

sangría /saŋ'gria/ f, sangria (wine); Surg. bloodletting; resin cut (on pines, etc.)

sangriento /saŋ'griento/ a bloody, bloodstained; bloodthirsty, cruel; mortal (insults, etc.); Poet. blood-colored

sangüesa /saŋ'guesa/ f, raspberry

sanguijuela /saŋgi'huela/ f, leech; Fig. Inf. sponger

sanguinaria /saŋgi'naria/ f, bloodstone

sanguinario /saŋgi'nario/ a vengeful, bloody, cruel

sanguíneo /saŋ'gineo/ a blood; sanguineous; sanguine, fresh-complexioned; blood-colored

sanguinolento /saŋgino'lento/ a. See **sangriento**

sanidad /sani'ðað/ f, safety, security; healthiness; health department. **s. interior,** Public Health. **S. militar,** army medical corps

sanitario /sani'tario/ a sanitary, hygienic. m, Mil. medical officer

sano /'sano/ a healthy; safe, secure; healthful, wholesome; unhurt, unharmed; upright, honest; sincere; Inf. entire, undamaged; sane. **s. y salvo,** safe and sound. Inf. **cortar por lo s.,** to cut one's losses

San Pablo /san 'paβlo/ São Paulo

sánscrito /'sanskrito/ a and m, Sanscrit

santa /'santa/ f, female saint

santamente /santa'mente/ adv in a saintly manner; simply

santero /san'tero/ **(-ra)** a given to image worship. n accomplice (of a burglar); caretaker (of a hermitage); beggar; Guatemala artisan who crafts figurines of saints

¡**Santiago!** /san'tiago/ interj St. James! (Spanish war cry). m, attack, assault

santiamén /santia'men/ m, Inf. split second

santidad /santi'ðað/ f, sanctity; saintliness; godliness. **Su S.,** His Holiness

santificación /santifika'sion; santifika'θion/ f, sanctification

santificador /santifika'ðor/ **(-ra)** a sanctifying. n sanctifier

santificar /santifi'kar/ vt to sanctify, make holy; consecrate; dedicate; keep (feast days)

santiguada /santi'guaða/ f, crossing oneself; rough treatment, harsh reproof

santiguar /santi'guar/ vt to make the sign of the cross over; Inf. beat, rain blows on; vr cross oneself; Inf. be dumbfounded

santísimo /san'tisimo/ a sup most saintly, most holy

santo /'santo/ a holy; saintly; saint (see **san**); consecrated; inviolate, sacred; Inf. simple, sincere, ingenuous. m, saint; image of a saint; saint's day, name day (of a person); Mil. password. **Santa Hermandad,** Holy Brotherhood (former name of the Spanish rural police force). **S. Oficio,** Holy Office, Inquisition. **S. y bueno,** Well and good, All right! Inf. **alzarse con el s. y la limosna,** to take the lot, make off with everything. **llegar y besar el s.,** to do in a trice. Inf. **No es s. de mi devoción,** I'm not very keen on him. Inf. **todo el s. día,** the whole blessed day

santón /san'ton/ m, dervish, santon. Inf. hypocrite, sham saint

santoral /santo'ral/ m, book of saints; calendar of saints; choir book

santuario /santu'ario/ m, sanctuary

santurrón /santu'rron/ **(-ona)** a sanctimonious; hypocritical; prudish. n hypocrite

santurronería /santurrone'ria/ f, sanctimoniousness

saña /'sana/ f, fury, blind rage; lust for revenge, cruelty

sañoso, sañudo /sa'ɲoso, sa'ɲuðo/ a furious, blind with rage; cruel

sapidez /sapi'ðes; sapi'ðeθ/ f, flavor, sapidity

sápido /'sapiðo/ a tasty, savory

sapiencia /sa'piensia; sa'pienθia/ *f*, wisdom; knowledge; erudition
sapino /sa'pino/ *m*, fir (tree)
sapo /'sapo/ *m*, toad
saque /'sake/ *m*, *Sports.* serve, service; service or bowling line; *Sports.* server; *Sports.* bowler; bowling (in cricket)
saqueador /sakea'ðor/ **(-ra)** *a* looting, pillaging. *n* pillager, plunderer
saquear /sake'ar/ *vt* to pillage, plunder, sack
saqueo /sa'keo/ *m*, plundering, pillage, sacking
sarampión /saram'pion/ *m*, measles
sarao /sa'rao/ *m*, soirée, evening party
sarape /sa'rape/ *m*, *Mexico* woolen shawl or blanket worn by males
sarcasmo /sar'kasmo/ *m*, sarcasm
sarcástico /sar'kastiko/ *a* sarcastic
sarcia /'sarsia; 'sarθia/ *f*, load, cargo
sarcófago /sar'kofago/ *m*, sarcophagus
sarda /'sarða/ *f*, mackerel
sardana /sar'ðana/ *f*, traditional Catalonian dance
sardina /sar'ðina/ *f*, sardine. **s. arenque,** herring. **como sardinas en banasta,** *Fig.* packed like sardines
sardinal /sarði'nal/ *m*, sardine net
sardinero /sarði'nero/ **(-ra)** *a* sardine. *n* sardine seller or dealer. *m*, famous district of Santander
sardineta /sarði'neta/ *f*, sprat; small sardine; *Mil.* chevron
sardónico /sar'ðoniko/ *a* sardonic
sarga /'sarga/ *f*, (silk) serge; willow
sargentear /sarhente'ar/ *vt* to be in charge as a sergeant; command, captain; *Inf.* boss
sargento /sar'hento/ *m*, sergeant
sarita /sa'rita/ *f. Peru* straw hat
sarmentoso /sarmen'toso/ *a* vine-like; twining
sarmiento /sar'miento/ *m*, vine shoot
sarna /'sarna/ *f*, scabies. **s. perruna,** mange. **más viejo que la s.,** *Inf.* older than the plague
sarnoso /sar'noso/ *a* itchy; mangy
sarraceno /sarra'seno; sarra'θeno/ **(-na)** *a* Saracen. *n* Saracen; Moor
sarracina /sarra'sina; sarra'θina/ *f*, scuffle
sarrillo /sa'rriyo; sa'rriʎo/ *m*, death rattle, rale; arum lily
sarro /'sarro/ *m*, furry encrustation, scale; film; tartar (on teeth)
sarta /'sarta/ *f*, string, link (of pearls, etc.); file, line
sartén /sar'ten/ *f*, frying pan. **tener la s. por el mango,** *Inf.* to be top dog
sastra /'sastra/ *f*, female tailor; tailor's wife
sastre /'sastre/ *m*, tailor. **ser buen s.,** *Inf.* to be an expert (in)
sastrería /sastre'ria/ *f*, tailoring; tailor's shop
Satanás /sata'nas/ *m*, Satan; devil
satánico /sa'taniko/ *a* satanic
satélite /sa'telite/ *m*, satellite; follower, admirer, sycophant
satén /sa'ten/ *m*, sateen
satinar /sati'nar/ *vt* to calender; glaze; satin (paper)
sátira /'satira/ *f*, satire
satírico /sa'tiriko/ *a* satiric
satirizar /satiri'sar; satiri'θar/ *vi* to write satires; *vt* satirize
sátiro /'satiro/ *m*, satyr; *Theat.* indecent play
satisfacción /satisfak'sion; satisfak'θion/ *f*, settlement, payment; atonement, expiation; satisfaction; gratification; amends; complacency, conceit; contentment; apology. **tomar s.,** to avenge oneself
satisfacer /satisfa'ser/ *vt irr* to pay, settle; atone for, expiate; gratify; quench; fulfill, observe; compensate, indemnify; discharge, meet; convince, persuade; allay, relieve; reward; explain; answer, satisfy; *vr* avenge oneself; satisfy oneself. *Pres. Ind.* **satisfago, satisfaces, etc.** *Fut.* **satisfaré, etc.** *Condit.* **satisfaría, etc.** *Preterite* **satisfice, etc.** *Past Part.* **satisfecho.** *Pres. Subjunc.* **satisfaga, etc.** *Imperf. Subjunc.* **satisficiese, etc.**
satisfactorio /satisfak'torio/ *a* satisfactory
satisfecho /satis'fetʃo/ *a* self-satisfied, complacent; happy, contented

sátrapa /'satrapa/ *m*, satrap; *Inf.* cunning fellow
saturación /satura'sion; satura'θion/ *f*, saturation
saturar /satu'rar/ *vt* to satiate, fill; saturate
saturnino /satur'nino/ *a* saturnine, melancholy, morose
saturnismo /satur'nismo/ *m*, saturnism, lead poisoning
Saturno /sa'turno/ *m*, Saturn
sauce /'sause; 'sauθe/ *m*, willow. **s. llorón,** weeping willow
saúco /sa'uko/ *m*, elder tree
saurio /'saurio/ *a* and *m*, saurian
savia /'saβia/ *f*, sap; energy, zest
sáxeo /'sakseo/ *a* stone, stony
saxófono /sak'sofono/ *or* **saxofón** *m*, saxophone
saya /'saya/ *f*, skirt; long tunic
sayal /sa'yal/ *m*, thick woolen material
sayo /'sayo/ *m*, loose smock; *Inf.* any garment. **cortar un s.** (a), *Inf.* to gossip behind a person's back
sayón /sa'yon/ *m*, executioner; *Inf.* hideous-looking man
sazón /sa'son; sa'θon/ *f*, ripeness, maturity; season; perfection, excellence; opportunity; taste, flavor; seasoning. **a la s.,** at that time, then. **en s.,** in season; opportunely
sazonador /sasona'ðor; saθona'ðor/ **(-ra)** *a* seasoning. *n* seasoner
sazonar /saso'nar; saθo'nar/ *vt Cul.* to season; mature; *vr* mature, ripen
se /se/ *object pron reflexive 3rd sing* and *pl mf* 1. Used as accusative (direct object) himself, herself, yourself, themselves, yourselves (e.g. *Juan se ha cortado,* John has cut himself). 2. Used as dative or indirect object to himself, at himself, herself, themselves, etc. (e.g. *María se mira al espejo,* Mary looks at herself in the mirror). Reciprocity is also expressed by reflexive (e.g. *No se hablan,* They do not speak to one another). When a direct object pron. (accusative) and an indirect object pron., both in the 3rd pers. (sing. or pl.), are used together, the indirect object pron. becomes **se** (instead of **le** or **les**) (e.g. *Se lo doy,* I give it to him). Many Spanish reflexive verbs have English equivalents that are not reflexive (e.g. *desayunarse,* to breakfast, *arrepentirse,* to repent, *quejarse,* to complain). Some intransitive (neuter) verbs have a modified meaning when used reflexively (e.g. *marcharse,* to go away, *dormirse,* to fall asleep). The passive may be formed by using **se** + 3rd pers. sing. of verb (e.g. *se dice,* it is said, people say). A number of impersonal phrases are also formed in this way (e.g. «*Se alquila,*» "To Let," «*Se vende,*» "For Sale"). The imperative is used in the same way (e.g. *Véase la página dos,* See page two)
sebáceo /se'βaseo; se'βaθeo/ *a* sebaceous
sebo /'seβo/ *m*, tallow; candle grease; fat, grease
seboso /se'βoso/ *a* tallowy; fat, greasy
seca /'seka/ *f*, drought; *Naut.* unsubmerged sandbank
secadero /seka'ðero/ *m*, drying place, drying room
secadora /seka'ðora/ *f*, dryer, drying machine, clothesdryer. **s. de cabello,** hairdryer
secafirmas /seka'firmas/ *m*, blotting pad
secamente /seka'mente/ *adv* tersely, brusquely, curtly; dryly
secamiento /seka'miento/ *m*, drying
secano /se'kano/ *m*, nonirrigated land; *Naut.* unsubmerged sandbank; anything very dry
secante /se'kante/ *a* drying. *a* and *f*, *Geom.* secant. **papel s.,** blotting paper
secar /se'kar/ *vt* to dry; desiccate; annoy, bore; *vr* dry; dry up (of streams, etc.); wilt, fade (of plants); become parched; grow thin, become emaciated; be very thirsty; become hard-hearted
sección /sek'sion; sek'θion/ *f*, act of cutting; section, part, portion; *Geom. Mil.* section. **s. cónica,** conic section. **s. de amenidades,** entertainment section (of a newspaper). **s. de reserva,** *Mil.* reserve list
seccionar /seksio'nar; sekθio'nar/ *vt* to divide into sections, section
seccionario /seksio'nario; sekθio'nario/ *a* sectional
secesión /sese'sion; seθe'sion/ *f*, secession

secesionista /sesesio'nista; seθesio'nista/ *a* and *mf* secessionist

seco /'seko/ *a* dry; dried up, parched; faded, wilted; dead (plants); dried (fruits); thin, emaciated; unadorned; barren, arid; brusque, curt; severe, strict; indifferent, unenthusiastic; sharp (sounds); dry (wines). **a secas,** only; solely; simply, just. **en s.,** on dry land; curtly. *Inf.* **dejar s.** (a), to dumbfound, petrify

secreción /sekre'sion; sekre'θion/ *f,* segregation, separation; *Med.* secretion

secreta /se'kreta/ *f, Law.* secret trial or investigation; *Eccl.* secret(s); toilet, water closet

secretar /sekre'tar/ *vt Med.* to secrete

secretaría /sekreta'ria/ *f,* secretaryship; secretary's office, secretariat

secretario /sekre'tario/ **(-ia)** *n* secretary; amanuensis, clerk. *m,* actuary; registrar. **s. de asuntos exteriores** *or* **s. de asuntos extranjeros,** foreign secretary. **s. particular,** private secretary

secretear /sekrete'ar/ *vi Inf.* to whisper, have secrets

secreteo /sekre'teo/ *m, Inf.* whispering, exchanging of secrets

secreto /se'kreto/ *m,* secret; secrecy, silence; confidential information; mystery; secret drawer. *a* secret; private, confidential. **en s.,** in secret, confidentially. **s. a voces,** open secret

secta /'sekta/ *f,* sect

sectario /sek'tario/ **(-ia)** *a* and *n* sectarian. *n* fanatical believer

sectarismo /sekta'rismo/ *m,* sectarianism

sector /sek'tor/ *m,* sector

secuaz /se'kuas; se'kuaθ/ *mf* follower, disciple

secuela /se'kuela/ *f,* sequel, result

secuencia /se'kuensia; se'kuenθia/ *f, Eccl.* sequence; (cinema) sequence

secuestrador /sekuestra'ðor/ **(-ra)** *a* sequestrating. *n* sequestrator

secuestrar /sekues'trar/ *vt* to sequester; kidnap

secuestro /se'kuestro/ *m,* sequestration; kidnapping; *Surg.* sequestrum

secular /seku'lar/ *a* secular, lay; centennial; age-old, ancient; *Eccl.* secular

secularización /sekularisa'sion; sekulariθa'θion/ *f,* secularization

secularizar /sekulari'sar; sekulari'θar/ *vt* to secularize; *vr* become secularized

secundar /sekun'dar/ *vt* to second, aid

secundario /sekun'dario/ *a* secondary; accessory, subordinate; *Geol.* mesozoic

sed /seð/ *f,* thirst; desire, yearning, appetite. **apagar** (*or* **matar**) **la s.,** to quench one's thirst. **tener s.,** to be thirsty

seda /'seða/ *f,* silk; bristle (boar, etc.). **s. cordelada,** twist silk. **s. ocal,** floss silk. **s. vegetal** *or* **s. artificial,** artificial silk. *Inf.* **como una s.,** as smooth as silk; sweet-tempered; achieved without any trouble

sedación /seða'sion; seða'θion/ *f,* calming, soothing

sedal /se'ðal/ *m,* fish line

sedar /se'ðar/ *vt* to soothe, calm

sedativo /seða'tiβo/ *a* and *m, Med.* sedative

sede /'seðe/ *f, Eccl.* see; bishop's throne; *Fig.* seat (of government, etc.); Holy See (also **Santa S.**)

sedentario /seðen'tario/ *a* sedentary

sedeño /se'ðeɲo/ *a* silky; silken, made of silk

sedería /seðe'ria/ *f,* silk goods; silks; silk shop

sedero /se'ðero/ **(-ra)** *a* silk. *n* silk weaver or worker; silk merchant

sedición /seði'sion; seði'θion/ *f,* sedition

sedicioso /seði'sioso; seði'θioso/ *a* seditious

sediento /se'ðiento/ *a* thirsty; parched, dry (land); eager (for), desirous (of)

sedimentación /seðimenta'sion; seðimenta'θion/ *f,* sedimentation

sedimentar /seðimen'tar/ *vt* to leave a sediment; *vr* settle, form a sediment

sedimento /seði'mento/ *m,* sediment; dregs, lees; scale (on boilers)

sedoso /se'ðoso/ *a* silky, silk-like

seducción /seðuk'sion; seðuk'θion/ *f,* seduction; temptation, blandishment, wile; charm, allurement

seducir /seðu'sir; seðu'θir/ *vt irr* to seduce; tempt, lead astray; charm, attract; corrupt, bribe. See **conducir**

seductivo /seðuk'tiβo/ *a* tempting; seductive, charming

seductor /seðuk'tor/ **(-ra)** *a* tempting; charming. *n* seducer; charming person

sefardí /sefar'ði/ *mf* Iberian Jew; *pl* Sephardim. *a* Sephardic

segadera /sega'ðera/ *f,* sickle

segador /sega'ðor/ *m,* reaper, harvester

segadora /sega'ðora/ *f,* mowing machine, harvester; woman harvester

segar /se'gar/ *vt irr* to scythe, cut down; reap, harvest; mow. See **cegar**

seglar /se'glar/ *a* secular, lay. *mf* layman

segmento /seg'mento/ *m,* segment; *Geom.* segment. **s. de émbolo,** piston ring

segoviano /sego'βiano/ **(-na)** *a* and *n* Segovian

segregación /segrega'sion; segrega'θion/ *f,* segregation

segregar /segre'gar/ *vt* to segregate, separate; *Med.* secrete

seguida /se'giða/ *f,* continuation, prolongation. **de s.,** continuously; immediately. **en s.,** at once, immediately

seguidamente /segiða'mente/ *adv* continuously; immediately

seguidilla /segi'ðiya; segi'ðiʎa/ *f,* popular Spanish tune and dance and verse sung to them; *Inf.* diarrhea

seguido /se'giðo/ *a* continuous, successive; direct, straight

seguidor /segi'ðor/ **(-ra)** *a* following. *n* follower, disciple

seguimiento /segi'miento/ *m,* following, pursuit; continuation, resumption

seguir /se'gir/ *vt irr* to follow; go after, pursue; prosecute, execute; continue, go on; accompany, go with; exercise (a profession); subscribe to, believe in; agree with; persecute; pester, annoy; imitate; *Law.* institute (a suit); handle, manage; *vr* result, follow as a consequence; follow in order, happen by turn; originate. *Pres. Part.* **siguiendo.** *Pres. Ind.* **sigo, sigues, sigue, siguen.** *Pres. Subjunc.* **siga, etc.** *Imperf. Subjunc.* **siguiese**

según /se'gun/ *adv* according to; as. **s. parece,** as it seems. **s. y como,** as, according to

segunda /se'gunda/ *f, Mus.* second

segundar /segun'dar/ *vt* to repeat, do again; *vi* be second, follow the first

segundero /segun'dero/ *a Agr.* of the second flowering or fruiting. *m,* second hand (of a watch)

segundo /se'gundo/ *a* second. *m,* second in command, deputy head; *Astron. Geom.* second. **segunda intención,** double meaning. **segunda velocidad,** *Auto.* second gear. **de segunda mano,** second-hand. **sin s.,** without peer or equal

segundogénito /segundo'henito/ **(-ta)** *a* and *n* secondborn

segundón /segun'don/ *m,* second son; any son but the eldest

segurador /segura'ðor/ *m,* surety, security (person)

seguramente /segura'mente/ *adv* securely, safely; surely, of course, naturally

seguridad /seguri'ðað/ *f,* security; safety; certainty; trustworthiness; *Com.* surety; *Mexico* clasp, lock (of a suitcase, trunk, etc) **con toda s.,** with complete safety, surely, absolutely. **de s.,** *a* safety

seguro /se'guro/ *a* secure; safe; certain, sure; firm, fixed; reliable, trustworthy; unfailing. *m,* clasp, fastener; certainty; haven, place of safety; *Mexico* safety pin; *Com.* insurance; permit; *Mech.* ratchet. **s. contra incendio, accidentes, robo,** fire, accident, burglary insurance. **s. sobre la vida,** life insurance. **de s.,** surely, certainly. **en s.,** in safety. **s. social** *Lat. Am.* social security

seis /seis/ *a* six; sixth. *m,* six; sixth (of the month); playing card or domino with six spots. **Son las s.,** It is six o'clock

seiscientos /seis'sientos; seis'θientos/ *a* six hundred; six-hundredth. *m*, six hundred
selección /selek'sion; selek'θion/ *f*, selection, choice.
s. natural, natural selection
seleccionar /seleksio'nar; selekθio'nar/ *vt* to select, choose
selectivo /selek'tiβo/ *a* selective
selecto /se'lekto/ *a* choice, select, excellent
sellado /se'jaðo; se'ʎaðo/ *m, Argentina* postage
sellador /seya'ðor; seʎa'ðor/ **(-ra)** *a* sealing, stamping. *n* sealer, stamper
selladura /seya'ðura; seʎa'ðura/ *f*, sealing, stamping
sellar /se'yar; se'ʎar/ *vt* to seal; stamp; end, conclude; close
sello /'seyo; 'seʎo/ *m*, seal; stamp. **s. fiscal,** stamp duty. **s. postal,** postage stamp. **s. y cruz** *Colombia,* heads or tails
selva /'selβa/ *f*, forest, wood; jungle. **s. tropical,** rainforest
Selva Negra, la /'selβa 'negra, la/ the Black Forest
selvático /sel'βatiko/ *a* sylvan, wood, forest; wild
selvoso /sel'βoso/ *a* wooded, sylvan
semafórico /sema'foriko/ *a* semaphoric
semáforo /se'maforo/ *m*, traffic light.
semana /se'mana/ *f*, week; week's salary. **S. Mayor** *or* **S. Santa,** Holy Week. **entre s.,** during the week, on weekdays; weekdays
semanal /sema'nal/ *a* weekly; of a week's duration
semanario /sema'nario/ *a* weekly. *m*, weekly periodical
semanero, -a /sema'nero/ *a* employed by the week; paid by the week; person employed by the week; person paid by the week
semántica /se'mantika/ *f*, semantics
semántico /se'mantiko/ *a* semantic
semblante /sem'βlante/ *m*, facial expression, countenance; face; appearance, look, aspect. **componer el s.,** to pull oneself together, straighten one's face. **mudar de s.,** to change color, change one's expression; alter (of circumstances)
semblanza /sem'βlansa; sem'βlanθa/ *f*, biographical sketch. **s. literaria,** short literary biography
sembradera /sembra'ðera/ *f*, sowing machine
sembradío /sembra'ðio/ *a Agr.* ready for sowing
sembrado /sem'βraðo/ *m*, sown land
sembrador /sembra'ðor/ **(-ra)** *a* sowing. *n* sower
sembradura /sembra'ðura/ *f, Agr.* sowing
sembrar /sem'βrar/ *vt irr Agr.* to sow; scatter, sprinkle; spread, disseminate. See **sentar**
semeja /se'meha/ *f*, resemblance, similarity; indication, sign (gen. *pl*)
semejante /seme'hante/ *a* like, similar; such a; *Math.* similar. *m*, fellow man
semejanza /seme'hansa; seme'hanθa/ *f*, similarity, likeness. **a s. de,** in the likeness of; like
semejar /seme'har/ **(se)** *vi* and *vr* to resemble
semen /'semen/ *m*, semen; *Bot.* seed
semental /semen'tal/ *a Agr.* seed; breeding (of male animals). *m*, stallion
sementar /semen'tar/ *vt Agr.* to sow
sementera /semen'tera/ *f, Agr.* sowing; sown land; seedbed; seedtime; *Fig.* hotbed, nursery, genesis
sementero /semen'tero/ *m*, seed bag; seed bed
semestral /semes'tral/ *a* biannual, half-yearly; lasting six months
semestre /se'mestre/ *a* biannual. *m*, half-year, period of six months; six months' salary; semester
semicírculo /semi'sirkulo; semi'θirkulo/ *m*, semicircle
semidifunto /semiði'funto/ *a* half-dead
semidormido /semiðor'miðo/ *a* half-asleep
semilla /se'miya; se'miʎa/ *f, Bot.* seed; *Fig.* germ, genesis
semillero /semi'yero; semi'ʎero/ *m*, seedbed; nursery; *Fig.* hotbed, origin
seminario /semi'nario/ *m*, seedbed; nursery; genesis, origin; seminary; tutorial. **s. conciliar,** theological seminary
seminarista /semina'rista/ *mf* seminarist

semiótica /semi'otika/ *f, Med.* symptomatology; semiotics
semita /se'mita/ *mf* Semite. *a* Semitic
semítico /se'mitiko/ *a* Semitic
semitismo /semi'tismo/ *m*, Semitism
semitono /semi'tono/ *m, Mus.* semitone
semitransparente /semitranspa'rente/ *a* semitransparent
semivivo /semi'βiβo/ *a* half-alive
sémola /'semola/ *f*, semolina
sempiterna /sempi'terna/ *f*, everlasting flower; thick woolen material
sempiterno /sempi'terno/ *a* eternal
sen /sen/ *m*, senna
Sena, el /'sena, el/ the Seine
sena /'sena, el/ *f, Bot.* senna; six-spotted die
senado /se'naðo/ *m*, senate; senate house; any grave assembly
senador /sena'ðor/ *m*, senator
senaduría /sena'ðuria/ *f*, senatorship
senario /se'nario/ *a* senary
senatorio /sena'torio/ *a* senatorial
sencillez /sensi'yes; senθi'ʎeθ/ *f*, simplicity; naturalness; easiness; ingenuousness, candor
sencillo /sen'siyo; sen'θiʎo/ *a* simple; unmixed; natural; thin, light (fabric); easy; ingenuous, candid; unadorned, plain; single; sincere
senda /'senda/ *f*, path, footpath; way; means
senderear /sendere'ar/ *vt* to conduct along a path; make a pathway; *vi* attain by tortuous means
sendero /sen'dero/ *m*, footpath, path
sendos, sendas /'sendos, 'sendas/ *a m*, and *f pl*, one each (e.g. *Les dio sendos lápices,* He gave them each a pencil)
senectud /senek'tuð/ *f*, old age
senescal /senes'kal/ *m*, seneschal
senil /se'nil/ *a* senile
senilidad /senili'ðað/ *f*, senility
seno /'seno/ *m*, hollow; hole; concavity; bosom, breast; chest; uterus, womb; any internal cavity of the body; bay, cove; lap (of a woman); interior (of anything), heart; gulf; *Math.* sine; *Anat.* sinus
sensación /sensa'sion; sensa'θion/ *f*, sensation
sensacional /sensasio'nal; sensaθio'nal/ *a* sensational
sensacionalista /sensasiona'lista; sensaθiona'lista/ *a* sensationalist
sensatez /sensa'tes; sensa'teθ/ *f*, prudence, good sense
sensato /sen'sato/ *a* prudent, wise
sensibilidad /sensiβili'ðað/ *f*, sensibility
sensibilizar /sensiβili'sar; sensiβili'θar/ *vt Photo.* to sensitize
sensible /sen'siβle/ *a* sensible, sensitive; tender, feeling; perceptible; noticeable, definite; sensitive; sad, regrettable
sensiblemente /sensiβle'mente/ *adv* appreciably; perceptibly; painfully, sadly
sensiblería /sensiβle'ria/ *f*, sentimentality, sentimentalism
sensiblero /sensi'βlero/ *a* oversentimental
sensitiva /sensi'tiβa/ *f*, sensitive plant, mimosa
sensitivo /sensi'tiβo/ *a* sensuous; sensitive, sensible
sensorio /sen'sorio/ *a* sensory. *m*, sensorium
sensual /sen'sual/ *a* sensual; sensitive, sensible; carnal, voluptuous
sensualidad /sensuali'ðað/ *f*, sensuality; sensualism
sensualismo /sensua'lismo/ *m*, sensualism; *Philos.* sensationalism
sensualista /sensua'lista/ *mf Philos.* sensationalist; sensualist
sentadera /senta'ðera/ *f, Lat. Am.* seat (of a chair)
sentadero /senta'ðero/ *m*, resting place, improvised seat
sentado /sen'taðo/ *a* prudent, circumspect
sentar /sen'tar/ *vt irr* to seat; *vi Inf.* suit, agree with (e.g. *No me sienta este clima (este plato),* This climate (dish) doesn't suit me); fit, become; *Inf.* please, satisfy, be agreeable to; *vr* sit down; *Inf.* leave a mark

on the skin. *Pres. Ind.* **siento, sientas, sienta, sientan.** *Pres. Subjunc.* **siente, sientes, siente, sienten**

sentencia /sen'tensia; sen'tenθia/ *f*, opinion, belief; maxim; *Law.* verdict, sentence; decision, judgment. *Law.* **fulminar** (*or* **pronunciar) la s.**, to pass sentence

sentenciador /sentensia'ðor; sentenθia'ðor/ *a Law.* sentencing

sentenciar /senten'siar; senten'θiar/ *vt Law.* to sentence; *Inf.* destine, intend

sentencioso /senten'sioso; senten'θioso/ *a* sententious

sentidamente /sentiða'mente/ *adv* feelingly; sadly, regretfully

sentido /sen'tiðo/ *m*, sense (hearing, seeing, touch, smell, taste); understanding, sense; meaning, interpretation, signification; perception, discrimination; judgment; direction, way. *a* and *past part* felt; expressive; hypersensitive, touchy. **s. común**, common sense. **costar un s.**, *Fig. Inf.* to cost a fortune. **perder el s.**, to lose consciousness

sentimental /sentimen'tal/ *a* emotional; sentimental; romantic

sentimentalismo /sentimenta'lismo/ *m*, emotional quality; sentimentalism

sentimiento /senti'miento/ *m*, feeling, sentiment; sensation, impression; feeling; grief, sorrow. **Le acompaño a usted en su s.**, I sympathize with you in your sorrow (bereavement)

sentina /sen'tina/ *f*, well (of a ship); *Naut.* bilge; cesspool; sink of iniquity

sentir /sen'tir/ *vt irr* to feel, experience; hear; appreciate; grieve, regret; believe, consider; envisage, foresee; *vr* complain; suffer; think or consider oneself; crack; feel, be; go rotten, decay (gen. with *estar* + *past part.*). *m*, view, opinion; feeling. **Lo siento,** I'm sorry. **Lo siento mucho,** I'm very sorry. **sin s.**, without feeling; without noticing. *Pres. Part.* **sintiendo.** *Pres. Ind.* **siento, sientes, siente, sienten.** *Preterite* **sintió, sintieron.** *Pres. Subjunc.* **sienta, sientas, sienta, sintamos, sintáis, sientan.** *Imperf. Subjunc.* **sintiese, etc.**

seña /'sena/ *f*, sign, mark; gesture; *Mil.* password; signal; *pl* address, domicile. **s. mortal,** definite or unmistakable sign. **dar señas,** to show signs, manifest. **hablar por señas,** to converse by signs

señal /se'nal/ *f*, mark, sign; boundary stone; landmark; scar; signal; trace, vestige; indication, symptom, token; symbol, sign; image, representation; prodigy, marvel; deposit, advance payment. **s. de aterrizaje,** *Aer.* landing signal. **s. de niebla,** fog signal. **señales horarias,** *Radio.* time signal. **en s.,** as a sign, in proof of. **s. luminosa de la circulación,** traffic light, traffic robot

señaladamente /senala'mente/ *adv* especially, particularly, notably

señalado /sena'laðo/ *a* famous, distinguished; important, notable

señalador /senala'ðor/ *m*, *Argentina* bookmark

señalamiento /senala'miento/ *m*, marking; pointing out; appointment, designation

señalar /sena'lar/ *vt* to mark; indicate, point out; fix; arrange; wound; signal; stamp; appoint (to office); *vr* excel

señero /se'nero/ *a* solitary, isolated

señor /se'nor/ *a Inf.* gentlemanly. *m*, owner, master; mister, esquire; **(S.)** the Lord; lord, sire. **s. de horca y cuchillo,** feudal lord, lord of life and death

señora /se'nora/ *f*, lady; owner, mistress; madam; wife. **s. de compañía,** chaperon; lady companion. **Nuestra S.,** Our Lady

señorear /senore'ar/ *vt* to control, run, manage; master; domineer; appropriate, seize; dominate, overlook; restrain (emotions); *vr* behave with dignity

señoría /seno'ria/ *f*, lordship (title and person); lordship, jurisdiction; area, territory; control, restraint

señoría /seno'ria/ *f*, dignity, sedateness; self-control

señorial /seno'rial/ *a* manorial; noble, dignified, lordly

señoril /seno'ril/ *a* lordly, noble, aristocratic

señorío /seno'rio/ *m*, lordship; jurisdiction, dominion

señorita /seno'rita/ *f*, young lady; miss; *Inf.* mistress of the house

señorito /seno'rito/ *m*, young gentleman; *Inf.* master of the house; master (address); *Inf.* young man about town

señuelo /se'nuelo/ *m*, decoy; bait; allurement, attraction. **caer en el s.,** *Fig. Inf.* to fall into the trap

sepancuantos /sepan'kuantos/ *m*, *Inf.* scolding, rebuke; spanking

separación /separa'sion; separa'θion/ *f*, separation

separado /sepa'raðo/ *a* separate

separador /separa'ðor/ **(-ra)** *a* separating. *n* separator. *m*, filter. **s. de aceite,** oil filter

separar /sepa'rar/ *vt* to separate; divide; dismiss (from a post); lay aside; *vr* retire, resign; separate

separatismo /separa'tismo/ *m*, separatism

separatista /separa'tista/ *a* and *mf* separatist

septeno /sep'teno/ *a*. See **séptimo**

septentrión /septen'trion/ *m*, *Astron.* Great Bear; north

septentrional /septentrio'nal/ *a* north; northern

septeto /sep'teto/ *m*, septet

septicemia /septi'semia; septi'θemia/ *f*, septicemia

séptico /'septiko/ *a* septic

septiembre /sep'tiembre/ *m*, September

septillo /sep'tiyo; sep'tiʎo/ *m*, *Mus.* septuplet

séptima /'septima/ *f*, *Mus.* seventh

séptimo /'septimo/ *a* and *m*, seventh

septuagenario /septuahe'nario/ **(-ia)** *a* and *n* septuagenarian

septuagésimo /septua'hesimo/ *a* seventieth; septuagesimal. *m*, seventieth

séptuplo /'septuplo/ *a* sevenfold

sepulcral /sepul'kral/ *a* sepulchral

sepulcro /se'pulkro/ *m*, sepulcher

sepultador /sepulta'ðor/ **(-ra)** *a* burying. *n* gravedigger; burier

sepultar /sepul'tar/ *vt* to inter, bury; hide, cover up

sepultura /sepul'tura/ *f*, interment; grave; tomb

sepulturero /sepultu'rero/ *m*, gravedigger

sequedad /seke'ðað/ *f*, dryness, barrenness; acerbity, sharpness

sequía /se'kia/ *f*, drought

séquito /'sekito/ *m*, following, suite, retinue; general approval, popularity

ser /ser/ *m*, essence, nature; being; existence, life. **El S. Supremo,** The Supreme Being, God

ser /ser/ *vi irr* to be (e.g. *El sombrero es azul*, The hat is blue). **Ser** may agree with either subject or complement, though when latter is *pl* the verb tends to be so too (e.g. *Son las once, (horas)*, It is eleven o'clock. **Cien dólares son poco dinero,** A hundred dollars is a small amount). If verbal complement is pers. pron., **ser** agrees with it both in number and person (e.g. *Son ellos*, It is they. *Soy yo*, It is I). In impers. phrases the pron. is not expressed (e.g. *Es difícil*, It is difficult. *Es sorprendente*, It is surprising). **ser** means to exist (e.g. *Pienso luego soy*, I think, therefore I am). **ser** (also **ser de** with nouns or obj. prons.) means to belong to, be the property of (e.g. *Este gato es mío*, This cat is mine. *El libro es de Juan*, The book belongs to John). Signifies to happen, occur (e.g. ¿*Cómo fue eso?* How did that happen?). Means to be suitable or fitting (e.g. *Este vestido no es para una señora mayor*, This dress is not suitable for an elderly lady). Expresses price, to be worth (e.g. ¿*A cuánto es el dólar?* How much is the dollar worth?) Means to be a member of, belong to (e.g. *Es de la Academia Española*, He is a member of the Spanish Academy). Means to be of use, be useful for (e.g. *Esta casa no es para una familia numerosa*, This house is no use for a large family). **Ser** expresses nationality (e.g. *Son francesas*, They are French. *Somos de Londres*, We are from London). *Auxiliary verb* used to form passive tense (e.g. *Esta historia ha sido leída por muchos*, This story has been read by many). *Fueron mandados al Japón*, They were sent to Japan. **s. de ver,** to be worth seeing. **s. para poco,** to be of little use, amount to little. **s. testigo de,** to witness. ¡*Cómo es eso!* How can that be! Surely not! ¡*Cómo ha de s.!* How should it be!; One must resign oneself. *Érase una vez or que érase,*

Once upon a time. *es a saber,* viz., that is to say. *un sí es no es,* a touch of, a suspicion of). *Pres. Part.* **siendo.** *Pres. Ind.* **soy, eres, es, somos, sois, son.** *Fut.* **seré, etc.** *Condit.* **sería, etc.** *Preterite* **fui, fuiste, fue, fuimos, fuisteis, fueron.** *Imperf.* **era, etc.** *Past Part.* **sido.** *Pres. Subjunc.* **sea, etc.** *Imperf. Subjunc.* **fuese, etc.** *Imperat.* **sé**

sera /'sera/ *f*, large frail

seráfico /se'rafiko/ *a* seraphic

serafín /sera'fin/ *m*, seraphim

serbal /ser'βal/ *m*, service tree

serena /se'rena/ *f*, serenade; *Inf.* dew

serenar /sere'nar/ *vt* to calm; soothe; clear; *vr* grow calm; clear up (weather); clear (liquids); be soothed or pacified

serenata /sere'nata/ *f*, serenade

serenidad /sereni'ðað/ *f*, serenity, composure, tranquility; Serene Highness (title)

sereno /se'reno/ *a* cloudless, fair; composed, serene. *m*, dew; night watchman. **al s.,** in the night air

sericultor /serikul'tor/ *m*, silk cultivator, sericulturist

sericultura /serikul'tura/ *f*, silk culture

serie /'serie/ *f*, series, sequence, succession; *Math.* progression; (*Biol. Elec.*) series; break (in billiards)

seriedad /serie'ðað/ *f*, seriousness, earnestness; gravity; austerity; sternness; importance; sincerity; solemnity

serigrafía /serigra'fia/ *f*, silkscreen printing

serio /'serio/ *a* serious, earnest; grave; austere; stern; important; sincere, genuine; solemn. **en s.,** seriously

sermón /ser'mon/ *m*, sermon; scolding. **dar un s.,** to give a sermon

sermonar /sermo'nar/ *vi* to preach

sermonear /sermone'ar/ *vi* to preach sermons; *vt* scold

sermoneo /sermo'neo/ *m*, *Inf.* scolding

seroja /se'roha/ *f*, withered leaves; brushwood

serpear /serpe'ar/ *vi* to wind, twist; wriggle, squirm; coil

serpenteado /serpente'aðo/ *a* winding

serpentear /serpente'ar/ *vi* to wind, twist, meander; stagger along; wriggle; coil; *Aer.* yaw

serpenteo /serpen'teo/ *m*, winding, twisting; wriggling; coiling; *Aer.* yaw

serpentín /serpen'tin/ *m*, *Chem.* worm; coil (in industry); *Mineral.* serpentine

serpentina /serpen'tina/ *f*, *Mineral.* serpentine; paper streamer

serpentino /serpen'tino/ *a* serpentine; *Poet.* winding, sinuous

serpiente /ser'piente/ *f*, snake, serpent; Satan, the Devil; *Astron.* Serpent. **s. de anteojos,** cobra. **s. de cascabel,** rattlesnake

serpollo /ser'poyo; ser'poʎo/ *m*, *Bot.* shoot, new branch; sprout; sucker

serrado /se'rraðo/ *a* serrate

serrallo /se'rrayo; se'rraʎo/ *m*, harem; seraglio; brothel

serranía /serra'nia/ *f*, mountainous territory

serrano /se'rrano/ **(-na)** *a* mountain, highland. *n* highlander, mountain dweller

serruchar /serru'tʃar/ *vt*, *Lat. Am.* to saw, saw off

serrucho /se'rrutʃo/ *m*, handsaw. **s. de calar,** fretsaw

Servia /'serβia/ Serbia

servible /ser'βiβle/ *a* serviceable; useful

servicial /serβi'sial; serβi'θial/ *a* useful, serviceable; obliging, obsequious

servicio /ser'βisio; ser'βiθio/ *m*, service; domestic service; cult, devotion; care, attendance; military service; set, service; department, section; present of money; cover (cutlery, etc., at table); domestic staff, servants. **s. informativo,** news service. **s. nocturno permanente,** all-night service. **hacer un flaco s. (a),** *Inf.* to do someone an ill turn. **prestar servicios,** to render service, serve

servidor /serβi'ðor/ **(-ra)** *n* servant, domestic; name by which one refers to oneself (e.g. *Un s. lo hará con mucho gusto,* I (your servant) will do it with much pleasure). *m*, wooer, lover; bowler (in cricket). **los servidores de una ametralladora,** the crew (of a

gun). **Quedo de Vd. atento y seguro s.,** I remain your obedient servant (in letters), Yours faithfully

servidumbre /serβi'ðumbre/ *f*, serfdom; servitude; servants, domestic staff; obligation, duty; enslavement (by passions); right of way; use, service

servil /ser'βil/ *a* servile; humble

servilismo /serβi'lismo/ *m*, servility; abjectness; absolutism (Spanish history)

servilleta /serβi'yeta; serβi'ʎeta/ *f*, table napkin. **s. higiénica,** sanitary napkin

servilletero /serβiye'tero; serβiʎe'tero/ *m*, napkin ring

servio /'serβio/ **(-ia)** *a* and *n* Serbian

servir /ser'βir/ *vi irr* to be employed (by), be in the service (of); serve (as), perform the duties (of); be of use; wait (on), be subject to. *Mil.* serve in the armed forces; wait at table; be suitable or favorable; *Sports.* serve; perform a service; follow the lead (cards); (*with de*) act as, be a deputy for; be a substitute for; *vt* serve; worship; do a favor to; woo, court; serve (food, drink); *vr* be pleased or willing, deign; help oneself to (food); (*with de*) make use of. **no s. para nada,** to be good for nothing, be useless. **No sirves para tales cosas,** You are no good at this sort of thing. **Para servirle,** At your service. **¡Sírvase de...!** (followed by infin.), Please! **s. de,** to serve as (e.g. *s. de base a,* to serve as a basis for). See **pedir**

sésamo /'sesamo/ *m*, sesame

sesenta /se'senta/ *a* and *m*, sixty; sixtieth

sesentavo /sesen'taβo/ *a* and *m*, sixtieth

sesentón /sesen'ton/ **(-ona)** *n Inf.* person of sixty

sesga /'sesga/ *f*, *Sew.* gore

sesgadamente /sesgaða'mente/ *adv* on the slant; askew; obliquely

sesgado /ses'gaðo/ *a* oblique, slanting

sesgar /ses'gar/ *vt Sew.* to cut on the bias; slant, slope; place askew, twist to one side

sesgo /'sesgo/ *a* slanting, oblique; serious-faced. *m*, slope, slant, obliquity; compromise, middle way. **al s.,** on the slant

sesión /se'sion/ *f*, session, meeting; conference, consultation; *Law.* sitting; term. **abrir la s.,** to open the meeting. **levantar la s.,** to adjourn the meeting

seso /'seso/ *m*, brain; prudence; *pl* brains. **perder el s.,** to go mad; *Fig.* lose one's head

sestear /seste'ar/ *vi* to take an afternoon nap; rest; settle

sesteo /ses'teo/ *m*, *Lat. Am.* nap, siesta

sesudez /sesu'ðes; sesu'ðeθ/ *f*, prudence, shrewdness

sesudo /se'suðo/ *a* sensible, prudent

seta /'seta/ *f*, mushroom. **s. venenosa,** poisonous toadstool

setal /se'tal/ *m*, mushroom bed, patch, or field

setecientos /sete'sientos; sete'θientos/ *a* and *m*, seven hundred; seven-hundredth

setenta /se'tenta/ *a* and *m*, seventy; seventieth

setentavo /seten'taβo/ *a* and *m*, seventieth

setentón /seten'ton/ **(-ona)** *n* septuagenarian

seter /'seter/ *m*, setter (dog)

setiembre /se'tiembre/ *m*. See **septiembre**

seto /'seto/ *m*, fence; hedge

seudo /'seuðo/ *a* pseudo

seudónimo /seu'ðonimo/ *m*, pseudonym

severamente /seβera'mente/ *adv* severely, harshly

severidad /seβeri'ðað/ *f*, severity; harshness; strictness, rigor; austerity, seriousness

severo /se'βero/ *a* severe; harsh; strict, rigid, scrupulous, exact; austere, serious

sevillanas /seβi'yanas; seβi'ʎanas/ *f pl*, Sevillian dance and its music

sevillano /seβi'yano; seβi'ʎano/ **(-na)** *a* and *n* of or from Seville, Sevillian

sexagenario /seksahe'nario/ **(-ia)** *n* sexagenarian

sexagésimo /seksa'hesimo/ *a* sixtieth

sexismo /sek'sismo/ *m*, sexism

sexo /'sekso/ *m*, sex; (sexual) organ

sexología /seksolo'hia/ *f*, sexology

sexólogo /sek'sologo/ **(-ga)** *n* sexologist

sexta /'seksta/ *f*, *Eccl.* sext; *Mus.* sixth

sexteto /seks'teto/ *m*, sextet

sexto /'seksto/ *a* sixth

sextuplicación /sekstuplika'sion; sekstuplika'θion/ *f*, multiplication by six

sextuplicar /sekstupli'kar/ *vt* to multiply by six, sextuple

séxtuplo /'sekstuplo/ *a* sixfold

sexualidad /seksuali'ðað/ *f*, sexuality

si /si/ *m*, *Mus.* B, seventh note of the scale. *conjunc* if; whether; even if, although. In conditional clause, **si,** meaning if, is followed by indicative tense unless statement be contrary to fact (e.g. *Si pierdes el tren, volverás a casa,* If you miss your train you will return home, but *Si hubieran venido habríamos ido al campo,* If they had come (but they didn't) we would have gone to the country). **Si** is used at the beginning of a clause to make expressions of doubt, desire, or affirmation more emphatic (e.g. *¡Si lo sabrá él, con toda su experiencia!* Of course he knows it, with all his experience. *¿Si será falsa la noticia?* Can the news be false?) **Si** also means whether (e.g. *Me preguntaron si era médico o militar,* They asked me whether I was a doctor or a soldier). Sometimes means even if, although (e.g. *Si viniesen no lo harían,* Even if they came they would not do it. *como si,* as if. *por si acaso,* in case, in the event of. *si bien,* although.

sí /si/ *pers pron reflexive 3rd pers m,* and *f, sing* and *pl* himself, herself, itself, themselves. Always used with prep. (e.g. *para sí,* for himself, herself, etc. *de por sí,* separately, on its own. *decir para sí,* to say to oneself)

sí /si/ *adv* yes. **sí** or **sí que** is frequently used to emphasize a verb generally in contrast to a previous negative (e.g. *Ellos no lo harán, pero yo sí,* They won't do it but I will). Often translated by "did" (e.g. *No lo vi todo, pero lo que sí vi,* I didn't see it all, but what I did see...). *m,* assent; yes; consent. **dar el sí,** to say yes; agree; accept an offer of marriage

siamés /sia'mes/ **(-esa)** *a* and *n* Siamese. *m,* Thai (language)

sibarita /siβa'rita/ *a* sybaritic. *mf* sybarite

sibarítico /siβa'ritiko/ *a* sybaritic; sensual

sibaritismo /siβari'tismo/ *m,* sybaritism

siberiano /siβe'riano/ **(-na)** *a* and *n* Siberian

sibila /si'βila/ *f,* sibyl

sibilante /siβi'lante/ *a* sibilant

sibilino /siβi'lino/ *a* sibylline

sicario /si'kario/ *m,* paid assassin

Sicilia /si'silia; si'θilia/ Sicily

siciliano /sisi'liano; siθi'liano/ **(-na)** *a* and *n* Sicilian

sicoanálisis /sikoa'nalisis/ *m,* psychoanalysis

sicoanalista /sikoana'lista/ *mf* psychoanalyst

sicoanalizar /sikoanali'sar; sikoanali'θar/ *vt* to psychoanalyze

sicofanta, sicofante /siko'fanta, siko'fante/ *m,* sycophant

sicología /sikolo'hia/ *f,* psychology

sicológico /siko'lohiko/ *a* psychological

sicólogo /si'kologo/ **(-ga)** *n* psychologist

sicomoro /siko'moro/ *m,* sycamore

sicopático /siko'patiko/ *a* psychopathic

sicosis /si'kosis/ *f, Med.* psychosis

sicoterapia /sikote'rapia/ *f,* psychotherapy

SIDA /'siða/ *m,* AIDS

sideral, sidéreo /siðe'ral, si'ðereo/ *a* sidereal

sidra /'siðra/ *f,* cider

siega /'siega/ *f,* reaping, harvesting; harvest time; harvest, crop

siembra /'siembra/ *f, Agr.* sowing; seedtime; sown field

siempre /'siempre/ *adv* always. **s. que,** provided that; whenever. **para s.,** forever. **por s. jamás,** for always, for ever and ever

siemprevivar /siempre'βiβa/ *f, Bot.* everlasting flower. **s. mayor,** houseleek

sien /sien/ *f, Anat.* temple

sierpe /'sierpe/ *f,* serpent, snake; anything that wriggles; kite (toy); *Bot.* sucker; hideous person

sierra /'sierra/ *f,* saw; ridge of mountains; sawfish; slope; hillside. **s. de cerrojero,** hacksaw. **s. de cinta,** handsaw

siervo /'sierβo/ **(-va)** *n* slave; servant; serf

siesta /'siesta/ *f,* noonday heat; afternoon nap

siete /'siete/ *a* seven; seventh. *m,* seven; seventh (days of the month); playing card with seven spots; number seven. **las s.,** seven o'clock. *Inf.* **más que s.,** more than somewhat, extremely

sietemesino /sieteme'sino/ **(-na)** *n* seven-month-old child; *Fig. Inf.* young cock

sífilis /'sifilis/ *f,* syphilis

sifilítico /sifi'litiko/ **(-ca)** *a* and *n* syphilitic

sifón /si'fon/ *m,* siphon; siphon bottle; soda water; *Mech.* trap

sigilar /sihi'lar/ *vt* to seal; hide, conceal

sigilo /si'hilo/ *m,* seal; secrecy, concealment; silence, reserve

sigiloso /sihi'loso/ *a* secret, silent

sigla /'sigla/ *f,* acronym

siglo /'siglo/ *m,* century; long time, age; social intercourse, age, world. **s. de oro,** golden age. **en** *or* **por los siglos de los siglos,** for ever and ever

signar /sig'nar/ *vt* to sign; make the sign of the cross over; *vr* cross oneself

signatario /signa'tario/ **(-ia)** *a* and *n* signatory

signatura /signa'tura/ *f, Print.* signature; mark, sign; *Mus.* signature

significación /signifika'sion; signifika'θion/ *f,* **significado** *m,* meaning; importance, significance

significante /signifi'kante/ *a* significant

significar /signifi'kar/ *vt* to signify, indicate; mean; publish, make known; *vi* represent, mean; be worth

significativo /signifika'tiβo/ *a* significant

signo /'signo/ *m,* sign, indication, token; sign, character; *Math.* symbol; sign of the zodiac; *Mus.* sign; *Med.* symptom; *Eccl.* gesture of benediction; destiny, fate

siguemepollo /sigeme'poyo; sigeme'poʎo/ *m, Inf.* streamer

siguiente /si'giente/ *a* following; next, subsequent. **el día s.,** the next day

sílaba /'silaβa/ *f,* syllable

silabario /sila'βario/ *m,* speller, spelling book

silabear /silaβe'ar/ *vi* and *vt* to pronounce by syllables, syllabize

silabeo /silaβe'o/ *m,* pronouncing syllable by syllable, syllabication

silábico /si'laβiko/ *a* syllabic

sílabo /'silaβo/ *m,* syllabus, list

silba /'silβa/ *f,* hissing (as a sign of disapproval)

silbador /silβa'ðor/ **(-ra)** *a* whistling; hissing. *n* whistler; one who hisses

silbar /sil'βar/ *vi* to whistle; whizz, rush through the air; *vi* and *vt Theat.* hiss

silbato /sil'βato/ *m,* whistle; air hole

silbido, silbo /sil'βiðo, 'silβo/ *m,* whistle, whistling; hiss, hissing

silenciador /silensia'ðor; silenθia'ðor/ *m,* (*Auto.* firearms) silencer

silenciar /silen'siar; silen'θiar/ *vt* to silence; keep secret

silenciario /silen'siario; silen'θiario/ *a* vowed to perpetual silence

silencio /si'lensio; si'lenθio/ *m,* silence; noiselessness, quietness; omission, disregard; *Mus.* rest. **en s.,** in silence; quietly; uncomplainingly. **pasar en s.** (una cosa), to pass over (something) in silence, omit. **s. de muerte,** deathly silence

silencioso /silen'sioso; silen'θioso/ *a* silent; noiseless; tranquil, quiet. *m,* (*Auto.* firearms) silencer

sílfide /'silfiðe/ *f,* **silfo** *m,* sylph

silicato /sili'kato/ *m, Chem.* silicate

sílice /'silise; 'siliθe/ *f, Chem.* silica

silla /'siya; 'siʎa/ *f,* chair; riding saddle; *Mech.* rest, saddle; *Eccl.* see. **s. de manos,** sedan chair. **s. de montar,** riding saddle. **s. de posta,** post chaise. **s. de ruedas,** wheelchair. **s. de tijera,** deck chair; campstool. **s. giratoria,** swivel chair. **s. poltrona,** easy chair. *Inf.* **pegársele la s.,** to overstay one's welcome

sillar /si'ʎar; si'ʎar/ *m,* ashlar, stone, quarry stone; horseback

sillería /siye'ria; siʎe'ria/ *f,* set of chairs; pew, choir stalls; chair factory; shop where chairs are sold; chair making; *Mas.* ashlar masonry

sillero /si'yero; si'ʎero/ **(-ra)** *n* chair maker or seller; saddler

silleta /si'yeta; si'ʎeta/ *f*, bedpan; fireman's lift

silletero /siye'tero; siʎe'tero/ *m*, runner, sedan chair carrier

sillín /si'yin; si'ʎin/ *m*, light riding saddle; seat, saddle (of bicycles, etc.)

sillón /si'yon; si'ʎon/ *m*, armchair; sidesaddle; *Lat. Am.* rocking chair. **s.-cama,** reclining chair. **s. de mimbres,** bamboo chair

silo /'silo/ *m, Agr.* silo; dark cavern, dark cave

silogismo /silo'hismo/ *m*, syllogism

silogístico /silo'histiko/ *a* syllogistic

silueta /si'lueta/ *f*, silhouette; figure

silúrico /si'luriko/ *a* silurian

siluro /si'luro/ *m*, catfish; *Nav.* self-propelling torpedo

silva /'silβa/ *f*, literary miscellany; metrical form

silvestre /sil'βestre/ *a Bot.* wild; sylvan; uncultivated; savage

silvicultor /silβikul'tor/ *m*, forester

silvicultura /silβikul'tura/ *f*, forestry

sima /'sima/ *f*, abyss, chasm

simbiosis /sim'biosis/ *f*, symbiosis

simbólico /sim'boliko/ *a* symbolical

simbolismo /simbo'lismo/ *m*, symbolism

simbolista /simbo'lista/ *mf* symbolist

simbolización /simbolisa'sion; simboliθa'θion/ *f*, symbolization

simbolizar /simboli'sar; simboli'θar/ *vt* to symbolize, represent

símbolo /'simbolo/ *m*, symbol. **s. de la fe,** *Eccl.* Creed

simetría /sime'tria/ *f*, symmetry

simétrico /si'metriko/ *a* symmetric; symmetrical

simetrizar /simetri'sar; simetri'θar/ *vt* to make symmetrical

símico /'simiko/ *a* simian

simiente /si'miente/ *f*, seed; semen; germ, genesis, origin

simiesco /si'miesko/ *a* apish, ape-like

símil /'simil/ *a* similar. *m*, comparison; simile

similar /simi'lar/ *a* similar

similitud /simili'tuð/ *f*, similarity

simio /'simio/ **(-ia)** *n* ape

simón /si'mon/ *m*, horse cab; cabdriver

simonía /simo'nia/ *f*, simony

simpatía /simpa'tia/ *f*, liking, understanding, affection; fellow feeling; sympathy

simpático /sim'patiko/ *a* friendly, nice, decent, congenial; sympathetic. **gran s.,** *Anat.* sympathetic

simpatizar /simpati'sar; simpati'θar/ *vi* to get on well, be congenial

simple /'simple/ *a* simple; single, not double; insipid; easy; plain, unadorned; stupid, silly; pure, unmixed; easily deceived, simple; naïve, ingenuous; mere; mild, meek. *mf* simpleton; fool

simpleza /sim'plesa; sim'pleθa/ *f*, foolishness, stupidity; simplicity

simplicidad /simplisi'ðað; simpliθi'ðað/ *f*, simplicity; candor, ingenuousness

simplicísimo /simpli'sisimo; simpli'θisimo/ *a sup* most simple, exceedingly simple

simplificable /simplifi'kaβle/ *a* simplifiable

simplificación /simplifika'sion; simplifika'θion/ *f*, simplification, simplifying

simplificador /simplifika'ðor/ *a* simplifying

simplificar /simplifi'kar/ *vt* to simplify

simplista /sim'plista/ *mf* herbalist

simulación /simula'sion; simula'θion/ *f*, pretense, simulation

simulacro /simu'lakro/ *m*, image, simulacrum; vision, fancy; *Mil.* mock battle

simuladamente /simulaða'mente/ *adv* pretendedly

simulador /simula'ðor/ **(-ra)** *a* feigned. *n* dissembler

simular /simu'lar/ *vt* to feign, pretend

simultanear /simultane'ar/ *vt* to perform simultaneously

simultaneidad /simultanei'ðað/ *f*, simultaneousness

simultáneo /simul'taneo/ *a* simultaneous

simún /si'mun/ *m*, sandstorm

sin /sin/ *prep* without (e.g. *Lo hizo s. hablar*, He did it without speaking). **s. embargo,** nevertheless. **s. fin,** endless. **s. hilos,** radio, wireless

sinagoga /sina'goga/ *f*, synagogue

sinapismo /sina'pismo/ *m, Med.* mustard plaster; *Inf.* pest, bore

sincerarse /sinse'rarse; sinθe'rarse/ *vr* to justify oneself; vindicate one's actions

sinceridad /sinseri'ðað; sinθeri'ðað/ *f*, sincerity

sincero /sin'sero; sin'θero/ *a* sincere

síncopa /'sinkopa/ *f, Mus.* syncopation; *Gram.* syncope

sincopar /sinko'par/ *vt* to syncopate; abbreviate

síncope /'sinkope/ *m*, syncope

sincrónico /sin'kroniko/ *a* synchronous

sincronismo /sinkro'nismo/ *m*, synchronism

sincronizar /sinkroni'sar; sinkroni'θar/ *vt* to synchronize; *Radio.* tune in

sindéresis /sin'deresis/ *f*, discretion, good sense

sindicación /sindika'sion; sindika'θion/ *f*, syndication

sindicado /sindi'kaðo/ *m*, syndicate

sindical /sindi'kal/ *a* syndical

sindicalismo /sindika'lismo/ *m*, syndicalism, trade unionism

sindicalista /sindika'lista/ *mf* syndicalist, trade unionist. *a* syndicalistic, trade unionist

sindicar /sindi'kar/ *vt* to accuse, charge; censure; syndicate

sindicato /sindi'kato/ *m*, syndicate; trade union. **s. gremial,** trade union. **S. Internacional de Trabajadoras de la Aguja,** International Ladies' Garment Workers' Union

sindicatura /sindika'tura/ *f*, (official) receivership

síndico /'sindiko/ *m, Com.* receiver, trustee

síndrome /'sindrome/ *m*, syndrome. **síndrome de inmunidad deficiente adquirida** acquired immunity deficiency syndrome

sinecura /sine'kura/ *f*, sinecure

sinergia /si'nerhia/ *f*, synergy

sinfín /sin'fin/ *m*, countless number

sinfonía /sinfo'nia/ *f*, symphony

sinfónico /sin'foniko/ *a* symphonic

sinfonista /sinfo'nista/ *mf* composer of symphonies, player in a symphony orchestra

sinfonola /sinfo'nola/ *f*, jukebox

singladura /siŋgla'ðura/ *f, Naut.* day's sailing; nautical twenty-four hours (beginning at midday)

singlar /siŋ'glar/ *vi Naut.* to sail a given course

singular /siŋgu'lar/ *a* singular, single; individual; extraordinary, remarkable. *a* and *m, Gram.* singular

singularidad /siŋgulari'ðað/ *f*, individuality, peculiarity; strangeness, remarkableness; oddness, eccentricity

singularizar /siŋgulari'sar; siŋgulari'θar/ *vt* to particularize, single out; *Gram.* make singular, singularize; *vr* distinguish oneself, stand out; be distinguished (by)

sinhueso /sin'ueso/ *f, Inf.* tongue (organ of speech)

siniestra /si'niestra/ *f*, left, lefthand

siniestro /si'niestro/ *a* left (side); vicious, perverse; sinister; unlucky. *m*, viciousness, depravity (gen. *pl*); shipwreck, sinking; disaster, catastrophe; *Com.* damage, loss

sinnúmero /sin'numero/ *m*, countless number

sino /'sino/ *m*, fate, destiny. *conjunc* but; except (e.g. *No lo hicieron ellos s. yo*, They didn't do it, I did. *no... s.*, not..., but); only (e.g. *No sólo lo dijo él s. ella*, Not only he said it, but she did too)

sínodo /'sinoðo/ *m*, (*Eccl. Astron.*) synod; council

sinología /sinolo'hia/ *f*, sinology

sinólogo /si'nologo/ *m*, sinologist

sinonimia /sino'nimia/ *f*, synonymy

sinónimo /si'nonimo/ *a* synonymous. *m*, synonym

sinopsis /si'nopsis/ *f*, synopsis

sinóptico /si'noptiko/ *a* synoptic

sinrazón /sinra'son; sinra'θon/ *f*, injustice, wrong

sinsabor /sinsa'βor/ *m*, unpleasantness, trouble; grief, anxiety

sintáctico /sin'taktiko/ *a* syntactic

sintaxis /sin'taksis/ *f*, syntax

síntesis /'sintesis/ *f*, synthesis

sintético /sin'tetiko/ *a* synthetic

sintetizar /sinteti'sar; sinteti'θar/ *vt* to synthesize

síntoma /'sintoma/ *m*, symptom

sintomático /sinto'matiko/ *a* symptomatic

sintomatología /sintomatolo'hia/ *f*, symptomatology

sintonización /sintonisa'sion; sintoniθa'θion/ *f*, *Radio.* tuning in

sintonizador /sintonisa'ðor; sintoniθa'ðor/ *m*, *Radio.* tuner

sintonizar /sintoni'sar; sintoni'θar/ *vt Radio.* to tune in

sinuosidad /sinuosi'ðað/ *f*, sinuosity

sinuoso /sin'uoso/ *a* sinuous, winding

sinvergüenza /simber'guensa; simber'guenθa/ *mf* rascal, knave, rogue

sinvergüenzada /simberguen'saða; simberguen'θaða/ *f*, *Lat. Am.* dirty thing (to do)

Sión /'sion/ Zion

sionismo /sio'nismo/ *m*, Zionism

sionista /sio'nista/ *a* and *mf* Zionist

siquiatra /si'kiatra/ *m*, psychiatrist

siquiatría /sikia'tria/ *f*, psychiatry

síquico /'sikiko/ *a* psychic

siquiera /si'kiera/ *conjunc* although, even if. **s.... s.**, whether... or. *adv* at least; even (e.g. *Hay que pedir mucho para tener s. la mitad*, One must ask a great deal to get even half). **ni s.**, not even (e.g. *No había nadie, ni s. un perro*, There was no one, not even a dog)

Siracusa /sira'kusa/ Syracuse

siracusano /siraku'sano/ **(-na)** *a* and *n* Syracusan

sirena /si'rena/ *f*, mermaid, siren; siren; foghorn

sirga /'sirga/ *f*, towline

sirgar /sir'gar/ *vt Naut.* to track, tow

Siria /'siria/ Syria

sirio /'sirio/ **(-ia)** *a* and *n* Syrian. *m*, Sirius

siroco /si'roko/ *m*, sirocco

sirte /'sirte/ *f*, sandbank, submerged rock

sirvienta /sir'βienta/ *f*, female servant

sirviente /sir'βiente/ *a* serving. *m*, servant

sisa /'sisa/ *f*, pilfering; *Sew.* dart. **s. dorada,** gold lacquer

sisador /sisa'ðor/ *a* filcher, pilferer

sisar /si'sar/ *vt* to pilfer, filch, steal; *Sew.* take in, make darts in

sisear /sise'ar/ *vi* and *vt* to hiss (disapproval); sizzle

sísmico /'sismiko/ *a* seismic

sismógrafo /sis'mografo/ *m*, seismograph

sismología /sismolo'hia/ *f*, seismology

sismológico /sismo'lohiko/ *a* seismological

sismómetro /sis'mometro/ *m*, seismometer

sistema /sis'tema/ *m*, system. **s. ferroviario,** railroad system. **s. métrico,** metric system

sistemático /siste'matiko/ *a* systematic

sistematización /sistematisa'sion; sistematiθa'θion/ *f*, systematization

sistematizar /sistemati'sar; sistemati'θar/ *vt* to systematize

sístole /'sistole/ *f*, systole

sitiador /sitia'ðor/ *a* besieging. *m*, besieger

sitiar /si'tiar/ *vt Mil.* to lay siege to; surround, besiege

sitio /'sitio/ *m*, place, spot; room, space; site; locality; *Mil.* siege, blockade; *Lat. Am.* taxi stand **No hay s.,** There's no room

sito /'sito/ *past part* situated, located

situación /situa'sion; situa'θion/ *f*, situation; position; circumstances; condition, state; location

situado /si'tuaðo/ *past part* situated, placed. *m*, income, interest

situar /si'tuar/ *vt* to situate, locate, place; assign funds; *vr* place oneself

snobismo /sno'βismo/ *m*, snobbery

so /so/ *prep* under (used only with **color, pena, pretexto, capa**) (e.g. *so color de*, under the pretext of). *interj* **¡So!** Whoa! (to horses); *Lat. Am.* Hush!

soba /'soβa/ *f*, rubbing; kneading; massage; beating; handling, touching

sobacal /soβa'kal/ *a* underarm, axillary

sobaco /so'βako/ *m*, armpit; *Bot.* axil

sobajar /soβa'har/ *vt* to squeeze, press

sobaquera /soβa'kera/ *f*, *Sew.* armhole; dress shield

sobar /so'βar/ *vt* to rub; knead; massage; beat, thrash; handle, touch, paw (persons); soften

soberanear /soβerane'ar/ *vi* to tyrannize, domineer

soberanía /soβera'nia/ *f*, sovereignty; dominance, sway, rule; dignity, majesty

soberano /soβe'rano/ **(-na)** *a* sovereign; superb; regal, majestic. *n* ruler, lord. *m*, sovereign (coin)

soberbia /so'βerβia/ *f*, arrogance, haughtiness; conceit, presumption; ostentation, pomp; rage, anger

soberbio /so'βerβio/ *a* haughty, arrogant; conceited; superb, magnificent; lofty, soaring; spirited (of horses)

sobón /so'βon/ *a Inf.* overdemonstrative, mushy; *Inf.* lazy

sobordo /so'βorðo/ *m*, *Naut.* manifest, freight list

sobornación /soβorna'sion; soβorna'θion/ *f*, bribing; bribery

sobornador /soβorna'ðor/ **(-ra)** *a* bribing. *n* briber

sobornar /soβor'nar/ *vt* to bribe

soborno /so'βorno/ *m*, bribing; bribe; inducement

sobra /'soβra/ *f*, excess, surplus; insult, outrage; *pl* leftovers (from a meal); remains, residue; rubbish, trash. **de s.,** in abundance; in excess, surplus; unnecessary, superfluous; too well

sobradamente /soβraða'mente/ *adv* abundantly; in excess

sobrado /so'βraðo/ *a* excessive; brazen; bold; wealthy, rich. *m*, garret

sobrante /so'βrante/ *a* surplus, leftover, remaining. *m*, remainder, surplus, excess

sobrar /so'βrar/ *vt* to exceed; have too much of (e.g. *Me sobran mantas*, I have too many blankets); *vi* be superfluous; remain, be left. *Inf.* **Aquí sobro yo,** I am in the way here, My presence is superfluous

sobrasada /soβra'saða/ *f*, spicy sausage

sobre /'soβre/ *prep* upon, on; above, over; concerning, about; apart from, besides; about (e.g. *s. las nueve*, at about nine o'clock) (indicates approximation); toward; after. *m*, envelope; address, superscription. **s. cero,** above freezing (Fahrenheit); above zero (Centigrade). **s. el nivel del mar,** above sea level. **s. manera,** excessively, extremely. **s. todo,** especially

sobreabundancia /soβreaβun'dansia; soβreaβun'danθia/ *f*, superabundance, excess

sobreabundante /soβreaβun'dante/ *a* superabundant

sobreabundar /soβreaβun'dar/ *vi* to be superabundant

sobreagudo /soβrea'guðo/ *a* and *m*, *Mus.* treble (pitch)

sobrealiento /soβrea'liento/ *m*, heavy, painful breathing

sobrealimentación /soβrealimenta'sion; soβrealimenta'θion/ *f*, overfeeding; *Auto.* supercharge

sobrealimentar /soβrealimen'tar/ *vt Auto.* to supercharge

sobreasar /soβrea'sar/ *vt* to roast or cook again

sobrecama /soβre'kama/ *f*, bedspread, quilt

sobrecarga /soβre'karga/ *f*, overload; rope, etc., for securing bales and packs; additional trouble or anxiety

sobrecargar /soβrekar'gar/ *vt* to overload; weigh down; *Sew.* oversew, fell

sobrecargo /soβre'kargo/ *m*, *Naut.* purser; flight attendant

sobrecarta /soβre'karta/ *f*, envelope (for a letter)

sobreceja /soβre'seha; soβre'θeha/ *f*, brow, lower forehead; frown

sobrecejo /soβre'seho; soβre'θeho/ *m*, frown

sobrecielo /soβre'sielo; soβre'θielo/ *m*, canopy

sobrecoger /soβreko'her/ *vt* to take by surprise; *vr* be frightened or apprehensive

sobrecogimiento /soβrekohi'miento/ *m*, fright, apprehension

sobrecomida /soβreko'miða/ *f*, dessert

sobrecoser /soβreko'ser/ *vt Sew.* to oversew, whip

sobrecrecer /soβrekre'ser; soβrekre'θer/ *vi irr* to grow too much. See **conocer**

sobrecubierta /soβreku'βierta/ *f*, second lid or cover; dust jacket (of a book); *Naut.* upper deck

sobrecuello /soβre'kueyo; soβre'kueʎo/ *m*, overcollar; loose collar

sobredicho /soβre'ðitʃo/ *a* aforementioned, aforesaid

sobredorar /soβreðo'rar/ *vt* to gild (metals); make excuses for

sobreedificar /soβreeðifi'kar/ *vt* to build upon or above

sobreexcitar /soβreekssi'tar; soβreeksθi'tar/ *vt* to overexcite

sobrefaz /soβre'fas; soβre'faθ/ *f*, surface, exterior

sobreganar /soβrega'nar/ *vt* to make an excess profit

sobreguarda /soβre'guarða/ *m*, head guard; extra or second guard

sobreherido /soβree'riðo/ *a* lightly wounded

sobrehilar /soβrei'lar/ *vt* to oversew or overcast. See **prohibir**

sobrehumano /soβreu'mano/ *a* superhuman

sobrellenar /soβreye'nar; soβreʎe'nar/ *vt* to fill full

sobrellevar /soβreye'βar; soβreʎe'βar/ *vt* to help in the carrying of a burden; endure, bear; make excuses for, overlook; help

sobremesa /soβre'mesa/ *f*, tablecloth; after-dinner conversation. **de s.**, *Fig.* at the dinner table

sobrenadar /soβrena'ðar/ *vi* to float

sobrenatural /soβrenatu'ral/ *a* supernatural; extraordinary, singular

sobrenombre /soβre'nombre/ *m*, additional surname; nickname

sobrentender /soβrenten'der/ *vt irr* to take for granted, understand as a matter of course; *vr* go without saying. See **entender**

sobrepaga /soβre'paga/ *f*, overpayment; extra pay

sobreparto /soβre'parto/ *m*, time after parturition; afterbirth

sobrepasar /soβrepa'sar/ *vt* to exceed; outdo, excel

sobrepelliz /soβrepe'yis; soβrepe'ʎiθ/ *f*, surplice

sobreponer /soβrepo'ner/ *vt irr* to place over; overlap; *vr* rise above (circumstances); dominate (persons). See **poner**

sobreprecio /soβre'presio; soβre'preθio/ *m*, extra charge, rise in price

sobreproducción /soβreproðuk'sion; soβreproðuk'θion/ *f*, overproduction

sobrepuerta /soβre'puerta/ *f*, curtain pelmet; door curtain

sobrepujar /soβrepu'har/ *vt* to excel, surpass, outdo

sobrequilla /soβre'kiya; soβre'kiʎa/ *f, Naut.* keelson

sobrerrealismo /soβrerrea'lismo/ *m*, surrealism

sobrerrealista /soβrerrea'lista/ *a* and *mf* surrealist

sobresaliente /soβresa'liente/ *a* overhanging; projecting; distinctive, outstanding; excellent, remarkable. *m*, "excellent" (mark in examinations). *mf Theat.* understudy

sobresalir /soβresa'lir/ *vi irr* to overhang, project; stand out; be conspicuous or noticeable; excel; distinguish oneself. See **salir**

sobresaltar /soβresal'tar/ *vt* to assail, rush upon; startle, frighten suddenly; *vi Art.* stand out, be striking; *vr* be startled or frightened

sobresalto /soβre'salto/ *m*, sudden attack; unexpected shock; agitation; sudden fear. **de s.**, unexpectedly

sobresanar /soβresa'nar/ *vi* to heal superficially but not deeply; conceal, dissemble

sobrescribir /soβreskri'βir/ *vt* to label; address, superscribe. *Past Part.* **sobrescrito**

sobrescrito /soβres'krito/ *m*, address, superscription

sobresello /soβre'seyo; soβre'seʎo/ *m*, second seal

sobrestante /soβres'tante/ *m*, overseer; supervisor; foreman; inspector

sobresueldo /soβre'sueldo/ *m*, additional salary, bonus

sobresuelo /soβre'suelo/ *m*, second flooring

sobretarde /soβre'tarðe/ *f*, early evening, late afternoon

sobretodo /soβre'toðo/ *m*, overcoat

sobrevenida /soβreβe'niða/ *f*, sudden arrival

sobrevenir /soβreβe'nir/ *vi irr* occur, take place; supervene. See **venir**

sobrevidriera /soβreβi'ðriera/ *f*, storm window; wiremesh window guard

sobrevienta /soβre'βienta/ *f*, gust of wind; fury, violence; shock, surprise. **a s.**, suddenly

sobreviviente /soβreβi'βiente/ *a* surviving. *mf* survivor

sobrevivir /soβreβi'βir/ *vi* to survive

sobriedad /soβrie'ðað/ *f*, sobriety, moderation

sobrina /so'βrina/ *f*, niece

sobrino /so'βrino/ *m*, nephew

sobrio /'soβrio/ *a* sober, moderate, temperate

socaliña /soka'liɲa/ *f*, cunning, craft

socaliñero /okali'ɲero/ **(-ra)** *a* cunning. *n* trickster

socalzar /sokal'sar; sokal'θar/ *vt Mas.* to underpin

socapa /so'kapa/ *f*, blind, pretext. **a s.**, secretly; cautiously

socarra /so'karra/ *f*, scorching, singeing; craftiness

socarrón /soka'rron/ *a* cunning, deceitful; malicious, sly (of humor, etc.)

socarronería /sokarrone'ria/ *f*, cunning, craftiness; slyness (of humor, etc.); knavish action

socava /so'kaβa/ *f*, undermining; *Agr.* hoeing round tree roots

socavar /soka'βar/ *vt* to undermine

sociabilidad /sosiaβili'ðað; soθiaβili'ðað/ *f*, sociability

sociable /so'siaβle; so'θiaβle/ *a* sociable; social

social /so'sial; so'θial/ *a* social

socialdemócrata /sosialde'mokrata; soθialde'mokrata/ *a* and *mf* social democrat

socialismo /sosia'lismo; soθia'lismo/ *m*, socialism

socialista /sosia'lista; soθia'lista/ *mf* socialist. *a* socialistic

socialización /sosialisa'sion; soθialiθa'θion/ *f*, socialization

socializar /sosiali'sar; soθiali'θar/ *vt* to socialize

sociedad /sosie'ðað; soθie'ðað/ *f*, society; association; *Com.* partnership; *Com.* company. *Com.* **s. anónima**, incorporated company, limited company. **S. de las Naciones**, League of Nations. **s. de socorros mutuos**, mutual aid society. **s. en comandita**, private company

socio /'sosio; 'soθio/ **(-ia)** *n* associate, partner; member. **s. comanditario**, *Com.* silent partner

sociología /sosiolo'hia; soθiolo'hia/ *f*, sociology

sociológico /sosio'lohiko; soθio'lohiko/ *a* sociological

sociólogo /so'siologo; so'θiologo/ **(-ga)** *n* sociologist

socollada /soko'yaða; soko'ʎaða/ *f, Naut.* flapping (of sails); pitching (of a ship)

socolor /soko'lor/ *m*, pretext. *adv* (also **so c.**) under pretext

socorredor /sokorre'ðor/ **(-ra)** *a* aiding, succoring. *n* helper

socorrer /soko'rrer/ *vt* to aid, succor, assist; pay on account

socorrido /soko'rriðo/ *a* helpful, generous, prompt to assist; well-equipped, well-furnished; well-supplied

socorro /so'korro/ *m*, aid, help, assistance; payment on account; *Mil.* relief (provisions or arms)

socrático /so'kratiko/ *a* a socratic

sodio /'soðio/ *m*, sodium

sodomía /soðo'mia/ *f*, sodomy

sodomita /soðo'mita/ *mf* sodomite. *a* sodomitic

soez /so'es; so'eθ/ *a* base, vile; vulgar

sofá /so'fa/ *m*, sofa, couch

sofaldar /sofal'dar/ *vt* to tuck up the skirts; disclose, reveal

sofisma /so'fisma/ *m*, sophism, fallacy

sofista /so'fista/ *a* sophistic. *mf* sophist, quibbler

sofistería /sofiste'ria/ *f*, sophistry

sofístico /so'fistiko/ a sophistic, fallacious

soflama /so'flama/ f, thin flame; glow; flush, blush; specious promise, deception

soflamar /sofla'mar/ vt to shame, make blush; promise with intent to deceive, swindle; vr Cul. burn

sofocación /sofoka'sion; sofoka'θion/ f, suffocation, smothering; shame; anger

sofocador, sofocante /sofoka'ðor, sofo'kante/ a suffocating; stifling

sofocar /sofo'kar/ vt to suffocate, smother; extinguish; dominate, oppress; pester, importune; shame, make blush, make angry; agitate; vr be ashamed; be angry

sofocleo /sofo'kleo/ a Sophoclean

sofoco /so'foko/ m, mortification, chagrin; shame; anger; suffocation, smothering; hot flush

sofreír /sofre'ir/ vt irr to fry lightly. See **reír**

sofrenada /sofre'naða/ f, sudden check, pulling up short (of horses); harsh scolding; moral restraint

sofrenar /sofre'nar/ vt to pull up, check suddenly (horses); scold harshly; restrain, repress (emotions)

sofrito /so'frito/ m, sauce of sautéed tomatoes, peppers, onions, and garlic

software /'sof0wer/ m, software

soga /'soga/ f, rope; land measure (varies in length). m, Inf. rogue, knave

soguería /soge'ria/ f, rope making; rope walk; rope shop; ropes

soguero /so'gero/ m, rope maker or seller

soja /'soha/ f, soybean

sojuzgador /sohusga'ðor; sohuθga'ðor/ (-ra) a conquering, oppressive. n conqueror, oppressor

sojuzgar /sohus'gar; sohuθ'gar/ vt to conquer, oppress, subdue

sol /sol/ m, sun; sunlight; day; Peruvian coin; Mus. G, fifth note of the scale, sol. **de s. a s.,** from sunrise to sunset. **hacer s.,** to be sunny. **morir uno sin s. sin luz y sin moscas,** Inf. to die abandoned by all. **no dejar a s. ni a sombra,** Inf. to follow everywhere; pester constantly. **tomar el s.,** to bask in the sun

solado /so'laðo/ m, paving; tile floor

solador /sola'ðor/ m, tiler

solamente /sola'mente/ adv only; exclusively; merely, solely. **s. que,** only that; nothing but

solana /so'lana/ f, sunny corner; Solarium

solanera /sola'nera/ f, sunburn; sunny spot

solapa /so'lapa/ f, lapel; excuse, pretext. **de s.,** Inf. secretly

solapado /sola'paðo/ a cunning, sly

solapar /sola'par/ vt Sew. to provide with lapels; Sew. cause to overlap; dissemble; vi Sew. overlap

solapo /so'lapo/ m, lapel; Inf. slap, buffet. **a s.,** Inf. secretly, slyly

solar /so'lar/ vt irr to pave; sole (shoes). m, family seat, manor house; building site; lineage, family. a solar. See **colar**

solariego /sola'riego/ a memorial; of an old and noble family

solas, a /'solas, a/ adv alone, in private

solaz /so'las; so'laθ/ m, consolation; pleasure; relief, relaxation. **a s.,** enjoyably, pleasantly

solazar /sola'sar; sola'θar/ vt to solace, comfort; amuse, entertain; rest; vr be comforted; find pleasure (in)

soldada /sol'daða/ f, salary, wages, emoluments; (Nav. Mil.) pay

soldadesca /solda'ðeska/ f, soldiering, military profession; troops. **a la s.,** in a soldier-like way

soldadesco /solda'ðesko/ a military, soldier

soldado /sol'daðo/ m, soldier; defender, partisan. **s. raso,** Mil. private

soldador /solda'ðor/ m, solderer, welder; soldering iron

soldadura /solda'ðura/ f, welding, soldering; correction, emendation

soldar /sol'dar/ vt irr to weld; mend by welding; correct, put right; Mil. wipe out, liquidate. See **contar**

solecismo /sole'sismo; sole'θismo/ m, solecism

soledad /sole'ðað/ f, solitude; loneliness; homesickness; pl melancholy Andalusian song and dance (also f pl. **soleares**)

solemne /so'lemne/ a solemn; magnificent; formal; serious, grave, important; pompous; Inf. downright, complete

solemnidad /solemni'ðað/ f, solemnity; magnificence; formality; gravity, seriousness; solemn ceremony; religious ceremony; legal formality

solemnización /solemnisa'sion; solemniθa'θion/ f, solemnization

solemnizar /solemni'sar; solemni'θar/ vt to solemnize, celebrate; extol

soler /so'ler/ vi irr defective to be in the habit, be used; happen frequently (e.g. Solía hacerlo los lunes, I generally did it on Mondays. Suele llover mucho aquí, It rains a great deal here). See **moler**

solercia /so'lersia; so'lerθia/ f, shrewdness, ability, astuteness

solevantado /soleβan'taðo/ a agitated; restless

solevantar /soleβan'tar/ vt to raise, push up; incite to rebellion. **s. con gatos,** Mech. to jack up

solfa /'solfa/ f, Mus. sol-fa

solfear /solfe'ar/ vt Mus. to sing in sol-fa; Inf. spank, buffet; Inf. scold

solfeo /sol'feo/ m, Mus. sol-fa, solfeggio; Inf. spanking, drubbing

solicitación /solisita'sion; soliθita'θion/ f, request; application; solicitation; wooing; search (for a post); attraction, inducement

solicitador /solisita'ðor; soliθita'ðor/ (-ra) a soliciting. n solicitor. m, agent; applicant

solicitante /solisi'tante; soliθi'tante/ mf applicant, candidate

solicitar /solisi'tar; soliθi'tar/ vt to solicit; request; apply for; make love to, court; seek (posts, etc.); try to, attempt to; manage (business affairs); Phys. attract; appeal to

solícito /so'lisito; so'liθito/ a solicitous; conscientious; careful

solicitud /solisi'tuð; soliθi'tuð/ f, diligence, conscientiousness; solicitude; request; application (forms); appeal, entreaty; petition; Com. demand. **a s.,** on request

solidaridad /soliðari'ðað/ f, solidarity

solidario /soli'ðario/ a Law. jointly responsible or liable

solideo /soli'ðeo/ m, Eccl. small skullcap

solidez /soli'ðes; soli'ðeθ/ f, solidity; Fig. force, weight (of arguments, etc.)

solidificación /soliðifika'sion; soliðifika'θion/ f, solidification

solidificar /soliðifi'kar/ (se) vt and vr to solidify

sólido /'soliðo/ a compact, solid; thick; fast or lasting (of colors); indisputable, convincing. m, (Geom. Phys.) solid; solidus (ancient coin)

soliloquiar /solilo'kiar/ vi Inf. to soliloquize, talk to oneself

soliloquio /soli'lokio/ m, soliloquy

solio /'solio/ m, throne

solista /so'lista/ mf soloist

solitario /soli'tario/ (-ia) a abandoned, deserted; solitary; secluded; solitude-loving. n recluse. m, solitaire diamond; hermit; solitaire (card game). **hacer solitarios,** to play solitaire (card game)

sólito /'solito/ a accustomed, wonted; customary, habitual

soliviantar /soliβian'tar/ vt to rouse, incite, excite

soliviar /soli'βiar/ vt to help to lift up; vr half get up, raise oneself

sollastre /so'ʎastre; so'ʎastre/ m, scullion; brazen rogue

sollozante /soyo'sante; soʎo'θante/ a sobbing

sollozar /soyo'sar; soʎo'θar/ vi to sob

sollozo /so'yoso; so'ʎoθo/ m, sob

solo /'solo/ a sole, only; alone; lonely; deserted, forsaken. m, solo performance; (cards) solo; solitaire (card game). **a solas,** alone; without help, unaided

sólo /'solo/ or **solo** adv only; merely, solely; exclusively

solomillo /solo'miyo; solo'miʎo/ *m*, sirloin; filet (of meat)

solsticio /sols'tisio; sols'tiθio/ *m*, solstice. **s. hiemal,** winter solstice. **s. vernal,** summer solstice

soltar /sol'tar/ *vt irr* to loosen; let go; disengage; untie; release; let drop; let out (a laugh, etc.); solve; *Inf.* utter; turn on (taps); set free; *vr* work loose; grow skillful; (*with prep. a* + *infin.*) begin to do (something). See **contar**

soltera /sol'tera/ *f*, spinster

soltería /solte'ria/ *f*, bachelorhood; spinsterhood

soltero /sol'tero/ *a* unmarried, single. *m*, bachelor

solterón /solte'ron/ *m*, confirmed bachelor

solterona /solte'rona/ *f*, confirmed old maid

soltura /sol'tura/ *f*, loosening; untying; freedom from restraint; ease, independence; impudence; immorality, viciousness; facility of speech; *Law.* release

solubilidad /soluβili'ðað/ *f*, solubility

soluble /so'luβle/ *a* soluble, dissolvable; solvable

solución /solu'sion; solu'θion/ *f*, dissolution, loosening; (*Math. Chem.*) solution; answer, solution; payment, satisfaction; *Lit.* climax; conclusion, end (of negotiations)

solucionar /solusio'nar; soluθio'nar/ *vt* to solve, find a solution for

solvencia /sol'βensia; sol'βenθia/ *f*, *Com.* solvency

solventar /solβen'tar/ *vt* to pay or settle accounts; solve (problems, difficulties)

solvente /sol'βente/ *a Com.* solvent

somático /so'matiko/ *a* somatic, corporeal

sombra /'sombra/ *f*, shadow; shade; darkness, dimness; specter, phantom; defense, refuge, protection; resemblance, likeness; defect; *Inf.* luck; gaiety, charm; trace, vestige; *Art.* shading, shadow. **sombras chinescas,** shadow show. **a la s.,** in the shade; *Inf.* in jail. **hacer s.,** to shade; *Fig.* stand in the light, be an obstacle; protect. **ni por s.,** by no means; without warning. **no tener s. de,** to have not a trace of.... **tener buena s.,** *Inf.* to be witty or amusing and agreeable. **tener mala s.,** *Inf.* to bring bad luck, exert an evil influence upon; be dull and disagreeable

sombrear /sombre'ar/ *vt* to shadow, shade; *Art.* shade; *vi* begin to show (of mustaches, beards)

sombrerera /sombre'rera/ *f*, milliner; hatbox

sombrerería /sombrere'ria/ *f*, hat shop or trade; hat factory

sombrerero /sombre'rero/ *m*, hatter; hat manufacturer

sombrerete /sombre'rete/ *m*, *Mech.* bonnet, cap; cowl

sombrero /som'βrero/ *m*, hat; *Mech.* cap, cowl; sounding board; head (of mushrooms, toadstools). **s. calañés,** Andalusian hat. **s. chambergo,** broad-brimmed plumed hat. **s. de canal** *or* **teja,** shovel hat (worn by clergymen). **s. de copa,** top hat. **s. de jipijapa,** Panama hat. **s. de pelo** *Lat. Am.* top hat. **s. de tres picos,** three-cornered hat, cocked hat. **s. flexible,** soft felt hat. **s. hongo,** bowler (hat)

sombría /som'βria/ *f*, shady spot

sombrilla /som'βriya; som'βriʎa/ *f*, sunshade

sombrío /som'βrio/ *a* dark; shadowy; overcast; *Art.* shaded; gloomy, melancholy

someramente /somera'mente/ *adv* superficially; briefly, summarily

somero /so'mero/ *a* superficial, shallow; summary, rudimentary, brief

someter /some'ter/ *vt* to put down, defeat; submit, place before; subject. **s. a votación,** to put to a vote. *vr* yield, surrender; (*with prep a*) undergo

sometimiento /someti'miento/ *m*, defeat; submission (to arbitration, etc.); subjection

somnambulismo /somnambu'lismo/ *m*, somnambulism, sleepwalking

somnámbulo /som'nambulo/ **(-la)** *a* somnambulistic. *n* somnambulist

somnífero /som'nifero/ *a* soporiferous

somnílocuo /som'nilokuo/ *a* somniloquous, sleep-talking

somnolencia /somno'lensia; somno'lenθia/ *f*, somnolence

son /son/ *m*, sound; rumor; reason, motive; means;

way; guise, manner. **al s. de,** to the sound of; to the music of. **en s. de,** in the manner of, as, like, under pretext of

sonadera /sona'ðera/ *f*, nose blowing

sonado /so'naðo/ *a* famous; much admired or talked of. **hacer una que sea sonada,** *Inf.* to cause a great scandal; do something noteworthy

sonaja /so'naha/ *f*, metal jingles on a tambourine; baby's rattle

sonajero /sona'hero/ *m*, baby's rattle

sonar /so'nar/ *vi irr* to sound; be quoted, be mentioned; ring; *Inf.* be familiar, remember (e.g. *No me suena el nombre,* I don't remember the name); (*with prep a*) be reminiscent of; *vt* sound; ring; play on; clink; *vr* be rumored, be reported; blow one's nose. *Pres. Ind.* **sueno, suenas, suena, suenan.** *Pres. Subjunc.* **suene, suenes, suene, suenen**

sonata /so'nata/ *f*, sonata

sonda /'sonda/ *f*, *Naut.* taking of soundings, heaving the lead; sound, plummet, lead; dragrope; probe, sound

sondar /son'dar/ *vt Naut.* to take soundings; probe; *Inf.* sound, try to find out; bore, drill

sondeable /sonde'aβle/ *a* fathomable

sondeo /son'deo/ *m*, *Naut.* sounding; *Mineral.* drilling; probing

sonetear, sonetizar /sonete'ar, soneti'sar; sonete'ar, soneti'θar/ *vi* to write sonnets

sonetista /sone'tista/ *mf* sonneteer

soneto /so'neto/ *m*, sonnet

sonido /so'niðo/ *m*, sound; literal meaning; rumor, report

sonochar /sono'tʃar/ *vi* to keep watch in the early hours of the night

sonoridad /sonori'ðað/ *f*, sonorousness

sonoro /so'noro/ *a* sounding; resonant; loud; sonorous

sonreir, sonereírse /son'reir, sone'reirse/ *vi* and *vr irr* to smile; *vi* look pleasant (landscape, etc.); look favorable (of circumstances). **sonreir tras la barba,** to laugh to oneself. See **reir**

sonriente /son'riente/ *a* smiling

sonrisa /son'risa/ *f*, smile

sonrojar /sonro'har/ *vt* to cause to blush; *vr* blush

sonrosado /sonro'saðo/ *a* rosy, rose-colored, pink

sonrosar /sonro'sar/ *vt* to make rose-colored; *vr* blush, flush

sonroseo /sonro'seo/ *m*, blush, flush

sonsaca /son'saka/ *f*, removal by stealth; pilfering; enticement; *Fig.* pumping (of a person for information)

sonsacar /sonsa'kar/ *vt* to remove by stealth; steal, pilfer; entice away; *Fig.* pump (a person for information), draw out

sonsonete /sonso'nete/ *m*, rhythmic tapping or drumming; monotonous sound (gen. unpleasant); sarcastic tone of voice

soñador /sona'ðor/ **(-ra)** *a* dreamy, sleepy. *n* dreamer

soñar /so'nar/ *vt* to dream; imagine, conjure up; (*with con*) dream of; (*with prep a*) fear (of persons)

soñoliento /sono'liento/ *a* sleepy, drowsy; soothing; slow, leisurely

¡Soo! /soo/ *interj* Whoa! (command to horses, etc.)

sopa /'sopa/ *f*, sop, piece of bread; soup. **s. boba,** beggar's portion; life of ease at others' expense. **andar a la s.,** to beg one's way. **hecho una s.,** *Inf.* wet through

sopapo /so'papo/ *m*, chuck under the chin; *Inf.* slap; valve

sopera /so'pera/ *f*, soup tureen

sopero /so'pero/ *m*, soup plate, soup bowl. *a* fond of soup

sopesar /sope'sar/ *vt* to try the weight of

sopetón /sope'ton/ *m*, blow, cuff. **de s.,** suddenly

soplada /so'plaða/ *f*, puff of wind

soplado /so'plaðo/ *a Inf.* overelegant; haughty, stiff. *m*, fissure, chasm

soplador /sopla'ðor/ **(-ra)** *a* instigatory. *m*, blower, fan. *n* instigator; blower

soplar /so'plar/ *vi* to blow; *vt* blow; blow away; inflate, blow up; filch, steal; instigate, inspire; accuse; fan; prompt, help out; *vr Inf.* eat and drink too much; *Inf.* be puffed up, grow haughty. *interj* ¡**Sopla!** *Inf.* You don't say so!

soplete /so'plete/ *m*, blowpipe

soplo /'soplo/ *m*, blow; blowing; instant, trice; *Inf.* hint, tip; *Inf.* accusation; *Inf.* tale-bearer; puff, breath (of wind)

soplón /so'plon/ **(-ona)** *a Inf.* tale-bearing, backbiting. *n* tale-bearer. *m, Auto.* scavenger

soponcio /so'ponsio; so'ponθio/ *m, Inf.* fainting fit

sopor /so'por/ *m*, stupor; deep sleep

soporífero /sopo'rifero/ *a* soporiferous

soportable /sopor'taβle/ *a* bearable

soportador /soporta'ðor/ **(-ra)** *a* supporting. *n* supporter

soportal /sopor'tal/ *m*, portico

soportar /sopor'tar/ *vt* to bear; carry, support; put up with, tolerate

soporte /so'porte/ *m*, rest, support; *Mech.* bearing; *Mech.* bracket, support; backup (of a computer file)

sorbedor /sorβe'ðor/ **(-ra)** *a* supping, sipping. *n* sipper

sorber /sor'βer/ *vt* to suck; imbibe; swallow; *Fig.* absorb eagerly (ideas); sip

sorbete /sor'βete/ *m*, sherbet, iced drink; French ice cream

sorbo /'sorβo/ *m*, sucking; imbibition; swallow; sip; mouthful, gulp

sordamente /sorða'mente/ *adv* secretly, quietly

sordera /sor'ðera/ *f*, deafness

sórdido /'sorðiðo/ *a* dirty, squalid; mean, niggardly; sordid

sordina /sor'ðina/ *f*, *Mus.* sordine, mute; *Mus.* damper. **a la s.,** on the quiet, in secret

sordo /'sorðo/ *a* deaf; silent, quiet; dull, muted (of sounds); insensible, inanimate; obdurate, uncompliant. **a la sorda** *or* **a lo s.** *or* **a sordas,** in silence, quietly

sordomudez /sorðomu'ðes; sorðomu'ðeθ/ *f*, deaf-muteness, deaf-mutism

sordomudo /sorðo'muðo/ **(-da)** *a* and *n* deaf-mute

sorna /'sorna/ *f*, slowness, sluggishness; craftiness, guile, knavery; malice

soroche /so'rotʃe/ *m, Peru* altitude sickness, mountain sickness

sorprendente /sorpren'dente/ *a* surprising, amazing

sorprender /sorpren'der/ *vt* to surprise, amaze

sorpresa /sor'presa/ *f*, surprise; amazement; shock

sorpresivo, -a /sorpre'siβo/ *a*, *Lat. Am.* sudden, unexpected; surprising

sortear /sorte'ar/ *vt* to raffle; draw lots for; avoid artfully (difficulties, etc.); fight (bulls)

sorteo /sor'teo/ *m*, raffle; casting lots

sortero /sor'tero/ **(-ra)** *n* sorcerer; holder of a draw ticket

sortija /sor'tiha/ *f*, ring (for a finger); ring (for a curtain, etc.); curl

sortilegio /sorti'lehio/ *m*, sorcery, magic

sortílego /sor'tilego/ **(-ga)** *a* magic. *n* sorcerer, fortuneteller

sosa /'sosa/ *f*, sodium carbonate, soda ash. **s. cáustica,** sodiumhydroxide, caustic soda, soda

sosegado /sose'gaðo/ *a* tranquil, peaceful, calm

sosegador /sosega'ðor/ **(-ra)** *a* soothing, calming. *n* appeaser, quieter

sosegar /sose'gar/ *vt irr* to soothe, quiet; reassure; appease, moderate; *vi* grow still; rest, sleep; *vr* grow quiet; calm down, be appeased; grow still. See **cegar**

sosería /sose'ria/ *f*, insipidness; lack of wit, dullness; stupidity

sosia /'sosia/ *m*, double, exact likeness (of persons)

sosiego /so'siego/ *m*, calm; peace, tranquility

soslayar /sosla'yar/ *vt* to slant, place in an oblique position; *Fig.* go around (a difficulty)

soslayo /sos'layo/ *a* slanting. **al s.,** obliquely, on the slant; askance

soso /'soso/ *a* saltless, insipid; dull, uninteresting; heavy (of people)

sospecha /sos'petʃa/ *f*, suspicion

sospechar /sospe'tʃar/ *vt* and *vi* to suspect

sospechoso /sospe'tʃoso/ *a* suspicious. *m*, suspect

sostén /sos'ten/ *m*, support; *Mech.* stand, support; brassiere, bra, bustier; steadiness (of a ship)

sostenedor /sostene'ðor/ **(-ra)** *a* supporting. *n* supporter

sostener /soste'ner/ *vt irr* to support; defend, uphold; bear, tolerate; help, aid; maintain, support. **s. una conversación,** to carry on a conversation. See **tener**

sostenido /soste'niðo/ *a Mus.* sostenuto, sustained. *a* and *m, Mus.* sharp

sostenimiento /losteni'miento/ *m*, support; defense; toleration, endurance; maintenance, sustenance

sota /'sota/ *f*, jack, knave (in cards); *Inf.* baggage, hussy. *m*, foreman, supervisor. *prep* deputy, substitute (e.g. *sotamontero*, deputy huntsman)

sotabanco /sota'βanko/ *m*, attic, garret

sotana /so'tana/ *f*, gown, cassock, robe

sótano /'sotano/ *m*, basement, cellar

sotavento /sota'βento/ *m*, leeward. **a s.,** on the lee

sotechado /sote'tʃaðo/ *m*, hut, shed

soterrar /sote'rrar/ *vt irr* to bury in the ground; hide, conceal. See **acertar**

sotileza /soti'lesa; soti'leθa/ *f*, fine cord for fishing (in Santander province)

soto /'soto/ *m*, thicket, grove, copse

soviético /so'βietiko/ *a* soviet

sovietismo /soβie'tismo/ *m*, sovietism

sovietizar /soβieti'sar; soβieti'θar/ *vt* to sovietize

sovoz, a /so'βos, a; so'βoθ, a/ *adv* in a low voice

su, sus /su, sus/ *poss pron 3rd pers mf sing* and *pl* his, her, its, one's, your, their

suasorio /sua'sorio/ *a* suasive, persuasive

suave /'suaβe/ *a* soft, smooth; sweet; pleasant, harmonious, quiet; slow, gentle; meek; delicate, subtle

suavidad /suaβi'ðað/ *f*, softness, smoothness; sweetness; pleasantness; quietness; gentleness; meekness; delicacy

suavizador /suaβisa'ðor; suaβiθa'ðor/ *a* softening, smoothing; soothing, quietening. *m*, razor strop

suavizar /suaβi'sar; suaβi'θar/ *vt* to soften; smooth; strop (a razor); moderate, temper; *Mech.* steady; quieten; ease

subalpino /suβal'pino/ *a* subalpine

subalternar /suβalter'nar/ *vt* to put down, subdue

subalterno /suβal'terno/ *a* subordinate. *m*, subordinate; *Mil.* subaltern

subarrendar /suβarren'dar/ *vt irr* to sublet. See **recomendar**

subarrendatario /suβarrenda'tario/ **(-ia)** *n* sublessee

subarriendo /suβa'rriendo/ *m*, sublease, sublet

subasta /su'βasta/ *f*, auction sale. **sacar a pública s.,** to sell by auction

subastar /suβas'tar/ *vt* to auction

subcentral /suβsen'tral; suβθen'tral/ *f*, substation

subclase /suβ'klase/ *f*, subclass

subcolector /suβkolek'tor/ *m*, assistant collector

subcomisión /suβkomi'sion/ *f*, subcommittee

subconsciencia /suβkons'siensia; suβkons'θienθia/ *f*, subconscious

subcutáneo /suβku'taneo/ *a* subcutaneous

subdelegar /suβðele'gar/ *vt* to subdelegate

subdirector /suβðirek'tor/ **(-ra)** *n* deputy, assistant director

súbdito /'suβðito/ **(-ta)** *a* dependent, subject. *n* subject (of a state)

subdividir /suβðiβi'ðir/ *vt* to subdivide

subdominante /suβðomi'nante/ *f, Mus.* subdominant

subgénero /suβ'henero/ *m*, subgenus

subgobernador /suβgoβerna'ðor/ *m*, deputy governor, lieutenant governor

subibaja /suβi'βaha/ *f*, seesaw, teetertotter

subida /su'βiða/ *f*, ascension, ascent; upgrade; rise; carrying up; raising (of a theater curtain)

subidero /suβi'ðero/ *m*, uphill road; mounting block; way up (to a higher level)

subido /su'βiðo/ *a* strong (of scents); deep (of colors); expensive, high-priced; best, finest

subidor /suβi'ðor/ *m*, porter, carrier; elevator

subintendente /suβinten'dente/ *m*, deputy or assistant intendant

subir /su'βir/ *vi* to ascend, climb, go up; mount; rise; *Com*. amount (to), reach; prosper, advance, be promoted; grow more acute (of illnesses); intensify; *Mus*. raise the pitch (of an instrument or voice); *vt* ascend, climb; pick up, take up; raise up; place higher; build up, make taller; straighten up, place in a vertical position; increase, raise (in price or value); *vr* ascend, climb. **s. a caballo**, to mount a horse. **subirse a la cabeza,** *Inf*. to go to one's head (of alcohol, etc.)

subitáneo /suβi'taneo/ *a* sudden

súbito /'suβito/ *a* unexpected, unforeseen; sudden; precipitate, impulsive. *adv* suddenly (also **de s.**)

subjefe /suβ'hefe/ *m*, deputy chief, second in command

subjetividad /suβhetiβi'ðað/ *f*, subjectivity

subjetivismo /suβheti'βismo/ *m*, subjectivism

subjetivo /suβhe'tiβo/ *a* subjective

subjuntivo /suβhun'tiβo/ *a* and *m*, subjunctive

sublevación /suβleβa'sion; suβleβa'θion/ *f*, **sublevamiento** *m*, rebellion, mutiny, uprising

sublevar /suβle'βar/ *vt* to rouse to rebellion; excite (indignation, etc.); *vr* rebel

sublimación /suβlima'sion; suβlima'θion/ *f*, sublimation

sublimado /suβli'maðo/ *m*, *Chem*. sublimate

sublimar /suβli'mar/ *vt* to exalt, raise up; *Chem*. sublimate

sublime /su'βlime/ *a* sublime

sublimidad /suβlimi'ðað/ *f*, sublimity, majesty, nobility

submarino /suβma'rino/ *a* submarine. *m*, submarine. **s. de bolsillo** *or* **s. enano,** midget submarine

suboficial /suβofi'sial; suβofi'θial/ *m*, *Mil*. subaltern; *Nav*. petty officer

subordinación /suβorðina'sion; suβorðina'θion/ *f*, dependence, subordination

subordinado /suβorði'naðo/ **(-da)** *a* and *n* subordinate

subordinar /suβorði'nar/ *vt* to subordinate

subprefecto /suβpre'fekto/ *m*, subprefect

subproducto /suβpro'ðukto/ *m*, by-product

subrayar /suβra'yar/ *vt* to underline; emphasize

subrepción /suβrep'sion; suβrep'θion/ *f*, underhand dealing; *Law*. subreption

subrepticio /suβrep'tisio; suβrep'tiθio/ *a* surreptitious; clandestine

subrogación /suβroga'sion; suβroga'θion/ *f*, surrogation

subrogar /suβro'gar/ *vt Law*. to surrogate, elect as a substitute

subs /suβs/ -- For words so beginning not found here, see **sus-**

subsanar /suβsa'nar/ *vt* to make excuses for; remedy, put right; indemnify

subscriptor /suβskrip'tor/ **(-ra)** *n* subscriber

subsección /suβsek'sion; suβsek'θion/ *f*, subsection

subsecretaría /suβsekreta'ria/ *f*, assistant secretaryship; assistant secretary's office

subsecretario /suβsekre'tario/ **(-ia)** *n* assistant secretary

subsecuente /suβse'kuente/ *a* subsequent

subsidiario /suβsi'ðiario/ *a* subsidized; subsidiary

subsidio /suβ'siðio/ *m*, subsidy

subsiguiente /suβsi'giente/ *a* subsequent; next

subsistencia /suβsis'tensia; suβsis'tenθia/ *f*, permanence; stability; subsistence, maintenance; livelihood

subsistir /suβsis'tir/ *vi* to last, endure; subsist, live; make a livelihood

subsuelo /suβ'suelo/ *m*, subsoil, substratum

subte /'suβte/ *m*, *Argentina*, *informal* subway

subteniente /suβte'niente/ *m*, *Mil*. second lieutenant

subterfugio /suβter'fuhio/ *m*, subterfuge, trick

subterráneo /suβte'rraneo/ *a* underground, subterranean. *m*, subterranean place

subtítulo /suβ'titulo/ *m*, subtitle; caption

subtropical /suβtropi'kal/ *a* subtropical

suburbano /suβur'βano/ **(-na)** *a* suburban. *n* suburbanite

suburbio /su'βurβio/ *m*, suburb

subvención /suββen'sion; suββen'θion/ *f*, subsidy, subvention, grant

subvencionar /suββensio'nar; suββenθio'nar/ *vt* to subsidize

subvenir /suββe'nir/ *vt irr* to help, succor; subsidize. See **venir**

subversivo /suββer'siβo/ *a* subversive

subvertir /suββer'tir/ *vt irr* to subvert, overturn, ruin. See **sentir**

subyugación /suβyuga'sion; suβyuga'θion/ *f*, subjugation

subyugador /suβyuga'ðor/ **(-ra)** *a* subjugating. *n* conqueror

subyugar /suβyu'gar/ *vt* to subjugate, overcome

succión /suk'sion; suk'θion/ *f*, suction

suceder /suse'ðer; suθe'ðer/ *vi* to follow, come after; inherit, succeed. *impers* happen, occur

sucedido /suse'ðiðo; suθe'ðiðo/ *m*, *Inf*. event, occurrence

sucesión /suse'sion; suθe'sion/ *f*, succession; series; offspring, descendants; *Law*. estate

sucesivo /suse'siβo; suθe'siβo/ *a* successive. **en lo s.,** in future

suceso /su'seso; su'θeso/ *m*, happening, occurrence; course (of time); outcome, result

sucesor /suse'sor; suθe'sor/ **(-ra)** *a* succeeding. *n* successor

suciedad /susie'ðað; suθie'ðað/ *f*, dirt; filth, nastiness; obscenity

sucinto /su'sinto; su'θinto/ *a* succinct, brief, concise

sucio /'susio; 'suθio/ *a* dirty, unclean; stained; easily soiled; *Fig*. sullied, spotted; obscene; dirty (of colors); *Fig*. tainted, infected. **jugar s.,** *Sports*. to play in an unsporting manner

suco /'suko/ *m*, juice

sucoso /su'koso/ *a* juicy

sucre /'sukre/ *m* sucre (monetary unit of Ecuador)

suculencia /suku'lensia; suku'lenθia/ *f*, succulence; juiciness

suculento /suku'lento/ *a* succulent; juicy

sucumbir /sukum'βir/ *vi* to yield, give in; die, succumb; lose a lawsuit

sucursal /sukur'sal/ *a* branch. *f*, *Com*. branch (of a firm)

sud /suð/ *m*, south (gen. **sur**). Used in combinations like **sudamericano**

sudadero /suða'ðero/ *m*, horse blanket; sudatorium, sweating bath

sudafricano /suðafri'kano/ **(-na)** *a* and *n* South African

Sudamérica /suða'merika/ *f* South America

sudamericano /suðameri'kano/ **(-na)** *a* and *n* South American

sudante /su'ðante/ *a* sweating, perspiring

sudar /su'ðar/ *vi* and *vt* to perspire, sweat; ooze; *vi Inf*. toil; *vt* bathe in sweat; *Inf*. give reluctantly. **s. frío,** to break out in a cold sweat. **s. la gota gorda,** *Fig*. *Inf*. to be in a stew

sudario /su'ðario/ *m*, shroud

sudeste /su'ðeste/ *m*, southeast; southeast wind

sudexpreso /suðeks'preso/ *m*, southern express

sudoeste /suðo'este/ *m*, southwest; southwest wind

sudor /su'ðor/ *m*, sweat, perspiration; toil; juice, moisture, sap, gum

sudoroso /suðo'roso/ *a* sweaty

sudsudeste /suðsu'ðeste/ *m*, southsoutheast

sudsudoeste /suðsuðo'este/ *m*, southsouthwest

Suecia /'suesia; 'sueθia/ Sweden

sueco /'sueko/ **(-ca)** *a* Swedish. *n* Swede. *m*, Swedish (language)

suegra /'suegra/ *f*, mother-in-law

suegro /'suegro/ *m*, father-in-law

suela /'suela/ *f*, sole (of a shoe); leather. **no llegarle a uno a la s. del zapato,** *inf* to be not fit to hold a candle to.

sueldo /'sueldo/ *m*, salary, wages; *Obs*. Spanish coin. **a s.,** for a salary, salaried

suelo /'suelo/ *m*, ground, earth; soil; bottom, base; sediment, dregs; site, plot; floor; flooring; story; land, territory; hoof (of horses); earth, world; *pl* chaff of grain. **s. natal,** native land; **besar el s.,** *Inf.* to fall flat. **dar consigo en el s.,** to fall down. **dar en el s. con,** to throw down; damage, spoil. *Inf.* **estar (una cosa) por los suelos,** to be dirt cheap

suelta /'suelta/ *f*, loosening, unfastening; hobble (for horses); relay of oxen. **dar s. a,** to let loose, allow to go out for a time

sueltista /suel'tista/ *mf*, *Lat. Am.* freelance journalist, stringer

suelto /'suelto/ *a* swift; competent, efficient; odd, separate; licentious; flowing, easy (style); loose, unbound. *m*, single copy (of a newspaper); loose change; newspaper paragraph

sueño /'sueɲo/ *m*, dream; sleep; drowsiness, desire for sleep; vision, fancy. **s. pesado,** deep sleep. **conciliar el s.,** to court sleep. **echar un s.,** *Inf.* to take a nap. **en sueños,** in a dream; while asleep. **entre sueños,** between sleeping and waking. **¡Ni por sueño!** *Inf.* Certainly not! I wouldn't dream of it!

suero /'suero/ *m*, serum. **s. de la leche,** whey

suerte /'suerte/ *f*, chance, luck; good luck; destiny, fate; condition, state; kind, species, sort; way, manner; bullfighter's maneuver; parcel of land. **de s. que,** so that; as a result. **echar suertes,** to draw lots. **tener buena s.,** to be lucky

sueste /'sueste/ *m*, southeast; sou'wester (cap); *Lat. Am.* southeast wind

suéter /'sueter/ *m*, sweater

suficiencia /sufi'siensia; sufi'θienθia/ *f*, sufficiency; talent, aptitude; pedantry. **a s.,** enough

suficiente /sufi'siente; sufi'θiente/ *a* sufficient, enough; suitable

sufijo /su'fiho/ *m*, suffix

sufragar /sufra'gar/ *vt* to assist, aid; favor; pay, defray

sufragio /su'frahio/ *m*, aid, assistance; *Eccl.* suffragium, pious offering; vote; suffrage

sufragista /sufra'hista/ *f*, suffragette

sufrible /su'friβle/ *a* bearable, endurable

sufrido /su'friðo/ *a* long-suffering, resigned; complaisant (of husbands); dirt-resistant (colors)

sufrimiento /sufri'miento/ *m*, suffering, pain; affliction; tolerance

sufrir /su'frir/ *vt* to suffer, undergo, experience; bear, endure; tolerate, put up with; allow, permit; resist, oppose; expiate; *vi* suffer

sugerir /suhe'rir/ *vt irr* to suggest. See **sentir**

sugestión /suhes'tion/ *f*, suggestion

sugestionable /suhestio'naβle/ *a* easily influenced, open to suggestion

sugestionador /suhestiona'ðor/ *a* suggestive

sugestionar /suhestio'nar/ *vt* to suggest hypnotically; dominate, influence

sugestivo /suhes'tiβo/ *a* suggestive, stimulating

suicida /sui'siða; sui'θiða/ *a* suicidal, fatal. *mf* suicide (person)

suicidarse /suisi'ðarse; suiθi'ðarse/ *vr* to commit suicide

suicidio /sui'siðio; sui'θiðio/ *m*, suicide (act)

Suiza /'suisa; 'suiθa/ Switzerland

suiza /'suisa; 'suiθa/ *f*, row, rumpus, scrap

suizo /'suiso; 'suiθo/ **(-za)** *a* and *n* Swiss

sujeción /suhe'sion; suhe'θion/ *f*, subjection, domination; fastening, fixture; obedience, conformity

sujetador /suheta'ðor/ *m*, clamp; clip

sujetar /suhe'tar/ *vt* to fasten, fix; hold down; grasp, clutch; subdue; *vr* (*with prep a*) conform to, obey. **s. con alfileres,** to pin up. **s. con tornillos,** to screw down

sujeto /su'heto/ *a* liable, subject. *m*, topic, subject; person, individual; *Gram. Philos.* subject

sulfatar /sulfa'tar/ *vt* to sulphate

sulfato /sul'fato/ *m*, sulphate

sulfurar /sulfu'rar/ *vt* to sulphurate; *vr* grow irritated, become angry

sulfúrico /sul'furiko/ *a* sulphuric

sulfuro /sul'furo/ *m*, sulphide

sulfuroso /sulfu'roso/ *a* sulphurous

sultán /sul'tan/ *m*, sultan

sultana /sul'tana/ *f*, sultana

suma /'suma/ *f*, total; amount, sum; *Math.* addition; summary, digest; computation. **en s.,** in brief, in short, finally. *Com.* **s. redonda,** lump sum

sumador /suma'ðor/ **(-ra)** *n* summarizer; computator, adder

sumamente /suma'mente/ *adv* extremely, most

sumar /su'mar/ *vt* to sum up, summarize; *Math.* add up

sumaria /su'maria/ *f*, written indictment

sumariamente /sumaria'mente/ *adv* concisely, in brief; *Law.* summarily

sumario /su'mario/ *a* brief, concise, abridged; *Law.* summary. *m*, summary, résumé, digest

sumergible /sumer'hiβle/ *a* sinkable; submergible. *m*, submarine

sumergir /sumer'hir/ *vt* to dip, immerse, sink, submerge; *Fig.* overwhelm (with grief, etc.); *vr* sink; dive; be submerged

sumersión /sumer'sion/ *f*, immersion, dive, submersion

sumidero /sumi'ðero/ *m*, cesspool; drain; sink; pit, gully

suministración /suministra'sion; suministra'θion/ *f*. See **suministro**

suministrador /suministra'ðor/ **(-ra)** *n* purveyor

suministrar /suminis'trar/ *vt* to purvey, supply, provide

suministro /sumi'nistro/ *m*, purveyance; provision; supply

sumir /su'mir/ *vt* to sink; submerge; *Eccl.* consummate; *Fig.* overwhelm (with grief, etc.); *vr* fall in, become sunken (of cheeks, etc.); sink; be submerged; *Lat. Am.* cower, cringe

sumisión /sumi'sion/ *f*, submission, obedience; *Com.* estimate, tender

sumiso /su'miso/ *a* submissive, docile

sumista /su'mista/ *mf* quick reckoner, computator. *m*, condenser, summarizer, abridger

sumo /'sumo/ *a* supreme; high; tremendous, extraordinary. **a lo s.,** at the most; even if, although. **en s. grado,** in the highest degree

suntuosidad /suntuosi'ðað/ *f*, magnificence, luxury

suntuoso /sun'tuoso/ *a* magnificent, luxurious, sumptuous

supeditación /supeðita'sion; supeðita'θion/ *f*, subjection

supeditar /supeði'tar/ *vt* to oppress; overcome, conquer; subordinate

superabundancia /superaβun'dansia; superaβun'danθia/ *f*, superabundance, excess; glut

superabundante /superaβun'dante/ *a* superabundant, excessive

superádito /supe'raðito/ *a* superadded

superar /supe'rar/ *vt* to overcome, conquer; surpass; do better than

superávit /supe'raβit/ *m*, *Com.* balance, surplus

superchería /supertʃe'ria/ *f*, trickery, guile

superchero /super'tʃero/ *a* guileful, wily

superconsciencia /superkons'siensia; superkons'θienθia/ *f*, higher consciousness

supereminencia /superemi'nensia; superemi'nenθia/ *f*, supereminence, greatest eminence

supereminente /superemi'nente/ *a* supereminent

superentender /superenten'der/ *vt irr* to supervise, superintend. See **entender**

supererogación /supereroga'sion; supereroga'θion/ *f*, supererogation

superestructura /superestruk'tura/ *f*, superstructure

superficial /superfi'sial; superfi'θial/ *a* surface, shallow; superficial, rudimentary; futile

superficialidad /superfisiali'ðað; superfiθiali'ðað/ *f*, superficiality; futility; shallowness

superficie /super'fisie; super'fiθie/ *f*, area; surface; outside, exterior. **s. de rodadura,** tire tread

superfino /super'fino/ *a* superfine

superfluidad /superflui'ðað/ *f*, superfluity

superfluo /su'perfluo/ *a* superfluous, redundant

superfortaleza volante /superforta'lesa bo'lante; superforta'leθa bo'lante/ f, Aer. superfortress

superhombre /super'ombre/ m, superman

superintendencia /superinten'densia; superinten'denθia/ f, supervision; superintendentship; higher administration

superintendente /superinten'dente/ mf superintendent; supervisor

superior /supe'rior/ a higher, upper; excellent, fine; superior; higher (education, etc.). m, head, director; superior

superiora /supe'riora/ f, mother superior

superioridad /superiori'ðað/ f, superiority

superlativo /superla'tiβo/ a and m, superlative

superno /su'perno/ a supreme

supernumerario /supernume'rario/ (-ia) a and n supernumerary

superposición /superposi'sion; superposi'θion/ f, superposition

superproducción /superproðuk'sion; superproðuk'θion/ f, overproduction; superproduction

superrealismo /superrea'lismo/ m, surrealism

superrealista /superrea'lista/ a surrealist

superstición /supersti'sion; supersti'θion/ f, superstition

supersticioso /supersti'sioso; supersti'θioso/ a superstitious

supervención /superβen'sion; superβen'θion/ f, Law. supervention

supervigilancia /superβihi'lansia; superβihi'lanθia/ f, Lat. Am. supervision

supervivencia /superβi'βensia; superβi'βenθia/ f, survival

superviviente /superβi'βiente/ a surviving. mf survivor

supino /su'pino/ a supine; foolish, stupid. m, Gram. supine

suplantación /suplanta'sion; suplanta'θion/ f, supplanting

suplantador /suplanta'ðor/ (-ra) a supplanting. n supplanter

suplantar /suplan'tar/ vt to forge, alter (documents); supplant

suplefaltas /suple'faltas/ mf Inf. scapegoat

suplementario /suplemen'tario/ a supplementary, additional

suplemento /suple'mento/ m, supplement; supply, supplying; newspaper supplement; Geom. supplement

suplente /su'plente/ m, substitute, proxy; Fig. makeweight

súplica /'suplika/ f, supplication, prayer; request

suplicación /suplika'sion; suplika'θion/ f, entreaty, supplication; Law. petition

suplicante /supli'kante/ a supplicatory; Law. petitioning. mf supplicator; Law. petitioner

suplicar /supli'kar/ vt to beg, supplicate; request; Law. appeal

suplicio /su'plisio; su'pliθio/ m, torment, torture; execution; place of torture or execution; affliction, anguish. **último s.,** capital punishment

suplir /su'plir/ vt to supply, furnish; substitute, take the place of; overlook, forgive

suponer /supo'ner/ vt irr to suppose, take for granted; simulate; comprise, include; vi carry weight, wield authority. See **poner**

suposición /suposi'sion; suposi'θion/ f, supposition; conjecture, assumption; distinction, talent, importance; falsity, falsehood

supositorio /suposi'torio/ m, suppository

suprasensible /suprasen'siβle/ a supersensible

supremacía /suprema'sia; suprema'θia/ f, supremacy

supremo /su'premo/ a supreme; matchless, incomparable; last

supresión /supre'sion/ f, suppression; destruction, eradication; omission

suprimir /supri'mir/ vt to suppress; destroy, eradicate; omit, leave out. **s. una calle al tráfico,** to close a street to traffic, ban traffic from a street

supuesto /su'puesto/ a supposed; so-called; reputed.

m, supposition, hypothesis. **por s.,** of course, presumably; doubtless

supurar /supu'rar/ vi to suppurate

suputar /supu'tar/ vt to calculate, compute

sur /sur/ m, south; south wind

surcador /surka'ðor/ m, plowman

surcar /sur'kar/ vt to plow furrows; furrow, line; cut, cleave (water, etc.)

surco /'surko/ m, furrow; wrinkle, line; groove, channel; rut

surgidero /surhi'ðero/ m, Naut. road, roadstead

surgir /sur'hir/ vi to spout, gush, spurt; Naut. anchor; appear, show itself; come forth, turn up

surrealismo /surrea'lismo/ m, surrealism

surrealista /surrea'lista/ a and mf surrealist

surtida /sur'tiða/ f, hidden exit; false door; Naut. slipway

surtidero /surti'ðero/ m, outlet, drain; jet, fountain

surtido /sur'tiðo/ a mixed, assorted. m, variety, assortment; stock, range. **de s.,** in everyday use

surtidor /surti'ðor/ (-ra) n purveyor, supplier. m, fountain, jet. **s. de gasolina,** gasoline pump, gas pump

surtimiento /surti'miento/ m, assortment; stock

surtir /sur'tir/ vt to provide, supply, furnish; vi spurt, gush

surto /'surto/ a calm, reposeful; Naut. anchored

susceptibilidad /susseptiβili'ðað; susθeptiβili'ðað/ f, susceptibility

susceptible /sussep'tiβle; susθep'tiβle/ a susceptible, open to; touchy, oversensitive

suscitar /sussi'tar; susθi'tar/ vt to cause, originate; provoke, incite; vr arise, take place

suscribir /suskri'βir/ vt to sign; agree to; vr subscribe, contribute; take out a subscription (to a periodical, etc.). Past Part. **suscrito**

suscripción /suskrip'sion; suskrip'θion/ f, subscription; agreement, accession

susodicho /suso'ðitʃo/ a aforesaid

suspender /suspen'der/ vt to suspend, hang up; postpone, defer, stop; amaze, dumbfound; suspend (from employment); fail (an exam); adjourn (meetings); vr rear (of horses)

suspensión /suspen'sion/ f, suspension; postponement, stoppage, deferment; amazement; failure (in an exam); adjournment (of a meeting); springs (of a car). Com. **s. de pagos,** suspension of payments. **con mala s.,** badly sprung (of a car)

suspensivo /suspen'siβo/ a suspensive

suspensivos /suspen'siβos/ m, pl suspension points, ellipsis points

suspenso /sus'penso/ a amazed, bewildered. m, failure slip (in an exam). **en s.,** in suspense

suspensor /suspen'sor/ m, Lat. Am. suspender (for pants)

suspicacia /suspi'kasia; suspi'kaθia/ f, suspiciousness; mistrust, uneasiness

suspicaz /suspi'kas; suspi'kaθ/ a suspicious, mistrustful

suspirado /suspi'raðo/ a eagerly desired, longed for

suspirar /suspi'rar/ vt and vi to sigh. **s. por,** to long for

suspiro /sus'piro/ m, sigh; breath; glass whistle; Mus. brief pause, pause sign. **último s.,** Inf. last leg, end

suspirón /suspi'ron/ a given to sighing

sustancia /sus'tansia; sus'tanθia/ f, substance, juice, extract, essence; Fig. core, pith; Fig. meat; wealth, estate; worth, importance; nutritive part; Inf. common sense. Anat. **s. gris,** gray matter. **en s.,** in short

sustanciación /sustansia'sion; sustanθia'θion/ f, substantiation

sustancial /sustan'sial; sustan'θial/ a substantial, real; important, essential; nutritive; solid

sustanciar /sustan'siar; sustan'θiar/ vt to substantiate; summarize, extract, abridge

sustancioso /sustan'sioso; sustan'θioso/ a substantial; nutritive

sustantivo /sustan'tiβo/ a and m, Gram. substantive, noun

sustentable /susten'taβle/ *a* arguable, defensible

sustentación /sustenta'sion; sustenta'θion/ *f,* maintenance; defense

sustentar /susten'tar/ *vt* to sustain, keep; support, bear; nourish, feed; uphold, advocate. **s. un ciclo de conferencias,** to give a series of lectures

sustento /sus'tento/ *m,* maintenance, preservation; nourishment, sustenance; support

sustitución /sustitu'sion; sustitu'θion/ *f,* substitution

sustituible /susti'tuiβle/ *a* substitutive, replaceable

sustituir /susti'tuir/ *vt irr* to substitute. See **huir**

sustitutivo /sustitu'tiβo/ *a* substitutive

sustituto /susti'tuto/ **(-ta)** *n* substitute

susto /'susto/ *m,* fright, shock; apprehension. **dar un s.** (a), to scare

sustracción /sustrak'sion; sustrak'θion/ *f,* subtraction

sustraer /sustra'er/ *vt irr* to remove, separate; rob, steal; *Math.* subtract; *vr* depart, remove oneself; avoid. See **traer**

sustrato /sus'trato/ *m,* substratum

susurrador /susurra'ðor/ **(-ra)** *a* whispering; murmuring; rustling. *n* whisperer

susurrante /susu'rrante/ *a* whispering; murmuring; rustling

susurrar /susu'rrar/ *vi* to whisper; murmur; rustle;

babble, purl, prattle (of water); *vi* and *vr* be whispered abroad

susurro /su'surro/ *m,* whispering, whisper; murmur; rustle; lapping

sutil /'sutil/ *a* fine, thin; penetrating, subtle, keen

sutileza, sutilidad /suti'lesa, sutili'ðað; suti'leθa, sutili'ðað/ *f,* fineness, thinness; subtlety, penetration. **sutileza de manos,** dexterity; light-fingeredness; sleight of hand

sutilizaciones /sutilisa'siones; sutiliθa'θiones/ *f, pl* casuistry, hairsplitting, quibbling

sutilizar /sutili'sar; sutili'θar/ *vt* to make thin, refine; *Fig.* finish, perfect; *Fig.* split hairs, make subtle distinctions

sutura /su'tura/ *f,* suture

suyo, suya /'suyo, 'suya/ *m,* and *f, pl* **suyos, suyas,** *poss pron* and *a 3rd pers* his; hers; its; yours; theirs; of his, of hers, etc. (e.g. *Este libro es suyo,* This book is his (hers, yours, theirs). **Este libro es uno de los suyos,** This book is one of his (hers, etc.). (**suyo** is often used with def. art. **el, la,** etc.) **los suyos,** his (hers, yours, etc.) family, following, adherents, etc. **de suyo,** of its very nature, of itself; spontaneously. **salirse con la suya,** to get one's own way. *Inf.* **ver la suyo,** to see one's opportunity

T

tabacal /taβa'kal/ *m,* tobacco plantation

tabacalero /taβaka'lero/ **(-ra)** *a* tobacco. *n* tobacco merchant; tobacco planter

tabaco /ta'βako/ *m,* tobacco plant, tobacco leaf; tobacco; cigar. **t. de pipa,** pipe tobacco. **t. flojo,** mild tobacco. **t. rubio,** Virginia tobacco

tabalear /taβale'ar/ **(se)** *vt* and *vr* to rock, sway, swing; *vi* drum with the fingers

tabaleo /taβa'leo/ *m,* swaying, rocking; drumming with the fingers

tabanco /ta'βanko/ *m,* market stall

tábano /'taβano/ *m, Ent.* horsefly, gadfly

tabanque /ta'βanke/ *m,* potter's wheel

tabaque /ta'βake/ *m,* small osier basket (for fruit, sewing, etc.); large tack

tabaquera /taβa'kera/ *f,* tobacco jar, tobacco tin; bowl of pipe tobacco; tobacco pouch; snuffbox

tabaquería /taβake'ria/ *f,* tobacconist's shop

tabaquero /taβa'kero/ **(-ra)** *n* tobacco grower; tobacco merchant; tobacco factory worker; tobacconist

tabaquismo /taβa'kismo/ *m,* nicotinism, nicotine poisoning

tabaquista /taβa'kista/ *mf* tobacco expert; heavy smoker

tabardillo /taβarðiyo; taβar'ðiʎo/ *m,* fever. **t. de tripas,** typhoid. **t. pintado,** typhus

tabardo /ta'βarðo/ *m,* tabard

taberna /ta'βerna/ *f,* public house, tavern

tabernáculo /taβer'nakulo/ *m,* tabernacle

tabernario /taβer'nario/ *a* public house, tavern; low, vulgar

tabernera /taβer'nera/ *f,* publican's wife; barmaid

tabernero /taβer'nero/ *m,* publican; barman, drawer

tabicar /taβi'kar/ *vt* to wall or board up; hide, cover up

tabique /ta'βike/ *m,* partition wall, inside wall; thin wall

tabla /'taβla/ *f,* plank of wood, board; *Metall.* plate; slab; flat side, face (of wood); *Sew.* box pleat; table (of contents, etc.); *Art.* panel; vegetable garden; butcher's slab; butcher's stall; *pl* tablets (for writing); (*Math.* etc.) tables; stalemate (chess, checkers); draw (in an election); *Theat.* boards, stage. **t. de armonía,** sounding board (of musical instruments). **t. de lavar,** washboard. **t. de materias,** table of contents. **t. de multiplicación,** multiplication table. **t. rasa,** clean sheet (of paper, etc.); complete ignorance. **T. Redonda,** Round Table (of King Arthur). **escapar** or **salvarse en una t.,** to have a narrow escape, escape in the nick of time

tablacho /ta'βlatʃo/ *m,* sluice gate. **echar el t.,** *Inf.* to interrupt the flow of someone's remarks

tablado /ta'βlaðo/ *m,* flooring; platform; *Theat.* stage; scaffold, gibbet. **sacar al t.,** to produce, put on the stage; to make known, publish

tablazón /taβla'son; taβla'θon/ *f,* planks, boards; flooring; *Naut.* deck planks or sheathing

tablear /taβle'ar/ *vt* to saw into planks; *Sew.* make box pleats in; hammer iron into sheets

tablero /ta'βlero/ *m,* board (of wood); paneling; boarding; slab; shop counter; board (checkers, chess). **t. de instrumentos,** dashboard; instrument panel

tableta /ta'βleta/ *f,* tablet; pastille, lozenge

tablilla /ta'βliya; ta'βliʎa/ *f,* small board; tablet; bulletin board, notice board

tablón /ta'βlon/ *m,* thick plank; wooden beam; *Inf.* drinking bout

tabú /ta'βu/ *m,* taboo

tabuco /ta'βuko/ *m,* miserable little room; hovel

taburete /taβu'rete/ *m,* stool; tabouret

tacañería /takaɲe'ria/ *f,* miserliness, niggardliness; craftiness

tacaño /ta'kaɲo/ *a* miserly, niggardly, *Inf.* cheap; crafty

tacha /'tatʃa/ *f,* imperfection, defect; spot, stain; fault; large tack. **poner t.,** to criticize, object to

tachable /ta'tʃaβle/ *a* censurable, blameworthy

tachar /ta'tʃar/ *vt* to criticize, blame; cross out, erase; charge, accuse

tacho de basura /'tatʃo de ba'sura/ *m, Argentina* garbage can

tachón /ta'tʃon/ *m,* round-headed ornamental nail; *Sew.* gold or silver studs, trimming; crossing out, erasure

tachonar /tatʃo'nar/ *vt* to stud with round-headed nails; *Sew.* trim with gold or silver studs or trimming

tachoso /ta'tʃoso/ *a* imperfect, defective, faulty; spotted, stained

tachuela /ta'tʃuela/ *f,* tack

tácito /'tasito; 'taθito/ *a* silent, unexpressed; tacit, implied

taciturnidad /tasiturni·oað; taθiturni'ðað/ *f,* taciturnity; reserve; melancholy

taciturno /tasi'turno; taθi'turno/ *a* taciturn; reserved; dismal, gloomy, melancholy

taco /'tako/ *m,* stopper, plug; billiard cue; rammer; wad, wadding (in a gun); pop gun; taco (filled tortilla); tear-off calendar; *Argentina,* heel (of a shoe) *Inf.* snack; obscenity, oath. **t. de papel,** writing tablet

tacón /ta'kon/ *m*, heel (of a shoe)

taconear /takone'ar/ *vi* to stamp with one's heels; walk heavily on one's heels; walk arrogantly

taconeo /tako'neo/ *m*, drumming or stamping of one's heels (gen. in dancing)

táctica /'taktika/ *f*, method, technique; *Mil.* tactics; policy, way, means

táctico /'taktiko/ *a* tactical. *m*, *Mil.* tactician

táctil /'taktil/ *a* tactile

tacto /'takto/ *m*, sense of touch; touch, feel; touching; skill; tact

tafetán /tafe'tan/ *m*, taffeta; *pl* flags, standards. **t. de heridas** *or* **t. inglés,** court plaster

tafilete /tafi'lete/ *m*, morocco leather

tahalí /taa'li/ *m*, sword shoulder belt

tahona /ta'ona/ *f*, horse mill; bakery; baker's shop

tahonero /tao'nero/ **(-ra)** *n* miller; baker

tahúr /ta'ur/ *m*, gambler; cardsharper

tahurería /taure'ria/ *f*, gambling den; gambling; cheating at cards

Tailandia /tai'landia/ Thailand

taimado /tai'maðo/ *a* knavish, crafty; obstinate, headstrong

taimería /taime'ria/ *f*, cunning, craftiness

taita /'taita/ *m*, daddy

taja /'taha/ *f*, cut, cutting; slice; washboard

tajada /ta'haða/ *f*, slice; strip, portion; steak, filet; *Inf.* cough; drinking bout; hoarseness

tajadera /taha'ðera/ *f*, cheese knife; chisel; *pl* sluice gate

tajado /ta'haðo/ *a* steep, sheer (of cliffs, etc.)

tajadura /taha'ðura/ *f*, cutting, dividing, dissection

tajar /ta'har/ *vt* to cut, chop; sharpen, trim (quill pens)

tajea /ta'hea/ *f*, culvert; aqueduct; drain; watercourse

tajear /tahe'ar/ *vt*, *Lat. Am.* to cut up

Tajo, el /'taho, el/ the Tagus

tajo /'taho, el/ *m*, cut, incision; task; cutting (in a mountain, etc.); cut, thrust (of sword); executioner's block; chopping board; washboard; steep cliff, precipice

tajón /ta'hon/ *m*, butcher block; chopping board

tal /tal/ *a pl* **tales,** such; said (e.g. *el t. Don Juan,* the so called Don Juan). **tal** is always used before nouns and (except when meaning "the said") without def. art. **un t.,** a certain (e.g. *un t. hombre,* a certain man). *pron* some, some people; someone; such a thing. *adv* so, thus. **t. para cual,** two of a kind, a well-matched pair; tit for tat. **con t. que,** *conjunc* on condition that, provided that. **No hay t.,** There is no such thing. *Inf.* **¿Qué t.?** How are you? What's the news? What's new? *Inf.* **fulano de t.,** whatsisname

tala /'tala/ *f*, felling or cutting down (of trees); cropping of grass (ruminants)

talabarte /tala'βarte/ *m*, sword belt

talabartería /talaβarte'ria/ *f*, saddlery

talador /tala'ðor/ **(-ra)** *a* felling, cutting; destructive. *n* feller, cutter; destroyer

taladrar /tala'ðrar/ *vt* to drill, bore, gouge holes; pierce, perforate; punch (a ticket); assail or hurt the ear (sounds); *Fig.* go into deeply (a subject)

taladro /ta'laðro/ *m*, drill, gimlet, gouge; drill hole, bore; puncher (for tickets, etc.)

tálamo /'talamo/ *m*, marriage bed; (*Bot. Anat.*) thalamus

talán /ta'lan/ *m*, peal, tolling (of a bell)

talanquera /talan'kera/ *f*, barricade; parapet, fence, wall; refuge, asylum; safety, security

talante /ta'lante/ *m*, mode of execution, technique; personal appearance, mien; disposition, temperament; wish, desire; aspect, appearance. **de buen (mal) t.,** willingly (unwillingly)

talar /ta'lar/ *a* full-length, long (of gowns, robes, etc.)

talar /ta'lar/ *vt* to fell, chop down (trees); ravage, lay waste; prune (gen. olive trees)

talco /'talko/ *m*, *Mineral.* talc; sequin, tinsel

talcualillo /talkua'liyo; talkua'liʎo/ *a Inf.* not too bad, fairly good; slightly better (of health)

taled /ta'leð/ *m*, prayer shawl, tales, tallit

talega /ta'lega/ *f*, sack, bag; sackful; money bag; *pl Inf.* cash wealth

talego /ta'lego/ *m*, narrow sack; *Inf.* dumpy person

talento /ta'lento/ *m*, talent (Greek coin); talent, gift, quality; intelligence, understanding; cleverness

talentoso /talen'toso/ *a* talented

talero /'talero/ *m*, *Argentina* whip

talión /ta'lion/ *m*, **(ley de)** law of retaliation

talismán /talis'man/ *m*, talisman

talla /'taya; 'taʎa/ *f*, carving (especially wood); cutting (of gems); reward for apprehension of a criminal; ransom; stature, height, size; height measuring rod

tallado /ta'yaðo; ta'ʎaðo/ *a* **bien** (or **mal**), well (or badly) carved; well (or badly) proportioned, of a good (or bad) figure

tallado /ta'yaðo; ta'ʎaðo/ *m*, carving

tallador /taya'ðor; taʎa'ðor/ *m*, metal engraver; die sinker

tallar /ta'yar; ta'ʎar/ *vt Art.* to carve; engrave; cut (gems); value, estimate; measure height (of persons)

tallarín /taya'rin; taʎa'rin/ *m*, (gen. *pl*) *Cul.* noodle

talle /'taye; 'taʎe/ *m*, figure, physique; waist; fit (of clothes); appearance, aspect. *Inf.* **largo de t.,** long-waisted; long drawn out, overlong. **tener buen t.,** to have a good figure

tallecer /taye'ser; taʎe'θer/ *vi irr Bot.* to sprout, shoot. See **conocer**

taller /ta'yer; ta'ʎer/ *m*, workshop; factory; mill; workroom, atelier; industrial school; school of arts and crafts; studio

tallista /ta'yista; ta'ʎista/ *mf* engraver; wood carver; sculptor

tallo /'tayo; 'taʎo/ *m*, *Bot.* stalk; shoot; slice of preserved fruit; cabbage. **t. rastrero,** *Bot.* runner

talludo /ta'yuðo; ta'ʎuðo/ *a* long-stalked; lanky, overgrown; no longer young, aging (of women); habit-ridden

talmúdico /tal'muðiko/ *a* Talmudic

talón /ta'lon/ *m*, heel; heel (of a shoe); *Com.* counterfoil; luggage receipt; *Com.* sight draft; coupon; heel (of a violin bow). *Inf.* **apretar los talones,** to take to one's heels. *Inf.* **pisarle (a uno) los talones,** to follow on a person's heels; rival successfully

talonada /talo'naða/ *f*, dig in with the spurs

talonario /talo'nario/ *m*, stub book

tamaño /ta'maɲo/ *a* more so big; so small (e.g. *La conocí tamaña,* I knew her when she was so high) (indicating her size with a gesture)); so great, so large (e.g. *tamaña empresa,* so great an undertaking). *m*, size

tamarindo /tama'rindo/ *m*, tamarind

tambaleante /tambale'ante/ *a* tottering, rickety; staggering

tambalear /tambale'ar/ **(se)** *vi* and *vr* to totter, sway, shake; reel, stagger

tambaleo /tamba'leo/ *m*, swaying; tottering; rocking; shaking; staggering, reeling

tambarillo /tamba'riyo; tamba'riʎo/ *m*, chest with an arched lid

también /tam'bien/ *adv* also, too; in addition, as well

tambor /tam'bor/ *m*, *Mus.* drum; drummer; embroidery frame; *Mech.* drum, cylinder; roaster (for coffee, chestnuts, etc.). **t. mayor,** drum major. **a t.** (or **con t.**) **>batiente,** with drums beating; triumphantly, with colors flying

tamborear /tambore'ar/ *vi* to totter, sway; stagger, reel

tamboreo /tambo'reo/ *m*, tottering, swaying; staggering, reeling

tamboril /tambo'ril/ *m*, tabor

tamborilada /tambori'laða/ *f*, *Inf.* slap on the back or face; *Inf.* fall on the bottom

tamborilear /tamborile'ar/ *vi* to play the tabor; *vt* eulogize, extol

tamborilero /tambori'lero/ *m*, tabor player

tamborín /tambo'rin/ *m*, tabor

Támesis, el /'tamesis, el/ the Thames

tamiz /ta'mis; ta'miθ/ *m*, sieve

tamizar /tami'sar; tami'θar/ *vt* to sieve

tamo /'tamo/ *m*, fluff; chaff
tampoco /tam'poko/ *adv* neither, not... either, nor... either; no more (e.g. *No lo ha hecho María t.*, Mary hasn't done it either)
tampón /tam'pon/ *m*, stamp moistener; *Surg.* tampon
tan /tan/ *adv abb* tanto so, as. Used before adjectives and adverbs, excepting **más, mejor, menos, peor,** which need **tanto. t.... como, as... as. t. siquiera,** even (see **siquiera**). **t. sólo,** only, solely (e.g. *No vengo t. sólo para saludarte,* I do not come merely to greet you). **qué... t.,** what a... (e.g. *¡Qué día t. hermoso!* What a lovely day!)
tanda /'tanda/ *f*, turn; opportunity; task; relay; game (of billiards); bad habit; collection, batch, group; round (of a game); (*Dance.*) set
tándem /'tandem/ *m*, tandem bicycle
tandeo /tan'deo/ *m*, allowance of irrigation water, turn for using water
Tangañica /taŋga'ɲika/ Tanganyika
tangente /tan'hente/ *a* and *f*, *Geom.* tangent
Tánger /'tanher/ Tangier
tangerino /tanhe'rino/ **(-na)** *a* and *n* of or from Tangier, Tangerine
tanque /'tanke/ *m*, *Mil.* tank; cistern, tank, reservoir; ladle, dipper
tanteador /tantea'ðor/ *m*, *Sports.* scorer, marker; scoreboard
tantear /tante'ar/ *vt* to measure, compare; consider fully; test, try out; *Fig.* probe, pump (persons); estimate roughly; *Art.* sketch, block in; *vt* and *vi Sports.* keep the score of
tanteo /tan'teo/ *m*, measurement, comparison; test; rough estimate; *Sports.* score
tanto /'tanto/ *a* so much; as much; very great; as great; *pl* **tantos,** so many; as many (e.g. *Tienen tantas flores como nosotros,* They have as many flowers as we). In comparisons **tanto** is used before **más, mejor, menos, peor,** but generally **tan** is used before adjectives and adverbs (e.g. *¡Tanto peor!* So much the worse!). *pron dem* that (e.g. *por lo t.,* therefore, on that account). *m,* so much, a certain amount; copy of a document; man, piece (in games); point (score in games); *Com.* rate (e.g. *el t. por ciento,* the percentage, the rate); *pl* approximation, odd (e.g. *Llegaron cien hombres y tantos,* A hundred-odd men arrived). *adv* so much; as much; so, in such a way. **t.... como,** the same as, as much as. **t.... cuanto,** as much as. **t. más,** the more. **t. menos,** the less (e.g. *Cuanto más (menos) dinero tiene t. más (menos) quiere,* The more (less) money he has, the more (less) he wants). **t. más (menos)... cuanto que,** all the more (less)... because. **algún t.,** a certain amount, somewhat. **al t. de (una cosa),** aware of, acquainted with (a thing). **en t.** *or* **entre t.,** meanwhile. **las tantas,** *Inf.* late hour, wee hours. **No es para t.,** *Inf.* It's not as bad as that, there's no need to make such a fuss; he (she, it) isn't equal to it. **otro t.,** the same, as much; as much more. **un t.,** a bit, somewhat
tañedor /taɲe'ðor/ **(-ra)** *n Mus.* player
tañer /ta'ɲer/ *vt irr Mus.* to play; *vi* sway, swing. **t. la occisa,** to sound the death (in hunting). *Pres. Part.* **tañendo.** *Preterite* **tañó, tañeron.** *Imperf. Subjunc.* **tañese, etc.**
tañido /ta'ɲiðo/ *m*, tune, sound, note; toll, peal; ring
taoísmo /tao'ismo/ *m*, Taoism
taoísta /tao'ista/ *mf* Taoist
tapa /'tapa/ *f*, lid; cover; cover (of books)
tapaboca /tapa'βoka/ *m*, blow on the mouth; *f*, scarf, muffler; *Inf.* remark that silences someone
tapada /ta'paða/ *f*, veiled woman, one whose face is hidden
tapadera /tapa'ðera/ *f*, loose lid, top, cover
tapadero /tapa'ðero/ *m*, stopper
tapado /ta'paðo/ *m*, *Argentina* coat, overcoat
tapador /tapa'ðor/ **(-ra)** *a* covering. *n* coverer. *m*, stopper; lid; cover
tapagujeros /tapagu'heros/ *m*, *Inf.* unskilled mason or bricklayer; *Fig. Inf.* stopgap (person)
tapar /ta'par/ *vt* to cover; cover with a lid; muffle up, veil; hide, keep secret; close up, stop up

taparrabo /tapa'rraβo/ *m*, loincloth; swimming trunks
tapete /ta'pete/ *m*, rug; tablecover. *Inf.* **t. verde,** gaming table. *Fig.* **estar sobre el t.,** to be on the carpet, be under consideration
tapia /'tapia/ *f*, adobe; mud wall; fence. *Inf.* **más sordo que una t.,** as deaf as a post
tapiar /ta'piar/ *vt* to wall up; put a fence around, fence in
tapicería /tapise'ria; tapiθe'ria/ *f*, set of tapestries; tapestry work; art of tapestry making; upholstery; tapestry storehouse or shop
tapicero /tapi'sero; tapi'θero/ *m*, tapestry weaver or maker; upholsterer; carpet layer; furnisher
tapioca /ta'pioka/ *f*, tapioca
tapisca /ta'piska/ *f Central America, Mexico* corn harvest
tapiz /ta'pis; ta'piθ/ *m*, tapestry; carpet
tapizar /tapi'sar; tapi'θar/ *vt* to cover with tapestry; cover, clothe; upholster; carpet; hang with tapestry; furnish with hangings or drapes
tapón /ta'pon/ *m*, stopper; cork (of a bottle); plug; *Surg.* tampon
taponar /tapo'nar/ *vt* to stopper, cork; plug; *Surg.* tampon; *Mil.* seal off
tapujarse /tapu'harse/ *vr* to wrap oneself up, muffle oneself
tapujo /ta'puho/ *m*, scarf, muffler, face covering; disguise; *Inf.* pretense, subterfuge
taquera /ta'kera/ *f*, rack (for billiard cues)
taquería /take'ria/ *f*, taco stand
taquigrafía /takigra'fia/ *f*, shorthand
taquigrafiar /takigra'fiar/ *vt* to write in shorthand
taquigráfico /taki'grafiko/ *a* shorthand
taquígrafo /ta'kigrafo/ **(-fa)** *n* shorthand writer, stenographer
taquilla /ta'kiya; ta'kiʎa/ *f*, booking office; box office; grille, window (in banks, etc.); rolltop desk, cupboard for papers; *Theat.* takings, cash
taquillero /taki'yero; taki'ʎero/ **(-ra)** *n* booking office clerk
tara /'tara/ *f*, tally stick; *Com.* tare
taracea /tara'sea; tara'θea/ *f*, inlaid work, marquetry
taracear /tarase'ar; taraθe'ar/ *vt* to inlay
tarambana /taram'bana/ *mf Inf.* madcap
tarántula /ta'rantula/ *f*, tarantula
tararear /tarare'ar/ *vt* to hum a tune
tarareo /tara'reo/ *m*, humming, singing under one's breath
tarasca /ta'raska/ *f*, figure of a dragon (carried in Corpus Christi processions); *Inf.* hag, trollop
tarascada /taras'kaða/ *f*, bite, nip; *Inf.* insolent reply
tarascar /taras'kar/ *vt* to bite; wound with the teeth
tardanza /tar'ðansa; tar'ðanθa/ *f*, delay, tardiness; slowness
tardar /tar'ðar/ *vi* to delay; be tardy, arrive late; take a long time. **a más t.,** at the latest
tarde /'tarðe/ *f*, afternoon. *adv* late. **¡Buenas tardes!** Good afternoon! **de t. en t.,** from time to time, sometimes. **hacerse t.,** to grow late. **Más vale t. que nunca,** Better late than never. **de la t. a la mañana,** overnight
tardecer /tarðe'ser/ *vi impers irr* to grow dusk. See **conocer**
tardecica, tardecita /tarðe'sika, tarðe'sita; tarðe'θika, tarðe'θita/ *f*, dusk, late afternoon
tardíamente /tar'ðiamente/ *adv* late; too late
tardío /tar'ðio/ *a* late; backward; behind; slow, deliberate
tardo /'tarðo/ *a* slow, slothful, tardy; late; dilatory; stupid, slow-witted; badly spoken, inarticulate
tarea /ta'rea/ *f*, task, work
tarifa /ta'rifa/ *f*, price list; tariff
tarifar /tari'far/ *vt* to put a tariff on
tarima /ta'rima/ *f*, stand, raised platform
tarín barín /ta'rin ba'rin/ *adv Inf.* more or less, about
tarja /'tarha/ *f*, large shield; ancient coin; tally stick. *Inf.* **beber sobre t.,** to drink on credit
tarjar /tar'har/ *vt* to reckon by tally; *Lat. Am.* cross out, erase

tarjeta /tar'heta/ f, buckler, small shield; *Archit.* tablet bearing an inscription; title (of maps and charts); visiting card; invitation (card). **t. de visita,** visiting card. **t. postal,** postcard, postal card

tarquín /tar'kin/ m, mud, mire

tárraga /'tarraga/ f, old Spanish dance

tarro /'tarro/ m, jar, pot; *Lat. Am.* top hat

tarso /'tarso/ m, *Anat.* tarsus, ankle; *Zool.* hock; *Ornith.* shank

tarta /'tarta/ f, cake pan; cake; tart

tártago /'tartago/ m, spurge; *Inf.* misfortune, disappointment

tartajear /tartahe'ar/ vi to stammer; stutter

tartajeo /tarta'heo/ m, stammering; stutter

tartajoso /tarta'hoso/ **(-sa)** a stammering; stuttering. n stutterer

tartalear /tartale'ar/ vi *Inf.* to stagger, totter; be speechless, be dumbfounded

tartamudear /tartamuðe'ar/ vi to stammer, stutter

tartamudeo /tartamu'ðeo/ m. **tartamudez** f, stammering; stuttering

tartamudo /tarta'muðo/ **(-da)** n stammerer

tartán /tar'tan/ m, tartan

tartana /tar'tana/ f, *Naut.* tartan; covered two-wheeled carriage

tartáreo /tar'tareo/ a *Poet.* infernal, hellish

tártaro /'tartaro/ **(-ra)** m, cream of tartar; tartar (on teeth); *Poet.* hell, hades. a and n Tartar

tartufo /tar'tufo/ m, hypocrite

tarugo /ta'rugo/ m, thick wooden peg; stopper; wooden block; a *Lat. Am.* dumb, stupid

tasa /'tasa/ f, assessment, valuation; valuation certificate; fixed price; standard rate; measure, rule. *Com.* **t. de cambio,** exchange rate

tasación /tasa'sion; tasa'θion/ f, valuation; assessment

tasador /tasa'ðor/ m, public assessor; valuer

tasajo /ta'saho/ m, salt meat; piece of meat

tasar /ta'sar/ vt to value; price; fix remuneration; tax; regulate; rate; dole out sparingly

tasca /'taska/ f, gambling den; tavern

tascar /tas'kar/ vt to dress (hemp, etc.); graze, crop the grass

tasquera /tas'kera/ f, *Inf.* quarrel, row, rumpus

tasquil /tas'kil/ m, wood splinter, chip

tata /'tata/ m, *Inf. West Hem.* daddy

tatarabuela /tatara'βuela/ f, great-great-grandmother

tatarabuelo /tatara'βuelo/ m, great-great-grandfather

tataradeudo /tatara'ðeuðo/ **(-da)** n very old relative; ancestor

tataranieta /tatara'nieta/ f, great-great-granddaughter

tataranieto /tatara'nieto/ m, great-great-grandson

tatas, andar a /'tatas, an'dar a/ vt to walk on all fours

¡tate! /'tate/ interj Stop!; Be careful!; Go slowly!; Now I understand!, Of course!

tatuaje /ta'tuahe/ m, tattooing

tatuar /tatu'ar/ vt to tattoo

taumaturgia /tauma'turhia/ f, thaumaturgy, wonder-working

taumaturgo /tauma'turgo/ m, thaumaturge, magician

taurino /tau'rino/ a taurine; pertaining to bullfights

Tauro /'tauro/ m, Taurus

tauromaquia /tauro'makia/ f, bullfighting, tauromachy

tautología /tautolo'hia/ f, tautology

taxi /'taksi/ m, taxi

taxidermia /taksi'ðermia/ f, taxidermy

taxidermista /taksiðer'mista/ mf taxidermist

taxista /tak'sista/ m, taxi driver

taxonomía /taksono'mia/ f, taxonomy

taza /'tasa; 'taθa/ f, cup; cupful; basin (of a fountain)

tazar /ta'sar; ta'θar/ **(se)** vt and vr to fray (of cloth)

taz a taz /tas a tas; taθ a taθ/ adv in exchange, without payment; even

tazón /ta'son; ta'θon/ m, large cup; bowl

te /te/ f, name of the letter T. mf dat. and acc. of pers pron 2nd pers sing thee; you; to thee, to you. Never used with a preposition

té /te/ m, tea

tea /tea/ f, torch; firebrand

teatral /tea'tral/ a theatrical

teatralidad /teatrali'ðað/ f, theatricality

teatro /te'atro/ m, theater; stage; dramatic works; dramatic art; drama, plays. **t. de variedades,** music hall. **t. por horas,** theater where short, one-act plays are staged hourly

teca /'teka/ f, teak

techado /te'tʃaðo/ m, ceiling; roof

techador /tetʃa'ðor/ m, roofer

techar /te'tʃar/ vt to roof

techo /'tetʃo/ m, roof; ceiling; dwelling, habitation

techumbre /te'tʃumbre/ f, ceiling; roof

tecla /'tekla/ f, key (of keyed instruments); typewriter, linotype, or calculating machine key; *Fig.* difficult or delicate point. *Inf.* **dar en la t.,** to hit on the right way of doing a thing

teclado /te'klaðo/ m, keyboard

tecleado /tekle'aðo/ m, *Mus.* fingering

teclear /tekle'ar/ vi to finger the keyboard; run one's fingers over the keyboard; *Inf.* drum or tap with the fingers; vt tap (the keys, etc.); *Inf.* try out various schemes

tecleo /te'kleo/ m, fingering the keys; *Inf.* drumming with the fingers; scheme, means

técnica /'teknika/ f, technique

tecnicismo /tekni'sismo; tekni'θismo/ m, technical jargon; technicality, technical term

técnico /'tekniko/ a technical. m, technician

tecnicolor /tekniko'lor/ m, technicolor

tecnología /teknolo'hia/ f, technology

tecnológico /tekno'lohiko/ a technological

tecnólogo /tek'nologo/ m, technologist

tecolote /teko'lote/ m, *Central America, Mexico* owl; *Mexico* cop (police officer)

tedero /te'ðero/ m, torch seller; torch holder

tedio /'teðio/ m, tedium, boredom, ennui

tedioso /te'ðioso/ a tedious, boring

teísmo /te'ismo/ m, theism

teísta /te'ista/ a theistic. mf theist

teja /'teha/ f, tile, slate. *Inf.* **de tejas abajo,** in the normal way; in the world of men. **de tejas arriba,** in a supernatural way; in heaven

tejadillo /teha'ðiyo; teha'ðiʎo/ m, roof (of a vehicle)

tejado /te'haðo/ m, roof

tejano, -a /te'hano/ a and m. Texan. **tejanos** jeans

tejar /te'har/ m, tile works. vt to roof with tiles

Tejas /'tehas/ m Texas

tejavana /teha'βana/ f, penthouse, open shed

tejedor /tehe'ðor/ **(-ra)** a weaving; *Inf.* scheming. n weaver; *Inf.* schemer

tejedura /tehe'ðura/ f, weaving; fabric; texture

tejeduría /teheðu'ria/ f, art of weaving; weaving shed or mill

tejemaneje /tehema'nehe/ m, *Inf.* cleverness, knack

tejer /te'her/ vt to weave; plait; spin a cocoon; arrange, regulate; concoct, hatch (schemes); wind in and out (in dancing)

tejero /te'hero/ m, tile manufacturer

tejido /te'hiðo/ m, texture, weaving; textile; *Anat.* tissue; fabric, material

tejo /'teho/ m, quoit, discus; metal disk; yew tree

tejón /te'hon/ m, *Zool.* badger

tela /'tela/ f, fabric, material, cloth; membrane; film (on liquids); spiderweb, cobweb; inner skin (of fruit, vegetables); film over the eye; matter, subject; scheme, plot. **t. metálica,** wire gauze. **en t. de juicio,** under consideration, in doubt. **llegarle a uno a las telas del corazón,** to hurt deeply, cut to the quick

telar /te'lar/ m, loom, weaving machine; *Theat.* gridiron

telaraña /tela'raɲa/ f, spider web, cobweb; mere trifle, bagatelle. *Inf.* **mirar las telarañas,** to be absent-minded. **Telaraña Global,** World Wide Web.

telarañoso /telara'ɲoso/ a cobwebby

telecomunicación /telekomunika'sion; telekomunika'θion/ f, telecommunication

telefonear /telefone'ar/ vt to telephone, call

telefonía /telefo'nia/ *f*, telephony. **t. sin hilos,** wireless telephony, broadcasting

telefónico /tele'foniko/ *a* telephonic

telefonista /telefo'nista/ *mf* telephone operator

teléfono /te'lefono/ *m*, telephone. **t. celular,** cellular phone. **llamar por t.** (a), to telephone, call

telefundir /telefun'dir/ *vt* to telecast

telegrafía /telegra'fia/ *f*, telegraphy. **t. sin hilos,** wireless telegraphy

telegrafiar /telegra'fiar/ *vt* to telegraph

telegráfico /tele'grafiko/ *a* telegraphic

telegrafista /telegra'fista/ *mf* telegraph operator

telégrafo /te'legrafo/ *m*, telegraph. **t. sin hilos,** wireless telegraph. *Inf.* **hacer telégrafos,** to talk by signs

telegrama /tele'grama/ *m*, telegram

telemetría /teleme'tria/ *f*, telemetry

telémetro /te'lemetro/ *m*, telemeter, rangefinder

teleología /teleolo'hia/ *f*, teleology

telepatía /telepa'tia/ *f*, telepathy

telepático /tele'patiko/ *a* telepathic

telescópico /teles'kopiko/ *a* telescopic

telescopio /teles'kopio/ *m*, telescope

telespectador /telespekta'ðor/ *m*, TV viewer, member of the television audience

teletipo /tele'tipo/ *m*, teleprinter

televisión /teleβi'sion/ *f*, television

telilla /te'liya; te'liʎa/ *f*, film (on liquids); thin fabric

telón /te'lon/ *m*, *Theat.* curtain; drop scene. **t. contra incendios, t. de seguridad,** *Theat.* safety curtain. **t. de boca,** drop curtain. **t. de foro,** drop scene

tema /'tema/ *m*, theme, subject; *Mus.* motif, theme; thesis, argument. *f*, obstinacy; obsession, mania; hostility, grudge, rancor

temático /te'matiko/ *a* thematic; pigheaded, obstinate

temblador /tembla'ðor/ **(-ra)** *a* trembling, shaking. *n* Quaker

temblante /tem'blante/ *a* shaking; quivering. *m*, bracelet

temblar /tem'blar/ *vi irr* to tremble, shake; wave, quiver; shiver with fear. See **acertar**

temblequear, tembletear /tembleke'ar, temblete'ar/ *vi Inf.* tremble; shake with fear

temblón /tem'blon/ *a Inf.* trembling, shaking. *m, Inf.* aspen

temblor /tem'blor/ *m*, shake, trembling, shiver. **temblor (de tierra)** earthquake

tembloroso, tembloso /temblo'roso, tem'bloso/ *a* trembling, shaking, shivering, quivering

temedero /teme'ðero/ *a* fearsome, dread

temedor /teme'ðor/ **(-ra)** *a* fearful. *n* fearer, dreader

temer /te'mer/ *vt* to fear, dread; suspect, imagine; *vi* be afraid

temerario /teme'rario/ *a* reckless, impetuous; thoughtless, hasty

temeridad /temeri'ðað/ *f*, recklessness, impetuosity, temerity; thoughtlessness; act of folly; rash judgment

temerón /teme'ron/ *a Inf.* swaggering, bombastic

temeroso /teme'roso/ *a* frightening, dread; fearful, timid; afraid, suspicious

temible /te'miβle/ *a* dread, awesome

temor /te'mor/ *m*, fear

temoso /te'moso/ *a* obstinate, headstrong

témpano /'tempano/ *m*, tabor; drumhead; block, flat piece; side of bacon. **t. de hielo,** iceberg, ice floe

temperación /tempera'sion; tempera'θion/ *f*, tempering

temperamento /tempera'mento/ *m*, temperament, nature; compromise; agreement

temperar /tempe'rar/ *vt* to temper; *Lat. Am.* spend the summer

temperatura /tempera'tura/ *f*, temperature

temperie /tem'perie/ *f*, weather conditions

tempestad /tempes'tað/ *f*, storm

tempestividad /tempestiβi'ðað/ *f*, opportuneness, seasonableness

tempestivo /tempes'tiβo/ *a* opportune, seasonable

tempestuoso /tempes'tuoso/ *a* stormy

templa /'templa/ *f*, tempera; *pl Anat.* temples

templado /tem'plaðo/ *a* moderate; temperate (of

regions); lukewarm; *Mus.* in tune; restrained (of style); *Inf.* brave, long-suffering. **estar bien** (*or* **mal**) **templado,** *Inf.* to be well (or badly) tuned (of musical instruments); be in a good (*or* bad) temper; be good- (*or* ill-) natured

templador /templa'ðor/ **(-ra)** *n* tuner. *m*, tuning key

templadura /templa'ðura/ *f*, tuning; tempering

templanza /tem'plansa; tem'planθa/ *f*, moderation; sobriety; mildness of climate

templar /tem'plar/ *vt* to tune; *Metall.* temper; moderate; warm; allay, appease; anneal; *Art.* harmonize, blend; *Naut.* trim the sails; *vr* control oneself, be moderate; *vi* grow warm

temple /'temple/ *m*, weather conditions; temperature; temper (of metals, etc.); nature, disposition; bravery; mean, average; *Mus.* tuning. **al t.,** in tempera

templete /tem'plete/ *m, dim* shrine; niche (for statues); kiosk, pavilion

templo /'templo/ *m*, temple

temporada /tempo'raða/ *f*, space of time, season, while. **de t.,** seasonal; temporary. **estar de t.,** to be out of town, on holiday

temporal /tempo'ral/ *a* temporal; temporary; secular, lay; transient, fugitive. *m*, storm, tempest; rainy period; seasonal laborer

temporalidad /temporali'ðað/ *f*, secular character; temporality secular possession (gen. *pl*)

temporáneo, temporario /tempora'neo, tempo'rario/ *a* temporary, impermanent, fleeting

témporas /'temporas/ *f pl*, Ember days

temporejar /tempore'har/ *vt Naut.* to lie to in a storm

temporero /tempo'rero/ *a* temporary (of work)

temporizar /tempori'sar; tempori'θar/ *vi* to while away the time; temporize

tempranal /tempra'nal/ *a* early fruiting

tempranear /temprane'ar/ *vi, Lat. Am.* to get up early

tempranero /tempra'nero/ *a* early

temprano /tem'prano/ *a* early. *adv* in the early hours; prematurely, too soon

temulento /temu'lento/ *a* intoxicated, drunken

tenacear /tenase'ar; tenaθe'ar/ *vi* to insist, be obstinate

tenacidad /tenasi'ðað; tenaθi'ðað/ *f*, adhesiveness; resistance, toughness; obstinacy, tenacity

tenacillas /tena'siyas; tena'θiʎas/ *f pl, dim* small tongs; candle snuffers; sugar tongs; curling irons; tweezers

tenaz /te'nas; te'naθ/ *a* adhesive; hard, resistant, unyielding; tenacious, obstinate

tenaza /te'nasa; te'naθa/ *f*, claw (of a lobster, etc.); *pl* pincers; pliers; dental forceps

tenazada /tena'saða; tena'θaða/ *f*, seizing with tongs; strong bite, snap; rattle of tongs

tenazón /tena'son; tena'θon/ (**a** or **de**) *adv* without taking aim, wildly; unexpectedly

tención /ten'sion; ten'θion/ *f*, retention, holding; grip

ten con ten /ten kon ten/ *m, Inf.* tact, diplomacy

tendal /ten'dal/ *m*, awning; sheet for catching olives; *Lat. Am.* heap, lot, pile, large amount, large number

tendedero /tende'ðero/ *m*, drying ground

tendedura /tende'ðura/ *f*, laying out; stretching

tendencia /ten'densia; ten'denθia/ *f*, tendency

tendencioso /tenden'sioso; tenden'θioso/ *a* tendentious, biased

tender /ten'der/ *vt irr* to hang out; unfold, spread out; extend, hold out; *Mas.* plaster; *vi* tend, incline; *vr* lie down at full length; place one's cards on the table; gallop hard (of horses). See **entender**

tendero /ten'dero/ **(-ra)** *n* shopkeeper; retailer. *m*, tent maker

tendido /ten'diðo/ *m*, row of seats in a bullfight arena; clothes hung out to dry; clear sky; *Mas.* plaster

tendón /ten'don/ *m*, tendon

tenducha /ten'dutʃa/ *f, Inf.* wretched little shop

tenebroso /tene'βroso/ *a* dark, gloomy

tenedero /tene'ðero/ *m, Naut.* anchoring ground, anchorage

tenedor /tene'ðor/ *m,* table fork; possessor, retainer; *Com.* holder; payee. **t. de libros,** bookkeeper

teneduría /teneðu'ria/ *f,* employment of a bookkeeper. **t. de libros,** bookkeeping

tenencia /te'nensia; te'nenθia/ *f,* possession; tenancy, occupation; lieutenancy

tener /te'ner/ *vt irr* to have; hold; grasp; possess, own; uphold, maintain; contain; include; hold fast, grip; stop; keep (promises); lodge, accommodate; (*with en*) value, estimate (e.g. *Le tengo en poco,* I have a poor opinion of him); (*with para*) be of the opinion that (e.g. *tengo para mí,* my opinion is); (*with por*) believe, consider; *vi* be wealthy; *vr* steady oneself; hold on to; lean (on); rest (on); defend oneself; uphold; rely on; (*with por*) consider oneself as. **tener** is used to express: 1. *Age* (e.g. *¿Cuántos años tiene Vd.?* How old are you?). 2. *Possession* (e.g. *Tenemos muchos sombreros,* We have a great many hats). 3. *Measurements* (e.g. *El cuarto tiene dieciocho metros de largo,* The room is eighteen meters long). Translated by "be" when describing some physical and mental states (e.g. *Tenemos miedo,* We are afraid. *Tengo sueño,* I am sleepy. *Tienen frío* (*calor*), They are cold (hot)). Used as *auxiliary verb* replacing *haber* in compound tenses of transitive verbs (e.g. *Tengo escritas las cartas,* I have written the letters). **t. a bien,** to think fit, please, judge convenient. **t. algo en cuenta a uno,** to hold something against someone. **t. a menos de hacer** (**una cosa),** to scorn to do (a thing). **t. cruda,** to have a hangover. **t. curiosidad por,** to be curious about. **t. curiosidad por que** + *subj* to be interested that. **t. en aprecio,** to appreciate, esteem, value. **t. en cuenta,** to bear in mind. **t. en menos** (**a**), to despise (a person). **t. gana,** to want, wish; feel disposed; have an appetite. **t. lugar,** to take place, occur. **t. muchas partes cruzadas,** to be well-traveled. **t. mucho colegio** to be well-educated. **t. muy en cuenta,** to certainly bear in mind. **t. poco colegio,** to have had little education. **t. presente,** to remember. **t. que,** to have to (e.g. *tengo que hacerlo,* I must do it). **t. que ver** (**con),** to have something to do (with), be related to. **no tenerlas todas consigo,** *Inf.* to have the jitters. *Pres. Indic.* **tengo, tienes, tiene, tenemos, tenéis, tienen.** *Preterite* **tuve, etc.** *Fut.* **tendré, etc.** *Condit.* **tendría, etc.** *Pres. Subjunc.* **tenga, etc.** *Imperf. Subjunc.* **tuviese, etc.**

tenguerengue, en /teŋgue'reŋgue, en/ *adv Inf.* rickety, insecure

tenia /'tenia/ *f,* tapeworm; *Archit.* fillet, narrow molding

teniente /te'niente/ *a* owning, holding; unripe (of fruit); *Inf.* slightly deaf; stingy, mean. *m,* deputy, substitute; *Mil.* first lieutenant, lieutenant. **t. coronel,** lieutenant colonel. **t. de navío,** naval lieutenant. **t. general,** *Mil.* lieutenant general. **t. general de aviación,** air marshal

tenis /'tenis/ *m,* tennis

tenor /te'nor/ *m,* import, contents (of a letter, etc.); constitution; composition; *Mus.* tenor

tenorio /te'norio/ *m,* rake, Don Juan, philanderer

tensar /ten'sar/ *vt* to tighten; tense

tensión /ten'sion/ *f,* tautness; tension; strain, stress; *Elec.* tension

tenso /'tenso/ *a* taut; tight; tense

tentación /tenta'sion; tenta'θion/ *f,* temptation; attraction, inducement

tentáculo /ten'takulo/ *m,* tentacle; feeler

tentadero /tenta'ðero/ *m,* yard for trying out young bulls for bullfighting

tentador /tenta'ðor/ (**-ra**) *a* tempting; attractive. *n* tempter. *m,* the Devil

tentalear /tentale'ar/ *vt* to examine by touch

tentar /ten'tar/ *vt irr* to touch, feel; examine by touch; incite, encourage; try, endeavor; test; tempt; *Surg.* probe. See **sentar**

tentativa /tenta'tiβa/ *f,* endeavor, attempt; preliminary exam (at some univs.)

tentativo /tenta'tiβo/ *a* tentative, experimental

tentemozo /tente'moso; tente'moθo/ *m,* support, prop; tumbler (toy)

tentempié /tentem'pie/ *m, Inf.* snack, bite

tenue /'tenue/ *a* thin; slender, delicate; trivial, worthless, insignificant; pale; faint

tenuidad /tenui'ðað/ *f,* slenderness; delicacy; triviality, insignificance; paleness; faintness

teñidura /teɲi'ðura/ *f,* dyeing, staining

teñir /te'ɲir/ *vt irr* to dye; *Art.* darken; color, tinge; *vr* be dyed; be tinged or colored. See **ceñir**

teocracia /teo'krasia; teo'kraθia/ *f,* theocracy

teocrático /teo'kratiko/ *a* theocratic

teodolito /teoðo'lito/ *m,* theodolite

telogal /teolo'gal/ *a* theological

teología /teolo'hia/ *f,* theology, divinity

teológico /teo'lohiko/ *a* theological

teologizar /teolohi'sar; teolohi'θar/ *vi* to theologize

teólogo /te'ologo/ *a* theological. *m,* theologian, divine; student of theology

teorema /teo'rema/ *m,* theorem

teoría /teo'ria/ *f,* theory

teórica /teo'orika/ *f,* theory

teórico /te'oriko/ *a* theoretical, speculative. *m,* theorist

teorizar /teori'sar; teori'θar/ *vt* to consider theoretically, theorize about

teoso /te'oso/ *a* resinous, gummy

teosofía /teoso'fia/ *f,* theosophy

teosófico /teo'sofiko/ *a* theosophical

teósofo /te'osofo/ *m,* theosophist

tepe /'tepe/ *m,* sod, cut turf

tequila /te'kila/ *f Mexico* tequila, maguey brandy

terapeuta /tera'peuta/ *mf* therapeutist

terapéutica /tera'peutika/ *f,* therapeutics

terapéutico /tera'peutiko/ *a* therapeutical

terapia /te'rapia/ *f,* therapy. **t. física,** physical therapy

teratología /teratolo'hia/ *f,* teratology

tercena /ter'sena; ter'θena/ *f,* warehouse for storing government monopoly goods (tobacco, etc.)

tercenista /terse'nista; terθe'nista/ *mf* person in charge of a tercena

tercer /ter'ser; ter'θer/ *a abb* of **tercero** third. Used before *m, sing* nouns

tercera /ter'sera; ter'θera/ *f,* procuress; *Mus.* third

tercería /terse'ria; terθe'ria/ *f,* arbitration, mediation; temporary occupation of a fortress, etc.

tercero /ter'sero; ter'θero/ (**-ra**) *a* third; mediatory. *n* third; mediator. *m,* pimp; *Eccl.* tertiary; tithes collector; third person. **¡A la tercera va la vencida!** Third time lucky!

terceto /ter'seto; ter'θeto/ *m,* tercet, triplet

tercia /'tersia; 'terθia/ *f,* one-third; *Eccl.* tierce, third hour; storehouse for tithes. **tercias reales,** royal share of ecclesiastical tithes

terciana /ter'siana; ter'θiana/ *f,* tertian fever

terciar /ter'siar; ter'θiar/ *vt* to slant; sling sideways; divide into three; equalize weight (on beasts of burden); plow or dig for the third time; *Agr.* prune; *vr* be opportune, come at the right time. *vi* mediate, arbitrate; make up a number (for cards, etc.); reach the third day (of the moon); take part, participate

tercio /'tersio; 'terθio/ *a* third. *m,* one-third; *Mil.* infantry regiment; *Obs.,* body of foreign volunteers; fishermen's association; *pl* brawny limbs of a man. **hacer t.,** to take part in; make up the number of.

hacer buen (*or* **mal**) **t. a alguien,** to do someone a good (*or* bad) turn

terciopelo /tersio'pelo; terθio'pelo/ *m,* velvet; velveteen

terco /'terko/ *a* pigheaded, obstinate; hard, tough

tergiversación /terhiβersa'sion; terhiβersa'θion/ *f,* tergiversation, vacillation

tergiversar /terhiβer'sar/ *vt* to tergiversate, shuffle, vacillate

termal /ter'mal/ *a* thermal

termas /'termas/ *f pl,* thermal springs, hot mineral baths; thermal

térmico /'termiko/ *a* thermic

terminable /termi'naβle/ *a* terminable

terminación /termina'sion; termina'θion/ *f,* conclusion, termination; end, finish; ending of a word; *Gram.* termination

terminador /termina'ðor/ **(-ra)** *a* concluding. *n* finisher

terminal /termi'nal/ *a* terminal; final. *m, Elec.* terminal. **t. de carga,** cargo terminal

terminante /termi'nante/ *a* conclusive, definite; categorical

terminar /termi'nar/ *vt* to end, conclude; complete; *vr* and *vi* end

término /'termino/ *m,* limit, end; term, expression; boundary marker; district, suburb; space, period; state, condition; boundary; object, aim; appearance, demeanor, behavior (gen. *pl*); completion; *Mus.* tone; (*Math., Law. Logic.*) term. **t. medio,** *Math.* average; medium; compromise, middle way. **correr el t.,** to lapse (of time). **en primer t.,** *Art.* in the foreground. **medios términos,** evasions, excuses. **primer t.,** (cinema) closeup

terminología /terminolo'hia/ *f,* terminology

termita /ter'mita/ *f,* thermite. *m,* termite

termodinámica /termoði'namika/ *f,* thermodynamics

termoeléctrico /termoe'lektriko/ *a* thermoelectric

termómetro /ter'mometro/ *m,* thermometer

termos /'termos/ *m,* thermos, vacuum bottle

termoscopio /termos'kopio/ *m,* thermoscope

termostático /termos'tatiko/ *a* thermostatic

termóstato /ter'mostato/ *m,* thermostat

terna /'terna/ *f,* triad, trio; set of dice

ternario /ter'nario/ *a* ternal, ternary

terne /'terne/ *a Inf.* bullying, braggartly; persistent, obstinate; robust. *mf* bully

ternera /ter'nera/ *f,* female calf; veal

ternero /ter'nero/ *m,* male calf

terneza /ter'nesa; ter'neθa/ *f,* tenderness, kindness; softness; softheartedness; endearment, caress, compliment (gen. *pl*)

ternilla /ter'niya; ter'niʎa/ *f,* cartilage, gristle

ternísimo /ter'nisimo/ *a sup* **tierno** most tender

terno /'terno/ *m,* triad; suit of clothes, three-piece suit; oath, curse

ternura /ter'nura/ *f,* softness; softheartedness; tenderness, kindness, sweetness

terquedad, terquería, terqueza /ter'kesa; terke'ðað, terke'ria, ter'keθa/ *f,* obstinacy, obduracy

terracota /terra'kota/ *f,* terra cotta

terrado /te'rraðo/ *m,* flat roof

Terranova /terra'noβa/ Newfoundland

terraplén /terra'plen/ *m,* embankment; *Mil.* terreplein

terraplenar /terraple'nar/ *vt* to fill up with earth; fill in (a hollow); make into an embankment; terrace

terrateniente /terrate'niente/ *mf* landowner

terraza /te'rrasa; te'rraθa/ *f,* terrace; flat roof; flower border (of a garden)

terrazgo /te'rrasgo; te'rraθgo/ *m,* tillable land; rent for farming land

terregoso /terre'goso/ *a* lumpy, full of clods (of soil)

terremoto /terre'moto/ *m,* earthquake

terrenal /terre'nal/ *a* terrestrial

terreno /te'rreno/ *a* terrestrial. *m,* ground, land; *Fig.* sphere; region; soil; plot of land. **ganar t.,** *Fig.* to win ground, make progress. **medir el t.,** *Fig.* to feel one's way

térreo /'terreo/ *a* earthy

terrero /te'rrero/ *a* earthly; low-flying, almost touching the ground; humble. *m,* flat roof; pile or mound of earth; deposit of earth, alluvium; target; mineral refuse

terrestre /te'rrestre/ *a* terrestrial, earthly

terrezuela /terre'suela; terre'θuela/ *f,* poor soil

terribilidad /terriβili'ðað/ *f,* terribleness, horribleness; rudeness

terribilísimo /terriβi'lisimo/ *a sup* most terrible

terrible /te'rriβle/ *a* terrible, horrible; rude, unsociable, ill-humored; enormous, huge

terrífico /te'rrifiko/ *a* terrible, frightful

territorial /territo'rial/ *a* territorial

territorialidad /territoriali'ðað/ *f,* territoriality

territorio /terri'torio/ *m,* territory; jurisdiction. **t. bajo mandato,** mandated territory

terrizo /te'rriso; te'rriθo/ *a* earthen

terrón /te'rron/ *m,* clod (of earth); lump; *pl* lands, landed property. **t. de azúcar,** lump of sugar

terrorismo /terro'rismo/ *m,* terrorism

terrorista /terro'rista/ *mf* terrorist

terrosidad /terrosi'ðað/ *f,* earthiness

terroso /te'rroso/ *a* earthy; earthen

terruño /te'rruɲo/ *m,* plot of ground; native earth; country; soil

terso /'terso/ *a* smooth, shiny, glossy; *Lit.* elegant, polished (style)

tersura /ter'sura/ *f,* smoothness, glossiness; elegance (of style)

tertulia /ter'tulia/ *f,* regular social meeting (gen. in cafés); conversational group; party; part of Spanish cafés set apart for players of chess, etc. **hacer t.,** to meet for conversation

tertuliano /tertu'liano/ **(-na)** *n* **tertuliante,** *mf* **tertulio (-ia),** *n* member of a tertulia

terzuelo /ter'suelo; ter'θuelo/ *m,* third, third part

Tesalia /te'salia/ Thessaly

tesar /te'sar/ *vt Naut.* to make taut; *vi* step backward, back (oxen)

tesela /te'sela/ *f,* tessera, square used in mosaic work

teselado /tese'laðo/ *a* tessellated

tesina /te'sina/ *f,* master's essay, thesis

tesis /'tesis/ *f,* thesis

teso /'teso/ *a* tight, taut, tense. *m,* hilltop; bulge, lump

tesón /te'son/ *m,* persistence, obstinacy, tenacity

tesonería /tesone'ria/ *f,* stubbornness, obstinacy

tesorería /tesore'ria/ *f,* treasury; treasuryship

tesorero /teso'rero/ **(-ra)** *n* treasurer

tesoro /te'soro/ *m,* treasure; public treasury; hoard; *Fig.* gem, excellent person; thesaurus. **t. de duende,** fairy gold

tespíades /tes'piaðes/ *f pl,* the muses

testa /'testa/ *f,* head; face, front; *Inf.* sense, acumen. **t. coronada,** crowned head

testación /testa'sion; testa'θion/ *f,* erasure, crossing out

testado /tes'taðo/ *a* testate

testador /testa'ðor/ **(-ra)** *n* testator

testaferro /testa'ferro/ *m, Fig.* figurehead, proxy

testamentar /testamen'tar/ *vt* to bequeath

testamentaria /testamen'taria/ *f,* execution of a will; *Law.* estate; executors' meeting

testamentario /testamen'tario/ *a* testamental, testamentary

testamento /testa'mento/ *m, Law.* will; testament. **Antiguo T.,** Old Testament. **ordenar** (*or* **otorgar) su t.,** to make one's will

testar /tes'tar/ *vi* to make a will; *vt* erase, cross out

testarada /testa'raða/ *f,* a blow with the head; pigheadedness, stubbornness

testarrón /testa'rron/ *a Inf.* pigheaded

testarudez /testaru'ðes; testaru'ðeθ/ *f,* obstinacy, obduracy

testarudo /testa'ruðo/ *a* stubborn, obstinate

testera /tes'tera/ *f,* front, face; front seat (in a vehicle); upper half of an animal's face; tester, canopy

testículo /tes'tikulo/ *m,* testicle

testificación /testifika'sion; testifika'θion/ *f,* testification

testificar /testifi'kar/ *vt* to testify; affirm, assert; attest, prove

testigo /tes'tigo/ *mf* witness. *m,* proof, evidence. *Law.* **t. de cargo,** witness for the prosecution. *Law.* **t. de descargo,** witness for the defense. **t. de vista,** eyewitness. *Law.* **hacer testigos,** to bring forward witnesses

testimonial /testimo'nial/ *a* confirmatory, proven

testimoniar /testimo'niar/ *vt* to attest, confirm, bear witness to

testimoniero /testimo'niero/ **(-ra)** *a* slanderous; hypocritical. *n* slanderer, hypocrite

testimonio /testi'monio/ *m,* testimony, proof; slander; affidavit

testuz /tes'tus; tes'tuθ/ *m*, front of the head (of some animals); nape (of animals)

teta /'teta/ *f*, mammary gland, breast; teat, dug, udder. **dar la t.** (a), to suckle

tétano, tétanos /'tetano, 'tetanos/ *m*, tetanus

tetera /te'tera/ *f*, teapot; teakettle; *Lat. Am.* (feeding) bottle

tetilla /te'tiya; te'tiʎa/ *f*, *dim* rudimentary teat or nipple; nipple (of a nursing bottle)

tétrico /'tetriko/ *a* gloomy; somber

teutón /teu'ton/ **(-ona)** *n* Teuton. *a* Teutonic

teutónico /teu'toniko/ *a* Teutonic

textil /teks'til/ *a* and *m*, textile

texto /'teksto/ *m*, text; quotation, citation; textbook

textorio /teks'torio/ *a* textile

textual /teks'tual/ *a* textual

textualista /tekstua'lista/ *mf* textualist

textura /teks'tura/ *f*, texture; weaving; structure (of a novel, etc.); animal structure

tez /tes; teθ/ *f*, complexion, skin

ti /ti/ *pers pron 2nd sing mf dat acc abl* thee, you. Always used with prep. (e.g. *por ti*, by thee (you))

tía /'tia/ *f*, aunt; *Inf.* wife, mother, dame; *Inf.* coarse creature. **t. abuela**, grandaunt, great-aunt. *Inf.* **quedarse para t.**, to be left an old maid

tianguis /'tiaŋguis/ *m*, *Central America, Mexico* open-air market

tiara /'tiara/ *f*, ancient Persian headdress; papal tiara; coronet; dignity and power of the papacy

tiberino /tiβe'rino/ *a* Tiberine

tibetano /tiβe'tano/ **(-na)** *a* and *n* Tibetan. *m*, Tibetan (language)

tibia /'tiβia/ *f*, flute; tibia

tibieza /ti'βiesa; ti'βieθa/ *f*, tepidity; indifference, lack of enthusiasm

tibio /'tiβio/ *a* tepid, lukewarm; indifferent, unenthusiastic

tiburón /tiβu'ron/ *m*, shark

ticket /'tikket/ *m*, ticket; pass, membership card

tico, -a /'tiko/ *mf inf* Costa Rican

tictac /tik'tak/ *m*, ticktock (of a clock)

tiempo /'tiempo/ *m*, time; season; epoch, period; chance, opportunity; leisure, free time; weather; *Mus.* tempo; *Gram.* tense; *Naut.* storm. **t. ha**, many years ago, long ago. **t. medio** *or* **medio t.**, *Sports.* halftime. **abrir el t.**, to clear up (of the weather). **ajustar los tiempos**, to fix the date (chronology). **a largo t.**, after a long time. **andando el t.**, in the course of time. **a su t.**, in due course, at the proper time. **a t.**, in time, at the right time. **a un t.**, simultaneously, at the same time. **cargarse el t.**, to cloud over (of the sky). **con t.**, in advance, with time; in time. **correr el t.**, to pass, move on (of time). **de t. en t.**, from time to time. **engañar** (*or* **entretener**) **el t.**, to kill time, while away the hours. *Inf.* **en t., de Maricastaña** *or* **del rey Perico**, long, long ago. **fuera de t.**, unseasonably, inopportunely; out of season. **ganar t.**, to gain time; *Inf.* hurry. **hacer t.**, to wait, cool one's heels; *Fig.* mark time. **perder el t.**, to waste time; misspend or lose time. **sentarse el t.**, to clear up (of the weather). **tomarse t. (para)**, to postpone, take time for (or to)

tienda /'tienda/ *f*, tent; *Naut.* awning, canopy; shop, store. **t. de abarrotes** *Lat. Am.* grocery store, grocery, grocer's. **t. de antigüedades**, antique shop. **t. de campaña**, bell tent, pavilion. **t. oxígena**, oxygen tent

tienta /'tienta/ *f*, astuteness; cleverness; *Surg.* probe; trying out young bulls for the bullring. **a tientas**, by touch, gropingly

tientaparedes /tientapa'reðes/ *mf* one who gropes one's way

tiento /'tiento/ *m*, touching, feeling; touch, feel; blind person's cane; tightrope walker's pole; manual control, steady hand; caution, care, tact; *Mus.* preliminary flourish; *Inf.* slap buffet; tentacle. **a t.**, by touch; unsurely, gropingly

tierno /'tierno/ *a* soft; tender; kind; sweet; delicate; softhearted; fresh, recent; affectionate

tierra /'tierra/ *f*, world, planet; earth; soil; ground; cultivated ground, land; homeland, native land; region; district, territory. **t. adentro**, inland. **t. de batán**, fuller's earth. **t. de Promisión**, Promised Land. **t. de Siena**, sienna. besar la **t.**, *Inf.* to fall down. **dar en t. con**, to throw down; demolish. **echar en t.**, *Naut.* to put ashore, land. **echar por t.**, *Fig.* to overthrow, destroy. **echar t. a**, *Fig.* to bury, forget. *Inf.* **la t. de María Santísima**, Andalusia. **por t.**, overland. **saltar en t.**, to land, disembark. **venir** (*or* **venirse**) **a t.**, to fall down, topple over

Tierra Santa /'tierra 'santa/ Holy Land

tieso /'tieso/ *a* hard, rigid, stiff; healthy, robust; taut; spirited, courageous; obstinate, stiff-necked; distant, formal. *adv* firmly, strongly

tiesto /'tiesto/ *m*, flowerpot; broken piece of earthenware

tiesura /tie'sura/ *f*, hardness, rigidity, stiffness; physical fitness; courageousness; obstinacy; formality, stiffness

tifoidea /tifoi'ðea/ *f*, typhoid

tifón /ti'fon/ *m*, typhoon

tifus /'tifus/ *m*, typhus. **t. exantemático**, trench fever

tigre /'tigre/ *m*, tiger; ferocious person; *Lat. Am.* jaguar

tijera /ti'hera/ *f*, scissors (gen. *pl*); any scissor-shaped instrument; shears; drainage channel; carpenter's horse; scandalmonger, gossip

tijeretada /tihere'taða/ *f*, cut or snip with scissors

tijeretear /tiherete'ar/ *vt* to cut with scissors; *Inf.* interfere arbitrarily

tijereteo /tihere'teo/ *m*, scissor cut; click of the scissors

tila /'tila/ *f*, lime tree or flower; linden tree or flower; infusion made of lime flowers

tildar /til'dar/ *vt* to cross out, erase; stigmatize; place a tilde over a letter

tilde /'tilde/ *mf*, bad reputation; tilde; *f*, jot, iota

tilín /ti'lin/ *m*, tinkle, peal (of a bell)

tillar /ti'yar; ti'ʎar/ *vt* to lay wood floors

tilo /'tilo/ *m*, lime tree

timador /tima'ðor/ **(-ra)** *n Inf.* swindler, sharper, cheat

timar /ti'mar/ *vt* to swindle, cheat, deceive; *vr Inf.* exchange looks or winks

timba /'timba/ *f*, *Inf.* casino, gambling den; game of chance

timbal /tim'bal/ *m*, kettledrum

timbalero /timba'lero/ *m*, kettledrum player

timbrador /timbra'ðor/ *m*, stamper; stamping machine; rubber stamp

timbrar /tim'brar/ *vt* to stamp; place the crest over a coat of arms

timbre /'timbre/ *m*, postage stamp; heraldic crest; excise stamp; bell, push-button; *Mus.* timbre; noble deed; personal merit; *Mexico* (postage) stamp; *Lat. Am.* description (of a person or goods)

timidez /timi'ðes; timi'ðeθ/ *f*, timidity, nervousness

tímido /'timiðo/ *a* timid, nervous

timo /'timo/ *m*, *Inf.* swindling, trick; thymus

timón /ti'mon/ *m*, *Naut.* helm; rudder; management, direction; stick of a rocket. **t. de dirección**, *Aer.* tailfin

timonear /timone'ar/ *vi Naut.* to steer

timonel, timonero /timo'nel, timo'nero/ *m*, helmsman, coxswain

timorato /timo'rato/ *a* godfearing; timid, vacillating

tímpano /'timpano/ *m*, *Anat.* eardrum, tympanum; *Mus.* kettledrum; *Archit.* tympanum; *Print.* tympan

tina /'tina/ *f*, vat; flour bin; large earthenware jar; wooden tub; bath

tinaco /ti'nako/ *m*, *Mexico* (water) tank

tinada /ti'naða/ *f*, woodpile; cow shed

tinaja /ti'naha/ *f*, large earthenware jar; jarful

tinajero /tina'hero/ *m*, seller of earthenware jars

tinelo /ti'nelo/ *m*, servants' hall

tinerfeño /tiner'feɲo/ **(-ña)** *a* and *n* of or from Tenerife

tinglado /tiŋ'glaðo/ *m*, overhanging roof; open shed; penthouse; intrigue

tiniebla /ti'nieβla/ *f*, gloom, darkness (gen. *pl*); *pl* profound ignorance; confusion of mind; *Eccl.* tenebrae

tino /'tino/ *m,* skilled sense of touch; good eye, accurate aim; judgment, shrewdness; *vat.* **sacar de t. (a),** to bewilder, confuse; irritate, exasperate. **sin t.,** without limit, excessively

tinta /'tinta/ *f,* color, tint; ink; staining, dyeing; dye, stain; *pl* shades, colors; *Art.* mixed colors ready for painting. **t. china,** India ink. **t. simpática,** invisible ink. **recargar las tintas,** *Fig.* to overpaint, lay the colors on too thick. *Inf.* **saber de buena t.** (**una cosa**), to learn (a thing) from a reliable source

tintar /tin'tar/ *vt* to dye; color, tinge, stain

tinte /'tinte/ *m,* dyeing, staining; color; dye; stain; dye house; pretext, disguise

tintero /tin'tero/ *m,* inkwell. *Inf.* **dejar** (*or* **quedársele a uno**) **en el t.,** to forget, omit (to say, write)

tintín /tin'tin/ *m,* ring, peal; clink; chink

tintinar /tinti'nar/ *vi* to ring, tinkle; clink; jingle

tintineo /tinti'neo/ *m,* ringing, tinkling; clinking; jingle

tinto /'tinto/ *a* red (of wine). *m,* red wine; dark red

tintorera /tinto'rera/ *f, Lat. Am.* shark

tintorería /tintore'ria/ *f,* dyeing industry; dyeing and dry-cleaning shop

tintorero /tinto'rero/ (**-ra**) *n* dyer; dry cleaner

tintura /tin'tura/ *f,* dyeing, staining; color, tint; dye; stain; tincture; smattering, slight knowledge

tinturar /tintu'rar/ *vt* to dye; color, tinge, stain; give a superficial notion of

tiña /'tiɲa/ *f,* ringworm; *Inf.* meanness, stinginess

tiñoso /ti'ɲoso/ *a* mangy; afflicted with ringworm; *Inf.* mean, stingy

tiñuela /ti'ɲuela/ *f,* shipworm

tío /'tio/ *m,* uncle; gaffer; fellow, chap; fool; stepfather; father-in-law. **t. abuelo,** granduncle, great-uncle

tiovivo /tio'βiβo/ *m,* merry-go-round

típico /'tipiko/ *a* typical

tiple /'tiple/ *m,* soprano or treble voice. *mf* soprano

tipo /'tipo/ *m,* model, pattern; type; print, type; species, group (of animals, etc.); *Inf.* guy, chap. *Com.* **t. de cambio,** exchange rate

tipografía /tipogra'fia/ *f,* typography

tipográfico /tipo'grafiko/ *a* typographical

tipógrafo /ti'pografo/ *m,* typographer

típula /'tipula/ *f,* daddy-longlegs

tiquismiquis /tikis'mikis/ *m pl,* ridiculous scruples; affected courtesies. *a Inf.* faddy, fussy

tira /'tira/ *f,* strip, band, ribbon; stripe, rib. **t. cómica,** comic strip

tirabotas /tira'βotas/ *m,* buttonhook

tirabuzón /tiraβu'son; tiraβu'θon/ *m,* corkscrew; ringlet, curl; hair curler

tirada /ti'raða/ *f,* throwing; drawing, pulling; cast, throw; distance, range; *Print.* edition, issue; circulation (of a newspaper, etc.); stroke (in golf); lapse, interval (of time). **t. aparte,** reprint (of an article, etc.)

tiradero /tira'ðero/ *m,* shooting butt

tirado /ti'raðo/ *a Inf.* dirt-cheap. *m,* wire drawing

tirador /tira'ðor/ (**-ra**) *n* thrower, caster; drawer, puller; marksman. *m,* handle, knob; *Mech.* trigger; bell rope, bell pull; *Print.* pressman. **t. de bota,** boot tag. **t. de gomas,** catapult. **t. de oro,** gold wire drawer

tiralíneas /tira'lineas/ *m,* ruling pen

tiramiento /tira'miento/ *m,* pulling; stretching

tiramira /tira'mira/ *f,* long, narrow mountain range; long line of persons or things; distance

tiranía /tira'nia/ *f,* tyranny, despotism

tiranicida /tirani'siða; tirani'θiða/ *mf* tyrannicide (person)

tiranicidio /tirani'siðio; tirani'θiðio/ *m,* tyrannicide (act)

tiránico /ti'raniko/ *a* tyrannical

tiranización /tiranisa'sion; tiraniθa'θion/ *f,* tyranny, tyrannization

tiranizar /tirani'sar; tirani'θar/ *vt* to tyrannize over

tirano /ti'rano/ (**-na**) *a* tyrannous, tyrannical; *Fig.* overwhelming, dominating. *n* tyrant

tirante /ti'rante/ *a* taut; tense, strained. *m,* trace (of a harness); shoulderstrap; suspender (gen. *pl*); *Archit.* tie

tirantez /tiran'tes; tiran'teθ/ *f,* tautness; tension, strain; straight distance between two points. **estado de t.,** *Polit.* strained relations

tiranuelo /tira'nuelo/ *m,* petty tyrant

tirar /ti'rar/ *vt* to throw, cast; fling, aim, toss; throw down, overthrow; pull; draw; discharge, shoot; stretch, pull out; rule, draw (lines); squander, waste; *Print.* print; *vi* attract; pull; (*with prep a*) turn to, turn in the direction of; incline, tend to; incline toward, have a tinge of (colors); try, aspire to; (*with de*) wield, unsheath, draw out (firearms, arms); *vr* cast oneself, precipitate oneself; throw oneself on. *Inf.* **ir tirando,** to carry on, get along somehow

tirilla /ti'riya; ti'riʎa/ *f, Sew.* shirt neckband

tiritaña /tiri'taɲa/ *f,* thin silk material; *Inf.* mere nothing, trifle

tiritar /tiri'tar/ *vi* to shiver with cold

tiritón /tiri'ton/ *m,* shiver, shudder

Tiro /'tiro/ Tyre

tiro /'tiro/ *m,* throwing; throw, cast; toss, fling; try (in football); shooting; piece of artillery; report, shot (of a gun); discharge (firearms); shooting range or gallery; team (of horses); range (of firearms, etc.); hoisting cable; flight (of stairs); *Mineral.* shaft; *Inf.* trick; robbery, theft; innuendo, insinuation; grave harm or injury; *pl* sword belt. **t. de pichón,** pigeon shooting. **t. par,** four-in-hand. **a t.,** within firing range; within reach. **de tiros largos,** *Inf.* in full regalia

tirocinio /tiro'sinio; tiro'θinio/ *m,* apprenticeship

tiroideo /tiroi'ðeo/ *a* thyroid

tiroides /ti'roiðes/ *f,* thyroid gland

tirón /ti'ron/ *m,* novice, beginner; pull, tug, heave. **de un t.,** with one tug; at one stroke, at one blow

tiroriro /tiro'riro/ *m, Inf.* sound of a wind instrument; *pl Inf.* wind instruments

tirotearse /tirote'arse/ *vr Mil.* to exchange fire; indulge in repartee

tiroteo /tiro'teo/ *m,* shooting, exchange of shots; crackle (of rifle fire)

Tirreno, el Mar /ti'rreno, el mar/ the Tyrrhenian Sea

tirria /'tirria/ *f, Inf.* hostility, grudge, dislike

tirulato /tiru'lato/ *a* dumbfounded, stupefied

tisana /ti'sana/ *f,* tisane

tísico /'tisiko/ (**-ca**) *a* tuberculous. *n* sufferer from tuberculosis, consumptive

tisis /'tisis/ *f,* tuberculosis

tisú /ti'su/ *m,* silver or gold tissue

titánico /ti'taniko/ *a* titanesque; colossal, huge

títere /'titere/ *m,* puppet; *Fig. Inf.* dummy, grotesque; *Inf.* fool; obsession, fixed idea; *pl Inf.* circus; Punch and Judy show. *Inf.* **echar los títeres a rodar,** to upset the whole show; quarrel, fall out with. *Inf.* **no dejar t. con cabeza,** to destroy entirely, smash up completely; leave no one

titerero /tite'rero/ (**-ra**), and **titiritero** (**-ra**), *n* **titerista** *mf* puppet showman; acrobat; juggler

tití /ti'ti/ *m,* marmoset

titilación /titila'sion; titila'θion/ *f,* quiver, tremor; twinkling, winking, gleam

titilador, titilante /titila'ðor, titi'lante/ *a* quivering, trembling; twinkling

titilar /titi'lar/ *vi* to quiver, tremble; twinkle

titiritaina /titiri'taina/ *f, Inf.* muffled strains of musical instruments; merrymaking, uproar

titiritar /titiri'tar/ *vi* to tremble, shiver, shudder

titiritero /titiri'tero/ (**-ra**) *n* puppet master; acrobat

titubear /tituβe'ar/ *vi* to totter, sway, rock; stutter, stammer; toddle; hesitate, vacillate

titubeo /titu'βeo/ *m,* tottering, swaying; stuttering; hesitation

titulado /titu'laðo/ *m,* titled person; one who holds an academic title

titular /titu'lar/ *a* titular. *vt* to entitle, call; *vi* obtain a title (of nobility); *vr* style oneself, call oneself

título /'titulo/ *m,* title; heading; inscription; pretext, excuse; diploma, certificate; claim, right; noble title and its owner; section, clause; (univ.) degree; *Com.*

stock certificate, bond; *Com.* title; caption; qualification, right, merit; basis of a claim or privilege; *pl Com.* securities, stocks. **t. de la columna,** *Print.* running title. **títulos de propiedad,** title deeds. **t. del reino,** title of nobility. **a t.,** under pretext

tiza /'tisa; 'tiθa/ *f,* chalk; whiting; calcined stag's antler

tiznar /tis'nar; tiθ'nar/ *vt* to make sooty; dirty, stain, begrime; *Fig.* sully, tarnish

tizne /'tisne; 'tiθne/ *m,* (sometimes *f*) soot; charcoal; stain (on one's honor, etc.); *Agr.* blight

tizón /ti'son; ti'θon/ *m,* firebrand; *Agr.* blight; *Fig.* stain (on one's honor, etc.)

tizona /ti'sona; ti'θona/ *f, Inf.* sword (by allusion to name of that of the Cid)

tizonear /tisone'ar; tiθone'ar/ *vi* to poke or rake the fire

toalla /to'aya; to'aʎa/ *f,* towel. **t. continua,** roller towel. **t. rusa,** Turkish towel

toallero /toa'yero; toa'ʎero/ *m,* towel rail

tobillera /toβi'yera; toβi'ʎera/ *f, Inf.* girl, flapper

tobillo /to'βiyo; to'βiʎo/ *m,* ankle

tobogán /toβo'gan/ *m,* toboggan; chute (in apartment buildings or amusement parks)

toca /'toka/ *f,* headdress; toque; wimple; coif

tocable /to'kaβle/ *a* touchable

tocado /to'kaðo/ *a Fig.* touched, half-crazy. *m,* headdress; coiffure, hairdressing

tocador /toka'ðor/ **(-ra)** *n Mus.* player. *m,* dressing table; kerchief; boudoir; cloakroom; dressing room; dressing case

tocamiento /toka'miento/ *m,* touching, feeling; touch; *Fig.* inspiration

tocante /to'kante/ *a* touching. **t. a,** concerning, with regard to

tocar /to'kar/ *vt* to touch, feel; *Mus.* play; knock, rap; summon; ring, peal; brush against; discover by experience; persuade, inspire; mention, touch upon; *Naut.* touch bottom; *Art.* retouch, touch up. *vi* belong; stop (at), touch at; be one's turn; concern, interest; be one's lot; adjoin, be near to; be opportune; be allied or closely related to; find the scent (of dogs). **t. en un puerto,** *Naut.* to touch at a port. **Ahora me toca a mí,** Now it's my turn. **Es un problema que me toca de cerca,** It is a problem that touches me very nearly. **a toca teja,** *Inf.* in ready cash

tocayo /to'kayo/ **(-ya)** *n* namesake

tochedad /totʃe'ðað/ *f,* boorishness, loutishness

tocho /'totʃo/ *a* boorish, loutish, countrified. *m,* iron bar

tocinería /tosine'ria; toθine'ria/ *f,* pork butcher's shop

tocinero /tosi'nero; toθi'nero/ *m,* pork butcher

tocino /to'sino; to'θino/ *m,* bacon; salt pork

tocología /tokolo'hia/ *f,* tokology, obstetrics

tocón /to'kon/ *m,* stump (of a tree or an amputated limb)

todavía /toða'βia/ *adv* still; even; nevertheless; yet. **No han venido t.,** They have not come yet. **Queda mucho que hacer t.,** There is still much to be done.

todo /'toðo/ *a* all; whole, entire; every, each. *m,* whole, entirety; whole word (in charades); all; *pl* all; everyone. *adv* wholly, entirely. **t. lo posible,** everything possible; all one can, one's best. **t. lo que,** all that which. **ante t.,** in the first place; especially, particularly. **así y t.,** nevertheless. **a t. esto,** in the meanwhile. **con t.** *or* **con t. esto** *or* **con t. y esto,** nevertheless, in spite of this. **del t.,** wholly, completely. **jugar el t. por el t.,** to risk everything on the outcome. **sobre t.,** especially. **y t.,** in addition, as well. **Todos somos hijos de Adán y Eva, sino que nos diferencia la lana y la seda,** We are all equal, but some of us are more equal than others

todopoderoso /toðopoðe'roso/ *a* all-powerful, almighty. *m,* the Almighty, God

toga /'toga/ *f,* toga; robe, gown

Tokio /'tokio/ Tokyo

tolda /'tolda/ *f* canvas; tent; shelter

toldadura /tolda'ðura/ *f,* awning; canopy; hanging, curtain

toldillo /tol'diyo; tol'diʎo/ *m,* covered litter or sedan chair; *West Hem.* mosquito net

toldo /'toldo/ *m,* awning; canopy; pomp, show

tole /'tole/ *m,* outcry, uproar, tumult

toledano /tole'ðano/ **(-na)** *a* and *n* Toledan

tolerable /tole'raβle/ *a* bearable, tolerable

tolerancia /tole'ransia; tole'ranθia/ *f,* tolerance, forbearance; permission

tolerante /tole'rante/ *a* tolerant, broad-minded

tolerantismo /toleran'tismo/ *m,* religious toleration

tolerar /tole'rar/ *vt* to put up with, bear, tolerate; overlook, allow, forgive

tolla /'toya; 'toʎa/ *f,* marsh, bog

tollina /to'yina; to'ʎina/ *f, Inf.* spanking, whipping

tolmo /'tolmo/ *m,* tor

tolondro /to'londro/ *a* stupid, heedless, reckless. *m,* bump, bruise

tolva /'tolβa/ *f,* chute (for grain, etc.)

toma /'toma/ *f,* taking; receiving; conquest, capture; dose (of medicine)

tomada /to'maða/ *f,* taking; take; capture

tomadero /toma'ðero/ *m,* handle, haft

tomadura /toma'ðura/ *f,* taking; receiving; dose (of medicine). *Inf.* **t. de pelo,** leg-pull, joke

tomar /to'mar/ *vt* to take; pick up; conquer; eat; drink; adopt, employ; contract (habits); engage (employees); rent; understand; steal; remove; buy; suffer; *Fig.* overcome (by laughter, sleep, etc.); choose; possess physically; *vi* (*with por*) go in the direction of; *vr* grow rusty; go moldy; (*with con*) quarrel with. **t. a chacota,** to take as a joke. **t. a pechos,** to take to heart. **t. el fresco,** to take the air. **tomarla con,** to contradict, oppose; bear a grudge. **t. la delantera,** to take the lead; excel, beat. **t. las de Villadiego,** *Inf.* to quit, show one's heels. **t. por su cuenta,** to undertake, take charge of; take upon oneself. **t. su despquite con,** to get even with. **Más vale un toma que dos te daré,** A little help is worth a lot of promises. **¡Toma!** *Inf.* Fancy! You don't say!; Of course! There's nothing new about this!

tomatal /toma'tal/ *m,* tomato bed, tomato patch; *Lat. Am.* tomato plant

tomate /to'mate/ *m,* tomato; tomato plant; *Mexico* small green tomato; *Inf.* hole, potato (in stockings, etc.)

tomatera /toma'tera/ *f,* tomato plant

tomatero /toma'tero/ **(-ra)** *n* tomato seller

tómbola /'tombola/ *f,* raffle (gen. for charity); jumble sale

tomillo /to'miyo; to'miʎo/ *m,* thyme

tomo /'tomo/ *m,* volume, book; importance, worth

ton /ton/ *m, abb* **tono. sin t. ni son,** *Inf.* without rhyme or reason

tonada /to'naða/ *f,* words of a song and its tune

tonadilla /tona'ðiya; tona'ðiʎa/ *f, dim* short song; comic song; *Theat.* musical interlude *Obs.*

tonadillero /tonaði'yero; tonaði'ʎero/ **(-ra)** *n* composer or singer of tonadillas

tonal /to'nal/ *a* tonal

tonalidad /tonali'ðað/ *f,* tonality

tonar /to'nar/ *vi Poet.* to thunder or lightning

tonel /to'nel/ *m,* barrel; cask; butt

tonelada /tone'laða/ *f,* ton

tonelería /tonele'ria/ *f,* cooperage; collection or stock of casks and barrels

tonelero /tone'lero/ *m,* cooper

tonga, tongada /'toŋga, toŋ'gaða/ *f,* layer, stratum; *Inf.* task

tónica /'tonika/ *f, Mus.* keynote

tónico /'toniko/ *a* tonic. *m, Med.* tonic; pick-me-up

tonificador, tonificante /tonifika'ðor, tonifi'kante/ *a* strengthening, invigorating tonic

tonillo /to'niyo; to'niʎo/ *m, dim* monotonous singsong voice; regional accent

tonina /to'nina/ *f,* tuna; dolphin

tono /'tono/ *m,* inflection, modulation; (*Mus. Med. Art.*) tone; pitch; resonance; energy, strength; style; manner, behavior; *Mus.* key; mode of speech. **bajar el t.,** *Fig. Inf.* to change one's tune. *Inf.* **darse t.,** to put on side, give oneself airs. **de buen (mal) t.**, in good (bad) taste

tonsila /ton'sila/ *f*, tonsil

tonsilitis /tonsi'litis/ *f*, tonsillitis

tonsura /ton'sura/ *f*, shearing; hair cutting; *Eccl.* tonsure

tonsurar /tonsu'rar/ *vt* to shear, clip; cut the hair off; *Eccl.* tonsure

tontaina /ton'taina/ *mf Inf.* ninny, fool

tontear /tonte'ar/ *vi* to behave foolishly; play the fool

tontería /tonte'ria/ *f*, foolishness, stupidity; piece of folly; trifle, bagatelle

tontillo /ton'tiyo; ton'tiʎo/ *m*, dress bustle; hoop (for dresses)

tontiloco /tonti'loko/ *a Inf.* crazy, daft

tontivano /tonti'βano/ *a* vain, conceited

tonto /'tonto/ **(-ta)** *a* silly, stupid, simple; foolish, absurd. *n* fool, idiot. *m*, short coat, stroller. **t. de capirote,** *Inf.* an utter fool. **a tontas y a locas,** without rhyme or reason, topsy-turvy. **volver t. (a),** *Fig. Inf.* to drive crazy

topacio /to'pasio; to'paθio/ *m*, topaz

topar /to'par/ *vt* (*with con*) to run into, collide with, hit; meet unexpectedly; come across, find; *vi* butt (of horned animals); take a bet (in cards); consist in (of obstacles); meet with (difficulties); *Inf.* be successful

tope /'tope/ *m*, projection, part that juts out; obstacle, impediment; collision, bump; crux, difficult point; quarrel, fight; *Mech.* stop; *Naut.* masthead; *Rail.* buffer; *Mexico* speed bump. **hasta el t.,** completely full, full to the brim

topera /to'pera/ *f*, molehill

topetada /tope'taða/ *f*, butt (of horned animals); *Inf.* knock, bang

topetar /tope'tar/ *vt* and *vi* to butt (of horned animals); *vt* meet, run into

topetón /tope'ton/ *m*, butt; collision, impact, bump; blow on the head

tópico /'topiko/ *a* topical. *m*, topic, theme

topo /'topo/ *m*, *Zool.* mole; *Inf.* clumsy or shortsighted person; dolt, ninny

topografía /topogra'fia/ *f*, topography

topográfico /topo'grafiko/ *a* topographical

topógrafo /to'pografo/ *m*, topographer

toque /'toke/ *m*, touch, touching; pealing, ringing (of bells); crux, essence; test, proof; touchstone; *Metall.* assay; warning; *Inf.* tap (on the shoulder, etc.); *Art.* touch. **t. de luz,** *Art.* light (in a picture). **t. de obscuro,** *Art.* shade (in a picture). **t. de queda,** curfew. **t. de tambor,** beating of a drum. **dar un t. a,** *Inf.* to put to the test; pump (for information)

toquero /to'kero/ **(-ra)** *n* manufacturer of headdresses

toquetear /tokete'ar/ *vt* to keep touching, handle repeatedly

toquilla /to'kiya; to'kiʎa/ *f*, hatband, hat trimming; kerchief; small shawl

torácico /to'rasiko; to'raθiko/ *a* thoracic

toral /to'ral/ *a* principal, chief, main

tórax /'toraks/ *m*, thorax

torbellino /torβe'yino; torβe'ʎino/ *m*, whirlwind; spate of things; *Inf.* madcap. **t. de ideas,** brainstorm

torcedero /torse'ðero; torθe'ðero/ *a* twisted, crooked

torcedor /torse'ðor; torθe'ðor/ *a* twisting. *m*, twister; cause of continual anxiety

torcedura /torse'ðura; torθe'ðura/ *f*, twisting; sprain, wrench

torcer /tor'ser; tor'θer/ *vt irr* to twist; bend; turn, bear (of roads, etc.); slant, slope, incline; misconstrue, pervert; dissuade; wrench, sprain (muscles); corrupt (justice). **t. el gesto,** to make a wry face. *vr* turn sour (of wine, milk); *Fig.* go astray; turn out badly (of negotiations). *Pres. Ind.* **tuerzo, tuerces, etc.** *Pres. Subjunc.* **tuerza, tuerzas, tuerza, tuerzan**

torcida /tor'siða; tor'θiða/ *f*, wick (of lamps, etc.)

torcido /tor'siðo; tor'θiðo/ *a* bent, crooked, sloping, inclined; curved; dishonest, tortuous. *m*, silk twist

torcijón /torsi'hon; torθi'hon/ *m*, stomachache

torcimiento /torsi'miento; torθi'miento/ *m*, twisting; twist, turn; circumlocution; digression

tordo /'torðo/ *a* piebald, black-and-white. *m*, *Ornith.* thrush. **t. de campanario** *or* **t. de Castilla,** starling

toreador /torea'ðor/ *m*, bullfighter

torear /tore'ar/ *vi* and *vt* to fight bulls; *vt* ridicule; exasperate, provoke; *Inf.* string along, deceive

toreo /to'reo/ *m*, bullfighting

torera /to'rera/ *f*, bullfighter's jacket

torero /to'rero/ *a Inf.* bullfighting. *m*, bullfighter

torete /to'rete/ *m*, *dim* small bull; *Inf.* problem, difficult question; engrossing topic of conversation

toril /to'ril/ *m*, pen for fighting bulls

torio /'torio/ *m*, thorium

tormenta /tor'menta/ *f*, storm; misfortune, calamity; indignation, agitation

tormento /tor'mento/ *m*, torment; torture; pain; anxiety, anguish. **dar t. (a),** to torture; inflict pain (on)

tormentoso /tormen'toso/ *a* stormy, tempestuous; *Naut.* pitching, rolling

torna /'torna/ *f*, return; restitution; backwater

tornaboda /torna'βoða/ *f*, day after a wedding; rejoicings of this day

tornada /tor'naða/ *f*, return home; return visit, revisit; *Poet.* envoy

tornadizo /torna'ðiso; torna'ðiθo/ **(-za)** *a Inf.* changeable. *n* turncoat

tornamiento /torna'miento/ *m*, return; change, transformation

tornar /tor'nar/ *vt* to return, give back; change, transform; *vi* return, go back; continue

tornasol /torna'sol/ *m*, sunflower; sheen, changing light; *Chem.* litmus

tornasolado /tornaso'laðo/ *a* shot (of silk, etc.)

tornasolar /tornaso'lar/ *vt* to look iridescent; change the color of, cause to appear variegated

tornátil /tor'natil/ *a* turned (in a lathe); inconstant, changeable; *Poet.* spinning, revolving

tornatrás /torna'tras/ *mf* half-caste

tornaviaje /torna'βiahe/ *m*, return journey

tornavoz /torna'βos; torna'βoθ/ *m*, soundboard, sounding board

torneador /tornea'ðor/ *m*, turner; jouster, fighter in a tournament

tornear /torne'ar/ *vt Sports.* to put a spin on (balls); turn in a lathe; *vi* turn around, spin; fight in a tournament; turn over in the mind

torneo /tor'neo/ *m*, tournament

tornería /torne'ria/ *f*, turnery

tornero /tor'nero/ *m*, turner; lathe maker; convent messenger

tornillero /torni'yero; torni'ʎero/ *m*, (*Inf. Mil.*) deserter

tornillo /tor'niyo; tor'niʎo/ *m*, screw; (*Inf. Mil.*) desertion

torniquete /torni'kete/ *m*, turnstile; tourniquet. **dar t. (a),** to pervert, misinterpret (meanings)

torniscón /tornis'kon/ *m*, *Inf.* slap, buffet, blow; pinch

torno /'torno/ *m*, lathe; turntable (of a convent, etc.); turn, rotation; windlass; dumbwaiter; axletree; spinning wheel; bend, loop (in a river). **en t.,** round about, around; in exchange

toro /'toro/ *m*, bull; Taurus; *pl* bullfight. *Inf.* **t. corrido,** tough nut to crack, wise guy. *Inf.* **Ciertos son los toros,** So it's true (gen. of bad news)

toronja /to'ronha/ *f*, grapefruit

toroso /to'roso/ *a* strong, vigorous, robust

torpe /'torpe/ *a* heavy, slow, encumbered; torpid; clumsy, unskilled; stupid, dull-witted; obscene, indecent; base, infamous; ugly

torpedeamiento /torpeðea'miento/ *m*, torpedoing, sinking

torpedear /torpeðe'ar/ *vt* to torpedo

torpedeo /torpe'ðeo/ *m*, torpedoing

torpedero /torpe'ðero/ *m*, torpedo boat

torpedo /tor'peðo/ *m*, *Ichth.* torpedo fish, electric ray; torpedo; sports car. **t. automóvil,** self-propelling torpedo

torpeza /tor'pesa; tor'peθa/ *f*, slowness, heaviness;

torpidity; stupidity; lack of skill, clumsiness; indecency; ugliness; baseness, infamy

tórpido /'torpiðo/ *a* torpid

torrar /to'rrar/ *vt* to toast, brown

torre /'torre/ *f*, tower; belfry, steeple; turret; rook (in chess); *Naut.* gun turret; stack, pile (of chairs, etc.); country house with a garden. **t. del tráfico,** traffic light. **t. de viento,** castle in the air, castle in Spain

torrefacción /torrefak'sion; torrefak'θion/ *f*, toasting (of coffee, etc.)

torrencial /torren'sial; torren'θial/ *a* torrential, rushing

torrente /to'rrente/ *m*, torrent; *Fig.* spate, rush; crowd

torrentoso, -a /torren'toso/ *a*, *Lat. Am.* = **torrencial**

torreón /to'rreon/ *m*, large fortified tower

torrero /to'rrero/ *m*, lighthouse keeper; gardener

torreznero /torres'nero; torreθ'nero/ **(-ra)** *n Inf.* lazybones, idler

torrezno /to'rresno; to'rreθno/ *m*, rasher of bacon

tórrido /'torriðo/ *a* torrid

torsión /tor'sion/ *f*, twisting, torsion

torta /'torta/ *f*, cake; pastry, tart; *Inf.* slap. **t. de reyes,** traditional Twelfth Night cake

tortada /tor'taða/ *f*, meat pie, game pie

tortedad /torte'ðað/ *f*, twistedness, crookedness

tortera /tor'tera/ *f*, cake pan; baking dish; whorl (of a spindle)

tortícolis /tor'tikolis/ *m*, crick (in the neck)

tortilla /tor'tiya; tor'tiʎa/ *f*, omelet; *Central America, Mexico* tortilla (corn pancake) **t. a la española,** potato omelet. **hacer t.,** to smash to atoms. **Se volvió la t.,** *Inf.* The tables are turned

tortillero, -a /torti'jero; torti'ʎero/ *mf Central America, Mexico* tortilla vendor

tórtola /'tortola/ *f*, turtledove

tórtolo /'tortolo/ *m*, male turtledove; *Inf.* devoted lover

tortuga /tor'tuga/ *f*, turtle; tortoise. **a paso de t.,** at a snail's pace

tortuosidad /tortuosi'ðað/ *f*, tortuousness; winding; indirectness; deceitfulness

tortuoso /tor'tuoso/ *a* tortuous; winding; disingenuous, deceitful

tortura /tor'tura/ *f*, twistedness; torture, torment; anguish, grief. **una t. china,** excruciating torture

torturador /tortura'ðor/ *a* torturing, tormenting

torturar /tortu'rar/ *vt* to torture

torva /'torβa/ *f*, squall of rain or snow

torzal /tor'sal; tor'θal/ *m*, sewing silk; twist, plait

tos /tos/ *f*, cough. **t. ferina,** whooping cough

tosco /'tosko/ *a* rough, unpolished; coarse; boorish, uncouth

toser /to'ser/ *vi* to cough

tósigo /'tosigo/ *m*, poison, venom; anguish; affliction

tosigoso /tosi'goso/ *a* poisoned, venomous

tosquedad /toske'ðað/ *f*, roughness, lack of polish; coarseness; boorishness, uncouthness

tostada /tos'taða/ *f*, *Cul.* toast

tostadera /tosta'ðera/ *f*, toasting fork

tostado /tos'taðo/ *a* golden brown, tanned. *m*, roasting (of coffee, etc.)

tostador /tosta'ðor/ **(-ra)** *n* toaster (of peanuts, etc.). *m*, toaster (utensil); coffee or peanut roaster

tostadura /tosta'ðura/ *f*, toasting; roasting (of coffee, etc.)

tostón /tos'ton/ *m*, buttered toast; anything overtoasted; roast pig; *Inf.* nuisance, bore

total /to'tal/ *a* total, entire, whole; general. *m*, total. *adv* in short; so, therefore

totalidad /totali'ðað/ *f*, whole; aggregate, entirety

totalitario /totali'tario/ *a* totalitarian

tótem /'totem/ *m*, totem

toxicidad /toksisi'ðað; toksiθi'ðað/ *f*, toxicity

tóxico /'toksiko/ *a* toxic. *m*, toxic substance

toxicología /toksikolo'hia/ *f*, toxicology

toxicológico /toksiko'lohiko/ *a* toxicological

tozo /'toso; 'toθo/ *a* dwarfish, small

tozudez /tosu'ðes; toθu'ðeθ/ *f*, obstinacy

tozudo /to'suðo; to'θuðo/ *a* obstinate, obdurate

tozuelo /to'suelo; to'θuelo/ *m*, scruff, fat nape (of animals)

traba /'traβa/ *f*, setting (of a saw's teeth); tether (for horses); difficulty, obstacle; fastening; bond, tie; shackle; *Law.* distraint

trabacuenta /traβa'kuenta/ *f*, mistake in accounts; argument, difference of opinion

trabajado /traβa'haðo/ *a* and *past part* wrought; fashioned; labored, exhausted, weary

trabajador /traβaha'ðor/ **(-ra)** *a* working; conscientious. *n* worker

trabajar /traβa'har/ *vi* to work; function; stand the strain, resist (of machines, etc.); exert oneself, strive; toil, labor; operate, work; produce, yield (the earth fruits, etc.); *vt* work; till, cultivate; exercise (a horse); worry, annoy, weary; operate, drive; *vr* make every effort, work hard

trabajo /tra'βaho/ *m*, work; toil, labor; operation, working; difficulty, obstacle; literary work; hardship, trouble; process; *pl* poverty; hardship. **t. a destajo,** piecework. **t. al ralenti,** go-slow tactics. **trabajos forzados** (*or* **forzosos**), *Law.* hard labor. **pasar trabajos,** to undergo hardships

trabajosamente /traβahosa'mente/ *adv* painstakingly

trabajoso /traβa'hoso/ *a* difficult, hard; ailing, delicate; needy; afflicted

trabalenguas /traβa'lenguas/ *m*, *Inf.* tongue twister, jawbreaker

trabamiento /traβa'miento/ *m*, joining, fastening; uniting; initiation, commencement; shackling; hobbling (of horses)

trabar /tra'βar/ *vt* to join, unite, fasten; grasp, seize; set the teeth (of a saw); thicken; begin, initiate; hobble (of horses); reconcile, bring together, harmonize; shackle; *Law.* distrain; *vr* speak with an impediment; stutter, hesitate. **t. amistad,** to make friends. **t. conversación,** to get into conversation. **Se me trabó la lengua,** I began to stutter

trabazón /traβa'son; traβa'θon/ *f*, join, union, fastening; connection; thickness, consistency

trabilla /tra'βiya; tra'βiʎa/ *f*, vest strap; dropped stitch (in knitting)

trabuca /tra'βuka/ *f*, squib, Chinese firecracker, riprap

trabucar /traβu'kar/ *vt* to turn upside down, upset; confuse, bewilder; mix up, confuse (news, etc.); pronounce or write incorrectly

trabucazo /traβu'kaso; traβu'kaθo/ *m*, shot or report of a blunderbuss; *Inf.* calamity, unexpected misfortune

trabuco /tra'βuko/ *m*, *Mil.* catapult; blunderbuss

trabuquete /traβu'kete/ *m*, catapult

tracalada /traka'laða/ *f*, *Lat. Am.* crowd (of people); lot (large amount)

tracamundana /trakamun'dana/ *f*, *Inf.* barter, exchange of trash; hubbub, uproar

tracción /trak'sion; trak'θion/ *f*, pulling, traction

tracoma /tra'koma/ *f*, trachoma

tracto /'trakto/ *m*, tract, area, expanse; lapse of time

tractor /trak'tor/ *m*, tractor. **t. de orugas,** caterpillar tractor

tractorista /trakto'rista/ *mf* driver of a tractor, tractor driver

tradición /traði'sion; traði'θion/ *f*, tradition

tradicional /traðisio'nal; traðiθio'nal/ *a* traditional

tradicionalismo /traðisiona'lismo; traðiθiona'lismo/ *m*, traditionalism

tradicionalista /traðisiona'lista; traðiθiona'lista/ *a* traditionalistic. *mf* traditionalist

traducción /traðuk'sion; traðuk'θion/ *f*, translation; interpretation, explanation

traducible /traðu'siβle; traðu'θiβle/ *a* translatable

traducir /traðu'sir; traðu'θir/ *vt irr* to translate; interpret, explain; express. See **conducir**

traductor /traðuk'tor/ **(-ra)** *n* translator; interpreter

traedizo /trae'ðiso; trae'ðiθo/ *a* portable, movable

traer /tra'er/ *vt irr* to bring; attract; cause, occasion; wear, have on; quote, cite (as proof); compel, force; persuade; conduct, lead (persons); be engaged in; *vr* dress (well or badly). **t. consigo,** to bring with it; have or carry or bring with one. **t. entre manos,** to have on hand. *Pres. Ind.* **traigo, traes, etc.** *Pres. Part.*

trayendo. *Preterite* **traje, trajiste, etc.** *Pres. Subjunc.* **traiga, etc.** *Imperf. Subjunc.* **trajese, etc.**

trafagador /trafaga'ðor/ *m*, dealer, trafficker, merchant

tráfago /'trafago/ *m*, traffic, trade; toil, drudgery

trafalmejas /trafal'mehas/ *a Inf.* rowdy, crazy, *mf Inf.* rowdy

traficante /trafi'kante/ *mf* dealer, merchant, trader

traficar /trafi'kar/ *vi* to trade; travel

tráfico /'trafiko/ *m*, traffic; trade, commerce

tragaderas /traga'ðeras/ *f pl*, throat, gullet. *Inf.* **tener buenas t.,** to be very credulous; be tolerant (of evil)

tragadero /traga'ðero/ *m*, throat, gullet; sink, drain; hole, plug

tragador /traga'ðor/ **(-ra)** *n* glutton, guzzler

tragahombres /traga'ombres/ *mf Inf.* braggart, bully

trágala /'tragala/ *m*, **(trágala tú, servilón),** title of Spanish Liberal song aimed at Absolutists; *Inf.* take that!

tragaleguas /traga'leguas/ *mf Inf.* fast walker

tragaluz /traga'lus; traga'luθ/ *m*, skylight; fan light

tragantón /tragan'ton/ **(-ona)** *a Inf.* guzzling, greedy. *n* glutton

tragantona /tragan'tona/ *f*, *Inf.* spread, large meal; swallowing with difficulty; *Fig. Inf.* hard pill to swallow

tragaperras /traga'perras/ *m*, *Inf.* vending machine, catchpenny

tragar /tra'gar/ *vt* to swallow; eat ravenously, devour; engulf, swallow up; believe, take in; tolerate, put up with; dissemble; consume, absorb

tragedia /tra'heðia/ *f*, tragedy

trágico /'trahiko/ **(-ca)** *a* tragic. *n* tragedian; writer of tragedies

tragicomedia /trahiko'meðia/ *f*, tragicomedy

tragicómico /trahi'komiko/ *a* tragicomic

trago /'trago/ *m*, swallow, gulp, draft; *Fig. Inf.* bitter pill. **a tragos,** *Inf.* little by little, slowly

tragón /tra'gon/ **(-ona)** *a Inf.* greedy, gluttonous. *n* glutton

tragonear /tragone'ar/ *vt Inf.* to devour, eat avidly

traición /trai'sion; trai'θion/ *f*, treason, treachery. **a t.,** treacherously

traicionar /traisio'nar; traiθio'nar/ *vt* to betray

traicionero /traisio'nero; traiθio'nero/ **(-ra)** *a* treacherous. *n* traitor

traída /tra'iða/ *f*, conduction. **t. de aguas,** water supply

traidor /trai'ðor/ **(-ra)** *a* treacherous. *n* traitor

traílla /tra'iya; tra'iʎa/ *f*, lead, leash (for animals)

traje /'trahe/ *m*, dress, apparel; outfit; costume; suit. **t. de americana,** lounge suit. **t. de baño,** swimsuit. **t. de ceremonia** *or* **t. de etiqueta,** full-dress uniform; evening dress (men). **t. de luces,** bullfighter's gala outfit. **t. de montar,** riding habit. **t. de noche,** evening dress (women). **t. paisano,** civilian dress; lounge suit

trajín /tra'hin/ *m*, carriage, transport; busyness, moving around; bustle; clatter

trajinar /trahi'nar/ *vt* to carry, transport; *Argentina* cheat, swindle; *vi* be busy, go about one's business

tralla /'traya; 'traʎa/ *f*, rope, cord; lash (of a whip); whip

trama /'trama/ *f*, woof, texture (of cloth); twisted silk; intrigue, scheme; *Lit.* plot; olive flower

tramar /tra'mar/ *vt* to weave; prepare, hatch (plots); *Fig.* prepare the way for; *vi* flower (of trees, especially olive)

tramitación /tramita'sion; tramita'θion/ *f*, transaction, conduct; procedure, method

tramitar /trami'tar/ *vt* to transact, conduct, settle

trámite /'tramite/ *m*, transit; negotiation; phase of a business deal; requirement, condition; *Inf. pl* red tape

tramo /'tramo/ *m*, plot of ground; flight of stairs, staircase; stretch, expanse, reach, tract

tramontana /tramon'tana/ *f*, north wind; arrogance, haughtiness

tramontano /tramon'tano/ *a* ultramontane, from beyond the mountains

tramontar /tramon'tar/ *vi* to cross the mountains;

sink behind the mountains (of the sun); *vr* run away, escape

tramoya /tra'moya/ *f*, *Theat.* stage machinery; trick, deception, hoax

tramoyista /tramo'yista/ *mf* stage carpenter; stagehand; scene-shifter; trickster, impostor, swindler

trampa /'trampa/ *f*, trap, snare; trapdoor; flap of a shop counter; trouser fly; trick, swindle; overdue debt. *Fig. Inf.* **caer en la t.,** to fall into the trap. *Inf.* **coger en la t.,** to catch in a trap; catch in the act

trampal /tram'pal/ *m*, bog, marsh

trampantojo /trampan'toho/ *m*, *Inf.* optical illusion, swindle

trampeador /trampea'ðor/ *a Inf.* swindling. *n* trickster, swindler

trampear /trampe'ar/ *vi Inf.* to obtain money on false pretenses; struggle on (against illness, etc.); keep oneself alive, make shift; *vt* defraud, swindle

trampolín /trampo'lin/ *m*, springboard; diving board; *Fig.* jumping-off place

tramposo /tram'poso/ **(-sa)** *n* debtor; cardsharper; swindler

tranca /'tranka/ *f*, thick stick, cudgel; bar (of a window, etc.)

trancada /tran'kaða/ *f*, stride

trancar /tran'kar/ *vt* to bar the door; *vi Inf.* oppose, resist; *vr, Lat. Am.* be constipated

trancazo /tran'kaso; tran'kaθo/ *m*, blow with a stick; influenza, flu

trance /'transe; 'tranθe/ *m*, crisis, difficult juncture; danger, peril. **t. de armas,** armed combat. **a todo t.,** at all costs, without hesitation

tranco /'tranko/ *m*, stride; threshold. *Inf.* **en dos trancos,** in a trice

tranquera /tran'kera/ *f*, stockade, palisade

tranquilar /tranki'lar/ *vt Com.* to check off

tranquilidad /trankili'ðað/ *f*, tranquility, peace, quietness; composure, serenity

tranquilizador /trankilisa'ðor; trankiliθa'ðor/ *a* tranquilizing, soothing

tranquilizar /trankili'sar; trankili'θar/ *vt* to calm, quiet; soothe

tranquilo /tran'kilo/ *a* tranquil, quiet, peaceful; serene, composed

tranquiza /tran'kisa; tran'kiθa/ *f*, *Mexico* beating, thrashing

transacción /transak'sion; transak'θion/ *f*, compromise, arrangement; transaction, negotiation, deal

transalpino /transal'pino/ *a* transalpine

transandino /transan'dino/ *a* transandean

transatlántico /transat'lantiko/ *a* transatlantic. *m*, (transatlantic) liner

transbordar /transβor'ðar/ *vt* to transship; transfer, remove goods from one vehicle to another

transbordo /trans'βorðo/ *m*, transshipment, transshipping; transfer, removal

transcendencia /transsen'densia; transθen'denθia/ *f* See **trascendencia**

transcendental /transsenden'tal; transθenden'tal/ *a*. See **trascendencia**

transcribir /transkri'βir/ *vt* to transcribe; copy. *Past Part.* **transcrito**

transcripción /transkrip'sion; transkrip'θion/ *f*, transcription; copy, transcript

transcurrir /transku'rrir/ *vi* to elapse, pass (time)

transcurso /trans'kurso/ *m*, passage, lapse, course (of time)

transepto /tran'septo/ *m*, transept

transeúnte /tran'seunte/ *a* transient, temporary. *mf* passerby; visitor, sojourner

transferencia /transfe'rensia; transfe'renθia/ *f*, transfer (from one place to another); *Law.* conveyance, transference. **t. bancaria,** bank draft

transferidor /transferi'ðor/ **(-ra)** *a* transferring. *n* transferrer; *Law.* transferor

transferir /transfe'rir/ *vt irr* to transfer, move from one place to another; *Law.* convey (property, etc.); postpone. See **sentir**

transfiguración /transfigura'sion; transfigura'θion/ *f*, transfiguration

transfigurar /transfigu'rar/ vt to transfigure

transfijo /trans'fiho/ a transfixed

transfixión /transfik'sion/ f, transfixion

transformable /transfor'maβle/ a transformable

transformación /transforma'sion; transforma'θion/ f, transformation

transformador /transforma'ðor/ a transformative. m, Elec. transformer

transformar /transfor'mar/ vt to transform; reform (persons); vr be transformed; reform, mend one's ways

transfregar /transfre'gar/ vt irr to rub, scrub. See **cegar**

transfretar /transfre'tar/ vt Naut. to cross the sea; vi spread

tránsfuga /'transfuga/ mf **tránsfugo** m, fugitive; political turncoat

transfundir /transfun'dir/ vt to transfuse, pour from one vessel to another; imbue, transmit

transfusor /transfu'sor/ a transfusive

transgredir /transgre'ðir/ vt to transgress, infringe

transgresión /transgre'sion/ f, infringement, violation, transgression

transgresor /transgre'sor/ **(-ra)** a infringing. n transgressor, violator

transición /transi'sion; transi'θion/ f, transition, change

transido /tran'siðo/ a exhausted, worn-out, spent; niggardly, mean

transigencia /transi'hensia; transi'henθia/ f, tolerance, forbearance, indulgence

transigente /transi'hente/ a tolerant, forbearing

transigir /transi'hir/ vi to be tolerant; be broadminded. vt put up with, tolerate

transitable /transi'taβle/ a passable, traversable

transitar /transi'tar/ vi to cross, pass through; travel

transitivo /transi'tiβo/ a transitive

tránsito /'transito/ m, passage, crossing; transit; stopping place; transition, change; gallery of a cloister; Eccl. holy death. **de t.,** temporarily; in transit (of goods). **hacer tránsitos,** to break one's journey, stop

transitorio /transi'torio/ a transitory, fugitive, fleeting

translimitación /translimita'sion; translimita'θion/ f, trespass; bad behavior; armed intervention in a neighboring state

translimitar /translimi'tar/ vt to overstep the boundaries (of a state, etc.); overstep the limits (of decency, etc.)

translucidez /translusi'ðes; transluθi'ðeθ/ f, translucence, semitransparency

translúcido /trans'lusiðo; trans'luθiðo/ a translucent, semitransparent

transmarino /transma'rino/ a transmarine

transmigración /transmigra'sion; transmigra'θion/ f, transmigration

transmigrar /transmi'grar/ vi to migrate; transmigrate (of the soul)

transmisión /transmi'sion/ f, transmission. **t. del pensamiento,** thought transference

transmisor /transmi'sor/ a transmitting. m, Elec. transmitter, sender

transmitir /transmi'tir/ vt to transmit; Mech. drive

transmutable /transmu'taβle/ a transmutable

transmutación /transmuta'sion; transmuta'θion/ f, transmutation, transformation, change

transmutar /transmu'tar/ vt to transmute, transform, change

transoceánico /transose'aniko; transoθe'aniko/ a transoceanic

transpacífico /transpa'sifiko; transpa'θifiko/ a transpacific

transparencia /transpa'rensia; transpa'renθia/ f, transparency; obviousness

transparentarse /transparen'tarse/ vr to be transparent; show through; Fig. reveal, give away (secrets)

transparente /transpa'rente/ a transparent; translucent; evident, obvious. m, windowshade, blind

transpiración /transpira'sion; transpira'θion/ f, perspiration

transpirar /transpi'rar/ vi to perspire

transponer /transpo'ner/ vt irr to move, transfer; transplant; transpose; vr hide behind; sink behind the horizon (of the sun, stars); be half-asleep. See **poner**

transportable /transpor'taβle/ a transportable

transportación /transporta'sion; transporta'θion/ f. See **transporte**

transportador /transporta'ðor/ **(-ra)** a transport. n transporter. m, Geom. protractor

transportamiento /transporta'miento/ m. See **transporte**

transportar /transpor'tar/ vt to transport; Mus. transpose; carry; vr Fig. be carried away by (anger, rapture)

transporte /trans'porte/ m, transport, carriage; cartage; Naut. transport; strong emotion, transport, ecstasy

transposición /transposi'sion; transposi'θion/ f, transposition

transpositivo /transposi'tiβo/ a transpositive

transubstanciación /transuβstansia'sion; transuβstanθia'θion/ f, transubstantiation

transubstanciar /transuβstan'siar; transuβstan'θiar/ vt to transubstantiate, transmute

transversal, transverso /transβer'sal, trans'βerso/ a transverse

tranvía /tram'bia/ m, street railway; streetcar. **t. de sangre,** horse-drawn streetcar.

tranviario /tram'biario/ a streetcar. m, streetcar employee

trapacear /trapase'ar; trapaθe'ar/ vi to cheat, swindle

trapacete /trapa'sete; trapa'θete/ m, Com. daybook

trapacista /trapa'sista; trapa'θista/ mf trickster, swindler, knave

trapajoso /trapa'hoso/ a ragged, shabby, tattered

trápala /'trapala/ f, noise, confusion, hubbub; noise of horse's hoofs, gallop; Inf. trick, swindle; prattling, babbling. mf Inf. babbler, prattler; trickster

trapalear /trapale'ar/ vi to walk noisily, tramp; Inf. chatter, babble

trapatiesta /trapa'tiesta/ f, Inf. brawl, row, quarrel

trapaza /tra'pasa; tra'paθa/ f, hoax, swindle

trapeador /trapea'ðor/ m, Lat. Am. (floor) mop

trapear /trape'ar/ vt, Lat. Am. to mop (the floor)

trapecio /tra'pesio; tra'peθio/ m, trapeze; Geom. trapezium, trapezoid

trapería /trape'ria/ f, old-clothes shop; old clothes, rags, trash, frippery

trapero /tra'pero/ **(-ra)** n old-clothes seller; rag merchant; ragpicker

trapezoide /trape'soiðe; trape'θoiðe/ m, trapezium, trapezoid

trapichear /trapitʃe'ar/ vi Inf. to make shift, endeavor

trapiento /tra'piento/ a ragged, shabby

trapillo /tra'piyo; tra'piʎo/ m, Inf. poverty-stricken lover; nest egg, savings. Inf. **de t.,** in a state of undress, in négligé

trapío /tra'pio/ m, Inf. spirit of a fighting bull; verve, dash, independent air (of women)

trapisonda /trapi'sonda/ f, Inf. uproar, brawl; hubbub, bustle; snare, fix

trapisondear /trapisonde'ar/ vi Inf. to be given to brawling; scheme, intrigue

trapisondista /trapison'dista/ mf brawler; schemer, trickster

trapo /'trapo/ m, rag; Naut. canvas; bullfighter's cape; pl garments, bits and pieces. Inf. **poner como un t.** (**a),** to dress down, scold. Inf. **soltar el t.,** to burst out crying or laughing

trapujo /tra'puho/ m, Inf. trick; subterfuge

traque /'trake/ m, report, bang (of a rocket, etc.); fuse (of a firework)

tráquea /'trakea/ f, trachea

traqueotomía /trakeoto'mia/ f, tracheotomy

traquetear /trakete'ar/ vi to crack, bang, go off with a report; rattle; jolt (of trains, etc.). vt shake, stir; Inf. paw, handle too much

traqueteo /trake'teo/ m, banging (of fireworks); creaking; rattling; jolting (of trains, etc.)

traquido /tra'kiðo/ *m*, report (of a gun); crack (of a whip); creak

tras /tras/ *prep* after; behind; following, in pursuit of; trans- (in compounds). *m*, *Inf*. buttock; sound of a blow, bang, bump. **t. t.,** knocking (at a door); banging

trasalcoba /trasal'koβa/ *f*, dressing room

trasbarrás /trasβa'rras/ *m*, bang, bump, noise

trasbocar /trasβo'kar/ *vt*, *Lat. Am.* to vomit

trascendencia /trassen'densia; trasθen'denθia/ *f*, transcendence, excellence; consequence, result

trascendental /trassenden'tal; trasθenden'tal/ *a* transcendental; important, farreaching

trascender /trassen'der; trasθen'der/ *vi irr* to spread to, influence; become known, leak out; exhale a scent; *vt* investigate, discover. See **entender**

trascocina /trasko'sina; trasko'θina/ *f*, back kitchen

trascolar /trasko'lar/ *vt irr* to filter, strain; cross over, traverse. See **colar**

trascordarse /traskor'ðarse/ *vr irr* to mix up, make a muddle of, forget. See **acordar**

trasechar /trase'tʃar/ *vt* to ambush, waylay

trasegar /trase'gar/ *vt irr* to upset, turn upside down; transfer, move from one place to another; empty, pour out, upset (liquids). See **cegar**

traseñalar /traseɲa'lar/ *vt* to re-mark, mark again

trasera /tra'sera/ *f*, rear, back, rear portion

trasero /tra'sero/ *a* rear, back. *m*, hindquarters, rump; buttocks, seat; *pl Inf*. ancestors

trasgo /'trasgo/ *m*, imp, sprite, puck

trashumante /trasu'mante/ *a* nomadic (of flocks)

trashumar /trasu'mar/ *vi* to go from winter to summer pasture (or vice versa) (of flocks). See **desahuciar.**

trasiego /tra'siego/ *m*, emptying, pouring out, upsetting (of liquids); decanting (of wines)

traslación /trasla'sion; trasla'θion/ *f*, removal, transfer; alteration (of the date for a meeting); metaphor

trasladable /trasla'ðaβle/ *a* removable, movable, transferable

trasladar /trasla'ðar/ *vt* to remove, transfer; move from one place to another; alter (the date of a meeting); translate; copy, transcribe; *vr* remove (from a place)

traslado /tras'laðo/ *m*, removal; transfer; transcription

traslapar /trasla'par/ *vt* to cover, overlap

traslapo /tras'lapo/ *m*, overlap, overlapping

traslucirse /traslu'sirse; traslu'θirse/ *vr irr* to be transparent or translucent; shine through; come out (of secrets); infer, gather. See **lucir**

traslumbramiento /traslumbra'miento/ *m*, dazzle, glare, brilliance

traslumbrar /traslum'βrar/ *vt* to dazzle; *vr* flicker, glimmer; fade quickly, disappear

trasluz /tras'lus; tras'luθ/ *m*, reflected light. **al t.,** against the light

trasminar /trasmi'nar/ *vt* to undermine, excavate; *vi* percolate, ooze; penetrate, spread

trasnochada /trasno'tʃaða/ *f*, previous night, last night; night's vigil; sleepless night; *Mil*. night attack

trasnochado /trasno'tʃaðo/ *a* stale, old; weary; hackneyed; drawn, pinched

trasnochador /trasnotʃa'ðor/ **(-ra)** *n* one who watches by night or stays up all night; *Inf*. night owl, reveler

trasnochar /trasno'tʃar/ *vi* to stay up all night; watch through the night; spend the night; *vt* sleep on, leave for the following day

trasnoche, trasnocho /tras'notʃe, tras'notʃo/ *m*, *Inf*. night out; night vigil

trasoir /traso'ir/ *vt irr* to hear incorrectly, misunderstand. See **oir**

trasojado /traso'haðo/ *a* haggard, tired-eyed

trasoñar /traso'ɲar/ *vt irr* to imagine, mistake a dream for reality. See **contar**

traspalar /traspa'lar/ *vt* to fork (grain); shovel; transfer, move

trasparencia /traspa'rensia; traspa'renθia/ *f*. See **transparencia**

traspasar /traspa'sar/ *vt* to transfer, move; cross; *Law*. convey, make over to; pierce; transgress, flout; exceed one's authority; *Fig*. go too far; reexamine, go over again; give intolerable pain (of illness, grief). **se traspasa,** to be disposed of (houses, etc.)

traspaso /tras'paso/ *m*, transport, transfer; *Law*. conveyance; property transferred; price agreed upon

traspatio /tras'patio/ *m*, *Lat. Am.* backyard

traspié /tras'pie/ *m*, slip, catching of the foot, stumble; heel of the foot. **dar traspiés,** *Inf*. to blunder

trasplantación /trasplanta'sion; trasplanta'θion/ *f*, **trasplante** *m*, transplantation; emigration

trasplantar /trasplan'tar/ *vt Agr*. to transplant; *vr* emigrate

trasplante /tras'plante/ *m*, planting out

traspuesta /tras'puesta/ *f*, transposition; back quarters; rear (of a house); back yard

traspunte /tras'punte/ *m*, *Theat*. prompter

traspuntín /traspun'tin/ *m*, *Auto*. folding seat

trasquilar /traski'lar/ *vt* to cut the hair unevenly; shear (sheep); *Inf*. cut down, diminish

trasquilón /traski'lon/ *m*, cropping (of hair); shearing; *Inf*. money stolen by pilfering

trastada /tras'taða/ *f*, *Inf*. dirty trick, mean act

traste /'traste/ *m*, fret (of stringed instruments); tasting cup. **dar al t. con,** to spoil, upset, damage. *Inf*. **sin trastes,** topsy-turvy, without method

trastear /traste'ar/ *vt* to play well (on the mandolin, etc.); *Inf*. manage tactfully; *vi* move around, change (furniture, etc.); discuss excitedly

trastejar /traste'har/ *vt* to repair the roof; renew slates; overhaul

trastienda /tras'tienda/ *f*, back of a shop; room behind a shop; *Inf*. wariness, caution

trasto /'trasto/ *m*, piece of furniture; (household) utensil; lumber, useless furniture; *Theat*. wing or set piece; *Inf*. useless person, ne'er-do-well; oddment, thing; *pl* implements, equipment

trastornable /trastor'naβle/ *a* easily overturned or upset; easily agitated

trastornar /trastor'nar/ *vt* to turn upside down; perturb, disturb; *Fig*. overpower (of scents, etc.); disorder, upset; dissuade; make mad; derange the mind

trastorno /tras'torno/ *m*, upset; perturbation, anxiety; disorder; mental derangement; confusion (of the senses)

trastrabillar /trastraβi'yar; trastraβi'ʎar/ *vi* to stumble, slip; totter, sway; hesitate; stutter, be tongue-tied

trastrás /tras'tras/ *m*, *Inf*. last but one (in games)

trastrocamiento /trastroka'miento/ *m*, alteration, change; disarrangement

trastrocar /trastro'kar/ *vt irr* to alter, change, disarrange; change the order of. See **contar**

trasudar /trasu'ðar/ *vt* to perspire

trasudor /trasu'ðor/ *m*, light perspiration

trasuntar /trasun'tar/ *vt* to copy, transcribe; summarize

trasunto /tra'sunto/ *m*, copy, transcript; imitation

trasver /tras'βer/ *vt irr* to see through or between; glimpse; see incorrectly. See **ver**

trasverter /trasβer'ter/ *vi irr* to overflow. See **entender**

trata /'trata/ *f*, slave trade. **t. de blancas,** white slave traffic

tratable /tra'taβle/ *a* easily accessible, sociable, unpretentious

tratadista /trata'ðista/ *mf* writer of a treatise; expert, writer on special subjects

tratado /tra'taðo/ *m*, pact, agreement; treaty; treatise

tratador /trata'ðor/ **(-ra)** *n* arbitrator

tratamiento /trata'miento/ *m*, treatment; courtesy title; address, style; *Med*. treatment; process

tratante /tra'tante/ *m*, merchant, dealer

tratar /tra'tar/ *vt* to handle, use; conduct, manage; have dealings with, meet, know (e.g. *Yo no le trato*, I don't know him); behave well or badly toward; care for, treat; discuss, deal with (e.g. *¿De qué trata el libro?* What is the book about?); propose, suggest; *Chem*. treat; (*with de*) address as, call; *vi* have amorous relations; (*with de*) try to, endeavor to; (*with* *en)* trade in; *vr* look after oneself; treat oneself; conduct oneself

trato /'trato/ *m,* use, handling; management; conduct, behavior; manner, demeanor; appellation, title; commerce, traffic; dealings, intercourse; treatment; agreement, arrangement. **t. colectivo,** collective bargaining

traumático /trau'matiko/ *a* traumatic

traumatismo /trauma'tismo/ *m,* traumatism

través /tra'βes/ *m,* slant, slope; mishap; *(Mil. Archit.)* traverse. **a t.** *or* **al t.,** across; through. **de t.,** athwart; through

travesaño /traβe'saɲo/ *m,* crossbar; bolster; rung (of a ladder); traverse

travesear /traβese'ar/ *vi* to run about, romp, be mischievous; lead a vicious life; speak wittily; move ceaselessly (of water, etc.)

travesía /traβe'sia/ *f,* crossing; traverse; crossroad; side road or street; distance, space; sea crossing; crosswise position; stretch of road within a town

travestido /traβes'tiðo/ *a* disguised, dressed up

travesura /traβe'sura/ *f,* romping, frolic; mischief; prank; quick-wittedness

traviesa /tra'βiesa/ *f,* sleeping car, sleeper (railroad); *Archit.* rafter; distance between two points

travieso /tra'βieso/ *a* transverse, crosswise; mischievous, willful; debauched; clever, subtle; ever-moving (of streams, etc.)

trayecto /tra'yekto/ *m,* run, distance, journey; stretch, expanse, tract; fare stage

trayectoria /trayek'toria/ *f,* trajectory; journey

traza /'trasa; 'traθa/ *f,* plan, design, draft; scheme, project; idea, proposal; aspect, appearance; means, manner. **Hombre pobre todo es trazas,** A poor man is full of schemes (for bettering himself)

trazado /tra'saðo; tra'θaðo/ *m,* designing, drawing; design, draft, model, plan; course, direction (of a canal, etc.)

trazador /trasa'ðor; traθa'ðor/ **(-ra)** *n* draftsman, designer; planner, schemer

trazar /tra'sar; tra'θar/ *vt* to plan, draft, design; make a drawing of; trace; describe; map out, arrange

trazo /'traso; 'traθo/ *m,* line, stroke; outline, contour, form, line; *Art.* fold in drapery; stroke of the pen

trebejar /treβe'har/ *vi* to frolic, skip, play

trebejo /tre'βeho/ *m,* chessman, chess piece; utensil, article (gen. *pl*); plaything

trébol /'treβol/ *m,* clover

trece /'trese; 'treθe/ *a* and *m,* thirteen, thirteenth. *m,* thirteenth (day of the month)

trecemesino /treseme'sino; treθeme'sino/ *a* thirteen months old

trecho /'tretʃo/ *m,* distance, space; interval (of time). **a trechos,** at intervals. **de t. en t.,** from time to time

trefe /'trefe/ *a* pliable, flexible; light; spurious (of coins)

tregua /'tregua/ *f,* truce; *Mil.* ceasefire; respite, rest. **dar treguas,** to afford relief, give a respite; give time

treinta /'treinta/ *a* and *m,* thirty; thirtieth. *m,* thirtieth (day of the month)

treintavo /trein'taβo/ *a* thirtieth

treintena /trein'tena/ *f,* thirtieth (part)

tremebundo /treme'βundo/ *a* fearsome, dread

tremedal /treme'ðal/ *m,* bog; quagmire

tremendo /tre'mendo/ *a* fearful, formidable; awesome; *Inf.* tremendous, enormous

trementina /tremen'tina/ *f,* turpentine

tremolar /tremo'lar/ *vt* and *vi* to wave, fly (of banners); *Fig.* make a show of

tremolina /tremo'lina/ *f,* noise of the wind; *Inf.* hubbub, confusion

trémulo /'tremulo/ *a* trembling, tremulous

tren /tren/ *m,* supply, provision; outfit; equipment; pomp, show; railroad train; following, train; *Mexico also* streetcar, trolley car, trolley **t. ascendente,** up train (from coast to interior). *Inf.* **t. botijo,** excursion train. **t. con coches corridos,** corridor train. **t. correo,** mail train. **t. descendente,** down train (from interior to coast). **t. mixto,** train carrying passengers

and freight. **t. ómnibus,** accommodation train, slow, stopping train. **t. rápido,** express

trencilla /tren'siya; tren'θiʎa/ *f,* braid, trimming

trencillar /trensi'yar; trenθi'ʎar/ *vt* to trim with braid, braid

trenza /'trensa; 'trenθa/ *f,* plait, braid; plait of hair; bread twist; *Lat. Am.* string (of onions). **en t.,** in plaits, plaited (of hair)

trenzadera /trensa'ðera; trenθa'ðera/ *f,* linen tape

trenzar /tren'sar; tren'θar/ *vt* to plait, braid; *vi* curvet, prance *Lat. Am.* **trenzarse (en...)** get involved (in...), e.g. *trenzarse en una disputa* get involved in a dispute

trepa /'trepa/ *f,* perforation, boring, piercing; climbing; creeping; *Inf.* half-somersault; grain, surface (of wood); craftiness, slyness; deception, fraud; beating, drubbing

trepador /trepa'ðor/ *a* climbing; crawling; *Bot.* creeping, climbing. *m,* climbing place

trepanación /trepana'sion; trepana'θion/ *f,* trepanning

trepanar /trepa'nar/ *vt* to trepan

trepante /tre'pante/ *a* creeping; *Bot.* twining, climbing

trepar /tre'par/ *vi* to climb, ascend; *Bot.* climb or creep; bore, perforate

trepatrepa /trepa'trepa/ *m,* jungle gym, monkey bars

trepidación /trepiða'sion; trepiða'θion/ *f,* trepidation, dread; vibration; jarring; shaking

trepidar /trepi'ðar/ *vi* to shiver, shudder; vibrate; shake; jar; *Lat. Am.* hesitate

trépido /'trepiðo/ *a* shuddering, shivering; vibrating

tres /tres/ *a* three; third. *m,* figure three; third (day of the month); three (of playing cards); trio. *Inf.* **como t. y dos son cinco,** as sure as two and two make four

trescientos /tres'sientos; tres'θientos/ *a* and *m,* three hundred; three-hundredth

tresillo /tre'siyo; tre'siʎo/ *m,* omber (card game); *Mus.* triplet

tresnal /tres'nal/ *m,* *Agr.* stook, cock, sheaf

treta /'treta/ *f,* scheme; trick, hoax; feint (in fencing)

trezavo /tre'saβo; tre'θaβo/ *a* thirteenth

tría /'tria/ *f,* selection, choice; worn place (in cloth)

triangulación /triaŋgula'sion; triaŋgula'θion/ *f,* triangulation

triángulo /tri'aŋgulo/ *a* triangular. *m,* (*Geom. Mus.*) triangle. **t. acutángulo,** acute triangle. **t. obtusángulo,** obtuse triangle. **t. rectángulo,** right-angled triangle

triar /triar/ *vt* to select, pick out; *vi* fly in and out of the hive (of bees); *vr* grow threadbare, become worn

tribu /'triβu/ *f,* tribe; species, family

tribulación /triβula'sion; triβula'θion/ *f,* tribulation, suffering

tribuna /tri'βuna/ *f,* tribune; platform, rostrum, pulpit; spectators' gallery; stand. **t. de la prensa,** press gallery. **t. del jurado,** jury box. **t. del órgano,** organ loft

tribunado /triβu'naðo/ *m,* tribunate

tribunal /triβu'nal/ *m,* law court; *Law.* bench; judgment seat; tribunal; board of examiners. **t. de menores,** children's court, juvenile court. *Naut.* **t. de presas,** prize court. **t. de primera instancia,** *Law.* petty sessions. **t. militar,** court-martial

tribuno /tri'βuno/ *m,* tribune; political speaker

tributar /triβu'tar/ *vt* to pay taxes; offer, render (thanks, homage, etc.)

tributario /triβu'tario/ **(-ia)** *a* tributary; tax-paying, contributive. *n* taxpayer. *m,* tributary (of a river)

tributo /tri'βuto/ *m,* contribution; tax; tribute, homage; census

tricenal /trise'nal; triθe'nal/ *a* of thirty years' duration; occurring every thirty years

tricentésimo /trisen'tesimo; triθen'tesimo/ *a* three-hundredth

triciclo /tri'siklo; tri'θiklo/ *m,* tricycle

tricolor /triko'lor/ *a* three-colored

tricorne /tri'korne/ *a* *Poet.* three-cornered, three-horned

tricornio /tri'kornio/ a three-cornered. m, three-cornered hat

tricotomía /trikoto'mia/ f, trichotomy, division into three

tricromía /trikro'mia/ f, three-color process

tridente /tri'ðente/ a tridentate, three-pronged. m, trident

trienal /trie'nal/ a triennial

trienio /'trienio/ m, space of three years

trifásico /tri'fasiko/ a three-phase

trifolio /tri'folio/ m, trefoil

trigal /tri'gal/ m, wheat field

trigésimo /tri'hesimo/ a thirtieth

trigo /'trigo/ m, wheat plant; ear of wheat; wheat field (gen. pl); wealth, money. **t. tremés** or **t. trechel** or **t. tremesino** or **t. de marzo**, summer wheat

trigonometría /trigonome'tria/ f, trigonometry

trigueño /tri'geɲo/ a brunette, dark

triguero /tri'gero/ a wheat; wheat-growing. m, grain sieve; grain merchant

trilátero /tri'latero/ a three-sided, trilateral

trilingüe /tri'liŋgue/ a trilingual

trilla /'triya; 'triʎa/ f, red mullet; Agr. harrow; threshing; threshing season

trillado /tri'yaðo; tri'ʎaðo/ a frequented, trodden, worn (of paths); hackneyed

trilladora /triya'ðora; triʎa'ðora/ f, threshing machine

trillar /tri'yar; tri'ʎar/ vt to thresh; Inf. frequent; ill-treat

trillo /'triyo; 'triʎo/ m, threshing machine; harrow

trillón /tri'yon; tri'ʎon/ m, trillion

trilogía /trilo'hia/ f, trilogy

trimestral /trimes'tral/ a quarterly; terminal (in schools, etc.)

trimestre /tri'mestre/ a quarterly; terminal. m, quarter, three months; term (in schools, etc.); quarterly payment; quarterly rent

trinado /tri'naðo/ m, Mus. trill; twittering, shrilling (of birds)

trinar /tri'nar/ vi Mus. to trill; twitter, shrill; Inf. get in a temper, be furious

trincapiñones /trinkapi'ɲones/ m, Inf. scatterbrained youth

trincar /trin'kar/ vt to fasten securely; tie tightly; pinion; Naut. lash, make fast; cut up, chop; Inf. tipple; vi Naut. sail close to the wind

trincha /'trintʃa/ f, vest strap

trinchante /trin'tʃante/ m, table carver; carving fork; stonecutter's hammer

trinchar /trin'tʃar/ vt to carve (at table); Inf. decide, dispose

trinche /'trintʃe/ m Mexico pitchfork; elsewhere in Lat. Am. fork

trinchera /trin'tʃera/ f, Mil. trench; cutting (for roads, etc.); trench coat

trinchero /trin'tʃero/ m, platter, trencher; serving table, side table

trineo /tri'neo/ m, sled, sledge, sleigh

trinidad /trini'ðað/ f, trinity

trinitaria /trini'taria/ f, Bot. pansy, heartsease

trinitario /trini'tario/ (-ia) a and n Eccl. Trinitarian

trino /'trino/ a triune; ternary. m, Mus. trill

trinomio /tri'nomio/ m, trinomial

trinquete /trin'kete/ m, Naut. mainmast; mainsail; Sports. rackets; Mech. ratchet

trinquis /'trinkis/ m, Inf. draft, drink

trío /'trio/ m, trio

tripa /'tripa/ f, entrail, gut; Inf. belly; inside (of some fruits). **hacer de tripas corazón**, Inf. to take heart, buck up. **revolver las tripas** (a), Fig. Inf. to make one sick

tripartición /triparti'sion; triparti'θion/ f, tripartition

tripartito /tripar'tito/ a tripartite

tripicallos /tripi'kayos; tripi'kaʎos/ m pl, Cul. tripe

triple /'triple/ a triple; three-ply (of yarn)

triplicación /triplika'sion; triplika'θion/ f, trebling

triplicar /tripli'kar/ vt to treble

trípode /'tripoðe/ m, (sometimes f) three-legged stool or table; tripod; trivet

tríptico /'triptiko/ m, triptych

triptongo /'triptoŋgo/ m, triphthong

tripulación /tripula'sion; tripula'θion/ f, crew (ships and aircraft)

tripulante /tripu'lante/ m, crew member

tripular /tripu'lar/ vt to provide with a crew, man; equip, furnish; serve in, work as the crew of

trique /'trike/ m, crack, creak. Inf. **a cada t.**, at every moment

triquiñuela /triki'ɲuela/ f, Inf. evasion, subterfuge

triquitraque /triki'trake/ m, tap, rap; crack; firework

tris /tris/ m, crack, noise of glass, etc., cracking; Inf. instant, trice. **estar en un t. (de)**, to be on the verge (of), within an inch (of)

trisar /tri'sar/ vt to crack, break, splinter (of glass); vi chirp, twitter (especially of swallows)

trisca /'triska/ f, cracking, crushing, crackling (of nuts, etc.); noise, tumult

triscar /tris'kar/ vi to make a noise with the feet; gambol, frolic; creak, crack; vt blend, mingle; set the teeth of a saw

trisecar /trise'kar/ vt to trisect

trisemanal /trisema'nal/ a three times weekly; every three weeks

trisílabo /tri'silaβo/ a trisyllabic

trismo /'trismo/ m, lockjaw, trismus

triste /'triste/ a unhappy, sorrowful; melancholy, gloomy; sad; piteous, unfortunate; useless, worthless; m, Lat. Am. sad love song

tristeza, tristura /tris'teθa, tris'tura; tris'tesa/ f, unhappiness; melancholy, gloom; sadness; piteousness

tritón /tri'ton/ m, merman

triturar /tritu'rar/ vt to crumble, crush; chew; masticate; ill-treat, bruise; refute, contradict

triunfada /triun'faða/ f, trumping (at cards)

triunfador /triunfa'ðor/ (-ra) a triumphant. n victor

triunfal /triun'fal/ a triumphal

triunfante /triun'fante/ a triumphant

triunfar /triun'far/ vi to triumph; be victorious, win; trump (at cards); spend ostentatiously

triunfo /'triunfo/ m, triumph; victory; trump card; success; booty, spoils of war; conquest

trivial /tri'βial/ a well-known, hackneyed; frequented, trodden; commonplace, mediocre; trivial, unimportant

trivialidad /triβiali'ðað/ f, banality, triteness; mediocrity; triviality

trivio /'triβio/ m, road junction

triza /'trisa; 'triθa/ f, fragment, bit; Naut. rope. **hacer trizas**, to smash to bits

trizar /tri'sar; tri'θar/ vt to smash up, destroy

trocable /tro'kaβle/ a exchangeable

trocada, a la /tro'kaða, a la/ adv contrariwise; in exchange

trocador /troka'ðor/ (-ra) n exchanger

trocar /tro'kar/ vt irr to exchange; vomit; distort, misconstrue, mistake; vr change, alter one's behavior; change places with another; be transferred. See **contar**

trocear /trose'ar; troθe'ar/ vt to divide into pieces

trocha /'trotʃa/ f, short cut; trail, path, track

trochemoche, a /trotʃe'motʃe, a/ adv Inf. without rhyme or reason, pell-mell

trofeo /tro'feo/ m, trophy; victory; military booty

troglodita /troglo'ðita/ a and mf troglodyte. m, Fig. savage, barbarian. mf glutton

troj /troh/ f, granary

trojero /tro'hero/ m, granary keeper

trola /'trola/ f, Inf. lie, nonsense, hoax

trole /'trole/ m, trolley

trolebús /trole'βus/ m, trolley car

trolero /tro'lero/ a Inf. deceiving, lying

tromba /'tromba/ f, waterspout

trombón /trom'bon/ m, trombone; trombone player.
¡Trombones y platillos! Great Scot!

trombosis /trom'bosis/ f, thrombosis

trompa /'trompa/ f, elephant's trunk; Mus. horn;

proboscis (of insects); waterspout; humming top. **t. de Falopio,** fallopian tube

trompada /trom'paða/ f, Inf. bang, bump; blow, buffet, slap; collision

trompazo /trom'paso; trom'paθo/ m, heavy blow, knock, bang

trompear /trompe'ar/ vi to play with a top; vt knock about

trompero /trom'pero/ m, top maker. a deceiving, swindling

trompeta /trom'peta/ f, trumpet; bugle. m, trumpeter; bugler; Inf. ninny. **t. de amor,** sunflower

trompetada /trompe'taða/ f, Inf. stupid remark, piece of nonsense

trompetazo /trompe'taso; trompe'taθo/ m, bray of a trumpet; bugle blast; Inf. stupid remark

trompetear /trompete'ar/ vi Inf. to play the trumpet or bugle

trompeteo /trompe'teo/ m, trumpeting, trumpet call; sound of the bugle

trompetería /trompete'ria/ f, collection of trumpets; metal organ pipes

trompetero /trompe'tero/ m, trumpet or bugle maker or player

trompetilla /trompe'tiya; trompe'tiʎa/ f, dim little trumpet; ear trumpet

trompicar /trompi'kar/ vt to make stumble, trip. vi stumble, trip up

trompicón /trompi'kon/ m, stumble

trompo /'trompo/ m, humming or spinning top; Inf. dolt, idiot

tronada /tro'naða/ f, thunderstorm

tronado /tro'naðo/ a worn-out; threadbare; old; poor, poverty-stricken; down at the heels

tronar /tro'nar/ v impers irr to thunder; vi growl, roar (of guns); Inf. go bankrupt, be ruined; Inf. protest against, attack; Central America, Mexico execute, shoot; (with con) quarrel with. Pres. Ind. **trueno, truenas, truena, truenan.** Pres. Subjunc. **truene, truenes, truena, truenen**

troncal /tron'kal/ a trunk; main, principal

troncha /'trontʃa/ f, Lat. Am. piece; slice

tronchar /tron'tʃar/ vt to break off, lop off (branches)

troncho /'trontʃo/ m, Bot. stem, stalk, branch

tronco /'tronko/ m, Anat. Bot. trunk; main body or line (of communications); trunk line; common origin, stock; Inf. blockhead; dolt; callous person. Fig. **estar hecho un t.,** to lie like a log; sleep like a log

tronera /tro'nera/ f, Naut. porthole; embrasure; slit window; pocket of a billiards table. mf Inf. madcap, harumscarum

tronido /tro'niðo/ m, roll of thunder

trono /'trono/ m, throne; Eccl. tabernacle; shrine; kingly might; pl thrones, hierarchy of angels

tronzador /tronsa'ðor; tronθa'ðor/ m, two-handled saw

tronzar /tron'sar; tron'θar/ vt to smash, break into bits; Sew. pleat; exhaust, overtire

tropa /'tropa/ f, crowd (of people); troops, military; Mil. call to arms; pl army. **t. de línea,** regiment of the line. **tropas de asalto,** storm troopers. **tropas de refresco,** fresh troops. **en t.,** in a crowd; in groups

tropel /tro'pel/ m, rush, surge (of crowds, etc.); bustle, confusion; crowd, multitude; heap, jumble (of things). **en t.,** in a rush; in a crowd

tropelía /trope'lia/ f, rush, dash; violence; outrage

tropezar /trope'sar; trope'θar/ vi irr to stumble, slip; (with con) meet unexpectedly or accidentally come up against, be faced with (difficulties); quarrel with or oppose; fall into (bad habits). See **empezar**

tropezón /trope'son; trope'θon/ m, stumbling, slipping; stumbling block, obstacle. **a tropezones,** Inf. stumblingly; by fits and starts

tropical /tropi'kal/ a tropical

trópicos /'tropikos/ m pl, tropics

tropiezo /tro'pieso; tro'pieθo/ m, stumble; stumbling block, obstacle; hitch; impediment; slip, peccadillo, fault; difficulty, embarrassment; fight, skirmish; quarrel

tropo /'tropo/ m, trope, figure of speech

troquel /tro'kel/ m, die, mold

trotaconventos /trotakom'bentos/ f, Inf. go-between, procuress

trotamundos /trota'mundos/ mf, Inf. globetrotter

trotar /tro'tar/ vi to trot; Inf. hurry, get a move on

trote /'trote/ m, trot; toil, drudgery. **t. corto,** jog-trot. **al t.,** with all speed

trotón /tro'ton/ (**-ona**) a trotting. m, horse. f, chaperone

trova /'troβa/ f, verse; song, lay, ballad; love song

trovador /troβa'ðor/ (**-ra**) m, troubadour, minstrel. n poet

trovadoresco /troβaðo'resko/ a pertaining to minstrels, troubadour

trovar /tro'βar/ vi to compose verses; write ballads; misconstrue, misinterpret

Troya /'troia/ Troy

troyano /tro'iano/ (**-na**) a and n Trojan

trozo /'troso; 'troθo/ m, part, fragment; piece, portion; Lit. selection. **t. de abordaje,** Nav. landing party

trucha /'trutʃa/ f, trout. **t. asalmonada,** salmon trout

truchuela /tru'tʃuela/ f, small trout; salt cod

truco /'truko/ m, trick, deception

truculencia /truku'lensia; truku'lenθia/ f, harshness, cruelty, truculence

truculento /truku'lento/ a fierce, harsh, truculent

trueco /'trueko/ m, exchange. **a t. de,** in exchange for; on condition that

trueno /'trueno/ m, thunder; report, noise (of firearms); Inf. rake, scapegrace

trueque /'trueke/ m, exchange. **a.** (or **en**) **t.,** in exchange

trufa /'trufa/ f, Bot. truffle; nonsense, idle talk

trufar /tru'far/ vt Cul. to stuff with truffles; vi Inf. lie, tell fibs

truhán /tru'an/ (**-ana**) a knavish, roguish, comic. n knave, rogue; clown, buffoon

truhanear /truane'ar/ vi to be a trickster, behave like a knave; play the clown

truhanería /truane'ria/ f, knavery, act of a rogue; clowning, buffoonery; collection of rogues

truhanesco /trua'nesko/ a knavish, scoundrelly; clownish

trujal /tru'hal/ m, oil or grape press; oil mill; vat for soap making

trujar /tru'har/ vt to partition off

trulla /'truya; 'truʎa/ f, uproar, tumult; crowd, throng

truncar /trun'kar/ vt to shorten, truncate; decapitate, mutilate; omit, cut out (words, etc.); curtail, abridge; mutilate, deform (texts, etc.)

truque /'truke/ m, card game; kind of hopscotch

trusa /'trusa/ f, Cuba, bathing suit

trust /trust/ m, Com. trust

tú /tu/ pers pron 2nd sing mf thou, you. **tratar de t.** (**a**), to address familiarly; be on intimate terms with

tu /tu/ poss pron mf thy, your. Used only before nouns

tuberculina /tuβerku'lina/ f, tuberculin

tubérculo /tu'βerkulo/ m, (Zool. Med.) tubercle; Bot. tubercle, tuber

tuberculoso /tuβerku'loso/ a tubercular, tuberculous

tubería /tuβe'ria/ f, piping, tubing; pipe system; pipe factory

tuberosa /tuβe'rosa/ f, tuberose

tuberoso /tuβe'roso/ a tuberous

tubo /'tuβo/ m, pipe, tube; lamp chimney; flue; Anat. duct, canal. **t. acústico,** speaking tube. **t. de ensayo,** test tube. **t. de escape,** exhaust pipe. **t. lanzatorpedos,** torpedo tube. **t. termiónico,** Radio. thermionic valve

tubular /tuβu'lar/ a tubular

tucán, tucano /tu'kan/ m toucan

tudesco /tu'ðesko/ a German

tueco /'tueko/ m, stump (of a tree); wormhole (in wood)

tuerca /'tuerka/ f, nut (of a screw)

tuerto /'tuerto/ a one-eyed. m, Law. tort; pl afterpains. **a t.,** unjustly

tueste /'tueste/ m, toasting

tuétano /'tuetano/ *m*, marrow. *Inf.* **hasta los tuétanos,** to the depths of one's being

tufillas /tu'fiyas; tu'fiʎas/ *mf Inf.* easily irritated person

tufo /'tufo/ *m*, strong smell, poisonous vapor; *Inf.* stink; side, airs, conceit (often *pl*); lock of hair over the ears

tugurio /tu'gurio/ *m*, shepherd's hut; miserable little room; *Inf.* haunt, low dive

tul /tul/ *m*, tulle

tulipa /tu'lipa/ *f*, small tulip; lampshade

tulipán /tuli'pan/ *m*, tulip

tullido /tu'yiðo; tu'ʎiðo/ *a* partially paralyzed; maimed, crippled

tullir /tu'yir; tu'ʎir/ *vt irr* to maim, cripple; paralyze; *vr* become paralyzed; be crippled. See **mullir**

tumba /'tumba/ *f*, tomb; tumble, overbalancing; somersault; Catherine wheel

tumbar /tum'bar/ *vt* to knock down; kill, drop; *Inf.* overpower, overcome (of odors, wine). *vi* fall down; *Naut.* run aground; *vr Inf.* lie down, stretch oneself out

tumbo /'tumbo/ *m*, tumble, overbalancing; undulation (of ground); rise and fall of sea waves; imminent danger; book containing deeds and privileges of monasteries and churches

tumbón /tum'bon/ *a Inf.* crafty, sly; idle, lazy. *m*, trunk with an arched lid

tumefacción /tumefak'sion; tumefak'θion/ *f*, swelling

tumefacto, túmido /tume'fakto, 'tumiðo/ *a* swollen

tumor /tu'mor/ *m*, tumor

túmulo /'tumulo/ *m*, tumulus; catafalque; mound of earth

tumulto /tu'multo/ *m*, riot, uprising; tumult, commotion, disturbance

tumultuario, tumultuoso /tumul'tuario, tumul'tuoso/ *a* noisy, tumultuous, confused

tuna /'tuna/ *f*, prickly pear tree or fruit; vagrant life; strolling student musicians (playing to raise money for charity)

tunante /tu'nante/ *a* rascally, roguish. *mf* rascal, scoundrel

tunantuelo /tunan'tuelo/ **(-la)** *n Inf.* imp, little rascal

tunda /'tunda/ *f*, shearing of cloth; *Inf.* sound beating, hiding

tundear /tunde'ar/ *vt* to beat, drub, buffet

tundidora /tundi'ðora/ *f*, woman who shears cloth; cloth-shearing machine; lawn mower

tundir /tun'dir/ *vt* to shear (cloth); mow (grass); *Inf.* beat, wallop

tunecino /tune'sino; tune'θino/ **(-na)** *a* and *n* Tunisian

túnel /'tunel/ *m*, tunnel

túnica /'tunika/ *f*, tunic, chiton; tunicle; robe

tuno /'tuno/ **(-na)** *a* knavish, rascally. *n* rascal, scoundrel

tupé /tu'pe/ *m*, forelock (of a horse); toupee; *Inf.* cheek, nerve

tupición /tupi'sion; tupi'θion/ *f*, *Lat. Am.* blockage, obstruction; cold (in the head)

tupido /tu'piðo/ *a* thick, dense; obtuse, dull, stupid; *Lat. Am.* blocked up, obstructed

tupir /tu'pir/ *vt* to thicken, make dense; press tightly; *vr* stuff oneself with food or drink

turba /'turβa/ *f*, crowd, multitude; peat

turbación /turβa'sion; turβa'θion/ *f*, disturbance; upset; perturbation; bewilderment, confusion; embarrassment

turbador /turβa'ðor/ **(-ra)** *a* disturbing, upsetting. *n* disturber, upsetter

turbamulta /turβa'multa/ *f*, *Inf.* mob, rabble

turbante /tur'βante/ *a* upsetting, perturbing. *m*, turban

turbar /tur'βar/ *vt* to disturb, upset; make turbid, muddy; bewilder, confuse; embarrass

turbera /tur'βera/ *f*, peat bog

turbiedad /turβie'ðað/ *f*, muddiness (of liquids); obscurity

turbina /tur'βina/ *f*, turbine

turbio /'turβio/ *a* turbid, muddy; troublous; turbulent, disturbed; obscure, confused (style); indistinct, blurred, *m pl*, lees, sediment (of oil)

turbión /tur'βion/ *m*, brief storm, squall; *Fig.* shower, rush

turbulencia /turβu'lensia; turβu'lenθia/ *f*, turbidity, muddiness; turbulence, commotion; disturbance, confusion

turbulento /turβu'lento/ *a* muddy, turbid; turbulent, disturbed; confused

turca /'turka/ *f*, *Inf.* drinking bout

turco /'turko/ **(-ca)** *a* Turkish. *n* Turk. *m*, Turkish (language)

turgencia /tur'hensia; tur'henθia/ *f*, swelling, turgidity

turgente /tur'hente/ *a Med.* turgescent; *Poet.* turgid, prominent, swollen

turismo /tu'rismo/ *m*, touring, tourist industry. **coche de t.,** touring car

turista /tu'rista/ *mf* tourist

turno /'turno/ *m*, turn. **por t.,** in turn

turquesa /tur'kesa/ *f*, turquoise

Turquía /tur'kia/ Turkey

turrón /tu'rron/ *m*, kind of nougat; almond paste; *Inf.* soft job, sinecure; civil service job

turulato /turu'lato/ *a Inf.* dumbfounded, speechless, inarticulate

¡tus! /tus/ *interj* word for calling dogs. **sin decir t. ni mus,** *Inf.* without saying anything

tusa /'tusa/ *f*, *Central America* corncob; whore; *Ar gentina* mane (of a horse)

tutear /tute'ar/ *vt* to address as tú (instead of the formal usted); treat familiarly

tutela /tu'tela/ *f*, guardianship; tutelage; protection, defense

tuteo /tu'teo/ *m*, the use in speaking to a person of the familiar tú instead of the formal usted

tutor /tu'tor/ **(-ra)** *n* guardian. *m*, stake (for plants); protector, defender

tutoría /tuto'ria/ *f*. See **tutela**

tuyo, tuya, tuyos, tuyas /'tuyo, 'tuya, 'tuyos, 'tuyas/ *poss pron 2nd sing* and *pl mf* thine, yours. Used sometimes with def. art. (e.g. *Este sombrero es el tuyo,* This hat is yours)

U

u /u/ *f*, letter U. *conjunc* Used instead of **o** or before words beginning with **o** or **ho** (e.g. *fragante u oloroso*)

ubérrimo /u'βerrimo/ *a sup* most fruitful; very abundant

ubicación /uβika'sion; uβika'θion/ *f*, situation, position, location

ubicar /uβi'kar/ *vt* to place, situate; *vi* and *vr* be situated

ubicuidad /uβikui'ðað/ *f*, ubiquity

ubicuo /u'βikuo/ *a* omnipresent; ubiquitous

ubre /'uβre/ *f*, udder

Ucrania /u'krania/ Ukraine

ucranio /u'kranio/ **(-ia)** *a* and *n* Ukrainian

¡uf! /uf/ *interj* ugh!

ufanarse /ufa'narse/ *vr* to pride oneself, put on airs

ufanía /ufa'nia/ *f*, pride, conceit

ufano /u'fano/ *a* conceited, vain; satisfied, pleased; expeditious, masterly

ujier /u'hier/ *m*, usher

úlcera /'ulsera; 'ulθera/ *f*, ulcer

ulcerar /ulse'rar; ulθe'rar/ **(se)** *vt* and *vr* to ulcerate

ulceroso /ulse'roso; ulθe'roso/ *a* ulcerous

ulpo /'ulpo/ *m*, *Chile, Peru* corn gruel

ulterior /ulte'rior/ *a* farther, ulterior; subsequent

ulteriormente /ulterior'mente/ *adv* subsequently, later

ultimación /ultima'sion; ultima'θion/ *f*, ending, finishing

ultimar /ulti'mar/ *vt* to end, conclude

ultimátum /ulti'matum/ *m*, ultimatum

último /'ultimo/ *a* last; farthermost; ultimate; top; final, definitive; most valuable, best; latter; recent. **«Última Hora.»** "Stop Press." **a última hora,** *Fig.* at the eleventh hour. **en estos últimos años,** in recent years. **a últimos de mes,** towards the end of the month. **el ú. piso,** the top floor. **por ú.,** finally. *Inf.* **estar en las últimas,** to be at the end, be finishing

ultra /'ultra/, *adv* besides; (with words like *mar*) beyond; (as prefix) excessively

ultrajar /ultra'har/ *vt* to insult; scorn, despise

ultraje /ul'trahe/ *m*, insult, outrage

ultrajoso /ultra'hoso/ *a* offensive, insulting, abusive

ultramar /ultra'mar/ *m*, overseas, abroad

ultramarino /ultrama'rino/ *a* oversea; ultramarine. *m*, foreign produce (gen. *pl*)

ultramontano /ultramon'tano/ *a* ultramontane

ultrarrojo /ultra'rroho/ *a* infrared

ultratumba /ultra'tumba/ *adv* beyond the grave

ultravioleta /ultraβio'leta/ *a* ultraviolet

úlula /'ulula/ *f*, screech owl

ululación /ulula'sion; ulula'θion/ *f*, screech, howl; hoot of an owl

ulular /ulu'lar/ *vi* to howl, shriek, screech; hoot (of an owl)

ululato /ulu'lato/ *m*, ululation

umbilical /umbili'kal/ *a* umbilical

umbral /um'bral/ *m*, threshold; *Fig.* starting point; *Archit.* lintel. **atravesar** (*or* **pisar**) **los umbrales,** to cross the threshold

umbría /um'bria/ *f*, shady place

umbrío /um'brio/ *a* shady, dark

umbroso /um'broso/ *a* shady

un /un/ *abb* of **uno, a,** one. Used before *m, sing f,* **una,** *indef art.* a, an; one

unánime /u'nanime/ *a* unanimous

unanimidad /unanimi'ðað/ *f,* unanimity. **por u.,** unanimously

unción /un'sion; un'θion/ *f,* anointing; *Eccl.* Extreme Unction; unction, fervor

uncir /un'sir; un'θir/ *vt* to yoke

undécimo /un'desimo; un'deθimo/ *a* eleventh

undísono /un'disono/ *a Poet.* sounding, sonorous (waves, etc.)

undoso /un'doso/ *a* wavy, rippling

undulación /undula'sion; undula'θion/ *f,* undulation; *Phys.* wave

undular /undu'lar/ *vi* to undulate; wriggle; float, wave (flags, etc.)

undulatorio /undula'torio/ *a* undulatory

ungimiento /unhi'miento/ *m,* anointment

ungir /un'hir/ *vt* to anoint

ungüento /uŋ'guento/ *m,* ointment; lotion; *Fig.* balm, unguent

unicelular /uniselu'lar; uniθelu'lar/ *a* unicellular

único /'uniko/ *a* unique; sole, solitary, only. **Lo ú. que se puede hacer es…,** The only thing one can do is…

unicolor /uniko'lor/ *a* of one color

unicornio /uni'kornio/ *m,* unicorn

unidad /uni'ðað/ *f,* unity; unit; (*Math. Mil.*) unit. **u. de bagaje,** piece of baggage. (of drama) **u. de lugar,** unity of place. **u. de tiempo,** unity of time

unidamente /uniða'mente/ *adv* jointly; harmoniously

unificación /unifika'sion; unifika'θion/ *f,* unification

unificar /unifi'kar/ **(se)** *vt* and *vr* to unify, unite

uniformación /uniforma'sion; uniforma'θion/ *f,* standardization

uniformar /unifor'mar/ *vt* to make uniform, standardize; put into uniform; *vr* become uniform

uniforme /uni'forme/ *a* uniform; same, similar. *m,* uniform

uniformidad /uniformi'ðað/ *f,* uniformity

unigénito /uni'henito/ *a* only-begotten. *m,* Christ

unilateral /unilate'ral/ *a* one-sided, unilateral

unión /u'nion/ *f,* union; correspondence, conformity; agreement; marriage; alliance, federation; composition, mixture; combination; proximity, nearness; (mystic) union

unionista /unio'nista/ *mf Polit.* unionist

Unión Soviética /u'nion so'βietika/ Soviet Union

unir /u'nir/ *vt* to unite, join; mix, combine; bind, fasten; connect, couple; bring together; marry; *Fig.* harmonize, conciliate; *vr* join together, unite; be combined; marry; (*with prep a* or *con*) be near to; associate with

unísono /u'nisono/ *a* unisonant. **al u.,** in unison; unanimously

unitario /uni'tario/ **(-ia)** *a* and *n* Unitarian

universal /uniβer'sal/ *a* universal; well-informed; widespread

universalidad /uniβersali'ðað/ *f,* universality

universalizar /uniβersali'sar; uniβersali'θar/ *vt* to make universal, generalize

universidad /uniβersi'ðað/ *f,* university; universality; universe

universitario /uniβersi'tario/ *a* university

universo /uni'βerso/ *a* universal. *m,* universe

uno /'uno/ (*f,* **una**) *a, n;* one; single, only; same; *pl* some; about, nearly. *m,* one (number). **Tiene unos doce años,** He is about twelve. **unas pocas manzanas,** a few apples. *pron* someone; one thing, same thing; *pl* some people. **No sabe uno qué creer,** One doesn't know what to believe. **Unos dicen que no, otros que sí,** Some (people) say no, others yes. **Juan no tiene libros y le voy a dar uno,** John has no books and I am going to give him one. **Todo es uno,** It's all the same. **u. a u.,** one by one. **u. que otro,** a few. **u. y otro,** both. **unos cuantos,** a few, some. **Es la una,** It is one o'clock

untar /un'tar/ *vt* to anoint; grease, oil; *Inf.* bribe; *vr* smear oneself with grease or similar thing; *Fig. Inf.* line one's pockets. **u. el carro,** *Fig.* to grease the wheels

unto /'unto/ *m,* grease; animal fat; *Fig.* balm; *Chile* shoe polish

untuoso /un'tuoso/ *a* fat, greasy

uña /'uɲa/ *f,* nail (of fingers or toes); hoof, trotter, claw; stinging tail of scorpion; thorn; stump of tree branch; *Naut.* fluke; *Fig. Inf.* light fingers (gen. *pl*). **afilarse las uñas,** to sharpen one's claws, prepare for trouble. **comerse las uñas,** to bite one's nails. **caer en las uñas de,** to fall into the clutches of. **hincar la u. (en),** to stick the claws into; to defraud, overcharge. **ser u. y carne,** to be devoted friends. **sacarle las uñas,** to use any means available

uñarada /uɲa'raða/ *f,* scratch with nails

uñero /u'ɲero/ *m,* ingrowing nail, ingrown nail

¡upa! /'upa/ *interj* Up you get! Up you go! Upsy daisy! (gen. to children)

uranio /u'ranio/ *m,* uranium

urbanidad /urβani'ðað/ *f,* civility, good manners, urbanity

urbanismo /urβa'nismo/ *m,* town planning; housing scheme

urbanización /urβanisa'sion; urβaniθa'θion/ *f,* urbanization

urbanizar /urβani'sar; urβani'θar/ *vt* to civilize, polish; urbanize

urbano /ur'βano/ *a* urban, city; urbane

urbe /'urβe/ *f,* city, metropolis

urbícola /ur'βikola/ *mf* city dweller

urdemalas /urðe'malas/ *mf,* schemer, intriguer

urdidera /urði'ðera/ *f,* warping-frame

urdimbre /ur'ðimbre/ *f,* warp; scheming, plotting

urdir /ur'ðir/ *vt* to warp; weave; scheme, intrigue

uréter /u'reter/ *m,* ureter

uretra /u'retra/ *f,* urethra

urgencia /ur'hensia; ur'henθia/ *f,* urgency; necessity; compulsion

urgente /ur'hente/ *a* urgent

urgir /ur'hir/ *vi* to be urgent; be valid, be in force (laws)

urinario /uri'nario/ a urinary. m, urinal
urna /'urna/ f, urn; ballot box; glass case
urraca /u'rraka/ f, magpie
Uruguay /uru'guai/ m Uruguay
uruguayo /uru'guayo/ **(-ya)** a and n Uruguayan
usado /u'saðo/ a worn out; accustomed, efficient. *Com.* **al u.**, in the usual form. **ropa usada,** secondhand clothing, worn clothing
usanza /u'sansa/ f, custom, usage
usar /u'sar/ vt to use; wear, make use of; follow (trade, occupation); vi be accustomed
usina /u'sina/ f, *Argentina* power plant
uso /'uso/ m, use; custom; fashion; habit; wear and tear. **al u.**, according to custom. **al u. de,** in the manner of
usted /us'teð/ mf you. pl **ustedes.** Often abbreviated to **Vd, V, Vds, VV** or **Ud, Uds**
usual /u'sual/ a usual; general, customary; sociable
usufructo /usu'frukto/ m, *Law.* usufruct; life-interest; profit
usura /u'sura/ f, usury; profiteering. **pagar con u.,** to pay back a thousandfold
usurario /usu'rario/ a usurious
usurear /usure'ar/ vi to lend or borrow with usury; profiteer, make excess profits
usurero /usu'rero/ **(-ra)** n usurer; profiteer

usurpación /usurpa'sion; usurpa'θion/ f, usurpation
usurpador /usurpa'ðor/ **(-ra)** a usurping. n usurper
usurpar /usur'par/ vt to usurp
utensilio /uten'silio/ m, utensil; tool, implement (gen. pl)
uterino /ute'rino/ a uterine
útero /'utero/ m, uterus
útil /'util/ a useful; profitable; *Law.* lawful (of days, etc.). m, usefulness, profit; pl **útiles,** utensils, tools
utilidad /utili'ðað/ f, utility; usefulness; profit
utilitario /utili'tario/ a utilitarian
utilitarismo /utilita'rismo/ m, utilitarianism
utilizable /utilisaβle; utili'θaβle/ a utilizable
utilización /utilisa'sion; utiliθa'θion/ f, utilization
utilizar /utili'sar; utili'θar/ vt to utilize
utillaje /uti'yahe; uti'ʎahe/ m, machinery
utópico /u'topiko/ a Utopian
uva /'uβa/ f, grape. **u. espina,** kind of gooseberry. **u. moscatel,** muscatel grape. *Inf.* **hecho una u.,** dead-drunk
uvero /u'βero/ **(-ra)** a pertaining or relating to grapes, grape. n grape seller
uxoricidio /uksori'siðio; uksori'θiðio/ m, uxoricide (act)
uxorio /uk'sorio/ a uxorious

V

---

v /be/ f, letter V. **v doble** or **doble v,** letter W. **V** or **Vd, VV,** abbs **vuestra (s) merced (es),** mf sing and pl you
vaca /'baka/ f, cow. **v. de San Antón,** *Ent.* ladybug
vacación /baka'sion; baka'θion/ f, vacation, holiday (gen. pl); vacancy; act of vacating (employment). **vacaciones retribuídas,** paid vacation
vacada /ba'kaða/ f, herd of cows
vacancia /ba'kansia; ba'kanθia/ f, vacancy
vacante /ba'kante/ a vacant. f, vacancy
vacar /ba'kar/ vi to be vacant; take a holiday; retire temporarily; (with prep a) dedicate oneself to, engage in
vaciadero /basia'ðero; baθia'ðero/ m, rubbish dump; sewer, drain
vaciado /ba'siaðo; ba'θiaðo/ m, plaster cast; *Archit.* excavation
vaciamiento /basia'miento; baθia'miento/ m, emptying; molding, casting; depletion
vaciar /ba'siar; ba'θiar/ vt to empty; drain, drink; mold, cast; *Archit.* excavate; hone; copy; vi flow (into) (rivers); vr Inf. blurt out
vaciedad /basie'ðað; baθie'ðað/ f, emptiness; foolishness, inanity
vacilación /basila'sion; baθila'θion/ f, swaying; tottering; staggering; hesitation, perplexity
vacilada /basi'laða; baθi'laða/ *Mexico,* f joke, trick (played on someone)
vacilante /basi'lante; baθi'lante/ a swaying; tottering; staggering; hesitating, vacillating
vacilar /basi'lar; baθi'lar/ vi to sway; totter; stagger; flicker; hesitate
vacío /ba'sio; ba'θio/ a empty, void; fruitless, vain; unoccupied, vacant, deserted; imperfect; hollow, empty; conceited, immature. m, hollow; *Anat.* flank; vacancy; shortage; *Phys.* vacuum. **v. de aire,** airpocket. **de v.,** unloaded (carts, etc.). **en v.,** in vacuo. *Inf.* **hacer el v. (a),** to send to Coventry
vacuidad /bakui'ðað/ f, emptiness; vacuity
vacuna /ba'kuna/ f, cowpox; vaccine. **v. antivariolosa,** smallpox vaccine
vacunación /bakuna'sion; bakuna'θion/ f, vaccination
vacunar /baku'nar/ vt to vaccinate; inoculate
vacuno /ba'kuno/ a bovine
vacuo /'bakuo/ a empty; vacant. m, void; vacuum
vadeable /baðe'aβle/ a fordable (rivers, etc.); *Fig.* surmountable
vadear /baðe'ar/ vt to ford, wade; *Fig.* overcome (ob-

stacles); *Fig.* sound, find out the opinion (of); vr behave
vademécum /baðe'mekum/ m, vade mecum; school satchel
vado /'baðo/ m, ford; expedient, help
vagabundear /bagaβunde'ar/ vi to wander, roam, loiter
vagabundeo /bagaβun'deo/ m, vagabondage
vagabundo /baga'βundo/ **(-da)** a roving, wandering; vagrant. n tramp, vagabond
vagamundear /bagamunde'ar/ vi. See **vagabundear**
vagancia /ba'gansia; ba'ganθia/ f, vagrancy
vagar /ba'gar/ m, leisure; interval, pause. vi be idle or at leisure; wander, roam
vagido /ba'hiðo/ m, cry, wail (infants)
vago /'bago/ **(-ga)** a vagrant, idle; vague; *Art.* indefinite, blurred. n idler. m, tramp; loafer. **en v.,** unsuccessfully, vainly
vagón /ba'gon/ m, wagon; (railway) coach. **v. comedor,** dining car
vagoneta /bago'neta/ f, open truck (railways, mines, etc.)
vaguear /bage'ar/ vi to roam, wander; loaf
vaguedad /bage'ðað/ f, vagueness; vague remark
vaharada /baa'raða/ f, whiff, exhalation
vahído /ba'iðo/ m, vertigo, dizzy spell
vaho /'bao/ m, vapor, fume
vaina /'baina/ f, scabbard; *Bot.* sheath, pod; case (scissors, etc.); *Dominican Republic* thing; *Colombia* hassle. **¡Qué vaina!** What a hassle!
vainilla /bai'niya; bai'niʎa/ f, *Bot.* vanilla; *Sew.* drawn-thread work
vaivén /bai'βen/ m, swing, sway, seesaw; instability, fluctuation
vajilla /ba'hiya; ba'hiʎa/ f, china; dinner service
val /bal/ m, abb **valle**
Valdepeñas /balde'peɲas/ m, red wine from Valdepeñas
vale /'bale/ m, *Com.* bond, I.O.U., promissory note; voucher; valediction; *Lat. Am.* buddy, pal
valedero /bale'ðero/ a valid, binding
valedor /bale'ðor/ **(-ra)** n protector; sponsor
valencia /ba'lensia; ba'lenθia/ f, valency
valenciano /balen'siano; balen'θiano/ **(-na)** a and n Valencian
valentía /balen'tia/ f, bravery; heroic deed; boast; (*Art. Lit.*) dash, imagination, fire; superhuman effort
valentón /balen'ton/ a boastful, blustering

valer /ba'ler/ *vt irr* to protect; defend; produce (income, etc.); cost; *vi* be worth; deserve; have power or authority; be of importance or worth; be a protection; be current (money); be valid; *vr* (*with de*) make use of. *m*, value, worth. **Vale, Spain** OK. **v. la pena,** to be worthwhile. **v. tanto como cualquiera,** to be as good as the next guy, be as good as the next fellow. **¡Válgame Dios!** Heavens! Bless me! **Más vale así,** It's better thus. **Vale más ser cola de león que cabeza de ratón.** Better a big frog in a small puddle than a small frog in a big puddle. *Pres. Ind.* **valgo, vales, etc.** *Fut.* **valdré, etc.** *Condit.* **valdría, etc.** *Pres. Subjunc.* **valga, etc.**

valeriana /bale'riana/ *f*, valerian

valeroso /bale'roso/ *a* active, energetic; courageous; powerful

valetudinario /baletuði'nario/ *a* valetudinarian

valía /ba'lia/ *f*, value, price; influence, worth; faction, party. **a las valías,** at the highest price

validación /baliða'sion; baliða'θion/ *f*, validation; force, soundness

validar /bali'ðar/ *vt* to make strong; validate

validez /bali'ðes; bali'ðeθ/ *f*, validity

valido /ba'liðo/ *a* favorite, esteemed. *m*, court favorite; prime minister

válido /ba'liðo/ *a* firm, sound, valid; strong, robust

valiente /ba'liente/ *a* strong, robust; courageous; active; excellent; excessive, enormous (gen. *Ironic.*); boastful

valija /ba'liha/ *f*, valise, suitcase, grip; mail bag; mail

valimiento /bali'miento/ *m*, value; favor; protection; influence

valioso /ba'lioso/ *a* valuable; powerful; wealthy

valisoletano /balisole'tano/ **(-na)** *a* and *n* of or from Valladolid

valla /'baya; 'baʎa/ *f*, barricade, paling; stockade; *Fig.* obstacle. **v. publicitaria,** billboard

vallado /ba'yaðo; ba'ʎaðo/ *m*, stockade; enclosure; *Mexico* deep ditch

valle /'baye; 'baʎe/ *m*, valley; vale; river-basin

valor /ba'lor/ *m*, worth, value; price; courage; validity; power; yield, income; insolence; *pl Com.* securities

valoración /balora'sion; balora'θion/ *f*, valuation; appraisement

valorar /balo'rar/ *vt* to value; appraise

valorización /balorisa'sion; baloriθa'θion/ *f*, valuation

valquiria /bal'kiria/ *f*, Valkyrie

vals /bals/ *m*, waltz

valsar /bal'sar/ *vi* to waltz

valuación /balua'sion; balua'θion/ *f*. See **valoración**

valuar /balu'ar/ *vt* to value; appraise; assess

valva /'balβa/ *f*, Zool. valve

válvula /'balβula/ *f*, Mech. valve. Auto. **v. de cámara (del neumático),** tire-valve. **v. de seguridad,** safety-valve

vampiro /bam'piro/ *m*, vampire; *Fig.* bloodsucker

vanagloria /bana'gloria/ *f*, vaingloriousness, conceit

vanagloriarse /banaglo'riarse/ *vr* to be conceited

vanaglorioso /banaglo'rioso/ **(-sa)** *a* conceited. *n* boaster

vanamente /bana'mente/ *adv* vainly; without foundation; superstitiously; arrogantly

vandálico /ban'daliko/ *a* Vandal

vandalismo /banda'lismo/ *m*, vandalism; destructiveness

vándalo /'bandalo/ **(-la)** *a* and *n* Vandal

vanguardia /baŋ'guarðia/ *f*, vanguard; *pl* outerworks. **a v.,** in the forefront

vanidad /bani'ðað/ *f*, vanity; ostentation; empty words; illusion. *Inf.* **ajar la v. de,** to take (a person) down a peg

vanidoso /bani'ðoso/ **(-sa)** *a* vain; ostentatious. *n* conceited person

vano /'bano/ *a* vain; hollow, empty; useless, ineffectual; unsubstantial, illusory. *m*, span (bridge). **v. único,** single span. **en v.,** uselessly, in vain

vapor /ba'por/ *m*, steam, vapor; fainting fit; steamboat; *pl* hysterics. **v. de ruedas, v. de paleta,** paddle

steamer. **v. volandero,** tramp steamer. **al v.,** full steam ahead; *Inf.* with all speed

vaporable /bapo'raβle/ *a* vaporizable

vaporación /bapora'sion; bapora'θion/ *f*, evaporation

vaporización /baporisa'sion; baporiθa'θion/ *f*, vaporization

vaporizador /baporisa'ðor; baporiθa'ðor/ *m*, vaporizer; spray, sprayer

vaporizar /bapori'sar; bapori'θar/ *vt* to vaporize; spray

vaporoso /bapo'roso/ *a* vaporous; ethereal; gauzy

vapulación /bapula'sion; bapula'θion/ *f*, **vapulamiento** *m*, whipping

vapular /bapu'lar/ *vt* to whip

vapuleo /bapu'leo/ *m*, whipping, spanking

vaquería /bake'ria/ *f*, herd of cattle; dairy; dairy farm

vaquero /ba'kero/ **(-ra)** *n* cowboy; **vaqueros,** *m*, *pl* jeans

vaquilla /ba'kiya; ba'kiʎa/ *f*, heifer

vara /'bara/ *f*, staff; rod; wand (of authority); vara (2.8 feet); shaft (of cart). **v. de aforar,** water gauge

varada /ba'raða/ *f*, Naut. running aground

varadero /bara'ðero/ *m*, shipyard

varar /ba'rar/ *vi* Naut. to run aground; *Fig.* be held up (negotiations, etc.); *vt* Naut. put in dry dock

varear /bare'ar/ *vt* to knock down (fruit from tree); beat (with a rod); measure with a rod; sell by the rod; *vr* grow thin

variabilidad /bariaβili'ðað/ *f*, variableness

variable /ba'riaβle/ *a* variable; changeable, inconsistent

variación /baria'sion; baria'θion/ *f*, variation

variado /ba'riaðo/ *a* varied; variegated

variante /ba'riante/ *a* varying. *f*, variant; discrepancy

variar /ba'riar/ *vt* to vary; change; *vi* change; be different

varice /ba'rise; ba'riθe/ *f*, varix

varicela /bari'sela; bari'θela/ *f*, chicken pox

varicoso /bari'koso/ *a* varicose

variedad /barie'ðað/ *f*, variety; change; inconstancy, instability; alteration; variation; *Biol.* variety

varilla /ba'riya; ba'riʎa/ *f*, *dim* rod; rib (fan, umbrella). **v. de virtudes,** conjurer's wand. *Mech.* **v. percusora,** tappet rod

vario /'bario/ *a* different, diverse; inconstant, changeable; variegated; *pl* some, a few

variopinto /bario'pinto/ *a* motley

varón /ba'ron/ *m*, male; man

varonil /baro'nil/ *a* male; manly

Varsovia /bar'soβia/ Warsaw

varsoviano /barso'βiano/ **(-na)** *a* and *n* of or from Warsaw

vasallaje /basa'yahe; basa'ʎahe/ *m*, vassalage; dependence; tribute money

vasallo /ba'sayo; ba'saʎo/ **(-lla)** *n* vassal. *a* vassal; dependent

vasco /'basko/ **(-ca), vascongado (-da)** *a* and *n* Basque

vascuence /bas'kuense; bas'kuenθe/ *m*, Basque (language); *Inf.* gibberish

vaselina /base'lina/ *f*, vaseline

vasija /ba'siha/ *f*, vessel, receptacle, jar

vaso /'baso/ *m*, receptacle; glass, tankard, mug; glassful; (*Naut. Anat. Bot.*) vessel; garden-urn; vase

vástago /'bastago/ *m*, stem, shoot; offspring, descendant; piston rod

vastedad /baste'ðað/ *f*, extensiveness, largeness, vastness

vasto /'basto/ *a* vast, extensive

vate /'bate/ *m*, bard; seer

vaticano /bati'kano/ *a* and *m*, Vatican

vaticinar /batisi'nar; batiθi'nar/ *vt* to prophesy, foretell

vaticinio /bati'sinio; bati'θinio/ *m*, prediction

vatímetro /ba'timetro/ *m*, water meter

vatio /'batio/ *m*, watt. **v. hora,** watt hour

ve /be/ *f*, name of the letter V. **v. doble** *or* **doble v.,** name of the letter W

vecinal /besi'nal; beθi'nal/ *a* neighboring, adjacent

vecindad /besin'daθ; beθin'daδ/ *f*, neighborhood; *Lat. Am.* slum. **buena v.,** good neighborliness. **hacer mala v.,** to be a nuisance to one's neighbors

vecindario /besin'dario; beθin'dario/ *m*, neighborhood; population of a district

vecino /be'sino; be'θino/ **(-na)** *a* neighboring; near; similar. *n* neighbor; citizen; inhabitant

vector /bek'tor/ *m*, carrier (of disease)

veda /'beδa/ *f*, close season; prohibition

vedamiento /beδa'miento/ *m*, prohibition

vedar /be'δar/ *vt* to forbid; prevent

vedija /be'δiha/ *f*, tangled lock of hair; piece of matted wool; curl (of smoke)

veedor /bee'δor/ **(-ra)** *a* prying. *n* busy-body. *m*, inspector; overseer

vega /'bega/ *f*, fertile lowland plain; meadow

vegada /be'gaδa/ *f*. See **vez**

vegetable /behe'taβle/ *a* and *m*, vegetable

vegetación /beheta'sion; beheta'θion/ *f*, vegetation

vegetal /behe'tal/ *a* vegetal; plant. *m*, vegetable, plant

vegetar /behe'tar/ *vi* to flourish, grow (plants); *Fig.* vegetate

vegetarianismo /behetaria'nismo/ *m*, vegetarianism

vegetariano /beheta'riano/ **(-na)** *a* and *n* vegetarian

vegetativo /beheta'tiβo/ *a* vegetative

vehemencia /bee'mensia; bee'menθia/ *f*, vehemence

vehemente /bee'mente/ *a* vehement; vivid

vehículo /be'ikulo/ *m*, vehicle; means, instrument

veinte /'beinte/ *a* and *m*, twenty; twentieth

veintena /bein'tena/ *f*, a score

veinticinco /beinti'sinko; beinti'θinko/ *a* and *m*, twenty-five; twenty-fifth

veinticuatro /beinti'kuatro/ *a* and *m*, twenty-four; twenty-fourth

veintidós /beinti'δos/ *a* and *m*, twenty-two; twenty-second

veintinueve /beinti'nueβe/ *a* and *m*, twenty-nine; twenty-ninth

veintiocho /bein'tiotʃo/ *a* and *m*, twenty-eight; twenty-eighth

veintiséis /beinti'seis/ *a* and *m*, twenty-six; twenty-sixth

veintisiete /beinti'siete/ *a* and *m*, twenty-seven; twenty-seventh

veintitrés /beinti'tres/ *a* and *m*, twenty-three; twenty-third

veintiuno /bein'tiuno/ *a* and *m*, twenty-one; twenty-first. Abbreviates to **veintiún** before a noun (even if one or more adjectives intervene)

vejación /beha'sion; beha'θion/ *f*, ill-treatment, persecution

vejamen /be'hamen/ *m*, irritation, provocation; taunt; lampoon

vejar /be'har/ *vt* to ill-treat, persecute; plague

vejatorio /beha'torio/ *a* vexing, annoying

vejete /be'hete/ *m*, *Inf.* silly old man

vejez /be'hes; be'heθ/ *f*, oldness; old age; platitude. **vejeces,** *pl* ailments of old age. *Inf.* **a la v., viruelas,** the older the madder

vejiga /be'higa/ *f*, bladder; blister. **v. natatoria,** float (of a fish)

vela /'bela/ *f*, vigil; watch; pilgrimage; sentinel, watchman; candle; *Naut.* sail; awning; night work, overtime. **v. de cangreja,** boom sail. **v. de mesana,** mizzen sail. **v. de trinquete,** foresail. **v. latina,** lateen sail. **a toda v.,** with all speed. **alzar velas,** to hoist sail. **en v.,** wakeful, without sleep. *Inf.* **estar entre dos velas,** to be tipsy

velación /bela'sion; bela'θion/ *f*, vigil; watch; marriage ceremony of veiling (gen. *pl*)

velada /be'laδa/ *f*, vigil; watch; evening party

velado /be'laδo/ *a* veiled; dim; (of voice) thick, indistinct

velador /bela'δor/ **(-ra)** *a* watchful; vigilant. *m*, candlestick; small round table; *Mexico* lampshade. *n* watcher, guard

velar /be'lar/ *vi* to watch, be wakeful; work overtime or at night; *Eccl.* watch; *Fig.* (with *por*) watch over,

defend; *vt* veil; conceal; *Photo.* blur; (with *prep a*) wake (corpse); sit with (patient at night)

veleidad /belei'δaδ/ *f*, velleity; fickleness

veleidoso /belei'δoso/ *a* inconstant, changeable

velero /be'lero/ **(-ra)** *m*, sailing ship; sailmaker. *n* candlemaker

veleta /be'leta/ *f*, weathercock; float, quill (fishing). *mf* changeable person

velís /be'lis/ *m*, *Mexico* suitcase.

vello /'beyo; 'beʎo/ *m*, down, soft hair

vellocino /beyo'sino; beʎo'θino/ *m*, wool; fleece

vellón /be'yon; be'ʎon/ *m*, fleece; copper and silver alloy formerly used in sense of "sterling"; *Obs.* copper coin

vellosidad /beyosi'δaδ; beʎosi'δaδ/ *f*, downiness, hairiness

velloso /be'yoso; be'ʎoso/ *a* downy, hairy

velludo /be'yuδo; be'ʎuδo/ *a* hairy, downy. *m*, plush, velvet

velo /'belo/ *m*, veil; curtain; *Eccl.* humeral veil; excuse, pretext; *Zool.* velum. **v. del paladar,** soft palate. **correr el v.,** to disclose a secret. **tomar el v.,** to take the veil, become a nun

velocidad /belosi'δaδ; beloθi'δaδ/ *f*, speed; *Mech.* velocity. *Aer.* **v. ascensional,** rate of climb. *Mech.* **v. del choque,** speed of impact. **en gran v.,** by passenger train. **en pequeña v.,** by goods train

velocímetro /belo'simetro; belo'θimetro/ *m*, *Mexico* speedometer

velódromo /be'loδromo/ *m*, velodrome

velón /be'lon/ *m*, oil lamp

velorio /be'lorio/ *m*, *Lat. Am.* (funeral) wake; dull party

veloz /be'los; be'loθ/ *a* swift; quick-thinking or acting

vena /'bena/ *f*, (*Bot. Anat.*) vein; streak, veining (in wood or stone); *Mineral.* seam; underground spring; inspiration. **estar de v.,** to be in the mood; be inspired

venablo /be'naβlo/ *m*, javelin

venado /be'naδo/ *m*, venison; deer

venal /be'nal/ *a* venous; saleable; venal

venalidad /benali'δaδ/ *f*, saleableness; venality

vencedor /bense'δor; benθe'δor/ **(-ra)** *a* conquering. *n* conqueror

vencer /ben'ser; ben'θer/ *vt* to conquer; defeat; overcome, rise above; outdo, excel; restrain, control (emotions); convince, persuade; *vi* succeed, triumph; *Com.* fall due, mature; *Com.* expire; *vr* control oneself; twist, incline; *Argentina* wear out. **La habitación vence a las doce,** Check-out time is twelve o'clock

vencible /ben'siβle; ben'θiβle/ *a* conquerable; superable

vencimiento /bensi'miento; benθi'miento/ *m*, defeat; conquest, victory; bend, twist (of things); *Com.* expiration; *Com.* maturity (of a bill)

venda /'benda/ *f*, bandage; fillet. **tener una v. en los ojos,** to be blind (to the truth)

vendaje /ben'dahe/ *m*, bandage

vendar /ben'dar/ *vt* to bandage; *Fig.* blind (generally passions)

vendaval /benda'βal/ *m*, strong wind

vendedor /bende'δor/ **(-ra)** *a* selling. *n* seller

vender /ben'der/ *vt* to sell; betray; *vr* sell oneself; be sold; risk all (for someone); *Fig.* give away (secret); (with *por*) sell under false pretences. **v. al contado,** to sell for cash. **v. al por mayor,** to sell wholesale. **v. al por menor,** to sell retail. **venderse caro,** to be unsociable

vendí /ben'di/ *m*, *Com.* certificate of sale

vendible /ben'diβle/ *a* purchasable; saleable

vendimia /ben'dimia/ *f*, vintage; profit, fruits

vendimiar /bendi'miar/ *vt* to harvest the grapes; take advantage of; *Inf.* kill

veneno /be'neno/ *m*, poison; venom; danger (to health or soul); evil passion

venenoso /bene'noso/ *a* poisonous, venomous

venera /be'nera/ *f*, scallop-shell (pilgrim's badge); badge, decoration

veneración /benera'sion; benera'θion/ f, respect, veneration

venerador /benera'ðor/ **(-ra)** a venerating. n venerator, respector

venerar /bene'rar/ vt to venerate; worship

venéreo /be'nereo/ a venereal

venero /be'nero/ m, spring of water; horary line on sundial; origin, genesis; Mineral. bed

venezolano /beneso'lano; beneθo'lano/ **(-na)** a and n Venezuelan

vengador /beŋga'ðor/ **(-ra)** a avenging. n avenger

venganza /beŋ'gansa; beŋ'ganθa/ f, revenge

vengar /beŋ'gar/ vt to avenge; vr avenge oneself

vengativo /beŋga'tiβo/ a vindictive

venia /'benia/ f, pardon, forgiveness; permission; inclination of head (in greeting); Law. license issued to minors to manage their own estate

venial /be'nial/ a venial

venialidad /beniali'ðað/ f, veniality

venida /be'niða/ f, arrival, coming; return; attack (fencing); precipitancy

venidero /beni'ðero/ a future. Poet. **la vida venidera,** the hereafter

venideros /beni'ðeros/ m pl, successors; posterity

venir /be'nir/ vi irr to come; arrive; turn up (at cards); fit, suit; consent, agree; Agr. grow; follow, come after, succeed; result, originate; occur (to the mind); feel, experience; (with prep a + infin.) happen finally, come to pass; (with en) decide, resolve; vr ferment. **v. a menos,** to deteriorate, decline; come upon evil days. **v. a pelo,** to come opportunely, be just right. **v. a ser,** to become. **venirse abajo,** to fall, collapse. **¿A qué viene este viaje?** What is the purpose of this journey? **el mes que viene,** next month. **El vestido te viene muy ancho,** The dress is too wide for you. **Me vino la idea de marcharme,** It occurred to me to leave. **en lo por venir,** in the future. Pres. Ind. **vengo, vienes, viene, venimos, venís, vienen.** Pres. Part. **viniendo.** Fut. **vendré, etc.** Condit. **vendría, etc.** Preterite **vine, viniste, vino, vinimos, vinisteis, vinieron.** Pres. Subjunc. **venga, etc.** Imperf. Subjunc. **viniese, etc.**

venta /'benta/ f, selling; sale; inn; Inf. wilderness; pl Com. turnover. **v. pública,** auction. **a la v.,** on sale. **la V. de la Mesilla,** the Gadsden Purchase

ventada /ben'taða/ f, gust of wind

ventaja /ben'taha/ f, advantage; profit

ventajoso /benta'hoso/ a advantageous; Lat. Am. unscrupulous

ventana /ben'tana/ f, window. **v. de guillotina,** sash window. **v. saladiza,** bay window. **echar algo por la v.,** to waste a thing

ventanal /benta'nal/ m, large window

ventanilla /benta'niya; benta'niλa/ f, small window (as in railway compartments); grill (ticket office, bank, etc.); nostril

ventarrón /benta'rron/ m, high wind

ventear /bente'ar/ v impers to blow (of the wind); vt sniff air (animals); air, dry; investigate; Lat. Am. brand (an animal); vr be spoiled by air (tobacco, etc.)

ventero /ben'tero/ **(-ra)** n innkeeper

ventilación /bentila'sion; bentila'θion/ f, ventilation; ventilator; current of air

ventilador /bentila'ðor/ m, ventilating fan; ventilator

ventilar /benti'lar/ vt to ventilate; shake, winnow; air; discuss

ventisca /ben'tiska/ f, snowstorm

ventiscar, ventisquear /bentis'kar, bentiske'ar/ v impers to snow with a high wind

ventisquero /bentis'kero/ m, glacier; snowfield, snowdrift; snowstorm

ventolera /bento'lera/ f, gust of wind; Inf. boastfulness; whim, caprice

ventolina /bento'lina/ f, Lat. Am. sudden gust (of wind)

ventor /ben'tor/ **(-ra)** n pointer (dog)

ventosa /ben'tosa/ f, vent (pipes, etc.); Zool. sucker; Surg. cupping glass

ventoso /ben'toso/ a windy; flatulent

ventrículo /ben'trikulo/ m, ventricle

ventrílocuo /ben'trilokuo/ **(-ua)** a ventriloquial. n ventriloquist

ventriloquia /bentri'lokia/ f, ventriloquism

ventrudo /ben'truðo/ a big-bellied

ventura /ben'tura/ f, happiness; chance, hazard; risk, danger. **a la v.,** at a venture. **buena v.,** good luck. **por v.,** perhaps; by chance; fortunately

venturoso /bentu'roso/ a fortunate

Venus /'benus/ m, Venus. f, beautiful woman, beauty

ver /ber/ vt irr to see; witness, behold; visit; inspect, examine; consider; observe; know, understand; Lat. Am. look at, watch (television, etc.) (with de + infin.) try to; vr be seen; show oneself, appear; experience, find oneself; exchange visits; meet. **v. mundo,** to travel. **V. y creer,** Seeing is believing. **A mi v.,** In my opinion. **¡A v.!** Let's see!; Wait and see! **no tener nada que v. con,** to have no connection with, nothing to do with. **Veremos,** Time will tell. **Verse en la casa,** to be a stay-at-home. **Ya se ve,** Of course, Naturally. Pres. Ind. **veo, ves, etc.** Imperf. **veía, etc.** Past Part. **visto.** Pres. Subjunc. **vea, etc.** Imperf. Subjunc. **viese, etc.**

vera /'bera/ f, edge; border; shore. **a la v.,** on the edge, on the verge

veracidad /berasi'ðað; beraθi'ðað/ f, truthfulness, veracity

veranadero /berana'ðero/ m, summer pasture

veraneante /berane'ante/ mf summer resident, summer vacationist, holiday-maker

veranear /berane'ar/ vi to spend the summer

veraneo /bera'neo/ m, summer vacation, summer holidays, summering

veraniego /bera'niego/ a summer; light, unimportant

verano /be'rano/ m, summer; dry season West Hem.

veras /'beras/ f pl, reality, truth; fervor, earnestness. **de v.,** really; in earnest

veraz /be'ras; be'raθ/ a truthful, veracious

verbal /ber'βal/ a verbal; oral

verbena /ber'βena/ f, Bot. verbena, vervain; fair held on eve of a saint's day

verbigracia /berβi'grasia; berβi'graθia/ adv for instance. m, example

verbo /'berβo/ m, word; vow; Gram. verb. **v. activo** or **v. transitivo,** active or transitive verb. **v. auxiliar,** auxiliary verb. **v. intransitivo** or **v. neutro,** intransitive or neuter verb. **v. reflexivo** or **v. recíproco,** reflexive verb

verbosidad /berβosi'ðað/ f, verbosity

verboso /ber'βoso/ a verbose, prolix

verdad /ber'ðað/ f, truth, veracity; reality. **a la v.,** indeed; without doubt. **en v.,** in truth; indeed. **cantar cuatro verdades a alguien,** to tell someone a few home truths. **la pura v.,** the plain truth

verdadero /berða'ðero/ a true; real; sincere; truthful

verdal /ber'ðal/ a green. **ciruela v.,** greengage

verde /'berðe/ a green; unripe; fresh (vegetables); youthful; immature, undeveloped; obscene, dissolute. m, green (color); verdure, foliage

verdear /berðe'ar/ vi to look green; be greenish; grow green

verdecer /berðe'ser; berðe'θer/ vi irr to grow green, be verdant. See **conocer**

verdegay /berðe'gai/ a and m, bright green

verdemar /berðe'mar/ a and m, sea-green

verdín /ber'ðin/ m, verdure; mold; verdigris

verdinegro /berði'negro/ a dark green

verdor /ber'ðor/ m, verdure; greenness; strength; youth (also pl)

verdoso /ber'ðoso/ a greenish

verdugo /ber'ðugo/ m, hangman, executioner; wale, mark; shoot of tree; switch; whip; Fig. scourge; tyrant

verdulera /berðu'lera/ f, greengrocer; market woman; Inf. harridan

verdulería /berðule'ria/ f, greengrocer's shop

verdulero /berðu'lero/ m, greengrocer

verdura /ber'ðura/ f, verdure; green garden produce, vegetables (gen. pl); Art. foliage; obscenity

verecundo /bere'kundo/ a bashful

vereda /be'reða/ f, footpath; sheep track; *Argentina, Chile, Peru* sidewalk

veredicto /bere'ðikto/ m, *Law.* verdict; judgment, considered opinion

verga /'berga/ f, steel bow of crossbow; *Naut.* yard; *Inf.* penis

vergajo /ber'gaho/ m, rod (for punishment)

vergel /ber'hel/ m, orchard

vergonzoso /bergon'soso; bergon'θoso/ **(-sa)** a shameful; bashful, shamefaced. n shy person

vergüenza /ber'guensa; ber'guenθa/ f, shame; self-respect; bashfulness, timidity; shameful act; public punishment

vericueto /beri'kueto/ m, narrow, stony path

verídico /be'riðiko/ a veracious; true, exact

verificación /berifika'sion; berifika'θion/ f, verification, checking; *Law.* **v. de un testamento,** probate

verificador /berifika'ðor/ **(-ra)** a verifying, checking. n inspector, checker

verificar /berifi'kar/ vt to prove; verify; vr take place, happen; check; come true. *Elec.* **v. las conexiones,** to check the connections

verisímil /beri'simil/ a credible, probable

verisimilitud /berisimili'tuð/ f, credibility

verismo /be'rismo/ m, realism; truthfulness

verja /'berha/ f, grating, grill; railing

vermífugo /ber'mifugo/ a and m, vermifuge

vermut /ber'mut/ m, vermouth

vernáculo /ber'nakulo/ a native, vernacular

vernal /ber'nal/ a vernal

verónica /be'ronika/ f, *Bot.* speedwell; veronica (bull-fighting)

verosímil /bero'simil/ a credible, probable

verosimilitud /berosimili'tuð/ f, verisimilitude, probability

verraco /be'rrako/ m, boar

verruga /be'rruga/ f, *Med.* wart; *Inf.* bore; defect

versar /ber'sar/ vi to revolve; (*with sobre*) concern, deal with (book, etc.); vr become versed (in). **La campaña versó en torno sobre tres temas,** The campaign revolved around three issues

versátil /ber'satil/ a *Zool.* versatile; changeable; fickle

versatilidad /bersatili'ðað/ f, *Zool.* versatility; changeableness; fickleness

versículo /ber'sikulo/ m, versicle; verse (of the Bible)

versificación /bersifika'sion; bersifika'θion/ f, versification

versificador /bersifika'ðor/ **(-ra)** n versifier

versificar /bersifi'kar/ vi to write verses; vt put into verse, versify

versión /ber'sion/ f, translation; version; account

verso /'berso/ m, poetry, verse; stanza; line (of a poem). **v. suelto,** blank verse

vertebrado /berte'βraðo/ a and m, *Zool.* vertebrate

vertedor /berte'ðor/ m, drain, sewer; chute

verter /ber'ter/ vt irr to pour, spill; empty; translate; vi flow. See **entender**

vertical /berti'kal/ a and f, vertical

verticalidad /bertikali'ðað/ f, verticality

vértice /'bertise; 'bertiθe/ m, vertex

vertiente /ber'tiente/ a emptying. mf, slope, incline; watershed; *Lat. Am.* also spring (of water)

vertiginoso /bertihi'noso/ a giddy; vertiginous

vértigo /'bertigo/ m, giddiness, faintness

vesícula /be'sikula/ f, blister; (*Anat. Bot.*) vesicle

vespertino /besper'tino/ a evening

vestíbulo /bes'tiβulo/ m, hall, vestibule foyer

vestido /bes'tiðo/ m, dress; clothes; *Panama, Peru* suit

vestidura /besti'ðura/ f, garment; pl vestments

vestigio /bes'tihio/ m, footprint; trace, mark; remains; *Fig.* vestige

vestir /bes'tir/ vt irr to clothe, dress; adorn; embellish (ideas); *Fig.* disguise (truth); simulate, pretend; vi be dressed; vr dress oneself; *Fig.* be covered. See **pedir**

vestuario /bes'tuario/ m, clothing, dress; *Theat.* wardrobe or dressing room; *Eccl.* vestry; *Mil.* uniform

Vesubio /be'suβio/ Vesuvius

veta /'beta/ f, vein; stripe, rib (fabric)

veterano /bete'rano/ **(-na)** a and n veteran

veterinaria /beteri'naria/ f, veterinary science

veterinario /beteri'nario/ a veterinary. m, veterinary surgeon

veto /'beto/ m, veto; prohibition

vetustez /betus'tes; betus'teθ/ f, antiquity, oldness

vetusto /be'tusto/ a ancient, very old

vez /bes; beθ/ f, time, occasion; turn; pl proxy, deputy, substitute. **a la v.,** simultaneously. **alguna v.,** sometime. **a su v.,** in its (her, his, their) turn. **a veces,** sometimes. **de una v.,** at the same time, all at once. **de v. en cuando,** from time to time. **en v. de,** instead of. **hacer las veces de,** to be a substitute for. **otra v.,** again. **Su cuarto es dos veces más grande que éste,** His room is twice as large as this one

vía /'bia/ f, way; road; railway track or gauge; *Anat.* tract; (mystic) way; route; conduct; pl procedure. **v. ancha,** broad gauge (railway). **v. angosta,** narrow gauge. **v. de agua,** *Naut.* leak. *Law.* **v. ejecutiva,** seizure, attachment. **v. férrea,** railway. **v. láctea,** Milky Way. **v. muerta,** railway siding. **v. principal,** main line. **v. pública,** public thoroughfare. **v. romana,** Roman road. **v. secundaria,** *Rail.* side line. **por v. aérea,** by air, by airplane

viabilidad /biaβili'ðað/ f, viability

viable /'biaβle/ a viable; practicable; workable; passable

viaducto /bia'ðukto/ m, viaduct

viajante /bia'hante/ mf traveling salesman, commercial traveler

viajar /bia'har/ vi to travel, journey, voyage

viaje /'biahe/ m, journey; voyage; water-supply; travel journal; *Naut.* **v. de ensayo,** trial trip. **v. redondo,** circular tour. **¡Buen v.!** Have a good trip! Bon voyage!

viajero /bia'hero/ **(-ra)** a traveling. n traveler; passenger

vianda /'bianda/ f, viand, victual (gen. pl); meal

viático /'biatiko/ m, *Eccl.* viaticum; provisions for a journey

víbora /'biβora/ f, viper; *Lat. Am.* poisonous snake

viborezno /biβo'resno; biβo'reθno/ m, young viper

vibración /biβra'sion; biβra'θion/ f, vibration; jar, jolt; thrill

vibrante /bi'βrante/ a shaking; vibrant; thrilling

vibrar /bi'βrar/ vt to shake, oscillate; vi vibrate; jar, jolt; quiver, thrill

vibratorio /biβra'torio/ a vibratory, vibrative

vicaría /bika'ria/ f, vicarage; vestry

vicario /bi'kario/ a vicarious. m, vicar; curate; deputy

vicecónsul /bise'konsul; biθe'konsul/ m, vice-consul

viceconsulado /bisekonsu'laðo; biθekonsu'laðo/ m, vice-consulate

vicepresidente /bisepresi'ðente; biθepresi'ðente/ **(-ta)** n vice president

vicesecretario /bisesekre'tario; biθesekre'tario/ **(-ia)** n assistant secretary

viciar /bi'siar; bi'θiar/ vt to corrupt; adulterate; forge; annul; interpret maliciously, misconstrue; vr become vicious

vicio /'bisio; 'biθio/ m, vice; defect; error, fraud; bad habit; excess, exaggerated desire; viciousness (animals); overgrowth (plants); mischief (children). **tener el v. de,** to have the bad habit of. **el v. del juego,** fondness for gambling

vicioso /bi'sioso; bi'θioso/ a vicious; vigorous, overgrown; abundant; *Inf.* spoiled (children)

vicisitud /bisisi'tuð; biθisi'tuð/ f, vicissitude

víctima /'biktima/ f, victim

victimar /bikti'mar/ vt, *Lat. Am.* to murder

victimario, -a /bikti'mario/ mf, *Lat. Am.* killer, murderer

¡víctor! /'biktor/ interj Victor!; Long live!; Hurrah!

victoria /bik'toria/ f, victory, triumph; victoria

victoriano /bikto'riano/ **(-na)** a and n Victorian

victorioso /bikto'rioso/ a victorious

vicuña /bi'kuɲa/ f vicuna

vid /bið/ f, vine

vida /'biða/ f, life; livelihood; human being;

biography; vivacity. **v. airada,** dissolute life. **la v. allende la muerte,** life after death. **de por v.,** for life. **darse buena v.,** to live comfortably; enjoy one's life. **dar mala v.,** to ill-treat. **en la v.,** in life; never. **ganarse la v.,** to make one's living

vidente /bi'ðente/ m, clairvoyant; seer

videocámara /biðeo'kamara/ f, video camera; camcorder.

videograbación /biðeograβa'sion; biðeograβa'θion/ f, videotape

vidriar /bi'ðriar/ vt to glaze (earthenware)

vidriera /bi'ðriera/ f, glass window (gen. stained or colored)

vidriero /bi'ðriero/ m, glazier. a made of glass

vidrio /'biðrio/ m, glass; anything made of glass; fragile thing; touchy person. **v. inastillable,** safetyglass. **v. jaspeado,** frosted glass. **v. pintado** or **v. de color,** stained glass. **v. plano,** plate glass. **v. soplado,** blown glass

vidrioso /bi'ðrioso/ a brittle; slippery; fragile; hypersensitive; *Fig.* glazed (eyes)

vieja /'bieha/ f, old woman

viejo /'bieho/ a old; ancient; former; old-fashioned; worn out. m, old man

Viena /'biena/ Vienna

vienés /bie'nes/ **(-esa)** a and n Viennese

viento /'biento/ m, wind; scent (of game, etc.); guy (rope); upheaval; vanity. **v. en popa,** *Naut.* following wind; without a hitch, prosperously. **vientos alisios,** trade-winds. **v. terral,** land wind. **a los cuatro vientos,** in all directions. **contra v. y marea,** *Fig.* against all obstacles. **correr malos vientos,** to be unfavorable (of circumstances). **refrescar el v.,** to stiffen (of the breeze)

vientre /'bientre/ m, stomach; belly; vitals; *Law.* venter

viernes /'biernes/ m, Friday. **V. Santo,** Good Friday

viga /'biga/ f, beam, rafter; girder; joist; mill beam. **v. maestra,** main beam or girder. **la v. de tu ojo,** the beam in your eye

vigente /bi'hente/ a valid; in force (laws, customs)

vigésimo /bi'hesimo/ a twentieth

vigía /bi'hia/ f, watch tower; (gen. m) look-out, watch

vigilancia /bihi'lansia; bihi'lanθia/ f, watchfulness, vigilance; watch patrol

vigilante /bihi'lante/ a watchful. m, watcher; watchman. **v. escolar,** truant officer

vigilar /bihi'lar/ vi to watch over; supervise

vigilia /bi'hilia/ f, vigil; wakefulness; night study; *Eccl.* vigil, eve; wake; *Mil.* watch. **día de v.,** fast-day

vigor /bi'gor/ m, strength; activity; vigor, efficiency; validity

vigorizar /bigori'sar; bigori'θar/ vt to invigorate; exhilarate; encourage

vigoroso /bigo'roso/ a strong, vigorous

vihuela /bi'uela/ f, lute

vil /bil/ a vile, infamous; base; despicable; untrustworthy

vileza /bi'lesa; bi'leθa/ f, baseness; vileness, infamy

vilipendiar /bilipen'diar/ vt to revile

vilipendio /bili'pendio/ m, vilification; contempt

villa /'biya; 'biʎa/ f, villa; country house; town. **v. miseria** *Argentina* slum

villancico /biyan'siko; biʎan'θiko/ m, carol

villanesco /biya'nesko; biʎa'nesko/ a peasant; rustic, country

villanía /biya'nia; biʎa'nia/ f, humbleness of birth; vileness; villainy

villano /bi'yano; bi'ʎano/ **(-na)** n peasant. a rustic, country; boorish; base

vilo, en /'bilo, en/ adv hanging in the air; *Fig.* in suspense

vilorta /bi'lorta/ f, hoop; *Mech.* washer

vilote /bi'lote/ mf, *Lat. Am.* chicken, coward

vinagre /bi'nagre/ m, vinegar

vinagrera /bina'grera/ f, vinegar bottle; table cruet; *Lat. Am.* heartburn

vinagreta /bina'greta/ f, vinegar sauce

vinagroso /bina'groso/ a vinegary; *Inf.* bad-tempered, acid

vinatero /bina'tero/ **(-ra)** n wine merchant. a wine

vincapervinca /binkaper'βinka/ f, *Bot.* periwinkle

vinculación /binkula'sion; binkula'θion/ f, *Law.* entail

vincular /binku'lar/ vt *Law.* to entail; *Fig.* base; vr perpetuate. a *Law.* entail

vínculo /'binkulo/ m, tie, bond; *Law.* entail

vindicación /bindika'sion; bindika'θion/ f, vindication; justification; excuse

vindicador /bindika'ðor/ **(-ra)** n vindicator. a vindicative

vindicar /bindi'kar/ vt to avenge; vindicate; justify; excuse

vindicativo /bindika'tiβo/ a avenging; vindicatory

vinería /bine'ria/ f, *Lat. Am.* wineshop

vinícola /bi'nikola/ a wine-growing; wine

vinicultor /binikul'tor/ **(-ra)** n wine grower, viniculturalist

vinicultura /binikul'tura/ f, wine-growing, viniculture

vinificación /binifika'sion; binifika'θion/ f, vinification

vinillo /bi'niyo; bi'niʎo/ m, thin, weak wine

vino /'bino/ m, wine; fermented fruit juice. **v. de Oporto,** port wine. **v. generoso,** well-matured wine. **v. tinto,** red wine

vinoso /bi'noso/ a vinous; fond of wine

viña /'biɲa/ f, vineyard

viñador /biɲa'ðor/ m, vineyard-keeper; vine-cultivator

viñedo /bi'ɲeðo/ m, vineyard

viñeta /bi'ɲeta/ f, vignette

viola /'biola/ f, *Mus.* viola; *Bot.* viola, pansy. mf viola player

violación /biola'sion; biola'θion/ f, violation; infringement; rape

violado /bio'laðo/ a violet

violador /biola'ðor/ **(-ra)** n violator seducer, rapist

violar /bio'lar/ vt to violate; infringe; rape; spoil, harm

violencia /bio'lensia; bio'lenθia/ f, violence; outrage; rape

violentar /biolen'tar/ vt to force; falsify, misinterpret; force an entrance; vr force oneself

violento /bio'lento/ a violent; repugnant; impetuous; hasty-tempered; unnatural, false; unreasonable

violeta /bio'leta/ f, *Bot.* violet. m, violet color. **v. de febrero,** snowdrop

violín /bio'lin/ m, violin

violinista /bioli'nista/ mf violinist

violón /bio'lon/ m, double-bass, bass viol; double-bass player

violoncelista /biolonse'lista; biolonθe'lista/ mf cellist

violoncelo /biolon'selo; biolon'θelo/ m, cello

viperino /bipe'rino/ a viperine; venomous, evil

vira /'bira/ f, welt (of a shoe); dart

viraje /bi'rahe/ m, *Auto.* change of direction; bend, turn

virar /bi'rar/ vt *Naut.* to put about; *Photo.* tone; vi *Naut.* tack; *Auto.* change direction. **v. de bordo,** *Naut.* to lay off

virgen /bir'hen/ mf virgin. f, *Astron.* Virgo

virginal /birhi'nal/ a virginal; pure, unspotted

virginidad /birhini'ðað/ f, virginity

virgulilla /birgu'liya; birgu'liʎa/ f, comma; cedilla; accent; apostrophe; fine line

viril /bi'ril/ a manly, virile. m, clear glass screen

virilidad /birili'ðað/ f, virility

virote /bi'rote/ m, arrow; shaft; *Inf.* young blood; *Mexico* roll (bread)

virreina /bi'rreina/ f, vicereine

virreinato /birrei'nato/ m, viceroyship

virrey /bi'rrei/ m, viceroy

virtual /bir'tual/ a virtual; implicit

virtualidad /birtuali'ðað/ f, virtuality

virtualmente /birtual'mente/ adv virtually; tacitly

virtud /bir'tuð/ f, virtue; power; strength, courage; efficacy. **en v. de,** in virtue of

virtuosidad /birtuosi'ðað/ *f*, virtuosity
virtuoso /bir'tuoso/ *a* virtuous; powerful, efficacious. *m*, virtuoso, artist
viruela /bi'ruela/ *f*, smallpox (gen. *pl*)
virulencia /biru'lensia; biru'lenθia/ *f*, virulence
virulento /biru'lento/ *a* virulent
virus /'birus/ *m*, virus
viruta /bi'ruta/ *f*, wood-shaving
visa /'bisa/ *f*, *Lat. Am.* visa
visado /bi'saðo/ *m*, *Spain* visa
visaje /bi'sahe/ *m*, grimace
visar /bi'sar/ *vt* to visa; endorse
vis cómica /bis 'komika/ *f*, the comic spirit
viscosidad /biskosi'ðað/ *f*, viscosity
viscoso /bis'koso/ *a* viscous, sticky
visera /bi'sera/ *f*, visor; eye-shade; peak (of a cap)
visibilidad /bisiβili'ðað/ *f*, visibility
visillo /bi'siyo; bi'siʎo/ *m*, window-blind
visión /bi'sion/ *f*, seeing, sight; queer sight; vision; hallucination; *Inf.* scarecrow, sight
visionario /bisio'nario/ (**-ia**) *a* and *n* visionary
visir /bi'sir/ *m*, vizier. **gran v.,** grand vizier
visita /bi'sita/ *f*, visit; visitor; inspection. **v. de cumplido,** formal call. **v. de sanidad,** health inspection. **hacer una v.,** to pay a call
visitación /bisita'sion; bisita'θion/ *f*, visitation; visit
visitador /bisita'ðor/ (**-ra**) *n* regular visitor. *m*, inspector. *a* visiting; inspecting
visitar /bisi'tar/ *vt* to visit; inspect; *Med.* attend; *Eccl.* examine. **v. los monumentos,** to see the sights, go sightseeing
visiteo /bisi'teo/ *m*, receiving or paying of visits
vislumbrar /bislum'βrar/ *vt* to glimpse; surmise, conjecture
vislumbre /bis'lumbre/ *f*, glimmer, glimpse; surmise, glimmering (gen. *pl*); semblance, appearance
viso /'biso/ *m*, view point, elevation; glare; shimmer, gleam; colored slip under transparent dress; semblance. **de v.,** prominent (persons)
visón /bi'son/ *m*, mink
víspera /'bispera/ *f*, eve; *Eccl.* day before festival; prelude, preliminary. *pl Eccl.* vespers. **en vísperas de,** on the eve of
vista /'bista/ *f*, vision, sight; view; eyes; eyesight; meeting, interview; *Law.* hearing (of a case); apparition; picture of a view; clear idea; connection (of things); proposition, intention; glance; *pl* window, door, skylight, opening for light. **v. corta,** short sight. **v. de lince,** sharp eyes. **a primera v.,** at first sight. **a v. de,** in sight of; in the presence of. **conocer de v.,** to know by sight. **dar una v.,** to take a look. **doble v.,** second sight; clairvoyance. **en v. de,** in view of, considering. **estar a la v.,** to be evident. *Inf.* **hacer la v. gorda,** to turn a blind eye. **¡Hasta la v.!** Good-bye! **perder de v.,** to lose sight of
vistazo /bis'taso; bis'taθo/ *m*, glance. **echar un v.,** to cast a glance. **Dale un v.,** Look it over
visto /'bisto/ *past part irr* **ver.** *Law.* whereas. **bien v.,** approved. **mal v.,** disapproved. **V. Bueno** (**Vº Bº**) Approved, Passed. **v. que,** since, inasmuch as
vistoso /bis'toso/ *a* showy, gaudy; beautiful
visual /bi'sual/ *a* visual
vital /bi'tal/ *a* vital; essential
vitalicio /bita'lisio; bita'liθio/ *a* lifelong. *m*, life-insurance
vitalidad /bitali'ðað/ *f*, vitality
vitamina /bita'mina/ *f*, vitamin
vitando /bi'tando/ *a* odious; bad; vital
vitela /bi'tela/ *f*, vellum
vitícola /bi'tikola/ *a* viticultural. *mf* viticulturist
viticultura /bitikul'tura/ *f*, viticulture
¡vítor! /'bitor/ *interj* Victor!; Hurrah!; Long live!
vitorear /bitore'ar/ *vt* to cheer; applaud, acclaim
vítreo /'bitreo/ *a* glassy, vitreous
vitrificar /bitrifi'kar/ (**se**) *vt* and *vr* to vitrify
vitrina /bi'trina/ *f*, show-case; display cabinet; *Argentina, Chile, Venezuela* (shop) window
vitriólico /bi'trioliko/ *a* vitriolic
vitriolo /bi'triolo/ *m*, vitriol

vitualla /bi'tuaya; bi'tuaʎa/ *f*, (gen. *pl*) victuals, provisions
vituperable /bitupe'raβle/ *a* blameworthy, vituperable
vituperador /bitupera'ðor/ (**-ra**) *a* vituperative. *n* vituperator
vituperar /bitupe'rar/ *vt* to censure, blame, vituperate
vituperio /bitu'perio/ *m*, vituperation
viuda /'biuða/ *f*, widow
viudedad /biuðe'ðað/ *f*, widow's pension
viudez /biu'ðes; biu'ðeθ/ *f*, widowhood
viudita /biu'ðita/ *f*, young widow
viudo /'biuðo/ *m*, widower
¡viva! /'biβa/ *interj* Long live!; Hurrah!
vivacidad /biβasi'ðað; biβaθi'ðað/ *f*, vivacity, gaiety; ardor, warmth; brightness
vivamente /biβa'mente/ *adv* quickly, lively
vivandera /biβan'dera/ *f*, vivandiere
vivandero /biβan'dero/ *m*, sutler
vivaque /bi'βake/ *m*, bivouac
vivaquear /biβake'ar/ *vi* to bivouac
vivar /bi'βar/ *m*, warren; aquarium; breeding ground; well (of a fishing boat); *vt*, *Lat. Am.* to cheer, shout hurrah (for...)
vivaracho /biβa'ratʃo/ *a Inf.* sprightly, cheery, lively
vivaz /bi'βas; bi'βaθ/ *a* vigorous; quick-witted; sprightly; *Bot.* perennial; vivid, bright
víveres /'biβeres/ *m pl*, provisions; *Mil.* stores
vivero /bi'βero/ *m*, *Bot.* nursery; vivarium; small marsh
viveza /bi'βesa; bi'βeθa/ *f*, quickness, briskness; vehemence; perspicuity; witticism; resemblance; brightness (eyes, colors); thoughtless word or act
vividero /biβi'ðero/ *a* habitable
vívido /bi'βiðo/ *a Poet.* vivid
vividor /biβi'ðor/ (**-ra**) *a* frugal, thrifty; dissolute. *n* liver; long-liver; libertine, rake
vivienda /bi'βienda/ *f*, dwelling
viviente /bi'βiente/ *a* living
vivificación /biβifika'sion; biβifika'θion/ *f*, vivification
vivificante /biβifi'kante/ *a* vivifying
vivificar /biβifi'kar/ *vt* to vivify; comfort
vivir /bi'βir/ *vi* to be alive, live; last, endure; (*with en*) inhabit. *m*, life. **¿Quién vive?** *Mil.* Who goes there? **v. a costillas ajenas,** to live at someone else's expense, live off someone else
vivisección /biβisek'sion; biβisek'θion/ *f*, vivisection
vivo /'biβo/ *a* alive; intense, strong; bright; *Mil.* active; subtle, ingenious; precipitate; *Fig.* lasting, enduring; diligent; hasty; persuasive, expressive. *m*, edge. **al v., a lo v.,** to the life; vividly
vizcaíno /bis'kaino; biθ'kaino/ (**-na**) *a* and *n* Biscayan
Vizcaya, el Golfo de /bis'kaya, el 'golfo de; biθ'kaya, el 'golfo de/ the Bay of Biscay
vizconde /bis'konde; biθ'konde/ *m*, viscount
vizcondesa /biskon'desa; biθkon'desa/ *f*, viscountess
vocablo /bo'kaβlo/ *m*, word
vocabulario /bokaβu'lario/ *m*, vocabulary
vocación /boka'sion; boka'θion/ *f*, vocation; trade, profession
vocal /bo'kal/ *a* vocal; oral. *f*, *Gram.* vowel. *mf* voting member
vocalización /bokalisa'sion; bokaliθa'θion/ *f*, vocalization
vocalizar /bokali'sar; bokali'θar/ *vi* to vocalize
voceador, -a /bosea'ðor; boθea'ðor/ *mf*, *Lat. Am.* newsvendor
vocear /bose'ar; boθe'ar/ *vi* to cry out, shout; *vt* proclaim; call for; acclaim
vocerío /bose'rio; boθe'rio/ *m*, shouting; clamor, outcry
vociferación /bosifera'sion; boθifera'θion/ *f*, vociferation, outcry
vociferar /bosife'rar; boθife'rar/ *vt* to boast (of); *vi* shout, vociferate
vocinglería /bosiŋgle'ria; boθiŋgle'ria/ *f*, clamor; babble, chatter

vocinglero /bosiŋ'glero/ a vociferous; prattling, babbling

vodca /'boðka/ m, vodka

volada /bo'laða/ f, short flight; *Mexico* flat tire, flat. *Mech.* **v. de grúa,** jib

voladura /bola'ðura/ f, explosion; blasting

volandas (en), volandillas (en) /bolan'diyas; bo'landas, bolan'diʌas/ adv in the air, as though flying; *Inf.* in a trice

volante /bo'lante/ a flying; wandering, restless. m, frill, flounce; screen; fan (of a windmill); *Mech.* flywheel; *Mech.* balance wheel (watches); coiner's stamp mill; shuttle-cock. *Auto.* **v. de dirección,** steering-wheel

volantón /bolan'ton/ **(-ona)** n fledgling

volar /bo'lar/ vi irr to fly (birds, insects, aviation); float in the air; hurry; disappear suddenly; burst, explode; jut out (buttresses, etc.); cleave (air) (arrows, etc.); *Fig.* spread (rumors); vt explode; blast; anger. See **contar**

volatería /bolate'ria/ f, fowling; fowls; poultry; flock of birds; *Fig.* crowd (of ideas)

volátil /bo'latil/ a volatile; inconstant

volatilizar /bolatili'sar; bolatili'θar/ vt to volatilize

volatinero /bolati'nero/ **(-ra)** n tight-rope walker, acrobat

volcán /bol'kan/ m, volcano; violent passion. **v. extinto,** extinct volcano

volcánico /bol'kaniko/ a volcanic

volcar /bol'kar/ vt irr to overturn, capsize; make dizzy; cause a change (of opinion); annoy; vi overturn. *Pres. Ind.* **vuelco, vuelcas, vuelca, vuelcan.** *Preterite* **volqué, volcaste, etc.** *Pres. Subjunc.* **vuelque, vuelques, vuelque, vuelquen**

volear /bole'ar/ vt to strike in the air, volley; *Agr.* sow broadcast

voleo /bo'leo/ m, volley (tennis, etc.); high kick; straight punch

volframio /bol'framio/ m, wolfram, tungsten

volición /boli'sion; boli'θion/ f, volition

volquete /bol'kete/ m, tip-cart

voltaico /bol'taiko/ a voltaic

voltaje /bol'tahe/ m, voltage

voltario /bol'tario/ a versatile; capricious, headstrong

volteador /boltea'ðor/ **(-ra)** n acrobat

voltear /bolte'ar/ vt to whirl, turn; overturn; change place (of); *Archit.* construct an arch or vault; vi revolve; tumble, twirl (acrobats)

volteo /bol'teo/ m, turning, revolution; whirl; overturning; twirling; *Elec.* voltage

voltereta /bolte'reta/ f, somersault

volteriano /bolte'riano/ a Voltairian

voltímetro /bol'timetro/ m, voltmeter

voltio /'boltio/ m, volt

volubilidad /boluβili'ðað/ f, inconstancy, fickleness

voluble /bo'luβle/ a easily turned; inconstant, changeable; *Bot.* twining

volumen /bo'lumen/ m, bulk, size; volume, book

voluminoso /bolumi'noso/ a voluminous, bulky

voluntad /bolun'tað/ f, volition; wish; decree; free will; intention; affection; free choice; consent. **a v.,** at will; by choice. **de buena v.,** of good will; willingly, with pleasure. **de su propia v.,** of one's own free will. **mala v.,** hostility, ill-will

voluntario /bolun'tario/ **(-ia)** a voluntary; strong-willed. n volunteer

voluntarioso /bolunta'rioso/ a self-willed

voluptuosidad /boluptuosi'ðað/ f, voluptuousness

voluptuoso /bolup'tuoso/ a voluptuous

volver /bol'βer/ vt irr to turn; turn over; return; pay back; direct, aim; translate; restore; change, alter; close (doors, etc.); vomit; reflect, reverberate; vi come back; continue (speech, etc.); bend, turn (roads); (*with prep* a + *infin.*) do something again (e.g. *v. a leer,* to read over again); (*with por* + *noun*)

protect; vr become; go sour; turn. **v. a las filas,** *Mil.* to reduce to the ranks. **v. en sí,** to regain consciousness. **v. la cabeza,** to turn one's head. **volverse atrás,** *Fig.* to back out. **volverse loco,** to go mad. See **resolver**

vomitar /bomi'tar/ vt to vomit; *Fig.* vomit forth; *Fig.* spit out (curses, etc.); *Inf.* burst into confidences

vomitivo /bomi'tiβo/ a and m, emetic

vómito /'bomito/ m, vomit

voracidad /borasi'ðað; boraθi'ðað/ f, voracity

vorágine /bo'rahine/ f, vortex, whirlpool

voraz /bo'ras; bo'raθ/ a voracious; *Mexico* bold

vórtice /'bortise; 'bortiθe/ m, whirlpool; *Fig.* vortex

vortiginoso /bortihi'noso/ a vortical

vos /bos/ *pers pron 2nd pers sing* and *pl* you; *Central America* you (familiar)

vosear /bose'ar/ vt to use the pronoun *vos*; address (someone) as *vos*

vosotros, vosotras /bo'sotros, bo'sotras/ *pers pron 2nd pers pl mf* you

votación /bota'sion; bota'θion/ f, voting

votador /bota'ðor/ **(-ra)** n voter; swearer

votar /bo'tar/ vi and vt to vote; make a vow; curse, swear. **v. una proposición de confianza,** to pass a vote of confidence

votivo /bo'tiβo/ a votive

voto /'boto/ m, vote; vow; voter; prayer; curse; desire; opinion. **v. de calidad,** casting vote. **v. de confianza,** vote of confidence

voz /bos; boθ/ f, voice; sound; noise; cry, shout (gen. *pl*); word; expression; *Mus.* singer or voice; *Gram.* mood; vote; rumor; instruction, order. **v. común,** general opinion. **a voces,** in a shout, loudly. **llevar la v. cantante,** *Inf.* to have the chief say

vuelco /'buelko/ m, overturning

vuelo /'buelo/ m, flight; wing; *Sew.* skirt-fullness; ruffle, frill; *Archit.* buttress. **v. a ciegas,** *Aer.* blind flying. **v. de distancia,** long-distance flight. **v. de patrulla,** patrol or reconnaissance flight. **v. de reconocimento,** reconnaissance flight. **v. nocturno,** *Aer.* night flying. **v. sin parar,** non-stop flight. **al v.,** on the wing; in passing; quickly. **alzar** (*or* **levantar**) **el v.,** to take flight

vuelta /'buelta/ f, revolution, turn; bend, curve; return; restitution; recompense; repetition; wrong side; beating; *Sew.* facing, cuff; change (money); conning (lessons, etc.); stroll, walk; change; vault, ceiling; *Sports.* round; *Mech.* **vueltas por minuto,** revolutions per minute. **a v. de correo,** by return mail, by return of post. **a la v.,** on returning; overleaf. **dar la v.,** to turn round, make a détour. **dar una v.,** to take a stroll. **dar vueltas,** to revolve; search (for); consider. **media v.,** half turn

vuelto /'buelto/ m, *Lat. Am.* change (money returned)

vuestro, vuestra, vuestros, vuestras /'buestro, 'buestra, 'buestros, 'buestras/ *poss pron 2nd pl mf* your, yours

vulcanizar /bulkani'sar; bulkani'θar/ vt to vulcanize

vulgar /bul'gar/ a popular; general, common; vernacular; mediocre

vulgaridad /bulgari'ðað/ f, vulgarity

vulgarismo /bulga'rismo/ m, vulgarism

vulgarización /bulgarisa'sion; bulgariθa'θion/ f, vulgarization; popularization

vulgarizar /bulgari'sar; bulgari'θar/ vt to vulgarize; popularize; translate into the vernacular; vr grow vulgar

vulgata /bul'gata/ f, Vulgate

vulgo /'bulgo/ adv commonly known as. mpl, the masses

vulnerabilidad /bulneraβili'ðað/ f, vulnerability

vulnerable /bulne'raβle/ a vulnerable

vulpeja /bul'peha/ f, vixen

vulpino /bul'pino/ a vulpine; crafty

WXYZ

wagneriano /wagne'riano/ *a* Wagnerian
wáter /'water/ *m*, toilet, water-closet
whisky /'wiski/ *m*, whiskey
xenofobia /seno'foβia/ *f*, xenophobia, hatred of foreigners
xilófago /si'lofago/ *a* xylophagous, wood-boring. *m*, wood-borer
xilófono /si'lofono/ *m*, xylophone
xilografía /silogra'fia/ *f*, xylography
y /i/ *conjunc* and. See **e**
ya /ya/ *adv* already; formerly; soon; now; finally; immediately; well, yes, quite. Used of past, present and future time, and in various idiomatic ways. **Ha venido ya,** He has already come. **¡Ya caerá!** His time will come!, He will get his comeuppance! **Ya vendrá,** He will come soon. **¡Ya voy!** Coming! **¡Ya verás!** You'll see! **¡Ya lo creo!** Of course!; I should think so! **¡Ya!** Quite!; I understand. **ya no,** no longer. **ya que,** since
yacaré /yaka're/ *m*, *Lat. Am.* alligator
yacente /ya'sente; ya'θente/ *a* recumbent, reclining (statues, etc.)
yacer /ya'ser; ya'θer/ *vi irr* to be lying at full length; lie (in the grave); be situated, be; lie (with), sleep (with); graze by night. *Pres. Ind.* **yazgo** *or* **yazco,** **yaces,** etc. *Pres. Subjunc.* **yazga** *or* **yazca,** etc.
yacija /ya'siha; ya'θiha/ *f*, bed; couch; tomb
yacimiento /yasi'miento; yaθi'miento/ *m*, *Geol.* bed, deposit
yacio /'yasio; 'yaθio/ *m*, india-rubber tree
yaguré /yagu're/ *m*, *Lat. Am.* skunk
yak /yak/ *m*, yak
yanqui /'yanki/ *a* and *mf contemptuous and offensive* North American (gen. U.S.A.)
yarda /'yarða/ *f*, yard (English measure)
yate /'yate/ *m*, *Naut.* yacht
ye /ye/ *f*, name of the letter Y
yegua /'yegua/ *f*, mare
yelmo /'yelmo/ *m*, helmet
yema /'yema/ *f*, bud; yolk (of egg); sweetmeat; *Fig.* best of anything. **y. del dedo,** finger-tip
yerba mate /'yerβa 'mate/ *m* mate (drink)
yermo /'yermo/ *a* uninhabited, deserted; uncultivated. *m*, wilderness, desert
yerno /'yerno/ *m*, son-in-law
yerro /'yerro/ *m*, error; mistake; fault
yerto /'yerto/ *a* stiff, rigid
yesca /'yeska/ *f*, tinder; fuel, stimulus
yeso /'yeso/ *m*, gypsum, calcium sulphate; plaster; plaster cast
yesquero /yes'kero/ *m*, *Lat. Am.* (cigarette) lighter
yídish /'yiðis/ *n* and *a* Yiddish
yip /yip/ *m* jeep
yo /yo/ *pers pron 1st sing mf* I. **el yo,** the ego
yodo /'yoðo/ *m*, iodine
yuca /'yuka/ *f*, yucca
yucateco /yuka'teko/ (**-ca**) *a* and *n* Yucatecan
yugo /'yugo/ *m*, yoke; nuptial tie; oppression; *Naut.* transom; *Fig.* **sacudir el y.,** to throw off the yoke
yugular /yugu'lar/ *a Anat.* jugular. *m*, jugular vein
Yukón, el /yu'kon, el/ the Yukon
yunque /'yunke/ *m*, anvil; patient, undaunted person; hard worker; *Anat.* incus
yunta /'yunta/ *f*, yoke (of oxen, etc.)
yute /'yute/ *m*, jute fiber or fabric
yuxtaponer /yukstapo'ner/ *vt irr* to juxtapose. See **poner**
yuxtaposición /yukstaposi'sion; yukstaposi'θion/ *f*, juxtaposition
zabarcera /saβar'sera; θaβar'θera/ *f*, vegetable seller
zaborda /sa'βorða; θa'βorða/ *f*, **zabordamiento** *m*, *Naut.* grounding, stranding
zabordar /saβor'ðar; θaβor'ðar/ *vi Naut.* to run aground, strand

zacatín /saka'tin; θaka'tin/ *m*, street or square where clothes are sold
zafadura /safa'ðura; θafa'ðura/ *f*, *Lat. Am.* dislocation, sprain
zafar /sa'far; θa'far/ *vt* to embellish, garnish, adorn; *Naut.* lighten (a ship); *vr* escape, hide oneself; (*with de*) excuse oneself, avoid; get rid of
zafarrancho /safa'rrantʃo; θafa'rrantʃo/ *m*, *Naut.* clearing the decks; *Inf.* damage; *Inf.* scuffle
zafiedad /safie'ðað; θafie'ðað/ *f*, rudeness, ignorance, boorishness
zafio /'safio; 'θafio/ *a* rude, unlettered, boorish
zafiro /sa'firo; θa'firo/ *m*, sapphire
zafra /'safra; 'θafra/ *f*, olive oil container; sugar crop or factory; *Mineral.* waste
zaga /'saga; 'θaga/ *f*, rear. *m*, last player. **en z.,** behind. *Inf.* **no quedarse en z.,** not to be left behind; be not inferior
zagal /sa'gal; θa'gal/ *m*, youth; strong, handsome lad; young shepherd; full skirt
zagala /sa'gala; θa'gala/ *f*, maiden, girl; young shepherdess
zagual /sa'gual; θa'gual/ *m*, paddle
zaguán /sa'guan; θa'guan/ *m*, entrance hall; vestibule
zaguero /sa'gero; θa'gero/ *a* loitering, straggling. *m*, *Sports.* back
zahareño /saa'reno; θaa'reno/ *a* untamable, wild (birds); unsociable, disdainful
zaherimiento /saeri'miento; θaeri'miento/ *m*, upbraiding; nagging
zaherir /sae'rir; θae'rir/ *vt irr* to upbraid, reprehend; nag. See **herir**
zahína /sa'ina; θa'ina/ *f*, *Bot.* sorghum
zahón /sa'on; θa'on/ *m*, leather apron (worn by cowboys)
zahorí /sao'ri; θao'ri/ *m*, soothsayer; waterfinder; sagacious person
zahúrda /sa'urða; θa'urða/ *f*, pigsty
zaino /'saino; 'θaino/ *a* treacherous; vicious (horses); chestnut (horses); black (cows)
zalagarda /sala'garða; θala'garða/ *f*, ambush; skirmish; snare, trap; *Inf.* trick, ruse; *Inf.* mock battle
zalamería /salame'ria; θalame'ria/ *f*, adulation, flattery
zalamero /sala'mero; θala'mero/ (**-ra**) *a* wheedling, flattering. *n* flatterer
zalea /sa'lea; θa'lea/ *f*, sheepskin
zalear /sale'ar; θale'ar/ *vt* to shake; frighten away (dogs)
zalema /sa'lema; θa'lema/ *f*, salaam
zamacuco /sama'kuko; θama'kuko/ *m*, *Inf.* oaf, dolt; *Inf.* drinking bout
zamarra /sa'marra; θa'marra/ *f*, sheepskin jacket
zamarrear /samarre'ar; θamarre'ar/ *vt* to worry, shake (prey); *Fig. Inf.* beat up; *Inf.* floor, confound
zambo /'sambo; 'θambo/ (**-ba**) *a* knock-kneed. *n*, *Lat. Am.* person of mixed African and indigenous origin
zambomba /sam'βomba; θam'βomba/ *f*, rustic drum
zambuco /sam'βuko; θam'βuko/ *m*, *Inf.* concealment (especially of cards)
zambullida /sambu'yiða; θambu'ʎiða/ *f*, plunge, submersion; thrust (in fencing)
zambullir /sambu'yir; θambu'ʎir/ *vt* to plunge in water, submerge; *vr* dive; hide oneself, cover oneself
zampar /sam'par; θam'par/ *vt* to conceal (one thing in another); eat greedily; (*with en*) arrive suddenly
zampatortas /sampa'tortas; θampa'tortas/ *mf Inf.* glutton
zampoña /sam'pona; θam'pona/ *f*, rustic flute; *Inf.* unimportant work
zanahoria /sana'oria; θana'oria/ *f*, carrot
zanca /'sanka; 'θanka/ *f*, long leg (birds); *Inf.* long thin leg; *Archit.* stringboard (of stairs)

zancada /san'kaða; θan'kaða/ f, swift stride
zancadilla /sanka'ðiya; θanka'ðiʎa/ f, trip (wrestling); *Inf.* trick, deceit. **echar la z.** (a), to trip up
zancajear /sankahe'ar; θankahe'ar/ vi to stride about
zancajo /san'kaho; θan'kaho/ m, heel-bone; torn heel (stocking, shoe); *Inf.* ill-shaped person. *Inf.* **no llegarle al z.,** to be immensely inferior to someone
zancajoso /sanka'hoso; θanka'hoso/ a flatfooted; slovenly
zanco /'sanko; 'θanko/ m, stilt. *Fig. Inf.* **andar** (or **estar) en zancos,** to have gone up in the world
zancudo /san'kuðo; θan'kuðo/ a long-legged
zangandungo /saŋgan'duŋgo; θaŋgan'duŋgo/ **(-ga)** n *Inf.* loafer
zanganear /saŋgane'ar; θaŋgane'ar/ vi *Inf.* to loaf
zángano /'saŋgano; 'θaŋgano/ m, *Ent.* drone; *Inf.* idler, parasite
zangolotear /saŋgolote'ar; θaŋgolote'ar/ vt *Inf.* to shake violently; vi fuss about, bustle; vr rattle (windows, etc.)
zangoloteo /saŋgolo'teo; θaŋgolo'teo/ m, shaking; rattling
zanguango /saŋ'guaŋgo; θaŋ'guaŋgo/ m, *Inf.* lazybones
zanja /'sanha; 'θanha/ f, trench, ditch; drain; furrow
zanjar /san'har; θan'har/ vt to excavate; *Fig.* remove (obstacles)
Zanzíbar /san'siβar; θan'θiβar/ Zanzibar
zapa /'sapa; 'θapa/ f, shovel, spade; *Mil.* sap; sandpaper
zapador /sapa'ðor; θapa'ðor/ m, *Mil.* sapper
zapapico /sapa'piko; θapa'piko/ m, pick-ax; mattock
zapaquilda /sapa'kilda; θapa'kilda/ f, *Inf.* she-cat
zapar /sa'par; θa'par/ vi *Mil.* to sap
zaparrastrar /saparras'trar; θaparras'trar/ vi *Inf.* to trail along the floor (dresses)
zapata /sa'pata; θa'pata/ f, half-boot; piece of leather used to stop creaking of a hinge; *Archit.* lintel; (*Naut. Mech.*) shoe
zapatazo /sapa'taso; θapa'taθo/ m, blow with a shoe; fall, thud; stamping (horses); flap (of sail)
zapateado /sapate'aðo; θapate'aðo/ m, dance in which rhythmic drumming of heels plays important part
zapatear /sapate'ar; θapate'ar/ vt to hit with a shoe; stamp feet; drum heels (in dancing); *Inf.* ill-treat; thump ground (rabbits); vi stamp (horses); *Naut.* flap (sails); vr *Fig.* stand one's ground
zapateo /sapa'teo; θapa'teo/ m, stamping; rhythmic drumming of heels
zapatera /sapa'tera; θapa'tera/ f, cobbler's wife; woman who makes or sells shoes
zapatería /sapate'ria; θapate'ria/ f, shoemaking; shoe shop
zapatero /sapa'tero; θapa'tero/ m, shoemaker; shoe seller. **z. remendón,** cobbler
zapateta /sapa'teta; θapa'teta/ f, caper, leap
zapatilla /sapa'tiya; θapa'tiʎa/ f, slipper; trotter, hoof
zapato /sa'pato; θa'pato/ m, shoe. **z. de hule** *Mexico,* galosh, rubber
zapatón /sapa'ton; θapa'ton/ m, *Lat. Am.* galosh, overshoe
¡zape! /'sape; 'θape/ interj *Inf.* shoo! Used for frightening away cats; exclamation of surprise or warning
zapear /sape'ar; θape'ar/ vt to scare away cats; *Inf.* frighten off
zaque /'sake; 'θake/ m, leather bottle, wineskin; *Inf.* drunkard, sot
zaquizamí /sakisa'mi; θakiθa'mi/ m, garret; dirty little house or room
zar /sar; θar/ m, tsar
zarabanda /sara'βanda; θara'βanda/ f, saraband; *Inf.* racket, row
zaragata /sara'gata; θara'gata/ f, *Inf.* fight, brawl
Zaragoza /sara'gosa; θara'goθa/ Saragossa
zaragozano /sarago'sano; θarago'θano/ **(-na)** a and n Saragossan
zaragüelles /sara'gueyes; θara'gueʎes/ m, pl wide pleated breeches

zaranda /sa'randa; θa'randa/ f, sieve, strainer, colander
zarandajas /saran'dahas; θaran'dahas/ f, pl *Inf.* odds and ends
zarandar /saran'dar; θaran'dar/ vt to sieve (grapes, grain); strain; *Inf.* pick out the best; vr *Inf.* move quickly
zarandillo /saran'diyo; θaran'diʎo/ m, small sieve; strainer; *Inf.* a live wire, energetic person; Spanish dance
zaraza /sa'rasa; θa'raθa/ f, chintz
zarcillo /sar'siyo; θar'θiʎo/ m, earring; *Bot.* tendril; *Agr.* trowel
zarco /'sarko; 'θarko/ a light blue (generally eyes or water)
zarpa /'sarpa; 'θarpa/ f, *Naut.* weighing anchor; paw
zarpada /sar'paða; θar'paða/ f, blow with a paw
zarpar /sar'par; θar'par/ vt and vi *Naut.* to weigh anchor, sail
zarza /'sarsa; 'θarθa/ f, *Bot.* bramble, blackberry bush
zarzal /sar'sal; θar'θal/ m, bramble patch
zarzamora /sarsa'mora; θarθa'mora/ f, blackberry
zarzaparrilla /sarsapa'rriya; θarθapa'rriʎa/ f, sarsaparilla
zarzo /'sarso; 'θarθo/ m, hurdle; wattle
zarzoso /sar'soso; θar'θoso/ a brambly
zarzuela /sar'suela; θar'θuela/ f, comic opera; musical comedy
zarzuelista /sarsue'lista; θarθue'lista/ mf writer or composer of comic operas
¡zas! /sas; θas/ m, sound of a bang or blow
zascandil /saskan'dil; θaskan'dil/ m, *Inf.* busybody
zatara /sa'tara; θa'tara/ f, raft
zeda /'seða; 'θeða/ f, name of the letter Z
zedilla /se'ðiya; θe'ðiʎa/ f, cedilla
zenit /'senit; 'θenit/ m. See **cenit**
zepelín /sepe'lin; θepe'lin/ m, Zeppelin
zeta /'seta; 'θeta/ f. See **zeda**
zigzag /sig'sag; θig'θag/ m, zigzag
zigzaguear /sigsage'ar; θigθage'ar/ vi to zigzag
zinc /sink; θink/ m, zinc
zipizape /sipi'sape; θipi'θape/ m, *Inf.* row, quarrel
zoca /'soka; 'θoka/ f, square
zócalo /'sokalo; 'θokalo/ m, *Archit.* socle; *Mexico* main square
Zócalo, el /'sokalo; 'θokalo/ m, the Main Square (of Mexico City)
zoclo /'soklo; 'θoklo/ m, clog, sabot
zoco /'soko; 'θoko/ m, square; market; clog, sabot
zodiaco /so'ðiako; θo'ðiako/ m, zodiac
zona /'sona; 'θona/ f, girdle, band; strip (of land); zone; *Med.* shingles. **z. de depresión,** air pocket. **z. templada,** temperate zone. **z. tórrida,** torrid zone
zonal /so'nal; θo'nal/ a zonal
zoncear /sonse'ar; θonθe'ar/ vi, *Lat. Am.* to behave stupidly
zonzo, -a /'sonso; 'θonθo/ a, *Lat. Am.* silly, stupid
zoología /soolo'hia; θoolo'hia/ f, zoology
zoológico /so'olohiko; θo'olohiko/ a zoological
zoólogo /so'ologo; θo'ologo/ m, zoologist
zopenco /so'penko; θo'penko/ a and *Inf.* oafish
zopo /'sopo; 'θopo/ a maimed, deformed (hands, feet)
zoquete /so'kete; θo'kete/ m, block; dowel; hunk of bread; *Inf.* short, ugly man; *Inf.* dunderhead
zorcico /sor'siko; θor'θiko/ m, Basque song and dance
zorra /'sorra; 'θorra/ f, vixen; fox; *Inf.* cunning person; *Inf.* prostitute; *Inf.* drinking bout; truck, dray
zorrera /so'rrera; θo'rrera/ f, foxhole
zorrería /sorre'ria; θorre'ria/ f, foxiness; *Inf.* cunning
zorro /'sorro; 'θorro/ m, fox; fox-skin; *Inf.* knave
zóster /'soster; 'θoster/ f, *Med.* shingles
zote /'sote; 'θote/ a dull, ignorant
zozobra /so'soβra; θo'θoβra/ f, *Naut.* foundering, capsizing; anxiety
zozobrar /soso'βrar; θoθo'βrar/ vi *Naut.* to founder, sink; *Naut.* plunge, shiver; be anxious, vacillate
zueco /'sueko; 'θueko/ m, sabot, clog

zulú /su'lu; θu'lu/ a and mf Zulu

zumaque /su'make; θu'make/ m, Bot. sumach tree; Inf. wine

zumba /'sumba; 'θumba/ f, cow bell; jest

zumbar /sum'βar; θum'βar/ vi to buzz, hum; ring (of the ears); whizz; twang (of a guitar, etc.); Fig. Inf. be on the brink

zumbido /sum'βiðo; θum'βiðo/ m, buzzing, humming; ringing (in the ears); whizz; twanging (of a guitar, etc.); Inf. slap, blow

zumbón /sum'βon; θum'βon/ a humming (motor), buzzing (insect); joke playing, teasing

zumo /'sumo; 'θumo/ m, sap; juice; profit, advantage

zumoso /su'moso; θu'moso/ a succulent, juicy

zupia /'supia; 'θupia/ f, wine lees; cloudy wine; Fig. dregs

zurcido /sur'siðo; θur'θiðo/ m, Sew. darn; mend

zurcidor /sursi'ðor; θurθi'ðor/ **(-ra)** n darner, mender. **z. de voluntades,** humorous pimp

zurcidura /sursi'ðura; θurθi'ðura/ f, darning; mending; darn

zurcir /sur'sir; θur'θir/ vt to darn; mend, repair; join; Fig. concoct, weave

zurdo /'surðo; 'θurðo/ a left-handed

zurra /'surra; 'θurra/ f, Tan. currying; Inf. spanking; Inf. quarrel

zurrador /surra'ðor; θurra'ðor/ m, Tan. currier, dresser

zurrapa /su'rrapa; θu'rrapa/ f, (gen. pl) sediment, lees, dregs

zurrar /su'rrar; θu'rrar/ vt to curry (leather); Inf. spank; Inf. dress down, scold

zurriagazo /surria'gaso; θurria'gaθo/ m, lash with a whip; Fig. blow of fate

zurriago /su'rriago; θu'rriago/ m, whip

zurribanda /surri'βanda; θurri'βanda/ f, Inf. whipping; fight, quarrel

zurriburri /surri'βurri; θurri'βurri/ m, Inf. ragamuffin; mob; uproar

zurrido /su'rriðo; θu'rriðo/ m, Inf. blow; dull noise

zurrir /su'rrir; θu'rrir/ vi to have a confused sound, hum, rattle

zurrón /su'rron; θu'rron/ m, shepherd's pouch; leather bag; Bot. husk

zutano /su'tano; θu'tano/ **(-na)** n Inf. so-and-so, such a one

English–Spanish
Dictionary

A

a /ei/ *n* (letter) a, *f*; *Mus.* la, *m*. **symphony in A major,** sinfonía en la mayor, *f*. **A1,** de primera clase; de primera calidad, excelente

a, an /ə/ ən; *when stressed* ei; æn/ *indef art.* (one) un, *m*; una, *f*; (with weights, quantities) el, *m*; la, *f*; (with weeks, months, years, etc.) por, al, *m*; a la, *f*. The indef. art. is omitted in Spanish before nouns expressing nationality, profession, rank, and generally before a noun in apposition. It is omitted also before certain words such as **mil, ciento, otro, semejante, medio,** etc. Not translated in book titles, e.g., *A History of Spain,* Historia de España. *prep* a. In phrases such as *to go hunting,* ir a cazar. As prefix, see *abed, ashore,* etc. *Madrid, a Spanish city,* Madrid, ciudad de España. *three times a month,* tres veces al mes. *ten dollars an hour,* diez dólares por hora. *thirty miles an hour,* treinta millas por hora. *a certain Mrs. Brown,* una tal Sra. Brown. *a thousand soldiers,* mil soldados. *half an hour later,* media hora después

aback /ə'bæk/ *adv Naut.* en facha; *Fig.* sorprendido, desconcertado. **to take a.,** desconcertar, coger desprevenido (a)

abacus /'æbəkəs/ *n* ábaco, *m*

abandon /ə'bændən/ *vt* abandonar; dejar; desertar, desamparar; renunciar; entregar. *n* entusiasmo, fervor, *m*; naturalidad, *f*. **to a. oneself to,** (despair, vice, etc.) entregarse a

abandoned /ə'bændənd/ *a* entregado a los vicios, vicioso

abandonment /ə'bændənmənt/ *n* abandono, *m*; renunciación, *f*; deserción, *f*

abase /ə'beis/ *vt* humillar; degradar; abatir

abasement /ə'beismənt/ *n* humillación, degradación, *f*; abatimiento, *m*

abash /ə'bæʃ/ *vt* avergonzar; confundir, desconcertar

abashed /ə'bæʃt/ *a* avergonzado, confuso, consternado

abate /ə'beit/ *vt* disminuir, reducir; (a price) rebajar; (suppress) suprimir, abolir; (remit) condonar, remitir; (annul) anular; (moderate) moderar; (of pain) aliviar. *vi* disminuir; moderarse; (of the wind and *Fig.*) amainar; cesar; apaciguarse, calmarse

abatement /ə'beitmənt/ *n* disminución, *f*; reducción, *f*; mitigación, *f*; (of price) rebaja, *f*; supresión, *f*; remisión, *f*; (annulment) anulación, *f*; (of the wind and of enthusiasm, etc.) amaine, *m*; (of pain, etc.) alivio, *m*

abattoir /'æbə,twɑr/ *n* matadero, *m*

abbey /'æbi/ *n* abadía, *f*

abbreviate /ə'brivi,eit/ *vt* abreviar; condensar, resumir

abbreviation /ə,brivi'eiʃən/ *n* abreviación, *f*; resumen, *m*, condensación, *f*; (of a word) abreviatura, *f*

abdicate /'æbdɪ,keit/ *vt* renunciar; (a throne) abdicar

abdication /,æbdɪ'keiʃən/ *n* renuncia, *f*; abdicación, *f*

abdomen /'æbdəmən/ *n* abdomen, *m*

abdominal /æb'dɒmənl/ *a* abdominal

abduct /æb'dʌkt/ *vt* raptar, secuestrar

abduction /æb'dʌkʃən/ *n* rapto, *m*; (*Anat. Philos.*) abducción, *f*

abductor /æb'dʌktər/ *n Anat.* abductor, *m*; raptor, *m*

aberration /,æbə'reiʃən/ *n* aberración (also *Astron. Phys. Biol.*), *f*

abet /ə'bet/ *vt* ayudar, apoyar, favorecer; incitar, alentar; (in bad sense) ser cómplice de

abetment /ə'betmənt/ *n* ayuda, *f*, apoyo, *m*; instigación, *f*

abettor /ə'betər/ *n* instigador (-ra); cómplice, *mf*

abeyance /ə'beiəns/ *n* suspensión, *f*; expectativa, esperanza, *f*. **in a.,** en suspenso; vacante; latente

abhor /æb'hɔr/ *vt* detestar, odiar, aborrecer; repugnar

abhorrence /æb'hɔrəns/ *n* detestación, *f*, odio, aborrecimiento, *m*; repugnancia, *f*

abhorrent /æb'hɔrənt/ *a* detestable, odioso, aborrecible; repugnante

abide /ə'baid/ *vi* morar, quedar. *vt* aguardar; *Inf.*

aguantar, sufrir. **to a. by,** atenerse a, cumplir; sostener

abiding /ə'baidɪŋ/ *a* permanente, constante, perenne

ability /ə'bɪliti/ *n* habilidad, facultad, *f*, poder, *m*; talento, *m*, capacidad, *f*. **to the best of my a.,** lo mejor que yo pueda

abject /'æbdʒekt/ *a* abyecto; vil; servil

abjure /æb'dʒʊr/ *vt* abjurar; renunciar; retractar

ablaze /ə'bleiz/ *adv* en llamas, ardiendo. *a* brillante; (with, of anger, etc.) dominado por

able /'eibəl/ *a* capaz (de); (clever) hábil; competente; en estado (de); *Law.* apto legalmente, capaz; bueno, excelente. **to be a. to,** poder; ser capaz de; (know how) saber. **a.-bodied,** fuerte, fornido. **a.-bodied seaman,** marinero práctico, *m*

abloom /ə'blum/ *adv* en flor

ablution /ə'bluʃən/ *n* ablución, *f*

ably /'eibli/ *adv* hábilmente; competentemente

abnegation /,æbnɪ'geiʃən/ *n* abnegación, *f*

abnormal /æb'nɔrməl/ *a* anormal; irregular

abnormality /,æbnɔr'mæliti/ *n* anormalidad, *f*; irregularidad, *f*

abnormally /æb'nɔrməli/ *adv* anormalmente; demasiado

aboard /ə'bɔrd/ *adv* a bordo. *prep* a bordo de. **to go a.,** embarcarse, ir a bordo. **All a.!** ¡Viajeros a bordo!; (a train) ¡Viajeros al tren!

abode /ə'boud/ *n* morada, habitación, *f*; residencia, *f*; (stay) estancia, *f*

abolish /ə'bolɪʃ/ *vt* abolir, suprimir, anular

abolition /,æbə'lɪʃən/ *n* abolición, supresión, *f*; anulación, *f*

abolitionist /,æbə'lɪʃənɪst/ *n* abolicionista, *mf*

abominable /ə'bɒmənəbəl/ *a* abominable, aborrecible; repugnante, execrable; *Inf.* horrible

abominably /ə'bɒmənəbli/ *adv* abominablemente

abominate /ə'bɒmə,neit/ *vt* abominar, aborrecer, detestar

abomination /ə,bɒmə'neiʃən/ *n* abominación, *f*; aborrecimiento, *m*; horror, *m*

aboriginal /,æbə'rɪdʒənl/ *a* aborigen; primitivo

aborigines /,æbə'rɪdʒə,niz/ *n pl* aborígenes, *m pl*

abort /ə'bɔrt/ *vi* abortar, malparir; *Fig.* malograrse

abortion /ə'bɔrʃən/ *n* aborto, *Colombia* avieso *m*; *Fig.* fracaso, malogro, *m*

abortive /ə'bɔrtɪv/ *a* abortivo

abound /ə'baund/ *vi* abundar (en)

about /ə'baut/ *adv* (around) alrededor; (round about) a la redonda, en torno; (all over) por todas partes; (up and down) acá y acullá; por aquí, por ahí; en alguna parte; por aquí; (in circumference) en circunferencia; (almost) casi, aproximadamente; (by turns) por turnos, en rotación. *prep* alrededor de; en torno; por; (near to) cerca de; (on one's person) sobre; (on the subject of) sobre; (concerning) acerca de; (over) a, a causa de; en; (of) de; (with time by the clock) a eso de, sobre; (towards) hacia; (engaged in) ocupado en; (on the point of) a punto de. **a. here,** por aquí. **a. nothing,** por nada. **a. supper time,** hacia la hora de cenar. **a. three o'clock,** a eso de las tres. **A. turn!** ¡Media vuelta! (a la izquierda or a la derecha). **He wandered a. the streets,** Vagaba por las calles. **somewhere a.,** en alguna parte. **to be a. to,** (tratar de + infin.), estar para, estar a punto de. **to bring a.,** ocasionar. **to come a.,** suceder. **to know a.,** saber de. **to set a.,** empezar, iniciar; (a person) acometer. **What are you thinking a.?** ¿En qué piensas?

above /ə'bʌv/ *adv* arriba; en lo alto; encima; (superior) superior; (earlier) antes; (higher up on a page, etc.) más arriba; (in heaven) en el cielo. *prep* encima de; por encima de; sobre; (beyond) fuera de; fuera del alcance de; (superior to) superior a; (more than) más de; (too proud to) demasiado orgulloso para; (too good to) demasiado bueno para; (in addition to) además de, en adición a; (with degrees of temperature) sobre. *a* anterior; (with past participles) antes. **from a.,** desde arriba. **a. all,** sobre todo. **over and a.,** además de. **a. board,** *adv* abiertamente, con las cartas boca arriba. *a* franco y abierto. **a. mentioned,** supradicho, susodicho, antes citado

abrasion /ə'breiʒən/ *n* abrasión, *f*; rozadura, *f*; *Geol.* denudación, *f*

abrasive /ə'breisɪv/ *a* abrasivo. *n* substancia abrasiva, *f*, abrasivo, *m*

abreast /ə'brɛst/ *adv* de frente, al lado uno de otro; *Naut.* por el través. **to keep a. of the times,** mantenerse al día. **to ride six a.,** cabalgar a seis de frente. **a. with,** al nivel de, a la altura de

abridge /ə'brɪdʒ/ *vt* abreviar; resumir, condensar, compendiar; disminuir; reducir

abridgment /ə'brɪdʒmənt/ *n* abreviación, *f*; resumen, *m*, sinopsis, *f*; disminución, *f*; reducción, *f*

abroad /ə'brɔd/ *adv* (out) fuera, afuera; (gone out) salido; ausente; (everywhere) en todas partes; (in foreign lands) en el extranjero. **to go a.,** ir al extranjero; (of rumors, etc.) propagarse, rumorearse

abrogation /ˌæbrə'geiʃən/ *n* abrogación, anulación, *f*

abrupt /ə'brʌpt/ *a* (precipitous) escarpado, precipitado, abrupto; (unexpected) repentino, inesperado; (of persons) brusco, descortés; (of style) seco

abruptly /ə'brʌptli/ *adv* bruscamente; repentinamente

abruptness /ə'brʌptnɪs/ *n* precipitación, *f*; brusquedad, *f*

abscess /'æbsɛs/ *n* absceso, *m*

abscond /æb'skɒnd/ *vi* evadirse; huir, escaparse; (with money) desfalcar

absence /'æbsəns/ *n* ausencia, *f*; alejamiento, *m*; (of mind) abstracción, *f*, ensimismamiento, *m*; (lack) falta, *f*. **leave of a.,** permiso para ausentarse, *m*; *Mil.* licencia, *f*, permiso, *m*

absent /*a* 'æbsənt; *v* æb'sɛnt/ *a* ausente; alejado (de); (in mind) abstraído, ensimismado, distraído. *vt* ausentarse; alejarse. **the a.,** los ausentes. **a.-mindedness,** ensimismamiento, *m*, abstracción, *f*

absentee /ˌæbsən'ti/ *n* ausente, *mf*

absenteeism /ˌæbsən'tiizəm/ *n* absentismo, *m*

absently /'æbsəntli/ *adv* distraídamente

absinthe /'æbsɪnθ/ *n* ajenjo, *m*

absolute /'æbsə,lut/ *a* absoluto; perfecto; puro; (unconditional) incondicional; (true) verdadero; (unlimited) ilimitado. **the a.,** lo absoluto

absolutely /ˌæbsə'lutli/ *adv* absolutamente; enteramente, completamente; realmente, categóricamente

absolution /ˌæbsə'luʃən/ *n* (*Eccl. Law.*) absolución, *f*

absolutism /'æbsəlu,tɪzəm/ *n* absolutismo, despotismo, *m*

absolutist /'æbsə,lutɪst/ *n* absolutista, *mf*

absolve /æb'zɒlv, -'sɒlv/ *vt* absolver; (free) exentar, eximir; librar; exculpar

absorb /æb'sɔrb, -'zɔrb/ *vt* absorber; (drink) beber; (use) gastar; (of shocks) amortiguar; (*Fig.* digest) asimilar; (engross) ocupar (el pensamiento, etc.). **to be absorbed in,** *Fig.* enfrascarse en, engolfarse en, estar entregado a

absorbent /æb'sɔrbənt, -'zɔr-/ *a* and *n* absorbente, *m*. **a. cotton,** algodón hidrófilo, *m*

absorbing /æb'sɔrbɪŋ, -'zɔr-/ *a* absorbente; *Fig.* sumamente interesante

absorption /æb'sɔrpʃən, -'zɔrp-/ *n* absorción, *f*; (*Fig.* digestion) asimilación, *f*; (engrossment) enfrascamiento, *m*, preocupación, abstracción, *f*

abstain /æb'stein/ *vi* abstenerse (de); evitar

abstemious /æb'stimiəs/ *a* abstemio, abstinente; sobrio; moderado

abstention /æb'stɛnʃən/ *n* abstención, *f*; abstinencia, *f*; privación, *f*

abstinence /'æbstənəns/ *n* abstinencia, *f*. **day of a.,** día de ayuno, *m*

abstinent /'æbstənənt/ *a* abstinente; sobrio

abstract /*a*, *v* æb'strækt, 'æbstrækt; *n* 'æbstrækt/ *a* abstracto. *n* extracto, resumen, *m*; abstracción, *f*. *vt* abstraer; separar; extraer; (précis) resumir; (steal) substraer. **in the a.,** en abstracto

abstraction /æb'strækʃən/ *n* abstracción, *f*; (of mind) preocupación, desatención, *f*; (stealing) substracción, *f*

abstruse /æb'strus/ *a* abstruso, ininteligible; obscuro; recóndito

absurd /æb'sɜrd/ *a* absurdo, grotesco; ridículo, disparatado; cómico

absurdity /æb'sɜrdɪti/ *n* absurdidad, ridiculez, *f*; disparate, *m*, tontería, *f*

abundance /ə'bʌndəns/ *n* abundancia, copia, *f*; muchedumbre (de), multitud (de), *f*; riqueza, *f*; prosperidad, *f*

abundant /ə'bʌndənt/ *a* abundante, copioso; rico

abundantly /ə'bʌndəntli/ *adv* en abundancia, abundantemente

abuse /*n* ə'byus; *v* ə'byuz/ *n* abuso, *m*; (bad language) insulto, *m*, injuria, *f*. *vt* (ill-use) maltratar; (misuse) abusar (de); (revile) insultar, injuriar; (deceive) engañar

abuser /ə'byuzər/ *n* abusador (-ra); injuriador (-ra); (defamer) denigrante, *mf*

abusive /ə'byusɪv/ *a* abusivo; (scurrilous) insultante, injurioso, ofensivo

abusively /ə'byusɪvli/ *adv* insolentemente, ofensivamente

abysmal /ə'bɪzməl/ *a* abismal

abyss /ə'bɪs/ *n* abismo, *m*, sima, *f*; (hell) infierno, *m*

acacia /ə'keiʃə/ *n* acacia, *f*

academic /ˌækə'dɛmɪk/ *a* académico

academician /ˌækədə'mɪʃən/ *n* académico, miembro de la Academia, *m*

academy /ə'kædəmi/ *n* academia, *f*; conservatorio, *m*; (school) colegio, *m*; (of riding, etc.) escuela, *f*. **A. of Music,** Conservatorio de Música, *m*

accede /æk'sid/ *vi* (to a throne) ascender (al trono); tomar posesión (de); (join) hacerse miembro (de); aceptar; (agree) acceder (a), consentir (en), convenir (en)

accelerate /æk'sɛlə,reit/ *vt* acelerar; apresurar; (shorten) abreviar

acceleration /æk,sɛlə'reiʃən/ *n* aceleración, *f*

accelerator /æk'sɛlə,reitər/ *n* (of a vehicle) acelerador, *m*

accent /'æksɛnt/ *n* acento (all meanings), *m*. *vt* acentuar

accentuate /æk'sɛntʃu,eit/ *vt* acentuar; dar énfasis a

accept /æk'sɛpt/ *vt* aceptar; (believe) creer; recibir; admitir; (welcome) acoger

acceptability /æk,sɛptə'bɪlɪti/ *n* aceptabilidad, *f*; mérito, *m*

acceptable /æk'sɛptəbəl/ *a* aceptable; admisible; agradable; (welcome) bien acogido

acceptably /æk'sɛptəbli/ *adv* aceptablemente; agradablemente

acceptance /æk'sɛptəns/ *n* aceptación, *f*. **a. speech** discurso aceptatorio; (approval) aprobación, *f*; (welcome) buena acogida, *f*; *Com.* aceptación, *f*

access /'æksɛs/ *n* acceso, *m*; entrada, *f*; (way) camino, *m*; *Med.* ataque, *m*; (fit) transporte, *m*; (advance) avance, *m*. **easy of a.,** accesible; fácil de encontrar. *vt* tener acceso a

accessibility /æk,sɛsə'bɪlɪti/ *n* accesibilidad, *f*

accessible /æk'sɛsəbəl/ *a* accesible; asequible

accession /æk'sɛʃən/ *n* (to the throne, etc.) advenimiento, *m*; aumento, *m*; (acquisition) adición, *f*; adquisición, *f*; *Law.* accesión, *f*

accessory /æk'sɛsəri/ *a* accesorio; secundario; suplementario, adicional, *m* accesorio, *m*; *Law.* cómplice, *mf*. **a. before the fact,** instigador (-ra). **a. after the fact,** encubridor (-ra)

accident /'æksɪdənt/ *n* accidente, *m*; (chance) casualidad, *f*; (mishap) contratiempo, *m*. **by a.,** por casualidad, accidentalmente. **a. insurance,** seguro contra accidentes, *m*

accidental /ˌæksɪ'dɛntl/ *a* accidental, casual, fortuito. *n Mus.* accidente, *m*

accidentally /ˌæksɪ'dɛntli/ *adv* accidentalmente; por casualidad; sin querer

acclaim /ə'kleim/ *vt* aclamar; proclamar; vitorear, aplaudir

acclamation /ˌæklə'meiʃən/ *n* aclamación, *f*; aplauso, *m*, vítor, *m*

acclimatization /ə'klaimətə,zeisnən/ *n* aclimatación, *f*

acclimatize /ə'klaimə,taiz/ vt aclimatar
accolade /'ækə,leid/ n acolada, f, espaldarazo, m
accommodate /ə'kɒmə,deit/ vt acomodar; ajustar; adaptar; (reconcile) reconciliar; (provide) proveer, proporcionar; (oblige) complacer; (fit) poner, instalar; (lodge) hospedar; (lend) prestar; (hold) tener espacio para, contener; (give a seat to) dar un sitio a. **to a. oneself to,** adaptarse a
accommodating /ə'kɒmə,deitɪŋ/ a acomodadizo; (obliging) servicial
accommodation /ə,kɒmə'deiʃən/ n acomodación, f; ajuste, m; adaptación, f; (arrangement) arreglo, m; (reconciliation) reconciliación, f; (lodging) alojamiento, m; (Aer. Naut.) partición, f; (space, room or seat) sitio, m; (loan) préstamo, m
accompaniment /ə'kʌmpənimənt/ n acompañamiento, m
accompanist /ə'kʌmpənist/ n acompañante (-ta)
accompany /ə'kʌmpəni/ vt acompañar
accompanying /ə'kʌmpəniiŋ/ a anexo n acompañamiento, m
accomplice /ə'kɒmplis/ n cómplice, comparte, mf
accomplish /ə'kɒmpliʃ/ vt llevar a cabo, efectuar; terminar; (fulfill) cumplir; perfeccionar; (achieve) conseguir, lograr
accomplished /ə'kɒmpliʃt/ a consumado; perfecto; culto; (talented) talentoso
accomplishment /ə'kɒmpliʃmənt/ n efectuación, f; realización, f, logro, m; (fulfilment) cumplimiento, m; (gift) prenda, f, talento, m; pl **accomplishments,** partes, dotes, f pl; conocimientos, m pl
accord /ə'kɔrd/ n acuerdo, m; unión, f; consentimiento, m; concierto, m, concordia, f; voluntad, f. vt otorgar, conceder. vi estar de acuerdo (con); armonizar (con). **of one's own a.,** espontáneamente. **with one a.,** unánimemente
accordance /ə'kɔrdns/ n acuerdo, m, conformidad, f; arreglo, m. **in a. with,** de acuerdo con, según, con arreglo a
according /ə'kɔrdiŋ/ adv según, conforme. **a. as,** conforme a, a medida que. **a. to,** según
accordingly /ə'kɔrdiŋli/ adv en consecuencia, por consiguiente; pues
accordion /ə'kɔrdiən/ n acordeón, m
accost /ə'kɔst/ vt abordar, molestar
account /ə'kaunt/ vt (judge) considerar, creer, juzgar, tener por. vi (for) explicar; (understand) comprender; (be responsible) responder de, dar razón de; justificar
account /ə'kaunt/ n (bill) cuenta, f; factura, f; (narrative) narración, relación, f; (description) descripción, f; historia, f; versión, f; (list) enumeración, f; (reason) motivo, m, causa, f; (importance) importancia, f; (weight) peso, m; (news) noticias, f pl; (advantage) provecho, m, ventaja, f. **by all accounts,** según lo que se oye, según voz pública. **outstanding a.,** cuenta pendiente, f. **on a.,** a cuenta. **on a. of,** a causa de, por motivo de. **on no a.,** de ninguna manera. **on that a.,** por lo tanto. **savings a.,** cuenta corriente, f. **to be of no a.,** ser insignificant; ser de poca importancia; Inf. ser la última mona. **to give an a.,** contar, hacer una relación (de). **to give an a. of oneself,** explicarse. **to keep a.,** llevar la cuenta. **to settle accounts,** ajustar cuentas. **to take into a.,** considerar. **to turn to a.,** sacar provecho de. **a. book,** libro de cuentas, m
accountability /ə,kauntə'biliti/ n responsabilidad, f
accountable /ə'kauntəbəl/ a responsable
accountancy /ə'kauntn̩si/ n contabilidad, f
accountant /ə'kauntn̩t/ n contador, m. **accountant's office,** contaduría, f
accouterment /ə'kutərmənt/ n atavío, m; equipo, m
accredit /ə'krɛdit/ vt acreditar
accretion /ə'kriʃən/ n acrecentamiento, aumento, m; Law. accesión, f
accrue /ə'kru/ vi resultar (de), proceder (de); originarse (en); aumentar
accumulate /ə'kyumyə,leit/ vt acumular; amontonar, atesorar. vi acumularse; aumentarse, crecer
accumulation /ə,kyumyə'leiʃən/ n acumulación, f; amontonamiento, m

accumulative /ə'kyumyə,leitɪv/ a acumulador; adquisitivo, ahorrador
accumulator /ə'kyumyə,leitər/ n Elec. acumulador, m
accuracy /'ækyərəsi/ n exactitud, correción
accurate /'ækyərit/ a exacto, correcto, fiel; (of persons) exacto, minucioso; (of apparatus) de precisión
accurately /'ækyəritli/ adv con exactitud, correctamente; con precisión
accursed /ə'kɜrsid, ə'kɜrst/ a maldito.
accusation /,ækyu'zeiʃən/ n acusación, f. **to lodge an a.,** querellarse ante el juez
accusatory /ə'kyuzə,tɔri/ a acusatorio
accuse /ə'kyuz/ vt acusar
accused /ə'kyuzd/ n Law. acusado (-da)
accuser /ə'kyuzər/ n acusador (-ra)
accustom /ə'kʌstəm/ vt acostumbrar (a), habituar (a)
accustomed /ə'kʌstəmd/ a acostumbrado, usual; general; característico
ace /eis/ n as, m; Fig. pelo, m
acerbity /ə'sɜrbiti/ n acerbidad, f; Fig. aspereza, f; severidad, f; sequedad, f
acetaminophen /ə,sitə'mɪnəfən/ n acetaminofén, m
acetate /'æsɪ,teit/ n acetato, m
acetic /ə'sitɪk/ a acético
acetylene /ə'sɛtl̩,in/ n acetileno, m. **a. lamp,** lámpara de acetileno, f
ache /eik/ n dolor, m; pena, f. vi doler. **My head aches,** Me duele la cabeza, Tengo dolor de cabeza
achievable /ə'tʃivəbəl/ a alcanzable, asequible; factible
achieve /ə'tʃiv/ vt conseguir, lograr; (reach) alcanzar; (obtain) obtener, ganar
achievement /ə'tʃivmənt/ n logro, m, realización, f; obtención, f; (deed) hazaña, f; (work) obra, f; (success) éxito, m; (discovery) descubrimiento, m; (victory) victoria, f
aching /'eikiŋ/ n dolor, m; pena, angustia, f. a doliente; afligido
achromatic /,eikrə'mætik/ a acromático
achromic /ei'kroumik/ a acrómico
acid /'æsid/ a and n ácido, m. **fatty a.,** ácido graso, m
acidify /ə'sidə,fai/ vt acidificar
acidity /ə'siditi/ n acidez, f
acidosis /,æsi'dousis/ n Med. acidismo, m
acid rain n lluvia ácida, f
acknowledge /æk'nɒlidʒ/ vt reconocer; confesar; (reply to) contestar a; (appreciate) agradecer. **to a. receipt,** Com. acusar recibo
acknowledgment /æk'nɒlidʒmənt/ n reconocimiento, m; confesión, f; (appreciation) agradecimiento, m; (reward) recompensa, f; (of a letter) acuse de recibo, m
acme /'ækmi/ n cumbre, f; Fig. auge, apogeo, m
acne /'ækni/ n acné, m
acolyte /'ækə,lait/ n acólito, monacillo (male) m, acólita, monacilla f, (female)
acorn /'eikɔrn/ n bellota, f. **a. cup,** capullo de bellota, m. **a.-shaped,** en forma de bellota, abellotado
acoustic /ə'kustik/ a acústico
acoustics /ə'kustiks/ n pl acústica, f
acquaint /ə'kweint/ vt dar a conocer, comunicar, informar (de), dar parte (de); familiarizar (con). **to be acquainted with,** conocer; saber. **to make oneself acquainted with,** familiarizarse con; entablar amistad con
acquaintance /ə'kweintns/ n conocimiento, m; (person) conocido (-da); pl **acquaintances,** amistades, f pl. **to make their a.,** conocer (a), llegar a conocer (a)
acquiesce /,ækwi'es/ vi asentir (en), consentir (a)
acquiescence /,ækwi'esəns/ n acquiescencia, f, consentimiento, m
acquiescent /,ækwi'esənt/ a conforme; resignado
acquire /ə'kwaɪər/ vt adquirir, obtener; (diseases, habits) contraer; ganar; (learn) aprender
Acquired Immune Deficiency Syndrome /ə'kwaɪərd/ n el Síndrome de Inmunodeficiencia Adquirida, f
acquirement /ə'kwaɪərmənt/ n adquisición, f; (learning) conocimiento, m; (talent) talento, m
acquirer /ə'kwaɪərər/ n adquisidor (-ra)
acquisition /,ækwə'ziʃən/ n adquisición, f

acquisitive /ə'kwɪzɪtɪv/ a adquisitivo
acquit /ə'kwɪt/ vt (a debt) pagar; exonerar; Law. absolver; (a duty) cumplir. **to a. oneself well (badly),** portarse bien (mal); salir bien (mal)
acquittal /ə'kwɪtl/ n (of a debt) pago, m; Law. absolución, f; (of a duty) cumplimiento, m
acquittance /ə'kwɪtn̩s/ n descargo, m; quitanza, f
acre /'eikər/ n (measure) acre, m; pl **acres,** terrenos, campos, m pl. **1.75 acres** Central America manzana f. **2.5 acres** Argentina manzana f
acreage /'eikərɪdʒ/ n acres, m pl
acrid /'ækrɪd/ a acre
acrimonious /ˌækrə'mouniəs/ a acrimonioso, áspero; mordaz, sarcástico
acrimony /'ækrəˌmouni/ n acrimonia, acritud, f; sarcasmo, m
acrobat /'ækrəˌbæt/ n acróbata. Lat. Am. also maromero (-ra) mf
acrobatic /ˌækrə'bætɪk/ a acrobático
acrobatics /ˌækrə'bætɪks/ n pl acrobacia, f
acronym /'ækrənɪm/ n sigla, f
acropolis /ə'krɒpəlɪs/ n acrópolis, f
across /ə'krɔs/ adv a través, de través, transversalmente; (on the other side) al otro lado; de una parte a otra; (of the arms, etc.) cruzados, m pl. prep a través de; al otro lado de; (upon) sobre; por. **He went a. the road,** Cruzó la calle. **to run a.,** correr por; tropezar con; dar con. **a. country,** a campo travieso. **a. the way,** en frente
acrostic /ə'krɒstɪk/ n (poema) acróstico, m, a acróstico
act /ækt/ n acción, obra, f, hecho, m; acto, m; Law. ley, f; Theat. acto, m. **in the act,** en el acto. **in the act (of doing),** en acto de (hacer algo). **in the very act,** en flagrante. **the Acts of the Apostles,** los Actos de los Apóstoles. **act of God,** fuerza mayor, f. **act of indemnity,** bill de indemnidad, m
act /ækt/ vt (a play) representar, hacer; (a part) desempeñar, hacer (un papel); (pretend) simular, fingir. vi obrar, actuar, Lat. Am. accionar; (behave) portarse, conducirse; (function) funcionar; producir su efecto; (feign) fingir; (as a profession) ser actor. **to act as,** hacer de; cumplir las funciones de. **to act as a second,** (in a duel) apadrinar. **to act for,** representar; ser el representante de. **to act upon,** obrar sobre; afectar; influir en
acting /'æktɪŋ/ n (of a play) representación (de una comedia), f; (of an actor) interpretación (de un papel), f; (as a hobby) el hacer comedia; (dramatic art) arte dramática, f. a interino, suplente; comanditario. **He is a. captain,** Está de capitán. **a. partner,** socio (-ia) comanditario (-ia)
action /'ækʃən/ n acción, f; función, f; operación, f; (movement) movimiento, m; (effect) efecto, m; influencia, f; Law. proceso, m; Mil. batalla, acción, f; Lit. acción, f. **in a.,** en actividad; en operación; Mil. en el campo de batalla. **man of a.,** hombre de acción, m. **to be killed in a.,** morir en el campo de batalla. **to bring an a. against,** pedir en juicio, entablar un pleito contra. **to put into a.,** hacer funcionar; introducir. **to take a.,** tomar medidas (para). **to take a. against,** prevenirse contra; Law. proceder contra
actionable /'ækʃənəbəl/ a procesable, punible
active /'æktɪv/ a activo; ágil; diligente; Mil. vivo; enérgico; Gram. activo. **be a.** Lat. Am. accionar. **to make a.,** activar, estimular
activity /æk'tɪvɪti/ n actividad, f
actor /'æktər/ n actor, m; (in comedy) comediante, m
actress /'æktrɪs/ n actriz, f; (in comedy) comediante, f
actual /'æktʃuəl/ a actual, existente; real, verdadero
actuality /ˌæktʃu'ælɪti/ n realidad, f
actually /'æktʃuəli/ adv en efecto, realmente, en realidad
actuary /'æktʃuˌɛri/ n actuario de seguros, m
actuate /'æktʃuˌeit/ vt mover, animar, excitar
acumen /ə'kyumən/ n cacumen, m, agudeza, sagacidad, f
acute /ə'kyut/ a agudo; (shrewd) perspicaz; (of a situation) crítico. **a. accent,** acento agudo, m. **a.-angled,** acutángulo

acutely /ə'kyutli/ adv agudamente; (deeply) profundamente
acuteness /ə'kyutnɪs/ n agudeza, f; (shrewdness) perspicacia, penetración, f
ad /æd/ n anuncio, m. See **advertisement**
adage /'ædɪdʒ/ n refrán, proverbio, decir, m
Adam /'ædəm/ n Adán, m. **Adam's apple,** nuez de la garganta, f
adamant /'ædəmənt/ a firme, duro, inexorable
adamantine /ˌædə'mæntin/ a adamantino
adapt /ə'dæpt/ vt adaptar; ajustar, acomodar; aplicar; (a play, etc.) refundir, arreglar; Mus. arreglar
adaptability /əˌdæptə'bɪlɪti/ n adaptabilidad, f
adaptable /ə'dæptəbəl/ a adaptable
adaptation /ˌædəp'teiʃən/ n adaptación, f; (of a play, etc.) refundición, f; (Mus. etc.) arreglo, m
adapter /ə'dæptər/ n (of a play, etc.) refundidor (-ra); Elec. enchufe de reducción, m
add /æd/ vt añadir; juntar; (up) sumar. **add insult to injury,** al mojado echarle agua, añadir a una ofensa otra mayor. **to add to,** añadir a; (increase) aumentar, acrecentar. **to add up,** sumar. **to add up to,** subir a; (mean) querer decir
adder /'ædər/ n víbora, serpiente, f
addict /'ædɪkt/ n adicto (-ta). **to a. oneself to,** dedicarse a, entregarse a
addicted /ə'dɪktɪd/ a aficionado (a), amigo (de), dado (a); adicto (a)
addiction /ə'dɪkʃən/ n afición, propensión, f; adicción, f
addition /ə'dɪʃən/ n añadidura, f; Math. adición, suma, f. **in a. (to),** además (de), también
additional /ə'dɪʃənl/ a adicional
addled /'ædl̩d/ a huero, podrido; Fig. confuso
address /n ə'drɛs, 'ædrɛs; v ə'drɛs/ n (on a letter) sobrescrito, m; (of a person) dirección, f, señas, f pl; (speech) discurso, m; (petition) memorial, m, petición, f; (dedication) dedicatoria, f; (invocation) invocación, f; (deportment) presencia, f; (tact) diplomacia, habilidad, f; pl **addresses,** corte, f. vt (a ball) golpear; (a letter) dirigir, poner el sobrescrito a, Mexico domiciliar; (words, prayers) dirigir (a); hablar, dirigirse a. **to a. oneself to a task,** dedicarse a (or entregarse a or emprender) una tarea. **to deliver an a.,** pronunciar un discurso. **to pay one's addresses to,** cortejar, hacer la corte (a), galantear
addressee /ˌædrɛ'si/ n destinatario (-ia)
adduce /ə'dus/ vt aducir, alegar; aportar
Aden /'ɑdn̩/ Adén m
adenoids /'ædn̩ˌɔidz/ n pl amígdalas, f pl
adept /ə'dɛpt; n 'ædɛpt/ a adepto, versado, consumado. n adepto, m
adequacy /'ædɪkwəsi/ n adecuación, f; suficiencia, f; competencia, f
adequate /'ædɪkwɪt/ a adecuado; proporcionado; suficiente; competente; a la altura (de)
adequately /'ædɪkwɪtli/ adv adecuadamente
adhere /æd'hiər/ vi adherirse; pegarse; ser fiel (a); persistir (en)
adherence /æd'hiərəns/ n Fig. adhesión, f
adherent /æd'hiərənt/ n partidario (-ia)
adhesion /æd'hiʒən/ n adherencia, f; (to a party, etc.) adhesión, f
adhesive /æd'hisɪv/ a adhesivo; (sticky) pegajoso. **a. tape,** esparadrapo, m; Elec. cinta aisladora adherente, f
adipose /'ædəˌpous/ a adiposo
adjacent /ə'dʒeisənt/ a próximo, contiguo, adyacente, vecino
adjective /'ædʒɪktɪv/ n adjetivo, m
adjoin /ə'dʒɔin/ vt estar contiguo a, lindar con; juntar. vi colindar
adjoining /ə'dʒɔinɪŋ/ a vecino, de al lado, adyacente; cercano
adjourn /ə'dʒɜrn/ vt aplazar, diferir; (a meeting, etc.) suspender, levantar. vi retirarse. **The debate was adjourned,** Se suspendió el debate. **to a. a meeting,** levantar la sesión
adjournment /ə'dʒɜrnmənt/ n aplazamiento, m; (of a meeting) suspensión (de la sesión), f
adjudicate /ə'dʒudɪˌkeit/ vt adjudicar; Law. declarar;

juzgar. *vi* ejercer las funciones del juez; fallar, dictar sentencia

adjudication /ə͵dʒudɪ'keɪʃən/ *n* adjudicación, *f*; *Law.* fallo, *m*, sentencia, *f*; (of bankruptcy) declaración (de quiebra), *f*; concesión, *f*, otorgamiento, *m*

adjudicator /ə'dʒudɪ͵keitər/ *n* adjudicador (-ra)

adjunct /'ædʒʌŋkt/ *n* atributo, *m*; accesorio, *m*; adjunto, *m*; *Gram.* adjunto, *m*

adjure /ə'dʒʊr/ *vt* conjurar; rogar encarecidamente

adjust /ə'dʒʌst/ *vt* ajustar; regular; arreglar; (correct) corregir; adaptar

adjustable /ə'dʒʌstəbəl/ *a* ajustable; regulable; desmontable; de quita y pon

adjustment /ə'dʒʌstmənt/ *n* ajuste, *m*; regulación, *f*; arreglo, *m*; (correction) corrección, *f*; adaptación, *f*; *Com.* prorrateo, *m*

adjutant /'ædʒətənt/ *n* *Mil.* ayudante, *m*

administer /æd'mɪnəstər/ *vt* administrar; (laws) aplicar; (blows, etc.) dar; (an office) ejercer; (govern) regir, gobernar; (provide) suministrar; (an oath) tomar; (justice) hacer; (the sacraments) administrar; (with to) contribuir a. **to a. an oath,** tomar juramento (a)

administration /æd͵mɪnə'streɪʃən/ *n* administración, *f*; (government) gobierno, *m*; dirección, *f*; (of laws) aplicación, *f*; distribución, *f*

administrative /æd'mɪnə͵streɪtɪv/ *a* administrativo; gubernativo

administrator /æd'mɪnə͵streɪtər/ *n* administrador (-ra)

admirable /'ædmərəbəl/ *a* admirable

admirably /'ædmərəbli/ *adv* admirablemente

admiral /'ædmərəl/ *n* almirante, *m*. **A. of the Fleet,** almirante supremo, *m*. **admiral's ship,** capitana, *f*

admiration /͵ædmə'reɪʃən/ *n* admiración, *f*

admire /æd'maɪᵊr/ *vt* sentir admiración por; (love) amar; (like) gustar; (respect) respetar

admirer /æd'maɪᵊrər/ *n* admirador (-ra); (amateur) aficionado (-da), apasionado (-da); (partisan) satélite, *m*; (lover) enamorado, amante, *m*

admiring /æd'maɪərɪŋ/ *a* admirativo, de admiración

admissible /æd'mɪsəbəl/ *a* admisible; aceptable; lícito, permitido

admission /æd'mɪʃən/ *n* admisión, *f*; recepción, *f*; entrada, *f*; confesión, *f*, reconocimiento, *m*. **Free a.,** Entrada libre. **No a.!** Entrada prohibida. **right of a.,** derecho de entrada, *m*. **a. ticket,** entrada, *f*

admit /æd'mɪt/ *vt* admitir; recibir; dejar entrar; hacer entrar, introducir; (hold) contener; (concede) conceder; (acknowledge) reconocer, confesar. **to a. of,** permitir; sufrir

admittance /æd'mɪtns/ *n* admisión, *f*; entrada, *f*. **No a.!** Prohibida la entrada. **to gain a.,** lograr entrar

admittedly /æd'mɪtɪdli/ *adv* según opinión general; sin duda

admonish /æd'mɒnɪʃ/ *vt* (advise) aconsejar; amonestar, advertir; (reprimand) reprender

admonition /͵ædmə'nɪʃən/ *n* amonestación, *f*; advertencia, *f*; admonición, *f*

admonitory /æd'mɒnɪ͵tɔri/ *a* amonestador

ad nauseam /'æd nɔziəm/ *adv* hasta la saciedad

ado /ə'du/ *n* (noise) ruido, *m*; (trouble) trabajo, *m*, dificultad, *f*; (fuss) barahúnda, *f*. **much ado about nothing,** mucho ruido y pocas nueces, nada entre dos platos. **without further ado,** sin más ni más

adolescence /͵ædḷ'esəns/ *n* adolescencia, *f*

adolescent /͵ædḷ'esənt/ *a* and *n* adolescente, *mf*

adopt /ə'dɒpt/ *vt* adoptar. **a. local customs** *Lat. Am.* acriollarse

adopted /ə'dɒptɪd/ *a* adoptivo

adoption /ə'dɒpʃən/ *n* adopción, *f*; (choice) elección, *f*

adoptive /ə'dɒptɪv/ *a* adoptivo

adorable /ə'dɔrəbəl/ *a* adorable

adoration /͵ædə'reɪʃən/ *n* adoración, *f*. **A. of the Magi,** Adoración de los Reyes, *f*

adore /ə'dɔr/ *vt* adorar

adorer /ə'dɔrər/ *n* adorador (-ra); amante, *m*

adoringly /ə'dɔrɪŋli/ *adv* con adoración

adorn /ə'dɔrn/ *vt* adornar, embellecer; (*Fig.* of persons) adornar con su presencia

adornment /ə'dɔrnmənt/ *n* adorno, *m*; ornamento, *m*; embellecimiento, *m*

adrenalin /ə'drenlɪn/ *n* adrenalina, *f*

Adriatic, the /͵eidri'ætɪk/ el (Mar) Adriático, *m*

adrift /ə'drɪft/ *a* and *adv* a merced de las olas; a la ventura. **to turn a.,** *Inf.* poner de patitas en la calle

adroit /ə'drɔit/ *a* hábil

adulate /'ædʒə͵leɪt/ *vt* adular

adulation /͵ædʒə'leɪʃən/ *n* adulación, *f*

adulatory /'ædʒələ͵tɔri/ *a* adulador

adult /ə'dʌlt/ *a* and *n* adulto (-ta)

adult education *n* educación de los adultos, *f*

adulterate /*v* ə'dʌltə͵reit; *a* ə'dʌltə͵reit; -tərɪt/ *vt* adulterar; falsificar; contaminar. *a* adulterado; falsificado; impuro

adulteration /ə͵dʌltə'reɪʃən/ *n* adulteración, *f*; falsificación, *f*; impureza, *f*; contaminación, *f*

adulterer /ə'dʌltərər/ *n* adúltero, *m*

adulteress /ə'dʌltərɪs/ *n* adúltera, *f*

adulterous /ə'dʌltərəs/ *a* adúltero

adultery /ə'dʌltəri/ *n* adulterio, *m*. **to commit a.,** cometer adulterio, adulterar

advance /æd'væns/ *n* avance, *m*; (progress) progreso, adelantamiento, *m*; (improvement) mejora, *f*; (of shares) alza, *f*; (of price) subida, *f*; (loan) préstamo, *m*; (in rank) ascenso, *m*; *pl* **advances,** (overtures) avances, *m pl*; (proposals) propuestas, *f pl*; (of love) requerimientos amorosos, *m pl.* **in a.,** de antemano, con anticipación, con tiempo, previamente; (of money) por adelantado. **a. guard,** *Mil.* avanzada, *f.* **a. payment,** anticipo, *m*, paga por adelantado, *f*

advance /æd'væns/ *vt* avanzar; (suggest) sugerir, proponer; (encourage) fomentar; (a person) ascender; (improve) mejorar; (of events, dates) adelantar; (of prices, stocks) hacer subir; (money) anticipar; (of steps) tomar. *vi* avanzar; (progress) progresar; (in rank, studies, etc.) adelantar; (of prices) subir

advanced /æd'vænst/ *a* avanzado; (developed) desarrollado; (mentally, of children) precoz; (course) superior. **a. research,** investigaciones superiores. **a. standing,** equivalencias, *f pl.* **a. views,** ideas avanzadas, *f pl*

advancement /æd'vænsmənt/ *n* adelantamiento, *m*; progreso, *m*; (encouragement) fomento, *m*; (in employment) promoción, *f*; prosperidad, *f*

advancing /æd'vænsɪŋ/ *a* que avanza; (of years) que pasan

advantage /æd'væntɪdʒ/ *n* ventaja, *f*; superioridad, *f*; (benefit) provecho, beneficio, *m*; interés, *m*; ocasión favorable, oportunidad, *f*; (tennis) ventaja, *f.* **to have the a. of,** tener la ventaja de. **to show to a.,** embellecer, realzar; aumentar la belleza (etc.) de. **to take a. of,** sacar ventaja de, aprovecharse de; (deceive) engañar. **to take a. of the slightest pretext,** asirse de un cabello

advantageous /͵ædvən'teidʒəs/ *a* ventajoso, provechoso. **to be a.,** ser de provecho

advent /'ædvent/ *n* advenimiento, *m*, llegada, *f*; *Eccl.* Adviento, *m*

adventitious /͵ædvən'tɪʃəs/ *a* adventicio (all uses)

adventure /æd'ventʃər/ *n* aventura, *f*; riesgo, *m*; (chance) casualidad, *f*; *Com.* especulación, *f*, *vt* aventurar, arriesgar. *vi* arriesgarse, osar

adventurer /æd'ventʃərər/ *n* aventurero (-ra); (one living by his or her wits) caballero de industria, *m*; (in commerce) especulador (-ra)

adventuresome /æd'ventʃərsəm/ *a* de aventura

adventurous /æd'ventʃərəs/ *a* aventurero; osado, audaz; (dangerous) peligroso, arriesgado

adverb /'ædvɜrb/ *n* adverbio, *m*

adversary /'ædvər͵seri/ *n* adversario (-ia)

adverse /æd'vɜrs/ *a* adverso; hostil (a); malo; desfavorable; (opposite) opuesto

adversity /æd'vɜrsiti/ *n* adversidad, *f*

advertise /'ædvər͵taiz/ *vt* anunciar. *vi* poner un anuncio; (oneself) llamar la atención

advertisement /͵ædvər'taizmənt, æd'vɜrtɪsmənt/ *n* anuncio, *m*; (poster) cartel, *m*; (to attract attention) reclamo, *m*. **to put an a. in the paper,** poner un anuncio en el periódico

advertiser /'ædvər͵taizər/ *n* anunciante, *mf*

advertising /'ædvər,taizɪŋ/ n anuncios, m pl; publicidad, propaganda, f; medios publicitarios, m pl
advice /æd'vais/ n consejo, m; (warning) advertencia, amonestación, f; (news) noticia, f, aviso, m; Com. comunicación, f; (belief) parecer, m, opinión, f. **piece of a.,** consejo, m. **to follow the a.** of, seguir los consejos de. **to give a.,** dar consejos
advisability /æd,vaizə'bɪlɪti/ n conveniencia, f; prudencia, f
advisable /æd'vaizəbəl/ a conveniente, aconsejable; prudente
advise /æd'vaiz/ vt aconsejar; (inform) avisar, informar
advised /æd'vaizd/ a avisado; premeditado. **ill-a.,** mal aconsejado; imprudente. **well-a.,** bien aconsejado; prudente
adviser /æd'vaizər/ n consejero (-ra), asesor
advisory /æd'vaizəri/ a asesor, consultivo, consultativo
advocacy /'ædvəkəsi/ n defensa, f; apología, f; abogacía, intercesión, f
advocate /n 'ædvəkɪt; v -,keit/ n Law. abogado (-da); defensor (-ra); (champion) campeón, m. vt abogar, defender; sostener, apoyar; recomendar
adze /ædz/ n azuela, f
Aegean, the /ə'dʒiən/ el (Mar) Egeo, m
aegis /'idʒɪs/ n égida, f; protección, f
aerated /'ɛə,reitɪd/ a aerado; (of lemonade, etc.) gaseoso. **a. waters,** aguas gaseosas, f pl
aeration /,ɛə'reiʃən/ n aeración, f
aerial /'ɛəriəl/ a aéreo, de aire; etéreo; fantástico. n (radio) antena, f. **indoor a.,** antena interior, f
aerobics /ɛə'roubɪks/ n aerobismo m
aerodynamics /,ɛəroudai'næmɪks/ n aerodinámica, f
aeronaut /'ɛərə,nɔt/ n aeronauta, mf
aeronautical /,ɛərə'nɔtɪkəl/ a aeronáutico
aeronautics /,ɛərə'nɔtɪks/ n aeronáutica, f
afar /ə'fɑr/ adv a lo lejos, en la distancia. **from a.,** desde lejos
affability /,æfə'bɪlɪti/ n afabilidad, condescendencia, urbanidad, f
affable /'æfəbəl/ a afable, condescendiente
affably /'æfəbli/ adv afablemente
affair /ə'fɛər/ n asunto, m, cosa, f; cuestión, f; (business) negocio, m; (Fam. applied to a machine, carriage, etc.) artefacto, m; (of the heart) amorío, m. **a. of honor,** lance de honor, m
affect /ə'fɛkt/ vt afectar; influir; Med. atacar; (move) impresionar, conmover; enternecer; (harm) perjudicar; (frequent) frecuentar; (like) gustar de; (love) amar; (wear) vestir; (use) gastar, usar; (feign) aparentar; (boast) hacer alarde de
affectation /,æfɛk'teiʃən/ n afectación, f
affected /ə'fɛktɪd/ a afectado; influido; Med. atacado; (moved) conmovido, impresionado; enternecido; (inclined) dispuesto, inclinado; (artificial) artificioso; amanerado, afectado; (of style) rebuscado, artificial
affecting /ə'fɛktɪŋ/ a conmovedor, emocionante
affection /ə'fɛkʃən/ n afecto, cariño, m; amor, m; apego, m; simpatía, f; (emotion) emoción, f, sentimiento, m; Med. afección, enfermedad, f
affectionate /ə'fɛkʃənɪt/ a afectuoso, cariñoso; mimoso; (tender) tierno; expresivo
affectionately /ə'fɛkʃənɪtli/ adv afectuosamente. **Yours a.,** tu cariñoso..., tu..., que te quiere
affective /'æfɛktɪv/ a afectivo
affidavit /,æfɪ'deivɪt/ n declaración jurada, declaración jurídica, f, atestiguación, f
affiliate /ə'fɪli,eit/ vt afiliar; adoptar; Law. imputar; Law. legitimar. n afiliado, socio, m
affiliation /ə,fɪli'eiʃən/ n afiliación, f; adopción, f; legitimación de un hijo, f
affinity /ə'fɪnɪti/ n afinidad, f
affirm /ə'fɜrm/ vt afirmar, aseverar, declarar; confirmar. vi Law. declarar ante un juez
affirmation /,æfər'meiʃən/ n afirmación, aserción, f; confirmación, f; Law. declaración, deposición, f
affirmative /ə'fɜrmətɪv/ a afirmativo. n afirmativa, f
affix /v ə'fɪks; n 'æfɪks/ vt fijar; pegar; añadir; (seal, one's signature) poner. n Gram. afijo, m

afflict /ə'flɪkt/ vt afligir, atormentar, aquejar
affliction /ə'flɪkʃən/ n aflicción, f; tribulación, pesadumbre, f; calamidad, f; miseria, f; (ailment) achaque, m
affluence /'æfluəns/ n afluencia, f; abundancia, f; riqueza, f; opulencia, f
affluent /'æfluənt/ a abundante; rico; opulento
afflux /'æflʌks/ n afluencia, f; Med. aflujo, m
afford /ə'fɔrd/ vt dar, proporcionar; producir; ofrecer; (bear) soportar; poder con; (financially) tener medios para; permitirse el lujo de; (be able) poder. **I could not a. to pay so much,** No puedo (podía) pagar tanto
afforest /ə'fɔrɪst/ vt convertir en bosque
afforestation /ə,fɔrə'steiʃən/ n conversión en bosque, f; plantación de un bosque, f
affray /ə'frei/ n riña, refriega, f
affront /ə'frʌnt/ n afrenta, f, insulto, agravio, m. vt insultar, ultrajar, afrentar; (offend) ofender
Afghan /'æfgæn/ a and n afgano (-na)
Afghanistan /æf'gænə,stæn/ Afganistán, m
afield /ə'fild/ adv en el campo; lejos. **to go far a.,** ir muy lejos
afire /ə'faiᵊr/ adv en fuego, en llamas; Fig. ardiendo
aflame /ə'fleim/ adv en llamas; Fig. encendido
afloat /ə'flout/ adv a flote; Naut. a bordo; (solvent) solvente; en circulación; (floating) flotante; (swamped) inundado; (in full swing) en marcha, en movimiento
afoot /ə'fut/ adv a pie; en marcha, en movimiento; en preparación. **to set a.,** iniciar, poner en marcha
aforementioned /ə'fɔr,mɛnʃənd/ a antedicho, mencionado
aforesaid /ə'fɔr,sɛd/ a consabido, dicho, susodicho
afraid /ə'freid/ a espantado; temeroso, miedoso. **I'm a. that...,** Me temo que.... **to be a.,** tener miedo. **to make a.,** dar miedo (a)
afresh /ə'frɛʃ/ adv de nuevo, otra vez
African /'æfrɪkən/ a and n africano (-na)
African-American /'æfrɪkən ə'mɛrɪkən/ n afroamericano (-na)
aft /æft/ adv en popa; a popa. **fore and aft,** de proa a popa
after /'æftər/ prep (of place) detrás de; (of time) después de; (behind) en pos de; (following) tras; (in spite of) a pesar de; (in consequence of) después de, a consecuencia de; (in accordance with) según; (in the style of) al estilo de, en imitación de. adv (later) después, más tarde; (subsequently) después (que); (when) cuando, a futuro, venidero. **day a. day,** día tras día. **on the day a.,** al día siguiente. **soon a.,** poco después. **to look a.,** cuidar de. **to go a.,** ir a buscar; seguir. **the day a. tomorrow,** pasado mañana. **What are you a.?** ¿Qué buscas? **a. all,** después de todo. **a. the manner of,** a la moda de, según la moda de. **a. the style of,** al estilo de. **a.-dinner conversation,** conversación de sobremesa, f. **a. glow,** resplandor crepuscular, reflejo del sol poniente en el cielo, m. **a. life,** vida futura, f. **a. pains,** dolores de sobreparto, m pl. **a. taste,** dejo, resabio, m
afterbirth /'æftər,bɜrθ/ n placenta, f
aftermath /'æftər,mæθ/ n consecuencias, f pl, resultado, m
afternoon /,æftər'nun/ n tarde, f. **Good a.!** ¡Buenas tardes! **a. nap,** siesta, f
afterthought /'æftər,θɔt/ n reflexión tardía, f; segunda intención, f. **to have an a.,** pensar en segundo lugar
afterwards /'æftərwərdz/ adv después; más tarde
again /ə'gɛn/ adv (once more) otra vez, de neuvo; por segunda vez, dos veces; (on the other hand) por otra parte; (moreover) además; (likewise) también; (returned) de vuelta. Sometimes translated by prefix **re** in verbs. **as much a.,** otro tanto. **never a.,** nunca más, no más. **now and a.,** de vez en cuando. **to do a.,** volver a hacer, hacer de nuevo. **a. and a.,** repetidas veces
against /ə'gɛnst/ prep (facing) enfrente de; contra; (in preparation for) para; (contrary to) contrario a; (opposed to) opuesto a; (near) cerca de. **to be a.,** oponer; estar enfrente de. **a. the grain,** a contrapelo
agate /'ægɪt/ n ágata, f; heliotropo, m

age /eidʒ/ *n* edad, *f*; (generation) generación, *f*; (epoch) siglo, período, *m*; época, *f*; (old age) vejez, *f*; (majority) mayoría de edad, *f*, *vi* envejecer. **at any age,** a cualquier edad. **the golden age,** la edad de oro; (in literature, etc.) el siglo de oro. **from age to age,** por los siglos de los siglos. **to be of age,** ser mayor de edad. **to be under age,** ser menor de edad. **to come of age,** llegar a la mayoría de edad. **She is six years of age,** Ella tiene seis años. **age-old,** secular

aged /eidʒd; 'eidʒɪd/ *a* de la edad de; (old) anciano, viejo. **a girl a. four,** una niña de cuatro años

ageless /'eidʒlɪs/ *a* siempre joven; eterno

agency /'eidʒənsi/ *n* órgano, *m*, fuerza, *f*; acción, *f*; influencia, *f*; intervención, *f*; mediación, *f*; *Com.* agencia, *f*. **through the a. of,** por la mediación (or influencia) de

agenda /ə'dʒendə/ *n* agenda, *f*

agent /'eidʒənt/ *n* agente, *m*; *Com.* representante, *mf*; *Law.* apoderado (-da). **business a.,** agente de negocios, *m*

agglomerate /ə'glɒmə,reit/ *vt and vi* aglomerar(se)

agglomeration /ə,glɒmə'reiʃən/ *n* aglomeración, *f*

agglutinate /ə'glutn,eit/ *vt and vi* aglutinar(se)

aggrandize /ə'grændaiz/ *vt* engrandecer

aggrandizement /ə'grændɪzmənt/ *n* engrandecimiento, *m*

aggravate /'ægrə,veit/ *vt* agravar, hacer peor; intensificar; (annoy) irritar, exasperar

aggravating /'ægrə,veitɪŋ/ *a* agravante, agravador; (tiresome) molesto; (annoying) irritante. **a. circumstance,** circunstancia agravante, *f*

aggravation /,ægrə'veiʃən/ *n* agravación, *f*, intensificación, *f*; (annoyance) irritación, *f*

aggregate /'ægrɪgɪt, -,geit/ *a* total. *n* agregado, conjunto, *m*. **in the a.,** en conjunto

aggression /ə'grɛʃən/ *n* agresión, *f*

aggressive /ə'grɛsɪv/ *a* agresivo

aggressiveness /ə'grɛsɪvnɪs/ *n* carácter agresivo, *m*, belicosidad, *f*

aggressor /ə'grɛsər/ *a and n* agresor (-ra)

aggrieved /ə'grivd/ *a* afligido; ofendido; lastimero

aghast /ə'gæst/ *a* horrorizado, espantado; (amazed) estupefacto

agile /'ædʒəl/ *a* ágil; ligero, *Mexico* alacre; vivo

agility /æ'dʒɪlɪti/ *n* agilidad, *f*; ligereza, *f*, *Mexico* alacridad

agitate /'ædʒɪ,teit/ *vt* agitar; excitar; inquietar, perturbar; discutir. **to a. for,** luchar por; excitar la opinión pública en favor de

agitating /'ædʒɪ,teitɪŋ/ *a* agitador

agitation /,ædʒɪ'teiʃən/ *n* agitación, *f*; perturbación, *f*; discusión, *f*

agitator /'ædʒɪ,teitər/ *n* agitador (-ra); (apparatus) agitador, *m*

aglow /ə'glou/ *a and adv* brillante, fulgente; encendido

agnostic /æg'nɒstɪk/ *a and n* agnóstico (-ca)

agnosticism /æg'nɒstə,sɪzəm/ *n* agnosticismo, *m*

ago /ə'gou/ *adv* hace. **a short while ago,** hace poco. **How long ago?** ¿Cuánto tiempo hace? **long ago,** hace mucho. **many years ago,** hace muchos años. **I last saw him ten years ago,** La última vez que le vi fue hace diez años

agog /ə'gɒg/ *a* agitado; ansioso; excitado; impaciente; curioso. *adv* con agitación; con ansia; con curiosidad

agonize /'ægə,naiz/ *vt* atormentar. *vi* sufrir intensamente; retorcerse de dolor

agonizing /'ægə,naizɪŋ/ *a* (of pain) intenso, atormentador

agonizingly /'ægə,naizɪŋli/ *adv* dolorosamente

agony /'ægəni/ *n* agonía, *f*; angustia, *f*; paroxismo, *m*. **a. column,** columna de los suspiros, *f*

agrarian /ə'grɛəriən/ *a* agrario

agree /ə'gri/ *vi* estar de acuerdo. **Do you a.?** ¿Estás de acuerdo?; convenir (en); acordar; ponerse de acuerdo, entenderse; (suit) sentar bien, probar; (consent) consentir (en); *Gram.* concordar, (get on well) llevarse bien; (correspond) estar conforme (con). **to**

a. to, convenir en, consentir en. **to a. with,** estar de acuerdo con, apoyar; dar la razón a; (suit) sentar bien; *Gram.* concordar

agreeable /ə'griəbəl/ *a* agradable; afable, amable; (pleasant) ameno, grato; conforme; dispuesto a (hacer algo); conveniente

agreeableness /ə'griəbəlnɪs/ *n* (of persons) afabilidad, amabilidad, *f*; amenidad, *f*; deleite, *m*; conformidad, *f*

agreeably /ə'griəbli/ *adv* agradablemente; de acuerdo (con), conforme (a)

agreed /ə'grid/ *a* convenido, acordado; (approved) aprobado. *interj* ¡convenido! ¡de acuerdo!

agreement /ə'grimənt/ *n* acuerdo, *m*; pacto, *m*; acomodamiento, concierto, *m*; contrato, *m*; *Com.* convenio, *m*; conformidad, *f*; consentimiento, *m*; *Gram.* concordancia, *f*. **in a.,** conforme. **in a. with,** de acuerdo con; según. **to reach an a.,** ponerse de acuerdo

agricultural /,ægrɪ'kʌltʃərəl/ *a* agrícola. **a. engineer,** ingeniero agrónomo, *m*. **a. laborer,** labriego, *m*. **a. show,** exposición agrícola, *f*

agriculturalist /,ægrɪ'kʌltʃərəlɪst/ *n* agrícola, *mf*

agriculture /'ægrɪ,kʌltʃər/ *n* agricultura, *f*

agronomist /ə'grɒnəmɪst/ *n* agrónomo, *m*

agronomy /ə'grɒnəmi/ *n* agronomía, *f*

aground /ə'graund/ *adv* *Naut.* varado, encallado. **running a.,** varada, *f*. **to run a.,** varar

ague /'eigyu/ *n* fiebre intermitente, *f*; *Fig.* escalofrío, *m*

ah! /ɑ/ *interj* ¡ah! ¡ay!

aha! /ɑ'hɑ/ *interj* ¡ajá!

ahead /ə'hɛd/ *adv* delante; enfrente; al frente (de); a la cabeza (de); adelante; hacia delante; *Naut.* por la proa. **Go a.!** ¡Adelante! **It is straight a.,** Está derecho. **to go straight a.,** ir hacia delante; seguir (haciendo algo)

ahoy! /ə'hɔi/ *interj* ¡ah del barco!

aid /eid/ *n* ayuda, *f*; socorro, auxilio, *m*; subsidio, *m*. *vt* ayudar; socorrer, auxiliar. **in aid of,** pro, en beneficio de. **first aid,** primera cura, *f*. **first aid post,** puesto de socorro, *m*. **to come or go to the aid of,** acudir en defensa de

aide-de-camp /'eid də 'kæmp/ *n* edecán, *m*

AIDS /eidz/ *n* el SIDA, *m*

ail /eil/ *vt* afligir, doler; pasar. *vi* estar indispuesto (or enfermo). **What ails you?** *Inf.* ¿Qué te pasa?

ailing /'eilɪŋ/ *a* enfermizo, enclenque, achacoso

ailment /'eilmənt/ *n* enfermedad, *f*, achaque, *m*

aim /eim/ *n* (of firearms) puntería, *f*; (mark) blanco, *m*; *Fig.* objeto, fin, *m*; *Fig.* intención, *f*, propósito, *m*, *vt* (a gun) apuntar; dirigir; (throw) lanzar; (a blow) asestar. *vi* apuntar (a); (a remark at) decir por; aspirar (a); intentar, proponerse. **Is your remark aimed at me?** ¿Lo dices por mí? **to aim high,** apuntar alto; *Inf.* picar alto. **to miss one's aim,** errar el tiro. **to take aim,** apuntar. **with the aim of,** con objeto de, a fin de

aimless /'eimlɪs/ *a,* **aimlessly,** *adv* sin objeto, a la ventura

air /ɛər/ *n* aire, *m*, (all meanings). **by air,** en avión; (of mail) por avión; (of goods) por vía aérea. **in the air,** al aire; al aire libre; (as though flying) en volandas. **in the open air,** al aire libre, al fresco, a la intemperie. **to be on the air,** *Radio.* hablar por radio. **to give oneself airs,** darse tono, tener humos. **to take the air,** tomar el fresco; despegar. **air balloon,** globo aerostático, *m*; (toy) globo, *m*. **air-base,** base aérea, *f*. **air-bed,** colchón de viento, *m*. **air-borne (to become),** levantar el vuelo, despegar. **air-brake,** *Mech.* freno neumático, *m*. **air-chamber,** cámara de aire, *f*. **air chief marshal,** general del ejército del aire, *m*. **air-cock,** válvula de escape de aire, *f*. **air commodore,** general de brigada de aviación, *m*. **air conditioning,** purificación de aire, *f*, *Lat. Am.* aclimación. **air-cooled,** enfriado por aire. **air crash,** accidente de aviación, *m*. **air current,** corriente de aire, *f*. **air-cushion,** almohadilla neumática, *f*. **air-field,** campo de aviación, *m*. **air fleet,** flotilla aérea, *f*. **air force,** fuerza aérea, flota aérea, *f*. **air-gun,** escopeta de viento, *f*. **air-hole,** respiradero, *m*. **air-hostess,** azafata, *f*. **air-lift,** puente aéreo, *m*. **air-liner,** avión de pasajeros, *m.* **airline** linea aérea, aerolínea, *f.* **airmail,** correo aéreo, *m.* **by airmail,** por avión. **air marshal,** teniente general de aviación, *m.* **air-pocket,** bolsa (or vacío, *m*) de aire, *f.* **air pollution** contaminación atmosférica, *f.* **air pump,** bomba neumática, *f.* **air raid,** bombardeo aéreo, *m.* **air-raid shelter,** refugio antiaéreo, *m.* **air-raid warning,** alarma aérea, *f.* **airroute,** vía aérea, *f.* **air-screw,** hélice de avión, *f.* **airshaft,** respiradero de mina, *m.* **air shuttle,** puente aéreo, *m.* **air squadron,** escuadrilla aérea, *f.* **air stream,** chorro de aire, *m.* **air taxi,** avión taxi, *m.* **air-tight,** herméticamente cerrado. **air valve,** válvula de aire, *f.* **air vice-marshal,** general de división de aviación, *m*

air /εər/ *vt* airear, orear; secar al aire; ventilar; *Fig.* sacar a lucir, emitir; *Fig.* ostentar

aircraft /'εər,kræft/ *n* aeronave, avión, *m.* **a. barrage,** cortina de fuego de artillería, *f.* **a.-carrier,** portaaviones, *m.* **a. factory,** fábrica de aeroplanos, *f*

airily /'εərəli/ *adv* ligeramente, sin preocuparse; alegremente

airiness /'εərinıs/ *n* airosidad, *f*; ventilación, *f*; situación airosa, *f*; (lightness) ligereza, *f*; alegría, *f*; frivolidad, *f*

airing /'εərıŋ/ *n* aireación, *f*; ventilación, *f*; secamiento, *m*; (walk) vuelta, *f*, paseo, *m.* **to take an a.,** dar una vuelta

airless /'εərlıs/ *a* sin aire; falto de ventilación; sofocante

airman /'εərmən/ *n* aviador, *m*

airplane /'εər,plein/ *n* aeroplano, avión, *m.* **jet-propelled a.,** aeroplano de reacción, *m.* **model a.,** aeroplano en miniatura, *m*

airport /'εər,pɔrt/ *n* aeropuerto, *m*

airsick /'εər,sık/ *a* mareado en el aire, mareado

airway /'εər,wei/ *n* vía aérea, *f*

airwoman /'εər,wʊmən/ *n* aviadora, *f*

airy /'εəri/ *a* aéreo; (breezy) airoso; ligero; vaporoso; alegre; (vain) vano; (flippant) frívolo

aisle /ail/ *n* nave lateral, ala, *f*

ajar /ə'dʒɑr/ *a* entreabierto, entornado. **to leave a.,** dejar entreabierto, entornar

akimbo /ə'kımbou/ *adv* en jarras. **with arms a.,** con los brazos en jarras

akin /ə'kın/ *a* consanguíneo, emparentado; análogo, relacionado; semejante

alabaster /'ælə,bæstər/ *n* alabastro, *m*, *a* alabastrino

alacrity /ə'lækrıti/ *n* alacridad, *f*

alarm /ə'lɑrm/ *n* alarma, *f*, toque de alarma, *m*; (tocsin) rebato, *m*; sobresalto, *m*, alarma, *f.* *vt* alarmar; *Mil.* dar la alarma (a); asustar. **to give the a.,** dar la alarma. **a. bell,** timbre de alarma, *m.* **a. clock,** despertador, *m.* **a. signal,** señal de alarma, *f*

alarming /ə'lɑrmıŋ/ *a* alarmante

alarmingly /ə'lɑrmıŋli/ *adv* de un modo alarmante; espantosamente

alarmist /ə'lɑrmıst/ *n* alarmista, *mf*

alas! /ə'læs/ *interj* ¡ay!

alb /ælb/ *n* alba, *f*

Albanian /æl'beiniən/ *a* and *n* albanés (-esa); (language) albanés, *m*

albatross /'ælbə,trɔs/ *n* albatros, *m*

albeit /ɔl'biit/ *conjunc* aunque, si bien; sin embargo

albinism /'ælbə,nızəm/ *n* albinismo, *m*

albino /æl'bainou/ *a* albino, *m*

album /'ælbəm/ *n* álbum, *m*

albumin /æl'byumən/ *n* albúmina, *f*

alchemist /'ælkəmıst/ *n* alquimista, *m*

alchemy /'ælkəmi/ *n* alquimia, *f*

alcohol /'ælkə,hɔl/ *n* alcohol, *m.* **industrial a.,** alcohol desnaturalizado, *m.* **wood a.,** alcohol metílico, alcohol de madera, *m*

alcoholic /,ælkə'hɔlık/ *a* alcohólico

alcoholism /'ælkəhɔ,lızəm/ *n* alcoholismo, *m*

alcove /'ælkouv/ *n* alcoba, *f*; nicho, *m*

alder /'ɔldər/ *n* (tree and wood) aliso, *m*

alderman /'ɔldərmən/ *n* concejal, *m*

ale /eil/ *n* cerveza, *f.* **ale-house,** cervecería, *f*

alert /ə'lɜrt/ *a* alerto; vigilante; despierto; vivo. *n* si-

rena, *f.* **to be on the a.,** estar sobre aviso; estar vigilante

alertly /ə'lɜrtli/ *adv* alertamente

alertness /ə'lɜrtnıs/ *n* vigilancia, *f*; viveza, *f*; prontitud, *f*

Alexandria /,ælıg'zændriə/ Alejandría, *f*

algae /'ældʒi/ *n* algas, *f pl*

algebra /'ældʒəbrə/ *n* álgebra, *f*

algebraic /,ældʒə'breiık/ *a* algebraico

Algeria /æl'dʒɪəriə/ Argelia, *f*

Algerian /æl'dʒɪəriən/ *a* and *n* argelino (-na)

Algiers /æl'dʒɪərz/ Argel, *m*

alias /'eiliəs/ *adv* alias, por otro nombre. *n* nombre falso, seudónimo, *m*

alibi /'ælə,bai/ *n* *Law.* coartada, *f.* **to prove an a.,** probar la coartada

alien /'eiliən/ *a* ajeno; (foreign) extranjero; extraño; contrario. *n* extranjero (-ra). **a. to,** ajeno a; repugnante a

alienable /'eiliənəbəl/ *a* enajenable

alienate /'eiliə,neit/ *vt* alejar, hacer indiferente; (property) enajenar, traspasar

alienation /,eiliə'neiʃən/ *n* desvío, *m*; enajenación, *f*; traspaso, *m*; enajenación mental, *f*

alight /ə'lait/ *vi* apearse (de), bajar (de); desmontar (de); (of birds, etc.) posarse (sobre)

align /ə'lain/ *vt* alinear

alignment /ə'lainmənt/ *n* alineación, *f*

alike /ə'laik/ *a* semejante; igual. *adv* del mismo modo; igualmente

alimentary /,ælə'mɛntəri/ *a* nutritivo; alimenticio. **a. canal,** tubo digestivo, *m*

alimentation /,æləmɛn'teiʃən/ *n* alimentación, *f*

alimony /'ælə,mouni/ *n* *Law.* alimentos, *m pl*, pensión alimenticia, *f*

alive /ə'laiv/ *a* viviente; vivo; del mundo; (busy) animado, concurrido; (aware) sensible; (alert) lleno de vida, enérgico, despierto. **He is still a.,** Aún vive. **He is the best man a.,** Es el mejor hombre que existe, Es el mejor hombre del mundo. **half-a.,** semivivo. **while a.,** en vida. **a. to,** consciente de, sensible de. **a. with,** plagado de, lleno de

alkali /'ælkə,lai/ *n* álcali, *m*

alkaline /'ælkə,lain/ *a* alcalino

alkaloid /'ælkə,lɔid/ *n* alcaloide, *m*

all /ɔl/ *a* todo, *m*; toda, *f*; todos, *m pl*; todas, *f pl*; (in games) iguales. *adv* enteramente, completamente; del todo; absolutamente. **after all,** después de todo; sin embargo. **at all,** nada; de ninguna manera; en absoluto. **fifteen all,** (tennis) quince iguales. **for good and all,** para siempre. **if that's all,** si no es más que eso. **in all,** en conjunto. **It is all one to me,** Me da igual. **not at all,** de ningún modo, nada de eso; nada; (never) jamás; (as a polite formula) No hay de qué. **once for all,** una vez por todas; por última vez. **That is all,** Eso es todo. **all along,** (of time) siempre, todo el tiempo; (of place) a lo largo de. **all to an extremo a otro de. all but,** (almost) casi, por poco; (except) todo menos. **all joking aside,** fuera de burla. **all of them,** todos ellos, *m pl*; todas ellas, *f pl*. **All right!** ¡Bien! ¡Está bien! ¡Entendido! **all that,** todo eso; (as much as) cuanto. **all that which,** todo lo que. **all those who,** todos los que, *m pl*; todas las que, *f pl*. **all the more,** cuanto más. **all the same,** sin embargo, a pesar de todo. **all the worse,** tanto peor

all /ɔl/ *n* todo, *m*; todos, *m pl*; todas, *f pl*; (everyone, all men) todo el mundo. **to lose one's all,** perder todo lo que se tiene. **All is lost,** Todo se ha perdido. **all told,** en conjunto

all /ɔl/ (*in compounds*) **all-absorbing,** que todo lo absorbe; sumamente interesante. **all-bountiful,** de suma bondad. **all-conquering,** invicto. **all-consuming,** que todo lo consume; irresistible; ardiente. **all-enduring,** resignado a todo. **All Fools' Day,** Día de los Inocentes, *m*, (December 28). **all-fours,** a cuatro patas; a gatas. **to go on all fours,** andar a gatas. **All hail!** ¡Salud! ¡Bienvenido! **all-important,** sumamente importante. **all-in insurance,** seguro contra todo riesgo, *m.* **all-in wrestling,** lucha libre, *f.* **all-loving,** de un amor infinito. **all-merciful,** de una compasión infinita, sumamente misericordioso. **all-powerful,** omnipotente, todo poderoso. **all-round,** completo, cabal; universal. **an all-round athlete,** un atleta completo. **All Souls' Day,** Día de las Ánimas, Día de los difuntos, *m.* **all-wise,** omniscio

allay /ə'leɪ/ *vt* calmar; (relieve) aliviar; apaciguar

allaying /ə'leɪɪŋ/ *n* alivio, *m;* apaciguamiento, *m*

allegation /ˌælɪ'geɪʃən/ *n* alegación, *f*

allege /ə'ledʒ/ *vt* afirmar, declarar; alegar

allegiance /ə'lidʒəns/ *n* lealtad, *f;* fidelidad, *f;* obediencia, *f*

allegorical /ˌælɪ'gɔrɪkəl/ *a* alegórico

allegory /'ælə,gɔri/ *n* alegoría, *f*

alleluia /ˌælə'luyə/ *n* aleluya, *mf*

allergic /ə'lərdʒɪk/ *a* alérgico

allergist /'ælərdʒɪst/ *n* alergólogo, *m*

allergy /'ælərdʒi/ *n* alergia, *f*

alleviate /ə'livi,eit/ *vt* aliviar

alleviation /ə,livi'eiʃən/ *n* alivio, *m;* mitigación, *f*

alley /'æli/ *n* callejuela, *f,* callejón, *m;* (skittle a.) pista de bolos, *f.* **a.-way,** *Naut.* pasadizo, *m*

alliance /ə'laiəns/ *n* alianza, *f;* parentesco, *m*

allied /'ælaid/ *a* aliado; allegado

alligator /'ælɪ,geitər/ *n* caimán, *m*

alliteration /ə,lɪtə'reiʃən/ *n* aliteración, *f*

allocate /'ælə,keit/ *vt* asignar, destinar; distribuir, repartir

allocation /,ælə'keiʃən/ *n* asignación, *f;* distribución, *f,* repartimiento, *m*

allotment /ə'lɒtmənt/ *n* repartimiento, *m,* distribución, *f;* porción, *f;* lote, *m;* parcela de tierra, huerta, *f*

allow /ə'lau/ *vt* permitir; autorizar; dejar; tolerar, sufrir; (provide) dar; conceder, otorgar; (acknowledge) admitir; confesar; (a pension) hacer; deducir. **to a. for,** tener en cuenta; ser indulgente con; deducir; dejar (espacio, etc.) para

allowable /ə'lauəbəl/ *a* admisible, permisible; lícito, legítimo

allowance /ə'lauəns/ *n* ración, *f;* (discount) descuento, *m;* pensión, *f;* concesión, *f,* excusa, *f;* (subsidy) subsidio, *m;* (bonus) abono, *m;* (monthly) mesada, *f.* **to make a. for,** tener presente; hacer excusas para, ser indulgente con

alloy /*n* 'ælɔi, *v* ə'lɔi/ *n* aleación, *f;* liga, *f;* mezcla, *f. vt* alear, ligar; mezclar

allspice /'ɔl,spais/ *n* guindilla de Indias, *f*

all-star game /'ɔl,star/ *n* juego de estrellas, *m*

allude /ə'lud/ *vi* aludir (a), referirse (a)

allure /ə'lʊr/ *vt* convidar, provocar; atraer; seducir, fascinar

allurement /ə'lʊrmənt/ *n* (snare) añagaza, *f;* atracción, *f;* tentación, seducción, *f*

alluring /ə'lʊrɪŋ/ *a* atractivo, seductor, tentador; (promising) halagüeño

allusion /ə'luʒən/ *n* alusión, referencia, *f;* insinuación, *f*

allusive /ə'lusɪv/ *a* alusivo

ally /*n* 'ælai, *v* ə'lai/ *n* aliado (-da), allegado (-da); asociado (-da); (state) aliado, *m. vt* unir. **to become allies,** aliarse

almanac /'ɔlmə,næk/ *n* almanaque, *m*

almighty /ɔl'maiti/ *a* omnipotente

almond /'amənd/ *n* almendra, *f;* (tree) almendro, *m.* **bitter a.,** almendra amarga, *f.* **green a.,** almendruco, *m.* **milk of almonds,** horchata de almendras, *f;* (for the hands) loción de almendras, *f.* **sugar a.,** almendra garapiñada, *f.* **a.-eyed,** con, or de, ojos rasgados. **a. paste,** pasta de almendras, *f.* **a.-shaped,** en forma de almendra, almendrado

almoner /'ælmənər, 'amə-/ *n* limosnero (-ra) *mf*

almost /'ɔlmoust/ *adv* casi; por poco

alms /amz/ *n* limosna, *f.* **to ask a.,** pedir limosna, mendigar. **to give a.,** dar limosna. **a.-box,** cepillo de limosna, *m*

almsgiving /'amz,gɪvɪŋ/ *n* caridad, *f*

aloe /'ælou/ *n* áloe, *m;* *pl* **aloes,** *Med.* acíbar, *m*

aloft /ə'lɔft/ *adv* arriba, en alto

alone /ə'loun/ *a* solo; solitario. *adv* a solas, sin compañía; solamente; únicamente. **to leave a.,** dejar solo; dejar en paz

along /ə'lɔŋ/ *adv* a lo largo; todo el tiempo. *prep* a lo

largo de; por; al lado (de); en compañía (de). **Come a.!** ¡Ven! **all a.,** todo el tiempo, desde el principio; a lo largo de. **a. with,** junto con; en compañía de

alongside /ə'lɔŋ'said/ *adv* al lado; *Naut.* al costado. *prep* junto a, al lado de; *Naut.* al costado de. **to bring a.,** *Naut.* abarloar. **to come a.,** *Naut.* acostarse

aloof /ə'luf/ *adv* a distancia; lejos. *a* altanero, esquivo; reservado. **to keep a.,** mantenerse alejado

aloofness /ə'lufnɪs/ *n* alejamiento, *m;* esquivez, *f;* reserva, *f*

aloud /ə'laud/ *adv* en alta voz, alto

alpaca /æl'pækə/ *n* alpaca, *f*

alphabet /'ælfə,bet/ *n* alfabeto, *m;* abecedario, *m*

alphabetical /,ælfə'betɪkəl/ *a* alfabético

Alpine /'ælpain/ *a* alpestre, alpino

Alps, the /'ælps/ los Alpes, *m*

already /ɔl'redi/ *adv* ya; previamente

Alsatian /æl'seiʃən/ *a* and *n* alsaciano (-nat. **A. dog,** perro policía, perro pastor alemán, perro lobo, *m*

also /'ɔlsou/ *adv* también, igualmente, además

altar /'ɔltər/ *n* altar, *m.* **high a.,** altar mayor, *m.* **to lead a woman to the a.,** llevar a una mujer a la iglesia. **a.-cloth,** mantel del altar, *m.* **a.-piece,** retablo, *m.* **a.-rail,** mesa del altar, *f*

altar boy *n* acólito, monaguillo, *m*

altar girl *n* acólita, monaguilla, *f*

altar server *n* acólito, monaguillo, *m* (male), acólita, monaguilla, *f* (female)

alter /'ɔltər/ *vt* cambiar; alterar; modificar; corregir; transformar; (clothes) arreglar. *vi* cambiar

alterable /'ɔltərəbəl/ *a* alterable

alteration /,ɔltə'reiʃən/ *n* cambio, *m,* alteración, *f;* modificación, *f;* corrección, *f;* innovación, *f;* (to buildings, etc.) reforma, *f;* renovación, *f;* arreglo, *m*

altercation /,ɔltər'keiʃən/ *n* altercación, *f*

alternate /*a* 'ɔltərnɪt/ *v* -,neit/ *a* alternativo; (Bot. and of rhymes) alterno. *vt* and *vi* alternar

alternately /'ɔltərnɪtli/ *adv* alternativamente; por turno

alternating /'ɔltər,neitɪŋ/ *a* alternador. **a. current,** *Elec.* corriente alterna, *f*

alternation /,ɔltər'neiʃən/ *n* alternación, *f;* (of time) transcurso, *m;* turno, *m*

alternative /ɔl'tərnətɪv/ *n* alternativa, *f,* a alternativo, alterno. **to have no a. but,** no poder menos de

alternatively /ɔl'tərnətɪvli/ *adv* alternativamente

alternative medicine *n* medicina alternativa; salud natural, *f*

alternator /'ɔltər,neitər/ *n Elec.* alternador, *m*

although /ɔl'ðou/ *conjunc* aunque, bien que; si bien; no obstante, a pesar de

altimeter /æl'tɪmɪtər/ *n Aer.* altímetro, *m*

altitude /'æltɪ,tud/ *n* altitud, elevación, *f;* altura, *f*

alto /'æltou/ *n* (voice) contralto, *m;* (singer) contralto, *mf;* viola, *f*

altogether /,ɔltə'geðər/ *adv* completamente; del todo; en conjunto

altruism /'æltru,ɪzəm/ *n* altruismo, *m*

altruist /'æltruɪst/ *n* altruista, *mf*

aluminum /ə'lumənəm/ *n* aluminio, *m*

aluminum foil *n* hoja de aluminio, *f*

alumna /ə'lʌmnə/ *n Lat. Am.* exalumna, *f*

alumnus /ə'lʌmnəs/ *n Lat. Am.* exalumno, *m*

always /'ɔlweiz/ *adv* siempre

amalgam /ə'mælgəm/ *n* amalgama, *f;* mezcla, *f*

amalgamate /ə'mælgə,meit/ *vt* amalgamar; combinar, unir. *vi* amalgamarse; combinarse, unirse

amalgamation /ə,mælgə'meiʃən/ *n* amalgamación, *f;* combinación, *f;* mezcla, *f*

amanuensis /ə,mænyu'ɛnsɪs/ *n* amanuense, *f;* secretario (-ia)

amass /ə'mæs/ *vt* acumular, amontonar

amateur /'æmə,tʃʊr/ *n* a aficionado (-da), (sports) no profesional. **a. theatricals,** función de aficionados, *f.* **a. band,** *Mexico* escoleta, *f*

amateurish /'æmə,tʃʊrɪʃ/ *a* no profesional; de aficionado; superficial; (clumsy) torpe

amatory /'æmə,tɔri/ *a* amatorio

amaze /ə'meiz/ *vt* asombrar, sorprender; pasmar; confundir

amazed /ə'meizd/ a asombrado; sorprendido; admirado; asustado

amazement /ə'meizmənt/ n asombro, pasmo, m; sorpresa, f; (wonderment) admiración, f; estupor, m

amazing /ə'meiziŋ/ a asombroso, pasmoso; sorprendente

amazingly /ə'meiziŋli/ adv asombrosamente

Amazon /'æmə,zɒn/ n amazona, f

Amazon River, the el (Río de las) Amazonas, m

ambassador /æm'bæsədər/ n embajador (-ra)

amber /'æmbər/ n ámbar, m, a ambarino

ambidextrous /ˌæmbɪ'dɛkstrəs/ a ambidextro

ambiguity /ˌæmbɪ'gyuɪti/ n ambigüedad, f

ambiguous /æm'bɪgyuəs/ a ambiguo, equivoco

ambition /æm'bɪʃən/ n ambición, f

ambitious /æm'bɪʃəs/ a ambicioso. **to be a. to,** ambicionar

amble /'æmbəl/ n (of a horse) paso de andadura, f; paso lento, m. vi (of a horse) andar a paso de andadura; andar lentamente

ambulance /'æmbyələns/ n ambulancia, f. **a. corps,** cuerpo de sanidad, m. **a. man,** sanitario, m

ambulatory /'æmbyələ,tɔri/ n paseo, m; claustro, m, a ambulante

ambush /'æmbʊʃ/ n acecho, m, asechanza, f; Mil. emboscada, f. vt acechar, asechar; Mil. emboscar; sorprender. **to be in a.,** emboscarse, estar en acecho

amelioration /ə,milyə'reiʃən/ n mejora, f

amen /'ei'mɛn, 'ɑ'mɛn/ n amén, m

amenable /ə'minəbəl/ a sujeto (a); responsable; dócil; fácil de convencer, dispuesto a ser razonable; dispuesto a escuchar. **to make a. to reason,** hacer razonable

amend /ə'mɛnd/ vt enmendar; modificar. vi reformarse

amendment /ə'mɛndmənt/ n enmienda, f; modificación, f

amends /ə'mɛndz/ n pl reparación, f; satisfacción, f; compensación, f. **to make a.,** dar satisfacción

amenity /ə'mɛniti/ n amenidad, f

America /ə'mɛrɪkə/ América, f

American /ə'mɛrɪkən/ n americano (-na); (U.S.A.) norteamericano (-na), Lat. Am. estadounidense. a americano, de América; norteamericano, de los Estados Unidos. **Central A.,** a and n centroamericano (-na). **A. bar,** bar americano, m

Americanism /ə'mɛrɪkə,nɪzəm/ n americanismo, m

Americanize /ə'mɛrɪkə,naiz/ vt americanizar

amethyst /'æməθɪst/ n amatista, f

amiability /ˌeimiə'bɪliti/ n amabilidad, afabilidad, cordialidad, f

amiable /'eimiəbəl/ a amable, afable, cordial

amiably /'eimiəbli/ adv amablemente, con afabilidad

amianthus /ˌæmi'ænθəs/ n amianto, m

amicable /'æmɪkəbəl/ a amigable, amistoso

amice /'æmɪs/ n amito, m

amid, amidst /ə'mɪd; ə'mɪdst/ prep en medio de; entre; rodeado por

amidships /ə'mɪd,ʃɪps/ adv en el centro del buque, en medio del navío

amiss /ə'mɪs/ adv mal; de más; (ill) indispuesto, enfermo; (inopportunely) inoportunamente. a malo

ammeter /'æm,mitər/ n Elec. amperímetro, m

ammonia /ə'mounyə/ n amoníaco, m

ammoniacal /ˌæmə'naiəkəl/ a amoniacal

ammunition /ˌæmyə'nɪʃən/ n munición, f. **a. box,** cajón de municiones, m

amnesia /æm'niʒə/ n amnesia, f

amnesty /'æmnɛsti/ n amnistía, f. **to concede an a. to,** amnistiar

amok /ə'mʌk/ **(to run a.)** atacar a ciegas

among /ə'mʌŋ/ prep en medio de; entre; con

amoral /ei'mɔrəl/ a amoral

amorality /ˌeimə'ræliti/ n amoralidad, f

amorous /'æmərəs/ a amoroso; (tender) tierno

amorousness /'æmərəsnɪs/ n erotismo, m; galantería, f

amorphous /ə'mɔrfəs/ a amorfo

amortization /ˌæmərtə'zeiʃən/ n amorcización, f

amortize /'æmər,taiz/ vt amortizar

amount /ə'maunt/ n importe, m, suma, f; cantidad, f. vi (to) subir a, ascender a, llegar a; valer; reducirse a. **gross a.,** importe bruto, m. **net a.,** importe líquido, importe neto, m. **It amounts to the same thing, then,** Es igual entonces, Viene a ser lo mismo pues. **What he says amounts to this,** Lo que dice se reduce a esto

amperage /'æmpərɪdʒ/ n amperaje, m

ampere /'æmpɪər/ n amper, amperio, m

amphibian /æm'fɪbiən/ n anfibio, m

amphibious /æm'fɪbiəs/ a anfibio

amphitheater /'æmfə,θiətər/ n anfiteatro, m

amphora /'æmfərə/ n ánfora, f

ample /'æmpəl/ a amplio; abundante; extenso, vasto; (sufficient) bastante, suficiente

amplification /ˌæmpləfɪ'keiʃən/ n amplificación, f

amplifier /'æmplə,faiər/ n amplificador, m

amplify /'æmplə,fai/ vt amplificar; aumentar, ampliar

amplitude /'æmplɪ,tud/ n amplitud, f; abundancia, f; extensión, f

amply /'æmpli/ adv ampliamente; abundantemente; suficientemente

amputate /'æmpyʊ,teit/ vt amputar

amputation /ˌæmpyʊ'teiʃən/ n amputación, f

amulet /'æmyəlɪt/ n amuleto, m

amuse /ə'myuz/ vt divertir, entretener, distraer. **to a. oneself,** divertirse; pasarlo bien

amusement /ə'myuzmənt/ n diversión, f, entretenimiento, m; (hobby) pasatiempo, m. **a. park,** parque de atracciones, m

amusing /ə'myuziŋ/ a divertido, entretenido; (of people) salado

amusingly /ə'myuziŋli/ adv de un modo divertido, entretenidamente

an. /ən/ See **a**

Anabaptism /ˌænə'bæptɪzəm/ n anabaptismo, m

Anabaptist /ˌænə'bæptɪst/ n anabaptista, mf

anachronism /ə'nækrə,nɪzəm/ n anacronismo, m

anachronistic /ə,nækrə'nɪstɪk/ a anacrónico

anagram /'ænə,græm/ n anagrama, m

analects /'ænl,ɛkts/ n pl analectas, f pl

analgesia /ˌænl'dʒiziə/ n analgesia, f

analgesic /ˌænl'dʒizɪk/ a and n analgésico, m

analogous /ə'næləgəs/ a análogo

analogy /ə'nælədʒi/ n analogía, f

analysis /ə'næləsɪs/ n análisis, m

analyst /'ænlɪst/ n analista, mf

analytical /ˌænl'ɪtɪkəl/ a analítico

analyze /'ænl,aiz/ vt analizar

anaphora /ə'næfərə/ n anáfora, f

anaphrodisiac /æn,æfrə'dizi,æk/ a anafrodisíaco

anarchic /æn'ɑrkɪk/ a anárquico

anarchism /'ænər,kɪzəm/ n anarquismo, m

anarchist /'ænərkɪst/ n anarquista, mf

anarchy /'ænərki/ n anarquía, f

anastigmatic /ˌænəstɪg'mætɪk/ a anastigmático

anathema /ə'næθəmə/ n anatema, mf

anathematize /ə'næθəmə,taiz/ vt anatematizar

anatomic /ˌænə'tɒmɪk/ a anatómico

anatomically /ˌænə'tɒmɪkli/ adv anatómicamente; físicamente

anatomist /ə'nætəmɪst/ n anatomista, mf

anatomy /ə'nætəmi/ n anatomía, f

ancestor /'ænsɛstər/ n antepasado, abuelo, m

ancestral /æn'sɛstrəl/ a de sus antepasados; de familia; hereditario. **a. home,** casa solariega, f

ancestry /'ænsɛstri/ n antepasados, m pl; linaje, abolengo, m; estirpe, f; nacimiento, m; origen, m

anchor /'æŋkər/ n ancla, f. Fig. áncora, f. vt sujetar con el ancla. vi anclar, echar anclas, fondear. a. **drag a.,** ancla flotante, ancla de arrastre, f. **sheet a.,** ancla de la esperanza, f; Fig. ancla de salvación, f. **to drop a.,** anclar. **to ride at a.,** estar al ancla. **to weigh a.,** levar el ancla

anchorage /'æŋkərɪdʒ/ n anclaje, m; ancladero, fondeadero, m; derechos de anclaje, m pl

anchovy /'æntʃouvi/ n anchoa, f, boquerón, m

ancient /'einʃənt/ a anciano; antiguo. n pl **ancients,**

los antiguos. **from** a. **times,** de antiguo. **most** a., antiquísimo

and /ænd, ənd/ *conjunc* y; (before stressed i or hi) e; (after some verbs and before infin.) de, a; que; (with) con; (often not translated before infins.). **Better and better,** Mejor que mejor. **I shall try and do it,** Trataré de hacerlo. **to come and see,** venir a ver. **We shall try and speak to him,** Procuraremos hablar con él

Andalusia /,ændḷ'uʒə/ Andalucía, *f*

Andalusian /,ændḷ'uʒən/ *a* andaluz. *n* andaluz (-za). **A. hat,** sombrero calañés, *m*

Andean /'ændiən/ *a* andino (-na), *Argentina, Chile also* corderillano (-na)

Andes, the /'ændiz/ los Andes, *f*

andiron /'ænd,aiᵊrn/ *n* morillo, *m*

Andorran /æn'dɔrən/ *a* and *n* andorrano (-na)

androgynous /æn'drɒdʒənəs/ *a* andrógino

anecdotal /'ænɪk,doutḷ/ *a* anecdótico

anecdote /'ænɪk,dout/ *n* anécdota, *f*

anemia /ə'nimiə/ *n* anemia, *f*

anemic /ə'nimɪk/ *a* anémico

anemometer /,ænə'mɒmɪtər/ *n* anemómetro, *m*

anemone /ə'nɛmə,ni/ *n* anémona, anémone, *f*

aneroid /'ænə,rɔid/ *a* aneroide. *n* barómetro aneroide, *m*

anesthesia /,ænəs'θiʒə/ *n* anestesia, *f*

anesthetic /,ænəs'θɛtɪk/ *a* and *n* anestésico, *m*.

anesthetist /ə'nɛsθɪtɪst/ *n* anestesiador (-ra)

anesthetize /ə'nɛsθɪ,taiz/ *vt* anestesiar

aneurism /'ænyə,rɪzəm/ *n* aneurisma, *mf*

angel /'eindʒəl/ *n* ángel, *m*

angelic /æn'dʒɛlɪk/ *a* angélico

angelica /æn'dʒɛlɪkə/ *n* angélica, *f*

anger /'æŋgər/ *n* cólera, ira, *f*, enojo, *m*, *vt* enojar, encolerizar; hacer rabiar, *Mexico* amuinar

angina /æn'dʒainə/ *n* angina, *f*. **a. pectoris,** angina de pecho, *f*

angle /'æŋgəl/ *n* ángulo, *m*; rincón, *m*; esquina, *f*; (of a roof) caballette, *m*; *Fig.* punto de vista, *m*, *vi* pescar con caña. **at an a.,** a un lado. **a.-iron,** hierro angular, *m*. **to a. for,** pescar; *Fig.* procurar obtener

Angle /'æŋgəl/ *a* and *n* anglo (-la)

angler /'æŋglər/ *n* pescador (-ra) de caña

Anglican /'æŋglɪkən/ *a* and *n* anglicano (-na)

Anglicanism /'æŋglɪkə,nɪzəm/ *n* anglicanismo, *m*

Anglicism /'æŋglə,sɪzəm/ *n* anglicismo, inglesismo, *m*

Anglicize /'æŋglə,saiz/ *vt* inglesar

angling /'æŋglɪŋ/ *n* pesca con caña, *f*

Anglo- (in compounds) anglo-. **A.-American,** *a* and *n* angloamericano (-na). **A.-Saxon,** *a* and *n* anglosajón (-ona); (language) anglosajón, *m*

anglomania /,æŋglə'meiniə/ *n* anglomanía, *f*

anglophile /'æŋglə,fail/ *n* anglófilo (la)

anglophobia /,æŋglə'foubiə/ *n* anglofobia, *f*

angora /æŋ'gɔrə/ *n* angora, *f*. **a. cat,** gato de angora, *m*. **a. rabbit,** conejo de angora, *m*

angrily /'æŋgrəli/ *adv* airadamente

angry /'æŋgri/ *a* (of persons) enfadado, enojado, airado; (of waves, etc.) furioso; *Med.* inflamado; (red) rojo; (scowling) cenudo; (dark) obscuro. **to be a.,** estar enojado. **to get angry, to grow a.,** enojarse, enfadarse, *Lat. Am.* entromparse; (of waves) encresparse; (of the sky) obscurecerse. **to make a.,** enojar

anguish /'æŋgwɪʃ/ *n* agonía, *f*, dolor, *m*; angustia, *f*. *vt* angustiar

angular /'æŋgyələr/ *a* angular; (of features, etc.) anguloso

angularity /,æŋgyə'lærɪti/ *n* angulosidad, *f*

anhydrous /æn'haidrəs/ *a* anhidro

aniline /'ænḷin/ *n* anilina, *f*

animal /'ænəməl/ *a* and *n* animal *m*. **a. fat,** grasa animal, *f*. **a. kingdom,** reino animal, *m*. **a. spirits,** *Philos.* espíritus animales, *m pl*

animalism /'ænəmə,lɪzəm/ *n* animalidad, *f*; sensualidad, *f*

animate /*v* 'ænə,meit; *a* -mɪt/ *vt* animar; inspirar. *a* animado; viviente

animated /'ænə,meitɪd/ *a* animado; vivo, lleno de vida

animation /,ænə'meiʃən/ *n* animación, *f*; vivacidad, *f*; calor, fuego, *m*

animism /'ænə,mɪzəm/ *n* animismo, *m*

animosity /,ænə'mɒsɪti/ *n* animosidad, hostilidad, *f*

aniseed /'ænə,sid/ *n* anís, *m*

anisette /,ænə'sɛt/ *n* (liqueur) anisete, *m*

ankle /'æŋkəl/ *n* tobillo, *m*. **a. bone,** hueso del tobillo, *m*. **a. sock,** calcetín corto, *m*

anklet /'æŋklɪt/ *n* brazalete para el tobillo, *m*; (support) tobillera, *f*

annals /'ænḷz/ *n pl* anales, *m pl*

anneal /ə'nil/ *vt* (metals) recocer; (glass) templar; (with oil) atemperar

annex /*v* ə'nɛks; 'ænɛks; *n* 'ænɛks/ *vt* unir, juntar; anexar. *n* anexo, *m*

annexation /,ænɪk'seiʃən/ *n* anexión, *f*

annihilate /ə'naiə,leit/ *vt* aniquilar

annihilation /ə,naiə'leiʃən/ *n* aniquilación, *f*

anniversary /,ænə'vɜrsəri/ *a* and *n* aniversario, *m*.

annotate /'ænə,teit/ *vt* anotar, acotar, comentar; hacer anotaciones a

annotation /,ænə'teiʃən/ *n* anotación, *f*; nota, *f*

annotator /'ænə,teitər/ *n* anotador (-ra), comentador (-ra)

announce /ə'nauns/ *vt* proclamar; declarar; publicar; anunciar

announcement /ə'naunsmənt/ *n* proclama, *f*; declaración, *f*; publicación, *f*; anuncio, *m*; (of a betrothal) participación, *f*

announcer /ə'naunsər/ *n* anunciador (-ra); (radio or TV) locutor (-ra)

annoy /ə'nɔi/ *vt* exasperar, irritar, disgustar; molestar, incomodar, *Lat. Am.* acatarrar, cargosear, engorrar

annoyance /ə'nɔiəns/ *n* disgusto, *m*, exasperación, *f*; molestia, *f*, fastidio, *m*

annoying /ə'nɔiɪŋ/ *a* enojoso, molesto, fastidioso, *Lat. Am.* cargoso

annual /'ænyuəl/ *a* anual. *n* anuario, *f*; calendario, *m*; planta anual, *f*

annually /'ænyuəli/ *adv* anualmente, cada año

annuitant /ə'nuitṇt/ *n* censualista, *mf*

annuity /ə'nuiti/ *n* anualidad, pensión vitalicia, *f*

annul /ə'nʌl/ *vt* anular

annulment /ə'nʌlmənt/ *n* anulación, *f*

annunciation /ə,nʌnsi'eiʃən/ *n* anunciación, *f*. **the A.,** la Anunciación

anodyne /'ænə,dain/ *a* and *n* anodino, *m*

anoint /ə'nɔint/ *vt* untar; (before death) olear; (a king, etc.) ungir

anointing /ə'nɔintɪŋ/ *n* unción, *f*

anomalous /ə'nɒmələs/ *a* anómalo

anomaly /ə'nɒməli/ *n* anomalía, *f*

anonymity /,ænə'nɪmɪti/ *n* anónimo, *m*

anonymous /ə'nɒnəməs/ *a* anónimo. **a. letter,** anónimo, *m*

anorexia /,ænə'rɛksiə/ *n* anorexia, *f*

another /ə'nʌðər/ *a* otro; (different) distinto. *n* otro, *m*; otra, *f*. **For one thing... and for a.,** En primer lugar... y además (y por otra cosa). **one after a.,** uno después de otro. **They love one a.,** Ellos se aman. **They sent from one to another,** Lo mandaron de uno a otro

answer /'ænsər, 'ɑn-/ *n* contestación, respuesta, *f*; (refutation) refutación, *f*; (pert reply) réplica, *f*; (solution) solución, *f*; *Math.* resultado, *m*; *Law.* contestación a la demanda, *f*

answer /'ænsər, 'ɑn-/ *vt* responder, contestar; (a letter, etc.) contestar a; (refute) refutar; (reply pertly) replicar; (write) escribir; (return) devolver; (suit) servir; (a bell, etc.) acudir a; (the door) abrir. *vi* contestar; (succeed) tener éxito; dar resultado. **to a. by return,** contestar a vuelta de correo, *m*. **to a. back,** replicar. **to a. for,** ser responsable por; ser responsable (de); (speak for) hablar por; (guarantee) garantizar, responder de

answerable /'ænsərəbəl/ *a* responsable; refutable; (adequate) adecuado. **to make a. for,** hacer responsable de

answering machine /'ænsərɪŋ/ n contestador telefónico, contestador, m
ant /ænt/ n hormiga, f. **ant-eater,** oso hormiguero, m. **ant-hill,** hormiguero, m
antagonism /æn'tægə,nɪzəm/ n antagonismo, m, hostilidad, oposición, f
antagonist /æn'tægənɪst/ n antagonista, mf
antagonistic /æn,tægə'nɪstɪk/ a antagónico, hostil
antagonize /æn'tægə,naiz/ vt contender; hacer hostil (a)
antarctic /ænt'ɑrktɪk/ a antártico. n polo antártico, m
antecedent /,æntə'sidn̩t/ a and n antecedente, m.
antechamber /'ænti,tʃeimbər/ n antecámara, antesala, f
antedate /'ænti,deit/ vt antedatar; anticipar
antediluvian /,æntidɪ'luviən/ a antediluviano
antelope /'ænt l̩,oup/ n antílope, m
antenna /æn'tɛnə/ n antena, f
anterior /æn'tɪəriər/ a anterior
anthem /'ænθəm/ n antífona, f
anthologist /æn'θɒlədʒɪst/ n antólogo, m
anthology /æn'θɒlədʒi/ n antología, floresta, f
anthracite /'ænθrə,sait/ n antracita, f, carbón mineral, m
anthrax /'ænθræks/ n ántrax, m
anthropological /,ænθrəpə'lɒdʒɪkəl/ a antropológico
anthropologist /,ænθrə'pɒlədʒɪst/ n antropólogo, m
anthropology /,ænθrə'pɒlədʒi/ n antropología, f
anti-aircraft /,ænti'ɛər,kræft, ,æntai-/ a antiaéreo. **A.A. gun,** cañon antiaéreo, m
antibody /'ænti,bɒdi/ n anticuerpo, m
antic /'æntɪk/ n travesura, f
Antichrist /'ænti,kraist/ n Anticristo, m
anticipate /æn'tɪsə,peit/ vt (foresee) prever; anticipar; adelantarse a; (hope) esperar; (frustrate) frustrar; (enjoy) disfrutar con anticipación de
anticipation /æn,tɪsə'peiʃən/ n anticipación, f; adelantamiento, m; esperanza, expectación, f. **in a. of,** en espera de
anticipatory /æn'tɪsəpə,tɔri/ a anticipador
anticlerical /,ænti'klɛrɪkəl, ,æntai-/ a anticlerical
anticlericalism /,ænti'klɛrɪkə,lɪzəm, ,æntai-/ n anticlericalismo, m
anticlimax /,ænti'klaimæks, ,æntai-/ n anticlímax, m
antidote /'ænti,dout/ n antídoto, contraveneno, m
antifreeze /'ænti,friz/ n anticongelante, m
Antilles, the /æn'tɪliz/ las Antillas, f
antimony /'æntə,mouni/ n antimonio, m
antipathetic /,æntɪpə'θɛtɪk/ a antipático
antipathy /æn'tɪpəθi/ n antipatía, f
antipode /'ænti,poud/ n pl antípodas, mf pl
antiquarian /,æntɪ'kwɛəriən/ a anticuario
antiquary /'ænti,kwɛri/ n anticuario, m
antiquated /'ænti,kweitid/ a anticuado
antique /æn'tik/ a antiguo. n antigüedad, antigualla, f. **a. dealer,** anticuario, m. **a. shop,** tienda de antigüedades, f
antiquity /æn'tɪkwɪti/ n antigüedad, f; ancianidad, f
antireligious /,æntiri'lɪdʒəs, ,æntai-/ a antirreligioso
anti-Semitic /,æntisə'mɪtɪk, ,æntai-/ a antisemita
anti-Semitism /,ænti'sɛmɪ,tɪzəm, ,æntai-/ n antisemitismo, m
antiseptic /,æntə'sɛptɪk/ a and n antiséptico, m
antisocial /,ænti'souʃəl, ,æntai-/ a antisocial
antithesis /æn'tɪθəsɪs/ n antítesis, f
antithetic /,ænti'θɛtɪk/ a antitético
antitoxin /,ænti'tɒksɪn/ n antitoxina, f
antler /'æntlər/ n asta, f
antonym /'æntənɪm/ n contrario, m
antrum /'æntrəm/ n antro, m
Antwerp /'æntwərp/ Amberes, m
anus /'einəs/ n ano, m
anvil /'ænvɪl/ n yunque, m, bigornia, f
anxiety /æŋ'zaiɪti/ n inquietud, intranquilidad, f; preocupación, f; ansiedad, f; curiosidad, f; impaciencia, f; (wish) deseo, afán, m
anxious /'æŋkʃəs, 'æŋʃəs/ a inquieto, intranquilo; preocupado; ansioso; impaciente; deseoso. **to be a.,** estar inquieto; apurarse. **to be a. to,** ansiar, tener de-

seos de. **to make a.,** preocupar, inquietar, intranquilizar
anxiously /'æŋkʃəsli, 'æŋʃəs-/ adv con inquietud; ansiosamente; impacientemente
any /'ɛni/ a cualquiera; (before the noun only) cualquier; (some) algún, m; alguna, f; (every) todo; (expressing condition or with interrogatives or negatives, following the noun) alguno, m; alguna, f, (is often not translated in a partitive sense, e.g. *Have you any butter?* ¿Tienes mantequilla?) pron algo; (with the relevant noun) algún, etc.; lo, m, and neut; la, f; los, m pl; las, f pl. **He hasn't any pity,** No tiene piedad alguna. **at any rate,** de todos modos; por lo menos. **If there is any,** Si lo (la, etc.) hay. **in any case,** venga lo que venga. **not any,** ninguno, m; ninguna, f. **Whether any of them...,** Si alguno de ellos... **any further,** más lejos. **any longer,** (ya no + infin.), **He doesn't drink any longer,** ya no toma; más largo; (of time) más tiempo. **any more,** nada más; nunca más
anybody /'ɛni,bɒdi/ n and pron (someone) alguien; cualquiera, mf; (everyone) todo el mundo; (with a negative) nadie; (of importance) persona de importancia, f. **hardly a.,** casi nadie
anyhow /'ɛni,hau/ adv de cualquier modo; (with a negative) de ningún modo; de cualquier manera; (at least) por lo menos, en todo caso; (carelessly) sin cuidado
anyone /'ɛni,wʌn/ n. See **anybody**
anything /'ɛni,θɪŋ/ n algo, m, alguna cosa, f; (negative) nada; cualquier cosa, f; todo (lo que). **a. but,** todo menos
anyway /'ɛni,wei/ adv de todos modos, con todo; venga lo que venga; (anyhow) de cualquier modo
anywhere /'ɛni,wɛər/ adv en todas partes, dondequiera; en cualquier parte; (after a negative) en (or a) ninguna parte
aorta /ei'ɔrtə/ n aorta, f
apart /ə'pɑrt/ adv aparte, a un lado; separadamente; separado (de); apartado (de). **a. from,** aparte de, dejando a un lado. **to keep a.,** mantener aislado; distinguir (entre). **to take a.,** desarmar. **wide a.,** muy distante
apartment /ə'pɑrtmənt/ n cuarto, m, habitación, f; piso, Argentina departamento m, elsewhere in Lat. Am. apartamento m
apathetic /,æpə'θɛtɪk/ a apático; indiferente
apathy /'æpəθi/ n apatía, f; indiferencia, f
ape /eip/ n simio, m
Apennines, the /'æpə,nainz/ los Apeninos, m
aperitive /ə'pɛrɪtɪv/ a and n aperitivo, m
aperture /'æpərtʃər/ n abertura, f; agujero, m; orificio, m
apex /'eipɛks/ n ápice, m
aphasia /ə'feiʒə/ n afasia, f
aphorism /'æfə,rɪzəm/ n aforismo, m
aphrodisiac /,æfrə'dizi,æk/ a and n afrodisíaco, m
apiary /'eipi,ɛri/ n colmenar, m
apiece /ə'pis/ adv cada uno; por persona
apish /'eipɪʃ/ a simiesco, de simio; (affected) afectado; (foolish) tonto
aplomb /ə'plɒm/ n confianza en sí, f, aplomo, m
apocalypse /ə'pɒkəlɪps/ n Apocalipsis, m
apocalyptic /ə,pɒkə'lɪptɪk/ a apocalíptico
apocopate /ə'pɒkə,peit/ vt apocopar
Apocrypha /ə'pɒkrəfə/ n libros apócrifos, m
apocryphal /ə'pɒkrəfəl/ a apócrifo
apogee /'æpə,dʒi/ n apogeo, m
apologetic /ə,pɒlə'dʒɛtɪk/ a apologético. n **apologetics,** apologética, f
apologist /ə'pɒlədʒɪst/ n apologista, mf
apologize /ə'pɒlə,dʒaiz/ vi presentar sus excusas; disculparse, excusarse; (regret) sentir
apology /ə'pɒlədʒi/ n excusa, disculpa, f; defensa, apología, f; (makeshift) substituto, m
apoplectic /,æpə'plɛktɪk/ a and n apoplético (-ca)
apoplexy /'æpə,plɛksi/ n apoplegía, f
apostasy /ə'pɒstəsi/ n apostasía, f
apostate /ə'pɒsteit/ n apóstata, mf. renegado (-da)
apostatize /ə'pɒstə,taiz/ vi apostatar, renegar

apostle /ə'pɒsəl/ n apóstol, m. **Apostles' Creed,** el Credo de los Apóstoles

apostolic /ˌæpə'stɒlɪk/ a apostólico

apostrophe /ə'pɒstrəfi/ n apóstrofe, mf; (punctuation mark) apóstrofo, m

apothecaries' weight /ə'pɒθəˌkɛriz/ peso de boticario, m

apothegm /'æpəˌθɛm/ n apotegma, m

apotheosis /əˌpɒθi'ousɪs/ n apoteosis, f

appall /ə'pɔl/ vt horrorizar, espantar, aterrar

appalling /ə'pɔlɪŋ/ a espantoso, horrible

apparatus /ˌæpə'rætəs/ n aparato, m; máquina, f; instrumentos, m pl

apparel /ə'pærəl/ n ropa, f; vestiduras, f pl; ornamento, m. vt vestir

apparent /ə'pærənt/ a aparente; visible; evidente, manifiesto; (of heirs) presunto. **to become a.,** manifestarse

apparently /ə'pærəntli/ adv al parecer, aparentemente

apparition /ˌæpə'rɪʃən/ n aparición, f, fantasma, espectro, m

appeal /ə'pil/ n súplica, f; llamamiento, m; (charm) atracción, f, encanto, m; Law. apelación, alzada, f. vi (to) suplicar (a); hacer llamamiento (a); poner por testigo (a); recurrir a; llamar la atención de; interesar (a); (attract) atraer, encantar; Law. apelar. **It doesn't a. to him,** No le atrae, No le gusta. **to allow an a.,** revocar una sentencia apelada. **without a.,** inapelable

appealing /ə'pilɪŋ/ a suplicante; atrayente

appealingly /ə'pilɪŋli/ adv de un modo suplicante

appear /ə'pɪər/ vi (of persons and things) aparecer; (seem) parecer; (before a judge) comparecer, presentarse (ante el juez); (of books) publicarse; (of lawyers) representar; (of the dawn) rayar; (of the sun, etc.) salir; (show itself) manifestarse. **to cause to a.,** hacer presentarse; (show) hacer ver; (prove) demonstrar, probar

appearance /ə'pɪərəns/ n aparición, f; (show, semblance or look, aspect) apariencia, f; presencia, f; aspecto, m; (in court of law) comparecencia, f; (of a book) publicación, f; (arrival) llegada, f; (view) perspectiva, f; (ghost) aparición, f, fantasma, m. **first a.,** (of an actor, etc.) debut, m; (of a play) estreno, m. **to all appearances,** según las apariencias. **to make one's first a.,** aparecer por primera vez; Theat. debutar. **Appearances are deceptive,** Las apariencias engañan

appease /ə'piz/ vt apaciguar, aplacar, pacificar; satisfacer

appeasement /ə'pizmənt/ n apaciguamiento, aplacamiento, m, pacificación, f; satisfacción, f

appellant /ə'pɛlənt/ a and n Law. apelante, mf

appellation /ˌæpə'leɪʃən/ n nombre, m; título, m; denominación, f

append /ə'pɛnd/ vt añadir; (a seal) poner; (enclose) incluir, anexar

appendage /ə'pɛndɪdʒ/ n accesorio, m; (Bot. Zool.) apéndice, m

appendicitis /əˌpɛndə'saɪtɪs/ n apendicitis, f

appendix /ə'pɛndɪks/ n apéndice, m

appertain /ˌæpər'teɪn/ vi pertenecer (a)

appetite /'æpɪˌtaɪt/ n apetito, m; Fig. hambre, f; deseo, m. **to have a bad a.,** no tener apetito, estar desganado. **to have a good a.,** tener buen apetito. **to whet the a.,** abrir el apetito

appetizer /'æpɪˌtaɪzər/ n aperitivo, m, Argentina ingrediente, m

appetizing /'æpɪˌtaɪzɪŋ/ a apetitoso

applaud /ə'plɔd/ vt and vi aplaudir; aclamar, ovacionar; celebrar

applause /ə'plɔz/ n aplauso, m; ovación, f; aprobación, alabanza, f

apple /'æpəl/ n manzana, f. **the a. of one's eye,** la niña de los ojos. **a. orchard,** manzanar, m. **a. sauce,** compota de manzanas, f. **a. tart,** pastel de manzanas, m. **a. tree,** manzano, m

appliance /ə'plaɪəns/ n aparato, m; instrumento, m; utensilio, m; máquina, f

applicability /ˌæplɪkə'bɪlɪti/ n aplicabilidad, f

applicable /'æplɪkəbəl/ a aplicable

applicant /'æplɪkənt/ n candidato, m; aspirante, m; solicitante, mf

application /ˌæplɪ'keɪʃən/ n aplicación, f; solicitud, f; petición, f; empleo, m. **on a.,** a solicitar

appliqué /ˌæplɪ'keɪ/ a aplicado. n aplicación, f

apply /ə'plaɪ/ vt aplicar; (use) emplear; (place) poner; (give) dar; (the brakes) frenar; vi ser aplicable; ser a propósito; dirigirse (a); acudir (a); (for a post) proponerse para. **a. for,** solicitar, pedir; (a post) proponerse para. **a. for admission (to...),** solicitar el ingreso (en...). **a. oneself to,** ponerse a; dedicarse a, consagrarse a

appoint /ə'pɔɪnt/ vt (prescribe) prescribir, ordenar; señalar; asignar; (furnish) amueblar; equipar; (create) crear, establecer; (to a post) nombrar, designar; (manage) gobernar; organizar. **at the appointed hour,** a la hora señalada. **well-appointed,** bien amueblado; bien equipado

appointive /ə'pɔɪntɪv/ a por nombramiento

appointment /ə'pɔɪntmənt/ n (assignation) cita, f; (to a post) nombramiento, m; (post, office) cargo, m; creación, f. **By Royal A.,** Proveedor de la Real Casa. **to make an a. with,** citar

apportion /ə'pɔrʃən/ vt dividir; distribuir; prorratear; (taxes) derramar

apportionment /ə'pɔrʃənmənt/ n repartimiento, m, distribución, f; división, f; prorrateo, m

apposite /'æpəzɪt/ a a propósito, pertinente, oportuno; justo

appositeness /'æpəzɪtnɪs/ n pertinencia, oportunidad, f

appraisal /ə'preɪzəl/ n valoración, valuación, f; estimación, f

appraise /ə'preɪz/ vt valorar, tasar; estimar

appraiser /ə'preɪzər/ n apreciador (-ra), avaluador (-ra)

appreciable /ə'priʃəbəl/ a apreciable, perceptible

appreciably /ə'priʃəbli/ adv sensiblemente

appreciate /ə'priʃiˌeɪt/ vt (understand) darse cuenta de, comprender; estimar; apreciar; (distinguish) distinguir. vi encarecer, aumentar en valor; (of shares) subir, estar en alza

appreciation /əˌpriʃi'eɪʃən/ n (understanding) comprensión, f; apreciación, f; (recognition, etc.) aprecio, reconocimiento, m; (in value) aumento (en valor), m; subida de precio, f

appreciative /ə'priʃətɪv/ a apreciativo

appreciatively /ə'priʃətɪvli/ adv con aprecio

appreciator /ə'priʃiˌeɪtər/ n apreciador (-ra)

apprehend /ˌæprɪ'hɛnd/ vt aprehender, prender; comprender, aprehender; (fear) temer

apprehension /ˌæprɪ'hɛnʃən/ n aprehensión, comprensión, f; (fear) aprensión, f; (seizure) aprehensión, presa, f

apprehensive /ˌæprɪ'hɛnsɪv/ a aprehensivo; (fearful) aprensivo

apprehensiveness /ˌæprɪ'hɛnsɪvnɪs/ n aprehensión, f; (fear) aprensión, f, temor, m

apprentice /ə'prɛntɪs/ n aprendiz (-za). **to bind a.,** poner de aprendiz

apprenticeship /ə'prɛntɪsˌʃɪp/ n aprendizaje, m. **to serve an a.,** hacer el aprendizaje

apprise /ə'praɪz/ vt dar parte (de), informar (de)

approach /ə'proutʃ/ vt acercarse a; aproximarse a; (pull, etc. nearer) acercar, aproximar; (resemble) parecerse a; ser semejante a; (speak to) hablar con; (entablar negociaciones con. vi acercarse, aproximarse. n acercamiento, m; (arrival) llegada, f; aproximación, f; (of night, etc.) avance, m; (entrance) entrada, f; avenida, f; vía, f; (step) paso, m; (to a subject) punto de vista (sobre), concepto (de), m; (introduction) introducción, f; pl **approaches,** (environs) alrededores, m pl, inmediaciones, f pl; (seas) mares, m pl; (overtures) avances, m pl

approachable /ə'proutʃəbəl/ a accesible

approaching /ə'proutʃɪŋ/ a venidero, próximo, cercano

approbation /ˌæprə'beɪʃən/ n asentimiento, m; aprobación, f

appropriate /a ə'proupriɪt; v -ˌeɪt/ a apropiado; con-

veniente; *vt* adueñarse de, tomar posesión de, apropiar
appropriately /ə'proupriıtli/ *adv* propiamente; convenientemente; justamente
appropriateness /ə'proupriıtnıs/ *n* conveniencia, *f*; justicia, *f*
appropriation /ə,proupri'eiʃən/ *n* apropiación, *f*; aplicación, *f*; empleo, *m*
approval /ə'pruvəl/ *n* aprobación, *f*; consentimiento, *m*. **on a.,** a prueba
approve /ə'pruv/ *vt* aprobar; confirmar; (sanction) autorizar, sancionar; ratificar; estar contento (de); (oneself) demostrarse. *vi* aprobar
approved /ə'pruvd/ *a* aprobado; bien visto; (on documents) Visto Bueno (V° B°)
approximate /a ə'prɒksəmıt/ *v* -,meit/ *a* aproximado. *vt* acercar. *vi* aproximarse (a)
approximately /ə'prɒksəmıtli/ *adv* aproximadamente, poco más o menos
approximation /ə,prɒksə'meiʃən/ *n* aproximación, *f*
appurtenance /ə'pɜrtn̩əns/ *n* accesorio, *m*, pertenencia, *f*
apricot /'æprı,kɒt/ *n* albaricoque, *m*. a. **tree,** albaricoquero, *m*
April /'eiprəl/ *n* abril, *m*, *a* abrileño. **A. Fool's Day,** el 1° de abril; (in Spain) el Día de los Inocentes (December 28)
apron /'eiprən/ *n* delantal, *m*; (of artisans and freemasons) mandil, *m*. **to be tied to a mother's a.-strings,** estar cosido a las faldas de su madre. **a.-stage,** proscenio, *m*. **a.-string,** cinta del delantal, *f*
apse /æps/ *n* ábside, *mf*
apt /æpt/ *a* apto, listo; propenso (a), inclinado (a); expuesto (a); (suitable) apropiado, oportuno
aptitude /'æptı,tud/ *n* aptitud, disposición, facilidad, *f*
aptly /'æptli/ *adv* apropiadamente; justamente, bien
aquamarine /,ækwəmə'rin/ *n* aguamarina, *f*
aquarelle /,ækwə'rɛl/ *n* acuarela, *f*
aquarellist /,ækwə'rɛlıst/ *n* acuarelista, *mf*
aquarium /ə'kwɛəriəm/ *n* acuario, *m*
Aquarius /ə'kwɛəriəs/ *n* Acuario, *m*
aquatic /ə'kwætık/ *a* acuático
aquatint /'ækwə,tınt/ *n* acuatinta, *f*
aqueduct /'ækwı,dʌkt/ *n* acueducto, *m*
aqueous /'ækwiəs/ *a* ácueo, acuoso
aquiline /'ækwə,lain/ *a* aguileño
Arab /'ærəb/ *a* árabe, *mf*
arabesque /,ærə'bɛsk/ *n* arabesco, *m*
Arabian /ə'reibiən/ *a* árabe, arábigo. **The A. Nights,** Las Mil y Una Noches
Arabic /'ærəbık/ *a* arábigo. *n* (language) arábigo, árabe, *m*
Arabist /'ærəbıst/ *n* arabista, *mf*
arable /'ærəbəl/ *a* cultivable, labrantío
Aragonese /,ærəgə'niz/ *a* and *n* aragonés (-esa)
arbiter /'arbıtər/ *n* árbitro (-ra), arbitrador (-ra)
arbitrariness /'arbı,trerınıs/ *n* arbitrariedad, *f*
arbitrary /'arbı,treri/ *a* arbitrario
arbitrate /'arbı,treit/ *vi* arbitrar, juzgar como árbitro; someter al arbitraje
arbitration /,arbı'treiʃən/ *n* arbitraje, *m*
arbitrator. /'arbı,treitər/ See **arbiter**
arbor /'arbər/ *n* glorieta, *f*, emparrado, *m*
arc /ark/ *n* arco, *m*. **arc-light,** lámpara de arco, *f*
arcade /ar'keid/ *n* arcada, *f*; galería, *f*; pasaje, *m*
arch /artʃ/ *n* arco, *m*; (vault) bóveda, *f*. *vt* abovedar; arquear; encorvar
arch /artʃ/ *a* (roguish) socarrón; (coy) coquetón
arch- *prefix* archi-
archaic /ar'keiık/ *a* arcaico
archaism /'arki,ızəm/ *n* arcaísmo, *m*
archangel /'ark,eindʒəl/ *n* arcángel, *m*
archbishop /'artʃ'bıʃəp/ *n* arzobispo, *m*
archenemy /'artʃ'ɛnəmi/ *n* mayor enemigo (-ga); Demonio, *m*
archeological /,arkiə'lɒdʒıkəl/ *a* arqueológico
archeologist /,arki'ɒlədʒıst/ *n* arqueólogo, *m*
archeology /,arki'ɒlədʒi/ *n* arqueología, *f*
archer /'artʃər/ *n* flechero, saltero, *m*; *Mil.* arquero, *m*

archery /'artʃəri/ *n* ballestería, *f*
archery range *n* campo de tiro con arco, *m*
archfiend /'artʃ'find/ *n* demonio, *m*
arching /'artʃıŋ/ *n* arqueo, *m*
archipelago /,arkə'pɛlə,gou/ *n* archipiélago, *m*
architect /'arkı,tɛkt/ *n* arquitecto, *m*
architectural /,arkı'tɛktʃərəl/ *n* arquitectónico
architecturally /,arkı'tɛktʃərəli/ *adv* arquitectónicamente; desde el punto de vista arquitectónico
architecture /'arkı,tɛktʃər/ *n* arquitectura, *f*
archive /'arkaiv/ *n* archivo, *m*
archivist /'arkəvıst/ *n* archivero, *m*
archness /'artʃnıs/ *n* coquetería, *f*; malicia, *f*
archway /'artʃ,wei/ *n* arcada, *f*, pasaje abovedado, *m*; arco, *m*
arctic /'arktık, 'artık/ *a* ártico; muy frío. **A. Circle,** Círculo ártico, *m*
ardent /'ardn̩t/ *a* ardiente; apasionado, vehemente; fogoso
ardently /'ardn̩tli/ *adv* ardientemente; con vehemencia, apasionadamente
ardor /'ardər/ *n* ardor, *m*
arduous /'ardʒuəs/ *a* arduo, difícil
arduousness /'ardʒuəsnıs/ *n* dificultad, arduidad, *f*
are /ar/ *pl* of present indicative of **be.** See **be. There are,** Hay
area /'ɛəriə/ *n* área, *f*; superficie, *f*; (extent) extensión, *f*; espacio, *m*; región, *f*; (of a house) patio, *m*; (of a concert hall, etc.) sala, *f*
area code *n* característica, *f*, (Chile) código territorial (Spain), prefijo (Spain), código interurbano, código (Argentina), *m*
arena /ə'rinə/ *n* arena, *f*
argent /'ardʒənt/ *n Poet.* blancura, *f*; *Herald.* argén, *m*
Argentina /,ardʒən'tinə/ Argentina
Argentinian /,ardʒən'tıniən/ *a* and *n* argentino (-na)
argonaut /'argə,nɔt/ *n* (*Zool.* and *Myth.*) argonauta, *m*
argot /'argou, -gət/ *n* jerga, *f*; (thieves') germanía, *f*
arguable /'argyuəbəl/ *a* discutible
argue /'argyu/ *vt* discutir; persuadir; (prove) demostrar. *vi* argüir, discutir; sostener. **to a. against,** hablar en contra de, oponer
arguing /'argyuıŋ/ *n* razonamiento *m*; argumentación, *f*, discusión, *f*
argument /'argyəmənt/ *n* argumento, *m*, *Argentina* arenga *f*
argumentative /,argyə'mɛntətıv/ *a* argumentador; contencioso
arid /'ærıd/ *a* árido, seco
aridity /ə'rıdıti/ *n* aridez, *f*
Aries /'ɛəriz/ *n* Aries, *m*
arise /ə'raiz/ *vi* levantarse; (appear) surgir, aparecer; ofrecerse, presentarse; (of sound) hacerse oír; provenir (de); proceder (de); (result) hacerse sentir; (rebel) sublevarse
aristocracy /,ærə'stɒkrəsi/ *n* aristocracia, *f*
aristocrat /ə'rıstə,kræt/ *n* aristócrata, *mf*
aristocratic /ə,rıstə'krætık/ *a* aristocrático
Aristotelian /,ærəstə'tilyən/ *a* aristotélico
arithmetic /ə'rıθmətık/ *n* aritmética, *f*
arithmetical /,ærıθ'mɛtıkəl/ *a* aritmético
ark /ark/ *n* arca, *f*. **Noah's ark,** arca de Noé, *f*. **Ark of the Covenant,** arca de la alianza, *f*
arm /arm/ *n* (*Anat. Geog. Mech.* of a chair, a cross, and *Fig.*) brazo, *m*; (lever) palanca, *f*; (of a tree) rama, *f*, brazo, *m*; (sleeve) manga, *f*; *Naut.* cabo de una verga, *m*; (weapon) arma, *f*; (of army, navy, etc.) ramo, *m*, *pl.* **arms,** *Herald.* armas, *f pl*, escudo, *m*. in arms, en brazos; armado; en oposición. **To arms!** ¡A las armas! **to keep at arm's length,** guardar las distancias; tratar fríamente. **to lay down arms,** rendir las armas. **to present arms,** presentar las armas. **to receive with open arms,** recibir con los brazos abiertos. **to take up arms,** alzarse en armas, empuñar las armas. **under arms,** sobre las armas. **with folded arms,** con los brazos cruzados. **arm in arm,** del brazo, de bracero. **arm of the sea,** brazo de mar, *m*. **arm-rest,** brazo, *m*
arm /arm/ *vt* armar; proveer (de); (*Fig.* fortify) fortificar. *vi* armarse

armada /ɑr'mɑdə/ n armada, f
armament /'ɑrməmənt/ n armamento, m
armchair /'ɑrm,tʃɛər/ n sillón, m, silla poltrona, f
armed /ɑrmd/ a armado
Armenian /ɑr'miniən/ a and n armenio (-ia); (language) armenio, m
armful /'ɑrm,fʊl/ n brazado, m
armhole /'ɑrm,houl/ n sobaquera, f
arming /'ɑrmɪŋ/ n armamento, m
armistice /'ɑrməstɪs/ n armisticio, m
armless /'ɑrmlɪs/ a sin brazos
armor /'ɑrmər/ n armadura, f; (for ships, etc.) blindaje, m. vt blindar, acorazar. **(to) a.-plate,** vt blindar. n coraza, plancha blindada, f
armored /'ɑrmərd/ a blindado, acorazado. **a. car,** carro blindado, m. **a. cruiser,** crucero acorazado, m
armory /'ɑrməri/ n armería, f
army /'ɑrmi/ n ejército, m; multitud, muchedumbre, f. **to be in the a.,** ser del ejército. **to go into the a.,** alistarse. **a. corps,** cuerpo del ejército, m. **a. estimates,** presupuesto del ejército, m. **a. list,** escalafón del ejército, m. **A. Medical Corps,** Sanidad Militar, f. **A. Supply Corps,** Cuerpo de Intendencia, m
aroma /ə'roumə/ n aroma, m
aromatic /,ærə'mætɪk/ a aromático
around /ə'raund/ prep alrededor de; por todas partes de; cerca de; (with words like corner) a la vuelta de. adv alrededor; a la redonda, en torno; por todas partes; de un lado para otro
arouse /ə'rauz/ vt despertar; excitar. **a. (someone's) suspicions,** despertar las sospechas (de fulano)
arpeggio /ɑr'pɛdʒi,ou/ n arpegio, m
arraign /ə'rein/ vt acusar; Law. procesar
arraignment /ə'reinmənt/ n acusación, f; Law. procesamiento, m
arrange /ə'reindʒ/ vt arreglar; acomodar; poner en orden, clasificar, Lat. Am. acotejar; (place) colocar; (order) ordenar, disponer; (contrive) agenciar; organizar; preparar; Mus. adaptar; (of differences) concertar, ajustar. vi convenir, concertarse; arreglar; hacer preparativos
arrangement /ə'reindʒmənt/ n arreglo, m; clasificación, f; disposición, f; (agreement) acuerdo, m; Mus. adaptación, f; pl **arrangements,** preparativos, m pl
array /ə'rei/ n (of troops) orden de batalla, mf; formación, f; colección, f; (dress) atavío, m, vt poner en orden de batalla; formar (las tropas, etc.); ataviar, adornar
arrears /ə'rɪərz/ n pl atrasos, m pl. **in a.,** atrasado
arrest /ə'rɛst/ vt detener, impedir; (the attention) atraer; (capture) arrestar, prender; (judgment) suspender. n (stop) interrupción, parada, f; (hindrance) estorbo, m; (detention) arresto, m, detención, f; (of a judgment) suspensión, f. **under a.,** bajo arresto
arresting /ə'rɛstɪŋ/ a que llama la atención, notable, muy interesante; asombroso, chocador
arrival /ə'raivəl/ n llegada, venida, f, advenimiento, m; Naut. arribada, f; entrada, f; el, m, (la, f), que llega. **on a.,** al llegar, a la llegada. **the new arrivals,** los recién llegados
arrive /ə'raiv/ vi llegar; aparecer; (happen) suceder; Naut. arribar; entrar. **to a. at,** (a place or conclusion) llegar a
arrogance /'ærəgəns/ n arrogancia, altivez, soberbia, f
arrogant /'ærəgənt/ a altivo, arrogante, soberbio
arrogate /'ærə,geit/ vt arrogar
arrow /'ærou/ n saeta, flecha, f. **a.-head,** punta de flecha, f. **a.-shaped,** en forma de flecha, sagital. **a. wound,** flechazo, saetazo, m
arsenal /'ɑrsənl/ n arsenal, m
arsenic /'ɑrsənɪk/ n arsénico, m
arson /'ɑrsən/ n incendio premeditado, m
art /ɑrt/ n arte, mf; (cleverness) habilidad, f; (cunning) artificio, m. **Faculty of Arts,** Facultad de Letras, f. **fine arts,** bellas artes, f pl. **art exhibition,** exposición de pinturas, f. **art gallery,** museo de pinturas, m. **art school,** colegio de arte, m
arterial /ɑr'tɪəriəl/ a arterial; (of roads) de primera clase. **a. forceps,** pinzas hemostáticas, f pl
artery /'ɑrtəri/ n arteria, f

artesian /ɑr'tiʒən/ a artesiano
artful /'ɑrtfəl/ a hábil, ingenioso; (crafty) astuto
artfully /'ɑrtfəli/ adv ingeniosamente; con astucia
artfulness /'ɑrtfəlnɪs/ n habilidad, ingeniosidad, f; astucia, maña, f
arthritic /ɑr'θrɪtɪk/ a artrítico
arthritis /ɑr'θraitɪs/ n artritis, f
artichoke /'ɑrtɪ,tʃouk/ n alcachofa, f. **Jerusalem a.,** aguaturma, f
article /'ɑrtɪkəl/ n artículo, m; (object) objeto, m, cosa, f; pl **articles,** escritura, f; contrato, m; estatutos, m pl. vt escriturar; contratar. **leading a.,** artículo de fondo, m. **articles of apprenticeship,** contrato de aprendizaje, m. **articles of association,** estatutos de asociación, m pl. **articles of war,** código militar, m
articulate /v ɑr'tɪkyə,leit/ a -lɪt/ vt articular; pronunciar, articular. vi estar unido por articulación; articular. a articulado; claro; expresivo
articulation /ɑr,tɪkyə'leiʃən/ n articulación, f, (all meanings)
artifice /'ɑrtəfɪs/ n artificio, m; arte, m, or f, habilidad, f
artificial /,ɑrtə'fɪʃəl/ a artificial; falso, fingido; afectado. **a. flowers,** flores de mano, f pl. **a. silk,** seda artificial, seda vegetal, f
artificial intelligence n inteligencia artificial, f
artificiality /,ɑrtə,fɪʃi'ælɪti/ n artificialidad, f; falsedad, f; afectación, f
artificially /,ɑrtə'fɪʃəli/ adv artificialmente; con afectación
artillery /ɑr'tɪləri/ n artillería, f. **field a.,** artillería volante (or ligera or montada), f. **a. practice,** ejercicio de cañón, m
artilleryman /ɑr'tɪlərimən/ n artillero, m
artisan /'ɑrtəzən/ n artesano (-na)
artist /'ɑrtɪst/ n artista, mf; (painter) pintor (-ra)
artistic /ɑr'tɪstɪk/ a artístico
artistically /ɑr'tɪstɪkli/ adv artísticamente
artistry /'ɑrtɪstri/ n habilidad artística, f, arte, mf
artless /'ɑrtlɪs/ a natural; sencillo, cándido, inocente
artlessly /'ɑrtlɪsli/ adv con naturalidad; con inocencia
artlessness /'ɑrtlɪsnɪs/ n naturalidad, f; sencillez, candidez, inocencia, f
art museum n museo de arte, m
Aryan /'ɛəriən/ a ario
as /æz/ adv conjunc rel pron como; así como; (followed by infin.) de; (in comparisons) tan... como; (while) mientras; a medida que; (when) cuando, al (followed by infin.); (since) puesto que, visto que; (because) porque; (although) aunque; por; (according to) según; en; (in order that) para (que). **as a rule,** por regla general. **Once as he was walking,** Una vez mientras andaba. **as... as,** tan... como. **as far as,** hasta; en cuanto a. **as from,** desde. **as good as,** tan bueno como. **as if,** como si. **as it were,** por decirlo así, en cierto modo. **as many,** otros tantos (e.g. six embassies as many countries, seis embajadas en otros tantos países). **as many as,** tantos... como; todos los que. **as soon as,** en cuanto, luego que, así que. **as soon as possible,** cuanto antes, Lat. Am. a la mayor brevedad posible. **as sure as can be,** sin duda alguna. **as to,** en cuanto a. **as usual,** como de costumbre. **as well,** también. **as well as,** (besides) además de. **as yet,** todavía.
asbestos /æs'bɛstəs/ n asbesto, amianto, m
ascend /ə'sɛnd/ vt and vi subir; (on, in) subir a; ascender; (rise) elevarse; (a river) remontar. **to a. the stairs,** subir las escaleras. **to a. the pulpit,** subir al púlpito. **to a. the throne,** subir al trono
ascendancy /ə'sɛndənsi/ n ascendiente, influjo, m
ascendant /ə'sɛndənt/ n elevación, f. a ascendente; predominante. **to be in the a.,** Fig. ir en aumento; predominar
ascending /ə'sɛndɪŋ/ a ascendente
ascension /ə'sɛnʃən/ n subida, ascensión, f; (of the throne) advenimiento (al trono), m. **The A.,** La Ascensión
ascent /ə'sɛnt/ n subida, f, ascenso, m; elevación, f; (slope) cuesta, pendiente, f
ascertain /,æsər'tein/ vt averiguar, descubrir

ascertainable /ˌæsərˈteinəbəl/ a averiguable, descubrible

ascertainment /ˌæsərˈteinmənt/ n averiguación, f

ascetic /əˈsɛtɪk/ a ascético. n asceta, mf

asceticism /əˈsɛtəˌsɪzəm/ n ascetismo, m

ascribable /əˈskraibəbəl/ a imputable, atribuible

ascribe /əˈskraib/ vt atribuir, adscribir, imputar

ascription /əˈskrɪpʃən/ n atribución, adscripción, f

asepsis /əˈsɛpsɪs/ n asepsia, f

aseptic /əˈsɛptɪk/ a aséptico

asexual /eiˈsɛkʃuəl/ a asexual

ash /æʃ/ n ceniza, f; cenizas, f pl; (tree and wood) fresno, m; pl **ashes,** cenizas, f pl; restos mortales, m pl. **mountain ash,** serbal, m. **ash-colored,** ceniciento. **ash grove,** fresneda, f. **ashtray,** cenicero, m. **Ash Wednesday,** miércoles de ceniza, m

ashamed /əˈʃeimd/ a avergonzado. **to be a. (of),** avergonzarse (de), Mexico apenarse (de). **to be a. of oneself,** avergonzarse, tener vergüenza de sí mismo

ashen /ˈæʃən/ a ceniciento; (of ash wood) de fresno; pálido como un muerto

ashlar /ˈæʃlər/ n sillar, m

ashore /əˈʃɔr/ adv a tierra; en tierra. **to go** or **put a.,** desembarcar

Asiatic /ˌeiʒiˈætɪk/ a and n asiático (-ca)

aside /əˈsaid/ adv a un lado; aparte. n Theat. aparte, m. **to set a.,** poner a un lado; (omit) dejar aparte; descontar; abandonar; (a judgment) anular. **to take a.,** llevar aparte

asinine /ˈæsəˌnain/ a asnal

ask /æsk/ vt (a question; enquire) preguntar; (request; demand) pedir; (beg) rogar; (invite) invitar. **to ask a question,** hacer una pregunta. **to ask about,** preguntar acerca de. **to ask after,** preguntar por. **to ask for,** pedir; preguntar por. **ask for the moon,** pedir cotofas en el golfo. **to ask in,** invitar (a alguien) a entrar. **to ask over,** invitar a bajar; invitar a visitar (a alguien)

askance /əˈskæns/ adv al (or de) soslayo, de reojo; con recelo

askew /əˈskyu/ adv oblicuamente; al lado; a un lado; sesgadamente

asleep /əˈslip/ a and adv dormido. **to be a.,** estar dormido. **to fall a.,** dormirse

asparagus /əˈspærəgəs/ n espárrago, m. **a. bed,** esparraguera, f

aspect /ˈæspɛkt/ n aspecto, m; vista, f; apariencia, f, semblante, m

asperity /əˈspɛriti/ n aspereza, f

aspersion /əˈspɜrʒən/ n Eccl. aspersión, f; calumnia, f; insinuación, f

asphalt /ˈæsfɔlt/ n asfalto, m, vt asfaltar

asphyxia /æsˈfɪksiə/ n asfixia, f

asphyxiate /æsˈfɪksiˌeit/ vt asfixiar

asphyxiating /æsˈfɪksiˌeitɪŋ/ a asfixiante

aspirant /ˈæspərənt/ n aspirante, candidato, m

aspirate /v ˈæspəˌreit; n -pərɪt/ vt aspirar. n letra aspirada, f

aspiration /ˌæspəˈreiʃən/ n aspiración, ambición, f; deseo, anhelo, m; Gram. aspiración, f

aspire /əˈspaiər/ vi aspirar (a), pretender, ambicionar; alzarse

aspirin /ˈæspərin/ n aspirina, f

ass /æs/ n asno, m

assail /əˈseil/ vt atacar, acometer, arremeter

assailable /əˈseiləbəl/ a atacable

assailant /əˈseilənt/ n asaltador (-ra)

assassin /əˈsæsin/ n asesino, mf

assassinate /əˈsæsəˌneit/ vt asesinar

assassination /əˌsæsəˈneiʃən/ n asesinato, m

assault /əˈsɔlt/ n asalto, m; acometida, embestida, f; Fig. ataque, m. vt asaltar; acometer, embestir; atacar. **to take by a.,** tomar por asalto

assay /n ˈæsei; v æˈsei/ n ensayo, m. vt ensayar, aquilatar

assayer /æˈseiər/ n ensayador, m

assaying /æˈseiiŋ/ n ensayo, m

assemblage /əˈsɛmblɪdʒ/ n reunión, f; (of a machine) montaje, m; (of people) muchedumbre, f, concurso, m; (of things) colección, f, grupo, m

assemble /əˈsɛmbəl/ vt (persons) reunir, convocar; (things and persons) juntar; (a machine, etc.) armar, ensamblar. vi reunirse, congregarse; acudir

assembly /əˈsɛmbli/ n asamblea, f; reunión, f; Eccl. concilio, m. **a. line,** cadena de montaje, línea de montaje, f. **a. room,** sala de reuniones, f; sala de baile, f

assent /əˈsɛnt/ n asentimiento, consentimiento, m; aprobación, f; (parliamentary, Law.) sanción, f. vi asentir (a), consentir (en); aprobar

assert /əˈsɜrt/ vt mantener, defender; declarar, afirmar; hacer valer, reclamar. **to a. oneself,** imponerse, hacerse sentir; hacer valer sus derechos

assertion /əˈsɜrʃən/ n aserción, afirmación, f; defensa, f; reclamación, f

assertive /əˈsɜrtɪv/ a afirmativo; dogmático

assess /əˈsɛs/ vt tasar, valorar; fijar, señalar; repartir (contribuciones, etc.)

assessment /əˈsɛsmənt/ n tasación, f; fijación, f; repartimiento, m

assessor /əˈsɛsər/ n Law. asesor (-ra); (of taxes) repartidor (-ra); (valuer) tasador, m. **publica.,** tasador, m

asset /ˈæsɛt/ n ventaja, f; adquisición, f; cualidad, f; pl **assets,** fondos, m pl; Com. activo, m, créditos activos, m pl, bienes m pl

assiduity /ˌæsɪˈdyuti/ n asiduidad, f

assiduous /əˈsɪdʒuəs/ a asiduo

assiduously /əˈsɪdʒuəsli/ adv asiduamente, con asiduidad

assign /əˈsain/ vt Law. ceder; señalar, asignar; (appoint) destinar; fijar; atribuir, imputar. n cesionario (-ia)

assignation /ˌæsɪgˈneiʃən/ n asignación, f; cita, f; Law. cesión, f

assignment /əˈsainmənt/ n (homework) tarea, f; Law. cesión, f; escritura de cesión, f; atribución, f; parte, porción, f

assimilable /əˈsɪmələbəl/ a asimilable

assimilate /əˈsɪməˌleit/ vt asimilar; incorporarse. vi mezclarse

assimilation /əˌsɪməˈleiʃən/ n asimilación, f; incorporación, f

assimilative /əˈsɪmələtɪv/ a asimilativo

assist /əˈsɪst/ vt ayudar; auxiliar, socorrer; (uphold) apoyar; (further) promover, fomentar. vi (be present) asistir (a)

assistance /əˈsɪstəns/ n ayuda, f; auxilio, socorro, m; apoyo, m; (furtherance) fomento, m. **public a.,** asistencia pública, f

assistant /əˈsɪstənt/ n ayudante, m; Eccl. asistente, m; (in a shop) dependiente (-ta); colaborador (-ra); (university) auxiliar, m; sub-. **a. secretary,** subsecretario (-ia). **a. secretaryship,** subsecretaría, f

associate /n, a əˈsousiɪt; v -siˌeit/ n asociado (-da); miembro, m; socio (-ia); compañero (-ra), amigo (-ga); colega, m; colaborador (-ra); (confederate) cómplice, mf. a asociado; auxiliar. vt asociar; unir, juntar. **to a. oneself with,** asociarse con; asociarse a. **to a. with,** frecuentar la compañía de, ir con

association /əˌsousiˈeiʃən/ n asociación, f; unión, f; sociedad, f; compañía, corporación, f; (connection) relación, f

assonance /ˈæsənəns/ n asonancia, f

assort /əˈsɔrt/ vt clasificar; mezclar

assorted /əˈsɔrtɪd/ a surtido, mezclado. **They are a well-a. pair,** Son una pareja bien avenida

assortment /əˈsɔrtmənt/ n clasificación, f, arreglo, m; surtido, m, mezcla, f

assuage /əˈsweidʒ/ vt mitigar; suavizar; calmar; aliviar

assume /əˈsum/ vt asumir; tomar; apropiarse; (wear) revestir; (suppose) suponer; poner por caso

assumed /əˈsumd/ a fingido, falso; supuesto

assumption /əˈsʌmpʃən/ n asunción, f; apropiación, arrogación, f; suposición, f. **Feast of the A.,** Fiesta de la Asunción, f

assurance /əˈʃurəns/ n garantía, f; promesa, f; confianza, seguridad, f; (in a good sense) aplomo, m, naturalidad, f; (in a bad sense) presunción frescura, f, descaro, m; Com. seguro, m

assure /əˈʃur/ vt asegurar

assured /əˈʃurd/ a aseguardo; seguro

assuredly /ə'ʃʊrıdli/ *adv* seguramente

asterisk /'æstərısk/ *n* asterisco, *m*

astern /ə'stɜrn/ *adv* a popa; de popa; en popa; atrás

asthma /'æzmə/ *n* asma, *f*

asthmatic /æz'mætık/ *a* asmático

astigmatic /,æstıg'mætık/ *a* astigmático

astigmatism /ə'stıgmə,tızəm/ *n* astigmatismo, *m*

astir /ə'stɜr/ *adv* en movimiento; (out of bed) levantado; excitado

astonish /ə'stɒnıʃ/ *vt* sorprender, asombrar

astonished /ə'stɒnıʃt/ *a* atónito, estupefacto

astonishing /ə'stɒnıʃıŋ/ *a* sorprendente, asombroso

astonishment /ə'stɒnıʃmənt/ *n* asombro, *m*, sorpresa, estupefacción, *f*

astound /ə'staund/ *vt* aturdir, pasmar. **to be astounded,** *Inf.* quedarse muerto

astounding /ə'staundıŋ/ *a* asombroso

astray /ə'strei/ *adv* desviado, extraviado; por el mal camino. **to go a.,** errar el camino, perderse; *Fig.* descarriarse

astride /ə'straid/ *adv* a horcajadas. *prep* a horcajadas sobre; a ambos lados de

astringent /ə'strındʒənt/ *a* astringente

astrologer /ə'strɒlədʒər/ *n* astrólogo (-ga)

astrological /,æstrə'lɒdʒıkəl/ *a* astrológico

astrology /ə'strɒlədʒi/ *n* astrología, *f*

astronaut /'æstrə,nɔt/ *n* astronauta, *mf*

astronomer /ə'strɒnəmər/ *n* astrónomo, *m*

astronomical /,æstrə'nɒmıkəl/ *a* astronómico

astronomy /ə'strɒnəmi/ *n* astronomía, *f*

astrophysics /,æstrou'fızıks/ *n* astrofísica, *f*

astute /ə'stut/ *a* astuto, sagaz; (with knave, etc.) redomado, pícaro

astuteness /ə'stutnıs/ *n* astucia, sagacidad, *f*

asunder /ə'sʌndər/ *adv* en dos; separadamente; lejos uno de otro

asylum /ə'sailəm/ *n* asilo, *m*; (for the insane) manicomio, *m*

asymmetrical /,eısı'mɛtrıkəl/ *a* asimétrico

asymmetry /ei'sımıtri/ *n* asimetría, *f*

at /æt/ *prep* a; en casa de; en; de; con; por; (before) delante de. Sometimes forms part of verb, e.g. *to aim at,* apuntar. *to look at,* mirar. May be translated by using pres. part., e.g. *They were at play,* Estaban jugando. *at a bound,* de un salto. *at peace,* en paz. *at the doctor's,* en casa del médico. *at the crack of dawn,* al rayar el alba, al romper el alba. *at the head,* a la cabeza. *John is at Brighton,* Juan está en Brighton. *at the house of...,* at...'s en casa de, *Lat. Am. also* donde (e.g., *My cousin is at my grandmother's* Mi primo está en casa de mi abuela, Mi primo está donde mi abuela) **at first,** el principio. **at last,** por fin. **at no time,** jamás. **at once,** en seguida. **at most,** a lo más. **at one go** *Lat. Am.* de una leída. **at all events,** en todo caso. **What is he getting at?** ¿Qué quiere saber? **at home,** en casa. **at-home day,** día de recibo, *m*

atavism /'ætə,vızəm/ *n* atavismo, *m*

atavistic /,ætə'vıstık/ *a* atávico

atheism /'eiθi,ızəm/ *n* ateísmo, *m*

atheist /'eiθiıst/ *n* ateo (-ea)

atheistic /,eiθi'ıstık/ *a* ateo

Athens /'æθınz/ Atenas, *f*

athlete /'æθlit/ *n* atleta, *m*

athletic /æθ'lɛtık/ *a* atlético

athletics /æθ'lɛtıks/ *n* atletismo, *m*

athwart /ə'θwɔrt/ *adv* de través. *prep* al través de; contra

Atlantic /æt'læntık/ *a* atlántico *m*. **A. Charter,** Carta del Atlántico, *f*. **A. liner,** transatlántico, *m*

Atlantis /æt'læntıs/ Atlántida, *f*

atlas /'ætləs/ *n* atlas, *m*

ATM *n* cajera automática, *f*

atmosphere /'ætməs,fıər/ *n* aire, *m*; atmósfera, *f*; *Fig.* ambiente, *m*

atmospheric /,ætməs'fɛrık/ *a* atmosférico

atmospherics /,ætməs'fɛrıks/ *n pl* perturbaciones eléctricas atmosféricas, *f pl*

atoll /'ætɒl/ *n* atolón, *m*

atom /'ætəm/ *n* átomo, *m*. **splitting of the a.,** escisión del átomo, *f*

atomic /ə'tɒmık/ *a* atómico. **a. bomb,** bomba atómica, *f*. **a. pile,** pila atómica, *f*. **a. theory,** teoría atómica, *f*

atomize /'ætə,maiz/ *vt* pulverizar

atomizer /'ætə,maizər/ *n* pulverizador, *m*

atone /ə'toun/ *vi* (for) expiar

atonement /ə'tounmənt/ *n* expiación, *f*

atonic /ə'tɒnık, ei'tɒn-/ *a* átono, atónico

atrocious /ə'trouʃəs/ *a* atroz; horrible

atrocity /ə'trɒsıti/ *n* atrocidad, *f*

atrophy /'ætrəfi/ *n* atrofia, *f*, *vi* atrofiarse

attach /ə'tætʃ/ *vt* (*Law.* of goods) embargar; (*Law.* of persons) arrestar; (fix) fijar; (tie) atar; (join) juntar; (stick) pegar; (connect) conectar; (hook) enganchar; (with a brooch, etc.) prender; (blame, etc.) imputar; (importance, etc.) dar, conceder; (assign) asignar; (attract) atraer; (enclose) adjuntar, incluir. *vi* pertenecer (a), ser indivisible (de). **to a. oneself to,** pegarse a; adherirse a, asociarse con; acompañar; hacerse inseparable de

attaché /ætæ'ʃei/ *n* agregado, *m*. **a. case,** maletín, *m*

attachment /ə'tætʃmənt/ *n* (*Law.* of goods) embargo, *m*, vía ejecutiva, *f*; (*Law.* of persons) arresto, *m*; unión, *f*; conexión, *f*; (hooking) enganche, *m*; (with a brooch, etc.) prendimiento, *m*; (tying) atadura, *f*; (fixing) fijación, *f*; (affection) apego, cariño, *m*; (friendship) amistad, *f*

attack /ə'tæk/ *n* ataque, *m*; *Mil.* ofensiva, *f*; (access) acceso, *m*. *vt* atacar

attacker /ə'tækər/ *n* atacador (-ra), asaltador (-ra)

attain /ə'tein/ *vt* alcanzar, conseguir, lograr. *vi* llegar a; alcanzar

attainable /ə'teinəbəl/ *a* asequible, realizable; accesible

attainment /ə'teinmənt/ *n* consecución, obtención, *f*; logro, *m*; *pl* **attainments,** prendas, dotes, *f pl*

attempt /ə'tɛmpt/ *vt* (try) procurar, tratar de, intentar; ensayar; querer; *Law.* hacer una tentativa (de), atentar. *n* tentativa, prueba, *f*; esfuerzo, ensayo, *m*; (criminal) atentado, *m*, tentativa, *f*

attend /ə'tɛnd/ *vi* prestar atención (a); escuchar; (look after) cuidar (de); (serve) servir; (accompany) acompañar; (await) esperar. *vt* (be present) asistir (a); (of a doctor) visitar; (accompany) acompañar; (bring) acarrear, traer; (follow) seguir. **to be attended with,** traer consigo, acarrear

attendance /ə'tɛndəns/ *n* asistencia, presencia, *f*; (those present) público, *m*, concurrencia, *f*; servicio, *m*; (train) acompañamiento, *m*; *Med.* asistencia, *f*, tratamiento médico, *m*. **to be in a.,** acompañar (a)

attendant /ə'tɛndənt/ *a* que acompaña; que sigue; concomitante. *n* criado (-da); (keeper) guardián (-ana); (nurse) enfermero (-ra); (in a cloakroom) guardarropa, *f*; (in a theater) acomodador (-ra); (on a train) mozo, *m*; (waiter) camarero, *m*; (at baths) bañero (-ra)

attention /ə'tɛnʃən/ ; ə,tɛn'ʃʌn/ *n* atención, *f*; cuidado, *m*. **A.!** ¡Atención!; *Mil.* ¡Firmes! **to pay a.,** prestar atención. **to stand at a.,** cuadrarse, permanecer en posición de firmes

attentive /ə'tɛntıv/ *a* atento; solícito; cortés, obsequioso

attentively /ə'tɛntıvli/ *adv* con atención, atentamente; solícitamente

attentiveness /ə'tɛntıvnıs/ *n* cuidado, *m*; cortesía, *f*

attenuate /ə'tɛnyu,eit/ *vt* atenuar

attenuating /ə'tɛnyu,eitıŋ/ *a* atenuante. **a. circumstance,** circunstancia atenuante, *f*

attenuation /ə,tɛnyu'eiʃən/ *n* atenuación, *f*

attest /ə'tɛst/ *vt* atestar. *vi* atestiguar, deponer, dar fe

attestation /,ætɛ'steiʃən/ *n* atestación, deposición, *f*; (certificate) certificado, *m*, fe, *f*

attic /'ætık/ *n* buhardilla, guardilla, *f*, desván, sotabanco, *m*

Attic /'ætık/ *a* ático

attire /ə'taiər/ *n* atavío, *m*; (dress) traje, *m*; (finery) galas, *f pl*, *vt* ataviar, vestir; engalanar

attitude /'ætı,tud/ *n* actitud, *f*; postura, *f*; posición, *f*

attorney /ə'tɜrni/ *n* (solicitor) abogado (-da); (agent) apoderado (-da); (public) procurador, *m*. **power of a.,** poderes, *m pl* procuración, *f*. **A.-general,** fiscal, *m*

attract /ə'trækt/ vt atraer; (charm) seducir, cautivar, apetecer; (invite) convidar; (goodwill, etc.) captar
attraction /ə'trækʃən/ n atracción, f; atractivo, aliciente, encanto, m
attractive /ə'træktɪv/ a atrayente; atractivo, seductivo; apetecible; encantador
attractively /ə'træktɪvli/ adv atractivamente
attributable /ə'trɪbyʊtəbəl/ a imputable, atribuible
attribute /v ə'trɪbyut; n 'ætrə,byut/ vt atribuir (a), achacar (a), imputar (a). n atributo, m
attribution /,ætrə'byuʃən/ n atribución, imputación, f; atributo, m
attrition /ə'trɪʃən/ n atrición, f
auburn /'ɔbərn/ a castaño, rojizo
auction /'ɔkʃən/ n subasta, almoneda, f; venta pública, pública subasta, f, vt subastar. **to put up to a.,** sacar a pública subasta
auctioneer /,ɔkʃə'nɪər/ n subastador (-ra), Lat. Am. also licitador (-ra)
audacious /ɔ'deɪʃəs/ a atrevido, audaz, osado, temerario; (shameless) descarado, impudente
audaciously /ə'deɪʃəsli/ adv osadamente; descaradamente
audacity /ɔ'dæsɪti/ n audacia, osadía, temeridad, f, atrevimiento, m; (shamelessness) descaro, m, desvergüenza, f
audibility /,ɔdə'bɪlɪti/ n audibilidad, perceptibilidad, f
audible /'ɔdəbəl/ a audible, oíble
audibly /'ɔdəbli/ adv en forma audible, perceptiblemente, en alta voz
audience /'ɔdiəns/ n (interview and Law.) audiencia, f; oyentes, m pl, auditorio, público, m. **to give a.,** dar audiencia. **a. chamber,** sala de recepción, f
audiofrequency /'ɔdiou,frikwɛnsi/ n audiofrecuencia, f
audit /'ɔdɪt/ vt intervenir, examinar (cuentas). n intervención, f, ajuste (de cuentas), m
audition /ɔ'dɪʃən/ n audición, f
auditor /'ɔdɪtər/ n (hearer) oyente, mf; interventor, contador, m
auditorium /,ɔdɪ'tɔriəm/ n sala de espectáculos, f
auditory /'ɔdɪ,tɔri/ a auditivo, auditorio
Augean /ɔ'dʒiən/ a de Augeas; muy sucio
auger /'ɔgər/ n taladro, m
aught /ɔt/ n algo. **For a. I know,** Por lo que yo sepa
augment /ɔg'mɛnt/ vt aumentar, acrecentar. vi aumentarse, acrecentarse
augmentation /,ɔgmɛn'teɪʃən/ n aumento, acrecentamiento, m; añadidura, f
augmentative /ɔg'mɛntətɪv/ a aumentativo
augur /'ɔgər/ n agorero (-ra). vt and vi presagiar, anunciar; pronosticar, agorar
augury /'ɔgyəri/ n predicción, f; agüero, presagio, pronóstico, m
August /'ɔgəst/ n agosto, m
august /ɔ'gəst/ a augusto
Augustan /ɔ'gʌstən/ a (of Roman emperor) augustal. **A. Age,** siglo de Augusto, m
Augustinian /,ɔgə'stɪniən/ a and n Eccl. agustino (-na)
aunt /ænt, ɑnt/ n tía, f. **great-a.,** tía abuela, f
aura /'ɔrə/ n exhalación, f; influencia psíquica, f; Med. aura, f
aural /'ɔrəl/ a auricular. **a. surgeon,** otólogo, m
auricle /'ɔrɪkəl/ n (of the heart) aurícula, ala del corazón, f; oreja, f, pabellón de la oreja, m
aurora /ɔ'rɔrə/ n aurora, f. **a. borealis,** aurora boreal, f
auspice /'ɔspɪs/ n auspicio, m
auspicious /ɔ'spɪʃəs/ a propicio, favorable, feliz
auspiciously /ɔ'spɪʃəsli/ adv prósperamente, felizmente
auspiciousness /ɔ'spɪʃəsnɪs/ n buenos auspicios, m pl; felicidad, f
austere /ɔ'stɪər/ a severo, austero, adusto; ascético; (of style) desnudo
austerity /ɔ'stɛrɪti/ n austeridad, severidad, f; ascetismo, m; (of style) desnudez, f
Australian /ɔ'streɪlyən/ a and n australiano (-na)
Austrian /'ɔstriən/ a and n austríaco (-ca)
authentic /ɔ'θɛntɪk/ a auténtico

authenticate /ɔ'θɛntɪ,keɪt/ vt autenticar
authentication /ɔ,θɛntɪ'keɪʃən/ n autenticación, f
authenticity /,ɔθɛn'tɪsɪti/ n autenticidad, f
author /'ɔθər/ n autor (-ra)
author index n índice de autores, m
authoritarian /ə,θɒrɪ'tɛəriən/ a autoritario
authoritative /ə'θɒrɪ,teɪtɪv/ a autoritario
authority /ə'θɒrɪti/ n autoridad, f; poder, m. **to have on the best a.,** tener de muy buena fuente
authorization /,ɔθərə'zeɪʃən/ n autorización, f
authorize /'ɔθə,raiz/ vt autorizar
authorship /'ɔθər,ʃɪp/ n profesión de autor, f; paternidad (literaria), f; origen, m
auto /'ɔtou/ n = **automobile**
autobiographical /,ɔtə,baiə'græfɪkəl/ a autobiográfico
autobiography /,ɔtəbai'ɒgrəfi/ n autobiografía, f
autocracy /ɔ'tɒkrəsi/ n autocracia, f
autocrat /'ɔtə,kræt/ n autócrata, mf
autocratic /,ɔtə'krætɪk/ a autocrático
autograph /'ɔtə,græf/ n autógrafo, m
autography /ɔ'tɒgrəfi/ n autografía, f
automatic /,ɔtə'mætɪk/ a automático. **a. gate,** (at level crossings, etc.) barrera de golpe, f. **a. pencil,** lapicero, m
automatically /,ɔtə'mætɪkəli/ adv automáticamente
automatism /ɔ'tɒmə,tɪzəm/ n automatismo, m
automaton /ɔ'tɒmə,tɒn/ n autómata, m
automobile /,ɔtəmə'bil/ n automóvil, coche, Lat. Am. carro, m
autonomous /ɔ'tɒnəməs/ a autónomo
autonomy /ɔ'tɒnəmi/ n autonomía, f
autopsy /'ɔtɒpsi/ n autopsia, f
autosuggestion /,ɔtousəg'dʒɛstʃən/ n autosugestión, f
autumn /'ɔtəm/ n otoño, m
autumnal /ɔ'tʌmnl/ a otoñal, de otoño
auxiliary /ɔg'zɪlyəri/ a auxiliar. n auxiliador, m. **a. verb,** verbo auxiliar
avail /ə'veil/ vi servir; valer; importar. vt aprovechar. **to a. oneself of,** valerse de, aprovecharse de. **to no a.,** en balde
availability /ə,veilə'bɪlɪti/ n utilidad, f; disponibilidad, f; provecho, m; (validity) validez, f
available /ə'veiləbəl/ a útil; disponible; aprovechable; válido
avalanche /'ævə,læntʃ/ n alud, lurte, m
avarice /'ævərɪs/ n avaricia, f
avaricious /,ævə'rɪʃəs/ a avaro, avaricioso
ave /'ɑvei/ interj ¡ave! n avemaría, f; despedida, f
avenge /ə'vɛndʒ/ vt vengar; vindicar. **to a. oneself for,** vengarse de
avenger /ə'vɛndʒər/ n vengador (-ra)
avenging /ə'vɛndʒɪŋ/ a vengador
avenue /'ævə,nyu/ n avenida, f
aver /ə'vɜr/ vt afirmar, asegurar
average /'ævərɪdʒ/ n promedio, término medio, m; (marine insurance) avería, f, a de promedio; típico; corriente; normal. vt hallar el término medio (de); prorratear, proporcionar; ser por término medio. **general a.,** (marine insurance) avería gruesa, f. **on the a.,** por término medio
averse /ə'vɜrs/ a opuesto (a); desinclinado (a); enemigo (de); repugnante. **to be a. to,** no gustar de; oponerse a; estar desinclinado a; ser enemigo de; repugnar
aversion /ə'vɜrʒən/ n aversión, f; repugnancia, f
avert /ə'vɜrt/ vt apartar; (avoid) evitar
aviary /'eivi,ɛri/ n avería, pajarera, f
aviation /,eivi'eiʃən/ n aviación, f
aviator /'eivi,eitər/ n aviador (-ra)
avid /'ævɪd/ a ávido
avidity /ə'vɪdɪti/ n avidez, f
avidly /'ævɪdli/ adv ávidamente, con avidez
avocado /,ævə'kɑdou, ,ɑvə-/ n aguacate, m
avocation /,ævə'keiʃən/ n pasatiempo, m, distracción, f; ocupación, f; profesión, f
avoid /ə'vɔid/ vt evitar; (pursuit) evadir, eludir; guardarse (de), rehuir; Law. anular
avoidable /ə'vɔidəbəl/ a evitable, eludible
avoidance /ə'vɔidns/ n evitación, f

avow /ə'vau/ vt confesar; declarar
avowal /ə'vauəl/ n confesión, admisión, f
avowedly /ə'vauıdli/ adv por confesión propia
avuncular /ə'vʌŋkyələr/ a avuncular
await /ə'weit/ vt aguardar, esperar
awake /ə'weik/ vt despertar. vi despertarse. a despierto; vigilante; consciente (de); atento (a)
awakening /ə'weikəniŋ/ n despertamiento, m
award /ə'wɔrd/ n sentencia, decisión, f; adjudicación, f; (prize) premio, m. vt adjudicar; otorgar, conceder. **She was awarded a professorship in Greek,** Ganó unas oposiciones para una cátedra de griego
aware /ə'weər/ a consciente, sabedor. **to be well a. of,** saber muy bien. **to make a. of,** hacer saber
awash /ə'wɒʃ/ adv a flor de agua
away /ə'wei/ adv a distancia, a lo lejos, lejos; (absent) ausente; (out) fuera; (unceasingly) sin parar, continuamente; (wholly) completamente; (visibly) a ojos vistas. In verbs of motion **a.** is rendered by the reflexive, e.g. to go a., marcharse, irse. to take a., quitar. interj ¡fuera de aquí! ¡márchese Vd.!; ¡vámonos! ¡adelante! **nine miles a.,** a nueve millas de distancia. **a. in the distance,** allá a lo lejos. **She sang a.,** Ella seguía cantando
awe /ɔ/ n temor reverente, m; horror, m; respeto, m; reverencia, f, vt intimidar, aterrar; infundir respeto (a). **to stand in awe of,** tener respeto (a), reverenciar
awesome /'ɔsəm/ a pavoroso, temible, aterrador; terrible; (august) augusto; (imposing) imponente
awestruck /'ɔ,strʌk/ a espantado, aterrado
awful /'ɔfəl/ a terrible, pavoroso; horrible; temible; atroz; Inf. enorme. **How a.!** Inf. ¡Qué barbaridad!

awfully /'ɔfəli, 'ɔfli/ adv terriblemente; horriblemente; Inf. muy
awfulness /'ɔfəlnıs/ n lo terrible; lo horrible; atrocidad, f; (of a crime, etc.) enormidad, f
awkward /'ɔkwərd/ a difícil; peligroso; delicado; embarazoso; (of time, etc.) inconveniente, inoportuno; (of things) incómodo; (clumsy) torpe, desmañado; desagradable; (ungraceful) sin gracia. **the a. age,** la edad difícil
awkwardly /'ɔkwərdli/ adv torpemente; incómodamente; mal; con dificultad; sin gracia. **He is a. placed,** Se encuentra en una situación difícil
awkwardness /'ɔkwərdnıs/ n dificultad, f; peligro, m; delicadeza, f; inconveniencia, inoportunidad, f; (clumsiness) torpeza, desmaña, f; (ungracefulness) falta de gracia, f
awl /ɔl/ n lezna, f, punzón, m
awning /'ɔniŋ/ n toldo, palio, m, Lat. Am. carpa f; Naut. toldilla, f
awry /ə'rai/ adv a un lado; oblicuamente; Fig. mal. a torcido; Fig. descarriado
ax /æks/ n hacha, f
axiom /'æksiəm/ n axioma, m
axiomatic /,æksiə'mætık/ a axiomático
axis /'æksıs/ n eje, m; Zool. axis, m. **A. power,** nacíon del Eje
axle /'æksəl/ n eje, m; peón, árbol (de una rueda), m. **back a.,** eje trasero, m. **differential a.,** eje diferencial, m. **front a.,** eje delantero, m
ay /ai/ interj sí. n voto afirmativo, m
azalea /ə'zeilyə/ n azalea, f
Aztec /'æztɛk/ a and n azteca, mf
azure /'æʒər/ n azul celeste, m

B

b /bi/ n (letter) be, f; Mus. si, m
baa /bæ, bɑ/ n balido, be, m, vi balar, dar balidos
babble /'bæbəl/ n (chatter) charla, f; (of a child) gorjeo, m; (confused sound) vocinglería, barbulla, f; rumor, m; (of water) murmullo, susurro, m. vi charlar; (of children) gorjearse; (incoherently) balbucir; (water) murmurar, susurrar; (a secret) descubrir
babbler /'bæblər/ n charlatán (-ana)
babbling /'bæbliŋ/ n garrulería, locuacidad, f; (incoherent speech) balbuceo, m. (of water) murmullo, m. a gárrulo, locuaz; balbuciente; murmurante
babel /'bæbəl/ n babel, m
baboon /bæ'bun/ n babuino, m
baby /'beibi/ n bebé, crío, m; niño (-ña) de pecho; Fig. gran bebé, m; niño mimado, m. a infantil. **b. blue,** azul claro, m. **b. doll,** muñeca bebé, f. **b. girl,** Argentina beba, f. **b. grand piano,** piano de media cola, m. **b. of the family,** Venezuela cuneco (-ca), mf
baby carriage n coche de niños, m
baby-faced /'beibi ,feist/ a con mejillas mofletudas
babyhood /'beibi,hʊd/ n infancia, niñez, f
babyish /'beibiiʃ/ a infantil, aniñado, pueril
babysitter /'beibi,sıtər/ n cuidaniños, mf
baccalaureate /,bækə'lɔriit, -'lɒr-/ n bachillerato, m
baccarat /,bɑkə'rɑ, ,bækə-/ n bacará, m
bachelor /'bætʃələr/ n soltero, célibe, m; (of a university) licenciado, bachiller, m; (as a title) caballero, m. **confirmed b.,** solterón, m. **degree of b.,** licenciatura, f. **to receive the degree of b.,** licenciarse, bachillerarse
bachelorhood /'bætʃələr,hʊd/ n soltería, f, celibato, m
bacillus /bə'sıləs/ n bacilo, m
back /bæk/ n Anat. espalda, f; (of an animal) lomo, espinazo, m; (reins, loins) riñones, m pl; (of chairs, sofas) respaldo, m; (of a book) lomo, m; (back, bottom) fondo, m; parte posterior, parte de atrás, f; (of a hand, brush and many other things) dorso, m; (of a coin) reverso, m; el otro lado de alguna cosa; (in football, hockey) defensa, m; Theat. foro, m; (of firearms) culata, f; (of a knife) canto, m; (upper portion) parte superior, f. a posterior, trasero; de atrás; (remote) alejado, apartado; inferior; (overdue) past; out

of date) atrasado; (earlier) anterior; Anat. dorsal. **at the b.,** detrás; en el fondo; en la última fila. **at the b. of one's mind,** por sus adentros, en el fondo del pensamiento. **behind one's b.,** a espaldas de uno, en ausencia de uno. **half-b.,** medio, m. **on one's b.,** boca arriba; a cuestas. **to see the b. of,** Inf. ver por última vez, desembarazarse de. **to turn one's b. on,** volver la espalda (a). **with one's b. to the engine,** de espaldas a la máquina. **b. to b.,** espalda con espalda
back /bæk/ vt empujar hacia atrás; (a vehicle) dar marcha atrás; hacer retroceder; (line) reforzar; (support) apoyar; (sign) endosar; (bind) forrar; (bet on) apostar a; (a sail) fachear. vi retroceder; dar marchar atrás; (of the wind) girar; (with on to) dar sobre, dominar; (with down) abandonar (una pretensión, etc.). **b. out,** salir, marcharse; volverse atrás; (retract) desdecirse
back /bæk/ adv detrás; atrás; otra vez, de nuevo; (returned) de vuelta; a las espaldas; (at home) en casa. interj ¡atrás! **A few weeks b.,** Hace unas semanas, Unas semanas atrás. **It stands b. from the road,** Está a alguna distancia del camino. **to go b. to,** (of families, etc.) remontar a. **to come b.,** regresar. **to come b. again,** regresar de nuevo, regresar por segunda vez
back axle n eje trasero, m
backbite /'bæk,bait/ vt cortar (a uno) un sayo, desollarle (a uno) vivo, murmurar de
backbiter /'bæk,baitər/ n mala lengua, f, murmurador (-ra)
backbiting /'bæk,baitiŋ/ n murmuración, detracción, maledicencia, f, a murmurador, detractor
backbone /'bæk,boun/ n espinazo, m, columna vertebral, f. **to the b.,** hasta la médula
backchat /'bæk,tʃæt/ n dimes y diretes, m pl; insolencia, f. **to indulge in b.-c.,** andar en dimes y diretes
back door n puerta trasera, puerta de servicio, f
backed /bækt/ a (lined) forrado, f; (in compounds; of persons) de espaldas, (of chairs) de respaldo
backer /'bækər/ n (better) apostador, m; protector (-ra, -triz)

backfire /'bæk͵faiᵊr/ n contrafuego m, falsa explosión, f
backgammon /'bæk͵gæmən/ n chaquete, m
back garden n jardín de atrás, m
background /'bæk͵graund/ n fondo, m; Art. último término, m. **in the b.**, en el fondo; Art. en último término; Fig. en las sombras; alejado, a distancia
backhand /'bæk͵hænd/ n Sports. revés, m
backhanded /'bæk͵hændɪd/ a de revés, dado con el revés de la mano; Fig. ambiguo, equívoco
backing /'bækɪŋ/ n forro, m; (lining) refuerzo, m; (of a vehicle) marcha atrás, f; retroceso, m; (betting) el apostar (a); (wagers) apuestas, f pl; (Fig. support) apoyo, m, ayuda, f; garantía, f
backlog /'bæk͵lɔg/ n Com. rezago de pedidos, m
back number n (of a periodical) número atrasado, m
back pedal vi contrapedalear
back premises /'prɛmɪsɪz/ n parte trasera (de una casa, etc.), f
backroom /'bæk'rum/ n cuarto interior, m, habitación trasera, f. **b. boy,** investigador ocupado en trabajos secretos para el gobierno, m
back seat n asiento trasero, m; fondo, m. **to take a b.-s.,** permanecer en el fondo, ceder el paso
back shop n trastienda, f
backside /'bæk͵said/ n trasero, m, posaderas, nalgas, f pl
backslide /'bæk͵slaid/ vi recaer, reincidir
backslider /'bæk͵slaidər/ n (in religion or politics) apóstata, mf; reincidente, mf
backsliding /'bæk͵slaidɪŋ/ n apostasía, f; reincidencia, f
backstage /'bæk'steidʒ/ n foro, fondo del escenario, m, adv hacia el foro; detrás de bastidores
back staircase n escalera de servicio, f; escalera secreta, f
backstairs /'bæk'stɛərz/ n escalera de servicio, f; Fig. vías secretas, f pl, a de cocina; Fig. secreto
backstitch /'bæk͵stɪtʃ/ n Sew. pespunte, m, vt and vi pespuntar
back street n calle secundaria, callejuela, f; pl **back streets,** barrios bajos, m pl
backstroke /'bæk͵strouk/ n reculada, f; Sports. revés, m
back tooth n muela, f
back view n vista de detrás, f
backward /'bækwərd/ a hacia atrás; vuelto hacia atrás; (in development) atrasado, poco avanzado; lento; negligente; (shy) modesto; (late) tardío; atrasado; retrógrado; (dull) torpe; retrospectivo. adv hacia atrás; atrás; al revés; (of falling) de espaldas; (of time) al pasado. **to go b. and forward,** ir y venir. **b. and forward,** de acá para allá
backwardness /'bækwərdnɪs/ n atraso, m; lentitud, f; negligencia, f; modestia, f; (lateness) tardanza, f; atraso, m; (dullness) torpeza, f; falta de progreso, f
backwards /'bækwərdz/ adv. See **backward**
backwash /'bæk͵wɒʃ/ n agua de rechazo, f
backwater /'bæk͵wɔtər/ n remanso, m
back wheel n rueda trasera, m, vi contrapedalear
backwoods /'bæk'wudz/ n monte, m, selva, f
back yard n corral, m
bacon /'beikən/ n tocino, m
bacteria /bæk'tɪəriə/ n bacteria, f
bacterial /bæk'tɪəriəl/ a bacterial, bacteriano
bactericide /bæk'tɪərə͵said/ n bactericida, m
bacteriological /bæk͵tɪəriə'lɒdʒɪkəl/ a bacteriológico
bacteriologist /͵bæktɪəri'ɒlədʒɪst/ n bacteriólogo, m
bacteriology /͵bæktɪəri'ɒlədʒi/ n bacteriología, f
bad /bæd/ a malo; (wicked) perverso; (ill) enfermo, malo (with estar); (naughty; undutiful) malo (with ser); (of coins) falso; (of debts) incobrable; (rotten) podrido; (harmful) nocivo; (dangerous) peligroso; (of pains, a cold) fuerte; intenso; (of a shot) errado; (mistaken) equivocado; (unfortunate) desgraciado. n el mal, lo malo; (persons) los malos. **extremely bad,** pésimo. **from bad to worse,** de mal en peor. **It's too bad!** ¡Esto es demasiado! **to go bad,** (fruit) macarse; (food) estropearse. **bad habit,** mala costumbre, f, vicio, m. **to have the bad habit of,** tener el vicio de.
bad temper, malhumor, mal genio, Lat. Am. catoche,

m. bad-tempered, malhumorado, Argentina cabrero.
bad turn, flaco servicio, m, mala pasada, f
badge /bædʒ/ n insignia, f; (decoration) condecoración, f; símbolo, emblema, m; (mark) marca, f
badger /'bædʒər/ n tejón, m, vt cansar, molestar
Bad Lands (of Nebraska and South Dakota) Tierras malas f pl; (of Argentina) la Travesía, f
badly /'bædli/ adv mal. **extremely b.,** pésimamente. **to want something b.,** necesitar algo con urgencia. **b. done,** mal hecho. **b. disposed,** malintencionado
badminton /'bædmɪntn/ n el juego del volante, m
badness /'bædnɪs/ n maldad, f; mala calidad, f; lo malo
bad-smelling /'bæd ͵smɛlɪŋ/ a maloliente
baffle /'bæfəl/ vt desconcertar; (bewilder) tener perplejo (a); contrariar, frustrar; (obstruct) impedir; (avoid) evitar. **to b. description,** no haber palabras para describir
baffling /'bæflɪŋ/ a desconcertante; difícil; confuso; perturbador; (of people) enigmático
bag /bæg/ n saco, m; talega, f; (hand) bolsa, f, saco (de mano), m; (for tools) capacho, m; (for sewing) costurero, m; (of bagpipes) fuelle, m; (saddle) alforja, f; (briefcase) cartera, f; (suitcase) maleta, f; (under the eye) ojera, f; (game shot) caza, f. vt entalegar; coger, cazar; matar; tomar. vi (of garments) arrugarse. **to clear out bag and baggage,** liar el petate. **a bag of bones,** (person) un manojo de huesos
bagatelle /͵bægə'tɛl/ n bagatela, friolera, f; (game) billar romano, m
bagful /'bægful/ n saco, m; bolsa, f
baggage /'bægɪdʒ/ n equipaje, m; Mil. bagaje, m; (madcap) pícara, f; (jade) mujerzuela, f. **b. master,** (railway) factor, m. **b. car,** furgón de equipajes, m
baggage rack n (of automobile) portaequipajes, m
baggy /'bægi/ a suelto; (creased, of trousers) con rodilleras, arrugado; (wide) bombacho
bagpipe /'bæg͵paip/ n gaita, f
bagpiper /'bæg͵paipər/ n gaitero, m
Bahamas, the /bə'haməz/ las Islas Bahamas, las Islas Lucayas, f
bail /beil/ n Law. fianza, caución, f; (person) fiador (-ra); (cricket) travesaño, m, barra, f. vt Law. poner en libertad bajo fianza; salir fiador (por); (a boat) achicar. **on b.,** en fiado. **to go b.,** dar fianza, fiar
bailiff /'beilɪf/ n Law. agente ejecutivo, m; alguacil, m; mayordomo, m; capataz, m
bait /beit/ n cebo, m; anzuelo, m; (fodder) pienso, m, vt cebar; (feed) dar pienso (a); azuzar; atormentar; (attract) atraer
baiting /'beitɪŋ/ n cebadura, f; combate, m; tormenta, f
bake /beik/ vt cocer; hacer (pan, etc.). **I like to bake cakes,** Me gusta hacer pasteles; Fig. endurecer. vi cocerse
bakelite /'beiklait/ n bakelita, f
baker /'beikər/ n panadero, hornero, m. **a baker's dozen,** la docena del fraile
bakery /'beikəri, 'beikri/ n panadería, f
baking /'beikɪŋ/ n cocimiento, m, cocción, f; (batch) hornada, f; el hacer (pan, etc.). a Inf. abrasador. **b.-dish,** tortera, f. **b.-powder,** levadura química, f
balance /'bæləns/ n balanza, f; equilibrio, m; Com. balance, saldo, m; (in a bank) saldo (a favor del cuentacorrentista), m; Math. resto, m; Astron. Libra, f; (pendulum) péndola, f; (counterweight) contrapeso, m. **credit b.,** saldo acreedor, m. **debit b.,** saldo deudor, m. **net b.,** saldo líquido, m. **to lose one's b.,** perder el equilibrio. **to strike a b.,** hacer balance. **b. of power,** equilibrio político, m. **b. of trade,** balanza de comercio, f. **b.-sheet,** balance, avanzo, Lat. Am. balance de situación, f. **b. wheel,** (of watches) volante, m
balance /'bæləns/ vt balancear, abalanzar; contrapesar; (accounts) saldar; equilibrar; comparar; considerar, examinar. vi balancearse; ser de igual peso; equilibrarse; (accounts) saldarse
balance of trade n balanza comercial, f
balancing /'bælənsɪŋ/ n balanceo, m; Com. balance, m. **b.-pole,** balancín, m

balconied /'bælkənid/ *a* con balcones, que tiene balcones
balcony /'bælkəni/ *n* balcón, *m*; galería, *f*; *Theat.* anfiteatro, *m*
bald /bɔld/ *a* calvo; (of style) seco, pobre; *Fig.* desnudo, árido, pelado; sin adorno; (simple) sencillo. **to grow b.,** ponerse calvo, encalvecer
balderdash /'bɔldər,dæʃ/ *n* galimatías, *m*, jerigonza, *f*; disparate, *m*
baldly /'bɔldli/ *adv* secamente; sencillamente
baldness /'bɔldnɪs/ *n* calvicie, *f*; (of style) sequedad, pobreza, *f*; (bareness) desnudez, aridez, *f*
bale /beil/ *n* (bundle) fardo, *m*; (of cotton, paper, etc.) bala, *f*
Balearic Islands, the /,bæli'ærɪk/ las Islas Baleares, *f*
baleful /'beilfəl/ *a* malicioso, siniestro, maligno
balk /bɔk/ *n* obstáculo, *m*; (beam) viga, *f*; (billiards) cabaña, *f. vi* frustrar; impedir. *vi* resistirse, rehusar
Balkans, the /'bɔlkənz/ los Balcanes, *m*
ball /bɔl/ *n* globo, *m*, esfera, *f*; (plaything) pelota, *f*; (as in billiards, cricket, croquet) bola, *f*; (in football, basket-ball) balón, *m*; (shot) bala, *f*; (of wool, etc.) ovillo, *m*; (of the eye) globo (del ojo), *m*; (of the thumb) yema (del pulgar), *f*; (of the foot) planta (del pie), *f*; (dance) baile, *m. vi* apelotonarse. **red b.,** (in billiards) mingo, *m.* **to play b.,** jugar a la pelota. **to roll oneself into a b.,** aovillarse, hacerse un ovillo. **b. -and-socket joint,** articulación esférica, *f.* **b.-bearing,** cojinete de bolas, *m*
ballad /'bæləd/ *n* romance, *m*; (song) balada, *f*
ballast /'bæləst/ *n* (*Naut.* and *Fig.*) lastre, *m*; *Rail.* balasto, *m. vt* lastrar; llenar de balasto
ballerina /,bælə'rinə/ *n* bailarina, *f*
ballet /bæ'lei/ *n* baile ruso, ballet, *m*; baile, *m.* **b. master,** director de ballet, *m*
ballistics /bə'lɪstɪks/ *n* balística, *f*
balloon /bə'lun/ *n* globo aerostático, *m*; *Chem.* balón, *m*; (toy) globo, *m*; *Archit.* bola, *f.* **captive b.,** globo cautivo, *m.* **b. barrage,** cortina de globos de intercepción, *f.* **b.-tire,** neumático balón, *m*
balloonist /bə'lunɪst/ *n* aeronauta, *mf*
ballot /'bælət/ *n* votación, *f*; papeleta para votar, cédula de votación, *f. vi* votar, balotar. **b. box,** urna electoral, *f*
ballpoint, ballpoint pen /'bɔl,pɔint/ *n Argentina* biro *m*, *Argentina, Uruguay* birome *m*, *Spain* bolígrafo *m*, *Mexico* bolilápiz *m*, *Colombia* esfero *m*, *Colombia* esferográfica *f*, *Cuba* estenógrafo *m*, *Argentina* lapicera *f*, *Central America, Colombia* lapicero *m*, *Paraguay*, *Peru* lápiz de bolilla *m*, *Chile* lápiz de pasta *m*, *Spain* pluma esférica *f*, *Spain* pluma esferográfica *f*, *Venezuela* plumilla *f*, *Spain* polígrafo *m*, *Bolivia* punto bola, punto-bola, puntobola *f*, pluma de bola *f*, pluma atómica *f*
ballroom /'bɔl,rum/ *n* salón de baile, *m*; salón de fiestas, *m*
ballroom dancing *n* baile de salón, *m*
balm /bɑm/ *n* bálsamo, *m*; *Fig.* ungüento, *m*
balminess /'bɑmɪnɪs/ *n* fragancia, *f*; aroma, *m*; (gentleness) suavidad, *f*
balmy /'bɑmi/ *a* balsámico; fragante; aromático; (soft) suave; (soothing) calmante
balsam /'bɔlsəm/ *n* bálsamo, *m*
Baltic, the /'bɔltɪk/ el (Mar) Báltico, *m*
balustrade /'bælə,streid/ *n* balaustrada, barandilla, *f*, antepecho, *m*
bamboo /bæm'bu/ *n* bambú, *m*
bamboozle /bæm'buzəl/ *vt* engatusar, embaucar
bamboozler /bæm'buzlər/ *n* embaucador (-ra)
ban /bæn/ *n* interdicción, *f*; prohibición, *f*; bando, *m. vt* prohibir; proscribir
banal /bə'næl/ *a* banal, vulgar, trivial
banality /bə'nælɪti/ *n* banalidad, vulgaridad, trivialidad, *f*
banana /bə'nænə/ *n* (tree and fruit) plátano, *m*; (fruit) banana, *f*, *Venezuela* cambur, *m.* **b. plantation,** platanar, *m*
band /bænd/ *n* lista, tira, *f*; zona, *f*; (black mourning) tira de gasa, *f*; (sash) faja, *f*; (ribbon) banda; cinta, *f*; (bandage) venda, *f*; *Mech.* correa, *f*; *Archit.* listón, *m*; *Mus.* banda, *f*; (group) pandilla, *f*, grupo,

m. vt congregar, reunir. *vi* reunirse, asociarse. **b.-saw,** sierra de cinta, *f*
bandage /'bændɪdʒ/ *n* venda, *f*, vendaje, *m*, *vt* vendar, poner un vendaje en (limbs, etc. or persons)
bandaging /'bændɪdʒɪŋ/ *n* vendaje, *m*
banderol /'bændə,rɔl/ *n* banderola, *f*
bandit /'bændɪt/ *n* bandido, bandolero, *m*
bandmaster /'bænd,mæstər/ *n* músico mayor, *m*; director de orquesta, *m*
bandsman /'bændzmən/ *n* músico, *m*
bandstand /'bænd,stænd/ *n* quiosco de música, *m*
bandy /'bændi/ *vt* cambiar, trocar; pasar de uno a otro
bandy-legged /'bændi ,lɛgɪd/ *a* estevado zanquituerto
bane /bein/ *n* (poison) veneno, *m*; perdición, ruina, *f*; (nuisance) plaga, *f*
baneful /'beinfəl/ *a* pernicioso, funesto; dañino; maligno
banefully /'beinfəli/ *adv* funestamente; malignamente
bang /bæŋ/ *n* golpe, golpazo, *m*; (of an explosive, fire-arm) estallido, *m*, detonación, *f*; (of a firework) traque, *m*; (of a door) portazo, *m*; (with the fist) puñetazo, *m*; (noise) ruido, *m*; (fringe) flequillo, *m. vt* golpear; (beat) sacudir; (throw) lanzar, arrojar con violencia; (a door, etc.) cerrar de golpe, cerrar con violencia. *vi* golpear; estallar; (thunder) retronar; (in the wind) cencerrear. *interj* ¡pum! ¡zas!
banging /'bæŋɪŋ/ *n* golpeadura, *f*; sacudidura, *f*; detonación, *f*; ruido, *m*
bangle /'bæŋgəl/ *n* pulsera, *f*; brazalete, *m*; (for ankles) ajorca, *f*
banish /'bænɪʃ/ *vt* desterrar; apartar; (from the mind) despedir, ahuyentar; (suppress) suprimir
banishment /'bænɪʃmənt/ *n* destierro, *m*; expulsión, *f*; relegación, *f*; (suppression) supresión, *f*
banister /'bænəstər/ *n* baranda, *f*, pasamano, *m*
banjo /'bændʒou/ *n* banjo, *m*
banjoist /'bændʒouɪst/ *n* tocador (-ra) de banjo
bank /bæŋk/ *n* (of rivers, etc.) ribera, orilla, *f*, margen, *m*; (of clouds) banda, capa, *f*; (of sand, fog, snow) banco, *m*; (embankment) terraplén, *m*; *Com.* banco, *m*; (gaming) banca, *f*; (for foreign exchange) casa de cambio, *f.* **b. account,** cuenta corriente, *f.* **b. book,** libreta de banco, *f.* **b. clerk,** empleado del banco, *m.* **b. holiday,** fiesta oficial, *f*, **b.-note,** billete de banco, *m.* **b. stock,** acciones de un banco, *f pl*
bank /bæŋk/ *vt* estancar, represar; amontonar; poner (dinero) en un banco, depositar en un banco. *vi* tener cuenta corriente en un banco; (gaming) tener la banca; ser banquero; *Aer.* inclinarse al virar
banker /'bæŋkər/ *n* bancario (-ia), banquero, *m*, (also at cards); (money-changer) cambista, *mf*
banking /'bæŋkɪŋ/ *n Com.* banca, *f*; *Aer.* vuelo inclinado, *m*, a *Com.* bancario. **b. house,** casa de banca, *f*
bankrupt /'bæŋkrʌpt/ *a* insolvente, quebrado. *n* quebrado (-da). **to go b.,** declararse en quiebra, hacer bancarrota
bankruptcy /'bæŋkrʌptsi/ *n* bancarrota, quiebra, *f*; *Fig.* pobreza, decadencia, *f.* **fraudulent b.,** quiebra fraudulenta, *f.* **b. court,** tribunal de quiebras, *m*
banner /'bænər/ *n* bandera, *f*
banns /bænz/ *n pl* amonestaciones, *f pl.* **to forbid the b.,** impedir las amonestaciones. **to publish the b.,** decir las amonestaciones
banquet /'bæŋkwɪt/ *n* banquete, *m*, *vt* and *vi* banquetear
banqueting /'bæŋkwɪtɪŋ/ *a* de banquetes. **b. hall,** sala de banquetes, *f*
bantam /'bæntəm/ *n* gallina enana, *f.* **b. weight,** (*Sports.*) *a* de peso gallo. *n* peso gallo, *m*
banter /'bæntər/ *n* chistes, *m pl*, burlas, *f pl. vt* and *vi* tomar el pelo (a). *n* chistes, *m pl*, burlas, *f pl*
baptism /'bæptɪzəm/ *n* bautismo, *m*; *Fig.* bautizo, *m*
baptist /'bæptɪst/ *n* bautista, *m.* **St. John the B.,** San Juan Bautista
baptistry /'bæptəstri/ *n* bautisterio, bautismo *m*
baptize /bæp'taiz/ *vt* bautizar

baptizing /bæp'taizɪŋ/ n bautizo, m
bar /bar/ n barra, f; (of chocolate, soap) pastilla, f;
Herald. banda, f; (on a window) reja, f; (of a door)
tranca, f, barrote, m; (bar lever) palanca, f; (of a balance) astil, m; *Mus.* barra, f; (in the sea, etc.) banco,
alfaque, m; (barrier) barrera, f; (legal profession)
foro, m, curia, f; *Fig.* tribunal, m; (in a court) barra,
f; *Fig.* impedimento, m; (of light) rayo, m; (stripe)
raya, f; (for refreshments) bar, m, *Lat. Am.* chingana,
f, mostrador del bar, m. vt atrancar, abarrotar; impedir, obstruir; prohibir; exceptuar, excluir; (streak)
rayar. **the b.,** el cuerpo de abogados. **to be called to
the b.,** ser recibido como abogado en los tribunales.
b.-tender, camarero del bar, m
bar association n colegio de abogados, m
barb /barb/ n púa, f; (of an arrow, fish-hook, etc.)
lengüeta, f; (of a lance) roquete, m; (of fish) barbilla,
f; (of a feather) barba, f; (horse) caballo berberisco,
m. vt proveer de púas; armar de lengüetas
Barbados /bar'beidouz/ Isla de Barbados, f
barbarian /bar'bɛəriən/ a bárbaro, barbárico. n bárbaro (-ra)
barbaric /bar'bærɪk/ a barbárico, salvaje
barbarism /'barbə,rɪzəm/ n barbarismo, salvajismo,
m; crueldad, f; (of style) barbarismo, m
barbarity /bar'bærɪti/ n barbaridad, ferocidad, f
barbarous /'barbərəs/ a feroz, cruel, salvaje; inculto
barbarously /'barbərəsli/ adv bárbaramente, cruelmente
barbarousness /'barbərəsnɪs/ n barbaridad, f; crueldad, ferocidad, f
barbecue /'barbɪ,kyu/ n alambre de púas, alambre espinoso, m
barbed wire /'barbd/ n alambre de púas, alambre espinoso, m
barber /'barbər/ n barbero, m. **barber shop,** barbería, f
Barcelona /,barsə'lounə/ (of or from) a and n barcelonés (-esa)
bar code n código de barras, m
bard /bard/ n bardo, vate, m
bare /bɛər/ a desnudo; descubierto; vacío; (mere)
mero, solo; (worn) raído; pelado, raso; (unadorned)
sencillo; (unsheathed) desnudo; (arid) árido; (curt)
seco; (unprotected) desabrigado; pobre. vt desnudar;
descubrir; revelar. **He bared his head,** Se descubrió.
to lay b., dejar al desnudo; revelar
bareback /'bɛər,bæk/ a que monta en pelo. adv en
pelo
barefaced /'bɛər,feist/ a descarado, desvergonzado,
cínico
barefoot /'bɛər,fʊt/ a descalzo
bareheaded /'bɛər,hɛdɪd/ a sin sombrero, descubierto
barelegged /'bɛər,lɛgɪd/ a en pernetas, en piernas
barely /'bɛərli/ adv apenas; escasamente; meramente,
solamente
bareness /'bɛərnɪs/ n desnudez, f; desadorno, m;
(aridity) aridez, f; pobreza, f
bargain /'bargən/ n contrato, m; pacto, acuerdo, m;
(purchase) ganga, f. vi negociar; (haggle) regatear.
into the b., de añadidura, también. **It is a b.,** Es una
ganga; Trato hecho. **to get the best of the b.,** salir
ganando. **to strike a b.,** cerrar un trato. **b. counter,**
sección de saldos, f. **b. sale,** venta de saldos, *Mexico*
barata f
bargainer /'bargənər/ n negociador (-ra); regatón
(-ona)
bargaining /'bargənɪŋ/ n negociación, gestión, f;
(haggling) regateo, m
barge /bardʒ/ n (for freight) barcaza, gabarra, f;
falúa, f; lancha, f. vi (into) tropezar con; dar empujones
baritone /'bærɪ,toun/ n barítono, m
barium /'bɛəriəm/ n *Chem.* bario, m
bark /bark/ n (of a tree) corteza, f; (quinine) quina,
f; (boat, *Poet.*) barca, f; *Naut.* buque de tres palos, m;
(of a dog) ladrido, m; (of a wolf) aullido, m; (of a
gun) ruido, m. vi (of a dog) ladrar; (of a wolf) aullar;
(of a gun) tronar
barking /'barkɪŋ/ n ladrido, m; (of stags) rebramo,
m; (of foxes) aullidos, m pl; (of guns) trueno, m

barley /'barli/ n cebada, f, a de cebada. **pearl b.,** cebada perlada, f. **b.-bin,** cebadera, f. **b. dealer,** cebadero, m. **b. field,** cebadal, m. **b.-water,** hordiate, m
barm /barm/ n (froth on beer) giste, m; (leaven)
levadura, f
barmaid /'bar,meid/ n moza de bar, camarera, f
barn /barn/ n pajar, granero, hórreo, m. **b.-owl,**
lechuza, f
barnacle /'barnəkəl/ n lapa, f, barnacla, m
barometer /bə'rɒmɪtər/ n barómetro, m
barometric /,bærə'mɛtrɪk/ a barométrico
baron /'bærən/ n barón, m
baroness /'bærənɪs/ n baronesa, f
Baron Munchausen /'bærən 'mʊntʃ,hauzən/ el
Barón de la Castaña
baroque /bə'rouk/ a barroco. **the b.,** lo barroco
barracks /'bærəks/ n *Mil.* cuartel, m, caserna, *Lat.
Am.* barraca f. **to quarter in b.,** acuartelar
barrage /bə'raʒ/ n *Mil.* presa de contención, f; *Mil.* cortina de fuego, f; (barrier) barrera, f; (of questions)
lluvia, f. **b. balloon,** globo de intercepción, m
barrel /'bærəl/ n barril, m; tonel, m, cuba, f; (of a
gun) cañón, m; *Mech.* cilindro, m; (of an animal)
cuerpo, m. vt embarrilar, entonelar. **b.-organ,** organillo, órgano de manubrio, m
barrelled /'bærəld/ a embarrilado, f; (of guns, generally
in compounds) de... cañones. **double-b. gun,** escopeta de dos cañones, f
barren /'bærən/ a estéril; (of ground) árido; (fruitless) infructuoso, yermo
barrenness /'bærən,nɪs/ n esterilidad, f; aridez, sequedad, f; (fruitlessness) inutilidad, f
barricade /'bærɪ,keid/ n barricada, f; barrera, f, vt
cerrar con barricadas; obstruir
barricading /'bærɪ,keidɪŋ/ n el cerrar con barricadas;
la defensa con barricadas (de)
barrier /'bæriər/ n barrera, f; impedimento, m; (for
customs duties) portazgo, m
barring /'barɪŋ/ prep salvo, excepto, con la excepción
de, menos
barrister /'bærəstər/ n abogado (-da)
barrow /'bærou/ n carretón, m; carretilla, f; (tumulus) túmulo, m
barter /'bartər/ n cambio, trueque, m; tráfico, m, vt
and vi cambiar, trocar; traficar
barterer /'bartərər/ n traficante, mf
basalt /bə'sɔlt/ n basalto, m
base /beis/ a bajo, vil, ruin; soez; indigno; impuro;
(of metals) de mala ley. n base, f; fundamento, m;
pie, m; *Archit.* pedestal, m; (*Mil. Chem. Geom.*) base,
f; (of a vase) asiento, m, vt basar; fundar. **b. action,**
bajeza, f. **b. line,** *Sports.* línea de base, f. **b. metal,**
metal común, m
baseball /'beis,bɔl/ n beisbol, m, pelota base, f
baseless /'beislɪs/ a sin base; sin fundamento; insostenible
basely /'beisli/ adv bajamente, vilmente
basement /'beismənt/ n sótano, m
baseness /'beisnɪs/ n bajeza, vileza, ruindad, f
bashful /'bæʃfəl/ a vergonzoso, ruboroso; tímido,
corto; (unsociable) huraño, esquivo
bashfully /'bæʃfəli/ adv vergonzosamente; tímidamente
bashfulness /'bæʃfəlnɪs/ n vergüenza, f, rubor, m;
encogimiento, m; timidez, cortedad, f; (unsociableness) hurañía, esquivez, f
basic /'beisɪk/ a básico; *Chem.* básico
basic commodity n artículo básico, producto primario, m
basilica /bə'sɪlɪkə/ n basílica, f
basilisk /'bæsəlɪsk/ n basilisco, m
basil (sweet) /'bæzəl, 'bei-/ n *Bot.* albahaca, f
basin /'beisən/ n vasija, f; (for washing) jofaina, f;
(barber's) bacía, f; (of a fountain) taza, f; *Anat.* baci-
nete, m; (of a harbor) concha, f; (of a river) cuenca,
f; (in the earth) hoya, f; (dock) dársena, f
basis /'beisɪs/ n base, f; fundamento, m; elemento
principal, m
bask /bæsk/ vi calentarse; (in the sun) tomar el sol
basket /'bæskɪt/ n cesta, f; canasta, capacha, f, *Lat.*

Am. jaba *f*; (frail) espuerta, *f*. **flat b.**, azafate, *m*.
large b., banasta, *f*. **b. with a lid**, excusabaraja, *f*. **b. ball**, baloncesto, *m*. **b. maker** or **dealer**, banastero, cestero, *m*. **b. work** or **shop** or **factory**, cestería, *f*. **b. work chair**, sillón de mimbres, *m*
basketful /'bæskɪt,fʊl/ *n* cesta, cestada, *f*
Basque /bæsk/ *a* and *n* vasco (-ca), vascongado (-da). *n* (language) vascuence, *m*; **B. Country**, el País Vasco
Basque Provinces, the las Provincias Vascongadas
bas-relief /ˌbɑrɪ'lif, ˌbæs-/ *n* bajo relieve, *m*
bass /beis/ *n Mus.* bajo, *m*; (for tying) esparto, *m*, *a Mus.* bajo. **double b.**, contrabajo, *m*. **figured b.**, bajo cifrado, *m*. **b. clef**, clave de fa, *f*. **b. string**, bordón, *m*. **b. voice**, voz baja, *f*
bassinet /ˌbæsə'nɛt/ *n* cochecito de niño, *m*
bassoon /bæ'sun/ *n Mus.* bajón, fagot, *m*
bassoonist /bæ'sunɪst/ *n* bajonista, fagotista, *mf*
bastard /'bæstərd/ *n* bastardo (-da), hijo (-ja) natural. *a* bastardo, ilegítimo; espurio
baste /beist/ *vt Sew.* bastear, hilvanar, embastar; *Cul.* enlardar, lardear
basting /'beistɪŋ/ *n Sew.* embaste, *m*; *Cul.* lardeamiento, *m*. **b. spoon**, cacillo, *m*. **b. stitch**, pasillo, *m*
bastion /'bæstʃən/ *n* bastión, baluarte, *m*. **to fortify with bastions**, abastionar
bastioned /'bæstʃənd/ *a* abastionado, con bastiones
bat /bæt/ *n Zool.* murciélago, *m*; (in baseball) bate, *m*; (in cricket) paleta, *f*; (in table tennis) pala, *f*. *vi* batear; (cricket) golpear con la paleta. See **without**
batch /bætʃ/ *n* (of loaves, etc.) hornada, *f*; lote, *m*; (of recruits) promoción, *f*
bath /bæθ/ *n* baño, *m*; (room) cuarto de baño, *m*; (vat) bañador, *m*; (for swimming) piscina cubierta, *f*; (in the open air) piscina al aire libre, *f*; *Photo.* baño, *m*, solución, *f*. *vt* bañar, lavar. **hot mineral baths**, termas, *f pl.* **Order of the B.**, Orden del Baño, *f*. **public baths**, casa de baños, *f*. **reinforcing b.**, *Photo.* reforzador, *m*. **to take a b.**, bañarse, tomar un baño. **b.-chair**, cochecillo de inválido, *m*. **b.-robe**, bata de baño, *f*, albornoz, *m*. **b. room**, cuarto de baño, *m*. **b. towel**, toalla del baño, *f*. **b. tub**, bañera, *f*, baño, *m*, bañadera *f*
bathe /beið/ *vt* bañar, lavar; (of light, etc.) bañar, envolver. *vi* bañarse. *n* baño, *m*
bather /'beiðər/ *n* bañista, *mf*; bañador (-ra)
bathing /'beiðɪŋ/ *a* de baño; balneario, *n* baño, *m*. **b. cap**, gorro de baño, *m*. **b. gown**, albornoz, *m*, bata de baño, *f*. **b. machine**, caseta de baños, *f*. **b.-pool**, piscina, *f*. **b.-resort**, estación balnearia, *f*. **b.-shoes**, calzado de baño, *m*. **b. suit**, traje de baño, *m*
bathos /'beiθɒs/ *n* paso de lo sublime a lo ridículo, *m*; anticlímax, *m*
batiste /bə'tist/ *n*; batista, *f*
baton /bə'tɒn/ *n* bastón de mando, *m*; *Mus.* batuta, *f*; (policeman's) porra, *f*
battalion /bə'tælyən/ *n* batallón, *m*
batter /'bætər/ *n Cul.* batido, *m*; pasta, *f*; *Sports.* lanzador, bateador, *m*. *vt* apalear, golpear; (demolish) derribar, demoler; (with artillery) cañonear; batir. **to coat with b.**, rebozar. **to b. down**, derribar
battering ram /'bætərɪŋ/ *n* ariete, *m*
battery /'bætəri/ *n* (*Mil. Nav.*) batería, *f*; *Elec.* pila, batería, *f*; *Law.* agresión, *f*. **dry b.**, batería de pilas, *f*. **storage b.**, acumulador, *m*. **b. cell**, pila de batería eléctrica, *f*
battle /'bætl/ *n* batalla, *f*; pelea, *f*, combate, *m*; (struggle) lucha, *f*. *vi* batallar; pelear; luchar. **b.-array**, orden de batalla, *f*. **b.-axe**, hacha de combate, *f*. **b.-cruiser**, acorazado, *m*. **b.-field**, campo de batalla, *m*. **b.-front**, frente de combate, *m*. **b.-piece**, *Art.* batalla, *f*. **b.-ship**, buque de guerra, *m*
battlement /'bætlmənt/ *n* almenaje, *m*; muralla almenada, *f*
bauble /'bɔbəl/ *n* (trifle) chuchería, fruslería, *f*; (fool's) cetro de bufón, *m*
bauxite /'bɔksait, 'bouzait/ *n* bauxita, *f*
Bavaria /bə'vɛəriə/ *n* Baviera, *f*
Bavarian /bə'vɛəriən/ *a* and *n* bávaro (-ra)
bawdy /'bɔdi/ *a* obsceno, indecente, escabroso
bawl /bɔl/ *vi* chillar, vocear
bawling /'bɔlɪŋ/ *n* vocerío, *m*, chillidos, *m pl*

bay /bei/ *n Geog.* bahía, *f*; (small) abra, *f*; *Bot.* laurel, *m*; (horse) bayo, *m*; (howl) aullido, *m*; *Archit.* abertura, *f*; *Rail.* andén, *m*. *a* (of horses) bayo, isabelino. *vi* aullar. **at bay**, en jaque, acorralado. **sick-bay**, enfermería, *f*. **to keep at bay**, tener a distancia; tener alejado; entretener. **bay rum**, ron de malagueta, *m*. **bay window**, ventana salediza, *f*
baying /'beiɪŋ/ *n* aullido, *m*
bayonet /'beiənɛt/ *n* bayoneta, *f*, *vt* herir o matar con bayoneta. **fixed b.**, bayoneta calada, *f*. **b. charge**, carga de bayoneta, *f*. **b. thrust**, bayonetazo, *m*
Bayonne /ba'yɔn/ Bayona, *f*
bazaar /bə'zɑr/ *n* bazar, *m*
be /bi/ *vi* ser; (of position, place, state, temporariness) estar; (exist) existir; (in impersonal expressions) haber; (of expressions concerning the weather and time) hacer; (remain) quedar; (leave alone) dejar; (do) hacer; (of one's health) estar; (of feeling cold, hot, afraid, etc. and of years of one's age) tener; (live) vivir; (belong) ser (de), pertenecer (a); (matter, concern) importar (a); (happen) ocurrir, suceder; (find oneself) hallarse, encontrarse, estar; (arrive) llegar (a); (cost) costar; (be worth) valer; (celebrate, hold) celebrarse, tener lugar; (forming continuous tense with present participle active or passive) estar; (with past participle forming passive) ser (this construction is often replaced by reflexive form when no ambiguity is entailed); (with infinitive expressing duty, intention) haber de; (must) tener que. **He is a soldier (doctor, etc.),** Es soldado (médico, etc.). **He is on guard,** Está de guardia. **They were at the door (in the house, etc.),** Estaban a la puerta (en la casa, etc.). **I am writing a letter,** Estoy escribiendo una carta (but this form is often replaced by a simple tense, e.g. escribo...). **It remains to be written,** Queda por escribir. **What is to be done?** ¿Qué hay que hacer? **Woe is me!** ¡Ay de mí! **to be hot (cold),** (of things) estar caliente (frío); (of weather) hacer calor (frío); (of persons) tener calor (frío). **How is John? He is well,** ¿Cómo está Juan? Está bien de salud. **It is daylight,** Es de día. **It is cloudy,** Está nublado. **She is 10,** Tiene diez años. **They are afraid,** Tienen miedo. **I am to go there tomorrow,** He de ir allí mañana. **It is to be will be,** Lo que tiene que ser será. **If John were to come we could go into the country,** Si viniera Juan podríamos ir al campo. **Be that as it may,** Sea como sea. **It is seven years since we saw him,** Hace siete años que no le vemos. **We have been here for three years,** Hace tres años que estamos aquí, Llevamos tres años aquí. **There is** or **there are,** Hay. **There will be many people,** Habrá mucha gente. **There are many people,** Hay mucha gente. **It is three miles to the next village,** Estamos a tres millas del pueblo próximo. **So be it!** Así sea. **Your pen is not to be seen,** Tu pluma no se ve. **It is to be hoped that...,** Se espera que...; ¡Ojalá que...! **The door is open,** La puerta está abierta. **The door was opened by Mary,** La puerta fue abierta por María. **He was accused of being a fascist,** Lo acusaron de fascista. **to be about to,** estar por; (of a more imminent action) estar para, estar a punto de. **to be in,** estar dentro; estar en casa. **to be off,** marcharse, irse. **Be off!** ¡Márchate! ¡Vete!; ¡Fuera! **to be out,** estar fuera; haber salido; no estar en casa; (of a light, etc.) estar apagado. **to be up,** estar levantado. **to be up to,** proyectar, traer entre manos; urdir, maquinar
beach /bitʃ/ *n* playa, *f*; costa, *f*. *vt* (a boat) encallar en la costa. **b. shoes,** playeras, *f pl.* **b. suit,** vestido de playa, *m*
beach club *n* club de playa, *m*
beacon /'bikən/ *n* (lighthouse) faro, *m*; (buoy) baliza, *f*, fanal, *m*; (watch-tower) atalaya, *f*; *Fig.* guía, *f*, *vt* iluminar. **b. fire,** almenara, *f*
bead /bid/ *n* cuenta, *f*; (of glass) abalorio, *m*; (drop) gota, *f*; *Archit.* perla, *f*; (bubble) burbuja, *f*; (foam) espuma, *f*; *pl* **beads,** rosario, *m*; *vt* adornar con abalorios. **to tell one's beads,** rezar el rosario. **b. work,** abalorio, *m*
beading /'bidɪŋ/ *n* abalorio, *m*; *Archit.* friso, listón, *m*
beadle /'bidl/ *n* bedel, *m*

beadleship /'bidəl‚ʃɪp/ n bedelía, f
beagle /'bigəl/ n perro sabueso, m
beak /bik/ n pico, m; punta, f; Naut. espolón, m. **to tap with the b.,** picotear
beaked /'bikt/ a que tiene pico; (in compounds) de... pico
beaker /'bikər/ n copa, f; Chem. vaso de precipitado, m
beam /bim/ n Archit. madero, m, viga, f; (width of a ship) manga, f; (of a balance) palanca, f; (of a plough) cama, f; (of light) rayo, destello, m; Phys. rayo, m; (smile) sonrisa brillante, f; pl **beams,** (of a building) envigado, m; (of a ship) baos, m pl. **main b.,** Archit. viga maestra, f. **b. of light,** rayo de luz, haz de luz, m
beam /bim/ vt lanzar, emitir; difundir. vi brillar, fulgurar, destellar; estar radiante, estar rebosando de alegría
beaming /'bimɪŋ/ a brillante; radiante
bean /bin/ n haba, f; judía, alubia, f; (of coffee) grano, m. **broad b.,** haba, f. **French, haricot, kidney b.,** judía, f. **string b.,** judía verde, f. **b. field,** habar, m. **beans,** Mexico frijoles, m; Dominican Republic habichuelas, f
bear /bɛər/ n Zool. oso, m; (she-bear) osa, f; (Stock Exchange) bajista, mf. **Great B.,** Astron. Osa Mayor, f, Septentrión, m. **Little B.,** Astron. Osa Menor, f. **polar b.,** oso blanco, m. **b.-cub,** osezno, m. **bear's den,** osera, f. **b.-hunting,** caza de osos, f. **b.-like,** osuno. **b.-pit,** recinto de los osos, m
bear /bɛər/ vt and vi (carry) llevar; (show) ostentar; (company, etc.) hacer; (profess) profesar; (of spite, etc. and of relation) guardar; (have) tener; (fruit) dar; (give birth to) parir; (support) sostener; (endure) aguantar; (suffer) padecer, sufrir; (tolerate) tolerar; (lean on) apoyarse en; (experience) experimentar; (produce) producir, dar; (enjoy) disfrutar de; (use) usar; (impel) empujar; (occupy, hold) ocupar; (go) dirigirse. **It was suddenly borne in on them that...,** De pronto vieron claro que... **I cannot b. any more,** No puedo más. **We cannot b. him,** No le aguantamos, No le sufrimos. **His language won't b. repeating,** Su lenguaje no puede repetirse. **to bring to b.,** ejercer (presión, etc.). **to b. a grudge,** guardar rencor (a), tener ojeriza (a). **to b. arms,** llevar armas; servir en el ejército o la milicia. **to b. company,** hacer compañía (a), acompañar (a). **to b. in mind,** tener en cuenta, tener presente; acordarse de. **to b. oneself,** conducirse, portarse. **to b. to the right,** ir hacia la derecha. **to b. witness,** atestiguar. **to b. false witness,** levantar falso testimonio. **to b. away,** llevarse; ganar. **to b. down,** hundir; derribar; bajar. **to b. down on,** avanzar rápidamente hacia; correr hacia; Naut. arribar sobre; (attack) caer sobre. **to b. in,** llevar adentro. **to b. off,** llevarse; ganar; Naut. apartarse de la costa. **to b. on, upon,** apoyarse en; (refer to) referirse a. **to b. out,** llevar fuera; confirmar; apoyar; justificar. **to b. up,** llevar arriba; llevar a la cumbre (de); sostener; (recover) cobrar ánimo; (against) resistir; hacer frente a. **to b. with,** soportar; sufrir; aguantar; llevar con paciencia; ser indulgente con
bearable /'bɛərəbəl/ a soportable; aguantable; tolerable
beard /bɪərd/ n barba, f; (of cereals) raspa, arista, f, vt desafiar. **thick b.,** barba bien poblada, f
bearded /'bɪərdɪd/ a con barba, barbudo
beardless /'bɪərdlɪs/ a barbilampiño, desbarbado, imberbe, lampiño
bearer /'bɛərər/ n llevador (-ra), portador (-ra); (of a bier) andero, m; Com. dador, portador, m. **good b.,** Agr. árbol fructífero, m. **to b.,** Com. al portador
bearing /'bɛərɪŋ/ n porte, m; postura, f; presencia, f; conducta, f; aspecto, m; relación, f; (meaning) significación, f; Naut. demora, orientación, f; Mech. cojinete, soporte, m; (endurance) tolerancia, f; pl **bearings,** (way) camino, m; Herald. escudo de armas, m. **ball b.,** cojinete de bolas, m; **to get one's bearings,** orientarse; encontrar el camino. **to lose one's bearings,** desorientarse; perderse. **to have a b. on,** tener relación con; tener que ver con; influir en
bearish /'bɛərɪʃ/ a osuno; rudo, áspero
bearskin /'bɛər‚skɪn/ n piel de oso, f; birretina, f

beast /bist/ n animal, bruto, m; cuadrúpedo, m; (cattle) res, f; bestia, f. **wild b.,** fiera, f. **b. of burden,** acémila, bestia de carga, f. **b. of prey,** animal de rapiña, m
beastliness /'bistlɪnɪs/ n bestialidad, brutalidad, f; obscenidad, f
beastly /'bistli/ a bestial, brutal; obsceno; Inf. horrible
beat /bit/ n latido, m, pulsación, f; golpe, m; (of a drum) toque (de tambor), m; (of a clock) tictac, m; sonido repetido, m; vibración, f
beat /bit/ vt and vi batir; golpear; (thrash) pegar, dar una paliza (a), Lat. Am. humear; (to remove dust, etc.) sacudir; (shake) agitar; (the wings) aletear; (hunting) batir; (excel) exceder, superar; ganar; (defeat) vencer; (of the rain, etc.) azotar; (a drum) tocar; (of the sun) batir, dar (en); (throb) latir, palpitar, pulsar. **to b. about the bush,** andarse por las ramas. **to stop beating about the bush,** dejarse de historias. **to b. a retreat,** Mil. emprender la retirada; batir. **to b. black and blue,** moler a palos. **to b. hollow,** vencer completamente; ganar fácilmente; aventajar con mucho. **to b. it,** Inf. escaparse corriendo. **to b. time,** Mus. llevar el compás; triunfar sobre la vejez. **to b. to it,** Inf. tomar la delantera. **to b. against,** golpear contra; chocar contra. **to b. back,** rechazar; (sobs, etc.) ahogar; reprimir. **to b. down,** (prices) regatear; (of the sun) caer de plomo, caer de plano; reducir; suprimir; destruir. **to b. out,** hacer salir; (metals) batir; (a tune) llevar el compás (de). **to b. up,** Cul. batir; (a mattress) mullir; asaltar; maltratar
beaten /'bitn/ a (of paths) trillado; (conquered) vencido; (of metals) batido; (dejected) deprimido; (trite) trivial, vulgar
beater /'bitər/ n batidor, m; (for carpets) sacudidor (de alfombras), m; Cul. batidor, m
beatific /‚biə'tɪfɪk/ a beatífico
beatification /bi‚ætɪ'keɪʃən/ n beatificación, f
beatify /bi'ætə‚faɪ/ vt beatificar
beating /'bitɪŋ/ n batimiento, m; vencimiento, m; (thrashing) paliza, f., Lat. Am. also azotera, f.; (of the heart, etc.) palpitación, f, latido, m; (of metals) batida, f; (of a drum) rataplán, toque de tambor, m; (of waves) embate, m; (of wings) aleteo, aletazo, m
beatitude /bi'ætɪ‚tud/ n beatitud, f
beau /bou/ n galán, m; (fop) petimetre, m
beautiful /'byutəfəl/ a bello, lindo, hermoso; magnífico; excelente; exquisito; elegante; encantador, delicioso
beautifully /'byutəfəli/ adv bellamente; (richly) ricamente; admirablemente; magníficamente; elegantemente
beautify /'byutə‚faɪ/ vt embellecer; hermosear; adornar. **to b. oneself,** arreglarse, ponerse elegante
beautifying /'byutə‚faɪɪŋ/ n embellecimiento, m; adorno, m
beauty /'byuti/ n belleza, hermosura, lindeza, f; magnificencia, f; excelencia, f; elegancia, f; encanto, m; (belle) beldad, Venus, f. **to lose one's b.,** desmejorarse, perder su hermosura. **b. contest,** concurso de belleza, m. **b. parlor,** salón de belleza, instituto de belleza, m. **b. sleep,** el primer sueño de la noche. **b. spot,** lunar, m; lunar postizo, m; (place) sitio hermoso, m. **b. treatment,** masaje facial, m
beaver /'bivər/ n castor, m; (hat) sombrero de copa, m; (of helmet) babera, f
because /bɪ'kɔz/ conjunc porque. **b. of,** debido a, a causa de
beckon /'bɛkən/ vt and vi hacer señas (a); llamar por señas, llamar con la mano
become /bɪ'kʌm/ vi volverse; llegar a ser, venir a ser; convertirse en; ponerse; hacerse; (befit) convenir; (suit) ir bien (a), favorecer. **He became red,** Se enrojeció. **The hat becomes you,** El sombrero te va bien. **He became king,** Llegó a ser rey. **What has b. of her?** ¿Qué es de ella? (Where is she?) ¿Qué se ha hecho de ella? **b. binding,** adquirir carácter de compromiso
becoming /bɪ'kʌmɪŋ/ a propio; correcto; decoroso; (suitable) conveniente; (of dress) que favorece, que

va bien. **This dress is b. to you,** Este vestido te favorece

becomingly /bɪˈkʌmɪŋli/ *adv* decorosamente

bed /bɛd/ *n* cama, *f*, lecho, *m*; (of sea) fondo, *m*; (of river) cauce, *m*; *Geol.* yacimiento, *m*; (in a garden) cuadro, macizo (de jardín), *m*; (of a machine) asiento, *m*; (of a building) cimiento, *m*; *Fig.* fundamento, *m*, base, *f*, *vt* (plants) plantar; (fix) fijar, poner. **double bed,** cama de matrimonio, *f*. **single bed,** cama de sencilla, *f*. **in bed,** en cama. **to be gone to bed,** haber ido a la cama. **to be in bed,** estar acostado. **to get into bed,** meterse en cama. **to get out of bed,** levantarse de la cama. **to go to bed,** acostarse, ir a la cama. **to make the beds,** hacer las camas. **to put to bed,** acostar. **to stay in bed,** quedarse en cama, guardar cama. **bed-bug,** chinche, *f*. **bed-clothes,** ropa de cama, *f*. **bed-cover,** cubrecama, colcha, *f*. **bed-head,** cabecera, *f*. **bed-pan,** silleta, *f*. **bed-sore,** úlcera de decúbito, *f*

bedaub, bedazzle. /bɪˈdɔb; bɪˈdæzəl/. See **daub, dazzle**

bedchamber /ˈbɛd,tʃeimbər/ *n* dormitorio, *m*, alcoba, *f*

bedded /ˈbɛdɪd/ *a* cama... cama(s). **a double-b. room,** un cuarto con dos camas; un cuarto con cama de matrimonio

bedding /ˈbɛdɪŋ/ *n* ropa de cama, *f*; cama para el ganado, *f*

bedeck /bɪˈdɛk/ *vt* embellecer, adornar, engalanar

bedfellow /ˈbɛd,fɛlou/ *n* compañero de almohada, compañero de cama

bedlam /ˈbɛdləm/ *n* belén, manicomio, *m*; *Fig.* babel, *m*

bedraggled /bɪˈdrægəld/ *a* mojado y sucio

bedridden /ˈbɛd,rɪdn/ *a* postrado en cama, inválido

bedrock /ˈbɛd,rɒk/ *n* lecho de roca, *m*; *Fig.* principios fundamentales, fundamentos, *m pl*

bedroom /ˈbɛd,rum/ *n* cuarto de dormir, dormitorio, *m*, habitación, *f*

bedside /ˈbɛd,said/ *n* lado de cama, *m*; cabecera, *f*. **b. manner,** mano izquierda, diplomacia, *f*. **b.-table,** mesa de noche, *f*

bedspread /ˈbɛd,sprɛd/ *n* colcha, cubrecama, sobrecama, *f*

bedstead /ˈbɛd,stɛd/ *n* cama, *f*

bedtime /ˈbɛd,taim/ *n* hora de acostarse, *f*

bee /bi/ *n* abeja, *f*; (meeting) reunión, *f*, *a* abejuno. **queen bee,** rey, *m*, abeja maestra, *f*. **to have a bee in one's bonnet,** tener una manía (o idea fija). **to make a bee-line for,** ir directamente a. **bee-eater,** *Ornith.* abejaruco, *m*. **bee hive,** colmena, *f*; abejar, *m*. **bee-keeper,** apicultor (-ra), colmenero (-ra), abejero (-ra). **bee's wax,** cera de abeja, *f*

beech /bitʃ/ *n* haya, *f*. **plantation of b. trees,** hayal, *m*. **b.-nut,** hayuco, *m*

beef /bif/ *n* carne de res, *f*; (flesh) carne, *f*; (strength) fuerza, *f*. **roast b.,** rosbif, *m*. **b.-tea,** caldo, *m*

beefsteak /ˈbif,steik/ *n* bistec, *Argentina* bife, *m*

beer /bɪər/ *n* cerveza, *f*. **b. barrel,** barril de cerveza, *m*. **b.-house,** cervecería, *f*. **b. mug,** jarro para la cerveza, *m*

beery /ˈbɪəri/ *a* de cerveza; (tipsy) achispado

beet /bit/ *n* remolacha, *f*. *Mexico* betabel, *m*. **b. sugar,** azúcar de remolacha, *Mexico* azúcar de betabel, *m*

beetle /ˈbitl/ *n* escarabajo, *m*. **b.-browed,** cejijunto

beetroot /ˈbit,rut/ *n* remolacha, *f*, *Mexico* betabel, *m*

befall /bɪˈfɔl/ *vi* acontecer, suceder, ocurrir. *vt* ocurrir (a), acontecer (a)

befit /bɪˈfɪt/ *vt* convenir (a), ser digno de

befitting /bɪˈfɪtɪŋ/ *a* conveniente, apropiado; digno; oportuno

before /bɪˈfɔr/ *adv* delante; al frente; (of time) antes, anteriormente; (of order) antes; (already) ya. *prep* delante de; en frente de; (of time, order) ante; (in the presence of) ante, en presencia de; (rather than) antes de. **b. going,** antes de marcharse. **B. I did it,** Antes de que lo hiciera; Antes de hacerlo. **as never b.,** como nunca. **b. long,** en breve, dentro de poco. **b.-mentioned,** antes citado. **b. the mast,** al pie del mástil, e.g. *two years b. the mast,* dos años al pie del mástil

beforehand /bɪˈfɔr,hænd/ *adv* previamente, de antemano

befoul /bɪˈfaul/ *vt* ensuciar; *Fig.* manchar, difamar

befriend /bɪˈfrɛnd/ *vt* proteger, ayudar, favorecer, amparar

beg /bɛg/ *vt* pedir, implorar, suplicar, rogar. *vi* mendigar, pordiosear; vivir de limosna. **I beg to propose,** Me permito proponer; Tengo el gusto de proponer; (the health of) Brindo a la salud de. **I beg your pardon!** ¡Vd. dispense!; (when passing in front of anyone, etc.) Con permiso; (in conversation for repetition of a word) ¿Cómo? **to beg the question,** dar por sentado lo mismo que se trata de probar. **His conduct begs description,** No hay palabras para su comportamiento

beget /bɪˈgɛt/ *vt* procrear, engendrar; causar; suscitar

begetter /bɪˈgɛtər/ *n* procreador (-ra); creador (-ra)

begetting /bɪˈgɛtɪŋ/ *n* procreación, *f*; origen, *m*, causa, *f*

beggar /ˈbɛgər/ *n* mendigo (-ga), pordiosero (-ra), *Lat. Am. also* llimosnero (-ra). **beggars can't be choosers,** a falta de pan, se conforma con tortillas (Mexico); *vt* empobrecer; arruinar. **to b. description,** no haber palabras para describir

beggarliness /ˈbɛgərlinɪs/ *n* mendicidad, *f*; pobreza, *f*

beggarly /ˈbɛgərli/ *a* miserable, pobre

beggary /ˈbɛgəri/ *n* miseria, pobreza, *f*

begging /ˈbɛgɪŋ/ *a* mendicante, pordiosero. *n* mendicidad, *f*, pordioseo, *m*. **to go b.,** andar mendigando. **b. letter,** carta pidiendo dinero, *f*

begin /bɪˈgɪn/ *vt* and *vi* empezar; comenzar; iniciar; (a conversation) entablar; (open) abrir; inaugurar; tener su principio; nacer. **to b. to,** empezar a; (start on) ponerse a; (with laughing, etc.) romper a. **to b. with,** empezar por; para empezar, en primer lugar

beginner /bɪˈgɪnər/ *n* principiante (-ta); (novice) novato (-ta); iniciador (-ra); autor (-ra)

beginning /bɪˈgɪnɪŋ/ *n* principio, comienzo, *Lat. Am.* empiezo, *m*; origen, *m*. **at the b.,** al principio; (of the month) a principios (de). **from the b. to the end,** desde el principio hasta el fin, *Inf.* de pe a pa. **in the b.,** al principio. **to make a b.,** comenzar, empezar

begone /bɪˈgɔn/ *interj* ¡fuera! ¡márchate! ¡vete!

begonia /bɪˈgounyə/ *n* begonia, *f*

begrudge /bɪˈgrʌdʒ/ *vt* envidiar

beguile /bɪˈgail/ *vt* engañar; defraudar; (time) entretener; (charm) encantar, embelesar

beguilement /bɪˈgailmənt/ *n* engaño, *m*; (of time) entretenimiento, *m*; (charm) encanto, *m*

beguilingly /bɪˈgailɪŋli/ *adv* encantadoramente

behalf /bɪˈhæf/ *n* (preceded by on or upon) por; (from) de parte (de); a favor (de); en defensa (de)

behave /bɪˈheiv/ *vi* (oneself) conducirse, portarse; (act) obrar, proceder. **to b. badly,** portarse mal; obrar mal. **B.!** ¡Pórtate bien!

behavior /bɪˈheivyər/ *n* conducta, *f*; comportamiento, *m*; proceder, *m*; (manner) modales, *m pl*; *Biol.* reacción, *f*. **b. science,** ciencias de la conducta, *f pl*

behaviorism /bɪˈheivyə,rizəm/ *n* *Psychol.* behaviorismo, *m*, conductismo, *m*

behead /bɪˈhɛd/ *vt* decapitar, descabezar

beheading /bɪˈhɛdɪŋ/ *n* decapitación, *f*

behest /bɪˈhɛst/ *n* precepto, mandato, *m*

behind /bɪˈhaind/ *adv* detrás; por detrás; atrás; hacia atrás; en pos; (of time and order) después; (late and in arrears) con retraso; (old-fashioned) atrasado. *prep* detrás de; por detrás de; inferior a; menos avanzado que. *n Inf.* trasero, *m*. **from b.,** por detrás. **to be b. time,** retrasarse; llegar tarde. **b. the back of,** a espaldas de. **b. the scenes,** entre bastidores. **b. the times,** *Fig.* atrasado de noticias; pasado de moda. **the ideology b. the French Revolution,** la ideología que informó la Revolución Francesa.

behold /bɪˈhould/ *vt* ver, mirar, contemplar; presenciar. *interj* ¡he aquí! ¡mira!

beholden /bɪˈhouldən/ *a* obligado, agradecido

beholder /bɪˈhouldər/ *n* espectador (-ra). **the beholders,** los que lo presenciaban

beholding /bɪˈhouldɪŋ/ *n* contemplación, vista, *f*

behoove /bɪˈhuv/ *vt* incumbir, tocar, corresponder

beige /beiʒ/ *n* beige, color arena, *m*

being /'biɪŋ/ n existencia, f; operación, f; ser, m; (spirit) alma, f, espíritu, m; esencia, f. **human b.,** ser humano, m, alma viviente, f. **for the time b.,** por ahora, por el momento

bejewel /bɪ'dʒuəl/ vt enjoyar, adornar con joyas

belabor /bɪ'leibər/ vt apalear, golpear

belated /bɪ'leitɪd/ a tardío

belay /bɪ'lei/ vt amarrar

belch /bɛltʃ/ n eructo, m; detonación, f; (of a volcano) erupción, f. vi eructar. vt vomitar; (curses, etc.) escupir; despedir, arrojar

belching /'bɛltʃɪŋ/ n eructación, f; (of smoke, etc.) vómito, m, emisión, f

beleaguer /bɪ'ligər/ vt sitiar

belfry /'bɛlfri/ n campanario, m

Belgian /'bɛldʒən/ a and n belga, mf

Belgium /'bɛldʒəm/ Bélgica, f

Belgrade /'bɛlgreid/ Belgrado, m

belie /bɪ'lai/ vt desmentir, contradecir; defraudar

belief /bɪ'lif/ n creencia, f; fe, f; opinión, f, parecer, m; (trust) confianza, f. **in the b. that,** creyendo que, en la creencia de que

believable /bɪ'livəbəl/ a creíble

believe /bɪ'liv/ vt and vi creer; opinar, ser de la opinión, parecer (a uno); confiar, tener confianza. **I b. not,** Creo que no, Me parece que no. **I b. so,** Creo que sí, Me parece que sí. **to make (a person) b.,** hacer (a uno) creer. **to b. in,** creer en; confiar en, tener confianza en

believer /bɪ'livər/ n persona que cree, f; creyente, mf

belittle /bɪ'lɪtl/ vt achicar; conceder poca importancia a

bell /bɛl/ n campana, f; (hand-bell) campanilla, f; (small, round) cascabel, m; (on cows, etc.) cencerro, m, esquila, f; (electric, push, or bicycle) timbre, m; (jester's) cascabeles, m pl; (cry of stag) bramido, m. vt poner un cascabel (a). vi (stags) bramar, roncar. **to ring the b.,** tocar el timbre; agitar la campanilla. **to ring the bells,** tocar las campanas. **to b. the cat,** ponerle el cascabel al gato, ponerle el collar al gato. **b.-boy,** botones, mozo de hotel, m. **b.-clapper,** badajo, m. **b.-flower,** campanilla, f. **b.-founder,** campanero, m. **b.-mouthed,** abocinado. **b.-pull,** tirador de campanilla, m. **b.-ringer,** campanero, m. **b.-shaped,** campanudo. **b.-tent,** pabellón, m. **b. tower,** campanario, m

belladonna /ˌbɛlə'dɒnə/ n belladona, f

belle /bɛl/ n beldad, f

belles-lettres /bɛl 'lɛtrə/ n pl bellas letras, f pl

bellicose /'bɛlɪˌkous/ a belicoso, agresivo

bellicosity /ˌbɛlɪ'kɒsɪti/ n belicosidad, f

belligerence /bə'lɪdʒərəns/ n beligerancia, f

belligerent /bə'lɪdʒərənt/ a beligerante; belicoso, guerrero. n beligerante, mf

bellow /'bɛlou/ n (shout) grito, m; rugido, bramido, m; (of guns) trueno, m. vi gritar, vociferar; rugir, bramar; tronar

bellowing /'bɛlouɪŋ/ n. See **bellow**

bellows /'bɛlouz/ n fuelle, m

belly /'bɛli/ n vientre, m, barriga, f; (of a jug, etc.) panza, f; estómago, m; (womb) seno, m. vt hinchar. vi hincharse

belong /bɪ'lɔŋ/ vi pertenecer (a); tocar (a), incumbir (a); (to a place) ser de; residir en

belongings /bɪ'lɔŋɪŋz/ n pl efectos, m pl; posesiones, f pl; (luggage) equipaje, m

beloved /bɪ'lʌvɪd/ a muy amado, muy querido. n querido (-da)

below /bɪ'lou/ adv abajo; (under) debajo; (further on) más abajo; (in hell) en el infierno; (in this world) en este mundo, aquí abajo. prep bajo; (underneath) debajo de; (after) después de; (unworthy of) indigno de; inferior a. **The valley lay b. us,** El valle se extendía a nuestros pies. **b. zero,** bajo cero

belt /bɛlt/ n cinturón, m; (of a horse) cincha, f; (corset) faja, f; Geog. zona, f; (of a machine) correa (de transmisión), f

beltway /'bɛltˌwei/ n anillo periférico, m

belvedere /'bɛlvɪˌdiər/ n mirador, m

bemoan /bɪ'moun/ vt deplorar, lamentar

bemoaning /bɪ'mounɪŋ/ n lamentación, f

bemuse /bɪ'myuz/ vt confundir, desconcertar

bench /bɛntʃ/ n banco, m; (with a back) escaño, m; mesa de trabajo, f; (carpenter's, shoemaker's, in a boat, in parliament) banco, m; (judges) tribunal, m

bend /bɛnd/ n corvadura, curva, vuelta, f; (in a river, street) recodo, m; (on a road) codo viraje, m; (of the knee) corva, f; (in a pipe) codo, m; Naut. nudo, m; Herald. banda, f. **sheet b.,** (knot) nudo de tejedor, m

bend /bɛnd/ vt encorvar; doblegar; torcer; (the head) bajar; (the body) inclinar; (steps) dirigir, encaminar; (the mind) aplicarse, dedicarse. vi encorvarse; doblegarse; torcerse; (arch) arquear; inclinarse. **to b. the knee,** arrodillarse. **on bended knee,** de rodillas. **to b. back,** vt redoblar. vi redoblarse; inclinarse hacia atrás. **to b. down,** agacharse; inclinarse. **to b. forward,** inclinarse hacia delante. **to b. over,** inclinarse encima de

bendable /'bɛndəbəl/ a que puede doblarse; plegadizo; flexible

bending /'bɛndɪŋ/ n doblamiento, m; flexión, f; inclinación, f. a doblado; inclinado

beneath /bɪ'niθ/ adv abajo; debajo; (at one's feet) a los pies de uno. prep bajo; debajo de; al pie de; (unworthy, inferior) indigno

Benedictine /ˌbɛnɪ'dɪktɪn; -tin/ a benedictino. n benedictino, m; (liqueur) benedictino, m

benediction /ˌbɛnɪ'dɪkʃən/ n bendición, f; gracia divina, merced, f

benefaction /'bɛnəˌfækʃən/ n beneficiación, f; buena obra, f; beneficio, favor, m

benefactor /'bɛnəˌfæktər/ n bienhechor, m; protector, m; patrono, m; fundador, m

benefactress /'bɛnəˌfæktrɪs/ n bienhechora, f; protectora, f; patrona, f; fundadora, f

benefice /'bɛnəfɪs/ n beneficio eclesiástico, m; prebenda, f

beneficence /bə'nɛfəsəns/ n beneficiencia, caridad, f; buenas obras, f pl

beneficent /bə'nɛfəsənt/ a benéfico, caritativo

beneficial /ˌbɛnə'fɪʃəl/ a beneficioso; provechoso, útil

beneficiary /ˌbɛnə'fɪʃiˌɛri/ n beneficiado (-da), beneficiario (-ia)

benefit /'bɛnəfɪt/ n beneficio, bien, m; provecho, m, utilidad, f; (favor) favor, m; Theat. beneficio, m; (help) ayuda, f, servicio, m. vt beneficiar; aprovechar; (improve) mejorar. vi (with by) sacar provecho de; ganar. **for the b. of,** para; en pro de, a favor de. **b. society,** sociedad benéfica, f

benevolence /bə'nɛvələns/ n benevolencia, bondad, f; liberalidad, f; caridad, f; favor, m

benevolent /bə'nɛvələnt/ a benévolo; bondadoso; caritativo. **b. society,** sociedad de beneficencia, f

benevolently /bə'nɛvələntli/ adv benignamente, con benevolencia

Bengal /bɛn'gɔl/ Bengala, f

benighted /bɪ'naitɪd/ a sorprendido por la noche; Fig. ignorante

benign, benignant /bɪ'nain; bɪ'nɪgnənt/ a benigno

bent /bɛnt/ n talento, m; inclinación, afición, f, a torcido, Mexico chueco; encorvado; resuelto

benumb /bɪ'nʌm/ See **numb**

bequeath /bɪ'kwið/ vt legar, dejar (en el testamento); transmitir

bequest /bɪ'kwɛst/ n legado, m

Berber /'bɑrbər/ a and n bereber, mf

bereave /bɪ'riv/ vt privar (de), quitar; arrebatar; afligir. **the bereaved parents,** los padres afligidos

bereavement /bɪ'rivmənt/ n privación, f; (by death) pérdida, f; aflicción, f

bereft /bɪ'rɛft/ a privado (de); desamparado; indefenso. **utterly b.,** completamente solo

beret /bə'rei/ n boina, f

Berlin /bər'lɪn/ a and n (of or from) berlinés (-esa). n (carriage) berlina, f

Bermudas, the /bər'myudəz/ m las Islas Bermudas

Bernard /bər'nɑrd/ n Bernardo, m. **St. B. dog,** perro de San Bernardo, m

Berne /bɜrn/ Berna, f

biddable

berry /'bɛri/ n baya, f; (of coffee, etc.) fruto, m, vi dar bayas; coger bayas
berth /bɜrθ/ n (bed) litera, f; (cabin) camarote, m; (anchorage) anclaje, fondeadero, m; (job) empleo, m, vt (a ship) fondear. **to give a wide b. to,** Naut. ponerse a resguardo de; apartarse mucho de; evitar
beseech /bɪ'sitʃ/ vt suplicar, rogar, implorar; (ask for) pedir con ahinco
beseeching /bɪ'sitʃɪŋ/ a suplicante, implorante. n súplica, f; ruego, m
beseechingly /bɪ'sitʃɪŋli/ adv suplicantemente
beset /bɪ'sɛt/ vt atacar, acosar; aquejar, acosar, perseguir. **beset by personal misfortune,** acosado por las desgracias personales; (block) obstruir; (surround) rodear, cercar
besetting /bɪ'sɛtɪŋ/ a usual, frecuente; obsesionante
beside, besides /bɪ'said; bɪ'saidz/ prep al lado de; cerca de; (compared with) en comparación de, comparado con; (in addition) además de; aparte de; excepto. adv además, también. **to be beside oneself,** estar fuera de sí
besiege /bɪ'sidʒ/ vt sitiar; (assail) asaltar, asediar; (surround) rodear; importunar
besieged /bɪ'sidʒd/ n sitiado (-da)
besieger /bɪ'sidʒər/ n sitiador, m
besieging /bɪ'sidʒɪŋ/ a sitiador. n sitio, asalto, m; asedio, m, importunación, f
besmear /bɪ'smɪər/ vt embadurnar, ensuciar
besotted /bɪ'sɒtɪd/ a estúpido; embrutecido; atontado
bespangled /bɪ'spæŋɡəld/ a adornado con lentejuelas; brillante (con); (studded) salpicado (de)
bespatter /bɪ'spætər/ vt manchar; derramar; salpicar
bespeak /bɪ'spik/ vt reservar; (goods) encargar; (signify) demostrar, indicar, significar; Poet. hablar
besprinkle /bɪ'sprɪŋkəl/ vt rociar
best /bɛst/ a sup of **good** and **well,** mejor; el (la) mejor, m, f., los (las) mejores, m pl, f pl. adv mejor; el mejor; (most) más. **as b. I can,** como mejor pueda. **at the b.,** cuando más, en el mejor caso. **He did it for the b.,** Lo hizo con la mejor intención. **the b.,** lo mejor. **to be at one's b.,** brillar; lucirse. **to do one's b.,** hacer todo lo posible. **to get the b. of,** llevar la mejor parte de; triunfar de (or sobre). **to make the b. of,** sacar el mayor provecho de. **The next b. thing to do is...,** Lo mejor que queda ahora por hacer es... **b. man,** padrino de boda, m. **to be b. man to,** apadrinar, ser padrino de. **b. seller,** libro que se vende más, libro favorito, m
bestial /'bɛstʃəl/ a bestial
bestiality /ˌbɛstʃi'ælɪti/ n bestialidad, f
bestir (oneself) /bɪ'stɜr/ vr menearse, moverse; preocuparse; (hurry) darse prisa
bestow /bɪ'stou/ vt (place) poner; (with upon) conferir, conceder, otorgar; (a present) regalar
bestowal /bɪ'stouəl/ n puesta, f; otorgamiento, m, concesión, f; (of a present) regalo, m, dádiva, f
bestride /bɪ'straid/ vt montar a horcajadas en; poner una pierna en cada lado de; cruzar de un tranco
bestseller /'bɛst'sɛlər/ n campeón de venta, éxito editorial, triunfo de librería, m
bet /bɛt/ n apuesta, postura, f, vi apostar; (gamble) jugar. **What do you bet?** ¿Qué apuesta Vd.?
bethink (oneself) /bɪ'θɪŋk/ vr pensar, reflexionar; (remember) recordar, hacer memoria; ocurrirse
Bethlehem /'bɛθlɪˌhɛm/ Belén, m
betray /bɪ'trei/ vt traicionar; revelar, descubrir; (a woman) seducir; (show) dejar ver
betrayal /bɪ'treiəl/ n traición, f; (of confidence) abuso (de confianza), m; (of a woman) seducción, f
betrayer /bɪ'treiər/ n traidor (-ra)
betroth /bɪ'trouð/ vt desposar(se) con, prometer(se). **to be betrothed to,** estar desposado con
betrothal /bɪ'trouðəl/ n desposorio, m, esponsales, m pl; (duration) noviazgo, m
betrothed /bɪ'trouðd/ n desposado (-da), futuro (-ra)
better /'bɛtər/ a comp of **good,** mejor; superior. adv mejor; más. vt mejorar; exceder. n apostador (-ra). **He has bettered himself,** Ha mejorado su situación. **It is b. to...,** Es mejor..., Vale más... (followed by infin.). **little b.,** poco mejor; algo mejor; poco más.

much b., mucho mejor. **so much the b.,** tanto mejor. **the b. to,** para mejor. **to be b.,** ser mejor; (of health) estar mejor. **to get b.,** mejorar. **to get the b. of,** triunfar sobre, vencer. **b. half,** Inf. media naranja, f. **b. off,** mejor situado, más acomodado
betterment /'bɛtərmənt/ n mejora, f, mejoramiento, m; adelantamiento, avance, m
betting /'bɛtɪŋ/ n apuesta, f
bettor /'bɛtər/ n apostador (-ra)
between /bɪ'twin/ prep entre; en medio de; de. **the break b. Mr. X and Mrs. Y,** el rompimiento del Sr. X y la Sra. Y. adv en medio; entre los dos. **far b.,** a grandes intervalos. **b. now and then,** desde ahora hasta entonces. **b. one thing and another,** entre una cosa y otra. **b. ourselves,** entre nosotros
bevel /'bɛvəl/ n bisel, m, vt abiselar
beverage /'bɛvərɪdʒ/ n brebaje, m, bebida, f
bevy /'bɛvi/ n grupo, m; (of birds) bandada, f; (of roes) manada, f
bewail /bɪ'weil/ vt lamentar, llorar
bewailing /bɪ'weilɪŋ/ n lamentación, f
beware /bɪ'wɛər/ vi guardarse (de); cuidar (de); desconfiar (de). interj ¡cuidado! ¡atención! **B. of imitations!** ¡Desconfiad de las imitaciones!
bewilder /bɪ'wɪldər/ vt aturdir, abobar; dejar perplejo (a); confundir
bewildered /bɪ'wɪldərd/ a aturdido, abobado; perplejo; confuso
bewildering /bɪ'wɪldərɪŋ/ a incomprensible; complicado
bewilderment /bɪ'wɪldərmənt/ n aturdimiento, m; perplejidad, f; confusión, f
bewitch /bɪ'wɪtʃ/ vt hechizar; fascinar, encantar
bewitching /bɪ'wɪtʃɪŋ/ a encantador, hechicero, fascinante. n embrujamiento, encantamiento, m
bewitchingly /bɪ'wɪtʃɪŋli/ adv de un modo encantador
bewitchment /bɪ'wɪtʃmənt/ n. See **bewitching**
beyond /bi'ɒnd/ prep más allá de; más lejos que; (behind) tras, detrás de; (of time) después de; Fig. fuera del alcance de; (without) fuera de; (above) encima de; (not including) aparte. adv más allá; más lejos; detrás. **b. doubt,** fuera de duda. **b. question,** indiscutible. **b. the sea,** allende el mar. **That is b. me,** Eso es demasiado para mí; Eso no está en mi mano; Eso está fuera de mi alcance. **the B.,** la otra vida
Bhután /bu'tɑn/ Bután, m
bias /'baiəs/ n sesgo, bies, través, m; Fig. prejuicio, m; parcialidad, f, vt influir; predisponer. **to cut on the b.,** cortar al sesgo
biased /'baiəst/ a parcial; tendencioso
bib /bɪb/ n babero, m; pechera, f, vi beber mucho, empinar el codo
Bible /'baibəl/ n Biblia, f
biblical /'bɪblɪkəl/ a bíblico. **b. history,** historia sagrada, f
bibliographer /ˌbɪbli'ɒɡrəfər/ n bibliógrafo (-fa)
bibliographical /ˌbɪblə'ɡræfɪkəl/ a bibliográfico
bibliography /ˌbɪbli'ɒɡrəfi/ n bibliografía, f
bibliophile /'bɪbliəˌfail/ n bibliófilo, m
bibulous /'bɪbyələs/ a bebedor, borrachín
bicarbonate /bai'kɑrbənɪt/ n bicarbonato, m
bicentenary /ˌbaisɛn'tɛnəri/ n segundo centenario, m
biceps /'baisɛps/ n bíceps, m
bicker /'bɪkər/ vi disputar, altercar; (of stream, etc.) murmurar, susurrar; (of flame) bailar, centellear
bickering /'bɪkərɪŋ/ n altercado, argumento, m
bicycle /'baisɪkəl/ n bicicleta, f, vi andar en bicicleta, ir de bicicleta
bicycle pump Lat. Am. inflador, m
bicycling /'baisɪklɪŋ/ n ciclismo, m
bicyclist /'baisɪklɪst/ n biciclista, mf
bid /bɪd/ n (at auction) postura, f; (bridge) puja, f; oferta, f, vt mandar, ordenar, invitar a; (at an auction) pujar, licitar. **to make a bid for,** (attempt) hacer un esfuerzo para; procurar. **to bid fair,** prometer; dar indicios de; dar esperanzas de. **to bid goodbye to,** decir adios (a), despedirse de. **to bid welcome,** dar la bienvenida (a)
biddable /'bɪdəbəl/ a obediente, dócil; manso

bidder /'bɪdər/ n postor, m, pujador (-ra). **the highest b.**, el mejor postor

bidding /'bɪdɪŋ/ n (order) orden, f; instrucción, f; invitación, f; (at an auction) postura, licitación, f. **to do a person's b.**, hacer lo que se le manda

bide /baɪd/ vt aguardar, esperar. **to b. by,** (fulfill) cumplir con

bidet /bi'dei/ n bidé, m

biennial /bai'ɛnɪəl/ a bianual, bienal

bier /bɪər/ n andas, f pl; féretro, ataúd, m

bifocal /bai'foukəl/ a bifocal

bifurcate /'baifər,keit/ vt and vi bifurcar(se)

bifurcation /,baifər'keiʃən/ n bifurcación, f

big /bɪg/ a grande; before n sing gran; grueso; (grown up) mayor; (tall) alto; voluminoso; (vast) extenso, vasto; (full) lleno (de); (with young) preñada; importante; tamaño. **to talk big**, echarla de importante. **big-boned,** huesudo. **big-end,** Auto. biela, f. **big game,** caza mayor, f. **big gun,** Inf. pájaro gordo, m

bigamist /'bɪgəmɪst/ n bígamo (-ma)

bigamous /'bɪgəməs/ a bígamo

bigamy /'bɪgəmi/ n bigamia, f

bight /bait/ n (in a rope) vuelta (de un cabo), f; (bay) ensenada, f

bigness /'bɪgnɪs/ n grandor, m; gran tamaño, m; altura, f; (tallness of a person) gran talle, m; (vastness) extensión, f; importancia, f

bigot /'bɪgət/ n fanático (-ca)

bigoted /'bɪgətɪd/ a fanático, intolerante

bigotry /'bɪgətri/ n fanatismo, m, intolerancia, f

bikini /bɪ'kini/ n bikini, m

bilberry /'bɪl,beri/ n arándano, m

bile /bail/ n bilis, hiel, f; mal humor, m, cólera, f

bilge /bɪldʒ/ n Naut. pantoque, m, sentina, f. **b. water,** agua de pantoque, f

bilingual /bai'lɪŋgwəl/ a bilingüe

bilious /'bɪlyəs/ a bilioso

bill /bɪl/ n (parliamentary) proyecto de ley, m; Law. escrito, m; Com. cuenta, f; (poster) cartel, m; (program) programa, m; (cast) repertorio, m; (bank note) billete de banco, m; (of a bird) pico, m; (for pruning) podadera, f. **due b.,** Com. abonaré, m. **Post no bills!** Se prohíbe fijar carteles. **b. of exchange,** letra de cambio, f. **b. of fare,** lista de platos, f; Fig. programa, m. **b. of health,** patente de sanidad, f. **b. of lading,** conocimiento de embarque, m. **b. of rights,** declaración de derechos, f. **b. of sale,** contrato de venta, m, carta de venta, f. **b.-broker,** agente de bolsa, agente de cambio, m. **b.-poster,** fijador de carteles, cartelero, m

bill /bɪl/ vt anunciar; publicar; poner en el programa; fijar carteles en. **to b. and coo,** (doves) arrullar; Inf. besuquearse

billboard /'bɪl,bɔrd/ n tablero publicitario, m

billed /bɪld/ a (in compounds) de pico

billet /'bɪlɪt/ n alojamiento, m; (of wood) pedazo (de leña), m; (job) empleo, destino, m, vt alojar (en or con)

billeting /'bɪlɪtɪŋ/ n alojamiento, m. **b. officer,** Mil. aposentador, m; oficial encargado de encontrar alojamiento, m

billiards /'bɪlyərdz/ n pl billar, m. **billiard ball,** bola de billar, f. **billiard cue,** taco, m. **billiard cushion,** baranda de la mesa de billar, f. **billiard marker,** marcador, m. **billiard match,** partida de billar, f. **billiard player,** jugador (-ra) de billar. **billiard pocket,** Lat. Am. buchaca, f. **billiard room,** sala de billar, f. **billiard table,** mesa de billar, f

billing /'bɪlɪŋ/ n facturación, f

billion /'bɪlyən/ n billón, m; (U.S.A. and France) mil millones, m pl

billionth /'bɪlyənθ/ a billonésimo; (U.S.A. and France) milmillonésimo

bill of particulars /pər'tɪkyələrz/ n relación detallada, f

billow /'bɪlou/ n oleada, f; Poet. ola, f; Fig. onda, f. vi hincharse, encresparse; ondular

billowy /'bɪloui/ a ondulante, ondeante

bimonthly /bai'mʌnθli/ a bimestral

bin /bɪn/ n hucha, f, arcón, m; recipiente, m; depósito, m; cajón, m; (for wine) estante, m

binary /'bainəri/ a binario

bind /baind/ vt atar; unir, ligar; amarrar; (in sheaves) agavillar; (bandage) vendar; sujetar; fijar; aprisionar; (a book) encuadernar; Sew. ribetear; (oblige) obligar; comprometer; (constipate) estreñir; contratar (como aprendiz). **I feel bound to,** Me siento obligado a. **to b. over,** obligar a comparecer ante el juez

binder /'baindər/ n encuadernador (-ra); Agr. agavilladora, f

binding /'baindɪŋ/ a válido, valedero; obligatorio; become **b.,** adquirir carácter de compromiso; Med. constrictivo. n atadura, ligación, f; (of books) encuadernación, f; Sew. ribete, m

binge /bɪndʒ/ n parranda, juerga, f. **to go on the b.,** ir de parranda, ir de picos pardos, ir de juerga

binnacle /'bɪnəkəl/ n Naut. bitácora, f

binocular /bɪ'nɒkyələr/ a binocular. n pl **binoculars,** binóculos, gemelos, m pl

binomial /bai'noumiəl/ a and n binomio m.

biochemist /,baiou'kɛmɪst/ n bioquímico, m

biochemistry /,baiou'kɛməstri/ n bioquímica, f

biodegradable /,baioudɪ'greidəbəl/ a biodegradable

biodiversity /,baioudɪ'vɜrsɪti/ n biodiversidad, f

biographer /bai'ɒgrəfər/ n biógrafo (-fa)

biographical /,baiə'græfɪkəl/ a biográfico

biography /bai'ɒgrəfi/ n biografía, vida, f

biological /,baiə'lɒdʒɪkəl/ a biológico

biologist /bai'ɒlədʒɪst/ n biólogo, m

biology /bai'ɒlədʒi/ n biología, f

bipartite /bai'partait/ a bipartido

biped /'baiped/ n bípedo, m, a bípedo, bípede

birch /bɜrtʃ/ n Bot. abedul, m; (rod) vara, f. a de abedul. vt pegar con una vara, dar una paliza (a)

bird /bɜrd/ n pájaro, m; ave, f. **Birds of a feather flock together,** Cada cual se arrima a su cada cual. **hen b.,** pájara, f. **b.-call,** voz del pájaro, f, canto del ave, m. **b. catcher or vendor,** pajarero, m. **bird's-eye view,** vista de pájaro, perspectiva aérea, f. **b.-like,** como un pájaro; de pájaro. **b.-lime,** liga, f. **to go b.-nesting,** ir a coger nidos de pájaros. **b. of paradise,** ave del paraíso, f. **b. of passage,** ave de paso, f. **b. of prey,** ave rapaz, f. **b.-seed,** alpiste, m. **b.-watcher,** aficionado (-da) a las aves; criador (-ra) de pájaros

birth /bɜrθ/ n nacimiento, m; (act of) parto, m; origen, m; (childhood) infancia, f; (family) linaje, m, familia, f; Fig. creación, f. **from b.,** de nacimiento. **to give b. to,** dar a luz, echar al mundo, parir. **b. certificate,** partida de nacimiento, certificación de nacimiento, f. **b. control,** anticoncepcionismo, m, regulación de la fecundidad, f. **b.-mark,** antojos, m pl. **b.-place,** lugar de nacimiento, m. **b.-rate,** natalidad, f

birthday /'bɜrθ,dei/ n cumpleaños, m

birthright /'bɜrθ,rait/ n derecho de nacimiento, m; herencia, f

Biscay, the Bay of /'bɪskei/ el Golfo de Vizcaya, m

Biscayan /bɪs'keiən/ a and n vizcaíno (-na)

biscuit /'bɪskɪt/ n galleta, f; bizcocho, m. **b. box or maker,** galletero, m. **b.-like,** abizcochado

bisect /bai'sɛkt/ vt dividir en dos partes iguales; Geom. bisecar

bisexual /bai'sɛkʃuəl/ a bisexual

bishop /'bɪʃəp/ n obispo, m; (in chess) alfil, m. **bishop's crozier,** báculo episcopal, cayado, m

bismuth /'bɪzməθ/ n bismuto, m

bison /'baisən/ n bisonte, m

bisque /bɪsk/ n porcelana blanca, f, bizcocho, m

bistoury /'bɪstəri/ n bisturí, m

bit /bɪt/ n pedazo, m; (of grass, etc.) brizna, f; (moment) instante, m; (quantity) cantidad, f; (of a drill) mecha, f; (part) parte, f; (passage) trozo, m; (horse's) bocado, m; Inf. miga, f. **a bit,** un :anto, algo, un poco. **A little bit,** Mexico un poquito. **in bits,** en pedazos. **Not a bit!** ¡Nada!; ¡Ni pizca!; ¡Claro que no! **bit by bit,** poco a poco, gradualmente. **To give someone a bit of one's mind,** contarle cuatro verdades. **to take the bit between one's teeth,** desbocarse; Fig. rebelarse. **Wait a bit!** ¡Espera un momento!

bitch /bɪtʃ/ n (female dog) perra, f; (fox) zorra, f; (wolf) loba, f

bite /bait/ n mordedura, f; mordisco, m; (mouthful, snack) bocado, m, Lat. Am. botana, f; (of fish and insects) picada, f; (hold) asimiento, m; (sting, pain) picadura, f; (pungency) resquemor, m; (offer) oferta, f; (Fig. mordancy) mordacidad, acritud, f. vt and vi morder; (gnaw) roer; (of fish, insects) picar; (of hot dishes) resquemar; (of acids) corroer; (deceive) engañar, defraudar; (of wheels, etc.) agarrar; (hurt, wound) herir. **to b. one's tongue,** morderse la lengua. **to b. the dust,** caer al suelo

biting /'baitiŋ/ a (stinging) picante; (mordant) mordaz, acre; (of winds, etc.) penetrante; satírico. n mordedura, f; roedura, f

bitter /'bitər/ a amargo; (sour) agrio, ácido; (of winds) penetrante; (of cold) intenso; cruel. **to the b. end,** hasta la muerte; hasta el último extremo. **b.-sweet,** agridulce

bitterly /'bitərli/ adv amargamente; intensamente; cruelmente

bitterness /'bitərnis/ n amargura, f; (sourness) acidez, f; (of cold) intensidad, f; crueldad, f

bitters /'bitərz/ n pl (drink) bíter, m, angostura, f

bitumen /bai'tumən/ n betún, m

bivouac /'bivu,æk/ n Mil. vivaque, m, vi vivaquear

bizarre /bi'zɑr/ a raro, extravagante; grotesco

black /blæk/ a negro; obscuro; (sad) triste, melancólico; funesto; perverso; (sullen) malhumorado. n (color) negro, m; (mourning) luto, m; (person) negro (-a), Lat. Am. moreno (-a). vt ennegrecer; tiznar. **in b. and white,** por escrito. **to look on the b. side,** verlo todo negro. **b. art,** nigromancia, f. **b.-currant,** grosella negra, f. **b.-eyed,** ojinegro, con ojos negros. **b.-haired,** pelinegro, de pelo negro. **b.-lead,** plombagina, f. **b.-list,** lista negra, f. **b.-market,** estraperlo, mercado negro, m. **b.-marketeer,** estraperlista, contrabandista, mf. **b.-out,** oscurecimiento, apagamiento, m. **b. panther,** pantera negra, f. **b.-pudding,** morcilla, f. **b. sheep,** oveja negra, f; Fig. oveja descarriada, f; (of a family) garbanzo negro, m. **b.-water fever,** melanuria, f

blackberry /'blæk,beri/ n mora, zarzamora, f; (bush) zarza, f, moral, m

blackbird /'blæk,bɜrd/ n mirlo, m

blackboard /'blæk,bɔrd/ n encerado, m, pizarra, f

black coffee n Spain café solo, Colombia café tinto, elsewhere in Lat. Am. café negro m

blacken /'blækən/ vt ennegrecer; tiznar; Fig. manchar, desacreditar. vi ennegrecerse

black eye n ojo como un tomate, ojo morado, m

blackguard /'blægɑrd/ n tipo de cuidado, perdido, m

blackhead /'blæk,hed/ n espinilla, f

blacking /'blækiŋ/ n betún, m

blackish /'blækiʃ/ a negruzco

blackmail /'blæk,meil/ n chantaje, m, vt hacer víctima de un chantaje; arrancar dinero por chantaje (a)

blackmailer /'blæk,meilər/ n chantajista, mf

blackness /'blæknis/ n negrura, f; obscuridad, f

blacksmith /'blæk,smiθ/ n herrero (-ra) mf, Lat. Am. also encasquillador (-ra) mf. **blacksmith's forge,** herrería, f

bladder /'blædər/ n Anat. vejiga, f; ampolla, f; (of sea-plants) vesícula, f; (of fish) vejiga natatoria, f

blade /bleid/ n (leaf) hoja, f; (of grass, etc.) brizna, f; (of sharp instruments) hoja, f; (of oar) pala, f; (of propeller) paleta, ala, f

bladed /'bleidid/ a de... hojas. **a two-b. knife,** un cuchillo de dos hojas

blame /bleim/ n culpa, f; responsabilidad, f; censura, f. vt culpar, echar la culpa (a); tachar, censurar, criticar; acusar. **You are to b. for this,** Vd. tiene la culpa de esto

blameless /'bleimlis/ a inculpable; inocente; intachable; elegante

blamelessness /'bleimlisnis/ n inculpabilidad, inocencia, f; elegancia, f

blameworthy /'bleim,wɜrði/ a culpable, digno de censura, vituperable

blanch /blæntʃ/ vt Cul. mondar; hacer palidecer. vi palidecer, perder el color

blanching /'blæntʃiŋ/ n palidecimiento, m; Cul. mondadura, f

blancmange /blə'mɑndʒ/ n manjar blanco, m

bland /blænd/ a afable, cortés; dulce, agradable

blandish /'blændiʃ/ vt adular, halagar, acariciar

blandishment /'blændiʃmənt/ n adulación, f, halago, m, caricia, f

blandness /'blændnis/ n afabilidad, urbanidad, f; dulzura, f

blank /blæŋk/ a en blanco; (empty) vacío; desocupado; pálido; (confused) confuso, desconcertado; (expressionless) sin expresión; (of verse) suelto; sin adorno. n blanco, hueco, m; papel en blanco, m; laguna, f; (form to be filled out) hoja f, Mexico esqueleto, m. **b. cartridge,** cartucho para salvas, cartucho de fogueo, m. **b. verse,** verso suelto, m

blanket /'blæŋkit/ n manta, frazada, Lat. Am. cobija f; (of a horse) sudadero, Lat. Am. mandil m; Fig. capa, f. vt cubrir con una manta. **to toss in a b.,** mantear. **wet b.,** aguafiestas, mf. **b. maker or seller,** mantero, m. **b. vote,** voto colectivo, m

blanketing /'blæŋkitiŋ/ n manteamiento, m

blankly /'blæŋkli/ adv con indiferencia; sin comprender; (flatly) categóricamente

blankness /'blæŋknis/ n confusión, f, desconcierto, m; (emptiness) vaciedad, f; indiferencia, f; incomprensión, f

blare /blɛər/ n sonido de la trompeta o del clarín, Poet. clangor, m; (of a car horn) ruido, m. vi sonar

blarney /'blɑrni/ n labia, f. vt lisonjear

blaspheme /blæs'fim/ vi blasfemar. vt renegar de, maldecir

blasphemer /blæs'fimər/ n blasfemador (-ra), blasfemo (-ma)

blasphemous /'blæsfəməs/ a blasfemo, blasfematorio

blasphemy /'blæsfəmi/ n blasfemia, f

blast /blæst/ n (of wind) ráfaga (de viento), f; (of a trumpet, etc.) trompetazo, son, m; (of a whistle) pitido, m; (draft) soplo, m; explosión, f; Fig. influencia maligna, f. vt (rock) barrenar, hacer saltar; (wither) marchitar, secar; Fig. destruir; (curse) maldecir. **in full b.,** en plena marcha. **b.-furnace,** alto horno, horno de cuba, m. **b. hole,** barreno, m

blaster /'blæstər/ n barrenero, m

blasting /'blæstiŋ/ n (of rock) voladura, f; (withering) marchitamiento, m; Fig. destrucción, ruina, f; (cursing) maldiciones, f pl. **a.** destructor; Fig. funesto. **b. charge,** carga explosiva, f

blatant /'bleitnt/ a ruidoso; agresivo; llamativo; (boastful) fanfarrón

blaze /bleiz/ n llama, f; fuego, m; conflagración, f; luz brillante, f; (of anger, etc.) acceso, m. vi llamear, encenderse en llamas; brillar, resplandecer. **a b. of color,** una masa de color. **Go to blazes!** ¡Vete al infierno!

blazon /'bleizən/ n Herald. blasón, m; Fig. proclamación, f, vt blasonar, adornar, proclamar

bleach /blitʃ/ n lejía, f. vt blanquear; descolorar. vi ponerse blanco; descolorarse

bleaching /'blitʃiŋ/ n blanqueo, f. **b. powder,** hipoclorito de cal, m

bleak /blik/ a yermo, desierto; frío; expuesto; (sad) triste; severo

bleakness /'bliknis/ n situación expuesta, f; desnudez, f; frío, m; (sadness) tristeza, f; severidad, f

bleary-eyed /'bliəri ,aid/ a legañoso, cegajoso

bleat /blit/ n balido, m, vt and vi balar, dar balidos

bleating /'blitiŋ/ a balador, que bala. n balido, m

bleed /blid/ vi sangrar, echar sangre; sufrir. vt sangrar; arrancar dinero a

bleeding /'blidiŋ/ n hemorragia, f; sangría, f, Lat. Am. desangre m

blemish /'blemiʃ/ n imperfección, f, defecto, m; (on fruit) maca, f; (stain) mancha, f, deshonra, f

blend /blend/ n mezcla, mixtura, f; combinación, f; fusión, f. vt mezclar; combinar. vi mezclarse; combinarse

blende /blend/ n Mineral. blenda, f

blending /'blendiŋ/ n mezcla, f; fusión, f

bless /bles/ vt bendecir; consagrar; (praise) alabar, glorificar; hacer feliz (a). **B. me!** ¡Válgame Dios!

blessed /'blesid/ a bendito; Eccl. beato, bienaventurado; (dear) querido; feliz; Inf. maldito

blessedness /ˈblɛsɪdnɪs/ n felicidad, f; bienaventuranza, f

blessing /ˈblɛsɪŋ/ n bendición, f; (grace) bendición de la mesa, f; (mercy) merced, gracia, f; favor, m; (good) bien, m. **He gave them his b.**, Les echó su bendición

Bless you! (to someone who has sneezed) ¡Salud!

blight /blaɪt/ n Agr. tizne, tizón, m; (of cereals) añublo, m; (mould) roña, f; (greenfly) pulgón, m; Fig. influencia maligna, f; (frustration) desengaño, m; (spoil-sport) aguafiestas, mf. vt atizonar; anublar; (wither) marchitar, secar; Fig. frustrar, destruir; malograr

blighter /ˈblaɪtər/ n bribón, m

blind /blaɪnd/ a ciego; (secret) secreto; (of a door, etc.) falso; (closed) cerrado, sin salida; (unaware) ignorante; sin apreciación (de). **to be b.**, ser ciego; Fig. tener una venda en los ojos. **to be b. in one eye**, ser tuerto. **to turn a b. eye**, hacer la vista gorda. **b. alley**, callejón sin salida, m. **b. as a bat**, más ciego que un topo. **b. flying**, Aer. vuelo a ciegas, m. **b. man**, ciego, hombre ciego, m. **b. obedience**, obediencia ciega, f. **b. side**, (of persons) lado débil, m. **b. woman**, ciega, mujer ciega, f

blind /blaɪnd/ vt cegar; poner una venda en los ojos (de); (dazzle) deslumbrar; hacer cerrar los ojos a; hacer ignorar

blind /blaɪnd/ n persiana, f; (Venetian) celosía, f; (deception) pretexto, m; velo, m

blindfold /ˈblaɪnd.foʊld/ vt vendar los ojos (a); Fig. poner una venda en los ojos (de). a and adv con los ojos vendados; a ciegas; con los ojos cerrados

blindly /ˈblaɪndli/ adv ciegamente; a ciegas; ignorantemente

blindman's buff /ˈblaɪnd.mænz ˈbʌf/ n gallina ciega, f

blindness /ˈblaɪndnɪs/ n ceguedad, f; ofuscación, f; ignorancia, f

blink /blɪŋk/ n parpadeo, m, guiñada, f; (of light) destello, m; reflejo, m; vi parpadear, pestañear; (of lights) destellar

blinkers /ˈblɪŋkərz/ n pl anteojeras, f pl

bliss /blɪs/ n felicidad, f; deleite, placer, m; Eccl. gloria, f

blissful /ˈblɪsfəl/ a feliz

blissfulness /ˈblɪsfəlnɪs/ n. See **bliss**

blister /ˈblɪstər/ n Med. vesícula, f; ampolla, f; (bubble) burbuja, f. vt ampollar; Fig. herir

blithe /blaɪð/ a alegre

blithely /ˈblaɪðli/ adv alegremente

blitheness /ˈblaɪðnɪs/ n alegría, f

blitzkrieg /ˈblɪts.krig/ n blitzkrieg, m, guerra relámpago, f

blizzard /ˈblɪzərd/ n ventisca, nevasca, f

bloated /ˈbloʊtɪd/ a abotagado, hinchado; orgulloso

bloater /ˈbloʊtər/ n arenque ahumado, m

blob /blɒb/ n masa, f; mancha, f; gota, f

block /blɒk/ n bloque, m; (log) leño, m; Naut. polea, f; (for beheading and of a butcher) tajo, m; (for mounting) apeadero, m; (of shares, etc.) lote, m; (of houses) manzana, Lat. Am. cuadra f; (jam) atasco, m; (obstruction) obstrucción, f; (for hats) forma, f. **A chip off the old b.**, De tal palo tal astilla. **b. and tackle**, Naut. polea con aparejo. **b.-hook**, grapa, f. **b.-house**, Mil. blocao, m

block /blɒk/ vt bloquear; cerrar (el paso); (stop up) atarugar, atascar; (a wheel) calzar; (a bill, etc.) obstruir; (hats) poner en forma. **to b. the way**, cerrar el paso.

blockade /blɒˈkeɪd/ n bloqueo, m, vt bloquear. **to run the b.**, violar el bloqueo

blockhead /ˈblɒk.hɛd/ n leño, zoquete, imbécil, m

blond(e) /blɒnd/ a (of hair) rubio; (of complexion) de tez blanca. n hombre rubio, m; (woman) rubia, mujer rubia, f. **peroxide b.**, rubia oxigenada, f. **b. lace**, blondina, f

blood /blʌd/ n sangre, f; (relationship) parentesco, m; (family) linaje, m, prosapia, f; (life) vida, f; (sap) savia, f; jugo, m; (horse) caballo de pura raza, m; (dandy) galán, m. vt sangrar. **bad b.**, mala sangre, f; odio, m; mala leche, f. **blue b.**, sangre azul, f. **in cold b.**, a sangre fría, f. **My b. is up**, Se me enciende

la sangre. **My b. runs cold**, Se me hiela la sangre. **to be in the b.**, llevar en la sangre. **b.-bank**, banco de sangre, m. **b.-bath**, matanza, f. **b.-colored**, de color de sangre, sanguíneo. **b.-feud**, venganza de sangre, f. **b.-guilt**, culpabilidad de homicidio, m. **b.-heat**, calor de sangre, m. **b.-letting**, sangría, f. **b. orange**, naranja dulce, f. **b.-plasma**, plasma sanguíneo, m. **b.-poisoning**, septicemia, f; infección, f. **b.-pressure**, presión sanguínea, f. **b. purity**, limpieza de sangre, f. **b.-red**, rojo como la sangre. **b.-relation**, pariente (-ta) consanguíneo(a). **b.-relationship**, consanguinidad, f. **b.-stain**, mancha de sangre, f. **b.-stained**, ensangrentado, manchado de sangre. **b.-stone**, sanguinaria, f. **b.-sucker**, sanguijuela, f; Fig. vampiro, m; (usurer) avaro (-ra). **b.-vessel**, vaso sanguíneo, m

blooded /ˈblʌdɪd/ a de sangre...; de casta...

bloodhound /ˈblʌd.haʊnd/ n sabueso, m

bloodily /ˈblʌdəli/ adv sangrientamente; cruentamente; con ferocidad, cruelmente

bloodiness /ˈblʌdɪnɪs/ n estado sangriento, m; crueldad, ferocidad, f

bloodless /ˈblʌdlɪs/ a exangüe; pálido; incruento; anémico; indiferente

bloodshed /ˈblʌdˌʃɛd/ n efusión de sangre, f; matanza, carnicería, f

bloodshot /ˈblʌdˌʃɒt/ a (of the eye) inyectado

bloodthirstiness /ˈblʌdˌθɜrstɪnɪs/ n sed de sangre, f

bloodthirsty /ˈblʌdˌθɜrsti/ a sanguinario, carnicero

bloody /ˈblʌdi/ a sangriento; (of battles) encarnizado; (cruel) sanguinario, cruel

bloom /blum/ n flor, f; florecimiento, m; (on fruit) flor, f; (prime) lozanía, f; (on the cheeks) color sano, m. vi florecer. **in b.**, en flor

blooming /ˈblumɪŋ/ a florido; en flor; fresco; lozano; brillante

blossom /ˈblɒsəm/ n flor, f. vi florecer. **to b. out into**, hacerse, llegar a ser; (wear) lucir; (buy) comprarse

blossomed /ˈblɒsəmd/ a con flores, de flores

blossoming /ˈblɒsəmɪŋ/ n floración, f

blot /blɒt/ n borrón, m; mancha, f. vt manchar; (erase) tachar; (dry) secar. **to b. out**, borrar; destruir; secar con papel secante

blotch /blɒtʃ/ n (on the skin, or stain) mancha, f

blotter /ˈblɒtər/ n Com. libro borrador, m; teleta, f

blotting paper /ˈblɒtɪŋ/ n papel secante, m

blouse /blaʊs/ n blusa, f

blow /bloʊ/ n golpe, m; bofetada, f; (with the fist) puñetazo, m; (with the elbow) codazo, m; (with a club) porrazo, m; (with a whip) latigazo, m; (blossoming) floración, f. **to come to blows**, venirse a las manos. **at a b.**, con un solo golpe; de una vez. **b. below the belt**, golpe bajo, m. **b. in the air**, golpe en vago, m. **b. of fate**, latigazo de la fortuna, m

blow /bloʊ/ vi (of wind) soplar (el viento); hacer viento, correr aire; (pant) jadear, echar resoplidos; (of fuses) fundirse. vt (wind instruments) tocar; soplar; (inflate) inflar; (swell) hinchar. **to b. a kiss**, tirar un beso. **to b. one's nose**, sonarse las narices. **to b. away**, disipar; ahuyentar; llevar (el viento). **to b. down**, echar por tierra, derribar (el viento). **to b. in**, llevar adentro, hacer entrar (el viento); (windows, etc.) quebrar. **to b. off**, quitar (el viento). **to b. open**, abrir (el viento). **to b. out**, hacer salir (el viento); llevar afuera (el viento); (a light) matar de un soplo, apagar soplando. **to b. over**, pasar de (el viento); soplar por; disiparse; olvidarse. **to b. up**, (inflate) inflar; (the fire) avivar (el fuego); (explode) volar; (swell) hinchar

blowing /ˈbloʊɪŋ/ n soplo, m; violencia, f; (blossoming) florecimiento, m. **b. up**, voleo, m; explosión, f

blow-up /ˈbloʊ ˌʌp/ n (photograph) fotografía ampliada, f

blubber /ˈblʌbər/ vi gimotear; berrear. n (of the whale) grasa de ballena, f. **b.-lip**, bezo, m. **b.-lipped**, bezudo

bludgeon /ˈblʌdʒən/ n cachiporra, porpa, f; garrote, m; estaca, f. vt golpear con una porra, dar garrotazos (a)

blue /blu/ a azul; (with bruises) amoratado; (sad)

deprimido, melancólico; (obscene) verde; (dark) sombrío; (traditionalist) conservador. *n* azul, *m*; (sky) cielo, *m*; (for clothes) añil de lavandera, *m*; *pl* **blues,** melancolía, depresión, *f*; (homesickness) morriña, *f*. *vt* (laundry) añilar. **to look b.,** parecer deprimido; (of prospects, etc.) ser poco halagüeño. **b. black,** azul negro, *m*; (of hair) azabache, *m*. **b.-bottle,** *Ent.* moscón, *m*. **b.-eyed,** con ojos azules. **b. gum,** eucalipto, *m*. **B. Peter,** bandera de salida, *f*. **b. print,** fotocopia, *f*; plan, *m*

bluebell /'blu₁bel/ *n* campanilla, *f*
bluestocking /'blu₁stɒkɪŋ/ *n* marisabidilla, doctora, *f*
bluff /blʌf/ *a* (of cliffs, etc.) escarpado; (of persons) franco, campechano, brusco
bluffer /'blʌfər/ *n* *Lat. Am.* blofista *mf*
bluffness /'blʌfnɪs/ *n* franqueza, brusquedad, *f*
bluish /'bluɪʃ/ *a* azulado
bluishness /'bluɪʃnɪs/ *n* color azulado, *m*
blunder /'blʌndər/ *n* desacierto, desatino, *m*; equivocación, *f*; (in a translation, etc.) falta, *f*. *vi* tropezar (con); desacertar; equivocarse; *Inf.* meter la pata. *vt* manejar mal; estropear
blunderer /'blʌndərər/ *n* desatinado (-da)
blundering /'blʌndərɪŋ/ *a* desacertado; equivocado; imprudente *n*. See **blunder**
blunt /blʌnt/ *a* romo, embotado; obtuso; (abrupt) brusco; franco; descortés; (plain) claro. *vt* enromar, embotar; (the point) despuntar; *Fig.* hacer indiferente; (pain) mitigar
bluntly /'blʌntli/ *adv* sin filo; sin punta; bruscamente, francamente; claramente
bluntness /'blʌntnɪs/ *n* embotamiento, *m*; *Fig.* brusquedad, franqueza, *f*; claridad, *f*
blur /blɜr/ *n* borrón, *m*; mancha, *f*; imagen indistinta, *f*. *vt* borrar; manchar; *Photo.* velar
blurred /blɜrd/ *a* borroso; indistinto; turbio, nebuloso
blurt (out) /blɜrt/ *vt* proferir bruscamente; revelar sin querer
blush /blʌʃ/ *n* rubor, *m*; rojo, *m*. *vi* enrojecerse, ruborizarse, ponerse colorado; avergonzarse (por)
blushing /'blʌʃɪŋ/ *a* ruboroso; púdico
bluster /'blʌstər/ *vi* (of the wind) soplar con furia; (of waves) encresparse, embravecerse; (of persons) bravear, fanfarronear. *n* furia, violencia, *f*; tumulto, *m*; fanfarronería, *f*
blustering /'blʌstərɪŋ/ *a* (of wind) violento, fuerte; (of waves) tumultuoso; (of people) fanfarrón, valentón
boar /bɔr/ *n* verraco, *m*; (wild) jabalí, *m*
board /bɔrd/ *n* tabla, *f*; (for notices) tablón, *m*; (b. residence) pensión, *f*; (table) mesa, *f*; (food) comida, *f*; (for chess, checkers) tablero, *m*; (sign) letrero, *m*; (of instruments) cuadro, *m*; (bookbinding) cartón, *m*; *Naut.* bordo, *m*; (committee) junta, dirección, *f*; tribunal, *m*; *pl* **boards** *Theat.* tablas, *f pl.* **above b.,** abiertamente, sin disimulo. **free on b.,** (f.o.b.) franco a bordo. **in boards,** (of books) encartonado. **managerial b.,** junta directiva, *f*. **on b.,** a bordo. **on the boards,** *Theat.* en las tablas. **room and b.,** pensión completa, casa y comida, *f*. **to go on b.,** ir a bordo. **b. of directors,** consejo de administración, *m*. **b. of examiners,** tribunal de exámenes, *m*. **b. of trade,** junta de comercio, *f*; ministerio de comercio, *m*
board /bɔrd/ *vt* entablar, enmaderar; embarcar en; (*Nav.* a ship) abordar; (lodge) alojar, tomar a pensión
boarder /'bɔrdər/ *n* huésped (-da); (at school) pensionista, *mf* alumno (-na) interno (-na)
boarding /'bɔrdɪŋ/ *n* entablado, *m*; (planking) tablazón, *f*; (of a ship) abordaje, *m*; (of a train) subida (al tren), *f*. **b.-house,** casa de huéspedes, pensión, *f*. **b.-school,** pensionado, *m*
boarding gate *n* puerta de embarque, *f*
boast /boust/ *n* jactancia, *f*; ostentación, *f*; (honor) gloria, *f*. *vi* jactarse, vanagloriarse, *Lat. Am.* dragonear, *Argentina* faramallear; alabarse; ostentar. **to b. about,** jactarse de; hacer gala de; gloriarse en
boaster /'boustər/ *n* vanaglorioso (-sa), jactancioso (-sa)
boastful /'boustfəl/ *a* vanaglorioso, jactancioso; ostentador

boastfulness /'boustfəlnɪs/ *n* vanagloria, jactancia, *f*; fanfarronería, *f*; ostentación, *f*
boasting /'boustɪŋ/ *n* alardeo, *m*; fanfarronería, *f*
boat /bout/ *n* barco, *m*; bote, *m*; (in a fun fair) columpio, *m*, lancha, *f*; (for sauce or gravy) salsera, *f*. *vi* ir en barco; (row) remar; navegar. **to b. down,** bajar en barco. **to b. up,** subir en barco. **b. building,** construcción de barcos, *f*. **b. club,** club náutico, *m*. **b. crew,** tripulación de un barco, *f*. **b.-hook,** bichero, garabato, *m*. **b.-house,** cobertizo de las lanchas, *m*. **b.-load,** barcada, *f*. **b.-race,** regata, *f*. **b.-scoop,** achicador, *m*. **b.-shaped,** en forma de barco. **b.-train,** tren que enlaza con un vapor, *m*
boating /'boutɪŋ/ *n* pasear en bote, *m*; manejo de un bote, *m*; (rowing) remo, *m*. **b.-pole,** botador, *m*
boatman /'boutmən/ *n* barquero, *m*
boatswain /'bousən/ *n* contramaestre, *m*. **boatswain's mate,** segundo contramaestre, *m*
bob /bɒb/ *n* (curtsey) reverencia, *f*; (woman's hair) pelo a la romana, *m*; (of bells) toque (de campana), *m*. *vi* saltar; moverse. *vt* cortar corto. **long bob,** (hair) melena, *f*. **to bob up,** ponerse de pie; surgir. **to bob up and down,** subir y bajar; bailar. **bob-tail,** rabo corto, *m*. **bob-tailed,** rabón
bobbin /'bɒbɪn/ *n* carrete, huso, *m*; (of wool, etc.) ovillo, *m*; (of looms, sewing machines) bobina, *f*; (in lace-making) bolillo, palillo, *m*
bobsled /'bɒb₁sled/ *n* trineo doble, *m*
bode /boud/ *vt* presagiar, prometer. **to b. ill,** prometer mal. **to b. well,** prometer bien
bodice /'bɒdɪs/ *n* corpiño, *m*
bodied /'bɒdid/ *a* (in compounds) de cuerpo
bodiless /'bɒdilɪs/ *a* incorpóreo
bodily /'bɒdli/ *a* del cuerpo; físico; corpóreo; real; material; (of fear) de su persona. *adv* corporalmente; en persona, personalmente; en conjunto, enteramente; en una pieza
boding /'boudɪŋ/ *a* ominoso, amenazador. *n* presagio, *m*; agüero, *m*
body /'bɒdi/ *n* *Anat.* cuerpo, *m*; (trunk) tronco, *m*; (corpse) cadáver, *m*; (of a vehicle) caja, *f*; (of a motor-car) carrocería, *f*; (of a ship) casco, *m*; (of a church) nave, *f*; (centre) centro, *m*; (of a book, persons, consistency and *Astron.*) cuerpo, *m*; (person) persona, *f*; corporación, *f*; grupo, *m*; (of an army) grueso (de ejercito), *m*; organismo, *m*. **in a b.,** en masa, juntos (juntas); en corporación. **to have enough to keep b. and soul together,** tener de que vivir. **b.-snatcher,** junta cadáveres *mf* ladrón de cadáveres, *m*. **b.-snatching,** robo de cadáveres, *m*
bodyguard /'bɒdi₁gɑrd/ *n* guardia de corps, *f*; guardia, *f*; (escort) escolta, *f*
body language *n* el lenguaje del cuerpo, *m*
bog /bɒg/ *n* pantano, marjal, *m*, marisma, *f*, *Central America* chagüe *m*
bogey /'bougi/ *n* duende, *m*; (to frighten children) coco, *m*; (nightmare) pesadilla, *f*
boggy /'bɒgi/ *a* pantanoso, fangoso
bogus /'bougəs/ *a* postizo, falso
Bohemian /bou'himiən/ *a* and *n* bohemio (-ia)
boil /bɔil/ *vi* bullir, hervir; (cook) cocer. *vt* hervir; cocer. *n* ebullición, *f*; *Med.* divieso, *m*. **to b. away,** consumirse hirviendo. *Chem.* evaporar a seco. **to b. over,** rebosar
boiler /'bɔilər/ *n* *Cul.* marmita, olla, *f*; (of a furnace) caldera, *f*. **double-b.,** baño de María, *m*. **steam-b.,** caldera de vapor, *f*. **b.-maker,** calderero, *m*. **b. room,** cámara de la caldera, *f*. **b.-suit,** mono, *m*
boiling /'bɔilɪŋ/ *n* ebullición, *f*, hervor, *m*; (cooking) cocción, *f*. *a* hirviente. **b. point,** punto de ebullición, *m*
boisterous /'bɔistərəs/ *a* (of persons) exuberante, impetuoso; (stormy) tempestuoso, borrascoso; violento
boisterously /'bɔistərəsli/ *adv* impetuosamente, ruidosamente; tempestuosamente; con violencia
boisterousness /'bɔistərəsnɪs/ *n* exuberancia, impetuosidad, *f*; violencia, *f*; tempestuosidad, borrascosidad, *f*
bold /bould/ *a* intrépido, audaz, *Argentina* agulludo; (determined) resuelto; (forward) atrevido; (showy) llamativo; (clear) claro. **b.-faced,** descarado, desvergonzado. **b.-faced type,** letra negra, *f*

boldly /'bouldli/ adv intrépidamente; descaradamente; resueltamente; claramente

boldness /'bouldnɪs/ n intrepidez, valentía, f; resolución, f; (forwardness) osadia, f, descaro, atrevimiento, m; claridad, f

Bolivia /bou'lɪviə/ Bolivia

Bolivian /bou'lɪviən/ a and n boliviano (-na)

Bolshevik /'boulʃəvɪk/ a and n bolchevique, mf

Bolshevist /'boulʃəvɪst/ n bolchevista, mf

bolster /'boulstər/ n travesaño, m. vt apuntalar; Fig. apoyar

bolt /boult/ n pasador, cerrojo, m; (pin) perno, m; (knocker) aldaba, f; (roll) rollo, m; (flight) huida, f; (of a crossbow) flecha, f; (from the blue) rayo, m. adv (upright) recto como una flecha; enhiesto; rígido. **nut and b.,** perno y tuerca, m

bolt /boult/ vt echar el cerrojo (a); empernar; (Fam. eat) zampar. vi huir; (horses) desbocarse, dispararse; (plants) cerner. **to b. down,** cerrar con cerrojo. **to b. in,** entrar corriendo, entrar de repente. **to b. off,** marcharse corriendo. **to b. out,** vi salir de golpe. vt cerrar fuera

bolus /'boulǝs/ n bolo, m

bomb /bɒm/ n bomba, f, vt bombardear. **to be a b.-shell,** Fig. caer como una bomba. **b.-carrier,** portabombas, m. **b. crater,** bombazo, m. **b.-release,** (Aer. Nav.) lanzabombas, m. **b.-sight,** mira de avión de bombardeo, f

bombard /bɒm'bɑrd/ vt bombardear, bombear; Fig. llover (preguntas, etc.) sobre

bombardier /,bɒmbər'dɪər/ n bombardero, m

bombardment /bɒm'bɑrdmənt/ n bombardeo, m

bombast /'bɒmbæst/ n ampulosidad, pomposidad, f

bombastic /bɒm'bæstɪk/ a bombástico, altisonante, pomposo

bomber /'bɒmər/ n avión de bombardeo, bombardero, m. **dive b.,** bombardero en picado, m. **heavy b.,** bombardero pesado, m. **light b.,** bombardero ligero, m. **b. command,** servicio de bombardero, m

bombproof /'bɒm,pruf/ a a prueba de bomba

bonafide /'bounə,faid/ a fidedigno

bonbon /'bɒn,bɒn/ n bombón, confite, dulce, m. **b. box,** bombonera, f

bond /bɒnd/ n lazo, vínculo, m; Chem. enlace, m; (financial) obligación, f; (security) fianza, f; (Customs) obligación, f; pl **bonds,** cadenas, f pl, a esclavo. **in b.,** en depósito. **bonds of interest,** intereses creados, m pl. **b.-holder,** obligacionista, m

bondage /'bɒndɪdʒ/ n esclavitud, f; servidumbre, f; cautiverio, m; prisión, f

bone /boun/ n hueso, m; (of fish) espina (de pez), f; (whale) ballena, f, pl **bones,** cuerpo, m, vt deshuesar; poner ballenas (a or en). **to be all skin and bones,** estar en los huesos. **to have a b. to pick with,** tener que arreglar las cuentas con. **b.-ash,** cendra, f

boned /bound/ a (in compounds) de huesos; deshuesado, sin hueso

boner /'bounər/ n (blunder) gazapo, m, patochada, plancha, f

bonfire /'bɒn,faiᵊr/ n fogata, hoguera, f

Bonn /bɒn/ Bonn, f

bonnet /'bɒnɪt/ n capota, f; (of babies) gorra, f; (of men) boina, f; (of chimney and of machines) sombrerete, m

bonus /'bounǝs/ n paga extraordinaria, bonificación, f; sobresueldo, m; (of food, etc.) ración extraordinaria, f

bon vivant /bɔ̃ vi'vɑ̃/ n alegre, vividor, m

bon voyage /bɔ̃ vwa'yaʒ/ interj ¡buen viaje! ¡feliz viaje!

bony /'bouni/ a huesudo, f; (of fish-bones) lleno de espinas; óseo

booby /'bubi/ n pazguato, bobo, m. **b.-prize,** último premio, m. **b.-trap,** trampa, f; Mil. mina, f

book /buk/ n libro, m; volumen, tomo, m; (of an opera) libreto, m, vt anotar en un libro; apuntar; (seats) tomar (localidades); (tickets) sacar (billetes); (of the issuing clerk) dar; (reserve) reservar; inscribir; consignar; (a suspect); (engage) contratar; (invite) comprometer. **to turn the pages of a b.,** hojear un

libro. **b.-ends,** sostén para libros, sujetalibros, m. **b.-keeper,** tenedor de libros, m. **b.-keeping,** teneduría de libros, f. **b.-maker,** apostador de profesión, m. **b. of reference,** libro de consulta, m. **b.-plate,** exlibris, m. **b.-post,** tarifa de impresos, f. **b.-shop,** librería, f. **b.-trade,** venta de libros, f; comercio de libros, m

bookbinder /'buk,baindər/ n encuadernador (-ra) de libros

bookbinding /'buk,baindɪŋ/ n encuadernación de libros, f

bookcase /'buk,keis/ n armario de libros, Lat. Am. librero m

booking /'bukɪŋ/ n (of rooms, etc.) reservación, f; (of tickets) toma, f; Com. asiento, m; (engagement) contratación, f. **b.-clerk,** vendedor (-ra) de billetes. **b.-office,** despacho de billetes, m; taquilla, f

bookish /'bukɪʃ/ a aficionado a los libros; docto, erudito

bookishness /'bukɪʃnɪs/ n afición a los libros, f; erudición, f

bookmark /'buk,mɑrk/ n marcador, m

bookseller /'buk,sɛlər/ n librero, m

bookselling /'buk,sɛlɪŋ/ n venta de libros, f; comercio de libros, m

bookshelf /'buk,ʃɛlf/ n estante para libros, m, Mexico repisa, f

bookstall /'buk,stɔl/ n puesto de libros, m

bookstrap /'buk,stræp/ n portalibros, m

bookworm /'buk,wɜrm/ n polilla que roe los libros, f; Fig. ratón de biblioteca, m

boom /bum/ n Naut. botavara, f; (of a crane) aguilón, m; (noise) ruido, m; (of the sea) bramido, m; (thunder) trueno, m; (in a port) cadena de puerto, f; Com. actividad, f; (Fig. peak) auge, m, vi sonar; bramar; tronar; Com. subir; ser famoso. **b. sail,** vela de cangreja, f

boomerang /'bumǝ,ræŋ/ n bumerang, m

boon /bun/ n favor, m, merced, f; bien, m, ventaja, f; don, m; privilegio, m, a (of friends) íntimo

boor /bʊr/ n monigote, patán, palurdo, m

boorish /'bʊrɪʃ/ a rudo, zafio, rústico, cerril

boorishness /'bʊrɪʃnɪs/ n zafiedad, patanería, tosquedad, f

boost /bust/ vt Elec. aumentar la fuerza de; Inf. empujar; subir; (advertise) dar bombo (a)

boot /but/ n bota, f; (of a car) compartimiento para equipaje, m. **button-boots,** botas de botones, f pl. **riding-boots,** botas de montar, f pl. **to b.,** además, de añadidura. **b.-maker,** zapatero, m. **b.-tag,** tirador de bota, m. **b.-tree,** horma de bota, f

bootblack /'but,blæk/ n limpiabotas, Mexico bolero (-ra), elsewhere in Lat. Am. embolador (-ra), lustrador (-ra)

booted /'butɪd/ a con botas, calzado con botas; (in compounds) de botas...

bootee /bu'ti/ n botín, m

booth /buθ/ n puesto, m, barraca, f

bootlace /'but,leis/ n cordón para zapatos, m

bootlegger /'but,lɛgər/ n contrabandista de alcohol, m

boots /buts/ n mozo de hotel, botones, m

booze /buz/ vi emborracharse. **b. up,** Argentina acatarrarse. n alcohol, m; borrachera, f

boozed up /buzd/ Lat. Am. apimplado (-da), Argentina acatarrado (-da), Central America azurumbado (-da)

boozer /'buzǝr/ n borracho (-cha)

boracic /bǝ'ræsɪk/ a bórico. a ácido bórico, m

borax /'bɔræks/ n bórax, m

Bordeaux /bɔr'dou/ a and n (of or from) bordelés (-esa). n (wine) vino de Burdeos, m

bordello /bɔr'dɛlou/ n burdel, m

border /'bɔrdər/ n borde, m; (of a lake, etc.) orilla, f; (edge) margen, m; (of a diploma, etc.) orla, f; Sew. ribete, m, orla, f; (fringe) franja, f; (garden) arriate, m; (territory) frontera, f; límite, confín, m. vt Sew. orlar, ribetear; ornar (de); (of land) lindar con. **to b. on,** (of land) tocar, lindar con; (approach) rayar en. **b. country,** región fronteriza, f

borderer /'bɔrdǝrǝr/ n habitante de una zona fronteriza, m; escocés (-esa) de la frontera con Inglaterra

borderland /'bɔrdər,lænd/ *n* zona fronteriza, *f*; lindes, *m pl*

borderline /'bɔrdər,lain/ *n* frontera, *f*; límite, *m*; margen, *m, a* fronterizo; lindero; (uncertain) dudoso, incierto

bore /bɔr/ *n* taladro, barreno, *m*; perforación, *f*; (hole) agujero, *m*; (of guns) calibre, *m*; (wave) oleada, *f*; (nuisance) fastidio, *m*; (dullness) aburrimiento, tedio, *m*; (person) pelmazo, *m*, machaca, *mf* *vt* taladrar, barrenar, horadar; perforar; hacer un agujero (en); (exhaust) aburrir; fastidiar. **It's a b.,** Es una lata. **to be bored,** aburrirse, fastidiarse

boredom /'bɔrdəm/ *n* aburrimiento, *m*; tedio, hastío, *m*

boring /'bɔrɪŋ/ *a* aburrido, pesado, tedioso; molesto, fastidioso. *n* taladro, *m*; horadación, *f*; sondeo, *m*; perforación, *f*

born /bɔrn/ *a* nacido; (by birth) de nacimiento; (b. to be) destinado a; natural (de). **He was b. in 1870.** Nació en 1870. **to be b.,** nacer, venir al mundo. **to be b. again,** *ecc.* nacido de nuevo, renacer, volver a nacer. **well-b.,** bien nacido. **b. with a silver spoon in one's mouth,** Nacido de pie, Nacido un domingo

-borne /-bɔrn/ trasmitido por... (e.g. *anthropod-b.,* trasmitido por los antrópodos)

borough /'bʌrou/ *n* burgo, *m*; villa, *f*; ciudad, *f*. **b. surveyor,** arquitecto municipal, *m*

borrow /'bɒrou/ *vt* pedir prestado; apropiarse, adoptar; copiar; (arithmetic) restar; (a book from a library) tomar prestado. **May I b. your pencil?** ¿Quieres prestarme tu lápiz?

borrower /'bɒrouər/ *n* el (la) que pide o toma prestado

borrowing /'bɒrouɪŋ/ *n* el pedir prestado, acto de pedir prestado, *m*

Bosnian /'bɒznɪən/ *n* bosnio

bosom /'buzəm/ *n* pecho, *m*; (heart) corazón, *m*; (of the earth, etc.) seno, *m*. **b. friend,** amigo (-ga) del alma, amigo (-ga) íntimo (-ma)

Bosphorus, the /'bɒsfərəs/ el Bósforo, *m*

boss /bɒs/ *n* (of a shield) corcova saliente, *f*; tachón, *m*; *Archit.* pinjante, *m. Inf.* amo, *m*; jefe, *m. vt* mandar; dominar. **political b.,** cacique, *m*

bossism /'bɒsɪzəm/ *n* caudillaje, *m*

bossy /'bɒsi/ *a* mandón, autoritario. **b. person,** *Lat. Am.* mandarín, *m*

botanical /bə'tænɪkəl/ *a* botánico. **b. garden,** jardín botánico, *m*

botanist /'bɒtn̩ɪst/ *n* botánico (-ca)

botany /'bɒtni/ *n* botánica, *f*

botch /bɒtʃ/ *n* (clumsy work) chapucería, *f*; remiendo, *m. vt* chapucear, chafallar; (patch) remendar

both /bouθ/ *a* and *pron* ambos, *m pl*; ambas, *f pl*; los dos, *m pl*; las dos, *f pl*, *adv* tan(to)... como; (and) y; a la vez, al mismo tiempo. **It appealed both to the young and the old,** Gustó tanto a los jóvenes como a los viejos. **b. of you,** ustedes dos, vosotros dos, vosotras dos. **b. pretty and useful,** bonito y útil a la vez

bother /'bɒðər/ *n* molestia, *f*, fastidio, *m*; (worry) preocupación, *f*; dificultad, *f*; (fuss) alboroto, *m*, *Lat. Am.* fregada *f. vt* molestar, fastidiar, *Lat. Am.* acatarrar; preocupar. *vi* preocuparse

bottle /'bɒtl/ *n* botella, *f*; (smaller) frasco, *m*; (babies) biberón, *m*; (for water) cantimplora, *f*, *vt* embotellar, envasar, enfrascar. **to b. up,** (liquids, capital, armies, navies) embotellar; (feelings) refrenar. **to bring up on the b.,** criar con biberón. **b.-green,** verde botella, *m*. **b.-neck,** (in an industry) embotellado, *m*; (in traffic) atascadero, *m*. **b.-washer,** fregaplatos, *mf*; (machine) máquina para limpiar botellas, *f*

bottle cap *n* corchalata, *f*

bottled /'bɒtl̩d/ *a* en botella; (of fruit, vegetables) conservado

bottleful /'bɒtl̩,ful/ *n* botella, *f*

bottler /'bɒtlər/ *n* embotellador (-ra)

bottling /'bɒtlɪŋ/ *n* embotellado, *m*; envase, *m*. **b. outfit,** embotelladora, *f*; (for fruit, etc.) aparato para conservar frutas o legumbres, *m*

bottom /'bɒtəm/ *n* base, *f*; (deepest part) fondo, *m*; (last place) último lugar, *m*; fundamento, *m*; (of a

chair) asiento, *m*; (of a page, table, mountain, etc.) pie, *m*; (posterior) culo, *m*; (of a river) lecho, *m*; (of the sea) fondo, *m*; (of a ship) casco, *m*; (of a skirt) orilla, *f*; (truth) realidad, verdad, *f*; (basis) origen, *m*, causa, *f*. **at b.,** en realidad. **at the b.,** en el fondo. **false b.,** fondo doble, fondo secreto, *m*. **to be at the b. of,** ocupar el último lugar en; ser el causante de. **to get to the b. of,** descubrir la verdad de; profundizar en, analizar. **to sink to the b.,** (of ships) irse a pique

bottomed /'bɒtəmd/ *a* (in compounds) de fondo...

bottomless /'bɒtəmlɪs/ *a* sin fondo; (of chairs, etc.) sin asiento; (unfathomable) insondable

boudoir /'budwɑr/ *n* tocador, gabinete de señora, *m*

bough /bau/ *n* rama, *f*, brazo (de un árbol) *m*

boulder /'bouldər/ *n* roca, peña, *f*; canto rodado, *f*; bloque de roca, *m*

boulevard /'bulə,vɑrd/ *n* bulevar, *m*

bounce /bauns/ *n* bote, rebote, *m*; salto, *m*; (boasting) fanfarronería, *f*, *vi* rebotar; saltar, brincar. *vt* hacer botar o saltar

bouncing /'baunsɪŋ/ *a* (healthy) sano, robusto; vigoroso, fuerte

bound /baund/ *n* límite, *m*; (jump) salto, brinco, *m*, *vt* limitar, confinar. *vi* saltar, brincar; (bounce) botar. **within bounds,** dentro del límite. **b. for,** con destino a; (of ships) con rumbo a

boundary /'baundəri/ *n* límite, lindero, término, *m*; frontera, *f*; raya, *f*. **b. stone,** mojón, *m*

bounden /'baundən/ *a* obligatorio, forzoso; indispensable

boundless /'baundlɪs/ *a* sin límites, infinito; inmenso

bounteous, bountiful /'bauntiəs; 'bauntɪfəl/ *a* dadivoso, generoso; bondadoso

bountifulness /'bauntɪfəlnɪs/ *n* munificencia, dadivosidad, generosidad, *f*

bounty /'baunti/ *n* generosidad, munificencia, *f*; don, *m*; (subsidy) subvención, *f*

bouquet /bou'kei, bu-/ *n* ramo, ramillete (de flores), *m*, *Lat. Am. also* maceta *f*; perfume, *m*; (of wine) nariz, *f*

Bourbon /'bɜrbən; 'bʊrbən/ *a* borbónico. *n* Borbón (-ona)

bourgeois /bur'ʒwɑ/ *a* and *n* burgués (-esa)

bourgeoisie /,burʒwɑ'zi/ *n* burguesía, mesocracia, *f*

bout /baut/ *n* turno, *m*; (in fencing, boxing, wrestling) asalto, *m*; (of illness, coughing) ataque, *m*; (fight) lucha, *f*, combate, *m*; (of drinking) borrachera, *f*

bovine /'bouvain/ *a* bovino, vacuno

bow /bou/ *n* (weapon) arco, *m*; (of a saddle) arzón (de silla), *m*; *Mus.* arco, *m*; (knot) lazo, *m*; (greeting) saludo, *m*; reverencia, inclinación, *f*; (of a boat) proa, *f*. **to tie a bow,** hacer un lazo. **bow and arrows,** arco y flechas, *m*. **bow-legged,** patizambo, *Central America* corveta, *f*, **bow window,** ventana saliente, *f*

bow /bau/ *vi* inclinarse; hacer una reverencia, saludar; (remove the hat) descubrirse; *Fig.* inclinarse (ante); (submit) someterse (a), reconocer; agobiarse; *Mus.* manejar el arco. *vt* (usher in) introducir en, conducir a; doblar; inclinar. **to bow down (to),** humillarse ante; obedecer; (worship) reverenciar, adorar. **to bow out,** despedir con una inclinación del cuerpo

bowel /'bauəl/ *n* intestino, *m*; *pl* **bowels,** *Fig.* seno, *m*, entrañas, *f pl*

bower /'bauər/ *n* (arbor) enramada, *f*; glorieta, *f*; (boudoir) tocador de señora, *m*

bowing /'bouɪŋ/ *n Mus.* arqueada, *f*; saludo, *m*, *a* (of acquaintance) superficial

bowl /boul/ *n* receptáculo, *m*; (of a fountain) taza, *f*; (of a pipe) cazoleta, *f*; (barber's) bacía, *f*; (for washing) jofaina, *f*; (for punch) ponchera, *f*; (goblet) copa, *f*; (for soup) escudilla, *f*; (for fruit) frutero, *m*; (of a spoon) paleta, *f*; (ball) boliche, *m*. *vt* tirar; (in cricket) sacar; (a hoop) jugar con; (in ninepins) tumbar con una bola. **to b. along,** recorrer; ir en coche o carruaje (por). **to b. over,** *Fig.* dejar consternado (a), desconcertar

bowler /'boulər/ *n* (in cricket) servidor, *m*; (hat) sombrero hongo, *m*; (skittle player) jugador de bolos, *m*

bowling /'boulɪŋ/ *n* (in cricket) saque, *m*; (skittles) (juego de) bolos, *m*, (juego de) boliche, *m*. **b. alley,**

bolera, pista de bolos, *f*, salón de boliche, *m*. **b.-green,** bolera en cesped, *f*

bowls /boulz/ *n* juego de boliche, *m*

bowsprit /'bausprɪt/ *n* bauprés, *m*

bowstring /'bou,strɪŋ/ *n* cuerda de arco, *f*

bow tie /bou/ *n* pajarita, *f*

bow-wow /'bau ,wau/ *n* guau, *m*

box /bɒks/ *n* caja, *f*; (case) estuche, *m*; (luggage) baúl, *m*, maleta, *f*; (for a hat) sombrerera, *f*; *Bot.* boj, *m*; *Theat.* palco, *m*, *Mexico* lumbrera, *f*; (for a sentry, signalman, etc.) garita, casilla, *f*; (on a carriage) pescante, *m*; (blow) cachete, *m*, bofetada, *f*; (for a horse) vagón, *m*. **post office box,** apartado de correos, *m*. **box-kite,** cometa celular, *f*. **box-maker,** cajero, *m*. **box office,** taquilla, *f*, *Lat. Am.* boletería *f*. **box-pleat,** *Sew.* tabla, *f*

box /bɒks/ *vt* encajonar, meter en una caja. *vi* box-ear. **to box the ears of,** calentar las orejas de. **to box up,** encerrar

boxer /'bɒksər/ *n Sports.* boxeador, pugilista, *m*

boxing /'bɒksɪŋ/ *n* encajonamiento, *m*; envase, *m*; *Sports.* boxeo, pugilato, *m*. **B. Day,** Día de San Esteban, *m*, (A Spanish child receives Christmas presents on the Día de Reyes (Twelfth Night).) **b.-gloves,** guantes de boxeo, *m pl*. **b.-ring,** cuadrilátero de boxeo, *m*

box-office success /'bɒks ,ɔfɪs/ *n* éxito de taquilla, *m*

boy /bɔi/ *n* muchacho, niño, rapaz, *m*; (older) chico, joven, *m*. **new boy,** nuevo alumno, *m*. **old boy,** (of a school) antiguo alumno, *m*; (*Fam.* address) chico. **small boy,** chiquillo, pequeño, crío, *m*. **b. doll,** muñeco, *m*. **boy scout,** muchacho explorador, *m*

boycott /'bɔikɒt/ *vt* boicotear. *n* boicot, *m*

boyhood /'bɔihʊd/ *n* muchachez, mocedad, *f*; (childhood) niñez, *f*

boyish /'bɔiɪʃ/ *a* muchachil; pueril; de niñez

brace /breis/ *n* (prop) puntal, barrote, *m*; abrazadera, *f*; berbiquí, *m*; viento, tirante, *m*; freno (for the teeth), *m*, (pair) par, *m*; *pl* **braces,** tirantes, *m pl*. *vt* apuntalar; asegurar; ensamblar; *Naut.* bracear; (trousers) tirar; *Fig.* fortalecer, refrescar

bracelet /'breislɪt/ *n* pulsera, *f*, brazalete, *m*, ajorca, *f*

bracing /'breisɪŋ/ *a* (of air, etc.) fortificante, tónico; estimulador

bracken /'brækən/ *n* helecho, *m*

bracket /'brækɪt/ *n* consola, *f*; *Archit.* repisa, *f*; soporte, *m*; (on furniture, etc.) cantonera, *f*; *Print.* paréntesis angular, *m*; (for a light) brazo (de alumbrado), *m*. *vt Print.* poner entre paréntesis; juntar. **in brackets,** entre paréntesis. **They were bracketed equal,** Fueron juzgados iguales

brackish /'brækɪʃ/ *a* salobre

brag /bræg/ *vi* jactarse, fanfarronear, *Lat. Am.* dragonear, *Argentina* faramallear. *n* jactancia, *f*. **to b. about,** hacer alarde de

braggart /'brægərt/ *a* baladrón, jactancioso. *n* jactancioso, fanfarrón, *m*

bragging /'brægɪŋ/ *n* jactancia, *f*

Brahmin /'bramɪn/ *n* brahmán, *m*

Brahminism /'bramɪ,nɪzəm/ *n* brahmanismo, *m*

braid /breid/ *n* trencilla, *f*, cordoncillo, *m*; (for trimming) galón, *m*; (plait) trenza, *f*. *vt* (hair) trenzar; (trim) galonear; acordonar, trencillar

brain /brein/ *n* cerebro, *m*; entendimiento, *m*, inteligencia, *f*; talento, *m*; (common sense) sentido común, *m*; *pl* **brains,** sesos, *m pl*, (animal and human); cacumen, *m*. *vt* romper la crisma (a). **to blow one's brains out,** levantarse la tapa de los sesos. **to rack one's brains,** devanarse los sesos. **Brains Trust,** masa cefálica, *f*; consorcio de inteligencias, *m*. **b.-box,** cráneo, *m*. **b.-fever,** fiebre cerebral, *f*. **b.-storm,** torbellino de ideas, *m*. **b.-wave,** idea luminosa, *f*. **b.-work,** trabajo intelectual, *m*

brainchild /'brein,tʃaild/ *n* engendro, *m*

brain drain *n* fuga de cerebros, *f*

brained /breind/ *a* de cabeza, de cerebro

brainless /'breinlɪs/ *a* sin seso; tonto

brainy /'breini/ *a* sesudo, inteligente, talentudo

braise /breiz/ *vt Cul.* asar

brake /breik/ *n* (of vehicles and *Fig.*) freno, *m*, *Chile*, *Peru* alitranca *f* (flax and hemp) caballete, *m*; (car-

riage) break, *m*; (thicket) matorral, *m*. *vt* (vehicles) frenar; (hemp, etc.) rastrillar. **foot-b.,** freno de pedal, *m*. **hand-b.,** freno de mano, *m*. **to b. hard,** frenar de repente. **to release the b.,** quitar el freno

bramble /'bræmbəl/ *n* zarza, *f*. **b. patch,** breña, *f*, zarzal, *m*

brambly /'bræmbli/ *a* zarzoso

bran /bræn/ *n* salvado, *m*

branch /bræntʃ, brɑntʃ/ *n* (of a tree, a family) rama, *f*; (of flowers, of learning) ramo, *m*; (of a river) tributario, afluente, *m*; (of roads, railways) ramal, *m*; (of a firm) sucursal, dependencia, *f. a* sucursal, dependiente; (of roads, railways) secundario. *vi* echar ramas; bifurcarse, dividirse; ramificarse. **to b. off,** bifurcarse, ramificarse. **to b. out,** extenderse; emprender cosas nuevas

branched /bræntʃt/ *a* con ramas; *Bot.* ramoso; (of candlesticks) de... brazos

branchiness /'bræntʃinɪs/ *n* ramaje, *m*, frondosidad, *f*

branching /'bræntʃiŋ/ *n* ramificación, *f*; división, *f*. **b. off,** bifurcación, *f*

brand /brænd/ *n* tizón, *m*; (torch) tea, *f*; (on cattle, etc.) hierro, *m*; (trademark) marca de fábrica, *f*; marca, *f*; (stigma) estigma, *m*. *vt* marcar con el hierro, herrar; marcar; estigmatizar, tildar. **b.-new,** flamante

branding /'brændiŋ/ *n* (of livestock) herradero, *m*; (of slaves, criminals) estigmatización, *f*; difamación, *f*. **b.-iron,** hierro de marcar, *m*

brandish /'brændiʃ/ *vt* blandir

brandy /'brændi/ *n* coñac, *m*

brass /bræs/ *n* latón, *m*; *Mus.* metal, *m*; (tablet) placa conmemorativa, *f*; *Inf.* dinero, *m*. **the b.,** *Mus.* el metal. **b. band,** banda de instrumentos de viento, *f*. **b.-neck,** *Inf.* cara dura, *f*. **b. works** or **shop,** latonería, *f*

brassiere /brə'zɪər/ *n* sostén, *f*

brat /bræt/ *n* crío, *m*

bravado /brə'vɑdou/ *n* bravata, *f*

brave /breiv/ *a* valiente, animoso, intrépido; espléndido, magnífico; bizarro. *n* valiente, *m*. *vt* desafiar, provocar; arrostrar

bravely /'breivli/ *adv* valientemente; espléndidamente; bizarramente

bravery /'breivəri/ *n* valentía, *f*, valor, *m*, intrepidez, *f*, coraje, *m*; esplendidez, suntuosidad, *f*; bizarría, *f*

bravo /'brɑvou/ *n* bandido, *m*; asesino pagado, *m*, *interj* ¡bravo! ¡ole!

bravura /brə'vyʊrə/ *n* bravura, *f*

brawl /brɔl/ *n* camorra, reyerta, pelotera, *Lat. Am.* follisca *f*. *vi* alborotar; (of streams) murmurar. **to start a b.,** armar camorra

brawler /'brɔlər/ *n* camorrista, *mf*

brawling /'brɔliŋ/ *n* alboroto, *m*, vocinglería, *f*; (of streams) murmullo, *m*

brawn /brɔn/ *n* *Cul.* embutido, *m*; músculo, *m*; (strength) fuerza, *f*

brawny /'brɔni/ *a* membrudo, musculoso, forzudo

bray /brei/ *n* rebuzno, *m*; (of trumpets) clangor, *m*, *vi* rebuznar; sonar

brazen /'breizən/ *a* de latón; (of voice) bronca; desvergonzado, descarado

brazier /'breiʒər/ *n* (fire) brasero, *m*; latonero, *m*

Brazil /brə'zɪl/ el Brasil, *m*

Brazilian /brə'zɪlyən/ *a* and *n* brasileño (-ña)

Brazil nut *n* nuez del Brasil, *f*

breach /britʃ/ *n* violación, contravención, *f*; (gap) abertura, *f*; *Mil.* brecha, *f*. *vt Mil.* hacer brecha (en); (in a line of defence) hacer mella (en). **b. of confidence,** abuso de confianza, *m*. **b. of promise,** incumplimiento de la palabra de casamiento, *m*. **b. of the peace,** alteración del orden público, *f*; quebrantamiento de la paz, *m*

bread /bred/ *n* pan, *m*. **to earn one's b. and butter,** ganarse el pan. **brown b.,** pan moreno, *m*. **unleavened b.,** pan ázimo, *m*. **b. and butter,** pan con mantequilla, *f*; *Fig.* sustento diario, *m*. **b.-basket,** cesta de pan, *f*; *Inf.* estómago, *m*. **b.-bin,** caja del pan, *f*. **b.-crumb,** miga, *f*; migaja, *f*. **b.-knife,** cuchillo para cortar el pan, *m*. **b. poultice,** cataplasma de miga de

pan, f. **b.-winner,** ganador (-ra) de pan, trabajador (-ra)
breadfruit tree /'brɛd,frut/ n árbol del pan, m
breadth /brɛdθ/ n anchura, f; latitud, f; liberalidad, f; *Sew.* ancho de una tela, m
breadthways /'brɛdθ,weiz/ adv a lo ancho
break /breik/ n rotura, f; (opening) abertura, f; *Geol.* rajadura, f; (fissure) grieta, f; solución de continuidad, f; interrupción, f; (billiards) serie, f; (change) cambio, m; (in a boy's voice) muda (de la voz), f; (blank) vacío, m; (in the market) baja, f; intervalo, m; descanso, m; pausa, f; (truce) tregua, f; (clearing) clara, f; *Mus.* quiebra (de la voz), f; (carriage) break, m; (*Fam.* folly) disparate, m. **with a b. in one's voice,** con voz entrecortada. **b. of day,** aurora, alba, f. **at the b. of day,** al despuntar el alba

break /breik/ vt romper; quebrar; quebrantar, fracturar; (breach) abrir brecha en; (in two) partir, dividir; (into pieces) hacer pedazos, despedazar; (into small pieces) desmenuzar; (into crumbs) desmigajar; (destroy) destrozar; (a blow) parar; (a law) infringir, violar; (the bank in gambling) quebrar; (a journey, etc.) interrumpir; (of a habit) desacostumbrar, hacer perder el vicio de; (a promise) no cumplir, faltar a; (a record) superar; (plow ground) roturar; (spoil) estropear; arruinar; *Com.* ir a la quiebra; (an official) degradar; (an animal) domar, amansar; (*Fig.* crush) subyugar; (betray) traicionar; (*Fig.* of silence, a spell, a lance, peace, the ranks) romper; (cushion) amortiguar; (lessen) mitigar; (disclose) revelar; *Elec.* interrumpir. **to b. one's promise,** faltar a su palabra. **to b. the ice,** *Fig.* romper el hielo. **to b. asunder,** romper en dos (partes); dividir. **to b. down,** echar abajo; destruir; (suppress) suprimir; subyugar; abolir; disolver. **to b. in,** (animals) domar, amaestrar; (persons) disciplinar; (new shoes) ahormar, romper. **to b. in two,** partir; dividir en dos; (split) hender. **to b. off,** separar, quitar; (a branch) desgajar; *Fig.* romper; interrumpir; cesar. **to b. open,** forzar, abrir a la fuerza. **to b. up,** hacer pedazos; (scatter) poner en fuga, dispersar; hacer levantar la sesión; (the ground) roturar; (parliament) disolver; (a ship) desguazar, deshacer (un buque)

break /breik/ vi romperse; quebrarse; quebrantarse; (of beads) desgranarse; (burst) reventar, estallar; (of abscesses) abrirse; (of a boy's voice) mudar; (*Fig.* and of clouds, etc.) romperse; desaparecer; (of the dawn) despuntar (el alba), amanecer; (sprout) brotar; (of a ball) torcerse; (of fine weather) terminar; (change) cambiar; (of a storm) estallar. **to b. loose,** desasirse; *Fig.* desencadenarse. **to b. away,** escaparse, fugarse; (from a habit) romper con, independizarse de (another country); disiparse. **to b. down,** (of machinery, cars) averiarse; (fail) frustrarse, malograrse; (weep) deshacerse en lágrimas; (lose one's grip) perder la confianza en sí; (in health) sufrir una crisis de salud. **The car broke down,** El auto tuvo una avería. **to b. in,** (of burglars) forzar la entrada; irrumpir (en), penetrar (en); exclamar. **to b. in on,** sorprender; entrar de sopetón; invadir; interrumpir; caer sobre; molestar. **to b. into,** (force) forzar; (utter) romper a, prorrumpir en; empezar (a); pasar de repente a; (of time, etc.) ocupar; hacer perder. **to b. off,** (of speech) interrumpirse; cesar; (detach) desprenderse, separarse; (of branches) desgajarse. **to b. out,** huir, escaparse; *Fig.* estallar; aparecer; declararse; (of fire) tomar fuego; derramarse; (of an eruption) salir. **to b. over,** derramarse por; bañar. **to b. through,** abrirse paso (por); abrirse salida (por); atravesar; *Fig.* penetrar; (of the sun, etc.) romper (por). **to b. up,** (depart) separarse (of meetings) levantarse la sesión; dispersarse; (smash) hacerse pedazos; disolverse; (of a school) cerrarse, empezar las vacaciones; (melt) fundir; desbandarse; (of a camp) levantar (el campo); (grow old) hacerse viejo; (be ill) estar agotado. **to b. with,** romper con; cesar; reñir con

breakable /'breikǝbǝl/ a quebradizo, frágil
breakage /'breikidʒ/ n rompimiento, quebrantamiento, m; cosa rota, f; fractura, f
breakdown /'breik,daun/ n accidente, m; (of a machine) avería, f; *Auto.* pane, f; (failure) fracaso, m,

falta de éxito, f; deterioración, f; (in health) crisis de salud, f
breaker /'breikǝr/ n oleada, f
breakfast /'brɛkfǝst/ n desayuno, m. vi desayunar(se), tomar el desayuno. **to have a good b.,** desayunar bien. **b.-cup,** tazón, m. **b.-time,** hora del desayuno, f
breaking /'breikɪŋ/ n rompimiento, m; quebrantamiento, m; fractura, f; ruptura, f; (in two) división, f; (into pieces) despedazamiento, m; (into small pieces) desmenuzamiento, m; (destruction) destrozo, m; (of a blow) parada, f; (of a law, etc.) violación, f; (of one's word) no cumplimiento, m; (of a journey, of sleep, etc.) interrupción, f; (escape) escape, m, huida, f; (of an animal) domadura, f; (of a boy's voice) muda (de la voz), f; (of news) revelación, f. **b. down,** demolición, f; (of negotiations) suspensión, f. **b. in,** irrupción, f; (of an animal) domadura, f; (training) entrenamiento, m. **b. open,** forzamiento, m; quebranto, m. **b. out,** huida, f, escape, m; *Fig.* estallido, m; aparición, f; declaración, f; (scattering) derramamiento, m; (of a rash) erupción, f. **b. up,** dispersión, f; disolución, f; fin, m; ruina, f; (of a school) cierre, m; (change in weather) cambio, m; (of a meeting) levantamiento (de una sesión), m; (of the earth) roturación, f
breakneck /'breik,nɛk/ a rápido, veloz, precipitado
breakwater /'breik,wɔtǝr/ n malecón, rompeolas, m
bream /brim/ n *Ichth.* sargo, m. **sea-b.,** besugo, m
breast /brɛst/ n pecho, m; (of birds) pechuga, f; (of female animals) teta, mama, f; (heart) corazón, m, vt (the waves) cortar (las olas); luchar con; *Fig.* arrostrar, hacer frente a. **b.-bone,** esternón, m. **b. high,** alto hasta el pecho. **b.-pin,** alfiler de pecho, m. **b.-pocket,** bolsillo de pecho, m. **b.-stroke,** estilo pecho, m
breast cancer n el cáncer del seno, m
breasted /'brɛstɪd/ a de pecho...; de pechuga...; de tetas... **a double-b. jacket,** una chaqueta cruzada. **a single-b. jacket,** una chaqueta
breastwork /'brɛst,wɜrk/ n *Mil.* parapeto, m
breath /brɛθ/ n aliento, m; suspiro, m; (phonetics) aspiración, f; (breeze) soplo (de aire), m; (of scandal, etc.) murmurio, m; (fragrance) perfume, m, fragancia, f; (life) vida, f. **in a b.,** de un aliento. **in the same b.,** sin respirar. **out of b.,** sin aliento. **under one's b.,** por lo bajo, entre dientes. **to draw b.,** tomar aliento. **to get one's b. back,** cobrar aliento. **to have bad b.,** tener mal aliento. **to hold one's b.,** contener el aliento. **to take one's b. away,** *Fig.* dejar consternado y-a
breathable /'briðǝbǝl/ a respirable
breathe /brið/ vi respirar; vivir; (of air, etc.) soplar; (take the air) tomar el fresco; (rest) tomar aliento. vt respirar; exhalar; dar aire (a); (whisper) murmurar; (convey) expresar, revelar; (infuse) infundir. **to b. forth fury,** echar rayos. **to b. hard,** jadear. **to b. one's last,** exhalar el último suspiro. **to b. in,** inspirar
breathing /'briðɪŋ/ n respiración, f; (of the air, etc.) soplo, m; (phonetics) aspiración, f. a que respira; viviente. **hard** or **heavy b.,** jadeo, resuello, resoplido, m. **b.-space,** *Fig.* respiro, m
breathless /'brɛθlɪs/ a jadeante, sin aliento; (dead) muerto; (sultry) sin un soplo de aire; intenso, profundo; (of haste) precipitado
breathlessly /'brɛθlɪsli/ adv anhelosamente; con expectación
breathlessness /'brɛθlɪsnɪs/ n falta de aliento, f; respiración difícil, f; (death) muerte, f; (of weather) falta de aire, f
bred /brɛd/ a criado. **ill (well) b.,** mal (bien) criado. **pure-b.,** de raza
breech /britʃ/ n *Anat.* trasero, m; (of fire-arms) recámara, f
breeches /'brɪtʃɪz/ n calzones, m pl; pantalones, m pl. **riding-b.,** pantalones de montar, m pl
breed /brid/ n casta, raza, f; tipo, m; clase, f, vt procrear; engendrar, crear; (bring up) educar; criar. vi reproducirse; sacar cría; multiplicarse. **to b. in-and-in,** procrear sin mezclar razas
breeder /'bridǝr/ n criador (-ra); animal reproductor, m

breeding /'bridɪŋ/ n reproducción, f; cría, f; (upbringing) crianza, f; educación, f; instrucción, f; producción, f; creación, f, a de cría; (of male animals) semental; prolífico. **bad b.**, mala crianza, f. **cross b.**, cruzamiento de razas, m. **good b.**, buena crianza, f. **b. farm**, criadero, m

breeze /briz/ n brisa, f, vientecillo, m, soplo de aire, m, Lat. Am. airecito m; (argument) altercación, f, argumento, m; (of coke) cisco de coque, m. **fresh b.**, brisa fresca, f. **light b.**, brisa floja, f. **strong b.**, viento fuerte, viento muy fresco, m

breezy /'brizi/ a con brisa, fresco; expuesto a la brisa; oreado; (of manner) animado, jovial

brethren /'brɛðrɪn/ n pl hermanos, m pl

Breton /'brɛtn/ a and n bretón (-ona). n (language) bretón, m

brevet /brə'vɛt/ n Mil. graduación honoraria, f; nombramiento honorario, m. vt Mil. graduar

breviary /'brivi,ɛri/ n breviario, m

brevity /'brɛvɪti/ n brevedad, f; concisión, f

brew /bru/ n mezcla, f; brebaje, m. vt hacer (cerveza, té, etc.); preparar, mezclar; Fig. urdir, tramar. vi prepararse; urdirse; (storm) gestarse.

brewer /'bruər/ n cervecero (-ra)

brewery /'bruəri/ n cervecería, fábrica de cerveza, f

brewing /'bruɪŋ/ n elaboración de cerveza, f

briar /'braiər/ n (wild rose) rosal silvestre, m; (heather) brezo, m. **b. pipe**, pipa de brezo, f

bribable /'braibəbəl/ a sobornable

bribe /braib/ n soborno, cohecho, m, Lat. Am. coima, f, Mexico mordida, f. vt sobornar, cohechar. **to take bribes**, dejarse sobornar

briber /'braibər/ n cohechador (-ra)

bribery /'braibəri/ n soborno, m

brick /brɪk/ n ladrillo, m; (for children) piedra de construcción, f; bloque, m; Inf. buen chico, m, joya, f, a de ladrillo. vt enladrillar. **b.-floor**, ladrillado, m; **b.-kiln**, horno de ladrillo, m. **b.-maker**, ladrillero, m. **b.-yard**, ladrillar, m

bricklayer /'brɪk,leiər/ n albañil, m

bricklaying /'brɪk,leiɪŋ/ n albañilería, f

brickwork /'brɪk,wɜrk/ n masonería, f

bridal /'braidl/ a nupcial; de la boda; de la novia. **b. bed**, tálamo, m. **b. cake**, torta de la boda, f. **b. shop**, tienda para novias, f. **b. shower**, despedida de soltera, despedida de soltería, f. **b. song**, epitalamio, m. **b. veil**, velo de la novia, velo nupcial, m. **b. wreath**, corona de azahar, f

bride /braid/ n novia, desposada, f; (after marriage) recién casada, f

bridegroom /'braid,grum/ n novio, m; (after marriage) recién casado, m

bridesmaid /'braidz,meid/ n madrina de boda, f; niña encargada de sostener la cola de la novia, f

bridge /brɪdʒ/ n (engineering, Mus. Naut.) puente, m; lomo (de la nariz), m; (game) bridge, m, vt construir un puente (sobre), pontear; (obstacles) salvar; evitar; (fill in) ocupar, llenar. **auction b.**, bridge por subasta, m. **contract b.**, bridge por contrato, m. **suspension-b.**, puente colgante, m. **toll b.**, pontazgo, m

bridgehead /'brɪdʒ,hed/ n cabeza de puente, f

bridle /'braidl/ n brida, f; freno, m. vt embridar, enfrenar; Fig. reprimir. vi (of horses) levantar la cabeza; (of persons) erguirse; hacer un gesto despreciativo. **snaffle b.**, bridón, m. **b. path**, camino de herradura, m

brief /brif/ a breve, corto; conciso; lacónico, seco; rápido; fugaz, pasajero. n (papal) breve, m; Law. relación, f; escrito, m. vt (a barrister) instruir. **to hold a b. for**, defender, abogar por. **b.-case**, portapapeles, m; cartera (grande), f

briefly /'brifli/ adv brevemente; en pocas palabras; sucintamente; (tersely) secamente

brier /'braiər/ n rosal silvestre, m; zarza, f

brigade /brɪ'geid/ n Mil. brigada, f; cuerpo, m; asociación, f

brigadier /,brɪgə'diər/ n brigadier, m

brigand /'brɪgənd/ n bandolero, bandido, m

brigandage /'brɪgəndɪdʒ/ n bandolerismo, m

bright /brait/ a brillante, reluciente; vivo; cristalino; subido; claro; optimista; alegre; inteligente; (quickwitted) agudo; ilustre; (smiling) risueño; (of future,

etc.) halagüeño. **to be as b. as a new pin**, estar como una ascua de oro. **b. blue**, azul subido, m. **b.-eyed**, con ojos vivos, con ojos chispeantes, ojialegre

brighten /'braitn/ vt hacer brillar; (polish) pulir; (make happy) alegrar; (improve) mejorar. vi (of the weather) aclarar, despejarse (el cielo); sentirse más feliz; mejorar

brightly /'braitli/ adv brillantemente; alegremente

brightness /'braitnɪs/ n brillo, m; claridad, f; esplendor, m; (of colors) brillantez, f; vivacidad, f; inteligencia, f; agudeza de ingenio, f

Bright's disease /braits/ n enfermedad de Bright, glomerulonefritis, f

brilliance /'brɪlyəns/ n fulgor, brillo, m, refulgencia, f; esplendor, m; lustre, m; talento, m; brillantez, gloria, f

brilliant /'brɪlyənt/ a brillante. n (gem) brillante, m. **to be b.**, (in conversation, etc.) brillar; (be clever) ser brillante

brilliantine /'brɪlyən,tin/ n brillantina, f

brim /brɪm/ n (of a glass, etc.) borde, m; (of a hat) ala, f; margen, m, orilla, f. **to be full to the b.**, estar lleno hasta los bordes; Fig. rebosar. **eyes brimming with tears**, ojos arrasados de lágrimas

brimful /'brɪm'fʊl/ a hasta el borde (or los bordes); Fig. rebosante

brimless /'brɪmlɪs/ a (of hats) sin ala

brimmed /brɪmd/ a (of hats) con ala

brimstone /'brɪm,stoun/ n azufre, m

brindled /'brɪndld/ a atigrado, abigarrado

brine /brain/ n salmuera, f; mar, m; Poet. lágrimas, f pl

bring /brɪŋ/ vt traer; llevar; transportar; (take a person or drive a vehicle) conducir; Fig. acarrear, traer; causar, ocasionar; producir; crear; (induce) persuadir; hacer (ver, etc.); (be worth) valer; (sell for) vender por; Law. entablar (un pleito, etc.): (before a judge) hacer comparecer (ante); (present) presentar; (attract) atraer; (place) poner. **to b. home**, llevar a casa; Fig. hacer ver, hacer sentir; demostrar; (a crime) probar contra. **to b. near**, acercar. **to b. about**, efectuar, poner por obra; causar, ocasionar; (achieve) lograr, conseguir. **to b. again**, traer otra vez, llevar de nuevo. **to b. around**, (from a swoon) sacar de un desmayo; curar; persuadir; conciliar. **to b. away**, llevarse. **to b. back**, devolver; traer; (of memories) recordar. **to b. down**, llevar abajo, bajar; (of persons) hacer bajar; (humble) humillar; hacer caer; (of prices) hacer bajar; arruinar; destruir. **to b. down the house**, Theat. hacer venirse el teatro abajo. **to b. forth**, (give birth to) dar a luz; producir; causar; sacar a luz. **to b. forward**, hacer adelantarse; empujar hacia adelante; Fig. avanzar; (allege) alegar; Com. llevar a nueva cuenta; presentar, producir. **brought forward**, Com. suma y sigue. **to b. in**, (things) traer adentro; (persons) hacer entrar; introducir; aparecer con, presentarse con; (meals) servir; producir; declarar; (a verdict) dictar (sentencia de), fallar. **to b. into being**, poner en práctica; dar origen (a). **to b. off**, (a ship) poner a flote; (rescue) salvar, rescatar; (carry out) efectuar, poner en práctica; (achieve) conseguir, lograr. **B. me the glass off the table**, Tráeme el vaso que hay en la mesa. **to b. on**, causar, inducir; acarrear; iniciar. **He brought a book on to the stage**, Entró en escena llevando un libro (or con un libro). **to b. out**, sacar; poner afuera; (a person) hacer salir; publicar; (a play) poner en escena; sacar a luz; (an idea, jewels, etc.) sacar a relucir; revelar; demostrar; hacer aparecer; (a girl in society) poner de largo (a). **to b. over**, llevar al otro lado; hacer venir; traer; conducir; hacer cruzar; (convert) convertir. **to b. through**, hacer atravesar; llevar a través de; ayudar a salir (de un apuro); (an illness) curar de. **to b. to**, traer a; llevar a; (from a swoon) hacer volver en sí; Naut. ponerse a la capa. **He cannot b. himself to**, No puede persuadirse a. **to b. together**, reunir; (things) juntar, amontonar; reconciliar, poner en paz. **to b. under**, someter; sojuzgar; incluir. **to b. up**, llevar arriba, subir; (a person) hacer subir; hacer avanzar; (a price) hacer subir; ir (a); andar; (breed) criar; (educate) educar, criar; (in a discussion) hacer notar; vomitar. **to b. up the rear**, ir al fin (de); Mil. ir a la retaguardia. **well** (or **badly**) **brought up**, bien (o mal) educado. **to b.** **upon oneself,** buscarse, incurrir (en). **to b.** **up-to-date,** poner al día; refrescar; rejuvenecer

bringing /'brɪŋɪŋ/ n acción de llevar o traer, f; conducción, f; transporte, m. **b.** **forth,** producción, f. **b.** **in,** introducción, f. **b.** **out,** producción, f; publicación, f; (of a girl in society) puesta de largo, f. **b.** **under,** reducción, f; subyugación, f. **b.** **up,** educación, crianza, f

brink /brɪŋk/ n borde, margen, m; (of water) orilla, f; Fig. margen, m. **on the b.,** al margen; a la orilla. **to be on the b.** **of,** (doing something) estar para, estar a punto de

briquette /brɪ'kɛt/ n briqueta, f, aglomerado de carbón, m

brisk /brɪsk/ a activo; vivo; animado; rápido, acelerado; enérgico

brisket /'brɪskɪt/ n falda, f

briskly /'brɪskli/ adv vivamente; enérgicamente; aprisa

briskness /'brɪsknɪs/ n actividad, f; viveza, f; animación, f; rapidez, f; energía, f

brisling /'brɪzlɪŋ/ n sardina noruega

bristle /'brɪsəl/ n cerda, seda, f, vi erizarse

bristly /'brɪsli/ a erizado, cerdoso; espinoso; hirsuto

Bristol board /'brɪstl/ n cartulina, f

British /'brɪtɪʃ/ a británico. **the B.,** el pueblo británico; los ingleses

British Commonwealth, the la Mancomunidad Británica, f

Briton /'brɪtn̩/ n inglés (-esa). **ancient B.,** britano (-na)

Brittany /'brɪtn̩i/ Bretaña, f

brittle /'brɪtl̩/ a frágil, quebradizo, deleznable, friable

brittleness /'brɪtl̩nɪs/ n fragilidad, friabilidad, f

broach /broutʃ/ n Cul. espetón, asador, m. vt espitar (un barril); abrir; Fig. introducir

broad /brɔd/ a ancho; grande; (extensive) vasto, extenso; **a b.** **confession,** una confesión amplia; (full) pleno; (of accents) marcado; (of words) lato; (clear) claro; (of the mind) liberal, tolerante; (of humor, etc.) grosero; (general) general, comprensivo. **in b.** **daylight,** en pleno día. **b.-brimmed,** de ala ancha. **b.-faced,** cariancho. **b.-mindedness,** tolerancia, liberalidad, f. **to be b.-minded,** ser tolerante, ser liberal, tener manga ancha. **b.-shouldered,** ancho de espaldas

broadcast /'brɔd,kæst/ n Agr. siembra al vuelo, f; Radio. radiodifusión, radiotransmisión, emisión, f, a radiado. adv por todas partes; extensamente. vt Agr. sembrar a vuelo; Radio. radiodifundir, radiar, transmitir por radio; (news, etc.) diseminar

broadcaster /'brɔd,kæstər/ n (lecturer) conferenciante, mf; radiodifusor (-ra); (announcer) locutor (-ra)

broadcasting /'brɔd,kæstɪŋ/ n radiación, radiodifusión, f; radio, f. **b.-station,** estación de radio, emisora, f. **b.-studio,** estudio de emisión, m

broaden /'brɔdn̩/ vt ampliar, ensanchar. vi ampliarse, ensancharse

broad-leaved /'brɔd,livd/ a frondoso

broadly /'brɔdli/ adv anchamente; con marcado acento dialectal; de una manera general

broadness /'brɔdnɪs/ n anchura, f; extensión, vastedad, f; tolerancia, f; liberalidad, f; grosería, f; (of accent) acento marcado, m

broadside /'brɔd,said/ n (of a ship) costado, m; (of guns) andanada, f; Fig. batería, f; Print. cara de un pliego, f. **to be b.** **on,** dar el costado

brocade /brou'keid/ a and n brocado m.. vt decorar con brocado. **imitation b.,** brocatel, m

brocaded /brou'keidid/ a decorado con brocado; de brocado

broccoli /'brɒkəli/ n brócoli, brécol, f

brochure /brou'ʃʊr/ n folleto, m

brogue /broug/ n acento, m; acento irlandés, m; (shoe) zapato grueso, m

broil /brɔil/ vt emparrillar, asar. vi asarse

broke /brouk/ a quebrado; (penniless) Peru calato

broken /'broukən/ a roto; quebrado; (spiritless) abatido, desalentado; (infirm) agotado, debilitado; (ru-

ined) arruinado; (of ground) desigual, escabroso; (of a language) chapucero; (spoiled) estropeado; imperfecto; incompleto; (loose) suelto; (of a horse, etc.) domado; (of the weather) variable; (of sleep) interrumpido; (of the heart, of shoes, etc.) roto; (of the voice, sobs, sighs) entrecortado; (of the voice through old age, etc.) cascada; (incoherent) incoherente. **b.-down,** (tired) rendido, agotado; arruinado; (not working) estropeado. **b.-hearted,** roto el corazón, angustiado. **b.-winged,** aliquebrado. **I speak broken Spanish,** Hablo el español chapuceramente

brokenly /'broukənli/ adv (of the voice) con voz entrecortada; a ratos; interrumpidamente

brokenness /'broukənnɪs/ n interrupción, f; (of the ground) desigualdad, f; (of speech) imperfección, f

broker /'broukər/ n corredor, m; (stock) corredor de bolsa, m

brokerage /'broukərɪdʒ/ n corretaje, m

bromide /'broumaid/ n bromuro, m

bromine /'broumin/ n bromo, m

bronchi /'brɒŋki/ n pl bronquios, m pl

bronchitis /brɒŋ'kaitɪs/ n bronquitis, f

broncopneumonia /'brɒŋkouniu'mouniə/ n bronconeumonía, f

Brontosaurus /,brɒntə'sɔrəs/ n brontosauro, m

bronze /brɒnz/ n bronce, m; objeto de bronce, m, a de bronce. vt broncear. **B. Age,** Edad de Bronce, f

brooch /broutʃ/ n broche, m; alfiler de pecho, m

brood /brud/ n (of birds) nidada, f; (of chickens) pollada, f; (other animals) cría, f; prole, f, vi empollar. **to b.** **over,** meditar sobre, rumiar; (of mountains, etc.) dominar

brook /brʊk/ n arroyo, riachuelo, m

broom /brum/ n escoba, f; Bot. retama, f; hiniesta, f. **common b.,** retama de escobas, f. **Spanish b.,** retama común, retama de olor, hiniesta, f. **b.-handle,** palo de escoba, m

broomstick /'brum,stɪk/ n palo de escoba, m

broth /brɔθ/ n caldo, m

brothel /'brɒθəl/ n burdel, lupanar, m, casa de trato, f

brother /'brʌðər/ n hermano, m; (colleague) colega, m; Inf. compañero, m. **foster-b.,** hermano de leche, m. **half-b.,** medio hermano, m. **step-b.,** hermanastro, m. **b.-in-law,** hermano político, cuñado, m. **b.-officer,** compañero de promoción, m

brotherhood /'brʌðər,hʊd/ n fraternidad, f; Eccl. cofradía, f; hermandad, f

brotherliness /'brʌðərlinɪs/ n fraternidad, f

brotherly /'brʌðərli/ a fraterno

brow /brau/ n frente, f; ceja, f; (of a hill) cresta, f; cumbre, f; (edge) borde, m. **to knit one's b.,** fruncir el ceño

browbeat /'brau,bit/ vt intimidar, amenazar

browbeating /'brau,bitɪŋ/ n intimidación, f

brown /braun/ a castaño; (gallicism often used of shoes, etc.) marrón; pardo; (of complexion, eyes, hair) moreno; (dark brown) bruno; (blackish) negruzco; (toasted) tostado; (burnt) quemado. n color moreno, m; color pardo, m; castaño, m; (from the sun) bronce, m, vt (toast) tostar; (a person) volver moreno, broncear; (meat) asar. vi tostarse; volverse moreno, broncearse; asarse. **b.** **bear,** oso pardo, m. **b.** **owl,** autillo, m. **b.** **paper,** papel de estraza, m. **b.** **sugar,** azúcar moreno (or quebrado), m

brownie /'brauni/ n duende benévolo, m

brownish /'braunɪʃ/ a rojenucho; que tira a castaño o a bruno; parduzco; trigueño

brownness /'braunnɪs/ n color moreno, m

browse /brauz/ vi pacer; (through a publication) hojear (un libro)

browsing /'brauzɪŋ/ n apacentamiento, m; hojeo (de un libro), m; lectura, f, estudio, m

Bruges /'brudʒɪz/ Brujas, f

bruise /bruz/ n cardenal, m. Lat. Am. magullón (m), abolladura, f; (in metal) bollo, m; (on fruit) maca, f; vt acardenalar, magullar; abollar; (fruit) macar

bruising /'bruzɪŋ/ n magullamiento, m; (of metal) abolladura, f; (crushing) machacadura, f; (boxing) boxeo, pugilato, m

brunette /bru'nɛt/ n trigueña, morena, f

brunt /brʌnt/ n peso, m; golpe, m; choque, m; esfuerzo, *m*. **to bear the b.,** soportar el peso; sufrir el choque; *Inf.* pagar el pato

brush /brʌʃ/ *n* cepillo, *m*; (broom) escoba, *f*; (for whitewashing, etc.) brocha, *f*; (for painting) pincel, *m*; (of a fox) cola (de zorro), *f*; (undergrowth) breñal, matorral, *m*; (fight) escaramuza, *f*; (argument) altercación, *f*. **scrubbing-b.,** cepillo para fregar, *m*. **shoe-b.,** cepillo para limpiar los zapatos, *m*. **stroke of the b.,** brochada, *f*; pincelada, *f*. **whitewash-b.,** brochón, *m*. **b. maker** or **seller,** escobero (-ra); pincelero (-ra)

brush /brʌʃ/ *vt* cepillar; (sweep) barrer; frotar; (touch) rozar; (touch lightly) acariciar. **to b. against,** rozar, tocar. **to b. aside,** echar a un lado; *Fig.* no hacer caso de; ignorar. **to b. off,** sacudir(se); quitar(se); (sweep) barrer. **to b. up,** cepillar; (wool) cardar; (tidy) asear; (a dispute) refrescar, repasar

brushing /'brʌʃɪŋ/ *n* acepilladura, *f*; (sweeping) barredura, *f*; (touching) roce, rozamiento, *m*; (of hair) peinadura, *f*

brushwood /'brʌʃ,wʊd/ *n* enjutos, *m pl*, chamarasca, *f*; matorral, *m*

brusque /brʌsk/ *a* brusco, seco

brusquely /'brʌskli/ *adv* secamente

brusqueness /'brʌsknɪs/ *n* brusquedad, *f*

Brussels /'brʌsəlz/ *a* bruselense; de Bruselas. **B. lace,** encaje de Bruselas, *m*

Brussels sprouts /sprauts/ *n pl* bretones, *m pl*

brutal /'brutl/ *a* bestial, brutal; salvaje, inhumano

brutality /bru'tælɪti/ *n* brutalidad, bestialidad, *f*; barbaridad, ferocidad, *f*

brutalize /'brutl,aiz/ *vt* embrutecer

brutally /'brutli/ *adv* brutalmente

brute /brut/ *n* bruto, animal, *m*; salvaje, bárbaro, *m*. **b. force,** la fuerza bruta

brutish /'brutɪʃ/ *a* bruto; sensual, bestial; grosero; salvaje; estúpido; ignorante. **to become b.,** embrutecerse

bubble /'bʌbəl/ *n* burbuja, *f*; borbollón, *m*, *vi* burbujear; borbollar, bullir, hervir

bubbling /'bʌbəlɪŋ/ *n* burbujeo, *m*; hervidero, *m*; (of brooks) murmullo, *m*, *a* burbujeante; hirviente; (of brooks) parlero; (of wine) espumoso, efervescente

bubonic /byu'bɒnɪk/ *a* bubónico. **b. plague,** peste bubónica, *f*

buccaneer /,bʌkə'nɪər/ *n* corsario, *m*; aventurero, *m*

Bucharest /'bukə,rɛst/ Bucarest, *m*

buck /bʌk/ *n* Zool. gamo, *m*; (male) macho, *m*; (fop) galán, petimetre, *m*, *vi* (of a horse) caracolear; fanfarronear. **to pass the b.,** *Inf.* echarle a uno el muerto. **b.-rabbit,** conejo, *m*. **to b. up,** hacer de tripas corazón

bucket /'bʌkɪt/ *n* cubo, balde, *m*, cubeta, *f*

buckle /'bʌkəl/ *n* hebilla, *f*. *vt* enhebillar, abrochar con hebilla. *vi* doblarse. **to b. to,** ponerse a hacer algo con ahínco

buckled /'bʌkəld/ *a* con hebillas

buckler /'bʌklər/ *n* broquel, *m*, rodela, tarjeta, *f*

buckram /'bʌkrəm/ *n* bocací, *m*

buckshot /'bʌk,ʃɒt/ *n* perdigón, *m*

buckskin /'bʌk,skɪn/ *n* ante, *m*

buckwheat /'bʌk,wit/ *n* alforfón, trigo sarraceno, *m*

bucolic /byu'kɒlɪk/ *a* bucólico, pastoril

bud /bʌd/ *n* brote, *m*; botón, capullo, *m*; (of vines) bollón, *m*; (of vegetables) gema, *f*. *vi* brotar, germinar. *vt* injertar de escudete

Buddhism /'budɪzəm/ *n* budismo, *m*

Buddhist /'budɪst/ *n* budista, *mf*

budding /'bʌdɪŋ/ *n* brotadura, *f*; (of roses, etc) injerto de escudete, *m*; *Fig.* germen, *m*

budge /bʌdʒ/ *vi* moverse, menearse. *vt* mover

budget /'bʌdʒɪt/ *n* presupuesto, *m*. *vi* presuponer

Buenos Aires /'bweiˈnəs aiˈrɪz/ (of or from the province of) *a* and *n* bonaerense, *mf*

buff /bʌf/ *n* color de ante, *m*; piel de ante, *f*. **b.-colored,** anteado. **in the buff = naked, nude**

buffalo /'bʌfə,lou/ *n* búfalo, *m*

buffer /'bʌfər/ *n* (railway) parachoques, *m*. **b. state,** estado tapón, *m*

buffet /bə'fei/ *n* bofetón, *m*; bofetada, *f*; bar, *m*. *vt* abofetear; golpear; luchar con las olas

buffoon /bə'fun/ *n* bufón, *m*

buffoonery /bə'funəri/ *n* bufonería, *f*

bug /bʌg/ *n* chinche, *f*. **bugs,** *Lat. Am.* bicherío, *m*

bugbear /'bʌg,bɛər/ *n* pesadilla, *f*

bugle /'byugəl/ *n* corneta, trompeta, *f*; (bead) abalorio, *m*. **b. blast,** trompetazo, *m*

bugler /'byuglər/ *n* trompetero, *m*

build /bɪld/ *vt* edificar; (engines, ships, organs, etc.) construir; (a nest and *Fig.*) hacer; (have built) hacer, edificar; crear; formar; fundar. *n* estructura, *f*; (of the body) hechura, *f*; talle, *m*. **to b. castles in Spain,** hacer castillos en el aire. **built-up area,** zona urbana, *f*. **to b. up,** construir, levantar; (block) tapar; (business, reputation) establecer, crear. **to b. upon,** *Fig.* contar con, confiar en; esperar de

builder /'bɪldər/ *n* constructor, *m*; maestro de obras, *m*; (laborer) albañil, *m*; creador (-ra), fundador (-ra); arquitecto, *m*

building /'bɪldɪŋ/ *n* edificación, *f*; construcción, *f*; edificio, *m*; fundación, *f*; creación, *f*. **b. contractor,** maestro de obras, *m*. **b. material,** material de construcción, *m*. **b. site,** solar, terreno, *m*. **b. timber,** madera de construcción, *f*

built-in /'bɪlt ,ɪn/ *a* empotrado. **b. closet,** armario empotrado, *m*

bulb /bʌlb/ *n* Bot. bulbo, *m*; (Elec. Phys.) bombilla, *f*; (of an oil lamp) cebolla, *f*

bulbous /'bʌlbəs/ *a* bulboso

Bulgarian /bʌl'gɛəriən/ *a* and *n* búlgaro (-ra)

bulge /bʌldʒ/ *n* bulto, *m*; hinchazón, *f*; protuberancia, *f*; *Mil.* bolsa (en el frente), *f*. *vi* hincharse; estar lleno (de)

bulging /'bʌldʒɪŋ/ *a* lleno (de); con bultos; hinchado (de)

bulimia /bu'limiə/ *n* bulimia, *f*

bulk /bʌlk/ *n* volumen, tamaño, *m*; bulto, *m*; (larger part) grueso, *m*; mayor parte, *f*; (of people) mayoría, *f*; (of a ship) capacidad, *f*. **in b.,** *Com.* en bruto, en grueso. **to b. large,** tener mucha importancia

bulkhead /'bʌlk,hɛd/ *n* Naut. mamparo, *m*

bulkiness /'bʌlkinɪs/ *n* abultamiento, *m*; volumen, tamaño, *m*

bulky /'bʌlki/ *a* voluminoso, grande, grueso

bull /bʊl/ *n* toro, *m*; Astron. Tauro, *m*; (of some animals) macho, *m*; (Stock Exchange) alcista, *mf*; (of the Pope) bula (del Papa), *f*. **a b. in a china shop,** un caballo loco en una cacharrería. **to fight bulls,** torear. **b.-calf,** ternero, *m*. **bull's eye,** blanco, *m*; acierto, *m*. **b. fight,** corrida de toros, *f*. **b. fighter's gala uniform,** traje de luces, *m*. **b.-ring,** plaza de toros, *f*

bulldog /'bʊl,dɔg/ *n* perro dogo, perro de presa, *m*

bulldozer /'bʊl,douzər/ *n* (excavator) tozodora, *f*

bullet /'bʊlɪt/ *n* bala, *f*. **spent b.,** bala fría, *f*. **stray b.,** bala perdida, *f*. **b.-proof,** a prueba de bala, blindado

bulletin /'bʊlɪtɪn/ *n* boletín, *m*

bulletin board *n* tablero de anuncios, tablero de avisos, tablón, *m*

bulletproof vest /'bʊlɪt,pruf/ *n* chaleco blindado, *m*

bullfighter /'bʊl,faitər/ *n* torero, *m* (on foot), toreador, *m* (on horseback)

bullfinch /'bʊl,fɪntʃ/ *n* pinzón real, *m*

bullion /'bʊlyən/ *n* Com. metálico, *m*; oro (or plata) en barras, *m*, *f*.

bullock /'bʊlək/ *n* becerro, *m*; buey, *m*

bullpen /'bʊl,pɛn/ *n* toril, *m* (bullfighting); calentador, *m* (baseball)

bully /'bʊli/ *n* valentón, perdonavidas, gallito, *m*; rufián, *Argentina* compadre *m*. *vt* intimidar; tratar mal. **b. beef,** vaca en lata, *f*

bulrush /'bʊl,rʌʃ/ *n* anea, *f*

bulwark /'bʊlwərk/ *n* baluarte, *m*; Naut. antepecho, *m*

bumblebee /'bʌmbəl,bi/ *n* abejorro, *m*

bump /bʌmp/ *n* golpe, *m*; ruido, *m*; choque, *m*; (bruise) chichón, *m*, roncha, *f*; Aer. sacudida, *f*, meneo, *m*. *vi* (into, against) tropezar con; (along) saltar en. *vt* chocar (contra)

bumper /'bʌmpər/ n (of a car) parachoques, m. **a b. harvest,** una cosecha abundante

bumpkin /'bʌmpkɪn/ n patán, villano, m

bumptious /'bʌmpfəs/ a fatuo, presuntuoso, presumido

bumpy /'bʌmpi/ n (of surface) desigual, escabroso; (of a vehicle) incómodo, con mala suspensión

bun /bʌn/ n buñuelo, bollo, m; (hair) moño, m

bunch /bʌntʃ/ n (of fruit) racimo, m; manojo, m; (of flowers) ramo, m, Lat. Am. also maceta f; (tuft) penacho, m; (gang) pandilla, f, vi arracimarse, agruparse

bundle /'bʌndl/ n atado, lío, m; (of papers) legajo, m; (of sticks) haz, m; (sheaf) fajo, m; (package) paquete, m; fardo, hatillo, m; (roll) rollo, m, vt atar, liar; envolver; empaquetar; (stuff) meter, introducir. **to b. in,** meter dentro (de). **to b. out,** despachar sin ceremonia, poner de patitas en la calle

bungalow /'bʌŋgə,lou/ n casa de un solo piso, f

bungle /'bʌŋgəl/ vt estropear; hacer mal. n equivocación, f, yerro, m; cosa (o obra) mal hecha, f

bungling /'bʌŋglɪŋ/ a chapucero, torpe

bunion /'bʌnyən/ n juanete (del pie), m

bunk /bʌŋk/ n litera, f, vi Inf. poner pies en polvorosa, pirarse

bunker /'bʌŋkər/ n Naut. pañol, m; (for coal) carbonera, f; (golf) hoya de arena, f

bunkum /'bʌŋkəm/ n patrañas, f pl

bunting /'bʌntɪŋ/ n gallardete, m

buoy /'bui/ n boya, baliza, f, vt boyar; abalizar; Fig. sostener. **light b.,** boya luminosa, f

buoyancy /'bɔiənsi/ n flotación, f; Fig. optimismo, m, alegría, f

buoyant /'bɔiənt/ a boyante; ligero

burden /'bɜrdṇ/ n carga, f, peso, m; (of a ship) tonelaje, m, capacidad, f; (of a song) estribillo, m; (gist) esencia, f. vt cargar. **to be a b. on,** pesar sobre

burdensome /'bɜrdṇsəm/ a pesado, oneroso, gravoso; abrumador

burdensomeness /'bɜrdṇsəmnɪs/ n pesadez, f; agobio, m

bureau /'byʊrou/ n buró, secreter, m; escritorio, m; (office) dirección, oficina, f; departamento, m

bureaucracy /byʊ'rɒkrəsi/ n burocracia, f

bureaucrat /'byʊrə,kræt/ n burócrata, mf; Inf. mandarín, m

bureaucratic /,byʊrə'krætɪk/ a burocrático

burgher /'bɜrgər/ n ciudadano (-na), vecino (-na)

burglar /'bɜrglər/ n ladrón de casas, escalador, m. **cat b.,** gato, m. **b. alarm,** alarma contra ladrones, f. **b. insurance,** seguro contra robo, m

burglary /'bɜrgləri/ n robo nocturno de una casa, m

burgle /'bɜrgəl/ vi robar una casa de noche. vt robar

burgundy /'bɜrgəndi/ n vino de Borgoña, borgoña, m

burial /'bɛriəl/ n entierro, m. **b.-ground,** campo santo, cementerio, m. **b. service,** misa de difuntos, f. **b. society,** sociedad de entierros, f

burlap /'bɜrlæp/ n arpillera, f

burlesque /bər'lɛsk/ a burlesco. n parodia. f. vt parodiar

burliness /'bɜrlɪnɪs/ n corpulencia, f

burly /'bɜrli/ a corpulento, fornido

burn /bɜrn/ vt quemar; calcinar; (bricks) cocer; cauterizar; (the tongue) picar; (dry up) secar; (the skin by sun or wind) tostar. vi quemar; arder; Fig. abrasarse (en). **b. at the stake,** vt quemar en la hoguera. **to b. to ashes,** reducir a cenizas. **to b. away,** consumir(se). **to b. oneself,** quemarse. **to b. the midnight oil,** Chile cranearse. **to b. up,** quemar del todo, consumir, f. **to b. with,** Fig. abrasarse en

burn /bɜrn/ n quemadura, f; (stream) arroyo, m

burnable /'bɜrnəbəl/ a combustible

burner /'bɜrnər/ n quemador (-ra); mechero, m

burning /'bɜrnɪŋ/ n quema, f; incendio, m; fuego, m; (inflammation) inflamación, f; (pain) quemazón, f; abrasamiento, m. a en llamas; ardiente; intenso; (notorious) notorio, escandaloso; abrasador; palpitante. **b. question,** cuestión palpitante, f

burnish /'bɜrnɪʃ/ n bruñido, m; lustre, brillo, m, vt

bruñir; pulir, pulimentar, dar brillo a; (weapons) acicalar. vi tomar lustre

burnisher /'bɜrnɪʃər/ n bruñidor, acicalador, m

burnishing /'bɜrnɪʃɪŋ/ n bruñido, m; pulimento, m; (of weapons) acicalado, m

burr /bɜr/ n Bot. cáliz de flor con espinas, m; Mech. rebaba, f; sonido fuerte de la erre, m

burrow /'bɜrou/ n madriguera, f, vivar, m; (for rabbits) conejera, f. vt amadrigar; minar

bursar /'bɜrsər/ n tesorero, m; becario, m

burst /bɜrst/ n estallido, m, explosión, f; (in a pipe) avería, f, (fit) acceso, m; transporte, m; (effort) esfuerzo, m; (expanse) extensión, f, panorama, m. **b. of applause,** salva de aplausos, f

burst /bɜrst/ vi estallar; reventar; quebrarse; romperse; (overflow) desbordar; (of seams) nacerse; derramarse (por); (into laughter) romper a; (into tears) deshacerse en. vt quebrar; romper; hacer estallar. **to b. into,** irrumpir en; (exclamations, etc.) prorrumpir en. **to b. into tears,** romper a llorar, deshacerse en lágrimas. **to b. on the scene,** aparecer de pronto. **to b. open,** abrir con violencia; forzar

bursting /'bɜrstɪŋ/ n estallido, m; quebrantamiento, m; (overflowing) desbordamiento, m

bury /'bɛri/ vt enterrar, sepultar; sumergir; (hide) esconder, ocultar; (forget) echar tierra a

bus /bʌs/ n (regular city bus) autobús m (Colombia, Spain, Venezuela), camión m (Mexico), camioneta f (Guatemala), casadoro m (Costa Rica), chiva f (Colombia, Panama, informal), colectivo m (Argentina, Bolivia), flota f (Colombia, informal), góndola f (Chile), guagua f (Canary Islands, Cuba), micro m (Chile), ómnibus m (Peru), omnibús m (Uruguay); (interurban bus), aerobús m (Venezuela), autobús (Argentina, Chile, Spain, Uruguay), camión, camión de primera clase m (Mexico), interprovincial m (Peru), pullmán m (Mexico; (interurban jitney bus) colectivo m (Colombia); (minibus) micro m (Colombia, Peru), liebre (Chile, informal) **double-decker bus,** ómnibus de dos pisos, m. **to travel by bus,** ir en autobús. **bus station,** estación de autobuses, Mexico camionera, f

busby /'bʌzbi/ n birretina, gorra de húsar, f

bush /bʊʃ/ n arbusto, matojo, m; (undergrowth) maleza, f; tierra virgen, f; Mech. manguito, m

bushel /'bʊʃəl/ n medida de áridos, f, (In England 8 gallons or 36.37 liters)

bushiness /'bʊʃɪnɪs/ n espesura, f; densidad, f

bushy /'bʊʃi/ a lleno de arbustos; denso; espeso; grueso; (eyebrows, etc.) poblado

busily /'bɪzəli/ adv diligentemente, solícitamente; afanosamente, laboriosamente. **He was b. occupied in...,** Estaba muy ocupado en...

business /'bɪznɪs/ n ocupación, f; quehaceres, m pl; (matter) asunto, m, cosa, f; empleo, oficio, m; Com. negocio(s), m, pl.; casa comercial, f; (trade) comercio, m; (clients, connection) clientela, f; (right) derecho, m; Theat. juego escénico, m, pantomima, f. **He had no b. to do that,** No tenía derecho a hacer eso. **Mind your own b.!** ¡No te metas donde no te llaman! **on b.,** por negocios. **to be in b. for oneself,** tener negocios por su propia cuenta. **to mean b.,** hacer algo en serio; estar resuelto. **to send about his b.,** mandar a paseo (a). **to set up in b.,** establecer un negocio. **b. affairs,** negocios, m pl. **b. agent,** agente de negocios, m. **b. hours,** horas de trabajo, f pl. **b.-like,** formal, práctico, sistemático. **b. man,** hombre de negocios, negociante, m

business administration n administración de empresas, f

bust /bʌst/ n Art. busto, bulto, m; pecho, m. **b. bodice,** sostén, m

bustard /'bʌstərd/ n avutarda, f

bustle /'bʌsəl/ n actividad, animación, f; confusión, f; (of a dress) polizón, tontillo, m. vi menearse, darse prisa. vt dar prisa (a)

bustling /'bʌslɪŋ/ a activo; ocupado, atareado; animado; bullicioso, ruidoso

busy /'bɪzi/ a ocupado; atareado; activo, diligente; (of places) animado, bullicioso; (of streets) de gran circulación; (officious) entremetido. **to b. oneself,**

ocuparse (en, con); dedicarse (a), entregarse (a); (interfere) entremeterse (con). **to be b.**, estar ocupado; estar atareado, tener mucho que hacer. **b.-body,** bullebulle, *mf.* entremetido (-da), chismoso (-sa), *Argentina* hurguete *mf*

busyness /'bɪzɪnɪs/ *n* ocupación, *f;* laboriosidad, *f;* actividad, *f*

but /bʌt/ *conjunc prep adv* pero; sino; (only) solamente; (except) menos; excepto; (almost) casi; que no; si no; (that) que; (nevertheless) sin embargo, empero, no obstante; (without) sin, sin que; (of time recently passed) no más que, tan recientemente. *n* pero, *m*. **He cannot choose but go,** No puede hacer otra cosa que marcharse. **to do nothing but...,** hacer únicamente..., no hacer más que... **but for,** a no ser por. **but yesterday,** solamente ayer. **but then (or but yet),** pero

butcher /'bʊtʃər/ *n* carnicero, *m. vt* matar reses; hacer una carnicería en. **butcher's boy,** mozo del carnicero, *m.* **butcher's shop,** carnicería, *f*

butchery /'bʊtʃəri/ *n* carnicería, *f;* matanza, *f*

butler /'bʌtlər/ *n* mayordomo, *m.* **butler's pantry,** despensa, repostería, *f*

butt /bʌt/ *n* (cask) tonel, *m,* pipa, *f;* (for water) barril, *m;* (of a cigarette, etc.) colilla, *f;* (of fire-arms) culata, *f;* (handle) mango, cabo, *m;* (billiards) mocho, *m;* (earthwork) terrero, *m;* (*Fig.* object) objeto (de), *m;* (of bulls, etc.) topetada, *f; pl* **butts,** campo de tiro, *m;* (target) blanco, *m. vt* (toss) topar, acornear; (meet) tropezar (con). **to b. in,** *Inf.* entrometerse, meter baza; encajarse

butter /'bʌtər/ *n* mantequilla, *f, vt* untar con mantequilla. **b.-dish,** mantequera, *f.* **b.-fingers,** torpe, *m.* **b.-knife,** cuchillo para mantequilla, *m.* **b.-milk,** suero de mantequilla, *m.* **b.-print,** molde para mantequilla, *m.* **b.-sauce,** mantequilla fundida, *f*

buttercup /'bʌtər,kʌp/ *n* ranúnculo, botón de oro, *m*

butterfly /'bʌtər,flai/ *n* mariposa, *f*

butterscotch /'bʌtər,skɒtʃ/ *n* dulce de azúcar y mantequilla, *m*

buttocks /'bʌtəks/ *n pl* nalgas, posaderas, *f pl*

button /'bʌtn̩/ *n* botón, *m; pl* **buttons,** botones, paje, *m. vt* abotonar, abrochar. *vi* abotonarse, abrocharse. **to press the b.,** apretar el botón. **b.-hook,** abotonador, *m*

buttonhole /'bʌtn̩,houl/ *n* ojal, *m;* flor que se lleva en el ojal, *f. vt Sew.* hacer ojales; (embroidery) hacer el festón; *Inf.* importunar

buttoning /'bʌtn̩ɪŋ/ *n* abrochamiento, *m*

buttress /'bʌtrɪs/ *n* estribo, macho, contrafuerte, *m; Fig.* apoyo, sostén, *m. vt* afianzar, estribar; *Fig.* apoyar, sostener. **flying-b.,** arbotante, *m*

buxom /'bʌksəm/ *a* (of a woman) fresca, frescachona

buxomness /'bʌksəmnɪs/ *n* frescura, *f*

buy /bai/ *vt* comprar; obtener; (achieve) lograr; (bribe) sobornar. **to buy on credit,** comprar al fiado. **to buy back,** comprar de nuevo; redimir; (ransom) rescatar. **to buy for,** (a price) comprar por; (purpose or destination) comprar para. **to buy in,** (at an auction) comprar por cuenta del dueño. **to buy off,** librarse de uno con dinero. **to buy out,** (of a business) comprar la parte de un socio. **to buy up,** comprar todo, acaparar

buyable /'baiəbəl/ *a* comprable, que se puede comprar

buyer /'baiər/ *n* comprador (-ra)

buying /'baiɪŋ/ *n* compra, *f.* **b. back,** rescate, *m.* **b. up,** acaparamiento, *m*

buying power *n* capacidad de compra, *f,* valor adquisitivo, *m*

buzz /bʌz/ *n* zumbido, *m;* (whisper) susurro, murmullo, *m;* (of a bell) sonido (del timbre), *m, vi* zumbar; susurrar

buzzer /'bʌzər/ *n* zumbador, *m;* sirena, *f;* (bell) timbre, *m*

buzzing /'bʌzɪŋ/ *a* zumbador, que zumba, *n.* See **buzz**

by /bai/ *prep* por; de; en; a; con; (of place) cerca de, al lado de; (according to) según, de acuerdo con; (in front of, past) delante (de); (at the latest) antes de, al más tardar; (expressing agency) por; (by means of) mediante; (through, along) por; (upon) sobre; (for) para; (under) bajo. **He will be here by Wednesday,** Estará aquí para el miércoles; (not later than) Estará aquí antes del miércoles (or el miércoles a lo más tardar). **How did he come by it?** ¿Cómo llegó a su poder? **He will come by train,** Vendrá en tren. **I know her by sight,** La conozco de vista. **There are three children by the first marriage,** Hay tres niños del primer matrimonio. **He goes by the name of Pérez,** Se le conoce por (or bajo) el nombre de Pérez. **six feet by eight,** seis pies por ocho. **They called her by her name,** La llamaron por su nombre. **two by two,** dos por dos. **The picture was painted by Cézanne,** El cuadro fue pintado por Cézanne. **drop by drop,** gota a gota. **by a great deal,** con mucho. **by all means,** naturalmente; de todos modos; cueste lo que cueste. **by chance,** por ventura. **by day (night),** de día (noche). **by daylight,** a la luz del día. **by doing it,** con hacerlo. **by myself,** solo; sin ayuda. **"By Appointment"** «Cita Previa». **by chance or by mischance,** por ventura o por desdicha. **an hour away by car,** a una hora de automóvil. **music by Brahms,** música de Brahms. **pull by the hair,** tirar por el pelo. **take by the hand,** llevar de la mano

by /bai/ *adv* (near) cerca; (before) delante; al lado; a un lado; aparte; (of time) pasado. **to put by,** (keep) guardar; (throw away) desechar; (accumulate) acumular; (put out of the way) arrinconar. **to pass by,** pasar; pasar delante de. **by and by,** luego, pronto; más tarde. **by now,** ya, antes de ahora. **by the way,** entre paréntesis, a propósito; de paso; al lado del camino. **by-election,** elección parcial, *f.* **by-law,** reglamento, *m.* **by-pass,** ruta de evitación, *f,* desvío, *m;* (*Mech. Elec.*) derivación, *f. vi* desviarse en; *Mil.* rebasar. **by-product,** derivado, *m; Fig.* consecuencia, *f;* resultado, *m*

bye /bai/ *n* (in cricket) meta, *f.* **by the bye,** a propósito, entre paréntesis

bye! *bai! interj. Argentina, Chile* ¡chao!

bygone /'bai,gɔn/ *a* pasado. **Let bygones be bygones,** Lo pasado pasado

byplay /'bai,plei/ *n* pantomima, *f,* gestos, *m pl; Theat.* juego escénico, *m,* escena muda, *f*

bystander /'bai,stændər/ *n* espectador (-ra); *pl* **bystanders,** los circunstantes

bystreet /'bai,strit/ *n* callejuela, *f;* calle pobre, *f*

byte /bait/ *n* octeto, byte, *m*

byway /'bai,wei/ *n* camino desviado, *m; Fig.* senda indirecta, *f; pl* **byways,** andurriales, *m pl*

byword /'bai,wɜrd/ *n* proverbio, *m;* objeto de burla o escándalo, *m*

Byzantine Empire, the /'bɪzən,tin/ el Imperio Bizantino, *m*

Byzantium /bɪ'zænʃiəm/ Bizancio, *m*

C

c /si/ *n* (letter) c, *f; Mus.* do, *m*

cab /kæb/ *n* (horse-drawn) simón, *m;* (taxi) coche de alquiler, *m;* (of a locomotive) cabina del conductor, *f.* **cab-rank,** punto de coches, *m*

cabala /'kæbələ/ *n* cábala, *f*

cabaret /,kæbə'rei/ *n* cabaret, *m;* taberna, *f*

cabbage /'kæbɪdʒ/ *n* col, berza, *f.* **red c.,** lombarda, *f.* **c. butterfly,** mariposa de col, *f*

cabin /'kæbɪn/ *n* cabaña, choza, *f; Naut.* camarote, *m;* (railway) garita, *f; Aer.* cabina, *f.* **c. boy,** grumete, galopín, mozo de cámara, *m.* **c. trunk,** baúl mundo, *m*

cabinet /'kæbənɪt/ *n* (piece of furniture) vitrina, *f;* colección, exposición, *f; Polit.* gabinete, *m;* (of a radio) cónsola, *f.* **c.-maker,** ebanista, *m.* **c.-making,**

ebanistería, *f*. **c. meeting,** consejo de ministros, *m*. **c. minister,** ministro, *m*
cable /'keibəl/ *n* amarra, maroma, *f*; cable, *m*; cable- (grama), *m*, *vt* cablegrafiar. **electric c.,** cable eléctrico, *m*. **overhead c.,** cable aéreo, *m*
cabman /'kæbmən/ *n* cochero de punto, simón, *m*
caboose /kə'bus/ *n Naut.* cocina, *f*
cache /kæʃ/ *n* escondite, escondrijo, *m*
cackle /'kækəl/ *vi* (of a hen) cacarear; (of a goose) graznar; (of humans) chacharear. *n* cacareo, *m*; graznido, *m*; cháchara, *f*
cacophony /kə'kɒfəni/ *n* cacofonía, *f*
cactus /'kæktəs/ *n* cacto, *m*
cad /kæd/ *n* sinvergüenza, *m*; tipo de cuidado, *m*
cadaverous /kə'dævərəs/ *a* cadavérico
caddish /'kædɪʃ/ *a* mal educado, grosero
caddy /'kædi/ *n* (for tea) cajita para té, *f*; (golf) cadi, *mf*
cadence /'keidn̩s/ *n* cadencia, *f*
cadet /kə'dɛt/ *n* hermano menor, *m*; *Mil.* cadete, *m*
cadge /kædʒ/ *vi* sablear. *vt* dar un sablazo (a)
cadger /'kædʒər/ *n* sablista, *mf*; mendigo, *m*; (loafer) golfo, *m*
Cadiz /'kɑdis/ Cádiz, *m*
cadmium /'kædmiəm/ *n* cadmio, *m*
café /kæ'fei/ *n* café, *m*
cafeteria /ˌkæfɪ'tɪəriə/ *n* bar automático, *m*
caffeine /kæ'fin/ *n* cafeína, *f*
cage /keidʒ/ *n* (animal's, bird's) jaula, *f*; (of a lift) camarín, *m*; (for transporting miners) jaula, *f*. *vt* enjaular; encerrar
Cain /kein/, **to raise** armar lo de Dios es Cristo
Cairo /'kairou/ el Cairo, *m*
cajole /kə'dʒoul/ *vt* lisonjear; engatusar, embromar; instar
cajolery /kə'dʒouləri/ *n* zalamerías, *f pl*; marrullería, *f*, engatusamiento, *m*
cake /keik/ *n Cul.* pastel, *m*, torta, *f*; (of chocolate, etc.) pastilla, *f*. *vt* and *vi* cuajar; formar costra; (with mud) enlodar. **to sell like hot cakes,** venderse como pan bendito. **to take the c.,** llevarse la palma. **c. of soap,** pastilla de jabón, *f*. **c.-shop,** pastelería, *f*
calamine /'kælə,main/ *n* calamina, *f*
calamitous /kə'læmɪtəs/ *a* calamitoso, desastroso
calamity /kə'læmɪti/ *n* calamidad, *f*; desastre, *m*, *Mexico also* funestidad *f*
calcium /'kælsiəm/ *n* calcio, *m*
calculate /'kælkyə,leit/ *vt* calcular; adaptar. **to c. on,** contar con
calculated /'kælkyə,leitɪd/ *a* premeditado. **to be c. to,** conducir a; ser a propósito para
calculatedly /'kælkyə,leitɪdli/ *adv* calculadamente
calculating /'kælkyə,leitɪŋ/ *n* cálculo, *m*, *a* calculador; (of persons) interesado; (shrewd) perspicaz; atento. **c. machine,** máquina de calcular, *f*, calculador, *m*
calculation /ˌkælkyə'leiʃən/ *n* cálculo, *m*; calculación, *f*
calculator /'kælkyə,leitər/ *n* calculador, *m*
calculus /'kælkyələs/ *n* cálculo, *m*
calendar /'kæləndər/ *n* calendario, *m*; almanaque, *m*; (university, etc.) programa, *m*
calender /'kæləndər/ *n* calandria, *f*, *vt* calandrar, cilindrar
calf /kæf/ *n* becerro (-rra), ternero (-ra); (young of other animals) hijuelo, *m*; (of the leg) pantorrilla, *f*; (leather) cuero de becerro, *m*; piel, *f*. **calf's-foot,** pie de ternera, *m*. **c. love,** amor de muchachos, *m*
caliber /'kæləbər/ *n* calibre, *m*
calibrate /'kælə,breit/ *vt* calibrar
calico /'kælɪ,kou/ *n* indiana, *f*; percal, *m*. **c.-printer,** fabricante de estampados, *m*
Californian /ˌkælə'fɔrnyən/ *a* californio. *n* californio (-ia)
caliph /'keilif/ *n* califa, *m*
calk. /kɔk/ See **caulk**
call /kɔl/ *n* llamada, *f*; (shout) grito, *m*; (of a bird) canto, *m*; (signal) señal, *f*; (visit) visita, *f*; (by a ship) escala, *f*; *Mil.* toque, *m*; (need) necesidad, *f*; (of religion, etc.) vocación, *f*; invitación, *f*; (demand) demanda, *f*; exigencia, *f*. **They came at my c.,** Acu-

dieron a mi llamada. **c. to arms,** llamada, llamada a filas, *f*. **port of c.,** puerto de escala, *m*. **telephone c.,** llamada telefónica, *f*. **to pay a c.,** hacer una visita. **within c.,** al alcance de la voz. **c.-box,** cabina del teléfono, *f*. **c.-boy,** ayudante del traspunte, *m*
call /kɔl/ *vi* llamar; gritar; dar voces; (visit) visitar, hacer una visita (a); venir; (stop) parar; (of a ship) hacer escala. *vt* llamar; (a meeting, etc.) convocar; (awaken) despertar, llamar; (say) decir; (appoint) nombrar; (at cards) declarar. **She is called Dorothy,** Se llama Dorotea. **Madrid calling!** ¡Aquí Madrid! **Will you c. me at eight o'clock, please?** Haga el favor de despertarme (llamarme) a las ocho. **to c. at a port,** hacer escala en un puerto. **to c. a halt,** hacer alto. **to c. a strike,** declarar una huelga. **to c. names,** vituperar, injuriar. **to c. to account,** pedir cuentas (a). **to c. to arms,** tocar el arma; alarmar. **to c. to mind,** acordarse (de); recordar. **to c. to witness,** hacer testigo (de). **to c. back,** *vt* llamar; hacer volver; (unsay) desdecir. *vi* (return) volver; venir a buscar; ir a buscar. **I called back for the parcel,** Volví a buscar el paquete. **to c. for,** pedir a gritos; llamar; (demand) pedir; exigir; (collect a person) pasar a buscar por (parcels, etc.) ir (or venir) a recoger. **He called for help,** Pidió socorro a gritos. **to c. forth,** producir; provocar; inspirar; revelar; (bring together) reunir. **to c. in,** hacer entrar; invitar; (a specialist, etc.) llamar; (worn coin) retirar de la circulación; recoger. **to c. in question,** poner en duda. **to c. off,** (dogs, etc.) llamar; (a strike) cancelar; parar; terminar; (a person) disuadir (de); (postpone) aplazar; suspender; (refrain) desistir (de). **to c. on,** (visit) hacer una visita (a), ir a ver, visitar; (a doctor) visitar; (a person to do something) recurrir (a); (for a speech) invitar (a hablar); (invoke) invocar. **I shall now c. on Mr. Martínez,** Doy la palabra al señor Martínez. **to c. out,** *vt* hacer salir; provocar; inspirar; (challenge) desafiar, retar. *vi* gritar. **c. the roll,** pasar lista. **to c. over,** (names) pasar lista (de). **to c. up,** hacer subir; (to the army) llamar a filas (a); (telephone) llamar por teléfono (a); (memories) evocar. **to c. upon.** See **to c. on**
caller /'kɔlər/ *n* visita, *f*; (telephone) la persona que llama, *f*
calligraphist /kə'lɪgrəfɪst/ *n* calígrafo, *m*
calligraphy /kə'lɪgrəfi/ *n* caligrafía, *f*
calling /'kɔlɪŋ/ *n* llamamiento, *m*; (occupation) profesión, *f*; empleo, *m*; vocación, *f*; (of a meeting) convocación, *f*
callipers /'kælɪpɔrz/ *n pl* compás de puntas, pie de rey, *m*
callisthenics /ˌkæləs'θɛnɪks/ *n pl* calistenia, *f*
callosity /kə'lɒsɪti/ *n* callosidad, *f*
callous /'kæləs/ *a* (of skin) calloso; *Fig.* insensible, duro, inhumano
callously /'kæləsli/ *adv* sin piedad
callousness /'kæləsnɪs/ *n* falta de piedad, inhumanidad, dureza, *f*
callow /'kælou/ *a* (of birds) implume; (inexperienced) bisoño, inexperto, novato
callus /'kæləs/ *n* callo, *m*
calm /kɑm/ *n* calma, *f*; paz, tranquilidad, *f*; sosiego, *m*; serenidad, *f. a* (of the sea) en calma; tranquilo; sereno; sosegado. *vt* calmar; tranquilizar; apaciguar. *vi* calmarse; tranquilizarse; sosegarse. **dead c.,** calma chicha, *f*
calming /'kɑmɪŋ/ *a* calmante
calmly /'kɑmli/ *adv* tranquilamente, sosegadamente; con calma
calmness /'kɑmnɪs/ *n* calma, tranquilidad, *f*; ecuanimidad, serenidad, *f*
caloric /kə'lɔrɪk/ *n* calórico
calorie /'kæləri/ *n* caloría, *f*
calumniation /kəˌlʌmni'eiʃən/ *n* calumnia, *f*
calumniator /kə'lʌmni,eitər/ *n* calumniador (-ra)
calumny /'kæləmni/ *n* calumnia, *f*
calvary /'kælvəri/ *n* calvario, *m*
calve /kæv/ *vi* (of a cow, etc.) parir
Calvinism /'kælvə,nɪzəm/ *n* calvinismo, *m*
Calvinist /'kælvənɪst/ *n* calvinista, *mf*
Calvinistic /ˌkælvə'nɪstɪk/ *a* calvinista
calyx /'keilɪks/ *n* cáliz, *m*

cam /kæm/ n Mech. leva, f. **camshaft,** árbol de levas, m

camaraderie /ˌkɑməˈrɑdəri/ n compañerismo, m

camber /ˈkæmbər/ n comba(dura), f

cambric /ˈkeimbrik/ n batista, f

camcorder /ˈkæmˌkɔrdər/ n videocámara, m

camel /ˈkæməl/ n camello (-lla). **c.-driver,** camellero, m. **camel's hair,** pelo de camello, m

camellia /kəˈmilyə/ n camelia, f

cameo /ˈkæmiˌou/ n camafeo, m

camera /ˈkæmərə/ n Photo. máquina fotográfica, f. **folding c.,** máquina fotográfica plegable, f. **in c.,** a puerta cerrada. **c. obscura,** cámara obscura, f

Cameroon /ˌkæməˈrun/ el Camerón, los Camerones, m

camouflage /ˈkæməˌflɑʒ/ n camuflaje, m, vt camuflar

camp /kæmp/ n campamento, m; campo, m; Fig. vida de cuartel, f; (for school children, etc.) colonia, f; (party) partido, m. vi acampar; vivir en tiendas de campaña. **to break c.,** levantar el campo. **c.-bed,** cama de campaña, f. **c.-stool,** silla de campaña, f

campaign /kæmˈpein/ n campaña, f. vi hacer una campaña

campaigner /kæmˈpeinər/ n veterano, m; propagandista, mf

campaigning /kæmˈpeiniŋ/ n campañas, f pl

camphor /ˈkæmfər/ n alcanfor, m

camphorated /ˈkæmfəˌreitid/ a alcanforado

campus /ˈkæmpəs/ n Puerto Rico recinto, m, ciudad universitaria, f, campus, m

can /kæn/ v auxil poder; (know how to) saber. **You can go to the village when you like,** Puedes ir al pueblo cuando quieras. **I cannot allow that,** No puedo permitir eso. **What can they mean?** ¿Qué quieren decir? **If only things could have been different!** ¡Si solamente las cosas hubiesen sido distintas! **Can you come to dinner on Saturday?** ¿Puede Vd. venir a cenar el sábado? **I can come later if you like,** Puedo (or Podría) venir más tarde si Vd. quiere. **Mary can** (knows how to) **play the piano,** María sabe tocar el piano **You can't eat your cake and have it too.** No hay rosa sin espinas

can /kæn/ n lata, f. vt conservar en latas. **can-opener,** abrelatas, m

Canada /ˈkænədə/ el Canadá, m

Canadian /kəˈneidiən/ a canadiense. n canadiense, mf

canaille /kəˈnai/ n gentualla, gentuza, f

canal /kəˈnæl/ n canal, m

canalization /ˌkænələˈzeifən/ n canalización, f

canalize /ˈkænlˌaiz/ vt canalizar

canary /kəˈneəri/ n canario (-ia); color de canario, m; vino de Canarias, m. **roller c.,** canario de raza flauta, m. **c.-seed,** alpiste, m

Canary Islands, the las Islas Canarias, f

cancel /ˈkænsəl/ vt cancelar; revocar; borrar; anular. **to c. out,** Math. anular

cancellation /ˌkænsəˈleifən/ n cancelación, f; revocación, f; anulación, f

cancer /ˈkænsər/ n Med. cáncer, m; Astron. Cáncer, m

cancerous /ˈkænsərəs/ a canceroso. **to become c.,** cancerarse

candelabrum /ˌkændlˈɑbrəm/ n candelabro, m

candescent /kænˈdɛsənt/ a candente

candid /ˈkændid/ a franco; sincero. **If I am to be c.,** Si he de decir la verdad, Si he de ser franco

candidate /ˈkændiˌdeit/ n candidato (-ta); aspirante, m

candidature /ˈkændidəˌtfʊr/ n candidatura, f

candidly /ˈkændidli/ adv francamente; sinceramente

candidness /ˈkændidnis/ n franqueza, f; sinceridad, f

candied /ˈkændid/ a (of peel, etc.) almibarado, garapiñado

candle /ˈkændl/ n vela, candela, f. **wax c.,** cirio, m. **You cannot hold a c. to him,** No llegas a la suela de su zapato, Ni llegas a sus pies, Ni le llegas a los pies. **The game is not worth the c.,** La cosa no vale la pena. **to burn the c. at both ends,** consumir la vida. **c.-grease,** sebo, m. **c.-light,** luz de las velas, f; luz artificial, f. **c.-maker,** candelero, m. **c.-power,** Elec. potencia luminosa, bujía, f. **c.-snuffer,** apagavelas, matacandelas, m

Candlemas /ˈkændlˌməs/ n candelaria, f

candlestick /ˈkændlˌstik/ n candelero, m, palmatoria, f; (processional) cirial, m

candor /ˈkændər/ n franqueza, f; sinceridad, f; candor, m

candy /ˈkændi/ n caramelo, bombón, m, vt garapiñar, almibarar

cane /kein/ n Bot. caña, f; (for chair seats, etc.) rejilla, f; (walking stick) bastón, m; (for punishment) vara, f. vt apalear, pegar. **sugar-c.,** caña de azúcar, f. **c.-break,** cañaveral, m. **c. chair,** sillón de mimbres, m. **c.-sugar,** azúcar de caña, m. **c.-syrup,** miel de caña, f

canine /ˈkeinain/ a canino. n (tooth) diente canino, f

caning /ˈkeiniŋ/ n paliza, f

canister /ˈkænəstər/ n bote, m, cajita, f

canker /ˈkæŋkər/ n úlcera, f; (in trees) cancro, m; Fig. cáncer, m, vt roer; Fig. corromper

canned /kænd/ a en lata

cannibal /ˈkænəbəl/ n caníbal, mf antropófago (-ga). a caníbal, antropófago

cannibalism /ˈkænəbəˌlizəm/ n canibalismo, m, antropofagía, f

canning /ˈkæniŋ/ n conservación en latas, f. **c. factory,** fábrica de conservas alimenticias, f

cannon /ˈkænən/ n (fire-arm) cañón, m; (billiards) carambola, f, vi carambolear. **to c. into,** chocar con. **c.-ball,** bala de cañón, f. **c.-shot,** cañonazo, m

cannonade /ˌkænəˈneid/ n cañoneo, m

canny /ˈkæni/ a cuerdo, sagaz

canoe /kəˈnu/ n canoa, f; piragua, f, vi ir en canoa

canoeist /kəˈnuist/ n canoero (-ra)

canon /ˈkænən/ n (Eccl. Mus. Print.) canón, m; (dignitary) canónigo, m; (criterion) criterio, m. **c. law,** derecho canónico, m

canonical /kəˈnɒnikəl/ a canónico

canonization /ˌkænənəˈzeifən/ n canonización, f

canonize /ˈkænəˌnaiz/ vt canonizar

canopy /ˈkænəpi/ n dosel, toldo, m; palio, m; Fig. capa, bóveda, f. **the c. of heaven,** la capa (or bóveda) del cielo

cant /kænt/ vt inclinar; ladear. vi inclinarse; (be a hypocrite) camandulear. n (slope) inclinación, f, sesgo, desplomo, m; (hypocrisy) gazmoñería, f

Cantabrian /kænˈteibriən/ a cántabrico

cantankerous /kænˈtæŋkərəs/ a irritable, intratable, malhumorado, Argentina cabrero

cantankerousness /kænˈtæŋkərəsnis/ n mal humor, m, irritabilidad, f

cantata /kənˈtɑtə/ n cantata, f

canteen /kænˈtin/ n cantina, f; (water bottle) cantimplora, f. **c. of cutlery,** juego de cubiertos, m

canter /ˈkæntər/ n medio galope, m, vi andar a galope corto

canticle /ˈkæntikəl/ n cántico, m

canto /ˈkæntou/ n canto, m

canton /ˈkæntn/ n (province and Herald.) cantón, m, vt (of soldiers) acantonar

cantonment /kænˈtɒnmənt/ n acantonamiento, cantón, m

cantor /ˈkæntər/ n Eccl. chantre, m

canvas /ˈkænvəs/ n lona, f; Art. lienzo, m; Naut. vela, f, paño, m. **under c.,** en tiendas de campaña; (of ships) a toda vela

canvass /ˈkænvəs/ vt (votes, etc.) solicitar

canvasser /ˈkænvəsər/ n solicitador (-ra) (de votos, etc.)

canvassing /ˈkænvəsiŋ/ n solicitación (de votos, etc.), f

canyon /ˈkænyən/ n cañón, m

canzonet /ˌkænzəˈnet/ n chanzoneta, f

cap /kæp/ n gorra, f; (with a peak) montera, f; (type of military headgear with brim at front) quépis, m; (cardinal's) birrete, m; Educ. bonete, m; (pointed) caperuza, f; (woman's old-fashioned) cofia, f; (jester's) gorro de bufón, m; (on a bottle) cápsula, tapa, f. vt Educ. conferir el grado (a). **cap and bells,** gorro de bufón, m. **cap and gown,** birrete y muceta, toga y birrete, toga y bonete. **to throw one's cap over the windmill,** echar la capa al toro. **to cap it all,** ser el colmo

capability /ˌkeipəˈbiliti/ n capacidad, f; aptitud, f

capable /'keɪpəbəl/ *a* capaz; competente; (of improvement) susceptible; (full of initiative) emprendedor

capably /'keɪpəbli/ *adv* competentemente

capacious /kə'peɪʃəs/ *a* espacioso; grande; extenso

capaciousness /kə'peɪʃəsnɪs/ *n* capacidad, *f*; amplitud, *f*

capacitate /kə'pæsɪˌteɪt/ *vt* capacitar

capacity /kə'pæsɪti/ *n* capacidad, *f*; calidad, *f*; aptitud, *f*. **in one's c. as**, en calidad de. **seating c.,** número de asientos, *m*; (in aircraft) número de plazas, *m*

caparison /kə'pærəsən/ *n* caparazón, *m*

cape /keɪp/ *n* (cloak) capa, *f*; (short) capotillo, *m*, capeta, *f*; (fur) cuello, *m*; *Geog.* cabo, promontorio, *m*. **c. coat,** capote, *m*

Cape Horn /'keɪp 'hɔrn/ Cabo de Hornos, *m*

caper /'keɪpər/ *vi* (gambol) brincar, saltar; cabriolar, corcovear; (play) juguetear. *n* travesura, *f*; zapateta, *f*; cabriola, *f*; (whim) capricho, *m*; *Bot.* alcaparra, *f*. **to c. about,** dar saltos, brincar; juguetear

capillarity /ˌkæpə'lærɪti/ *n* capilaridad, *f*

capillary /'kæpəˌleri/ *a* capilar. *n* vaso capilar, *m*

capital /'kæpɪtl/ *a* capital; mortal; de muerte; de vida; principal; (of letters) mayúscula; (very good) excelente; (of the capital city) *Lat. Am.* capitalino *n* (city) capital, *f*; (letter) (letra) mayúscula, *f*; *Com.* capital, *m*; *Archit.* capitel, chapitel, *m*. **floating c.,** capital fluctuante, *m*. **idle c.,** fondos inactivos, *m pl.* **c. punishment,** pena de muerte, pena capital, pena de la vida, *f*. **C.!** ¡Estupendo! ¡Excelente! **to make c. out of,** aprovecharse de, sacar ventaja de

capitalism /'kæpɪtlˌɪzəm/ *n* capitalismo, *m*

capitalist /'kæpɪtlɪst/ *n* capitalista, *mf*

capitalistic /ˌkæpɪtl'ɪstɪk/ *a* capitalista

capitalization /ˌkæpɪtələ'zeɪʃən/ *n* capitalización, *f*

capitalize /'kæpɪtlˌaɪz/ *vt* capitalizar, (letters) escribir con mayúsculas

capitally /'kæpɪtli/ *adv* estupendamente

capitation /ˌkæpɪ'teɪʃən/ *n* capitación, *f*

Capitol /'kæpɪtl/ *n* Capitolio, *m*. **C. Hill,** el Congreso de los EEUU

capitulate /kə'pɪtʃəˌleɪt/ *vi* capitular

capitulation /kəˌpɪtʃə'leɪʃən/ *n* capitulación, *f*

capon /'keɪpɒn/ *n* capón, *m*

caprice /kə'pris/ *n* capricho, *m*

capricious /kə'prɪʃəs/ *a* caprichoso

capriciousness /kə'prɪʃəsnɪs/ *n* carácter inconstante, *m*; lo caprichoso

Capricorn /'kæprɪˌkɔrn/ *n* Capricornio, *m*

capsize /'kæpsaɪz/ *vt Naut.* hacer zozobrar; volcar. *vi Naut.* zozobrar; volcarse

capsizing /'kæpˌsaɪzɪŋ/ *n Naut.* zozobra, *f*; vuelco, *m*

capsule /'kæpsəl/ *n* (*Bot. Med. Chem. Zool.*) cápsula, *f*

captain /'kæptən/ *n* (*Mil. Nav. Aer.* and *Sports.*) capitán, *m*, *vt* capitanear. **to c. a team,** ser el capitán de un equipo. **group c.,** *Aer.* capitán de aviación, *m*

captaincy /'kæptənsi/ *n* capitanía, *f*

caption /'kæpʃən/ *n* (arrest) arresto, *m*; (heading) encabezamiento, título, pie, *m*; (cinema) subtítulo, *m*

captious /'kæpʃəs/ *a* capcioso; caviloso

captivate /'kæptəˌveɪt/ *vt* cautivar, seducir

captivating /'kæptəˌveɪtɪŋ/ *a* encantador, seductor

captive /'kæptɪv/ *a* cautivo, *n* cautivo (-va), prisionero (-ra), preso (-sa). **c. balloon,** globo cautivo, globo de observación, *m*

captivity /kæp'tɪvɪti/ *n* cautiverio, *m*

captor /'kæptər/ *n* el, *m*, (*f*, la) que hace prisionero (-ra), captor (-ra)

capture /'kæptʃər/ *n* captura, *f*; presa, toma, *f*; *Law.* captura, *f*. *vt* prender, capturar; tomar

car /kɑr/ *n* (chariot) carro, *m*; (tram) tranvía, *m*; (motor) automóvil, coche, *Lat. Am.* carro *m*; (on a train) coche vagón, *m*. **sleeping car,** coche camas, *m*. **car park,** parque de automóviles, *m*

carafe /kə'ræf/ *n* garrafa, *f*

caramel /'kærəməl/ *n* caramelo, *m*; azúcar quemado, *m*

carat /'kærət/ *n* quilate, *m*

caravan /'kærəˌvæn/ *n* caravana, *f*; coche de gitanos, *m*; coche habitación, *m*

caraway /'kærəˌweɪ/ *n* alcaravea, *f*

carbarn /'kɑrˌbɑrn/ *n* encierro, *m* (Mexico), cochera, cochera de tranvías, *f*, cobertizo, cobertizo para tranvías, *m*

carbide /'kɑrbaɪd/ *n* carburo, *m*

carbine /'kɑrbɪn/ *n* carabina, *f*

carbohydrate /ˌkɑrbou'haɪdreɪt/ *n* hidrato de carbono, *m*

carbolic /kɑr'bɒlɪk/ *a* carbólico. **c. acid,** ácido fénico, *m*

carbon /'kɑrbən/ *n* carbono, *m*. **c. copy,** copia en papel carbón, *f*. **c. dioxide,** anhídrido carbónico, *m*. **c. monoxide,** óxido de carbono, *m*. **c. paper,** papel carbón, papel de calcar, *m*

carbonate /'kɑrbəˌneɪt/ *n* carbonato, *m*

carbonated /'kɑrbəˌneɪtɪd/ *a* (beverage) carbónico (formal), con gas (informal)

carbonic /kɑr'bɒnɪk/ *a* carbónico

carbonization /ˌkɑrbənə'zeɪʃən/ *n* carbonización, *f*

carbonize /'kɑrbəˌnaɪz/ *vt* carbonizar

carbuncle /'kɑrbʌŋkəl/ *n Med.* carbunco, *m*; (stone) carbúnculo, *m*

carburetor /'kɑrbəˌreɪtər/ *n* carburador, *m*

carcass /'kɑrkəs/ *n* (animal) res muerta, *f*; (corpse) cadáver, *m*; (body) cuerpo, *m*; (of a ship) casco, *m*

carcinoma /ˌkɑrsə'noumə/ *n* carcinoma, *m*

card /kɑrd/ *n* (playing) naipe, *m*; (pasteboard) cartulina, *f*; (visiting, postal, etc.) tarjeta, *f*; (index) ficha, *f*; (for wool, etc.) carda, *f*. *vt* (wool, etc.) cardar. **I still have a c. up my sleeve,** Me queda todavía un recurso. **to lay one's cards on the table,** poner las cartas boca arriba. **to play one's cards well,** *Fig.* jugar el lance. **admission c.,** billete de entrada, *m*. **post c.,** tarjeta postal, *f*. **visiting c.,** tarjeta de visita, *f*. **c.-case,** tarjetero, *m*. **c.-index,** fichero, *m*. *vt* poner en el fichero. **c.-sharper,** fullero, *m*. **c.-table,** mesa de juego, *f*. **c. trick,** juego de manos con cartas, *m*

cardboard /'kɑrdˌbɔrd/ *n* cartón, *m*, a de cartón

cardiac /'kɑrdiˌæk/ *a* cardíaco. **c. arrest,** infarto, *m*

cardigan /'kɑrdɪgən/ *n* rebeca, chaqueta de punto, *f*

cardinal /'kɑrdnl/ *a* cardinal. *n* cardenal, *m*. **c. number,** número cardinal, *m*. **c. points,** puntos cardinales, *m pl*

cardinalate /'kɑrdnlˌeɪt/ *n* cardenalato, *m*

carding /'kɑrdɪŋ/ *n* (of wool, etc.) cardadura, *f*. **c. machine,** carda mecánica, *f*

cardiogram /'kɑrdiəˌgræm/ *n* cardiograma, *m*

care /keər/ *n* cuidado, *m*; atención, *f*; inquietud, ansia, *f*; (charge) cargo, *m*. *vi* preocuparse; tener interés; (suffer) sufrir. **I couldn't c. less,** No se me da un bledo. **I don't c.,** Me es igual; No me importa. **They don't c. for eggs,** No les gustan los huevos. **We don't c. what his opinion is,** Su opinión nos tiene sin cuidado (or no nos importa). **to c. for,** cuidar, mirar por; (love) querer (a); (like) gustar. **Take c.!** ¡Cuidado! ¡Ojo! **Take c. not to spoil it!** ¡Ten cuidado que no lo estropees! **Would you c. to...?** ¿Le gustaría...? ¿Tendría inconveniente en...? **c. of,** (on a letter, etc.) en casa de. **c.-free,** a libre de cuidados

careen /kə'rin/ *vt* carenar. *vi* dar a la banda

careening /kə'rinɪŋ/ *n* carena, *f*

career /kə'rɪər/ *n* carrera, *f*; curso, *m*. *vi* correr a carrera tendida; galopar

careful /'keərfəl/ *a* cuidadoso (de); atento (a); prudente. **Careful!, Be careful!** ¡Cuidado! **to be c.,** tener cuidado

carefully /'keərfəli/ *adv* con cuidado. **drive c.,** manejar con cuidado; cuidadosamente; prudentemente; atentamente

carefulness /'keərfəlnɪs/ *n* cuidado, *m*; atención, *f*; prudencia, *f*

careless /'keərlɪs/ *a* sin cuidado; indiferente (a); insensible (a); negligente; (of mistakes, etc.) de (or por) negligencia

carelessly /'keərlɪsli/ *adv* indiferentemente; negligentemente; descuidadamente

carelessness /'keərlɪsnɪs/ *n* indiferencia, *f*; negligencia, *f*; descuido, *m*; omisión, *f*

caress /kə'res/ *n* caricia, *f*, *vt* acariciar

caressing /kə'resɪŋ/ a acariciador
caretaker /'kɛər,teikər/ n (of museums, etc.) guardián (-ana); (of apartments, etc.)
careworn /'kɛər,wɔrn/ a devorado de inquietud, ansioso
cargo /'kɑrgou/ n cargamento, m, carga, f. **c.-boat,** barco de carga, m
Caribbean /,kærə'biən, kə'rɪbi-/ a caribe
Caribbean Sea, the el Mar Caribe, m
caricature /'kærɪkətʃər/ n caricatura, f, vt caricaturizar
caricaturist /'kærɪkə,tʃʊrɪst/ n caricaturista, mf
carious /'kɛəriəs/ a cariado. **to become c.,** cariarse
Carmelite /'kɑrmə,lait/ a carmelita. n carmelita, mf
carmine /'kɑrmɪn/ n carmín, m, a de carmín
carnage /'kɑrnɪdʒ/ n carnicería, f
carnal /'kɑrnl/ a carnal; sensual
carnality /kɑr'næliti/ n carnalidad, f
carnally /'kɑrnli/ adv carnalmente
carnation /kɑr'neiʃən/ n clavel, m
carnival /'kɑrnəvəl/ n carnaval, m, a de carnaval, carnavalesco
carnivore /'kɑrnə,vɔr/ n carnívoro, m
carnivorous /kɑr'nɪvərəs/ a carnívoro
carol /'kærəl/ n villancico, m; canto, m. vi cantar alegremente; (of birds) trinar, gorjear
Carolingian /,kærə'lɪndʒiən/ a carolingio
carotid /kə'rɒtɪd/ n carótida, f
carousal /kə'rauzəl/ n borrachera, f; holgorio, m, jarana, f
carouse /kə'rauz/ vi emborracharse. n borrachera, orgía, f
carp /kɑrp/ n carpa, f, vi criticar, censurar
Carpathian Mountains, the /kɑr'peiθiən/ los Montes Carpotes, m
carpel /'kɑrpəl/ n carpelo, m
carpenter /'kɑrpəntər/ n carpintero, m, vi carpintear. **carpenter's bench,** banco de carpintero, m. **carpenter's shop,** carpintería, f
carpentry /'kɑrpəntri/ n carpintería, f
carpet /'kɑrpɪt/ n alfombra, f; Fig. tapete, m. vt cubrir de una alfombra, alfombrar; entapizar. **to be on the c.,** estar sobre el tapete. **c.-beater,** sacudidor de alfombras, m. **c. merchant,** alfombrista, m. **c. slippers,** zapatillas de fieltro, f pl. **c.-sweeper,** aspirador de polvo, m
carpeting /'kɑrpɪtɪŋ/ n alfombrado, m
carping /'kɑrpɪŋ/ a capcioso, criticón
carriage /'kærɪdʒ/ n (carrying) transporte, porte, m; (deportment) porte, continente, m, presencia, f; (vehicle) carruaje, m; carroza, f; coche, m; (railway) departamento, m; (chassis) chasis, bastidor, m; (of a typewriter, etc.) carro, m. **c. door,** portezuela, f. **c.-forward,** porte debido. **c.-free,** franco de porte. **c.-paid,** porte pagado
carrier /'kæriər/ n el, m, (f, la) que lleva; portador (-ra); Com. mensajero, m; (on a car, bicycle) portaequipajes, m; (of a disease) vector, m; (aircraft) portaaviones, m. **c.-pigeon,** paloma mensajera, f
carrion /'kæriən/ n carroña, f. **c.-crow,** chova, f
carrot /'kærət/ n zanahoria, f
carry /'kæri/ vt llevar; transportar; traer; conducir; (Mil. of arms) portar; (have with one) tener consigo; (an enemy position) tomar, ganar; (a motion) aprobar; (oneself) portarse; (one's point, etc.) ganar; (in the mind) retener; (conviction) convencer; (involve) implicar; (influence) influir; (send) despachar, enviar; (contain) incluir, comprender. vi (of the voice, etc.) alcanzar, llegar. **The noise of the guns carried a long way,** El ruido de los cañones se oía desde muy lejos. **to fetch and c.,** traer y llevar. **to c. into effect,** poner en efecto. **to c. one's audience with one,** captar (or cautivar) su auditorio. **to c. oneself well,** tener buena presencia. **to c. on one's back,** llevar a cuestas. **to c. the day,** quedar victorioso, quedar señor del campo. **to c. weight,** Fig. ser de peso. **to c. along,** llevar; (drag) arrastrar; conducir; acarrear. **to c. away,** llevar; llevarse, llevar consigo; (kidnap) robar, secuestrar; (of emotions) dominar; (by enthusiasm) entusiasmar; (inspire) inspirar. **to c. forward,** llevar a cabo; avanzar; fomentar; (bookkeeping) pasar a cuenta nueva. **to c. off,** (things) llevarse; (per-

sons) llevar consigo (a); (abduct or steal) robar; (kill) matar; (a prize) ganar. **to c. (a thing) off well,** llevar la mejor parte, salir vencedor. **to c. on,** vt (a discussion, etc.) seguir, continuar. **c. on a conversation,** llevar una conversación; mantener; (a business, etc.) tener; dirigir. vi ir tirando; seguir trabajando. **to c. out,** realizar, llevar a cabo; hacer, ejecutar, efectuar; (a promise) cumplir. **to c. through,** llevar a cabo
carrying /'kærɪŋ/ n transporte, m; (of a motion) adopción, f
cart /kɑrt/ n carro, m. vt acarrear; llevar. **c.-horse,** caballo de tiro, m. **c.-load,** carretada, f, carro, m. **c.-wheel,** rueda de carro, f; (somersault) voltereta, f
cartage /'kɑrtɪdʒ/ n carretaje, transporte, porte, m
carte blanche /'kɑrt 'blɑntʃ/ n carta blanca, f
cartel /kɑr'tel/ n cartel, m
carter /'kɑrtər/ n carretero, m
Cartesian /kɑr'tiʒən/ a cartesiano. n cartesiano (-na)
Carthage /'kɑrθɪdʒ/ Cartago, m
Carthaginian /,kɑrθə'dʒɪniən/ a cartaginés. n cartaginés (-esa)
car thief n. Lat. Am. autero (-ra)
cartilage /'kɑrtl̩ɪdʒ/ n cartílago, m
cartilaginous /,kɑrtl̩'ædʒənəs/ a cartilaginoso
cartographer /kɑr'tɒgrəfər/ n cartógrafo, m
cartography /kɑr'tɒgrəfi/ n cartografía, f
cartomancy /'kɑrtəmænsi/ n cartomancia, f
carton /'kɑrtn̩/ n caja de cartón, f
cartoon /kɑr'tun/ n (design for tapestry, etc.) cartón, m; caricatura, f
cartoonist /kɑr'tunɪst/ n caricaturista, mf
cartridge /'kɑrtrɪdʒ/ n cartucho, m. **blank c.,** cartucho sin bala, m. **c.-belt,** cartuchera, canana, f. **c.-case,** cápsula de proyectil, f
carve /kɑrv/ vt tallar, labrar; grabar; cortar; (meat, etc.) trinchar; (a career, etc.) hacer, forjarse
carver /'kɑrvər/ n tallador, m; (at table) trinchador, m; (implement) trinchante, m
carving /'kɑrvɪŋ/ n talla, f; (design) tallado, m. **c.-knife,** trinchante, m
cascade /kæs'keid/ n cascada, catarata, f, salto de agua, m; Fig. chorro, m. vi chorrear
case /keis/ n caso, m; Law. proceso, m, causa, f; Gram. caso, m; Med. caso, m; enfermo (-ma); (box) caja, f; (for scissors, etc.) vaina, f; (for a cushion, etc.) funda, f; (for jewels, manicure implements, etc.) estuche, m; (of a piano, watch and Print.) caja, f; (for documents) carpeta, f; (glass) vitrina, f; (for a book) sobrecubierta, f; (dressing) neceser, m. vt cubrir; forrar; resguardar. **packing-c.,** caja de embalaje, f. **c. of goods,** caja de mercancías, f; bulto, m. **in any c.,** en todo caso; venga lo que venga. **in c.,** por si acaso. **in c. of emergency,** en caso de urgencia. **in such a c.,** en tal caso. **in the c. of,** en el caso de; respecto a. **lower c.,** Print. caja baja, f. **upper c.,** Print. caja alta, f. **c.-hardened,** (of iron) templado; Fig. endurecido, indiferente
case closed! ¡asunto concluido!
casement window /'keismənt/ n ventana, f
cash /kæʃ/ n efectivo, metálico, m; dinero contante, m; Inf. dinero, m; Com. caja, f. vt cobrar; pagar, hacer efectivo. **hard or ready c.,** dinero contante, m. **to pay c.,** pagar al contado. **c. on delivery,** (C.O.D.) contra reembolso. **c. on hand,** efectivo en caja, m. **c.-book,** libro de caja, m. **c.-box,** caja, f. **c.-desk,** caja, f. **c. down,** pago al contado, m. **c. prize,** premio en metálico, m. **c.-register,** caja registradora, f. **petty c.,** caja chica, f
cashew /'kæʃu/ n anacardo, m
cashier /kæ'ʃiər/ n cajero (-ra). vt degradar. **cashier's desk,** caja, f
cash machine n cajera automática, f
cashmere /'kæʒmɪər/ n cachemira, f
casino /kə'sinou/ n casino, m
cask /kæsk/ n pipa, barrica, f, tonel, m; cuba, f
casket /'kæskɪt/ n cajita, arquilla, f, cofrecito, m
Caspian Sea, the /'kæspiən/ el (Mar) Caspio, m
casserole /'kæsə,roul/ n cacerola, f
cassock /'kæsək/ n sotana, f
cast /kæst/ vt arrojar, tirar; (in fishing, the anchor,

dice, darts, lots, a net, glances, blame, etc.) echar; (skin) mudar; (lose) perder; (a shadow, etc.) proyectar; (a vote) dar; (mold) vaciar; (accounts) echar, calcular; (a horoscope) hacer; (the parts in a play) repartir; (an actor for a part) dar el papel de; (metals) colar, fundir. **the shadow c. by the wall,** la sombra proyectada por el muro. **to c. anchor,** echar anclas, anclar. **to c. in one's lot with,** compartir la suerte de. **to c. something in a person's teeth,** echar en cara (a). **to c. lots,** echar suertes. **to c. about,** meditar, considerar; imaginar; (devise) inventar. **to c. aside,** desechar; poner a un lado; abandonar. **to c. away,** tirar lejos; desechar; (money) derrochar, malgastar. **to be c. away,** *Naut.* naufragar. **to c. down,** (overthrow) derribar, destruir; (eyes) bajar; (depress) desanimar, deprimir; (humiliate) humillar. **to be c. down,** estar deprimido. **to c. iron,** n hierro colado, hierro fundido, m. **c.-iron,** a de hierro colado; *Fig.* inflexible. **to c. off,** quitarse; desechar; (a wife) repudiar; (desert) abandonar; (free oneself) librarse (de). **c.-off,** n desecho, m. **c.-off clothing,** ropa de desecho, f. **to c. out,** echar fuera; hacer salir; excluir. **to c. up,** echar; vomitar; (a sum) sumar; (something at a person) reprochar

cast /kæst/ n (of dice, fishing-line) echada, f; (of a net) redada, f; (worm) molde, m; (of a play) reparto, m, Lat. Am. elenco, m; (of mind) inclinación, f; (in the eye) defecto en la mirada, m; (of color) matiz, tinte, m. **c. of features,** facciones, f pl, fisonomía, f. **plaster c.,** vaciado, m

castanets /ˌkæstə'nɛts/ n pl castañuelas, f pl

castaway /'kæstəˌwei/ n náufrago (-ga); *Fig.* perdido (-da)

caste /kæst/ n casta, f; clase social, f. **to lose c.,** desprestigiarse

castigate /'kæstɪˌgeit/ vt castigar

Castile /kæ'stil/ Castilla, f

Castilian /kæ'stɪlyən/ a castellano. n castellano (-na); (language) castellano, m

casting /'kæstɪŋ/ n lanzamiento, m; (of metals) fundición, colada, f; obra de fundición, f. **c.-net,** esparavel, m. **c.-vote,** voto de calidad, m

castle /'kæsəl/ n castillo, m; (in chess) torre, f, roque, m. **to build castles in Spain,** hacer castillos en el aire

castor /'kæstər/ n *Zool.* castor, m; (for sugar) azucarero, m; (cruet) convoy, m; (on chairs, etc.) ruedecilla, roldana, f. **c.-oil,** aceite de ricino, m. **c.-sugar,** azúcar en polvo, m

castrate /'kæstreit/ vt castrar, capar

castration /kæs'treiʃən/ n castración, capadura, f

casual /'kæʒuəl/ a fortuito, accidental; ligero, superficial; *Inf.* despreocupado. **c. clothing,** ropa de sport, f. **c. worker,** jornalero, m

casually /'kæʒuəli/ adv por casualidad; de paso; negligentemente

casualness /'kæʒuəlnɪs/ n *Inf.* negligencia, despreocupación, f

casualty /'kæʒuəlti/ n víctima, f; herido, m; *Mil.* baja, f; pl **casualties,** heridos, m pl; muertos, m pl. **c.-list,** lista de víctimas, f; *Mil.* lista de bajas, f

casuist /'kæʒuɪst/ n casuista, mf

casuistry /'kæʒuəstri/ n casuística, f

cat /kæt/ n gato (-ta). **She is an old cat,** Ella es una vieja chismosa. **to be like a cat on hot bricks,** estar como en brasas. **to let the cat out of the bag,** tirar de la manta. **to lead a cat-and-dog life,** vivir como perros y gatos. **cat's-cradle,** (game) cunas, f pl. **cat's paw,** (person) hombre de paja, m; *Naut.* bocanada de viento, f. **cat o' nine tails,** gato de siete colas, m, penca, f. **catwhisker,** *Radio.* detector, m

cataclysm /'kætəˌklɪzəm/ n cataclismo, m

catacombs /'kætəˌkoumz/ n pl catacumbas, f pl

catafalque /'kætəˌfɔk/ n catafalco, m

Catalan /'kætlˌæn/ a catalán (-ana). n catalán; (language) catalán, m

catalepsy /'kætlˌɛpsi/ n catalepsia, f

catalogue /'kætlˌɔg/ n catálogo, m, vt catalogar

catalysis /kə'tæləsɪs/ n catálisis, f

cat-and-mouse /'kæt n 'maus/ n el juego de ratón, m

catapult /'kætəˌpʌlt/ n *Mil.* catapulta, f; *Aer.* catapulta (para lanzar aviones), f; (toy) tirador de go-

---

mas, m. vt tirar con una catapulta (or con un tirador de gomas); (throw) lanzar

cataract /'kætəˌrækt/ n catarata, cascada, f, salto de agua, m; (of the eye) catarata, f

catarrh /kə'tɑr/ n catarro, m; constipado, resfriado, m

catastrophe /kə'tæstrəfi/ n catástrofe, f, desastre, m, Mexico also funestidad; (in drama) desenlace, m

catastrophic /ˌkætəs'trɒfɪk/ a catastrófico

catcall /'kætˌkɔl/ n silbido, m

catch /kætʃ/ vt coger; agarrar, asir; (capture) prender, haber; (a disease) contraer; (habit) tomar; (on a hook, etc.) enganchar; (surprise) sorprender; (understand) comprender; (hear) oír; (with blows, etc.) dar. vi (of a lock) encajarse; (become entangled) engancharse; (of a fire) encenderse. **to c. a glimpse of,** ver por un instante (a); alcanzar a ver, entrever. **to c. at,** asir; agarrarse (a); echar mano de; procurar asir; alargar la mano hacia; (an idea, etc.) adoptar con entusiasmo. **to c. on,** (be popular) tener éxito; (understand) comprender. **to c. out,** coger en el acto; coger en un error; *Sports.* coger. **to c. up,** coger; interrumpir. **to c. up with,** (a person) alcanzar; (news) ponerse al corriente de

catch /kætʃ/ n presa, f; (of fish) redada, pesca, f; (of a window, etc.) cerradura, f; (latch) pestillo, m; (trick) trampa, f; *Mus.* canon, m. **a good c.,** (matrimonial) un buen partido. **to have a c. in one's voice,** hablar con voz entrecortada. **c.-as-c.-can,** lucha libre, f

catching /'kætʃɪŋ/ a contagioso

catchment /'kætʃmənt/ n desagüe, m

catchword /'kætʃˌwɜrd/ n reclamo, m; (theater cue) pie, apunte, m; (slogan) mote, m

catchy /'kætʃi/ a atractivo. **It's a c. tune,** Es una canción que se pega

catechism /'kætɪˌkɪzəm/ n catequismo, m

categorical /ˌkætɪ'gɔrɪkəl/ a categórico

category /'kætɪˌgɔri/ n categoría, f

cater /'keitər/ vi proveer, abastecer. **to c. to all tastes,** atender a todos los gustos

caterer /'keitərər/ n despensero (-ra)

catering /'keitərɪŋ/ n provisión, f

caterpillar /'kætərˌpɪlər/ n oruga, Argentina isoca f. **c. tractor,** tractor de orugas, m

caterwaul /'kætərˌwɔl/ vi (of a cat) maullar

caterwauler /'kætərˌwɔlər/ n (violinist, etc.) rascatripas, m

caterwauling /'kætərˌwɔlɪŋ/ n maullidos, m pl; música ratonera, f

catfish /'kætˌfɪʃ/ n siluro, m

catgut /'kætˌgʌt/ n *Surg.* catgut, m; *Mus.* cuerda, f

catharsis /kə'θɑrsɪs/ n *Med.* purga, f; *Fig.* catarsis, f

cathedral /kə'θidrəl/ n catedral, f

Catherine wheel /'kæθrɪn/ n *Archit.* rosa, f; (firework) rueda de Santa Catalina, f; (somersault) tumba, f

catheter /'kæθɪtər/ n catéter, m

cathode /'kæθoud/ n cátodo, m. **c. rays,** rayos catódicos, m pl. **c. ray tube,** tubo de rayos catódicos, m

cathodic /kæ'θɒdɪk/ a catódico

catholic /'kæθəlɪk/ a católico

Catholicism /kə'θɒləˌsɪzəm/ n catolicismo, m

catlike /'kætˌlaik/ a gatuno

cattle /'kætl/ n ganado vacuno, m; ganado, m; animales, m pl. **c.-dealer,** ganadero, m. **c.-lifter,** hurtador de ganado, m. **c.-pen,** corral, m. **c.-raiser,** criador de ganado, m. **c.-raising,** ganadería, f. **c.-ranch,** hacienda de ganado, estancia, Argentina cabaña f. **c.-show,** exposición de ganado, f. **c.-truck,** vagón de ferrocarril para ganado, m

cattle rustler /'rʌslər/ n abigeo, cuatrero, ladrón de ganado, m

cattle rustling n abigeato, m

catty /'kæti/ a gatuno; malicioso, chismoso

Caucasian /kɔ'keiʒən/ a and n caucáseo (-ea)

cauldron /'kɔldrən/ n caldera, f

cauliflower /'kɔləˌflauər/ n coliflor, f

caulk /kɔk/ vt calafatear

caulker /'kɔkər/ n calafate, m

caulking /'kɔkɪŋ/ n calafateado, m. **c. iron,** calador, m

causality /kɔ'zælɪti/ n causalidad, f

causative /'kɔzətɪv/ a causante

cause /kɔz/ n causa, f; (reason) motivo, m, razón, f; (lawsuit) proceso, m. vt causar; ocasionar; suscitar; (oblige) hacer, obligar (a). **final c.,** Philos. causa final, f. **to have good c. for,** tener buen motivo para

causeway /'kɔz,wei/ n dique, m; acera, f

caustic /'kɔstɪk/ a cáustico; Fig. mordaz. **c. soda,** sosa cáustica, f

caustically /'kɔstɪkli/ adv mordazmente, con sarcasmo

causticity /kɔ'stɪsɪti/ n causticidad, f

cauterization /,kɔtərə'zeiʃən/ n cauterización, f

cauterize /'kɔtə,raiz/ vt cauterizar

cautery /'kɔtəri/ n cauterio, m

caution /'kɔʃən/ n prudencia, cautela, f; (warning) amonestación, f; aviso, m. vt amonestar. **to proceed with c.,** ir con prudencia; ir despacio

"Caution" /'kɔʃən/ (road sign) «Atención»

cautionary /'kɔʃə,nɛri/ a (of tales) de escarmiento

cautious /'kɔʃəs/ a cauteloso, cauto; prudente, circunspecto

cautiously /'kɔʃəsli/ adv cautamente; prudentemente. **to go c.,** Inf. ir con pies de plomo

cavalcade /,kævəl'keid/ n cabalgata, f

cavalier /,kævə'lɪər/ n jinete, m; caballero, m; galán, m, a arrogante, altanero

cavalry /'kævəlri/ n caballería, f. **c.-man,** jinete, soldado de a caballo, m

cave /keiv/ n cueva, caverna, f. **to c. in,** hundirse; desplomarse; Fig. rendirse. **c.-man,** hombre cavernícola, m

caveat /'kævi,ɑt/ n aviso, m; advertencia, f

cavern /'kævərn/ n caverna, f

cavernous /'kævərnəs/ a cavernoso

caviar /'kævi,ɑr/ n caviar, m

cavil /'kævəl/ vi cavilar

cavity /'kævɪti/ n cavidad, f; hoyo, m; hueco, m; (in a lung) caverna, f; (in teeth) caries, f

cavy /'keivi/ n cobayo (-ya), conejillo (-lla) de las Indias

caw /kɔ/ n graznido, m, vi graznar, grajear

cawing /'kɔɪŋ/ n graznidos, m pl

cayenne /kai'ɛn/ n pimentón, m

cease /sis/ vi cesar (de), dejar de; parar. vt cesar de; parar de; (payments, etc.) suspender; discontinuar. **c.-fire,** tregua, f. **C. fire!** ¡Cesar fuego!

ceaseless /'sislɪs/ a incesante,continuo, sin cesar

ceaselessly /'sislɪsli/ adv sin cesar, incesantemente

ceasing /'sisɪŋ/ n cesación, f. **without c.,** sin cesar

cedar /'sidər/ n (tree and wood) cedro, m. **red c.,** cedro dulce, m

cede /sid/ vt ceder, traspasar; (admit) conceder

cedilla /sɪ'dɪlə/ n zedilla, f

ceiling /'silɪŋ/ n techo, m; Aer. altura máxima, f. **c. price,** máximo precio, m

celebrant /'sɛləbrənt/ n Eccl. celebrante, m

celebrate /'sɛlə,breit/ vt celebrar; solemnizar. **Their marriage was celebrated in the autumn,** Su casamiento se solemnizó en el otoño

celebrated /'sɛlə,breitɪd/ a célebre, famoso

celebration /,sɛlə'breiʃən/ n celebración, f; festividad, f

celebrity /sə'lɛbrɪti/ n celebridad, f

celerity /sə'lɛrɪti/ n celeridad, f

celery /'sɛləri/ n apio, m

celestial /sə'lɛstʃəl/ a celestial

celibacy /'sɛləbəsi/ n celibato, m

celibate /'sɛləbɪt/ a célibe. n célibe, mf

cell /sɛl/ n celda, f; (Bot. Biol.) célula, f; (bees, wasps) celdilla, f; Elec. elemento, m

cellar /'sɛlər/ n sótano, m; (wine) bodega, f

cellist /'tʃɛlɪst/ n violoncelista, mf

cello /'tʃɛlou/ n violoncelo, m

cellophane /'sɛlə,fein/ n (papel) celofán, m

cellular /'sɛlyələr/ a celular, celuloso

cellular phone n teléfono celular, m

cellule /'sɛlyul/ n célula, f

celluloid /'sɛlyə,lɔid/ n celuloide, f

cellulose /'sɛlyə,lous/ n celulosa, f

Celt /kɛlt, sɛlt/ n celta, mf

Celtic /'kɛltɪk, 'sɛl-/ a celta

cement /sɪ'mɛnt/ n cemento, m, vt cementar

cemetery /'sɛmɪ,teri/ n cementerio, m

cenotaph /'sɛnə,tæf/ n cenotafio, m

cenote /sə'nouti/ n cenote m

cense /sɛns/ vt incensar

censer /'sɛnsər/ n incensario, m, botafumeiro, m

censor /'sɛnsər/ n censor, m, vt censurar. **banned by the c.,** prohibido por la censura

censorious /sɛn'sɔriəs/ a severo; crítico

censoriousness /sɛn'sɔriəsnɪs/ n severidad, propensión a censurar, f

censorship /'sɛnsər,ʃɪp/ n censura, f

censure /'sɛnʃər/ vt censurar, culpar, criticar

census /'sɛnsəs/ n censo, m. **to take the c.,** formar el censo, levantar el censo, tomar el censo, empadronar

census-taking /'sɛnsəs ,teikɪŋ/ n la formación del censo, la formación de los censos, f, el levantamiento del censo, el levantamiento de los censos, m

cent /sɛnt/ n (coin) centavo, m. Lat. Am. cobre (of copper) m. **per c.,** por ciento. **not to have a c., not to have a c. to one's name,** no tener donde caer muerto

centaur /'sɛntɔr/ n centauro, m

centavo /sɛn'tavou/ n centavo, Lat. Am. cobre (of copper) m

centenarian /,sɛntṇ'ɛəriən/ a and n centenario (-ia)

centenary /sɛn'tɛnɛri/ n centenario, m, a centenario

center /'sɛntər/ n centro, m; medio, m. a central; centro. vt centrar; concentrar (en). **nervous centers,** centros nerviosos, m pl. **c.-forward,** Sports. delantero centro, m. **c.-half,** Sports. medio centro, m. **c. of gravity,** centro de gravedad, m. **c.-piece,** centro, m

centerfold /'sɛntər,fould/ n páginas centrales, f pl

centigrade /'sɛntɪ,greid/ a centígrado

centigram /'sɛntɪ,græm/ n centigramo, m

centiliter /'sɛntl,itər/ n centilitro, m

centime /'santim/ n céntimo, m

centimeter /'sɛntə,mitər/ n centímetro, m. **cubic c.,** centímetro cúbico, m

centipede /'sɛntə,pid/ n ciempiés, m

central /'sɛntrəl/ a central; céntrico. **The house is very c.,** La casa es muy céntrica. **C. America** n Centroamérica f **C. American,** a and n centroamericano (-na). **c. depot,** central, f. **c. heating,** calefacción central, f

centralism /'sɛntrə,lɪzəm/ n centralismo, m

centralist /'sɛntrəlɪst/ n centralista, mf

centralization /,sɛntrələ'zeiʃən/ n centralización, f

centralize /'sɛntrə,laiz/ vt centralizar

centrally /'sɛntrəli/ adv centralmente; céntricamente

centric /'sɛntrɪk/ a céntrico; central

centrifugal /sɛn'trɪfyəgəl/ a centrífugo

centripetal /sɛn'trɪpɪtḷ/ a centrípeto

centuple /'sɛn'tupəl/ a céntuplo

centuplicate /sɛn'tupli,keit/ vt centuplicar

centurion /sɛn'tyuriən/ n centurión, m

century /'sɛntʃəri/ n siglo, m, centuria, f

ceramic /sə'ræmɪk/ a cerámico

ceramics /sə'ræmɪks/ n cerámica, f

cereal /'sɪəriəl/ a cereal. n cereal, m

cerebellum /,sɛrə'bɛləm/ n cerebelo, m

cerebral /sə'ribrəl/ a cerebral

cerebrospinal /sə,ribrou'spainḷ/ a cerebroespinal

cerebrum /sə'ribrəm/ n cerebro, m

ceremonial /,sɛrə'mouniəl/ a ceremonial; de ceremonia. n ceremonial, m

ceremonially /,sɛrə'mouniəli/ adv ceremonialmente; con ceremonia

ceremonious /,sɛrə'mouniəs/ a ceremonioso

ceremoniously /,sɛrə'mouniəsli/ adv ceremoniosamente

ceremoniousness /,sɛrə'mouniəsnɪs/ n ceremonia, formalidad, f

ceremony /'sɛrə,mouni/ n ceremonia, f. **to stand on c.,** gastar cumplidos. **without c.,** sin cumplidos

certain /'sɜrtṇ/ a (sure) seguro; cierto; (unerring) certero. **a c. man,** cierto hombre. **I am c. that...,** Estoy seguro de que... **to know for c.,** saber con toda seguridad, saber a ciencia cierta. **to make c. of,** asegurarse de

certainly /'sɜrtṇli/ adv seguramente; ciertamente; (as

a reply) sin duda; naturalmente. **c. not,** no, por cierto; claro que no

certainty /'sɜrtn̩ti/ n certidumbre, f; seguridad, f; convicción, f. **of a c.,** seguramente

certificate /n sər'tɪfɪkɪt/ v -,keit/ n certificado, m; fe, f; partida, f; Com. bono, título, m; diploma, m. vt certificar. **birth c.,** partida de nacimiento, f. **death c.,** partida de defunción, f. **marriage c.,** partida de casamiento, f

certificated /sər'tɪfɪ,keitɪd/ a (of teachers, etc.) con título

certify /'sɜrtə,fai/ vt certificar; atestiguar; declarar

certitude /'sɜrtɪ,tyud/ n certeza, certidumbre, f

cerulean /sə'ruliən/ a cerúleo

Cervantine /sər'væntin/ a cervantino

cervix /'sɜrvɪks/ n Anat. cerviz, f

Cesarean /sə'zɛəriən/ a cesáreo

cessation /sɛ'seiʃən/ n cesación, f

cession /'sɛʃən/ n cesión, f

cessionary /'sɛʃənɛri/ n cesionario (-ia)

cesspool /'sɛs,pul/ n sumidero, m

cetacean /sɪ'teiʃən/ a cetáceo. n cetáceo, m

Ceylon /sɪ'lɒn/ n Ceilán, m

cf. cfr.

chafe /tʃeif/ vt (rub) frotar; (make sore) escocer, rozar. vi raerse, desgastarse; escocerse; Fig. impacientarse; Fig. irritarse, enojarse

chaff /tʃæf/ n (of grain) ahechadura, f; (in a general sense and Fig.) paja, f; tomadura de pelo, burla, f. vt (a person) tomar el pelo (a), burlarse de

chaffinch /'tʃæfɪntʃ/ n pinzón, m

chafing /'tʃeifɪŋ/ n frotación, f; (soreness) excoriación, f; Fig. impaciencia, f. **c.-dish,** escalfador, m

chagrin /ʃə'grɪn/ n mortificación, decepción, f, disgusto, m, vt mortificar

chain /tʃein/ n cadena, f, vt encadenar. **c. of mountains,** cadena de montañas, cordillera, f. **c.-gang,** cadena de presidiarios, f. **c.-mail,** cota de malla, f. **c.-stitch,** cadeneta, f. **c.-stores,** empresa con sucursales, f. **in chains,** cargado de cadenas (e.g., prisoners in chains, prisioneros cargados de cadenas)

chair /tʃɛər/ n silla, f; Educ. cátedra, f; (of a meeting) presidencia, f. vt llevar en hombros (a). **C.!** ¡Orden! **easy-c.,** (silla) poltrona, f. **to be in the c.,** ocupar la presidencia; presidir. **to take a c.,** sentarse, tomar asiento. **to take the c.,** presidir. **swivel-c.,** silla giratoria, f. **wheel-c.,** silla de ruedas, f; (of a child) respaldo de una silla, m

chairman /'tʃɛərmən/ n presidente (-ta). **to act as c.,** presidir

chairmanship /'tʃɛərmən,ʃɪp/ n presidencia, f

chaise longue /'ʃeiz 'lɒŋ/ n meridiana, tumbona, f

Chaldea /kæl'diə/ Caldea, f

Chaldean /kæl'diən/ a caldeo

chalet /ʃæ'lei/ n chalet, m

chalice /'tʃælɪs/ n cáliz, m

chalk /tʃɔk/ n creta, f; (for writing, etc.) tiza, f, yeso, m. vt marcar con tiza; dibujar con tiza. **to c. up,** apuntar. **not by a long c.,** no con mucho

chalky /'tʃɔki/ a cretáceo; cubierto de yeso; (of the complexion) pálido

challenge /'tʃælɪndʒ/ n provocación, f; (of a sentry) quién vive, m; (to a duel, etc.) desafío, reto, m; Law. recusación, f; concurso, m. vt (of a sentry) dar el quién vive (a); desafiar; provocar; Law. recusar

challenger /'tʃælɪndʒər/ n desafiador (-ra)

challenging /'tʃælɪndʒɪŋ/ a desafiador, provocador

chamber /'tʃeimbər/ n cuarto, m; sala, f; (bed-) dormitorio, m, alcoba, f; cámara, f; Mech. cilindro, m; (in a gun) cámara, f. **c. concert,** concierto de música de cámara, m. **c.-maid,** camarera, f. **c. music,** música de cámara, f. **c. of commerce,** cámara de comercio, f. **c.-pot,** orinal, m

chamberlain /'tʃeimbərlɪn/ n camarero, m. **court c.,** chambelán, m. **Lord C.,** camarero mayor, m

chameleon /kə'miliən/ n camaleón, m

chamfer /'tʃæmfər/ n chaflán, bisel, m

chamois /'ʃæmi/ n gamuza, f, rebeco, m. **c. leather,** piel de gamuza, f

chamomile /'kæmə,mail/ n camomila, manzanilla, f

champagne /ʃæm'pein/ n (vino de) champaña, m

champion /'tʃæmpiən/ n campeón, m; defensor (-ra)

championship /'tʃæmpiən,ʃɪp/ n campeonato, m; (of a cause) defensa, f

chance /tʃæns/ n casualidad, f; suerte, fortuna, f; posibilidad, f; probabilidad, f; esperanza, f; (opportunity) ocasión, oportunidad, f. a fortuito; accidental. vi impers suceder, acontecer. vt Inf. arriesgar; probar. **by c.,** por casualidad; por ventura. **if by c.,** si acaso. **If it chances that...,** Si sucede que; Si a mano viene que... **The chances are that...,** Las probabilidades son que... **There is no c.,** No hay posibilidad; No hay esperanza. **to let the c. slip,** perder la ocasión. **to take a c.,** aventurarse, arriesgarse. **to c. to do,** hacer algo por casualidad. **to c. upon,** encontrar por casualidad.

chancel /'tʃænsəl/ n antealtar, entrecoro, m

chancellery /'tʃænsələri/ n cancillería, f

chancellor /'tʃænsələr/ n canciller, m; Educ. cancelario, m. **C. of the Exchequer,** Ministro de Hacienda, m

chancellorship /'tʃænsələrʃɪp/ n cancillería, f

chancery /'tʃænsəri, 'tʃɑn-/ n chancillería, f; (papal) cancelaría, f

chandelier /,ʃændl̩'ɪər/ n araña de luces, f

chandler /'tʃændlər/ n velero, m

change /tʃeindʒ/ vt cambiar; transformar; modificar; (clothes) mudarse (de); (one thing for another) trocar; sustituir (por). vi cambiar; (clothes) mudarse. **All c.!** ¡Cambio de tren! **to c. a check,** cambiar un cheque. **to c. color,** cambiar de color; (of persons) mudar de color. **to c. countenance,** demudarse. **to c. front,** Fig. cambiar de frente. **to c. hands,** (of shops, etc.) cambiar de dueño. **to c. one's clothes,** cambiar de ropa, mudarse de ropa. **to c. one's mind,** cambiar de opinión. **to c. one's tune,** cambiar de tono. **to c. the subject,** cambiar de conversación. **to c. trains,** cambiar de trenes

change /tʃeindʒ/ n cambio, m; transformación, f; modificación, f; variedad, f; (of clothes, feathers) muda, f; (Theat. of scene) mutación, f; (money) cambio, m; (small coins) suelto, m; (stock) bolsa, f; lonja, f; vicisitud, f; (of bells) toque (de campanas), m. **for a c.,** para cambiar, como un cambio; para variar. **small c.,** suelto, m; moneda suelta, f. **c. for the better,** cambio para mejor, m. **c. for the worse,** cambio para peor, m. **c. of clothes,** cambio de ropa, m; **c. of front,** Fig. cambio de frente, m. **c. of heart,** cambio de sentimientos, m; conversión, f. **c. of life,** menopausia, f. **c.-over,** cambio, m

changeability /,tʃeindʒə'bɪlɪti/ n mutabilidad, f; inconstancia, volubilidad, f

changeable /'tʃeindʒəbəl/ a voluble; variable; cambiable

changeless /'tʃeindʒlɪs/ a immutable; constante

changeling /'tʃeindʒlɪŋ/ n niño (-ña) cambiado (-da) por otro

changing /'tʃeindʒɪŋ/ a cambiante. **c.-room,** vestuario, m

channel /'tʃænl̩/ n (of a river, etc.) cauce, m; canal, m; (irrigation) acequia, f; (strait) estrecho, m; Fig. conducto, m; (furrow) surco, m, estría, f; (of information, etc.) medio, m. vt acanalar; (furrow) surcar; (conduct) encauzar

chant /tʃænt/ n canto llano, m; salmo, m. vt salmodiar; cantar; recitar

chantey /'ʃænti/ n saloma, f

chaos /'keiɒs/ n caos, m

chaotic /kei'ɒtɪk/ a caótico, desordenado

chaotically /kei'ɒtɪkli/ adv en desorden

chap /tʃæp/ vt agrietar. vi agrietarse. n Inf. chico, m

chapbook /'tʃæp,bʊk/ n librito de cordel, m

chapel /'tʃæpəl/ n capilla, f; templo disidente, m

chaperon /'ʃæpə,roun/ n dama de compañía, señora de compañía, dueña, f, vt acompañar

chaplain /'tʃæplɪn/ n capellán, m

chaplaincy /'tʃæplɪnsi/ n capellanía, f

chaplet /'tʃæplɪt/ n guirnalda, f; rosario, m; (necklace) collar, m

chapter /'tʃæptər/ n (in a book) capítulo, m; Eccl. cabildo, capítulo, m. **a c. of accidents,** una serie de desgracias. **c. house,** sala capitular, f

char /tʃɑr/ vt (a house, etc.) fregar, hacer la limpieza de; (of fire) carbonizar. n Inf. fregona, asistenta, f

character /'kærɪktər/ n carácter, m; (of a play) personaje, m; (role) papel, m; (eccentric) tipo, m. **Gothic characters,** caracteres góticos, m pl. **in c.,** característico; apropiado. **in the c. of,** en el papel de. **out of c.,** nada característico; no apropiado. **principal c.,** protagonista, mf. **c. actor,** actor de carácter, m. **c. actress,** actriz de carácter

characteristic /ˌkærɪktəˈrɪstɪk/ a característico, típico. n característica, peculiaridad, f, rasgo, m

characterization /ˌkærɪktərəˈzeɪʃən/ n caracterización, f

characterize /'kærɪktəˌraɪz/ vt caracterizar

characterless /'kærɪktərlɪs/ a sin carácter; insípido, soso

charade /ʃəˈreɪd/ n charada, f

charcoal /'tʃɑrˌkoʊl/ n carbón de leña, m; (for blacking the face, etc.) tizne, m; Art. carboncillo, m. **c. burner,** carbonera, f. **c. crayon,** carboncillo, m. **c. drawing,** dibujo al carbón, m

charge /tʃɑrdʒ/ vt cargar; (enjoin) encargar; (accuse) acusar (de); (with price) cobrar; (with a mission, etc.) encomendar, confiar; Mil. acometer, atacar. vi Mil. atacar; (a price) cobrar, pedir. **How much do you c.?** ¿Cuánto cobra Vd.? **to c. with a crime,** acusar de un crimen

charge /tʃɑrdʒ/ n (load) carga, f; (price) precio, m; gasto, m; (on an estate, etc.) derechos, m pl; (task) encargo, m; (office or responsibility) cargo, m; (guardianship) tutela, f; (care) cuidado, m; exhortación, f; Law. acusación, f; Mil. ataque, m. **He is in c. of...,** Está encargado de...; Es responsable de... **The diamonds are in the c. of...,** Los diamantes están a cargo de. **depth c.,** carga de profundidad, f. **extra c.,** gasto suplementario, m; (on a train) suplemento, m. **free of c.,** gratis. **c. for admittance,** entrada, f. **to bring a c. against,** acusar de. **to give (someone) in c.,** entregar (una persona) a la policía. **to take c. of,** encargarse de

chargé d'affaires /ʃɑrˈʒeɪ dəˈfɛər/ n encargado de negocios, m

charger /'tʃɑrdʒər/ n caballo de guerra, corcel, m

chariness /'tʃɛərɪnɪs/ n cautela, f

chariot /'tʃærɪət/ n carro, m

charioteer /ˌtʃærɪəˈtɪər/ n auriga, m

charitable /'tʃærɪtəbəl/ a caritativo, limosnero; benéfico

charitableness /'tʃærɪtəbəlnɪs/ n caridad, f

charity /'tʃærɪti/ n caridad, f; beneficencia, f; (alms) limosna, f. **c. child,** niño (-ña) de la doctrina

charlatan /'ʃɑrlətn̩/ n charlatán (-ana); (quack) curandero, m

charlatanism /'ʃɑrlətn̩ˌɪzəm/ n charlatanismo, m; curanderismo, m

charm /tʃɑrm/ n hechizo, m; ensalmo, m; (amulet) amuleto, m; (trinket) dije, m; (general sense) encanto, atractivo, m. vt encantar, hechizar, fascinar

charming /'tʃɑrmɪŋ/ a encantador; atractivo, seductor, fascinador

charm school n academia de buenos modales, f

chart /tʃɑrt/ n Naut. carta de marear, f; (graph) gráfica, f, (table) tabla, f. vt poner en una carta

charter /'tʃɑrtər/ n carta, f; (of a city, etc.) fuero, m; cédula, f. vt (a ship) fletar; (hire) alquilar. **royal c.,** cédula real, f

Chartism /'tʃɑrtɪzəm/ n el cartismo, m

chartist /'tʃɑrtɪst/ n cartista, mf

charwoman /'tʃɑrˌwʊmən/ n fregona, asistenta; mujer de hacer faenas, Mexico fregandera f

chary /'tʃɛəri/ a cauteloso; desinclinado; frugal

chase /tʃeɪs/ n caza, f; seguimiento, m. vt cazar; dar caza (a); perseguir; (drive off) ahuyentar; Fig. disipar, hacer desaparecer; (engrave) cincelar. **to give c. to,** dar caza (a). **to go on a wild goose c.,** buscar pan de trastrigo

chasm /'kæzəm/ n sima, f, precipicio, m; Fig. abismo, m

chassis /'tʃæsi/ n chasis, m

chaste /tʃeɪst/ a casto

chasten /'tʃeɪsən/ vt castigar; corregir; humillar, mortificar

chastened /'tʃeɪsənd/ a sumiso, dócil

chastise /tʃæsˈtaɪz/ vt castigar

chastisement /tʃæsˈtaɪzmənt/ n castigo, m

chastity /'tʃæstɪti/ n castidad, f

chat /tʃæt/ vi charlar, conversar. n conversación, charla, f. **They are having a c.,** Están charlando, Están de palique

chattels /'tʃætəlz/ n pl bienes muebles, efectos, m pl

chatter /'tʃætər/ vi charlar; hablar por los codos, chacharear; (of water) murmurar; (of birds) piar; (of monkeys, etc.) chillar; (of teeth) rechinar; (of a person's teeth) dar diente con diente. n charla, f; cháchara, parla, f; (of water) murmurio, m; (of birds) gorjeo, m; (of monkeys, etc.) chillidos, m pl

chatterbox /'tʃætˌbɒks/ n badajo, m, cotorra, f

chattering /'tʃætərɪŋ/ n charla, cháchara, f; (of teeth) rechinamiento, m, a gárrulo, chacharero, locuaz

chauffeur /'ʃoʊfər/ n chófer, m

cheap /tʃip/ a barato; (of works of art) cursi. adv barato. **dirt c.,** baratísimo. **to be dirt c.,** estar por los suelos. **to hold (something) c.,** tener en poco, estimar en poco

cheapen /'tʃipən/ vt disminuir el valor de; reducir el precio de

cheaply /'tʃipli/ adv barato; a bajo precio

cheapness /'tʃipnɪs/ n baratura, f; precio módico, m; mal gusto, m, vulgaridad, f

cheat /tʃit/ n engaño, fraude, m, estafa, f; (person) fullero (-ra), trampista, mf embustero (-ra). vt engañar; defraudar; (at cards) hacer trampas. **He cheated me out of my property,** Me defraudó de mi propiedad

cheating /'tʃitɪŋ/ n engaño, m; fraude, m; (at cards) fullerías, f pl

check /tʃɛk/ n (chess) jaque, m; revés, m; impedimento, m; contratiempo, m; (of a bridle) cama, f; (control) freno, m; control, m; (checking) verificación, f; (ticket) papeleta, f; (counterfoil) talón, m; (square) cuadro, m; (bill) cuenta, f, Argentina adición f; (bank) cheque, m. vt (chess) jaquear; (hamper) refrenar; detener; contrarrestar; (test) verificar. vi detenerse. **to c. off,** marcar. **to c. oneself,** detenerse; contenerse. **to c. up,** comprobar. **crossed c.,** cheque cruzado, m. **c. book,** libro de cheques, m

checked /tʃɛkt/ a (cloth) a cuadros

checker /'tʃɛkər/ vt escaquear; (variegate) motear, salpicar; diversificar. **a checkered career,** una vida accidentada

checkerboard /'tʃɛkərˌbɔrd/ n tablero de damas, m

checkers /'tʃɛkərz/ n pl damas, f pl

checking /'tʃɛkɪŋ/ n represión, f; control, m; verificación, f; comprobación, f

checkmate /'tʃɛkˌmeɪt/ n mate, jaque, mate, m. vt dar mate (a); (plans, etc.) frustrar

checks and balances n pl frenos y contrapesos, m pl

cheek /tʃik/ n mejilla, f; Inf. descaro, m; insolencia, Lat. Am. impavidez f. **They have plenty of c.,** Tienen mucha cara dura. **c. by jowl,** cara a cara; al lado de. **c.-bone,** pómulo, m

cheekiness /'tʃikɪnɪs/ n cara dura, insolencia, Lat. Am. impavidez f

cheeky /'tʃiki/ a insolente, descarado, Lat. Am. impávido, Peru lisurero; (pert) respondón

cheer /tʃɪər/ n alegría, f, regocijo, m; vítor, m; aplauso, m. vt animar, alegrar, regocijar; vitorear, aplaudir. **to be of good c.,** estar alegre; ser feliz. **C. up!** ¡Ánimo! **to c. up,** animarse, cobrar ánimo

cheerful /'tʃɪərfəl/ a alegre; jovial; de buen humor

cheerfully /'tʃɪərfəli/ adv alegremente; (willingly) con mucho gusto, de buena gana

cheerfulness /'tʃɪərfəlnɪs/ n alegría, f; jovialidad, f; buen humor, m

cheering /'tʃɪərɪŋ/ n vítores, m pl, aclamaciones, f pl, a animador

cheerleader /'tʃɪərˌlidər/ n porro, m

cheerless /'tʃɪərlɪs/ a triste; sin alegría; (dank) obscuro, lóbrego

cheese /tʃiz/ n queso, m. **cream c.,** queso de nata, m. **grated c.,** queso rallado, m. **c.-dish,** quesera, f. **c.-**

mite, cresa, *f*. **c.-paring**, *n* corteza de queso, *f. a Inf.* tacaño. **c.-vat**, quesera, *f*

cheesecake /'tʃiːzˌkeik/ *n Lat. Am.* alfandoque, *m*

cheesy /'tʃizi/ *a* caseoso

chemical /'kɛmɪkəl/ *a* químico. **c. warfare**, defensa química, *f*

chemicals /'kɛmɪkəlz/ *n pl* productos químicos, *m pl*

chemise /ʃə'miz/ *n* camisa (de mujer), *f*

chemist /'kɛmɪst/ *n* químico, *m*. **chemist's shop**, farmacia, *f*; droguería, *f*

chemistry /'kɛməstri/ *n* química, *f*

chemotherapy /ˌkimou'θɛrəpi/ *n* quimioterapia, *f*

cherish /'tʃɛrɪʃ/ *vt* amar, querer; (a hope, etc.) abrigar, acariciar

cherry /'tʃɛri/ *n* (fruit) cereza, *f*; (tree and wood) cerezo, *m*. **c. brandy**, aguardiente de cerezas, *m*. **c. orchard**, cerezal, *m*

cherub /'tʃɛrəb/ *n* querub(e), querubín, *m*

cherubic /tʃə'rubɪk/ *a* querúbico

chess /tʃɛs/ *n* ajedrez, *m*. **c.-board**, tablero de ajedrez, *m*

chessman /'tʃɛsˌmæn/ *n* pieza de ajedrez, *f*

chest /tʃɛst/ *n* arca, *f*, cofre, *m*; cajón, *m*; *Anat.* pecho, *m*. **to throw out one's c.**, inflar el pecho. **c.-expander**, extensor, *m*. **c. of drawers**, cómoda, *f*

chested /'tʃɛstɪd/ *a* (in compounds) de pecho...

chestnut /'tʃɛsˌnʌt/ *n* (tree) castaño, *m*; (fruit) castaña, *f*; (color) castaño, color castaño, *m*; (horse) caballo castaño, *m*; (joke) chiste del tiempo de Maricastaña, *m*, *a* castaño. **horse-c. tree**, castaño de Indias, *m*

chevron /'ʃɛvrən/ *n Herald.* cabrio, *m*; (*Mil.* etc.) sardineta, *f*

chew /tʃu/ *vt* mascar, mascullar; (ponder) masticar

chewing /'tʃuɪŋ/ *n* masticación, *f*. **c.-gum**, chicle, *m*

chianti /ki'anti/ *n* (wine) quianti, *m*

chiaroscuro /ki,ɑrə'skyʊrou/ *n* claroscuro, *m*

chic /ʃik/ *n* chic, *m*, elegancia, *f*

chicanery /ʃi'keinəri/ *n* sofistería, *f*

chicken /'tʃikən/ *n* pollo, *m*. **c.-hearted**, medroso, cobarde, timorato. **c.-pox**, varicela, *f*

chickenwire /'tʃikənˌwai³r/ *n* alambrillo, *m*

chickpea /'tʃikˌpi/ *n* garbanzo, *m*

chickweed /'tʃikˌwid/ *n* pamplina, *f*

chicory /'tʃikəri/ *n* chicoria, *f*

chide /tʃaid/ *vt* reprender, reñir

chidingly /'tʃaidɪŋli/ *adv* en tono de represión

chief /tʃif/ *n* jefe, *m*, a principal; primero; en jefe; mayor. **c.-of-staff**, jefe de estado mayor, *m*

chiefly /'tʃifli/ *adv* principalmente; sobre todo

chieftain /'tʃiftən/ *n* caudillo, *m*; (of a clan) cabeza, jefe, *m*

chiffon /ʃi'fɒn/ *n* chifón, *m*, gasa, *f*

chiffonier /ˌʃifə'nɪər/ *n* cómoda, *f*

chignon /'ʃinyɒn/ *n* moño, *m*

child /tʃaild/ *n* niño (-ña); hijo (-ja), *Mexico* escuincle *mf*. **from a c.**, desde niño, desde la niñez. **with c.**, encinta, embarazada. **How many children do you have?** ¿Cuántos hijos tiene Vd.? **child's play**, juegos infantiles, *m pl*; *Fig.* niñerías, *f pl*. **c. welfare**, puericultura, *f*

childbirth /'tʃaildˌbɜrθ/ *n* parto, *m*

childhood /'tʃaildhʊd/ *n* niñez, infancia, *f*. **from his c.**, desde su niñez, desde niño

childish /'tʃaildɪʃ/ *a* de niño; aniñado; pueril; fútil. **to grow c.**, chochear

childishly /'tʃaildɪʃli/ *adv* como un niño

childishness /'tʃaildɪʃnɪs/ *n* puerilidad, *f*; futilidad, *f*

child labor *n* trabajo de menores, trabajo infantil, *m*

childless /'tʃaildlɪs/ *a* sin hijos; sin niños

childlike /'tʃaildˌlaik/ *a* de niño, aniñado; pueril

children. /'tʃildrən/ See **child**

Chilean /'tʃilian/ *a* and *n* chileno (-na)

chili /'tʃili/ *n* chile, pimento de cornetilla, *Lat. Am.* ají *m*. **c. sauce** *Lat. Am.* ají *m*

chill /tʃil/ *n* frío, *m*; (of fear, etc.) estremecimiento, *m*, (illness) resfriado, *m*; (unfriendliness) frialdad, frigidez, *f*, *a* frío; (unfriendly) frígido. *vt* enfriar; helar; (with fear, etc.) dar escalofríos (de). *vi* tener frío; tener escalofríos. **to take the c. off**, templar, calentar un poco

chilliness /'tʃilinis/ *n* frío, *m*; (unfriendliness) frialdad, frigidez, *f*

chilly /'tʃili/ *a* frío; (sensitive to cold) friolero; (of politeness, etc.) glacial, frígido

chime /tʃaim/ *n* juego de campanas, *m*; repique, campaneo, *m*; armonía, *f*. *vi* (of bells) repicar; *Fig.* armonizar. **to c. the hour**, dar la hora

chimera /kɪ'mɪərə/ *n* quimera, *f*

chimerical /kɪ'mɛrɪkəl/ *a* quimérico

chimney /'tʃɪmni/ *n* chimenea, *f*; (of a lamp) tubo (de lámpara), *m*. **c.-corner**, rincón de chimenea, *m*. **c.-pot**, sombrerete de chimenea, *m*. **c.-stack**, chimenea, *f*. **c.-sweep**, limpiador de chimeneas, deshollinador, *m*

chimpanzee /ˌtʃimpæn'zi, tʃim'pænzi/ *n* chimpancé, *m*

chin /tʃin/ *n* barbilla, barba, *f*, mentón, *m*. **c.-rest**, mentonera, *f*. **c.-strap**, barboquejo, *m*; venda para la barbilla, *f*

china /'tʃainə/ *n* china, porcelana, *f*; loza, *f. a* de porcelana; de loza. **China**, China, *f*. **c. cabinet**, chinero, *f*

chinchilla /tʃin'tʃilə/ *n* (animal and fur) chinchilla, *f*

Chinese /tʃai'niz/ *a* and *n* chino (-na); (language) chino, *m*. **C. lantern**, farolillo de papel, *m*. **C. white**, óxido blanco de cinc, *m*

chink /tʃiŋk/ *n* resquicio, *m*, grieta, hendidura, *f*; (clink) retintín, tintineo, *m*. *vi* tintinar

chintz /tʃints/ *n* zaraza, *f*

chip /tʃip/ *n* astilla, *f*; (counter) ficha, *f. vt* picar; cincelar. **a c. off the old block**, de tal palo tal astilla. **c. potatoes**, patatas fritas, *f pl*

chiromancy /'kairə,mænsi/ *n* quiromancia, *f*

chiropodist /kɪ'rɒpədɪst/ *n* pedicuro, *m*, callista, *mf*

chiropody /kɪ'rɒpədi/ *n* pedicura, *f*

chiropractor /'kairə,præktər/ *n* quiropráctico, *m*

chirp /tʃɜrp/ *vi* piar, gorjear. *n* pío, gorjeo, *m*

chirping /'tʃɜrpɪŋ/ *n* piada, *f*, a gárrulo, piante

chisel /'tʃizəl/ *n* escoplo, cincel, *m*, *vt* cincelar. **cold c.**, cortafrío, *m*

chitchat /'tʃit,tʃæt/ *n* charla, *f*

chitterlings /'tʃitlinz/ *n* asadura, *f*

chivalrous /'ʃivəlrəs/ *a* caballeroso

chivalry /'ʃivəlri/ *n* caballería, *f*; caballerosidad, *f*k. **novel of c.**, novela de caballería, *f*

chive /tʃaiv/ *n Bot.* cebollana, *f*, cebollino, *m*

chloral /'klɔrəl/ *n* cloral, *m*

chlorate /'klɔreit/ *n* clorato, *m*

chloride /'klɔraid/ *n* cloruro, *m*

chlorine /'klɔrin/ *n* cloro, *m*

chloroform /'klɔrə,fɔrm/ *n* cloroformo, *m*, *vt* cloroformizar

chlorophyll /'klɔrəfil/ *n* clorófila, *f*

chock-full /'tʃɒk 'fʊl/ *a* lleno de bote en bote

chocolate /'tʃɒkəlit/ *n* chocolate, *m*, *a* de chocolate. **thick drinking-c.**, chocolate a la española, *f*. **thin drinking-c.**, chocolate a la francesa, *m*. **c. shop**, chocolatería, *f*

choice /tʃɔis/ *n* selección, *f*; preferencia, *f*; elección, *f*; opción, *f*; alternativa, *f*; lo más escogido. *a* escogido, selecto; excelente. **for c.**, con preferencia

choir /kwai³r/ *n* coro, *m*. **c.-boy**, niño del coro, *m*. **c.-master**, maestro de capilla, *m*

choke /tʃouk/ *vi* ahogarse; atragantarse; obstruirse. *vt* ahogar; estrangular. **to c. with laughter**, ahogarse de risa. **to c. back**, (words) tragar. **to c. off**, (a person) disuadir (de); quitarse de encima(a). **to c. up**, obstruir, cerrar, obturar; (hide) cubrir, tapar

choking /'tʃoukɪŋ/ *a* asfixiante, sofocante. *n* ahogamiento, *m*, sofocación, *f*

cholera /'kɒlərə/ *n* cólera, *m*

choleric /'kɒlərɪk/ *a* colérico

cholesterol /kə'lɛstə,roul/ *n* colesterina, *f*

choline /'koulin/ *n* colina, *f*

choose /tʃuz/ *vt* escoger; elegir; optar por; (wish) querer, gustar. **They will do it when they c.**, Lo harán cuando les parezca bien. **If you c.**, Si Vd. quiere; Sl Vd. gusta. **He was chosen as Mayor**, Fue elegido alcalde. **There is nothing to c. between them**, No hay diferencia entre ellos; Tanto vale el uno como el otro. **You cannot c. but love her**, No puedes menos de quererla

choosing /'tʃuzɪŋ/ n selección, f; (for an office, etc.) elección, f

chop /tʃɒp/ vt cortar; (mince) picar; (split) hender, partir. n (meat) chuleta, f; (jaw) quijada, f. **to c. about, round,** (of the wind) girar, virar. **to c. down,** (trees) talar. **to c. off,** separar; cortar; tajar. **to c. up,** cortar en pedazos

chopper /'tʃɒpər/ n hacha, f; (helicopter) helicóptero, m

choppy /'tʃɒpi/ a picado, agitado

chopstick /'tʃɒp,stɪk/ n palillo chino, m

choragus /kə'reigəs/ n corega, corego, m

choral /'kɔrəl/ a coral

chord /kɔrd/ n cuerda, f, lazo, m; Mus. acorde, m; **the right c.,** Fig. la cuerda sensible

choreographer /,kɔri'ɒɡrəfər/ n coreógrafo, m

choreographic /,kɔriə'ɡræfɪk/ a coreográfico

choreography /,kɔri'ɒɡrəfi, ,kour-/ n coreografía, f

chorister /'kɔrəstər/ n corista, m

chorus /'kɔrəs/ n coro, m; (in revues) comparsa, f, acompañamiento, m; (of a song) refrán, m. **to sing in c.,** cantar a coro. **c. girl,** corista, f

chosen /'tʃouzən/ a escogido; elegido. **the c.,** los elegidos

chrestomathy /kres'tɒməθi/ n crestomatía, f

Christ /kraist/ n Cristo, Jesucristo, m

christen /'krɪsən/ vt bautizar

Christendom /'krɪsəndəm/ n cristianismo, m, cristiandad, f

christening /'krɪsənɪŋ/ n bautizo, m, a bautismal, de bautizo

Christian /'krɪstʃən/ a cristiano. n cristiano (-na). **C. name,** nombre de pila, m

christianity /,krɪstʃi'ænɪti/ n cristianismo, m

Christmas /'krɪsməs/ n Navidad, f. **A Merry C.!** ¡Felices Pascuas (de Navidad)! **Father C.,** Padre Noel, m; (Sp. equivalent) Los Reyes Magos. **C. box,** regalo de Navidad, m. **C. card,** felicitación de Navidad, f. **C. carol,** villancico de Navidad, m. **C. Day,** día de Navidad, m. **C. Eve,** Nochebuena, f. **C.-tide,** Navidades, f pl. **C. tree,** árbol de Navidad, m

Christopher Columbus /'krɪstəfər kə'lʌmbəs/ Cristóbal Colón, m

chromate /'kroumeit/ n cromato, m

chromatic /krou'mætɪk/ a cromático

chrome /kroum/ n cromo, m. **c. yellow,** amarillo de cromo, m

chromic /'kroumɪk/ a crómico

chromium /'kroumiəm/ n cromo, m. **c.-plated,** cromado

chromosome /'kroumə,soum/ n cromosoma, m

chronic /'krɒnɪk/ a crónico; inveterado

chronicle /'krɒnɪkəl/ n crónica, f. vt narrar

chronicler /'krɒnɪklər/ n cronista, mf

chronological /,krɒnl'ɒdʒɪkəl/ a cronológico. **in c. order,** por orden cronológico

chronology /krə'nɒlədʒi/ n cronología, f

chronometer /krə'nɒmɪtər/ n cronómetro, m

chrysalis /'krɪsəlɪs/ n crisálida, f

chrysanthemum /krɪ'sænθəməm/ n crisantemo, m

chubbiness /'tʃʌbinɪs/ n gordura, f

chubby /'tʃʌbi/ a regordete, gordito. **c.-cheeked,** mofletudo

chuck /tʃʌk/ vt (throw) lanzar, arrojar; (discontinue) abandonar, dejar. n (in a lathe) mandril, m. **to c. under the chin,** acariciar la barbilla (a). **to c. away,** derrochar; malgastar, perder. **to c. out,** echar, poner en la calle

chuckle /'tʃʌkəl/ vi reír entre dientes. n risa ahogada, f; risita, f

chum /tʃʌm/ n compinche, camarada, mf. **to c. up with,** ser camarada de

chunk /tʃʌŋk/ n pedazo, trozo, m

church /tʃɜrtʃ/ n iglesia, f; (Protestant) templo, m. vt (a woman) purificar. **poor as a c. mouse,** más pobre que las ratas. **the Roman Catholic C.,** la iglesia católica. **to go to c.,** ir a misa; ir al templo. **c. music,** música sagrada, f

churchyard /'tʃɜrtʃ,yɑrd/ n cementerio, m

churl /tʃɜrl/ n patán, m

churlish /'tʃɜrlɪʃ/ a grosero, cazurro; (mean) tacaño, ruin

churn /tʃɜrn/ n mantequera, f. vt (cream) batir; Fig. azotar, agitar

chute /ʃut/ n (for grain, etc.) manga de tolva, f; vertedor, m; (in apartment buildings and amusement parks) tobogán, deslizadero, m

ciborium /sɪ'bɔriəm/ n (chalice) copón, m; (tabernacle) sagrario, m; Archit. ciborio, m

cicada /sɪ'keidə/ n cigarra, f

cicatrice /'sɪkətrɪs/ n cicatriz, f

cicatrization /,sɪkətrə'zeiʃən/ n cicatrización, f

cicatrize /'sɪkə,traiz/ vt cicatrizar. vi cicatrizarse

cider /'saidər/ n sidra, f

cigar /sɪ'ɡɑr/ n cigarro, m. **c.-box,** cigarrera, f. **c.-case,** petaca, cigarrera, f. **c.-cutter,** corta-puros, m

cigarette /,sɪɡə'rɛt/ n cigarrillo, pitillo, Lat. Am. cigarro m. **c.-butt,** colilla, f. **c.-case,** pitillera, f. **c.-holder,** boquilla, f. **c.-lighter,** encendedor de cigarrillos, m. **c.-paper,** papel de fumar, m

cinch /sɪntʃ/ n (of a saddle) cincha, f; Inf. ganga, f; Inf. seguridad, f. **c.-strap,** látigo, m

cinchona /sɪŋ'kounə/ n quina, cinchona, f

cinder /'sɪndər/ n ceniza, f; carbonilla, f. **red-hot c.,** rescoldo, m. **c.-track,** pista de ceniza, f

cinema, cinematograph /'sɪnəmə/ n cine, cinematógrafo, m

cinematographic /,sɪnə,mætə'ɡræfɪk/ a cinematográfico

cinematography /,sɪnəmə'tɒɡrəfi/ n cinematografía, f

cinemogul /,sɪnə'mouɡəl/ n magnate del cine, mf

cinnamon /'sɪnəmən/ n (spice) canela, f; (tree) canelo, m; color de canela, m

cipher /'saifər/ n Math. cero, m; Fig. nulidad, f; (code) cifra, f; monograma, m. **to be a mere c.,** ser un cero

Circassian /sər'kæʃən/ a circasiano. n circasiano (-na)

circle /'sɜrkəl/ n círculo, m; (revolution) vuelta, f; (group) grupo; m; (club, etc.) centro, m; (cycle) ciclo, m. vt dar vueltas alrededor de; rodear; ceñir; (on an application, examination, etc.) encerrar en un círculo. vi dar vueltas; (aircraft) volar en círculo; (of a hawk, etc.) cernerse. **dress-c.,** Theat. anfiteatro, m. **the family c.,** el círculo de la familia. **to come full c.,** dar la vuelta. **upper c.,** Theat. segundo piso, m. **vicious c.,** círculo vicioso, m

circlet /'sɜrklɪt/ n (of flowers, etc.) corona, f; (ring) anillo, m

circuit /'sɜrkɪt/ n circuito, m; (tour) gira, f; (revolution) vuelta, f; (radius) radio, m. **short c.,** corto circuito, m. **c.-breaker,** corta-circuitos, m

circuit court of appeals /ə'pilz/ n tribunal colegial de circuito, m

circuitous /sər'kyuɪtəs/ a indirecto; tortuoso

circuitously /sər'kyuɪtəsli/ adv indirectamente

circular /'sɜrkyələr/ a circular; redondo. n carta circular, f; circular, f. **c. tour,** viaje redondo, m

circularize /'sɜrkyələ,raiz/ vt enviar circulares (a)

circulate /'sɜrkyə,leit/ vi circular. vt hacer circular; poner en circulación; (news, etc.) divulgar, diseminar

circulating library /'sɜrkyə,leitɪŋ/ n biblioteca por subscripción, f

circulation /,sɜrkyə'leiʃən/ n circulación, f; (of a newspaper, etc.) tirada, circulación, f. **c. of the blood,** circulación de la sangre, f

circulatory /'sɜrkyələ,tɔri/ a circulatorio

circumcise /'sɜrkəm,saiz/ vt circuncidar

circumcised /'sɜrkəm,saizd/ a circunciso

circumcision /,sɜrkəm'sɪʒən/ n circuncisión, f

circumference /sər'kʌmfərəns/ n circunferencia, f

circumflex /'sɜrkəm,flɛks/ a circunflejo. **c. accent,** acento circunflejo, m; (informal) capucha, f

circumlocution /,sɜrkəmlou'kyuʃən/ n circunlocución, f

circumnavigate /,sɜrkəm'nævɪ,geit/ vt circunnavegar

circumnavigation /'sɜrkəm,nævə'geiʃən/ n circunnavegación, f

circumscribe /'sɜrkəm,skraib/ vt circunscribir; Fig. limitar

clean

circumscribed /'sɜrkəm₁skraibd/ *a* circunscripto; *Fig.* limitado

circumscription /₁sɜrkəm'skrıpʃən/ *n* circunscripción, *f*; *Fig.* limitación, restricción, *f*

circumspect /'sɜrkəm₁spɛkt/ *a* circunspecto; discreto, correcto; prudente

circumspection /₁sɜrkəm'spɛkʃən/ *n* circunspección, *f*; prudencia, *f*

circumspectly /'sɜrkəm₁spɛktli/ *adv* con circunspección; prudentemente

circumstance /'sɜrkəm₁stæns/ *n* circunstancia, *f*; detalle, *m*. **aggravating c.,** circunstancia agravante, *f*. **attenuating c.,** circunstancia atenuante, *f*. **in the circumstances,** en las circunstancias. **in easy circumstances,** en buena posición, acomodado. **Do you know what his circumstances are?** ¿Sabes cuál es su situación económica? **under the circumstances,** bajo las circunstancias

circumstantial /₁sɜrkəm'stænʃəl/ *a* circunstancial; detallado. **c. evidence,** prueba de indicios, *f*

circumvent /₁sɜrkəm'vɛnt/ *vt* frustrar; impedir

circumvention /₁sɜrkəm'vɛnʃən/ *n* frustración, *f*

circumvolution /₁sɜrkəmvə'luʃən/ *n* circunvolución, *f*

circus /'sɜrkəs/ *n* circo, *m*; plaza redonda, *f*; (traffic) redondel, *m*

cirrhosis /sɪ'rousɪs/ *n* cirrosis, *f*

cirrus /'sɪrəs/ *n* (all meanings) cirro, *m*

cistern /'sɪstərn/ *n* tanque, *m*; cisterna, *f*, aljibe, *m*

citadel /'sɪtədḷ/ *n* ciudadela, *f*

citation /sai'teɪʃən/ *n* *Law.* citación, *f*; cita, *f*

citation dictionary *n* diccionario de autoridades, *m*

cite /sait/ *vt* citar

citizen /'sɪtəzən/ *n* ciudadano (-na); vecino (-na); natural, *mf*. **fellow c.,** conciudadano, *m*; compatriota, *mf*

citizenship /'sɪtəzən₁ʃɪp/ *n* ciudadanía, *f*

citrate /'sɪtreit/ *n* citrato, *m*

citric /'sɪtrɪk/ *a* cítrico

citrine /'sɪtrin/ *a* cetrino

citron /'sɪtrən/ *n* (fruit) cidra, *f*; (tree) cidro, *m*

city /'sɪti/ *n* ciudad, *f*, a municipal

city-state /'sɪti₁steit/ *n* ciudad-estado, *f*, (plural: ciudades-estado)

civet /'sɪvɪt/ *n* algalia, *f*

civic /'sɪvɪk/ *a* cívico; municipal

civics /'sɪvɪks/ *n* civismo, *m*

civil /'sɪvəl/ *a* civil; doméstico; (polite) cortés, atento; (obliging) servicial. **c. defense,** defensa civil, *f*. **c. engineer,** ingeniero de caminos, canales y puertos, *m*. **C. Service,** cuerpo de empleados del Estado, *m*

civilian /sɪ'vɪlyən/ *a* civil. *n* ciudadano (-na). **c. dress,** traje paisano, *m*

civility /sɪ'vɪlɪti/ *n* civilidad, cortesía, *f*

civilization /₁sɪvələ'zeɪʃən/ *n* civilización, *f*

civilize /'sɪvə₁laiz/ *vt* civilizar

civilized /'sɪvə₁laizd/ *a* civilizado

civilizing /'sɪvə₁laizɪŋ/ *a* civilizador

civilly /'sɪvəli/ *adv* civilmente, cortésmente

clad /klæd/ *a* vestido

claim /kleim/ *vt* reclamar; pretender exigir; *Law.* demandar; (assert) afirmar. *vi Law.* pedir en juicio. *n* reclamación, *f*; pretensión, *f*; *Law.* demanda, *f*; (in a gold-field, etc.) concesión, *f*; (right) derecho, *m*. **to lay c. to,** pretender a; exigir. **to put in a c. for,** reclamar

claimant /'kleimənt/ *n Law.* demandante, *mf*; pretendiente (-ta); *Com.* acreedor (-ra)

clairvoyance /klɛr'vɔiəns/ *n* doble vista, *f*, clarividencia, *f*

clairvoyant /klɛr'vɔiənt/ *n* vidente, *m*

clam /klæm/ *n* almeja, chirla, *f*

clamber /'klæmbər/ *vi* trepar, encaramarse. *n* subida difícil, *f*

clamminess /'klæmɪnɪs/ *n* viscosidad, humedad, *f*

clammy /'klæmi/ *a* viscoso; húmedo, mojado

clamor /'klæmər/ *n* clamor, estruendo, *m*; gritería, vocería, *f*. *vi* gritar, vociferar. **to c. against,** protestar contra. **to c. for,** pedir a voces

clamorous /'klæmərəs/ *a* clamoroso, ruidoso, estrepitoso

clamp /klæmp/ *n* grapa, *f*; abrazadera, *f*; tornillo, *m*; (pile) montón, *m*. *vt* empalmar; sujetar, lañar

clan /klæn/ *n* clan, *m*; familia, *f*; partido, grupo, *m*

clandestine /klæn'dɛstɪn/ *a* clandestino, furtivo

clandestinely /klæn'dɛstɪnli/ *adv* en secreto, clandestinamente

clang /klæŋ/ *vi* sonar; (of a gate, etc.) rechinar. *vt* hacer sonar. *n* sonido metálico, *m*; estruendo, *m*

clank /klæŋk/ *vi* dar un ruido metálico; crujir. *vt* hacer sonar; (glasses) hacer chocar. *n* ruido metálico, *m*; el crujir

clannish /'klænɪʃ/ *a* exclusivista

clansman /'klænzmən/ *n* miembro de un clan, *m*

clap /klæp/ *vt* (hands) batir; (spurs, etc.) poner rápidamente; (one's hat on) encasquetarse (el sombrero); (shut) cerrar apresuradamente. *vi* aplaudir. *n* (of the hands) palmada, *f*; (of thunder) trueno, *m*; (noise) ruido, *m*. **to c. eyes on,** echar la vista encima de. **to c. someone on the back,** dar una palmada en la espalda (a). **to c. the hands,** batir las palmas

clapper /'klæpər/ *n* (of a bell) badajo, *m*

clapping /'klæpɪŋ/ *n* aplausos, *m pl*

claque /klæk/ *n* claque, *f*

claret /'klærɪt/ *n* clarete, *m*

clarification /₁klærəfə'keiʃən/ *n* clarificación, *f*; elucidación, *f*

clarify /'klærə₁fai/ *vt* clarificar; elucidar, aclarar

clarinet /₁klærə'nɛt/ *n* clarinete, *m*

clarinettist /₁klærə'nɛtɪst/ *n* clarinete, *m*

clarion /'klæriən/ *n* clarín, *m*

clarity /'klærɪti/ *n* claridad, *f*; lucidez, *f*

clash /klæʃ/ *vi* chocar; encontrarse; (of events) coincidir; (of opinions, etc.) oponerse, estar en desacuerdo; (of colors) desentonar, chocar. *n* estruendo, fragor, *m*; choque, *m*; *Mil.* encuentro, *m*; (of opinions, etc.) desacuerdo, *m*; disputa, *f*

clasp /klæsp/ *n* (a brooch, etc.) abrochar, enganchar; (embrace) abrazar; (of plants, etc.) ceñir. *n* (brooch) broche, *m*; (of a belt) hebilla, *f*; (of a necklace, handbag, book) cierre, *m*; (for the hair) pasador, *m*. **to c. someone in one's arms,** tomar en los brazos (a), abrazar. **c.-knife,** navaja, *f*

class /klæs/ *n* clase, *f*; (kind) especie, *f*; (of exhibits, etc.) categoría, *f*. *vt* clasificar. **in a c. by itself,** único en su línea. **the lower classes,** las clases bajas. **the middle classes,** la clase media. **the upper classes,** la clase alta. **c.-mate,** condiscípulo (-la). **c.-room,** sala de clase, *f*, salón de clase, *f*. **c. war,** lucha de clases, *f*

classic /'klæsɪk/ *a* clásico. *n* clásico, *m*

classical /'klæsɪkəl/ *a* clásico

classicist /'klæsəsɪst/ *a* and *n* clasicista, *mf*

classifiable /'klæsə₁faiəbəl/ *a* clasificable

classification /₁klæsəfɪ'keiʃən/ *n* clasificación, *f*

classified /'klæsə₁faid/ *a* (secreto) reservado, secreto; (advertisement) por palabras

classified advertisement *n* anuncio por palabras, *m*

classify /'klæsə₁fai/ *vt* clasificar

clatter /'klætər/ *vi* hacer ruido; (knock) golpear; (of loose horseshoes) chacolotear. *vt* hacer ruido con; chocar (una cosa contra otra). *n* ruido, *m*; (hammering) martilleo, *m*; (of horseshoes) chacoloteo, *m*; (of a crowd) estruendo, *m*, bulla, *f*. **John clattered along the street,** Los pasos de Juan resonaban por la calle

clause /klɔz/ *n Gram.* cláusula, *f*; *Law.* condición, estipulación, cláusula, *f*

claustrophobia /₁klɔstrə'foubiə/ *n* claustrofobia, *f*

clavichord /'klævɪ₁kɔrd/ *n* clavicordio, *m*

clavicle /'klævɪkəl/ *n* clavícula, *f*

claw /klɔ/ *n* garra, *f*; (of a lobster, etc.) tenaza, *f*; (hook) garfio, gancho, *m*. *vt* arañar, clavar las uñas en; (tear) desgarrar. **c.-hammer,** martillo de orejas, *m*

clay /klei/ *n* arcilla, *f*; barro, *m*; (pipe) pipa de barro, *f*. **c.-pit,** barrizal, *m*

clayey /'kleii/ *a* arcilloso

clean /klin/ *a* limpio; puro, casto. *adv* limpio; completamente; exactamente. **to make a c. sweep (of),** no dejar títere con cabeza. **to make a c. breast of,** confesar sin tormento, no quedarse con nada en el pecho. **to show a c. pair of heels,** tomar las de Villadiego. **c. bill of health,** patente de sanidad, *m*. **c.-cut,**

clean

bien definido; claro. **c.-limbed,** bien proporcionado, gallardo. **c.-shaven,** lampiño; sin barba, bien afeitado
clean /klin/ *vt* limpiar; (streets) barrer; (a floor) fregar; (dryclean) lavar al seco. **to c. one's hands (teeth),** limpiarse las manos (los dientes). **to c. up,** limpiar; (tidy) asear; poner en orden
cleaner /'klinər/ *n* limpiador (-ra); (charwoman) fregona, *f*; (stain remover) sacamanchas, *m*; (drycleaner, person) tintorero (-ra)
cleaning /'klinɪŋ/ *n* limpieza, *f*, *a* de limpiar. **dry-c.,** lavado al seco, *m*. **c. rag,** trapo de limpiar, *m*. **c. woman** *Mexico* fregandera
cleanliness /'klɛnlɪnɪs/ *n* limpieza, *f*; aseo, *m*
cleanse /klɛnz/ *vt* lavar; purgar; purificar
cleansing /'klɛnzɪŋ/ *n* limpieza, *f*; lavamiento, *m*; purgación, *f*; purificación, *f*
clear /klɪər/ *a* claro; (of the sky) sereno, despejado; transparente; (free (from)) libre (de); (open) abierto; (of profit, etc.) neto; (of thoughts, etc.) lúcido; (apparent) evidente; explícito; (of images) distinto; absoluto; (whole) entero, completo. **c. majority,** mayoría absoluta, *f*. **c. profit,** beneficio neto, *m*. **c.-cut,** bien definido. **c.-headed,** perspicaz; inteligente. **c.-sighted,** clarividente
clear /klɪər/ *vt* aclarar; despejar; limpiar; librar (de); quitar; (one's throat) carraspear; (*Com.* stock) liquidar; (of a charge) absolver; (one's character) vindicar; (avoid, miss) evitar; (jump) salvar, saltar; (a court, etc.) desocupar; (a debt) satisfacer; (an account) saldar; (a mortgage) cancelar; (win) ganar; hacer un beneficio de; (through customs) despachar en la aduana. *vi* (of sky, etc.) serenarse; escampar; (of wine, etc.) aclararse; despacharse en la aduana. **to c. the table,** levantar la mesa, levantar los manteles. **to c. the underbrush from** *Lat. Am.* desmalezar. **to c. the way,** abrir calle; *Fig.* abrir paso. **to c. away,** *vt* quitar; disipar. *vi* disiparse. **to c. off,** *vt* (finish) terminar; (debts) pagar; (discharge) despedir. *vi* (of rain) despejarse, escampar; marcharse. **to c. out,** *vt* limpiar; (a drain, etc.) desatascar; vaciar; echar. *vi* marcharse, escabullirse. **C. out!** ¡Fuera! **to c. the decks,** hacer zafarrancho. **to c. the decks for action,** hacer zafarrancho. **to c. up,** *vt* poner en orden; (a mystery, etc.) aclarar, resolver, *vi* (of weather) serenarse, escampar, despejarse
clearance /'klɪərəns/ *n* (of trees, etc.) desmonte, *m*; eliminación, *f*; expulsión, *f*; *Mech.* espacio muerto, *m*; despacho de aduana, *m*. **to make a c. of,** deshacerse de. **c. sale,** liquidación, venta de saldos, *f*
clearing /'klɪərɪŋ/ *n* (in a wood) claro, *m*, *Argentina* abra *f*; desmonte, *m*; (of one's character) vindicación, *f*. **c.-house,** casa de compensación, *f*
clearness /'klɪərnɪs/ *n* claridad, *f*
cleavage /'klivɪdʒ/ *n* hendimiento, *m*; (in views, etc.) escisión, *f*
cleave /kliv/ *vt* partir; abrir; (air, water, etc.) surcar, hender. *vi* partirse; (stick) pegarse, adherirse
cleaver /'klivər/ *n* partidor, *m*; hacha, *f*
clef /klɛf/ *n* clave, *f*. **treble c.,** clave de sol, *f*
cleft /klɛft/ *n* hendedura, fisura, rendija, abertura, *f*. **c.-palate,** paladar hendido, *m*
clematis /'klɛmətɪs/ *n* clemátide, *f*
clemency /'klɛmənsi/ *n* (of weather) benignidad, *f*; (of character, etc.) clemencia, *f*
clement /'klɛmənt/ *a* (of weather) benigno; (of character, etc.) clemente, benévolo
clench /klɛntʃ/ *vt* agarrar; (teeth, etc.) apretar; (a bargain) cerrar, concluir
clergy /'klɜrdʒi/ *n* clero, *m*, clérigos, *m pl*
clergyman /'klɜrdʒimən/ *n* clérigo, *m*
cleric /'klɛrɪk/ *n* eclesiástico, *m*
clerical /'klɛrɪkəl/ *a* clerical; de oficina. **c. error,** error de oficina, *m*. **c. work,** trabajo de oficina, *m*
clericalism /'klɛrɪkə,lɪzəm/ *n* clericalismo, *m*
clerk /klɜrk/ *n* (clergyman) clérigo, *m*; (in an office) oficinista, escribiente, *m*; oficial, *m*; secretario, *m*
clerkship /'klɜrkʃɪp/ *n* puesto de oficinista, *m*; escribanía, *f*; secretaría, *f*
clever /'klɛvər/ *a* listo, inteligente; ingenioso; hábil; (dexterous) diestro

cleverly /'klɛvərli/ *adv* hábilmente; diestramente, con destreza
cleverness /'klɛvərnɪs/ *n* talento, *m*; inteligencia, *f*; habilidad, *f*; (dexterity) destreza, *f*
cliché /kli'ʃei/ *n* frase hecha, frase de cajón, *f*, cliché, *m*
click /klɪk/ *vi* (of the tongue) dar un chasquido; (of a bolt, etc.) cerrarse a golpe; hacer tictac. *vt* (one's tongue) chascar; (a bolt, etc.) cerrar a golpe. *n* golpe seco, *m*; tictac, *m*; (of the tongue) chasquido, *m*. **to c. one's heels together,** hacer chocar los talones
client /'klaiənt/ *n* cliente, *mf*; (customer) parroquiano (-na), *Lat. Am. also* marchante (-ta) *mf*
clientele /,klaiən'tɛl/ *n* clientela, *f*
cliff /klɪf/ *n* acantilado, *m*, roca, escarpa, *f*
cliff dweller *n* hombre de la roca, hombre de las rocas, *m*, mujer de la roca, mujer de las rocas, *f*
climate /'klaimɪt/ *n* clima, *m*
climatic /klai'mætɪk/ *a* climático
climatology /,klaimə'tɒlədʒi/ *n* climatología, *f*
climax /'klaimæks/ *n* culminación, *f*; (rhetoric) clímax, *m*; gradación, *f*; punto más alto, apogeo, cenit, *m*; (of a play, etc.) desenlace, *m*
climb /klaim/ *vt* and *vi* trepar; escalar; montar; subir; ascender. **rate of c.,** *Aer.* velocidad ascensional, *f*. **to c. down,** bajar; *Fig.* echar el pie atrás. **to c. over,** (obstacles) salvar. **to c. up,** encaramarse por; subir por; montar
climber /'klaimər/ *n* alpinista, *mf*; (plant) trepadera, enredadera, *f*; (social) arribista, *mf*
clinch /klɪntʃ/ *vt* (nails, etc.) remachar, rebotar; (a bargain, etc.) cerrar; (an argument, etc.) remachar. *n* (wrestling) cuerpo a cuerpo, *m*
cling /klɪŋ/ *vi* pegarse (a); agarrarse (a); (of scents) pegarse; (follow) seguir. **They clung together for an instant,** Quedaron abrazados un instante
clinging /'klɪŋɪŋ/ *a* tenaz; (of plants, etc.) trepador; (of persons) manso, dócil. **to be a c. vine,** *Inf.* ser una malva
clinic /'klɪnɪk/ *n* clínica, *f*
clinical /'klɪnɪkəl/ *a* clínico.
clink /klɪŋk/ *vi* retiñir; (of glasses) chocarse. *vt* hacer sonar; (glasses) chocar. *n* retintín, *m*; (of a hammer) martilleo, *m*; sonido metálico, *m*; (of glasses) choque, *m*; (jail) *Argentina, Chile* capacha *f*
clip /klɪp/ *vt* (grasp) agarrar; (sheep, etc.) esquilar; (trim) recortar, cercenar; (prune) podar; (a ticket) taladrar. *n* pinza, *f*; (paper-clip) sujetapapeles, *Central America* ataché, *elsewhere in Lat. Am.* broche *m*; *Mech.* grapa, escarpia, *f*; (for ornament) sujetador, *m*. **to c. a person's wings,** *Fig.* cortar (o quebrar) las alas (a)
clipper /'klɪpər/ *n* (person) esquilador (-ra); (*Naut.* and *Aer.*) clíper, *m*; *pl* **clippers,** tenazas de cortar, *f pl*; (for pruning) podaderas, *f pl*; (punch) taladro, *m*
clipping /'klɪpɪŋ/ *n* (of sheep, etc.) esquileo, *m*; (of a newspaper, etc.) recorte, *m*
clique /klik/ *n* camarilla, *f*, grupito *m*
cliquish /'klikɪʃ/ *a* exclusivista
cliquishness /'klikɪʃnɪs/ *n* famiguismo, *m*
cloak /klouk/ *n* capa, *f*; manto, *m*; *Fig.* velo, *m*. *vt* encapotar; embozar; (conceal) ocultar, encubrir. **c. and sword play,** comedia de capa y espada, *f*. **c.-room,** guardarropa, *m*; (ladies') tocador, *m*; (on a station) consigna, *f*
clock /klɒk/ *n* reloj, *m*; (of a stocking) cuadrado, *m*. **It is six o'clock,** Son las seis. **c.-face,** esfera de reloj, *f*. **c.-maker,** relojero, *m*. **c.-making,** relojería, *f*. **c.-work,** aparato de relojería, *m*. **to go like c.-work,** ir como un reloj. **c.-work train,** tren de cuerda, *m*
clockwise /'klɒk,waiz/ *a* and *adv* en el sentido de las agujas del reloj; de derecha a izquierda
clod /klɒd/ *n* (of earth) terrón, *m*; (corpse) tierra, *f*; (person) zoquete, *m*. **c.-hopper,** patán, *m*
clog /klɒg/ *n* (shoe) zueco, zoclo, *m*; (obstacle) estorbo, obstáculo, *m*. *vt* embarazar; estorbar, impedir; (block) obturar, cerrar; *Fig.* paralizar
cloister /'klɔistər/ *n* claustro, *m*; convento, *m*. *vt* enclaustrar
cloistered /'klɔistərd/ *a* enclaustrado; retirado, aislado
close /klous/ *a* estrecho; (of a prisoner) incomuni-

cado; (reticent) reservado; (niggardly) tacaño, avaro; (scarce) escaso; (of friends) íntimo; (equal) igual; (lacking space) apretado; (dense) denso; (thick) tupido; compacto; (of a copy, etc.) fiel, exacto; (thorough) concienzudo; (careful) cuidadoso; (attentive) atento; (to the roots) a raíz; (of shaving) bueno; (of weather) pesado, sofocante; (of rooms) mal ventilado. **at c. quarters,** de cerca. **It is c. to eight o'clock,** Son casi las ocho. **to press c.,** perseguir de cerca; fatigar. **c. at hand, c. by,** cerca; al lado; a mano. **c.-cropped,** (of hair) al rape. **c. fight,** lucha igualada, *f.* **c.-fisted,** tacaño, apretado. **c.-fitting,** ajustado, ceñido al cuerpo; pequeño. **c. season,** veda, *f.* **c.-up,** *n* (cinema) primer plano, *m*

close /klouz/ *n* (end) fin, *m*, conclusión, *f*; (of day) caída, *f*; *Mus.* cadencia, *f*; (enclosure) cercado, *m*; (square) plazoleta, *f*; (alley) callejón, *m*; (of a cathedral) patio, *m*. **at the c. of day,** a la caída de la tarde. **to bring to a c.,** terminar; llevar a cabo. **to draw to a c.,** tocar a su fin; estar terminando

close /klouz/ *vt* cerrar; (end) concluir, terminar; poner fin a. *vi* cerrar(se); (of a wound) cicatrizarse, cerrarse; (end) terminar(se), acabar, concluir. **to c. the ranks,** cerrar filas. **to c. about,** (surround) rodear, cercar; (envelop) envolver. **to c. down,** *vt* cerrar. *vi* cerrar; *Radio.* cerrarse. **to c. halfway** entrecerrar **to c. in,** (surround) cercar; (of night) cerrar; (envelop) envolver; (of length of days) acortarse. **to c. in on,** cercar. **to c. round,** envolver; (of water) tragar. **to c. up,** *vt* cerrar; cerrar completamente; obstruir. *vi* (of persons) acercarse; (of a wound) cicatrizarse; cerrarse

closed /klouzd/ *a* cerrado. "**Road C.,**" Paso Cerrado. **to have a c. mind,** ser cerrado de mollera; sufrir de estrechez de miras

closely /'klousli/ *adv* estrechamente; de cerca; (carefully) cuidadosamente; (exactly) exactamente; (attentively) con atención, atentamente

closeness /'klousnıs/ *n* estrechez, *f*; densidad, *f*; (nearness) proximidad, *f*; (of a copy, etc.) fidelidad, exactitud, *f*; (stuffiness) falta de aire, *f*; (of friendship) intimidad, *f*; (stinginess) tacañería, *f*; (reserve) reserva

closet /'klɒzıt/ *n* camarín, *m*; (cupboard) alacena, *f*; (water) excusado, *m*; (clothes) ropero, *m*

closing /'klouzıŋ/ *n* cerramiento, *m*; (of an account) saldo, *m*. **c. time,** cierre, *m*, hora de cerrar, *f*

closure /'klouʒər/ *n* conclusión, *f*; *Polit.* clausura, *f*

clot /klɒt/ *n* coágulo, grumo, *m*. *vt* coagular. *vi* coagularse, cuajarse

cloth /klɔθ/ *n* tela, *f*; paño, *m*; (table) mantel, *m*; (clergy) clero, *m*. **She cleaned the books with a c.,** Ella limpió los libros con un paño. **in c.,** (of books) en tela

clothe /klouð/ *vt* vestir; cubrir; (with authority, etc.) revestir. **to c. oneself,** vestirse

clothes /klouz/ *n pl* vestidos, *m pl*, ropa, *f*. **a suit of c.,** un traje. **old c. shop,** ropavejería, *f*. **c.-basket,** cesta de la colada, *f*. **c.-brush,** cepillo para ropa, *m*. **c.-hanger,** percha, *f*. **c.-horse,** enjugador, *m*. **c.-line,** cuerda de la ropa, *f*. **c.-peg,** pinza de la ropa, *f*. **c.-prop,** palo para sostener la cuerda de la colada, *m*

clothier /'klouðiər/ *n* ropero, *m*. **clothier's shop,** ropería, *f*

clothing /'klouðıŋ/ *n* vestidos, *m pl*, ropa, *f*. **article of c.,** prenda de vestir, *f*

clotted /'klɒtıd/ *a* grumoso

cloud /klaud/ *n* nube, *f*. *vt* anublar, oscurecer; empañar; (blot out) borrar. *vi* anublarse. **to be under a c.,** estar bajo sospecha. **summer c.,** nube de verano, *f*. **storm-c.,** nubarrón, *m*. **c.-burst,** nubada, *f*, chaparrón, *m*. **c.-capped,** coronado de nubes

cloudiness /'klaudınıs/ *n* nebulosidad, *f*; obscuridad, *f*; (of liquids) turbiedad, *f*

cloudless /'klaudlıs/ *a* sin nubes, despejado; sereno, claro

cloudy /'klaudi/ *a* nublado, nubloso; obscuro; (of liquids) turbio

clout /klaut/ *n* Central America, Mexico arranque, *m*

clove /klouv/ *n* clavo de especia, *m*; (of garlic) diente de ajo, *m*. **c.-tree,** clavero, *m*

cloven /'klouvən/ *a* hendido. **to show the c. hoof,** enseñar la oreja. **c. hoof,** pezuña, *f*

clover /'klouvər/ *n* trébol, *m*. **to be in c.,** nadar en la abundancia

clown /klaun/ *n* patán, *m*; bufón, tonto, *m*; (in a circus) payaso, *m*. *vi* hacer el tonto, hacer el payaso

clowning /'klaunıŋ/ *n* payasada, *f*

clownish /'klaunıʃ/ *a* grosero; palurdo, zafio; bufón

cloy /klɔi/ *vt* empalagar

cloying /'klɔiıŋ/ *a* empalagoso

club /klʌb/ *n* porra, cachiporra, clava, *f*; (gymnastic) maza, *f*; (hockey) bastón de hockey, *m*; (golf) palo de golf, *m*; (in cards) basto, *m*; (social) club, *m*. *vt* golpear. **to c. together,** asociarse, unirse. **We clubbed together to buy him a present,** Entre todos le compramos un regalo. **c.-house,** club, *m*

clubfoot /'klʌb,fut/ *n* pie calcáneo, pie contrahecho, pie de piña, pie equino, pie talo, pie zambo, *m*

club member *n* miembro de un club, *m*

cluck /klʌk/ *vi* cloquear. *n* cloqueo, *m*

clucking /'klʌkıŋ/ *n* cloqueo, *m*

clue /klu/ *n* indicio, *m*; (to a problem) clave, *f*; (of a crossword) indicación, *f*; idea, *f*

clump /klʌmp/ *n* bloque, pedazo, *m*; (of trees) grupo, *m*; (of feet) ruido, *m*. *vi* caminar pisando fuerte

clumsily /'klʌmzəli/ *adv* torpemente; pesadamente

clumsiness /'klʌmzınıs/ *n* torpeza, *f*; falta de maña, *f*; pesadez, *f*

clumsy /'klʌmzi/ *a* torpe; desmañado; chapucero, sin arte; (lumbering) pesado; (in shape) disforme

cluster /'klʌstər/ *n* (of currants, etc.) racimo, *m*; (of flowers) ramillete, *m*; grupo, *m*. *vi* arracimarse; agruparse. **They clustered around him,** Se agrupaban a su alrededor

clutch /klʌtʃ/ *vt* agarrar; sujetar, apretar. *n Mech.* embrague, *m*; (of eggs) nidada, *f*; *Fig.* garras, *f pl*. **to fall into the clutches of,** caer en las garras de. **to make a c. at,** procurar agarrar. **to throw in the c.,** *Mech.* embragar. **to throw out the c.,** *Mech.* desembragar. **c. pedal,** pedal de embrague, *m*

clutter /'klʌtər/ *n* desorden, *m*, confusión, *f*, *vt* desordenar

coach /koutʃ/ *n* carroza, *f*; charabán, *m*; *Rail.* vagón, coche, *m*; (hackney) coche de alquiler, *m*; *Sports.* entrenador, *m*; (tutor) profesor particular, *m*. *vt Sports.* entrenar; (teach) preparar, dar lecciones particulares (a). **through c.,** coche directo, *m*. **c.-box,** pescante, *m*. **c.-house,** cochera, *f*

coaching /'koutʃıŋ/ *n Sports.* entrenamiento, *m*; lecciones particulares, *f pl*

coachman /'koutʃmən/ *n* cochero, *m*

coagulate /kou'ægyə,leit/ *vi* coagularse. *vt* coagular, cuajar

coagulation /kou,ægyə'leiʃən/ *n* coagulación, *f*

coal /koul/ *n* carbón, *m*; pedazo de carbón, *m*; (burning) brasa, *f*. *vi* carbonear, hacer carbón. *vt* proveer de carbón; carbonear. **to carry coals to Newcastle,** llevar leña al monte, elevar aqua al mar. **to rake a person over the coals,** reprender a alguien. **c.-barge,** (barco) carbonero, *m*. **c.-black,** negro como el azabache, *m*. **c.-cellar, house,** carbonera, *f*. **c.-dust,** cisco, *m*. **c.-field,** yacimiento de carbón, *m*. **c.-gas,** gas de hulla, *m*. **c.-heaver,** cargador de carbón, *m*. **c.-merchant,** carbonero, *m*. **c.-mine,** mina de carbón, *f*. **c.-miner,** minero de carbón, *m*. **c.-scuttle,** carbonera, *f*. **c.-tar,** alquitrán mineral, *m*

coalesce /,kouə'les/ *vi* fundirse; unirse; incorporarse

coalescence /,kouə'lesəns/ *n* fusión, *f*; unión, *f*; incorporación, *f*

coalition /,kouə'lıʃən/ *n* coalición, *f*

coarse /kɔrs/ *a* (in texture) basto, burdo; tosco; (gross) grosero; vulgar. **c.-grained,** de fibra gruesa, (of persons) vulgar, poco fino. **c. woolen cloth** Chile litro *m*

coarsen /'kɔrsən/ *vt* (of persons) embrutecer. *vi* embrutecerse; (of the skin) curtirse

coarseness /'kɔrsnıs/ *n* basteza, *f*; tosquedad, *f*; (of persons) grosería, indelicadeza, *f*; vulgaridad, *f*

coast /koust/ *n* costa, *f*; litoral, *m*. *vi* costear; deslizarse en un tobogán; dejar muerto el motor. **The c. is**

not clear, Hay moros en la costa. **c.-guard,** guardacostas, *m*. **c.-line,** litoral, *m*
coastal /'koʊstl̩/ *a* costanero, costero. **c. defences,** defensas costeras, *f pl*
coaster /'koʊstər/ *n Naut.* barco costanero, barco de cabotaje, *m*
coasting /'koʊstɪŋ/ *n Naut.* cabotaje, *m*
coat /koʊt/ *n* abrigo, *m*; gabán, *m*; chaqueta, *f*; (animal's) capa, *f*; (of paint) mano, *f*. *vt* recubrir; (with paint, etc.) dar una mano de. **fur c.,** abrigo de pieles, *m*. **sports c.,** Americana sport, *f*. **c. of arms,** escudo de armas, *m*. **c. of mail,** cota de malla, *f*. **c.-hanger,** percha, *f*
coating /'koʊtɪŋ/ *n* (of paint, etc.) capa, mano, *f*
co-author /,koʊ'ɔθər/ *n* coautor, *m*
coax /koʊks/ *vt* instar; halagar, engatusar, *Lat. Am. also* engaratusar; persuadir (a)
coaxing /'koʊksɪŋ/ *n* ruegos, *m pl*; mimos, *m pl*, caricias, *f pl*; persuasión, *f*. *a* mimoso, zalamero; persuasivo
cob /kɒb/ *n* (horse) jaca, *f*; (lump) pedazo, *m*; (swan) cisne macho, *m*
cobalt /'koʊbɔlt/ *n* cobalto, *m*. **c. blue,** azul cobalto, *m*
cobble /'kɒbəl/ *n* (stone) guijarro, *m*, *vt* (with stones) empedrar con guijarros; (shoes) remendar
cobbler /'kɒblər/ *n* zapatero remendón, *m*. **cobbler's last,** horma, *f*. **cobbler's wax,** cerote, *m*
cobblestone /'kɒbəl,stoʊn/ *n* guijarro, *m*, piedra, *f*
cobelligerent /,koʊbə'lɪdʒərənt/ *n* cobeligerante, *mf*
cobra /'koʊbrə/ *n* cobra, serpiente de anteojos, *f*
cobweb /'kɒb,wɛb/ *n* telaraña, *f*
cobwebby /'kɒb,wɛbi/ *a* cubierto de telarañas; transparente; de gasa
cocaine /koʊ'keɪn/ *n* cocaína, *f*
coccyx /'kɒksɪks/ *n* cóccix, *m*, *inf* rabadilla, *f*
cochlea /'kɒkliə/ *n* caracol (del oído), *m*
cock /kɒk/ *n* gallo, *m*; (male) macho, *m*; (tap) grifo, *m*, espita, *f*; (of a gun) martillo, *m*; (weather-vane) veleta, *f*; (of hay) montón, *m*. *vt* (a gun) amartillar; (a hat) ladear; (raise) erguir, enderezar. **a cocked hat,** un sombrero de tres picos. **at half c.,** (of a gun) desamartillada *f*. **He cocked his head,** Erguió la cabeza. **The dog cocked its ears,** El perro aguzó las orejas. **to c. one's eye at,** lanzar una mirada (a). **c.-a-doodle-doo,** quiquiriquí, *m*. **c.-a-hoop,** triunfante, jubiloso; arrogante. **c.-crow,** canto del gallo, *m*. **c.-fight,** riña de gallos, *f*. **c.-of-the-walk,** gallito, *m*. **c.-sure,** pagado de sí mismo; completamente convencido
cockerel /'kɒkərəl/ *n* gallo joven, gallito, *m*
cocker spaniel /,kɒkər 'spænyəl/ *n* cóquer, *m*
cockle /'kɒkəl/ *n* (bivalve) bucarda, *f*. *vi* arrugarse; (warp) torcerse; doblarse. **c.-shell,** (pilgrims') concha, *f*; (boat) cascarón de nuez, *m*
Cockney /'kɒkni/ *a* londinense, de Londres. *n* londinense, *mf*
cockpit /'kɒk,pɪt/ *n* gallería, *f*; *Aer.* casilla del piloto, *f*; *Fig.* arena, *f*
cockroach /'kɒk,roʊtʃ/ *n* cucaracha, *f*
cockscomb /'kɒks,koʊm/ *n* cresta de gallo, *f*
cocktail /'kɒk,teɪl/ *n* (drink) cótel, coctel, *m*. **to shake a c.,** mezclar un coctel. **c. party,** coctel *m*. **c. shaker,** cotelera, *f*
cocky /'kɒki/ *a* fatuo; presuntuoso
cocoa /'koʊkoʊ/ *n* cacao, *m*
coconut /'koʊkə,nʌt/ *n* coco, *m*; *Inf.* cabeza, *f*. **c. milk,** agua de coco, *f*. **c. shy,** pim, pam, pum, *m*. **c. tree,** cocotero, *m*
cocoon /kə'kun/ *n* capullo, *m*
cod /kɒd/ *n* bacalao, *m*. **cod-liver oil,** aceite de hígado de bacalao, *m*
coddle /'kɒdl̩/ *vt* criar con mimo, mimar, consentir
code /koʊd/ *n* código, *m*; clave, *f*; (secret) cifra, *f*. *vt* poner en cifra. **signal c.,** *Naut.* código de señales, *m*. **c. word,** palabra de clave, *f*
codeine /'koʊdin/ *n* codeína, *f*
codex /'koʊdɛks/ *n* códice, *m*
codicil /'kɒdɪsɪl/ *n* codicilio, *m*
codification /,kɒdəfɪ'keɪʃən/ *n* codificación, *f*
codify /'kɒdə,faɪ/ *vt* codificar

coeducation /,koʊɛdʒʊ'keɪʃən/ *n* coeducación, *f*
coefficient /,koʊə'fɪʃənt/ *n* coeficiente, *m*
coequality /,koʊɪ'kwɒlɪti/ *n* coigualdad, *f*
coerce /koʊ'ɜrs/ *vt* forzar, obligar; constreñir
coercion /koʊ'ɜrʃən/ *n* coerción, coacción, *f*
coercive /koʊ'ɜrsɪv/ *a* coercitivo, coactivo
coeval /koʊ'ivəl/ *a* coevo
coexist /,koʊɪg'zɪst/ *vi* coexistir
coexistence /,koʊɪg'zɪstəns/ *n* coexistencia, *f*
coffee /'kɔfi/ *n* café, *m*. **black c.,** café solo, *m*. **white c.,** café con leche, *m*. **c.-bean,** grano de café, *m*. **c.-cup,** taza para café, *f*. **c.-house,** café, *m*. **c.-mill,** molinillo de café, *m*. **c.-plantation,** cafetal, *m*. **c.-pot,** cafetera, *f*. **c.-set,** juego de café, *m*. **c.-tree,** cafeto, *m*
coffer /'kɔfər/ *n* cofre, *m*; arca, caja, *f*
coffin /'kɔfɪn/ *n* ataúd, féretro, *m*; caja, *f*
cog /kɒg/ *n Mech.* diente (de rueda), *m*
cogency /'koʊdʒənsi/ *n* fuerza, *f*
cogent /'koʊdʒənt/ *a* convincente, fuerte; urgente
cogitate /'kɒdʒɪ,teɪt/ *vi* pensar, considerar, meditar
cogitation /,kɒdʒɪ'teɪʃən/ *n* reflexión, meditación, consideración, *f*
cognac /'koʊnyæk/ *n* coñac, *m*
cognate /'kɒgneɪt/ *a* (of stock) consanguíneo; afín; análogo; semejante
cognition /kɒg'nɪʃən/ *n* cognición, *f*
cognitive /'kɒgnɪtɪv/ *a* cognoscitivo. **c. science,** las ciencias cognoscitivas, *f pl*
cognizance /'kɒgnəzəns/ *n* conocimiento, *m*; jurisdicción, *f*
cogwheel /'kɒg,wil/ *n* rueda dentada, *f*
cohabit /koʊ'hæbɪt/ *vi* cohabitar
cohabitation /koʊ,hæbɪ'teɪʃən/ *n* cohabitación, *f*
coheir /koʊ'ɛr/ *n* coheredero, *m*
coheiress /koʊ'ɛrɪs/ *n* coheredera, *f*
cohere /koʊ'hɪər/ *vi* pegarse, adherirse; unirse
coherent /koʊ'hɪərənt/ *a* coherente; consecuente
cohesion /koʊ'hiʒən/ *n* cohesión, *f*; coherencia, *f*
cohort /'koʊhɔrt/ *n* cohorte, *f*
coif /kwɑf/ *n* cofia, *f*; toca, *f*
coiffure /kwɑ'fyʊr/ *n* peinado, *m*; tocado, *m*
coil /kɔɪl/ *vt* arrollar; (*Naut.* of ropes) adujar. *vi* arrollarse; enroscarse; serpentear. *n* rollo, *m*; (of a serpent and ropes) anillo, *m*; (of hair) trenza, *f*; *Elec.* carrete, *m*. **coil of smoke,** nube de humo, *f*. **to c. up,** hacerse un ovillo
coiling /'kɔɪlɪŋ/ *n* arrollamiento, *m*; serpenteo, *m*
coin /kɔɪn/ *n* moneda, *f*; *Inf.* dinero, *m*. *vt* acuñar; (a new word) inventar. **to pay back in the same c.,** pagar en la misma moneda
coinage /'kɔɪnɪdʒ/ *n* acuñación, *f*; moneda, *f*; sistema monetario, *m*; invención, *f*; (new word) neologismo, *m*
coincide /,koʊɪn'saɪd/ *vi* coincidir (con); estar conforme, estar de acuerdo
coincidence /koʊ'ɪnsɪdəns/ *n* coincidencia, *f*; (chance) casualidad, *f*
coiner /'kɔɪnər/ *n* acuñador de moneda, *m*; monedero falso, *m*; (of phrases, etc.) inventor, *m*
coitus /'koʊɪtəs/ *n* coito, *m*
coke /koʊk/ *n* (carbón de) coque, *m*
colander /'kɒləndər/ *n* colador, *m*
cold /koʊld/ *a* frío. *n* frío, *m*; *Med.* catarro, constipado, *m*. **I am c.,** Tengo frío. **It is c.,** Está frío. (weather) Hace frío. **to catch a c.,** acatarrarse, resfriarse. **to grow c.,** enfriarse; (of the weather) empezar a hacer frío. **in c. blood,** a sangre fría. **c.-blooded,** (fishes, etc.) de sangre fría; (chilly, of persons) friolero; (pitiless) insensible, sin piedad; (of actions) a sangre fría, premeditado. **c.-chisel,** cortafrío, *m*. **c. cream,** crema (para el cutis), *f*. **c.-hearted,** seco, insensible. **c.-shoulder,** *n* frialdad, *f*. *vt* tratar con frialdad (a). **c.-storage,** conservación refrigerada, *f*
coldly /'koʊldli/ *adv* fríamente
coldness /'koʊldnɪs/ *n* frío, *m*; (of one's reception, etc.) frialdad, *f*; (of heart) inhumanidad, *f*
coleopterous /,koʊli'ɒptərəs/ *a* coleóptero
colic /'kɒlɪk/ *n* cólico, *m*
coliseum /,kɒlɪ'siəm/ *n* coliseo, *m*
colitis /kə'laɪtɪs/ *n* colitis, *f*
collaborate /kə'læbə,reɪt/ *vi* colaborar (con)

collaboration /kə,læbə'reɪʃən/ n colaboración, f
collaborationist /kə,læbə'reɪʃənɪst/ n colaboracionista, mf
collaborator /kə'læbə,reɪtər/ n colaborador (-ra); (quisling) colaboracionista, mf
collapse /kə'læps/ n derrumbamiento, m; desplome, m; Med. colapso, m; (of buildings and Fig.) hundimiento, m; (of plans) frustración, f; (failure) fracaso, m. vi derrumbarse; (of buildings, etc.) hundirse, venirse abajo; (of persons, fall) desplomarse; Med. sufrir colapso; (of plans, etc.) frustrarse, venirse abajo. **George came to us after the c. of France,** Jorge vino a quedarse con nosotros después del hundimiento de Francia
collapsible /kə'læpsəbəl/ a plegable
collar /'kɒlər/ n (of a garment and of fur) cuello, m; (of a dog, etc., and necklace) collar, m. vt (seize) agarrar. **detachable c.,** cuello suelto, m. **high c.,** alzacuello, m. **c.-bone,** clavícula, f
collate /kou'leit/ vt cotejar; (to a benefice) colacionar
collateral /kə'lætərəl/ a colateral
collation /kə'leiʃən/ n colación, f
colleague /'kɒlig/ n colega, m; compañero (-ra)
collect /'kɒlekt/ vt (assemble) reunir; (catch) coger; acumular; (call for) pasar a buscar, ir (or venir) a buscar; (pick up) recoger; (taxes, etc.) recaudar; coleccionar; (one's strength, etc. and debts, etc.) cobrar; (letters) recoger. vi reunirse, congregarse; acumularse. n Eccl. colecta, f. **to c. oneself,** reponerse
collected /kə'lektɪd/ a (of persons) seguro de sí.
collection /kə'lekʃən/ n reunión, f; (of data, etc.) acumulación, f; (of pictures, stamps, etc.) colección, f; (of a debt, etc.) cobranza, f; (of taxes, etc.) recaudación, f; (from a mail box) recogida, f; (of laws, etc.) compilación, f; Eccl. ofertorio, m; (of donations) colecta, f
collection agency n agencia de cobros de cuentas, f
collective /kə'lektɪv/ a colectivo. **c. bargaining,** regateo colectivo, trato colectivo, m
collectivism /kə'lektə,vɪzəm/ n colectivismo, m
collector /kə'lektər/ n (of pictures, etc.) coleccionador (-ra), coleccionista, mf; cobrador, m; Elec. colector, m
college /'kɒlɪdʒ/ n colegio, m; escuela, f; universidad, f. **C. of Cardinals,** Colegio de Cardenales, m
collegiate /kə'lidʒɪt/ a colegial, colegiado. **c. church,** iglesia colegial, f
collide /kə'laid/ vi chocar (contra), topar (con); estar en conflicto (con). **c. head-on,** chocar frontalmente
collie /'kɒli/ n perro de pastor escocés, m
collier /'kɒlyər/ n minero de carbón, m; (barco) carbonero, m
collision /kə'lɪʒən/ n choque, m, colisión, f; (of interests, etc.) antagonismo, conflicto, m. **to come into c. with,** chocar con
colloid /'kɒlɔid/ a coloide. n coloide, m
colloquial /kə'loukwiəl/ a familiar
colloquialism /kə'loukwiə,lɪzəm/ n expresión familiar, f
colloquially /kə'loukwiəli/ adv en lenguaje familiar; familiarmente
colloquy /'kɒləkwi/ n coloquio, m
collusion /kə'luʒən/ n colusión, f. **to be in c.,** Law. coludir; conspirar, estar de manga
Colombia /kə'lʌmbiə/ Colombia, f
Colombian /kə'lʌmbiən/ a colombiano. n colombiano (-na)
colon /'koulən/ n Anat. colon, m; (punctuation) dos puntos, m pl
colonel /'kɜrnl/ n coronel, m
colonial /kə'louniəl/ a colonial. n habitante de las colonias, m. **c. government,** Lat. Am. coloniaje, m. **C. Office,** Ministerio de Asuntos Coloniales, m. **c. period,** Lat. Am. coloniaje, m
colonist /'kɒlənɪst/ n colono, m; colonizador (-ra)
colonization /,kɒlənə'zeɪʃən/ n colonización, f
colonize /'kɒlə,naiz/ vt colonizar. vi establecerse en una colonia
colonizer /'kɒlə,naizər/ n colonizador (-ra)
colonizing /'kɒlə,naizɪŋ/ n colonización, f, a colonizador

colonnade /,kɒlə'neid/ n columnata, f
colony /'kɒləni/ n colonia, f
color /'kʌlər/ n color, m; colorido, m; tinta, f; materia colorante, f; pl **colors,** insignia, f; bandera, f, estandarte, m; Naut. pabellón, m. vt colorar; pintar; iluminar; (influence) influir, afectar. vi colorarse; ruborizarse; encenderse. **fast c.,** color estable, color sólido, m. **regimental colors,** bandera del regimiento, f. **with colors flying,** con tambor batiente, a banderas desplegadas. **to be off c.,** estar malucho, estar indispuesto. **to change c.,** (of persons) mudar de color, mudar de semblante. **to give c. to,** (a story, etc.) hacer verosímil. **to lay the colors on too thick,** recargar las tintas. **to pass with flying colors,** salir triunfante. **under c. of,** so color de, a pretexto de. **c.-blind,** daltoniano. **c.-blindness,** daltonismo, m
Colorado beetle /,kɒlə'rɑdou/ n escarabajo de la patata, m
colored /'kʌlərd/ a colorado; de color
coloring /'kʌlərɪŋ/ n (substance) colorante, m; (act of) coloración, f; Art. colorido, m; (of complexion) colores, m pl
colorist /'kʌlərɪst/ n colorista, mf
colorless /'kʌlərlɪs/ a sin color, incoloro; Fig. insípido
colossal /kə'lɒsəl/ a colosal, gigantesco; enorme; Inf. estupendo
colossus /kə'lɒsəs/ n coloso, m
colt /koult/ n potro, m; (boy) muchacho alegre, m
colt's-foot /'koults,fut/ n Bot. fárfara, f
columbine /'kɒləm,bain/ n Bot. aguileña, f; (in pantomime) Colombina, f
column /'kɒləm/ n columna, f. **Fifth c.,** quinta columna, f
columned /'kɒləmd/ a con columnas
columnist /'kɒləmnɪst/ n periodista, m
coma /'koumə/ n coma, m
comatose /'koumə,tous/ a comatoso
comb /koum/ n peine, m; (for flax) carda, f; (curry) almohaza, f; (of cock) cresta, carúncula, f; (of a wave) cima, cresta, f; (honey) panal, m, vt (hair) peinar; (flax) rastrillar, cardar. **c. and brush,** cepillo y peine. **high c.,** peineta, f. **to c. one's hair,** peinarse
combat /v kəm'bæt; n 'kɒmbæt/ vt luchar contra, combatir, resistir. vi combatir, pelear. n combate, m; lucha, batalla, f. **in single c.,** cuerpo a cuerpo
combatant /kəm'bætnt/ n combatiente, m, a combatiente
combative /kəm'bætɪv/ a belicoso, pugnaz
combination /,kɒmbə'neiʃən/ n combinación, f; mezcla, f; unión, f; asociación, f; pl **combinations,** camisa pantalón, f. **c. lock,** cerradura de combinación, f
combine /v kəm'bain; n 'kɒmbain/ vt combinar; reunir, juntar; Chem. combinar. vi combinarse; asociarse (con); Com. fusionarse. n asociación, f; Com. monopolio, m
combustible /kəm'bʌstəbəl/ a combustible. n combustible, m
combustion /kəm'bʌstʃən/ n combustión, f. **rapid c.,** combustión rápida, f. **spontaneous c.,** combustión espontánea, f
come /kʌm/ vi venir; llegar; avanzar; acercarse; (happen) suceder, acontecer; (result) resultar; (find oneself) encontrarse, hallarse; (become) llegar a ser; (begin to) ponerse (a), empezar (a). **Coming!** ¡Voy! ¡Allá voy! **C., c.!** ¡Vamos! ¡No es para tanto! ¡Ánimo! **I am ready whatever comes,** Estoy preparado venga lo que venga. **He comes of a good family,** Es (Viene) de buena familia. **I came to know him well,** Llegué a conocerle bien. **I don't know what came over me,** No sé lo que me pasó. **When I came to it,** Cuando me puse a considerarlo. **The bill comes to six thousand pesetas,** La cuenta sale a seis mil pesetas. **He comes up before the judge tomorrow,** Ha de comparecer ante el juez mañana. **What you say comes to this,** Lo que dice Vd. se reduce a esto. **What is the world coming to?** ¿A dónde va parar el mundo? **It does not b within my scope,** No está dentro de mi alcance. **to c. apart,** deshacerse; romperse; dividirse. **to c. home to,** Fig. impresionar mucho, tocar en lo más íntimo; hacer comprender

(a). **to c. into bloom,** empezar a tener flores, florecer. **to c. into one's head,** venir a las mientes. **to c. into the world,** venir al mundo. **to c. near,** acercarse; aproximarse, estar próximo. **to c. next,** venir después; suceder luego. **to c. to an end,** terminar, acabarse. **to c. to blows,** venir a las manos. **to c. to grief,** salir mal parado; (of schemes, etc.) malograrse. **to c. to hand,** venir a mano; (of letters) llegar a las manos (de). **to c. to life,** despertar; animarse; resucitarse. **to c. to nothing,** frustrarse; no quedar en nada. **to c. to pass,** suceder; realizarse. **to c. to terms,** ponerse de acuerdo. **to c. true,** cumplirse, verificarse. **to c. about,** suceder, acontecer, tener lugar; (of the wind) girar. **to c. across,** dar con, encontrar por casualidad; tropezar con. **to c. after,** (a situation) solicitar; (follow) seguir (a); venir más tarde (que); (succeed) suceder. **to c. again,** volver. **to c. along,** caminar (por); andar (por); (arrive) llegar. **C. along!** ¡Vamos! ¡Andamos! **to c. at,** alcanzar; (attack) embestir, atacar; (gain) obtener, adquirir. **to c. away,** irse, marcharse; (break) deshacerse. **to c. back,** volver, regresar, *Lat. Am.* devolverse **c.-back,** *Inf.* respuesta, *f;* contraataque, *m.* **to c. before,** llegar antes; preceder (a). **to c. between,** interponerse (entre), intervenir. **to c. by,** pasar por, pasar junto a; (acquire) obtener, adquirir; (achieve) conseguir. **to c. down,** bajar, descender; (in the world) venir a menos; (be demolished) demolerse; (collapse) derrumbarse, hundirse; (of prices) bajar; (of traditions, etc.) llegar e.g. *This work has c. down to us in two fifteenth-century manuscripts* Esta obra nos ha llegado en dos manuscritos del siglo quince; (fall) caer. **c.-down,** *n* caída, *f;* frustración, *f;* desengaño, *m;* desprestigio, *m;* pérdida de posición, *f.* **to c. down on a person,** cantar la cartilla (a). **to c. down with altitude sickness** *Peru* asorocharse **to c. forward,** avanzar, adelantarse; (offer) ofrecerse; presentarse. **to c. in,** entrar; (of money) ingresar; (of trains, etc.) llegar; (of the tide) crecer; (of the new year) empezar; (of fashion) ponerse de moda; (be useful) servir (para). **C. in!** ¡Adelante! ¡Pase Vd.! **to c. into,** (a scheme) asociarse con; (property) heredar; (the mind) presentarse a la imaginación, ocurrirse (a). **to c. off,** (happen) tener lugar; realizarse, efectuarse; (be successful) tener éxito; (break off) separarse (de); romperse. **to c. off well,** tener éxito; (of persons) salir bien. **c. off the press,** salir de prensas. **to c. on,** avanzar; (of actors) salir a la escena; (progress) hacer progresos; (develop) desarrollarse; (of pain, etc.) acometer (a); (arrive) llegar; (of a lawsuit) verse. **C. on!** ¡Vamos! ¡En marcha! **to c. out,** salir; (of stars) nacer; (of buds, etc.) brotar; (of the moon, etc.) asomarse; (of stains) borrarse; (of a book) ver la luz, publicarse; (of secrets) divulgarse, saberse; (of a girl, in society) ponerse de largo; (on strike) declararse en huelga; (of fashions, etc.) aparecer. **to c. out with,** (a remark) soltar; (oaths, etc.) prorrumpir (en); (disclose) revelar, hacer público. **to c. round,** (to see someone) venir a ver (a); (coax) engatusar; (after a faint, etc.) volver en sí; (after illness) reponerse; (to another's point of view) aceptar, compartir. **to c. through,** pasar por; (trials, etc.) salir; salir de; (of liquids) salirse. **to c. to,** volver en sí. **to c. together,** reunirse, juntarse; venir juntos; unirse. **to c. under,** venir (o estar) bajo la jurisdicción de; (the influence of) estar dominado por; (figure among) figurar entre, estar comprendido en. **to c. up,** subir; (of sun, moon) salir; (of plants) brotar; (of problems, etc.) surgir; (in conversation) discutirse; (before a court) comparecer. **to c. up to,** (equal) igualar, ser igual (a); rivalizar con; (in height) llegar hasta. **He came up to them in the street,** Les abordó (o se les acercó) en la calle. **We have c. up against many difficulties,** Hemos tropezado con muchas dificultades. **This novel does not c. up to his last,** Esta última novela no es tan buena como la anterior. **The party did not c. up to their expectations,** La reunión no fue tan divertida como esperaban. **to c. up with,** idear, (a person) alcanzar (a). **to c. upon,** encontrar, hallar; tropezar con; encontrar por casualidad. **to c. upon evil days,** venir a menos

comedian /kə'midiən/ *n* actor cómico, comediante, *m*

comedy /'kɒmɪdi/ *n* comedia, *f.* **c. of manners,** comedia de costumbres, *f*

comeliness /'kʌmlinɪs/ *n* hermosura, *f*

comely /'kʌmli/ *a* hermoso

comer /'kʌmər/ *n* el, *m,* (*f,* la) que viene. **all comers,** todo el mundo. **first c.,** primer (-ra) venido (-da)

comet /'kɒmɪt/ *n* cometa, *m*

comfort /'kʌmfərt/ *vt* consolar, confortar; (encourage) animar; (reassure) alegrar. *n* consuelo, *m;* satisfacción, *f;* comodidad, *f;* bienestar, *m.* **He lives in great c.,** Vive con mucha comodidad. **c.-loving,** comodón

comfortable /'kʌmftəbəl/ *a* cómodo; (with income) suficiente; (consoling) consolador. **to make oneself c.,** ponerse cómodo

comfortably /'kʌmftəbli/ *adv* cómodamente; suficientemente; fácilmente; con facilidad; (well) bien. **He is c. off,** Está bien de dinero

comforter /'kʌmfərtər/ *n* consolador (-ra); (scarf) bufanda, *f*

comforting /'kʌmfərtɪŋ/ *a* consolador

comfortless /'kʌmfərtlɪs/ *a* incómodo, sin comodidad; desconsolador; (of persons) inconsolable, desconsolado

comic /'kɒmɪk/ *a* cómico; bufo; satírico. *n* cómico, *m;* *pl* **comics,** (printed) historietas cómicas, *f pl.* **c. opera,** ópera cómicas, *f*

comical /'kɒmɪkəl/ *a* cómico; divertido, gracioso

coming /'kʌmɪŋ/ *a* (with year, etc.) próximo, que viene; (promising) de porvenir; (approaching) que se acerca. *n* venida, *f;* llegada, *f;* advenimiento, *m.* **c.-out party,** puesta de largo, *f.* **comings and goings,** entradas y salidas, *f pl*

comma /'kɒmə/ *n* coma, *f.* **inverted commas,** comillas, *f pl*

command /kə'mænd/ *vt* mandar, ordenar; (silence, respect, etc.) imponer; (an army, fleet, etc.) comandar; capitanear; (one's emotions) dominar; (have at one's disposal) disponer de; (a military position, view) dominar; (sympathy, etc.) despertar, merecer; (of price) venderse por. *vi* mandar. *n* orden, *f;* (*Mil. Nav.*) mando, *m;* (of an army, etc.) comandancia, *f;* (of one's emotions, etc.) dominio, *m;* (of a military position, etc.) dominación, *f;* disposición, *f.* **At your c.,** A sus órdenes. **By Royal C.,** Por Real Orden; (of shops, etc.) Proveedor de la Real Casa. **word of c.,** orden, *f*

commandant /,kɒmən'dænt/ *n* comandante, *m*

commandeer /,kɒmən'dɪər/ *vt* (conscript) reclutar; *Mil.* requisar; expropiar

commander /kə'mændər/ *n* *Mil.* comandante, *m;* *Nav.* capitán de fragata, *m;* (of order of Knighthood) comendador, *m.* **c.-in-chief,** generalísimo, *m.* **C. of the Faithful,** Comendador de los creyentes, *m*

commanding /kə'mændɪŋ/ *a* *Mil.* comandante; imponente; (of manner) imperioso; dominante. **c. officer,** comandante en jefe, *m*

commandment /kə'mændmənt/ *n* precepto, mandamiento, *m.* **the Ten Commandments,** los diez mandamientos

commando /kə'mændou/ *n* *Mil.* comando, *m*

commemorate /kə'mɛmə,reit/ *vt* conmemorar

commemoration /kə,mɛmə'reiʃən/ *n* conmemoración, *f*

commemorative /kə'mɛmə,reitɪv/ *a* conmemorativo

commence /kə'mɛns/ *vt* comenzar, empezar, principiar. *vi* comenzar. **He commenced to eat,** Empezó a comer

commencement /kə'mɛnsmənt/ *n* principio, comienzo, *m*

commend /kə'mɛnd/ *vt* (entrust) encomendar; recomendar; alabar

commendable /kə'mɛndəbəl/ *a* loable; recomendable

commendation /,kɒmən'deiʃən/ *n* aprobación, alabanza, *f,* aplauso, *m*

commendatory /kə'mɛndə,tɔri/ *a* (of letters) comendatorio

commensurable /kə'mɛnsərəbəl/ *a* conmensurable

commensurate /kə'mɛnsərɪt/ *a* proporcionado (a); conforme (a)

comment /'kɒmɛnt/ *n* observación, *f;* (on a work)

comento, *m*; explicación, nota, *f*. *vi* hacer una observación (sobre); (a work) comentar, anotar. **to c. unfavorably on,** criticar
commentary /'kɒmən,teri/ *n* comentario, *m*; (on a person, etc.) comentos, *m pl*, observaciones, *f pl*
commentator /'kɒmən,teitər/ *n* comentador (-ra); (of a work) comentarista, *mf*
commerce /'kɒmərs/ *n* comercio, *m*; negocios, *m pl*; (social) trato, *m*
commercial /kə'mɜrʃəl/ *a* comercial; mercantil. **c. traveler,** viajante, *mf*
commercialism /kə'mɜrʃə,lɪzəm/ *n* mercantilismo, *m*
commercialize /kə'mɜrʃə,laiz/ *vt* hacer objeto de comercio
commercially /kə'mɜrʃəli/ *adv* comercialmente
commingle /kə'mɪŋgəl/ *vt* mezclar. *vi* mezclarse
commiserate /kə'mɪzə,reit/ *vi* compadecerse (de), apiadarse (de)
commiseration /kə,mɪzə'reiʃən/ *n* conmiseración, compasión, *f*
commissariat /,kɒmə'sɛəriət/ *n* comisaría, *f*; *Inf*. despensa, *f*
commissary /'kɒmə,sɛri/ *n* comisario, *m*
commission /kə'mɪʃən/ *n* comisión, *f*; *Mil*. graduación de oficial, *f*. *vt* comisionar; (a ship) poner en servicio activo, armar; (appoint) nombrar. **in c.,** en servicio, activo. **out of c.,** (of ships) inutilizado; inservible. **c. agent,** comisionista, *mf* **to gain one's c.,** *Mil*. graduarse de oficial. **to put out of c.,** retirar del servicio; poner fuera de combate; estropear
commissionaire /kə,mɪʃə'nɛər/ *n* portero, *m*
commissioned /kə'mɪʃənd/ *a* comisionado. **c. officer,** oficial, *m*
commissioner /kə'mɪʃənər/ *n* comisario, *m*. **High C.,** alto comisario, *m*. **c. for oaths,** notario, *m*. **c. of police,** jefe de policía, *m*
commit /kə'mɪt/ *vt* entregar (a); (a crime) cometer; (to prison) encarcelar; (for trial) remitir. **to c. oneself,** comprometerse. **to c. to memory,** aprender de memoria. **to c. to writing,** poner por escrito
commitment /kə'mɪtmənt/ *n* (financial, etc.) obligación, responsabilidad, *f*; compromiso, *m*
committal /kə'mɪtl/ *n* (of an offense) comisión, *f*; (placing, entrusting) entrega, *f*; (to prison) encarcelamiento, *m*; (legal procedure) auto de prisión, *m*
committee /kə'mɪti/ *n* comité, *m*; comisión, junta, *f*; consejo, *m*. **They decided in c.,** Tomaron la resolución en comité. **c. of management,** consejo de administración, *m*
commodious /kə'moudiəs/ *a* espacioso, grande
commodiousness /kə'moudiəsnɪs/ *n* espaciosidad, *f*
commodity /kə'mɒdɪti/ *n* artículo, *m*, mercancía, *f*
commodore /'kɒmə,dɔr/ *n* *Nav*. jefe de escuadra, *m*; comodoro, *m*
common /'kɒmən/ *a* común; general, corriente; universal; vulgar; (disparaging) cursi; (elementary) elemental. *n* pastos comunes, *m pl*. **He is not a c. man,** No es un hombre cualquiera; No es un hombre vulgar. **in c.,** en común. **the c. man,** el hombre medio. **the c. people,** el pueblo. **c. sense,** sentido común, *m*. **c. soldier,** soldado raso, *m*. **c. speech,** lenguaje vulgar, *m*. **c. usage,** uso corriente, *m*
commoner /'kɒmənər/ *n* plebeyo (-ya)
commonly /'kɒmənli/ *adv* comúnmente, por lo general
commonness /'kɒmənnɪs/ *n* frecuencia, *f*; vulgaridad, *f*
commonplace /'kɒmən,pleis/ *n* lugar común, *m*; trivialidad, *f*. *a* trivial
commons /'kɒmənz/ *n* el pueblo; (House of) Cámara de los Comunes, *f*; (food) provisiones, *f pl*. **to be on short c.,** comer mal, estar mal alimentado
Commonwealth /'kɒmən,wɛlθ/ *n* estado, *m*; república, *f*; comunidad (de naciones), *f*; mancomunidad, *f*. **the Commonwealth of Puerto Rico,** el Estado Libre Asociado de Puerto Rico, *m*
commotion /kə'mouʃən/ *n* confusión, *f*; conmoción, perturbación, *f*; tumulto, *m*
communal /kə'myunl/ *a* comunal
commune /'kɒmyun/ *n* comuna, *f*. *vi* conversar (con). **to c. with oneself,** hablar consigo

communicable /kə'myunɪkəbəl/ *a* comunicable
communicant /kə'myunɪkənt/ *n* *Eccl*. comulgante, *mf*; (of information) informante, *mf*
communicate /kə'myunɪ,keit/ *vt* comunicar; (diseases) transmitir. *vi* comunicarse (con); *Eccl*. comulgar
communication /kə,myunɪ'keiʃən/ *n* comunicación, *f*. **lines of c.,** comunicaciones, *f pl*. **to get into c. with,** ponerse en comunicación con. **c.-cord,** (in a railway carriage) timbre de alarma, *m*
communicative /kə'myunɪ,keitɪv/ *a* comunicativo; expansivo
communicativeness /kə'myunɪ,keitɪvnɪs/ *n* carácter expansivo, *m*; locuacidad, *f*
communion /kə'myunyən/ *n* comunión, *f*. **Holy c.,** comunión, *f*. **to take c.,** comulgar. **c. card,** cédula de comunión, *f*. **c. cup,** cáliz, *f*. **c. table,** sagrada mesa, *f*; altar, *m*
communiqué /kə,myunɪ'kei/ *n* comunicación, parte, *f*. **to issue a c.,** dar parte
communism /'kɒmyə,nɪzəm/ *n* comunismo, *m*
communist /'kɒmyənɪst/ *n* comunista, *mf*. *a* comunista
community /kə'myunɪti/ *n* comunidad, *f*. **the c.,** la nación; el público. **c. center,** centro social, *m*
commutation /,kɒmyə'teiʃən/ *n* conmutación, *f*; reducción, *f*
commute /kə'myut/ *vt* conmutar; reducir
compact /*n* 'kɒmpækt; *a* kəm'pækt/ *n* (pact) acuerdo, pacto, *m*; (powder) polvorera, *f*. *a* compacto; firme; sólido; apretado, cerrado; (of persons) bien hecho; (of style) conciso, sucinto
compact disc (CD) *n* disco compacto, *m*
compactness /kəm'pæktnɪs/ *n* compacidad, *f*; (of style) concisión, *f*
companion /kəm'pænyən/ *n* compañero (-ra); camarada, *mf*; (of an Order) caballero, *m*, dama, *f*. *vt* acompañar. **lady c.,** señora de compañía, *f*. **c.-hatch,** cubierta de escotilla, *f*. **c.-ladder,** escala de toldilla, *f*
companionable /kəm'pænyənəbəl/ *a* sociable, amistoso
companionably /kəm'pænyənəbli/ *adv* sociablemente, amistosamente
companionship /kəm'pænyən,ʃɪp/ *n* compañía, *f*; compañerismo, *m*
company /'kʌmpəni/ *n* (*Com. Mil.* etc.) compañía, *f*; (ship's) tripulación, *f*. **I will keep you c.,** Te haré compañía. **to part c. with,** separarse de. **Present c. excepted!** ¡Mejorando lo presente! **They are not very good c.,** No son muy divertidos
company store *n* tienda de raya, *f* (Mexico)
comparable /'kɒmpərəbəl/ *a* comparable
comparably /'kɒmpərəbli/ *adv* comparablemente
comparative /kəm'pærətɪv/ *a* comparativo; relativo
comparatively /kəm'pærətɪvli/ *adv* comparativamente; relativamente
compare /kəm'pɛər/ *vt* comparar. *vi* compararse; poder compararse. ser comparable. **beyond c.,** sin comparación; sin igual. **to c. favorably with,** no perder por comparación con. **to c. notes,** cambiar impresiones
comparison /kəm'pærəsən/ *n* comparación, *f*. **in c. with,** comparado con
compartment /kəm'partmənt/ *n* compartimiento, *m*; *Rail*. departamento, *m*
compass /'kʌmpəs/ *n* circuito, *m*; límites, *m pl*; alcance, *m*; (of a voice) gama, *f*; *Naut*. brújula, *f*; *pl* **compasses,** compás, *m*, *vt* (achieve) conseguir; (plan) idear, **mariner's c.,** compás de mar, *m*, rosa de los vientos, *f*. **pocket c.,** brújula de bolsillo, *f*. **to c. about,** cercar, rodear
compassion /kəm'pæʃən/ *n* compasión, *f*. **to have c. on,** apiadarse de, compadecerse de
compassionate /kəm'pæʃənɪt/ *a* compasivo, piadoso. **c. leave,** permiso, *m*
compassionately /kəm'pæʃənɪtli/ *adv* compasivamente, con piedad
compatibility /kəm,pætə'bɪlɪti/ *n* compatibilidad, *f*
compatible /kəm'pætəbəl/ *a* compatible, conciliable
compatriot /kəm'peitriət/ *n* compatriota, *mf*
compel /kəm'pɛl/ *vt* obligar (a), forzar (a); exigir;

imponer. **His attitude compels respect,** Su actitud impone el respeto

compelling /kəm'pelɪŋ/ a compulsivo

compendious /kəm'pɛndiəs/ a compendioso, sucinto

compendium /kəm'pɛndiəm/ n compendio, m; resumen, m

compensate /'kɒmpən,seit/ vt compensar; (reward) recompensar; (for loss, etc.) indemnizar. **to c. for,** compensar; indemnizar contra

compensation /,kɒmpən'seiʃən/ n compensación, f; (reward) recompensa, f; (for loss, etc.) indemnización, f

compensatory /kəm'pɛnsə,tɔri/ a compensatorio

compete /kəm'pit/ vi competir (con); rivalizar; ser rivales; (in a competition) concurrir

competence /'kɒmpɪtəns/ n aptitud, f; capacidad, f; competencia, f

competent /'kɒmpɪtənt/ a competente; capaz

competently /'kɒmpɪtəntli/ adv competentemente

competition /,kɒmpɪ'tɪʃən/ n competencia, competición, rivalidad, f; emulación, f; (contest, etc.) concurso, m. **spirit of c.,** espíritu de competencia, m

competitive /kəm'pɛtɪtɪv/ a competidor; de competición. **c. examination,** oposición, f

competitor /kəm'pɛtɪtər/ n competidor (-ra)

compilation /,kɒmpə'leiʃən/ n compilación, f

compile /kəm'pail/ vt compilar

compiler /kəm'pailər/ n compilador (-ra)

complacence /kəm'pleisəns/ n complacencia, satisfacción, f; contento de sí mismo, m

complacent /kəm'pleisənt/ a satisfecho; pagado de sí mismo

complacently /kəm'pleisəntli/ adv con satisfacción

complain /kəm'plein/ vi quejarse; lamentarse; Law. querellarse. **He complains about everything,** Se queja de todo

complainant /kəm'pleinənt/ n Law. demandante, mf

complaint /kəm'pleint/ n queja, f; lamento, m; Law. demanda, f; (illness) enfermedad, f. **to lodge a c. (against),** quejarse (de)

complaisance /kəm'pleisəns/ n afabilidad, cortesía, f

complaisant /kəm'pleisənt/ a complaciente, cortés, afable; (of husbands) consentido, sufrido

complement /n 'kɒmpləmənt; v -,mɛnt/ n complemento, m; total, número completo, m. vt completar

complementary /,kɒmplə'mɛntəri/ a complementario

complete /kəm'plit/ a entero; completo; perfecto; acabado. vt completar; acabar; (happiness, etc.) coronar, poner el último toque (a); (years) cumplir; (forms) llenar

completely /kəm'plitli/ adv completamente, enteramente

completeness /kəm'plitnɪs/ n entereza, f; totalidad, f

completion /kəm'pliʃən/ n terminación, f, fin, m

complex /a kəm'plɛks; n 'kɒmplɛks/ a complejo. n complejo, m. **inferiority c.,** complejo de inferioridad, m

complexion /kəm'plɛkʃən/ n tez, f, cutis, m; Fig. carácter, m

complexity /kəm'plɛksɪti/ n complejidad, f

compliance /kəm'plaiəns/ n condescendencia, f; (subservience) sumisión, f; obediencia, f. **in c. with,** de acuerdo con, en conformidad con

compliant /kəm'plaiənt/ a condescendiente; sumiso, dócil; obediente

complicate /'kɒmplɪ,keit/ vt complicar

complicated /'kɒmplɪ,keitɪd/ a complejo; complicado; enredado

complication /,kɒmplɪ'keiʃən/ n complicación, f

complicity /kəm'plɪsɪti/ n complicidad, f. **c. in a crime,** complicidad en un crimen

compliment /n 'kɒmpləmənt; v -,mɛnt/ n cumplido, m, cortesía, f; requiebro, Inf. piropo, m; favor, m; honor, m; (greeting) saludo, m; (congratulation) felicitación, f. vt cumplimentar; requebrar; (flatter) adular, lisonjear; (congratulate) felicitar. **They did him the c. of reading his book,** Le hicieron el honor de leer su libro. **to pay compliments,** hacer cumplidos; Inf. echar piropos

complimentary /,kɒmplə'mɛntəri/ a lisonjero; galante. **c. ticket,** billete gratuito, m

comply /kəm'plai/ vi (with) cumplir, obedecer; conformarse (con); consentir

component /kəm'pounənt/ a componente. n componente, m

comport /kəm'pɔrt/ vt (oneself), comportarse

comportment /kəm'pɔrtmənt/ n comportamiento, m, conducta, f

compose /kəm'pouz/ vt (all meanings) componer. **to c. oneself,** serenarse, calmarse. **to c. one's features,** componer el semblante

composed /kəm'pouzd/ a sereno, tranquilo, sosegado

composer /kəm'pouzər/ n compositor (-ra)

composite /kəm'pɒzɪt/ a compuesto; mixto. n compuesto, m; Bot. planta compuesta, f

composition /,kɒmpə'zɪʃən/ n (all meanings) composición, f

compositor /kəm'pɒzɪtər/ n Print. cajista, mf

compost /'kɒmpoust/ n abono; estiércol, m

composure /kəm'pouʒər/ n tranquilidad, serenidad, calma, f; sangre fría, f, aplomo, m

compote /'kɒmpout/ n compota, f

compound /'kɒmpaund/ vt mezclar, componer; concertar. a compuesto. n compuesto, m; mixtura, f. **c. interest,** interés compuesto, m

comprehend /,kɒmprɪ'hɛnd/ vt comprender

comprehensible /,kɒmprɪ'hɛnsəbəl/ a comprensible

comprehensibly /,kɒmprɪ'hɛnsəbli/ adv comprensiblemente

comprehension /,kɒmprɪ'hɛnʃən/ n comprensión, f

comprehensive /,kɒmprɪ'hɛnsɪv/ a comprensivo

comprehensiveness /,kɒmprɪ'hɛnsɪvnɪs/ n alcance, m, extensión, f

compress /v kəm'prɛs; n 'kɒmprɛs/ vt comprimir; condensar; reducir, abreviar. n compresa, f

compression /kəm'prɛʃən/ n compresión, f

compressor /kəm'prɛsər/ n compresor, m

comprise /kəm'praiz/ vt comprender, abarcar, incluir

compromise /'kɒmprə,maiz/ n compromiso, m, transacción, f; componenda, f. vt (settle) componer, arreglar; (jeopardize) arriesgar; comprometer. vi transigir. **to c. oneself,** comprometerse

compromising /'kɒmprə,maizɪŋ/ a comprometedor

compulsion /kəm'pʌlʃən/ n compulsión, fuerza, f. **under c.,** a la fuerza

compulsory /kəm'pʌlsəri/ a obligatorio. **c. measures,** medidas obligatorias, f pl. **c. powers,** poderes absolutos, m pl

compunction /kəm'pʌŋkʃən/ n compunción, f, remordimiento, m; escrúpulo, m. **without c.,** sin escrúpulo

computable /kəm'pyutəbəl/ a calculable

computation /,kɒmpyu'teiʃən/ n computación, f, cómputo, m

compute /kəm'pyut/ vt computar, calcular

computer /kəm'pyutər/ m West. Hem. computador (-ra), Spain ordenador, m

computer center n centro calculador, centro de computación, m

comrade /'kɒmræd/ n camarada, mf compañero (-ra)

comradeship /'kɒmræd,ʃɪp/ n compañerismo, m

con /kɒn/ vt estudiar; leer con atención, m; Naut. gobernar (el buque)

concatenation /kɒn,kætṇ'eiʃən/ n concatenación, f

concave /kɒn'keiv/ a cóncavo

conceal /kən'sil/ vt esconder, ocultar; (the truth, etc.) encubrir, callar; disimular

concealed /kən'sild/ a oculto; escondido; disimulado. **c. lighting,** iluminación indirecta, f. **c. turning,** (on a road) viraje oculto, m

concealment /kən'silmənt/ n ocultación, f; encubrimiento, m; (place of) escondite, m; secreto, m

concede /kən'sid/ vt conceder

conceit /kən'sit/ n presunción, vanidad, fatuidad, f, envanecimiento, m

conceited /kən'sitɪd/ a presumido, fatuo, vanidoso. **to be c.,** estar pagado de sí mismo, ensimismado. **to become c.** Lat. Am. ensimismarse

conceivable /kən'sivəbəl/ a concebible, imaginable

conceivably /kən'sivəbli/ *adv* posiblemente
conceive /kən'siv/ *vt* concebir; (affection, etc.) tomar; (an idea, etc.) formar; (plan) formular, idear. *vi* concebir; (understand) comprender; (suppose) imaginar, suponer
concentrate /'kɒnsənˌtreit/ *vt* concentrar. *vi* concentrarse; (on, upon) dedicarse (a), entregarse (a); prestar atención (a), concentrar atención (en)
concentrated /'kɒnsənˌtreitɪd/ *a* concentrado
concentration /ˌkɒnsən'treifən/ *n* concentración, *f*. **c. camp,** campo de concentración, *m*
concentric /kən'sɛntrɪk/ *a* concéntrico
concept /'kɒnsɛpt/ *n* concepto, *m*
conception /kən'sɛpfən/ *n* concepción, *f*; conocimiento, *m*; idea, *f*, concepto, *m*. **to have not the remotest c. of,** no tener la menor idea de
conceptualism /kən'sɛptfuəˌlɪzəm/ *n* conceptualismo, *m*
concern /kən'sɜrn/ *vt* tocar, tener que vercon, importar, concernir; interesar; referirse (a); tratar (de); (trouble) preocupar, inquietar; (take part in) ocuparse (de or con). *n* asunto, *m*, cosa, *f*; (share) interés, *m*; (anxiety) inquietud, *f*; solicitud, *f*; (business) casa comercial, firma, *f*. **as concerns...,** en cuanto a..., respecto a... **It concerns the date of the next meeting,** Es cuestión de la fecha de la próxima reunión. **It is no c. of yours,** No tiene nada que ver contigo. **The book is concerned with the adventures of two boys,** El libro trata de las aventuras de dos muchachos
concerned /kən'sɜrnd/ *a* ocupado (en); afectado; (in a crime) implicado (en); (troubled) preocupado; inquieto, agitado
concerning /kən'sɜrnɪŋ/ *prep* tocante a, con respecto a, referente a, sobre
concert /'kɒnsərt/ *n* acuerdo, concierto, *m*, armonía, *f*; *Mus.* concierto, *m*, *vt* concertar, acordar. **in c. with,** de acuerdo con. **c. hall,** sala de conciertos, *f*
concerted /kən'sɜrtɪd/ *a* concertado
concertina /ˌkɒnsər'tinə/ *n* concertina, *f*
concerto /kən'tʃertou/ *n* concierto, *m*
concession /kən'sɛfən/ *n* concesión, *f*; privilegio, *m*
concessionaire /kənˌsɛfə'nɛər/ *n* concesionario, *m*
concierge /ˌkɒnsi'ɛarʒ/ *n* conserje, *m*
conciliate /kən'sɪli,eit/ *vt* conciliar
conciliation /kənˌsɪli'eifən/ *n* conciliación, *f*
conciliatory /kən'sɪliəˌtɔri/ *a* conciliador
concise /kən'sais/ *a* conciso, breve, sucinto
concisely /kən'saisli/ *adv* concisamente
concision /kən'sɪʒən/ *n* concisión, *f*
conclave /'kɒnkleiv/ *n* conciliábulo, *m*; (of cardinals) conclave, *m*
conclude /kən'klud/ *vt* concluir. *vi* concluirse
conclusion /kən'kluʒən/ *n* conclusión, *f*. **in c.,** en conclusión, para terminar. **to come to the c. that...,** concluir que...
conclusive /kən'klusɪv/ *a* conclusivo, concluyente, decisivo
conclusively /kən'klusɪvli/ *adv* concluyentemente
conclusiveness /kən'klusɪvnɪs/ *n* carácter decisivo, *m*, lo concluyente
concoct /kɒn'kɒkt/ *vt* confeccionar; inventar
concoction /kɒn'kɒkfən/ *n* confección, *f*; mezcla, *f*; invención, *f*; (of a plot) maquinación, *f*
concomitant /kɒn'kɒmɪtənt/ *a* concomitante. *n* concomitante, *m*
concord /'kɒnkɔrd/ *n* concordia, buena inteligencia, armonía, *f*; (*Mus. Gram.*) concordancia, *f*; (of sounds) armonía, *f*
concordance /kɒn'kɔrdns/ *n* concordia, armonía, *f*; (book) concordancias, *f pl*
concordat /kɒn'kɔrdæt/ *n* concordato, *m*
concourse /'kɒnkɔrs/ *n* concurrencia, muchedumbre, *f*
concrete /'kɒnkrit/ *a* concreto; de hormigón. *n* hormigón, *m*. *vt* concretar; cubrir de hormigón. **reinforced c.,** hormigón armado, *m*
concretion /kɒn'krifən/ *n* concreción, *f*
concubine /'kɒŋkyəˌbain/ *n* concubina, manceba, *f*
concur /kən'kɜr/ *vi* coincidir, concurrir; estar de acuerdo, convenir (en)

concurrence /kən'kɜrəns/ *n* (agreement) acuerdo, consentimiento, *m*, aprobación, *f*
concurrent /kən'kɜrənt/ *a* concurrente; unánime; coincidente
concurrently /kən'kɜrəntli/ *adv* concurrentemente
concussion /kən'kʌfən/ *n* concusión, *f*; *Med.* concusión cerebral, *f*
condemn /kən'dɛm/ *vt* condenar; censurar, culpar; (forfeit) confiscar. **condemned cell,** celda de los condenados a muerte, *m*
condemnation /ˌkɒndɛm'neifən/ *n* condenación, *f*; censura, *f*
condensation /ˌkɒndɛn'seifən/ *n* condensación, *f*
condense /kən'dɛns/ *vt* condensar. *vi* condensarse
condenser /kən'dɛnsər/ *n* (*Elec. Mech. Chem.*) condensador, *m*
condescend /ˌkɒndə'sɛnd/ *vi* dignarse; (in a bad sense) consentir (en); (with affability) condescender
condescending /ˌkɒndə'sɛndɪŋ/ *a* condescendiente
condescendingly /ˌkɒndə'sɛndɪŋli/ *adv* con condescendencia
condescension /ˌkɒndə'sɛnfən/ *n* condescendencia, *f*; afabilidad, *f*
condign /kən'dain/ *a* condigno
condiment /'kɒndəmənt/ *n* condimento, *m*
condition /kən'dɪfən/ *n* condición, *f*; estado, *m*; *pl* **conditions,** condiciones, *f pl*; circunstancias, *f pl*. **on c. that,** con tal que; siempre que, dado que. **to be in no c. to,** no estar en condiciones de. **to change one's c.,** cambiar de estado. **to keep oneself in c.,** mantenerse en buena forma
conditional /kən'dɪfənl/ *a* condicional. **to be c. on,** depender de
conditionally /kən'dɪfənli/ *adv* condicionalmente
conditioned /kən'dɪfənd/ *a* acondicionado. **c. reflex,** reflejo acondicionado, *m*
condole /kən'doul/ *vi* condolerse (de); (on a bereavement) dar el pésame
condolence /kən'douləns/ *n* condolencia, *f*. **to present one's condolences,** dar el pésame
condom /'kɒndəm/ *n* condón, *m*, *Argentina* forro, *m*
condone /kən'doun/ *vt* condonar, perdonar
conduce /kən'dus/ *vi* contribuir, conducir
conducive /kən'dusɪv/ *a* que contribuye, conducente; favorable
conduct /*n* 'kɒndʌkt; *v* kən'dʌkt/ *n* conducta, *f*. *vt* conducir; guiar; *Mus.* dirigir; (oneself) portarse, conducirse; *Phys.* conducir. *vi Mus.* dirigir (una orquesta, etc.); *Phys.* ser conductor. **conducted tour,** excursión acompañada, *f*; viaje acompañado, *m*
conduction /kən'dʌkfən/ *n* conducción, *f*
conductive /kən'dʌktɪv/ *a* conductivo
conductivity /ˌkɒndʌk'tɪvɪti/ *n* conductibilidad, *f*
conductor /kən'dʌktər/ *n* (guide) guía, *mf*; (of an orchestra) director, *m*; (on a tram, etc.) cobrador, *m*; *Phys.* conductor, *m*
conduit /'kɒnduɪt/ *n* conducto, *m*; cañería, *f*; canal, *m*
cone /koun/ *n* (*Bot. Geom.* etc.) cono, *m*
confabulation /kənˌfæbyə'leifən/ *n* confabulación, *f*
confection /kən'fɛkfən/ *n* confección, *f*, *vt* confeccionar
confectioner /kən'fɛkfənər/ *n* confitero (-ra); pastelero (-ra)
confectionery /kən'fɛkfəˌnɛri/ *n* confitería, pastelería, repostería, *f*
confederate /*a, n* kən'fɛdərɪt; *v* -'fɛdəˌreit/ *a* confederado; aliado. *n* confederado, *m*; (in crime) cómplice, *mf*. *vt* confederar. *vi* confederarse; aliarse
confederation /kənˌfɛdə'reifən/ *n* confederación, *f*
confer /kən'fɜr/ *vt* conceder, conferir; (an honor, etc.) otorgar, investir (con). *vi* consultar (con); deliberar, considerar
conference /'kɒnfərəns/ *n* conferencia, consulta, *f*; conversación, *f*
conferment /kən'fɜrmənt/ *n* otorgamiento, *m*; concesión, *f*
confess /kən'fɛs/ *vt* confesar, reconocer; *Inf.* admitir; (of a priest) confesar; (of a penitent) confesarse. *vi* hacer una confesión; (one's sins) confesarse. **I c. that I was surprised,** No puedo negar que me sorprendió

confessed /kənˈfɛst/ a confesado, declarado
confession /kənˈfɛʃən/ n confesión, f; reconocimiento, m; declaración, f; religión, f; (creed) credo, m. **to go to c.**, confesarse. **to hear a c.**, confesar (a)
confessional /kənˈfɛʃənl/ n confesionario, m
confessor /kənˈfɛsər/ n confesor, m
confetti /kənˈfɛti/ n pl confeti, papel picado m, serpentina, f
confidant /ˈkɒnfɪˌdænt/ n confidente, m
confidante /ˌkɒnfɪˈdænt/ n confidenta, f
confide /kənˈfaɪd/ vi confiar (a or en). vt confiar
confidence /ˈkɒnfɪdəns/ n confianza, f; seguridad, f; (revelation) confidencia, f. **in c.**, en confianza. **over-c.**, presunción, f. **to have c. in**, tener confianza en. **c. man**, caballero de industria, estafador, m. **c. trick**, timo, m
confident /ˈkɒnfɪdənt/ a confiado; seguro; (conceited) presumido
confidential /ˌkɒnfɪˈdɛnʃəl/ a confidencial; de confianza. **c. clerk**, empleado (-da) de confianza. **c. letter**, carta confidencial, f
confidentially /ˌkɒnfɪˈdɛnʃəli/ adv en confianza, confidencialmente
confidently /ˈkɒnfɪdəntli/ adv confiadamente
confiding /kənˈfaɪdɪŋ/ a confiado
confidingly /kənˈfaɪdɪŋli/ adv con confianza
configuration /kənˌfɪɡjəˈreɪʃən/ n configuración, f
confine /kənˈfaɪn/ vt limitar; (imprison) encerrar. **confined space**, espacio limitado, m. **to be confined**, (of a woman) estar de parto, parir. **to be confined to one's room**, no poder dejar su cuarto. **to c. oneself to**, limitarse a
confinement /kənˈfaɪnmənt/ n encierro, m, prisión, f; reclusión, f; (of a woman) parto, m. **to suffer solitary c.**, estar incomunicado
confines /ˈkɒnfaɪnz/ n pl límites, m pl; confines, m pl; fronteras, f pl
confirm /kənˈfɜrm/ vt confirmar; corroborar; Eccl. confirmar
confirmation /ˌkɒnfərˈmeɪʃən/ n confirmación, f; (of a treaty) ratificación, f; Eccl. confirmación, f
confirmatory /kənˈfɜrməˌtɔri/ a confirmatorio
confirmed /kənˈfɜrmd/ a inveterado
confiscate /ˈkɒnfəˌskeɪt/ vt confiscar
confiscation /ˌkɒnfəˈskeɪʃən/ n confiscación, f
conflagration /ˌkɒnfləˈɡreɪʃən/ n conflagración, f, incendio, m
conflict /n ˈkɒnflɪkt; v kənˈflɪkt/ n conflicto, m; lucha, f. vi estar opuesto (a), estar en contradicción (con)
conflicting /kənˈflɪktɪŋ/ a opuesto; incompatible; (of evidence) contradictorio
confluence /ˈkɒnfluəns/ n confluencia, f
conform /kənˈfɔrm/ vt ajustar, conformar. vi ajustarse (a), amoldarse (a); conformarse (a); adaptarse (a)
conformation /ˌkɒnfərˈmeɪʃən/ n conformación, f
conformity /kənˈfɔrmɪti/ n conformidad, f. **in c. with**, en conformidad con, con arreglo a
confound /kɒnˈfaʊnd/ vt confundir. **C. it!** ¡Demonio!
confounded /kɒnˈfaʊndɪd/ a perplejo; Inf. maldito
confraternity /ˌkɒnfrəˈtɜrnɪti/ n cofradía, hermandad, f
confront /kənˈfrʌnt/ vt hacer frente (a), afrontar; salir al paso; confrontar
Confucianism /kənˈfyuʃəˌnɪzəm/ n el confucianismo, m
confuse /kənˈfyuz/ vt turbar, aturdir; confundir (con); (the issue) obscurecer; (disconcert) desconcertar; dejar confuso (a); dejar perplejo (a). **You have confused one thing with another**, Has confundido una cosa con otra. **My mind was confused**, Mis ideas eran confusas; Tenía la cabeza trastornada
confused /kənˈfyuzd/ a confuso
confusing /kənˈfyuzɪŋ/ a turbador; desconcertante. **It is all very c.**, Todo ello es muy difícil de comprender
confusion /kənˈfyuʒən/ n confusión, f. **covered with c.**, confuso, avergonzado. **to be in c.**, estar confuso; estar en desorden

confute /kənˈfyut/ vt (a person) confundir; (by evidence) refutar, confutar
congeal /kənˈdʒil/ vt congelar; (blood) coagular. vi congelarse, helarse; coagularse
congealment /kənˈdʒilmənt/ n congelación, f; (of blood) coagulación, f
congenial /kənˈdʒinyəl/ a (of persons) simpático; propicio, favorable; agradable
congenital /kənˈdʒenɪtl/ a congénito
congest /kənˈdʒɛst/ vt atestar; amontonar; Med. congestionar
congested /kənˈdʒɛstɪd/ a Med. congestionado; (of places) atestado de gente; de mayor población; concurrido. **c. area**, área de mayor densidad de población, f
congestion /kənˈdʒɛstʃən/ n Med. congestión, f; densidad del tráfico, f; mayor densidad de población, f
conglomerate /kənˈɡlɒmərɪt/ a conglomerado. n conglomerado, m
conglomeration /kənˌɡlɒməˈreɪʃən/ n conglomeración, f
congratulate /kənˈɡrætʃəˌleɪt/ vt felicitar, dar la enhorabuena (a); congratular
congratulation /kənˌɡrætʃəˈleɪʃən/ n felicitación, enhorabuena, f; congratulación, f
congratulatory /kənˈɡrætʃələˌtɔri/ a de felicitación, congratulatorio
congregate /ˈkɒŋɡrɪˌɡeɪt/ vi congregarse, reunirse, juntarse
congregation /ˌkɒŋɡrɪˈɡeɪʃən/ n congregación, f; asamblea, reunión, f; (in a church) fieles, m pl; (parishioners) feligreses, m pl
congress /ˈkɒŋɡrɪs/ n congreso, m. **C.-member**, miembro del Congreso, m, congresista, mf
conical /ˈkɒnɪkəl/ a cónico
conifer /ˈkounəfər/ n conífera, f
coniferous /kouˈnɪfərəs/ a conífero
conjectural /kənˈdʒɛktʃərəl/ a conjetural
conjecture /kənˈdʒɛktʃər/ n conjetura, f, vt conjeturar
conjoint /kənˈdʒɔɪnt/ a asociado, conjunto
conjointly /kənˈdʒɔɪntli/ adv juntamente, en común
conjugal /ˈkɒndʒəɡəl/ a conyugal
conjugate /ˈkɒndʒəˌɡeɪt/ vt conjugar. vi conjugarse
conjugation /ˌkɒndʒəˈɡeɪʃən/ n conjugación, f
conjunction /kənˈdʒʌŋkʃən/ n conjunción, f. **in c. with**, de acuerdo con
conjunctive /kənˈdʒʌŋktɪv/ a conjuntivo. n conjunción, f
conjunctivitis /kənˌdʒʌŋktəˈvaɪtɪs/ n conjuntivitis, f
conjure /ˈkɒndʒər/ vt (implore) rogar, suplicar. vi (juggle) hacer juegos de manos. **a name to c. with**, un nombre todopoderoso. **to c. up**, (spirits) conjurar; Fig. evocar
conjurer, conjuror /ˈkɒndʒərər/ n (magician) nigromante, m; prestidigitador, m. **conjuror's wand**, varilla de virtudes, f
conjuring /ˈkɒndʒərɪŋ/ n prestidigitación, f, juegos de manos, m pl. **c. trick**, juego de manos, m. **c. up**, evocación, f
connect /kəˈnɛkt/ vt juntar, unir; (relate) relacionar; asociar; (Elec. and Mech.) conectar. vi juntarse, unirse; relacionarse; asociarse; (of events) encadenarse; (of trains) enlazar. **This train connects with the Madrid express**, Este tren enlaza con el expreso de Madrid. **They are connected with the Borgia family**, Están emparentados con los Borgia, Son parientes de los Borgia
connected /kəˈnɛktɪd/ a conexo; (coherent) coherente; relacionado; asociado; (in a crime) implicado; (by marriage, etc.) emparentado
connectedly /kəˈnɛktɪdli/ adv coherentemente
connecting /kəˈnɛktɪŋ/ a que une; (Mech. and Elec.) conectivo; (of doors, etc.) comunicante. **c.-link**, Mech. varilla de conexión, f; Fig. lazo, m. **c.-rod**, biela, f
connection /kəˈnɛkʃən/ n conexión, f; unión, f; (of ideas) relación, f; (junction) empalme, m; (of trains, boats) enlace, m; (intimacy) intimidad, f; (relative) pariente, m; (of a firm, etc.) clientela, f; Elec. conexión, f. **in c. with**, con referencia a; en asociación con. **in this c.**, respecto a esto

conning tower /'kɒnɪŋ/ n torre de mando, f
connivance /kə'naivəns/ n consentimiento, m; complicidad, f
connive (at) /kə'naiv/ vi hacer la vista gorda, ser cómplice (en)
connotation /ˌkɒnə'teiʃən/ n connotación, f
connote /kə'nout/ vt connotar
connubial /kə'nubiəl/ a conyugal
conquer /'kɒŋkər/ vt conquistar; vencer. vi triunfar
conquering /'kɒŋkərɪŋ/ a conquistador, vencedor; triunfante, victorioso
conqueror /'kɒŋkərər/ n conquistador, m; vencedor, m
conquest /'kɒnkwɛst/ n conquista, f. **to make a c. of,** conquistar
consanguineous /ˌkɒnsæŋ'gwɪniəs/ a consanguíneo
consanguinity /ˌkɒnsæŋ'gwɪnɪti/ n consanguinidad, f
conscience /'kɒnʃəns/ n conciencia, f. **in all c.,** en verdad. **with a clear c.,** con la conciencia limpia. **c.-stricken,** lleno de remordimientos
conscienceless /'kɒnʃənslɪs/ a desalmado, falto de conciencia, sin conciencia
conscientious /ˌkɒnʃi'ɛnʃəs/ a concienzudo; diligente. **c. objector,** objetor de conciencia, m
conscientiously /ˌkɒnʃi'ɛnʃəsli/ adv concienzudamente
conscientiousness /ˌkɒnʃi'ɛnʃəsnɪs/ n conciencia, diligencia, f; rectitud, f
conscious /'kɒnʃəs/ a consciente. n Psychol. consciente, m. **to become c.,** (after unconsciousness) volver en sí. **to become c. of,** darse cuenta de
consciously /'kɒnʃəsli/ adv conscientemente, a sabiendas
consciousness /'kɒnʃəsnɪs/ n conciencia, f; conocimiento, sentido, m. **to lose c.,** perder el conocimiento, perder el sentido. **to recover c.,** recobrar el sentido, volver en sí
conscript /n 'kɒnskrɪpt/ v kən'skrɪpt/ n conscripto, m, a conscripto. vt reclutar
conscription /kən'skrɪpʃən/ n conscripción, f
consecrate /'kɒnsɪˌkreit/ vt consagrar; bendecir
consecration /ˌkɒnsɪ'kreiʃən/ n consagración, f; dedicación, f
consecutive /kən'sɛkyətɪv/ a consecutivo
consecutively /kən'sɛkyətɪvli/ adv consecutivamente
consensus /kən'sɛnsəs/ n consenso, m, unanimidad, f. **c. of opinion,** opinión general, f
consent /kən'sɛnt/ vi consentir. n consentimiento, m; permiso, m, aquiescencia, f. **by common c.,** de común acuerdo
consequence /'kɒnsɪˌkwɛns/ n consecuencia, f; resultado, m; importancia, f, **in c.,** por consiguiente. **in c. of,** de resultas de. **of no c.,** sin importancia
consequences /'kɒnsɪˌkwɛnsɪz/ n (game) cartas rusas, f pl
consequent /'kɒnsɪˌkwɛnt/ a consecuente, consiguiente
consequential /ˌkɒnsɪ'kwɛnʃəl/ a consecuente; (of persons) fatuo, engreído
consequently /'kɒnsɪˌkwɛntli/ adv por consiguiente, en consecuencia
conservation /ˌkɒnsər'veiʃən/ n conservación, f. **c. of energy,** conservación de energía, f
conservatism /kən'sɜrvəˌtɪzəm/ n conservadurismo, m
conservative /kən'sɜrvətɪv/ a preservativo; conservador. n conservador (-ra). **c. party,** partido conservador, m
conservatoire /kənˌsɜrvə'twɑr/ n conservatorio de música, m
conservatory /kən'sɜrvəˌtɔri/ n invernáculo, invernadero, m
conserve /kən'sɜrv/ vt conservar
consider /kən'sɪdər/ vt considerar, pensar meditar; tomar en cuenta; examinar; (deem) juzgar; (believe) creer, estar convencido de (que); (of persons) considerar. **all things considered,** considerando todos los puntos, después de considerarlo todo
considerable /kən'sɪdərəbəl/ a considerable
considerably /kən'sɪdərəbli/ adv considerablemente

considerate /kən'sɪdərɪt/ a considerado, solícito
considerately /kən'sɪdərɪtli/ adv con consideración, solícitamente
consideration /kənˌsɪdə'reiʃən/ n consideración, f; reflexión, deliberación, f; remuneración, f. **out of c. for,** en consideración de; por consideración a. **to take into c.,** tomar en cuenta, tomar en consideración
considered /kən'sɪdərd/ a considerado
considering /kən'sɪdərɪŋ/ prep en consideración de, considerando, en vista de
consign /kən'sain/ vt consignar; Fig. enviar. **to c. to oblivion,** sepultar en el olvido
consignee /ˌkɒnsai'ni/ n consignatorio, m
consignment /kən'sainmənt/ n consignación, f; envío, m
consignor /kən'sainər/ n consignador, m
consist /kən'sɪst/ vi consistir (en); ser compatible (con). **to c. of,** componerse de, consistir de
consistence, consistency /kən'sɪstəns; kən'sɪstənsi/ n consistencia, f; compatibilidad, f; lógica, f; (of persons) consecuencia, f
consistent /kən'sɪstənt/ a compatible; lógico; (of persons) consecuente
consistently /kən'sɪstəntli/ adv conformemente (a); consecuentemente
consolation /ˌkɒnsə'leiʃən/ n consuelo, m, consolación, f
console /v kən'soul; n 'kɒnsoul/ vt consolar; confortar. n Archit. cartela, f. **c. table,** consola, f
consolidate /kən'sɒlɪˌdeit/ vt consolidar. vi consolidarse
consolidation /kənˌsɒlɪ'deiʃən/ n consolidación, f
consoling /kən'soulɪŋ/ a consolador; confortador
consols /'kɒnsɒlz, kən'sɒlz/ n pl (títulos) consolidados, m pl
consonance /'kɒnsənəns/ n consonancia, f
consonant /'kɒnsənənt/ a consonante
consort /n 'kɒnsɔrt; v kən'sɔrt/ n consorte, mf. **to c. with,** frecuentar la compañía de; ir con; acompañar (a). **prince c.,** príncipe consorte, m
conspicuous /kən'spɪkyuəs/ a conspicuo; prominente; notable. **to be c.,** destacarse; llamar la atención. **to make oneself c.,** ponerse en evidencia, llamar la atención
conspicuously /kən'spɪkyuəsli/ adv visiblemente; muy en evidencia
conspiracy /kən'spɪrəsi/ n conspiración, f; complot, m
conspirator /kən'spɪrətər/ n conspirador (-ra)
conspire /kən'spaiᵊr/ vi conspirar
constable /'kɒnstəbəl/ n agente de policía, m; (historical) condestable, m. **chief c.,** jefe de policía, m
constabulary /kən'stæbyəˌlɛri/ n policía, f
constancy /'kɒnstənsi/ n constancia, f
constant /'kɒnstənt/ a constante; incesante. n constante, m
Constantinople /ˌkɒnstæntn̩'oupəl/ Constantinopla, f
constantly /'kɒnstəntli/ adv constantemente
constellation /ˌkɒnstə'leiʃən/ n constelación, f
consternation /ˌkɒnstər'neiʃən/ n consternación, f; espanto, terror, m
constipate /'kɒnstəˌpeit/ vt estreñir
constipation /ˌkɒnstə'peiʃən/ n estreñimiento, m, constipación de vientre, f
constituency /kən'stɪtʃuənsi/ n distrito electoral, m
constituent /kən'stɪtʃuənt/ a constituyente. n constituyente, m; componente, m; elector (-ra)
constitute /'kɒnstɪˌtut/ vt constituir; nombrar; autorizar
constitution /ˌkɒnstɪ'tuʃən/ n constitución, f
constitutional /ˌkɒnstɪ'tuʃənl/ a constitucional
constitutionally /ˌkɒnstɪ'tuʃənli/ adv constitucionalmente
constrain /kən'strein/ vt obligar, forzar. **I felt constrained to help them,** Me sentí obligado a ayudarles
constrained /kən'streind/ a (of smiles, etc.) forzado; (of silences) violento; (of persons) avergonzado
constraint /kən'streint/ n fuerza, compulsión, f; (of atmosphere) tensión, f; (reserve) reserva, f; vergüenza, f
constrict /kən'strɪkt/ vt apretar, estrechar

constriction /kən'strɪkʃən/ n constricción, f
construct /kən'strʌkt/ vt edificar; construir
construction /kən'strʌkʃən/ n construcción, f; interpretación, f. **to put a wrong c. on,** interpretar mal
constructional /kən'strʌkʃənl/ a construccional
constructive /kən'strʌktɪv/ a constructivo
constructor /kən'strʌktər/ n constructor, m
construe /kən'stru/ vt construir; (translate) traducir; Fig. interpretar
consul /'kɒnsəl/ n cónsul, m
consular /'kɒnsələr/ a consular
consular fees n pl derechos consulares, m pl
consulate /'kɒnsəlɪt/ n consulado, m. **c. general,** consulado general, m
consult /kən'sʌlt/ vt consultar. vi consultar (con), aconsejarse (con)
consultant /kən'sʌltənt/ n (Med. and other uses) especialista, m
consultation /ˌkɒnsəl'teɪʃən/ n consulta, f
consultative /kən'sʌltətɪv/ a consultativo
consulting /kən'sʌltɪŋ/ a consultor. **c. hours,** horas de consulta, f pl. **c. rooms,** consultorio, m
consume /kən'sum/ vt consumir; (eat) comerse, tragarse. vi consumirse. **to be consumed by envy,** estar consumido por la envidia. **to be consumed by thirst,** estar muerto de sed
consumer /kən'sumər/ n consumidor (-ra)
consummate /a 'kɒnsəmɪt; v -ˌmeɪt/ a consumido, perfecto. vt consumar
consummation /ˌkɒnsə'meɪʃən/ n consumación, f
consumption /kən'sʌmpʃən/ n consumo, m; gasto, m; Med. tuberculosis, f. **fuel c.,** consumo de combustible, m
consumptive /kən'sʌmptɪv/ a destructivo; Med. tísico, hético. n tísico (-ca)
contact /'kɒntækt/ n contacto, m, vt ponerse en contacto con. **to be in c. with,** estar en contacto con
contact lens n lente de contacto, m
contagion /kən'teɪdʒən/ n contagio, m
contagious /kən'teɪdʒəs/ a contagioso
contain /kən'teɪn/ vt contener; incluir; Geom. encerrar; (arithmetic) ser divisible por; (oneself) dominarse. **I could not c. myself,** No pude dominarme
container /kən'teɪnər/ n recipiente, m; envase, m; (box) caja, f
contaminate /kən'tæməˌneɪt/ vt contaminar; corromper
contamination /kənˌtæmə'neɪʃən/ n contaminación, f
contemplate /'kɒntəmˌpleɪt/ vt contemplar; meditar, considerar; (plan) tener intención de, pensar, proponerse
contemplation /ˌkɒntəm'pleɪʃən/ n contemplación, f; meditación, f; expectación, esperanza, f; (plan) proyecto, m. **to have something in c.,** proyectar algo
contemplative /kən'templətɪv/ a contemplativo, meditabundo
contemplatively /kən'templətɪvli/ adv contemplativamente; atentamente
contemporaneous /kənˌtempə'reɪniəs/ a contemporáneo
contemporary /kən'tempəˌreri/ a contemporáneo; (of persons) coetáneo; (of events, etc.) actual. n contemporáneo (-ea)
contempt /kən'tempt/ n desprecio, menosprecio, m; desdén, m. **c. of court,** falta de respeto a la sala, f
contemptible /kən'temptəbəl/ a menospreciable, despreciable, vil
contemptibly /kən'temptəbli/ adv vilmente
contempt of court n rebeldía a la corte, f
contempt of law n rebeldía a la ley, f
contemptuous /kən'temptʃuəs/ a desdeñoso; despectivo; de desprecio. **to be c. of,** desdeñar; menospreciar, tener en poco (a)
contemptuously /kən'temptʃuəsli/ adv con desprecio, desdeñosamente
contend /kən'tend/ vi contender; (affirm) sostener, mantener. **He contended that...,** Sostuvo que...; **contending party,** Law. parte litigante, f
content /n 'kɒntent; a, v kən'tent/ n contenido, m; capacidad, f; (emotion) contento, m; satisfacción, f. a

contento; satisfecho (de). vt contentar; satisfacer. **to one's heart's c.,** a pedir de boca; a gusto de uno; cuanto quisiera
contented /kən'tentɪd/ a satisfecho, contento
contentedly /kən'tentɪdli/ adv con satisfacción, contentamente
contention /kən'tenʃən/ n disputa, controversia, discusión, f; argumento, m, opinión, f
contentious /kən'tenʃəs/ a contencioso
contentment /kən'tentmənt/ n contentamiento, m; contento, m
contest /v kən'test; n 'kɒntest/ vt disputar; (a suit) defender; (a match, an election, etc.) disputar. n disputa, f; combate, m, lucha, f; (competition) concurso, m
contestant /kən'testənt/ n contendiente, mf
context /'kɒntekst/ n contexto, m
contiguity /ˌkɒntɪ'gyuɪti/ n contigüidad, f
contiguous /kən'tɪgyuəs/ a contiguo, lindero, adyacente
continence /'kɒntn̩əns/ n continencia, f
continent /'kɒntn̩ənt/ a continente. n continente, m
continental /ˌkɒntn̩'entl/ a continental
continental shelf n plataforma continental, f
contingency /kən'tɪndʒənsi/ n contingencia, f
contingent /kən'tɪndʒənt/ a contingente. n Mil. contingente, m. **to be c. on,** (of events) depender de
continual /kən'tɪnyuəl/ a continuo
continually /kən'tɪnyuəli/ adv continuamente
continuance /kən'tɪnyuəns/ n continuación, f
continuation /kənˌtɪnyu'eɪʃən/ n continuación, f; prolongación, f
continue /kən'tɪnyu/ vi continuar; seguir; prolongarse; durar. vt continuar; seguir; proseguir; perpetuar; (in an office) retener. **to be continued,** se continuará, continuará, seguirá
continuer /kən'tɪnyuər/ n continuador (-ra)
continuity /ˌkɒntn̩'uti/ n continuidad, f
continuous /kən'tɪnyuəs/ a continuo. **c. performance,** sesión continua, f
continuously /kən'tɪnyuəsli/ adv de continuo, continuamente
contort /kən'tɔrt/ vt retorcer
contortion /kən'tɔrʃən/ n contorsión, f
contortionist /kən'tɔrʃənɪst/ n contorsionista, m
contour /'kɒntʊr/ n contorno, m; curva de nivel, f. **c. map,** mapa con curvas de nivel, m
contraband /'kɒntrəˌbænd/ n contrabando, m
contrabandist /'kɒntrəˌbændɪst/ n contrabandista, mf
contrabass /'kɒntrəˌbeɪs/ n contrabajo, m
contraception /ˌkɒntrə'sepʃən/ n anticoncepción, f
contraceptive /ˌkɒntrə'septɪv/ n anticonceptivo, m
contract /v kən'trækt; n 'kɒntrækt/ n pacto, m; (Com. and Law.) contrato, m; (betrothal) esponsales, m pl; (marriage) capitulaciones, f pl; (cards) "Bridge," m vt contraer; (acquire) adquirir, contraer; (a marriage, etc.) contraer; (be betrothed to) desposarse con; (by formal contract) contratar; pactar. vi (shrink) contraerse, encogerse; comprometerse por contrato. **breach of c.,** el no cumplimiento de contrato, m. **c. party,** (of matrimony) contrayente, mf
contractile /kən'træktl/ a contráctil
contraction /kən'trækʃən/ n contracción, f (act or process); forma contracta, f (like isn't or can't)
contractor /'kɒntræktər/ n contratista, mf
contradict /ˌkɒntrə'dɪkt/ vt contradecir; desmentir
contradiction /ˌkɒntrə'dɪkʃən/ n contradicción, f; negación, f
contradictory /ˌkɒntrə'dɪktəri/ a contradictorio; opuesto (a), contrario (a)
contralto /kən'træltou/ n (voice) contralto, m; (woman) contralto, f
contraption /kən'træpʃən/ n Inf. artefacto, m
contrapuntal /ˌkɒntrə'pʌntl/ a Mus. de contrapunto
contrariness /'kɒntrerinɪs/ n Inf. testarudez, terquedad, f
contrariwise /'kɒntreriˌwaiz/ adv al contrario; al revés
contrary /'kɒntreri/ a contrario; opuesto (a); desfavorable, poco propicio; (of persons) difícil, terco. n contraria, f; (logic) contrario, m, adv en contra, con-

trariamente. **on the c.,** al contrario. **to be c.,** (of persons) llevar la contraria

contrast /n 'kɒntræst; v kən'træst/ n contraste, m. vt contrastar (con). vi contrastar (con), hacer contraste (con)

contravene /ˌkɒntrə'vin/ vt contravenir; atacar, oponerse (a)

contravention /ˌkɒntrə'vɛnʃən/ n contravención, f

contribute /kən'trɪbyut/ vt contribuir; (an article) escribir

contribution /ˌkɒntrə'byuʃən/ n contribución, f; (to a review, etc.) artículo, m

contributor /kən'trɪbyətər/ n contribuyente, mf; (to a journal) colaborador (-ra)

contributory /kən'trɪbyə,tɔri/ a contribuyente

contrite /kən'trait/ a penitente, arrepentido, contrito

contritely /kən'traitli/ adv contritamente

contrition /kən'trɪʃən/ n contrición, penitencia, f, arrepentimiento, m

contrivance /kən'traivəns/ n invención, f; (scheme) treta, idea, estratagema, f; (machine) aparato, mecanismo, artefacto, m

contrive /kən'traiv/ vt inventar; idear, proyectar. vi (succeed in) lograr, conseguir; (manage) arreglárselas

control /kən'troul/ n autoridad, f; dominio, m; gobierno, m; dirección, f; regulación, f; (restraint) freno, m; (Biol. and Spirit.) control, m; (of a vehicle) conducción, f; manejo, m, manipulación, f; pl **controls,** Mech. mando, m. vt dirigir, regir; regular; usar, manejar, manipular; controlar; (dominate) dominar; (curb) refrenar, reprimir; (command) mandar. **He lost c. of the car,** Perdió el mando (or control) del automóvil. **out of c.,** fuera de mando, fuera de control. **remote c.,** mando a distancia, m. **to c.** **oneself,** dominarse, contenerse. **to lose c. of oneself,** no lograr dominarse, perder el control. **c. stick,** Aer. palanca de mando, f. **c. tower,** Aer. torre de mando, f

controller /kən'troulər/ n interventor, m; (device) regulador, m

controlling /kən'troulɪŋ/ n See **control.** a regulador

controversial /ˌkɒntrə'vɜrʃəl/ a debatible, discutible

controversy /'kɒntrə,vɜrsi/ n controversia, f; argumento, m; altercación, disputa, f

contumacious /ˌkɒntʊ'meiʃəs/ a contumaz

contumacy /'kɒntʊməsi/ n contumacia, f

contumely /'kɒntʊməli/ n contumelia, f

contusion /kən'tuʒən/ n herida contusa, f

conundrum /kə'nʌndrəm/ n acertijo, rompecabezas, m; problema, m

convalesce /ˌkɒnvə'lɛs/ vi convalecer, estar convaleciente

convalescence /ˌkɒnvə'lɛsəns/ n convalecencia, f

convalescent mf. **c. home,** casa de convalecencia, f

convalescent /ˌkɒnvə'lɛsənt/ a convaleciente. n convaleciente, mf. **c. home,** casa de convalecencia, f

convene /kən'vin/ vt (a meeting) convocar; (person) citar. vi reunirse

convenience /kən'vinyəns/ n conveniencia, f; (comfort) comodidad, f; utilidad, f; (advantage) ventaja, f; (public) retretes, m pl. **at one's c.,** cuando le sea conveniente a uno. **to make a c. of,** abusar de. **with all modern conveniences,** con todo el confort moderno

convenient /kən'vinyənt/ a conveniente; apropiado; cómodo. **I shall make it c. to see him at 6 p.m.,** Arreglaré mis asuntos para verle a las seis

conveniently /kən'vinyəntli/ adv cómodamente, oportunamente; sin inconveniente

convent /'kɒnvɛnt/ n convento, m

convention /kən'vɛnʃən/ n convención, f

conventional /kən'vɛnʃənl/ a convencional

conventual /kən'vɛntʃuəl/ a conventual. n conventual, m

converge /kən'vɜrdʒ/ vi convergir

convergence /kən'vɜrdʒəns/ n convergencia, f

convergent /kən'vɜrdʒənt/ a convergente

conversance /kən'vɜrsəns/ n familiaridad, f, conocimiento, m

conversant /kən'vɜrsənt/ a familiar, versado, conocedor. **c. with,** versado en

conversation /ˌkɒnvər'seiʃən/ n conversación, f. **to engage in c. with,** entablar conversación con

conversational /ˌkɒnvər'seiʃənl/ a de conversación; (talkative) locuaz

conversationally /ˌkɒnvər'seiʃənli/ adv en tono familiar; familiarmente; en conversación

converse /kən'vɜrs/ vi conversar. **to c. by signs,** hablar por señas

conversely /kən'vɜrsli/ adv recíprocamente

conversion /kən'vɜrʒən/ n conversión, f

convert /v kən'vɜrt; n 'kɒnvɜrt/ vt convertir; transformar. n converso (-sa). **to become a c.,** convertirse

convertible /kən'vɜrtəbəl/ a convertible; transformable

convex /kɒn'vɛks/ a convexo

convey /kən'vei/ vt transportar; conducir, llevar; (a meaning, etc.) comunicar, dar a entender; expresar; Law. traspasar

conveyance /kən'veiəns/ n transporte, m; conducción, f; medio de transporte, m; vehículo, m; carruaje, m; (of property) traspaso, m; (document) escritura de traspaso, f. **public c.,** coche de alquiler, m; ómnibus, m

convict /n 'kɒnvɪkt; v kən'vɪkt/ n convicto, m; presidiario, m. vt Law. condenar; culpar. **c. settlement,** colonia penal, f

conviction /kən'vɪkʃən/ n (of a prisoner) condenación, f; (belief) convencimiento, m, convicción, f

convince /kən'vɪns/ vt convencer

convincing /kən'vɪnsɪŋ/ a convincente

convivial /kən'vɪviəl/ a convivial

conviviality /kən,vɪvi'æliti/ n jovialidad, f

convocation /ˌkɒnvə'keiʃən/ n convocación, f

convoke /kən'vouk/ vt convocar

convolution /ˌkɒnvə'luʃən/ n circunvolución, f; espira, f

convoy /'kɒnvɔi/ vt convoyar, escoltar. n convoy, m. **to sail in a c.,** navegar en convoy

convulse /kən'vʌls/ vt agitar; sacudir; estremecer. **to be convulsed with laughter,** desternillarse de risa, morirse de risa

convulsion /kən'vʌlʃən/ n convulsión, f; conmoción, f

convulsive /kən'vʌlsɪv/ a convulsivo

coo /ku/ vi arrullar; (of infants) gorjearse. n arrullo, m

cooing /'kuɪŋ/ n arrullo, m

cook /kʊk/ n cocinero (-ra). vt guisar, cocer, cocinar; (falsify) falsear

cookbook /'kʊk,bʊk/ n libro de cocina, m

cooker /'kʊkər/ n cocina, f. **gas c.,** cocina de gas, f

cookery /'kʊkəri/ n cocina, f

cookie /'kʊki/ n galleta, f

cooking /'kʊkɪŋ/ n arte de guisar, m, or f; cocina, f; (of accounts, etc.) falsificación, f. **c. range,** cocina económica, f. **c.-stove,** cocina, f. **c. utensils,** batería de cocina, f

cool /kul/ a fresco; bastante frío; (not ardent and of receptions, etc.) frío; (calm) sereno, imperturbable. n fresco, m. vi enfriarse; (of love, etc.) resfriarse; (of the weather) refrescar; (of persons) refrescarse. vt refrescar; enfriar. **to grow cooler,** (of weather) refrescarse; (of persons) tener menos calor. **It is c.,** Hace fresco. **to be as c. as a cucumber,** tener sangre fría. **c. drink,** bebida fría, f. **c.-headed,** sereno, imperturbable

coolie /'kuli/ n culí, m

cooling /'kulɪŋ/ n enfriamiento, m, a refrescante

coolly /'kuli/ adv frescamente; fríamente, con frialdad; imperturbablemente; (impudently) descaradamente

coolness /'kulnɪs/ n frescura, f; (of a welcome, etc.) frialdad, f; (sangfroid) sangre fría, serenidad, f; aplomo, m

coop /kup/ n gallinero, m; caponera, f, vt enjaular; encerrar. **to keep** (someone) **cooped up,** tener encerrado (a)

cooper /'kupər/ n tonelero, barrilero, m, vt hacer barriles

cooperate /kou'ɒpə,reit/ vi cooperar; colaborar

cooperation /kou,ɒpə'reiʃən/ n cooperación, f

cooperative /kou'ɒpərətɪv/ a cooperativo. **c. society,** cooperativa, f

coopt /kou'ɒpt/ vt elegir por votación
coordinate /v kou'ɔrdn̩ˌeit/ n, a kou'ɔrdn̩ɪt/ vt coordinar. n Math.
coordination /kou,ɔrdn̩'eiʃən/ n coordinación, f
coot /kut/ n fúlica, f
cop /kɒp/ n (police officer) polizonte, mf, Ecuador, chapa, Mexico cuico (-ca)
copartner /kou'pɑrtnər/ n copartícipe, mf; socio (-ia)
cope /koup/ n Eccl. capa, f; (of heaven) dosel, m, bóveda, f. **to c. with,** contender con; (a difficulty) hacer cara a, arrostrar
copeck /'koupɛk/ n copec, m
Copenhagen /,koupən'heigən, -'hagən/ Copenhague, m
copier /'kɒpiər/ n copiador (-ra)
coping /'koupɪŋ/ n Archit. albardilla, f. **c.-stone,** teja cumbrera, f; Fig. coronamiento, m
copious /'koupiəs/ a copioso, abundante
copiously /'koupiəsli/ adv en abundancia
copiousness /'koupiəsnɪs/ n abundancia, f
copper /'kɒpər/ n cobre, m; (coin) calderilla, f; (vessel) caldera, f. a de cobre. **c.-colored,** cobrizo. **c.-smith,** calderero, m. **c.-sulfate,** sulfato de cobre, m
copperplate /'kɒpər,pleit/ n lámina de cobre, f; grabado en cobre, m
coppery /'kɒpəri/ a cobrizo
coppice /'kɒpɪs/ n soto, bosquecillo, m. **c. with standards,** monte medio, m
coproprietor /,kouprə'praiɪtər/ n copropietario, m
copse /kɒps/ n arboleda, f, bosquecillo, m
copulate /'kɒpyə,leit/ vi copularse
copulation /,kɒpyə'leiʃən/ n cópula, f
copy /'kɒpi/ n copia, f; (of a book) ejemplar, m; (of a paper) número, m; manuscrito, m; (subject-matter) material, m. vt copiar; imitar; tomar como modelo (a). **rough c.,** borrador, m. **c.-book,** cuaderno de escritura, m
copy editor n redactor de textos, m
copying /'kɒpiɪŋ/ n imitación, f; transcripción, f. **c. ink,** tinta de copiar, f
copyist /'kɒpiɪst/ n copiador (-ra); (plagiarist) copiante, mf
copyright /'kɒpi,rait/ n derechos de autor, m pl; depósito legal, m; propiedad literaria, f. a protegido por los derechos de autor. vt registrar como propiedad literaria. **C. reserved,** Derechos reservados, Queda hecho el depósito que marca la ley
copywriter /'kɒpi,raitər/ n escritor de anuncios, m
coquet /kou'kɛt/ vi coquetear; Fig. jugar (con)
coquetry /'koukɪtri/ n coquetería, f
coquette /kou'kɛt/ n coqueta, f
coquettish /kou'kɛtɪʃ/ a coquetón; atractivo
coral /'kɔrəl/ n coral, m; (polyp) coralina, f. a de coral, coralino. **white c.,** madrépora, f. **c. beads,** corales, m pl. **c.-island,** atalón, m. **c.-reef,** escollo de coral, m. **c. snake,** coral, f
corbel /'kɔrbəl/ n Archit. ménsula, f
cord /kɔrd/ n cuerda, f; cordel, m; cordón, m. vt encordelar. **spinal c.,** médula espinal, f. **umbilical c.,** cordón umbilical, m
cordial /'kɔrdʒəl/ a cordial; sincero, fervoroso. n cordial, m
cordiality /'kɔrdn̩'dʒælɪti/ n cordialidad, f
cordon /'kɔrdn̩/ n cordón, m; cinto, m. **to c. off,** acordonar
Cordova /'kɔrdəvə/ Córdoba, f
cordovan /'kɔrdəvən/ a cordobés, m (leather) cordobán, m
corduroy /'kɔrdə,rɔi/ n pana de cordoncillo, f
core /kɔr/ n (of a fruit) corazón, m; (of a rope) alma, f, centro, m; (of an abscess) foco, m; (of a corn) ojo, m; Fig. núcleo, m; esencia, f; lo esencial
corespondent /,kouri'spɒndənt/ n cómplice en un caso de divorcio, mf
Corinth /'kɔrɪnθ/ Corinto, m
Corinthian /kə'rɪnθiən/ a corintio. n corintio (-ia)
cork /kɔrk/ n corcho, m; (of a bottle) tapón, m, a de corcho. vt tapar con corcho, taponar; (wine) encorchar; (the face) tiznar con corcho quemado. **pop of a**

c., taponazo, m. **to draw a c.,** descorchar. **c.-jacket,** chaleco salvavidas, m. **c. tree,** alcornoque, m
corkscrew /'kɔrk,skru/ n sacacorchos, m
cormorant /'kɔrmərənt/ n cormorán, m
corn /kɔrn/ n grano, cereal, m; (wheat) trigo, m; (maize) maíz, m; (single seed) grano, m; (on the foot, etc.) callo, m. **Indian c.,** maíz, m. **c. cure,** callicida, m. **c.-exchange,** bolsa de granos, f. **c.-field,** campo de trigo, m. **c.-flower,** aciano, m. **c. liquor,** Lat. Am. chicha, f
cornea /'kɔrniə/ n córnea, f
corner /'kɔrnər/ n ángulo, m; (of a street or building) esquina, f; (of a room) rincón, Mexico ancón m; Auto. viraje, m; Com. monopolio, m; (of the eye) rabo, m; (soccer) "corner," m. vt arrinconar; acorralar; Com. acaparar. **the four corners of the earth,** los cuatro ángulos de la tierra. **a tight c.,** un lance apretado, un apuro. **to drive into a c.,** Fig. poner entre la espada y la pared. **to look out of the c. of the eye,** mirar de reojo. **to turn the c.,** doblar la esquina; Fig. pasar la crisis. **c.-cupboard,** rinconera, f. **c. seat,** asiento del rincón, m. **c. shop,** Lat. Am. esquina, f. **c.-stone,** piedra angular, f.
cornered /'kɔrnərd/ a (of a person) acorralado, en aprieto; (of hats) de... picos. **three-c. hat,** sombrero de tres picos, m
cornet /kɔr'nɛt/ n (musical instrument) corneta, f; Mil. corneta, m; (paper) cucurucho, m. **c. player,** cornetín, m
cornflour /'kɔrn,flauər/ n harina de maíz, f
cornice /'kɔrnɪs/ n cornisa, f
Cornish /'kɔrnɪʃ/ a de Cornualles
cornucopia /,kɔrnə'koupiə/ n cornucopia, f
corollary /'kɔrə,lɛri/ n corolario, m
corona /kə'rounə/ n (Astron. Archit.) corona, f
coronation /,kɔrə'neiʃən/ n coronación, f
coroner /'kɔrənər/ n juez de guardia, mf, médico forense, m
coronet /,kɔrə'nɛt/ n (of a peer, etc.) corona, f; tiara, f; guirnalda, f
corporal /'kɔrpərəl/ a corporal, n Mil. cabo, m; (altar-cloth) corporal, m. **c. punishment,** castigo corporal, m
corporate /'kɔrpərɪt/ a corporativo
corporation /,kɔrpə'reiʃən/ n corporación, f; concejo, cabildo municipal, m; Com. sociedad anónima, f
corporeal /kɔr'pɔriəl/ a corpóreo
corps /kɔr/ n cuerpo, m
corpse /kɔrps/ n cadáver, m
corpulence /'kɔrpyələns/ n gordura, obesidad, f
corpulent /'kɔrpyələnt/ a corpulento, grueso, gordo
corpus /'kɔrpəs/ n cuerpo, m. **C. Christi,** Corpus, m. **c. delicti,** cuerpo del delito, m
corpuscle /'kɔrpəsəl/ n corpúsculo, m
correct /kə'rɛkt/ a correcto; exacto, justo. vt corregir; rectificar; amonestar, reprender
correction /kə'rɛkʃən/ n corrección, f; rectificación, f
corrective /kə'rɛktɪv/ a correctivo. n correctivo, m
correctness /kə'rɛktnɪs/ n corrección, f; exactitud, f; justicia, f
correlate /'kɔrə,leit/ vt poner en correlación. vi tener correlación
correlation /,kɔrə'leiʃən/ n correlación, f
correspond /,kɔrə'spɒnd/ vi corresponder (a); (by letter) escribirse, corresponderse
correspondence /,kɔrə'spɒndəns/ n correspondencia, f; Com. correo, m. **c. course,** curso por correspondencia, m
correspondent /,kɔrə'spɒndənt/ n correspondiente, mf; (Com. and journalist) corresponsal, mf. **special c.,** corresponsal extraordinario, m
corresponding /,kɔrə'spɒndɪŋ/ a correspondiente. **c. member,** miembro correspondiente, m
corridor /'kɔrɪdər/ n corredor, pasillo, m; (railway) pasillo, m; Polit. corredor, m. **c. train,** tren con coches corridos, m
corroborate /kə'rɒbə,reit/ vt corroborar, confirmar
corroboration /kə,rɒbə'reiʃən/ n corroboración, confirmación, f

corroborative /kə'rɒbə,reitɪv/ *a* corroborativo, confirmatorio
corrode /kə'roud/ *vt* corroer, morder; *Fig.* roer
corrosion /kə'rouʒən/ *n* corrosión, *f*
corrosive /kə'rousɪv/ *a* corrosivo; mordaz
corrugate /'kɔrə,geit/ *vt* arrugar. *vi* arrugarse
corrugated /'kɔrə,geitɪd/ *a* arrugado; ondulado. **c. iron,** chapa canaleta, *f*
corrugation /,kɔrə'geiʃən/ *n* corrugación, *f*, arrugamiento, *m*
corrupt /kə'rʌpt/ *a* corrompido; vicioso, desmoralizado. *vt* corromper. *vi* corromperse
corrupter /kə'rʌptər/ *n* corruptor (-ra)
corruption /kə'rʌpʃən/ *n* corrupción, *f*
corsage /kɔr'sɑʒ/ *n* corpiño, *m*
corset /'kɔrsɪt/ *n* corsé, *m*, *vt* encorsetar. **c. shop,** corsetería, *f*
Corsica /'kɔrsɪkə/ Córcega, *f*
Corsican /'kɔrsɪkən/ *a* corso. *n* corso (-sa)
cortege /kɔr'tɛʒ/ *n* séquito, acompañamiento, *m*; desfile, *m*
cortex /'kɔrtɛks/ *n Bot. Anat.* corteza, *f*
cortisone /'kɔrtə,zoun/ *n* (drug) cortisona, *f*
Corunna /kə'runyə/ La Coruña, *f*
coruscation /,kɔrə'skeiʃən/ *n* brillo, *m*
corvette /kɔr'vet/ *n* corbeta, *f*
cosignatory /kou'sɪgnə,tɔri/ *n* cosignatario (-ia)
cosine /'kousain/ *n* coseno, *m*
cosiness /'kouzinɪs/ *n* comodidad, *f*
cosmetic /kɒz'mɛtɪk/ *a* cosmético. *n* afeite, cosmético, *m*
cosmic /'kɒzmɪk/ *a* cósmico
cosmographer /kɒz'mɒgrəfər/ *n* cosmógrafo, *m*
cosmography /kɒz'mɒgrəfi/ *n* cosmografía, *f*
cosmopolitan /,kɒzmə'pɒlɪtṇ/ *a* cosmopolita. *n* cosmopolita, *mf*
cosmopolitanism /,kɒzmə'pɒlɪtṇ,izəm/ *n* cosmopolitismo, *m*
cosmos /'kɒzməs/ *n* cosmos, universo, *m*
Cossack /'kɒsæk/ *a* cosaco. *n* cosaco (-ca)
cosset /'kɒsɪt/ *vt* mimar, consentir
cost /kɔst/ *vi* costar. *n* costa, *f*, coste, precio, *m*; *Fig.* costa, *f*; *pl* **costs,** *Law.* costas, *f pl.* **at all costs,** cueste lo que cueste, a toda costa. **to my c.,** a mi costa. **c. of living,** coste de la vida, *m*. **to c. a fortune,** costar un sentido
Costa Rican /'kɒstə 'rikən/ *a* and *n* costarricense, *mf*
coster /'kɔstər/ *n* vendedor (-ra) ambulante
costliness /'kɔstlinɪs/ *n* alto precio, *m*; suntuosidad, *f*
costly /'kɔstli/ *a* costoso; suntuoso, magnífico
costume /'kɒstum/ *n* traje, *m*; (fancy-dress) disfraz, *m*; (tailored) traje sastre, *m*; **"Costume,"** (among credits in films and plays) «Vestuario»
costumier /,kɒstu'miər/ *n* modista, *mf*; sastre, *m*
cot /kɒt/ *n* (hut) choza, cabaña, *f*; (child's) camita, *f*
coterie /'koutəri/ *n* círculo, grupo, *m*; (clique) camarilla, *f*
cotillion /kə'tilyən/ *n* cotillón, *m*
cottage /'kɒtɪdʒ/ *n* cabaña, choza, *f*; casita, *f*, hotelito, *m*; torre, villa, *f*. **c. cheese** *Mexico* asadero *m*
cotter /'kɒtər/ *n* chaveta, llave, *f*
cotton /'kɒtṇ/ *n* algodón, *m*, *a* de algodón. **I don't c. to the idea at all,** No me gusta nada la idea; la idea no me seduce. **sewing-c.,** hilo de coser, *m*. **c. goods,** géneros de algodón, *m pl.* **c. mill,** hilandería de algodón, algodonería, *f*. **c. plantation,** algodonal, *m*. **c.-seed oil,** aceite de semilla de algodón, *m*. **c.-spinner,** hilandero (-ra) de algodón. **c.-wool,** algodón en rama, *m*. **c.-yarn,** hilo de algodón, *m*
couch /kautʃ/ *n* sofá, canapé, *m*; (bed) lecho, *m*; (lair) cama, *f*. *vt* (lay down) acostar, echar; (a lance) enristrar; (express) expresar, redactar. *vi* acostarse; (crouch) agacharse; estar en acecho
cough /kɔf/ *vi* toser. *n* tos, *f*. **to c. up,** escupir, expectorar. **c.-drop,** pastilla para la tos, *f*
coughing /'kɔfɪŋ/ *n* tos, *f*
could. /kʊd/. **See can**
council /'kaunsəl/ *n* consejo, *m*; junta, *f*; *Eccl.* concilio, *m*. **Privy C.,** consejo privado, *m*. **to hold c.,** celebrar un consejo; aconsejarse (con); consultarse

town c., ayuntamiento, *m*. **c. chamber,** sala consistorial, *f*; sala de actos, *f*. **c. houses,** casas baratas, *f pl.* **c. of war,** consejo de guerra, *m*
councilor /'kaunsələr/ *n* concejal, *m*; miembro de la junta, *m*
counsel /'kaunsəl/ *n* consultación, *f*; deliberación, *f*; consejo, *m*; *Law.* abogado, *m*. *vt* aconsejar. **a c. of perfection,** un ideal imposible. **to keep one's own c.,** no decir nada, callarse, guardar silencio. **to take c. with,** consultar (a), aconsejarse con
counselor /'kaunsələr/ *n* consejero, *m*. **c. of state,** consejero de estado, *m*
count /kaunt/ *vt* contar; calcular; (consider) creer, considerar. *vi* contar. *n* cuenta, *f*; (of votes) escrutinio, *m*; *Law.* capítulo, *m*. **John simply doesn't c.,** Juan no cuenta para nada. **Erudition alone counts for very little,** La mera erudición sirve para muy poco. **to keep c. of,** tener cuenta de. **to lose c. of,** perder cuenta de. **to c. on,** contar con; (doing something) esperar. **to c. up,** contar
count /kaunt/ *n* (title) conde, *m*
countenance /'kauntṇəns/ *n* semblante, *m*; expresión de la cara, *f*; aspecto, *m*; (favor) apoyo, *m*, ayuda, *f*. *vt* autorizar, aprobar; apoyar, ayudar. **to put (a person) out of c.,** desconcertar (a)
counter /'kauntər/ *n* (in a bank) contador, *m*; (in a shop) mostrador, *m*; (in games) ficha, *f*, *adv* contra, al contrario; al revés. *a* opuesto (a), contrario (a). *vt* parar; contestar. **to run c. to my inclinations,** oponerse a mis deseos. **to c. with the left,** (boxing) contestar con la izquierda. **c.-attack,** contraataque, *m*. **c.-attraction,** atracción contraria, *f*. **c.-offensive,** contraofensiva, *f*. **c.-reformation,** contrarreforma, *f*. **c.-revolution,** contrarevolución, *f*
counteract /,kauntər'ækt/ *vt* neutralizar; frustrar
counterbalance /'kauntər,bæləns/ *n* contrapeso, *m*, *vt* contrabalancear; compensar, igualar
counterblast /'kauntər,blæst/ *n* denunciación, *f*; respuesta, *f*
countercharge /'kauntər,tʃɑrdʒ/ *n* recriminación, *f*. *vt* recriminar; *Law.* reconvenir
counterfeit /'kauntər,fit/ *a* falso, espurio; fingido. *n* falsificación, *f*; imitación, *f*; moneda falsa, *f*; (person) impostor (-ra). *vt* imitar; (pretend) fingir; (coins, handwriting, etc.) falsificar
counterfeiter /'kauntər,fitər/ *n* falsario (-ia)
counterfoil /'kauntər,fɔil/ *n* talón, *m*
countermand /v ,kauntər'mænd; *n* 'kauntər,mænd/ *vt* contramandar; (an order) revocar, cancelar. *n* contraorden, *f*; revocación, *f*
countermeasure /'kauntər,mɛʒər/ *n* contramedida, *f*
counterpane /'kauntər,pein/ *n* sobrecama, colcha, *f*
counterpart /'kauntər,pɑrt/ *n* contraparte, *f*; (of a document) duplicado, *m*
counterplot /'kauntər,plɒt/ *n* contratreta, *f*
counterpoint /'kauntər,pɔint/ *n Mus.* contrapunto, *m*
counterpoise /'kauntər,pɔiz/ *n* contrapeso, *m*; equilibrio, *m*, *vt* contrabalancear, contrapesar
countersign /'kauntər,sain/ *n* contraseña, *f*, *vt* refrendar
countess /'kauntɪs/ *n* condesa, *f*
counting /'kauntɪŋ/ *n* cuenta, *f*; numeración, *f*; (of votes) escrutinio, *m*. **c.-house,** contaduría, *f*
countless /'kauntlɪs/ *a* innumerable. **a c. number,** un sinfín, un sinnúmero
countrified /'kʌntrə,faid/ *a* rústico, campesino
country /'kʌntri/ *n* país, *m*; (fatherland) patria, *f*; región, campiña, tierra, *f*; (as opposed to town) campo, *m*. *a* del campo; campesino, campestre, rústico. **He lives in the c.,** Vive en el campo. **c. club,** club campestre, *m*. **c. cousin,** provinciano (-na). **c.-dance,** baile campestre, *m*. **c. gentleman,** hacendado, *m*. **c. girl,** campesina, *f*; aldeana, *f*. **c.-house,** finca, *f*; casa de campo, *f*. **c. life,** vida del campo, *f*. **c.-seat,** finca, *f*
countryman /'kʌntrimən/ *n* campesino, *m*; hombre del campo, *m*; compatriota, *m*
countryside /'kʌntri,said/ *n* campo, *m*; campiña, *f*
countrywoman /'kʌntri,wʊmən/ *n* campesina, *f*; compatriota, *f*
county /'kaunti/ *n* condado, *m*; provincia, *f*. **c. coun-**

cil, diputación provincial, *f.* **c. town,** cabeza de partido, *f;* ciudad provincial, *f*
county seat *n* cabecera municipal, cabeza de partido, *f*
coup /ku/ *n* golpe, *m.* **c. d'état,** golpe de estado, *m*
coupe /kup/ *n* cupé, *m*
couple /'kʌpəl/ *n* par, *m;* (in a dance, etc.) pareja, *f.* *vt* enganchar, acoplar; (in marriage) casar; (animals) aparear; (ideas) asociar; (names) juntar. **the young (married) c.,** el matrimonio joven
couplet /'kʌplɪt/ *n* copla, *f*
coupling /'kʌplɪŋ/ *n* enganche, acoplamiento, *m;* (of railway carriages) enganche, *m;* (of ideas) asociación, *f*
coupon /'kupɒn/ *n* talón, *m;* cupón, *m*
courage /'kɜrɪdʒ/ *n* valor, *m.* **C.!** ¡Ánimo! **to muster up c.,** cobrar ánimo
courageous /kə'reɪdʒəs/ *a* valiente
courageously /kə'reɪdʒəsli/ *adv* valientemente
courier /'kɜriər/ *n* correo, *m,* estafeta, *f;* (guide) guía, *m;* (newspaper) estafeta, *f*
course /kɔrs/ *n* curso, *m;* (of time) transcurso, *m;* (of events) marcha, *f;* (of a river, etc.) cauce, *m;* (of stars) carrera, *f,* curso, *m;* (of a ship) derrota, *f,* rumbo, *m;* (way) camino, *m,* ruta, *f;* (of conduct) línea de conducta, *f;* actitud, *f;* (of study) curso, *m;* (of a meal) plato, *m;* (of an illness) desarrollo, *m; Med.* tratamiento, *m.* **He took it as a matter of c.,** Lo tomó sin darle importancia. **in due c.,** a su tiempo debido. **in the c. of time,** andando el tiempo, en el transcurso de los años. **of c.,** claro está; naturalmente; por supuesto. **Are you coming tomorrow? Of c.!** ¿Vienes mañana? ¡Ya lo creo! **the best c. to take,** lo mejor que se puede hacer, el mejor plantamiento, *m*
course /kɔrs/ *vt* cazar, perseguir; *Poet.* correr por, cruzar. *vi* (of blood, etc.) correr; cazar
court /kɔrt/ *n* (yard) patio, *m;* (tennis) campo de tenis, *m;* (fives, racquets) cancha, *f;* (royal) corte, *f;* (of justice) tribunal, *m;* (following) séquito, acompañamiento, *m. vt* hacer la corte (a); cortejar, pretender; solicitar; (sleep) conciliar. **to c.,** (a woman) galantear, pretender; (a person) hacer la rueda (a), *Lat. Am.* afilar. **to respect the c.,** *Law.* guardar sala. **c. of appeal,** sala de apelación, *f.* **c. of justice,** sala de justicia, *f;* tribunal de justicia, *m.* **supreme c.,** tribunal supremo, *m.* **c. house,** palacio de justicia, *m.* **c. jester,** bufón, *m.* **c.-martial,** tribunal militar, *m.* **room,** sala de justicia, *f*
courteous /'kɜrtiəs/ *a* cortés
courteousness /'kɜrtiəsnɪs/ *n* cortesía, *f*
courtesy /'kɜrtəsi/ *n* cortesía, *f;* favor, *m,* merced, *f;* permiso, *m*
courtier /'kɔrtiər/ *n* cortesano, palaciego, *m*
courtliness /'kɔrtlinɪs/ *n* cortesía, urbanidad, *f;* dignidad, *f;* elegancia, *f*
courtly /'kɔrtli/ *a* cortés, galante; digno; elegante
courtship /'kɔrtʃɪp/ *n* noviazgo, *m;* galanteo, *m*
courtyard /'kɔrt,yard/ *n* patio, *m*
cousin /'kʌzən/ *n* primo (-ma). **first c.,** primo (-ma) carnal. **second c.,** primo (-ma) segundo (-da)
cove /kouv/ *n* cala, abra, ensenada, *f,* ancón *m*
covenant /'kʌvənənt/ *n* contrato, *m;* estipulación, *f;* pacto, *m;* alianza, *f. vt* prometer; estipular
Coventry, to send to, /'kʌvəntri/ hacer el vacío (a)
cover /'kʌvər/ *vt* cubrir; abrigar; (dissemble) disimular; (a distance) recorrer; (comprise) comprender, abarcar; (with confusion, etc.) llenar (de); (with a revolver, etc.) amenazar (con); (an overdraft, etc.) garantizar; (of stallions) cubrir; (of a hen and eggs) empollar; (a story, journalism) investigar. *n* cubierta, *f;* (for a chair, umbrella, etc.) funda, *f;* (of a saucepan, jar, etc.) tapa, *f;* (dish-cover) tapadera, *f;* (of a book) cubierta, tapa, *f;* (of a letter) sobre, *m;* (shelter) abrigo, *m;* protección, *f;* (undergrowth) maleza, *f; Fig.* velo, manto, *m;* (pretence) pretexto, *m; Com.* garantía, *f.* **outer c.,** (of tire) cubierta de neumático, *f.* **to c. oneself with glory,** cubrirse de gloria. **to c. up,** cubrir(se) del todo; (with clothes) arropar; (wrap up) envolver. **to c. with a revolver,** amenazar con un revólver. **to read a book from c. to c.,** leer un libro del principio al fin. **to take c.,** refugiarse, tomar abrigo. **under c.,** bajo tejado; al abrigo

cover charge *n* consumo mínimo, precio del cubierto, *m*
covering /'kʌvərɪŋ/ *n* cubrimiento, *m;* cubierta, *f;* envoltura, *f;* capa, *f,* abrigo, *m.* **c. letter,** carta adjunta, *f*
coverlet /'kʌvərlɪt/ *n* colcha, sobrecama, *f*
covert /a 'kouvərt; *n* 'kʌvərt/ *n* guarida, *f. a* oculto; furtivo
covertly /'kouvərtli/ *adv* secretamente, furtivamente
covet /'kʌvɪt/ *vt* codiciar; ambicionar, suspirar por
covetous /'kʌvɪtəs/ *a* codicioso; ávido; ambicioso
covetously /'kʌvɪtəsli/ *adv* codiciosamente; ávidamente
covetousness /'kʌvɪtəsnɪs/ *n* codicia, avaricia, *f;* avidez, *f;* ambición, *f*
cow /kau/ *vt* intimidar, acobardar
cow /kau/ *n* vaca, *Lat. Am. also* lechera *f;* (of other animals) hembra, *f.* **c.-bell,** cencerro, *m,* zumba, *f.* **c.-catcher,** *Auto.* salvavidas, *m.* **c.-hide,** cuero, cuero de vaca, zurriago, *m;* penca, *f.* **c.-house,** establo, *m,* boyera, *f.* **c.-pox,** vacuna, *f*
coward /'kauərd/ *n* cobarde, *m,* a cobarde
cowardice /'kauərdɪs/ *n* cobardía, *f, Argentina* canillera, *f*
cowardly /'kauərdli/ *a* cobarde, *Mexico, Venezuela* correlón
cowboy /'kau,bɔi/ *n* vaquero, *m;* gaucho, "cowboy," *m*
cower /'kauər/ *vi* temblar, acobardarse
cowherd /'kau,hɜrd/ *n* vaquero, boyero, *m*
cowl /kaul/ *n* capucha, *f;* (of a chimney) sombrerete, *m*
coworker /'kou,wɜrkər, kou'wɜr-/ *n* colaborador (-ra)
cowshed /'kau,ʃɛd/ *n* establo, *m*
cowslip /'kauslɪp/ *n* prímula, *f*
cox /kɒks/ *n* timonel, *m*
coxcomb /'kɒks,koum/ *n* (of a jester) gorra de bufón, *f;* mequetrefe, *m*
coxswain /'kɒksən/ *n* patrón, *m;* (of a rowboat) timonel, *m*
coy /kɔi/ *a* modoso, tímido; coquetón
coyly /'kɔili/ *adv* tímidamente; con coquetería
coyness /'kɔinɪs/ *n* timidez, modestia, *f;* coquetería, *f*
cozy /'kouzi/ *a* cómodo; agradable; caliente. **You are very c. here,** Estás muy bien aquí
crab /kræb/ *n* (sea) cangrejo de mar, cámbaro, *m, Lat. Am. also* jaiba *m;* (river) cangrejo, *m; Astron.* Cáncer, *m. vt* (thwart) frustrar. **hermit c.,** cangrejo ermitaño, *m.* **c.-apple,** manzana silvestre, *f.* **c.-louse,** ladilla, *f*
crabbed /'kræbɪd/ *a* áspero, hosco, desabrido, arisco; (of handwriting) apretado, metido
crack /kræk/ *vt* hender; quebrantar, romper; (nuts) cascar; (a whip and fingers) chasquear; (a bottle of wine) abrir. *vi* (of earth, skin, etc.) agrietarse; romperse, quebrarse; (of the voice) romper; (of the male voice) mudar. *n* hendedura, rendija, *f;* quebraja, *f;* (of a whip) chasquido, *m;* (of a rifle) estallido, *m;* (blow) golpe, garrotazo, *m, a* excelente, de primera categoría; estupendo. **to c. a joke,** decir un chiste. **to c. up,** *vt* dar bombo (a), alabar. *vi* (in health) quebrantarse; (airplane) cuartearse, estrellarse. **c.-brained,** descalabrado; estúpido, loco
cracked /krækt/ *a* grietado; (of a bell, etc.) hendido; (of the voice) cascada; (of a person) chiflado
cracker /'krækər/ *n* (firework) petardo, *m;* buscapiés, *m*
crackle /'krækəl/ *vi* (of burning wood, etc.) crepitar, (rustle) crujir; (of rifle fire) tirotear. *n* crepitación, *f;* crujido, *m;* (of rifle fire) tiroteo, *m*
crackling /'kræklɪŋ/ *n.* See **crackle;** *Cul.* chicharrón, *m*
cradle /'kreidl/ *n* cuna, *f; Fig.* niñez, infancia, *f;* (for a limb) arco de protección, *m;* (for winebottle) cesta, *f. vt* mecer. **c.-song,** canción de cuna, *f*
craft /kræft/ *n* (guile) astucia, *f;* (skill) habilidad, *f;* arte, *mf;* (occupation) oficio manual, *m;* profesión, *f;* (guild) gremio, *m;* (ship, plane) nave, *f,* embarcación, *f*
craftily /'kræftli/ *adv* astutamente
craftiness /'kræftinɪs/ *n* astucia, *f*
craftsman /'kræftsmən/ *n* artífice, *m;* arte sano, *m;* artista, *m*

craftsmanship /'kræftsmən‚ʃɪp/ n arte, m, or f; habilidad, f; artificio, m
crafty /'kræfti/ a astuto, taimado, Lat. Am. macuco.
c. person Mexico fistol m
crag /kræg/ n peña, f, risco, despeñadero, m
cragginess /'kræginɪs/ n escabrosidad, aspereza, fragosidad, f
craggy /'krægi/ a escabroso, escarpado, peñascoso, riscoso
cram /kræm/ vt henchir; atestar; (one's mouth) llenar (de); (poultry) cebar; (a pupil) preparar para un examen; (a subject) empollar. vi (with food) atracarse. **The room was crammed with people,** La sala estaba atestada de gente
cramp /kræmp/ n Med. calambre, m; (numbness) entumecimiento, m; (rivet) grapa, f. vt dar calambre (a); (numb) entumecer; (fasten) lañar; (Fig. hamper) estorbar. **to c. someone's style,** cortar los vuelos (a). **writer's c.,** calambre del escribiente, m
cramped /kræmpt/ a (of space) apretado, estrecho; (of writing) menuda
cranberry /'kræn‚bɛri/ n arándano, m
crane /krein/ n Ornith. grulla, f; (machine) grúa, f. **jib c.,** grúa de pescante, f. **travelling c.,** grúa móvil, f. **to c. one's neck,** estirar el cuello. **crane's bill,** pico de cigüeña, m
cranium /'kreiniəm/ n cráneo, m
crank /kræŋk/ n (handle) manivela, f; (person) maniático (-ca). vt poner en marcha (un motor) con la manivela
crankiness /'kræŋkinɪs/ n (crossness) irritabilidad, f, mal humor, m; (eccentricity) excentricidad, f
cranky /'kræŋki/ a (cross) irritable, malhumorado; (eccentric) chiflado, maniático, excéntrico
cranny /'kræni/ n hendedura, grieta, f
crape /kreip/ n crespón, m
crash /kræʃ/ vi caer estrepitosamente; romperse; estallarse; (of aircraft, cars) estrellarse; Fig. hundirse, arruinarse. n estrépito, estruendo, m; estallido, m; (of aircraft) accidente de aviación, m; (car) accidente, m, (or choque, m) de automóviles; (financial) ruina, f; Fig. hundimiento, m. **to c. into,** estrellarse contra, chocar con. **c. helmet,** casco, m. **c.-landing,** aterrizaje violento, m
crass /kræs/ a craso
crassness /'kræsnɪs/ n estupidez, f
crate /kreit/ n (box) caja de embalaje, f; (basket) canasto, m, banasta, Mexico jaba f
crater /'kreitər/ n cráter, m
cravat /krə'væt/ n corbata, f
crave /kreiv/ vt suplicar, implorar. **to c. for,** perecer por, suspirar por, anhelar
craven /'kreivən/ a cobarde, pusilánime. n poltrón, cobarde, m
craving /'kreivɪŋ/ n deseo vehemente, m, sed, f
crawfish /'krɔ‚fɪʃ/ n cangrejo de río, m; cigala, f
crawl /krɔl/ vi arrastrarse; andar a gatas; andar a paso de tortuga; (abase oneself) humillarse; (be full of) abundar (en). n paso de tortuga, m; (swimming) arrastne m
crayfish /'krei‚fɪʃ/ n cangrejo de río, m; cigala, f
crayon /'kreiən/ n carbón, m; pastel, m; (pencil) lápiz de color, m. vt dibujar con pastel, etc. **c. drawing,** dibujo al carbón, m
craze /kreiz/ vt enloquecer, volver loco (a). n manía, f, capricho, entusiasmo, m; (fashion) moda, f
crazily /'kreizəli/ adv locamente
craziness /'kreizinɪs/ n locura, f
crazy /'kreizi/ a loco; chiflado; (of structure) dilapidado. **He is c. about music,** Está loco por la música. **to be completely c.,** (of persons) ser un loco de atar; ser completamente loco. **to drive c.,** volver loco (a)
creak /krik/ vi (of shoes, chairs, etc.) crujir; (of gates, etc.) rechinar, chirriar. n crujido, m; chirrido, m
creaking /'krikɪŋ/ n. See **creak**
creaky /'kriki/ a crujiente, que cruje; chirriador
cream /krim/ n crema, f; nata, f; Fig. flor, nata, f. a de nata. **whipped c.,** nata batida, f. **c. cake,** pastel de nata, m. **c.-cheese,** queso de nata, m. **c.-colored,** de color crema. **c.-jug,** jarro para crema, m. **c. of tartar,** cremor, tártaro, m

creamery /'krimәri/ n lechería, f
creamy /'krimi/ a cremoso
crease /kris/ n (wrinkle) arruga, f; (fold) pliegue, m; (in trousers) raya, f; (in cricket) línea de la meta, f. vt (wrinkle) arrugar; (fold) plegar; (trousers) poner la raya en. vi arrugarse
create /kri'eit/ vt crear; (appoint) nombrar; (produce) suscitar, producir
creation /kri'eiʃən/ n creación, f; establecimiento, m; (appointment) nombramiento, m
creative /kri'eitɪv/ a creador; de la creación
creativeness /kri'eitɪvnɪs/ n facultad creativa, inventiva, f
creator /kri'eitər/ n creador (-ra)
creature /'kritʃər/ n criatura, f; animal, m. **c. comforts,** bienestar material, m
crèche /krɛʃ/ n casa cuna, f
credence /'kridns/ n crédito, m, fe, creencia, f; Eccl. credencia, f. **to give c. to,** dar crédito (a), creer
credentials /krɪ'dɛnʃəlz/ n pl credenciales, f pl
credibility /‚krɛdə'bɪlɪti/ n credibilidad, verosimilitud, f
credible /'krɛdəbəl/ a creíble, verosímil; (of persons) digno de confianza
credibly /'krɛdəbli/ adv creíblemente
credit /'krɛdɪt/ n crédito, m; reputación, f; honor, m; (Com. and banking) crédito, m; (in bookkeeping) data, f. vt dar fe (a), dar crédito (a); creer; atribuir; (bookkeeping) acreditar. **It does them c.,** Les hace honor. **on c.,** a crédito, al fiado. **open c.,** Com. letra abierta, f. **to give on c.,** dar fiado. **c. balance,** haber, m
creditable /'krɛdɪtəbəl/ a loable, honroso, digno de alabanza
creditably /'krɛdɪtəbli/ adv honrosamente
creditor /'krɛdɪtər/ n acreedor (-ra); (bookkeeping) haber, m
credulity /krə'dulɪti/ n credulidad, f
credulous /'krɛdʒələs/ a crédulo, Lat. Am. creído
credulously /'krɛdʒələsli/ adv con credulidad, crédulamente
creed /krid/ n credo, m
creek /krik/ n caleta, abra, f
creel /kril/ n (for fish) cesta de pescador, f
creep /krip/ vi arrastrarse; (of plants and birds) trepar; (of infants) andar a gatas; (totter) hacer pinitos; (slip) deslizarse; (cringe) lisonjear, rebajarse; (of one's flesh) sentir hormigueo. **to c. about on tiptoe,** andar de puntillas. **to c. into a person's favor,** insinuarse en el favor de. **to c. in,** entrar sin ser notado (en); deslizarse en. **to c. on,** (of time) avanzar lentamente; (of old age, etc.) acercarse insensiblemente. **to c. out,** salir sin hacer ruido; escurrirse. **to c. up,** trepar por; subir a gatas
creeper /'kripər/ n Bot. enredadera, f; Ornith. trepador, m; Zool. reptil, m
creeping /'kripɪŋ/ a Bot. trepante; Zool. trepador; (servile) rastrero
cremate /'krimeit/ vt incinerar
cremation /krɪ'meiʃən/ n cremación, f
crematorium /‚krimə'tɔriəm/ n crematorio, m; horno de incineración, m, inhumadora, f
creole /'krioul/ a criollo. n criollo (-lla)
creolize /'kriə‚laiz/ vt acriollar
crescent /'krɛsənt/ n media luna, f; Herald. creciente, m; calle en forma de semicírculo, f. a en forma de media luna; Poet. creciente
cress /krɛs/ n Bot. berro, m
crest /krɛst/ n (of a cock, etc.) cresta, f; (plume) penacho, m; (of a helmet) cimera, f; (of a hill) cumbre, cima, f; (of a wave) cresta, f. **family c.,** blasón, escudo, m
crested /'krɛstɪd/ a Lat. Am. copetudo (-da)
crestfallen /'krɛst‚fɔlən/ a cabizbajo, cariacontecido
cretan /'kritn/ a cretense. n cretense, mf
cretin /'kritn/ n cretino (-na)
crevasse /krə'væs/ n grieta en un ventisquero, f
crevice /'krɛvɪs/ n intersticio, m, rendija, grieta, f
crew /kru/ n (of ships, boats, aircraft) tripulación, f; (of a gun) servidores de una ametralladora, m pl; (gang) pandilla, cuadrilla, f
crib /krɪb/ n pesebre, m; (child's) camita de niño, m;

(plagiary) plagio, *m. vt* (plagiarize) plagiar; (steal) hurtar

crick /krɪk/ *n* (in the neck) tortícolis, *m*

cricket /'krɪkɪt/ *n Ent.* grillo, *m*; (game) cricquet, *m.* **c. ball,** pelota de cricquet, *f.* **c. bat,** paleta de cricquet, *f.* **c. ground,** campo de cricquet, *m.* **c. match,** partido de cricquet, *m*

cricketer /'krɪkɪtər/ *n* jugador de cricquet, *m*

crier /'kraɪər/ *n* (town) pregonero, *m*

crime /kraɪm/ *n* crimen, *m*; ofensa, *f*, delito, *m*

criminal /'krɪmənḷ/ *a* criminal. *n* criminal, *m*; reo, *mf* **C. Investigation Department,** (nearest equivalent) policía secreta, *f.* **c. laws,** código penal, *m*

criminally /'krɪmənḷi/ *adv* criminalmente

criminologist /,krɪmə'nɒlədʒɪst/ *n* criminalista, *m*

criminology /,krɪmə'nɒlədʒi/ *n* criminología, *f*

crimson /'krɪmzən, -sən/ *n* carmesí, *m. a* de carmesí. *vt* teñir de carmesí. *vi* enrojecerse

cringe /krɪndʒ/ *vi* temblar; asustarse, acobardarse; inclinarse (ante)

cringing /'krɪndʒɪŋ/ *a* servil, humilde; adulador, *Mexico also* lambioche

crinkle /'krɪŋkəl/ *vi* arrugarse; rizarse. *vt* arrugar. *n* arruga, *f*

crinoline /'krɪnḷɪn/ *n* crinolina, *f*, miriñaque, guardainfante, *m*

cripple /'krɪpəl/ *n* tullido (-da); cojo (-ja). *vt* lisiar, tullir, estropear; *Fig.* paralizar

crisis /'kraɪsɪs/ *n* crisis, *f*

crisp /krɪsp/ *a* (of hair and of leaves) crespo; (fresh) fresco; (stiff) tieso; (of style) nervioso, vigoroso; (of manner) decidido; (of repartee) chispeante; (of tone) incisivo

crisscross /'krɪs,krɒs/ *vt* entrecruzar

criterion /kraɪ'tɪəriən/ *n* criterio, *m*

critic /'krɪtɪk/ *n* crítico, *m*; censor, *m*

critical /'krɪtɪkəl/ *a* crítico

criticism /'krɪtə,sɪzəm/ *n* crítica, *f*

criticize /'krɪtə,saiz/ *vt* criticar; censurar

critique /krɪ'tik/ *n* crítica, *f*

croak /krouk/ *vi* (of frogs) croar; (of ravens) graznar; (of persons) lamentarse, gruñir

croaking /'kroukɪŋ/ *n* canto de la rana, *m*; graznido, *m*

Croat /'krouæt/ *a* croata. *n* croata, *mf*

Croatia /krou'eɪʃə/ Crocia, *f*

crochet /krou'ʃeɪ/ *n* ganchillo, *m*, *vi* hacer ganchillo. *vt* hacer (algo) de ganchillo. **c. hook,** aguja de gancho, *f*, ganchillo, *m.* **c. work,** croché, ganchillo, *m*

crockery /'krɒkəri/ *n* loza, *f*, cacharros, *m pl.* **c. store,** cacharrería, *f*

crocodile /'krɒkə,daɪl/ *n* cocodrilo, *m. m.* **c. tears,** lágrimas de cocodrilo, *f pl*

crocus /'kroukəs/ *n* azafrán de primavera, *m*

croft /krɒft/ *n* campillo, *m*; (farm) heredad, *f*

crony /'krouni/ *n* compinche, *mf*

crook /krʊk/ *n* curva, *f*; (staff) cayado, *m*; (swindler) caballero de industria, estafador, *m*, *vt* doblar, encorvar

crooked /'krʊkɪd/ *a* curvo; encorvado; torcido, *Mexico* chueco; ladeado; (deformed) contrahecho; (of paths, etc.) tortuoso; (dishonest) torcido, tortuoso

crookedly /'krʊkɪdli/ *adv* torcidamente; de través

crookedness /'krʊkɪdnɪs/ *n* encorvadura, *f*; tortuosidad, *f*; sinuosidad, *f*

croon /krun/ *vt* and *vi* canturrear; cantar

crooner /'krunər/ *n* cantante, *m*

crop /krɒp/ *n* (of birds) buche, *m*; (whip) látigo, *m*, fusta, *f*; (handle) mango, *m*; (harvest) cosecha, *f*; (of the hair) cortadura, *f. vt* cortar; (nibble) rozar; (hair) rapar. **Eton c.,** pelo a la garçonne, *m.* **to c. up,** aparecer, surgir

crop rotation *n* la rotación de cultivos, *f*

croquet /krou'keɪ/ *n* juego de la argolla, juego de croquet, *m*

croquette /krou'kɛt/ *n Cul.* croqueta, *f*

crosier /'kroʊʒər/ *n* báculo, cayado del obispo, *m*

cross /krɒs/ *n* cruz, *f*; *Biol.* cruzamiento, *m*; (Sew. bias) bies, *m.* **in the shape of a c.,** en cruz. **the Red C.,** la Cruz Roja. **c.-bearer,** *Eccl.* crucero, *m*

cross /krɒs/ *vt* cruzar; atravesar; pasar por; (a check

and animals) cruzar; (thwart) contrariar. **It did not c. my mind,** No se me ocurrió. **Our letters must have crossed,** Nuestras cartas deben haberse cruzado. **to c. oneself,** *Eccl.* persignarse. **to c. out,** tachar, rayar. **to c. over,** *vt* atravesar, cruzar. *vi* ir al otro lado

cross /krɒs/ *a* transversal; cruzado; oblicuo; (contrary) opuesto (a); (bad-tempered) malhumorado. **c.-breed,** *a* mestizo, atravesado. **c.-country,** *a* a campo travieso. **c.-examination,** *Law.* repregunta, *f*, contrainterrogatorio, *m.* **c.-examine,** *vt Law.* repreguntar; interrogar. **c.-eyed,** bizco. **c.-fire,** *Mil.* fuego cruzado, *m sing* fuegos cruzados, *m pl; Fig.* tiroteo, *m.* **c.-grained,** (of wood) vetisesgado; (of persons) áspero, intratable, desabrido. **c.-legged,** con las piernas cruzadas. **c.-purpose,** despropósito, *m.* **at c.-purposes,** a despropósito. **c.-question,** *vt Law.* repreguntar; interrogar. **c. reference,** contrarreferencia, *f.* **c. section,** sección transversal, *f.* **c.-stitch,** punto cruzado, *m.* **c.-word puzzle,** crucigrama, *m*

crossbar /'krɒs,bɑr/ *n* travesaño, *m*

crossbeam /'krɒs,bim/ *n* viga transversal, *f*

crossbench /'krɒs,bɛntʃ/ *a* atravesado

crossbred /'krɒs,brɛd/ *a* cruzado, mestizo; híbrido

crossbreed /'krɒs,brid/ *n* mestizo (-za); híbrido, *m*

crossing /'krɒsɪŋ/ *n* cruzamiento, *m*; (of the sea) travesía, *f*; (intersection) cruce, *m*; paso, *m.* **level c.,** paso a nivel, *m.* **pedestrian c.,** paso para peatones, *m.* **c.-sweeper,** barrendero, *m*

crossly /'krɒsli/ *adv* con mal humor, con displicencia, irritablemente

crossness /'krɒsnɪs/ *n* irritabilidad, *f*, mal humor, *m*

crossroad /'krɒs,roud/ *n* travesía, *f*; cruce, *m*; *pl* **crossroads,** cruce, cruce de caminos, *m sing* encrucijada, *f sing*

crosswise /'krɒs,waiz/ *adv* en cruz; a través

crotch /krɒtʃ/ *n* (of a tree) bifurcación, *f*; *Anat.* horcajadura, *f*; (of trousers) entrepiernas, *f pl*

crotchet /'krɒtʃɪt/ *n Mus.* semínima, *f*; (fad) capricho, *m*; extravagancia, excentricidad, *f*

crotchety /'krɒtʃɪti/ *a* caprichoso; raro, excéntrico; difícil

crouch /krautʃ/ *vi* acurrucarse, agacharse, acuclillarse

croup /krup/ *n* (disease) crup, garrotillo, *m*; (of a horse) grupa, anca, *f*

croupier /'krupiər/ *n* coime, crupié, *m*

crow /krou/ *n Ornith.* cuervo, *m*; *Ornith.* grajo, *m*; (of a cock) canto del gallo, cacareo, *m*; (of an infant) gorjeo, *m. vi* (of a cock) cantar, cacarear. **as the c. flies,** en línea recta. **to c. over,** gallear, cantar victoria. **crow's-foot,** pata de gallo, *f.* **crow's-nest,** *Naut.* gavias, *f pl*

crowbar /'krou,bɑr/ *n* alzaprima, palanca, *f*

crowd /kraud/ *n* multitud, muchedumbre, *f*; concurso, *m*; vulgo, *m*; (majority) mayoría, *f*; *Theat.* acompañamiento, *m. vi* reunirse, congregarse; agolparse, remolinarse, apiñarse. *vt* (fill) llenar; atestar. **in a c.,** en tropel. **So many ideas crowded in on me,** Se me ocurrieron tantas ideas a la vez. **to follow the c.,** seguir la multitud; *Fig.* ir con la mayoría. **to c. in,** entrar en tropel. **to c. round,** cercar, agruparse alrededor de. **to c. together,** apiñarse. **to c. up,** subir en masa, subir en tropel

crowded /'kraudɪd/ *a* lleno; atestado, apiñado; (weighed down) agobiado; (of hours, etc.) lleno

crowing /'krouɪŋ/ *n* cacareo, canto del gallo, *m*; (boasting) jactancia, *f*

crown /kraun/ *n* corona, *f*; (of the head) coronilla, corona, *f*; (of a hat) copa, *f*; *Archit.* coronamiento, *m. vt* coronar. **c. prince,** príncipe heredero, *m*

crowning /'kraunɪŋ/ *n* coronamiento, *m*; *Archit.* remate, *m*, *a* final; supremo

crozier /'krouʒər/ *n.* See **crosier**

crucial /'kruʃəl/ *a* decisivo, crítico; difícil

crucible /'krusəbəl/ *n* crisol, *m*

crucifix /'krusəfɪks/ *n* crucifijo, *m*

crucifixion /,krusə'fɪkʃən/ *n* crucifixión, *f*

cruciform /'krusə,fɔrm/ *a* cruciforme

crucify /'krusə,faɪ/ *vt* crucificar

crude /krud/ *a* crudo; (of colors) chillón, llamativo; (uncivilized) cerril, inculto; (vulgar) cursi; (of truth, etc.) desnudo

crudity /'kruditi/ n crudeza, f
cruel /'krual/ a cruel
cruelty /'krualti/ n crueldad, f
cruet /'kruit/ n ánfora, vinagrera, f; (stand) angarillas, f pl, convoy, m
cruise /kruz/ vi cruzar, navegar; (of cars) correr. n viaje por mar, m
cruiser /'kruzər/ n crucero, m
crumb /krʌm/ n miga, f; (spongy part of bread) migaja, f. vt (bread) desmigajar; desmenuzar. **c. brush,** recogemigas, m
crumble /'krʌmbəl/ vt desmigajar, desmenuzar. vi desmoronarse, desmigajarse; Fig. hundirse, derrumbarse; Fig. desaparecer
crumbling /'krʌmblɪŋ/ n (of buildings, etc.) desmoronamiento, m; Fig. destrucción, f
crumple /'krʌmpəl/ vt arrugar, ajar. vi arrugarse. **to c. up,** vt (crush) estrujar; (persons) dejar aplastado. vi (collapse) hundirse, derrumbarse; (of persons) desplomarse; (despair) desalentarse
crunch /krʌntʃ/ vt mascar; hacer crujir. vi crujir
crupper /'krʌpər/ n baticola, f
crusade /kru'seid/ n cruzada, f
crusader /kru'seidər/ n cruzado, m
crush /krʌʃ/ vt aplastar; (to powder) moler, triturar; (grapes, etc.) exprimir; (crease) arrugar; (opposition, etc.) vencer; (annihilate) aniquilar, destruir; (abash) humillar, confundir; (hope, etc.) matar; (of sorrow, etc.) agobiar. **We all crushed into his dining room,** Fuimos en tropel a su comedor. **to c. up,** machacar, moler; (paper, etc.) estrujar
crushing /'krʌʃɪŋ/ a (of defeats and replies) aplastante; (of sorrow, etc.) abrumador
crust /krʌst/ n (of bread, pie) corteza, f; (scab) costra, f; (of the earth, snow) capa, f. vt encostrar. vi encostrarse. **c. of bread,** mendrugo de pan, m
crustacean /krʌ'steiʃən/ a crustáceo. n crustáceo, m
crustily /'krʌstḷi/ adv irritablemente, malhumoradamente
crustiness /'krʌstinis/ n mal humor, m, aspereza, f
crusty /'krʌsti/ a costroso; (of persons) malhumorado, irritable; áspero
crutch /krʌtʃ/ n muleta, f; (fork) horquilla, f; (crotch) horcajadura, f
crux /krʌks/ n problema, m; (knotty point) nudo, m
cry /krai/ vi (weep) llorar; (shout) gritar; (exclaim) exclamar. vt (one's wares) pregonar. n grito, m. **to cry for help,** pedir socorro a voces. **to cry to high heaven,** poner el grito en el cielo. **to cry one's eyes out,** llorar a mares. **to cry down,** desacreditar. **to cry off,** desdecirse; volverse atrás. **to cry out,** vt gritar. vi dar gritos; gritar; Fig. clamar. **cry-baby,** niño (-ña) llorón (-ona)
crying /'kraiɪŋ/ a urgente; notorio. n gritos, m pl; (weeping) llanto, m, lamentaciones, f pl; (tears) lágrimas, f pl
crypt /kript/ n cripta, f
cryptic /'kriptik/ a secreto, oculto
cryptography /krip'tɒgrəfi/ n criptografía, f
crystal /'kristḷ/ n cristal, m. **c. set,** Radio. receptor de galena, m
crystal ball n bola de cristal, esfera de cristal, f
crystalline /'kristḷin/ a cristalino
crystallization /ˌkristḷə'zeiʃən/ n cristalización, f
crystallize /'kristḷˌaiz/ vt and vi cristalizar
crystallography /ˌkristḷ'ɒgrəfi/ n cristalografía, f
cub /kʌb/ n cachorro (-rra)
Cuba Cuba
Cuban /'kyubən/ a cubano. n cubano (-na)
cubbyhole /'kʌbiˌhoul/ n refugio, m; garita, f; cuarto pequeño, m; chiribitil, m
cube /kyub/ n cubo, m; (of sugar) terrón, m. vt cubicar. **c. root,** raíz cúbica, f
cubic /'kyubik/ a cúbico
cubicle /'kyubikəl/ n cubículo, m
cubism /'kyubizəm/ n cubismo, m
cuckold /'kʌkəld/ n cornudo, m
cuckoo /'kuku/ n cuclillo, m; (cry) cucú, m. **c.-clock,** reloj de cuclillo, m
cucumber /'kyukʌmbər/ n cohombro, m

cud /kʌd/ n rumia, f. **to chew the cud,** rumiar
cuddle /'kʌdḷ/ vt abrazar. n abrazo, m. **to c. up together,** estar abrazados
cudgel /'kʌdʒəl/ n porra, estaca, tranca, f, vt aporrear, apalear
cue /kyu/ n Theat. pie, m; (lead) táctica, f; (hint) indicación, f; (of hair) coleta, f; (billiard) taco (de billar), m. **to take one's cue from,** tomar como modelo (a); seguir el ejemplo de
cueca /'kueka/ n cueca f
cuff /kʌf/ vt abofetear. n (blow) bofetón, m; (of sleeve) puño, m, bocamanga, valenciana, f.
cufflink /'kʌf,lɪŋk/ n gemelo m, Central America mancuerna, mancuernilla f, Chile collera f, Colombia mancorna f
cuisine /kwi'zin/ n cocina, f
cul-de-sac /'kʌldə'sæk/ n callejón sin salida, m
culinary /'kyulə,nɛri/ a culinario
cullender /'kʌləndər/ n colador, m
culminate /'kʌlmə,neit/ vi culminar (en), terminar (en). **culminating point,** punto culminante, m
culmination /ˌkʌlmə'neiʃən/ n culminación, f; Fig. apogeo, punto culminante, m
culpability /ˌkʌlpə'biliti/ n culpabilidad, f
culpable /'kʌlpəbəl/ a culpable
culpably /'kʌlpəbli/ adv culpablemente
culprit /'kʌlprit/ n culpado (-da)
cult /kʌlt/ n culto, m
cultivable /'kʌltəvəbəl/ a cultivable, labradero
cultivate /'kʌltə,veit/ vt cultivar
cultivated /'kʌltə,veitid/ a cultivado; (of persons) culto, fino
cultivation /ˌkʌltə'veiʃən/ n cultivación, f; (of the land) cultivo, m; (of persons, etc.) cultura, f
cultivator /'kʌltə,veitər/ n cultivador (-ra); (machine) cultivador, m
cultural /'kʌltʃərəl/ a cultural
culture /'kʌltʃər/ n cultura, f; (bacteriology) cultivo, m, vt (bacteriology) cultivar
cultured /'kʌltʃərd/ a culto
culvert /'kʌlvərt/ n alcantarilla, f
cumbersome /'kʌmbərsəm/ a pesado; incómodo
cumulative /'kyumyəlɑtɪv/ a cumulativo
cumulus /'kyumyələs/ n cúmulo, m
cuneiform /kyu'niə,fɔrm/ a cuneiforme
cunning /'kʌnɪŋ/ a astuto, taimado, Lat. Am. macuco n (skill) habilidad, f; astucia, f
cup /kʌp/ n taza, f; (Eccl. and Bot.) cáliz, m; Sports. copa, f; (hollow) hoyo, m, hondonada, f. **c.-final,** Sports. final de la copa, m. **c.-tie,** Sports. partido eliminatorio, m
cup-and-ball /'kʌpən'bɔl/ n boliche, m
cupboard /'kʌbərd/ n armario, m; (in the wall) alacena, f. **c. love,** amor interesado, m
cupful /'kʌpful/ n taza, f
cupidity /kyu'piditi/ n avaricia, codicia, f
cup of sorrow n ramito de amargura, m
cupola /'kyupələ/ n cúpula, f
cur /kɜr/ n perro mestizo, m; canalla, m
curable /'kyʊrəbəl/ a curable
curableness /'kyʊrəbəlnis/ n curabilidad, f
curative /'kyʊrɑtɪv/ a curativo, terapéutico
curator /kyʊ'reitər/ n (of a museum) director, m; (Scots law) curador, m
curb /kɜrb/ n (of a bridle) barbada, f; Fig. freno, m; (stone) bordillo, m, guarnición, f. vt (a horse) enfrenar; Fig. refrenar, reprimir; (limit) limitar
curd /kɜrd/ n requesón, m; cuajada, f
curdle /'kɜrdḷ/ vi coagularse; (of blood) helarse. vt coagular; (blood) helar
cure /kyʊr/ n cura, f; Eccl. curato, m. vt curar; (leather) zurrar; (salt) salar; Fig. remediar. **to take a c.,** tomar una cura. **c.-all,** panacea, f. **c. of souls,** cura de almas, f
curer /'kyʊrər/ n (of fish, etc.) salador, m; (of evils, etc.) remediador, m
curfew /'kɜrfyu/ n toque de queda, m
curing /'kyʊrɪŋ/ n curación, f; (salting) saladura, f
curio /'kyʊri,ou/ n curiosidad, antigüedad, f
curiosity /ˌkyʊri'ɒsiti/ n curiosidad, f

curious /'kyʊriəs/ a (all meanings) curioso
curiously /'kyʊriəsli/ adv curiosamente
curl /kɜrl/ n (of hair) rizo, bucle, m; (of smoke) penacho, m. vt rizar. vi rizarse; Sports. jugar al curling. **in c.,** rizado. **to c. one's lip,** hacer una mueca de desdén. **to c. up,** vt arrollar; Fig. dejar fuera de combate (a). vi hacerse un ovillo, enroscarse; (of leaves) abarquillarse; Fig. desplomarse; desanimarse. **c.-paper,** papillote, m
curlew /'kɜrlu/ n Ornith. zarapito, m
curling /'kɜrlɪŋ/ n (game) curling, m, a rizado. **c.-tongs,** encrespador, m
curly /'kɜrli/ a rizado, crespo
curmudgeon /kər'mʌdʒən/ n erizo, misántropo, cara de viernes, m
currant /'kɜrənt/ n (dry) pasa de Corinto, f; (fresh) grosella, f. **black c.,** grosella negra, f; (bush) grosellero negro, m. **c.-bush,** grosellero, m
currency /'kɜrənsi/ n uso corriente, m; moneda corriente, f, dinero, m; dinero en circulación, m; valor corriente, m; estimación, f
current /'kɜrənt/ a corriente; presente, de actualidad; (of money) en circulación. n (of water, etc., Fig. Elec.) corriente, f. **alternating c.,** Elec. corriente alterna, f. **direct c.,** Elec. corriente continua, f. **the c. number of a magazine,** el último número de una revista. **c. events,** actualidades, f pl
currently /'kɜrəntli/ adv actualmente, corrientemente, generalmente
curricle /'kɜrɪkəl/ n carriola, f
curriculum /kə'rɪkyələm/ n plan de estudios, m; curso, m
curriculum vitae /'vaiti/ n hoja de vida, f
curry /'kɜri/ vt (a horse) almohazar; Cul. condimentar con cari. **to c. favor with,** insinuarse en el favor de. **c.-comb,** almohaza, f
curse /kɜrs/ n maldición, f; blasfemia, f; (ruin) azote, castigo, m. vt maldecir; (afflict) castigar. vi blasfemar, echar pestes
cursed /'kɜrsɪd, kɜrst/ a maldito; abominable, odioso
cursing /'kɜrsɪŋ/ n maldición, f; blasfemias, f pl
cursorily /'kɜrsərəli/ adv rápidamente; de prisa; superficialmente
cursory /'kɜrsəri/ a rápido; apresurado; superficial
curt /kɜrt/ a seco, brusco; corto
curtail /kər'teil/ vt abreviar; reducir; disminuir
curtailment /kər'teilmənt/ n abreviación, f; reducción, f; disminución, f
curtain /'kɜrtn/ n cortina, f; Theat. telón, m. vt poner cortinas (a) **drop c.,** telón de boca, m. **iron c.,** Polit. telón de acero, m. **to c. off,** separar por cortinas. **c.-lecture,** reprimenda conyugal, f. **c.-raiser,** entremés, m. **c.-ring,** anilla, f
curtly /'kɜrtli/ adv secamente, bruscamente
curtness /'kɜrtnɪs/ n brusquedad, sequedad, f
curtsey /'kɜrtsi/ n reverencia, cortesía, f, vi hacer una reverencia
curvature /'kɜrvətʃər/ n curvatura, f
curve /kɜrv/ n curva, f; Mech. codo, m; (Auto. of a road) viraje, m. vt encorvar, torcer. vi encorvarse, torcerse; (of a road) hacer un viraje.
curved /kɜrvd/ a curvo
curvet /'kɜrvɪt/ n corveta, cabriola, f, vi corvetear, corcovear, cabriolar
curvilinear /ˌkɜrvə'lɪniər/ a curvilíneo
cushion /'kʊʃən/ n almohada, f; cojín, m; (billiards) banda, f; (of fingers, etc.) pulpejo, m. vt proveer de almohadas; (a shock) amortiguar; suavizar
custard /'kʌstərd/ n flan, m, natillas, f pl
custodian /kʌ'stoudiən/ n custodio, m; guardián, m; (of a museum, etc.) director, m
custody /'kʌstədi/ n custodia, f; guarda, f; prisión, f. **in safe c.,** en lugar seguro. **to take** (a person) **into c.,** arrestar
custom /'kʌstəm/ n costumbre, f; uso, m; Com. parroquia, clientela, f; (sales) ventas, f pl; pl **Customs,** aduana, f. **to go through the Customs,** pasar por la aduana. **Customs duty,** derechos de aduana, m pl. **Customs officer,** aduanero, m. **c.-house,** aduana, f

customarily /ˌkʌstə'mɛrəli/ adv habitualmente, por lo general
customary /'kʌstəˌmɛri/ a acostumbrado, usual, habitual
customer /'kʌstəmər/ n cliente, mf parroquiano (-na), Lat. Am. also marchante (-ta)
customs barrier /'kʌstəmz/ n barrera aduanera, barrera arancelaria, f
cut /kʌt/ vt cortar; (diamonds) tallar; (hay, etc.) segar; (carve) labrar, tallar; (engrave) grabar; (a lecture, etc.) no asistir a; (cards) destajar, cortar; (Fig. wound) herir; (reduce) reducir; abreviar; (teeth) echar; (of lines) cruzar. vi cortar; cortar bien; (Fam. go) marcharse a prisa y corriendo. **I must get my hair cut,** He de hacerme cortar el pelo. **That cuts both ways,** Es una arma de dos filos. **His opinion cuts no ice,** Su opinión no cuenta. **Mary cut him dead,** María hizo como si no le reconociera. **to cut a caper,** dar saltos; hacer cabriolas. **to cut a person short,** echar el tablacho (a). **to cut and run,** poner los pies en polvorosa. **to cut for deal,** (cards) cortar para ver quién da las cartas. **to cut short,** (a career) terminar. **to cut to the quick,** herir en lo más vivo. **to cut across,** cortar al través; (fields, etc.) atravesar; tomar por un atajo. **to cut away,** vt quitar. vi Inf. poner pies en polvorosa. **to cut down,** derribar; (by the sword) acuchillar; (by death, etc.) segar, malograr; (expenses, etc.) reducir; (gambling) abreviar, abreviar. **to cut off,** bloquear, cortar, separar; amputar; (on a telephone) cortar la comunicación; (gas, water, etc.) cortar; (supply of food, etc.) interrumpir; (of death) llevarse. **to cut out,** (dresses, etc.) cortar; (oust) suplantar. **He is not cut out for medicine,** No tiene la disposición para la medicina. **to cut up,** trinchar, cortar en pequeños trozos, Lat. Am. destajar; (afflict) entristecer, afligir. **to cut up rough,** Inf. ponerse furioso

cut /kʌt/ a cortado. **well-cut features,** facciones regulares, f pl. **cut and dried opinion,** opinión hecha, idea fija, f; ideas cerradas, f pl. **cut glass,** cristal tallado, m
cut /kʌt/ n corte, m; (with a whip) latigazo, m; (with a sword) cuchillada, f; (with a sharp instrument) tajo, m; cortadura, f; (in prices, etc.) reducción, f; (engraving) grabado, m; clisé, m; (of cards) corte, m. **short cut,** atajo, m. **the cut of a coat,** el corte de un abrigo. **to give** (someone) **the cut direct,** pasar cerca de (una persona) sin saludarle. **cut-out,** n (paper) recortado, m; Elec. cortacircuitos, m. **cut-throat,** n asesino, m
cutaneous /kyu'teiniəs/ a cutáneo
cute /kyut/ a guapo, cuco, listo; mono, Mexico chulo
cuteness /'kyutnɪs/ n cuquería, inteligencia, f; monería, f
cuticle /'kyutɪkəl/ n cutícula, f
cutlass /'kʌtləs/ n alfanje m
cutler /'kʌtlər/ n cuchillero, m
cutlery /'kʌtləri/ n cuchillería, f
cutlet /'kʌtlɪt/ n chuleta, f
cutter /'kʌtər/ n cortador, m; Naut. cúter, m; escampavía, f
cutting /'kʌtɪŋ/ n corte, m; (of diamonds) talla, f; (in a mountain, etc.) tajo, m; Agr. plantón, m; (of cloth) retazo, m; (newspaper) recorte, m. a cortante; (of remarks) mordaz. **newspaper c.,** recorte de periódico. **c. down,** (of trees) tala, f; reducción, f
cuttingly /'kʌtɪŋli/ adv mordazmente, con malicia
cuttlefish /'kʌtl,fɪʃ/ n jibia, f
cyanide /'saiə,naid/ n cianuro, m
cyberspace /'saibər,speis/ n ciberespacio, m
cycle /'saikəl/ n ciclo, m; período, m; (bicycle) bicicleta, f. vi ir en bicicleta
cyclic /'saiklɪk/ a cíclico
cycling /'saiklɪŋ/ n ciclismo, m
cyclist /'saiklɪst/ n ciclista, mf
cyclone /'saikloun/ n ciclón, m
cygnet /'sɪgnɪt/ n pollo del cisne, m
cylinder /'sɪlɪndər/ n cilindro, m; Mech. tambor, m. **c. head,** culata, f
cylindrical /sɪ'lɪndrɪkəl/ a cilíndrico
cymbal /'sɪmbəl/ n címbalo, platillo, m

cymbalist /'sɪmbəlɪst/ n cimbalero (-ra)
cynic /'sɪnɪk/ n cínico, m
cynical /'sɪnɪkəl/ a cínico
cynicism /'sɪnə͵sɪzəm/ n cinismo, m
cynosure /'sainə͵ʃʊr/ n Astron. Osa Menor, f; blanco, m
cypress /'saiprəs/ n (tree and wood) ciprés, m. **c. grove,** cipresal, m

Cypriot /'sɪpriət/ a chipriota. n chipriota, mf
Cyprus /'saiprəs/ Isla de Chipre, f
cyst /sɪst/ n quiste, m
cystic /'sɪstɪk/ a cístico
Czech /tʃɛk/ a checo. n checo (-ca); (language) checo, m
Czechoslovak /'tʃɛkə'slouvæk/ n checoslovaco (-ca)

D

d /di/ n (letter) de, f; Mus. re, m
dab /dæb/ vt golpear suavemente, tocar; (sponge) esponjar; (moisten) mojar. n golpecito, golpe blando, m; (small piece) pedazo pequeño, m; (blob) borrón, m; (peck) picotazo, m; Inf. experto (-ta). **to dab at one's eyes,** secarse los ojos
dabble /'dæbəl/ vt mojar (en). vi chapotear; (engage in) entretenerse en; (meddle in) meterse en; (speculate in) especular en. **to d. in politics,** meterse en política
dabbler /'dæblər/ n aficionado (-da)
dace /deis/ n dardo, albur, m
dachshund /'dɑks͵hʊnt/ n perro pachón, m
daddy /'dædi/ n papaíto, m. **d.-longlegs,** típula, f
daffodil /'dæfədɪl/ n narciso trompón, m
daft /dæft/ a bobo, tonto, chiflado; loco
dagger /'dægər/ n daga, f, puñal, m; Print. cruz, f. **to be at daggers drawn,** estar a matar. **to look daggers (at),** lanzar miradas de odio (hacia), mirar echando chispas. **d. thrust,** puñalada, f
daguerreotype /də'gɛrə͵taip/ n daguerrotipo, m
dahlia /'dælyə/ n dalia, f
daily /'deili/ a diario, de todos los días; cotidiano. adv diariamente, cada día, todos los días; cotidianamente. n (paper) diario, m. **d. bread,** pan cotidiano, pan de cada día, m. **d. help,** (person) asistenta, f. **d. pay,** jornal, m; Mil. pre, m
daintily /'deintʃi/ adv delicadamente; elegantemente; con primor
daintiness /'deintinɪs/ n delicadeza, f; elegancia, f; (beauty) primor, m
dainty /'deinti/ a delicado; elegante; primoroso, exquisito; (fastidious) melindroso, difícil. n bocado exquisito, m, golosina, f
dairy /'dɛəri/ n lechería, f. **d. cattle,** vacas lecheras, f pl. **d.-farm,** granja, f. **d.-farmer,** granjero (-ra). **d.-farming,** industria lechera, f
dairymaid /'dɛəri͵meid/ n lechera, f
dairyman /'dɛərimən/ n lechero, m
dais /'deiɪs/ n estrado, m
daisy /'deizi/ n margarita, f
dale /deil/ n valle, m
dalliance /'dæliəns/ n (delay) tardanza, f; (play) jugueteo, m; diversiones, f pl; (caresses) caricias, f pl, abrazos, m pl
dally /'dæli/ vi tardar, perder el tiempo; entretenerse, divertirse; (make love) holgar (con); (with an idea) entretenerse con, jugar con
Dalmatian /dæl'meiʃən/ a dalmático, dálmata. n dálmata, mf. **D. dog,** perro dálmata, m
dalmatic /dæl'mætɪk/ n dalmática, f
daltonism /'dɔltn͵ɪzəm/ n daltonismo, m
dam /dæm/ n (of animals) madre, f; (of a river, etc.) presa, f, embalse, m; (mole) dique, m; pared de retención, f. vt represar, embalsar; cerrar; (restrain) contener, reprimir
damage /'dæmɪdʒ/ n daño, perjuicio, m; mal, m; avería, f; pérdida, f; (Fam. price) precio, m; pl **damages,** Law. daños y perjuicios, m pl. vt dañar, perjudicar, Lat. Am. afectar; estropear; deteriorar; (reputation, etc.) comprometer
damageable /'dæmɪdʒəbəl/ a que puede ser dañado; frágil
damaging /'dæmɪdʒɪŋ/ a perjudicial; comprometedor
damascene /'dæməsin/ vt damasquinar
Damascus /də'mæskəs/ Damasio, m
damask /'dæməsk/ n (cloth) damasco, m; (steel)

acero damasquino, m. a de damasco; damasquino. vt (metals) damasquinar; (cloth) adamascar. **d.-like,** adamascado. **d. rose,** rosa de Damasco, f
dame /deim/ n dama, señora, f; Inf. madre, f; (schoolmistress) amiga, f. **to attend a d. school,** ir a la amiga
damming /'dæmɪŋ/ n embalse, m, represa, f; retención, f; represión, f
damn /dæm/ vt condenar al infierno; maldecir; vituperar. **D. it!** ¡Maldito sea!
damnable /'dæmnəbəl/ a detestable, infame; Inf. horrible
damnably /'dæmnəbli/ adv abominablemente; Inf. horriblemente
damnation /dæm'neiʃən/ n condenación, perdición, f; maldición, f; vituperación, f
damned /dæmd/ a condenado; maldito; detestable, odioso
damning /'dæmɪŋ/ a que condena; irresistible
damp /dæmp/ a húmedo. n humedad, f; (mist) niebla, f; exhalación, f; (gas) mofeta, f; Fig. tristeza, depresión, f. vt humedecer, mojar; apagar, amortiguar; (depress) deprimir, entristecer; (stifle) ahogar; (lessen) moderar; (trouble) turbar. **d.-proof,** impermeable
damper /'dæmpər/ n (of a chimney) registro de humos, m; (of a piano) batiente, m; (for stamps) mojador, m; (gloom) depresión, tristeza, f; (restraint) freno, m
dampish /'dæmpɪʃ/ a algo húmedo
dampness /'dæmpnɪs/ n humedad, f
damsel /'dæmzəl/ n chica, muchacha, f; damisela, f, Poet. doncella, f
damson /'dæmzən/ n ciruela damascena, f. **d. tree,** ciruelo damasceno, m
dance /dæns/ n danza, f; baile, m. vi bailar, danzar; saltar, brincar. vt bailar; hacer saltar. **to d. attendance on,** servir humildemente; hacer la rueda (a). **to lead someone a d.,** hacer bailar. **d. band,** orquestina, f; orquesta de jazz, f. **d. floor,** pista de baile, f. **d. hall,** salón de baile, m. **d. music,** música bailable, f. **d.-number,** (in a theater) bailable, m. **d. of death,** danza de la muerte, f
dancer /'dænsər/ n bailarín (-ina); danzador (-ra), bailador (-ra); pl **dancers,** (partners) parejas de baile, f pl
dancing /'dænsɪŋ/ n baile, m, danza, f. **d.-girl,** bailarina, f; (Indian) bayadera, f. **d.-master,** maestro de baile, m. **d. school,** academia de baile, f. **d. slipper,** zapatilla de baile, f
dandelion /'dændl͵aiən/ n diente de león, m
dandle /'dændl/ vt mecer, hacer saltar sobre las rodillas, hacer bailar
dandruff /'dændrəf/ n caspa, f
dandy /'dændi/ n dandi, petimetre, barbilindo, m
Dane /dein/ n danés (-esa). **Great D.,** perro danés, m
danger /'deindʒər/ n peligro, m; riesgo, m. **out of d.,** fuera de peligro. **to be in d.,** correr peligro, peligrar, estar en peligro
dangerous /'deindʒərəs/ a peligroso; arriesgado; nocivo
dangerously /'deindʒərəsli/ adv peligrosamente
dangerousness /'deindʒərəsnɪs/ n peligro, m
dangle /'dæŋgəl/ vi colgar, pender. vt dejar colgar; oscilar; (show) mostrar
Danish /'deinɪʃ/ a danés, de Dinamarca. n (language) danés, m

dank /dæŋk/ a húmedo

dankness /'dæŋknɪs/ n humedad, f

dapper /'dæpər/ a apuesto, aseado; activo, vivaz

dapple /'dæpəl/ vt motear, salpicar, manchar. **d.-grey,** a rucio

dappled /'dæpəld/ a (of horses) rodado, empedrado

Dardanelles, the /,dardn̩'ɛlz/ los Dardanelos, m

dare /dɛər/ vi atreverse, osar. vt arriesgar; desafiar, provocar; hacer frente a, arrostrar. n reto, m. **I d. say!** ¡Ya lo creo! ¡No lo dudo! **I d. say that...,** No me sorprendería que...; Supongo que... **d.-devil,** calavera, m; atrevido (-da), valeroso (-sa)

daring /'dɛərɪŋ/ a intrépido, audaz; atrevido, *Argentina* agalludo (dangerous) arriesgado, peligroso. n audacia, osadia, f, atrevimiento, m; peligro, m

daringly /'dɛərɪŋli/ adv atrevidamente

dark /dɑrk/ a oscuro; (of complexion, etc.) moreno; negro; lóbrego; (of colors) oscuro; misterioso; enigmático; secreto, escondido; (sad) funesto, triste; (evil) malo, malévolo. n oscuridad, f; (shade) sombra, f; ignorancia, f. **after d.,** a nocturno. adv después del anochecer. **in the d.,** a oscuras; de noche; *Fig.* be in the d., quedarse en la luna. **to become d.,** oscurecerse; (cloud over) anublarse; (become night) anochecer. **to keep d.,** vt tener secreto. vi esconderse. **d. ages,** los siglos de la ignorancia y de la superstición. **d.-eyed,** de ojos negros, ojinegro. **d. horse,** caballo desconocido, m; *Polit.* batacazo, m. **d. lantern,** linterna sorda, f. **d. room,** cuarto oscuro, m; *Photo.* laboratorio fotográfico, m; (optics) cámara oscura, f

darken /'dɑrkən/ vt obscurecer; sombrear; (of color) hacer más oscuro; (sadden) entristecer. vi obscurecerse; (of the sky) anublarse; (of the face with emotion) inmutarse.

darkening /'dɑrkənɪŋ/ n oscurecimiento, m

darkly /'dɑrkli/ adv oscuramente; misteriosamente; con malevolencia; secretamente; (archaic) indistintamente

darkness /'dɑrknɪs/ n oscuridad, f, tinieblas, f pl; sombra, f; (of color) oscuro, m; (of the complexion) color moreno, m; (of eyes, hair) negrura, f; (night) noche, f; (ignorance) ignorancia, f; (privacy) secreto, m. **Prince of d.,** el príncipe de las tinieblas

darling /'dɑrlɪŋ/ a querido, amado; (greatest) mayor. n querido (-da); (favorite) el predilecto, la predilecta, el favorito, la favorita. **My d.!** ¡Amor mío! ¡Vida mía! ¡Pichoncito mío!

darn /dɑrn/ vt zurcir, remendar. n zurcido, remiendo, m

darner /'dɑrnər/ n zurcidor (-ra); (implement) huevo de zurcir, m

darning /'dɑrnɪŋ/ n zurcidura, f; zurcido, recosido, m. **d.-needle,** aguja de zurcir, f. **d. wool,** lana de zurcir, f

dart /dɑrt/ n dardo, m; movimiento rápido, m; avance rápido, m; *Sew.* sisa, f. vi lanzarse, abalanzarse (sobre); volar; correr, avanzar rápidamente. vt lanzar, arrojar; dirigir. **to make darts in,** *Sew.* sisar

Darwinian /dɑr'wɪniən/ a darviniano. n darvinista, mf

Darwinism /'dɑrwə,nɪzəm/ n darvinismo, m

dash /dæʃ/ n (spirit) fogosidad, f, brío, m; energía, f; (impact) choque, golpe, m; (mixture) mezcla, f; (of a liquid) gota, f; (of the pen) rasgo, m; (attack) ataque, m; avance rápido, m; (a little) algo, un poco (de); *Gram.* raya, f; (show) ostentación, f. **He made a d. for the door,** Se precipitó a la puerta, Corrió hacia la puerta. **to cut a d.,** hacer gran papel. **d.-board,** tablero de instrumentos, m

dash /dæʃ/ vt arrojar con violencia; (break) quebrar, estrellar; (sprinkle) rociar (con), salpicar (con); (mix) mezclar; (knock) golpear; (disappoint) frustrar, destruir; (confound) confundir; (depress) desanimar. vi (rush) precipitarse; quebrarse, estrellarse; chocar (contra); (of waves) romperse. **to d. to pieces,** hacer añicos, estrellar. **to d. along,** avanzar rápidamente; correr. **to d. away,** vi marcharse apresuradamente. vt apartarse bruscamente. **to d. down,** vi bajar aprisa. vt derribar. (overturn) volcar; (throw) tirar. **to d. off,** vi marcharse apresuradamente; vt hacer apresuradamente; (a

letter, etc.) escribir de prisa; (sketch) bosquejar rápidamente. **to d. out,** vi salir precipitadamente; lanzarse a la calle. vt (erase) borrar; hacer saltar. **to d. through,** atravesar rápidamente; hacer de prisa. **to d. up,** llegar a prisa; (sprout) saltar

dashing /'dæʃɪŋ/ a valiente; (spirited) fogoso, gallardo; majo, brillante. n choque, m; (breaking) quebrantamiento, m; (of the waves) embate, m

dastardly /'dæstərdli/ a cobarde

data /'deitə/ n pl datos, m pl

database /'deitəbeis/ n base de datos, f

data entry n entrada de datos, f

data processing /'prɒsɛsɪŋ/ n elaboración electrónica de datos, f, recuento de datos, m

date /deit/ n fecha, f; (period) época, f; (term) plazo, m; (duration) duración, f; (appointment) cita, f; *Bot.* dátil, m. vt fechar, datar; poner fecha a; asignar. vi datar (de), remontar (a). **out of d.,** anticuado; pasado de moda; (of persons) atrasado de noticias. **to be up to d.,** ser nuevo; ser de última moda; (of persons) estar al día. **to bring up to d.,** renovar; (of persons) poner al corriente. **to fix the d.,** señalar el día; (chronologically) ajustar los tiempos. **to d.,** hasta la fecha. **under d. (of),** con fecha (de). **up to d.,** hasta hoy, hasta ahora. **What is the d.?** ¿Qué fecha es? ¿A cómo estamos hoy? ¿A cuántos estamos hoy? **d. palm,** datilera, f

date of expiration n fecha de vencimiento, f

daub /dɔb/ vt barrar, embadurnar; manchar, ensuciar; untar; (paint) pintorrear. n embadurnamiento, m; (picture) aleluya, f

dauber /'dɔbər/ n chafalmejas, pintamonas, mf pintor (-ra) de brocha gorda

daughter /'dɔtər/ n hija, f. **adopted d.,** hija adoptiva, f. **little d.,** hijuela, f. **d.-in-law,** nuera, f

daughterly /'dɔtərli/ a de hija

daunt /dɔnt, dɑnt/ vt intimidar, acobardar; dar miedo (a), espantar; (dishearten) desanimar

dauntless /'dɔntlɪs/ a impávido, intrépido

dauphin /'dɔfɪn/ n delfín, m

dawdle /'dɔdl̩/ vi perder el tiempo; haraganear, gandulear

dawdler /'dɔdlər/ n gandul (-la)

dawdling /'dɔdlɪŋ/ a perezoso, lento

dawn /dɔn/ n alba, madrugada, primera luz, f; *Fig.* aurora, f. vi amanecer, alborear, romper el día; (appear) mostrarse, asomar. **at d.,** a primera luz, al amanecer de madrugada, al alba. **It had not dawned on me,** No me había ocurrido

day /dei/ n día, m; luz del día, f; (day's work) jornada, f; (battle) batalla, f; (victory) victoria, f; pl **days,** (time) tiempos, m pl, época, f; (life) vida, f; (years) años, m pl, a diario. **all day long,** durante todo el día. **any day,** cualquier día. **by day,** de día. **by the day,** al día. **every day,** todos los días, cada día. **every other day,** un día sí y otro no, cada dos días. **from this day forward,** desde hoy en adelante. **from day to day,** de día en día. **Good day!** ¡Buenos días! **in these days,** en estos días. **in olden days,** en la antigüedad; *Inf.* en tiempos de Maricastaña. **in the days of,** en los tiempos de; durante los años de; durante la vida de. **next day,** al día siguiente. **(on) the next day,** al día siguiente, al otro día. **one of these days,** un día de éstos. **some fine day,** el mejor día, de un día a otro. **the day after tomorrow,** pasado mañana. **the day before yesterday,** anteayer. **the day before,** la víspera. **to win the day,** ganar el día, salir victorioso. **day after day,** cada día, día tras día. **day by day,** día por día. **day in, day out,** sin cesar, día tras día. **day-book,** *Com.* libro diario, m. **day's holiday,** día de asueto, m; día libre, m. **day laborer,** jornalero, m. **day nursery,** guardería de niños, f. **day-pupil,** alumno (-na) externo (-na). **day-school,** externado, m. **day shift,** turno de día, m. **day-star,** lucero del alba, m. **day ticket,** billete de excursión, m

daybreak /'dei,breik/ n alba, f, amanecer, m. **at d.,** al romper el día, al amanecer

daydream /'dei,drim/ n ensueño, m; ilusión, f; fantasía, visión, f. vi *Lit.* soñar despierto, dejar volar sus pensamientos; *Fig.* hacerse ilusiones

daydreamer /'dei,drimər/ *n* soñador (-ra); visionario (-ia)

daylight /'dei,lait/ *n* luz del día, *f*, día, *m*; (contrasted with artificial light) luz natural, *f*. **in broad d.,** a plena calle, a plena luz, en plena luz del día. **It's d. robbery!** ¡Es un desuello! **d.-saving,** hora de verano, *f*

daytime /'dei,taim/ *n* día, *m*. **in the d.,** durante el día

daze /deiz/ *vt* aturdir, confundir; (dazzle) deslumbrar. *n* aturdimiento, *m*, confusión, *f*; perplejidad, *f*

dazzle /'dæzəl/ *vt* (camouflage) disfrazar; deslumbrar, ofuscar. *n* deslumbramiento, *m*; brillo, *m*, refulgencia, *f*

dazzling /'dæzlɪŋ/ *a* deslumbrador; brillante

deacon /'dikən/ *n* diácono, *m*

deaconess /'dikənɪs/ *n* diaconisa, *f*

dead /dɛd/ *a* and *past part* muerto; inanimado; (withered) marchito; (deep) profundo; (unconscious) inerte, inmóvil; insensible; (numb) entumecido; (complete) absoluto, completo; (sure) certero, excelente; (useless) inútil; (of color and human character) apagado; sin espíritu, inactivo; (of eyes) mortecino; (of sound) sordo, opaco; (of villages, etc.) desierto, despoblado; (quiet) silencioso; (empty) vacío; (monotonous) monótono; (of fire) apagado; (with weight, language) muerto; *Elec.* interrumpido; *Law.* muerto civilmente. *adv* completamente, enteramente; del todo; directamente; exactamente; profundamente. **the d.,** los muertos. **in the d. of night,** en las altas horas de la noche. **to be d.,** estar muerto; haber muerto. **to be d. against,** estar completamente opuesto a. **to drop d.,** caer muerto; morir de repente. **to rise from the d.,** resucitar. **to sham d.,** hacer la mortecina, fingirse muerto. **to speak ill of the d.,** hablar mal de los muertos; *Inf.* desenterrar los muertos. **d. ball,** pelota fuera de juego, *f*. **d.-beat,** delincuente. **d. body,** cadáver, cuerpo muerto, *m*. **d. calm,** calma profunda, *f*; *Naut.* calma chicha, *f*. **d. certainty,** seguridad completa, *f*. **d.-drunk,** hecho una uva. **d. end,** callejón sin salida, *m*. **d. heat,** empate, *m*. **d. language,** lengua muerta, *f*. **d.-letter,** letra muerta, *f*; carta devuelta o no reclamada, *f*. **d.-lock,** punto muerto, *m*. **to reach a d.-lock,** llegar a un punto muerto. **d. march,** marcha fúnebre, *f*. **d. set,** empeñado (en). **d. shot,** (person) tirador (-ra) certero (-ra) (shot) tiro certero, *m*. **d. silence,** silencio profundo, *m*. **d. stop,** parada en seco, *f*. **d. tired,** rendido. **d. weight,** peso muerto, *m*. **d. wood,** leña seca, *f*; material inútil, *m*

deaden /'dɛdn̩/ *vt* amortiguar; (of pain) calmar; (remove) quitar; (of colors) apagar

deadening /'dɛdn̩ɪŋ/ *n* amortiguamiento, *m*

deadliness /'dɛdlɪnɪs/ *n* carácter mortal, *m*; implacabilidad, *f*

deadly /'dɛdli/ *a* mortal; implacable; *Inf.* insoportable. *adv* mortalmente. **He was d. pale,** Estaba pálido como un muerto. **the seven d. sins,** los siete pecados capitales. **d. nightshade,** belladona, *f*

deadness /'dɛdnɪs/ *n* falta de vida, *f*; inercia, *f*; marchitez, *f*; (numbness) entumecimiento, *m*; desanimación, *f*; parálisis, *f*

Dead Sea, the el mar Muerto, *m*

Dead Sea Scrolls, the /skroulz/ los rollos del mar Muerto, *m pl*

deaf /dɛf/ *a* sordo. **d. people,** los sordos. **to be d.,** ser sordo; padecer sordera. **to be as d. as a post,** ser más sordo que una tapia. **to become d.,** ensordecer, volverse sordo. **to fall on d. ears,** caer en saco roto. **to turn a d. ear,** hacerse el sordo. **d. aid,** audífono, *m*. **d.-mute,** sordomudo (-da). **d.-mutism,** sordomudez, *f*

deafen /'dɛfən/ *vt* asordar, ensordecer

deafening /'dɛfənɪŋ/ *a* ensordecedor

deafly /'dɛfli/ *adv* sordamente

deafness /'dɛfnɪs/ *n* sordera, *f*

deal /dil/ *n* (transaction) negocio, trato, *m*; (at cards) reparto, *m*; (wood) pino, *m*, (plank) tablón de pino, *m*. **a d., a great d.,** mucho. **a very great d.,** muchísimo. **to conclude a d.,** cerrar un trato

deal /dil/ *vt* repartir; (a blow) asestar, dar; (cards) dar; (justice) dispensar. **to d. a blow at,** asestar un golpe; *Fig.* herir (en); *Fig.* destruir de un golpe. **to d. in,** comerciar en, traficar en; ocuparse en; meterse en. **to d. out,** dispensar. **to d. with,** (buy from) comprar de; tener relaciones con, tratar; entenderse con; portarse con; (of affairs) ocuparse en, arreglar, dirigir; (contend) luchar con; (discuss) discutir, tratar de; (of books) versar sobre. **d. regularly with,** *Lat. Am.* amarchantarse con. **to make a d.,** hacer un arreglo

dealer /'dilər/ *n* traficante, *mf* mercader, *m*, *Lat. Am.* marchante (-ta); (at cards) el que da las cartas

dealing /'dilɪŋ/ *n* conducta, *f*; proceder, *m*; trato, *m*; tráfico, *m*; *pl* **dealings,** relaciones, *f pl*; transacciones, *f pl*

dean /din/ *n* *Eccl.* deán, *m*; *Educ.* decano, *m*

dear /dɪər/ *a* (beloved) querido, amado; (charming) encantador, simpático; (in letters) estimado, querido; (favorite) predilecto; (expensive) caro. *n* querido (-da); persona querida, *f*, bien amado (-da). *adv* caro. **Oh d.!** ¡Dios mío! ¡Ay!

dearly /'dɪərli/ *adv* tiernamente, entrañablemente; caro

dearness /'dɪərnɪs/ *n* cariño, afecto, *m*, ternura, *f*; (of price) precio alto, *m*

dearth /dɜrθ/ *n* carestía, *f*; (of news, etc.) escasez, *f*

death /dɛθ/ *n* muerte, *f*; (*Law.* and in announcements) fallecimiento, *m*, defunción, *f*. **to be at death's door,** estar a la muerte. **to sentence to d.,** ajusticiar. **to the d.,** a muerte. **untimely d.,** muerte repentina, *f*; malogro, *m*. **death's head,** calavera, *f*. **d. certificate,** partida de defunción, *f*. **d.-duties,** derechos de herencia, *m pl*. **d.-like,** cadavérico. **d.-mask,** mascarilla, *f*. **d. penalty,** pena de muerte, *f*. **d.-rate,** mortalidad, *f*. **d.-trap,** lugar peligroso, *m*; *Fig.* trampa, *f*. **d.-warrant,** sentencia de muerte, *f*. **d.-watch beetle,** reloj de la muerte, *m*

deathbed /'dɛθ,bɛd/ *n* lecho mortuorio, lecho de muerte, *m*. **on one's d.,** en su lecho de muerte

deathblow /'dɛθ,blou/ *n* golpe mortal, *m*

deathly /'dɛθli/ *a* mortal

death toll *n* (of a bell) doble, toque de difuntos, *m*; (casualties) número de muertos, saldo de muertos, *m*

debacle /də'bɑkəl/ *n* *Fig.* ruina, *f*

debar /dɪ'bɑr/ *vt* excluir, privar

debase /dɪ'beis/ *vt* degradar, humillar, envilecer; (the coinage) alterar (la moneda)

debasement /dɪ'beismənt/ *n* degradación, humillación, *f*, envilecimiento, *m*; (of the coinage) alteración (de la moneda), *f*

debasing /dɪ'beisɪŋ/ *a* degradante, humillante

debatable /dɪ'beitəbəl/ *a* discutible

debate /dɪ'beit/ *n* debate, *m*; discusión, *f*; disputa, *f*. *vt* and *vi* debatir; discutir; disputar; considerar

debater /dɪ'beitər/ *n* discutidor (-ra); orador (-ra).

debating /dɪ'beitɪŋ/ *n* discusión, *f*; argumentación, *f*

debauch /dɪ'bɔtʃ/ *vt* corromper, pervertir; (a woman) seducir, violar. *n* libertinaje, *m*; borrachera, *f*

debauched /dɪ'bɔtʃt/ *a* vicioso, licencioso

debauchee /,dɛbɔ'tʃi, -'ʃi/ *n* libertino, vicioso, *m*

debauchery /dɪ'bɔtʃəri/ *n* libertinaje, mal vivir, *m*, viciosidad, licencia, *f*

debenture /dɪ'bɛntʃər/ *n* obligación, *f*. **d. holder,** obligacionista, *mf*

debilitate /dɪ'bɪlɪ,teit/ *vt* debilitar

debilitating /dɪ'bɪlɪ,teitɪŋ/ *a* debilitante

debilitation /dɪ,bɪlɪ'teiʃən/ *n* debilitación, *f*

debility /dɪ'bɪlɪti/ *n* debilidad, *f*

debit /'dɛbɪt/ *n* débito, cargo, *m*; saldo deudor, *m*; "debe" de una cuenta, *m*. *vt* adeudar. **d. and credit,** el cargo y la data. **d. balance,** saldo deudor, *m*

debonair /,dɛbə'nɛər/ *a* gallardo, gentil, donairoso; alegre

debonairly /,dɛbə'nɛərli/ *adv* gallardamente; alegremente

debris /də'bri/ *n* escombros, desechos, *m pl*; ruinas, *f pl*; *Geol.* despojos, *m pl*

debt /dɛt/ *n* deuda, *f*, *Lat. Am. also* dita *f*. **a bad d.,** una deuda incobrable. **to be in the d. of,** ser en cargo a; deber dinero a; *Fig.* sentirse bajo una obligación. **to get into d.,** adeudarse, contraer deudas, *Lat. Am.* enditarse

debtor /'dɛtər/ *n* deudor (-ra); *Com.* debe, *m*

debunk /dɪ'bʌŋk/ vt demoler
debut /dei'byu/ n (of a debutante) puesta de largo, f; (of a play, etc.) estreno, m. **to make one's d.**, ponerse de largo, presentarse en sociedad
debutante /'debyu̱,tant/ n debutante, f
decade /'dɛkeid/ n década, f, decenio, m; (of the rosary) decena, f
decadence /'dɛkədəns/ n decadencia, f
decadent /'dɛkədənt/ a decadente
decaffeinated /di'kæfə,neitɪd/ a descafeinado
decagram /'dɛkə,græm/ n decagramo, m
decaliter /'dɛkə,litər/ n decalitro, m
decalogue /'dɛkə,lɔg/ n decálogo, m
decameter /'dɛkə,mitər/ n decámetro, m
decamp /dɪ'kæmp/ vi Mil. decampar; escaparse, fugarse
decant /dɪ'kænt/ vt decantar
decanter /dɪ'kæntər/ n garrafa, f
decapitate /dɪ'kæpɪ,teit/ vt decapitar, descabezar
decapitation /dɪ,kæpɪ'teiʃən/ n decapitación, f
decarbonization /dɪ,kɑrbənə'zeiʃən/ n descarburación, f
decarbonize /di'kɑrbə,naiz/ vt descarbonizar
decay /dɪ'kei/ vi (rot) pudrirse; degenerar; marchitarse; (of teeth) cariarse; (crumble) desmoronarse, caer en ruinas; decaer, declinar; (come down in the world) venir a menos, arruinarse. n pudrición, putrefacción, f; (of teeth) caries, f; (withering) marchitez, f; degeneración, f; desmoronamiento, m; ruina, f; (oldness) vejez, f; decadencia, declinación, f; (fall) caída, f
decease /dɪ'sis/ n fallecimiento, m, defunción, f, vi fallecer
deceased /dɪ'sist/ n finado (-da), difunto (-ta). a difunto
deceit /dɪ'sit/ n engaño, fraude, m; duplicidad, f
deceitful /dɪ'sitfəl/ a engañoso, falso; embustero, mentiroso; ilusorio
deceitfully /dɪ'sitfəli/ adv engañosamente
deceitfulness /dɪ'sitfəlnɪs/ n falsedad, duplicidad, f
deceivable /dɪ'sivəbəl/ a fácil a engañar, engañadizo
deceive /dɪ'siv/ vt engañar; (disappoint) decepcionar, desilusionar; frustrar. **If my memory does not d. me,** Si la memoria no me engaña, Si mal no me acuerdo
deceiver /dɪ'sivər/ n engañador (-ra); seductor, m
deceiving /dɪ'sivɪŋ/ a engañador
December /dɪ'sɛmbər/ n diciembre, m
decency /'disənsi/ n decoro, m, decencia, f; pudor, m , modestia, f; conveniencias, f pl; Inf. bondad, f; (manners) cortesía, f, buenos modales, m pl
decennial /dɪ'sɛniəl/ a decenal
decent /'disənt/ a decente; decoroso, honesto; púdico; (likable) simpático; (of things) bastante bueno; (honorable) honrado
decently /'disəntli/ adv decentemente
decentralization /di,sɛntrələ'zeiʃən/ n descentralización, f
decentralize /di'sɛntrə,laiz/ vt descentralizar
deception /dɪ'sɛpʃən/ n engaño, m; ilusión, f
deceptive /dɪ'sɛptɪv/ a engañoso, mentiroso, ilusorio
deceptively /dɪ'sɛptɪvli/ adv engañosamente
decide /dɪ'said/ vt decidir; Law. determinar. vi decidir, resolver; acordar, quedar en; juzgar; Law. dictar sentencia, fallar
decided /dɪ'saidɪd/ a decidido; (downright) categórico, inequívoco; resuelto; positivo; definitivo
decidedly /dɪ'saidɪdli/ adv decididamente; categóricamente; definitivamente
deciduous /dɪ'sɪdʒuəs/ a Bot. caedizo
decigram /'dɛsɪ,græm/ n decigramo, m
decimal /'dɛsəməl/ a decimal. **d. fraction,** fracción decimal, f. **d. point,** punto decimal, m. **d. system,** sistema métrico, m
decimate /'dɛsə,meit/ vt diezmar, asolar
decimation /,dɛsə'meiʃən/ n gran mortandad, f; matanza, f
decimeter /'dɛsə,mitər/ n decímetro, m
decipher /dɪ'saifər/ vt descifrar; deletrear
decipherable /dɪ'saifərəbəl/ a descifrable

decipherer /dɪ'saifərər/ n descifrador, m
decipherment /dɪ'saifərmənt/ n el descifrar; deletreo, m
decision /dɪ'sɪʒən/ n decisión, determinación, f; Law. sentencia, f, fallo, m; (agreement) acuerdo, m; (of character) firmeza, resolución, f
decisive /dɪ'saisɪv/ a decisivo; terminante, conclusivo; crítico
decisively /dɪ'saisɪvli/ adv decisivamente
decisiveness /dɪ'saisɪvnɪs/ n carácter decisivo, m; firmeza, resolución, f; decisión, f
deck /dɛk/ n cubierta, f; (of cards) baraja (de naipes), f. vt adornar, ataviar; decorar. **between decks,** entrecubiertas, f pl. **lower d.,** cubierta, f. **promenade d.,** cubierta de paseo, f. **upper d.,** cubierta superior, f. **d.-cabin,** camarote de cubierta, m. **d.-chair,** silla de cubierta, silla de tijera, silla extensible, f. **d.-hand,** marinero, estibador, m
decked /dɛkt/ a ornado, ataviado; engalanado; Naut. de... puentes
declaim /dɪ'kleim/ vt recitar. vi perorar, declamar
declamation /,dɛklə'meiʃən/ n declamación, f
declamatory /dɪ'klæmə,tɔri/ a declamatorio
declaration /,dɛklə'reiʃən/ n declaración, f; manifiesto, m; proclamación, f
declarative /dɪ'klærətɪv/ a declaratorio, declarativo
declare /dɪ'klɛər/ vt declarar; proclamar; afirmar; manifestar; confesar. vi declarar; Law. deponer, testificar. **to d. war (on)** declarar la guerra (a)
declaredly /dɪ'klɛərɪdli/ adv declaradamente, explícitamente, abiertamente
declension /dɪ'klɛnʃən/ n declinación, f
declination /,dɛklə'neiʃən/ n declinación, f
decline /dɪ'klain/ n declinación, decadencia, f; disminución, f; debilitación, f; (of the day) caída, f; (of stocks, shares) depresión, f; (illness) consunción, f; (Fig. setting) ocaso, m, vi declinar; inclinarse; decaer; disminuir; debilitarse; (refuse) negarse (a). vt (refuse) rechazar, rehusar; Gram. declinar; (avoid) evitar
declining /dɪ'klainɪŋ/ a declinante. **in one's d. years,** en sus últimos años
declivity /dɪ'klɪvɪti/ n cuesta, pendiente, f, declive, m
declutch /di'klʌtʃ/ vi desembragar
decoction /dɪ'kɒkʃən/ n decocción, f
decode /di'koud/ vt descifrar
decoder /di'koudər/ n descifrador, m
décolletee /,deikɒlə'tei/ a escotado
decoloration /di,kʌlə'reiʃən/ n decoloración, f
decompose /,dikəm'pouz/ vt descomponer. vi descomponerse
decomposition /di,kɒmpə'zɪʃən/ n descomposición, f
decompressor /,dikəm'prɛsər/ n decompresor, m
decontaminate /,dikən'tæmə,neit/ vt descontaminar
decontamination /,dikən,tæmə'neiʃən/ n descontaminación, f
decontrol /,dikən'troul/ vt suprimir las restricciones sobre
decorate /'dɛkə,reit/ vt adornar (con), embellecer; (by painting, etc.) decorar, pintar; (honor) investir (con), condecorar
decoration /,dɛkə'reiʃən/ n decoración, f; Theat. decorado, m; (honor) condecoración, f; ornamento, m
decorative /'dɛkərətɪv/ a decorativo
decorator /'dɛkə,reitər/ n decorador, m; (interior) adornista, m
decorous /'dɛkərəs/ a decoroso, decente; correcto
decorum /dɪ'kɔrəm/ n decoro, m; corrección, f
decoy /n 'dikɔi; v/ vt de'kɔi/ n señuelo, m; añagaza, f; (trap) lazo, m, trampa, f; Fig. añagaza, f. vt (birds) reclamar, atraer con señuelo; Fig. tentar (con), seducir (con). **d. bird,** pájaro de reclamo, m
decrease /n 'dikris; v vt/di'kris/ n disminución, f; baja, f; reducción, f; (of the moon, waters) mengua, f. vi decrecer, disminuir; bajar; menguar. vt disminuir; reducir
decreasingly /dɪ'krisɪŋli/ adv de menos en menos
decree /dɪ'kri/ n decreto, m; edicto, m. vi and vt decretar, mandar
decrepit /dɪ'krɛpɪt/ a decrépito

decry /dɪ'kraɪ/ vt desacreditar, rebajar
dedicate /'dɛdɪ,keɪt/ vt dedicar; consagrar; destinar; aplicar; (a book, etc.) dedicar. **to d. oneself to,** dedicarse a, consagrarse a, entregarse a
dedication /,dɛdɪ'keɪʃən/ n dedicación, f; consagración, f; (of a book, etc.) dedicatoria, f
dedicatory /'dɛdɪkə,tɔri/ a dedicatorio
deduce /dɪ'dus/ vt derivar; deducir, inferir
deduct /dɪ'dʌkt/ vt deducir; descontar
deduction /dɪ'dʌkʃən/ n deducción, f; descuento, m
deductive /dɪ'dʌktɪv/ a deductivo
deed /did/ n acción, f; hecho, acto, m; hazaña, f; (reality) realidad, f; Law. escritura, f; Law. contrato, m. **d. of gift,** escritura de donación, f
deem /dim/ vt juzgar, creer, estimar
deep /dip/ a profundo; (low) bajo; (of colors) subido; (of sounds) grave, profundo; (immersed (in)) absorto (en); (of the mind) penetrante; (secret) secreto; (intense) intenso, hondo; (cunning) astuto, artero; (dark) oscuro; (of mourning) riguroso. n Poet. piélago, mar, m; profundidad, f; abismo, m, adv profundamente; a una gran profundidad. **to be in d. waters,** Fig. estar con el agua al cuello. **to be three feet d.,** tener tres pies de profundidad. **to be d. in,** estar absorto en; (of debt) estar cargado de. **three d.,** tres de fondo. **d. into the night,** hasta las altas horas de la noche. **d.-felt,** hondamente sentido. **d. mourning,** luto riguroso, m. **d.-rooted,** arraigado. **d.-sea fishing,** pesca mayor, f. **d.-sea lead,** escandallo, m. **d.-seated,** íntimo, profundo; arraigado. **d.-set,** hundido
deepen /'dipən/ vt profundizar, ahondar; (broaden) ensanchar; (intensify) intensificar; (increase) aumentar; (of colors) aumentar el tono de, intensificar. vi hacerse más profundo, hacerse más hondo; intensificarse; aumentarse; (of sound) hacerse más grave
deeply /'dipli/ adv profundamente; intensamente; fuertemente
deepness /'dipnɪs/ n (cunning) astucia, f; see **depth**
deer /dɪər/ n ciervo (-va), venado, m, a cervuno. **d.-hound,** galgo de cazar venados, m. **d.-hunting,** caza del ciervo, f. **d.-skin,** piel de venado, f
deface /dɪ'feɪs/ vt desfigurar, mutilar; estropear; (erase) borrar
defacement /dɪ'feɪsmənt/ n desfiguración, mutilación, f; afeamiento, m; borradura, f
defamation /,dɛfə'meɪʃən/ n difamación, denigración, f
defamatory /dɪ'fæmə,tɔri/ a difamatorio, denigrante
defame /dɪ'feɪm/ vt difamar, denigrar, calumniar
default /dɪ'fɔlt/ n omisión, f, descuido, m; falta, f; ausencia, f; Law. rebeldía, f. vi dejar de cumplir; faltar; no pagar. vt Law. condenar en rebeldía. **in d. of,** en la ausencia de
defaulter /dɪ'fɔltər/ n el, m, (f, la) que no cumple sus obligaciones; delincuente, mf; desfalcador (-ra); Law. rebelde, mf
defeat /dɪ'fit/ vt vencer, derrotar; frustrar; (reject) rechazar; (elude) evitar; Fig. vencer, triunfar sobre. n derrota, f; vencimiento, m; frustración, f; rechazamiento, m. **to d. one's own ends,** defraudar sus intenciones
defeatism /dɪ'fitɪzəm/ n derrotismo, m
defeatist /dɪ'fitɪst/ n derrotista, mf
defecate /'dɛfɪ,keɪt/ vi vt defecar
defecation /,dɛfɪ'keɪʃən/ n defecación, f
defect /'difɛkt/ n defecto, m; imperfección, f; falta, f
defection /dɪ'fɛkʃən/ n defección, f; deserción, f; (from a religion) apostasía, f
defective /dɪ'fɛktɪv/ a defectuoso; Gram. defectivo; falto; imperfecto; (mentally) anormal. n persona anormal, f, anormal, m
defectiveness /dɪ'fɛktɪvnɪs/ n imperfección, f; deficiencia, f; defecto, m
defend /dɪ'fɛnd/ vt defender; proteger; preservar; sostener; (a thesis) sustentar
defendant /dɪ'fɛndənt/ n Law. acusado (-da), procesado (-da), demandado (-da)
defender /dɪ'fɛndər/ n defensor (-ra); (of a thesis) sustentante, mf
defense /dɪ'fɛns/ n defensa, f; justificación, f; pl **defenses,** defensas, f pl; obras de fortificación, f pl. **for**

the d., (of witnesses) de descargo; (of counsel) para la defensa. **in d. of,** en defensa de. **in one's own d.,** en su propia defensa. **d. in depth,** Mil. defensa en fondo, f
defenseless /dɪ'fɛnslɪs/ a indefenso, sin defensa
defenselessness /dɪ'fɛnslɪsnɪs/ n incapacidad de defenderse, f; debilidad, f, desvalimiento, m
defensible /dɪ'fɛnsəbəl/ a defendible; justificable
defensive /dɪ'fɛnsɪv/ a defensivo. n defensiva, f. **to be on the d.,** estar a la defensiva
defensively /dɪ'fɛnsɪvli/ adv defensivamente
defer /dɪ'fər/ vt (postpone) diferir, aplazar; suspender. vi (yield) deferir, ceder; (delay) tardar, aguardar. **deferred payment,** pago a plazos, m
deference /'dɛfərəns/ n deferencia, f, respeto, m; consideración, f
deferential /,dɛfə'rɛnʃəl/ a deferente, respetuoso
deferment /dɪ'fərmənt/ n aplazamiento, m; suspensión, f
defiance /dɪ'faɪəns/ n desafío, m; provocación, f; oposición, f; insolencia, f. **in d. of,** en contra de
defiant /dɪ'faɪənt/ a provocativo; insolente
defiantly /dɪ'faɪəntli/ adv de un aire provocativo; insolentemente
deficiency /dɪ'fɪʃənsi/ n falta, deficiencia, f; imperfección, f; defecto, m; omisión, f; (scarcity) carestía, f; (in accounts) déficit, m
deficient /dɪ'fɪʃənt/ a deficiente; falto, incompleto; imperfecto; pobre; defectuoso; (not clever at) débil (en); (mentally) anormal. **to be d. in,** carecer de; ser pobre en
deficit /'dɛfəsɪt/ n déficit, m; descubierto, m
defile /dɪ'faɪl/ n desfiladero, m. vt contaminar; profanar; manchar; deshonrar. vi Mil. desfilar
defilement /dɪ'faɪlmənt/ n contaminación, f; corrupción, f; profanación, f
definable /dɪ'faɪnəbəl/ a definible
define /dɪ'faɪn/ vt definir; (throw into relief) destacar; fijar; Law. determinar
definite /'dɛfənɪt/ a definido; positivo; categórico; exacto; concreto. **d. article,** artículo definido, m
definitely /'dɛfənɪtli/ adv positivamente; claramente. **definitely not!** ¡definitivamente no!
definiteness /'dɛfənɪtnɪs/ n carácter definido, m; exactitud, f; lo categórico
definition /,dɛfə'nɪʃən/ n definición, f
definitive /dɪ'fɪnɪtɪv/ a definitivo
deflate /dɪ'fleɪt/ vt desinflar. vi desinflarse, deshincharse
deflation /dɪ'fleɪʃən/ n desinflación, f
deflect /dɪ'flɛkt/ vt desviar; apartar. vi desviarse; apartarse
deflection /dɪ'flɛkʃən/ n desviación, f; apartamiento, m
defloration /,dɛflə'reɪʃən/ n desfloración, f
deflower /dɪ'flauər/ vt desflorar
deforestation /dɪ,fɔrɪ'steɪʃən/ n desforestación, desmontadura, despoblación forestal, f
deform /dɪ'fɔrm/ vt deformar, desfigurar; afear
deformation /,difɔr'meɪʃən/ n deformación, f
deformed /dɪ'fɔrmd/ a deformado; contrahecho
deformity /dɪ'fɔrmɪti/ n deformidad, f
defraud /dɪ'frɔd/ vt defraudar
defrauder /dɪ'frɔdər/ n defraudador (-ra)
defrauding /dɪ'frɔdɪŋ/ n defraudación, f
defray /dɪ'freɪ/ vt sufragar, costear, pagar
defrayal /dɪ'freɪəl/ n pago, m
defrost /dɪ'frɔst/ vt deshelar
deft /dɛft/ a diestro; hábil
deftly /'dɛftli/ adv con destreza; hábilmente
deftness /'dɛftnɪs/ n destreza, f; habilidad, f
defunct /dɪ'fʌŋkt/ a and n difunto (-ta)
defy /dɪ'faɪ/ vt desafiar; (face) arrostrar; (violate) contravenir
degeneracy /dɪ'dʒɛnərəsi/ n degeneración, f; depravación, perversión, f; degradación, f
degenerate /a, dɪ'dʒɛnərɪt; v -,reɪt/ a and n degenerado (-da). vi degenerar
degeneration /dɪ,dʒɛnə'reɪʃən/ n degeneración, f

degradation /ˌdɛgrɪ'deiʃən/ n degradación, f; abyección, f

degrade /dɪ'greid/ vt degradar; envilecer, deshonrar

degrading /dɪ'greidɪŋ/ a degradante

degree /dɪ'gri/ n grado, m; (academic) título; punto, m; clase social, f. **by degrees,** poco a poco, gradualmente, **five degrees below zero,** cinco grados bajo cero. **in the highest d.,** en sumo grado, en grado superlativo. **to a certain d.,** hasta cierto punto. **to receive a d.,** graduarse

degree-granting institution /dɪ'gri ˌgræntɪŋ/ n plantel habilitado para expedir títulos, m

dehydrate /di'haidreit/ vt deshidratar

dehydration /ˌdihai'dreiʃən/ n deshidratación, f

de-ice /di'ais/ vt deshelar

deification /ˌdiəfɪ'keiʃən/ n deificación, f

deify /'diəˌfai/ vt deificar, endiosar

deign /dein/ vi dignarse. vt conceder

deism /'diːzəm/ n deísmo, m

deist /'diist/ n deísta, mf

deity /'diiti/ n deidad, divinidad, f; dios, m

dejected /dɪ'dʒɛktɪd/ a abatido, desanimado, deprimido

dejectedly /dɪ'dʒɛktɪdli/ adv tristemente, abatidamente

dejection /dɪ'dʒɛkʃən/ n abatimiento, desaliento, m, melancolía, f

delay /dɪ'lei/ n retraso, m, dilación, tardanza, demora, f. vt retrasar, demorar; (a person) entretener; (postpone) aplazar; (obstruct) impedir. vi tardar; entretenerse. **without more d.,** sin más tardar

delectable /dɪ'lɛktəbəl/ a deleitoso, delicioso

delectably /dɪ'lɛktəbli/ adv deliciosamente

delectation /ˌdilek'teiʃən/ n delectación, f, deleite, m

delegacy /'dɛlɪgəsi/ n delegación, f

delegate /n 'dɛlɪgɪt; v -ˌgeit/ n delegado (-da). vt delegar, diputar

delegation /ˌdɛlɪ'geiʃən/ n delegación, f

delete /dɪ'lit/ vt suprimir, borrar

deleterious /ˌdɛlɪ'tɪəriəs/ a deletéreo

deletion /dɪ'liʃən/ n supresión, borradura, f

deliberate /a dɪ'lɪbərɪt; v -əˌreit/ a premeditado, intencionado; (slow) pausado, lento. vi and vt deliberar, discurrir, considerar

deliberately /dɪ'lɪbərɪtli/ adv (intentionally) con premeditación, a sabiendas, Central America adifés; (slowly) pausadamente, lentamente

deliberation /dɪˌlɪbə'reiʃən/ n reflexión, deliberación, consideración, f; (slowness) lentitud, pausa, f

deliberative /dɪ'lɪbərətɪv/ a deliberativo, de liberante

delicacy /'dɛlɪkəsi/ n delicadeza, f; fragilidad, f; suavidad, f; sensibilidad, f; escrupulosidad, f; (of health) debilidad, delicadez, f; (difficulty) dificultad, f; (food) manjar exquisito, m, golosina, f

delicate /'dɛlɪkɪt/ a delicado; fino; frágil; suave; exquisito; delicado (de salud); (of situations) difícil

delicatessen /ˌdɛlɪkə'tɛsən/ n (store) fiambrería, f

delicious /dɪ'lɪʃəs/ a delicioso

deliciously /dɪ'lɪʃəsli/ adv deliciosamente

deliciousness /dɪ'lɪʃəsnɪs/ n deleite, m, lo delicioso; excelencia, f; delicias, f pl

delict /dɪ'lɪkt/ n delito, m

delictive /dɪ'lɪktɪv/ a delictivo

delight /dɪ'lait/ n deleite, regocijo, m; encanto, m, delicia, f; placer, gozo, m. vt deleitar, encantar; halagar. vi deleitarse, complacerse. **to be delighted with,** estar encantado con. **to d. in,** deleitarse en, complacerse en; tomar placer en

delightful /dɪ'laitfəl/ a delicioso, precioso, encantador

delightfully /dɪ'laitfəli/ adv deliciosamente

delimit /dɪ'lɪmɪt/ vt delimitar

delimitation /dɪˌlɪmɪ'teiʃən/ n delimitación, f

delineate /dɪ'lɪni,eit/ vt delinear, diseñar; Fig. pintar, describir

delineation /dɪˌlɪni'eiʃən/ n delineación, f; retrato, m; Fig. descripción, f

delineator /dɪ'lɪnieitər/ n diseñador, m

delinquency /dɪ'lɪŋkwənsi/ n delincuencia, f; criminalidad, f; culpa, f; delito, m

delinquent /dɪ'lɪŋkwənt/ a delincuente. n delincuente, mf

deliquescence /ˌdɛlɪ'kwɛsəns/ n delicuescencia, f

deliquescent /ˌdɛlɪ'kwɛsənt/ a delicuescente

delirious /dɪ'lɪəriəs/ a delirante; desvariado; Inf. loco. **to be d.,** delirar, desvariar

delirium /dɪ'lɪəriəm/ n delirio, desvarío, m. **d. tremens,** delírium tremens, m

deliver /dɪ'lɪvər/ vt librar (de); salvar (de); (distribute) repartir; (hand over) entregar; (recite) recitar, decir; (a speech) pronunciar; comunicar; (send) despachar, expedir; (a blow) asestar; (give) dar; (bring) traer; (battle, a lecture) dar; (a woman, of a doctor) asistir en el parto (a); (a child) traer al mundo; (a judgment) pronunciar. **to be delivered (of a child),** dar a luz. **to d. oneself up,** entregarse. **delivered free,** porte pagado.

deliverance /dɪ'lɪvərəns/ n libramiento, rescate, m; redención, salvación, f; (of a judgment) pronuncia, f

deliverer /dɪ'lɪvərər/ n libertador (-ra); salvador (-ra); (distributor) repartidor (-ra); entregador (-ra)

delivery /dɪ'lɪvəri/ n (distribution) reparto, m, distribución, f; entrega, f; Law. cesión, f; (of a judgment) pronuncia, f; (of a speech) pronunciación, f; (manner of speaking) declamación, f; dicción, f; (of a child) parto, m. **on d.,** al entregarse. **The letter came by the first d.,** La carta llegó en el primer reparto. **d. man,** mozo de reparto, m. **d. note,** nota de entrega, f. **d. van,** camión de reparto, m

delivery truck n camioneta de reparto, furgoneta, f; sedán de reparto, m

dell /dɛl/ n hondonada, f; pequeño valle, m

delouse /di'laus/ vt despiojar, espulgar

Delphi /'dɛlfai/ Delfos, m

delta /'dɛltə/ n (Greek letter) delta, f; (of a river) delta, m

delude /dɪ'lud/ vt engañar; ilusionar. **to d. oneself,** engañarse

deluded /dɪ'ludɪd/ a iluso, engañado, ciego

deluge /'dɛlyudʒ/ n diluvio, m. vt diluviar; inundar (con)

delusion /dɪ'luʒən/ n engaño, m, ceguedad, f; error, m; ilusión, f

delve /dɛlv/ vt and vi cavar; Fig. ahondar (en), penetrar (en), investigar

demagogic /ˌdɛmə'gɒdʒɪk/ a demagógico

demagogue /'dɛmə,gɒg/ n demagogo (-ga)

demagogy /'dɛmə,goudʒi/ n demagogia, f

demand /dɪ'mænd/ n exigencia, f; Com. demanda, f; petición, f; Polit. Econ. consumo, m. vt exigir; requerir; pedir; (claim) reclamar. **in d.,** en demanda. **on d.,** al solicitarse. **to be in d.,** ser popular. **d. note,** apremio, m

demanding /dɪ'mændɪŋ/ a exigente

demarcate /dɪ'markeit/ vt demarcar

demarcation /ˌdimar'keiʃən/ n demarcación, f

demean (oneself) /dɪ'min/ vr degradarse, rebajarse

demeanor /dɪ'minər/ n conducta, f; continente, porte, aire, m; (manners) modales, m pl

demented /dɪ'mɛntɪd/ a demente, loco

demerit /dɪ'mɛrɪt/ n demérito, m

demi- prefix semi; casi. **d.-tasse,** taza cafetera, jícara, f

demigod /'dɛmi,gɒd/ n semidios, m

demigoddess /'dɛmi,gɒdɪs/ n semidiosa, f

demijohn /'dɛmɪ,dʒɒn/ n damajuana, f

demilitarize /di'mɪlɪtə,raiz/ vt desmilitarizar

demise /dɪ'maiz/ n Law. traslación de dominio, f; sucesión de la corona, f; (death) óbito, fallecimiento, m

demisemiquaver /ˌdɛmi'sɛmi,kweivər/ n fusa, f

demobilization /di,moubələ'zeiʃən/ n desmovilización, f

demobilize /di'moubə,laiz/ vt desmovilizar

democracy /dɪ'mɒkrəsi/ n democracia, f

democrat /'dɛmə,kræt/ n demócrata, mf

democratic /ˌdɛmə'krætɪk/ a democrático. **to make d.,** democratizar

Democratic Party n Partido Democrático, m

demolish /dɪ'mɒlɪʃ/ vt demoler, derribar; Fig. destruir; (eat) engullir, devorar

demolisher /dɪ'mɒlɪʃər/ n demoledor, m; Fig. destructor (-ra)

demolition /ˌdɛmə'lɪʃən/ n demolición, f; derribo, m, a demoledor; de demolición. **d. squad,** pelotón de demolición, m

demon /'dimən/ n demonio, diablo, m

demonetization /diˌmɒnɪtə'zeɪʃən/ n desmonetización, f

demonetize /diˈmɒnɪˌtaiz/ vt desmonetizar

demoniacal /ˌdimə'naiɪkəl/ a demoníaco

demonology /ˌdimə'nɒlədʒi/ n demonología, f

demonstrable /dɪ'mɒnstrəbəl, 'dɛmən-/ a demonstrable

demonstrably /dɪ'mɒnstrəbli/ adv demostrablemente

demonstrate /'dɛmənˌstreɪt/ vt demostrar; mostrar, probar. vi hacer una demostración

demonstration /ˌdɛmən'streɪʃən/ n demostración, f; manifestación, f

demonstrative /də'mɒnstrətɪv/ a demostrativo; (of persons) expresivo, mimoso. **d. pronoun,** pronombre demostrativo, m

demonstrator /'dɛmənˌstreɪtər/ n demostrador (-ra)

demoralization /dɪˌmɔrələ'zeɪʃən/ n desmoralización, f

demoralize /dɪ'mɔrəˌlaiz, -'mɒr-/ vt desmoralizar

demoralizing /dɪ'mɔrəˌlaizɪŋ/ a desmoralizador

demur /dɪ'mɜr/ vi dudar, vacilar; objetar, protestar; poner dificultades. n objeción, protesta, f

demure /dɪ'myʊr/ a serio, modoso recatado; púdico; de una coquetería disimulada

demurely /dɪ'myʊrli/ adv modestamente; con recato; con coquetería disimulada

demureness /dɪ'myʊrnɪs/ n seriedad, f, recato, m; modestia fingida, coquetería disimulada, f

den /dɛn/ n madriguera, guardia, f; (of thieves) cueva, f; (in a zoo) cercado, recinto, m; (study) gabinete, m; (squalid room) cuartucho, m

denaturalization /diˌnætʃərələ'zeɪʃən/ n desnaturalización, f

denaturalize /diˈnætʃərəˌlaiz/ vt desnaturalizar

denial /dɪ'naiəl/ n negación, f; rechazo, m; contradicción, f; negativa, f

denizen /'dɛnəzən/ n habitante, m; ciudadano (-na)

Denmark /'dɛnmark/ Dinamarca, f

denominate /dɪ'nɒməˌneit/ vt denominar, nombrar

denomination /diˌnɒmə'neɪʃən/ n denominación, f; secta, f; clase, f

denominational /dɪˌnɒmə'neɪʃənl/ a sectario

denominator /dɪ'nɒməˌneitər/ n Math. denominador, m

denote /dɪ'nout/ vt denotar, indicar; significar

dénouement /ˌdeinu'mã/ n desenlace, desenredo, m; solución, f

denounce /dɪ'nauns/ vt denunciar; delatar, acusar

denouncer /dɪ'naunsər/ n denunciante, mf delator (-ra)

dense /dɛns/ a denso; espeso, compacto; tupido; impenetrable; Inf. estúpido

densely /'dɛnsli/ adv densamente; espesamente. **d. populated,** con gran densidad de población

density /'dɛnsɪti/ n densidad, f; espesor, m; consistencia, f; Inf. estupidez, f

dent /dɛnt/ n mella, f; (in metal) abolladura, f, vt mellar; abollar

dental /'dɛntl̩/ a dental. n letra dental, f. **d. forceps,** gatillo, m. **d. mechanic,** mecánico dentista, m. **d. surgeon,** odontólogo, m

dental floss n seda dental, f

dentifrice /'dɛntəfrɪs/ n dentífrico, m

dentist /'dɛntɪst/ n dentista, mf; odontólogo, m

dentistry /'dɛntəstri/ n odontología, f

dentition /dɛn'tɪʃən/ n dentición, f

denture /'dɛntʃər/ n dentadura, f

denudation /dinu'deɪʃən/ n denudación, f

denude /dɪ'nud/ vt denudar, despojar, privar (de)

denunciation /dɪˌnʌnsi'eiʃən/ n denuncia, f; acusación, delación, f

denunciatory /dɪ'nʌnsiəˌtɔri/ a denunciatorio

Denver boot /'dɛnvər/ n cepo, m

deny /dɪ'nai/ vt negar; desmentir; rehusar; rechazar;

renegar (de); (give up) renunciar, sacrificar. **to d. oneself,** privarse (de); sacrificar; negarse

deodorant /di'oudərənt/ a and n desodorante m

deodorize /di'oudəˌraiz/ vt desinfectar, destruir el olor de

depart /dɪ'part/ vi marcharse, irse, partir; (of trains, etc., and meaning go out) salir; (deviate) desviarse (de), apartarse (de); (go away) alejarse; (leave) dejar; (disappear) desaparecer; (alter) cambiar; (die) morir

departed /dɪ'partɪd/ a (past) pasado; desaparecido; (dead) difunto, muerto. n difunto (-ta)

department /dɪ'partmənt/ n departamento, m; sección, f; (of learning) ramo, m. **d. store,** grandes tiendas, f pl, (Argentina), grandes almacenes, m pl

departmental /dɪˌpart'mɛntl̩/ a departamental

departure /dɪ'partʃər/ n partida, ida, f, Lat. Am. egreso, m; (going out, and of trains, etc.) salida, f; (deviation) desviación, el apartarse. **d. from the rules,** el apartarse de las reglas, f; (disappearance) desaparición, f; (change) cambio, m; (giving up) renuncia, f; (death) muerte, f. **to take one's d.,** marcharse

depend /dɪ'pɛnd/ vi depender. **to d. on,** depender de; (rest on) apoyarse en; (count on) contar con; (trust) fiarse de; tener confianza en, estar seguro de. **That depends!** ¡Eso depende!

dependable /dɪ'pɛndəbəl/ a digno de confianza; seguro

dependence, dependency /dɪ'pɛndəns; dɪ'pɛndənsi/ n dependencia, f; subordinación, f; (trust) confianza, f

dependent /dɪ'pɛndənt/ a dependiente; subordinado; condicional. n dependiente, m. **to be d. on,** depender de

depict /dɪ'pɪkt/ vt representar; pintar; dibujar; Fig. describir, retratar

depiction /dɪ'pɪkʃən/ n representación, f; pintura, f; dibujo, m; Fig. descripción, f

depilate /'dɛpəˌleit/ vt depilar

depilatory /dɪ'pɪləˌtɔri, -ˌtouri/ a and n depilatorio m

deplete /dɪ'plit/ vt agotar; disipar

depletion /dɪ'pliʃən/ n agotamiento, m

deplorable /dɪ'plɔrəbəl/ a lamentable, deplorable

deplorably /dɪ'plɔrəbli/ adv lamentablemente

deplore /dɪ'plɔr/ vt deplorar, lamentar

deploy /dɪ'plɔi/ vt desplegar. vi desplegarse. n despliegue, m

deployment /dɪ'plɔimənt/ n despliegue, m

deponent /dɪ'pounənt/ n Law. declarante, deponente, mf a deponente. **d. verb,** verbo deponente, m

depopulate /di'pɒpyəˌleit/ vt despoblar

depopulation /diˌpɒpyə'leiʃən/ n despoblación, f

deport /dɪ'pɔrt/ vt deportar

deportation /ˌdipɔr'teiʃən/ n deportación, f

deportment /dɪ'pɔrtmənt/ n comportamiento, m; porte, aire, m; conducta, f

depose /dɪ'pouz/ vt destronar; (give evidence) testificar, declarar

deposit /dɪ'pɒzɪt/ n depósito, m; Geol. yacimiento, filón, m; sedimento, m. vt depositar. **to leave a d.,** dejar un depósito. **d. account,** cuenta corriente, f

deposition /ˌdɛpə'zɪʃən/ n deposición, f; Law. testimonio, m, declaración, Lat. Am. constancia f; (from the Cross) descendimiento, m, (de la Cruz)

depositor /dɪ'pɒzɪtər/ n depositador (-ra)

depository /dɪ'pɒzɪˌtɔri/ n depositaría, f, almacén, m; (of knowledge, etc.) pozo, m

depot /'dipou/ n almacén, m; (military headquarters) depósito, m; (for army vehicles, m etc.) parque, m; (for buses, etc.) estación, f

depravation /ˌdɛprə'veiʃən/ n depravación, f

depraved /dɪ'preivd/ a depravado, perverso, vicioso

depravity /dɪ'prævɪti/ n corrupción, maldad, perversión, f

deprecate /'dɛprɪˌkeit/ vt desaprobar, criticar; lamentar, deplorar

deprecatingly /'dɛprɪˌkeitiŋli/ adv con desaprobación, críticamente

deprecation /ˌdɛprɪ'keiʃən/ n deprecación, f; desaprobación, crítica, f

deprecatory /'dɛprɪkə,tɔri/ a deprecativo; de desaprobación, de crítica

depreciate /dɪ'priʃi,eit/ vt depreciar, rebajar; Fig. tener en poco, menospreciar. vi depreciarse, deteriorarse; bajar de precio

depreciatingly /dɪ'priʃi,eitɪŋli/ adv con desprecio

depreciation /dɪ,priʃi'eiʃən/ n (in value) amortización, depreciación, f; Fig. desprecio, m

depreciatory /dɪ'priʃiə,tɔri/ a Fig. despectivo, despreciativo

depredation /,dɛprə'deiʃən/ n depredación, f

depress /dɪ'prɛs/ vt deprimir; (weaken) debilitar; (humble) humillar; (dispirit) abatir, entristecer; (trade) desanimar, paralizar

depressed /dɪ'prɛst/ a deprimido, desalentado, melancólico, triste; (of an area) necesitado

depressing /dɪ'prɛsɪŋ/ a melancólico, triste; pesimista

depressingly /dɪ'prɛsɪŋli/ adv con tristeza; con pesimismo

depression /dɪ'prɛʃən/ n depresión, f; (hollow) hoyo, m; (sadness) desaliento, abatimiento, m, melancolía, f; (in prices) baja, f; (in trade) desanimación, parálisis, f; Astron. depresión, f

deprivation /,dɛprə'veiʃən/ n privación, f; pérdida, f

deprive /dɪ'praiv/ vt privar (de), despojar (de); defraudar (de); Eccl. destituir (de)

depth /dɛpθ/ n profundidad, f; (thickness) espesor, m; fondo, m; (of night, winter, the country) medio, m; (of sound) gravedad, f; (of colour, feeling) intensidad, f; (abstruseness) dificultad, f; (sagacity) sagacidad, f; pl **depths,** profundidades, f pl; abismo, m; lo más hondo; lo más íntimo. **to be 4 feet in d.,** tener cuatro pies de profundidad. **to the depths of one's being,** hasta lo más íntimo de su ser; hasta los tuétanos. **d. charge,** carga de profundidad, f

deputation /,dɛpyə'teiʃən/ n deputación, delegación, f

deputize (for) /'dɛpyə,taiz/ vi desempeñar las funciones de, substituir

deputy /'dɛpyəti/ n (substitute) lugarteniente, m; (agent) representante, m; apoderado, m; (parliamentary) diputado, m; (in compounds) sub, vice. **d.-governor,** subgobernador, m. **d.-head,** subjefe, m; (of a school) subdirector (-ra)

derail /di'reil/ vt (hacer) descarrilar, Lat. Am. desrielar

derailment /di'reilmənt/ n descarrilamiento, m

derange /dɪ'reindʒ/ vt desordenar; desorganizar; turbar; (mentally) trastornar, hacer perder el juicio (a)

derangement /dɪ'reindʒmənt/ n desorden, m; turbación, f; (mental) trastorno, m, locura, f

derby /'dərbi/ n carrera del Derby, f; (hat) sombrero hongo, m

deregulate /di'rɛgyə,leit/ vt desregular

deregulation /di,rɛgyə'leiʃən/ n desregulación, f

derelict /'dɛrəlɪkt/ a abandonado, derrelicto. n derrelicto, m

dereliction /,dɛrə'lɪkʃən/ n abandono, m; omisión, negligencia, f; descuido, m

deride /dɪ'raid/ vt burlarse de, mofarse de; ridiculizar

derision /dɪ'rɪʒən/ n escarnio, f, menosprecio, m

derisive /dɪ'raisɪv/ a irrisorio; irónico

derisively /dɪ'raisɪvli/ adv irrisoriamente; con ironía, irónicamente

derivation /,dɛrə'veiʃən/ n derivación, f

derivative /dɪ'rɪvətɪv/ a derivativo. n derivado, m

derive /dɪ'raiv/ vt derivar; obtener; extraer; Fig. sacar, hallar. vi (from) derivar de; proceder de; remontar a

dermatitis /,dərmə'taitɪs/ n dermatitis, f

dermatologist /,dərmə'tɒlədʒɪst/ n dermatólogo, m

dermatology /,dərmə'tɒlədʒi/ n dermatología, f

derogatory /dɪ'rɒgə,tɔri/ a despectivo, despreciativo; deshonroso

derrick /'dɛrɪk/ n grúa, machina, f; abanico, m

descant /n 'dɛskænt; v dɛs'kænt/ n Mus. discante, m. vi Mus. discantar; discurrir (sobre), disertar (sobre)

descend /dɪ'sɛnd/ vt descender, bajar; (be inherited) pasar a; (fall) caer; (of the sun) ponerse. vt bajar. **to d. from,** descender de. **to d. to,** (lower oneself) rebajarse; (consider) venir a, considerar. **to d. upon,** caer

sobre; (arrive unexpectedly) llegar inesperadamente, invadir

descendant /dɪ'sɛndənt/ n descendiente, mf; pl **descendants,** descendencia, f

descent /dɪ'sɛnt/ n descenso, m; bajada, f; (slope) pendiente, cuesta, f; (attack) invasión, f, ataque, m; (lineage) descendencia, alcurnia, procedencia, f; (inheritance) herencia, f; transmisión, f. **D. from the Cross,** Descendimiento de la Cruz, m

describable /dɪ'skraibəbəl/ a descriptible

describe /dɪ'skraib/ vt describir; pintar

description /dɪ'skrɪpʃən/ n descripción, f

descriptive /dɪ'skrɪptɪv/ a descriptivo

desecrate /'dɛsɪ,kreit/ vt profanar

desecration /,dɛsɪ'kreiʃən/ n profanación, f

desegregation /,disɛgrɪ'geiʃən/ n desegregación, f

desert /dɪ'zərt/ vt abandonar; dejar; (Mil. etc.) desertar. vi desertar

desert /'dɛzərt/ n desierto, m

desert /dɪ'zərt/ n (merit) mérito, m **to receive one's deserts,** llevar su merecido

deserted /dɪ'zərtɪd/ a abandonado; desierto; solitario; inhabitado, despoblado

deserter /dɪ'zərtər/ n desertor, m

desertion /dɪ'zərʃən/ n abandono, m, deserción, f; (Mil. etc.) deserción, f

deserve /dɪ'zərv/ vt and vi merecer

deservedly /dɪ'zərvɪdli/ adv merecidamente

deserving /dɪ'zərvɪŋ/ a merecedor; meritorio. **to be d. of,** merecer

desiccate /'dɛsɪ,keit/ vt desecar. vi desecarse

design /dɪ'zain/ n proyecto, m; plan, m; intención, f, propósito, m; objeto, m; modelo, m; (pattern) diseño, dibujo, m; arte del dibujo, mf. vt idear; proyectar; (destine) destinar, dedicar; diseñar, dibujar, delinear; planear. **by d.,** expresamente, intencionalmente

designate /v 'dɛzɪg,neit/ a -nɪt/ vt señalar; designar; (appoint) nombrar. a electo

designation /,dɛzɪg'neiʃən/ n designación, f; nombramiento, m

designedly /dɪ'zainɪdli/ adv de propósito

designer /dɪ'zainər/ n inventor (-ra), autor (-ra); delineador (-ra); dibujante, mf; (of public works, etc.) proyectista, mf

designing /dɪ'zainɪŋ/ a intrigante, astuto

desirability /dɪ,zaiʳə'bɪliti/ n lo deseable; conveniencia, f; ventaja, f

desirable /dɪ'zaiʳəbəl/ a deseable; conveniente; ventajoso; agradable; apetecible

desire /dɪ'zaiʳr/ vt desear; querer; ansiar, ambicionar; (request) rogar, pedir; (order) mandar. n deseo, m; ansia, aspiración, f; ambición, f; impulso, m; (will) voluntad, f. **to d. ardently,** perecerse por; suspirar por

desirous /dɪ'zaiʳrəs/ a deseoso (de); ambicioso (de); ansioso (de); impaciente (a); curioso (de)

desist /dɪ'sɪst/ vi desistir; dejar (de)

desk /dɛsk/ n pupitre, m; escritorio, buró, m; mesa de trabajo, f; (cashier's) caja, f; (teacher's, lecturer's; pulpit) cátedra, f

desolate /a 'dɛsəlɪt; v -,leit/ a solitario; desierto; deshabitado; abandonado; arruinado; árido; (afflicted) desolado, angustiado. vt desolar; despoblar

desolation /,dɛsə'leiʃən/ n desolación, f; aflicción, f, angustia, f, desconsuelo, m

despair /dɪ'spɛər/ n desesperación, f. vi perder toda esperanza. **He despaired of life,** Se ha perdido la esperanza de salvarle (la vida). **to be in d.,** estar desesperado

despairing /dɪ'spɛərɪŋ/ a desesperado

despairingly /dɪ'spɛərɪŋli/ adv sin esperanza

desperate /'dɛspərɪt/ a desesperado; sin esperanza; irremediable; furioso; violento; (dangerous) arriesgado, peligroso; terrible

desperately /'dɛspərɪtli/ adv desesperadamente; furiosamente; terriblemente

desperation /,dɛspə'reiʃən/ n desesperación, f; furia, violencia, f

despicable /'dɛspɪkəbəl/ a vil, despreciable; insignificante

despise /dɪ'spaiz/ *vt* despreciar; desdeñar
despiser /dɪ'spaizər/ *n* menospreciador (-ra)
despite /dɪ'spait/ *prep* a pesar de
despoil /dɪ'spɔil/ *vt* despojar, desnudar
despoiler /dɪ'spɔilər/ *n* despojador (-ra)
despoliation /dɪˌspouli'eiʃən/ *n* despojo, *m*
despondency /dɪ'spɒndənsi/ *n* abatimiento, desaliento, *m*, desesperación, *f*
despondent /dɪ'spɒndənt/ *a* abatido, desanimado, deprimido
despondently /dɪ'spɒndəntli/ *adv* con desaliento
despot /'dɛspət/ *n* déspota, *m*
despotic /dɛs'pɒtɪk/ *a* despótico
despotism /'dɛspəˌtɪzəm/ *n* despotismo, *m*
dessert /dɪ'zɜrt/ *n* postre, *m*, *a* de postre. **d. plate,** plato para postre, *m*. **d.-spoon,** cuchara de postre, *f*
destination /ˌdɛstə'neiʃən/ *n* destinación, *f*
destine /'dɛstɪn/ *vt* destinar; dedicar; predestinar
destiny /'dɛstəni/ *n* destino, *m*
destitute /'dɛstɪˌtut/ *a* indigente, menesteroso; desnudo (de); privado (de); desprovisto (de), falto (de); desamparado
destitution /ˌdɛstɪ'tuʃən/ *n* destitución, indigencia, miseria, *f*; privación, falta, *f*; desamparo, *m*
destroy /dɪ'strɔi/ *vt* destruir; demoler; deshacer; (kill) matar; exterminar; (finish) acabar con
destroyer /dɪ'strɔiər/ *n* destructor (-ra); *Nav.* destructor, cazatorpedero, *m*
destructible /dɪ'strʌktəbəl/ *a* destructible, destruible
destruction /dɪ'strʌkʃən/ *n* destrucción, *f*; demolición, *f*; ruina, *f*; pérdida, *f*; muerte, *f*; exterminio, *m*; perdición, *f*
destructive /dɪ'strʌktɪv/ *a* destructivo, destructor; (of animals) dañino. **d. animal,** animal dañino, *m*, alimaña, *f*
destructiveness /dɪ'strʌktɪvnɪs/ *n* destructividad, *f*; instinto destructor, *m*
desultory /'dɛsəlˌtɔri/ *a* inconexo; sin método, descosido; irregular
detach /dɪ'tætʃ/ *vt* separar, desprender; (unstick) despegar; *Mil.* destacar
detachable /dɪ'tætʃəbəl/ *a* separable, de quita y pon
detached /dɪ'tætʃt/ *a* suelto, separado; (Fig. with outlook, etc.) imparcial; indiferente, despegado. **d. house,** hotelito, *m*
detachment /dɪ'tætʃmənt/ *n* separación, *f*; *Mil.* destacamento, *m*; (Fig. of mind) imparcialidad, *f*; independencia (de espíritu, etc.), *f*; indiferencia, *f*
detail /dɪ'teil/ *n* detalle, *m*; particularidad, *f*; circunstancia, *f*; *Mil.* destacamento, *m*. *vt* detallar; particularizar, referir con pormenores; *Mil.* destacar. **in d.,** detalladamente, *f*; *Inf.* ce por be. **to go into details,** entrar en detalles
detain /dɪ'tein/ *vt* detener; (arrest) arrestar, prender; (withhold) retener; (prevent) impedir
detect /dɪ'tɛkt/ *vt* descubrir; averiguar; (discern) discernir, percibir; *Elec.* detectar
detectable /dɪ'tɛktəbəl/ *a* perceptible
detection /dɪ'tɛkʃən/ *n* descubrimiento, *m*; averiguación, *f*; percepción, *f*
detective /dɪ'tɛktɪv/ *n* detective, *m*, *a* de detectives, policíaco. **d. novel,** novela policíaca, *f*
detector /dɪ'tɛktər/ *n* descubridor, *m*; *Elec.* detector, *m*; *Mech.* indicador, *m*
detention /dɪ'tɛnʃən/ *n* detención, *f*; (arrest) arresto, *m*; (confinement) encierro, *m*
deter /dɪ'tɜr/ *vt* desanimar, desalentar; acobardar; (dissuade) disuadir; (prevent) impedir
detergent /dɪ'tɜrdʒənt/ *a* detersorio. *n* detersorio, *m*
deteriorate /dɪ'tɪəriəˌreit/ *vt* deteriorar. *vi* deteriorarse; empeorar
deterioration /dɪˌtɪəriə'reiʃən/ *n* deterioración, *f*; empeoramiento, *m*
determinable /dɪ'tɜrmənəbəl/ *a* determinable
determination /dɪˌtɜrmə'neiʃən/ *n* determinación, *f*; definición, *f*; resolución, decisión, *f*; *Law.* fallo, *m*; *Med.* congestión, *f*
determine /dɪ'tɜrmɪn/ *vt* determinar; definir; decidir; resolver; concluir; (fix) señalar; *Law.* sentenciar. *vi*

resolverse, decidirse; (insist (on)) empeñarse en, insistir en
determined /dɪ'tɜrmɪnd/ *a* determinado; resuelto, decidido; (of price) fijo
determining /dɪ'tɜrmənɪŋ/ *a* determinante
determinism /dɪ'tɜrməˌnɪzəm/ *n* determinismo, *m*
deterministic /dɪˌtɜrmə'nɪstɪk/ *a* determinista
deterrent /dɪ'tɜrənt/ *a* disuasivo. *n* freno, *m*. **to act as a d.,** servir como un freno. **d. capability,** poder de disuasión, *m*
detest /dɪ'tɛst/ *vt* detestar, abominar, aborrecer
detestable /dɪ'tɛstəbəl/ *a* detestable, aborrecible, abominable
detestation /ˌdite'steiʃən/ *n* detestación, abominación, *f*, aborrecimiento, *m*
dethrone /di'θroun/ *vt* destronar
detonate /'dɛtņˌeit/ *vt* hacer detonar. *vi* detonar, estallar
detonation /ˌdɛtņ'eiʃən/ *n* detonación, *f*
detonator /'dɛtņˌeitər/ *n* detonador, *m*; señal detonante, *f*
detour /'ditur/ *n* rodeo, *m*; desvío, *m*, desviación, *f*
detract /dɪ'trækt/ *vt* quitar; (diminish) disminuir; (slander) detraer, denigrar
detraction /dɪ'trækʃən/ *n* detracción, denigración, *f*
detractor /dɪ'træktər/ *n* detractor (-ra); infamador (-ra)
detriment /'dɛtrəmənt/ *n* detrimento, *m*; perjuicio, *m*; daño, *m*
detrimental /ˌdɛtrə'mɛntļ/ *a* perjudicial
deuce /dus/ *n* (dice, cards) dos, *m*; (tennis) "dos," *m*. **The d.!** ¡Diantre! **to be the d. of a row,** haber moros y cristianos. **D. take it!** ¡Demonios!
Deuteronomy /ˌdutə'rɒnəmi/ *n* Deuteronomio, *m*
devaluation /diˌvælyu'eiʃən/ *n* desvalorización, *f*
devalue /di'vælyu/ *vt* rebajar el valor de
devastate /'dɛvəˌsteit/ *vt* devastar, asolar
devastation /ˌdɛvə'steiʃən/ *n* devastación, *f*
develop /dɪ'vɛləp/ *vt* desarrollar; (make progress) avanzar, fomentar; perfeccionar; *Photo.* revelar. *vi* desarrollarse; crecer; avanzar, progresar; evolucionar
developer /dɪ'vɛləpər/ *n* *Photo.* revelador, *m*
development /dɪ'vɛləpmənt/ *n* desarrollo, *m*; evolución, *f*; progreso, avance, *m*; (encouragement) fomento, *m*; (event) acontecimiento, suceso, *m*; (product) producto, *m*; (working) explotación, *f*; *Photo.* revelación, *f*
deviate /'diviˌeit/ *vi* desviarse (de); (disagree) disentir (de)
deviation /ˌdivi'eiʃən/ *n* desviación, *f*
device /dɪ'vais/ *n* (contrivance) aparato, artefacto, mecanismo, *m*; (invention) invento, *m*; (trick) expediente, artificio, *m*; (scheme) proyecto, *m*; (design) dibujo, emblema, *m*; (motto) divisa, leyenda, *f*; *pl* **devices,** placeres, caprichos, *m pl*
devil /'dɛvəl/ *n* diablo, Satanás, *m*; demonio, *m*; (printer's) aprendiz de impresor, *m*. **Go to the d.!** ¡Vete enhoramala! **He is a poor d.,** Es un pobre diablo. **little d.,** diablillo, *m*. **The devil's abroad,** Anda el diablo suelto. **The d. take it!** ¡Lléveselo el diablo! **to play the d. with,** arruinar por completo. **What the d.!** ¡Qué diablos! **d.-possessed,** endemoniado
devilish /'dɛvəlɪʃ/ *a* diabólico, demoníaco; infernal
devilry /'dɛvəlri/ *n* diablura, *f*; magia, *f*; monología, *f*; (wickedness) maldad, *f*; crueldad, *f*
devious /'diviəs/ *a* desviado; tortuoso
deviousness /'diviəsnɪs/ *n* tortuosidad, *f*
devise /dɪ'vaiz/ *vt* idear, inventar; fabricar; *Law.* legar
deviser /dɪ'vaizər/ *n* inventor (-ra)
devitalize /di'vaitļˌaiz/ *vt* restar vitalidad, privar de vitalidad
devoid /dɪ'vɔid/ *a* desprovisto (de), privado (de); libre (de), exento (de)
devolve /dɪ'vɒlv/ *vt* traspasar, transmitir. *vi* (on, upon) incumbir (a), corresponder (a), tocar (a)
devote /dɪ'vout/ *vt* dedicar; consagrar. **to d. oneself to,** darse a, dedicarse a; consagrarse a

devoted /dɪ'voutɪd/ *a* fervoroso, apasionado; (faithful) fiel, leal
devotedly /dɪ'voutɪdli/ *adv* con devoción
devotee /ˌdɛvə'ti/ *n* devoto (-ta), admirador (-ra); aficionado (-da)
devotion /dɪ'vouʃən/ *n* devoción, *f*; dedicación, *f*; (zeal) celo, *m*; afición, *f*; (loyalty) lealtad, *f*; *pl* **devotions,** rezos, *m pl,* oraciones, *f pl*
devotional /dɪ'vouʃənl/ *a* devoto, religioso, de devoción. **devotional literature,** literatura de devoción, *f*
devour /dɪ'vaur/ *vt* devorar; consumir
devourer /dɪ'vaurər/ *n* devorador (-ra)
devouring /dɪ'vaurɪŋ/ *a* devorador; absorbente
devout /dɪ'vaut/ *a* devoto, piadoso, practicante (e.g., *a d. Catholic,* un católico practicante)
devoutly /dɪ'vautli/ *adv* piadosamente
devoutness /dɪ'vautnɪs/ *n* piedad, devoción, *f*
dew /du/ *n* rocío, sereno, relente, *m; Fig.* rocío, *m, vt* rociar; humedecer; (refresh) refrescar. **d.-drop,** aljófar, *m,* gota de rocío, *f*
dewlap /'duˌlæp/ *n* papada, *f,* papo, *m*
dewy /'dui/ *a* rociado, lleno de rocío; húmedo; (of eyes) lustroso
dexterity /dɛk'stɛrɪti/ *n* destreza, *f*
dextrine /'dɛkstrɪn/ *n* dextrina, *f*
dextrose /'dɛkstrous/ *n* dextrosa, glucosa, *f*
dextrous /'dɛkstrəs/ *a* diestro; hábil, listo
diabetes /ˌdaɪə'bitɪs/ *n* diabetes, *f*
diabetic /ˌdaɪə'bɛtɪk/ *a* diabético
diabolical /ˌdaɪə'bɒlɪkəl/ *a* diabólico
diadem /'daɪəˌdɛm/ *n* diadema, *f*
diagnose /'daɪəgˌnous/ *vt* diagnosticar
diagnosis /ˌdaɪəg'nousɪs/ *n* diagnóstico, *m,* diagnosis, *f*
diagnostician /ˌdaɪəgnɒ'stɪʃən/ *n* diagnóstico, *m*
diagonal /daɪ'ægənl/ *n* diagonal, *f*
diagram /'daɪəˌgræm/ *n* diagrama, *m;* esquema, *f;* gráfico, *m*
diagrammatic /ˌdaɪəgrə'mætɪk/ *a* esquemático
dial /'daɪəl/ *n* (sundial) reloj de sol, *m;* (of clocks, gas-meter) esfera, *f;* (of machines) indicador, *m;* (of a wireless set) cuadrante graduado, *m;* (of a telephone) marcador, disco, *m. vt* (a telephone number) marcar. **d. telephone,** teléfono automático, *m*
dialect /'daɪəˌlɛkt/ *n* dialecto, *m,* habla, *f, a* dialectal
dialectic /ˌdaɪə'lɛktɪk/ *a* dialéctico. *n* dialéctica, *f*
dialectics /ˌdaɪə'lɛktɪks/ *n* dialéctica, *f*
dialogue /'daɪəˌlɔg/ *n* diálogo, *m.* **to hold a d.,** dialogar
dialysis /daɪ'æləsɪs/ *n* diálisis, *f*
diameter /daɪ'æmɪtər/ *n* diámetro, *m*
diametrical /ˌdaɪə'mɛtrɪkəl/ *a* diametral
diamond /'daɪmənd/ *n* diamante, *m;* brillante, *m;* (tool) cortavidrios, *m;* (cards) oros (de baraja), *m pl.* **rough d.,** diamante bruto, *m.* **d.-bearing,** diamantífero. **d. cutter,** diamantista, *mf* **d. cutting,** talla de diamantes, *f.* **d. edition,** edición diamante, *f.* **d.-like,** adiamantado. **d. wedding,** bodas de diamante, *f pl*
diapason /ˌdaɪə'peɪzən/ *n* diapasón, *m*
diaper /'daɪpər/ *n* lienzo adamascado, *m;* (baby's) pañal, *m;* (woman's) servilleta higiénica, *f*
diaphanous /daɪ'æfənəs/ *a* diáfano, transparente
diaphragm /'daɪəˌfræm/ *n* diafragma, *m*
diarist /'daɪərɪst/ *n* diarista, *mf*
diarrhea /ˌdaɪə'riə/ *n* diarrea, *f*
diary /'daɪəri/ *n* diario, *m*
diastase /'daɪəˌsteɪs/ *n* diastasa, *f*
diastole /daɪ'æstl̩/ *n* diástole, *f*
diatribe /'daɪəˌtraɪb/ *n* diatriba, denunciación violenta, *f*
dibble /'dɪbəl/ *n* plantador, *m, vt and vi* plantar con plantador
dice /daɪs/ *n pl* dados, *m pl.* **to load the d.,** cargar los dados
dicky /'dɪki/ *n* (front) pechera postiza, *f;* (seat) trasera, *f;* (apron) delantal, *m.* **d. seat,** *Inf.* ahí te pudras, *m*
dictaphone /'dɪktəˌfoun/ *n* dictáfono, *m*
dictate /'dɪkteɪt/ *vt* dictar; mandar. *n* (order) dictamen, *m; Fig.* dictado, *m*

dictation /dɪk'teɪʃən/ *n* dictado, *m.* **to write from d.,** escribir al dictado
dictator /'dɪkteɪtər/ *n* dictador, *m*
dictatorial /ˌdɪktə'tɔriəl/ *a* dictatorial, dictatorio, imperioso
dictatorship /dɪk'teɪtərˌʃɪp/ *n* dictadura, *f*
diction /'dɪkʃən/ *n* dicción, *f*
dictionary /'dɪkʃəˌnɛri/ *n* diccionario, *m*
dictum /'dɪktəm/ *n* dictamen, *m;* (saying) sentencia, *f; Law.* fallo, *m*
didactic /daɪ'dæktɪk/ *a* didáctico
die /daɪ/ *vi* morir; fallecer, finar; (wither) marchitarse; (disappear) desvanecerse, desaparecer; (of light) palidecer; extinguirse; (end) cesar; (desire) ansiar, perecerse (por). **Never say die!** ¡Mientras hay vida, hay esperanza! **to die early,** morir temprano; malograrse. **to die a violent death,** tener una muerte violenta, *Inf.* morir vestido. **to die from natural causes,** morir por causas naturales; *Inf.* morir en la cama. **to die hard,** luchar contra la muerte; tardar en morir; tardar en desaparecer. **to die of a broken heart,** morir con el corazón destrozado, morir de pena. **to die away,** desaparecer gradualmente; extinguirse poco a poco; dejar de oírse poco a poco; cesar; pasar. **to die down,** extinguirse gradualmente; palidecer; dejar de oírse; desaparecer; (of the wind) amainar; perder su fuerza. **to die out,** desaparecer; olvidarse; dejar de existir; pasarse de moda
die /daɪ/ *n* dado, *m; Fig.* suerte, *f;* (stamp) cuño, troquel, *m; Archit.* cubo, *m.* **The die is cast,** La suerte está echada. **die-sinker,** grabador en hueco, *m*
diehard /'daɪˌhɑrd/ *n* valiente, *m;* tradicionalista empedernido, *m;* partidario (-ia) entusiasta
dieresis /daɪ'ɛrəsɪs/ *n* diéresis, crema, *f*
diesel /'dizəl, -səl/ *a* Diesel. **d. engine,** motor Diesel, *m*
diet /'daɪɪt/ *n* dieta, *f,* régimen dietario, *m;* (assembly) dieta, *f. vi* estar a dieta, hacer régimen
dietetic /ˌdaɪɪ'tɛtɪk/ *a* dietético
dietetics /ˌdaɪɪ'tɛtɪks/ *n* dietética, *f*
dietician /ˌdaɪɪ'tɪʃən/ *n* dietista, *mf*
differ /'dɪfər/ *vi* diferenciarse; (contradict) contradecir; (disagree) no estar de acuerdo; disentir
difference /'dɪfərəns/ *n* diferencia, *f;* disparidad, *f;* contraste, *m;* (of opinion) disensión, *f;* controversia, disputa, *f.* **to make no d.,** no hacer diferencia alguna; no afectar; dar lo mismo, no importar
different /'dɪfərənt/ *a* distinto; diferente; vario, diverso
differential /ˌdɪfə'rɛnʃəl/ *a* diferencial. **d. calculus,** cálculo diferencial, *m*
differentiate /ˌdɪfə'rɛnʃiˌeɪt/ *vt* diferenciar, distinguir. *vi* diferenciarse, distinguirse
differentiation /ˌdɪfəˌrɛnʃi'eɪʃən/ *n* diferenciación, *f*
differently /'dɪfərəntli/ *adv* diferentemente
difficult /'dɪfɪˌkʌlt/ *a* difícil. **to make d.,** hacer difícil, dificultar
difficulty /'dɪfɪˌkʌlti/ *n* dificultad, *f.* **d. in breathing,** opresión de pecho, *f*
diffidence /'dɪfɪdəns/ *n* modestia, timidez, *f;* huraña, *f;* falta de confianza en sí mismo, *f*
diffident /'dɪfɪdənt/ *a* modesto, tímido; huraño; sin confianza en sí mismo
diffidently /'dɪfɪdəntli/ *adv* tímidamente; vergonzosamente
diffract /dɪ'frækt/ *vt* difractar
diffraction /dɪ'frækʃən/ *n* difracción, *f*
diffractive /dɪ'fræktɪv/ *a* difrangente
diffuse /*v* dɪ'fyuz; *a* -'fyus/ *vt* difundir. *a* difuso; (long-winded) prolijo
diffuseness /dɪ'fyusnɪs/ *n* difusión, *f;* prolijidad, *f*
diffusion /dɪ'fyuʒən/ *n* difusión, *f;* esparcimiento, *m;* diseminación, *f*
diffusive /dɪ'fyusɪv/ *a* difusivo
dig /dɪg/ *vt* and *vi* cavar; excavar; (of animals) escarbar; (mine) zapar, minar; (into a subject) ahondar (en); (with the spurs) aguijonear, dar con las espuelas; (poke) clavar. **to dig one's heels in,** *Lat. Am.* encabestrarse. **to dig in,** enterrarse; *Mil.* abrir trincheras; *Inf.* arreglarse las cosas. **to dig out,** excavar; sacar cavando; sacar con azadón; extraer. **to dig up,** desenterrar; descubrir

digest /v dɪ'dʒɛst, dai-/ n 'daidʒɛst/ vt (food, also chem. and fig. tolerate and think over) digerir; (of knowledge and territory) asimilar. vi digerir. n compendio, resumen, m; Law. digesto, m; recopilación, f. **This food is easy to d.**, Este alimento es fácil de digerir; Este alimento es muy ligero

digestibility /dɪ,dʒɛstə'bɪlɪti, dai-/ n digestibilidad, f

digestible /dɪ'dʒɛstəbəl, dai-/ a digerible, digestible

digestion /dɪ'dʒɛstʃən, dai-/ n digestión, f; (of ideas) asimilación, f; Chem. digestión, f

digestive /dɪ'dʒɛstɪv, dai-/ a digestivo

digger /'dɪgər/ n cavador (-ra)

digging /'dɪgɪŋ/ n cavadura, f; excavación, f; pl **diggings**, minas, f pl; excavaciones, f pl; Inf. alojamiento, m, posada, f

digit /'dɪdʒɪt/ n dígito, m, Anat. dedo.

digital /'dɪdʒɪtl/ a digital, dígito

digitalin /,dɪdʒɪ'tælɪn/ n digitalina, f

digitalis /,dɪdʒɪ'tælɪs/ n digital, f

dignified /'dɪgnə,faid/ a serio, grave; majestuoso; (worthy) digno; solemne; altivo; noble

dignify /'dɪgnə,fai/ vt dignificar, honrar; exaltar; dar dignidad (a); ennoblecer

dignitary /'dɪgnɪ,tɛri/ n dignatario, m; dignidad, f

dignity /'dɪgnɪti/ n dignidad, f; (rank) rango, m; (post) cargo, puesto, m; (honor) honra, f; (stateliness) majestad, f; mesura, seriedad, f; (haughtiness) altivez, f; (nobility) nobleza, f. **to stand on one's d.**, darse importancia

digress /dɪ'grɛs, dai-/ vi divagar

digression /dɪ'grɛʃən, dai-/ n digresión, divagación, f

dike /daik/ n dique, m; (ditch) acequia, f; canal, m; (embankment) zanja, f, vt represar

dilapidated /dɪ'læpɪ,deitid/ a arruinado, destartalado; (of fortune) dilapidado; (of persons, families) venido a menos; (shabby) raído

dilapidation /dɪ,læpə'deiʃən/ n deterioración, f; ruina, f, estado ruinoso, m

dilatation /,dɪlə'teiʃən/ n dilatación, f; ensanche, m

dilate /dai'leit/ vt dilatar; ensanchar. vi dilatarse. **to d. upon**, extenderse sobre, dilatarse en

dilator /dai'leitər/ n dilatador, m

dilatoriness /'dɪlətɔrinɪs/ n tardanza, f; (slowness) lentitud, f

dilatory /'dɪlə,tɔri/ a dilatorio, tardo; (slow) lento

dilemma /dɪ'lɛmə/ n dilema, m

dilettante /'dɪlɪ,tɑnt/ n diletante, m; aficionado (-da)

dilettantism /'dɪlɪtɑn,tɪzəm/ n diletantismo, m

diligence /'dɪlɪdʒəns/ n diligencia, f; asiduidad, f; (care) cuidado, m; (coach) diligencia, f

diligent /'dɪlɪdʒənt/ a diligente, asiduo, aplicado, industrioso; (painstaking) concienzudo

dilute /dɪ'lut, dai-/ vt diluir; Fig. adulterar. a diluido

dilution /dɪ'luʃən, dai-/ n dilución, f; Fig. adulteración, f

diluvian /dɪ'luviən/ a diluviano

dim /dɪm/ a (of light) apagado, débil, tenue; (of sight) turbio; (dark) sombrío, oscuro; (blurred, etc.) empañado; indistinto, confuso. vt obscurecer; empañar; (dazzle) ofuscar; (eclipse) eclipsar; reducir la intensidad (de una luz); (of memories) borrar. **dim intelligence**, de brumoso seso

dimension /dɪ'mɛnʃən/ n dimensión, f; (size) tamaño, m; (scope) extensión, f, alcance, m

dimensional /dɪ'mɛnʃənl/ a dimensional

diminish /dɪ'mɪnɪʃ/ vt disminuir; reducir; debilitar, atenuar. vi disminuir; reducirse; debilitarse, atenuarse

diminishing /dɪ'mɪnɪʃɪŋ/ a menguante

diminution /,dɪmə'nuʃən/ n disminución, f; reducción, f; atenuación, f

diminutive /dɪ'mɪnyətɪv/ a diminutivo. n diminutivo, m

diminutiveness /dɪ'mɪnyətɪvnɪs/ n pequeñez, f

dimly /'dɪmli/ adv obscuramente; vagamente; indistintamente. **dimly lit**, apenas alumbrado

dimness /'dɪmnɪs/ n oscuridad, f; deslustre, f; (of light) tenuidad (de la luz), f; confusión, f

dimple /'dɪmpəl/ n hoyuelo, m

dimpled /'dɪmpəld/ a con hoyuelos, que tiene hoyuelos

din /dɪn/ n estrépito, estruendo, ruido, m; algarabía, barahúnda, f, vt ensordecer

dine /dain/ vi (in the evening) cenar; (at midday) comer, almorzar. vt convidar a cenar or a comer. **to d. out**, cenar or comer fuera

diner /'dainər/ n (on a train) coche comedor, coche restaurante, m; cenador, m; comedor, m

ding-dong /'dɪŋ,dɔŋ/ n tintín, m

dinghy /'dɪŋgi/ n lancha, f; canoa, f, bote, m. **rubber d.**, canoa de goma, f

dinginess /'dɪndʒinɪs/ n deslustre, m; suciedad, f; oscuridad, f; (of a person) desaseo, m

dingy /'dɪndʒi/ a deslucido, empañado; sucio; oscuro; (of persons) desaseado

dining car /'dainɪŋ/ n coche comedor, vagón restaurante, m

dining room /'dainɪŋ/ n comedor, m; refectorio, m

dining table n mesa del comedor, f

dinner /'dɪnər/ n (in the evening) cena, f; (at midday) comida, f. **over the d. table**, de sobremesa. **d.-jacket**, smoking, m. **d. party**, cena, f. **d. plate**, plato, m. **d. roll**, panecillo, m. **d. service**, vajilla, f

dinosaur /'dainə,sɔr/ n dinosauro, m

diocesan /dai'ɒsəsən/ a diocesano

diocese /'daiəsɪs/ n diócesis, f

Dionysus Thrax /dai'naisəs 'θræks/ Dionisio el Tracio, m

dioxide /dai'ɒksaid, -sɪd/ n dióxido, m

dip /dɪp/ n inmersión, f; baño, m; (in the ground) declive, m; (in the road) columpio, m, depresión, f; (slope) pendiente, f; (candle) vela de sebo, f; (of the horizon) depresión (del horizonte), f; (of the needle) inclinación (de la aguja), f. vt sumergir; bañar; (put) poner. vi inclinarse hacia abajo. **to dip into a book,** hojear un libro. **to dip the colors,** saludar con la bandera

diphtheria /dɪf'θɪəriə/ n difteria, f

diphthong /'dɪfθɔŋ/ n diptongo, m

diploma /dɪ'ploumə/ n diploma, m

diplomacy /dɪ'ploʊməsi/ n diplomacia, f; tacto, m

diploma mill n fábrica de títulos académicos, f

diplomat /'dɪplə,mæt/ n diplomático, m

diplomatic /,dɪplə'mætɪk/ a diplomático. **d. bag,** valija diplomática, f. **d. corps,** cuerpo diplomático, m

diplomatically /,dɪplə'mætɪkəli/ adv diplomáticamente

dipper /'dɪpər/ n (ladle) cazo, m. **Big Dipper,** Osa Mayor, f

dipsomania /,dɪpsə'meiniə/ n dipsomanía, f

dipsomaniac /,dɪpsə'meiniæk/ n dipsómano (-na)

diptych /'dɪptɪk/ n díptica, f

dire /dair/ a espantoso, horrible; cruel; funesto

direct /dɪ'rɛkt, dai-/ a directo; claro, inequívoco; (of descent) recto; (of electric current) continuo; exacto. adv directamente. vt dirigir; (command) ordenar, encargar; dar instrucciones. **d. action,** acción directa, f. **d. current,** corriente continua, f. **d. line,** línea directa, f; (of descent) línea recta, f. **d. object,** acusativo, m. **d. speech,** oración directa, f

direct dialing /'daiəlɪŋ/ n discado directo, m

direction /dɪ'rɛkʃən/ 'dai-/ n dirección, f; rumbo, m; instrucción, f; (on a letter) sobrescrito, m; señas, f pl. **in the d. of,** en la dirección de; hacia; Naut. con rumbo a. **in all directions,** por todas partes; a los cuatro vientos. **to go in the d. of,** ir en la dirección de; tomar por. **Directions for use,** Direcciones para el uso. **d. indicator, d. signal,** (on car) indicador de dirección, m

directive /dɪ'rɛktɪv, dai-/ a directivo, director. n orden, m

directly /dɪ'rɛktli, dai-/ adv directamente; inmediatamente, en seguida

directness /dɪ'rɛktnɪs, dai/ n derechura, f

director /dɪ'rɛktər, dai-/ n director (-triz, -ora), **managing d.,** director gerente, m

directorate /dɪ'rɛktərɪt, dai-/ n directorio, m, junta directiva, f; cargo de director, m

directory /dɪ'rɛktəri, dai-/ *n* directorio, *m*, guía, *f*.
telephone d., guía de teléfonos, *f*

dirge /dɜrdʒ/ *n* endecha, *f*, lamento, *m*; canto fúnebre, *m*

dirt /dɜrt/ *n* mugre, suciedad, *f*; (mud) lodo, *m*; (earth) tierra, *f*; (dust) polvo, *m*; *Fig.* inmundicia, *f*. **to be d. cheap,** (of goods) estar por los suelos. **d.-track,** pista de ceniza, *f*. **d.-track racing,** carreras en pista de ceniza, *f pl*

dirtiness /'dɜrtinɪs/ *n* suciedad, *f*; (untidiness) desaseo, *m*; sordidez, *f*; (meanness) bajeza, *f*

dirty /'dɜrti/ *a* sucio, *Central America* descacharrado; (untidy) desaseado; (muddy) enlodado; (dusty) polvoriento; (of weather) borrascoso; (sordid) sórdido; (base, mean) vil; (indecent) indecente, verde, obsceno. *vt* ensuciar. **d. trick,** mala pasada, *Lat. Am.* chancada *f*

disability /,dɪsə'bɪlɪti/ *n* incapacidad, *f*; impotencia, *f*; desventaja, *f*

disable /dɪs'eibəl/ *vt* (cripple) estropear, tullir; hacer incapaz (de), incapacitar; imposibilitar; (destroy) destruir; *Law.* incapacitar legalmente

disabled /dɪs'eibəld/ *a* inválido; impedido, lisiado; (in the hand) manco; incapacitado; (of ships, etc.) fuera de servicio, estropeado. **d. soldier,** inválido, *m*

disablement /dɪs'eibəlmənt/ *n* (physical) invalidez, *f*; inhabilitación, *f*; *Law.* impedimento, *m*

disabuse /,dɪsə'byuz/ *vt* desengañar, sacar de un error

disadvantage /,dɪsəd'væntɪdʒ/ *n* desventaja, *f*. **to be under the d. of,** sufrir la desventaja de

disadvantaged /,dɪsəd'væntɪdʒd/ *a* (financially) de escasos recursos

disadvantageous /dɪs,ædvən'teidʒəs/ *a* desventajoso

disaffected /,dɪsə'fɛktɪd/ *a* desafecto

disaffection /,dɪsə'fɛkʃən/ *n* desafecto, descontento, *m*

disagree /,dɪsə'gri/ *vi* no estar de acuerdo; diferir; (quarrel) reñir; (not share the opinion of) no estar de la opinión (de); (of food, etc.) sentar mal; no probar. **The meat disagreed with me,** La carne me sentó mal

disagreeable /,dɪsə'griəbəl/ *a* desagradable; repugnante; (of persons) antipático, displicente

disagreeableness /,dɪsə'griəbəlnɪs/ *n* lo desagradable; (of persons) displicencia, *f*

disagreeably /,dɪsə'griəbli/ *adv* desagradablemente; con displicencia

disagreement /,dɪsə'grimənt/ *n* desacuerdo, *m*; diferencia, *f*; desavenencia, *f*; discordia, *f*; (quarrel) riña, disputa, *f*; discrepancia, *f*

disallow /,dɪsə'lau/ *vt* negar; rechazar

disappear /,dɪsə'pɪər/ *vi* desaparecer. **to cause to d.,** hacer desaparecer

disappearance /,dɪsə'pɪərəns/ *n* desaparición, *f*

disappoint /,dɪsə'pɔint/ *vt* desilusionar; frustrar; (hopes) defraudar; (deprive) privar de; (annoy) contrariar; (break a promise) faltar (a la palabra); *Lat. Am.* decepcionar

disappointedly /,dɪsə'pɔintɪdli/ *adv* con desilusión, con desengaño

disappointing /,dɪsə'pɔintɪŋ/ *a* desengañador; pobre; triste; poco halagüeño

disappointment /,dɪsə'pɔintmənt/ *n* desengaño, *m*, decepción, *f*; frustración, *f*; desilusión, *f*; (vexation) contrariedad, *f*; contratiempo, *m*. **to suffer a d.,** sufrir un desengaño; *Inf.* llevarse un chasco

disapproval /,dɪsə'pruvəl/ *n* desaprobación, *f*

disapprove /,dɪsə'pruv/ *vt* desaprobar

disapproving /,dɪsə'pruvɪŋ/ *a* de desaprobación, severo

disapprovingly /,dɪsə'pruvɪŋli/ *adv* con desaprobación

disarm /dɪs'ɑrm/ *vt* desarmar. *vi* desarmarse; deponer las armas

disarmament /dɪs'ɑrməmənt/ *n* desarme, *m*

disarrange /,dɪsə'reindʒ/ *vt* desarreglar; descomponer, desajustar; (hair) despeinar

disarrangement /,dɪsə'reindʒmənt/ *n* desarreglo, *m*; desajuste, *m*; desorden, *m*

disarray /,dɪsə'rei/ *n* desorden, desarreglo, *m*; confusión, *f*. *vt* desordenar, desarreglar

disarticulate /,dɪsɑr'tɪkyə,leit/ *vt* desarticular

disarticulation /,dɪsɑr,tɪkyə'leiʃən/ *n* desarticulación, *f*

disaster /dɪ'zæstər/ *n* desastre, *m*; catástrofe, *m*; infortunio, *m*

disastrous /dɪ'zæstrəs/ *a* desastroso; funesto, trágico

disastrously /dɪ'zæstrəsli/ *adv* desastrosamente

disastrousness /dɪ'zæstrəsnɪs/ *n* carácter desastroso, *m*

disavow /,dɪsə'vau/ *vt* repudiar; retractar

disavowal /,dɪsə'vauəl/ *n* repudiación, *f*

disband /dɪs'bænd/ *vt* licenciar. *vi* desbandarse, dispersarse

disbelief /,dɪsbɪ'lif/ *n* incredulidad, *f*; desconfianza, *f*

disbelieve /,dɪsbɪ'liv/ *vt* and *vi* descreer, no creer; desconfiar (de)

disburse /dɪs'bɜrs/ *vt* desembolsar, pagar

disbursement /dɪs'bɜrsmənt/ *n* desembolso, *m*

disc /dɪsk/ *n* disco, *m*

discard /v dɪ'skɑrd; *n* 'dɪskɑrd/ *vt* desechar, arrinconar, *Lat. Am.* botar; despedir; (at cards) descartar. *n* (at cards) descarte, *m*

discern /dɪ'sɜrn/ *vt* discernir, distinguir, percibir

discerner /dɪ'sɜrnər/ *n* discernidor (-ra)

discernible /dɪ'sɜrnəbəl/ *a* distinguible, perceptible

discerning /dɪ'sɜrnɪŋ/ *a* perspicaz, discernidor

discernment /dɪ'sɜrnmənt/ *n* discernimiento, *m*

discharge /dɪs'tʃɑrdʒ/ *vt* descargar; (a gun) disparar, tirar; (an arrow) lanzar; *Elec.* descargar; emitir; (dismiss) destituir, despedir; arrojar; *Mil.* licenciar; (exempt) dispensar (de); (exonerate) absolver, exonerar; (free) dar libertad (a); (from hospital) dar de baja (a); *Law.* revocar; (perform) cumplir, ejecutar; (pay) pagar, saldar; (of an abscess, etc.) supurar

discharge /'dɪtʃɑrdʒ/ *n* (of firearms) disparo, tiro, *m*; (of artillery) descarga, *f*; (of goods, cargo) descargue, *m*; *Elec.* descarga, *f*; (from a wound, etc.) pus, *m*, supuración, *f*; (from the intestine) flujo, *m*; (of a debt) pago, m.; *Com.* descargo, *m*; (receipt) carta de pago, quitanza, *f*; *Mil.* licencia absoluta, *f*; (dismissal) despedida, destitución, *f*; (exoneration) exoneración, *f*; (freeing) liberación, *f*; (from hospital) baja, *f*; (performance) cumplimiento, *m*; ejecución, *f*

disciple /dɪ'saipəl/ *n* discípulo (-la)

disciplinarian /,dɪsəplə'nɛəriən/ *n* disciplinario (-ia)

disciplinary /'dɪsəplə,nɛri/ *a* disciplinario

discipline /'dɪsəplɪn/ *n* disciplina, *f*. *vt* disciplinar

disclaim /dɪs'kleim/ *vt* renunciar (a); (repudiate) rechazar, repudiar

disclaimer /dɪs'kleimər/ *n* *Law.* renunciación, *f*; repudiación, *f*

disclose /dɪ'sklouz/ *vt* descubrir, revelar

disclosure /dɪ'sklouʒər/ *n* descubrimiento, *m*, revelación, *f*

discolor /dɪs'kʌlər/ *vt* descolorar. *vi* descolorarse

discoloration /dɪs,kʌlə'reiʃən/ *n* descoloramiento, *m*

discomfit /dɪs'kʌmfɪt/ *vt* desconcertar

discomfiture /dɪs'kʌmfɪtʃər/ *n* desconcierto, *m*

discomfort /dɪs'kʌmfərt/ *n* falta de comodidades, *f*; incomodidad, *f*; malestar, *m*; molestia, *f*; inquietud, *f*; dolor, *m*

discomposure /,dɪskəm'pouʒər/ *n* confusión, agitación, inquietud, *f*

disconcert /,dɪskən'sɜrt/ *vt* desconcertar, turbar; (of plans, etc.) frustrar

disconnect /,dɪskə'nɛkt/ *vt* separar; (of railway engines, etc.) desacoplar, desconectar; (of electric plugs) desenchufar

disconnected /,dɪskə'nɛktɪd/ *a* inconexo; incoherente, deshilvanado

disconnectedness /,dɪskə'nɛktɪdnɪs/ *n* inconexión, *f*; incoherencia, *f*

disconsolate /dɪs'kɒnsəlɪt/ *a* desconsolado, triste

disconsolately /dɪs'kɒnsəlɪtli/ *adv* desconsoladamente, tristemente

disconsolateness /dɪs'kɒnsəlɪtnɪs/ *n* desconsuelo, *m*

discontent /,dɪskən'tɛnt/ *n* descontento, disgusto, *m*, *vt* descontentar, desagradar

discontented /,dɪskən'tɛntɪd/ *a* descontentadizo, descontento, disgustado

discontinuance /ˌdɪskən'tɪnyuəns/ n descontinuación, cesación, f; interrupción, f

discontinue /ˌdɪskən'tɪnyu/ vt descontinuar; cesar; interrumpir; (of payments, etc.) suspender. vi cesar

discontinuous /ˌdɪskən'tɪnyuəs/ a descontinuo; interrumpido; intermitente

discord /'dɪskɔrd/ n discordia, f; Mus. disonancia, f, desentono, m

discordant /dɪs'kɔrdənt/ a discorde, poco armonioso; incongruo; Mus. disonante, desentonado. **to be d.**, discordar; ser incongruo; Mus. disonar

discount /'dɪskaunt; v also dɪs'kaunt/ n descuento, m; rebaja, f. vt descontar; rebajar; balancear; (disconsider) desechar. **at a d.**, al descuento; bajo la par; fácil de obtener; superfluo; Fig. en disfavor, en descrédito. **rate of d.**, tipo de descuento, m. **d. for cash**, descuento por venta al contado, m

discourage /dɪ'skʌrɪdʒ/ vt desalentar, desanimar; oponerse a; disuadir; frustrar

discouragement /dɪ'skʌrɪdʒmənt/ n desaliento, m; desaprobación, oposición, f; disuasión, f; (obstacle) estorbo, m

discouraging /dɪ'skʌrɪdʒɪŋ/ a poco animador, que ofrece pocas esperanzas; (with prospect, etc.) nada halagüeño

discourse /n 'dɪskɔrs; v dɪs'kɔrs/ n discurso, m; plática, f; (treatise) disertación, f. vi (converse) platicar, conversar; (with on, upon) disertar sobre, discurrir sobre; tratar de

discourteous /dɪs'kɜrtiəs/ a descortés, desconsiderado

discourtesy /dɪs'kɜrtəsi/ n descortesía, f

discover /dɪ'skʌvər/ vt descubrir; (see) ver; (realize) darse cuenta de; (show) manifestar; revelar

discoverable /dɪ'skʌvərəbəl/ a que se puede descubrir; averiguable; distinguible, perceptible

discoverer /dɪ'skʌvərər/ n descubridor (-ra); revelador (-ra)

discovery /dɪ'skʌvəri/ n descubrimiento, m; revelación, f

discredit /dɪs'krɛdɪt/ n descrédito, m; des honra, f; duda, f. vt dudar (de), no creer (en); desacreditar; deshonrar

discreditable /dɪs'krɛdɪtəbəl/ a deshonroso, ignominioso, vergonzoso

discreetly /dɪ'skritli/ adv discretamente; prudentemente

discrepancy /dɪ'skrɛpənsi/ n discrepancia, diferencia, f; contradicción, f

discrepant /dɪ'skrɛpənt/ a discrepante; contradictorio, inconsistente

discretion /dɪ'skrɛʃən/ n discreción, f; prudencia, circunspección, f; juicio, m; voluntad, f. **at one's own d.**, a voluntad (de uno). **years of d.**, edad de discreción, f

discriminate /dɪ'skrɪm,əneit/ vi distinguir (entre); hacer una distinción (en favor de or en perjuicio de). vt distinguir

discriminating /dɪ'skrɪmə,neitɪŋ/ a discerniente, que sabe distinguir, juicioso; culto; diferencial

discrimination /dɪ,skrɪmə'neiʃən/ n discernimiento, m; gusto, m; distinción, f; discriminación, f

discursive /dɪ'skɜrsɪv/ a discursivo; digresivo

discus /'dɪskəs/ n disco, m. **d. thrower**, discóbolo, m

discuss /dɪ'skʌs/ vt discutir; hablar de; debatir; (deal with) tratar; (Fam. a dish) probar; (a bottle of wine) vaciar

discussion /dɪ'skʌʃən/ n discusión, f; debate, m

disdain /dɪs'dein/ n desdén, m; altivez, f. vt desdeñar, desairar, despreciar. **to d. to**, desdeñarse de

disdainful /dɪs'deinfəl/ a desdeñoso; altivo

disdainfully /dɪs'deinfəli/ adv desdeñosamente

disease /dɪ'ziz/ n enfermedad, f; Fig. mal, m. **infectious d.**, enfermedad contagiosa, f

diseased /dɪ'zizd/ a enfermo; (of fruit, etc.) malo

disembark /ˌdɪsɛm'bɑrk/ vt and vi desembarcar

disembarkation /dɪs,ɛmbɑr'keiʃən/ n desembarque, m; Mil. desembarco (de tropas), m

disembodied /ˌdɪsɛm'bɒdid/ a incorpóreo

disembowel /ˌdɪsɛm'bauəl/ vt desentrañar, destripar

disenchant /ˌdɪsɛn'tʃænt/ vt desencantar; deschechizar; desilusionar

disenchantment /ˌdɪsɛn'tʃæntmənt/ n desencanto, m; desilusión, f

disengage /ˌdɪsɛn'geidʒ/ vt desasir; soltar; (gears) desembragar; (uncouple) desacoplar; (free) librar

disengaged /ˌdɪsɛn'geidʒd/ a (free) libre

disentangle /ˌdɪsɛn'tæŋgəl/ vt (undo) desatar, desanudar; separar; (of threads, etc., and Fig.) desenredar, desenmarañar. vi desenredarse

disentanglement /ˌdɪsɛn'tæŋgəlmənt/ n desatadura, f; separación, f; desenredo, m

disestablish /ˌdɪsɪ'stæblɪʃ/ vt separar (la Iglesia del Estado)

disestablishment /ˌdɪsɪ'stæblɪʃmənt/ n separación (de la Iglesia del Estado), f

disfavor /dɪs'feivər/ n disfavor, m; (disapproval) desaprobación, f. vt desaprobar

disfigure /dɪs'fɪgyər/ vt desfigurar, afear; deformar; (mar) estropear

disfigurement /dɪs'fɪgyərmənt/ n desfiguración, f; deformidad, f; defecto, m

disfranchise /dɪs'fræntʃaiz/ vt privar de los derechos civiles (a)

disfranchisement /dɪs'fræntʃaizmənt/ n privación de los derechos civiles, privación del derecho de votar, f

disgrace /dɪs'greis/ n desgracia, vergüenza, ignominia, f; deshonra, f; (insult) afrenta, f; (scandal) escándalo, m; disfavor, m. vt deshonrar; despedir con ignominia. **in d.**, fuera de favor; desacreditado; (of children and animals) castigado

disgraceful /dɪs'greisfəl/ a deshonroso; ignominioso; escandaloso, desgraciado

disgracefully /dɪs'greisfəli/ adv escandalosamente

disgracefulness /dɪs'greisfəlnəs/ n ignominia, vergüenza, f; deshonra, f

disgruntled /dɪs'grʌntld/ a refunfuñador, enfurruñado, malhumorado

disguise /dɪs'gaiz/ n disfraz, m; (mask) máscara, f. vt disfrazar; cubrir, tapar; (Fig. conceal) ocultar. **in d.**, disfrazado

disgust /dɪs'gʌst/ n repugnancia, aversión, f; aborrecimiento, m; asco, m. vt repugnar, inspirar aversión; disgustar; dar asco (a)

disgusted /dɪs'gʌstid/ a asqueado; disgustado; furioso; (bored) aburrido

disgusting /dɪs'gʌstɪŋ/ a repugnante; odioso, horrible; asqueroso

dish /dɪʃ/ n (for meat, vegetables, fruit, etc.) fuente, f; (food) plato, m; pl **dishes**, platos, m pl, vajilla, f. vt servir; Inf. frustrar. **cooked d.**, guiso, m. **special d. for today**, plato del día, m. **to wash the dishes**, fregar los platos, m. **d.-cloth**, (for washing) fregador, m; (for drying) paño de los platos, m. **d.-cover**, cubreplatos, m. **d.-rack**, escurre-platos, m. **d.-washer**, lavaplatos, lavavajillas, m. **d.-water**, agua de lavar los platos, f

disharmony /dɪs'hɑrməni/ n falta de armonía, f; (disagreement) discordia, desavenencia, f; incongruencia, f; Mus. disonancia, f

dishearten /dɪs'hɑrtn/ vt desalentar, desanimar; desesperar; disuadir (de)

disheveled /dɪ'ʃɛvəld/ a despeinado, desgreñado; (untidy) desaseado

dishonest /dɪs'ɒnɪst/ a deshonesto, falto de honradez, tramposo; fraudulento; falso, desleal, Lat. Am. also flequetero

dishonestly /dɪs'ɒnɪstli/ adv de mala fe, sin honradez; fraudulentamente; deslealmente

dishonesty /dɪs'ɒnəsti/ n deshonestidad, falta de honradez, falta de integridad, f; fraude, m; falsedad, deslealtad, f

dishonor /dɪs'ɒnər/ n deshonra, f. vt deshonrar; Com. no pagar, o no aceptar, un giro

dishonorable /dɪs'ɒnərəbəl/ a deshonroso

dishonorer /dɪs'ɒnərər/ n deshonrador (-ra); profanador (-ra)

disillusion /ˌdɪsɪ'luʒən/ vt desengañar, desilusionar

disillusionment /ˌdɪsɪ'luʒənmənt/ n desilusión, f, desengaño, desencanto, m

disinclination /dɪs,ɪnklə'neiʃən/ n aversión, f

disincline /ˌdɪsɪn'klaɪn/ *vt* desinclinar
disinfect /ˌdɪsɪn'fekt/ *vt* desinfectar
disinfectant /ˌdɪsɪn'fektənt/ *a* and *n* desinfectante *m*.
disinfection /ˌdɪsɪn'fekʃən/ *n* desinfección, *f*
disingenuous /ˌdɪsɪn'dʒɛnyuəs/ *a* tortuoso, doble, falso, insincero
disinherit /ˌdɪsɪn'herɪt/ *vt* desheredar
disinheritance /ˌdɪsɪn'herɪtəns/ *n* desheredación, *f*
disintegrate /dɪs'ɪntəˌgreɪt/ *vt* despedazar, disgregar. *vi* disgregarse; desmoronarse
disintegration /dɪsˌɪntə'greɪʃən/ *n* disgregación, *f*; disolución, *f*; desmoronamiento, *m*
disinter /ˌdɪsɪn'tɜr/ *vt* desenterrar
disinterested /dɪs'ɪntəˌrestɪd, -trɪstɪd/ *a* desinteresado
disinterestedness /dɪs'ɪntəˌrestɪdnɪs, -trɪstɪd-/ *n* desinterés, *m*
disinterment /ˌdɪsɪn'tɜrmənt/ *n* desenterramiento, *m*
disjointed /dɪs'dʒɔɪntɪd/ *a* dislocado; desarticulado; incoherente, inconexo; (of a speech, etc.) descosido
disjointedness /dɪs'dʒɔɪntɪdnɪs/ *n* descoyuntamiento, desencajamiento, *m*; incoherencia, *f*
disk /dɪsk/ *n* disco, *m*
diskette /dɪ'skɛt/ *n* disquete, *m*, disco flexible, *m*
dislike /dɪs'laɪk/ *n* aversión, *f*; antipatía, *f*; (hostility) animosidad, *f*. *vt* desagradar, no gustar; repugnar. **I d. the house,** No me gusta la casa. **I d. them,** No me gustan
dislocate /'dɪslouˌkeɪt/ *vt* dislocar, descoyuntar; *Fig.* interrumpir
dislocation /ˌdɪslou'keɪʃən/ *n* dislocación, *f*, descoyuntamiento, *m*; *Fig.* interrupción, *f*
dislodge /dɪs'lɒdʒ/ *vt* desalojar
dislodgement /dɪs'lɒdʒmənt/ *n* desalojamiento, *m*
disloyal /dɪs'lɔɪəl/ *a* desleal, infiel, falso
disloyalty /dɪs'lɔɪəlti/ *n* deslealtad, infidelidad, falsedad, *f*
dismal /'dɪzməl/ *a* lóbrego, sombrío; lúgubre; funesto; triste
dismantle /dɪs'mæntl/ *vt* (a ship or fort) desmantelar; (a machine) desmontar; (a house, etc.) desamueblar
dismantling /dɪs'mæntlɪŋ/ *n* desmantelamiento, *m*
dismay /dɪs'meɪ/ *n* desmayo, desaliento, *m*; consternación, *f*; espanto, terror, *m*. *vt* desanimar; consternar; espantar, horrorizar
dismember /dɪs'mɛmbər/ *vt* desmembrar
dismemberment /dɪs'mɛmbərmənt/ *n* desmembración, *f*
dismiss /dɪs'mɪs/ *vt* (from a job) despedir (de); (from an official position) destituir (de) *Chile* desahuciar (de); (bid good-bye to) despedirse de; (after military parade) dar la orden de romper filas; (thoughts) apartar de sí, ahuyentar; (discard) desechar, descartar; (omit) pasar por alto de; (disregard) rechazar; (a parliament, etc.) disolver; (a law case) absolver de la instancia. **to d. in a few words,** tratar someramente; hablar brevemente de
dismissal /dɪs'mɪsəl/ *n* despedida, *f*; (from an official post) destitución, *f*, *Chile* desahúcio *m*; apartamiento, *m*; (discard) descarte, *m*; (of a parliament, etc.) disolución, *f*
dismount /dɪs'maunt/ *vi* apearse, desmontar, echar pie a tierra; bajar. *vt* desmontar; (dismantle) desarmar
disobedience /ˌdɪsə'bidiəns/ *n* desobediencia, *f*
disobedient /ˌdɪsə'bidiənt/ *a* desobediente
disobey /ˌdɪsə'beɪ/ *vt* and *vi* desobedecer
disobliging /ˌdɪsə'blaɪdʒɪŋ/ *a* poco servicial
disobligingly /ˌdɪsə'blaɪdʒɪŋli/ *adv* descortésmente
disorder /dɪs'ɔrdər/ *n* desorden, *m*; confusión, *f*; (unrest) perturbación del orden público, *f*, motín, *m*; (disease) enfermedad, *f*; (mental) enajenación mental, *f*; trastorno, *m*. *vt* desordenar, desarreglar; (of health) perjudicar; (the mind) trastornar. **in d.,** en desorden, desarreglado; (helter-skelter) atropelladamente
disordered /dɪs'ɔrdərd/ *a* en desorden; irregular, desordenado; (of the mind and bodily organs) trastornado; (ill) enfermo; (confused) confuso
disorganization /dɪsˌɔrgənə'zeɪʃən/ *n* desorganización, *f*
disorganize /dɪs'ɔrgəˌnaɪz/ *vt* desorganizar

disorientate /dɪs'ɔriənˌteɪt/ *vt* desorientar
disorientation /dɪsˌɔriən'teɪʃən/ *n* desorientación, *f*
disown /dɪs'oun/ *vt* repudiar; negar; renegar de
disparage /dɪ'spærɪdʒ/ *vt* menospreciar; desacreditar; denigrar; (spoil) perjudicar; (scorn) despreciar
disparagement /dɪ'spærɪdʒmənt/ *n* menosprecio, *m*; denigración, *f*; desprecio, *m*
disparagingly /dɪ'spærɪdʒɪŋli/ *adv* con desprecio
disparity /dɪ'spærɪti/ *n* disparidad, *f*
dispassionate /dɪs'pæʃənɪt/ *a* desapasionado, sereno; imparcial; moderado
dispassionately /dɪs'pæʃənɪtli/ *adv* con imparcialidad; serenamente; con moderación
dispatch /dɪ'spætʃ/ *n* despacho, *m*; *Com.* envío, *m*; (message) mensaje, *m*; (communiqué) parte, *f*; (cable) telegrama, *m*; (promptness) prontitud, presteza, *f*; (execution) ejecución, muerte, *f*. *vt* despachar; enviar, remitir; (*Fam.* kill) despachar. **d.-case,** cartera, *f*. **d.-rider,** mensajero motociclista, *m*
dispel /dɪ'spɛl/ *vt* disipar
dispensable /dɪ'spɛnsəbəl/ *a* dispensable
dispensary /dɪ'spɛnsəri/ *n* dispensario, *m*
dispensation /ˌdɪspən'seɪʃən/ *n* dispensación, *f*; (of the Pope, etc.) dispensa, *f*; (decree) ley, *f*, decreto, *m*; (of justice) administración, *f*
dispense /dɪ'spɛns/ *vt* dispensar; (of justice) administrar. **to d. with,** pasar sin, prescindir de
dispenser /dɪ'spɛnsər/ *n* dispensador (-ra); administrador (-ra)
dispersal /dɪ'spɜrsəl/ *n* dispersión, *f*; disipación, *f*; esparcimiento, *m*
disperse /dɪ'spɜrs/ *vt* dispersar; disipar; esparcir. *vi* dispersarse disiparse
dispirited /dɪ'spɪrɪtɪd/ *a* abatido, desanimado, deprimido; lánguido
dispiritedly /dɪ'spɪrɪtɪdli/ *adv* desanimadamente, con desaliento; lánguidamente
displace /dɪs'pleɪs/ *vt* desalojar; cambiar de situación; (of liquids) desplazar; (oust) quitar el puesto (a), destituir
displacement /dɪs'pleɪsmənt/ *n* desalojamiento, *m*; cambio de situación, *m*; (of liquid) desplazamiento, *m*; (from a post) destitución, *f*
display /dɪ'spleɪ/ *n* exhibición, *f*; ostentación, *f*; presentación, *f*; (development) desarrollo, *m*; manifestación, *f*; (naval or military) maniobras, *f pl*; espectáculo, *m*; (pomp) pompa, *f*; fausto, *m*. *vt* exhibir; mostrar, manifestar; ostentar; (unfold) desplegar, extender; (develop) desarrollar. **d. cabinet,** vitrina, *f*
displease /dɪs'pliz/ *vt* desagradar; ofender; enojar
displeasing /dɪs'plizɪŋ/ *a* desagradable
displeasure /dɪs'plɛʒər/ *n* desagrado, *m*; disgusto, *m*; disfavor, *m*; indignación, *f*; enojo, *m*; (grief) angustia, *f*
disposable /dɪ'spouzəbəl/ *a* desechable
disposal /dɪ'spouzəl/ *n* disposición, *f*; (transfer) cesión, enajenación, *f*; (sale) venta, *f*; (gift) donación, *f*. **I am at your d.,** Estoy a la disposición de Vd. **the d. of the troops,** la disposición de las tropas
dispose /dɪ'spouz/ *vt* disponer; inclinar. *vi* disponer. **to d. of,** disponer de; (finish) terminar, concluir; (get rid of) deshacerse de, botar; (give away) regalar; (sell) vender; (transfer) ceder; (of houses, etc.) traspasar; (kill) matar; (send) enviar; (use) servirse de; (refute) refutar. **"To be disposed of,"** (a business, etc.) «Se traspasa»
disposed /dɪ'spouzd/ *a* (in compounds) intencionado, dispuesto. **well-d.,** bien intencionado
disposition /ˌdɪspə'zɪʃən/ *n* disposición, *f*; (temperament) naturaleza, índole, *f*, temperamento, carácter, *m*; (humor) humor, *m*
dispossess /ˌdɪspə'zɛs/ *vt* desposeer (de); privar (de); desahuciar
dispossession /ˌdɪspə'zɛʃən/ *n* desposeimiento, *m*; desahúcio, *m*
disproportion /ˌdɪsprə'pɔrʃən/ *n* desproporción, *f*
disproportionate /ˌdɪsprə'pɔrʃənɪt/ *a* desproporcionado
disproportionately /ˌdɪsprə'pɔrʃənɪtli/ *adv* desproporcionadamente
disprovable /dɪs'pruvəbəl/ *a* refutable

disprove /dɪs'pruv/ *vt* refutar
disputable /dɪ'spyutəbəl/ *a* disputable; discutible
disputant /dɪ'spyutənt/ *n* disputador (-ra)
dispute /dɪ'spyut/ *n* disputa, controversia, *f*; altercación, *f*; discusión, *f*; debate, *m*. *vt* and *vi* disputar. **beyond d.,** *a* incontestable. *adv* incontestablemente; fuera de duda
disqualification /dɪs,kwɒləfɪ'keiʃən/ *n* incapacidad, *f*; inhabilitación, *f*; impedimento, *m*; *Sports.* descalificación, *f*
disqualify /dɪs'kwɒlə,fai/ *vt* incapacitar; inhabilitar; *Sports.* descalificar
disquiet /dɪs'kwaiit/ *n* desasosiego, *m*; intranquilidad, inquietud, agitación, *f*. *vt* desasosegar, intranquilizar, perturbar, agitar
disquieting /dɪs'kwaiitɪŋ/ *a* intranquilizador, perturbador
disquisition /,dɪskwə'zɪʃən/ *n* disquisición, *f*
disregard /,dɪsrɪ'gɑrd/ *n* indiferencia, *f*; omisión, *f*; descuido, *m*; (scorn) desdén, *m*. *vt* no hacer caso de, desatender; omitir; desconocer; descuidar; despreciar
disregardful /,dɪsrɪ'gɑrdfəl/ *a* indiferente; negligente; desatento; desdeñoso
disrepair /,dɪsrɪ'pɛər/ *n* deterioro, mal estado, *m*
disreputable /dɪs'rɛpyətəbəl/ *a* de mala fama; (shameful) vergonzoso, vil; (compromising) comprometedor; de mal aspecto, horrible; ruin
disreputably /dɪs'rɛpyətəbli/ *adv* ruinmente; vergonzosamente
disrepute /,dɪsrɪ'pyut/ *n* disfavor, *m*; mala fama, *f*; deshonra, *f*; descrédito, *m*. **to come into d.,** caer en disfavor; perder su reputación
disrespect /,dɪsrɪ'spɛkt/ *n* falta de respeto, *f*; irreverencia, *f*
disrespectful /,dɪsrɪ'spɛktfəl/ *a* irrespetuoso, irreverente
disrobe /dɪs'roub/ *vt* desnudar. *vi* desnudarse
disrupt /dɪs'rʌpt/ *vt* quebrar; desorganizar; interrumpir; separar
disruption /dɪs'rʌpʃən/ *n* quebrantamiento, *m*; desorganización, *f*; interrupción, *f*; separación, *f*
dissatisfaction /,dɪssætɪs'fækʃən/ *n* descontento, desagrado, disgusto, *m*
dissatisfied /dɪs'sætɪs,faid/ *a* descontentado, malcontento, no satisfecho
dissect /dɪ'sɛkt/ *vt* disecar; *Fig.* analizar
dissecting table /dɪ'sɛktɪŋ/ *n* mesa de disección, *f*
dissection /dɪ'sɛkʃən/ *n* disección, *f*; análisis, *m*
dissector /dɪ'sɛktər/ *n* disector, *m*; *Fig.* analizador (-ra)
dissemble /dɪ'sɛmbəl/ *vt* and *vi* disimular, fingir
dissembler /dɪ'sɛmblər/ *n* hipócrita, *mf*; disimulador (-ra)
disseminate /dɪ'sɛmə,neit/ *vt* diseminar; propagar, sembrar
dissemination /dɪ,sɛmə'neiʃən/ *n* diseminación, *f*; propagación, *f*
dissension /dɪ'sɛnʃən/ *n* disensión, *f*; disidencia, *f*
dissent /dɪ'sɛnt/ *n* disentimiento, *m*, *vi* disentir, disidir
dissenter /dɪ'sɛntər/ *n* disidente, *mf*
dissertation /,dɪsər'teiʃən/ *n* disertación, *f*, tesis, *f*
disservice /dɪs'sɜrvɪs/ *n* deservicio, *m*
dissimilar /dɪ'sɪmələr/ *a* disímil, desemejante, diferente
dissimilarity /dɪ,sɪmə'lærɪti/ *n* desemejanza, diferencia, disparidad, *f*
dissimulation /dɪ,sɪmyə'leiʃən/ *n* disimulación, *f*, disimulo, *m*
dissipate /'dɪsə,peit/ *vt* disipar; dispersar; (waste) derrochar, desperdiciar. *vi* disiparse; dispersarse; (vanish) desvanecerse; (of persons) ser disoluto
dissipated /'dɪsə,peitid/ *a* (of persons) disipado, disoluto, vicioso
dissipation /,dɪsə'peiʃən/ *n* disipación, *f*; (waste) derroche, *m*; libertinaje, *m*
dissociate /dɪ'souʃi,eit/ *vt* disociar
dissociation /dɪ,sousi'eiʃən/ *n* disociación, *f*
dissoluble /dɪ'sɒlyəbəl/ *a* disoluble
dissolute /'dɪsə,lut/ *a* disoluto, vicioso, licencioso

dissoluteness /'dɪsə,lutnɪs/ *n* disolución, inmoralidad, *f*
dissolution /,dɪsə'luʃən/ *n* disolución, *f*; separación, *f*; muerte, *f*
dissolvable /dɪ'zɒlvəbəl/ *a* soluble
dissolve /dɪ'zɒlv/ *vt* disolver; derretir; (of parliament) prorrogar; (a marriage, etc.) anular; *Fig.* disipar. *vi* disolverse; derretirse; (vanish) desvanecerse, disiparse, evaporarse. **to d. into tears,** deshacerse en lágrimas
dissolvent /dɪ'zɒlvənt/ *a* disolutivo. *n* disolvente, *m*
dissonance /'dɪsənəns/ *n* disonancia, *f*; *Fig.* discordia, falta de armonía, *f*
dissonant /'dɪsənənt/ *n* disonancia, *f*, *a* disonante
dissuade /dɪ'sweid/ *vt* disuadir (de), apartar (de)
dissuasion /dɪ'sweiʒən/ *n* disuasión, *f*
distaff /'dɪstæf/ *n* rueca, *f*
distance /'dɪstəns/ *n* distancia, *f*; lontananza, *f*; lejanía, *f*; trecho, *m*; (of time) intervalo, *m*; (difference) diferencia, *f*. **at a d.,** a alguna distancia; lejos; (from afar) desde lejos. **from a d.,** desde (or de) lejos. **in the d.,** a lo lejos, en lontananza. **to keep at a d.,** mantener lejos; guardar las distancias (con). **to keep one's d.,** mantenerse a distancia; no intimarse, guardar las distancias. **What is the d. from London to Madrid?** ¿Qué distancia hay desde Londres a Madrid?
distant /'dɪstənt/ *a* distante; lejano; remoto; (of manner) frío, reservado; (slight) ligero; (of references, etc.) indirecto. **He is a d. relation,** Es un pariente lejano. **They are always rather d. with her,** La tratan siempre con bastante frialdad
distantly /'dɪstəntli/ *adv* a distancia; a lo lejos; desde lejos; remotamente; (of manner) con frialdad; (slightly) ligeramente
distaste /dɪs'teist/ *n* aversión, repugnancia, *f*; disgusto, hastío, *m*
distasteful /dɪs'teistfəl/ *a* desagradable
distemper /dɪs'tɛmpər/ *n* enfermedad, *f*; (in animals) moquillo, *m*; *Fig.* mal, *m*; (for walls) pintura al temple, *f*. *vt* desordenar, perturbar; (walls) pintar al temple
distend /dɪ'stɛnd/ *vt* ensanchar; dilatar; inflar, henchir; *Med.* distender. *vi* ensancharse, etc.
distension /dɪs'tɛnʃən/ *n* dilatación, *f*; inflación, *f*; henchimiento, *m*; *Med.* distensión, *f*
distill /dɪ'stɪl/ *vt* destilar; extraer. *vi* destilar; exudar
distillation /,dɪstl'eiʃən/ *n* destilación, *f*; extracción, *f*; exudación, *f*
distiller /dɪ'stɪlər/ *n* destilador (-ra)
distillery /dɪ'stɪləri/ *n* destilería, *f*, destilatorio, *m*
distinct /dɪ'stɪŋkt/ *a* distinto; diferente; claro; notable, evidente
distinction /dɪ'stɪŋkʃən/ *n* distinción, *f*
distinctive /dɪ'stɪŋktɪv/ *a* distintivo; característico
distinctive feature *n Ling.* rasgo pertinente, m
distinctly /dɪ'stɪŋktli/ *adv* claramente; distintamente
distinctness /dɪ'stɪŋktnɪs/ *n* claridad, *f*; distinción, *f*; carácter distintivo, *m*
distinguish /dɪ'stɪŋgwɪʃ/ *vt* distinguir; discernir; caracterizar; (honor) honrar. *vi* distinguir, diferenciar
distinguishable /dɪ'stɪŋgwɪʃəbəl/ *a* distinguible; perceptible, discernible
distinguished /dɪ'stɪŋgwɪʃt/ *a* distinguido; eminente; famoso, ilustre, egregio
distinguishing /,dɪ'stɪŋgwɪʃɪŋ/ *a* distintivo
distort /dɪ'stɔrt/ *vt* (twist) torcer; deformar; falsear; pervertir
distorting mirror /dɪ'stɔrtɪŋ/ *n* (at fairs) espejo de la risa, *m*; espejo deformador, *m*
distortion /dɪ'stɔrʃən/ *n* deformación, *f*; torcimiento, *m*; contorsión, *f*; perversión, *f*; *Radio.* deformación, *f*
distract /dɪ'strækt/ *vt* distraer; interrumpir; perturbar; (turn aside) desviar, apartar; (madden) enloquecer; volver loco (a)
distracted /dɪ'stræktid/ *a* aturdido; demente, loco
distractedly /dɪ'stræktidli/ *adv* locamente; perdidamente
distraction /dɪ'strækʃən/ *n* distracción, *f*; (amusement) diversion, *f*, pasatiempo, *m*; (bewilderment)

confusión, f, aturdimiento, m; (madness) locura, f; frenesí, m. **to drive to d.**, trastornar, sacar de quicio.

distraught /dɪ'strɔt/ a aturdido; desesperado; enloquecido

distress /dɪ'strɛs/ n dolor, m, aflicción, f; pena, f; miseria, penuria, f; (exhaustion) fatiga, f, cansancio, m; (pain) dolor, m; (misfortune) desdicha, f; apuro, m; (danger) peligro, m; Law. embargo, m. vt afligir, dar pena (a), llenar de angustia; cansar, fatigar; (pain) doler

distressed /dɪ'strɛst/ a afligido; necesitado, pobre

distressing /dɪ'strɛsɪŋ/ a congojoso, doloroso, penoso

distributable /dɪ'strɪbyʊtəbəl/ a repartible

distribute /dɪ'strɪbyut/ vt (of justice, etc.) administrar; distribuir; repartir

distribution /ˌdɪstrə'byuʃən/ n (of justice) administración, f; distribución, f; reparto, m

distributive /dɪ'strɪbyətɪv/ a distributivo

distributor /dɪ'strɪbyətər/ n distribuidor (-ra); repartidor (-ra). **d. of false money,** expendedor (-ra) de moneda falsa

district /'dɪstrɪkt/ n distrito, m; comarca, f; (of a town) barrio, m; (judicial) partido judicial, m, Lat. Am. comuna f; jurisdicción, f; región, zona, f

distrust /dɪs'trʌst/ n desconfianza, f; recelo, m, sospecha, f. vt desconfiar de, sospechar

distrustful /dɪs'trʌstfəl/ a desconfiado, receloso, suspicaz

distrustfully /dɪs'trʌstfəli/ adv desconfiadamente, con recelo

disturb /dɪ'stɜrb/ vt perturbar; interrumpir; incomodar; (make anxious) inquietar; (alter) cambiar; (disarrange) desordenar, desarreglar. **to d. the peace,** perturbar el orden público

disturbance /dɪ'stɜrbəns/ n perturbación, f; disturbio, m, conmoción, f; incomodidad, f; agitación, f; confusión, f; tumulto, m; desorden, m; Radio. parásitos, m pl

disturber /dɪ'stɜrbər/ n perturbador (-ra)

disturbing /dɪ'stɜrbɪŋ/ a perturbador; inquietador; conmovedor, impresionante, emocionante

disunion /dɪs'yunyən/ n desunión, f; discordia, f

disunite /ˌdɪsyu'nait/ vt desunir; separar, dividir. vi separarse

disuse /n dɪs'yus; v -'yuz/ n desuso, m. vt desusar; desacostumbrar. **to fall into d.,** caer en desuso

ditch /dɪtʃ/ n zanja, f; (for defense, etc.) foso, m; (irrigation) acequia, f. vt zanjar; abarrancar. **to die in the last d.,** morir en la brecha

ditto /'dɪtou/ adv ídem; también

ditty /'dɪti/ n canción, cantinela, f

diuretic /ˌdaiə'rɛtɪk/ a diurético

divan /dɪ'væn/ n diván, m

dive /daiv/ n buceo, m; Aer. picada, f; Inf. (bar) antro, m. vi bucear; sumergirse (en); Aer. volar en picado; penetrar (en); (into a book) enfrascarse en. **to d. out,** salir precipitadamente. **to d.-bomb,** bombardear en picado. **d.-bomber,** avión en picado, m. **d.-bombing,** bombardeo en picado, m

diver /'daivər/ n buceador, m; buzo, m; (bird) somorgujo, m

diverge /dɪ'vɜrdʒ/ vi divergir

divergence /dɪ'vɜrdʒəns/ n divergencia, f

divergent /dɪ'vɜrdʒənt/ a divergente

diverse /dɪ'vɜrs/ a diverso, vario

diversify /dɪ'vɜrsəˌfai/ vt diversificar

diversion /dɪ'vɜrʒən/ n diversión, f; entretenimiento, m, recreación, f; pasatiempo, m; placer, m; Mil. diversión, f

diversity /dɪ'vɜrsɪti/ n diversidad, variedad, f

divert /dɪ'vɜrt/ vt desviar; (amuse) divertir, entretener

divide /dɪ'vaid/ vt dividir; partir; separar; (cut) cortar; (share) repartir, distribuir; (hair) hacer la raya (del pelo); (of voting) provocar una votación. vi dividirse; separarse; (of roads, etc.) bifurcarse; (of voting) votar. **divided skirt,** n falda pantalón, f

dividend /'dɪvɪˌdɛnd/ n dividendo, m. **d. warrant,** cupón de dividendo, m

dividers /dɪ'vaidərz/ n pl compás de puntas, m

dividing /dɪ'vaidɪŋ/ a divisorio, divisor

divination /ˌdɪvə'neiʃən/ n adivinación, f

divine /dɪ'vain/ a divino; sublime; Inf. estupendo. n teólogo, m. vt (foretell) vaticinar, pronosticar; presentir; (guess) adivinar

diving /'daivɪŋ/ n buceo, m; Aer. picado, m. **d.-bell,** campana de bucear, f. **d.-board,** (low) trampolín, m; (high) palanca, f. **d.-suit,** escafandra, f. **scuba d.,** buceo, m

diving rod /dɪ'vainɪŋ/ n vara divinatoria, f

divinity /dɪ'vɪnɪti/ n divinidad, f; teología, f

divisibility /dɪˌvɪzə'bɪlɪti/ n divisibilidad, f

divisible /dɪ'vɪzəbəl/ a divisible

division /dɪ'vɪʒən/ n división, f; separación, f; (distribution) repartimiento, m; (Mil. Math.) división, f; sección, f; grupo, m; (voting) votación, f; (discord) discordia, desunión, f. **without a d.,** por unanimidad, sin votar

divisor /dɪ'vaizər/ n Math. divisor, m

divorce /dɪ'vɔrs/ n divorcio, m. vt divorciarse de; Fig. divorciar, separar. **to file a petition of d.,** poner una petición de divorcio

divorcee /dɪvɔr'sei/ n (wife) divorciada, f; (husband) divorciado, m

divulge /dɪ'vʌldʒ/ vt divulgar, revelar

dizzily /'dɪzəli/ adv vertiginosamente

dizziness /'dɪzɪnɪs/ n vértigo, m; mareo, m; (bewilderment) aturdimiento, m, confusión, f

dizzy /'dɪzi/ a vertiginoso; mareado; confuso, perplejo, aturdido

DNA n DNA, m

do /du/ vt hacer; ejecutar; (one's duty, etc.) cumplir con; concluir; (cause) causar; (homage) rendir; (commit) cometer; (arrange) arreglar; (cook) cocer, guisar; (roast) asar; (Fam. cheat) engañar; (suit) convenir; (suffice) bastar; (act) hacer el papel (de); (Fam. treat) tratar (bien o mal); (learn) aprender; (exhaust) agotar; (walk) andar; (travel, journey) recorrer; (translate) traducir; (prepare) preparar. vi hacer; (behave) conducirse; (of health) estar (bien o mal); (act) obrar; (get on) ir; (be suitable, suit) convenir; (suffice) bastar; (of plants) florecer; (cook) cocerse; (last) durar. **Don't!** ¡No lo hagas! ¡Quieto! ¡Calla! **How do you do?** ¿Cómo está Vd.? ¡Buenos días! **It will do you good,** Te conviene; Te hará bien; Te sentará bien. **It will do you no harm,** No te perjudicará; No te hará daño. **I could do with one,** Me gustaría (tener) uno; (of drinks) Me bebería uno con mucho gusto. **That is not done (customary),** Eso no se hace. **That will do,** Eso basta; Se puede servirse de eso; Está bien así; (leave it alone) ¡Déjate de eso! (be quiet!) ¡No digas más! ¡Cállate! **That won't do,** Eso no es bastante; Eso no sirve; Eso no se hace así. **That will never do,** (when buying an article) Me quedaré con éste; Me serviré de esto; Esto basta; Esto será suficiente; (is all right) Está bien así. **Thy will be done!** ¡Hágase tu voluntad! **to be doing,** estar haciendo; estar ocupado en (or con) hacer; (of food) estar cocinando. **to be done for,** estar perdido; estar muerto. **to do better,** hacer mejor (que); (mend one's ways) enmendarse, corregirse; (improve) mejorar, hacer progresos; (in health) encontrarse mejor. **to do business with,** Lat. Am. amarchantarse con. **to do nothing,** no hacer nada. **to do reverence,** rendir homenaje; inclinarse. **to do violence to,** Fig. hacer fuerza a. **to do well,** hacer bien; obrar bien; (be successful) tener éxito; hacer buena impresión; (prosperous) tener una buena posición. **to do wonders,** hacer maravillas. **to have done with,** renunciar (a); dejar de usar; dejar de hacer, cesar; concluir, terminar; no tener más que ver (con), (forsake) abandonar; (a person) romper con. **d.-it-yourself,** no tener nada que ver con; (of people) no tratar; (end a friendship) romper su amistad con, dejar de ver. **well done,** bien hecho; (of food) bien guisado; (of meat) bien asado. **What is to be done?** ¿Qué hay que hacer? ¿Qué se puede hacer? **What is there to do?** ¿Qué pasa? ¿Qué hay? **When he had done speaking,** Cuando hubo terminado de hablar. **to do again,** hacer de nuevo, volver a hacer, rehacer; repetir. **He**

will not do it again, No lo hará más. **to do away with,** quitar; eliminar; suprimir; hacer desaparecer; poner fin a; hacer cesar; destruir; matar. **to do by,** tratar (a), portarse con. **to do for,** arruinar; matar; (suffice) bastar para; ser a propósito para, servir para; (look after) cuidar; (as a housekeeper) dirigir la casa para. **to do out of,** quitar; privar de; (steal) robar.

to do up, (tie) atar; (fold) enrollar, plegar; envolver; (parcel) empaquetar; (arrange) arreglar; decorar; poner en orden; poner como nuevo; (iron) planchar; (launder) lavar y planchar; (tire) fatigar. **to do with,** (of people) tratar; (of things) tener que ver con; (put up with) poder con; poder sufrir. **to do without,** prescindir de; pasarse sin

do /du/ as an auxiliary verb is not translated in Spanish, e.g. *I do believe,* creo. *Do not do that,* no hagas eso. *I did not know,* no sabía When it is used for emphasis, *do* is translated by *sí, ciertamente, claro* and similar words, e.g.: *She did not know, but he did,* Ella no lo sabía pero él sí *You do paint well,* Pintas muy bien por cierto *Do come this time,* No dejes de venir esta vez

docile /'dɒsəl/ *a* dócil

dock /dɒk/ *n* dique, *m,* dársena, *f;* (wharf) muelle, *m;* (in a law court) banquillo de los acusados, *m; Bot.* romaza, *f. vt* (a tail) descolar; cortar, cercenar; reducir; (money) descontar; (a ship) poner en dique. *vi* entrar en dársena, entrar en dique, entrar en muelle. **dry-d.,** dique seco, *m.* **floating-d.,** dique flotante, *m.* **d.-dues,** muellaje, *m.* **d. rat,** (thief) raquero, *m*

docker /'dɒkər/ *n* estibador, descargador del muelle, *m*

docket /'dɒkɪt/ *n* (bundle) legajo, *m;* extracto, *m;* minuta, *f;* (label) etiqueta, *f,* marbete, *m*

dockyard /'dɒk,yɑrd/ *n* arsenal, astillero, *m*

doctor /'dɒktər/ *n* doctor (-ra); (medical practitioner) médico (-ca), asistir; (repair) reparar, componer; adulterar; mezclar drogas con; falsificar. *vi* ejercer la medicina. **family d.,** médico de cabecera, *m.* **to graduate as a d.,** doctorarse. **d. of divinity, laws, medicine,** doctor (-ra) en teología, en derecho, en medicina, *m*

doctoral /'dɒktərəl/ *a* doctoral

doctorate /'dɒktərɪt/ *n* doctorado, *m*

doctrinaire /,dɒktrə'nɛər/ *a* and *n* doctrinario (-ia)

doctrinal /'dɒktrənļ/ *a* doctrinal

doctrine /'dɒktrɪn/ *n* doctrina, *f*

document /n 'dɒkyəmənt; v -,mɛnt/ *n* documento, *m. vt* documentar; probar con documentos. **d.-case,** carpeta, *f*

documentary /,dɒkyə'mɛntəri/ *a* documental; escrito, auténtico. **d. film,** película documental, *f*

documentation /,dɒkyəmɛn'teiʃən/ *n* documentación, *f*

Dodecanese, the /dou,dɛkə'nis, -'niz, ,doudɛkə-/ el Dodecaneso, *m*

dodge /dɒdʒ/ *n* esguince, regate, *m;* evasiva, *f;* (trick) estratagema, *m,* maniobra, *f;* artefacto, *m. vt* esquivar, evadir

doe /dou/ *n* gama, *f.* **doe rabbit,** coneja, *f*

doer /'duər/ *n* hacedor (-ra); autor (-ra)

doeskin /'dou,skɪn/ *n* ante, *m,* piel de gama, *f*

doff /dɒf/ *vt* quitar; (of hats, etc.) quitarse; desnudarse de

dog /dɔg/ *n* perro, *m;* (male) macho, *m;* (andiron) morillo, *m; Astron.* Can Mayor (or Menor), Sirio, *m. vt* perseguir; seguir los pasos de; espiar. **You can't deceive an old dog,** A perro viejo no hay tus tus. **to go to the dogs,** ir a las carreras de galgos; *Fig.* ir en cuesta abajo. **mongrel dog,** perro mestizo, *m.* **thoroughbred dog,** perro de raza pura, *m.* **dog-collar,** collar de perro, *m; Eccl.* alzacuello, *m.* **dog-days,** días caniculares, *m pl,* canícula, *f.* **dog-eared** (of books) con las puntas de las hojas dobladas. **dog-fight,** lucha de perros, *f;* combate aéreo, *m.* **dog-fish,** lija, *f,* cazón, *m.* **dog in the manger,** el perro del hortelano, *m.* **dog-kennel,** perrera, *f.* **dog-latin,** bajo latín, *m.* **dog license,** matrícula de perros, *f.* **dog-racing,** carrera de galgos, *f.* **dog-rose,** escaramujo, *m.* **dog show,** exposición canina, *f.* **dog-tooth,** *Archit.* diente de perro, *m.:* **dog-vane,** *Naut.* cataviento, *m*

doge /doudʒ/ *n* dux, *m*

dogged /'dɔgɪd/ *a* persistente, tenaz, pertinaz, obstinado

doggedly /'dɔgɪdli/ *adv* tenazmente

doggedness /'dɔgɪdnɪs/ *n* pertinacia, tenacidad, terquedad, persistencia, *f*

doggerel /'dɔgərəl/ *n* malos versos, *m pl;* aleluyas, coplas de ciego, *f pl, a* malo, irregular

dogma /'dɔgmə/ *n* dogma, *m*

dogmatic /dɔg'mætɪk/ *a* dogmático

dogmatize /'dɔgmə,taiz/ *vt* and *vi* dogmatizar; mostrarse dogmático

doh /dou/ *n Mus.* do, *m*

doily /'dɔili/ *n* carpeta, *f,* pañito de adorno, *m*

doings /'duɪŋz/ *n pl* acciones, *f pl;* (deeds) hechos, *m pl;* (behavior) conducta, *f;* (happenings) acontecimientos, *m pl;* (works) obras, *f pl;* (things) cosas, *f pl*

doldrums /'douldrəmz/ *n pl* calmas ecuatoriales, *f pl*

dole /doul/ *n* limosna, *f;* porción, *f.* **to d. out,** repartir; distribuir en porciones pequeñas; racionar; dar contra la voluntad de uno.

doleful /'doulfəl/ *a* triste, lúgubre, melancólico; doloroso

dolefulness /'doulfəlnɪs/ *n* tristeza, melancolía, *f;* dolor, *m*

doll /dɒl/ *n* muñeca, *f*

dollar /'dɒlər/ *n* dólar, *m*

dolly /'dɒli/ *n* muñeca, *f;* (trolley) carrito, *m* (for clothes) moza, *f*

dolphin /'dɒlfɪn/ *n* delfín, *m*

dolt /doult/ *n* cabeza de alcornoque, *mf,* zamacuco, *m*

domain /dou'mein/ *n* territorio, *m;* heredad, posesión, propiedad, *f;* (empire) dominio, *m*

dome /doum/ *n* cúpula, *f;* bóveda, *f;* (palace) palacio, *m*

domestic /də'mɛstɪk/ *a* doméstico; familiar; (home-loving) casero; (of animals) doméstico; (national) interior, nacional. *n* doméstico, sirviente, *m;* criada, *f.* **d. economy,** economía doméstica, *f*

domesticate /də'mɛstɪ,keit/ *vt* domesticar

domesticated /də'mɛstɪ,keitɪd/ *a* (of animals) domesticado; (of persons) casero

domestication /də,mɛstɪ'keiʃən/ *n* domesticación, *f*

domesticity /,doumɛ'stɪsɪti/ *n* domesticidad, *f*

domicile /'dɒmə,sail/ *n* domicilio, *m, vt* domiciliar

domiciliary /,dɒmə'sɪli,ɛri/ *a* domiciliario

dominant /'dɒmənənt/ *a* dominante; imperante. *n Mus.* dominante, *f.* **to be d.,** prevalecer

dominate /'dɒmə,neit/ *vt* and *vi* dominar

domination /,dɒmə'neiʃən/ *n* dominación, *f*

domineer /,dɒmə'nɪər/ *vi* dominar, tiranizar. **to d. over,** mandar en

domineering /,dɒmə'nɪərɪŋ/ *a* dominante, mandón, tiránico. **d. person,** *Lat. Am.* mandarín *m*

Dominican /də'mɪnɪkən/ *a* dominicano. *n* dominicano, *m*

Dominican Republic, the /də'mɪnɪkən/ la República Dominicana, *f*

dominion /də'mɪnyən/ *n* dominio, *m;* autoridad, soberanía, *f;* imperio, *m; pl* **dominions,** *Eccl.* dominaciones, *f pl*

Dominions, the /də'mɪnyənz/ los Dominios, *m*

domino /'dɒmə,nou/ *n* dominó, *m.* **to go d.,** nacer domino

don /dɒn/ *n* (Spanish and Italian title) don, *m;* señor, *m. vt* ponerse, vestirse

donation /dou'neiʃən/ *n* donación, dádiva, *f;* contribución, *f*

done /dʌn/ *a* and *past part* hecho; (of food) cocido; (roasted) asado; (tired) rendido; (*Fam.* deceived) engañado. **Well d.!** ¡Bien hecho! **d. for,** arruinado; muerto; perdido; vencido; (spoilt) estropeado

donkey /'dɒŋki/ *n* borrico (-ca), burro (-rra). **d.-engine,** máquina auxiliar, *f*

donor /'dounər/ *n* donador (-ra); dador (-ra)

doodle /'dudļ/ *v* borrajear, garabatear, hacer garabatos

doom /dum/ *n* condena, *f;* (fate) suerte, *f;* (judgment) destino, *m;* ruina, *f;* juicio, *m. vt* sentenciar; condenar

doomsday /'dumz,dei/ *n* día del juicio final, *m*

door /dɔr/ n puerta, f; entrada, f. **front d.,** puerta de entrada, f. **next d.,** la casa vecina; la puerta de al lado, la puerta vecina. **next d. neighbor,** vecino (-na) de al lado. **out of doors,** al aire libre; en la calle. **to knock at the d.,** llamar a la puerta. **to slam the d.** in a person's face, dar con la puerta en las narices de alguien. **d.-bell,** timbre (non-electric, campanilla, f) de llamada, m. **d.-jamb,** quicial, m. **d. keeper,** portero, m. **d.-knob,** tirador, m. **d.-knocker,** manija, f; picaporte, m, aldaba, f. **d.-plate,** placa, f. **d.-shutter,** cierre metálico, m. **d.-step,** peldaño de la puerta, m; umbral, m. **d.-way,** portal, m

dope /doup/ n drogas, f pl, narcóticos, m pl; (news) información, f. **d. fiend,** morfinómano (-na)

dope-pusher /'doup ˌpʊʃər/ n narcotraficante, mf

Doric /'dɒrɪk/ a dórico

dormant /'dɔrmənt/ a durmiente; latente; secreto; inactivo. **to go d.,** dormirse

dormer window /'dɔrmər/ n lumbrera, f

dormitory /'dɔrmɪˌtɔri/ n dormitorio, m

dormouse /'dɔrˌmaus/ n lirón, m

dorsal /'dɔrsəl/ a dorsal

dory /'dɔri/ n (fish) dorado, m

dose, dosage /dous; 'dousɪdʒ/ n; dosis, f

dossier /'dɒsiˌei/ n documentación, f

dot /dɒt/ n punto, m; Mus. puntillo, m; pl **dots,** Gram. puntos suspensivos, m pl. vt poner punto (a una letra); (scatter) salpicar. **on the dot,** (of time) en punto. **to dot one's i's,** poner los puntos sobre las íes

dotage /'doutɪdʒ/ n senectud, chochera, f

dotard /'doutərd/ n viejo chocho, m; vieja chocha, f; Inf. carcamal, m

dote /dout/ vi chochear. **to d. on,** adorar en, idolatrar

doting /'doutɪŋ/ a chocho

double /'dʌbəl/ a and adv doble; dos veces; (in a pair) en par; en dos; doblemente; (deceitful) doble, de dos caras, falso; ambiguo. n doble, m; duplicado, m; Theat. contrafigura, f; pl **doubles,** (tennis) dobles, m pl, juego doble, m. vt doblar; duplicar; (fold) doblegar; (the fist) cerrar (el puño); (Theat. and Naut.) doblar. vi doblarse; (dodge) volverse atrás, hacer un rodeo, dar una vuelta; esquivarse. **to d. up,** vt envolver; arrollar; (a person) doblar. vi doblegarse; arrollarse; (collapse) desplomarse. **on the d.,** corriendo. **He was doubled up with pain,** El dolor le hacía retorcerse. **mixed doubles,** parejas mixtas, f pl; dobles mixtos, m pl. **double two,** (telephone) dos dos. **with a d. meaning,** con segunda intención. **d.-barrelled,** de dos cañones. **d.-bass,** contrabajo, m. **d. bed,** cama de matrimonio, f. **d.-bedded,** con cama de matrimonio; con dos camas. **d.-breasted,** cruzado. **d.-chin,** papada, f. **d.-dealing,** duplicidad, f. **d.-edged,** de doble filo. **d.-entry,** Com. partida doble, f. **d.-faced,** de dos caras. **d.-jointed,** con articulaciones dobles

double room Mexico cuarto doble, m

double-spaced /'dʌbəl 'speist/ a a doble espacio, a dos espacios

doublet /'dʌblɪt/ n (garment) jubón, justillo, m; pareja, f, par, m

doubling /'dʌblɪŋ/ n doblamiento, m; doblez, plegadura, f; duplicación, f; (dodging) evasiva, f, esguince, m

doubloon /dʌ'blun/ n doblón, m

doubly /'dʌbli/ adv doblemente; con duplicidad

doubt /daut/ n duda, f; incertidumbre, f; sospecha, f. vt and vi dudar; sospechar; titubear, hesitar; temer. **beyond all d.,** fuera de duda. **no d.,** sin duda. **There is no d. that,** No hay duda de que, No cabe duda de que. **When in d....,** En caso de duda...

doubter /'dautər/ n incrédulo (-la)

doubtful /'dautfəl/ a dudoso; incierto; perplejo; ambiguo; (of places) sospechoso

doubtfully /'dautfəli/ adv dudosamente; inciertamente; irresolutamente; ambiguamente

doubtfulness /'dautfəlnɪs/ n duda, incertidumbre, f; ambigüedad, f

doubtless /'dautlɪs/ adv sin duda, por supuesto; probablemente

dough /dou/ n pasta, masa, f; (money) lana, f

dour /dʊr/ a huraño, adusto, austero

dourly /'dʊrli/ adv severamente

douse /daus/ vt zambullir; (a sail) recoger; Inf. apagar

dove /dʌv/ n paloma, f. **d.-cote,** palomar, m

dovetail /'dʌvˌteil/ n cola de milano, f, vt machihembrar, empalmar; Fig. encajar

dowager /'dauədʒər/ n viuda, f; matrona, f. **d. countess,** condesa viuda, f

dowager empress n emperatriz viuda, f

dowdiness /'daudinɪs/ n desaliño, desaseo, m; falta de elegancia, f

dowdy /'daudi/ a desaliñado, desaseado; poco elegante. n mujer poco elegante, f

dowel /'dauəl/ n espiga, clavija, f, zoquete, m, vt enclavijar

down /daun/ n (of a bird) plumón, m; (on a peach, etc.) pelusilla, f; (hair) vello, m; (before the beard) bozo, m; (of a thistle, etc.) vilano, m. **ups and downs,** vicisitudes, f pl

down /daun/ a pendiente; (of trains, etc.) descendente. adv abajo; hacia abajo; (lowered) bajado; (of the eyes) bajos; (on the ground) en tierra, por tierra; (stretched out) tendido a lo largo; (depressed) triste, abatido; (ill) enfermo; (fallen) caído; (of the wind) cesado; (closed) cerrado; (exhausted) agotado; Com. al contado; (of temperature) más bajo. prep abajo de; abajo; en la dirección de; abajo a lo largo de; por. **"Down"** (on elevators) «Para bajar». interj ¡Abajo!; ¡A tierra! **He went d. the hill,** Bajaba la colina. **He is d. now,** Ha bajado ahora; Está abajo ahora; Está derribado ahora. **The sun has gone d.,** Se ha puesto el sol. **His stock has gone d.,** Fig. Inf. Ha caído en disfavor. **Prices have come d.,** Los precios han bajado. **Their numbers have gone d.,** Sus números han disminuido. **to be d. and out,** estar completamente arruinado, ser pobre de solemnidad. **to boil d.,** reducir hirviendo. **to come d. in the world,** venir a menos. **while I was going d. the river,** mientras iba río abajo, mientras bajaba al río. **d. below,** allá abajo; abajo; en el piso de abajo. **D. on your knees!** ¡De rodillas! **d. to,** hasta. **d. spout,** tubo de bajada, m. **d. with!** ¡Abajo! ¡Muera! **d.-stream,** agua abajo. **d. train,** tren descendente, m

down /daun/ vt derribar; vencer. **to d. tools,** declararse en huelga

downcast /'daunˌkæst/ a bajo; cabizbajo, deprimido, abatido

downfall /'daunˌfɔl/ n caída, f; derrumbamiento, m; (failure) fracaso, m; (Fig. ruin) decadencia, ruina, f

downhearted /'daunˈhɑrtɪd/ a descorazonado, alicaído, desalentado

downhill /adv 'daunˈhɪl; a 'daunˌhɪl/ adv cuesta abajo, hacia abajo. a en declive, inclinado. **to go d.,** ir cuesta abajo

downiness /'dauninɪs/ n vellosidad, f

download /'daunˌloud/ vt (computer) bajar, descargar

down payment Mexico enganche, m

downpour /'daunˌpɔr/ n chubasco (Mexico), aguacero, chaparrón, m

downright /'daunˌrait/ a franco, sincero; categórico; terminante; absoluto. adv muy; completamente

downstairs /'daunˈstɛərz/ adv escalera abajo; al piso de abajo; en el piso bajo; abajo. a del piso de abajo. n planta baja, f; piso de abajo, m. **to go d.,** bajar la escalera; ir al piso de abajo

downtrodden /'daunˌtrɒdn̩/ a oprimido, esclavizado

downward /'daunwərd/ a descendente; inclinado. adv hacia abajo

downy /'dauni/ a velloso; (Fam. of persons) con más conchas que un galápago

dowry /'dauri/ n dote, mf. **to give as a d.,** dotar

dowse /dauz/ vt. see **douse**

doze /douz/ vi dormitar. n sueño ligero, m

dozen /'dʌzən/ n docena, f

drab /dræb/ a pardo, parduzco, grisáceo; Fig. gris, monótono. n (slut) pazpuerca, f; (prostitute) ramera, f

drachma /'drækmə/ n dracma, f

draft /dræft/ n (detachment) destacamento, m; Com. giro, m, letra de cambio, f; (for the army, navy) conscripción, leva, *f*; (outline) bosquejo, *m*; proyecto, *m*; borrador, *m*; (act of drawing) tiro, *m*; (of liquid) trago, *m*; (glass) vaso, *m*; (of a ship) calando, *m*; (of air) corriente de aire, *f*, *Lat. Am.* chiflón *m*; (party) destacamento, *m*. *vt* (detach) destacar; (recruit) reclutar; (outline) bosquejar, delinear; (draw up) redactar; proyectar. **on d.**, (of beer, etc.) por vaso. **d. horse,** caballo de tiro, *m*. **d. screen,** cancel, *m*

draft card *n* cartilla (Mexico), libreta de enrolamiento (Argentina), *m*

draft dodger /'dɔdʒər/ *n* emboscado, prófugo, *m*

drafting /'dræftɪŋ/ *n* (*Mil. Nav.*) reclutamiento, *m*; (of a bill, etc.) redacción, *f*; (wording) términos, *m pl*

draftsman /'dræftsmən/ *n* dibujante, *m*; delineante, *m*; redactor, *m*

draftsmanship /'dræftsmən,ʃɪp/ *n* arte del dibujo lineal, *mf*; redacción (de un proyecto de ley), *f*

drafty /'dræfti/ *a* que tiene corriente de aire; expuesto a los vientos. **This room is d.,** Hay corriente de aire en esta habitación

drag /dræg/ *n* (for dredging) draga, *f*; (harrow) rastrillo, *m*; (break) freno, *m*; (obstacle) estorbo, *m*; *Aer.* sonda, *f*. *vt* arrastrar; (fishing nets) rastrear; (harrow) rastrillar. *vi* (of the anchor) garrar; arrastrarse por el suelo; (of time) pasar lentamente; ir más despacio (que); (of interest) decaer, disminuir. **d.-hook,** garfio, *m*. **d.-net,** brancada, *f*

dragging /'drægɪŋ/ *n* arrastre, *m*; (of lakes, etc.) rastreo, *m*, a rastrero; cansado

draggled /'drægəld/ *a* mojado y sucio

dragon /'drægən/ *n* dragón, *m*. **d.-fly,** libélula, *f*, caballito del diablo, *m*

dragoon /drə'gun/ *n Mil.* dragón, *m*, *vt* someter a una disciplina rigurosa; obligar a la fuerza (a)

drain /drein/ *n* desaguadero, *m*; (sewer) cloaca, alcantarilla, *f*; sumidero, *m*; *Agr.* acequia, *f*. *vt* desaguar; sanear; (lakes, etc.) desangrar; secar; (bail) achicar; (empty and drink) vaciar; (swallow) tragar; (*Fig.* of sorrow, etc.) apurar; (despoil) despojar; (deprive) privar (de); (impoverish) empobrecer; (exhaust) agotar. *vi* desaguarse; vaciarse; (with off) escurrirse. **to be well drained,** tener buen drenaje. **to d. the sump,** vaciar la culata. **to d. away,** vaciar. **d.-pipe,** tubo de desagüe, *m*

drainage /'dreinidʒ/ *n* (of land) drenaje, *m*; desagüe, *m*; (of wounds) drenaje, *m*; (sewage) aguas del alcantarillado, *f pl*. **main d.,** drenaje municipal, *m*

draining /'dreinɪŋ/ *a* de desagüe; de drenaje. **d.-board,** escurridor, *m*

drake /dreik/ *n* ánade macho, *m*

drama /'drɑmə, 'dræmə/ *n* drama, *m*

dramatic /drə'mætɪk/ *a* dramático

dramatically /drə'mætɪkli/ *adv* dramáticamente

dramatis personae /'dræmətɪs pər'souni/ *n pl* personajes, *m pl*

dramatist /'dræmətɪst, 'drɑmə-/ *n* dramaturgo, *m*

dramatization /ˌdræmətə'zeiʃən, ˌdrɑmə-/ *n* versión escénica, *f*; descripción dramática, *f*; (of emotions) dramatización, *f*

dramatize /'dræmə,taiz, 'drɑmə-/ *vt* dramatizar

drape /dreip/ *vt* colgar, cubrir; vestir

draper /'dreipər/ *n* pañero (-ra)

drapery /'dreipəri/ *n* colgaduras, *f pl*; ropaje, *m*, ropas, *f pl*; pañería, *f*

drastic /'dræstɪk/ *a* drástico; enérgico, fuerte; **a drastic measure,** una medida avanzada, *f*

draw /drɔ/ *vt* tirar; arrastrar; traer; (pluck) arrancar; (attract) atraer; (extract) extraer; sacar; hacer salir; (unsheath) desenvainar; (a bow-string) tender; (cards, dominoes) tomar, robar; (threads) deshilar; (disembowel) destripar; (a check, etc.) girar, librar; (of a ship) calar; (of lines) hacer (rayas); (curtains) correr; (to draw curtains back) descorrer; (salary, money) cobrar, percibir; (obtain) obtener; (persuade) persuadir, inducir; (inhale) respirar; (a sigh) dar; (win) ganar; (a conclusion) deducir, inferir; (a distinction) hacer formular; *Sports.* empatar; (a number, etc.) sortear; (suck) chupar; (tighten) estirar; (lengthen) alargar; (comfort, etc.) tomar; (inspiration) inspirarse en; (obtain money) procurarse (recursos); (withdraw funds) retirar; (write) escribir; (draw) di-

bujar; (trace) trazar; (provoke) provocar. **to be drawn,** (of tickets in a lottery and cards) salir. **to d. lots,** echar suertes. **to d. water,** sacar agua. **to d. along,** arrastrar; conducir. **to d. aside,** tomar a un lado, tomar aparte; quitar de en medio, poner a un lado; (curtains) descorrer. **to d. away,** (remove) quitar; (a person) llevarse (a); apartar. **to d. back,** hacer recular; hacer retirarse; hacer volverse atrás; (curtains) descorrer. **to d. down,** hacer bajar; tirar a lo largo de (or por); bajar; (attract) atraer. **to d. forth,** hacer salir; hacer avanzar; tirar hacia adelante; conducir; (develop) desarrollar; sacar; hacer aparecer; (comment, etc.) suscitar. **to d. in,** tirar hacia adentro; sacar; acercar; atraer. **to d. off,** sacar; retirar; quitar; (water from pipes, etc.) vaciar; *Print.* tirar; (turn aside) desviar. **to d. out,** sacar fuera; hacer salir; tirar (de); (extract) extraer; (trace) trazar; (a person) hacer hablar. **to d. over,** poner encima de; arrastrar por; hacer acercarse (a), tirar hacia; atraer; persuadir. **to d. prestige (from),** cobrar prestigio (de). **to d. round,** poner alrededor de. **to d. together,** reunir; acercar. **to d. up,** tirar hacia arriba; subir; sacar; extraer; (raise) levantar, alzar; (bring) traer; (bring near) acercar; (order) ordenar; *Mil.* formar; (a document) redactar; formular. **to d. oneself up,** erguirse

draw /drɔ/ *vi* tirar; (shrink) encogerse; (wrinkle) arrugarse; (of chimneys, etc.) tirar; (a picture) dibujar; *Sports.* empatar; (move) moverse; avanzar, adelantarse; (of a ship) calar; (a sword) desnudar (la espada); (lots) echar suertes; (attract people) atraer gente; *Com.* girar. **to d. aside,** ponerse a un lado; retirarse. **to d. back,** retroceder, recular; retirarse; vacilar. **to d. in,** retirarse; (of days) hacerse corto; (of dusk) caer. **to d. off,** alejarse; apartarse, retirarse. **to d. on,** (approach) acercarse; avanzar; *Com.* girar contra; inspirarse en. **to d. out,** hacerse largo; (of a vehicle) ponerse en marcha, empezar a andar. **to d. round,** ponerse alrededor; reunirse alrededor. **to d. together,** reunirse. **to d. up,** parar.

draw /drɔ/ *n* tirada, *f*; (of lotteries) sorteo, *m*; *Sports.* empate, *m*; atracción, *f*; (*Fig.* feeler) tanteo, *m*. **to be a big d.,** ser una gran atracción

drawback /'drɔ,bæk/ *n* desventaja, *f*, inconveniente, *m*

drawbridge /'drɔ,brɪdʒ/ *n* puente levadizo, *m*

drawee /drɔ'i/ *n Com.* girado, *m*

drawer /'drɔr/ *n* (receptacle) cajón, *m*; *pl* **drawers,** (men's) calzoncillos, *m pl*; (women's) pantalones, *m pl*

drawing /'drɔɪŋ/ *n* (pulling) tiro, *m*, atracción, *f*; (extraction) extracción, *f*; saca, *f*; (in raffles, etc. and of lots) sorteo, *m*; (of money) percibo, *m*; *Com.* giro, *m*; (sketch) dibujo, *m*; (plan) esquema, *f*. **free-hand d.,** dibujo a pulso, *m*. **d. from life,** dibujo del natural, *m*. **d.-board,** tablero de dibujo, *m*. **d.-paper,** papel para dibujar, *m*. **d.-pin,** chinche, *f*. **d.-room,** salón, *m*

drawl /drɔl/ *vi* hablar arrastrando las palabras

drawn /drɔn/ *past part* See **draw.** *a* (tired) ojeroso, con ojeras, con un aspecto de cansancio; (with pain) desencajado. **long d. out,** demasiado largo. **d. sword,** espada desnuda, *f*. **d.-thread work,** deshilados, *m pl*

dread /drɛd/ *n* pavor, temor, terror, espanto, *m*; trepidación, *f*, miedo, *m*. *a* temible, espantoso, terrible; augusto. *vt* temer. *vi* tener miedo, temer. **in d. of,** con miedo de, con terror de

dreader /'drɛdər/ *n* el, *m*, (*f*, la) que teme, temedor (-ra)

dreadful /'drɛdfəl/ *a* terrible, pavoroso, espantoso, horroroso; formidable; augusto

dreadfully /'drɛdfəli/ *adv* terriblemente, horriblemente

dreadfulness /'drɛdfəlnɪs/ *n* horror, *m*

dream /drim/ *n* sueño, *m*; ilusión, *f*; ensueño, *m*; fantasía, *f*. *vt* and *vi* soñar; imaginar. **He dreamed away the hours,** Pasaba las horas soñando. **I wouldn't d. of it!** ¡Ni por sueño! **in a d.,** en sueños; (waking) como en sueños; mecánicamente. **Sweet dreams!** ¡Duerme bien! **to d. of,** soñar con

dreamer /'drimər/ *n* soñador (-ra); visionario (-ia)

dreamily /'driməli/ *adv* como en sueños; soñolientamente; vagamente

dreaming /'drimɪŋ/ *n* sueños, *m pl*

dreamland /'drim,lænd/ n reino de los sueños, m
dreamy /'drimi/ a soñador; soñoliento; fantástico; (empty) vació
dreariness /'drɪərɪnɪs/ n tristeza, f; melancolía, f; lobreguez, f
dreary /'drɪəri/ a triste; melancólico; lóbrego
dredge /drɛdʒ/ vt dragar; (with sugar, etc.) espolvorear
dredger /'drɛdʒər/ n draga, f; (for sugar) azucarera, f; (for flour) harinero, m
dredging /'drɛdʒɪŋ/ n dragado, m; (sprinkling) salpicadura, f. **d. bucket,** cangilón, m
dregs /drɛgz/ n pl heces, f pl, posos, m pl, Lat. Am. concho m **to drain to the d.,** vaciar hasta las heces
drench /drɛntʃ/ vt mojar, calar. **He is drenched to the skin,** Está calado hasta los huesos
dress /drɛs/ vt (with clothes) vestir; (arrange) arreglar; (the hair) peinar(se); (a wound) curar; (hides); adobar; (cloth) aprestar; (flax) rastrillar; (stone) labrar; (wood) desbastar; (prune) podar; (a garden) cultivar; (manure) abonar; Cul. aderezar; preparar; (season) condimentar; (a table) poner; (adorn) ataviar, adornar; revestir; (a dead body) amortajar. vi vestirse; ataviarse; (of troops) alinearse. **all dressed up and nowhere to go,** compuesta y sin novio. **dress to kill, dress to the nines** Lat. Am. arriscarse, Central America empavonarse **dressed up to the nines,** vestido de veinticinco alfileres. **Left (Right) d.!** ¡A la izquierda (A la derecha) alinearse! **to d. down,** (scold) poner como un trapo (a), dar una calada (a). **to d. up,** vt ataviar; (disguise) disfrazar. vi ponerse muy elegante; disfrazarse
dress /drɛs/ n (in general) el vestir; (clothes) ropa, f; (frock) vestido, traje, m; (uniform) uniforme, m; (Fig. covering) hábitos, m pl; (appearance) aspecto, m; forma, f. **full d.,** (uniform) uniforme de gala, m; (civilian, man's) traje de etiqueta, m; (woman's) traje de gala, m. **morning d.,** (man's) traje de paisano, m; (woman's) vestido de todos los días, m; (man's formal dress) chaqué, m. **ready-made d.,** traje hecho, m. **d. allowance,** alfileres, m pl. **d.-circle,** anfiteatro, m. **d.-coat,** frac, m. **d. protector,** sobaquera, f. **d. rehearsal,** ensayo general, m. **d. shirt,** camisa de pechera dura, f. **d. suit,** (with white tie) traje de frac, m; (with black tie) smoking, m. **d. sword,** espada de gala, f. **d. tie,** corbata de smoking (or de frac), f
dresser /'drɛsər/ n el que aderaza; (of wounds) practicante (de hospital), m; (valet) ayuda de cámara, m; (maid) doncella, f; (of skins) adobador de pieles, m; (furniture) aparador, m; (in the kitchen) armario de la cocina, m
dressing /'drɛsɪŋ/ n el vestir(se); aderezamiento, m; (for cloth) apresto, m; (of leather) adobo, m; (of wood) desbaste, m; (of stone) labrado, m; (manuring) estercoladura, f; (sauce) salsa, f; (seasoning) condimentación, f; (of a wound) cura, f; (bandage) apósito, m, vendaje, m. **d.-case,** neceser, saco de noche, m. **d.-down,** Inf. rapapolvo, m. **d.-gown,** (woman's) salto de cama, quimono, m; (man's) batín, m. **d.-jacket,** chambra, f, peinador, m. **d.-room,** Theat. camarín, m; (in a house) trasalcoba, recámara, f. **d.-station,** puesto de socorro, m. **d.-table,** tocador, m, mesa de tocador, f
dressmaker /'drɛs,meikər/ n modista, mf
dressmaking /'drɛs,meikɪŋ/ n confección de vestidos, f; arte de la modista, m
dribble /'drɪbəl/ vi gotear; (slobber) babear. vt (in football) regatear. n (in football) regate, m
dried /draid/ a seco; (of fruit) paso. **d. up,** (withered) marchito; (of people) enjuto. **d. fish,** cecial, m. **d. meat,** cecina, f
drift /drɪft/ n (in a ship or airplane's course) deriva, f; (of a current) velocidad, f; (tendency) tendencia, f; (meaning) significación, f; (heap) montón, m; (aim) objeto, propósito, fin, m; Mineral. galería, f; (of dust, etc.) nube, f; (shower) lluvia, f; (impulsion) impulso, m; violencia, f. vi flotar, ir arrastrado por la corriente; amontonarse; Naut. derivar; Aer. abatir. vt llevar; amontonar. **continental d.,** deriva continental. **drifts of sand,** arena movediza, f. **to d. into,** (war, etc.) entrar sin querer en; (habits) dar en la flor de; (a room, etc.) deslizarse en. **d.-wood,** madera de deriva, f

drill /drɪl/ n (instrument) taladro, perforador, m, barrena, f; ejercicio, m, educación física, f; Mil. instrucción militar, f; (cloth) dril, m; Agr. sembradora mecánica, f; (for seeds) hilera, f; (discipline) disciplina, f; (teaching) instrucción, f. vt taladrar, barrenar; enseñar el ejercicio (a); enseñar la instrucción; disciplinar; (seed) sembrar en hileras. vi hacer el ejercicio; hacer la instrucción militar. **d. ground,** (in a barracks) patio de un cuartel, m; (in a school) patio de recreo, m. **d.-sergeant,** sargento instructor, m
drilling /'drɪlɪŋ/ n (boring) perforación, f, barrenamiento, m; (of seeds) sembradura en hileras, f; ejercicios, m pl; (maneuvers) maniobras, f pl
drink /drɪŋk/ n bebida, f; (glass of wine, etc.) copita, f; (of water, etc.) vaso, m. vt beber; tomar; (empty) vaciar. vi beber. **to d. to,** beber a la salud de, brindar por. **to give someone a d.,** dar a beber. **Would you like a d.?** ¿Quieres tomar algo? **to d. in,** absorber. **to d. off, up,** beber de un trago
drinkable /'drɪŋkəbəl/ a potable, bebedero
drinker /'drɪŋkər/ n bebedor (-ra)
drinking /'drɪŋkɪŋ/ n acción de beber, f; el beber, m; (alcoholism) bebida, f. a que bebe; aficionado a la bebida; (of things) para beber; (drinkable) potable; (tavern) de taberna. **d.-fountain,** fuente pública para beber agua, f. **d. place,** bebedero, m; bar, m. **d.-song,** canción de taberna, f. **d.-trough,** abrevadero, m; **d.-water,** agua potable, f
drip /drɪp/ vi and vt chorrear, gotear; caer gota a gota; escurrir; destilar; chorrear. n goteo, m; gota, f; Archit. goterón, m
dripping /'drɪpɪŋ/ n goteo, m; chorreo, m; (fat) grasa, f, a que gotea; mojado; que chorrea agua. **d.-pan,** grasera, f
drive /draiv/ vt empujar; arrojar; conducir; (grouse, etc.) batir; (a ball) golpear; (a nail, etc.) clavar; (oblige) compeler, forzar a; (a horse, plow, car, etc.) manejar; (Mech. work) mover; (cause to work, of machines) hacer funcionar; (a tunnel, etc.) abrir, construir; (a bargain, etc.) hacer; (cause) impulsar, hacer; (mad, etc.) volver. vi lanzarse; (of rain) azotar; (a vehicle) conducir; (in a vehicle) ir en (coche, etc.). **to let d. at,** (aim) asestar. **to d. a wedge,** hacer mella. **to d. home a point,** convencer; hacer convincente. **What is he driving at?** ¿Qué se propone?; ¿Qué quiere?; ¿Qué quiere decir con sus indirectas? ¿A dónde quiere llegar con esto? **to d. along,** ir en coche o carruaje por; pasearse en coche o carruaje; conducir un auto, etc., por. **to d. away,** vt echar; (chase) cazar; (flies, etc.) sacudirse, espantar; (care, etc.) ahuyentar; (of persons) apartar, alejar. vi (depart) marcharse en coche, etc.). **to d. back,** vt rechazar; (a ball) devolver. vi volver (en auto, etc.); (arrive) llegar. **to d. crazy, d. insane,** enloquecer, Lat. Am. also idiotizar, **to d. down,** hacer bajar; arrojar hacia abajo; (in a vehicle) bajar (por). **to d. in, into,** vt hacer entrar; (of teeth, etc.) hincar; (nails) clavar; Fig. introducir. vt entrar (en coche, carruaje); llegar (en coche, etc.). **to d. off,** See **away**. **to d. off the stage,** hacer dejar la escena, silbar. **to d. on,** vt empujar; hacer avanzar; (attack) atacar. vi seguir su marcha; seguir avanzando; emprender la marcha. **to d. out,** vt expulsar; hacer salir; (chase) cazar. vi salir (en coche, etc.). **to d. up,** vi llegar (en coche, etc.); parar. **to d. up to,** avanzar hasta, llegar hasta; conducir (el coche, etc.) hasta
drive /draiv/ n paseo (en coche, etc.), m; (avenue) avenida, f, camino m; (distance) trayecto, m; (journey) viaje, m; Mech. acción, f; conducción, f; m; Mil. ataque, m; (of a person) energía, f; campaña vigorosa, f; impulso, m. **left (right) hand d.,** conducción a la izquierda (derecha). **to take a d.,** dar un paseo en auto, etc.). **to take for a d.,** llevar a paseo en (auto, etc.)
drive-in /'draiv,ɪn/ n autocine, autocinema, m
drivel /'drɪvəl/ n vaciedades, patrañas, f pl, disparates, m pl, vi decir disparates, chochear
driver /'draivər/ n conductor (-ra); chófer, m; (of an engine) maquinista, m; (of a cart) carretero, m; (of a coach, carriage) cochero, m; (of cattle, etc.) ganadero, m; (golf) conductor, m
driver's license /'draivərz/ Spain carné de chofer, Ar-

gentina carné de conductor, *m, elsewhere in Lat. Am.* licencia de manejar, *f*

driveway /'draiv,wei/ *n* camino, *m*, entrada para coches *f*

driving /'draiviŋ/ *n* conducción, *f*; modo de conducir, *m*; paseo (en coche, etc.), *m*; impulsión, *f. a* de conducir; de chófer; para choferes; motor; propulsor; impulsor; de transmisión; *Fig.* impulsor; (violent) violento, impetuoso. **to go d.,** ir de paseo (en auto o carruaje). **d. mirror,** espejo retrovisor, *m.* **d. seat,** asiento del conductor, *m*; (of an old-fashioned coach, etc.) pescante, *m.* **d.-shaft,** *Mech.* árbol motor, *m.* **d. test,** examen para choferes, *m.* **d.-wheel,** volante, *m*; rueda motriz, *f*

drizzle /'drizəl/ *n* llovizna, *f, vi* lloviznar, *Lat. Am.* briznar

droll /droul/ *a* chusco, gracioso. *n* bufón, *m*

drone /droun/ *n* abejón, *m*; *Fig.* zángano, *m*; (hum) zumbido, *m*; (of a song, voice) salmodia, *f, vt and vi* (hum) zumbar; (of a song, voice) salmodiar; (idle) zanganear

droop /drup/ *vi* inclinarse; colgar; caer; (wither) marchitarse; (fade) consumirse; (pine) desanimarse. *vt* bajar; dejar caer. *n* caída, *f*; inclinación, *f*

drooping /'drupiŋ/ *a* caído; debilitado; lánguido; (of ears) gacho; (depressed) alicaído, deprimido

drop /drɒp/ *n* gota, *f*; (tear) lágrima, *f*; (for the ear) pendiente, *m*; (sweet) pastilla, *f*; (of a chandelier) almendra, *f*; (fall) caída, *f*; (in price, etc.) baja, *f*; (slope) pendiente, cuesta, *f.* **by drops,** a gotas. **d. bottle,** frasco cuentagotas, *m.* **d.-curtain,** telón de boca, *m.* **d.-hammer,** martinete, *m.* **d.-head coupé,** cupé descapotable, *m.* **d.-scene,** telón de foro, *m*

drop /drɒp/ *vt* verter a gotas; destilar; (sprinkle) salpicar, rociar; dejar caer; soltar; (lower) bajar; (of clothes, etc.) desprenderse de, quitar; (lose) perder; (a letter in a mailbox) echar; (leave) dejar; (give up) renunciar (a); desistir (de); abandonar; (kill) tumbar; (a hint) soltar; (a curtsey) hacer. *vi* gotear, caer en gotas, destilar; (descend) bajar, descender; caer muerto; caer desmayado; (sleep) dormirse; (fall) caer; (of the wind) amainar; (of prices, temperature) bajar. **to let the matter d.,** poner fin a una cuestión. **to d. a course,** bajar un curso. **to d. a line,** poner unas líneas. **to d. anchor,** anclar. **to d. behind,** quedarse atrás. **to d. down,** caer (a tierra). **to d. in,** entrar al pasar. **d. in on somebody,** pasarse por casa de fulano, pasarse por el despacho de (etc.). **to d. off,** separarse (de); disminuir; (sleep) quedar dormido; (die) morir de repente. **to d. out,** separarse; (from a race, etc.) retirarse (de); quedarse atrás; desaparecer; ausentarse, apartarse; (decrease) disminuir; decaer. **He has dropped out of my life,** Le he perdido de vista. **to d. through,** caer por; frustrarse; no dar resultado

dropping /'drɒpiŋ/ *n* gotera, *f*; gotas, *f pl*; (fall) caída, *f*; *pl* **droppings** (of a candle) moco, *m*; (dung) cagadas, *f pl.* **Constant d. wears away the stone,** La gotera cava la piedra

dropsy /'drɒpsi/ *n* hidropesía, *f*

dross /drɔs/ *n* escoria, *f*; (rubbish) basura, *f*

drought /draut/ *n* aridez, *f*; (thirst) sed, *f*; (dry season) sequía, *f*

drove /drouv/ *n* manada, *f*, hato, *m*; (of sheep) rebaño, *m*; (crowd) muchedumbre, *f*

drown /draun/ *vi* ahogarse. *vt* ahogar; sumergir; inundar; (*Fig.* of cries, sorrow, etc.) ahogar

drowning /'drauniŋ/ *n* ahogamiento, *m*; sumersión, *f*; inundación, *f. a* que se ahoga

drowse /drauz/ *vi* adormecerse

drowsily /'drauzəli/ *adv* soñolientamente

drowsiness /'drauzinis/ *n* somnolencia, *f*; sueño, *m*; (laziness) indolencia, pereza, *f*

drowsy /'drauzi/ *a* soñoliento; adormecedor, soporífero; (heavy) amodorrado. **to grow d.,** adormecerse. **to make d.,** adormecer

drudgery /'drʌdʒəri/ *n* trabajo arduo, *m*, faena monótona, *f*

drug /drʌg/ *n* droga, *f*; medicamento, *m*; narcótico, *m. vt* mezclar con drogas; administrar drogas (a); narcotizar. *vi* tomar drogas. **d. trade,** comercio de

drogas, *m.* **d. traffic,** contrabando de drogas, narcotráfico *m*

drug addict *n* drogadicto (-ta), *Lat. Am.* adicto *mf*

drug addiction *n* toxicomanía, *f*

druggist /'drʌgist/ *n* droguero (-ra)

drum /drʌm/ *n* tambor, *m*; (of the ear) tímpano (del oído), *m*; (cylinder) cilindro, *m*; (box) caja, *f*; *Archit.* cuerpo de columna, *m.* **drums,** batería, *f.* **bass d.,** bombo, *m.* **with drums beating,** con tambor batiente. **d.-head,** parche (del tambor), *m.* **d.-head service,** misa de campaña, *f.* **d.-major,** tambor mayor, *m*

drum /drʌm/ *vt and vi* tocar el tambor; (with the fingers) tabalear, teclear; (with the heels) zapatear; (into a person's head) machacar. **to d. out,** *Mil.* expulsar a tambor batiente

drummer /'drʌmər/ *n* tambor, *m*

drumming /'drʌmiŋ/ *n* ruido del tambor, *m*; (of the heels) taconeo, *m*; (of the fingers) tabaleo, tecleo, *m*

drumstick /'drʌm,stik/ *n* palillo (de tambor), *m*

drunk /drʌŋk/ *a* borracho, ebrio, *Lat. Am. also* iluminado, *Central America* azunumbaso *n* borracho, *m.* **to be d.,** estar borracho. **to get d.,** emborracharse, *Lat. Am. also* iluminarse; *Inf.* pillar un lobo, (on wine) *Mexico* envinarse. **to make d.,** emborrachar

drunkard /'drʌŋkərd/ *n* borracho (-cha)

drunken /'drʌŋkən/ *a* borracho, ebrio

drunkenness /'drʌŋkənnıs/ *n* embriaguez, borrachera, ebriedad, *f*

dry /drai/ *vi* secarse. *vt* secar; desaguar; (wipe) enjugar. **to dry one's tears,** enjugarse las lágrimas; *Fig.* secarse las lágrimas. **to dry up,** secarse; (of persons) acecinarse; (with old age) apergaminarse; (of ideas, etc.) agotarse; (be quiet) callarse

dry /drai/ *a* seco; árido; estéril; (thirsty) sediento; (of wine) seco; (U.S.A.) prohibicionista; (squeezed) exprimido; (of toast) sin mantequilla; (*Fig.* chilly) aburrido; (sarcastic) sarcástico; (of humor) agudo. **on dry land,** en seco. **dry battery,** pila seca, *f.* **to dry-clean,** lavar al seco, *m.* **dry-cleaner,** tintorero (-ra). **dry-cleaning,** lavado al seco, *m.* **dry-cleaning shop,** tintorería, *f.* **dry goods,** lencería, *f.* **dry land,** tierra firme, *f.* **dry measure,** medida para áridos, *f.* **dry-nurse,** ama seca, *f.* **dry-point,** punta seca, *f.* **dry-rot,** carcoma, *f.* **dry-shod,** con los pies secos

drying /'drai·iŋ/ *n* secamiento, *m*; desecación, *f. a* secante; seco; para secar. **d. ground,** tendedero, *m.* **d. machine,** secadora, *f*; (for the hair) secadora de cabello, *f.* **d. room,** secadero, *m*

dryly /'draili/ *adv* secamente

dryness /'drainis/ *n* sequedad, *f*; aridez, *f*; (of humor) agudeza, *f*

dual /'duəl/ *a* doble; *Gram.* dual. **d. control,** mandos gemelos, *m pl.* **d. personality,** conciencia doble, *f*

dualism /'duə,lizəm/ *n* dualismo, *m*

duality /du'ælti/ *n* dualidad, *f*

dub /dʌb/ *vt* (a knight) armar caballero; (call) apellidar; (nickname) motejar, apodar

dubbing /'dʌbiŋ/ *n* (of films) doblaje, *m*

dubious /'dubiəs/ *a* dudoso, incierto; indeciso; problemático; ambiguo

dubiously /'dubiəsli/ *adv* dudosamente

dubiousness /'dubiəsnıs/ *n* carácter dudoso, *m*; incertidumbre, *f*; ambigüedad, *f*

Dublin /'dʌblin/ Dublín, *f*

Dubliner /'dʌblənər/ *n* dublinés (-esa)

ducat /'dʌkət/ *n* ducado, *m*

duchess /'dʌtʃıs/ *n* duquesa, *f*

duchy /'dʌtʃi/ *n* ducado, *m*

duck /dʌk/ *n* pato (-ta), ánade, *mf*; *Sports.* cero, *m*; (darling) vida mía, querida, *f*; (jerk) agachada, *f*; (under the water) chapuz, *m*; (material) dril, *m*; *Mil.* auto anfibio, *m. vi* agacharse; (under water) chapuzarse. *vt* zabullir, sumergir; bajar, inclinar

ducking /'dʌkiŋ/ *n* chapuz, *m*; *Naut.* chapuzar, *f.* **d.-stool,** silla de chapuzar, *f*

duckling /'dʌkliŋ/ *n* anadino (-na)

duct /dʌkt/ *n* conducto, canal, *m*; *Bot.* tubo, *m*

ductile /'dʌktļ/ *a* dúctil

ductility /dʌk'tıliti/ *n* ductilidad, *f*

ductless /'dʌktlɪs/ a sin tubos
due /du/ a debido; (payable) pagadero; (fallen due) vencido; (fitting) propio; (expected) esperado. n impuesto, m; derecho, m. **in due form,** en regla. **in its due time,** a su tiempo debido. **to fall due,** vencerse. **due bill,** *Com.* abonaré, m. **due west,** poniente derecho, m
duel /'dual/ n duelo, lance de honor, m; *Fig.* lucha, f. **to fight a d.,** batirse en duelo
dueling /'dualɪŋ/ n el (batirse en) duelo
duelist /'dualɪst/ n duelista, m
duenna /du'ɛnə/ n dueña, f
duet /du'ɛt/ n dúo, m
duettist /du'ɛtɪst/ n duetista, mf
dug /dʌg/ n teta, f
dugout /'dʌg,aut/ n trinchera, f
duke /duk/ n duque, m
dukedom /'dukdəm/ n ducado, m
dulcet /'dʌlsɪt/ a dulce
dulcimer /'dʌlsəmər/ n dulcémele, m
dull /dʌl/ a (stupid) lerdo, estúpido, obtuso; (boring, tedious) aburrido; (of pain, sounds) sordo; (of colors and eyes) apagado; (of light, beams, etc.) sombrío; (not polished) mate; (pale) pálido; (insipid) insípido, insulso; (of people) soso, poco interesante; (dreary, sad) triste; (gray) gris; (of mirrors, etc.) empañado; (of weather) anublado; (of hearing) duro; (slow) lento; lánguido; insensible; (blunt) romo; *Com.* encalmado, inactivo. **to find life d.,** encontrar la vida aburrida. **d. of hearing,** duro de oído, algo sordo. **d. pain,** dolor sordo, m. **d.-witted,** lerdo
dull /dʌl/ vt (make stupid) entontecer; (lessen) mitigar; (weaken) debilitar; (pain) calmar, aliviar; (sadden) entristecer; (blunt) embotar; (spoil) estropear; (a mirror, etc.) empañar; (a polished surface) hacer mate, deslustrar; (of enthusiasm, etc.) enfriar; (tire) fatigar; (obstruct) impedir
dullness /'dʌlnɪs/ n (stupidity) estupidez, f; (boredom) aburrimiento, m; (heaviness) pesadez, f; (drowsiness) somnolencia, f; (insipidity) insipidez, insulsez, f; (of literary style) prosaísmo, m; (of persons) sosería, f; (of a surface) deslustre, m; (laziness) pereza, languidez, f; (slowness) lentitud, f; (tiredness) cansancio, m; (sadness) tristeza, f; (bluntness) embotamiento, m; (of hearing) dureza, f; *Com.* desanimación, f
dully /'dʌli/ adv (stupidly) estúpidamente; sin comprender; (insipidly) insípidamente; (not brightly) sin brillo; (slowly) lentamente; (sadly) tristemente; (tiredly) con cansancio; (of sound) sordamente
duly /'duli/ adv debidamente; puntualmente
dumb /dʌm/ a mudo; callado; silencioso; *Inf.* tonto, estúpido, *Lat. Am.* also baboso, *Central America* azurumbado. **to become d.,** enmudecer. **to strike d.,** dejar sin habla. **d.-bell,** barra con pesas, f. **d. waiter,** bufete, m
dumbfound /dʌm'faund/ vt dejar sin habla; confundir; pasmar
dumbness /'dʌmnɪs/ n mudez, f, mutismo, m; silencio, m
dummy /'dʌmi/ n (tailor's, etc.) maniquí, m; (puppet) títere, m; cabeza para pelucas, f; (figurehead) hombre de paja, testaferro, m; (baby's) chupador, m; (at cards) el muerto. a fingido. **to be d.,** (at cards) ser el muerto
dump /dʌmp/ n depósito, m; vaciadero, m. vt depositar; (goods on a market) inundar (con)
dumping /'dʌmpɪŋ/ n depósito, m; vaciamiento, m; (of goods on a market) inundación, f. **"D. prohibited,"** «Se prohibe arrojar la basura»
dun /dʌn/ vt apremiar, importunar
dunce /dʌns/ n asno, bobo, zoquete, m. **dunce's cap,** coroza, f
dun-colored /'dʌn,kʌlərd/ a pardo
dune /dun/ n duna, f
dung /dʌŋ/ n estiércol, m; (of rabbits, mice, deer, sheep, goats) cagarruta, f; (of cows) boñiga, f; (of hens) gallinaza, f. **d.-cart,** carro de basura, m
dungarees /ˌdʌŋgə'riz/ n mono, m, pantalones-vaquero, m pl
dungeon /'dʌndʒən/ n mazmorra, f, calabozo, m

dunghill /'dʌŋ,hɪl/ n muladar, m
duodenum /ˌduə'dinəm/ n duodeno, m
dupe /dup/ n víctima, f; tonto (-ta). vt embelecar, engañar. **to be a d.,** *Inf.* hacer el primo
duplicate /a, n 'duplɪkɪt; v -ˌkeɪt/ a duplicado, doble. n duplicado, m; copia, f. vt duplicar
duplication /ˌduplɪ'keɪʃən/ n duplicación, f
duplicator /'duplɪˌkeɪtər/ n copiador, m
duplicity /du'plɪsɪti/ n duplicidad, f
durability /ˌdʊrə'bɪlɪti/ n duración, f. **This is a cloth of great d.,** Este es un paño que dura mucho, Este es un paño muy duradero
durable /'dʊrəbəl/ a duradero
duration /dʊ'reɪʃən/ n duración, f
duress /dʊ'rɛs/ n compulsión, f
during /'dʊrɪŋ/ prep durante
dusk /dʌsk/ n atardecer, anochecer, m; (twilight) crepúsculo, m; (darkness) oscuridad, f. **at d.,** al atardecer, a la caída de la tarde
dusky /'dʌski/ a (dim, dark) oscuro; (of colors) sucio
dust /dʌst/ n polvo, m; (cloud of dust) polvareda, f; (ashes) cenizas, f pl; (of coal) cisco, m; (sweepings) barreduras, f pl; (of grain) tamo, m. vt desempolvar, quitar (or sacudir) el polvo de; (cover with dust) polvorear; (scatter) salpicar; (sweep) barrer; (clean) limpiar. **d.-bin,** basurero, m. **d.-cart,** carro de la basura, m. **d. cloud,** polvareda, f. **d. jacket,** (books) sobrecubierta, f. **d.-pan,** recogedor de basura, m. **d.-sheet,** guardapolvo, m. **d. storm,** vendaval de polvo, m
duster /'dʌstər/ n el, m, que quita el polvo; paño (para quitar el polvo), m; (of feathers) plumero, m
dustiness /'dʌstɪnɪs/ n empolvoramiento, m; estado polvoriento, m
dusting /'dʌstɪŋ/ n limpieza, f; (sweeping) barredura, f; (powder) polvos antisépticos, m pl
dusty /'dʌsti/ a polvoriento, polvoroso, empolvado; del color del polvo; (of colors) sucio. **It is very d.,** Hay mucho polvo. **to get d.,** llenarse (or cubrirse) de polvo
Dutch /dʌtʃ/ a holandés. **the D.,** los holandeses. **double D.,** griego, galimatías, m. **D. cheese,** queso de bola, m. **D. courage,** coraje falso, m. **D. woman,** holandesa, f
Dutchman /'dʌtʃmən/ n holandés, m
dutiable /'dutiəbəl/ a sujeto a derechos de aduana
dutiful /'dutəfəl/ a que cumple con sus deberes; obediente, sumiso; respetuoso; excelente, muy bueno
dutifully /'dutəfəli/ adv obediente; respetuosamente
dutifulness /'dutəfəlnɪs/ n obediencia, docilidad, f; respeto, m
duty /'duti/ n deber, m; obligación, f; (greetings) respetos, m pl; (charge, burden) carga, f; (tax) derecho, impuesto, m; *Mil.* servicio, m; (guard) guardia, f. **off d.,** libre. **on d.,** de servicio. **to be on sentry d.,** estar de guardia. **to do d. as,** servir como. **to do one's d.,** hacer (or cumplir con) su deber. **to pay d. on,** pagar derechos de aduana sobre. **d.-free,** franco de derechos
dwarf /dwɔrf/ a enano. n enano (-na). vt impedir el crecimiento de; empequeñecer
dwarfish /'dwɔrfɪʃ/ a enano
dwell /dwɛl/ vi vivir, habitar; (with on, upon) (think about) meditar sobre, pensar en; (deal with) tratar de; hablar largamente de; (insist on) insister en; apoyarse en, hacer hincapié en; (pause over) detenerse en
dweller /'dwɛlər/ n habitante, mf; (more poetic) morador (-ra)
dwelling /'dwɛlɪŋ/ n vivienda, f; (abode) morada, habitación, f; residencia, f; casa, f; (domicile) domicilio, m. **d.-house,** casa, f
dwindle /'dwɪndl/ vi disminuirse; consumirse; (decay) decaer; (degenerate) degenerar. **to d. to,** reducirse a
dwindling /'dwɪndlɪŋ/ n disminución, f
dye /daɪ/ vt teñir, colorar. vi teñirse. n tinte, m; (colour) color, m. **fast dye,** tinte estable, m. **dye-house,** tintorería, f. **dye-stuff,** materia colorante, f. **dye-works,** tintorería, f
dyed-in-the-wool /'daɪd ən ðə 'wʊl/ a de pies a cabeza

dyeing /'daiɪŋ/ n teñidura, tintura, f; (as a trade) tintorería, f. **d. and dry-cleaning shop,** tintorería, f
dyer /'daiər/ n tintorero (-ra)
dyestuff /'dai‚stʌf/ n materia colorante, materia de tinte, materia tintórea, f
dying /'daiɪŋ/ a moribundo, agonizante; de la muerte; (of light) mortecino; (last) último; supremo; (languishing) lánguido; (deathbed) hecho en su lecho mortuorio. **to be d.,** estar agonizando; (of light) fenecer. **to be d. for,** estar muerto por

dynamic /dai'næmɪk/ a dinámico
dynamics /dai'næmɪks/ n dinámica, f
dynamite /'dainə‚mait/ n dinamita, f
dynamo /'dainə‚mou/ n dinamo, f
dynastic /dai'næstɪk/ a dinástico
dynasty /'dainəsti/ n dinastía, f
dysentery /'dɪsən‚tɛri/ n disentería, f
dyslexia /dɪs'lɛksiə/ n dislexia, f
dyspepsia /dɪs'pɛpʃə/ n dispepsia, f
dyspeptic /dɪs'pɛptɪk/ a dispéptico. n dispéptico (-ca)

E

e /i/ n (letter) e, f; Mus. mi, m
each /itʃ/ a cada (invariable), todo. pron cada uno, m; cada una, f. **e. other,** el uno al otro. **e. of them,** cada uno de ellos. **They help e. other,** Se ayudan mutuamente, Se ayudan entre sí. **to love e. other,** amarse
eager /'igər/ a impaciente; ansioso, deseoso; ambicioso
eagerly /'igərli/ adv con impaciencia; con ansia; ambiciosamente
eagerness /'igərnɪs/ n impaciencia, f; ansia, f, deseo, m; (promptness) alacridad, f; (zeal) fervor, m
eagle /'igəl/ n águila, f. **royal e.,** águila caudal, águila real, f. **e.-eyed,** con ojos de lince, de ojo avizor. **have the eyes of an e.,** tener ojos de lince, tener vista de lince
ear /iər/ n (outer ear) oreja, f; (inner ear and sense of hearing) oído, m; Bot. espiga, panoja, f. **to begin to show the ear,** (grain) espigar. **to be all ears,** ser todo oídos. **to give ear,** dar oído. **to have a good ear,** tener buen oído. **to play by ear,** tocar de oído. **to turn a deaf ear,** hacerse el sordo. **ear-ache,** dolor de oídos, m. **ear-drum,** tímpano (del oído), m. **ear-flap,** orejera, f. **ear-phone, ear-piece,** auricular, m. **ear-piercing,** penetrante, agudo. **ear-shot,** alcance del oído, m. **to be within ear-shot,** estar al alcance del oído. **ear-trumpet,** trompetilla, f. **ear wax,** cerilla, f
eared /iərd/ a con orejas; de orejas; Bot. con espigas
earl /ɜrl/ n conde, m
earldom /'ɜrldəm/ n condado, m
earlier, earliest /'ɜrliər; 'ɜrliist/ a comp and sup más temprano; más primitivo; más antiguo; (first, of time) primero. adv más temprano; más pronto; antes
earliness /'ɜrlinɪs/ n lo temprano; antigüedad, f, lo primitivo; (precocity) precocidad, f. **The e. of his arrival,** Su llegada de buena hora
early /'ɜrli/ a temprano; primitivo; (of fruit, etc.) temprano, adelantado; (movement) primero (e.g. early Romanticism, el primer romanticismo); (person) de la primera época (e.g. the early Cervantes, Cervantes de la primera época); (work) un primer (e.g. an early work of Unamuno's, una primera obra de Unamuno); (advanced) avanzado; (precocious) precoz; (first, of time) primero; (in the morning) matutino; (near) próximo; cercano; (premature) prematuro; (of child's age) tierno; joven. **in the e. hours,** en las primeras horas; en las altas horas (de la noche). **e. age,** edad temprana, tierna edad, f. **e.-fruiting,** Agr. tempranal. **e. riser,** madrugador (-ra). **e.-rising,** a madrugador. **e. years,** primeros años, años de la niñez, m pl
early /'ɜrli/ adv temprano; al principio (de); en los primeros días (de); desde los primeros días (de); (in the month, year) a principios (de); (in time) a tiempo; (in the day) de buena hora; (soon) pronto; (among the first) entre los primeros (de). **as e. as possible,** lo más temprano posible; lo más pronto posible. **to be e.,** llegar antes de tiempo; llegar de buena hora. **to get up e.,** madrugar. **to go to bed e.,** acostarse temprano. **too e.,** demasiado temprano, muy temprano. **e. in the morning,** de madrugada
earmark /'iər‚mɑrk/ vt marcar; Fig. destinar, reservar
earn /ɜrn/ vt ganar; obtener, adquirir; (deserve) merecer
earnable /'ɜrnəbəl/ a ganable

earnest /'ɜrnɪst/ a serio; fervoroso; diligente; sincero. **to be in e. about something,** tomarlo en serio; ser sincero (en). **e. money,** arras, f pl
earnestly /'ɜrnɪstli/ adv seriamente; fervorosamente; con diligencia; sinceramente, de buena fe
earnestness /'ɜrnɪstnɪs/ n seriedad, f; fervor, celo, m; diligencia, f; sinceridad, buena fe, f
earnings /'ɜrnɪŋz/ n pl Com. ingresos, m pl; (salary) salario, m; estipendio, m; (of a workman) jornal, m
earring /'iər‚rɪŋ/ n pendiente, arete, Lat. Am. also aro m
earth /ɜrθ/ n tierra, f; (of a badger, etc.) madriguera, f; Radio. tierra, f. vt cubrir con tierra; Radio. conectar con tierra. **clod of e.,** terrón, m. **half the e.,** Inf. medio mundo, m. **on e.,** en este mundo, sobre la tierra
earthen /'ɜrθən/ a terrizo, terroso; (of mud) de barro
earthenware /'ɜrθən‚wɛər/ n alfar, m, a de loza, de barro
earthiness /'ɜrθinɪs/ n terrosidad, f
earthly /'ɜrθli/ a terrestre, terrenal; de la tierra; (fleshly) carnal; (worldly) mundano; material. **There is not an e. chance,** No hay la más mínima posibilidad
earthquake /'ɜrθ‚kweik/ n terremoto, temblor de tierra, m
earth tremor movimiento sísmico, m
earthwork /'ɜrθ‚wɜrk/ n terraplén, m
earthworm /'ɜrθ‚wɜrm/ n gusano de tierra, m
earthy /'ɜrθi/ a térreo, terroso
earwig /'iər‚wɪg/ n tijereta, f
ease /iz/ n bienestar, m; tranquilidad, f; descanso, m; (leisure) ocio, m; (comfortableness) comodidad, f; (freedom from embarrassment) naturalidad, f, desembarazo, desenfado, m; (from pain) alivio, m; (simplicity) facilidad, f. vt (widen) ensanchar; aflojar; (pain) aliviar; (lighten) aligerar; (moderate) moderar; (soften) suavizar; (free) librar; (one's mind) tranquilizar. **in my moments of e.,** en mis ocios, en mis momentos de ocio. **Stand at e.!** Mil. ¡En su lugar descansen! **to be at e.,** estar a sus anchas; encontrarse bien; comportarse con toda naturalidad. **with e.,** fácilmente. **to e. off,** vt (Naut. cables, sails) arriar. vi sentirse menos, cesar
easel /'izəl/ n caballete (de pintor) m
easily /'izəli/ adv fácilmente. **The engine runs e.,** El motor marcha bien
easiness /'izinɪs/ n facilidad, f; sencillez, f; (of manner) desembarazo, m, naturalidad, f
east /ist/ n este, m; oriente, m, (of countries) Oriente, m; Levante, m. a del este; del oriente; (of countries) de Oriente, oriental; levantino. **e. North e.,** estenordeste, m. **e. South e.,** estesudeste, m. **e. wind,** viento del este, m
Easter /'istər/ n Pascua de Resurrección, f. **E. egg,** huevo de Pascua, m. **E. Saturday,** sábado de gloria, m. **E. Sunday,** domingo de Pascua, m
easterly /'istərli/ a del este; al este. adv hacia el este
eastern /'istərn/ a del este; de Oriente; oriental. n oriental, m
easternmost /'istərn‚moust/ a situado más al este
East Indies /'ɪndiz/ Indias Orientales, f pl
eastward /'istwərd/ adv hacia el este, hacia oriente
easy /'izi/ a fácil; sencillo; (comfortable) cómodo; (free from pain) aliviado; Com. flojo; (well-off) acomodado, holgado; (calm) tranquilo; tolerante; natu-

ral; afable, condescendiente; (of virtue, women) fácil. *adv* con calma; despacio. **to take it e.,** tomarlo con calma. **e.-chair,** (silla) poltrona, *f*. **easy come, easy go,** lo que por agua, agua (Mexico and Colombia), los dineros del sacristán cantando vienen y cantando se van (Spain). **e.-going,** acomodadizo; indolente; (morally) de manga ancha; (casual) descuidado

eat /it/ *vt* comer; (meals, soup, refreshments) tomar; (with a good, bad appetite) hacer; consumir; (corrode) corroer; desgastar. *vi* comer; (*Fam.* of food) ser de buen (or mal) comer. **to eat one's breakfast (lunch),** tomar el desayuno, desayunar (almorzar). **to eat one's words,** retractarse. **to eat away,** comer; consumir; corroer. **to eat into,** (of chemicals) morder; (a fortune) consumir; gastar. **eat out of s. b.'s hand,** comer de la mano de fulano, comer en la mano de fulano. **to eat up,** devorar (also *Fig.*)

eatable /'itəbəl/ *a* comestible, comedero. *n pl* **eatables,** comestibles, *m pl*

eater /'itər/ *n* el, *m*, (*f*, la) que come

eating /'itɪŋ/ *n* el comer; comida, *f*. **e. and drinking,** el comer y beber. **e.-house,** casa de comidas, *f*

eau de cologne /'ou də kə'loun/ *n* agua de Colonia, *f*

eaves /ivz/ *n* rafe, alero, *m*. **under the e.,** debajo del alero

eavesdrop /'ivz,drɒp/ *vi* escuchar a las puertas; fisgonear, espiar

eavesdropper /'ivz,drɒpər/ *n* fisgón (-ona)

eavesdropping /'ivz,drɒpɪŋ/ *n* fisgoneo, *m*

ebb /ɛb/ *n* (of the tide) reflujo, *m*; menguante, *f*; *Fig.* declinación, *f*; *Fig.* decadencia, *f*; (of life) vejez, *f*; *vi* (of tide) menguar; declinar; decaer. **to ebb and flow,** fluir y refluir. **to ebb away from,** dejar; dejar aislado. **ebb-tide,** marea menguante, *f*

ebonite /'ɛbə,nait/ *n* ebonita, *f*

ebony /'ɛbəni/ *n* ébano, *m*

ebullience /ɪ'bʌlyəns/ *n* efervescencia, exuberancia, *f*

ebullient /ɪ'bʌlyənt/ *a* efervescente, exuberante

ebullition /,ɛbə'lɪʃən/ *n* (boiling) ebullición, *f*, hervor, *m*; *Fig.* efervescencia, *f*, estallido, *m*

eccentric /ɪk'sɛntrɪk/ *a* Geom. excéntrico; raro, original; extravagante, excéntrico, *Lat. Am.* ideático. *n* persona excéntrica, *f*, original, *m*

eccentrically /ɪk'sɛntrɪkəli/ *adv* excéntricamente

eccentricity /,ɛksən'trɪsɪti/ *n* Geom. excentricidad, *f*; rareza, extravagancia, excentricidad, *f*

Ecclesiastes /ɪ,klizi'æstiz/ *n* Eclesiastés, *m*

ecclesiastic /ɪ,klizi'æstɪk/ *a* eclesiástico. *n* eclesiástico, clérigo, *m*

echo /'ɛkou/ *n* eco, *m*; reverberación, resonancia, *f*. *vt* repercutir; *Fig.* repetir. *vi* resonar, retumbar, reverberar

echoing /'ɛkouɪŋ/ *a* retumbante. *n* eco, *m*

eclectic /ɪ'klɛktɪk/ *a* and *n* ecléctico (-ca)

eclecticism /ɪ'klɛktə,sɪzəm/ *n* eclecticismo, *m*

eclipse /ɪ'klɪps/ *n* Astron. eclipse, *m*, *vt* eclipsar, hacer eclipse a. **to be in e.,** estar en eclipse

ecliptic /ɪ'klɪptɪk/ *n* Astron. eclíptica, *f*, *a* eclíptico

eclogue /'ɛklɔg/ *n* égloga, *f*

ecologist /ɪ'kɒlədʒɪst/ *n* ecólogo (-ga)

ecology /ɪ'kɒlədʒi/ *n* ecología, *f*

economic /,ɛkə'nɒmɪk, ,ikə-/ *a* económico

economical /,ɛkə'nɒmɪkəl, ,ikə-/ *a* económico

economics /,ɛkə'nɒmɪks, ,ikə-/ *n* economía política, *f*

economist /ɪ'kɒnəmɪst/ *n* economista, *mf*

economize /ɪ'kɒnə,maiz/ *vt* economizar, ahorrar. *vi* hacer economías

economy /ɪ'kɒnəmi/ *n* economía, *f*. **domestic e.,** economía doméstica, *f*. **political e.,** economía política, *f*

ecosystem /'ɛkou,sɪstəm/ *n* ecosistema, *m*

ecstasy /'ɛkstəsi/ *n* éxtasis, arrebato, *m*; transporte, *m*. **to be in e.,** estar en éxtasis

ecstatic /ɛk'stætɪk/ *a* extático

Ecuador /'ɛkwə,dɔr/ *n* el Ecuador

Ecuadorian /,ɛkwə'dɔriən/ *a* and *n* ecuatoriano (-na)

ecumenical /'ɛkyu'mɛnɪkəl/ *a* ecuménico

eczema /'ɛksəmə/ *n* eczema, *f*

eddy /'ɛdi/ *n* remolino, *m*, *vi* remolinar; *Fig.* remolinear

edelweiss /'eidl,wais/ *n* inmortal de las nieves, *f*

edema /ɪ'dimə/ *n* edema, *m*

Eden /'idn/ *n* Edén, *m*

edge /ɛdʒ/ *n* (of sharp instruments) filo, *m*; (of a skate) cuchilla, *f*; margen, *mf*; (shore) orilla, *f*; (of two surfaces) arista, *f*; (of books) borde, *m*; (of a coin) canto, *m*; (of a chair, a precipice, a forest, a curb, etc.) borde, *m*; (extreme) extremidad, *f*. **on e.,** de canto; *Fig.* ansioso. **to be on e.,** *Fig.* tener los nervios en punta. **to set on e.,** poner de canto; (of teeth) dar dentera

edge /ɛdʒ/ *vt* (sharpen) afilar; *Sew.* ribetear; orlar; poner un borde (a); (cut) cortar. **to e. away,** escurrirse. **to e. into,** *vt* insinuarse. *vi* deslizarse en. **to e. out,** salir poco a poco

edged /ɛdʒd/ *a* afilado, cortante; (in compounds) de... filos; (bordered) bordeado; (of books) de bordes...

edgewise /'ɛdʒwaiz/ *adv* de lado; de canto. **He couldn't get a word in e.,** No pudo meter baza en la conversación

edging /'ɛdʒɪŋ/ *n* borde, *m*; ribete, *m*

edibility /,ɛdə'bɪlɪti/ *n* el ser comestible

edible /'ɛdəbəl/ *a* comestible

edict /'idɪkt/ *n* edicto, *m*

edification /,ɛdəfɪ'keiʃən/ *n* edificación, *f*

edifice /'ɛdəfɪs/ *n* edificio, *m*

edify /'ɛdə,fai/ *vt* edificar

edifying /'ɛdə,faiɪŋ/ *a* edificante, edificador, de edificación

Edinburgh /'ɛdn,bərə/ *n* Edinburgo, *m*

edit /'ɛdɪt/ *vt* editar; (a newspaper, journal) ser director de; (prepare for press) redactar; (correct) corregir

editing /'ɛdɪtɪŋ/ *n* trabajo editorial, *m*; redacción, *f*; dirección, *f*; corrección, *f*

edition /ɪ'dɪʃən/ *n* edición, *f*; *Print.* tirada, *f*. **first e.,** edición príncipe, *f*. **miniature e.,** edición diamante, *f*

editor /'ɛdɪtər/ *n* (of a book) editor (-ra); (of a newspaper, journal) director (-ra)

editorial /,ɛdɪ'tɔriəl/ *n* artículo de fondo, *m*. **e. staff,** redacción, *f* editorial, *a* editorial. *n* editorial board consejo de redacción, *m*

editorship /'ɛdɪtər,ʃɪp/ *n* dirección (de un periódico, de una revista), *f*

educability /,ɛdʒəkə'bɪlɪti/ *n* educabilidad, *f*

educable /'ɛdʒəkəbəl/ *a* educable

educate /'ɛdʒə,keit/ *vt* educar; formar; (accustom) acostumbrar

educated /'ɛdʒə,keitɪd/ *a* culto

education /,ɛdʒə'keiʃən/ *n* educación, *f*; enseñanza, *f*; pedagogía, *f*. **chair of e.,** cátedra de pedagogía, *f*. **early e.,** primeras letras, *f pl*. **higher e.,** enseñanza superior, *f*

educational /,ɛdʒə'keiʃənļ/ *a* educativo; pedagógico; instructivo

educationalist /,ɛdʒə'keiʃənļɪst/ *n* pedagogo (-ga)

educative /'ɛdʒə,keitɪv/ *a* educativo

educator /'ɛdʒə,keitər/ *n* educador (-ra)

educe /ɪ'dus/ *vt* educir; deducir; *Chem.* extraer

eduction /ɪ'dʌkʃən/ *n* educción, *f*

eel /il/ *n* anguila, *f*. **electric eel,** gimnoto, *m*. **eel-basket,** nasa para anguilas, *f*

eerie /'ɪəri/ *a* misterioso, fantástico; sobrenatural; lúgubre

eerily /'ɪərəli/ *adv* fantásticamente; de modo sobrenatural

eeriness /'ɪərɪnɪs/ *n* ambiente de misterio, *m*; efecto misterioso, *m*

efface /ɪ'feis/ *vt* borrar, destruir; quitar. **to e. one-self,** retirarse; permanecer en el fondo

effacement /ɪ'feismənt/ *n* borradura, *f*

effect /ɪ'fɛkt/ *n* efecto, *m*; impresión, *f*; (result) resultado, *m*, consecuencia, *f*; (meaning) substancia, *f*, significado, *m*; *pl* **effects,** efectos, bienes, *m pl*. **to** efectuar; producir. **in e.,** en efecto, efectivamente. **of no e.,** inútil. **striving after e.,** efectismo, *m*. **to feel the effects of,** sentir los efectos de; padecer las consecuencias de. **to put into e.,** poner en práctica; hacer efectivo. **to take e.,** producir efecto; ponerse en vigor

effective /ɪ'fɛktɪv/ *a* eficaz; (striking) de mucho efecto, poderoso, vistoso. **to make e.**, llevar a efecto
effectively /ɪ'fɛktɪvli/ *adv* eficazmente; (strikingly) con gran efecto; efectivamente, en efecto
effectiveness /ɪ'fɛktɪvnɪs/ *n* eficacia, *f*; efecto, *m*
effectuate /ɪ'fɛktʃu,eit/ *vt* efectuar
effeminacy /ɪ'fɛmənəsi/ *n* afeminación, *f*
effeminate /ɪ'fɛmənɪt/ *a* afeminado, adamado. **to make e.**, afeminar
efferent /'ɛfərənt/ *a* eferente
effervesce /,ɛfər'vɛs/ *vi* estar efervescente, hervir
effervescence /,ɛfər'vɛsəns/ *n* efervescencia, *f*
effervescent /,ɛfər'vɛsənt/ *a* efervescente
effete /ɪ'fit/ *a* gastado; estéril; decadente
effeteness /ɪ'fitnɪs/ *n* decadencia, *f*; esterilidad, *f*
efficacious /,ɛfɪ'keiʃəs/ *a* eficaz
efficacy /'ɛfɪkəsi/ *n* eficacia, *f*
efficiency /ɪ'fɪʃənsi/ *n* eficiencia, *f*; buen estado, *m*; habilidad, *f*; *Mech.* rendimiento, *m*
efficient /ɪ'fɪʃənt/ *a* (e.g. medicine) eficaz; eficiente; (person) competente, capaz
efficiently /ɪ'fɪʃəntli/ *adv* eficientemente; eficazmente; competentemente
effigy /'ɛfɪdʒi/ *n* efigie, imagen, *f*
efflorescence /,ɛflə'rɛsəns/ *n Chem.* eflorescencia, *f*; *Bot.* florescencia, *f*
effluvium /ɪ'fluviəm/ *n* efluvio, *m*
effort /'ɛfərt/ *n* esfuerzo, *m*. **to make an e.**, hacer un esfuerzo. **make every effort to**, hacer lo posible por + *inf*; empeñar sus máximos esfuerzos en el sentido de + *inf*
effortless /'ɛfərtlɪs/ *a* sin esfuerzo
effrontery /ɪ'frʌntəri/ *n* descaro, *m*, insolencia, *f*
effulgence /ɪ'fʌldʒəns/ *n* esplendor, fulgor, *m*
effulgent /ɪ'fʌldʒənt/ *a* fulgente, resplandeciente
effusion /ɪ'fyuʒən/ *n* efusión, *f*
effusive /ɪ'fyusɪv/ *a* efusivo, expansivo
egg /ɛg/ *n* huevo, *m*. **to egg on**, incitar (a). **boiled egg**, huevo cocido, *m*. **fried egg**, huevo frito, *m*. **hard egg**, huevo duro, *m*. **poached egg**, huevo escalfado, *m*. **scrambled egg**, huevos revueltos, *m pl*. **soft egg**, huevo pasado por agua, *m*. **to lay eggs**, poner huevos. **to put all one's eggs in one basket,** *Fig.* poner toda la carne en el asador. **egg-cup,** huevera, *f*. **egg dealer**, vendedor (-ra) de huevos. **egg flip**, huevo batido con ron, *m*. **eggplant,** berenjena, *f*. **egg-shaped,** aovado. **egg-shell,** cascarón, *m*, cáscara de huevo, *f*. **egg-shell china,** loza muy fina, *f*. **egg-spoon,** cucharita para comer huevos, *f*. **egg-whisk,** batidor de huevos, *m*
ego /'igou/ *n* (psychology) el yo, *m*
egoism /'igou,ɪzəm/ *n* egoísmo, *m*
egoist /'igouɪst/ *n* egoísta, *mf*
egoistic /,igou'ɪstɪk/ *a* egoísta
egoistically /,igou'ɪstɪkəli/ *adv* egoístamente
egotism /'igə,tɪzəm/ *n* egotismo, *m*, egolatría, *f*
egotist /'igətɪst/ *n* egotista, *mf*
egotistic /,igə'tɪstɪk/ *a* egotista
egregious /ɪ'gridʒəs/ *a* notorio, atroz
egress /'igrɛs/ *n* salida, *f*
Egypt /'idʒɪpt/ Egipto, *m*
Egyptian /ɪ'dʒɪpʃən/ *a* egipcio. *n* egipcio (-ia); cigarrillo egipcio, *m*
Egyptologist /,idʒɪp'tɒlədʒɪst/ *n* egiptólogo (-ga)
Egyptology /,idʒɪp'tɒlədʒi/ *n* egiptología, *f*
eh? /ei/ *interj* ¿eh? ¿qué?
eider /'aidər/ *n Ornith.* pato de flojel, *m*
eiderdown /'aidər,daun/ *n* edredón, *m*
eight /eit/ *a* and *n* ocho *m*. **He is e. years old,** Tiene ocho años. **It is e. o'clock,** Son las ocho. **e.-day clock,** reloj con cuerda para ocho días, *m*. **e. hundred,** *a* and *n* ochocientos *m.*. **e.-syllabled,** octosilábico
eighteen /'ei'tin/ *a* and *n* diez y ocho, *m*
eighteenth /'ei'tinθ/ *a* décimoctavo; (of the month) (el) diez y ocho, diecíocho; (of monarchs) diez y ocho. *n* décimoctava parte, *f*. **e. century,** el siglo diez y ocho
eightfold /'eit,fould/ *a* óctuple

eighth /eitθ, eiθ/ *a* octavo, *m*; (of the month) (el) ocho; (of monarchs) octavo. *n* octavo, *m*
eighthly /'eitθli/ *adv* en octavo lugar
eightieth /'eitiiθ/ *a* octogésimo
eighty /'eiti/ *a* and *n* ochenta, *m*.
either /'iðər/ *a* and *pron* uno u otro, cualquiera de los dos; ambos (-as). *conjunc* o (becomes **u** before words beginning with **o** or **ho**). *adv* tampoco. **I do not like e.,** No me gusta ni el uno ni el otro (ni la una ni la otra). **e.... or,** o... o
ejaculate /ɪ'dʒækyə,leit/ *vt* exclamar, lanzar; *Med.* eyacular
ejaculation /ɪ,dʒækyə'leiʃən/ *n* exclamación, *f*; *Med.* eyaculación, *f*
ejaculatory /ɪ'dʒækyələ,tɔri/ *a* jaculatorio
eject /ɪ'dʒɛkt/ *vt* echar, expulsar; *Law.* desahuciar; (emit) despedir, emitir
ejection /ɪ'dʒɛkʃən/ *n* echamiento, *m*, expulsión, *f*; *Law.* desahúcio, *m*; (emission) emisión, *f*
eke out /ik/ *vt* (make funds last) hacer alcanzar. **e. out a living,** ganarse la vida a duras penas.
elaborate /*a* ɪ'læbərɪt; *v* -ə,reit/ *a* elaborado; primoroso; elegante; complicado; (detailed) detallado; (of meals) de muchos platos; (of courtesy, etc.) estudiado. *vt* elaborar; amplificar
elaborately /ɪ'læbərɪtli/ *adv* primorosamente; elegantemente; complicadamente; con muchos detalles
elaborateness /ɪ'læbərɪtnɪs/ *n* primor, *m*; elegancia, *f*; complicación, *f*; (care) cuidado, *m*; minuciosidad, *f*
elaboration /ɪ,læbə'reiʃən/ *n* elaboración, *f*
elapse /ɪ'læps/ *vi* transcurrir, andar, pasar
elastic /ɪ'læstɪk/ *a* elástico. *n* elástico, *m*. **e. band,** anillo de goma, *m*; cinta de goma, *f*. **e. girdle,** faja elástica, *f*
elasticity /ɪlæ'stɪsɪti/ *n* elasticidad, *f*
elate /ɪ'leit/ *vt* alegrar; animar
elatedly /ɪ'leitɪdli/ *adv* alegremente; triunfalmente
elation /ɪ'leiʃən/ *n* alegría, *f*, júbilo, *m*; triunfo, *m*
elbow /'ɛlbou/ *n* codo, *m*; ángulo, *m*; (of a chair) brazo, *m*. *vt* codear, dar codazos (a). **at one's e.,** a la mano. **nudge with the e.,** codazo, *m*. **to be out at e.,** enseñar los codos, tener los codos raídos; ser harapiento. **to e. one's way,** abrirse paso a codazos. **e.-chair,** silla de brazos, *f*. **e.-grease,** jugo de muñeca, *m*. **e.-piece** or **patch,** codera, *f*. **e. room,** libertad de movimiento, *f*
elder /'ɛldər/ *a comp* mayor. *n* persona mayor, *f*; señor mayor, *m*; (among Jews and in Christian Church) anciano, *m*; *Bot.* saúco, *m*
elderly /'ɛldərli/ *a* mayor
eldest /'ɛldɪst/ *a sup* mayor (el, la, etc.) mayor. **e. daughter,** hija mayor, *f*. **e. son,** hijo mayor, *m*
elect /ɪ'lɛkt/ *vt* elegir. *a* elegido; predestinado. *n* electo, *m*; elegido, *m*
election /ɪ'lɛkʃən/ *n Theol.* predestinación, *f*; elección, *f*. **by-e.,** elección parcial, *f*
electioneer /ɪ,lɛkʃə'nɪər/ *vi* solicitar votos; hacer propaganda electoral
electioneering /ɪ,lɛkʃə'nɪərɪŋ/ *n* solicitación de votos, *f*; propaganda electoral, *f*
elective /ɪ'lɛktɪv/ *a* electivo. *n* (subject at school) materia optativa, *f*
elector /ɪ'lɛktər/ *n* elector (-ra); (prince) elector, *m*
electoral /ɪ'lɛktərəl/ *a* electoral. **e. register,** lista electoral, *f*
electoral college colegio de compromisarios, *m*
electorate /ɪ'lɛktərɪt/ *n* electorado, *m*
electric, electrical /ɪ'lɛktrɪk; ɪ'lɛktrɪkəl/ *a* eléctrico; *Fig.* vivo, instantáneo. **e. arc,** arco voltaico, *m*. **e. engineer,** ingeniero electricista, *m*. **electric fan,** (Spain) ventilador (Western Hemisphere) ventilador eléctrico, *m*. **e. fire,** estufa eléctrica, *f*. **e. immersion heater,** calentador de agua eléctrico, *m*. **e. light,** luz eléctrica, *f*. **e. pad,** alfombrilla eléctrica, *f*. **e. shock,** conmoción eléctrica, *f*. **e. washing-machine,** lavadora eléctrica, *f*. **e. wire** or **cable,** conductor eléctrico, *m*
electrically /ɪ'lɛktrɪkəli/ *adv* por electricidad
electrician /ɪlɛk'trɪʃən/ *n* electricista, *mf*
electricity /ɪlɛk'trɪsɪti/ *n* electricidad, *f*
electrification /ɪ,lɛktrəfɪ'keiʃən/ *n* electrificación, *f*

electrify /ɪ'lektrə,fai/ vt electrificar; Fig. electrizar

electro- prefix (in compounds) electro. **e.-chemistry,** electroquímica, f. **e.-dynamics,** electrodinámica, f. **e.-magnet,** electroimán, m. **e.-magnetic,** electromagnético. **e.-plate,** vt galvanizar, platear. n artículo galvanizado, m. **e.-therapy,** electroterapia, f

electrocute /ɪ'lektrə,kyut/ vt electrocutar

electrocution /ɪ,lektrə'kyuʃən/ n electrocución, f

electrode /ɪ'lektroud/ n electrodo, m

electrolysis /ɪlek'trɒləsɪs/ n electrólisis, f

electrolyte /ɪ'lektrə,lait/ n electrólito, m

electrolyze /ɪ'lektrə,laiz/ vt electrolizar

electrometer /ɪlek'trɒmɪtər/ n electrómetro, m

electromotive /ɪ,lektrə'moutɪv/ a electromotriz. **e. force,** fuerza electromotriz, f

electron /ɪ'lektrɒn/ n electrón, m

electroscope /ɪ'lektrə,skoup/ n electroscopio, m

elegance /'elɪgəns/ n elegancia, f

elegant /'elɪgənt/ a elegante; bello

elegantly /'elɪgəntli/ adv elegantemente, con elegancia

elegiac /,elɪ'dʒaiək/ a elegíaco

elegy /'elɪdʒi/ n elegía, f

element /'eləmənt/ n elemento, m; factor, m; ingrediente, m; Elec. par, elemento, m; Chem., Phys. cuerpo simple, m; pl **elements,** rudimentos, m pl, nociones, f pl; (weather) intemperie, f; (Eucharist) el pan y el vino. **to be in one's e.,** estar en su elemento

elemental /,elə'mɛntl/ a elemental; rudimentario, lo elemental

elementariness /,elə'mɛntərinɪs/ n el carácter, elemental

elementary /,elə'mɛntəri/ a elemental; rudimentario; primario. **e. education,** enseñanza primaria, f

elephant /'eləfənt/ n elefante (-ta). **e. keeper** or **trainer,** naire, m

elephantiasis /,eləfən'taiəsɪs/ n elefantíasis, f

elephantine /,elə'fæntin/ a elefantino

elevate /'elə,veit/ vt (the Host) alzar; elevar; (the eyes, the voice) levantar; (honor) enaltecer

elevated /'elə,veitɪd/ a noble, elevado, sublime; edificante; (drunk) achispado

elevation /,elə'veiʃən/ n elevación, f; enaltecimiento, m; (of style, thought) nobleza, sublimidad, f; (hill) eminencia, altura, f

elevator /'elə,veitər/ n (lift) ascensor, m; (for grain, etc.) montacargas, m

elevator shaft caja, f, hueco pozo, m

eleven /ɪ'levən/ a once. n once, m. **It is e. o'clock,** Son las once

eleventh /ɪ'levənθ/ a onceno, undécimo; (of month) (el) once; (of monarchs) once. n onzavo, m; undécima parte, f. **at the e. hour,** Fig. a última hora.

Louis the E., Luis once (XI)

elf /elf/ n elfo, duende, m; (child) trasgo, m; (dwarf) enano, m

elfin /'elfɪn/ a de duendes; de hada

elicit /ɪ'lɪsɪt/ vt sacar; hacer contestar; hacer confesar; descubrir

elicitation /ɪ,lɪsɪ'teiʃən/ n descubrimiento, m

elide /ɪ'laid/ vt elidir

eligibility /,elɪdʒə'bɪlɪti/ n elegibilidad, f

eligible /'elɪdʒəbəl/ a elegible; deseable

eliminate /ɪ'lɪmə,neit/ vt eliminar; quitar

elimination /ɪ,lɪmə'neiʃən/ n eliminación, f

eliminatory /ɪ'lɪmənə,tɔri/ a eliminador

elision /ɪ'lɪʒən/ n elisión, f

elite /ɪ'lit/ n élite, elite, f

elitism /ɪ'litɪzəm/ n elitismo, m

elixir /ɪ'lɪksər/ n elixir, m

Elizabethan /ɪ,lɪzə'biθən/ a de la época de la Reina Isabel I de Inglaterra

elk /elk/ n ante, m

ell /el/ n (measure) ana, f

ellipse /ɪ'lɪps/ n Geom. elipse, f; óvalo, m

ellipsis /ɪ'lɪpsɪs/ n Gram. elipsis, f

elliptic /ɪ'lɪptɪk/ a Geom., Gram. elíptico

elm /elm/ n olmo, m. **e. grove,** olmeda, f

elocution /,elə'kyuʃən/ n elocución, f; (art of elocution) declamación, f

elocutionist /,elə'kyuʃənɪst/ n recitador (-ra), declamador (-ra)

elongate /ɪ'lɔŋgeit/ vt alargar; extender. vi alargarse; extenderse. a alargado; (of face) perfilado

elongation /ɪlɔŋ'geiʃən/ n alargamiento, m; prolongación, f; extensión, f

elope /ɪ'loup/ vi evadirse, huir; fugarse (con un amante)

elopement /ɪ'loupmənt/ n fuga, f

eloquence /'eləkwəns/ n elocuencia, f

eloquent /'eləkwənt/ a elocuente

eloquently /'eləkwəntli/ adv elocuentemente

else /els/ adv (besides) más; (instead) otra cosa, más; (otherwise) si no, de otro modo. **anyone e.,** (cualquier) otra persona; alguien más. **Anything e.?** ¿Algo más? **everyone e.,** todos los demás. **everything e.,** todo lo demás. **nobody e.,** ningún otro, nadie más. **nothing e.,** nada más. **or e.,** o bien, de otro modo; si no. **someone e.,** otra persona, otro. **somewhere e.,** en otra parte. **There's nothing e. to do,** No hay nada más que hacer; No hay más remedio

elsewhere /'els,wɛər/ adv a, or en, otra parte

elucidate /ɪ'lusɪ,deit/ vt elucidar, aclarar

elucidation /ɪ,lusɪ'deiʃən/ n elucidación, aclaración, f

elucidatory /ɪ'lusɪdə,tɔri/ a aclaratorio

elude /ɪ'lud/ vt eludir, evitar

elusive /ɪ'lusɪv/ a (of persons) esquivo; fugaz; difícil de comprender

elusiveness /ɪ'lusɪvnɪs/ n esquivez, f; fugacidad, f

Elysian /ɪ'lɪʒən/ a elíseo. **E. Fields,** campos elíseos, m pl

Elysium /ɪ'lɪʒiəm/ n elíseo, m

emaciate /ɪ'meiʃi,eit/ vt extenuar, demacrar, enflaquecer

emaciated /ɪ'meiʃi,eitɪd/ a extenuado, demacrado. **to become e.,** demacrarse

emaciation /ɪ,meiʃi'eiʃən/ n demacración, emaciación, f; Med. depauperación, f

e-mail /'i,meil/ n correo electrónico, m. **e. message,** mensaje de correo electrónico, m

emanate /'emə,neit/ vi emanar (de), proceder (de)

emanation /,emə'neiʃən/ n emanación, f; exhalación, f

emancipate /ɪ'mænsə,peit/ vt emancipar

emancipated /ɪ'mænsə,peitɪd/ a emancipado

emancipation /ɪ,mænsə'peiʃən/ n emancipación, f

emancipator /ɪ'mænsə,peitər/ n emancipador (-ra), libertador (-ra)

emasculate /a ɪ'mæskyəlɪt/ v -,leit/ a afeminado. vt emascular; Fig. afeminar; mutilar

emasculation /ɪ,mæskyə'leiʃən/ n emasculación, f

embalm /ɛm'bam/ vt embalsamar; Fig. conservar el recuerdo de; perfumar

embalmer /ɛm'bamər/ n embalsamador, m

embalmment /ɛm'bammənt/ n embalsamamiento, m

embankment /ɛm'bæŋkmənt/ n declive, m; ribera, f; terraplén, m; dique, m; (quay) muelle, m

embargo /ɛm'bargou/ n embargo, m, vt embargar. **to put an e. on,** embargar. **to remove an e.,** sacar de embargo

embark /ɛm'bark/ vi embarcarse; lanzarse (a). vt embarcar

embarkation /,embar'keiʃən/ n (of persons) embarcación, f; (of goods) embarque, m

embarrass /ɛm'bærəs/ vt avergonzar, impedir; (financially) apurar; (perplex) tener perplejo; (worry) preocupar; (confuse) desconcertar, turbar; (annoy) molestar

embarrassed /ɛm'bærəst/ a avergonzado, turbado

embarrassing /ɛm'bærəsɪŋ/ a avergonzoso, embarazoso; desconcertante; molesto

embarrassingly /ɛm'bærəsɪŋli/ adv de un modo desconcertante; demasiado

embarrassment /ɛm'bærəsmənt/ n bochorno, m; vergüenza, f; pena, f; (financial) apuro, m; (obligation) compromiso, m; (perplexity) perplejidad, f; (worry) preocupación, f; (confusion) turbación, f

embassy /'ɛmbəsi/ n embajada, f

embattled /ɛm'bæt̬ld/ *a* en orden de batalla; *Herald.* almenado
embed /ɛm'bɛd/ *vt* empotrar, enclavar; fijar
embellish /ɛm'bɛlɪʃ/ *vt* embellecer; adornar
embellishment /ɛm'bɛlɪʃmənt/ *n* embellecimiento, *m*; adorno, *m*
ember /'ɛmbər/ *n* rescoldo, *m*. **E. days**, témporas, *f pl*
embezzle /ɛm'bɛzəl/ *vt* desfalcar
embezzlement /ɛm'bɛzəlmənt/ *n* desfalco, *m*
embezzler /ɛm'bɛzlər/ *n* desfalcador (-ra)
embitter /ɛm'bɪtər/ *vt Fig.* amargar; envenenar
embittering /ɛm'bɪtərɪŋ/ *a* amargo
embitterment /ɛm'bɪtərmənt/ *n* amargura, *f*
emblazon /ɛm'bleizən/ *vt* blasonar; *Fig.* ensalzar
emblem /'ɛmbləm/ *n* emblema, *m*
emblematic /ˌɛmblə'mætɪk/ *a* emblemático
embodiment /ɛm'bɒdimənt/ *n* incarnación, *f*; expresión, *f*; personificación, *f*; símbolo, *m*; síntesis, *f*
embody /ɛm'bɒdi/ *vt* encarnar; expresar; personificar; incorporar; contener; formular; sintetizar. **to be embodied in,** quedar plasmado en
embolden /ɛm'bouldən/ *vt* animar, dar valor (a)
embolism /'ɛmbə,lizəm/ *n Med.* embolia, *f*
emboss /ɛm'bɔs/ *vt* repujar, abollonar; estampar en relieve
embossment /ɛm'bɔsmənt/ *n* abolladura, *f*; relieve, *m*
embrace /ɛm'breis/ *n* abrazo, *m. vt* abrazar, dar un abrazo (a); (*Fig.*. seize) aprovechar; (accept) aceptar; adoptar; (engage in) dedicarse a; (comprise) incluir, abarcar; (comprehend) comprender. **They embraced,** Se abrazaron
embroider /ɛm'brɔidər/ *vt* bordar; embellecer; (a tale, etc.) exagerar; *vi* hacer bordado
embroiderer /ɛm'brɔidərər/ *n* bordador (-ra)
embroidery /ɛm'brɔidəri, -dri/ *n* bordado, *m*; labor, *f*. **e.-frame,** bastidor, *m*. **e. silk,** hilo de bordar, *m*
embroil /ɛm'brɔil/ *vt* enredar, embrollar; desordenar
embryo /'ɛmbri,ou/ *n* embrión, *m*; *Fig.* germen, *m. a* embrionario
embryology /ˌɛmbri'blədʒi/ *n* embriología, *f*
embryonic /ˌɛmbri'ɒnɪk/ *a* embrionario
emend /ɪ'mɛnd/ *vt* enmendar; corregir
emendation /ˌimən'deiʃən/ *n* enmienda, *f*; corrección, *f*
emerald /'ɛmərəld/ *n* esmeralda, *f*, *a* de color de esmeralda. **e. green,** verde esmeralda, *m*
emerge /ɪ'mɜrdʒ/ *vi* emerger; surgir; *Fig.* salir; aparecer
emergence /ɪ'mɜrdʒəns/ *n* emergencia, *f*; salida, *f*; aparición, *f*
emergency /ɪ'mɜrdʒənsi/ *n* urgencia, *f*; necesidad, *f*; emergencia, *f*; aprieto, *m*. **e. exit,** salida de urgencia, *f*. **e. port,** *Naut.* puerto de arribada, *m*
emergent /ɪ'mɜrdʒənt/ *a* emergente; que sale; naciente
emery /'ɛməri/ *n* esmeril, *m*. **to polish with e.,** esmerilar. **e.-paper,** papel de lija, *m*
emetic /ɪ'mɛtɪk/ *a* and *n* emético, vomitivo, *m*.
emigrant /'ɛmigrənt/ *a* emigrante. *n* emigrante, *mf* emigrado, *m*
emigrate /'ɛmi,greit/ *vi* emigrar; *Inf.* trasladarse
emigration /ˌɛmə'greiʃən/ *n* emigración, *f*. **e. officer,** oficial de emigración, *m*
eminence /'ɛmənəns/ *n* (hill) elevación, prominencia, *f*; eminencia (also as title), *f*; distinción, *f*
eminent /'ɛmənənt/ *a* distinguido, eminente; famoso, ilustre; notable; conspicuo
eminently /'ɛmənəntli/ *adv* eminentemente
emir /ə'mɪər/ *n* amir, *m*
emissary /'ɛmə,sɛri/ *n* emisario (-ia); embajador (-ra), agente, *m*
emission /ɪ'mɪʃən/ *n* emisión, *f*
emit /ɪ'mɪt/ *vt* despedir; exhalar; emitir
emollient /ɪ'mɒlyənt/ *a* emoliente, lenitivo. *n* emoliente, *m*
emolument /ɪ'mɒlyəmənt/ *n* emolumento, *m*
emotion /ɪ'mouʃən/ *n* emoción, *f*. **to cause e.,** emocionar

emotional /ɪ'mouʃənl/ *a* emocional, sentimental; emocionante
emotionalism /ɪ'mouʃənlˌizəm/ *n* sentimentalismo, *m*
emotionalize /ɪ'mouʃənlˌaiz/ *vt* considerar bajo un punto de vista sentimental
emotionally /ɪ'mouʃənlˌi/ *adv* con emoción, sentimentalmente
emotionless /ɪ'mouʃənlɪs/ *a* sin emoción
emotive /ɪ'moutɪv/ *a* emotivo
emperor /'ɛmpərər/ *n* emperador, *m*
emphasis (on) /'ɛmfəsɪs/ *n* énfasis (en), *mf*; insistencia especial (en), especial atención (a), *f*; accentuación, *f*
emphasize /'ɛmfə,saiz/ *vt* subrayar, dar énfasis a, poner de relieve, hacer resaltar, dar importancia a; acentuar; insistir en, hacer hincapié (en)
emphatic /ɛm'fætɪk/ *a* enfático
emphatically /ɛm'fætɪkəli/ *adv* con énfasis
empire /'ɛmpaiⁱr/ *n* imperio, *m*
empirical /ɛm'pɪrɪkəl/ *a* empírico
empiricism /ɛm'pɪrə,sɪzəm/ *n* empirismo, *m*
employ /ɛm'plɔi/ *n* empleo, *m*; servicio, *m. vt* emplear; ocupar; tomar; servirse de, usar. **How do you e. yourself?** ¿Cómo te ocupas? ¿Cómo pasas el tiempo?
employable /ɛm'plɔiəbəl/ *a* empleable; utilizable
employee /ɛm'plɔii/ *n* empleado (-da)
employer /ɛm'plɔiər/ *n* el, *m*, (*f*, la) que emplea; dueño (-ña), amo (-a); patrón (-ona)
employment /ɛm'plɔimənt/ *n* empleo, *m*; uso, *m*; ocupación, *f*; aprovechamiento, *m*; (post) puesto, cargo, *m*; (situation) colocación, *f*. **e. exchange,** bolsa de trabajo, *f*
emporium /ɛm'pɔriəm/ *n* emporio, *m*; (store) almacén, *m*
empower /ɛm'pauər/ *vt* autorizar; permitir; ayudar (a); dar el poder (para)
empress /'ɛmprɪs/ *n* emperatriz, *f*
emptiness /'ɛmptinɪs/ *n* vaciedad, *f*; futilidad, *f*; vacuidad, *f*; (verbosity) palabrería, *f*
empty /'ɛmpti/ *a* vacío; (of a house, etc.) deshabitado, desocupado; (deserted) desierto; (vain) vano, inútil; frívolo; (hungry) hambriento. *n* envase vacío, *m. vt* vaciar; descargar. *vi* vaciarse; (river, etc.) desembocar, venir a morir en. **e.-handed,** con las manos vacías. **e.-headed,** casquivano
emptying /'ɛmptiɪŋ/ *n* vaciamiento, *m*; abandono, *m*; *pl* **emptyings,** heces de la cerveza, *f pl*
emu /'imyu/ *n* emu, *m*
emulate /'ɛmyə,leit/ *vt* emular
emulation /ˌɛmyə'leiʃən/ *n* emulación, *f*
emulative /'ɛmyə,leitɪv/ *a* emulador
emulsify /ɪ'mʌlsifai/ *vt* emulsionar
emulsion /ɪ'mʌlʃən/ *n* emulsión, *f*
emulsive /ɪ'mʌlsɪv/ *a* emulsivo
enable /ɛn'eibəl/ *vt* (to) hacer capaz (de); ayudar (a); autorizar (para); permitir (de)
enact /ɛn'ækt/ *vt Law.* promulgar; decretar; (a part) hacer, desempeñar (un papel); (a play) representar; (happen) ocurrir, tener lugar
enaction /ɛn'ækʃən/ *n Law.* promulgación, *f*
enamel /ɪ'næməl/ *n* esmalte, *m*, *vt* esmaltar
enameler /ɪ'næmələr/ *n* esmaltador (-ra)
enameling /ɪ'næməlɪŋ/ *n* esmaltadura, *f*
enamor /ɪ'næmər/ *vt* enamorar. **to be enamored of,** estar enamorado de; estar aficionado a
encamp /ɛn'kæmp/ *vt* and *vi* acampar
encampment /ɛn'kæmpmənt/ *n* campamento, *m*
encase /ɛn'keis/ *vt* encajar; encerrar; (line) forrar
encasement /ɛn'keismənt/ *n* encaje, *f*; encierro, *m*
encephalitis /ɛn,sefə'laitis/ *n* encefalitis, *f*. **e. lethargica,** encefalitis letárgica, *f*
enchant /ɛn'tʃænt/ *vt* encantar, hechizar; fascinar; embelesar, deleitar
enchanter /ɛn'tʃæntər/ *n* encantador, *m*
enchanting /ɛn'tʃæntɪŋ/ *a* encantador, fascinador
enchantment /ɛn'tʃæntmənt/ *n* encantamiento, *m*; fascinación, *f*; encanto, deleite, *m*
enchantress /ɛn'tʃæntrɪs/ *n* bruja, *f*; *Fig.* mujer seductora, *f*

encircle /ɛn'sɜrkəl/ vt cercar; rodear; dar la vuelta (a)

enclose /ɛn'klouz/ vt cercar; meter dentro de; encerrar; (with a letter, etc.) incluir, adjuntar

enclosed /ɛn'klouzd/ a (of letters) adjunto

enclosure /ɛn'klouʒər/ n cercamiento, m; cercado, m; recinto, m; (wall) tapia, cerca, f; (with a letter) contenido adjunto, m

encomium /ɛn'koumiəm/ n encomio, m

encompass /ɛn'kʌmpəs/ vt cercar, rodear

encore /'ɑŋkɔr/ n repetición, f, interj ¡bis!

encounter /ɛn'kauntər/ n encuentro, m; combate, m; conflicto, m; lucha, f. vt encontrar; atacar; tropezar con

encourage /ɛn'kʌrɪdʒ/ vt animar; alentar; darle ánimo a; estimular; incitar; ayudar; (approve) aprobar; (foster) fomentar

encouragement /ɛn'kʌrɪdʒmənt/ n ánimos, m pl; estímulo, incentivo, m; ayuda, f; (approval) aprobación, f; (promotion) fomento, m

encourager /ɛn'kʌrɪdʒər/ n instigador (-ra); ayudador (-ra); aprobador (-ra); fomentador (-ra)

encouraging /ɛn'kʌrɪdʒɪŋ/ a alentador; estimulante; fomentador; (favorable) halagüeño, favorable

encouragingly /ɛn'kʌrɪdʒɪŋli/ adv de un modo alentador; con aprobación

encroach /ɛn'kroutʃ/ vi usurpar; abusar (de); invadir; robar; (of sea, river) hurtar

encroaching /ɛn'kroutʃɪŋ/ a usurpador; invadiente

encroachment /ɛn'kroutʃmənt/ n usurpación, f; abuso, m; invasión, f

encrust /ɛn'krʌst/ vt encostrar; incrustar

encumber /ɛn'kʌmbər/ vt impedir, estorbar; llenar; (burden) cargar; (mortgage) hipotecar; (overwhelm) agobiar

encumbrance /ɛn'kʌmbrəns/ n impedimento, estorbo, m; gravamen, m; carga, f; (mortgage) hipoteca, f

encyclical /ɛn'sɪklɪkəl/ n encíclica, f

encyclopedia /ɛn,saɪklə'pidiə/ n enciclopedia, f

encyclopedic /ɛn,saɪklə'pidɪk/ a enciclopédico

encyclopedist /ɛn,saɪklə'pidɪst/ n enciclopedista, m

end /ɛnd/ n fin, m; extremidad, f; extremo, m; conclusión, f; (point) punta, f; cabo, m; (district) barrio, m; cabeza, f; (death) muerte, f; (aim) objeto, intento, m; (purpose) propósito, m; (issue) resultado, m; (bit) fragmento, pedazo, m; (of a word) terminación, f. vi terminar; acabar; concluir; cesar; (in) terminar en; resultar en; (with) terminar con. vt terminar; acabar, dar fin a. **at an end,** terminado. **at the end,** al cabo (de); al extremo (de). **end of quotation,** fin de cita, final de la cita, m. **from end to end,** de un extremo a otro; de un cabo a otro. **in the end,** por fin, finalmente. **on end,** de pie, de cabeza, derecho; de punta; (of hair) erizado. **no end of,** un sinnúmero de. **to make both ends meet,** pasar con lo que se tiene. **to make an end of,** acabar con. **to put an end to,** poner fin a. **to the end that,** a fin de que, para que; con objeto de. **toward the end of,** (months, years, etc.) a fines de, a últimos de; hacia el fin de. **two hours on end,** dos horas seguidas. **end-paper,** guarda, f

endanger /ɛn'deɪndʒər/ vt arriesgar, poner en peligro

endear /ɛn'dɪər/ vt hacer querer

endearing /ɛn'dɪərɪŋ/ a que inspira cariño; atrayente; cariñoso

endearment /ɛn'dɪərmənt/ n cariño, amor, m; caricia, terneza, f; palabra de cariño, f

endeavor /ɛn'dɛvər/ vi procurar, intentar, hacer un esfuerzo. n esfuerzo, m; tentativa, f

endemic /ɛn'dɛmɪk/ a Med. endémico

ending /'ɛndɪŋ/ n fin, m; conclusión, f; Gram. terminación, f; cesación, f; (climax) desenlace, m

endive /'ɛndaɪv/ n Bot. escarola, f

endless /'ɛndlɪs/ a eterno; inacabable; infinito; sin fin; interminable; incesante

endlessly /'ɛndlɪsli/ adv sin fin; incesantemente; sin parar

endlessness /'ɛndlɪsnɪs/ n eternidad, f; infinidad, f; continuidad, f

endocrine /'ɛndəkrɪn/ a endocrino. n secreción interna, f

endocrinology /,ɛndoukrə'nɒlədʒi/ n endocrinología, f

end-of-season /'ɛnd əv 'sizən/ a por final de temporada (e.g., end-of-season reductions, rebajas por final de temporada, m pl. end-of-season sale, liquidación por final de temporada, f)

endogenous /ɛn'dɒdʒənəs/ a endógeno

endorse /ɛn'dɔrs/ vt Com. endosar; garantizar; (uphold) apoyar; confirmar

endorsee /ɛndɔr'si/ n endosatario (-ia)

endorsement /ɛn'dɔrsmənt/ n Com. endoso, m; aval, m, garantía, f; corroboración, confirmación, f

endorser /ɛn'dɔrsər/ n Com. endosante, m

endow /ɛn'dau/ vt dotar; fundar; crear

endowment /ɛn'daumənt/ n dotación, f; fundación, f; creación, f; (mental) inteligencia, f; cualidad, f, don, m. **e. policy,** póliza dotal, f

endurable /ɛn'durəbəl/ a sufrible, soportable; tolerable

endurance /ɛn'durəns/ n aguante, m; resistencia, f; sufrimiento, m; tolerancia, f; paciencia, f; (lasting-ness) duración, continuación, f. **beyond e.,** intolerable, inaguantable. **e. test,** prueba de resistencia, f

endure /ɛn'dur/ vt soportar; tolerar; aguantar; sufrir; resistir. vi sufrir; (last) durar, continuar

enduring /ɛn'durɪŋ/ a permanente, perdurable; continuo; constante

enduringness /ɛn'durɪŋnɪs/ n (lastingness) permanencia, f; paciencia, f; aguante, m

enema /'ɛnəmə/ n lavativa, enema, f

enemy /'ɛnəmi/ n enemigo (-ga); adversario (-ia); (in war) enemigo, m. a del enemigo, enemigo. **to be one's own e.,** ser enemigo de sí mismo. **to become an e. of,** enemistarse con; hacerse enemigo de, volverse hostil a

energetic /,ɛnər'dʒɛtɪk/ a enérgico

energy /'ɛnərdʒi/ n energía, fuerza, f, vigor, m

enervate /v 'ɛnər,veit/ a 'ɪnɜrvɪt/ vt enervar; debilitar. a enervado

enervation /,ɛnər'veɪʃən/ n enervación, f; debilitación, f

enfeeble /ɛn'fibəl/ vt debilitar

enfeeblement /ɛn'fibəlmənt/ n debilitación, f, desfallecimiento, m

enfold /ɛn'fould/ vt envolver; abrazar

enforce /ɛn'fɔrs/ vt (a law) poner en vigor; (impose) imponer a la fuerza; hacer cumplir; conseguir por fuerza; (demonstrate) demostrar

enforcement /ɛn'fɔrsmənt/ n (of a law) ejecución (de una ley), m; imposición a la fuerza, f; observación forzosa, f

enfranchise /ɛn'fræntʃaiz/ vt emancipar; conceder derechos civiles (a)

enfranchisement /ɛn'fræntʃaizmənt/ n emancipación, f; concesión de derechos civiles, f

engage /ɛn'geɪdʒ/ vt empeñar; contratar; tomar en alquiler; tomar a su servicio; (seats, etc.) reservar; (occupy) ocupar; (attention) atraer; (in) aplicarse a, dedicarse a; Mil. combatir con, librar batalla con; atacar; (of wheels) endentar con. vi obligarse; dedicarse (a); tomar parte (en); (bet) apostar; Mil. librar batalla; (fight) venir a las manos. **to be engaged in,** traer entre manos, ocuparse en. **to become engaged,** comprometerse

engaged /ɛn'geɪdʒd/ a ocupado; (betrothed) prometido; reservado. **I have an e. at two o'clock.** Tengo una cita a las dos

engagement gift regalo de esponsales, m

engagement /ɛn'geɪdʒmənt/ n obligación, f; compromiso, m; (date) cita, f; (betrothal) palabra de casamiento, f; (battle) combate, m, batalla, f.

engaging /ɛn'geɪdʒɪŋ/ a simpático, atractivo

engagingly /ɛn'geɪdʒɪŋli/ adv de un modo encantador

engender /ɛn'dʒɛndər/ vt Fig. engendrar; excitar

engine /'ɛndʒən/ n máquina, f; motor, m; (locomotive) locomotora, f; (pump) bomba, f. **to sit with one's back to the e.,** estar sentado de espaldas a la máquina (or locomotora). **e. builder,** constructor de máquinas, m. **e. driver,** maquinista, mf. **e. room,**

cuarto de máquinas, *m*. **e. works,** taller de maquinaria, *m*

engineer /ˌɛndʒə'nɪər/ *n* ingeniero, *m*; mecánico, *m*. *vt Fig*. gestionar, arreglar. **civil e.,** ingeniero de caminos, canales y puertos, *m*. **Royal Engineers,** Cuerpo de Ingenieros, *m*

engineering /ˌɛndʒə'nɪərɪŋ/ *n* ingeniería, *f; Fig*. manejo, *m. a* de ingeniería

England /'ɪŋglənd/ Inglaterra, *f*

English /'ɪŋglɪʃ/ *a* inglés. *n* (language) inglés, *m*. **in E. fashion,** a la inglesa. **to speak E.,** hablar inglés. **to speak plain E.,** hablar sin rodeos. **E.-speaking,** anglohablante. **E. Church,** iglesia anglicana, *f*. **E.-teacher,** maestro (-ra) de inglés. **English-translator,** traductor al inglés, *m*

English Channel, the el Canal de la Mancha

Englishman /'ɪŋglɪʃmən/ *n* inglés, *m*

Englishwoman /'ɪŋglɪʃˌwʊmən/ *n* inglesa, *f*

engrain /ɛn'greɪn/ *vt* inculcar

engrave /ɛn'greɪv/ *vt* grabar; esculpir, cincelar; *Fig*. grabar

engraver /ɛn'greɪvər/ *n* grabador (-ra); (tool) cincel, *m*

engraving /ɛn'greɪvɪŋ/ *n* grabadura, *f*; (picture) grabado, *m*. **e. needle,** punta seca, *f*

engross /ɛn'grous/ *vt* (a document) poner en limpio; redactar; (absorb) absorber

engrossing /ɛn'grousɪŋ/ *a* absorbente

engulf /ɛn'gʌlf/ *vt* hundir, sumir, sumergir

enhance /ɛn'hæns/ *vt* realzar; intensificar; aumentar; mejorar

enhancement /ɛn'hænsmənt/ *n* realce, *m*; intensificación, *f*; aumento, *m*; mejoría, *f*

enigma /ə'nɪgmə/ *n* enigma, *m*

enigmatic /ˌɛnɪg'mætɪk/ *a* enigmático

enjoin /ɛn'dʒɔɪn/ *vt* imponer; ordenar, mandar; encargar

enjoy /ɛn'dʒɔɪ/ *vt* disfrutar; gustar de; gozar de; poseer, tener. **to e. oneself,** recrearse, regocijarse; (amuse oneself) divertirse; entretenerse; pasarlo bien. **Did you e. yourself?** ¿Lo pasaste bien? **E. your meal,** Buen provecho

enjoyable /ɛn'dʒɔɪəbəl/ *a* agradable; divertido, entretenido

enjoyableness /ɛn'dʒɔɪəbəlnɪs/ *n* lo agradable; lo divertido

enjoyably /ɛn'dʒɔɪəbli/ *adv* de un modo muy agradable

enjoyer /ɛn'dʒɔɪər/ *n* el, *m*, (*f*, la) que disfruta; poseedor (-ra); (amateur) aficionado (-da)

enjoyment /ɛn'dʒɔɪmənt/ *n* posesión, *f*; goce, disfruto, *m*; (pleasure) placer, *m*; aprovechamiento, *m*; utilización, *f*; (satisfaction) satisfacción, *f*

enlarge /ɛn'lardʒ/ *vt* agrandar; aumentar; ensanchar; extender; *Photo*. ampliar; dilatar; (the mind, etc.) ensanchar. *vi* agrandarse; ensancharse; aumentarse; extenderse. **an enlarged heart,** dilatación del corazón, *f*. **to e. upon,** tratar detalladamente, explayarse en

enlargement /ɛn'lardʒmənt/ *n* engrandecimiento, *m*; ensanchamiento, *m; Photo*. ampliación, *f; Med*. dilatación, *f*; aumento, *m*; amplificación, *f*; (of a town, etc.) ensanche, *m*

enlarger /ɛn'lardʒər/ *n Photo*. ampliadora, *f*

enlighten /ɛn'laɪtn̩/ *vt* iluminar; aclarar; informar

enlightened /ɛn'laɪtn̩d/ *a* culto; ilustrado; inteligente

enlightening /ɛn'laɪtn̩ɪŋ/ *a* instructivo

enlightenment /ɛn'laɪtn̩mənt/ *n* ilustración, *f*; cultura, civilización, *f*

enlist /ɛn'lɪst/ *vt Mil*. reclutar; alistar; obtener, conseguir. *vi Mil*. sentar plaza, sentar plaza de soldado; engancharse; alistarse

enlistment /ɛn'lɪstmənt/ *n Mil*. enganche, *m*; reclutamiento, *m*; alistamiento, *m*

enliven /ɛn'laɪvən/ *vt* animar; avivar; alegrar

enmity /'ɛnmɪti/ *n* enemistad, enemiga, hostilidad, *f*

ennoble /ɛn'noubəl/ *vt* ennoblecer; ilustrar

ennui /ɑn'wi/ *n* tedio, *m*; aburrimiento, *m*

enormity /ɪ'nɔrmɪti/ *n* enormidad, *f*; gravedad, *f*; atrocidad, *f*

enormous /ɪ'nɔrməs/ *a* enorme, colosal

enormously /ɪ'nɔrməsli/ *adv* enormemente

enormousness /ɪ'nɔrməsnɪs/ *n* enormidad, *f*

enough /ɪ'nʌf/ *a* bastante, suficiente. *n* lo bastante, lo suficiente. *adv* bastante; suficientemente. *interj* ¡bastante! ¡basta! **to be e.,** ser suficiente; bastar. **two are enough,** con dos tenemos bastante, con dos tengo bastante

enquire. /ɛn'kwaɪər/ See **inquire**

enrage /ɛn'reɪdʒ/ *vt* enfurecer, hacer furioso; *Inf*. hacer rabiar

enraged /ɛn'reɪdʒd/ *a* furioso

enrapture /ɛn'ræptʃər/ *vt* entusiasmar, extasiar; (intoxicate) embriagar; (charm) encantar, deleitar

enrich /ɛn'rɪtʃ/ *vt* enriquecer; (adorn) adornar, embellecer; (the land) fertilizar

enrichment /ɛn'rɪtʃmənt/ *n* enriquecimiento, *m*; embellecimiento, *m*; (of the land) abono, *m*

enroll /ɛn'roul/ *vt* alistar; matricular; inscribir; (perpetuate) inmortalizar

enrollment /ɛn'roulmənt/ *n* alistamiento, *m*; inscripción, *f*

ensconce /ɛn'skɒns/ *vt* acomodar, colocar; ocultar

ensemble /ɑn'sɑmbəl/ *n* conjunto, *m*

enshrine /ɛn'ʃraɪn/ *vt* poner en sagrario; guardar con cuidado; *Fig*. guardar como una reliquia

enshroud /ɛn'ʃraud/ *vt* amortajar; envolver; esconder

ensign /'ɛnsən/ *n* (badge) insignia, *f*; (flag) enseña, bandera, *f*; pabellón, *m*; bandera de popa, *f; Mil*. alférez, *m*; (U.S.A. navy) subteniente, *m*

enslave /ɛn'sleɪv/ *vt* esclavizar

enslavement /ɛn'sleɪvmənt/ *n* esclavitud, *f*

ensue /ɛn'su/ *vi* conseguir. *vi* resultar; suceder, sobrevenir

ensuing /ɛn'suɪŋ/ *a* (next) próximo; (resulting) resultante

ensure /ɛn'ʃʊr/ *vt* asegurar; estar seguro de que; garantizar

entail /ɛn'teɪl/ *vt* traer consigo, acarrear; *Law*. vincular; *n Law*. vinculación, *f*; herencia, *f*

entangle /ɛn'tæŋgəl/ *vt* enredar; coger; *Fig*. embrollar

entanglement /ɛn'tæŋgəlmənt/ *n* enredo, *m*; complicación, *f*; intriga, *f*; (*Mil*. of wire) alambrada, *f*

entangling /ɛn'tæŋglɪŋ/ *a* enmarañador (e.g., *entangling alliances,* alianzas enmarañadoras, *f pl*)

enter /'ɛntər/ *vt* entrar en; penetrar; (of thoughts) ocurrirse; (join) ingresar en; entrar en; (become a member of) hacerse miembro de; (enroll) alistarse; (a university) matricularse; (inscribe) inscribir, poner en la lista; (note) anotar, apuntar; (a protest) hacer constar; (make) hacer; formular. *vi* entrar; *Theat*. salir (a la escena); penetrar; *Com*. anotarse. **to e. for,** *vt* inscribir. *vi* inscribirse; tomar parte en. **to e. into,** entrar en; formar parte de; (conversation) entablar (conversación); (negotiations) iniciar; considerar; (another's emotion) acompañar en; (an agreement, etc.) hacer; (sign) firmar; (bind oneself) obligarse a, comprometerse a; tomar parte en; (undertake) emprender; empezar; adoptar. **to e. up,** anotar; poner en la lista; registrar. **to e. upon,** comenzar, emprender; tomar posesión de; encargarse de, asumir; inaugurar, dar principio a

enteric /ɛn'tɛrɪk/ *a* entérico

enteritis /ˌɛntə'raɪtɪs/ *n* enteritis, *f*

enterprise /'ɛntərˌpraɪz/ *n* empresa, *f*; aventura, *f*; (spirit) iniciativa, *f*, empuje, *m*

enterprising /'ɛntərˌpraɪzɪŋ/ *a* emprendedor, acometedor; de mucha iniciativa

entertain /ˌɛntər'teɪn/ *vt* (an idea, etc.) acariciar, abrigar; considerar; (as a guest) agasajar, obsequiar; recibir en casa; (amuse) divertir, entretener. *vi* ser hospitalario; tener invitados en casa; dar fiestas

entertaining /ˌɛntər'teɪnɪŋ/ *a* entretenido, divertido

entertainingly /ˌɛntər'teɪnɪŋli/ *adv* entretenidamente; (witty) graciosamente

entertainment /ˌɛntər'teɪnmənt/ *n* convite, *m*; fiesta, *f*; reunión, *f*; banquete, *m*; (hospitality) hospitalidad, *f*; (amusement) diversión, *f*, entretenimiento, *m*; espectáculo, *m*; función, *f*; concierto, *m*

enthrall /ɛn'θrɔl/ *vt* seducir, atraer, encantar; absorber, captar la atención

enthralling /ɛn'θrɔlɪŋ/ *a* absorbente; atrayente, halagüeño
enthrallment /ɛn'θrɔlmənt/ *n* absorción, *f*; atracción, *f*
enthrone /ɛn'θroun/ *vt* entronizar
enthronement /ɛn'θrounmənt/ *n* entronización, *f*
enthusiasm /ɛn'θuzi,æzəm/ *n* entusiasmo, *m*
enthusiast /ɛn'θuzi,æst, -ɪst/ *n* entusiasta, *mf*
enthusiastic /ɛn,θuzi'æstɪk/ *a* entusiasta. **to make e.,** entusiasmar. **to be e.,** entusiasmarse
enthusiastically /ɛn,θuzi'æstɪkəli/ *adv* con entusiasmo
entice /ɛn'tais/ *vt* tentar, inducir; atraer, seducir
enticement /ɛn'taismənt/ *n* tentación, *f*; atractivo, *m*
enticing /ɛn'taisɪŋ/ *a* seduciente, atrayente; halagüeño
entire /ɛn'taiˀr/ *a* entero; completo; intacto; absoluto; perfecto; íntegro; total
entirely /ɛn'taiˀrli/ *adv* enteramente; completamente; integralmente; totalmente
entirety /ɛn'taiˀrti/ *n* totalidad, *f*; integridad, *f*; todo, *m*
entitle /ɛn'taitl/ *vt* (designate) intitular; dar derecho (a); autorizar. **to be entitled to,** tener derecho a
entity /'ɛntɪti/ *n* entidad, *f*; ente, ser, *m*
entombment /ɛn'tummənt/ *n* sepultura, *f*, entierro, *m*
entomological /,ɛntəmə'lɒdʒɪkəl/ *a* entomológico
entomologist /,ɛntə'mɒlədʒɪst/ *n* entomólogo, *m*
entomology /,ɛntə'mɒlədʒi/ *n* entomología, *f*
entourage /,antu'raʒ/ *n* séquito, *m*; (environment) medio ambiente, *m*
entr'acte /ɑn'trækt/ *n* entreacto, *m*
entrails /'ɛntreilz/ *n* entrañas, tripas, *f pl*, intestinos, *m pl*
entrance /'ɛntrəns/ *n* entrada, *f*; *Theat.* salida (a la escena), *f*; (into a profession, etc.) ingreso, *m*; alistamiento, *m*; (beginning) principio, *m*; (door) puerta, *f*; (porch) portal, *m*; (of a cave) boca, *f*. **e. fee,** cuota de entrada, *f*. **e. hall,** zaguán, *m*. **e. money,** entrada, *f*
entrance /ɛn'træns/ *vt* *Fig.* encantar, fascinar; ecstasiar
entrancing /ɛn'trænsɪŋ/ *a* encantador
entreat /ɛn'trit/ *vt* suplicar, implorar, rogar
entreating /ɛn'tritɪŋ/ *a* suplicante, implorante
entreatingly /ɛn'tritɪŋli/ *adv* de un modo suplicante; insistentemente
entreaty /ɛn'triti/ *n* súplica, instancia, *f*, ruego, *m*
entree /'ɑntrei/ *n* entrada, *f*
entrench /ɛn'trɛntʃ/ *vt* atrincherar
entrenchment /ɛn'trɛntʃmənt/ *n* atrincheramiento, *m*; *Mil.* parapeto, *m*; (encroachment) invasión, *f*
entresol /'ɛntər,sɒl/ *n* entresuelo, *m*
entrust /ɛn'trʌst/ *vt* confiar a (or en), encomendar a; encargar
entry /'ɛntri/ *n* entrada, *f*; (passage) callejuela, *f*; (note) inscripción, apuntación, *f*; *Com.* partida, *f*; (registration) registro, *m*. **double e.,** *Com.* partida doble, *f*. **single e.,** *Com.* partida simple, *f*
entwine /ɛn'twain/ *vt* entrelazar, entretejer
enumerate /ɪ'numə,reit/ *vt* enumerar
enumeration /ɪ,numə'reiʃən/ *n* enumeración, *f*
enumerative /ɪ'numə,reitɪv/ *a* enumerativo
enunciate /ɪ'nʌnsi,eit/ *vt* enunciar; articular
enunciation /ɪ,nʌnsi'eiʃən/ *n* enunciación, *f*; articulación, *f*
envelop /ɛn'vɛləp/ *vt* envolver, cubrir
envelope /'ɛnvə,loup/ *n* sobre, *m*
envelopment /ɛn'vɛləpmənt/ *n* envolvimiento, *m*; cubierta, *f*
enviable /'ɛnviəbəl/ *a* envidiable
envious /'ɛnviəs/ *a* envidioso. **an e. look,** una mirada de envidia
enviously /'ɛnviəsli/ *adv* con envidia
environment /ɛn'vairənmənt/ *n* medio ambiente, *m*
environmental /ɛn,vairən'mɛntl/ *a* ambiental
environs /ɛn'vairənz/ *n* inmediaciones, *f pl*, alrededores, *m pl*
envisage /ɛn'vɪzɪdʒ/ *vt* hacer frente a; contemplar; imaginar
envoy /'ɛnvɔi/ *n* enviado, *m*; mensajero (-ra)

envy /'ɛnvi/ *n* envidia, *f*, *vt* envidiar
enzyme /'ɛnzaim/ *n* fermento, *m*, enzima, *f*
eon /'iən/ *n* eón, *m*
epaulette /'ɛpə,lɛt/ *n* hombrera, *f*
ephemeral /ɪ'fɛmərəl/ *a* efímero; *Fig.* fugaz, pasajero
Ephesus /'ɛfəsəs/ Efiso, *m*
Ephraim /'ifriəm/ Efraín, *m*
epic /'ɛpɪk/ *a* épico. *n* epopeya, *f*
epicenter /'ɛpə,sɛntər/ *n* epicentro, *m*
epicure /'ɛpɪ,kyʊr/ *n* epicúreo (-ea)
epicurean /,ɛpɪkyʊ'riən/ *a* epicúreo
Epicureanism /,ɛpɪkyʊ'riə,nɪzəm/ *n* epicureísmo, *m*
epidemic /,ɛpɪ'dɛmɪk/ *n* epidemia, *f*; plaga, *f*, *a* epidémico
epidermis /,ɛpɪ'dɜrmɪs/ *n* epidermis, *f*
epiglottis /,ɛpɪ'glɒtɪs/ *n* epiglotis, *f*
epigram /'ɛpɪ,græm/ *n* epigrama, *m*
epigrammatic /,ɛpɪgrə'mætɪk/ *a* epigramático
epigraph /'ɛpɪ,græf/ *n* epígrafe, *m*
epigraphy /ɪ'pɪgrəfi/ *n* epigrafía, *f*
epilepsy /'ɛpə,lɛpsi/ *n* epilepsia, alferecía, *f*
epileptic /,ɛpə'lɛptɪk/ *a* and *n* epiléptico (-ca). **e. fit,** ataque epiléptico, *m*. **e. aura,** aura epiléptica, *f*
epilogue /'ɛpə,lɔg/ *n* epílogo, *m*
epiphany /ɪ'pɪfəni/ *n* epifanía, *f*
episcopacy /ɪ'pɪskəpəsi/ *n* episcopado, *m*
episcopal /ɪ'pɪskəpəl/ *a* episcopal
Episcopalianism /ɪ,pɪskə'peilyə,nɪzəm/ *n* episcopalismo, *m*
episode /'ɛpə,soud/ *n* suceso, incidente, *m*; *Lit.* episodio, *m*
episodic /,ɛpə'sɒdɪk/ *a* episódico
epistle /ɪ'pɪsəl/ *n* epístola, *f*
epistolary /ɪ'pɪstl,ɛri/ *a* epistolar
epitaph /'ɛpɪ,tæf/ *n* epitafio, *m*
epithet /'ɛpə,θɛt/ *n* epíteto, *m*
epitome /ɪ'pɪtəmi/ *n* epítome, *m*
epitomize /ɪ'pɪtə,maiz/ *vt* resumir, abreviar
epoch /'ɛpək/ *n* época, edad, *f*
epode /'ɛpoud/ *n* épodo, *f*
Epsom salts /'ɛpsəm/ *n* sal de la Higuera, *f*
equability /,ɛkwə'bɪlɪti/ *n* igualdad (de ánimo), ecuanimidad, *f*; uniformidad, *f*
equable /'ɛkwəbəl/ *a* igual, ecuánime; uniforme
equably /'ɛkwəbli/ *adv* con ecuanimidad; igualmente; uniformemente
equal /'ikwəl/ *a* igual; uniforme; imparcial; equitativo, justo. *n* igual, *mf*. *vt* ser igual a; equivaler a; igualar; *Sports.* empatar. **to be e. to,** (of persons) ser capaz de; servir para; atreverse a; (circumstances) estar al nivel de; sentirse con fuerzas para. **without e.,** sin igual; (of beauty, etc.) sin par. **e. sign,** *Math.* igual, *m*
equality /ɪ'kwɒlɪti/ *n* igualdad, *f*; uniformidad, *f*
equalization /,ikwələ'zeiʃən/ *n* igualación, *f*
equalize /'ikwə,laiz/ *vt* igualar
equalizing /'ikwə,laizɪŋ/ *a* igualador; compensador
equally /'ikwəli/ *adv* igualmente; imparcialmente
equanimity /,ikwə'nɪmɪti/ *n* ecuanimidad, *f*
equation /ɪ'kweiʒən/ *n* ecuación, *f*
equator /ɪ'kweitər/ *n* ecuador, *m*
equatorial /,ikwə'tɔriəl/ *a* ecuatorial
equestrian /ɪ'kwɛstriən/ *a* ecuestre
equiangular /,ikwi'æŋgyələr/ *a* equiángulo
equidistance /,ikwɪ'dɪstəns/ *n* equidistancia, *f*
equidistant /,ikwɪ'dɪstənt/ *a* equidistante
equilateral /,ikwə'lætərəl/ *a* equilátero
equilibrist /ɪ'kwɪləbrɪst/ *n* equilibrista, *mf*
equilibrium /,ikwə'lɪbriəm/ *n* equilibrio, *m*
equine /'ikwain/ *a* equino; hípico; de caballo
equinoctial /,ikwə'nɒkʃəl/ *a* equinoccial. **e. gale,** tempestad equinoccial,
equinox /'ikwə,nɒks/ *n* equinoccio, *m*
equip /ɪ'kwɪp/ *vt* proveer; pertrechar; equipar
equipage /'ɛkwəpɪdʒ/ *n* (train) séquito, tren, *m*; (carriage) carruaje, *m*
equipment /ɪ'kwɪpmənt/ *n* habilitación, *f*; equipo, *m*; pertrechos, *m pl*; material, *m*; aparatos, *m pl*; armamento, *m*

equitable /'ɛkwɪtəbəl/ *a* equitativo, justo
equitableness /'ɛkwɪtəbəlnɪs/ *n* equidad, justicia, *f*
equitably /'ɛkwɪtəbli/ *adv* equitativamente, con justicia
equity /'ɛkwɪti/ *n* equidad, *f*; imparcialidad, justicia, *f*
equivalence /ɪ'kwɪvələns/ *n* equivalencia, *f*
equivalent /ɪ'kwɪvələnt/ *a* and *n* equivalente, *m*. **to be e. to,** equivaler a
equivocal /ɪ'kwɪvəkəl/ *a* equívoco, ambiguo
equivocally /ɪ'kwɪvəkəli/ *adv* equivocadamente
equivocate /ɪ'kwɪvə,keɪt/ *vi* usar frases equívocas, emplear equívocos, tergiversar
equivocation /ɪ,kwɪvə'keɪʃən/ *n* equívoco, *m*
era /'ɪərə, 'ɛrə/ *n* época, era, *f*
eradiation /ɪ,reidi'eɪʃən/ *n* irradiación, *f*
eradicable /ɪ'rædɪkəbəl/ *a* erradicable
eradicate /ɪ'rædɪ,keɪt/ *vt* erradicar; destruir, extirpar; suprimir
eradication /ɪ,rædɪ'keɪʃən/ *n* erradicación, *f*; destrucción, *f*; supresión, *f*
erasable /ɪ'reisəbəl/ *a* borrable
erase /ɪ'reɪs/ *vt* borrar; tachar
eraser /ɪ'reisər/ *n* goma de borrar, *f*. **ink e.,** goma para tinta, *f*
erasure /ɪ'reiʃər/ *n* borradura, *f*; tachón, *m*
ere /ɛər/ *conjunc* antes de (que), antes de. *prep* antes de
erect /ɪ'rɛkt/ *a* (upright) derecho; erguido; vertical; (uplifted) levantado; (standing) de pie; (firm) firme, resuelto; (alert) vigilante. *vt* (build) edificar, construir; instalar; (raise) alzar; convertir
erectile /ɪ'rɛktl/ *a* eréctil
erection /ɪ'rɛkʃən/ *n* erección, *f*; construcción, edificación, *f*; (building) edificio, *m*; (structure) estructura, *f*; instalación, *f*; (assembling) montaje, *m*
erectly /ɪ'rɛktli/ *adv* derecho
erectness /ɪ'rɛktnɪs/ *n* derechura, *f*
erg /ɜrg/ *n Phys.* ergio, *m*
ermine /'ɜrmɪn/ *n* armiño, *m*, *a* de armiño
erode /ɪ'roud/ *vt* corroer; comer; *Geol.* denudar
erosion /ɪ'rouʒən/ *n* erosión, *f*
erotic /ɪ'rɒtɪk/ *a* erótico
eroticism /ɪ'rɒtə,sɪzəm/ *n* erotismo, *m*
err /ɜr, ɛr/ *vi* desviarse; errar; desacertar; pecar
errand /'ɛrənd/ *n* mensaje, recado, *m*; encargo, *m*; misión, *f*. **e.-boy,** mandadero, mensajero, motril, mozo, recadero, *m*
errant /'ɛrənt/ *a* errante; (of knights) andante
erratic /ɪ'rætɪk/ *a* (of conduct) excéntrico, irresponsable; (of thoughts, etc.) errante; *Med.* errático
erratum /ɪ'rɑtəm/ *n* errata, *f*
erring /'ɛrɪŋ/ *a* extraviado; pecaminoso
erroneous /ə'rouniəs/ *a* erróneo; falso; injusto
erroneously /ə'rouniəsli/ *adv* erróneamente; falsamente; injustamente
erroneousness /ə'rouniəsnɪs/ *n* falsedad, *f*
error /'ɛrər/ *n* error, *m*; equivocación, *f*, desacierto, *m*; (sin) pecado, *m*. **in e.,** por equivocación
erudite /'ɛryʊ,daɪt/ *a* erudito; sabio
erudition /,ɛryʊ'dɪʃən/ *n* erudición, *f*
erupt /ɪ'rʌpt/ *vi* entrar en erupción, estar en erupción; *Fig.* salir con fuerza
eruption /ɪ'rʌpʃən/ *n* erupción, *f*
escalade /,ɛskə'leɪd/ *n* escalada, *f*, *vt* escalar
escalator /'ɛskə,leɪtər/ *n* escalera automática, escalera eléctrica, escalera mecánica, escalera móvil, escalera rodante, *f*
escapable /ɪ'skeipəbəl/ *a* evitable, eludible
escapade /'ɛskə,peɪd/ *n* escapada, *f*; aventura, *f*
escape /ɪ'skeɪp/ *n* huida, fuga, *f*; evasión, evitación, *f*; (leak) escape, *m*; *Fig.* salida, *f*. *vt* eludir, evitar; (of cries, groans, etc.) dar, salir de. *vi* huir, fugarse, escapar; (slip away) escurrirse; librarse; salvarse; (leak) escaparse. **His name escapes me,** Se me escapa (or se me olvida) su nombre. **to e. notice,** pasar inadvertido. **to have a narrow e.,** salvarse en una tabla. **to e. from,** escaparse de; librarse de; huir de
escape clause *n* cláusula de salvaguardia, *f*
escaping /ɪ'skeɪpɪŋ/ *a* fugitivo
escarpment /ɪ'skɑrpmənt/ *n* escarpa, *f*

eschew /ɛs'tʃu/ *vt* evitar
eschewal /ɛs'tʃuəl/ *n* evitación, *f*
escort /*n* 'ɛskɔrt; *v* ɪ'skɔrt/ *n Mil.* escolta, *f*; (of ships) convoy, *m*; acompañamiento, *m*; acompañante, *m*. *vt Mil.* escoltar; (of ships) convoyar; acompañar
escudo /ɛ'skudou/ *n* escudo, *m*
escutcheon /ɪ'skʌtʃən/ *n* escudo, blasón, *m*
Eskimo /'ɛskə,mou/ *a* and *n* esquimal *mf*
esoteric /,ɛsə'tɛrɪk/ *a* esotérico
esparto /ɪ'spɑrtou/ *n* esparto, *m*
especial /ɪ'spɛʃəl/ *a* especial; particular
especially /ɪ'spɛʃəli/ *adv* especialmente; en particular
Esperantist /,ɛspə'rɑntɪst/ *n* esperantista, *mf*
Esperanto /,ɛspə'rɑntou/ *n* esperanto, *m*
espionage /'ɛspiə,nɑʒ/ *n* espionaje, *m*
esplanade /'ɛsplə,nɑd/ *n Mil.* explanada, *f*; bulevar, paseo, *m*
espousal /ɪ'spauzəl/ *n* desposorio, *m*; *Fig.* adhesión (a una causa), *f*
espouse /ɪ'spauz/ *vt* desposar; (a cause) abrazar; defender
espy /ɪ'spai/ *vt* divisar, ver, observar
esquire /'ɛskwaiər/ *n* escudero, *m*; (landowner) hacendado, *m*; (as a title) don (before given name)
essay /*n* 'ɛsei; *v* ɛ'sei/ *n* tentativa, *f*; *Lit.* ensayo, *m*, *vt* probar; procurar; (on an examination) tema, *m*. **essay question,** tema, *m*
essayist /'ɛseiist/ *n* ensayista, *mf*
essence /'ɛsəns/ *n* esencia, *f*
essential /ə'sɛntʃəl/ *a* esencial; indispensable, imprescindible; intrínseco. *n* artículo de primera necesidad, *m*; elemento necesario, *m*
essentially /ə'sɛntʃəli/ *adv* esencialmente
establish /ɪ'stæblɪʃ/ *vt* establecer; fundar; crear; erigir, *Lat. Am. also* instaurar; (constitute) constituir; (order) disponer; (prove) demostrar, probar; (take root, settle) arraigarse
established /ɪ'stæblɪʃt/ *a* establecido; arraigado; (proved) demostrado; bien conocido; (author) consagrado; (of churches) oficial
establishment /ɪ'stæblɪʃmənt/ *n* establecimiento, *m*; fundación, *f*; creación, *f*, *Lat. Am. also* instauración; institución, *f*; (building) erección, *f*; arraigo, *m*; (house) casa, *f*; (church) iglesia oficial, *f*; demostración, *f*; reconocimiento, *m*
estate /ɪ'steit/ *n* estado, *m*; clase, *f*; condición, *f*; (land) propiedad, finca, *f*; fortuna, *f*; (inheritance) heredad, *f*, patrimonio, *m*; *Law.* bienes, *m* pl. **personal e.,** bienes muebles, *m pl*; fortuna personal, *f*. **third e.,** estado llano, *m*. **e. agent,** agente de fincas, *m*; agente de casas, *m*
esteem /ɪ'stim/ *n* estima, *f*, aprecio, *m*; consideración, *f*, *vt* estimar, apreciar; creer, juzgar
ester /'ɛstər/ *n Chem.* éster, *m*
esthete /'ɛsθit/ *n* estético, *m*
esthetic /ɛs'θɛtɪk/ *a* estético
esthetically /ɛs'θɛtɪkli/ *adv* estéticamente
esthetics /ɛs'θɛtɪks/ *n* estética, *f*
estimable /'ɛstəməbəl/ *a* apreciable, estimable
estimableness /'ɛstəməbəlnɪs/ *n* estimabilidad, *f*
estimate /*n* 'ɛstəmɪt; *v* -,meit/ *n* estimación, tasa, *f*; cálculos, *m pl*; apreciación, *f*; opinión, *f*; *pl* **estimates,** presupuesto, *m*. *vt* (value) avalorar, tasar; calcular, computar; considerar. *vi* hacer un presupuesto
estimation /,ɛstə'meiʃən/ *n* opinión, *f*; cálculo, cómputo, *m*; (esteem) aprecio, *m*, estima, *f*
estrange /ɪ'streindʒ/ *vt* enajenar; ofender
estrangement /ɪ'streindʒmənt/ *n* enajenación, alienación, *f*
estuary /'ɛstʃu,ɛri/ *n* estuario, *m*, ría, *f*
etcetera /ɛt'sɛtərə/ etcétera. (Used as noun, *f*)
etch /ɛtʃ/ *vt* grabar al agua fuerte
etcher /'ɛtʃər/ *n* grabador (-ra) al agua fuerte
etching /'ɛtʃɪŋ/ *n* aguafuerte, *f*; grabado al agua fuerte, *m*. **e. needle,** punta seca, aguja de grabador, *f*
eternal /ɪ'tɜrnl/ *a* eterno; incesante. *n* (E.) el Eterno
eternally /ɪ'tɜrnli/ *adv* eternamente
eternity /ɪ'tɜrnɪti/ *n* eternidad, *f*

eternize /ɪ'tɜrnaiz/ vt eternizar
ether /'iθər/ n éter, m
ethereal /ɪ'θɪəriəl/ a etéreo; vaporoso, aéreo
etheric /ɪ'θɛrɪk/ a etéreo
etherize /'iθə,raiz/ vt eterizar
ethical /'ɛθɪkəl/ a ético, moral; n droga de ordenanza, f
ethics /'ɛθɪks/ n ética, f; (filosofía) moral, f
Ethiopia /,iθi'oupiə/ Etiopia, f
ethnic /'ɛθnɪk/ a étnico
ethnographic /,ɛθnou'græfɪk/ a etnográfico
ethnography /ɛθ'nɒgrəfi/ n etnografía, f
ethnologist /ɛθ'nɒlədʒɪst/ n etnólogo, m
ethnology /ɛθ'nɒlədʒi/ n etnología, f
ethyl /'ɛθəl/ n Chem. etilo, m
ethylene /'ɛθə,lin/ n Chem. etileno, m
etiquette /'ɛtɪkɪt/ n etiqueta, f
Etruscan /ɪ'trʌskən/ a and n etrusco (-ca)
etymological /,ɛtəmə'lɒdʒɪkəl/ a etimológico
etymologist /,ɛtə'mɒlədʒɪst/ n etimólogo, m, etimologista, mf
etymology /,ɛtə'mɒlədʒi/ n etimología, f
eucalyptus /,yukə'lɪptəs/ n eucalipto, m
Eucharist /'yukərɪst/ n Eucaristía, f
eucharistic /,yukə'rɪstɪk/ a eucarístico
eugenic /yu'dʒɛnɪk/ a eugenésico
eugenics /yu'dʒɛnɪks/ n eugenesia, f
eulogist /'yulədʒɪst/ n elogiador (-ra), loador (-ra)
eulogistic /,yulə'dʒɪstɪk/ a elogiador
eulogize /'yulə,dʒaiz/ vt elogiar, alabar, encomiar
eulogy /'yulədʒi/ n elogio, encomio, m; alabanza, f; panegírico, m
eunuch /'yunək/ n eunuco, m
euphemism /'yufə,mɪzəm/ n eufemismo, m
euphonious /yu'founiəs/ a eufónico
euphony /'yufəni/ n eufonía, f
euphuistic /,yufyu'ɪstɪk/ a alambicado, gongorino
Eurasian /yʊ'reiʒən/ a and n eurasio (-ia)
eurhythmic /yʊ'rɪðmɪk/ a eurítmico
eurhythmics /yʊ'rɪðmɪks/ n euritmia, f
European /,yʊrə'piən/ a and n europeo (-ea)
europeanize /,yʊrə'piə,naiz/ vt europeanizar
euthanasia /,yuθə'neiʒə, -ʒiə, -ziə/ n eutanasia, f
evacuate /ɪ'vækyu,eit/ vt evacuar
evacuation /ɪ,vækyu'eiʃən/ n evacuación, f
evade /ɪ'veid/ vt evadir, eludir; evitar, esquivar; rehuir
evaluate /ɪ'vælyu,eit/ vt evaluar, estimar; calcular
evaluation /ɪ,vælyu'eiʃən/ n evaluación, estimación, f
evanescent /,ɛvə'nɛsənt/ a transitorio, fugaz, pasajero
evangelical /,ivæn'dʒɛlɪkəl/ a evangélico
evangelicalism /,ivæn'dʒɛlɪkə,lɪzəm/ n evangelismo, m
evangelist /ɪ'vændʒəlɪst/ n evangelista, m
evangelize /ɪ'vændʒə,laiz/ vt evangelizar
evaporate /ɪ'væpə,reit/ vi evaporarse; desvanecerse. vt evaporar
evaporation /ɪ,væpə'reiʃən/ n evaporación, f; desvanecimiento, m
evaporative /ɪ'væpə,reitɪv/ a evaporatorio
evasion /ɪ'veiʒən/ n (escape) fuga, f; evasión, f; evasiva, f, efugio, m, Lat. Am. esquivada, f
evasive /ɪ'veisɪv/ a evasivo, ambiguo
evasively /ɪ'veisɪvli/ adv evasivamente
evasiveness /ɪ'veisɪvnɪs/ n carácter evasivo, m
eve /iv/ n víspera, f; Eccl. vigilia, f. **on the eve of,** la víspera de; Fig. en vísperas de
even /'ivən/ a (flat) llano; (smooth) liso; igual; (level with) al mismo nivel (de); uniforme; (of numbers) par; (approximate, of sums) redondo; rítmico; invariable, constante; (of temper) apacible; (just) imparcial; (monotonous) monótono, igual; (paid) pagado; (Com. of date) mismo. **to get e. with,** pagar en la misma moneda, vengarse de. **to be e. (with...)** Lat. Am. estar a mano (con...)
even /'ivən/ adv siquiera; aun; hasta; (also) también. **not e.,** ni siquiera. **e. as,** así como, del mismo modo que. **e. if,** aun cuando, si bien. **e. now,** aun ahora;

ahora mismo. **e. so,** aun así; (nevertheless) sin embargo. **e. though,** aunque; suponiendo que
even /'ivən/ vt igualar; (level) allanar, nivelar; (accounts) desquitar; compensar; hacer uniforme
evening /'ivnɪŋ/ n tarde, f, atardecer, m; noche, f; Fig. fin, m, a vespertino, de la tarde. **Good e.!** ¡Buenas tardes! ¡Buenas noches! **in the e.,** al atardecer. **tomorrow e.,** mañana por la tarde. **yesterday e.,** ayer por la tarde. **e. class,** clase nocturna, f. **e. dress,** (women) traje de noche, m; (men) traje de etiqueta, m. **e. meal,** cena, f. **e. paper,** periódico (or diario) de la noche, m. **e. primrose,** hierba del asno, onagra, f. **e. star,** estrella vespertina, estrella de la tarde, f; (Venus) lucero de la tarde, m
evenly /'ivənli/ adv igualmente; (on a level) a nivel; uniformemente; imparcialmente; (of speech) con suavidad
evenness /'ivənnɪs/ n igualdad, f; (smoothness) lisura, f; uniformidad, f; imparcialidad, f; (of temper) ecuanimidad, serenidad, f
evensong /'ivən,sɔŋ/ n vísperas, f pl
event /ɪ'vɛnt/ n incidente, suceso, acontecimiento, m; (result) consecuencia, f; resultado, m; caso, m; (athletics) prueba, f; (race) carrera, f. **at all events,** de todas maneras. **in such an e.,** en tal caso. **in the e. of,** en el caso de
eventful /ɪ'vɛntfəl/ a lleno de acontecimientos; accidentado; memorable
eventual /ɪ'vɛntʃuəl/ a eventual; final, último
eventuality /ɪ,vɛntʃu'ælɪti/ n eventualidad, f
eventually /ɪ'vɛntʃuəli/ adv a la larga, al fin
ever /'ɛvər/ adv siempre; (at any time) jamás; alguna vez; nunca; (even) siquiera; (very) muy; (in any way) en modo alguno. **As fast as e. he can,** Lo más aprisa que pueda. **Be it e. so big,** Por grande que sea. **Did you e.!** ¡Habráse visto! ¡Qué cosa! **for e.,** para siempre. **for e. and e.,** para siempre jamás; (mostly ecclesiastical) por los siglos de los siglos; eternamente. **He is e. so nice,** Es muy simpático. **Hardly e.,** casi nunca. **I don't think I have e. been there,** No creo que haya estado nunca allí. **if e.,** si alguna vez; (rarely) raramente. **nor... e.,** ni nunca. **not... e.,** nunca. **e. after,** desde entonces; (afterward) después. **e. and anon,** de vez en cuando. **e. so little,** siquiera un poco; muy poco
evergreen /'ɛvər,grin/ a siempre verde. n planta vivaz, f. **e. oak,** encina, f
everlasting /,ɛvər'læstɪŋ/ a eterno, perpetuo; (of colors) estable; incesante. **e. flower,** perpetua, f
evermore /,ɛvər'mɔr/ adv eternamente
every /'ɛvri/ a todo; cada (invariable); todos los, m pl; todas las, f pl. **e. day,** todos los días, cada día. **e. now and then,** de cuando en cuando. **e. other day,** cada dos días
everybody /'ɛvri,bɒdi, -,bʌdi/ n todo el mundo, m; todos, m pl; todas, f pl; cada uno, m; cada una, f
everyday /'ɛvri,dei/ a diario, cotidiano; corriente, de cada día, usual
everything /'ɛvri,θɪŋ/ n todo, m; (e. that) todo lo (que). **e. possible,** todo lo posible
everywhere /'ɛvri,wɛər/ adv por todas partes
evict /ɪ'vɪkt/ vt desahuciar; expulsar
eviction /ɪ'vɪkʃən/ n evicción, f, desahúcio, m; expulsión, f
evidence /'ɛvɪdəns/ n Law. testimonio, m, deposición, f; indicios, m pl; evidencia, f; prueba, f; hecho, m, vt patentizar, probar. **to give e.,** dar testimonio, deponer
evident /'ɛvɪdənt/ a evidente, patente, manifiesto; claro. **to be e.,** ser patente, estar a la vista
evidently /'ɛvɪdəntli/ adv evidentemente; claramente
evil /'ivəl/ a malo; malvado, perverso; de maldad; (unfortunate) aciago; de infortunio; (of spirits) diabólico, malo. n mal, m; maldad, perversidad, f; (misfortune) desgracia, f. **the E. one,** el Malo. **e.-doer,** malhechor (-ra). **e. eye,** mal de ojo, aojo, m. **e.-minded,** mal pensado; malintencionado. **e.-speaking,** maledicencia, calumnia, f. **e. spirit,** demonio, espíritu malo, m
evince /ɪ'vɪns/ vt evidenciar; mostrar
eviscerate /ɪ'vɪsə,reit/ vt destripar, desentrañar

evocation /ˌɛvə'keiʃən/ n evocación, f

evocative /ɪ'vɒkətɪv/ a evocador

evoke /ɪ'vouk/ vt evocar

evolution /ˌɛvə'luʃən/ n evolución, f; desarrollo, m; (Nav., Mil.) maniobra, f; Math. extracción de una raíz, f; (revolution) revolución, vuelta, f

evolutionary /ɛvə'luʃənˌɛri/ a evolucionario

evolve /ɪ'vɒlv/ vi evolucionar; desarrollarse. vt producir por evolución; desarrollar; pensar

ewe /yu/ n oveja, f. ewe lamb, cordera, f

ewer /'yuər/ n aguamanil, m

exacerbate /ɪg'zæsərˌbeit/ vt exacerbar; agravar, empeorar

exacerbation /ɪgˌzæsər'beiʃən/ n exacerbación, f; agravación, f

exact /ɪg'zækt/ a exacto; fiel; metódico; estricto. vt exigir

exacting /ɪg'zæktɪŋ/ a exigente; severo, estricto; (hard) agotador, arduo

exaction /ɪg'zækʃən/ n exigencia, f; extorsión, exacción, f

exactly /ɪg'zæktli/ adv exactamente; precisamente

exactness /ɪg'zæktnɪs/ n exactitud, f

exaggerate /ɪg'zædʒə,reit/ vt exagerar; acentuar. vi exagerar

exaggerated /ɪg'zædʒə,reitɪd/ a exagerado

exaggeration /ɪgˌzædʒə'reiʃən/ n exageración, f

exaggerator /ɪg'zædʒə,reitər/ n exagerador (-ra)

exalt /ɪg'zɔlt/ vt exaltar; enaltecer, elevar; (praise) glorificar, magnificar; (intensify) realzar; intensificar

exaltation /ˌɛgzɔl'teiʃən/ n exaltación, elevación, f; alegría, f, júbilo, m; (ecstasy) éxtasis, arrobamiento, m; (of the Cross) exaltación, f

exalted /ɪg'zɔltɪd/ a exaltado, eminente

exaltedness /ɪg'zɔltɪdnɪs/ n exaltación, f

exam /ɪg'zæm/ n examen, m

examination /ɪgˌzæmə'neiʃən/ n examen, m; inspección, f; investigación, f; Law. interrogatorio, m; prueba, f. to sit an e., examinarse. written e., prueba escrita, f

examine /ɪg'zæmɪn/ vt examinar; inspeccionar; investigar; Law. interrogar; (search) reconocer; (by touch) tentar; observar; analizar. to e. into, examinar; considerar detenidamente; ahondar en

examinee /ɪgˌzæmə'ni/ n examinando (-da)

examiner /ɪg'zæmɪnər/ n examinador (-ra); inspector (-ra)

examinership /ɪg'zæmɪnərˌʃɪp/ n cargo de examinador, m

examining /ɪg'zæmɪnɪŋ/ a que examina; de examen; Law. interrogante

example /ɪg'zæmpəl/ n ejemplo, m; ilustración, f; (parallel) ejemplar, m; (warning) escarmiento, m. for e., por ejemplo. to set an e., dar ejemplo, dar el ejemplo.

exasperate /ɪg'zæspə,reit/ vt exasperar, irritar; (increase) aumentar; (worsen) agravar

exasperating /ɪg'zæspə,reitɪŋ/ a exasperante, irritante, provocador

exasperation /ɪgˌzæspə'reiʃən/ n exasperación, irritación, f; (worsening) agravación, f; enojo, f

excavate /'ɛkskə,veit/ vt excavar; (hollow) vaciar

excavation /ˌɛkskə'veiʃən/ n excavación, f; Archit. vaciado, m

excavator /'ɛkskə,veitər/ n excavador (-ra); (machine) excavadora, f

exceed /ɪk'sid/ vt exceder; (excel) superar, aventajar; (one's hopes, etc.) sobrepujar. vi excederse. e. all expectations, exceder a toda ponderación. to e. one's rights, abusar de sus derechos, ir demasiado lejos

exceedingly /ɪk'sidɪŋli/ adv sumamente, extremadamente; sobre manera

excel /ɪk'sɛl/ vt aventajar, superar; vencer. vi sobresalir; distinguirse, señalarse; ser superior

excellence /'ɛksələns/ n excelencia, f; superioridad, f; perfección, f; mérito, m; buena calidad, f

excellency /'ɛksələnsi/ n (title) Excelencia, f. Your E., Su Excelencia

excellent /'ɛksələnt/ a excelente; superior; perfecto; magnífico; (in examinations) sobresaliente

excellently /'ɛksələntli/ adv excelentemente; perfectamente; magníficamente

except /ɪk'sɛpt/ vt exceptuar; omitir

except, excepting /ɪk'sɛpt/ prep excepto, con excepción de; exceptuando; menos; salvo; fuera de. conjunc a menos que. except for, si no fuese por; con excepción de; fuera de

exception /ɪk'sɛpʃən/ n excepción, f; objeción, protesta, f. to make an e., hacer una excepción. to take e. to, protestar contra; tachar, criticar; desaprobar

exceptional /ɪk'sɛpʃənl/ a excepcional

excerpt /n 'ɛksɜrpt; v ɪk'sɜrpt/ n excerpta, f, extracto, m. vt extraer

excess /ɪk'sɛs, 'ɛksɛs/ n exceso, m; superabundancia, f; demasía, f; Com. superávit, m. in e., en exceso, de sobra. in e. of, en exceso de; arriba de. to e., excesivamente, demasiado. e. fare, suplemento, m. e. luggage, exceso de equipaje, m; (overweight) exceso de peso, m

excessive /ɪk'sɛsɪv/ a excesivo; superabundante; inmoderado, desmesurado; exagerado

excessively /ɪk'sɛsɪvli/ adv excesivamente; exageradamente

excessiveness /ɪk'sɛsɪvnɪs/ n exceso, m; superabundancia, f; exageración, f

exchange /ɪks'tʃeindʒ/ n cambio, trueque, m; (of prisoners) canje, m; (financial) cambio, m; (building) bolsa, lonja, f; (telephone) oficina central de teléfonos, f. vt cambiar (for, por); trocar; (replace) reemplazar; (prisoners) canjear; (of blows) darse; (pass from, into) pasar de... a. vi hacer un cambio. in e. for, en cambio de, a trueque de; por. to e. greetings, saludarse; cambiar saludos. They exchanged looks, Se miraron. What is the rate of e.? ¿Cuál es el tipo de cambio? e. of prisoners, canje de prisioneros, m

exchangeable /ɪks'tʃeindʒəbəl/ a cambiable; trocable

exchequer /'ɛkstʃɛkər/ n (public finance) Hacienda pública, f; tesorería, f; (funds) fondos, m pl. Chancellor of the E., Ministro de Hacienda, m

excise /n 'ɛksaiz; v ɪk'saiz/ n contribución indirecta, f; (customs and e.) Aduana, f. vt (cut) cortar, extirpar; imponer una contribución. e. duty, derecho de aduana, m

excise tax arbitrios, m pl

excision /ɛk'sɪʒən/ n excisión, f; extirpación, f

excitability /ɪkˌsaitə'bilɪti/ n excitabilidad, f

excitable /ɪk'saitəbəl/ a excitable

excitation /ˌɛksai'teiʃən/ n excitación, f

excite /ɪk'sait/ vt emocionar; conmover; agitar; excitar; suscitar, provocar; incitar, instigar; (attention, interest) despertar; estimular. to become excited, emocionarse; exaltarse; (annoyed) acalorarse; (upset) agitarse

excitedly /ɪk'saitɪdli/ adv con emoción; acaloradamente; agitadamente

excitement /ɪk'saitmənt/ n conmoción, f; agitación, f, Central America embullo m; (annoyance) acaloramiento, m; emoción, f; estímulo, m; instigación, f, fomento, m; (amusement) placer, m

exciting /ɪk'saitɪŋ/ a emocionante; conmovedor; agitador; muy interesante

exclaim /ɪk'skleim/ vt and vi exclamar. to e. against, clamar contra

exclamation /ˌɛksklə'meiʃən/ n exclamación, f. e. mark, punto de exclamación, m

exclamatory /ɪk'sklæmə,tɔri/ a exclamatorio

exclude /ɪk'sklud/ vt excluir; exceptuar; evitar; (refuse) rechazar

exclusion /ɪk'skluʒən/ n exclusión, f; exceptuación, f; eliminación, f

exclusive /ɪk'sklusɪv/ a exclusivo; (snobbish) exclusivista. e. of, no incluido; aparte de

exclusively /ɪk'sklusɪvli/ adv exclusivamente; únicamente

exclusivism /ɪk'sklusə,vɪzəm/ n exclusivismo, m

exclusivist /ɪk'sklusəvɪst/ n exclusivista, mf

excommunicate /ˌɛkskə'myunɪˌkeit/ a -kɪt/ vt excomulgar. a excomulgado

excommunication /ˌɛkskəˌmyunɪ'keiʃən/ *n* excomunión, *f*

excrement /'ɛkskrəmənt/ *n* excremento, *m*

excrescence /ɪk'skrɛsəns/ *n* excrecencia, *f*

excrescent /ɪk'skrɛsənt/ *a* que forma excrecencia; superfluo

excrete /ɪk'skrit/ *vt* excretar

excretion /ɪk'skriʃən/ *n* excreción, *f*

excretory /'ɛkskrɪ,tɔri/ *a* excretorio

excruciating /ɪk'skruʃiˌeitɪŋ/ *a* atormentador, angustioso; (of pain) agudísimo

excursion /ɪk'skɜrʒən/ *n* excursión, *f*; expedición, *f*; (digression) digresión, *f*. **e. ticket,** billete de excursión, *m*. **e. train,** tren de excursionistas, *m*

excursionist /ɪk'skɜrʒənɪst/ *n* excursionista, *mf*; turista, *mf*

excusable /ɪk'skyuzəbəl/ *a* disculpable, excusable

excusably /ɪk'skyuzəbli/ *adv* excusablemente

excuse /ɪk'skyus/ *n* excusa, *f*; disculpa, *f*; pretexto, *m*; justificación, defensa, *f*. **to give as an e.,** pretextar

excuse /ɪk'skyuz/ *vt* disculpar, excusar; dispensar (de); librar (de); (forgive) perdonar; (defend) justificar, defender; (minimize) paiar; (oneself) disculparse. **E. me!** ¡Con permiso!; ¡Perdone Vd.!; ¡Dispense Vd.!

execrable /'ɛksɪkrəbəl/ *a* execrable, abominable

execrate /'ɛksɪ,kreit/ *vt* execrar, abominar. *vi* maldecir

execration /ˌɛksɪ'kreiʃən/ *n* execración, abominación, *f*; maldición, *f*

execute /'ɛksɪ,kyut/ *vt* (perform) ejecutar, poner en efecto, realizar; (*Art., Mus.*) ejecutar; (part in a play) hacer, desempeñar; (fulfil) cumplir; *Law.* otorgar (un documento); (kill) ajusticiar

execution /ˌɛksɪ'kyuʃən/ *n* efectuación, realización, *f*; (*Art., Mus.*) ejecución, *f*; (of part in a play) desempeño (de un papel), *m*; (fulfilment) cumplimiento, *m*; *Law.* otorgamiento (de un documento), *m*; (killing) suplicio, *m*, ejecución de la pena de muerte, *f*; (*Law.* seizure) ejecución, *f*

executioner /ˌɛksɪ'kyuʃənər/ *n* verdugo, *m*

executive /ɪg'zɛkyətɪv/ *a* ejecutivo; administrativo. *n* poder ejecutivo, *m*

executor /ɪg'zɛkyətər/ *n* administrador testamentario, *m*

executrix /ɪg'zɛkyətrɪks/ *n* administradora testamentaria, *f*

exegesis /ˌɛksɪ'dʒisɪs/ *n* exégesis, *f*

exegetical /ˌɛksɪ'dʒɛtɪkəl/ *a* exegético

exemplary /ɪg'zɛmpləri/ *a* ejemplar

exemplification /ɪgˌzɛmpləfɪ'keiʃən/ *n* ejemplificación, ilustración, demostración, *f*

exemplify /ɪg'zɛmplə,fai/ *vt* ejemplificar; ilustrar, demostrar

exempt /ɪg'zɛmpt/ *vt* exentar, eximir; librar; dispensar, excusar. *a* exento; libre; excusado; inmune

exemption /ɪg'zɛmpʃən/ *n* exención, *f*; libertad, *f*; inmunidad, *f*

exercise /'ɛksər,saiz/ *n* ejercicio, *m*; uso, *m*; (essay) ensayo, *m*; *pl* **exercises,** (on land or sea) maniobras, *f pl*. *vt* ejercer; usar, emplear; (train) ejercitar, entrenar; adiestrar; pasear, dar un paseo; (worry) preocupar. *vi* hacer ejercicio; ejercitarse; adiestrarse. **spiritual exercises,** ejercicios espirituales, *m pl*. **to take e. in the open air,** tomar ejercicio al aire libre. **to write an e.,** escribir un ejercicio. **e. book,** cuaderno de ejercicios, *m*

exert /ɪg'zɜrt/ *vt* hacer uso de, emplear, ejercer, poner en juego; (deploy) desplegar. **to e. oneself,** hacer un esfuerzo (para); esforzarse (de); trabajar mucho; tratar (de); apurarse, tomarse mucha molestia; preocuparse

exertion /ɪg'zɜrʃən/ *n* esfuerzo, *m*; uso, *m*; (exercise) ejercicio, *m*; (good offices) diligencias, gestiones, *f pl*; buenos oficios, *m pl*

exhalation /ˌɛkshə'leiʃən/ *n* exhalación, *f*; efluvio, *m*; vapor, *m*; humo, *m*

exhale /ɛks'heil/ *vt* exhalar; emitir, despedir. *vi* evaporarse; disiparse

exhaust /ɪg'zɔst/ *vt* agotar; (empty) vaciar; (end) acabar; apurar; consumir; (tire) rendir, cansar mucho;

(weaken) debilitar; (a subject) tratar detalladamente. *n Mech.* escape, *m*; emisión de vapor, *f*; vapor de escape, *m*. **e. pipe,** tubo de escape, *m*

exhaustible /ɪg'zɔstəbəl/ *a* agotable

exhausting /ɪg'zɔstɪŋ/ *a* cansado, agotador

exhaustion /ɪg'zɔstʃən/ *n* agotamiento, *m*; rendimiento, cansancio, *m*; lasitud, *f*; postración, *f*

exhaustive /ɪg'zɔstɪv/ *a* completo; minucioso

exhaustively /ɪg'zɔstɪvli/ *adv* detenidamente; detalladamente; minuciosamente

exhaustiveness /ɪg'zɔstɪvnɪs/ *n* lo completo; minuciosidad, *f*

exhibit /ɪg'zɪbɪt/ *vt* exhibir; manifestar, ostentar; velar, descubrir; presentar. *vi* exhibir, ser expositor. *n* exposición, *f*, objeto exhibido, *m*; *Law.* prueba, *f*

exhibition /ˌɛksə'bɪʃən/ *n* exposición, *f*; (performance) función, *f*; espectáculo, *m*; exhibición, *f*; (showing) manifestación, *f*; (grant) bolsa de estudio, beca, *f*

exhibitionism /ˌɛksə'bɪʃəˌnɪzəm/ *n* exhibicionismo, *m*

exhibitionist /ˌɛksə'bɪʃənɪst/ *n* exhibicionista, *mf*

exhibitor /ɪg'zɪbɪtər/ *n* expositor (-ra)

exhilarate /ɪg'zɪlə,reit/ *vt* alegrar, alborozar

exhilarating /ɪg'zɪlə,reitɪŋ/ *a* alegre; estimulador, vigorizador, tonificante

exhilaration /ɪgˌzɪlə'reiʃən/ *n* alegría, *f*, alborozo, regocijo, *m*

exhort /ɪg'zɔrt/ *vt* and *vi* exhortar

exhortation /ˌɛgzɔr'teiʃən/ *n* exhortación, *f*

exhumation /ˌɛkshyu'meiʃən/ *n* exhumación, *f*

exhume /ɪg'zum/ *vt* exhumar

exigence /'ɛksɪdʒəns/ *n* exigencia, *f*; urgencia, *f*; (need) necesidad, *f*

exigent /'ɛksɪdʒənt/ *a* exigente; urgente

exiguous /ɪg'zɪgyuəs/ *a* exiguo

exiguousness /ɪg'zɪgyuəsnɪs/ *n* exigüidad, *f*

exile /'ɛgzail/ *n* destierro, *m*; (person) desterrado (-da), *Lat. Am.* exiliado (-da) *mf vt* desterrar, *Lat. Am.* exiliar

exist /ɪg'zɪst/ *vi* existir

existence /ɪg'zɪstəns/ *n* existencia, *f*; (being) ser, *m*; (life) vida, *f*. **to bring into e.,** causar; producir

existentialism /ˌɛgzɪ'stɛnʃəˌlɪzəm/ *n* existencialismo, *m*

existing /ɪg'zɪstɪŋ/ *a* existente

exit /'ɛgzɪt, 'ɛksɪt/ *n* salida, *f*; partida, *f*; (death) muerte, *f*; *Theat.* mutis, *m*. *vi Theat.* hacer mutis. **to make one's e.,** salir; marcharse; irse; morir; *Theat.* hacer mutis

exodus /'ɛksədəs/ *n* éxodo, *m*; salida, *f*; emigración, *f*; **E.,** Éxodo, *m*

exonerate /ɪg'zɒnə,reit/ *vt* exonerar

exoneration /ɪgˌzɒnə'reiʃən/ *n* exoneración, *f*

exorbitance /ɪg'zɔrbɪtəns/ *n* exorbitancia, *f*

exorbitant /ɪg'zɔrbɪtənt/ *a* exorbitante

exorcism /'ɛksɔr,sɪzəm/ *n* exorcismo, *m*

exorcist /'ɛksɔrsɪst/ *n* exorcista, *m*

exorcize /'ɛksər,saiz/ *vt* exorcizar, conjurar

exotic /ɪg'zɒtɪk/ *a* exótico. *n* planta exótica, *Fig.* flor de estufa, *f*

expand /ɪk'spænd/ *vt* extender; abrir; (wings, etc.) desplegar; (the chest, etc.) expandir; dilatar; (amplify) ampliar; (an edition) ampliar, aumentar; (develop) desarrollar; *Fig.* ensanchar; (increase) aumentar. *vi.* dilatarse; hincharse; abrirse; extenderse; *Fig.* ensancharse; (increase) aumentarse

expanse /ɪk'spæns/ *n* extensión, *f*

expansibility /ɪkˌspænsə'bɪlɪti/ *n Phys.* expansibilidad, *f*; dilatabilidad, *f*

expansible /ɪk'spænsəbəl/ *a Phys.* expansible; dilatable

expansion /ɪk'spænʃən/ *n* expansión, *f*; extensión, *f*; dilatación, *f*; (amplification) ampliación, *f*; (development) desarrollo, *m*; *Fig.* ensanchamiento, *m*; (increase) aumento, *m*

expansionism /ɪk'spænʃəˌnɪzəm/ *n* expansionismo, *m*

expansive /ɪk'spænsɪv/ *a* expansivo; (of persons) efusivo, expresivo, comunicativo, afable

expansiveness /ɪk'spænsɪvnɪs/ *n* expansibilidad, *f*; (of persons) afabilidad, *f*

expatiate /ɪk'speiʃi,eit/ **(upon)** *vi* extenderse en
expatiation /ɪk,speiʃi'eiʃən/ *n* discurso, *m*; digresión, *f*
expatriation /ɛks,peitri'eiʃən/ *n* expatriación, *f*
expect /ɪk'spɛkt/ *vt* esperar; (await) aguardar; (suppose) suponer; (demand) exigir; (count on) contar con. *vi* creer
expectance /ɪk'spɛktəns/ *n* expectación, *f*; esperanza, *f*
expectant /ɪk'spɛktənt/ *a* expectante; (hopeful) esperanzudo; (pregnant) embarazada
expectantly /ɪk'spɛktəntli/ *adv* con expectación
expectation /,ɛkspɛk'teiʃən/ *n* expectación, *f*; (hope) esperanza, expectativa, *f*; probabilidad, *f*
expectorate /ɪk'spɛktə,reit/ *vt* expectorar. *vi* escupir
expectoration /ɪk,spɛktə'reiʃən/ *n* expectoración, *f*
expedience /ɪk'spidiəns/ *n* conveniencia, *f*; oportunidad, *f*; aptitud, *f*; (self-interest) egoísmo, *m*
expedient /ɪk'spidiənt/ *a* conveniente; oportuno; apto; prudente; político. *n* expediente, recurso, medio, *m*
expedite /'ɛkspɪ,dait/ *vt* acelerar; facilitar; (send off) despachar
expedition /,ɛkspɪ'diʃən/ *n* expedición, *f*; (haste) celeridad, diligencia, *f*
expeditionary /,ɛkspɪ'diʃə,nɛri/ *a* expedicionario. **e. force,** fuerza expedicionaria, *f*
expeditious /,ɛkspɪ'diʃəs/ *a* expedito, pronto
expeditiously /,ɛkspɪ'diʃəsli/ *adv* expeditamente, prontamente
expeditiousness /,ɛkspɪ'diʃəsnɪs/ *n* prontitud, *f*
expel /ɪk'spɛl/ *vt* expeler, expulsar; echar, arrojar; despedir
expend /ɪk'spɛnd/ *vt* gastar, expender; (time) perder
expenditure /ɪk'spɛndɪtʃər/ *n* gasto, desembolso, *m*, *Lat. Am.* erogación *f*; (of time) pérdida, *f*
expense /ɪk'spɛns/ *n* gasto, *m*; pérdida, *f*; costa, *f*; *pl* **expenses,** expensas, *f pl*, gastos, *m pl.* **at the e. of,** a costa de. **e. account,** cuenta de gastos, *f*. **to be put to great e.,** tener que gastar mucho. **to pay one's expenses,** pagar sus gastos
expensive /ɪk'spɛnsɪv/ *a* costoso; caro
expensively /ɪk'spɛnsɪvli/ *adv* costosamente
expensiveness /ɪk'spɛnsɪvnɪs/ *n* lo costoso; costa, *f*
experience /ɪk'spɪəriəns/ *n* experiencia, *f*. *vt* experimentar; sentir; sufrir. **by e.,** por experiencia
experienced /ɪk'spɪəriənst/ *a* experimentado; experto; hábil; (lived) vivido
experiment /n ɪk'spɛrəmənt; v -,mɛnt/ *n* experimento, *m*; prueba, *f*; ensayo, *m*, tentativa, *f*. *vi* experimentar; hacer una prueba
experimental /ɪk,spɛrə'mɛntl/ *a* experimental; tentativo
experimentally /ɪk,spɛrə'mɛntli/ *adv* experimentalmente; por experimentación
expert /'ɛkspɜrt/ *a* experto; perito; hábil; (finished) acabado. *n* experto, *m*, especialista, *mf*
expertise /,ɛkspər'tiz/ *n* destreza, *f*
expertly /'ɛkspɜrtli/ *adv* expertamente; hábilmente
expertness /'ɛkspɜrtnɪs/ *n* pericia, *f*; maestría, *f*; habilidad, *f*; (knowledge) conocimiento, *m*
expiable /'ɛkspiəbəl/ *a* que se puede expiar
expiate /'ɛkspi,eit/ *vt* expiar; reparar
expiation /,ɛkspi'eiʃən/ *n* expiación, *f*
expiatory /'ɛkspiə,tɔri/ *a* expiatorio
expiration /,ɛkspə'reiʃən/ *n* (breathing out) espiración, *f*; (ending) expiración, *f*; terminación, *f*; *Com.* vencimiento, *m*; (death) muerte, *f*
expiration date fecha de vencimiento, *f*
expire /ɪk'spai°r/ *vi* (exhale) espirar; (die) morir, dar el último suspiro; (of fire, light) extinguirse; (end) expirar; terminar; *Com.* vencer
expiry /ɪk'spai°ri/ *n* terminación, *f*; expiración, *f*; *Com.* vencimiento, *m*
explain /ɪk'splein/ *vt* explicar; aclarar; demostrar; exponer; (justify) justificar, defender. *vi* explicarse. **to e. away,** explicar; justificar
explainable /ɪk'spleinəbəl/ *a* explicable
explanation /,ɛksplə'neiʃən/ *n* explicación, *f*; aclaración, *f*

explanatory /ɪk'splænə,tɔri/ *a* explicativo; aclaratorio
expletive /'ɛksplitɪv/ *a* expletivo. *n* interjección, *f*
explicable /'ɛksplɪkəbəl/ *a* explicable
explicit /ɪk'splɪsɪt/ *a* explícito
explode /ɪk'sploud/ *vi* estallar; detonar; reventar. *vt* hacer estallar; (a mine) hacer saltar; (a belief, etc.) hacer abandonar; desechar
exploit /ɪk'splɔit/ *n* hazaña, proeza, *f*; aventura, *f*. *vt* explotar
exploitation /,ɛksplɔi'teiʃən/ *n* explotación, *f*
exploiter /ɪk'splɔitər/ *n* explotador (-ra)
exploration /,ɛksplə'reiʃən/ *n* exploración, *f*
exploratory /ɪk'splɔrə,tɔri/ *a* exploratorio
explore /ɪk'splɔr/ *vt* explorar; examinar; averiguar; investigar; (Med. Surg.) explorar
explorer /ɪk'splɔrər/ *n* explorador (-ra)
explosion /ɪk'splouʒən/ *n* explosión, *f*; estallido, *m*, detonación, *f*
explosive /ɪk'splousɪv/ *a* and *n* explosivo, *m*. **high e.,** explosivo violento, *m*. **explosives chamber,** recámara, *f*
explosiveness /ɪk'splousɪvnɪs/ *n* propiedad explosiva, *f*; lo explosivo; violencia, *f*
exponent /ɪk'spounənt/ *a* and *n* exponente, *mf*
export /n 'ɛkspɔrt; v ɪk'spɔrt/ *n* exportación, *f*. *vt* exportar. **e. license,** permiso de exportación, *m*. **e. trade,** comercio de exportación, *m*
exportation /,ɛkspɔr'teiʃən/ *n* exportación, *f*
exporter /ɪk'spɔrtər/ *n* exportador (-ra)
expose /ɪk'spouz/ *vt* exponer; arriesgar; (exhibit) exhibir, (unmask) desenmascarar; descubrir; revelar; *Photo.* exponer; (ridicule) ridiculizar
exposed /ɪk'spouzd/ *a* descubierto; no abrigado; expuesto, peligroso
exposition /,ɛkspə'zɪʃən/ *n* explicación, interpretación, *f*; declaración, *f*; (exhibition) exposición, *f*
expostulate /ɪk'spɒstʃə,leit/ *vi* protestar, **to e. with,** reprochar; reconvenir
expostulation /ɪk,spɒstʃə'leiʃən/ *n* protesta, *f*; reconvención, *f*
exposure /ɪk'spouʒər/ *n* exposición, *f*; (aspect) orientación, *f*; (scandal) revelación, *f*, escándalo, *m*; peligro, *m*; exposición al frío o al calor, *f*
expound /ɪk'spaund/ *vt* exponer, explicar; comentar
expounder /ɪk'spaundər/ *n* intérprete, *mf*; comentador (-ra)
express /ɪk'sprɛs/ *a* (clear) categórico, explícito; claro; expreso; (exact) exacto; (quick) rápido. *n* (messenger, post) expreso, *m*; (train) (tren) expreso, (tren) rápido, *m*; (goods) expreso, *m*. *vt* expresar; (a letter, etc.) mandar por expreso
expressible /ɪk'sprɛsəbəl/ *a* decible
expression /ɪk'sprɛʃən/ *n* expresión, *f*
expressionless /ɪk'sprɛʃənlɪs/ *a* sin expresión
expressive /ɪk'sprɛsɪv/ *a* expresivo; que expresa
expropriate /ɛks'proupri,eit/ *vt* expropiar
expropriation /ɛks,proupri'eiʃən/ *n* expropiación, *f*
expulsion /ɪk'spʌlʃən/ *n* expulsión, *f*
expunge /ɪk'spʌndʒ/ *vt* borrar; testar; omitir
expunging /ɪk'spʌndʒɪŋ/ *n* borradura, *f*; testación, *f*; omisión, *f*
expurgate /'ɛkspər,geit/ *vt* expurgar
expurgator /'ɛkspər'geiʃən/ *n* expurgación, *f*
expurgatory /ɪk'spɜrgə,tɔri/ *a* expurgatorio
exquisite /ɪk'skwɪzɪt/ *a* exquisito, precioso; primoroso; excelente; (acute) agudo, intenso; (keen) vivo. *n* elegante, petimetre, *m*
exquisitely /ɪk'skwɪzɪtli/ *adv* primorosamente, pulcramente; a la perfección
exquisiteness /ɪk'skwɪzɪtnɪs/ *n* primor, *m*; pulcritud, perfección, *f*; excelencia, *f*; (of pain) intensidad, *f*; (keenness) viveza, *f*
extant /'ɛkstənt/ *a* estante; existente; viviente
extemporize /ɪk'stɛmpə,raiz/ *vt* and *vi* improvisar
extend /ɪk'stɛnd/ *vt* extender; (hold out) tender, alargar; (lengthen) prolongar; (a period of time) prorrogar, diferir; (make larger) ensanchar; (increase) aumentar; dilatar; ampliar; (offer) ofrecer; *vi* extenderse; dilatarse; continuar; (give) dar de sí, esti-

rarse; (last) prolongarse, durar; (become known) propagarse

extensible /ɪk'stɛnsəbəl/ a extensible

extension /ɪk'stɛnʃən/ n extensión, f; expansión, f; (increase) aumento, m; prolongación, f; ampliación, f; Com. prórroga, f; (telephone number) extensión, f, interno, m

extension cord n cordón de extensión, m; ladrón m, (Mexico; slang)

extensive /ɪk'stɛnsɪv/ a extenso, ancho, vasto; grande, considerable; (comprehensive) comprensivo

extensively /ɪk'stɛnsɪvli/ adv extensamente; generalmente

extensiveness /ɪk'stɛnsɪvnɪs/ n extensión, f; amplitud, f

extensor /ɪk'stɛnsər, -sɔr/ n Anat. extensor, m

extent /ɪk'stɛnt/ n extensión, f; (degree) punto, m; (limit) límite, m. **to a great e.**, en gran parte; considerablemente. **to some e.**, hasta cierto punto. **to the full e.**, en toda su extensión; completamente. **to what e.?** ¿hasta qué punto?

extenuate /ɪk'stɛnyu,eit/ vt atenuar, desminuir, mitigar, paliar

extenuating /ɪk'stɛnyu,eitɪŋ/ a atenuante

extenuation /ɪk,stɛnyu'eiʃən/ n atenuación, mitigación, f

exterior /ɪk'stɪəriər/ a exterior, externo; de fuera; (foreign) extranjero. n exterior, m; aspecto, m; forma, f

exterminate /ɪk'stɜrmə,neit/ vt exterminar

extermination /ɪk,stɜrmə'neiʃən/ n exterminio, m

exterminator /ɪk'stɜrmə,neitər/ n exterminador (-ra)

exterminatory /ɪk'stɜrmənə,tɔri/ a exterminador

external /ɪk'stɜrnl/ a externo, exterior; (foreign) extranjero. n pl **externals**, apariencias, f pl; aspecto exterior, m; comportamiento, m

externally /ɪk'stɜrnli/ adv exteriormente

exterritorial /,ɛkstɛrɪ'tɔriəl/ a extraterritorial

exterritoriality /,ɛkstɛrɪtɔri'ælɪti/ n extraterritorialidad, f

extinct /ɪk'stɪŋkt/ a extinto; (of light, fire) extinguido; suprimido

extinction /ɪk'stɪŋkʃən/ n extinción, f

extinguish /ɪk'stɪŋgwɪʃ/ vt extinguir; apagar; Fig. eclipsar

extinguishable /ɪk'stɪŋgwɪʃəbəl/ a apagable

extinguisher /ɪk'stɪŋgwɪʃər/ n apagador (-ra); (for fires) extintor, m; (snuffer) matacandelas, m

extinguishment /ɪk'stɪŋgwɪʃmənt/ n apagamiento, m; extinción, f; abolición, f; (destruction) aniquilamiento, m

extirpate /'ɛkstər,peit/ vt extirpar

extirpation /,ɛkstər'peiʃən/ n extirpación, f

extol /ɪk'stoul/ vt elogiar, encomiar, alabar; cantar

extoller /ɪk'stoulər/ n alabador (-ra)

extort /ɪk'stɔrt/ vt arrancar, sacar por fuerza; exigir por amenazas

extortion /ɪk'stɔrʃən/ n extorsión, f; exacción, f

extortionate /ɪk'stɔrʃənɪt/ a injusto; opresivo; (of price) exorbitante, excesivo

extra /'ɛkstrə/ a and adv adicional; extraordinario; suplementario; (spare) de repuesto. prefix (in compounds) extra. n extra, m; suplemento, m; (of a paper) hoja extraordinaria, f; (actor) supernumerario (-ia). **e. charge**, gasto suplementario, m; (on the railway, etc.) suplemento, m. **e.-mural**, a de extramuros.

extract /v ɪk'strækt; n 'ɛkstrækt/ vt sacar; (Chem. Math.) extraer; arrancar; (obtain) obtener. n Chem. extracto, m; (excerpt) cita, f

extraction /ɪk'strækʃən/ n saca, f; extracción, f; obtención, f

extradite /'ɛkstrə,dait/ vt entregar por extradición

extradition /,ɛkstrə'dɪʃən/ n extradición, f

extraneous /ɪk'streiniəs/ a extraño; (irrelevant) ajeno (a)

extraordinarily /ɪk,strɔrdṇ'ɛrəli/ adv extraordinariamente, singularmente

extraordinariness /ɪk'strɔrdṇ,ɛrinɪs/ n lo extraordinario; singularidad, f; (queerness) rareza, f

extraordinary /ɪk'strɔrdṇ,ɛri/ a extraordinario; singular; (queer) raro, excéntrico; (incredible) increíble

extraterrestrial /,ɛkstrətə'rɛstriəl/ a Lat. Am. extraterrenal

extravagance /ɪk'strævəgəns/ n (in spending) prodigalidad, f, derroche, m; (of dress, speech) extravagancia, f; (foolishness) disparate, m; (luxury) lujo, m

extravagant /ɪk'strævəgənt/ a extravagante; (queer) extraño, raro; (wasteful) pródigo; (of persons) gastador, manirroto; (of price) exorbitante; excesivo

extravagantly /ɪk'strævəgəntli/ adv extravagantemente; de un modo extraño; pródigamente; profusamente; excesivamente

extreme /ɪk'strim/ a extremo. n extremo, m. **in e.**, extremamente, en extremo, en sumo grado. **to carry to extremes**, llevar a extremos; **E. Unction**, Extremaunción, f

extremely /ɪk'strimli/ adv sumamente; Inf. muy

extremism /ɪk'stri,mɪzəm/ n extremismo, m

extremist /ɪk'strimɪst/ a and n extremista, mf

extremity /ɪk'strɛmɪti/ n extremidad, f; (point) punta, f; necesidad, f; pl **extremities**, Anat. extremidades, f pl; (measures) medidas extremas, f pl

extricate /'ɛkstrɪ,keit/ vt desenredar; librar; sacar

extrication /,ɛkstrɪ'keiʃən/ n liberación, f

extrinsic /ɪk'strɪnsɪk/ a extrínseco

extrovert /'ɛkstrə,vɜrt/ n Psychol. extravertido, m

exuberance /ɪg'zubərəns/ n exuberancia, f

exuberant /ɪg'zubərənt/ a exuberante

exudation /,ɛksyʊ'deiʃən/ n exudación, f

exude /ɪg'zud/ vt exudar; rezumar; sudar. vi exudar; rezumarse

exult /ɪg'zʌlt/ vi exultar; alegrarse

exultant /ɪg'zʌltənt/ a exultante, triunfante

exultantly /ɪg'zʌltəntli/ adv con exultación; triunfalmente

exultation /,ɛgzʌl'teiʃən/ n exultación, f; triunfo, m

eye /ai/ n ojo, m; (sight) vista, f; (look) mirada, f; atención, f; (opinion) opinión, f, juicio, m; (of a needle, of cheese) ojo, m; (of a hook) corcheta, f; Bot. yema, f; (of a potato) grillo, m. vt ojear; fijar los ojos en; examinar, mirar detenidamente. **bright eyes**, ojos vivos, m pl. **prominent eyes**, ojos saltones, m pl. He couldn't keep his eyes off Mary, Se le fueron los ojos tras María. **as far as the eye can reach**, hasta donde alcanza la vista. **before one's eyes**, a la vista de uno, ante los ojos de uno. **in my (etc.) eyes**, Fig. según creo yo, en mi opinión. **in the twinkling of an eye**, en un abrir y cerrar de ojos. **with an eye to**, pensando en. **with my own eyes**, con mis propios ojos. **with the naked eye**, con la simple vista. **to keep an eye on**, vigilar. **to make eyes at**, guiñar el ojo; mirar con ojos de enamorado. **to have one's eyes opened**, Fig. caérsele la venda. **eye-bath**, ojera, f. **eye-opener**, revelación, sorpresa, f. **eye-pencil**, pincel para las cejas, m. **eye-piece**, objetivo, ocular, m. **eye-shade**, visera, f. **eye-tooth**, colmillo, m. **eye-witness**, testigo ocular, testigo de vista, testigo presencial, mf

eyeball /'ai,bɔl/ n globo ocular, m

eyebrow /'ai,brau/ n ceja, f

eye care atención de la vista, f

eyed /aid/ a que tiene ojos; (in compounds) de ojos..., con ojos...; con los ojos; (of a needle) con el ojo... **She is a blue-eyed child**, Es una niña de ojos azules

eyeglass /'ai,glæs/ n lente, m. **eyeglasses**, gafas, f pl, anteojos, m pl, Puerto Rico espejuelos, m pl

eyelash /'ai,læʃ/ n pestaña, f

eyeless /'ailɪs/ a sin ojos

eyelet /'ailɪt/ n ojete, m

eyelid /'ai,lɪd/ n párpado, m

eyesight /'ai,sait/ n vista, f

eyewash /'ai,wɔʃ/ n colirio, m; Inf. camelo, m. **That's all e.!** ¡Eso es un camelo!

eyrie /'ɛəri/ n nido (of any bird of prey), nido de águila (eagle's) m

F

f /ɛf/ n (letter) efe, f; Mus. fa, m. **f sharp,** fa sostenido, m
fa /fɑ/ n Mus. fa, m
fable /'feibəl/ n fábula, leyenda, historia, f, apólogo, cuento, m; (untruth) invención, mentira, f
fabled /'feibəld/ a celebrado, famoso
fabric /'fæbrɪk/ n obra, fábrica, f; estructura, construcción, f; (making) manufactura, f; (cloth) tejido, paño, m; textura, f
fabricate /'fæbrɪˌkeit/ vt fabricar, construir; (invent) fingir, inventar
fabrication /ˌfæbrɪ'keiʃən/ n fabricación, manufactura, f; construcción, f; (lie) invención, ficción, f
fabulous /'fæbyələs/ a fabuloso
façade /fə'sɑd/ n fachada, frente, f
face /feis/ n superficie, f; (of persons) cara, f, rostro, m; (look) semblante, aire, m; (of coins) anverso, m; (grimace) mueca, f, gesto, m; (dial) esfera, f; (of gems) faceta, f; (of a wall) paramento, m; (front) fachada, frente, f; (effrontery) cara dura, f, descaro, m. **in the f. of,** ante; en presencia de. Mil. **Left f.!** ¡Izquierda! **on the f. of it,** juzgando por las apariencias. **to bring f. to f.,** confrontar (con). **to laugh in a person's f.,** reírse a la cara (de). **to make a f.,** hacer muecas. **to my f.,** en mi cara, en mis barbas. **to put a good f. on,** Fig. poner (or hacer) buena cara a. **to set one's f. against,** oponerse resueltamente a. **to straighten one's f.,** componer el semblante. **to wash one's f.,** lavarse la cara. **f. card,** figura (de la baraja), f. **f.-cloth,** paño para lavar la cara, m. **f. down,** boca abajo. **f. lift,** operación estética facial, f. **f. of the waters,** faz de las aguas, f. **f. powder,** polvos de arroz, m pl. **f. to f.,** cara a cara, de persona a persona; frente a frente. **f. value,** significado literal, m; Com. valor nominal, m
face /feis/ vt mirar hacia; confrontar, hacer cara (a); (of buildings, etc.) mirar a, caer a (or hacia); Fig. arrostrar, enfrentarse con; Sew. guarnecer, aforrar. vi estar orientado. **to f. the facts,** enfrentarse con la realidad. **to f. the music,** Fig. arrostrar las consecuencias. **to f. up to,** Fig. hacer cara a
faced /feist/ a con cara..., de cara...; Sew. forrado (de). **to be two-f.,** Fig. ser de dos haces
facer /'feisər/ n puñetazo en la cara, m; Fig. dificultad insuperable, f, problema muy grande, m
facet /'fæsɪt/ n faceta, f
facetious /fə'siʃəs/ a chancero, chistoso, jocoso
facetiousness /fə'siʃəsnɪs/ n jocosidad, festividad, f
facial /'feiʃəl/ a facial. **f. expression,** expresión de la cara, f, semblante, m
facile /'fæsɪl/ a (frivolous) ligero (e.g., a deduction or inference)
facilitate /fə'sɪlɪˌteit/ vt facilitar
facilitation /fəˌsɪlɪ'teiʃən/ n facilitación, f
facility /fə'sɪlɪti/ n facilidad, f; habilidad, destreza, f
facing /'feisɪŋ/ n Sew. vuelta, f; (of a building) paramento, m; (of lumber) chapa f; encaramiento, m
facsimile /fæk'sɪməli/ n facsímile, m
fact /fækt/ n (event) hecho, suceso, m; (datum) dato, m; realidad, verdad, f. **as a matter of f.,** en realidad. **in f.,** en efecto, en realidad. **I know as a f.,** Tengo por cierto. **The f. is...,** La verdad es (que)... **the f. that,** el hecho de que
fact-finding /'fækt ˌfaindɪŋ/ informador (e.g. send s.b. on a fact-finding mission, enviar a fulano en misión informadora)
faction /'fækʃən/ n facción, f, partido, bando, m; (tumult) alboroto, m
factional /'fækʃənl/ a partidario
factious /'fækʃəs/ a faccioso, sedicioso
factiousness /'fækʃəsnɪs/ n espíritu de facción, m; rebeldía, f
factitious /fæk'tɪʃəs/ a falso; artificial
factor /'fæktər/ n (fact) factor, elemento, m; consideración, f; Math. factor, m; Com. agente, factor, m

factory /'fæktəri/ n fábrica, manufactura, f; taller, m. **F. Act,** ley de trabajadores industriales, f. **f. hand,** operario (-ia)
factual /'fæktʃuəl/ a basado en hechos, objetivo
faculty /'fækəlti/ n facultad, f; (talent) habilidad, f, talento, m; (university division) facultad, f; (teachers as a group) claustro de profesores, claustro, profesorado, m; (authorization) privilegio, m, autoridad, f
fad /fæd/ n capricho, m, chifladura, f, dengue, m
faddiness /'fædɪnɪs/ n manías, f pl, excentricidad, f
faddist /'fædɪst/ n chiflado (-da)
faddy /'fædi/ a caprichoso, dengoso, difícil, excéntrico
fade /feid/ vi (of plants) marchitarse, secarse; (of color) palidecer, descolorarse; (vanish) disiparse, desaparecer; (of persons) desmejorarse; (of stains) salir. vt descolorar. **to f. away,** desvanecer; (of persons) consumirse. **f.-out,** n (cinema) desaparecimiento gradual, m
faded /'feidɪd/ a (of plants) seco, marchito, mustio; (of colors) descolorado, pálido; (of people) desmejorado
fadeless /'feidlɪs/ a de colores resistentes; eterno, no olvidado; siempre joven
fading /'feidɪŋ/ a que palidece, (of flowers) medio marchito; (of light) mortecino, pálido; decadente. n desaparecimiento, m, marchitez, f; decadencia, f
faggot /'fægət/ n haz (or gavilla) de leña, f
faience /fai'ɑns/ n fayenza, f
fail /feil/ vi faltar; fracasar, malograrse; no tener éxito, salir mal; (of strength) decaer, acabarse; (be short of) carecer (de); Com. hacer bancarrota, suspender pagos. vt abandonar; (disappoint) decepcionar, engañar; (in exams) suspender. **Do not f. to see her,** No dejes de verla. **He failed to do his duty,** Faltó a su deber
fail /feil/ n without f., sin falta
failing /'feilɪŋ/ n falta, f; (shortcoming) vicio, flaco, m, debilidad, f; malogro, fracaso, m; decadencia, f
failure /'feilyər/ n fracaso, m; falta de éxito, f; (in exams) suspensión, f; (of power) no funcionamiento, m; omisión, f, descuido, m; Com. quiebra, bancarrota, f; (decay) decadencia, f. **on f. of,** al fracasar; bajo pena de
fain /fein/ a deseoso, muy contento. **He was f. to...,** Se sintió obligado a...; Quería
faint /feint/ a débil; (dim) indistinto, vago, borroso; (of colors) pálido, desmayado; (weak) lánguido, desfallecido; (slight) superficial, rudimentario. vi perder el sentido, desmayarse. n desmayo, m. **to be f. with hunger,** estar muerto de hambre. **to cause to f.,** hacer desmayar. **f.-hearted,** pusilánime, medroso. **f.-heartedness,** pusilanimidad, f
faintly /'feintli/ adv débilmente; en voz débil; indistintamente
faintness /'feintnɪs/ n languidez, debilidad, f; (swoon) desmayo, m; lo indistinto; lo borroso
fair /fɛər/ n feria, f; (sale) mercado, m; (exhibition) exposición, f
fair /fɛər/ a (beautiful) hermoso, lindo, bello; (of hair) rubio; (of skin) blanco; (clear, fresh) limpio, claro; (good) bueno; (favorable) favorable, propicio, próspero; (of weather) despejado, sereno; (just) imparcial; (straightforward) honrado, recto, justo; (passable) regular, mediano; (of writing) legible; (proper) conveniente. adv honradamente; (politely) cortésmente; exactamente. **by f. means,** por medios honrados. **It's not f.!** ¡No hay derecho! **to become f.,** (of weather) serenarse. **to give a f. trial,** juzgar imparcialmente; dar una buena oportunidad; Law. procesar imparcialmente. **to make a f. copy,** poner en limpio. **f.-haired,** de pelo rubio, rubio. **f. one,** una beldad, f. **f. play,** Sports. juego limpio, m; proceder leal, m. **f.-skinned,** de tez blanca, rubio, güero. **f.-weather,** buen tiempo, m, bonanza, f. **f.-weather friends,** amigos de los días prósperos, m pl

fairing /'fɛərɪŋ/ *n Brit* regalo de feria, *m*. **to give fairings,** feriar

fairly /'fɛərli/ *adv* (justly) con imparcialidad; (moderately) bastante; totalmente, enteramente. **f. good,** bastante bueno; regular

fairness /'fɛərnɪs/ *n* belleza, hermosura, *f*; (of skin) blancura, *f*; (justness) imparcialidad, *f*; (reasonableness) justicia, equidad, *f*; (of hair) color rubio, oro, *m*

fairway /'fɛər,wei/ *n Naut.* canalizo, paso, *m*; (golf) terreno sin obstáculos, *m*

fairy /'fɛəri/ *n* hada, *f*, duende, *m*, *a* de hada, de duendes; *Fig.* delicado. **f.-gold,** tesoro de duendes, *m*; **f.-light,** lucecillo, *m*; luminaria, *f*. **f.-like,** aduendado, como una hada. **f.-ring,** círculo mágico, *m*. **f.-tale,** cuento de hadas, *m*; patraña, *f*, cuento de viejas, *m*

fairyland /'fɛəri,lænd/ *n* país de las hadas, *m*

faith /feiθ/ *n* fe, *f*; confianza, *f*; (doctrine) creencia, religión, filosofía, *f*; (honor) palabra, *f*. **in good f.,** de buena fe. **to break f.,** faltar a la palabra dada. **f.-healing,** curanderismo, *m*

faithful /'feiθfəl/ *a* fiel, leal; (accurate) exacto; (trustworthy) veraz. **the f.,** los creyentes

faithfully /'feiθfəli/ *adv* fielmente, lealmente; (accurately) con exactitud. **Yours f.,** Queda de Vd. su att. s.s.

faithfulness /'feiθfəlnɪs/ *n* fidelidad, lealtad, *f*; (accuracy) exactitud, *f*

faithless /'feiθlɪs/ *a* infiel, desleal, pérfido.

faithlessness /'feiθlɪsnɪs/ *n* infidelidad, deslealtad, traición, *f*

fake /feik/ *vt* imitar, falsificar. *n* imitación, falsificación, *f*. **to f. up,** inventar

Falangist /fei'lɑndʒɪst/ *a* and *n* falangista *mf*

falcon /'fɔlkən/ *n* halcón, *m*, (literary) azor, *m*. **f. gentle,** *Ornith.* neblí, *m*

falconry /'fɔlkənri/ *n* cetrería, *f*

Falkland Islands, the /'fɔklənd/ *pl* las Malvinas, *fpl*

fall /fɔl/ *n* caída, *f*; (of temperature, mercury) baja, *f*; (of water) salto de agua, *m*, catarata, cascada, *f*; (in value) depreciación, *f*; (in price and Stock Exchange) baja, *f*; (descent) bajada, *f*; (autumn) otoño, *m*; (declivity) declinación, *f*, declive, desnivel, *m*; (ruin) ruina, *f*, destrucción, *f*; (of night, etc.) caída (de la noche, *f*; (of snow) nevada, *f*; (of rain) golpe, *m*; (*Theat.* of curtain) caída, bajada, *f*; (surrender) capitulación, rendición, *f*; (of earth) desprendimiento de tierras, *m*; (of the tide) reflujo, *m*

fall /fɔl/ *vi* caer; (of mercury, temperature) bajar; (collapse) desplomarse, hundirse, derrumbarse; (die) caer muerto; (descend) descender; (*Theat.* of the curtain) bajar, caer; (of a river into the sea, etc.) desembocar, desaguar; (of hair, draperies) caer; (decrease) disminuir; (of spirits) ponerse triste, sentirse deprimido; (sin) caer; (come upon) sobrevenir; (of dusk, etc.) caer, llegar; (strike, touch) tocar; (as a share) tocar en suerte; (as a duty, responsibility) tocar, corresponder; (of seasons) caer en; (of words from the lips) caer de (los labios); (say) decir, pronunciar palabras; (of exclamations) escaparse; (become) venir a ser; (happen) suceder; (be) ser. **fallen upon evil days,** venido a menos. **His face fell. on a Thursday this year,** Navidad cae en jueves este año. **to let f.,** dejar caer. **to f. a-** (followed by verb) empezar a. **He fell a-crying,** Empezó a llorar. **to f. again,** volver a caer, recaer. **to f. among,** caer entre. **to f. away,** (leave) abandonar, dejar; (grow thin) enflaquecer; (crumble) desmoronarse. **to f. back,** retroceder, volver hacia atrás. **to f. back upon,** recurrir a; *Mil.* replegarse hacia. **to f. backward,** caer de espaldas, caer hacia atrás. **to f. behind,** quedarse atrás. **to f. down,** venirse a tierra; venirse abajo, dar consigo en el suelo, caer. **to f. due,** vencer. **to f. flat,** caer de bruces; (be unsuccessful) no tener éxito. **to f. in,** caer en; (collapse) desplomarse; *Mil.* alinearse; (expire) vencer. **to f. into,** caer en. **to f. in with,** tropezar con; reunirse con, juntarse con; (agree) convenir en; **to f. off,** caer de; (of leaves, etc.) desprenderse de, separarse de; (abandon) abandonar; (diminish) disminuir. **to f. on,** caer de (e.g. *to f. on one's back,* caer de espaldas); (of seasons) caer en; (attack) echarse encima de, atacar. **to f. out,** (of a

window, etc.) caer por; (happen) acontecer, suceder; (quarrel) pelearse, reñir; *Mil.* romper filas. **to f. out with,** reñir con. **to f. over,** volcar, caer; (stumble) tropezar con. **to f. short,** faltar; carecer, ser deficiente; (fail) malograrse, no llegar a sus expectaciones; (of shooting) errar el tiro. **to f. through,** caer por; (fail) malograrse, fracasar. **to f. to,** empezar a, ponerse a; (be incumbent on) tocar a, corresponder a; (attack) atacar. **to f. under,** caer debajo; caer bajo; sucumbir, perecer; (incur) incurrir en, merecer. **to f. upon,** (attack) caer sobre, acometer; acaecer, tener lugar; (be incumbent) tocar a

fallacious /fə'leifəs/ *a* falaz, engañoso, ilusorio

fallaciousness /fə'leifəsnɪs/ *n* falacia, *f*, engaño, *m*

fallacy /'fæləsi/ *n* error, *m*, ilusión, *f*

fallen /'fɔlən/ *a* caído; arruinado; degradado. **f. angel,** ángel caído, *m*. **f. woman,** perdida, mujer caída, *f*

fallibility /,fælə'bɪlɪti/ *n* falibilidad, *f*

fallible /'fæləbəl/ *a* falible

falling /'fɔlɪŋ/ *a* que cae, cayente. *n* caída, *f*; (of mercury, temperature) baja, *f*; (crumbling) desmoronamiento, *m*; (collapse) hundimiento, derrumbamiento, *m*; (of tide) reflujo, *m*; (of water level) bajada, *f*; (in value) depreciación, *f*; (of prices and Stock Exchange) baja, *f*; (diminishment) disminución, *f*; (in level of earth) declinación, *f*; (*Com.* expiry) vencimiento, *m*; (*Theat.* of curtain) bajada, caída, *f*. **f. away,** (crumbling) desmoronamiento, *m*; desprendimiento de tierras, *m*; (desertion) deserción, *f*, abandono, *m*. **f. back,** retirada, *f*, retroceso, *m*. **f. down,** caída, *f*; derrumbamiento, *m*. **f. due,** vencimiento, *m*. **f. in,** hundimiento, *m*; (crumbling) desmoronamiento, *m*. **f. off,** caída, *f*; (disappearance) desaparición, *f*; (diminution) disminución, *f*; (deterioration) deterioración, *f*. **f. out,** caída por, *f*, disensión, *f*. **f. short,** falta, *f*; carácter inferior, *m*; frustración, *f*. **f. star,** estrella fugaz, *f*

fallout /'fɔl,aut/ caída radiactiva, lluvizna radiactiva, precipitación radiactiva, *f*

fallow /'fælou/ *a* (of color) leonado; *Agr.* barbechado; descuidado. *n* barbecho, *m*. *vt* barbechar. **to leave f.,** dejar en barbecho. **f. deer,** corzo (-za)

false /fɔls/ *a* incorrecto, erróneo, equivocado; falso; (unfounded) infundado; (disloyal) infiel, traidor, desleal; (not real) postizo; artificial; de imitación; *Mus.* desafinado; (pretended) fingido; engañoso, mentiroso. **to play a person f.,** traicionar (a). **f. bottom,** fondo doble, *m*; **f. claim,** pretensión infundada, *f*. **f. door,** surtida, *f*. **f.-hearted,** pérfido, desleal. **f. teeth,** dientes postizos, *m pl*, dentadura postiza, *f*

falsehood /'fɔlshʊd/ *n* mentira, *f*

falseness /'fɔlsnɪs/ *n* falsedad, *f*; (disloyalty) duplicidad, perfidia, traición, *f*

falsetto /fɔl'sɛtou/ *n* falsete, *m*, voz de cabeza, *f*

falsification /,fɔlsəfɪ'keifən/ *n* falsificación, *f*; (of texts) corrupción, *f*

falsifier /'fɔlsəfaiər/ *n* falsificador (-ra)

falsify /'fɔlsəfai/ *vt* falsear, falsificar; (disappoint) defraudar, frustrar, contrariar

falter /'fɔltər/ *vi* (physically) titubear; (of speech) balbucir, tartamudear; (of action) vacilar. **to f. out,** balbucir; hablar con voz entrecortada; decir con vacilación

faltering /'fɔltərɪŋ/ *a* titubeante; (of speech) entrecortado; vacilante. *n* temblor, *m*; vacilación, *f*

falteringly /'fɔltərɪŋli/ *adv* (of speech) balbuciente, en una voz temblorosa; con dificultad, vacilantemente

fame /feim/ *n* fama, *f*; reputación, *f*; (renown) celebridad, *f*, renombre, *m*. **of ill f.,** de mala fama

famed /feimd/ *a* reputado; renombrado, célebre, famoso

familiar /fə'mɪlyər/ *a* íntimo, familiar; afable, amistoso; (ill-bred) insolente, demasiado familiar; (usual) corriente, usual, común; conocido. *n* amigo (-ga), íntimo (-ma); *Eccl.* familiar, *m*; demonio familiar, *m*. **to be f. with,** (a subject) estar versado en, conocer muy bien; (a person) tratar con familiaridad. **to become f. with,** acostumbrarse a; familiarizarse con; (a person) hacerse íntimo de

familiarity /fə,mɪli'ærɪti/ *n* intimidad, familiaridad, confianza, *f*; (friendliness) afabilidad, *f*; (over-familiarity) insolencia, demasiada familiaridad, *f*; (with a subject) conocimiento (de), *m*, experiencia (de), *f*

familiarize /fə'mɪlyə,raiz/ *vt* familiarizar, acostumbrar, habituar. *vr* familiarizarse

familiarly /fə'mɪlyərli/ *adv* familiarmente; amistosamente

family /'fæməli/ *n* familia, *f*; (lineage) linaje, abolengo, *m*; (*Bot. Zool.*) familia, *f*; (of languages) grupo, *m. a* de familia; familiar; casero. **f. doctor,** médico de cabecera, *m*. **f. life,** vida de familia, *f*; hogar, *m*. **f. man,** padre de familia, *m*. **f. name,** apellido, *m*. **f. seat,** casa solar, *f*. **f. tree,** árbol genealógico, *m*

family quarrel disputa de familia, *f*

famine /'fæmɪn/ *n* hambre, *f*; carestía, escasez, *f*

famish /'fæmɪʃ/ *vt* matar de hambre. *vi* morirse de hambre

famished /'fæmɪʃt/ *a* hambriento

famous /'feiməs/ *a* famoso, célebre, renombrado; insigne, distinguido; *Inf.* excelente

famously /'feiməsli/ *adv Inf.* muy bien, excelentemente

fan /fæn/ *n* abanico, *m*; *Agr.* aventador, *m*; *Mech.* ventilador, *m*; (on a windmill) volante, *m*; (amateur) aficionado (-da); (admirer) admirador (-ra); *Archit.* abanico, *m. vt* abanicar; *Agr.* aventar; ventilar. **fan oneself,** hacerse viento. **tap with a f.,** abanicazo, golpecito con el abanico, *m*. **f.-belt,** *Mech.* correa de transmisión del ventilador, *f*. **f.-light,** tragaluz, *m*. **f. maker** or **seller,** abaniquero (-ra). **f.-shaped,** en abanico, abanicado, en forma de abanico

fanatic /fə'nætɪk/ *a* and *n* fanático (-ca)

fanaticism /fə'nætə,sɪzəm/ *n* fanatismo, *m*

fanaticize /fə'nætə,saiz/ *vt* fanatizar

fancied /'fænsid/ *a* imaginario

fancier /'fænsiər/ *n* aficionado (-da); (of animals) criador (-ra)

fanciful /'fænsifəl/ *a* romántico, caprichoso; fantástico

fancifulness /'fænsifəlnɪs/ *n* extravagancia, *f*; romanticismo, *m*

fancy /'fænsi/ *n* fantasía, imaginación, *f*; (idea) idea, *f*, ensueño, *m*; (caprice) capricho, antojo, *m*; (liking) afecto, cariño, *m*; gusto, *m*, afición, *f*; (wish) deseo, *m*; (fantasy) quimera, *f*, *a* imaginario; elegante, ornado; *Com.* de capricho, de fantasía; fantástico, extravagante. *vt* imaginar, figurarse; (like) gustar de; aficionarse a; antojarse. **I have a f. for...,** Se me antoja.... **Just f.!** ¡Toma! ¡Quia! ¡Parece mentira! **to take a f. to,** (things) tomar afición a; (people) tomar cariño (a). **f.-dress,** disfraz, *m*. **f.-dress ball,** baile de trajes, *m*

fane /fein/ *n* templo, *m*

fanfare /'fænfeər/ *n* tocata de trompetas, *f*

fang /fæŋ/ *n* colmillo, *m*; raíz de un diente, *f*

fanged /fæŋd/ *a* que tiene colmillos; (of teeth) acolmillado

fangless /'fæŋlɪs/ *a* sin colmillos

fanner /'fænər/ *n* abanicador (-ra); *Agr.* aventador, *m*

fanning /'fænɪŋ/ *n* abanique, *m*; *Agr.* avienta, *f*

fantastic /fæn'tæstɪk/ *a* fantástico; extravagante

fantastically /fæn'tæstɪkəli/ *adv* fantásticamente; extravagantemente

fantasy /'fæntəsi/ *n* imaginación, *f*; fantasía, quimera, visión, *f*; creación imaginativa, *f*

far /fɑr/ *adv* lejos; a lo lejos; (much, greatly) mucho, en alto grado; (very) muy; (mostly) en gran parte. *a* lejano, distante; (farther) ulterior. **as far as,** tan lejos como; (up to, until) hasta; en cuanto, por lo que, según que. (e.g. *As far as we know,* Por lo que nosotros sepamos. *As far as we are concerned,* En cuanto a nosotros toca). **by far,** con mucho. **from far and near,** de todas partes. **from far off,** desde lejos. **He read far into the night,** Leyó hasta las altas horas de la noche. **how far?** ¿a qué distancia?; (to what extent) ¿hasta qué punto? ¿hasta qué dónde? **How far is it to...?** ¿Qué distancia hay a...? **in so far as,** en tanto que. **on the far side,** al lado opuesto; al otro extremo. **so far,** tan lejos; (till now) hasta ahora. **to go far,** ir lejos. **far away,** *a* distante, remoto, lejano; *Fig.*

abstraído. *adv* muy lejos. **far beyond,** mucho más allá. **far-fetched,** increíble, improbable. **far-off,** *a* distante. *adv* a lo lejos, en lontananza. **far-reaching,** de gran alcance. **far-sighted,** sagaz, presciente, previsor. **far-sightedness,** sagacidad, previsión, *f*

farce /fɑrs/ *n* farsa, *f*, *vt Cul.* embutir, rellenar

farcical /'fɑrsɪkəl/ *a* burlesco, cómico, sainetesco; absurdo, grotesco, ridículo

fare /feər/ *n* (price) pasaje, precio del billete, *m*; (traveler) viajero (-ra), pasajero (-ra); (food) comida, *f*. *vi* pasarlo (e.g. *to f. well,* pasarlo bien). **bill of f.,** menú, *m*. **full f.,** billete entero, *m*. **f. stage,** trayecto, *m*

farewell /,feər'wɛl/ *n* despedida, *f*, adiós, *m*. *a* de despedida. *interj* ¡adiós! ¡quede Vd. con Dios! **to bid f. to,** despedirse de

farewell address *n* discurso de despedida *m*

farflung /'fɑr'flʌŋ/ de gran alcance, extenso, vasto; (empire) dilatado

farina /fə'rinə/ *n* harina (de cereales), *f*; *Chem.* fécula, *f*, almidón, *m*; *Bot.* polen, *m*

farm /fɑrm/ *n* granja, hacienda, quintería, finca, chacra, *f*, cortijo, *m. vt* cultivar, labrar (la tierra); (taxes) arrendar. *vi* ser granjero. **to f. out,** (taxes) dar en arriendo. **f. girl,** labradora, *f*. **f. house,** alquería, casa de labranza, granja, *f*. **f. laborer,** labriego, peón, *m*. **f. yard,** corral de una granja, *m*

farmer /'fɑrmər/ *n* granjero, hacendado, quintero, *m*, agrícola, *mf*; (small) colono, labrador, *m*; (of taxes) arrendatario, *m*

farmers' movement /'fɑrmərz/ *Mexico* agrarismo *m*

farmhand /'fɑrm,hænd/ gañán, mozo, mozo de granja, peón *m*

farming /'fɑrmɪŋ/ *n* labranza, *f*, cultivo, *m*; agricultura, labor agrícola, *f*; (of taxes) arriendo, *m. a* de labranza, labradoril; agrícola

faro /'feərou/ *n* (card game) faraón, *m*

farouche /fə'ruʃ/ *a* huraño, esquivo

farrago /fə'rɑgou/ *n* fárrago, *m*, mezcla, *f*

farrier /'færiər/ *n* herrador, *m*

farther /'fɑrðər/ *adv* más lejos; (beyond) más adelante; (besides) además. *a* ulterior; más distante. **at the f. end,** al otro extremo; en el fondo. **f. on,** más adelante; más allá

farthest /'fɑrðɪst/ *adv* más lejos. *a* más lejano, más distante; extremo

farthing /'fɑrðɪŋ/ *n* cuarto, *m*; *Fig.* ardite, maravedí, *m*. **He hasn't a brass f.,** No tiene dos maravedís

fascinate /'fæsə,neit/ *vt* fascinar; encantar, hechizar, seducir

fascinating /'fæsə,neitɪŋ/ *a* fascinador; encantador, seduciente

fascination /,fæsə'neiʃən/ *n* fascinación, *f*; encanto, hechizo, *m*

Fascism /'fæʃ,ɪzəm/ *n* fascismo, *m*

Fascist /'fæʃɪst/ *a* and *n* fascista *mf*

fashion /'fæʃən/ *n* (form) forma, hechura, *f*; (way) modo, *m*; (custom) costumbre, *f*, uso, *m*; (vogue) moda, *f*; (high life) alta sociedad, *f*; (tone) buen tono, *m. vt* hacer, labrar; inventar. **in Spanish f.,** a la española, al uso de España. **the latest f.,** la última moda. **to be in f.,** estar de moda. **to go out of f.,** dejar de ser de moda, perder la popularidad. **f. book,** revista de modas, *f*. **f. plate,** figurín, *m*

fashionable /'fæʃənəbəl/ *a* de moda; elegante; de buen tono. **to be in f.,** estar en boga, ser de moda. **f. world,** mundo elegante, mundo de sociedad, *m*

fashionableness /'fæʃənəbəlnɪs/ *n* buen tono, *m*; elegancia, *f*

fashionably /'fæʃənəbli/ *adv* a la moda, elegantemente

fashion show desfile de modas, *m*, exhibición de modas, *f*

fast /fæst/ *a* (firm) firme; (secure) seguro; (strong) fuerte; (fixed) fijo; (closed) cerrado; (of boats) amarrado; (tight) apretado; (of colors) estable; (of trains) rápido; (of sleep) profundo; (of friends) leal, seguro; (quick) rápido, veloz; (of a watch) adelantado; (dissipated) disoluto. *adv* firmemente, seguramente; (quickly) rápidamente; (of sleep) profundamente; (tightly) estrechamente, apretadamente; (of rain) (llover) a cántaros; (ceaselessly) continuamente; (of-

ten) frecuentemente; (entirely) completamente. **to be f.,** (clocks) adelantar. **to make f.,** *Naut.* amarrar, trincar. **f. asleep,** profundamente dormido. **f. color,** color estable, color sólido, *m*
fast /fæst/ *n* ayuno, *m, vi* ayunar. **to break one's f.,** romper el ayuno. **f.-day,** día de ayuno, día de vigilia, *m*
fasten /'fæsən/ *vt* (tie) atar; (fix) fijar; sujetar; (stick) pegar; (a door) cerrar; (bolt) echar el cerrojo; *Naut.* trincar; (together) juntar, unir; (with buttons, hooks, etc.) abrochar; (on, upon) fijar en; *Fig.* imputar (a). *vi* fijarse; pegarse; (upon) agarrarse a, asir. **to f. one's eyes on,** fijar los ojos en. **to f. up,** cerrar; atar; (nail) clavar
fastener /'fæsənər/ *n* (bolt) pasador, *m*; (for bags, jewelry, etc.) cierre, *m*; (buckle) hebilla, *f*; (of a coat, etc.) tiador, *m*; (of a book, file) sujetador, *m*; (lock) cerrojo, *m.* **paper-f.,** sujetador de papeles, *m.* **patent-f.,** botón automático, *m*
fastening /'fæsənɪŋ/ *n* atadura, *f*; sujeción, *f*, afianzamiento, *m*; (together) unión, *f*; (of a garment) brochadura, *f*; (of a handbag) cierre, *m*
fastidious /fæ'stɪdɪəs/ *a* dengoso, melindroso, desdeñoso; (sensitive) sensitivo, delicado; (critical) discerniente, crítico
fastidiously /fæs'tɪdɪəsli/ *adv* melindrosamente
fastidiousness /fæs'tɪdɪəsnɪs/ *n* dengues, melindres, *m pl*, nimiedad, *f*, desdén, *m*; sensibilidad, delicadeza, *f*; sentido crítico, *m*
fasting /'fæstɪŋ/ *n* ayuno, *m. a* and *part* de ayuno; en ayunas
fastness /'fæstnɪs/ *n* firmeza, solidez, *f*; (stronghold) fortaleza, *f*; (retreat) refugio, *m*; (speed) velocidad, rapidez, *f*; (dissipation) disipación, *f*, libertinaje, *m*
fat /fæt/ *a* (stout) gordo, grueso; mantecoso, graso, seboso; (greasy) grasiento; (rich) fértil, pingüe; (productive) lucrativo. *n* (stoutness) gordura, *f*; (for cooking) manteca, *f*; (lard) lardo, *m*; (of animal or meat) grasa, *f*; sebo, saín, *m*; *Fig.* riqueza, *f*; *Fig.* fertilidad, *f.* **to grow fat,** engordarse, ponerse grueso
fatal /'feitl/ *a* fatal, mortal; funesto
fatalism /'feitl,ɪzəm/ *n* fatalismo, *m*
fatalist /'feitlɪst/ *n* fatalista, *mf*
fatalistic /,feitl'ɪstɪk/ *a* fatalista
fatality /fei'tælɪti/ *n* fatalidad, *f*; infortunio, *m*, calamidad, *f*; muerte, *f*
fatally /'feitli/ *adv* mortalmente, fatalmente; inevitablemente
fate /feit/ *n* destino, sino, hado, *m*, providencia, *f*; fortuna, suerte, *f*; destrucción, ruina, *f*; muerte, *f.* **the Three Fates,** las Parcas
fated /'feitɪd/ *a* fatal, destinado; predestinado
fateful /'feitfəl/ *a* decisivo, fatal; aciago, ominoso
father /'faðər/ *n* padre, *m. vt* prohijar, adoptar; (on or upon) atribuir (a), imputar (a). **Eternal F.,** Padre Eterno, *m.* **Holy F.,** Padre Santo, *m.* **indulgent f.,** padre indulgente, padrazo, *m.* **Like f. like son,** De tal palo tal astilla. **f. confessor,** *Eccl.* director espiritual, *m.* **f.-in-law,** suegro, *m*
fatherhood /'faðər,hʊd/ *n* paternidad, *f*
fatherland /'faðər,lænd/ *n* patria, madre patria, *f*
fatherless /'faðərlɪs/ *a* sin padre, huérfano de padre
fatherliness /'faðərlinɪs/ *n* amor paternal, *m*; sentimiento paternal, *m*
fatherly /'faðərli/ *a* paternal, de padre
fathom /'fæðəm/ *n Naut.* braza, *f. vt* sondear; *Fig.* profundizar, tantear; (a mystery) desentrañar
fathomless /'fæðəmlɪs/ *a* insondable; *Fig.* incomprensible, impenetrable
fatigue /fə'tig/ *n* fatiga, *f*, cansancio, *m*; *Mil.* faena, *f*; *Mech.* pérdida de resistencia, *f. vt* fatigar, cansar. **to be fatigued,** estar cansado, cansarse, fatigarse. **f. party,** *Mil.* pelotón de castigo, *m*
fatiguing /fə'tigɪŋ/ *a* fatigoso
fatness /'fætnɪs/ *n* (stoutness) gordura, carnosidad, *f*; grasa, *f*, gordo, *m*; (richness) fertilidad, *f*; lo lucrativo
fatten /'fætn/ *vt* engordar; (animals) cebar, sainar; (land) abonar, fertilizar. *vi* ponerse grueso, echar carnes
fatty /'fæti/ *a* untoso, grasiento; *Chem.* graso. **f. acid,** ácido graso, *m.* **f. degeneration,** degeneración grasienta, *f*

fatuity /fə'tuɪti/ *n* fatuidad, necedad, *f*
fatuous /'fætʃuəs/ *a* fatuo, necio, lelo
faucet /'fɔsɪt/ *n* canilla, llave, *f*, grifo, *m*
fault /fɔlt/ *n* defecto, *m*, imperfección, *f*; (blame) culpa, *f*; (mistake) falta, *f*, error, *m*; (in cloth) canilla, barra, *f*; *Geol.* falla, quiebra, *f*; *Elec.* avería, *f*; *Sports.* falta, *f*, *vi Sports.* cometer una falta. **to a f.,** excesivamente. **to be at f.,** (to blame) tener la culpa; (mistaken) estar equivocado; (puzzled) estar perplejo; (of dogs) perder el rastro. **to find f.,** tachar, culpar, criticar. **Whose f. is it?** ¿Quién tiene la culpa?
faultfinder /'fɔlt,faindər/ *n* criticón (-ona)
faultiness /'fɔltinɪs/ *n* defectuosidad, imperfección, *f*
faultless /'fɔltlɪs/ *a* sin faltas; perfecto, sin tacha; impecable
faulty /'fɔlti/ *a* defectuoso, imperfecto
fauna /'fɔnə/ *n* fauna, *f*
favor /'feivər/ *n* favor, *m*; (protection) amistad, protección, *f*, amparo, *m*; (permission) permiso, *m*, licencia, *f*; (kindness) merced, gracia, *f*; (gift) obsequio, *m*; (favoritism) favoritismo, *m*, preferencia, *f*; (benefit) beneficio, *m*; (badge) colores, *m pl*; *Com.* grata, atenta, *f. vt* favorecer, apoyar; mirar con favor, mostrar parcialidad (hacia); (suit) favorecer; (be advantageous) ser propicio (a); (contribute to) contribuir a, ayudar; (resemble) parecerse a. **Circumstances f. the idea,** Las circunstancias son propicias a la idea, Las circunstancias militan en pro de la idea. **I f. the teaching of modern languages,** Soy partidario de la enseñanza de lenguas vivas. **in f. of,** a favor de, en pro de. **in the f. of,** en el favor de. **out of f.,** fuera de favor; (not fashionable) fuera de moda. **to count on the f. of,** tener de su parte (a), contar con el apoyo de. **to do a f.,** hacer un favor. **to enjoy the f. of,** gozar del favor de. **to fall out of f.,** caer en desgracia; (go out of fashion) pasar de moda. **to grow in f.,** aumentar en favor
favorable /'feivərəbəl/ *a* favorable; propicio, próspero
favorableness /'feivərəbəlnɪs/ *n* lo favorable; lo propicio; benignidad, benevolencia, *f*
favored /'feivərd/ *a* favorecido; predilecto; (in compounds) parecido, encarado
favoring /'feivərɪŋ/ *a* favorecedor, propicio
favorite /'feivərɪt/ *a* favorito; predilecto, preferido. *n* favorito (-ta). **court f.,** valido, privado, *m*; (mistress) querida (de un rey), *f*; (lover) amante (de una reina), *m.* **to be a f.,** ser favorito
favoritism /'feivəri,tɪzəm/ *n* favoritismo, *m*
fawn /fɔn/ *n Zool.* cervato, *m*; (color) color de cervato, color de ante, *m. a* de color de cervato, anteado, pardo; (of animals) rucio, pardo. *vt* and *vi* parir la cierva. *vi* acariciar; (on, upon) adular, lisonjear
fawning /'fɔnɪŋ/ *n* adulación, *Lat. Am.* aduloneríanf, *a* adulador, lisonjero, *Lat. Am. also* incondicional, *Mexico* lambioche
fax /fæks/ *n* facsimile, *m*, fax, *m.* **fax machine,** máquina fax, *f. vt* mandar un fax, pasar el tono
fear /fɪr/ *n* miedo, temor, *m*, *Argentina* canillera *f*; (apprehension) ansiedad, aprensión, *f*, recelo, *m*; (respect) veneración, *f. vt* temer; recelar; (respect) reverenciar. *vi* tener miedo; estar receloso, estar con cuidado. **for f. of,** por miedo de. **for f. that,** por temor de que, por miedo de que. **from f.,** por miedo. **There is no f. of...,** No hay miedo de (que)...
fearer /'fɪrər/ *n* temedor (-ra), el (la) que teme
fearful /'fɪrfəl/ *a* miedoso, aprensivo, receloso; (cowardly) tímido, pusilánime; (terrible) horrible, espantoso, pavoroso; *Inf.* tremendo, enorme
fearfully /'fɪrfəli/ *adv* con miedo; tímidamente (terribly) horriblemente; *Inf.* enormemente
fearfulness /'fɪrfəlnɪs/ *n* temor, miedo, *m*; (horribleness) lo horrible
fearless /'fɪrlɪs/ *a* sin miedo, intrépido, audaz
fearlessness /'fɪrlɪsnɪs/ *n* intrepidez, valentía, *f*
fearsome /'fɪrsəm/ *a* temible, horrible, espantoso
feasibility /,fizə'bɪlɪti/ *n* practicabilidad, posibilidad, *f*
feasible /'fizəbəl/ *a* factible, hacedero, practicable, ejecutable
feast /fist/ *n Eccl.* fiesta, *f*; banquete, *m*; *Fig.* abun-

dancia, *f, vi* regalarse. *vt* festejar, agasajar; (delight) recrear, deleitar. **immovable f.,** *Eccl.* fiesta fija, *f.* **movable f.,** fiesta movible, *f.* **f. day,** día de fiesta, *m,* festividad, *f*

feasting /'fistɪŋ/ *n* banquetes, *m pl;* fiestas, *f pl*

feat /fit/ *n* hazaña, proeza, *f,* hecho, *m;* (accomplishment) logro, *m*

feather /'fɛðər/ *n* pluma, *f;* (of the tail) pena, *f; pl* **feathers,** plumaje, *m;* plumas, *f pl. vt* emplumar; adornar con plumas; (rowing) poner casi horizontal la pala del remo. **to f.** one's **nest,** *Inf.* hacer su agosto. **f.-bed,** plumón, colchón de plumas, *m.* **f.-brained,** casquivano, alocado, aturdido. **f.-duster,** plumero, *m.* **f.-stitch,** *Sew.* diente de perro, *m.* **f. weight,** (boxing) peso pluma, *m*

feathered /'fɛðərd/ *a* plumado, plumoso; adornado con plumas; (winged) alado

feathery /'fɛðəri/ *a* plumoso; como plumas

feature /'fitʃər/ *n* rasgo, *m,* característica, *f;* (cinema) número de programa, *m; pl* **features** (of the face) facciones, *f pl. vt* dar importancia (a); (cinema) presentar. **f. film,** documentaria, *f*

febrile /'fibrəl/ *a* febril

February /'fɛbru,ɛri, 'fɛbyu-/ *n* febrero, *m*

fecal /'fikəl/ *a* fecal

feces /'fisiz/ *n* heces, *f pl;* excremento, *m*

fecund /'fikʌnd/ *a* fecundo, fértil

fecundate /'fikən,deit/ *vt* fecundar

fecundity /fɪ'kʌndɪti/ *n* fecundidad, fertilidad, *f*

federal /'fɛdərəl/ *a* federal, federalista

federalism /'fɛdərə,lɪzəm/ *n* federalismo, *m*

federalist /'fɛdərəlɪst/ *n* federalista, federal, *mf*

federate /v 'fɛdə,reit; *a* -ərɪt/ *vt* confederar. *vi* confederarse. *a* confederado

federation /,fɛdə'reiʃən/ *n* confederación, federación, *f;* liga, unión, asociación, *f*

fed up /fɛd/ *a* *Argentina, Chile* incomódo, *elsewhere in Lat. Am.* harto

fee /fi/ *n* (duty) derecho, *m;* (professional) honorario, estipendio, *m;* (to a servant) gratificación, *f;* (entrance, university, etc.) cuota, *f;* (payment) paga, *f.* **registration f.,** matrícula, *f*

feeble /'fibəl/ *a* débil; lánguido; enfermizo; (of light, etc.) tenue; *Fig.* flojo. **to grow f.,** debilitarse; disminuir. **f.-minded,** anormal

feebleness /'fibəlnɪs/ *n* debilidad, *f; Fig.* flojedad, *f*

feebly /'fibli/ *adv* débilmente; lánguidamente

feed /fid/ *n* alimento, *m;* (meal) comida, *f;* (of animals) pienso, forraje, *m; Mech.* alimentación, *f. vt* alimentar; dar de comer (a); (animals) cebar; *Mech.* alimentar; mantener; *Fig.* nutrir. *vi* comer, alimentarse; (graze) pastar. **to be fed up,** *Inf.* estar hasta la coronilla, estar harto. **to f. on,** alimentarse de; *Fig.* nutrirse de. **f. pipe,** tubo de alimentación, *m*

feedback /'fid,bæk/ *n* retrocomunicación, *f*

feeder /'fidər/ *n* el, *m,* (*f,* la) que da de comer a; (eater) comedor (-ra); (of a river) tributario, afluente, *m;* (bib) babero, *m; Mech.* alimentador, *m;* (cup for invalids) pistero, *m*

feeding /'fidɪŋ/ *n* alimentación, *f, a* alimenticio, de alimentación. **f.-bottle,** biberón, *m.* **f.-cup,** pistero, *m.* **f.-trough,** pesebre, *m*

feel /fil/ *n* (touch) tacto, *m;* (feeling) sensación, *f;* (instinct) instinto, *m,* percepción innata, *f*

feel /fil/ *vt* (touch) tocar, tentar, palpar; (experience) sentir, experimentar; (understand) comprender; (believe) creer; (be conscious of) estar consciente de; (the pulse) tomar; examinar. *vi* sentir, ser sensible; sentirse, encontrarse; (to the touch) ser... *a* tal, estar. **How do you f.?** ¿Cómo se siente Vd.? **I f. cold,** Tengo frío. **I f. for you,** Lo siento en el alma; Estoy muy consciente de ello. **I f. strongly that...,** Estoy convencido de que... **I f. that it is a difficult question,** Me parece una cuestión difícil. **It feels like rain,** Creo que va a llover. **to f. at home,** sentirse a sus anchas, sentirse como en su casa. **to f. hungry (thirsty),** tener hambre (sed). **to f. one's way,** ir a tientas; *Fig.* medir el terreno. **to f. soft,** ser blando al tacto. **to make itself felt,** hacerse sentir. **Your hands f. cold,** Tus manos están frías

feeler /'filər/ *n* (of insects) palpo, *m,* antena, *f;* tentáculo, *m; Fig.* tentativa, *f,* balón de ensayo, *m*

feeling /'filɪŋ/ *n* (touch) tacto, *m;* (sensation) sensación, *f;* (sentiment) sentimiento, *m;* emoción, *f;* (premonition) corazonada, intuición, premonición, *f;* (tenderness) ternura, *f;* (perception) sensibilidad, percepción, *f;* (passion) pasión, *f;* (belief) opinión, *f,* sentir, *m. a* sensible; tierno; (compassionate) compasivo; apasionado; (moving) conmovedor

feelingly /'filɪŋli/ *adv* con emoción; (strongly) enérgicamente, vivamente; (understandingly) comprensivamente

feign /fein/ *vt* fingir; (invent) inventar, imaginar; simular; (allege) pretextar; (dissemble) disimular. *vi* disimular

feint /feint/ *n* artificio, engaño, *m;* (in fencing) treta, finta, *f. vi* hacer finta

feldspar /'fɛld,spɑr/ *n* *Mineral.* feldespato, *m*

felicitate /fɪ'lɪsɪ,teit/ *vt* felicitar, congratular, dar el parabién (a)

felicitation /fɪ,lɪsɪ'teiʃən/ *n* felicitación, *f,* parabién, *m*

felicitous /fɪ'lɪsɪtəs/ *a* feliz, dichoso, afortunado; (of phrases, etc.) feliz, acertado; oportuno

felicity /fɪ'lɪsɪti/ *n* felicidad, dicha, *f*

feline /'filain/ *a* felino, gatuno, de gato. *n* felino, *m*

fell /fɛl/ *n* (skin) piel, *f;* (upland) altura, cuesta de montaña, *f. a* cruel, feroz; (unhappy) aciago, funesto. *vt* talar, cortar; (knock down) derribar; *Sew.* sobrecoser

feller /'fɛlər/ *n* talador, leñador, *m*

felling /'fɛlɪŋ/ *n* corta, tala, *f*

fellow /'fɛlou/ *n* compañero (-ra); (equal) igual, *mf;* (in crime) cómplice, *mf;* (man) hombre, *m;* (boy, youth) chico, *m;* (colleague) colega, *m;* (of a society) miembro, *m;* (of a pair of objects) pareja, *f; Inf.* tipo, chico, *m.* **He's a good f.,** Es un buen chico. **How are you, old f.?** ¡Hombre! ¿Cómo estás? **f.-citizen,** conciudadano (-na). **f.-countryman,** compatriota, *m;* paisano (-na). **f.-creature,** semejante, *mf.* **f.-feeling,** simpatía, comprensión mutua, *f.* **f.-member,** compañero (-ra); colega, *m.* **f.-passenger,** compañero (-ra) de viaje. **f.-prisoner,** compañero (-ra) de prisión. **f.-student,** condiscípulo (-la). **f.-worker,** compañero (-ra) de trabajo; (collaborator) colaborador (-ra); (colleague) colega, *m*

fellowship /'felouʃɪp/ *n* coparticipación, *f;* (companionship, religious) compañerismo, *m;* (brotherhood) comunidad, confraternidad, *f;* (society) asociación, *f;* (grant) beca, *f;* (of a university) colegiatura, *f*

felon /'fɛlən/ *n* reo, criminal, *m;* felón (-ona) malvado (-da); (swelling) panadizo, *m*

felonious /fə'lounɪəs/ *a* criminal; pérfido, traidor

felony /'fɛləni/ *n* felonía, *f*

felt /fɛlt/ *n* fieltro, *m. a* **f. hat,** un sombrero de fieltro

female /'fimeil/ *n* hembra, *f, a* femenino. (**f.** is often rendered in Sp. by the feminine ending of the noun, e.g. *a f. cat,* una gata; *a f. friend,* una amiga.) **This is a f. animal,** Este animal es una hembra. **f. screw,** hembra de tornillo, tuerca, *f*

feminine /'fɛmənɪn/ *a* femenino; mujeril, afeminado. **in the f. gender,** en el género femenino

feminism /'fɛmə,nɪzəm/ *n* feminismo, *m*

feminist /'fɛmənɪst/ *n* feminista, *mf*

feministic /,fɛmə'nɪstɪk/ *a* feminista

femur /'fimər/ *n* *Anat.* fémur, *m*

fen /fɛn/ *n* marjal, pantano, *m*

fence /fɛns/ *n* cerca, *f;* (of stakes) estacada, palizada, *f;* (hedge) seto, *m;* (fencing) esgrima, *f; Mech.* guía, *f; Inf.* comprador (-ra) de efectos robados. *vi* esgrimir; *Fig.* defenderse; *Inf.* recibir efectos robados. *vt* cercar; estacar; *Fig.* defender; proteger. **to sit on the f.,** *Fig.* estar a ver venir

fencer /'fɛnsər/ *n* esgrimidor, *m*

fencesitter /'fɛns,sɪtər/ *n* bailarín de la cuerda flaja, *m*

fencing /'fɛnsɪŋ/ *n* esgrima, *f;* palizada, empalizada, *f.* **f. mask,** careta, *f.* **f. master,** maestro de esgrima, maestro de armas, *m.* **f. match,** asalto de esgrima, *m*

fend /fɛnd/ **(off)** *vt* parar; defenderse de, guardarse de. *vi* (for) mantener, cuidar de. **to f. for oneself,** ganarse la vida; defenderse

fender /'fɛndər/ n (round hearth) guardafuegos, m; *Naut.* espolón, m, defensas, f pl; *Auto.* parachoques, m

fennel /'fɛnl/ n *Bot.* hinojo, m

ferment /n 'fɜrmɛnt; v fər'mɛnt/ n fermento, m; fermentación, f; *Fig.* agitación, conmoción, efervescencia f. *vt* hacer fermentar; *Fig.* agitar, excitar. *vi* fermentar, estar en fermentación; *Fig.* hervirse, agitarse, excitarse

fermentation /ˌfɜrmɛn'teiʃən/ n fermentación, f

fern /fɜrn/ n helecho, m

ferocious /fə'rouʃəs/ a feroz, bravo, salvaje

ferocity /fə'rɒsɪti/ n ferocidad, braveza, fiereza, f

ferreous /'fɛriəs/ a férreo

ferret /'fɛrɪt/ n *Zool.* hurón (-ona); **to f. out,** cazar con hurones; (discover) husmear, descubrir

Ferris wheel /'fɛrɪs/ n estrella giratoria, gran rueda, novia, rueda de feria, f

ferroconcrete /ˌfɛrou'kɒnkrit/ n hormigón armado, m

ferrous /'fɛrəs/ a ferroso

ferruginous /fə'rudʒənəs/ a ferruginoso; aherrumbrado, rojizo

ferrule /'fɛrəl/ n herrete, regatón, m, contera, f; garrucha de tornillos, f

ferry /'fɛri/ n barca de transporte, f; barca de pasaje, f, transbordador, m. *vt* transportar de una a otra orilla, llevar en barca. *vi* cruzar un río en barca. **ferry across** *vt* transbordar. **F.-Command,** servicio de entrega y transporte de aeroplanos, m

ferryman /'fɛrimən/ n barquero, m

fertile /'fɜrtl/ a fértil, fecundo; (rich) pingüe; *Fig.* prolífico, abundante

Fertile Crescent, the el Creciente Fértil m

fertility /fər'tɪlɪti/ n fertilidad, fecundidad, f

fertilization /ˌfɜrtlə'zeiʃən/ n *Biol.* fecundación, f; *Agr.* fertilización, f, abono, m

fertilize /'fɜrtlˌaiz/ *vt* *Biol.* fecundar; *Agr.* fertilizar, abonar

fertilizer /'fɜrtlˌaizər/ n abono, m

ferule /'fɛrəl/ n palmatoria, palmeta, férula, f

fervent /'fɜrvənt/ a ardiente; fervoroso, intenso; (enthusiastic) entusiasta, apasionado

fervently /'fɜrvəntli/ adv con fervor, con vehemencia

fervor /'fɜrvər/ n ardor, fervor, m, pasión, f; (enthusiasm) entusiasmo, celo, m; vehemencia, f

festal /'fɛstl/ a de fiesta; alegre, festivo, regocijado

fester /'fɛstər/ *vi* ulcerarse, enconarse; *Fig.* inflamarse, amargarse. *vt* ulcerar

festival /'fɛstəvəl/ a de fiesta. n festividad, f; *Eccl.* fiesta, f; (musical, etc.) festival, m

festive /'fɛstɪv/ a de fiesta; festivo, alegre

festivity /fɛ'stɪvɪti/ n festividad, fiesta, f; (merriment) alegría, f, júbilo, m

festoon /fɛ'stun/ n festón, m, guirnalda, f. *vt* festonear

festschrift /'fɛstˌʃrift/ n libro de homenaje, libro jubilar, m

fetal /'fitl/ a fetal

fetch /fɛtʃ/ *vt* traer; ir a buscar; ir por; llevar; (conduct) conducir; (of tears) hacer derramar lágrimas, hacer saltársele las lágrimas; (blood) hacer correr la sangre; (produce, draw) sacar; (a blow, a sigh) dar; (acquire) conseguir; (charm) fascinar; (of price) venderse por. **to go and f.,** ir a buscar

fetid /'fɛtɪd/ a fétido, hediondo

fetidness /'fɛtɪdnɪs/ n fetidez, f, hedor, m

fetish /'fɛtɪʃ/ n fetiche, m

fetishism /'fɛtɪˌʃizəm/ n fetichismo, m

fetter /'fɛtər/ n grillete, m; pl **fetters,** grillos, m pl, cadenas, f pl; prisión, cárcel, f. *vt* encadenar, atar

fettle /'fɛtl/ n condición, f, estado, m

fetus /'fitəs/ n feto, m

feud /fyud/ n enemistad, riña, f; (feudal law) feudo, m

feudal /'fyudl/ a feudal. **f. lord,** señor feudal, señor de horca y cuchillo, m

feudalism /'fyudlˌizəm/ n feudalismo, m

feudatory /'fyudəˌtɔri/ a and n feudatario (-ia)

fever /'fivər/ n fiebre, f; calentura, f; (enthusiasm) pasión, afición, f. **to be in a f.,** tener fiebre; (agitated) estar muy agitado. **to be in a f. to,** estar muy

impaciente de. **puerperal f.,** fiebre puerperal, f. **tertian f.,** fiebre terciana, f. **yellow f.,** fiebre amarilla, f

feverish /'fivərɪʃ/ a febril; *Fig.* ardiente, febril, vehemente. **to grow f.,** empezar a tener fiebre, acalenturarse

feverishness /'fivərɪʃnɪs/ n calentura, f; (impatience) impaciencia, f

few /fyu/ a and n pocos, m pl; pocas, f pl; algunos, m pl; algunas, f pl; (few in number) número pequeño (de), m. **a good f.,** bastantes, mf pl. **not a f.,** no pocos, m pl, (pocas, f pl). **the f.,** la minoría, f. **f. and far between,** raramente, en raras ocasiones; pocos y contados

fewer /'fyuər/ a comp menos. **The f. the better,** Cuantos menos mejor

fewest /'fyuɪst/ a sup (el) menos, m; el menor número (de), m; (el) menos posible de, m

fewness /'fyunɪs/ n corto número, m

fiancé(e) /ˌfiɑn'sei/ n novio (-ia); desposado (-da), prometido (-da)

fiasco /fi'æskou/ n fiasco, mal éxito, fracaso, malogro, m

fiat /'fiat/ n fiat, mandato, m, orden, f

fib /fɪb/ n mentirilla, f, *Peru* bacho m *vt*, decir mentirillas, mentir

fibber /'fɪbər/ n embustero (-ra), mentiroso (-sa)

fiber /'faibər/ n fibra, f; filamento, n, hebra, f; (of grass, etc.) brizna, f; *Fig.* naturaleza, f

fibroid /'faibrɔid/ a fibroso. n fibroma, m

fibrous /'faibrəs/ a fibroso

fibula /'fɪbyələ/ n *Anat.* peroné, m

fichu /'fiʃu/ n pañoleta, f, fichú, m

fickle /'fɪkəl/ a inconstante; mudable; (of persons) liviano, ligero, voluble, falaz

fickleness /'fɪkəlnɪs/ n inconstancia, f; mudanza, f; liviandad, ligereza, veleidad, volubilidad, f

fiction /'fɪkʃən/ n ficción, f; invención, f; literatura narrativa, f; novelas, f pl. **legal f.,** ficción legal, ficción de derecho, f

fictitious /fɪk'tɪʃəs/ a ficticio; imaginario; fingido

fictitiousness /fɪk'tɪʃəsnɪs/ n carácter ficticio, m; falsedad, f

fiddle /'fɪdl/ n violín, m. *vt* tocar... en el violín. *vi* tocar el violín; (fidget) jugar; perder el tiempo. **to play second f.,** tocar el segundo violín; *Fig.* ser plato de segunda mesa

fiddler /'fɪdlər/ n violinista, mf

fiddling /'fɪdlɪŋ/ a insignificante, trivial, frívolo

fidelity /fɪ'dɛlɪti/ n fidelidad, f

fidget /'fɪdʒɪt/ *vi* estar nervioso, estar inquieto; impacientarse; trajinar; (with) jugar con. *vt* molestar; impacientar

fidgetiness /'fɪdʒɪtinɪs/ n inquietud, nerviosidad, f

fidgety /'fɪdʒiti/ a inquieto, nervioso. **to be f.,** tener hormiguillo

fiduciary /fɪ'duʃiˌɛri/ a fiduciario. n fideicomisario (-ia)

fief /fif/ n feudo, m

field /fild/ n campo, m; (meadow) prado, m, pradera, f; (sown field) sembrado, m; (*Phys., Herald.*) campo, m; (of ice) banco, m; *Mineral.* yacimiento, m; (background) fondo, m; (campaign) campaña, f; (battle) batalla, lucha, f; (space) espacio, m; (of knowledge, etc.) especialidad, esfera, f; (hunting) caza, f; *Sports.* campo, m; (competitors) todos los competidores en una carrera, etc.; (horses in a race) el campo. a campal, pradeño; de campo; de los campos. *vt* *Sports.* parar y devolver la pelota. **in the f.,** *Mil.* en el campo de batalla, en campaña. **magnetic f.,** campo magnético, m. **to take the f.,** entrar en campaña. **f.-artillery,** artillería ligera, artillería montada, f. **f.-day,** (holiday) día de asueto, m; (day out) día de campo, m; *Mil.* día de maniobras, m. **f.-glasses,** anteojos, gemelos, m pl. **f.-hospital,** hospital de sangre, m; ambulancia fija, f. **f.-kitchen,** cocina de campaña, f. **f.-marshal,** capitán general de ejército, m. **f.-mouse,** ratón silvestre, m. **f. of battle,** campo de batalla, m. **f. of vision,** campo visual, m. **f.-telegraph,** telégrafo de campaña, m

fielder /'fildər/ n (baseball) jardinero (-ra)

field work prácticas de campo, f pl

fiend /find/ n diablo, demonio, m; malvado (-da); (addict) adicto (-ta)
fiendish /'findɪʃ/ a diabólico, infernal; malvado, cruel, malévolo
fiendishness /'findɪʃnɪs/ n perversidad, crueldad, f
fierce /fɪərs/ a salvaje, feroz, cruel; (of the elements) violento, furioso; (intense) intenso, vehemente
fiercely /'fɪərsli/ adv ferozmente; violentamente, con furia; intensamente, con vehemencia
fierceness /'fɪərsnɪs/ n ferocidad, fiereza, f; violencia, furia, f; intensidad, vehemencia, f
fieriness /'faiərinɪs/ n ardor, m; (flames) las llamas, f pl; (redness) rojez, f; (irritability) ferocidad, irritabilidad, f; (vehemence) pasión, vehemencia, f; (of horses) fogosidad, f
fiery /'faiəri/ a ardiente; (red) rojo; (irritable) feroz, colérico, irritable; (vehement) apasionado, vehemente; (of horses) fogoso
fife /faif/ n Mus. pífano, pito, m
fifteen /'fɪf'tin/ a and n quince m.; (of age) quince años, m pl
fifteenth /'fɪf'tinθ/ a and n décimoquinto m.; (part) quinzavo, m, décimoquinta parte, f; (of the month) (el) quince, m; (of monarchs) quince; Mus. quincena, f
fifth /fɪfθ/ a quinto; (of monarchs) quinto; (of the month) (el) cinco. n quinto, m; (part) quinto, m, quinta parte, f; Mus. quinta, f, **Charles V,** Carlos quinto. **f. column,** quinta columna, f
fifthly /'fɪfθli/ adv en quinto lugar
fiftieth /'fɪftiiθ/ a quincuagésimo; (part) quincuagésima parte, f, cincuentavo, m
fifty /'fɪfti/ a and n cincuenta m.; (of age) cincuenta años, m pl
fiftyfold /'fɪfti,fould/ a and adv cincuenta veces
fig /fɪg/ n higo, m; (tree) higuera, f; Fig. bledo, ardite, m. **green fig,** higo, m, breva, f. **fig-leaf,** hoja de higuera, f; Fig. hoja de parra, f
fight /fait/ n lucha, pelea, f, combate, m; batalla, f; (struggle) lucha, f; (quarrel) riña, pelea, Argentina arenga f; (conflict) conflicto, m; (valor) coraje, brío, m. **hand-to-hand f.,** cachetina, f. **in fair f.,** en buena lid. **to have a f.,** tener una pelea. **to show f.,** mostrarse agresivo
fight /fait/ vt luchar contra, batirse con; (a battle) dar (batalla); (oppose) oponer, Mexico desafiar; (defend) defender, pelear por; hacer batirse. vi luchar, batirse, pelear; (with words) disputar; (struggle) luchar; (make war) hacer la guerra; (in a tournament) tornear. **to f. one's way,** abrirse paso con las armas. **to f. against,** luchar contra. **to f. off,** librarse de; sacudirse. **to f. with,** luchar con; pelear con; reñir con
fighter /'faitər/ n luchador (-ra); combatiente, m; guerrero, m; duelista, m; (boxer) boxeador, m; Aer. (avión de) caza, m. **night f.,** Aer. (avión de) caza nocturno, m. **f.-bomber,** Aer. caza bombardero, m. **F. Command,** Aer. servicio de aviones de caza, m
fighting /'faitɪŋ/ n lucha, f, combate, m; el pelear; (boxing) boxeo, m, a combatiente; (bellicose) agresivo, belicoso. **f.-man,** combatiente, guerrero, m
figment /'fɪgmənt/ n ficción, invención, f
figurative /'fɪgyərətɪv/ a figurado, metafórico; figurativo; simbólico
figuratively /'fɪgyərətɪvli/ adv en sentido figurativo; metafóricamente
figure /'fɪgyər/ n figura, f; (statue) estatua, figura, f; (of a person) silueta, f; talle, m; (number) cifra, f, número, m; (quantity) cantidad, f; (price) precio, m; Geom., Gram., Dance. (skating) figura, f; (appearance) presencia, f, aire, m; (picture) imagen, m; (on fabric) diseño, m; Mus. cifra, f; pl **figures,** aritmética, f, matemáticas, f pl. vt figurar; (imagine) figurarse, imaginar; Mus. cifrar. vi figurar, hacer un papel; (calculate) calcular, hacer cuentas. **to f. out,** calcular; (a problem, etc.) resolver. **a fine f. of a woman,** Inf. una real hembra. **to be good at figures,** estar fuerte en matemáticas. **to cut a f.,** Fig. hacer figura. **to have a good f.,** tener buen talle. **f. of speech,** figura retórica, figura de dicción f; (manner of speaking) metáfora f. **f. dance,** baile de

figuras, m, contradanza, f. **f.-head,** Naut. mascarón, m, (or figura, f) de proa; Fig. figura decorativa, f
figured /'fɪgyərd/ a estampado, con diseños, labrado
figurine /,fɪgyə'rin/ n figurilla, f
filament /'fɪləmənt/ n filamento, m; hebra, f
filbert /'fɪlbərt/ n avellana, f; (tree) avellano, m
filch /fɪltʃ/ vt sisar, ratear
filching /'fɪltʃɪŋ/ n sisa, f
file /fail/ n (line) fila, hilera, sarta, línea, f; Mil. fila, f; (tool) lima, f; (rasp) escofina, f; (list) lista, f, catálogo, m; (for documents) carpeta, f, cartapacio, m; (bundle of papers) legajo, m; (for bills, letters, etc.) clasificador, m; archivo, m; (in an archives) expediente m. **in a f.,** en fila; en cola
file /fail/ vt hacer marchar en fila; (smooth) limar; (literary work) pulir; (classify) clasificar; (note particulars) fichar; (keep) guardar; (a petition, etc.) presentar, registrar. vi marchar en fila. **to f. in,** entrar en fila. **to f. off,** desfilar. **to file a brief,** presentar un escrito. **to f. letters,** clasificar correspondencia. **to f. past,** Mil. desfilar
filial /'fɪliəl/ a filial
filiation /,fɪli'eiʃən/ n filiación, f
filibuster /'fɪlə,bʌstər/ n filibustero, pirata, m
filigree /'fɪlə,gri/ n filigrana, f, a afiligranado
filing /'failɪŋ/ n (with a tool) limadura, f; clasificación, f; (of a petition, etc.) presentación, f registro, m; pl **filings,** limaduras, f pl, retales, m pl. **f.-cabinet,** fichero, m. **f.-card,** ficha, f
fill /fɪl/ vt llenar; (stuff) rellenar; (appoint to a post) proveer; (occupy a post) desempeñar; (imbue) henchir; (saturate) saturar; (occupy) ocupar; (a tooth) empastar, Argentina emplomar; (fulfil) cumplir; (charge, fuel) cargar; (with food) hartar. vi llenarse. **fill an order,** servir un pedido. **fill a prescription,** surtir una receta. **to f. the chair,** ocupar la presidencia; (university) ocupar la cátedra. **to f. the place of,** ocupar el lugar de; substituir; suplir. **It will be difficult to find someone to f. his place,** Será difícil de encontrar uno que haga lo que hizo él. **to f. to the brim,** llenar hasta los bordes. **to f. in, f. out,** (a form) llenar (or completar) (una hoja); (insert) insertar, añadir; (a hollow) terraplenar. **to f. out,** vi hinchar. vi hincharse; echar carnes; (of the face) redondearse. **to f. up,** colmar, llenar hasta los bordes; (an office) proveer; (block) macizar; (a form) completar, llenar
fillet /'fɪlɪt/ n venda, cinta, f; (of meat or fish) filete, m; (of meat) solomillo, m; Archit. filete, m. vt atar con una venda o cinta; Cul. cortar en filetes
filling /'fɪlɪŋ/ n envase, m; (swelling) henchimiento, m; (of a tooth) empastadura, f; (in or up, of forms, etc.) llenar, m. **f. station,** depósito de gasolina, f
filly /'fɪli/ n jaca, potra, f
film /fɪlm/ n (on liquids) tela, f; membrana, f; (coating) capa ligera, f; (on eyes) tela, f; (cinema) película, cinta, f; Photo. película, f; Fig. velo, m; nube, f, vi cubrirse de un velo, etc. vt cubrir de un velo, etc.; filmar, fotografiar para el cine. **roll f.,** película fotográfica, f. **silent f.,** película muda, f. **talking f.,** película sonora, f. **to shoot a f.,** hacer una película. **to take part in a f.,** actuar, en tomar parte, en una película. **f. pack,** película en paquetes f. **f. star,** estrella de la pantalla (or del cine), f
film industry industria fílmica, f
filminess /'fɪlminɪs/ n transparencia, diafanidad, f
filmy /'fɪlmi/ a transparente, diáfano
filter /'fɪltər/ n filtro, m. vt filtrar. vi infiltrarse; (Fig. of news) trascender, divulgarse. **f.-bed,** filtro, m. **f.-paper,** papel filtro, m
filth /fɪlθ/ n inmundicia, suciedad, f; Fig. corrupción, f; Fig. obscenidad, f
filthiness /'fɪlθinɪs/ n suciedad, f; escualidez, f; Fig. asquerosidad, f. Fig. obscenidad, f
filthy /'fɪlθi/ a inmundo, sucio; escuálido, Argentina cascarriento; Central America descacharrado; Fig. asqueroso; Fig. obsceno
filtrate /'fɪltreit/ n filtrado, m, vt filtrar
filtration /fɪl'treiʃən/ n filtración, f
fin /fɪn/ n (of fish) aleta, ala, f; (of whale) barba, f; Aer. aleta, f

final /'fainḷ/ *a* último, final; (conclusive) conclusivo, decisivo, terminante. *n Sports.* finales, *m pl; Educ.* último examen, *m.* **f. blow,** *Fig.* golpe decisivo, *m.* **f. cause,** *Philos.* causa final, *f*

finale /fɪ'næli/ *n* final, *m*

finalist /'fainḷɪst/ *n* finalista, *mf*

finality /fai'nælɪti/ *n* finalidad, *f*; (decision) determinación, resolución, decisión, *f*

finally /'fainḷi/ *adv* por fin, finalmente, por último, a la postre; (irrevocably) irrevocablemente

finance /'fainæns/ *n* hacienda pública, *f*, asuntos económicos, *m pl*; finanzas, *f pl. vt* financiar

financial /fɪ'nænʃəl/ *a* financiero, monetario. **f. year,** año económico, *m*

financially /fɪ'nænʃəli/ *adv* del punto de vista financiero

financier /ˌfɪnən'sɪər, ˌfainən-/ *n* financiero, *m*

find /faind/ *vt* encontrar, hallar; (discover) descubrir, dar con; (invent) inventar, crear; (supply) facilitar, proporcionar; (provide) proveer; (instruct) instruir; *Law.* declarar. *vi Law.* fallar, dar sentencia. *n* hallazgo, *m*; descubrimiento, *m.* **I found him out a long time ago,** *Fig.* Hace tiempo que me di cuenta de cómo era él. **I found it possible to go out,** Me fue posible salir. **The judge found them guilty,** El juez les declaró culpables. **to f. a verdict,** *Law.* dar sentencia, fallar. **to f. one's way,** encontrar el camino. **to f. oneself,** hallarse, verse, encontrarse. **to f. out,** averiguar, descubrir, saber (especially in preterite). **to f. out about,** informarse sobre (or de)

finder /'faindər/ *n* hallador (-ra); (inventor) inventor (-ra), descubridor (-ra); (telescope, camera) buscador, *m*

finding /'faindɪŋ/ *n* hallazgo, *m*; (discovery) descubrimiento, *m; Law.* fallo, *m*, sentencia, *f*

fine /fain/ *n* multa, *f*; (end) fin, *m.* **in f.,** en fin, en resumen

fine /fain/ *vt* multar, cargar una multa de

fine /fain/ *a* (thin) delgado; (sharp) agudo; (delicate) fino, delicado; (minute) menudo; (refined) refinado, puro; (healthy) saludable; (of weather) bueno; magnífico; (beautiful) hermoso, lindo, excelente; (perfect) perfecto; (good) bueno; elegante; (showy) ostentoso, vistoso; (handsome) guapo; (subtle) sutil; (acute) agudo; (noble) noble; (eminent, accomplished) distinguido, eminente; (polished) pulido; (affected) afectado; (clear) claro; (transparent) transparente, diáfano. *adv* muy bien. **a f. upstanding young man,** un buen mozo. **a f. upstanding young woman,** una real moza. **He's a f. fellow,** (ironically) Es una buena pieza. **That is all very f. but...,** Todo eso está muy bien pero.... **to become f.,** (weather) mejorar

finely /'fainli/ *adv* finamente; menudamente; elegantemente; (ironically) lindamente

fineness /'fainnɪs/ *n* (thinness) delgadez, *f*; (excellence) excelencia, *f*; delicadeza, *f*; (softness) suavidad, *f*; elegancia, *f*; (subtlety) sutileza, *f*; (acuteness) agudeza, *f*; (perfection) perfección, *f*; (nobility) nobleza, *f*; (beauty) hermosura, *f*

finery /'fainəri/ *n* galas, *f pl*, atavíos magníficos, *m pl*; adornos, *m pl*; primor, *m*, belleza, *f*

finesse /fɪ'nɛs/ *n* sutileza, diplomacia, *f*; estratagema, artificio, *m*; (cunning) astucia, *f*, *vi* valerse de estratagemas y artificios

finger /'fɪŋgər/ *n* dedo, *m*; (of a clock, etc.) manecilla, *f*; (measurement) dedada, *f*; *Fig.* mano, *f. vt* manosear, tocar; (soil) ensuciar con los dedos; (steal) sisar; (Mus. a keyed instrument) teclear, (a stringed instrument) tocar. **first f.,** dedo índice, *m.* **fourth f.,** dedo anular, *m.* **little f.,** dedo meñique, *m.* **second f.,** dedo de en medio, dedo del corazón, *m.* **to burn one's fingers,** quemarse los dedos; *Fig.* cogerse los dedos. **to have at one's f.-tips,** *Fig.* saber al dedillo. **f.-board,** (of piano) teclado, *m*; (of stringed instruments) diapasón, *m.* **f.-bowl,** lavadedos, lavafrutas, *m.* **finger's breadth,** dedo, *m.* **f.-mark,** huella digital, *f.* **f.-nail,** uña del dedo, *f.* **f.-print,** impresión digital, *f.* **f.-stall,** dedil, *m.* **f.-tip,** punta del dedo, yema del dedo, *f.* **f.-wave,** peinado al agua, *m*

fingered /'fɪŋgərd/ *a* (in compounds) con dedos, que tiene los dedos...

fingering /'fɪŋgərɪŋ/ *n* (touching) manoseo, *m; Mus.* digitación, *f*; (Mus. the keys) tecleo, *m*; (wool) estambre, *m*

finial /'fɪniəl/ *n* pináculo, *m*

finicky /'fɪnɪki/ *a* (of persons) dengoso, remilgado; (of things) nimio

finish /'fɪnɪʃ/ *n* fin, *m*, conclusión, terminación, *f*; (final touch) última mano, *f*; perfección, *f*; (of an article) acabado, *m; Sports.* llegada, (horse race) meta, *f. vt* terminar, acabar, concluir; llevar a cabo, poner fin a; (perfect) perfeccionar; (put finishing touch to) dar la última mano a; (kill) matar; (exhaust) agotar, rendir; (overcome) vencer. *vi* acabar; concluirse. **to f. off,** acabar, terminar; (kill) matar, acabar con; (destroy) destruir. **to f. up,** acabar; (eat) comer; (drink) beber

finishable /'fɪnɪʃəbəl/ *a* acabable

finished /'fɪnɪʃt/ *a* acabado, terminado, completo; perfecto; (careful) cuidadoso

finished goods *n pl* bienes terminados, *m pl*

finisher /'fɪnɪʃər/ *n* terminador (-ra), acabador (-ra); pulidor (-ra); (final blow) golpe de gracia, *m*

finishing /'fɪnɪʃɪŋ/ *a* concluyente. *n* terminación, *f*, fin, *m*; perfección, *f*; (last touch) última mano, *f.* **to put the f. touch,** dar la última pincelada

finite /'fainait/ *a* finito

Finland /'fɪnlənd/ Finlandia, *f*

Finn /fɪn/ *n* finlandés (-esa)

Finnish /'fɪnɪʃ/ *a* finlandés. *n* (language) finlandés, *m*

fir /fɜr/ *n* abeto, sapino, pino, *m.* **red fir,** pino silvestre, *m.* **fir-cone,** piña de abeto, *f.* **fir grove,** abetal, *m*

fire /fair/ *n* fuego, *m*; (conflagration) incendio, *m*; (on the hearth) lumbre, *f*, fuego, *m; Fig.* ardor, *m*, pasión, *f*; (shooting) fuego, tiro, *m.* **by f. and sword,** a sangre y fuego. **by the f.,** cerca del fuego; (in a house) al lado de la chimenea. **long-range f.,** *Mil.* fuego de largo alcance, *m.* **short-range f.,** *Mil.* fuego de corto alcance, *m.* **on f.,** en fuego, ardiendo, en llamas; *Fig.* impaciente; *Fig.* lleno de pasión. **to make a f.,** encender un fuego. **to miss f.,** no dar en el blanco, errar el tiro. **to open f.,** *Mil.* hacer una descarga. **to set on f.,** prender fuego a, incendiar. **to take f.,** encenderse. **under f.,** bajo fuego. **f.-alarm,** alarma de incendios, *f.* **f.-arm,** arma de fuego, *f.* **f.-box,** hogar, *m.* **f.-brand,** tea, *f.* **f.-damp,** aire detonante, grisú, *m*, mofeta, *f.* **f.-department,** cuerpo de bomberos, *m.* **f.-dog,** morillo, *m.* **f.-drill,** (firefighters') instrucción de bomberos, *f*, (others') simulacro de incendio, *m.* **f.-engine,** autobomba, bomba, de incendios, *f.* **f.-escape,** escalera de incendios, *f.* **f.-extinguisher,** apagador de incendio, extintor, matafuego, *m.* **f.-guard,** vigilante de incendios, *m*; alambrera, *f.* **f.-hose,** manguera de incendios, *f.* **f.-insurance,** seguro contra incendios, *m.* **f.-irons,** badil *m.* y tenazas *f pl.* **f.-lighter,** encendedor, *m.* **f.-screen,** pantalla, *f.* **f.-ship,** brulote, *m.* **f.-shovel,** badil, *m*, paleta, *f.* **f.-spotter,** vigilante de incendios, *m.* **f.-sprite,** salamandra, *f.* **f.-watching,** servicio de vigilancia de incendios, *m*

fire /fair/ *vt* incendiar, prender (or pegar) fuego a; quemar; (bricks) cocer; (fire-arms) disparar; (cauterize) cauterizar; (Fig. stimulate) estimular, excitar; (inspire) inspirar; (Inf. of questions) disparar; (Inf. sack) despedir. *vi* encenderse; (shoot) hacer fuego, disparar (un tiro); (Inf. away) disparar; (up) enojarse. **to f. a salute,** disparar una salva. *Mil.* **F.!** ¡Fuego!

firecracker /'fairˌkrækər/ *n* buscapiés *m*

fire department *n* parque de bomberos, servicio de bomberos, servicio de incendios, parque de bombas (Puerto Rico), *m*

firefly /'fairˌflai/ *n* cocuyo, *m*, luciérnaga, *f*

fireman /'fairmən/ *n* bombero, *m*; (of an engine, etc.) fogonero, *m.* **fireman's lift,** silleta, *f*

fireplace /'fairˌpleis/ *n* chimenea francesa, chimenea, *f*, *Mexico* brasero *m*; (hearth) hogar, *m*

fireproof /'fairˌpruf/ *a* a prueba de incendios; incombustible

firer /'fairər/ *n* disparador, *m*

firewood /'fairˌwʊd/ *n* leña, *Lat. Am.* charamusca *f.* **f. dealer,** leñador (-ra), vendedor (-ra) de leña

firework /'faiᵊr,wᵊrk/ *n* fuego artificial, *m*
firing /'faiᵊrɪŋ/ *n* (of fire-arms) disparo, *m*; (burning) incendio, *m*, quema, *f*; (of bricks, etc.) cocimiento, *m*; (of pottery) cocción, *f*; (cauterization) cauterización, *f*; (fuel) combustible, *m*; (*Inf.* sacking) despedida, *f*. **within f. range,** a tiro. **f.-line,** línea de fuego, *f*. **f.-oven,** (pottery) horno alfarero, *m*. **f.-squad,** pelotón de ejecución, *m*
firm /fᵊrm/ *a* firme; (strong) fuerte; (secure) seguro; sólido; (resolute) inflexible, resoluto; severo; (steady) constante; (persistent) tenaz. *n Com.* casa (de comercio), empresa, *f*; razón social, *f*
firmament /'fᵊrməmənt/ *n* firmamento, *m*
firmly /'fᵊrmli/ *adv* firmemente; inflexiblemente; constantemente
firmness /'fᵊrmnɪs/ *n* firmeza, *f*; solidez, *f*; inflexibilidad, resolución, *f*; severidad, *f*; constancia, *f*; tenacidad, *f*
first /fᵊrst/ *a* primero (primer before *m sing* nouns); (of monarchs) primero; (of dates) (el) primero. *n* primero, *m*; (beginning) principio, *m*. *adv* primero, en primer lugar; (before, of time) antes; (for the first time) por primera vez; (at the beginning) al principio; (ahead) adelante. **at f.,** al principio. **from the very f.,** desde el primer momento. **to appear for the f. time,** aparecer (or presentarse) por primera vez; *Theat.* debutar. **to go f.,** ir delante de todos, ir a la cabeza; ir adelante. **f. and foremost,** en primer lugar; ante todo. **f.-aid,** primera cura, *f*. **f.-aid post,** casa de socorro, *f*. **f.-aider,** practicante, *m*. **f.-born,** *a* and *n* primogénito (-ta). **f.-class,** *a* de primera clase; *Fig.* excelente. **f.-cousin,** primo (-ma) carnal, primo (-ma) hermano (-na). **f. edition,** edición príncipe, *f*. **f. floor,** primer piso, *m*. **f. fruits,** frutos primerizos, *m pl*; *Fig.* primicias, *f pl*. **f.-hand,** a original, de primera mano. **f. letters,** primeras letras, *f pl*. **f. night,** *Theat.* estreno, *m*. **f. of all,** primero, ante todo. **f.-rate,** *a* de primera clase
firstly /'fᵊrstli/ *adv* en primer lugar, primero
firth /fᵊrθ/ *n* ría, *f*
fiscal /'fɪskəl/ *a* and *n* fiscal *m..* **f. year,** año económico, *m*
fish /fɪʃ/ *n* pez, *m*; (out of the water) pescado, *m*; *Inf.* tipo, indivíduo, *m*. *vt* pescar; (out) sacar. *vi* pescar; *Fig.* buscar. **fried f.,** pescado frito, *m*. **to be neither f. nor fowl,** no ser ni carne ni pescado. **to feel like a f. out of water,** sentirse fuera de su ambiente. **to f. in troubled waters,** A río revuelto ganancia de pescadores. **f.-eating,** *a* ictiófago. **f.-fork,** tenedor de pescado, *m*. **f.-glue,** cola de pescado, *f*. **f.-hook,** anzuelo, *m*. **f.-knife,** cuchillo de pescado, *m*. **f.-like,** de pez; como un pez, parecido a un pez. **f. roe,** hueva, *f*. **f.-server,** pala para pescado, *f*
fishbone /'fɪʃ,boun/ *n* espina de pescado, raspa de pescado, *f*
fisherman /'fɪʃərmən/ *n* pescador, *m*
fishery /'fɪʃəri/ *n* pesquería, *f*
fishing /'fɪʃɪŋ/ *n* pesca, *f*, *a* de pescar. **to go f.,** ir de pesca. **f.-boat,** barco de pesca, *m*. **f.-floats,** levas, *f pl*. **f.-line,** sedal, *m*. **f.-net,** red de pesca, *f*. **f.-reel,** carretel, carrete, *m*. **f.-rod,** caña de pescar, *f*. **f.-tackle,** aparejo de pesca, *m*. **f.-village,** pueblo de pescadores, *m*
fishmeal /'fɪʃ,mil/ *n* harina de pescado, *f*
fishmonger /'fɪʃ,mʌŋgər/ *n* pescadero (-ra).
fishpond /'fɪʃ,pɒnd/ *n* vivero, *m*, piscina, *f*
fishy /'fɪʃi/ *a* de pescado; (of eyes, etc.) de pez, como un pez; (in smell) que huele a pescado; *Inf.* sospechoso; (of stories) inverosímil
fissure /'fɪʃər/ *n* grieta, hendidura, rendija, *f*; (*Anat.*, *Geol.*) fisura, *f*
fissured /'fɪʃərd/ *a* hendido
fist /fɪst/ *n* puño, *m*; *Print.* manecilla, *f*; (handwriting) letra, *f*. **with clenched fists,** a puño cerrado
fisticuff /'fɪstɪ,kʌf/ *n* puñetazo, *m*; *pl* **fisticuffs,** agarrada, riña, *f*
fit /fɪt/ *n* espasmo, paroxismo, *m*; ataque, *m*; (impulse) acceso, arranque, *m*; (whim) capricho, *m*; (of a garment) corte, *m*; (adjustment) ajuste, encaje, *m*. **by fits and starts,** a tropezones, espasmódicamente, *m*. **fit of fainting** *Argentina, Venezuela* insulto *m*
fit /fɪt/ *a* a propósito (para), bueno (para); (oppor-

tune) oportuno; (proper) conveniente; apto; (decent) decente; (worthy) digno; (ready) preparado, listo; (adequate) adecuado; (capable) capaz, en estado (de); (appropriate) apropiado; (just) justo. **It is not in a fit state to be used,** No está en condiciones para usarse. **to be not fit for,** no servir para; (through ill-health) no tener bastante salud para. **to think fit,** creer (or juzgar) conveniente. **fit for use,** usable. **fit to eat,** comestible
fit /fɪt/ *vt* ajustar, acomodar, encajar; adaptar (a); (furnish) proveer (de), surtir (con); (of tailor, dressmaker) entallar, probar; (of shoemaker) calzar; (of garments, shoes) ir (bien o mal); (prepare) preparar; (go with) ser apropiado (a); (adapt itself to) adaptarse a. *vi* ajustarse, acomodarse, encajarse; adaptarse; (clothes) ir (bien o mal). **to fit in,** *vt* encajar; incluir. *vi* encajarse; caber; adaptarse. **to fit out,** equipar; proveer (de); preparar. **to fit up,** montar, instalar; proveer (de). **to fit with,** proveer de
fitful /'fɪtfəl/ *a* intermitente; espasmódico; caprichoso
fitfully /'fɪtfəli/ *adv* por intervalos, a ratos; caprichosamente
fitly /'fɪtli/ *adv* adecuadamente; justamente; apropiadamente
fitness /'fɪtnɪs/ *n* conveniencia, *f*; aptitud, capacidad, *f*; oportunidad, *f*; salud, *f*; (good health) vigor, *m*
fitted /'fɪtɪd/ *a* (of clothes) ajustado
fitter /'fɪtər/ *n* ajustador, *m*; (mechanic) armador, mecánico, *m*; (tailoring) cortador, *m*; (dressmaking) probador (-ra)
fitting /'fɪtɪŋ/ *n* encaje, ajuste, *m*; adaptación, *f*; (of a garment) prueba, *f*; (size) medida, *f*; (installation) instalación, *f*; *pl.* **fittings,** guarniciones, *f pl*; instalaciones, *f pl*; accesorios, *m pl*. *a* conveniente, justo; apropiado; adecuado; (worthy) digno; (of coats, etc.) ajustado. **f. room,** cuarto de pruebas, *m*. **f. in,** encaje, *m*. **f. out,** equipo, *m*. **f. up,** arreglo, *m*; (of machines) montaje, *m*; (of a house) mueblaje, *m*
five /faiv/ *a* and *n* cinco *m.*; (of the clock) las cinco, *f pl*; (of age) cinco años, *m pl*. **to be f.,** tener cinco años. **f. feet deep,** de cinco pies de profundidad. **f. feet high,** cinco pies de altura. **f.-finger exercises,** ejercicios de piano, *m pl*. **F.-Year Plan,** Plan Quinquenal, *m*
fivefold /'faiv,fould/ *a* quíntuplo
fix /fɪks/ *n* aprieto, apuro, *m*; callejón sin salida, *m*. *vt* fijar; sujetar, afianzar; (bayonets) calar; (with nails) clavar; (*Photo.*, *Chem.*, *Med.*) fijar; (decide) establecer; (a date) señalar; (eyes, attention) clavar; (on the mind) grabar, estampar; (one's hopes) poner; (base) basar, fundar; (*Inf.* put right) arreglar, componer. *vi* fijarse; establecerse; determinarse. **to get in a fix,** hacerse un lío. **to fix a price,** fijar un precio. **to fix on, upon,** elegir, escoger; decidir, determinar. **to fix up,** arreglar; decidir; organizar; (differences) olvidar (sus disensiones)
fixation /fɪk'seiʃən/ *n* obsesión, idea fija, *f*; (scientific) fijación, *f*
fixative /'fɪksətɪv/ *n* (*Med.*, *Photo.*) fijador, *m*; (dyeing) mordiente, *m*. *a* que fija
fixed /fɪkst/ *a* fijo; inmóvil; permanente; (of ideas) inflexible. **f. bayonet,** bayoneta calada, *f*. **f. price,** precio fijo, *m*. **f. star,** estrella fija, *f*
fixedly /'fɪksɪdli/ *adv* fijamente; resueltamente; firmemente
fixing /'fɪksɪŋ/ *n* fijación, *f*; afianzamiento, *m*; arreglo, *m*; (of a date) señalamiento, *m*. **f. bath,** *Photo.* baño fijador, *m*
fixity /'fɪksɪti/ *n* permanencia, *f*; inmovilidad, *f*; invariabilidad, *f*; firmeza, *f*
fixture /'fɪkstʃər/ *n* instalación, *f*; accesorio fijo, *m*; *Sports.* partido, *m*; *Inf.* permanencia, *f*. **f. card,** *Sports.* calendario deportivo, *m*
fizz /fɪz/ *n* espuma, *f*; chisporroteo, *m*. *Inf.* champaña, *m*. *vi* (liquids) espumear; (sputter) chisporrotear
fizzle /'fɪzəl/ *n* (failure) fiasco, fracaso, *m*. *vi* chisporrotear; (out) apagarse; (fail) fracasar, no tener éxito
fjord /fjᵊrd/ *n* fiordo, *m*
flabbergast /'flæbər,gæst/ *vt* dejar con la boca abierta, dejar de una pieza

flabbiness, flaccidity /'flæbɪnɪs; flæk'sɪdɪtɪ/ n flaccidez, flojedad, f; Med. reblandecimiento, m; (of character) debilidad, flaqueza del ánimo, f

flabby, flaccid /'flæbɪ; 'flæksɪd/ a fláccido, flojo; Fig. débil

flag /flæg/ n bandera, f; pabellón, estandarte, m; (small) banderola, f; (iris) (yellow) cala, f, (purple) lirio cárdeno, m; (stone) losa, f. **to dip the f.,** saludar con la bandera. **to hoist the f.,** izar la bandera. **to strike the f.,** bajar la bandera; (in defeat) rendir la bandera. **f. bearer,** portaestandarte, abanderado, m. **f.-day,** día de la banderita, m; día de la bandera, m. **f.-officer,** almirante, m; vicealmirante, m; jefe de escuadra, m. **f. of truce,** bandera blanca, bandera de paz, f

flag /flæg/ vi flaquear, debilitarse; languidecer; (wither) marchitarse; decaer, disminuir. vt adornar con banderas; (signal) hacer señales con una bandera; (for a race, etc.) marcar con banderas; (with stones) enlosar, embaldosar.

flagellant /'flædʒələnt/ n flagelante, m

flagellate /'flædʒə,leit/ vt flagelar

flagellation /,flædʒə'leiʃən/ n flagelación, f

flageolet /,flædʒə'let/ n Mus. caramillo, m, chirimía, f. **f. player,** chirimía, m

flagging /'flægɪŋ/ n pavimentación, f; (floor) enlosado, m. a lánguido, flojo

flagon /'flægən/ n frasco, m; botella, f

flagrancy /'fleigrənsɪ/ n escándalo, m, notoriedad, f

flagrant /'fleigrənt/ a escandaloso, notorio

flagship /'flæg,ʃɪp/ n capitana, f

flagstaff /'flæg,stæf/ n asta de bandera, f

flagstone /'flæg,stoun/ n losa, lancha, Lat. Am. laja f

flail /fleil/ n mayal, m

flair /flɛər/ n instinto natural, m, comprensión innata, f; habilidad natural, f

flak /flæk/ n Aer. cortina (or barrera) antiaérea, f; (criticism) críticas, f pl

flake /fleik/ n escama, f; laminilla, hojuela, f; (of snow) copo, m; (of fire) chispa, f. vt cubrir con escamas, etc.; exfoliar; (crumble) hacer migas de, desmigajar. vi escamarse; (off) exfoliarse; caer en copos

flaky /'fleiki/ a escamoso; en laminillas; (of pastry) hojaldrado. **f. pastry,** hojaldre, f

flamboyance /flæm'bɔiəns/ n extravagancia, f, Lit. ampulosidad, f

flamboyant /flæm'bɔiənt/ a Archit. flamígero; extravagante, llamativo, rimbombante; (of style) ampuloso. **f. gothic,** gótico florido, m

flame /fleim/ n llama, f; Fig. fuego, m. Inf. amorío, m, vi flamear, llamear; arder, abrasarse; (shine) brillar; (up, Fig.) inflamarse; acalorarse. **f.-colored,** de color de llama, anaranjado. **f.-thrower,** lanzallamas, m

flaming /'fleimɪŋ/ a llameante; abrasador; (of colors) llamativo, chillón; (of feelings) ardiente, fervoroso, apasionado

flamingo /flə'mɪŋgou/ n Ornith. flamenco, m

Flanders /'flændərz/ flandes, m

flange /flændʒ/ n Mech. reborde, m, vt rebordear

flank /flæŋk/ n (of animal) ijada, f; (human) costado, m; (of hill, etc.) lado, m, falda, f; Mil. flanco, m. a (Mil. Nav.) por el flanco. vt lindar con, estar contiguo a; (Mil., Nav.) flanquear. vi estar al lado de; tocar a, lindar con.

flannel /'flænl/ n franela, f, a de franela

flannelette /,flænl'ɛt/ n moletón, m

flap /flæp/ n golpe, m; (of a sail) zapatazo, m, sacudida, f; (of a pocket) cartera, tapa, f; (of skin) colgajo, m; (of a shoe, etc.) oreja, f; (of a shirt, etc.) falda, f; (of a hat) ala, f; (of trousers) bragueta, f; (rever) solapa, f; (of a counter) trampa, f; (of a table) hoja plegadiza, f; (of the wings) aletazo, m; vt sacudir, golpear, batir; agitar; (the tail) menear. vi agitarse; (of wings) volar con un batir de alas, aletear; (of sails) zapatear, sacudirse; colgar. **f.-eared,** de orejas grandes y gachas

flapjack /'flæp,dʒæk/ n Cul. torta de sartén, f; (for powder) polvorera, f

flapper /'flæpər/ n Inf. polla, tobillera, chica "topolino,"

flapping /'flæpɪŋ/ n batimiento, m; (waving) ondulación, f; (of sails) zapatazo, m; (of wings) aleteo, m

flare /flɛər/ n fulgor, m, llama, f; hacha, f; Aer. cohete de señales, m; Sew. vuelo, m. vi relampaguear, fulgurar; brillar; (of a lamp) llamear; (up) encolerizarse, salirse de tino; (of epidemic) declararse; (war, etc.) desencadenarse

flash /flæʃ/ n relámpago, centelleo, m, ráfaga de luz, f; brillo, m; (from a gun) fuego, fogonazo, m; (of wit, genius) rasgo, m; (of joy, etc.) acceso, m. vi relampaguear, fulgurar, centellear; brillar; cruzar rápidamente, pasar como un relámpago. vt hacer relampaguear; hacer brillar; (a look, etc.) dar; lanzar; (light) encender; (powder) quemar; transmitir señales por heliógrafo; Inf. sacar a relucir, enseñar. **shoulder-f.,** Mil. emblema, m. **to be gone like a f.,** desaparecer como un relámpago. **to f. out,** brillar, centellear. **f. of lightning,** relámpago, rayo, m. **f. of wit,** agudeza, f, rasgo de ingenio, m

flashback /'flæʃ,bæk/ n episodio intercalado, m, retrospección, f

flashily /'flæʃəli/ adv llamativamente, ostentosamente

flashing /'flæʃɪŋ/ n centelleo, m, llamarada, f. a centellador, relampagueante; brillante; chispeante

flashlight /'flæʃ,lait/ n luz de magnesio, f; (torch) lamparilla eléctrica, f, Mexico rayo, m; **f. photograph,** magnesio, m

flashy /'flæʃi/ a llamativo, charro, Lat. Am. figuroso; frívolo, superficial

flask /flæsk/ n frasco, m, redoma, botella, f; (for powder) frasco, m; (vacuum) termos, m

flat /flæt/ a llano; (smooth) liso; (lying) tendido, tumbado; (flattened) aplastado; (destroyed) arrasado; (stretched out) extendido; (of nose, face) chato, romo; (of tire) desinflado; (uniform) uniforme, (depressed) desanimado; (uninteresting) monótono; (boring) aburrido; Com. paralizado; (downright) categórico; absoluto; (net) neto; Mus. bemol; (of boats) de fondo plano. adv See **flatly.** n planicie, f; (of a sword) hoja, f; (of the hand) palma, f; (land) llanura, f; (apartment) piso, m; Mus. bemol, m. **to fall f.,** caer de bruces; Fig. no tener éxito. **to make f.,** allanar. **to sing f.,** desafinar. **f. boat,** barco de fondo plano. **f.-footed,** de pies achatados; Fig. pedestre. **f.-iron,** plancha, f. **f. roof,** azotea, f

flatly /'flætli/ adv de plano; a nivel; (plainly) llanamente, netamente; (dully) indiferentemente; (categorically) categóricamente

flatness /'flætnɪs/ n planicie, f; llanura, f; (smoothness) lisura, f; (evenness) igualdad, f; (uninterestingness) insulsez, insipidez, f; aburrimiento, m; (depression) desaliento, abatimiento, m

flatten /'flætn/ vt aplanar, allanar; aplastar; (smooth) alisar; (even) igualar; (destroy) derribar, arrasar, destruir; (dismay) desconcertar; (out) extender. vi aplanarse, allanarse; aplastarse

flattening /'flætnɪŋ/ n achatamiento, m, allanamiento, m; aplastamiento, m; igualación, f

flatter /'flætər/ vt adular, lisonjear, halagar, engatusar, Lat. Am. also adular, engaratusar; (of a dress, photograph, etc.) favorecer, (please the senses) regalar, deleitar; (oneself) felicitarse

flatterer /'flætərər/ n adulador (-ra), lisonjero (-ra), Guatemala barbero (-ra) mf

flattering /'flætərɪŋ/ a adulador, lisonjero; (promising) halagüeño; favoreciente; deleitoso

flattery /'flætəri/ n adulación, f. Lat. Am. adulonería f

flat tire llanta desinflada, f

flatulence /'flætʃələns/ n flatulencia, f

flatulent /'flætʃələnt/ a flatulento

flaunt /flɔnt/ vi (flutter) ondear; (boast) pavonearse. vt desplegar; ostentar, sacar a relucir; enseñar

flaunting /'flɔntɪŋ/ n ostentación, f; alarde, m. a ostentoso; magnífico; (fluttering) ondeante

flautist /'flɔtɪst/ n flautista, mf

flavor /'fleivər/ n sabor, gusto, m; Cul. condimento, m; Fig. dejo, m. vt Cul. sazonar, condimentar; dar un gusto (de), hacer saborear (de); Fig. dar un dejo (de)

flavored /'fleivərd/ a (in compounds) de sabor...; sazonado; que tiene sabor de...

flavoring /'fleivərɪŋ/ n Cul. condimento, m; Fig. sabor, dejo, m

flavorless /'fleivərlɪs/ a insípido, soso, sin sabor

flaw /flɔ/ n desperfecto, m, imperfección, f; (crack) grieta, hendedura, f; (in wood, metals) quebraja, f; (in gems) pelo, m; (in fruit) maca, f; (in cloth) gabarro, m; Fig. defecto, error, m; (wind) ráfaga de viento, f

flawless /'flɔlɪs/ a sin defecto; perfecto; impecable

flax /flæks/ n lino, m. **to dress f.**, rastrillar lino. **f.- comb**, rastrillo, m. **f. field**, linar, m

flaxen /'flæksən/ a de lino; (fair) rubio, blondo. **f.- haired**, de pelo rubio

flay /flei/ vt desollar; (criticize) despellejar

flaying /'fleiɪŋ/ n desuello, m, desolladura, f

flea /fli/ n pulga, f. **f. bite**, picada de pulga, f

fleck /flɛk/ n pinta, mancha, f, lunar, m; (of sun) mota, f; (speck) partícula, f; (freckle) peca, f. vt abigarrar; manchar; (dapple) salpicar, motear

fledged /flɛdʒd/ a emplumecido, plumado; alado; Fig. maduro

fledgling /'flɛdʒlɪŋ/ n volantón, m; Fig. niño (-ña); Fig. novato (-ta)

flee /fli/ vi huir, fugarse, escapar; (vanish) desaparecer; (avoid) evitar, huir de. vt abandonar

fleece /flis/ n vellón, m; lana, f; toisón, m. vt esquilar; Fig. Inf. pelar. **Order of the Golden F.**, Orden del Toisón de Oro, f

fleecy /'flisi/ a lanudo, lanar; (white) blanquecino; (of clouds) borreguero. **f. clouds**, borregos, m pl

fleet /flit/ n (navy) armada, f; escuadra, flota, f; Fig. serie, f, a alado, rápido, veloz. **f.-footed**, ligero de pies

fleeting /'flitɪŋ/ a fugaz, momentáneo, efímero, pasajero

flesh /flɛʃ/ n carne, f; (mankind) género humano, m, humanidad, f; (of fruit) pulpa, f. **a man of f. and blood**, un hombre de carne y hueso. **of one's own f. and blood**, de la misma sangre de uno. **to make one's k. creep**, dar carne de gallina (a). **f.-colored**, encarnado, de color de carne. **f.-eating**, carnívoro. **f. wound**, herida superficial, f

fleshiness /'flɛʃɪnɪs/ n carnosidad, gordura, f

fleshpot /'flɛʃˌpɒt/ n marmita, f; Fig. olla, f. **the fleshpots of Egypt**, las ollas de Egipto

fleshy /'flɛʃi/ a carnoso, grueso; (of fruit) pulposo; suculento

fleur-de-lis /ˌflɜrdl̩'i/ n flor de lis, f

flex /flɛks/ n Elec. flexible, m, vt doblar. vi doblarse

flexibility /ˌflɛksə'bɪlɪti/ n flexibilidad, f; (of style) plasticidad, f; docilidad, f

flexible /'flɛksəbəl/ a flexible; dúctil, maleable; (of style) plástico; of) voice) quebradizo; adaptable; dócil

flexion /'flɛkʃən/ n flexión, f; Gram. inflexión, f; Gram. flexión, f

flexor /'flɛksər/ n Anat. músculo flexor, m

flick /flɪk/ n golpecito, toque, m; (of the finger) capirotazo, m; Inf. cine, m, vt dar un golpecito a; dar ligeramente con un látigo; sacudir. **f. one's wrist**, hacer girar la muñeca. **to f. over the pages of**, hojear

flicker /'flɪkər/ n estremecimiento, temblor, m; fluctuación, f; (of bird) aleteo, m; (of flame) onda (de una llama), f; (of eyelashes) pestañeo, m; (of a smile) indicio, f, vi agitarse; (of flags) ondear; vacilar

flickering /'flɪkərɪŋ/ a tenue; vacilante

flier /'flaiər/ n volador (-ra); aviador (-ra); piloto, m; fugitivo (-va)

flight /flait/ n vuelo, m; (of bird of prey) colada, f; (flock of birds) bandada, f; (migration) migración, f; (of time) transcurso, m; (of imagination, etc.) arranque, m; (volley) lluvia, f; (of airplanes) escuadrilla (de aviones), f; (of stairs) tramo, tiro, m; (staircase) escalera, f; (of locks on canal, etc.) ramal, m; (escape) huida, fuga, f. **long-distance f.**, Aer. vuelo de distancia, m. **non-stop f.**, Aer. vuelo sin parar, m. **reconnaissance f.**, Aer. vuelo de reconocimiento, vuelo de patrulla, m. **test f.**, Aer. vuelo de pruebas, m. **to put to f.**, ahuyentar, poner en fuga. **to take f.**, alzar

el vuelo. **f.-lieutenant**, teniente aviador, m. **f.- sergeant**, sargento aviador, m

flight attendant sobrecarbo, Lat. Am. aeromozo (-za), cabinero (-ra) mf

flightiness /'flaitinɪs/ n frivolidad, veleidad, ligereza, f

flighty /'flaiti/ a frívolo, inconstante, veleidoso

flimsiness /'flɪmzinɪs/ n falta de solidez, endeblez, f; fragilidad, f; (of arguments) futilidad, f

flimsy /'flɪmzi/ a endeble; frágil; fútil, insubstancial

flinch /flɪntʃ/ vi echarse atrás, retirarse (ante); vacilar, titubear. **without flinching**, sin vacilar; sin quejarse

fling /flɪŋ/ vt arrojar, echar, tirar; lanzar; (scatter) derramar; (oneself) echarse; (oneself upon) echarse encima; Fig. confiar en. vi lanzarse; marcharse precipitadamente; saltar. n tiro, m; (of dice, etc.) echada, f; (gibe) sarcasmo, m, burla, chufleta, f; (of horse) respingo, brinco, m; baile escocés, m. **in full f.**, en plena operación; en progreso. **to have a f.**, darse un verde amorío, correrla. **to f. away**, vt desechar; (waste) desperdiciar, malgastar, perder. vi marcharse enfadado; marcharse rápidamente. **to f. back**, (a ball) devolver; (the head) echar atrás. **to f. down**, tirar al suelo; arrojar; derribar. **to f. off**, vt rechazar; apartar; (a garment, etc.) quitar. vi marcharse sin más ni más. **to f. oneself down**, tumbarse, echarse; despeñarse (por). **to f. oneself headlong**, despeñarse. **to f. open**, abrir violentamente, abrir de repente. **to f. out**, vt echar a la fuerza; (a hand) alargar, extender. vi salir apresuradamente. **to f. over**, (upset) volcar; arrojar por; abandonar. **to f. up**, lanzar al aire; levantar, erguir; renunciar (a), abandonar; dejar

flint /flɪnt/ n pedernal, m; (for producing fire) piedra de encendedor, f

flinty /'flɪnti/ a pedernalino, f; Fig. endurecido

flippancy /'flɪpənsi/ n levedad, ligereza, f; frivolidad, f; impertinencia, f

flippant /'flɪpənt/ a poco serio, ligero; frívolo; impertinente

flipper /'flɪpər/ n aleta, f

flirt /flɜrt/ n (man) coquetón, castigador, m; (woman) coqueta, castigadora, f. vt (shake) sacudir; (move) agitar; (wave) menear. vi flirtear, coquetear; (toy with) jugar con; divertirse con

flirtation /flɜr'teiʃən/ n flirteo, amorío, m

flirtatious /flɜr'teiʃəs/ a (of men) galanteador, castigador; (of women) coqueta

flit /flɪt/ vi revolotear, mariposear; (move silently) deslizarse, pasar silenciosamente; (depart) irse, marcharse; mudarse por los aires. **to f. about**, ir y venir silenciosamente. **to f. past**, pasar como una sombra

float /flout/ n masa flotante, f; (raft) balsa, f; Mech. flotador, m; (of fishing rod or net) corcho, m; (of fish) vejiga natatoria, f; (for swimming) nadadera, calabaza, f; (for tableaux) carroza, f; pl **floats**, Theat. candilejas, f pl. vi flotar; (flags, hair, etc.) ondear; (wander) vagar; Naut. boyar. vt poner a flote; hacer flotar; (a grounded ship) desencallar; (Com. a company) fundar; (a loan, etc.) emitir, poner en circulación; (launch a ship) botar; (flood) inundar

floating /'floutɪŋ/ n flotación, f, flote, m; Com. fundación (de una compañía), f; (of a loan) emisión, f; (of a ship) botadura, f. a flotante; boyante; Com. en circulación, flotante; fluctuante, variable. **f. capital**, capital fluctuante, m. **f. debt**, deuda flotante, f. **f. dock**, dique flotante, m. **f. light**, buque faro, m. **f. population**, población flotante, f. **f. rib**, costilla flotante, f

flock /flɒk/ n rebaño, m, manada, f; (of birds) bandada, f; Fig. grey, f; (crowd) multitud, muchedumbre, f; (parishioners) congregación, f; (of wool or cotton) vedija (de lana or de algodón), f; pl **flocks**, (for stuffing) borra, f. vi concurrirse, reunirse, congregarse; ir en tropel, acudir; (birds) volar en bandada. **f.-bed**, colchón de borra, m

floe /flou/ n banco de hielo, m

flog /flɒg/ vt azotar; castigar

flogging /'flɒgɪŋ/ n azotamiento, vapuleo, m

flood /flʌd/ n inundación, f; (Bible) diluvio, m; (of the tide) flujo, m; Fig. torrente, m; (abundance) copia, abundancia, f; (fit) paroxismo, m. vt inundar; sumergir; (of tears) mojar. vi desbordar. **f. lighting,** iluminación intensiva, f

floodgate /'flʌd,geit/ n compuerta (de esclusa), f

flooding /'flʌdɪŋ/ n inundación, f; desbordamiento, m; Med. hemorragia uterina, f

floodtide /'flʌd,taid/ n marea creciente, f

floor /flɔr/ n suelo, piso, m; (wooden) entarimado, m; (story) piso, m; (of a cart) cama, f; Agr. era, f. vt entablar; echar al suelo, derribar; Fig. desconcertar, confundir. **on the f.,** en el suelo. **on the ground f.,** en el piso bajo. **to take the f.,** Fig. tener la palabra. **f. mop** Lat. Am. lampazo m. **f.-polisher,** lustrador de piso, m

flooring /'flɔrɪŋ/ n tablado, m, tablazón, f; piso, m

flop /flɒp/ n golpe, m; ruido sordo, m; (splash) chapoteo, m; Inf. fiasco, m. vi dejarse caer

flora /'flɔrə/ n flora, f

floral /'flɔrəl/ a floral. **f. games,** juegos florales, m pl

Florence /'flɔrəns/ Florencia, f

Florentine /'flɔrən,tin/ a and n florentino (-na)

florescence /flɔ'rɛsəns/ n florescencia, f

florid /'flɔrɪd/ a florido; demasiado ornado, cursi, llamativo; (of complexion) rubicundo

floridness /'flɔrɪdnɪs/ n floridez, f, estilo florido, m; demasiada ornamentación, vulgaridad, f, mal gusto, m; (of complexion) rubicundez, f

florin /'flɔrɪn/ n florín, m

florist /'flɔrɪst/ n florista, mf

floss /flɔs/ n seda floja, filoseda, f; (of maize) penacho, m; (of a cocoon) cadarzo, m. **f. silk,** seda floja, f

flotilla /flou'tɪlə/ n flotilla, f

flotsam /'flɒtsəm/ n pecio, m

flounce /flauns/ n volante, m, vi saltar de impaciencia. **to f. out,** salir airadamente

flounder /'flaundər/ n (nearest equivalent) Ichth. platija, f; tumbo, m. vi tropezar; revolcarse; andar dificultosamente; (wander) errar, vagar

flour /flauər/ n harina, f, vt enharinar. **f.-bin,** tina, f, harinero, m. **f. merchant,** harinero, m

flourish /'flɜrɪʃ/ n movimiento, m; gesto, saludo, m; (of a pen) plumada, f; (on the guitar, in fencing) floreo, m; preludio, m; (fanfare) tocata (de trompetas), f; (of a signature) rúbrica, f; (in rhetoric) floreo, m. vi (of plants) vegetar; (prosper) prosperar, medrar; florecer; (of the guitar, in fencing) florear; Mus. preludiar; (with a pen) hacer plumadas (or rasgos de pluma); (of a signature) firmar con rúbrica; (sound a fanfare) hacer una tocata (de trompetas). vt agitar en el aire, blandir

flourishing /'flɜrɪʃɪŋ/ a (of plants) lozano; floreciente; (prosperous) próspero; (happy) feliz

flourmill /'flauər,mɪl/ n molino de harina, m, fábrica de harina, f, molina harinero, m

floury /'flauəri/ a harinoso

flout /flaut/ vt burlarse de; despreciar, no hacer caso de

flow /flou/ n flujo, m; corriente, f; chorro, m; (of water) caudal, m; (output) producción total, cantidad, f; (of the tide) flujo (de la marea), m; (of words) facilidad, f. vi fluir, manar; correr; (of the tide) crecer (la marea); (pass) pasar, correr; (result) resultar (de); provenir (de); (of hair, drapery) caer, ondular; (abound) abundar (en). **to f. away,** escaparse, salir. **to f. back,** refluir. **to f. down,** descender, fluir hacia abajo; (of tears) correr por. **to f. from,** dimanar de; manar de; Fig. provenir de. **to f. in,** llegar en abundancia. **to f. into,** (rivers) desaguar en, desembocar en. **to f. over,** derramarse por. **to f. through,** fluir por; atravesar; (water) regar. **to f. together,** (rivers) confluir

flower /'flauər/ n flor, f; (best) flor y nata, crema, f. vi florecer. **in f.,** en flor. **No flowers by request,** (for a funeral) No flores por deseo del finado. **f.-bud,** capullo, m. **f.-garden,** jardín, m. **f. girl,** florista, vendedora de flores, f. **f. market,** mercado de flores, m. **f.-piece,** florero, m. **f. pot,** tiesto, m, maceta, f; Lat. Am. macetero m. **f. show,** exposición de flores, f. **f. vase,** florero, m

flowerbed /'flauər,bɛd/ n cuadro, macizo, m

flower car coche portacoronas, m

flowered /'flauərd/ a (in compounds) con flores; con dibujos de flores

floweriness /'flauərɪnɪs/ n abundancia de flores, f; (of style) floridez, f, estilo florido, m

flowering /'flauərɪŋ/ n florecimiento, m. a floreciente; con flores; (of shrubs) de adorno. **f. season,** época de la floración, f

flowery /'flauəri/ a florido

flowing /'flouɪŋ/ n flujo, m; derrame, m. a fluente, corriente; (of tide) creciente; (waving) ondeante; suelto; (of style) flúido

flow of capital corriente de capital, f

fluctuate /'flʌktʃu,eit/ vi fluctuar, vacilar; variar

fluctuating /'flʌktʃu,eitɪŋ/ a fluctuante, vacilante; variable; (hesitating) irresoluto, dudoso

fluctuation /,flʌktʃu'eiʃən/ n fluctuación, f; cambio, m, variación, f; (hesitancy) indecisión, vacilación, f

flue /flu/ n (of a chimney) cañón, m; (of a boiler) tubo, m

fluency /'fluənsi/ n fluidez, f

fluent /'fluənt/ a flúido; fácil

fluently /'fluəntli/ adv corrientemente, con facilidad, de corrido

fluff /flʌf/ n borra, pelusa, f, tamo, m

fluffy /'flʌfi/ a velloso; (feathered) plumoso; (woolly) lanudo; (of hair) encrespado

fluid /'fluɪd/ n flúido, líquido, m, a flúido

fluidity /flu'ɪdɪti/ n fluidez, f

fluke /fluk/ n (in billiards) chiripa, f; Naut. uña, f; Inf. carambola, chiripa, chambonada, f. **by a f.,** de carambola, por suerte. **f.-worm,** duela del hígado, f

flunkey /'flʌŋki/ n lacayo, m; Fig. adulador, m

fluorescence /flʊ'rɛsəns/ n fluorescencia, f

fluorescent /flʊ'rɛsənt/ a fluorescente

fluorine /'flʊrin/ n Chem. flúor, m

fluorite /'flʊrait/ n fluorita, f

flurry /'flɜri/ n (of wind) ráfaga, f; (squall) chubasco, m; agitación, f; conmoción, f. vt agitar

flush /flʌʃ/ n rubor, m; (in the sky) arrebol, rojo, color de rosa, m; emoción, f, acceso, m; sensación, f; (at cards) flux, m; vigor, m; (flowering) floración, f; abundancia, f; (of youth, etc.) frescura, f. a (level) igual, parejo; abundante; (generous) pródigo, liberal; (rich) adinerado. vi ruborizarse, enrojecerse, ponerse colorado; (flood) inundarse, llenarse (de agua, etc.); (of sky) arrebolarse. vt inundar, limpiar con un chorro de agua, etc., lavar; (of blood) circular por; (redden) enrojecer; (make blush) hacer ruborizarse; (exhilarate) excitar, animar; (inflame) inflamar, encender; (make level) igualar, nivelar. **f. with,** a ras de

flushing /'flʌʃɪŋ/ n rojez, f; (cleansing) limpieza, lavadura, f; (flooding) inundación, f

fluster /'flʌstər/ n agitación, confusión, f, aturdimiento, m. vt agitar, poner nervioso (a), aturdir; (oneself) preocuparse. vi agitarse; estar nervioso, estar perplejo; (with drink) estar entre dos velas

flute /flut/ n flauta, f; Archit. estría, f; (organ-stop) flautado, m. vi tocar la flauta, flautear; tener la voz flauteada. vt tocar (una pieza) en la flauta; (groove) encanutar, acanalar, estriar. **f. player,** flautista, mf

fluted /'flutɪd/ a (grooved) acanalado

fluting /'flutɪŋ/ n Mus. son de la flauta, m; (of birds) trinado, m; Archit. estría, f; Sew. rizado, m

flutter /'flʌtər/ n (of wings) aleteo, m; (of leaves, etc.) murmurio, m; (of eyelashes) pestañeo, m; (of flags, etc.) ondeo, m, ondulación, f; (excitement) agitación, f; (stir) sensación, f; (gamble) jugada, f. vi (of birds) aletear; revolotear; (of butterflies) mariposear; (of flags) ondear; palpitar; (of persons) estar agitado. vt agitar; (the eyelashes) pestañear; (agitate) agitar, alarmar, azorar

fluttering /'flʌtərɪŋ/ n mariposeo, m; revoloteo, m; (of birds) aleteo, m; (of leaves, etc.) murmurio, m; (of flags, etc.) ondeo, m, ondulación, f; (of eyelashes) pestañeo, m

fluvial /'fluviəl/ a fluvial

flux /flʌks/ n flujo, m

fly /flai/ n (insect) mosca, f; (on a fishhook) mosca artificial, f; (carriage) calesín, m; (of trousers) bragueta, *f*; *Theat.* bambalina, *f*; (of a tent) toldo, *m*; (flight) vuelo, *m*; (of a flag) vuelo, *m*. **fly-blown,** manchado por las moscas. **fly-by-night,** trasnochador (-ra). **fly-catcher,** *Ornith.* papamoscas, *m*; matamoscas, *m*. **fly-fishing,** pesca con moscas artificiales, *f*. **fly-leaf,** guarda (de un libro), *f*. **fly-paper,** papel matamoscas, *m*. **fly-swatter,** matamoscas, *m*. **fly-wheel,** *Mech.* volante, *m*

fly /flai/ *vi* volar; (flutter) ondear; (jump) saltar; (rush) lanzarse, precipitarse; (pass away) pasar volando, volar; (run off) marcharse a toda correr; (escape) huir, escapar; (seek refuge) refugiarse; (to the head, of intoxicants) subirse; (vanish) desaparecer. *vt* hacer volar; hacer ondear, enarbolar; (an airplane) pilotar, dirigir; (flee from) huir de; evitar. **to let fly (at),** descargar, tirar; *Fig.* saltar la sinhueso. **to fly about,** volar en torno de; revolotear. **to fly at,** lanzarse sobre; acometer, asaltar. **to fly away,** emprender el vuelo. **to fly back,** volar hacia el punto de partida; (of doors, etc.) abrir, o cerrar, de repente. **to fly down,** volar abajo. **to fly in,** volar dentro de; volar adentro; (of airplanes) llegar (el avión). **to fly into a rage,** montarse en cólera. **to fly low,** rastrear; *Aer.* volar a poca altura. **to fly off,** emprender el vuelo; (hasten) marcharse volando; (of buttons, etc.) saltar (de), separarse (de). **to fly open,** abrirse de repente. **to fly over,** volar por, volar por encima de. **to fly to pieces,** hacerse pedazos. **to fly upwards,** volar hacia arriba; subir

flying /ˈflaiiŋ/ *n* vuelo, *m*. *a* volante, volador; que vuela; de volar; volátil; (hasty) rápido; (flowing) ondeante, ondulante. **to shoot f.,** tirar al vuelo. **with f. colors,** con banderas desplegadas, triunfante. **f.-boat,** hidroavión, *m*. **f.-buttress,** botarel, arbotante, *m*. **f.-column,** *Mil.* cuerpo volante, *m*. **f.-fish,** (pez) volador, *m*. **f.-fortress,** *Aer.* fortaleza volante, *f*. **f.-officer,** oficial de aviación, *m*. **f.-sickness,** mal de altura, *m*. **f.-squad,** escuadra ligera, *f*. **f.-test,** *Aer.* examen de pilotaje, *m*

foal /foul/ *n* potro (-ra). *vi* and *vt* parir una yegua

foam /foum/ *n* espuma, *f*. *vi* espumar; (of horses, etc.) echar espumarajos. **to f. and froth,** (of the sea) hervir. **f. at the mouth,** echar espuma por la boca.

foam rubber *n* caucho esponjoso, *m*, espuma de caucho, *f*, espuma sintética, *f*

foamy /ˈfoumi/ *a* espumoso

fob /fɒb/ *n* bolsillo del reloj, *m*; faltriquera pequeña, *f*. *vt* (off) engañar con

focal /ˈfoukəl/ *a* focal

focus /ˈfoukəs/ *n* foco, *m*; centro, *m*. *vt* enfocar; concentrar. *vi* convergir. **in f.,** en foco

fodder /ˈfɒdər/ *n* *Agr.* pienso, forraje, *m*. *vt* dar forraje (a)

foe /fou/ *n* enemigo, *m*

fog /fɒg/ *n* neblina, niebla, *f*; *Fig.* confusión, *f*; *Fig.* perplejidad, *f*, *vt* obscurecer; *Photo.* velar; *Fig.* ofuscar. *vi* hacerse nebuloso; *Photo.* velarse. **fog-signal,** señal de niebla, *f*

fogbound /ˈfɒgˌbaund/ *a* rodeado de niebla; detenido por la niebla

fogey /ˈfougi/ *n* obscurantista, *m*. **He is an old f.,** Es un señor chapado a la antigua

fogginess /ˈfɒginɪs/ *n* oscuridad, neblina, *f*

foggy /ˈfɒgi/ *a* nebuloso; *Photo.* velado. **It is f.,** Hay niebla

foghorn /ˈfɒgˌhɔrn/ *n* sirena, *f*; bocina, *f*

foible /ˈfɔibəl/ *n* flaco, *m*, debilidad, *f*

foil /fɔil/ *n* (sword) florete, *m*; (coat) hoja, *f*; (of a mirror) azogado, *m*. *vt* frustrar. **f. a plot,** desbaratar un complot

foiling /ˈfɔiliŋ/ *n* frustración, *f*

foist /fɔist/ *vt* imponer; insertar, incluir; engañar (con)

fold /fould/ *n* doblez, *f*, pliegue, *m*; arruga, *f*; *Sew.* cogido, *m*; (for sheep) redil, aprisco, *m*; *Fig.* iglesia, congregación de los fieles, *f*; (in compounds) vez, *f*. *vt* doblar, plegar, doblegar; (the arms) cruzar (los brazos); (embrace) abrazar; (wrap) envolver; (clasp) entrelazar; (sheep) meter en redil, encerrar. *vi* doblarse, plegarse; cerrarse

folder /ˈfouldər/ *n* doblador (-ra); plegadera (-ra)

folding /ˈfouldiŋ/ *n* plegadura, *f*, doblamiento, *m*; (of sheep) encerramiento, *m*, a plegadizo. **f.-door,** puerta plegadiza, *f*. **f.-machine,** plegador, *m*. **f.-seat,** *Auto.* traspuntín, *m*. **f.-table,** mesa de tijeras, *f*; mesa plegadiza, *f*

foliage /ˈfouliidʒ/ *n* follaje, *m*, frondas, *f pl.* **thick f.,** frondosidad, *f*

folio /ˈfouliˌou/ *n* folio, *m*; (a volume) infolio, *m*. *a* de infolio. *vt* foliar

folk /fouk/ *n* (nation) pueblo, *m*, nación, *f*; gente, *f*; *pl* **folks,** *Inf.* familia, *f*; parientes, *m pl.* **f.-dance,** danza popular, *f*

folklore /ˈfoukˌlɔr/ *n* folclore, *m*, tradiciones folclóricas, *f pl*

folklorist /ˈfoukˌlɔrɪst/ *n* folclorista, *mf*

folksong /ˈfoukˌsɔŋ/ *n* canción popular, *f*; romance, *m*; copla, *f*

folktale /ˈfoukˌteil/ *n* conseja, *f*, cuento popular, *m*

follicle /ˈfɒlikəl/ *n* (*Anat.*, *Bot.*) folículo, *m*

follow /ˈfɒlou/ *vt* seguir; (pursue) perseguir; (hunt) cazar; (adopt) adoptar; (understand) comprender; (notice) observar. *vi* ir, o venir, detrás; (of time) venir después; (gen. impers.) seguir, resultar; seguirse. **as follows,** como sigue. **I shall f. your advice,** Seguiré tus consejos. **to f. on the heels of,** *Fig.* pisar los talones (a). **to f. suit,** (at cards) asistir, jugar el mismo palo; *Fig.* imitar. **to f. up,** proseguir; continuar; (pursue) perseguir; (enhance) reforzar. **f.-me-lads,** *Inf.* siguemepollo, *m*

follower /ˈfɒlouər/ *n* seguidor (-ra); adherente, secuaz, *mf*; (imitator) imitador (-ra); (lover) novio, *m*; *pl* **followers,** acompañamiento, séquito, *m*

following /ˈfɒlouiŋ/ *n* séquito, acompañamiento, *m*, comitiva, *f*; partidarios, *m pl*, adherentes, *mf pl.* *a* siguiente; próximo. **f. wind,** viento en popa, *m*

folly /ˈfɒli/ *n* locura, extravagancia, absurdidad, tontería, *f*, disparate, *m*

foment /fouˈmɛnt/ *vt* (poultice) fomentar; provocar, incitar, instigar; (assist) fomentar, proteger, promover

fomentation /ˌfoumenˈteiʃən/ *n* *Med.* fomentación, *f*; provocación, instigación, *f*; fomento, *m*, protección, *f*

fomenter /ˈfoumentər/ *n* fomentador (-ra), instigador (-ra)

fond /fɒnd/ *a* (doting) demasiado indulgente; (loving) cariñoso, tierno, afectuoso; (addicted to) aficionado a, adicto a, amigo de. **to be f. of,** (things) tener afición a, estar aficionado de; (people) tener cariño (a). **to grow f. of,** (things) aficionarse a; (people) tomar cariño (a)

fondle /ˈfɒndl/ *vt* mimar, acariciar; jugar (con.)

fondly /ˈfɒndli/ *adv* cariñosamente, tiernamente

fondness /ˈfɒndnɪs/ *n* cariño, afecto, *m*; (for things) afición, inclinación, *f*; gusto, *m*

font /fɒnt/ *n* pila bautismal, *f*; *Poet.* fuente, *f*; *Print.* fundición, *f*

food /fud/ *n* alimento, *m*; comida, *f*, el comer, *m*; (of animals) pasto, *m*; *Fig.* pábulo, *m*; materia, *f*. **She gave him f.** Le dio de comer. **You have given me f. for thought,** Me has dado en qué pensar. **f.-card,** cartilla de racionamiento, *f*. **food, clothing, and shelter** comida, abrigo y vivienda, *f*. **F. Ministry,** Ministerio de Alimentación, *m*. **f. value,** valor nutritivo, *m*

food poisoning, intoxicación alimenticia, *f*

foodstuffs /ˈfudˌstʌfs/ *n pl* comestibles, víveres, *m pl*

fool /ful/ *n* tonto (-ta), mentecato (-ta), majadero (ra) necio (-ia); (jester) bufón, *m*; (butt of jest) hazmerreír, *m*; víctima, *f*; *Cul.* compota de frutas con crema, *f*, *vi* tontear, hacer tonterías. *vt* poner en ridículo (a); (deceive) engañar, embaucar; (with) jugar con. **to make a f. of oneself,** ponerse en ridículo. **to f. about,** vi perder el tiempo, vagabundear. **to f. away,** malgastar, malbaratar. **fool's bauble,** cetro de bufón, *m*. **fool's cap,** gorro de bufón, *m*

foolhardiness /ˈfulˌhardinɪs/ *n* temeridad, *f*

foolhardy /ˈfulˌhardi/ *a* temerario, atrevido

fooling /ˈfuliŋ/ *n* payasada, bufonada, *f*; (deceiving) engaño, *m*, burla, *f*

foolish /ˈfuliʃ/ *a* imprudente; estúpido; tonto; ridículo, absurdo; imbécil

foolishly /ˈfuliʃli/ *adv* imprudentemente; tontamente; imbécilmente

foolishness /'fulɪʃnɪs/ *n* imprudencia, *f*; estupidez, tontería, *f*, disparate, *m*; ridiculez, *f*; imbecilidad, *f*
foolproof /'ful͵pruf/ *a* (of utensils, etc.) con garantía absoluta
fool's gold /fulz/ *n* pirita amarilla, *f*, sulfuro de hierro *m*
foot /fʊt/ *n* pie, *m*; (of animals, furniture) pata, *f*; (of bed, sofa, grave, ladder, page, etc.) pie, *m*; (hoof) pezuña, *f*; (metric unit and measure) pie, *m*; *Mil.* infantería, *f*; (base) base, *f*; (step) paso, *m. a Mil.* de a pie; a pie. *vi* ir a pie; venir a pie; bailar. *vt* hollar; (account) pagar (una cuenta); (stockings) poner pie (a). **on f.,** a pie; (of soldiers) de a pie; (in progress) en marcha. **to go on f.,** ir a pie, andar. **to put one's best f. forward,** apretar el paso; *Fig.* hacer de su mejor. **to put one's f. down,** poner pies en pared, pararle fulano el alto. **to put one's f. in it,** meter la pata. **to rise to one's feet,** ponerse de pie. **to set f. on,** pisar, hollar. **to set on f.,** poner en pie; *Fig.* poner en marcha. **to trample under f.,** pisotear. **f.-and-mouth disease,** glosopeda, *f.* **f.-brake,** freno de pedal, *m.* **f.-pump,** fuelle de pie, *m.* **f.-rule,** (nearest equivalent) doble decímetro, *m.* **f.-soldier,** soldado de a pie, infante, *m*
football /'fʊt͵bɔl/ *n* (game) fútbol americano, *m*; (ball) pelota de fútbol, *f.* **f. field,** campo de fútbol, *m.* **f. match,** partida de fútbol, *f.* **f. pools,** apuestas de fútbol, *f pl*; (in Spain) apuestas benéficas de fútbol, *f pl*
football player *n* fútbolista, *m*
footbath /'fʊt͵bæθ/ *n* baño de pies, *m*
footbridge /'fʊt͵brɪdʒ/ *n* puente para peatones, *m*
footed /'fʊtɪd/ *a* con pies; de pies...; de patas...
footfall /'fʊt͵fɔl/ *n* pisada, *f*, paso, *m*
foothills /'fʊt͵hɪlz/ *n pl* faldas de la montaña, *f pl*
foothold /'fʊt͵hoʊld/ *n* hincapié, *m*; posición establecida, *f*
footing /'fʊtɪŋ/ *n* hincapié, *m*; posición firme, *f*; condiciones, *f pl*; relaciones, *f pl.* **on a peacetime f.,** en pie de paz. **to be on an equal f.,** estar en pie de igualdad, estar en iguales condiciones. **to miss one's f.,** resbalar
footlights /'fʊt͵laɪts/ *n pl* canilejas, candilejas, *f pl.* **to get across the f.,** hacer contacto con el público
footman /'fʊtmən/ *n* lacayo, *m*
footnote /'fʊt͵noʊt/ *n* llamada a pie de página, nota a pie de página, *f*, cita, *f*
footpath /'fʊt͵pæθ/ *n* senda, vereda, *f*, sendero, *m*
footprint /'fʊt͵prɪnt/ *n* huella, pisada, *f*, vestigio, *m*
footsore /'fʊt͵sɔr/ *a* con los pies lastimados
footstep /'fʊt͵stɛp/ *n* paso, *m*; (trace) pisada, huella, *f.* **to follow in the footsteps of,** *Fig.* seguir las pisadas de
footstool /'fʊt͵stul/ *n* escabel, banquito, *m*
footwarmer /'fʊt͵wɔrmər/ *n* calientapiés, *m*
footwear /'fʊt͵wɛər/ *n* calzado, *m*
for /fɔr; *unstressed* fər/ *prep* (expressing exchange, price or penalty of, instead of, in support or favor of, on account of) por; (expressing destination, purpose, result) para; (during) durante, por; (for the sake of) para; (because of) a causa de; (in spite of) a pesar de; (as) como; (with) de; (in favor of) en favor de; (in election campaign) con (e.g., "Ecuadorians for Martínez!" ¡Ecuatorianos con Martínez!) (toward) hacia; (that) que, para que (with *subjunc*); a, (before) antes de; (searching for) en busca de; (bound for) con rumbo a; (regarding) en cuanto a; (until) hasta. What's for dinner? ¿Qué hay de comida? **center for...** centro de... (e.g., *Center for Applied Linguistics,* Centro de Lingüística Aplicada). **He is in business for himself,** Tiene negocios por su propia cuenta. **It is raining too hard for you to go there,** Llueve demasiado para que vayas allí. **It is not for him to decide,** No le toca a él el decidirlo. **Were it not for...,** Si no fuese por... **She has not been to see me for a week,** Hace una semana que no viene a verme. **It is impossible for them to go out,** Les es imposible salir. **but for all that,** pero con todo. **for ever,** por (or para) siempre. **for fear that,** por miedo de que. **for myself,** en cuanto a mí, personalmente. **for the present,** por ahora. **for what reason?** ¿para qué? ¿por cuál motivo? **for brevity's sake,** for the sake of

brevity, por causa de la brevedad. **For such a young girl, she plays the piano well,** Para una niña tan joven toca bien el piano
for /fɔr; *unstressed* fər/ *conjunc* porque; visto que, pues, puesto que, en efecto, ya que
forage /'fɔrɪdʒ/ *n* forraje, *m. vt* and *vi* forrajear. **to f. for,** buscar. **f. cap,** gorra de cuartel, *f*
forager /'fɔrɪdʒər/ *n* forrajeador, *m*
foraging /'fɔrɪdʒɪŋ/ *n* forraje, *m*
forasmuch as /͵fɔrəz'mʌtʃ ͵æz/ *conjunc* puesto que, como que, ya que, por tanto que
foray /'fɔreɪ/ *n* correría, cabalgada, *f*; saqueo, *m*
forbear /'fɔr͵bɛər/ *vt* and *vi* dejar (de), guardarse (de); abstenerse de; evitar; reprimirse (de); rehusarse (de); (cease) cesar (de); (be patient) ser paciente; ser tolerante
forbearance /fɔr'bɛərəns/ *n* abstención, *f*; tolerancia, transigencia, *f*; indulgencia, *f*; paciencia, *f*
forbearing /fɔr'bɛərɪŋ/ *a* tolerante, transigente; generoso, magnánimo; paciente
forbid /fər'bɪd/ *vt* prohibir, defender (de); impedir. **I f. you to do it,** Te prohibo hacerlo. **The game is forbidden,** El juego está prohibido. **They have forbidden me to...,** Me han defendido de... **Heaven f.!** ¡Dios no lo quiera!
forbidden /fər'bɪdn̩/ *a* prohibido; ilícito. **f. fruit,** fruto prohibido, *m*
forbidding /fər'bɪdɪŋ/ *a* repugnante, horrible; antipático, desagradable; (dismal) lúgubre; (threatening) amenazador. *n* prohibición, *f*
force /fɔrs/ *n* fuerza, *f*; violencia, *f*; vigor, *m*; (efficacy) eficacia, *f*; (validity) validez, *f*; (power) poder, *m*; (motive) motivo, *m*, razón, *f*; (weight) peso, *m*, importancia, *f*; (police) policía, *f*; *pl* **forces,** *Mil.* fuerzas, tropas, *f pl.* **by main f.,** por fuerza mayor. **in f.,** vigente, en vigor. **to be in f.,** estar vigente
force /fɔrs/ *vt* forzar; (compel) obligar, constreñir, precisar; (ravish) violar; *Cul.* rellenar; (impose) imponer; (plants) forzar; (the pace) apresurar; (cause) hacer; (a lock, etc.) forzar. **to f. oneself into,** entrar a la fuerza en; (a garment) ponerse con dificultad; imponerse a la fuerza. **to f. oneself to,** esforzarse a. **to f. the pace,** forzar el paso. **to f. away,** ahuyentar. **to f. back,** hacer retroceder; rechazar; (a sigh, etc.) ahogar. **to f. down,** hacer bajar, obligar a bajar; (make swallow) hacer tragar; (of airplanes) hacer tomar tierra. **to f. in,** introducir a la fuerza; obligar a entrar. **to f. into,** meter a la fuerza, obligar a entrar (en). **to f. on, upon,** imponer. **to f. open,** abrir a la fuerza; (a lock) romper, forzar. **to f. out,** hacer salir; empujar hacia fuera; (words) pronunciar con dificultad. **to f. up,** obligar a subir; hacer subir; hacer vomitar
forced /fɔrst/ *a* forzado; forzoso; afectado. **f. landing,** *Aer.* aterrizaje forzoso, *m.* **f. march,** *Mil.* marcha forzada, *f*
forceful /'fɔrsfəl/ *a* See **forcible**
forceps /'fɔrsəps/ *n* fórceps, *m pl*; pinzas, *f pl.* **arterial f.,** pinzas hemostáticas, *f pl*
forcible /'fɔrsəbəl/ *a* fuerte; a la fuerza; violento; enérgico, vigoroso; poderoso; *Lit.* vívido, gráfico, vehemente. **f. feeding,** alimentación forzosa, *f*
forcibleness /'fɔrsəbəlnɪs/ *n* fuerza, *f*; vigor, *m*, energía, *f*; vehemencia, *f*
forcibly /'fɔrsəbli/ *adv* a la fuerza
forcing /'fɔrsɪŋ/ *n* forzamiento, *m*; compulsión, *f*. **f. frame,** semillero, *m*, especie de invernadero, *f*
ford /fɔrd/ *n* esguazo, vado, *m. vt* esguazar, vadear
fordable /'fɔrdəbəl/ *a* esguazable, vadeable
fore /fɔr/ *a* delantero; *Naut.* de proa *adv* delante; *Naut.* de proa. **f.-and-aft,** *Naut.* de popa a proa.
forearm /'fɔr'ɑrm/ *n* antebrazo, *m. vt* armar de antemano; preparar
forebear /'fɔr͵bɛər/ *n* antecesor, *m*, ascendiente, *mf*
forebode /fɔr'boʊd/ *vt* presagiar, augurar, anunciar; presentir
foreboding /fɔr'boʊdɪŋ/ *n* presagio, augurio, *m*; presentimiento, *m*, corazonada, *f*
forecast /'fɔr͵kæst/ *n* pronóstico, *m*; proyecto, plan, *m*, *vt* pronosticar; proyectar. **weather f.,** pronóstico del tiempo, *m*

forecastle /'fouksəl/ n Naut. castillo de proa, m
foreclose /fɔr'klouz/ vt excluir; impedir; vender por orden judicial; anticipar el resultado de; decidir de antemano
foreclosure /fɔr'klouʒər/ n venta por orden judicial, f; juicio hipotecario, m
foredoom /fɔr'dum/ vt predestinar
forefather /'fɔr,faðər/ n antepasado, antecesor, m
forefinger /'fɔr,fɪŋgər/ n índice, dedo índice, m
forefoot /'fɔr,fʊt/ n pata delantera, f
forefront /'fɔr,frʌnt/ n delantera, primera línea, f; frente, m; vanguardia, f. **in the f.,** en la vanguardia; en el frente
foregoing /fɔr'gouɪŋ/ a precedente, anterior
foregone /fɔr'gɔn/ a decidido de antemano; previsto
foreground /'fɔr,graund/ n primer plano, primer término, frente, m. **in the f.,** Art. en primer término
forehand /'fɔr,hænd/ a derecho. **f. stroke,** golpe derecho, m
forehead /'fɔrɪd/ n frente, f
foreign /'fɔrɪn/ a extranjero; extraño; exótico; exterior; (alien) ajeno. **f. affairs,** asuntos extranjeros, m pl. **f. body,** cuerpo extraño, m. **f. debt,** deuda exterior, f. **F. Legion,** tercio extranjero, m. **F. Office,** Ministerio de Relaciones Extranjeras, m. **f. parts,** extranjero, m. **f. policy,** política internacional, f. **F. Secretary,** Secretario de Asuntos Extranjeros, Secretario de Asuntos Exteriores, Ministro de Relaciones Extranjeras, m. **f. trade,** comercio con el extranjero, m
foreigner /'fɔrənər/ n extranjero (-ra), Argentina, Chile also cuico (-ca), Mexico also fuereño (-ña) mf
foreignness /'fɔrənnɪs/ n extranjerismo, m; (strangeness) extrañeza, f; lo exótico
foreknowledge /'fɔr,nɒlɪdʒ/ n presciencia, precognición, f
foreland /'fɔr,lænd/ n promontorio, cabo, m
forelock /'fɔr,lɒk/ n guedeja, vedeja, f; (of a horse) copete, tupé, m. **to take time by the f.,** asir la ocasión por la melena
foreman /'fɔrmən/ n (of jury) presidente (del jurado), m; (of a farm) mayoral, m; (in a works) capataz, m
foremost /'fɔr,moust/ a delantero; de primera fila; más importante. adv en primer lugar; en primera fila
forensic /fə'rɛnsɪk/ a forense, legal. **f. medicine,** medicina legal, f
foreordained /,fɔrɔr'deind/ a predestinado
forerunner /'fɔr,rʌnər/ n precursor (-ra), predecessor (-ra); (presage) anuncio, presagio, m
foresee /fɔr'si/ vt prever, anticipar
foreseeing /fɔr'siɪŋ/ a presciente, sagaz
foreseer /fɔr'siər/ n previsor (-ra)
foreshadow /fɔr'ʃædou/ vt anunciar, prefigurar; simbolizar; hacer sentir.
foresight /'fɔr,sait/ n presciencia, f; previsión, prudencia, f; (of gun) punto de mira, m; (optical) croquis de nivel, m
forest /'fɔrɪst/ n bosque, m, selva, f. vt arbolar
forestall /fɔr'stɔl/ vt anticipar, saltear; prevenir; Com. acaparar
forestalling /fɔr'stɔlɪŋ/ n anticipación, f
forestation /,fɔrə'steiʃən/ n repoblación forestal, f
forester /'fɔrəstər/ n silvicultor, guardamonte, ingeniero forestal, m; habitante de los bosques, m
forest fire incendio forestal, m
forestry /'fɔrəstri/ n silvicultura, f
foresworn /fɔr'swɔrn/ a perjuro
foretaste /n 'fɔr,teist; v fɔr'teist/ n muestra, f; presagio, m. vt gustar con anticipación
foretell /fɔr'tɛl/ vt predecir, profetizar; anunciar, presagiar
foreteller /fɔr'tɛlər/ n profeta, m; presagio, m
foretelling /fɔr'tɛlɪŋ/ n profecía, predicción, f
forethought /'fɔr,θɔt/ n presciencia, previsión, f; prevención, f
forewarn /fɔr'wɔrn/ vt prevenir, advertir
forewarning /fɔr'wɔrnɪŋ/ n presagio, m
forewoman /'fɔr,wʊmən/ n encargada, f; primera oficiala, f
foreword /'fɔr,wɜrd/ n prefacio, m, introducción, f

forfeit /'fɔrfɪt/ n pérdida, f; (fine) multa, f; (in games) prenda, f; (of rights, goods, etc.) confiscación, f. a confiscado. vt perder; perder el derecho o el título de
forfeiture /'fɔrfɪtʃər/ n pérdida, f; confiscación, f; secuestro, m
forge /fɔrdʒ/ n fragua, f; (smithy) herrería, f. vt and vi fraguar, forjar; (fabricate) inventar, fabricar; falsificar; (advance) avanzar lentamente. **to f. ahead,** abrirse camino; avanzar
forged /fɔrdʒd/ a (of iron) forjado; (of checks, etc.) falso, falsificado
forger /'fɔrdʒər/ n falsificador (-ra), falsario (-ia); (creator) artífice, mf
forgery /'fɔrdʒəri/ n falsificación, f
forget /fər'gɛt/ vt olvidar; descuidar. vi olvidarse. **to f. about,** olvidarse de, desacordarse de. **to f. oneself,** olvidarse de sí mismo; propasarse; (in anger) perder los estribos. **I forgot my key,** Se me olvidó la llave
forgetful /fər'gɛtfəl/ a olvidadizo; descuidado, negligente
forgetfulness /fər'gɛtfəlnɪs/ n olvido, m; descuido, m; falta de memoria, f
forging /'fɔrdʒɪŋ/ n fraguado, m; falsificación, f
forgivable /fər'gɪvəbəl/ a perdonable, excusable
forgive /fər'gɪv/ vt perdonar, disculpar; condonar; (debts) remitir
forgiveness /fər'gɪvnɪs/ n perdón, m; condonación, f; (remission) remisión, f
forgiving /fər'gɪvɪŋ/ a misericordioso, clemente, dispuesto a perdonar
forgo /fɔr'gou/ vt renunciar, sacrificar, privarse de; abandonar, ceder
forgoing /fɔr'gouɪŋ/ n renunciación, f; sacrificio, m; cesión, f
"For Immediate Occupancy" «De Ocupación Inmediata»
fork /fɔrk/ n Agr. horca, horquilla, f; (table fork) tenedor, m; bifurcación, f; (of rivers) confluencia, f; (of branches) horcadura, f; (of legs) horcajadura, f; (for supporting trees, etc.) horca, f; Mus. diapasón normal, m. vi hacinar con horca. vi bifurcarse; ramificarse
forked /fɔrkt/ a bifurcado, hendido, ahorquillado. **f. lightning,** relámpago, m. **f. tail,** cola hendida, f
forlorn /fɔr'lɔrn/ a abandonado, desamparado, desesperado. **f. hope,** aventura desesperada, f
forlornness /fɔr'lɔrnnɪs/ n desamparo, m, miseria, f; desolación, f; desconsuelo, m
form /fɔrm/ n forma, f; figura, f; (shadowy) bulto, m; (formality) formalidad, f; ceremonia, f; Eccl. rito, m; método, m; regla, f; (in a school) clase, f; (lair) cama, f; (seat) banco, m; (system) sistema, m; (ghost) espectro, m; aparición, f; (to fill out) documento, m; hoja, f, Mexico esqueleto m; (state) condición, f; Lit. construcción, forma, f. **It is a matter of f.,** Es una pura formalidad. **in due f.,** en debida forma, en regla. **in the usual f.,** Com. al usado. **It is not good f.,** No es de buena educación
form /fɔrm/ vt formar; (a habit) contraer; (an idea) hacerse (una idea). vi formarse. **to f. fours,** Mil. formar a cuatro
formal /'fɔrməl/ a esencial; formal; ceremonioso, solemne; (of person) etiquetero, formalista. **f. call,** visita de cumplido, f
formaldehyde /fɔr'mældə,haid/ n formaldehído, m
formalism /'fɔrmə,lɪzəm/ n formalismo, m
formality /fɔr'mælɪti/ n formalidad, f; ceremonia, solemnidad, f
formally /'fɔrməli/ adv formalmente
format /'fɔrmæt/ n formato, m
formation /fɔr'meiʃən/ n formación, f; disposición, f; arreglo, m; (organization) organización, f; (Mil., Geol.) formación, f
formative /'fɔrmətɪv/ a formativo
former /'fɔrmər/ a primero; antiguo; anterior; pasado. **in f. times,** antes, antiguamente. **the f.,** ése, aquél, m; ésa, aquélla, f; aquéllos, m pl; aquéllas, f pl
former /'fɔrmər/ n formador (-ra); creador (-ra), autor (-ra)
formerly /'fɔrmərli/ adv antiguamente, antes

formidable /'fɔrmɪdəbəl/ a formidable; terrible, espantoso

formless /'fɔrmlɪs/ a informe

formlessness /'fɔrmlɪsnɪs/ n falta de forma, f

formula /'fɔrmyələ/ n fórmula, f. **standard f.**, (*Math., Chem.*) fórmula clásica, f

formulate /'fɔrmyə,leit/ vt formular

fornicate /'fɔrnɪ,keit/ vi fornicar

fornication /,fɔrnɪ'keiʃən/ n fornicación, f

fornicator /'fɔrnɪ,keitər/ n fornicador (-ra)

forsake /fɔr'seik/ vt dejar, desertar; abandonar, desamparar; separarse de; (of birds, the nest) aborrecer; (one's faith) renegar de

forsaker /fɔr'seikər/ n el, m, (la, f) que abandona; desertor, m; renegado (-da) **"For Sale"** «Se Vende»

forsooth /fɔr'suθ/ adv ciertamente, claro está

forswear /fɔr'swɛər/ vt abjurar; renunciar a. **to f. oneself,** perjurarse

forswearing /fɔr'swɛərɪŋ/ n abjuración, f; renuncia, f; perjurio, m

fort /fɔrt/ n fortaleza, f, fuerte, m

forte /'fɔrtei/ n fuerte, m. a Mus. fuerte

forth /fɔrθ/ adv (on) adelante, hacia adelante; (out) fuera; (in time) en adelante, en lo consecutivo; (show) a la vista. **and so f.**, y así en lo sucesivo; etcétera

forthcoming /'fɔrθ'kʌmɪŋ/ a próximo; futuro; en preparación

forthwith /,fɔrθ'wɪθ/ adv en seguida, sin tardanza

fortieth /'fɔrtiɪθ/ a cuadragésimo; cuarenta. n cuarentavo, m

fortifiable /'fɔrtə,faiəbəl/ a fortificable

fortification /,fɔrtəfɪ'keiʃən/ n fortificación, f

fortify /'fɔrtə,fai/ vt fortificar; fortalecer; confirmar; *Fig.* proveer (de)

fortitude /'fɔrtɪ,tud/ n aguante, m, fortaleza, f, estoicismo, m

fortnight /'fɔrt,nait/ n quince días, m pl, dos semanas, f pl; quincena, f. **a f. ago,** hace quince días. **a f. tomorrow,** mañana en quince. **in a f.,** dentro de quince días; al cabo de quince días. **once a f.,** cada quince días

fortress /'fɔrtrɪs/ n fortaleza, plaza fuerte, f

fortuitous /fɔr'tuɪtəs/ a fortuito, accidental

fortuitously /fɔr'tuɪtəsli/ adv accidentalmente

fortuity /fɔr'tuɪti/ n casualidad, f; accidente, m

fortunate /'fɔrtʃənɪt/ a dichoso, feliz; afortunado; próspero. **to be f.,** (of persons) tener suerte

fortunately /'fɔrtʃənɪtli/ adv afortunadamente, por dicha, felizmente

fortune /'fɔrtʃən/ n suerte, fortuna, f, destino, m; (money) caudal, m, fortuna, f; bienes, m pl; buena ventura, f. **good f.,** buena fortuna, dicha, f. **ill f.,** mala suerte, f. **to cost a f.,** costar un sentido. **to make one's f.,** enriquecerse; *Inf.* hacer su pacotilla. **to tell fortunes,** echar las cartas. **f. hunter,** buscador de dotes, cazador de dotes, cazador de fortunas, aventurero, m. **f.-teller,** adivinadora, f; echadora de cartas, f. **f.-telling,** buenaventura, f

forty /'fɔrti/ a and n cuarenta, m. **He is turned f.,** Ha cumplido los cuarenta. **person of f.,** cuarentón (-ona). **She is f.,** Tiene cuarenta años. **She's over f.,** Ella pasó las cuarenta años

forum /'fɔrəm/ n foro, tribuna f, (e.g., *to serve as a forum for discussion*, servir de tribuna de discusión)

forward /'fɔrwərd/ a avanzado; adelantado; (of position) delantero; (ready) preparado; (eager) pronto, listo, impaciente; activo, emprendedor; (of persons, fruit, etc.) precoz; (pert) insolente, desenvuelto, atrevido. adv adelante; hacia adelante; (of time) en adelante; (farther on) más allá; hacia el frente; en primera línea. vt ayudar, promover; adelantar; (letters) hacer seguir; *Com.* expedir, remitir; (a parcel) despachar; (hasten) apresurar; (plants) hacer crecer. n *Sports.* delantero, m. **center-f.,** *Sports.* delantero centro, m. **from this time f.,** de hoy en adelante. **Please f.,** ¡Haga seguir! **putting f. of the clock,** el adelanto de la hora. **to carry f.,** *Com.* pasar a cuenta nueva. **to go f.,** adelantarse; estar en marcha,

estar en preparación. **f. line,** *Sports.* delantera, f. **F.!** ¡Adelante!

forwarder /'fɔrwərdər/ n promotor (-ra); *Com.* remitente, m

forwarding /'fɔrwərdɪŋ/ n fomento, m, promoción, f; *Com.* expedición, f, envío, m

forwardness /'fɔrwərdnɪs/ n progreso, adelantamiento, m; (haste) apresuramiento, m; (of persons, fruit, etc.) precocidad, f; (pertness) desenvoltura, insolencia, frescura, f, descaro, m; (eagerness) impaciencia, f

fossil /'fɒsəl/ a and n fósil, m.

fossilization /,fɒsələ'zeiʃən/ n fosilización, f

fossilize /'fɒsə,laiz/ vt fosilizar; petrificar. vi fosilizarse

foster /'fɒstər/ vt provocar, promover, suscitar; (favor) favorecer, ser propicio a. **f.-brother,** hermano de leche, m. **f.-child,** hijo (-ja) de leche. **f.-father,** padre adoptivo, m. **f.-mother,** ama de leche, f. **f.-sister,** hermana de leche, f

foul /faul/ a sucio, asqueroso, puerco; (evil-smelling) hediondo, fétido; (of air) viciado; impuro; (language) ofensivo; (coarse) indecente, obsceno; (harmful) nocivo, dañino; (wicked) malvado; infame; vil; (unfair) injusto; *Sports.* sucio; (ugly) feo; (entangled) enredado; (with corrections) lleno de erratas; (choked) atascado; (of weather) borrascoso, tempestuoso; malo, desagradable; (repulsive) repugnante. n *Sports.* juego sucio, *Lat. Am.* faul m. vt ensuciar; *Naut.* chocar, abordar; (block) atascar; (the anchor) enredar; *Sports., Lat. Am.* faulear; (dishonor) deshonrar. vi atascarse; (anchor) enredarse; *Naut.* chocar. **to fall f. of,** *Naut.* abordar (un buque); *Fig.* habérselas con. **by fair means or f.,** a las buenas o a las malas. **f. breath,** aliento fétido, aliento corrompido, m. **f. brood,** peste de las abejas, f. **f. language,** palabras ofensivas, f pl; lenguaje obsceno, m. **f. play,** juego sucio, m. **f. weather,** mal tiempo, tiempo borrascoso, m

found /faund/ vt fundar; (metal, glass) fundir; (create, etc.) establecer

foundation /faun'deiʃən/ n fundación, f; establecimiento, m; creación, f; *Archit.* cimiento, embasamiento, m; (basis) base, f; (cause) causa, f, origen, principio, m; (endowment) dotación, f; *Sew.* refuerzo, m. **to lay the f.,** poner las fundaciones. **f. stone,** piedra angular, f; *Fig.* primera piedra, f. **to lay the f. stone,** poner la piedra angular

founder /'faundər/ n fundador (-ra); (of metals) fundidor, m. vt (a ship) hacer zozobrar. vi zozobrar, irse a pique; *Fig.* fracasar

foundering /'faundərɪŋ/ n *Naut.* zozobra, f

founding /'faundɪŋ/ n fundación, f; establecimiento, m; (of metals) fundición, f

foundling /'faundlɪŋ/ n hijo (-ja) de la cuna, expósito (-ta). **f. hospital** or **home,** casa de cuna, casa de expósitos, inclusa, f

foundry /'faundri/ n fundición, f

fountain /'fauntɪn/ n fuente, f; (spring) manantial, m; (jet) chorro, m; (artificial) fuente, f, surtidero, m; (source) origen, principio, m. **f.-head,** fuente, f. **Fountain of Youth,** Fuente de la juventud, Fuente de Juvencio, f. **f. pen,** pluma estilográfica, f

four /fɔr/ a and n cuatro, m. **It is f. o'clock,** Son las cuatro. **She is f.,** Tiene cuatro años. **on all fours,** a gatas. **f.-course,** (of meals) de cuatro platos. **f.-engined,** cuadrimotor. **f.-engined plane,** cuadrimotor, m. **f.-footed,** cuadrúpedo. **f.-horse,** de cuatro caballos. **f. hundred,** cuatrocientos. **f.-inhand,** tiro par, m. **f.-part,** (of a song) a cuatro voces. **f.-wheel brakes,** freno en las cuatro ruedas, m

fourfold /'fɔr,fould/ a cuádruple

fourscore /'fɔr'skɔr/ a and n ochenta, m.

foursome /'fɔrsəm/ n partido de cuatro personas, m

fourteen /'fɔr'tin/ a and n catorce, m. **He is f.,** Tiene catorce años

fourteenth /'fɔr'tinθ/ a and n décimocuarto m.; (of the month) (el) catorce, m; (of monarchs) catorce. **April f.,** El 14 (catorce) de abril

fourth /fɔrθ/ a cuarto; (of the month) el cuatro; (of monarchs) cuarto. n (fourth part) cuarta parte, f;

Mus. cuarta, f. **f. dimension,** cuarta dimensión, f. **f. term,** *Polit.* cuarto mandato, m

fourthly /'fɔrθli/ *adv* en cuarto lugar

fowl /faul/ n gallo. m; gallina, f; (chicken) pollo, m; (bird) ave, f; (barndoor.) ave de corral, f. *vi* cazar aves. **f.-house or run,** gallinero, m

fox /fɒks/ n zorro, m; (vixen) zorra, raposa, *Argentina* chilla f; *Fig.* zorro, taimado, m. *vi* disimular. *vt* (books) descolorar. **f.-brush,** cola de raposa, f. **f.-earth,** zorrera, f. **f.-hunting,** caza de zorras, f. **f. terrier,** fox-térrier, m

foxhound /'fɒks,haund/ n perro zorrero, m

foxiness /'fɒksɪnɪs/ n zorrería, astucia, f

foxtrot /'fɒks,trɒt/ n foxtrot, m

foxy /'fɒksi/ a de zorro; zorrero, astuto

foyer /'fɔiər/ n foyer, salón de descanso, m

fraction /'frækʃən/ n *Math.* fracción, f, número quebrado, m; pequeña parte, f; fragmento, m. **improper f.,** *Math.* fracción impropia, f. **proper f.,** *Math.* fracción propia, f

fractional /'frækʃənl/ a fraccionario

fractious /'frækʃəs/ a malhumorado, enojadizo

fractiousness /'frækʃəsnɪs/ n mal humor, m

fracture /'fræktʃər/ n *Surg.* fractura, f. *vt* fracturar. **compound f.,** fractura conminuta, f

fragile /'frædʒəl/ a frágil, quebradizo; (of persons) delicado

fragility /frə'dʒɪlɪti/ n fragilidad, f

fragment /'frægmənt/ n fragmento, m; trozo, pedazo, m. **to break into fragments,** hacer pedazos, hacer añicos

fragmentary /'frægmən,tɛri/ a fragmentario

fragrance /'freigrəns/ n fragancia, f, buen olor, perfume, aroma, m

fragrant /'freigrənt/ a fragante, oloroso. **to make f.,** perfumar

frail /freil/ a frágil, quebradizo; débil, endeble. n capacho, m, espuerta, f

frailty /'freilti/ n fragilidad, f; debilidad, f

frame /freim/ n constitución, f; sistema, m; organización, f; (of the body) figura, f, talle, m; (of window, picture) marco, m; (of machine, building) armadura, f; (of a bicycle) cuadro (de bicicleta), m; *Agr.* cajonera, f; (embroidery) bastidor (para bordar), m; (skeleton) esqueleto, m; *Lit.* composición, construcción, f; (of eyeglasses) armadura, f; (of mind) disposición (de ánimo), f; humor, m. *vt* formar; construir; arreglar; ajustar; (a picture) enmarcar; componer; hacer; (draw up) redactar; (think up) idear, inventar; (words) articular, pronunciar. **f. a constitution,** elaborar una constitución

framer /'freimər/ n fabricante de marcos, m; autor (-ra), creador (-ra), inventor (-ra)

framework /'freim,wɜrk/ n armadura, armazón, f, esqueleto, m; organización, f; (basis) base, f

franc /fræŋk/ n (coin) franco, m

France /fræns/ Francia, f

Franche-Comté /frɑ̃ʃ kɔ̃'tei/ Franco-Condado, m

franchise /'fræntʃaiz/ n (retail) franquicia, f, concesión, f; privilegio, m; (vote) derecho de sufragio, m; (citizenship) derecho político, m

Franciscan /fræn'sɪskən/ a and n franciscano (-na)

Franco- (in compounds) franco-... a (referring to General Franco) franquista

Francophile /'fræŋkə,fail/ a and n afrancesado (-da)

frank /fræŋk/ a franco, cándido, sincero; abierto. *vt* franquear

frankincense /'fræŋkɪn,sɛns/ n incienso, m

frankly /'fræŋkli/ *adv* francamente; sinceramente; cara a cara; sin rodeos, claramente; abiertamente. **to speak f.,** hablar claro, hablar sin rodeos

frankness /'fræŋknɪs/ n franqueza, f; sinceridad, f; candor, m

frantic /'fræntɪk/ a frenético, furioso, loco. **He drives me f.,** Me vuelve loco

fraternal /frə'tɜrnl/ a fraterno, fraternal

fraternity /frə'tɜrnɪti/ n fraternidad, hermandad, f

fraternization /,frætərnə'zeiʃən/ n fraternización, f

fraternize /'frætər,naiz/ *vi* fraternizar

fratricidal /,frætrɪ'saidl/ a fratricida

fratricide /'frætrɪ,said/ n (person) fratricida, mf; (action) fratricidio, m

fraud /frɔd/ n fraude, m; engaño, embuste, *Argentina* also forro m; (person) farsante, m, embustero (-ra)

fraudulence /'frɔdʒələns/ n fraudulencia, fraude, f

fraudulent /'frɔdʒələnt/ a fraudulento

fraught /frɔt/ a (with) cargado de; lleno de, preñado de

fray /frei/ n refriega, riña, f; combate, m, batalla, f; (rubbing) raedura, f. *vt* raer, tazar. *vi* tazarse, deshilarse

frayed /freid/ a raído

fraying /'freiɪŋ/ n raedura, deshiladura, f

freak /frik/ n monstruo, m; fenómeno, m; (whim) capricho, m

freakish /'frikɪʃ/ a monstruoso; caprichoso; extravagante; raro, singular

freakishness /'frikɪʃnɪs/ n carácter raro, m; extravagancia, f; rareza, extrañeza, f

freckle /'frɛkəl/ n peca, f. *vi* tener pecas; salir pecas (a la cara, etc.)

freckled /'frɛkəld/ a pecoso, con pecas

free /fri/ a (in most senses) libre; independiente; emancipado; desembarazado; abierto; limpio (de); franco; (voluntary) voluntario; (self-governing) autónomo, independiente; accesible; (disengaged) desocupado; (vacant) vacío; (exempt) exento (de); (immune) immune (de); ajeno; gratuito; (loose) suelto; (generous) generoso, liberal; (vicious) disoluto, licencioso; (bold) atrevido; (impudent) insolente, demasiado familiar. *adv* gratis, gratuitamente. **There are two f. seats in the train,** Hay dos asientos libres en el tren. **to get f.,** libertarse. **to make f. with,** tomarse libertades con; usar como si fuera suyo. **to set f.,** poner en libertad. **f. agent,** libre albedrío, m. **f. and easy,** familiar, sin ceremonia. **f. gift,** *Com.* objeto de reclamo, m. **f.-hand drawing,** dibujo a pulso, m. **f. kick,** *Sports.* golpe franco, m. **f. love,** amor libre, m. **f. port,** puerto franco, m. **f. rein,** rienda suelta, f; *Mech.* holgura, f. **f. speech,** libertad de palabra, f. **f. thought,** libre pensamiento, m. **f. ticket,** *Theat.* billete de favor, m. **f. trade,** a librecambista. n librecambio, m. **f. trader,** librecambista, mf. **North American Free Trade Agreement (NAFTA),** Tratado libre de comercio (TLC), m. **f. verse,** verso libre, m; verso suelto, m. **f.-wheeling,** desenfrenado, libre. **f. will,** propia voluntad, f; (theology) libre albedrío, m

free /fri/ *vt* libertar, poner en libertad (a); librar (de); (slave) salvar; emancipar; exentar (of obstacles, difficulties) desembarazar; **to f. from,** libertar de; librar de; (clean) limpiar de

freebooter /'fri,butər/ n pirata, filibustero, m

freeborn /'fri,bɔrn/ a nacido libre, libre por herencia

freedman /'fridmən/ n liberto, m

freedom /'fridəm/ n libertad, f; independencia, f; exención, f; inmunidad, f; soltura, facilidad, f; franqueza, f; (over-familiarity) insolencia, f; (boldness) audacia, intrepidez, f; (of customs) licencia, f. **to receive the f. of a city,** ser recibido como ciudadano de honor. **f. of speech,** libertad de palabra, f. **f. of the press,** libertad de la prensa, f. **f. of worship,** libertad de cultos, f

freehold /'fri,hould/ n feudo franco, m

freeing /'friɪŋ/ n liberación, f; emancipación, f; salvación, f; (from obstruction) desembarazo, m; limpieza, f

freelance /'fri,læns/ n *Mil.* soldado libre, m; *Polit.* independiente, m; aventurero (-ra). **f. journalist,** periodista libre, m

freely /'frili/ *adv* libremente; francamente; generosamente; sin reserva

freeman /'frimən/ n hombre libre, m; (of a city) ciudadano de honor, m

freemason /'fri,meisən/ n francmasón, m. **freemason's lodge,** logia masónica, f

freemasonry /'fri,meisənri/ n francmasonería, masonería, f

freethinker /'fri'θɪŋkər/ n librepensador (-ra)

freeze /friz/ *vt* helar; (meat, etc.) congelar; *Fig.* helar. *vi* helarse; congelarse; (impers. of the weather) helar. **to f. to death,** morir de frío

freezing /'frizɪŋ/ n hielo, m; congelación, f. a glacial;

congelante, frigorífico. **f. mixture,** mezcla frigorífica, *f*. **f. of assets,** bloqueo de los depósitos bancarios, *m*. **f.-point,** punto de congelación, *m*. **above f.-point,** sobre cero. **below f.-point,** bajo cero

freight /freit/ *n* flete, *m*; porte, *m*. *vt* fletar

freighter /'freitər/ *n* fletador, *m*; (ship) buque de carga, *m*

French /frɛntʃ/ *a* francés. *n* (language) francés, *m*; (people) los franceses, *m pl*. **in F. fashion,** a la francesa. **to take F. leave,** despedirse a la inglesa. **What is the F. for "hat"?** ¿Cómo se dice «sombrero» en francés? **F. spoken,** Se habla francés. **F. bean,** judía, *f*. **F. chalk,** jabón de sastre, *m*. **F. horn,** trompa, *f*. **F. lesson,** lección de francés, *f*. **F. marigold,** flor del estudiante, *f*. **F. polish,** barniz de muebles, *m*. **F. poodle,** perro (-rra) de aguas. **F. roll,** panecillo, *m*. **F. window,** puerta ventana, *f*

Frenchify /'frɛntʃə,fai/ *vt* afrancesar

Frenchman /'frɛntʃmən/ *n* francés, *m*. **a young F.,** un joven francés

Frenchwoman /'frɛntʃ,wʊmən/ *n* francesa, mujer francesa, *f*. **a young F.,** una joven francesa, una muchacha francesa, *f*

frenzied /'frɛnzid/ *a* frenético

frenzy /'frɛnzi/ *n* frenesí, delirio, paroxismo, *m*

frequency /'frikwənsi/ *n* frecuencia, *f*. **high f.,** alta frecuencia, *f*. **low f.,** baja frecuencia, *f*

frequent /'frikwənt/ *v* frɪ'kwɛnt/ *a* frecuente; (usual) común, corriente. *vt* frecuentar

frequentation /,frikwən'teiʃən/ *n* frecuentación, *f*

frequenter /'frikwəntər/ *n* frecuentador (-ra)

frequently /'frikwəntli/ *adv* frecuentemente, con frecuencia, muchas veces; comúnmente

fresco /'freskou/ *n* Art. fresco, *m*, pintura al fresco, *f*. *vt* pintar al fresco

fresh /frɛʃ/ *a* fresco; nuevo; reciente; (newly arrived) recién llegado; (inexperienced) inexperto, bisoño; (of water, not salt) dulce; puro; (healthy) sano; (brisk) vigoroso, enérgico; (vivid) vivo, vívido; (bright) brillante; (cheeky) fresco, *Lat. Am.* impávido. *adv* nuevamente, recién (with past participle). **He came to us f. from school,** Vino a nosotros recién salido de su colegio. **We are going to get some f. air,** Vamos a tomar el fresco. **The milk is not f.,** La leche no está fresca. **f.-complexioned,** de buenos colores. **f. news,** noticias nuevas, *f pl*. **f. troops,** tropas nuevas, *f pl*, (reinforcements) tropas de refuerzo, *f pl*. **f. water,** agua fresca, *f*; (not salt) agua dulce, *f*. **f.-water shrimp** *Mexico* acocil *m*. **f. wind,** viento fresco, *m*

freshen /'frɛʃən/ *vt* refrescar; (remove salt) desalar. *vi* (wind) refrescar. **to f. up,** renovar; refrescar; (of dress, etc.) arreglar

freshly /'frɛʃli/ *adv* nuevamente; recientemente

freshness /'frɛʃnɪs/ *n* frescura, *f*; (newness) novedad, *f*; (vividness, brightness) intensidad, *f*; pureza, *f*; (beauty) lozanía, hermosura, *f*; (cheek) frescura, *f*, descaro, *m*

freshwater /'frɛʃ,wɔtər/ *n* agua dulce, *f*. **f. sailor,** marinero de agua dulce, *m*

fret /frɛt/ *n* agitación, *f*; ansiedad, preocupación, *f*; *Archit.* greca, *f*; (of stringed instrument) traste, *m*. *vt* roer; (of a horse) bocezar; (corrode) desgastar, corroer; (of the wind, etc.) rizar; (worry) tener preocupado (a); irritar, enojar; (lose) perder; (oneself) apurarse, consumirse; *Archit.* calar. *vi* torturarse, preocuparse, inquietarse; (complain) quejarse; (mourn) lamentarse, estar triste

fretful /'frɛtfəl/ *a* mal humorado, mohíno, quejoso, irritable

fretfully /'frɛtfəli/ *adv* irritablemente, con mal humor

fretwork /'frɛt,wɜrk/ *n* calado, *m*

Freudian /'frɔidiən/ *a* freudiano

friar /'fraiər/ *n* fraile, *m*. **Black f.,** dominicano, *m*. **Gray f.,** franciscano, *f*. **White f.,** carmelita, *m*. **f.-like,** frailesco

friction /'frɪkʃən/ *n* frote, frotamiento, roce, *m*; *Phys.* rozamiento, *m*; fricción, *f*. **to make f.,** friccionar, dar fricciones (a). **f. gearing,** engranaje de fricción, *m*. **f. glove,** guante de fricciones, *m*

Friday /'fraidei/ *n* viernes, *m*. **Good F.,** Viernes Santo, *m*

fried /fraid/ *a* frito. **f. egg,** huevo frito, *m*

friend /frɛnd/ *n* amigo (-ga); (acquaintance) conocido (-da); (Quaker) cuáquero (-ra); (follower) adherente, *m*; partidario (-ia); (ally) aliado (-da); *pl* **friends,** amistades, *f pl*; amigos, *m pl*. **a f. of yours,** un amigo tuyo, uno de tus amigos. **to make friends,** hacer amigos; (become friends) hacerse amigos; (after a quarrel) hacer las paces. **Friends!** (to sentinel) ¡Gente de paz!

friendless /'frɛndlɪs/ *a* sin amigos; desamparado

friendliness /'frɛndlinɪs/ *n* amabilidad, afabilidad, cordialidad, amigabilidad, *f*

friendly /'frɛndli/ *a* amistoso, amigable, amigo; afable, acogedor, simpático; propicio, favorable. **to be f. with,** ser amigo de. **f. society,** sociedad de socorros, *f*

friendship /'frɛndʃɪp/ *n* amistad, intimidad, *f*

frieze /friz/ *n* friso, *m*; (cloth) frisa, jerga, *f*

frigate /'frɪgɪt/ *n* *Nav.* fragata, *f*

fright /frait/ *n* terror, susto, *m*; (guy) espantajo, *m*. *vt* asustar. **to have a f.,** tener un susto. **to take f.,** asustarse

frighten /'fraitn/ *vt* espantar, dar un susto (a), alarmar, asustar; horrorizar; (overawe) acobardar. **to be frightened out of one's wits,** estar muerto de miedo. **to f. away,** ahuyentar, espantar

frightened /'fraitnd/ *a* miedoso, tímido, medroso, nervioso

frightening /'fraitnɪŋ/ *a* que da miedo; alarmante, amedrentador; horrible

frightful /'fraitfəl/ *a* horrible, espantoso, horroroso; *Inf.* tremendo, enorme

frightfully /'fraitfəli/ *adv* horrorosamente; *Inf.* enormemente

frigid /'frɪdʒɪd/ *a* frío; helado; *Med.* impotente

frigidity /frɪ'dʒɪdɪti/ *n* frialdad, frigidez, *f*; *Med.* impotencia, *f*

frigidly /'frɪdʒɪdli/ *adv* fríamente

frill /frɪl/ *n* *Sew.* volante, *m*; (jabot) chorrera, *f*; (round a bird's neck) collarín de plumas, *m*; (of paper) frunce, *m*. *vt* alechugar; fruncir

fringe /frɪndʒ/ *n* fleco, *m*, franja, *f*, *Lat. Am.* cerquillo *f*; (of hair) flequillo, *m*; (edge) borde, *m*, margen, *mf*. *vt* guarnecer con fleco, franjar; adornar; (grow by) crecer al margen (de)

Frisian /'frɪʒən/ *a* and *n* frisón (-ona); (language) frisón, *m*

frisk /frɪsk/ *vi* retozar, brincar

friskiness /'frɪskinɪs/ *n* viveza, agilidad, *f*

frisky /'frɪski/ *a* retozón, juguetón

fritter /'frɪtər/ *n* *Cul.* fruta de sartén, *f*. *vt* (away) malgastar, desperdiciar; perder

frivolity /frɪ'vɒlɪti/ *n* frivolidad, ligereza, *f*; futilidad, *f*

frivolous /'frɪvələs/ *a* frívolo, ligero, liviano; (futile) trivial, fútil

frizz /frɪz/ *vt* (cloth) frisar; (hair) rizar

frizzy /'frɪzi/ *a* (of hair) crespo, rizado

fro /frou/ *adv* hacia atrás. **movement to and fro,** vaivén, *m*. **to and fro,** de un lado a otro. **to go to and fro,** ir y venir

frock /frɒk/ *n* vestido, *m*; (of a monk) hábito, *m*; (of priest) sotana, *f*. **f.-coat,** levita, *f*

frog /frɒg/ *n* rana, *f*. **to have a f. in the throat,** padecer carraspera

frolic /'frɒlɪk/ *n* (play) juego, *m*; (mischief) travesura, *f*; (folly) locura, extravagancia, *f*; (joke) chanza, *f*; (amusement) diversión, *f*; (wild party) holgorio, *m*, parranda, *f*. *vi* retozar, juguetear; divertirse

frolicsome /'frɒlɪksəm/ *a* retozón, juguetón

from /frʌm, frɒm; *unstressed* frəm/ *prep* de; desde; (according to) según; (in the name of, on behalf of) de parte de; (through, by) por; (beginning on) a contar de; (with) con; **F.** (on envelope) Remite, Remitente. **He is coming here f. the dentist's,** Vendrá aquí desde casa del dentista. **Give him this message f. me,** Dale este recado de mi parte. **Judging f. his appearance,** Juzgando por su apariencia. **prices f. five hundred pesetas upward,** precios desde quinientos pesetas en adelante. **f. what I hear,** según mi información, según lo que oigo. **f. above,** desde arriba. **f. among,** de entre. **f. afar,** de lejos; desde lejos. **f. time to time,** de cuando en cuando, de vez en cuando

frond /frɒnd/ *n Bot.* fronda, *f*

front /frʌnt/ *n* frente, *f*; cara, *f*; *Mil.* frente, *m*; (battle line) línea de combate, *f*; (of a building) fachada, *f*; (of shirt) pechera, *f*; (at the seaside) playa, *f*; (promenade) paseo de la playa, *m*; (forefront) primera línea, *f*; (forepart) parte delantera, *f*; *Theat.* auditorio, *m*; (organization) organización de fachada, *f*; (impudence) descaro, *m*, *a* delantero; anterior; de frente; primero. *adv* hacia delante. *vi* mirar a, dar a; hacer frente a. **in f.,** en frente. **in f. of,** en frente de; (in the presence of) delante de, en la presencia de. **to face f.,** hacer frente. **to put on a bold f.,** hacer de tripas corazón. **f. door,** puerta de entrada, puerta principal, *f*. **f. line,** *Mil.* línea del frente, *f*; primera línea, *f*. **f. seat,** (at an entertainment, etc.) delantera, *f*. **f. organization,** organización de fachada *f*. **f. tooth,** diente incisivo, *m*. **f. view,** vista de frente, *f*; vista de cerca, *f*

frontage /'frʌntɪdʒ/ *n* (of a building) fachada, *f*; (site) terreno de... metros de fachada, *m*

frontal /'frʌntl/ *a Mil.* de frente; *Anat.* frontal

frontier /frʌn'tɪər/ *n* frontera, *f*; *Fig.* límite, *m*. *a* fronterizo

frontispiece /'frʌntɪsˌpis/ *n* (of a building) frontispicio, *m*, fachada, *f*; (of a book) portada, *f*

frost /frɔst/ *n* escarcha, *f*; helada, *f*. *vt* helar; *Cul.* escarchar; (glass) deslustrar; *Fig.* escarchar. *vi* helar. **f.-bitten,** helado

frostbite /'frɔstˌbait/ *n* efectos del frío, *m pl*

frosted /'frɔstɪd/ *a* escarchado; helado; (of glass) deslustrado, opaco; *Cul.* escarchado

frostily /'frɔstəli/ *adv Fig.* glacialmente, con frialdad

frostiness /'frɔstɪnɪs/ *n*; frío glacial, *m*

frosting /'frɔstɪŋ/ *n* escarcha, *f*; (of glass) deslustre, *m*; *Cul.* cobertura, escarcha, *f*

frosty /'frɔsti/ *a* helado; de hielo; (of hair) canoso; *Fig.* glacial, frío. **It was f. last night,** Anoche heló

froth /frɔθ/ *n* espuma, *f*; *Fig.* frivolidad, vanidad, *f*, *vi* espumar, hacer espuma; echar espuma. *vt* hacer espumar; hacer echar espuma

frothiness /'frɔθɪnɪs/ *n* espumosidad, *f*; *Fig.* frivolidad, superficialidad, vaciedad, *f*

frothy /'frɔθi/ *a* espumoso, espumajoso; *Fig.* frívolo, superficial

frown /fraun/ *n* ceño, *m*; cara de juez, expresión severa, *f*; desaprobación, *f*; (of fortune) revés, golpe, *m*. *vi* fruncir el ceño. **to f. at, on, upon,** mirar con desaprobación, ver con malos ojos; ser enemigo de; desaprobar

frowning /'frauniŋ/ *a* ceñudo; severo; amenazador

frowningly /'frauniŋli/ *adv* severamente

frozen /'frouzən/ *a* helado; cubierto de hielo; con gelado; (*Geog.* and *Fig.*) glacial. **to be f. up,** estar helado. **f. meat,** carne congelada, *f*

frugal /'frugəl/ *a* económico; frugal; sobrio

frugality /fru'gælɪti/ *n* economía, *f*; frugalidad, sobriedad, *f*

fruit /frut/ *n* (in general sense) fruto, *m*; (off a tree or bush) fruta, *f*; *Fig.* fruto, *m*; resultado, *m*, consecuencia, *f*. *vi* frutar, dar fruto. **bottled f.,** fruta en almíbar, *f*. **candied f.,** fruta azucarada, *f*. **dried f.,** fruta seca, *f*. **first fruits,** primicias, *f pl*. **soft f.,** frutas blandas, *f pl*. **stone f.,** fruta de hueso, *f*. **f.-bearing,** frutal. **f.-cake,** pastel de fruta, *m*. **f.-dish,** frutero, *m*. **f. farming,** fruticultura, *f*. **f.-knife,** cuchillo de postres, *m*. **f. shop,** frutería, *f*. **f. tree,** frutal, *m*

fruitful /'frutfəl/ *a* fructuoso, fértil; prolífico, fecundo; provechoso

fruitfulness /'frutfəlnɪs/ *n* fertilidad, *f*; fecundidad, *f*; provecho, *m*

fruition /fru'ɪʃən/ *n* fruición, *f*

fruitless /'frutlɪs/ *a* infructuoso, estéril; inútil

fruitlessness /'frutlɪsnɪs/ *n* infructuosidad, esterilidad, *f*; inutilidad, *f*

fruity /'fruti/ *a* de fruta; (wines) vinoso; (of voice) melodioso

frump /frʌmp/ *n* estantigua, *f*

frumpish /'frʌmpɪʃ/ *a* estrafalario; fuera de moda

frustrate /'frʌstreit/ *vt* frustrar; defraudar; malograr; destruir; anular

frustration /frʌ'streiʃən/ *n* frustración, *f*; defraudación, *f*; malogro, *m*; destrucción, *f*; desengaño, *m*

fry /frai/ *n Cul.* fritada, *f*, *vt* freír. *vi* freírse. **small fry,** *Inf.* gente menuda, *f*

frying /'fraiiŋ/ *n* fritura, *f*, el freír. **to fall out of the f.-pan into the fire,** ir de mal en peor, andar de zocos en colodros, ir de Guatemala en Guatapeor. **f.-pan,** sartén, *f*

fuchsia /'fyuʃə/ *n* fuscia, *Lat. Am.* aljaba *f*

fuddle /'fʌdl/ *vt* atontar, aturdir; embriagar, emborrachar

fudge /fʌdʒ/ *n* patraña, tontería, *f*, disparate, *m*; (food) *Lat. Am.* manjar *m*. *interj* ¡qué disparate! ¡qué va!

fuel /'fyuəl/ *n* combustible, *m*; *Fig.* cebo, pábulo, *m*. *vt* cebar, echar combustible en. *vi* tomar combustible. **to add f. to the flame,** echar leña al fuego. **f. consumption,** consumo de combustible, *m*. **f.-oil,** aceite combustible, aceite de quemar, *m*. **f.-tank,** depósito de combustible, *m*

fueling /'fyuəliŋ/ *n* aprovisionamiento de combustible, *m*

fugitive /'fyudʒɪtɪv/ *a* fugitivo; pasajero, perecedero; transitorio, efímero, fugaz. *n* fugitivo (-va); (from justice) prófugo (-ga); *Mil.* desertor, *m*; (refugee) refugiado (-da)

fugue /fyug/ *n Mus.* fuga, *f*

fulcrum /'fulkrəm/ *n Mech.* fulcro, *m*

fulfill /fʊl'fɪl/ *vt* cumplir; (satisfy) satisfacer; (observe) observar; guardar. **to be fulfilled,** cumplirse, realizarse

fulfillment /fʊl'fɪlmənt/ *n* cumplimiento, *m*; desempeño, ejercicio, *m*; (satisfaction) satisfacción, realización, *f*; (observance) observancia, *f*

full /fʊl/ *a* lleno; colmado; todo; pleno; (crowded) atestado; (replete) harto; abundante; (intent on) preocupado con, pensando en; (loose) amplio; (plentiful) copioso; (occupied) ocupado; completo; (resonant) sonoro; (mature) maduro; puro; perfecto; (satiated) saciado (de); (of the moon, sails) lleno; (weighed down) agobiado, abrumado; (detailed) detallado; (with uniform, etc.) de gala; (with years, etc.) cumplido. *n* colmo, *m*; totalidad, *f*. *adv* muy; completamente, totalmente. **at f. gallop,** a galope tendido. **at f. speed,** a todo correr; a toda velocidad. **His hands are f.,** Sus manos están llenas. **The moon was f.,** La luna estaba llena. **in f.,** por completo; sin abreviaciones; integralmente. **in f. swing,** en plena actividad. **in f. vigor,** en pleno vigor. **to the f.,** completamente; hasta la última gota; a la perfección. **to be f. to the brim,** estar lleno hasta el tope. **f.-blooded,** sanguíneo; de pura raza; *Fig.* viril, vigoroso; *Fig.* apasionado. **f.-blown,** en plena flor, abierto. **f. dress,** *a* de gala. *n* traje de etiqueta, traje de ceremonia, *m*. **f.-face,** de cara, *f*. **f.-flavored,** (wine) abocado. **f.-grown,** adulto; completamente desarrollado. **f.-length,** de cuerpo entero. **f. moon,** luna llena, *f*; plenilunio, *m*. **f. name,** nombre y apellidos, *m*. **f. powers,** plenos poderes, *m pl*. **f. scale,** tamaño natural, *m*. **f. scope,** carta blanca, *f*; todo clase de facilidades. **f. steam ahead,** a todo vapor. **f. stop,** *Gram.* punto final, *m*

full-color /'fʊl 'kʌlər/ *a* a todo color. **full-color plates,** láminas a todo color

fuller /'fʊlər/ *n* batanero, *m*. **fuller's earth,** tierra de batán, galactita, *f*

fulling /'fʊliŋ/ *n* abatanadura, *f*. **f.-mill,** batán, *m*

fullness /'fʊlnɪs/ *n* abundancia, *f*; plenitud, *f*; (repletion) hartura, *f*; (of clothes) amplitud, *f*; (stoutness) gordura, *f*; (swelling) hinchazón, *f*. **She wrote with great f. of all that she had seen,** Describía muy detalladamente todo lo que había visto. **in the f. of time,** andando el tiempo

full-page /'fʊl 'peidʒ/ *a* a toda plana. **full-page advertisement,** anuncio a toda plana.

full-time /'fʊl 'taim/ *a* de tiempo completo

fully /'fʊli/ *adv* plenamente; enteramente. **It is f. six years since...,** Hace seis años bien cumplidos que... **It is f. 9 o'clock,** Son las nueve bien sonadas. **f. dressed,** completamente vestido

fulminant /'fʌlmənənt/ *a* fulminante

fulminate /'fʌlmə,neit/ n Chem. fulminato, m. vi estallar; fulminar. vt volar; fulminar

fulminous /'fʌlmənəs/ a fulmíneo, fulminoso

fulsome /'fulsəm/ a servil; insincero, hipócrita; asqueroso, repugnante

fumble /'fʌmbəl/ vi (grope) ir a tientas; procurar hacer algo; chapucear (con); (for a word) titubear

fumbling /'fʌmbliŋ/ n hesitación, f; tacto incierto, m. a incierto; vacilante

fumblingly /'fʌmbliŋli/ adv de manera incierta; a tientas

fume /fyum/ n vaho, humo, gas, m; emanación, f; mal olor, m, fetidez, f; Fig. vapor, m; (state of mind) agitación, f; frenesí, m. vi humear; refunfuñar, echar pestes, Lat. Am. estar hecho un ají

fumigate /'fyumɪ,geit/ vt fumigar, Lat. Am. also humear; sahumar, perfumar; desinfectar

fumigation /,fyumə'geifən/ n fumigación, f; sahumerio, m

fumigator /'fyumɪ,geitər/ n fumigador (-ra); (apparatus) fumigador, m

fumigatory /'fyuməgə,tɔri/ a fumigatorio

fuming /'fyumiŋ/ n refunfuño, m. a refunfuñador

fumy /'fyumi/ a humoso

fun /fʌn/ n diversión, f, entretenimiento, m; (joke) chanza, broma, f. for fun, para divertirse; en chanza. in fun, de burlas. to have fun, divertirse. to poke fun at, burlarse de, mofarse de, ridiculizar

function /'fʌŋkʃən/ n función, f. vi funcionar

functional /'fʌŋkʃənl/ a funcional

functionary /'fʌŋkʃə,nɛri/ n funcionario, m. a funcional

functioning /'fʌŋkʃəniŋ/ n funcionamiento, m

fund /fʌnd/ n fondo, m; pl **funds,** fondos, m pl; Inf. dinero, m. **public funds,** fondos públicos, m pl. **sinking f.,** fondo de amortización, m

fundamental /,fʌndə'mɛntl/ a fundamental, básico; esencial. n fundamento, m

fundamentally /,fʌndə'mɛntli/ adv fundamentalmente, básicamente

funeral /'fyunərəl/ a funeral, fúnebre, funerario. n funerales, m pl; entierro, m. to attend the f. (of), asistir a los funerales (de). f. feast, banquetes fúnebres, m pl. f. director, f. furnisher, director de pompas fúnebres, m. f. procession, cortejo fúnebre, m. f. pyre, pira funeraria, f. f. service, misa de difuntos, f

funereal /fyu'niəriəl/ a fúnebre, lúgubre

fungicide /'fʌndʒə,said/ n anticriptógamo, m

fungous /'fʌŋgəs/ a fungoso

fungus /'fʌŋgəs/ n hongo, m

funicular /fyu'nɪkyələr/ a funicular. f. railway, ferrocarril funicular, m

funnel /'fʌnl/ n Chem. embudo, m; Naut. chimenea, f; (of a chimney) cañón (de chimenea), m. f.-shaped, en forma de embudo

funnily /'fʌnli/ adv de un modo raro, curiosamente

funniness /'fʌninis/ n lo divertido; rareza, extrañeza, f

funny /'fʌni/ a cómico, gracioso; divertido; (strange) curioso, extraño, raro; (mysterious) misterioso. **It struck me as f.,** (amused me) Me hizo gracia; (seemed strange) Me pareció raro. **f.-bone,** hueso de la alegría, m

fur /fɜr/ n piel, f; depósito, sarro, m; (on tongue) saburra, f. a hecho de pieles. vt forrar, or adornar, or cubrir, con pieles; depositar sarro sobre; (the tongue) ensuciar la lengua. vi estar forrado, or adornado, or cubierto, con pieles; formarse incrustaciones; (of the tongue) tener la lengua sucia. **fur cap,** gorra de pieles, f. **fur cape,** cuello de piel, m; capa de pieles, f. **fur trade,** peletería, f

furbish /'fɜrbiʃ/ vt pulir; renovar; limpiar

furious /'fyuriəs/ a furioso. **to become f.,** ponerse furioso, enfurecerse

furiously /'fyuriəsli/ adv furiosamente, con furia

furiousness /'fyuriəsnis/ n furia, f

furl /fɜrl/ vt plegar; enrollar; Naut. aferrar

furlong /'fɜrlɔŋ/ n estadio, m

furlough /'fɜrlou/ n Mil. permiso, m. vt conceder un permiso (a). **on f.,** de permiso

furnace /'fɜrnis/ n horno, m; (of steam boiler) fogón,

m; (for central heating) caldera de calefacción central, f; (for smelting) cubilote, m

furnish /'fɜrniʃ/ vt proveer (de), equipar (de), suplir (de); amueblar; (an opportunity) proporcionar; producir

furnished /'fɜrniʃt/ a amueblado, con muebles. **f. house,** casa amueblada, f

furnisher /'fɜrniʃər/ n decorador, m; proveedor (-ra)

furnishing /'fɜrniʃiŋ/ n provisión, f, equipo, m; pl **furnishings,** accesorios, m pl; mobiliario, mueblaje, m

furniture /'fɜrnitʃər/ n muebles, m pl, mobiliario, mueblaje, Central America, Mexico amoblado m; ajuar, equipo, m; avíos, m pl; Naut. aparejo, m. **a piece of f.,** un mueble. **to empty of f.,** desamueblar, quitar los muebles (de). **f. dealer** or **maker,** mueblista, mf. **f. factory,** mueblería, f. **f. polish,** crema para muebles, f. **f. mover,** transportador de muebles, m; (packer) embalador, m. **f. repository,** guardamuebles, m. **f. van,** carro de mudanzas, m

furor /'fyuror/ n furor, m

furred /fɜrd/ a forrado or cubierto or adornado de piel; (of the tongue) sucia

furrier /'fɜriər/ n peletero, m. **furrier's shop,** peletería, f

furrow /'fɜrou/ n surco, m; muesca, f; Archit. estría, f; (wrinkle) arruga, f. vt surcar

furry /'fɜri/ a cubierto de piel; parecido a una piel; hecho de pieles

further /'fɜrðər/ a ulterior, más distante; (other) otro; opuesto; adicional, más. adv más lejos; más allá; además; también; por añadidura. vt promover, fomentar; ayudar. **on the f. side,** al otro lado. **till f. orders,** hasta nueva orden. **f. on,** más adelante; más allá

furtherance /'fɜrðərəns/ n fomento, m, promoción, f; progreso, avance, m

furthermore /'fɜrðər,mɔr/ adv además, por añadidura

furthest /'fɜrðist/ a (el, la, lo) más lejano or más distante; extremo. adv más lejos

furtive /'fɜrtiv/ a furtivo

furtively /'fɜrtivli/ adv furtivamente, a hurtadillas. **to look at f.,** mirar de reojo

fury /'fyuri/ n furor, enfurecimiento, m, rabia, f; violencia, f; frenesí, arrebato, m; furia, f. **like a f.,** hecho una furia. **to breathe forth f.,** echar rayos

fuse /fyuz/ n (of explosives) espoleta, mecha, f; Elec. fusible, m. vi (metals) fundir; fusionar, mezclar. vi (metals) fundirse; mezclarse. **safety-f.,** espoleta de seguridad, f. **time-f.,** espoleta de tiempo, f. **to blow a f.,** fundir un fusible. **f. box,** caja de fusibles, f. **f. wire,** fusible, m

fuselage /'fyusə,laʒ/ n Aer. fuselaje, m

fusible /'fyuzəbəl/ a fusible

fusillade /'fyusə,lad/ n descarga cerrada, f

fusion /'fyuʒən/ n fusión, f; unión, f; (melting) fundición, f

fuss /fʌs/ n agitación, f; (bustle) conmoción, bulla, f; bullicio, m. vi agitarse, preocuparse. vt poner nervioso. **There's no need to make such a f.,** No es para tanto. **to make a f. of,** (a person) hacer la rueda (a), ser muy atento (a); (spoil) mimar mucho (a). **to f. about,** andar de acá para allá

fussily /'fʌsəli/ adv nerviosamente; de un aire importante

fussy /'fʌsi/ a meticuloso, nimio; nervioso; (of style) florido, hinchado; (of dress) demasiado adornado

fusty /'fʌsti/ a (moldy) mohoso; mal ventilado; mal oliente; (of views, etc.) pasado de moda

futile /'fyutl/ a fútil, superficial, frívolo; inútil

futility /fyu'tiliti/ n futilidad, superficialidad, frivolidad, f; (action) tontería, estupidez, f

future /'fyutʃər/ a futuro, venidero. n futuro, porvenir, m. **in the f.,** en adelante, en lo venidero, en lo sucesivo. **for f. reference,** para información futura. **f. perfect tense,** Gram. futuro perfecto, m. **f. tense,** Gram. futuro, m

futurism /'fyutʃə,rizəm/ n futurismo, m

futurist /'fyutʃərist/ n futurista, mf

futuristic /,fyutʃə'ristik/ a futurístico

fuzz /fʌz/ n tamo, m, pelusa, f. **f.-ball,** Bot. bejín, m

fuzzy /'fʌzi/ a crespo rizado; velloso

G

g /dʒi/ n (letter) ge, f; *Mus.* sol, m. **G clef,** clave de sol, f

gab /gæb/ n *Inf.* labia, f. **to have the gift of the gab,** tener mucha labia

gabardine /'gæbər,din/ n gabardina, f

gabble /'gæbəl/ vi chacharear, garlar; hablar indistintamente; (of goose and some birds) graznar. vt decir indistintamente; decir rápidamente; (a language) chapurrear; mascullar. n cháchara, f; vocerío, m; (of goose and some birds) graznido, m

gabbler /'gæblər/ n charlatán (-ana), chacharero (-ra)

gabbling /'gæblɪŋ/ n See **gabble**

gable /'geibəl/ n *Archit.* gablete, hastial, m. **g.-end,** alero, m

gad /gæd/ vi corretear, callejear. **to gad about,** correr por todos lados; divertirse.

gadabout /'gædə,baut/ n azotacalles, mf; gandul (-la), vagabundo (-da)

gadding /'gædɪŋ/ a callejero; vagabundo. n vagancia, f; vida errante, f; gandulería, f

gadfly /'gæd,flai/ n *Ent.* tábano, m; *Inf.* moscardón, m

gadget /'gædʒɪt/ n accesorio, m; aparato, m; chuchería, f

Gael /geil/ n escocés (-esa) del norte; celta, mf

Gaelic /'geilɪk/ a gaélico. n gaélico, m

gaff /gæf/ n (hook) garfio, m; *Naut.* pico de cangrejo, m; *Theat.* teatrucho, m

gaffer /'gæfər/ n viejo, tío, abuelo, m

gag /gæg/ n mordaza, f; *Theat.* morcilla, f. vt amordazar; *Fig.* hacer callar. vi *Theat.* meter morcillas

gage /geidʒ/ n prenda, fianza, f; (symbol of challenge) guante, m; (challenge) desafío, m. See **gauge**

gagging /'gægɪŋ/ n amordazamiento, m

gaggle /'gægəl/ n (cry) graznido, m; (of geese) manada (de ocas), f. vi graznar; cacarear

gaiety /'geiiti/ n alegría, f; animación, vivacidad, f; (entertainment) diversión, festividad, f

gaily /'geili/ adv alegremente

gain /gein/ n ganancia, f; provecho, beneficio, m; (increase) aumento, m; (riches) riqueza, f. vt ganar; (acquire) conseguir; adquirir; obtener; conquistar; captar; (friends) hacerse; (reach) llegar a, alcanzar. vi ganar; (improve) mejorar; (of a watch) adelantarse. **What have they gained by going to Canada?** ¿Qué han logrado con marcharse al Canadá? **to g. ground,** *Fig.* ganar terreno. **to g. momentum** adquirir velocidad **to g. time,** ganar tiempo. **to g. on, upon,** acercarse a; (overtake) alcanzar; (outstrip) dejar atrás, pasar; (of sea) invadir; (of habits) imponerse

gainful /'geinfəl/ a ganancioso, lucrativo; ventajoso

gainfully /'geinfəli/ adv ventajosamente; lucrativamente

gainsay /'gein,sei/ vt contradecir; oponer; negar

gainsaying /'gein,seiiŋ/ n contradicción, f; oposición, f; negación, f

gait /geit/ n porte, andar, m; paso, m, andadura, f

gaiter /'geitər/ n polaina, f; (spat) botín, m

gala /'geilə/ n gala, fiesta, f. **g.-day.** día de fiesta, m. **g.-dress,** traje de gala, m

galaxy /'gæləksi/ n *Astron.* vía láctea, f; *Fig.* constelación, f; grupo brillante, m

gale /geil/ n vendaval, ventarrón, m; (storm) temporal, m; tempestad, f

Galician /gə'lɪʃən/ a and n gallego (-ga).

Galilean /,gælə'leiən/ a and n galileo (-ea)

Galilee /'gælə,li/ n Galilea, f

gall /gɔl/ n (on horses) matadura, f; (abrasion) rozadura, f; hiel, bilis, f; *Fig.* hiel, amargura, f; rencor, m; (impudence) descaro, m, impertinencia, f; *Bot.* agalla, f. vt rozar; *Fig.* mortificar, herir. **g.-bladder,** vejiga de la hiel, f. **g.-stone,** cálculo hepático, m

gallant /'gælənt/ a hermoso; (imposing) imponente; majestuoso; (brave) valiente, gallardo, valeroso, intrépido; (chivalrous) caballeroso; noble; (attentive to ladies, or amorous) galante. n galán, m. vt galantear, cortejar

gallantly /'gæləntli/ adv (bravely) valientemente; caballerosamente; cortésmente; galantemente

gallantry /'gæləntri/ n (bravery) valentía, f, valor, m; heroísmo, m, proeza, f; (chivalry) gallantería, cortesía, f; (toward women, or amorousness) galantería, f

galleon /'gæliən/ n galeón, m

gallery /'gæləri/ n galería, f; pasillo, m; (of a cloister) tránsito, m; (cloister) claustro, m; (for spectators) tribuna, f; *Theat.* paraíso, gallinero, m; (theater audience) galería, f; (of portraits, etc.) galería, colección, f; (*Mineral.*, *Mil.*) galería, f; (building) museo, m. **art g.,** museo de pinturas, f

galley /'gæli/ n (*Naut.*, *Print.*) galera, f; (kitchen) cocina, f; (rowboat) falúa de capitán, f. **to condemn to the galleys,** echar a galeras. **wooden g.,** *Print.* galerín, m. **g.-proof,** galerada, f. **g.-slave,** galeote, m

Gallic /'gælɪk/ a gálico, galicano; francés

gallicism /'gælɪsɪzəm/ n galicismo, m

galling /'gɔlɪŋ/ a *Fig.* irritante; mortificante

gallivant /'gælə,vænt/ vi callejear, corretear; divertirse; ir de parranda

gallon /'gælən/ n galón, m

gallop /'gæləp/ n galope, m. vi galopar; ir aprisa. vt hacer galopar, **at full g.,** a rienda suelta, a galope tendido. **to g. back,** volver a galope. **to g. down,** bajar a galope. **to g. off,** marcharse galopando; alejarse corriendo. **to g. past,** desfilar a galope ante. **to g. through,** cruzar a galope. **to g. up,** vt subir a galope. vi llegar a galope

gallopade /,gælə'peid/ n (dance) galop, m

galloping /'gæləpɪŋ/ n galope, m; galopada, f. a que va a galope; *Med.* galopante. **g. consumption,** tisis galopante, f

gallows /'gælouz/ n patíbulo, m, horca, f; (framework) montante, m. **g.-bird,** criminal digno de la horca, m

galop /'gæləp/ n galop, m

galore /gə'lɔr/ adv a granel, en abundancia (e.g. *sunshine galore,* sol a granel)

galosh /gə'lɒʃ/ n chanclo, m

galvanic /gæl'vænɪk/ a *Elec.* galvánico; espasmódico

galvanize /'gælvə,naiz/ vt galvanizar

gambit /'gæmbɪt/ n (chess) gambito, m; *Fig.* táctica, f

gamble /'gæmbəl/ n juego de azar, m; jugada, f; aventura, f; *Com.* especulación, f. vi jugar por dinero; especular; (with) *Fig.* aventurar, arriesgar. **to g. on the Stock Exchange,** jugar en la bolsa. **to g. away,** perder al juego

gambler /'gæmblər/ n jugador (-ra), *Mexico* dadista mf

gambling /'gæmblɪŋ/ n juego, m. a jugador; de juego. **g.-den,** casa de juego, f, garito, m

gambol /'gæmbəl/ n salto, brinco, retozo, m; cabriola, f; juego, m. vi saltar, brincar, retozar; juguetear

game /geim/ n juego, m; (match) partido, m; (jest) chanza, f; (trick) trampa, f; (birds, hares, etc.) caza menor, f; (tigers, lions, etc.) caza mayor, f; (flesh of game) caza, f; pl **games,** deportes, m pl. a de caza; (courageous) valiente, animoso, brioso; resuelto. vi jugar por dinero. **He is g. for anything,** Se atreve a todo. **big g. hunting,** caza mayor, f. **head of g.,** pieza de caza, f. **It is a g. at which two can play,** Donde las dan las toman. **The g. is not worth the candle,** La cosa no vale la pena. **The g. is up,** *Fig.* El proyecto se ha frustrado. **to make g. of,** (things) burlarse de; (persons) tomar el pelo a; mofarse de. **to play the g.,** *Fig.* jugar limpio. **to g. away,** perder al juego. **g. of cards,** juego de naipes, m. **g. of chance,** juego de azar, m. **g.-bag,** morral, m. **g. drive,** batida de caza, f. **g.-laws,** leyes de caza, f pl. **g.-license,** licencia de caza, f. **g.-pie,** tortada, f. **g. preserve,** coto de caza, m

gamekeeper /'geim,kipər/ n guardabosque, m

gamely /'geimli/ adv valientemente
gameness /'geimnis/ n valentía, resolución, fortaleza, f
gamete /'gæmit/ n gameto, m
gaming /'geimiŋ/ n juego, m, a de juego. **g.-house**, garito, m. **g.-table**, mesa de juego, f; Fig. juego, m
gamut /'gæmət/ n gama, f
gander /'gændər/ n ganso, m
gang /gæŋ/ n cuadrilla, pandilla, banda, Mexico carpanta f; (squad) pelotón, m; (of workers) brigada, cuadrilla, f; group, m. **g.-plank**, plancha, f
ganglion /'gæŋgliən/ n ganglio, m; Fig. centro, m
gangrene /'gæŋgrin/ n gangrena, f. vt gangrenar. vi gangrenarse
gangrenous /'gæŋgrinəs/ a gangrenoso
gangster /'gæŋstər/ n pistolero, gángster, bandito, m
gangway /'gæŋ,wei/ n pasillo, m; Naut. plancha, f, pasamano, m; (opening in ship's side) portalón, m. **midship g.**, crujía, f
gap /gæp/ n brecha, f; abertura, f; (hole) boquete, m; (pass) desfiladero, paso, m; (ravine) hondonada, barranca, f; (blank) laguna, f, vacío, m; (crack) intersticio, m, hendedura, f, resquicio, m. **to fill a gap**, llenar un boquete; llenar un vacío
gape /geip/ vi estar con la boca abierta, papar moscas. **to g. at**, mirar con la boca abierta
gaping /'geipiŋ/ n huelgo, m; abertura, f, a que bosteza; boquiabierto; abierto
garage /gə'rɑʒ/ n garaje, m. vt poner (un coche, etc.) en un garaje. **g. owner**, garajista, mf
garb /gɑrb/ n traje, vestido, m, ropa f; uniforme, m; Herald. espiga, f. vt vestir, ataviar
garbage /'gɑrbidʒ/ n basura, inmundicia, f
garbage can basurero, tarro de la basura, m
garbage dump Lat. Am. basural m
garble /'gɑrbəl/ vt falsear, mutilar, pervertir
garden /'gɑrdn/ n jardín, m; huerto, m; (fertile region) huerta, f. a de jardín. vi trabajar en el jardín, cultivar un huerto. **g. city**, ciudad jardín, f. **g.-frame**, semillero, m. **g. mold**, tierra vegetal, f. **g.-party**, fiesta de jardín, f. **g.-plot**, terraza, f. **g. produce**, hortalizas, legumbres, f pl. **g. roller**, rodillo, m. **g.-seat**, banco de jardín, m. **g. urn**, jarrón, m
gardener /'gɑrdnər/ n jardinero, m
gardenia /gɑr'dinyə/ n gardenia, f, jazmín de la India, m
gardening /'gɑrdnɪŋ/ n jardinería, f; horticultura, f. a de jardinería
gargantuan /gɑr'gæntʃuən/ a gargantuesco; tremendo, enorme
gargle /'gɑrgəl/ n (liquid) gargarismo, m; gárgaras, f pl. vi hacer gárgaras, gargarizar
gargling /'gɑrglɪŋ/ n gargarismo, m
gargoyle /'gɑrgɔil/ n gárgola, f
garish /'geərɪʃ/ a cursi, llamativo, charro, chillón
garishness /'geərɪʃnɪs/ n cursería, ostentación, f, lo llamativo
garland /'gɑrlənd/ n guirnalda, f; corona, f; (anthology) florilegio, m; Archit. festón, m. vt enguirnaldar
garlic /'gɑrlɪk/ n ajo, m
garment /'gɑrmənt/ n prenda de vestir, f; traje, vestido, m; Fig. vestidura, f; (Fig. cloak) capa, f
garner /'gɑrnər/ n granero, m; tesoro, m; colección, f. vt atesorar, guardar
garnet /'gɑrnɪt/ n granate, m
garnish /'gɑrnɪʃ/ n Cul. aderezo, m; adorno, m. vt Cul. aderezar; embellecer, adornar
garnishing /'gɑrnɪʃɪŋ/ n. See **garnish**
garret /'gærɪt/ n guardilla, buhardilla, f, desván, m
garrison /'gærəsən/ n guarnición, f, presidio, m. vt guarnecer, presidiar. **g. town**, plaza de armas, f
garrote /gə'rɒt/ n garrote, m. vt agarrotar, dar garrote (a)
garrulity /gə'ruliti/ n garrulidad, locuacidad, charlatanería, f
garrulous /'gærələs/ a gárrulo, locuaz, charlatán
garter /'gɑrtər/ n liga, f; (G.) Jarretera, f, a atar con liga; investir con la Jarretera
gas /gæs/ n gas, m; Fig., Inf. palabrería, f; (fuel) gasolina, f, a de gas; con gas; para gases. vt asfixiar

con gas; Mil. atacar con gas; saturar de gas. **gas attack**, ataque con gases asfixiantes, m. **gas-bag**, bolsa de gas, f; Inf. charlatán (-ana). **gas-burner**, mechero de gas, m. **gas-chamber**, cámara de gas, f. **gas detector**, detector de gases, m. **gas-fire**, estufa de gas, f. **gas-fitter**, gasista, m. **gas-fittings**, lámparas de gas, f pl. **gas-light**, luz de gas, f; mechero de gas, m. **gas-main**, cañería maestra de gas, f **gas-man**, gasista, m. **gas-mantle**, camiseta incandescente, f. **gas-mask**, máscara para gases, f. **gas-meter**, contador de gas, m. **gas-pipes**, cañerías (or tuberías) de gas, f pl. **gas-ring**, fogón de gas, m. **gas-shell**, obús de gases asfixiantes, m. **gas-stove**, cocina de gas, f. **gas warfare**, guerra química, f. **gas-works**, fábrica de gas, f
gaseous /'gæsiəs/ a gaseoso
gash /gæʃ/ n cuchillada, f; herida extensa, f. vt acuchillar; herir extensamente
gasket /'gæskɪt/ n aro de empaquetadura, m
gasoline /,gæsə'lin/ n gasolina, f; bencina, f
gasp /gæsp/ n boqueada, f. vi boquear. **to be at the last g.**, estar agonizando. **to g. for breath**, luchar por respirar. **to g. out**, decir anhelante, decir con voz entrecortada
gastric /'gæstrɪk/ a gástrico
gastritis /gæ'straitis/ n gastritis, f
gastronome /'gæstrə,noum/ n gastrónomo (-ma)
gastronomic /,gæstrə'nɑmɪk/ a gastronómico
gastronomy /gæ'strɒnəmi/ n gastronomía, f
gate /geit/ n puerta, f; cancela, verja, f; entrada, f; (of a lock, etc.) compuerta, f; (across a road, etc.) barrera, f; (money) entrada, f; Fig. puerta, f. **automatic g.**, (at level crossings, etc.) barrera de golpe, f. **g.-keeper**, portero, m; guardabarrera, mf **g.-money**, entrada, f. **g.-post**, soporte de la puerta, m
gateway /'geit,wei/ n entrada, f; puerta, f; paso, m; vestíbulo, m; Fig. puerta, f
gather /'gæðər/ vt (assemble) reunir; (amass) acumular, amontonar; (acquire) obtener, adquirir; hacer una colección (de); cobrar; (harvest) cosechar, recolectar; (pick up) recoger; (pluck) coger; (infer) sacar en limpio, aprender; Sew. fruncir (the brows) fruncir (el ceño). vi reunirse, congregarse; amontonarse; (threaten) amenazar; (sadden) amargar; (Fig. hover over) cernerse (sobre); (increase) aumentar, crecer; (be covered) cubrirse; (fester) supurar. n Sew. frunce, pliegue, m. **to g. breath**, tomar aliento. **to g. speed**, ganar velocidad. **to g. strength**, cobrar fuerzas. **I g. from Mary that they are going abroad**, Según lo que me ha dicho María, van al extranjero. **to g. in**, juntar; reunir; (harvest) cosechar; coger. **to g. together**, vt reunir. vi reunirse. **to g. up**, recoger; coger; tomar; (one's limbs) encoger. **to g. up the threads**, Fig. recoger los hilos.
gatherer /'gæðərər/ n cogedor, colector, m; (harvester) segador, m; (of grapes) vendimiador (-ra) (f taxes) recaudador, m
gathering /'gæðərɪŋ/ n cogedura, f; (fruit, etc.) recolección, f; (of taxes) recaudación, f; amontonamiento, m; colección, f; Med. absceso, m; Sew. fruncimiento, m; (assembly) reunión, asamblea, f; (crowd) concurrencia, muchedumbre, f
gathers /'gæðərz/ n Sew. fruncidos, pliegues, m pl
gauche /gouʃ/ a torpe, huraño
gaudily /'gɔdəli/ adv ostentosamente; brillantemente
gaudiness /'gɔdɪnɪs/ n ostentación, f; brillantez, f
gaudy /'gɔdi/ a llamativo, vistoso, brillante, ostentoso
gauge /geidʒ/ n (of gun) calibre, m; (railway) entrevía, f; (for measuring) indicator, m; regla de medir, f; Naut. calado, m; Fig. medida, f; (test) indicación, f; (model) norma, f. vt calibrar; medir; estimar; (ship's capacity) arquear; (judge) juzgar; (size up) tomar la medida (de); Fig. interpretar; Sew. fruncir; (liquor) aforar. **broad (narrow) g. railway**, ferrocarril de vía ancha (estrecha), m. **pressure g.**, manómetro, m. **water g.**, indicador del nivel de agua, m
gauging /'geidʒɪŋ/ n medida, f; (of ship's capacity) arqueo, m; (of liquor) aforamiento, f; Fig. apreciación, f; interpretación, f
gaunt /gɔnt/ a anguloso, huesudo, desvaído; (of houses, etc.) lúgubre
gauntlet /'gɔntlɪt/ n guante de manopla, m; (part of

armor) manopla, *f*, guantelete, *m*. **to throw down the g.,** echar el guante, desafiar

gauntness /'gɔntnɪs/ *n* angulosidad, flaqueza, *f*

gauze /gɔz/ *n* gasa, *f*; (mist) bruma, *f*. **wire-g.,** tela metálica, *f*

gauziness /'gɔzinɪs/ *n* diafanidad, *f*

gauzy /'gɔzi/ *a* diáfano; de gasa

gavotte /gə'vɒt/ *n* gavota, *f*

gawkiness /'gɔkinɪs/ *n* torpeza, desmaña, *f*

gawky /'gɔki/ *a* anguloso, desgarbado, torpe

gay /gei/ *a* alegre; festivo, animado; ligero de cascos, disipado; homosexual; (of colors) brillante, llamativo

Gaza Strip /'gɑzə/ la franja de Gaza, *f*

gaze /geiz/ *n* mirada, *f*; mirada fija, *f*. *vi* mirar; mirar fijamente, contemplar

gazelle /gə'zɛl/ *n* gacel (-la)

gazer /'geizər/ *n* espectador (-ra)

gazette /gə'zɛt/ *n* gaceta, *f*. *vt* publicar en la gaceta.

gazing /'geizɪŋ/ *n* contemplación, *f*, *a* contemplador; que presencia, que asiste a

gear /gɪər/ *n* (apparel) atavíos, *m pl*; (harness) guarniciones, *f pl*, arneses, *m pl*; (tackle) utensilios, *m pl*, herramientas, *f pl*; *Naut.* aparejo, *m*; *Mech.* engranaje, *m*; juego, *m*, marcha, *f*. *vt* aparejar, enjaezar; *Mech.* poner en marcha, hacer funcionar. *vi Mech.* engranar, endentar. **low g.,** pimera velocidad, *f*. **neutral g.,** punto muerto, *m*. **reverse g.,** marcha atrás, *f*. **second g.,** segunda velocidad, *f*. **three-speed g.,** cambio de marchas de tres velocidades, *m*. **top g.,** tercera (or cuarta--according to gear-box) velocidad, *f*. **to change g.,** cambiar de marcha, cambiar de velocidad. **to throw out of g.,** *Fig.* desquiciar. **g.-box,** caja de velocidades, *f*. **g.-changing,** cambio de velocidad, *m*. **g.-changing lever,** palanca de cambio de velocidad, palanca de cambio de marchas, *f*

gearing /'gɪərɪŋ/ *n* engranaje, *m*

gehenna /gɪ'hɛnə/ *n* gehena, *m*

geisha /'geiʃə/ *n* geisha, *f*

gelatin /'dʒɛlətṇ/ *n* gelatina, *f*. **cooking g.,** gelatina seca, *f*

gelatinous /dʒə'lætṇəs/ *a* gelatinoso

geld /gɛld/ *vt* capar, castrar

gelder /'gɛldər/ *n* castrador, *m*

gelding /'gɛldɪŋ/ *n* castración, capadura, *f*; caballo castrado, *m*; animal castrado, *m*

gem /dʒɛm/ *n* piedra preciosa, *f*; joya, alhaja, *f*; *Fig.* joya, *f*. *vt* adornar con piedras preciosos; enjoyar

Gemini /'dʒɛmə,nai/ *n* (los) Gemelos

gender /'dʒɛndər/ *n Gram.* género, *m*; sexo, *m*

gene /dʒin/ *n Biol.* gene, *m*

genealogical /,dʒiniə'lɒdʒikəl/ *a* genealógico. **g. tree,** árbol genealógico, *m*

genealogist /,dʒini'ɒlədʒɪst/ *n* genealogista, *mf*

genealogy /,dʒini'ɒlədʒi/ *n* genealogía, *f*

general /'dʒɛnərəl/ *a* general; universal; común; corriente; (usual) acostumbrado, usual; del público, público. *n* lo general; (*Mil.*, *Eccl.*) general, *m*; *Inf.* criada para todo, *f*. **in g.,** por lo general, en general, generalmente. **to become g.,** generalizarse. **to make g.,** generalizar, hacer general. **g. average,** (marine insurance) avería gruesa, *f*. **g. election,** elección general, *f*. **g. meeting,** pleno, mitin general, *m*. **g. option,** voz común, opinión general, *f*. **G. Post Office,** Oficina Central de Correos, *f*. **g. practitioner,** médico (-ca) general. **g. public,** público, *m*. **the general reader,** el lector de tipo general

generalissimo /,dʒɛnərə'lɪsə,mou/ *n* generalísimo, *m*

generality /,dʒɛnə'rælɪti/ *n* generalidad, *f*

generalization /,dʒɛnərələ'zeiʃən/ *n* generalización, *f*

generalize /'dʒɛnərə,laiz/ *vt and vi* generalizar

generally /'dʒɛnərəli/ *adv* en general, por lo general, generalmente; comúnmente, por lo común

generalship /'dʒɛnərəl,ʃip/ *n Mil.* generalato, *m*; (strategy) táctica, estrategia, *f*; dirección, jefatura, *f*

generate /'dʒɛnə,reit/ *vt* (beget) engendrar, procrear; (*Phys.*, *Chem.*) generar; *Fig.* producir, crear

generation /,dʒɛnə'reiʃən/ *n* procreación, *f*; generación, *f*; *Fig.* producción, creación, *f*. **the younger g.,** los jóvenes

generative /'dʒɛnərətɪv/ *a* generador

generator /'dʒɛnə,reitər/ *n Mech.* generador, *m*; dínamo, *f*

generic /dʒə'nɛrɪk/ *a* genérico

generosity /,dʒɛnə'rɒsɪti/ *n* generosidad, *f*; liberalidad, *f*

generous /'dʒɛnərəs/ *a* generoso; liberal, dadivoso, limosnero, *Lat. Am.* maniabierto; magnánimo; (plentiful) abundante; (of wines) generoso

generously /'dʒɛnərəsli/ *adv* generosamente; abundantemente

genesis /'dʒɛnəsɪs/ *n* principio, origen, *m*; (G.) Génesis, *m*

genetic /dʒə'nɛtɪk/ *a* genético

genetics /dʒə'nɛtɪks/ *n* genética, *f*

Geneva /dʒə'nivə/ Ginebra, *f*

genial /'dʒinyəl/ *a* (of climate) agradable, bueno; (of persons) afable, bondadoso; de buen humor, bonachón

geniality /'dʒini'ælɪti/ *n* afabilidad, bondad, *f*; buen humor, *n*

genially /'dʒinyəli/ *adv* afablemente

genie /'dʒini/ *n* genio, *m*

genital /'dʒɛnɪtḷ/ *a* genital, sexual. *n pl* **genitals,** genitales, *m pl*

genitive /'dʒɛnɪtɪv/ *a* and *n Gram.* genitivo *m*

genius /'dʒinyəs/ *n* genio, *m*; carácter, *m*, índole, *f*; ingenio, *m*; *Inf.* talento, *m*

Genoa /'dʒɛnouə/ Genova, *f*

Genoese /,dʒɛnou'iz/ *a* and *n* genovés (-esa)

genre /'ʒɑnrə/ *n* género, *m*. **g. painting,** cuadro de género, *m*

genteel /dʒɛn'til/ *a* fino; (affected) remilgado, melindroso; de buen tono; de buena educación

gentile /'dʒɛntail/ *a* and *n* gentil, *mf*

gentility /dʒɛn'tɪlɪti/ *n* aristocracia, *f*; respetabilidad, *f*

gentle /'dʒɛntḷ/ *a* noble, bien nacido, de buena familia; amable; suave; ligero; dulce; (docile) manso, dócil; (affectionate) cariñoso; bondadoso; sufrido, paciente; cortés; pacífico, tolerante. **He was a man of g. birth,** Era un hombre bien nacido. **"G. reader,"** «Querido lector». **g. wind,** *Lat. Am.* airecito, *m*

gentlefolk /'dʒɛntḷ,fouk/ *n pl* gente de bien, gente fina, *f*; gente de buena familia, *f*

gentleman /'dʒɛntḷmən/ *n* caballero, señor, *m*; gentilhombre, *m*. **Ladies and gentlemen,** Señoras y caballeros, Señores. **young g.,** señorito, *m*. **to be a perfect g.,** ser un caballero perfecto. **g.-inwaiting,** gentilhombre de la cámara, *m*

gentlemanliness /'dʒɛntḷmənlinɪs/ *n* caballerosidad, *f*

gentlemanly /'dʒɛntḷmənli/ *a* caballeroso

gentleness /'dʒɛntḷnɪs/ *n* amabilidad, *f*; suavidad, *f*; dulzura, *f*; mansedumbre, docilidad, *f*; bondad, *f*; paciencia, *f*; cortesía, *f*; tolerancia, *f*

gentlewoman /'dʒɛntḷ,wumən/ *n* dama, *f*; dama de servicio, *f*

gently /'dʒɛntli/ *adv* suavemente; dulcemente; silenciosamente, sin ruido; (slowly) despacio, poco a poco. **g. born,** bien nacido

gentry /'dʒɛntri/ *n* pequeña aristocracia, alta clase media, *f*; (disparaging) gentle, *f*

genuflect /'dʒɛnyu,flɛkt/ *vi* doblar la rodilla

genuflection /,dʒɛnyu'flɛkʃən/ *n* genuflexión, *f*

genuine /'dʒɛnyuɪn/ *a* puro; genuino; verdadero; real; sincero; auténtico

genuinely /'dʒɛnyuɪnli/ *adv* genuinamente; verdaderamente; realmente; sinceramente

genuineness /'dʒɛnyuɪnnɪs/ *n* pureza, *f*; autenticidad, *f*; verdad, *f*; sinceridad, *f*

genus /'dʒinəs/ *n* género, *m*

geodesic /,dʒiə'dɛsɪk/ *a* geodésico

geodesy /dʒi'ɒdəsi/ *n* geodesia, *f*

geographer /dʒi'ɒgrəfər/ *n* geógrafo, *m*

geographical /,dʒiə'græfikəl/ *a* geográfico

geographically /,dʒiə'græfikəli/ *adv* geográficamente; desde el punto de vista geográfico

geography /dʒi'ɒgrəfi/ *n* geografía, *f*

geological /,dʒiə'lɒdʒikəl/ *a* geológico

geologically /,dʒiə'lɒdʒikəli/ *adv* geológicamente; desde el punto de vista geológico

geologist /dʒi'ɒlədʒɪst/ n geólogo, m
geologize /dʒi'ɒlə,dʒaiz/ vi estudiar la geología. vt estudiar desde un punto de vista geológico
geology /dʒi'ɒlədʒi/ n geología, f
geometric /,dʒiə'mɛtrɪk/ a geométrico
geometry /dʒi'ɒmɪtri/ n geometría, f
geophysics /,dʒiou'fɪzɪks/ n geofísica, f
Georgian /'dʒɔrdʒən/ a Geog. georgiano; Lit. del principio del siglo diez y nueve
georgic /'dʒɔrdʒɪk/ n geórgica, f
geotropism /dʒi'ɒtrə,pɪzəm/ n geotropismo, m
geranium /dʒə'reiniəm/ n geranio, m
germ /dʒɜrm/ n embrión, germen, m; microbio, bacilo, m; Fig. germen, m. **g.-cell,** célula germinal, f
German /'dʒɜrmən/ a alemán; germánico. n alemán (-ana); (language) alemán, m; germano (-na), germánico (-ca). **Sudeten G.,** alemán (-ana) sudete. **G. measles,** rubeola, f. **G. silver,** alpaca, f, melchor m, plata alemana f
germander /dʒər'mændər/ n Bot. camedrio, m
germane /dʒər'mein/ a pertinente (a), a propósito (a)
Germanic /dʒər'mænɪk/ a germánico. n (language) germánico, m
Germanization /,dʒɜrmənɪ'zeiʃən/ n germanización, f
Germanize /'dʒɜrmə,naiz/ vt germanizar. vi germanizarse
Germanophile /dʒər'mænə,fail/ n germanófilo (-la)
Germany /'dʒɜrməni/ Alemania, f
germicidal /,dʒɜrmə'saidḷ/ a bactericida
germicide /'dʒɜrmə,said/ n desinfectante, m
germinal /'dʒɜrmənḷ/ a germinal. n (G.) germinal, m
germinate /'dʒɜrmə,neit/ vi germinar, brotar. vt hacer germinar
germination /,dʒɜrmə'neiʃən/ n germinación, f
germinative /'dʒɜrmə,neitɪv/ a germinativo
gerund /'dʒɛrənd/ n gerundio, m
gerundive /dʒə'rʌndɪv/ n gerundio adjetivado, m
Gestapo /gə'stɑpou/ n Gestapo, f
gestation /dʒɛ'steiʃən/ n gestación, f
gesticulate /dʒɛ'stɪkyə,leit/ vi gesticular, hacer gestos; accionar. vt expresar por gestos
gesticulation /dʒɛ,stɪkyə'leiʃən/ n gesticulación, f
gesticulatory /dʒɛ'stɪkyələ,tɔri/ a gesticular
gesture /'dʒɛstʃər/ n movimiento, m; gesticulación, f; (of the face) gesto, m, mueca, f; ademán, m, acción, f. vi gesticular. vt decir por gestos; acompañar con gestos
get /gɛt/ vt (obtain) obtener; (acquire) adquirir; (buy) comprar; (take) tomar; (receive) recibir; (gain, win) ganar; (hit) acertar, dar; (place) poner; (achieve) alcanzar, lograr; (make) hacer; (call) llamar; (understand) comprender; (catch) coger; (procreate) procrear, engendrar; (induce) persuadir; (invite) convidar, invitar; (cause) hacer; (with have and past part.) tener; (with have and past part. followed by infin.) tener que; (followed by noun and past part.) hacer; (fetch) buscar, ir a buscar; (order) mandar, disponer; (procure) procurar; (bring) traer; (money) hacer; (a reputation, etc.) hacerse; (a prize, an advantage) llevar; (learn) aprender; (be) ser. vi (become) hacerse; ponerse; venir a ser; (old) envejecerse; (angry) montar (en cólera), enojarse; (arrive) llegar a; (attain) alcanzar; (accomplish) conseguir, lograr; (drunk) emborracharse; (hurt) hacerse daño; (wet) mojarse; (cool) enfriarse; (money) hacer (dinero); (of health) ponerse; (find oneself) hallarse, encontrarse; (late) hacerse (tarde); (dark) empezar a caer (la noche), empezar a caer (la noche), empezar a oscurecer; (put oneself) meterse; (grow, be) estar; (on to or on top of) montar sobre, subir a. **He has got run over,** Ha sido atropellado. **It gets on my nerves,** Se me pone los nervios en punta. **Let's get it over!** ¡Vamos a concluir de una vez! **How do you get on with her?** ¿Cómo te va con ella? **She must be getting on for twenty,** Tendrá alrededor de veinte años. **to get a suit made,** mandar hacerse un traje. **to get altitude sickness,** Peru asorocharse. **to get better,** (in health) mejorar de salud; hacer progresos adelantar. **to get dark,** obscurecer. **to get depressed,** Lat. Am. amurrarse. **to get into conversa-**

tion with, trabar conversación con. **to get into bad company,** frecuentar malas compañías. **to get into the habit of,** acostumbrarse a. **to get married,** casarse. **to get near,** acercarse. **to get one's own way,** salir con la suya. **to get oneself up as,** disfrazarse de. **to get out in a hurry,** salir apresuradamente; marcharse rápidamente, Inf. salir pitando. **to get out of the way,** quitarse de en medio, apartarse. **to get rid of,** desembarazarse de, librarse de; salir de; perder. tener; padecer. **Get on!** ¡Adelante!; (to a horse) ¡Arre!; (continue) ¡Sigue! **Get out!** ¡Fuera! ¡Largo de aquí! ¡Sal! **to get the blues = to get depressed. Get up!** ¡Levántate!; (to a horse) ¡Arre! **to get about,** moverse mucho; andar mucho; (attend to business affairs) ir a sus negocios; (travel) viajar; (get up from sick bed) levantarse; (go out) salir; (be known) saberse, divulgarse, hacerse público. **to get above,** subir a un nivel más alto (de). **to get across,** vi cruzar, atravesar. vt hacer cruzar. **to get along,** vi (depart) marcharse; (continue) seguir, vivir; (manage) ir, ir tirando. vt llevar; traer; hacer andar por. **How are you getting along?** ¿Cómo le va? **I am getting along all right, thank you,** Voy tirando, gracias. **to get along without,** pasarse sin. **to get angry** vi Central America empurrarse **to get at,** (remove) sacar; (find) encontrar; (reach) llegar a; alcanzar; (discover) descubrir; (allude to) aludir a; (understand) comprender. **to get away,** vi dejar (un lugar); marcharse, irse; (escape) escaparse. vt ayudar a marcharse; ayudar a escaparse. **to get away with,** llevarse, marcharse con; Inf. salir con la suya. **to get back,** vi regresar, volver; (get home) volver a casa; (be back) estar de vuelta. vt (recover) recobrar; (receive) recibir; (find again) hallar de nuevo. **to get depressed,** Central America acuilmarse. **to get down,** vi bajar, descender. vt bajar; (take off a hook) descolgar; (swallow) tragar; (note) anotar; escribir. **to get down on all fours,** ponerse en cuatro patas. **to get down to,** ponerse a (estudiar, trabajar, etc.). **to get in,** vi entrar en; lograr entrar en; (slip in) colarse en; (of political party) entrar en el poder; (of a club) hacerse socio de; (return) regresar; (home) volver a casa; (find oneself) hallarse, estar; (a habit) adquirir. vt hacer entrar en; (a club, etc.) hacer socio de; (a word) decir. **to get in line,** Mexico formarse. **to get into.** See to get in. **to get off,** vt apearse de; bajar de; (send) enviar; (from punishment) librar; (bid goodbye) despedirse de; (remove) quitar, sacar. vi apearse; bajar; (from punishment) librarse de; (leave) ponerse en camino, marcharse. **to get on,** vi (wear) tener puesto; (progress) hacer progresos, adelantar; (prosper) medrar, prosperar; (succeed) tener éxito; avanzar; seguir el camino; (agree) avenirse. vt (push) empujar; (place) poner; (cause) hacer; (clothes) ponerse; (mount) subir a. **to get open,** abrir. **to get out,** vt hacer salir; sacar; (publish) publicar; divulgar. vi salir; escapar; **to get out of a jam,** salir de un paso; (descend) bajar de. **to get over,** (cross) atravesar, cruzar; (an illness, grief, etc.) reponerse de; (excuse) perdonar; (surmount) superar; (ground) recorrer. **to get round,** (a person) persuadir; (surround) rodear; (avoid) evitar; (difficulties) superar, vencer. **to get one's degree,** Lat. Am. diplomarse. **to get through,** pasar por; (time) pasar; (finish) terminar, acabar; (pierce or enter) penetrar; (communicate) comunicar (con); (difficulties) vencer; (an exam) aprobar. **to get the blues,** Central America acuilmarse. **to get to,** llegar a; encontrar; (begin) empezar. **to get together,** vt reunir, juntar. vi reunirse, juntarse. **to get under,** ponerse debajo de; (control) dominar. **to get up,** vt (raise) alzar, levantar; (carry up things) subir; hacer subir; organizar; preparar; (learn) aprender; (linen) blanquear, colar; (ascend) subir; (dress) ataviar; (steam) generar; (a play) ensayar; poner en escena. vi levantarse; (on a horse) montar a caballo; (of the wind) refrescarse; (of the fire) avivarse; (of the sea) embravecerse. **to get up to,** llegar a; alcanzar

getting /'gɛtɪŋ/ n adquisición, f; (of money) ganancia, f. **g. up,** preparación, f; organización, f; (of a play) representación (de una comedia), puesta en escena, f

get-up /'gɛt ˌʌp/ n atavío, m; (of a book, etc.) aspecto, m

geyser /'gaizər/ n géiser, m; (for heating water) calentador (de agua), m

ghastliness /'gæstlinɪs/ n horror, m; palidez mortal, f; aspecto miserable, m; (boringness) tedio, aburrimiento, m; lo desagradable

ghastly /'gæstli/ a horrible; de una palidez mortal; cadavérico; (boring) aburrido; muy desagradable

ghetto /'gɛtou/ n gueto m

ghost /goust/ n fantasma, espectro, aparecido, m; (spirit) alma, f, espíritu, m; (shadow) sombra. f; (writer) mercenario, m. **Holy G.**, Espíritu Santo, m. **to give up the g.**, entregar el alma; perder la esperanza, desesperarse. **to look like a g.**, parecer un fantasma

ghostliness /'goustlinɪs/ n espiritualidad, f; lo misterioso; palidez, f; tenuidad, f

ghostly /'goustli/ a espiritual; espectral; misterioso; pálido; vaporoso, tenue; indistinto

ghost town n pueblo-fantasma, m

ghost word n palabra-fantasma, f

ghoul /gul/ n vampiro, m

ghoulish /'gulɪʃ/ a insano; cruel; sádico

giant /'dʒaiənt/ n gigante, m; Fig. coloso, m, a gigantesco; de gigantes; de los gigantes. **g.-killer,** matador de gigantes, m. **g.-stride,** (gymnastics) paso volante, m

gibber /'dʒɪbər/ vi hablar incoherentemente, hablar entre dientes; farfullar, hablar atropelladamente; decir disparates

gibberish /'dʒɪbərɪʃ/ n galimatías, m; jerigonza, f, griego, m

gibbet /'dʒɪbɪt/ n horca, f, patíbulo, m. **to die on the g.,** morir ahorcado

gibbon /'gɪbən/ n Zool. gibón, m

gibe /dʒaib/ n improperio, escarnio, m, burla, mofa, f. vi criticar. **to g. at,** burlarse de, ridiculizar, mofarse de

gibing /'dʒaibɪŋ/ a burlón, mofador. n mofas, burlas, f pl

gibingly /'dʒaibɪŋli/ adv burlonamente, con sorna

giblets /'dʒɪblɪts/ n menudillos, m pl

giddily /'gɪdli/ adv vertiginosamente; frívolamente, atolondradamente

giddiness /'gɪdinɪs/ n vértigo, m; atolondramiento, m; inconstancia, f; frivolidad, ligereza de cascos, f

giddy /'gɪdi/ a vertiginoso; mareado; atolondrado, casquivano, frívolo; inconstante. **She felt very g.,** Se sintió muy mareada. **to make g.,** dar vértigo (a), marear

gift /gɪft/ n regalo, m, dádiva, f; (quality) don, talento, m; prenda, f; poder, m; Law. donación, f; (offering) ofrenda, oblación, f. vt dotar. **deed of g.,** Law. escritura de donación, f. **in the g. of,** en el poder de, en las manos de. **I wouldn't have it as a g.,** No lo tomaría ni regalado. **Never look a g. horse in the mouth,** A caballo regalado no se le mira el diente. **g. of tongues,** don de las lenguas, genio de las lenguas, m

gifted /'gɪftɪd/ a talentoso

gig /gɪg/ n (carriage) carrocín, m; (boat) falúa, lancha, f; (for wool) máquina de cardar paño, f; (harpoon) arpón, m, (performance) actuación, f

gigantic /dʒai'gæntɪk/ a gigantesco; colosal, enorme

giggle /'gɪgəl/ vi reírse sin motivo; reírse disimuladamente. n risa disimulada, f

giggling /'gɪglɪŋ/ n risa estúpida, f; risa nerviosa, f

gigolo /'dʒɪgəˌlou/ n gigolo, mantenido, jinetero (Cuba), m

gild /gɪld/ vt dorar; (metals) sobredorar; embellecer. **to g. the pill,** dorar la píldora

gilder /'gɪldər/ n dorador, m

gilding /'gɪldɪŋ/ n dorado, m, doradura, f; embellecimiento, m

Gileadite /'gɪliəˌdait/ n and a galaadita, mf

gill /gɪl/ n (of fish) agalla, branquia, f; (ravine) barranco, m;

gill /dʒɪl/ n (measure) cierta medida de líquidos, f, ($\frac{1}{8}$ litro)

gilt /gɪlt/ n dorado, m; pan de oro, m; relumbrón, f;

Fig. encanto, m, a dorado, áureo. **g.-edged,** (of books) con los bordes dorados. **g.-edged security,** papel del Estado, m; valores de toda confianza, m pl

gimcrack /'dʒɪmˌkræk/ n chuchería, f. a de baratillo, cursi; mal hecho

gimlet /'gɪmlɪt/ n barrena, f, taladro, m

gin /dʒɪn/ n (drink) ginebra, f; (snare) trampa, f. vt (snare) coger con trampa. **g. block,** Mech. garrucha, f

ginger /'dʒɪndʒər/ n jengibre, m; Inf. energía, f, brío, m, a rojo. vt sazonar con jengibre; Inf. animar, estimular. **g.-beer,** gaseosa, f

gingerly /'dʒɪndʒərli/ adv con gran cuidado; delicadamente

gingham /'gɪŋəm/ n guinga, f

gingivitis /ˌdʒɪndʒə'vaitɪs/ n gingivitis, f

gipsy /'dʒɪpsi/ n. See **gypsy**

giraffe /dʒə'ræf/ n jirafa, f

gird /gɜrd/ vt ceñir; (invest) investir; (surround) cercar, rodear; (put on) revestir. **to g. oneself for the fray,** prepararse para la lucha

girder /'gɜrdər/ n viga, jácena, f. **main g.,** viga maestra, f

girdle /'gɜrdl̩/ n (belt) cinturón, m; (corset) faja, f; circunferencia, f; zona, f. vt ceñir; Fig. cercar, rodear

girl /gɜrl/ n niña, f; chica, muchacha, f; (maidservant) criada, muchacha, f; (young lady) señorita, f. **a young g.,** una jovencita; (a little older) una joven. **old g.,** (of a school) antigua alumna, f; Inf. vieja, f; (Inf. affectionate) chica, f. **g. friend,** amiguita, f. **g. guide, girl scout,** exploradora, f. **girls' school,** colegio de niñas, colegio de señoritas, m

girlhood /'gɜrlhʊd/ n niñez, f; juventud, f

girlish /'gɜrlɪʃ/ a de niña, de muchacha; (of boys) afeminado; joven

girth /gɜrθ/ n (of horse, etc.) cincha, f; circunferencia, f; (of person) talle, m; (obesity) corpulencia, obesidad, f

gist /dʒɪst/ n esencia, substancia, f, importe, m

give /gɪv/ vt dar; (a present) regalar; (infect) contagiar; (impart) comunicar; (grant) otorgar; (allow, concede) conceder; (assign) asignar, señalar; (appoint) nombrar; (a toast) brindar (a la salud de); (a party, ball, etc.) dar; (a bill) presentar; (wish) desear; (punish) castigar; (pay) pagar; (hand over) entregar; (names at baptism) imponer; (produce) producir; (cause) causar; (of judicial sentences) condenar a; (evoke) proporcionar; (provoke) provocar; (devote) dedicar, consagrar; (sacrifice) sacrificar; (evidence, an account, orders, a lesson, a performance, a concert) dar; (a cry, shout) lanzar, proferir; (a laugh) soltar; (describe) describir; (paint) pintar; (write) escribir; (offer) ofrecer; (show) mostrar; (transmit) transmitir; (heed, pain) hacer; (a speech) pronunciar, hacer; (award, adjudge) adjudicar; (ear) prestar (oído (a)). vi dar; ser dadivoso, mostrarse generoso; (give in) ceder; (be elastic) dar de sí; ablandarse; (collapse) hundirse. **G. them my best wishes!** ¡Dales mis mejores recuerdos! **G. us a song!** ¡Cántanos algo! **I can g. him a lift in my car,** Puedo ofrecerle un asiento en mi auto. **I g. you my word,** Os doy mi palabra. **to g. a good account of oneself,** defenderse bien; hacer bien; salir bien. **to g. a person a piece of one's mind,** contarle cuatro verdades. **to g. chase,** dar caza (a). **to g. it to a person,** poner a uno como nuevo; reprender; (beat) pegar, dar de palos. **to g. of oneself,** dar de sí. **to g. rise to,** dar lugar a, ocasionar, causar. **to g. way,** no poder resistir; (break) romperse; (yield) ceder; (collapse) hundirse; (retreat) retroceder. **to g. way to,** (retreat before) retirarse ante; (abandon oneself to) entregarse a, abandonarse a. **to g. away,** enajenar; dar; regalar; (sell cheaply) vender a un precio muy bajo; (get rid of) deshacerse de; (sacrifice) sacrificar; (a secret) revelar; (betray) traicionar; (expose) descubrir; (tell) contar; (a bride) conducir al altar. **He gave himself away,** Reveló su pensamiento sin querer. **to g. back,** vt devolver; restituir. vi retirarse, cejar. **to g. forth,** divulgar, publicar; (scatter) derramar; (emit) emitir, despedir; (smoke, rays) echar. **to g. in,** vt entregar; presentar. vi darse por vencido. **to g. in to,** (agree with) asentir a, consentir en; rendirse ante. **Mary always gives in to George,** María hace siempre lo que Jorge quiere. **to g. off,** (of odors, etc.) emitir, exhalar, despedir. **to g. out,** *vt* (distribute) distribuir, repartir; (allocate) asignar; (publish) publicar; (announce) anunciar; (reveal) divulgar; (allege) afirmar, hacer saber; (emit) emitir. *vi* (be exhausted) agotarse; (end) acabarse; (be lacking) faltar. **to g. over,** *vt* entregar; (transfer) traspasar; cesar de. *vi* cesar. **to g. up,** entregar; ceder; (renounce) renunciar (a); (sacrifice) sacrificar; (abandon) abandonar; (cease) dejar de; (as lost) dar por perdido; (of a patient) desahuciar; (a post) dimitir de; (return) devolver, restituir; (a problem) renunciar (a resolver un problema); (lose hope) perder la esperanza; (give in) darse por vencido. **I had given up on you,** (didn't expect you), Creí que no ibas a venir. **to g. oneself up to,** entregarse a; dedicarse a; *Mil.* rendirse a. **to g. up one's seat,** ceder su sitio (or asiento). **to g. upon,** (overlook) dar sobre

give /gɪv/ *n* elasticidad, *f*; el dar de sí; (concession) concesión, *f.* **g. and take,** concesiones mutuas, *f pl.* **g. away,** *Inf.* revelación indiscreta, *f*
given /'gɪvən/ *a* dado; especificado; convenido; (with to) dado a, adicto a. **in a g. time,** en un tiempo dado. **g. that,** dado que
giver /'gɪvər/ *n* dador (-ra); donador (-ra)
giving /'gɪvɪŋ/ *a* = **generous**
gizzard /'gɪzərd/ *n* molleja, *f.* **It sticks in my g.,** *Inf.* No lo puedo tragar
glacial /'gleɪʃəl/ *a* glacial
glacier /'gleɪʃər/ *n* glaciar, *m*
glad /glæd/ *a* feliz, alegre; contento, satisfecho; *Inf.* elegante. **to be g.,** alegrarse, estar contento; estar satisfecho. **to give the g. eye,** hacer ojos
gladden /'glædn/ *vt* alegrar, regocijar
glade /gleɪd/ *n* claro, *m*; rasa, *f*
gladiator /'glædi,eɪtər/ *n* gladiador, *m*
gladiolus /,glædi'oʊləs/ *n* *Bot.* gladíolo, gladio, *m*; espadaña, *f*
gladly /'glædli/ *adv* alegremente; con mucho gusto, gustoso, de buena gana
gladness /'glædnɪs/ *n* alegría, felicidad, *f*, contento, *m*; placer, *m*
glamorous /'glæmərəs/ *a* exótico; garboso
glamour /'glæmər/ *n* encanto, *m*, fascinación, *f*; garbo, *m*. **g. girl,** belleza exótica, *f*
glance /glæns/ *n* (of a projectile) desviación, *f*; (of light) vislumbre, *m*; relumbrón, centelleo, *m*; (look) vistazo, *m*, ojeada, *f*; mirada, *f*, *vi* desviarse; relumbrar, centellear, brillar; (with at) ojear, echar un vistazo a, lanzar miradas a; (a book) hojear; mirar; mirar de reojo; *Fig.* indicar brevemente. **at a g.,** con un vistazo; en seguida. **at the first g.,** a primera vista. **to g. off,** desviarse (al chocar). **to g. over,** repasar, echar un vistazo a; (a book) hojear
glancing /'glænsɪŋ/ *a* (of a blow) que roza
gland /glænd/ *n* (*Anat., Bot.*) glándula, *f*; (in the neck) ganglio, *m.* **to have swollen glands,** tener inflamación de los ganglios
glandular /'glændʒələr/ *a* glandular
glare /glɛər/ *n* brillo, fulgor, *m*; luminosidad, *f*; reflejo, *m*; (look) mirada feroz, *f. vi* relumbrar, centellear; (stare) mirar con ferocidad, mirar fijamente
glaring /'glɛərɪŋ/ *a* deslumbrante, brillante; (of colors) chillón, llamativo; (of looks) de mirada feroz; (flagrant) notorio, evidente
glaringly /'glɛərɪŋli/ *adv* brillantemente; con mirada feroz; notoriamente
glass /glæs/ *n* vidrio, *m*; cristal, *m*; (glassware) artículos de vidrio, *m pl*; cristalería, *f*; (for drinking) vaso, *m*, copa, *f*; (pane) cristal, *m*; (mirror) espejo, *m*; (telescope) telescopio, *m*; catalejo, *m*; (barometer) barómetro, *m*; (hour-glass) reloj de arena, *m*; (of a watch) vidrio (de reloj), *m*; *pl* **glasses,** (binoculars) anteojos, *m pl*; (eyeglasses) gafas, lentes, *m pl*; (opera glasses) gemelos de teatro, *m pl*, *a* de vidrio; de cristal. *vt* vidriar. **John wears glasses,** Juan lleva gafas. **The g. is falling (rising),** El barómetro baja (sube). **to clink glasses,** trincar las copas. **to look in the g.,** mirarse en el espejo. **clear g.,** vidrio trasparente, *m.* **cut g.,** cristal tallado, *m.* **frosted g.,** vidrio jaspeado, *m.* **plate-g.,** vidrio plano, *m.* **safety g.,** vidrio inastillable, *m.* **stained**

g., vidrio de color, vidrio pintado, *m.* **under g.,** bajo vidrio; en invernáculo. **g. bead,** abalorio, *m*; cuenta de vidrio, *f.* **g.-blower,** soplador de vidrio, *m.* **g.-blowing,** el soplar de vidrio. **g. case,** escaparate, *m.* **g.-cloth,** paño para vasos, *m.* **g. eye,** ojo de cristal, *m.* **g. paper,** papel de vidrio, *m.* **g. roof,** techo de cristal, *m.* **g. window,** vidriera, *f*
glasscutter /'glæs,kʌtər/ *n* cortador de vidrio, *m*
glassful /'glæsfʊl/ *n* contenido de un vaso, *m*; vaso, vaso lleno, *m*, copa, *f*
glasshouse /'glæs,haʊs/ *n* fábrica de vidrio, *f*; vidriería, *f*; invernáculo, invernadero, *m*, estufa, *f*
glassware /'glæs,wɛər/ *n* cristalería, *f*
glassy /'glæsi/ *a* vítreo; (of eyes) vidrioso; *Fig.* cristalino; (smooth) liso, raso
glaze /gleɪz/ *n* barniz, *m*: luster, brillo, *m. vt* poner vidrios (a); vidriar; barnizar; (paper, leather, etc.) satinar. *vi* (of eyes) vidriarse, ponerse vidrioso
glazier /'gleɪʒər/ *n* vidriero, *m*
glazing /'gleɪzɪŋ/ *n* vidriado, *m*; barnizado, satinado, *m*; (material) barniz, *m*
gleam /glim/ *n* rayo, destello, *m*; (of color) viso, *m*, mancha, *f*; *Fig.* rayo, *m*; (in the eye) chispa, *f. vi* relucir, centellear, resplandecer; brillar; reflejar la luz; *Fig.* brillar. **g. of hope,** rayo de esperanza, *m*
gleaming /'glimɪŋ/ *a* reluciente, centelleante; brillante. *n* see **gleam**
glean /glin/ *vt* espigar, rebuscar; recoger. *vi* espigar
gleaner /'glinər/ *n* espigador, *m*; recogedor (-ra)
gleaning /'glinɪŋ/ *n* espigueo, *m*; rebusca, recolección, *f*; *pl* **gleanings,** fragmentos, *m pl*
glee /gli/ *n* alegría, *f*, júbilo, alborozo, *m*; *Mus.* canción para voces solas, *f*
gleeful /'glifəl/ *a* alegre, jubiloso, gozoso
gleefully /'glifəli/ *adv* alegremente, con júbilo
glen /glɛn/ *n* cañada, *f*, cañón, *m*, hondonada, *f*
glib /glɪb/ *a* locuaz, voluble; (easy) fácil
glibness /'glɪbnɪs/ *n* locuacidad, volubilidad, *f*; (easiness) facilidad, *f*
glide /glaɪd/ *n* deslizamiento, *m*; *Aer.* planeo, *m. vi* deslizarse; resbalar; *Aer.* planear. **to g. away,** escurrirse; desaparecer silenciosamente
glider /'glaɪdər/ *n* *Aer.* deslizador, planeador, *m*
gliding /'glaɪdɪŋ/ *n* *Aer.* vuelo sin motor, *m*
glimmer /'glɪmər/ *n* luz trémula, luz débil, *f*, tenue resplandor, *m*; vislumbre, *m. vi* brillar con luz trémula, rielar *Fig.*; tener vislumbres (de)
glimpse /glɪmps/ *n* vistazo, *m*; vislumbre, *m*; indicio, *m*; impresión, *f*; vista, *f. vt* entrever, divisar; tener una vista (de); ver por un instante; vislumbrar
glint /glɪnt/ *n* tenue resplandor, *m*; lustre, *m*; centelleo, *m*; reflejo, *m*; (in the eye) chispa, *f. vi* relucir, destellar, rutilar; reflejar
glisten /'glɪsən/ *vi* brillar, relucir
glistening /'glɪsənɪŋ/ *a* coruscante; brillante, reluciente
glitter /'glɪtər/ *n* brillo, resplandor, *m*, rutilación, *f. vi* brillar, resplandecer, relucir; rutilar. **All that glitters is not gold,** Todo lo que reluce no es oro
glittering /'glɪtərɪŋ/ *a* reluciente, resplandeciente, *Fig.* brillante
gloat (over) /gloʊt/ *vi* recrearse en, gozarse en, deleitarse en
globe /gloʊb/ *n* globo, *m*; esfera, *f*; (for fish) pecera, *f*; (for gas, electric light) globo, *m.* **geographical g.,** globo terráqueo, *m*, globo mapamundi, *m.* **g.-trotter,** trotamundos, *mf*
globular /'glɒbyələr/ *a* globular, esférico
globule /'glɒbyul/ *n* glóbulo, *m*
gloom /glum/ *n* obscuridad, *f*; lobreguez, *f*, tinieblas, *f pl*; *Fig.* melancolía, tristeza, *f*; taciturnidad, *f. vi Fig.* ponerse melancólico; ser taciturno
gloomily /'gl`uməli/ *adv* obscuramente; *Fig.* tristemente; taciturnamente
gloomy /'glumi/ *a* obscuro; sombrío, lóbrego; melancólico, triste; taciturno; (of prospects, etc.) poco halagüeño, nada atrayente
glorification /,glɔrəfɪ'keɪʃən/ *n* glorificación, *f*
glorify /'glɔrə,faɪ/ *vt* glorificar; exaltar; alabar

glorious /'glɔːriəs/ *a* glorioso; espléndido, magnífico; insigne; *Inf.* estupendo

glory /'glɔːri/ *n* gloria, *f*; esplendor, *m*, magnificencia, *f*; *Art.* gloria, *f*. *vi* recrearse, gozarse; glorificarse, jactarse. **to be in one's g.,** estar en la gloria. **to g. in,** hacer gala de, glorificarse en

gloss /glɒs/ *n* (sheen) lustre, brillo, *m*; *Fig.* apariencia, *f*; (note) glose, *m*; (excuse) disculpa, *f*. *vt* pulir; glosar. **to g. over,** (faults) disculpar, excusar

glossary /'glɒsəri/ *n* glosario, *m*

glossiness /'glɒsinis/ *n* lustre, *m*, tersura, *f*; brillo, *m*

glossy /'glɒsi/ *a* lustroso, terso; brillante; (of hair) liso

glottal stop /'glɒtl/ *n* choque glótica, golpe de glotis, *m*

glottis /'glɒtis/ *n Anat.* glotis, *f*

glove /glʌv/ *n* guante. **evening gloves,** guantes largos, *m pl.* **to be hand in g. with,** juntar diestra con diestra. **to fit like a g.,** sentar como un guante. **to put on one's gloves,** ponerse los guantes. **g. shop,** guantería, *f*. **g.-stretcher,** ensanchador (-ra) de guantes, abridor (-ra) de guantes *mf*

glove compartment gaveta, guantera, *f*, guantero, portaguantes *m*

glove-compartment light /'glʌv kəm'pɑrtmənt/ luz de portaguantes, *f*

glover /'glʌvər/ *n* guantero (-ra)

glow /glou/ *n* incandescencia, *f*; claridad, *f*; luz difusa, *f*; (heat) calor, *m*; (of color) intensidad, *f*; color vivo, *m*; (enthusiasm) ardor, entusiasmo, *m*; (redness) rojez, *f*; (in the sky) arrebol, *m*; (of pleasure, etc.) sentimiento de placer, *m*; sensación de bienestar, *f*. *vi* estar incandescente; arder; abrasarse; sentir entusiasmo; mostrarse rojo; experimentar un sentimiento de placer o una sensación de bienestar. **to g. with health,** estar rebosando de salud. **g.-worm,** luciérnaga, *f*

glower /'glauər/ *n* ceño, *m*; mirada amenazadora, *f*. *vi* poner cara de pocos amigos, mirar airadamente; tener los ojos puestos (en)

glowing /'glouɪŋ/ *a* candente, incandescente; ardiente; entusiasta; satisfecho; intenso; (bright) vivo; (red) encendido; (with health) rebosante de salud. *n* see **glow**

glowingly /'glouɪŋli/ *adv* encendidamente; *Fig.* con entusiasmo

glucose /'glukous/ *n* glucosa, *f*

glue /glu/ *n* engrudo, *m*, cola, *f*. *vt* encolar, engrudar; pegar; *Fig.* fijar, poner. **He kept his eyes glued on them,** Tenía los ojos fijados (or pegados) en ellos. **g.-pot,** pote de cola, *m*

gluey /'glui/ *a* gomoso; pegajoso, viscoso

glueyness /'gluinis/ *n* viscosidad, *f*

gluing /'gluɪŋ/ *n* encoladura, *f*

glum /glʌm/ *a* deprimido, taciturno, sombrío

glumly /'glʌmli/ *adv* taciturnamente

glut /glʌt/ *n* superabundancia, *f*, exceso, *m*. *vt* (satiate) hartar; *Fig.* saciar; (the market) inundar

gluteal /'glutiəl/ *a* glúteo

glutinous /'glutnəs/ *a* glutinoso, pegajoso, viscoso

glutton /'glʌtn/ *n* glotón (-ona); *Fig.* ávido (-da)

gluttonous /'glʌtnəs/ *a* glotón, comilón

gluttony /'glʌtni/ *n* glotonería, gula, *f*

glycerin /'glisərin/ *n* glicerina, *f*

gnarled /nɑrld/ *a* nudoso; (of human beings) curtido

gnash /næʃ/ *vt* rechinar, crujir (los dientes)

gnashing /'næʃiŋ/ *n* rechinamiento (de dientes), *n*

gnat /næt/ *n* mosquito, *m*

gnaw /nɔ/ *vt* roer; morder; (of wood by worms) carcomer; *Fig.* roer

gnawing /'nɔiŋ/ *n* roedura, *f*; mordedura, *f*, *a* roedor; mordedor

gnome /noum/ *n* nomo, *m*

gnostic /'nɒstik/ *a* nóstico (-ca)

gnosticism /'nɒstisizəm/ *n* nosticismo, *m*

go /gou/ *vi* ir; (depart) irse, marcharse; (go toward) dirigirse a, encaminarse a; (lead to, of roads, etc.) conducir a, ir a; (vanish) desaparecer; (leave) dejar, salir de; (lose) perder; (pass) pasar; (of time) transcurrir, pasar; (be removed) quitarse; (be prohibited) prohibirse; (fall) caer; (collapse) hundirse; (be torn

off) desprenderse; desgajarse; *Mech.* funcionar, trabajar, andar; (sound) sonar; (of the heart) palpitar, latir; (follow) seguir; (gesture) hacer un gesto; (be stated) decirse, afirmarse; (live) vivir; (wear) llevar; (turn out) salir, resultar; (improve) mejorar; (prosper) prosperar; (turn, become) ponerse; volverse; (to sleep) dormirse; (into a faint) desmayarse; (decay) echarse a perder, estropearse; (turn sour) agriarse; (become, adopt views, etc.) hacerse; (be sold) venderse; (be decided) decidirse, ser decidido; (have) tener; (by will) pasar; (belong) pertenecer; (receive) recibir; (have its place) estar; (put) ponerse; (going plus infin.) ir a; (die) morir, irse; (do a journey, a given distance) hacer; (a pace, step) dar; (take) tomar; (escape) escaparse, (contribute) contribuir (a); (harmonize) armonizar (con); (be current) ser válido; (be) ser; (of a document, etc., run) rezar; (attend) asistir a; (be broken) estar roto; (be worn) estar raído; (be granted) darse, otorgarse. **It's gone five,** Ya dieron las cinco. **It's time to be going,** Es hora de marcharse. **Let's go!** ¡Vamos! **These two colors go well together,** Estos colores armonizan bien. **Well, how goes it?** Bueno, ¿qué tal? ¿Cómo te va? **Who goes there?** *Mil.* ¡Quién va? **to go and fetch,** ir a buscar. **to let go,** soltar; dejar ir. **to go one's way,** seguir su camino. **to go wrong,** salir mal, fracasar; (sin) descarriarse. **"Go!"** (traffic sign) «¡Siga!» **Go on!** ¡Adelante!; (continue) ¡Siga!; *Inf.* ¡Qué va! **to go about,** dar la vuelta a; rodear; recorrer; (undertake) emprender, hacer; intentar; (of news, etc.) circular; *Naut.* virar de bordo. **Go about your business!** ¡Métete en lo que to importa! **to go abroad,** ir al extranjero; salir a la calle; publicarse, divulgarse. **to go across,** cruzar, atravesar; pasar. **to go after,** andar tras; seguir; (seek) ir a buscar; (persecute) perseguir. **to go again,** ir de nuevo; (be present) asistir otra vez; volver. **to go against,** ir contra; militar contra; oponerse a; ser desfavorable a. **to go ahead,** adelantar, avanzar; progresar; prosperar; (lead) ir a la cabeza (de), conducir; *Naut.* marchar hacia adelante. **to go along,** andar por; recorrer; (depart) irse, marcharse. **go apartment-hunting,** ir en busca de piso. **to go along with,** acompañar (a). **to go aside,** quitarse de en medio; apartarse, retirarse. **to go astray,** perderse; extraviarse, descarriarse. **to go at,** atacar, acometer; (undertake) emprender; empezar a. **to go at it again,** *Inf.* volver a la carga. **to go away,** irse, marcharse; ausentarse; (on abode) llevarse. **to go back,** volver, regresar; (an) retroceder; (retreat) retroceder, volverse atrás; (in history) remontarse a. **to go back on,** (a promise, etc.) faltar a; (retract) retractarse; (betray) traicionar. **to go backwards,** retroceder, cejar; desandar lo andado; *Fig.* deteriorarse, empeorar. **to go backwards and forwards,** ir y venir; oscilar. **to go before,** (lead) ir a la cabeza de, conducir; anteceder; proceder; (a judge, etc.) comparecer ante. **to go behind,** ir detrás de; esconderse detrás de; seguir; (evidence, etc.) mirar más allá de. **to go between,** ponerse entre; interponerse; (as a mediator) mediar; (insert) intercalarse; (travel) ir entre; llevar cartas entre, ser mensajero de. **to go beyond,** ir más allá; exceder. **to go by,** pasar; dejar pasar cerca de, pasar junto a; ir por; (of time) transcurrir, pasar; (follow) seguir; guiarse por, atenerse a; (judge by) juzgar por; (a name) pasar por; tomar el nombre de. **to go down,** bajar, descender; (of the sun) ponerse; (sink) hundirse; sumergirse; (fall) caer; (be remembered) ser recordado; (believe) tragar; ser creído. **to go down again,** bajar de nuevo; volver a caer. **go Dutch,** ir a escote, ir a la gringa, ir a la par, ir a limón. **to go far,** ir lejos; influir mucho (en); impresionar mucho; (contribute) contribuir (a). **to go fetch,** (seek) ir en busca de; procurar tener; (attack) echarse encima de, atacar. **to go for a ride (by car, bicycle, on horseback),** dar un paseo (en coche, en bicicleta, a caballo). **to go forth,** salir; publicarse. **to go forward,** adelantar, avanzar; progresar; continuar; (happen) tener lugar. **to go from,** dejar, abandonar; separarse de, apartarse de; marcharse de. **to go in,** entrar en; (a railway carriage, etc.) subir a; (compete) concurrir. **to go in again,** volver a entrar en, entrar de nuevo en. **to go in and out,** entrar y salir; ir y venir.

to go in for, entrar a buscar; dedicarse a, entregarse a; (buy) comprarse; tomar parte en; (an examination) tomar (un examen); (for a competition) entrar en (un concurso); (try) ensayar; arriesgar. **to go into,** entrar en; examinar; investigar; ocuparse con. **to go native,** *Lat. Am.* acriollarse. **to go near,** acercarse a. **to go off,** marcharse; (explode) estallar; (of fire-arms) dispararse; (of the voice, etc.) perder (la voz, etc.); (run away) huir, fugarse. **to go off badly,** salir mal, fracasar, no tener éxito. **to go off well,** salir bien, tener éxito. **to go on,** subirse a; continuar; durar; avanzar; proseguir su marcha; progresar; prosperar; *Theat.* entrar en escena; (of clothes) ponerse; (rely on) apoyarse en. **to go on an excursion, go on an outing, go on a trip,** *Lat. Am.* excursionarse. **Don't go on like that,** No seas así, No te pongas así. **This glove will not go on me,** No puedo ponerme este guante. **to be gone on a person,** *Inf.* estar loco por. **I went on to say...,** Después dije; Continuando mi discurso dije... **It was going on six o'clock when...** Serían alrededor de las seis cuando... **He is going on fifty,** Raya en los cincuenta años. **to go on foot,** ir a pie. **to go on with,** continuar con; empezar. **to go out,** salir; (descend) bajar; (of fires, lights) extinguirse, apagarse; (of fashion, etc.) pasar (de); (the tide) menguar; (retire) retirarse; (in society) frecuentar la alta sociedad; (die) morir; (arouse) excitar. **to go out of** salir de, *Lat. Am. also* egresar de. **to go out of fashion,** pasar de moda. **to go out of one's way (to),** dejar su camino (para); (lose oneself) perder el camino, extraviarse; (take trouble) desvivirse (por), tomarse molestia (para). **to go over,** cruzar; pasar por encima; (to another party or to the other side) pasarse a; (read) repasar; examinar. **to go past,** pasar; pasar en frente de. **to go round,** dar la vuelta a; (revolve) girar; (surround) rodear; (of news, etc.) divulgarse; (be enough) ser suficiente para todos. **to go through,** ir por, pasar por; recorrer; (pierce) penetrar, atravesar; (examine) examinar; (suffer) padecer, sufrir; (experience) experimentar; (live) vivir; (of time) pasar; (of money) malgastar, derrochar. **to go through with,** llevar a cabo; terminar. **to go to,** ir a, encaminarse a; (a person) acercarse a, dirigirse a; (help, be useful) servir para; (be meant for) destinarse a; (rise of price) subir a; (find) encontrar; (of a bid) subir una apuesta hasta. **to go to war,** declarar la guerra. **to go together,** ir juntos (juntas). **to go toward,** encaminarse hacia; ir hacia; (help) ayudar a. **to go under,** pasar por debajo de; (sink) hundirse; (fail) fracasar; (be bankrupt) arruinarse, declarare en quiebra; (the name of) hacerse pasar por. **to go up,** subir; ir arriba; (a tree) trepar; (a ladder, etc.) subir; (a river) ir río arriba; (to town) ir a; (explode) estallar. **to go up and down,** subir y bajar; oscilar; ir de una parte a otra. **to go upon,** subirse a; (rely on) apoyarse en; obrar según; emprender. **to go upstairs,** ir arriba; (to another story, as in an apartment) subir al otro piso; subir la escalera. **to go up to,** acercarse a; (of a bid) subir una apuesta hasta. **to go with,** acompañar; (agree with) estar de acuerdo con; (of principles) seguir, ser fiel a; (harmonize) armonizar con; (be suitable to) convenir a; bien con; convenir a; (*Inf.* get along) ir. **to go without,** marcharse sin; (lack) pasarse sin. **It goes without saying that...,** Huelga decir que.... **Where are you going with this?** (What do you mean?) ¿A dónde quieres llegar con esto?

go /gou/ *n* (fashion) moda, boga, *f*; (happening) suceso, *m*; (fix) apuro, *m*; (energy) energía, *f*, empuje, brío, *m*; (turn) turno, *m*; (attempt) tentativa, *f*; (action) movimiento, *m*, acción, *f*; (bargain) acuerdo, *m*. **It's a go!** (agreed) ¡Trato hecho! ¡Acordado! ¡Entendidos! ¡Entendidas! **It is all the go,** Hace furor, Es la gran moda. **It is no go,** No puede ser, Es imposible. **Now it's my go,** Ahora me toca a mí, Ahora es mi turno. **on the go,** en movimiento; entre manos; ocupado. **to have a go,** probar suerte; procurar, tratar de; tener un turno

goad /goud/ *n* garrocha, aguijada, *f*, aguijón, *m*, *Lat. Am.* lanceta *f*; *Fig.* acicate, estímulo, *m*. *vt* aguijar, picar; *Fig.* incitar, estimular, empujar. **prick with a g.,** aguijonazo, *m*

go-ahead /'gou ə,hɛd/ *a* emprendedor; progresivo

goal /goul/ *n* (posts in football, etc.) meta, portería, *f*, *Lat. Am.* arco, *m*; (score) gol, *m*; (in racing) meta, *f*; (destination) destinación, *f*; *Fig.* ambición, *f*; (purpose, objective) fin, objeto, *m*. **to score a g.,** marcar un gol. **g.-keeper,** guardameta, *m*, portero (-ra). **g.-post,** palo de la portería, *m*

goat /gout/ *n* cabra, *f*; *Astron.* capricornio, *m*. **he-g.,** cabrón, *m*. **young g.,** cabrito, *m*, chivo (-va). **g.-herd,** cabrero, *m*. **g. skin,** piel de cabra, *f*; (wineskin) odre, *m*

goatee /gou'ti/ *n* pera, perilla, *f*

goatish /'goutɪʃ/ *a* cabruno; de cabra; lascivo

gobble /'gɒbəl/ *vt* and *vi* engullir, tragar. *vi* (of turkey) gluglutear. *n* glugluteo, *m*, voz del pavo, *f*

go-between /'gou bɪ,twin/ *n* trotaconventos, *f*; alcahuete, *m*; (mediator) medianero (-ra)

goblet /'gɒblɪt/ *n* copa, *f*

goblin /'gɒblɪn/ *n* trasgo, duende, *m*

go-cart /'gou ,kɑrt/ *n* andaderas, *f pl*; pollera, *f*; cochecito de niño, *m*

god /gɒd/ *n* dios, *m*; *pl* **gods**, dioses, *m pl*; (in a theater) público del paraíso, *m*; paraíso, *m*. **By God!** ¡Vive Dios! **For God's sake,** ¡Por el amor de Dios!; ¡Por Dios! **Please God,** ¡Plegue a Dios! **Thank God!** ¡Gracias a Dios! **God Bless You!** (to someone who has sneezed) ¡Salud! **God forbid!** ¡No lo quiera Dios! **God grant it!** ¡Dios lo quiera! **God keep you!** ¡Dios le guarde! ¡Vaya Vd. con Dios! **God willing,** Dios mediante. **My father, God rest his soul, was...,** Mi padre, que Dios perdone, era...

godchild /'gɒd,tʃaild/ *n* ahijado (-da)

goddess /'gɒdɪs/ *n* diosa, *f*; *Poet.* dea, *f*

godfather /'gɒd,faðər/ *n* padrino, *m*. **to be a g. to,** ser padrino de, sacar de pila (a)

godfearing /'gɒd,fɪərɪŋ/ *a* timorato, temeroso de Dios; religioso

godforsaken /'gɒdfər,seikən/ *a* dejado de la mano de Dios; (of places) remoto, solitario

Godhead /'gɒd,hɛd/ *n* divinidad, *f*

godless /'gɒdlɪs/ *a* impío, irreligioso; sin Dios

godlessness /'gɒdlɪsnɪs/ *n* impiedad, irreligiosidad, *f*

godlike /'gɒd,laik/ *a* divino

godliness /'gɒdlinɪs/ *n* piedad, *f*; santidad, *f*

godling /'gɒdlɪŋ/ *n* diosecillo, *m*

godly /'gɒdli/ *a* devoto, piadoso, religioso

godmother /'gɒd,mʌðər/ *n* madrina, *f*. **fairy g.,** hada madrina, *f*. **to be a g. to,** ser madrina de

godparent /'gɒd,pɛərənt/ *n* padrino, *m*; madrina, *f pl*. **godparents,** padrinos, *m pl*

godsend /'gɒd,sɛnd/ *n* bien, *m*; buena suerte, *f*; fortuna, *f*

go-getter /'gou ,gɛtər/ *n* buscavidas, *mf*

goggle /'gɒgəl/ *n* mirada fija, *f*; *pl* **goggles,** anteojos, *m pl*; gafas, *f pl*; (of a horse) anteojeras, *f pl*. *vi* mirar fijamente; salirse a uno los ojos de la cabeza. **g.-eyed,** de ojos saltones. **g.-eyes,** ojos saltones, *m pl*

going /'gouɪŋ/ *n* ida, *f*; (departure) partida, marcha, *f*; salida, *f*; (pace) paso, *m*; (speed) velocidad, *f*. **It was heavy g.,** El avance era lento; El progreso era lento; (of parties, etc.) Era aburrido. **The g. was difficult on those mountainous roads,** El conducir (or el ir o el andar) era difícil en aquellos caminos de montaña. **g. back,** vuelta, *f*, regreso, *m*. **g. down,** bajada, *f*, descenso, *m*; (of the sun, etc.) puesta, *f*. **g. forward,** avance, *m*; progreso, *m*. **g. in,** entrada, *f*. **g. in and out,** idas y venidas, *f pl*. **g. out,** salida, *f*; (of a fire, light) apagamiento, *m*

going /'gouɪŋ/ *a* and *pres part* que va, yendo; que funciona. **G., g., gone** (at an auction) A la una, a las dos, a las tres. **goings-on,** (tricks) trapujos, *m pl*; (conduct) conducta, *f*. **g. concern,** empresa próspera, *f*. **g. to,** con destino a

going-away present /'gouɪŋ ə,wei/ *n* regalo de despedida, *m*

goiter /'gɔitər/ *n* bocio, *m*

gold /gould/ *n* oro, *m*; color de oro, *m*. *a* de oro; áureo. **All that glitters is not g.,** No es oro todo lo que reluce. **cloth of g.,** tela de oro, *f*. **dull g.,** oro mate, *m*. **light g.,** oro pálido, *m*. **old g.,** oro viejo, *m*. **g.-beater,** batidor de oro, *m*. **g.-digger,** minero de oro, *m*; (woman) aventurera, *f.* **g. dust,** oro en polvo, *m.* **g.-fever,** fiebre de oro, *f.* **g. lace,** galón de oro, *m.* **g. lacquer,** sisa dorada, *f.* **g. leaf,** pan de oro, oro batido, *m.* **g.-mine,** mina de oro, *f.* **g. piece,** moneda de oro, *f.* **g. plate,** vajilla de oro, *f.* **g. stand-ard,** patrón oro, *m.* **g.-thread,** hilo de oro, *m.* **g.-yielding,** *a* aurífero

golden /'gouldən/ *a* de oro; dorado; áureo; amarillo; *Fig.* feliz; excelente. **to become g.,** dorarse. **g. age,** edad de oro, *f.* **G. Age,** (Spanish literature) El Siglo de Oro, *m.* **g.-crested wren,** abadejo, *m.* **g. hair,** cabellos dorados (or de oro), *m pl.* **G. Legend,** leyenda áurea, *f.* **g. mean,** justo medio, *m.* **g. rose,** rosa de oro, *f.* **g. rule,** regla áurea, *f.* **g. syrup,** jarabe de arce, *m.* **g. voice,** voz de oro, *f.* **g. wedding anniversary,** bodas de oro, *f pl*

goldfinch /'gould,fɪntʃ/ *n* jilguero, *m*

goldfish /'gould,fɪʃ/ *n* carpa dorada, *f.* **g. bowl,** pecera, *f*

goldrush /'gould,rʌʃ/ *n* carrera de oro, *f*

goldsmith /'gould,smɪθ/ *n* orfebre, oribe, orífice, *m*

golf /gɒlf/ *n* golf, *m.* **g.-club,** (stick) palo de golf, *m*; (organization) club de golf, *m.* **g.-course,** campo de golf, *m*

golfer /'gɒlfər/ *n* jugador (-ra) de golf

gonad /'gounæd/ *n* gonada, *f*

gondola /'gɒndlə/ *n* góndola, *f*

gondolier /,gɒndl'ɪər/ *n* gondolero, *m*

gone /gɒn/ *a* and *past part* ido; (lost) perdido; (ruined) arruinado; (dead) muerto; (past) pasado; (disappeared) desaparecido; (fainted) desmayado; (suppressed) suprimido; (drunk) borracho; (ended) terminado; (exhausted) agotado; (ill) enfermo. **far g.,** avanzado; (in years) de edad avanzada; (of illness) cerca de la muerte, muy enfermo; (in love) loco de amor; (drunk) muy borracho. **It is all g.,** No hay más. **It is g. seven o'clock,** Son las siete y pico, Son las siete ya

gong /gɒŋ/ *n* gong, *m*; (Chinese) batintín, *m*

gonorrhea /,gɒnə'riə/ *n* gonorrea, *f*

good /gud/ *a* bueno (before *m sing* nouns) buen; agradable; afortunado; (appropriate) apropiado, oportuno; (beneficial) provechoso, ventajoso; (wholesome) sano, saludable; (suitable) apto; (useful) útil; (kind) bondadoso; (much) mucho; (obliging) amable; (virtuous) virtuoso; (skilled) experto; (fresh) fresco; (genuine) genuino, legítimo; verdadero. *adv* bien. *interj* ¡bueno! ¡bien! **a g. deal,** mucho. **a g. many,** bastantes. **a g. turn,** un favor. **a g. way,** (distance) un buen trecho; mucho. **a g. while,** un buen rato. **as g. as,** tan bueno como. **Be so g. as to...!** Haga el favor de, Tenga Vd. la bondad de (followed by infin.). **fairly g.,** *a* bastante bueno. *adv* bastante bien. **I'm g. for another five miles,** Tengo fuerzas para cinco mi llas más. **It was g. of you to do it,** Vd. fue muy amable de hacerlo, Vd. tuvo mucha bondad de hacerlo. **to be no g. at this sort of thing,** no servir para tales cosas. **to have a g. time,** pasarlo bien. **to make g.,** reparar; indemnizar; (accomplish) llevar a cabo, poner en práctica; justificar; (a promise) cumplir. **very g.,** *a* muy bueno. *adv* muy bien. **g.-feeling,** buena voluntad, *f.* **g.-fellowship,** compañerismo, *m*; buena compañía, *f.* **g.-for-nothing,** papanatas, badulaque, *m.* **to be g.-for-nothing,** no servir para nada. **g. luck,** buena suerte, *Lat. Am. also* derechura, leche *f.* **g. manners,** buenos modales, *m pl*; buena crianza, educación, *f.* **g. nature,** buen humor, *m.* **g.-natured,** de buen natural; de buen humor, bonachón. **g. offices,** buenos oficios, *m pl.* **g.-tempered,** de buen humor

good /gud/ *n* bien, *m*; provecho, *m*; utilidad, *f*; *pl* **goods.** See separate entry. **I am saying this for your g.,** Lo digo para tu bien. **Much g. may it do you!** ¡Buen provecho te haga! **for g. and all,** para siempre jamás. **It is no g.,** Es inútil; No vale la pena. **the g.,** el bien; (people) los buenos. **They have gone for g.,** Se han marchado para no volver. **to do one g.,** hacer bien a uno; mejorar; ser provechoso (a uno); (suit) sentar bien (a uno). **What is the g. of...?** ¿Para qué sirve...?; ¿Qué vale...? **g. and evil,** el bien y el mal

good-bye /,gud 'bai/ *interj* ¡adiós! *n* adiós, *m*, despedida, *f.* **to bid g.-b.,** decir adiós. **G.-b. for the**

present! ¡Hasta la vista! ¡Hasta luego! **G.-b. until to-morrow, then,** Hasta mañana pues, adiós, Hasta mañana entonces

goodness /'gudnɪs/ *n* bondad, *f*; (of quality) buena calidad, *f*; (of persons) amabilidad, benevolencia, *f*; (essence) esencia, substancia, *f*; bien, *m*: excelencia, *f*; *interj* ¡Jesús! ¡Dios mío! **For g. sake!** ¡Por Dios! **I wish to g. that,** ¡Ojalá que...!

goods /gudz/ *n pl* bienes, efectos, *m pl*; artículos, *m pl*; *Com.* mercancías, *f pl*, géneros, *m pl.* **by g.-train,** en pequeña velocidad. **stolen g.,** objetos robados, *m pl.* **g. lift,** montacargas, *m.* **g. office,** depósito de mercancías, *m.* **g. station,** estación de carga, *f.* **g.-train,** tren de mercancías, *m.* **g. van,** furgón, *m.* **g. wagon,** vagon de mercancías, *m*

good-smelling /'gud ,smelɪŋ/ *a* oloroso

goodwill /'gud'wɪl/ *n* benevolencia, *f*; buena voluntad, *f*; (of a business) clientela, *f*

goose /gus/ *n* oca, *f*, ganso (-sa); plancha de sastre, *f. a* de oca. **g.-flesh,** *Fig.* carne de gallina, *f.* **g. girl,** ansarera, *f.* **g.-step,** paso de oca, *m*

gooseberry /'gus,beri/ *n* uva espina, *f*

Gordian /'gɔrdiən/ *a* gordiano. **G. knot,** nudo gordiano, *m*

gore /gɔr/ *n* sangre, *f*; *Sew.* sesga, nesga, *f. vt* acornear; desgarrar; herir (con arma blanca)

gorge /gɔrdʒ/ *n* (valley) cañón, barranco, *m*; (heavy meal) comilona, *f*, atracón, *m. vt* engullir, tragar. *vi* hartarse, atracarse

gorgeous /'gɔrdʒəs/ *a* magnífico; espléndido, suntuoso; *Inf.* maravilloso, estupendo

gorgeously /'gɔrdʒəsli/ *adv* magníficamente

gorgeousness /'gɔrdʒəsnɪs/ *n* magnificencia, *f*; suntuosidad, *f*, esplendor, *m*

gorilla /gə'rɪlə/ *n* gorila, *m*

gormandize /'gɔrmən,daiz/ *vi* glotonear

gormandizer /'gɔrmən,daizər/ *n* glotón (-ona)

gory /'gɔri/ *a* ensangrentado; sangriento

gosh /gɒʃ/ *interj* ¡caray! ¡caramba!

goshawk /'gɒs,hɔk/ *n* *Ornith.* azor, *m*

gosling /'gɒzlɪŋ/ *n* ansarino, *m*

gospel /'gɒspəl/ *n* evangelio, *m*; doctrina, *f.* **The G. according to St. Mark,** El Evangelio según San Marcos. **to believe in g. truth,** creer como si fuese el evangelio. **to preach the G.,** predicar el evangelio

gossamer /'gɒsəmər/ *n* hilo de araña, *m*, red de araña, telaraña, *f*; (filmy material) gasa, *f*; hilo finísimo, *m*, *a* de gasa; sutil, delgado, fino

gossip /'gɒsəp/ *n* murmurador (-ra), chismoso (-sa), hablador (-ra); (scandal) chisme, *m*, *Lat. Am. also* lengüeterías *fpl*; habladuría, murmuración, *f*; (obsolete, of a woman) comadre, *f*; (talk) charla, *f. vi* charlar, conversar; (in bad sense) murmurar, chismear; criticar. **to g. about,** charlar de; poner lenguas en, cortar un sayo (a); hablar mal de (alguien). **g. column,** gacetilla, *f*

gossiping /'gɒsəpɪŋ/ *a* charlatán, hablador; chismoso, murmurador. *n* See **gossip**

Goth /gɒθ/ *n* godo (-da); bárbaro (-ra)

Gothic /'gɒθɪk/ *a Art.* gótico; (of race) godo; bárbaro. *n* (language) gótico, *m*; arquitectura gótica, *f.* **G. characters,** letra gótica, *f*

gouge /gaudʒ/ *n* gubia, *f. vt* escoplear. **to g. out,** vaciar; sacar

gourd /gɔrd/ *n* calabaza, *f*

gourmand /gur'mɑnd/ *n* glotón, *m*

gourmet /gur'mei/ *n* gastrónomo, *m*

gout /gaut/ *n Med.* gota, *f*

gouty /'gauti/ *a* gotoso

govern /'gʌvərn/ *vt* gobernar; regir; (guide) guiar; dominar; domar, refrenar; *Gram.* regir; (regulate) regular

governable /'gʌvərnəbəl/ *a* gobernable; manejable; dócil

governess /'gʌvərnɪs/ *n* institutriz, *f*; (in a school) maestra, *f*

governing /'gʌvərnɪŋ/ *a* gubernativo; director; (with principle, etc.) directivo. *n* See **government**

government /'gʌvərnmənt, -ərmənt/ *n* gobierno, *m*; dirección, *f*; autoridad, *f.* **g. bond,** bono del gobierno,

m. **g. house,** palacio del gobernador, *m.* **g. office,** oficina del gobierno, *f.* **g. stock,** papel del Estado, *m*
governmental /ˌgʌvərn'mentl̩, ˌgʌvər-/ *a* gubernamental, gubernativo.

Government Printing Office Talleres Gráficos de la Nación, *m pl*
governor /'gʌvərnər/ *n* gobernador (-ra); vocal de la junta de gobierno, *mf*; (of a prison) director (-ra) (de una prisión); *Mech.* regulador, *m.* **g.-general,** gobernador general, *m*
governorship /'gʌvərnərˌʃɪp/ *n* gobierno, *m*; dirección, *f*
gown /gaun/ *n* toga, *f*; (cassock) sotana, *f*; (dressing-g.) bata, *f*; (for sleeping) camisa de noche, *f*; (bathing-wrap) albornoz, *m*; (dress) vestido, traje, *m*
Goyesque /gɔi'esk/ *a* goyesco
grab /græb/ *n* asimiento, *m*, presa, *f*; *Mech.* gancho, *m. vt* arrebatar, asir, agarrar; *Fig.* alzarse con, tomar
grabber /'græbər/ *n* cogedor (-ra); codicioso (-sa)
grace /greis/ *n* elegancia, *f*; simetría, armonía, *f*; gracia, gentileza, *f*, donaire, *m*; encanto, *m*; (goodness) bondad, *f*; gracia, *f*; merced, *f*, favor, *m*; (period of time) plazo, *m*; (privilege) privilegio, *m*; *Theol.* gracia divina, *f*; (at table) bendición de la mesa, *f*; (as a title) excelentísimo, (to an archbishop) ilustrísimo. *vt* adornar; favorecer; honrar. **airs and graces,** humos, *m pl.* **the Three Graces,** las Gracias. **three days' g.,** plazo de tres días, *m.* **to get into a person's good graces,** congraciarse con; caer en gracia con. **to say g.,** bendecir la mesa. **with a bad g.,** a regañadientes. **with a good g.,** de buena gana. **g.-note,** *Mus.* nota de adorno, *f*
graceful /'greisfəl/ *a* airoso, gentil, gracioso; elegante; bonito
gracefully /'greisfəli/ *adv* airosamente, gentilmente; con gracia; elegantemente
gracefulness. /'greisfəlnɪs/ See **grace**
graceless /'greislɪs/ *a* réprobo; dejado de la mano de Dios; sin gracia
gracious /'greiʃəs/ *a* (merciful) piadoso, clemente; (urbane) afable, condescendiente, agradable. **Good g.!** ¡Vamos!, ¡Dios mío!
graciously /'greiʃəsli/ *adv* afablemente; con benevolencia. **to be g. pleased,** tener a bien
graciousness /'greiʃəsnɪs/ *n* amabilidad, afabilidad, condescendencia, *f*
gradation /grei'deiʃən/ *n* graduación, *f*; *Mus.* gradación, *f*; paso gradual, *m*; seno, *f*
grade /greid/ *n* grado, *m*; (quality) calidad, clase, *f*; (class in school) clase, *f*, (evaluation of coursework) nota, *f*; (gradient) pendiente, *f*, declive, *m. vt* graduar, clasificar; (cattle breeding) cruzar. **down g.,** cuesta abajo. **up g.,** cuesta arriba. **highest g.,** *n* primera clase, *f. a* de primera clase; de calidad excelente
gradient /'greidiənt/ *n* declive, *m.* cuesta, pendiente, *f*
gradual /'grædʒuəl/ *a* gradual. *n Eccl.* gradual, *m*
gradually /'grædʒuəli/ *adv* gradualmente; poco a poco
graduate /*n,* *a* 'grædʒuɪt; *v* -,eit/ *n* licenciado (-da), *Lat. Am.* exalumno (na) *mf a* graduado. *vt* graduar. *vi* graduarse; (as a doctor) doctorarse. **to g. as,** recibirse de. **be graduated from...** *Lat. Am.* egresar de...
graduation /ˌgrædʒu'eiʃən/ *n* graduación, *f*, *Lat. Am.* egreso *m*
graft /græft/ *n Bot.* injerto, *m*; *Surg.* injerto de piel, *m*; (swindle) estafa, *f*; (bribery) soborno, *m. vt Bot.* injertar; *Surg.* injertar un trozo de piel, *Fig.* injerir
grafting /'græftɪŋ/ *n Bot.* injerto, *m*; *Surg.* injerto de piel, *m*; *Fig.* inserción, *f*
grain /grein/ *n* (corn) grano, *m*; (cereal) cereal, *m*, or *f*; (seed, weight) grano, *m*; (trace) pizca, *f*; (of wood, etc.) hila, *m*, fibra, hebra, veta, *f*; (of leather) flor, *f*; (texture) textura, *f. vt* granear; granular; (wood, marble, etc.) vetear. **against the g.,** a contrapelo. **g. lands,** mieses, *f pl*
gram /græm/ *n* gramo, *m*
grammar /'græmər/ *n* gramática, *f*. **g. school,** instituto de segunda enseñanza, *m*
grammarian /grə'meəriən/ *n* gramático, *m*
grammatical /grə'mætɪkəl/ *a* gramático

grammatically /grə'mætɪkəli/ *adv* gramaticalmente, como la gramática lo quiere. (e.g., *She now speaks Catalan g.,* Ahora habla el catalán como la gramática lo quiere)
grammaticalness /grə'mætɪkəlnɪs/ *n* corrección gramatical, *f*
gramophone /'græməˌfoun/ *n* gramófono, *m.*
granary /'greinəri/ *n* granero, hórreo, *m*, troj, *f*, *Mexico* espiguero *m.* **g. keeper,** trojero, *m*
grand /grænd/ *a* magnífico, soberbio; imponente; (of dress) espléndido, vistoso; (of people) distinguido, importante; aristocrático; (proud) orgulloso; (of style) elevado, sublime; (morally) noble; augusto; (main) principal; (full) completo; *Inf.* estupendo, magnífico; (with duke, etc.) gran. *n* piano de cola, *m.* **g.-aunt,** tía abuela, *f.* **g. cross,** gran cruz, *f.* **g. duchess,** gran duquesa, *f.* **g. duke,** gran duque, *m.* **g. lodge,** (of freemasons) Gran Oriente, *m.* **g. master,** gran maestre, *m.* **g.-nephew,** resobrino, *m.* **g.-niece,** resobrina, *f.* **g. opera,** ópera, *f.* **g. piano,** piano de cola, *m.* **g.-stand,** tribuna, *f.* **g.-uncle,** tío abuelo, *m.* **g. vizier,** gran visir, *m*
grandchild /'græn,tʃaild/ *n* nieto (-ta). **great-g.,** biznieto (-ta). **great-great-g.,** tataranieto (-ta)
granddaughter /'græn,dɔtər/ *n* nieta, *f.* **great-g.,** bisnieta, *f.* **great-great-g.,** tataranieta, *f*
grandee /græn'di/ *n* grande (de España, grande de Portugal), *m*
grandeur /'grændʒər/ *n* magnificencia, *f*; grandiosidad, *f*; magnitud, grandeza, *f*; (pomp) pompa, *f*, fausto, *m*
grandfather /'græn,fɑðər/ *n* abuelo, *m.* **great-g.,** bisabuelo, *m.* **great-great-g.,** tatarabuelo, *m*
grandfather clock reloj de péndulo, *m*
grandfatherly /'græn,fɑðərli/ *a* de abuelo
grandiloquence /græn'dɪləkwəns/ *n* grandilocuencia, *f*
grandiloquent /græn'dɪləkwənt/ *a* grandílocuo
grandiose /'grændi,ous/ *a* grandioso, sublime; impresionante; imponente; (in a bad sense) extravagante; (of style) bombástico, hinchado
grand jury *n* jurado de acusación, jurado de juicio, *m*
grandmother /'græn,mʌðər/ *n* abuela, *f.* **great-g.,** bisabuela, *f.* **great-great-g.,** tatarabuela, *f*
grandness /'grændnɪs/ *n* magnificencia, *f*; aristocracia, *f*; (pride) orgullo, *m*; grandiosidad, *f*; (of style) sublimidad, *f*; (of character) nobleza, *f*
grandparent /'græn,peərənt/ *n* abuelo, *m*; abuela, *f*, *pl* **grandparents,** abuelos, *m pl.* **great-grandparents,** bisabuelos, *m pl.* **great-great-grandparents,** tatarabuelos, *m pl*
grandson /'græn,sʌn/ *n* nieto, *m.* **great-g.,** biznieto, *m.* **great-great-g.,** tataranieto, *m*
grange /greindʒ/ *n* granja, *f*; casa de campo, *f*
granite /'grænɪt/ *n* granito, *m*
granny /'græni/ *n* abuelita, nana, *f*; abuela, *f.* **g. knot,** nudo al revés, *m*
grant /grænt/ *n* concesión, *f*; otorgamiento, *m*; donación, *f*; privilegio, *m*; (for study) beca, bolsa de estudio, *f*; (transfer) traspaso, *m.* cesión, *f. vt* conceder; (bestow) otorgar, dar; donar; (agree to) acceder a, asentir en; permitir; (transfer) traspasar; (assume) suponer. **to g. a degree,** expedir un título. **to g. a motion,** dar por entrada a una moción. **to take for granted,** descontar, dar por hecho, dar por sentado. **God g. it!** ¡Dios lo quiera! **granted that,** dado que
grantee /græn'ti/ *n* cesionario (-ia), adjudicatorio (-ia)
grantor /'græntər/ *n* cesionista, *mf*; otorgador (-ra)
granulated /'grænyə,leitid/ *a* granulado
granule /'grænyul/ *n* gránulo, *m*
granulous /'grænyələs/ *a* granuloso
grape /greip/ *n* uva, *f.* **bunch of grapes,** racimo de uvas, *m.* **muscatel g.,** uva moscatel, *f.* **sour grapes,** uvas agrias, *f pl*; (phrase) ¡están verdes! **g.-fruit,** toronja, *f.* **g. gatherer,** vendimiador (-ra). **g. harvest,** vendimia, *f.* **g. juice,** mosto, *m.* **g.-shot,** metralla, *f.* **g. stone,** granuja, *f.* **g.-sugar,** glucosa, *f.* **g.-vine,** vid, parra, *f*
graph /græf/ *n* gráfica, *f*; diagrama, *m*
graphic /'græfɪk/ *a* gráfico

graphite /'græfait/ *n* grafito, *m*
graphology /græ'fɒlədʒi/ *n* grafología, *f*
grapple /'græpəl/ *n Naut.* rezón, arpeo, *m*; lucha a brazo partido, *f. vt Naut.* aferrar; asir, agarrar. *vi Naut.* aferrarse. **to g. with,** luchar a brazo partido (con); *Fig.* luchar con
grappling /'græplɪŋ/ *n Naut.* aferramiento, *m*; lucha cuerpo a cuerpo, *f*; (with a problem) lucha con, *f*
grasp /græsp/ *n* agarro, *m*; (reach) alcance, *m*; (of a hand) apretón, *m*; (power) garras, *f pl*, poder, *m*; (understanding) comprensión, *f*; inteligencia, capacidad intelectual, *f. vt* agarrar, asir; empuñar; abrazar; *Fig.* comprender, alcanzar; (a hand) estrechar. *vi* agarrarse. **within one's g.,** al alcance de uno. **to g. at,** asirse de
grasping /'græspɪŋ/ *n* asimiento, *m*; (understanding) comprensión, *f, a* codicioso, tacaño, mezquino
graspingness /'græspɪŋnɪs/ *n* codicia, *f*
grass /græs/ *n* hierba, *f*; (pasture) pasto, herbaje, *m*; (sward) césped, *m. vt* cubrir de hierba; sembrar de hierba; apacentar. **to hear the g. grow,** sentir crecer la hierba. **to let the g. grow,** *Fig.* dejar crecer la hierba. **to turn out to g.,** echar al pasto. **g.-blade,** brizna de hierba, *f.* **g.-green,** *a* and *n* verde como la hierba *m..* **g.-grown,** cubierto de hierba. **g.-land,** pradera, *f.* **g.-snake,** culebra *f.* **g. widow,** mujer cuyo marido está ausente
grasshopper /'græs,hɒpər/ *n* saltamontes, *m.* **grasshopper's chirp,** chirrido (del saltamontes), *m*
grassy /'græsi/ *a* parecido a la hierba, como la hierba; cubierto de hierba; de hierba
grate /greit/ *n* parrilla, *f*; (grating) reja, *f. vt* raspar, raer; *Cul.* rallar; (make a noise) hacer rechinar. *vi* rozar; rechinar, chirriar. **to g. on, upon,** (of sounds) irritar, molestar; chocar con. **to g. on the ear,** herir el oído
grateful /'greitfəl/ *a* agradecido, reconocido; (pleasant) agradable, grato
gratefully /'greitfəli/ *adv* agradecidamente; gratamente
gratefulness /'greitfəlnɪs/ *n* agradecimiento, *m*, gratitud, *f*; (pleasantness) agrado, *m*
grater /'greitər/ *n Cul.* rallador, *m*
gratification /,grætəfɪ'keiʃən/ *n* satisfacción, *f*; (pleasure) placer, gusto, *m*
gratified /'grætə,faid/ *a* satisfecho, contento
gratify /'grætə,fai/ *vt* satisfacer; (please) gratificar, agradar
gratifying /'grætə,faiɪŋ/ *a* satisfactorio, agradable
grating /'greitɪŋ/ *n* reja, *f*; rejilla, *f*; *Naut.* jareta, *f*; (optics) retículo, *m*; (sound) rechinamiento, chirrido, *m. a* rechinante, chirriador; áspero
gratis /'grætɪs/ *a* and *adv* gratis
gratitude /'græti,tud/ *n* agradecimiento, *m*, gratitud, *f*
gratuitous /grə'tuitəs/ *a* gratuito
gratuitousness /grə'tuitəsnɪs/ *n* gratuidad, *f*
gratuity /grə'tuiti/ *n* gratificación, propina, *f*
grave /greiv/ *n* (hole) sepultura, fosa, *f*; (monument) tumba, *f*, sepulcro, *m*; *Fig.* muerte, *f.* **g.-digger,** enterrador, sepulturero, *m*
grave /greiv/ *a* grave; importante; serio; sobrio; (anxious) preocupado; (of accent) grave. *n* (grave accent) acento grave, *m*
gravel /'grævəl/ *n* grava, *f*; cascajo, casquijo, *m*; *Med.* arenillas, *f pl*, cálculo, *m*
gravely /'greivli/ *adv* gravemente; seriamente
Graves' disease /greivz/ *n* bocio exoftálmico, *m*
gravestone /'greiv,stoun/ *n* lápida mortuoria, *f*
graveyard /'greiv,yɑrd/ *n* camposanto, cementerio, *m*
gravitate /'grævi,teit/ *vi* gravitar; tender
gravitation /,grævi'teiʃən/ *n* gravitación, *f*; tendencia, *f*
gravitational /,grævi'teiʃənḷ/ *a* de gravitación, gravitacional, gravitatorio
gravitational pull *n* atracción gravitatoria, *f*
gravity /'græviti/ *n Phys.* gravedad, *f*; seriedad, *f*; solemnidad, *f*; gravedad, *f*; (weight) peso, *m*; importancia, *f*; (enormity) enormidad, *f*; (danger) peligro, *m.* **center of g.,** centro de gravedad, *m.* **law of g.,** ley de la gravedad, *f.* **specific g.,** peso específico, *m*

gravy /'greivi/ *n* salsa, *f*; jugo (de la carne), *m.* **g.-boat,** salsera, *f*
gray /grei/ *a* gris; (of animals) rucio. *n* color gris, gris, *m*; caballo gris, *m.* **g. hairs,** canas, *f.* **His hair is turning g.,** Se le está saliendo canas. **g.-haired,** de pelo gris. **g. matter,** materia gris, *f*; cacumen, *m.* **g. mullet,** *Ichth.* mújol, *m.* **g. squirrel,** gris, *m.* **g. wolf,** lobo gris, *m*
grayish /'greiɪʃ/ *a* grisáceo, agrisado; (of hair) entrecano
grayness /'greinɪs/ *n* color gris, gris, *m*; *Fig.* monotonía, *f*
graze /greiz/ *n* abrasión, *f*; (brush) roce, *m*, *vi* pacer, apacentarse. *vt* pastorear, apacentar; (brush) rozar
grazing /'greizɪŋ/ *n Agr.* apacentamiento, pastoreo, *m*; (brushing) rozadura, *f. a* que pace, herbívoro; (of land) pacedero. **g. land,** pasto, *m*
grease /gris/ *n* grasa, *f*; (dirt) mugre, *f*; (of a candle) sebo, *m*, cera, *f. vt* engrasar; manchar con grasa; *Fig. Inf.* untar. **to g. the wheels,** *Fig.* untar el carro. **g.-box,** *Mech.* caja de sebo, *f.* **g.-gun,** engrasador de compresión, *m.* **g.-paint,** afeites de actor (or de actriz), *m pl.* **g.-proof paper,** papel impermeable, *m.* **g. spot,** lámpara, mancha de grasa, *f*, saín, *m*
greaser /'grisər/ *n* engrasador, *m*
greasiness /'grisinɪs/ *n* graseza, *f*; lo aceitoso; untuosidad, *f*
greasing /'grisɪŋ/ *n* engrasado, *m*
greasy /'grisi/ *a* grasiento; (oily) aceitoso; (grubby) mugriento, bisunto, *Argentina* cascarriento, *f. Fig.* lisonjero. **g. pole,** cucaña, *f*
great /greit/ *a* gran; grande; enorme; vasto; (much) mucho; (famous) famoso, ilustre; noble, sublime; (intimate) íntimo; importante; principal; poderoso; magnífico, impresionante; *Inf.* famoso, estupendo; (of time) largo; (clever) fuerte. **Alexander the G.,** Alejandro Magno. **the G. Mogul,** el Gran Mogul. **a g. deal,** mucho. **a g. man,** un grande hombre, un hombre famoso. **a g. many,** muchos (muchas). **He lived to a g. age,** Vivió hasta una edad avanzada. **so g.,** tan grande, tamaño. **the g.,** los grandes hombres. **g. on,** aficionado a. **g.-aunt,** tía abuela, *f.* **g.-grandchild,** etc. See **grandchild,** etc. **g.-hearted,** valeroso; magnánimo, generoso. **g. power,** gran poder, *m.* **G. Britain,** Gran Bretána, *f.* **G. War,** Gran Guerra, *f.* **the Great Schism,** el Gran Cisma, *m*
greater /'greitər/ *a* comp. of **great,** mayor; más grande. **to make g.,** agrandar
greatest /'greitɪst/ *a* sup. of **great,** más grande; mayor; máximo; más famoso; sumo
greatly /'greitli/ *adv* mucho; con mucho; (very) muy; noblemente
greatness /'greitnɪs/ *n* grandeza, *f*; grandiosidad, *f*; extensión, vastedad, *f*; importancia, *f*; poder, *m*; majestad, *f*; esplendor, *m*; (intensity) intensidad, *f*; (enormity) enormidad, *f*
Greco- *prefix* (in compounds) greco-, greco
Greece /gris/ *n* Grecia, *f*
greed /grid/ *n* (cupidity) codicia, rapacidad, avaricia, *f*; avidez, ansia, *f*; (of food) gula, glotonería, *f*
greedily /'gridali/ *adv* codiciosamente; con avidez; (of eating) vorazmente
greedy /'gridi/ *a* (for food) glotón; codicioso; ambicioso; ávido; deseoso
Greek /grik/ *a* and *n* griego (-ga); (language) griego, *m.* **It's all G. to me,** Para mí es como si fuese en latín, Me es chino. **G. tunic,** peplo, *m*
green /grin/ *a* verde; (inexpert) inexperto, bisoño; (recent) nuevo, reciente; (fresh) fresco; (of complexion) pálido, descolorido; (flowery) floreciente; (vigorous) lozano; (young) joven; (unripe) verde; (credulous) crédulo; (raw) crudo; (of wood, vegetables) verde. *n* verde, color verde, *m*; (vegetables) verdura, *f*; (meadow) prado, *m*; (turf) césped, *m*; (grass) hierba, *f*; (bowling) campo de juego, *m. vt* teñir de verde; pintar) de verde. **bright g.,** verdegay, verde claro, *m.* **dark g.,** *n* verdinegro, *m.* **light g.,** *n* verde pálido, *m.* **to grow** or **look g.,** verdear. **g.-eyed,** de ojos verdes. **g. peas,** guisantes, *m pl.* **g. table,** tapete verde, *m*
greenery /'grinəri/ *n* follaje, *m*; verdura, *f*

greengrocery /'grin,grousəri/ n verdulería, f
greenhorn /'grin,hɔrn/ n bisoño (-ña); papanatas, m
greenhouse /'grin,haus/ n invernáculo, invernadero, Lat. Am. conservatorio m
greenish /'griniʃ/ a verdoso. **g.-yellow,** cetrino
Greenland /'grinlənd/ Groenlandia, f
Greenlander /'grinləndər/ n groenlandés (-esa)
greenness /'grinnis/ a lo verde; verdor, m, verdura, f; (inexperience) falta de experiencia, f; (vigor) vigor, m, lozanía, f; (newness) novedad, f; (of wood, fruit) falta de madurez, f
greenroom /'grin,rum/ n Theat. saloncillo, m
greenstuff /'grin,stʌf/ n hortalizas, legumbres, f pl
greet /grit/ vt saludar; recibir; (express pleasure) dar la bienvenida (a)
greeting /'gritiŋ/ n salutación, f, saludo, m; recepción, f; (welcome) bienvenida, f; pl **greetings,** recuerdos, m pl
gregarious /grɪ'gɛəriəs/ a gregario
gregariousness /grɪ'gɛəriəsnɪs/ n gregarismo, m
Gregorian /grɪ'gɔriən/ a gregoriano
grenade /grɪ'neid/ n granada, bomba, f. **hand-g.,** bomba de mano, f
grey /grei/ See **gray**
greyhound /'grei,haund/ n galgo, lebrel, m. **g. bitch,** galga, f; **g. racing,** carreras de galgos, f pl
grid /grid/ n (of electric power) red, f; rejilla, f; (for water, etc.) alcantarilla, f
gridiron /'grid,aiərn/ n Cul. parrilla, f; (of electric power) red, f; Theat. telar, m
grief /grif/ n angustia, pena, aflicción, f; dolor, suplicio, m. **to come to g.,** pasarlo mal, tener un desastre
grievance /'grivəns/ n injusticia, f; motivo de queja, m
grieve /griv/ vt entristecer, afligir, angustiar; atormentar. vi entristecerse, afligirse, acongojarse. **to g. for,** lamentar; echar de menos
grievous /'grivəs/ a (heavy) oneroso, gravoso; opresivo; doloroso, penoso; lamentable; cruel. **g. error,** error lamentable
grievousness /'grivəsnɪs/ n (weight) peso, m; carácter opresivo, m; dolor, m, aflicción, f; enormidad, f; crueldad, f
griffin /'grifin/ n grifo, m; (Fig. chaperon) carabina, f; (dog) grifón, m
grill /gril/ n Cul. parrilla, f; (grating) rejilla, f; (before a window) reja, f; (food) asado a la parrilla, m. vt Cul. asar a la parrilla; (burn) quemar; (question) interrogar; (torture) torturar. vi Cul. asarse a la parrilla; (be burnt) quemarse. **g.-room,** parrilla, f
grille /gril/ n reja, f; rejilla, f; (screen) verja, f
grilled /grild/ a Cul. a la parrilla; con rejilla
griller /'grilər/ n Cul. parrilla, f
grim /grim/ a (fierce) feroz, salvaje; (severe) severo, ceñudo, adusto; inflexible; (frightful) horrible
grimace /'griməs/ n mueca, f, gesto, mohín, visaje, m, vi hacer muecas
grime /graim/ n mugre, f; suciedad, f. **to cover with g.,** enmugrecer
grimly /'grimli/ adv severamente; sin sonreír; inflexiblemente; (without retreating) sin cejar; (frightfully) horriblemente; de un modo espantoso
grimness /'grimnɪs/ n (ferocity) ferocidad, f; (severity) severidad, f; inflexibilidad, f; (frightfulness) horror, m, lo espantoso
grimy /'graimi/ a mugriento, sucio
grin /grin/ n sonrisa grande, f; sonrisa burlona, f; (grimace) mueca, f. vi sonreír mostrando los dientes; sonreír bonachonamente; sonreír de un modo burlón
grind /graind/ vt (to powder) pulverizar; moler; (break up) quebrantar; (oppress) agobiar, oprimir; (sharpen) afilar, amolar; (a barrel-organ) tocar (un manubrio); (the teeth) crujir, rechinar (los dientes); (into) reducir a; (Inf. teach) empollar. vi moler; Inf. trabajar laboriosamente. n Inf. trabajo pesado, m; Inf. estudiantón, m
grinder /'graindər/ n (of scissors, etc.) afilador, m; (of an organ) organillero; (mill-stone) piedra de moler, f; (molar) muela, f
grinding /'graindiŋ/ a (tedious) cansado, aburrido; opresivo; (of pain) incesante. n pulverización, f;

amoladura, f; (of grain) molienda, f; (polishing) pulimento, bruñido, m; (oppression) opresión, f; (of teeth) rechinamiento, m
grindstone /'graind,stoun/ n amoladera, afiladera, piedra de amolar, f. **to have one's nose to the g.,** batir el yunque
grinning /'griniŋ/ a sonriente; riente; (mocking) burlón
grip /grip/ n asimiento, agarro, m; (claws, clutches) garras, f pl; (hand) mano, f; (of shaking hands) apretón de manos, m; (of a weapon, etc.) empuñadura, f; (reach) alcance, m; (understanding) comprensión, f; (control) dominio, m; (bag) portamanteo, m; maleta, f. vt asir, agarrar; (of wheels) agarrarse; Mech. morder; (a sword, etc.) empuñar; (pinch) pellizcar; (surround) cercar; (understand) comprender; (press; to grip the hand and Fig. the heart) apretar; (fill) llenar; (the attention) atraer, llamar; (sway, hold) dominar
gripe /graip/ n (Inf. pain) retortijón (de tripas), m. vi quejarse (de)
grisly /'grizli/ a espantoso; repugnante
grist /grist/ n molienda, f. **Everything is g. to their mill,** Sacan partido de todo
gristle /'grisəl/ n cartílago, m, ternilla, f
gristly /'grisli/ a cartilaginoso
grit /grit/ n cascajo, m; polvo, m; Fig. firmeza (de carácter), f; (courage) valor, m; (endurance) aguante, m
gritty /'griti/ a arenoso, arenisco
grizzled /'grizəld/ a (of hair, etc.) gris; canoso; grisáceo
grizzly bear /'grizli/ n oso (-sa) pardo (-da)
groan /groun/ n gemido, m. vi gemir; (creak) crujir. **to g. out,** decir (or contar) entre gemidos. **to g. under,** sufrir bajo, gemir bajo; (of weight) crujir bajo
groaning /'grouniŋ/ n gemidos, m pl. a que gime, gemidor; (under a weight) crujiente
grocer /'grousər/ n abacero (-ra) vendedor (-ra) de comestibles, Lat. Am. abarrotero (-ra). **grocer's shop,** tienda de comestibles, bodega, f, Mexico abarrotería, f
grocery /'grousəri/ n tienda de comestibles, tienda de ultramarinos, abarrotería, lonja, bodega, f, negocio de comestibles, m; pl **groceries,** provisiones, f pl, comestibles, m pl, Lat. Am. abarrotes mpl
groin /grɔin/ n Anat. ingle, f
groom /grum/ n (in a royal household) gentilhombre, m; lacayo, m; mozo de caballos, m; (of a bride) novio, m. vt (a horse) cuidar; (oneself) arreglarse. **She is always well groomed,** Está siempre muy bien arreglada
groomsman /'grumzmən/ n padrino de boda, m
groove /gruv/ n ranura, muesca, f; estría, f; surco, m; Fig. rutina, f. vt entallar; estriar
grooved /gruvd/ a con ranura; estriado
grope /group/ vi andar a tientas; (with for) buscar a tientas; procurar, encontrar, buscar. **to g. one's way toward,** avanzar a tientas hacia; Fig. avanzar poco a poco hacia
gropingly /'groupiŋli/ adv a tientas; irresolutamente
gross /grous/ n Com. gruesa, f; totalidad, f, a grueso; denso, espeso; (unrefined) grosero; (great) grande; (crass) craso; total; Com. bruto; (tremendous) enorme. **in g.,** en grueso. **g. amount,** total, m; Com. importe bruto, m. **g. weight,** peso bruto, m
grossly /'grousli/ adv groseramente; (much) enormemente
grossness /'grousnɪs/ n gordura, f; (vulgarity) grosería, f; obscenidad, f; (enormity) enormidad, f
grotesque /grou'tɛsk/ a grotesco; extravagante, estrambótico; ridículo. n grotesco, m
grotesqueness /grou'tɛsknɪs/ n lo grotesco; ridiculez, f
grotto /'grotou/ n gruta, f
ground /graund/ n suelo, m; (of water and Naut.) fondo, m; (earth) tierra, f; Fig. terreno, m; (strata) capa, f; Sports. campo, m; (parade) plaza (de armas), f; (background) fondo, m; (basis) base, f, fundamento, m; (reason) causa, f; motivo, m; (excuse) pretexto, m; pl **grounds,** jardines, m pl, parque, m; (sediment) sedimento, m, heces, f pl; (reason) causa, f. vi Naut. varar, encallar. vt poner en tierra; Naut.

hacer varar; *Elec.* conectar con tierra; (base) fundar (en), basar (en); (teach) enseñar los rudimentos (de). **a** molido; en polvo; (of floors, stories) bajo; (of glass) deslustrado; *Bot.* terrestre. **common g.,** tierra comunal, *f*; *Fig.* tierra común, *f*. **He is on his own g.,** Está en terreno propio. **It fell to the g.,** Cayó al suelo; *Fig.* Fracasó. **It is on the g.,** Está en el suelo. **It suits me to the g.,** Me viene de perilla. **to break fresh g.,** *Fig.* tratar problemas nuevos. **to be well grounded in,** conocer bien los elementos (or rudimentos) de. **to cover g.,** cubrir terreno; recorrer; (in discussion) tocar muchos puntos. **to cut the g. from beneath one's feet,** hacer perder la iniciativa (a). **to give g.,** retroceder; perder terreno. **to raze to the g.,** echar por tierra, arrasar. **to stand one's g.,** resistir el ataque; no darse por vencido; *Fig.* mantenerse firme, mantenerse en sus trece. **to win g.,** ganar terreno. **g. coffee,** café molido, *m*. **g.-color,** (of paint) primera capa, *f*; (color de) fondo, *m*; **g.-floor,** piso bajo, *m*. **g. glass,** vidrio deslustrado, *m*. **g.-ivy,** hiedra terrestre, *f*. **g. nut,** cacahuete, *m*. **g.-plan,** *Archit.* planta, *f*. **g.-rent,** censo, *m*. **g.-sheet,** tela impermeable, *f*; **g. staff,** *Aer.* personal del aeropuerto, *m*. **g.-swell,** mar de fondo, *m*

grounded /'ɡraundɪd/ *a* fundado. **The airplanes are g.,** Los aviones están sin volar. **His suspicions are well g.,** Tiene motivos para sus sospechas

grounding /'ɡraundɪŋ/ *n* *Naut.* encalladura, *f*; (teaching) instrucción en los rudimentos, *f*

groundless /'ɡraundlɪs/ *a* sin fundamento, inmotivado, sin causa, sin motivo

groundwork /'ɡraund,wɜrk/ *n* fundamento, *m*; base, *f*; principio, *m*

group /ɡrup/ *n* grupo, *m*. *vt* agrupar. *vi* agruparse. **g. captain,** coronel de aviación, *m*

grouping /'ɡrupɪŋ/ *n* agrupación, *f*

grouse /ɡraus/ *n* *Ornith.* ortega, *f*. *vi* rezongar, refunfuñar

grove /ɡrouv/ *n* soto, boscaje, *m*; arboleda, *f*

grovel /'ɡrɒvəl/ *vi* arrastrarse; *Fig.* humillarse

groveling /'ɡrɒvəlɪŋ/ *a* *Fig.* servil; ruin

grow /ɡrou/ *vi* crecer; (increase) aumentar; (become) hacerse; empezar a; llegar a; (turn) volverse, ponerse; (flourish) progresar, adelantar; (develop) desarrollarse; (extend) extenderse. *vt* cultivar; dejar crecer. **I grew to fear it,** Llegué a temerlo. **to g. cold,** ponerse frío; enfriarse; (of weather) empezar a hacer frío. **to g. fat,** engordar. **to g. hard,** ponerse duro; *Fig.* endurecerse. **to g. hot,** ponerse caliente; calentarse; (of weather) empezar a hacer calor. **to g. like Topsy,** crecer a la buena de Dios. **to g. old,** envejecer. **to g. tall,** crecer mucho; ser alto. **to g. again,** crecer de nuevo. **to g. into,** hacerse, llegar a ser; venir a ser. **to g. out of,** brotar de; originarse en; (a habit) desacostumbrarse poco a poco. **He is growing out of his clothes,** La ropa se le hace pequeña. **to g. up,** (of persons) hacerse hombre (mujer); desarrollarse; (of a custom, etc.) imponerse. **to g. on, upon,** crecer sobre; llegar a dominar; (make think) hacer creer, empezar a pensar; (of a habit) arraigar en

grower /'ɡrouər/ *n* cultivador (-ra)

growing /'ɡrouɪŋ/ *n* crecimiento, *m*; desarrollo, *m*; (increase) aumento, *m*; (of flowers, etc.) cultivación, *f*, *a* creciente

growing pains /peinz/ *n pl* crisis de desarrollo, *f*

growl /ɡraul/ *n* gruñido, *m*; reverberación, *f*; trueno, *m*. *vi* gruñir; (of guns) tronar; (of thunder) reverberar. **to g. out,** decir gruñendo

grown /ɡroun/ *a* crecido; maduro; adulto. **a g. up,** una persona mayor. **to be full-g.,** estar completamente desarrollado; haber llegado a la madurez. **g. over with,** cubierto de

growth /ɡrouθ/ *n* crecimiento, *m*; (development) desarrollo, *m*; (progress) progreso, adelanto, *m*; (increase) aumento, *m*; (cultivation) cultivo, *m*; (vegetation) vegetación, *f*; *Med.* tumor, *m*. **He has a week's g. on his chin,** Tiene una barba de una semana

grub /ɡrʌb/ *n* larva, *f*, gusano, *m*; *Inf.* *Argentina* (food) morfe, papeo, *m*. *vt* (with up, out) desarraigar; cavar; desmalezar; *Fig.* *Inf.* buscar

grubbiness /'ɡrʌbinɪs/ *n* suciedad, *f*; (untidiness) desaliño, *m*

grubby /'ɡrʌbi/ *a* lleno de gusanos; sucio; bisunto; desaliñado

grudge /ɡrʌdʒ/ *n* motivo de rencor, *m*; rencor, resentimiento, *m*, ojeriza, *f*; mala voluntad, *f*; aversión, *f*. *vt* envidiar. **to bear a g.,** tener ojeriza

grudging /'ɡrʌdʒɪŋ/ *a* (niggardly) mezquino; envidioso; poco generoso; de mala gana; nada afable

grudgingly /'ɡrʌdʒɪŋli/ *adv* de mala gana, contra su voluntad; con rencor; a regañadientes

gruel /'ɡruəl/ *n* gachas, *f pl*

gruesome /'ɡrusəm/ *a* pavoroso, horrible; macabro

gruff /ɡrʌf/ *a* (of the voice) bronco, grave, áspero; (of manner) brusco, malhumorado

gruffly /'ɡrʌfli/ *adv* en una voz bronca (or áspera); bruscamente, con impaciencia, malhumoradamente

gruffness /'ɡrʌfnɪs/ *n* aspereza, bronquedad, *f*; brusquedad, sequedad, impaciencia, *f*, mal humor, *m*

grumble /'ɡrʌmbəl/ *n* ruido sordo, trueno, *m*; estruendo, *m*; (complaint) refunfuño, rezongo, *m*. *vi* tronar; refunfuñar, rezongar; hablar entre dientes; quejarse; protestar (contra). *vt* decir refunfuñando

grumbler /'ɡrʌmblər/ *n* murmurador (-ra), refunfuñador (-ra)

grumbling /'ɡrʌmblɪŋ/ *a* gruñón, refunfuñador; regañón; descontento. *n* See **grumble**

grumblingly /'ɡrʌmblɪŋli/ *adv* a regañadientes, refunfuñando

grumpiness /'ɡrʌmpinɪs/ *n* mal humor, *m*, irritabilidad, *f*

grumpy /'ɡrʌmpi/ *a* malhumorado, irritable

grunt /ɡrʌnt/ *n* gruñido, *m*. *vi* gruñir

grunting /'ɡrʌntɪŋ/ *a* gruñidor

guarantee /ˌɡærənˈti/ *n* *Law.* persona de quien otra sale fiadora, *f*; garantía, *f*; abono, *m*. *vt* garantizar; responder de; abonar; (assure) asegurar, acreditar

guarantor /'ɡærən,tɔr/ *n* garante, *mf*

guard /ɡard/ *n* (watchfulness) vigilancia, *f*; (in fencing) guardia, *f*; (of a sword) guarnición, *f*; (sentry) centinela, *m*; (soldier) guardia, *m*; (body of soldiers) guardia, *f*; (escort) escolta, *f*; (keeper) guardián, *m*; (protection) protección, defensa, *f*; (of a train) jefe de tren, *m*. *vt* guardar; proteger, defender; vigilar; (escort) escoltar. **to g. against,** guardarse de. **the changing of the g.,** el relevo de la guardia. **to be on g.,** *Mil.* estar de guardia; (in fencing) estar en guardia. **to be on one's g.,** estar prevenido, estar alerta. **to be off one's g.,** estar desprevenido. **to mount g.,** *Mil.* montar la guardia; vigilar. **guard's van,** furgón de equipajes, *m*. **g.-house,** cuerpo de guardia, *m*; prisión militar, *f*

guarded /'ɡardɪd/ *a* (reticent) reservado, circunspecto, prudente, discreto

guardedly /'ɡardɪdli/ *adv* prudentemente, con circunspección, discretamente

guardian /'ɡardiən/ *n* protector (-ra); guardián (-ana); *Law.* tutor, *m*. *a* que guarda; tutelar. **g. angel,** ángel de la guarda, ángel custodio, *m*; deidad tutelar, *f*

guardianship /'ɡardiən,ʃɪp/ *n* protección, *f*; patronato, *m*; *Law.* curaduría, tutela, *f*

guardsman /'ɡardzmən/ *n* guardia, *m*

Guatemalan /ˌɡwɑtəˈmɑlən/ *a* and *n* guatemalteco (-ca)

guava /'ɡwɑvə/ *n* *Bot.* guayaba, *f*

guerrilla /ɡəˈrɪlə/ *n* guerrilla, *f*; (soldier) guerrillero, *m*. *a* de guerrilla. **g. warfare,** guerra de guerrillas, *f*

guess /ɡɛs/ *n* adivinación, *f*; estimación, *f*; conjetura, *f*; sospecha, *f*. *vt* and *vi* adivinar; conjeturar; sospechar; imaginar; (suppose) suponer, creer; calcular. **to g. at,** formar una opinión sobre; imaginar. **a rough g.,** estimación aproximada, *f*. **at a g.,** a poco más o menos, a ojo de buen cubero. **g.-work,** conjeturas, suposiciones, *f pl*

guest /ɡɛst/ *n* (at a meal) convidado (-da), invitado (-da); (at a hotel, etc.) cliente (-da); *Lat. Am.* (house guest) alojado (-da); *Biol.* parásito, *m*. **g.-room,** alcoba de respeto, alcoba de honor, alcoba de huéspedes, *f*, cuarto de amigos, cuarto para invitados, *m*

guffaw /gʌ'fɔ/ n carcajada, f. vi reírse a carcajadas, soltar el trapo

Guiana /gɪ'ænə/ Guayana, f

guidance /'gaidn̩s/ n dirección, f; gobierno, m; (advice) consejos, m pl; inspiración, f

guide /gaid/ n (person) guía, mf; (girl g.) exploradora, f; (book and Fig.) guía, f; mentor, m; modelo, m; (inspiration) norte, m; Mech. guía, f. vt guiar; conducir; encaminar; dirigir; (govern) gobernar. **g.-book,** guía (de turistas), f. **g.-post,** poste indicador, m

guided tour /'gaidɪd/ n visita explicada, visita programada, f

guideline /'gaid,lain/ Lit. falsarregla, falsilla, f; Fig. pauta, f

guiding /'gaidɪŋ/ a que guía; directivo; decisivo. n See **guidance**

guild /gɪld/ n gremio, m. a gremial. **g. member,** gremial, m

guilder /'gɪldər/ n (coin) florín holandés, m

guile /gail/ n astucia, superchería, maña, f

guileful /'gailfəl/ a astuto

guileless /'gaillɪs/ a cándido, sin malicia, inocente

guilelessly /'gaillɪsli/ adv inocentemente

guilelessness /'gaillɪsnɪs/ n inocencia, candidez, f

guillotine /'gɪlə,tin/ n guillotina, f. vt guillotinar

guilt /gɪlt/ n culpabilidad, f; crimen, m; (sin) pecado, m

guilt complex complejo de culpa, m

guiltily /'gɪltəli/ adv culpablemente; como si fuese culpable

guiltless /'gɪltlɪs/ a libre de culpa, inocente; puro; ignorante

guilty /'gɪlti/ a culpable; delincuente; criminal. **to find g.,** encontrar culpable. **to plead g.,** confesarse culpable. **g. party,** culpable, m

Guinea /'gɪni/ Guinea, f

guinea /'gɪni/ n guinea, f. **g.-fowl,** gallina de Guinea, f. **g.-pig,** conejillo de Indias, cobayo, m

guise /gaiz/ n manera, guisa, f; (garb) traje, m; máscara, f; Fig. pretexto, m. **under the g. of,** bajo el pretexto de; bajo la apariencia de

guitar /gɪ'tɑr/ n guitarra, f

guitarist /gɪ'tɑrɪst/ n guitarrista, mf

gulf /gʌlf/ n golfo, m, abismo, m

Gulf Stream, the la Corriente del Golfo

gull /gʌl/ n Ornith. gaviota, f; (dupe) primo, m. vt engañar, timar, defraudar

gullet /'gʌlɪt/ n esófago, m; garganta, f

gullibility /,gʌlə'bɪlɪti/ n credulidad, f

gullible /'gʌləbəl/ a crédulo

gully /'gʌli/ n hondonada, barranca, f; (gutter) arroyo, m

gulp /gʌlp/ n trago, sorbo, m. vt engullir, tragar; (repress) ahogar; (believe) tragar. **to g. up,** vomitar

gum /gʌm/ n (of the mouth) encía, f; goma, f. vt engomar; pegar con goma. **gum arabic,** goma arábiga, f. **gum boots,** botas de goma, f. **gum-resin,** gomorresina, f. **gum starch,** aderezo, m. **gum tree,** eucalipto, m

gummy /'gʌmi/ a gomoso

gumption /'gʌmpʃən/ n sentido común, seso, m

gun /gʌn/ n arma de fuego, f; (handgun) fusil, m; (sporting g.) escopeta, f; (pistol) pistola, f, revólver, m; (cannon) cañón, m; (firing) cañonazo, m. **big gun,** Inf. pájaro gordo, m. **heavy gun,** cañón de grueso calibre, m. **gun-barrel,** cañón de escopeta, m. **gun-carriage,** cureña, f. **gun-cotton,** pólvora de algodón, f. **gun-fire,** cañonazos, m pl, fuego, m. **gunmetal,** bronce de cañón, m; pavón, m. **gun-room,** ar-

mería, f; (on a ship) polvorín, m. **gun-running,** contrabanda de armas, f. **gun-turret,** torre, f. **gun wound,** balazo, m

gunboat /'gʌn,bout/ n cañonero, m, lancha bombardera, f

gunflint /'gʌn,flɪnt/ n piedra de escopeta, f

gunman /'gʌnmən/ n escopetero, armero, m; bandido armado, m; gángster, apache, m

gunner /'gʌnər/ n artillero, m; escopetero, m

gun permit n licencia de armas, f, permiso de armas, m

gunpowder /'gʌn,paudər/ n pólvora, f

gunshot /'gʌn,ʃɒt/ n escopetazo, m; tiro de fusil, m

gunsmith /'gʌn,smɪθ/ n escopetero, armero, m

gunwale /'gʌnl/ n Naut. regala, borda, f

gurgle /'gɜrgəl/ n murmullo, murmurio, gorgoteo, m; gluglú, m; (of a baby) gorjeo, m. vi murmurar; hacer gluglú; (of babies) gorjear

gurgling /'gɜrglɪŋ/ a murmurante; (of babies) gorjeador. n See **gurgle**

gush /gʌʃ/ n chorro, m; (of words) torrente, m; (of emotion) efusión, f. vi chorrear, borbotar; surtir, surgir. **to g. out,** saltar, brotar a borbotones, salir a borbollones, salira borbotones. **to g. over,** Fig. hablar con efusión de

gushing /'gʌʃɪŋ/ a hirviente; (of people) efusivo, extremoso, empalagoso

gusset /gʌsɪt/ n Sew. escudete, m

gust /gʌst/ n (of wind) ráfaga, bocanada (de aire), f; Fig. arrebato, acceso, m

gusto /'gʌstou/ n brío, m; entusiasmo, m

gusty /'gʌsti/ a borrascoso

gut /gʌt/ n intestino, m, tripa, f; (catgut) cuerda de tripa, f; Naut. estrecho, m; pl **guts,** tripas, f pl; (content) meollo, m, substancia, f; (stamina) aguante, espíritu, m. vt (of fish, etc.) destripar; (plunder) saquear; destruir por completo; quemar completamente

gutter /'gʌtər/ n canal, m; (of a street) arroyo (de la calle), m; (ditch) zanja, f; Fig. hampa, f. vt surcar. vi gotear; (of a candle) cerotear, gotear la cera. **g. spout,** canalón, m

guttersnipe /'gʌtər,snaip/ n golfillo, m, niño (-ña) del hampa

guttural /'gʌtərəl/ a gutural. n letra gutural, f

guy /gai/ n (rope) viento, m; Naut. guía, f; (effigy) mamarracho, m; (scarecrow) espantajo, m; Inf. (fellow) tipo, Mexico chavo. vt sujetar con vientos o guías; burlarse de

guzzle /'gʌzəl/ vt tragar, engullir. vi atracarse, engullir; emborracharse. n comilón, m; borrachera, f

guzzler /'gʌzlər/ n tragador (-ra); borracho (-cha)

gymnasium /dʒɪm'nɑziəm/ n gimnasio, m

gymnast /'dʒɪmnæst/ n gimnasta, mf

gymnastic /dʒɪm'næstɪk/ a gimnástico. **g. rings,** anillas, f pl

gymnastics /dʒɪm'næstɪks/ n gimnasia, f

gynecological /,gainɪkə'lɒdʒɪkəl/ a ginecológico

gynecologist /,gainɪ'kɒlədʒɪst/ n ginecólogo (-ga)

gynecology /,gainɪ'kɒlədʒi/ n ginecología, f

gypsum /'dʒɪpsəm/ n yeso, m

gypsy /'dʒɪpsi/ n gitano (-na). a gitano, gitanesco; (music) flamenco

gyrate /'dʒaireit/ vi girar, rodar

gyration /dʒai'reiʃən/ n giro, m, vuelta, f

gyratory /'dʒairə,tɔri/ a giratorio

gyro-compass /'dʒairou ,kʌmpəs/ n brújula giroscópica, f

gyroscope /'dʒairə,skoup/ n Phys. giroscopio, m

H

h /eitʃ/ n (letter) hache, f
ha /hɑ/ interj ¡ah!
ha, ha! /hɑ/ interj ¡ja, ja!
haberdasher /'hæbər,dæʃər/ n mercero, m
haberdashery /'hæbər,dæʃəri/ n mercería, f
habiliment /hə'bɪləmənt/ n vestidura, f; pl **habiliments**, indumentaria, f
habilitate /hə'bɪlɪˌteit/ vt habilitar
habilitation /hə,bɪlɪ'teiʃən/ n habilitación, f
habit /'hæbɪt/ n costumbre, f, hábito, m; (temperament) temperamento, carácter, m; (use) uso, m; (of body) complexión, constitución, f; Eccl. hábito, m. **to be in the h. of,** soler, acostumbrar, estar acostumbrado a. **to have bad habits,** estar malacostumbrado. **to have the bad h. of,** tener el vicio (or la mala costumbre) de. **to contract the h. of,** contraer la costumbre de. **h. maker,** sastre de trajes de montar, m
habitable /'hæbɪtəbəl/ a habitable, vividero
habitat /'hæbɪˌtæt/ n (Bot., Zool.) medio, m, habitación, f
habitation /ˌhæbɪ'teiʃən/ n habitación, f
habit-forming /'hæbɪt,fɔrmɪŋ/ a enviciador, que crea vicio
habitual /hə'bɪtʃuəl/ a habitual, acostumbrado, usual; constante; común
habitually /hə'bɪtʃuəli/ adv habitualmente; constantemente; comúnmente
habituate /hə'bɪtʃuˌeit/ vt habituar, acostumbrar
habituation /hə,bɪtʃu'eiʃən/ n habituación, f
habitué /hə'bɪtʃuˌei/ n parroquiano (-na); veterano (-na)
hack /hæk/ n caballo de alquiler, m; rocín, jaco, m; (writer) escritor mercenario, m. vt acuchillar; tajar, cortar. vi cortar. **to h. to pieces,** cortar en pedazos; pasar a cuchillo
hacker /'hækər/ n (computer) violador de seguridades, m
hacking /'hækɪŋ/ a (of coughs) seco
hackle /'hækəl/ n (for flax, hemp) rastrillo, m
hackney carriage /'hækni/ n coche de plaza, coche de alquiler, m
hackneyed /'hæknid/ a gastado, trillado, muy usado, repetido, resobado
hacksaw /'hæk,sɔ/ n sierra de cerrajero, sierra para metal, f
hackwork /'hæk,wɜrk/ n trabajo de rutina, m
haddock /'hædək/ n merlango, m, pescadilla, f
Hades /'heidiz/ n Hades, m; Inf. el infierno, m
haft /hæft/ n mango, tomadero, m, manija, f; puño, m
hag /hæg, hɑg/ n bruja, f
haggard /'hægərd/ a ojeroso, trasnochado, trasojado
haggardly /'hægərdli/ adv ansiosamente
haggardness /'hægərdnɪs/ n aspecto ojeroso, m
haggle /'hægəl/ vi regatear; vacilar
haggling /'hæglɪŋ/ n regateo, m, a regatón
hagiographer /ˌhægi'ɒgrəfər/ n hagiógrafo, m
hagiography /ˌhægi'ɒgrəfi/ n hagiografía, f
hail /heil/ n (salutation) saludo, m; (shout) grito, m; aclamación, f; (frozen rain) granizo, m; (of blows) lluvia, f. interj ¡salve! vt saludar; llamar; aclamar; Fig. lanzar, echar. vi (hailstones) granizar; (blows, etc.) llover. **to h. from,** proceder de, ser natural de. **within h.,** al habla. **H. Mary,** Salve Regina, Avemaría, f
hailstone /'heil,stoun/ n granizo, pedrisco, m
hailstorm /'heil,stɔrm/ n granizada, f
hair /hɛər/ n (single h.) cabello, m; (Zool., Bot.) pelo, m; (of horse's mane) crin, f; (head of h.) cabellera, m; mata de pelo, f, pelo, m; (superfluous) vello, m; (fiber) fibra, f, filamento, m; (on the pen) raspa, f, pelo, m; Fig. pelo, m. **lock of h.,** bucle, rizo, m; mecha, f. **to dress one's h.,** peinarse. **to have one's h. cut,** hacerse cortar el pelo. **to part the h.,** hacer(se) la raya del pelo. **to put up one's h.,** hacerse el moño; (to "come out") ponerse de largo. **to tear one's h.,** mesarse los cabellos.

h. combings, peinaduras, f pl. **h.-curler,** tirabuzón, m. **h. dryer,** secadora de cabello, f. **h. dye,** tinte para el pelo, m. **h.-net,** redecilla, f, Mexico invisible m. **h.-oil,** brillantina, f. **h.-raising,** horripilante, espeluznante. **h.-ribbon,** cinta para el pelo, f. **h.-shirt,** cilicio, m. **h. slide,** pasador, m. **h.-splitting,** sofistería, argucia, f; mez quinas argucias, quis quillas, f pl. **h.-spring,** muelle del volante, m. **h.-switch,** añadido, m. **h.-trigger,** pelo de una pistola, m
hairband /'hɛər,bænd/ m Lat. Am. bincha, f
hairbrush /'hɛər,brʌʃ/ n cepillo para el cabello, m
hairdresser /'hɛər,drɛsər/ n peluquero (-ra), peinadora, f
hairdressing /'hɛər,drɛsɪŋ/ n peinado, m. **h. establishment** or **trade,** peluquería, f
haired /hɛərd/ a peludo, con pelo; (in compounds) de pelo...
hairless /'hɛərlɪs/ a sin pelo; calvo
hairlike /'hɛər,laik/ a filiforme
hairpin /'hɛər,pɪn/ n horquilla, f, Argentina invisible m. **h. bend,** viraje en horquilla, m
hairsbreadth /'hɛərz,brɛdθ/ n pelo, m. **to have a h. escape,** escapar por un pelo.
hairsplitting arguments /'hɛər,splitɪŋ/ 'ɑrgyəmənts/ Lat. Am. abogaderas, abogaderías pl
hairy /'hɛəri/ a peludo; velloso; Bot. hirsuto
Haiti /'heiti/ Haití, m
Haitian /'heiʃən/ a and n haitiano (-na)
hake /heik/ n merluza, f
halcyon /'hælsiən/ n alción, martín pescador, m. a Fig. feliz, sereno, tranquilo
hale /heil/ a fuerte, sano, robusto. vt hacer comparecer
half /hæf/ n mitad, f; (school term) trimestre, semestre, m. a medio; semi. adv a medias; mitad; (almost) casi; insuficientemente; imperfectamente. **It is h.-past two,** Son las dos y media. **an hour and a h.,** una hora y media. **better h.,** Inf. media naranja, cara mitad, f. **by halves,** a medias. **in h.,** en dos mitades. **one h.,** la mitad. **to go halves,** ir a medias. **to h. close,** entreabrir. **to h. open,** entreabrir. **h. a bottle,** media botella, f. **h. a crown,** media corona, f. **h.-alive,** semivivo. **h. an hour,** media hora, f. **h.-and-h.,** mitad y mitad; en partes iguales. **h.-asleep,** semidormido, medio dormido. **h.-awake,** medio despierto, entre duerme y vela. **h.-back,** Sports. medio, m. **h.-baked,** medio cocido, crudo; Fig. poco maduro. **h.-binding,** encuadernación en media pasta, f. **h.-breed,** a mestizo. n cruce, m. **h.-brother,** hermanastro, hermano de padre, hermano de madre, m. **h. circle,** semicírculo, m. **h.-closed,** entreabierto; medio cerrado. **h.-dead,** medio muerto; más muerto que vivo. **h.-done,** hecho a medias, sin acabar. **h.-dozen,** media docena, f. **h.-dressed,** medio desnudo. **h. fare,** medio billete, m. **h.-full,** medio lleno. **h.-hearted,** débil, poco eficaz, lánguido; indiferente, sin entusiasmo. **h.-heartedness,** debilidad, f; indiferencia, f. **h.-hourly,** cada media hora, f. **h.-length,** (portrait) de medio cuerpo. **h.-length coat,** abrigo de tres cuartos, m. **h.-light,** media luz, f. **h.-mast,** a media asta. **h.-measure,** medida poco eficaz, f. **h.-moon,** a media luna, f; Astron. semilunio, m; (of a nail) blanco (de la uña), m. **h.-mourning,** medio luto, m. **h.-pay,** media paga, f. **h.-price,** a mitad de precio. **h.-seas-over,** Inf. entre dos velas. **h.-sister,** hermanastra, hermana de padre, hermana de madre, f. **h.-time,** Sports. media parte, f, medio tiempo, m. **h.-tone,** de medio tono. **h.-truth,** verdad a medias, f. **h.-turn,** media vuelta, f. **h.-way,** a medio camino; medio. **h.-witted,** medio loco, tonto, imbécil, m. **h.-year,** medio año, m. **h.-yearly,** semestral
half close vt entrecerrar
half title anteportada, falsa portada, portadilla, preportada, f
halibut /'hæləbət/ n halibut, m; (genus) hipogloso, m
halitosis /ˌhæli'tousɪs/ n halitosis, f

hall /hɔl/ *n* (mansion) mansión, casa de campo, *f*, caserón, *m*; (public building) edificio, *m*, casa (de); (town h.) casa del ayuntamiento, *f*; (room) sala, *f*; (entrance) vestíbulo, *m*; (dining room) comedor, *m*; (of residence for students) residencia, *f*. **h. door,** portón, *m*, puerta del vestíbulo, *f*. **h. porter,** conserje, *m*. **h.-stand,** perchero, *m*

hallelujah /ˌhælə'luyə/ *n* aleluya, *f*

hallmark /'hɔl,mɑrk/ *n* marca de ley, *f*; *Fig.* señal, *f*; indicio, *m*. *vt* poner la marca de ley sobre; *Fig.* sellar

halloo /hə'lu/ *vt* (hounds) azuzar; perseguir dando voces; (call) llamar

hallow /'hælou/ *vt* santificar; reverenciar; (consecrate) consagrar

Halloween /ˌhælə'win/ *n* la víspera de Todos los Santos, *f*

hallucination /hə,lusə'neiʃən/ *n* alucinación, ilusión, *f*; visión, *f*; fantasma, *m*

hallucinatory /hə'lusənə,tɔri/ *a* alucinador

halo /'heilou/ *n* halo, nimbo, *m*

halogen /'hælədʒən/ *n Chem.* halógeno, *m*

halt /hɔlt/ *n Mil.* alto, *m*; cesación, *f*; interrupción, *f*; (on a railway) apeadero, *m*; (for trams, buses) parada, *f*. *vt* parar, detener. *vi* pararse, detenerse; *Mil.* hacer alto; cesar; interrumpirse; (in speech) titubear; (of verse) estar cojo; (doubt) dudar; (limp) cojear. **H.!** *Mil.* ¡Alto!

halter /'hɔltər/ *n* ronzal, cabestro, *m*; (for hanging) dogal, *m*. *vt* encabestrar, cabestrar

halting /'hɔltɪŋ/ *n* parada, *f*; interrupción, *f*. *a* (of gait) cojo; incierto; vacilante; (of speech) titubeante

halve /hæv/ *vt* partir (o dividir) en dos mitades

ham /hæm/ *n* jamón, *m*; *Anat.* pernil, *m*; (radio-operator) radioaficionado, *m*

hamburger /'hæm,bɜrgər/ *n* hamburguesa, *f*

hamlet /'hæmlɪt/ *n* aldea, *f*, pueblecito, *m*

hammer /'hæmər/ *n* martillo, *m*; (stone cutter's) maceta, *f*; (mason's) piqueta, *f*; (of fire-arms) percusor, *m*; (of piano) macillo, *m*. *vt* amartillar, martillar, batir. **to throw the h.,** lanzar el martillo. **under the h.,** en subasta, al remate. **h. blow,** martillazo, *m*

hammering /'hæmərɪŋ/ *n* martilleo, martillazo, *m*. **by h.,** a martillo

hammock /'hæmək/ *n* hamaca, *f*; *Naut.* coy, *m*

hamper /'hæmpər/ *n* banasta, canasta, *f*, cesto grande, *m*. *vt* estorbar, dificultar, impedir; *Fig.* embarazar

hamster /'hæmstər/ *n Zool.* hámster, *m*, marmota de Alemania, rata del trigo, *f*

hand /hænd/ *n* mano, *f*; (of animal) pata, mano, *f*; (worker) operario (-ia); obrero (-ra); (skill) habilidad, *f*; (side) mano, *f*, lado, *m*; (measure) palmo, *m*; (of a clock) manecilla, *f*; (of instruments) aguja, *f*; (applause) aplauso, *m*; (power) poder, *m*; las manos; (at cards) mano, *f*; (card player) jugador, *m*; (signature) firma, *f*; (handwriting) letra, escritura, *f*; (influence) influencia, parte, mano, *f*. **old h.,** veterano; perro viejo. **at h.,** a mano, al lado, cerca. **have at hand,** tener a la mano. **at the hands of,** de manos de. **by h.,** a mano; (on the bottle) con biberón. **from h. to h.,** de mano a mano. **in h.,** entre manos; (of money) de contado. **in the hands of,** *Fig.* en el poder de. **"Hands wanted,"** «Se desean trabajadores.» **h. over h.,** mano sobre mano. **hand's breadth,** palmo, *m*. **Hands off!** ¡Fuera las manos! **Hands up!** ¡Manos arriba! **lost with all hands,** (of a ship) perdido con toda su tripulación. **off one's hands,** despachado; (of a daughter) casada. **on all hands,** por todas partes. **on h.,** entre manos; (of goods) existente; (present) presente. **on one's hands,** a cargo de uno. **on the one h.,** por un lado; a un lado. **on the other h.,** por otra parte; en cambio. **out of h.,** luego, inmediatamente; revoltoso. **to get one's h. in,** ejercitarse. **to have a h. in,** tener parte en; intervenir en. **to have no h. in,** no tener arte ni parte en. **to have on h.,** traer entre manos. **to have the upper h.,** tener la sartén por el mango, llevar la ventaja. **to hold one's h.,** abstenerse; detenerse. **to hold hands,** cogerse de las manos. **to lay hands on,** tocar; poner mano en; echar manos a. **to set one's h. to,** emprender; (sign) firmar. **to shake hands,** estrechar la mano. **to stretch out one's hands,** tender las manos. **to take one's hands off,** no tocar. **with folded hands,** mano sobre mano. **with his hands behind his back,** con las manos en la espalda. **h.-in-h.,** cogidos (cogidas) de las manos. **h.-lever,** manija, *f*. **h.-loom,** telar de mano, *m*. **h. luggage,** equipaje de mano, *m*. **h.-made,** hecho a mano. **h.-mill,** molinillo, *m*. **h.-pump,** *n Naut.* sacabuche, *m*. **h. rail,** pasamano, *m*, baranda, balustrada, *f*. **h.-sewn,** cosido a mano. **h.-to-h.,** de mano en mano; (of a fight) a brazo partido, cuerpo a cuerpo. **h.-to-h. fight,** cachetina, *f*. **h.-to-mouth,** precario. **to live from h.-to-mouth,** vivir de día en día

hand /hænd/ *vt* dar; entregar; alargar. **to h. down,** bajar; (a person) ayudar a bajar; transmitir. **to h. in,** entregar; (a person) ayudar a entrar; (one's resignation) dimitir; (send) mandar, enviar. **to h. on,** transmitir. **to h. out,** *vt* distribuir; (a person) ayudar a salir; (from a vehicle) ayudar a bajar. *vi Inf.* pagar. **to h. over,** *vt* traspasar. *vi Mil.* traspasar los poderes (a). **to h. around,** pasar de mano en mano; pasar; ofrecer. **to h. up,** subir; (a person) ayudar a subir

handbag /'hænd,bæg/ *n* bolso, saco, monedero, *m*, cartera, *Mexico* bolsa, *f*

handbill /'hænd,bɪl/ *n* anuncio, *m*

handbook /'hænd,bʊk/ *n* manual, compendio, tratado, *m*; anuario, *m*; (guide) guía, *f*

handcart /'hænd,kɑrt/ *n* carretilla de mano, *f*, carretón, *m*

handcuff /'hænd,kʌf/ *n* esposa, *f*, grillo, *m*, (gen. *pl*). *vt* poner las esposas (a), maniatar

handed /'hændɪd/ *a* (in compounds) que tiene manos; de manos...; con manos... **four-h.,** *Sports.* de cuatro personas. **one-h.,** manco

handful /'hændfʊl/ *n* puño, puñado, manojo, *m*. **to be a h.,** *Inf.* tener el diablo en el cuerpo. **in handfuls,** a manojos

handgrip /'hænd,grɪp/ *n* apretón de manos, *m*

handicap /'hændi,kæp/ *n* desventaja, *f*; obstáculo, *m*; *Sports.* handicap, *m*; ventaja, *f*. *vt Fig.* perjudicar, impedir, dificultar. **the handicapped,** los lisiados, *m pl*

handicraft /'hændi,kræft/ *n* mano de obra, *f*; (skill) destreza manual, *f*

handiwork /'hændi,wɜrk/ *n* mano de obra, *f*; trabajo manual, *m*; obra, *f*; (deed) acción, *f*, hecho, *m*

handkerchief /'hæŋkərtʃɪf/ *n* pañuelo, *m*

handle /'hændl/ *n* mango, puño, *m*, *Lat. Am.* also manivela, *f*; (lever) palanca, *f*; (of baskets, dishes, jugs) asa, *f*; (of doors, windows, drawers) pomo, *m*, (of a car door) picaporte, *m*; (to one's name) designación, *f*; título, *m*; (excuse) pretexto, *m*. *vt* (touch) tocar; manejar, manipular; (treat) tratar; **h. with kid gloves,** tratar con guantes de seda; (deal in) comerciar en; tomar; (paw) manosear; (direct) dirigir; (control) gobernar; (pilot) pilotar; (a theme) explicar, tratar de. **h.-bar grip,** puño en un manillar, *m*

handlebars /'hændl,bɑrz/ *npl Spain* guia, *f sing*, manillar, *m sing*, *Lat. Am.* manubrio, *m sing*

handless /'hændlɪs/ *a* sin manos; manco; *Fig.* torpe

handling /'hændlɪŋ/ *n* manejo, *m*; manipulación, *f*; (treatment) trato, *m*, relaciones (con), *f pl*; (thumbing) manoseo, *m*; interpretación, *f*; *Art.* tratamiento, *m*, técnica, *f*

handmaid /'hænd,meid/ *n* sirvienta, criada, *f*; *Fig.* mayordomo, *m*

handsaw /'hænd,sɔ/ *n* sierra de mano, *f*, serrucho, *m*

handsbreadth /'hændz,bredθ/ *n* palmo, *m*

handshake /'hænd,ʃeik/ *n* apretón de manos, *m*

handsome /'hænsəm/ *a* (generous) generoso; magnánimo; considerable; hermoso, bello; elegante; (of people) guapo, distinguido; excelente; (flattering) halagüeño, *Lat. Am.* buen mozo. **He was a very h. man,** Era un hombre muy guapo

handsomely /'hænsəmli/ *adv* generosamente; con magnanimidad; elegantemente; bien

handsomeness /'hænsəmnɪs/ *n* generosidad, *f*; magnanimidad, *f*; hermosura, *f*; elegancia, *f*; distinción, *f*

handspring /'hænd,sprɪŋ/ *n* voltereta sobre las manos, *f*

handwork /'hænd,wɜrk/ *n* obra hecha a mano, *f*, trabajo a mano, *m*; (needlework) labor de aguja, *f*

handworked /'hænd,wɜrkt/ *a* hecho a mano; (embroidered) bordado

handwriting /'hænd,raitɪŋ/ *n* caligrafía, letra, escritura, *f*. **the h. on the wall,** la mano que escribía en la pared, *f*

handy /'hændi/ *a* (of persons) diestro, mañoso, hábil; (of things) conveniente; útil; (near) cercano, a mano. *adv* cerca. **h.-man,** hombre de muchos oficios, *m*; factótum, *m*

hang /hæŋ/ *vt* colgar; suspender; (execute) ahorcar; (the head) bajar; dejar caer; (upholster) entapizar; (with wallpaper) empapelar; (drape) poner colgaduras en; (place) poner; (cover) cubrir. *vi* colgar, pender; estar suspendido; (be executed) ser ahorcado; (of garments) caer. *n* (of garments) caída, *f*; (of a machine) mecanismo, *m*; (meaning) sentido, *m*, significación, *f*. **to h. by a thread,** pender de un hilo. **to h. in the balance,** estar en la balanza. **to h. fire,** estar (una cosa) en suspenso. **to h. loose,** caer suelto; (clothes) venir ancho. **to h. about,** (surround) rodear, pegarse a; (frequent) frecuentar; (haunt) rondar; (be imminent) ser inminente, amenazar; (embrace) abrazar. **to h. back,** retroceder; quedarse atrás; *Fig.* vacilar, titubear. **to h. down,** colgar, pender; estar caído; caerse. **to h. on,** seguir agarrado (a); apoyarse en; *Fig.* persistir; (a person's words) estar pendiente de, beber; (remain) quedarse. **to h. out,** *vt* tender. *vi* (lean out) asomarse (por); (*Inf.* live) habitar. **to h. over,** colgar por encima; (brood) cernerse sobre; (lean over) inclinarse sobre; quedarse cerca de; (overhang) sobresalir; (overarch) abovedar; (threaten) amenazar. **to h. together,** (of persons) permanecer unidos; (of things) tener cohesión; (be consistent) ser lógico, ser consistente. **to h. up,** colgar; suspender; *Fig.* dejar pendiente, interrumpir. **to h. upon,** apoyarse en; (a person's words) beber las palabras de uno

hangar /'hæŋər/ *n* cobertizo; *aer* hangar, *m*

hanger /'hæŋər/ *n* colgadero, *m*; percha *f*. **h.-on,** parásito, *m*; dependiente, *m*

hanging /'hæŋɪŋ/ *n* colgamiento, *m*; (killing) ahorcamiento, *m*; *pl* **hangings,** colgaduras, *f pl*, cortinajes, *m pl*. *a* pendiente colgante; péndulo; (of gardens) pensil. **It's not a h. matter,** No es una cuestión de vida y muerte. **h. bridge,** puente colgante, *m*. **h. committee,** junta (de una exposición,) *f*. **h. lamp,** lámpara de techo, *f*

hangman /'hæŋmən/ *n* verdugo, *m*

hangnail /'hæŋ,neil/ *n* padrastro, *m*

hangover /'hæŋ,ouvər/ *n* (after drinking) resaca, cruda (Mexico), *f*

hank /hæŋk/ *n* madeja, *f*

hanker /'hæŋkər/ *vi* (with after) ansiar, ambicionar; (with for) anhelar, suspirar por, desear con vehemencia

hankering /'hæŋkərɪŋ/ *n* ambición, *f*; deseo vehemente, *m*

hanky-panky /'hæŋki 'pæŋki/ *n* superchería, *f*; engaño, *m*

hap /hæp/ *n* casualidad, suerte, *f*; suceso fortuito, *m*

haphazard /*n* 'hæp,hæzərd; *a* hæp'hæzərd/ *n* casualidad, *f*. *a* fortuito, casual

hapless /'hæplɪs/ *a* desgraciado, desdichado

haplessness /'hæplɪsnɪs/ *n* desgracia, desdicha, *f*

happen /'hæpən/ *vi* suceder, acontecer, ocurrir, pasar; (to be found, be) hallarse por casualidad; (take place) tener lugar, verificarse; (arise) sobrevenir. **Do you know what has happened to...?** ¿Sabes qué se ha hecho de...? **as if nothing had happened,** como si no hubiese pasado nada. **He turned up as if nothing had happened,** Se presentó como si tal cosa. **How did it h.?** ¿Cómo fue esto? **If they h. to see you,** Si acaso te vean. **I happened to be in London,** Me hallaba por casualidad en Londres. **It won't h. again,** No volverá a suceder. **whatever happens,** venga lo que venga. *Inf.* **What's happening?** ¿Qué pasa?

happening /'hæpənɪŋ/ *n* suceso, acontecimiento, hecho, *m*, ocurrencia, *f*

happily /'hæpəli/ *adv* felizmente; por suerte

happiness /'hæpinɪs/ *n* felicidad, dicha, *f*; alegría, *f*, regocijo, *m*

happy /'hæpi/ *a* (lucky) afortunado; (felicitous) feliz, oportuno; feliz, dichoso; alegre, regocijado. **to be h.,** estar contento, ser feliz. **to be h. about,** alegrarse de. **to make h.,** hacer feliz, alegrar. **h.-go-lucky,** irresponsable, descuidado

harangue /hə'ræŋ/ *n* arenga, *f*. *vt* arengar. *vi* pronunciar una arenga

harass /hə'ræs/ *vt* hostigar, acosar; atormentar; preocupar; *Mil.* picar. **to h. the rear-guard,** picar la retaguardia

harbinger /'harbɪndʒər/ *n Fig.* precursor, heraldo, *m*; presagio, anuncio, *m*. *vt* anunciar, presagiar

harbor /'harbər/ *n* puerto, *m*; (bay) bahía, *f*; (haven) asilo, refugio, *m*. *vt* dar refugio (a), albergar, acoger; (cherish) abrigar, acariciar; (conceal) esconder. **inner h.,** puerto, *m*. **outer h.,** rada del puerto, *f*. **to put into h.,** entrar en el puerto. **h. bar,** barra del puerto, *f*. **h.-dues,** derechos de puerto, *m pl*. **h.-master,** capitán de puerto, contramaestre de puerto, *m*

harborer /'harbərər/ *n* amparador (-ra), protector (-ra); (criminal) encubridor (-ra)

hard /hard/ *a* duro; (firm) firme; difícil; laborioso, agotador; violento; poderoso; arduo; fuerte, recio; vigoroso, robusto; insensible, inflexible; cruel; (of weather) inclemente, severo; (unjust) injusto, opresivo; (stiff) tieso; (of water) cruda; (of wood) brava. *adv* duro; duramente; con ahínco; con fuerza; de firme; difícilmente; (of gazing) fijamente; severamente; (firmly) firmemente; vigorosamente; (of raining) a cántaros, mucho; (quickly) rápidamente; excesivamente; (much) mucho; (of bearing misfortune) a pechos; (attentively) atentamente; (heavily) pesadamente; (badly) mal; (closely) de cerca, inmediatamente. **It was a h. blow,** Fue un golpe recio. **to be h. put to,** encontrar difícil. **to go h.,** endurecerse. **to go h. with,** irle mal a uno. **to have a h. time,** pasar apuros, pasarlo mal. **to look h. at,** mirar atentamente, examinar detenidamente; mirar fijamente. **to be a h. drinker,** ser un bebedor empedernido. **h. and fast rule,** regla inalterable, *f*. **h.-bitten,** de carácter duro. **a h.-boiled egg,** un huevo duro. **h. breathing,** resuello, *m*. **h. cash,** efectivo, *m*. **h.-earned,** difícilmente conseguido; ganado con el sudor de la frente. **h.-featured,** de facciones duras. **h.-fisted,** tacaño. **h.-fought,** arduo, reñido. **h.-headed,** práctico, perspicaz. **h.-hearted,** duro de corazón, insensible. **h.-heartedness,** insensibilidad, *f*. **h. labor,** *Law.* trabajos forzados, *m pl*, presidio, *m*. **h.-mouthed,** (of horses) boquiduro. **h. of hearing,** duro de oído. **h.-up,** apurado. **to be very h.-up,** ser muy pobre; *Inf.* estar a la cuarta pregunta. **h.-wearing,** duradero; sufrido. **h.-won,** See **h.-earned.** **h.-working,** trabajador, hacendoso, diligente

harden /'hardṇ/ *vt* endurecer; (metal) templar; robustecer; (to war) aguerrir; (make callous) hacer insensible. *vi* endurecerse; hacerse duro; templarse, robustecerse; (of shares) entonarse

hardening /'hardṇɪŋ/ *n* endurecimiento, *m*; (of metal) temple, *m*. **h. of the arteries,** arteriosclerosis, *f*

hardiness /'hardinɪs/ *n* vigor, *m*, fuerza, robustez, *f*; audacia, *f*

hardly /'hardli/ *adv* duramente; difícilmente; (badly) mal; severamente; (scarcely) apenas, casi. **h. ever,** casi nunca

hardness /'hardnɪs/ *n* dureza, *f*; severidad, *f*; inhumanidad, insensibilidad, *f*; (stiffness) tiesura, *f*; (difficulty) dificultad, *f*; (of water) crudeza, *f*; (of hearing) dureza de oído, *f*

hardship /'hardʃɪp/ *n* penas, *f pl*, trabajos, *m pl*; infortunio, *m*, desdicha, *f*; (suffering) sufrimiento, *m*; (affliction) aflicción, *f*; (privation) privación, *f*. **to undergo h.,** pasar trabajos

hardware /'hard,wɛr/ *n* ferretería, *f*

hardwood /'hard,wʊd/ *n* madera brava, *f*

hardy /'hardi/ *a* audaz, intrépido; (strong) fuerte, robusto; *Bot.* resistente

hare /hɛər/ *n* liebre, *f*. **young h.,** lebrato, *m*. **h. and hounds,** rally paper, *m*, caza de papelitos, *f*. **h.-brained,** casquivano, atronado, con cabeza de chorlito. **hare's foot,** mano de gato, *f*. **h.-lip,** labio leporino, *m*. **h.-lipped,** labihendido

harebell /'hɛər,bɛl/ *n* campanilla, campánula, *f*

harem /'hɛərəm/ *n* harén, serrallo, *m*

haricot /'hærə,kou/ n (green bean) judia, f; (dried bean) alubia, f
hark /hɑrk/ vt escuchar; oír. **to h. back,** volver al punto de partida; volver a la misma canción
harlequin /'hɑrləkwɪn/ n arlequín, m
harlequinade /,hɑrləkwɪ'neid/ n arlequinada, f
harlot /'hɑrlət/ n ramera, prostituta, meretriz, f
harlotry /'hɑrlətri/ n prostitución, f
harm /hɑrm/ n mal, m; daño, m; perjuicio, m; (danger) peligro, m; (detriment) menoscabo, m; (misfortune) desgracia, f, vt hacer mal (a); dañar, hacer daño (a); perjudicar. **And there's no h. in that,** Y en eso no hay mal. **to keep out of harm's way,** evitar el peligro; guardarse del mal
harmful /'hɑrmfəl/ a malo; dañino, perjudicial, nocivo; (dangerous) peligroso. **to be h.,** (of food, etc.) hacer mal (a); (of pests) ser dañino; (of behavior, etc.) perjudicar
harmfulness /'hɑrmfəlnɪs/ n lo malo; perniciosidad, f; daño, m; peligro, m
harmless /'hɑrmlɪs/ a innocuo; inofensivo; inocente
harmlessness /'hɑrmlɪsnɪs/ n innocuidad, f; inocencia, f
harmonic /hɑr'mɒnɪk/ n (Phys. Math.) harmónica, f; Mus. armónico, m, a Mus. armónico
harmonica /hɑr'mɒnɪkə/ n armónica, f
harmonics /hɑr'mɒnɪks/ n armonía, f; (tones) armónicos, m pl
harmonious /hɑr'mouniəs/ a armonioso
harmoniously /hɑr'mouniəsli/ adv armoniosamente; Fig. en armonía
harmoniousness /hɑr'mouniəsnɪs/ n armonía, f
harmonium /hɑr'mouniəm/ n armonio, m
harmonization /,hɑrmənɪ'zeifən/ n armonización, f
harmonize /'hɑrmə,naiz/ vt armonizar. vi armonizarse, estar en armonía
harmony /'hɑrməni/ n armonía, f; Fig. paz, f, buenas relaciones, f pl; música, f. **to live in h.,** vivir en paz
harness /'hɑrnɪs/ n guarniciones, f pl, jaeces, m pl; (armor) arnés, m. vt enjaezar; (yoke) enganchar; (water) represar. **to die in h.,** Fig. morir en la brecha. **h. maker,** guarnicionero, m. **h. room,** guadarnés, m
harp /hɑrp/ n arpa, f. **to h. on,** volver a la misma canción, volver a repetir
harpist /'hɑrpɪst/ n arpista, mf
harpoon /hɑr'pun/ n arpón, m. vt arponear
harpooner /hɑr'punər/ n arponero, m
harpsichord /'hɑrpsɪ,kɔrd/ n arpicordio, m
harpy /'hɑrpi/ n arpía, f
harridan /'hærədn̩/ n bruja, f
harrow /'hærou/ n Agr. rastra, f, escarificador, m. vt Agr. escarificar; Fig. lastimar, atormentar
harrowing /'hærouɪŋ/ a patibulario, conmovedor, atormentador, angustioso
harry /'hæri/ vt devastar, asolar; (persons) robar; perseguir; (worry) atormentar; (annoy) molestar
harsh /hɑrʃ/ a áspero; (of voice) ronco; (of sound) discordante; (of colors) áspero; duro; chillón; severo; duro; (of features) duro; (of taste) ácido, acerbo
harshly /'hɑrʃli/ adv severamente
harshness /'hɑrʃnɪs/ n (roughness) aspereza, f; (of voice) ronquedad, aspereza, f; (of sound) disonancia, f; (of colors) aspereza, f; severidad, f; dureza, f; (of taste) acidez, f
harum-scarum /'hɛərəm 'skɛərəm/ n tronera, saltabarrancos, mf molino, m, a irresponsable
harvest /'hɑrvɪst/ n cosecha, siega, f; recolección, f; Fig. producto, fruto, m. vt cosechar; recoger. **h. festival,** fiesta de la cosecha, f
harvester /'hɑrvəstər/ n segador, m, cosechero (-ra), mf; (machine) segadora, f
hash /hæʃ/ n Cul. picado, m. vt Cul. picar
hashish /'hæʃɪʃ/ n hachich, hachís, quif, m
hasp /hæsp/ n pasador, m; sujetador, m
hassle /'hæsəl/ n Lat. Am. fregada, f
hassock /'hæsək/ n cojín, m
haste /heist/ n prisa, rapidez, f; precipitación, f; urgencia, f. vt dar prisa (a); acelerar; precipitar. vi darse prisa; acelerarse; precipitarse. **in h.,** de prisa,

aprisa. **to be in h.,** estar de prisa, llevar prisa. **in great h.,** muy aprisa, aprisa y corriendo, precipitadamente; con mucha prisa. **More h. less speed,** (Spanish equivalent. Words said by Charles III of Spain to his valet) ¡Vísteme despacio que voy de prisa!
hasten /'heisən/ vt acelerar, apresurar; precipitar. vi darse prisa, apresurarse; moverse con rapidez; correr. **to h. one's steps,** apretar el paso. **to h. away,** marcharse rápidamente. **to h. back,** regresar apresuradamente. **to h. down,** bajar rápidamente. **to h. on,** seguir el camino sin descansar; seguir rápidamente. **to h. out,** salir rápidamente. **to h. towards,** ir rápidamente hacia; correr hacia. **to h. up,** subir aprisa, correr hacia arriba; darse prisa
hastily /'heistli/ adv de prisa, rápidamente; con precipitación, precipitadamente; (angrily) impacientemente, airadamente; (thoughtlessly) sin reflexión
hastiness /'heistinɪs/ n rapidez, f; precipitación, f; (anger) impaciencia, irritación, f
hasty /'heisti/ a rápido, apresurado; precipitado; (superficial) superficial, ligero; (ill-considered) desconsiderado, imprudente; (angry) impaciente, irritable; violento, apasionado
hat /hæt/ n sombrero, m. **to pass round the h.,** pasar el platillo. **Andalusian h.,** sombrero calañés, m. **bowler h.,** sombrero hongo, m. **broad-brimmed h.,** sombrero chambergo, m. **Panama h.,** sombrero de jipijapa, m. **picture h.,** pamela, f. **shovel h.,** sombrero de teja, m. **soft felt h.,** sombrero flexible, m. **straw h.,** sombrero de paja, m. **three-cornered h.,** sombrero de tres picos, m. **top-h.,** sombrero de copa, m. **h. shop** or **trade,** sombrerería, f
hatband /'hæt,bænd/ n cinta de sombrero, f, cintillo, m
hatbox /'hæt,bɒks/ n sombrerera, f
hatbrush /'hæt,brʌʃ/ n cepillo para sombreros, m
hatch /hætʃ/ n (wicket) compuerta, f; (trap-door) puerta caediza, f; Naut. escotilla, f; compuerta de esclusa, f; (of chickens) pollada, f; (of birds) nidada, f. vt (birds) empollar; incubar, encobar; Fig. tramar, urdir. vi empollarse, salir del cascarón; incubarse; Fig. madurarse. **to h. a plot,** urdir un complot, conspirar. **to h. chickens,** sacar pollos
hatchet /'hætʃɪt/ n hacha pequeña, f, machado, m. **to bury the h.,** hacer la paz. **h.-faced,** de cara de cuchillo
hatching /'hætʃɪŋ/ n incubación, f; (of a plot) maquinación, f
hatchway /'hætʃ,wei/ n Naut. escotilla, f
hate /heit/ n odio, aborrecimiento, m, aversión, f; abominación, f. vt odiar, aborrecer, detestar; repugnar; saber mal, sentir. **I h. to trouble you,** Me sabe mal molestarle, Siento mucho molestarle. **to h. the sight of,** Inf. no poder ver (a)
hateful /'heitfəl/ a odioso, aborrecible; repugnante
hatefulness /'heitfəlnɪs/ n odiosidad, f, lo odioso; maldad, f
hater /'heitər/ n aborrecedor (-ra)
hatful /'hætfəl/ n un sombrero lleno (de)
hatless /'hætlɪs/ a sin sombrero, descubierto
hatpin /'hæt,pɪn/ n horquilla de sombrero, f
hatred /'heitrɪd/ n odio, aborrecimiento, m, detestación, f; aversión, enemistad, f
hatstand /'hæt,stænd/ n perchera, f
hatter /'hætər/ n sombrerero, m. **as mad as a h.,** loco como una cabra
haughtiness /'hɔtinɪs/ n altanería, arrogancia, altivez, soberbia, f, orgullo, m
haughty /'hɔti/ a altanero, arrogante, altivo, orgulloso, Lat. Am. copetudo, Mexico also alzado
haul /hɔl/ n (pull) tirón, m; (of fish) redada, f; (booty) botín, m. vt arrastrar, tirar de; Naut. halar. **to h. at, upon,** (ropes, etc.) aflojar, soltar, arriar. **to h. down,** (flags, sails) arriar
haulage /'hɔlɪdʒ/ n transporte, acarreo, m; coste de transporte, m. **h. contractor,** contratista de transporte, m
haunch /hɔntʃ/ n anca, culata, f; (of meat) pierna, f.
haunt /hɔnt/ n punto de reunión, lugar frecuentado (por), m; (lair) cubil, nido, m, guarida, f. vt frecuen-

tar; rondar; (of ideas) perseguir; (of ghosts) aparecer, visitar. **It is a h.** of thieves, Es una cueva de ladrones

haunted /'hɔntɪd/ a (by spirits) encantado

haunter /'hɔntər/ n frecuentador (-ra); (ghost) fantasma, espectro, m

haunting /'hɔntɪŋ/ n frecuentación, f; aparición de un espectro, f. a persistente

hautboy /'houbɔi, 'oubɔi/ n oboe, m

hauteur /hou'tər/ n altivez, f

Havana /hə'vænə/ la Habana, f. n (cigar) habano, m. (native) habanero (-ra), habano (-na)

have /hæv; unstressed həv, əv/ vt tener; poseer; (suffer) padecer; (spend) pasar; (eat or drink) tomar; (eat) comer; (a cigarette) fumar; (a bath, etc.) tomar; (a walk, a ride) dar; (cause to be done) mandar (hacer), hacer (hacer); (deceive) engañar; (defeat) vencer; (catch) coger; (say) decir; (allow) permitir; (tolerate) tolerar, sufrir; (obtain) lograr, conseguir; (wish) querer; (know) saber; (realize) realizar; (buy) comprar; (acquire) adquirir. As an auxiliary verb, haber (e.g. I h. done it, Lo he hecho, etc.). **As fate would h. it,** Según quiso la suerte. **Do you h. to go?** ¿Tiene Vd. que marcharse? **H. him come here,** Hazle venir aquí. **I h. been had,** Me han engañado. **I h. a good mind to...,** Tengo ganas de... **I had all my books stolen,** Me robaron todos los libros. **You had better go,** Es mejor que te vayas. **I had rather,** Preferiría, Me gustaría más bien. **I h. had a suit made,** Mandé hacerme un traje, Hice hacerme un traje. **I would not h. had it otherwise,** No lo hubiese querido de otra manera. **I will not h. it,** No lo quiero; No quiero tomarlo; (object) No lo permitiré. **If we had known,** Si lo hubiésemos sabido. **It has to do with the sun,** Está relacionado con el sol, Tiene que ver con el sol. **Have a good trip!** ¡Buen viaje!, ¡Feliz viaje! **What are you going to h.?** ¿Qué quiere Vd. tomar? **Will you h. some jam?** ¿Quiere Vd. mermelada? **to h. breakfast,** desayunar. **to h. dinner, supper,** cenar. **to h. lunch,** almorzar. **to h. for tea,** invitar a tomar el té; (of food) merendar. **to h. tea,** tomar el té. **to h. it out with,** habérselas con. **to h. just,** acabar de. **I h. just done it,** Acabo de hacerlo. **to h. on hand,** traer entre manos. **to h. one's eye on,** no perder de vista (a), vigilar. **to h. one's fist between one's legs,** ir rabo entre piernas. **to h. to,** tener que; deber. **It has to be so,** Tiene que ser así. **to h. too much of,** sobrar, tener demasiado de. **He has too much time,** Le sobra tiempo. **to h. about one,** tener (or llevar) consigo. **to h. back,** aceptar; recibir. **to h. down,** hacer bajar. **She had her hair down,** El pelo le caía por las espaldas. **to h. in,** hacer entrar. **to h. on,** vestir, llevar puesto; (engagements) tener (compromisos). **to h. out,** hacer salir; llevar a paseo; llevar fuera; (have removed) hacerse sacar; quitar. **to h. up,** (persons) hacer subir; (things) subir; Law. llevar a (ante) los tribunales. **to h. with one,** tener consigo. **I h. her with me,** La tengo conmigo, Ella me acompaña

haven /'heivən/ n puerto, m, abra, f; Fig. oasis, abrigo, refugio, m

haversack /'hævər,sæk/ n mochila, f, morral, m

havoc /'hævək/ n destrucción, ruina, f; Fig. estrago, m. **to wreak h. among,** destruir; Fig. hacer estragos entre (or en)

Hawaii /hə'waii/ Hawai, m

Hawaiian /hə'waiən/ a and n hawaiano; n (language) hawaiano, m

hawk /hɔk/ n halcón, m; gavilán, milano, m. vi cazar con halcón. vt vender mercancías por las calles; Fig. difundir. **h.-eyed**, de ojos de lince. **h.-nosed**, de nariz aguileña

hawker /'hɔkər/ n halconero, m; (vendor) buhonero, m, vendedor (-ra) ambulante

hawking /'hɔkɪŋ/ n caza con halcones, cetrería, f; (expectorating) gargajeo, m; (selling) buhonería, f

hawser /'hɔzər/ n maroma, f, calabrote, m

hawthorn /'hɔ,θɔrn/ n espino, m. **white h.,** espino blanco, m

hay /hei/ n, heno, m. **to make hay while the sun shines,** hacer su agosto. **hay fever,** fiebre del heno, f.

hay-fork, horca, f

hayloft /'hei,lɔft/ n henil, m

haymaker /'hei,meikər/ n segador (-ra); (machine) segadora, f

haymaking /'hei,meikɪŋ/ n recolección del heno, f

haystack /'hei,stæk/ n almiar, m, niara, f

hazard /'hæzərd/ n peligro, azar, m, suerte, f; riesgo, peligro, m; (game) juego de azar, m. vt arriesgar, aventurar. **at all hazards,** a todo riesgo

hazardous /'hæzərdəs/ a azaroso, arriesgado, peligroso

haze /heiz/ n bruma, f, confusión, f

hazel /'heizəl/ n avellano, m. **h.-nut,** avellana, f

hazy /'heizi/ a brumoso, calinoso; confuso

he /hi/ pers. pron él. n (of humans) varón, m; (of animals) macho, m. **he who,** el que, quien. **he-goat,** macho cabrío, m. **he-man,** todo un hombre, hombre cabal, m

head /hɛd/ vt golpear con la cabeza; encabezar; (lead) capitanear; (direct) dirigir, guiar; (wine) cabecear. vi irse a, estar a la cabeza de; dirigirse a. **headed for,** con rumbo a, en dirección a. **to h. off,** interceptar; desviar; Fig. distraer

head /hɛd/ n Anat. cabeza, f; (upper portion) parte superior, f; (of a coin) cara, f; (hair) cabellera, f; (individual) persona, f; (of cattle) res, f; (of a mountain) cumbre, f; (of a ladder) último peldaño, m; (of toadstools) sombrero, m; (of trees) copa, f; (of a stick) puño, m; (of a cylinder) culata, f; (of a river, etc.) manantial, origen, m; (of a bed) cabecera, f; (of nails, pins) cabeza, f; (froth) espuma, f; (flower) flor, f; (leaves) hojas, f pl; (first place) primer puesto, m; (of game, fish) pieza, f; (of a page, column) cabeza, f; (cape) cabo, m; (of an arrow, dart, lance) punta, f; (front) frente, m; (leader) jefe, cabeza, m; (chief) director (-ra), superior (-ra); presidente (-ta); (of a school) director (-ra); (of a cask) fondo, m; Mech. cabezal, m; (of an ax) filo, m; (of a bridge) cabeza, f; (of a jetty, pier) punta, f; (of a ship) proa, f; (of a flower) cabezuela, f; (of asparagus) punta, f; (of a table) cabeza, f; (of the family) jefe, cabeza, m; (seat of honor) cabecera, f; (title) título, m; (aspect) punto de vista, m; (division) capítulo, m; (management, direction) dirección, f; (talent) talento, m, cabeza, f; (intelligence) inteligencia, f. a principal; primero; en jefe. **at the h. of,** a la cabeza de. **crowned h.,** testa coronada, f. **from h. to foot,** de pies a cabeza; de hito en hito; de arriba abajo. **He took it into his h. to...,** Se le ocurrió de... **This story has neither h. nor tail,** Este cuento no tiene pies ni cabeza. **with h. held high,** con la frente levantada. **to come to a h.,** llegar a la crisis; llegar al punto decisivo. **to get an idea out of a person's h.,** quitar una idea a uno de la cabeza. **to keep one's h.,** conservar la sangre fría, no perder la cabeza. **to lose one's h.,** Fig. perder la cabeza. **to put into a person's h.,** Fig. meter (a uno) en la cabeza. **to run one's h. against,** golpear la cabeza contra. **h. first,** de cabeza. **h. of cattle,** res, f. **h. office,** central, f. **h. of hair,** cabellera, f; mata de pelo, f. **h.-on,** de cabeza. **h. opening,** (of a garment) cabezón, m. **heads or tails,** cara o cruz (Spain), águila o sol (Mexico), cruz o sello (Argentina, Chile). **h. over heels,** de patas arriba. **h. over heels in love,** calado hasta los huesos. **h.-dress,** tocado, m; peinado, m; sombrero, m. **h. voice,** voz de cabeza, f. **h. waiter,** encargado de comedor, jefe de camareros, m

headache /'hɛd,eik/ n dolor de cabeza, m; Fig. quebradero de cabeza, m

headboard /'hɛd,bɔrd/ n cabecera (de una cama), f

headed /'hɛdɪd/ a con cabeza...; que tiene la cabeza...; de cabeza...; (of an article) intitulado. **large h.,** cabezudo

header /'hɛdər/ n caída de cabeza, f; salto de cabeza, m

headgear /'hɛd,gɪər/ n tocado, m; sombrero, gorro, m

head-hunting /'hɛd,hʌntɪŋ/ n la caza de cabezas, f

heading /'hɛdɪŋ/ n Naut. el poner la proa en dirección (a); el guiar en dirección (a); (of a book, etc.) título, encabezamiento, m; (soccer) golpe de cabeza, m. **to come under the h. of,** estar incluido entre; clasificarse bajo

headland /'hɛdlənd/ n cabo, promontorio, m

headlight /'hɛd,lait/ *n* *Auto.* faro, *m*; (*Rail.*, *Naut.*) farol, *m*. **to dim the headlights,** bajar los faros. **to switch on the headlights,** encender los faros (or los faroles)

headline /'hɛd,lain/ *n* (of a newspaper) titular, *m*; (to a chapter) título de la columna, *m*

headlong /'hɛd,lɔŋ/ *a* precipitado; despeñado. *adv* de cabeza; precipitadamente. **to fall h.,** caer de cabeza

headman /'hɛd'mæn/ *n* cacique, cabecilla, *m*; (foreman) capataz, contramaestre, *m*

headmaster /'hɛd'mæstər/ *n* director de colegio, rector, *m*

headmistress /'hɛd'mɪstrɪs/ *n* directora de colegio, rectora, *f*

head nurse enfermero-jefe, *m*

head-on collision /'hɛd ,ɒn/ *n* choque frontal, *m*

headphones /'hɛd,foundz/ *n pl* auriculares, *m pl*

headquarters /'hɛd,kwɔrtərz/ *n* *Mil.* cuartel general, *m*; oficina central, *f*; jefatura, *f*; centro, *m*

headrest /'hɛd,rɛst/ *n* respaldo, *m*; apoyo para la cabeza, *m*

headstone /'hɛd,stoun/ *n* piedra mortuoria, *f*

headstrong /'hɛd,strɔŋ/ *a* impetuoso, terco, testarudo

headway /'hɛd,wei/ *n* marcha, *f*; *Fig.* progreso, avance, *m*. **to make h.,** avanzar; *Fig.* hacer progresos; *Fig.* prosperar

headwind /'hɛd,wɪnd/ *n* viento en contra, *m*

heady /'hɛdi/ *a* apasionado, violento; impetuoso, precipitado; (obstinate) terco; (of alcohol) encabezado; *Fig.* embriagador

heal /hil/ *vt* curar, sanar; (flesh) cicatrizar. *vi* curar, sanar; cicatrizarse; (superficially) sobresanar

healable /'hiləbəl/ *a* curable

healer /'hilər/ *n* sanador (-ra), curador (-ra); curandero, *m*

healing /'hiliŋ/ *a* curador, sanador; médico. *n* curación, *f*; cura, *f*, remedio, *m*

health /hɛlθ/ *n* salud, *f*; higiene, sanidad, *f*. **Here's to your very good h.!** ¡Salud y pesetas! **He is in good h.,** Disfruta de buena salud. **to drink a person's h.,** beber a la salud de. **to enjoy good h.,** gozar de buena salud. **to look full of h.,** vender salud. **h.-giving,** saludable. **h. inspection,** visita de sanidad, *f*. **h. officer,** inspector de sanidad, *m*. **h. resort,** balneario, *m*

healthiness /'hɛlθinɪs/ *n* buena salud, *f*; sanidad, salubridad, *f*

healthy /'hɛlθi/ *a* sano; con buena salud; (healthful) saludable. **to be h.,** tener buena salud

heap /hip/ *n* montón, *m*; rima, pila, *f*, acervo, *m*; (of people) muchedumbre, *f*, tropel, *m*. *vt* amontonar; apilar; colmar. **in heaps,** a montones. **We have heaps of time,** Nos sobra tiempo, Tenemos tiempo de sobra. **to h. together,** juntar, mezclar. **to h. up, upon,** colmar; amontonar; *Agr.* hacinar; *Fig.* acumular

hear /hɪər/ *vt* oír; (listen) escuchar; (attend) asistir a; (give audience) dar audiencia (a); (a lawsuit) ver (un pleito); (speak) hablar; (be aware of, feel) sentir. *vi* oír; tener noticias; (learn) enterarse de; (allow) permitir. **H.! H.!** ¡Muy bien! ¡Bravo! **I have heard it said that...** He oído decir que... **Let me h. from you!** ¡Mándame noticias tuyas! **They were never heard of again,** No se volvió a saber de ellos, No se supo más de ellos. **to h. about,** oír de; (know) saber de, tener noticias de; recibir información sobre. **to h. from,** ser informado por; tener noticias de: recibir carta de. **to h. of,** enterarse de, saber; recibir información sobre; (allow) permitir

hearer /'hɪərər/ *n* oyente, *mf*

hearing /'hɪərɪŋ/ *n* (sense of) oído, *m*; alcance del oído, *m*; presencia, *f*; audición, *f*; *Law.* vista (de una causa) *f*. **It was said in my h.,** Fue dicho en mi presencia. **out of h.,** fuera del alcance del oído. **within h.,** al alcance del oído. **have a h. problem,** ser parcialmente sordo

hearing aid acústica, aparato auditivo, aparato acústico, *m*

hearsay /'hɪər,sei/ *n* fama, *f*, rumor, *m*. **by h.,** de oídas

hearse /hɜrs/ *n* coche fúnebre, *m*

heart /hɑrt/ *n* corazón, *m*; (feelings) entrañas, *f pl*; (of the earth, etc.) seno, corazón, *m*; (of lettuce, etc.) cogollo, repollo, *m*; (suit in cards) copas, *f pl*; *Bot.* médula, *f*; (soul) alma, *f*; (courage) valor, *m*; ánimo, *m*. **at h.,** en el fondo, esencialmente. **by h.,** de memoria. **from the h.,** con toda sinceridad, de todo corazón. **He is a man after my own h.,** Es un hombre de los que me gustan. **I have no h. to do it,** No tengo valor de hacerlo. **in the h. of the country,** en medio del campo. **to break one's h.,** partirse el corazón. **to have one's h. in one's mouth,** tener el alma en un hilo, estar muerto de miedo. **to have no h.,** *Fig.* no tener entrañas. **to lose h.,** desanimarse, descorazonarse. **to set one's h. on,** poner el corazón en. **to take h.,** cobrar ánimo; *Inf.* hacer de tripas corazón. **to take to h.,** tomar a pechos. **to wear one's h. on one's sleeve,** tener el corazón en la mano. **with all my h.,** con toda el alma. **h.-ache,** angustia, pena, *f*; **h.-beat,** latido del corazón, *m*. **h.-breaker,** (woman) coqueta, *f*; (man) ladrón de corazones, *m*. **h. disease,** enfermedad del corazón, enfermedad cardíaca, *f*. **h. failure,** colapso cardíaco, *m*. **h.-rending,** desgarrador, angustioso. **h.-searching,** examen de conciencia, *m*. **h.-shaped,** acorazonado, en forma de corazón. **h.-strings,** fibras del corazón, *f pl*. **h.-to-h. talk,** conversación íntima, *f*

heartbreaking /'hɑrt,breikiŋ/ *a* desgarrador, angustioso, doloroso, lastimoso

heartbroken /'hɑrt,broukən/ *a* acongojado, afligido, transido de dolor

heartburn /'hɑrt,bɜrn/ *n* acidez del estómago, acedia, pirosis, rescoldera, *f*

heartburning /'hɑrt,bɜrniŋ/ *n* rencor, *m*, animosidad, envidia, *f*

hearted /'hɑrtɪd/ *a* de corazón... que tiene el corazón... **kind-h.,** de buen corazón, bondadoso

hearten /'hɑrtṇ/ *vt* alentar, animar

heartfelt /'hɑrt,fɛlt/ *a* hondo; de todo corazón, sincero; más expresivo

hearth /hɑrθ/ *n* hogar, *m*; chimenea, *f*; *Fig.* hogar, *m*

heartily /'hɑrtḷi/ *adv* cordialmente; sinceramente; enérgicamente; con entusiasmo; (of eating) con buen apetito; (very) muy, completamente. **I am h. sick of it all,** *Inf.* Estoy harto hasta los dientes

heartiness /'hɑrtinɪs/ *n* cordialidad, *f*; sinceridad, *f*; energía, *f*, vigor, *m*; vehemencia, *f*; entusiasmo, *m*; (of appetite) buen diente, buen apetito, *m*

heartless /'hɑrtlɪs/ *a* sin corazón, sin piedad, despiadado, inhumano, cruel

heartlessness /'hɑrtlɪsnɪs/ *n* falta de corazón, inhumanidad, crueldad, *f*

hearty /'hɑrti/ *a* cordial; sincero; enérgico; vigoroso; robusto; (frank) campechano; (of appetite) voraz; bueno; (big) grande

heat /hit/ *n* calor, *m*; (in animals) celo, *m*; (of an action) calor, *m*; *Fig.* vehemencia, fogosidad, *f*; *Fig.* fuego, *m*; (passion) ardor, *m*, pasión, *f*; (of a race) carrera eliminatoria, *f*. *vt* calentar; (excite) conmover, acalorar, excitar; (annoy) irritar. *vi* calentarse. **dead h.,** empate, *m*. **in h.,** en celo. **in the h. of the moment,** en el calor del momento. **to become heated,** *Fig.* acalorarse, exaltarse. **white h.,** candencia, incandescencia, *f*. **h. lightning,** fucilazo, *m*. **h. spot,** pápula, *f*; terminación sensible, *f*. **h. stroke,** insolación, *f*. **h. wave,** onda de calor, *f*

heated /'hitɪd/ *a* calentado; caliente; excitado; apasionado

heatedly /'hitɪdli/ *adv* con vehemencia, con pasión

heater /'hitər/ *n* calentador, *m*; calorífero, *m*; (stove) estufa, *f*; (for plates) calientaplatos, *m*. **water-h.,** calentador de agua, *m*

heath /hiθ/ *n* brezal, *m*; yermo, páramo, *m*; *Bot.* brezo, *m*

heathen /'hiðən/ *a* pagano (-na); idólatra, *mf*; ateo (-ea), descreído (-da). *a* pagano; ateo; bárbaro

heathenism /'hiðə,nɪzəm/ *n* paganismo, *m*; idolatría, *f*; ateísmo, *m*

heather /'hɛðər/ *n* brezo, *m*

heating /'hitiŋ/ *n* calefacción, *f*, *a* calentador; (of drinks) fortificante. **central h.,** calefacción central, *f*

heave /hiv/ *vt* alzar, levantar; *Naut.* izar; (the anchor, etc.) virar; (throw) arrojar, lanzar; elevar; (extract) extraer; (emit) dar, exhalar. *vi* subir y bajar; palpitar; agitarse. *n* tirón, *m*; (of the sea) vaivén, *m*. **to h. in sight,** aparecer, surgir. **to h. out sail,** *Naut.* desenvergar. **to h. the lead,** *Naut.* escandallar. **to h. to,** *Naut.* estarse a la capa

heaven /'hɛvən/ *n* cielo, *m*; firmamento, *m*; paraíso, *m*. **Heavens!** ¡Cielos! ¡Por Dios! **Thank H.!** ¡Gracias a Dios! **h.-born,** celeste. **h.-sent,** *Fig.* providencial

heavenliness /'hɛvənlinɪs/ *n* carácter celestial, *m*; delicia, *f*

heavenly /'hɛvənli/ *a* celeste, celestial; divino; *Fig.* delicioso. **h. body,** astro, *m*

heavily /'hɛvəli/ *adv* pesadamente; torpemente; penosamente; (slowly) lentamente; severamente; excesivamente; (of sighing) hondamente; (sadly) tristemente; (of rain, etc.) reciamente, fuertemente; (of wind) con violencia. **He fell h.,** Cayó de plomo. **to lie h. upon,** pesar mucho sobre. **to rain h.,** llover mucho, diluviar

heaviness /'hɛvɪnɪs/ *n* peso, *m*; (lethargy) torpor, letargo, *m*; sueño, *m*, languidez, *f*; (clumsiness) torpeza, *f*; (severity) severidad, *f*; importancia, responsabilidad, *f*; dificultad, *f*; (gravity) gravedad, *f*; tristeza, melancolía, *f*; (boredom) sosería, insulsez, *f*; (of style) monotonía, ponderosidad, *f*

heavy /'hɛvi/ *a* pesado; torpe; sin gracia; (slow) lento; (thick) grueso; (strong) fuerte; (hard) duro; grave; difícil; oneroso; responsable, importante; (oppressive) opresivo; penoso; grande; (sad) triste, melancólico; (of the sky) anublado; (of food) indigesto; (tedious) aburrido, soso; (pompous) pomposo; (of roads) malo; (of scents) fuerte, penetrante; (of sleep, weather) pesado; (weary) rendido; (charged with) cargado de; (of a meal) grande, abundante; (violent) violento; (of a cold, etc.) malo; (drowsy) soñoliento; (torpid) tórpido; (of rain, snow, hail) fuerte, recio; (of firing) intenso; (of sighs) profundo; (of soil) recio, de mucha miga; (*Phys. Chem.*) pesado. **How h. are you?** ¿Cuánto pesa Vd.? **h.-armed,** pesado; armado hasta los dientes. **h.-eyed,** con ojeras. **h. guns,** artillería pesada, *f*. **h.-handed,** de manos torpes; *Fig.* tiránico, opresivo. **h.-hearted,** triste, apesadumbrado. **h. industry,** la gran industria, la industria pesada, *f*. **h.-laden,** muy cargado. **h. losses,** *Mil.* pérdidas cuantiosas, *f pl*. **h.weight,** *Sports.* peso pesado, *m*

Hebraic /hɪ'breɪɪk/ *a* hebraico, hebreo, judaico

Hebraist /'hibreiɪst/ *n* hebraísta, *m*

Hebrew /'hibru/ *n* hebreo (-ea), judío (-ía): (language) hebreo, *m*

Hebrides, the /'hɛbrɪ,diz/ las Hébridas

heckle /'hɛkəl/ *vt* *Fig.* interrumpir, importunar con preguntas

heckler /'hɛklər/ *n* perturbador (-ra)

heckling /'hɛklɪŋ/ *n* interrupción, *f*

hectare /'hɛktɛər/ *n* hectárea, *f*

hectic /'hɛktɪk/ *a* (consumptive) hético; (feverish) febril; *Fig. Inf.* agitado

hector /'hɛktər/ *vt* intimidar, amenazar

hectoring /'hɛktərɪŋ/ *a* imperioso; amenazador

hectowatt /'hɛktə,wɑt/ *n* *Elec.* hectovatio, *m*

hedge /hɛdʒ/ *n* seto, *m*; barrera, *f*. *vt* cercar con un seto; rodear. *vi* *Fig.* titubear, vacilar. **h.-hopping,** *Aer.* vuelo a ras de tierra, *m*. **h.-sparrow,** acentor de bosque, *m*

hedgehog /'hɛdʒ,hɒg/ *n* erizo, *m*. **h. position,** *Mil.* puesto fuerte, *m*

hedonism /'hidn,ɪzəm/ *n* hedonismo, *m*

hedonist /'hidnɪst/ *n* hedonista, *mf*

heed /hid/ *n* atención, *f*, cuidado, *m*. *vt* atender; observar, considerar; escuchar. *vi* hacer caso

heedful /'hidfəl/ *a* atento; cuidadoso

heedless /'hidlɪs/ *a* desatento; descuidado, negligente; distraído

heedlessly /'hidlɪsli/ *adv* sin hacer caso; negligentemente; distraídamente

heedlessness /'hidlɪsnɪs/ *n* desatención, distracción, *f*; descuido, *m*; negligencia, *f*; inconsideración, *f*

heel /hil/ *n* *Anat.* talón, calcañar, *m*; (of shoe) tacón, *m*; (of a violin, etc., bow) talón, *m*; (remains) restos, *m pl*. *vt* poner tacón a; poner talón a; *Naut.* hacer zozobrar. *vi Naut.* zozobrar. **rubber h.,** tacón de goma, *m*. **She let him cool his heels for half an hour,** le dio un plantón de media hora. **to follow on a person's heels,** pisarle (a uno) los talones. **to be down at h.,** (of shoes) estar gastados los tacones; estar desaseado. **to take to one's heels,** apretar a correr, poner pies en polvorosa. **to turn on one's h.,** dar media vuelta. **h.-bone,** zancajo, *m*. **h.-piece,** talón, *m*

heeltap /'hil,tæp/ *n* tapa de tacón, *f*; escurridura, *f*

heft /hɛft/ *vt* sopesar, tomar al peso

hegemony /hɪ'dʒɛməni/ *n* hegemonía, *f*

heifer /'hɛfər/ *n* ternera, vaquilla, *f*

heigh /hei/ *interj* (calling attention) ¡oye! ¡ioiga! **h.-ho!** ¡ay!

height /hait/ *n* altura, *f*; elevación, *f*; altitud, *f*; (stature) estatura, *f*; (high ground) cerro, *m*, colina, *f*; (sublimity) sublimidad, excelencia, *f*; colmo, *m*; (zenith) auge, *m*, cumbre, *f*

heighten /'haitn/ *vt* hacer más alto; (enhance) realzar; (exaggerate) exagerar; (perfect) perfeccionar; (intensify) intensificar

heightening /'haitnɪŋ/ *n* elevación, *f*; (enhancement) realce, *m*; (exaggeration) exageración, *f*; (perfection) perfección, *f*; (intensification) intensificación, *f*

heinous /'heinəs/ *a* atroz, nefando, horrible.

heinousness /'heinəsnɪs/ *n* atrocidad, enormidad, *f*

heir /ɛər/ *n* heredero, *Lat. Am.* asignatario *m*. **h. apparent,** heredero aparente, *m*. **h.-at-law,** heredero forzoso, *m*. **h. presumptive,** presunto heredero, *m*

heiress /'ɛərɪs/ *n* heredera, *Lat. Am.* asignataria *f*

heirloom /'ɛər,lum/ *n* reliquia de familia, *f*; *Fig.* herencia, *f*

helicopter /'hɛli,kɒptər/ *n* helicóptero, *m*

helium /'hiliəm/ *n* *Chem.* helio, *m*

helix /'hilɪks/ *n* *Geom.* hélice, *m*; (*Archit. Geom.*) espira, *f*

hell /hɛl/ *n* infierno, *m*. **h.-fire,** fuego del infierno, *m*, llamas del infierno, *f pl*

Hellenic /hɛ'lɛnɪk/ *a* helénico

Hellenism /'hɛlə,nɪzəm/ *n* helenismo, *m*

Hellenist /'hɛlənɪst/ *n* helenista, *mf*

Hellenize /'hɛlə,naiz/ *vt* helenizar

hellish /'hɛlɪʃ/ *a* infernal; *Inf.* horrible, detestable

hello /hɛ'lou/ *interj* ¡hola!; (on telephoning someone) ¡oiga! ¡alo!; (answering telephone) *Spain* ¡diga!, ¡alo!, *Colombia* ¡a ver!, *Mexico* ¡bueno!

helm /hɛlm/ *n* caña del timón, *f*; timón, gobernalle, *m*. **to obey the h.,** obedecer al timón. **to take the h.,** gobernar el timón; ponerse a pilotar

helmet /'hɛlmɪt/ *n* casco, *m*; (in olden days) yelmo, capacete, *m*; (sun) casco colonial, *m*

helmsman /'hɛlmzmən/ *n* timonero, *m*

help /hɛlp/ *n* ayuda, *f*; auxilio, socorro, *m*; (protection) favor, *m*, protección, *f*; (remedy) remedio, *m*; (cooperation) cooperación, *f*, concurso, *m*; (domestic) criada, *f*. **A little h. is worth a lot of sympathy,** Más vale un toma que dos te daré. **There's no h. for it,** No hay más remedio. **to call for h.,** pedir socorro a gritos. **without h.,** a solas, sin la ayuda de nadie

help /hɛlp/ *vt* ayudar; socorrer, auxiliar; (favor) favorecer; (mitigate) aliviar; (contribute to) contribuir a, facilitar; (avoid) evitar. *vi* ayudar. **He cannot h. worrying,** No puede menos de preocuparse. **God h. you!** ¡Dios te ampare! **So h. me God!** ¡Así Dios me salve! **to h. one another,** ayudarse mutuamente, ayudarse los unos a los otros. **to h. oneself,** (to food) servirse. **to h. down, off,** ayudar a bajar; ayudar a apearse. **to h. in,** ayudar a entrar. **to h. along, forward, on,** avanzar, fomentar, promover; contribuir a. **Shall I h. you on with the dress?** ¿Quieres que te ayude a ponerte el vestido? **to h. out,** ayudar a salir; (from a vehicle) ayudar a bajar; (of a difficulty, etc.) sacar; suplir la falta de; ayudar. **to h. over,** ayudar a cruzar; (a difficulty) ayudar a salir (de un apuro); ayudar a vencer (un obstáculo, etc.); (a period) ayudar a pasar. **to h. to,** contribuir a, ayudar en; (food) servir. **to h. up,** ayudar a subir; ayudar a levantarse, levantar

helper /'hɛlpər/ n auxiliador (-ra); asistente (-ta); (protector) favorecedor (-ra); bienhechor (-ra), *Argentina* *also* ladero m; (colleague) colega, m; (coworker) colaborador (-ra). **He thanked all his helpers,** Dio las gracias a todos los que le habían ayudado
helpful /'hɛlpfəl/ a útil, provechoso; (obliging) servicial, atento, *Lat. Am.* acomedido; (favorable) favorable; (healthy) saludable
helpfulness /'hɛlpfəlnɪs/ n utilidad, f; bondad, f
helping /'hɛlpɪŋ/ n ayuda, f; (of food) porción, ración, f, plato, m. **Won't you have a second h.?** ¿No quiere usted servirse más (or otra vez)? ¿No quiere usted repetir? **to lend a h.** hand (to), prestar ayuda (a)
helpless /'hɛlplɪs/ a desamparado, abandonado; (through infirmity) imposibilitado; impotente, sin fuerzas (para); (shiftless) incompetente, inútil
helplessness /'hɛlplɪsnɪs/ n desamparo, m; invalidez, debilidad, f; impotencia, f; incompetencia, f
helter-skelter /'hɛltər 'skɛltər/ adv atropelladamente; en desorden. n barahunda, f
hem /hɛm/ n *Sew.* dobladillo, filete, m, bastilla, f; (edge) orilla, f. *interj* ¡ejem! vt hacer dobladillo en, dobladillar. vi (cough) fingir toser. **false hem,** *Sew.* dobladillo falso, m. **running hem,** *Sew.* jareta, f. **to hem and haw,** tartamudear; vacilar. **to hem in,** cercar, sitiar
hematology /,himə'tɒlədʒi/ n hematología, f
hemisphere /'hɛmɪ,sfɪər/ n hemisferio, m
hemispherical /,hɛmɪ'sfɛrɪkəl/ a hemisférico, semiesférico
hemlock /'hɛm,lɒk/ n *Bot.* cicuta, f
hemoglobin /'himə,gloubɪn/ n *Chem.* hemoglobina, f
hemophilia /,himə'filiə/ n *Med.* hemofilia, f
hemorrhage /'hɛmərɪdʒ/ n hemorragia, f, flujo de sangre, m
hemorrhoids /'hɛmə,rɔidz/ n pl *Med.* hemorroides, f
hemp /hɛmp/ n cáñamo, m. **h. cloth,** lienzo, m. **h.-seed,** cañamón, m
hemstitch /'hɛm,stɪtʃ/ n vainica, f. vt hacer vainica en
hen /hɛn/ n gallina, f; (female bird) hembra, f. **the hen pheasant,** la hembra del faisán. **hen bird,** pájara, f. **hen-coop** or **house,** gallinero, m. **hen party,** *Inf.* reunión de mujeres, f. **hen-roost,** nidal, ponedero, m
hence /hɛns/ adv (of place) de aquí; (of time) de ahora, de aquí a, al cabo de, en; (therefore) por eso, por lo tanto, por consiguiente. *interj* ¡fuera! ¡fuera de aquí! **I shall come to see you a month h.,** Vendré a verte en un mes (or al cabo de un mes). **ten years h.,** de aquí a diez años. **h. the fact that...,** de aquí que.... **H. it happens that...,** Por eso sucede que...
henceforth /,hɛns'fɔrθ/ adv desde aquí en adelante, de hoy en adelante
henchman /'hɛntʃmən/ n escudero, m; satélite, secuaz, m
henna /'hɛnə/ n alheña, f
henpecked /'hɛn,pɛkt/ a gobernado por su mujer, que se deja mandar por su mujer
hepatitis /,hɛpə'taitɪs/ n hepatitis, m
her /hər/ *unstressed* hər, ər/ *pers pron direct object* la; (with prepositions) ella. *pers. pron indirect object* le, a ella. *poss* a su, mf; sus, mf pl, de ella. **I saw her on Wednesday,** La vi el miércoles. **The message is for her,** El recado es para ella. **It is her book,** Es su libro, Es el libro de ella
herald /'hɛrəld/ n heraldo, m; presagio, anuncio, m. vt proclamar; anunciar, presagiar
heraldic /hɛ'rældɪk/ a heráldico
heraldry /'hɛrəldri/ n heráldica, f
herb /ɜrb/ *esp. Brit.* hɜrb/ n hierba, f
herbaceous /hɜr'beifəs, ɜr-/ a herbáceo
herbage /'ɜrbɪdʒ, 'hɜr-/ n herbaje, m; pasto, m
herbal /'ɜrbəl, 'hɜr-/ a herbario. n herbolaria, f
herbalist /'hɜrbəlɪst, 'ɜr-/ n herbario, m, simplista, mf
herbarium /hɜr'bɛəriəm, ɜr-/ n herbario, m
herbivorous /hɜr'bɪvərəs, ɜr-/ a herbívoro
herby /'ɜrbi, 'hɜr-/ a herbáceo
Herculean /,hɜrkyə'liən/ a hercúleo
herd /hɜrd/ n manada, f; (of cattle) hato, m; (race)

raza, f; (*Fig.* contemptuous) populacho, m, masa, f. vt reunir en manadas; reunir en hatos; (sheep) reunir en rebaños; guiar las manadas, etc. vi ir en manadas, hatos o rebaños; asociarse, reunirse. **h.-instinct,** instinto gregario, m; instinto de las masas, m
herdsman /'hɜrdzmən/ n ganadero, pastor, manadero, m; (head herdsman) rabadán, m
here /hɪər/ adv aquí; (at roll-call) ¡presente!; acá; en este punto; ahora. n presente, m. **And h. he looked at me,** Y a este punto me miró. **Come h.!** ¡Ven acá! **in h.,** aquí dentro. **h. below,** aquí abajo, en la tierra. **h. and there,** aquí y allá. **h., there and everywhere,** en todas partes. **H. I am,** Heme aquí. **h. is...,** he aquí.... **H. they are,** Aquí los tienes, Aquí están. **Here's to you!** (on drinking) ¡Salud y pesetas! ¡A tu salud!
hereabouts /'hɪərə,bauts/ adv por aquí cerca
hereafter /hɪər'æftər/ adv en lo futuro; desde ahora; en adelante. n futuro, m. **the H.,** la otra vida, la vida venidera
hereat /hɪər'æt/ adv en esto
hereby /hɪər'bai/ adv por esto, por las presentes
hereditarily /hə,rɛdɪ'tɛrəli/ adv hereditariamente, por herencia
hereditary /hə'rɛdɪ,tɛri/ a hereditario
heredity /hə'rɛdɪti/ n herencia, f
herein /hɪər'ɪn/ adv por en esto; aquí dentro; incluso
hereinafter /,hɪərɪn'æftər/ adv después, más abajo, más adelante, en adelante, en lo sucesivo
hereinbefore /,hɪərɪnbɪ'fɔr/ adv en la anterior, en lo arriba citado, en lo antes mencionado, en lo precedente
hereof /hɪər'ʌv/ adv de esto
heresy /'hɛrəsi/ n herejía, f
heretic /'hɛrɪtɪk/ n hereje, mf
heretical /hə'rɛtɪkəl/ a herético
hereupon /,hɪərə'pɒn/ adv en esto, en seguida
herewith /hɪər'wɪθ/ adv junto con esto, con esto; ahora, en esta ocasión
heritage /'hɛrɪtɪdʒ/ n herencia, f
hermaphrodite /hɜr'mæfrə,dait/ a and n hermafrodita, mf
hermetic /hɜr'mɛtɪk/ a hermético
hermit /'hɜrmɪt/ n ermitaño, m. **h. crab,** paguro, cangrejo ermitaño, m
hernia /'hɜrniə/ n hernia, f
hero /'hɪərou/ n héroe, m. **h.-worship,** culto a los héroes, m
heroic /hɪ'rouɪk/ a heroico, épico
heroin /'hɛrouɪn/ n *Chem.* heroína, f
heroine /'hɛrouɪn/ n heroína, f
heroism /'hɛrou,ɪzəm/ n heroísmo, m
heron /'hɛrən/ n garza, f
herpes /'hɜrpiz/ n pl herpes, mf pl
herring /'hɛrɪŋ/ n arenque, m
hers /hɜrz/ poss pron 3rd sing (el) suyo, m; (la) suya, f; (los) suyos, m pl; (las) suyas, f pl; de ella. **This book is h.,** Este libro es suyo, Este libro es de ella. **This book is h., not mine,** Este libro es el suyo no el mío. **a sister of h.,** una de sus hermanas, una hermana suya
herself /hər'sɛlf/ pron sí misma, sí; ella misma; (with reflexive verb) se. **She has done it by h.,** Lo ha hecho por sí misma. **She told me so,** Ella misma me lo dijo. **She is by h.,** Está a solas, Está sola
hesitancy. /'hɛzɪtənsi/ See **hesitation**
hesitant /'hɛzɪtənt/ a indeciso, vacilante, irresoluto. **to be h.,** mostrarse irresoluto
hesitate /'hɛzɪ,teit/ vi vacilar, dudar; titubear. **I do not h. to say...,** No vacilo en decir... **He hesitated over his reply,** Tardaba en dar su respuesta
hesitatingly /'hɛzɪ,teitɪŋli/ adv irresolutamente; titubeando
hesitation /,hɛzɪ'teifən/ n vacilación, hesitación, f; irresolución, indecisión, f; (reluctance) aversión, repugnancia, f; titubeo, m
heterodox /'hɛtərə,dɒks/ a heterodoxo
heterodoxy /'hɛtərə,dɒksi/ n heterodoxia, f
heterogeneity /,hɛtəroudʒə'niiti/ n heterogeneidad, f
heterogeneous /,hɛtərə'dʒiniəs/ a heterogéneo

heterosexual /ˌhɛtərəˈsɛkʃuəl/ n and a heterosexual, mf

hew /hyu/ vt cortar, tajar; (trees) talar; (a career, etc.) hacerse

hewer /ˈhyuər/ n partidor, talador, m

hexagon /ˈhɛksəˌgɒn/ n hexágono, m

hey /hei/ interj ¡he! ¡oye!

heyday /ˈheiˌdei/ n apogeo, colmo, m; buenos tiempos, m pl; reinado, m; pleno vigor, m

hi /hai/ interj ¡oye! ¡hola!

hiatus /haiˈeitəs/ n hiato, m; laguna, f, vacío, m

hibernate /ˈhaibərˌneit/ vi invernar

hibernation /ˌhaibərˈneiʃən/ n invernada, f

hibiscus /haiˈbiskəs/ n Bot. hibisco, m

hiccup /ˈhɪkʌp/ n hipo, m. vi hipar. vt decir con hipo

hidden /ˈhɪdn̩/ a escondido, secreto, oculto

hide /haid/ n piel, f; pellejo, cuero, m

hide /haid/ vt esconder, ocultar; (cover) cubrir, tapar; (dissemble) disimular; (meaning) obscurecer. vi esconderse; ocultarse, Mexico atejonarse; refugiarse. **to h. from each other,** esconderse el uno del otro. **h.-and-seek,** escondite, dormirlas, m

hidebound /ˈhaidˌbaund/ a Fig. muy conservador, reaccionario, de ideas muy tradicionales

hideous /ˈhɪdiəs/ a horrible, repulsivo, horroroso; repugnante, odioso

hideously /ˈhɪdiəsli/ adv horriblemente. **to be h. ugly,** (of people) ser más feo que Picio

hideousness /ˈhɪdiəsnɪs/ n fealdad, horribilidad, f; repugnancia, f

hiding /ˈhaidɪŋ/ n ocultación, f; encubrimiento, m; refugio, m; Inf. paliza, tunda, f. **h.-place,** escondite, m; escondrijo, m

hierarchical /ˌhaiəˈrɑrkɪkəl/ a jerárquico

hierarchy /ˈhaiəˌrɑrki/ n jerarquía, f

hieroglyph /ˈhaiərəˌglɪf/ n jeroglífico, m

higgledy-piggledy /ˈhɪgəldi ˈpɪgəldi/ adv revueltamente, en confusión; en montón, en desorden

high /hai/ a alto; elevado; (with altar, Mass, street, festival) mayor; grande; eminente; aristocrático; (of shooting) fijante; (of quality) superior; excelente; (haughty) orgulloso; (solemn) solemne; (good) bueno; noble; supremo; sumo; (of price) subido; Mus. agudo; (of the sea) tempestuoso, borrascoso; (of wind and explosives) violento, fuerte; (of polish) brillante; (with speed) grande; (with tension, frequency) alto; (with number, etc.) importante, grande; (with colors) subido; (of food) pasado; (angry) enojado, airado; (of cheek bones) saliente, prominente; (well-seasoned) picante; (flattering) lisonjero. adv alto; hacia arriba; arriba; (deeply) profundamente, fuertemente; con violencia; (of price) a un precio elevado; (luxuriously) lujosamente, Mus. agudo. **a room 12 ft. h.,** un cuarto de doce pies de altura. **I knew her when she was so h.,** La conocí tamaña. **It is h. time he came,** Ya es hora de que viniese. **on h.,** en alto, arriba; en los cielos. **h. altar,** altar mayor, m. **h. and dry,** en la playa, varado; Fig. en seco. **h. and low,** de arriba abajo; por todas partes. **h.-born,** aristocrático, de alta alcurnia. **h.-bred,** (of people) de buena familia; (of animals) de buena raza. **h.-class,** de buena clase; de alta calidad. **h. collar,** alzacuello, m. **h. colored,** de colores vivos; Fig. exagerado. **h. command,** (Mil., Nav.) alto mando, m. **h. court,** tribunal supremo, m. **h. day,** día festivo, m. **h. explosive,** explosivo violento, m. **h.-flown,** hinchado, retumbante, altisonante. **h. frequency,** alta frecuencia, f. **h.-handed,** arbitrario, dominador, despótico. **h.-heeled,** a de tacón alto. **h. jump,** salto de altura, m. **h. land,** tierras altas, f pl; eminencia, f. **h. life** Lat. Am. jáilaif m. **h. light,** Art. realce, m; acontecimiento de más interés, m; momento culminante, m. **h. mass,** misa mayor, f. **h.-minded,** de nobles pensamientos; arrogante. **h.-necked,** con cuello alto. **h.-pitched,** de tono alto, agudo. **h.-powered,** de alta potencia. **h.-powered car,** coche de muchos caballos, m. **h. precision,** suma precisión, f. **h. pressure,** alta presión, f; Fig. urgencia, f; n de alta presión; Fig. urgente. **h.-priced,** caro. **h. priest,** sumo pontífice, sumo sacerdote, alto sacerdote, m. **h. relief,** alto relieve, m. **h. road,** carretera mayor, f. **h. school,** instituto de

segunda enseñanza, instituto, colegio, liceo, m; colegio, liceo, instituto, m, escuela secundaria, secundaria, f. **h. sea,** marejada, f. **h. seas,** alta mar, f. **h.-seasoned,** picante. **h. society,** alta sociedad, f. **h.-sounding,** altisonante, bombástico. **h.-speed,** de alta velocidad. **h.-spirited,** brioso; alegre. **h.-strung,** nervioso, excitable, sensitivo. **h. tension,** alta tensión, f. **h. tide,** marea alta, f. **h.-toned,** Mus. agudo; Inf. de alto copete; aristocrático. **h. treason,** alta traición, f. **h. water,** marea alta, pleamar, f. **h.-water mark,** límite de la marea, m; Fig. colmo, m; apogeo, m

High Andes, the el Altiplano m

highball /ˈhaiˌbɔl/ m Spain güisquisoda, f, Lat. Am. jáibol, m

highbrow /ˈhaiˌbrau/ a and n intelectual, mf

high-ceilinged /ˈhai ˈsilɪŋd/ a alto de techo

higher /ˈhaiər/ a comp of **high,** más alto; más elevado; superior. **on a h. plane,** en un nivel más alto. **h. education,** enseñanza superior, f. **h. mathematics,** la alta matemática, f. **h. criticism,** la alta crítica. **h. up,** más arriba. **h. up the river,** río arriba

highest /ˈhaiɪst/ a superl of **high,** el más alto; la más alta; los más altos; las más altas; sumo, supremo; excelente. **h. common factor,** Math. máximo común divisor, m. **h. references,** (of cook, gardener, etc.) informes inmejorables, m pl; Com. referencias excelentes, f pl

highland /ˈhailənd/ n altiplanicie, f; montañas, f pl, distrito montañoso, m. a montañoso

highlight /ˈhaiˌlait/ vtr dar relieve a, destacar

highly /ˈhaili/ adv altamente; mucho; muy; extremadamente; grandemente; bien; favorablemente; con lisonja, lisonjeramente. **h. seasoned,** picante. **h. strung,** nervioso, excitable

highness /ˈhainɪs/ n altura, f; elevación, f; excelencia, f; nobleza, f; (title) Alteza, f. **His Royal H., Her Royal Highness,** Su Alteza Real

high-ranking /ˈhai ˈræŋkɪŋ/ a de alta jerarquía, de alto rango

highway /ˈhaiˌwei/ n camino real, m, carretera, f. **h. code,** código de la vía pública (or de la circulación), m. **h. robbery,** salteamiento de caminos, atraco, m. **highwayman** /ˈhaiˌweimən/ n salteador de caminos, m

highways and byways /ˈhaiˌweiz ən ˈbaiˌweiz/ caminos y veredas

hike /haik/ vi ir de excursión. n marcha con equipo, f

hiker /ˈhaikər/ n excursionista, mf

hiking /ˈhaikɪŋ/ n excursionismo, m; marcha con equipo, f

hilarious /hɪˈlɛəriəs/ a alegre

hilarity /hɪˈlærɪti/ n hilaridad, f

hill /hɪl/ n colina, f, cerro, otero, m; monte, m, montaña, f; (pile) montón, m. **h.-side,** falda de montaña, ladera de una colina, f. **h.-top,** cumbre de una colina, f

hilliness /ˈhɪlinɪs/ n montuosidad, f, lo montañoso

hillman /ˈhɪlˌmæn/ n montañés, m

hillock /ˈhɪlək/ n altozano, montículo, collado, m

hilly /ˈhɪli/ a montañoso

hilt /hɪlt/ n puño, m, empuñadura, f

him /hɪm/ pers pron 3rd sing direct object le, lo; (with prep.) él; indirect object se, a él; (with a direct obj. in 3rd person) se. **I gave him the magazine,** Le di la revista. **I gave it to him,** Se lo di a él. **This is for him,** Esto es para él

Himalayan /ˌhɪməˈleiən/ a himalayo

Himalayas, the /ˌhɪməˈleiəz, hɪˈmɑlyəz/ los Himalayas, m pl

himself /hɪmˈsɛlf/ pron él; sí mismo; él mismo; (reflexive) se. **He did it by h.,** Lo hizo por sí mismo. For more examples see **herself**

hind /haind/ n corza, cierva, f. a trasero, posterior. **h.-quarters,** cuarto trasero, m; (of a horse) ancas, f pl

hinder /ˈhaindər/ a trasero, posterior

hinder /ˈhɪndər/ vt impedir, estorbar; embarazar, dificultar; interrumpir. vi ser un obstáculo; formar un obstáculo

hinderer /ˈhɪndərər/ n estorbador (-ra); interruptor (-ra)

hindmost /ˈhaindˌmoust/ a posterior, postrero, último

hindrance /'hɪndrəns/ n obstáculo, estorbo, impedimento, m; perjuicio, m; interrupción, f

Hindu /'hɪndu/ a hindú, mf

Hinduism /'hɪndu,ɪzəm/ n indoísmo, m

Hindustani /,hɪndʊ'stɑni/ a indostanés. n (language) indostani, m

hinge /hɪndʒ/ n gozne, pernio, m, bisagra, f; articulación, f; Fig. eje, m. vi moverse (or abrirse) sobre goznes; Fig. depender (de). vt engoznar

hinged /hɪndʒd/ a con goznes

hint /hɪnt/ n indirecta, insinuación, sugestión, f; (advice) consejo, m. vt dar a entender, decir con medias palabras, insinuar, sugerir. vi insinuar. **to take the h.,** darse por aludido

hinterland /'hɪntər,lænd/ n interior (de un país), m

hip /hɪp/ n Anat. cadera, f; Bot. fruto del rosal silvestre, m. **h.-bath,** baño de asiento, m. **h.-bone,** hueso ilíaco, m. **h.-joint,** articulación de la cadera, f. **h.-pocket,** faltriquera, f

hipped /hɪpt/ a de caderas

hippodrome /'hɪpə,droum/ n hipódromo, m

hippopotamus /,hɪpə'pɒtəməs/ n hipopótamo, m

hire /haɪər/ n (employee) empleado (-da); salario, m. vt emplear; (person) contratar; tomar a su servicio. **to h. out,** alquilar. **for** or **on h.,** de alquiler.

hireling /'haɪərlɪŋ/ n mercenario, m

hirer /'haɪərər/ n alquilador (-ra), arrendador (-ra)

hirsute /'hɜrsut/ a hirsuto. **non-h.** Bot. lampiño

his /hɪz/ unstressed ɪz/ poss pron 3rd sing (el) suyo, m; (la) suya, f; (los) suyos, m pl; (las) suyas, f pl; de él. poss a su, mf; sus, mf pl; de él. **his handkerchiefs,** sus pañuelos. **his mother,** su madre, la madre de él. **a sister of his,** una de sus hermanas, una hermana suya. See **hers** for more examples.

Hispanic /hɪ'spænɪk/ n and a hispano (-na)

Hispanism /'hɪspə,nɪzəm/ n hispanismo, m

Hispanist /'hɪspənɪst/ n hispanista, mf

hispanize /'hɪspə,naɪz/ vt españolizar

Hispano-American /hɪs'pænou ə'mɛrɪkən/ a hispano-americano

hiss /hɪs/ n silbido, m; (sputter) chisporroteo, m. vi silbar

hissing /'hɪsɪŋ/ n silbido, m; chisporroteo, m. a silbante

hist /hɪst/ interj ¡chist!

histologist /hɪs'tɒlədʒɪst/ n histólogo, m

histology /hɪ'stɒlədʒi/ n histología, f

historian /hɪ'stɔriən/ n historiador (-ra)

historic /hɪ'stɒrɪk/ a histórico

historical /hɪ'stɒrɪkəl/ a histórico. **h. truth,** verdad histórica, f

historically /hɪs'tɒrɪkəli/ adv históricamente

historiographer /hɪ,stɔri'ɒgrəfər/ n historiógrafo, m

historiography /hɪ,stɔri'ɒgrəfi/ n historiografía, f

history /'hɪstəri/ n historia, f. **Biblical h.,** historia sagrada, f. **natural h.,** historia natural, f

histrionic /,hɪstri'ɒnɪk/ a histriónico

hit /hɪt/ n golpe, m; Aer. impacto, m; (success) éxito, m; (piece of luck) buena suerte, f; (satire) sátira, f. vt golpear; (buffet) abofetear, pegar; (find) dar con, tropezar con; (attain) acertar; (guess) adivinar; (attract) atraer; (deal) lanzar, dar; (wound) herir, hacer daño (a). **The sun hits me right in the eyes,** El sol me da en la cabeza. **direct hit,** Aer. impacto de lleno, m. **lucky hit,** acierto, m. **to hit a straight left,** (boxing) lanzar un directo con la izquierda. **to hit the mark,** dar en el blanco; Fig. dar en el clavo. **hit or miss,** acierto o error. **to hit against,** dar contra, estrellar contra. **to hit back,** defenderse; devolver golpe por golpe. **to hit off,** imitar; (a likeness) coger. **to hit out,** abofetear; Fig. atacar; golpear (la pelota) fuera. **to hit upon,** dar con; tropezar con; encontrar por casualidad; (remember) acordarse de

hitch /hɪtʃ/ n nudo fácil de soltar, m; Fig. obstáculo, m; Fig. dificultad, f; (lift, ride) Mexico aventón m. vt sacudir; (a chair, etc.) arrastrar, empujar; amarrar, enganchar; atar. vi (along a seat, etc.) correrse (en); (get entangled) enredarse, cogerse; (rub) rascarse. **without a h.,** sin dificultad alguna, viento en popa; (smoothly) a pedir de boca

hitchhike /'hɪtʃ,haɪk/ vi ir a dedo (Argentina), pedir aventón (Mexico), pedir botella (Cuba), hacer autostop, ir por autostop (Spain)

hither /'hɪðər/ adv acá, hacia acá; a citerior, más cercano. **h. and thither,** acá y aculla allá

hitherto /'hɪðər,tu/ adv hasta ahora, hasta el presente

Hitlerian /hɪt'lɛəriən/ a hitleriano, nacista

Hitlerism /'hɪtlə,rɪzəm/ n hitlerismo, nacismo, m

hive /haɪv/ n (for bees) colmena, f; (swarm) enjambre, m; Fig. centro, m. vt (bees) enjambrar. **h. of industry,** centro de industria

hoard /hɔrd/ n acumulación, f; provisión, f; tesoro, m. vt acumular, amasar, amontonar; guardar

hoarder /'hɔrdər/ n acaparador (-ra)

hoarding /'hɔrdɪŋ/ n amontonamiento, m; acaparamiento, m; (fence) empalizada, cerca, f; palizada de tablas, f

hoarfrost /'hɔr,frɒst/ n escarcha, helada blanca, f

hoariness /'hɔrinɪs/ n (of the hair) canicie, f; blancura, f; (antiquity) vejez, vetustez, f

hoarse /hɔrs/ a ronco; discordante. **to be h.,** tener la voz ronca. **to grow h.,** enronquecer

hoarsely /'hɔrsli/ adv roncamente

hoarseness /'hɔrsnɪs/ n ronquera, f; Inf. carraspera, f

hoary /'hɔri/ a (of the hair) canoso; blanco; (old) vetusto, antiguo, viejo

hoax /houks/ n estafa, f, engaño, m; broma pesada, f; burla, f. vt estafar, engañar; burlar

hoaxer /'houksər/ n burlador (-ra); estafador (-ra)

hobble /'hɒbəl/ n (gait) cojera, f; traba, maniota, f. vi cojear. vt manear. **h. skirt,** falda muy estrecha, f

hobby /'hɒbi/ n pasatiempo, m, recreación, f; manía, afición, f. **h.-horse,** caballo de cartón, m; Fig. caballo de batalla, m

hobgoblin /'hɒb,gɒblɪn/ n trasgo, duende, m

hobnail /'hɒb,neɪl/ n clavo de herradura, clavo de botas, m

hobnailed /'hɒb,neɪld/ a (of boots) con clavos

hobnob /'hɒb,nɒb/ vi codearse, tratar con familiaridad

hock /hɒk/ n Anat. pernil, m; (wine) vino del Rin, m

hockey /'hɒki/ n hockey, chueca, m. **h. ball,** bola, pelota de chueca, f. **h. stick,** bastón de chueca, m

hocus-pocus /'houkəs 'poukəs/ n juego de pasa pasa, m; engaño, m, treta, f

hod /hɒd/ n cuezo, m

hodgepodge /'hɒdʒ,pɒdʒ/ n mezcolanza, f, fárrago, m

hoe /hou/ n azadón, m, Chile, Peru lampa f. vt azadonar; sachar

hoeing /'houɪŋ/ n cavadura con azadón, f; sachadura, f

hog /hɒg/ n cerdo, puerco, Peru cuchí m. **to go the whole hog,** ir al extremo. **hogskin,** piel de cerdo, f

hoggish /'hɒgɪʃ/ a porcuno; (greedy) comilón, tragón; (selfish) egoísta

hoist /hɔɪst/ n levantamiento, m; (lift) montacargas, m; (winch) cabria, f; (crane) grúa, f. vt levantar, alzar; (flags) enarbolar; suspender; Naut. izar

hoity-toity /'hɔɪti 'tɔɪti/ a picajoso, quisquilloso; presuntuoso

hold /hould/ n asimiento, agarro, m, presa, f; asidero, m; Fig. autoridad, f, poder, m; Fig. comprensión, f; (of a ship) cala, bodega, f. **to loose one's h.,** aflojar su presa. **to lose one's h.,** perder su presa. **to seize h. of,** asirse de, echar mano de. **h.-all,** funda, f. **h.-up,** (robbery) atraco, robo a mano armada, m; (in traffic) atasco (or obstáculo) en el tráfico, m; (in work) parada, cesación (de trabajo), f

hold /hould/ vt tener; asir, agarrar; coger; retener; (embrace) abrazar; (a post) ocupar; (a meeting, etc.) celebrar; (bear weight of) aguantar, soportar; (own) poseer; Mil. ocupar, defender; (contain) contener; (have in store) reservar; tener capacidad para; (retain) retener; (believe) creer, sostener; (consider) opinar, tener para (mí, etc.); juzgar; (restrain) detener; contener; (of attention, etc.) mantener; (maneuvers) hacer; (observe) guardar. vi resistir, aguantar; (be valid) ser válido; regir; (apply) aplicarse; (last) continuar, seguir. interj ¡tente! ¡para! **The room won't h. more,** En este cuarto no caben más. **They h. him in**

great respect, Le tienen mucho respeto. **The theory does not h.** water, La teoría es falsa, La teoría no es lógica. **to h. one's own,** defenderse, mantenerse en sus trece. **to h. one's breath,** contener la respiración. **to h. one's tongue,** callarse. **to h. sway,** mandar; reinar. **to h. tightly,** agarrar fuertemente; (clasp) estrechar. **H. the line!** (telephone) ¡Aguarde un momento! **to h. back,** vt detener; contener; retener; esconder; abstenerse de entregar. vi quedarse atrás; vacilar, dudar; tardar en. **to h. by,** seguir; basarse en, apoyarse en. **to h. down,** sujetar; (oppress) oprimir. **to h. fast,** vt sujetar fuertemente. vi mantenerse firme; Fig. estar agarrado (a). **to h. forth,** vt ofrecer; expresar. vi hacer un discurso, perorar. **to h. in,** vt contener; retener. vi contenerse. **to h. off,** vt apartar, alejar. vi apartarse, alejarse, mantenerse alejado. **to h. on,** seguir, persistir en; aguantar. **to h. out,** vt alargar, extender; ofrecer. vi aguantar; durar, resistir. **to h. over,** tener suspendido sobre; (postpone) aplazar; Fig. amenazar con. **to h. to,** agarrarse a; atenerse a. **to h. together,** vt unir; juntar. vi mantenerse juntos. **to h. up,** vt (display) mostrar, enseñar; levantar; sostener, soportar; (rob) atracar, saltear; (delay) atrasar; (stop) interrumpir, parar. vi mantenerse en pie; (of weather) seguir bueno. **The train has been held up by fog,** El tren viene con retraso a causa de la niebla

holder /'houldər/ n el m, (f, la) que tiene; poseedor (-ra); Com. tenedor (-ra); inquilino (-na); propietario (-ia); (support) soporte, m; mango, m; asa, f; (in compounds) porta...

holding /'houldɪŋ/ n tención, f; posesión, f; propiedad, f; (leasing) arrendamiento, m; (celebration) solemnización, f; (of a meeting) el celebrar, el tener; pl **holdings,** Com. valores habidos, m pl

holding company n compañía de cartera, f

hole /houl/ n hoyo, m, Lat. Am. also foramen m; boquete, m; agujero, m; cavidad, f; (hollow) depresión, f, hueco, m; orificio, m; (tear) roto, desgarro, m; (eyelet) punto, m; (in cheese) ojo, m; (in stocking) rotura, f, punto, m; (lair) madriguera, f; (nest) nido, m; (golf) hoyo, m; (fix) aprieto, m. vt agujerear: excavar; (bore) taladrar; Sports. meter la pelota (en). **to h. out,** (golf) meter la pelota en el hoyo. **h.-and-corner,** a Inf. bajo mano, secreto

hole-puncher /'houl ˌpʌntʃər/ n agujereadora, f

holiday /'hɒlɪˌdei/ n día feriado, m; día de fiesta, día festivo, m; a festivo, alegre; hacer fiesta.

holiness /'houlɪnɪs/ n santidad, f

Holland /'hɒlənd/ Holanda, f

holland /'hɒlənd/ n lienzo crudo. a holandés. **H. gin,** ginebra holandesa, f

hollow /'hɒlou/ a hueco; cóncavo; (empty) vacío; (of eyes, etc.) hundido; (of sound) sordo; (of a cough) cavernoso; (echoing) retumbante; (Fig. unreal) vacío, falso; insincero. adv vacío; Inf. completamente. n hueco, m; concavidad, f; (hole) hoyo, m; cavidad, f; (valley) hondonada, f, barranco, m; (groove) ranura, f; (depression) depresión, f; (in the back) curvadura, f. vt excavar, ahuecar; vaciar. **h.-cheeked,** con las mejillas hundidas. **h.-eyed,** con los ojos hundidos, de ojos hundidos

hollowness /'hɒlounɪs/ n concavidad, f; (falseness) falsedad, f; insinceridad, f

holly /'hɒli/ n acebo, agrifolio, m

holocaust /'hɒləˌkɔst/ n holocausto, m

holograph /'hɒləˌgræf/ n hológrafo, m

holster /'houlstər/ n pistolera, f

holy /'houli/ a santo; sagrado; (blessed) bendito. **most h.,** a santísimo. **to make h.,** santificar. **H. Father,** Padre Santo, el Papa, m. **H. Ghost,** Espíritu Santo, m. **H. Office,** Santo Oficio, m, Inquisición, f. **H. Orders,** órdenes sagradas, f pl. **h. places,** santos lugares, m pl. **H. Scripture,** Sagrada Escritura, f. **H. See,** Cátedra de San Pedro, f. **h. water,** agua bendita, f. **H. Souls,** las Ánimas Benditas. **h. water stoup,** acetre, m. **H. Week,** Semana Santa, f

Holy Land, the la Tierra Santa, f.

homage /'hɒmɪdʒ/ n homenaje, m; culto, m; reverencia, f. **to pay h.,** rendir homenaje

home /houm/ n casa, f; hogar, m; domicilio, m; residencia, f; (institution) asilo, m; (haven) refugio, m; (habitation) morada, f; (country of origin) país de origen, m; (native land) patria, f; (environment) ambiente natural, m; Sports. meta, f. a casero, doméstico; nativo; nacional, del país; indígena. adv a casa, hacia casa; (in one's country) en su patria; (returned) de vuelta; (of the feelings) al corazón, al alma; (to the limit) al límite. **at h.,** en casa; Fig. en su elemento; (of games) en campo propio; de recibo. **at-h. day,** día de recibo, m. **He shot the bolt h.,** Echó el cerrojo. **one's long h.,** su última morada. **to be at h.,** estar en casa; estar de recibo. **to be away from h.,** estar fuera de casa; estar ausente. **to bring h.,** traer (or llevar) a casa; hacer ver; convencer; llegar al alma; (a crime) probar (contra). **to go h.,** volver a casa; volver a la patria; (be effective) hacer su efecto; (move) herir en lo más vivo. **to make oneself at h.,** ponerse a sus anchas, sentirse como en casa de uno. **Please make yourself at home!** ¡Ha tomado posesión de su casa! **to strike h.,** dar en el blanco; herir; (hit) golpear; herir en lo más vivo; hacerse sentir. **h. affairs,** asuntos domésticos, m pl, (Ministry of) Gobernación, f. **h.-bred,** criado en el país. **h.-brewed,** fermentado en el país; fermentado en casa. **h.-coming,** regreso al hogar, m. **h. farm,** residencia del propietario de una finca, f. **h. for the aged,** asilo de ancianos, m. **h. front,** frente doméstico, m. **h. life,** vida de familia, f. **h.-made** casero, de fabricación casera, hecho en casa. **H. Rule,** autonomía, f. **h. stretch,** último trecho (de una carrera), m. **h. truth,** verdad, Inf. fresca, f. **to tell someone a few h. truths,** contarle cuatro verdades

homeless /'houmlɪs/ a sin casa; sin hogar. **the h.,** los sin techo

homeliness /'houmlinɪs/ n comodidad, f; sencillez, f; (ugliness) fealdad, f

homely /'houmli/ a doméstico; familiar; (unpretentious) sencillo; llano; (ugly) feo; desabrido

homemaker /'houmˌmeikər/ n ama de casa, f

homeopath /'houmiəˌpæθ/ n homeópata, mf

homeopathic /ˌhoumiə'pæθɪk/ a homeópata

homeopathy /ˌhoumi'ɒpəθi/ n homeopatía, f

home page n página web, f

Homeric /hou'mɛrɪk/ a homérico

home run n (sports) jonrón, m

homesick /'houmˌsɪk/ a nostálgico. **to be h.,** tener morriña

homesickness /'houmˌsɪknɪs/ n nostalgia, añoranza, morriña, f

homespun /'houmˌspʌn/ n tejido en casa; hecho en casa; basto, grueso

homestead /'houmstɛd/ n hacienda, f; casa solariega, f; casa, f

homeward /'houmwərd/ adv hacia casa, en dirección al hogar; de vuelta; hacia la patria. **h.-bound,** en dirección a casa; (of ships) con rumbo al puerto de origen; (of other traffic) de vuelta

homicidal /ˌhɒmə'saidl/ a homicida

homicide /'hɒməˌsaid/ n (act) homicidio, m; (person) homicida, mf

homily /'hɒməli/ n Eccl. homilía, f; sermón, m

homing pigeon /'houmɪŋ/ n palomo (-ma) mensajero (-ra)

homogeneity /ˌhoumədʒə'niːti/ n homogeneidad, f

homogeneous /ˌhoumə'dʒiniəs/ a homogéneo

homologous /hə'mɒləgəs/ a homólogo

homonym /'hɒmənɪm/ n homónimo, m

homonymous /hə'mɒnəməs/ a homónimo

homosexual /ˌhoumə'sɛkʃuəl/ a and n homosexual, mf

Honduran /hɒn'durən/ a and n hondureño (-ña)

Honduras /hɒn'durəs/ Honduras

hone /houn/ n piedra de afilar, f. vt afilar, vaciar

honest /'ɒnɪst/ a honrado; decente, honesto; (chaste) casto; (loyal) sincero, leal; (frank) franco; imparcial. **an h. man,** un hombre de buena fe, un hombre honrado, un hombre decente

honesty /'ɒnəsti/ n honradez, f; honestidad, f; (chastity) castidad, f; sinceridad, f; rectitud, imparcialidad, f

honey /'hʌni/ n miel, f. **h.-bee,** abeja obrera, f. **h.-colored,** melado. **h.-pot,** jarro de miel, m. **h.-tongued,** melifluo; de pico de oro

honeycomb /'hʌni,koum/ n panal, m
honeycombed /'hʌni,koumd/ a apanalado
honeydew /'hʌni,du/ n mielada, f; Fig. ambrosia, f
honeyed /'hʌnid/ a de miel; Fig. meloso, adulador
honeymoon /'hʌni,mun/ n luna de miel, f; viaje de novios, viaje nupcial, m. vi hacer un viaje nupcial
honeysuckle /'hʌni,sʌkəl/ n madreselva, f
honor /'ɒnər/ n honor, m; honra, f; honradez, rectitud, integridad, f; pl **honors,** honores, m pl; condecoraciones, f pl; (last h.) honras, pompas fúnebres, f pl. vt honrar; (God) glorificar; (decorate) condecorar, laurear; (respect) respetar; reverenciar; Com. aceptar; (a toast) beber. **On my h.,** A fe mía. **point of h.,** punto de honor, pundonor, m. **word of h.,** palabra de honor, f. **Your H.,** (to a judge) Excelentísimo Señor Juez
honorable /'ɒnərəbəl/ a honorable; glorioso; digno; ilustre; (sensitive of honor) pundonoroso
honorable mention n accésit, m
honorableness /'ɒnərəbəlnıs/ n honradez, f
honorably /'ɒnərəbli/ adv honorablemente; dignamente
honorarium /,ɒnə'rɛəriəm/ n honorario, m
honorary /'ɒnə,rɛri/ a honorario, honorífico. **h. member,** socio (-ia) honorario (-ia). **h. mention,** mención honorífica, f
hood /hʊd/ n capucha, caperuza, f; (folding, of vehicles) capota, cubierta, cubierta del motor f; (of a carriage) caparazón, fuelle, m; (of a car) capó, m, (university) muceta, f; (of a fireplace) campana (de hogar), f; (cowl of chimney) sombrerete (de chimenea), m. vt cubrir con capucha; cubrir; (the eyes) ocultar, cubrir, velar
hooded /'hʊdid/ a con capucha
hoodwink /'hʊd,wıŋk/ vt vendar (los ojos); Fig. engañar, embaucar, burlar
hoof /hʊf/ n casco, m; (cloven) pezuña, f
hoofed /hʊft/ a ungulado
hoof it ir a golpe de calcetín
hook /hʊk/ n gancho, garfio, m; (boat-) bichero, m; (fish-) anzuelo, m; (on a dress) corchete, m; (hanger) colgadero, m; (claw) garra, f. vt enganchar; (a dress) abrochar; (fish) pescar, coger; (nab) atrapar, pescar. **by h. or by crook,** a tuertas o a derechas. **left h.,** (boxing) izquierdo, m. **right h.,** (boxing) derecho, m. **to catch oneself on a h.,** engancharse. **h. and eye,** los corchetes. **h.-nosed,** con nariz de gancho, con nariz aguileña. **h.-up,** Radio. circuito, m; transmisión en circuito, f
hooked /hʊkt/ a con ganchos; corvo, ganchoso
hooking /'hʊkıŋ/ n enganche, m; (of a dress) abrochamiento, m; (of fish and Inf.) pesca, f
hookworm /'hʊk,wɜrm/ n anquilostoma, m
hooligan /'huligən/ n rufián, m
hoop /hup/ n aro, arco, m; (of a skirt) miriñaque, m; (croquet) argolla, f; (toy) aro, m; círculo, m. vt poner aros a; Fig. rodear
hoot /hut/ n (of owls) ululación, f grito, m; (whistle) silbido, m; ruido, clamor, m. vi (of owls) ulular, gritar; silbar; Auto. avisar con la bocina. **to h. off the stage,** hacer abandonar la escena. **to h. down,** silbar
hooting /'hutıŋ/ n See **hoot**
hop /hɒp/ n salto, brinco, m; Bot. lúpulo, m; Bot. flores de oblón, f pl; (dance) baile, m. vi saltar con un pie; andar dando brincos; saltar; (limp) cojear; recoger lúpulo; (of plant) dar lúpulo. vt saltar. **hop-garden,** huerto de lúpulo, m. **hop-kiln,** horno para secar lúpulo, m. **hop-picker,** recolector (-ra) de lúpulo. **hop-picking,** recolección de lúpulos, f
hope /houp/ n esperanza, f; (faith) confianza, f; (expectation) anticipación, expectación, f; (probability) probabilidad, f; (illusion) ilusión, f; sueño, m. vi esperar. **to live in h. that,** vivir con la esperanza de que. **to lose h.,** desesperarse. **to h. against h.,** esperar sin motivo, esperar lo imposible. **to h. for,** desear. **to h. in,** confiar en
hopeful /'houpfəl/ a lleno de esperanzas, confiado; optimista; (Fig.) risueño. n Inf. la esperanza de la casa. **to look h.,** Fig. prometer bien
hopefully /'houpfəli/ adv con esperanza

hopefulness /'houpfəlnıs/ n optimismo, m; Fig. aspecto prometedor, m
hopeless /'houplıs/ a desesperado, sin esperanza; irremediable; (of situations) imposible; (of disease) incurable. **to be h.,** (lose hope) desesperarse; (have no remedy) ser irremediable; (of disease) no tener cura. **to make h.,** hacer perder la esperanza, desesperar; dejar sin remedio; (a situation) hacer imposible; (an illness) hacer imposible de curar
hopelessly /'houplısli/ adv sin esperanza; sin remedio; imposiblemente; incurablemente
hopelessness /'houplısnıs/ n desesperación, f; (of an illness) imposibilidad de curar, f; lo irremediable; imposibilidad, f
hopscotch /'hɒp,skɒtʃ/ n infernáculo, m, rayuela, f
horde /hɔrd/ n horda, f
horizon /hə'raizən/ n horizonte, m
horizontal /,hɔrə'zɒntl/ a horizontal. **h. suspension,** (gymnastics) plancha, f
horizontality /,hɔrəzɒn'tælıtı/ n horizontalidad, f
horizontally /,hɔrə'zɒntlı/ adv horizontalmente
hormone /'hɔrmoun/ n hormona, f
horn /hɔrn/ n (of bull, etc.) cuerno, m; (antler) asta, f; (of an insect) antena, f; (of a snail) tentáculo, m; Mus. cuerno, m; trompa, f; (of motor and phonograph) bocina, f, Mexico kláxon m; (of moon) cuerno (de la luna), m. **article made of h.,** objeto de cuerno, m. **on the horns of a dilemma,** entre la espada y la pared. **h. of plenty,** cuerno de abundancia, m; cornucopia, f. **h.-rimmed spectacles,** anteojos de concha, m pl. **h. thrust,** cornada, f
horned /hɔrnd/ a cornudo; (antlered) enastado
hornet /'hɔrnıt/ n avispón, abejón, m
horny /'hɔrni/ a córneo; calloso; duro; Inf. (sexually excited) caliente
horoscope /'hɔrə,skoup/ n horóscopo, m
horrible /'hɔrəbəl/ a horrible, repugnante, espantoso; (of price) enorme; Inf. horrible
horribleness /'hɔrəbəlnıs/ n horribilidad, f, horror, m, lo espantoso
horribly /'hɔrəbli/ adv horriblemente
horrid /'hɔrıd/ a horroroso; desagradable
horridness /'hɔrıdnıs/ n horror, m; lo desagradable
horrific /hɔ'rıfık/ a horrífico, horrendo
horrify /'hɔrə,fai/ vt horrorizar; escandalizar
horrifying /'hɔrə,faiıŋ/ a horroroso, horripilante
horror /'hɔrər/ n horror, m. **h.-stricken,** horrorizado
hors d'oeuvres /'ɔr dɜrvz/ n pl entremeses, m pl
horse /hɔrs/ n caballo, m, Lat. Am. cuaco m; (cavalry) caballería, f; (frame) caballete, m; (gymnastics and as punishment) potro, m. a caballar, caballuno. vt montar a caballo. **pack of horses,** caballada, f. **to ride a h.,** cabalgar, montar a caballo. **h. blanket,** manta para caballos, f; sudadero, m, Lat. Am. mandil m. **h.-block,** montador, m. **h.-box,** vagón para caballos, m. **h.-breaker,** domador de caballos, m. **h.-cab,** simón, m. **h.-chestnut,** castaña pilonga, f. **h.-chestnut flower,** candela, f. **h.-collar,** collera, f, collerón m. **h.-dealer,** chalán, m. **h.-doctor,** veterinario, m. **h.-flesh,** carne de caballo, f. **h.-fly,** tábano, m. **h.-latitudes,** calmas de Cáncer, f pl. **h.-laugh,** carcajada, f. **h.-master,** maestro de equitación, m. **h. meat,** carne de caballo, f. **h. pistol,** pistola de arzón, f. **h.-play,** payasada, f. **h.-power,** caballo de vapor, m; potencia, f. **a twelve-h.p. car,** un coche de doce caballos. **h.-race,** carrera de caballos, f. **h.-radish,** rábano picante, raíz amarga, m. **h.-sense,** sentido común, m; gramática parda, f. **h. show,** exposición de caballos, feria equina f; concurso de caballos, m. **h.-trainer,** entrenador de caballos, m. **h. tram,** tranvía de sangre, m. **h. trappings,** monturas, f pl. **That's a horse of a different color** Es harina de otro costal, Argentina, Peru Esas son otras cuarenta
horseback /'hɔrs,bæk/ n lomo de caballo, m. **on h.,** a caballo. **to ride on h.,** ir a caballo
horseman /'hɔrsmən/ n jinete, cabalgador, m
horsemanship /'hɔrsmən,ʃıp/ n equitación, f, manejo del caballo, m
horseshoe /'hɔrs,ʃu/ n herradura, f. **h. arch,** arco de herradura, arco morisco, m
horsewoman /'hɔrs,wʊmən/ n amazona, f

horticultural /ˌhɔrtɪ'kʌltʃərəl/ a horticultural. **h. show,** exposición de flores, f
horticulturalist /ˌhɔrtɪ'kʌltʃərɪst/ n horticultor (-ra)
horticulture /'hɔrtɪˌkʌltʃər/ n horticultura, f
hosanna /hou'zænə/ n hosanna, m
hose /houz/ n (tube) manga, f; (breeches) calzón, m; (stockings) medias, f pl; (socks) calcetines, m pl. **h. man,** manguero, m. **h.-pipe,** manga de riego, manguera, f
hosier /'houʒər/ n calcetero (-ra)
hosiery /'houʒəri/ n calcetería, f. **h. trade,** calcetería, f
hospice /'hɒspɪs/ n hospicio, m; asilo, refugio, m
hospitable /'hɒspɪtəbəl/ a hospitalario
hospitableness /'hɒspɪtəbəlnɪs/ n hospitalidad, f
hospital /'hɒspɪtl̩/ n hospital, m; (school) colegio, m. **h. nurse,** enfermera, f. **h. ship,** buque hospital, m
hospital bed cama hospitalaria, f
hospitality /ˌhɒspɪ'tælɪti/ n hospitalidad, f
host /houst/ n huésped, convidador, (of radio or tv program) presentador, m; (at an inn) patrón, mesonero, m; (army) ejército, m; (crowd) multitud, muchedumbre, f; Eccl. hostia, f; pl hosts, huestes, f pl. **h.-plant,** planta huésped, f
hostage /'hɒstɪdʒ/ n rehén, m; Fig. prenda, f
host country n (of an organization) país-sede, m
hostel /'hɒstl̩/ n hostería, f; club, m; residencia de estudiantes, f
hostelry /'hɒstl̩ri/ n hospedería, f; parador, mesón, m
hostess /'houstɪs/ n ama de la casa, f; la que recibe a los invitados; la que convída; (of an inn) patrona, mesonera, f
hostile /'hɒstl̩/ a enemigo; hostil, contrario (a); (of circumstances, etc.) desfavorable
hostility /hɒ'stɪlɪti/ n enemistad, f, antagonismo, m, mala voluntad, f; hostilidad, guerra, f. **suspension of hostilities,** suspensión de hostilidades, f
hot /hɒt/ a caliente; (of a day, etc.) caluroso; (piquant) picante; ardiente; vehemente, impetuoso; violento; impaciente; colérico; entusiasta; lleno de deseo; Art. intenso; (great) grande, mucho; (vigorous) enérgico. **It is hot,** Está caliente; (of weather) Hace calor. **to grow hot,** calentarse; Fig. acalorarse; (of weather) empezar a hacer calor. **to make hot,** calentar; dar calor a (a); Inf. dar vergüenza. **hot-blooded,** de sangre caliente; apasionado; colérico. **hot-foot,** aprisa, apresuradamente, impetuoso. **hot-plate,** Elec. calientaplatos, m. **hot springs,** termas, f pl. **hot-tempered,** colérico, irascible. **hot water,** agua caliente, f. **hot-water bottle,** bolsa de goma, f. **hot-water pipes,** las cañerías del agua caliente
hotbed /'hɒtˌbed/ n semillero, vivero, m; Fig. semillero, foco, m
hotchpotch /'hɒtʃˌpɒtʃ/ n potaje, m
hotel /hou'tɛl/ n hotel, m. **h.-keeper,** hotelero (-ra)
hothead /'hɒtˌhed/ n exaltado (-da), fanático (-ca)
hothouse /'hɒtˌhaus/ n invernáculo, m, estufa, f. **h. plant,** Fig. planta de estufa, f
hotly /'hɒtli/ adv calurosamente; con vehemencia; coléricamente
hough /hɒk/ n Zool. pernil, m; (in man) corva, f
hound /haund/ n perro de caza, sabueso de artois, m; perro, Inf. canalla, m. vt cazar con perros; Fig. perseguir; Fig. incitar. **master of hounds,** montero, m. **pack of hounds,** jauría, f
hour /auər/ n hora, f; momento, m; ocasión, oportunidad, f pl. horas, horas, f pl; after hours, fuera de horas. **at the eleventh h.,** en el último minuto. **by the h.,** por horas; horas enteras. **small hours,** altas horas de la noche, Inf. las tantas, f pl. **to keep late hours,** acostarse tarde. **to strike the h.,** dar la hora. **h.-glass,** reloj de arena, m. **h.-hand,** horario, m. **h. of death,** hora suprema, hora de la muerte, f. **till all hours,** hasta la madrugada
hourly /'auərli/ a cada hora; por hora; continuo. adv a cada hora; de un momento a otro
house /n haus; v hauz/ n casa, f; (home) hogar, m; (lineage) familia, f, abolengo, m; Theat. sala, f, teatro, m; Com. casa comercial, f; (takings) entrada, f; (audience) público, m; (of Lords, Commons) cámara, f; (college) colegio, m; (parliament) parla-

mento, m; (building) edificio, m. a de casa; de la casa; doméstico. vt dar vivienda (a); alojar, recibir (or tener) en casa de uno; (store) poner, guardar. **The cottage will not h. them all,** No habrá bastante lugar para todos ellos en la cabaña, No cabrán todos en la cabaña. **country-h.,** finca, f; casa de campo, f. **full h.,** casa llena, f; Theat. lleno, m. **to bring down the h.,** Theat. hacer venirse el teatro abajo. **to keep open h.,** llevar la casa; ser ama de casa. **to keep open h.,** tener mesa puesta, ser hospitalario. **to set up h.,** poner casa. **h. of cards,** castillo de naipes, m. **H. of Commons,** Cámara de los Comunes, f. **H. of Lords,** Cámara de los Lores, f. **H. of Representatives,** Cámara de Representantes (de Diputados. **h.-agent,** agente de casas, m. **h.-boat,** barco-habitación, m, casa flotante, f. **h.-dog,** perro de guardia, m; perro de casa, m. **h.-fly,** mosca doméstica, f. **h. furnisher,** mueblista, mf. **h. painter,** pintor de brocha gorda, m. **h. party,** reunión en casa de campo, f. **h.-physician,** médico (-ca) interno (-na). **h. porter,** portero, m. **h. property,** propiedad inmueble, f. **h.-room,** capacidad de una casa, f. **h. slipper,** zapatilla, f, pantuflo, m. **h.-surgeon,** cirujano interno, m. **h.-to-h.,** de casa en casa. **h.-warming,** reunión para colgar la cremallera, f. **publishing h.,** editorial, f
housebreaker /'hausˌbreikər/ n ladrón de casas, m
housebreaking /'hausˌbreikɪŋ/ n robo de una casa, m
houseful /'hausful/ n casa, f
house furnishings /'fɜrnɪʃɪŋz/ n pl artefactos para el hogar, accesorios caseros, aparatos electrodomésticos, m pl
household /'hausˌhould/ n casa, f; familia, f; hogar, m. a de la casa; doméstico; del hogar. **to be a h. word,** andar en lenguas. **h. accounts,** cuentas de la casa, f pl. **h. duties,** labores de la casa, f pl. **h. gods,** penates, m pl. **h. goods,** ajuar, mobiliario, m. **h. management,** gobierno de la casa, m
householder /'hausˌhouldər/ n padre de familia, m; dueño (-ña) (or inquilino (-na)) de una casa
housekeeper /'hausˌkipər/ n ama de llaves, f; mujer de su casa, f
housekeeping /'hausˌkipɪŋ/ n gobierno de la casa, m; economía doméstica, f. a de casa. **to set up h.,** poner casa
housemaid /'hausˌmeid/ n camarera, sirvienta, f. **housemaid's knee,** rodilla de fregona, f
house of ill repute /rɪ'pyut/ n burdel, m; casa de citas, casa de zorras, casa pública, f; lupanar, m
housetops /'hausˌtɒps/ n pl azotea, f; (flat roof) azotea, m. **to shout from the h.,** pregonar a los cuatro vientos
housewife /'hausˌwaif/ n madre de familia, mujer de su casa, f; (sewing-bag) neceser de costura, m
housewifely /'hausˌwaifli/ a propio de una mujer de su casa; doméstico; (of a woman) hacendosa
housing /'hauzɪŋ/ n provisión de vivienda, f; (storage) almacenaje, m; alojamiento, m; Inf. casa, vivienda, f. **h. scheme,** urbanización, f. **h. shortage,** crisis de vivienda, f, déficit habitacional, m
hovel /'hʌvəl/ n casucha, f
hover /'hʌvər/ vi revolotear; (of hawks, etc.) cernerse; estar suspendido; rondar; seguir de cerca, estar al lado (de); Fig. vacilar, dudar
hovering /'hʌvərɪŋ/ n revoloteo, m; (of birds of prey) calada, f; Fig. vacilación, f. a revolante, que revolotea; que se cierne (sobre); (menacing) que amenaza, inminente
how /hau/ adv cómo; (by what means, in what manner) de qué modo; (at what price) a qué precio; qué; cuánto. n el cómo. **to know how,** saber. **For how long?** ¿Por cuánto tiempo? **How are you?** ¿Cómo está Vd.? Inf. ¿Qué tal? **How do you do!** ¡Mucho gusto (en conocerlo/conocerla/conocerlos/conocerlas)! **How old are you?** ¿Qué edad tiene Vd.? **How beautiful!** ¡Qué hermoso! **How big!** ¡Cuán grande! **How early?** ¿Cuán temprano? ¿Cuánto a más tardar? **How far?** ¿A qué distancia? ¿Hasta qué punto? ¿Hasta dónde? **How fast?** ¿A qué velocidad? **How few!** ¡Qué pocos! **How little!** ¡Qué pequeño!; ¡Qué poco! **How long?** ¿Cuánto tiempo? **How many?** ¿Cuántos? m pl; ¿Cuántas? f pl. **How much is it?** ¿Cuánto vale? **How much cloth do you want?** ¿Cuánta tela quieres? **How**

often? ¿Cuán a menudo? ¿Cuántas veces? **How would you like to go for a walk?** ¿Te gustaría pasearte? **How are you going to Lisbon?** ¿En qué vas a Lisboa?

however /hau'ɛvər/ *adv* como quiera (que) (followed by subjunctive); por más que (followed by subjunctive); por... que (followed by subjunctive). *conjunc* (nevertheless) sin embargo, no obstante. **h. good it is,** por bueno que sea. **h. he does it,** como quiera que lo haga. **h. it may be,** sea como sea. **h. much,** por mucho que

howl /haul/ *n* aullido, *m*; (groan) gemido, *m*; (cry) grito, *m*; (roar) rugido, bramido, *m*; lamento, *m*. *vi* aullar; gemir; gritar; rugir, bramar. *vt* chillar. **Each time he opened his mouth he was howled down,** Cada vez que abrió la boca se armó una bronca

howler /'haulər/ *n* aullador (-ra); *Zool.* mono (-na) chillón (-ona); (blunder) coladura, plancha, *f*. **h. monkey** *Lat. Am.* araguato *m*

howling /'haulɪŋ/ *a* aullante; gemidor; (crying) que llora; bramante, rugiente. *n* los aullidos; (groaning) el gemir, los gemidos; (crying) los gritos; (weeping) el lloro; (roaring) los bramidos, el rugir; los lamentos

hub /hʌb/ *n* (of a wheel) cubo (de rueda) *m*; *Fig.* centro, *m*. **hub cap,** tapa de cubo, *f*

hubbub /'hʌbʌb/ *n* algarada, barahúnda, *f*

huckster /'hʌkstər/ *n* revendedor (-ra). *vi* revender; (haggle) regatear

huddle /'hʌdl/ *n* (heap) montón, *m*; colección, *f*; (group) corrillo, grupo, *m*; (mixture) mezcla, *f*. *vt* arrebujar, amontonar; acurrucar, arrebujar; (throw on) echarse. *vi* amontonarse; apiñarse; acurrucarse, arrebujarse

hue /hyu/ *n* color, *m*; matiz, tono, *m*; (of opinion) matiz, *m*; (clamor) clamor, *m*, gritería, *f*. **hue and cry,** alarma, *f*

huff /hʌf/ *n* acceso de cólera, *m*

huffily /'hʌfəli/ *adv* malhumoradamente; petulantemente

huffiness /'hʌfɪnɪs/ *n* mal humor, *m*; petulancia, *f*; arrogancia, *f*

hug /hʌg/ *n* abrazo, *m*. *vt* abrazar, apretujar; *Fig.* acariciar; *Naut.* navegar muy cerca de. **to hug oneself,** *Fig.* congratularse

huge /hyudʒ/ *a* enorme, inmenso; gigante; vasto

hugely /'hyudʒli/ *adv* inmensamente, enormemente

hugeness /'hyudʒnɪs/ *n* inmensidad, enormidad, *f*; vastedad, *f*

Huguenot /'hyugə,nɒt/ *a* and *n* hugonote (-ta)

hulk /hʌlk/ *n* barco viejo, *m*; pontón, *m*

hulking /'hʌlkɪŋ/ *a* pesado, desgarbado

hull /hʌl/ *n* *Naut.* casco (de un buque), *m*; (shell) cáscara, *f*; (pod) vaina, *f*, *vt* mondar

hullabaloo /'hʌləbə,lu/ *n* alboroto, tumulto, *m*; vocerío, *m*

hum /hʌm/ *n* zumbido, *m*; ruido confuso, *m*. *vi* (sing) canturrear; zumbar; (confused sound) zurrir; (hesitate) vacilar. *vt* (a tune) tararear

human /'hyumən/ *a* humano. **the h. touch,** el don de gentes. **h. being,** ser humano, hombre, *m*

humane /hyu'mein/ *a* humanitario, humano

humanely /hyu'meinli/ *adv* humanitariamente

humaneness /hyu'meinnɪs/ *n* humanidad, *f*

humanism /'hyumə,nɪzəm/ *n* humanismo, *m*

humanist /'hyumənɪst/ *n* humanista, *mf*

humanistic /,hyumə'nɪstɪk/ *a* humanista

humanitarian /hyu,mænɪ'tɛəriən/ *a* humanitario

humanitarianism /hyu,mænɪ'tɛəriə,nɪzəm/ *n* humanitarismo, *m*

humanity /hyu'mænɪti/ *n* humanidad, *f*; raza humana, *f*. **the humanities,** las humanidades

humanize /'hyumə,naiz/ *vt* humanizar; (milk) maternizar. *vi* humanizarse

humanly /'hyumənli/ *adv* humanamente

humble /'hʌmbəl/ *a* humilde; modesto; (cringing) servil; sumiso; pobre. *vt* humillar; mortificar. **to h. oneself,** humillarse

humbleness /'hʌmbəlnɪs/ *n* humildad, *f*; modestia, *f*; (abjectness) servilismo, *m*; sumisión, *f*; pobreza, *f*; (of birth, etc.) obscuridad, *f*

humbling /'hʌmblɪŋ/ *n* humillación, *f*; mortificación, *f*

humbly /'hʌmbli/ *adv* humildemente; modestamente; servilmente

humbug /'hʌm,bʌg/ *n* (fraud) embuste, engaño, *m*; (nonsense) disparate, *m*, tontería, *f*; mentira, *f*; (person) farsante, charlatán, *m*; (sweetmeat) caramelo de menta, *m*. *vt* engañar, embaucar; burlarse de

humdrum /'hʌm,drʌm/ *a* monótono; aburrido

humeral /'hyumərəl/ *a* humeral. *n* *Eccl.* velo humeral, *m*

humerus /'hyumərəs/ *n* *Anat.* húmero, *m*

humid /'hyumɪd/ *a* húmedo

humidity /hyu'mɪdɪti/ *n* humedad, *f*

humiliate /hyu'mɪli,eit/ *vt* humillar, mortificar. **to h. oneself,** humillarse

humiliating /hyu'mɪli,eitɪŋ/ *a* humillante; degradante

humiliation /hyu,mɪli'eiʃən/ *n* humillación, mortificación, *f*; degradación, *f*

humility /hyu'mɪlɪti/ *n* humildad, *f*; modestia, *f*

humming /'hʌmɪŋ/ *n* zumbido, *m*; (of a tune) tarareo, *m*. *a* zumbador. **h.-bird,** pájaro mosca, colibrí, *m*. **h.-top,** trompa, *f*

humor /'hyumər/ *n* humor, *m*; humorismo, *m*; (temperament) disposición, *f*, carácter, *m*; (whim) capricho, *m*. *vt* seguir el humor (a), complacer; satisfacer, consentir en; (a lock, etc.) manejar. **in a good (bad) h.,** de buen (mal) humor. **I am not in the h. to...** No estoy de humor para... **sense of h.,** sentido de humor, *m*

humored /'hyumərd/ *a* (in compounds) de humor... **good-h.,** de buen humor. **ill-h.,** malhumorado, de mal humor

humoresque /,hyumə'rɛsk/ *n* *Mus.* capricho musical, *m*

humorist /'hyumərɪst/ *n* humorista, *mf*

humorless /'hyumərlɪs/ *a* sin sentido humorístico, sin sentido de humor

humorous /'hyumərəs/ *a* humorístico; cómico, risible

humorously /'hyumərəsli/ *adv* humorísticamente; cómicamente

humorousness /'hyumərəsnɪs/ *n* humorismo, *m*; lo cómico

hump /hʌmp/ *n* joroba, giba, *f*; (hillock) montecillo, *m*; *Inf.* depresión, *f*

humpback /'hʌmp,bæk/ *n* giba, joroba, *f*; (person) jorobado (-da), giboso (-sa)

humpbacked /'hʌmp,bækt/ *a* jorobado, giboso, corcovado

humph /an inarticulate expression resembling a snort or grunt; spelling pron. hʌmf/ *interj* ¡qué va!; ¡patrañas!

humus /'hyuməs/ *n* humus, mantillo, *m*

hunch /hʌntʃ/ *n*: **I have a hunch that...** *Mexico* Me late que...

hunchback /'hʌntʃ,bæk/ *n* joroba, giba, *f*; (person) jorobado (-da), corcovado (-da), giboso (-sa)

hunchbacked /'hʌntʃ,bækt/ *a* jorobado, giboso, corcovado

hundred /'hʌndrɪd/ *n* ciento, *m*; centenar, *m*, centena, *f*. *a* ciento; (before nouns and adjectives, excluding numerals, with the exception of mil and millón) cien. **a h. thousand,** cien mil. **one h. and one,** ciento uno. **by the h.,** a centenares. **hundreds of people,** centenares de personas, *m pl.* **h.-millionth,** *a* and *n* cienmillonésimo *m*. **h.-thousandth,** *a* and *n* cienmilésimo *m*

hundredfold /'hʌndrɪd,fould/ *adv* cien veces. *n* céntuplo, *m*

hundredth /'hʌndrɪdθ/ *a* centésimo, céntimo. *n* centésimo, *m*, centésima parte, *f*

Hungarian /hʌŋ'gɛəriən/ *a* and *n* húngaro (-ra); (language) húngaro, *m*

Hungary /'hʌŋgəri/ Hungría, *f*

hunger /'hʌŋgər/ *n* hambre, *f*; apetito, *m*; (craving) deseo, *m*, ansia, *f*. *vi* estar hambriento, tener hambre. **to h. for,** desear, ansiar. **h.-strike,** huelga de hambre, *f*

hungrily /'hʌŋgrəli/ *adv* hambrientamente, con hambre; ansiosamente

hungry /'hʌŋgri/ *a* hambriento; (of land) pobre;

(anxious) deseoso. **to be h.,** tener hambre. **to make h.,** dar hambre

hunk /hʌŋk/ n rebanada, f, pedazo, m

hunt /hʌnt/ n caza, cacería, montería, f; grupo de cazadores, m; (search) busca, f; (pursuit) persecución, f. vt cazar; cazar a caballo; (search) buscar; rebuscar, explorar; (pursue) perseguir. **to h. down,** perseguir. **to h. for,** buscar. **to h. out,** buscar; descubrir, desenterrar

hunter /'hʌntər/ n cazador, m; caballo de caza, m; (watch) saboneta, f

hunting /'hʌntɪŋ/ n caza, f; caza a caballo, f; persecución, f. a cazador, de caza. **to go h.,** ir a cazar. **h.-box,** pabellón de caza, m. **h.-cap,** gorra de montar, f. **h.-crop,** látigo para cazar, m. **h.-ground,** coto de caza, terreno de caza, m. **h.-horn,** cuerno de caza, m, corneta de monte, f. **h. party,** partido de caza, m, cacería, f

huntsman /'hʌntsmən/ n cazador, montero, m

huntsmanship /'hʌntsmən,ʃɪp/ n montería, arte de cazar, f

hurdle /'hɜrdl/ n valla, f; zarzo, m. **h.-race,** carrera de obstáculos, f; carrera de vallas, f

hurdy-gurdy /'hɜrdi'gɜrdi/ n organillo, m

hurl /hɜrl/ vt lanzar, tirar, arrojar, echar. **to h. oneself,** lanzarse. **to h. oneself against,** arrojarse a (or contra). **to h. oneself upon,** abalanzarse sobre

hurly-burly /'hɜrli'bɜrli/ n alboroto, tumulto, m

hurrah /hə'rɑ/ interj ¡hurra! ¡viva! n vítor, m. **H. for...!** ¡Viva...!, ¡Vivan...! **to shout h.,** vitorear

hurricane /'hɜrɪ,kein/ n huracán, m. **h.-lamp,** lámpara sorda, f

hurried /'hɜrid/ a apresurado, precipitado; hecho a prisa; superficial

hurriedly /'hɜridli/ adv apresuradamente, precipitadamente, con prisa; superficialmente; (of writing) a vuela pluma

hurry /'hɜri/ n prisa, f; precipitación, f; urgencia, f; confusión, f; alboroto, m. **in a h.,** aprisa. **in a great h.,** aprisa y corriendo. **to be in a h.,** llevar prisa, estar de prisa. **There is no h.,** No corre prisa, No hay prisa

hurry /'hɜri/ vt apresurar, dar prisa, Lat. Am. apurar (a); llevar aprisa; hacer andar aprisa; enviar apresuradamente; precipitar; acelerar. vi darse prisa; apresurarse. **to h. after,** correr detrás de, seguir apresuradamente. **to h. away,** vi marcharse aprisa, marcharse corriendo; huir; salir precipitadamente. vt hacer marcharse aprisa; llevar con prisa. **to h. back,** vi volver aprisa, apresurarse a volver. vt hacer volver aprisa. **to h. in,** vi entrar aprisa, entrar corriendo. vt hacer entrar aprisa. **to h. off.** See **to h. away. to h. on,** vi apresurarse. vt apresurar, precipitar. **to h. out,** salir rápidamente. **to h. over,** hacer rápidamente; concluir aprisa; despachar aprisa; (travel over) atravesar aprisa; pasar rápidamente por. **to h. toward,** llevar rápidamente hacia; arrastrar hacia; impeler hacia. **to h. up,** vi darse prisa. vt apresurar, precipitar, Lat. Am. apurar; estimular

hurt /hɜrt/ n herida, f; (harm) daño, mal, m; perjuicio, m. vt (wound) herir; (cause pain) doler; hacer daño (a); hacer mal (a); (damage) perjudicar, estropear, Lat. Am. afectar; (offend) ofender; (the feelings) mortificar, lastimar, herir. vi doler; hacer mal; perjudicarse, estropearse. **I haven't h. myself,** No me he hecho daño. **Does it still h. you?** ¿Te duele todavía? **to h. deeply,** Fig. herir en el alma. **to h. a person's feelings,** herirle (a uno) el amor propio, lastimar, ofender

hurtful /'hɜrtfəl/ a nocivo, dañino; injurioso, pernicioso

hurtfulness /'hɜrtfəlnɪs/ n nocividad, f; perniciosidad, f

hurtle /'hɜrtl/ vt lanzar. vi lanzarse; volar; caer

husband /'hʌzbənd/ n esposo, marido, m. vt economizar, ahorrar. **h. and wife,** los esposos, los cónyuges

husbandry /'hʌzbəndri/ n labor de los campos, agricultura, f; (thrift) frugalidad, parsimonia, f

hush /hʌʃ/ n silencio, m, tranquilidad, f. interj ¡chitón! ¡calla! ¡silencio! vt silenciar, hacer callar, imponer silencio (a); (a baby) adormecer; Fig. sosegar, calmar. vi callarse, enmudecer. **to h. up,** mantener secreto, ocultar. **h.-h.,** secreto. **h. money,** soborno, chantaje, m

hushaby /'hʌʃə,bai/ interj ¡duerme!

husk /hʌsk/ n (of grain) cascabillo, m; zurrón, m; cáscara, f; (of chestnut) erizo, m; vt Lat. Am. deshojar (corn)

huskily /'hʌskəli/ adv roncamente

huskiness /'hʌskɪnɪs/ n ronquera, f; Inf. robustez, f

husky /'hʌski/ a (of voice) ronco; Bot. cascarudo; (Eskimo) esquimal; Inf. robusto, fuerte. n perro esquimal, m

hussy /'hʌsi/ n pícara, bribona, f

hustle /'hʌsəl/ vt empujar, codear; Fig. precipitar; Inf. acelerar. vi codearse; andarse de prisa

hut /hʌt/ n choza, cabaña, barraca, f, Mexico jacal, elsewhere in Lat. Am. bohío m

hutch /hʌtʃ/ n (chest) arca, f, cofre, m; (cage) jaula, f; (for rabbits) conejera, f; (for rats) ratonera, f; Inf. choza, f

hyacinth /'haiəsɪnθ/ n jacinto, m

hybrid /'haibrid/ a híbrido; mestizo, mixto. n híbrido, m

hybridism /'haibrɪ,dɪzəm/ n hibridismo, m

hybridization /,haibrɪdə'zeiʃən/ n hibridación, f

hybridize /'haibrɪ,daiz/ vt cruzar. vi producir (or generar) híbridos

hydrangea /hai'dreindʒə/ n Bot. hortensia, f

hydrant /'haidrənt/ n boca de riego, f

hydrate /'haidreit/ n Chem. hidrato, m. vt hidratar

hydraulic /hai'drɔlɪk/ a hidráulico. **h. engineering,** hidrotecnia, f

hydraulics /hai'drɔlɪks/ n hidráulica, f

hydrocarbon /,haidrə'karbən/ n Chem. hidrocarburo, m

hydrochloric /,haidrə'klɔrɪk/ a clorhídrico. **h. acid,** ácido clorhídrico, m

hydrogen /'haidrədʒən/ n hidrógeno, m. **h. peroxide,** agua oxigenada, f

hydrogenation /,haidrədʒə'neiʃən/ n hidrogenación, f

hydrogenize /'haidrədʒə,naiz/ vt hidrogenizar

hydrolysis /hai'drɔləsɪs/ n hidrólisis, f

hydromel /'haidrə,mɛl/ n aguamiel, f, hidromel, m

hydropathic /,haidrə'pæθɪk/ a hidropático. **h. establishment,** balneario, m

hydrophobia /,haidrə'foubiə/ n hidrofobia, rabia, f

hydrophobic /,haidrə'foubɪk/ a hidrofóbico, rabioso

hydroplane /'haidrə,plein/ n hidroplano, m

hydrotherapic /,haidrou'θəræpɪk/ a hidroterápico

hydrotherapy /,haidrə'θɛrəpi/ n hidroterapia, f

hyena /hai'inə/ n hiena, f

hygiene /'haidʒin/ n higiene, f. **personal h.,** higiene privada, f

hygienic /,haidʒi'ɛnɪk/ a higiénico

hymen /'haimən/ n Anat. himen, m; himeneo, m

hymeneal /,haimə'niəl/ a nupcial

hymn /hɪm/ n himno, m. **h.-book,** himnario, m

hyperbole /hai'pɜrbəli/ n hipérbole, f

hyperbolical /,haipər'bɒlɪkəl/ a hiperbólico

hypercorrection /,haipərkə'rɛkʃən/ n seudocultismo, m, ultracorrección, f

hypercritic /,haipər'krɪtɪk/ n hipercrítico, m

hypercritical /,haipər'krɪtɪkəl/ a hipercrítico, criticón

hypersensitive /,haipər'sɛnsɪtɪv/ a vidrioso, quisquilloso

hypertension /,haipər'tɛnʃən/ n hipertensión, f

hypertrophy /hai'pɜrtrəfi/ n hipertrofia, f. vi hipertrofiarse

hyphen /'haifən/ n guión, m

hypnosis /hɪp'nousɪs/ n hipnosis, f

hypnotic /hɪp'nɒtɪk/ a hipnótico. n (person) hipnótico (-ca); (drug) hipnótico, narcótico, m

hypnotism /'hɪpnə,tɪzəm/ n hipnotismo, m

hypnotist /'hɪpnətɪst/ n hipnotizador (-ra)

hypnotization /,hɪpnətə'zeiʃən/ n hipnotización, f

hypnotize /'hɪpnə,taiz/ vt hipnotizar

hypo /ˈhaipəu/ n (sodium hyposulfite) hiposulfito sólido, m
hypochondria /ˌhaipəˈkɒndriə/ n hipocondria, f
hypochondriac /ˌhaipəˈkɒndri,æk/ n hipocondríaco (-ca)
hypochondriacal /ˌhaipoukənˈdraiəkəl/ a hipocondríaco
hypocrisy /hɪˈpɒkrəsi/ n hipocresía, f; mojigatería, gazmoñería, f
hypocrite /ˈhɪpəkrɪt/ n hipócrita, mf; mojigato (-ta). **to be a h.**, ser hipócrita
hypocritical /ˌhɪpəˈkrɪtɪkəl/ a hipócrita; mojigato, gazmoño

hypocritically /ˌhɪpəˈkrɪtɪkəli/ adv hipócritamente, con hipocresía
hypodermic /ˌhaipəˈdɜrmɪk/ a hipodérmico. **h. syringe,** jeringa de inyecciones, f
hypotenuse /haiˈpɒtn̩us/ n Geom. hipotenusa, f
hypothesis /haiˈpɒθəsɪs/ n hipótesis, f
hypothetical /ˌhaipəˈθɛtɪkəl/ a hipotético
hysterectomy /ˌhɪstəˈrɛktəmi/ n Surg. histerectomía, f
hysteria /hɪˈstɛriə/ n Med. histerismo, m; histeria, f, ataque de nervios, m
hysterical /hɪˈstɛrɪkəl/ a histérico. **to become h.,** tener un ataque de nervios. **hysterics,** n pl ataque de nervios, m

I

i /ai/ n (letter) i. *1st pers pron* yo. **It is I,** Soy yo. Normally omitted, the verb alone being used except when **yo** is needed for emphasis, e.g. *Hablo a María,* I speak to Mary, *but Yo toco el violín, pero Juan toca el piano,* I play the violin, but *John* plays the piano
Iberia /aiˈbiriə/ Iberia
Iberian /aiˈbɪəriən/ a ibero, ibérico. n ibero (-ra)
Iberian Peninsula, the la Peninsula Ibérica
ibex /ˈaibɛks/ n Zool. íbice, m
ice /ais/ n hielo, m; (ice cream) helado, m. vt helar; cubrir de hielo; congelar, cuajar; (a cake, etc.) garapiñar, escarchar, alcorzar. **to ice up,** (Aer., Auto.) helarse. **to be as cold as ice,** Inf. estar hecho un hielo. **His words cut no ice,** Sus palabras ni pinchan ni cortan. **ice-age,** edad del hielo, f. **ice-ax,** piolet, m. **ice-box,** nevera, f. **ice-cream,** helado, mantecado, m. **ice-cream cone,** cucurucho de helado, m. **ice-cream freezer,** heladora, f. **ice-cream vendor,** mantequero (-ra). **ice-field,** campo de hielo, m. **ice hockey,** hockey sobre patines, m. **ice-pack,** bolsa para hielo, f. **ice-skates,** patines de cuchilla, m pl. **ice water,** agua helada, f
iceberg /ˈaisbɜrg/ n iceberg, témpano de hielo, banco de hielo, m
icebound /ˈaisˌbaund/ a aprisionado por el hielo; atascado en el hielo; (of roads, etc.) helado
iced /aist/ a helado; congelado, cuajado; (cakes) garapiñado, escarchado; (of drinks) con hielo. **i. drink,** sorbete, m
Iceland /ˈaislənd/ Islandia, f
Icelander /ˈaisˌlændər/ n islandés (-esa)
icelandic /aisˈlændɪk/ a islandes, islándico. n (language) islandés, m
icicle /ˈaisɪkəl/ n carámbano, canelón, cerrión, m
icily /ˈaisəli/ adv fríamente; Fig. frígidamente, con indiferencia, con frialdad
iciness /ˈaisinɪs/ n frialdad, frigidez, f; Fig. indiferencia, frigidez, f
icing /ˈaisɪŋ/ n helada, f, hielo, m; (on a cake, etc.) alcorza, capa de azúcar, f
icon /ˈaikɒn/ n icono, m
iconoclast /aiˈkɒnə,klæst/ n iconoclasta, mf
iconoclastic /ai,kɒnəˈklæstɪk/ a iconoclasta
iconography /ˌaikəˈnɒgrəfi/ n iconografía, f
iconology /ˌaikəˈnɒlədʒi/ n iconología, f
icy /ˈaisi/ a helado; glacial, frío; Med. álgido; Fig. indiferente, desabrido; Poet. frígido, gélido
idea /aiˈdiə/ n idea, f, concepto, m; (opinion) juicio, m, opinión, f; (notion) impresión, noción, f; (plan) proyecto, plan, designio, m. **to form an i.** of, hacerse una idea de, formar un concepto de. **to have an i. of,** tener una idea de; tener nociones de. **An i. struck me,** Se me ocurrió una idea. **full of ideas,** preñado (or lleno) de ideas. **I had no i. that...** No tenía la menor idea de que... No sabía que... **What an i.!** ¡Qué idea!
ideal /aiˈdiəl/ a ideal; excelente, perfecto; (utopian) utópico; (imaginary) imaginario, irreal, ficticio. n ideal, m; modelo, prototipo, m
idealism /aiˈdiə,lɪzəm/ n idealismo, m
idealist /aiˈdiəlɪst/ n idealista, mf
idealistic /ai,diəˈlɪstɪk/ a idealista

idealization /ai,diəlɪˈzeiʃən/ n idealización, f
idealize /aiˈdiə,laiz/ vt idealizar
ideally /aiˈdiəli/ adv idealmente
ideation /ˌaidiˈeiʃən/ n Philos. ideación, f
idem /ˈaidɛm/ adv ídem
identical /aiˈdɛntɪkəl/ a idéntico, mismo, igual; muy parecido, semejante
identically /aiˈdɛntɪkəli/ adv idénticamente
identifiable /ai,dɛntɪˈfaiəbəl/ a identificable
identification /ai,dɛntəfɪˈkeiʃən/ n identificación, f. **i. number,** placa de identidad, f
identify /aiˈdɛntə,fai/ vt identificar. **to i. oneself with,** identificarse con
identity /aiˈdɛntɪti/ n identidad, f. **i. card,** cédula personal, f; carnet de identidad, m. **i. disc,** disco de identidad, m
ideogram, ideograph /ˈidiə,græm; ˈidiə,græf/ n ideograma, m
ideography /ˌidiˈɒgrəfi/ n ideografía, f
ideological /ˌaidiəˈlɒdʒɪkəl/ a ideológico
ideologist /ˌaidiˈɒlədʒɪst/ n ideólogo (-ga)
ideology /ˌaidiˈɒlədʒi/ n ideología, f
Ides /aidz/ n pl idus, m pl
idiocy /ˈɪdiəsi/ n idiotez, imbecilidad, f; (foolishness) necedad, tontería, sandez, f
idiom /ˈɪdiəm/ n idiotismo, m; modismo, m, locución, f; (language) habla, f; lenguaje, m
idiomatic /ˌɪdiəˈmætɪk/ a idiomático
idiopathy /ˌɪdiˈɒpəθi/ n Med. idiopatía, f
idiosyncrasy /ˌɪdiəˈsɪŋkrəsi/ n idiosincrasia, f
idiosyncratic /ˌɪdiousɪnˈkrætɪk/ a idiosincrásico
idiot /ˈɪdiət/ n idiota, imbécil, mf; (fool) necio (-ia), tonto (-ta), mentecato (-ta)
idiotic /ˌɪdiˈɒtɪk/ a idiota, imbécil; (foolish) necio, tonto, sandío
idle /ˈaidl/ a desocupado; indolente, ocioso; (unemployed) cesante, sin empleo; (lazy) perezoso, holgazán; (of machines) parado, inactivo; (useless) vano, inútil, sin efecto; (false) falso, mentiroso, infundado; (stupid) fútil, frívolo. vi holgar, estar ocioso; holgazanear, haraganear, gandulear. **to i. away,** malgastar, perder. **to i. away the time,** pasar el rato, matar el tiempo. **i. efforts,** vanos esfuerzos, m pl. **i. fancies,** ilusiones, fantasías, f pl, sueños, m pl. **i. hours,** horas desocupadas, f pl, ratos perdidos, m pl. **i. question,** pregunta ociosa, f. **i. tale,** cuento de viejas, m. **i. threat,** reto vacuo, m
idleness /ˈaidlnɪs/ n ociosidad, indolencia, inacción, f; pereza, holgazanería, gandulería, f; (uselessness) inutilidad, futilidad, f
idler /ˈaidlər/ n ocioso (-sa); haragán (-ana); perezoso (-sa), holgazán (-ana), gandul (-la), Lat. Am. aplanacalles m
idly /ˈaidli/ adv ociosamente, perezosamente; (uselessly) vanamente
idol /ˈaidl/ n ídolo, m. **a popular i.,** el ídolo de las masas, m
idolater /aiˈdɒlətər/ n idólatra, mf; (admirer) amante, mf esclavo (-va), admirador (-ra)
idolatrous /aiˈdɒlətrəs/ a idólatra, idolátrico

idolatrously /ai'dɒlətrəsli/ *adv* idolatradamente, con idolatría

idolatry /ai'dɒlətri/ *n* idolatría, *f*; (devotion) adoración, pasión, *f*

idolization /ˌaidlə'zeiʃən/ *n* idolatría, *f*

idolize /'aidlˌaiz/ *vt* idolatrar, adorar

idyll /'aidl/ *n* idilio, *m*

idyllic /ai'dɪlɪk/ *a* idílico

if /ɪf/ *conjunc* si; (even if) aunque, aun cuando; (whenever) cuando, en caso de que; (whether) si. **as if,** como si (foll. by subjunc.). **If he comes, we shall tell him,** Si viene se lo diremos. **If he had not killed the tiger, she would be dead,** Si él no hubiera matado al tigre, ella estaría muerta. **If ever there was one,** Si alguna vez lo hubiera. **if necessary,** si fuese necesario. **if not,** si no, si no es que (e.g., *Poet and philosopher are twins, if not one and the same,* Poeta y filósofo son hermanos gemelos, si no es que la misma cosa). **If only!** ¡Ojalá que! (foll. by subjunc.)

igloo /'iglu/ *n* iglú, *m*

igneous /'ɪgniəs/ *a* ígneo

ignite /ɪg'nait/ *vt* encender, pegar fuego (a), incendiar. *vi* prender fuego, incendiarse; arder

ignition /ɪg'nɪʃən/ *n* ignición, *f*; *Auto.* encendido, *m*. **i. coil,** *Auto.* carrete de inducción del encendido, *m*. **i. key,** *Auto.* llave del contacto, *f*

ignoble /ɪg'noubəl/ *a* innoble, vil, indigno

ignobly /ɪg'noubli/ *adv* bajamente, vilmente

ignominious /ˌɪgnə'mɪniəs/ *a* ignominioso

ignominiously /ˌɪgnə'mɪniəsli/ *adv* ignominiosamente

ignominy /'ɪgnəˌmɪni/ *n* ignominia, deshonra, afrenta, *f*

ignoramus /ˌɪgnə'reiməs/ *n* ignorante, *mf*

ignorance /'ɪgnərəns/ *n* ignorancia, *f*; (unawareness) desconocimiento, *m*. **to plead i.,** pretender ignorancia

ignorant /'ɪgnərənt/ *a* ignorante; inculto. **He is an i. fellow,** Es un ignorante. **to be i. of,** no saber, ignorar. **to be very i.,** ser muy ignorante, *Inf.* ser muy burro

ignorantly /'ɪgnərəntli/ *adv* ignorantemente, por ignorancia; neciamente

ignore /ɪg'nɔr/ *vt* no hacer caso de, desatender; (omit) pasar por alto de, ignorar; *Law.* rechazar; (pretend not to recognize) hacer semblante de no reconocer; (not recognize) no reconocer

iguana /ɪ'gwɑnə/ *n Zool.* iguana, *f*

ileac /'ɪliæk/ *a Anat.* ilíaco

ileum /'ɪliəm/ *n Anat.* íleon, *m*

Iliad /'ɪliəd/ *n* Ilíada, *f*

ilium /'ɪliəm/ *n Anat.* ilion, *m*

ill /ɪl/ *n* mal, *m. a* (sick) enfermo, malo; (bad) malo; (unfortunate) desdichado, funesto. *adv* mal. **to be ill,** estar malo. **to be taken ill,** caer enfermo. **ill-advised,** mal aconsejado; desacertado, imprudente. **ill-advisedly,** imprudentemente. **ill at ease,** incómodo. **ill-bred,** mal criado, mal educado, mal nacido. **ill-breeding,** mala crianza, mala educación, *f*. **ill-disposed,** malintencionado. **ill fame,** mala fama, *f*. **ill-fated,** malhadado, malaventurado, aciago, fatal. **ill-favored,** mal parecido, feúcho. **ill-feeling,** hostilidad, *f*, rencor, *m*. **ill-gotten,** maladquirido. **ill-humor,** mal humor, *m*. **ill-humored,** de mal humor, malhumorado. **ill-luck,** desdicha, mala suerte, malaventura, *f*; infortunio, *m*. **ill-mannered,** mal educado. **ill-natured,** malévolo, perverso. **ill-naturedly,** malignamente. **ill-omened,** nefasto. **ill-spent,** malgastado, perdido. **ill-spoken,** mal hablado. **ill-suited,** malavenido. **ill-timed,** inoportuno, intempestivo. **ill-treat,** maltratar, malparar, tratar mal. **ill-treated,** que ha sido tratado mal; maltrecho. **ill-treatment,** maltratamiento, *m*, crueldad, *f*. **ill-turn,** mala jugada, *f*. **to do an ill-turn,** hacer un flaco servicio. **ill will,** mala voluntad, *f*; rencor, *m*, ojeriza, *f*. **to bear a person ill will,** guardarle rencor

illegal /ɪ'ligəl/ *a* ilegal; indebido, ilícito

illegality /ˌɪli'gælɪti/ *n* ilegalidad, *f*

illegally /ɪ'ligəli/ *adv* ilegalmente

illegibility /ɪˌledʒə'bɪlɪti/ *n* ilegibilidad, *f*

illegible /ɪ'ledʒəbəl/ *a* ilegible, indescifrable

illegibly /ɪ'ledʒəbli/ *adv* de un modo ilegible

illegitimacy /ˌɪlɪ'dʒɪtəməsi/ *n* ilegitimidad, *f*; falsedad, *f*

illegitimate /ˌɪlɪ'dʒɪtəmɪt/ *a* ilegítimo, bastardo; falso; ilícito, desautorizado

illegitimately /ˌɪlɪ'dʒɪtəmɪtli/ *adv* ilegítimamente

illiberal /ɪ'lɪbərəl/ *a* iliberal; intolerante, estrecho de miras; (mean) avaro, tacaño, ruin

illiberally /ɪ'lɪbərəli/ *adv* avariciosamente, ruinmente

illicit /ɪ'lɪsɪt/ *a* ilícito, indebido, ilegal

illicitly /ɪ'lɪsɪtli/ *adv* ilícitamente, ilegalmente

illicitness /ɪ'lɪsɪtnɪs/ *n* ilicitud, ilegalidad, *f*

illimitable /ɪ'lɪmɪtəbəl/ *a* ilimitado, sin límites, infinito

illiteracy /ɪ'lɪtərəsi/ *n* analfabetismo, *m*

illiterate /ɪ'lɪtərɪt/ *a* and *n* analfabeto (-ta), iliterato (-ta)

illness /'ɪlnɪs/ *n* enfermedad, dolencia, *f*, mal, *m*

illogical /ɪ'lɒdʒɪkəl/ *a* ilógico; absurdo, irracional

illogicality /ɪˌlɒdʒɪ'kælɪti/ *n* falta de lógica, *f*; absurdo, *m*, irracionalidad, *f*

illuminant /ɪ'lumənənt/ *a* iluminador, alumbrador

illuminate /ɪ'lumə,neit/ *vt* iluminar, alumbrar; *Art.* iluminar; (explain) aclarar, ilustrar

illuminated /ɪ'lumə,neitid/ *a* iluminado, encendido; *Art.* iluminado. **i. sign,** letrero luminoso, *m*

illuminati /ɪˌlumə'nɑti/ *n pl* secta de los alumbrados, *f*

illuminating /ɪ'lumə,neitɪŋ/ *a* iluminador; (explanatory) aclaratorio. *n Art.* iluminación, *f*

illumination /ɪˌlumə'neiʃən/ *n* iluminación, *f*, alumbrado, *m*; (for decoration) luminaria, *f*; *Art.* iluminación, *f*; *Fig.* inspiración, *f*

illuminator /ɪ'lumə,neitər/ *n Art.* iluminador (-ra)

illumine /ɪ'lumɪn/ *vt* encender, alumbrar; *Fig.* inspirar

illusion /ɪ'luʒən/ *n* ilusión, *f*, engaño, *m*; (dream) esperanza, ilusión, *f*, ensueño, *m*. **to harbor illusions,** tener ilusiones

illusive /ɪ'lusɪv/ *a* ilusivo, engañoso, falso

illusively /ɪ'lusɪvli/ *adv* falsamente, aparentemente

illusoriness /ɪ'lusərɪnɪs/ *n* ilusión, falsedad, *f*, engaño, *m*

illusory /ɪ'lusəri/ *a* ilusorio, deceptivo, falso, irreal

illustrate /'ɪlə,streit/ *vt* ilustrar, aclarar, explicar, elucidar; *Art.* ilustrar; (prove) probar, demostrar

illustration /ˌɪlə'streiʃən/ *n* ejemplo, *m*; ilustración, *f*; *Art.* grabado, *m*; estampa, *f*; (explanation) elucidación, aclaración, *f*

illustrative /ɪ'lʌstrətɪv/ *a* ilustrativo, ilustrador, explicativo, aclaratorio

illustrator /'ɪlə,streitər/ *n* ilustrador (-ra), grabador (-ra)

illustrious /ɪ'lʌstriəs/ *a* ilustre, famoso, renombrado, distinguido

illustriously /ɪ'lʌstriəsli/ *adv* ilustremente, noblemente

illustriousness /ɪ'lʌstriəsnɪs/ *n* eminencia, *f*, renombre, *m*, grandeza, *f*

image /'ɪmɪdʒ/ *n* (optics) imagen, *f*; efigie, imagen, *f*; (religious) imagen, estatua, *f*; *Art.* figura, *f*; (metaphor) metáfora, expresión, *f*; (of a person) retrato, *m*. **to be the i. of,** ser el retrato de. **sharp i.,** imagen nítida, *f*. **i. breaker,** iconoclasta, *mf*. **i. vendor,** vendedor (-ra) de imágenes

imagery /'ɪmɪdʒri/ *n Art.* imaginería, *f*; (style) metáforas, *f pl*

imaginable /ɪ'mædʒənəbəl/ *a* imaginable

imaginary /ɪ'mædʒə,nɛri/ *a* imaginario; fantástico, de ensueño

imagination /ɪˌmædʒə'neiʃən/ *n* imaginación, *f*; imaginativa, fantasía, inventiva, *f*, ingenio, *m*

imaginative /ɪ'mædʒənɪtɪv/ *a* imaginativo; fantástico

imagine /ɪ'mædʒɪn/ *vt* imaginar, concebir; idear, proyectar, inventar; figurarse, suponer. **Just i.!** ¡Imagínese usted!

imam /ɪ'mɑm/ *n* imán, *m*

imbecile /'ɪmbəsɪl/ *a* imbécil; (foolish) necio, estúpido, tonto. *n* imbécil, *mf*; (fool) necio (-ia), tonto (-ta), estúpido (-da)

imbecility /ˌɪmbə'sɪlɪti/ *n* imbecilidad, *f*; (folly) necedad, sandez, *f*

imbibe /ɪm'baɪb/ *vt* embeber, absorber; (drink) sorber, chupar; empaparse de

imbibing /ɪm'baɪbɪŋ/ *n* imbibición, absorción, *f*

imbroglio /ɪm'broʊlyoʊ/ *n* embrollo, lío, *m*

imbue /ɪm'byu/ *vt* imbuir, calar, empapar; teñir. **to i. with,** infundir de

imitable /'ɪmɪtəbəl/ *a* imitable

imitate /'ɪmɪˌteɪt/ *vt* imitar; copiar, reproducir; (counterfeit) contrahacer

imitation /ˌɪmɪ'teɪʃən/ *n* imitación, *f*; copia, *f*; remedo, traslado, *m*. *a* imitado; falso, artificial

imitative /'ɪmɪˌteɪtɪv/ *a* imitativo; imitador

imitativeness /'ɪmɪˌteɪtɪvnɪs/ *n* facultad imitativa (or de imitacion), *f*

imitator /'ɪmɪˌteɪtər/ *n* imitador (-ra); contrahacedor (-ra), falsificador (-ra)

immaculate /ɪ'mækyəlɪt/ *a* inmaculado, puro; (of dress) elegante. **I. Conception,** la Purísima Concepción

immaculately /ɪ'mækyəlɪtli/ *adv* inmaculadamente; elegantemente

immaculateness /ɪ'mækyəlɪtnɪs/ *n* pureza, *f*; (of dress) elegancia, *f*

immanence /'ɪmənəns/ *n* inmanencia, inherencia, *f*

immanent /'ɪmənənt/ *a* inmanente; inherente

immaterial /ˌɪmə'tɪəriəl/ *a* inmaterial, incorpóreo; sin importancia. **It is i. to me,** Me es indiferente, No me importa, Me da lo mismo, Me da igual

immateriality /ˌɪmə,tɪəri'ælɪti/ *n* inmaterialidad, *f*

immature /ˌɪmə'tʃʊr/ *a* inmaduro; precoz; (of fruit) verde

immaturity /ˌɪmə'tʃʊrɪti/ *n* falta de madurez, *f*; precocidad, *f*

immeasurability /ɪ,mɛʒərə'bɪlɪti/ *n* inmensurabilidad, inmensidad, *f*

immeasurable /ɪ'mɛʒərəbəl/ *a* inmensurable, inmenso, imponderable

immeasurably /ɪ'mɛʒərəbli/ *adv* inmensamente, enormemente

immediate /ɪ'midiɪt/ *a* (of place) inmediato, cercano, contiguo; (of time) próximo, inmediato, directo; (of action) inmediato, perentorio; (on letters) urgente. **to take i. action,** tomar acción inmediata

immediately /ɪ'midiɪtli/ *adv* inmediatamente, (of place) próximamente, contiguamente; (of time) luego, seguidamente, en el acto, ahora mismo, enseguida; directamente; (as soon as) así que

immemorial /ˌɪmə'mɔriəl/ *a* inmemorial, inmemorable

immemorially /ˌɪmə'mɔriəli/ *adv* desde tiempo inmemorial

immense /ɪ'mɛns/ *a* inmenso, enorme; vasto, extenso; infinito

immensely /ɪ'mɛnsli/ *adv* inmensamente, enormemente

immensity /ɪ'mɛnsɪti/ *n* inmensidad, *f*; extensión, vastedad, *f*

immerse /ɪ'mɜrs/ *vt* sumergir, hundir en, zambullir; bautizar por sumersión. *Fig.* **to be immersed in,** estar absorto en

immersion /ɪ'mɜrʒən/ *n* sumersion, *f*, hundimiento, *m*; *Astron.* inmersión, *f*

immigrant /'ɪmɪgrənt/ *a and n* inmigrante, *mf*

immigrate /'ɪmɪˌgreɪt/ *vi* inmigrar

immigration /ˌɪmɪ'greɪʃən/ *n* inmigración, *f*, (US Immigration and Naturalization Service) *Inf.* La Migra

imminence /'ɪmənəns/ *n* inminencia, *f*

imminent /'ɪmənənt/ *a* inminente

immobile /ɪ'moʊbəl/ *a* inmóvil, inmoble; impasible, imperturbable

immobility /ˌɪmou'bɪlɪti/ *n* inmovilidad, *f*; impasibilidad, imperturbabilidad, *f*

immobilization /ɪ,moʊbələ'zeɪʃən/ *n* inmovilización, *f*

immobilize /ɪ'moʊbəˌlaɪz/ *vt* inmovilizar

immoderate /ɪ'mɒdərɪt/ *a* inmoderado, excesivo, indebido

immoderately /ɪ'mɒdərɪtli/ *adv* inmoderadamente, excesivamente

immoderateness /ɪ'mɒdərɪtnɪs/ *n* inmoderación, *f*, exceso, *m*

immodest /ɪ'mɒdɪst/ *a* inmodesto; indecente, deshonesto; (pert) atrevido, descarado

immodestly /ɪ'mɒdɪstli/ *adv* impúdicamente, inmodestamente

immodesty /ɪ'mɒdɪsti/ *n* inmodestia, impudicia, *f*; deshonestidad, licencia, *f*; (forwardness) descaro, atrevimiento, *m*

immolate /'ɪməˌleɪt/ *vt* inmolar, sacrificar

immolation /ˌɪmə'leɪʃən/ *n* inmolación, *f*, sacrificio, *m*

immolator /'ɪməˌleɪtər/ *n* inmolador (-ra)

immoral /ɪ'mɔrəl/ *a* inmoral; licencioso, vicioso; incontinente

immorality /ˌɪmə'rælɪti/ *n* inmoralidad, *f*

immortal /ɪ'mɔrtl̩/ *a* inmortal; perenne, eterno, imperecedero. *n* inmortal, *mf*

immortality /ˌɪmɔr'tælɪti/ *n* inmortalidad, *f*; fama inmortal, *f*

immortalize /ɪ'mɔrtl̩ˌaɪz/ *vt* inmortalizar, perpetuar

immortally /ɪ'mɔrtl̩i/ *adv* inmortalmente, eternamente, para siempre

immovability /ɪ,muvə'bɪlɪti/ *n* inamovibilidad, inmovilidad, *f*; (of purpose) inflexibilidad, tenacidad, constancia, *f*

immovable /ɪ'muvəbəl/ *a* inmoble, fijo, inmóvil; (of purpose) inconmovible, inalterable, constante. *n pl.* **immovables,** *Law.* bienes inmuebles, *m pl.* **i. feast,** *Eccl.* fiesta fija, *f*

immovably /ɪ'muvəbli/ *adv* inmóvilmente, fijamente

immune /ɪ'myun/ *a* inmune, libre; *Med.* inmune. **i. from,** exento de; libre de

immunity /ɪ'myunɪti/ *n* inmunidad, libertad, *f*; exención, *f*; *Med.* inmunidad, *f*

immunization /ɪ,myunə'zeɪʃən/ *n* *Med.* inmunización, *f*

immunize /'ɪmyəˌnaɪz/ *vt* inmunizar

immure /ɪ'myʊr/ *vt* emparedar, recluir, encerrar

immutability /ɪ,myutə'bɪlɪti/ *n* inmutabilidad, inalterabilidad, *f*

immutable /ɪ'myutəbəl/ *a* inmutable, inalterable, constante

immutably /ɪ'myutəbli/ *adv* inmutablemente

imp /ɪmp/ *n* trasgo, diablillo, duende, *m*; (child) picaruelo (-la)

impact /'ɪmpækt/ *n* impacto, *m*, impacción, *f*; choque, *m*, colisión, *f*

impair /ɪm'pɛər/ *vt* perjudicar, echar a perder, deteriorar, empeorar, desmejorar. **to be impaired,** deteriorarse, perjudicarse

impairment /ɪm'pɛərmənt/ *n* deterioración, perjuicio, empeoramiento. *m*

impale /ɪm'peɪl/ *vt* (punishment) empalar; (with a sword) atravesar, espetar

impalement /ɪm'peɪlmənt/ *n* (punishment) empalamiento, *m*; atravesamiento, *m*, transfixión, *f*

impalpability /ɪm,pælpə'bɪlɪti/ *n* impalpabilidad, intangibilidad, *f*

impalpable /ɪm'pælpəbəl/ *a* impalpable, intangible; incorpóreo

impart /ɪm'part/ *vt* comunicar, dar parte (de); conferir

impartial /ɪm'parʃəl/ *a* imparcial, ecuánime

impartiality /ɪm,parʃi'ælɪti/ *n* imparcialidad, ecuanimidad, entereza, *f*, desinterés, *m*

impartially /ɪm'parʃəli/ *adv* imparcialmente, con desinterés

impassability /ɪm,pæsə'bɪlɪti/ *n* impracticabilidad, *f*

impassable /ɪm'pæsəbəl/ *a* intransitable, impracticable; (of water) invadeable

impasse /'ɪmpæs/ *n* callejón sin salida, *m*

impassibility /ɪm,pæsə'bɪlɪti/ *n* impasibilidad, imperturbabilidad, indiferencia, *f*

impassible /ɪm'pæsəbəl/ *a* impasible, insensible; indiferente, imperturbable

impassion /ɪm'pæʃən/ *vt* apasionar, conmover

impassioned /ɪm'pæʃənd/ *a* apasionado, vehemente, ardiente

impassive /ɪm'pæsɪv/ *a* impasible, insensible; indiferente, imperturbable; apático

impassively /ɪm'pæsɪvli/ *adv* indiferentemente

impassivity /ˌɪmpæˈsɪvɪti/ n impasibilidad, f; indiferencia, f; apatía, f

impatience /ɪmˈpeɪʃəns/ n impaciencia, f

impatient /ɪmˈpeɪʃənt/ a impaciente; intolerante. **to make i.,** impacientar. **to grow i.,** impacientarse, perder la paciencia. **to grow i. at,** impacientarse ante. **to grow i. to,** impacientarse a or por. **to grow i. under,** impacientarse bajo

impatiently /ɪmˈpeɪʃəntli/ adv con impaciencia, impacientemente

impeach /ɪmˈpitʃ/ vt Law. denunciar, delatar, acusar, hacer juicio político (Argentina); censurar, criticar, tachar

impeachable /ɪmˈpitʃəbəl/ a Law. delatable, denunciable, acusable; censurable

impeacher /ɪmˈpitʃər/ n acusador (-ra), denunciador (-ra), delator (-ra)

impeachment /ɪmˈpitʃmənt/ n Law. acusación, denuncia, f; reproche, m, queja, f

impeccability /ɪmˌpɛkəˈbɪlɪti/ n (perfection) impecabilidad, perfección, f; elegancia, f

impeccable /ɪmˈpɛkəbəl/ a impecable, intachable, perfecto; elegante

impeccably /ɪmˈpɛkəbli/ adv perfectamente; elegantemente

impecuniosity /ˌɪmpəˌkyuniˈɒsɪti/ n indigencia, pobreza, f

impecunious /ˌɪmpəˈkyuniəs/ a indigente, pobre

impede /ɪmˈpid/ vt impedir, obstruir, estorbar; Fig. dificultar, embarazar

impediment /ɪmˈpɛdəmənt/ n obstáculo, estorbo, m; Fig. dificultad, f; Law. impedimento, m. **to have an i. in one's speech,** tener una dificultad en el hablar

impel /ɪmˈpɛl/ vt impulsar, impeler; Fig. estimular, obligar, mover, constreñir. **I felt impelled (to),** Me sentí obligado (a)

impend /ɪmˈpɛnd/ vi ser inminente, amenazar

impending /ɪmˈpɛndɪŋ/ a inminente, pendiente

impenetrability /ɪmˌpɛnɪtrəˈbɪlɪti/ n impenetrabilidad, f; Fig. enigma, secreto, misterio, m

impenetrable /ɪmˈpɛnɪtrəbəl/ a impenetrable; intransitable; denso, espeso; Fig. enigmático, insondable, secreto

impenetrably /ɪmˌpɛnɪtrəˈbɪlɪti/ adv impenetrablemente, densamente

impenitence /ɪmˈpɛnɪtəns/ n impenitencia, f

impenitent /ɪmˈpɛnɪtənt/ a impenitente, incorregible

impenitently /ɪmˈpɛnɪtəntli/ adv sin penitencia

imperative /ɪmˈpɛrətɪv/ a imperioso, perentorio; Gram. imperativo; (necessary) esencial, urgente. n mandato, m, orden, f; Gram. imperativo, m. **in the i.,** en el imperativo

imperatively /ɪmˈpɛrətɪvli/ adv imperativamente

imperativeness /ɪmˈpɛrətɪvnɪs/ n perentoriedad, f; urgencia, importancia, f

imperceptible /ˌɪmpərˈsɛptəbəl/ a imperceptible, insensible

imperceptibly /ˌɪmpərˈsɛptəbli/ adv imperceptiblemente

imperceptive /ˌɪmpərˈsɛptɪv/ a insensible

imperfect /ɪmˈpɜrfɪkt/ a imperfecto; incompleto, defectuoso. a and n Gram. imperfecto m

imperfection /ˌɪmpərˈfɛkʃən/ n imperfección, f; defecto, desperfecto, m; falta, tacha, f

imperfectly /ɪmˈpɜrfɪktli/ adv imperfectamente

imperial /ɪmˈpɪəriəl/ a imperial, imperatorio. n (beard) pera, f. **i. preference,** preferencia dentro del Imperio, f

imperial /ɪmˈpɪəriəl/ vt arriesgar, poner en peligro, aventurar

imperialism /ɪmˈpɪəriəˌlɪzəm/ n imperialismo, m

imperialist /ɪmˈpɪəriəlɪst/ n imperialista, mf

imperialistic /ɪmˌpɪəriəˈlɪstɪk/ a imperialista

imperious /ɪmˈpɪəriəs/ a imperioso, altivo, arrogante; (pressing) urgente, apremiante

imperiously /ɪmˈpɪəriəsli/ adv imperiosamente, con arrogancia

imperiousness /ɪmˈpɪəriəsnɪs/ n autoridad, arrogancia, altivez, f; necesidad, urgencia, f, apremio, m

imperishability /ɪmˌpɛrɪʃəˈbɪlɪti/ n (immortality) inmortalidad, perennidad, f

imperishable /ɪmˈpɛrɪʃəbəl/ a imperecedero, inmarchitable, perenne, eterno

impermanence /ɪmˈpɜrmənəns/ n inestabilidad, interinidad, f; brevedad, fugacidad, f

impermanent /ɪmˈpɜrmənənt/ a interino, no permanente

impermeability /ɪmˌpɜrmiəˈbɪlɪti/ n impermeabilidad, f

impermeable /ɪmˈpɜrmiəbəl/ a impermeable

impersonal /ɪmˈpɜrsənl/ a impersonal, objetivo; Gram. impersonal

impersonality /ɪmˌpɜrsəˈnælɪti/ n objetividad, f

impersonally /ɪmˈpɜrsənli/ adv impersonalmente

impersonate /ɪmˈpɜrsəˌneɪt/ vt personificar, simbolizar; Theat. representar

impersonation /ɪmˌpɜrsəˈneɪʃən/ n personificación, simbolización, f; Theat. representación, f

impertinence /ɪmˈpɜrtnəns/ n impertinencia, majadería, insolencia, f; inoportunidad, f; despropósito, m

impertinent /ɪmˈpɜrtnənt/ a impertinente, insolente; (unseasonable) intempestivo, inoportuno; (irrelevant) fuera de propósito

impertinently /ɪmˈpɜrtnəntli/ adv con insolencia, impertinentemente

imperturbability /ˌɪmpərtɜrbəˈbɪlɪti/ n imperturbabilidad, serenidad, impasibilidad, f; impavidez, f

imperturbable /ˌɪmpərˈtɜrbəbəl/ a imperturbable, impasible, sereno; impávido

imperturbably /ˌɪmpərˈtɜrbəbli/ adv con serenidad, imperturbablemente

impervious /ɪmˈpɜrviəs/ a impermeable, impenetrable; Fig. insensible. **He is i. to arguments,** No hace caso de argumentos

imperviousness /ɪmˈpɜrviəsnɪs/ n impermeabilidad, impenetrabilidad, f; Fig. insensibilidad, f

impetigo /ˌɪmpɪˈtaɪgoʊ/ n Med. impétigo, m

impetuosity /ɪmˌpɛtʃuˈɒsɪti/ n impetuosidad, temeridad, irreflexión, f

impetuous /ɪmˈpɛtʃuəs/ a impetuoso, temerario, irreflexivo; violento, vehemente

impetuously /ɪmˈpɛtʃuəsli/ adv impetuosamente; con vehemencia

impetus /ˈɪmpɪtəs/ n Mech. ímpetu, m, impulsión, f; Fig. incentivo, estímulo, impulso, m

impiety /ɪmˈpaɪɪti/ n impiedad, irreligión, irreligiosidad, f

impinge (upon) /ɪmˈpɪndʒ/ vi chocar con, tropezar con

impious /ˈɪmpiəs/ a impío, irreligioso, sacrílego; (wicked) malvado, perverso, malo

impish /ˈɪmpɪʃ/ a travieso, revoltoso, enredador

implacability /ɪmˌplækəˈbɪlɪti/ n implacabilidad, f

implacable /ɪmˈplækəbəl/ a implacable, inexorable, inflexible, riguroso

implacably /ɪmˈplækəbli/ adv implacablemente

implant /ɪmˈplænt/ vt Fig. implantar, inculcar, instilar

implantation /ˌɪmplænˈteɪʃən/ n Fig. implantación, instilación, inculcación, f

implement /n ˈɪmpləmənt/ v also -ˌmɛnt/ n instrumento, utensilio, m, herramienta, f; (of war) elemento, m. vt cumplir, hacer efectivo; llevar a cabo

implicate /ˈɪmplɪˌkeɪt/ vt enredar, envolver; (imply) implicar, contener, llevar en sí; (in a crime) comprometer. **to be implicated in a crime,** estar implicado en un crimen

implication /ˌɪmplɪˈkeɪʃən/ n implicación, inferencia, repercusión, sugestión, f; (in a crime) complicidad, f

implicit /ɪmˈplɪsɪt/ a implícito, virtual, tácito; (absolute) ciego, absoluto, implícito. **with i. faith,** con fe ciega

implicitness /ɪmˈplɪsɪtnɪs/ n carácter implícito, m, lo implícito

implied /ɪmˈplaɪd/ a tácito, implícito

implore /ɪmˈplɔr/ vt implorar, suplicar

imploring /ɪmˈplɔrɪŋ/ a suplicante, implorante

imploringly /ɪmˈplɔrɪŋli/ adv con encarecimiento, a súplica, de un modo suplicante

imply /ɪmˈplaɪ/ vt implicar, indicar, presuponer;

(mean) querer decir, significar; (hint) insinuar, sugerir

impolite /ˌɪmpəˈlait/ *a* descortés, mal educado

impolitely /ˌɪmpəˈlaitli/ *adv* con descortesía

impoliteness /ˌɪmpəˈlaitnɪs/ *n* descortesía, falta de urbanidad, *f*

impolitic /ɪmˈpɒlɪtɪk/ *a* impolítico

imponderability /ɪmˌpɒndərəˈbɪlɪti/ *n* imponderabilidad, *f*

imponderable /ɪmˈpɒndərəbəl/ *a* imponderable

import /*v* ɪmˈpɔrt; *a, n* ˈɪmpɔrt/ *vt Com.* importar; (mean) significar, querer decir. *a Com.* importado, de importación. *n Com.* importación, *f*; (meaning) significado, sentido, *m*; (value) importe, valor, *m*; (contents) contenido, tenor, *m*; importancia, *f*. **i. duty,** derechos de importación derechos de entrada, *m pl,* gravamen a la importación, *m*. **i. licence,** permiso de importación, *m*. **i. trade,** negocios de importación, *m pl*

importable /ɪmˈpɔrtəbəl/ *a* importable, que se puede importar

importance /ɪmˈpɔrtns/ *n* importancia, *f*; valor, alcance, *m*, magnitud, *f*; consideración, eminencia, *f*. **to be fully conscious of one's i.,** tener plena conciencia de su importancia

important /ɪmˈpɔrtnt/ *a* importante; distinguido; presuntuoso, vanidoso. **to be i.,** importar, ser importante. **i. person,** personaje, *m*, persona importante, *f*

importantly /ɪmˈpɔrtntli/ *adv* importantemente, con importancia

importation /ˌɪmpɔrˈteiʃən/ *n* importación, *f*; *Com.* introducción (or importación) de géneros extranjeros, *f*

importer /ɪmˈpɔrtər/ *n* importador (-ra)

importunate /ɪmˈpɔrtʃənɪt/ *a* (of a demand) insistente, importuno; (of persons) impertinente, pesado

importunately /ɪmˈpɔrtʃənɪtli/ *adv* importunadamente

importune /ˌɪmpɔrˈtun/ *vt* importunar, asediar, perseguir

importuning /ˌɪmpɔrˈtunɪŋ/ *n* persecución, importunación, *f*

importunity /ˌɪmpɔrˈtunɪti/ *n* importunidad, insistencia, impertinencia, *f*

impose /ɪmˈpouz/ *vt* (on, upon) imponer, infligir, cargar; *Print.* imponer. *vi* (on, upon) (deceive) engañar, embaucar

imposing /ɪmˈpouzɪŋ/ *a* imponente, impresionante; (of persons) majestuoso, importante

imposition /ˌɪmpəˈzɪʃən/ *n* imposición, *f*; (burden) impuesto, tributo, *m*, carga, *f*; (*Print., etc.*) imposición, *f*; (trick) fraude, engaño, *m*, decepción, *f*

impossibility /ɪmˌpɒsəˈbɪlɪti/ *n* imposibilidad, *f*

impossible /ɪmˈpɒsəbəl/ *a* imposible. **Nothing is i.,** No hay nada imposible, *Inf.* De menos no hizo Dios. **to do the i.,** hacer lo imposible

impostor /ɪmˈpɒstər/ *n* impostor (-ra), bribón (-ona), embustero (-ra)

imposture /ɪmˈpɒstʃər/ *n* impostura, *f*, engaño, fraude, *m*

impotence /ˈɪmpətəns/ *n* impotencia, *f*

impotent /ˈɪmpətənt/ *a* impotente

impound /ɪmˈpaund/ *vt* acorralar; (water) embalsar; (goods) confiscar

impoverish /ɪmˈpɒvərɪʃ/ *vt* empobrecer, depauperar, arruinar; (health) debilitar; (land) agotar

impoverished /ɪmˈpɒvərɪʃt/ *a* indigente, necesitado; (of land) agotado

impoverishment /ɪmˈpɒvərɪʃmənt/ *n* empobrecimiento, *m*, ruina, *f*; (of land) agotamiento, *m*

impracticability /ɪmˌpræktɪkəˈbɪlɪti/ *n* impracticabilidad, imposibilidad, *f*

impracticable /ɪmˈpræktɪkəbəl/ *a* impracticable, no factible, imposible

imprecation /ˌɪmprɪˈkeiʃən/ *n* imprecación, maldición, *f*

imprecatory /ˈɪmprɪkəˌtɔri/ *a* imprecatorio, maldiciente

impregnable /ɪmˈprɛgnəbəl/ *a* inexpugnable, inconquistable

impregnate /ɪmˈprɛgneit/ *vt* impregnar, empapar; *Biol.* fecundar. **to become impregnated,** impregnarse

impregnation /ˌɪmprɛgˈneiʃən/ *n* impregnación, *f*; *Biol.* fecundación, fertilización, *f*; *Fig.* inculcación, *f*

impresario /ˌɪmprəˈsɑri,ou/ *n* empresario, *m*

imprescriptible /ˌɪmprəˈskrɪptəbəl/ *a* imprescriptible, inalienable

impress /*v* ɪmˈprɛs; *n* ˈɪmprɛs/ *vt* imprimir; (on the mind) impresionar; inculcar, imbuir; (with respect) imponer; *Mil.* reclutar; (of goods) confiscar. *n* impresión, marca, señal, huella, *f*

impression /ɪmˈprɛʃən/ *n* impresión, *f*; marca, señal, huella, *f*; *Print.* impresión, *f*; efecto, *m*; idea, noción, *f*. **He has the i. that they do not like him,** Sospecha que no les es simpático. **to be under the i.,** tener la impresión

impressionability /ɪmˌprɛʃənəˈbɪlɪti/ *n* susceptibilidad, sensibilidad, *f*

impressionable /ɪmˈprɛʃənəbəl/ *a* susceptible, impresionable, sensitivo

impressionism /ɪmˈprɛʃəˌnɪzəm/ *n* impresionismo, *m*

impressionist /ɪmˈprɛʃənɪst/ *n* impresionista, *mf*

impressionistic /ɪmˌprɛʃəˈnɪstɪk/ *a* impresionista

impressive /ɪmˈprɛsɪv/ *a* impresionante; emocionante; imponente, majestuoso; enfático

impressively /ɪmˈprɛsɪvli/ *adv* solemnemente, de modo impresionante; enfáticamente

impressiveness /ɪmˈprɛsɪvnɪs/ *n* efecto impresionante, *m, Lat. Am.* imponencia *f*; grandiosidad, pompa, *f*; majestuosidad, *f*; fuerza, *f*

imprint /*n* ˈɪmprɪnt; *v* ɪmˈprɪnt/ *n* impresión, señal, marca, huella, *f*; *Print.* pie de imprenta, *m*. *vt* imprimir; (on the mind) grabar, fijar

imprison /ɪmˈprɪzən/ *vt* encerrar, encarcelar, aprisionar

imprisonment /ɪmˈprɪzənmənt/ *n* encarcelación, prisión, *f*, encierro, *m*

improbability /ɪmˌprɒbəˈbɪlɪti/ *n* improbabilidad, *f*; inverosimilitud, *f*

improbable /ɪmˈprɒbəbəl/ *a* improbable; inverosímil

improbity /ɪmˈproubɪti/ *n* improbidad, *f*

impromptu /ɪmˈprɒmptu/ *a* indeliberado, impremeditado, espontáneo. *adv* de improviso, in promptu. *n* improvisación, *f*

improper /ɪmˈprɒpər/ *a* impropio, inadecuado; incorrecto; indebido; indecente, indecoroso. **i. fraction,** *Math.* quebrado impropio, *m*

improperly /ɪmˈprɒpərli/ *adv* impropiamente, incorrectamente; indecorosamente

impropriety /ˌɪmprəˈpraiti/ *n* inconveniencia, *f*; incorrección, *f*; (style) impropiedad, *f*; falta de decoro, *f*

improvable /ɪmˈpruvəbəl/ *a* mejorable, perfectible

improve /ɪmˈpruv/ *vt* mejorar; perfeccionar; (beautify) embellecer, hermosear; (land) bonificar; *Lit.* corregir, enmendar; (cultivate) cultivar; (increase) aumentar; (an opportunity) aprovechar; (strengthen) fortificar; (business) sacar provecho de, explotar. *vi* mejorar; perfeccionarse; (progress) hacer progresos, progresar, adelantarse; *Com.* subir; (become beautiful) hacerse hermoso, embellecerse; (increase) aumentarse. **to i. upon,** mejorar, perfeccionar; pulir

improvement /ɪmˈpruvmənt/ *n* mejora, *f*; perfeccionamiento, *m*; aumento, *m*; adelantamiento, progreso, *m*; (in health) mejoría, *f*; embellecimiento, *m*; cultivación, *f*; (of land) abono, *m*

improver /ɪmˈpruvər/ *n* aprendiz (-za)

improvidence /ɪmˈprɒvɪdəns/ *n* imprevisión, *f*; improvidencia, *f*

improvident /ɪmˈprɒvɪdənt/ *a* impróvido, desprevenido

improvidently /ɪmˈprɒvɪdəntli/ *adv* impróvidamente

improvisation /ɪmˌprɒvəˈzeiʃən/ *n* improvisación, *f*

improvise /ˈɪmprəˌvaiz/ *vt* improvisar

improviser /ˈɪmprəˌvaizər/ *n* improvisador (-ra)

imprudence /ɪmˈprudns/ *n* imprudencia, *f*; desacierto, *m*, indiscreción, *f*

imprudent /ɪmˈprudnt/ *a* imprudente; desacertado, indiscreto, mal avisado, irreflexivo

imprudently /ɪmˈprudntli/ *adv* imprudentemente; sin pensar

impudence /'ɪmpyədəns/ n impudencia, f, descaro, m, insolencia, desvergüenza, f, atrevimiento, m
impudent /'ɪmpyədənt/ a impudente, descarado, insolente, desvergonzado, atrevido, Peru lisurero
impudently /'ɪmpyədəntli/ adv descaradamente, con insolencia
impugn /ɪm'pyun/ vt impugnar, contradecir, atacar
impugnable /ɪm'pyunəbəl/ a impugnable, atacable
impugnment /ɪm'pyunmənt/ n impugnación, f
impulse /'ɪmpʌls/ n ímpetu, m, impulsión, f; impulso, estímulo, m; incitación, instigación, f; motivo, m; (fit) arranque, arrebato, acceso, m
impulsion /ɪm'pʌlʃən/ n ímpetu, m, impulsión, f; empuje, m, arranque, m
impulsive /ɪm'pʌlsɪv/ a impelente; irreflexivo, impulsivo
impulsively /ɪm'pʌlsɪvli/ adv por impulso
impulsiveness /ɪm'pʌlsɪvnɪs/ n irreflexión, f; carácter impulsivo, m
impunity /ɪm'pyunɪti/ n impunidad, f. **with i.,** impunemente
impure /ɪm'pyʊr/ a impuro; adulterado, mezclado; (indecent) deshonesto, indecente; (dirty) turbio, sucio
impurity /ɪm'pyʊrɪti/ n impureza, f; adulteración, mezcla, f; deshonestidad, liviandad, f; suciedad, turbiedad, f
imputable /ɪm'pyutəbəl/ a imputable, atribuible
imputation /ˌɪmpyʊ'teɪʃən/ n imputación, atribución, f; (in a bad sense) acusación, f, reproche, m
impute /ɪm'pyut/ vt imputar, achacar, atribuir; acusar, reprochar
in /ɪn/ prep en; a; (of duration) durante, mientras; (with) con; (through) por; dentro de; (under) bajo; (following a superlative) de; (of specified time) dentro de, de aquí a; (with afternoon, etc.) por; (out of) sobre. **course in medieval Catalan literature,** curso de literatura catalana medioeval. **dressed in black,** vestido de negro. **in New York,** en Nueva York. **in the morning,** por la mañana; (in the course of) durante la mañana. **in time,** a tiempo; dentro de algún tiempo. **in a week,** dentro de una semana. **in the best way,** del mejor modo. **in writing,** por escrito. **in anger,** con enojo. **in one's hand,** en la mano. **in addition to,** además de, a más de. **in case,** por si acaso, en caso de que. **in order to,** a fin de, para (foll. by infin.). **in order that,** para que (foll. by subjunc.). **in so far as,** en cuanto. **in spite of,** a pesar de. **in the distance,** a lo lejos, en lontananza. **in the meantime,** entre tanto. **in the middle of,** en el medio de; a la mitad de. **in the style of,** al modo de; a la manera de, a la (francesa, etc.)
in /ɪn/ adv adentro, dentro; (at home) en casa; (of sun) escondido; (of fire) alumbrado; (in power) en el poder; (of harvest) cosechado; (of boats) entrado (with haber); (of trains) llegado (with haber). **to be in,** estar dentro; haber llegado; estar en casa. **in for,** estar expuesto a, correr el riesgo de. **to be in with a person,** ser muy amigo de, estar muy metido con. **Come in!** ¡Adelante!; ¡Pase usted! **ins and outs,** sinuosidades, f pl; (of river) meandros, m pl; (of an affair) pormenores, detalles, m pl. **in less time than you can say Jack Robinson,** en menos de Jesús, en un credo, en menos que canta un gallo, en menos que se persigna un cura loco. **in the middle of nowhere,** donde Cristo dio las tres voces, (Western Hemisphere) donde el diablo perdió el poncho.
in /ɪn/ a interno. **in-law** /ʊf (of relations) político. **in-patient,** enfermo (-ma) de hospital
inability /ˌɪnə'bɪlɪti/ n incapacidad, inhabilidad, ineptitud, incompetencia, f; impotencia, f
inaccessibility /ˌɪnək,sɛsə'bɪlɪti/ n inaccesibilidad, f
inaccessible /ˌɪnək'sɛsəbəl/ a inaccesible
inaccuracy /ɪn'ækyərəsi/ n inexactitud, incorrección, f
inaccurate /ɪn'ækyərɪt/ a inexacto, incorrecto
inaccurately /ɪn'ækyərɪtli/ adv inexactamente, erróneamente
inaction /ɪn'ækʃən/ n inacción, f
inactive /ɪn'æktɪv/ a inactivo, pasivo; (of things) inerte; (lazy) perezoso, indolente; (machinery) parado; (motionless) inmóvil; (at leisure) desocupado, sin empleo

inactivity /ˌɪnæk'tɪvɪti/ n inactividad, pasividad, f; (of things) inercia, f; pereza, indolencia, f; (of machinery) paro, m; inmovilidad, f; (leisure) desocupación, f
inadaptable /ˌɪnə'dæptəbəl/ a inadaptable, no adaptable
inadequacy /ɪn'ædɪkwəsi/ n insuficiencia, escasez, f; imperfección, f, defecto, m
inadequate /ɪn'ædɪkwɪt/ a inadecuado, insuficiente, escaso; imperfecto, defectuoso
inadequately /ɪn'ædɪkwɪtli/ adv inadecuadamente
inadmissible /ˌɪnəd'mɪsəbəl/ a inadmisible, no admisible
inadvertence /ˌɪnəd'vɜrtn̩s/ n inadvertencia, f, equivocación, f, descuido, m
inadvertent /ˌɪnəd'vɜrtn̩t/ a inadvertido, accidental, casual; negligente
inadvertently /ˌɪnəd'vɜrtn̩tli/ adv inadvertidamente, sin querer
inalienability /ɪnˌeɪlyənə'bɪlɪti/ n inalienabilidad, f
inalienable /ɪn'eɪlyənəbəl/ a inajenable, inalienable
inalterability /ɪnˌɔltərə'bɪlɪti/ n inalterabilidad, f
inalterable /ɪn'ɔltərəbəl/ a inalterable
inalterably /ɪn'ɔltərəbli/ adv inalterablemente, sin alteración
inane /ɪ'neɪn/ a lelo, fatuo, vacío, necio
inanimate /ɪn'ænəmɪt/ a (of matter) inanimado; sin vida, exánime, muerto
inanity /ɪ'nænɪti/ n vacuidad, fatuidad, necedad, f
inappeasable /ˌɪnə'pizəbəl/ a implacable, riguroso
inapplicability /ɪnˌæplɪkə'bɪlɪti/ n no aplicabilidad, f
inapplicable /ɪn'æplɪkəbəl/ a inaplicable
inapposite /ɪn'æpəzɪt/ a fuera de propósito, no pertinente, inoportuno
inappreciable /ˌɪnə'priʃəbəl/ a inapreciable, imperceptible
inappreciation /ˌɪnəpriʃi'eɪʃən/ n falta de apreciación, f
inappreciative /ˌɪnə'priʃətɪv/ a desagradecido, ingrato. **i. of,** insensible a, indiferente a
inapproachable /ˌɪnə'proutʃəbəl/ a inaccesible, huraño, adusto
inappropriate /ˌɪnə'proupriɪt/ a impropio, inconveniente, inadecuado, incongruente; inoportuno
inappropriately /ˌɪnə'proupriɪtli/ adv impropiamente, inoportunamente
inappropriateness /ˌɪnə'proupriɪtnɪs/ n impropiedad, inconveniencia, incongruencia, f; inoportunidad, f
inapt /ɪn'æpt/ a inepto, inhábil; impropio
inaptitude /ɪn'æptɪˌtud/ n ineptitud, inhabilidad, f; impropiedad, f
inarticulate /ˌɪnɑr'tɪkyəlɪt/ a (of speech) inarticulado; (reticent) inexpresivo, reservado; indistinto; Anat. inarticulado
inarticulately /ˌɪnɑr'tɪkyəlɪtli/ adv indistintamente, de un modo inarticulado
inarticulateness /ˌɪnɑr'tɪkyəlɪtnɪs/ n inexpresión, reserva, f; silencio, m
inartistic /ˌɪnɑr'tɪstɪk/ a antiartístico, antiestético
inartistically /ˌɪnɑr'tɪstɪkli/ adv sin gusto (estético)
inasmuch (as) /ˌɪnəz'mʌtʃ/ adv puesto que, visto que, dado que
inattention /ˌɪnə'tɛnʃən/ n desatención, inaplicación, abstracción, f; falta de solicitud, f
inattentive /ˌɪnə'tɛntɪv/ a desatento, distraído; poco solícito, no atento
inattentively /ˌɪnə'tɛntɪvli/ adv sin atención, distraídamente
inaudibility /ɪnˌɔdə'bɪlɪti/ n imposibilidad de oír, f
inaudible /ɪn'ɔdəbəl/ a inaudible, no audible, ininteligible
inaudibly /ɪn'ɔdəbli/ adv indistintamente, de modo inaudible
inaugurate /ɪn'ɔgyəˌreit/ vt inaugurar; (open) estrenar, abrir, dedicar; (install) investir, instalar; (initiate) originar, iniciar, dar lugar (a)
inauguration /ɪnˌɔgyə'reɪʃən/ n inauguración, f; (opening) estreno, m, apertura, f; (investiture) instalación, investidura, f
inauspicious /ˌɪnɔ'spɪʃəs/ a poco propicio, desfavorable; ominoso, triste, infeliz

inauspiciously /ˌɪnɔ'spɪʃəsli/ *adv* en condiciones desfavorables, desfavorablemente; infelizmente, bajo malos auspicios

inauspiciousness /ˌɪnɔ'spɪʃəsnɪs/ *n* condiciones desfavorables, *f pl*; infelicidad, *f*; malos auspicios, *m pl*

inborn /'ɪn'bɔrn/ *a* innato, instintivo, inherente

inbred /'ɪn'brɛd/ *a* innato, inherente, instintivo

Inca /'ɪŋkə/ *a* incaico, de los incas, *Lat. Am. also* incásico. *n* inca, *m*

incalculability /ɪn,kælkələ'bɪlɪti/ *n* imposibilidad de calcular, *f*; (of persons) volubilidad, veleidad, *f*; infinidad, immensidad, *f*

incalculable /ɪn'kælkyələbəl/ *a* incalculable, innumerable; (of persons) voluble, veleidoso, caprichoso; infinito, immenso

incalculably /ɪn'kælkyələbli/ *adv* enormemente, infinitamente; caprichosamente

incandescence /ˌɪnkən'dɛsəns/ *n* incandescencia, candencia, *f*

incandescent /ˌɪnkən'dɛsənt/ *a* incandescente, candente. **i. light,** luz incandescente, *f*. **to make i.,** encandecer

incantation /ˌɪnkæn'teɪʃən/ *n* hechizo, *m*, encantación, *f*, ensalmo, *m*

incapability /ɪn,keɪpə'bɪlɪti/ *n* incapacidad, *f*; inhabilidad, ineptitud, incompetencia, *f*

incapable /ɪn'keɪpəbəl/ *a* incapaz; inhábil, incompetente; (physically) imposibilitado

incapacitate /ˌɪnkə'pæsɪ,teɪt/ *vt* imposibilitar, incapacitar, inutilizar; (disqualify) inhabilitar, incapacitar

incapacitation /ˌɪnkə,pæsɪ'teɪʃən/ *n* inhabilitación, *f*

incapacity /ˌɪnkə'pæsɪti/ *n* incapacidad, inhabilidad, *f*

incarcerate /ɪn'kɑrsə,reɪt/ *vt* encarcelar

incarceration /ɪn,kɑrsə'reɪʃən/ *n* encarcelación, prisión, *f*

incarnate /a ɪn'kɑrnɪt/ *v* -neit/ *a* encarnado. *vt* encarnar

incarnation /ˌɪnkɑr'neɪʃən/ *n* encarnación, *f*

incautious /ɪn'kɔʃəs/ *a* incauto, imprudente

incautiously /ɪn'kɔʃəsli/ *adv* incautamente

incautiousness /ɪn'kɔʃəsnɪs/ *n* imprudencia, negligencia, falta de cautela, *f*

incendiary /ɪn'sɛndi,ɛri/ *a* incendiario. **i. bomb,** incendiaria, *f*

incense /ɪn'sɛns/ *n* incienso, *m*; *Fig.* adulación, *f*. *vt Eccl.* incensar; (annoy) irritar, exasperar, enojar. **i. burner,** incensario, *m*

incentive /ɪn'sɛntɪv/ *n* incentivo, estímulo, motivo, *m*. *a* estimulador, incitativo

inception /ɪn'sɛpʃən/ *n* comienzo, principio, *m*; inauguración, *f*

incertitude /ɪn'sɜrtɪ,tud/ *n* incertidumbre, *f*

incessant /ɪn'sɛsənt/ *a* incesante, continuo, constante

incessantly /ɪn'sɛsəntli/ *adv* incesantemente, sin cesar

incest /'ɪnsɛst/ *n* incesto, *m*

incestuous /ɪn'sɛstʃuəs/ *a* incestuoso

inch /ɪntʃ/ *n* pulgada, *f*. **every i. a man,** hombre hecho y derecho. **Not an i.!** ¡Ni pizca! **within an i. of,** a dos dedos de. **i. by i.,** palmo a palmo, paso a paso. **i. tape,** cinta métrica, *f*

inchoate /ɪn'koʊɪt/ *a* rudimentario; imperfecto, incompleto

incidence /'ɪnsɪdəns/ *n* incidencia, *f*

incident /'ɪnsɪdənt/ *a* propio, característico, incidental. *n* incidente, acontecimiento, *m*, ocurrencia, *f*

incidental /ˌɪnsɪ'dɛntl/ *a* incidente, incidental; accidental, accesorio, no esencial. **i. expense,** gasto imprevisto, *m*

incidentally /ˌɪnsɪ'dɛntli/ *adv* (secondarily) incidentalmente; (by the way) de propósito

incident of navigation *n* accidente de navegación, *m*

incinerate /ɪn'sɪnə,reɪt/ *vt* incinerar

incineration /ɪn,sɪnə'reɪʃən/ *n* incineración, cremación, *f*

incinerator /ɪn'sɪnə,reɪtər/ *n* incinerador, *m*

incipient /ɪn'sɪpiənt/ *a* incipiente, naciente, rudimentario

incision /ɪn'sɪʒən/ *n* incisión, *f*; corte, tajo, *m*; *Med.* abscisión, *f*

incisive /ɪn'saɪsɪv/ *a* (of mind) agudo, penetrante; (of words) mordaz, incisivo, punzante

incisively /ɪn'saɪsɪvli/ *adv* en pocas palabras; mordazmente, incisivamente

incisiveness /ɪn'saɪsɪvnɪs/ *n* (of mind) agudeza, penetración, *f*; (of words) mordacidad, *f*, sarcasmo, *m*

incisor /ɪn'saɪzər/ *n* diente incisivo, *m*

incite /ɪn'saɪt/ *vt* incitar, estimular, animar; provocar, tentar. **to i. to,** mover a, incitar a

incitement /ɪn'saɪtmənt/ *n* incitación, instigación, *f*; estímulo, *m*; tentación, *f*; aliciente, *m*

incivility /ˌɪnsə'vɪlɪti/ *n* incivilidad, descortesía, *f*

inclemency /ɪn'klɛmənsi/ *n* inclemencia, *f*, rigor, *m*

inclement /ɪn'klɛmənt/ *a* inclemente, riguroso, borrascoso

inclination /ˌɪnklə'neɪʃən/ *n* inclinación, *f*; (slope) declive, *m*, pendiente, cuesta, *f*; (tendency) propensión, tendencia, *f*; (liking) afición, *f*; amor, *m*; (bow) reverencia, *f*; *Geom.* inclinación, *f*

incline /v ɪn'klaɪn; n 'ɪnklaɪn/ *vt* inclinar, torcer; doblar; (cause) inclinar (a), hacer. *vi* inclinarse, torcerse; (tend) tender, propender, inclinarse; (colors) tirar (a). *n* declive, *m*, pendiente, cuesta, inclinación, *f*. **I am inclined to believe it,** Me inclino a creerlo. **I am inclined to do it,** Estoy por hacerlo, Creo que lo haré

inclined /ɪn'klaɪnd/ *a* torcido, inclinado, doblado; *Fig.* propenso, adicto. **i. plane,** plano inclinado, *m*

include /ɪn'klud/ *vt* incluir, contener, encerrar; comprender, abrazar

including /ɪn'kludɪŋ/ *present part* incluso, inclusive. **not i.,** no comprendido

inclusion /ɪn'kluʒən/ *n* inclusión, *f*

inclusive /ɪn'klusɪv/ *a* inclusivo. **January 2 to January 12 i.,** del 2 al 12 de enero, ambos inclusivos. **not i. of,** sin contar, exclusivo de. **i. of,** que incluye. **i. terms,** todo incluido, todos los gastos incluidos

incognito /ˌɪnkɒg'nitou/ *a and adv and n* incógnito, *m*

incoherence /ˌɪnkou'hɪərəns/ *n* incoherencia, inconsecuencia, *f*

incoherent /ˌɪnkou'hɪərənt/ *a* incoherente, inconexo, inconsecuente. **an i. piece of writing,** un escrito sin pies ni cabeza

incoherently /ˌɪnkou'hɪərəntli/ *adv* con incoherencia

incombustibility /ˌɪnkəm,bʌstə'bɪlɪti/ *n* incombustibilidad, *f*

incombustible /ˌɪnkəm'bʌstəbəl/ *a* incombustible

income /'ɪnkʌm/ *n* renta, *f*, ingreso, *m*; *Com.* rédito, *m*. **i.-tax,** impuesto sobre la renta, *m*. **i.-tax agents,** inspectores de impuestos de utilidades, *m pl.* **i.-tax return,** declaración de utilidades, *f*

incoming /'ɪn,kʌmɪŋ/ *a* entrante; nuevo. *n* entrada, llegada, *f. n pl* **incomings,** ingresos, *m pl*

incommensurability /ˌɪnkə,mɛnsərə'bɪlɪti/ *n* inconmensurabilidad, *f*

incommensurable /ˌɪnkə'mɛnsərəbəl/ *a* inconmensurable, no conmensurable

incommensurate /ˌɪnkə'mɛnsərɪt/ *a* desproporcionado, desmedido

incommodious /ˌɪnkə'moudiəs/ *a* estrecho; incómodo, inconveniente

incommodiousness /ˌɪnkə'moudiəsnɪs/ *n* estrechez, *f*; incomodidad, *f*

incommunicable /ˌɪnkə'myunɪkəbəl/ *a* incommunicable, indecible, inexplicable

incommunicative /ˌɪnkə'myunɪkətɪv/ *a* insociable, intratable, adusto, huraño

incomparable /ɪn'kɒmpərəbəl/ *a* incomparable; sin par, sin igual, excelente

incomparableness /ɪn'kɒmpərəbəlnɪs/ *n* excelencia, perfección, *f*

incomparably /ɪn'kɒmpərəbli/ *adv* incomparablemente, con mucho

incompatibility /ˌɪnkəm,pætə'bɪlɪti/ *n* incompatibilidad, *f*

incompatible /ˌɪnkəm'pætəbəl/ *a* incompatible

incompetence /ɪn'kɒmpɪtəns/ *n* incompetencia, ineptitud, inhabilidad, *f*; *Law.* incapacidad, *f*

incompetent /ɪn'kɒmpɪtənt/ *a* incompetente, incapaz, inepto, inhábil; *Law.* incapaz

incompetently /ɪn'kɒmpɪtəntli/ *adv* inhábilmente

incomplete /ˌɪnkəm'plit/ a incompleto; imperfecto, defectuoso; (unfinished) sin terminar, inacabado, inconcluso. **incomplete sentence,** frase que queda colgando, f
incompletely /ˌɪnkəm'plitli/ adv incompletamente; imperfectamente
incompleteness /ˌɪnkəm'plitnɪs/ n estado incompleto, m; imperfección, f; inconclusión, f
incomprehensibility /ˌɪnkɒmprɪˌhɛnsə'bɪlɪti/ n incomprensibilidad, f
incomprehensible /ˌɪnkɒmprɪ'hɛnsəbəl/ a incomprensible
incomprehension /ˌɪnkɒmprɪ'hɛnʃən/ n incomprensión, falta de comprensión, f
inconceivable /ˌɪnkən'sivəbəl/ a inconcebible, inimaginable
inconclusive /ˌɪnkən'klusɪv/ a inconcluyente, cuestionable, dudoso, no convincente
inconclusiveness /ˌɪnkən'klusɪvnɪs/ n carácter inconcluso, m, falta de conclusiones, f
incongruity /ˌɪnkən'gruɪti/ n incongruencia, desproporción, disonancia, f
incongruous /ɪn'kɒŋgruəs/ a incongruente, incongruo; chocante, desproporcionado, disonante
incongruously /ɪn'kɒŋgruəsli/ adv incongruentemente, incongruamente
inconsequence /ɪn'kɒnsɪ,kwɛns/ n inconsecuencia, f
inconsequent, inconsequential /ɪn'kɒnsɪ,kwɛnt; ɪnˌkɒnsɪ'kwɛnʃəl/ a inconsecuente, ilógico; inconsistente
inconsiderable /ˌɪnkən'sɪdərəbəl/ a insignificante
inconsiderate /ˌɪnkən'sɪdərɪt/ a desconsiderado, irreflexivo, irrespetuoso
inconsiderately /ˌɪnkən'sɪdərɪtli/ adv sin consideración, desconsideradamente
inconsiderateness /ˌɪnkən'sɪdərɪtnɪs/ n desconsideración, falta de respeto, f
inconsistency /ˌɪnkən'sɪstənsi/ n inconsistencia, inconsecuencia, incompatibilidad, contradicción, anomalía, f
inconsistent /ˌɪnkən'sɪstənt/ a inconsistente, inconsiguiente, incompatible, contradictorio, anómalo
inconsistently /ˌɪnkən'sɪstəntli/ adv contradictoriamente
inconsolable /ˌɪnkən'souləbəl/ a inconsolable, desconsolado. **to be i.,** estar inconsolable, (Inf. of a woman) estar hecha una Magdalena
inconsolably /ˌɪnkən'souləbli/ adv desconsoladamente
inconspicuous /ˌɪnkən'spɪkyuəs/ a que no llama la atención; insignificante, humilde, modesto
inconspicuously /ˌɪnkən'spɪkyuəsli/ adv humildemente, modestamente
inconspicuousness /ˌɪnkən'spɪkyuəsnɪs/ n modestia, humildad, f
inconstancy /ɪn'kɒnstənsi/ n inconstancia, movilidad, f; mudanza, veleidad, f
inconstant /ɪn'kɒnstənt/ a inconstante, mudable, variable; veleidoso, volátil, voluble
incontestable /ˌɪnkən'tɛstəbəl/ a incontestable, evidente, indisputable
incontinence /ɪn'kɒntnəns/ n incontinencia, f
incontinent /ɪn'kɒntnənt/ a incontinente
incontrollable /ˌɪnkən'trouləbəl/ a ingobernable, indomable
incontrovertible /ˌɪnkɒntrə'vɜrtəbəl/ a incontrovertible, incontrastable
inconvenience /ˌɪnkən'vinyəns/ n incomodidad, inconveniencia, f; (of time) inoportunidad, f. vt incomodar, causar inconvenientes (a)
inconvenient /ˌɪnkən'vinyənt/ a incómodo, inconveniente, molesto, embarazoso; (of time) inoportuno. **at an i. time,** a deshora
inconveniently /ˌɪnkən'vinyəntli/ adv incómodamente; (of time) inoportunamente
incorporate /v ɪn'kɔrpə,reit/ a -pərɪt/ vt incorporar, agregar; comprender, incluir, encerrar. vi asociarse, incorporarse. a incorpóreo, inmaterial; incorporado, asociado

incorporation /ɪnˌkɔrpə'reiʃən/ n incorporación, agregación, f; asociación, f
incorporeal /ˌɪnkɔr'pɔriəl/ a incorpóreo, inmaterial
incorporeity /ɪnˌkɔrpə'riɪti/ n incorporeidad, inmaterialidad, f
incorrect /ˌɪnkə'rɛkt/ a incorrecto; inexacto, erróneo, falso
incorrectness /ˌɪnkə'rɛktnɪs/ n incorrección, f
incorrigibility /ɪnˌkɒrɪdʒə'bɪlɪti/ n incorregibilidad, f
incorrigible /ɪn'kɒrɪdʒəbəl/ a incorregible, empecatado
incorrigibly /ɪn'kɒrɪdʒəbli/ adv incorregiblemente, obstinadamente
incorrupt /ˌɪnkə'rʌpt/ a incorrupto; recto, honrado
incorruptibility /ˌɪnkəˌrʌptə'bɪlɪti/ n incorruptibilidad, f; honradez, probidad, f
incorruptible /ˌɪnkə'rʌptəbəl/ a incorrupto; honrado, incorruptible
incorruption /ˌɪnkə'rʌpʃən/ n incorrupción, f
increase /v ɪn'kris; n 'ɪnkris/ vt aumentar, acrecentar; (in numbers) multiplicar; (extend) ampliar, extender; (of price) encarecer, aumentar. vi aumentar, crecer; multiplicarse; extenderse; encarecerse, aumentar. n aumento, crecimiento, m; multiplicación, f; (in price) encarecimiento, m, alza, f; (of water) crecida, f; (of moon) creciente, f. **It is on the i.,** Va en aumento. **to i. and multiply,** crecer y multiplicar
increasingly /ɪn'krisɪŋli/ adv más y más; en creciente, en aumento
incredibility /ɪnˌkrɛdə'bɪlɪti/ n incredibilidad, f
incredible /ɪn'krɛdəbəl/ a increíble; fabuloso, extraordinario. **It seems i.,** Es increíble, Inf. Parece mentira
incredibly /ɪn'krɛdəbli/ adv increíblemente
incredulity /ˌɪnkrɪ'dulɪti/ n incredulidad, f, escepticismo, m
incredulous /ɪn'krɛdʒələs/ a incrédulo, escéptico
incredulously /ɪn'krɛdʒələsli/ adv con incredulidad, escépticamente
increment /'ɪnkrəmənt/ n aumento, incremento, m; adición, añadidura, f; Math. incremento, m. **unearned i.,** plusvalía, mayor valía, f
incriminate /ɪn'krɪmə,neit/ vt incriminar
incriminating /ɪn'krɪmə,neitɪŋ/ a incriminante, acriminador
incrust /ɪn'krʌst/ vt incrustar, encostrar
incrustation /ˌɪnkrʌ'steiʃən/ n incrustación, f; (scab) costra, f
incubate /'ɪnkyə,beit/ vt empollar; Med. incubar
incubation /ˌɪnkyə'beiʃən/ n empolladura, incubación, f; Med. incubación, f
incubator /'ɪnkyə,beitər/ n incubadora, f
incubus /'ɪnkyəbəs/ n incubo, m; (burden) carga, f
inculcate /ɪn'kʌlkeit/ vt inculcar, implantar, instilar
inculcation /ˌɪnkʌl'keiʃən/ n inculcación, implantación, instilación, f
incumbency /ɪn'kʌmbənsi/ n posesión, duración de, posesión, duración (de cualquier puesto), f
incumbent /ɪn'kʌmbənt/ a obligatorio. n Eccl. beneficiado, m. **to be i. on,** incumbir a, ser de su obligación
incur /ɪn'kɜr/ vi incurrir (en), incidir (en). **to i. an obligation,** contraer una obligación
incurability /ɪnˌkyʊrə'bɪlɪti/ n incurabilidad, f
incurable /ɪn'kyʊrəbəl/ a incurable, insanable; Fig. sin solución, irremediable. n incurable, mf
incurably /ɪn'kyʊrəbli/ adv incurablemente, irremediablemente
incurious /ɪn'kyʊriəs/ a indiferente, sin interés, incurioso, negligente, descuidado
incursion /ɪn'kɜrʒən/ n incursión, invasión, irrupción, f, acometimiento, m
indebted /ɪn'dɛtɪd/ a empeñado, adeudado; (obliged) reconocido
indebtedness /ɪn'dɛtɪdnɪs/ n deuda, f; (gratitude) obligación, f; agradecimiento, m
indecency /ɪn'disənsi/ n indecencia, f
indecent /ɪn'disənt/ a indecente; obsceno, deshonesto

indecently /ɪn'diːsntli/ *adv* torpemente, indecentemente

indecision /ˌɪndɪ'sɪʒən/ *n* indecisión, vacilación, irresolución, *f*

indecisive /ˌɪndɪ'saɪsɪv/ *a* indeciso, irresoluto, vacilante

indeclinable /ˌɪndɪ'klaɪnəbəl/ *a* indeclinable

indecorous /ɪn'dɛkərəs/ *a* indecoroso, indecente, indigno

indecorum /ˌɪndɪ'kɔrəm/ *n* indecoro, *m*, indecencia, *f*; incorrección, *f*

indeed /ɪn'diːd/ *adv* en efecto, de veras, a la verdad, realmente, por cierto, claro está. *interr* ¿de veras? ¿es posible? **I shall be very glad i.**, Estaré contento de veras. **It is i. an excellent book,** Es en efecto un libro excelente. **There are differences i. between this house and the other,** Hay diferencias, claro está, entre esta casa y la otra

indefatigability /ˌɪndɪˌfætɪɡə'bɪlɪti/ *n* resistencia, *f*, aguante, *m*, tenacidad, *f*

indefatigable /ˌɪndɪ'fætɪɡəbəl/ *a* incansable, infatigable, resistente

indefatigably /ˌɪndɪ'fætɪɡəbli/ *adv* infatigablemente

indefensible /ˌɪndɪ'fɛnsəbəl/ *a* indefendible, insostenible

indefinable /ˌɪndɪ'faɪnəbəl/ *a* indefinible

indefinite /ɪn'dɛfənɪt/ *a* indefinido, incierto; (delicate) sutil, delicado; *Gram.* indefinido; (vague) vago. *Gram.* **i. article,** artículo indefinido, *m*

indefinitely /ɪn'dɛfənɪtli/ *adv* indefinidamente

indefiniteness /ɪn'dɛfənɪtnɪs/ *n* lo indefinido, el carácter indefinido, *m*; vaguedad, *f*

indelibility /ɪnˌdɛlə'bɪlɪti/ *n* resistencia, *f*, lo indeleble; *Fig.* duración, tenacidad, *f*

indelible /ɪn'dɛləbəl/ *a* indeleble, imborrable; *Fig.* inolvidable

indelibly /ɪn'dɛləbli/ *adv* indeleblemente

indelicacy /ɪn'dɛlɪkəsi/ *n* falta de buen gusto, grosería, *f*; (tactlessness) indiscreción, falta de tacto, *f*

indelicate /ɪn'dɛlɪkɪt/ *a* grosero, descortés; indecoroso, inmodesto; (tactless) inoportuno, indiscreto

indemnification /ɪnˌdɛmnəfɪ'keɪʃən/ *n* indemnización, compensación, *f*

indemnify /ɪn'dɛmnəˌfaɪ/ *vt* indemnizar, compensar

indemnity /ɪn'dɛmnɪti/ *n* indemnización, reparación, *f*

indent /ɪn'dɛnt/ *vt* endentar, mellar; *Print.* sangrar

indentation /ˌɪndɛn'teɪʃən/ *n* impresión, depresión, *f*; corte, *m*, mella, *f*; línea quebrada, *f*, zigzag, *m*

indenture /ɪn'dɛntʃər/ *n* escritura, *f*, instrumento, *m*. *vt* escriturar

independence /ˌɪndɪ'pɛndəns/ *n* independencia, libertad, *f*; (autonomy) autonomía, *f*. **I. Day,** El Día de la Independencia, *m*. **i. movement,** movimiento en favor de la independencia, *m*

independent /ˌɪndɪ'pɛndənt/ *a* independiente; libre; (autonomous) autónomo; **i. of,** libre de; aparte de. **a person of i. means,** una persona acomodada

independently /ˌɪndɪ'pɛndəntli/ *adv* independientemente

indescribability /ˌɪndɪˌskraɪbə'bɪlɪti/ *n* imposibilidad de describir, *f*, lo indescriptible

indescribable /ˌɪndɪ'skraɪbəbəl/ *a* indescriptible; indefinible, indecible, inexplicable; incalificable

indestructibility /ˌɪndɪˌstrʌktə'bɪlɪti/ *n* indestructibilidad, *f*

indestructible /ˌɪndɪ'strʌktəbəl/ *a* indestructible

indeterminable /ˌɪndɪ'tɜrmənəbəl/ *a* indeterminable

indeterminate /ˌɪndɪ'tɜrmənɪt/ *a* indeterminado, indefinido, vago; *Math.* indeterminado

indetermination /ˌɪndɪˌtɜrmə'neɪʃən/ *n* irresolución, indecisión, duda, vacilación, *f*

index /'ɪndɛks/ *n* (forefinger) dedo índice, *m*; (of book) tabla de materias, *f*, índice, *m*; (on instruments) manecilla, aguja, *f*; *Math.* índice, *m*; (sign) señal, indicación, *f*. *vt* poner índice (a); poner en el índice. **i. card,** ficha, *f*. **I. expurgatorius,** Índice expurgatorio, *m*

India /'ɪndiə/ *n* la India, *f*. **I. paper,** papel de China, *m*. **i.-rubber,** *Bot.* caucho, *m*; (eraser) goma de borrar, *f*. **i.-rubber tree,** yacio, *m*

Indian /'ɪndiən/ *a* and *n* indio (-ia). **I. chief,** cacique, *m*. **I. club,** maza, *f*. **I. corn,** maíz, *m*. **I. ink,** tinta china, *f*. **I. summer,** veranillo, veranillo de San Martín, *m*

Indian Ocean, the el Océano Indico, *m*

indicate /'ɪndɪˌkeɪt/ *vt* indicar, señalar; (show) denotar, mostrar, anunciar

indication /ˌɪndɪ'keɪʃən/ *n* indicación, *f*; señal, *f*, indicio, síntoma, *m*; prueba, *f*

indicative /ɪn'dɪkətɪv/ *a* indicador, indicativo, demostrativo; *Gram.* indicativo. *n Gram.* indicativo, *m*. **to be i. of,** indicar, señalar

indicator /'ɪndɪˌkeɪtər/ *n* indicador, señalador, *m*

indict /ɪn'daɪt/ *vt* acusar; *Law.* demandar, enjuiciar

indictable /ɪn'daɪtəbəl/ *a* procesable, denunciable, enjuiciable

indictment /ɪn'daɪtmənt/ *n* acusación, *f*; *Law.* procesamiento, *m*

indifference /ɪn'dɪfərəns/ *n* indiferencia, apatía, *f*, desinterés, desapego, *m*; imparcialidad, neutralidad, *f*; (coldness) frialdad, tibieza, *f*

indifferent /ɪn'dɪfərənt/ *a* indiferente, apático; imparcial, neutral; frío; (ordinary) regular, ordinario, ni bien ni mal

indifferently /ɪn'dɪfərəntli/ *adv* con indiferencia; imparcialmente; friamente

indigence /'ɪndɪdʒəns/ *n* indigencia, necesidad, penuria, *f*

indigenous /ɪn'dɪdʒənəs/ *a* indígena, nativo, natural

indigent /'ɪndɪdʒənt/ *a* indigente, necesitado, menesteroso

indigestible /ˌɪndɪ'dʒɛstəbəl/ *a* indigesto

indigestion /ˌɪndɪ'dʒɛstʃən/ *n* indigestión, *f*, *Mexico* insulto *m*; *Fig.* empacho, ahíto, *m*

indignant /ɪn'dɪɡnənt/ *a* indignado. **to make i.,** indignar

indignantly /ɪn'dɪɡnəntli/ *adv* con indignación

indignation /ˌɪndɪɡ'neɪʃən/ *n* indignación, cólera, *f*

indignity /ɪn'dɪɡnɪti/ *n* indignidad, *f*; ultraje, *m*

indigo /'ɪndɪˌɡoʊ/ *n* añil, índigo, *m*

indirect /ˌɪndə'rɛkt/ *a* indirecto; oblicuo; tortuoso; *Gram.* **i. case,** caso oblicuo, *m*

indirectness /ˌɪndə'rɛktnɪs/ *n* (of route) rodeo, *m*, desviación, *f*; oblicuidad, *f*; (falsity) tortuosidad, *f*

indiscernible /ˌɪndɪ'sɜrnəbəl/ *a* imperceptible

indiscipline /ɪn'dɪsəplɪn/ *n* indisciplina, falta de disciplina, *f*

indiscreet /ˌɪndɪ'skriːt/ *a* indiscreto, imprudente, impolítico

indiscretion /ˌɪndɪ'skrɛʃən/ *n* indiscreción, imprudencia, *f*; (slip) desliz, *m*

indiscriminate /ˌɪndɪ'skrɪmənɪt/ *a* general, universal; indistinto, promiscuo

indiscriminately /ˌɪndɪ'skrɪmənɪtli/ *adv* promiscuamente

indiscrimination /ˌɪndɪˌskrɪmə'neɪʃən/ *n* universalidad, indistinción, *f*

indispensability /ˌɪndɪˌspɛnsə'bɪlɪti/ *n* indispensabilidad, precisión, necesidad, *f*

indispensable /ˌɪndɪ'spɛnsəbəl/ *a* imprescindible, indispensable, insustituible

indispensably /ˌɪndɪ'spɛnsəbli/ *adv* forzosamente, indispensablemente

indispose /ˌɪndɪ'spoʊz/ *vt* indisponer. **to be indisposed,** estar indispuesto, indisponerse

indisposed /ˌɪndɪ'spoʊzd/ *a* indispuesto, enfermo, destemplado; (reluctant) maldispuesto

indisposition /ˌɪndɪspə'zɪʃən/ *n* indisposición, enfermedad, *f*

indisputability /ˌɪndɪˌspyutə'bɪlɪti/ *n* verdad manifiesta, certeza, evidencia, *f*

indisputable /ˌɪndɪ'spyutəbəl/ *a* innegable, incontestable; irrefutable, evidente

indisputably /ˌɪndɪ'spyutəbli/ *adv* indisputablemente

indissolubility /ˌɪndɪˌsɒlyə'bɪlɪti/ *n* indisolubilidad, *f*

indissoluble /ˌɪndɪ'sɒlyəbəl/ *a* indisoluble

indistinct /ˌɪndɪ'stɪŋkt/ *a* indistinto; confuso, vago

indistinctly /ˌɪndɪ'stɪŋktli/ *adv* indistintamente; confusamente, vagamente

indistinctness /ˌɪndɪ'stɪŋktnɪs/ n incertidumbre, vaguedad, indistinción, indeterminación, f
indistinguishable /ˌɪndɪ'stɪŋgwɪʃəbəl/ a indistinguible
individual /ˌɪndə'vɪdʒuəl/ a (single) solo, único; individual, individuo, particular, propio; personal. n individuo, m, particular, mf
individualism /ˌɪndə'vɪdʒuə,lɪzəm/ n individualismo, m
individualist /ˌɪndə'vɪdʒuəlɪst/ n individualist, mf
individualistic /ˌɪndə,vɪdʒuə'lɪstɪk/ a individualista
individuality /ˌɪndə,vɪdʒu'ælɪti/ n individualidad, personalidad, f; carácter, m, naturaleza, f
individualize /ˌɪndə'vɪdʒuə,laiz/ vt particularizar, individuar
individually /ˌɪndə'vɪdʒuəli/ adv individualmente, particularmente
indivisibility /ˌɪndə,vɪzə'bɪlɪti/ n indivisibilidad, f
indivisible /ˌɪndə'vɪzəbəl/ a incompartible, impartible, indivisible
indivisibly /ˌɪndə'vɪzəbli/ adv indivisiblemente
Indo /'ɪndou/ (in compounds) indo. **I.-China,** n indochina. **I.-European,** indoeuropeo
indocile /ɪn'dɒsɪl/ a indócil, desobediente, rebelde
indocility /ˌɪndɒ'sɪlɪti/ n indocilidad, desobediencia, falta de docilidad, f
indolence /'ɪndləns/ n indolencia, pereza, desidia, f
indolent /'ɪndlənt/ a indolente, perezoso, holgazán; *Med.* indoloro
indolently /'ɪndləntli/ adv perezosamente
indomitable /ɪn'dɒmɪtəbəl/ a indomable, indómito
indoor /'ɪn,dɔr/ a de casa; de puertas adentro, interno. **i. swimming pool,** piscina bajo techo, f. **i. tennis,** tenis en pistas cubiertas, tenis bajo techo, m
indoors /ɪn'dɔrz/ adv en casa; adentro, bajo techo
indorsee /ɪndɔr'si/ n endosatario (-ia)
indubitable /ɪn'dubɪtəbəl/ a indudable
indubitably /ɪn'dubɪtəbli/ adv indudablemente, sin duda
induce /ɪn'dus/ vt inducir, mover; instigar, incitar; producir, ocasionar; *Elec.* inducir. **Nothing would i. me to do it,** Nada me induciría a hacerlo
inducement /ɪn'dusmənt/ n incitamiento, m; estímulo, m; aliciente, atractivo, m; tentación, f
induct /ɪn'dʌkt/ vt instalar; introducir, iniciar
induction /ɪn'dʌkʃən/ n instalación, f; iniciación, introducción, f; *Phys.* inducción, f. **i. coil,** carrete de inducción, m
inductive /ɪn'dʌktɪv/ a (of reasoning) inductivo; *Phys.* inductor
indulge /ɪn'dʌldʒ/ vt (children) consentir, mimar; (a desire) satisfacer, dar rienda suelta a; (with a gift) agasajar (con), dar gusto (con). **to i. in,** vt consentir en. vi entregarse a, permitirse, gustar de
indulgence /ɪn'dʌldʒəns/ n (of children) mimo, cariño excesivo, m; (of a desire) propensión (a), afición (a), f; (toward others) tolerancia, transigencia, f; *Eccl.* indulgencia, f
indulgent /ɪn'dʌldʒənt/ a indulgente; tolerante, transigente
indult /ɪn'dʌlt/ n *Eccl.* indulto, m
industrial /ɪn'dʌstriəl/ a industrial. **i. alcohol,** alcohol desnaturalizado, m. **i. school,** escuela de artes y oficios, f, *Com.* **i. shares,** valores industriales, m pl
industrialism /ɪn'dʌstriə,lɪzəm/ n industrialismo, m
industrialist /ɪn'dʌstriəlɪst/ n industrial, m
industrialization /ɪn,dʌstriəlɪ'zeɪʃən/ n industrialización, f
industrialize /ɪn'dʌstriə,laiz/ vt industrializar
industrious /ɪn'dʌstriəs/ a industrioso, aplicado, diligente
industriously /ɪn'dʌstriəsli/ adv industriosamente, diligentemente
industriousness /ɪn'dʌstriəsnɪs/ n industria, laboriosidad, f
industry /'ɪndəstri/ n diligencia, aplicación, f; (work) trabajo, m, labor, f; *Com.* industria, f
inebriate /a, n i'nibriɪt; vi -bri,eit/ a borracho, ebrio. n borracho (-cha). vt embriagar, emborrachar
inebriation /ɪ,nibri'eiʃən/ n embriaguez, borrachera, f
inedible /ɪn'ɛdəbəl/ a incomible, no comestible

inedited /ɪn'ɛdɪtɪd/ a inédito
ineffable /ɪn'ɛfəbəl/ a indecible, inefable
ineffaceable /ˌɪnɪ'feisəbəl/ a imborrable, indeleble
ineffective /ˌɪnɪ'fɛktɪv/ a ineficaz; vano, fútil. **to be i.,** (of persons) no pinchar ni cortar. **to prove i.,** quedar sin efecto; no tener influencia
ineffectiveness /ˌɪnɪ'fɛktɪvnɪs/ n ineficacia, f; futilidad, f
inefficiency /ˌɪnɪ'fɪʃənsi/ n ineficacia, incompetencia, ineptitud, f
inefficient /ˌɪnɪ'fɪʃənt/ a ineficaz, incapaz
inefficiently /ˌɪnɪ'fɪʃəntli/ adv ineficazmente
inelastic /ˌɪnɪ'læstɪk/ a inelástico
inelegance /ɪn'ɛlɪgəns/ n inelegancia, fealdad, vulgaridad, f
inelegant /ɪn'ɛlɪgənt/ a inelegante, ordinario, de mal gusto
inelegantly /ɪn'ɛlɪgəntli/ adv sin elegancia
ineligibility /ɪn,ɛlɪdʒə'bɪlɪti/ n ineligibilidad, f
ineligible /ɪn'ɛlɪdʒəbəl/ a inelegible
inept /ɪn'ɛpt/ a inepto, inoportuno; absurdo, ridículo; (of persons) incompetente, ineficaz
ineptitude /ɪn'ɛptɪ,tud/ n ineptitud, f; necedad, f; (of persons) incapacidad, incompetencia, f
ineptly /ɪn'ɛptli/ adv ineptamente, neciamente
inequality /ˌɪnɪ'kwɒlɪti/ n desigualdad, desemejanza, disparidad, f; (of surface) escabrosidad, aspereza, f; *Fig.* injusticia, f; (of opportunity) diferencia, f
inequitable /ɪn'ɛkwɪtəbəl/ a desigual, injusto
inequity /ɪn'ɛkwɪti/ n injusticia, desigualdad, f
ineradicable /ˌɪnɪ'rædɪkəbəl/ a indeleble, imborrable
ineradicably /ˌɪnɪ'rædɪkəbli/ adv indeleblemente
inert /ɪn'ɜrt/ a inerte, inactivo, pasivo; ocioso, flojo, perezoso
inertia /ɪn'ɜrʃə/ n inercia, inacción, f; abulia, pereza, f; *Phys.* inercia, f
inertly /ɪn'ɜrtli/ adv indolentemente, sin mover, pasivamente
inescapable /ˌɪnə'skeipəbəl/ a ineludible, inevitable
inessential /ˌɪnɪ'sɛnʃəl/ a no esencial
inestimable /ɪn'ɛstəməbəl/ a inestimable
inevitability /ɪn,ɛvɪtə'bɪlɪti/ n fatalidad, necesidad, f; lo inevitable
inevitable /ɪn'ɛvɪtəbəl/ a inevitable, necesario, fatal, forzoso, ineludible
inevitably /ɪn'ɛvɪtəbli/ adv inevitablemente, necesariamente, forzosamente
inexact /ˌɪnɪg'zækt/ a inexacto, incorrecto
inexactitude /ˌɪnɪg'zæktɪ,tud/ n inexactitud, f
inexcusable /ˌɪnɪk'skyuzəbəl/ a imperdonable, inexcusable, irremisible
inexcusableness /ˌɪnɪk'skyuzəbəlnɪs/ n enormidad, f; lo inexcusable
inexcusably /ˌɪnɪk'skyuzəbli/ adv inexcusablemente
inexhaustible /ˌɪnɪg'zɔstəbəl/ a inagotable, inexhausto
inexorability /ɪn,ɛksərə'bɪlɪti/ n inflexibilidad, inexorabilidad, f
inexorable /ɪn'ɛksərəbəl/ a inexorable, inflexible, duro
inexorably /ɪn'ɛksərəbli/ adv inexorablemente, implacablemente
inexpediency /ˌɪnɪk'spidiənsi/ n inoportunidad, inconveniencia, imprudencia, f
inexpedient /ˌɪnɪk'spidiənt/ a inoportuno; inconveniente; impolítico, imprudente. **to deem i.,** creer inoportuno
inexpensive /ˌɪnɪk'spɛnsɪv/ a poco costoso, barato
inexpensiveness /ˌɪnɪk'spɛnsɪvnɪs/ n baratura, f, bajo precio, m
inexperience /ˌɪnɪk'spɪəriəns/ n inexperiencia, falta de experiencia, f
inexperienced /ˌɪnɪk'spɪəriənst/ a inexperto, novato
inexpert /ɪn'ɛkspɜrt/ a inexperto, imperito
inexpertly /ɪn'ɛkspɜrtli/ adv sin habilidad
inexpertness /ɪn'ɛkspɜrtnɪs/ n impericia, torpeza, f
inexpiable /ɪn'ɛkspiəbəl/ a inexpiable
inexplicable /ˌɪnɪk'splɪkəbəl/ a inexplicable
inexplicit /ˌɪnɪk'splɪsɪt/ a no explícito
inexplosive /ˌɪnɪk'splousɪv/ a inexplosible

inexpressible /ˌɪnɪk'spresəbəl/ a inexplicable, indecible, inefable

inexpressive /ˌɪnɪk'spresɪv/ a inexpresivo; (of persons) reservado, callado, poco expresivo, retraído

inexpressiveness /ˌɪnɪk'spresɪvnɪs/ n falta de expresión, f; (of persons) reserva, f, silencio, retraimiento, m

inexpugnable /ˌɪnɪk'spʌgnəbəl/ a inexpugnable

inextinguishable /ˌɪnɪk'stɪŋgwɪʃəbəl/ a inapagable, inextinguible

inextricable /ɪn'ɛkstrɪkəbəl/ a inextricable, intrincado, enmarañado

inextricably /ɪn'ɛkstrɪkəbli/ adv intrincadamente

infallibility /ɪnˌfælə'bɪlɪti/ n infalibilidad, f

infallible /ɪn'fæləbəl/ a infalible

infamous /'ɪnfəməs/ a infame, torpe, vil, ignominioso; odioso, repugnante

infamously /'ɪnfəməsli/ adv infamemente

infamy /'ɪnfəmi/ n infamia, torpeza, vileza, ignominia, f; deshonra, f

infancy /'ɪnfənsi/ n infancia, niñez, f; Law. minoridad, f

infant /'ɪnfənt/ n criatura, f; crío (-ía), niño (-ña); Law. menor, mf. **i. school,** escuela de párvulos, f

infanticidal /ɪnˌfæntə'saidl/ a infanticida

infanticide /ɪn'fæntə,said/ n (act) infanticidio, m; (person) infanticida, mf

infantile /'ɪnfən,tail/ a infantil. **i. paralysis,** parálisis infantil, f

infantry /'ɪnfəntri/ n Mil. infantería de la guerra, f

infantryman /'ɪnfəntrimən/ n Mil. infante, soldado, peón, m

infatuate /ɪn'fætʃu,eit/ vt infatuar, embobar

infatuation /ɪnˌfætʃu'eiʃən/ n infatuación, f, encaprichamiento, m

infect /ɪn'fɛkt/ vt infectar, contagiar; Fig. pegar, influir; (Fig. in a bad sense) corromper, pervertir, inficionar. **to become infected,** infectarse

infected /ɪn'fɛktɪd/ a infecto

infection /ɪn'fɛkʃən/ n infección, f, contagio, m; Fig. influencia, f; (Fig. in a bad sense) corrupción, perversión, f

infectious /ɪn'fɛkʃəs/ a infeccioso, contagioso; (Fig. in a bad sense) corruptor; Fig. contagioso

infectiousness /ɪn'fɛkʃəsnɪs/ n contagiosidad, f

infelicitous /ˌɪnfə'lɪsɪtəs/ a poco apropiado, desacertado

infelicity /ˌɪnfə'lɪsɪti/ n infelicidad, desdicha, f, infortunio, m; desacierto, m, inoportunidad, f

infer /ɪn'fɜr/ vt inferir, concluir, educir, deducir, implicar

inferable /ɪn'fɜrəbəl/ a deducible, demostrable

inference /'ɪnfərəns/ n inferencia, deducción, conclusión, f

inferential /ˌɪnfə'rɛnʃəl/ a ilativo, deductivo

inferior /ɪn'fɪəriər/ a inferior; (in rank) subordinado, subalterno; (of position) inferior. n inferior, mf subordinado (-da). **to be not i.,** no ser inferior, Inf. no quedarse en zaga

inferiority /ɪnˌfɪəri'ɔrɪti/ n inferioridad, f. **i. complex,** complejo de inferioridad, m

infernal /ɪn'fɜrnl/ a infernal; Poet. inferno, tartáreo

infernally /ɪn'fɜrnli/ adv infernalmente

inferno /ɪn'fɜrnou/ n infierno, m

infertile /ɪn'fɜrtl/ a infértil, infecundo, estéril

infertility /ˌɪnfər'tɪlɪti/ n infertilidad, infecundidad, esterilidad, f

infest /ɪn'fɛst/ vt infestar. **to be infested with,** plagarse de

infestation /ˌɪnfɛs'teiʃən/ n infestación, f

infidel /'ɪnfɪdl/ n infiel, gentil, mf pagano (-na); (atheist) descreído (-da), ateo (-ea). a pagano; infiel, descreído, ateo

infidelity /ˌɪnfɪ'dɛlɪti/ n infidelidad, alevosía, perfidia, f

infiltrate /ɪn'fɪltreit/ vt infiltrar. vi infiltrarse

infiltration /ˌɪnfɪl'treiʃən/ n infiltración, f

infinite /'ɪnfənɪt/ a infinito, ilimitado; inmenso, enorme; (of number) innumerable, infinito. n infinito, m

infinitely /'ɪnfənɪtli/ adv infinitamente

infinitesimal /ˌɪnfɪnɪ'tɛsəməl/ a infinitesimal. **i. calculus,** cálculo infinitesimal, m

infinitive /ɪn'fɪnɪtɪv/ a and n Gram. infinitivo, m.

infinitude, infinity /ɪn'fɪnɪtud; ɪn'fɪnɪti/ n infinidad, infinitud, f; (extent) inmensidad, f; (of number) sinfín, m; Math. infinito, m

infirm /ɪn'fɜrm/ a achacoso, enfermizo, enclenque; (shaky) inestable, inseguro; (of purpose) irresoluto, vacilante

infirmary /ɪn'fɜrməri/ n enfermería, f, hospital, m

infirmity /ɪn'fɜrmɪti/ n achaque, m, enfermedad, dolencia, f; (fault) flaqueza, falta, f

inflame /ɪn'fleim/ vt encender; (excite) acalorar, irritar, provocar; Med. inflamar. vi encenderse, arder; acalorarse, irritarse; Med. inflamarse

inflammability /ɪnˌflæmə'bɪlɪti/ n inflamabilidad, f

inflammable /ɪn'flæməbəl/ a inflamable

inflammation /ˌɪnflə'meiʃən/ n inflamación, f

inflammatory /ɪn'flæmə,tɔri/ a inflamador; Med. inflamatorio

inflate /ɪn'fleit/ vt inflar, hinchar; (with pride) engreír, ensoberbecer

inflation /ɪn'fleiʃən/ n inflación, hinchazón, f; Com. inflación, f

inflationism /ɪn'fleiʃə,nɪzəm/ n inflacionismo, m

inflator /ɪn'fleitər/ n Mech. bomba para inflar, f

inflect /ɪn'flɛkt/ vt torcer; (voice) modular; Gram. conjugar, declinar

inflection /ɪn'flɛkʃən/ n dobladura, f; (of voice) tono, acento, m, modulación, f; Gram. conjugación, declinación, f

inflexibility /ɪnˌflɛksə'bɪlɪti/ n inflexibilidad, dureza, rigidez, f

inflexible /ɪn'flɛksəbəl/ a inflexible, rígido; Fig. inexorable, inalterable

inflexibly /ɪn'flɛksəbli/ adv inflexiblemente

inflict /ɪn'flɪkt/ vt infligir, imponer

infliction /ɪn'flɪkʃən/ n imposición, f; castigo, m

inflorescence /ˌɪnflɔ'rɛsəns/ n Bot. inflorescencia, f

inflow /'ɪn,flou/ n afluencia, f, flujo, m

influence /'ɪnfluəns/ n influencia, f, influjo, m; ascendiente, m; (importance) influencia, importancia, f. vt influir, afectar; persuadir, inducir. **to have i. over,** (a person) tener ascendiente sobre. Law. **undue i.,** influencia indebida, f

influential /ˌɪnflu'ɛnʃəl/ a influyente; (of person) prestigioso, importante

influenza /ˌɪnflu'ɛnzə/ n Med. gripe, f, trancazo, m

influx /'ɪn,flʌks/ n influjo, m; (of rivers) desembocadura, afluencia, f

inform /ɪn'fɔrm/ vt (fill) infundir, llenar; (tell) informar, enterar, advertir; instruir; (with about) poner al corriente de, participar. vi (with against) delatar (a), denunciar. **to i. oneself,** informarse, enterarse. **to be informed about,** estar al corriente de

informal /ɪn'fɔrməl/ a irregular; sin ceremonia, de confianza; (meeting) no oficial, extraoficial

informality /ˌɪnfɔr'mælɪti/ n irregularidad, f; falta de ceremonia, sencillez, f; intimidad, f

informally /ɪn'fɔrməli/ adv sin ceremonia

informant /ɪn'fɔrmənt/ n informante, mf; informador (-ra)

information /ˌɪnfɔr'meiʃən/ n información, instrucción, f; noticia, f, aviso, m; Law. denuncia, delación, f. **piece of i.,** información, f. **i. bureau,** oficina de información, f

informative /ɪn'fɔrmətɪv/ a informativo

informer /ɪn'fɔrmər/ n delator (-ra), denunciador (-ra)

infraction /ɪn'frækʃən/ n contravención, infracción, transgresión, f

infrared /ˌɪnfrə'rɛd/ a Phys. infrarrojo, ultrarrojo

infrequency /ɪn'frikwənsi/ n infrecuencia, rareza, irregularidad, f

infrequent /ɪn'frikwənt/ a infrecuente, raro, irregular

infrequently /ɪn'frikwəntli/ adv rara vez, infrecuentemente

infringe /ɪn'frɪndʒ/ vt infringir, violar, contravenir, quebrantar

infringement /ɪn'frɪndʒmənt/ n contravención, violación, infracción, f
infringer /ɪn'frɪndʒər/ n infractor (-ra), contraventor (-ra), violador (-ra), transgresor (-ra)
infuriate /ɪn'fyʊri,eit/ vt enfurecer, enloquecer, enojar. **to be infuriated,** estar furioso
infuse /ɪn'fyuz/ vt vaciar, infiltrar; Fig. infundir, inculcar, instilar
infusible /ɪn'fyuzəbəl/ a infundible
infusion /ɪn'fyuʒən/ n infusión, f; Fig. instilación, inculcación, f
ingathering /ɪn'gæðərɪŋ/ n cosecha, recolección, f
ingenious /ɪn'dʒinyəs/ a ingenioso; mañoso, hábil
ingeniously /ɪn'dʒinyəsli/ adv ingeniosamente, hábilmente
ingenuity /,ɪndʒə'nuiti/ n ingeniosidad, inventiva, listeza, habilidad, f
ingenuous /ɪn'dʒɛnyuəs/ a ingenuo, franco, sincero, cándido, sencillo, inocente
ingenuousness /ɪn'dʒɛnyuəsnɪs/ n ingenuidad, franqueza, sinceridad, f; candor, m
ingest /ɪn'dʒɛst/ vt ingerir
ingestion /ɪn'dʒɛstʃən/ n ingestión, f
ingoing /'ɪn,gouɪŋ/ a entrante, que entra. n ingreso, m, entrada, f; Com. **i. and outgoing,** entradas y salidas, f pl
ingot /'ɪŋgət/ n pepita, f, lingote, m; (of any metal) barra, f
ingrained /ɪn'greind, 'ɪn,greind/ a innato, natural
ingratiate /ɪn'greiʃi,eit/ vt (oneself with) congraciarse con, captarse la buena voluntad de, insinuarse en el favor de
ingratiating /ɪn'greiʃi,eitɪŋ/ a obsequioso
ingratitude /ɪn'græti,tud/ n ingratitud, f, desagradecimiento, m
ingredient /ɪn'gridiənt/ n ingrediente, m
ingress /'ɪngrɛs/ n ingreso, m; derecho de entrada, m
ingrowing /'ɪn,grouɪŋ/ a que crece hacia adentro. **i. nail,** uñero, m
inhabit /ɪn'hæbɪt/ vt habitar, ocupar, vivir en, residir en
inhabitable /ɪn'hæbɪtəbəl/ a habitable, vividero
inhabitant /ɪn'hæbɪtənt/ n habitante, residente, m; vecino (-na)
inhabited /ɪn'hæbɪtɪd/ a habitado, poblado
inhalation /,ɪnhə'leiʃən/ n inspiración, f; Med. inhalación, f
inhale /ɪn'heil/ vt aspirar; Med. inhalar
inharmonious /,ɪnhɑr'mouniəs/ a Mus. disonante, inarmónico; desavenido, discorde, desconforme. **to be i.,** disonar; (of people) llevarse mal
inhere /ɪn'hɪər/ vi ser inherente; pertenecer (a), residir (en)
inherence /ɪn'hɪərəns/ n inherencia, f
inherent /ɪn'hɪərənt/ a inherente; innato, intrínseco, natural
inherently /ɪn'hɪərəntli/ adv intrínsecamente
inherit /ɪn'hɛrɪt/ vt heredar
inheritance /ɪn'hɛrɪtəns/ n herencia, f; patrimonio, abolengo, m
inheritor /ɪn'hɛrɪtər/ n heredero (-ra)
inhibit /ɪn'hɪbɪt/ vt inhibir, impedir; Eccl. prohibir. **be inhibited, became inhibited,** cohibirse
inhibition /,ɪnɪ'bɪʃən/ n inhibición, f
inhibitory /ɪn'hɪbɪ,tɔri/ a inhibitorio
inhospitable /ɪn'hɒspɪtəbəl/ a inhospitalario
inhospitably /ɪn'hɒspɪtəbli/ adv desabridamente
inhuman /ɪn'hyumən/ a inhumano; cruel, bárbaro
inhumanity /,ɪnhyu'mænɪti/ n inhumanidad, crueldad, f
inhumanly /ɪn'hyumənli/ adv inhumanamente, cruelmente
inhume /ɪn'hyum/ vt inhumar, sepultar
inimical /ɪ'nɪmɪkəl/ a enemigo, hostil, opuesto, contrario
inimically /ɪ'nɪmɪkəli/ adv hostilmente
inimitable /ɪ'nɪmɪtəbəl/ a inimitable
inimitably /ɪ'nɪmɪtəbli/ adv inimitablemente
iniquitous /ɪ'nɪkwɪtəs/ a inicuo, malvado, perverso, nefando; Inf. diabólico

iniquity /ɪ'nɪkwɪti/ n iniquidad, maldad, injusticia, f
initial /ɪ'nɪʃəl/ a inicial. n inicial, letra inicial, f. vt firmar con las iniciales
initially /ɪ'nɪʃəli/ adv al principio, en primer lugar
initiate /a ɪ'nɪʃiɪt; v ɪ'nɪʃi,eit/ a iniciado. vt iniciar, poner en pie, empezar, entablar; (a person) admitir
initiation /ɪ,nɪʃi'eiʃən/ n principio, m; (of a person) iniciación, admisión, f
initiative /ɪ'nɪʃiətɪv/ n iniciativa, f. **to take the i.,** tomar la iniciativa
initiator /ɪ'nɪʃi,eitər/ n iniciador (-ra)
inject /ɪn'dʒɛkt/ vt inyectar
injection /ɪn'dʒɛkʃən/ n inyección, f. **i. syringe,** jeringa de inyecciones, f
injudicious /,ɪndʒu'dɪʃəs/ a imprudente, indiscreto
injudiciously /,ɪndʒu'dɪʃəsli/ adv imprudentemente
injudiciousness /,ɪndʒu'dɪʃəsnɪs/ n imprudencia, indiscreción, f
injunction /ɪn'dʒʌŋkʃən/ n precepto, mandato, m; Law. embargo, m
injure /'ɪndʒər/ vt perjudicar, dañar, Lat. Am. afectar; menoscabar, deteriorar; (hurt) lastimar, lisiar. **to i. oneself,** hacerse daño
injured /'ɪndʒərd/ a (physically) lisiado; (morally) ofendido
injurer /'ɪndʒərər/ n perjudicador (-ra)
injurious /ɪn'dʒʊriəs/ a dañoso, perjudicial, malo; ofensivo, injurioso
injuriously /ɪn'dʒʊriəsli/ adv perjudicialmente
injury /'ɪndʒəri/ n perjuicio, daño, m; (physical) lesión, Lat. Am. also lastimadura f; (insult) agravio, insulto, m
injustice /ɪn'dʒʌstɪs/ n injusticia, desigualdad, f. **You do him an i.,** Le juzgas mal
ink /ɪŋk/ n tinta, f. vt entintar. **copying-ink,** tinta de copiar, f. **marking-ink,** tinta indeleble, f. **printer's ink,** tinta de imprenta, f. **ink-stand** or **ink-well,** tintero, m
inker /'ɪŋkər/ n Print. rodillo, m
inkling /'ɪŋklɪŋ/ n sospecha, noción, f
inky /'ɪŋki/ a manchado de tinta
inland /'ɪnlænd/ n el interior de un país, a interior, mediterráneo; del país, regional. adv tierra adentro. **to go i.,** internarse en un país. **I. Revenue,** delegación de contribuciones, f. **i. town,** ciudad del interior, f
inlay /'ɪn,lei/ vt taracear, ataracear, embutir; incrustar. n taracea, f, embutido, m
inlet /'ɪnlet/ n entrada, admisión, f; Geog. ensenada, f. **i. valve,** válvula de admisión, f
inmate /'ɪn,meit/ n residente, habitante, m; (of hospital) paciente, mf; enfermo (-ma) (of prison) prisionero
inmost /'ɪnmoust/. See **innermost**
inn /ɪn/ n posada, fonda, venta, f, mesón, m
innate /ɪ'neit/ a innato, inherente, instintivo, nativo
innately /ɪ'neitli/ adv naturalmente, instintivamente
innavigable /ɪ'nævɪgəbəl/ a innavegable
inner /'ɪnər/ a interior, interno. **i. tube** Auto. cámara de neumatico, cámara de aire, f
innermost /'ɪnər,moust/ a más adentro; Fig. más íntimo, más hondo
innings /'ɪnɪŋz/ n (sport) turno, m
innkeeper /'ɪn,kipər/ n fondista, mf; tabernero (-ra), mesonero (-ra), posadero (-ra)
innocence /'ɪnəsəns/ n inocencia, f; pureza, f; (guilelessness) simplicidad, f; candor, m
innocent /'ɪnəsənt/ a inocente, puro; (guiltless) inocente, inculpable; (foolish) simple, tonto, candoroso, inocentón; (harmless) innocuo. n inocente, mf **Holy Innocents,** Santos Inocentes, m pl
innocuous /ɪ'nɒkyuəs/ a innocuo, inofensivo
innocuousness /ɪ'nɒkyuəsnɪs/ n inocuidad, f
innovate /'ɪnə,veit/ vt innovar
innovation /,ɪnə'veiʃən/ n innovación, f
innovative /'ɪnə,veitɪv/ a innovador
innovator /'ɪnə,veitər/ n innovador (-ra)
innuendo /,ɪnyu'endou/ n indirecta, insinuación, f
innumerable /ɪ'numərəbəl/ a innumerable, incalculable. **i. things,** un sinfín de cosas

inobservance /ˌɪnəb'zɜrvəns/ *n* inobservancia, *f*, incumplimiento, *m*

inoculate /ɪ'nɒkyəˌleit/ *vt* inocular

inoculation /ɪˌnɒkyə'leiʃən/ *n* inoculación, *f*

inoculator /ɪ'nɒkyəˌleitər/ *n* inoculador, *m*

inodorous /ɪn'oudərəs/ *a* inodoro

inoffensive /ˌɪnə'fɛnsɪv/ *a* inofensivo, innocuo; (of people) pacífico, apacible, manso

inoffensively /ˌɪnə'fɛnsɪvli/ *adv* inofensivamente

inoffensiveness /ˌɪnə'fɛnsɪvnɪs/ *n* inocuidad, *f*; (of people) mansedumbre, *f*

inoperable /ɪn'ɒpərəbəl/ *a* inoperable

inoperative /ɪn'ɒpərətɪv/ *a* ineficaz, impracticable, inútil

inopportune /ɪnˌɒpər'tun/ *a* inoportuno, intempestivo, inconveniente

inopportunely /ɪnˌɒpər'tunli/ *adv* inoportunamente, a destiempo

inopportuneness /ɪnˌɒpər'tunnɪs/ *n* inoportunidad, inconveniencia, *f*

inordinate /ɪn'ɔrdn̩ɪt/ *a* desordenado, excesivo

inordinately /ɪn'ɔrdn̩tli/ *adv* desmedidamente

inorganic /ˌɪnɔr'gænɪk/ *a* inorgánico

inoxidizable /ɪn'ɒksɪˌdaizəbəl/ *a* inoxidable

input /'ɪnˌpʊt/ *n* capacidad instalada, *f*, insumo, *m*

inquest /'ɪnkwɛst/ *n Law.* indagación, investigación, *f*

inquietude /ɪn'kwaiɪˌtud/ *n* inquietud, *f*, desasosiego, *m*, agitación, preocupación, *f*

inquire /ɪn'kwaiᵊr/ *vt and vi* preguntar, averiguar, indagar. **to i. about,** (persons) preguntar por; (things) hacer preguntas sobre. **to i. into,** investigar, examinar, averiguar. **to i. of,** preguntar a. **"I. within,"** «Se dan informaciones»

inquirer /ɪn'kwaiᵊrər/ *n* indagador (-ra), inquiridor (-ra)

inquiring /ɪn'kwaiᵊrɪŋ/ *a* indagador, inquiridor

inquiringly /ɪn'kwaiᵊrɪŋli/ *adv* interrogativamente

inquiry /ɪn'kwaiᵊri/ *n* interrogación, pregunta, *f*; indagación, pesquisa, investigación, *f*; examen, *m*. **i. office,** oficina de informaciones, *f*. **on i.,** al preguntar

inquisition /ˌɪnkwə'zɪʃən/ *n* investigación, indagación, *f*; inquisición, *f*. **Holy I.,** Santo Oficio, *m*, Inquisición, *f*

inquisitive /ɪn'kwɪzɪtɪv/ *a* curioso, inquiridor; preguntador, impertinente, mirón

inquisitively /ɪn'kwɪzɪtɪvli/ *adv* con curiosidad, impertinentemente

inquisitiveness /ɪn'kwɪzɪtɪvnɪs/ *n* curiosidad, *f*; impertinencia, *f*

Inquisitor /ɪn'kwɪzɪtər/ *n Eccl.* inquisidor, *m*

inquisitorial /ɪnˌkwɪzɪ'tɔriəl/ *a* inquisitorial, inquisidor

inroad /'ɪnˌroud/ *n* incursión, *f*

insalubrious /ˌɪnsə'lubriəs/ *a* malsano, insalubre

insane /ɪn'sein/ *a* loco, demente, insano; (senseless) insensato, ridículo. **to become i.,** enloquecer, volverse loco, perder la razón. **to drive i.,** volver a uno el juicio, enloquecer, trastornar. **i. person,** demente, *mf.* loco (-ca)

insanely /ɪn'seinli/ *adv* locamente

insanitary /ɪn'sænɪˌtɛri/ *a* antihigiénico, malsano

insanity /ɪn'sænɪti/ *n* demencia, locura, *f*; enloquecimiento, *m*; (folly) insensatez, ridiculez, *f*

insatiability /ɪnˌseiʃə'bɪlɪti/ *n* insaciabilidad, *f*

insatiable /ɪn'seiʃəbəl/ *a* insaciable

insatiably /ɪn'seiʃəbli/ *adv* insaciablemente

inscribe /ɪn'skraib/ *vt* inscribir

inscription /ɪn'skrɪpʃən/ *n* inscripción, *f*; letrero, *m*; (of a book) dedicatoria, *f*; *Com.* inscripción, anotación, *f*, asiento, *m*

inscrutability /ɪnˌskrutə'bɪlɪti/ *n* enigma, misterio, *m*; incomprensibilidad, *f*

inscrutable /ɪn'skrutəbəl/ *a* enigmático, insondable, incomprensible, inescrutable

inscrutably /ɪn'skrutəbli/ *adv* incomprensiblemente, enigmáticamente

insect /'ɪnsɛkt/ *n* insecto, *m*. bichería, *m*. **i. powder,** polvos insecticidas, *m pl*

insecticide /ɪn'sɛktəˌsaid/ *a* and *n* insecticida *m*.

insecure /ˌɪnsɪ'kyʊr/ *a* inseguro, precario

insecurely /ˌɪnsɪ'kyʊrli/ *adv* inseguramente

insecurity /ˌɪnsɪ'kyʊrɪti/ *n* inseguridad, *f*; incertidumbre, inestabilidad, *f*

inseminate /ɪn'sɛməˌneit/ *vt Fig.* implantar; *Med.* fecundar

insemination /ɪnˌsɛmə'neiʃən/ *n Fig.* implantación, *f*; *Med.* fecundación, *f*

insensate /ɪn'sɛnseit/ *a* (unfeeling) insensible, insensitivo; (stupid) insensato, sin sentido, necio

insensibility /ɪnˌsɛnsə'bɪlɪti/ *n* insensibilidad, inconsciencia, *f*; (stupor) sopor, letargo, *m*; impasibilidad, indiferencia, *f*

insensible /ɪn'sɛnsəbəl/ *a* insensible, inconsciente; indiferente, impasible, duro de corazón; (scarcely noticeable) imperceptible. **to make i.,** (to sensations) hacer indiferente (a); insensibilizar

insensibly /ɪn'sɛnsəbli/ *adv* insensiblemente, imperceptiblemente

insensitive /ɪn'sɛnsɪtɪv/ *a* insensible, insensitivo; (person) hecho un tronco, hecho un leño

insensitiveness /ɪn'sɛnsɪtɪvnɪs/ *n* insensibilidad, *f*

insentient /ɪn'sɛnʃiənt/ *a* insensible

inseparability /ɪnˌsɛpərə'bɪlɪti/ *n* inseparabilidad, *f*

inseparable /ɪn'sɛpərəbəl/ *a* inseparable

insert /ɪn'sɜrt/ *vt* insertar, intercalar; (introduce) meter dentro, introducir, encajar; (in a newspaper) publicar

insertion /ɪn'sɜrʃən/ *n* inserción, intercalación, *f*; (introduction) introducción, *f*; metimiento, encaje, *m*; *Sew.* entredós, *m*; (in a newspaper) publicación, *f*

inshore /ɪn'ʃɔr/ *a* cercano a la orilla. *adv* cerca de la orilla. **i. fishing,** pesca de arrastre, *f*

inside /ˌɪn'said/ *a* interior, interno. *adv* adentro, dentro. *n* interior, *m*; (contents) contenido, *m*; (lining) forro, *m*; (*Inf.* stomach) entrañas, *f pl.* **to turn i. out,** volver al revés. **to walk on the i. of the pavement,** andar a la derecha de la acera. **from the i.,** desde el interior; por dentro. **on the i.,** por dentro, en el interior. **i. information,** información confidencial, *f*. **i. out,** al revés, de dentro afuera

insidious /ɪn'sɪdiəs/ *a* insidioso, enganoso, traidor

insidiously /ɪn'sɪdiəsli/ *adv* insidiosamente

insidiousness /ɪn'sɪdiəsnɪs/ *n* insidia, *f*; engaño, *m*, traición, *f*

insight /'ɪnˌsait/ *n* percepción, perspicacia, intuición, *f*. atisbo, *m*

insignia /ɪn'sɪgniə/ *n pl* insignias, *f pl*

insignificance /ˌɪnsɪg'nɪfɪkəns/ *n* insignificancia, futilidad, pequeñez, *f*

insignificant /ˌɪnsɪg'nɪfɪkənt/ *a* insignificante; fútil, trivial

insincere /ˌɪnsɪn'sɪər/ *a* insincero, hipócrita, falso

insincerely /ˌɪnsɪn'sɪərli/ *adv* falsamente, hipócritamente

insincerity /ˌɪnsɪn'sɛrɪti/ *n* insinceridad, hipocresía, falsedad, falta de sinceridad, doblez, *f*

insinuate /ɪn'sɪnyuˌeit/ *vt* insinuar, introducir; (hint) soltar una indirecta, sugerir; (oneself) insinuarse, introducirse con habilidad

insinuation /ɪnˌsɪnyu'eiʃən/ *n* insinuación, introducción, *f*; (hint) indirecta, *f*

insipid /ɪn'sɪpɪd/ *a* insípido, insulso; (dull) soso

insipidity /ˌɪnsə'pɪdɪti/ *n* insipidez, insulsez, *f*, desabor, *m*; (dullness) sosería, *f*

insist /ɪn'sɪst/ *vi* insistir; persistir, obstinarse. **to i. on,** insistir en; obstinarse en, hacer hincapié en, aferrarse en (or a)

insistence /ɪn'sɪstəns/ *n* insistencia, *f*, obstinación, pertinacia, *f*

insistent /ɪn'sɪstənt/ *a* insistente; porfiado, obstinaz

insistently /ɪn'sɪstəntli/ *adv* con insistencia, porfiadamente

insobriety /ˌɪnsə'braiɪti/ *n* falta de sobriedad, *f*; embriaguez, ebriedad, *f*

insole /'ɪnˌsoul/ *n* (of shoes) plantilla, *f*

insolence /'ɪnsələns/ *n* insolencia, altanería, majadería, frescura, *f*, atrevimiento, descaro, *m*

insolent /'ɪnsələnt/ *a* insolente, arrogante, atrevido, descarado, desmesurado, fresco

insolently /'ɪnsələntli/ *adv* insolentemente, con descaro

insolubility /ɪn,sɒljə'bɪlɪti/ *n* insolubilidad, *f*

insoluble /ɪn'sɒljəbəl/ *a* insoluble

insolvency /ɪn'sɒlvənsi/ *n* in olvencia, *f*

insolvent /ɪn'sɒlvənt/ *a* insolvente

insomnia /ɪn'sɒmnɪə/ *n* insomnio, *m*

insomuch /,ɪnsə'mʌtʃ/ *adv* (gen. with as or that) de modo (que), así (que), de suerte (que)

inspect /ɪn'spɛkt/ *vt* examinar, investigar, inspeccionar; (officially) registrar, reconocer

inspection /ɪn'spɛkʃən/ *n* inspección, investigación, *f*; examen, *m*; (official) reconocimiento, registro, *m*

inspector /ɪn'spɛktər/ *n* inspector, *m*, veedor, interventor, *m*

inspectorate /ɪn'spɛktərɪt/ *n* inspectorado, *m*; cargo de inspector, *m*

inspiration /,ɪnspə'reɪʃən/ *n* (of breath) inspiración, aspiración, *f*; numen, *m*, inspiración, vena, *f*. **to find i. in,** inspirarse en

inspire /ɪn'spaɪər/ *vt* (inhale) aspirar, inspirar; (stimulate) animar, alentar, iluminar; (suggest) sugerir, inspirar; infundir. **to i. enthusiasm,** entusiasmar. **to i. hope,** dar esperanza, esperanzar

inspired /ɪn'spaɪərd/ *a* inspirado, intuitivo, iluminado; (of genius) genial

inspirer /ɪn'spaɪərər/ *n* inspirador (-ra)

inspiring /ɪn'spaɪərɪŋ/ *a* alentador, animador; inspirador

inspirit /ɪn'spɪrɪt/ *vt* alentar, inspirar, estimular, animar

inspiriting /ɪn'spɪrɪtɪŋ/ *a* alentador, estimulador

instability /,ɪnstə'bɪlɪti/ *n* inestabilidad, mutabilidad, inconstancia, *f*

install /ɪn'stɔl/ *vt* (all meanings) instalar. **to i. oneself,** instalarse, establecerse

installation /,ɪnstə'leɪʃən/ *n* (all meanings) instalación, *f*

installment /ɪn'stɔlmənt/ *n* (of a story) entrega, *f*; *Com.* plazo, *m*, cuota, *f*. **by installments,** *Com.* a plazos. **i. plan,** pago a plazos, pago por cuotas, *m*

instance /'ɪnstəns/ *n* ejemplo, caso, *m*; (request) solicitación, *f*, ruego, *m*; *Law.* instancia, *f*. *vt* citar como ejemplo, mencionar; demostrar, probar. **for i.,** por ejemplo, verbigracia. **in that i....,** en el caso... **in the first i.,** en primer lugar, primero

instant /'ɪnstənt/ *a* immediato, urgente; *Com.* corriente, actual. *n* instante, momento, *m*; *Inf.* tris, santiamén, *m*. *Com.* **the 2nd i.,** el 2º (segundo) del corriente. **this i.,** (immediately) en seguida

instantaneous /,ɪnstən'teɪnɪəs/ *a* instantáneo. *Photo.* **i. exposure,** instantánea, *f*

instantaneously /,ɪnstən'teɪnɪəsli/ *adv* instantáneamente

instantaneousness /,ɪnstən'teɪnɪəsnɪs/ *n* instantaneidad, *f*

instantly /'ɪnstəntli/ *adv* en seguida, al instante, inmediatamente

instead /ɪn'stɛd/ *adv* en cambio; (with of) en vez de, en lugar de

instep /'ɪn,stɛp/ *n* empeine, *m*

instigate /'ɪnstɪ,geɪt/ *vt* instigar, incitar, aguijar, animar, provocar; fomentar

instigating /'ɪnstɪ,geɪtɪŋ/ *a* instigador, provocador, fomentador

instigation /,ɪnstɪ'geɪʃən/ *n* instigación, incitación, *f*; estímulo, *m*

instigator /'ɪnstɪ,geɪtər/ *n* instigador (-ra), provocador (-ra), fomentador (-ra)

instill /ɪn'stɪl/ *vt* instilar; (ideas) inculcar, infundir

instillment /ɪn'stɪlmənt/ *n* inculcación, implantación, insinuación, *f*

instinct /ɪn'stɪŋkt/ *n* instinto, *m*. **i. with,** imbuido de, lleno de. **by i.,** por instinto, movido por instinto

instinctive /ɪn'stɪŋktɪv/ *a* instintivo, espontáneo

instinctively /ɪn'stɪŋktɪvli/ *adv* por instinto

institute /'ɪnstɪ,tut/ *vt* instituir, fundar, establecer; (an inquiry) iniciar, empezar. *n* instituto, *m*; *pl* **institutes,** *Law.* instituta, *f*

institution /,ɪnstɪ'tuʃən/ *n* (creation) fundación, crea-

ción, *f*; institución, *f*, instituto, *m*; (beginning) comienzo, *m*, iniciación, *f*; (charitable) asilo, *m*; (custom) uso, *m*, costumbre, tradición, *f*

institutional /,ɪnstɪ'tuʃən]/ *a* institucional

instruct /ɪn'strʌkt/ *vt* (teach) instruir, enseñar; (order) mandar, dar orden (a)

instruction /ɪn'strʌkʃən/ *n* (teaching) instrucción, enseñanza, *f*; *pl* **instructions,** (orders) instrucciones, *f pl* orden, *f*, mandato, *m*

instructive /ɪn'strʌktɪv/ *a* instructivo, instructor, informativo

instructively /ɪn'strʌktɪvli/ *adv* instructivamente

instructiveness /ɪn'strʌktɪvnɪs/ *n* el carácter informativo, lo instructivo

instructor /ɪn'strʌktər/ *n* instructor, preceptor, *m*

instrument /'ɪnstrəmənt/ *n* instrumento, *m*; (tool) herramienta, *f*, utensilio, aparato, *m*; (agent) órgano, agente, medio, *m*; *Law.* instrumento, *m*, escritura, *f*. *vt Mus.* instrumentar. **percussion i.,** instrumento de percusión, *m*. **scientific i.,** instrumento científico, *m*. **stringed i.,** instrumento de cuerda, *m*. **wind i.,** instrumento de viento, *m*

instrumental /,ɪnstrə'mɛnt]/ *a* instrumental; influyente. **to be i. in,** contribuir a

instrumentalist /,ɪnstrə'mɛntlɪst/ *n Mus.* instrumentista, *m*

instrumentality /,ɪnstrəmɛn'tælɪti/ *n* mediación, intervención, agencia, *f*, buenos oficios, *m pl*

instrumentation /,ɪnstrəmɛn'teɪʃən/ *n Mus.* instrumentación, *f*; mediación, *f*

insubordinate /,ɪnsə'bɔrdnɪt/ *a* insubordinado, rebelde, desobediente, refractario

insubordination /,ɪnsə,bɔrdn'eɪʃən/ *n* insubordinación, rebeldía, desobediencia, *f*

insubstantial /,ɪnsəb'stænʃəl/ *a* irreal; insubstancial

insubstantiality /,ɪnsəb,stænʃi'ælɪti/ *n* irrealidad, *f*; insubstancialidad, *f*

insufferable. /ɪn'sʌfərəbəl/. See **intolerable**

insufficiency /,ɪnsə'fɪʃənsi/ *n* insuficiencia, falta, carestía, *f*

insufficient /,ɪnsə'fɪʃənt/ *a* insuficiente, falto. "**I. Postage,**" «Falta de franqueo»

insufficiently /,ɪnsə'fɪʃəntli/ *adv* insuficientemente

insular /'ɪnsələr/ *a* isleño, insular; (narrow-minded) intolerante, liberal

insularity /,ɪnsə'leərɪti/ *n* carácter isleño, *m*; (narrow-mindedness) iliberalidad, intolerancia, *f*

insulate /'ɪnsə,leɪt/ *vt* aislar

insulating /'ɪnsə,leɪtɪŋ/ *a* aislador. **i. tape,** *Elec.* cinta aisladora, *f*

insulation /,ɪnsə'leɪʃən/ *n* aislamiento, *m*

insulator /'ɪnsə,leɪtər/ *n Elec.* aislador, *m*

insulin /'ɪnsəlɪn/ *n Med.* insulina, *f*

insult /*n.* 'ɪnsʌlt; *v.* ɪn'sʌlt/ *n* insulto, agravio, ultraje, *m*, afrenta, ofensa, *f*. *vt* insultar, ofender, afrentar. **He was insulted,** Fue insultado; Se mostró ofendido

insulter /ɪn'sʌltər/ *n* insultador (-ra)

insulting /ɪn'sʌltɪŋ/ *a* insultante, injurioso, ofensivo. **He was very i. to them,** Les insultó, Les trató con menosprecio

insultingly /ɪn'sʌltɪŋli/ *adv* con insolencia, ofensivamente

insuperability /ɪn,supərə'bɪlɪti/ *n* dificultades insuperables, *f pl*, imposibilidad, *f*, lo insuperable

insuperable /ɪn'supərəbəl/ *a* insuperable, invencible

insuperably /ɪn'supərəbli/ *adv* invenciblemente

insupportable /,ɪnsə'pɔrtəbəl/ *a* insoportable, inaguantable, intolerable, insufrible

insupportably /,ɪnsə'pɔrtəbli/ *adv* insufriblemente, insoportablemente

insurable /ɪn'ʃʊrəbəl/ *a* asegurable

insurance /ɪn'ʃʊrəns/ *n* aseguramiento, *m*; *Com.* seguro, *m*; aseguración, *f*. **accident i.,** seguro contra accidentes, *m*. **fire-i.,** seguro contra incendio, *m*. **life i.,** seguro sobre la vida, *m*. **maritime i.,** seguro marítimo, *m*. **National I. Act,** Ley del Seguro Nacional Obligatorio, *f*. **i. broker,** corredor de seguros, *m*. **i. company,** compañía de seguros, *f*. **i. policy,** póliza de seguros, *f*. **i. premium,** prima de seguros, *f*

insure /ɪn'ʃʊr, -'ʃɜr/ *vt Com.* asegurar. **to i. oneself,** asegurarse. **the insured,** (person) el asegurado
insurer /ɪn'ʃʊrər/ *n* asegurador (-ra)
insurgent /ɪn'sɜrdʒənt/ *a* insurgente, rebelde; (of sea) invasor. *n* rebelde, *mf,* insurrecto (-ta)
insurmountable /ˌɪnsər'maʊntəbəl/ *a* insalvable, insuperable, invencible, intransitable
insurrection /ˌɪnsə'rɛkʃən/ *n* insurrección, sublevación, *f,* levantamiento, *m*
insurrectionary /ˌɪnsə'rɛkʃəˌnɛri/ *a* rebelde, amotinado, insurgente
insusceptible /ˌɪnsə'sɛptəbəl/ *a* no susceptible, indiferente, insensible
intact /ɪn'tækt/ *a* intacto, íntegro, indemne
intake /'ɪnˌteik/ *n* (of a stocking) menguado, *m; Mech.* aspiración, *f;* válvula de admisión, *f; Aer.* admisión, toma, *f;* orificio de entrada, *m*
intangibility /ɪnˌtændʒə'bɪliti/ *n* intangibilidad, *f*
intangible /ɪn'tændʒəbəl/ *a* intangible; incomprensible
integer /'ɪntɪdʒər/ *n Math.* número entero, *m*
integral /'ɪntɪgrəl/ *a* íntegro, intrínseco, inherente; *Math.* entero. *n Math.* integral, *f.* **i. calculus,** cálculo integral, *m*
integrate /'ɪntɪˌgreit/ *vt* integrar, completar; formar en un todo; *Math.* integrar
integrity /ɪn'tɛgrɪti/ *n* integridad, honradez, rectitud, entereza, *f*
intellect /'ɪntḷˌɛkt/ *n* intelecto, entendimiento, *m*
intellectual /ˌɪntḷ'ɛktʃuəl/ *a* intelectual, mental. *n* intelectual
intellectualism /ˌɪntḷ'ɛktʃuəˌlɪzəm/ *n* intelectualismo, *m,* intelectualidad, *f*
intellectually /ˌɪntḷ'ɛktʃuəli/ *adv* intelectualmente, mentalmente
intelligence /ɪn'tɛlɪdʒəns/ *n* inteligencia, comprensión, mente, *f;* (quickness of mind) agudeza, perspicacia, *f;* (news) noticia, *f,* conocimiento, informe, *m.* **the latest i.,** las últimas noticias. **i. quotient,** cociente de inteligencia, *m.* **I. Service,** Inteligencia, *f;* policía secreta, *f.* **i. test,** prueba de inteligencia, *f*
intelligent /ɪn'tɛlɪdʒənt/ *a* inteligente
intelligentsia /ɪnˌtɛlɪ'dʒɛntsiə/ *n* clase intelectual, intelectualidad, *f, Inf.* masa cefálica, *f*
intelligibility /ɪnˌtɛlɪdʒə'bɪliti/ *n* comprensibilidad, *f,* inteligibilidad, *f*
intelligible /ɪn'tɛlɪdʒəbəl/ *a* inteligible, comprensible
intelligibly /ɪn'tɛlɪdʒəbəl/ *adv* inteligiblemente
intemperance /ɪn'tɛmpərəns/ *n* intemperancia, inmoderación, *f;* exceso en la bebida, *m*
intemperate /ɪn'tɛmpərɪt/ *a* intemperante, destemplado, descomedido; inmoderado; bebedor en exceso
intemperately /ɪn'tɛmpərɪtli/ *adv* inmoderadamente
intend /ɪn'tɛnd/ *vt* intentar, proponerse, pensar; destinar, dedicar; (mean) querer decir. **to be intended,** estar destinado; tener por fin; querer decir
intendant /ɪn'tɛndənt/ *n* intendente, *m*
intended /ɪn'tɛndɪd/ *a* pensado, deseado. *n Inf.* novio (-ia), futuro (-ra), prometido (-da)
intense /ɪn'tɛns/ *a* intenso, vivo, fuerte; (of emotions) profundo, hondo, vehemente; (of colors) subido, intenso; (great) extremado, sumo, muy grande
intensification /ɪnˌtɛnsəfɪ'keiʃən/ *n* intensificación, *f;* aumento, *m*
intensify /ɪn'tɛnsəˌfai/ *vt* intensar, intensificar; aumentar
intensity /ɪn'tɛnsɪti/ *n* intensidad, fuerza, *f;* (of emotions) profundidad, vehemencia, violencia, *f;* (of colors) intensidad, *f*
intensive /ɪn'tɛnsɪv/ *a* intensivo
intensive-care unit /ɪn'tɛnsɪv'kɛər/ *n* sala de terapia intensiva, unidad de cuidados intensivos, unidad de vigilancia intensiva, *f*
intent /ɪn'tɛnt/ *n* intento, propósito, deseo, *m. a* atento; (absorbed) absorto, interesado; (on doing) resuelto a, decidido a. **to all intents and purposes,** en efecto, en realidad. **to be i. on,** (reading, etc.) estar absorto en, entregarse a. **with i. to defraud,** con el propósito deliberado de defraudar

intention /ɪn'tɛnʃən/ *n* intención, voluntad, *f,* propósito, pensamiento, proyecto, *m*
intentional /ɪn'tɛnʃənḷ/ *a* intencional, deliberado, premeditado
intentionally /ɪn'tɛnʃənḷi/ *adv* a propósito, intencionalmente, de pensado
intentioned /ɪn'tɛnʃənd/ *a* intencionado
intently /ɪn'tɛntli/ *adv* atentamente
inter /ɪn'tɜr/ *vt* enterrar, sepultar
inter- *prefix* inter, entre. **i.-allied,** interaliado, de los aliados. **i.-denominational,** intersectario. **i.-university,** interuniversitario. **i.-urban,** interurbano
interaction /ˌɪntər'ækʃən/ *n* interacción, acción recíproca, acción mutua, *f*
intercalate /ɪn'tɜrkəˌleit/ *vt* intercalar, interpolar
intercede /ˌɪntər'sid/ *vi* interceder, mediar. **to i. for,** hablar por
intercept /ˌɪntər'sɛpt/ *vt* interceptar, detener; entrecoger, atajar
interception /ˌɪntər'sɛpʃən/ *n* interceptación, detención, *f*
intercession /ˌɪntər'sɛʃən/ *n* mediación, intercesión, *f*
intercessor /ˌɪntər'sɛsər/ *n* intercesor (-ra), mediador (-ra)
interchange /*n.* 'ɪntərˌtʃeindʒ; *v.* ˌɪntər'tʃɛndʒ/ *n* intercambio, *f;* (of goods) comercio, tráfico, *m. vt* cambiar, trocar; alternar
interchangeable /ˌɪntər'tʃeindʒəbəl/ *a* intercambiable
intercom /'ɪntərˌkɒm/ *n* teléfono interior, *m*
intercommunicate /ˌɪntərkə'myunɪˌkeit/ *vi* comunicarse
intercommunication /ˌɪntərkəˌmyunɪ'keiʃən/ *n* comunicación mutua, *f;* comercio, *m*
intercostal /ˌɪntər'kɒstḷ/ *a Anat.* intercostal
intercourse /'ɪntərˌkɔrs/ *n* (social) trato, *m,* relaciones, *f pl; Com.* comercio, tráfico, *m;* (of ideas) intercambio, *m;* (sexual) coito, trato sexual, *m*
interdependence /ˌɪntərdɪ'pɛndəns/ *n* dependencia mutua, mutualidad, *f*
interdependent /ˌɪntərdɪ'pɛndənt/ *a* mutuo
interdict /*n* 'ɪntərˌdɪkt; *v* ˌɪntər'dɪkt/ *n* interdicto, veto, *m,* prohibición, *f; Eccl.* entredicho, *m. vt* interdecir, prohibir, privar; *Eccl.* poner entredicho
interdiction /ˌɪntər'dɪkʃən/ *n* interdicción, prohibición, *f*
interest /'ɪntərɪst/ *n* interés, *m;* provecho, *m; Com.* premio, rédito, interés, *m;* (in a firm) participación, *f;* (curiosity) interés, *m;* curiosidad, *f;* simpatía, *f;* (influence) influencia, *f. n. pl* **interests,** (commercial undertakings) empresas, *f pl,* intereses, negocios, *m pl. vt* interesar. **to be interested in,** interesarse en, (on behalf of) por. **to be in one's own i.,** ser en provecho de uno, ser en su propio interés. **to bear eight per cent. i.,** dar interés del ocho por ciento. **to pay with i.,** pagar con creces. **to put out at i.,** dar a interés. **in the interests of,** en interés de. **compound i.,** interés compuesto. **simple i.,** interés sencillo, *m.* **vested interests,** intereses creados, *m pl*
interesting /'ɪntərɪstɪŋ/ *a* interesante, curioso, atractivo
interestingly /'ɪntərɪstɪŋli/ *adv* amenamente, de modo interesante
interfere /ˌɪntər'fɪər/ *vi* intervenir, meterse, entremeterse, mezclarse; *Inf.* mangonear, meter las narices; (with) meterse con; (impede) estorbar, impedir
interference /ˌɪntər'fɪərəns/ *n* intervención, *f,* entrometimiento, *m;* (obstacle) estorbo, obstáculo, *m; Phys.* interferencia, *f; Radio.* parásitos, *m pl*
interfering /ˌɪntər'fɪərɪŋ/ *a* entremetido, oficioso, *Inf.* mangoneador
interim /'ɪntərəm/ *n* ínterin, intermedio, *Lat. Am. also* interregno. *a* interino, provisional. **in the i.,** entre tanto, en el ínterin. *Com.* **i. dividend,** dividendo interino, *m*
interior /ɪn'tɪəriər/ *a* interior, interno; doméstico. *n* interior, *m*
interject /ˌɪntər'dʒɛkt/ *vt* interponer
interjection /ˌɪntər'dʒɛkʃən/ *n* exclamación, interjección, *f;* interposición, *f*
interlace /ˌɪntər'leis/ *vt* entrelazar, entretejer
interleave /ˌɪntər'liv/ *vt* interfoliar, interpaginar

interline /'ɪntər‚laɪn/ vt entrerrenglonar, interlinear
interlinear /‚ɪntər'lɪniər/ a interlineal
interlineation /‚ɪntər‚lɪni'eiʃən/ n interlineación, f
interlining /'ɪntər‚laɪnɪŋ/ n entretela, f
interlock /‚ɪntər'lɒk/ vt (of wheels, etc.). endentar; trabar; cerrar. vi endentarse; entrelazarse, unirse; cerrar
interlocutor /‚ɪntər'lɒkyətər/ n interlocutor (-ra)
interloper /'ɪntər‚loupər/ n intruso (-sa); Com. intérlope, m
interloping /‚ɪntər'loupɪŋ/ a intérlope
interlude /'ɪntər‚lud/ n intervalo, intermedio, m; Mus. interludio, m; Theat. entremés, m
intermarriage /‚ɪntər'mærɪdʒ/ n casamiento entre parientes próximos, entre razas distintas, o entre grupos étnicos distintos, m
intermarry /‚ɪntər'mæri/ vi contraer matrimonio entre parientes próximos, entre personas de razas distintas, o entre grupos étnicos distintos
intermediary /‚ɪntər'midi‚eri/ a and n intermediario (-ia)
intermediate /‚ɪntər'midi‚eit/ a intermedio, medio, medianero. n sustancia intermedia, f. vi intervenir, mediar
interment /ɪn'tɜrmənt/ n entierro, m
intermezzo /‚ɪntər'mɛtsou/ n Theat. intermedio, m; Mus. intermezzo, m
interminable /ɪn'tɜrmənəbəl/ a interminable, inacabable
interminably /ɪn'tɜrmənəbli/ adv interminablemente, sin fin, sin cesar
intermingle /‚ɪntər'mɪŋgəl/ vt entremezclar, entreverar. vi mezclarse
intermission /‚ɪntər'mɪʃən/ n intermisión, interrupción, pausa, f; Theat. entreacto, m. **without i.,** sin pausa, sin tregua
intermittence /‚ɪntər'mɪtns/ n intermitencia, alternación, f
intermittent /‚ɪntər'mɪtnt/ a intermitente, discontinuo; (of fever) intermitente
intermittently /‚ɪntər'mɪtntli/ adv a intervalos, a ratos, a pausas
intern /ɪn'tɜrn/ n Med. practicante de hospital m, interino (-na), interno (-na), interno de hospital, alumno interno, m. vt confinar, encerrar
internal /ɪn'tɜrnl/ a interno, interior; (of affairs) doméstico, civil; intrínseco; íntimo. **i.-combustion engine,** motor de combustión interna, m
internally /ɪn'tɜrnli/ adv interiormente
international /‚ɪntər'næʃənl/ a internacional. n Sports. un partido internacional. **i. law,** derecho internacional, m. **i. studies,** estudios internacionales
internationalism /‚ɪntər'næʃənl‚ɪzəm/ n internacionalismo, m
internationalist /‚ɪntər'næʃənlɪst/ n internacionalista, mf
internationalization /‚ɪntər‚næʃənlə'zeiʃən/ n internacionalización, f
internationalize /‚ɪntər'næʃənl‚aiz/ vt hacer internacional, poner bajo un control internacional
internecine /‚ɪntər'nisin/ a sanguinario, feroz
internee /‚ɪntər'ni/ n internado (-da)
Internet /'ɪntər‚nɛt/ n Internet, m
internment /ɪn'tɜrnmənt/ n internamiento, m. **i. camp,** campo de internamiento, m
internship /'ɪntɜrn‚ʃɪp/ n interino, m
interoceanic /‚ɪntər‚ouʃi'ænɪk/ a interoceánico
interpolate /ɪn'tɜrpə‚leit/ vt interpolar, intercalar, interponer
interpolation /ɪn‚tɜrpə'leiʃən/ n interpolación, inserción, añadidura, f
interpolator /ɪn'tɜrpə‚leitər/ n interpolador (-ra)
interpose /‚ɪntər'pouz/ vt interponer; (a remark) interpolar. vi interponerse, intervenir; (interfere) entrometerse; interrumpir
interposition /‚ɪntərpə'zɪʃən/ n interposición, f; entrometimiento, m
interpret /ɪn'tɜrprɪt/ vt interpretar; (translate) traducir; (explain) explicar, descifrar. vi interpretar.

interpretation /ɪn‚tɜrprɪ'teiʃən/ n interpretación, f; (translation) traducción, f; (explanation) explicación, f
interpretative /ɪn'tɜrprɪ‚teitɪv/ a interpretativo, interpretador
interpreter /ɪn'tɜrprɪtər/ n intérprete, mf
interregnum /‚ɪntər'rɛgnəm/ n interregno, m
interrelation /‚ɪntərrɪ'leiʃən/ n relación mutua, f
interrogate /ɪn'tɛrə‚geit/ vt interrogar, examinar, preguntar
interrogating /ɪn'tɛrə‚geitɪŋ/ a interrogante
interrogation /ɪn‚tɛrə'geiʃən/ n interrogación, f, examen, m; pregunta, f. **mark of i.,** punto de interrogación, m
interrogative /‚ɪntə'rɒgətɪv/ a interrogativo. n palabra interrogativa, f
interrogatively /‚ɪntə'rɒgətɪvli/ adv interrogativamente
interrogator /ɪn'tɛrə‚getər/ n examinador (-ra), interrogador (-ra)
interrogatory /‚ɪntə'rɒgə‚tɔri/ a interrogativo. n interrogatorio, m
interrupt /‚ɪntə'rʌpt/ vt interrumpir
interruptedly /‚ɪntə'rʌptɪdli/ adv interrumpidamente
interrupter /‚ɪntə'rʌptər/ n interruptor (-ra); Elec. interruptor, m
interruption /‚ɪntə'rʌpʃən/ n interrupción, f
intersect /‚ɪntər'sɛkt/ vt cruzar. vi cruzarse, intersecarse
intersection /‚ɪntər'sɛkʃən/ n intersección, f; cruce, m, (of streets) bocacalle, Lat. Am. cruza f
intersperse /‚ɪntər'spɜrs/ vt diseminar, esparcir; interpolar, entremezclar
interstice /ɪn'tɜrstɪs/ n intervalo, intermedio, m; (chink) intersticio, m, hendedura, f
intertwine /‚ɪntər'twain/ vt entretejer, entrelazar. vi entrelazarse
interval /'ɪntərvəl/ n intervalo, intermedio, m, pausa, f; Theat. entreacto, m, intermisión, f; (in schools) recreo, m. **at intervals,** a trechos, de vez en cuando. **lucid i.,** intervalo claro, intervalo lúcido, m
intervene /‚ɪntər'vin/ vi intervenir, tomar parte (en); mediar; (occur) sobrevenir, acaecer; Law. interponerse
intervening /‚ɪntər'vinɪŋ/ a intermedio; interventor
intervention /‚ɪntər'vɛnʃən/ n intervención, mediación, f
interventionist /‚ɪntər'vɛnʃənɪst/ n Polit. partidario (-ia) de la intervención
interview /'ɪntər‚vyu/ n entrevista, f, interviú, m. vt entrevistarse con
interviewer /'ɪntər‚vyuər/ n interrogador (-ra); (reporter) reportero, periodista, m
interweave /‚ɪntər'wiv/ vt entretejer, entrelazar
interweaving /‚ɪntər'wivɪŋ/ n entretejimiento, m
intestacy /ɪn'tɛstəsi/ n ausencia de un testamento, f
intestate /ɪn'tɛsteit/ a and n intestado (-da)
intestinal /ɪn'tɛstənl/ a intestinal, intestino. **i. worm,** lombriz intestinal, f
intestine /ɪn'tɛstɪn/ n intestino, m. **large i.,** intestino grueso, m. **small i.,** intestino delgado, m
intimacy /'ɪntəməsi/ n intimidad, f, familiaridad, f; (of nobility and others) privanza, f
intimate /'ɪntəmɪt/ a íntimo; (of relations) entrañable, estrecho; intrínseco, esencial; (of knowledge) profundo, completo, detallado. n amigo (-ga) de confianza. vt intimar, dar a entender, indicar. **to become i.,** intimarse. **to be on i. terms with,** tratar de tú (a), ser amigo íntimo de
intimately /'ɪntəmɪtli/ adv íntimamente, al fondo
intimation /‚ɪntə'meiʃən/ n intimación, indicación, f; (hint) insinuación, indirecta, f
intimidate /ɪn'tɪmɪ‚deit/ vt intimidar, aterrar, infundir miedo (a), espantar, acobardar, amedrentar
intimidation /ɪn‚tɪmɪ'deiʃən/ n intimidación, f
intimidatory /ɪn'tɪmɪdə‚tɔri/ a aterrador, amenazador
into /'ɪntu; unstressed -tʊ, -tə/ prep en; a, al, a la; dentro, adentro; (of pouring, forming, etc.) a. **Throw it i. the fire,** Échalo al (or en el) fuego. **She went i. the house,** Entró en la casa. **to look i.,** mirar dentro de; mirar hacia el interior (de); investigar

intolerable /ɪn'tɒlərəbəl/ a intolerable, insufrible, inaguantable, insoportable, inllevable

intolerableness /ɪn'tɒlərəbəlnɪs/ n intolerabilidad, f

intolerably /ɪn'tɒlərəbli/ adv intolerablemente, insufriblemente

intolerance /ɪn'tɒlərəns/ n intolerancia, intransigencia, f

intolerant /ɪn'tɒlərənt/ a intolerante, intransigente; Med. intolerante

intonation /ˌɪntou'neɪʃən/ n entonación, f

intone /ɪn'toun/ vt entonar; Eccl. salmodiar

intoxicant /ɪn'tɒksɪkənt/ a embriagador. n bebida alcohólica, f

intoxicate /ɪn'tɒksɪˌkeɪt/ vt emborrachar, embriagar; Med. intoxicar, envenenar; (excite) embriagar, embelesar

intoxicated /ɪn'tɒksɪˌkeɪtɪd/ a borracho; (excited) ebrio, embriagado; Med. intoxicado

intoxicating /ɪn'tɒksɪˌkeɪtɪŋ/ a embriagador

intoxication /ɪnˌtɒksɪ'keɪʃən/ n borrachera, embriaguez, f; Med. intoxicación, f, envenenamiento, m; (excitement) entusiasmo, m, ebriedad, f

intractability /ɪnˌtræktə'bɪlɪti/ n insociabilidad, hurañería, f

intractable /ɪn'træktəbəl/ a intratable, insociable, huraño

intramural /ˌɪntrə'myʊrəl/ adv intramuros

intransigence /ɪn'trænsɪdʒəns/ n intransigencia, intolerancia, f

intransigent /ɪn'trænsɪdʒənt/ a intransigente, intolerante

intransitive /ɪn'trænsɪtɪv/ a intransitivo, neutro

intrauterine /ˌɪntrə'yutərɪn/ a Med. intrauterino

intravenous /ˌɪntrə'vinəs/ a Med. intravenoso

intrepid /ɪn'trepɪd/ a intrépido, osado, audaz

intrepidity /ˌɪntrə'pɪdɪti/ n intrepidez, osadía, audacia, f

intrepidly /ɪn'trepɪdli/ adv intrépidamente, audazmente

intricacy /'ɪntrɪkəsi/ n intrincación, complejidad, f

intricate /'ɪntrɪkɪt/ a intrincado, complejo

intricately /'ɪntrɪkɪtli/ adv intrincadamente

intrigue /ɪn'trig/ n. also 'ɪntrig/ n intriga, maquinación, f, enredo, m; (amorous) lío, m. vi intrigar, enredar; (amorous) tener un lío. vt (interest) atraer, interesar; (with) intrigar con. **to be intrigued** Lat. Am. intrigarse

intriguer /ɪn'trigər/ n intrigante, mf. urdemalas, m, enredador (-ra)

intriguing /ɪn'trigɪŋ/ a enredador; (attractive) atrayente, interesante, seductor

intrinsic /ɪn'trɪnsɪk/ a intrínseco, innato, inherente, esencial

intrinsically /ɪn'trɪnsɪkli/ adv intrínsecamente, esencialmente

introduce /ˌɪntrə'dus/ vt introducir; hacer entrar; insertar, injerir; (a person) presentar; poner de moda, introducir; (a bill) presentar; (a person to a thing) llamar la atención sobre. **Allow me to i. my friend,** Permítame que le presente mi amigo

introduction /ˌɪntrə'dʌkʃən/ n introducción, f; (of a book) prefacio, prólogo, m, advertencia, f; (of a person) presentación, f; inserción, f

introductory /ˌɪntrə'dʌktəri/ a introductor, preliminar, preparatorio

intromission /ˌɪntrə'mɪʃən/ n intromisión, f

introspection /ˌɪntrə'spɛkʃən/ n introspección, f

introspective /ˌɪntrə'spɛktɪv/ a introspectivo

introversion /ˌɪntrə'vɜrʒən/ n Psychol. introversión f

introvert /'ɪntrəˌvɜrt/ a and n Psychol. introverso (-sa)

intrude /ɪn'trud/ vt introducir, imponer. vi entremeterse, inmiscuirse. **Do I i.?** ¿Estorbo?

intruder /ɪn'trudər/ n intruso (-sa)

intrusion /ɪn'truʒən/ n intrusión, f; Geol. intromisión, f

intrusive /ɪn'trusɪv/ a intruso

intuition /ˌɪntu'ɪʃən/ n intuición, f. **to know by i.,** intuir, saber por intuición

intuitive /ɪn'tuɪtɪv/ a intuitivo

inundate /'ɪnənˌdeɪt/ vt inundar, anegar; Fig. abrumar

inundation /ˌɪnən'deɪʃən/ n inundación, anegación, f; Fig. diluvio, m, abundancia, f

inure /ɪn'yʊr/ vt endurecer, habituar

inurement /ɪn'yʊrmənt/ n habituación, f

invade /ɪn'veɪd/ vt invadir, irrumpir, asaltar; Med. invadir

invader /ɪn'veɪdər/ n invasor (-ra), acometedor (-ra), agresor (-ra)

invading /ɪn'veɪdɪŋ/ a invasor, irruptor

invalid /ɪn'vælɪd/ a inválido, nulo. **to become i.,** caducar

invalid /ɪn'vælɪd/ n inválido (-da), enfermo (-ma). **to become an i.,** quedarse inválido. **to i. out of the army,** licenciar por invalidez. **i. carriage,** cochecillo de inválido, m

invalidate /ɪn'vælɪˌdeɪt/ vt invalidar, anular

invalidation /ɪnˌvælɪ'deɪʃən/ n invalidación, f

invalidity /ˌɪnvə'lɪdɪti/ n invalidez, nulidad, f

invaluable /ɪn'vælyuəbəl/ n inestimable

invariability /ɪnˌvɛəriə'bɪlɪti/ n invariabilidad, invariación, inalterabilidad, inmutabilidad, f

invariable /ɪn'vɛəriəbəl/ a invariable, inmutable, inalterable

invariably /ɪn'vɛəriəbli/ adv invariablemente, inmutablemente

invariant /ɪn'vɛəriənt/ n Math. invariante, m

invasion /ɪn'veɪʒən/ n invasión, irrupción, f; Med. invasión, f

invective /ɪn'vɛktɪv/ n invectiva, diatriba, f

inveigh (against) /ɪn'veɪ/ vi desencadenarse (contra), prorrumpir en invectivas (contra)

inveigle /ɪn'veɪgəl/ vt seducir, engatusar, persuadir

invent /ɪn'vɛnt/ vt inventar, descubrir, originar; (a falsehood) fingir; (create) idear, componer

invention /ɪn'vɛnʃən/ n invención, f, invento, descubrimiento, m; (imagination) ingeniosidad, inventiva, f; (falsehood) ficción, mentira, f; (finding) invención, f, hallazgo, m

inventive /ɪn'vɛntɪv/ a inventor, inventivo; ingenioso, despejado

inventiveness /ɪn'vɛntɪvnɪs/ n inventiva, f

inventor /ɪn'vɛntər/ n inventor (-ra), autor (-ra)

inventory /'ɪnvənˌtɔri/ n inventario, m; descripción, f. vt inventariar

inverse /ɪn'vɜrs/ a inverso. **i. proportion,** razón inversa, f

inversely /ɪn'vɜrsli/ adv inversamente, a la inversa

inversion /ɪn'vɜrʒən/ n inversión, f, trastrocamiento, m; Gram. hipérbaton, m

invert /ɪn'vɜrt/ vt invertir, trastornar, trastrocar. **inverted commas,** comilla, f

invertebrate /ɪn'vɜrtəbrɪt/ a and n invertebrado m.

invest /ɪn'vɛst/ vt Com. invertir; Mil. sitiar, cercar; (foll. by with) poner, cubrir con; (of qualities) conferir, otorgar, dar. vi (with in) poner dinero en, echar caudal en; Inf. comprar

investigable /ɪn'vɛstɪgəbəl/ a averiguable

investigate /ɪn'vɛstɪˌgeɪt/ vt investigar, estudiar; examinar, averiguar; explorar. **to i. closely** Lat. Am. interiorizar

investigation /ɪnˌvɛstɪ'geɪʃən/ n investigación, f, estudio, m; examen, m, averiguación, f; encuesta, pesquisa, f

investigator /ɪn'vɛstɪˌgeɪtər/ n investigador (-ra), averiguador (-ra)

investigatory /ɪn'vɛtɪgəˌtɔri/ a investigador

investiture /ɪn'vɛstɪtʃər/ n investidura, instalación, f

investment /ɪn'vɛstmənt/ n (Com. of money) inversión, f, empleo, m; Mil. cerco, m; (investiture) instalación, f; pl **investments,** Com. acciones, f pl, fondos, m pl

investor /ɪn'vɛstər/ n inversionista, m; accionista, mf, Lat. Am. inversor (-ra) mf

inveteracy /ɪn'vɛtərəsi/ n antigüedad, f, lo arraigado

inveterate /ɪn'vɛtərɪt/ a inveterado, antiguo, arraigado, incurable

invidious /ɪn'vɪdiəs/ a odioso, repugnante, injusto

invidiousness /ɪn'vɪdiəsnɪs/ n injusticia, f, lo odioso

invigorate /ɪn'vɪgə,reit/ vt vigorizar, dar fuerza (a), avivar

invigorating /ɪn'vɪgə,reitɪŋ/ a fortaleciente, fortificador, vigorizador

invincibility /ɪn,vɪnsə'bɪlɪti/ n invencibilidad, f

invincible /ɪn'vɪnsəbəl/ a invencible, indomable; Fig. insuperable

inviolability /ɪn,vaiələ'bɪlɪti/ n inviolabilidad, f

inviolable /ɪn'vaiələbəl/ a inviolable

inviolate /ɪn'vaiəlɪt/ a inviolado

invisibility /ɪn,vɪzə'bɪlɪti/ n invisibilidad, f

invisible /ɪn'vɪzəbəl/ a invisible. **i. ink,** tinta simpática, f. **i. mending,** zurcido invisible, m

invitation /,ɪnvɪ'teiʃən/ n invitación, f; convite, m; (card) tarjeta de invitación, f

invite /ɪn'vait/ vt invitar, convidar; (request) pedir, rogar; (of things) incitar, tentar.

inviting /ɪn'vaitɪŋ/ a atrayente, incitante; (of food) apetitoso; (of looks) provocativo

invocation /,ɪnvə'keiʃən/ n invocación, f

invocatory /ɪn'vɒkətɔri/ a invocatorio, invocador

invoice /'ɪnvɔis/ n Com. factura, f. vt facturar. **proforma i.,** factura simulada, f. **shipping i.,** factura de expedición, f. **i. book,** libro de facturas, m

invoke /ɪn'vouk/ vt invocar; suplicar, implorar; (Law) acogerse (a)

involuntarily /ɪn,vɒlən'tɛərəli/ adv sin querer, involuntariamente

involuntariness /ɪn'vɒlən,tɛrɪnɪs/ n involuntariedad, f

involuntary /ɪn'vɒlən,tɛri/ a involuntario; instintivo, inconsciente

involve /ɪn'vɒlv/ vt (entangle) enredar, embrollar, enmarañar; (implicate) comprometer; (imply) implicar, ocasionar, suponer, traer consigo

involved /ɪn'vɒlvd/ a complejo, intrincado; (of style) confuso, obscuro

invulnerability /ɪn,vʌlnərə'bɪlɪti/ n invulnerabilidad, f

invulnerable /ɪn'vʌlnərəbəl/ a invulnerable

inward /'ɪnwərd/ a interior, interno; íntimo, espiritual. adv adentro

inwardly /'ɪnwərdli/ adv interiormente; para sí, entre sí

inwards /'ɪnwərdz/ adv hacia dentro; adentro

iodine /'aiə,dain/ n yodo, m. **i. poisoning,** yodismo, m

ion /'aiən/ n Chem. ion, m

Ionian /ai'ouniən/ a and n jónico (-ca)

Ionic /ai'ɒnɪk/ a jónico. **i. foot** Poet. jónico, m

iota /ai'outə/ n (letter) iota, f; jota, pizca, f, ápice, m. **not an i.,** ni pizca

I.O.U. n Com. abonaré, m

ipecacuanha /,ɪpɪ,kækyə'wany'ə/ n ipecacuana, f

Iranian /ɪ'reiniən/ a and n iranio (-ia)

irascibility /ɪ,ræsə'bɪlɪti/ n irascibilidad, iracundia, irritabilidad, f

irascible /ɪ'ræsəbəl/ a irascible, iracundo, irritable

irate /ai'reit/ a airado, colérico, enojado

ire /aiᵊr/ n ira, cólera, furia, f

Ireland /'aiᵊrlənd/ Irlanda, f

iridescence /,ɪrɪ'dɛsəns/ n iridiscencia, f

iridescent /,ɪrɪ'dɛsənt/ a iridiscente. **to look i.,** irisar, tornasolarse

iridium /ɪ'rɪdiəm/ n Chem. iridio, m

iris /'airɪs/ n Anat. iris, m; Bot. irídea, f

Irish /'airɪʃ/ a and n irlandés (-esa). **the I.,** los irlandeses

Irish Sea Mar de Irlanda, f

irksome /'ɜrksəm/ a fastidioso, tedioso, aburrido

irksomeness /'ɜrksəmnɪs/ n tedio, fastidio, aburrimiento, m

iron /'aiərn/ n hierro, m; (for clothes) plancha, f; (tool) utensilio, m, herramienta, f; (golf) hierro, m; pl **irons,** m pl, cadenas, f pl. a de hierro, férreo; Fig. duro, severo. vt (linen) planchar; (with out) allanar. **to have too many irons in the fire,** tener demasiados asuntos entre manos. **to put in irons,** echar grillos (a). **to strike while the i. is hot,** A hierro caliente batir de repente. **cast-i.,** hierro colado, m. **scrap i.,** hierro viejo, m. **sheet i.,** hierro en planchas, m. **wrought i.,** hierro dulce, m. **i. age,** edad de hierro, f. **i.-foundry,** fundición de hierro, f. **i. lung,**

Med. pulmón de hierro, pulmón de acero, m. **i.-mold,** mancha de orín, f. **i. smelting furnace,** alto horno, m. **i. tonic,** Med. reconstituyente ferruginoso, m. **i. will,** voluntad de hierro, f

ironclad /a 'aiərn'klæd; n -,klæd/ a blindado, acorazado. n buque de guerra blindado, acorazado, m

ironer /'aiərnər/ n planchador (-ra)

ironical /ai'rɒnɪkəl/ a irónico

ironically /ai'rɒnɪkli/ adv con ironía, irónicamente

ironing /'aiərnɪŋ/ n planchado, m; ropa por planchar, f. a de planchar. **i. board,** tabla de planchar, f

ironist /'airənɪst/ n ironista, mf

ironmonger /'aiərn,mʌŋgər/ n ferretero (-ra). **ironmonger's shop,** ferretería, f

ironmongery /'aiərn,mʌŋgəri/ n ferretería, quincallería, f

iron sulphide /'sʌlfaid/ sulfuro de hierro, m

ironwork /'aiərn,wɜrk/ n herraje, m; obra de hierro, f

ironworks /'aiərn,wɜrks/ n herrería, f

irony /'airəni/ n ironía, f. a (like iron) ferruginoso

Iroquois /'ɪrə,kwɔi/ a and n iroqués (-esa)

irradiate /ɪ'reidi,eit/ vt irradiar; Fig. iluminar, aclarar

irradiation /ɪ,reidi'eiʃən/ n irradiación, f; Fig. iluminación, f

irrational /ɪ'ræʃənl/ a ilógico, ridículo, irracional

irrationality /ɪ,ræʃə'nælɪti/ n irracionalidad, f

irreclaimable /,ɪri'kleiməbəl/ a irrecuperable, irredimible; (of land) inservible, improductivo; irreformable

irreconcilable /ɪ'rɛkən,sailəbəl/ a irreconciliable

irreconcilably /ɪ'rɛkən,sailəbli/ adv irremediablemente

irrecoverable /,ɪri'kʌvərəbəl/ a irrecuperable, incobrable

irredeemable /,ɪri'diməbəl/ a irredimible, perdido. **i. government loan,** deuda perpetua, f

irredeemably /,ɪri'diməbli/ adv perdidamente

irreducible /,ɪri'dusəbəl/ a irreducible

irrefutability /ɪ,rɛfyətə'bɪlɪti/ n verdad, f

irrefutable /ɪ'rɛfyətəbəl/ a irrefutable, indisputable, innegable, irrebatible

irregular /ɪ'rɛgyələr/ a irregular, anormal; (of shape) disforme; desordenado; Gram. irregular; (of surface) desigual, escabroso

irregularity /ɪ,rɛgyə'lærɪti/ n irregularidad, f; anormalidad, f; (of shape) desproporción, irregularidad, f; (of surface) escabrosidad, desigualdad, f; exceso, m, demasía, f

irrelevance /ɪ'rɛləvəns/ n inconexión, f; inoportunidad, f; futilidad, poca importancia, f; (stupidity) desatino, m, impertinencia, f

irrelevant /ɪ'rɛləvənt/ a inaplicable, fuera de propósito; inoportuno; sin importancia, fútil; (stupid) impertinente

irreligion /,ɪri'lɪdʒən/ n irreligión, impiedad, f

irreligious /,ɪri'lɪdʒəs/ a irreligioso, impío

irremediable /,ɪri'midiəbəl/ a irremediable, irreparable

irremediably /,ɪri'midiəbli/ adv sin remedio, irremediablemente

irreparable /ɪ'rɛpərəbəl/ a irreparable

irreplaceable /,ɪri'pleisəbəl/ a irreemplazable

irrepressible /,ɪri'prɛsəbəl/ a incontrolable, indomable

irreproachable /,ɪri'proutʃəbəl/ a irreprochable, intachable

irresistible /,ɪri'zɪstəbəl/ a irresistible

irresistibleness /,ɪri'zɪstəbəlnɪs/ n superioridad, f

irresolute /ɪ'rɛzə,lut/ a irresoluto, indeciso, vacilante

irresoluteness /ɪ'rɛzə,lutnɪs/ n irresolución, indecisión, f

irrespective /,ɪri'spɛktɪv/ a (with of) independiente de, aparte de, sin contar

irresponsibility /,ɪrɪ,spɒnsə'bɪlɪti;/ n irresponsabilidad, f

irresponsible /,ɪri'spɒnsəbəl/ a irresponsable

irretrievable /,ɪri'trivəbəl/ a irrecuperable

irretrievably /,ɪri'trivəbli/ adv irreparablemente, sin remedio

irreverence /ɪ'rɛvərəns/ n irreverencia, f

irreverent /ɪ'rɛvərənt/ a irreverente, irrespetuoso

irrevocability /ɪˌrevəkə'bɪlɪti/ *n* irrevocabilidad, *f*
irrevocable /ɪ'revəkəbəl/ *a* irrevocable; inquebrantable
irrigable /'ɪrɪgəbəl/ *a* regadío
irrigate /'ɪrɪˌgeit/ *vt Agr.* poner en regadío, regar; *Med.* irrigar
irrigation /ˌɪrɪ'geiʃən/ *n Agr.* riego, *m*; *Med.* irrigación, *f.* **i. channel,** cacera, acequia, *f*, canal de riego, *m*
irritability /ˌɪrɪtə'bɪlɪti/ *n* irritabilidad, iracundia, *f*
irritable /'ɪrɪtəbəl/ *a* irritable, irascible, iracundo
irritably /'ɪrɪtəbli/ *adv* con irritación, airadamente
irritant /'ɪrɪtnt/ *a* irritante, irritador. *n* irritador, *m*; *Med.* medicamento irritante, *m*
irritate /'ɪrɪˌteit/ *vt* provocar, estimular; irritar, molestar, exasperar; *Med.* irritar
irritating /'ɪrɪˌteitɪŋ/ *a* irritador, irritante
irritatingly /'ɪrɪˌteitɪŋli/ *adv* de un modo irritante
irritation /ˌɪrɪ'teiʃən/ *n* irritación, *f*, enojo, *m*; *Physiol.* picazón, *f*, picor, *m*
irruption /ɪ'rʌpʃən/ *n* irrupción, invasión, *f*
isinglass /'aizənˌglæs/ *n* cola de pescado, *f*
Islamic /ɪs'læmɪk/ *a* islámico
Islamism /ɪs'lɑmɪzəm/ *n* islamismo, *m*
Islamite /ɪs'læmait/ *a* and *n* islamita *mf*
island /'ailənd/ *n* isla, *f*, a isleño
islander /'ailəndər/ *n* isleño (-ña)
islet /'ailɪt/ *n* isleta, *f*; isolote, *m*
isobaric /ˌaisə'bærɪk/ *a* isobárico
isolate /'aisəˌleit/ *vt* aislar, apartar
isolated /'aisəˌleitɪd/ *a* aislado, apartado, solitario; único, solo
isolation /ˌaisə'leiʃən/ *n* aislamiento, apartamiento, *m*, soledad, *f*
isolationism /ˌaisə'leiʃəˌnɪzəm/ *n Polit.* aislacionismo, aislamientismo, *m*
isolationist /ˌaisə'leiʃənɪst/ *a* and *n Polit.* aislacionista, aislamientista, *mf*
isomerism /ai'sɒməˌrɪzəm/ *n Chem.* isomería, *f*
isometric /ˌaisə'mɛtrɪk/ *a* isométrico
isosceles /ai'sɒsəˌliz/ *a* isósceles
isotope /'aisəˌtoup/ *n* isotope, isotopo, *m*
Israelite /'ɪzriəˌlait/ *a* and *n* israelita *mf*
issue /'ɪʃu/ *n* salida, *f*; (result) resultado, *m*, consecuencia, *f*; (of a periodical) número, *m*; *Print.* edición, tirada, *f*; (offspring) prole, sucesión, *f*; (of notes, bonds) emisión, *f*; *Med.* flujo, *m*; cuestión, *f*, problema, *m*. *vi* salir, fluir, manar; nacer, originarse; resultar, terminarse. *vt* (an order) expedir, emitir, dictar; publicar, dar a luz; (of notes, bonds) poner en

circulación, librar. **at i.,** en disputa, en cuestión. **to join i.,** llevar la contraria, oponer
isthmian /'ɪsmiən/ *a* ístmico
isthmus /'ɪsməs/ *n* istmo, *m*
it /ɪt/ *pron* (as subject) él, *m*; ella, *f*; (gen. omitted with all verbs in Sp.); (as object) lo, *m*; la, *f*; (as indirect object) le (se with an object in 3rd pers.); (meaning that thing, that affair) eso, ello. Sometimes omitted in other cases, e.g. *He has thought it necessary to stay at home,* Ha creído necesario de quedarse en casa. *We heard it said that...,* Oímos decir que... *to make it perfectly clear that...,* dejar bien claro que... *n* (slang) garbo, aquél, *m*; atractivos, *m pl.* **Is it not so?** ¿No es así? **That is it,** Eso es. **It's me,** Soy yo
Italian /ɪ'tælyən/ *a* and *n* italiano (-na) (language) italiano, *m. Art.* **I. School,** escuela italiana, *f*
italic /ɪ'tælɪk/ *a* (of Italy) itálico; *Print.* itálico, bastardillo. *n* letra bastardilla, bastardilla, letra itálica, *f.* **italics mine,** el subrayado es mío, los subrayados son míos
italicize /ɪ'tæləˌsaiz/ *vt* imprimir en bastardilla; dar énfasis (a)
Italy /'ɪtli/ Italia, *f*
itch /ɪtʃ/ *n* sarna, *f*; *Fig.* picazón, *f*; prurito, capricho, *m. vi* picar; *Fig.* sentir picazón; (with to) rabiar por, suspirar por.
itching /'ɪtʃɪŋ/ *n* picazón, *f*, picor, *m. a* sarnoso, picante; *Med.* pruriginoso. **to have an i. palm,** *Fig.* ser de la virgen del puño
item /*n* 'aitəm; *adv* 'aitɛm/ *n* ítem, artículo, *m*; *Com.* partida, *f*; punto, detalle, *m*; (of a program) número, *m*; asunto, *m. adv* ítem
iterative /'ɪtəˌreitɪv/ *a* iterativo
Ithaca /'ɪθəkə/ Ítaca, *f*
itinerant /ai'tɪnərənt/ *a* nómada, errante
itinerary /ai'tɪnəˌrɛri/ *n* itinerario, *m*, ruta, *f*
its /ɪts/ *poss a* su (with pl. obj.) sus. **a book and its pages,** un libro y sus páginas.
itself /ɪt'sɛlf/ *pron* él mismo, *m*; ella misma, *f*; (with prep.) sí; (with reflex. verb) se; (with noun) el mismo, la misma; (meaning alone) solo. **in i.,** en sí
ivied /'aivid/ *a* cubierto de hiedra
ivory /'aivəri/ *n* marfil, *m. a* ebúrneo, de marfil, marfileño. **vegetable i.,** marfil vegetal, *m.* **i. carving,** talla de marfil, *f*
ivory tower /'aivəri 'tauər/ *n* torre de marfil, *f*
ivory-tower /'aivəri 'tauər/ *a* de torre de marfil
ivy /'aivi/ *n* hiedra, *f*

J

j /dʒei/ *n* (letter) jota, *f*
jab /dʒæb/ *vt* (with a hypodermic needle, etc.) pinchar; introducir (en); clavar (con); (scrape) hurgar; (place) poner. *n* pinchazo, *m*; golpe, *m.* **He jabbed his pistol in my ribs,** Me puso la pistola en las costillas
jabber /'dʒæbər/ *vt* and *vi* chapurrear; (of monkeys) chillar
jabbering /'dʒæbərɪŋ/ *n* chapurreo, *m*; (of monkeys) chillidos, *m pl*
Jack /dʒæk/ *n* Juan, *m*; (man) hombre, *m*; (sailor) marinero, *m*; (in cards) sota, *f*; (for raising weights) gato, *m*; (of a spit) torno, *m*; (of some animals) macho, *m*; (bowls) boliche, *m. vt* (with up) solevantar con gatos. **Union J.,** pabellón británico, *m.* **j.-boot,** bota de montar, *f.* **J.-in-office,** mandarín, funcionario impertinente, *m.* **J.-in-the-box,** faca, *f.* **j.-knife,** navaja, *f.* **J. of all trades,** hombre de muchos oficios, *m.* **jack of all trades, master of none,** aprendiz de todo, oficial de nada. **j.-rabbit,** liebre americana, *f.* **J.-tar,** marinero, *m*
jackal /'dʒækəl/ *n* chacal, adive, *m*
jackass /'dʒækˌæs/ *n* asno, *m*; (fool) tonto, asno, *m.* **laughing j.,** martín pescador, *m*
jacket /'dʒækɪt/ *n* chaqueta, *f*; americana, *f*; (for boil-

ers, etc.) camisa, *f*; (of a book) forro, *m*, sobrecubierta, *f.* **strait j.,** camisa de fuerza, *f*
jacks /dʒæks/ *n* (game) matatenas, *f pl*, cantillos, *m pl*
jade /dʒeid/ *n Mineral.* jade, *m*; (horse) rocín, *m*; (woman) mala pécora, *f*; (saucy wench) mozuela, picaruela, *f*
jaded /'dʒeidɪd/ *a* fatigado, agotado, rendido; (of the palate) saciado
jagged /'dʒægɪd/ *a* dentado
jaguar /'dʒægwɑr/ *n* jaguar, *m*
jai alai /'hai ˌlai/ *n Mexico* frontón, *m*
jail /dʒeil/ *n* cárcel, prisión, *f*; encierro, *m. vt* encarcelar. *a* carcelario, carcelero.
jailbird /'dʒeilˌbɜrd/ *n* malhechor; presidiario, *m*
jailer /'dʒeilər/ *n* carcelero (-ra)
jalopy /dʒə'lopi/ *n* carcacho, *m*, (Mexico), cafetera rusa, *f*, (Spain)
jalousie /'dʒælə,si/ *n* celosía, *f*
jam /dʒæm/ *vt* (ram) apretar; apiñar; estrujar; (a machine) atascar; (radio) causar interferencia (a); (preserve) hacer confitura de. *vi* atascarse. *n* (of people) agolpamiento, *m*; (traffic) atasco, *m*; (preserve) confitura, mermelada, compota, *f.* **He jammed his hat on,** Se encasquetó el sombrero. **She suddenly jammed**

down on the brakes, Frenó de repente. **jam-dish,** compotera, *f*. **jam-jar,** pote para confitura, *m*

Jamaican /dʒəˈmeikən/ *a* jamaicano, *n* jamaicano (-na)

jamboree /ˌdʒæmbəˈri/ *n* campamento, *m* .

jamming /ˈdʒæmɪŋ/ *n Radio.* interferencias, *f pl*

jangle /ˈdʒæŋɡəl/ *vi* cencerrear; chocar; rechinar. *n* cencerreo, *m*; choque, *m*; rechinamiento, *m*

janissary /ˈdʒænəˌsɛri/ *n* jenízaro, *m*

janitor /ˈdʒænɪtər/ *n* portero, *m*; (in a university, etc.) bedel, *m*

January /ˈdʒænyuˌɛri/ *n* enero, *m*

Japan /dʒəˈpæn/ el Japón, *m*

Japanese /ˌdʒæpəˈniz/ *a* japonés. *n* japonés (-esa); (language) japonés, *m*

jar /dʒɑr/ *n* chirrido, *m*; choque, *m*; sacudida, *f*; vibración, trepidación, *f*; (quarrel) riña, *f*; (receptacle) jarra, *f*; (for tobacco, honey, cosmetics, etc.) pote, *m*; (Leyden) botella (de Leyden), *f*. *vi* chirriar; vibrar, trepidar; chocar; (of sounds) ser discorde; (of colors) chillar. *vt* sacudir; hacer vibrar. **It jarred on my nerves,** Me atacaba los nervios. **It gave me a nasty jar,** *Fig.* Me hizo una impresión desagradable. **on the jar,** entreabierto

jardiniere /ˌdʒɑrdnˈɪər/ *n* jardinera, *f*

jargon /ˈdʒɑrɡən/ *n* jerga, jerigonza, *f*; monserga, *f*; (technical) lenguaje especial, *m*

jarring /ˈdʒɑrɪŋ/ *a* discorde, disonante; en conflicto, opuesto; (to the nerves) que ataca a los nervios

jasmine /ˈdʒæzmɪn/ *n* jazmín, *m*. **yellow j.,** jazmín amarillo, *m*

jasper /ˈdʒæspər/ *n Mineral.* jaspe, *m*

jaundice /ˈdʒɔndɪs/ *n* ictericia, *f*

jaundiced /ˈdʒɔndɪst/ *a* envidioso; desengañado, desilusionado

jaunt /dʒɔnt/ *n* excursión, *f*, *vi* ir de excursión

jauntily /ˈdʒɔntļi/ *adv* airosamente, con garbo

jauntiness /ˈʒɔntɪnɪs/ *n* garbo, *m*, gentileza, ligereza, *f*

jaunty /ˈdʒɔnti/ *a* garboso, airoso

Javanese /ˌdʒævəˈniz/ *a* javanés. *n* javanés (-esa)

javelin /ˈdʒævlɪn/ *n* jabalina, *f*. **j. throwing,** lanzamiento de la jabalina, *m*

jaw /dʒɔ/ *n* quijada, *f*; maxilar, *m*; *pl* **jaws,** boca, *f*; (of death, etc.) garras, *f pl*; *Mech.* quijada, *f*; (narrow entrance) boca, abertura, *f*. **jaw-bone,** mandíbula, *f*, *Anat.* hueso maxilar, *m*

jay /dʒei/ *n* arrendajo, *m*

jazz /dʒæz/ *n* jazz, *m*. *vi* bailar el jazz. **j. band,** orquesta de jazz, *f*

jealous /ˈdʒɛləs/ *a* celoso; envidioso. **to be j. of,** tener celos de. **to make j.,** dar celos (a)

jealously /ˈdʒɛləsli/ *adv* celosamente

jealousy /ˈdʒɛləsi/ *n* celos, *m pl*

jeans /dʒinz/ *n* vaqueros, *m pl*

jeep /dʒip/ *n Mil.* yip, *m*

jeer /dʒɪr/ *n* burla, mofa, *f*; insulto, *m*, *vi* burlarse; (with at) mofarse de

jeerer /ˈdʒɪərər/ *n* mofador (-ra)

jeering /ˈdʒɪərɪŋ/ *a* mofador. *n* burlas, *f pl*; insultos, *m pl*

jeeringly /ˈdʒɪərɪŋli/ *adv* burlonamente

jellied /ˈdʒɛlid/ *a* en gelatina

jelly /ˈdʒɛli/ *n* jalea, *f*; gelatina, *f*, *vi* solidificarse. **j.-bag,** manga, *f*. **j.-fish,** aguamala, aguaviva, malagna, medusa, *f*

jeopardize /ˈdʒɛpərˌdaiz/ *vt* arriesgar, poner en juego; comprometer

jeopardy /ˈdʒɛpərdi/ *n* peligro, *m*

jeremiad /ˌdʒɛrəˈmaiəd/ *n* jeremiada, *f*

jerk /dʒɜrk/ *n* sacudida, *f*. *vt* sacudir; dar una sacudida (a); lanzar bruscamente; (pull) tirar de; (push) empujar. *vi* moverse a sacudidas. **I jerked myself free,** Me libré de una sacudida

jerkily /ˈdʒɜrkəli/ *adv* con sacudidas; espasmódicamente; nerviosamente

jerkin /ˈdʒɜrkɪn/ *n* justillo, *m*

jerky /ˈdʒɜrki/ *a* espasmódico; nervioso (also of style)

jerry-built /ˈdʒɛriˌbɪlt/ *a* mal construido, de pacotilla

jersey /ˈdʒɜrzi/ *n* jersey, *m*. *a* de jersey; de Jersey.

football j., camiseta de fútbol, *f*, jersey de fútbol, *m*. **J. cow,** vaca jerseysa, *f*

Jerusalem /dʒɪˈrusələm/ Jerusalén, *m*

jest /dʒɛst/ *n* broma, chanza, *f*; (joke) chiste, *m*; (laughingstock) hazmerreír, *m*. *vi* bromear; burlarse (de). **in j.,** en broma, de guasa

jester /ˈdʒɛstər/ *n* burlón (-ona); (practical joker, etc.) bromista, *mf*; (at a royal court) bufón, *m*

jesting /ˈdʒɛstɪŋ/ *n* bromas, *f pl*; chistes, *m pl*; burlas, *f pl*. *a* de broma; burlón

jestingly /ˈdʒɛstɪŋli/ *adv* en broma

Jesuit /ˈdʒɛʒuɪt/ *n* Jesuita, *m*

Jesuitical /ˌdʒɛʒuˈɪtɪkəl/ *a* jesuítico

jet /dʒɛt/ *n Mineral.* azabache, *m*; (stream) chorro, *m*; (pipe) surtidero, *m*; (burner) mechero, *m*, *vi* chorrear. **jet-black,** negro como el azabache, de azabache. **jet-propelled engine,** motor de retroacción, *m*. **jet-propelled plane,** aeroplano de reacción, *m*

jetsam /ˈdʒɛtsəm/ *n* echazón, *f*, *Fig.* víctima, *f*

jettison /ˈdʒɛtəsən/ *n* echazón, *f*. *vt* echar (mercancías) al mar; *Fig.* librarse de, abandonar

jetty /ˈdʒɛti/ *n* dique, malecón, *m*; (landing pier) embarcadero, muelle, *m*

Jew /dʒu/ *n* judío (-ía). **Jew's harp,** birimbao, *m*

jewel /ˈdʒuəl/ *n* joya, alhaja, *f*; (of a watch) rubí, *m*; *Fig.* alhaja, *f*. *vt* enjoyar, adornar con piedras preciosas. **j.-box, -case,** joyero, *m*

jeweled /ˈdʒuəld/ *a* adornado con piedras preciosas, enjoyado; (of a watch) con rubíes

jeweler /ˈdʒuələr/ *n* joyero (-ra). **jeweler's shop,** joyería, *f*

jewelry /ˈdʒuəlri/ *n* joyas, *f pl*; artículos de joyería, *m pl*

Jewish /ˈdʒuɪʃ/ *a* judío

Jewry /ˈdʒuri/ *n* judería, *f*

jib /dʒɪb/ *n Naut.* foque, *m*. *vi* (of a horse) plantarse; (refuse) rehusar. **to jib at,** vacilar en; mostrarse desinclinado. **jib-boom,** *Naut.* botalón de foque, *m*

jiffy /ˈdʒɪfi/ *n* instante, credo, *m*. **in a j.,** en un decir Jesús, en un credo, en un santiamén

jig /dʒɪɡ/ *n* (dance) jiga, *f*. *vi* bailar una jiga; bailar, agitarse, sacudirse. *vt* agitar, sacudir; (sieve) cribar

jigger /ˈdʒɪɡər/ *n Naut.* cangreja de mesana, *f*; aparejo de mano, *m*; jigger, *m*

jigsaw puzzle /ˈdʒɪɡˌsɔ/ *n* rompecabezas, *m*

jilt /dʒɪlt/ *vt* dar calabazas (a)

jingle /ˈdʒɪŋɡəl/ *n* tintineo, *m*; ruido, *m*; verso, *m*; estribillo, *m*. *vi* tintinar; sonar; rimar

jingoism /ˈdʒɪŋɡouˌɪzəm/ *n* jingoísmo, *m*

jitters, to have the /ˈdʒɪtərz/ *no* tenerlas todas consigo, no saber dónde meterse

job /dʒɒb/ *n* tarea, *f*; trabajo, *m*; empleo, *m*; (affair) asunto, *m*; (thing) cosa, *f*; (unscrupulous transaction) intriga, *f*. **It is a good (bad) job that…,** Es una buena (mala) cosa que… **He has done a good job,** Ha hecho un buen trabajo. **He has lost his job,** Ha perdido su empleo, Le han declarado cesante. **odd-job man,** factótum, *m*. **job-lot,** colección miscelánea, *f*; *Com.* saldo de mercancías, *m*

jobber /ˈdʒɒbər/ *n* (workman) destajista, *m*; (in stocks) agiotista, *m*; *Com.* corredor, *m*

jobless /ˈdʒɒblɪs/ *a* sin trabajo

jockey /ˈdʒɒki/ *n* jockey, *m*. *vt* engañar; (with into) persuadir, hacer; (with out of) quitar, robar. **j. cap,** gorra de jockey, *f*. **J. Club,** jockey-club, *m*

jocose /dʒouˈkous/ *a* jocoso, gracioso, guasón

jocosity /dʒouˈkɒsɪti/ *n* jocosidad, *f*

jocular /ˈdʒɒkyələr/ *a* gracioso, alegre; chistoso, zumbón

jocularity /ˌdʒɒkyəˈlærɪti/ *n* alegría, jocosidad, *f*

jocularly /ˈdʒɒkyələrli/ *adv* en broma; alegremente

jocund /ˈdʒɒkənd/ *a* alegre, jovial; jocundo

jocundity /dʒouˈkʌndɪti/ *n* alegría, *f*; jocundidad, *f*

jog /dʒɒɡ/ *vt* empujar; (the memory) refrescar. *vi Sport.* correr, ir despacio; andar a trote corto. *n* empujón, *m*. **He jogged me with his elbow,** Me dio con el codo. **jog-trot,** trote corto, *m*

joie de vivre /ʒwɑdəˈvivrə/ *n* goce de vivir, arregosto de vivir, *m*

join /dʒɔin/ *vt* juntar; unir; añadir; (railway lines)

empalmar; juntarse con; (meet) encontrarse (con); reunirse (con); (a club, etc.) hacerse miembro (de); (share) acompañar; (regiments, ships) volver (a). *vi* juntarse; unirse; asociarse. *n* unión, *f*; (railway) empalme, *m*; (roads) bifurcación, *f*. **At what time will you j. me?** ¿A qué hora me vendrás a buscar? **He has joined his ship,** Ha vuelto a su buque. **Will you j. me in a drink?** ¿Me quieres acompañar en una bebida? **to j. battle,** librar batalla. **to j. forces,** combinar; *Inf.* juntar meriendas. **to j. in,** tomar parte en, participar en. **to j. together,** *vt* unir, juntar. *vi* juntarse; asociarse. **to j. up,** alistarse

joiner /'dʒɔinər/ *n* carpintero, ensamblador, *m*,

joinery /'dʒɔinəri/ *n* ensambladuría, *f*; carpintería, *f*

joining /'dʒɔiniŋ/ *n* juntura, conjunción, *f*; (etc.) ensambladura, *f*; *Fig.* unión, *f*

joint /dʒɔint/ *n* juntura, junta, *f*; *Anat.* coyuntura, articulación, *f*; (knuckle) nudillo, *m*; (of meat) cuarto, *m*; (hinge) bisagra, *f*; *Bot.* nudo, *m*, *a* unido; combinado; colectivo; mixto; mutuo; (in compounds) co. *vt* juntar; (meat) descuartizar. **out of j.,** dislocado; (of the times) fuera de compás. **j. account,** cuenta corriente mutua, *f*. **j.-heir,** coheredero, *m*. **j. stock company,** compañía por acciones, sociedad anónima, *f*

jointed /'dʒɔintid/ *a* articulado; (foldable) plegadizo

jointly /'dʒɔintli/ *adv* juntamente, en común, colectivamente

joist /dʒɔist/ *n* sopanda, viga, *f*

joke /dʒouk/ *n* chiste, *m*; burla, broma, *f*. *vi* bromear, chancearse. *vt* burlarse (de). **Can he take a j.?** ¿Sabe aguantar una broma? **practical j.,** broma pesada, *f*. **to play a j.,** gastar una broma, hacer una burla

joker /'dʒoukər/ *n* bromista, *Argentina also* fomista, *mf*; (in cards) comodín, *m*

joking /'dʒoukiŋ/ *n* chistes, *m pl*, bromas, *f pl*. *a* chistoso; cómico

jokingly /'dʒoukiŋli/ *adv* en broma, de guasa

jollification /ˌdʒɒləfɪ'keiʃən/ *n* regocijo, *m*; festividades, fiestas, *f pl*

jollity /'dʒɒliti/ *n* alegría, *f*, regocijo, *m*

jolly /'dʒɒli/ *a* alegre, jovial; (tipsy) achispado; (amusing) divertido; (nice) agradable. *adv* muy. **He is a j. good fellow,** Es un hombre estupendo. **I am j. glad,** Estoy contentísimo, Me alegro mucho

jolt /dʒoult/ *n* sacudida, *f*. *vt* sacudir. *vi* (of a vehicle) traquetear

jolting /'dʒoultiŋ/ *n* sacudidas, *f pl*, sacudimiento, *m*; (of a vehicle) traqueteo, *m*

jonquil /'dʒɒŋkwil/ *n Bot.* junquillo, *m*

Jordan /'dʒɔrdn/ Jordania, *f*

jostle /'dʒɒsəl/ *vt* empujar, empellar. *vi* dar empujones, codear

jot /dʒɒt/ *n* jota, pizca, *f*. *vt* (down) apuntar. **not a jot,** ni jota, ni pizca. **to be not worth a jot,** no valer un comino

jotter /'dʒɒtər/ *n* taco para notas, *m*; (exercise book) cuaderno, *m*

jotting /'dʒɒtiŋ/ *n* apunte, *m*; observación, *f*

journal /'dʒɜrnl/ *n* (diary) diario, *m*; (ship's) diario de navegación, *m*; (newspaper) periódico, *m*; (review) revista, *f*

journalese /ˌdʒɜrnl'iz/ *n* lenguaje periodístico, *m*

journalism /'dʒɜrnlˌizəm/ *n* periodismo, *Lat. Am. also* diarismo, *m*

journalist /'dʒɜrnlist/ *n* periodista, *mf*

journalistic /ˌdʒɜrnl'istik/ *a* periodístico

journey /'dʒɜrni/ *n* viaje, *m*; expedición, *f*; trayecto, *m*; camino, *m*. *vi* viajar. **j. by sea,** viaje por mar. **Pleasant j.!** ¡Buen viaje! ¡Feliz viaje! **outward j.,** viaje de ida, *m*. **return j.,** viaje de regreso, *m*

Jove /dʒouv/ *n* Júpiter, *m*. **By J.!** ¡Pardiez! ¡Caramba!

jovial /'dʒouviəl/ *a* jovial

joviality /ˌdʒouvi'æliti/ *n* jovialidad, *f*

jowl /dʒaul/ *n* (cheek) carrillo, *m*; (of cattle, etc.) papada, *f*; (jaw) quijada, *f*

joy /dʒɔi/ *n* alegría, *f*; felicidad, *f*; deleite, placer, *m*, *vi* alegrarse. **I wish you joy,** Te deseo la felicidad.

joy-ride, excursión en coche, *f*; vuelo en avión, *m*.

joy-stick, (of an airplane) palanca de gobierno, *f*

joyful /'dʒɔifəl/ *a* alegre

joyfulness /'dʒɔifəlnis/ *n* alegría, *f*

joyless /'dʒɔilis/ *a* sin alegría, triste

joylessness /'dʒɔilisnis/ *n* falta de alegría, tristeza, *f*

joyous. /'dʒɔiəs/. See **joyful**

jubilant /'dʒubələnt/ *a* jubiloso; triunfante

jubilantly /'dʒubələntli/ *adv* con júbilo, alegremente; triunfalmente

jubilation /ˌdʒubə'leiʃən/ *n* júbilo, *m*, alegría, *f*; ruido triunfal, *m*

jubilee /'dʒubə,li/ *n* jubileo, *m*

jubilee volume *n* libro de homenaje, libro jubilar, *m*

Judaic /dʒu'deiik/ *a* judaico

Judaism /'dʒudi,izəm/ *n* judaísmo, *m*

Judas /'dʒudəs/ *n* (traitor and hole) judas, *m*

Judezmo /dʒu'dezmou/ *n* el judesmo, el ladino, *m*

judge /dʒʌdʒ/ *n* juez, *m*; (connoisseur) conocedor (-ra) (de); (umpire) arbitro, *m*. *vt* juzgar; considerar, tener por. *vi* servir como juez; juzgar. **judging by,** a juzgar por. **to be a good j. of,** ser buen juez de. **to j. for oneself,** formar su propia opinión

judgment /'dʒʌdʒmənt/ *n Law.* fallo, *m*; sentencia, *f*; juicio, *m*; (understanding) entendimiento, discernimiento, *m*; (opinion) opinión, *f*, parecer, *m*. **In my j....,** Según mi parecer,... Según creo yo... **Last J.,** Juicio Final, *m*. **to pass j. on,** *Law.* pronunciar sentencia (en or sobre); dictaminar sobre; juzgar. **to sit in j. on,** ser juez de; juzgar. **j.-day,** Día del Juicio, *m*. **seat,** tribunal, *m*

judicature /'dʒudɪˌkeitʃər/ *n* judicatura, *f*; (court) juzgado, *m*

judicial /dʒu'dɪʃəl/ *a* judicial; legal; (of the mind) juicioso. **j. inquiry,** investigación judicial, *f*. **j. separation,** separación legal, *f*

judiciary /dʒu'dɪʃi,ɛri/ *a* judicial. *n* judicatura, *f*

judicious /dʒu'dɪʃəs/ *a* juicioso, prudente

judiciously /dʒu'dɪʃəsli/ *adv* prudentemente, juiciosamente

judiciousness /dʒu'dɪʃəsnis/ *n* juicio, *m*, prudencia, sensatez, *f*

judo /'dʒudou/ *n* yudo, *m*

judoka /'dʒudou,ka/ *n* yudoca, *mf*

jug /dʒʌg/ *n* jarro, *m*; cántaro, *m*; pote, *m*; (jail) *Argentina, Chile* capacha *f*. *vt Cul.* estofar. *vi* (of nightingale) trinar, cantar. **jugged hare,** *n* liebre en estofado, *f*

juggle /'dʒʌgəl/ *vi* hacer juegos malabares. **to j. out of,** (money, etc.) quitar con engaño, estafar. **to j. with,** *Fig.* (facts, etc.) tergiversar, falsificar; (person) engañar

juggler /'dʒʌglər/ *n* malabarista, *mf*; (deceiver) estafador (-ra)

jugglery /'dʒʌgləri/ *n* prestidigitación, *f*; juegos malabares, *m pl*; (imposture) engaño, *m*, estafa, *f*; trampas, *f pl*

jugular /'dʒʌgyələr/ *a Anat.* yugular. **j. vein,** yugular, *m*

juice /dʒus/ *n* jugo, *m*; *Fig.* zumo, *m*. **digestive j.,** jugo digestivo, *m*

juiciness /'dʒusinis/ *n* jugosidad, *f*; suculencia, *f*

juicy /'dʒusi/ *a* jugoso; suculento

jukebox /'dʒuk,bɒks/ *n* tocadiscos, vitrola, sinfonola, *f*

July /dʒu'lai/ *n* julio, *m*

jumble /'dʒʌmbəl/ *vt* mezclar, confundir. *n* mezcla confusa, colección miscelánea, confusión, *f*. **j. sale,** tómbola, *f*

jump /dʒʌmp/ *n* salto, *m*; (in prices, etc.) aumento, *m*. **at one j.,** de un salto. **high j.,** salto de altura, *m*. **long j.,** salto de longitud, *m*. **In my j. of the j.,** *Inf.* estar nervioso, tener los nervios en punta

jump /dʒʌmp/ *vi* saltar; dar un salto; brincar; (of tea-cups, etc.) bailar; (throb) pulsar. *vt* saltar; hacer saltar; (a child) brincar; (omit) pasar por alto de, omitir. **The train jumped the rails,** El tren se descarriló. **to j. out of bed,** saltar de la cama. **to j. to the conclusion that...,** darse prisa a concluir que... **to j. about,** dar saltos, brincar; revolverse, moverse de un lado para otro. **to j. at,** saltar sobre; precipitarse sobre, abalanzarse hacia; (an offer) apresurarse a aceptar; (seize) coger con entusiasmo. **to j. down,** bajar de un salto. **to j. over,** saltar; saltar por encima de. **to j. up,** saltar; (on to a horse, etc.) montar rápidamente; levantarse apresuradamente. **to j. with,** (agree) convenir en, estar conforme con

jumper /'dʒʌmpər/ n saltador (-ra); (sailor's) blusa, f; jersey, suéter m, Lat. Am. chompa, f

jumpiness /'dʒʌmpinɪs/ n nerviosidad, f

jumping /'dʒʌmpɪŋ/ n saltos, m pl. a saltador. **j.-off place,** base avanzada, f; Fig. trampolín, m. **j.-pole,** pértiga, f

jumpy /'dʒʌmpi/ a nervioso, agitado

junction /'dʒʌŋkʃən/ n unión, f; (of roads) bifurcación, f; (railway) empalme, m; (connection) conexión, f

juncture /'dʒʌŋktʃər/ n coyuntura, f; momento, m; crisis, f, momento crítico, m; (joint) junta, f

June /dʒun/ n junio, m

jungle /'dʒʌŋgəl/ n selva, f. **j.-fever,** fiebre de los grandes bosques, f

junior /'dʒunyər/ a joven; hijo; más joven; menos antiguo; subordinado, segundo. n joven, mf **Carmen is my j. by three years,** Carmen es tres años más joven que yo. **James Thomson, Jr.,** James Thomson, hijo. **the j. school,** los pequeños. **j. partner,** socio menor, m

juniper /'dʒunəpər/ n Bot. enebro, m

junk /dʒʌŋk/ n trastos viejos, m pl; (nonsense) patrañas, f pl; Naut. junco, m; (salt meat) tasajo, m. **j.-shop,** tienda de trastos viejos, f

junk bond bono-basura, m

junketing /'dʒʌŋkɪtɪŋ/ n festividades, f pl

junk mail n correo basura, m

juridical /dʒʊ'rɪdɪkəl/ a jurídico

jurisconsult /,dʒʊrɪskən'sʌlt/ n jurisconsulto, m

jurisdiction /,dʒʊrɪs'dɪkʃən/ n jurisdicción, f; competencia, f

jurisprudence /,dʒʊrɪs'prudns/ n jurisprudencia, f

jurist /'dʒʊrɪst/ n jurista, legista, mf

juror /'dʒʊrər/ n (miembro del) jurado, m

jury /'dʒʊri/ n jurado, m. **to be on the j.,** formar parte del jurado. **j.-box,** tribuna del jurado, f

juryman /'dʒʊrimən/ n miembro del jurado, m

just /dʒʌst/ a justo; justiciero; exacto; fiel. **Peter the J.,** Pedro el justiciero

just /dʒʌst/ adv justamente, exactamente; precisamente; (scarcely) apenas; (almost) casi; (entirely) completamente; (simply) meramente, solamente, tan sólo; nada más; Mexico no más; (newly) recién (followed by past part.), recientemente. **He only j. missed being run over,** Por poco le atropellan. **It is j. near,** Está muy cerca. **It is j. the same to me,** Me es completamente igual. **J. as he was leaving,** Cuando estaba a punto de marcharse, En el momento de marcharse. **Just as you arrive in Spain, you must...** Nada más llegar a España, tienes que... **That's j. it!** ¡Eso es! ¡Exactamente! **to have j.,** acabar de. **They have j. dined,** Acaban de cenar. **J. as you wish,** Como Vd. quiera. **j. at that moment,** precisamente en aquel momento. **j. by,** muy cerca; al lado. **j. now,** ahora mismo; hace poco; pronto, dentro de poco. **j. yet,** todavía. **They will not come j. yet,** No vendrán todavía. **Just looking** (browser to shopkeeper) Estoy viendo, Estamos viendo

justice /'dʒʌstɪs/ n justicia, f; (judge) juez, m; (magistrate) juez municipal, m. **to bring to j.,** llevar ante el juez (a). **to do j. to,** (a person) hacer justicia (a); (a meal) hacer honor (a). **to do oneself j.,** quedar bien

justifiable /'dʒʌstə,faiəbəl/ a justificable

justifiably /'dʒʌstə,faiəbli/ adv con justicia, justificadamente

justification /,dʒʌstəfɪ'keiʃən/ n justificación, f

justify /'dʒʌstə,fai/ vt justificar, vindicar; (excuse) disculpar; Print. justificar. **to be justified (in),** tener derecho (a), tener motivo (para), tener razón (en)

justly /'dʒʌstli/ adv justamente; con justicia; con derecho; con razón; exactamente; debidamente

justness /'dʒʌstnɪs/ n justicia, f; exactitud, f

jute /dʒut/ n yute, m

jut (out) /dʒʌt/ vi salir, proyectar; sobresalir

juvenile /'dʒuvənl/ a juvenil; de la juventud; para la juventud; joven; de niños; para niños. n joven, mf. **j. court,** tribunal de menores, m. **j. lead,** Theat. galancete, galán joven, m. **j. offender,** delincuente infantil, m

juxtapose /'dʒʌkstə,pouz/ vt yuxtaponer

juxtaposition /,dʒʌkstəpə'zɪʃən/ n yuxtaposición, f

K

k /kei/ n (letter) ka, f

kaiser /'kaizər/ n káiser, emperador, m. **the K.** el emperador alemán, m

kaleidoscope /kə'laidə,skoup/ n calidoscopio, m

kaleidoscopic /kə,laidə'skɒpik/ a calidoscópico

kangaroo /,kæŋgə'ru/ n canguro, m

kaolin /'keiəlin/ n caolín, m

kapok /'keipɒk/ n miraguano, m

keel /kil/ n quilla, f. vt carenar. **to k. over,** volcar; caer; Naut. zozobrar

keelson /'kɛlsən/ n sobrequilla, f

keen /kin/ a (of edges) afilado; agudo; (of feeling) vivo; sutil; ardiente; celoso, entusiasta; mordaz; (desirous) ansioso; (of appetite) grande, bueno. **He is a k. tennis player,** Es tenista entusiasta. **Joan has a very k. ear,** Juana tiene un oído muy agudo. **I'm not very k. on apples,** No me gustan mucho las manzanas

keenly /'kinli/ adv agudamente; vivamente; (of feeling) hondamente; (of looking) atentamente

keenness /'kinnɪs/ n (of a blade) afiladura, f; agudeza, f; viveza, f; sutileza, f; perspicacia, f; (enthusiasm) entusiasmo, m, afición, f; (desire) ansia, f

keep /kip/ vt guardar; tener; quedarse con; retener; conservar; mantener; (a shop, hotel, etc.) dirigir; tener; (a school) ser director de; (a promise, etc.) cumplir; (the law, etc.) observar, guardar; (celebrate) solemnizar; (a secret) guardar; (books, accounts, a house, in step) llevar; (sheep, etc., one's bed) guardar; (a city, etc.) defender; (domestic animals, cars, etc.) tener; (lodge) alojar; (detain) detener; (reserve) reservar; (cause) hacer. **They had kept this room for me,** Me habían reservado este cuarto. **Dorothy has kept the blue dress,** Dorotea se ha quedado con el vestido azul. **The government could not k. order,** El gobierno no sabía mantener el orden. **I did not know how to k. their attention,** No sabía retener su atención. **Carmen kept quiet,** Carmen guardó silencio, Carmen se calló. **Can you k. a secret?** ¿Sabes guardar un secreto? **to k. an appointment,** acudir a una cita. **to k. in repair,** conservar en buen estado. **to k. someone from doing something,** evitar que uno haga algo. **to k. someone waiting,** hacer que espere uno. **to k. something from someone,** ocultar algo de uno. **We were kept at night and day,** Nos hacían trabajar día y noche. **I always k. it by me,** Lo tengo siempre a mi lado (or conmigo). **to k. away,** alejar; mantener a distancia; no dejar venir. **to k. back,** (a crowd, etc.) detener; cortar el paso (a); no dejar avanzar; (retain) guardar, retener; reservar; (tears, words) reprimir, contener; (evidence, etc.) callar, suprimir. **to k. down,** no dejar subir (a); sujetar; (a nation, etc.) oprimir, subyugar; (emotions) dominar; (prices, expenses) mantener bajo; (check) moderar, reprimir. **to k. in,** (feelings) contener; reprimir; (the house) hacer quedarse en casa, no dejar salir; (imprison) encerrar; (school) hacer quedar en la escuela (a). **to k. off,** alejar; tener a distancia (a); cerrar el paso (a), no dejar avanzar; no andar sobre; no tocar; (a subject) no tratar de, no tocar. **K. your hands off!** ¡No toques! **to k. on,** guardar; retener; (eyes) fijar en, poner en. **to k. out,** no dejar entrar; excluir. **It is difficult to k. him out of trouble,** Es difícil de evitar que se meta en líos. **to k. to,** seguir; limitarse a; adherirse a; **K. to the Left,** «Tome su izquierda», **K. to the right,** «Tome su derecha»; (a path, etc.) seguir por; (one's bed) guardar; (fulfil) cumplir; (oblige) hacer, obligar. **to k. under,** subyugar, oprimir; dominar; controlar. **to k. up,** mantener; (appearances) guardar; conservar; persistir en; (prices) sostener; (in good repair) conservar en buen estado; (go on doing) continuar. **He kept me up late last night,** Anoche me entretuvo hasta muy tarde; Ayer me hizo trasnochar; Anoche me hizo velar. **to k. one's end up,** volver por sí, hacerse fuerte. **to k. up one's spirits,** no desanimarse

keep /kip/ *vi* quedar; (be) estar; (continue) seguir, continuar; mantenerse; (at home, etc.) quedarse, permanecer; (be accustomed) acostumbrar, soler; (persist) perseverar; (of food) conservarse fresco. **How is he keeping?** ¿Cómo está? **to k. in with someone,** cultivar a alguien. **to k. up with the times,** mantenerse al corriente. **to k. at,** seguir; persistir; perseverar; (pester) importunar. **John keeps at it,** Juan trabaja sin descansar. **to k. away,** mantenerse apartado; mantenerse a distancia; no acudir. **to k. back,** hacerse a un lado, apartarse, alejarse. **to k. down,** quedarse tumbado; seguir acurrucado; no levantarse; esconderse. **to k. from,** (doing something) guardarse de. **to k. off,** mantenerse a distancia. **If the storm keeps off,** Si no estalla una tempestad. **If the rain keeps off,** Si no empieza a llover, Si no hay lluvia. **to k. on,** continuar; seguir. **to k. straight on,** seguir derecho. **I'm tired, but I still k. on,** Estoy cansado, pero sigo trabajando. **to k. out,** quedarse fuera. **to k. out of,** (quarrels, trouble, etc.) no meterse en, evitar. **to k. out of sight,** no dejarse ver, no mostrarse, mantenerse oculto. **to k. together,** quedarse juntos; reunirse

keep /kip/ *n* (of a castle) mazmorra, *f*; (maintenance) subsistencia, *f*; comida, *f*. **for keeps,** para siempre jamás

keeper /'kipər/ *n* guarda, *mf*; (in a park, zoo, of a lunatic) guardián, *m*; (of a museum, etc.) director, *m*; (of animals) criador (-ra); (gamekeeper) guardabosque, *m*; (of a boardinghouse, shop, etc.) dueño (-ña); (of accounts, books) tenedor, *m*. **Am I my brother's k.?** ¿Soy yo responsable por mi hermano?

keeping /'kipɪŋ/ *n* guarda, *f*; conservación, *f*; protección, *f*; (of a rule) observación, *f*; (of an anniversary, etc.) celebración, *f*; (of a person) mantenimiento, *m*. **in k. with,** en armonía con; de acuerdo con. **out of k. with,** en desacuerdo con. **to be in safe k.,** estar en buenas manos; estar en un lugar seguro. **k. back,** retención, *f*

keepsake /'kip,seik/ *n* recuerdo, *m*

keg /kɛg/ *n* barrilete, *m*

ken /kɛn/ *n* alcance de la vista, *m*; vista, *f*; comprensión, *f*

kennel /'kɛnl/ *n* (of a dog) perrera, *f*; (of hounds) jauría, *f*; (dwelling) cuchitril, *m*; (gutter) arroyo, *m*. **k. man,** perrero, *m*

kepi /'keipi/ *n* quepis, *m*

Kepler /'kɛplər/ Keplero

kerchief /'kɜrtʃif/ *n* pañuelo, *m*; pañoleta, *f*. **brightly-colored k.,** pañuelo de hierbas, *m*

kernel /'kɜrnl/ *n* almendra, semilla, *f*; *Fig.* meollo, *m*, esencia, *f*

kerosene /'kɛrə,sin/ *n* petróleo de lámpara, *m*; kerosén, *m*

ketchup /'kɛtʃəp/ *n* salsa de tomate y setas, *f*

kettle /'kɛtl/ *n* caldero, *m*, *Mexico* marmita, *f*. **pretty k. of fish,** olla de grillos, *f*. **k.-drum,** timbal, *m*. **k.-drum player,** timbalero, *m*

key /ki/ *n* llave, *f*; (*Fig. Archit., Mus.*) clave, *f*; (tone) tono, *m*; (of a piano, typewriter, etc.) tecla, *f*; *Mech.* chaveta, *f*; (of a wind instrument) pistón, *m*; (winged fruit) sámara, *f*; *Elec.* conmutador, *m*. **major (minor) key,** tono mayor (menor), *m*. **latch-key,** llave de la puerta, *f*; (Yale) llavín, *m*. **master key,** llave maestra, *f*. **skeleton key,** ganzúa, *f*. **He is all keyed up,** Tiene los nervios en punta. **key industry,** industria clave, *f*. **key man,** hombre indispensable, *m*. **key point,** punto estratégico, *m*. **key-ring,** llavero, *m*. **key signature,** *Mus.* clave, *f*. **key word,** palabra clave, *f*

keyboard /'ki,bɔrd/ *n* teclado, *m*

keyhole /'ki,houl/ *n* ojo de la cerradura, *m*. **through the k.,** por el ojo de la cerradura

keynote /'ki,nout/ *n Mus.* tónica, *f*; *Fig.* piedra clave, idea fundamental, *f*

keystone /'ki,stoun/ *n* piedra clave, *f*

khaki /'kæki/ *n* caqui, *m*

kick /kɪk/ *vt* dar un puntapié (a); golpear; (a goal) chutar. *vi* (of horses, etc.) dar coces, cocear; (of guns) recular. **to k. one's heels,** hacer tiempo. **to k. the bucket,** palmarla, *Lat. Am.* arrancarse. **to k. up a row,** hacer un ruido de mil diablos; (quarrel) armar camorra. **to k. about,** dar patadas (a). **to k. away,** quitar con el pie; lanzar con el pie. **to k. off,** quitar con el pie; lanzar; sacudirse. **k.-off,** *n* golpe de salida, puntapié inicial, saque, *m*. **to k. out,** echar a puntapiés

kick /kɪk/ *n* puntapié, *m*; golpe, *m*; coz, *f*; (of guns) culatazo, *m*. **free k.,** golpe franco, *m*

kicking /'kɪkɪŋ/ *n* coces, *f pl*; acoceamiento, *m*; pataleo, *m*; golpeamiento, *m*

kid /kɪd/ *n* cabrito, *m*, chivo (-va); carne de cabrito, *f*; (leather) cabritilla, *f*; *Inf.* crío, *m*. **kid gloves,** guantes de cabritilla, *m pl*

kidnap /'kɪdnæp/ *vt* secuestrar

kidnapper /'kɪdnæpər/ *n* secuestrador (-ra); ladrón (-ona) de niños

kidnapping /'kɪdnæpɪŋ/ *n* secuestro, *m*

kidney /'kɪdni/ *n* riñón, *m*; *Fig.* especie, índole, *f*. **k.-bean,** (plant) judía, *f*; (fruit) habichuela, judía, *f*, fréjol, *Mexico* calamaco, *m*

kill /kɪl/ *vt* matar; destruir; suprimir. **to k. off,** exterminar. **to k. time,** entretener el tiempo, pasarse las horas muertas. **to k. two birds with one stone,** matar dos pájaros de un tiro. **k.-joy,** aguafiestas, *mf*

killer /'kɪlər/ *n* matador (-ra); (murderer) asesino, *mf*

killing /'kɪlɪŋ/ *n* matanza, *f*; (murder) asesinato, *m*. *a* matador; destructivo; (comic) cómico; ridículo, absurdo; (ravishing) irresistible

kiln /kɪl/ *n* horno de cerámica, horno, *m*

kilo /'kilou/ *n* kilo, *m*

kilocycle /'kɪlə,saikəl/ *n Elec.* kilociclo, *m*

kilogram /'kɪlə,græm/ *n* kilogramo, *m*

kiloliter /'kɪlə,litər/ *n* kilolitro, *m*

kilometer /kɪ'lɒmɪtər/ *n* kilómetro, *m*

kilometric /ˌkɪlə'mɛtrɪk/ *a* kilométrico

kilowatt /'kɪlə,wɒt/ *n Elec.* kilovatio, *m*

kin /kɪn/ *n* parientes, *m pl*; familia, *f*; clase, especie, *f*. **the next of kin,** los parientes próximos, la familia

kind /kaɪnd/ *n* género, *m*, clase, *f*; especie, *f*; *Inf.* tipo, *m*. **He is a queer k. of person,** Es un tipo muy raro. **What k. of cloth is it?** ¿Qué clase de tela es? **Nothing of the k!** ¡Nada de eso! **payment in k.,** pago en especie, *m*

kind /kaɪnd/ *a* bondadoso, bueno; cariñoso, tierno; amable; favorable, propicio. **Will you be so k. as to...** Tenga Vd. la bondad de... **With k. regards,** Con un saludo afectuoso. **You have been very k. to her,** Vd. ha sido muy bueno para ella. **k.-hearted,** bondadoso. **k.-heartedness,** bondad, benevolencia, *f*

kindergarten /'kɪndər,gɑrtn/ *n* jardín de la infancia, kindergarten, *m*

kindle /'kɪndl/ *vt* encender; hacer arder; *Fig.* avivar. *vi* prender, empezar a arder; encenderse; *Fig.* inflamarse

kindliness /'kaɪndlɪnɪs/ *n* bondad, *f*

kindling /'kɪndlɪŋ/ *n* encendimiento (del fuego), *m*; (wood) leña menuda, *Lat. Am.* charamusca, *f*

kindly /'kaɪndli/ *a* bondadoso; bueno; benévolo; propicio, favorable; (of climate) benigno. *adv* con bondad, bondadosamente; fácilmente. **K. sit down,** Haga el favor de sentarse

kindness /'kaɪndnɪs/ *n* bondad, *f*; benevolencia, *f*; amabilidad, *f*; cariño, *m*; favor, *m*, atención, *f*

kindred /'kɪndrɪd/ *n* parentesco, *m*; parientes, *m pl*; familia, *f*; afinidad, *f*, a emparentado; hermano

king /kɪŋ/ *n* (ruler, important person, chess, cards) rey, *m*; (in checkers) dama, *f*. **king's evil,** escrófula, *f*. **k.-bolt,** perno real, *m*. **k.-craft,** arte de reinar, *m*, or *f*. **k.-cup,** *Bot.* botón de oro, *m*. **K.-of-Arms,** rey de armas, *m*. **k.-post,** pendolón, *m*

kingdom /'kɪŋdəm/ *n* reino, *m*. **animal k.,** reino animal, *m*

kingfisher /'kɪŋ,fɪʃər/ *n* martín pescador, alción, *m*

kink /kɪŋk/ n nudo, m; pliegue, m; (curl) rizo, m; Fig. peculiaridad, f
kinsfolk /'kɪnz,fouk/ n parientes, m pl, familia, f
kinship /'kɪnʃɪp/ n parentesco, m; afinidad, f
kinsman /'kɪnzmən/ n pariente, deudo, m
kinswoman /'kɪnz,womən/ n parienta, f
kiosk /'kiɒsk/ n quiosco, m
kipper /'kɪpər/ n arenque ahumado, m. vt ahumar
kiss /kɪs/ n beso, m; (in billiards) pelo, m. vt besar; dar un beso (a); (of billiard balls) tocar. **to k. each other,** besarse. **k.-curl,** rizo de la sien, m, sortijilla, f
kit /kɪt/ n (tub) cubo, m; (for tools, etc.) cajita, caja, f; (soldier's) equipo, m. **kit-bag,** mochila, f
kitchen /'kɪtʃən/ n cocina, f. **k.-boy,** pinche (de cocina), m. **k.-garden,** huerta, f. **k.-maid,** fregona, f. **k.-range,** cocina económica, f. **k.-sink,** fregadero, Chile, Mexico, also lavaplatos, m. **k.-stove,** horno de cocina, m. **k. utensils,** batería de cocina, f
kitchenette /,kɪtʃə'nɛt/ n cocinilla, f
kite /kait/ n Ornith. milano, m; cometa, pájara, f. **to fly a k.,** hacer volar una cometa. **box-k.,** cometa celular, f
kith and kin /kɪθ/ n pl parientes y amigos, m pl
kitten /'kɪtn/ n gatito (-ta). vi (of a cat) parir
kittenish /'kɪtnɪʃ/ a de gatito; juguetón
kitty /'kɪti/ n michito, m; (in card games) platillo, m
kleptomania /,klɛptə'meiniə/ n cleptomanía, f
kleptomaniac /,klɛptə'meiniæk/ a cleptómano. n cleptómano (-na)
knack /næk/ n destreza, f; talento, m; (trick) truco, m
knapsack /'næp,sæk/ n mochila, f; Mil. alforja, f
knave /neiv/ n bellaco, truhán, tunante, m; (at cards) sota, f
knavery /'neivəri/ n bellaquería, truhanería, f
knavish /'neivɪʃ/ a de bribón; taimado, truhanesco
knead /nid/ vt amasar; (massage) sobar; Fig. formar
kneading /'nidɪŋ/ n amasijo, m; (massaging) soba, f. **k.-trough,** amasadera artesa f
knee /ni/ n rodilla, f; Fig. ángulo, codillo, m. **on bended k.,** de hinojos. **on one's knees,** de rodillas, arrodillado. **to go down on one's knees,** arrodillarse, ponerse de rodillas. **k.-cap,** rótula, f. **k.-deep,** hasta las rodillas. **k.-joint,** articulación de la rodilla, f; Mech. junta de codillo, f. **k.-pad,** rodillera, f
kneel (down) /nil/ vi arrodillarse, hincarse de rodillas, ponerse de rodillas
kneeling /'nilɪŋ/ a arrodillado, de rodillas
knell /nɛl/ n toque de difuntos, tañido fúnebre, m; toque de campanas, m; Fig. muerte, f. vi tocar a muerto. vt Fig. anunciar, presagiar
knickerbockers /'nɪkər,bɒkərz/ n pl bragas, f pl; calzón corto, m; (women's) pantalones, m pl
knickknack /'nɪk,næk/ n chuchería, f
knife /naif/ n cuchillo, m. **to have one's k. in someone,** tener enemiga (a), querer mal (a). **war to the k.,** guerra a muerte, f. **k.-edge,** filo de cuchillo, m; fiel de soporte, m. **k. grinder,** amolador, m. **k.-handle,** mango de cuchillo, m. **k. thrust,** cuchillada, f
knife, fork, and spoon /naif/ cuchara, tenedor, y cuchillo
knight /nait/ n caballero, m; (chess) caballo, m. vt armar caballero, calzar la espuela; (in modern usage) dar el título de caballero. **untried k.,** caballero novel, m. **k. commander,** comendador, m. **k.-errant,** caballero andante, m. **k.-errantry,** caballería andante, f. **Knight of Labor,** Caballero del Trabajo m. **k. of the rueful countenance,** el caballero de la triste figura
knighthood /'naithʊd/ n caballería, f; (in modern usage) título de caballero, m
knightly /'naitli/ a caballeresco; de caballero; de caballería
knit /nɪt/ vt and vi hacer calceta, hacer de punto, hacer media; juntar, ligar; unir. **Isabel is knitting me a jumper,** Isabel me hace un jersey de punto de media. **to k. one's brows,** fruncir el ceño
knitted /'nɪtɪd/ a de punto. **k. goods,** géneros de punto, m pl
knitter /'nɪtər/ n calcetero (-ra); (machine) máquina de hacer calceta, f
knitting /'nɪtɪŋ/ n acción de hacer calceta, f; trabajo de punto, m, labor de calceta, f; unión, f. **k.-**

machine, máquina de hacer calceta, f. **k.-needle,** aguja de media, aguja de hacer calceta, f
knob /nɒb/ n protuberancia, f; (of a door, etc.) perilla, borlita, f; (ornamental) bellota, f; (of sugar) terrón, m; (of a stick) puño, m
knock /nɒk/ n golpe, m; choque, m; (with a knocker) aldabado, f
knock /nɒk/ vt golpear; chocar (contra). vi llamar a la puerta; (of an engine) picar. **to k. one's head against,** chocar con la cabeza contra, dar con la cabeza contra. **to k. about,** vt pegar; aporrear. vi viajar; vagar, rodar; callejear. **to k. against,** golpear contra; chocar contra. **to k. down,** derribar; (of vehicles) atropellar, Mexico antellevar; (houses, etc.) demoler; (an argument, etc.) destruir; (a tender, etc.) rebajar; (of an auctioneer) rematar al mejor postor. **to k. in,** (nails, etc.) clavar. **to k. into one another,** toparse. **to k. off,** hacer caer; sacudir; quitar; (from price) descontar; (from speed, etc.) reducir; (finish) terminar pronto; (runs in cricket) hacer. **to k. on or at the door,** tocar (a) la puerta. **to k. out,** (remove) quitar; (boxing) dejar fuera de combate, noquear; (Fig. stun) atontar; (an idea, etc.) bosquejar. **to k. over,** volcar. **to k. up against,** chocar contra; tropezar con. **k.-kneed,** a patiabierto. **k.-out,** "knock-out," m
knocker /'nɒkər/ n (on a door) aldaba, f. **k.-up,** despertador, m
knocking /'nɒkɪŋ/ n golpes, m pl, golpeo, m; (with a knocker) aldabeo, m. **k. over,** vuelco, m; (by a vehicle) atropello, m
knoll /noul/ n altillo, otero, m
knot /nɒt/ n nudo, m; (bow) lazo, m; (of hair) moño, m; Naut. nudo, m, milla náutica, f; (of people) corrillo, grupo, m; (on timber) nudo, m. vt anudar. vi hacer nudos; enmarañarse. **to tie a k.,** hacer un nudo
knotted /'nɒtɪd/ a nudoso
knotty /'nɒti/ a nudoso; Fig. intrincado, difícil, complicado. **a k. problem,** problema espinoso
know /nou/ vt conocer; saber; (understand) comprender; (recognize) reconocer. **I k. her very well by sight,** La conozco muy bien de vista. **John knows Latin,** Juan sabe latín. **How can I k.?** ¿Cómo lo voy a saber yo? **I knew you at once,** Te reconocí en seguida. **They always k. best,** Siempre tienen razón. **Did you k. about Philip?** ¿Has oído lo de Felipe? **to be in the k.,** estar bien informado, saber de buena tinta. **to get to k.,** (a person) llegar a conocer, trabar amistad con. **to make known,** dar a conocer; manifestar; **Who knows?** ¿Quién sabe? **to k. by heart,** saber de coro. **to k. how,** (to do something) saber. **to k. oneself,** conocerse a sí mismo. **k.-it-all,** sabelotodo, mf, marisabidilla, f
knowing /'nouɪŋ/ a inteligente; malicioso; (of animals) sabio. **There is no k.,** No hay modo de saberlo. **worth k.,** digno de saberse
knowingly /'nouɪŋli/ adv a sabiendas, de intento; conscientemente; (cleverly) hábilmente; (with look, etc.) de un aire malicioso
knowledge /'nɒlɪdʒ/ n conocimiento, m. **To the best of my k.** the book does not exist, El libro no existe que yo sepa. **He has a thorough k. of...,** Conoce a fondo... **lack of k.,** ignorancia, f. **He did it without my k.,** Lo hizo sin que lo supiera yo. **It is a matter of common k. that...,** Es notorio que...
knowledgeable /'nɒlɪdʒəbəl/ a sabedor
known /noun/ a conocido
knuckle /'nʌkəl/ n (of a finger) nudillo, m, articulación del dedo, f; (of meat) jarrete, m. **He knuckled down to his work,** Se puso a trabajar con ahínco. **to k. under,** someterse. **k.-duster,** rompecabezas, m
kopeck /'koupɛk/ n copec, f
Koran /kɔ'ran/ n Corán, Alcorán, m
Korea /kə'riə/ Corea, f
kosher /'kouʃər/ a cosher; (slang) genuino
kowtow /'kau'tau/ vi saludar humildemente, m; Fig. bajar la cerviz
Kremlin /'krɛmlɪn/ n Kremlín, m
kudos /'kudouz/ n prestigio, m, gloria, f
Kurdish /'kɜrdɪʃ/ a curdo
kyrie eleison /'kɪəri,ei ɛ'leiə,sɒn/ n kirieleisón, m

L

l /ɛl/ n (letter) ele, f
la /lɑ/ n Mus. la, m
label /ˈleibəl/ n etiqueta, (on a garment), rótula, m, (on a can), f; (on a museum specimen, etc.) letrero, m; Fig. calificación, f. vt poner etiqueta en; marcar, rotular; Fig. calificar, designar, clasificar
labial /ˈleibiəl/ a labial. n letra labial, f
labor /ˈleibər/ n trabajo, m; labor, f; fatiga, pena, f; clase obrera, f; (manual workers) mano de obra, f; (effort) esfuerzo, m; (of childbirth) dolores de parto, m pl. vi trabajar; (strive) esforzarse, afanarse; (struggle) forcejar, luchar; (try) procurar, tratar de; avanzar con dificultad; (in childbirth) estar de parto. vt elaborar; pulir, perfeccionar. **to l. under,** sufrir; tener que luchar contra. **hard l.,** trabajo arduo, m; Law. trabajos forzosos, m pl, presidio, m. **Ministry of L.,** Ministerio de Trabajo, m. **to be in l.,** estar de parto. **to l. in vain,** trabajar en balde, arar en el mar. **to l. under a delusion,** estar en el error, estar equivocado. **L. Exchange,** Bolsa de Trabajo, f. **l. leader,** dirigente sindical, m. **L. party,** partido laborista, partido obrero, m. **l. question,** cuestión obrera, f; (domestic) problema del servicio, m. **l.-saving,** a que ahorra trabajo. **l. union,** sindicato, m
laboratory /ˈlæbrə,tɔri/ n laboratorio, m
labored /ˈleibərd/ a (of style) premioso, artificial; forzado; (of breathing) fatigoso; (slow) torpe, lento
laborer /ˈleibərər/ n obrero, m; (on the land) labrador, labriego, m; (on the roads, etc.) peón, m; (by the day) jornalero, m
laborious /ləˈbɔriəs/ a laborioso; arduo, difícil, penoso
laboriously /ləˈbɔriəsli/ adv laboriosamente; con dificultad, penosamente
laboriousness /ləˈbɔriəsnɪs/ n laboriosidad, f; dificultad, f
Labrador dog /ˈlæbrə,dɔr/ n perro de Labrador, m
labyrinth /ˈlæbərɪnθ/ n laberinto, m
labyrinthine /,læbəˈrɪnθɪn/ a laberíntico; intrincado
lace /leis/ n (of shoes, corsets, etc.) cordón, m; (tape) cinta, f; encaje, m; (narrow, for trimming) puntilla, f; (of gold or silver) galón, m. vt and vi (shoes, etc.) atarse los cordones, (trim) guarnecer con encajes, etc.; Fig. ornar; (a drink) echar (coñac, etc.) en. **blond l.,** blonda, f. **gold l.,** galón de oro, m. **point l.,** encaje de aguja, m. **l. curtain,** cortina de encaje, f; (of net) visillo, m. **l. maker or seller,** encajero (-ra), mf. **l. making,** obra de encaje, f. **l.-pillow,** almohadilla para encajes, f. **l. shoes,** zapatos con cordones, m pl
lacerate /ˈlæsə,reit/ vt lacerar
laceration /,læsəˈreiʃən/ n laceración, f
lachrymal /ˈlækrəməl/ a lagrimal, lacrimal
lachrymose /ˈlækrə,mous/ a lacrimoso
lack /læk/ n falta, f. **l. of evidence,** falta de pruebas, f; carestía, escasez, f; (absence) ausencia, f; (need) necesidad, f. vt carecer de; no tener; necesitar. vi hacer falta; necesitarse. **to l. confidence in oneself,** no tener confianza en sí mismo, carecer de confianza en sí mismo. **l.-luster,** (of eyes) apagado, mortecino. **l. of evidence,** falta de pruebas, f
lackadaisical /,lækəˈdeizikəl/ a lánguido; indiferente; (dreamy) ensimismado, distraído
lackey /ˈlæki/ n lacayo, m
laconic /ləˈkɒnɪk/ a lacónico
lacquer /ˈlækər/ n laca, f, vt dar laca (a), barnizar con laca. **gold l.,** sisa dorada, f. **l. work,** laca, f
lacquering /ˈlækərɪŋ/ n barnizado de laca, m; laca, capa de barniz de laca, f
lactate /ˈlækteit/ n lactato, m, vi lactar
lactation /lækˈteiʃən/ n lactancia, f
lacteal /ˈlæktiəl/ a lácteo
lactic /ˈlæktɪk/ a láctico
lactose /ˈlæktous/ n lactosa, f
lacuna /ləˈkyunə/ n laguna, f

lacy /ˈleisi/ a de encaje; parecido a encaje; Fig. transparente, etéreo
lad /læd/ n muchacho, joven, mozalbete, m; zagal, m; (stable, etc.) mozo, m. **He's some l.!** ¡Qué tío que es! **l. of the village,** chulo, m
ladder /ˈlædər/ n escalera de mano, f; Naut. escala, f; (in a stocking, etc.) carrera, f. **companion l.,** escala de toldilla, f. **to l. one's stocking,** escurrirse un punto de las medias
Ladies and gentlemen /ˈleidiz/ n. pl Señoras y señores, Damas y caballeros. **ladies' man,** hombre de salón, Perico entre ellas, mujeriego, m
lading /ˈleidɪŋ/ n flete, m, carga, f
ladle /ˈleidl/ n cucharón, cazo, m. vt servir con cucharón; (a boat) achicar; Inf. distribuir, repartir
lady /ˈleidi/ n dama, f; señora, f; (English title) milady, f; (woman) mujer, f. **to be a l.,** ser una señora. **leading l.,** Theat. dama primera, f. **Our L.,** Nuestra Señora. **young l.,** señorita, f; Inf. novia, f. **lady's maid,** doncella, f. **l. of the house,** señora de la casa, f. **l. bug,** Ent. catalina mariquita, vaca de San Antonio, f. **L. Chapel,** capilla de la Virgen, f. **L. Day,** de la Anunciación (de Nuestra Señora), m. **l.-help,** asistenta, f. **l.-in-waiting,** dama de servicio, f. **l.-killer,** ladrón de corazones, castigador, tenorio, m. **l.-love,** querida, amada, f. **ladies' room,** baño para damas, m
ladylike /ˈleidi,laik/ a de dama; elegante; distinguido; bien educado; delicado; (of men) afeminado
ladyship /ˈleidi,ʃɪp/ n señoría, f. **Your L.,** Su Señoría
lag /læg/ vt recubrir; aislar. vi retrasarse; quedarse atrás; ir (or andar) despacio; rezagarse; Naut. roncear. n retraso, m; Mech. retardación de movimiento, f
laggard /ˈlægərd/ n holgazán (-ana), haragán (-ana)
lagoon /ləˈgun/ n laguna, f
laid /leid/ past part of verb **to lay. l. up,** (ill) enfermo; Naut. inactivo; (of cars, etc.) fuera de circulación
lair /lɛər/ n cubil, m; guarida, madriguera, f
laity /ˈleiti/ n legos, m pl
lake /leik/ n lago, m; (pigment) laca, f. **small l.,** laguna, f. **l. dwelling,** vivienda palustre, f
lama /ˈlɑmə/ n lama, m
lamb /læm/ n cordero (-ra). vi parir corderos. **lamb's wool,** lana de cordero, f
lambent /ˈlæmbənt/ a ondulante, vacilante; centelleante
lamblike /ˈlæm,laik/ a manso como un cordero; inocente
lambskin /ˈlæm,skɪn/ n corderina, piel de cordero, f
lame /leim/ a estropeado, lisiado; (in the feet) cojo; (of meter) que cojea, malo; (of arguments) poco convincente; frívolo, flojo. vt lisiar; hacer cojo. **to be l.,** (in the feet) (permanently) ser cojo; (temporarily) estar cojo
lamely /ˈleimli/ adv cojeando, con cojera, f; Fig. sin convicción; mal
lameness /ˈleimnɪs/ n cojera, f; falta de convicción, f
lament /ləˈment/ n lamento, m; queja, lamentación, f. vi lamentarse; quejarse. vt lamentar, deplorar, llorar
lamentable /ləˈmentəbəl/ a lamentable, deplorable; lastimero
lamentation /,læmənˈteiʃən/ n lamentación, f, lamento, m. **Book of Lamentations,** Libro de los lamentos, m
lamenting /ləˈmentɪŋ/ n lamentación, f
lamina /ˈlæmənə/ n lámina, f
laminate /ˈlæmə,neit/ a laminado, laminar. vt laminar
lamp /læmp/ n lámpara, f; (on vehicles, trains, ships and in the street) farol, m; luz, f; (oil) candil, m, lámpara de aceite, f. **safety-l.,** lámpara de seguridad, lámpara de los mineros, f. **street l.,** farol (de las calles), m. **l.-black,** negro de humo, m. **l.-chimney,**

tubo de una lámpara, *m*. **l. factory** or **shop**, lamparería, *f*. **l.-holder**, portalámpara, *f*. **l.-lighter**, farolero, lamparero, *m*. **l.-post**, farola, *f*. **l.-shade**, pantalla (de lámpara,) *f*. **l. stand**, pie de lámpara, *m*

lamplight /'læmp,lait/ *n* luz de la lámpara, *f*; luz artificial, *f*. **in the l.**, a la luz de la lámpara; en luz artificial

lampoon /læm'pun/ *n* pasquinada, *f*, pasquín, *m*, *vt* pasquinar, satirizar

lampooner /læm'punər/ *n* escritor (-ra) de pasquinadas, libelista, *m*

lamprey /'læmpri/ *n* lamprea, *f*

lance /læns/ *n* lanza, *f*; (soldier) lancero, *m*. *vt* alancear; *Med.* lancinar. **l. in rest**, lanza en ristre, *f*. **l. thrust**, lanzada, *f*. **l.-corporal**, soldado de primera clase, *m*

lancer /'lænsər/ *n* *Mil.* lancero, *m*; *pl* lancers, (dance and music) lanceros, *m pl*

lancet /'lænsɪt/ *n* apostemero, *m*, lanceta, *f*. **l. arch**, arco puntiagudo, *m*

land /lænd/ *n* tierra, *f*; terreno, *m*; (country) país, *m*; (region) región, *f*; territorio, *m*; (estate) bienes raíces, *m pl*, tierras, fincas, *f pl*. *vt* desembarcar; echar en tierra; (*Fig.* place) poner; *Inf.* dejar plantado (con); (obtain) obtener; (a fish) sacar del agua; (a blow) dar (un golpe); (leave) dejar. *vi* desembarcar; saltar en tierra; (of a plane) aterrizar; (arrive) llegar; (fall) caer. **to l. on water** *Lat. Am.* acuatizar. **cultivated l.**, tierras cultivadas, *f pl*. **dry l.**, (not sea) tierra firme, *f*. **native l.**, patria, *f*; suelo natal, *m*. **on l.**, en tierra. **Promised Land**, la tierra prometida. **to see how the l. lies**, *Fig.* tantear el terreno. **l. of milk and honey**, jauja, *f*, paraíso, *m*. **l. agent**, procurador de fincas, *m*. **l. breeze**, brisa de tierra, *f*. **l. forces**, fuerzas terrestres, *f pl*. **l. law**, leyes agrarias, *f pl*. **l.-locked**, cercado de tierra, mediterráneo **l.-lubber**, marinero de agua dulce, *m*. **l. mine**, mina terrestre, *f*. **l. surveying**, agrimensura, *f*. **l. surveyor**, agrimensor, *m*. **l. tax**, contribución territorial, *f*

landau /'lændɔ/ *n* landó, *m*

landed /'lændɪd/ *a* hacendado. **l. gentry**, hacendados, terratenientes, *m pl*. **l. property**, bienes raíces, *m pl*

landfall /'lænd,fɔl/ *n* derrumbamiento de tierras, *m*

landing /'lændɪŋ/ *n* desembarque, desembarco, *m*; (landing place) desembarcadero, *m*; *Aer.* aterrizaje, *m*; (of steps) descanso, rellano, *m*, mesa, mesilla, *f*. **forced l.**, aterrizaje forzoso, *m*. **l. certificate**, *Com.* tornaguía, *f*. **l. craft**, barcaza de desembarco, *f*. **l. field**, campo de aterrizaje, *m*, pista de vuelo, *f*. **l.-net**, salabardo, *m*. **l. party**, trozo de abordaje, *m*. **l. signal**, *Aer.* señal de aterrizaje, *f*. **l.-stage**, desembarcadero, *m*; (jetty) atracadero, *m*

landlady /'lænd,leidi/ *n* patrona, huéspeda, *f*

landlord /'lænd,lɔrd/ *n* (of houses, land) propietario, *m*; hotelero, patrón, *m*

landmark /'lænd,mɑrk/ *n* (of a hill or mountain) punto destacado, *m*; lugar conocido, *m*; característica, *f*; *Fig.* monumento, *m*

landmass /'lænd,mæs/ *n* unidad territorial, *f*

landowner /'lænd,ounər/ *n* hacendado, terrateniente, *m*

landscape /'lænd,skeip/ *n* paisaje, *m*; perspectiva, *f*. **l. gardener**, arquitecto de jardines, *m*. **l. painter**, paisajista, *mf*

landslide /'lænd,slaid/ *n* desprendimiento de tierras, *m*; *Fig.* cambio brusco de la opinión pública, *m*

landward /'lændwərd/ *adv* hacia tierra

lane /lein/ *n* vereda, senda, *f*; (of traffic) carril, *m*, *Argentina, Spain,* línea, *f*

language /'læŋgwɪdʒ/ *n* lenguaje, *m*; lengua, *f*, idioma, *m*. **modern l.**, lengua viva, *f*. **strong l.**, palabras mayores, *f pl*

languid /'læŋgwɪd/ *a* lánguido

languidness /'læŋgwɪdnɪs/ *n* languidez, *f*

languish /'læŋgwɪʃ/ *vi* languidecer

languishing /'læŋgwɪʃɪŋ/ *a* lánguido; amoroso, sentimental

languishingly /'læŋgwɪʃɪŋli/ *adv* lánguidamente; amorosamente

languor /'læŋgər/ *n* languidez, *f*

languorous /'læŋgərəs/ *a* lánguido

languorously /'læŋgərəsli/ *adv* con langor

lank /læŋk/ *a* flaco, descarnado, alto y delgado; (of hair) lacio

lankiness /'læŋkinɪs/ *n* flacura, *f*

lanky /'læŋki/ *a* larguirucho, descarnado, *Lat. Am.* largucho

lanolin /'lænlɪn/ *n* lanolina, *f*

lantern /'læntərn/ *n* linterna, *f*; (*Naut.* and of a lighthouse) farol, *m*; *Archit.* linterna, *f*; (small) farolillo, *m*. **dark l.**, linterna sorda, *f*. **magic l.**, linterna mágica, *f*. **l.-jawed**, carilargo. **l. maker**, farolero, *m*. **l. slide**, diapositiva, *f*

lap /læp/ *n* regazo, *m*; falda, *f*; (knees) rodillas, *f pl*; (lick) lamedura, *f*; (of water) murmurio, susurro, *m*; (in a race) vuelta, *f*; (stage) etapa, *f*. *vt* (wrap) envolver; (cover) cubrir; (fold) plegar; (lick) lamer; (swallow) tragar. *vi* (overlap) traslaparse; estar replegado; (lick) lamer; (of water) murmurar, susurrar, besar. **l.-dog**, perro de faldas, perro faldero, *m*

lapel /lə'pɛl/ *n* solapa, *f*

lapidary /'læpɪˌdɛri/ *a* lapidario

lapidate /'læpɪˌdeit/ *vt* lapidar

lapis lazuli /'læp'ɪs læzʊli/ *n* lapislázuli, *m*

Laplander /'læp,lændər/ *n* lapón (-ona)

lapping /'læpɪŋ/ *n* (licking) lamedura, *f*; (of water) murmurio, susurro, chapaleteo, *m*

lapse /læps/ *n* lapso, *m*; (fault) desliz, *m*, falta, *f*; (of time) transcurso, intervalo, *m*; (fall) caída, *f*; (*Law.* termination) caducidad, *f*. **lapse (into)**, *vi* caer (en), recaer (en), reincidir (en); volver a, caer de nuevo (en); (*Law.* cease) caducar; (*Law.* pass to) pasar (a); dejar de existir, desaparecer. **after the l. of three days**, después de tres días, al cabo de tres días. **with the l. of years**, en el transcurso de los años

laptop /'læp,tɔp/ *n* laptop, *m*, ordenador portátil, *m*

larceny /'lɑrsəni/ *n* latrocinio, *m*

lard /lɑrd/ *n* manteca, *f*; lardo, *m*. *vt* *Cul.* lardear, mechar; *Fig.* sembrar (con), adornar (con)

larder /'lɑrdər/ *n* despensa, *f*

large /lɑrdʒ/ *a* grande; grueso; amplio; vasto, extenso; (wide) ancho; considerable; (in number) numeroso; (main, chief) principal; liberal; magnánimo. **at l.**, en libertad, suelto. **on the l. side**, algo grande. **l.-headed**, cabezudo. **l.-hearted**, que tiene un gran corazón, magnánimo. **l. mouth**, boca grande, boca rasgada, *f*. **l.-nosed**, narigudo. **l. scale**, en gran escala, *f*. **l.-sized**, de gran tamaño. **l.-toothed**, dentudo, que tiene dientes grandes. **l. type**, letras grandes, *f pl*

largely /'lɑrdʒli/ *adv* grandemente; en gran manera; en so mayor parte, considerablemente; muy; ampliamente; liberalmente; extensamente

largeness /'lɑrdʒnɪs/ *n* gran tamaño, *m*; (of persons) gran talle, *m*; amplitud, *f*; vastedad, extensión, *f*; (width) anchura, *f*; liberalidad, *f*; (generosity) magnanimidad, *f*; grandeza de ánimo, *f*

larger /'lɑrdʒər/ *a comp* más grande, etc. See **large**. **to grow l.**, crecer, aumentarse. **to make l.**, hacer más grande; aumentar

largesse /lɑr'dʒɛs/ *n* liberalidad, prodigalidad, *f*

largo /'lɑrgou/ *n* and *adv* *Mus.* largo, *m*

lariat /'læriət/ *n* lazo, *m*

lark /lɑrk/ *n* alondra, *f*; (spree) juerga, *f*; (joke) risa, *f*. **to rise with the l.**, levantarse con las gallinas

larva /'lɑrvə/ *n* larva, *f*

laryngeal /lə'rɪndʒiəl/ *a* laríngeo

laryngitis /ˌlærən'dʒaitɪs/ *n* laringitis, *f*

larynx /'lærɪŋks/ *n* laringe, *f*

lascivious /lə'sɪviəs/ *a* lascivo, lujurioso

lasciviousness /lə'sɪviəsnɪs/ *n* lujuria, lascivia, *f*

lash /læʃ/ *n* (thong) tralla, *f*; (whip) látigo, *m*; (blow) latigazo, *m*; azote, *m*; (of the eye) pestaña, *f*. *vt* dar latigazos (a); azotar; (of waves) romper contra; (of hail, rain) azotar; (excite) provocar; (the tail) agitar (la cola); (scold) fustigar; (fasten) sujetar, atar; *Naut.* trincar. **to l. out**, (of horses, etc.) dar coces; (in words) prorrumpir (en)

lashing /'læʃɪŋ/ *n* (whipping) azotamiento, *m*; (tying) ligadura, atadura, *f*; amarradura, *f*

lass /læs/ *n* muchacha, chica, mozuela, *f*; zagala, *f*; niña, *f*

lassitude /'læsɪˌtud/ n lasitud, f
lasso /'læsou/ n lazo, m, mangana, *Argentina* armada, f, vt lazar, manganear, *Lat. Am.* lacear
last /læst/ vi durar; subsistir, conservarse; continuar
last /læst/ a último; (with month, week, etc.) pasado; (supreme) extremo, (el) mayor. adv al fin; finalmente; por último; después de todos; por última vez; la última vez. n el, m, (f, la) último (-ma); los últimos, m pl, (f pl, las últimas); (end) fin, m; (for shoes) horma, f. **at l.**, en fin; por fin, a la postre. **at the l. moment,** a última hora. **I have not been there these l. five years,** Hace cinco años que no voy allá. **John spoke l.**, Juan habló el último. **She came at l.**, Por fin llegó. **to the l.**, hasta el fin. **l. but one,** penúltimo (-ma). **l. hope,** última esperanza, f; último recurso, m. **l. kick,** *Inf.* último suspiro, m. **l. night,** anoche. **l. week,** la semana pasada
lasting /'læstɪŋ/ a permanente, perdurable; duradero; constante; (of colours) sólido
lastly /'læstli/ adv en conclusión, por fin, finalmente, por último
latch /lætʃ/ n pestillo, m, vt cerrar con pestillo. **l.-key,** llave de la puerta, f; (Yale) llavín, m
late /leit/ a tardío; (advanced) avanzado; (last) último; reciente; (dead) difunto; (former) antiguo, ex...; (new) nuevo. adv tarde. **Better l. than never,** Más vale tarde que nunca. **Helen arrived l.**, Elena llegó tarde. **The train arrived five minutes l.**, El tren llegó con cinco minutos de retraso. **He keeps l. hours,** Se acuesta muy tarde, Se acuesta a las altas horas de la noche (*Inf.* a las tantas). **of l.**, últimamente. **to grow l.**, hacerse tarde. **l.-eighteenth-century poetry,** la poesía de fines del siglo diez y ocho; llorado, malogrado (e.g. the l. Mrs. Smith, la llorada Sra. Smith, la malograda Sra. Smith);
lateen /læ'tin/ a latino. **l. sail,** vela latina, f
lately /'leitli/ adv recientemente; últimamente, hace poco
latency /'leitn̩si/ n estado latente, m
lateness /'leitnɪs/ n lo tarde; lo avanzado; retraso, m. **the l. of the hour,** la hora avanzada
latent /'leitn̩t/ a latente
later /'leitər/ a más tarde; posterior; más reciente. adv más tarde; (afterwards) luego, después; posteriormente. **sooner or l.**, tarde o temprano. **l. on,** más tarde
lateral /'lætərəl/ a lateral, ladero
late registration n matrícula tardía, f
latest /'leitɪst/ a and adv sup último; más reciente, etc. See **late. at the l.**, a lo más tarde, a más tardar. **l. fashion,** última moda, f. **l. news,** últimas noticias, f pl; novedad, f
latex /'leiteks/ n (*Bot. Chem.*) látex, m
lath /læθ/ n listón, m. **to be as thin as a l.**, no tener más que el pellejo, estar en los huesos
lathe /leið/ n torno, m
lather /'læðər/ n espuma de jabón, f, jabonaduras, f pl; (of sweat) espuma, f. vt enjabonar; *Inf.* zurrar. vi hacer espuma
lathering /'læðərɪŋ/ n jabonadura, f; *Inf.* tunda, zurra, f
Latin /'lætn̩/ n latín, m, a latino. **Low L.**, bajo latín, m. **L.-American,** a latinoamericano. n latinoamericano (-na)
Latin America Latinoamérica
Latinism /'lætn̩ˌɪzəm/ n latinismo, m
Latinist /'lætn̩ɪst/ n latinista, mf
latitude /'lætɪˌtud/ n latitud, f; libertad, f
latitudinal /ˌlætɪ'tudn̩l/ a latitudinal
latrine /lə'trin/ n letrina, f
latter /'lætər/ a más reciente: último, posterior; moderno. **the l.**, éste, m; ésta, f; esto, neut; éstos, m pl; éstas, f pl. **the l. half,** la segunda mitad. **toward the l. end of the year,** hacia fines del año. **L.-Day Saint,** santo de los últimos días m, santa de los últimos días, f
latterly /'lætərli/ adv recientemente, últimamente; en los últimos tiempos; hacia el fin
lattice /'lætɪs/ n rejilla, f; celosía, reja, f. vt poner celosía (a); entrelazar. **l.-work,** enrejado, m
latticed /'lætɪst/ a (of windows, etc.) con reja
Latvia /'lætviə/ Latvia, Letonia, f

Latvian /'lætviən/ a latvio. n latvio (-ia)
laud /lɔd/ n alabanza, f; pl. **lauds,** *Eccl.* laudes, f pl. vt alabar, elogiar
laudability /ˌlɔdə'bɪlɪti/ n mérito, m, lo meritorio
laudable /'lɔdəbəl/ a loable, meritorio
laudably /'lɔdəbli/ adv laudablemente
laudatory /'lɔdəˌtɔri/ a laudatorio
laugh /læf/ n risa, f; carcajada, f. vi reír; (smile) sonreír; reírse. **loud l.**, risa estrepitosa, f. **to l. in a person's face,** reírsele a uno en las barbas. **to l. loudly,** reírse a carcajadas. **to l. to oneself,** reírse interiormente. **to l. to scorn,** poner en ridículo. **to l. at,** reírse de; burlarse de, ridiculizar
laughable /'læfəbəl/ a risible, irrisible, ridículo, absurdo
laughing /'læfɪŋ/ a risueño, alegre; (absurd) risible, n risa, f. **to burst out l.**, reírse a carcajadas. **l.-gas,** gas hilarante, m. **l.-stock,** hazmerreír, m
laughingly /'læfɪŋli/ adv riendo
laughter /'læftər/ n risa, f; (in a report) risas, f pl. **burst of l.**, carcajada, f. **to burst into l.**, soltar el trapo, reírse a carcajadas, desternillarse de risa
launch /lɔntʃ/ n botadura (de un buque), f; lancha, f; bote, m; canoa, f. vt (throw) lanzar; (a blow) asestar; (a vessel) botar, echar al agua; (begin) iniciar, dar principio a; (make) hacer. **to l. an offensive,** *Mil.* emprender una ofensiva. **to l. into,** arrojarse en; entregarse a. **motor l.**, canoa automóvil, f. **steam l.**, bote de vapor, m
launching /'lɔntʃɪŋ/ n botadura (de un buque), f; (throwing) lanzamiento, m; (beginning) iniciación, f; inauguración, f; (of a loan, etc.) emisión, f. **l. site,** rampa, f
launder /'lɔndər/ vt lavar y planchar (ropa)
laundress /'lɔndrɪs/ n lavandera, f
laundromat /'lɔndrəˌmæt/ n lavandería automática, f
laundry /'lɔndri/ n lavadero, m, lavandería, f; (washing) colada, f; *Inf.* ropa lavada or ropa para lavar, f. **l.-man,** lavandero, m
laureate /'lɔriit/ a laureado. n poeta laureado, m
laurel /'lɔrəl/ n laurel, cerezo, m, a láureo. **to crown with l.**, laurear. **l. wreath,** lauréola, f
Lausanne /lou'zæn/ Lausana, Losana, f
lava /'lɑvə/ n lava, f
lavabo /lə'veibou/ n lavabo, m; *Eccl.* lavatorio, m
lavatory /'lævəˌtɔri/ n lavabo, m; retrete, excusado, m
lavender /'lævəndər/ n espliego, m, lavanda, f. **l.-water,** agua de lavanda, f
lavish /'lævɪʃ/ a pródigo; profuso, abundante; (spender) *Mexico* disparador. vt prodigar
lavishly /'lævɪʃli/ adv pródigamente; en profusión
lavishness /'lævɪʃnɪs/ n prodigalidad, f; profusión, abundancia, f
law /lɔ/ n ley, f; derecho, m; jurisprudencia, f; código de leyes, m. **according to law,** según derecho. **canon law,** derecho civil, m. **constitutional law,** derecho político, m. **criminal law,** derecho penal, m. **in law,** por derecho, de acuerdo con la ley; desde el punto de vista legal. **international law,** derecho internacional, m. **maritime law,** código marítimo, m. **sumptuary law,** ley suntuaria, f. **to be the law,** ser la ley. **to go to law,** pleitear (sobre). **to sue at law,** pedir en juicio, poner pleito. **to take the law into one's own hands,** tomar la ley por su propia mano. **law-abiding,** observante de la ley; amigo del orden. **law-breaker,** transgresor (-ra). **law court,** tribunal de justicia, m; palacio de justicia, m. **law of nature,** ley natural, f. **law report,** revista de tribunales, f. **law school,** escuela de derecho, f. **law student,** estudiante de derecho, mf
lawful /'lɔfəl/ a legítimo; legal; lícito; válido
lawfully /'lɔfəli/ adv legalmente, legítimamente, lícitamente
lawfulness /'lɔfəlnɪs/ n legalidad, f; legitimidad, f
lawgiver /'lɔˌgɪvər/ n legislador (-ra)
lawless /'lɔlɪs/ a ilegal; desordenado; ingobernable, rebelde
lawlessness /'lɔlɪsnɪs/ n ilegalidad, f; desorden, m; rebeldía, f
lawn /lɔn/ n césped, prado, m; (cloth) estopilla, f. **l.-**

mower, cortacésped *m*, tundidora de césped, *f*, máquina segadora del césped, *f*. **l.-tennis,** tenis (en pista de hierba), *m*

lawsuit /'lɔ,sut/ *n* pleito, litigio, *m*, causa, acción, *f*, *Lat. Am.* demanda, *f*

lawyer /'lɔyər/ *n* abogado (-da). **lawyer's office** or **practice,** bufete, *m*

lax /læks/ *a* laxo; indisciplinado; vago; descuidado

laxative /'læksətɪv/ *n* laxante, *m*, purga, *f*, *a* laxativo

laxity /'læksɪti/ *n* laxitud, *f*; descuido, *m*; indiferencia, *f*

lay /lei/ *a* laico, seglar, lego; profano. *n* poema, *m*, trova, *f*; romance, *m*; (song) canción, *f*. **the lay of the land,** la configuración del terreno. **lay brother,** confeso, monigote, *m*. **lay figure,** maniquí, *m*. **lay sister,** (hermana) lega, *f*

lay /lei/ *vt and vi* poner; colocar; dejar; (strike) tumbar; (demolish) derribar; (the dust) matar; (pipes, etc.) instalar; (hands on) asentar (la mano en); (deposit) depositar; (beat down corn, etc.) encamar, abatir; (eggs, keel) poner; (the table) cubrir, poner; (stretch) extender(se); (bury) depositar en el sepulcro; (a bet) hacer; (wager) apostar; (an accusation) acusar; (the wind, etc.) sosegar, amainar; (a ghost) exorcizar; (impute) atribuir, imputar; (impose) imponer; (prepare) prepara; (make) hacer; (open) abrir; (blame, etc.) echar; (claim) reclamar; (reveal) revelar. **Don't lay the blame on me!** ¡No me eches la culpa! **We laid our plans,** Hicimos nuestros planes; Hicimos nuestros preparativos. **to lay siege to,** asediar. **to lay the colors on too thick,** *Fig.* recargar las tintas. **to lay the foundations,** abrir los cimientos; *Fig.* crear, establecer; fundar. **to lay about one,** dar garrotazos de ciego. **to lay aside,** poner a un lado; arrinconar; (save) ahorrar; (cast away) desechar; abandonar; (reserve) reservar; (a person) apartar de sí; (incapacitate) incapacitar. **lay something at somebody's feet,** embutir algo en el guante de fulano. **to lay before,** mostrar; presentar; poner a la vista; revelar. **to lay by,** See **to lay aside. to lay down,** acostar; depositar; (a burden) posar; (arms) rendir; (one's life); entregar; (give up) renunciar (a); (sketch out) trazar, dibujar; (plan) proyectar; (keep) guardar; (as a principle) establecer, sentar; (the law) dictar. **to lay oneself down,** echarse, tumbarse. **to lay in,** (a stock) proveerse de, hacer provisión de; (hoard) ahorrar; (buy) compara. **to lay off,** *Naut.* virar de bordo; *Inf.* quitarse de encima. **to lay on,** *vt* colocar sobre; (thrash) pegar; (blows) descargar; (paint, etc.) dar; (water, etc.) instalar; (impose) imponer; (exaggerate) exagerar. *vi* atacar. **to lay open,** abrir; descubrir, revelar; manifestar; exponer. **to lay oneself open to attack,** exponerse a ser atacado. **to lay out,** poner; arreglar; (the dead) amortajar; (one's money) invertir, emplear; (at interest) poner a rédito; (plan) planear; (knock down) derribar. **to lay oneself out to,** esforzarse a; tomarse la molestia de. **to lay over,** cubrir; sobreponer; extender sobre. **to lay to,** *vi Naut.* estar a la capa. **to lay up,** guardar, acumular, atesorar; poner a un lado; (a ship) desarmar; (a car) poner fuera de circulación; (a person) obligar a guardar cama, incapacitar

layabout /'leiə,baut/ *n* = **lazybones**

layer /'leiər/ *n* capa, *f*; *Geol.* estrato, *m*; *Mineral.* manto, *m*; (bird) gallina (pata, etc.) ponedera, *f*; (one who bets) apostador (-ra); *Agr.* acodo, *m*. *vt* (of plants) acodar

laying /'leiɪŋ/ *n* colocación, *f*; puesta, *f*; (of an egg) postura, *f*. **l. down,** depósito, *m*; conservación, *f*; (explanation) exposición, *f*. **l. on of hands,** imposición de manos, *f*. **l. out,** tendedura, *f*; (of money) empleo, *m*; inversión, *f*; (arrangement) arreglo, *m*

layman /'leimən/ *n* seglar, *mf*; profano (-na)

layout /'lei,aut/ *n* plan, *m*; diagramación, disposición, *f*; distribución, *f*; esquema, *m*

laze /leiz/ *vi* holgazanear, gandulear, no hacer nada; encontrarse a sus anchas

lazily /'leizəli/ *adv* perezosamente; indolentemente; lentamente

laziness /'leizɪnɪs/ *n* pereza, holgazanería, *f*; indolencia, *f*; lentitud, *f*

lazy /'leizi/ *a* perezoso, holgazán; indolente. **l.bones,** gandul (-la), *Lat. Am.* aplanacalles, *Mexico* flojo, *mf*

lead /lɛd/ *n* (metal) plomo, *m*; (in a pencil) mina, *f*; (plummet) sonda, *f*; *Print.* interlínea, *f*; *pl* **leads,** (roofs) tejados, *m pl*. *vt* emplomar; guarnecer con plomo; *Print.* interlinear. **black-l.,** grafito, *m*. **deep-sea l.,** *Naut.* escandallo, *m*. **white l.,** albayalde, *m*. **to heave the l.,** echar el escandallo, sondar. **l.-colored,** de color de plomo, plomizo. **l.-footed,** pesado; lento. **l. mine,** mina de plomo, *f*. **l. poisoning,** saturnismo, *m*

lead /lid/ *n* delantera, *f*; primer lugar, *m*; dirección, *f*, mando, *m*; (suggestion) indicación, *f*; (influence) influencia, *f*; (dog's) traílla, *f*; *Theat.* protagonista, *mf*; *Theat.* papel principal, *m*; (at cards) mano, *f*

lead /lid/ *vt and vi* (conduct) conducir, llevar; guiar; (induce) mover, persuadir, inducir; inclinar; (cause) hacer, causar; (captain) capitanear, encabezar; dirigir; (channel) encauzar; (with life) llevar; (give) dar; (head) ir a la cabeza de; *Mil.* mandar; (at cards) salir; (at games) jugar en primer lugar; tomar la delantera; *Fig.* superar a los demás; (of roads) conducir. **to take the l.,** ir delante; ir a la cabeza, tomar la delantera; tomar la iniciativa. **to l. one to think,** hacer pensar. **to l. the way,** mostrar el camino; ir adelante. **to l. along,** llevar (por la mano, etc.), conducir; conducir por; guiar. **to l. astray,** descarriar; desviar (de), seducir (de). **to l. away,** conducir (a otra parte); llevarse (a). **to l. back,** conducir de nuevo; hacer volver. **This path leads back to the village,** Por esta senda se vuelve al pueblo. **to l. in, into,** conducir a (or ante); introducir en, hacer entrar en; invitar a entrar en; (of rooms) comunicarse con; (sin, etc.) inducir a. **to l. off,** *vi* ir adelante; (begin) empezar; (of rooms) comunicarse con. *vt* hacer marcharse, llevarse (a). **to l. on,** *vt* conducir; guiar; hacer pensar en; (make talk) dar cuerda (a). *vi* ir a la cabeza; tomar la delantera. **to l. out,** conducir afuera; (to dance) sacar. **to l. to,** conducir a; desembocar en, salir a; (cause) dar lugar a, causar; (make) hacer; (incline) inclinar. **This street leads to the square,** Por esta calle se va a la plaza, Esta calle conduce a la plaza. **to l. up to,** conducir a; (in conversation, etc.) preparar el terreno para; preparar; tener lugar antes de, ocurrir antes de

leaden /'lɛdn/ *a* hecho de plomo, plúmbeo; (of skies, etc.) plomizo, de color de plomo, aplomado

leader /'lidər/ *n* conductor (-ra); guía, *mf*; jefe (-fa); general, *m*; director (-ra); (in a journal) artículo de fondo, *m*; (of an orchestra) primer violín, *m*. **follow-the-l.,** (game) juego de seguir la fila, *m*

leadership /'lidər,ʃɪp/ *n* dirección, *f*; jefatura, *f*; *Mil.* mando, *m*

lead-in /'lid ,ɪn/ *a Radio.* de entrada. *n Radio.* conductor de entrada, *m*

leading /'lɛdɪŋ/ (leadwork) emplomadura, *f*

leading /'lidɪŋ/ *n* (guidance) dirección, *f*. *a* principal; primero; importante; eminente. **l. article,** artículo de fondo, *m*; editorial, *m*. **l. card,** primer naipe, *m*. **l. counsel,** abogado (-da) principal, *m*. **l. lady,** *Theat.* dama primera, primera actriz, *f*; (cinema) estrella (de la pantalla), *f*. **l. man,** *Theat.* primer galán, *m*. **l. question,** pregunta que sugiere la respuesta, *f*; cuestión importante, *f*. **l. strings,** andadores, *m pl*; *Fig.* tutelaje, *m*

leaf /lif/ *n* (Bot. and of a page, door, window, table, screen, etc.) hoja, *f*; (petal) pétalo, *m*, *vi* echar hojas. **gold l.,** pan de oro, *m*. **to turn over a new l.,** volver la hoja, hacer libro nuevo, hacer vida nueva. **to turn over the leaves of a book,** hojear (un libro). **l.-bud,** yema, *f*. **l.-mold,** abono verde, *m*. **l. tobacco,** tabaco en hoja, *m*

leafiness /'lifinɪs/ *n* frondosidad, *f*

leafless /'liflɪs/ *a* sin hojas

leaflet /'liflɪt/ *n* hojuela, *f*; (pamphlet) folleto, *m*

leafy /'lifi/ *a* frondoso

league /lig/ *n* (measure) legua, *f*; liga, federación, sociedad, *f*; (football) liga, *f*. *vt* aliar; asociar. *vi* aliarse; asociarse, confederarse. **to be in l.,** *Inf.* estar de manga. **L. of Nations,** Sociedad de las Naciones, *f*. **the Ivy L.,** las universidades prestigiosas, *f pl*

leak /lik/ *n* (hole) agujero, *m*, grieta, *f*; *Naut.* vía de agua, *f*; (of gas, liquids, etc.) escape, *m*; (in a roof, etc.) gotera, *f; Elec.* resistencia de escape, *f. vi Naut.* hacer agua; (gas, liquids, etc.) escaparse, salirse; (drip) gotear. **to l. out,** (of news, etc.) trascender, saberse. **to spring a l.,** aparecer una vía de agua, hacer agua

leakage /'likɪdʒ/ *n* (of gas, liquids) escape, *m,* fuga, *f;* derrame, *m;* pérdida, *f;* (of information) revelación, *f*

leaky /'liki/ *a Naut.* que hace agua; agujereado; poroso; que tiene goteras

lean /lin/ *a* magro, seco, enjuto, delgado; (of meat) magro; *Fig.* pobre, estéril. *n* carne magra, *f,* magro, *m.* **to grow l.,** enflaquecer

lean /lin/ *vi* inclinarse; apoyarse (en). *vt* apoyar (en). dejar arrimado (en). **to l. out of the window,** asomarse a la ventana. **to l. against,** apoyarse en, recostarse en (or contra). **to l. back,** echarse hacia atrás; recostarse. **to l. over,** inclinarse. **to l. upon,** apoyarse en; descansar sobre

leaning /'linɪŋ/ *n* inclinación, tendencia, *f;* predilección, afición, *f*

leanness /'linnɪs/ *n* magrura, flaqueza, *f;* (of meat) magrez, *f; Fig.* pobreza, *f*

leap /lip/ *n* salto, *m;* brinco, *m;* (caper) zapateta, *f; Fig.* salto, *m. vi* saltar, dar un salto; brincar. *vt* saltar; hacer saltar. **at one l.,** en un salto. **by leaps and bounds,** en saltos. **My heart leaped,** Mi corazón dio un salto. **to l. to the conclusion that...,** saltar a la conclusión de que... **to l. to the eye,** saltar a la vista. **l. frog,** salto, salto de la muerte, *m,* pídola *f.* **l. year,** año bisiesto, *m,* salta cabrillas, *f pl*

leaping /'lipɪŋ/ *a* saltador. *n* saltos, *m pl*

learn /lɜrn/ *vt and vi* aprender; instruirse; enterarse de. **to l. by heart,** aprender de memoria. **to l. from a reliable source,** saber de buena tinta. **to l. from experience,** aprender por experiencia

learned /'lɜrnɪd/ *a* sabio, docto; erudito; (of professions) liberal; versado (en), entendido (en). **a l. society,** una sociedad erudita

learner /'lɜrnər/ *n* aprendedor (-ra)

learning /'lɜrnɪŋ/ *n* saber, *m;* conocimientos, *m pl;* erudición, *f;* estudio, *m;* (literature) literatura, *f*

lease /lis/ *n* arrendamiento, arriendo, *m;* contrato de arrendamiento, *m. vt* dar en arriendo, arrendar. **on l.,** en arriendo. **To take a new l. on life,** recobrar su vigor. **Lend L. Act,** ley de préstamo y arriendo, *f*

leaseholder /'lis,houldər/ *n* concesionario, *m;* arrendatario (-ia)

leash /lif/ *n* (of a dog) traílla, *f*

least /list/ *a sup* little, mínimo; el (la, etc.) menor; más pequeño. *adv* menos. *n* lo menos. **at l.,** siquiera; por lo menos, al menos. **at the very l.,** a lo menos. **not in the l.,** de ninguna manera, nada. **to say the l. of,** sin exagerar, para no decir más

leather /'lɛðər/ *n* cuero, *m;* piel, *f, a* de cuero; de piel. **patent l.,** charol, *m.* **Spanish l.,** cordobán, *m.* **tanned l.,** curtido, *m.* **l. apron,** mandil, *m.* **l. bag,** saco de cuero, *m.* **l. bottle,** bota, *f.* **l. breeches,** pantalón de montar, *m.* **l. jerkin,** coleto, *m.* **l. shield,** adarga, *f.* **l. strap,** correa, *f.* **l. trade,** comercio en cueros, *m*

leatherette /,lɛðə'rɛt/ *n* cartón cuero, *m*

leathery /'lɛðəri/ *a* de cuero; (of the skin) curtido por la intemperie; (tough) correoso

leave /liv/ *n* (permission) permiso, *m;* (Mil. etc.) licencia, *f;* (farewell) despedida, *f. vt and vi* dejar; abandonar; salir (de), quitar, marcharse (de), *Lat. Am.* egresar (de...); (as surety) empeñar; (by will) legar, mandar; (an employment) darse de baja (de), dejar; (give into the keeping of) entregar; (bid farewell) despedirse (de). **By your l.,** Con permiso de Vd. (Vds.). Con la venia de Vd. (Vds.). **on l.,** de permiso. **l.-taking,** despedidas, *f pl.* **to be left,** quedar. **to be left over,** quedar; sobrar. **Two from four leaves two,** De cuatro a dos van dos. **to take French l.,** despedirse a la inglesa. **to take l. of,** despedirse de. **to take one's l.,** marcharse; despedirse. **to l. a deep impression,** *Fig.* impresionar mucho; quedar grabado (en). **to l. undone,** dejar de hacer, no hacer; dejar sin terminar. **to l. about,** dejar por todas partes. *vi* (of time) marcharse a eso de... **to l. ajar,** entreabrir, (when opening), entrecerrar (when closing), entornar. **to l. alone,** dejar a solas; dejar en paz; no molestar,

no meterse con. **to l. aside,** omitir; prescindir de; olvidar. **to l. behind,** dejar atrás; olvidar. **l. much to be desired,** tener mucho que desear. **to l. off,** *vt* dejar de; abandonar; (garments) no ponerse, quitarse. *vi* terminar. **to l. out,** dejar fuera; dejar a un lado; descontar; omitir; pasar por; (be silent about) callar; suprimir. **to l. to,** dejar para; dejar hacer

leaven /'lɛvən/ *n* levadura, *f,* fermento, *m, vt* fermentar; (Fig. permeate) penetrar (en), infiltrar en, imbuir; (a speech) salpimentar (con)

leaving /'livɪŋ/ *n* salida, partida, marcha, *f, Lat. Am.* egreso, *m; pl* **leavings,** sobras, *f pl;* desechos, *m pl*

lecherous /'lɛtʃərəs/ *a* lascivo, lujurioso

lechery /'lɛtʃəri/ *n* lascivia, lujuria, *f*

lectern /'lɛktərn/ *n* atril, *m;* (in a church) facistol, *m*

lecture /'lɛktʃər/ *n* conferencia, *f;* (in a university) lección, clase, *f;* discurso, *m;* (Inf. scolding) sermoneo, *m. vi* dar una conferencia; (in a university) dar clase. *vt* (Inf. scold) predicar, sermonear. **l. room,** sala de conferencias, *f;* (in a university) sala de clase, aula, *f*

lecturer /'lɛktʃərər/ *n* conferenciante, *Lat. Am.* conferencista, *mf;* (university rank) auxiliar, *m;* (professor) catedrático (-ca), profesor (-ra)

lectureship /'lɛktʃər,ʃɪp/ *n* auxiliaría, *f*

ledge /lɛdʒ/ *n* borde, *m;* capa, *f;* (of a window) alféizar, *m;* (shelf) anaquel, *m*

ledger /'lɛdʒər/ *n* libro mayor, *m*

leech /litʃ/ *n* sanguijuela, *f*

leek /lik/ *n* puerro, *m*

leer /lɪər/ *vi* mirar de soslayo; guiñar el ojo; mirar con los ojos llenos de deseo. *n* mirada de soslayo, *f;* mirada de lascivia, *f*

lees /liz/ *n pl* heces, *f pl;* sedimento, *m*

leeward /'liwərd/ *n* sotavento, *m.* **on the l. side,** a sotavento

leeway /'li,wei/ *n Naut.* deriva, *f; Fig.* amplitud, margen de holgura, márgenes de maniobra, *f pl.* **to give someone l.,** darle espacio a alguien

left /lɛft/ *past part* dejado, etc. See **leave.** *a* izquierdo. *adv* a la izquierda; hacia la izquierda. *n* izquierda, *f.* **on the l.,** a la izquierda. **the L.,** *Polit.* las izquierdas. **the Left Bank** (of Paris) la Ribera izquierda, la Orilla izquierda **L. face!** ¡Izquierda! **l.-hand,** mano izquierda, *f;* izquierda, *f.* **l.-hand drive,** conducción a la izquierda, *f.* **l.-handed,** zurdo. **l. luggage office,** consigna, *f.* **l.-overs,** sobras, *f pl,* desperdicios, *m pl*

leg /lɛg/ *n* pierna, *f;* (of animals, birds, furniture) pata, *f;* (of a triangle) cateto, *m;* (of a pair of compasses, trousers, lamb, veal) pierna, *f;* (of boots, stockings) caña, *f;* (of pork) pernil, *m;* (support) pie, *m;* (stage) etapa, *f.* **to be on one's last legs,** estar en las últimas; estar acabándose; estar sin recursos. **to pull a person's leg,** tomar el pelo (a). **leg-pull,** tomadura de pelo, *f.* **leg-of-mutton sleeve,** manga de pernil, *f*

legacy /'lɛgəsi/ *n* legado, *m,* manda, *f;* herencia, *f*

legal /'ligəl/ *a* legal; de derecho; jurídico; (lawful, permissible) legítimo, lícito; (of a lawyer) de abogado. **l. expenses,** litisexpensas, *f pl.* **l. inquiry,** investigación jurídica, *f*

legalistics /,ligə'lɪstɪks/ *n. Lat. Am.* abogaderas, abogaderías, *f pl*

legality /li'gæliti/ *n* legalidad, *f*

legalization /,ligələ'zeiʃən/ *n* legalización, *f*

legalize /'ligə,laiz/ *vt* legalizar; autorizar, legitimar

legally /'ligəli/ *adv* según la ley; según derecho; legalmente

legal tender *n* moneda de curso liberatorio, *f*

legate /'lɛgɪt/ *n* legado, *m.* **papal l.,** legado papal, *m*

legatee /,lɛgə'ti/ *n* legatario (-ia), *Lat. Am.* asignatario (-ia)

legation /lɪ'geiʃən/ *n* legación, *f*

legend /'lɛdʒənd/ *n* leyenda, *f*

legendary /'lɛdʒən,dɛri/ *a* legendario

legerdemain /,lɛdʒərdə'mein/ *n* juegos de manos, *m pl*

legged /'lɛgɪd/ *a* con piernas; de piernas...; de patas... **a three-l. stool,** un taburete de tres patas. **long l.,** zancudo

leggings /'lɛgɪŋz/ *n pl* polainas, *f pl*

legibility /ˌlɛdʒəˈbɪlɪti/ n legibilidad, f
legible /ˈlɛdʒəbəl/ a legible
legion /ˈlidʒən/ n legión, f. **L. of Honor,** Legión de Honor, f
legionary /ˈlidʒəˌnɛri/ a legionario. n legionario, m
legislate /ˈlɛdʒɪsˌleit/ vt legislar
legislation /ˌlɛdʒɪsˈleiʃən/ n legislación, f
legislative /ˈlɛdʒɪsˌleitɪv/ a legislativo, legislador
legislator /ˈlɛdʒɪsˌleitər/ n legislador (-ra)
legislature /ˈlɛdʒɪsˌleitʃər/ n legislatura, f
legitimacy /lɪˈdʒɪtəməsi/ n legitimidad, f; justicia, f
legitimate /lɪˈdʒɪtəmɪt/ a legítimo; justo
legitimation /lɪˌdʒɪtəˈmeiʃən/ n legitimación, f
leisure /ˈliʒər/ n ocio, m, desocupación, f; tiempo libre, m. **at one's l.,** con sosiego, despacio. **You can do it at your l.,** Puedes hacerlo cuando tengas tiempo. **to be at l.,** estar desocupado, no tener nada que hacer. **l. moments,** ratos perdidos, momentos de ocio, m pl
leisured /ˈliʒərd/ a desocupado, libre; sin ocupación; (wealthy) acomodado
leisurely /ˈliʒərli/ a pausado, lento, deliberado; tardo
lemon /ˈlɛmən/ n limón, m; (tree) limonero, m, a limonado, de color de limón; hecho o sazonado con limón. **l. drop,** pastilla de limón, f. **l.-grove,** limonar, m. **l.-squash,** limonada natural, f. **l.-squeezer,** exprime limones, m, exprimidera, f
lemonade /ˌlɛməˈneid/ n limonada, f. **l. powder,** limonada seca, f
lemur /ˈlimər/ n lemur, m
lend /lɛnd/ vt prestar. **to l. an ear to,** prestar atención a. **It does not l. itself to...,** No se presta a... **to l. a hand,** echar una mano, dar una mano
lender /ˈlɛndər/ n el, m, (f, la) que presta; prestador (-ra); (of money) prestamista, mf; Com. mutuante, mf
lending /ˈlɛndɪŋ/ n prestación, f, préstamo, m. **l.-library,** biblioteca circulante, f
length /lɛŋkθ/ n largo, m; longitud, f; (of fabric) corte, m; (of a ship) eslora, f; (in racing) largo, m; distancia, f; (in time) duración, f; alcance, m. **at l.,** por fin, finalmente; (in full) extensamente, largamente. **by a l.,** por un largo. **full-l.,** de cuerpo entero. **three feet in l.,** tres pies de largo. **to go the l. of...,** llegar al extremo de...
lengthen /ˈlɛŋkθən/ vt alargar; prolongar; extender. vi alargarse; prolongarse; extenderse; (of days) crecer
lengthening /ˈlɛŋkθənɪŋ/ n alargamiento, m; prolongación, f; crecimiento, m
lengthily /ˈlɛŋkθəli/ adv largamente
lengthiness /ˈlɛŋkθinɪs/ n largueza, f; prolijidad, f
lengthy /ˈlɛŋkθi/ a largo; demasiado largo, larguísimo; (of speech) prolijo; verboso
leniency /ˈliniənsi/ n lenidad, f; indulgencia, f
lenient /ˈliniənt/ a indulgente; poco severo
leniently /ˈliniəntli/ adv con indulgencia
Leningrad /ˈlɛnɪnˌgræd/ Leningrado, m
lenitive /ˈlɛnɪtɪv/ a lenitivo. n lenitivo, m
lens /lɛnz/ n lente, m; (of the eye) cristalino, m
Lent /lɛnt/ n Cuaresma, f
Lenten /ˈlɛntṇ/ a de Cuaresma, cuaresmal
lentil /ˈlɛntɪl/ n lenteja, f
lentitude /ˈlɛntɪˌtud/ n lentitud, f
Leo /ˈliou/ n León, m
leonine /ˈliəˌnain/ a leonino
leopard /ˈlɛpərd/ n leopardo, m
leper /ˈlɛpər/ n leproso (-sa). **l. colony,** colonia de leprosos, f
leprosy /ˈlɛprəsi/ n lepra, f
leprous /ˈlɛprəs/ a leproso
lesbian /ˈlɛzbiən/ a and n lesbiana
lesion /ˈliʒən/ n lesión, f
less /lɛs/ a menor; más pequeño; menos; inferior. adv menos; sin. **l. than,** menos de (que). **more or l.,** poco más o menos. **no l.,** nada menos. **none the l.,** sin embargo. **to grow l.,** disminuir. **l. and l.,** cada vez menos
lessee /lɛˈsi/ n arrendatario (-ia); inquilino (-na)
lessen /ˈlɛsən/ vi disminuir; reducirse. vt disminuir; reducir; (lower) rebajar; (disparage) menospreciar
lessening /ˈlɛsənɪŋ/ n disminución, f; reducción, f

lesser /ˈlɛsər/ a comp menor; más pequeño. See **little**
lesson /ˈlɛsən/ n lección, f. **to give a l.,** dar lección, dar clase; Fig. dar una lección (a). **to hear a l.,** tomar la lección
lessor /ˈlɛsɔr/ n arrendador (-ra)
lest /lɛst/ conjunc para que no; por miedo de (que), no sea que. **I did not do it l. they should not like it,** No lo hice por miedo de que no les gustase
let /lɛt/ vt dejar, permitir; (lease) arrendar. vi alquilarse, ser alquilado. **Let** as an expression of the imperative is rendered in Spanish by the subjunctive or the imperative, e.g. Let them go! ¡Que se vayan! ¡Déjalos marchar! He let them go, Les dejó marchar. **to let fall,** dejar caer. **to let go,** dejar marchar; soltar; poner en libertad (a). **to let loose,** dar suelta a; Fig. desencadenar. **to let one know,** hacer saber, comunicar. **to let the cat out of the bag,** tirar de la manta. **to let th chance slip,** perder la ocasión. **to let alone,** (a thing) no tocar; (a person) dejar en paz, dejar tranquilo; (an affair) no meterse (en or con); (omit) no mencionar, omitir toda mención de. **to let down,** bajar; (by a rope) descolgar; (hair, etc.) dejar caer; (a dress, etc.) alargar; Naut. calar; (disappoint) dejar plantado. **to let in,** dejar entrar; hacer entrar; invitar a entrar; recibir; (insert) insertar. **to let into,** (initiate) iniciar en, admitir en; (a secret) revelar. Other meanings, see **to let in. to let off,** dejar salir; dejar en libertad; exonerar; perdonar; (a gun) disparar; (fireworks, etc.) hacer estallar. **to let out,** dejar salir; poner en libertad; (from a house) acompañar a la puerta; abrir la puerta; Sew. ensanchar; (fire) alquilar; (the fire, etc.) dejar extinguirse. **to let up,** dejar subir; (decrease) disminuir; (end) terminar
let /lɛt/ n estorbo, impedimento, obstáculo, m. **without let or hindrance,** sin estorbo ni obstáculo
lethal /ˈliθəl/ a letal. **l. weapon,** instrumento de muerte, m
lethargic /ləˈθɑrdʒɪk/ a aletargado; letárgico
lethargy /ˈlɛθərdʒi/ n letargo, m; Med. letargía, f
letter /ˈlɛtər/ n (of the alphabet) letra, f; (epistle) carta, f; Print. carácter, m; (lessor) arrendador (-ra); pl **letters,** letras, f pl; (correspondence) correo, m; correspondencia, f. vt inscribir; imprimir. **capital l.,** letra mayúscula, f. **first letters,** Fig. primeras letras, f. **l. registered l.,** carta certificada, f, certificado, m. **small l.,** letra minúscula, f. **the l. of the law,** la ley escrita. **to be l.-perfect,** saber de memoria. **to the l.,** Fig. a la letra. **letters patent,** patente, f; título de privilegio, m. **l.-balance,** pesacartas, m. **l.-book,** Com. libro copiador, m. **l.-box,** buzón de correos, m. **l.-card,** tarjeta postal del gobierno, f. **l. of credit,** carta de crédito, f. **l. of introduction,** carta de presentación, f. **l.-writer,** escritor (-ra) de cartas
lettered /ˈlɛtərd/ a culto, instruido; (printed) impreso
lettering /ˈlɛtərɪŋ/ n inscripción, f; letrero, rótulo, m
letterpress /ˈlɛtərˌprɛs/ n imprenta, f; (not illustrations) texto, m
letting /ˈlɛtɪŋ/ n (hiring) arrendamiento, m
lettuce /ˈlɛtɪs/ n lechuga, f. **l. plant,** lechuguino, m. **l. seller,** lechuguero (-ra)
Leuven /ˈluvən/ Lovaina, f
Levant, the /lɪˈvænt/ el Levante, m
Levantine /ˈlɛvənˌtain/ a and n levantino (-na)
levee /ˈlɛvi/ n besamanos, m, recepción, f, dique, m
level /ˈlɛvəl/ n nivel, m; ras, m, flor, f; llano, m; (plain) llanura, f; (instrument) nivel, m, a llano; igual; al nivel (de); uniforme; imparcial. adv a nivel; igualmente. vt nivelar; igualar; allanar; (a blow) asestar; (a gun) apuntar; (raze) arrasar, derribar; adaptar; hacer uniforme. **on the l.,** a nivel; Fig. de buena fe. **l. spirit,** nivel de burbuja, m. **to make l. again,** rellanar. **l. country,** campaña, llanura, f. **l. with the ground,** a ras de la tierra. **l. with the water,** a flor de agua. **l. crossing,** paso a nivel, m. **l.-headed,** sensato, cuerdo. **l. stretch,** rellano, m; llanura, f
leveler /ˈlɛvələr/ n nivelador (-ra)
leveling /ˈlɛvəlɪŋ/ n nivelación, f; allanamiento, m; (to the ground) arrasamiento, m; igualación, f
levelness /ˈlɛvəlnɪs/ n nivel, m; planicie, f; igualdad, f

lever /'lɛvər/ n palanca, f; (handle) manivela, f; escape de reloj, m; (excuse) pretexto, m; (means) modo, m. vt sopalancar. **control l.,** Aer. palanca de mando, f. **hand-l.,** palanca de mano, f
leverage /'lɛvərɪdʒ/ n sistema de palancas, m; acción de palanca, f; Fig. influencia, fuerza, f, poder, m
Leviathan /lɪ'vaiəθən/ n leviatán, m
levitation /,lɛvɪ'teiʃən/ n levitación, f
Levite /'livait/ n levita, m
Levitical /lɪ'vɪtɪkəl/ a levítico
Leviticus /lɪ'vɪtɪkəs/ n Levítico, m
levity /'lɛvɪti/ n levedad, frivolidad, ligereza, f
levy /'lɛvi/ n exacción (de tributos), f; impuesto, m; (of a fine) imposición, f; Mil. leva, f. vt (taxes) exigir; (a fine) imponer; (troops) reclutar, enganchar
levying /'lɛviŋ/ n (of a tax) exacción (de tributos), f; (of a fine) imposición, f; (of troops) leva, f
lewd /lud/ a lascivo, lujurioso, impúdico
lewdness /'ludnɪs/ n lascivia, lujuria, impudicia, f
lexicographer /,lɛksɪ'kɒgrəfər/ n lexicógrafo, m
lexicography /,lɛksɪ'kɒgrəfi/ n lexicografía, f
lexicon /'lɛksɪ,kɒn/ n léxico, m
liability /,laiə'bɪlɪti/ n responsabilidad, obligación, f; tendencia, f; riesgo, m; pl **liabilities**, obligaciones, f pl; Com. pasivo, m
liable /'laiəbəl/ a responsable; propenso (a); expuesto (a); sujeto (a)
liaison /li'eizən/ n lío, m; coordinación, f. **l. officer,** oficial de coordinación, m
liar /'laiər/ n mentiroso (-sa)
libation /lai'beiʃən/ n libación, f
libel /'laibəl/ n libelo, m; difamación, f, vt difamar, calumniar
libeler /'laibələr/ n libelista, mf difamador (-ra)
libelous /'laibələs/ a difamatorio
liberal /'lɪbərəl/ a liberal; generoso; abundante. n liberal, mf **l. profession,** carrera liberal, f. **l.-minded,** tolerante. **l.-mindedness,** tolerancia, f
liberalism /'lɪbərə,lɪzəm/ n liberalismo, m
liberality /,lɪbə'rælɪti/ n liberalidad, f; generosidad, f
liberalize /'lɪbərə,laiz/ vt liberalizar
liberate /'lɪbə,reit/ vt (a prisoner) poner en libertad; librar (de); (a gas, etc.) dejar escapar
liberation /,lɪbə'reiʃən/ n liberación, f; (of a captive) redención, f; (of a slave) manumisión, f
liberator /'lɪbə,reitər/ n libertador (-ra)
libertinage /'lɪbər,tinɪdʒ/ n libertinaje, m
libertine /'lɪbər,tin/ n libertino, m
libertinism /'lɪbərti,nɪzəm/ n libertinaje, m
liberty /'lɪbərti/ n libertad, f; (familiarity) familiaridad, f; (right) privilegio, m, prerrogativa, f; (leave) permiso, m. **at l.,** en libertad; desocupado, libre. **I have taken the l. of giving them your name,** Me he tomado la libertad de darles su nombre. **to set at l.,** poner en libertad (a). **to take liberties with,** tratar con familiaridad; (a text) tergiversar. **l. of speech,** libertad de palabra, libertad de expresión, f. **l. of thought,** libertad de pensamiento, f
libidinous /lɪ'bɪdnəs/ a libidinoso
Libra /'librə/ n Libra, f
librarian /lai'brɛəriən/ n bibliotecario (-ia)
librarianship /lai'brɛəriən,ʃɪp/ n carrera f, or empleo m, de bibliotecario
library /'lai,brɛri/ n biblioteca, f; (book shop) librería, f. **l. catalog,** catálogo de la biblioteca, m
librettist /lɪ'brɛtɪst/ n libretista, mf
libretto /lɪ'brɛtou/ n libreto, m
Libya /'lɪbiə/ Libia, f
Libyan /'lɪbiən/ a and n libio (-ia)
license /'laisəns/ n licencia, f, permiso, m; autorización, f; (driving) carnet de chófer, permiso de conducción, m; (of a car) permiso de circulación, m; (for a wireless, etc.) licencia, f; (marriage) licencia de casamiento, f; (excess) libertinaje, desenfreno, m. **import l.,** permiso de importación, m. **poetic l.,** licencia poética, f. **l. number,** (of a car) número de matriculación, m. vt licenciar; autorizar; (a car) sacar la licencia del automóvil
licensee /,laisən'si/ n concesionario (-ia)
licentiate /lai'sɛnʃiit/ n licenciado (-da)

licentious /lai'sɛnʃəs/ a licencioso, disoluto
licentiousness /lai'sɛnʃəsnɪs/ n libertinaje, m, disipación, f
lichen /'laikən/ n liquen, m
licit /'lɪsɪt/ a lícito
lick /lɪk/ vt lamer; (of waves) besar; (of flames) bailar; (thrash) azotar; (defeat) vencer. **to l. one's lips,** relamerse los labios, chuparse los dedos. **to l. the dust,** morder el polvo
licking /'lɪkɪŋ/ n lamedura, f; (beating) paliza, tunda, f; (defeat) derrota, f
licorice /'lɪkərɪʃ, -rɪs/ n regaliz, m
lid /lɪd/ n cobertera, f; tapa, f; (of the eye) párpado, m
lie /lai/ n mentira, f; invención, falsedad, f; mentís, m, vi mentir. **to tell a barefaced lie,** mentir por la mitad de la barba. **white lie,** mentira oficiosa, f
lie /lai/ vi estar tumbado, estar echado; estar recostado; descansar, reposar; (in the grave) yacer; (be) estar; (be situated) hallarse, estar situado; (stretch) extenderse; (sleep) dormir; (depend) depender; (consist) consistir, estribar; (as an obligation) incumbir. **Here lies...,** Aquí descansa..., Aquí yace... **It does not lie in my power,** No depende de mí. **to let lie,** dejar; dejar en paz. **to lie at anchor,** estar anclado. **to lie fallow,** estar en barbecho; Fig. descansar. **to lie about,** estar esparcido por todas partes; estar en desorden. **to lie along,** estar tendido a lo largo de; Naut. dar a la banda. **to lie back,** recostarse; apoyarse (en). **to lie by,** estar acostado al lado de; (of things, places) estar cerca (de); descansar. **to lie down,** tenderse, tumbarse, echarse, acostarse; reposar. **Lie down!** (to a dog) ¡Echate! **to lie down under,** tenderse bajo; (an insult) tragar, sufrir. **to lie in,** consistir en; depender de; (of childbirth) estar de parto. **to lie open,** estar abierto; estar expuesto (a); estar al descubierto, estar a la vista. **to lie over,** (be postponed) quedar aplazado. **to lie to,** Naut. estarse a la capa, ponerse en facha. **to lie under,** estar bajo, hallarse bajo; estar bajo el peso de; (be exposed) estar expuesto a. **to lie with,** (concern) tocar (a); corresponder (a)
lie /lai/ n configuración, f; disposición, f; posición, f. **the lie of the land,** la configuración del terreno
lieu /lu/ n lugar, m. **in l. of,** en lugar de, en vez de
lieutenant /lu'tɛnənt/ n teniente, lugarteniente, m; (naval) alférez, m. **first l.,** (in the army) primer teniente, teniente, m; (in the navy) alférez de navío, m. **naval l.,** teniente de navío, m. **second l.,** (in the army) segundo teniente, m; (in the navy) alférez de fragata, m. **l.-colonel,** teniente coronel
life /laif/ n vida, f; (being) ser, m; (society) mundo, m, sociedad, f; (vitality) vitalidad, f; vigor, m, a de vida; (of annuities, etc.) vitalicio; (life-saving) de salvamento. **for l.,** de por vida. **from l.,** del natural. **high l.,** gran mundo, m, alta sociedad, f. **low l.,** vida del hampa, vida de los barrios bajos, f. **to the l.,** al vivo. **to lay down one's l.,** entregar la vida. **to take one's l. in one's hands,** jugarse la vida. **l. annuity,** fondo vitalicio, m. **l.-belt,** (cinturón) salvavidas, m. **l.-blood,** sangre vital, f; Fig. nervio, m; vigor, m. **l.-boat,** (on a ship) bote salvavidas, m; (on the coast) lancha de salvamento, f. **l.-boat station,** estación de salvamento, f. **l.-giving,** vivificante, que da vida; tonificante. **l.-guard,** (soldier) guardia militar, f; Guardia de Corps, f; (at beach or swimming pool) guardavidas, mf. **l.-insurance,** seguro sobre la vida, m. **l.-interest,** usufructo, m. **l.-jacket,** chaleco salvavidas, m. **l.-like,** natural. **l.-line,** cable de salvamento, m. **l.-saving,** a de salvamento; curativo. **l.-saving apparatus,** aparato salvavidas, m. **l.-sized,** de tamaño natural
life cycle n ciclo vital, m
life imprisonment n reclusión perpetua, f
life jacket n chaleco salvavidas, f
lifeless /'laiflɪs/ a sin vida, muerto; inanimado; Fig. desanimado
lifelessness /'laiflɪsnɪs/ n falta de animación; inercia
lifelong /'laifˌlɔŋ/ a de toda la vida
lifetime /'laif,taim/ n vida, f
lift /lɪft/ n esfuerzo para levantar, m; acción de levantar, f; alza, f; (blow) golpe, m; (help) ayuda, f;

(hitch, ride) *Mexico* aventón; *m*, (elevator) ascensor, *m*; (for goods) montacargas, *m*; *pl* **lifts,** *Naut.* balancines, *m pl.* **to give a l. to,** (help) ayudar; (hitchhiker etc.) dar un aventón.

lift /lɪft/ *vt* levantar; alzar, elevar; (pick up) coger; (one's hat) quitarse; (steal) hurtar; exaltar. *vi* (of mist) disiparse; desaparecer. **to l. the elbow,** empinar el codo. **to l. down,** quitar (de); (a person) bajar en brazos. **to l. up,** alzar; erguir, levantar; levantar en brazos

lifting /'lɪftɪŋ/ *n* acción de levantar, *f*; levantamiento, alzamiento, *m*

ligament /'lɪgəmənt/ *n* ligamento, *m*

ligature /'lɪgətʃər/ *n* (*Surg. Mus.*) ligadura, *f*

light /lait/ *a* (not dark) claro, con mucha luz, bañado de luz; (of colors) claro; (not heavy, and of sleep, food, troops, movements) ligero; (of reading) de entretenimiento; (irresponsible) frívolo; (easy) fácil; (slight) leve; (of hair) rubio; (happy) alegre; (fickle) inconstante, liviano; (of complexion) blanco. *adv* ligero. **to be l.,** no pesar mucho; estar de día. **to grow l.,** (dawn) clarear; iluminarse. **to make l. of,** no tomar en serio; no preocuparse de; (suffering) sufrir sin quejarse. **l.-colored,** (de color) claro. **l.-fingeredness,** sutileza de manos, *f*. **l.-footed,** ligero de pies. **l.-haired,** de pelo rubio. **l.-headed,** casquivano, ligero de cascos; delirante. **l.-headedness,** ligereza de cascos, frivolidad, *f*; delirio, *m*. **l.-hearted,** alegre (de corazón). **l.-heartedness,** alegría, *f*. **l. horse,** *Mil.* caballería ligera, *f*. **l. troops,** tropas ligeras, *f pl.* **l.-weight,** *n* (*Box.*) peso ligero, *m*, *a* de peso ligero

light /lait/ *n* luz., *f*; (day) día, *m*; (match) cerilla, *f*; (of a cigarette, etc.) fuego, *m*; (of a window) cristal, vidrio, *m*; (point of view) punto de vista, *m*; (in a picture) toque de luz, *m*; *pl* **lights,** (offal) bofes, *m pl.* **against the l.,** al trasluz. **by the l. of,** a la luz de; según. **half-l.,** media luz, *f*. **high light** (**s**), *Art.* claros, *m pl*; *Fig.* momento culminante, *m*; acontecimiento de más interés, *m*. **to come to l.,** descubrirse. **to put a l. to the fire,** encender el fuego. **l.-year,** año de luz, *m*

light /lait/ *vt* (a lamp, fire, etc.) encender; iluminar. *vi* encenderse; iluminarse; *Fig.* animarse; brillar. **to l. upon,** encontrar por casualidad; tropezar con

lighten /'laitn/ *vt* (illuminate) iluminar; (of weight) aligerar; (cheer) alegrar; (mitigate) aliviar. *vi* (grow light) clarear; (of lightning) relampaguear; (become less heavy) disminuir de peso, aligerarse; volverse más alegre

lightening /'laitnɪŋ/ *n* aligeramiento, *m*; (easing) alivio, *m*; luz, *f*

lighter /'laitər/ *n* (boat) lancha, barcaza, gabarra, *f*; (device) encendedor, *m*. **pocket l.,** encendedor de bolsillo, *m*. **l. man,** gabarrero, *m*

light-fingered /lait 'fɪŋgərd/ *a* ligero de manos

lighthouse /'lait,haus/ *n* faro, *m*. **l.-keeper,** guardafaro, *m*

lighting /'laitɪŋ/ *n* iluminación, *f*; alumbrado, *m*. **flood l.,** iluminación intensiva, *f*. **l.-up time,** hora de encender los faros, *f*

lightly /'laitli/ *adv* ligeramente; fácilmente; (slightly) levemente; ágilmente; sin seriedad. **l. wounded,** levemente herido

lightness /'laitnɪs/ *n* ligereza, *f*; poco peso, *m*; agilidad, *f*; (brightness) claridad, *f*; (inconstancy) liviandad, inconstancia, *f*; frivolidad, *f*

lightning /'laitnɪŋ/ *n* relámpago, rayo, *m*. **as quick as l.,** como un relámpago. **to be struck by l.,** ser herido por un relámpago. **l.-rod,** pararrayos, *m*

lightship /'lait,ʃɪp/ *n* buque faro, *m*

ligneous /'lɪgniəs/ *a* leñoso

lignite /'lɪgnait/ *n* lignito, *m*

likable /'laikəbəl/ *a* simpático

like /laik/ *a* semejante; parecido; igual, mismo; (characteristic) típico, característico; (likely) probable; (equivalent) equivalente. *adv* como; igual (que); del mismo modo (que). *n* semejante, igual, *mf*; tal cosa, *f*; cosas semejantes, *f pl.* **Don't speak to me l. that,** No me hables así. **He was l. a fury,** Estaba hecho una furia. **They are very l. each other,** Se parecen

mucho. **to be l.,** parecerse (a), semejar. **to look l.,** parecer ser (que); tener el aspecto de; (of persons) parecerse (a). **to return l. for l.,** pagar en la misma moneda

like /laik/ *vt* gustar, agradar; estar aficionado (a), gustar de; (wish) querer. **I l. coffee and Adam likes tea,** A mí me gusta café y a Adán le gusta té. **Do you l. coffee?** ¿Te gusta café? **I don't like hot drinks,** No me gustan las bebidas calientes. **As you l.,** Como te parezca bien, Como quieras. **If you l.,** Si quieres. **James likes painting,** Jaime está aficionado a la pintura. **Judith does not l.** the north of England, A Judit no le gusta el norte de Inglaterra. **I don't l. to do it,** No me gusta hacerlo. **I should l. him to go to Madrid,** Quisiera que fuera a Madrid

likelihood /'laikli,hʊd/ *n* posibilidad, *f*; probabilidad, *f*

likely /'laikli/ *a* probable; verosímil, creíble, plausible; posible; (suitable) satisfactorio, apropiado; (handsome) bien parecido. *adv* probablemente. **They are not l. to come,** No es probable que vengan

liken /'laikən/ *vt* comparar

likeness /'laiknɪs/ *n* parecido, *m*, semejanza, *f*; (portrait) retrato, *m*

likewise /'laik,waiz/ *adv* igualmente, asimismo, también. *conjunc* además

liking /'laikɪŋ/ *n* (for persons) simpatía, *f*, cariño, *m*; (for things) gusto, *m*, afición, *f*; (appreciation) aprecio, *m*. **I have a l. for old cities,** Me gustan (or me atraen) las viejas ciudades. **to take a l. to,** (things) aficionarse a; (persons) prendarse de, tomar cariño (a)

lilac /'lailək/ *n* lila, *f*. **l. color,** color de lila, *m*

Lilliputian /,lɪlɪ'pyuʃən/ *a* liliputiense. *n* liliputiense, *mf*

lilt /lɪlt/ *n* canción, *f*; ritmo, *m*; armonía, *f*

lily /'lɪli/ *n* lirio, *m*, azucena, *f*; (of France) flor de lis, *f*. **l. of the valley,** lirio de los valles, muguete, *m*. **l.-white,** blanco como la azucena

limb /lɪm/ *n Anat.* miembro, *m*; (of a tree) rama, *f*

limbless /'lɪmlɪs/ *a* mutilado

limbo /'lɪmbou/ *n* limbo, *m*

lime /laim/ *n Chem.* cal, *f*; (for catching birds) liga, hisca, *f*; (linden tree) tilo, *m*; (tree like a lemon) limero, *m*; (fruit) lima, *f*. *vt* (whiten) encalar; *Agr.* abonar con cal. **slaked l.,** cal muerta, *f*. **l.-flower,** flor del tilo, tila, *f*. **flor del limero,** *f*. **l.-juice,** jugo de lima, *m*. **l.-kiln,** calera, *f*. **l.-pit,** pozo de cal, *m*. **l. tree** *Lat. Am.* limo, *m*

limelight /'laim,lait/ *n* luz de calcio, *f*; *Fig.* centro de atención, *m*; publicidad, *f*. **to be in the l.,** ser el centro de atención, estar a la vista (de público)

limestone /'laim,stoun/ *n* piedra caliza, *f*. **l. deposit,** calar, *m*

limit /'lɪmɪt/ *n* límite, *m*; confín, *m*; linde, *m* or *f*; limitación, *f*, *vt* limitar; fijar; (restrict) restringir. **This is the l.!** ¡Este es el colmo! ¡No faltaba más!

limitation /,lɪmɪ'teiʃən/ *n* limitación, *f*; restricción, *f*

limitative /'lɪmɪ,teitɪv/ *a* restrictivo, limitativo

limited /'lɪmɪtɪd/ *a* limitado; restringido; escaso; (of persons) de cortos alcances; *Com.* anónimo. **l. company,** sociedad anónima, *f*

limited monarchy *n* monarquía moderada, *f*

limiting adjective /'lɪmɪtɪŋ/ *n* adjetivo determinativo, *m*

limitless /'lɪmɪtlɪs/ *a* sin límites; ilimitado, inmenso

limousine /'lɪmə,zin/ *n* limousina, *f*, coche cerrado, *m*

limp /lɪmp/ *a* flojo; débil; fláccido; lánguido. *n* cojera, *f*. *vi* cojear. **to l. off,** marcharse cojeando. **to l. up,** acercarse cojeando; subir cojeando

limpid /'lɪmpɪd/ *a* límpido, cristalino, puro

limpidity /lɪm'pɪdɪti/ *n* limpidez, *f*

limping /'lɪmpɪŋ/ *a* cojo

limply /'lɪmpli/ *adv* flojamente; débilmente; lánguidamente

limpness /'lɪmpnɪs/ *n* flojedad, *f*; debilidad, *f*; languidez, *f*

linchpin /'lɪntʃ,pɪn/ *n* pezonera, *f*

linden /'lɪndən/ *n* tilo, *m*, (tea) tilia americana, *f*

line /lain/ *vt* (furrow) surcar; (troops, etc.) poner en fila; alinear; (clothes, nests, etc.) forrar; (building) revestir; (one's pocket) llenar. *vi* estar en línea, alinearse

line /lain/ *n* (most meanings) línea, *f*; (cord) cuerda, *f*; *Naut.* cordel, *m*; (fishing) sedal, *m*; (railway) vía, *f*; (wrinkle) surco, *m*; arruga, *f*; (row) hilera, ringlera, fila, *f*; (of verse) verso, *m*; *Print.* renglón, *m*; (of business) ramo, *m*; profesión, *f*; (interest) especialidad, *f*. **bowling** or **serving l.,** línea de saque, *f*; **hard lines,** mala suerte, *f*; apuro, *m*, situación difícil, *f*. **in a l.,** en fila; en cola. **in direct l.,** (of descent) en línea recta. **It is not in my l.,** No es una especialidad mía; No es uno de mis intereses. **on the lines of,** conforme a; parecido a. **to cross the l.,** (equator) pasar la línea; (railway) cruzar la vía. **to drop a l.,** escribir unas líneas, poner unas líneas. **to read between the lines,** leer entre líneas. **l.-drawing,** dibujo de líneas, *m*. **l. of battle,** línea de batalla, *f*

lineage /'lɪnɪdʒ/ *n* linaje, *m*, familia, raza, *f*

lineal /'lɪnɪəl/ *a* lineal

lineament /'lɪnɪəmənt/ *n* lineamento, *m*; (of the face) facciones, *f pl*

linear /'lɪnɪər/ *a* lineal. **l. equation,** ecuación de primer grado, *f*

lined /laind/ *a* rayado, con líneas; (of the face) surcado, arrugado; (of gloves, etc.) forrado. **lined paper,** papel rayado, *m*

linen /'lɪnən/ *n* lino, *m*; *Inf.* ropa blanca, *f*; *a* de lino. **clean l.,** ropa limpia, *f*. **dirty l.,** ropa sucia, *f*; ropa para lavar, *f*. **table-l.,** mantelería, *f*. **l. cupboard,** armario para ropa blanca, *m*. **l. draper,** lencero (-ra). **l.-draper's shop,** lencería, *f*. **l. room,** lencería, *f*. **l. tape,** trenzadera, *f*. **l. thread,** hilo de lino, *m*

liner /'lainər/ *n* (ship) transatlántico, *m*; buque de vapor, *m*; *Aer.* avión de pasaje, *m*

linesman /'lainzmən/ *n* soldado de línea, *m*; *Sports.* juez de línea, *m*

ling /lɪŋ/ *n Bot.* brezo, *m*; *Ichth.* especie de abadejo, *f*

linger /'lɪŋgər/ *vi* (remain) quedarse; tardar en marcharse; ir lentamente; hacer algo despacio

lingerie /,lanʒə'rei/ *n* ropa blanca, *f*

lingering /'lɪŋgərɪŋ/ *a* lento; largo, prolongado; melancólico, triste

lingeringly /'lɪŋgərɪŋli/ *adv* lentamente; largamente; melancólicamente

linguist /'lɪŋgwɪst/ *n* lingüista, *mf*

linguistic /lɪŋ'gwɪstɪk/ *a* lingüístico

linguistics /lɪŋ'gwɪstɪks/ *n* lingüística, *f*

liniment /'lɪnəmənt/ *n* linimento, *m*

lining /'lainɪŋ/ *n* (of a garment, etc.) forro, *m*; (building) revestimiento, *m*

link /lɪŋk/ *n* (in a chain) eslabón, *m*; (of beads) sarta, *f*; *Fig.* enlace, *m*, cadena, *f*; conección, *f*; *Mech.* corredera, *f*; (torch) hacha de viento, *f*. *vt* enlazar, unir; *Fig.* encadenar. **missing l.,** *Fig.* eslabón perdido, *m*. **to l. arms,** cogerse del brazo

linking /'lɪŋkɪŋ/ *n* encadenamiento, *m*; *Fig.* conección, *f*

links /lɪŋks/ *n pl* campo de golf, *m*

linoleum /lɪ'nouliəm/ *n* linóleo, *m*

linotype /'lainə,taip/ *n* linotipia, *f*

linseed /'lɪn,sid/ *n* linaza, *f*. **l. cake,** bagazo, *m*. **l.-oil,** aceite de linaza, *m*

lint /lɪnt/ *n Med.* hilas, *f pl*; (fluff) borra, *f*

lintel /'lɪntl/ *n* dintel, *m*; (threshold) umbral, *m*

lion /'laiən/ *n* león, *m*; *Fig.* celebridad, *f*. **l. cage** or **den,** leonera, *f*. **l.-hearted,** valeroso. **l.-hunter,** cazador (-ra) de leones. **l.-keeper,** leonero (-ra). **lion's mane,** melena, *f*. **l.-tamer,** domador (-ra) de leones

lioness /'laiənɪs/ *n* leona, *f*

lionize /'laiə,naiz/ *vt* dar bombo (a), hacer la rueda (a), tratar como a una celebridad (a)

lion's share *n* parte del león, tajada del león, *f*

lip /lɪp/ *n* labio, *m*; (of a vessel) pico, *m*; (of a crater) borde, *m*; *Fig.* boca, *f*. **to open one's lips,** abrir la boca. **to smack one's lips,** chuparse los dedos. **lip reading,** lectura labial, *f*. **lip-service,** amor fingido, *m*; promesas hipócritas, *f pl*. **lip stick,** lápiz para los labios, *m*

liposuction /'lɪpə,sʌkʃən, 'laipə-/ *n* liposucción, *f*

lipped /lɪpt/ *a* (in compounds) con labios..., que tiene labios; (of vessels in compounds) con... picos

liquefaction /,lɪkwə'fækʃən/ *n* licuefacción, *f*

liquefiable /'lɪkwə,faiəbəl/ *a* liquidable

liquefy /'lɪkwə,fai/ *vt* liquidar. *vi* liquidarse

liqueur /lɪ'kɜr/ *n* licor, *m*. **l.-glass,** copita de licor, *f*. **l.-set,** licorera, *f*

liquid /'lɪkwɪd/ *n* líquido, *m*, *a* líquido; límpido. **l. air,** aire líquido, *m*. **l. measure,** medida para líquidos, *f*

liquidate /'lɪkwɪ,deit/ *vt* liquidar; saldar (cuentas); *Mil.* soldar

liquidation /,lɪkwɪ'deiʃən/ *n* liquidación, *f*

liquidness /'lɪkwɪdnɪs/ *n* liquidez, *f*; fluidez, *f*

liquor /'lɪkər/ *n* licor, *m*. **l. shop,** aguardentería, *f*. **l. traffic,** negocio de vinos y licores, *m*; contrabando, *m*

lira /'lɪərə/ *n* lira, *f*

Lisbon /'lɪzbən/ Lisboa, *f*

lisp /lɪsp/ *n* ceceo, *m*; balbuceo, *m*, *vi* cecear; balbucir

lisping /'lɪspɪŋ/ *a* ceceoso; balbuciente. *n* ceceo, *m*; (of a child, etc.) balbuceo, *m*

lissom /'lɪsəm/ *a* flexible; ágil

list /lɪst/ *n* lista, *f*; catálogo, *m*; matrícula, *f*; *Naut.* recalcada, *f*; inclinación, *f*; (tournament) liza, *f*. *vt* hacer una lista de; catalogar; matricular, inscribir. *vi Naut.* recalcar; inclinarse a un lado. **to enter the lists,** entrar en liza. **l. of wines,** lista de vinos, *f*

listen /'lɪsən/ *vi* escuchar; (attend) attender. **Don't you want to l. to the music?** ¿No quieres escuchar la música? **to l. in,** (to the radio) escuchar la radio; (eavesdrop) escuchar a hurtadillas

listener /'lɪsənər/ *n* oyente, *mf*; (to radio) radioyente, *mf*

listless /'lɪstlɪs/ *a* lánguido, apático, indiferente

listlessly /'lɪstlɪsli/ *adv* lánguidamente, indiferentemente

listlessness /'lɪstlɪsnɪs/ *n* apatía, languidez, indiferencia, inercia, *f*

litany /'lɪtni/ *n* letanía, *f*

liter /'lɪtər/ *n* litro, *m*

literal /'lɪtərəl/ *a* literal. **l.-minded,** sin imaginación

literalness /'lɪtərəlnɪs/ *n* literalidad, *f*

literary /'lɪtə,reri/ *a* literario

literary executor *n* depositario de la obra literaria, *m*

literate /'lɪtərɪt/ *a* and *n* literato (-ta)

literature /'lɪtərətʃər/ *n* literatura, *f*

lithe /laið/ *a* flexible; sinuoso y delgado; ágil

litheness /'laiðnɪs/ *n* flexibilidad, *f*; sinuosidad, *f*; delgadez, *f*; agilidad, *f*

lithograph /'lɪθə,græf/ *n* litografía, *f*, *vt* litografiar

lithographer /lɪ'θɒgrəfər/ *n* litógrafo, *m*

lithographic /,lɪθə'græfɪk/ *a* litográfico

lithography /lɪ'θɒgrəfi/ *n* litografía, *f*

Lithuania /,lɪθu'einiə/ Lituania, *f*

Lithuanian /,lɪθu'einiən/ *a* lituano, lituano (-na); (language) lituano, *m*

litigant /'lɪtɪgənt/ *n* litigante, *mf*

litigate /'lɪtɪ,geit/ *vi* and *vt* litigar, pleitear

litigation /,lɪtɪ'geiʃən/ *n* litigación, *f*

litigious /lɪ'tɪdʒəs/ *a* litigioso

litmus /'lɪtməs/ *n* tornasol, *m*. **l. paper,** papel de tornasol, *m*

litter /'lɪtər/ *n* litera, *f*; (stretcher) camilla, *f*; (bed) lecho, *m*; cama de paja, *f*; (brood) camada, cría, *f*; (rubbish) cosas en desorden, *f pl*; (papers) papeletas, *f pl*; (untidiness) desarreglo, desorden, *m*, confusión, *f*, *vt* poner en desorden

little /'lɪtl/ *a* pequeño; poco; (scanty) escaso; insignificante; bajo; mezquino. *adv* poco. **a l.,** un poco (de); un tanto. **in l.,** en pequeño. **not a l.,** no poco; bastante. **l. by l.,** poco a poco. **l. or no,** poco o nada. **however l.,** por pequeño que. **as l. as possible,** lo menos posible. **to make l. of,** no dar importancia a; sacar poco en claro de, no comprender bien; no hacer caso de; (persons) acoger mal. **l. by l.,** poco a poco. **l. finger,** dedo meñique, *m*. **l. one,** pequeñuela, *f*, pequeñín, *m*

littleness /'lɪtlnɪs/ *n* pequeñez, *f*; poquedad, *f*; mezquindad, *f*; trivialidad, *f*

littoral /'lɪtərəl/ *a* and *n* litoral, *m*

liturgical /lɪ'tɜrdʒɪkəl/ *a* litúrgico. **l. calendar,** calendario litúrgico, *m*

liturgical vestment *n* paramento litúrgico, *m*
liturgy /'lɪtərdʒi/ *n* liturgia, *f*
live /laiv/ *a* vivo, viviente; (alight) encendido; (of a wire, etc.) cargado de electricidad. **l. cartridge,** cartucho con bala, *m*. **l. coal,** ascua, *f*. **l.-stock,** ganadería, *f*. **l. wire,** conductor eléctrico, *m*; *Fig.* fuerza viva, *f*
live /lɪv/ *vi* vivir; residir, habitar; (of ships) mantenerse a flote; salvarse; subsistir. *vt* (one's life) llevar, pasar. **Long l.!** ¡Viva! **to have enough to l. on,** tener de que vivir. **to l. together,** convivir. **to l. again,** volver a vivir. **to l. at,** vivir en, habitar. **to l. down,** sobrevivir a; (a fault) lograr borrar. **to l. on,** vivir de. **to l. up to,** vivir con arreglo a, vivir en conformidad con; estar al nivel de, merecer. **to l. up to one's income,** vivir al día, gastarse toda la renta
live broadcast *n* emisión en directo, *f*
livelihood /'laivli,hʊd/ *n* vida, subsistencia, *f*. **to make a l.,** ganarse la vida
liveliness /'laivlinɪs/ *n* vivacidad, vida, *f*; animación, *f*; alegría, *f*
livelong /'lɪv,lɔŋ/ *a* entero, todo; eterno. **all the l. day,** todo el santo día
lively /'laivli/ *a* vivo; vivaracho; brioso, enérgico; alegre; bullicioso; animado; (fresh) fresco; (of colours) brilliante; intenso
liver /'lɪvər/ *n* vividor (-ra), el, *m*, (*f*, la) que vive; habitante, *m*; *Anat.* hígado, *m*. **l. cancer,** cáncer del hígado, *m*. **l. complaint,** mal de hígado, *m*. **l. extract,** extracto de hígado, *m*
livery /'lɪvəri/ *n* librea, *f*; uniforme, *m*; *Poet.* vestiduras, *f pl*. **l. stables,** pensión de caballos, *f*; cochería de alquiler, *f*
livid /'lɪvɪd/ *a* lívido; cárdeno, amoratado
lividness /'lɪvɪdnɪs/ *n* lividez, *f*
living /'lɪvɪŋ/ *a* viviente; vivo, vital. *n* vida, *f*; modo de vivir, *m*; beneficio eclesiástico, *m*. **the l.,** los vivos. **to make one's l.,** ganarse la vida. **l. memory,** memoria de personas vivientes, memoria de los que aún viven, *f*. **l.-room,** sala de estar, *f*. **l. soul,** ser viviente; *Inf.* bicho viviente, *m*. **l. wage,** jornal básico, *m*
lizard /'lɪzərd/ *n* lagarto (-ta). **giant l.,** dragón, *m*. **wall l.,** lagartija, *f*. **l. hole,** lagartera, *f*
llama /'lɑmə/ *n* llama, *f*
load /loud/ *n* carga, *f*; peso, *m*; (cart) carretada, *f*; *Elec.* carga, *f*; (quantity) cantidad, *f*. *vt* cargar (con); (with honors) llenar (de); (*Fig.* weigh down) agobiar (con); (a stick with lead) emplomar; (*Elec.* and of dice) cargar; (wine) mezclar vino con un narcótico. **to be loaded with fruit,** estar cargado de fruta. **to l. oneself with,** cargarse de. **to l. the dice,** cargar los dados. **to l. again,** recargar
loader /'loudər/ *n* cargador, *m*
loading /'loudɪŋ/ *n* carga, *f*. **l. depot,** cargadero, *m*
loaf /louf/ *n* pan, *m*; (French) barra de pan, *f*. *vi* golfear, vagabundear, gandulear. **l. sugar,** azúcar de pilón, *m*
loafer /'loufər/ *n* vago (-ga); azotacalles, *mf*; gandul (-la); golfo (-fa)
loafing /'loufɪŋ/ *n* gandulería, *f*, vagabundeo, *m*
loam /loum/ *n* marga, *f*
loamy /'loumi/ *a* margoso
loan /loun/ *n* empréstito, *m*; (lending) prestación, *f*; préstamo, *m*. *vt* prestar. **l. fund,** caja de empréstitos, *f*. **l. company office,** casa de préstamos, *f*
loath /louθ/ *a* desinclinado, poco dispuesto
loathe /louð/ *vt* abominar, detestar, odiar, aborrecer; repugnar
loather /'louðər/ *n* el, *m*, (*f*, la) que odia; aborrecedor (-ra)
loathing /'louðɪŋ/ *n* aborrecimiento, odio, *m*; repugnancia, aversión, *f*
loathsome /'louðsəm/ *a* odioso, aborrecible; asqueroso; repugnante
loathsomeness /'louðsəmnɪs/ *n* carácter repugnante, *m*; asquerosidad, *f*
lobby /'lɒbi/ *n* pasillo, *m*; antecámara, *f*; (in a hotel, house) vestíbulo, recibidor, *m*; (waiting-room) sala de espera, *f*; (in Parliament) sala de los pasos perdidos, *f*. *vt* and *vi* cabildear

lobe /loub/ *n* *Bot.* lobo, *m*; (*Anat. Archit.*) lóbulo, *m*
lobster /'lɒbstər/ *n* langosta, *f*; bogavante, *m*. **l.-pot,** cambín, *m*, nasa, *f*
local /'loukəl/ *a* local; de la localidad. **l. anesthetic,** anestésico local, *m*. **l. color,** color local, *m*
locale /lou'kæl/ *n* local, *m*
locality /lou'kælɪti/ *n* localidad, *f*; situación, *f*
localization /,loukələ'zeiʃən/ *n* localización, *f*
localize /'loukə,laiz/ *vt* localizar
locate /'loukeit/ *vt* situar; colocar; localizar. **to be located,** situarse; hallarse
location /lou'keiʃən/ *n* colocación, *f*; emplazamiento, *m*; localidad, *f*; situación, posición, *f*
loch /lɒk/ *n* lago, *m*
lock /lɒk/ *n* cerradura (of a door, including a vehicle) *f*; (of a gun) cerrojo, *m*; (in wrestling) llave, *f*; (on rivers, canals) presa, *f*; (at a dock) esclusa, *f*; (of hair) mechón, *m*, guedeja, *f*; (ringlet) bucle, *m*; *pl* **locks,** (hair) cabellos, *m pl*, pelo, *m*. **spring l.,** cerradura de golpe, *f*. **to put a l. on,** poner cerradura a. **under l. and key,** bajo cuatro llaves. **l.-jaw,** trismo, *m*. **l. keeper,** esclusero (-ra) *mf*. **l.-out strike,** huelga patronal, *f*
lock /lɒk/ *vt* cerrar con llave; *Fig.* encerrar; (embrace) abrazar estrechamente; (of wheels, etc.) trabar; (twine) entrelazar. *vi* cerrarse con llave. **to l. in,** cerrar con llave; encerrar. **to l. out,** cerrar la puerta (a); dejar en la calle (a). **to l. up,** encerrar; (imprison) encarcelar
locker /'lɒkər/ *n* (drawer) cajón, *m*; (cupboard) armario, *m*; *Naut.* cajonada, *f*
locket /'lɒkɪt/ *n* guardapelo, *m*; medallón, *m*
locksmith /'lɒk,smɪθ/ *n* cerrajero, *m*. **locksmith's trade,** cerrajería, *f*
locomotion /,loukə'mouʃən/ *n* locomoción, *f*
locomotive /,loukə'moutɪv/ *a* locomotor. *n* locomotora, *f*
locum tenens /'loukəm 'tinɛnz/ *n* interino (-na)
locust /'loukəst/ *n* langosta migratoria, *f*
locution /lou'kyuʃən/ *n* locución, *f*
lode /loud/ *n* filón, *m*
lodestar /'loud,stɑr/ *n* estrella polar, *f*; *Fig.* norte, *m*
lodge /lɒdʒ/ *n* casita, garita, *f*; casa de guarda, *f*; (freemason's) logia, *f*; (porter's) portería, *f*, *vi* hospedarse, alojarse, vivir, parar; penetrar; entrar (en); fijarse (en). *vt* hospedar, alojar; albergar; (a blow) asestar; (a complaint) hacer, dar; (money, etc.) depositar. **to l. an accusation against,** querellarse contra, quejarse de. **l.-keeper,** conserje, *m*
lodger /'lɒdʒər/ *n* huésped (-eda), *Lat. Am.* alojado (-da)
lodging /'lɒdʒɪŋ/ *n* hospedaje, alojamiento, *m*; (inn) posada, *f*; residencia, *f*; casa, *f*. **l.-house,** casa de huéspedes, *f*
loft /lɒft/ *n* desván, sotabanco, *m*; pajar, *m*
loftily /'lɒftli/ *adv* en alto; (proudly) con arrogancia, con altanería
loftiness /'lɒftinɪs/ *n* altura, *f*; sublimidad, *f*; nobleza, *f*; dignidad, *f*; (haughtiness) altanería, soberbia, *f*
lofty /'lɒfti/ *a* alto; sublime; noble; eminente; (haughty) altanero, soberbio
log /lɔg/ *n* madero, tronco, *m*; palo, *m*; leño, *m*; *Naut.*, diario de a bordo *m*, barquilla, *f*. **to lie like a log,** estar hecho un tronco. **log-book,** *Naut.* cuaderno de bitácora, *m*. **log-cabin,** cabañas de troncos, *m*. **log-wood,** palo campeche, *m*
logarithm /'lɔgə,rɪðəm/ *n* logaritmo, *m*
logarithmic /,lɔgə'rɪðmɪk/ *a* logarítmico
logic /'lɒdʒɪk/ *n* lógica, *f*
logical /'lɒdʒɪkəl/ *a* lógico
logician /lou'dʒɪʃən/ *n* lógico (-ca)
loin /lɔin/ *n* ijar, *m*; (of meat) falda, *f*; *pl* **loins,** lomos, riñones *m pl*. **to gird up one's loins,** *Fig.* arremangarse los faldones. **l.-cloth,** taparrabo, *m*
loiter /'lɔitər/ *vi* vagabundear, vagar, errar; haraganear; rezagarse
loiterer /'lɔitərər/ *n* haragán (-ana) *m*, vago (-ga), rezagado (-da)
loll /lɒl/ *vi* recostarse (en), apoyarse (en). *vt* (the tongue) sacar

London /'lʌndən/ Londres, *m*
Londoner /'lʌndənər/ *n* londinense, *mf*
lone /loun/ *a* solitario, (only) único
loneliness /'lounlinis/ *n* soledad, *f*; aislamiento, *m*
lonely /'lounli/ *a* solitario; solo; aislado, remoto; desierto
lonesome /'lounsəm/ *a* solo, solitario
long /lɔŋ/ *a* largo; prolongado; de largo; (extensive) extenso; (big) grande; (much) mucho. **a l. time,** mucho tiempo. **It is five feet l.,** Tiene cinco pies de largo. **l.-armed,** que tiene los brazos largos. **l.-boat,** falúa, *f.* **l. clothes,** (infant's) mantillas, *f pl.* **l.-distance call,** conferencia telefónica, *f.* **l.-distance race,** carrera de fondo, *f.* **l.-eared,** de orejas largas. **l.-faced,** de cara larga, carilargo. **l.-forgotten,** olvidado hace mucho tiempo. **l.-haired,** que tiene el pelo largo. **l.-headed,** dolicocéfalo; *Fig.* astuto, sagaz. **l.-legged,** zanquilargo, zancudo. **l.-lived,** que vive hasta una edad avanzada; longevo; duradero. **l.-lost,** perdido hace mucho tiempo. **l.-sighted,** présbita; previsor; sagaz. **l.-standing,** viejo, de muchos años. **l.-suffering,** sufrido, paciente. **l.-tailed,** de cola larga. **l.-waisted,** de talle largo. **l.-winded,** prolijo
long /lɔŋ/ *adv* mucho tiempo; mucho; durante mucho tiempo. **as l. as,** mientras (que). **before l.,** dentro de poco. **the l. and the short of it,** en resumidas cuentas. **How l. has she been here?** ¿Cuánto tiempo hace que está aquí? **not l. before,** poco tiempo antes. **l. ago,** tiempo ha, muchos años ha
long /lɔŋ/ *vi* anhelar, suspirar (por), desear con vehemencia
longanimity /ˌlɔŋgə'nimiti/ *n* longanimidad, *f*
longer /'lɔŋgər/ *a comp* más largo. *adv comp* más tiempo. **How much l. must we wait?** ¿Cuánto tiempo más hemos de esperar? **He can no l. walk as he used,** Ya no puede andar como antes
longevity /lɒn'dʒevɪti/ *n* longevidad, *f*
longing /'lɔŋɪŋ/ *a* anheloso, ansioso; de envidia. *n* anhelo, *m*, ansia, *f*; deseo vehemente, *m*; envidia, *f*
longingly /'lɔŋɪŋli/ *adv* con ansia; impacientemente; con envidia
longish /'lɔŋɪʃ/ *a* algo largo
longitude /'lɒndʒɪˌtud/ *n* longitud, *f*
longitudinal /ˌlɒndʒə'tudn̩l/ *a* longitudinal
loofah /'lufə/ *n* esponja vegetal, *f*
look /lʊk/ *n* mirada, *f*; (glance) vistazo, *m*, ojeada, *f*; (air) semblante, aire, porte, *m*; (appearance) aspecto, *m*; apariencia, *f.* **good looks,** buen parecer, *m*; guapeza, *f.* **the new l.,** la nueva línea, la nueva silueta, la nueva moda. **to be on the l.-out,** andar a la mira
look /lʊk/ *vi* and *vt* mirar; considerar, contemplar; (appear, seem) parecer; tener aire (de); tener aspecto (de); hacer el efecto (de); (show oneself) mostrarse; (of buildings, etc.) caer (a), dar (a); mirar (a.); (seem to be) revelar (e.g., *You don't l. thirty,* No revelas treinta años) **to l. alike,** parecerse. **to l. hopeful,** *Fig.* prometer bien. **to l. out of the corner of the eye,** mirar de reojo. **to l. (a person) up and down,** mirar de hito en hito. **to l. about one,** mirar a su alrededor; observar. **to l. after,** tener la mirada puesta en, mirar; (care for) cuidar; (watch) vigilar; mirar por. **to l. at,** mirar; considerar; examinar. **He looked at his watch,** Miró su reloj. **He looked at her,** La miró. **to l. away,** desviar los ojos, apartar la mirada. **to l. back,** mirar hacia atrás, volver la cabeza; (in thought) pensar en el pasado. **to l. down,** bajar los ojos; mirar el suelo; mirar hacia abajo. **to l. down upon,** dominar, mirar a; (scorn) despreciar; mirar de arriba para abajo. **to l. for,** buscar; buscar con los ojos; (await) aguardar; (expect) esperar. **to l. forward,** mirar hacia el porvenir; pensar en el futuro; esperar con ilusión. **to l. in,** entrar por un instante, hacer una visita corta. **to l. into,** mirar dentro de; mirar hacia el interior de; estudiar, investigar, *Lat. Am. also* interiorizar. **to l. on,** *vt* mirar; considerar; (of buildings, etc.) dar a. *vi* ser espectador. **to l. on to,** dar a, mirar a. **to l. out,** *vi* (be careful) tener cuidado; (look through) mirar por; asomarse a. *vt* (search) buscar; (find) hallar; (choose) escoger, elegir. **L. out!** ¡Atención! ¡Ojo!, *Mexico* ¡abusado! **to l. out for,** buscar; (await) aguardar, esperar; (be careful) tener cuidado con. **to l. out**

of, mirar por; asomarse a. **to l. over,** mirar bien; (persons) mirar de hito en hito; examinar; visitar; (a house) inspeccionar; (a book) hojear; mirar superficialmente. **to l. around,** *vt* (a place) visitar. *vi* volver la cabeza, volverse; mirar hacia atrás. **to l. around for,** buscar con los ojos; buscar por todas partes. **to l. through,** mirar por; mirar a través de; examinar; (search) registrar; (understand) registrar. **to l. to,** (be careful of) tener cuidado de; (attend to) atender a; (care for) cuidar de; (count on) contar con; (resort to) acudir a; (await) esperar. **to l. toward,** mirar hacia, mirar en la dirección de; caer a. **to l. up,** *vi* mirar hacia arriba; (aspire) aspirar; (improve) mejorar. *vt* visitar, ir (or venir) a ver; (turn up) buscar; averiguar. **to l. upon,** mirar. Other meanings see **to l. on.** **They l. upon her as their daughter,** La miran como una hija suya. **to l. up to,** *Fig.* respetar
looking /'lʊkɪŋ/ *a* (in compounds) de... aspecto, de... apariencia. **dirty-l.,** de aspecto sucio. **l.-glass,** espejo, *m*
lookout /'lʊkˌaut/ vigilancia, observación, *f*; (view) vista, *f*, panorama, *m*; (viewpoint) miradero, *m*; *Mil.* atalaya, *m*; *Naut.* gaviero, *m*; (*Fig.* prospect) perspectiva, *f*
loom /lum/ *n* telar, *m*, *vi* asomar, aparecer
loop /lup/ *n* (turn) vuelta, *f*; (in rivers, etc.) recodo, *m*, curva, *f*; (fold) pliegue, *m*; bucle, *m*; (fastening) fiador, *m*, presilla, *f*; *Aer.* rizo, *m*; (knot) nudo corredizo, *m.* **to l. the l.,** *Aer.* hacer el rizo, hacer rizos. **l.-line,** empalme de ferrocarril, *m*
loophole /'lupˌhoul/ *n* saetera, aspillera, *f*; *Fig.* escapatoria, *f*; pretexto, *m*, excusa, *f*
loose /lus/ *a* suelto; (free) libre; (slack) flojo; (of garments) holgado; (untied) desatado; (unfastened) desprendido; movible; (unchained) desencadenado; en libertad; (of the bowels) suelto (de vientre); (pendulous) colgante; (of a nail, tooth, etc.) inseguro; poco firme; que se mueve; (of knots, etc.) flojo; (of the mind, etc.) incoherente, ilógico; poco exacto; (of style, etc.) vago, impreciso; (of conduct) disoluto, vicioso; (careless) negligente, descuidado. *vt* (untie) desatar; desprender; soltar; aflojar; (of a priest) absolver; *Fig.* desencadenar. **to break l.,** desprenderse; soltarse; libertarse; escapar; *Fig.* desencadenarse. **to let l.,** desatar; aflojar; poner en libertad; soltar; *Fig.* desencadenar; (interject) lanzar. **to turn l.,** poner en libertad; dar salida (a); echar de casa, poner en la calle. **to give someone l. reins,** darle reinda suelta. **to work l.,** desprenderse; aflojarse; desvencijarse. **l.-box,** caballeriza, *f.* **l. change,** suelto, *m.* **l.-leaf note-book,** libreta de hojas sueltas, *f*
loosely /'lusli/ *adv* flojamente; sueltamente; (vaguely) vagamente; incorrectamente; incoherentemente; (carelessly) negligentemente; (viciously) disolutamente
loosen /'lusən/ *vt* (untie) desatar; aflojar; soltar; desasir; (the tongue) desatar; *Fig.* hacer menos riguroso, ablandar
looseness /'lusnis/ *n* flojedad, *f*; (of clothing) holgura, *f*; soltura, *f*; relajación, *f*; (of the bowels) diarrea, *f*; (viciousness) licencia, *f*, libertinaje, *m*; (vagueness) vaguedad, *f*; incoherencia, *f*
loosening /'lusənɪŋ/ *n* desprendimiento, *m*; desasimiento, *m*; aflojamiento, *m*
loot /lut/ *n* botín, *m*, *vt* saquear
looter /'lutər/ *n* saqueador (-ra)
looting /'lutɪŋ/ *n* saqueo, pillaje, *m*, *a* saqueador
lop /lɒp/ *vt* mochar; podar; destroncar; cortar de un golpe. *a* (of ears) gacho. **to lop off the ends,** cercenar. **to lop off the top,** desmochar. **lop-sided,** desproporcionado; desequilibrado
lopping /'lɒpɪŋ/ *n* desmoche, *m*; poda, *f*
loquacious /lou'kweiʃəs/ *a* locuaz, gárrulo
loquacity /lou'kwæsiti/ *n* locuacidad, garrulidad, *f*
lord /lɔrd/ *n* señor, *m*; (husband) esposo, *m*; (English title) lord, *m*, (*pl* lores) (Christ) Señor, *m.* **feudal l.,** señor de horca y cuchillo, *m.* **my l.,** milord. **my lords,** milores. **Our L.,** Nuestro Señor. **the Lord's Prayer,** el Padrenuestro. **to l. it over,** mandar como señor, mandar a la baqueta
lordliness /'lɔrdlinis/ *n* suntuosidad, *f*; liberalidad,

munificencia, *f*; dignidad, *f*; (haughtiness) altivez, arrogancia, *f*

lordly /'lɔrdli/ *a* señorial, señoril; altivo, arrogante

lordship /'lɔrdʃɪp/ *n* señoría, *f*; señorío, poder, *m*. **his l.,** su señoría

lore /lɔr/ *n* saber, *m*; erudición, *f*; tradiciones, *f pl* olvidar. *vi* perder; (of clocks) atrasar. **to be lost in**

lose /luz/ *vt* perder; hacer perder, quitar; (forget) olvidar. *vi* perder; (of clocks) atrasar. **to be lost in thought,** estar ensimismado, estar absorto. **to l. oneself (in)** perderse (en); abstraerse (en); entregarse (a). **to l. one's footing,** resbalar. **to l. one's way,** extraviarse, perder el camino. **to l. one's self-control,** perder el tino. **to l. one's head,** perder la cabeza. **to l. ground,** perder terreno. **to l. one's voice,** perder la voz. **to l. patience,** perder la paciencia, perder los estribos

loser /'luzər/ *n* perdedor (-ra), *Inf.* desdichado (-da)

losing /'luzɪŋ/ *a* perdedor. *n* pérdida, *f*

loss /lɔs/ *n* pérdida, *f*. **at a l., Com.** con pérdida; perplejo, dudoso. **heavy losses,** *Mil.* pérdidas cuantiosas, *f pl.* **loss of blood** *Lat. Am.* desangre *m*. **We are at a l. for words...,** No tenemos palabras para...

lot /lɒt/ *n* suerte, *f*; fortuna, *f*; lote, *m*; parte, porción, cuota, *f*; (for building) solar, *m*. **a lot of people,** muchas personas. **Our lot would have been very different,** Nuestra suerte hubiera sido muy distinta, Otro gallo nos cantara. **to draw lots,** echar suertes, sortear. **to take the lot,** *Inf.* alzarse con el santo y la limosna

lotion /'louʃən/ *n* loción, *f*

lottery /'lɒtəri/ *n* lotería, *f*. **l. ticket,** billete de la lotería, *m*

lotus /'loutəs/ *n* loto, *m*. **l.-eating,** lotofagía, *f*; *Fig.* indolencia, pereza, *f*

loud /laud/ *a* fuerte; (noisy) ruidoso, estrepitoso; alto; (gaudy) chillón, llamativo, cursi, *Lat. Am. also* figuroso. *adv* ruidosamente. **l.-speaker,** *Radio.* altavoz, *Mexico* magnavoz. *m*

loudly /'laudli/ *adv* en alta voz; fuertemente; ruidosamente, con estrépito

loudness /'laudnɪs/ *n* (noise) ruido, *m*; sonoridad, *f*; (force) fuerza, *f*; (of colors, etc.) mal gusto, *m*, vulgaridad, *f*

lounge /laundʒ/ *n* sala de estar, *f*; salón, *m*, *vi* reclinarse, ponerse a sus anchas; apoyarse (en); gandulear; vagar. **l. chair,** poltrona, *f*. **l.-lizard,** *Inf.* pollo pera, *m*. **l.-suit,** traje americano, *m*

lounger /'laundʒər/ *n* holgazán (-ana); golfo (-fa), azotacalles, *mf*

louse /laus/ *n* piojo, *m*

lousy /'lauzi/ *a* piojoso

lout /laut/ *n* patán, zamacuco, *m*

loutish /'lautɪʃ/ *a* rústico

lovable /'lʌvəbəl/ *a* amable; simpático

lovableness /'lʌvəbəlnɪs/ *n* amabilidad, *f*

love /lʌv/ *n* amor, *m*; (friendship) amistad, *f*; (enthusiasm, liking) afición, *f*; (in tennis) cero, *m*, *vt* querer; amar; gustar mucho; tener afición (a). *vi* estar enamorado. **I should l. to dine with you,** Me gustaría mucho cenar con Vds. **to be in l. with,** estar enamorado de. **to fall in l. with,** enamorarse de. **They l. each other,** Se quieren. **to make l. to,** hacer el amor (a), galantear. **l. affair,** amorío, lance de amor, *m*. **l.-bird,** periquito, *m*. **l.-letter,** carta amatoria, carta de amor, *f*. **l.-making,** galanteo, *m*. **l.-philtre,** filtro, *m*. **l.-song,** canción de amor, *f*. **l.-story,** historia de amor, *f*. **l.-token,** prenda de amor, *f*

loveless /'lʌvlɪs/ *a* sin amor

loveliness /'lʌvlinɪs/ *n* hermosura, belleza, *f*; encanto, *m*; amabilidad, *f*

lovely /'lʌvli/ *a* hermoso, bello; delicioso; amable; *Inf.* estupendo

lover /'lʌvər/ *n* amante, *mf*; aficionado (-da)

lovesick /'lʌv,sɪk/ *a* enfermo de amor, enamorado

loving /'lʌvɪŋ/ *a* amoroso; cariñoso; (friendly) amistoso; de amor

low /lou/ *a* bajo; de poca altura; (of dresses, etc.) escotado; (of musical notes) grave; (soft) suave; (feeble) débil; (depressed) triste, abatido; (plain) sencillo; (of a fever) lento; (of a bow) profundo; pequeño; inferior; humilde; (ill) enfermo;

(vile) vil, ruin; obsceno, escabroso. *adv* bajo; cerca de la tierra; en voz baja; (cheaply) barato, a bajo precio. **in a low voice,** en voz baja, paso. **to lay low,** (kill) tumbar; (knock down) derribar; incapacitar. **to lie low,** descansar; estar muerto; esconderse, agacharse; callar. **to run low,** escasear. **low-born,** de humilde cuna. **low-brow,** nada intelectual. **low comedy,** farsa, *f*. **low flying,** *n* bajo vuelo, *m*, a que vuela bajo; terrero, rastrero; que vuela a ras de tierra. **low frequency,** baja frecuencia, *f*. **low Latin,** bajo latín, *m*. **Low Mass,** misa rezada, *f*. **low neck,** escote, *m*. **low-necked,** escotado. **low-pitched,** grave. **low-spirited,** deprimido. **Low Sunday,** domingo de Cuasimodo, *m*. **low tension,** baja tensión, *f*. **low trick,** mala pasada, *f*. **low water,** marea baja, bajamar, *f*; (of rivers) estiaje, *m*

low /lou/ *vi* berrear, mugir. *n* berrido, mugido, *m*

low-ceiling /'lou 'silɪŋ/ *a* bajo de techo.

lower /'louər/ *vt* bajar; descolgar; disminuir; (price) rebajar; (a boat, sails) arriar. *vi* (of persons) fruncir el ceño, mostrarse malhumorado; (of the sky) encapotarse, cargarse; (menace) amenazar. **to l. a boat,** arriar un bote. **to l. oneself,** (by a rope, etc.) descolgarse. **to l. the flag,** abatir la bandera

lower /'louər/ *a comp* más bajo; menos alto; bajo; inferior. **l. classes,** clase obrera, *f*, clases bajas, *f pl.* **l. down,** más abajo. cámara baja, *f*. **l. jaw,** mandíbula inferior, *f*. **l. story,** piso bajo, *m*; piso de abajo, *m*

lowering /'louərɪŋ/ *n* abajamiento, *m*; descenso, *m*; (of prices) baja, *f*; (of a boat) arriada, *f*; (of the flag) abatimiento, *m*, *a* (of persons) ceñudo; (of the sky) anublado, encapotado; (threatening) amenazador

lowest /'louɪst/ *a sup* el (la, etc.) más bajo; el (la, etc.) más profundo; ínfimo

lowing /'lauɪŋ/ *n* berrido, mugido, *m*

lowland /'loulənd/ *n* tierra baja, *f*. **the Lowlands,** las tierras bajas de Escocia

lowliness /'loulinɪs/ *n* humildad, *f*; modestia, *f*

lowly /'louli/ *a* humilde

lowness /'lounɪs/ *n* poca altura, *f*; situación poco elevada, *f*; pequeñez, *f*; (of musical notes) gravedad, *f*; (softness) suavidad, *f*; (feebleness) debilidad, *f*; (sadness) tristeza, *f*, abatimiento, *m*; (of price) baratura, *f*; inferioridad, *f*; humildad, *f*; (vileness) bajeza, *f*; obscenidad, *f*

loyal /'lɔiəl/ *a* leal, fiel

loyalist /'lɔiəlɪst/ *n* realista, *mf*; defensor (-ra) del gobierno legítimo

loyalty /'lɔiəlti/ *n* lealtad, fidelidad, *f*

loyalty oath *n* (approximate equivalent) certificado de adhesión, *m*

lozenge /'lɒzɪndʒ/ *n* pastilla, *f*

lubricant /'lubrɪkənt/ *a and n* lubricante *m*

lubricate /'lubrɪ,keit/ *vt* lubricar, engrasar

lubricating oil /'lubrɪ,keitɪŋ/ *n* aceite lubricante, *m*

lubrication /,lubrɪ'keiʃən/ *n* lubricación, *f*, engrasado, *m*

lubricator /'lubrɪ,keitər/ *n* lubricador, *m*; engrasador, *m*

Lucerne /lu'sɜrn/ Lucerna, *f*

lucid /'lusɪd/ *a* lúcido; claro

lucidity /lu'sɪdɪti/ *n* lucidez, *f*; claridad, *f*

lucidly /'lusɪdli/ *adv* claramente

luck /lʌk/ *n* destino, azar, *m*; (good) buenaventura, suerte, *f*. **to bring bad l.,** traer mala suerte. **to try one's l.,** probar fortuna

luckily /'lʌkəli/ *adv* por fortuna, afortunadamente, felizmente

luckless /'lʌklɪs/ *a* desdichado

lucky /'lʌki/ *a* afortunado; dichoso, venturoso, *Lat. Am. also* lechudo; feliz. **to be l.,** tener buena suerte

lucrative /'lukrətɪv/ *a* lucrativo

lucre /'lukər/ *n* lucro, *m*

lucubration /,lukyu'breiʃən/ *n* lucubración, *f*

ludicrous /'ludɪkrəs/ *a* absurdo, risible, ridículo

ludicrousness /'ludɪkrəsnɪs/ *n* ridiculez, *f*

lug /lʌg/ *n* tirón, *m*; (ear and projection) oreja, *f*, *vt* tirar (de); arrastrar. **to lug about,** arrastrar (por); llevar con dificultad. **to lug in,** arrastrar adentro; introducir; hacer entrar. **to lug out,** arrastrar afuera; hacer salir

luggage /'lʌgɪdʒ/ n equipaje, m. **excess l.**, exceso de equipaje, m. **piece of l.**, bulto, m. **to register one's l.**, facturar el equipaje. **l. carrier,** (on buses, etc.) baca, f; (on a car) portaequipajes, m. **l. porter,** mozo de equipajes, m. **l. rack,** (on a car) portaequipajes, m; (in a train) rejilla para el equipaje, f. **l. receipt,** talón de equipaje, m. **l. room,** consigna, f. **l. van,** furgón de equipaje, m

lugubrious /lʊ'gubriəs/ a lúgubre

lukewarm /'luk'wɔrm/ a tibio, templado; Fig. indiferente, frío

lukewarmness /'luk'wɔrmnɪs/ n tibieza, f; Fig. indiferencia, frialdad, f

lull /lʌl/ n momento de calma, m; tregua, f; silencio, m, vt (a child) arrullar, adormecer; (soothe) sosegar, calmar; disminuir, mitigar

lullaby /'lʌlə,bai/ n canción de cuna, f

lumbago /lʌm'beigou/ n lumbago, m

lumbar /'lʌmbər/ a lumbar

lumber /'lʌmbər/ n (wood) maderas de sierra, f pl; (rubbish) trastos viejos, m pl. vt amontonar trastos viejos; obstruir. vi andar pesadamente; avanzar ruidosamente, avanzar con ruido sordo. **l.-jack,** maderero, ganchero, m. **l.-room,** leonera, f. **l.-yard,** maderería, f, depósito de maderas, m

lumbering /'lʌmbərɪŋ/ a pesado

luminary /'lumə,nɛri/ n lumbrera, f

luminosity /,lumə'nɒsɪti/ n luminosidad, f

luminous /'lumənəs/ a luminoso

lump /lʌmp/ n masa, f; bulto, m; pedazo, m; (of sugar) terrón m; (swelling) hinchazón, f; protuberancia, f. vt amontonar. **to l. together,** mezclar; incluir. **in the l.,** en la masa; en grueso. **Let him l. it!** ¡Que se rasque! **l. in one's throat,** nudo en la garganta, m. **l. of sugar,** terrón de azúcar, m. **l. sum,** cantidad gruesa, f

lumpishness /'lʌmpɪʃnɪs/ n hobachonería, f

lunacy /'lunəsi/ n locura, f

lunar /'lunər/ a lunar

lunatic /'lunətɪk/ n loco (-ca); demente, mf a de locos; loco. **l. asylum,** manicomio, m

lunch, luncheon /lʌntʃ; lʌntʃən/ n almuerzo, m, Mexico fajina, f; (snack) merienda, f. vi almorzar. **l. basket** or **pail,** fiambrera, f

lunch counter, luncheonette Mexico almuercería, elsewhere in Lat. Am. lonchería, f

lunette /lu'nɛt/ n (Archit. Mil.) luneta, f

lung /lʌŋ/ n pulmón, m

lunge /lʌndʒ/ n (fencing) estocada, f; embestida, f, vi dar una estocada; abalanzarse sobre

lurch /lɜrtʃ/ n sacudida, f; Naut. guiñada, f, tambaleo, m; movimiento brusco, m. vi Naut. guiñar; tambalearse; andar haciendo eses. **to leave in the l.,** dejar plantado

lure /lʊr/ n añagaza, f; reclamo, m; aliciente, atractivo, m; seducción, f. vt atraer, tentar

lurid /'lʊrɪd/ a misterioso, fantástico; cárdeno; ominoso; funesto, triste; (orange) anaranjado; (vicissitudinous) accidentado

lurk /lɜrk/ vi acechar, espiar; esconderse

lurking /'lɜrkɪŋ/ a (in ambush) en acecho; (of fear, etc.) vago

luscious /'lʌʃəs/ a delicioso; suculento; meloso; atractivo, apetitoso; sensual

lusciousness /'lʌʃəsnɪs/ n suculencia, f; melosidad, f; atractivo, m; sensualidad, f

lush /lʌʃ/ a jugoso; fresco y lozano; maduro

lust /lʌst/ n lujuria, lascivia, f; codicia, f; deseo, m. **l. for revenge,** deseo de venganza, m

luster /'lʌstər/ n lustre, brillo, m; brillantez, f

lusterless /'lʌstərlɪs/ a sin brillo; mate, deslustrado; (of eyes) apagado

lustful /'lʌstfəl/ a lujurioso, lúbrico, lascivo

lustrous /'lʌstrəs/ a lustroso

lusty /'lʌsti/ a vigoroso, fuerte, lozano

lute /lut/ n laúd, m, vihuela, f. **l.-player,** vihuelista, mf

Lutheran /'luθərən/ a luterano. n luterano (-na)

Lutheranism /'luθərə,nɪzəm/ n luteranismo, m

luxation /lʌk'seiʃən/ n luxación, f

luxuriance /lʌg'ʒuriəns/ n lozanía, f; exuberancia, superabundancia, f

luxuriant /lʌg'ʒuriənt/ a lozano; fértil; exuberante

luxuriate /lʌg'ʒuri,eit/ vi crecer con exuberancia; complacerse (en); disfrutar (de), gozar (de)

luxurious /lʌg'ʒuriəs/ a lujoso

luxuriously /lʌg'ʒuriəsli/ adv lujosamente, con lujo

luxury /'lʌkʃəri/ n lujo, m. **l. goods,** artículos de lujo, m pl

lyceum /lai'siəm/ n liceo, m

lye /lai/ n lejía, f

lying /'laiɪŋ/ a (recumbent) recostado; (untrue) mentiroso, falso. n mentiras, f pl. **l.-in,** parto, m

lymph /lɪmf/ n linfa, f; vacuna, f

lymphatic /lɪm'fætɪk/ a linfático; flemático

lynch /lɪntʃ/ vt linchar

lynching /'lɪntʃɪŋ/ n linchamiento, m

lynx /lɪŋks/ n lince, m. **l.-eyed,** de ojos de lince

lyre /lair/ n lira, f. **l.-bird,** pájaro lira, m

lyric /'lɪrɪk/ n poesía lírica, f; poema lírico, m; letra (de una canción,) f

lyrical /'lɪrɪkəl/ a lírico

lyricism /'lɪrə,sɪzəm/ n lirismo, m

M

m /ɛm/ n (letter) eme, f

ma'am /mæm/ n señora, f

macabre /mə'kɑbrə/ a macabro

macadam /mə'kædəm/ n macadán, m, a de macadán

macadamize /mə'kædə,maiz/ vt macadanizar

macaroni /,mækə'rouni/ n macarrones, m pl

macaronic /,mækə'rɒnɪk/ a macarrónico

macaroon /,mækə'run/ n macarrón de almendras, m

macaw /mə'kɔ/ n macagua, f, guacamayo, m

mace /meis/ n maza, f; Cul. macis, f. **m.-bearer,** macero, m

Macedonian /,mæsɪ'douniən/ a macedón, macedonio. n macedonio (-ia)

macerate /'mæsə,reit/ vt macerar. vi macerarse

machete /mə'ʃɛti/ n Mexico alfanje, elsewhere machete, m

Machiavellian /,mækiə'vɛliən/ a maquiavélico

Machiavellism /,mækiə'vɛlizəm/ n maquiavelismo, m

machination /,mækə'neiʃən/ n maquinación, f

machine /mə'ʃin/ n máquina, f; mecanismo, m; aparato, m; instrumento, m; organización, f, vt trabajar a máquina; Sew. coser a máquina. **m.-gun,** n ametralladora, f. vt ametrallar. **m.-gun carrier,** portametralladoras, m. **m.-gunner,** ametrallador, m. **m.-made,** hecho a máquina. **m.-oil,** aceite de motores, m. **m.-shop,** taller de maquinaria, m, Lat. Am. maestranza, f. **m.-tool,** máquina herramienta, f

machinery /mə'ʃinəri/ n maquinaria, f; mecanismo, m; organización, f; sistema, m

machinist /mə'ʃinɪst/ n maquinista, mf; Sew. costurera a máquina, f

mackerel /'mækərəl/ n caballa, f. **m. sky,** cielo aborregado, m

mackintosh /'mækɪn,tɒʃ/ n impermeable, m

macrocosm /'mækrə,kɒzəm/ n macrocosmo, m

mad /mæd/ a loco; fuera de sí; (of a dog, etc.) rabioso; furioso. **as mad as a hatter,** loco como una cabra. **to drive mad,** volver loco (a). **to go mad,** volverse loco, enloquecer, perder el seso. **mad with joy (pain),** loco de alegría (dolor). **mad dog,** perro rabioso, m

madam /'mædəm/ n señora, f; (French form) madama, f. **Yes, m.,** Sí señora

madcap /'mæd,kæp/ n locuelo (-la), f, botarate, m; tarambana, mf

madden /'mædn̩/ *vt* enloquecer; enfurecer, exasperar
maddening /'mædn̩ɪŋ/ *a* exasperante, irritador
madder /'mædər/ *n Bot.* rubia, *f*
made /meid/ *past part* and *a* hecho; formado. **self-m. man,** un hombre hecho y derecho. **m.-to-measure,** hecho a la medida. **m.-up,** compuesto; (of clothes) confeccionado, ya hecho; (of the face) pintado; (fictitious) inventado, ficticio; artificial
Madeira /mə'dɪərə/ *n* vino de Madera, *m, a* de Madera
madhouse /'mæd,haus/ *n* casa de locos, *f*, manicomio, *m*
madly /'mædli/ *adv* locamente; furiosamente
madman /'mæd,mæn/ *n* loco, *m*
madness /'mædnɪs/ *n* locura, *f*; (of a dog, etc.) rabia, *f*; furia, *f*
Madonna /mə'dɒnə/ *n* Madona, *f*
madrigal /'mædrɪgəl/ *n* madrigal, *m*
Madrilenian /ˌmædrə'liniən/ *a* madrileño, matritense. *n* madrileño (-ña)
madwoman /'mæd,wʊmən/ *n* loca, *f*
Maecenas /mi'sinəs/ *n* mecenas, *m*
maelstrom /'meilstrəm/ *n* remolino, vórtice, *m*
magazine /ˌmægə'zin/ *n* (store) almacén, *m*; (for explosives) polvorín, *m*, santabárbara, *f*; (periodical) revista, *f*. **m. rifle,** rifle de repetición, *m*
Magdalen /'mægdə,lin/ *n* magdalena, *f*
magenta /mə'dʒɛntə/ *n* color magenta, *m*
maggot /'mægət/ *n* gusano, *m*, cresa, *f*; *Fig.* manía, *f*, capricho, *m*
maggoty /'mægəti/ *a* gusanoso
Magi, the /'meidʒai/ *n pl* los reyes magos
magic /'mædʒɪk/ *n* magia, *f*; mágica, *f*; *Fig.* encanto, *m, a* mágico. **as if by m.,** por ensalmo. **m. lantern,** linterna mágica, *f*
magically /'mædʒɪkli/ *adv* por encanto
magician /mə'dʒɪʃən/ *n* mago, mágico, brujo, *m*; (conjurer) jugador de manos, *m*
magisterial /ˌmædʒə'stɪəriəl/ *a* magistral
magistracy /'mædʒəstrəsi/ *n* magistratura, *f*
magistrate /'mædʒə,streit/ *n* magistrado, *m*; juez municipal, *m*
Magna Charta /'mægnə 'kartə/ *n* Carta Magna, *f*
magnanimity /ˌmægnə'nɪmɪti/ *n* magnanimidad, generosidad, *f*
magnanimous /mæg'nænəməs/ *a* magnánimo, generoso
magnanimously /mæg'nænəməsli/ *adv* magnánimamente
magnate /'mægneit/ *n* magnate, *m*
magnesia /mæg'niʒə/ *n* magnesia, *f*
magnesium /mæg'niziəm/ *n* magnesio, *m*. **m. light,** luz de magnesio, *f*
magnet /'mægnɪt/ *n* imán, *m*
magnetic /mæg'nɛtɪk/ *a* magnético; *Fig.* atractivo. **m. field,** campo magnético, *m*. **m. needle,** brújula, *f*
magnetics /mæg'nɛtɪks/ *n* la ciencia del magnetismo, *f*
magnetism /'mægnɪ,tɪzəm/ *n* magnetismo, *m*
magnetization /ˌmægnɪtɪ'zeiʃən/ *n* imanación, magnetización, *f*
magnetize /'mægnɪ,taiz/ *vt* magnetizar, imanar; (hypnotize) magnetizar; *Fig.* atraer
magnification /ˌmægnəfɪ'keiʃən/ *n* (by a lens, etc.) aumento, *m*; exageración, *f*
magnificence /mæg'nɪfəsəns/ *n* magnificencia, *f*
magnificent /mæg'nɪfəsənt/ *a* magnífico
magnify /'mægnə,fai/ *vt* (by lens) aumentar; exagerar; (praise) magnificar
magnifying /'mægnə,faiɪŋ/ *a* de aumento, vidrio de aumento. **m. glass,** lente de aumento, *m*
magniloquence /mæg'nɪləkwəns/ *n* grandilocuencia, *f*
magniloquent /mæg'nɪləkwənt/ *a* grandílocuo
magnitude /'mægnɪ,tud/ *n* magnitud, *f*
magnolia /mæg'noulyə/ *n* magnolia, *f*
magnum /'mægnəm/ *n* botella de dos litros, *f*
magpie /'mæg,pai/ *n* marica, picaza, *f*
maharaja /ˌmahə'radʒə/ *n* maharajá, *m*
mahogany /mə'hɒgəni/ *n* caoba, *f, a* de caoba
maid /meid/ *n* doncella, muchacha, *f*; virgen, *f*; sol-

tera, *f*; (servant) criada, *f*; (daily) asistenta, *f*. **old m.,** solterona, *f*. **m.-of-all-work,** criada para todo, *f*. **m.-of-honor,** dama de honor, *f*
maiden /'meidn̩/ *n* doncella, joven, soltera, *f*; virgen, *f*; zagala, *f. a* de soltera; soltera *f*; virginal; (of speeches, voyages, etc.) primero. **m. lady,** dama soltera, *f*. **m.-name,** apellido de soltera, *m*. **m. speech,** primer discurso, *m*
maidenhood /'meidn̩,hʊd/ *n* doncellez, virginidad, *f*
maidenly /'meidn̩li/ *a* virginal; modesto, modoso; tímido
maidservant /'meid,sɜrvənt/ *n* criada, sirvienta, *f*
mail /meil/ *n* correo, *m*; correspondencia, *f*; (armor) cota de malla, *f. vt* mandar por correo, enviar por correo; armar con cota de malla. **coat of m.,** cota de malla, *f. royal m.,** malla real, *f*. **m.-bag,** valija de correo, *f*; portacartas, *m*. **m.-boat,** buque correo, *m*. **m.-cart,** ambulancia de correos, *f*. **m.-clad,** vestido de cota de malla; armado. **m.-coach,** coche correo, *m*, diligencia, *f*. **m.-order,** pedido postal, *m*. **m.-order business,** negocio de ventas por correo, *m*. **m.-plane,** avión postal, *m*. **m. service,** servicio de correos, *m*. **m. steamer,** vapor correo, *m*. **m. train,** tren correo, *m*. **m. van,** (on a train) furgón postal, *m*
mailed /meild/ *a* de malla; armado. **m. fist,** *Fig.* puño de hierro, *m*
maim /meim/ *vt* mancar; mutilar, tullir; estropear
maimed /meimd/ *a* manco; tullido, mutilado
main /mein/ *a* mayor; principal; más importante, esencial; maestro. *n* (mainland) continente, *m*; (sea) océano, *m*; (pipe) cañería maestra, *f*. **by m. force,** por fuerza mayor. **in the m.,** en general, generalmente; en su mayoría. **m. beam,** viga maestra, *f*. **m. body,** (of a building) ala principal, *f*; (of a church) cuerpo (de iglesia), *m*; (of an army) cuerpo (del ejército), *m*; mayor parte, mayoría, *f*. **m. line,** línea principal, *f*. **m. mast,** palo mayor, *m*. **m. thing,** cosa principal, *f*, lo más importante. **m. wall,** pared maestra, *f*
mainland /'mein,lænd/ *n* continente, *m*; tierra firme, *f*
mainly /'meinli/ *adv* principalmente; en su mayoría; generalmente
mainsail /'mein,seil/ *n* vela mayor, *f*
mainspring /'mein,sprɪŋ/ *n* (of a watch) muelle real, *m*; motivo principal, *m*; origen, *m*
mainstay /'mein,stei/ *n* estay mayor, *m*; *Fig.* sostén principal, *m*
maintain /mein'tein/ *vt* mantener; sostener; tener; guardar; afirmar
maintainable /mein'teinəbəl/ *a* sostenible; defendible
maintenance /'meintənəns/ *n* mantenimiento, *m*; manutención, *f*, sustento, *m*; conservación, *f*, subsistencia, *f*
maize /meiz/ *n* maíz, *m*. **m. field,** maizal, *m*
majestic /mə'dʒɛstɪk/ *a* majestuoso
majesty /'mædʒəsti/ *n* majestad, *f*; majestuosidad, *f*. **His** or **Her M.,** Su Majestad
majolica /mə'dʒɒlɪkə/ *n* mayólica, *f*
major /'meidʒər/ *a* mayor; principal. *n* mayor de edad, *m*; *Mil.* comandante. **anthropology major,** alumno con la especialidad en antropología *m*. **m.-domo,** mayordomo, *m*. **m.-general,** general de división, *m*. **m. road,** carretera, *f*; ruta de prioridad, *f*. **m. scale,** escala mayor, *f*
Majorca /mə'dʒɔrkə/ *n* Mallorca, *f*
majority /mə'dʒɒrɪti/ *n* mayoría, *f*; mayor número, *m*; generalidad, *f*. **to have attained one's m.,** ser mayor de edad
make /meik/ *vt* hacer; crear, formar; (manufacture) fabricar, confeccionar; construir; (produce) producir; causar; (prepare) preparar; (a bed, a fire, a remark, poetry, friends, enemies, war, a curtsey) hacer; (earn, win) ganar; (a speech) pronunciar; (compel) obligar (a), forzar (a); inclinar (a); (arrive at) alcanzar, llegar (a); (calculate) calcular; (arrange) arreglar; deducir (be) ser; (equal) ser igual a; (think) creer; (appoint as) constituir (en), hacer; (behave) portarse (como). *vi* (begin) ir (a), empezar (a); (make as though) hacer (como si); (of the tide) crecer; contribuir (a); tender (a). **He made as if to go,** Hizo como si de

marchara. **to m. as though...,** aparentar, fingir. **It made me ill,** Me hizo sentir mal. **They have made up,** Han hecho las paces. **They m. a great deal of money,** Hacen (or ganan) mucho dinero. **You cannot m. me believe it,** No puedes hacerme creerlo. **He is making himself ridiculous,** Se está poniendo en ridículo. **to m. ready,** preparar. **to m. the tea,** hacer el té; preparar el té. **Two and two m. four,** Dos y dos son cuatro. **to m. oneself known,** darse a conocer. **to m. one of...,** ser uno de... **to m. after,** seguir; correr detrás de. **to m. again,** hacer de nuevo, rehacer. **to m. angry,** *Mexico.* amuinar. **to m. away with,** quitar; suprimir; destruir; (kill) matar; (squander) derrochar; (steal) llevarse; hurtar. **to m. away with oneself,** quitarse la vida, suicidarse. **to m. for,** encaminarse a, dirigirse a; (attack) abalanzarse sobre, atacar; (tend to) contribuir a, tender a. **to m. off,** marcharse corriendo, largarse; huir, escaparse. **to m. out,** (discern) distinguir; descifrar; (understand) comprender; (prove) probar, justificar; (draw up) redactar; (fill in a form) completar, llenar; (a check, etc.) extender; (an account) hacer; (get on, succeed or otherwise) ir (with bien or mal); (convey) dar la impresión de que; sugerir. **I cannot m. it out,** No lo puedo comprender. **How did you m. out** (get on)**?** ¿Cómo te fue? **to m. over,** hacer de nuevo, rehacer; (transfer) ceder, traspasar. **to m. up,** hacer; acabar; concluir; (clothes) confeccionar; fabricar; (the face) pintarse, maquillarse; (the fire) echar carbón, etc. a; *Print.* compaginar; (invent) inventar; (lies) fabricar; (compose) formar; (package) empaquetar; reparar; indemnizar; compensar; (an account) ajustar; preparar; arreglar; (conciliate) conciliar; enumerar; *Theat.* caracterizarse. **to m. up for,** reemplazar; compensar; (lost time, etc.) recobrar. **to m. up to,** compensar; indemnizar; (flatter) adular, halagar; procurar congraciarse con, procurar obtener el favor de; (court) galantear (con). **m. an impression (on),** dejar(le a fulano) una impresión

make /meik/ *n* forma, *f*; hechura, *f*; estructura, *f*; confección, *f*; manufactura, *f*; producto, *m*; (trade name) marca, *f*; (character) carácter, temperamento, *m*. **m.-believe,** *m* artificio, pretexto, *m*, a fingido, *vi* fingir. **land of m.-believe,** reino de los sueños, *m*. **m. -up,** (for the face, etc.) maquillaje, *m*; *Theat.* caracterización, *f*; *Print.* imposición, *f*; (whole) conjunto, *m*; (character) carácter, modo de ser, *m*

maker /'meikər/ *n* creador, *m*; autor (-ra); artífice, *mf*; (manufacturer) fabricante, *m*; constructor, *m*; (of clothes, etc.) confeccionador (-ra); (worker) obrero (-ra)

makeshift /'meik,ʃift/ *n* expediente, *m*, a provisional
makeweight /'meik,weit/ *n* añadidura (de peso), *f*, contrapeso, *m*; *Fig.* suplente, *m*

making /'meikiŋ/ *n* creación, *f*; hechura, *f*; (manufacture) fabricación, *f*; construcción, *f*; (of clothes, etc.) confección, *f*; formación, *f*; preparación, *f*; estructura, *f*; composición, *f*; *pl* **makings,** (profits) ganancias, *f pl*; (elements) elementos, *m pl*; germen, *m*; rasgos esenciales, *m pl*, características, *f. pl.* **m.-up,** (of clothes) confección, *f*; *Print.* ajuste, *m*; (of the face) maquillaje, *m*; (invention) invención, *f*; fabricación, *f*

maladjustment /,mælə'dʒʌstmənt/ *n* mal ajuste, *m*; inadaptación, *f*
maladministration /,mæləd,mɪnə'streiʃən/ *n* desgobierno, *m*, mala administración, *f*; (of funds) malversación, *f*
maladroit /,mælə'drɔit/ *a* torpe
maladroitness /,mælə'drɔitnɪs/ *n* torpeza, *f*
malady /'mælədi/ *n* enfermedad, *f*; mal, *m*
Malaga /'mæləgə/ *n* Málaga, (wine) vino de Málaga, *m*
malaria /mə'lɛəriə/ *n* paludismo, *m*
malarial /mə'lɛəriəl/ *a* palúdico. **m. fever,** fiebre palúdica, *f*
Malaya /mə'leiə/ Malasia, *f*, Archipiélago Malayo, *m*
Malayan /mə'leiən/ *a* malayo. *n* malayo (-ya)
malcontent /,mælkən'tɛnt/ *n* malcontento (-ta). *a* descontento
Maldives /'mɔldivz/ Maldivas, *f pl*
male /meil/ *a* macho; masculino. *n* macho, *m*;

varón, *m*. **m. child,** niño, *m*; niño varón, *m*; (son) hijo varón, *m*. **m. flower,** flor masculina, *f*. **m. issue,** sucesión masculina, *f*. **m. nurse,** enfermero, *m*. **m. sex,** sexo masculino, *m*
malediction /,mælɪ'dɪkʃən/ *n* maldición, *f*
malefactor /'mælə,fæktər/ *n* malhechor (-ra)
malefic /mə'lɛfɪk/ *a* maléfico
malevolence /mə'lɛvələns/ *n* malevolencia, *f*
malevolent /mə'lɛvələnt/ *a* malévolo, maligno
malformation /,mælfɔr'meiʃən/ *n* formación anormal, deformidad, deformación congénita, *f*
malice /'mælɪs/ *n* malicia, *f*; *Law.* alevosía, *f*. **to bear m.,** guardar rencor
malicious /mə'lɪʃəs/ *a* malicioso; maligno, rencoroso
maliciousness /mə'lɪʃəsnɪs/ *n* malicia, mala intención, *f*
malign /mə'lain/ *vt* calumniar, difamar. *a* maligno; malévolo
malignancy /mə'lɪgnənsi/ *n* malignidad, *f*; malevolencia, *f*
malignant /mə'lɪgnənt/ *a* maligno; malévolo; *Med.* maligno
malinger /mə'lɪŋgər/ *vi* fingirse enfermo
malingerer /mə'lɪŋgərər/ *n* enfermo (-ma) fingido (-da)
malingering /mə'lɪŋgəriŋ/ *n* enfermedad fingida, *f*
mallard /'mælərd/ *n* pato (-ta), silvestre
malleability /,mæliə'bɪlɪti/ *n* maleabilidad, *f*
malleable /'mæliəbəl/ *a* maleable
mallet /'mælɪt/ *n* mazo, *m*; (in croquet) pala, *f*, mazo, *m*; (in polo) maza (de polo), *f*
mallow /'mælou/ *n* malva, *f*
malmsey /'mɑmzi/ *n* (wine) malvasía, *f*
malnutrition /,mælnu'triʃən/ *n* desnutrición, alimentación deficiente, *f*
malodorous /mæl'oudərəs/ *a* de mal olor, hediondo, fétido
malpractice /mæl'præktɪs/ *n* (wrongdoing) maleficencia, *f*; (by a doctor) tratamiento equivocado, perjudicial o ilegal, *m*; (malversation) malversación, *f*; inmoralidad, *f*
malt /mɔlt/ *n* malta, *m*. *vt* preparar el malta. **m.-house,** fábrica de malta, *f*. **m. vinegar,** vinagre de malta, *m*
malted milk /'mɔltɪd/ *n* leche malteada, *f*
Maltese /mɔl'tiz/ *a* maltés. *n* maltés (-esa). **M. cat,** gato maltés, *m*. **M. cross,** cruz de Malta, *f*. **M. dog,** perro maltés, *m*
Malthusian /mæl'θuʒən/ *a* maltusiano
Malthusianism /mæl'θuʒə,nɪzəm/ *n* maltusianismo, *m*
maltose /'mɔltous/ *n* maltosa, *f*
maltreat /mæl'trit/ *vt* maltratar
maltreatment /mæl'tritmənt/ *n* maltrato, *m*,
malt shop *n* café-nevería, *m*
mamma /'mæmə for 1; 'mamə for 2/ *n Anat.* mama, *f*; (mother) mamá, *f*
mammal /'mæməl/ *n* mamífero, *m*
mammalian /mə'meiliən/ *a* mamífero
mammary /'mæməri/ *a* mamario. **m. gland,** mama, teta, *f*
mammon /'mæmən/ *n* becerro de oro, *m*
mammoth /'mæməθ/ *n* mamut, *m*, a gigantesco, enorme
man /mæn/ *n* hombre, *m*; varón, *m*; persona, *f*; (servant) criado, *m*; (workman) obrero, *m*; (soldier) soldado, *m*; (sailor) marinero, *m*; (humanity) raza humana, *f*; (husband) marido, *m*; (chess) peón, *m*; (checkers) dama, *f*; (a ship) buque, *m*. **no man,** nadie; ningún hombre. **young man,** joven, *m*. **to a man,** como un solo hombre. **to come to man's estate,** llegar a la edad viril. **Man overboard!** ¡Hombre al agua! **man and wife,** marido y mujer, *m*, cónyuges, esposos, *m pl*. **man about town,** hombre de mundo, señorito, *m*. **man-at-arms,** hombre de armas, *m*. **man-eater,** caníbal, *mf*; tigre, *m*. **man-eating,** *a* antropófago. **man hater,** misántropo, *m*; mujer que odia a los hombres, *f*. **man-hole,** pozo, *m*. **man-hunter,** caníbal, *mf*; (woman) castigadora, *f*. **man in charge,** encargado, *m*. **man in the moon,** mujer de

la luna, *f*. **man in the street,** hombre de la calle, hombre medio, *m*. **man of letters,** hombre de letras, literato, *m*; **man of straw,** bausán, *m*; (figure-head) testaferro, *m*. **man of the world,** hombre del mundo, *m*. **man of war,** buque de guerra, *m*. **man-power,** mano de obra, *f*, brazos, *m pl*, (e.g. *lack of manpower,* falta de brazos, *f*). **man servant,** criado, *m*

man /mæn/ *vt* armar; *Mil.* poner guarnición (a); ocupar; *Naut.* tripular; dirigir; *Fig.* fortificar

manacle /'mænəkəl/ *n* manilla, *f*; *pl* **manacles,** esposas, *f pl*; grillos, *m pl*. *vt* poner esposas (a)

manage /'mænɪdʒ/ *vt* manejar; (animals) domar; dirigir; gobernar; administrar; (arrange) agenciar, arreglar; (work) explotar; (do) hacer; (eat) comer. *vi* arreglárselas (para); (get along) ir tirando; (know how) saber hacer; (succeed in) lograr; (do) hacer

manageability /ˌmænɪdʒə'bɪlɪti/ *n* lo manejable; flexibilidad, *f*; (of animals, persons) docilidad, mansedumbre, *f*

manageable /'mænɪdʒəbəl/ *a* manejable; flexible; (of persons, animals) dócil

management /'mænɪdʒmənt/ *n* manejo, *m*; dirección, *f*; gobierno, *m*; administración, *f*; arreglo, *m*; (working) explotación, *f*; *Com.* gerencia, *f*; *Theat.* empresa, *f*; conducta, *f*; (economy) economía, *f*; (skill) habilidad, *f*; prudencia, *f*. **the m.,** la dirección, el cuerpo de directores. **domestic m.,** economía doméstica, *f*

manager /'mænɪdʒər/ *n* director (-ra); administrador (-ra); jefe (-fa); *Theat.* empresario (-ria); *Com.* gerente, *mf*; regente, *mf*. **She is not much of a m.,** No es muy mujer de su casa. **manager's office,** dirección, *f*

managerial /ˌmænɪ'dʒɪəriəl/ *a* directivo; administrativo. **m. board,** junta directiva, *f*

managership /'mænɪdʒərˌʃɪp/ *n* puesto de director, *m*; jefatura, *f*

managing /'mænɪdʒɪŋ/ *a* directivo; (officious) mandón, dominante; (niggardly) tacaño

manatee /'mænəˌti/ *n* manatí, *m*

mandarin /'mændərɪn/ *n* mandarín, *m*; (language) mandarina, *f*. **m. orange,** mandarina, *f*

mandate /'mændeit/ *n* mandato, *m*. **mandated territory,** territorios bajo mandato, *m pl*

mandatory /'mændəˌtɔri/ *a* obligatorio

mandible /'mændəbəl/ *n* mandíbula, *f*

mandolin /'mændlɪn/ *n* bandolín, *m*, bandurria, *f*

mandrake /'mændreik, -drɪk/ *n* mandrágora, *f*

mandrill /'mændrɪl/ *n* mandril, *m*

mane /mein/ *n* melena, *f*; (of a horse) crines, *f pl*

maned /meind/ *a* (in compounds) con melena...; con crines...

maneuver /mə'nuvər/ *n* maniobra, *f*. *vi* maniobrar, hacer maniobras. *vt* hacer maniobrar; manipular

maneuvering /mə'nuvərɪŋ/ *n* maniobras, *f pl*; maquinaciones, intrigas, *f pl*

manfully /'mænfəli/ *adv* valientemente; vigorosamente

manganate /'mæŋgəneit/ *n* manganato, *m*

manganese /'mæŋgəˌnis, -ˌniz/ *n* manganeso, *m*

mange /meindʒ/ *n* sarna, *f*; (in sheep) roña, *f*

manger /'meindʒər/ *n* pesebre, *m*

manginess /'meindʒinɪs/ *n* estado sarnoso, *m*

mangle /'mæŋgəl/ *n* (for clothes) exprimidor de la ropa, *m*. *vt* pasar por el exprimidor; (mutilate) mutilar, lacerar, magullar; (a text) mutilar

mangling /'mæŋglɪŋ/ *n* (mutilation) mutilación, laceración, *f*

mango /'mæŋgou/ *n* mango, *m*

mangy /'meindʒi/ *a* sarnoso

manhandle /'mæn,hændl/ *vt* maltratar

manhood /'mænhʊd/ *n* virilidad, *f*; edad viril, *f*; masculinidad, *f*; los hombres; (manliness) hombradía, *f*, valor, *m*

mania /'meiniə/ *n* manía, *f*; obsesión, *f*; capricho, *m*, chifladura, *f*, *Lat. Am.* barreno, *m*

maniac /'meini,æk/ *n* maníaco (-ca). *a* maníaco, maniático

manicure /'mæni,kyʊr/ *n* manicura, *f*. *vt* arreglar las uñas. **m.-set,** estuche de manicura, *m*

manicurist /'mænɪ,kyʊrɪst/ *n* manicuro (-ra)

manifest /'mænə,fest/ *n* *Naut.* manifiesto, *m*. *vt* mostrar; hacer patente, probar; manifestarse. *vi* publicar un manifiesto; (of spirits) manifestarse. *a* manifiesto, evidente, claro, patente. **to make m.,** poner de manifiesto

manifestation /ˌmænəfə'steiʃən/ *n* manifestación, *f*

manifestly /'mænə,festli/ *adv* evidentemente, manifiestamente

manifesto /ˌmænə'festou/ *n* manifiesto, *m*

manifold /'mænə,fould/ *a* múltiple; numeroso; diverso, vario

manikin /'mænɪkɪn/ *n* enano, *m*; muñeco, *m*; *Art.* maniquí, *m*

Manila /mə'nɪlə/ *n* Manila, *f*; cigarro filipino, *m*. **M. hemp,** cáñamo de Manila, *m*

maniple /'mænəpəl/ *n* manípulo, *m*

manipulate /mə'nɪpyə,leit/ *vt* manipular

manipulation /mə,nɪpyə'leiʃən/ *n* manipulación, *f*

manipulative /mə'nɪpyə,leitɪv/ *a* manipulador

mankind /'mæn'kaind/ *n* humanidad, raza humana, *f*, género humano, *m*

manlike /'mæn,laik/ *a* de hombre, masculino; varonil; (of a woman) hombruno

manliness /'mænlinɪs/ *n* masculinidad, hombradía, *f*; virilidad, *f*; valor, *m*; (of a woman) aire hombruno, *m*

manly /'mænli/ *a* masculino, de hombre; varonil, viril; valiente; fuerte. **to be very m.,** ser muy hombre, ser todo un hombre

manna /'mænə/ *n* maná, *m*

mannequin /'mænɪkɪn/ *n* manequín, modelo, *f*. **m. parade,** exposición de modelos, *f*

manner /'mænər/ *n* manera, *f*, modo, *m*; aire, porte, *m*; conducta, *f*; (style) estilo, *m*; (sort) clase, *f*; *Gram.* modo, *m*; *pl* **manners,** modales, *m pl*, crianza, educación, *f*; (customs) costumbres, *f pl*. **after the m. of,** en (or según) el estilo de. **in a m. of speaking,** en cierto modo, para decirlo así. **in this m.,** de este modo. **to have bad (good) manners,** tener malos (buenos) modales, ser mal (bien) criado. **the novel of manners,** la novela de costumbres

mannered /'mænərd/ *a* amanerado; (in compounds)... educado, de... modales; de costumbres... **well-m.,** bien educado, de buenos modales

mannerism /'mænə,rɪzəm/ *n* amaneramiento, *m*; afectación, *f*; *Theat.* latiguillo, *m*. **to acquire mannerisms,** amanerarse

manneriness /'mænərinɪs/ *n* cortesía, buena educación, urbanidad, *f*

mannerly /'mænərli/ *a* cortés, bien educado, atento

mannish /'mænɪʃ/ *a* (of a woman) hombruno; de hombre, masculino

manor /'mænər/ *n* feudo, *m*; finca, hacienda, *f*; casa solariega, *f*; señorío, *m*

manorial /mə'nɔriəl/ *a* señorial

mansion /'mænʃən/ *n* mansión, *f*; casa solariega, *f*; hotel, *m*. **m.-house,** casa solariega, *f*; residencia del alcalde de Londres, *f*

manslaughter /'mæn,slɔtər/ *n* homicidio, *m*; *Law.* homicidio sin premeditación, *m*

mantelpiece /'mæntl,pis/ *n* repisa de chimenea, *f*

mantilla /mæn'tilə/ *n* mantilla, *f*

mantle /'mæntl/ *n* capa, *f*, manto, *m*; *Fig.* cobertura, *f*; (gas) camiseta, *f*, manguito, *m*; *Zool.* manto, *m*. *vt* cubrir; envolver; ocultar. *vi* extenderse; (of blushes) inundar, subirse (a las mejillas)

Mantuan /'mæntʃuən/ *a* mantuano

manual /'mænyuəl/ *a* manual. *n* manual, *m*; *Mus.* teclado de órgano, *m*. **m. work,** trabajo manual, *m*

manufactory /ˌmænyə'fæktəri/ *n* fábrica, *f*, taller, *m*

manufacture /ˌmænyə'fæktʃər/ *n* fabricación, *f*; manufactura, *f*. *vt* manufacturar, fabricar

manufacturer /ˌmænyə'fæktʃərər/ *n* fabricante, industrial, *m*. **manufacturer's price,** precio de fábrica, *m*

manufacturing /ˌmænyə'fæktʃərɪŋ/ *a* manufacturero, fabril. *n* fabricación, *f*

manure /mə'nʊr/ *n* estiércol, abono, *m*. *vt* estercolar, abonar. **m. heap,** estercolero, *m*

manuring /mə'nʊrɪŋ/ *n* estercoladura, *f*

manuscript /'mænyə,skrɪpt/ n manuscrito, m, a manuscrito

many /'meni/ a muchos (-as); numeroso; diversos (-as); varios (-as). n muchos (-as); la mayoría; las masas; muchedumbre, multitud, f. **a great m.,** muchísimos, m pl, muchísimas, f pl; un gran número. **as m. as...,** tantos como... **How m. are there?** ¿Cuántos hay? ¿Cuántas hay? **m. a time,** muchas veces. **three too m.,** tres de más. **for m. long years,** por largos años. **m.-colored,** multicolor. **m.-headed,** con muchas cabezas. **m.-sided,** multilátero; polifacético; complicado

Maori /'mauri/ n maorí, m, (pl maoríes)

map /mæp/ n mapa, m; plano, m; (chart) carta, f. vt hacer un mapa (or plano) de. **to map out,** Surv. apear; trazar; (plan) proyectar. **ordnance map,** mapa del estado mayor, m. **map of the world,** mapamundi, mapa del mundo, m. **map-making,** cartografía, f

maple /'meipəl/ n (tree) arce, m; (wood) madera de arce, f. **m.-syrup,** jarabe de arce, m

mapping /'mæpɪŋ/ n cartografía, f

maquiladora /mə,kilə'dɔrə/ n maquiladora, f

mar /mɑr/ vt estropear; desfigurar; (happiness) destruir, aguar; frustrar

maraca /mə'rɑkə/ n Lat. Am. alfandoque, m

maraschino /,mærə'skinou/ n marrasquino, m. **m. cherry,** cerezas en marrasquino, f pl

maraud /mə'rɔd/ vi merodear

marauder /mə'rɔdər/ n merodeador, m

marauding /mə'rɔdɪŋ/ a merodeador, n merodeo, m

marble /'mɑrbəl/ n mármol, m; (for playing with) canica, f, a de marmol, marmóreo; Fig. insensible; (of paper, etc.) jaspeado. vt jaspear. **m. cutter,** marmolista, m. **m. works,** marmolería, f

marbled /'mɑrbəld/ a jaspeado

March /mɑrtʃ/ n marzo, m. **as mad as a M. hare,** loco como una cabra, loco de atar

march /mɑrtʃ/ n marcha, f; (step) paso, m; Fig. marcha, f, progreso, m. **forced m.,** marcha forzada, f. **quick m.,** paso doble, m. **to steal a m. on,** tomar la delantera (a), ganar por la mano (a). **to strike up a m.,** batir la marcha. **m.-past,** desfile, m

march /mɑrtʃ/ vi marchar; (of properties) lindar (con). vt hacer marchar, poner en marcha (a). **to m. back,** vi regresar (or volver) a pie. vt hacer volver a pie. **to m. in,** entrar (a pie) en. **to m. off,** marcharse. **to m. on,** seguir marchando; seguir adelante; avanzar. **to m. past,** desfilar ante

marching /'mɑrtʃɪŋ/ n marcha, f. a en marcha; de marcha. **to receive one's m. orders,** recibir la orden de marchar; Inf. ser despedido. **m. order,** orden de marcha, m. **m. song,** canción de marcha, f

mardi gras /'mɑrdi ,grɑ/ n martes de carnaval, m

mare /mɛər/ n yegua, f

margarine /'mɑrdʒərɪn/ n margarina, f

margin /'mɑrdʒɪn/ n borde, lado, m; orilla, f; (of a page) margen, mf; reserva, f; sobrante, m. **in the m.,** al margen

marginal /'mɑrdʒənl/ a marginal. **m. note,** acotación, nota marginal, f

marigold /'mærɪ,gould/ n caléndula, maravilla, f

marijuana /,mærə'wɑnə/ n marijuana, f. Lat. Am. cáñamo, m

marine /mə'rin/ a marino, de mar; marítimo; naval. n (fleet) marina, f; (soldier) soldado de marina, m. **Tell that to the marines!** ¡Cuéntaselo a tu tía! **mercantile m.,** marina mercante, f. **m. forces,** infantería de marina, f. **m. insurance,** seguro marítimo, m

mariner /'mærənər/ n marinero, marino, m. **mariner's compass,** aguja de marear, brújula, f

marionette /,mæriə'nɛt/ n marioneta, f, títere, m

marital /'mærɪtl/ a marital

maritime /'mærɪ,taim/ a marítimo

mark /mɑrk/ n marca, f; señal, f; mancha, f; impresión, f; (target) blanco, m; (standard) norma, f; (level) nivel, m; (distinction) importancia, distinción, f; (in examinations) nota, f; calificación, f; (signature) cruz, f; (coin) marco, m. vt marcar; señalar; (price) poner precio (a); (notice) observar, darse cuenta (de); (characterize) caracterizar. **trade-m.,**

marca de fábrica, f. **to be beside the m.,** no dar en el blanco; errar el tiro; Fig. no tener nada que ver con; equivocarse. **to hit the m.,** dar en el blanco; Fig. dar en el clavo. **to make one's m.,** firmar con una cruz; distinguirse. **to m. time,** marcar el paso; Fig. hacer tiempo. **to m. down,** (a person) señalar; escoger; (in price) rebajar. **to m. out,** marcar; trazar; definir; (erase) borrar; (a person) escoger; destinar. **m. somebody absent,** ponerle a alguien su ausencia. **m. somebody present,** ponerle a alguien su asistencia.

Mark /mɑrk/ n Marcos. **the Gospel according to St. M.,** el Evangelio de San Marcos

marked /mɑrkt/ a marcado; señalado; notable; acentuado; particular, especial. **He speaks with a m. Galician accent,** Habla con marcado acento gallego

markedly /'mɑrkɪdli/ adv marcadamente; notablemente; especialmente, particularmente

marker /'mɑrkər/ n (billiards) marcador, m; (football, etc.) tanteador, m

market /'mɑrkɪt/ n mercado, m; tráfico, m; venta, f; (price) precio, m; (shop) bazar, emporio, m. vt and vi comprar en un mercado; vender en un mercado. **black m.,** mercado negro, estraperlo, m. **open m.,** mercado al aire libre, m; Fig. mercado libre, m. **m. day,** día de mercado, m. **m. garden,** huerto, m, huerta, f. **m. gardener,** hortelano, m. **m.-place,** plaza de mercado, f; Fig. mercado, m. **m. price,** precio corriente, m. **m. stall,** tabanco, puesto de mercado, m. **m.-woman,** verdulera, f

marketable /'mɑrkɪtəbəl/ a comerciable, vendible; corriente

marketing /'mɑrkɪtɪŋ/ n venta, f; compra en un mercado, f; mercado, m. **to go m.,** ir al mercado

marking /'mɑrkɪŋ/ n marca, f; (spot on animals, etc.) pinta, f. **m.-ink,** tinta de marcar, f. **m.-iron,** ferrete, hierro de marcar, m

marksman /'mɑrksmən/ n tirador (-ra)

marksmanship /'mɑrksmən,ʃɪp/ n puntería, f

marl /mɑrl/ n marga, f

marmalade /'mɑrmə,leid/ n mermelada de naranjas amargas, f

marmoset /'mɑrmə,zɛt/ n tití, m

marmot /'mɑrmət/ n Zool. marmota, f

maroon /mə'run/ n (color) marrón, m; (slave) cimarrón (-ona); (firework) petardo, m. a de marrón. vt abandonar, dejar

marquee /mɑr'ki/ n marquesina, f

marqueterie /'mɑrkɪtri/ n marquetería, f

marquis /'mɑrkwɪs/ n marqués, m

marriage /'mærɪdʒ/ n matrimonio, m; unión, f; (wedding) boda, f, casamiento, m. **by m.,** (of relationship) político. **She is an aunt by m.,** tía política. **m. articles,** capitulaciones (matrimoniales) f pl. **m. contract,** contrato matrimonial, m. **m. license,** licencia de casamiento, f. **m. portion,** dote, mf. **m. rate,** nupcialidad, f. **m. register,** acta matrimonial, f. **m. song,** epitalamio, m

marriageable /'mærɪdʒəbəl/ a casadero

married /'mærid/ past part and a casado; matrimonial, conyugal. **newly-m. couple,** los recién casados. **to get m. to,** casarse con. **m. couple,** matrimonio, m, cónyuges, m pl. **m. life,** vida conyugal, f. **married name** n nombre de casada, f

marrow /'mærou/ n tuétano, m, médula, f; Fig. meollo, m. **to the m. of one's bones,** hasta los tuétanos

marrowbone /'mærou,boun/ n hueso medular, m. **on one's marrowbones,** de rodillas

marry /'mæri/ vt casarse con, contraer matrimonio con; casar; (of a priest) unir en matrimonio; Fig. juntar, unir. vi casarse. **to m. again,** volver a casarse

Marseillaise /,mɑrsei'ɛz/ n marsellesa, f

Marseilles /mɑr'sei/ Marsella, f

marsh /mɑrʃ/ n marjal, pantano, Central America chagüe, m. **m.-mallow,** Bot. malvavisco, m. **m. marigold,** calta, f

marshal /'mɑrʃəl/ n mariscal, m, vt poner en orden, arreglar; dirigir. **field-m.,** capitán general de ejército, m

marshaling /'mɑrʃəlɪŋ/ n ordenación, f; dirección, f. **m.-yard,** (railway) apartadero ferroviario, m

marshy /'marʃî/ a pantanoso

mart /mart/ n Poet. plaza de mercado, f; mercado, m; emporio, m; (auction rooms) martillo, m

marten /'martn̩/ n marta, f

martial /'marʃəl/ a militar; marcial, belicoso. **m. array,** orden de batalla, m. **m. law,** derecho militar, m; estado de guerra, m. **m. spirit,** marcialidad, f, espíritu belicoso, m

martially /'marʃəli/ adv militarmente; marcialmente

Martian /'marʃən/ a marciano

martinet /,martn̩'et/ n Mil. ordenancista, m; rigorista, mf

Martinique /,martn̩'ik/ Martinica, f

Martinmas /'martn̩məs/ n día de San Martín, m

martyr /'martər/ n mártir, mf vt martirizar

martyrdom /'martərdəm/ n martirio, m

martyrize /'martə,raiz/ vt martirizar

marvel /'marvəl/ n maravilla, f. **to m. at,** maravillarse de, admirarse de

marvelous /'marvələs/ a maravilloso

marvelousness /'marvələsnɪs/ n maravilla, f, carácter maravilloso, m, lo maravilloso

Marxism /'marksɪzəm/ n marxismo, m

Marxist /'marksɪst/ a and n marxista, mf

marzipan /'marzə,pæn/ n mazapán, m

mascot /'mæskɒt/ n mascota, f

masculine /'mæskyəlɪn/ a masculino; varonil, macho; de hombre; (of a woman) hombruno. n masculino, m

masculinity /,mæskyə'lɪnɪti/ n masculinidad, f

mash /mæʃ/ n mezcla, f; amasijo, m; pasta, f, puré, m. vt mezclar; amasar. **mashed potatoes,** puré de patatas (de papas), m

mask /mæsk/ n máscara, f; antifaz, m; (death) mascarilla, f; (person) máscara, mf. vt enmascarar; Fig. encubrir, disimular. vi ponerse una máscara; disfrazarse. **masked ball,** n baile de máscaras, m

masker /'mæskər/ n máscara, mf

masochism /'mæsə,kɪzəm/ n masoquismo, m

mason /'meisən/ n albañil, m; (freemason) francmasón, masón, m

masonic /mə'sɒnɪk/ a masónico. **m. lodge,** logia de francmasones, f

masonry /'meisənri/ n (trade) albañilería, f; mampostería, f

masque /mæsk/ n mascarada, f

masquerade /,mæskə'reid/ n mascarada, f

masquerader /,mæskə'reidər/ n máscara, mf

mass /mæs/ n misa, f. **to hear m.,** oír misa. **to say m.,** celebrar misa. **high m.,** misa mayor, f. **low m.,** misa rezada, f. **m. book,** libro de misa, m

mass /mæs/ n masa, f; (shape) bulto, m; (heap) montón, m; (great number) muchedumbre, f; (cloud of steam, etc.) nube, f. vt amasar; Mil. concentrar. vi congregarse en masa. **in a m.,** en masa; en conjunto. **the m.** (**of**)..., la mayoría (de)... **the masses,** las masas, el vulgo, el pueblo. **m. formation,** columna cerrada, f. **m.-meeting,** mitin, mitin popular, m. **m.-production,** fabricación en serie, f

massacre /'mæsəkər/ n matanza, carnicería, f, vt hacer una carnicería (de)

massage /mə'saʒ/ n masaje, m; (friction) fricción, f. vt dar un masaje (a)

masseur, masseuse /mə'sɜr; mə'sus/ n masajista, mf

massive /'mæsɪv/ a macizo; sólido

massively /'mæsɪvli/ adv macizamente; sólidamente

massiveness /'mæsɪvnɪs/ n maciez, f; solidez, f

mast /mæst/ n Naut. palo, árbol, m; (for wireless) mástil, m; poste, m; (beech) hayuco, m; (oak) bellota, f. vt Naut. arbolar. **at half-m.,** a media asta. **m.-head,** calcés, tope, m

masted /'mæstɪd/ a arbolado; (in compounds) de... palos

master /'mæstər/ n (of the house, etc.) señor, amo, m; maestro, m; Naut. patrón, m; (owner) dueño, m; (teacher) profesor, maestro, m; (young master and as address) señorito, m; director, m; jefe, m; (expert) perito, m; (of a military order) maestre, m, a maestro; superior. vt dominar; ser maestro en; dominar, conocer a fondo. **This picture is by an old m.,** Este cuadro es de un gran maestro antiguo. **to be m. of**

oneself, ser dueño de sí. **to be one's own m.,** ser dueño de sí mismo; trabajar por su propia cuenta; ser independiente; estar libre. **m. builder,** maestro de obras, m. **m. hand,** mano maestra, f. **M. of Arts,** (academic degree) maestría en artes. **master's degree,** la maestría. **M. of Ceremonies,** maestro de ceremonias, m. **m.-key,** llave maestra, f. **m. mind,** águila, f, ingenio, m. **m. stroke,** golpe maestro, m

masterful /'mæstərfəl/ a imperioso, dominante; autoritario, arbitrario

masterfulness /'mæstərfəlnɪs/ n imperiosidad, f; arbitrariedad, f

masterless /'mæstərlɪs/ a sin amo

masterliness /'mæstərlɪnɪs/ n maestría, f; excelencia, f; perfección, f

masterly /'mæstərli/ a maestro; excelente; perfecto. **m. performance,** obra maestra, f; Theat. representación perfecta, f; ejecución excelente, f

masterpiece /'mæstər,pis/ n obra maestra, f

master plan n plan regulador, m

masterstroke /'mæstər,strouk/ n golpe magistral, golpe de maestro, m

mastery /'mæstəri/ n dominio, m; autoridad, f; poder, m; ventaja, f; superioridad, maestría, f; conocimiento profundo, m. **to gain the m. of,** hacerse el señor de; llegar a dominar

mastic /'mæstɪk/ n masilla, almáciga, f

masticate /'mæstɪ,keit/ vt masticar, mascar

mastication /,mæstɪ'keiʃən/ n masticación, f

mastiff /'mæstɪf/ n mastín, alano, m

mastodon /'mæstə,dɒn/ n mastodonte, m

mastoid /'mæstɔid/ a mastoides. n apófisis mastoides, f

masturbate /'mæstər,beit/ vi masturbarse

masturbation /,mæstər'beiʃən/ n masturbación, f

mat /mæt/ n esterilla, f; alfombrilla, f; (on the table) tapete individual, m. vt (tangle) enmarañar, desgreñar. vi enmarañarse

match /mætʃ/ n Sports. partido, m. (wrestling, boxing) lucha, f; (fencing) asalto, m; (race) carrera, f; (contest) concurso, m; (equal) igual, mf; (pair) pareja, f; compañero (-ra); (marriage) boda, f, casamiento, m; (for lighting) cerilla, f, fósforo, Mexico cerillo, m; (for guns) mecha, f. vt competir con; (equal) igualar; ser igual (a); hacer juego con; emparejar, aparear; armonizar. vi ser igual; hacer juego; armonizarse. **good m.,** Inf. buen partido, m. **as thin as a m.,** más delgado que una cerilla. **to meet one's m.,** dar con la horma de su zapato. **to play a m.,** jugar un partido. **m.-box,** cajita de cerillas, fosforera, f. **m.-seller,** fosforero (-ra)

matchless /'mætʃlɪs/ a incomparable, sin igual, sin par

matchwood /'mætʃ,wʊd/ n madera para cerillas, f

mate /meit/ n compañero, camarada, m; (spouse) compañero (-ra); pareja, f; (on merchant ships) piloto, m; (assistant) ayudante, m; (at chess) mate, m. vt (marry) casar, desposar; (animals, birds) aparear, acoplar; (chess) dar jaque mate (a). vi casarse; aparearse, acoplarse

maté /'matei/ n maté, té del Paraguay, m

materfamilias /,meitərfə'mɪliəs/ n madre de familia, f

material /mə'tɪriəl/ a material; importante, esencial; considerable, sensible, notable; grave. n material, m; materia, f; (fabric) tela, f; tejido, m. **raw materials,** materias primas, f pl. **writing materials,** utensilios de escritorio, m pl; papel de escribir, m

materialism /mə'tɪriə,lɪzəm/ n materialismo, m

materialist /mə'tɪriəlɪst/ n materialista, mf

materialistic /mə,tɪriə'lɪstɪk/ a materialista

materiality /mə,tɪri'ælɪti/ n materialidad, f; importancia, f

materialization /mə,tɪriələ'zeiʃən/ n materialización, f

materialize /mə'tɪriə,laiz/ vt materializar

maternal /mə'tɜrnl/ a materno, maternal. **m. grandparents,** abuelos maternos, m pl

maternity /mə'tɜrnɪti/ n maternidad, f. **m. center,** centro de maternidad, m. **m. hospital,** casa de maternidad, f

mathematical /,mæθə'mætɪkəl/ a matemático

mathematician /ˌmæθəmə'tɪʃən/ n matemático, m
mathematics /ˌmæθə'mætɪks/ n pl; matemáticas, f pl.
applied m., matemáticas prácticas, f pl. **higher m.,**
matemáticas superiores, f pl. **pure m.,** matemáticas
teóricas, f pl
matinee /ˌmætn̩'ei/ n función de tarde, f
mating /'meitɪŋ/ n (of animals) apareamiento, acoplamiento, m; unión, f; casamiento, m
matins /'mætn̩z/ n pl Eccl. maitines, m pl
matriarch /'meitriˌɑrk/ n matriarca, f
matriarchal /ˌmeitri'ɑrkəl/ a matriarcal
matriarchy /'meitriˌɑrki/ n matriarcado, m
matricide /'mætrɪˌsaid/ n (crime) matricidio, m; (person) matricida, mf
matriculate /mə'trɪkyəˌleit/ vt matricular. vi matricularse
matriculation /məˌtrɪkyə'leiʃən/ n matriculación, f
matrimonial /ˌmætrə'mouniəl/ a matrimonial, de
matrimonio; marital. **m. agency,** agencia de matri-
monios, f
matrimony /'mætrəˌmouni/ n matrimonio, m
matrix /'meitrɪks/ n matriz, f
matron /'meitrən/ n matrona, mujer casada, madre
de familia, f; (of a hospital) matrona, f; (of a school)
ama de llaves, f; directora, f. **m. of honor,** (at a wedding) madrina, f
matronly /'meitrənli/ a de matrona, matronal; respetable; serio
matte /mæt/ a mate
matted /'mætɪd/ a enmarañado, enredado
matter /'mætər/ n materia, f; substancia, f; caso, m;
cuestión, f; asunto, m; causa, f; (distance) distancia,
f; (amount) cantidad, f; (duration) espacio de tiempo,
m; (importance) importancia, f; Med. pus, m; pl
matters, asuntos, m pl, etc.; situación, f. **as if nothing were the m.,** como si no hubiese pasado nada.
for that m., en cuanto a eso. **gray m.,** substancia
gris, f. **in the m. of,** en el caso de. **It is a m. of
taste,** Es cuestión de gusto. **printed m.,** impresos, m
pl. **What is the m.?** ¿Qué pasa? ¿Qué hay? **What is
the m. with him?** ¿Qué tiene? ¿Qué le pasa? **m.-of-
course,** cosa natural, f. **m.-of-fact,** práctico; sin
imaginación; positivista. **m. of fact,** n hecho positivo,
m, realidad, f. **As a m. of fact...,** En realidad..., El
caso es que ... **m. of form,** cuestión de fórmula, f;
pura formalidad, f
matter /'mætər/ vi importar; (discharge) supurar.
What does it m.? ¿Qué importa? **It doesn't m.,** Es
igual, No importa, Da lo mismo
Matterhorn, the /'mætərˌhɔrn/ el Matterhorn, m
matting /'mætɪŋ/ n estera, f
mattress /'mætrɪs/ n colchón, m. **spring-m.,** colchón
de muelles, m. **m.-maker,** colchonero, m
mature /mə'tʃʊr/ a maduro/ Com. vencido. vt madurar. vi madurarse; Com. vencer
maturity /mə'tʃʊriti/ n madurez, f; edad madura, f;
(Com. of a bill) vencimiento, m
matutinal /mə'tutn̩l/ a matutino
maudlin /'mɔdlɪn/ a sensiblero; lacrimoso; (tipsy)
calamocano
maul /mɔl/ vt maltratar; herir
Maundy Thursday /'mɔndi/ n Jueves Santo, m
Mauritius /mɔ'rɪʃəs/ Mauricio, m, Isla de Francia, f
mausoleum /ˌmɔsə'liəm/ n mausoleo, m
mauve /mouv/ n color purpúreo delicado, color de
malva, m, a de color de malva
maw /mɔ/ n (of a ruminant) cuajar, m; (of a bird)
buche, m; Fig. abismo, m
mawkish /'mɔkɪʃ/ a insípido, insulso; sensiblero; asqueroso
mawkishness /'mɔkɪʃnɪs/ n insipidez, insulsez, f;
sensiblería, f; asquerosidad, f
maxilla /mæk'sɪlə/ n hueso maxilar, maxilar, m
maxillary /'mæksəˌlɛri/ a maxilar
maxim /'mæksɪm/ n máxima, f
maximum /'mæksəməm/ a máximo. n máximo, m
may /mei/ v aux poder; ser posible; (expressing
wish, hope) ojalá que..., Dios quiera que..., or the
present subjunctive may be used, e.g. May you live
many years! ¡(qué) Viva Vd. muchos años! (to denote

uncertainty, the future tense of the verb is often used,
e.g. You may perhaps remember the date, Vd. quizás
se acordará de la fecha. Who may he be? ¿Quién
será?) **May God grant it!** ¡(que) Dios lo quiera! **It
may be that...,** Puede ser que..., Es posible que...,
Quizás... **He may come on Saturday,** Es posible que
venga el sábado; Puede venir el sábado. **May I come
in?** ¿Puedo entrar? ¿Se puede entrar? **May I come and
see you?** ¿Me das permiso para hacerte una visita?
¿Me dejas venir a verte? **May I go then?** ¿Puedo irme
pues? ¿Tengo permiso para marcharme entonces?
May /mei/ n mayo, m; Fig. abril, m; Bot. espina
blanca, f. **May Day,** primero de mayo, m. **mayflower,** flor del cuclillo, f. **mayfly,** cachipolla, f. **May
queen,** maya, f
maybe /'meibi/ adv quizás, tal vez
mayonnaise /ˌmeiə'neiz/ n mayonesa, f. **m. sauce,**
salsa mayonesa, f
mayor /'meiər/ n alcalde, m, alcaldesa, f, Argentina
intendente, m
mayoral /'meiərəl/ a de alcalde
mayoralty /'meiərəlti/ n Argentina intendencia, f
maypole /'mei,poul/ n mayo, m. **m. dance,** danza de
cintas, f
maze /meiz/ n laberinto, m; Fig. perplejidad, f. vt dejar perplejo, aturdir
mazurka /mə'zɜrkə/ n mazurca, f
me /mi/ pron me; (after a preposition only) mí. **They
sent it for me,** Lo mandaron para mí. **Dear me!** ¡Ay
de mí!
meadow /'mɛdou/ n prado, m, pradera, f. **m.-sweet,**
reina de los prados, f
meager /'migər/ a magro, enjuto, flaco; (scanty) exiguo, escaso, insuficiente; pobre; Fig. árido
meagerness /'migərnɪs/ n exigüidad, escasez, f; pobreza, f; Fig. aridez, f
meal /mil/ n comida, f; (flour) harina, f. **to have a
good m.,** comer bien. **test m.,** Med. comida de
prueba, f. **m.-time,** hora de comida, f
mealy /'mili/ a harinoso; (of the complexion) pastoso
mean /min/ a (middle) mediano; (average) mediano; (humble) humilde; pobre; inferior; bajo, vil,
ruin; (avaricious) tacaño, mezquino, Argentina agalludo, Chile, Peru coñete, **m.-spirited,** vil, de alma
ruin
mean /min/ n medio, m; medianía, f; pl means, medio, m; expediente, m; medios, m pl; (financial) recursos, m pl; modo, m, manera, f. **by all means,** por
todos los medios; (certainly) ¡ya lo creo! ¡no faltaba
más! ¡naturalmente! **by means of,** mediante, por medio de; con la ayuda de. **by no means,** de ningún
modo; nada. **by some means,** de algún modo, de alguna manera
mean /min/ vt destinar (para); pretender, proponerse; intentar, pensar, querer decir, significar; importar; (wish) querer; (concern, speak about) tratarse
(de). vi tener el propósito, tener la intención. **I did
not m. to do it,** Lo hice sin querer. **What does this
word m.?** ¿Qué significa esta palabra? **What do you
m. by that?** ¿Qué quieres decir con eso? **This portrait
is meant to be Joan,** Este retrato quiere ser Juana.
What do they m. to do? ¿Qué piensan (or se pro-
ponen) hacer? **Do you really m. it?** ¿Lo dices en
serio? **Charles always means well,** Carlos siempre
tiene buenas intenciones
meander /mi'ændər/ n meandro, serpenteo, m;
camino tortuoso, m, vi serpentear; errar, vagar; (in
talk) divagar
meandering /mi'ændərɪŋ/ n meandros, m pl, serpenteo, m; (in talk) divagaciones, f pl, a serpentino,
tortuoso
meaning /'minɪŋ/ n intención, voluntad, f; significación, f, significado, m; (of words) acepción, f; (sense)
sentido, m; (thought) pensamiento, m. a significante.
double m., doble intención, f. **He gave me a m.
look,** Me miró con intención. **What is the m. of it?**
¿Qué significa? ¿Qué quiere decir?
meaningful /'minɪŋfəl/ a significante
meaningless /'minɪŋlɪs/ a sin sentido; insensato; insignificante
meanness /'minnɪs/ n pobreza, f; inferioridad, f; me-

diocridad, *f*; bajeza, ruindad, *f*; (stinginess) mezquindad, tacañería, *Lat. Am. also* lechería, *f*

meantime, meanwhile /'min,taim/ 'min,wail/ *n* ínterin, *m, adv* entre tanto, mientras tanto, a todo esto. **in the m.,** mientras tanto, en el ínterin

measles /'mizəlz/ *n* sarampión, *m*. **German m.,** rubéola, *f*

measurable /'mɛʒərəbəl/ *a* mensurable

measure /'mɛʒər/ *n* medida, *f*; capacidad, *f*; (for measuring) regla, *f*; número, *m*; proporción, *f*; (limit) límite, *m*; (*Fig.* step) medida, *f*; (meter) metro, *m*; *Mus.* compás, *m*; (degree) grado, *m*; manera, *f*; (parliamentary) proyecto (de ley), *m. vt* medir; proporcionar, distribuir; (water) aforar; (land) apear; (height of persons) tallar; (for clothes) tomar las medidas (a); (judge) juzgar; (test) probar; (*Poet.* traverse) recorrer. **a suit made to m.,** un traje hecho a medida. **in great m.,** en gran manera, en alto grado. **in some m.,** hasta cierto punto. **to m. one's length,** caer tendido. **to take a person's m.,** *Fig.* tomar las medidas (a). **to m. up to,** *Fig.* estar al nivel de, ser igual a

measured /'mɛʒərd/ *a* mesurado, moderado; uniforme; limitado. **to walk with m. tread,** andar a pasos contados

measurement /'mɛʒərmənt/ *n* medición, *f*; medida, *f*; dimensión, *f*

meat /mit/ *n* carne, *f*; (food) alimento, *m*; (meal) comida, *f*; *Fig.* substancia, *f*. **to sit at m.,** estar a la mesa. **cold meats,** fiambres, *m pl*. **m.-ball,** albóndiga, *f*. **m.-chopper,** picador, *m*. **m.-dish,** fuente, *f*. **m.-eater,** comedor (-ra) de carne. **m. extract,** carne concentrada, *f*. **m.-market,** carnicería, *f*. **m.-pie,** pastel de carne, *m*. **m.-safe,** fresquera, *f*

meaty /'miti/ *a* carnoso; *Fig.* substancial

Mecca /'mɛkə/ la Meca, *f*

mechanic /mə'kænɪk/ *n* mecánico, *m*

mechanical /mə'kænɪkəl/ *a* mecánico; maquinal

mechanically /mə'kænɪkli/ *adv* mecánicamente; maquinalmente

mechanical pencil *n* lapicero, *m*

mechanics /mə'kænɪks/ *n* mecánica, *f*

mechanism /'mɛkə,nɪzəm/ *n* mecanismo, *m*; (philosophy) mecanicismo, *m*

mechanize /'mɛkə,naiz/ *vt* convertir en máquina; (gen. *Mil.*) mecanizar; motorizar

medal /'mɛdl/ *n* medalla, *f*

medallion /mə'dælyən/ *n* medallón, *m*

medallist /'mɛdlɪst/ *n* grabador de medallas, *m*; el, *m*, (*f*, la) que recibe una medalla

meddle /'mɛdl/ *vi* tocar; meterse (con or en); entremeterse, inmiscuirse; intrigar

meddler /'mɛdlər/ *n* entremetido (-da); intrigante, *mf*

meddlesome /'mɛdlsəm/ *a* entremetido; oficioso; impertinente; enredador, intrigante. **to be very m.,** meterse en todo

meddlesomeness /'mɛdlsəmnɪs/ *n* entremetimiento, *m*; oficiosidad, *f*; impertinencia, *f*; intrigas, *f pl*

media, the /'midiə/ los medios informativos, *m pl*

median /'midiən/ *a* del medio

mediate /*v* 'midi,eit/ *a* -ɪt/ *vi* intervenir, mediar, arbitrar; abogar (por). *a* medio; interpuesto

mediation /,midi'eiʃən/ *n* mediación, intervención, *f*; intercesión, *f*; interposición, *f*

mediator /'midi,eitər/ *n* mediador (-ra); arbitrador (-ra); intercesor (-ra)

mediatory /'midiə,tɔri/ *a* de mediador; intercesor

medical /'mɛdɪkəl/ *a* médico; de medicina; de médico. *n Inf.* estudiante de medicina, *m*. **Army M. Service,** Servicio de Sanidad Militar, *m*. **M. books,** libros de medicina, *m pl*. **m. examination,** examen médico, *m*, exploración médica, *f*. **m. jurisprudence,** medicina legal, *f*. **m. knowledge,** conocimientos médicos, *m pl*. **m. practitioner,** médico (-ca). **m. school,** escuela de medicina, *f*

medicate /'mɛdɪ,keit/ *vt* medicar; medicinar

medicated /'mɛdɪ,keitɪd/ *a* medicado

medication /,mɛdɪ'keiʃən/ *n* medicación, *f*, *Lat. Am.* medicamentos, *m pl*

medicinal /mə'dɪsənl/ *a* medicinal

medicine /'mɛdəsɪn/ *n* medicina, *f*; medicamento, *m*; (charm) ensalmo, hechizo, *m*. **patent m.,** específico

farmacéutico, *m*. **m. ball,** balón medical, *m*. **m. chest,** botiquín, *m*. **m. man,** hechizador, *m*

medico- *prefix* médico-. **m.-legal,** médicolegal

medieval /,midi'ivəl/ *a* medieval

medievalism /,midi'ivə,lɪzəm/ *n* afición a la edad media, *f*; espíritu medieval, *m*

mediocre /,midi'oukər/ *a* mediocre

mediocrity /,midi'ɒkrɪti/ *n* mediocridad, *f*; medianía, *f*

meditate /'mɛdɪ,teit/ *vt* idear, proyectar, meditar. *vi* meditar, reflexionar; pensar, intentar

meditation /,mɛdɪ'teiʃən/ *n* meditación, *f*

meditative /'mɛdɪ,teitɪv/ *a* meditabundo, contemplativo; de meditación

meditatively /'mɛdɪ,teitɪvli/ *adv* reflexivamente

Mediterranean /,mɛdɪtə'reiniən/ *a* mediterráneo. *n* Mar Mediterráneo, *m*

medium /'midiəm/ *n* medio, *m*; (cooking) término medio, a medio cocer, a medio asar, *m*; (environment) medio ambiente, *m*; (agency) intermediario, *m*; (spiritualism) médium, *m*; *Art.* medio, *m, a* mediano; regular; mediocre. **through the m. of,** por medio de. **m.-sized,** de tamaño regular

medlar /'mɛdlər/ *n* (fruit) níspola, *f*; (tree) níspero, *m*

medley /'mɛdli/ *n* mezcla, *f*; miscelánea, *f, a* mezclado, mixto

medulla /mə'dʌlə/ *n* medula, *f*

meek /mik/ *a* dulce, manso; humilde; modesto; pacífico

meekly /'mikli/ *adv* mansamente; humildemente; modestemente

meekness /'miknɪs/ *n* mansedumbre, *f*; humildad, *f*; modestia, *f*

meet /mit/ *vt* encontrar; encontrarse con; tropezar con; (by arrangement) reunirse con; (make the acquaintance of) conocer (a); (satisfy) satisfacer; cumplir (con); (a bill) pagar, saldar; (refute) refutar; (fight) batirse (con); (confront) hacer frente (a). *vi* juntarse; encontrarse; reunirse; verse; (of rivers) confluir. *n* montería, *f, a* conveniente. **I shall m. you at the station,** Te esperaré en la estación. **Until we m. again!** ¡Hasta la vista! **to go to m.,** ir al encuentro de. **to m. half-way,** encontrar a la mitad del camino; partir la diferencia (con); hacer concesiones (a). **to m. the eye,** saltar a la vista. **to m. with,** encontrar; experimentar; sufrir

meeting /'mitɪŋ/ *n* encuentro, *m*; reunión, *f*; (interview) entrevista, *f*; (of rivers, etc.) confluencia, *f*; (public, etc.) mitin, *m*; (council) concilio, *m*; concurso, *m*; (race) concurso de carreras de caballos, *m*. **creditors',** concurso de acreedores, *m*. **m.-house,** templo de los Cuáqueros, *m*. **m.-place,** lugar de reunión, *m*; lugar de cita, *m*; centro, *m*. **to adjourn the m.,** levantar la sesión. **to call a m.,** convocar una sesión. **to open the m.,** abrir la sesión

megalomania /,mɛgəlou'meiniə/ *n* megalomanía, *f*; monomanía de grandezas, *f*

megalomaniac /,mɛgəlou'meiniæk/ *n* megalómano (-na)

megaphone /'mɛgə,foun/ *n* megáfono, portavoz, *m*

Meknès /mɛk'nɛs/ Mequínez, *f*

melancholy /'mɛlən,kɒli/ *a* melancólico. *n* melancolía, *f*

mellifluence /mə'lɪfluəns/ *n* melifluidad, *f*

mellifluous /mə'lɪfluəs/ *a* melifluo; dulce

mellow /'mɛlou/ *a* maduro; dulce; (of wine) rancio; blando; suave; (of sound) melodioso; (slang) alegre; (tipsy) entre dos luces. *vt* madurar; ablandar; suavizar. *vi* madurarse

mellowing /'mɛlouɪŋ/ *n* maduración, *f*

mellowness /'mɛlouɪs/ *n* madurez, *f*; dulzura, *f*; (of wine) ranciedad, *f*; blandura, *f*; suavidad, *f*; melodía, *f*

melodic /mə'lɒdɪk/ *a* melódico

melodious /mə'loudiəs/ *a* melodioso

melodiously /mə'loudiəsli/ *adv* melodiosamente

melodiousness /mə'loudiəsnɪs/ *n* melodía, *f*

melodrama /'mɛlə,drɑmə/ *n* melodrama, *m*

melodramatic /,mɛlədrə'mætɪk/ *a* melodramático

melody /'mɛlədi/ *n* melodía, *f*

melon /'mɛlən/ *n* melón, *m*; sandía, *f*. **slice of m.,**

raja de melón, *f.* **m. bed,** sandiar, *m.* **m.-shaped,** amelonado

melt /mɛlt/ *vi* derretirse; deshacerse; disolverse; evaporarse; desaparecer; (of money, etc.) hacerse sal y agua; (relent) enternecerse, ablandarse. *vt* fundir; (snow, etc.) derretir; (*Fig.* soften) ablandar. **He melted away,** *Inf.* Se escurrió. **to m. into tears,** deshacerse en lágrimas. **to m. down,** fundir

melting /'mɛltɪŋ/ *a* fundente; (forgiving) indulgente; (tender) de ternura; lánguido; dulce. *n* fusión, *f*; derretimiento, *m.* **m. point,** punto de fusión, *m.* **m. pot,** *Metall.* crisol, *m*; *Fig.* caldera de razas, *f, m*

member /'mɛmbər/ *n* miembro, *m*; (of a club, etc.) socio (-ia). **M. of Congress,** representante del Congreso de los Estados Unidos, congresista, *mf*

membership /'mɛmbərˌʃɪp/ *n* calidad de miembro, socio(-ia); número de miembros (*or* socios), *m*, composición, integración, *f*

membrane /'mɛmbrein/ *n* membrana, *f*

membranous /'mɛmbrənəs/ *a* membranoso

memento /mə'mɛntou/ *n* recuerdo, *m*

memoir /'mɛmwɑr/ *n* memoria, *f*

memorable /'mɛmərəbəl/ *a* memorable

memorably /'mɛmərəbli/ *adv* memorablemente

memorandum /ˌmɛmə'rændəm/ *n* memorándum, *m*

memorial /mə'mɔriəl/ *a* conmemorativo. *n* monumento conmemorativo, *m*; memorial, *m*

memorize /'mɛməˌraiz/ *vt* aprender de memoria

memory /'mɛməri/ *n* memoria, *f*; recuerdo, *m.* **from m.,** de memoria. **If my m. does not deceive me,** Si mal no me acuerdo. **in m. of,** en conmemoración de; en recuerdo de

memory span *n* retentiva memorística, *f*

menace /'mɛnɪs/ *n* amenaza, *f*, *vt* amenazar

menacing /'mɛnəsɪŋ/ *a* amenazador

menacingly /'mɛnəsɪŋli/ *adv* con amenazas

menagerie /mə'nædʒəri/ *n* colección de fieras, *f*; casa de fieras, *f*

mend /mɛnd/ *vt* remendar; componer; reparar; (darn) zurcir; (rectify) remediar; reformar; enmendar; (a fire) echar carbón (or leña, etc.) a; (one's pace) avivar. *vi* (in health and of the weather) mejorar. *n* remiendo, *m*; (darn) zurcido, *m.* **to be on the m.,** ir mejorando. **to m. one's ways,** reformarse, enmendarse

mendacious /mɛn'deiʃəs/ *a* mendaz

mendacity /mɛn'dæsɪti/ *n* mendacidad, *f*

Mendelism /'mɛndl̩ˌɪzəm/ *n* mendelismo, *m*

mender /'mɛndər/ *n* componedor (-ra); (darner) zurcidor (-ra); reparador (-ra); (cobbler and tailor) remendón, *m*

mendicancy /'mɛndɪkənsi/ *n* mendicidad, *f*

mendicant /'mɛndɪkənt/ *a* mendicante. *n* mendicante, *mf.* **m. friar,** fraile mendicante, *m*

mending /'mɛndɪŋ/ *n* compostura, *f*; reparación, *f*; (darning) zurcidura, *f*; ropa por zurcir, *f*

menial /'miniəl/ *a* doméstico; servil; bajo, ruin. *n* criado (-da); lacayo, *m*

meningeal /ˌmɛnɪn'dʒiəl/ *a* meningeo

meningitis /ˌmɛnɪn'dʒaitɪs/ *n* meningitis, *f*

menopause /'mɛnəˌpɔz/ *n* menopausia, *f*

menses /'mɛnsiz/ *n* menstruación, *f*

menstrual /'mɛnstruəl/ *a* menstrual

menstruate /'mɛnstruˌeit/ *vi* menstruar

menstruation /ˌmɛnstru'eiʃən/ *n* menstruación, *f*

mental /'mɛntl̩/ *a* mental; intelectual. **m. derangement,** enajenación mental, *f.* **m. hospital,** manicomio, *m*

mentality /mɛn'tæliti/ *n* mentalidad, *f*

mentally /'mɛntl̩i/ *adv* mentalmente. **m. deficient,** anormal

menthol /'mɛnθɔl/ *n* mentol, *m*

mention /'mɛnʃən/ *n* mención, *f*; alusión, *f. vt* hacer mención (de), mencionar, mentar, hablar (de); aludir (a); (quote) citar; (in dispatches) nombrar. **Don't m. it!** (keep silent) ¡No digas nada!; (you're welcome) ¡No hay de que!

mentor /'mɛntɔr/ *n* mentor, *m*

menu /'mɛnyu/ *n* menú, *m*; lista de platos, *f*

meow /mi'au/ *vi* maullar. *n* maullido, *m*

Mephistophelean /ˌmɛfəstə'filiən/ *a* mefistofélico

mercantile /'mɜrkənˌtil/ *a* mercantil; mercante. *m.* **law,** derecho mercantil, *m.* **m. marine,** marina mercante, *f*

mercantilism /'mɜrkəntɪˌlɪzəm/ *n* mercantilismo, *m*

mercenariness /'mɜrsəˌnɛrinɪs/ *n* lo mercenario

mercenary /'mɜrsəˌnɛri/ *a* mercenario. *n* (soldier) mercenario, *m*

mercer /'mɜrsər/ *n* mercero, *m*

mercerize /'mɜrsəˌraiz/ *vt* mercerizar

mercery /'mɜrsəri/ *n* mercería, *f*

merchandise /'mɜrtʃənˌdaiz/ *n* mercancía, *f*

merchant /'mɜrtʃənt/ *n* traficante (en), *mf*, negociante (en), *m*; comerciante, *mf. Lat. Am.* marchante (-ta), *mf* mercader, *m. a* mercante. **The M. of Venice,** El Mercader de Venecia. **m. navy, service,** marina mercante, *f.* **m. ship,** buque mercante, *m*

merchantman /'mɜrtʃəntmən/ *n* buque mercante, *m*

merciful /'mɜrsɪfəl/ *a* misericordioso, piadoso; compasivo; clemente; indulgente

mercifully /'mɜrsɪfəli/ *adv* misericordiosamente; compasivamente; con indulgencia

mercifulness /'mɜrsɪfəlnɪs/ *n* misericordia, *f*; compasión, *f*; indulgencia, *f*

merciless /'mɜrsɪlɪs/ *a* despiadado, inhumano

mercilessly /'mɜrsɪlɪsli/ *adv* sin piedad

mercilessness /'mɜrsɪlɪsnɪs/ *n* inhumanidad, *f*; falta de compasión, *f*

mercurial /mər'kyʊriəl/ *a* mercurial; (changeable) volátil; (lively) vivo

mercury /'mɜrkyəri/ *n* mercurio, *m*; (*Astron.* and *Myth.*) Mercurio, *m.* **Mercury's wand,** caduceo, *m*

mercy /'mɜrsi/ *n* misericordia, *f*; compasión, *f*; clemencia, *f*; indulgencia, *f*; merced, *f.* **at the m. of the elements,** a la intemperie. **to be at the m. of,** estar a la merced de

mere /miər/ *a* mero; simple; no más que, solo. *n* lago, *m*

merely /'miərli/ *adv* meramente, solamente; simplemente, sencillamente

meretricious /ˌmɛrɪ'trɪʃəs/ *a* (archaic) meretricio; (flashy) de oropel; llamativo, charro

meretriciousness /ˌmɛrɪ'trɪʃəsnɪs/ *n* mal gusto, *m*

merge /mɜrdʒ/ *vt* fundir; *Com.* fusionar; mezclar. *vi* fundirse; *Com.* fusionarse; mezclarse

merger /'mɜrdʒər/ *n* combinación, *f*; *Com.* fusión, *f*

meridian /mə'rɪdiən/ *n* (*Geog. Astron.*) meridiano, *m*; (noon) mediodía, *m*; (peak) apogeo, *m*

meringue /mə'ræŋ/ *n* merengue, *m, Lat. Am.* espumilla, *f*

merino /mə'rinou/ *a* de merino; merino. *n* (fabric and sheep) merino, *m*

merit /'mɛrɪt/ *n* mérito, *m*, *vt* merecer, ser digno de

meritorious /ˌmɛrɪ'tɔriəs/ *a* meritorio

meritoriously /ˌmɛrɪ'tɔriəsli/ *adv* merecidamente

meritoriousness /ˌmɛrɪ'tɔriəsnɪs/ *n* mérito, *m*

merlon /'mɜrlən/ *n* merlón, *m*, almena, *f*

mermaid /'mɜrˌmeid/ *n* sirena, *f*

merrily /'mɛrɪli/ *adv* alegremente

merriment /'mɛrimənt/ *n* alegría, *f*; júbilo, *m*; regocijo, *m*; diversión, *f*; juego, *m*

merry /'mɛri/ *a* alegre; jovial; feliz; regocijado, divertido; (tipsy) calamocano. **to make m.,** divertirse. **to make m. over,** reírse de. **M. Christmas!** ¡Felices Navidades! **m.-go-round,** caballitos, *m pl*, tiovivo, *m, Lat. Am.* calesita, *f.* **m.-making,** festividades, fiestas, *f pl*

meseta /me'seta/ *n* meseta, *f*

mesh /mɛʃ/ *n* malla, *f*; *Mech.* engranaje, *m*; (network) red, *f*; (snare) lazo, *m. vt* coger con red; *Mech.* endentar

mesmerism /'mɛzməˌrɪzəm/ *n* mesmerismo, *m*

mesmerize /'mɛzməˌraiz/ *vt* hipnotizar

mess /mɛs/ *n* (of food) plato de comida, *m*; porción, ración, *f*; rancho, *m*; (mixture) mezcla, *f*; (disorder) desorden, *m*; suciedad, *f*; *Inf.* reguero, *m*; (failure) fracaso, *m. vt* (dirty) ensuciar; desordenar; (mismanage) echar a perder. **to be in a m.,** *Inf.* estar aviado. **to get in a m.,** *Inf.* hacerse un lío. **to make a m. of,** ensuciar; desordenar; (spoil) echarlo todo a rodar

message /'mɛsɪdʒ/ *n* mensaje, *m*; recado, *m*; (telegraphic) parte, *m*. **I have to take a m.**, Tengo que hacer un recado

messenger /'mɛsəndʒər/ *n* mensajero (-ra); (of telegrams) repartidor, *m*; heraldo, *m*; anuncio, *m*

Messiah /mɪ'saiə/ *n* Mesías, *m*

Messianic /ˌmɛsi'ænɪk/ *a* mesiánico

messrs. /'mɛsərz/ *n pl* (abbreviation) sres. (from señores), *m pl*

metabolism /mə'tæbəˌlɪzəm/ *n* metabolismo, *m*

metabolize /mə'tæbəˌlaiz/ *va* metabolizar

metal /'mɛtl/ *n* metal, *m*; vidrio en fusión, *m*; (road) grava, *f*; *Herald.* metal, *m*; (mettle) temple, temperamento, *m*; brío, fuego, *m*; *pl* metals, (of a railway) rieles, *m pl*. **m. engraver**, grabador en metal, *m*. **m. polish**, limpiametales, *m*. **m. shavings**, cizallas, *f pl*. **m. work**, metalistería, *f*. **m. worker**, metalario, *m*

metallic /mə'tælɪk/ *a* metálico

metalloid /'mɛtlˌɔid/ *n* metaloide, *m*

metallurgic /ˌmɛtl'ɜrdʒɪk/ *a* metalúrgico

metallurgist /'mɛtlˌɜrdʒɪst/ *n* metalúrgico, *m*

metallurgy /'mɛtlˌɜrdʒi/ *n* metalurgia, *f*

metamorphosis /ˌmɛtə'mɔrfəsɪs/ *n* metamorfosis, *f*

metaphor /'mɛtəˌfɔr/ *n* metáfora, *f*

metaphorical /ˌmɛtə'fɔrɪkəl/ *a* metafórico

metaphysical /ˌmɛtə'fɪzɪkəl/ *a* metafísico

metaphysician /ˌmɛtəfə'zɪʃən/ *n* metafísico, *m*

metaphysics /ˌmɛtə'fɪzɪks/ *n* metafísica, *f*

metathesis /mə'tæθəsɪs/ *n* metátesis, *f*

mete /mit/ *vt* repartir, distribuir

metempsychosis /məˌtɛmsə'kousɪs/ *n* metempsicosis, *f*

meteor /'mitiər/ *n* meteoro, *m*

meteoric /ˌmiti'ɔrɪk/ *a* meteórico

meteorite /'mitiəˌrait/ *n* meteorito, *m*

meteorological /ˌmitiərə'lɒdʒɪkəl/ *a* meteorológico

meteorologist /ˌmitiə'rɒlədʒɪst/ *n* meteorologista, *mf*

meteorology /ˌmitiə'rɒlədʒi/ *n* meteorología, *f*

meter /'mitər/ *n* (for gas, etc.) contador, *m*; (verse and measure) metro, *m*

methane /'mɛθein/ *n* metano, *m*

method /'mɛθəd/ *n* método, *m*; técnica, *f*; táctica, *f*

methodical /mə'θɒdɪkəl/ *a* metódico; ordenado, sistemático

Methodism /'mɛθəˌdɪzəm/ *n* metodismo, *m*

Methodist /'mɛθədɪst/ *n* metodista, *mf*

methyl /'mɛθəl/ *n* metilo, *m*. **m. alcohol**, alcohol metílico, *m*

methylated spirit /'mɛθəˌleitɪd/ *n* alcohol desnaturalizado, *m*

meticulous /mə'tɪkyələs/ *a* meticuloso; minucioso

meticulously /mə'tɪkyələsli/ *adv* con meticulosidad

meticulousness /mə'tɪkyələsnɪs/ *n* meticulosidad, *f*; minuciosidad, *f*

metric /'mɛtrɪk/ *a* métrico. **m. system**, sistema métrico, *m*

metrics /'mɛtrɪks/ *n* métrica, *f*

metronome /'mɛtrəˌnoum/ *n* metrónomo, *m*

metropolis /mɪ'trɒpəlɪs/ *n* metrópoli, *f*; capital, *f*

metropolitan /ˌmɛtrə'pɒlɪtn/ *a* metropolitano; de la capital. *n Eccl.* metropolitano, *m*

mettle /'mɛtl/ *n* temple, temperamento, *m*; fuego, brío, *m*; valor, *m*

mew /myu/ *n* (gull) gaviota, *f*; (of a cat) maullido, *m; (of sea-birds) alarido, m. *vi* (of a cat) maullar; (of sea-birds) dar alaridos. **to mew up**, encerrar

mews /myuz/ *n* establos, *m pl*, caballeriza, *f*

Mexican /'mɛksɪkən/ *a* mexicano, mejicano. *n* mexicano (-na), mejicano (-na)

Mexico /'mɛksɪˌkou/ México, Méjico, *m*

mezzanine /'mɛzəˌnin/ *n* entresuelo, *m*

mezzosoprano /'mɛtsou sə'prænou/ *n* mezzosoprano

mi /mi/ *n Mus.* mi, *m*

miaow /mi'au/ *n* miau, *m*, *vi* maullar

miasma /mai'æzmə/ *n* miasma, *m*

miasmatic /ˌmaiəz'mætɪk/ *a* miasmático

mica /'maikə/ *n* mica, *f*

microbe /'maikroub/ *n* microbio, *m*

microbial /mai'kroubiəl/ *a* microbiano

microbiologist /ˌmaikroubai'ɒlədʒɪst/ *n* microbiólogo, *m*

microbiology /ˌmaikroubai'ɒlədʒi/ *n* microbiología, *f*

microchip /'maikrouˌtʃɪp/ *n* microchip *m*, microplaqueta, *f*

microcosm /'maikrəˌkɒzəm/ *n* microcosmo, *m*

microphone /'maikrəˌfoun/ *n* micrófono, *m*

microscope /'maikrəˌskoup/ *n* microscopio, *m*

microscopic /ˌmaikrə'skɒpɪk/ *a* microscópico

microwave /'maikrouˌweiv/ *n* microonda, *f*

mid /mɪd/ *a* medio. *prep* entre; en medio de; a mediados de. **from mid May to August**, desde mediados de mayo hasta agosto. **a mid-fourteenth century castle**, un castillo de mediados del siglo catorce. **in mid air**, en medio del aire. **in mid channel**, en medio del canal. **in mid winter**, en medio del invierno

midday /'mɪd'dei/ *n* mediodía, *m*, *a* del mediodía, meridional. **at m.**, a mediodía

middle /'mɪdl/ *a* medio; en medio de; del centro; intermedio; (average) mediano. *n* medio, *m*; mitad, *f*; centro, *m*; (waist) cintura, *f*. **in the m. of**, en medio de. **in the m. of nowhere**, donde Cristo dio las tres voces. **toward the m. of the month**, a mediados del mes. **m. age**, edad madura, *f*. **m.-aged**, de edad madura, de cierta edad. **M. Ages**, edad media, *f*. **m. class**, clase media, burguesía, *f*, a de la clase media, burgués. **m. distance**, término medio, *m*. **m. ear**, oído medio, *m*. **m. finger**, dedo de en medio (or del corazón), *m*. **m. way**, *Fig.* término medio, *m*. **weight**, peso medio, *m*

Middle East, the el Medio Oriente, el Oriente Medio, el Levante, *m*

middleman /'mɪdlˌmæn/ *n* agente de negocios, *m*; (retailer) revendedor, *m*; intermediario, *m*

middling /'mɪdlɪŋ/ *a* mediano; mediocre; regular; así, así

midge /mɪdʒ/ *n* mosquito, *m*, mosca de agua, *f*

midget /'mɪdʒɪt/ *n* enano (-na). **m. submarine**, submarino de bolsillo, *m*

midnight /'mɪdˌnait/ *n* medianoche, *f*. *a* de medianoche; nocturno. **at m.**, a medianoche. **to burn the m. oil**, quemarse las cejas. **m. mass**, misa del gallo, *f*

midriff /'mɪdrɪf/ *n* diafragma, *m*

midship /'mɪdˌʃɪp/ *a* maestro *n* medio del buque, *m*. **m. beam**, bao maestro, *m*. **m. gangway**, crujía, *f*

midshipman /'mɪdˌʃɪpmən/ *n* guardiamarina, *m*

midst /mɪdst/ *n* medio, *m*; seno, *m*, *prep* entre. **in the m. of**, en medio de. **There is a traitor in our m.**, Hay un traidor entre nosotros (or en nuestra compañía)

midstream /'mɪd'strim/ *n* **in m.**, en medio de la corriente, *m*

midsummer /'mɪd'sʌmər/ *n* pleno verano, *m*; solsticio estival, *m*; fiesta de San Juan, *f*. **A M. Night's Dream**, El Sueño de la Noche de San Juan

midway /*adv*, *a* 'mɪd'wei; *n* -ˌwei/ *a* and *adv* situado a medio camino; a medio camino, a la mitad del camino; entre. *n* mitad del camino, *f*; medio, *m*. **m. between...**, equidistante de..., entre

midwife /'mɪdˌwaif/ *n* comadrona, partera, *f*

midwifery /mɪd'wɪfəri/ *n* obstetricia, *f*

midwinter /'mɪd'wɪntər/ *n* medio del invierno, *m*

mien /min/ *n* aire, *m*; porte, semblante, *m*

might /mait/ *vi* poder. **It m. or m. not be true.**, Podría o no podría ser verdad. **How happy Mary have been!** ¡Qué feliz pudo haber sido María! **I thought that you m. have seen him in the theater,** Creí que pudieras haberle visto en el teatro. **That I m....!** ¡Que yo pudiese...! **This m. have been avoided if...**, Esto podía haberse evitado si...

might /mait/ *n* fuerza, *f*; poder, *m*. **with m. and main**, con todas sus fuerzas

mightily /'maitli/ *adv* fuertemente; poderosamente; *Inf.* muchísimo; sumamente

mightiness /'maitinɪs/ *n* fuerza, *f*; poder, *m*; grandeza, *f*

mighty /'maiti/ *a* fuerte, vigoroso; poderoso; grande; *Inf.* enorme; (proud) arrogante. *adv Inf.* enormemente, muy

migraine /'maigrein/ *n* migraña, jaqueca, *f*

migrant /'maigrənt/ *a* migratorio, de paso. *n* ave migratoria, ave de paso, *f*
migrate /'maigreit/ *vi* emigrar
migration /mai'greiʃən/ *n* migración, *f*
migratory /'maigrə,tɔri/ *a* migratorio, de paso; (of people) nómada, pasajero
migratory worker *n* trabajador golondrino, *m*
Milanese /,milə'niz/ *a* milanés. *n* milanés (-esa)
milch /miltʃ/ *a f*, (of cows) lechera
mild /maild/ *a* apacible, pacífico; manso; dulce; suave; (of the weather) blando; *Med.* benigno; (light) leve; (of drinks) ligero; (weak) débil
mildew /'mil,du/ *n* mildiu, añublo, *m*; moho, *m*. *vt* anublar; enmohecer. *vi* anublarse; enmohecerse
mildly /'maildli/ *adv* suavemente; dulcemente; con indulgencia
mildness /'maildnis/ *n* apacibilidad, *f*; mansedumbre, *f*; suavidad, *f*; (of weather) blandura, *f*; dulzura, *f*; indulgencia, *f*; (weakness) debilidad, *f*
mile /mail/ *n* milla, *f*
mileage /'mailidʒ/ *n* distancia en millas, *f*; kilometraje, *m*
milestone /'mail,stoun/ *n* hito, *m*, piedra miliaria, *f*; mojón kilométrico, *m*
milfoil /'mil,fɔil/ *n Bot.* milenrama, *f*
militancy /'militənsi/ *n* carácter militante, *m*; belicosidad, *f*
militant /'militənt/ *a* militante, combatiente; belicoso; agresivo. *n* combatiente, *mf*
militarily /,mili'terəli/ *adv* militarmente
militariness /'mili,terinis/ *n* lo militar, el carácter militar
militarism /'milita,rizəm/ *n* militarismo, *m*
militarist /'militarist/ *n* militarista, *mf*
militaristic /,milita'ristik/ *a* militarista
militarization /,militari'zeiʃən/ *n* militarización, *f*
militarize /'milita,raiz/ *vt* militarizar
military /'mili,teri/ *a* militar; de guerra. **the m.,** los militares. **m. academy,** colegio militar, *m*. **m. camp,** campo militar, *m*. **m. law,** código militar, *m*. **m. man,** militar, *m*. **m. police,** policía militar, *f*. **m. service,** servicio militar, *m*
militate (against) /'mili,teit/ *vi* militar contra
militia /mi'liʃə/ *n* milicia, *f*
militiaman /mi'liʃəmən/ *n* miliciano, *m*
milk /milk/ *n* leche, *f*. *a* de leche; lácteo. *vt* ordeñar. *vi* dar leche. **to have m. and water in one's veins,** tener sangre de horchata. **condensed m.,** leche condensada, leche en lata, *f*. **m.-can,** lechera, *f*. **m.-cart,** carro de la leche, *m*. **m. chocolate,** chocolate con leche, *m*. **m. of magnesia,** leche de magnesia, *f*. **m.-pail,** ordeñadero, *m*. **m.-tooth,** diente de leche, *m*. **m.-white,** blanco como la leche
milkiness /'milkinis/ *n* lactescencia, *f*; carácter lechoso, *m*; (whiteness) blancura, *f*
milking /'milkiŋ/ *n* ordeño, *m*. **m.-machine,** máquina ordeñadora, *f*. **m.-stool,** taburete, banquillo, *m*
milkmaid /'milk,meid/ *n* lechera, *f*
milkman /'milk,mæn/ *n* lechero, *m*
milky /'milki/ *a* lechero; de leche; lechoso, como leche; *Astron.* lácteo. **the Milky Way** la Vía láctea
mill /mil/ *n* molino, *m*; (for coffee, etc.) molinillo, *m*; (factory) fábrica, *f*; taller, *m*; (textile) hilandería, *f*; fábrica de tejidos, *f*; (fight) riña a puñetazos, *f*; pugilato, *m*. *vt* (grind) moler; (coins) acordonar; (cloth) abatanar; (chocolate) batir. **cotton m.,** hilandería de algodón, *f*. **hand-m.,** molinillo, *m*. **paper-m.,** fábrica de papel, *f*. **saw-m.,** serrería, *f*. **spinning m.,** hilandería, *f*. **water m.,** molino de agua, *m*. **m.-course,** saetín, canal de molino, *m*. **m.-dam,** esclusa de molino, *f*. **m.-hand,** obrero (-ra). **m.-pond,** cubo, *m*. **m.-race,** caz, *m*. **m.-wheel,** rueda de molino, *f*
millennial /mi'leniəl/ *a* milenario
millennium /mi'leniəm/ *n* milenario, *m*
miller /'milər/ *n* molinero, *m*. **miller's wife,** molinera
millet /'milit/ *n* mijo, *m*
milligram /'mili,græm/ *n* miligramo, *m*
milliliter /'milə,litər/ *n* mililitro, *m*
millimeter /'milə,mitər/ *n* milímetro, *m*

milliner /'milənər/ *n* sombrerero (-ra), modista, *mf*
milliner's shop, sombrerería, tienda de modista, *f*
millinery /'milə,neri/ *n* sombreros, *m pl*; modas, *f pl*; tienda de modista, *f*
milling /'miliŋ/ *n* molienda, *f*; acuñación, *f*; (edge of coin) cordoncillo, *m*. **m. machine,** fresadora, *f*
million /'milyən/ *n* millón, *m*. **the m.,** las masas
millionaire /,milyə'nɛər/ *a* millonario. *n* millonario, *m*
millionairess /,milyə'nɛəris/ *n* millonaria, *f*
millionth /'milyənθ/ *a* millonésimo
millstone /'mil,stoun/ *n* piedra de moler, muela, *f*
mime /maim/ *n* (Greek farce and actor) mimo, *m*; (mimicry) mímica, *f*; pantomima, *f*. *vi* hacer en pantomima
mimetic /mi'metik/ *a* mímico, imitativo
mimic /'mimik/ *a* mímico; (pretended) fingido. *n* imitador (-ra). *vt* imitar, contrahacer; *Biol.* imitar, adaptarse a
mimicry /'mimikri/ *n* mímica, imitación, *f*; *Biol.* mimetismo, *m*
minaret /,minə'ret/ *n* minarete, *m*; (of a mosque) alminar, *m*
minatory /'minə,tɔri, -,touri/ *a* amenazador
mince /mins/ *vt* desmenuzar; (meat) picar; (words) medir (las palabras). *vi* andar con pasos menuditos; andar o moverse con afectación; hacer remilgos. **m.-meat,** carne picada, *f*; (sweet) conserva de fruta y especias, *f*
mincing /'minsiŋ/ *a* afectado. *n* acción de picar carne, *m*. **m. machine,** máquina de picar carne, *f*
mincingly /'minsiŋli/ *adv* con afectación; con pasos menuditos
mind /maind/ *n* inteligencia, *f*; espíritu ánimo, *m*; imaginación, *f*; alma, *f*; (memory) memoria, *f*, recuerdo, *m*; (understanding) entendimiento, *m*; (genius) ingenio, *m*; (cast of mind) mentalidad, *f*; (opinion) opinión, *f*; (liking) gusto, *m*; (thoughts) pensamiento, *m*; (intention) propósito, *m*, intención, *f*; (tendency) propensión, inclinación, *f*. **I have a good m. to go away,** Por poco me marcho; Tengo ganas de marcharme. **I have changed my m.,** He cambiado de opinión. **out of m.,** olvidado. **I shall give him a piece of my m.,** Le diré cuatro verdades. **It had quite gone out of my m.,** Lo había olvidado completamente. **I can see it in my mind's eye,** Está presente a mi imaginación. **I shall bear it in m.,** Lo tendré en cuenta. **I thought in my own m. that...,** Pensé por mis adentros que... **We are both of the same m.,** Ambos somos de la misma opinión. **to be out of one's m.,** estar fuera de juicio. **to call to m.,** acordarse de. **to have something on one's m.,** estar preocupado. **to make up one's m.** (**to),** resolverse (a), decidirse (a), determinar; animarse (a). **m.-reader,** adivinador (-ra) del pensamiento
mind /maind/ *vt* (remember) recordar, no olvidar; (heed) atender a; hacer caso de; tener cuidado de; (fear) tener miedo de; (obey) obedecer; preocuparse de; (object to) molestar; importar; (care for) cuidar. *vi* tener cuidado; molestar; (feel) sentir; (fear) tener miedo; (be the same thing) ser igual, (be bothered by) molestar. **Do you m. being quiet a moment?** ¿Quieres hacer el favor de callarte un momento? **Do you m. if I smoke?** ¿Le molesta si fumo? **They don't m.,** No les importa, Les da igual. **Never m.!** ¡No se moleste!; ¡No se preocupe!; ¡No importa! ¡Vaya! **M. what you are doing!** ¡Cuidado con lo que haces! **M. your own business!** ¡No te metas donde no te llaman!
minded /'maindid/ *a* dispuesto, inclinado; de... pensamientos, de... disposición
mindful /'maindfəl/ *a* atento a (a), cuidadoso (de); que se acuerda (de)
mine /main/ *a poss* mío, *m*, (mía, *f*; míos, *m pl*; mías, *f pl*); el mío, *m*, (la mía, *f*; lo mío, *neut*; los míos, *m pl*; las mías, *f pl*); mi (*pl* mis). **a friend of m.,** un amigo mío; uno de mis amigos
mine /main/ *n* mina, *f*. *vt* minar; extraer; sembrar minas en, colocar minas en. *vi* minar; hacer una mina; dedicarse a la minería. **drifting m.,** mina a la deriva, *f*. **land m.,** mina terrestre, *f*. **magnetic m.,** mina magnética, *f*. **to lay mines,** colocar (or sembrar)

minas. **m.-sweeper,** dragaminas, buque barreminas, *m*

minefield /'main,fild/ *n* campo de minas, *m*; barrera de minas, *f*

minelayer /'main,leiər/ *n* barca plantaminas, *f*, barco siembraminas, lanzaminas, *m*

miner /'mainər/ *n* minero, *m*; *Mil.* zapador minador, *m*

mineral /'mɪnərəl/ *n* mineral, *m*, *a* mineral. **m. baths,** baños, *m pl.* **m. water,** agua mineral, *f*; gaseosa, *f*

mineralogical /,mɪnərə'lɒdʒɪkəl/ *a* mineralógico

mineralogist /,mɪnə'ɒlədʒɪst/ *n* mineralogista, *m*

mineralogy /,mɪnə'rɒlədʒi/ *n* mineralogía, *f*

mingle /'mɪŋgəl/ *vt* mezclar; confundir. *vi* mezclarse; confundirse

mingling /'mɪŋglɪŋ/ *n* mezcla, *f*

miniature /'mɪniətʃər/ *n* miniatura, *f*. *a* en miniatura. **m. edition,** edición diamante, *f*

miniature golf *n* minigolf, *m*

miniaturist /'mɪniətʃərɪst/ *n* miniaturista, *mf*

minibus /'mɪni,bʌs/ *n* micro, microbús, *Mexico* combi, *m*

minimize /'mɪnə,maiz/ *vt* aminorar, reducir al mínimo; mitigar; (underrate) tener en menos, despreciar

minimum /'mɪnəməm/ *n* mínimo, *m*, *a* mínimo

mining /'mainɪŋ/ *n* minería, *f*, *a* minero; de mina; de minas; de minero. **m. engineer,** ingeniero de minas, *m*

minion /'mɪnyən/ *n* favorito (-ta); satélite, *m*; *Print.* miñona, *f*

minister /'mɪnəstər/ *n* ministro, *m*. *vi* servir; suministrar, proveer de; (contribute) contribuir (a). **m. of health,** ministro de sanidad, *m*. **m. of war,** ministro de la guerra, *m*

ministration /,mɪnə'streiʃən/ *n Eccl.* ministerio, *m*; servicio, *m*; agencia, *f*

ministry /'mɪnəstri/ *n* ministerio, *m*. **m. of food,** Ministerio de Abastecimientos, *m*

mink /mɪŋk/ *n* visón, *m*

minnow /'mɪnou/ *n* pez pequeño de agua dulce, *m*

minor /'mainər/ *a* menor. *n* menor de edad, *m*; (logic) menor, *f*; *Mus.* tono menor, *m*; *Eccl.* menor, *m*. **to be a m.,** ser menor de edad. **m. key,** tono menor, *m*. **m. orders,** *Eccl.* órdenes menores, *f pl.* **m. scale,** escala menor, *f*

Minorca /mɪ'nɔrkə/ Menorca, *f*

minority /mɪ'nɔrɪti/ *a* minoritario. *n* minoría, *f*; (of age) minoridad, *f*. **in the m.,** en la minoría

minster /'mɪnstər/ *n* catedral, *f*; monasterio, *m*

minstrel /'mɪnstrəl/ *n* trovador, juglar, *m*; músico, *m*; cantante, *m*

minstrelsy /'mɪnstrəlsi/ *n* música, *f*; canto, *m*; arte del trovador, *m*, or *f*; gaya ciencia, *f*

mint /mɪnt/ *n Bot.* menta, hierbabuena, *f*; casa de moneda, casa de la moneda, ceca, *f*; *Fig.* mina, *f*; (source) origen, *m*. *vt* (money) acuñar; *Fig.* inventar, *a* (postage stamp) en estado nuevo

minter /'mɪntər/ *n* acuñador, *m*; *Fig.* inventor (-ra)

minting /'mɪntɪŋ/ *n* (of coins) acuñación, *f*; *Fig.* invención, *f*

minuet /,mɪnyu'ɛt/ *n* minué, *m*

minus /'mainəs/ *a* menos; negativo; desprovisto de; sin. *n* signo menos, *m*; cantidad negativa, *f*

minute /mai'nut/ *a* menudo, diminuto; insignificante; minucioso

minute /'mɪnɪt/ *n* minuto, *m*; momento, *m*; instante, *m*; (note) minuta, *f*; *pl* **minutes,** actas, *f pl.* **in a m.,** en un instante. **m.-book,** libro de actas, minutario, *m*. **m.-hand,** minutero, *m*

minutely /mai'nutli/ *adv* minuciosamente; en detalle; exactamente

minuteness /mai'nutnɪs/ *n* suma pequeñez, *f*; minuciosidad, *f*

minx /mɪŋks/ *n* picaruela, *f*; coqueta, *f*

miracle /'mɪrəkəl/ *n* milagro, *m*. **m.-monger,** milagrero (-ra). **m. play,** milagro, *m*

miraculous /mɪ'rækyələs/ *a* milagroso

miraculously /mɪ'rækyələsli/ *adv* milagrosamente, por milagro

miraculousness /mɪ'rækyələsnɪs/ *n* carácter milagroso, *m*, lo milagroso

mirage /mɪ'rɑʒ/ *n* espejismo, *m*

mire /mai⁸r/ *n* fango, lodo, *m*; (miry place) lodazal, *m*

mirror /'mɪrər/ *n* espejo, *m*. *vt* reflejar. **to look in the m.,** mirarse al espejo. **full-length m.,** espejo de cuerpo entero, *m*. **small m.,** espejuelo, *m*

mirth /mərθ/ *n* alegría, *f*, júbilo, *m*; risa, *f*; hilaridad, *f*

mirthful /'mɛrθfəl/ *a* alegre

mirthless /'mɛrθlɪs/ *a* sin alegría, triste

miry /'mai⁸ri/ *a* lodoso, fangoso, cenagoso

misadventure /,mɪsəd'vɛntʃər/ *n* desgracia, *f*; accidente, *m*

misanthrope /'mɪsən,θroup/ *n* misántropo, *m*

misanthropic /,mɪsən'θrɒpɪk/ *a* misantrópico

misanthropy /mɪs'ænθrəpi/ *n* misantropía, *f*

misapplication /,mɪsæplɪ'keiʃən/ *n* mala aplicación, *f*; mal uso, *m*; abuso, *m*

misapply /,mɪsə'plai/ *vt* aplicar mal; hacer mal uso de; abusar de

misapprehend /,mɪsæprɪ'hɛnd/ *vt* comprender mal; equivocarse sobre

misapprehension /,mɪsæprə'hɛnʃən/ *n* concepto erróneo, *m*; equivocación, *f*, error, *m*

misappropriate /,mɪsə'proupri,eit/ *vt* malversar

misappropriation /,mɪsəproupri'eiʃən/ *n* malversación, *f*

misbehave /,mɪsbɪ'heiv/ *vi* portarse mal; (of a child) ser malo

misbehavior /,mɪsbɪ'heivyər/ *n* mala conducta, *f*

miscalculate /mɪs'kælkyəleit/ *vt* calcular mal; engañarse (sobre)

miscalculation /,mɪskælkyə'leiʃən/ *n* mal cálculo, error, *m*; desacierto, *m*

miscall /mɪs'kɔl/ *vt* mal nombrar; llamar equivocadamente; (abuse) insultar

miscarriage /mɪs'kærɪdʒ/ *n Med.* aborto, *m*; (failure) malogro, fracaso, *m*; (of goods) extravío, *m*

miscarriage of justice *n* yerro en la administración de la justicia, *m*

miscarry /mɪs'kæri/ *vi Med.* abortar, malparir; (fail) malograrse, frustrarse; (of goods) extraviarse

miscellaneous /,mɪsə'leiniəs/ *a* misceláneo; vario, diverso

miscellany /'mɪsə,leini/ *n* miscelánea, *f*

mischance /mɪs'tʃæns/ *n* mala suerte, *f*; infortunio, *m*, desgracia, *f*; accidente, *m*

mischief /'mɪstʃɪf/ *n* daño, *m*; mal, *m*; (wilfulness) travesura, *f*; (person) diablillo, *m*. **m.-maker,** enredador (-ra), chismoso (-sa); alborotador, *m*; malicioso (-sa). **m.-making,** *a* enredador; chismoso; malicioso; alborotador

mischievous /'mɪstʃəvəs/ *a* dañino, perjudicial, malo; malicioso; chismoso; (wilful) travieso; juguetón; (of glances, etc.) malicioso

mischievously /'mɪstʃəvəsli/ *adv* maliciosamente; con (or por) travesura

mischievousness /'mɪstʃəvəsnɪs/ *n* mal, *m*; malicia, *f*; maleficencia, *f*; travesura, *f*

misconceive /,mɪskən'siv/ *vt* formar un concepto erróneo de; concebir mal, juzgar mal

misconception /,mɪskən'sɛpʃən/ *n* concepto erróneo, *m*, idea falsa, *f*; error, *m*, equivocación, *f*; engaño, *m*

misconduct /*n* mɪs'kɒndʌkt; *v* ,mɪskən'dʌkt/ *n* mala conducta, *f*. **to m. oneself,** portarse mal

misconstruction /,mɪskən'strʌkʃən/ *n* mala interpretación, *f*; falsa interpretación, *f*; tergiversación, *f*; mala traducción, *f*

misconstrue /,mɪskən'stru/ *vt* interpretar mal; entender mal; tergiversar; traducir mal

miscount /*v* mɪs'kaunt; *n* 'mɪs,kaunt/ *vt* contar mal, equivocarse en la cuenta de; calcular mal. *n* error, *m*; yerro de cuenta, *m*

miscreant /'mɪskriənt/ *n* malandrín, *m*; bribón, *m*, *a* vil, malandrín

misdeed /mɪs'did/ *n* delito, malhecho, crimen, *m*

misdemeanor /,mɪsdɪ'minər/ *n* mala conducta, *f*; *Law.* delito, *m*; ofensa, *f*, malhecho, *m*

misdirect /,mɪsdɪ'rɛkt/ *vt* informar mal (acerca del

camino); (a letter) dirigir mal, poner unas señas incorrectas en

miser /'maizər/ n avaro (-ra)

miserable /'mɪzərəbəl/ a infeliz, desgraciado; miserable; despreciable; sin valor

miserably /'mɪzərəbli/ adv miserablemente

miserliness /'maizərlinɪs/ n avaricia, tacañería, f

miserly /'maizərli/ a avaro, tacaño

misery /'mɪzəri/ n miseria, f; sufrimiento, m; dolor, tormento, m

misfire /mɪs'fɪᵊr/ vi no dar fuego; (of a car, etc.) hacer falsas explosiones, errar el encendido

misfit /mɪs'fɪt/ 'mɪs,fɪt for person/ n traje que no cae bien, m; zapato que no va bien, m; (person) inadaptado, m

misfortune /mɪs'fɔrtʃən/ n infortunio, m, mala suerte, adversidad, f; desdicha, desgracia, f; mal, m

misgive /mɪs'gɪv/ vt hacer temer; llenar de duda; hacer recelar; hacer presentir

misgiving /mɪs'gɪvɪŋ/ n temor, m; duda, f; recelo, m; presentimiento, m

misgovern /mɪs'gʌvərn/ vt gobernar mal; administrar mal; dirigir mal

misgovernment /mɪs'gʌvərnmənt/ n desgobierno, m; mala administración, f

misguided /mɪs'gaidɪd/ a mal dirigido; extraviado; engañado; (blind) ciego

misguidedly /mɪs'gaidɪdli/ adv equivocadamente

mishap /'mɪshæp/ n desgracia, f; contratiempo, accidente, m. **to have a m.**, sufrir una desgracia; tener un accidente

misinform /,mɪsɪn'fɔrm/ vt informar mal; dar informes erróneos a

misinformation /,mɪsɪnfər'meiʃən/ n noticia falsa, f; información errónea, f

misinterpret /,mɪsɪn'tɜrprɪt/ vt interpretar mal; entender mal; torcer; tergiversar; traducir mal

misinterpretation /,mɪsɪn,tɜrprɪ'teiʃən/ n mala interpretación, f; interpretación falsa, f; tergiversación, f; mala traducción, f

misjudge /mɪs'dʒʌdʒ/ vt juzgar mal; equivocarse (en or sobre); tener una idea falsa de

misjudgment /mɪs'dʒʌdʒmənt/ n juicio errado, m; idea falsa, f; juicio injusto, m

mislay /mɪs'lei/ vt extraviar, perder

mislead /mɪs'lid/ vt extraviar; llevar a conclusiones erróneas, despistar; engañar

misleading /mɪs'lidɪŋ/ a de falsas apariencias; erróneo, falso; engañoso

mismanage /mɪs'mænɪdʒ/ vt administrar mal, dirigir mal; echar a perder

mismanagement /mɪs'mænɪdʒmənt/ n mala administración, f; desgobierno, m

misname /mɪs'neim/ vt mal nombrar; llamar equivocadamente

misnomer /mɪs'noumər/ n nombre equivocado, m; nombre inapropiado, m

misogynist /mɪ'sɒdʒənɪst/ n misógino, m

misogyny /mɪ'sɒdʒəni/ n misoginia, f

misplace /mɪs'pleis/ vt colocar mal; poner fuera de lugar

misplaced /mɪs'pleist/ a mal puesto; inoportuno; equivocado

misprint /n. 'mɪs,prɪnt/ v. mɪs'prɪnt/ n error de imprenta, m, errata, f, vt imprimir con erratas

mispronounce /,mɪsprə'nouns/ vt pronunciar mal

mispronunciation /,mɪsprənʌnsi'eiʃən/ n mala pronunciación, f

misquotation /,mɪskwou'teiʃən/ n cita errónea, f

misquote /mɪs'kwout/ vt citar mal, citar erróneamente

misrepresent /,mɪsreprɪ'zɛnt/ vt desfigurar; tergiversar; falsificar

misrepresentation /mɪs,rɛprɪzɛn'teiʃən/ n desfiguración, f; tergiversación, f; falsificación, f

misrule /mɪs'rul/ vt gobernar mal. n mal gobierno, desgobierno, m; confusión, f

miss /mɪs/ n señorita, f

miss /mɪs/ vt (one's aim) errar (el tiro, etc.); no acertar (a); (let fall) dejar caer; (lose a train, the post,

etc., one's footing, an opportunity, etc.) perder; (fall short of) dejar de; no ver; no notar; pasar por alto de; omitir; echar de menos; notar la falta de; no encontrar. vi errar; (fail) salir mal, fracasar. **I m. you,** Te echo de menos. **to be missing,** faltar; estar ausente; haberse marchado; haber desaparecido. **to m. one's mark,** errar el blanco. **to m. out,** omitir, pasar por alto de. **She doesn't miss a beat,** (fig.) No se le escapa nada

missal /'mɪsəl/ n misal, m

misshapen /mɪs'ʃeipən/ a deforme

missile /'mɪsəl/ n arma arrojadiza, f; proyectil, m

missing /'mɪsɪŋ/ a que falta; perdido; ausente; Mil. desaparecido

mission /'mɪʃən/ n misión, f

missionary /'mɪʃə,nɛri/ n misionero, m

missionize /'mɪʃə,naiz/ vi misionar

missis /'mɪsəz/ n señora, f; Inf. mujer, f

Mississippi /,mɪsə'sɪpi/ el Misisipí, m

missive /'mɪsɪv/ n misiva, f

Missouri /mɪ'zʊri/ el Misuri, m

misspend /mɪs'spɛnd/ vt malgastar; desperdiciar; perder

mist /mɪst/ n bruma, neblina, f; vapor, m; (drizzle) llovizna, f; Fig. nube, f. vt anublar, empañar. vi lloviznar

mistakable /mɪ'steikəbəl/ a confundible

mistake /mɪ'steik/ vt comprender mal; equivocarse sobre; errar; (with for) confundir con, equivocarse con. n equivocación, f; error, m; inadvertencia, f; (in an exercise, etc.) falta, f. **And no m.!** Inf. Sin duda alguna. **by m.,** por equivocación; (involuntarily) sin querer. **If I am not mistaken,** Si no me engaño, Si no estoy equivocado. **to make a m.,** equivocarse

mistaken /mɪ'steikən/ a (of persons and things) equivocado; (of things) erróneo; incorrecto

mistakenly /mɪ'steikənli/ adv equivocadamente; injustamente, falsamente

mister /'mɪstər/ n señor, m

mistily /'mɪstəli/ adv a través de la neblina; obscuramente; indistintamente, vagamente

mistimed /mɪs'taimd/ a intempestivo; inoportuno

mistiness /'mɪstinɪs/ n neblina, bruma, f; vaporosidad, f; obscuridad, f

mistletoe /'mɪsəl,tou/ n muérdago, m

mistranslate /,mɪstrænz'leit/ vt traducir mal; interpretar mal

mistranslation /,mɪstrænz'leiʃən/ n mala traducción, f; traducción inexacta, f

mistress /'mɪstrɪs/ n señora, f; maestra, f; (fiancée) prometida, f; (beloved) amada, dulce dueña, f; (concubine) amiga, querida, f. **M. (Mrs.) Gómez,** Sra Gómez. **m. of the robes,** camarera mayor, f

mistrust /mɪs'trʌst/ vt desconfiar de, no tener confianza en; dudar de. n desconfianza, f; recelo, m, suspicacia, f; aprensión, f

mistrustful /mɪs'trʌstfəl/ a desconfiado; receloso, suspicaz. **to be m. of,** recelarse de

misty /'mɪsti/ a brumoso, nebuloso; vaporoso; (of the eyes) anublado; (of windows, etc.) empañado

misunderstand /,mɪsʌndər'stænd/ vt comprender mal; tomar en sentido erróneo; interpretar mal

misunderstanding /,mɪsʌndər'stændɪŋ/ n concepto erróneo, error, m; equivocación, f; (disagreement) desavenencia, f

misuse /n mɪs'yus; v -'yuz/ vt emplear mal; abusar de; (funds) malversar; (ill-treat) tratar mal. n abuso, m; (of funds) malversación, f

mite /mait/ n (coin) ardite, m; (trifle) pizca, f; óbolo, m; Ent. ácaro, m

miter /'maitər/ n mitra, f; inglete, m, vt cortar ingletes en

mitigate /'mɪtɪ,geit/ vt (pain) aliviar; mitigar; suavizar

mitigation /,mɪtɪ'geiʃən/ n (of pain) alivio, m; mitigación, f

mitten /'mɪtn/ n mitón, m

mix /mɪks/ vt mezclar; (salad) aderezar; (concrete, etc.) amasar; combinar, unir; (sociably) alternar (con); (confuse) confundir. vi mezclarse; frecuentar la compañía (de); frecuentar; (get on well) llevarse bien

mixed /mɪkst/ a mezclado; vario, surtido; mixto; (confused) confuso. **m. doubles,** parejas mixtas, f pl. **m. up,** (in disorder) revuelto; confuso. **m. up with,** implicado en; asociado con

mixer /'mɪksər/ n mezclador, m; (person) mezclador (-ra); Inf. persona sociable, f. **electric m.,** mezclador eléctrico, m

mixture /'mɪkstʃər/ n mezcla, f; (medicine) poción, medicina, f

mizzen /'mɪzən/ n mesana, f. **m.-mast,** palo de mesana, m. **m.-sail,** vela de mesana, f. **m.-topsail,** sobremesana, f

mnemonics /nɪ'mɒnɪks/ n mnemotecnia, f

moan /moun/ vt lamentar; llorar. vi gemir; quejarse, lamentarse. n gemido, m; lamento, m; quejido, m

moaning /'mouniŋ/ n gemidos, m pl

moat /mout/ n foso, m

mob /mɒb/ n (crowd) muchedumbre, multitud, f; (rabble) populacho, m, gentuza, f. vt atropellar; atacar. **mob-cap,** cofia, f

mobile /'moubil/ a móvil; ambulante; (fickle) voluble. **m. canteen,** cantina ambulante, f

mobility /mou'bɪlɪti/ n movilidad, f

mobilization /,moubələ'zeɪʃən/ n movilización, f

mobilize /'moubə,laiz/ vt movilizar. vi movilizarse

moccasin /'mɒkəsɪn, -zən/ n mocasín, m

mocha /'moukə/ n café de Moca, m

mock /mɒk/ vt ridiculizar; burlarse (de), mofarse (de); (cause to fail) frustrar; (mimic) imitar; (delude) engañar. vi mofarse, burlarse, reírse. a cómico, burlesco; falso; fingido; imitado. **to make a m. of,** poner en ridículo; hacer absurdo; burlarse de. **m.-heroic,** heroico-cómico. **m.-orange,** Bot. jeringuilla, f. **m.-turtle soup,** sopa hecha con cabeza de ternera a imitación de tortuga, f

mocker /'mɒkər/ n mofador (-ra); el, m, (f, la) que se burla de

mockery /'mɒkəri/ n mofa, burla, f; ridículo, m; ilusión, apariencia, f. **to make a m. of,** mofarse de; hacer ridículo

mocking /'mɒkiŋ/ a burlón. **m. bird,** pájaro burlón, m

mockingly /'mɒkiŋli/ adv burlonamente

modality /mou'dælɪti/ n modalidad, f

mode /moud/ n modo, m; manera, f; (fashion) moda, f; uso, m, costumbre, f

model /'mɒdl/ n modelo, m; (artist's) modelo vivo, m, a modelo; en miniatura. vt modelar; moldear; formar; hacer; planear. **m. display,** (hats, etc.) exposición de modelos, f. **m. railway,** ferrocarril en miniatura, m

modeler /'mɒdlər/ n modelador (-ra); disenador, m

modeling /'mɒdlɪŋ/ n modelado, m; modelo, m. **m. wax,** cera para moldear, f

modem /'moudəm/ n módem, m

moderate /a, n. 'mɒdərɪt v. -ə,reit/ a moderado; (of prices, etc.) módico; (fair, medium) regular, mediano; razonable; mediocre. n moderado, m. vt moderar; modificar; calmar. vi moderarse; calmarse

moderately /'mɒdərɪtli/ adv moderadamente; módicamente; medianamente; bastante; razonablemente; mediocremente

moderation /,mɒdə'reiʃən/ n moderación, f. **in m.,** en moderación

moderator /'mɒdə,reitər/ n moderador, m; (Church of Scotland) presidente, m; Educ. examinador, m; Educ. inspector de exámenes, m. **m. lamp,** lámpara de regulador, f

modern /'mɒdərn/ a moderno. n modernista, mf. **in the m. way,** a la moderna. **m. language,** lengua viva, f

modernism /'mɒdər,nɪzəm/ n modernismo, m

modernist /'mɒdərnɪst/ n modernista, mf

modernistic /,mɒdər'nɪstɪk/ a modernista

modernity /mɒ'dɜrnɪti/ n modernidad, f

modernization /,mɒdərnə'zeɪʃən/ n modernización, f

modernize /'mɒdər,naiz/ vt modernizar

modernness /'mɒdərnnɪs/ n modernidad, f

modest /'mɒdɪst/ a modesto; (of a woman) púdico

modesty /'mɒdəsti/ n modestia, f; (of a woman) pudor, m

modicum /'mɒdɪkəm/ n porción pequeña, f; poco, m

modifiable /,mɒdə'faiəbəl/ a modificable

modification /,mɒdəfɪ'keɪʃən/ n modificación, f

modify /'mɒdə,fai/ vt modificar. **It has been much modified,** Se ha modificado mucho; Se han hecho muchas modificaciones

modifying /'mɒdə,faiɪŋ/ a modificante, modificador

modish /'moudɪʃ/ a de moda en boga; elegante

modishness /'moudɪʃnɪs/ n elegancia, f

modiste /mou'dist/ n modista, mf

modulate /'mɒdʒə,leit/ vt and vi modular

modulation /,mɒdʒə'leiʃən/ n modulación, f

modus vivendi /'moudəs vɪ'vɛndi, -dai/ n modo de conveniencia, m

Mogul /'mougəl/ a mogol. n mogol (-la). **the Great M.,** el Gran Mogol

Mohammedan /mo'hæmɪdn, mou-/ a mahometano, agareno

Mohican /mou'hikən/ n mohican, m

moiety /'mɔiti/ n mitad, f

moiré /mwɑ'rei, mɔ-/ n muaré, m

moist /mɔist/ a húmedo

moisten /'mɔisən/ vt humedecer, mojar

moisture /'mɔistʃər/ n humedad, f

molar /'moulər/ n muela, f, a molar

molasses /mə'læsɪz/ n pl melaza, f

mold /mould/ n (fungus) moho, m; (humus) mantillo, m; (iron-mold) mancha de orín, f; (matrix) molde, m, matriz, f; Cul. cubilete, m; Naut. gálibo, m; (for jelly, etc.) molde, m; Archit. moldura, f; (temperament) temple, m, disposición, f. vt moldear; (cast) vaciar; moldurar; Naut. galibar; Fig. amoldar, formar; Agr. cubrir con mantillo. **to m. oneself on,** modelarse sobre. **m.-board,** (of a plow) orejera, f

Moldavian /moul'deiviən/ a moldavo. n moldavo (-va)

molder /'mouldər/ n moldeador, m; Fig. amolador (-ra); creador (-ra). vi desmoronarse, convertirse en polvo; Fig. decaer, desmoronarse; vegetar

moldiness /'mouldɪnɪs/ n moho, m

molding /'mouldɪŋ/ n amoldamiento, m; vaciado, m; Archit. moldura, f; Fig. formación, f

moldy /'mouldi/ a mohoso, enmohecido; Fig. anticuado

mole /moul/ n (animal) topo, m; (spot) lunar, m; (breakwater) dique, malecón, m; muelle, m

molecular /mə'lɛkyələr/ a molecular

molecule /'mɒlɪ,kyul/ n molécula, f

molehill /'moul,hɪl/ n topera, f

moleskin /'moul,skɪn/ n piel de topo, f

molest /mə'lɛst/ vt molestar; perseguir, importunar; faltar al respeto (a)

molestation /,moulə'steiʃən/ n importunidad, persecución, f; molestia, incomodidad, f

mollification /,mɒləfɪ'keɪʃən/ n apaciguamiento, m; mitigación, f

mollify /'mɒlə,fai/ vt apaciguar, calmar, mitigar

mollusk /'mɒləsk/ n molusco, m

mollycoddle /'mɒli,kɒdl/ n alfeñique, mírame y no me toques, m; niño (-ña), mimado (-da)

Moloch /'moulɒk/ n Moloch, Moloc, m

molt /moult/ vi mudar, n muda, f

molten /'moultn/ a fundido; derretido

Moluccas, the /mə'lʌkəz/ las Malucas, f pl

moment /'moumənt/ n momento, m; instante m; (importance) importancia, f. **at this m.,** en este momento. **Do it this m.!** ¡Hazlo al instante (or en seguida)!

momentarily /,moumən'tɛrəli, 'moumən,tɛr-/ adv momentáneamente; cada momento

momentariness /'moumən,tɛrinɪs/ n momentaneidad, f

momentary /'moumən,tɛri/ a momentáneo

momentous /mou'mɛntəs/ a de suma importancia; crítico; grave

momentousness /mou'mɛntəsnɪs/ n importancia, f; gravedad, f

momentum /mou'mɛntəm/ n momento, m, velocidad adquirida *f*; *Fig.* ímpetu, *m*. **to gather m.**, cobrar velocidad, acelerar

monarch /'mɒnərk/ *n* monarca, *m*

monarchic /mə'narkık/ *a* monárquico

monarchism /'mɒnər,kızəm/ *n* monarquismo, *m*

monarchist /'mɒnərkıst/ *n* monárquico (-ca)

monarchy /'mɒnərki/ *n* monarquía, *f*

monastery /'mɒnə,stɛri/ *n* monasterio, *m*

monastic /mə'næstık/ *a* monástico. **m. life,** vida de clausura, *f*

monasticism /mə'næstə,sızəm/ *n* vida monástica, *f*

Monday /'mʌndei, -di/ *n* lunes, *m*

monetary /'mɒnı,tɛri/ *a* monetario

monetization /,mɒnıtı'zeiʃən/ *n* monetización, *f*

money /'mʌni/ *n* dinero, *m*; (coin) moneda, *f*; sistema monetario, *m*. **paper m.,** papel moneda, *m*. **ready m.,** dinero contante, *m*. **to make m.,** ganar (or hacer) dinero; enriquecerse. **m.-bag,** talega, *f*; (person) ricacho (-cha). **m.-bags,** riqueza, *f*. **m.-box,** alcancía, hucha, *f*. **m.-changer,** cambista, *mf* **m.-lender,** prestamista, *mf* **m.-making,** *n* el hacer dinero; prosperidad, ganancia, *f*. *a* lucrativo, *Lat. Am.* libranza de correos, libranza postal, *f*. **m.-order,** giro postal, *m* (postal)

moneyed /'mʌnid/ *a* adinerado; acomodado

mongoose /'mɒŋ,gus/ *n* mangosta, *f*

mongrel /'mʌŋgrəl/ *a* mestizo, atravesado. *n* perro mestizo, *m*; (in contempt) bastardo, *m*

monitor /'mɒnıtər/ *n* monitor, *m*

monitory /'mɒnı,tɔri/ *a* monitorio. *n* *Eccl.* monitorio, *m*

monk /mʌŋk/ *n* monje, *m*. **to become a m.,** hacerse monje, tomar el hábito. **monk's-hood,** acónito, *m*

monkey /'mʌŋki/ *n* mono (-na); (imp) diablillo, *m*; (of a pile-driver) pilón de martinete, *m*; (in glass-making) crisol, *m*. **m. business,** disparates, *m pl*, tretas, *f pl*. **to m. with,** meterse con; entremeterse. **m. nut,** cacahuete, *m*. **m.-puzzle,** (tree) araucaria, *f*. **m. tricks,** monadas, travesuras, diabluras, *f pl*. **m.-wrench,** llave inglesa, *f*

monkish /'mʌŋkıʃ/ *a* monacal, de monje; monástico

monochromatic /,mɒnəkrou'mætık/ *a* monocromo

monochrome /'mɒnə,kroum/ *n* monocromo, *m*

monocle /'mɒnəkəl/ *n* monóculo, *m*

monogamist /mə'nɒgəmıst/ *n* monógamo (-ma)

monogamous /mə'nɒgəməs/ *a* monógamo

monogamy /mə'nɒgəmi/ *n* monogamia, *f*

monogram /'mɒnə,græm/ *n* monograma, *m*

monograph /'mɒnə,græf/ *n* monografía, *f*, opúsculo, *m*

monolith /'mɒnəlıθ/ *n* monolito, *m*

monolithic /,mɒnə'lıθık/ *a* monolítico

monologue /'mɒnə,lɔg/ *n* monólogo, *m*

monomania /,mɒnə'meiniə/ *n* monomanía, *f*

monomaniac /,mɒnə'meini,æk/ *n* monomaníaco (-ca)

monomial /mou'noumiəl/ *n* monomio, *m*, *a* de un solo término

monoplane /'mɒnə,plein/ *n* monoplano, *m*

monopolist /mə'nɒpəlıst/ *n* monopolista, *mf*; acaparador (-ra)

monopolization /mə,nɒpələ'zeiʃən/ *n* monopolio, *m*

monopolize /mə'nɒpə,laiz/ *vt* monopolizar

monopoly /mə'nɒpəli/ *n* monopolio, *m*

monotheism /'mɒnəθi,ızəm/ *n* monoteísmo, *m*

monotheist /'mɒnə,θiıst/ *n* monoteísta, *mf*

monotone /'mɒnə,toun/ *n* monotonía, *m*

monotonous /mə'nɒtnəs/ *a* monótono

monotony /mə'nɒtni/ *n* monotonía, *f*

monoxide /mɒn'ɒksaid/ *n* monóxido, *m*

Monroe doctrine /mən'rou/ *n* monroísmo, *m*

monsignor /mɒn'sinyər/ *n* monseñor, *m*

monsoon /mɒn'sun/ *n* monzón, *m*

monster /'mɒnstər/ *n* monstruo, *m*

monstrosity /mɒn'strɒsıti/ *n* monstruosidad, *f*

monstrous /'mɒnstrəs/ *a* monstruoso; horrible, atroz; enorme

montage /mɒn'tɑʒ/ *n* montaje, *m*

month /mʌnθ/ *n* mes, *m*. **He arrived a m. ago,** Llegó hace un mes. **a m. later** *Lat. Am.* al mes

monthly /'mʌnθli/ *a* mensual. *adv* mensualmente, cada mes. *n* revista (or publicación) mensual, *f*; *pl* **monthlies,** menstruación, regla, *f*. **m. salary** or **payment,** mensualidad, *f*

monument /'mɒnyəmənt/ *n* monumento, *m*

monumental /,mɒnyə'mɛntļ/ *a* monumental

moo /mu/ *vi* (of cattle) mugir. *n* mugido, *m*

mood /mud/ *n* humor, *m*; espíritu, *m*; *Gram.* modo, *m*

moodily /'mudļi/ *adv* taciturnamente; tristemente, pensativamente

moodiness /'mudınıs/ *n* mal humor, *m*, taciturnidad, *f*; melancolía, tristeza, *f*

moody /'mudi/ *a* taciturno, de mal humor; triste, melancólico, pensativo

mooing /'muıŋ/ *n* (of cattle) mugido, *m*

moon /mun/ *n* luna, *f*; satélite, *m*; mes lunar, *m*; luz de la luna, *f*. **full m.,** plenilunio, *m*; luna llena, *f*. **new m.,** novilunio, *m*, luna nueva, *f*

moonbeam /'mun,bim/ *n* rayo de luna, *m*

moonless /'munlıs/ *a* sin luna

moonlight /'mun,lait/ *n* luz de la luna, *f*. **in the m.,** a la luz de la luna. **to do a m. flit,** *Inf.* mudarse por el aire

moonlighting /'mun,laitıŋ/ *n* el pluriempleo, *m*

moonlit /'mun,lıt/ *a* iluminado por la luna. **moonlit night,** noche de luna, *f*

moonshine /'mun,ʃain/ *n* claridad de la luna, *f*; *Fig.* música celestial, ilusión, *f*

moonstone /'mun,stoun/ *n* adularia, *f*

moonstruck /'mun,strʌk/ *a* lunático

Moor /mʊr/ *n* moro (-ra)

moor /mʊr/ *n* páramo, brezal, *m*; (marsh) pantano, *m*; (for game) coto, *m*. *vt* amarrar, aferrar; afirmar con anclas o cables. **m.-hen,** polla de agua, *f*

mooring /'mʊrıŋ/ *n* amarre, *m*. **m.-mast,** *Aer.* poste de amarre, *m*

moorings /'mʊrıŋz/ *n pl* amarradero, *m*

Moorish /'mʊrıʃ/ *a* moro; árabe. **M. architecture,** arquitectura árabe, *f*. **M. girl,** mora, *f*

moorland /'mʊrlənd/ *n* páramo, brezal, *m*

moose /mus/ *n* anta, *f*

moot /mut/ *n* junta, *f*; ayuntamiento, *m*. *a* discutible. *vt* (bring up) suscitar; (discuss) discutir, debatir

mop /mɒp/ *n* (implement) trapeador, *m*, *Ecuador,* escoba con fleco, *f*, *elsewhere in Lat. Am.* lampazo, *m*; (of hair) mata (de pelo), *f*. *vt* trapear *Ecuador;* (dry) enjugar, secar. **to mop up,** *Inf.* limpiar; *Mil.* acabar con (el enemigo)

mope /moup/ *vi* replace by tristear. **to m. about,** vagar tristemente

moquette /mou'ket/ *n* moqueta, *f*

moral /'mɔrəl/ *a* moral; (chaste) casto, virtuoso; honrado. *n* (maxim) moraleja, *f*; *pl* **morals,** moralidad, *f*; ética, *f*; moral, *f*; (conduct) costumbres, *f pl*. **m. philosophy,** filosofía moral, *f*. **m. support,** apoyo moral, *m*. **m. tale,** apólogo, *m*

morale /mə'ræl/ *n* moral, *f*

moralist /'mɔrəlıst/ *n* moralista, *m*

morality /mə'rælıti/ *n* moralidad, *f*; virtud, *f*; castidad, *f*. **m. play,** moralidad, *f*, drama alegórico, *m*

moralization /,mɔrələ'zeiʃən/ *n* moralización, *f*

moralize /'mɔrə,laiz/ *vt and vi* moralizar

moralizer /'mɔrə,laizər/ *n* moralizador (-ra)

moralizing /'mɔrə,laizıŋ/ *a* moralizador

morally /'mɔrəli/ *adv* moralmente

morals. /'mɔrəlz/. See **moral**

morass /mə'ræs/ *n* marisma, ciénaga, *f*

moratorium /,mɔrə'tɔriəm/ *n* moratoria, *f*

Moravian /mə'reiviən/ *a* moravo. *n* moravo (-va)

morbid /'mɔrbid/ *a* mórbido, mórboso; (of the mind, etc.) insano

morbidezza /,mɔrbı'dɛtsə/ *n* (*Art.* and *Lit.*) morbidez, *f*

morbidity /mɔr'bıdıti/ *n* morbidez, *f*

mordacity /mɔr'dæsıti/ *n* mordacidad, *f*

mordant /'mɔrdņt/ *a* mordaz; (of acid) mordiente. *n* mordiente, *m*

more /mɔr/ *a* and *adv* más. **The m. he earns, the**

less he saves, Cuanto más gana, menos ahorra. **the m. the better,** cuanto más, tanto mejor. **without m. ado,** sin más ni más; sin decir nada. **Would you like some m.?** ¿Quiere Vd. más? **más?** (of food) ¿Quiere Vd. repetir? **no m.,** no más; (never) nunca más; (finished) se acabó. **once m.,** otra vez, una vez más. **m. and m.,** cada vez más, más y más. **m. or less,** más o menos; (about) poco más o menos

moreover /mɔr'ouvər/ *adv* además, también; por otra parte

morganatic /ˌmɔrgə'nætɪk/ *a* morganático

morgue /mɔrg/ *n* depósito de cadáveres, *m*

moribund /'mɔrəˌbʌnd/ *a* moribundo

Mormon /'mɔrmən/ *a* mormónico. *n* mormón (-ona)

Mormonism /'mɔrməˌnɪzəm/ *n* mormonismo, *m*

morning /'mɔrnɪŋ/ *n* mañana, *f*, *a* matutino, de la mañana. **Good m.!** ¡Buenos días! **the next m.,** la mañana siguiente. **very early in the m.,** muy de mañana. **m. coat,** chaqué, *m*. **m. dew,** rocío de la mañana, *m*. **m. paper,** periódico de la mañana, *m*. **m. star,** lucero del alba, *m*. **m. suit,** chaqué, *m*

Moroccan /mə'rɒkən/ *a* marroquí, marrueco. *n* marrueco (-ca), marroquí, *mf*

Morocco /mə'rɒkou/ Marruecos, *m*

morocco /mə'rɒkou/ *n* (leather) marroquí, tafilete, *m*

morose /mə'rous/ *a* sombrío, taciturno, malhumorado

morosely /mə'rousli/ *adv* taciturnamente

moroseness /mə'rousnɪs/ *n* taciturnidad, *f*; mal humor, *m*

morpheme /'mɔrfim/ *n* morfema, *f*

morphine /'mɔrfin/ *n* morfina, *f*. **m. addict,** morfinómano (-na)

morphology /mɔr'fɒlədʒi/ *n* morfología, *f*

morrow /'mɔrou/ *n* mañana, *f*; día siguiente, *m*

Morse code /mɔrs/ *n* la clave telegráfica de Morse, *f*, el alfabeto de Morse, *m*

morsel /'mɔrsəl/ *n* pedazo, *m*; (mouthful) bocado, *m*

mortal /'mɔrtl̩/ *a* mortal. *n* mortal, *mf*. **m. sin,** pecado mortal, pecado capital, *m*

mortality /mɔr'tælɪti/ *n* mortalidad, *f*

mortally wounded /'mɔrtl̩i/ *adv* herido de muerte

mortar /'mɔrtər/ *n* (for building) argamasa, *f*; (for mixing and *Mil.*) mortero, *m*. **m. and pestle,** mortero y majador, *m*. **m.-board,** (in building) cuezo, *m*; (academic cap) birrete, *m*

mortgage /'mɔrgɪdʒ/ *n* hipoteca, *f*. *vt* hipotecar. *a* hipotecario. **to pay off a m.,** redimir una hipoteca

mortgageable /'mɔrgɪdʒəbəl/ *a* hipotecable

mortgaged debt /'mɔrgɪdʒd/ *n* deuda garantizada con una hipoteca, *f*

mortgagee /ˌmɔrgə'dʒi/ *n* acreedor (-ra) hipotecario (-ia)

mortgagor /'mɔrgədʒər/ *n* deudor (-ra) hipotecario (-ia)

mortification /ˌmɔrtəfɪ'keɪʃən/ *n* mortificación, *f*; humillación, *f*; *Med.* gangrena, *f*

mortify /'mɔrtəˌfaɪ/ *vt* mortificar; humillar. *vi Med.* gangrenarse

mortifying /'mɔrtəˌfaɪɪŋ/ *a* humillante

mortise /'mɔrtɪs/ *n* muesca, *f*. *vt* hacer muescas (en); ensamblar

mortuary /'mɔrtʃuˌɛri/ *a* mortuorio. *n* depósito de cadáveres, *m*

Mosaic /mou'zeiɪk/ *a* mosaico

mosaic /mou'zeiɪk/ *n* mosaico, *m*

Moscow /'mɒskou,-kau/ Moscú, *m*

mosque /mɒsk/ *n* mezquita, *f*

mosquito /mə'skitou/ *n* mosquito, *m*. **m. net,** mosquitero, *m*

moss /mɔs/ *n* musgo, *m*; moho, *m*; (swamp) marjal, *m*

mossgrown /'mɔsˌgroun/ *a* musgoso, cubierto de musgo; *Fig.* anticuado

mossiness /'mɔsinɪs/ *n* estado musgoso, *m*

mossy /'mɔsi/ *a* musgoso

most /moust/ *a* el (la, los, etc.) más; la mayor parte de; la mayoría de; (el, etc.) mayor. *adv* más; el (la, etc.) más; (extremely) sumamente; (very) muy; (before adjectives sometimes expressed by superlative), e.g. *m. reverend,* reverendísimo, *m. holy,* santísimo,

etc.). *n* (highest price) el mayor precio; la mayor parte; el mayor número; lo más. **m. of all,** sobre todo. **m. people,** la mayoría de la gente. **at the m.,** a lo más, a lo sumo. **for the m. part,** en su mayor parte; casi todos; generalmente, casi siempre. **to make the m. of,** sacar el mayor partido posible de; aprovechar bien; exagerar

mostly /'moustli/ *adv* principalmente; en su mayoría; en su mayor parte; casi siempre; en general, generalmente

mote /mout/ *n* átomo, *m*; mota, *f*. **to see the m. in our neighbor's eye and not the beam in our own,** ver la paja en el ojo del vecino y no la viga en el nuestro

moth /mɔθ/ *n* mariposa nocturna, *f*; polilla, *f*. **m.ball,** bola de naftalina, *f*. **m.-eaten,** apolillado

mother /'mʌðər/ *n* madre, *f*; madre de familia, *f*; (of alcoholic beverages) madre, *f*. *vt* cuidar como una madre (a); servir de madre (a); (animals) ahijar. **M. Church,** madre iglesia, *f*; iglesia metropolitana, *f*. **m.-in-law,** suegra, *f*. **m. land,** (madre) patria, *f*. **m.-of-pearl,** *n* madreperla, *f*, nácar, *m*. *a* nacarado, nacáreo. **M. Superior,** (madre) superiora, *f*. **m. tongue,** lengua materna, *f*

motherhood /'mʌðərˌhʊd/ *n* maternidad, *f*

motherless /'mʌðərlɪs/ *a* huérfano de madre, sin madre

motherlike /'mʌðərˌlaik/ *a* de madre, como una madre

motherliness /'mʌðərlinɪs/ *n* cariño maternal, *m*

motherly /'mʌðərli/ *a* maternal

motif /mou'tif/ *n* motivo, *m*; tema, *m*; *Sew.* adorno, *m*

motion /'mouʃən/ *n* movimiento, *m*; *Mech.* marcha, operación, *f*; mecanismo, *m*; (sign) seña, señal, *f*; (gesture) ademán, gesto, *m*; (carriage) aire, porte, *m*; (of the bowels) movimiento del vientre, *m*, deyección, *f*; (will) voluntad, *f*, deseo, *m*; (proposal in an assembly or debate) proposición, moción, *f*; *Law.* pedimento, *m*. *vt* hacer una señal (a). *vi* hacer señas. **to set in m.,** poner en marcha. **m. picture,** fotografía cinematográfica, película, *f*. **m.-picture theater,** cine, *m*

motionless /'mouʃənlɪs/ *a* inmóvil

motivate /'moutəˌveit/ *vt* motivar

motive /'moutɪv/ *n* motivo, *m*. *a* motor; motivo. **with no m.,** sin motivo. **m. power,** fuerza motriz, *f*

motley /'mɒtli/ *a* abigarrado, multicolor; (mixed) diverso, vario. *n* traje de colores, *m*, botarga, *f*

motor /'moutər/ *n* motor, *m*; automóvil, *m*, a motor; movido por motor; con motor; (traveling) de viaje. *vi* ir en automóvil. *vt* llevar en automóvil (a). **m.boat,** lancha automóvil, *f*. **m.bus,** autobús, ómnibus, *m*. **m. car,** automóvil, *m*. **m.-coach,** autobús, *m*. **m.cycle,** motocicleta, *f*. **m.cyclist,** motociclista, *mf* **m.-launch,** canoa automóvil, *f*. **m.oil,** aceite para motores, *m*. **m.-road,** autopista, *f*. **m.-rug,** manta de viaje, *f*. **m.-scooter,** bicicleta con motor, *f*. **m.-spirit,** bencina, *f*

motoring /'moutərɪŋ/ *n* automovilismo, *m*

motorist /'moutərɪst/ *n* automovilista motorizada, *mf*

mottled /'mɒtl̩d/ *a* abigarrado; (of marble, etc.) jaspeado, esquizado; manchado (con), con manchas (de); pintado (con)

motto /'mɒtou/ *n Herald.* divisa, *f*; mote, *m*; (in a book, etc.) lema, *m*

mound /maund/ *n* montón, *m*; (knoll) altozano, *m*; (for defence) baluarte, *m*; (for burial) túmulo, *m*

mount /maunt/ *n* (hill, and in palmistry) monte, *m*; (for riding) caballería, *f*; montadura, *f*; (for a picture) borde, *m*. *vt* subir; (machines, etc.) montar; (jewels) engastar; (a picture) poner un borde a; (a play) poner en escena; poner a caballo; proveer de caballo. *vi* montar; subir; (increase) aumentar. **to m. a horse,** subir a caballo, montar. **to m. guard,** *Mil.* montar la guardia. **to m. the throne,** subir al trono

mountain /'mauntn̩/ *n* montaña, *f*; (mound) montón, *m*. *a* de montaña(s); montañés; alpino, alpestre. **to make a m. out of a molehill,** convertir un grano de arena en una montaña. hacer de una pulga un camello. hacer de una pulga un elefante. **m.-chain,** cadena de montañas, *f*. **m. climber,** *Lat. Am.* andinista, *mf*. **m. climbing,** *Lat. Am.* andinismo, *m*. **m.**

dweller, montañés (-esa). **m. railway,** ferrocárril de cremallera, *m*. **m.-side,** falda de una montaña, *f*
mountaineer /ˌmauntṇˈɪər/ *n* (inhabitant) montañés (-esa); (climber) alpinista, *mf*. *vi* hacer alpinismo
mountaineering /ˌmauntṇˈɪərɪŋ/ *n* alpinismo, *m*
mountainous /ˈmauntṇəs/ *a* montañoso; (huge) enorme
mountebank /ˈmauntəˌbæŋk/ *n* saltabanco, *m*; charlatán, *m*
mounting /ˈmauntɪŋ/ *n* (ascent) subida, *f*; ascensión, *f*; (of machinery, etc.) armadura, *f*; montadura, *f*; (of a precious stone) engaste, *m*. **m.-block,** subidero, *m*
mourn /mɔrn/ *vi* afligirse, lamentarse; (wear mourning) estar de luto. *vt* llorar; lamentar; llevar luto por
mourner /ˈmɔrnər/ *n* lamentador (-ra); (paid) plañidera, *f*; el, *m*, (*f*, la) que acompaña al féretro
mournful /ˈmɔrnfəl/ *a* triste, acongojado; funesto, lúgubre; fúnebre; lamentable
mournfully /ˈmɔrnfəli/ *adv* tristemente
mournfulness /ˈmɔrnfəlnɪs/ *n* tristeza, *f*; melancolía, aflicción, *f*, pesar, *m*
mourning /ˈmɔrnɪŋ/ *n* aflicción, *f*; lamentación, *f*; luto, *m*. **deep m.,** luto riguroso, *m*. **half m.,** medio luto, *m*. **to be in m.,** estar de luto. **to be in m. for,** llevar luto por. **to come out of m.,** dejar el luto. **m.-band,** (on the hat) tira de gasa, *f*; (on the arm) brazal de luto, *m*. **m.-coach,** coche fúnebre, *m*
mouse /maus/ *n* ratón (-na); *Naut.* barrilete, *m*. *vi* cazar ratones. **m.-colored,** de color de rata. **m.-hole, m.-trap,** ratonera, *f*
mouser /ˈmauzər/ *n* gato ratonero, *m*
mousing /ˈmausɪŋ/ *n* caza de ratones, *f*
mousy /ˈmausi/ *a* ratonesco, ratonil
mouth /*n.* mauθ; *v.* mauð/ *n* (*Anat.* human being, of a bottle, cave) boca, *f*; (entrada, *f*; (of a river) desembocadura, *f*; (of a channel) embocadero, *m*; (of a wind-instrument) boquilla, *f*. *vt* pronunciar con afectación; (chew) mascar. *vi* clamar a gritos, vociferar. **It makes my m. water,** Se me hace la boca agua. **large m.,** boca rasgada, *f*. **m.-gag,** abrebocas, *m*. **m.-organ,** armónica, *f*. **m.-wash,** antiséptico bucal, *m* (Argentina), enjuague, *m*
mouthed /mauðd, mauθt/ *a* que tiene boca...; de boca... **open-m.,** boquiabierto
mouthful /ˈmauθˌful/ *n* bocado, *m*; (of smoke, air) bocanada, *f*
mouthpiece /ˈmauθˌpis/ *n* (of wind-instruments, tobacco-pipe, waterpipe) boquilla, *f*; (of a wineskin) brocal, *m*; (spokesman) portavoz, *m*; intérprete, *mf*
movable /ˈmuvəbəl/ *a* movible; (of goods) mobiliario. **m. feast,** fiesta movible, *f*
movables /ˈmuvəbəlz/ *n pl* bienes muebles, efectos, *m pl*
movable type *n* tipos sueltos, *m pl*
move /muv/ *n* movimiento, *m*; (of household effects) mudanza, *f*; (motion) marcha, *f*; (in a game) jugada, *f*; (*Fig.* step) paso, *m*; (device) maniobra, *f*. **Whose m. is it?** ¿A quién le toca jugar? **to be on the m.,** estar en movimiento; estar de viaje. **to be always on the m.,** *Inf.* parecer una lanzadera
move /muv/ *vt* mover; poner en marcha; (furniture) trasladar; cambiar de lugar; (stir) remover; (shake) agitar, hacer temblar; (transport) transportar; (a piece in chess, etc.) jugar; (pull) arrancar; (impel) impulsar; (incline) inclinar, disponer; (affect emotionally) conmover, emocionar, enternecer; impresionar. *vi* moverse; ponerse en marcha; (walk) andar; ir; avanzar; (a step forward, etc.) dar; (move house) trasladarse; (act) entrar en acción; (in games) hacer una jugada; (progress) progresar; (shake) agitarse, temblar; removerse; (propose in an assembly) hacer una proposición; (in a court of law) hacer un pedimento; (grow) crecer. **to m. about,** pasearse; ir y venir; (of traffic) circular; (remove) trasladarse; (stir, tremble) agitarse. **to m. along,** caminar por; avanzar por. **to m. aside,** *vt* apartar; poner a un lado; (curtains) descorrer. *vi* ponerse a un lado; quitarse de en medio. **to m. away,** *vt* alejar. *vi* alejarse; marcharse; trasladarse; mudar de casa. **to m. back,** retroceder, volver hacia atrás. **to m. down,** bajar, descender. **to m. forward,** adelantarse; avanzar; progresar. **to m. in,** en-

trar (en); tomar posesión de una casa. **to m. off,** *vt* quitar. *vi* marcharse; ponerse en marcha; alejarse, apartarse. **to m. on,** avanzar; ponerse en marcha; circular; (of time) pasar, correr. **to m. out,** *vt* sacar, quitar. *vi* salir; (from a house) mudarse, abandonar (una casa, etc.). **to m. round,** dar vueltas, girar; (turn round) volverse. **to m. to,** (make) hacer, animar (a); causar. **to m. up,** *vt* montar, subir. *vi* montar; avanzar
movement /ˈmuvmənt/ *n* movimiento, *m*; *Mech.* mecanismo, *m*; (Stock Exchange) actividad, *f*. **encircling m.,** *Mil.* movimiento envolvente, *m*
mover /ˈmuvər/ *n* motor, *m*; móvil, *m*; promotor (-ra); (of a motion, proposer) autor (-ra) de una moción
movie /ˈmuvi/ *n* *Inf.* cine, *m*. **m. camera,** máquina de impresionar, *f*. **m. star,** estrella de la pantalla, *f*
moving /ˈmuvɪŋ/ *a* móvil; motor; (affecting) emocionante, conmovedor; impresionante; patético. *n* movimiento, *m*; traslado, *m*; cambio de domicilio, *m*. **m. picture,** fotografía cinematográfica, *f*. **m. staircase,** escalera móvil, *f*
movingly /ˈmuvɪŋli/ *adv* con emoción; patéticamente
mow /mou/ *vt* segar. *vi* (grimace) hacer muecas
mowing /ˈmouɪŋ/ *n* siega, *f*. **m.-machine,** segadora, *f*
Mr. /ˈmɪstər/ See **mister**
Mrs. /ˈmɪsəz/ See **mistress**
much /mʌtʃ/ *a* mucho. *adv* mucho; (by far) con mucho; (with past part.) muy; (pretty nearly) casi, más o menos. **m. of a size,** más o menos del mismo tamaño. **I was m. angered,** Estuve muy enfadado. **as m. as,** tanto como. **as m. more,** otro tanto. **How m. is it?** ¿Cuánto cuesta? **however m....,** por mucho que... **not m.,** no mucho. **not to think m. of,** tener en poco (a). **so m. so that,** tanto que. **too m.,** demasiado. **to make m. of,** dar grande importancia a; (a person) apreciar, querer; agasajar; (a child) mimar, acariciar
mucilage /ˈmyusəlɪdʒ/ *n* mucílago, *m*
muck /mʌk/ *n* (dung) estiércol, *m*; (filth) porquería, inmundicia, *f*; suciedad, *f*; (rubbish, of a literary work, etc.) porquería, *f*. **to m. up,** ensuciar; (spoil) estropear por completo
mucky /ˈmʌki/ *a* muy sucio; puerco; asqueroso, repugnante
mucosity /muˈkɒsɪti/ *n* mucosidad, *f*
mucous /ˈmyukəs/ *a* mucoso. **m. membrane,** mucosa, *f*
mucus /ˈmyukəs/ *n* mucosidad, *f*; (from the nose) moco, *m*
mud /mʌd/ *n* lodo, barro, fango, *m*. **to stick in the mud,** (of a ship, etc.) atrancarse. **mudbath,** baño de barro, *m*. **mud wall,** tapia, *f*
muddiness /ˈmʌdɪnɪs/ *n* estado fangoso, *m*; (of liquids) turbiedad, *f*; suciedad, *f*
muddle /ˈmʌdl/ *vt* (bewilder) dejar perplejo, aturdir; (intoxicate) emborrachar; (stupefy) entontecer; (spoil) estropear; embarullar, dejar en desorden; hacer un lío de. *n* desorden, *m*; confusión, *f*; lío, embrollo, *m*. **in a m.,** en desorden; en confusión. **to make a m.,** armar un lío. **to m. away,** derrochar sin ton ni son
muddled /ˈmʌdld/ *a* desordenado; confuso; estúpido; torpe; (drunk) borracho
muddy /ˈmʌdi/ *a* fangoso, lodoso, barroso; cubierto de lodo; (of liquids, etc.) turbio; (of the complexion) cetrino. *vt* enlodar, cubrir de lodo; ensuciar; (liquids) enturbiar
muezzin /myuˈɛzɪn, muˈ/ *n* almuecín, almuédano, *m*
muff /mʌf/ *n* manguito, *m*; (for a car radiator) cubierta para radiador, *m*; (*Inf.* at games, etc.) maleta, *m*. *vt* dejar escapar (una pelota); (an opportunity) perder
muffin /ˈmʌfɪn/ *n* mollete, *m*
muffle /ˈmʌfəl/ *vt* embozar, arrebozar; envolver; encubrir, ocultar, tapar; (stifle sound of) apagar; (oars, bells) envolver con tela para no hacer ruido; *Fig.* ahogar. **to m. oneself up,** embozarse
muffled /ˈmʌfəld/ *a* (of sound) sordo; confuso; apagado. **m. drum,** tambor enlutado, *m*
muffler /ˈmʌflər/ *n* (furnace) mufla, *f*; (of a car ra-

diator) mofle, *m*, cubierta para radiador, *f*; (silencer) silencioso, *m*

mufti /'mʌfti/ *n* mufti, *m*

mug /mʌg/ *n* vaso, *m*; (tankard) pichel, tarro, *m*; (face) jeta, *f*; (dupe) primo, *m*; (at games, etc.) maleta, *m*

mulatto /mə'lætou/ *a* mulato. *n* mulato (-ta). **m.-like,** amulatado

mulberry /'mʌl,bɛri/ *n* (fruit) mora, *f*; (bush) morera, *f*. **m. plantation,** moreral, *m*

mule /myul/ *n* mulo (-la); (slipper) mula, chinela, *f*; (spinning-jenny) huso mecánico, *m*

mulish /'myulɪʃ/ *a* mular; terco como una mula

mulishness /'myulɪʃnɪs/ *n* terquedad de mula, *f*

mullet /'mʌlɪt/ *n* (red) salmonete, *m*, trilla, *f*; (grey) mújol, *m*

multicolored /'mʌlti,kʌlərd/ *a* multicolor

multifarious /,mʌltə'fɛəriəs/ *a* numeroso, mucho; diverso, vario

multiform /'mʌltə,fɔrm/ *a* multiforme

multilateral /,mʌltɪ'lætərəl/ *a* multilátero

multimillionaire /,mʌltɪ'mɪlyə,nɛər/ *a* archimillonario, multimillonario, *n* multimillonario, *m*

multiple /'mʌltəpəl/ *a* múltiple, múltiplo. *n* múltiplo, *m*

multiple-choice question /'mʌltəpəl 'tʃɔis/ *n* pregunta optativa, *f*

multiplicand /,mʌltəplɪ'kænd/ *n* multiplicando, *m*

multiplication /,mʌltəplɪ'keiʃən/ *n* multiplicación, *f*. **m. table,** tabla de multiplicación, *f*

multiplicity /,mʌltə'plɪsɪti/ *n* multiplicidad, *f*

multiplier /'mʌltə,plaiər/ *n* Math. multiplicador, *m*; máquina de multiplicar, *f*

multiply /'mʌltəpli/ *vt* multiplicar. *vi* multiplicarse

multitude /'mʌltɪ,tud/ *n* multitud, *f*. **the m.,** las masas

multitudinous /,mʌltɪ'tudṇəs/ *a* muy numeroso

mumble /'mʌmbəl/ *vi* and *vt* musitar, hablar entre dientes; refunfuñar; (chew) mascullar

mummer /'mʌmər/ *n* momero (-ra); máscara, *mf*

mummery /'mʌməri/ *n* momería, *f*; mascarada, *f*

mummification /,mʌməfɪ'keiʃən/ *n* momificación, *f*

mummify /'mʌmə,fai/ *vt* momificar. *vi* momificarse

mummy /'mʌmi/ *n* momia, *f*; carne de momia, *f*; **m. case,** sarcófago, *m*

mumps /mʌmps/ *n pl* parotiditis, papera, *f*

munch /mʌntʃ/ *vt* masticar, mascullar, mascar

mundane /mʌn'dein/ *a* mundano

municipal /myu'nɪsəpəl/ *a* municipal. **m. charter,** fuero municipal, *m*. **m. government,** gobierno municipal, *m*

municipality /myu,nɪsə'pælɪti/ *n* municipio, *m*

munificence /myu'nɪfəsəns/ *n* munificencia, *f*

munificent /myu'nɪfəsənt/ *a* munífico, generoso

munition /myu'nɪʃən/ *n* munición, *f*. *vt* municionar. **m. dump,** depósito de municiones, *m*. **m. factory,** fábrica de municiones, *f*. **m. worker,** obrero (-ra) de una fábrica de municiones

mural /'myurəl/ *a* mural. *n* pintura mural, *f*

murder /'mɜrdər/ *n* asesinato, *m*. *vt* asesinar; dar muerte (a), matar; (a work, etc.) degollar. **He was murdered,** Fue asesinado. **willful m.,** homicidio premeditado, *m*

murderer /'mɜrdərər/ *n* asesino, *m*

murderess /'mɜrdərɪs/ *n* asesina, *f*

murderous /'mɜrdərəs/ *a* homicida; cruel, sanguinario; fatal; imposible, intolerable

murderously /'mɜrdərəsli/ *adv* con intento de asesinar; (with look) con ojos asesinos; cruelmente

murkiness /'mɜrkɪnɪs/ *n* obscuridad, lobreguez, *f*, tinieblas, *f pl*

murky /'mɜrki/ *a* lóbrego, negro, obscuro; (of one's past, etc.) negro, accidentado

murmur /'mɜrmər/ *n* murmullo, *m*; rumor, *m*; susurro, *m*; (grumble) murmurio, *m*. *vi* murmurar, susurrar; (complain) murmurar, quejarse. *vt* murmurar, decir en voz baja

murmuring /'mɜrmərɪŋ/ *n* murmurio, *m*, *a* que murmura, susurrante

muscatel /,mʌskə'tɛl/ *a* moscatel. *n* moscatel, *m*. **m. grape,** uva moscatel, *f*

muscle /'mʌsəl/ *n* músculo, *m*

Muscovite /'mʌskə,vait/ *a* moscovita. *n* moscovita, *mf*

muscular /'mʌskyələr/ *a* muscular, musculoso; (brawny) membrudo, fornido. **m. pains,** (in the legs, etc.) agujetas, *f pl*

muscularity /,mʌskyə'lærɪti/ *n* fuerza muscular, *f*

musculature /'mʌskyələtʃər/ *n* musculatura, *f*

Muse /myuz/ *n* musa, *f*

muse /myuz/ *n* meditación, *f*. *vi* meditar, reflexionar, rumiar; mirar las musarañas, estar distraído. **to m. on,** meditar en (or sobre)

museum /myu'ziəm/ *n* museo, *m*

museum of arms *n* museo de armas, *m*, aloteca, *f*

mushroom /'mʌʃrum/ *n Bot.* seta, *f*, hongo, *m*. *a* de setas; de forma de seta; (upstart) advenedizo; (ephemeral) efímero, de un día. **m.-bed,** setal, *m*. **m.-spawn,** esporas de setas, *f pl*

music /'myuzɪk/ *n* música, *f*; armonía, *f*; melodía, *f*. *a* de música. **to set to m.,** poner en música. **m.-hall,** teatro de variedades, *m*; salón de conciertos, *m*. **m. master,** profesor de música, *m*. **m. publisher,** editor de obras musicales, *m*. **m. stand,** atril, *m*; tablado para una orquesta, *m*. **m. stool,** taburete de piano, *m*

musical /'myuzɪkəl/ *a* musical; de música; armonioso, melodioso. **She is very m.,** Es muy aficionada a la música; Tiene mucho talento para la música. **m.-box,** caja de música, *f*. **m. comedy,** zarzuela, *f*. **m. instrument,** instrumento de música, *m*

musical chairs *n* escobas, *f pl*, el juego de sillas, *m sg*

musically /'myuzɪkli/ *adv* musicalmente; melodiosamente

musician /myu'zɪʃən/ *n* músico (-ca)

musing /'myuzɪŋ/ *n* meditación, *f*; ensueños, *m pl*, *a* pensativo, meditabundo

musingly /'myuzɪŋli/ *adv* reflexivamente

musk /mʌsk/ *n* (substance) almizcle, *m*; perfume de almizcle, *m*. *a* de almizcle; almizclero; (of scents) almizcleño. **m.-deer,** almizclero, *m*. **m.-rat,** rata almizclera, *f*

musket /'mʌskɪt/ *n* mosquete, *m*

musketeer /,mʌskɪ'tɪər/ *n* mosquetero, *m*

Muslim /'mʌzlɪm/ *a* musulmán, mahometano. *n* musulmán (-ana)

muslin /'mʌzlɪn/ *n* muselina, *f*, *a* de muselina

mussel /'mʌsəl/ *n* mejillón, *m*. **m.-bed,** criadero de mejillones, *m*

must /mʌst/ *vi* haber de; tener que; deber; (expressing probability) deber de, ser. **This question m. be settled without delay,** Esta cuestión debe ser resuelta sin demora. **You m. do it at once,** Tienes que hacerlo en seguida. **I m. have seen him in the street sometime,** Debo haberle visto en la calle alguna vez. **One m. eat to live,** Se ha de comer para vivir. **Well, go if you m.,** Bueno, vete si no hay más remedio. **It m. be a difficult decision for him,** Debe ser una decisión difícil para él. **It m. have been about twelve o'clock when...,** Serían las doce cuando...

must /mʌst/ *n* mosto, zumo de la uva, *m*; (mould) moho, *m*

mustache /'mʌstæʃ, mə'stæʃ/ *n* bigote, mostacho, *m*

mustang /'mʌstæŋ/ *n* potro mesteño, *m*

mustard /'mʌstərd/ *n* mostaza, *f*. **m. gas,** iperita, *m*. **m. plaster,** sinapismo, *m*. **m. pot,** mostacera, *f*. **m. spoon,** cucharita para la mostaza, *f*

muster /'mʌstər/ *n* lista, *f*, rol, *m*; revista, *f*; reunión, *f*, *vt* pasar lista (de); pasar revista (a); reunir. *vi* juntarse, reunirse. **to m. out,** (from the army) dar de baja (a). **to m. up sufficient courage,** cobrar ánimos suficientes. **to pass m.,** pasar revista; ser aceptado. **m.-roll,** *Mil.* revista, *f*; *Naut.* rol de la tripulación, *m*

mustiness /'mʌstɪnɪs/ *n* moho, *m*; ranciedad, *f*; (of a room, etc.) olor de humedad, *m*

musty /'mʌsti/ *a* mohoso; rancio; que huele a humedad. **to go m.,** enmohecerse

mutability /,myutə'bɪlti/ *n* mutabilidad, *f*; inconstancia, inestabilidad, *f*

mutable /'myutəbəl/ *a* mudable; inconstante, inestable

mutation /myu'teiʃən/ n mutación, f
mute /myut/ a mudo; silencioso. n mudo (-da); *Mus.* sordina, f; (phonetics) letra muda, f. **deaf m.**, sordomudo (-da)
muted /'myutɪd/ a (of sounds) sordo, apagado
mutely /'myutli/ adv mudamente; en silencio
muteness /'myutnɪs/ n mudez, f; silencio, m
mutilate /'myutḷˌeit/ vt mutilar; estropear
mutilation /ˌmyutḷ'eiʃən/ n mutilación, f
mutineer /ˌmyutn̩'ɪər/ n amotinador, rebelde, m
mutinous /'myutn̩əs/ a amotinado; rebelde, sedicioso; turbulento
mutiny /'myutn̩i/ n motín, m; sublevación, insurrección, f, vi amotinarse, sublevarse
mutt /mʌt/ n chucho, m
mutter /'mʌtər/ vt and vi murmurar, musitar; mascullar, decir (or hablar) entre dientes; gruñir, refunfuñar; (of thunder, etc.) tronar, retumbar. n murmurio, m; rumor, m; retumbo, m
mutton /'mʌtn̩/ n carnero, m, a de carnero. **m.-chop**, chuleta, f
mutual /'myutʃuəl/ a mutuo, recíproco; común. **by m. consent**, de común acuerdo. **m. aid society**, sociedad de socorros mutuos, f. **m. insurance company**, sociedad de seguros mutuos, f
mutual fund n fondo de inversiones rentables, m
mutualism /'myutʃuəˌlɪzəm/ n mutualismo, m
mutuality /ˌmyutʃu'ælɪti/ n mutualidad, f
mutually /'myutʃuəli/ adv mutuamente, recíprocamente
muzzle /'mʌzəl/ n (snout) hocico, m; (for a dog) bozal, m; (of a gun) boca, f. vt abozalar, poner un bozal (a); (Fig. gag) amordazar, imponer silencio (a)
muzzling /'mʌzlɪŋ/ n acción de abozalar, f; (Fig. gagging) amordazamiento, m
my /mai/ a poss mi, mf; mis, mf pl **my relatives,** mis parientes. **My goodness!** ¡Dios mío!
myelitis /ˌmaiə'laitɪs/ n mielitis, f
myopia /mai'oupiə/ n miopía, f
myopic /mai'ɒpɪk/ a miope
myriad /'mɪriəd/ n miríada, f
myrmidon /'mɜrmɪˌdɒn/ n rufián, m; asesino, m; secuaz, m
myrrh /mɜr/ n mirra, f
myrtle /'mɜrtḷ/ n mirto, arrayán, m
myself /mai'sɛlf/ pron yo mismo; (as a reflexive with a preposition) mí; (with a reflexive verb) me. **I m. sent it,** yo mismo (-ma) lo mandé
mysterious /mɪ'stiəriəs/ a misterioso
mysteriousness /mɪ'stiəriəsnɪs/ n misterio, m, lo misterioso
mystery /'mɪstəri/ n misterio, m. **m. play,** (religious) misterio, drama litúrgico, m; (thriller) comedia de detectives, f. **m. story,** novela policíaca, f; novela de aventuras, f
mystic /'mɪstɪk/ a místico
mysticism /'mɪstəˌsɪzəm/ n misticismo, m
mystification /ˌmɪstəfɪ'keiʃən/ n mistificación, f
mystify /'mɪstəˌfai/ vt mistificar
myth /mɪθ/ n mito, m
mythical /'mɪθɪkəl/ a mítico
mythologist /mɪ'θɒlədʒɪst/ n mitólogo, m
mythology /mɪ'θɒlədʒi/ n mitología, f

N

n /ɛn/ n (letter) ene, f
nab /næb/ vt Inf. atrapar, apresar, agazapar
nabob /'neibɒb/ n nabab, m; ricacho, m
nacre /'neikər/ n nácar, m, madreperla, f
nadir /'neidər/ n nadir, m
nag /næg/ n jaca, f; (wretched hack) rocín, jamelgo, penco, m. vt zaherir, echar en cara, regañar; (of one's conscience) remorder; *Lat. Am.* majaderear (pester) vi criticar, regañar
nagging /'nægɪŋ/ n zaherimiento, m. a zaheridor, criticón; (pain) continuo, incesante, constante
naiad /'neiæd/ n Myth. náyade, f
nail /neil/ vt clavar, enclavar; (for ornament) clavetear, tachonar, adornar con clavos. n uña, f; Mech. clavo, m; (animal's) garra, f. **to n. down,** sujetar (or cerrar) con clavos. **to n. to (on to),** clavar en. **to n. together,** fijar con clavos. Inf. **on the n.,** en el acto, en seguida. Inf. **to hit the n. on the head,** dar en el clavo. **brass-headed n.,** tachón, m. **French n.,** punta de París, f. **headless n.,** puntilla, f. **hob-n.,** clavo de herradura, m. **hook n.,** gancho, m. **round-headed n.,** bellota, f. **n.-brush,** cepillo para las (or de) uñas, m. **n.-file,** lima para las uñas, f. **n. head,** cabeza de un clavo, f. **n. polish,** barniz para las uñas, m. **n.-puller,** sacaclavos, arrancaclavos, botador, m. **n.-scissors,** tijeras para las uñas, f pl. **n. trade,** ferretería, f
nailed /neild/ a adornado con clavos, claveteado
nailer /'neilər/ n fabricante de clavos, chapucero, m
nailing /'neilɪŋ/ n enclavación, f
naive /nɑ'iv/ a ingenuo, candoroso, espontáneo
naively /na'ivli/ adv ingenuamente, espontáneamente
naiveté /nɑiv'tei, -'ivtei, -'ivə-/ n ingenuidad, naturalidad, franqueza, f; candor, m
naked /'neikɪd/ a desnudo, nudo, Peru calato, elsewhere in Lat. Am. encuerado; desabrigado, indefenso, desamparado; (birds) implume; calvo; (truth) simple, sencillo, puro; evidente, patente. **stark n.,** en cueros vivos, tal como le parió su madre. **with the n. sword,** con la espada desnuda. **n. eye,** simple vista, f. **n. light,** llama descubierta, f
nakedly /'neikɪdli/ adv nudamente; desabrigadamente; abiertamente, claramente
nakedness /'neikɪdnɪs/ n desnudez, f; Fig. desabrigo, m, aridez, f; Fig. claridad, f. **the truth in all its n.,** la verdad desnuda
namby-pamby /'næmbi'pæmbi/ a soso, insípido, ñoño
name /neim/ n nombre, m; título, m; fama, opinión, f; renombre, crédito, m; autoridad, f; apodo, mal nombre, m. vt nombrar, llamar, imponer el nombre de, apellidar; mencionar, señalar; (appoint) designar, elegir; (ships) bautizar. **by n.,** por nombre. **Christian n.,** nombre de pila, m. **in his n.,** en nombre de él, en nombre suyo; de parte de él. **in n. only,** nada más que en nombre. **to be named,** llamarse. **to call** (a person) **names,** poner como un trapo (a). **to go under the n. of,** vivir bajo el nombre de. **to have a good n.,** tener buena fama. **What is her n.?** ¿Cómo se llama? **n. day,** santo, m. **n. plate,** (machinery) placa de fábrica, f; (streets) rótulo, m; (professional) placa profesional, f
nameless /'neimlɪs/ a anónimo; desconocido; (inexpressible) vago, indecible
namely /'neimli/ adv a saber, es decir
namesake /'neim,seik/ n tocayo (-ya)
naming /'neimɪŋ/ n bautizo, m; nombramiento, m; designación, f
nannygoat /'næni,gout/ n cabra, f
nap /næp/ n (cloth) pelusa, f, pelo, tamo, m; (plants) vello, m, pelusilla, f; (sleep) siesta, f, sueño, m; (cards) napolitana, f. **to take a nap,** vi dormitar, echar un sueño, echar una siesta. **to take an afternoon nap,** dormir la siesta. **to be caught napping,** estar desprevenido
nape /neip/ n nuca, f, cogote, m; (animal's) testuz, m
naphtha /'næfθə, 'næp-/ n Chem. nafta, f. **wood n.,** alcohol metílico, m
naphthalene /'næfθə,lin, 'næp-/ n Chem. naftalina, f
napkin /'næpkɪn/ n (table) servilleta, f; (babies') pañal, m. **n.-ring,** servilletero, m
Naples /'neipəlz/ Nápoles, m
Napoleonic /nə,pouli'ɒnɪk/ a napoleónico
narcissism /'nɑrsə,sɪzəm/ n narcisismo, m
narcissus /nɑr'sɪsəs/ n narciso, m
narcosis /nɑr'kousɪs/ n Med. narcosis, f

narcotic /nɑr'kɒtɪk/ a Med. narcótico, calmante, soporífero. n Med. narcótico, m, opiata, f
nard /nɑrd/ n Bot. nardo, m, tuberosa, f
narrate /'næreɪt/ vt narrar, contar; referir, relatar
narration /næ'reɪʃən/ n narración, narrativa; relación, descripción, f, relato, m
narrative /'nærətɪv/ a narrador, narrativo, narratorio. n narrativa, f; descripción, f
narrator /'næreɪtər/ n narrador (-ra), relator (-ra), descriptor (-ra)
narrow /'nærou/ vt estrechar, angostar; reducir, limitar. vi reducirse, hacerse más estrecho; (eyes) entornarse; (knitting) menguar. a estrecho, angosto; limitado, restringido, reducido, corto; (avaricious) ruin, avaro, mezquino; (ideas) intolerante, intransigente. "Narrow Road," «Camino Estrecho». n pl **narrows,** Naut. estrecho, m; desfiladero, paso estrecho, m. **to have a n. escape,** escapar en una tabla. **n.-brimmed** (hats), de ala estrecha. **n.-gauge railway,** ferrocarril de vía estrecha (or de vía angosta), m. **n. life,** vida de horizontes estrechos, f. **n. majority,** escasa mayoría, f. **n.-minded,** cerrado al mundo, intolerante, intransigente. **n.-mindedness,** intolerancia, intransigencia, estrechez de miras, f
narrowing /'nærouɪŋ/ n estrechez, f, estrechamiento, m; reducción, limitación, f; (in knitting) menguado, m
narrowly /'nærouli/ adv estrechamente; por poco, con dificultad; atentamente, cuidadosamente. **I n. escaped being run over,** Por poco me atropellan
narrowness /'nærounɪs/ n estrechez, angostura, f; (of means) pobreza, miseria, f; (of ideas) intolerancia, intransigencia, f
nasal /'neɪzəl/ a nasal, gangoso. n letra nasal, f
nasally /'neɪzəli/ adv nasalmente. **to speak n.,** hablar por las narices, ganguear
nascent /'næsənt, 'neɪsənt/ a naciente
nastily /'næstəli/ adv suciamente; ofensivamente, de un modo insultante; maliciosamente, con malignidad
nastiness /'næstɪnɪs/ n suciedad, inmundicia, porquería, f; (indecency) obscenidad, indecencia, f; (rudeness) insolencia, impertinencia, grosería, f; (difficulty) dificultad, f, lo malo
nasturtium /nə'stɜrʃəm/ n mastuerzo, m, capuchina, f
nasty /'næsti/ a nauseabundo, repugnante; asqueroso, inmundo, sucio; (obscene) indecente, obsceno; desagradable, malo; (malicious) rencoroso, malicioso; violento; malévolo, amenazador; peligroso; difícil. Fig. **to be in a n. mess,** tener el agua al cuello. **to turn n.,** Inf. ponerse desagradable
nation /'neɪʃən/ n nación, f, estado, país, m; (people) pueblo, m
national /'næʃənl/ a nacional; público; patriótico. n nacional, mf. **n. anthem,** himno nacional, m. **n. debt,** deuda pública, f. **n. schools,** escuelas públicas, f pl. **n. socialism,** nacionalsocialismo, m. **n. socialist,** a and n nacionalsocialista mf. **n. syndicalism,** Polit. nacionalsindicalismo, m. **n. syndicalist,** a and n Polit. nacionalsindicalista, mf
nationalism /'næʃənl,ɪzəm/ n nacionalismo, patriotismo, m
nationalist /'næʃənlɪst/ a and n nacionalista, mf
nationality /,næʃə'nælɪti/ n nacionalidad, f; nación, f
nationalization /,næʃənlə'zeɪʃən/ n nacionalización, f
nationalize /'næʃənl,aɪz, 'næʃnə,laɪz/ vt nacionalizar, Lat. Am. also estatizar
National Labor Relations Board n Junta Nacional de Relaciones Laborales
nationally /'næʃənli/ adv nacionalmente, como nación; del punto de vista nacional
native /'neɪtɪv/ a (of a place) nativo, natal, oriundo; indígena; nacional, típico, del país; (vocabulary) patrimonial (as opposed to borrowed vocabulary); (of genius) natural, innato, instintivo; Mineral. nativo; (language) vernáculo. n nacional, mf; natural, mf; ciudadano (-na) indígena, aborigen (gen. pl.), mf; producto nacional, m. **He is a n. of Madrid,** Nació en Madrid, Es natural de Madrid, Es madrileño. **Native American commune** (in Peru) ayllu, m. **native informant,** sujeto, m. **n. land,** patria, tierra. **n. of the capital** Lat. Am. capitalino, n. of Rio de Janeiro ca-

rioca, mf. **n. place,** lugar natal, m. **n. region,** patria chica, f. **n. soil,** terruño, m. **n. tongue,** lengua materna, f
Native American n (Indian) indígena, mf
Native American movement n Lat. Am. indigenismo, m
nativity /nə'tɪvɪti/ n navidad, natividad, f; (manger) nacimiento, m
natty /'næti/ a Inf. chulo, majo; coquetón
natural /'nætʃərəl/ a natural; (wild) virgen, salvaje; nativo; (of products) crudo; normal; (usual) acostumbrado, corriente, natural; (of likeness) fiel, verdadero; (illegitimate) ilegítimo, bastardo; (of qualities) innato, instintivo; físico; característico, propio; (of people) inafectado, sencillo, genuino; Mus. natural. n Mus. becuadro, m; Mus. nota natural, f; imbécil, mf n. **features,** geografía física, f. **n. history,** historia natural, f. **n. philosophy,** filosofía natural, f. **n. science,** ciencias naturales, f pl. **n. selection,** selección natural, f. **n. state,** estado virgen, m
natural child n hijo natural, m
naturalism /'nætʃərə,lɪzəm/ n naturalismo, m
naturalist /'nætʃərəlɪst/ n (Lit. and Science.) naturalista, mf
naturalistic /,nætʃərə'lɪstɪk/ a naturalista
naturalization /,nætʃərələ'zeɪʃən/ n naturalización, f; aclimatación, f. **n. papers,** carta de naturaleza, f
naturalize /'nætʃərə,laɪz/ vt naturalizar; aclimatar. **to become naturalized,** naturalizarse
naturally /'nætʃərəli/ adv naturalmente, por naturaleza; normalmente; sin afectación; instintivamente, por instinto; (without art) al natural. **n. curly hair,** Guatemala colocho, m
naturalness /,nætʃərəlnɪs/ n naturalidad, f; sencillez, desenvoltura, f; desembarazo, m
nature /'neɪtʃər/ n naturaleza, f; (of people) carácter, fondo, temperamento, genio, natural, modo de ser, m; (kind) género, m, especie, f; (essence) condición, esencia, cualidad, f, Art. **from n.,** del natural. **good n.,** bondad natural, afabilidad, f. **ill n.,** mala índole, f. **nature cure,** naturismo, m. **n. curist,** naturista, mf. **n. study,** historia natural, f. **n. worship,** panteísmo, culto de la naturaleza, m
natured /'neɪtʃərd/ a de carácter, de índole, con un modo de ser, de condición
naught /nɔt/ n nada, f; cero, m. a inútil, sin valor. **all for n.,** todo en balde. **to come to n.,** malograrse. **to set at n.,** tener en menos; despreciar
naughtily /'nɔtli/ adv traviesamente; con picardía, con malicia
naughtiness /'nɔtinɪs/ n travesura, picardía, mala conducta, f; malicia, f
naughty /'nɔti/ a travieso, pícaro, revoltoso, malo; salado, escabroso, verde (stories, etc.). **to be n.,** (children) ser malo
nausea /'nɔziə, -ʒə/ n náusea, f, bascas, f pl, mareo, m; Fig. asco, m; repugnancia, f
nauseate /'nɔzi,eɪt, -ʒi-/ vt dar náuseas; Fig. repugnar, dar asco
nauseating /'nɔzi,eɪtɪŋ, -ʒi-/ a repugnante, horrible; asqueroso
nauseous /'nɔʃəs/ a nauseabundo, asqueroso; Fig. repugnante
nauseousness /'nɔʃəsnɪs/ n náusea, asquerosidad, f; Fig. repugnancia, f, asco, m
nautical /'nɔtɪkəl/ a náutico, marítimo. **n. day, twenty-four hours,** singladura, f
naval /'neɪvəl/ a naval; de marina, marítimo. **n. base,** base naval, f. **n. engagement,** batalla naval, f. **n. hospital,** hospital de marina, m. **n. law,** código naval, m. **n. officer,** oficial de marina, m. **n. power,** poder marítimo, m. **n. reservist,** marinero de reserva, m. **n. yard,** arsenal, m
Navarre /nə'vɑr/ Navarra, f
nave /neɪv/ n Archit. nave, f; (of wheels) cubo, m
navel /'neɪvəl/ n ombligo, m. **n. string,** cordón umbilical, m
navigability /,nævɪgə'bɪlɪti/ n navegación, practicabilidad de navegar, f
navigable /'nævɪgəbəl/ a navegable, practicable

navigate /'nævɪˌgeɪt/ *vt* navegar, marear, dirigir (unbuque); *Fig.* conducir, guiar. *vi* navegar
navigation /ˌnævɪ'geɪʃən/ *n* navegación, *f*; (science of) náutica, marina, *f*. **n. company,** empresa naviera, *f*. **n. laws,** derecho marítimo, *m*. **n. lights,** luces de navegación, *f pl*
navigator /'nævɪˌgeɪtər/ *n* navegador, navegante, *m*; piloto, *m*
navvy /'nævi/ *n* peón, bracero, jornalero, *m*; *Mech.* máquina, excavadora, *f*. **road n.,** peón caminero, *m*. **to work like a n.,** estar hecho un azacán, sudar la gota gorda
navy /'neivi/ *n* marina, *f*; armada, *f*; (color) azul marino, *m*. **n. board,** consejo de la armada, *m*. **n. department** ministerio de marina, *m*. **n. estimates,** presupuesto de marina, *m*. **n. list,** escalafón de marina, *m*
nay /nei/ *adv* no; al contrario, más bien, mejor dicho. *n* negativa, *f*, voto contrario, *m*
Nazarene /ˌnæzə'rin/ *a* and *n* nazareno (-na)
Nazareth /'næzərəθ/ Nazaret, *m*
Nazi /'nɑtsi/ *a* and *n* nacionalsocialista, naci, *mf*
Nazism /'nɑtsɪzəm/ *n* nacismo, *m*
n.d. (no date) *s.f.* (sin fecha)
Neapolitan /ˌniə'pɒlɪtn̩/ *a* and *n* neapolitano (-na)
near /nɪər/ *vi* acercarse, aproximarse. *a* cercano, inmediato, contiguo; (of time) inminente, próximo; (relationship) cercano, consanguíneo; (of friends) íntimo, entrañable; (mean) tacaño, avariento
near /nɪər/ *prep* cerca de, junto a; hacia, en la dirección de; (of time) cerca de, casi. *adv* cerca, *Central America, Chile, Mexico* lueguito; (time) cerca, próximamente. **to be n. to,** estar cerca de. **to bring n.,** acercar, aproximar. **It was a n. thing,** Escapamos por un pelo. **n. at hand,** a la mano; (time) cerca, inminente. **n.-by,** *a* cercano, inmediato, *Central America, Chile, Mexico* lueguito. *adv* cerca, *m*. **n. side,** (of vehicles) lado de la acera, *m*. **n.-sighted,** corto de vista, miope. **n.-sightedness,** miopía, cortedad de vista, *f*
nearest /'nɪərɪst/ *a comp* and *sup* más cercano, más cerca; más corto. **the n. way,** el camino más corto, el camino directo
nearly /'nɪərli/ *adv* casi; cerca de, aproximadamente; estrechamente; íntimamente. **It touches me n.,** Me toca de cerca, Es de sumo interés para mí. **They n. killed me,** Por poco me matan. **to be n.,** (of age) frisar en, rayar en
nearness /'nɪərnɪs/ *n* (of place) cercanía, proximidad, contigüidad, *Argentina* adyacencia, *f*; (of time) inminencia, proximidad, *f*; (relationship) consanguinidad, *f*; (avarice) avaricia, tacañería, *f*; (dearness) intimidad, amistad estrecha, *f*
neat /nit/ *a* limpio, ordenado, sencillo, de buen gusto; (of the body) bien hecho, airoso, esbelto; aseado; (of handwriting) legible, bien proporcionado; pulido, esmerado, acabado; hábil, astuto, diestro; *Zool.* vacuno; (of liquor, spirits) puro, solo. **to make a n. job of,** hacer (algo) bien
neatly /'nitli/ *adv* sencillamente, con elegancia, con primor; con aseo, limpiamente; bien (proporcionado); diestramente, hábilmente
neatness /'nitnɪs/ *n* aseo, *m*, limpieza, *f*; elegancia, sencillez, *f*; buen gusto, *m*; destreza, habilidad, *f*; (aptness) pertinencia, *f*
nebula /'nɛbyələ/ *n Astron.* nebulosa, *f*
nebulosity /ˌnɛbyə'lɒsɪti/ *n* nebulosidad, *f*; *Astron.* nebulosa, *f*; vaguedad, imprecisión, *f*
nebulous /'nɛbyələs/ *a* nebuloso; vago, impreciso, confuso
necessarily /ˌnɛsə'sɛərəli/ *adv* necesariamente; inevitablemente, sin duda
necessary /'nɛsəˌsɛri/ *a* necesario, inevitable; imprescindible, preciso, indispensable, esencial; obligatorio, debido, forzoso. *n* requisito esencial, *m*. **if n.,** en caso de necesidad; si fuera necesario. **to be n.,** hacer falta; necesitarse
necessitate /nə'sɛsɪˌteɪt/ *vt* necesitar, exigir, requerir, obligar
necessitous /nə'sɛsɪtəs/ *a* pobre, indigente, miserable, necesitado
necessity /nə'sɛsɪti/ *n* necesidad, *f*; menester, *m*, (e.g., *an indispensable n.,* un menester imprescindible); consecuencia, *f*, resultado, efecto, *m*; inevitabilidad, fatalidad, *f*; (poverty) indigencia, pobreza, *f*. **Fire and clothing are necessities,** El fuego y el vestir son cosas necesarias. **from n.,** por necesidad. **in case of n.,** si fuese necesario, en caso de necesidad. **of n.,** de necesidad, sin remedio. **physical necessities,** menesteres físicos, *m pl*. **prime n.,** artículo de primera necesidad, *m*. **to be under the n. of,** tener que, tener la necesidad de
Necessity is the mother of invention La necesidad es una gran inventora, La necesidad aguza el ingenio
neck /nɛk/ *n* cuello, *m*, garganta, *f*; (of bottles) gollete, cuello, *m*; (of animals) pescuezo, *m*; *Geog.* istmo, *m*, lengua de tierra, *f*; (of musical instruments) clavijero, mástil, *m*; *Sew.* escote, *m*. **low-necked,** (of dresses) escotado. **She fell on his n.,** Se colgó de su cuello. **He won by a n.,** Ganó por un cuello; *Fig.* Ganó por un tris. **to break anyone's n.,** romperle el pescuezo. **to wring the n. of,** torcer el pescuezo (a). **n. and n.,** parejos. **n. or nothing,** todo o nada, perdiz o no comenta. **n. stock,** alzacuello, *m*
neckband /'nɛkˌbænd/ *n* tirilla de camisa, *f*
necklace /'nɛklɪs/ *n* collar, *m*
necklet /'nɛklɪt/ *n* collar, *m*; (of fur) cuello, *m*
necktie /'nɛkˌtai/ *n* corbata, *f*
necrological /ˌnɛkrə'lɒdʒɪkəl/ *a* necrológico
necrology /nə'krɒlədʒi/ *n* necrología, *f*
necropolis /nə'krɒpəlɪs/ *n* necrópolis, *f*
nectar /'nɛktər/ *n* néctar, *m*
nectarine /'nɛktə'rin/ *n Bot.* variedad de melocotón, *f*
need /nid/ *vt* necesitar, haber menester, requerir, exigir. *vi* ser necesario, hacer falta, carecer; haber (de). **N. I obey?** ¿He de obedecer? **You need to write carefully,** Hay que escribir con cuidado. **The work n. not be done for tomorrow,** No es preciso hacer el trabajo para mañana
need /nid/ *n* necesidad, *f*; cosa necesaria, *f*; falta, *f*; (poverty) indigencia, pobreza, *f*; urgencia, *f*; (shortage) escasez, carestía, *f*. **in case of n.,** en caso de necesidad, en caso de urgencia. **I have n. of two more books,** Me hacen falta dos libros más
needful /'nidfəl/ *a* necesario, preciso; indispensable, esencial. **the n.,** lo necesario
needfulness /'nidfəlnɪs/ *n* necesidad, falta, *f*
neediness /'nidinɪs/ *n* pobreza, penuria, miseria, estrechez, *f*
needle /'nidl̩/ *n Sew.* aguja, *f*; (of compass) brújula, aguja imanada, *f*; (monument) obelisco, *m*; (of scales) field, *m*, lengüeta, *f*; (of phonograph) púa, *f*, (of measuring instruments) índice, *m*; *Med.* aguja de inyecciones, *f*. *Inf.* **to be as sharp as a n.,** no tener pelo de tonto. **pack n.,** aguja espartera, *f*. **n.-case,** alfiletero, agujero, *m*. **n. maker,** fabricante de agujas, *m*. **n.-shaped,** en forma de aguja, acicular. *vt Lat. Am.* engorrar
needle and thread hilo y aguja
needless /'nidlɪs/ *a* innecesario, supérfluo. **n. to say,** claro está que..., huelga decir que...
needlessly /'nidlɪsli/ *adv* innecesariamente, inútilmente; en vano, de balde
needlessness /'nidlɪsnɪs/ *n* superfluidad, *f*, lo innecesario
needlewoman /'nidl̩ˌwʊmən/ *n* (professional) cosedora, *f*; costurera, *f*. **She is a good n.,** Cose bien (or es una buena cosedora)
needlework /'nidl̩ˌwɜrk/ *n* labor de aguja, labor blanca, costura, *f*; bordado, *m*. **to do n.,** hacer costura
needs /nidz/ *adv* necesariamente, sin remedio *n pl* necesidades, *f pl*. **if must n.,** si hace falta
needy /'nidi/ *a* necesitado, menesteroso, corto de medios, pobre, apurado
ne'er-do-well /'nɛərduˌwɛl/ *n* calavera, perdido, *m*. **to be a n.,** ser de mala madera
nefarious /nɪ'fɛəriəs/ *a* nefario, vil, nefando
nefariously /nɪ'fɛəriəsli/ *adv* vilmente, nefariamente *f*
negation /nɪ'geɪʃən/ *n* negación, *f*
negative /'nɛgətɪv/ *vt* negar, denegar; votar en contra (de), oponerse (a); (prevent) impedir, imposibilitar. *a* negativo. *n* negativa, negación, *f*; repulsa, denegación, *f*; *Photo.* negativo, *m*, prueba negativa, *f*; *Elec.*

electricidad negativa, f. **to reply in the n.**, dar una respuesta negativa

negativeness /'nɛgətɪvnɪs/ n el carácter negativo, m

neglect /nɪ'glɛkt/ vt descuidar, desatender; abandonar, dejar; (ignore) despreciar, no hacer caso (de); omitir, olvidar. n descuido, m, desatención, f; inobservancia, f; abandono, olvido, m; desdén, m, frialdad, f. **to fall into n.**, caer en desuso. **to n. one's obligations**, descuidar sus obligaciones

neglectful /nɪ'glɛktfəl/ a negligente, descuidado, omiso

negligee /,nɛglɪ'ʒei/ n salto de cama, quimono, m, bata, f

negligence /'nɛglɪdʒəns/ n negligencia, f, descuido, m; flojedad, pereza, f; (of dress) desaliño, m

negligent /'nɛglɪdʒənt/ a negligente, descuidado; remiso, flojo, perezoso

negligently /'nɛglɪdʒəntli/ adv negligentemente; con indiferencia

negligible /'nɛglɪdʒəbəl/ a insignificante, escaso, insuficiente; sin importancia, desdeñable

negotiable /nɪ'goʊʃiəbəl, -ʃəbəl/ a negociable; (of a road) practicable, transitable

negotiate /nɪ'goʊʃi,eit/ vt gestionar, agenciar, tratar; (a bend) tomar; (an obstacle) salvar, franquear; vi negociar. **to n. a bill of exchange**, descontar una letra de cambio. **to n. for a contract**, tratar un contrato

negotiation /nɪ,goʊʃi'eiʃən/ n negociación, f; Com. gestión, transacción, f; (of a bend) toma, f; (of an obstacle) salto, m

negotiator /nɪ'goʊʃi,eitər/ n negociador (-ra)

neigh /nei/ vi relinchar. n relincho, relinchido, m

neighbor /'neibər/ n vecino (-na); (biblical) prójimo (-ma)

neighborhood /'neibər,hʊd/ n vecindad, f, vecindario, m; cercanía, f, afueras, f pl, alrededores, m pl; a de barrio (e.g. neighborhood moviehouse, cine del barrio)

neighboring /'neibərɪŋ/ a vecino; cercano, inmediato, adyacente

neighborliness /'neibərlinɪs/ n buena vecindad, f

neighborly /'neibərli/ a amistoso, sociable, bondadoso. **to be n.**, ser de buena vecindad.

neither /'niðər, 'nai-/ a ningún; ninguno de los dos, e.g. N. explanation is right, Ninguna de las dos explicaciones es correcta. conjunc ni, tampoco, e.g. N. Mary nor John, Ni María ni Juan. N. will he give it to her, Tampoco se lo dará. pron ni uno ni otro, ninguno, e.g. N. of them heard it, Ni uno ni otro lo oyó.

nemesis /'nɛməsɪs/ n némesis, f; justicia, f

neo- prefix neo. **neo-Catholic**, a and n neo-católico (-ca). **neo-Platonic**, neoplatónico. **neo-Platonism**, neoplatonismo, m

neolithic /,niə'lɪθɪk/ a neolítico

neologism /ni'ɒlə,dʒɪzəm/ n neologismo, m

neon /'niɒn/ n Chem. neón, m

neon sign anuncio luminoso, m

neophyte /'niə,fait/ n neófito (-ta); aspirante, mf

nephew /'nɛfyu/ n sobrino, m

nephritis /nə'fraitɪs/ n Med. nefritis, f

nepotism /'nɛpə,tɪzəm/ n nepotismo, m

nerve /nɜrv/ n (Anat. Bot.) nervio, m; valor, ánimo, m; vitalidad, f; Inf. descaro, m, desvergüenza, frescura, f. vt animar, alentar, envalentonar; esforzar; dar fuerza (a). vi animarse, esforzarse (a). **My nerves are all on edge, Se me crispan los nervios. n.-cell**, neurona, f. **to lose one's n.**, perder la cabeza; perder los nervios. **to strain every n.**, hacer un esfuerzo supremo. **n. center**, centro nervioso, m. **n.-racking**, espantoso, horripilante. **n. strain**, tensión nerviosa, f

nerveless /'nɜrvlɪs/ a sin nervio; enervado

nerviness /'nɜrvinɪs/ n nervosidad, f

nervous /'nɜrvəs/ a nervioso, asustadizo, tímido; agitado, excitado; (of style) vigoroso. **n. breakdown**, crisis nerviosa, f. **n. system**, sistema nervioso, m

nervously /'nɜrvəsli/ adv nerviosamente; tímidamente

nervousness /'nɜrvəsnɪs/ n nervosidad, timidez, f; agitación, f; (of style) vigor, m; energía, f

nervy /'nɜrvi/ a valeroso; Inf. descarado

nest /nɛst/ vi anidar, hacerse un nido. n (bird's) nido, m; (animal's) madriguera, f; (of drawers) juego, m, serie, f; (of thieves) cueva, guarida, f; Inf. casita, f, hogar, m. **to feather one's n.**, hacer su agosto. **n.-egg**, Fig. nidal, m. **n. of eggs**, nidada de huevos, f

nestle /'nɛsəl/ vt apoyar. vi apiñarse, hacerse un ovillo. **to n. up to a person**, apretarse contra

nestling /'nɛstlɪŋ/ n pichón, pollo, m; pajarito, m

net /nɛt/ vt coger con redes; obtener, coger; cubrir con redes. vi hacer redes. n red, f; (mesh) malla, f; (fabric) tul, m. **net making**, manufactura de redes, f

net /nɛt/ a Com. líquido, neto, limpio; (of fabric) de tul. **net amount**, importe líquido, importe neto, m. **net balance**, saldo líquido, m. **net cost**, precio neto, m. **net profit**, beneficio neto (or líquido), m

nether /'nɛðər/ a inferior, bajero, más bajo. **n. regions**, infierno, m

Netherland /'nɛðərlənd/ a neerlandés, holandés

Netherlander /'nɛðər,lændər/ n neerlandés (-esa), holandés (-esa)

Netherlands, the /'nɛðərləndz/ los Países Bajos m pl

nethermost /'nɛðər,moust/ a lo más bajo, ínfimo, más hondo

netting /'nɛtɪŋ/ n red, (obra de) malla, f; Naut. jareta, f; manufactura de redes, f; pesca con redes, f. **wire-n.**, tela metálica, malla de alambre, f

nettle /'nɛtl/ vt picar; Fig. irritar, picar, fastidiar, disgustar. n ortiga, f. **n.-rash**, urticaria, f

network /'nɛt,wɜrk/ n red, malla, randa, f; (of communications) sistema, m, red, f

neuralgia /nʊ'rældʒə/ n neuralgia, f

neuralgic /nʊ'rældʒɪk/ a neurálgico

neurasthenia /,nʊrəs'θiniə/ n neurastenia, f

neurasthenic /,nʊrəs'θɛnɪk/ a and n neurasténico (-ca)

neuritis /nʊ'raitɪs/ n neuritis, f

neurologist /nʊ'rɒlədʒɪst/ n neurólogo, m

neurology /nʊ'rɒlədʒi/ n neurología, f

neuropath /'nʊrə,pæθ/ n neurópata, m

neuropathic /,nʊrə'pæθɪk/ a neuropático

neurosis /nʊ'rousɪs/ n neurosis, f

neurosurgeon /'nʊrou,sɜrdʒən/ n neurocirujano, m

neurotic /nʊ'rɒtɪk/ a and n neurótico (-ca)

neuter /'nutər/ a neutro; (of verbs) intransitivo; (Zool. Bot.) sin sexo

neutral /'nutrəl/ a neutral; (Chem. Mech.) neutro; (of colors) indeciso, indeterminado; (of persons) imparcial, indiferente. n neutral, mf Mech. **to go into n.**, pasar a marcha neutra

neutrality /nu'trælɪti/ n neutralidad, f; indiferencia, f; imparcialidad, f

neutralization /,nutrələ'zeiʃən/ n neutralización, f

neutralize /'nutrə,laiz/ vt neutralizar

never /'nɛvər/ adv nunca, jamás; de ningún modo, no; ni aun, ni siquiera. **Better late than n.**, Más vale tarde que nunca. **Never look a gift horse in the mouth**, A caballo regalado no se le mira el diente. **Were the hour n. so late**, Por más tarde que fuese la hora. **n. again**, nunca jamás. **n. a one**, ni siquiera uno. **n. a whit**, ni pizca. **N. mind!** ¡No importa! ¡No te preocupes! ¡No hagas caso! ¡Olvídatelo! **n.-ceasing**, continuo, incesante. **n.-ending**, inacabable, eterno, sin fin. **n.-failing**, infalible. **n.-to-be-forgotten**, inolvidable

nevermore /,nɛvər'mɔr/ adv nunca jamás

nevertheless /,nɛvərðə'lɛs/ adv sin embargo, no obstante, con todo

new /nu/ a nuevo; novel, fresco, distinto, diferente; moderno; (inexperienced) novato, no habituado; reciente. adv (in compounds) recién. **as good as new**, como nuevo. **brand-new**, flamante, nuevecito. **new-born**, recién nacido. **new-comer**, recién llegado (-da). **new-fashioned**, de última moda. **new-found**, recién hallado. **new moon**, luna nueva, f, novilunio, m. **new rich**, ricacho (-cha); indio, m. **new student**, alumno de nuevo ingreso, m. **New Testament**, Nuevo Testamento, m. **New World**, Nuevo Mundo, m. **New**

York (er), *a* and *n* neoyorquino (-na). **New Zealand (er),** *a* and *n* neozelandés (-esa)

newel /'nuəl/ *n* (of stair) alma, *f*, árbol, nabo, *m*. **n.-post,** pilarote (de escalera), *m*

newest /'nuɪst/ *a sup* novísimo; más reciente

Newfoundland /'nufənlənd/ Terranova, *f*. **N. dog,** perro de Terranova, *m*

newish /'nuɪʃ/ *a* bastante nuevo

newly /'nuli/ *adv* nuevamente; hace poco, recientemente. The abb. form **recién** is used only with past part, e.g. *the n. painted door,* la puerta recién pintada. *the n.-weds,* los desposados, los recién casados

newness /'nunɪs/ *n* novedad, *f*; inexperiencia, falta de práctica, *f*; innovación, *f*

New Orleans /'ɔrliənz, ɔr'linz/ Nueva Orleans, *f*

news /nuz/ *n pl* noticias, *f pl*; nueva, *f*; reporte, aviso, *m*; novedad, *f*. **No n. is good n.,** Falta de noticias, buena señal. **piece of n.,** noticia, *f*. **What's the n.?** ¿Qué hay de nuevo? **n. agency,** agencia de noticias, agencia periodística, *f*. **n.-agent,** agente de la prensa, *m*; vendedor (-ra) de periódicos. **n. bulletin,** *Radio.* boletín de noticias, *m*. *Inf.* **n.-hound,** gacetillero (-ra). **n. item,** noticia de actualidad, *f*. **n.-print,** papel para periódicos, *m*. **n.-room,** gabinete de lectura, *m*. **n. reel,** película noticiera, revista cinematográfica, *f*, noticiario cinematográfico, noticiero *m*, actualidades, *f pl*. **n.-stand,** puesto de periódicos, quiosco de periódicos, *m*

newsboy /'nuz,bɔi/ *n Lat. Am.* canillito, *m*

newscast /'nuz,kæst/ *n* noticiario, *m*

newsgirl /'nuz,gɜrl/ *n Lat. Am.* canillita, *f*

newsletter circular /'nuz,letər/ noticiera, relación de sucesos, *f*

newspaper /'nuz,peipər/ *n* periódico, diario, noticiero, *m*. **n. clipping, n. cutting,** recorte de periódico, *m*. **n. paragraph,** suelto, *m*. **n. reporter,** reportero (-ra); periodista, *mf* **n. reporting,** reporterismo, *m*. **n. serial,** folletín, *m*, novela por entregas, *f*. **n. vendor,** vendedor (-ra) de periódicos, *m*

news report *n* reportaje, *m*

newsy /'nuzi/ *a Inf.* lleno de noticias, noticioso

newt /nut/ *n* tritón, *m*

Newtonian /nu'touniən/ *a* neutoniano

New York /yɔrk/ Nueva York, *f*

New Zealand /'zilənd/ Nueva Zelandia, *f*

next /nɛkst/ *a* (of place) siguiente, vecino, contiguo; (of time) próximo, siguiente. **on the n. page,** en la página siguiente. **the n. day,** el día siguiente. **the n.-door house,** la casa vecina. **the n. life,** la otra vida. **n. month (yesar),** el mes (año) próximo (or que viene). **n. time,** otra vez, la próxima vez

next /nɛkst/ *adv* (of time) luego, en seguida; (of place) inmediatamente después. **I come n.,** Ahora me toca a mí. **It is n. to a certainty that...,** Es casi seguro que... **the n. best,** el segundo. **the n. of kin,** los pariente más cercarro, *m*, parientes más cercanos, *m pl*. **to wear n. to the skin,** llevar sobre la piel. **n. to,** al lado de, junto a; primero después de; casi. **n. to nothing,** casi nada, muy poco. **What n.?** ¿Qué más?; ¿Y ahora qué?

nib /nɪb/ *n* punto, tajo (de una pluma), *m*

nibble /'nɪbəl/ *vt* mordiscar, mordisquear, roer; (horses) rozar; (fish) picar; *Fig.* considerar, tantear; *vi* picar. *n* mordisco, *m*; roedura, *f*

Nicaragua /,nɪkə'rɑgwə/ Nicaragua

Nicaraguan /,nɪkə'rɑgwən/ *a* and *n* nicaragüeño (-ña)

Nice /nis/ Niza, *f*

nice /nais/ *a* escrupuloso, minucioso, exacto; (of persons) simpático, afable, amable; fino; (of things) agradable, bonito; bueno; sutil, delicado; (*Inf. Ironic.*) bonito. **a n. point,** un punto delicado. **a n. view,** una vista agradable (or bonita). **n.-looking,** guapo. **n. people,** gente fina, *f*; gente simpática, *f*

nicely /'naisli/ *adv* muy bien; con elegancia; primorosamente; con amabilidad, gentilmente; agradablemente

Nicene /nai'sin/ *a* niceno

niceness /'naisnɪs/ *n* exactitud, minuciosidad, *f*; (of persons) bondad, amabilidad, *f*; amenidad, hermosura, *f*; lo bonito; sutileza, *f*; refinamiento, *m*

nicety /'naisɪti/ *n* exactitud, *f*; sutileza, *f*; refina-

miento, *m*. **niceties,** *n pl* detalles, *m pl*. **to a n.,** con la mayor precisión; a la perfección

niche /nɪtʃ/ *n* nicho, templete, *m*; (vaulted) hornacina, *f*, *Fig.* **to find a n. for oneself,** encontrarse una buena posición; situarse

nick /nɪk/ *vt* cortar en muescas, mellar, tarjar. *n* mella, muesca, *f*. **in the n. of time,** en el momento oportuno, a tiempo

nickel /'nɪkəl/ *n* níquel, *m*; *Com.* moneda de níquel, *f*. **n.-plated,** niquelado

nickname /'nɪk,neim/ *vt* apodar, motejar, apellidar. *n* apodo, sobrenombre, mote, mal nombre, *m*

nicotine /'nɪkə,tin/ *n* nicotina, *f*

nictitating membrane /'nɪktɪ,teitɪŋ/ *n Anat.* membrana nictitante, *f*

niece /nis/ *n* sobrina, *f*

niggardliness /'nɪgərdlinɪs/ *n* tacañería, avaricia, parsimonia, mezquindad, *f*

niggardly /'nɪgərdli/ *a* tacaño, avaricioso, mezquino, ruin, miserable

niggling /'nɪglɪŋ/ *a* nimio, meticuloso; escrupuloso, minucioso

nigh /nai/ *adv* See **near**

night /nait/ *n* noche, *f*; *Fig.* oscuridad, *f*, tinieblas, *f pl*. **all n.,** toda la noche, la noche entera. **all n. service,** servicio nocturno permanente, *m*. **at** or **by n.,** de noche. **every n.,** todas las noches, cada noche. **Good n.!** ¡Buenas noches! **last n.,** ayer por la noche, anoche, la noche pasada. **restless n.,** noche mala, noche toledana, *f*. **the n. before last,** anteayer por la noche, *m*. **to-n.,** esta noche. **tomorrow n.,** mañana por la noche. **to be n.,** ser de noche. **to spend the n.,** pernoctar, pasar la noche. **n.-bird,** pájaro nocturno, *m*; *Inf.* trasnochador (-ra). **n.-blindness,** nictalopia, *f*. **n.-cap,** gorro de dormir, *m*. **n. clothes,** traje de dormir, *m*. **n. club,** cabaré *m*. **n. dew,** relente, sereno, *m*. **n. flying,** vuelo nocturno, *m*. **n.-jar,** *Ornith.* chotacabras, *m*. **n.-light,** mariposa, lamparilla, *f*. **n. mail,** último correo, *m*; tren correo de la noche, *m*. **n. school,** escuela nocturna, *f*. **n. shift,** turno de noche, *m*. **n. table** *Mexico* buró, *m*. **n. watch,** ronda de noche, *f*; *Naut.* sonochada, *f*. **n. watchman,** (in the street) sereno, *m*; (of a building) vigilante nocturno, *m*

nightfall /'nait,fɔl/ *n* anochecer, crepúsculo, atardecer, *m*

nightgown /'nait,gaun/ *n* camisa de noche, *f*

nightingale /'naitn̩,geil, 'naitɪŋ-/ *n* ruiseñor, *m*

nightly /'naitli/ *a* de noche; nocturno, nocturnal. *adv* todas las noches, cada noche

nightmare /'nait,mɛər/ *n* pesadilla, *f*

nightmarish /'nait,mɛərɪʃ/ *a* de pesadilla, horrible

nightshade /'nait,ʃeid/ *n Bot.* hierba mora, *f*, solano, *m*

nihilism /'naiə,lɪzəm, 'ni-/ *n* nihilismo, *m*

nihilist /'naiəlɪst, 'ni-/ *n* nihilista, *mf*

Nile, the /nail/ el Nilo, *m*

nimble /'nɪmbəl/ *a* ágil, activo, *Mexico* alacre; vivo, listo. **n.-fingered,** ligero de dedos. **n.-witted,** despierto, vivo

nimbleness /'nɪmbəlnɪs/ *n* agilidad, actividad, *Mexico* alacridad, *f*; viveza, habilidad, *f*

nimbly /'nɪmbli/ *adv* ágilmente, ligeramente

nimbus /'nɪmbəs/ *n* nimbo, *m*, aureola, *f*

nincompoop /'nɪnkəm,pup, 'nɪŋ-/ *n* papirote, *m*, papanatas, *mf* tonto (-ta)

nine /nain/ *a* and *n* nueve, *m*. **He is n.,** Tiene nueve años. **the N.,** las nueve Musas. **n. o'clock,** las nueve. **to be dressed up to the nines,** estar hecho un brazo de mar

ninefold /a 'nain,fould/ *adv.* 'nain'fould/ *a* and *adv* nueve veces

ninepins /'nain,pɪnz/ *n* juego de bolos, *m*

nineteen /'nain'tin/ *a* and *n* diez y nueve, diecinueve *m*

nineteenth /'nain'tinθ/ *a* décimonono. *n* (of month) el diez y nueve; (of monarchs) diez y nueve. **the n. century,** el siglo diez y nueve

ninetieth /'naintiəθ/ *a* nonagésimo, noventa

ninety /'nainti/ *a* and *n* noventa *m*. **n.-one,** noventa y uno. **n.-two,** noventa y dos. **the n.-first chapter,** el capítulo noventa y uno

ninny /'nɪni/ *n* parapoco, chancleta, *mf*; mentecato (-ta)

ninth /nainθ/ a noveno, nono. n nueve, m; (of the month) el nueve (of sovereigns) nono. **one n.,** un noveno

ninthly /'nainθli/ adv en noveno (or nono) lugar

nip /nɪp/ vt pellizcar, pinchar; mordiscar, morder; (wither) marchitar; (freeze) helar; (run) correr. vi pinchar; picar (el viento). n pellizco, pinchazo, m; mordisco, m; (of spirits) trago, m; copita, f; (in the air) viento frío, hielo, m. **to nip in,** colarse dentro, deslizarse en. **to nip off,** pirarse, mudarse. *Fig.* **to nip in the bud,** cortar en flor

nippers /'nɪpərz/ n pl alicates, m pl; tenacillas, pinzas, f pl

nipping /'nɪpɪŋ/ n pinchadura, f; mordedura, f. a punzante; helado, glacial, mordiente. **n. off,** (of a point) despuntadura, f

nipple /'nɪpəl/ n pezón, m; pezón artificial, m

nit /nɪt/ n Ent. liendre, f

niter /'naitər/ n salitre, m

nitrate /'naitreit/ n Chem. nitrato, m

nitric /'naitrɪk/ a nítrico

nitrite /'naitrait/ n Chem. nitrito, m

nitro- prefix Chem. nitro. **n.-cellulose,** algodón pólvora, m. **n.-glycerine,** nitroglicerina, f

nitrogen /'naitrədʒən/ n Chem. nitrógeno, m

no /nou/ a ningún, ninguno, ninguna, e.g. by no means, de ningún modo. No is often not translated in Sp., e.g. I have no time, No tengo tiempo. adv no. n voto negativo, no, m. to be of no account, no tener importancia; no significar nada. to be no good for, no servir para. to be of no use, ser inútil. to have no connection with, no tener nada que ver con. for no reason, sin motivo alguno. "No Admittance," «Entrada Prohibida.» no, indeed, Cierto que no. no-man's land, tierra de nadie, f. no more, no más. No more of this! ¡No hablemos más de eso! no one, nadie, ninguno. no sooner, no bien, tan pronto (como). no such thing, no tal. **"No Thoroughfare,"** «Prohibido el Paso.» whether or not, sea o no sea

Noah's Ark /'nouəz/ n arca de Noé, f

nobility /nou'bɪlɪti/ n nobleza, f; (of rank) aristocracia, nobleza, f; (of conduct) caballerosidad, hidalguía, generosidad, bondad, f; (grandeur) grandeza, sublimidad, f. **the higher n.,** los nobles de primera clase

noble /'noubəl/ a noble; (in rank) aristocrático, noble, linajudo; (of conduct) caballeroso, generoso; (of buildings) sublime, magnífico. n noble, m, aristócrata, mf **to make n.,** ennoblecer. **n.-mindedness,** generosidad, grandeza de alma, f. **n. title,** título de nobleza, título del reino, m

noblewoman /'noubəl,wʊmən/ n dama noble, mujer noble, aristócrata, f

nobly /'noubli/ adv noblemente, generosamente. **n. born,** noble de nacimiento

nobody /'nou,bɒdi/ n nadie, ninguno. There was n. there, No había nadie allí. Inf. **a n.,** un (una) cualquiera, una persona insignificante. **n. else,** nadie más, ningún otro

nocturnal /nɒk'tɜrnl/ a nocturno, nocherniego, nocturnal

nocturne /'nɒktɜrn/ n Mus. nocturno, m

nod /nɒd/ vt inclinar la cabeza; hacer una señal (or señas) con la cabeza; vi dar cabezadas; cabecear; (of trees) mecerse, inclinarse; inclinar la cabeza. n señal (or seña) con la cabeza, f; inclinación de la cabeza, f; cabeceo, m, cabezada, f. Lat. Am. cabeceada, f. **A nod is as good as a wink,** A buen entendedor pocas palabras. **He nodded to me as he passed,** Me saludó con la cabeza al pasar. **He signed to me with a nod,** Me hizo una señal con la cabeza

nodding /'nɒdɪŋ/ a que cabecea; Bot. colgante, inclinado; temblante. n cabeceo, m; saludo con la cabeza, m

noddle /'nɒdl/ n mollera, f

node /noud/ n (Bot. Med.) nudo, m

nodule /'nɒdʒul/ n nódulo, m; nudillo, m

noise /nɔiz/ n ruido, son, m; tumulto, clamor, estruendo, alboroto, f; Central America embullo, m. **to make a n.,** hacer ruido. **to n. abroad,** divulgar, publicar

noiseless /'nɔizlɪs/ a silencioso, callado, sin ruido

noiselessness /'nɔizlɪsnɪs/ n silencio, m, falta de ruido, f

noisily /'nɔizəli/ adv ruidosamente

noisiness /'nɔizinɪs/ n ruido, estrépito, tumulto, clamor, m; (of voices) gritería, f

noisome /'nɔisəm/ a ofensivo; fétido, apestoso

noisy /'nɔizi/ a ruidoso; estruendoso; estrepitoso, clamoroso

nomad /'noumæd/ a nómada, errante; (of flocks) trashumante. n nómada, mf

nomadism /'noumædɪzəm/ n nomadismo, m

nomenclature /'noumən,kleitʃər/ n nomenclatura, f

nominal /'nɒmənl/ a nominal; titular; insignificante, de poca importancia. **the n. head,** el director en nombre

nominalism /'nɒmənl,ɪzəm/ n nominalismo, m

nominally /'nɒmənli/ adv nominalmente, en nombre

nominate /'nɒmə,neit/ vt nombrar, designar, elegir; fijar, señalar

nominating /'nɒmə,neitɪŋ/ a nominador

nomination /,nɒmə'neiʃən/ n nombramiento, m, nominación, f; señalamiento, m

nominator /'nɒmə,neitər/ n nominador (-ra)

nominee /,nɒmə'ni/ n nómino propuesto, m

non /nɒn/ adv non; des-; in-; falta de. **nonacceptance,** rechazo, m. **non-acquaintance,** ignorancia, f. **non-admission,** no admisión, f; denegación, f, rechazo, m. **non-aggression,** no agresión, f. **nonalcoholic,** no alcohólico. **non-appearance,** ausencia, f; Law. no comparecencia, contumacia, f. **nonarrival,** ausencia, f; falta de recibo, f. **nonattendance,** falta de asistencia, ausencia, f. **noncarbonated,** sin gas. **non-combatant,** no combatiente. **non-commissioned officer,** oficial subalterno, m. **non-committal,** evasivo, equívoco, ambiguo. **noncompliance,** falta de obediencia, f. **non-concurrence,** falta de acuerdo, f. **non-conducting,** no conductivo. **non-conductor,** mal conductor, m; Elec. aislador, m. **non-contagious,** no contagioso. **non-cooperation,** Polit. resistencia pasiva, f; no cooperación, f. **nondelivery,** falta de entrega, f. **non-essential,** no esencial, prescindible. **non-execution,** no cumplimiento, m. **non-existence,** no existencia, f. **non-existent,** inexistente, no existente. **non-intervention,** no intervención, f. **non-manufacturing,** no industrial. **nonmember,** visitante, mf **non-observance,** incumplimiento, m; violación, f. **non-payment,** falta de pago, f. **non-performance,** falta de ejecución, f. **nonpoisonous,** no venenoso, innocuo. **non-resistance,** falta de resistencia, f; obediencia pasiva, f. **non-skid,** antideslizante, antirresbaladizo. **non-smoking,** que no fuma; (of a railway compartment, etc.) para no fumadores. **non-stop,** continuo, incesante; directo, sin parar; Aer. sin escalas

nonagenarian /,nɒnədʒə'nɛəriən/ a and n nonagenario (-ia)

non-aligned /,nɒn ə'laind/ a no abanderado

non-alignment /,nɒn ə'lainmənt/ n no abanderamiento m

nonce word /nɒns/ n palabra ocasional, f

nonchalance /,nɒnʃə'lɑns/ n aplomo, m, indiferencia, frialdad, calma, f

nonchalant /,nɒnʃə'lɑnt/ a indiferente, frío, impasible

nonchalantly /,nɒnʃə'lɑntli/ adv con indiferencia

nonconformist /,nɒnkən'fɔrmɪst/ a and n disidente mf; a inconforme, m, inconformista, mf

nonconformity /,nɒnkən'fɔrmɪti/ n disidencia, f

nondescript /,nɒndɪ'skrɪpt/ a indeterminado, indefinido, indeciso, mediocre

none /nʌn/ pron nadie, ninguno; nada. a and n ninguno (-na). adv no; de ningún modo, de ninguna manera. **I have n.,** No lo tengo, No tengo ninguno. **We have n. of your things,** No tenemos ninguna de tus cosas. **I was n. the worse,** No me hallaba peor. **N. can read his account with pleasure,** Nadie puede leer su narración con gusto. **n. the less,** no menos; sin embargo

nonentity /nɒn'ɛntɪti/ n persona sin importancia, medianía, f, cero, m

nones /nounz/ n pl Eccl. nona, f; (Roman Calendar) nonas, f pl,

nonplussed /nɒn'plʌst/ a cortado, perplejo, confuso

non-profit /nɒn 'prɒfɪt/ a sin fines de lucro, sin fines lucrativos

non-self-governing /'nɒn sɛlf'gʌvərnɪŋ/ a no autónomo

nonsense /'nɒnsɛns/ n disparate, despropósito, desatino, m, absurdidad, f; Inf. galimatías, m; pamplina, patraña, f. **to talk n.,** hablar sin ton ni son. **N.!** ¡A otro perro con este hueso! ¡Patrañas!

nonsensical /nɒn'sɛnsɪkəl/ a absurdo, ridículo, disparatado

noodle /'nudl/ n Cul. tallarín, m; Inf. mentecato (-ta), bobo (-ba)

nook /nʊk/ n escondrijo, lugar retirado, rincón, m

noon /nun/ n mediodía, m; Fig. punto culminante, apogeo, m, a de mediodía, meridional. **at n.,** a mediodía

noose /nus/ vt coger con lazos. n lazo corredizo, dogal, m

nopal /'noupəl/ n Bot. nopal, m

No Parking «Se Prohibe Estacionar,» «Estacionarse Prohibido»

nor /nɔr; unstressed nər/ conjunc ni, no, tampoco. **He removed neither his coat nor his hat,** No se quitó ni el gabán ni el sombrero. **Nor was this the first time,** Y no fue ésta la primera vez. **Nor I,** Ni yo tampoco

Nordic /'nɔrdɪk/ a and n nórdico (-ca)

norm /nɔrm/ n modelo, m, norma, regla, pauta, f; (of size) marca, f; (Bot. Zool.) tipo, m

normal /'nɔrməl/ a normal; común, natural, corriente, regular; Math. perpendicular, normal. n condición normal, f, estado normal, m; Math. normal, f. **to become n.,** normalizarse, hacerse normal. **to make n.,** normalizar. **n. school,** escuela normal, f

normality /nɔr'mælɪti/ n normalidad, f

normalization /ˌnɔrmələ'zeiʃən/ n normalización, f

normalize /'nɔrməˌlaiz/ vt normalizar

normally /'nɔrməli/ adv normalmente

Norman /'nɔrmən/ a and n normando (-da)

Normandy /'nɔrməndi/ Normandía, f

Norse /nɔrs/ n noruego (language), m, a escandinavo

Norseman /'nɔrsmən/ n normando, viking (pl -os), hombre del norte, m

north /nɔrθ/ n norte, m. a del norte, septentrional. **n. by west,** norte, cuarta noroeste. **n. of the city,** al norte de la ciudad. **N.-American,** a and n norteamericano (-na). **n.-east,** a and n nordeste m. **n.-easter,** viento del nordeste, m. **n.-easterly,** del nordeste (winds). **n.-eastern,** del nordeste (places). **n.-eastward,** hacia el nordeste. **n.-n.-east,** nornordeste, m. **n.-n.-west,** nornorueste, m. **n.-polar,** árctico. **N. Star,** estrella del norte, estrella polar, f. **n.-west,** noroeste, m. **n.-wester,** viento del noroeste, m. **n.-westerly,** del noroeste (winds). **n.-westerly gale,** temporal del noroeste, m. **n.-western,** del noroeste; situado al noroeste. **n.-westwards,** hacia el noroeste. **n. wind,** el viento del norte, el cierzo

North America Norteamérica, América del Norte, f

northern /'nɔrðərn/ a del norte, septentrional, norteño; (of races) nórdico. **N. Cross,** crucero, m. **N. lights,** aurora boreal, f

northerner /'nɔrðərnər/ n hombre del norte, m, habitante del norte, mf

northernmost /'nɔrðərnˌmoust/ a sup al extremo norte, más septentrional

northwards /'nɔrθwərdz/ adv hacia el norte

Norway /'nɔrwei/ Noruega, f

Norwegian /nɔr'widʒən/ a and n noruego (-ga); (language) noruego, m

nose /nouz/ n nariz, f; (of animals) hocico, m; (sense of smell) olfato, m; (of ships) proa, f; (of jug) pico, m, boca, f; (projecting piece) cuerno, m, nariz, f; (of airplane) cabeza, f, vt acariciar con la nariz; avanzar lentamente. vi husmear, olfatear. **to n. into,** Inf. meter las narices, poner baza. **to n. out,** descubrir, averiguar. **to bleed at the n.,** echar sangre por las narices. **to blow one's n.,** sonar (o limpiarse) las narices. **to keep one's n. to the grindstone,** estar sobre el yunque, batir el cobre. Fig. **to lead by the n.,** tener a uno agarrado por las narices. **to pay through the n.,** costar un ojo de la cara. **to speak through the n.,** ganguear. **to turn up one's n.,** Fig. hacer gestos (a), volver la cara. **flat n.,** nariz chata, f. **snub n.,** nariz respingona, f. **well-shaped n.,** nariz perfilada, f. **under one's n.,** bajo las narices de uno. **n.-bag,** cebadera, mochila, f; morral, m. **n.-bleeding,** Med. epistaxis, f; hemorragia de las narices, f. **n.-dive,** Aer. descenso de cabeza, picado, m. vi picar. **n.-piece,** (of microscope) ocular, m. **n.-ring,** (of a bull, etc.) narigón, m

-nosed /nouzd/ a de nariz..., con la nariz...

nosegay /'nouzˌgei/ n ramillete, m

nosey Parker /'nouzi 'pɑrkər/ n Inf. mequetrefe, m; cócora, Lat. Am. averigüetas, Argentina hurguete, mf

No Smoking «Prohibido Fumar», Se Prohibe Fumar

nostalgia /nɒ'stældʒə/ n nostalgia, añoranza, f

nostalgic /nɒ'stældʒɪk/ a nostálgico

nostril /'nɒstrəl/ n ventana de la nariz, f, n pl **nostrils,** narices, f pl

nostrum /'nɒstrəm/ n panacea, f, curalotodo, m; medicina patentada, f

not /nɒt/ adv no; sin; ni, ni siquiera. **Is it not true? We think not,** ¿No es verdad? No lo creemos. **You have seen Mary, have you not?** Vd. ha visto a María, ¿verdad? **not caring whether he came or not,** sin preocuparse de que viniese o no. **not that he will come,** no es decir que venga. **not at all,** de ningún modo; (courtesy) ¡de nada! **not even,** ni siquiera. **not guilty,** no culpable. **not one,** ni uno. **not so much as,** no tanto como; ni siquiera. **It is not so much that, as it is...** No es tanto eso, cuanto que... **not to say,** por no decir. **notability** /ˌnoutə'bɪliti/ n notabilidad, f; (person) notable, mf persona de importancia, f

notable /'noutəbəl/ a notable, señalado, memorable; digno de atención. n persona eminente, f, notable, m

notably /'noutəbli/ adv notablemente, señaladamente

notary /'noutəri/ n notario, escribano, m

notation /nou'teiʃən/ n notación, f

notch /nɒtʃ/ vt cortar muescas (en); mellar, ranurar, entallar. n muesca, mella, ranura, entalladura, f

note /nout/ vt notar, observar; anotar, apuntar; advertir, hacerse cuenta de. n Mus. nota, f; son, acento, m; (letter) recado, billete, m; anotación, glosa, f; apuntación, f, apunte, m, nota, f; (importance) importancia, distinción, f; Com. vale, abonaré, m; (sign) marca, señal, f. **to n. down,** anotar. **worthy of note,** digno de atención. **n.-book,** libro de apuntes, cuaderno, m, libreta, f. **n.-case,** cartera, f, Com. **n. of hand,** pagaré, m. **n.-paper,** papel de escribir, m. **n.-taker,** apuntador (-ra)

noted /'noutɪd/ a célebre, famoso, ilustre, eminente, insigne

noteworthy /'noutˌwɜrði/ a digno de nota, notable, digno de atención

nothing /'nʌθɪŋ/ n nada, f; la nada; cero, m. adv en nada. **to come to n.,** anonadarse, fracasar. **to do n.,** no hacer nada. **to do n. but,** no hacer más que. **to have n. to do with,** no tener nada que ver con; Inf. no tener arte ni parte en. **There is n. else to do,** No hay nada más que hacer. No hay más remedio. **There is n. to fear,** No hay de que tener miedo. **We could make n. of the book,** No llegamos a comprender el libro. **for n.,** de balde, en vano; gratis. **next to n.,** casi nada. **n. else or more,** nada más. **n. like,** ni con mucho. **n. much,** poca cosa. **n. new,** nada nueva. **n. similar,** nada semejante. **to speak of,** poca cosa

nothingness /'nʌθɪŋnɪs/ n nada, f

notice /'noutɪs/ vt observar, reparar en, darse cuenta (de); marcar, caer en la cuenta (de), fijarse (en). n observación, atención, f; aviso, m, notificación, f; anuncio, m; (term) plazo, m; (review) crítica, f. **at short n.,** a corto aviso. **until further n.,** hasta nuevo aviso (or orden). **to attract n.,** atraer la atención. **I hadn't noticed,** No me había fijado. **to be beneath one's n.,** no merecer su atención. **to be under n.,** estar dimitido. **to bring to the n. of,** dar noticia de. **to escape n.,** pasar desapercibido. **to give n.,** hacer saber, informar; (of employer) despedir (a); (of employee) dimitir, dar la dimisión. **to take n. of,** notar, darse cuenta de; hacer caso, atender (a). **n. board,** letrero, tablero de anuncios, *m*. **n. to quit,** desahúcio, *m*

noticeable /'noutɪsəbəl/ *a* perceptible, evidente; digno de observación, notable

noticeably /'noutɪsəbli/ *adv* perceptiblemente; notablemente

notifiable /ˌnoutə'faiəbəl/ *a* declarable, notificable

notification /ˌnoutəfɪ'keiʃən/ *n* notificación, intimación, advertencia, *f*, aviso, *m*

notify /'noutə,fai/ *vt* notificar, comunicar, avisar, intimar, hacer saber

notion /'nouʃən/ *n* noción, idea, *f*, concepto, *m*; (view) opinión, *f*, parecer, *m*; (novelty) novedad, *f*; artículo de fantasía, *m*. **I have a n. that...,** Tengo la idea de que..., Sospecho que... **I haven't a n.,** No tengo idea

No Tipping /'tipɪŋ/ «No Se Admiten Propinas»

notoriety /ˌnoutə'raiɪti/ *n* notoriedad, publicidad, *f*; escándalo, *m*; persona notoria, *f*

notorious /nou'tɔriəs/ *a* notorio, famoso, conocido; escandaloso, sensacional

notoriously /nou'tɔriəsli/ *adv* notoriamente

notwithstanding /ˌnɒtwið'stændɪŋ/ *prep* a pesar de. *adv* sin embargo, no obstante. *conjunc* aunque, bien que, por más que

nougat /'nugət/ *n* turrón, *m*

nought /nɔt/ *n* Math. cero, *m*; nada, *f*

noun /naun/ *n* substantivo, nombre, *m*

nourish /'nɜrɪʃ/ *vt* sustentar, alimentar, nutrir; *Fig.* fomentar, favorecer

nourishing /'nɜrɪʃɪŋ/ *a* nutritivo, alimenticio, nutricio

nourishment /'nɜrɪʃmənt/ *n* nutrición, *f*; sustento, *m*; alimento, *m*; *Fig.* fomento, pasto, *m*

Nova Scotia /'nouvə 'skouʃə/ Nueva Escocia, *f*

novel /'nɒvəl/ *a* nuevo, original, inacostumbrado. *n* novela, *f*. **n. of roguery,** novela picaresca, *f*

novelette /ˌnɒvə'lɛt/ *n* novela corta, *f*

novelist /'nɒvəlɪst/ *n* novelista, *mf*

novelty /'nɒvəlti/ *n* novedad, *f*; innovación, *f*; cambio, *m*

November /nou'vɛmbər/ *n* noviembre, *m*

novice /'nɒvɪs/ *n* Eccl. novicio (-ia); comenzante, principiante, *mf*, aspirante, *m*, Lat. Am. advenedizo (-za)

novocain /'nouvə,kein/ *n* Med. novocaína, *f*

now /nau/ *adv* ahora, actualmente, al presente, a la fecha; en seguida, ahora, inmediatamente; poco ha, hace poco; pues bien. *interj* ¡A ver! ¡Vamos! *conjunc* pero, mas. *n* presente, *m*, actualidad, *f*. **before now,** antes, en otras ocasiones, ya, previamente. **just now,** ahora mismo, hace poco. **now... now,** ya... ya; sucesivamente, en turno. **now and then,** de vez en cuando, de tarde en tarde. **now that,** ya que, ahora que, dado que. **until now,** hasta el presente, hasta aquí, hasta ahora

nowadays /'nauə,deiz/ *adv* hoy en día, actualmente, en nuestros días

nowhere /'nou,wɛər/ *adv* en ninguna parte. **in the middle of n.,** en tierra de nadie. **n. else,** en ninguna otra parte. *Inf.* **n. near,** ni con mucho; muy lejos (de) alguno, de ninguna manera

nowise /'nou,waiz/ *adv* de ningún modo, en modo alguno, de ninguna manera

noxious /'nɒkʃəs/ *a* dañoso, nocivo; pestífero

noxiousness /'nɒkʃəsnɪs/ *n* nocividad, *f*

nozzle /'nɒzəl/ *n* (of a hose-pipe) boquilla, *f*; *Mech.* gollete, *m*; tubo de salida, *m*, tobera, *f*; inyector, *m*

n.p. (no place) s.l. (sin lugar)

nuance /'nuɑns/ *n* matiz, *m*, gradación, sombra, *f*

nubile /'nubɪl, -bail/ *a* núbil

nuclear /'nukliər/ *a* nuclear

nucleus /'nukliəs/ *n* núcleo, *m*; centro, foco, *m*

nude /nud/ *a* desnudo, nudo, Peru calato, *elsewhere in Lat. Am.* encuerado

nudge /nʌdʒ/ *vt* dar un codazo (a). *n* codazo, *m*

nudism /'nudɪzəm/ *n* nudismo, *m*

nudist /'nudɪst/ *n* nudista, *mf*

nudity /'nuditi/ *n* desnudez, *f*

nugget /'nʌgɪt/ *n* Mineral. pepita, *f*

nuisance /'nusəns/ *n* molestia, incomodidad, *f*, fastidio, *m*; *Inf.* tostón, *m*, lata, Lat. Am. fregada, Colom-

bia vaina, *f*. **to make a n. of oneself,** meterse donde no le llaman, ser un pelmazo. **What a n.!** ¡Qué lata! ¡Qué fastidio!, Colombia ¡Qué vaina!

null /nʌl/ *a* nulo, inválido, sin fuerza legal. **n. and void,** nulo, írrito

nullification /ˌnʌləfɪ'keiʃən/ *n* anulación, invalidación, *f*

nullity /'nʌlɪti/ *n* nulidad, *f*

numb /nʌm/ *vt* entumecer, entorpecer. *a* entumecido; torpe, dormido; paralizado; *Fig.* insensible, pasmado. **n. with cold,** entumecido de frío

number /'nʌmbər/ *vt* numerar, contar; poner número (a); (pages of a book) foliar; ascender a. *n* número, *m*; (figure) cifra, *f*; (crowd) multitud, muchedumbre, *f*; cantidad, *f*; (of a periodical) ejemplar, *m*; *Gram.* número, *m*; *pl* versos, *m pl.* **Numbers,** (Bible) Números, *m pl*; **to be numbered among,** figurar entre. **among the n. of,** entre la muchedumbre de. **a n. of,** varios, muchos, una cantidad de. **in great n.,** en gran número; en su mayoría. **6 Peace Street,** Calle de la Paz nº (número) 6. **one of their n.,** uno entre ellos. **n. board,** (racing) indicador, *m.* **n. plate,** Auto. chapa de identidad, placa de número, *f*

numbering /'nʌmbərɪŋ/ *n* numeración, *f*

numberless /'nʌmbərlɪs/ *a* innumerable, sin número, sin fin, infinito

numbness /'nʌmnɪs/ *n* entumecimiento, entorpecimiento, *m*; *Fig.* insensibilidad, *f*

numeral /'numərəl/ *a* numeral. *n* número, *m*, cifra, *f*; *Gram.* nombre o adjetivo numeral, *m*

numerator /'numə,reitər/ *n* numerador

numerical /nu'mɛrɪkəl/ *a* numérico

numerous /'numərəs/ *a* numeroso; nutrido, grande; muchos (-as)

numerousness /'numərəsnɪs/ *n* numerosidad, multitud, muchedumbre, *f*

numismatic /ˌnumɪz'mætɪk/ *a* numismático. *n pl* **numismatics,** numismática, *f*

numismatist /nu'mɪzmətɪst/ *n* numismático, *m*

numskull /'nʌm,skʌl/ *n* zote, topo, *m*

nun /nʌn/ *n* monja, religiosa, *f*. **to become a nun,** profesar, tomar el hábito, meterse monja, hacer los votos

nuncio /'nʌnʃiˌou/ *n* nuncio, *m*. **acting n.,** pronuncio, *m*

nunnery /'nʌnəri/ *n* convento de monjas, *m*

nuptial /'nʌpʃəl/ *a* nupcial. *n pl* **nuptials,** nupcias, *f pl*, enlace, *m*. **n. mass,** Eccl. misa de velaciones, *f*. **n. song,** epitalamio, *m*

nurse /nɜrs/ *vt* criar; dar de mamar (a), amamantar; (the sick) cuidar, asistir; (fondle) acariciar, mecer; *Fig.* fomentar, promover. *vi* trabajar como enfermera. *n* (of the sick) enfermera, *f*; (wet) nodriza, ama de leche, Lat. Am. criandera, *f*; (children's) niñera, *f*; *Fig.* fomentador, *m*. **male n.,** enfermero, *m*

nursery /'nɜrsəri/ *n* Agr. plantel, vivero semillero, criadero, *m*; (children's room) cuarto de los niños, *m*; *Fig.* sementera, *f*; semillero, *m*. **n. governess,** aya, *f*. **n. rhyme,** canción infantil, *f*

nurseryman /'nɜrsərimən/ *n* horticultor, *m*; jardinero, *m*

nursing /'nɜrsɪŋ/ *n* lactancia, crianza, *f*; (of the sick) asistencia, *f*, cuido, *m*. **n. home,** clínica, *f*. **n. mother,** madre lactante, *f*

nurture /'nɜrtʃər/ *vt* alimentar; criar, educar. *n* nutrición, alimentación, *f*; crianza, educación, *f*

nut /nʌt/ *n* Bot. nuez, *f*; *Mech.* tuerca, hembra de tornillo, *f*, *Inf.* **to be a tough nut to crack,** ser un tío de cuidado. **to crack nuts,** cascar nueces. **to go nutting,** coger nueces. **cashew nut,** anacardo, *m.* **loose nut,** Mech. tuerca aflojada, *f*. **nut-brown,** castaño. **nut tree,** nogal, *m*

nutcrackers /'nʌt,krækərz/ *n pl* cascanueces, quebrantanueces, *m*

nutmeg /'nʌtmɛg/ *n* nuez moscada, nuez de especia, *f*

nutria /'nutriə/ *n* Zool. nutria, *f*

nutriment /'nutrəmənt/ *n* nutrimento, alimento, *m*

nutrition /nu'trɪʃən/ *n* nutrición, alimentación, *f*

nutritious, nutritive /nu'trɪʃəs; 'nutrɪtɪv/ *a* nutritivo, alimenticio, alible

nutshell /'nʌt‚ʃɛl/ n cáscara de nuez, f. **to put in a n.**, decir en resumidas cuentas, decir en forma apastillada

nutty /'nʌti/ a de nuez

nuzzle /'nʌzəl/ vt acariciar con la nariz

nylon /'nailɒn/ n nilón, nylon, m. **n. stockings,** medias de cristal (or de nilón), f pl

nymph /nɪmf/ n ninfa, f; Ent. crisálida, f. **n.-like,** como una ninfa; de ninfa

nymphomania /‚nɪmfə'meiniə/ n ninfomanía, f, furor uterino, m

O

o /ou/ n (letter) o, f, interj ¡o! **O that...!** ¡Ojalá que!

oaf /ouf/ n zoquete, zamacuco, m

oafish /'oufɪʃ/ a lerdo, torpe

oafishness /'oufɪʃnɪs/ n torpeza, estupidez, f

oak /ouk/ n (tree and wood) roble, m, a de roble. **carved oak,** roble tallado, m. **holm-oak,** encina, f. **oak-apple,** agalla, f. **oak grove,** robledo, m

oakum /'oukəm/ n estopa, f

oar /ɔr/ n remo, m. **to lie on the oars,** cesar de remar. **to pull at the oars,** bogar, remar. **to put in one's oar,** Inf. meter baza. **to ship the oars,** armar los remos. **to unship the oars,** desarmar los remos. **oar-stroke,** palada, f

oarsman /'ɔrzmən/ n remero, bogador, m

oarsmanship /'ɔrzmən‚ʃɪp/ n arte de remar, m, or f

oasis /ou'eisɪs/ n oasis, m

OAS (Organization of American States) OEA (Organización de los Estados Americanos)

oast /oust/ n horno para secar el lúpulo, m

oat /out/ n Bot. avena, f. **wild oat,** avena silvestre, f. **to sow one's wild oats,** correrla, andarse a la flor del berro. **oat field,** avenal, m

oath /ouθ/ n juramento, m; (curse) blasfemia, f, reniego, m. **on o.,** bajo juramento. **to break an o.,** violar el juramento. **to put on o.,** tomar juramento, hacer prestar juramento. **to take an o.,** prestar (or hacer) juramento. **to take the o. of allegiance,** jurar la bandera

oatmeal /'out‚mil/ n harina de avena, f

obduracy /'ɒbdurəsi/ n obduración, obstinación, terquedad, f

obdurate /'ɒbdurɪt/ a obstinado, terco, porfiado. **He is o. to our requests,** Es sordo a nuestros ruegos

obedience /ou'bidiəns/ n obediencia, sumisión, docilidad, f. **blind o.,** obediencia ciega, f. **in o. to,** conforme a, de acuerdo con

obedient /ou'bidiənt/ a obediente, sumiso, dócil. **to be o. to,** ser obediente (a), obedecer (a)

obediently /ou'bidiəntli/ adv obedientemente, dócilmente. **Yours o.,** Su atento servidor (su att. s.)

obeisance /ou'beisəns, ou'bi-/ n reverencia, cortesía, f, saludo, m; (homage) homenaje, m

obelisk /'ɒbəlɪsk/ n obelisco, m

obese /ou'bis/ a obeso, corpulento, grueso, gordo

obesity /ou'bisɪti/ n obesidad, gordura, corpulencia, f

obey /ou'bei/ vt and vi obedecer. vt (carry out) cumplir, observar. **to be obeyed,** ser obedecido

obfuscate /'ɒbfə‚skeit/ vt ofuscar, cegar

obfuscation /‚ɒbfə'skeiʃən/ n ofuscamiento, m, confusión, f

obituary /ou'bɪtʃuˌɛri/ a mortuorio, necrológico. n obituario, m, necrología, f. **o. column,** (in newspaper) sección necrológica, f. **o. notice,** esquela de defunción, f

object /n. 'ɒbdʒɪkt; v. əb'dʒɛkt/ n objeto, artículo, m, cosa, f; (purpose) propósito, intento, m; (aim) fin, término, m; Gram. complemento, m; Inf. individuo, m. vt objetar, poner reparos (a). vi oponerse, poner objeciones. **I o. to that remark,** Protesto contra esa observación. **If you don't o,** Si Vd. no tiene inconveniente. **o. finder,** objetivo, m. **o. lesson,** lección de cosas, f; lección práctica, f. **direct o.,** complemento directo, m. **indirect o.,** complemento indirecto, m. **o. of the preposition,** complemento circunstancial

objection /əb'dʒɛkʃən/ n objeción, protesta, f, reparo, m; (obstacle) dificultad, f, inconveniente, m. **to have no o.,** no tener inconveniente. **to raise an o.,** hacer constar una protesta, poner una objeción

objectionable /əb'dʒɛkʃənəbəl/ a censurable, reprensible; desagradable, molesto

objective /əb'dʒɛktɪv/ a objetivo; Gram. acusativo. n objeto, propósito, m; destinación, f; Mil. objetivo, m, Gram. **o. case,** caso acusativo, m,

objectivism /əb'dʒɛktə‚vɪzəm/ n Philos. objetivismo, m

objectivity /‚ɒbdʒɪk'tɪvɪti/ n objetividad, f

objector /ɒb'dʒɛktər/ n objetante, mf, impugnador (-ra). **conscientious o.,** (dissident) el, m, (f, la) que protesta contra; (pacifist) pacifista, mf

oblation /ɒ'bleiʃən/ n oblación, ofrenda, f

obligation /‚ɒblɪ'geiʃən/ n obligación, f; deber, m, precisión, f; compromiso, m. **of o.,** de deber; de precepto. **to be under an o.,** estar bajo una obligación; deber un favor. **to place under an o.,** poner bajo una obligación

obligatory /ə'blɪɡəˌtɔri/ a obligatorio, forzoso

oblige /ə'blaidʒ/ vt (insist on) obligar, hacer, forzar; (gratify) hacer un favor (a), complacer. **He obliged me with a match,** Me hizo el favor de una cerilla. **They are much obliged to you,** Le están muy reconocidos. **Much obliged!** ¡Se agradece!

obliging /ə'blaidʒɪŋ/ a atento, condescendiente, complaciente, servicial, Lat. Am. acomedido

obligingly /ə'blaidʒɪŋli/ adv cortésmente

obligingness /ə'blaidʒɪŋnɪs/ n cortesía, amabilidad, bondad, f

oblique /ə'blik/ a oblicuo, sesgado; (indirect) indirecto, evasivo; Gram. oblicuo

obliquely /ə'blikli/ adv oblicuamente, al sesgo, sesgadamente; indirectamente. **to place o.,** poner al sesgo

obliquity /ə'blɪkwɪti/ n oblicuidad, f, sesgo, m; (of conduct, etc.) tortuosidad, f

obliterate /ə'blɪtəˌreit/ vt borrar; destruir, aniquilar. **to be obliterated,** borrarse; quedar destruido

obliteration /əˌblɪtə'reiʃən/ n testación, f; destrucción, f. **o. raid,** bombardeo de saturación, m

oblivion /ə'blɪviən/ n olvido, m. **to cast into o.,** echar al olvido

oblivious /ə'blɪviəs/ a olvidadizo, descuidado

oblong /'ɒb‚lɒŋ/ a oblongo, cuadrilongo, rectangular. n rectángulo, cuadrilongo, m

obloquy /'ɒbləkwi/ n infamia, maledicencia, deshonra, f

obnoxious /əb'nɒkʃəs/ a odioso, ofensivo, aborrecible

obnoxiously /əb'nɒkʃəsli/ adv odiosamente

obnoxiousness /əb'nɒkʃəsnɪs/ n odiosidad, f

oboe /'oubou/ n Mus. oboe, m. **o. player,** oboe, m

obol /'ɒbəl/ n óbolo, m

obscene /əb'sin/ a indecente, obsceno, escabroso

obscenely /əb'sinli/ adv obscenamente, escabrosamente

obscenity /əb'sɛnɪti/ n indecencia, obscenidad, f

obscurantism /əb'skyʊrənˌtɪzəm/ n obscurantismo, m

obscurantist /əb'skyʊrəntɪst/ a and n obscurantista mf

obscure /əb'skyʊr/ a (indistinct) obscuro, indistinto; (dark) lóbrego, tenebroso; (remote) retirado, apartado; (puzzling) confuso; (unknown) desconocido; humilde; (difficult to understand) abstruso, obscuro; (vague) vago. vt obscurecer; (hide) esconder; (eclipse) eclipsar. **to o. the issue,** hacer perder de vista el problema

obscurely /əb'skyʊrli/ adv obscuramente; humildemente, retiradamente; confusamente; vagamente

obscurity /əb'skyʊrɪti/ n (darkness) obscuridad, lobreguez, f; (difficulty of meaning) ambigüedad, confusión, vaguedad, f; humildad, f

obsequies /'ɒbsɪkwiz/ n pl exequias, f pl, ritos fúnebres, m pl

obsequious /əb'sikwiəs/ a servil, empalagoso, zalamero

obsequiously /əb'sikwiəsli/ adv servilmente

obsequiousness /əb'sikwiəsnɪs/ n servilismo, m, sumisión, f

observable /əb'zɜrvəbəl/ a observable, perceptible, visible; notable

observably /əb'zɜrvəbli/ adv notablemente

observance /əb'zɜrvəns/ n observancia, f, cumplimiento, m; práctica, costumbre, f; (religious) rito, m

observant /əb'zɜrvənt/ a observador; obediente, atento. **o. of,** observador de; atento a

observation /ˌɒbzər'veiʃən/ n observación, f, examen, escrutinio, m; (experience) experiencia, f; (remark) advertencia, f, comento, m. **to escape o.,** no ser advertido. **o. car.,** vagón-mirador, m, **o. post,** puesto de observación, m

observatory /əb'zɜrvəˌtɔri/ n observatorio, m

observe /əb'zɜrv/ vt (laws) cumplir; (holy days, etc.) guardar; (notice) observar, mirar, notar, ver, reparar en; (remark) decir, advertir; (examine) vigilar, atisbar, examinar; Astron. observar. vi ser observador. **to o. silence,** guardar silencio

observer /əb'zɜrvər/ n observador (-ra)

obsess /əb'sɛs/ vt obsesionar, obcecar

obsessed /əb'sɛst/ a obseso

obsession /əb'sɛʃən/ n obsesión, obcecación, idea fija, manía, f

obsidian /əb'sɪdiən/ n Mineral. obsidiana, f

obsolescent /ˌɒbsə'lɛsənt/ a que se hace antiguo, que cae en desuso

obsolete /ˌɒbsə'lit/ a obsoleto, anticuado; Biol. rudimentario, atrofiado

obstacle /'ɒbstəkəl/ n obstáculo, impedimento, m; dificultad, f, inconveniente, m. **to put obstacles in the way of,** Fig. dificultar, hacer difícil. **o. race,** carrera de obstáculos, f

obstetric /əb'stɛtrɪk/ a obstétrico

obstetrician /ˌɒbstɪ'trɪʃən/ n obstétrico (-ea), médico (-ca) partero (-ra)

obstetrics /əb'stɛtrɪks/ n obstetricia, tocología, f

obstinacy /'ɒbstənəsi/ n obstinación, terquedad, tenacidad, porfía, f, tesón, m; persistencia, f

obstinate /'ɒbstənɪt/ a terco, porfiado, obstinado, tenaz; refractario; persistente, pertinaz. **to be o. about,** ser terco; porfiar. **to be o. about,** obstinarse en

obstinately /'ɒbstənɪtli/ adv tercamente

obstreperous /əb'strɛpərəs/ a turbulento, ruidoso

obstruct /əb'strʌkt/ vt obstruir: impedir; cerrar; (thwart) estorbar; (hinder) dificultar, embarazar; (the traffic) obstruir, atascar. vi estorbar. **to become obstructed,** obstruirse, cerrarse

obstruction /əb'strʌkʃən/ n obstrucción, f; estorbo, obstáculo, m. **to cause a street o.,** obstruir el tráfico

obstructionism /əb'strʌkʃəˌnɪzəm/ n obstruccionismo, m

obstructionist /əb'strʌkʃənɪst/ n obstruccionista, mf

obstructive /əb'strʌktɪv/ a estorbador, obstructor

obtain /əb'tein/ vt obtener, conseguir, lograr; recibir; (by threats) arrancar. vi existir en boga, estar en vigor, predominar. **to o. on false pretenses,** conseguir por engaño

obtainable /əb'teinəbəl/ a asequible, alcanzable. **easily o.,** fácil a obtener

obtainer /əb'teinər/ n conseguidor (-ra), adquisidor (-ra)

obtainment /əb'teinmənt/ n obtención, f, logro, m

obtrude /əb'trud/ vt imponer

obtrusion /əb'truʒən/ n imposición, f; importunidad, f

obtrusive /əb'trusɪv/ a importuno; entremetido; pretencioso

obtrusiveness /əb'trusɪvnɪs/ n importunidad, f; entremetimiento, m

obtuse /əb'tus/ a (blunt) obtuso, romo; (stupid) estúpido, torpe, lerdo. **o. angle,** obtusángulo, m

obtuseness /əb'tusnɪs/ n (bluntness) embotamiento, m; (stupidity) estupidez, torpeza, f

obverse / a. ɒb'vɜrs; n. 'ɒbvɜrs/ a del anverso. n anverso, m

obviate /'ɒbviˌeit/ vt obviar, evitar

obvious /'ɒbviəs/ a evidente, manifiesto, patente, obvio, aparente, transparente; poco sutil

obviously /'ɒbviəsli/ adv evidentemente, patentemente

obviousness /'ɒbviəsnɪs/ n evidencia, transparencia, f

occasion /ə'keiʒən/ n ocasión, f; oportunidad, f, momento oportuno, tiempo propicio, m; (reason) motivo, origen, m, causa, razón, f; (need) necesidad, f. vt ocasionar, causar, producir. **as o. demands,** cuando las circunstancias lo exigen, en caso necesario. **for the o.,** para la ocasión. **on one o.,** una vez. **on the o. of,** en la ocasión de. **on that o.,** en tal ocasión, en aquella ocasión. **He has given me no o. to say so,** No me ha dado motivos de decirlo. **There is no o. for it,** No hay necesidad para ello. **to have o. to,** haber de, tener que, necesitar. **to lose no o.,** no perder ripio (or oportunidad). **to rise to the o.,** estar al nivel de las circunstancias. **to take this o.,** aprovechar esta oportunidad

occasional /ə'keiʒənl/ a (occurring at times) de vez en cuando, intermitente; poco frecuente, infrecuente; (of verse) de ocasión. **o. table,** mesilla, f

occasionally /ə'keiʒənli/ adv de vez en cuando, de cuando en cuando

occiput /'ɒksəˌpʌt/ n Anat. occipucio, m

occlude /ə'klud/ vt obstruir, cerrar; Med. ocluir; Chem. absorber

occlusion /ə'kluʒən/ n cerramiento, m; Med. oclusión, f; Chem. absorción de gases, f

occlusive /ə'klusɪv/ a oclusivo

occult /ə'kʌlt/ a oculto, escondido, misterioso; mágico. **o. sciences,** creencias ocultas, f pl

occultation /ˌɒkʌl'teiʃən/ n Astron. ocultación, f; eclipse, m

occultism /ə'kʌltɪzəm/ n ocultismo, m

occultist /ə'kʌltɪst/ n ocultista, mf

occupancy /'ɒkyəpənsi/ n ocupación, posesión, f; (tenancy) tenencia, f

occupant /'ɒkyəpənt/ n habitante, mf; ocupante, mf; (tenant) inquilino (-na)

occupation /ˌɒkyə'peiʃən/ n ocupación f; (tenure) inquilinato, m, tenencia, f; (work) trabajo, quehacer, m, labor, m; (employment) empleo, oficio, m; profesión, f

occupational /ˌɒkyə'peiʃənl/ a de oficio. **o. disease,** enfermedad profesional, f

occupier /'ɒkyəˌpaiər/ n ocupante, mf, inquilino (-na)

occupy /'ɒkyəˌpai/ vt ocupar; (live in) vivir en, habitar; (time) emplear, pasar; (take over) apoderarse de, ocupar. **to o. oneself in or with,** ocuparse en, ocuparse con. **to be occupied in or with,** estar ocupado con, ocuparse en

occur /ə'kɜr/ vi (happen) suceder, tener lugar, acaecer; (exist) encontrarse, existir; (of ideas) ocurrirse, venirse. **to o. to one's mind,** venírsele a las mientes. **to o. again,** volver a suceder, ocurrir de nuevo. **An idea occurred to her,** Se le ocurrió una idea

occurrence /ə'kɜrəns/ n ocurrencia, f; incidente, suceso, acontecimiento, m. **to be of frequent o.,** ocurrir con frecuencia, acontecer a menudo

ocean /'ouʃən/ n océano, m; Fig. mar, abundancia, f. **o.-going vessel,** buque de alta mar, m

Oceania /ˌouʃi'æniə/ el Mundo Novísmo, m

oceanic /ˌouʃi'ænɪk/ a oceánico

oceanography /ˌouʃə'nɒgrəfi/ n oceanografía, f

ocelot /'ɒsəˌlɒt/ n Zool. ocelote, m

ocher /'oukər/ n ocre, m

octagon /'ɒktəˌgɒn/ n octágono, m

octagonal /ɒk'tægənl/ a octagonal

octave /'ɒktɪv/ n (Eccl. metrics, Mus.) octava, f

octavo /ɒk'teivou, -'tɑ-/ n Print. libro, etc. en octavo (8°), m. **in o.,** en octavo. **large o.,** octavo mayor, m. **small o.,** octavo menor, m

octet /ɒk'tɛt/ n Mus. octeto, m

October /ɒk'toubər/ n octubre, m. **October 2, 1996,** el segundo (2°) de octubre de mil novecientos noventa y seis, **October 2, 2000,** el segundo de octubre del dos mil

octogenarian /ˌɒktədʒəˈnɛəriən/ a and n octogenario (-ia)

octopus /ˈɒktəpəs/ n pulpo, m

ocular /ˈɒkyələr/ a ocular, visual. n ocular, m

oculist /ˈɒkyəlɪst/ n oculista, mf

odd /ɒd/ a (of numbers) impar; (of volumes, etc.) suelto; (strange) raro, curioso, extraño, extravagante; (casual) casual, accidental; (extra) y pico, y tantos, sobrante; (of gloves, etc.) sin pareja. **at odd moments,** en momentos de ocio. **at odd times,** de vez en cuando. **thirty odd,** treinta y pico. **odd number,** número impare, m. **odd or even,** pares o impares. **odd trick,** (at cards) una baza más

oddity /ˈɒdɪti/ n excentricidad, rareza, extravagancia, f; (person) ente singular, m; (curio) objeto curioso, m, antigüedad, f

oddly /ˈɒdli/ adv singularmente, curiosamente

oddment /ˈɒdmənt/ n bagatela, baratija, f

oddness /ˈɒdnɪs/ n singularidad, rareza, extravagancia, f

odds /ɒdz/ n pl diferencia, desigualdad, f; (superiority) ventaja, superioridad, f; (quarrel) disputa, riña, f. **The o. are that...,** Lo más probable es que... **to fight against dreadful o.,** luchar contra fuerzas muy superiores. **o. and ends,** (remains) sobras y picos, f pl; (trifles) ñaques, m pl, chucherías, f pl

Odessa /ouˈdɛsə/ Odesa, f

odious /ˈoudiəs/ a odioso, detestable, aborrecible, repugnante

odiousness /ˈoudiəsnɪs/ n odiosidad, f

odium /ˈoudiəm/ n odio, m

odor /ˈoudər/ n olor, m, (fragrance) perfume, aroma, m, fragancia, f; Fig. sospecha, f. **in bad o.,** Fig. en disfavor. **o. of sanctity,** olor de santidad, m

odoriferous /ˌoudəˈrɪfərəs/ a odorífero; (perfumed) oloroso, perfumado

odorless /ˈoudərlɪs/ a inodoro

odorous /ˈoudərəs/ a fragante, oloroso

odyssey /ˈɒdəsi/ n odisea, f

Oedipus complex /ˈɛdəpəs/ n complejo de Edipo, m

of /əv/ prep de. **of** has many idiomatic translations which are given as far as possible under the heading of the word concerned. It is also not translated. **I robbed him of his reward,** Le robé su recompensa. **I was thinking of you,** Pensaba en tí. **It was very good of you to...,** Vd. ha tenido mucha bondad de... **Your naming of the child Mary,** El que Vd. haya dado el nombre de María al niño. **29th of Sept., 1936,** el 29 de septiembre de 1936. **Of course!** ¡Claro está! ¡Ya lo creo! ¡Naturalmente! **of late,** última mente. **of the** (before m, sing) del; (before f, sing) de la; (before m pl) de los; (before f pl) de las. **to dream of,** soñar con. **to smell of,** oler a tener olor de. **to taste of, etc.,** saber a, tener gusto de.

off /ɔf/ prep de; fuera de; cerca de; desde; Naut. a la altura de. **from off,** de. **Take your gloves off the table!** ¡Quítate los guantes de la mesa! **The wheel was off the car,** La rueda se había desprendido del coche. **to be off duty,** no estar de servicio; Mil. no estar de guardia. **to lunch off cold meat,** almorzar de carne fría. **off one's head,** chiflado

off /ɔf/ a (contrasted with near) de la derecha, derecho; (unlikely) improbable, remoto. adv (with intransitive verbs of motion) se (e.g. He has gone off, Se ha marchado); (contrasted with on) de (e.g. He has fallen off the horse, Ha caído del caballo); (of place at a distance) lejos, a distancia de; (of time) generally a verb is used (e.g. The wedding is three months off, Faltan tres meses para la boda); (completely) enteramente. **Off** is often not translated in Sp. (e.g. to put off, aplazar, to cut off, cortar). **day off,** día libre, día de asueto, m. **How far off is the house from here? The house is five miles off.** ¿Cuántas millas está la casa de aquí? La casa está a cinco millas de aquí. **His hat is off,** Está sin sombrero, Se ha quitado el sombrero. **The cover is off,** La cubierta está quitada. **The party is off,** Se ha anulado la reunión. **6% off,** un descuento de seis por ciento. interj **Off with you!** ¡Márchate! ¡Fuera! **off and on,** de vez en cuando, espasmódicamente. **off color,** (ill) malucho; (of jokes)

verde. **off season,** estación muerta, f. **off-shore,** a vista de tierra. **off-stage,** entre bastidores

offal /ˈɔfəl/ n (butchers') menudencias, f pl, asadura, f, menudos, despojos, m pl; desperdicio, m

offend /əˈfɛnd/ vt ofender; agraviar, insultar; herir; desagradar, disgustar; vi ofender, pecar. **to be offended,** resentirse, insultarse. **This offends my sense of justice,** Esto ofende mi sentimiento de justicia. **to o. against,** pecar contra; violar

offender /əˈfɛndər/ n delincuente, mf; agraviador (-ra), pecador (-ra), transgresor (-ra). **old o.,** Law. criminal inveterado, m

offense /əˈfɛns/ n ofensa, transgresión, violación, f; pecado, m; Law. delito, crimen, m; (insult) agravio, m, afrenta, f. **the first o.,** el primer delito, m. **fresh o.,** nuevo delito, m. **political o.,** crimen político, m. **technical o.,** Law. cuasidelito, m. **to commit an o. against,** ofender contra. **to take o.,** resentirse, darse por ofendido

offensive /əˈfɛnsɪv/ a ofensivo, desagradable, repugnante; (insulting) injurioso, agraviador, agresivo. n Mil. ofensiva, f. **to take the o.,** tomar la ofensiva

offensiveness /əˈfɛnsɪvnɪs/ n lo desagradable; (insult) ofensa, f; lo injurioso

offer /ˈɔfər/ n oferta, f; ofrecimiento, m; (of help) promesa, f; proposición, f; Com. oferta, f. vt ofrecer; prometer; (opportunities, etc.) deparar, brindar; tributar. vi ofrecerse, ocurrir, surgir. **to o. up,** ofrecer; inmolar, sacrificar. **He did not offer to go,** No hizo ademán de marcharse. **to o. resistance,** oponer resistencia. **o. of marriage,** oferta de matrimonio, f

offerer /ˈɔfərər/ n ofrecedor (-ra)

offering /ˈɔfərɪŋ/ n ofrecimiento, m; Eccl. ofrenda, oblación, f, sacrificio, m; regalo, don, m, dádiva, f

offhand /ˈɔfˈhænd/ a sin preparación, de repente; (casual) casual, despreocupado; (discourteous) brusco, descortés

offhandedly /ˈɔfˈfɪfəˈhændɪdli/ adv sin preparación, espontáneamente; negligentemente; bruscamente

office /ˈɔfɪs/ n oficina, m; (post) cargo, puesto, destino, m; (state department) ministerio, m; (of a Cabinet minister) cartera, f; (room) oficina, f; despacho, escritorio, m; (of a newspaper) redacción, f; (lawyer's) bufete, m; departamento, m; Eccl. oficio, m. **offices,** negocio, m; oficinas, f pl; (prayers) rezos, m pl; Eccl. oficios, m pl. **domestic offices,** dependencias, f pl. **good offices,** Fig. buenos oficios, m pl. **head o.,** casa central, oficina principal, f. **private o.,** despacho particular, m. **to be in o.,** estar en el poder. **o.-bearer,** miembro de la junta, m; funcionario, m. **o.-boy,** mozo de oficina, m. **o. employee,** oficinista, mf. **o. hours,** horas de oficina, f pl; (professions) horas de consulta, f pl. **o.-seeker,** aspirante, m; pretendiente, m. **o. work,** trabajo de oficina, m

officer /ˈɔfəsər/ n oficial, funcionario, m; (police) agente de policía, m; (of the Church) dignatario, m; (Mil. Nav. Aer.) oficial, m. vt mandar. **commissioned o.,** oficial, m. **non-commissioned o.,** oficial subalterno, m. **to be well officered,** tener buena oficialidad. **Officers' Training Corps,** Escuela de Oficiales, f

office worker n oficinista, mf

official /əˈfɪʃəl/ a oficial; autorizado; ceremonioso, grave. n funcionario, m; oficial público, m. **high o.,** funcionario importante. m. **o. mourning,** duelo oficial, m. **o. receiver,** fiscal de quiebras, m

officialdom /əˈfɪʃəldəm/ n funcionarismo, m; círculos oficiales, m pl

officiant /əˈfɪʃiənt/ n oficiante, m

officiate /əˈfɪʃiˌeit/ vi celebrar; oficiar, funcionar

officiating /əˈfɪʃiˌeitɪŋ/ a oficiante; celebrante. **o. priest,** sacerdote oficiante, celebrante, m

officious /əˈfɪʃəs/ a oficioso, entremetido

officiousness /əˈfɪʃəsnɪs/ n oficiosidad, f

offing /ˈɔfɪŋ/ n Naut. mar afuera, m. **in the o.,** cerca

off season fuera de temporada

offset /n. ˈɔfˌsɛt; v. ˌɔfˈsɛt/ n compensación, f, vt compensar, neutralizar

offshoot /ˈɔfˌʃut/ n renuevo, vástago, m

offside /ˈɔfˈsaid/ a (of a car) del lado derecho (or izquierda); Sports. fuera de juego

offspring /'ɔf,sprɪŋ/ n vástago, m; descendiente, mf; prole, f; hijos, m pl

often /'ɔfən/ adv a menudo, mucho, con frecuencia, frecuentemente, muchas veces. **as o. as,** tan a menudo como, siempre que. **as o. as not,** no pocas veces. **How o.?** ¿Cuántas veces? **It is not o. that...,** No ocurre con frecuencia que... **so o.,** tantas veces, con frecuencia. **Do you go there o.?** ¿Va Vd. allí con frecuencia (or frecuentemente)? **Not o.,** Voy rara vez allá

ogival /'oudʒaivəl/ a Archit. ojival

ogive /'oudʒaiv/ n Archit. ojiva, f

ogle /'ougəl/ vt and vi comer(se) con los ojos (a), ojear, guiñar el ojo (a). n ojeada, f, guiño, m

ogling /'ouglɪŋ/ n guiño, m, ojeada, f

ogre /'ougər/ n ogro, m

oh! /ou/ interj ¡o! **O no!** ¡Ca! ¡Claro que no!

ohm /oum/ n Elec. ohmio, m

oil /ɔil/ n aceite, m; petróleo, m; óleo, m. vt aceitar, engrasar, Argentina enaceitar; olear, ungir, untar; (bribe) sobornar, untar la mano; Fig. suavizar. a aceitero; petrolero. **to pour oil on troubled waters,** echar aceite sobre aguas turbulentas. **to strike oil,** encontrar un pozo de petróleo; Fig. encontrar un filón. **crude oil,** petróleo bruto, m. **heavy oil,** aceite pesado, m. **thin oil,** aceite ligero, m. Art. **in oils,** al óleo. **oil-bearing,** petrolífero. **oil-box,** engrasador, m. **oil-burner,** quemador de petróleo, m. **oil-can,** aceitera, f. **oil-colors,** pinturas al óleo, f pl. **oil field,** yacimiento petrolífero, campo de petróleo, m. **oil-filter,** separador de aceite, m. **oil-gauge,** nivel de aceite, m. **oil lamp,** velón, candil, quinqué, m. **oil of turpentine,** aceite de trementina, aguarrás, m. esencia de trementina, f. **oil-painting,** pintura al óleo, f. **oil pipeline,** oleoducto, m. **oil shop,** aceitería, f. **oil-silk,** encerado, m. **oil stove,** estufa de petróleo, f. **oil tanker,** Naut. petrolero, m. **oil-well,** pozo de petróleo, m

oilcake /'ɔil,keik/ n bagazo, m

oilcloth /'ɔil,klɔθ/ n hule, m; linóleo, m

oiler /'ɔilər/ n (can) aceitera, f; Naut. petrolero, m; lubricador, m

oiliness /'ɔilinɪs/ n oleaginosidad, untuosidad, f

oiling /'ɔilɪŋ/ n engrasado, m

oil seed n semilla oleaginosa, f

oilskin /'ɔil,skɪn/ n encerado, m

oily /'ɔili/ a aceitoso, grasiento

ointment /'ɔintmənt/ n ungüento, m, pomada, f

old /ould/ a viejo; antiguo, anciano; (of wines, etc.) añejo; (worn out) usado, gastado; (inveterate) arraigado, inveterado. **How old are you?** ¿Cuántos años tiene usted? **to be sixteen years old,** tener dieciséis años. **He is old enough to know his own mind,** Tiene bastante edad para saber lo que quiere. **to grow old,** envejecer. **of old,** antiguamente. **prematurely old,** revejido averiado. **old age,** vejez, senectud, f. **old bachelor,** solterón, m. **old clothes,** ropa vieja (or usada), ropa de segunda mano, f. **old-clothes dealer,** ropavejero (-ra). **old-clothes shop,** ropavejería, f. **old-established,** viejo. **old-fashioned,** pasado de moda, viejo; (of people) chapado a la antigua. **old lady,** anciana, dama vieja, f. **old-looking,** de aspecto viejo, avejentado. **old maid,** solterona, f. **old-maidish,** remilgado. **old man,** viejo, m; Theat. barba, m. **old salt,** lobo de mar, m; **Old Testament,** Antiguo Testamento, m. **old wives' tale,** cuento de viejas, m. **old woman,** vieja, f. **Old World,** Viejo Mundo, mundo antiguo, m

old-age home /'ould 'eidʒ/ n asilo de ancianos, m

olden /'ouldən/ a antiguo. **o. days,** días pasados, m pl

older /'ouldər/ a comp más viejo, mayor. **The older the madder,** A la vejez viruelas

old hat n viejo conocido

oldish /'ouldɪʃ/ a bastante viejo, de cierta edad

oldness /'ouldnɪs/ n antigüedad, ancianidad, edad, f

oleaginous /,ouli'ædʒənəs/ a oleaginoso

oleander /'ouli,ændər/ n Bot. adelfa, f, baladre, m

olfactory /ɒl'fæktəri/ a olfatorio, olfativo

oligarchic /,ɒlɪ'gɑrkɪk/ a oligárquico

oligarchy /'ɒlɪ,gɑrki/ n oligarquía, f

olive /'ɒlɪv/ n (tree) olivo, m; (fruit) aceituna, oliva,

f, a aceitunado, Lat. Am. aceituno. **wild o. tree,** acebuche, m. **o.-complected,** con tez aceitunada. **o. green,** verde oliva, m. **o. grove,** olivar, m. **o. oil,** aceite de oliva, m

olympiad /ə'lɪmpi,æd/ n olimpíada, f

olympian /ə'lɪmpiən/ a olímpico

olympic /ə'lɪmpɪk/ a olímpico. **o. games,** juegos olímpicos, m pl

olympus /ə'lɪmpəs/ n olimpo, m

omasum /ou'meisəm/ n Zool. librillo, libro, m

omber /'ɒmbər/ n tresillo, hombre, m

omega /ou'migə, ou'mei-/ n omega, f

omelet /'ɒmlɪt/ n tortilla, f. **sweet o.,** tortilla dulce, f

omen /'oumən/ n pronóstico, presagio, agüero, m, vt agorar, anunciar

ominous /'ɒmənəs/ a ominoso, azaroso, siniestro, amenazante

ominously /'ɒmənəsli/ adv ominosamente, con amenazas

omission /ou'mɪʃən/ n omisión, f; olvido, descuido, m; supresión, f

omit /ou'mɪt/ vt omitir; olvidar, descuidar; (suppress) suprimir, excluir, callar, dejar a un lado

omitting /ou'mɪtɪŋ/ pres part salvo, excepto

omnibus /'ɒmnə,bʌs/ n ómnibus, autobús, m. **o. conductor,** cobrador de autobús, m. **o. driver,** conductor de autobús, m. **o. route,** trayecto de autobús, m. **o. service,** servicio de autobuses, m. **o. volume,** volumen de obras coleccionadas, m

omnipotence /ɒm'nɪpətəns/ n omnipotencia, f

omnipotent /ɒm'nɪpətənt/ a omnipotente, todopoderoso

omnipresence /,ɒmnə'prɛzəns/ n omnipresencia, ubicuidad, f

omnipresent /,ɒmnə'prɛzənt/ a ubicuo

omniscience /ɒm'nɪʃəns/ n omnisciencia, f

omniscient /ɒm'nɪʃənt/ a omniscio, omnisciente

omnivorous /ɒm'nɪvərəs/ a omnívoro

on /ɒn/ prep (upon) sobre, en, encima de; (concerning) de, acerca de, sobre; (against) contra; (after) después; (according to) según; (with gerund) en; (with infin.) al; (at) a; (connected with, employed in) de; (by means of) por, mediante; (near to) cerca de, sobre; (into) en. Untranslated before days of week, dates of month or time of day (e.g. on Monday, el lunes. on Friday afternoons, los viernes por la tarde). **She has a bracelet on her wrist,** Tiene una pulsera en la muñeca. **He will retire on a good income,** Se jubilará con una buena renta. **on my uncle's death,** después de la muerte (o a la muerte) de mi tío, a morir. **On seeing them, he stopped,** Al verles se paró. **on leave,** con licencia, en uso de licencia. **on the next page,** en la página siguiente. **on this occasion,** en esta ocasión. **on the other hand,** en cambio. **on second thoughts,** luego de pensarlo bien. **on the way,** en camino. **on one side,** a un lado. **on the left,** a la izquierda. **on time,** a tiempo. **on my honor,** bajo palabra de honor. **on pain of death,** so pena de muerte, bajo pena de muerte. **on an average,** por término medio. **on his part,** por su parte. **on and after,** desde, a partir de. **on credit,** de fiado. **on fire,** ardiendo, en llamas. **on foot,** a pie. **on purpose,** a propósito; con intención. **on,** adv puesto (e.g. She has her gloves on, Tiene los guantes puestos); (forward) adelante, hacia adelante; (continue, with a verb) seguir, continuar (e.g. He went on talking, Siguió hablando). Often on is included in Sp. verb (e.g. The new play is on, Se ha estrenado la nueva comedia. The fight is on, Ya ha empezado la lucha). **On!** interj ¡Adelante! **and so on,** y así sucesivamente. **to have on,** llevar puesto. **on and off,** de vez en cuando. **on and on,** sin cesar

onanism /'ouna,nɪzəm/ n onanismo, m

once /wʌns/ adv una vez; (formerly) en otro tiempo, antiguamente; conjunc si (e.g. O. you give him the opportunity, Si le das la oportunidad). **all at o.,** todo junto, a un mismo tiempo; simultáneamente; (suddenly) súbitamente, de repente. **at o.,** en seguida, inmediatamente, Lat. Am. also lueguito. **for o.,** por una vez. **more than o.,** más de una vez. **not o.,** ni siquiera una vez. **o. before,** una vez antes. **o. and for**

all, una vez para siempre; por última vez. **o. in a while,** de vez en cuando. **o. more,** otra vez. **o. or twice,** una vez o dos, algunas veces. **o. too often,** una vez demasiado. **O. upon a time,** En tiempos pasados, En tiempos de Maricastaña; (as beginning of a story) Érase una vez, Había una vez, Hubo una vez **once in a blue moon** a cada muerte de un obispo
one /wʌn/ *a* un, uno, una; (first) primero; (single) único, solo; (indifferent) igual, indiferente; (some, certain) algún, cierto, un (e.g. *one day,* cierto día). *n* uno; (hour) la una; (of age) un año. Often not translated in Sp. (e.g. *I shall take the blue one,* Tomaré el azul). *pron* se; uno. **one's,** su, de uno (e.g. *one's work,* el trabajo de uno). **I for one do not think so,** Yo por uno no lo creo. **It is all one,** Es igual, No hace diferencia alguna. **only one,** un solo. **that one,** ése, *m*, ésa, *f*, eso, *neut.* **this one,** éste, *m*, ésta, *f*, esto, *neut.* **these ones,** éstos, etc. **those ones,** ésos, etc. **the one,** el (que), *m*, la (que), *f.* **with one accord,** unánimemente. **one and all,** todos. **one another,** se, uno a otro, mutuamente. **one by one,** uno a uno. **one day,** un día; un día de éstos, algún día. **one-eyed,** tuerto. **one-handed,** manco. **one-sided,** parcial. **one-way street,** *Spain* calle de dirección única, *Argentina* calle de una sola mano, *Mexico* calle de un sentido, calle de una corrida, *f.* **one-way traffic,** tráfico en una sola dirección, *m*
oneiric /ouˈnairɪk/ *a* onírico
oneness /ˈwʌnɪs/ *n* unidad, *f*
onerous /ˈɒnərəs/ *a* oneroso, pesado, molesto, gravoso
onerousness /ˈɒnərəsnɪs/ *n* pesadez, molestia, dificultad, inconveniencia, *f*
one-seater /wʌn ˈsitər/ *n* avión de una plaza, *m*
oneself /wʌnˈsɛlf/ *pron* se, uno mismo (una misma); (after prep.) sí mismo, sí. **It must be done by o.,** Uno mismo ha de hacerlo
onion /ˈʌnyən/ *n* cebolla, *f.* **string of onions,** ristra de cebollas, *f.* **young o.,** babosa, *f.* **o. bed,** cebollar, *m.* **o. seed,** cebollino, *m.* **o. seller,** cebollero (-ra)
on-line /ˈɒnˈlain, ˈɒn-/ *a* conectado, en línea
onlooker /ˈɒnˌlʊkər/ *n* espectado (-ra), observador (-ra); testigo, *mf*
only /ˈounli/ *a* único, solo. *adv* únicamente, sólo; no... más (que), tan sólo; con la excepción de, salvo. *conjunc* pero, salvo (que), si no fuera (que). **I shall o. give you three,** No te daré más de tres. **The o. thing one can do,** Lo único que se puede hacer. **I o. wished to see her,** Quería verla nada más. **if o.,** ¡ojalá (que)! **not o....,** no sólo... **o.-begotten,** *a* unigénito. **o. child,** hijo (-ja) único (-ca)
onomatopoeia /ˌɒnəˌmætəˈpiə/ *n* onomatopeya, *f*
onomatopoeic /ˌɒnəˌmætəˈpiːk/ *a* onomatopéyico
onrush /ˈɒnˌrʌʃ/ *n* asalto, ataque, acometimiento, *m*, acometida, embestida, *f*; (of water, etc.) acceso, *m*; torrente, *m*, corriente, *f*
onset /ˈɒnˌsɛt/ *n* ataque, *m*, acometida, *f*; (beginning) principio, *m.* **at the first o.,** al primer ímpetu
onslaught /ˈɒnˌslɔt/ *n* asalto, ataque, *m*
onus /ˈounəs/ *n* responsabilidad, *f.* **o. of proof,** obligación de probar, *f*
onward /ˈɒnwərd/ *a* progresivo. *adv* adelante, hacia adelante; (as a command) ¡Adelante!
onyx /ˈɒnɪks/ *n* ónice, *m*
ooze /uz/ *n* légamo, limo, fango, *m*, lama, *f. vi* exudar, rezumarse; manar; *vt* sudar. **to o. satisfaction,** caérsele (a uno) la baba. **to o. away,** (of money, etc.) desaparecer, volar. **to o. out,** (news) divulgarse
oozing /ˈuzɪŋ/ *a* fangoso, legamoso, lamoso
opacity /ouˈpæsɪti/ *n* opacidad, *f*
opal /ˈoupəl/ *n* ópalo, *m*
opalescence /ˌoupəˈlɛsəns/ *n* opalescencia, *f*
opalescent /ˌoupəˈlɛsənt/ *a* opalescente, iridiscente
opaline /ˈoupəlin/ *a* opalino
opaque /ouˈpeik/ *a* opaco
opaqueness /ouˈpeiknɪs/ *n* opacidad, *f*
op. cit. /ˈɒp ˈsɪt/ (opere citato) obra cit. (obra citada)
open /ˈoupən/ *vt* abrir; (a package) desempaquetar, desenvolver; (remove lid) destapar; *Lat. Am.* desenlatar (canned food); (unfold) desplegar; (inaugurate)

inaugurar; iniciar, empezar; establecer; (an abscess) cortar; (with arms, heart, eyes) abrir; (with mind, thought) descubrir, revelar; (make accessible) franquear, hacer accesible; (tear) romper; *vi* abrirse; empezar, comenzar; (of a view, etc.) aparecer, extenderse; inaugurarse; (of a career, etc.) prepararse. **to o. fire against,** abrir el fuego contra. **to o. into,** comunicar con, salir a. **to o. into each other,** (of rooms) comunicarse. **to o. on,** mirar a, dar a, caer a. **to o. out,** *vt* abrir; desplegar; revelar. *vi* extenderse; revelarse. **to o. the eyes of,** *Fig.* desengañar, desilusionar. **to o. up,** abrir; explorar, hacer accesible; revelar; *Fig. Inf.* desabrocharse. **to o. with** or **by,** empezar con
open /ˈoupən/ *a* abierto; descubierto; expuesto; (unfenced) descercado; (not private) público; libre; (unfolded) desplegado, extendido; (persuasible) receptivo; no resuelto, pendiente; (frank) franco, candoroso; (with sea) alto; (liberal) generoso, hospitalario; sin prejuicios; *Com.* abierto, pendiente; sin defensa; (of weather) despejado; (of a letter) sin sellar; (without a lid) destapado; (well-known) manifiesto, bien conocido. *n* aire libre, *m.* **in the o.,** al descubierto. **in the o. air,** al aire libre, al raso, a cielo abierto. **to break o.,** forzar. **to cut o.,** abrir de un tajo, cortar. **to leave o.,** dejar abierto. **wide o.,** muy abierto; (of doors) de par en par. **half o.,** entreabierto. **o. boat,** barco descubierto, *m.* **o. car,** coche abierto, *m.* **o. carriage,** carruaje descubierto, *m.* **o. cast,** *Mineral.* roza abierta, *f.* **o.-eyed,** con los ojos abiertos. **o.-handed,** generoso, dadivoso, *Lat. Am. also* maniabierto. **o.-letter,** carta abierta, *f.* **o.-minded,** imparcial. **o.-mouthed,** con la boca abierta, boquiabierto. **o. question,** cuestión por decidir, cuestión discutible, *f.* **o. secret,** secreto a voces, *m.* **o. sea,** alta mar, *f.* **o. town,** ciudad abierta, *f.* **o. tramcar,** jardinera, *f.* **o. truck,** vagoneta, *f.* **o.-work,** *Sew.* calado, enrejado, *m*
opener /ˈoupənər/ *n* abridor, *m*
opening /ˈoupənɪŋ/ *n* abertura, brecha, *f*; orificio, *m*; inauguración, apertura, *f*; principio, *m*; (chance) oportunidad, *f*; (employment) puesto, *m.* **o. price,** *Com.* (on Exchange) precio de apertura, *m*, primer curso *m*
openly /ˈoupənli/ *adv* abiertamente, francamente; públicamente
openness /ˈoupənnɪs/ *n* situación expuesta, *f*; espaciosidad, *f*; franqueza, *f*, candor, *m*; imparcialidad, *f*
opera /ˈɒprə/ *n* ópera, *f.* **comic o.,** zarzuela, *f.* **o.-cloak,** abrigo de noche, *m.* **o.-glasses,** gemelos de teatro, *m pl.* **o.-hat,** clac, *m.* **o.-house,** teatro de la ópera, *m.* **o. singer,** cantante de ópera, operista, *mf*
operate /ˈɒpəˌreit/ *vi* funcionar, trabajar; obrar; (with on, upon) producir efecto sobre; influir; *Surg.* operar; (on Exchange) especular, jugar a la bolsa; *vt* hacer funcionar, manejar; mover, impulsar; dirigir
operatic /ˌɒpəˈrætɪk/ *a* de ópera, operístico
operating /ˈɒpəˌreitɪŋ/ *a* (of surgeons) operante; de operación. **o. table,** mesa de operaciones, *f.* **o. theater,** anfiteatro, *m*; sala de operaciones, *f*
operation /ˌɒpəˈreiʃən/ *n* funcionamiento, *m*, acción, *f*; *Surg.* intervención quirúrgica, operación, *f*; (*Mil. Naut.*) maniobra, *f*; manipulación, *f.* **to come into o.,** ponerse en práctica; hacerse efectivo. **to continue in o.,** (*Law*) seguir en vigor. **to perform an o.,** *Surg.* operar, praticar una intervención quirúrgica; hacer una maniobra. **to put into o.,** poner en práctica
operative /ˈɒpərətiv/ *a* operativo, activo. *n* operario (-ia), obrero (-ra). **to become o.,** tener efecto
operator /ˈɒpəˌreitər/ *n* operario (-ia); (telephone) telefonista, *mf*; (machines, engines) maquinista, *mf*; *Surg.* operador, *m*
operetta /ˌɒpəˈrɛtə/ *n* opereta, *f*
ophthalmologist /ˌɒfθəlˈmɒlədʒɪst/ *n* oftalmólogo, *m*
ophthalmology /ˌɒfθəlˈmɒlədʒi/ *n* oftalmología, *f*
opiate /ˈoupiət/ *n* opiata, *f*, narcótico, *m*, *a* opiado
opinion /əˈpɪnyən/ *n* opinión, *f*, parecer, juicio, *m*; concepto, *m*, idea, *f.* **in my o.,** según mi parecer. **to be of the o. that,** ser de la opinión que, opinar que. **to be of the same o.,** estar de acuerdo, concurrir. **public o.,** opinión (or voz) pública, *f*
opinionated /əˈpɪnyəˌneitid/ *a* terco, obstinado

opium /'oupiəm/ *n* opio, *m*. **o. addict,** opiónamo (-ma). **o. den,** fumadero de opio, *m*. **o. eater,** mascador de opio, opiófago, *m*. **o. smoker,** fumador (-ra) de opio

Oporto /ou'pɔrtou/ Oporto, Porto, *m*

opponent /ə'pounənt/ *n* antagonista, *mf*, enemigo (-ga); contrario (-ia), adversario (-ia), competidor (-ra)

opportune /,ɒpər'tun/ *a* oportuno, tempestivo, conveniente, a propósito. **to be o.,** venir al caso. **o. moment,** momento oportuno, *m*; hora propicia, *f*

opportunely /,ɒpər'tunli/ *adv* oportunamente. **to come o.,** venir a pelo

opportuneness /,ɒpər'tunnɪs/ *n* oportunidad, tempestividad, conveniencia, *f*

opportunism /,ɒpər'tunɪzəm/ *n* oportunismo, *m*

opportunist /,ɒpər'tunɪst/ *n* oportunista, *Lat. Am. also* maromero (-ra), *mf*

opportunity /,ɒpər'tunɪti/ *n* oportunidad, ocasión, posibilidad, *f*. **to give an o. for,** dar margen para. **to open new opportunities,** abrir nuevos horizontes. **to take the o.,** tomar la oportunidad

opposable /ə'pouzəbəl/ *a* oponible

oppose /ə'pouz/ *vt* (counterbalance) oponer, contrarrestar; combatir; hacer frente (a), contrariar, pugnar contra, oponerse (a)

opposed (to) /ə'pouzd/ *a* opuesto a, enemigo de, contra

opposing /ə'pouzɪŋ/ *a* opuesto; enemigo, contrario

opposite /'ɒpəzɪt/ *a* (facing) de cara a, frente a, del otro lado de; opuesto; (antagonistic) contrario, antagónico; otro, diferente. *n* contraria, *f*, lo opuesto; antagonista, *mf*; adversario (-ia). **the o. sex,** el otro sexo. **o. leaves,** *Bot.* hojas opuestas, *f pl*. **o. to,** frente a; distinto de

opposition /,ɒpə'zɪʃən/ *n* oposición, *f*; (obstacle) estorbo, impedimento, *m*, dificultad, *f*; resistencia, hostilidad, *f*; (*Astron. Polit.*) oposición, *f*; (difference) contraste, *m*, diferencia, *f*. *a* de la oposición. **in o.,** en oposición; *Polit.* en la oposición. **to be in o.,** estar en oposición; *Polit.* ser de la oposición, estar en la oposición

oppress /ə'pres/ *vt* oprimir, tiranizar, sojuzgar, apremiar; (of moral causes) abrumar, agobiar, desanimar; (of heat, etc.) ahogar

oppression /ə'preʃən/ *n* opresión, tiranía, crueldad, *f*; (moral) agobio, sufrimiento, *m*, ansia, *f*; (difficulty in breathing) sofocación, *f*, ahogo, *m*

oppressive /ə'presɪv/ *a* opresivo, tiránico, cruel; (taxes, etc.) gravoso; (of heat) sofocante, asfixiante; agobiador, abrumador

oppressor /ə'presər/ *n* opresor (-ra), sojuzgador (-ra), tirano (-na)

opprobrious /ə'proubriəs/ *a* oprobioso, vituperioso; infame

opprobrium /ə'proubriəm/ *n* oprobio, *m*, ignominia, *f*

opt /ɒpt/ *vi* optar, escoger, elegir

optic, optical /'ɒptɪk; 'ɒptɪkəl/ *a* óptico. **o. illusion,** ilusión óptica, *f*; engaño a la vista, trampantojo, *m*. **o. nerve,** nervio óptico, *m*

optician /ɒp'tɪʃən/ *n* óptico, *m*

optics /'ɒptɪks/ *n* óptica, *f*

optimism /'ɒptə,mɪzəm/ *n* optimismo, *m*

optimist /'ɒptəmɪst/ *n* optimista, *mf*

optimistic /,ɒptə'mɪstɪk/ *a* optimista

optimum /'ɒptəməm/ *n* lo óptimo; (used as adjective) óptimo

option /'ɒpʃən/ *n* opción, *f*, (all meanings)

optional /'ɒpʃənl/ *a* discrecional, facultativo

opulence /'ɒpyələns/ *n* opulencia, riqueza, magnificencia, *f*; (abundance) abundancia, copia, *f*

opulent /'ɒpyələnt/ *a* opulento, rico, acaudalado; abundante

opus /'oupəs/ *n* obra, composición, *f*

opuscule /ou'pʌskyul/ *n* opúsculo, *m*

or /ɔr/ *conjunc* o; (before a word beginning with o or ho) u; (negative) ni. *n Herald.* oro, *m*. **an hour or so,** una hora más o menos, alrededor de una hora. **either... or,** o... o. **or else,** o bien. **whether... or,** que... que, siquiera... siquiera, ya... ya. **without... or,** sin... ni

oracle /'ɔrəkəl/ *n* oráculo, *m*

oracular /ɔ'rækyələr/ *a* profético, vatídico; ambiguo, misterioso, sibilino; dogmático, magistral

oral /'ɔrəl/ *a* verbal, hablado; *Anat.* oral, bucal

oral cavity *n* cavidad bucal, *f*

orange /'ɔrɪndʒ/ *n* (tree) naranjo, *m*; (fruit) naranja, *f*; **bitter o.,** naranja amarga, *f*. **blood o.,** naranja dulce, *f*. **tangerine o.,** naranja mandarina, *f*. **o. blossom,** azahar, *m*. **o. color,** color de naranja, *m*. **o.-colored,** de color de naranja, anaranjado. **o.-flower water,** agua de azahar, *f*. **o. grove,** naranjal, *m*. **o. grower** (or **seller**), naranjero (-ra). **o. peel,** piel de naranja, *f*. **o.-stick,** (for nails) limpiauñas, *m*

orangeade /,ɔrɪndʒ'eid/ *n* naranjada, *f*; (mineral water) gaseosa, *f*

orangery /'ɔrɪndʒri/ *n* naranjal, *m*

orangutan /ɔ'ræŋʊ,tæn/ *n* *Zool.* orangután, *m*

oration /ɔ'reiʃən/ *n* oración, declamación, *f*, discurso, *m*

orator /'ɔrətər/ *n* orador (-ra), declamador (-ra)

oratorical /,ɔrə'tɔrɪkəl/ *a* oratorio, declamatorio, retórico

oratorio /,ɔrə'tɔri,ou/ *n* *Mus.* oratorio, *m*

oratory /'ɔrə,tɔri/ *n* oratoria, elocuencia, *f*; *Eccl.* oratorio, *m*, capilla, *f*

orb /ɔrb/ *n* orbe, *m*; esfera, *f*, globo, *m*; astro, *m*; *Poet.* ojo, *m*

orbit /'ɔrbɪt/ *n* *Astron.* órbita, *f*; *Anat.* órbita, cuenca del ojo, *f*

orbital /'ɔrbɪtl/ *a* *Anat.* orbital

orchard /'ɔrtʃərd/ *n* huerto, vergel, *m*; (especially of apples) pomar, *m*

orchestra /'ɔrkəstrə/ *n* orquesta, *f*. **with full o.,** con gran orquesta. *Theat.* **o. seat, o. stall,** butaca de platea, *f*

orchestral /ɔr'kestrəl/ *a* orquestal, instrumental

orchestrate /'ɔrkə,streit/ *vt* orquestar, instrumentar

orchestration /,ɔrkə'streiʃən/ *n* orquestración, instrumentación, *f*

orchid /'ɔrkɪd/ *n* orquídea, *f*

orchitis /ɔr'kaitɪs/ *n* *Med.* orquitis, *f*

ordain /ɔr'dein/ *vt* mandar, disponer, decretar; *Eccl.* ordenar. **to be ordained as,** *Eccl.* ordenarse de

ordeal /ɔr'dil/ *n* *Hist.* ordalías, *f pl*; prueba severa, *f*

order /'ɔrdər/ *n* (most meanings) orden, *m*; (command) precepto, mandamiento, decreto, *m*; orden, *f*; (rule) regla, *f*; (for money) libranza postal, *f*; (for goods) pedido, encargo, *m*; (arrangement) método, arreglo, *m*, clasificación, *f*; (condition) estado, *m*; *Archit.* estilo, *m*; (*Zool. Bot.*) orden, *m*; (sort) clase, especie, *f*; (rank) clase social, *f*; *Eccl.* orden, *f*; (badge) condecoración, insignia, *f*; (association) sociedad, asociación, compañía, *f*; (to view a house, etc.) permiso, *m*; (series) serie, *f*. **His liver is out of o.,** No está bien del hígado. **in good o.,** en buen estado; arreglado. **in o.,** (alphabetical, etc.) en orden; arreglado; (parliamentary) en regla. **in o. that,** para que, a fin de que. **in o. to,** a fin de, para. **out of o.,** estropeado, descompuesto; (on a notice) No funciona; (parliamentary) fuera del orden del dia. **till further o.,** hasta nueva orden. **to o.,** *Com.* por encargo especial. **to give an o.,** dar una orden; *Com.* poner un pedido. **to go out of o.,** descomponerse. **to keep in o.,** mantener en orden. **to put in o.,** poner en orden, ordenar. **to take holy orders,** tomar órdenes sagradas. **O.!** ¡Orden! **O. in Council,** orden real, *f*. **o. of knighthood,** orden de caballería, *f*. **o. of the day,** orden del día, *f*. **o. paper,** orden del día, *f*; reglamento, *m*

order /'ɔrdər/ *vt* disponer; arreglar; (command) mandar; (request) rogar, pedir; (direct) dirigir, gobernar; *Com.* encargar, cometer; (a meal, a taxi) encargar. **I ordered them to do it,** Les mandé hacerlo. **to o. about,** mandar. **to o. back,** hacer volver, mandar que vuelva. **to o. down,** hacer bajar, pedir (a uno) que baje. **to o. in,** mandar entrar. **to o. off,** despedir, decir (a uno) que se vaya. **to o. out,** mandar salir; (the troops) hacer salir la tropa; echar. **to o. up,** mandar subir, hacer subir

orderliness /'ɔrdərlinɪs/ *n* orden, aseo, método, *m*; limpieza, *f*; buena conducta, formalidad, *f*; buena administración, *f*

orderly /'ɔrdərli/ *a* bien arreglado, metódico; aseado, en orden; (of behaviour) formal, bien disciplinado. *n Mil.* ordenanza, *m;* ayudante de hospital *m*
ordinal /'ɔrdn̩əl/ *a* and *n* ordinal *m*
ordinance /'ɔrdn̩əns/ *n* ordenanza, *f,* reglamento, *m; Archit.* ordenación, *f; Eccl.* rito, *m*
ordinarily /,ɔrdn̩'ɛərəli/ *adv* de ordinario, ordinariamente, comúnmente
ordinary /'ɔrdn̩,ɛri/ *a* (usual) corriente, común, usual, ordinario, normal; (average) mediano, mediocre; (somewhat vulgar) ordinario, vulgar. *n Eccl.* ordinario, *m.* **out of the o.,** excepcional; poco común. **o. seaman,** marinero, *m.* **o. share,** *Com.* acción ordinaria, *f*
ordination /,ɔrdn̩'eiʃən/ *n Eccl.* ordenación, *f*
ordnance /'ɔrdnəns/ *n* artillería, *f,* cañones, *m pl;* pertrechos de guerra, *m pl.* **o. survey map,** mapa del estado mayor, *m.* **o. survey number,** acotación, *f*
ore /ɔr/ *n Mineral.* mena, *f,* quijo, *Lat. Am.* llampo, *m*
organ /'ɔrgən/ *n* (all meanings) órgano, *m.* **barrel-o.,** organillo, órgano de manubrio, *m.* **o.-blower,** entonador (-ra). **o.-grinder,** organillero (-ra). **o.-loft,** tribuna del órgano, *f.* **o.-pipe,** cañón de órgano, *m.* **o.-stop,** registro de órgano, *m*
organdy /'ɔrgəndi/ *n* organdí, *m*
organic /ɔr'gænɪk/ *a* orgánico. **o. chemistry,** química orgánica, *f*
organism /'ɔrgə,nɪzəm/ *n* organismo, *m*
organist /'ɔrgənɪst/ *n* organista, *mf*
organization /,ɔrgənə'zeiʃən/ *n* organización, *f;* grupo, *m,* asociación, sociedad, *f;* organismo, *m*
organize /'ɔrgə,naiz/ *vt* organizar; arreglar. *vi* organizarse; asociarse, constituirse
organizer /'ɔrgə,naizər/ *n* organizador (-ra)
organizing /'ɔrgə,naizɪŋ/ *a* organizador
orgasm /'ɔrgæzəm/ *n Med.* orgasmo, *m*
orgiastic /,ɔrdʒi'æstɪk/ *a* orgiástico
orgy /'ɔrdʒi/ *n* orgía, *f*
oriel /'ɔriəl/ *n Archit.* mirador, *m*
orient /'ɔriənt/ *a Poet.* naciente, oriental. *n* Oriente, Este, *m.* **pearl of fine o.,** perla de hermoso oriente, *f*
oriental /,ɔri'ɛntl̩/ *a* and *n* oriental, *mf*
orientalism /,ɔri'ɛntl̩ɪzəm/ *n* orientalismo, *m*
orientalist /,ɔri'ɛntl̩ɪst/ *n* orientalista, *mf*
orientate /'ɔriən,teit/ *vt* orientar; dirigir, guiar. *vi* mirar (or caer) hacia el este; orientarse
orientation /,ɔriən'teiʃən/ *n* orientación, *f*
orifice /'ɔrəfɪs/ *n* orificio, *m;* abertura, boca, *f*
origin /'ɔrɪdʒɪn/ *n* origen, génesis, *m;* raíz, causa, *f;* principio, comienzo, *m;* (extraction) descendencia, procedencia, familia, *f,* nacimiento, *m*
original /ə'rɪdʒənl̩/ *a* original; primitivo, primero; ingenioso. *n* original, *m;* prototipo, modelo, *m.* **o. sin,** pecado original, *m*
originality /ə,rɪdʒə'nælɪti/ *n* originalidad, *f*
originally /ə'rɪdʒənli/ *adv* originalmente; al principio; antiguamente
originate /ə'rɪdʒə,neit/ *vt* (produce) ocasionar, producir, suscitar, iniciar, engendrar; (create) inventar, crear. *vi* originarse, surgir, nacer. **to o. in,** tener su origen en, surgir de, emanar de, venir de
origination /ə,rɪdʒə'neiʃən/ *n* origen, principio, génesis, *m*
originator /ə'rɪdʒə,neitər/ *n* iniciador (-ra), fundador (-ra); autor (-ra), creador (-ra)
oriole /'ɔri,oul/ *n Ornith.* oropéndola, *f*
Orion /ə'raiən/ *n Astron.* Orión, *m*
Orkneys, the /'ɔrkniz/ las Orcades, *f pl*
ornament /*n.* 'ɔrnəmənt; *v.* -,mɛnt/ *n* adorno, *m;* decoración, *f; Fig.* ornamento, *m;* (trinket) chuchería, *f, n pl.* **ornaments,** *Eccl.* ornamentos, *m pl. vt* ornar, adornar, decorar, embellecer
ornamental /,ɔrnə'mɛntl̩/ *a* ornamental, decorativo
ornamentation /,ɔrnəmɛn'teiʃən/ *n* ornamentación, decoración, *f*
ornate /ɔr'neit/ *a* vistoso, ornado en demasía, barroco
ornateness /ɔr'neitnɪs/ *n* elegancia, vistosidad, magnificencia, *f*
ornithological /,ɔrnəθə'lɒdʒɪkəl/ *a* ornitológico

ornithologist /,ɔrnə'θɒlədʒɪst/ *n* ornitólogo, *m*
ornithology /,ɔrnə'θɒlədʒi/ *n* ornitología, *f*
orphan /'ɔrfən/ *a* and *n* huérfano (-na)
orphanage /'ɔrfənɪdʒ/ *n* orfanato, hospicio, *m*
orphanhood /'ɔrfən,hʊd/ *n* orfandad, *f*
Orphean /ɔr'fiən/ *a* órfico
orthodox /'ɔrθə,dɒks/ *a* ortodoxo
orthodoxy /'ɔrθə,dɒksi/ *n* ortodoxia, *f*
orthographic /,ɔrθə'græfɪk/ *a* ortográfico
orthography /ɔr'θɒgrəfi/ *n* ortografía, *f*
orthopedic /,ɔrθə'pidɪk/ *a* ortopédico
orthopedics /,ɔrθə'pidɪks/ *n* ortopedia, *f*
orthopedist /,ɔrθə'pidɪst/ *n* ortopedista, *mf* ortopédico (-ca)
oscillate /'ɒsə,leit/ *vi* oscilar, fluctuar; (hesitate) dudar, vacilar. *vt* hacer oscilar
oscillation /,ɒsə'leiʃən/ *n* oscilación, fluctuación, vibración, *f; Elec.* oscilación, *f*
oscillator /'ɒsə,leitər/ *n* oscilador, *m*
oscillatory /'ɒsələ,tɔri/ *a* oscilante
osculation /,ɒskyə'leiʃən/ *n* ósculo, *m*
osier /'ouʒər/ *n Bot.* mimbre, *m,* or *f.* **o. bed,** mimbrera, *f*
osmic /'ɒzmɪk/ *a Chem.* ósmico
osmosis /ɒz'mousɪs/ *n* (*Phys. Chem.*) ósmosis, *f*
osprey /'ɒspri, -prei/ *n Ornith.* quebrantahuesos, *m*
osseous /'ɒsiəs/ *a* óseo
ossification /,ɒsəfɪ'keiʃən/ *n* osificación, *f*
ossify /'ɒsə,fai/ *vt* osificar; *vi* osificarse
ossuary /'ɒʃu,ɛri/ *n* osario, *m*
osteitis /,ɒsti'aitɪs/ *n Med.* osteítis, *f*
Ostend /ɒs'tɛnd/ Ostende, *m*
ostensible /ɒ'stɛnsəbəl/ *a* ostensible; aparente, engañoso, ilusorio
ostensibly /ɒ'stɛnsəbli/ *adv* en apariencia, ostensiblemente
ostentation /,ɒstɛn'teiʃən/ *n* ostentación, *f;* aparato, fausto, boato, alarde, *m,* soberbia, *f*
ostentatious /,ɒstɛn'teiʃəs/ *a* ostentoso; aparatoso, fastuoso, rumboso
ostentatiously /,ɒstɛn'teiʃəsli/ *adv* con ostentación
osteology /,ɒsti'ɒlədʒi/ *n* osteología, *f*
osteomyelitis /,ɒstiou,maiə'laitɪs/ *n Med.* osteomielitis, *f*
osteopath /'ɒstiə,pæθ/ *n* osteópata, *m*
osteopathy /,ɒsti'ɒpəθi/ *n* osteopatía, *f*
osteoplasty /'ɒstiə,plæsti/ *n Surg.* osteoplastia, *f*
ostler /'ɒslər/ *n* mozo de cuadras, establero, *m*
ostracism /'ɒstrə,sɪzəm/ *n* ostracismo, *m*
ostracize /'ɒstrə,saiz/ *vt* desterrar; excluir del trato, echar de la sociedad
ostrich /'ɒstrɪtʃ/ *n* avestruz, *m.* **o. farm,** criadero de avestruces, *m*
otalgia /ou'tældʒiə/ *n Med.* otalgia, *f,* dolor de oídos, *m*
other /'ʌðər/ *a* otro. *pron* el otro, *m;* la otra, *f;* lo otro, *neut adv* (with than) de otra manera que, de otro modo que; otra cosa que. **this hand, not the o.,** esta mano, no la otra. **every o. day,** un día sí y otro no, cada dos días. **no o.,** ningún otro, *m;* otra ninguna, *f.* **someone o. o.,** alguien. **the others,** los (las) demás, *m, f pl;* los otros, *m pl;* las otras, *f pl.* **o. people,** otros, los demás
otherwise /'ʌðər,waiz/ *adv* de otra manera, de otro modo, otramente; (in other respects) por lo demás, por otra parte; (if not) si no
otitis /ou'taitɪs/ *n Med.* otitis, *f*
otologist /ou'tɒlədʒɪst/ *n* otólogo, *m*
otology /ou'tɒlədʒi/ *n* otología, *f*
otter /'ɒtər/ *n Zool.* nutria, *f.* **o. hound,** perro para cazar la nutria
ottoman /'ɒtəmən/ *a* otomano, turco. *n* otomana, *f*
ouch! /autʃ/ *interj* ¡ax!, ¡huy!
ought /ɔt/ *v aux* deber, tener la obligación (de); ser conveniente, convenir; ser necesario (que), tener que. **I o. to have done it yesterday,** Debía haberlo hecho ayer. **She o. not to come,** No debe (debiera, debería) venir. **He o. to see them tomorrow,** (should) Conviene que les vea mañana; Tiene la obligación de verles mañana; (must) Es necesario que les vea mañana, Tiene que verles mañana.

ounce /auns/ *n* (animal and weight) onza, *f*. **He hasn't an o. of common sense,** No tiene pizca de sentido común

our /auᵊr/ *unstressed* ɑr/ *a* nuestro.

ours /auᵊrz/ *pron* nuestro, *m*; nuestra, *f*; nuestros, *m pl*; nuestras, *f pl*; de nosotros, *m pl*; de nosotras, *f pl*; el nuestro, *m*; la nuestra, *f*; lo nuestro, *neut*; los nuestros, *m pl*; las nuestras, *f pl*. **This book is ours,** Este libro es nuestro (or el nuestro)

ourselves /ɑr'sɛlvz/ *pron pl* nosotros mismos, *m pl*; nosotras mismas, *f pl*

oust /aust/ *vt* despedir, desahuciar, expulsar, echar

out /aut/ *adv* afuera; hacia fuera; (gone out) fuera, salido, ausente; (invested) puesto; (published) publicado, salido; (discovered) conocido, descubierto; (on strike) en huelga; (mistaken) en error, equivocado; (of journeys) de ida, (on ships) de navegación (e.g. *on the second day out,* al segundo día de navegación); (of fire, etc.) extinguido; (at sea) en el mar; (of girls in society) puesta de largo, que ha entrado en sociedad; (of fashion) fuera de moda; (of office) fuera del poder; (in holes) roto, agujereado, andrajoso; (exhausted) agotado; (expired) vencido; (of a watch) llevar... minutos (horas) de atraso or de adelanto; (unfriendly) reñido; (way out) salida, *f*; (sport) fuera de juego; (of flowers) abierto; (of chickens) empollado. **a scene out of one of Shakespeare's plays,** una escena de una de las comedias de Shakespeare. **I am out $6,** He perdido seis dólares. **I am out of tea,** Se me ha acabado el té. **to drink out of a glass,** beber de un vaso. **to read out of a book,** leer en un libro. **to speak out,** hablar claro. **Murder will out,** El asesinato se descubrirá. **out-and-out,** completo; (with rogue, etc.) redomado. **out of,** fuera de; (beyond) más allá de; (through, by) por; (with) con; (without) sin; (from among) entre; (in) en; (with a negative sense) no. **out of breath,** jadeante, sin aliento. **out of character,** impropio. **out of commission,** fuera de servicio. **out of danger,** fuera de peligro. **out of date,** anticuado. **out of hand,** en seguida; indisciplinado. **out of money,** sin dinero. **out of necessity,** por necesidad. **out of one's mind,** loco, demente. **out of order.** See **out. out of print,** agotado. **out of reach,** fuera de alcance, inasequible. **out of season,** fuera de temporada. **out of sight,** fuera del alcance de la vista; invisible. **Out of sight, out of mind,** Ojos que no ven, corazón que no siente. **out of sorts,** indispuesto. **out of temper,** de mal genio. **out of the question,** imposible. **out of the way,** *adv* (of work) terminado, hecho; (remote) fuera del camino; (put aside) arrinconado; donde no estorbe. **out-of-the-way,** *a* remoto, aislado; (unusual) extraordinario, singular. **out of this world,** lo máximo, lo último. **out of touch with,** alejado de; sin relaciones con; sin simpatía con. **out of work,** sin empleo, sin trabajo, en paro forzoso. **out-patient,** enfermo (-ma) de un dispensario. **Out!** *interj* ¡Fuera! ¡Fuera de aquí! ¡Márchate! **Out with it!** ¡Hable Vd.! sin rodeos! ¡Hablen claro!

outbalance /ˌaut'bæləns/ *vt* exceder, sobrepujar

outbid /ˌaut'bɪd/ *vt* pujar, mejorar, ofrecer más dinero

outbidding /ˌaut'bɪdɪŋ/ *n* puja, mejora, *f*

outbreak /'aut,breik/ *n* (of war) declaración, *f*; comienzo, *m*; (of disease) epidemia, *f*; (of crimes, etc.) serie, *f*

outbuilding /'aut,bɪldɪŋ/ *n* dependencia, *f*, edificio accesorio, anexo, *m*

outburst /'aut,bᵊrst/ *n* acceso, arranque, *m*, explosión, *f*

outcast /'aut,kæst/ *n* paria, *mf*; desterrado (-da), proscripto (-ta)

outclass /ˌaut'klæs/ *vt* aventajar, ser superior (a), exceder

outcome /'aut,kʌm/ *n* consecuencia, *f*, resultado, *m*

outcry /'aut,krai/ *n* clamor, grito, *m*; protesta, *f*

outdistance /ˌaut'dɪstəns/ *vt* dejar atrás

outdo /ˌaut'du/ *vt* eclipsar, aventajar, sobrepujar

outdoor /'aut,dɔr/ *a* externo; (of activities) al aire libre; fuera de casa

outdoors /ˌaut'dɔrz/ *adv* fuera de casa; al aire libre

outer /'autər/ *a* externo, exterior

outermost /'autər,moust/ *a* sup (el, etc.) más externo, más exterior; extremo, de más allá

outer space *n* espacio extraatmosférico, espacio extraterrestre, espacio exterior, espacio sideral, espacio sidéreo, espacio ultraterrestre, *m*

outfit /'aut,fɪt/ *n* equipo, *m*; (of clothes) traje, *m*; (of furniture or trousseau) ajuar, *m*; (gear) pertrechos, avíos, *m pl*. *vt* aviar equipar

outfitter /'aut,fɪtər/ *n* proveedor (-ra), abastecedor (-ra)

outflank /ˌaut'flæŋk/ *vt* Mil. flanquear; ser más listo (que)

outgoing /'aut,gouɪŋ/ *a* saliente, que sale; cesante. **outgoings,** *n pl* gastos, *m pl*

outgrow /'aut'grou/ *vt* hacerse demasiado grande para; crecer más que; (ideas) perder; (illness) curarse de, curarse con la edad; pasar de la edad de, ser ya viejo para. **to o. one's clothes,** quedársele a uno chica la ropa. **to o. one's strength,** estar demasiado crecido para su edad

outgrowth /'aut,grouθ/ *n* excrecencia, *f*; resultado, fruto, *m*, consecuencia, *f*

outhouse /'aut,haus/ *n* edificio accesorio, *m*

outing /'autɪŋ/ *n* excursión, vuelta, *f*, paseo, *m*

outlandish /aut'lændɪʃ/ *a* extraño, singular, raro; absurdo, ridículo

outlast /ˌaut'læst/ *vt* durar más que; (outlive) sobrevivir a

outlaw /'aut,lɔ/ *n* bandido, proscrito, *m*, *vt* proscribir

outlay /'aut,lei/ *n* gasto, desembolso, *m*

outlet /'autlɛt/ *n* salida, *f*; orificio de salida, *m*; (of drains, etc.) desagüe, *m*; (of streets, rivers) desembocadura, *f*; *Fig.* escape, *m*, válvula de seguridad, *f*

outline /'aut,lain/ *n* perfil, contorno, *m*; (drawing) esbozo, bosquejo, *m*; idea general, *f*; plan general, *m*, *vt* esbozar, bosquejar. **in o.,** en esbozo; en perfil. **to be outlined** (against), dibujarse (contra), destacarse (contra)

outlive /ˌaut'lɪv/ *vt* sobrevivir (a); (live down) hacer olvidar

outlook /'aut,lʊk/ *n* (view) perspectiva, vista, *f*; (opinion) actitud, *f*, punto de vista, *m*; aspecto, *m*, apariencia, *f*; (for trade, etc.) perspectiva, *f*, posibilidades, *f pl*. **o. tower,** atalaya, *f*

outlying /'aut,laiɪŋ/ *a* remoto, lejano, distante. **o. areas,** los alrededores, *m pl*

outmaneuver /ˌautmə'nuvər/ *vt* superar en estrategia

outmatch /ˌaut'mætʃ/ *vt* aventajar, superar

outmoded /ˌaut'moudɪd/ *a* anticuado, pasado de moda

outnumber /ˌaut'nʌmbər/ *vt* ser más numerosos que, exceder en número

out-of-court settlement /'aut əv ˌkɔrt/ *n* arreglo pacífico, *m*

out-of-town /'aut əv 'taun/ *a* de las provincias

outpost /'aut,poust/ *n* Mil. avanzada, *f*, puesto avanzado, *m*

outpouring /'aut,pɔrɪŋ/ *n* derramamiento, *m*; efusión, *f*

output /'aut,pʊt/ *n* producción, *f*. **o. capacity,** capacidad de producción, *f*

outrage /'autreidʒ/ *n* barbaridad infamia, atrocidad, *f*; rapto, *m*, violación, *f*. *vt* ultrajar; violar; violentar

outrageous /aut'reidʒəs/ *a* atroz, terrible; desaforado, monstruoso; injurioso; ridículo

outrageousness /aut'reidʒəsnıs/ *n* lo atroz; violencia, furia, *f*; escándalo, *m*; enormidad, *f*; lo excesivo; lo horrible

outré /u'trei/ *a* cursi, extravagante

outride /ˌaut'raid/ *vt* cabalgar a más prisa que

outright /adv. 'aut'rait; a. 'aut,rait/ *adv* (frankly) de plano (e.g. *to reject outright,* rechazar de plano), francamente, sin reserva; (immediately) en seguida, inmediatamente, *a* completo; franco

outrival /ˌaut'raivəl/ *vt* vencer, superar

outrun /ˌaut'rʌn/ *vt* correr más que

outset /'aut,sɛt/ *n* principio, comienzo, *m*

outshine /ˌaut'fain/ *vt* brillar más que, eclipsar en brillantez; superar, eclipsar

outside /adv., prep., a. ˌaut'said; n. 'aut'said/ *adv*

afuera, fuera. *prep* fuera de, al otro lado de, al exterior de; (besides) aparte de, fuera de. *a* externo, exterior; (of labor, etc.) desde fuera; máximo; ajeno. *n* exterior, *m*; superficie, *f*; aspecto, *m*, apariencia, *f*. **at the o.,** a lo sumo, cuando más. **from the o.,** de (or desde) fuera. **on the o.,** (externally) por fuera. **o. the door,** a la puerta

outsider /,aut'saidər/ *n* forastero (-ra); desconocido (-da), *Argentina, Chile also* cuico (-ca); caballo desconocido, *m*; persona poco deseable, *f*

outsize /'aut,saiz/ *n* artículo de talla mayor que las corrientes, *m*

outskirts /'aut,skərts/ *n pl* alrededores, *m pl*, afueras, immediaciones, cercanías, *f pl*

outspoken /'aut'spoukən/ *a* franco. **to be o.,** decir lo que se piensa, no tener pelos en la lengua

outspokenness /'aut'spoukənnɪs/ *n* franqueza, *f*,

outspread /'aut,sprɛd/ *a* extendido; (of wings) desplegadas

outstanding /,aut'stændɪŋ/ *a* excelente; sobresaliente, conspicuo; *Com.* pendiente, sin pagar. **to be o.,** *Com.* estar pendiente; *Fig.* sobresalir. **o. account,** *Com.* cuenta pendiente, *f*

outstay /,aut'stei/ *vt* quedarse más tiempo que. **to o. one's welcome,** pegársele la silla

outstretched /,aut'strɛtʃt/ *a* extendido

outstrip /,aut'strɪp/ *vt* dejar atrás, pasar; aventajar, superar

outvote /,aut'vout/ *vt* emitir más votos que; rechazar por votación

outward /'autwərd/ *a* exterior, externo; aparente, visible. *adv* exteriormente; hacia fuera; superficialmente. **o. bound,** con rumbo a... **o. voyage,** el viaje de ida

outwardly /'autwərdli/ *adv* exteriormente; hacia fuera; en apariencia

outwear /,aut'wɛar/ *vt* durar más que; gastar

outweigh /,aut'wei/ *vt* exceder, valer más que

outwit /,aut'wɪt/ *vt* ser más listo que; vencer

outworn /'aut'wɔrn/ *a* anticuado, ya viejo

oval /'ouvəl/ *n* óvalo, *m*, *a* oval, ovalado, aovado

ovarian /ou'vɛariən/ *a* (*Bot. Zool.*) ovárico

ovary /'ouvəri/ *n* ovario, *m*

ovation /ou'veiʃən/ *n* ovación, recepción entusiasta, *f*

oven /'ʌvən/ *n* horno, *m*. **o. peel,** pala de horno, *f*. **o. rake,** hurgón, *m*

over /'ouvər/ *prep* (above, upon, over) sobre, encima de; (on the other side) al otro lado de; (across) allende, a través de; (more than) más de; (beyond) más allá de; (of rank) superior a; (during) durante; (in addition) además de; (through) por. *n* (cricket) serie de saques, *f*, *adv* encima; en; por encima; al otro lado; de un lado a otro; enfrente; al lado contrario; de un extremo a otro; (finished) terminado; (ruined) arruinado, perdido; (more) más; (excessively) demasiado, excesivamente; (covered) cubierto (de); (extra) en exceso; (completely) enteramente; (from head to foot) de pies a cabeza, de hito en hito; (of time) pasado. **over** is also used as a prefix. Indicating excess, it is generally translated by demasiado or excesivamente. In other meanings, it is either not translated or its meaning forms part of the verb, being translated as re-, super-, trans-, ultra. Very often a less literal translation is more successful than the employment of the above prefixes. **all o.,** (everywhere) en todas partes; (finished) todo acabado; (covered) cubierto (de); (up and down) de pies a cabeza. **all the world o.,** en todo el mundo. **embroidered all o.,** todo bordado. **He is o. in Germany,** Está en Alemania. **He trembled all o.,** Estaba todo tembloroso. **that which is o.,** el exceso, lo que queda. **to read o.,** leer, repasar. **o. again,** de nuevo. **o. and above,** por encima de, fuera de, en exceso de. **o. and o.,** repetidamente, muchas veces. **o. my signature,** bajo mi firma. **o. six months since...,** más de seis meses desde que...

overabundance /,ouvərə'bʌndəns/ *n* sobreabundancia, *f*

overabundant /,ouvərə'bʌndənt/ *a* sobreabundante

overact /,ouvər'ækt/ *vt* exagerar (un papel)

overall /'ouvər,ɔl/ *n* bata, *f*; guardapolvo, *m*; *a* de

conjunto (e.g., *overall assessment*, evaluación de conjunto) *pl* **overalls,** mono, *m*

overanxious /,ouvər'æŋkʃəs/ *a* demasiado ansioso; demasiado inquieto. **to be o.-a.,** preocuparse demasiado

overarch /,ouvər'artʃ/ *vt* abovedar

overawe /,ouvər'ɔ/ *vt* intimidar, acobardar

overbalance /,ouvər'bæləns/ *vt* hacer perder el equilibrio. hacer caer; preponderar. *vi* perder el equilibrio, caer

overbalancing /'ouvər,bælənsɪŋ/ *n* pérdida del equilibrio, caída, *f*; preponderancia, *f*

overbearing /,ouvər'bɛarɪŋ/ *a* dominante, autoritario, imperioso

overboard /'ouvər,bɔrd/ *adv* al agua, al mar, *Fig.* en exceso

overburden /,ouvər'bərdn/ *vt* sobrecargar, agobiar

overcast /*a.* 'ouvər'kæst; *v.* ,ouvər'kæst/ *a* anublado, cerrado, encapotado. *vt Sew.* sobrehilar. **to become o.,** anublarse

overcharge /*n.* 'ouvər,tʃardʒ; *v.* ,ouvər'tʃardʒ/ *n* recargo, *m*; (price) recargo de precio, precio excesivo, *m*. *vt* recargar, cobrar un precio excesivo; *Elec.* sobrecargar. *vi* cobrar demasiado

overcloud /,ouvər'klaud/ *vt* anublar; *Fig.* entristecer

overcoat /'ouvər,kout/ *n* abrigo, sobretodo, gabán, *m*

overcome /,ouvər'kʌm/ *vt* vencer, rendir, subyugar; (difficulties) triunfar de, allanar, dominar. *vi* saber vencer. *a* (by sleep, etc.) rendido; (at a loss) turbado, confundido; (by kindness) agradecidísimo

overconfidence /,ouvər'kɒnfɪdəns/ *n* confianza excesiva, *f*

overcooked /'ouvər,kʊkt/ *a* recocido, demasiado cocido

overcrowd /,ouvər'kraud/ *vt* atestar, llenar de bote en bote; (over-populate) sobrepoblar

overcrowding /,ouvər'kraudɪŋ/ *n* sobrepoblación, *f*

overdo /,ouvər'du/ *vt* exagerar; ir demasiado lejos, hacer demasiado; *Cul.* recocer; (overtire) fatigarse demasiado

overdose /'ouvər,dous/ *n* dosis excesiva, *f*

overdraft /'ouvər,dræft/ *n Com.* giro en descubierto, *m*

overdraw /,ouvər'drɔ/ *vt* and *vi Com.* girar en descubierto

over-dressed /'ouvər 'drɛst/ *a* que viste demasiado; cursi

overdue /,ouvər'du/ *a* atrasado; *Com.* vencido y no pagado

overeat /,ouvər'it/ *vi* comer demasiado, atracarse, *Lat. Am.* jambarse

overestimate /,ouvər'ɛstə,meit/ *vt* estimar en valor excesivo; exagerar, sobreestimar, *n* presupuesto excesivo, *m*; estimación excesiva, *f*

overexcite /,ouvərɪk'sait/ *vt* sobreexcitar

overexposure /,ouvərɪk'spouʒər/ *n Photo.* exceso de exposición, *m*

overfatigue /,ouvərfə'tig/ *vt* fatigar demasiado. *n* cansancio excesivo, *m*

overfeeding /,ouvər,fidɪŋ/ *n* sobrealimentación, *f*

overflow /*v.* ,ouvər'flou; *n.* 'ouvər,flou/ *vt* inundar, derramarse por; *Fig.* cubrir, llenar; desbordarse. *vi* (with) rebosar de. *n* inundación, *f*, desbordamiento, derrame, *m*; *Fig.* residuo, resto, exceso, *m*; (plumbing) sumidero, vertedero, *m*, descarga, *f*. **The river overflowed its banks,** El río se desbordó, El río salió de cauce

overflowing /,ouvər'flouɪŋ/ *a* rebosante; superabundante; (its banks) *Lat. Am.* desbocado. **filled to o.,** lleno hasta los bordes. **o. with health,** rebosante de salud, vendiendo salud

overgrown /,ouvər'groun/ *a* (gawky) talludo; (plants) exuberante, vicioso; frondoso, cubierto de verdura

overhang /,ouvər'hæŋ/ *vt* caer a, mirar a; colgar; *Fig.* amenazar. *vi* colgar, sobresalir; *Fig.* amenazar

overhanging /,ouvər'hæŋɪŋ/ *a* saledizo, sobresaliente; colgante, pendiente

overhaul /*v.* ,ouvər'hɔl; *n.* 'ouvər,hɔl/ *vt* examinar, investigar; componer, hacer una inspección general de; (of boats overtaking) alcanzar. *n* examen, *m*, investigación, *f*; *Med.* exploración general, *f*

overhead /'ouvər'hɛd/ *adv* arriba, en lo alto, encima de la cabeza. *a* aéreo, elevado; general, fijo. **o. cable,** cable eléctrico, *m*. **o. expenses,** gastos generales, *m pl*. **o. railway,** ferrocarril aéreo (or elevado), *m*

overhear /,ouvər'hɪər/ *vt* (accidentally) oír por casualidad, oír sin querer; (on purpose) alcanzar a oír, lograr oír

overheat /,ouvər'hit/ *vt* acalorar, hacer demasiado caliente, recalentar. *vi* (in argument) acalorarse; hacerse demasiado caliente

overheating /,ouvər'hitɪŋ/ *n* recalentramiento, *m*

overindulge /,ouvərɪn'dʌldʒ/ *vt* mimar demasiado; dedicarse a algo con exceso; tomar algo con exceso. *vi* darse demasiada buena vida

overjoyed /'ouvər,dʒɔid/ *a* contentísimo, lleno de alegría, encantado

overland /'ouvər,lænd/ *adv* por tierra. *a* terrestre, trascontinental

overlap /v. ,ouvər'læp; *n*. 'ouvər,læp/ *vi* traslaparse; coincidir. *n* traslapo, *m*

overlay /,ouvər'lei/ *vt* cubrir, dar una capa; (with silver) platear; (with gold) dorar. *n* capa, *f*; cubierta, *f*

overleaf /'ouvər,lif/ *adv* a la vuelta

overload /v. ,ouvər'loud; *n*. 'ouvər,loud/ *vt* sobrecargar, recargar. *n* sobrecarga, *f*

overlook /,ouvər'lʊk/ *vt* (face) dar a, mirar a, dominar; (supervise) vigilar, examinar, inspeccionar; (not notice) no notar, pasar por alto, no hacer, caso de, no fijarse en; (neglect) desdeñar; (ignore) no darse cuenta de, ignorar; (excuse) perdonar, tolerar, hacer la vista gorda

overlord /'ouvər,lɔrd/ *n* señor de horca y cuchillo, señor, jefe, *m*

overmuch /'ouvər'mʌtʃ/ *adv* demasiado, en exceso

overnight /adv. 'ouvər'nait; *a*. 'ouvər,nait/ *adv* la noche pasada, durante la noche; toda la noche. *a* de la víspera, nocturno. **to stay o. with,** pasar la noche con

overpass /'ouvər,pæs/ *n* pasaje elevado, viaducto, *m*

overpay /,ouvər'pei/ *vt* pagar demasiado

overpayment /'ouvər,peimənt/ *n* pago excesivo, *m*

overpopulate /,ouvər'pɒpyə,leit/ *vt* sobrepoblar, become overpopulated recargarse de habitantes (with people), recargarse de animales (with animals)

overpower /,ouvər'pauər/ *vt* vencer, subyugar; (of scents, etc.) trastornar; rendir, dominar

overpowering /,ouvər'pauərɪŋ/ *a* irresistible

overpraise /,ouvər'preiz/ *vt* encarecer, alabar mucho

overproduce /,ouvərprə'dus/ *vt* and *vi* sobreproducir

overproduction /,ouvərprə'dʌkʃən/ *n* sobreproducción, *f*

overrate /,ouvər'reit/ *vt* exagerar el valor de; (of property) sobrevalorar

overreach /,ouvər'ritʃ/ *vt* sobrealcanzar. **to o. oneself,** sobrepasarse, ir demasiado lejos

override /,ouvər'raid/ *vt* (trample) pasar por encima (de); *Fig.* rechazar, poner a un lado; (bully) dominar; (a horse) fatigar, reventar

overripe /'ouvər'raip/ *a* demasiado maduro

overrule /,ouvər'rul/ *vt* *Law.* denegar, no admitir; vencer

overrun /,ouvər'rʌn/ *vt* (flood) inundar; (ravage) invadir; (infest) plagar, infestar; desbordarse, derramarse

overseas /a. 'ouvər'siz; adv. ,ouvər'siz/ *a* ultramarino, de ultramar. *adv* en ultramar, allende los mares

oversee /,ouvər'si/ *vt* vigilar, inspeccionar

overseer /'ouvər,siər/ *n* capataz, mayoral, sobrestante, contramaestre, *m*; inspector (-ra), veedor (-ra)

oversell /,ouvər'sɛl/ *vt* and *vi* vender en exceso

oversensitive /,ouvər'sɛnsɪtɪv/ *a* demasiado sensitivo; vidrioso; susceptible

oversew /'ouvər,sou/ *vt* sobrecoser

overshadow /,ouvər'ʃædou/ *vt* sombrear; *Fig.* eclipsar, obscurecer; (sadden) entristecer

overshoe /'ouvər,ʃu/ *n* chanclo, *m*; (for snow) galocha, *f*

overshoot /,ouvər'ʃut/ *vt* tirar más allá del blanco; *Fig.* exceder, rebasar el límite conveniente, **overshoot**

the target (fig.) ir más allá del blanco, ir más allá de lo razonable. **to o. oneself,** exagerar; propasarse, descomedirse

oversight /'ouvər,sait/ *n* inadvertencia, omisión, equivocación, *f*; descuido, *m*

oversimplify /,ouvər'sɪmplə,fai/ *vt* simplificar en exceso

oversleep /,ouvər'slip/ *vi* dormir demasiado; *Inf.* pegárselle a uno las sábanas, levantarse demasiado tarde

overspend /,ouvər'spɛnd/ *vt* and *vi* gastar demasiado

overspread /,ouvər'sprɛd/ *vt* desparramar, salpicar, esparcir, sembrar; cubrir

overstate /,ouvər'steit/ *vt* exagerar, encarecer, ponderar

overstatement /,ouvər'steitmənt/ *n* exageración, ponderación, *f*

overstep /,ouvər'stɛp/ *vt* exceder, pasar, violar; rebasar, pasar más allá (de)

overstrain /,ouvər'strein/ *vt* fatigar demasiado, agotar. *n* fatiga, *f*. **to o. oneself,** esforzarse demasiado, cansarse demasiado

overstrung /,ouvər'strʌŋ/ *a* nervioso, excitable; (piano) de cuerdas cruzadas

oversubscribe /,ouvərsəb'skraib/ *vt* subscribir en exceso

overt /ou'vɜrt/ *a* abierto, público; manifiesto, evidente

overtake /,ouvər'teik/ *vt* alcanzar, pasar, dejar atrás; adelantarse (a); (surprise) coger, sorprender; (overwhelm) vencer, dominar

overtax /,ouvər'tæks/ *vt* oprimir de tributos; agobiar, cansar demasiado

overthrow /v. ,ouvər'θrou; *n*. 'ouvər,θrou/ *vt* volcar, echar por tierra, derribar; *Fig.* vencer, destruir, destronar. *n* vuelco, derribo, *m*; *Fig.* destrucción, ruina, *f*

overtime /'ouvər,taim/ *adv* fuera de las horas estipuladas. *n* horas extraordinarias de trabajo, *f pl.* **to work o.,** trabajar horas extraordinarias

overtone /'ouvər,toun/ *n* *Mus.* armónico, *m*

overtop /,ouvər'tɒp/ *vt* dominar, sobresalir, elevarse encima de

overture /'ouvərtʃər/ *n* *Mus.* obertura, *f*

overturn /,ouvər'tɜrn/ *vt* volcar, derribar, echar a rodar, echar abajo; (upset) revolver, desordenar. *vi* volcar, venirse abajo, allanarse; estar revuelto

overturning /,ouvər'tɜrnɪŋ/ *n* vuelco, salto de campana, *m*

overweening /'ouvər'winɪŋ/ *a* arrogante, insolente, altivo

overweight /'ouvər,weit/ *n* sobrepeso, exceso en el peso, *m*. **to be o.,** pesar más de lo debido

overwhelm /,ouvər'wɛlm/ *vt* (conquer) vencer, aplastar, derrotar; (of waves, etc.) sumergir, hundir, inundar, engolfar; (in argument) confundir, dejar confuso, avergonzar; (of grief, etc.) vencer, postrar, dominar; (of work) inundar

overwhelming /,ouvər'wɛlmɪŋ/ *a* irresistible, invencible, abrumador, apabullante

overwind /,ouvər'waind/ *vt* (a watch) dar demasiada cuerda a; romper la cuerda de

overwork /v. ,ouvər'wɜrk; *n*. 'ouvər,wɜrk/ *vt* hacer trabajar demasiado (or con exceso); esclavizar. *vi* trabajar demasiado. *n* exceso de trabajo, demasiado trabajo, *m*

overwrought /'ouvər'rɔt/ *a* (overworked) agotado por el trabajo, rendido, muy cansado; nerviosísimo, sobreexcitado, exaltado, muy agitado

ovine /'ouvain/ *a* ovejuno

ovoid /'ouvɔid/ *a* ovoide

ovulation /,ɒvyə'leiʃən/ *n* *Med.* ovulación, *f*

owe /ou/ *vt* deber, tener deudas (de); deber, estar agradecido (por), estar obligado (a). *vi* estar en deuda, estar endeudado, tener deudas. **He owes his tailor \$30,** Le debe treinta dólares a su sastre. **I owe him thanks for his help,** Le estoy agradecido por su ayuda (*or* Le debo las gracias por...). **He owes his success to good fortune,** Su éxito se debe a la suerte

owing /'ouɪŋ/ *a* por pagar. **o.** *a*, debido a, a causa de, por. **We had to stay in o. to the rain,** Tuvimos que quedarnos en casa a causa de la lluvia. **What is o. to you now?** ¿Cuánto se le debe ahora?

owl /aul/ *n* búho, mochuelo, *Peru* carancho, *m*. **barn or screech owl,** lechuza, *f*. **brown owl,** autillo, *m*
owlish /'aulɪʃ/ *a* parecido a un búho, de búho
own /oun/ *a* propio. *n* (dearest) bien, *m*. *vt* poseer, tener, ser dueño de; (recognize) reconocer; (admit) confesar. *vi* confesar. **my (thy, his, our, your) own,** mi (tu, su, nuestro, vuestro) propio, *m*, (*f*, propia); mis (tus, sus, nuestros, vuestros) propios, *m pl*, (*f pl*, propias); (when not placed before a noun) el mío (tuyo, suyo, nuestro, vuestro), la mía (tuya, etc.), los míos (tuyos, etc.), las mías (tuyas, etc.); (relations) los suyos. **in his own house,** en su propia casa. **my (thy, his, etc.) own self,** yo (tú, él) mismo, *m*, (*f*, misma, *m pl*, mismos, *f pl*, mismas). **a room of one's own,** un cuarto para sí (or para uno mismo). **to be on one's own,** ser independiente; estar a solas. **to hold one's own,** mantenerse en sus trece. **to own up,** confesar

owner /'ounər/ *n* dueño (-ña), propietario (-ia), posesor (-ra)
ownerless /'ounərlɪs/ *a* sin dueño, sin amo
ownership /'ounər,ʃɪp/ *n* posesión, *f*, dominio, *m*; propiedad, *f*
ox /ɒks/ *n* buey (*pl* bueyes), *m*. **oxeye daisy,** margarita, *f*. **oxstall,** boyera, *f*
oxidation /,ɒksɪ'deiʃən/ *n Chem*. oxidación, *f*
oxide /'ɒksaid/ *n Chem*. óxido, *m*
oxidization /,ɒksədɪ'zeiʃən, -,dai-/ *n* oxidación, *f*
oxidize /'ɒksɪ,daiz/ *vt Chem*. oxidar; *vi* oxidarse
oxygen /'ɒksɪdʒən/ *n* oxígeno, *m*. **o. mask,** máscara de oxígeno, *f*. **o. tent,** tienda de oxígeno, *f*
oxygenate /'ɒksɪdʒə,neit/ *vt Chem*. oxigenar
oxygenation /,ɒksɪdʒə'neiʃən/ *n Chem*. oxigenación, *f*
oyster /'ɔistər/ *n* ostra, *f*, *Lat. Am*. ostión, *m*. **o. bed,** pescadero (or criadero) de ostras, *m*. **o. culture,** ostricultura, *f*
ozone /'ouzoun/ *n* ozono, *m*

P

p /pi/ *n* (letter) pe, *f*. **to mind one's p's and q's,** poner tus puntos sobre las íes; ir con pies de plomo
pabulum /'pæbyələm/ *n* pábulo, *m*; sustento, *m*
pace /peis/ *n* paso, *m*; (gait) andar, *m*, marcha, *f*; (of a horse) andadura, *f*; (speed) velocidad, *f*. *vi* pasear-(se), andar; (of a horse) amblar. *vt* recorrer, andar por; marcar el paso para; (with out) medir a pasos. **at a good p.,** a un buen paso. **to keep p. with,** ajustarse al paso de, ir al mismo paso que; andar al paso de; (events) mantenerse al corriente de. **to p. up and down,** pasearse, dar vueltas. **p.-maker,** el que marca el paso
paced /peist/ *a* de andar...; (of a horse) de andadura...; de paso...
pachyderm /'pækɪ,dɜrm/ *n* paquidermo, *m*
Pacific, the /pə'sɪfɪk/ *n* el (Océano) Pacífico, *m*
pacific /pə'sɪfɪk/ *a Geog*. pacífico; sosegado, tranquilo, pacífico. **He is of a p. disposition,** Es amigo de la paz
pacification /,pæsəfɪ'keiʃən/ *n* pacificación, *f*
pacificatory /pə'sɪfɪkə,tɔri/ *a* pacificador
pacifier /'pæsə,faiər/ *n* pacificador (-ra)
pacifism /'pæsə,fɪzəm/ *n* pacifismo, *m*
pacifist /'pæsəfɪst/ *a* pacifista. *n* pacifista, *mf*
pacify /'pæsə,fai/ *vt* pacificar; calmar, tranquilizar; aplacar, conciliar
pack /pæk/ *n* (bundle) fardo, lio, *m*; paquete, *m*; (load) carga, *f*; (of hounds) jauría, *f*; (herd) hato, *m*; (of seals) manada, *f*; (of cards) baraja (de naipes), *f*; (of rogues) cuadrilla, *f*; (of lies, etc.) colección, *f*; masa, *f*, (of ice) témpanos flotantes, *m pl*; (Rugby football) delanteros, *m pl*; (for the face) compresa, *f*. **p.-horse,** caballo de carga, *m*. **p.-needle,** aguja espartera, *f*. **p.-saddle,** albarda, *f*. **p.-thread,** bramante, *m*
pack /pæk/ *vt* embalar; empaquetar; envasar; encajonar; (a suit-case, etc.) hacer; (cram) apretar; (crowd) atestar, llenar; (a pipe joint, etc.) empaquetar; (an animal) cargar. *vi* llenar; (one's luggage) hacer el equipaje, hacer el baúl, arreglar el equipaje. **packed like sardines,** como sardinas en banasta. **The train was packed,** El tren estaba lleno de bote en bote. **to p. off,** (a person) despachar; poner de partitas en la calle. **to p. up,** hacer el equipaje; empaquetar; embalar; *Inf*. liar el hato
package /'pækɪdʒ/ *n* paquete, *m*; bulto, *m*; (bundle) fardo, *m*
packer /'pækər/ *n* embalador, *m*; envasador (-ra)
packet /'pækɪt/ *n* paquete, *m*; (of cigarettes, etc.) cajetilla, *f*; (boat) paquebote, *m*. **to make one's p.,** *Inf*. hacer su pacotilla
packing /'pækɪŋ/ *n* embalaje, *m*; envoltura, *f*; envase, *m*; (on a pipe, etc.) guarnición, *f*. **I must do my p.,** Tengo que hacer las maletas. **p.-case,** caja de embalaje, *f*. **p.-needle,** aguja espartera, *f*
pact /pækt/ *n* pacto, convenio, *m*. **to make a p.,** pactar

pad /pæd/ *n* almohadilla, *f*, cojinete, *m*; (on a bed, chair) colchoneta, *f*; (on a wound) cabezal, *m*; (for polishing) muñeca, *f*; (hockey) defensa, *f*; (cricket) espinillera, *f*; (writing) bloque, *m*; (of a calendar) taco, *m*; (blotting) secafirmas, *m*; (of a quadruped's foot) pulpejo, *m*; (of fox, hare) pata, *f*; (leaf) hoja grande, *f*, *vt* almohadillar; acolchar; rellenar, forrar; (out, a book, etc.) meter paja en. **inking-pad,** almohadilla de entintar, *f*. **padded cell,** celda acolchonada, *f*. **shoulder-pad,** (in a garment) hombrera, *f*
padding /'pædɪŋ/ *n* relleno, *m*, almohadilla, *f*; (material) borra, *f*, algodón, *m*; *Fig*. paja, *f*, ripio, *m*,
paddle /'pædl/ *n* (oar) canalete, zagual, *m*; paleta, *f*; (flipper) aleta, *f*, *vt* and *vi* remar con canalete; (dabble) chapotear. **double p.,** remo doble, *m*. **p.-steamer,** vapor de ruedas, vapor de paleta, *m*. **p.-wheel,** rueda de paletas, *f*
paddler /'pædlər/ *n* remero (-ra); el, *m*, (*f*, la) que chapotea
paddling /'pædlɪŋ/ *n* chapoteo, chapaleo, *m*
paddock /'pædək/ *n* prado, *m*, dehesa, *f*; parque, *m*; (near a racecourse) en silla dero, picadero, *m*; (toad) sapo, *m*
padlock /'pæd,lɒk/ *n* candado, *m*, *vt* cerrar con candado, acerrojar
paean /'piən/ *n* himno de alegría, *m*
pagan /'peigən/ *a* and *n* pagano (-na)
paganism /'peigənɪzəm/ *n* paganismo, *m*
page /peidʒ/ *n* (boy) paje, *m*; (squire) escudero, *m*; (of a book, etc.) página, *f*; *Fig*. hoja, *f*. *vt* compaginar; (a person) vocear. **on p. nine,** en la página nueve. **to turn the p.,** *Fig*. volver la hoja
pageant /'pædʒənt/ *n* espectáculo, *m*; (procession) desfile, *m*; representación teatral, *f*; fiesta, *f*; *Fig*. pompa, *f*, aparato, *m*
pageantry /'pædʒəntri/ *n* pompa, *f*, aparato, *m*, magnificencia, *f*
paginate /'pædʒə,neit/ *vt* paginar
pagination /,pædʒə'neiʃən/ *n* paginación, *f*
pagoda /pə'goudə/ *n* pagoda, *f*
paid /peid/ *a* pagado; (on a parcel) porte pagado. **p. mourner,** plañidera, *f*. **p.-up share,** acción liberada, *f*
pail /peil/ *n* cubo, pozal, *m*, cubeta, *f*
pailful /'peil,fol/ *n* cubo (de agua, etc.), *m*
pain /pein/ *n* dolor, *m*; sufrimiento, *m*; (mental) tormento, *m*, angustia, *f*; *Law*. pena, *f*, *pl* **pains,** (effort) trabajo, esfuerzo, *m*. *vt* doler; atormentar, afligir. **dull p.,** dolor sordo, *m*. **I have a p. in my head,** Me duele la cabeza. **on p. of death,** so pena de muerte. **to be in great p.,** sufrir mucho. **to take pains,** tomarse trabajo, esforzarse, esmerarse
pained /peind/ *a* dolorido; afligido; de angustia
painful /'peinfəl/ *a* doloroso; angustioso; fatigoso; (troublesome) molesto; (embarrassing) embarazoso; difícil; (laborious) arduo

painfully /'peinfəli/ adv dolorosamente; penosamente; fatigosamente; con angustia; laboriosamente
painfulness /'peinfəlnıs/ n dolor, m; angustia, aflicción, f; tormento, m; dificultad, f
painless /'peinlıs/ a sin dolor, indoloro
painlessly /'peinlısli/ adv sin dolor; sin sufrir
painlessness /'peinlısnıs/ n falta de dolor, f
painstaking /'peinz,teikıŋ, 'pein,stei-/ a concienzudo; diligente, industrioso; cuidadoso. n trabajo, m; diligencia, industria, f; cuidado, m
paint /peint/ n pintura, f; (for preserving metal) pavón, m; (rouge) colorete, m. vt pintar. vi pintar; pintarse. **The door is painted blue,** La puerta está pintada de azul. **p.-box,** caja de pinturas, f. **p.-brush,** pincel, m; (for house painting) brocha, f
painter /'peintər/ n pintor (-ra); (house) pintor de brocha gorda, pintor de casas, m; (of a boat) boza, f. **sign-p.,** pintor de muestras, m
painting /'peintıŋ/ n pintura, f; (picture) cuadro, m, pintura, f
pair /pɛər/ n par, m; (of people) pareja, f; (of oxen) yunta, f. vt parear, emparejar; (persons) unir, casar; (animals) aparear. vi parearse; casarse; aparearse. **a carriage and p.,** un landó con dos caballos. **a p. of steps,** una escalera de mano. **a p. of pants, a p. of trousers,** unos pantalones. **in pairs,** de dos en dos; por parejas. **to p. off,** vi formar pareja; Inf. casarse
pal /pæl/ n camarada, compinche, mf; amigote, m, Carribean pana, mf
palace /'pælıs/ n palacio, m
paladin /'pælədın/ n paladín, m
palatable /'pælətəbəl/ a sabroso, apetitoso; Fig. agradable, aceptable
palatableness /'pælıtəbəlnıs/ n buen sabor, gusto agradable, m; Fig. lo agradable
palatably /'pælıtəbli/ adv agradablemente
palatal /'pælətḷ/ a paladial. n letra paladial, f
palatalize /'pælətḷ,aiz/ vt palatizar
palate /'pælıt/ n paladar, m. **hard p.,** paladar, m. **soft p.,** velo del paladar, m
palatial /pə'leiʃəl/ a (of a palace) palaciego; (sumptuous) magnífico, suntuoso
pale /peil/ n (stake) estaca, f; límite, m; Herald. palo, m, a pálido; (wan) descolorido, Lat. Am. also lívido; (of colors) claro, desmayado; (of light) tenue, mortecino; (lusterless) sin brillo, muerto. vi palidecer, perder el color; Fig. eclipsarse
palely /'peilli/ adv pálidamente; vagamente, indistintamente
paleness /'peilnıs/ n palidez, f; (wanness) descoloramiento, m, amarillez, f; (of light) tenuidad, f
paleographer /,peili'ɒɡrəfər/ n paleógrafo, m
paleography /,peili'ɒɡrəfi/ n paleografía, f
paleolithic /,peiliə'lıθık/ a paleolítico
paleology /,peili'ɒlədʒi/ n paleología, f
paleontology /,peiliən'tɒlədʒi/ n paleontología, f
palette /'pælıt/ n paleta, f. **p.-knife,** espátula, f
palimpsest /'pælımp,sest/ n palimpsesto, m
palindrome /'pælın,droum/ n capicúa f, (of numbers), palíndromo m
paling /'peilıŋ/ n palizada, estacada, valla, f
palisade /,pælə'seid/ n palenque, m, tranquera, palizada, f; Mil. estacada, f
palish /'peiliʃ/ a algo pálido; paliducho
pall /pɔl/ n (on a coffin) paño mortuorio, m; (Fig. covering) manto, m, capa, f; Eccl. palio, m; (over a chalice) palia, f. vi perder el sabor, hacerse insípido; saciarse (de); aburrirse (de), cansarse (de). **The music of Bach never palls on me,** No me canso nunca de la música de Bach
palladium /pə'leidiəm/ n Mineral. paladio, m; (safeguard) paladión, m
pallet /'pælıt/ n jergón, m; camilla, f; Mech. fiador de rueda, m; torno de alfarero, m
palliate /'pæli,eit/ vt (pain) paliar, aliviar; mitigar; (excuse) disculpar, excusar
palliation /,pæli'eiʃən/ n paliación, f; mitigación, f; disculpa, f
palliative /'pæli,eitıv, -iətıv/ a paliativo; (extenuating) atenuante. n paliativo, m

pallid /'pælıd/ a pálido, Lat. Am. also lívido
pallidness /'pælıdnıs/ n palidez, f
pallor /'pælər/ n palidez, f
palm /pɑm/ n (of the hand, and Fig., victory) palma, f; (measurement) ancho de la mano, m; (tree) palma, f. vt (a card, etc.) empalmar; (with off) defraudar (con); dar gato por liebre (a). **to bear away the p.,** llevar la palma. **p. branch,** palma, f. **p. grove,** palmar, m. **p.-oil,** aceite de palma, m; (bribe) soborno, m. **P. Sunday,** Domingo de Ramos, m. **p. tree,** palmera, Lat. Am. chonta, f
palmate /'pælmeit, -mıt, 'pɑl-, 'pɑmeit/ a palmeado
palmer /'pɑmər, 'pɑl-/ n peregrino, m; (caterpillar) oruga velluda, f
palming /'pɑmıŋ/ n (in conjuring, etc.) empalme, m
palmist /'pɑmıst/ n quiromántico (-ca)
palmistry /'pɑmıstri/ n quiromancía, f
palmy /'pɑmi/ a palmar; (flourishing) floreciente; (happy) dichoso, feliz; (prosperous) próspero; triunfante
Palmyra /pæl'mairə/ Palmira, f
palp /pælp/ n palpo, m
palpability /,pælpə'bılıti/ n palpabilidad, f
palpable /'pælpəbəl/ a palpable
palpate /'pælpeit/ vt palpar
palpation /pæl'peiʃən/ n palpación, f
palpitate /'pælpı,teit/ vi palpitar
palpitating /'pælpı,teitıŋ/ a palpitante
palpitation /,pælpı'teiʃən/ n palpitación, f
palsied /'pɔlzid/ a paralítico
palsy /'pɔlzi/ n parálisis, perlesía, f. vt paralizar. **cerebral p.,** perlesía cerebral
paltriness /'pɔltrinıs/ n mezquindad, pequeñez, f
paltry /'pɔltri/ a mezquino, insignificante, pobre
paludism /'pælyə,dizəm/ n Med. paludismo, m
pampas /'pæmpəz/ attributively 'pæmpəs/ n pampa, f
pamper /'pæmpər/ vt mimar, consentir demasiado; criar con mimos, regalar; alimentar demasiado bien
pampered /'pæmpərd/ a mimado, consentido; demasiado bien alimentado
pamphlet /'pæmflıt/ n folleto, m
pamphleteer /,pæmflı'tıər/ n folletinista, mf
pan /pæn/ n (vessel) cazuela, f; cacerola, f; (brain) cráneo, m; (of a balance) platillo, m; (of a firelock) cazoleta, f, Cinema. toma panorámica f, prefix pan-. **to pan off,** separar el oro en una gamella. **to pan out,** Inf. Fig. suceder. **Pan-Americanism,** panamericanismo, m. **Pan-American Highway,** la carretera panamericana, f
Pan /pæn/ n Pan, m. **pipes of Pan,** flauta de Pan, f
panacea /,pænə'siə/ n panacea, f
panache /pə'næʃ/ n penacho, m
panada /pə'nɑdə/ n Cul. panetela, f
Panama /'pænə,mɑ/ el Panamá, m
Panama /'pænə,mɑ/ a panameño. (-ña). **P. hat,** sombrero de jipijapa, panamá m
pancake /'pæn,keik/ n fruta de sartén, hojuela, f. **p. landing,** Aer. aterrizaje brusco, m. **P. Tuesday,** martes de Carnaval, m
panchromatic /,pænkrou'mætık, -krə-/ a pancromático
pancreas /'pænkriəs, 'pæŋ-/ n páncreas, m
pancreatic /,pænkri'ætık/ a pancreático
panda /'pændə/ n Zool. panda, mf
pandemic /pæn'demık/ a pandémico
pandemonium /,pændə'mouniəm/ n pandemonio, m
pander /'pændər/ n alcahuete, m, vi alcahuetear. **to p. to,** prestarse a; favorecer, ayudar
pandore /pæn'dɔr/ n Mus. bandola, f
pane /pein/ n hoja de vidrio, hoja de cristal, f; cuadro, m
panegyric /,pænı'dʒırık/ a panegírico. n panegírico, m
panel /'pænḷ/ n panel, entrepaño, m; Art. tabla, f; (in a dress) paño, m; (list) lista, f, registro, m; (jury) jurado, m; lista de jurados, f, vt labrar a entrepaños; artesonar. **p. doctor,** médico (-ca) de seguros
paneled /'pænḷd/ a entrepañado; (of ceilings) artesonado. **p. ceiling,** artesonado, m
paneling /'pænḷıŋ/ n entrepaños, m pl; artesonado, m
panful /'pæn,fʊl/ n cazolada, f

pang /pæŋ/ n punzada (de dolor), f, dolor agudo, m; dolor, m; (anguish of mind) angustia, f, tormento, m; (of conscience) remordimiento, m
panic /'pænɪk/ n pánico, m; pavor, espanto, m; terror súbito, m, a pánico. *vi* espantarse. **p.-monger,** alarmista, *mf* **p.-stricken,** aterrorizado, despavorido
panicky /'pænɪki/ a *Inf.* lleno de pánico; nervioso
pannier /'pænyər/ n (basket) alforja, f; cesto, m; (bustle) caderillas, f pl
panoply /'pænəpli/ n panoplia, f
panorama /,pænə'ræmə, -'rɑmə/ n panorama, m
panoramic /,pænə'ræmɪk/ a panorámico
pansy /'pænzi/ n pensamiento, m, trinitaria, f
pant /pænt/ *vi* jadear; (of dogs) hipar; resollar; (of the heart) palpitar. n jadeo, m; palpitación, f. **to p. after,** suspirar por
pantaloon /,pæntl'un/ n (trouser) pantalón, m; (Pantaloon) Pantalón, m
pantheism /'pænθi,ɪzəm/ n panteísmo, m
pantheist /'pænθiɪst/ n panteísta, mf
pantheistic /,pænθi'ɪstɪk/ a panteísta
pantheon /'pænθi,ɒn, -ən/ n panteón, m
panther /'pænθər/ n pantera, f
panties /'pæntiz/ n pl pantalones, m pl
panting /'pæntɪŋ/ a jadeante, sin aliento. n jadeo, m; resuello, m, respiración difícil, f; palpitación, f
pantomime /'pæntə,maim/ n pantomima, f; revista, f. **in p.,** en pantomima; por gestos
pantry /'pæntri/ n despensa, f
pants /pænts/ n pl calzoncillos, m pl; (trousers) pantalones, m pl. **p.** buttoned down the sides *Mexico* calzoneras, f pl
panzer division /'pænzər/ n división motorizada, f
pap /pæp/ n (nipple) pezón, m; (soft food) papilla, f
papa /'pɑpə, pə'pɑ/ n papá, m
papacy /'peipəsi/ n papado, pontificado, m
papal /'peipəl/ a papal, pontificio. **p. bull,** bula pontificia, f. **p. nuncio,** nuncio del Papa, nuncio apostólico, m. **p. see,** sede apostólica, f
papaya /pə'paɪə/ n *Cuba* fruta bomba, f
paper /'peipər/ n papel, m; hoja de papel, f; documento, m; (lecture) comunicación, f; (newspaper) periódico, m; (journal) revista, f; (exam.) examen escrito, trabajo, m; ejercicio, m; pl **papers,** (credentials) documentación, f, credenciales, f pl; *Com.* valores negociables, m pl; (packet) paquete, m, a de papel; para papeles; parecido al papel. *vt* (a room) empapelar; (a parcel) envolver. **daily p.,** diario, m. **in p. covers,** (of books) en rústica. **slip of p.,** papeleta. f. **to send in one's papers,** entregar su dimisión. **p. bag,** saco de papel, m. **p.-chase,** rally-paper, m. **p. clip,** prendedero de oficina, sujetapapeles, *Central America* ataché, *elsewhere in Lat. Am.* broche, m. **p.-cutting machine,** guillotina, f. **p. folder,** plegadera, f. **p.-hanger,** empapelador, m. **p.-hanging,** empapelado, m. **p.-knife,** cortapapel, m. **p.-maker,** fabricante de papel, m. **p.-making,** manufactura de papel, f. **p.-mill,** fábrica de papel, f. **p.-money,** papel moneda, m. **p.-pulp,** pasta, f. **p.-streamer,** serpentina, f. **p.-weight,** pisapapeles, m
papering /'peipərɪŋ/ n (of a room) empapelado, m
papery /'peipəri/ a semejante al papel
papier-mâché /,peipərmə'ʃei, pɑ,pyei-/ n cartón piedra, m
papillary /'pæpə,lɛri/ a papilar
paprika /pæ'prikə, pə-, pɑ-, 'pæprɪkə/ n pimienta húngara, f
papyrus /pə'paɪrəs/ n papiro, m
par /pɑr/ n par, f. **at par,** *Com.* a la par. **above (below) par,** *Com.* por encima (or debajo) de la par. **He is a little below par,** No está muy bien de salud. **to be on par with,** ser el equivalente de; ser igual a. **par excellence,** por excelencia
parable /'pærəbəl/ n parábola, f
parabola /pə'ræbələ/ n *Geom.* parábola, f
parachute /'pærə,ʃut/ n paracaídas, m; *Bot.* vilano, m. **to p. down,** lanzarse en paracaídas. **p. troops,** cuerpo de paracaidistas, m
parachutist /'pærə,ʃutɪst/ n paracaidista, mf
parade /pə'reid/ n alarde, m; *Mil.* parada, revista, f;

(procession) desfile, m, procesión, f; (promenade) paseo, m. *vt* (display) hacer alarde de, hacer gala de, ostentar; (troops) formar en parada; pasar revista (a); (patrol) recorrer. *vi Mil.* tomar parte en una parada; desfilar. **to p. up and down,** pasearse. **p.-ground,** campo de instrucción, m; plaza de armas, f
paradigm /'pærə,daim/ n paradigma, m
paradise /'pærə,dais/ n paraíso, edén, m; *Fig.* jauja, f. **bird of p.,** ave del paraíso, f
paradisiac /,pærə'dizi,æk/ a paradisíaco
paradox /'pærə,dɒks/ n paradoja, f
paradoxical /,pærə'dɒksɪkəl/ a paradójico
paradoxicality /,pærə,dɒksɪ'kælɪti/ n lo paradójico
paraffin /'pærəfɪn/ n parafina, f. *vt* parafinar. **p.-oil,** parafina líquida, f
paragon /'pærə,gɒn/ n modelo perfecto, dechado, m
paragraph /'pærə,græf/ n párrafo, m; (in a newspaper) suelto, m, *vt* dividir en párrafos; escribir un suelto sobre. **new p.,** párrafo aparte, m
Paraguay /'pærə,gwai, -,gwei/ el Paraguay, m
Paraguayan /,pærə'gwaiən/ a and n paraguayo (-ya)
parakeet /'pærə,kit/ n *Ornith.* perico, m
parallel /'pærə,lɛl/ a paralelo; igual; semejante, análogo. n línea paralela, f; paralelo, m; *Mil.* paralela, f; *Geog.* paralelo, m; *Print.* pleca, f. *vt* poner en paralelo; cotejar, comparar; igualar. **to run p. to,** ser paralelo a; ser conforme a. **p. bars,** paralelas, f pl
parallelism /'pærəlɛ,lɪzəm/ n paralelismo, m
parallelogram /,pærə'lɛlə,græm/ n paralelogramo, m
paralysis /pə'ræləsɪs/ n parálisis, f
paralytic /,pærə'lɪtɪk/ a and n paralítico (-ca)
paralyze /'pærə,laiz/ *vt* paralizar
paramount /'pærə,maunt/ a supremo, sumo
paramour /'pærə,mʊr/ n amante, querido, m; querida, amiga, f
paranoia /,pærə'nɔiə/ n paranoia, f
paranoiac /,pærə'nɔiæk/ n paranoico, m
parapet /'pærəpɪt, -,pɛt/ n (*Archit.* and *Mil.*) parapeto, m
paraphernalia /,pærəfər'neilyə, -fə'neil-/ n *Law.* bienes parafernales, m, p; (finery) atavíos, adornos, m pl; equipo, m; arreos, m pl; insignias, f pl
paraphrase /'pærə,freiz/ n paráfrasis, f, *vt* parafrasear
parasite /'pærə,sait/ n parásito, m; *Inf.* zángano, m, gorrista, mf, *Mexico* arrimado, m
parasitic /,pærə'sɪtɪk/ a parásito, parasitario; *Med.* parasítico
parasitology /,pærəsai'tɒlədʒi, -sɪ-/ n parasitología, f
parasol /'pærə,sɔl, -,sɒl/ n parasol, quitasol, f
parathyroid /,pærə'θairɔid/ a paratiroides. n paratiroides, f pl
paratroops /'pærə,trups/ n pl paracaidistas, m pl
paratyphoid /,pærə'taifɔid/ n paratifoidea, f
parboil /'pɑr,bɔil/ *vt* sancochar
parcel /'pɑrsəl/ n paquete, m; fardo, m; (of land) parcela, f. **to p. out,** repartir, distribuir; dividir. **to p. up,** envolver, empaquetar. **p. post,** servicio de paquetes, m
parceling /'pɑrsəlɪŋ/ n empaque, m; (out) reparto, m, distribución, f; división, f
parch /pɑrtʃ/ *vt* secar; abrasar, quemar; (roast) tostar. *vi* secarse; quemarse, abrasarse
parched /pɑrtʃt/ a seco, sediento. **p. with thirst,** muerto de sed
parchedness /'pɑrtʃɪdnɪs/ n sequedad, aridez, f
parchment /'pɑrtʃmənt/ n pergamino, m; (of a drum) parche, m. **p.-like,** apergaminado
pardon /'pɑrdn/ n perdón, m; *Eccl.* indulgencia, f. *vt* perdonar; indultar, amnistiar. **a general p.,** una amnistía. **I beg your p.!** ¡Vd. dispense!; ¡Perdone Vd.! **to beg p.,** pedir perdón; disculparse. **P.?** ¿Cómo?
pardonable /'pɑrdnəbəl/ a perdonable, disculpable, excusable
pardonableness /'pɑrdnəbəlnɪs/ n disculpabilidad, f
pardonably /'pɑrdnəbli/ adv disculpablemente, excusablemente
pardoner /'pɑrdnər/ n vendedor de indulgencias, m; perdonador (-ra)
pardoning /'pɑrdnɪŋ/ n perdón, m; remisión, f
pare /pɛər/ *vt* (one's nails) cortar; (fruit) mondar;

(potatoes, etc.) pelar; (remove) quitar; (reduce) reducir

parent /'pɛərənt, 'pær-/ n padre, m; madre, f; (ancestor) antepasado, m; (origin) origen, m, fuente, f; (cause) causa, f; (author) autor, m; autora, f; pl **parents,** padres, m pl. a madre, materno; principal

parentage /'pɛərəntɪdʒ, 'pær-/ n parentela, f; linaje, m, familia, alcurnia, f; procedencia, f, nacimiento, origen, m

parental /pə'rɛntl/ a paternal; maternal, de madre

parentally /pə'rɛntli/ adv como un padre; como una madre

parenthesis /pə'rɛnθəsɪs/ n paréntesis, m

parenthetical /ˌpɛərən'θɛtɪkəl/ a entre paréntesis; de paréntesis

parenthood /'pɛərəntˌhʊd, 'pær-/ n paternidad, f; maternidad, f

pariah /pə'raiə/ n paria, mf

parietal /pə'raiɪtl/ a parietal

paring /'pɛərɪŋ/ n (act) raedura, f; peladura, mondadura, f; (shred) brizna, f; (refuse) desecho, desperdicio, m. **p.-knife,** trinchete, m

Paris /'pærɪs/ París, m

parish /'pærɪʃ/ n parroquia, f; feligresía, f, a parroquial. **p. church,** parroquia, f. **p. clerk,** sacristán de parroquia, m. **p. priest,** párroco, m. **p. register,** registro de la parroquia, m

parishioner /pə'rɪʃənər/ n parroquiano (-na); feligrés (-esa)

Parisian /pə'rɪʒən, -'rɪʒən, -'rɪziən/ a parisiense. n parisiense, mf

parity /'pærɪti/ n paridad, f

park /park/ n parque, m; jardín, m. vt (vehicles) estacionar; (dump) depositar. **car p.,** parque de automóviles, m. **p.-keeper,** guardián del parque, m

parking /'parkɪŋ/ n (of vehicles) estacionamiento, m; (dumping) depósito, m. **p. lights,** Auto. luces de estacionamiento, f pl. **p. place,** parque de estacionamiento, m

parking meter n Mexico estacionómetro, m, Argentina, Spain parquímetro, m, elsewhere in Lat. Am. parcómetro, m, Spain reloj de estacionamiento, m

parlance /'parləns/ n lenguaje, m. **in common p.,** en lenguaje vulgar

parley /'parli/ n plática, conversación, f; discusión, f; Mil. parlamento, m. vi Mil. parlamentar; discutir; conversar. vt hablar

parliament /'parləmənt/ n parlamento, m; cortes, f pl; cuerpo legislativo, m

parliamentarian /ˌparləmɛn'tɛəriən/ a and n parlamentario; (of an academy) censor, m

parliamentarianism /ˌparləmɛn'tɛəriənɪzəm/ n parlamentarismo, m,

parliamentary /ˌparlə'mɛntəri, -tri/ a parlamentario. **p. immunity,** inviolabilidad parlamentaria, f

parlor /'parlər/ n salón, gabinete, m; sala de recibo, f; (in a convent) locutorio, m. **p. games,** diversión de salón, f, juego de sociedad, m. **p.-maid,** camarera, f

parlous /'parləs/ a crítico, malo. adv sumamente, muy

Parmesan /'parməˌzan, ˌparmə'zan/ a parmesano, de Parma. n parmesano (-na). **P. cheese,** queso de Parma, m

Parnassian /par'næsiən/ a del parnaso; parnasiano. n parnasiano, m

Parnassus /par'næsəs/ n Parnaso, m

parochial /pə'roukiəl/ a parroquial, parroquiano; Fig. provincial

parochialism /pə'roukiəˌlɪzəm/ n provincialismo, m

parochially /pə'roukiəli/ adv por parroquias

parodist /'pærədɪst/ n parodista, mf

parody /'pærədi/ n parodia, f, vt parodiar

parole /pə'roul/ n (of convict) libertad vigilada, f

paroxysm /'pærəkˌsɪzəm/ n paroxismo, m; ataque, m, acceso, m

parquet /par'kei/ (floor) entarimado m; (of theater) platea, f

parricide /'pærəˌsaid/ n (act) parricidio, m; (person) parricida, mf

parrot /'pærət/ n papagayo, loro, m, Lat. Am. cata, f

parry /'pæri/ vt (a blow, and in fencing) parar; rechazar; evitar. n parada, f; (in fencing) quite, m, parada, f

parse /pars, parz/ vt analizar

Parsee /'parsi, par'si/ n parsi, m

parsimonious /ˌparsə'mouniəs/ a parsimonioso

parsimoniously /ˌparsə'mouniəsli/ adv con parsimonia

parsimony /'parsəˌmouni/ n parsimonia, f

parsley /'parsli/ n perejil, m

parsnip /'parsnɪp/ n chirivía, f

parson /'parsən/ n párroco, cura, m; (clergyman) clérigo, m

parsonage /'parsənɪdʒ/ n rectoría, f

part /part/ n parte, f; porción, f; trozo, m; Mech. pieza, f; (Gram. and of a literary work) parte, f; (of a living organism) miembro, m; (duty) deber, m, obligación, f; Theat. papel, m; Mus. voz, f; pl **parts,** (region) partes, f pl, lugar, m; (talents) partes, dotes, f pl. **foreign parts,** países extranjeros, m pl, el extranjero. **For my p....,** Por lo que a mí toca, Por mi parte. **for the most p.,** en su mayoría. **from all parts,** de todas partes. **in p.,** en parte; parcialmente. **spare p.,** pieza de recambio, f. **The funny p. of it is...,** Lo cómico del asunto es... **the latter p. of the month,** los últimos días del mes, la segunda quincena del mes. **to form p. of,** formar parte de. **to play a p.,** hacer un papel; desempeñar un papel. **to take a person's p.,** apoyar a alguien, ser partidario de alguien. **to take in good p.,** tomar bien. **to take p. in,** tomar parte en, participar en. **p. of speech,** parte de la oración, f. **p.-owner,** copropietario (-ia). **p.-time job,** trabajo de unas cuantas horas, m, trabajo de mediotiempo, m

part /part/ vt distribuir, repartir; dividir; separar (de); (open) abrir. vi partir, marcharse; despedirse; (of roads, etc.) bifurcarse; dividirse; (open) abrirse. **to p. one's hair,** hacerse la raya. **to p. from,** (things) separarse de; (people) despedirse de. **to p. with,** separarse de; deshacerse de; perder; (dismiss) despedir (a)

partake /par'teik/ vt participar de, compartir; tomar parte en. vi tomar algo (de comer, de beber). **to p. of,** comer (beber) de; tener rasgos de

partaker /par'teikər/ n partícipe, mf

Parthian /'parθiən/ a parto. n parto (-ta). **P. shot,** la flecha del parto

partial /'parʃəl/ a parcial; (fond of) aficionado (a). **p. eclipse,** eclipse parcial, m

partiality /ˌparʃi'ælɪti, par'ʃæl-/ n parcialidad, f; preferencia, predilección, f

partially /'parʃəli/ adv en parte, parcialmente; (with bias) con parcialidad

participant /par'tɪsəpənt/ a participante. n partícipe, mf

participate /par'tɪsəˌpeit/ vi participar (de), compartir; tomar parte (en)

participation /parˌtɪsə'peiʃən/ n participación, f

participial /ˌpartə'sɪpiəl/ a Gram. participial

participle /'partəˌsɪpəl, -səpəl/ n Gram. participio, m. **past p.,** participio pasado (or pretérito o pasivo), m. **present p.,** participio activo (or presente), m

particle /'partɪkəl/ n partícula, f; Fig. átomo, grano, m, pizca, f; Gram. partícula, f

parti-colored /'partiˌkʌlərd/ a bicolor

particular /pər'tɪkyələr/ a particular; especial; individual; singular; cierto; exacto; escrupuloso; difícil, exigente. n detalle, pormenor, m; circunstancia, f; caso particular, m; pl **particulars,** informes, detalles, m pl. **further particulars,** más detalles. **in p.,** en particular; sobre todo. **He is very p. about...,** Es muy exigente en cuanto a...; Le es muy importante..., Le importa mucho...

particularize /pər'tɪkyələˌraiz/ vt particularizar, detallar; especificar

particularly /pər'tɪkyələrli/ adv en particular; particularmente; sobre todo

parting /'partɪŋ/ n despedida, f; partida, f; separación, f; (of the hair) raya, crencha, f; (cross roads) bifurcación, f. a de despedida. **at p.,** al despedirse. **to reach the p. of the ways,** Fig. llegar al punto decisivo

partisan /'pɑrtəzən, -sən/ n partidario (-ia); (fighter) guerrillero, m, a partidario; de guerrilleros

partisanship /'pɑrtə,zənʃɪp/ n partidarismo, m

partition /pɑr'tɪʃən, pər-/ n partición, f; división, f; (wall) pared, f, tabique, m. **the p. of Ireland,** la división de Irlanda. vt **to p. off,** Lat. Am. entabicar

partly /'pɑrtli/ adv en parte

partner /'pɑrtnər/ n asociado (-da); Com. socio (-ia); (dancing) pareja, f; (in games, and companion) compañero (-ra); (spouse) consorte, mf; (in crime) delincuente, mf **sleeping p.,** socio comanditario, m. **working p.,** socio industrial, m

partnership /'pɑrtnər,ʃɪp/ n asociación, f; Com. sociedad, compañía, f. **deed of p.,** artículos de sociedad, m pl. **to take into p.,** tomar como socio (a). **to form a p.,** asociarse

partridge /'pɑrtrɪdʒ/ n Ornith. perdiz, f. **young p.,** perdigón, m

parturient /pɑr'tʊriənt/ a f, parturienta. n parturienta, f

parturition /,pɑrtʊ'rɪʃən, -tʃʊ-/ n parto, m

party /'pɑrti/ n partido, m; grupo, m; (of pleasure, etc.) partida, f; reunión, fiesta, f; Mil. pelotón, destacamento, m; Law. parte, f; (person) interesado (-da); (accessory) cómplice, mf. **rescue p.,** pelotón de salvamento, m. **to be a p. to,** prestarse a; ser cómplice en. **to give a p.,** dar una fiesta, dar una reunión. **p.-spirit,** espíritu del partido, m. **p.-wall,** pared medianera, f

parvenu /'pɑrvə,nu/ n advenedizo (-za)

parvis /'pɑrvɪs/ n Archit. atrio, m

Paschal /pæ'skæl/ a pascual

pass /pæs/ n (in an exam.) aprobación, f; (crisis) crisis, situación crítica, f; estado, m; (with the hands) pase, m; (permit) permiso, m; Mil. licencia, f; (safeconduct) salvoconducto, m; (in football, etc.) pase, m; (membership card) carnet, m; (defile) desfiladero, paso, puerto, m; Naut. rebasadero, m; (fencing) estocada, f. **free p.,** billete de favor, m. **p.-book,** libreta de banco, f. **p. certificate,** (in exams.) aprobado, m. **p.-key,** llave maestra, f

pass /pæs/ vi pasar; (of time) correr, pasar, transcurrir; (happen) ocurrir, tomar lugar; (end) cesar, desaparecer; (die) morir. vt pasar; hacer pasar; (the butter, etc.) dar, alargar; (in football, hockey) pasar; (excel) aventajar, exceder; (a bill, an examination) aprobar; (sentence) fallar, pronunciar; (a remark) hacer; (transfer) traspasar; (tolerate) sufrir, tolerar; evacuar. **He passed in psychology,** Aprobó sicología. **to allow to p.,** ceder el paso (a). **to bring to p.,** ocasionar. **to come to p.,** suceder. **to let p.,** (put up with) dejar pasar; no hacer caso de; (forgive) perdonar. **to p. a vote of confidence,** votar una proposición de confianza. **to p. the buck,** Inf. echarle a uno el muerto. **to p. the hat, to p. the plate,** hacer la gorra. **to p. along,** pasar por; pasar. **to p. away,** pasar; desaparecer; (die) morir, fallecer; (of time) transcurrir. **to p. by,** pasar por, pasar delante de, pasar al lado de; (omit) pasar por alto de, omitir; (ignore) pasar sin hacer caso de. **to p. for,** pasar por. **to p. in,** entrar. **to p. in and out,** entrar y salir. **to p. off,** vi cesar, acabarse; desaparecer; evaporarse, disiparse; (of events) tener lugar. vt (oneself) darse por; dar por, hacer pasar por. **to p. a cat off as hare,** dar gato por liebre. **to p. on,** vi pasar; seguir su camino, continuar su marcha. vt pasar algo de uno a otro. **to p. out,** salir. **to p. over,** pasar por encima de; pasar; cruzar, atravesar; (transfer) traspasar; (disregard) pasar por alto de, dejar a un lado; omitir. **to p. over in silence,** pasar en silencio (por). **to p. around,** circular. **to p. through,** cruzar, atravesar, pasar por; (pierce) traspasar; Fig. experimentar

passable /'pæsəbəl/ a transitable, pasadero; (fairly good) regular, mediano; tolerable

passably /'pæsəbli/ adv medianamente, pasaderamente, tolerablemente

passage /'pæsɪdʒ/ n pasaje, m; paso, tránsito, m; (voyage) viaje, m, travesía, f; (corridor) pasillo, m; (entrance) entrada, f; (way) camino, m; (alley) callejón, m; (in a mine) galería, f; (of time) transcurso, m; (of birds) pasa, f; (in a book, and Mus.) pasaje, m; (occurrence) episodio, incidente, m; (of a bill) apro-

bación, f. **p. money,** pasaje, m. **p. of arms,** lucha, f, combate, m; disputa, f

passementerie /pæs'mentri/ n pasamanería, f

passenger /'pæsəndʒər/ n viajero (-ra); (on foot) peatón, m. **by p. train,** en gran velocidad

passerby /'pæsər'bai/ n transeúnte, paseante, mf

passing /'pæsɪŋ/ a pasajero; fugitivo; momentáneo. adv sumamente, extremadamente. n pasada, f; paso, m; (death) muerte, f; (disappearance) desaparición, f; (of a law) aprobación, f. **in p.,** de paso. **p.-bell,** toque de difuntos, m. **p. grade,** calificación mínima aprobatoria, f

passion /'pæʃən/ n pasión, f; (Christ's) Pasión, f; (anger) cólera, f. **to fly into a p.,** montar en cólera. **p.-flower,** pasionaria, granadilla, f. **P. play,** drama de la Pasión, m. **P. Sunday,** Domingo de Pasión, m. **P. Week,** Semana Santa, f

passionate /'pæʃənɪt/ a apasionado; (quick-tempered) irascible, colérico; (fervid) vehemente, intenso, ardiente

passionately /'pæʃənɪtli/ adv con pasión, apasionadamente; (irascibly) coléricamente; (fervidly) con vehemencia, ardientemente

passionless /'pæʃənlɪs/ a sin pasión, frío; impasible; imparcial

passive /'pæsɪv/ a pasivo. n Gram. pasiva, f. **p. resistance,** resistencia pasiva, f

passivity /pæ'sɪvɪti/ n pasividad, f

Passover /'pæs,ouvər/ n Pascua de los judíos, f

passport /'pæspɔrt/ n pasaporte, m

password /'pæs,wɜrd/ n contraseña, f

past /pæst/ a pasado; último; (expert) consumado; (former) antiguo, ex-. n pasado, m; historia, f, antecedentes, m pl, prep después de; (in front of) delante de; (next to) al lado de; (beyond) más allá de; (without) sin; fuera de; (of age) más de; (no longer able to) incapaz de. adv más allá. (The translation of **past** as an adverb is often either omitted, or included in the verb, e.g. The years flew p., Los años transcurrieron. for centuries p., durante siglos.) **I am p. caring,** Nada me importa ya. **It is a quarter p. ten,** Son las diez y cuarto. **It is p. four o'clock,** Son las siete pasadas. Son después de las cuatro. **what's p. is p.,** lo pasado, pasado. **p. doubt,** fuera de duda. **p. endurance,** insoportable. **p. help,** sin remedio, irremediable. **p. hope,** sin esperanza. **p.-master,** maestro, consumado, experto, m. **p. participle,** participio pasado, m. **p. president,** ex-presidente, m. **p. tense,** (tiempo) pasado, m

paste /peist/ n pasta, f; (gloy) engrudo, m. vt (affix) pegar; (glue) engomar, engrudar

pasteboard /'peist,bɔrd/ n cartón, m, cartulina, f, a de cartón, de cartulina

pastel /pæ'stel/ n Art. pastel, m. **p. drawing,** pintura al pastel, f

pastelist /pæ'stelist/ n pastelista, mf

pasteurization /,pæstʃərə'zeiʃən/ n pasteurización, f

pasteurize /'pæstʃə,raiz/ vt pasteurizar

pastille /pæ'stil/ n pastilla, f

pastime /'pæs,taim/ n pasatiempo, entretenimiento, m, diversión, recreación, f

pastor /'pæstər/ n pastor, m

pastoral /'pæstərəl/ a pastoril; Eccl. pastoral. n Eccl. pastoral, f; (Poet. Mus.) pastorela, f

pastorate /'pæstərɪt/ n pastoría, f

pastry /'peistri/ n (dough) pasta, f; pastel, m, torta, f; pastelería, f. **p.-cook,** repostero, m, pastelero (-ra)

pasturage /'pæstʃərɪdʒ/ n (grass, etc.) pasto, m; pasturaje, m; pastoreo, m

pasture /'pæstʃər/ n (grass, etc.) pasto, herbaje, m; pasturaje, m; (field) prado, m, pradera, dehesa, f. vi pacer; pastar. vt apacentar, pastar, Argentina costear

pasty /'pæsti/ a pastoso; (pale) pálido. n empanada, f

pat /pæt/ n toque, m; caricia, f; (for butter) molde (de mantequilla), m. vt tocar; acariciar, pasar la mano (sobre). adv a propósito; oportunamente; fácilmente. **pat of butter,** pedacito de mantequilla, m. **pat on the back,** golpe en la espalda, m; Fig. elogio, m

Patagonian /,pætə'gouniən/ a and n patagón (-ona)

patch /pætʃ/ n (mend) remiendo, m; (piece) pedazo, m; (plaster and Auto., etc.) parche, m; (beauty spot)

lunar postizo, *m*; (of ground) parcela, *f*; (of flowers, etc.) masa, *f*; (stain, and *Fig.*) mancha, *f*. *vt* (mend) remendar; poner remiendo (a); pegar; (roughly) chafallar; (the face) ponerse lunares postizos. **p. of blue sky,** pedazo de cielo azul. **patch of green grass,** mancha de hierba verde. **to be not a p. on,** no ser de la misma clase que; (of persons) no llegarle a los zancajos de. **to p.** up a quarrel, hacer las paces **patchwork** /'pætʃ,wɜrk/ *n* labor de retazos, obra de retacitos, *f*; *Fig.* mezcla, mezcolanza, *f*. **p. quilt,** centón, *m*
patchy /'pætʃi/ *a* desigual; manchado
patella /pə'tɛlə/ *n Anat.* rótula, *f*
patency /'peitn̩si/ *n* evidencia, claridad, *f*
patent /'pætn̩t/ *a* evidente, patente; patentado. *n* patente, *f*. *vt* patentar. **p. of nobility,** carta de hidalguía, ejecutoria, *f*. **"P. Applied For,"** «Patente Solicitada.» **Patent Pending** marca en trámite. **p. leather,** *n* charol, *m*. *a* de charol. **p. medicine,** específico farmacéutico, *m*
patentee /,pætn̩'ti/ *n* el, *m*, (*f*, la) que obtiene una patente; inventor (-ra)
patently /'pætn̩tli/ *adv* evidentemente, claramente
paterfamilias /,peitərfə'miliəs, ,pɑ-, ,pætər-/ *n* padre de familia, *m*
paternal /pə'tɜrn̩l/ *a* paterno, paternal
paternally /pə'tɜrn̩li/ *adv* paternalmente
paternity /pə'tɜrniti/ *n* paternidad, *f*
path /pæθ/ *n* senda, vereda, *f*, sendero, *m*; camino, *m*; (track) pista, *f*; (trajectory) trayectoria, *f*. **the beaten p.,** el camino trillado
pathetic /pə'θɛtik/ *a* patético, desgraciado, desafortunado
pathless /'pæθlɪs/ *a* sin senda
pathogenic /,pæθə'dʒɛnik/ *a Med.* patógeno
pathological /,pæθə'lɒdʒɪkəl/ *a* patológico
pathologist /pə'θɒlədʒɪst/ *n* patólogo, *m*
pathology /pə'θɒlədʒi/ *n* patología, *f*
pathos /'peiθɒs/ *n* lo patético
patience /'peiʃəns/ *n* paciencia, *f*. **He tries my p. very much,** Me cuesta mucho no impacientarme con él. **to lose p.,** perder la paciencia; (grow angry) perder los estribos. **to play p.,** hacer solitarios
patient /'peiʃənt/ *a* paciente. *n* paciente, *mf*; (ill person) enfermo (-ma); (of a physician) cliente, *mf*
patiently /'peiʃəntli/ *adv* con paciencia, pacientemente
patina /'pætnə, pə'tinə/ *n* pátina, *f*
patriarch /'peitri,ɑrk/ *n* patriarca, *m*
patriarchal /,peitri'ɑrkəl/ *a* patriarcal
patriarchy /'peitri,ɑrki/ *n* patriarcado, *m*
patrician /pə'trɪʃən/ *a* and *n* patricio (-ia)
patrimonial /,pætrə'mouniəl/ *a* patrimonial
patrimony /'pætrə,mouni/ *n* patrimonio, *m*
patriot /'peitriət/ *n* patriota, *mf*
patriotic /,peitri'ɒtik/ *a* patriótico
patriotism /'peitriə,tɪzəm/ *n* patriotismo, *m*
patrol /pə'troul/ *n* patrulla, *f*; ronda, *f*, *vi* and *vt* patrullar; rondar; recorrer. **p. boat,** lancha escampavía, *f*. **p. flight,** vuelo de patrulla, *m*
patron /'peitrən/ *n* (of a freed slave) patrono, *m*; (of the arts, etc.) mecenas, protector, *m*; (customer) parroquiano (-na), cliente, *mf*. **p. saint,** santo (-ta) patrón (-ona)
patronage /'peitrənɪdʒ/ *n* (protection) patrocinio, *m*; protección, *f*; *Eccl.* patronato, *m*; (regular custom) clientela, *f*; (of manner) superioridad, *f*
patroness /'peitrənɪs/ *n* patrona, *f*; protectora, *f*; (of a charity, etc.) patrocinadora, *f*; (of a regiment, etc.) madrina, *f*
patronize /'peitrə,naiz/ *vt* patrocinar; proteger, favorecer; (a shop) ser parroquiano de; (treat arrogantly) tratar con superioridad
patronizing /'peitrə,naizɪŋ/ *a* (with air, behavior, etc.) de superioridad, de altivez
patten /'pætn̩/ *n* zueco, chanclo, *m*
patter /'pætər/ *n* (jargon) jerga, *f*; charla, *f*; (of rain) azotes, *m pl*; (of feet) son, *m*; golpecitos, *m pl*. *vt* (repeat) decir mecánicamente. *vi* (chatter) charlar; (of rain) azotar, bailar; correr ligeramente

pattern /'pætərn/ *n* modelo, *m*; (*Sew.* and dressmaking) patrón, *m*; (in founding) molde, *m*; (templet) escantillón, *m*; (of cloth, etc.) muestra, *f*; (design) dibujo, diseño, *m*; (example) ejemplar, *m*. *vt* diseñar; estampar. **p. book,** libro de muestras, *m*
patty /'pæti/ *n* empanada, *f*, pastelillo, *m*
paucity /'pɔsiti/ *n* poquedad, *f*; corto número, *m*; insuficiencia, escasez, *f*
paunch /pɔntʃ/ *n* panza, barriga, *f*
pauper /'pɔpər/ *n* pobre, *mf*
pauperism /'pɔpə,rɪzəm/ *n* pauperismo, *m*
pauperization /,pɔpərə'zeiʃən/ *n* empobrecimiento, *m*
pauperize /'pɔpə,raiz/ *vt* empobrecer, reducir a la miseria
pause /pɔz/ *n* pausa, *f*; intervalo, *m*; silencio, *m*; interrupción, *f*; *Mus.* pausa, *f*. *vi* pausar, hacer una pausa; detenerse, interrumpirse; vacilar. **to give p. to,** hacer vacilar (a)
pave /peiv/ *vt* empedrar, enlosar. **to p. the way for,** facilitar el paso de, preparar el terreno para, abrir el camino de
pavement /'peivmənt/ *n* pavimento, *m*, *Mexico* escarpa, *f*; (sidewalk) acera, *f*. **p.-artist,** pintor callejero, *m*
pavilion /pə'vɪlyən/ *n* pabellón, *m*; (for a band, etc.) quiosco, *m*; (tent) tienda de campaña, *f*
paving /'peivɪŋ/ *n* pavimentación, *f*; empedrado, *m*; see **pavement. p.-stone,** losa, *f*
paw /pɔ/ *n* pata, *f*; (with claws) garra, *f*, *Inf.* manaza, *f*. *vt* tocar con la pata; (scratch) arañar; (handle) manosear. *vi* (of a horse) piafar
pawing /'pɔɪŋ/ *n* (of a horse) el piafar; (handling) manoseo, *m*
pawn /pɔn/ *n* (chess) peón (de ajedrez), *m*; empeño, *m*; *Fig.* prenda, *f*. *vt* empeñar, pignorar; dar en prenda. **p.-ticket,** papeleta de empeño, *f*
pawnbroker /'pɔn,broukər/ *n* prestamista, *mf*
pawnshop /'pɔn,ʃɒp/ *n* casa de préstamos, casa de empeño, *f*, monte de piedad, *m*
pay /pei/ *n* paga, *f*; (*Mil. Nav.*) soldada, *f*; salario, *m*; (of a workman) jornal, *m*; (reward) recompensa, compensación, *f*; (profit) beneficio, provecho, *m*. **pay-day,** día de paga, *m*. **pay-office,** pagaduría, *f*. **pay list, pay-sheet,** nómina, *Mexico* lista de raya, *f*
pay /pei/ *vt* pagar; (a debt) satisfacer; (spend) gastar; (recompense) remunerar, recompensar; (hand over) entregar; (yield) producir; (a visit) hacer; (attention) prestar; (homage) rendir; (one's respects) presentar. *vi* pagar; producir ganancia; sacar provecho; ser una ventaja, ser provechoso. **It would not pay him to do it,** No le saldría a cuenta hacerlo. **This job doesn't pay,** Este trabajo no da dinero. **to pay a compliment (to),** cumplimentar, decir alabanzas (a), echar una flor (a). **to pay attention,** prestar atención; hacer caso. **to pay cash,** pagar al contado. **to pay in advance,** pagar adelantado, *Lat. Am.* aprontar. **to pay in full,** saldar. **to pay off old scores,** ajustar cuentas viejas. **to pay one's addresses to,** hacer la corte (a), pretender en matrimonio (a). **to pay the penalty,** sufrir el castigo, hacer penitencia. **to pay with interest,** *Fig.* pagar con creces. **to pay again,** volver a pagar, pagar de nuevo. **to pay back,** devolver, restituir; (money only) reembolsar; *Fig.* pagar en la misma moneda, vengarse (de). **to pay down,** pagar al contado. **to pay for,** pagar, costear; satisfacer. **to pay in,** ingresar. **to pay off,** (persons) despedir; (a debt) saldar; (a mortgage) cancelar, redimir. **to pay out,** (persons) vengarse de; (money) pagar; (ropes, etc.) arriar. **to pay up,** pagar; pagar por completo; (shares, etc.) redimir
payable /'peiəbəl/ *a* pagadero; a pagar; que puede ser pagado
payee /pei'i/ *n* tenedor, *m*
payer /'peiər/ *n* pagador (-ra)
paying /'peiɪŋ/ *a*. See **payment**
paymaster /'pei,mæstər/ *n* pagador, *m*; tesorero, *m*. **P.-General,** ordenador general de pagos, *m*
payment /'peimənt/ *n* pago, *m*; paga, *f*, *Lat. Am. also* entero, *m*; remuneración, *f*; *Fig.* recompensa, satisfacción, *f*; *Fig.* premio, *m*. **in p. of,** en pago de. **on**

p. of, mediante el pago de. **p. in advance,** pago adelantado, anticipo, *m*

pea /pi/ *n* guisante, *m*, *Lat. Am.* alverjana, arveja, *f*. **dry or split pea,** guisante seco, *m*. **sweet pea,** guisante de olor, *m*. **pea-flour,** harina de guisantes, *f*. **pea-green,** verde claro, *m*. **pea-jacket,** chaquetón de piloto, *m*. **pea-shooter,** cerbatana, *f*

peace /pis/ *n* paz, *f*; tranquilidad, quietud, *f*, sosiego, *m*; *Law.* orden público, *m*. **P.!** ¡Silencio! **to hold one's p.,** callarse, guardar silencio. **to make p.,** hacer las paces. **P. be upon this house!** ¡Paz sea en esta casa! **p.-footing,** pie de paz, *m*. **p.-loving,** pacífico. **p.-offering,** sacrificio propiciatorio, *m*; satisfacción, oferta de paz, *f*

peaceable /ˈpisəbəl/ *a* pacífico; apacible; tranquilo, sosegado

peaceableness /ˈpisəbəlnɪs/ *n* paz, *f*; apacibilidad, *f*; tranquilidad, quietud, *f*, sosiego, *m*

peaceably /ˈpisəbli/ *adv* pacíficamente; tranquilamente

peaceful /ˈpisfəl/ *a* pacífico; tranquilo; silencioso. **to come with p. intentions,** venir de paz

peacefully /ˈpisfəli/ *adv* en paz; pacíficamente; tranquilamente

peacefulness /ˈpisfəlnɪs/ *n* paz, *f*; tranquilidad, calma, quietud, *f*; silencio, *m*; carácter pacífico, *m*

peacemaker /ˈpisˌmeikər/ *n* pacificador (-ra); conciliador (-ra)

peach /pitʃ/ *n* (fruit) melocotón, *m*; (tree) melocotonero, melocotón, *m*; (girl) breva, *f*. **p.-colour,** color de melocotón, *m*

peacock /ˈpiˌkɒk/ *n* pavo real, pavón, *m*. *vi* pavonearse; darse humos. **The p. spread its tail,** El pavo real hizo la rueda

peahen /ˈpiˌhɛn/ *n* pava real, *f*

peak /pik/ *n* punta, *f*; (of a cap) visera, *f*; (of a mountain) peñasco, *m*, cumbre, cima, *f*; (mountain itself) pico, *m*; (*Naut.* of a hull) pico, *m*; *Fig.* auge, apogeo, *m*; punto más alto, *m*. *vi* consumirse, enflaquecer. **p. hours,** horas de mayor tráfico, *f pl*

peaked /ˈpikɪd/ *a* en punta; puntiagudo; picudo; (of a cap) con visera; (wan) ojeroso; (thin) delgaducho, macilento, consumido

peal /pil/ *n* toque (or repique) de campanas, *m*; campanillazo, *m*; carillón, *m*; (noise) estruendo, ruido, *m*; (of thunder) trueno, *m*; (of an organ) sonido, *m*. *vi* repicar; sonar. *vt* tañer; echar a vuelo (las campanas); (of a bell that one presses) hacer sonar, tocar. **a p. of laughter,** una carcajada

peanut /ˈpiˌnʌt/ *n* cacahuete, *m*, *Dominican Republic* maní, *m*. **p. butter,** mantequilla de cacahuete, *f*

pear /pɛər/ *n* pera, *f*. **p.-shaped,** piriforme, de figura de pera. **p. tree,** peral, *m*

pearl /pɜrl/ *n* perla, *f*; (mother-of-pearl) nácar, *m*, *a* de perla; perlero. *vt* (dew) rociar, aljofarar. *vi* pescar perlas; formar perlas. **seed p.,** aljófar, *f*. **p.-ash,** carbonato potásico, *m*. **p.-barley,** cebada perlada, *f*. **p.-button,** botón de nácar, *m*. **p.-fisher,** pescador de perlas, *m*. **p.-fishery,** pescadería de perlas, *f*. **p.-gray,** gris de perla, *m*

pearly /ˈpɜrli/ *a* perlino; de perla; nacarado; (dewy) aljofarado

peasant /ˈpɛzənt/ *n* campesino (-na), labrador (-ra). *a* campesino

peasant movement *n Mexico* agrarismo, *m*

peasantry /ˈpɛzəntri/ *n* campesinos, *m pl*, gente del campo, *f*

peat /pit/ *n* turba, *f*. **p.-bog,** turbera, *f*

pebble /ˈpɛbəl/ *n* guijarro, *m*, pedrezuela, guija, *f*; (gravel) guijo, *m*; cristal de roca, *m*; lente de cristal de roca, *m*

pebbled, pebbly /ˈpɛbəld/; ˈpɛbli/ *a* guijarroso, enguijarrado

peccadillo /ˌpɛkəˈdɪlou/ *n* pecadillo, *m*

peck /pɛk/ *n* (of a bird) picotazo, *m*, picada, *f*; (kiss) besito, *m*; (large amount) montón, *m*; multitud, *f*. *vt* (of a bird) picotear; sacar (or coger) con el pico; (kiss) besar rápidamente. *vi* (with at) picotear; picar

pectoral /ˈpɛktərəl/ *a* pectoral

peculiar /pɪˈkyulyər/ *a* particular, peculiar, individual;

propio, característico; (marked) especial; (unusual) extraño, raro, extraordinario

peculiarity /pɪˌkyuliˈærɪti/ *n* peculiaridad, particularidad, *f*; singularidad, *f*; (eccentricity) excentricidad, rareza, *f*

peculiarly /pɪˈkyulyərli/ *adv* particularmente, peculiarmente; especialmente; extrañamente

pecuniarily /pɪˌkyuniˈɛərəli/ *adv* pecuniariamente

pecuniary /pɪˈkyuniˌɛri/ *a* pecuniario

pedagogic /ˌpɛdəˈgɒdʒɪk/ *a* pedagógico

pedagogy /ˈpɛdəˌgoudʒi, -ˌgɒdʒi/ *n* pedagogía, *f*

pedal /ˈpɛdl/ *a Zool.* del pie. *n* pedal, *m*. *vi* pedalear

pedant /ˈpɛdnt/ *n* pedante, *mf*

pedantic /pəˈdæntɪk/ *a* pedante

pedantically /pəˈdæntɪkli/ *adv* con pedantería, pedantescamente

pedantry /ˈpɛdn̩tri/ *n* pedantería, *f*

peddle /ˈpɛdl/ *vi* ser buhonero. *vt* revender

peddling /ˈpɛdlɪŋ/ *n* buhonería, *f*. *a* trivial, insignificante; mezquino

pedestal /ˈpɛdəstl/ *n* pedestal, *m*; *Fig.* fundamento, *m*, base, *f*. **to put on a p.,** *Fig.* poner sobre un pedestal

pedestrian /pəˈdɛstriən/ *n* peatón, peón, *m*, *a* pedestre; *Fig.* patoso. **p. traffic,** circulación de los peatones, *f*

pedestrian crosswalk /ˈkrɔsˌwɔk/ *n* cruce peatonal, *Argentina* cruce de peatones, *m*

pediatrician /ˌpidiəˈtrɪʃən/ *n* pediatra, *mf*

pedigree /ˈpɛdɪˌgri/ *n* genealogía, *f*; raza, *f*; (of words) etimología, *f*. *a* (of animals) de raza, de casta. **p. dog,** perro de casta, *m*

pediment /ˈpɛdəmənt/ *n Archit.* frontón, *m*

pedlar /ˈpɛdlər/ *n* buhonero (-ra), *Lat. Am.* marchante (-ta), *mf*

pedometer /pəˈdɒmɪtər/ *n* pedómetro, cuentapasos, *m*

peel /pil/ *n* (baker's) pala, *f*; (of fruit, etc.) piel, *f*, hollejo, *m*. *vt* pelar, mondar; (bark) descortezar; *Lat. Am.* deshojar (fruit). *vi* descascararse, desconcharse; (of the bark of a tree) descortezarse

peeling /ˈpilɪŋ/ *n* (of fruit, etc.) peladura, monda, *f*; (of bark) descortezadura, *f*; (of paint, etc.) desconchadura, *f*

peep /pip/ *vi* (of birds) piar; (of mice) chillar; (peer) atisbar, mirar a hurtadillas; (appear) asomar; mostrarse; (of the dawn) despuntar. *n* (of birds) pío, *m*; (of mice) chillido, *m*; (glimpse) vista, *f*; (glance) ojeada, mirada furtiva, *f*; **at the p. of day,** al despuntar el día. **p.-hole,** mirilla, *f*, atisbadero, *m*; escucha, *f*. **p.-show,** óptica, *f*

peeper /ˈpipər/ (eye) avizón *m*

peer /pɪər/ *n* par, *m*; igual, *mf*. *vi* atisbar; escudriñar; *Fig.* asomar, aparecer

peerage /ˈpɪərɪdʒ/ *n* nobleza, aristocracia, *f*; dignidad de par, *f*

peeress /ˈpɪərɪs/ *n* paresa, *f*

peerless /ˈpɪərlɪs/ *a* sin par, incomparable, sin igual

peevish /ˈpivɪʃ/ *a* displicente, malhumorado; picajoso, vidrioso, enojadizo

peevishness /ˈpivɪʃnɪs/ *n* displicencia, *f*, mal humor, *m*; impaciencia, *f*

peg /pɛg/ *n* clavija, *f*; (of a tent) estaca, *f*; (of a barrel) estaquilla, *f*; (of a violin, etc.) clavija, *f*; (for coats, etc.) colgadero, *m*; (of whisky, etc.) trago, *m*; *Fig.* pretexto, *m*. *vt* clavar, enclavijar, empernar. **to take down a peg,** bajar los humos (a). **to peg away,** batirse el cobre. **to peg down,** fijar con clavijas; (a tent) sujetar con estacas; (prices) fijar

peignoir /pein'wɑr/ *n* peinador, salto de cama, *m*, bata, *f*

pekinese /ˌpikəˈniz/ *n* perro (-rra) pequinés (-esa)

pelican /ˈpɛlɪkən/ *n* pelícano, *m*

pellagra /pəˈlægrə/ *n Med.* pelagra, *f*

pellet /ˈpɛlɪt/ *n* bolita, *f*; (pill) píldora, *f*; (shot) perdigón, *m*

pellmell /ˈpɛlˈmɛl/ *adv* a trochemoche; atropelladamente

pellucid /pəˈlusɪd/ *a* diáfano

Peloponnesian /ˌpɛləpəˈniʒən/ *a* and *n* peloponense, *mf*

pelota /pə'loutə/ n pelota vasca, f. **p. player,** pelotari, m
pelt /pɛlt/ n pellejo, m; cuero, m; (fur) piel, f; (blow) golpe, m. vt llover (piedras, etc.) sobre, arrojar... sobre; (questions) disparar; (throw) tirar. vi (of rain) azotar, diluviar
pelvic /'pɛlvɪk/ a pélvico, pelviano
pelvis /'pɛlvɪs/ n pelvis, f
pen /pɛn/ n (for sheep, etc.) aprisco, m; corral, m; (paddock) parque, m; (for hens) pollera, f; (for writing and Fig., author, etc.) pluma, f. vt (shut up) acorralar; encerrar; (write) escribir (con pluma). **pen-and-ink drawing,** dibujo a la pluma, m. **pen-holder,** portaplumas, m. **pen-name,** seudónimo, m. **pen-wiper,** limpiaplumas, m
penal /'pinl/ a penal. **p. code,** código penal, m. **p. colony,** colonia penal, f. **p. servitude,** trabajos forzados (or forzosos), m pl. **p. servitude for life,** cadena perpetua, f
penalization /,pinlə'zeifən/ n castigo, m
penalize /'pinl,aiz/ vt penar, imponer pena (a); castigar
penalty /'pɛnlti/ n Law. penalidad, f; castigo, m; (fine) multa, f; (risk) riesgo, m; Sports. sanción, m. **the p. of,** la desventaja de. **under p. of,** so pena de. **p. kick,** (football) penalty, m
penance /'pɛnəns/ n penitencia, f. **to do p.,** hacer penitencia
penchant /'pɛntʃənt/ n tendencia, f; inclinación, f
pencil /'pɛnsəl/ n lápiz, m; (automatic) lapicero, m. vt escribir (or dibujar or marcar) con lápiz. **p.-case,** estuche para lápices, m. **p.-holder,** lapicero, m. **p.-sharpener,** cortalápices, afilalápices, m
pendant /'pɛndənt/ n (jewel) pendiente, m; Archit. culo de lámpara, m; (Naut. rope) amantillo, m; (flag) gallardete, m
pending /'pɛndɪŋ/ a pendiente. prep durante. **to be p.,** pender; amenazar
pendulous /'pɛndʒələs/ a péndulo; colgante; oscilante
pendulum /'pɛndʒələm/ n péndola, f, péndulo, m
penetrability /,pɛnɪtrə'bɪlɪti/ n penetrabilidad, f
penetrable /'pɛnɪtrəbəl/ a penetrable
penetrate /'pɛnɪ,treit/ vt and vi penetrar
penetrating /'pɛnɪ,treitɪŋ/ a penetrante
penetration /,pɛnɪ'treifən/ n penetración, f
penguin /'pɛŋgwɪn/ n pingüino, pájaro bobo, m
penicillin /,pɛnə'sɪlɪn/ n penicilina, f
peninsula /pə'nɪnsələ, -'nɪnsyələ/ n península, f
peninsular /pə'nɪnsələr, -'nɪnsyələr/ a peninsular. **P. War,** Guerra de la Independencia, f
penis /'pinɪs/ n pene, m
penitence /'pɛnɪtəns/ n penitencia, f
penitent /'pɛnɪtənt/ a penitente. n penitente, mf
penitential /,pɛnɪ'tɛnʃəl/ a penitencial
penitentiary /,pɛnɪ'tɛnʃəri/ n Eccl. penitenciaria, f; casa de corrección, f; penitenciaría, f, presidio, m; cárcel modelo, f, a penitenciario
penknife /'pɛn,naif/ n cortaplumas, m
penmanship /'pɛnmən,ʃɪp/ n caligrafía, f
pennant /'pɛnənt/ n Naut. gallardete, m; banderola, f; (ensign) insignia, bandera, f
penniless /'pɛnɪlɪs/ a sin un penique, sin blanca; indigente, pobre de solemnidad, Peru calato. **to leave p.,** dejar en la miseria; Inf. dejar sin camisa
pennilessness /'pɛnɪlɪsnɪs/ n falta de dinero, extrema pobreza, f
penning /'pɛnɪŋ/ n escritura, f; (drawing up) redacción, f; (of bulls, etc.) acorralamiento, m
pennon /'pɛnən/ n pendón, m, banderola, f; (ensign) bandera, insignia, f
Pennsylvanian /,pɛnsəl'veinyən/ a and n pensilvano (-na)
penny /'pɛni/ n de un centavo, penique, m; perra gorda, f. a de un penique. **p.-a-liner,** gacetillero, m. **p. dreadful,** folletín, m, novela por entregas, m. **p.-in-the-slot machine,** tragaperras, m
pennyworth /'pɛni,wɜrθ/ n penique, valor de un penique, m
pension /'pɛnʃən/ n pensión, f; Mil. retiro, m;

(grant) beca, f; (boardinghouse) pensión de familia, f. vt pensionar, dar una pensión (a); (with off) jubilar. **old age p.,** pensión para la vejez, f. **retirement p.,** pensión vitalicia, f
pensioner /'pɛnʃənər/ n pensionista, mf; (Mil. and Nav.) inválido, m
pensive /'pɛnsɪv/ a pensativo, meditabundo; cabizbajo, triste
pensively /'pɛnsɪvli/ adv pensativamente; tristemente
pensiveness /'pɛnsɪvnɪs/ n reflexión, meditación profunda, f; tristeza, melancolía, f
pentagon /'pɛntə,gɒn/ n pentágono, m
Pentateuch /'pɛntə,tuk/ n pentateuco, m
Pentecost /'pɛntɪ,kɒst/ n Pentecostés, m
pentecostal /,pɛntɪ'kɒstl/ a de Pentecostés, pascual. n (religious movement) pentecostal, mf
penthouse /'pɛnt,haus/ n cobertizo, tinglado, m, tejavana, f
pent-up /pɛnt 'ʌp/ a encerrado; enjaulado; (of emotion) reprimido
penultimate /pɪ'nʌltəmɪt/ a penúltimo. n penúltimo, m
penurious /pə'nʊriəs/ a pobre; escaso; (stingy) tacaño, avaro
penury /'pɛnyəri/ n penuria, f
peony /'piəni/ n peonía, f, saltaojos, m, rosa albardera, rosa montés, f
people /'pipəl/ n pueblo, m; nación, f; gente, f; personas, f pl; (used disparagingly, mob) populacho, vulgo, m; (inhabitants) habitantes, m pl; (subjects) súbditos, m pl; (relations) parientes, m pl; familia, f. vt poblar. **little p.,** (children) gente menuda, f. **respectable p.,** gente de bien, f. **the p. of Burgos,** los habitantes de Burgos. **P. say,** Se dice, La gente dice. **Very few p. think as you do,** Hay muy pocas personas que opinan como Vd. **How are your p.** (family)? ¡Cómo están los de tu casa? ¿Cómo está tu familia? **"People Working"** «Trabajadores»
peopling /'piplɪŋ/ n población, f; colonización, f
pep /pɛp/ n Inf. energía, f, ánimo, m. **p. talk,** discurso estimulante, m. **p. up,** animar
peplum /'pɛpləm/ n peplo, m
pepper /'pɛpər/ n pimienta, f; (plant) pimentero, pimiento, m, vt sazonar con pimienta; (pelt) acribillar; (with questions) disparar; (a literary work with quotations, etc.) salpimentar. **black p.,** pimienta negra, f. **red p.,** pimiento, m; (cayenne) pimentón, m. **p.-castor,** pimentero, m
peppercorn /'pɛpər,kɔrn/ n grano de pimienta, m
peppermint /'pɛpər,mɪnt/ n menta, f. **p. drop,** pastilla de menta, f
peppery /'pɛpəri/ a picante; (irascible) colérico, irascible
pepsin /'pɛpsɪn/ n Chem. pepsina, f
peptic /'pɛptɪk/ a péptico
per /pɜr/ unstressed prep por. **ninety miles per hour,** noventa millas por hora. **ten pesetas per dozen,** diez pesetas la docena. **$60 per annum,** sesenta dólares al año. **per cent.,** por ciento
perambulate /pər'æmbyə,leit/ vt recorrer
perambulator /pər'æmbyə,leitər/ n cochecito para niños, m
percale /pər'keil/ n percal, m
percaline /,pɜrkə'lin/ n percalina, f
perceive /pər'siv/ vt percibir, comprender, darse cuenta de; percibir, discernir
percentage /pər'sɛntɪdʒ/ n tanto por ciento, m; porcentaje, m
perceptible /pər'sɛptəbəl/ a perceptible, visible; sensible
perceptibly /pər'sɛptəbli/ adv visiblemente; sensiblemente
perception /pər'sɛpʃən/ n percepción, f; sensibilidad, f
perceptive /pər'sɛptɪv/ a perceptivo
perch /pɜrtʃ/ n Ichth. perca, f; (for birds) percha, f; (measure) pértiga, f. vi posarse (en or sobre). vt posar (en or sobre)
percolate /'pɜrkə,leit/ vi filtrar; Fig. penetrar. vt filtrar, colar
percolation /,pɜrkə'leifən/ n filtración, f

percolator /'pɜrkə,leitər/ n filtro, m. **coffee p.**, colador de café, m
percussion /pər'kʌʃən/ n percusión, f; choque, m. **p. cap**, fulminante, m. **p. instrument**, instrumento de percusión, m
perdition /pər'dıʃən/ n perdición, f; ruina, f
peregrination /,perıgrə'neıʃən/ n peregrinación, f
peremptorily /pə'remptərəli/ adv perentoriamente
peremptoriness /pə'remptərınıs/ n perentoriedad, f
peremptory /pə'remptəri/ a perentorio; (of manner, etc.) imperioso, autoritario
perennial /pə'reniəl/ a Bot. vivaz; perenne; eterno, perpetuo. n planta vivaz, f
perennially /pə'reniəli/ adv perennemente
perfect /a., n. 'pɜrfıkt/ v. pər'fekt/ a perfecto; (of a work) acabado; completo. n Gram. (tiempo) perfecto, m. vt perfeccionar; (oneself) perfeccionarse. **to have a p. knowledge of...**, conocer a fondo... **They are p. strangers to me**, Me son completamente desconocidos
perfectible /pər'fektəbəl/ a perfectible
perfecting /pər'fektıŋ/ n perfeccionamiento, m; terminación, f
perfection /pər'fekʃən/ n perfección, f; excelencia, f. **to p.**, a la perfección, a las mil maravillas
perfectionist /pər'fekʃənıst/ n perfeccionista, mf
perfidious /pər'fıdiəs/ a pérfido
perfidy /'pɜrfıdi/ n perfidia, f
perforate /'pɜrfə,reit/ vt perforar, agujerear
perforating /'pɜrfə,reitıŋ/ a perforador
perforation /,pɜrfə'reiʃən/ n perforación, f; agujero, m
perform /pər'fɔrm/ vt hacer; poner por obra, llevar a cabo; desempeñar, cumplir; ejercer; (a piece of music, etc.) ejecutar; realizar; (a play) representar, dar; (a part in a play) desempeñar (el papel de...); (Divine Service) oficiar. vi Theat. trabajar, representar un papel; (a musical instrument) tocar; (sing) cantar; (of animals) hacer trucos
performable /pər'fɔrməbəl/ a hacedero, practicable, ejecutable; Theat. que puede representarse; Mus. tocable
performance /pər'fɔrməns/ n ejecución, realización, f; desempeño, ejercicio, m; cumplimiento, m; acción, f; hazaña, f; (work) obra, f; Theat. función, representación, f; (Theat. acting of a part) interpretación, f; Mus. ejecución, f; Mech. potencia, f. **first p.**, Theat. estreno, m
performer /pər'fɔrmər/ n Mus. ejecutante, mf, músico, m; Theat. actor (-triz), representante, mf; artista, mf
performing /pər'fɔrmıŋ/ a (of animals) sabio. **p. dog**, perro sabio, m
perfume /n. 'pɜrfyum/ v. pər'fyum/ n perfume, m; fragancia, f; aroma, m. vt perfumar; embalsamar, aromatizar, llenar con fragancia. **p. burner**, perfumador, m
perfumer /pər'fyumər/ n perfumista, mf
perfumery /pər'fyuməri/ n perfumería, f
perfuming /'pɜrfyumıŋ/ n acción de perfumar, f, a que perfuma
perfunctorily /pər'fʌŋktərəli/ adv perfunctoriamente, sin cuidado; superficialmente
perfunctoriness /pər'fʌŋktərınıs/ n descuido, m, negligencia, f; superficialidad, f
perfunctory /pər'fʌŋktəri/ a perfunctorio, negligente; superficial; ligero, de cumplido
pergola /'pɜrgələ/ n emparrado, cenador, m
perhaps /pər'hæps/ adv quizá, quizás(s), tal vez
peril /'perəl/ n peligro, m; riesgo, m. vt poner en peligro; arriesgar. **at one's p.**, a su riesgo. **in p.**, en peligro
perilous /'perələs/ a peligroso, arriesgado
perimeter /pə'rımıtər/ n perímetro, m
perineum /,perə'niəm/ n Anat. perineo, m
period /'pıəriəd/ n período, m; época, f; edad, f, tiempo, m; duración, f; término, plazo, m; Gram. período, m; (full stop) punto final, m; Med. menstruación, regla, f. **p. furniture**, muebles de época, m pl
periodic /,pıəri'ɒdık/ a periódico

periodical /,pıəri'ɒdıkəl/ a periódico. n publicación periódica, revista, f
periodicity /,pıəriə'dısıti/ n periodicidad, f
peripatetic /,perəpə'tetık/ a peripatético
peripheral /pə'rıfərəl/ a periférico
periphery /pə'rıfəri/ n periferia, f
periphrastic /,perə'fræstık/ a perifrástico
periscope /'perə,skoup/ n periscopio, m
perish /'perıʃ/ vi perecer; marchitarse; desaparecer, acabar. **to be perished with cold**, estar muerto de frío
perishable /'perıʃəbəl/ a perecedero, frágil
peritoneum /,perıtn'iəm/ n peritoneo, m
peritonitis /,perıtn'aitıs/ n peritonitis, f
periwig /'perı,wıg/ n peluca, f
periwinkle /'perı,wıŋkəl/ n Zool. caracol marino, m; Bot. vincapervinca, f
perjure /'pɜrdʒər/ vt perjurar. **to p. oneself**, perjurarse
perjurer /'pɜrdʒərər/ n perjuro (-ra); perjurador (-ra)
perjury /'pɜrdʒəri/ n perjurio, m. **to commit p.**, jurar en falso, perjurar
perkiness /'pɜrkinıs/ n desenvoltura, gallardía, f, despejo, m
perk (up) /pɜrk/ vi levantar la cabeza; recobrar sus bríos, alzar la cabeza; sacar la cabeza
perky /'pɜrki/ a desenvuelto, gallardo; coquetón; atrevido; (gay) alegre
permanence /'pɜrmənəns/ n permanencia, f; estabilidad, f
permanent /'pɜrmənənt/ a permanente; estable; (of posts, etc.) fijo. **p. wave**, ondulación permanente, f. **p. way**, Rail. vía, f
permanganate /pər'mæŋgə,neit/ n permanganato, m
permeability /,pɜrmiə'bılıti/ n permeabilidad, f
permeable /'pɜrmiəbəl/ a permeable
permeate /'pɜrmi,eit/ vt penetrar; impregnar; Fig. infiltrar (en)
permeation /,pɜrmi'eiʃən/ n penetración, f; impregnación, f; Fig. infiltración, f
permissible /pər'mısəbəl/ a permisible, admisible; lícito
permission /pər'mıʃən/ n permiso, m, licencia, f
permissive /pər'mısıv/ a permisivo, tolerado; (optional) facultativo
permit /v pər'mıt; n 'pɜrmıt/ vt permitir; dar permiso (a), dejar; tolerar, sufrir; admitir. n permiso, m; licencia, f; pase, m. **Will you p. me to smoke?** ¿Me permites fumar?
permutation /,pɜrmyʊ'teiʃən/ n permutación, f
permute /pər'myut/ vt permutar
pernicious /pər'nıʃəs/ a pernicioso. **p. anemia**, anemia perniciosa, f
perniciousness /pər'nıʃəsnıs/ n perniciosidad, f
peroration /,perə'reiʃən/ n peroración, f
peroxide /pə'rɒksaid/ n peróxido, m
perpendicular /,pɜrpən'dıkyələr/ a perpendicular. n perpendicular, f
perpendicularity /,pɜrpən,dıkyə'lærıti/ n perpendicularidad, f
perpendicularly /,pɜrpən'dıkyələrli/ adv perpendicularmente
perpetrate /'pɜrpı,treit/ vt Law. perpetrar; cometer
perpetration /,pɜrpı'treiʃən/ n Law. perpetración, f; comisión, f
perpetrator /'pɜrpı,treitər/ n el, m, (f, la) que comete; Law. autor (-ra); perpetrador (-ra)
perpetual /pər'petʃuəl/ a perpetuo, perdurable, eterno; incesante, constante; (life-long) perpetuo
perpetually /pər'petʃuəli/ adv perpetuamente; sin cesar; continuamente; constantemente
perpetuate /pər'petʃu,eit/ vt perpetuar, eternizar; inmortalizar
perpetuation /pər,petʃu'eiʃən/ n perpetuación, f
perpetuity /,pɜrpı'tuti/ n perpetuidad, f. **in p.**, para siempre
perplex /pər'pleks/ vt dejar perplejo, aturdir, confundir; embrollar
perplexed /pər'plekst/ a perplejo, irresoluto; confuso; (of questions, etc.) complicado, intrincado

perplexedly /pər'plɛksɪdli/ *adv* perplejamente
perplexing /pər'plɛksɪŋ/ *a* difícil; complicado; confuso
perplexity /pər'plɛksɪti/ *n* perplejidad, *f*; confusión, *f*
perquisites /'pɜrkwəzɪts/ *n pl* emolumentos, *m pl*; gajes, percances, *m pl*; (tips) propinas, *f pl*
persecute /'pɜrsɪˌkyut/ *vt* perseguir; importunar, molestar
persecution /ˌpɜrsɪ'kyufən/ *n* persecución, *f*
persecutor /'pɜrsɪˌkyutər/ *n* perseguidor (-ra)
perseverance /ˌpɜrsə'vɪərəns/ *n* perseverancia, *f*
persevere /ˌpɜrsə'vɪər/ *vi* perseverar
persevering /ˌpɜrsə'vɪərɪŋ/ *a* perseverante
perseveringly /ˌpɜrsə'vɪərɪŋli/ *adv* con perseverancia, perseverantemente
Persia /'pɜrʒə/ (la) Persia, *f*
Persian /'pɜrʒən/ *a* persa; de Persia; pérsico. *n* persa, *mf*; (language) persa, *m*. **P. blinds,** persianas, *f pl.* **P. cat,** gato (-ta) de Angora
persist /pər'sɪst/ *vi* persistir; persistir (en), empeñarse (en), obstinarse (en)
persistence /pər'sɪstəns/ *n* persistencia, *f*
persistent /pər'sɪstənt/ *a* persistente
persistently /pər'sɪstəntli/ *adv* con persistencia, persistentemente
person /'pɜrsən/ *n* persona, *f*. **first p.,** *Gram.* primera persona, *f*. **in p.,** en persona. **no p.,** nadie
personable /'pɜrsənəbəl/ *a* bien parecido
personage /'pɜrsənɪdʒ/ *n* personaje, *m*
personal /'pɜrsənļ/ *a* personal; íntimo; particular; en persona; (movable) mueble. **He is to make a p. appearance,** Va a estar presente en persona. **p. column,** (in a newspaper) columna de los suspiros, *f*. **p. equation,** ecuación personal, *f*. **p. estate,** (goods) bienes muebles, *m pl*
personality /ˌpɜrsə'nælɪti/ *n* personalidad, *f*; (insult) personalismo, *m*. **dual p.,** conciencia doble, *f*
personification /pərˌsɒnəfɪ'keifən/ *n* personificación, *f*
personify /pər'sɒnəˌfai/ *vt* personificar
personnel /ˌpɜrsə'nɛl/ *n* personal, *m*
perspective /pər'spɛktɪv/ *n* perspectiva, *f*, *a* en perspectiva
perspicacious /ˌpɜrspɪ'keifəs/ *a* perspicaz, clarividente, sagaz
perspicacity /ˌpɜrspɪ'kæsɪti/ *n* perspicacia, clarividencia, sagacidad, *f*
perspicuity /ˌpɜrspɪ'kyuɪti/ *n* perspicuidad, claridad, lucidez, *f*
perspicuous /pər'spɪkyuəs/ *a* perspicuo, claro
perspiration /ˌpɜrspə'reifən/ *n* sudor, *m*
perspire /pər'spaiᵊr/ *vi* sudar, transpirar
persuadable /pər'sweidəbəl/ *a* persuasible
persuade /pər'sweid/ *vt* persuadir; inducir (a), instar (a), mover (a), inclinar (a)
persuasion /pər'sweiʒən/ *n* persuasión, *f*; persuasiva, *f*; opinión, *f*; creencia, *f*; religión, *f*; secta, *f*
persuasive /pər'sweisɪv/ *a* persuasivo. *n* persuasión, *f*; aliciente, atractivo, *m*
persuasively /pər'sweisɪvli/ *adv* de un modo persuasivo, persuasivamente
persuasiveness /pər'sweisɪvnɪs/ *n* persuasiva, *f*
pert /pɜrt/ *a* petulante; respondón, desparpajado
pertain /pər'tein/ *vi* pertenecer (a); tocar (a), incumbir (a), convenir (a); estar relacionado (con)
pertinacious /ˌpɜrtņ'eifəs/ *a* pertinaz
pertinaciously /ˌpɜrtņ'eifəsli/ *adv* con pertinacia
pertinacity /ˌpɜrtņ'æsɪti/ *n* pertinacia, *f*
pertinence /'pɜrtņəns/ *n* pertinencia, *f*
pertinent /'pɜrtņənt/ *a* pertinente, atinado
pertinently /'pɜrtņəntli/ *adv* atinadamente
pertly /'pɜrtli/ *adv* con petulancia; con descaro
pertness /'pɜrtnɪs/ *n* petulancia, *f*; desparpajo, descaro, *m*
perturb /pər'tɜrb/ *vt* perturbar, agitar, turbar, inquietar
perturbation /ˌpɜrtər'beifən/ *n* perturbación, agitación, inquietud, *f*; confusión, *f*; desorden, *m*
perturbed /pər'tɜrbd/ *a* perturbado, agitado, ansioso, intranquilo

perturbing /pər'tɜrbɪŋ/ *a* perturbador, inquietador
Peru /pə'ru/ el Perú
peruke /pə'ruk/ *n* peluca, *f*
perusal /pə'ruzəl/ *n* lectura, *f*; examen, *m*
peruse /pə'ruz/ *vt* leer con cuidado, estudiar, examinar
Peruvian /pə'ruviən/ *a* and *n* peruano (-na)
pervade /pər'veid/ *vt* penetrar; llenar, saturar; difundirse por; reinar en
pervasion /pər'veiʒən/ *n* penetración, *f*
pervasive /pər'veisɪv/ *a* penetrante
perverse /pər'vɜrs/ *a* (wicked) perverso, depravado; obstinado; travieso; intratable
perversion /pər'vɜrʒən/ *n* perversión, *f*
perversity /pər'vɜrsɪti/ *n* (wickedness) perversidad, *f*; obstinacia, *f*; travesura, *f*
perversive /pər'vɜrsɪv/ *a* perversivo
pervert /pər'vɜrt/ *vt* pervertir; (words, etc.) torcer, tergiversar
pervious /'pɜrviəs/ *a* penetrable; permeable
pessimism /'pɛsəˌmɪzəm/ *n* pesimismo, *m*
pessimist /'pɛsəmɪst/ *n* pesimista, *mf*
pessimistic /ˌpɛsə'mɪstɪk/ *a* pesimista
pessimistically /ˌpɛsə'mɪstɪkli/ *adv* con pesimismo
pest /pɛst/ *n* insecto nocivo, *m*; animal dañino, *m*; parásito, *m*; (pestilence) peste, *f*; *Fig.* plaga, *f*; (person) mosca, *f*
pester /'pɛstər/ *vt* importunar, molestar, incomodar, *Lat. Am.* acatorrar, cargosear, majaderear. **to p. constantly,** *Inf.* no dejar a sol ni a sombra
pestering /'pɛstərɪŋ/ *n* importunaciones, *f pl*; *a* = annoying
pestilence /'pɛstļəns/ *n* pestilencia, peste, *f*; plaga, *f*
pestilential /ˌpɛstļ'ɛnfəl/ *a* pestilente, pestífero; pernicioso
pestle /'pɛsəl/ *n* mano de mortero, *f*, *vt* pistar, machacar, majar
pet /pɛt/ *n* animal doméstico, *m*; niño (-ña) mimado (-da); favorito (-ta); (dear) querido (-da); (peevishness) despecho, malhumor, *m*. *vt* acariciar; (spoil) mimar. **to be a great pet,** ser un gran favorito
petal /'pɛtļ/ *n* pétalo, *m*, hoja, *f*
peter (out) /'pitər/ *vi* desaparecer; agotarse
petition /pə'tɪfən/ *n* petición, *f*; súplica, *f*; instancia, solicitud, *f*; memorial, *m*. *vt* suplicar; pedir, demandar; dirigir un memorial (a). **to file a p.,** elevar una instancia
petitioner /pə'tɪfənər/ *n* peticionario (-ia)
pet peeve /piv/ *Lat. Am.* barreno, *m*
Petrarchan /pɪ'trɑrkən/ *a* petrarquista
petrifaction /ˌpɛtrə'fækfən/ *n* petrificación, *f*
petrify /'pɛtrəˌfai/ *vt* petrificar; *Inf.* dejar seco. **to become petrified,** petrificarse
petrol /'pɛtrəl/ *n* bencina, gasolina, *f*. *a* de gasolina, de bencina.
petroleum /pə'trouliəm/ *n* petróleo, *m*. *a* petrolero; de petróleo. **p. works,** refinería de petróleo, *f*
petrology /pɪ'trɒlədʒi/ *n* petrografía, *f*
petrous /'pɛtrəs/ *a* pétreo
petticoat /'pɛtiˌkout/ *n* enagua, *f*; *pl* **petticoats,** (slang) faldas, *f pl*. *a* de faldas, de mujeres; de mujer
pettifogger /'pɛtiˌfɒgər/ *n* (lawyer) picapleitos, *m*, rábula, *mf*; (quibbler) sofista, *mf*
pettifogging /'pɛtiˌfɒgɪŋ/ *a* charlatán, mezquino, trivial
pettiness /'pɛtinɪs/ *n* trivialidad, insignificancia, *f*; pequeñez, *f*; mezquindad, *f*; ruindad, bajeza, *f*
petty /'pɛti/ *a* trivial, sin importancia, insignificante; inferior; pequeño; mezquino; ruin; bajo. **p. cash,** gastos menores de caja, *m pl*. **p. expense,** gasto menudo, *m*. **p. officer,** suboficial, *m*. **p. thief,** ratero (-ra)
petulance /'pɛtfələns/ *n* mal humor, *m*, displicencia, irritabilidad, *f*
petulant /'pɛtfələnt/ *a* malhumorado, displicente, enojadizo, irritable
petulantly /'pɛtfələntli/ *adv* displicentemente, con mal humor
petunia /pɪ'tunyə/ *n* petunia, *f*

pew /pyu/ *n* banco (de iglesia), *m*. **p.-opener,** sacristán, *m*
pewter /'pyutər/ *n* peltre, *m*, *a* de peltre
phalange /'fæləndʒ/ *n* falange, *f*
phalanx /'feilæŋks/ *n* falange, *f*
phallic /'fælɪk/ *a* fálico
phallus /'fæləs/ *n* falo, *m*
phantasmagoria /fæn,tæzmə'gɔriə/ *n* fantasmagoría, *f*
phantasmagoric /fæn,tæzmə'gɔrɪk/ *a* fantasmagórico
phantom /'fæntəm/ *n* fantasma, espectro, *m*; sombra, ficción, *f*; visión, *f*
Pharisaical /,færə'seiɪkəl/ *a* farisaico
Pharisee /'færə,si/ *n* fariseo, *m*
pharmaceutical /,farmə'sutɪkəl/ *a* farmacéutico; *n* producto farmacéutico, *m*
pharmacist /'farməsɪst/ *n* farmacéutico, *m*
pharmacological /,farməkə'lɒdʒɪkəl/ *a* farmacológico
pharmacologist /,farmə'kɒlədʒɪst/ *n* farmacólogo, *m*
pharmacology /,farmə'kɒlədʒi/ *n* farmacología, *f*
pharmacopoeia /,farmə'koupiə/ *n* farmacopea, *f*
pharmacy /'farməsi/ *n* farmacia, *f*
pharyngeal /fə'rɪndʒiəl/ *a* faríngeo
pharyngitis /,færɪn'dʒaitɪs/ *n* faringitis, *f*
pharynx /'færɪŋks/ *n* faringe, *f*
phase /feiz/ *n* fase, *f*; aspecto, *m*; *Astron.* fase, *f*
pheasant /'fezənt/ *n* faisán, *m*. **hen p.,** faisana, *f*. **p. shooting,** caza de faisanes, *f*
phenic /'finɪk/ *a* fénico
phenol /'finɔl/ *n* fenol, *m*
phenomenal /fɪ'nɒmənl/ *a* fenomenal
phenomenon /fɪ'nɒmə,nɒn/ *n* fenómeno, *m*
phial /'faiəl/ *n* redoma, *f*
philander /fɪ'lændər/ *vi* galantear
philanderer /fɪ'lændərər/ *n* Tenorio, galanteador, *m*
philandering /fɪ'lændərɪŋ/ *n* galanteo, *m*
philanthropic /,fɪlən'θrɒpɪk/ *a* filantrópico
philanthropist /fɪ'lænθrəpɪst/ *n* filántropo, *m*
philanthropy /fɪ'lænθrəpi/ *n* filantropía, *f*
philatelic /,fɪlə'tɛlɪk/ *a* filatélico
philatelist /fɪ'lætlɪst/ *n* filatelista, *mf*
philately /fɪ'lætli/ *n* filatelia, *f*
philharmonic /,fɪlhɑr'mɒnɪk/ *a* filarmónico
Philippine /'fɪlə,pin/ *a* and *n* filipino (-na)
Philippines, the /'fɪlə,pinz/ las (Islas) Filipinas, *f pl*
Philistine /'fɪlə,stin/ *a* and *n* filisteo (-ea)
philological /,fɪlə'lɒdʒɪkəl/ *a* filológico
philologist /fɪ'lɒlədʒɪst/ *n* filólogo, *m*
philology /fɪ'lɒlədʒi/ *n* filología, *f*
philosopher /fɪ'lɒsəfər/ *n* filósofo, *m*. **philosopher's stone,** piedra filosofal, *f*
philosophical /,fɪlə'sɒfɪkəl/ *a* filosófico
philosophize /fɪ'lɒsə,faiz/ *vi* filosofar
philosophy /fɪ'lɒsəfi/ *n* filosofía, *f*. **moral p.,** filosofía moral, *f*. **natural p.,** filosofía natural, *f*
phlebitis /flə'baitɪs/ *n* flebitis, *f*
phlebotomist /flə'bɒtəmɪst/ *n* sangrador, flebotomiano, *m*
phlebotomy /flə'bɒtəmi/ *n* flebotomía, *f*
phlegm /flɛm/ *n* flema, *f*, *Lat. Am.* desgarro, *m*
phlegmatic /fleg'mætɪk/ *a* flemático
phlox /flɒks/ *n* flox, *m*
Phoenician /fɪ'nɪʃən/ *a* and *n* fenicio (-ia)
phoenix /'finɪks/ *n* fénix, *f*
phonetic /fə'netɪk/ *a* fonético
phoneticist /fe'netəsɪst/ *n* fonetista, *mf*
phonetics /fə'netɪks, fou-/ *n* fonética, *f*
phonograph /'founə,græf/ *n* fonógrafo, *m*
phonological /,fɒn|ɒdʒɪkəl/ *a* fonológico
phonology /fə'nɒlədʒi/ *n* fonología, *f*
phony /'founi/ *a* falso; espurio. **p. war,** guerra tonta, guerra falsa, *f*
pyorrhea /,paiə'riə/ *n* piorrea, *f*
phosphate /'fɒsfeit/ *n* fosfato, *m*
phosphoresce /,fɒsfə'res/ *vi* fosforecer, ser fosforescente
phosphorescence /,fɒsfə'resəns/ *n* fosforescencia, *f*
phosphorescent /,fɒsfə'resənt/ *a* fosforescente
phosphoric /fɒs'fɔrɪk/ *a* fosfórico

phosphorus /'fɒsfərəs/ *n* fósforo, *m*
photo /'foutou/ *n* foto, *f*
photochemistry /,foutou'kɛməstri/ *n* fotoquímica, *f*
photocopy /'foutə,kɒpi/ *n* fotocopia, *f*. *vt* fotocopiar, sacar copias
photogenic /,foutə'dʒenɪk/ *a* fotogénico
photograph /'foutə,græf/ *n* fotografía, *f*. *vt* fotografiar, retratar. **to have one's p. taken,** hacerse retratar
photographer /fə'tɒgrəfər/ *n* fotógrafo, *m*
photographic /,foutə'græfɪk/ *a* fotográfico
photography /fə'tɒgrəfi/ *n* fotografía, *f*
photogravure /,foutəgrə'vyʊr/ *n* fotograbado, *m*
photostat /'foutə,stæt/ *n* fotostato, *m*
photosynthesis /,foutə'sɪnθəsɪs/ *n* fotosíntesis, *f*
phrase /freiz/ *n* frase, *f*; *Mus.* frase musical, *f*. *vt* expresar, frasear; redactar. **p.-book,** libro de frases, *m*
phraseology /,freizi'ɒlədʒi/ *n* fraseología, *f*
phrasing /'freizɪŋ/ *n* (drawing up) redacción, *f*; (style) estilo, *m*; *Mus.* frases, *f pl*
phrenetic /frɪ'netɪk/ *a* frenético
Phrygian /'frɪdʒiən/ *a* and *n* frigio (-ia)
Phrygian cap *n* gorro frigio, *m*
phthisis /'θaisɪs/ *n* tisis, *f*
phylactery /fɪ'læktəri/ *n* filactria, *f*
phylloxera /fɪ'lɒksərə/ *n* filoxera, *f*
physical /'fɪzɪkəl/ *a* físico. **p. fitness,** buen estado físico, *m*. **p. geography,** geografía física, *f*. **p. jerks,** ejercicios físicos, *m pl*. **p. sciences,** ciencias físicas, *f pl*. **p. training,** educación física, *f*
physician /fɪ'zɪʃən/ *n* médico (-ca)
physicist /'fɪzəsɪst/ *n* físico, *m*
physics /'fɪzɪks/ *n* física, *f*
physiognomist /,fɪzi'ɒgnəmɪst/ *n* fisonomista, *mf*
physiognomy /,fɪzi'ɒgnəmi/ *n* fisonomía, *f*
physiological /,fɪziə'lɒdʒɪkəl/ *a* fisiológico
physiologist /,fɪzi'ɒlədʒɪst/ *n* fisiólogo, *m*
physiology /,fɪzi'ɒlədʒi/ *n* fisiología, *f*
physiotherapy /,fɪziou'θɛrəpi/ *n* fisioterapia, *f*
physique /fɪ'zik/ *n* físico, *m*
pianist /pi'ænɪst, 'piənɪst/ *n* pianista, *mf*
piano /pi'ænou/ *n* piano, *m*. **baby grand p.,** piano de media cola, *m*. **grand p.,** piano de cola, *m*. **upright p.,** piano vertical, *m*. **p. maker,** fabricante de pianos, *m*. **p. stool,** taburete de piano, *m*. **p. tuner,** afinador de pianos, *m*
pianola /,piə'noulə/ *n* piano mecánico, *m*
picaresque /,pɪkə'resk/ *a* picaresco
piccolo /'pɪkə,lou/ *n* flautín, *m*
pick /pɪk/ *n* (tool) pico, zapapico, *m*; (mattock) piqueta, *f*; (choice) selección, *f*; derecho de elección, *m*; (best) lo mejor, lo más escogido; (*Fig.* cream) flor, nata, *f*. **tooth-p.,** mondadientes, *m*. **p.-a-back,** sobre los hombros, a cuestas. **p.-ax,** zapapico, *m*, alcotana, *f*. **p.-me-up,** tónico, *m*; trago, *m*
pick /pɪk/ *vt* (with a pick-ax, make a hole) picar; (pluck, pick up) coger; (remove) sacar; (clean) limpiar; (one's teeth) mondarse (los dientes); (one's nose) hurgarse (las narices); (a bone) roer; (a lock) abrir con ganzúa; (a pocket) bolsear, robar del bolsillo; (peck) picotear; (choose) escoger; (a quarrel) buscar. *vi* (steal) hurtar, robar; (nibble) picar. **I have a bone to p. with you,** Tengo que ajustar unas cuentas contigo. **Take your p.!** ¡Escoja! **to p. and choose,** mostrarse difícil. **to p. to pieces,** *Fig.* criticar severamente. **to p. one's way through,** abrirse camino entre; andar con precaución por; andar a tientas por. **to p. off,** coger; arrancar; quitar; (shoot) disparar; fusilar. **to p. out,** entresacar; escoger; (recognize) reconocer; (understand) llegar a comprender; (a tune) tocar de oídas; (a song) cantar de oídas; (of colors) contrastar, resaltar. **to p. up,** *vt* (ground, etc.) romper con pico; coger; tomar; recoger; (raise) levantar, alzar; (information, etc.) cobrar, adquirir; (a living) ganar; (make friends with) trabar amistad con; (recover) recobrar; (find) encontrar, hallar; (buy) comprar; (learn) aprender; (a wireless message) interceptar; (a radio station) oír, tener. *vi* recobrar la salud; reponerse; mejorar. *n Mech.* recobro, *m*
picket /'pɪkɪt/ *n* estaca, *f*; (*Mil.* and during strikes) pi-

quete, *m*. *vt* cercar con estacas; poner piquetes ante (or alrededor de); poner de guardia; estacionar

picking /'pɪkɪŋ/ *n* (gathering) recolección, *f*; (choosing) selección, *f*; (pilfering) robo, *m*; *pl* **pickings,** desperdicios, *m pl*; (perquisites) gajes, *m pl*; ganancias, *f pl*

pickle /'pɪkəl/ *n* (solution) escabeche, *m*; (vegetable, etc.) encurtido, *m*; (plight) apuro, *m*; (child) diablillo, *m*. *vt* encurtir, escabechar

picklock /'pɪk,lɒk/ *n* (thief and instrument) ganzúa, *f*

pickpocket /'pɪk,pɒkɪt/ *n* carterista, *mf* ratero (-ra)

picnic /'pɪknɪk/ *n* partida de campo, jira, *f*, picnic, *m*. *vi* llevar la merienda al campo, hacer un picnic

picnicker /'pɪknɪkər/ *n* excursionista, *mf*

pictorial /pɪk'tɔriəl/ *a* pictórico; ilustrado. *n* revista ilustrada, *f*

pictorially /pɪk'tɔriəli/ *adv* pictóricamente; en grabados; por imágenes

picture /'pɪktʃər/ *n* cuadro, *m*; (of a person) retrato, *m*; imagen, *f*; (illustration) grabado, *m*, lámina, *f*; fotografía, *f*; (outlook) perspectiva, *f*; idea, *f*. *vt* pintar; describir; imaginar. **to go to the pictures,** ir al cine. **motion p.,** película, *f*. **talking p.,** película sonora, *f*. **p. book,** libro con láminas, *m*. **p. frame,** marco, *m*. **p. gallery,** museo de pinturas, *m*; galería de pinturas, *f*. **p. hat,** pamela, *f*. **p. postcard,** tarjeta postal, *f*. **p. restorer,** restaurador de cuadros, *m*. **p. writing,** pictografía, *f*

picturesque /,pɪktʃə'rɛsk/ *a* pintoresco

picturesqueness /,pɪktʃə'rɛsknɪs/ *n* carácter pintoresco, *m*, lo pintoresco; pintoresquismo, *m*

pie /pai/ *n* (savory) empanada, *f*; (sweet) pastel, *m*, torta, *f*; (of meat) pastelón, *m*; *Print.* pastel, *m*. **apple pie,** torta de manzanas, *f*. **to eat humble pie,** bajar las orejas. **to have a finger in the pie,** meter baza

piebald /'pai,bɔld/ *a* pío; tordo

piece /pis/ *n* pedazo, *m*; trozo, *m*; parte, porción, *f*; (literary, artistic work, coin, of fabric, at chess, etc. and slang) pieza, *f*; (of luggage) bulto, *m*; (of paper) hoja, *f*; (of ground) parcela, *f*; (of money) moneda, *f*, *vt* remendar; unir, juntar. **a p. of advice,** un consejo. **a p. of bread,** un pedazo de pan; una rebanada de pan. **a p. of folly,** un acto de locura. **a p. of furniture,** un mueble. **a p. of insolence,** una insolencia. **a p. of news,** una noticia. **a p. of paper,** un papel, una hoja de papel, una cuartilla. **a p. of poetry,** una poesía. **to break in pieces,** *vt* hacer pedazos, romper. *vi* hacerse pedazos, romperse. **to come or fall to pieces,** deshacerse; (of machines) desarmarse. **to cut in pieces,** cortar en pedazos; (an army) destrozar. **to give a p. of one's mind (to),** decir cuatro verdades (a), decir cuántas son cinco (a). **to go to pieces,** (of persons) hacerse pedazos. **to take to pieces,** (a machine) desmontar; deshacer. **to tear or pull to pieces,** hacer pedazos, despedazar; desgarrar. **p. goods,** géneros en piezas, *m pl*. **p.-work,** trabajo a destajo, *m*. **to do p.-work,** trabajar a destajo. **p.-worker,** destajista, *mf*

piecemeal /'pis,mil/ *adv* en pedazos; a remiendos; en detalle; poco a poco

piecrust /'pai,krʌst/ *n* pasta, *f*

pied /paid/ *a* bicolor; abigarrado, de varios colores

pier /pɪər/ *n* (jetty) dique, *m*; embarcadero, *m*; malecón, *m*; (of a bridge) pila, *f*; (pillar) columna, *f*; (between windows, etc.) entrepaño, *m*. **p.-glass,** espejo de cuerpo entero, *m*. **p. head,** punta del dique, *f*. **p. table,** consola, *f*

pierce /pɪərs/ *vt* penetrar; (of sorrow, etc.) traspasar, herir; (bore) agujerear, taladrar. *vi* penetrar

pierced ear /pɪərst/ *n* oreja perforada, *f*

piercing /'pɪərsɪŋ/ *a* penetrante; (of the wind, etc.) cortante; (of the voice, etc.) agudo. *n* penetración, *f*

piercingly /'pɪərsɪŋli/ *adv* de un modo penetrante, agudamente

pietism /'paiɪ,tɪzəm/ *n* pietismo, *m*

pietist /'paiɪtɪst/ *n* pietista, *mf*

pietistic /,paiɪ'tɪstɪk/ *a* pietista

piety /'paiɪti/ *n* piedad, devoción, *f*

piezometer /,paiə'zɒmɪtər/ *n* piezómetro, *m*

piffle /'pɪfəl/ *n* patrañas, tonterías, *f pl*

pig /pɪg/ *n* puerco, cerdo, *m*, *Lat. Am.* chancho, *m*; *Inf.*

cochino, *m*; (metal) lingote, *m*. **to buy a p. in a poke,** cerrar un trato a ciegas. **p.-eyed,** de ojos de cerdo. **p.-iron,** arrabio; hierro colado en barras, lingote de fundición, *m*

pigeon /'pɪdʒən/ *n* paloma, *f*, palomo, *m*; *Inf.* primo, *m*. *vt* embaucar, engañar. **carrier p.,** paloma mensajera, *f*. **clay p.,** pichón de barro, platillo de arcilla, *m*. **male p.,** pichón, *m*. **pouter p.,** paloma buchona, *f*. **young p.,** palomino, *m*. **p. fancier,** palomero, *m*. **p.-hole,** casilla, *f*. *vt* encasillar. **set of p.-holes,** encasillado, *m*. **p.-shooting,** tiro de pichón, *m*. **p.-toed,** patituerto

piggy bank /'pɪgi/ *n* alcancía, *f*

pigheaded /'pɪg,hɛdɪd/ *a* terco, testarudo, *Lat. Am.* empecinado

pigheadedness /'pɪg,hɛdɪdnɪs/ *n* terquedad, testarudez, *f*

piglet /'pɪglɪt/ *n* cerdito, *m*

pigment /'pɪgmənt/ *n* pigmento, *m*

pigmentation /,pɪgmən'teiʃən/ *n* pigmentación, *f*

pigskin /'pɪg,skɪn/ *n* piel de cerdo, *f*

pigsty /'pɪg,stai/ *n* pocilga, *f*

pigtail /'pɪg,teil/ *n* coleta, *f*

pike /paik/ *n* *Mil.* pica, *f*, chuzo, *m*; (peak) pico, *m*

pilaster /pɪ'læstər/ *n* pilastra, *f*

pile /pail/ *n* estaca, *f*; poste, *m*; (engineering) pilote, *m*; (heap) pila, *f*, montón, *m*; (pyre) pira, *f*; (building) edificio grande, *m*; *Elec.* pila, *f*; (hair) pelo, *m*; (nap) pelusa, *f*; *pl* **piles,** *Med.* almorranas, *f pl*. *vt* clavar pilotes en; apoyar con pilotes; (heap) amontonar; (load) cargar. **to make one's p.,** *Inf.* hacer su pacotilla. **to p. arms,** poner los fusiles en pabellón. **to p. on,** (coal, etc.) echar; (increase) aumentar. **to p. it on,** exagerar, intensificar; (a table) cargar. **to p. up,** *vi* amontonarse; acumularse; *vt Lat. Am.* empilonar; (of a ship) encallar. **p.-driver,** machina, *f*; martinete, *m*. **p. dwelling,** vivienda palustre, sostenida por pilares, *f*

pilfer /'pɪlfər/ *vt* sisar, sonsacar, hurtar, ratear, *Mexico* chalequear

pilferer /'pɪlfərər/ *n* sisador (-ra), ratero (-ra)

pilfering /'pɪlfərɪŋ/ *n* sisa, ratería, *f*

pilgrim /'pɪlgrɪm/ *n* peregrino (-na). **pilgrim's staff,** bordón, *m*

pilgrimage /'pɪlgrəmɪdʒ/ *n* peregrinación, *f*; romería, *f*. **to make a p.,** hacer una peregrinación, peregrinar; ir en romería

piling /'pailɪŋ/ *n* amontonamiento, *m*; (of buildings) pilotaje, *m*

pill /pɪl/ *n* píldora, *f*. **to gild the p.,** *Fig.* dorar la píldora. **p.-box,** caja de píldoras, *f*; casamata, *f*, *Mil.* nido de ametralladoras, *m*

pillage /'pɪlɪdʒ/ *vt* pillar, saquear. *n* saqueo, *m*

pillager /'pɪlɪdʒər/ *n* saqueador (-ra)

pillaging /'pɪlɪdʒɪŋ/ *n* pillaje, *m*, a pillador, saqueador

pillar /'pɪlər/ *n* pilar, *m*, columna, *f*; (person) sostén, soporte, *m*. **from p. to post,** de Ceca en Meca. **p. of salt,** estatua de sal, *f*. **the Pillars of Hercules,** las Columnas de Hércules. **to be a p. of strength,** *Inf.* ser una roca. **p.-box,** buzón, *m*

pillared /'pɪlərd/ *a* con columnas, sostenido por columnas; en columnas

pillion /'pɪlyən/ *n* (on a horse, etc.) grupera, *f*; (on a motor-cycle) grupa, *f*. **to ride p.,** ir a la grupa

pillory /'pɪləri/ *n* picota, argolla, *f*. *vt* empicotar; *Fig.* poner en ridículo; censurar duramente

pillow /'pɪlou/ *n* almohada, *f*; (for lace-making) cojín, *m*; (of a machine) cojinete, *m*. *vt* apoyar; reposar; servir como almohada. **to take counsel of one's p.,** consultar con la almohada. **p.-case,** funda de almohada, *f*

pilot /'pailət/ *n* piloto, *m*; *Naut.* práctico, piloto (de puerto), *m*. *vt* guiar, conducir; (*Naut. Aer.*) pilotar, pilotear. **p. boat,** vaporcito del práctico, *m*. **p. jacket,** chaquetón de piloto, *m*. **p. officer,** oficial de aviación, *m*

pilotage /'pailətɪdʒ/ *n* pilotaje, *m*; *Naut.* practicaje, *m*

pilotless /'pailətlɪs/ *a* sin piloto

pimento /pɪ'mɛntou/ *n* pimiento, *m*

pimp /pɪmp/ *n* rufián, alcahuete, *m*, *vi* alcahuetear

pimple /'pɪmpəl/ n grano, m

pimply /'pɪmpli/ a con granos

pin /pɪn/ n alfiler, m; prendedor, m; clavija, f; clavo, m, chaveta, f; (bolt) perno, m. vt prender con alfileres; (with a peg) enclavijar; fijar; sujetar. **to pin up,** sujetar con alfileres; (the hair) sujetar con horquillas. **to be on pins,** estar en ascuas. **to suffer from pins and needles,** tener aguijones. **pin-head,** cabeza de alfiler, f. **pin-money,** alfileres, m pl. **pin-oak,** Bot. pincarrasco, m, carrasca, f. **pin point,** punta de alfiler, f. **pin-prick,** alfilerazo, m

pinafore /'pɪnə,fɔr/ n delantal de niño, m

pince-nez /'pæns,nei/ n quevedos, m pl

pincers /'pɪnsərz/ n pl pinzas, tenazas, f pl, alicates, m pl; (of crustaceans) pinzas, f pl. **p. movement,** movimiento de pinzas, m

pinch /pɪntʃ/ vt pellizcar; (crush) estrujar; aplastar; apretar; (of the cold) helar; (steal) hurtar, birlar; (arrest) coger, prender. n pellizco, torniscón, m; pulgarada, f; (of snuff) polvo, m; (distress) miseria, f; (pain) dolor, m, angustia. f. **at a p.,** en caso de apuro. **to know where the shoe pinches,** saber dónde te aprieta el zapato

pinched /pɪntʃt/ a (by the cold) helado; (wan) marchito, descolorido

pincushion /'pɪn,kʊʃən/ n acerico, m

Pindaric /pɪn'dærɪk/ a pindárico

pine /pain/ n Bot. pino, m. vi languidecer, marchitarse, consumirse. **to p. for,** anhelar, suspirar por, perecer por. **pitch-p.,** pino de tea, m. **p.-apple,** piña de las Indias, f, ananás, m. **p. cone,** piña, f. **p. kernel,** piñón, m. **p. needle,** pinocha, f. **p. wood,** pinar, m, pineda, f

pineal /'pɪnɪəl/ a en figura de piña; Anat. pineal

ping /pɪŋ/ n silbido de una bala, m; zumbido, m. **p. pong,** tenis de mesa, pingpong, m

pinion /'pɪnyən/ n (wing) ala, f; (small feather) piñón, m; (in carving) alón, m; (wheel) piñón, m. vt atar las alas de; cortar un piñón de; (a person) atar; (the arms of) trincar, asegurar

pink /pɪŋk/ n Bot. clavel, m; color de rosa, m; (perfection) modelo, m; colmo, m; (hunting) color rojo, m; levitín rojo de caza, m. a de color de rosa, rosado. vt Sew. picar; (pierce) penecrar, atravesar. vi (of an engine) picar

pinking /'pɪŋkɪŋ/ n Sew. picadura, f

pinkish /'pɪŋkɪʃ/ a rosáceo

pinky /'pɪŋki/ n (finger) meñique, m

pinnacle /'pɪnəkəl/ n Naut. pinaza, f

pinnacle /'pɪnəkəl/ n pináculo, m

pinpoint /'pɪn,pɔint/ vt precisar

pint /paint/ n (measure) pinta, f

pintle /'pɪntl/ n (pin) perno, m

pioneer /,paiə'nɪər/ n pionero, explorador, m; introductor, m. **to be a p. in...,** ser el primero en (or a)... **pioneering role,** papel de iniciador (e.g. She played a pioneering role, jugó un papel de iniciadora)

pious /'paiəs/ a pío, devoto, piadoso

piously /'paiəsli/ adv piadosamente, devotamente

pip /pɪp/ n (of fruit) pepita, f; (on cards, dice) punto, m; (disease) moquillo, m; (of an army, etc.) officer) insignia, f

pipe /paip/ n (for tobacco) pipa (de fumar), Argentina cachimba, f; Mus. caramillo, m; (boatswain's) pito, m; (of a bird) trino, m; (voice) voz aguda, f; tubo, m; (for water, etc.) cañería, f; (of a hose) manga, f; (of an organ) cañón, m; (of wine) pipa, f; pl **pipes,** Mus. gaita, f. vi tocar el caramillo (or la gaita); empezar a cantar; silbar; (of birds) trinar. vt (a tune) tocar; (sing) cantar; (whistle) llamar con pito; conducir con cañerías; instalar cañerías en. **He smokes a p.,** Fuma una pipa. **I smoked a p.** (of tobacco) **before I went to bed,** Fumé una pipa antes de acostarme. **Put that in your p. and smoke it!** ¡Chúpate eso! **p. clay,** blanquizal, m. **p. cleaner,** limpiapipas, m. **p. layer,** cañero, fontanero, m. **p. laying,** instalación de cañerías, f. **p.-line,** cañería, f; (oil) oleoducto, m. **p. tobacco,** tabaco de pipa, m

pipeful /'paipfʊl/ n pipa, f

piper /'paipər/ n (bagpiper) gaitero, m; flautista, mf

pipette /pai'pɛt/ n Chem. pipeta, f

piping /'paipɪŋ/ n sonido del caramillo, m; música de la flauta, etc., f; (of birds) trinos, m pl; voz aguda, f; (for water, etc.) cañería, tubería, f; Sew. cordoncillo, m. **p.-hot,** hirviente

pipkin /'pɪpkɪn/ n ollita de barro, f

piquant /'pɪkənt/ a picante

pique /pik/ n (resentment, and score in game) pique, m. **to p. oneself upon,** preciarse de, jactarse de. **to be piqued,** estar enojado; Inf. amoscarse

piquet /pɪ'kei/ n juego de los cientos, m

piracy /'pairəsi/ n piratería, f

pirate /'pairət/ n pirata, mf. vi piratear. vt publicar una edición furtiva de. **p. edition,** edición furtiva, f

pirouette /,pɪru'ɛt/ n pirueta, f

Pisces /'paisiz/ n pl peces, m pl

pisciculture /'pɪsɪ,kʌltʃər/ n piscicultura, f

Pisgah /'pɪzgə/ Fasga, f

pistachio /pɪ'stæʃi,ou/ n pistacho, m

pistil /'pɪstl/ n Bot. pistilo, m

pistol /'pɪstl/ n pistola, f. **p. belt,** charpa, f, cinto de pistolas, m. **p. case,** pistolera, f. **p. shot,** pistoletazo, m

piston /'pɪstən/ n Mech. émbolo, pistón, m; Mus. pistón, m, llave, f. **p. ring,** anillo de émbolo, segmento de émbolo, m. **p. rod,** biela, f. **p. stroke,** carrera del émbolo, f

pit /pɪt/ n hoyo, m; foso, m; (in a garage) foso de reparación, m; Theat. platea, f; (trap) trampa, f; (scar) hoyo, m; precipicio, m; (hell) infierno, m. vt (with smallpox) marcar con viruelas; (against) competir con. **pithead,** boca de mina, f. **pit of the stomach,** boca del estómago, f. **pit stall,** butaca de platea, f

pitch /pɪtʃ/ n Chem. pez, brea, f, alquitrán, m; (place) puesto, m; (throwing) lanzamiento, m; (distance thrown) alcance, m; (for cricket) cancha, f; (bowling) saque, m; (slope) pendiente, inclinación, f; (height) elevación, f; Mus. tono, m; (Fig. degree) grado, extremo, m; (Naut. Aer.) cabeceo, m; (of threads of a screw, etc.) paso, m. vt (camp) asentar; (a tent, etc.) colocar, poner; (throw) lanzar, arrojar, tirar; (cricket, etc.) lanzar; (fix in) clavar; Mus. graduar el tono de; (tell) narrar. vi (fall) caer; Naut. cabecear, zozobrar; Aer. cabecear. **to paint with p.,** embrear. **to p. into,** (attack) acometer, atacar; (scold) desatarse contra; (food) engullir. **p.-black,** negro como la pez; oscuro como boca de lobo. **p.-pine,** pino de tea, m. **p.-pipe,** diapasón vocal, m

pitched battle /pɪtʃt/ n batalla campal, f

pitcher /'pɪtʃər/ n jarro, cántaro, m; (in baseball) lanzador de pelota, m

pitcherful /'pɪtʃər,fʌl/ n jarro (de), m

pitchfork /'pɪtʃ,fɔrk/ n horquilla, f, aventador, m. vt levantar con horquilla; Fig. lanzar

pitching /'pɪtʃɪŋ/ n (pavement) adoquinado, m; (of a ship) socollada, f; cabeceo, m

piteous /'pɪtiəs/ a lastimero; triste; plañidero; compasivo, tierno

piteousness /'pɪtiəsnɪs/ n estado lastimero, m; tristeza, f; compasión, ternura, f

pitfall /'pɪt,fɔl/ n trampa, f; Fig. añagaza, f, lazo, peligro, m

pith /pɪθ/ n Bot. médula, f; médula espinal, f; Fig. meollo, m; fuerza, f, vigor, m; substancia, f; quinta esencia, f; importancia, f

pithiness /'pɪθɪnɪs/ n jugosidad, f; fuerza, f, vigor, m

pithy /'pɪθi/ a meduloso; Fig. jugoso; enérgico, vigoroso

pitiable /'pɪtiəbəl/ a lastimoso, digno de compasión; (paltry) despreciable

pitiful /'pɪtɪfəl/ a piadoso, compasivo; conmovedor, doloroso, lastimero; (contemptible) miserable

pitifully /'pɪtɪfəli/ adv lastimosamente

pitiless /'pɪtɪlɪs/ a sin piedad, despiadado

pitilessness /'pɪtɪlɪsnɪs/ n crueldad, inhumanidad, f

pitman /'pɪtmən/ n minero, m; aserrador de foso, m

pittance /'pɪtns/ n pitanza, f; pequeña porción, f; ración de hambre, f

pitted /'pɪtɪd/ a picoso

pituitary /pɪ'tuɪ,teri/ a pituitario

pity /'pɪti/ n piedad, compasión, f; lástima. f. vt compadecerse de, tener lástima (a); compadecer. **It is a p.**

that..., Es lástima que... **Have p.!** ¡Ten piedad! **to take p. on,** tener lástima (de). **to move to p.,** dar lástima (a), enternecer
pityingly /'pɪtiɪŋli/ adv con lástima
pivot /'pɪvət/ n pivote, m; eje, m; Fig. punto de partida, m, vi girar sobre un pivote o eje
pivotal /'pɪvətl/ a Fig. cardinal, principal, fundamental
pixy /'pɪksi/ n duende, m. **p. hood,** caperuza, f
pizzicato /,pɪtsɪ'kɑtou/ a pichigato
placability /,plækə'bɪlɪti/ n placabilidad, f
placable /'plækəbəl/ a aplacable, placable
placard /'plækɑrd/ n cartel, m. vt fijar carteles (en); publicar por carteles
placate /'pleikeit/ vt aplacar, ablandar, apaciguar
placatory /'pleikə,tɔri/ a placativo
place /pleis/ n lugar, m; sitio, m; (position) puesto, m; (seat) asiento, m; (laid at table) cubierto, m; (square) plaza, f; (house) residencia, f; (in the country) casa de campo, finca, f; (in a book) pasaje, m; (in an examination) calificación, f; (rank) posición, f, rango, m; situación, f; (employment) empleo, m, colocación, f. vt poner; colocar; (in employment) dar empleo (a); (appoint) nombrar; (an order) dar; (money) invertir; (remember) recordar, traer a la memoria; (size up) fijar; (confidence) poner. **in p.,** en su lugar; apropiado. **in p. of,** en vez de, en lugar de. **in the first p.,** en primer lugar, primero. **in the next p.,** luego, después. **out of p.,** fuera de lugar; inoportuno. **It is not my p. to...,** No me toca a mí de... **to give p. to,** ceder el paso (a); ceder (a). **to take p.,** verificarse, tener lugar, ocurrir. **p. of business,** establecimiento, local de negocios, m. **p. of worship,** edificio de culto, m
placenta /plə'sɛntə/ n placenta, f
placid /'plæsɪd/ a plácido, apacible; calmoso; sereno, sosegado; dulce
placidity /plə'sɪdɪti/ n placidez, f; serenidad, tranquilidad, f, sosiego, m
placidly /'plæsɪdli/ adv plácidamente
placing /'pleisɪŋ/ n colocación, f; posición, f; localización, f
placket /'plækɪt/ n abertura (en una falda), f
plagiarism /'pleidʒə,rɪzəm/ n plagio, m
plagiarist /'pleidʒərɪst/ n plagiario (-ia)
plagiarize /'pleidʒə,raiz/ vt plagiar, hurtar
plague /pleig/ n plaga, f; peste, pestilencia, f. vt importunar, atormentar; plagar
plaid /plæd/ n manta escocesa, f; género de cuadros, m, a a cuadros
plain /plein/ a claro; evidente; (simple) sencillo; llano; sin adorno; (flat) liso, igual; (candid) franco; (with truth, etc.) desnudo; mero; puro, sin mezcla; (of words) redondo; (ugly) feo. adv claramente; llanamente; sencillamente; francamente. n llanura, f, llano, m. **the p. truth,** la pura verdad. **p. clothes,** traje de paisano, m. **p. clothes man,** detective, m. **p. cooking,** cocina sencilla, cocina casera, f. **p. dealing,** buena fe, sinceridad, f. **p. dweller,** llanero (-ra). **p. living,** vida sencilla, f. **p. people,** gente sencilla, f. **p. sailing,** Fig. camino fácil, m. **p. sewing,** costura, f. **p.-song,** canto llano, m. **p. speaking,** franqueza, f. **p.-spoken,** franco. **in p. English,** sin rodeos, en cristiano (e.g. Speak in p. English! Habla sin rodeos! Habla en cristiano!)
plainly /'pleinli/ adv claramente; sencillamente; llanamente; francamente; rotundamente
plainness /'pleinnis/ n claridad, f; sencillez, f; llaneza, f; franqueza, f; (ugliness) fealdad, f
plainsman /'pleinzmən/ n hombre de las llanuras, m
plaintiff /'pleintɪf/ n demandante, mf, actor, m, parte actora, actora, f
plaintive /'pleintɪv/ a quejumbroso, dolorido; patético
plaintively /'pleintɪvli/ adv quejumbrosamente
plaintiveness /'pleintɪvnɪs/ n melancolía, tristeza, f; voz quejumbrosa, f
plait /pleit/ n trenza, f. vt trenzar; tejer. **in plaits,** (of hair) en trenzas
plan /plæn/ n plan, m; (map) plano, m; proyecto, m. vt planear; proyectar; proponerse. **the Marshall P.,** el

Plan Marshall. **to make a p. of,** trazar un plano de. **to make plans,** hacer planes
planchette /plæn'ʃɛt/ n mesa giratoria, f
plane /plein/ n (tree) plátano, m; (tool) cepillo, m; Geom. plano, m; (level) nivel, m; Aer. avión, m; plano. vt acepillar, alisar. vi Aer. planear
planet /'plænɪt/ n planeta, m
planetarium /,plænɪ'tɛəriəm/ n planetario, m
planetary /'plænɪ,tɛri/ a planetario
planing /'pleinɪŋ/ n acepilladura, alisadura, f,
plank /plæŋk/ n tabla, f; Fig. fundamento, principio, m; pl **planks,** tablazón, f. vt entablar, enmaderar
planking /'plæŋkɪŋ/ n entablado, m, tablazón, f
plankton /'plæŋktən/ n plancton, m
planned /plænd/ a proyectado, planeado; dirigido. **p. economy,** economía dirigida, f
planner /'plænər/ n proyectista, mf; autor (-ra) de un plan; (appointment book) agenda, f
planning /'plænɪŋ/ n proyecto, m; concepción, f
plant /plænt/ n Bot. planta, f; instalación, f, material, m. vt plantar; (place) colocar; fijar; (a blow) asestar; (people) establecer; (instill) inculcar, imbuir (con); (conceal) esconder. **p. pot,** florero, m. **p. stand,** jardinera, f
plantain /'plæntɪn/ n Bot. llantén, plátano, m
plantation /plæn'teiʃən/ n plantación, f; plantío, m; Fig. colonia, f; introducción, f, establecimiento, m
planter /'plæntər/ n plantador, cultivador, m
planting /'plæntɪŋ/ n plantación, f; Fig. colonia, f; introducción, f. **p. out,** trasplante, m
plantlike /'plænt,laik/ a como una planta; de planta
plaque /plæk/ n placa, f; medalla, f
plash /plæʃ/ n (puddle) charco, m; (sound) chapaleteo, m. vt and vi chapotear, chapalear
plasma /'plæzmə/ n plasma, m
plaster /'plæstər/ n (for walls, etc.) argamasa, f; yeso, m; Med. parche, emplasto, m. vt (walls, etc.) enlucir, enyesar; poner emplastos (a or en); (daub) embadurnar manchar; (cover) cubrir. **p. cast,** vaciado, yeso, m. **p. of Paris,** escayola, f
plasterer /'plæstərər/ n yesero, m
plastering /'plæstərɪŋ/ n revoque, enyesado, guarnecido, m. **p. trowel,** fratás, m
plastic /'plæstɪk/ a plástico. n plástica, f; pl **plastics,** materias plásticas, f pl. **p. surgery,** cirugía plástica, cirugía estética, f
plasticine /'plæstə,sin/ n plasticina, f
plasticity /plæ'stɪsɪti/ n plasticidad, f
plate /pleit/ n plancha, chapa, f; (engraving and Phot., of a doctor, etc.) placa, f; (illustration) lámina, f; (cutlery, etc.) vajilla, f; (for eating) plato, m; (for money) platillo, m; electrotipo, m; (dental) dentadura postiza, f. vt (with armor) blindar; (with metal) planchear; (silver) platear; (electro-plate) niquelar. **silver p.,** vajilla de plata, plata, f. **p.-armor,** armadura, f; (of a ship) blindaje, m. **p.-draining rack,** escurreplatos, m. **p.-glass,** vidrio plano, m. **p.-rack,** escurridero para platos, m. **p. warmer,** calientaplatos, m
plateau /plæ'tou/ n meseta, altiplanicie, f, Lat. Am. altiplano, m
plateful /'pleit,fʌl/ n plato (de), m
plater /'pleitər/ n plateador, m; platero, m
plateresque /,plætə'rɛsk/ a Archit. plateresco
platform /'plætfɔrm/ n plataforma, f; (railway) andén, m. **p. ticket,** billete de andén, m
plating /'pleitɪŋ/ n niquelado, m; electrogalvanización, f; (with armor) blindaje, m
platinum /'plætnəm/ n platino, m. **p. blonde,** rubia platino, f
platitude /'plætɪ,tud/ n perogrullada, f, lugar común, m; trivialidad, vulgaridad, f
platitudinous /,plætɪ'tudnəs/ a lleno de perogrulladas; trivial
platonic /plə'tɒnɪk/ a platónico
Platonism /'pleitṇ,ɪzəm/ n platonismo, m
Platonist /'pleitṇɪst/ n platonista, mf
platoon /plə'tun/ n Mil. pelotón, m
platter /'plætər/ n fuente, f, trinchero, m; plato, m
plaudit /'plɔdɪt/ n aplauso, m, aclamación, f; (praise) elogio, m, alabanza, f

plausibility /ˌplɔzə'bɪlɪti/ n plausibilidad, f
plausible /'plɔzəbəl/ a plausible
plausibly /'plɔzəbli/ adv plausiblemente
play /plei/ vi jugar; (frolic) juguetear, retozar; recrearse, divertirse; Mech. moverse; (on a musical instrument) tocar; (wave) ondear, flotar; Theat. representar; (behave) conducirse. vt jugar; (of a searchlight, etc.) enfocar; (direct) dirigir; (a fish) agotar; (a joke, etc.) hacer; (a piece in a game) mover; (a musical instrument or music) tocar; (a string instrument) tañer; (a character in a play) hacer el papel de; (a drama, etc.) representar, poner en escena. **to p. a joke,** gastar una broma, hacer una burla. **to p. fair,** jugar limpio. **to p. false,** jugar sucio, engañar. **to p. the fool,** hacerse el tonto, hacerse el mayor. **to p. at,** jugar a; (pretend) fingir; hacer sin entusiasmo. **to p. off,** confrontar, contraponer. **to p. for,** (a person) tocar para. **to p. upon,** tocar; (a person's fears, etc.) explotar. **to p. up to,** (a person) adular, hacer la rueda (a). **to p. with,** jugar con; burlarse de; (an idea) acariciar play, n juego, m; diversión, f, recreo, m; (reflection) reflejo, m; movimiento libre, m; (to the imagination, etc.) rienda suelta, f; Mech. holgura, f; Lit. pieza dramática, comedia, f; (performance) función, representación, f; (Theat.) teatro, m. **fair p.,** juego limpio, m. **foul p.,** juego sucio, m; traición, perfidia, f. **to bring into p.,** poner en juego. **to come into p.,** entrar en juego. **to give p. to,** dar rienda a. **p. on words,** juego de palabras, m. **p.-pen,** cuadro enrejado, m
playact /'plei,ækt/ vi hacer la comedia
playbill /'plei,bɪl/ n cartel, m; programa, m
played-out /ˌpleid 'aut/ a agotado; viejo
player /'pleiər/ n jugador (-ra); Theat. actor (-triz), representante, mf; Mus. músico (-ca), tocador (-ra)
playfellow /'plei,felou/ n camarada, mf; compañero (-ra) de juego, compañero de juegos
playful /'pleifəl/ a juguetón; travieso; alegre
playfully /'pleifəli/ adv en juego, de broma; alegremente
playfulness /'pleifəlnɪs/ n carácter juguetón, m; travesuras, f pl; alegría, f
playgoer /'plei,gouər/ n persona que frecuenta los teatros, f; espectador de comedias, m
playground /'plei,graund/ n patio de recreo, m
playing /'pleiɪŋ/ n juego, m. **p.-cards,** naipes, m pl, cartas, f pl. **p.-field,** campo de deportes, m
playlet /'pleilɪt/ n comedia corta, f
playmate. /'plei,meit/. See **playfellow**
plaything /'plei,θɪŋ/ n juguete, m
playtime /'plei,taim/ n recreación, f; (in schools) hora de recreo, f, recreo, m
playwright /'plei,rait/ n dramaturgo, m, autor (-ra) de comedias
plea /pli/ n Law. informe, m; declaración, f; Law. acción, f, proceso, m; (excuse) pretexto, m, excusa, f; (entreaty) súplica, f. **under p. of,** bajo pretexto de, con excusa de
plead /plid/ vi Law. pleitear; Law. declarar; suplicar; (of counsel, etc.) abogar (por); interceder (por). vt defender en juicio; aducir, alegar; pretender. **to p. guilty,** confesarse culpable. **to p. not guilty,** negar la acusación. **to p. ignorance,** pretender ignorancia
pleading /'plidɪŋ/ n súplicas, f pl; Law. defensa, f; pl **pleadings,** alegatos, m pl, a implorante
pleasant /'plezənt/ a agradable; placentero; ameno; encantador; dulce; alegre; (of persons) simpático, amable; bueno; divertido
pleasantly /'plezəntli/ adv agradablemente; de un modo muy amable; alegremente
pleasantness /'plezəntnɪs/ n agrado, m; placer, m; amabilidad, f; alegría, f
pleasantry /'plezəntri/ n jocosidad, f; broma, chanza, f
please /pliz/ vi dar placer, gustar, dar gusto, agradar; parecer bien, querer, servirse; tener a bien, placer. vt deleitar, agradar, gustar; halagar; contentar, satisfacer; (polite request) por favor. **I will do what I p.,** Haré lo que me parezca bien. **If you p.,** Si te parece bien, Con tu permiso. **She is very easy to p.,** Es muy fácil de darle placer. **When you p.,** Cuando Vd. quiera, Cuando a Vd.

le venga bien Cuando Vd. guste. **"Please Do Not Disturb,"** «No Molesten.» **P. sit down!** ¡Haga el favor de sentarse! ¡Sírvase de sentarse! **P. God!** ¡Plegue a Dios!
pleased /plizd/ a contento (de or con); encantado (de); alegre (de); satisfecho (de or con). **I am p. with my new house,** Estoy contento con mi nueva casa. **I'm p. to meet you,** Mucho gusto (en conocerle), Mucho gusto (en conocerla). **to be p.,** estar contento; complacerse de
pleasing /'plizɪŋ/ a agradable, grato; placentero; halagüeño
pleasurable /'plezərəbəl/ a agradable; divertido, entretenido
pleasure /'plezər/ n placer, m; gusto, m; satisfacción, f; (will) voluntad, f; recreo, m; diversión, distracción, f. **to give p. (to),** dar placer (a); deleitar, agradar; complacer. **to take p. in,** gustar de, disfrutar de; complacerse en. **I shall do it with great p.,** Lo haré con mucho gusto, Lo haré con mucho placer. **p.-boat,** barco de recreo, m. **p.-ground,** parque de atracciones, m. **p.-seeking,** amigo de placeres, frívolo. **p. trip,** viaje de recreo, m; excursión, f
pleasure craft n barco de recreo, m, (one vessel); barcas de recreo (collectively), m pl
pleat /plit/ n pliegue, m, vt plegar, hacer pliegues en
pleating /'plitɪŋ/ n plegado, m
plebeian /plɪ'biən/ a plebeyo. n plebeyo (-ya)
plebiscite /'plebə,sait/ n plebiscito, m. **to take a p.,** hacer un plebiscito
plectrum /'plektrəm/ n plectro, m
pledge /pledʒ/ n prenda, f; empeño, m; garantía, f; (hostage) rehén, m; (toast) brindis, m. vt empeñar; dar en prenda; garantizar; brindar por; prometer. **to p. oneself,** comprometerse. **to p. support for,** prometer apoyo para
Pleiades /'pliə,diz/ n pl pléyades, f pl
plenary /'plinəri/ a pleno; plenario. **p. indulgence,** indulgencia plenaria, f. **p. session,** sesión plenaria, f
plenipotentiary /ˌplenəpə'tenʃi,eri/ a plenipotenciario. n plenipotenciario, m
plenitude /'plenɪ,tud/ n plenitud, f
plentiful /'plentəfəl/ a copioso, abundante. **to be p.,** abundar
plentifully /'plentəfəli/ adv en abundancia
plenty /'plenti/ n abundancia, f; en abundancia, de sobra; mucho. adv Inf. bastante. **There is p. of food,** Hay comida en abundancia. **We have p. of time,** Tenemos tiempo de sobra
pleonasm /'pliə,næzəm/ n pleonasmo, m
plethora /'pleθərə/ n plétora, f
pleurisy /'plʊrəsi/ n pleuresía, f
plexus /'pleksəs/ n plexo, m
pliability /ˌplaiə'bɪlɪti/ n flexibilidad, f; docilidad, f
pliable, pliant /'plaiəbəl, 'plaiənt/ a flexible; dócil
pliers /'plaiərz/ n pinzas, f pl, alicates, m pl, tenazas, f pl
plight /plait/ n (fix) aprieto, apuro, m. **the p. of the poor,** la situación de los pobres
plinth /plɪnθ/ n Archit. plinto, m
Pliny the Elder /'plɪni/ Plinio el Antiguo, Plinio el Mayor
Pliny the Younger /'plɪni/ Plinio el Menor
plod /plɒd/ vi andar despacio, caminar con trabajo; Fig. trabajar con ahínco
plodder /'plɒdər/ n trabajador lento y concienzudo, m; (student) empollón (-ona)
plot /plɒt/ n (of land) parcela, f; terreno, solar, m; (plan) proyecto, m; estratagema, m; (literary) intriga, trama, f; (story) argumento, m; (conspiracy) conjuración, f, complot, m. vt trazar (un plano, etc.); urdir, tramar. vi conspirar, intrigar
plotter /'plɒtər/ n conspirador (-ra conjurado (-da)
plotting /'plɒtɪŋ/ n trazado (de un plano, una gráfica), m; (conspiracy) conspiración, f; maquinaciones, f pl; (hatching) trama, f
plover /'plʌvər, 'plouvər/ n ave fría, f, chorlito, m
plow /plau/ n arado, m; Astron. el Carro, la Osa Mayor; (in an examination) escabechina, f. vt and vi arar; Fig. surcar; (in examinations) escabechar, dar calabazas (a), suspender. **plow the sands,** arar en el mar. **p. handle,** esteva, f. **to p. up,** roturar

plowman /'plaʊmən/ n arador, surcador, m; (peasant) labrador, m

plowshare /'plaʊˌʃeər/ n reja de arado, f

pluck /plʌk/ vt (pick) coger; (a bird) desplumar; Mus. puntear; (in an examination) calabacear escabechar. vi tirar (de). n (tug) tirón, m; (of an animal) asadura, f; (courage) coraje, m. **to p. up courage,** tomar coraje, sacar ánimos. **to p. off,** quitar. **to p. out,** arrancar; quitar

pluckily /'plʌkɪli/ adv valientemente

pluckiness /'plʌkɪnɪs/ n coraje, valor, m

plucky /'plʌki/ a valiente, esforzado, resuelto, animoso

plug /plʌg/ n tapón, tarugo, m; (in building) nudillo, m; (of a switchboard) clave, f; Elec. enchufe, m; (of a w.c.) tirador, m; (of a bath, etc.) tapón, m; (of tobacco) rollo, m. vt atarugar, taponar, obturar; (in building) rellenar. vi (with away) batirse el cobre, sudar la gota gorda. **to p. in,** enchufar

plum /plʌm/ n (tree) ciruelo, m; (fruit) ciruela, f; (raisin) pasa, f; (Inf. prize) breva, golosina, f. **p. cake,** pastel de fruta, m

plumage /'pluːmɪdʒ/ n plumaje, m

plumb /plʌm/ n plomada, f; (sounding-lead) escandallo, m. a perpendiculo; recto; completo. adv a plomo, verticalmente; exactamente. vt aplomar; Naut. sondar; (Fig. pierce) penetrar; (understand) comprender. vi trabajar como plomero. **p.-line,** plomada, f

plumbago /plʌm'beigou/ n plombagina, f

plumber /'plʌmər/ n plomero, fontanero, m; instalador de cañerías, m

plumbic /'plʌmbɪk/ a Chem. plúmbico

plumbing /'plʌmɪŋ/ n plomería, fontanería, f; instalación de cañerías, f

plumbless /'plʌmlɪs/ a Poet. insondable

plume /pluːm/ n pluma, f; penacho, m. vt adornar con plumas; desplumar; Fig. **to p. itself,** (of a bird) limpiarse las plumas. **to p. oneself on,** echárselas de, hacer alarde de; jactarse de

plumed /pluːmd/ a plumado; con plumas; empenachado

plumelet /'pluːmlɪt/ n agujas, f pl

plummet /'plʌmɪt/ n plomada, f; (weight) plomo, m; (sounding-lead) sonda, f. vi sondear

plump /plʌmp/ a gordito, llenito; rollizo; hinchado. adv de golpe; claramente. vt (swell) hinchar, rellenar; (make fall) hacer (or dejar) caer. vi (swell) hincharse; engordar; (fall) caer a plomo; dejarse caer. **to p. for,** escoger, dar apoyo (a); votar por. **p.-cheeked,** mofletudo

plumpness /'plʌmpnɪs/ n gordura, f; lo rollizo

plumy /'pluːmi/ a como una pluma; plumado

plunder /'plʌndər/ vt saquear; pillar, despojar. n saqueo, pillaje, m; (booty) botín, despojo, m

plunderer /'plʌndərər/ n saqueador (-ra); ladrón (-ona)

plundering /'plʌndərɪŋ/ n saqueo, m; despojo, m. a saqueador

plunge /plʌndʒ/ vt chapuzar; sumergir; hundir; meter. vi sumergirse; (into water) zambullirse; (rush) precipitarse, lanzarse; Naut. zozobrar; (of a horse) encabritarse; (gamble) jugarse el todo. n sumersión, f; zambullida, f; chapuz, m; (rush) salto, m; (Fig. step) paso, m

plunger /'plʌndʒər/ n Mech. émbolo, m

plunging /'plʌndʒɪŋ/ n (of a ship) zozobra, f; (of a horse) cabriolas, f pl; saltos, m pl, For other meanings, see **plunge**

plural /'plʊrəl/ a plural. n plural, m. **in the p.,** en el plural. **to make p.,** poner en plural

plurality /plʊ'rælɪti/ n pluralidad, f

pluralize /'plʊrəˌlaiz/ vt pluralizar

plus /plʌs/ prep and a más; (Math. Elec.) positivo. n signo más, m; Math. cantidad positiva, f. **p. fours,** pantalones de golf, m pl

plush /plʌʃ/ n felpa, f; velludo, m

plushy /'plʌʃi/ a felpudo; de felpa

Pluto /'pluːtou/ n Plutón, m; (pipe-line) oleoducto, m

plutocracy /plu'tɒkrəsi/ n plutocracia, f

plutocrat /'pluːtəˌkræt/ n plutócrata, mf

plutocratic /ˌpluːtə'krætɪk/ a plutocrático

pluviometer /ˌpluvi'ɒmɪtər/ n pluviómetro, m

ply /plai/ n cabo, m. vt emplear, usar; manejar; ejercer; ofrecer, servir (con); importunar (con). vi hacer el trayecto; hacer el servicio; ir y venir; hacer viajes. **to ply for hire,** tomar viajeros; ofrecerse para ser alquilado

plywood /'plaiˌwʊd/ n madera contrachapada, f

pneumatic /nʊ'mætɪk/ a neumático. n (tire) neumático, m. **p. drill,** barreno neumático, m

pneumococcus /ˌnuːmə'kɒkəs/ n neumococo, m

pneumonia /nʊ'mounyə/ n pulmonía, f. **double p.,** pulmonía doble, f

poach /poutʃ/ vt cazar (or pescar) en vedado. vt robar caza de un vedado; Fig. invadir; (Fig. steal) hurtar; (eggs) escalfar. **to p. upon another's preserves,** meterse en los asuntos de otro

poacher /'poutʃər/ n cazador furtivo, m

poaching /'poutʃɪŋ/ n caza (or pesca) furtiva, f

pock /pɒk/ n pústula, f. **p.-mark,** hoyo, m. **p.-marked,** picado de viruelas

pocket /'pɒkɪt/ n bolsillo, m; bolsillo del reloj, m; faltriquera, f; Mineral. bolsa, f, depósito, m; Fig. bolsa, f; (in billiards) tronera, f. vt meter (or poner) en el bolsillo; (an insult) tragarse; (in billiards) entronerar; (a profit) ganar; apropiarse. **air-p.,** bolsa de aire, f. **to be out of p.,** haber perdido, tener una pérdida. **to have a person in one's p.,** calzarse a una persona. **to p. one's pride,** olvidarse de su orgullo. **p. battleship,** acorazado de bolsillo, m. **p.-book,** cartera, f. **p. dictionary,** diccionario de bolsillo, m. **p.-flap,** portezuela, f. **p.-handkerchief,** pañuelo (de bolsillo), m. **p.-knife,** cortaplumas, m. **p.-lighter,** encendedor de bolsillo, m. **p.-money,** alfileres, m pl, dinero del bosillo, m. **p. picking,** ratería de carterista, f

pocketful /'pɒkɪtˌfʊl/ n bolsillo lleno (de), m; lo que cabe en un bolsillo

pocket of resistance n foco de resistencia, m

pod /pɒd/ n Bot. vaina, f; (of a silkworm) capullo, m. vt desvainar; mondar. vi hincharse, llenarse

podgy /'pɒdʒi/ a gordo, grueso

poem /'pouəm/ n poema, m; pl **poems,** poesías, f pl, versos, m pl

poet /'pouɪt/ n poeta, m. **p. laureate,** poeta laureado, m

poetaster /'pouɪtˌæstər/ n poetastro, m

poetess /'pouɪtɪs/ n poetisa, f

poetic /pou'ɛtɪk/ a poético. **p. license,** licencia poética, f

poeticize /pou'ɛtəˌsaiz/ vt poetizar; hacer un poema (de)

poetics /pou'ɛtɪks/ n poética, f

poetry /'pouɪtri/ n poesía, f; versos, poemas, m pl

pogrom /pə'grʌm/ n pogrom, m

poignancy /'pɔinyənsi/ n (of emotions) profundidad, violencia, f, lo patético; (of a retort, etc.) mordacidad, acerbidad, f

poignant /'pɔinyənt/ a (moving) conmovedor, hondo, agudo; patético; (mordant) mordaz, agudo

poignantly /'pɔinyəntli/ adv de un modo conmovedor, patéticamente; mordazmente

poinsettia /pɔin'setiə/ n flor de nochebuena, f

point /pɔint/ n (usual meanings and ast., math., in cards, in a speech, piece) punto, m; característica, f; cualidad, f; (purpose) motivo, fin, m; (question) cuestión, f; asunto, m; (wit) agudeza, f; (significance) significación, f; (detail) detalle, m; (in rationing) cupón, m; (sharp end) punta, f; (of a shawl, etc.) pico, m; (of land) promontorio, cabo, m; (engraving) buril, m; (railway) aguja, f; (of horses) cabo, m. **Mary has many good points,** María tiene muchas cualidades buenas. **There is no p. in being angry,** No hay para que enfadarse. **in p.,** en cuestión; a propósito. **in p. of fact,** en efecto, en verdad. **on the p. of,** a punto de. **to be to the p.,** venir al caso; ser apropiado. **to carry one's p.,** salir con la suya. **to come to the p.,** ir al grano, ir al mollo del asunto. **to make a p. of,** insistir en; tener por principio. **to win on points,** (boxing) ganar por puntos. **p. at issue,** cuestión bajo consideración, f, punto en cuestión, m. **p.-blank,** a boca de jarro. **p.-duty,** regulación de tráfico, f. **p. lace,** encaje de aguja, m. **p. of honor,** punto de honor, m; cuestión de honor, f. **p. or order,** cuestión de orden, f. **p. of view,** punto de vista, m. **What's your p.?** ¿A dónde quieres llegar con esto?

point /pɔint/ vt sacar punta (a), afilar; (a moral, etc.) inculcar; (in building) rejuntar; Gram. puntuar; (of dogs) mostrar la caza. **He pointed his gun at them,** Les apuntó con su fusil. **The hands of the clock pointed to seven o'clock,** Las agujas del reloj marcaban las siete. **to p. with the finger,** señalar con el dedo. **to p. at,** señalar, indicar; (with a gun) apuntar; dirigir. **to p. out,** señalar, indicar; enseñar, mostrar; advertir

pointed /'pɔintɪd/ a (sharpened) afilado; (in shape) puntiagudo; picudo; Archit. ojival; Fig. mordaz; satírico; (of a remark, etc.) directo; personal; aparente, evidente

pointedly /'pɔintɪdli/ adv explícitamente, categóricamente; mordazmente; directamente; satíricamente

pointedness /'pɔintɪdnɪs/ n forma puntiaguda, f; (incisiveness) mordacidad, aspereza, f; claridad, f

pointer /'pɔintər/ n (of a clock, weighing-machine, etc.) aguja, f; (of a balance) fiel, m; (wand) puntero, m; Fig. índice, m; (dog) perro de muestra, m

pointillism /'pwantl,ɪzem/ n Art. puntillismo, m

pointing /'pɔintɪŋ/ n (in building) rejuntado, m; (of a gun) puntería, f

pointless /'pɔintlɪs/ a sin motivo, innecesario; fútil; sin importancia

pointlessly /'pɔintlɪsli/ adv sin motivo, sin necesidad; fútilmente

pointsman /'pɔintsmən/ n (railway) guardagujas, m; (policeman) guardia del tráfico, m

poise /pɔiz/ vt balancear; pesar. vi balancearse; posar, estar suspendido. n equilibrio, m; (of mind) serenidad de ánimo, sangre fría, f; aplomo, m; (bearing) porte, aire, m

poison /'pɔizən/ n veneno, m; Fig. ponzoña, f, veneno, m. vt envenenar; intoxicar; Fig. emponzoñar. **p. gas,** gas asfixiante, m

poisoner /'pɔizənər/ n envenenador (-ra); Fig. corruptor (-ra)

poisoning /'pɔizənɪŋ/ n envenenamiento, m; intoxicación, f

poisonous /'pɔizənəs/ a venenoso; tóxico; Fig. ponzoñoso, pernicioso. **p. snake,** serpiente venenosa

poisonousness /'pɔizənəsnɪs/ n venenosidad, f; toxicidad, f; Fig. veneno, m, ponzoña, f

poke /pouk/ vt (thrust) clavar; (make) hacer; (the fire) atizar; hurgar; (push) empujar; (put away) arrinconar. vi andar a tientas; meterse. **Don't p. your nose into other people's business!** ¡No te metas donde no te llaman! **They poked his eyes out,** Le saltaron los ojos. **to p. fun at,** burlarse de, mofarse de. **to p. the fire,** atizar la lumbre (o el fuego). **to p. about for,** buscar a tientas. **p.-bonnet,** capelina, f

poker /'poukər/ n (game) póker, m; (for the fire) hurgón, atizador, m. **p. work,** pirograbado, m

poky /'pouki/ a estrecho, ahogado, pequeño; miserable

Poland /'poulənd/ Polonia, f

polar /'poulər/ a polar. **p. bear,** oso (-sa) blanco (-ca). **p. lights,** aurora boreal, f

polarimeter /,poulə'rɪmitər/ n polarímetro, m

polarity /pou'lærɪti/ n polaridad, f

polarization /,poulərə'zeiʃən/ n polarización, f

polarize /'poulə,raiz/ vt polarizar

pole /poul/ n palo largo, m; poste, m; (of a tent) mástil, m; (of a cart) pértiga, f; Sports. pértiga, garrocha, f; (measurement) percha, f; (Astron. Geog. Biol. Math. Elec.) polo, m. vt (a punt) impeler con pértiga. **from p. to p.,** de polo a polo. **greasy p.,** cucaña, f. **under bare poles,** Naut. a palo seco. **p.-ax,** hachuela de mano, f; hacha de marinero, f; (butcher's) mazo, m. **p. jumping,** salto de pértiga, salto a la garrocha, m. **p.-star,** estrella polar, f

Pole /poul/ n polaco (-ca)

polemic /pə'lɛmɪk/ n polémica, f

polemical /pə'lɛmɪkəl/ a polémico

police /pə'lis/ n policía, f. vt mantener servicio de

policía en; mantener el orden público en; administrar, regular. **mounted p.,** policía montada, f. **p. constable,** (agente de) policía, guardia urbano, m. **p. court,** tribunal de la policía, m. **p. dog,** perro de policía, m. **p. force,** cuerpo de policía, m, policía, f. **p. magistrate,** juez municipal, m. **p. station,** comisaría de policía, f. **p. trap,** puesto oculto de la policía del tráfico, m. **p. woman,** policía, f

policeman /pə'lismən/ n policía, guardia, Lat. Am. cívico, m

policy /'pɒlɪsi/ n política, f; táctica, f; sistema, m; norma de conducta, f; ideas, f pl, principios, m pl; prudencia, f; (insurance) póliza, f. **fixed premium p.,** póliza a prima fija, f. **p.-holder,** asegurado (-da), tenedor (-ra) de una póliza, m

poliomyelitis /,pouliou,maiə'laitɪs/ n poliomielitis, f

polish /'pɒlɪʃ/ vt (metals and wood) pulir; (furniture and shoes) dar brillo (a); (Lit. works) pulir, limar; (persons) descortezar, civilizar. n (shine) brillo, m; (furniture) cera para los muebles, f; (metal, silver) líquido para limpiar metales, m; (for shoes) betún para zapatos, m; (varnish) barniz, m; (of lit. works) pulidez, elegancia, f; (of persons) urbanidad, cultura, f. **to p. off,** terminar a prisa; (a person) acabar con; (food) engullir

Polish /'poulɪʃ/ a polaco, polonés. n (language) polaco, m

polished /'pɒlɪʃt/ a (of verses, etc.) pulido, elegante; (of person) culto, distinguido; (of manners) fino, cortés, (shined) brillante

polisher /'pɒlɪʃər/ n (machine) pulidor, m; lustrador, m. **floor-p.,** lustrador de piso, m. **French p.,** barnizador, m

polite /pə'lait/ a cortés, bien educado; atento; elegante

politely /pə'laitli/ adv cortésmente; atentamente

politeness /pə'laitnɪs/ n cortesía, f. **for p. sake,** por cortesía

politic /'pɒlɪtɪk/ a político

political /pə'lɪtɪkəl/ a político. **p. agent,** agente político, m. **p. economist,** hacendista, mf **p. economy,** economía política, f

politically /pə'lɪtɪkli/ adv políticamente

politician /,pɒlɪ'tɪʃən/ n político (-ca)

politics /'pɒlɪtɪks/ n política, f. **to dabble in p.,** meterse en política

polity /'pɒlɪti/ n forma de gobierno, constitución política, f

polka /'poulkə/ n polca, f

polka-dot /'poukə,dɒt/ a con puntos

poll /poul/ n (head of person) cabeza, f; (voters' register) lista electoral, f; (voting) votación, f; (counting of votes) escrutinio, m. vt (trees) desmochar; (vote) votar, dar su voto (a); (obtain votes) obtener, recibir; (count votes) escrutar. **p.-tax,** capitación, f

pollard /'pɒlərd/ vt desmochar. n (tree) árbol desmochado, m

pollen /'pɒlən/ n polen, m

pollinate /'pɒlə,neit/ vt fecundar con polen

pollination /,pɒlə'neiʃən/ n polinización, f

polling /'poulɪŋ/ n votación, f. **p. booth,** colegio electoral, m

pollute /pə'lut/ vt contaminar; ensuciar; profanar; (corrupt morally) corromper

polluter /pə'lutər/ n profanador (-ra), corruptor (-ra)

pollution /pə'luʃən/ n contaminación, f; profanación, f; corrupción, f

polo /'poulou/ n polo, m. **p. mallet,** maza de polo, f. **p. player,** jugador de polo, m, polista, mf

polonaise /,pɒlə'neiz/ n polonesa, f

poltroon /pɒl'trun/ n cobarde, m

polychrome /'pɒli,kroum/ a policromo

polygamist /pə'lɪgəmɪst/ n polígamo (-ma)

polygamous /pə'lɪgəməs/ a polígamo

polygamy /pə'lɪgəmi/ n poligamia, f

polygenesis /,pɒli'dʒɛnəsɪs/ n poligenismo, m

polyglot /'pɒli,glɒt/ n poligloto (-ta). **p. Bible,** poliglota, f

polygon /'pɒli,gɒn/ n polígono, m

Polynesia /,pɒlə'niʒə/ n Polinesia, f

polyp /'pɒlɪp/ n pólipo, m
polyphonic /,pɒli'fɒnɪk/ a polifónico
polyphony /pə'lɪfəni/ n polifonía, f
polytechnic /,pɒli'tɛknɪk/ a politécnico
polytheism /'pɒliθi,ɪzəm/ n politeísmo, m
polytheistic /,pɒliθi'ɪstɪk/ a politeísta
pomade /pɒ'meid/ n pomada, f
pomegranate /'pɒm,grænɪt/ n granada, f
Pomeranian /,pɒmə'reiniən/ a pomerano. **P. dog,** perro pomerano, m
pommel /'pʌməl/ n pomo, m, vt aporrear
pomp /pɒmp/ n pompa, magnificencia, f, fausto, aparato, m; ostentación, f
Pompeii /pɒm'pei/ Pompeya, f
pompom /'pɒm,pɒm/ n pompón, m
pomposity /pɒm'pɒsɪti/ n pomposidad, presunción, f; (of language) ampulosidad, f
pompous /'pɒmpəs/ a pomposo, ostentoso; (of style) ampuloso, hinchado; importante. **to be p.,** (of persons) darse tono
pond /pɒnd/ n charca, f, estanque, m
ponder /'pɒndər/ vt ponderar, estudiar, considerar. vi meditar (sobre), reflexionar (sobre)
ponderable /'pɒndərəbəl/ a ponderable
ponderous /'pɒndərəs/ a pesado; macizo, abultado; grave; (dull) pesado, aburrido
ponderously /'pɒndərəsli/ adv pesadamente; gravemente
ponderousness /'pɒndərəsnɪs/ n pesadez, f; gravedad, importancia, f
pontiff /'pɒntɪf/ n pontífice, m
pontifical /pɒn'tɪfɪkəl/ a pontificio
pontificate /pɒn'tɪfɪ,kɪt/ n pontificado, m
pontonier /,pɒntn'ɪər/ n pontonero, m
pontoon /pɒn'tun/ n pontón, m. **p. bridge,** puente de pontones, m
pony /'pouni/ n jaca, f
poodle /'pudl/ n perro (-rra) de aguas, perro de lanas, perro lanudo
pooh-pooh /'pu'pu/ vt despreciar, desdeñar. **Pooh!** ¡Bah!
pool /pul/ n (in a river) rebalsa, f; charca, f, estanque, m; (of blood, etc.) charco, m; (swimming) Spain piscina, Lat. Am. alberca, f; (in cards) baceta, f; Com. asociación, f; Fig. fuente, f; pl **pools,** (football) apuestas benéficas de fútbol, f pl. vt (resources, etc.) combinar; juntar
poop /pup/ n Naut. popa, f. **p. lantern,** fanal, m
poor /pʊr/ a pobre; malo; (insignificant or unfortunate) infeliz, desgraciado. **the p.,** los pobres. **to be in p. health,** estar mal de salud. **to be p. stuff,** ser de pacotilla. **to be poorer than a church mouse,** ser más pobre que las ratas. **to have a p. opinion of,** tener en poco (a). **P. me!** ¡Ay de mí! ¡Pecador de mí! **p.-box,** cepillo, m. **p.-law,** ley de asistencia pública, f. **p.-spirited,** apocado
poorhouse /'pʊr,haus/ n asilo, m
poorly /'pʊrli/ adv pobremente; mal. a indispuesto, malo
poorness /'pʊrnɪs/ n pobreza, f; mala calidad, f; (lack) carestía, f; (of soil) infertilidad, f; (of character) mezquindad, f
pop /pɒp/ n (of a cork) taponazo, m; (of a gun) detonación, f; (drink) gaseosa, f, adv ¡pum! vi (of a cork) saltar; (of guns) detonar. vt (corks) hacer saltar; (a gun, a question, etc.) disparar. **popgun,** escopeta de aire comprimido, f. **to pop down,** bajar a presuradamente. **to pop in,** (visit) dejarse caer; entrar rápidamente. **to pop off,** marcharse a prisa; (die) estirar la pata, Lat. Am. arrancarse. **to pop up,** subir corriendo; aparecer de pronto
popcorn /'pɒp,kɔrn/ nsg palomitas (de maíz), rosetas (de maíz) fpl (Spain), cabritos mpl (Chile), alborotos mpl (Argentina, Central America, Peru), cabritas fpl (elsewhere)
pope /poup/ n Papa, m
poplar /'pɒplər/ n (black) chopo, álamo, m; (white) álamo blanco, m. **p. grove,** alameda, f
poplin /'pɒplɪn/ n popelina, f
poppy /'pɒpi/ n amapola, adormidera, f

populace /'pɒpyələs/ n pueblo, m; (scornful) populacho, m
popular /'pɒpyələr/ a popular; en boga, de moda; común. **He is a p. hero,** Es un héroe popular
popularity /,pɒpyə'lærɪti/ n popularidad, f
popularization /,pɒpyələrə'zeiʃən/ n vulgarización, f
popularize /'pɒpyələ,raiz/ vt popularizar, vulgarizar
popularly /'pɒpyələrli/ adv popularmente
populate /'pɒpyə,leit/ vt poblar
population /,pɒpyə'leiʃən/ n población, f
populous /'pɒpyələs/ a populoso; muy poblado
porcelain /'pɔrsəlɪn/ n porcelana, f
porch /pɔrtʃ/ n pórtico, m; (of a house) portal, m
porcine /'pɔrsain/ a porcino, porcuno
porcupine /'pɔrkyə,pain/ n puerco espín, m
pore /pɔr/ n poro, m. **to p. over,** estar absorto en; examinar cuidadosamente
pork /pɔrk/ n carne de cerdo, f. **salt p.,** tocino, m. **p. butcher,** tocinero, m. **p. pie,** pastel de carne de cerdo, m
pornographic /,pɔrnə'græfɪk/ a pornográfico
pornography /pɔr'nɒgrəfi/ n pornografía, f
porosity /pɔ'rɒsɪti/ n porosidad, f
porous /'pɔrəs/ a poroso
porphyry /'pɔrfəri/ n pórfido, m
porpoise /'pɔrpəs/ n marsopa, f, puerco marino, m
porridge /'pɒridʒ/ n gachas, f pl, m
port /pɔrt/ n puerto, m; (in a ship) porta, f; (larboard) babor, m; (wine) vino de Oporto, m; (mien) porte, m, presencia, f. vt (the helm) poner a babor; Mil. llevar un fusil terciado. **to put into p.,** tomar puerto. **to stop at a p.,** hacer escala en un puerto. **p. dues,** derechos de puerto, m pl
portable /'pɔrtəbəl/ a portátil; móvil. **p. typewriter,** máquina de escribir portátil (or de viaje), f. **p. wireless,** radio portátil, f
portal /'pɔrtl/ n portal, m
portcullis /pɔrt'kʌlɪs/ n rastrillo, m
portend /pɔr'tɛnd/ vt presagiar, anunciar
portent /'pɔrtɛnt/ n augurio, presagio, m; portento, m
portentous /pɔr'tɛntəs/ a ominoso; portentoso; importante
porter /'pɔrtər/ n (messenger) mozo de cordel, m; (of a university, hotel) portero, m; (of apartments) conserje, m; (railway) mozo de estación, Argentina changador, m; (drink) cerveza negra, f. **porter's lodge,** portería, f; conserjería, f
porterage /'pɔrtərɪdʒ/ n porte, m
portfolio /pɔrt'fouli,ou/ n carpeta, f; (Polit. of a minister) cartera, f; (Polit. ministry) ministerio, m
porthole /'pɔrt,houl/ n tronera, f
portico /'pɔrtɪ,kou/ n pórtico, m
portion /'pɔrʃən/ n porción, f; parte, f; (marriage) dote, mf; (piece) pedazo, m; (in a restaurant) ración, f; (in life) fortuna, f. vt dividir; repartir; (dower) dotar
portliness /'pɔrtlɪnɪs/ n corpulencia, f
portly /'pɔrtli/ a corpulento, grueso
portmanteau /pɔrt'mæntou/ n maleta, f
portmanteau word n palabra de acarreo, f
portrait /'pɔrtrɪt/ n retrato, m. **p. painter,** pintor (-ra) de retratos
portraiture /'pɔrtrɪtʃər/ n retratos, m pl; descripción, pintura, f
portray /pɔr'trei/ vt retratar; pintar, representar; (in words) describir, pintar
portrayal /pɔr'treiəl/ n pintura, f; retrato, m; (in words) descripción, f
portrayer /pɔr'treiər/ n retratista, mf, pintor (-ra)
portress /'pɔrtrɪs/ n portera, f; (in a convent) tornera, f
Portugal /'pɔrtʃəgəl/ Portugal
Portuguese /,pɔrtʃə'giz/ a portugués. n portugués (-esa); (language) portugués, m
pose /pouz/ vt colocar; (a problem, etc.) plantear; (a question) hacer; vi colocarse; (with as) echárselas de, dárselas de, fingir ser; hacerse pasar por. n actitud, postura, f; (affected) pose, f; (deception) engaño, m
poser /'pouzər/ n problema difícil, m; (in an examination) pega, f; pregunta embarazosa, f
position /pə'zɪʃən/ n posición, f; situación, f; actitud,

postura, *f*; condición, *f*, estado, *m*; (post) puesto, empleo, *m*. **He is not in a p. to...**, No está en condiciones de..., No está para... **to place in p.**, poner en posición, colocar

positive /'pɒzɪtɪv/ *a* positivo; absoluto; (convinced) convencido, seguro; (downright) categórico; *Inf.* completo. *n* realidad, *f*; *Photo.* (prueba) positiva, *f*

positively /'pɒzɪtɪvli/ *adv* positivamente; categóricamente

positiveness /'pɒzɪtɪvnɪs/ *n* certitud, seguridad, *f*; terquedad, obstinacia, *f*

positivism /'pɒzɪtə,vɪzəm/ *n* positivismo, *m*

posse /'pɒsi/ *n* pelotón, *m*; multitud, muchedumbre, *f*

possess /pə'zɛs/ *vt* poseer; gozar (de); (of ideas, etc.) dominar. **to p. oneself of,** apoderarse de, apropiarse. **What possessed you to do it?** ¿Qué te hizo hacerlo?

possession /pə'zɛʃən/ *n* posesión, *f*. **to take p. of,** tomar posesión de; hacerse dueño de, apoderarse de; (a house, etc.) entrar en, ocupar

possessive /pə'zɛsɪv/ *a* posesivo. *n* posesivo, *m*

possessor /pə'zɛsər/ *n* poseedor (-ra); dueño (-ña); propietario (-ia)

possibility /,pɒsə'bɪlɪti/ *n* posibilidad, *f*

possible /'pɒsəbəl/ *a* posible. **as soon as p.,** cuanto antes, lo más pronto posible. **to make p.,** hacer posible, posibilitar

possibly /'pɒsəbli/ *adv* posiblemente; (perhaps) quizás. **I shall come as soon as I p. can,** Vendré lo más pronto posible

post /poust/ *n* (pole) poste, *m*; (of a sentry, etc.) puesto, *m*; (employment) empleo, *m*; (mail) correo, *m*; *Mil.* toque, *m*. *vt* (a notice) fijar; anunciar; (to an appointment) destinar; (letters, etc.) echar al correo; *Com.* pasar al libro mayor; (inform) tener al corriente. *vi* viajar en posta. **"P. no bills!"** «Se prohibe fijar carteles.» **registered p.,** correo certificado, *m*. **p. card,** tarjeta postal, *f*. **p.-chaise,** silla de posta, *f*. **p.-date,** posfecha, *f*. **p.-free,** franco de porte. **p.-haste,** con gran celeridad. **p.-horse,** caballo de posta, *m*. **p.-impressionism,** post-impresionismo, *m*. **p.-mortem,** *n* autopsia, *f*. **p.-natal,** post-natal. **p.-nuptial,** postnupcial. **p. office,** correo, *m*, correos, *m pl*; (on a train) ambulancia de correos, *f*. **p. office box,** *Spain* apartado de correos, *m*, *Lat. Am.* casilla, *f*. **p. office savings bank,** caja postal de ahorros, *f*. **p.-paid,** porte pagado; franco. **p.-war,** *n* postguerra, *f*. *a* de la postguerra

postage /'poustɪdʒ/ *n* porte de correos, franqueo, *m*. **p. stamp,** sello postal, *m*, *Mexico* timbre, m, *elsewhere in Lat. Am.* estampilla, *f*

postage meter *n* franqueadora, *f*

postal /'poustḷ/ *a* postal. **p. money order** *Spain* giro postal, *m*, *Lat. Am.* libranza de correos, libranza postal, *f*. **p. order,** orden postal de pago, *f*. **p. packet,** paquete postal, *m*

poster /'poustər/ *n* cartel, *m*. *vt* fijar carteles (a o en); anunciar por carteles. **bill-p.,** fijador de carteles, *m*

poste restante /,poust rɛ'stɑnt/ *n* lista de correos, *f*

posterior /pɒ'stɪəriər/ *a* posterior. *n* trasero, *m*, asentaderas, *f pl*

posteriority /pɒ,stɪəri'ɒrɪti/ *n* posterioridad, *f*

posterity /pɒ'stɛrɪti/ *n* posteridad, *f*

postgraduate /poust'grædʒuɪt/ *n* posgraduado (-da), estudiante graduado que hace estudios avanzados, *m*. *a* avanzado; para estudiantes graduados

posthumous /'pɒstʃəməs/ *a* póstumo

posthumously /'pɒstʃəməsli/ *adv* después de la muerte

postman /'poustmən/ *n* cartero, *m*

postmark /'poust,mɑrk/ *n* matasellos, *m*, *vt* poner matasellos (a)

postmaster /'poust,mæstər/ *n* administrador de correos, *m*

postmistress /'poust,mɪstrɪs/ *n* administradora de correos, *f*

postpone /poust'poun/ *vt* aplazar, diferir; retrasar; (subordinate) postergar

postponement /poust'pounmənt/ *n* aplazamiento, *m*; tardanza, *f*

postscript /'poust,skrɪpt/ *n* posdata, *f*, *Mexico* aumento, *m*

---

postulate /*n*. 'pɒstʃəlɪt; *v.* -,leit/ *n* postulado, *m*, *vt* postular

posture /'pɒstʃər/ *n* postura, actitud, *f*; (of affairs) estado, *m*, situación, *f*. *vi* tomar una postura

posy /'pouzi/ *n* (nosegay) ramillete de flores, *m*; flor, *f*; (motto) mote, *m*

pot /pɒt/ *n* pote, *m*; tarro, *m*; (flower-) tiesto, *m*; (for cooking) olla marmita, *f*; jarro, *m*. *vt* plantar en tiestos; conservar en potes. **pot-bellied,** panzudo. **pot-boiler,** obra literaria escrita con el sólo propósito de ganar dinero, *f*. **pot-herb,** hierba que se emplea para sazonar, hortaliza, *f*. **pot-hole,** bache, *m*. **pot-luck,** comida ordinaria, *f*. **pot-shot,** tiro fácil, *m*; tiro al azar, *m*

potage /pou'tɑʒ/ *n* potaje, *m*

potash /'pɒt,æʃ/ *n* potasa, *f*. **caustic p.,** potasa cáustica, *f*

potassium /pə'tæsiəm/ *n* potasio, *m*

potato /pə'teitou/ *n* patata, *f*. **sweet p.,** batata, *f*. **p. beetle,** coleóptero de la patata, *m*. **p. omelet,** tortilla a la española, *f*. **p. patch,** patatal, *m*. **p. peeler,** pela-patatas, *f*

potency /'poutnsi/ *n* potencia, *f*; fuerza, eficacia, *f*

potent /'poutnt/ *a* potente, fuerte; eficaz

potentate /'poutn,teit/ *n* potentado, *m*

potential /pə'tɛnʃəl/ *a* potencial; virtual; (*Phys. Gram.*) potencial, *n* poder, *m*; *Gram.* modo potencial, *m*; *Phys.* energía potencial, *f*; *Elec.* tensión potencial, *f*

potentiality /pə,tɛnʃi'ælɪti/ *n* potencialidad, *f*

pothook /'pɒt,hʊk/ *n* garabato de cocina, *m*; palote, *m*; (scrawl) garabato, *m*

potion /'pouʃən/ *n* poción, *f*,

potpourri /,poupʊ'ri/ *n* popurrí, *m*

potter /'pɒtər/ *n* alfarero, *m*. *vi* gandulear. *vt* perder. **potter's clay,** barro de alfarero, *m*. **potter's wheel,** tabanque, *m*. **potter's workshop,** alfar, *m*

pottery /'pɒtəri/ *n* alfarería, *f*; (china) loza, porcelana, *f*

pouch /pautʃ/ *n* bolsa, *f*; *Zool.* bolsa marsupial, *f*; (for tobacco) tabaquera, *f*; (for cartridges) cartuchera, *f*. *vt* embolsar. *vi* bolsear

poulterer /'poultərər/ *n* pollero (-ra)

poultice /'poultɪs/ *n* apósito, emplasto, *m*, *vt* poner emplastos (a o en)

poultry /'poultri/ *n* volatería, *f*. **p. dealer,** gallinero (-ra) vendedor (-ra) de volatería. **p. manure** *Mexico* cuitla, *f*. **p. yard,** gallinero, *m*

poultry farming *n* avicultura, *f*

pounce /pauns/ *n* (swoop) calada, *f*. *vi* (swoop) calarse; saltar (sobre); agarrar, hacer presa (en); *Fig.* atacar; descubrir, hacer patente

pound /paund/ *n* (weight and currency) libra, *f*; (for cattle) corral de concejo, *m*; (thump) golpe, *m*. *vt* (break up) machacar, pistar; (beat) batir; (thump) golpear, aporrear. **p. sterling,** libra esterlina, *f*. **p. troy,** libra medicinal, *f*

pounding /'paundɪŋ/ *n* machucamiento, *m*; batimiento, *m*

pour /pɔr/ *vt* vaciar, verter; derramar. *vi* correr; (of rain) diluviar, llover a cántaros; (fill) llenar; (of crowds, words, etc.) derramarse. **to p. out the tea,** servir el té. **The crowd poured in,** La multitud entró en tropel

pouring /'pɔrɪŋ/ *a* (of rain) torrencial

pout /paut/ *vi* torcer el gesto; hacer pucheritos

poverty /'pɒvərti/ *n* pobreza, *f*. **p.-stricken,** menesteroso, indigente, necesitado

powder /'paudər/ *n* polvo, *m*; (face) polvos de arroz, *m pl*; (gun) pólvora, *f*. *vt* polvorear; (crush) reducir a polvo, pulverizar. *vi* convertirse en polvos. **p.-flash,** fogonazo, *m*. **p.-flask,** polvorín, *m*. **p.-magazine,** santabárbara, *f*. **p.-mill,** fábrica de pólvora, *f*. **p.-puff,** polvera, borla de empolvarse, *f*

powdered /'paudərd/ *a* en polvo

powdery /'paudəri/ *a* polvoriento; friable

power /'pauər/ *n* poder, *m*; facultad, capacidad, *f*; vigor, *m*, fuerza, *f*; (*Polit.* and *Math.*) potencia, *f*; *Mech.* fuerza, *f*; influencia, *f*. **as far as lies within my p.,** en cuanto me sea posible. **It does not lie within my p.,** No está dentro de mis posibilidades, No está en mi poder. **the Great Powers,** las grandes

potencias. **the powers that be,** los que mandan. **to be in p.,** estar en el poder. **p.-house, p.-station,** central eléctrica, f. **p. of attorney,** poderes, m pl, procuración, f. **to grant p.** of attorney (to), dar poderes (a)
powerful /'pauərfəl/ a poderoso; fuerte; eficaz; potente; (of arguments, etc.) convincente
powerfully /'pauərfəli/ adv poderosamente; fuertemente
powerless /'pauərlıs/ a impotente
power steering n dirección asistida f (Spain), servo dirección f
powwow /'pau,wau/ n conferencia, f; conversación, f
pox /pɒks/ n sífilis, f; (smallpox) viruelas, f pl; (chicken-pox) viruelas falsas, f pl
practicability /,præktıkə'bılıti/ n factibilidad, f
practicable /'præktıkəbəl/ a practicable, factible, posible; viable, transitable
practical /'præktıkəl/ a (doable) factible; práctico; virtual. **p. joke,** burla de consecuencias
practically /'præktıkli/ adv prácticamente; en práctica; virtualmente; (in fact) en efecto. **p. nothing,** casi nada
practicalness /'præktıkəlnıs/ n carácter práctico, m
practice /'præktıs/ n (custom) costumbre, f; práctica, f; ejercicio, m; (of a doctor, etc.) clientela, f; profesión, f; (religious) rito, m, ceremonias, f pl; (experience) experiencia, f. **It is not his p. to...,** No es su costumbre de... **to be out of p.,** estar desentrenado. **to put into p.,** poner en práctica. **P. makes perfect,** El ejercicio hace maestro. vt tener la costumbre de; practicar; (a profession) ejercer; (a game) entrenarse en; (work at) estudiar; (a musical instrument) tocar; (accustom) acostumbrar. **to p. what one preaches,** predicar con el ejemplo
practiced /'præktıst/ a experimentado; experto
practitioner /præk'tıʃənər/ n médico (-ca). **general p.,** médico (-ca) general
pragmatic /præg'mætık/ a pragmatista; (historical) pragmático; práctico
pragmatism /'prægmə,tızəm/ n pragmatismo, m
pragmatist /'prægmətıst/ n pragmatista, mf
Prague /prɑg/ Praga, f
prairie /'preəri/ n pradera, sabana, pampa, f, a de la pradera, etc.
praise /preiz/ vt alabar; ensalzar, glorificar; elogiar. n alabanza, f; elogio, m; glorificación, f, ensalzamiento, m. **to p. to the skies,** poner en los cuernos de la luna poner por las nubes, poner sobre las estrellas hacerse lenguas de
praiseworthiness /'preiz,wɜrðınıs/ n mérito, m
praiseworthy /'preiz,wɜrði/ a digno de alabanza, laudable
prance /præns/ vi (of a horse) caracolear, encabritarse, cabriolar, saltar; andar airosamente. n corveta, cabriola, f; salto, m
prank /præŋk/ n travesura, diablura, f. **to play pranks,** hacer diabluras
prankster /'præŋstər/ n juguetón (-ona), burlón (-ona)
prate, prattle /preit; 'prætl/ vi charlar, chacharear; (lisp) balbucir; (of brooks, etc.) murmurar, susurrar. vt divulgar. n charla, cháchara, f; balbuceo, m
prattler /'prætlər/ n parlanchín (-ina); (gossip) chismoso (-sa); (child) niño (-ña)
prattling /'prætlıŋ/ n charla, f; (lisping) balbuceo, m; (of brooks, etc.) murmullo, susurro, ruido armonioso, m. a charlatán, gárrulo; balbuciente; (of brooks, etc.) parlero
prawn /prɔn/ n camarón, m
pray /prei/ vt and vi suplicar; implorar; rezar, orar. **P. be seated,** Haga el favor de sentarse
prayer /'preiər/ n rezo, m, plegaria, oración, f; súplica, f; Law. petición, f. **p. book,** libro de devociones, devocionario, m. **p.-meeting,** reunión para rezar, f. **p.-rug,** alfombra de rezo, f
praying /'preiıŋ/ n rezo, m; suplicación, f
pre- prefix de antes de (e.g. pre-World-War-1 publications, publicaciones de antes de la Primera Guerra Mundial)
preach /pritʃ/ vt and vi predicar

preacher /'pritʃər/ n predicador (-ra). **to turn p.,** meterse a predicar
preaching /'pritʃıŋ/ n predicación, f, a predicador
preamble /'pri,æmbəl/ n preámbulo, m
prearrange /,priə'reindʒ/ vt preparar de antemano, predisponer
precarious /prı'kɛəriəs/ a precario; inseguro; incierto, arriesgado
precariousness /prı'kɛəriəsnıs/ n condición precaria, f; inseguridad, f; incertidumbre, f
precaution /prı'kɔʃən/ n precaución, f. **to take precautions,** tomar precauciones
precautionary /prı'kɔʃə,nɛri/ a de precaución; preventivo
precede /prı'sid/ vt preceder (a), anteceder (a); tomar precedencia (a), exceder en importancia (a). vi ir delante; tener la precedencia
precedence /'prɛsıdəns/ n precedencia, f; prioridad, f; superioridad, f. **to take p. over,** tomar precedencia (a), preceder (a)
precedent /n. 'prɛsıdənt; a. prı'sidnt/ n precedente, m, a precedente. **without p.,** sin precedente
preceding /prı'sidıŋ/ a anterior, precedente
precept /'prisɛpt/ n precepto, m
preceptor /prı'sɛptər/ n preceptor, m
precinct /'prisıŋkt/ n (police station) Argentina comisaría de sección, Mexico delegación, f
precincts /'prisıŋkts/ n pl recinto, m; ámbito, m; distrito, barrio, m
preciosity /,prɛʃi'ɒsıti/ n afectación, f
precious /'prɛʃəs/ a precioso; de gran valor; hermoso; amado; muy querido; (with rogue, etc.) redomado; completo. **p. little,** muy poco. **p. stone,** piedra preciosa, f
preciousness /'prɛʃəsnıs/ n preciosidad, f; gran valor, f
precipice /'prɛsəpıs/ n precipicio, m
precipitancy /prı'sıpıtənsi/ n precipitación, f
precipitant /prı'sıpıtənt/ a precipitado
precipitate /v. prı'sıpı,teit; n., a. -tıt/ vt precipitar, despeñar, arrojar; acelerar; Chem. precipitar. vi precipitarse. n precipitado, m. a precipitado, súbito. **to p. oneself,** tirarse, lanzarse
precipitately /prı'sıpıtıtli/ adv precipitadamente
precipitation /prı,sıpı'teiʃən/ n Chem. precipitación, f; Chem. precipitado, m; (rain, etc.) precipitación pluvial, f
precipitous /prı'sıpıtəs/ a precipitoso, escarpado, acantilado
precipitously /prı'sıpıtəsli/ adv en precipicio
precise /prı'sais/ a preciso; exacto; justo; puntual; escrupuloso; formal; claro; pedante, afectado; ceremonioso
precisely /prı'saisli/ adv precisamente; exactamente, puntualmente; escrupulosamente; claramente; con afectación; ceremoniosamente. **at six o'clock p.,** a las seis en punto
precision /prı'sıʒən/ n precisión, f; exactitud, f; puntualidad, f; escrupulosidad, f; claridad, f; afectación, f; ceremonia, f
preclude /prı'klud/ vt excluir; impedir, hacer imposible
preclusion /prı'kluʒən/ n exclusión, f; imposibilidad, f
precocious /prı'kouʃəs/ a precoz
precocity /prı'kɒsıti/ n precocidad, f
preconceived /,prikən'sivd/ a preconcebido
preconception /,prikən'sɛpʃən/ n idea preconcebida, f; (prejudice) prejuicio, m
preconcerted /,prikən'sɜrtıd/ a concertado de antemano
precursor /prı'kɜrsər/ n precursor (-ra)
precursory /prı'kɜrsəri/ a precursor
predatory /'prɛdə,tɔri/ a rapaz; de rapiña; voraz
predecease /,pridı'sis/ vt morir antes (de o que); Law. premorir. n Law. premuerto, m
predecessor /'prɛdə,sɛsər/ n predecesor (-ra); (ancestor) antepasado, m
predestination /prı,dɛstə'neiʃən/ n predestinación, f
predestine /prı'dɛstın/ vt predestinar

predetermination /ˌpridɪˌtɜrmɪ'neɪʃən/ n predeterminación, f
predetermine /ˌpridɪ'tɜrmɪn/ vt predeterminar
predicament /prɪ'dɪkəmənt/ n /'prɛdɪkəmənt/ (logic) predicamento, m; situación, f; (fix) apuro, m; pl **predicaments,** categorías, f pl
predicate /v. 'prɛdɪˌkeɪt/ n. -kɪt/ vt afirmar. n (logic, Gram.) predicado, m
predict /prɪ'dɪkt/ vt predecir, pronosticar, profetizar
prediction /prɪ'dɪkʃən/ n predicción, f; pronóstico, vaticinio, m; profecía, f
predilection /ˌprɛdl'ɛkʃən/ n predilección, f
predispose /ˌpridɪ'spouz/ vt predisponer
predisposition /ˌpridɪspə'zɪʃən/ n predisposición, f
predominance /prɪ'dɒmənəns/ n predominio, m
predominant /prɪ'dɒmənənt/ a predominante
predominate /prɪ'dɒmə,neɪt/ vi predominar
preeminence /pri'ɛmənəns/ n preeminencia, f; primacia, superioridad, f
preeminent /pri'ɛmənənt/ a preeminente; superior; extraordinario
preeminently /pri'ɛmənəntli/ adv preeminentemente; extraordinariamente; por excelencia; entre todos
preen /prin/ vt (of birds) limpiarse; (of people) darse humos, jactarse
preexist /ˌpriɪg'zɪst/ vi preexistir
preexistence /ˌpriɪg'zɪstəns/ n preexistencia, f
prefabricated /pri'fæbrɪˌkeɪtɪd/ a prefabricado
preface /'prɛfɪs/ n prólogo, m; Eccl. prefacio, m; introducción, f. vt dar principio (a), empezar. **He prefaced his remarks by...,** Dijo a modo de introducción
prefatory /'prɛfəˌtɔri/ a preliminar, introductorio; a manera de prólogo
prefect /'prifɛkt/ n prefecto, m
prefecture /'prifɛktʃər/ n prefectura, f
prefer /prɪ'fɜr/ vt preferir, gustar más (a); (promote) ascender, elevar; (a charge, etc.) presentar. **to p. a charge against,** pedir en juicio (a). **I p. oranges to apples,** Me gustan más las naranjas que las manzanas, Prefiero las naranjas a las manzanas
preferable /ˌprɛfərə'bɪlɪti/ n preferencia, ventaja, f
preferable /'prɛfərəbəl/ a preferible
preferably /'prɛfərəbli/ adv preferiblemente, con preferencia
preference /'prɛfərəns/ n preferencia, f; privilegio, m. **p. share,** acción privilegiada, acción preferente, f
preferential /ˌprɛfə'rɛnʃəl/ a preferente
preferment /prɪ'fɜrmənt/ n promoción, f, ascenso, m; puesto eminente, m
preferred /prɪ'fɜrd/ a preferente; favorito, predilecto. **p. share,** acción preferente, f
prefix /'prifɪks/ vt anteponer, prefijar; (to a word) poner prefijo (a). n prefijo, m
pregnancy /'prɛgnənsi/ n embarazo, m, preñez, f
pregnant /'prɛgnənt/ a embarazada, encinta, preñada, f; Fig. fértil; Fig. preñado
prehensile /prɪ'hɛnsɪl/ a prensil
prehistoric /ˌprihɪ'stɔrɪk/ a prehistórico
prehistory /pri'hɪstəri/ n prehistoria, f
prejudge /pri'dʒʌdʒ/ vt prejuzgar
prejudice /'prɛdʒədɪs/ n prejuicio, m; Law. perjuicio, m. vt influir, predisponer; (damage) perjudicar. **without p.,** sin perjuicio
prejudiced /'prɛdʒədɪst/ a parcial; con prejuicios
prejudicial /ˌprɛdʒə'dɪʃəl/ a perjudicial
prelacy /'prɛləsi/ n prelacía, f; episcopado, m
prelate /'prɛlɪt/ n prelado, m
preliminarily /prɪˌlɪmə'nɛərəli/ adv preliminarmente
preliminary /prɪ'lɪmə,nɛri/ a preliminar. n preliminar, m
prelude (to) /'prɛlyud/ n preludio (de) m; presagio (de) m, vt and vi preludiar
premature /ˌprimə'tʃʊr/ a prematuro
prematurely /ˌprimə'tʃʊrli/ adv prematuramente
prematureness /'primə'tʃʊrnɪs/ n lo prematuro
premeditate /pri'mɛdɪ,teɪt/ vt premeditar
premeditatedly /pri'mɛdɪˌteɪtɪdli/ adv premeditadamente, con premeditación
premeditation /prɪˌmɛdɪ'teɪʃən/ n premeditación, f
premier /prɪ'mɪər/ a primero, principal. n primer

ministro, m; (in Spain) presidente del Consejo de Ministros, m
premiere /prɪ'mɪər/ n estreno, m
premiership /prɪ'mɪərʃɪp/ n puesto de primer ministro, m; in Spain presidencia del Consejo de Ministros, f
premise /'prɛmɪs/ n (logic) premisa, f; pl **premises,** local, m; recinto, m; establecimiento, m; propiedad, f; tierras, f pl. **on the premises,** en el local; en el establecimiento
premium /'primiəm/ n (prize) premio, m, recompensa, f; Com. prima, f; precio, m. **at a p.,** a premio; a una prima; (of shares) sobre la par; Fig. en boga, muy solicitado, en gran demanda
premonition /ˌprimə'nɪʃən/ n presentimiento, presagio, m
premonitory /prɪ'mɒnɪˌtɔri/ a premonitorio
prenatal /pri'neɪtl/ a prenatal, antenatal
preoccupation /priˌɒkyə'peɪʃən/ n preocupación, f
preoccupied /pri'ɒkyə,paɪd/ a preocupado; abstraído, absorto
preoccupy /pri'ɒkyə,paɪ/ vt preocupar
prepaid /pri'peɪd/ a porte pagado, franco de porte
preparation /ˌprɛpə'reɪʃən/ n preparación, f; preparativo, m, disposición, f; (patent food) preparado, m. **I have made all my preparations,** He hecho todos mis preparativos. **The book is in p.,** El libro está en preparación
preparative /prɪ'pærətɪv/ a preparativo. n preparativo, m
preparatory /prɪ'pærəˌtɔri/ a preparatorio, preparativo; preliminar. **p. school,** escuela preparatoria, f, m. **p. to,** como preparación para; antes de
prepare /prɪ'pɛər/ vt preparar; aparejar, aviar; equipar; (cloth) aprestar. vi prepararse; hacer preparativos
preparedness /prɪ'pɛərɪdnɪs/ n estado de preparación, m; preparación, f, apercibimiento, m
prepay /pri'peɪ/ vt pagar adelantado, Lat. Am. aprontar; (a letter, etc.) franquear
prepayment /pri'peɪmənt/ n pago adelantado, m; (of a letter, etc.) franqueo, m
preponderance /prɪ'pɒndərəns/ n preponderancia, f
preponderant /prɪ'pɒndərənt/ a preponderante, predominante
preponderantly /prɪ'pɒndərəntli/ adv predominantemente; en su mayoría
preponderate /prɪ'pɒndəˌreɪt/ vi preponderar; prevalecer (sobre), predominar (sobre)
preposition /ˌprɛpə'zɪʃən/ n preposición, f
prepossess /ˌprɛpə'zɛs/ vt predisponer; causar buena impresión, f
prepossessing /ˌprɛpə'zɛsɪŋ/ a atractivo
preposterous /prɪ'pɒstərəs/ a ridículo, absurdo
preposterously /prɪ'pɒstərəsli/ adv absurdamente
preposterousness /prɪ'pɒstərəsnɪs/ n ridiculez, f
Prep School /prɛp/ n preparatoria, f
prepuce /'pripyus/ n prepucio, m
prerequisite /pri'rɛkwəzɪt/ n requisito necesario, esencial, m, a previamente necesario, esencial
prerogative /prɪ'rɒgətɪv/ n prerrogativa, f
presage /'prɛsɪdʒ/ n presagio, m; anuncio, m. vt presagiar; anunciar
Presbyterian /ˌprɛzbɪ'tɪəriən/ a and n presbiteriano (-na)
prescience /'prɛʃəns/ n presciencia, previsión, f
prescient /'prɛʃənt/ a presciente
prescind /prɪ'sɪnd/ vt prescindir (de); separar (de). vi separar
prescribe /prɪ'skraɪb/ vt and vi prescribir; Med. recetar; dar leyes; Law. prescribir
prescription /prɪ'skrɪpʃən/ n prescripción, f; Med. receta, f
presence /'prɛzəns/ n presencia, f; (ghost) aparición, f. **in the p. of,** en presencia de, delante; a vista de. **p. of mind,** presencia de ánimo, serenidad de ánimo, f
present /'prɛzənt/ n presente, m; actual; (with month) corriente; Gram. presente. **at p.,** al presente, actualmente. **at the p. day,** a la fecha, en la actualidad, hoy día. **P. company excluded!** ¡Mejorando lo presente! **the present writer,** el que suscribe, el que

esto escribe, el que estas líneas traza. **to be p.** at, presenciar, ser testigo de; asistir a, acudir a; hallarse en. **p.-day,** de hoy, actual. **p. tense,** *Gram.* tiempo presente, *m*

present /'prɛzənt/ *n* (time) presente, *m;* actualidad, *f; Gram.* tiempo presente, *m;* (gift) regalo, *m,* dádiva, *f.* **By these presents...,** *Law.* Por estas presentes... **to make a p. of,** regalar. **Jane made me a p. of a watch,** Juana me regaló un reloj

present /prɪ'zɛnt/ *vt* presentar; ofrecer; manifestar; (a gift) regalar, dar; (*Eccl. Mil.*) presentar. **New problems presented themselves,** Nuevos problemas surgieron. **to p. arms,** presentar las armas. **He presented himself in the office,** Se presentó en la oficina. **He presented his friend Mr. Moreno to me,** Me presentó a su amigo el Sr. Moreno

presentable /prɪ'zɛntəbəl/ *a* presentable

presentation /,prɛzən'teɪʃən/ *n* presentación, *f;* homenaje, *m;* (exhibition) exposición, *f.* **on p.,** *Com.* a la presentación

presentiment /prɪ'zɛntəmənt/ *n* presentimiento, *m,* corazonada, *f.* **I had a p. that...,** Tuve el presentimiento de que..., Tuve una corazonada que... **to have a p. about,** presentir

presently /'prɛzəntli/ *adv* pronto; en seguida; dentro de poco

preservation /,prɛzər'veɪʃən/ *n* conservación, *f;* (from harm) preservación, *f*

preservative /prɪ'zɜrvətɪv/ *a* preservativo. *n* preservativo, *m*

preserve /prɪ'zɜrv/ *vt* preservar (de); guardar; proteger; conservar; *Cul.* hacer conservas de; (in syrup) almibarar. *n Cul.* conserva, *f;* (of fruit) compota, confitura, *f;* (covert) coto, *m.* **preserved fruit, p. dish,** compotera, *f*

preserver /prɪ'zɜrvər/ *n* conservador (-ra); (savior) salvador (-ra); (benefactor) bienhechor (-ra)

preserving /prɪ'zɜrvɪŋ/ *n* (from harm) preservación, *f;* conservación, *f.* **p. pan,** cazuela para conservas, *f*

preside /prɪ'zaɪd/ *vi* (over) presidir; dirigir, gobernar. **He presided at the meeting,** Presidió la reunión

presidency /'prɛzɪdənsi/ *n* presidencia, *f*

president /'prɛzɪdənt/ *n* presidente (-ta); (of a college) rector (-ra)

presidential /,prɛzɪ'dɛnʃəl/ *a* presidencial

presidentship /'prɛzɪdənt,ʃɪp/ *n* presidencia, *f*

press /prɛs/ *vt* prensar; (juice out of) exprimir; (clothes) planchar; (a bell, a hand, and of a shoe, etc.) apretar, *Mexico* apachurrar; (embrace) dar un abrazo (a); (a stamp, a kiss, etc.) imprimir; (an enemy) hostigar, acosar; (in a game) apretar; (crowd upon) oprimir; (emphasize) insistir en; (urge) instar, instigar; (compel) obligar; apremiar; (oppress) abrumar, agobiar; (paper) satinar; (an advantage) aprovecharse de. **Lola pressed his hand,** Lola le apretó la mano. **Time presses,** El tiempo es breve. **I did not p. the point,** No insistí. **to p. against,** pegar(se) contra. **to p. down,** comprimir; *Fig.* agobiar. **to p. for,** exigir, reclamar. **to p. forward, on,** avanzar; seguir el camino, continuar la marcha; (hurry) apretar el paso

press /prɛs/ *n* (pressure) apretón, *m;* (push) golpe, *m;* (throng) muchedumbre, *f;* (of business, etc.) urgencia, *f;* (apparatus) prensa, *f;* (printing press and publishing firm) imprenta, *f;* (cupboard) armario, *m.* **Associated P.,** Prensa Asociada, *f.* **freedom of the p.,** libertad de la prensa, *f.* **in p., in the p.,** en prensa. **in the p. of battle,** en lo más reñido de la batalla. **to go to p.,** entrar en prensa. **p.-agent,** agente de publicidad, *m.* **p.-box,** tribuna de la prensa, *f.* **p. clipping, p.-cutting,** recorte de prensa, *m.* **p.-gallery,** tribuna de la prensa, *f.* **p.-gang,** ronda de enganche, *f.* **p.-mark,** número de catálogo, *m.* **p. proof,** prueba de imprenta, *f.* **p.-room,** taller de imprenta, *m.* **p. conference,** rueda de prensa, entrevista de prensa, conferencia de pensa, *f*

pressing /'prɛsɪŋ/ *a* urgente, apremiante; importuno. *n* prensado, *m,* prensadura, *f;* expresión, *f;* (of a garment) planchado, *m*

pressingly /'prɛsɪŋli/ *adv* urgentemente, con urgencia; importunamente

pressman /'prɛsmən/ *n* tirador, *m;* (journalist) periodista, *m*

pressure /'prɛʃər/ *n* presión, *f;* (of the hand) apretón, *m;* apremio, *m;* opresión, *f;* (weight) peso, *m;* (force) fuerza, *f;* urgencia, *f.* **p.-cooker,** cazuela de presión, olla de presión, *f,* presto, *m.* **p.-gauge,** manómetro, *m*

prestidigitation /,prɛstɪ,dɪdʒɪ'teɪʃən/ *n* prestidigitación, *f,* juegos de manos, *m pl*

prestige /prɛ'stiʒ/ *n* prestigio, *m*

prestigious /prɛ'stɪdʒəs/ *a* prestigiado

presumable /prɪ'zuməbəl/ *a* presumible

presume /prɪ'zum/ *vt* presumir; suponer, sospechar; (attempt) pretender. *vi* presumir; tomarse libertades; abusar (de)

presumption /prɪ'zʌmpʃən/ *n* presunción, *f;* suposición, *f;* (effrontery) atrevimiento, *m;* insolencia, *f*

presumptive /prɪ'zʌmptɪv/ *a* presuntivo; (with heir, etc.) presunto

presumptuous /prɪ'zʌmptʃuəs/ *a* presumido, insolente, presuntuoso; atrevido

presumptuously /prɪ'zʌmptʃuəsli/ *adv* presuntuosamente

presumptuousness /prɪ'zʌmptʃuəsnɪs/ *n* presunción, presuntuosidad, *f;* atrevimiento, *m*

presuppose /,prisə'pouz/ *vt* presuponer

presupposition /,prisʌpə'zɪʃən/ *n* presuposición, *f*

pretence /prɪ'tɛns/ *n* (claim) pretensión, *f;* afectación, *f;* (simulation) fingimiento, *m;* pretexto, *m.* **false pretences,** apariencias fingidas, *f pl;* engaño, *m,* estafa, *f.* **to make a p. of,** fingir. **under p. of,** bajo pretexto de

pretend /prɪ'tɛnd/ *vt* dar como pretexto de; aparentar, fingir, simular, hacer el papel (de). *vi* pretender (a); tener pretensiones (de); ser pretendiente (a); fingir

pretended /prɪ'tɛndɪd/ *a* supuesto, fingido; falso

pretender /prɪ'tɛndər/ *n* pretendiente, *m;* hipócrita, *mf*

pretension /prɪ'tɛnʃən/ *n* pretensión, *f;* afectación, simulación, *f*

pretentious /prɪ'tɛnʃəs/ *a* pretencioso; (of persons) presumido

pretentiousness /prɪ'tɛnʃəsnɪs/ *n* pretensiones, *f pl,* lo pretencioso

preterite /'prɛtərɪt/ *n* (tiempo) pretérito, *m, a* pretérito, pasado

pretext /'pritɛkst/ *n* pretexto, *m. vt* pretextar. **under p. of,** bajo pretexto de, so color de

prettily /'prɪtli/ *adv* lindamente; con gracia; agradablemente

prettiness /'prɪtɪnɪs/ *n* lo bonito; elegancia, *f;* gracia, *f*

pretty /'prɪti/ *a* bonito; (of women, children) guapo, mono; (of men) lindo; elegante; excelente; *Ironic.* bueno. *adv* bastante; medianamente; (very) muy; (almost) casi. **p. good,** bastante bueno. **p. ways,** monerías, *f pl*

prevail /prɪ'veɪl/ *vi* prevalecer, predominar; ser la costumbre. **to p. against or over,** triunfar de, vencer (a). **to p. on, upon,** inducir, convencer, persuadir. **to be prevailed upon to,** dejarse persuadir a

prevailing /prɪ'veɪlɪŋ/ *a* prevaleciente; dominante; predominante, reinante; general; común; (fashionable) en boga

prevalence /'prɛvələns/ *n* predominio, *m;* existencia, *f;* (habit) costumbre, *f;* (fashion) boga, *f*

prevalent /'prɛvələnt/ *a* prevaleciente; predominante; general; común; corriente; (fashionable) en boga

prevaricate /prɪ'værɪ,keɪt/ *vi* tergiversar; *Law.* prevaricar

prevarication /prɪ,værɪ'keɪʃən/ *n* tergiversación, *f,* equívoco, *m*

prevaricator /prɪ'værɪ,keɪtər/ *n* tergiversador (-ra)

prevent /prɪ'vɛnt/ *vt* evitar; (hinder) impedir (a)

preventable /prɪ'vɛntəbəl/ *a* evitable

prevention /prɪ'vɛnʃən/ *n* prevención, *f;* (preventive) estorbo, obstáculo, *m*

preventive /prɪ'vɛntɪv/ *a* preventivo. *n* preservativo, *m*

preview /'pri,vyu/ *n* vista de antemano, *f;* (of a film) avances, *m pl* (Cuba, Mexico), colas, *f pl* (Argentina), cortos *m pl* (Venezuela), sinopsis, *f* (Uruguay), tráiler, *m* (Spain)

previous /'priviəs/ *a* previo, anterior. **p. to,** antes de

previously /'priviəsli/ *adv* anteriormente, antes, previamente

previousness /'priviəsnıs/ *n* anterioridad, *f*; inoportunidad, *f*

prevision /prı'vıʒən/ *n* previsión, *f*

prewar /'pri'wɔr/ *a* de antes de la guerra

prey /prei/ *n* presa, *f*; *Fig.* víctima, *f*; (booty) botín, *m*. *vi* (of animals) devorar; (plunder) robar, pillar; (of sorrow, etc.) hacer presa (de); agobiar, consumir; (sponge on) vivir a costa de. **to fall p. to,** ser víctima de

price /prais/ *n* precio, *m*; valor, *m*; costa, *f*. *vt* evaluar, tasar; poner precio a; preguntar el precio de; fijar el precio de. **at any p.,** a cualquier precio; (whatever the cost) cueste lo que cueste. **at a reduced p.,** a precio reducido. **fixed p.,** precio fijo, *m*. **p. ceiling,** precio máximo, precio tope, *m*. **p. control,** control de precios, *m*. **price list,** lista de precios, *f*; tarifa, *f*; (of shares, etc.) boletín de cotización, *m*. **Prices are subject to change without notice,** Los precios están sujetos a variación sin previo aviso.

priceless /'praislıs/ *a* sin precio; (amusing) divertidísimo. **These jewels are p.,** Estas joyas no tienen precio

prick /prık/ *n* pinchazo, *m*; picadura, *f*; punzada, *f*; (prickle) espina, *f*; (with a goad) aguijonazo, *m*; (with a pin) alfilerazo, *m*; (with a spur) espolada, *f*; (of conscience) remordimiento, escrúpulo, *m*. *vt* pinchar, punzar; picar; (with remorse) atormentar, causar remordimiento (a); (urge on) incitar. **to p. the ears,** aguzar las orejas

pricking /'prıkıŋ/ *n* picadura, *f*; punzada, *f*. **prickings of conscience,** remordimientos, *m pl*

prickle /'prıkəl/ *n* espina, *f*; (irritation) escozor, *m*

prickly /'prıkli/ *a* espinoso; erizado. **p. heat,** salpullido causado por exceso de calor, *m*. **p. pear,** higo chumbo, *m*, chumbera, *f*

pride /praid/ *n* orgullo, *m*; arrogancia, *f*; (splendour) pompa, *f*, fausto, aparato, *m*; belleza, *f*; vigor, *m*; (of lions) manada, *f*. **to take p. in,** estar orgulloso de. **to p. oneself,** sentirse orgulloso, ufanarse. **to p. oneself upon,** jactarse de, preciarse de

prie-dieu /'pri'dyʊ/ *n* reclinatorio, *m*

prier /'praiər/ *n* espía, *mf*; curioso (-sa)

priest /prist/ *n* sacerdote, *m*; cura, *m*. **high-p.,** sumo sacerdote, *m*. **p.-ridden,** dominado por el clero

priestess /'pristıs/ *n* sacerdotisa, *f*

priesthood /'pristhʊd/ *n* sacerdocio, *m*

priestly /'pristli/ *a* sacerdotal

prig /prıg/ *n* fatuo (-ua), mojigato (-ta)

priggish /'prıgıʃ/ *a* fatuo, gazmoño

priggishness /'prıgıʃnıs/ *n* gazmoñería, fatuidad, *f*

prim /prım/ *a* almidonado, etiquetero; peripuesto; afectado

primacy /'praiməsi/ *n* primacía, *f*

prima donna /,primə 'dɒnə/ *n* cantatriz, *f*

primarily /prai'meərəli/ *adv* en primer lugar principalmente

primary /'praimeri/ *a* primario; primitivo; principal. **p. education,** enseñanza primaria, *f*. **p. color,** color primario, *m*. **p. school,** escuela primaria, *f*. **p. election,** elección interna (dentro de un partido), *f*

primate /'praimeit/ *n* primado, *m*

prime /praim/ *a* primero; principal; excelente; de primera calidad; de primera clase. *n* (spring) primavera, *f*; (of life, etc.) flor, *f*, vigor, *m*; (best) nata, crema, *f*; *Eccl.* prima, *f*; (number) número primo, *m*. *vt* preparar, aprestar; (fire-arms) cebar. **p. the pump,** cebar la bomba; (with paint, etc.) imprimar; (instruct) dar instrucciones (a), informar. **in his p.,** en la flor de su edad. **of p. quality,** de primera calidad. **P. Minister,** Primer Ministro, *m*. **p. necessity,** artículo de primera necesidad, *m*

primer /'praimər/ *n* cartilla, *f*, abecedario, *m*; libro de lectura, *m*; (prayer book) devocionario, *m*

primeval /prai'mivəl/ *a* primevo, primitivo

priming /'praimıŋ/ *n* preparación, *f*; (of fire-arms) cebo, *m*; (of paint, etc.) imprimación, *f*; instrución, *f*

primitive /'prımıtıv/ *a* primitivo; anticuado. *n* primitivo, *m*

primitiveness /'prımıtıvnıs/ *n* lo primitivo; carácter primitivo, *m*

primly /'prımli/ *adv* afectadamente, con afectación; gravemente

primness /'prımnıs/ *n* afectación, *f*; gravedad, *f*

primogeniture /,praimə'dʒenıtʃər/ *n* primogenitura, *f*

primordial /prai'mɔrdiəl/ *a* primordial

primrose /'prım,rouz/ *n* *Bot.* vellorita, primavera, *f*; color amarillo pálido, *m*

prince /prıns/ *n* príncipe, *m*. **P. Consort,** príncipe consorte, *m*. **P. of Wales,** (Britain) príncipe heredero, *m*; (Spanish equivalent) Príncipe de Asturias, *m*. **p. regent,** príncipe regente, *m*. **P. Charming,** el Príncipe Azul, *m*

princeliness /'prınslınıs/ *n* magnificencia, *f*; nobleza, *f*

princely /'prınsli/ *a* principesco; magnífico; noble

princess /'prınsıs/ *n* princesa, *f*

principal /'prınsəpəl/ *a* principal; fundamental; mayor. *n* principal, jefe, *m*; (of a university) rector, *m*; (of a school) director (-ra); *Law.* causante, *m*; *Com.* capital, *m*

principality /,prınsə'pælıti/ *n* principado, *m*

principally /'prınsəpli/ *adv* principalmente

principle /'prınsəpəl/ *n* principio, *m*. **in p.,** en principio

principled /'prınsəpəld/ *a* de principios...

print /prınt/ *n* (mark) impresión, marca, *f*; (type) letra de molde, *f*, tipo, *m*; (of books) imprenta, *f*; (fabric) estampado, *m*; (picture) grabado, *m*; (photograph) positiva impresa, *f*; (mold) molde, *m*. *vt* marcar; imprimir; (on the mind) grabar; *Print.* imprimir, hacer una tirada (de); (in photography) tirar una prueba (de); (publish) sacar a luz, publicar; (fabrics) estampar. **in p.,** impreso; publicado; **He likes to see his name in print,** Le gusta ver su nombre en letras de molde; (available) existente. **to be out of p.,** estar agotado. **p. dress,** vestido estampado, *m*. **p. fabric,** estampado, *m*. **p. matter,** impresos, *m pl*

printer /'prıntər/ *n* impresor, *m*; tipógrafo, *m*. **printer's devil,** aprendiz de impresor, *m*. **printer's ink,** tinta de imprenta, tinta tipográfica, *f*. **printer's mark,** pie de imprenta, *m*

printing /'prıntıŋ/ *n* imprenta, *f*; impresión, *f*; (of fabrics) estampación, *f*; (art of) tipografía, *f*. **p. house,** imprenta, *f*. **p. machine,** máquina de imprimir, *f*. **p. press,** prensa tipográfica, *f*. **p. types,** caracteres de imprenta, *m pl*

prior /'praiər/ *n* prior, *m*, *a* anterior, previo. **p. to,** anterior a, antes de

prioress /'praiərıs/ *n* priora, *f*

priority /prai'ɔrıti/ *n* prioridad, *f*

prism /'prızəm/ *n* prisma, *m*; espectro solar, *m*

prismatic /prız'mætık/ *a* prismático

prison /'prızən/ *n* prisión, cárcel, *f*. **p.-breaking,** huida de la prisión, *f*. **p. camp,** campo de prisioneros, *m*. **p. van,** coche celular, *m*. **p. yard,** patio de la prisión, *m*

prisoner /'prızənər/ *n* prisionero (-ra), preso (-sa). **to take p.,** prender, hacer prisionero

pristine /'prıstin/ *a* pristino, original

privacy /'praivəsi/ *n* privacidad, soledad, *f*, aislamiento, retiro, *m*; intimidad, *f*; secreto, *m*

private /'praivıt/ *a* particular; privado; secreto; confidencial; reservado; íntimo; personal; doméstico; (of hearings, etc.) a puertas cerradas, secreto; (own) propio, *n* (soldier) soldado raso, *m*. **in p.,** en secreto; confidencialmente, de persona a persona. **They wish to be p.,** Quieren estar a solas. **p. company,** sociedad en comandita, *f*. **p. hotel,** pensión, *f*. **p. house,** casa particular, *f*. **p. individual,** particular, *mf*. **p. interview,** entrevista privada, *f*. **p. life,** vida privada, *f*. **p. office,** despacho particular, *m*. **p. secretary,** secretario (-ia) particular. **p. viewing, (of a film)** función privada, *f*; **(of an exhibition)** día de inauguración, *m*

privateer /,praivə'tıər/ *n* corsario, *m*

privately /'praivıtli/ *adv* privadamente; en secreto; personalmente; confidencialmente; (of hearings) a puertas cerradas

privation /praɪˈveɪʃən/ *n* privación, *f*; carencia, escasez, *f*

privet /ˈprɪvɪt/ *n* alheña, *f*

privilege /ˈprɪvəlɪdʒ/ *n* privilegio, *m*; derecho, *m*; inmunidad, *f. vt* privilegiar

privileged /ˈprɪvəlɪdʒd/ *a* privilegiado; confidencial

privy /ˈprɪvi/ *a* privado; cómplice; enterado; personal, particular. *n* (latrine) retrete, *m*. **p. council,** consejo privado, *m*

prize /praɪz/ *n* premio, *m*; recompensa, *f*, galardón, *m*; (capture) presa, *f. a* que ha ganado un premio; premiado; (huge) enorme; (complete) de primer orden. *vt* estimar, apreciar. **to p. open,** abrir con una palanca. **to carry off the p.,** ganar el premio. **cash p.,** premio en metálico, *m*. **first p.,** primer premio, *m*; (in a lottery) premio gordo, *m*. **p. court,** tribunal de presas, *m*. **p. fight,** partido de boxeo, *m*. **p. fighter,** boxeador, *m*. **p. giving,** distribución de premios, *f*. **p. money,** premio en metálico, *m*; (boxing) bolsa, *f*

pro /prou/ *prep* pro. **pro forma invoice,** factura simulada, *f*

probability /ˌprɒbəˈbɪlɪti/ *n* probabilidad, *f*

probable /ˈprɒbəbəl/ *a* probable

probably /ˈprɒbəbli/ *adv* probablemente

probate /ˈproubeɪt/ *n* verificación de un testamento, *f*

probation /prouˈbeɪʃən/ *n* probación, *f*; *Law.* libertad vigilada, *f*

probationary /prouˈbeɪʃəˌnɛri/ *a* de probación; de prueba

probationer /prouˈbeɪʃənər/ *n* novicio, *m*; estudiante de enfermera, *f*; candidato, *m*; aspirante, *m*

probe /proub/ *n Surg.* sonda, cala, tienta, *f. vt Surg.* tentar; escudriñar

probing /ˈproubɪŋ/ *n* sondeo, *m*

probity /ˈproubɪti/ *n* probidad, integridad, *f*

problem /ˈprɒbləm/ *n* problema, *m*; cuestión, *f. a* **p. play,** drama de tesis, *m*

problematic /ˌprɒbləˈmætɪk/ *a* problemático

problem child *n* niño problemático, *m* (male), niña problemática, *f* (female)

proboscis /prouˈbɒsɪs/ *n* (of an elephant) trompa, *f*; (of an insect) trompetilla, *f*

Probus /ˈproubəs/ Probo, *m*

procedure /prəˈsidʒər/ *n* procedimiento, *m*

proceed /prəˈsid/ *vi* seguir el camino, continuar la marcha; avanzar; seguir adelante; ir; proceder; ponerse (a); empezar (a); (say) proseguir; (come to) llegar a, ir a; (of a play, etc.) desarrollarse. **Before we p. any further...** Antes de ir más lejos... **to p. to blows,** llegar a las manos. **to p. against,** proceder contra, procesar. **to p. from,** venir de. **to p. with,** proseguir; poner por obra; usar

proceeding /prəˈsidɪŋ/ *n* modo de obrar, *m*; conducta, *f*; procedimiento, *m*; transacción, *f*; *pl*

proceedings, (measures) medidas, *f pl*, actos, *m pl*; (of a learned society or a conference) actas, *f pl.* **to take proceedings against,** *Law.* procesar

proceeds /ˈprousidz/ *n pl* producto, *m*; ganancias, *f pl*; beneficios, *m pl.* **net p.,** producto neto, *m*

process /ˈprɒsɛs/ *n* proceso, *m*; (method) procedimiento, *m*; (course) curso, *m*; marcha, *f*; (*Law., Zool.*) proceso, *m. vt* beneficiar (ore), trasformar, elaborar. **in p. of,** en curso de. **in the p. of time,** con el tiempo marchando el tiempo

processing industry /ˈprɒsɛsɪŋ/ *n* industria de trasformación, industria de elaboración, *f*

procession /prəˈsɛʃən/ *n* desfile, *m*; cortejo, *m*; (religious) procesión, *f.* **funeral p.,** cortejo fúnebre, *m.* **to walk in p.,** desfilar

processional /prəˈsɛʃənl/ *a* procesional

proclaim /prouˈkleɪm/ *vt* proclamar; publicar, pregonar; anunciar; (reveal) revelar; (outlaw) denunciar

proclamation /ˌprɒkləˈmeɪʃən/ *n* proclamación, *f*; proclama, *f*, anuncio, *m*; declaración, *f*

proclivity /prouˈklɪvɪti/ *n* proclividad, propensión, *f*

procrastinate /prouˈkræstəˌneɪt/ *vi* tardar (en decidirse), aplazar su decisión; vacilar; perder el tiempo

procrastination /prouˌkræstəˈneɪʃən/ *n* dilación, tardanza, *f*; vacilación, *f*; pereza, *f*

procrastinator /prouˈkræstəˌneɪtər/ *n* perezoso (-sa)

procreate /ˈproukriˌeɪt/ *vt* procrear

procreation /ˌproukriˈeɪʃən/ *n* procreación, *f*

procreator /ˈproukriˌeɪtər/ *n* procreador (-ra)

proctor /ˈprɒktər/ *n* procurador, *m*; *Educ.* censor, *m*

procurable /prouˈkyʊrəbəl/ *a* procurable; asequible

procure /prouˈkyʊr/ *vt* obtener, conseguir, lograr

procurement /prouˈkyʊrmənt/ *n* obtención, *f*, logro, *m*

procurer /prouˈkyʊrər/ *n* alcahuete, *m*

procuress /prouˈkyʊrɪs/ *n* alcahueta, celestina, trotaconventos, *f*

prod /prɒd/ *n* (with a bayonet, etc.) punzada, *f*; *Fig.* pinchazo, *m. vt* punzar; (in the ribs, etc.) clavar; *Fig.* pinchar

prodigal /ˈprɒdɪɡəl/ *a and n* pródigo (-ga)

prodigality /ˌprɒdɪˈɡælɪti/ *n* prodigalidad, *f*

prodigally /ˈprɒdɪɡəli/ *adv* pródigamente

prodigious /prəˈdɪdʒəs/ *a* prodigioso

prodigiousness /prəˈdɪdʒəsnɪs/ *n* prodigiosidad, *f*; enormidad, *f*

prodigy /ˈprɒdɪdʒi/ *n* prodigio, *m*; portento, *m*. **child p.,** niño prodigio

produce /*v.* prəˈdus; *n.* ˈprɒdus, ˈproudus/ *vt* producir; dar frutos; (show) mostrar, presentar; (take out) sacar; (occasion) causar, traer consigo, ocasionar; (goods) fabricar, manufacturar; (of shares, etc.) rendir; *Geom.* prolongar; (a play) poner en escena. *n* producto, *m*; víveres, comestibles, *m pl*

producer /prəˈdusər/ *n* productor (-ra); *Theat.* director de escena, *m*

product /ˈprɒdəkt/ *n* producto, *m*; (result) fruto, resultado, *m*, consecuencia, *f*; *Math.* producto, *m*

production /prəˈdʌkʃən/ *n* producción, *f*; producto, *m*; *Geom.* prolongación, *f*; (of a play) dirección escénica, *f*; (performance) producción, *f.* **p. cost,** coste de producción, *m*

productive /prəˈdʌktɪv/ *a* productivo

productivity /ˌproudʌkˈtɪvɪti/ *n* productividad, *f*

profanation /ˌprɒfəˈneɪʃən/ *n* profanación, *f*

profane /prəˈfeɪn/ *a* profano; sacrílego, blasfemo. *vt* profanar

profaner /prəˈfeɪnər/ *n* profanador (-ra)

profanity /prəˈfænɪti/ *n* profanidad, *f*; blasfemia, *f*

profess /prəˈfɛs/ *vt* (assert) afirmar, manifestar; declarar; (a faith, a profession, teach) profesar; (feign) fingir; (pretend) tener pretensiones de. *vi* (as a monk or nun) tomar estado, entrar en religión. **He professed himself surprised,** Se declaró sorprendido

professed /prəˈfɛst/ *a* declarado; *Eccl.* profeso; ostensible, fingido

profession /prəˈfɛʃən/ *n* profesión, *f*; carrera, *f*; declaración, *f.* **p. of faith,** profesión de fe, *f.* **the learned professions,** las carreras liberales

professional /prəˈfɛʃənl/ *a* profesional; de la profesión; de profesión; de carrera. **p. diplomat,** diplomático (-ca) de carrera. **p. etiquette,** etiqueta profesional, *f.* **p. man,** hombre profesional, *m*; hombre de carrera liberal, *m*

professor /prəˈfɛsər/ *n* catedrático (-ca), profesor (-ra)

professorate /prəˈfɛsərɪt/ *n* profesorado, *m*

professorial /ˌproufəˈsɔriəl/ *a* de catedrático; de profesor

professorship /prəˈfɛsərˌʃɪp/ *n* cátedra, *f*

proffer /ˈprɒfər/ *vt* proponer; ofrecer. *n* oferta, *f*

proficiency /prəˈfɪʃənsi/ *n* pericia, habilidad, *f*

proficient /prəˈfɪʃənt/ *a* proficiente, experto, adepto, perito

profile /ˈproufaɪl/ *n* perfil, *m. vt* perfilar. **in p.,** de perfil

profit /ˈprɒfɪt/ *n* provecho, *m*; utilidad, *f*; ventaja, *f*; *Com.* ganancia, *f*, lucro, *m*, *vt* aprovechar. *vi* ganar; *Com.* sacar ganancia. **to p. by,** aprovechar. **gross p.,** ganancia total, *f.* **p. and loss,** lucros y daños, *f pl.* **p. sharing,** participación en las ganancias, participación de utilidades, *f.* **non-p. organization,** compañía sin fines de lucro

profitable /ˈprɒfɪtəbəl/ *a* provechoso, útil, ventajoso; lucrativo. **p. use,** aprovechamiento, *m*

profitably /ˈprɒfɪtəbli/ *adv* con provecho, provechosamente; lucrativamente

profiteer /ˌprɒfɪˈtɪər/ *n* estraperlista, *mf*

profit incentive *n* acicate del lucro, *m*
profitless /'prɒfɪtlɪs/ *a* sin provecho, infructuoso, inútil
profligacy /'prɒflɪgəsɪ/ *n* libertinaje, *m*
profligate /'prɒflɪgɪt/ *a* licencioso, disoluto. *n* libertino, *m*
profound /prə'faund/ *a* profundo
profundity /prə'fʌndɪtɪ/ *n* profundidad, *f*
profuse /prə'fyus/ *a* profuso; pródigo; lujoso
profusely /prə'fyuslɪ/ *adv* profusamente; pródigamente; lujosamente
profusion /prə'fyuʒən/ *n* profusión, abundancia, *f*; prodigalidad, *f*; exceso, *m*
progenitor /prou'dʒɛnɪtər/ *n* progenitor, *m*; (ancestor) antepasado, *m*
progeny /'prɒdʒənɪ/ *n* prole, *f*
prognosis /prɒg'nousɪs/ *n* prognosis, *f*; presagio, *m*; *Med.* pronóstico, *m*
prognosticate /prɒg'nɒstɪ,keit/ *vt* pronosticar, presagiar
prognostication /prɒg,nɒstɪ'keiʃən/ *n* pronosticación, *f*; pronóstico, presagio, augurio, *m*
program /'prougræm/ *n* programa, *m*
programmer /'prougræmər/ *n* programador (-ra)
progress /*n*. 'prɒgrɛs/ *v*. prə'grɛs/ *n* progreso, *m*; avance, *m*; (betterment) mejora, *f*, (of events) marcha, *f*. *vi* avanzar, marchar; (improve) progresar, adelantar; mejorar. **to make p.,** adelantarse; hacer progresos
progression /prə'grɛʃən/ *n* progresión, *f*
progressive /prə'grɛsɪv/ *a* progresivo; avanzado; *Polit.* progresista. *n Polit.* progresista, *mf*
progressiveness /prə'grɛsɪvnɪs/ *n* carácter progresivo, *m*
prohibit /prou'hɪbɪt/ *vt* prohibir; defender; (prevent) impedir, privar. **His health prohibited him from doing it,** Su salud le impidió hacerlo
prohibition /,prouə'bɪʃən/ *n* prohibición, *f*; interdicción, *f*; (of alcohol) prohibicionismo, *m*
prohibitionist /,prouə'bɪʃənɪst/ *n* prohibicionista, *mf*
prohibitive /prou'hɪbɪtɪv/ *a* prohibitivo, prohibitorio
project /*v*. prə'dʒɛkt; *n*. 'prɒdʒɛkt/ *vt* (all meanings) proyectar. *vi* sobresalir; destacarse. *n* proyectil, plan, *m*
projectile /prə'dʒɛktɪl/ *n* proyectil, *m*, *a* arrojadizo
projecting /prə'dʒɛktɪŋ/ *a* saliente; (of teeth) saltón
projection /prə'dʒɛkʃən/ *n* (hurling) lanzamiento, *m*; prominencia, protuberancia, *f*; (other meanings) proyección, *f*
projector /prə'dʒɛktər/ *n* proyectista, *mf*; proyector, *m*
proletarian /,proulɪ'tɛarɪən/ *a* proletario
proletariate /,proulɪ'tɛarɪɪt/ *n* proletariado, *m*
prolific /prə'lɪfɪk/ *a* prolífico; fecundo, fértil
prolix /prou'lɪks/ *a* prolijo
prolixity /prou'lɪksɪtɪ/ *n* prolijidad, *f*
prolog /'prou,lɒg/ *n* prólogo, *m*, *vt* prologar
prolong /prə'lɒŋ/ *vt* prolongar
prolongation /,proulɒŋ'geiʃən/ *n* prolongación, *f*
promenade /,prɒmə'neid, -'nɑd/ *n* paseo, *m*; bulevar, *m*; avenida, *f*. *vi* pasearse. *vt* recorrer, andar por, pasearse por. **p. deck,** cubierta de paseo, *f*
Promethean /prə'miθiən/ *a* de Prometeo
prominence /'prɒmənəns/ *n* prominencia, *f*; protuberancia, *f*; eminencia, *f*; importancia, *f*
prominent /'prɒmənənt/ *a* prominente, saliente; (of eyes, teeth) saltón; (distinguished) eminente, distinguido. **They placed the vase in a p. position,** Pusieron el florero muy a la vista. **to play a p. part,** desempeñar un papel importante. **p. eyes, ojos** saltones, *m pl*
promiscuous /prə'mɪskyuəs/ *a* promiscuo
promiscuousness /prə'mɪskyuəsnɪs/ *n* promiscuidad, *f*
promise /'prɒmɪs/ *n* promesa, *f*; (hope) esperanza, *f*; (word) palabra, *f*; (future) porvenir, *m*. *vt* and *vi* prometer. **a young man of p.,** un joven de porvenir. **to break one's p.,** faltar a su palabra; no cumplir una promesa. **to keep one's p.,** guardar su palabra; cumplir su promesa. **to p. and do nothing,** apuntar y no

dar. **under p. of,** bajo palabra de. **p. of marriage,** palabra de matrimonio, *f*
promised /'prɒmɪst/ *a* prometido. **P. Land,** Tierra de promisión, *f*
promising /'prɒməsɪŋ/ *a* que promete bien, que promete mucho; prometedor; (of the future, etc.) halagüeño; (of persons) que llegará
promissory /'prɒmə,sɔrɪ/ *a* promisorio. **p. note,** pagaré, abonaré, *m*
promontory /'prɒmən,tɔrɪ/ *n* promontorio, *m*
promote /prə'mout/ *vt* fomentar, promover; provocar; (aid) favorecer, proteger; avanzar; estimular; (to a post) ascender; (an act bill) promover; *Com.* negociar
promoter /prə'moutər/ *n* promotor (-ra); instigador (-ra); (*Theat.* etc.) empresario, *m*
promotion /prə'mouʃən/ *n* (encouragement) fomento, *m*; (furtherance) adelanto, *m*; protección, *f*, favorecimiento, *m*; (in employment, etc.) promoción, *f*, ascenso, *m*; (of a company, etc.) creación, *f*
prompt /prɒmpt/ *a* pronto; diligente; presuroso; puntual; rápido; *Com.* inmediato. *vt* impulsar, incitar, mover; dictar; insinuar; *Theat.* apuntar; (remind) recordar. **He came at five o'clock p.,** Vino a las cinco en punto. **p. book,** libro del traspunte, *m*. **p. box,** concha (del apuntador), *f*
prompter /'prɒmptər/ *n Theat.* apuntador, (in the wings) traspunte, *m*
prompting /'prɒmptɪŋ/ *n* sugestión, *f*; instigación, *f*; *pl* **promptings,** impulso, *m*; (of the heart, etc.) dictados, *m pl*
promptitude /'prɒmptɪ,tud/ *n* prontitud, presteza, *f*; prisa, expedición, *f*; puntualidad, *f*
promptly /'prɒmptlɪ/ *adv* inmediatamente, en seguida; con prontitud, con celeridad; puntualmente
promptness /'prɒmptnɪs/ *n* See **promptitude**
promulgate /'prɒməl,geit/ *vt* promulgar; divulgar, diseminar
promulgation /'prɒməl'geiʃən/ *n* promulgación, *f*; divulgación, diseminación, *f*
prone /proun/ *a* postrado; inclinado, propenso
proneness /'prounɪs/ *n* postración, *f*; inclinación, tendencia, propensión, *f*
prong /prɒŋ/ *n* (pitchfork) horquilla, *f*; (of a fork) diente, *m*, púa, *f*
pronged /prɒŋd/ *a* dentado, con púas
pronoun /'prou,naun/ *n* pronombre, *m*
pronounce /prə'nauns/ *vt* pronunciar; declarar; articular
pronounced /prə'naunst/ *a* marcado; perceptible; bien definido
pronouncement /prə'naunsmənt/ *n* pronunciamiento, *m*
pronunciation /prə,nʌnsi'eiʃən/ *n* pronunciación, *f*; articulación, *f*
proof /pruf/ *n* prueba, *f*; demostración, *f*; ensayo, *m*; *Law.* testimonio, *m*; (*Photo. Print.*) prueba, *f*; *Math.* comprobación, *f*, a hecho a prueba (de); impenetrable (a); *Fig.* insensible (a). *vt* (raincoats, etc.) impermeabilizar. **in p. whereof,** en fe de lo cual. **p. against bombs,** a prueba de bombas. **p. reading,** corrección de pruebas, *f*
prop /prɒp/ *n* apoyo, puntal, estribadero, *m*; (for a tree) horca, *f*, rodrigón, *m*; *Naut.* escora, *f*, *Fig.* báculo, *m*, columna, *f*, apoyo, *m*. *vt* apoyar; apuntalar; (a tree) ahorquillar; (a building) acodalar; *Naut.* escorar; *Fig.* sostener. **He propped himself against the wall,** Se apoyó en el muro, Se arrimó al muro
propaganda /,prɒpə'gændə/ *n* propaganda, *f*
propagandist /,prɒpə'gændɪst/ *n* propagandista, *mf*
propagate /'prɒpə,geit/ *vt* propagar. *vi* propagarse
propagation /,prɒpə'geiʃən/ *n* propagación, *f*
propagator /'prɒpə,geitər/ *n* propagador (-ra)
propel /prə'pɛl/ *vt* propulsar, empujar, mover
propeller /prə'pɛlər/ *n* propulsor, *m*; *Mech.* hélice, *f*
propelling /prə'pɛlɪŋ/ *n* propulsión (a), *f*. **p. pencil,** lapicero, *m*
propensity /prə'pɛnsɪtɪ/ *n* propensión, tendencia, inclinación, *f*
proper /'prɒpər/ *a* propio; apropiado; correcto; decente; (prim) afectado; serio, formal; (exact) justo,

exacto; (suitable (for)) bueno (para), apto (para); (true) verdadero; (characteristic) peculiar; *Herald.* natural; (with rascal, etc.) redomado; (handsome) guapo. **If you think it p.,** Si te parece bien. **p. noun,** nombre propio, *m*
properly /'prɒpərli/ *adv* decentemente; correctamente; propiamente; bien. **to do (a thing) p.,** hacer algo bien. **p. speaking,** propiamente dicho, hablando con propiedad
propertied /'prɒpərtid/ *a* propietario, hacendado; (rich) pudiente, adinerado
property /'prɒpərti/ *n* propiedad, *f*; (belongings) bienes, *m pl*; posesiones, *f pl*; (estate) hacienda, *f*; (quality) cualidad, *f*; *pl* **properties,** *Theat.* accesorios, *m pl.* **personal p.,** bienes muebles, *m pl*; cosas personales, *f pl.* **real p.,** bienes raíces, *m pl.* **p. man,** *Theat.* encargado de los accesorios, *m.* **p. owner,** propietario (-ia). **p. tax,** contribución sobre la propiedad, *f*
prophecy /'prɒfəsi/ *n* profecía, *f*; predicción, *f*
prophesier /'prɒfə,siər/ *n* See **prophet**
prophesy /'prɒfə,sai/ *vt* profetizar; presagiar, predecir. *vi* hacer profecías
prophet /'prɒfit/ *n* profeta, *m*
prophetess /'prɒfitis/ *n* profetisa, *f*
prophetic /prə'fɛtɪk/ *a* profético
prophylactic /,proufə'læktɪk/ *a* and *n* profiláctico, *m*
propinquity /prou'pɪŋkwɪti/ *n* propincuidad, proximidad, *f*; (relationship) parentesco, *m*
propitiate /prə'pɪʃi,eit/ *vt* propiciar; apaciguar, conciliar
propitiation /prə,pɪʃi'eiʃən/ *n* propiciación, *f*
propitiator /prə'pɪʃi,eitər/ *n* propiciador (-ra)
propitiatory /prə'pɪʃiə,tɔri/ *a* propiciador
propitious /prə'pɪʃəs/ *a* propicio, favorable
propitiousness /prə'pɪʃəsnɪs/ *n* lo propicio
proportion /prə'pɔrʃən/ *n* proporción, *f*; parte, *f*; porción, *f*; *pl* **proportions,** proporciones, *f pl*; dimensiones, *f pl.* *vt* proporcionar; repartir, distribuir. **in p.,** en proporción; conforme (a), según; *Com.* a prorrata. **in p. as,** a medida que. **out of p.,** desproporcionado. **He has lost all sense of p.,** Ha perdido su equilibrio (mental)
proportional /prə'pɔrʃənḷ/ *a* proporcional; en proporción (a); proporcionado (a). **p. representation,** representación proporcional, *f*
proportionally /prə'pɔrʃənḷi/ *adv* proporcionalmente, en proporción
proportionate /*a.* prə'pɔrʃənɪt; *v.* -,neit/ *a* proporcionado; proporcional. *vt* proporcionar
proportionately /prə'pɔrʃənɪtli/ *adv* See **proportionally**
proposal /prə'pouzəl/ *n* proposición, *f*; oferta, *f*; (plan) propósito, proyecto, *m.* **p. of marriage,** oferta de matrimonio, *f*
propose /prə'pouz/ *vt* proponer; ofrecer; (a toast) dar, brindar. *vi* pretender, intentar, tener la intención de; pensar; (marriage) declararse
proposer /prə'pouzər/ *n* proponente, *m*; (of a motion) autor (-ra) de una proposición
proposition /,prɒpə'zɪʃən/ *n* proposición, *f*; (plan) proyecto, propósito, *m*
propound /prə'paund/ *vt* proponer; plantear, presentar
proprietary /prə'praiɪ,tɛri/ *a* propietario; de propiedad
proprietor /prə'praiɪtər/ *n* propietario, *m*; dueño, *m*
proprietorship /prə'praiɪtərˌʃɪp/ *n* propiedad, pertenencia, *f*
proprietress /prə'praiɪtrɪs/ *n* propietaria, *f*; dueña, *f*
propriety /prə'praiɪti/ *n* decoro, *m*; conveniencia, *f*; corrección, *f*
propulsion /prə'pʌlʃən/ *n* propulsión, *f*
propulsive /prə'pʌlsɪv/ *a* propulsor
prorogation /,prourou'geiʃən/ *n* prorrogación, *f*
prorogue /prou'roug/ *vt* prorrogar, suspender (la sesión de una asamblea legislativa)
prosaic /prou'zeiɪk/ *a* prosaico
pros and cons /'prouz ən 'kɒnz/ el pro y el contra
proscenium /prou'siniəm/ *n* proscenio, *m*

proscribe /prou'skraib/ *vt* proscribir
proscription /prou'skrɪpʃən/ *n* proscripción, *f*
prose /prouz/ *n* prosa, *f.* **p. writer,** prosista, *mf*
prosecute /'prɒsɪ,kyut/ *vt* proseguir, llevar adelante; (*Law.* a person) procesar; (*Law.* a claim) pedir en juicio
prosecution /,prɒsɪ'kyuʃən/ *n* prosecución, *f*; cumplimiento, *m*; *Law.* acusación, *f*; (*Law.* party) parte actora, *f.* **in the p. of his duty,** en el cumplimiento de su deber
prosecutor /'prɒsɪ,kyutər/ *n* demandante, actor, *m.* **public p.,** fiscal, *m*
proselyte /'prɒsə,lait/ *n* prosélito, *m*
proselytism /'prɒsəlɪ,tɪzəm/ *n* proselitismo, *m*
prose writer *n* prosador, *m*
prosody /'prɒsədi/ *n* prosodia, *f*
prospect /'prɒspɛkt/ *n* perspectiva, *f*; esperanza, *f*; probabilidad, *f*; (in mining) indicio de filón, *m*; criadero (de oro, etc.), *m.* *vi* explorar; (of a mine) prometer (bien), dar buenas esperanzas. *vt* explorar, inspeccionar; examinar. **He is a man with good prospects,** Es un hombre de porvenir
prospecting /'prɒspɛktɪŋ/ *n* la prospección, *f*
prospective /prə'spɛktɪv/ *a* en expectativa, futuro; previsor
prospector /'prɒspɛktər/ *n* explorador, operador, *m*
prospectus /prə'spɛktəs/ *n* prospecto, programa, *m*
prosper /'prɒspər/ *vi* prosperar. *vt* favorecer, prosperar
prosperity /prɒ'spɛrɪti/ *n* prosperidad, *f*
prosperous /'prɒspərəs/ *a* próspero; favorable
prostate /'prɒsteit/ *n* próstata, *f*
prostitute /'prɒstɪ,tut/ *n* prostituta, *f*, *vt* prostituir
prostitution /,prɒstɪ'tuʃən/ *n* prostitución, *f*
prostrate /'prɒstreit/ *a* tendido; postrado; abatido. *vt* derribar; arruinar; (by grief, etc.) postrar; (oneself) postrarse
prostration /prɒ'streiʃən/ *n* postración, *f*; abatimiento, *m.* **nervous p.,** neurastenia, *f*
protagonist /prou'tægənɪst/ *n* protagonista, *mf*
protean /'proutiən/ *a* proteico
protect /prə'tɛkt/ *vt* proteger
protection /prə'tɛkʃən/ *n* protección, *f*; defensa, *f*; garantía, *f*; abrigo, *m*; refugio, *m*; (passport) salvoconducto, *m*; *Polit.* proteccionismo, *m*
protectionism /prə'tɛkʃə,nɪzəm/ *n* proteccionismo, *m*
protectionist /prə'tɛkʃənɪst/ *n* proteccionista, *mf*
protective /prə'tɛktɪv/ *a* protector; *Polit.* proteccionista
protector /prə'tɛktər/ *n* protector, *m*
protectorate /prə'tɛktərɪt/ *n* protectorado, *f*
protectress /prou'tɛktrɪs/ *n* protectriz, *f*
protégé /'proutə,ʒei/ *n* protegido (-da)
protein /'proutin, -tiɪn/ *n* proteína, *f*
protest /*v.* prə'tɛst, 'proutɛst; *n.* 'proutɛst/ *vt* protestar; *Law.* hacer el protesto de una letra de cambio. *vi* declarar; insistir (en); hacer una protesta. *n* protesta, *f*; *Law.* protesto, *m.* **under p.,** bajo protesta. **to p. against,** protestar contra
Protestant /'prɒtəstənt/ *a* and *n* protestante, *mf*
Protestantism /'prɒtəstən,tɪzəm/ *n* protestantismo, *m*
protestation /,proutɛ'steiʃən/ *n* protestación, *f*
protester /'proutɛstər/ *n* el, *m*, (*f*, la) que protesta
protest literature *n* literatura de denuncia, *f*
protocol /'proutə,kɒl/ *n* protocolo, *m*, *vt* protocolizar
protoplasm /'proutə,plæzəm/ *n* protoplasma, *m*
prototype /'proutə,taip/ *n* prototipo, *m*
protract /prou'trækt/ *vt* prolongar; dilatar
protracted /prou'træktɪd/ *a* prolongado; largo
protraction /prou'trækʃən/ *n* prolongación, *f*
protractor /prou'træktər/ *n* (*Geom.* and *Surv.*) transportador, *m.* **p. muscle,** músculo extensor, *m*
protrude /prou'trud/ *vt* sacar fuera. *vi* salir fuera; sobresalir
protuberance /prou'tubərəns/ *n* protuberancia, *f*
protuberant /prou'tubərənt/ *a* protuberante, prominente
proud /praud/ *a* orgulloso; arrogante; noble; glorioso; magnífico; soberbio, *Mexico* alzado. **to be p.,** enorgullecerse. **to make p.,** enorgullecer; hacer

orgulloso. **to be p. of,** ser orgulloso de, pagarse de, gloriarse en

proudly /'praudli/ *adv* con orgullo, orgullosamente

provable /'pruvəbəl/ *a* demostrable

prove /pruv/ *vt* probar; demostrar; (experience) experimentar, sufrir; poner a prueba; (a will) verificar; (show) mostrar; confirmar. *vi* resultar, salir (bien o mal)

provenance /'provənəns/ *n* origen, *m*

Provençal /ˌprouvən'sɑl, ˌprɔvɑ̃-/ *a* provenzal. *n* provenzal, *mf;* (language) provenzal, *m*

Provence /prə'vɑns/ Provenza, *f*

provender /'provəndər/ *n* forraje, *m; Inf.* provisiones, *f pl*

proverb /'provɜrb/ *n* refrán, *m;* proverbio, *m.* **collection of proverbs,** refranero, *m.* **Book of Proverbs,** Proverbios, *m pl*

proverbial /prə'vɜrbiəl/ *a* proverbial

proverbially /prə'vɜrbiəli/ *adv* proverbialmente

provide /prə'vaid/ *vt* proporcionar, dar; proveer, surtir, suplir; (stipulate) estipular; preparar (por); tomar precauciones (contra); sufragar los gastos (de); proporcionar medios de vida (a); señalar una pensión (a). **to p. oneself with,** proveerse de

provided (that) /prə'vaidid/ *conjunc* si; a condición de que, siempre que, con tal que

providence /'providəns/ *n* providencia, *f*

provident /'providənt/ *a* próvido, previsor, prudente; económico

providential /ˌprovi'dɛnʃəl/ *a* providencial

providentially /ˌprovi'dɛnʃəli/ *adv* providencialmente

providently /'providəntli/ *adv* próvidamente, prudentemente

provider /prə'vaidər/ *n* proveedor (-ra)

province /'provins/ *n* provincia, *f;* esfera, *f;* función, incumbencia, *f*

provincial /prə'vinʃəl/ *a* provincial, de provincia; provinciano. *n* provinciano (-na); *Eccl.* provincial, *m*

provincialism /prə'vinʃəˌlizəm/ *n* provincialismo, *m*

provision /prə'viʒən/ *n* provisión, *f;* (stipulation) estipulación, *f; pl* **provisions,** provisiones, *f pl;* víveres, comestibles, *m pl. vt* abastecer, aprovisionar. **to make p. for,** hacer provisión para, proveer de. **to make p. for one's family,** asegurar el porvenir de su familia. **p. merchant,** vendedor (-ra) de comestibles

provisional /prə'viʒənl/ *a* provisional, interino

provisioning /prə'viʒəniŋ/ *n* aprovisionamiento, abastecimiento, *m*

proviso /prə'vaizou/ *n* condición, estipulación, disposición, *f*

provisory /prə'vaizəri/ *a* provisional; condicional

provocation /ˌprovə'keiʃən/ *n* provocación, *f*

provocative /prə'vɒkətiv/ *a* provocativo, provocador

provocatively /prə'vɒkətivli/ *adv* de un modo provocativo

provoke /prə'vouk/ *vt* provocar; suscitar; incitar, excitar; (irritate) sacar de madre (a), indignar

provoker /prə'voukər/ *n* provocador (-ra); instigador (-ra)

provoking /prə'voukiŋ/ *a* provocativo; (irritating) enojoso, irritante

provost /'prouvoust *or, esp. in military usage,* 'prouvou/ *n* preboste, *m;* (of a college) director, *m;* (in Scotland) alcalde, *m.* **p.-marshal,** capitán preboste, *m*

prow /prau/ *n* proa, *f*

prowess /'prauis/ *n* valor, *m,* destreza, *f;* proeza, *f*

prowl /praul/ *vi* and *vt* rondar; cazar al acecho

prowler /'praulər/ *n* rondador (-ra); ladrón (-ona)

proximity /prok'simiti/ *n* proximidad, *Argentina* adyacencia, *f*

proxy /'proksi/ *n* poder, *m;* delegación, *f;* apoderado, *m;* delegado (-da); substituto (-ta). **to be married by p.,** casarse por poderes

prude /prud/ *n* mojigata, beata, *f*

prudence /'prudns/ *n* prudencia, *f*

prudent /'prudnt/ *a* prudente

prudently /'prudntli/ *adv* con prudencia

prudery /'prudəri/ *n* mojigatería, beatería, damería, gazmoñería, *f*

prudish /'prudiʃ/ *a* mojigato, gazmoño, remilgado

prune /prun/ *n* ciruela pasa, *f;* color de ciruela, *m, vt* podar; (cut) cortar; reducir

pruning /'pruniŋ/ *n* poda, *f;* reducción, *f.* **p. knife,** podadera, *f*

prurient /'pruriənt/ *a* lascivo, lujurioso, salaz

prussic acid /'prʌsik/ *n* acido prúsico, *m*

pry /prai/ *vi* escudriñar; acechar, espiar, fisgonear; (meddle) entremeterse, meterse donde no le llaman. *vt* See **prize**

prying /'praiiŋ/ *n* fisgoneo, *m;* curiosidad, *f, a* fisgón, curioso

psalm /sɑm/ *n* salmo, *m.* **to sing psalms,** salmodiar

psalmist /'sɑmist/ *n* salmista, *m*

psaltery /'sɔltəri/ *n* salterio, *m*

pseudo- *a* seudo. **p.-learned,** erudito a la violeta

pseudonym /'sudnim/ *n* seudónimo, *m*

psychiatrist /si'kaiətrist, sai-/ *n* sicoanalista, *m*

psychiatry /si'kaiətri, sai-/ *n* siquiatría, *f*

psychic /'saikik/ *a* síquico

psychoanalysis /ˌsaikouə'næləsis/ *n* sicoanálisis, *m*

psychoanalyst /ˌsaikou'ænlist/ *n* sicoanalista, *mf*

psychoanalyze /ˌsaikou'ænlˌaiz/ *vt* sicoanalizar

psychological /ˌsaikə'lodʒikəl/ *a* sicológico

psychologist /sai'kolədʒist/ *n* sicólogo (-ga)

psychology /sai'kolədʒi/ *n* sicología, *f*

psychopathic /ˌsaikə'pæθik/ *a* sicopático

psychosis /sai'kousis/ *n* sicosis, *f*

psychotherapy /ˌsaikou'θɛrəpi/ *n* sicoterapia, *f*

ptomaine poisoning /'toumein/ *n* intoxicación por tomaínas, *f*

puberty /'pyubərti/ *n* pubertad, *f*

pubescent /pyu'besənt/ *a* púber

pubic /'pyubik/ *a* púbico

pubis /'pyubis/ *n* pubis, *m*

public /'pʌblik/ *a* and *n* público *m.* **in p.,** en público. **p. assistance,** asistencia pública, *f.* **p. funds,** hacienda pública, *f.* **p. health,** higiene pública, *f.* **p.-house,** taberna, *f.* **p. opinion,** opinión pública, *f. Inf.* el qué dirán. **p.-spirited,** patriótico. **p. thoroughfare,** vía pública, *f.* **p. works,** obras públicas, *f pl*

publican /'pʌblikən/ *n* tabernero, *m*

publication /ˌpʌbli'keiʃən/ *n* publicación, *f*

publicist /'pʌbləsist/ *n* publicista, *mf*

publicity /pʌ'blisiti/ *n* publicidad, *f*

publicity agent *n* publicista, *mf*

publish /'pʌbliʃ/ *vt* publicar, divulgar, difundir; (a book, etc.) dar a luz, dar a la prensa, publicar; (of a publisher) editar. **to p. abroad,** pregonar a los cuatro vientos. **to p. banns of marriage,** correr las amonestaciones

publisher /'pʌbliʃər/ *n* publicador (-ra); (of books) editor (-ra)

publishing /'pʌbliʃiŋ/ *n* publicación, *f.* **p. house,** casa editorial, *f.* **the p. world,** el mundo de la edición, *m*

puck /pʌk/ *n* trasgo, *m;* diablillo, picaruelo, *m*

pucker /'pʌkər/ *vt* (one's brow, etc.) fruncir; (crease) arrugar. *vi* arrugarse. *n* frunce, *m;* arruga, *f;* (fold) bolsa, *f*

puckering /'pʌkəriŋ/ *n* fruncido, *m;* arrugas, *f pl*

puckish /'pʌkiʃ/ *a* travieso

pudding /'pudiŋ/ *n* pudín, budín, *m.* **black p.,** morcilla, *f*

puddle /'pʌdl/ *n* charco, *m*

puerile /'pyuəril/ *a* pueril

puerperal /pyu'ɜrpərəl/ *a* puerperal. **p. fever,** fiebre puerperal, *f*

Puerto Rican /'pwɛrtə 'rikən, 'pɔr-/ *a* and *n* puertorriqueño (-ña), *a* boricua, *n* borinqueño (-ña)

Puerto Rico /'pwɛrtə 'rikou/ Puerto Rico *m*

puff /pʌf/ *vt* and *vi* (blow) soplar; (at a pipe, etc.) chupar; (smoke) lanzar bocanadas de humo; (make pant) hacer jadear; (advertise) dar bombo a; (distend) hinchar; (make conceited) envanecerse; (of a train, etc.) bufar; resoplar. *n* soplo, *m;* (of smoke, etc.) bocanada, *f;* (of an engine, etc.) resoplido, bufido, *m;* (for powder) borla (para polvos), *f;* (pastry) bollo, *m;* (advertisement) bombo, *m.* **to be puffed up,** *Fig.* hincharse, inflarse. **p. of wind,** ráfaga de

aire, *f.* **p.-ball,** bejín, *m.* **p.-pastry,** hojaldre, *m,* or *f.*
p.-sleeve, manga de bullón, *f*
puffiness /'pʌfɪnɪs/ *n* hinchazón, *f*
puffy /'pʌfi/ *a* (of the wind) a ráfagas; (panting) jadeante; (swollen) hinchado
pug /pʌg/ *n* (dog) doguino, *m.* **p.-nosed,** de nariz respingona
pugilism /'pyudʒə,lɪzəm/ *n* boxeo, pugilato, *m*
pugilist /'pyudʒəlɪst/ *n* pugilista, *mf,* boxeador, *m*
pugnacious /pʌg'neɪʃəs/ *a* pugnaz, belicoso
pugnacity /pʌg'næsɪti/ *n* pugnacidad, belicosidad, *f*
pull /pʊl/ *n* tirón, *m;* sacudida, *f;* golpe, *m;* (row) paseo en barco, *m;* (with the oars) golpe (de remos), *m;* (at a bell) tirón, *m;* (bell-rope) tirador, *m;* (at a bottle) trago, *m;* (strain) fuerza, *f;* atracción, *f;* (struggle) lucha, *f;* (advantage) ventaja, *f;* (influence) influencia, *f, Central America, Mexico* arranque *m.* **to give a p.,** tirar (de), dar un tirón (a). **to have plenty of p.,** *Inf.* tener buenas aldabas
pull /pʊl/ *vt* tirar (de); (drag) arrastrar; (extract) sacar; (a boat) remar; (gather) coger; *Print.* imprimir. **He pulled the trigger (of his gun),** Apretó el gatillo. **to p. a person's leg,** tomar el pelo (a). **to p. oneself together,** componer el semblante, serenarse; recobrar el aplomo; (tidy oneself) arreglarse. **to p. apart,** *vt* separar; romper en dos. *vi* separarse; romperse en dos. **to p. away,** *vt* arrancar; quitar. *vi* tirar con esfuerzo. **to p. back,** tirar hacia atrás; hacer retroceder (a); retener. **to p. down,** hacer bajar, obligar a bajar; (objects) bajar; (buildings) derribar, demoler; (humble) humillar; degradar; (weaken) debilitar. **to p. in,** tirar hacia dentro; hacer entrar; (a horse) enfrenar; (expenditure) reducir. **to p. off,** arrancar; (clothes) quitarse; (a deal) cerrar (un trato), concluir con éxito; (win) ganar. **to p. on,** *vt* (gloves, etc.) meterse, ponerse. *vi* seguir remando. **to p. open,** abrir; abrir rápidamente. **to p. out,** hacer salir; obligar a salir; (teeth, daggers, etc.) sacar; (hair) arrancar. **to p. round, through,** *vt* ayudar a reponerse (a); sacar de un aprieto. *vi* restablecerse; reponerse, cobrar la salud, sanar. **to p. together,** obrar de acuerdo; (get on) llevarse (bien or mal). **He pulled himself together very quickly,** Se repuso muy pronto. **to p. up,** *vt* montar, subir; (a horse) sofrenar; (stop) parar; (by the root) desarraigar, extirpar; (interrupt) interrumpir; (scold) reñir. *vi* parar(se); (restrain oneself) reprimirse, contenerse
pullet /'pʊlɪt/ *n* polla, *f*
pulley /'pʊli/ *n* polea, *f; Naut.* garrucha, *f.* **p. wheel,** roldana, *f*
pulling /'pʊlɪŋ/ *n* tracción, *f;* tirada, *f;* arranque, *m*
pullover /'pʊl,oʊvər/ *n* jersey, *m, Lat. Am.* chompa, *f*
pullulate /'pʌlyə,leɪt/ *vi* pulular
pulmonary /'pʌlmə,nɛri/ *a* pulmonar
pulp /pʌlp/ *n* pulpa, *f;* (of fruit) carne, *f;* (paper) pasta, *f;* (of teeth) bulbo dentario, *m. vt* reducir a pulpa; deshacer (el papel). **to beat to a p.,** *Inf.* poner como un pulpo
pulpit /'pʊlpɪt, 'pʌl-/ *n* púlpito, *m*
pulpy /'pʌlpi/ *a* pulposo; *Bot.* carnoso
pulsate /'pʌlseɪt/ *vi* pulsar, latir
pulsation /pʌl'seɪʃən/ *n* pulsación, *f,* latido, *m*
pulsatory /'pʊlsə,tɔri/ *a* pulsante, pulsativo, latiente
pulse /pʌls/ *n* pulso, *m;* pulsación, *f,* latido, *m;* vibración, *f;* (vegetable) legumbre, *f, vi* pulsar, latir; vibrar. **to take a person's p.,** tomar el pulso (a)
pulverization /,pʊlvərə'zeɪʃən/ *n* pulverización, *f*
pulverize /'pʌlvə,raiz/ *vt* pulverizar
puma /'pyumə, 'pu-/ *n* puma, *f, Lat. Am.* león, *m*
pumice /'pʌmɪs/ *n* piedra pómez, *f*
pummel /'pʌməl/ *vt* aporrear
pump /pʌmp/ *n Mech.* bomba, *f;* (for water, etc.) aguatocha, *f; Naut.* pompa, *f;* (slipper) escarpín, *m, vt* bombear, extraer por medio de una bomba; (inflate) inflar; (for information) sondear, sonsacar. **hand-p.,** bomba de mano, *f.* **to work a p.,** darle a la bomba
pumpkin /'pʌmpkɪn/ *n* calabaza, *f, Central America* ayote, *m, Chile* zapallo, *m;* (plant) calabacera, *f*
pun /pʌn/ *n* retruécano, *m*
punch /pʌntʃ/ *n* (drink) ponche, *m;* (blow) puñetazo,

golpe, *m; Mech.* punzón, *m;* (for tickets, etc.) taladro, *m; Inf.* fuerza, *f. vt* (perforate) taladrar, punzar; estampar; (hit) dar un puñetazo (a). **p.-ball,** pelota de boxeo, *f.* **p.-bowl,** ponchera, *f*
punctilious /pʌŋk'tɪliəs/ *a* formal, puntual, puntilloso
punctiliousness /pʌŋk'tɪliəsnɪs/ *n* formalidad, puntualidad, *f*
punctual /'pʌŋktʃuəl/ *a* puntual
punctually /'pʌŋktʃuəli/ *adv* puntualmente
punctuate /'pʌŋktʃu,eit/ *vt* puntuar
punctuation /,pʌŋktʃu'eiʃən/ *n* puntuación, *f*
puncture /'pʌŋktʃər/ *n* pinchazo, *m;* perforación, *f; Surg.* punción, *f. vt* pinchar; perforar; punzar. **We have a p. in the right tire,** Tenemos un pinchazo en el neumático derecho
pungency /'pʌndʒənsi/ *n* picante, *m;* acerbidad, *f,* mordacidad, *f*
pungent /'pʌndʒənt/ *a* picante; acerbo, mordaz
Punic /'pyunɪk/ *a* púnico, cartaginés
punish /'pʌnɪʃ/ *vt* castigar; maltratar
punishable /'pʌnɪʃəbəl/ *a* punible
punishment /'pʌnɪʃmənt/ *n* castigo, *m;* pena, *f;* maltrato, *m*
punitive /'pyunɪtɪv/ *a* punitivo
punt /pʊnt/ *n* batea, *f. vt* impeler una batea con una pértiga; ir en batea; (a ball) golpear, dar un puntapié (a)
puny /'pyuni/ *a* débil, encanijado; insignificante; pequeño
pup /pʌp/ *n* cachorro (-rra). *vi* parir la perra
pupa /'pyupə/ *n* crisálida, *f*
pupil /'pyupəl/ *n* alumno (-na), discípulo (-la); (of the eye) pupila, niña (del ojo), *f; Law.* pupilo (-la). *a* escolar. **day p.,** alumno (-na) externo (-na). **p. teacher,** maestro (-tra) alumno (-na)
puppet /'pʌpɪt/ *n* títere, *m,* marioneta, *f;* muñeca, *f;* (person) maniquí, *m.* **p. show,** función de títeres, *f.* **p. showman,** titiritero, titerero, *m*
puppy /'pʌpi/ *n* perrito (-ta), cachorro (-rra)
purblind /'pɜr,blaind/ *a* ciego; (short-sighted and *Fig.*) miope
purchasable /'pɜrtʃəsəbəl/ *a* comprable, que puede comprarse; *Fig.* sobornable
purchase /'pɜrtʃəs/ *vt* comprar; adquirir; *Fig.* lograr, conseguir. *n* compra, *f;* adquisición, *f; Mech.* apalancamiento, *m;* fuerza, *f;* (lever) palanca, *f,* aparejo, *m; Fig.* influencia, *f.* **p. tax,** impuesto de lujo, *m*
purchaser /'pɜrtʃəsər/ *n* comprador (-ra)
purchasing /'pɜrtʃəsɪŋ/ *n* See **purchase. p. power,** poder de adquisición, *m*
pure /pyʊr/ *a* puro. **p.-bred,** de raza
purgation /pɜr'geiʃən/ *n* purgación, *f*
purgative /'pɜrgətɪv/ *a* purgativo. *n* purga, *f*
purgatorial /,pɜrgə'tɔriəl/ *a* del purgatorio; (expiatory) purgatorio
purgatory /'pɜrgə,tɔri/ *n* purgatorio, *m*
purge /pɜrdʒ/ *n* purgación, *f;* (laxative) purga, *f; Polit.* depuración, *f;* purificación, *f. vt* purgar; *Polit.* depurar; purificar; expurgar
purging /'pɜrdʒɪŋ/ *n* purgación, *f; Polit.* depuración, *f; Fig.* purificación, *f*
purification /,pyʊrəfɪ'keiʃən/ *n* purificación, *f*
purificatory /pyu'rɪfɪkə,tɔri/ *a* purificador, purificatorio, que purifica
purifier /'pyʊrə,faiər/ *n* purificador (-ra)
purify /'pyʊrə,fai/ *vt* purificar; (metals) acrisolar; refinar; depurar; (purge) purgar
purist /'pyʊrɪst/ *n* purista, *mf*
puritan /'pyʊrɪtn/ *a* and *n* puritano (-na)
Puritanism /'pyʊrɪtn,ɪzəm/ *n* puritanismo, *m*
purity /'pyʊrɪti/ *n* pureza, *f*
purl /pɜrl/ *vi* (of a stream, etc.) murmurar, susurrar. *n* (of a stream, etc.) susurro, murmullo, *m*
purling /'pɜrlɪŋ/ *a* murmurante, que susurra, parlero. *n* murmullo, susurro, *m*
purloin /pər'lɔin/ *vt* hurtar, robar
purple /'pɜrpəl/ *n* púrpura, *f,* a purpúreo. *vt* purpurar, teñir de púrpura. *vi* purpurear
purplish /'pɜrplɪʃ/ *a* purpurino, algo purpúreo
purport /v. pər'pɔrt; n. 'pɜrpɔrt/ *vt* dar a entender,

querer decir; significar; indicar; parecer; tener el objeto de; pretender. *n* importe, *m*; sentido, significado, *m*; objeto, *m*

purpose /'pɜrpəs/ *n* objeto, *m*; propósito, fin, *m*; intención, *f*; proyecto, *m*; designio, *m*; determinación, voluntad, *f*; efecto, *m*; ventaja, utilidad, *f*, *vi* and *vt* proponerse; pensar, tener el propósito (de), intentar. **It will serve my p.**, Servirá para lo que yo quiero. **for the p. of...**, con el propósito de..., con el fin de... **for purposes of...** para efectos de... **on p.**, de propósito, expresamente, *Central America* adifés. **to no p.**, inútilmente; en vano

purposeful /'pɜrpəsfəl/ *a* resuelto; de substancia

purposeless /'pɜrpəslɪs/ *a* irresoluto, vacilante, vago; sin objeto; inútil

purposely /'pɜrpəsli/ *adv* expresamente, de intento

purr /pɜr/ *vi* ronronear. *n* ronroneo, *m*

purse /pɜrs/ *n* bolsa, *f*; monedero, portamonedas, *m*. **to p. one's lips,** apretar los labios

purser /'pɜrsər/ *n* Naut. contador, sobrecargo, *Argentina* comisario, *m*. **purser's office,** contaduría, *f*

pursuance /pər'suəns/ *n* cumplimiento, desempeño, *m*, prosecución, *f*. **in p. of,** en cumplimiento de; en consecuencia de

pursuant /pər'suənt/ *a* and *adv* según; conforme (a), de acuerdo (con); en consecuencia (de)

pursue /pər'su/ *vt* perseguir; seguir; (search) buscar; (hunt) cazar; (a submarine, etc.) dar caza (a); (continue) proseguir, continuar; (an occupation) dedicarse (a), ejercer

pursuer /pər'suər/ *n* perseguidor (-ra)

pursuit /pər'sut/ *n* perseguimiento, *m*; (search) busca, *f*; (hunt) caza, *f*; (performance) prosecución, *f*, desempeño, *m*; (employment) ocupación, *f*. **in p. of,** en busca de. **p. plane,** avión de caza, *m*

purulence /'pyʊrələns/ *n* purulencia, *f*

purulent /'pyʊrələnt/ *a* purulento

purvey /pər'vei/ *vt* proveer, surtir, suministrar; abastecer; procurar

purveyance /pər'veiəns/ *n* suministro, abastecimiento, *m*; provisión, *f*

purveyor /pər'veiər/ *n* suministrador (-ra), proveedor (-ra), abastecedor (-ra)

pus /pʌs/ *n* pus, *m*

push /pʊʃ/ *n* empujón, *m*; empellón, *m*; impulso, *m*; (of a person) empuje, *m*, energía, *f*; (attack) ataque, *m*; ofensiva, *f*; (effort) esfuerzo, *m*; crisis, *f*, momento crítico, *m*. **at a push,** *Inf.* en caso de necesidad; en un aprieto, si llegara el caso. **to give the p. to,** *Inf.* despedir (a). **p.-bicycle,** bicicleta, *f*. **p.-button,** botón, *m*; botón de llamada, *m*. **p.-cart,** carretilla de mano, *f*; (child's) cochecito de niño, *m*

push /pʊʃ/ *vt* empujar; (jostle) empellar, dar empellones (a); (a finger in one's eye, etc.) clavar; (a button) apretar; (*Fig.* a person) proteger, ayudar; dar publicidad (a); (a claim, etc.) insistir en; (compel) obligar. *vi* empujar; dar empujones, empellar. **I have pushed my finger in my eye,** Me he clavado el dedo en el ojo. **to p. against,** empujar contra; lanzarse contra; empellar, dar empellones (a). **to p. aside, away,** apartar con la mano; rechazar, alejar. **to p. back,** (hair, etc.) echar hacia atrás; (people) hacer retroceder; rechazar. **to p. by,** pasar. **to p. down,** hacer bajar; hacer caer; (demolish) derribar. **to p. forward,** *vt* empujar hacia delante, hacer avanzar; (a plan, etc.) llevar adelante. *vi* adelantarse a empujones; avanzar; seguir el camino. **to p. oneself forward,** *Fig.* abrirse camino; entrometerse; darse importancia. **to p. in,** *vt* empujar; hacer entrar; clavar, hincar. *vi* entrar a la fuerza; entremeterse. **to p. off,** *vt* apartar con la mano (a); *Inf.* quitar de encima (a). *vi* *Naut.* desatracar; *Inf.* ponerse en camino. **to p. open,** empujar, abrir. **to p. out,** *vt* empujar hacia fuera; hacer salir; echar. *vi* *Naut.* zarpar. **to p. through,** *vt* (business, etc.) despachar rápidamente; (a crowd) abrirse camino por. *vi* aparecer, mostrarse. **to p. to,** cerrar. **to p. up,** empujar; hacer subir; (windows, etc.) levantar.

pushing /'pʊʃɪŋ/ *a* enérgico, emprendedor; ambicioso; agresivo. **by p. and shoving,** a empellones, a empujones

pusillanimity /ˌpyusələ'nɪmɪti/ *n* pusilanimidad, *f*

pusillanimous /ˌpyusə'lænəməs/ *a* pusilánime

puss /pʊs/ *n* micho (-cha). **P.! P.!** ¡Miz, Miz!

pustule /'pʌstʃʊl/ *n* pústula, *f*

put /pʊt/ *vt* poner; colocar; (pour out) echar; aplicar; emplear; (estimate) calcular; presentar; (ask) preguntar; (say) decir; (express) expresar; (a question) hacer; (a problem) plantear; (the weight) lanzar; (rank) estimar. **As the Spanish put it,** Como dicen los españoles. **If I may put it so,** Si puedo expresarlo así, Por así decirlo. **hard put to it,** en dificultades, apurado. **How will you put it to her?** ¿Cómo se lo vas a explicar a ella? **to put ashore,** echar en tierra (a). **to put a child to bed,** acostar a un niño. **to put in order,** arreglar; ordenar, *Lat. Am.* acotejar. **to put out of joint,** dislocar. **to put out of order,** estropear. **to put to death,** matar; (judicially) ajusticiar. **to put about,** *vt* (a rumor) diseminar, divulgar; (worry) preocupar. *vi* *Naut.* virar, cambiar de rumbo **to put a roof on = roof** *vt*. **to put aside,** poner a un lado; descartar; (omit) omitir, pasar por alto de; (fears, etc.) desechar. **to put away,** quitar; guardar; poner en salvo; arrinconar; (thoughts) desechar, ahuyentar; (save) ahorrar; (banish) despedir, alejar; (a wife) repudiar, divorciar; (food) tragar. **to put back,** *vt* echar hacia atrás; hacer retroceder; (replace) devolver, restituir; (the clock) retrasar; (retard) retardar, atrasar. *vi* volver; *Naut.* volver a puerto. **to put down,** depositar; poner en el suelo; (the blinds) bajar; (an umbrella) cerrar; (a rebellion) sofocar; (gambling, etc.) suprimir; (humble) abatir, humillar; degradar; (silence) hacer callar; (reduce) reducir, disminuir; (write) apuntar, anotar; (a name) inscribir; (to an account) poner a la cuenta de; (estimate) juzgar, creer; (impute) atribuir. **The book is so interesting that it's hard to put down,** El libro es tan interesante que es difícil dejarlo. **to put forth,** (leaves, flowers, sun's rays) echar; (a book) publicar, dar a luz; (a hand) alargar; (an arm) extender; (show) manifestar, mostrar; (strength, etc.) desplegar; (use) emplear. **to put forward,** avanzar; (a clock) adelantar; (a suggestion, etc.) hacer; (propose) proponer; (a case) presentar. **to put oneself forward,** ponerse en evidencia. **to put in,** poner dentro; (a hand, etc.) introducir; (liquids) echar en; (a government) poner en el poder; (an employment) nombrar, colocar; (insert) insertar; (a claim) presentar; (say) decir. **I shall put in two hours' work before bedtime,** Trabajaré por dos horas antes de acostarme. **He put in a good word for you,** Habló en tu favor. **to put in writing,** poner por escrito. **to put in for,** (an employment) solicitar (un empleo); (as a candidate) presentarse como candidato para. **to put into,** meter dentro (de); (words) expresar; (port) arribar, hacer escala en (un puerto). **to put off,** desechar; (garments) quitarse, despojarse (de); (postpone) diferir, aplazar; (evade) evadir, entretener; quitarse de encima (a), desembarazarse (de); (confuse) desconcertar; (discourage) desanimar; quitar el apetito (a). **to put on,** poner sobre; (clothes) ponerse; (pretend) fingir, afectar; poner; (a play) poner en escena; (the hands of a clock) adelantar; (weight) engordar, poner carnes; (add) añadir; (*Sports.* score) hacer; (bet) apostar; (the light) encender; (assume) tomar; (the brake) frenar; (abuse) abusar (de). **He put the kettle on the fire,** Puso la tetera en el fuego. **to put on airs and graces,** darse humos. **to put on probation,** dar el azul a, poner a prueba a. **to put on more trains,** poner más trenes. **put one's foot down,** ponerle a fulano el alto. **to put out,** *vt* (eject) echar, expulsar; hacer salir; poner en la calle; (a tenant) desahuciar; (one's hand) alargar; (one's arm) extender; (one's tongue) sacar; (eyes) saltar; (fire, light) apagar, extinguir; (leaves, etc.) echar; (horns) sacar; (head) asomar, sacar; (use) emplear; (give) entregar, dar; (at interest) dar a interés; (finish) terminar; (dislocate) dislocar; (worry) desconcertar; turbar; poner los nervios en punta (a); (anger) enojar; (inconvenience) incomodar; (a book) publicar; (a boat) echar al mar. *vi* (of a ship) hacerse a la vela, zarpar. **to put out to grass,** We put out to sea, Nos hicimos a la mar. **to put the cart before the horse,** poner la carreta por delante de los bueyes. **to put through,**

(perform) desempeñar; concluir, terminar; (thrust) meter; (subject to) someter a; (exercise) ejercitar; (on the telephone) poner en comunicación (con). **to put together,** juntar; (a machine, etc.) montar, armar. **to put two and two together,** atar cabos. **to put up,** *vt* (sails, a flag) izar; (raise a window) levantar, cerrar; (open a window, or an umbrella) abrir; (one's hands, etc.) poner en alto; (one's fists) alzar; (a prayer) ofrecer, hacer; (as a candidate) nombrar; (for sale) poner (a la venta); (the price) aumentar; (a prescription) preparar; (food) conservar; (pack) empaquetar; (a sword) envainar; (lodge) alojar; (a petition) presentar; (build) construir; *Mech.* montar; (*Inf.* plan) arreglar. *vi* alojarse. **to put upon,** abusar (de); oprimir; (accuse) imputar, acusar (de). **to put up to,** incitar (a), instigar (a); dar informaciones sobre; poner al corriente (de). **to put up with,** tolerar, soportar, aguantar; resignarse a; contentarse con, conformarse con

putative /'pyutətɪv/ *a* supuesto; (of relationship) putativo

putrefaction /ˌpyutrə'fækʃən/ *n* putrefacción, *f*

putrefy /'pyutrəˌfai/ *vt* pudrir. *vt* pudrirse, descomponerse

putrid /'pyutrɪd/ *a* pútrido; *Inf.* apestoso

putt /pʌt/ *vt* and *vi* patear.

putting /'pʊtɪŋ/ *n* acción de poner, *f*; colocación, *f*. **p. forward of the clock,** adelanto de la hora, *m*. **p. off,** tardanza, dilación, *f*. **p. the weight,** lanzamiento del peso, *m*. **p. up,** (for office) candidatura, *f*. **p. green,** pista de golf en miniatura, *f*

putty /'pʌti/ *n* masilla, *f*, *vt* enmasillar, rellenar con masilla

puzzle /'pʌzəl/ *vt* dejar perplejo; desconcertar; confundir; embrollar. *n* problema, *m*; dificultad, *f*; enigma, *m*; (perplexity) perplejidad, *f*; (game) rompecabezas, *m*. **to p. out,** procurar resolver; encontrar la solución de. **to p. over,** pensar en, meditar sobre. **I am puzzled by...,** Me trae (or tiene) perplejo.... **to be puzzled** *Lat. Am.* intrigarse

pygmy /'pɪgmi/ *a* and *n* pigmeo (-ea)

pyjamas /pə'dʒɑməz, -'dʒæməz/ *n* pijama, *m*

pylon /'pailɒn/ *n* pilón, *m*; poste, *m*; (at an airport) poste de señales, *m*

pylorus /pai'lɔrəs/ *n* píloro, *m*

pyramid /'pɪrəmɪd/ *n* pirámide, *f*

pyramidal /pɪ'ræmɪdl/ *a* piramidal

pyre /paiər/ *n* pira, *f*

Pyrenean /ˌpiərə'niən/ *a* pirineo, pirenaico

Pyrenees, the /'pirəˌniz/ los Pirineos, *m pl*

pyromancy /'pairəˌmænsi/ *n* piromancia, *f*

pyrotechnic /ˌpairə'teknɪk/ *a* pirotécnico

pyrotechnics /ˌpairə'tekniks/ *n* pirotecnia, *f*

pyrotechnist /ˌpairə'teknɪst/ *n* pirotécnico, *m*

Pyrrhic /'pirɪk/ *a* pírrico

Pythagorean /pɪˌθægə'riən/ *a* and *n* pitagórico (-ca)

Pythian /'pɪθiən/ *a* pitio

python /'paiθɒn/ *n* pitón, *m*

pythoness /'paiθənɪs/ *n* pitonisa, *f*

Q

q /kyu/ *n* (letter) cu, *f*

quack /kwæk/ *vi* (of a duck) graznar. *n* (of a duck) graznido, *m*; (charlatan) charlatán, farsante, *m*; curandero, *m*. **q. doctor,** matasanos, medicastro, curandero, *m*. **q. medicine,** curanderismo, *m*

quackery /'kwækəri/ *n* charlatanería, *f*, charlatanismo, *m*

quadrangle /'kwɒdˌræŋgəl/ *n* cuadrángulo, *m*; (courtyard) patio, *m*

quadrangular /kwɒd'ræŋgyələr/ *a* cuadrangular

quadratic /kwɒ'drætɪk/ *a* cuadrático. **q. equation,** cuadrática, ecuación de segundo grado, *f*

quadrature /'kwɒdrətʃər/ *n* (*Math. Astron.*) cuadratura, *f*

quadrennial /kwɒ'drɛniəl/ *a* cuadrienal

quadrilateral /ˌkwɒdrə'lætərəl/ *a* and *n* cuadrilátero *m*

quadrille /kwɒ'drɪl/ *n* cuadrilla, *f*; (card game) cuatrillo, *m*

quadruped /'kwɒdrʊˌped/ *a* and *n* cuadrúpedo *m*

quadruple /kwɒ'drupəl/ *a* cuádruple. *vt* cuadruplicar. *n* cuádruplo, *m*

quadruplet /kwɒ'drʌplɪt/ *n* serie de cuatro cosas, *f*; bicicleta de cuatro asientos, *f*; uno (una) de cuatro niños (-as) gemelos (-as)

quadruplication /kwɒˌdruplɪ'keiʃən/ *n* cuadruplicación, *f*

quagmire /'kwægˌmaiər/ *n* tremedal, pantano, *m*; *Fig.* cenagal, *m*

quail /kweil/ *n* codorniz, *f*; parpayuela, *f*. *vi* cejar, retroceder; temblar, acobardarse

quaint /kweint/ *a* pintoresco; curioso, raro; (eccentric) excéntrico, extravagante

quaintly /'kweintli/ *adv* de un modo pintoresco; curiosamente; con extravagancia

quaintness /'kweintnɪs/ *n* lo pintoresco; rareza, singularidad, *f*; (eccentricity) extravagancia, *f*

quake /kweik/ *vi* estremecerse, vibrar; temblar. *n* estremecimiento, *m*; (of the earth) terremoto, *m*. **to q. with fear,** temblar de miedo

Quaker /'kweikər/ *n* cuáquero (-ra)

quaking /'kweikɪŋ/ *a* tembloroso; tembloroso. *n* temblor, *m*; estremecimiento, *m*. **q. ash,** álamo temblón, *m*

qualifiable /'kwɒləˌfaiəbəl/ *a* calificable

qualification /ˌkwɒləfɪ'keiʃən/ *n* calificación, *f*; requisito, *m*; capacidad, aptitud, *f*; (reservation) reservación, salvedad, *f*

qualified /'kwɒləˌfaid/ *a* apto, competente; (of professions) con título universitario; habilitado; limitado

qualify /'kwɒləˌfai/ *vt* habilitar; calificar; modificar; suavizar; *vi* habilitarse; prepararse; llenar los requisitos

qualifying /'kwɒləˌfaiɪŋ/ *a Gram.* calificativo

qualitative /'kwɒlɪˌteitɪv/ *a* cualitativo

quality /'kwɒlɪti/ *n* cualidad, *f*; calidad, *f*; propiedad, *f*. **This cloth is of good q.,** Esta tela es de buena calidad. **the q.,** la alta sociedad, la aristocracia

qualm /kwɑm/ *n* náusea, *f*; mareo, desmayo, *m*; (of conscience) escrúpulo, remordimiento, *m*

quandary /'kwɒndəri/ *n* incertidumbre, perplejidad, *f*; dilema, apuro, *m*. **to be in a q.,** estar perplejo

quantitative /'kwɒntɪˌteitɪv/ *a* cuantitativo

quantity /'kwɒntɪti/ *n* cantidad, *f*; gran cantidad, *f*. **unknown q.,** incógnita, *f*

quantum /'kwɒntəm/ *n* cantidad, *f*; tanto, *m*. **q. theory,** teoría de la quanta, *f*

quarantine /'kwɔrənˌtin/ *n* cuarentena, *f*, *vt* someter a cuarentena

quarrel /'kwɔrəl/ *vi* pelear, disputar; (scold) reñir; (find fault) criticar. *n* pelea, disputa, *Argentina* arenga, *f*; (glazier's) diamante de vidriero, *m*. **to pick a q. with,** armar pleito con, reñir con, *Chile, Peru* cruzar. **to q. with,** reñir con, romper con; quejarse de

quarreller /'kwɔrələr/ *n* reñidor (-ra)

quarrelling /'kwɔrəlɪŋ/ *n* disputas, altercaciones, *f pl*

quarrelsome /'kwɔrəlsəm/ *a* pendenciero, peleador, belicoso

quarrelsomeness /'kwɔrəlsəmnɪs/ *n* belicosidad, pugnacidad, *f*

quarry /'kwɔri/ *n* cantera, *f*, pedrera *f*; *Fig.* mina, *f*; (prey) presa, *f*; víctima, *f*. *vt* explotar una cantera; examinar

quarrying /'kwɔriɪŋ/ *n* explotación de canteras, *f*; cantería, *f*

quarryman /'kwɔrimən/ *n* cantero, *m*, picapedrero, *m*

quart /kwɔrt/ *n* cuarto de galón, *m*

quartan /'kwɔrtn̩/ *a* cuartanal. *n* (fever) cuartana, *f*

quarter /'kwɔrtər/ *n* (fourth part) cuarta parte, *f*, cuarto, *m*; (of a year) trimestre, *m*; (of an hour, the moon, a ton, an animal, etc.) cuarto, *m*; (of the compass) cuarta, *f*; *Naut.* cuartelada, *f*; (of a town) barrio, *m*; (mercy) cuartel, *m*; *Herald.* cuartel, *m*; dirección, *f*; origen, *m*, fuente, *f*; *pl* **quarters,** vivienda, *f*; alojamiento, *m*; (barracks) cuartel, *m*. *vt* cuartear; (a body) descuartizar, hacer cuartos (a); (troops) alojar; (in barracks) acuartelar; *Herald.* cuartelar. **a q. of an hour,** un cuarto de hora. **at close quarters,** de cerca. **hind quarters,** cuartos traseros, *m pl*. **It is a q. to four,** Son las cuatro menos cuarto. **It is a q. past four,** Son las cuatro y cuarto. **q.-day,** primer día de un trimestre, *m*. **q.-deck,** alcázar, *m*; cuerpo de oficiales de un buque, *m*. **q.-mile,** cuarto de milla, *m*. **q.-plate,** cuarto de placa, *m*. **q.-sessions,** sesión trimestral de los juzgados municipales, *f*. **q.-staff,** barra, *f*. **q.-tone,** cuarto de tono, *m*

quartering /'kwɔrtərɪŋ/ *n* (punishment) descuartizamiento, *m*; *Herald.* cantón, *m*

quarterly /'kwɔrtərli/ *a* trimestral, trimestre. *n* publicación trimestral, *f*, *adv* trimestralmente

quartermaster /'kwɔrtər,mæstər/ *n* *Mil.* cabo furriel, *m*; *Nav.* maestre de víveres, cabo de mar, *m*. **q.-general,** intendente de ejército, *m*

quartet /kwɔr'tɛt/ *n* cuarteto, *m*

quarto /'kwɔrtou/ *n* papel en cuarto, *m*; libro en cuarto, *m*. **in q.,** en cuarto

quartz /kwɔrts/ *n* cuarzo, *m*

quash /kwɒʃ/ *vt* *Law.* anular, derogar; *Inf.* sofocar, reprimir

quasi /'kweizai, 'kwɑsi/ *a* and *adv* cuasi

quasimodo /,kwɑsə'moudou/ *n* cuasimodo, *m*

quatrain /'kwɒtrein/ *n* cuarteta, *f*

quaver /'kweivər/ *vi* temblar; temblar; (trill) trinar, hacer quiebros. *vt* decir con voz temblorosa. *n* vibración, *f*; trémolo, *m*; (trill) trino, *m*; (musical note) corchea, *f*

quaveringly /'kweivərɪŋli/ *adv* con voz temblorosa

quavery /'kweivəri/ *a* trémulo, tembloroso

quay /ki, kei/ *n* muelle, *m*

queasiness /'kwizinɪs/ *n* náusea, *f*; escrupulosidad, *f*

queasy /'kwizi/ *a* propenso a la náusea; nauseabundo; delicado, escrupuloso

Quechua /'kɛtʃwɑ/ *n* and *a* quechua, *mf*

queen /kwin/ *n* reina, *f*; (in a Spanish pack of cards) caballo, *m*; (in a French or English pack and in chess) reina, *f*. **to q. it,** conducirse como una reina; mandar. **q. bee,** maestra, abeja reina, *f*. **q. cell,** maestril, *m*. **q. mother,** reina madre, *f*. **q. regent,** reina regente, *f*

queenliness /'kwinlinɪs/ *n* majestad de reina, *f*

queenly /'kwinli/ *a* de reina; regio

queer /kwɪər/ *a* raro; extraño, singular; ridículo; (shady) sospechoso; (ill) malucho, algo enfermo; (mad) chiflado

queerly /'kwɪərli/ *adv* extrañamente; ridiculamente

queerness /'kwɪərnɪs/ *n* rareza, extrañeza, singularidad, *f*; ridiculez, *f*

quell /kwɛl/ *vt* subyugar; reprimir; apaciguar, calmar

quench /kwɛntʃ/ *vt* apagar; calmar; satisfacer. **to q. one's thirst,** apagar la sed

quenching /'kwɛntʃɪŋ/ *n* apagamiento, *m*; satisfacción, *f*

querulous /'kwɛrələs/ *a* quejumbroso

querulousness /'kwɛrələsnɪs/ *n* hábito de quejarse, *m*; quejumbre, *f*

query /'kwɪəri/ *n* pregunta, *f*; duda, *f*; punto de interrogación, *m*. *vt* preguntar; dudar (de); poner en duda. *vi* hacer una pregunta; expresar una duda

quest /kwɛst/ *n* busca, *f*; (adventure) demanda, *f*. **in q. of,** en busca de

question /'kwɛstʃən/ *n* pregunta, *f*; problema, *m*; asunto, *m*; cuestión, *f*; (discussion) debate, *m*, discusión, *f*. *vt* and *vi* interrogar; examinar; poner en duda, dudar de; preguntarse; hacer preguntas. **beyond q.,** fuera de duda. **to ask a q.,** hacer una pregunta. **without q.,** sin duda. **It is out of the q.,** Es completamente imposible. **It is a q. of whether...,** Se trata de si... **q.-mark,** punto interrogante, *m*

questionable /'kwɛstʃənəbəl/ *a* cuestionable, discutible; dudoso; equívoco, sospechoso

questionableness /'kwɛstʃənəbəlnɪs/ *n* lo discutible; carácter dudoso, *m*; carácter sospechoso, *m*

questioner /'kwɛstʃənər/ *n* preguntador (-ra); interrogador (-ra)

questioning /'kwɒstʃənɪŋ/ *n* preguntas, *f pl*; interrogatorio, *m*

questioningly /'kwɛstʃənɪŋli/ *adv* interrogativamente

questionnaire /,kwɛstʃə'nɛər/ *n* cuestionario, *m*

quetzal /kɛt'sɑl/ *n* (money and *Ornith.*) quetzal, *m*

queue /kyu/ *n* coleta, *f*; cola, *f*, *vi* formar cola; hacer cola

quibble /'kwɪbəl/ *n* equívoco, subterfugio, *m*; sutileza, *f*; (pun) retruécano, *m*. *vi* hacer uso de subterfugios; sutilizar

quibbler /'kwɪblər/ *n* sofista, *mf*

quibbling /'kwɪblɪŋ/ *n* sofistería, *f*, sofismas, *m pl*, sutilezas, *f pl*

quick /kwɪk/ *a* vivo; agudo; penetrante; sagaz; rápido, veloz; (ready) pronto; ágil, activo; (light) ligero. *adv* rápidamente; (soon) pronto. *n* carne viva, *f*; *Fig.* lo vivo. **Be q.!** ¡Date prisa! **He was very q.,** Lo hizo muy aprisa; Volvió (or Fue, according to sense) rápidamente. **the q. and the dead,** los vivos y los muertos. **to cut to the q.,** herir en lo más vivo. **q. march,** paso doble, *m*. **q.-sighted,** de vista aguda; perspicaz. **q. step,** paso rápido, *m*. **q.-tempered,** de genio vivo, colérico. **q. time,** compás rápido, *m*; *Mil.* paso doble, *m*. **q.-witted,** de ingenio agudo

quicken /'kwɪkən/ *vt* vivificar; animar; acelerar; excitar, avivar. *vi* vivificarse; despertarse; renovarse; acelerarse; (stir) moverse. **to q. one's step,** acelerar el paso

quicklime /'kwɪk,laim/ *n* cal viva, *f*

quickly /'kwɪkli/ *adv* rápidamente; (soon) pronto; (immediately) en seguida; (promptly) con presteza; vivamente

quickness /'kwɪknɪs/ *n* viveza, *f*; (of wit, etc.) agudeza, *f*; rapidez, velocidad, *f*; (promptness) prontitud, *f*; agilidad, *f*; (lightness) ligereza, *f*; (understanding) penetración, sagacidad, *f*

quicksand /'kwɪk,sænd/ *n* arena movediza, *f*; *Fig.* cenagal, *m*

quicksilver /'kwɪk,sɪlvər/ *n* azogue, mercurio, *m*, *vt* azogar

quiescence /kwi'ɛsəns/ *n* reposo, *m*; quietud, tranquilidad, *f*; inactividad, *f*; pasividad, *f*

quiescent /kwi'ɛsənt/ *a* quieto; inactivo; pasivo

quiet /'kwaiit/ *a* tranquilo; quieto; silencioso; quedo; monótono; inactivo; (informal) sin ceremonia; (simple) sencillo; (of the mind) sereno; (of colours, etc.) suave. *n* tranquilidad, quietud, *f*; silencio, *m*; paz, *f*; (of mind) serenidad, *f*. *vt* tranquilizar, sosegar; calmar. **to be q.,** callarse; no hacer ruido. **Be q.!** ¡Estate quieto! ¡A callar!

quietism /'kwaii,tizəm/ *n* quietismo, *m*

quietist /'kwaiitɪst/ *n* quietista, *mf*

quietistic /,kwaii'tɪstɪk/ *a* quietista

quietly /'kwaiitli/ *adv* tranquilamente; en silencio; sin ruido; en calma; (simply) sencillamente; dulcemente

quietness /'kwaiitnɪs/ *n* tranquilidad, quietud, *f*; calma, *f*; paz, *f*; silencio, *m*

quietus /kwai'itəs/ *n* (quittance) quitanza, *f*, finiquito, *m*; golpe de gracia, *m*; muerte, *f*

quill /kwɪl/ *n* pluma de ave, *f*; (of a feather) cañón, *m*; (pen) pluma, *f*; (of a porcupine) púa, *f*. **q.-driver,** cagatintas, *mf*

quilt /kwɪlt/ *n* colcha, *f*, edredón, *m*. *vt* acolchar. **q. maker,** colchero, *m*

quilting /'kwɪltɪŋ/ *n* acolchamiento, *m*; colchadura, *f*

quince /kwɪns/ *n* (tree and fruit) membrillo, *m*. **q. cheese,** carne de membrillo, *f*. **q. jelly,** jalea de membrillo, *f*

quincentenary /,kwɪnsɛn'tɛnəri/ *n* quinto centenario, *m*

quinine /'kwainən/ *n* quinina, *f*

quinsy /'kwɪnzi/ *n* angina, *f*

quintessence /kwɪn'tɛsəns/ *n* quinta esencia, *f*

quintessential /,kwɪntə'sɛnʃəl/ *a* quintaesenciado

quintet /kwɪn'tɛt/ *n* quinteto, *m*

quintuple /kwɪn'tupəl/ *a* quíntuplo

quintuplet /kwɪn'tʌplɪt/ *n* quintupleto, *m*; uno (una) de cinco niños (-as) gemelos (-as)

quip /kwɪp/ n agudeza, salida, f; (hint) indirecta, f; donaire, m, chanza, burla, f
quire /kwaiᵊr/ n (of paper) mano (de papel), f
quirk /kwɜrk/ n (quip) agudeza, salida, f; (quibble) sutileza, evasiva, f, (gesture) gesto, m
quit /kwɪt/ vt abandonar; dejar; renunciar (a). vi marcharse, Inf. tomar las de Villadiego, poner pies en polvorosa; (slang) dejar de, cesar de. **notice to q.**, aviso de desahúcio, m
quite /kwait/ adv completamente, enteramente; totalmente; del todo; (very) muy; (fairly) bastante. **It is not q. the thing to do,** Esto es algo que no se hace. **Q. so!** ¡Claro!; ¡Eso es! Se comprende. **It is not q. so good as we hoped,** No es tan bueno como esperábamos. **Peter is q. grown-up,** Pedro está hecho un hombre (or es todo un hombre)
quits /kwɪts/ adv quito, descargado
quittance /'kwɪtns/ n quitanza, f; recibo, m; recompensa, f
quitter /'kwɪtər/ n desertor (-ra); cobarde, mf
quiver /'kwɪvər/ vi temblar; vibrar; estremecerse; palpitar; (of light) titilar. n (for arrows) aljaba, f, carcaj, m. See also **quivering**

quivering /'kwɪvərɪŋ/ a tremulante; vibrante; palpitante. n temblor, m; estremecimiento, m
quixotic /kwɪk'sɒtɪk/ a quijotesco
quixotism /'kwɪksə,tɪzəm/ n quijotismo, m
quiz /kwɪz/ n examen parcial, m. vt tomar el pelo (a); burlarse (de); (stare) mirar de hito en hito (a)
quizzical /'kwɪzɪkəl/ a burlón; cómico; estrafalario
quizzically /'kwɪzɪkli/ adv burlonamente; cómicamente
quoin /kɔin, kwɔin/ n piedra angular, f; ángulo, m; (wedge) cuña, f. vt meter cuñas (a)
quoit /kwɔit/ n tejo, m; pl **quoits,** juego de tejos, m
quondam /'kwɒndəm/ a antiguo
quorum /'kwɔrəm/ n quórum, m. **to form a q.,** hacer un quórum
quota /'kwouta/ n cuota, f
quotable /'kwoutəbəl/ a citable; (Stock Exchange) cotizable
quota system n tablas diferenciales, f pl
quotation /kwou'teiʃən/ n citación, f; cita, f; Com. cotización, f. **q. mark,** comilla, f
quote /kwout/ vt citar; Com. cotizar. n Inf. comilla, f
quoth /kwouθ/ vt **q. I,** dije yo. **q. he,** dijo él
quotient /'kwouʃənt/ n cociente, m. **intelligence q.,** cociente intelectual, m

R

r /ar/ n (letter) erre, f
rabbet /'ræbɪt/ n ranura, f, rebajo, m. vt ensamblar a rebajo, m. **r.-joint,** junta a rebajo, f
rabbi /'ræbai/ n rabí, rabino, m. **grand r.,** gran rabino, m
rabbinical /rə'bɪnɪkəl/ a rabínico
rabbinism /'ræbə,nɪzəm/ n rabinismo, m
rabbit /'ræbɪt/ n conejo (-ja). a conejuno, de conejo. vi cazar conejos. **young r.,** gazapo, m. **r.-hutch,** jaula para conejos, f. **r.-warren,** conejera, f
rabble /'ræbəl/ n populacho, vulgo, m, plebe, f
rabid /'ræbɪd/ a rabioso; fanático; furioso, violento
rabies /'reibiz/ n rabia, hidrofobia, f
raccoon /ræ'kun/ n mapache, m
race /reis/ n carrera, f; (current) corriente, f; (prize) premio, m; (breed) raza, f; casta, estirpe, f; (family) linaje, m, familia, f; (scornful) ralea, f; (struggle) lucha, f. vi tomar parte en una carrera; correr de prisa; asistir a concursos de carreras de caballos; (of a machine) dispararse. vt (hacer) correr; competir en una carrera (con); desafiar a una carrera. **flat r.,** carrera llana, f. **mill-r.,** caz, m. **to run a r.,** tomar parte en una carrera; Fig. hacer una carrera. **r.-card,** programa de carreras de caballos, m. **r. hatred,** odio de razas, m. **r.-meeting,** concurso de carreras de caballos, m. **r. suicide,** suicidio de la raza, m. **r.-track,** pista, f
racecourse /'reis,kɔrs/ n hipódromo, m; estadio, m
racehorse /'reis,hɔrs/ n caballo de carrera, m
racer /'reisər/ n (horse) caballo de carreras, m; (person) carrerista, mf; (car) coche de carreras, m; (boat) yate de carreras, m; (bicycle) bicicleta de carreras, f
rachitic /rə'kɪtɪk/ a raquítico
racial /'reiʃəl/ a racial, de raza
racialism /'reiʃə,lɪzəm/ n rivalidad de razas, f
raciness /'reisɪnɪs/ n sabor, m; savia, f, picante, m
racing /'reisɪŋ/ n carreras, f pl; Mech. disparo, m, a de carreras; hípico. **r. calendar,** calendario de concursos de carreras de caballos, m. **r. car,** coche de carreras, m. **r. cycle,** bicicleta de carreras, f
racism /'reisɪzəm/ n racismo, m
racist /'reisɪst/ n racista, mf
rack /ræk/ n (for hay) percha (del pesebre), f; (in a railway compartment) rejilla, f; (for billiard cues) taquera, f; (for clothes) percha, f; (for torture) potro, m; Mech. cremallera, f. vt poner en el potro, torturar; atormentar. **to be on the r.,** estar en el potro **to r. one's brains,** devanarse los sesos, quebrarse la cabeza. **r. and ruin,** ruina total, f. **r. railway,** ferrocarril de cremallera, m,
racket /'rækɪt/ n Sports. raqueta, f; (din) barahúnda,

f; ruido, estrépito, m; confusión, f; (bustle) bullicio, m, agitación, f; (swindle) estafa, f; (binge) parranda, f. **to play rackets,** jugar a la raqueta
racking /'rækɪŋ/ n tortura, f; (of wine) trasiego, m, a torturante; (of a pain or cough) persistente
racoon /ræ'kun/ n mapache, m
racquet /'rækɪt/ n See **racket**
racy /'reisi/ a picante; sabroso
radar /'reidar/ n radar, m
raddled /'rædl̩d/ a pintado de almagre; mal pintado
radial /'reidiəl/ a radial
radiance /'reidiəns/ n resplandor, brillo, m, luminosidad, f
radiant /'reidiənt/ a radiante; brillante, luminoso. n Geom. línea radial, f. **r. heat,** calor radiante, m
radiantly /'reidiəntli/ adv con resplandor; brillantemente; con alegría
radiate /'reidi,eit/ vi radiar. vt irradiar
radiation /,reidi'eiʃən/ n irradiación, f; Geom. radiación, f
radiator /'reidi,eitər/ n (for central heating and of a car) radiador, m; (stove) calorífero, m
radical /'rædɪkəl/ a radical. n (Math. Chem.) radical, m; Politt. radical, mf
radicalism /'rædɪkə,lɪzəm/ n radicalismo, m
radio /'reidi,ou/ n radio, f; radiocomunicación, f. **r. amateur, r. enthusiast,** radioaficionado (-da). **r. announcer,** locutor (-ra). **r. broadcast,** radioemisión, radiodifusión, f. **r. listener,** radiooyente, mf **r. receiver,** (technical) radiorreceptor, m; (usual word) aparato de radio, m. **r. transmitter,** radiotransmisor, m
radioactive /,reidiou'æktɪv/ a radioactivo
radioactive fallout n caída radiactiva, llovizna radiactiva, precipitación radiactiva, f
radioactivity /,reidiouæk'tɪvɪti/ n radiactividad, f
radiofrequency /,reidiou'frikwənsi/ n radiofrecuencia, f
radiolocation /,reidioulou'keiʃən/ n radiolocación, f
radiologist /,reidi'ɒləgɪst/ n radiólogo, m
radiology /reidi'ɒlədʒi/ n radiología, f
radiometer /,reidi'ɒmɪtər/ n radiómetro, m
radiometry /,reidi'ɒmɪtri/ n radiometría, f
radioscopy /,reidi'ɒskəpi/ n radioscopia, f
radiotherapy /,reidiou'θɛrəpi/ n radioterapia, f
radish /'rædɪʃ/ n rábano, m. **horse-r.,** rábano picante, m
radium /'reidiəm/ n radio, m
radius /'reidiəs/ n (Geom. Anat.) radio, m; (of a wheel) rayo, m; (scope) alcance, m
raffia /'ræfiə/ n rafia, f

raffish /'ræfɪʃ/ *a* disoluto, libertino

raffle /'ræfəl/ *n* rifa, *f*, sorteo, *m*; lotería, *f*. *vt* rifar, sortear

raffling /'ræflɪŋ/ *n* sorteo, *m*, rifa, *f*

raft /ræft/ *n* balsa, *f*; (timber) armadía, *f*. *vt* transportar en balsa; cruzar en balsa

rafter /'ræftər/ *n* (of a roof) viga, traviesa, *f*; (raftsman) balsero, *m*

raftered /'ræftərd/ *a* con vigas

rag /ræg/ *n* jirón, guiñapo, *m*; (for cleaning) paño, trapo, *m*; (for papermaking) estraza, *f*; (of smoke, etc.) penacho, *m*; (newspaper) papelucho, *m*; *pl* **rags,** harapos, *m pl*; *Inf.* viejos hábitos, *m pl*. *vt* (tease) tomar el pelo (a); burlarse de; hacer una broma pesada (a). **r.-and-bone-man, ragpicker,** andrajero, trapero (Mexico), pepinador, *m*. **r. doll,** muñeca de trapo, *f*

ragamuffin /'rægə,mʌfɪn/ *n* galopín, *m*

rage /reidʒ/ *n* (anger) cólera, rabia, ira, *f*; (of the elements) furia, violencia, *f*; (ardor) entusiasmo, ardor, *m*; (fashion) boga, moda, *f*; (craze) manía, *f*; (of the poet) furor, *m*. *vi* (be angry) rabiar, estar furioso; (of the sea) encresparse, alborotarse, enfurecerse; (of wind, fire, animals) bramar, rugir; (of pain) rabiar; (be prevalent) prevalecer, desencadenarse. **to r. against,** protestar furiosamente contra; culpar amargamente (de). **to be all the r.,** *Inf.* ser la ultima moda. **to fly into a r.,** montar en cólera. **to put into a r.,** hacer rabiar

ragged /'rægɪd/ *a* harapiento, andrajoso; roto; (uneven) desigual; (rugged) peñascoso, áspero, escabroso; (serrated) serrado; dentellado; (of a coastline) accidentado; (unfinished) inacabado, sin terminar; (of style) descuidado, sin pulir

raggedness /'rægɪdnɪs/ *n* harapos, *m pl*; estado andrajoso, *m*; aspereza, escabrosidad, *f*; lo serrado; lo accidentado; (of style) falta de elegancia, tosquedad, *f*

raging /'reidʒɪŋ/ *a* furioso, rabioso; violento; (roaring) bramante; (of the sea) bravío; intenso. *n* furia, *f*; violencia, *f*; intensidad, *f*

raglan /'ræglən/ *n* raglán, *m*. **r. sleeve,** manga raglán, *f*

ragout /ræ'gu/ *n* estofado, *m*

ragpicker /'ræg,pɪkər/ *n* trapero (-ra)

ragtime /'ræg,taɪm/ *n* música sincopada, *f*

raid /reid/ *n* incursión, correría, *f*; asalto, ataque, *m*; (by the police) razzia, *f*; (by aircraft) bombardeo, *m*, *vt* invadir; atacar, asaltar; apoderarse de; hacer una razzia en; (by aircraft) bombear, bombardear; (pillage) pillar, saquear. **obliteration r.,** bombardeo de saturación, *m*

raider /'reidər/ *n* corsario, *m*; atacador, asaltador, *m*; (aircraft) avión enemigo, *m*

rail /reil/ *n* barra, *f*; antepecho, *m*; (of a staircase) barandilla, *f*, pasamano, *m*; (track) riel, *m*; (railway) ferrocarril, *m*; (of a ship) barandilla, *f*; (of a chair) travesaño, *m pl*. **rails, (fence)** cerca, barrera, palizada, *f*. *vt* cercar con una palizada, poner cerca a; mandar por ferrocarril. **by r.,** por ferrocarril. **to run off the rails,** descarrilar. **to r. at,** protestar contra; prorrumpir en invectivas contra, injuriar de palabra (a)

railing /'reilɪŋ/ *n* barandilla, *f*; antepecho, *m*, enrejado, *m*; (grille) reja, *f*; (jeers) burlas, *f pl*; insultos, *m pl*, injurias, *f pl*; quejas, *f pl*

raillery /'reiləri/ *n* jocosidad, tomadura de pelo, *f*; sátiras, *f pl*

railway /'reil,wei/ *n* ferrocarril, *m*; vía férrea, *f*, camino de hierro, *m*, *a* de ferrocarril, ferroviario. **elevated r.,** ferrocarril aéreo, *m*. **narrow gauge r.,** ferrocarril de vía estrecha, *m*. **r. buffet,** fonda, *f*, (or restaurante, *m* de estación. **r. carriage,** departamento de tren, *m*. **r. company,** compañía de ferrocarriles, *f*. **r. crossing,** paso a nivel, *m*. **r. engine,** locomotora, *f*. **r. guard,** jefe del tren, *m*. **r. guide,** guía de ferrocarriles, *f*. **r. line,** vía férrea, *f*. **r. marshalling yard,** apartadero ferroviario, *m*. **r. passenger,** viajero (-ra) en un tren. **r. platform,** andén, *m*. **r. porter,** mozo de estación, *m*. **r. siding,** vía muerta, *f*. **r. signal,** disco de señales, *m*. **r. station,** estación (de ferrocarril), *f*. **r. system,** sistema ferroviario, *m*. **r. ticket,** billete de tren, *m*

railwayman /'reil,weimən/ *n* ferroviario, empleado de los ferrocarriles, *m*

raiment /'reimənt/ *n* ropa, *f*; *Poet.* hábitos, *m pl*

rain /rein/ *n* lluvia, *f*. *vi* and *vt* llover. **a r. of arrows,** una lluvia de flechas. **fine r.,** llovizna, *f*. **to r. cats and dogs,** llover a cántaros. **to r. hard,** diluviar. **r. cloud,** nubarrón, *m*. **r.-gauge,** pluviómetro, *m*

rainbow /'rein,bou/ *n* arco iris, arco de San Martín, *m*

raincoat /'rein,kout/ *n* abrigo impermeable, *m*

raindrop /'rein,drɒp/ *n* gota de lluvia, *f*

rainfall /'rein,fɔl/ *n* cantidad llovida, *f*; (shower) aguacero, *m*

rainless /'reinlɪs/ *a* sin lluvia, seco

rainstorm /'rein,stɔrm/ *n* chaparrón, *m*, tempestad de lluvia, *f*

rainwater /'rein,wɔtər/ *n* lluvia, *f*; agua lluvia, *f*

rainy /'reini/ *a* lluvioso. **r. day,** día de lluvia, *m*; *Fig.* tiempo de escasez, *m*

raise /reiz/ *vt* levantar; alzar; (the hat) quitar; solevantar; (dough) fermentar; (erect) erigir, edificar; (dust) levantar; elevar; (promote) ascender; (increase) aumentar; hacer subir; (spirits, memories) evocar; (the dead) resucitar; (cause) causar; dar lugar (a); hacer concebir; (a question, a point) hacer; plantear; (breed or educate) criar; (a crop) cultivar; (an army) alistar; (gather together) juntar; (a subscription) hacer; (money, etc.) obtener, hallar; (a siege, etc.) levantar, alzar; (a laugh, a protest, etc.) suscitar, provocar; (utter) poner, dar; (a fund) abrir. **to r. oneself,** incorporarse. **He succeeded in raising himself,** Logró alzarse; Logró mejorar su posición. **He raised their hopes unduly,** Les hizo concebir esperanzas desmesuradas. **to r. an objection (to),** poner objeción (a). **to r. an outcry,** armar un alboroto. **to r. a point,** hacer una observación; plantear una cuestión. **to r. a siege,** levantar un sitio. **to r. Cain,** armar un alboroto. **to r. one's voice,** alzar la voz

raised /reizd/ *a* (in relief) en relieve; (embossed) de realce

raiser /'reizər/ *n* (breeder) criador (-ra); (cultivator) cultivador (-ra); (educator) educador (-ra); autor (-ra); fundador (-ra); (of objections, etc.) suscitador (-ra)

raisin /'reizɪn/ *n* pasa, *f*

raising /'reizɪŋ/ *n* levantamiento, *m*; alzamiento, *m*; (of a building, monument) erección, *f*; elevación, *f*; (increase) aumento, *m*; provocación, *f*; fundación, *f*; (breeding or education) crianza, *f*; (of spirits) evocación, *f*; (of the dead) resucitación, *f*; producción, *f*; (of crops) cultivo, *m*

rake /reik/ *n Agr.* rastrillo, *m*, rastra, *f*; (for the fire) hurgón, *m*; (croupier's) raqueta, *f*; (of a mast, funnel) inclinación, *f*; (person) tenorio, calavera, *m*. *vt Agr.* rastrillar; (a fire, etc.) hurgar; (sweep) barrer; recoger; (ransack) buscar (en); (with fire) enfilar, tirar a lo largo de; (scan) escudriñar. *vi* trabajar con el rastrillo; (slope) inclinarse. **r. off,** tajada, *f*. **to r. together,** juntar con el rastrillo; amontonar; ahorrar. **to r. up,** (revive) resucitar, desenterrar

raking /'reikɪŋ/ *n* rastrillaje, *m*; (the fire, etc.) hurgonada, *f*

rakish /'reikɪʃ/ *a* (of a ship) de palos muy inclinados, (dissolute) disoluto, libertino; (dashing) elegante

rakishly /'reikɪʃli/ *adv* disolutamente; elegantemente

rakishness /'reikɪʃnɪs/ *n* (licentiousness) libertinaje, *m*, disipación, disolución, *f*; (elegance) elegancia, *f*

rally /'ræli/ *vt* reunir; *Mil.* rehacer; (faculties) concentrar; (tease) tomar el pelo (a). *vi* reunirse; *Mil.* rehacerse; (revive) mejorar, recobrar las fuerzas; (of markets, etc.) mejorar *n* reunión, *f*

rallying /'ræliɪŋ/ *n* reunión, *f*; (of faculties, etc.) concentración, *f*; (recovery) mejora, *f*. **r. point,** punto de reunión, *m*

ram /ræm/ *n Zool.* carnero, morueco, *m*; *Astron.* Aries, Carnero, *m*; (*Mil.* etc.) ariete, *m*; (tool) pisón, *m*; *Nav.* espolón, *m*. *vt* golpear con ariete o espolón; (of a gun) atacar; apisonar; meter a la fuerza; hacer tragar a la fuerza; (squeeze) apretar; (crowd) atestar

Ramadan /ˌræmə'dɑn/ *n* ramadán, *m*

ramble /'ræmbəl/ *vi* vagar, vagabundear; hacer una excursión. *vt* errar por

rambler /'ræmblər/ n excursionista, mf; paseante, mf; Bot. rosa trepante, f
rambling /'ræmblɪŋ/ a (of houses) encantado; laberíntico; (straggly) disperso; (of thought, etc.) incoherente, inconexo. n vagabundeo, m; excursiones, f pl; paseo, m; (digression) digresiones, f pl; (delirium) desvaríos, m pl
ramification /ˌræməfɪ'keiʃən/ n ramificación, f
ramify /'ræməˌfai/ vi ramificarse, tener ramificaciones. vt ramificar; dividir en ramales
rammer /'ræmər/ n pisón de empedrador, m; baqueta (de fusil), f; (of a ship) espolón, m
ramp /ræmp/ n rampa, f; (swindle) estafa, f; (storm, commotion) tormenta, f
rampage /'ræmpeidʒ/ n alboroto, m. vi alborotarse; bramar
rampant /'ræmpənt/ a salvaje; Herald. rampante; (of persons) impaciente, furioso; (of plants, growth) lozano, exuberante; desenfrenado; (rife) prevaleciente, predominante
rampart /'ræmpɑrt/ n muralla, f; terraplén, m; Fig. baluarte, m. vt abaluartar, abastionar
ramrod /'ræmˌrɒd/ n baqueta, f
ramshackle /'ræmˌʃækəl/ a destartalado, ruinoso; desvencijado; (badly made) mal hecho
ranch /ræntʃ/ n rancho, m, hacienda (de ganado), Lat. Am. estancia, f
rancher /'ræntʃər/ n ranchero (-ra), Lat. Am. estanciero (-ra) mf
rancid /'rænsɪd/ a rancio
rancor /'ræŋkər/ n rencor, encono, m
rancorous /'ræŋkərəs/ a rencoroso
random /'rændəm/ n azar, m, a fortuito, al azar; sin orden ni concierto. **at r.,** a la ventura, al azar; sin pensar; (of shooting) sin apuntar. **to talk at r.,** hablar a trochemoche
randomly /'rændəmli/ adv al azar, por casualidad
range /reindʒ/ n línea, hilera, f; (of mountains) cadena, f; serie, f; clase, f; variedad, f; (of goods) surtido, m; (of a gun, voice, vision, etc.) alcance, m; (area) extensión, área, f; esfera de actividad, f; (scope) alcance, m; (of voice, musical instrument) compás, m; (of colors) gama, f; (for shooting) campo de tiro, m; (for cooking) cocina económica, f. **at close r.,** de cerca. **out of r.,** fuera de alcance. **within r.,** al alcance. **r.-finder,** (of guns, cameras) telémetro, m. **r. of mountains,** cadena de montañas, f; sierra, f
range /reindʒ/ vt clasificar; (a gun, etc.) apuntar; (place oneself) ponerse; sumarse (a); (roam) recorrer; (scan) escudriñar. vi extenderse; (roam) vagar; (of plants) crecer (en); variar, fluctuar; oscilar, vacilar; (of guns, etc.) alcanzar; (of the mind) pasar (por); (include) incluir
ranger /'reindʒər/ n (wanderer) vagabundo, m; (keeper) guardabosque, m; Mil. batidor, m
ranging /'reindʒɪŋ/ n clasificación, f; (roving) vida errante, f
rank /ræŋk/ n línea, f; fila, f; grado, m; clase, f; rango, m; categoría, f; posición, f; calidad, f; distinción, f. vt ordenar; clasificar; (estimate) estimar; poner (entre). vi ocupar un puesto; tener un grado, rango, etc.; estar al nivel (de); ser igual (a); contarse (entre). a (luxuriant) lozano, exuberante; fértil; (thick) espeso; (rancid) rancio; (complete) consumado; completo; (foul-smelling) fétido; Fig. repugnante, aborrecible; (very) muy. **of the first r.,** de primera calidad; de primera clase; de distinción. **the r. and file,** los soldados, la tropa; las masas, hombres de filas, m pl, mujeres de fila, f pl, la mayoría; los socios ordinarios (de un club, etc.). **to break ranks,** Mil. romper filas. **to rise from the ranks,** ascender de las filas. **to r. high,** ocupar alta posición; ser de los mejores (de). **to r. with,** estar al nivel de; (be numbered among) contarse entre, figurar entre
rankle /'ræŋkəl/ vi Fig. irritar, molestar; envenenarse la vida, hacerse odioso
rankly /'ræŋkli/ adv ranciamente, lozanamente; con exuberancia; abundantemente; groseramente
rankness /'ræŋknɪs/ n rancidez, f; olor rancio, m; fertilidad, lozanía, f; exuberancia, f, vigor, m; enormidad, f

ransack /'rænsæk/ vt (search) registrar; (pillage) saquear; Fig. buscar en
ransacking /'rænsækɪŋ/ n (searching) registro, m; (sacking) saqueo, m
ransom /'rænsəm/ n rescate, m, redención, f; liberación, f. vt rescatar, redimir
ransomer /'rænsəmər/ n rescatador (-ra)
ransoming /'rænsəmɪŋ/ n redención, f; liberación, f
rant /rænt/ vi declamar a gritos, vociferar; despotricar (contra); desvariar; hablar por hablar, hablar sin ton ni son. n declamación, vociferación, f; desvarío, m
ranter /'ræntər/ n declamador (-ra); agitador popularchero, m; predicador chillón, m
rap /ræp/ n golpecito, m; toque, m; (with the knocker) aldabada, f; (worthless trifle) ardite, maravedí, m. vt and vi golpear; tocar. **He doesn't care a rap,** No le importa un ardite. **to rap at the door,** tocar a la puerta. **to rap with the knuckles,** golpear con los nudillos. **to rap out an oath,** proferir una blasfemia
rapacious /rə'peiʃəs/ a rapaz
rapacity /rə'pæsɪti/ n rapacidad, f
rape /reip/ n violación, f, (carrying off) rapto, m. **the Rape of the Sabine Women,** el Rapto de las Sabinas, m; Law. estupro, m; violación, f; Bot. nabo silvestre, m. vt (carry off) raptar, robar; violar, forzar
rapid /'ræpɪd/ a rápido. n rápido, m. **r. combustion,** combustión activa, f
rapidity /rə'pɪdɪti/ n rapidez, f
rapidly /'ræpɪdli/ adv rápidamente, con rapidez
rapids /'ræpɪdz/ npl Argentina correntada, f sg
rapier /'reipiər/ n estoque, m; espadín, m
rapine /'ræpɪn/ n rapiña, f
rapist /'reipɪst/ n violador (-ra)
rapping /'ræpɪŋ/ n golpecitos, m pl; golpeo, m; toques, m pl; (of the knocker) aldabeo, m
rapscallion /ræp'skælyən/ n bribón, m
rapt /ræpt/ past part and a arrebatado; absorto; extático, extasiado
rapture /'ræptʃər/ n arrebato, m; éxtasis, m; transporte, m; embriaguez, f; entusiasmo, m; Eccl. El Retorno de Cristo
rapturous /'ræptʃərəs/ a embelesado, extático; entusiasta
rapturously /'ræptʃərəsli/ adv extáticamente; con entusiasmo
rare /rɛər/ a raro; extraordinario; exótico; infrecuente
raree show /'rɛəri/ n barracón de los fenómenos, barracón de las atracciones, m
rarefaction /ˌrɛərə'fækʃən/ n rarefacción, f
rarefy /'rɛərəˌfai/ vt rarefacer. vi rarefacerse
rareness /'rɛərnɪs/ n rareza, f; singularidad, f; infrecuencia, f
rarity /'rɛərɪti/ n raridad, f; (uncommonness and rare object) rareza, f
rascal /'ræskəl/ n sinvergüenza, m; truhán, bribón, pícaro, m; (affectionately) picaruelo, m
rascality /ræ'skælɪti/ n bellaquería, truhanería, f
rascally /'ræskəli/ a redomado; vil, ruin, canallesco
rash /ræʃ/ a temerario, precipitado; imprudente. n erupción, f, salpullido, m
rasher /'ræʃər/ n magra, f; (of bacon) torrezno, m
rashly /'ræʃli/ adv temerariamente, precipitadamente; imprudentemente, con imprudencia
rashness /'ræʃnɪs/ n temeridad, precipitación, f; imprudencia, f
rasp /ræsp/ n escofina, f, rallo, m; sonido áspero, m. vt raspar, escofinar; (get on one's nerves) poner los nervios en punta (a)
raspberry /'ræzˌbɛri/ n frambuesa, f. **r.-cane,** frambueso, m. **r. jam,** mermelada de frambuesa, f
rasping /'ræspɪŋ/ a (of the voice) áspero, estridente
rat /ræt/ n rata, f; desertor, m; (black leg) esquirol, m. vi cazar ratas; ser desertor; ser esquirol. **rat-catcher,** cazador de ratas, m. **rat poison,** matarratas, m, raticida, f. **rat-trap,** ratonera, f
ratable /'reitəbəl/ a sujeto a contribución; imponible; valuable
ratafia /ˌrætə'fiə/ n ratafía, f
rataplan /ˌrætə'plæn/ n rataplán, m

ratchet /'rætʃɪt/ *n* Mech. trinquete, *m*; (of a watch) disparador, *m*. **r.-drill,** carraca, *f*. **r.-wheel,** rueda dentada con trinquete, *f*

rate /reit/ *n* velocidad, *f*; razón, proporción, *f*; (of exchange) tipo, *m*; tanto, *m*; precio, *m*; clase, *f*; modo, *m*, manera, *f*; Naut. clasificación, *f*; (tax) contribución, *f*, impuesto, *m*; *pl* **rates,** (of a house) inquilinato, *m*. *vt* tasar; estimar; fijar el precio (a); Naut. clasificar; imponer una contribución (de); (scold) reñir. **at a great r.,** rápidamente, velozmente. **at a r. of,** a razón de; a una velocidad de. **at any r.,** de todos modos; por lo menos; sea como fuere. **at this r.,** de este modo; a este paso; a esa cuenta; en esta proporción; (with seguir) así. **first-r.,** de primera clase. **rates and taxes,** contribuciones e impuestos, *f pl*. **r. of climb,** Aer. velocidad ascensional, *f*. **r. of exchange,** tipo de cambio, *m*. **r.-payer,** contribuyente, *mf*

rather /'ræðər/ *adv* más bien; antes; (more willingly) de mejor gana; (somewhat) algo, un poco; (perhaps) quizás; mejor dicho; (fairly) bastante; (very) muy; mucho; al contrario. **or r.,** o más bien. **anything r. than...,** todo menos... **He had r.,** Preferiría. **r. than,** antes que, en vez de

ratification /,rætɪfɪ'keiʃən/ *n* ratificación, *f*; (of a bill) aprobación, *f*

ratifier /'rætə,faiər/ *n* ratificador (-ra)

ratify /'rætə,fai/ *vt* ratificar

ratifying /'rætə,faiɪŋ/ *n* ratificación, *f*, *a* ratificatorio

rating /'reitɪŋ/ *n* tasación, *f*; valuación, *f*; clasificación, *f*; impuesto, *m*, contribución, *f*; repartición de impuestos, *f*; (of a ship's company) graduación, *f*; (scolding) represión, *f*

ratio /'reiʃou/ *n* razón, *f*; proporción, *f*. **in direct r.,** en razón directa

ratiocinate /,ræʃi'ɒsə,neit/ *vi* raciocinar

ratiocination /,ræʃi,ɒsə'neiʃən/ *n* raciocinación, *f*

ration /'ræʃən, 'reiʃən/ *n* ración, *f*. *vt* racionar. **r.-book,** cartilla de racionamiento, *f*

rational /'ræʃənl/ *a* racional; razonable, juicioso. *n* ser racional, *m*

rationalism /'ræʃənl,ɪzəm/ *n* racionalismo, *m*

rationalist /'ræʃənlɪst/ *n* racionalista, *mf*

rationalistic /,ræʃənl'ɪstɪk/ *a* racionalista

rationality /,ræʃə'næliti/ *n* racionalidad, *f*; justicia, *f*

rationalization /,ræʃənlə'zeiʃən/ *n* racionalización, *f*; justificación, *f*

rationalize /'ræʃənl,aiz/ *vt* hacer racional; concebir racionalmente; Math. quitar los radicales (a); justificar

rationing /'ræʃənɪŋ, 'rei-/ *n* racionamiento, *m*

rattan /ræ'tæn/ *n* rota, *f*, bejuco, *m*; junquillo, *m*

ratteen /ræ'tin/ *n* ratina, *f*

ratter /'rætər/ *n* perro ratonero, *m*; gato que caza ratas, *m*

ratting /'rætɪŋ/ *n* caza de ratas, *f*; deserción, *f*

rattle /'rætl/ *vi* hacer ruido; rechinar, crujir; (of loose windows, etc.) zangolotearse; (knock) golpear; tocar; (patter) bailar; sonar; (of the dying) dar un estertor. *vt* (shake) sacudir; hacer vibrar; (jolt) traquetear; (do rapidly) acabar rápidamente; (confuse) aturdir, hacer perder la cabeza (a); desconcertar. **to r. along,** deslizarse (or correr) rápidamente. **to r. off,** (repeat) decir rápidamente; terminar apresuradamente. **to r. on about,** charlar mucho de, hablar sin cesar sobre

rattle /'rætl/ *n* rechinamiento, crujido, *m*; zangoloteo, *m*; ruido, *m*; son (de la lluvia, etc.), *m*; (in the throat) estertor, *m*; (of a rattlesnake) cascabel, *m*; (child's) sonajero, *m*; matraca, *f*; carraca, *f*; (chatter) charla, *f*. **r.-headed,** de cabeza de chorlito, casquivano

rattlesnake /'rætl,sneik/ *n* serpiente de cascabel, *f*, crótalo, *m*

rattling /'rætlɪŋ/ *n* See **rattle**

raucous /'rɔkəs/ *a* ronco, estridente

raucousness /'rɔkəsnɪs/ *n* ronquedad, *f*, estridor, *m*

ravage /'rævɪdʒ/ *vt* devastar; (pillage) saquear; destruir; (spoil) estropear. *n* devastación, *f*; destrucción, *f*; estrago, *m*

ravager /'rævɪdʒər/ *n* devastador (-ra); saqueador (-ra)

rave /reiv/ *vi* desvariar, delirar; (of the elements) bramar, rugir. **to r. about,** hablar con entusiasmo de; delirar por. **to r. against,** vociferar contra, despotricarse contra

ravel /'rævəl/ *vt* deshilar, destejer; Fig. enredar. **to r. out,** deshilarse; Fig. desenredarse, desenmarañarse

raven /'reivən/ *n* cuervo, *m*, *a* negro como el azabache

ravening /'rævənɪŋ/ *a* rapaz, salvaje

ravenous /'rævənəs/ *a* voraz

ravenously /'rævənəsli/ *adv* vorazmente

ravenousness /'rævənəsnɪs/ *n* voracidad, *f*

ravine /rə'vin/ *n* cañada, *f*, barranco, cañón, *m*

raving /'reivɪŋ/ *n* delirio, *m*, desvaríos, *m pl*. *a* delirante; violento; bravío

ravioli /,rævi'ouli/ *n pl* ravioles, *m pl*

ravish /'rævɪʃ/ *vt* (carry off) arrebatar, raptar; extasiar, encantar; (rape) violar, forzar

ravisher /'rævɪʃər/ *n* raptador, *m*; violador, *m*

ravishing /'rævɪʃɪŋ/ *n* violación, *f*, *a* encantador

ravishment /'rævɪʃmənt/ *n* violación, *f*; arrobamiento, *m*; transporte, éxtasis, *m*

raw /rɔ/ *a* (of meat, etc., silk, leather, weather) crudo; bruto; (inexpert) bisoño; (of flesh) vivo; Com. en bruto. **raw-boned,** huesudo. **raw hand,** novato (-ta). **raw material,** primera materia, *f*. **raw materials,** materias primas, *f pl*. **raw score,** puntuación bruta, *f*. **raw silk,** seda cruda, seda en rama, *f*. **raw sugar,** azúcar bruto, *m*

rawhide /'rɔ,haid/ *a* de cuero crudo

rawness /'rɔnɪs/ *n* crudeza, *f*; inexperiencia, *f*; (of weather) humedad, *f*

ray /rei/ *n* rayo, *m*; (line) raya, *f*; (radius) radio, *m*; (fish) raya, *f*. **cathode rays,** rayos catódicos, *m pl*

rayon /'reiɒn/ *n* rayón, *m*

raze /reiz/ *vt* arrasar, asolar; demoler; (erase) borrar, tachar

razor /'reizər/ *n* navaja, *f*. **electric r.,** máquina de afeitar eléctrica, *f*. **safety r.,** máquina de afeitar, *f*. **slash with a r.,** navajada, *f*. **r. blade,** hoja de afeitar, *f*. **r. case,** navajero, *m*. **r. strop,** suavizador, *m*

re /ri, rei/ *n* Mus. re, *m*; *prep* Law. causa, *f*; Com. concerniente a

re *prefix* (attached to verb) re-; (after the verb) de nuevo; (followed by infin.) volver a... **to re-count,** volver a contar, contar de nuevo, recontar

reabsorb /,riəb'sɔrb, -'zɔrb/ *vt* resorber

reabsorption /,riəb'sɔrpʃən, -'zɔrp-/ *n* reabsorción, resorción, *f*

reach /ritʃ/ *vt* (stretch out) alargar; extender; alcanzar; llegar hasta; (arrive at) llegar a; (achieve) lograr, obtener. *vi* extenderse; alcanzar; penetrar. *n* alcance, *m*; extensión, *f*; poder, *m*; capacidad, *f*; (of a river) tabla, *f*. **as far as the eye could r.,** hasta donde alcanzaba la vista. **He reached home very soon,** Llegó muy pronto a casa. **out of r.,** fuera de alcance. **to r. a deadlock,** llegar a un punto muerto. **within r.,** al alcance. **within easy r.,** de fácil acceso; a corta distancia. **to r. after,** procurar alcanzar; hacer esfuerzos para obtener. **to r. back,** (of time) remontarse. **to r. down,** bajar.

react /ri'ækt/ *vi* reaccionar. *vt* hacer de nuevo; Theat. volver a representar

reaction /ri'ækʃən/ *n* reacción, *f*

reactionary /ri'ækʃə,neri/ *a* and *n* reaccionario (-ia)

reactive /ri'æktɪv/ *a* reactivo

read /rid/ *vt* leer; (a riddle, etc.) adivinar; descifrar; interpretar; (study) estudiar; (the Burial Service, etc.) decir; (correct) corregir; (of thermometers, etc.) marcar. *vi* leer; estudiar; (be written) estar escrito, decir. **The play acts better than it reads,** La comedia es mejor representada que leída. **to r. aloud,** leer en voz alta. **to r. between the lines,** leer entre líneas. **to r. proofs,** corregir pruebas. **to r. to oneself,** leer para sí. **to r. about,** leer (learn) enterarse de. **to r. again,** volver a leer, leer otra vez. **to r. on,** continuar leyendo. **to r. out,** leer en alta voz. **to r. over,** leer; leerlo todo. **to r. over and over again,** leer muchas veces, leer y releer.

read /red/ *past part* leído, etc. **well-r.,** releído; instruido, culto

readability /ˌridəˈbɪlɪti/ n legibilidad, f; interés, m, amenidad, f
readable /ˈridəbəl/ a legible; interesante
readdress /ˌriəˈdrɛs/ vt dirigir de nuevo (una carta, etc.); poner la nueva dirección en (una carta, etc.)
reader /ˈridər/ n lector (-ra); Eccl. lector, m; (proof) corrector de pruebas, m; (citation collector for a dictionary) cedulista, mf; (university) profesor (-ra) auxiliar a cátedra; (book) libro de lectura, m. **to be a great r.,** leer mucho. **the Spanish r.** (reader of Spanish books) el lector de español
readily /ˈrɛdli/ adv fácilmente; en seguida, inmediatamente; de buena gana, con placer
readiness /ˈrɛdinɪs/ n prontitud, expedición, f; buena voluntad, f; (of speech, etc.) facilidad, f. **in r.,** preparado. **r. of wit,** viveza de ingenio, f
reading /ˈridɪŋ/ n lectura, Lat. Am. also leída, f; (erudition) conocimientos, m pl; (recital) declamación, f; (lecture) conferencia, f; (study) estudio, m; interpretación, f; (of a thermometer, etc.) registro, m; (of a will) apertura, f. **at one reading,** Lat. Am. de una leída. **r.-book,** libro de lectura, m. **r.-desk,** atril, m. **r.-glass,** lente para leer, m, carlita, f. **r.-lamp,** lámpara de sobremesa, f. **r.-matter,** material de lectura, m. **r.-room,** gabinete de lectura, m, sala de lectura, f
readjourn /ˌriəˈdʒɜrn/ vt (a meeting) suspender (la sesión) de nuevo
readjust /ˌriəˈdʒʌst/ vt reajustar, reacomdar; vi reacomodarse
readjustment /ˌriəˈdʒʌstmənt/ n reajuste, m, reacomodación, f
readmission /ˌriədˈmɪʃən/ n readmisión, f
ready /ˈrɛdi/ a listo, preparado; dispuesto; pronto; (on the point of) a punto de; (easy) fácil; (near at hand) a la mano; (with money) contante; (with wit, etc.) vivo; (available) disponible; (nimble) ágil, ligero. **I am r. to do it,** Estoy dispuesto a hacerlo. **in r. cash,** en dinero contante. **to get r.,** prepararse; (dress) vestirse. **to make r.,** vt preparar; aprestar; Print. imponer. vi prepararse, disponerse. **r.-made,** hecho; confeccionado. **r.-made clothing,** ropa hecha, f. **r. money,** dinero contante, m. **r.-witted,** de ingenio vivo
reaffirm /ˌriəˈfɜrm/ vt afirmar de nuevo; reiterar, volver a repetir
reaffirmation /ˌriæfərˈmeɪʃən/ n reiteración, f
reagent /riˈeɪdʒənt/ n reactivo, m
real /reiˈɑl/ a real; verdadero; efectivo; (with silk, etc.) puro; sincero. **r. estate, r. property,** bienes raíces, m pl
realism /ˈriəˌlɪzəm/ n realismo, m
realist /ˈriəlɪst/ n realista, mf
realistic /ˌriəˈlɪstɪk/ a realista
reality /riˈælɪti/ n realidad, f; verdad, f
realizable /ˌriəˈlaizəbəl/ a realizable; factible
realization /ˌriələˈzeɪʃən/ n realización, f; comprensión, f
realize /ˈriəˌlaiz/ vt (understand) darse cuenta de, hacerse cargo de; realizar; (make real) dar vida a; (accomplish) llevar a cabo; Com. realizar; (gain) adquirir
really /ˈriəli/ adv realmente; en verdad; en realidad; en efecto; (frankly) francamente. **R.?** ¿De veras?
realm /rɛlm/ n reino, m, dominios, m pl; Fig. esfera, f
realty /ˈriəlti/ n bienes raíces, m pl
ream /rim/ n resma, f
reanimate /ˌriˈænəˌmeit/ vt reanimar
reap /rip/ vt segar; Fig. cosechar, recoger
reaper /ˈripər/ n segador (-ra); (machine) segadora mecánica, f
reaping /ˈripɪŋ/ n siega, f; Fig. cosecha, f. **r.-machine,** segadora mecánica, f
reappear /ˌriəˈpɪər/ vi reaparecer
reappearance /ˌriəˈpɪərəns/ n reaparición, f
reapplication /ˌriæplɪˈkeɪʃən/ n nueva aplicación, f; (of paint, etc.) otra capa, f; (for a post, etc.) neuva solicitud, f
reapply /ˌriəˈplai/ vt aplicar de nuevo; (paint, etc.) dar otra capa (de); (for a post, etc.) mandar una nueva solicitud
reappoint /ˌriəˈpɔint/ vt designar de nuevo

rear /rɪər/ vt (lift) alzar, levantar; (breed, educate) criar; (build) erigir, construir. vi (of horses) encabritarse, corcovear
rear /rɪər/ n cola, f; parte de atrás, f; parte posterior, f; última fila, f; (background) fondo, m; Inf. trasera, f; Mil. retaguardia, f. a de atrás; trasero; último; posterior; de última fila; Mil. de retaguardia. **in the r.,** por detrás; a la cola; a retaguardia. **to bring up the r.,** cerrar la marcha. **r.-admiral,** contra almirante, m. **r.-axle,** eje trasero, m. **r.-guard,** retaguardia, f. **r. lamp,** faro trasero, m. **r. rank,** última fila, f. **r. view, lamp,** faro trasero, m. **r. rank,** última fila, f. **r. view,** vista por detrás, f; vista posterior, f
rearing /ˈrɪərɪŋ/ n (breeding) cría, f; (education) crianza, f
rearm /riˈɑrm/ vt rearmar. vi rearmarse
rearmament /riˈɑrməmənt/ n rearmamento, m
rearrange /ˌriəˈreindʒ/ vt volver a arreglar; arreglar de otra manera; (a literary work) refundir, adaptar
rearrangement /ˌriəˈreindʒmənt/ n nuevo arroglo, m; (of a literary work) refundición, adaptación, f
reascend /ˌriəˈsɛnd/ vi and vt subir de nuevo, subir otra vez; montar de nuevo (sobre)
reason /ˈrizən/ n razón, f. **I have plenty of r. to...** No me faltarían motivos para... vi and vt razonar. **to r. out of,** disuadir de. **by r. of,** a causa de, con motivo de; en virtud de. **for this r.,** por esto, por esta razón. **out of all r.,** fuera de razón. **to stand to r.,** ser lógico, estar puesto en razón. **with r.,** con razón. **r. of state,** razón de estado, f
reasonable /ˈrizənəbəl/ a razonable; racional
reasonableness /ˈrizənəbəlnɪs/ n lo razonable; moderación, f; justicia, f; racionalidad, f
reasonably /ˈrizənəbli/ adv razonablemente; con razón; bastante
reasoning /ˈrizənɪŋ/ n razonamiento, m
reassemble /ˌriəˈsɛmbəl/ vt reunir otra vez. vi juntarse de nuevo
reassert /ˌriəˈsɜrt/ vt afirmar de nuevo, reiterar
reassertion /ˌriəˈsɜrʃən/ n reiteración, f
reassess /ˌriəˈsɛs/ vt tasar de nuevo; repartir de nuevo; (a work of art) hacer una nueva apreciación (de)
reassessment /ˌriəˈsɛsmənt/ n nueva tasación, f; nuevo repartimiento, m; (of a work of art) nueva estimación, f
reassume /ˌriəˈsum/ vt reasumir
reassumption /ˌriəˈsʌmpʃən/ n reasunción, f
reassurance /ˌriəˈsʊrəns/ n afirmación repetida, f; confianza restablecida, f
reassure /ˌriəˈʃʊr/ vt asegurar de nuevo; tranquilizar, confortar
reassuring /ˌriəˈʃʊrɪŋ/ a tranquilizador, consolador
rebate /ˈribeit/ n rebaja, f, descuento, m; reducción, f. vt rebajar, descontar; reducir. **to r. pro rata,** ratear
rebec /ˈribɛk/ n Mus. rabel, m
rebel /ˈrɛbəl; v. rɪˈbɛl/ n rebelde, mf, insurrecto (-ta). vi rebelarse, sublevarse. **r. leader,** cabecilla, m
rebellion /rɪˈbɛlyən/ n rebelión, f
rebellious /rɪˈbɛlyəs/ a rebelde; revoltoso; refractario
rebelliousness /rɪˈbɛlyəsnɪs/ n rebeldía, f
rebind /riˈbaind/ vt atar de nuevo; (a book) reencuadernar
rebirth /riˈbɜrθ/ n renacimiento, m
rebore /riˈbɔr/ vt (an engine) descarbonizar
reboring /riˈbɔrɪŋ/ n (of an engine) descarburación, f
reborn, to be /riˈbɔrn/ vi renacer; ser reincarnado, (Christianity) ser naciado (-da) de nuevo
rebound /v. rɪˈbaund; n. ˈriˌbaund/ a (of books) reencuadernado; vi rebotar; repercutir; (envy) reavivarse. n rebote, resalto, m; Mil. reacción, f, rechazo, m
rebuff /rɪˈbʌf/ n repulsa, f, desaire, m; contrariedad, f. vt rechazar; contrariar
rebuild /riˈbɪld/ vt reedificar
rebuilding /riˈbɪldɪŋ/ n reedificación, f
rebuke /rɪˈbyuk/ n reconvención, reprensión, censura, f, reproche, m, vt reprender, censurar, reprochar
rebukingly /rɪˈbyukɪŋli/ adv en tono de censura; con reprensión, con reprobación
rebut /rɪˈbʌt/ vt refutar
rebuttal /rɪˈbʌtl/ n refutación, f

recalcitrance /rɪˈkælsɪtrəns/ n terquedad, obstinacia, f; rebeldía, f
recalcitrant /rɪˈkælsɪtrənt/ a reacio, recalcitrante
recall / v. rɪˈkɔl; n. also ˈrikɔl/ vt llamar; hacer volver; (dismiss) destituir; (ambassador, etc.) retirar; (remind or remember) recordar; (revoke) revocar. n llamada, f; Mil. toque de llamada, m; (of ambassadors, etc.) retirada, f; (dismissal) destitución, f. **beyond r.**, irrevocable; (forgotten) olvidado
recant /rɪˈkænt/ vt retractar, retirar. vi desdecirse (de), retractarse
recantation /ˌrikænˈteiʃən/ n recantación, f
recapitulate /ˌrikəˈpɪtʃəˌleit/ vt recapitular, resumir
recapitulation /ˌrikəˌpɪtʃəˈleiʃən/ n recapitulación, f
recapture /riˈkæptʃər/ vt volver a prender, hacer prisionero nuevamente; (a place) volver a tomar; (a ship) represar
recast /riˈkæst/ vt (metals, a literary work) refundir; (alter) cambiar; (reckon) volver a calcular
recasting /riˈkæstɪŋ/ n (metals, a literary work) refundición, f
recede /riˈsid/ vi retroceder; alejarse (de), separarse (de); desviarse (de); retirarse; desaparecer; (diminish) disminuir; (of prices) bajar
receding /riˈsidɪŋ/ a que retrocede, etc.
receipt /rɪˈsit/ n recibo, m; (for money) recibí, m; (recipe) receta, f; pl **receipts**, ingresos, m pl. vt firmar (or extender) recibo. **on r. of**, al recibir. **to acknowledge the r. of**, acusar recibo de. **r. book**, libro talonario, m
receive /rɪˈsiv/ vt and vi recibir; admitir, aceptar; acoger; (money) percibir, cobrar; (lodge) hospedar, alojar; (contain) contener. **to r. one's degree**, Lat. Am. diplomarse. **to be well received**, tener buena acogida
receiver /rɪˈsivər/ n recibidor (-ra); (of stolen goods) receptador (-ra); (in bankruptcies) síndico, m; (for other legal business) receptor, m; (of a telephone) auricular, m; Elec. receptor, m; Radio. radiorreceptor, m. **to hang up (the r.)**, colgar (el auricular)
receivership /rɪˈsivərˌʃip/ n sindicatura, f; receptoría, f
receiving /rɪˈsivɪŋ/ n recibimiento, m; (of money, etc.) cobranza, f, percibo, m; (of stolen goods) encubrimiento, m. a que recibe; recipiente; de recepción. **r. set**, aparato de radio, m
recency /ˈrisənsi/ n lo reciente; novedad, f
recent /ˈrisənt/ a reciente; nuevo. **in r. years**, en estos últimos años
recently /ˈrisəntli/ adv recientemente; (before past participles) recién. **until r.**, hasta hace poco. **r. painted**, recién pintado
receptacle /rɪˈsɛptəkəl/ n receptáculo, recipiente, m; Bot. receptáculo, m
reception /rɪˈsɛpʃən/ n recepción, f; recibo, m; (welcome) acogida, f; (of evidence) recepción, f. **r. room**, pieza de recibo, f, gabinete, m
receptive /rɪˈsɛptɪv/ a receptivo; susceptible
receptiveness /rɪˈsɛptɪvnɛs/ n sensibilidad, susceptibilidad, f
recess /rɪˈsɛs, ˈrisɛs/ n (holiday) vacaciones, f pl; (during school hours) hora de recreo, f; (Fig. heart) seno, m, entrañas, f pl; (of the soul, heart) hondón, m; (in a coastline, etc.) depresión, f; (in a wall) nicho, m; (alcove) alcoba, f. **parliamentary r.**, interregno parlamentario, m
recessional /rɪˈsɛʃən/ n himno que se canta mientras se retiran los eclesiásticos y el coro, m
recharge /riˈtʃɑrdʒ/ vt (a gun, etc.) recargar; acusar de nuevo
recipe /ˈrɛsəpi/ n receta, f
recipient /rɪˈsɪpiənt/ n recibidor (-ra); el, m, (f, la) que recibe. a recipiente; receptivo
reciprocal /rɪˈsɪprəkəl/ a recíproco
reciprocate /rɪˈsɪprəˌkeit/ vt reciprocar; Mech. producir movimiento de vaivén. vi Mech. oscilar, tener movimiento alternativo; corresponder; ser recíproco
reciprocation /rɪˌsɪprəˈkeiʃən/ n reciprocación, f; reciprocidad, correspondencia, f
reciprocity /ˌrɛsəˈprɒsəti/ n reciprocidad, f
recital /rɪˈsaitl/ n narración, relación, f; enumeración, f; recitación, f; Mus. recital, m

recitation /ˌrɛsɪˈteiʃən/ n recitación, f
recitative /ˌrɛsɪtəˈtiv/ n recitado, m
recite /rɪˈsait/ vt recitar, repetir; narrar; declamar. vi decir una recitación
reciter /rɪˌsaitər/ n recitador (-ra); declamador (-ra)
reckless /ˈrɛklɪs/ a temerario, audaz; precipitado; descuidado (de); indiferente (a); excesivo; imprudente
recklessly /ˈrɛklɪsli/ adv temerariamente; descuidadamente; imprudentemente
recklessness /ˈrɛklɪsnɪs/ n temeridad, audacia, f; descuido, m; imprudencia, f; indiferencia, f
reckon /ˈrɛkən/ vt calcular, computar; contar; enumerar; (believe) considerar, juzgar; (attribute) atribuir; (think) creer (que). **to r. up**, echar cuentas, calcular. **to r. with**, contar con; tomar en serio
reckoner /ˈrɛkənər/ n calculador (-ra). **ready r.**, tablas matemáticas, f pl
reckoning /ˈrɛkənɪŋ/ n cálculo, m, calculación, f; cuenta, f; Fig. retribución, f, castigo, m; Naut. estima, f. **the day of r.**, el día de ajuste de cuentas; el día del juicio final. **to be out in one's r.**, equivocarse en el cálculo; engañarse en el juicio
reclaim /rɪˈkleim/ vt (land) entarquinar; (reform) reformar; (tame) domesticar; (claim) reclamar; (restore) restaurar
reclamation /ˌrɛkləˈmeiʃən/ n (of land) entarquinamiento, m; cultivo, m; (reform) reformación, f; (restoration) restauración, f; (claiming) reclamación, f
recline /rɪˈklain/ vt apoyar; recostar; reclinar; descansar, reposar. vi recostarse, reclinarse; estar tumbado; apoyarse; descansar
reclining /rɪˈklainɪŋ/ a reclinación, f. a inclinado; acostado; (of statues) yacente
recluse /ˈrɛklus, rɪˈklus/ a solitario, n recluso (-sa); solitario (-ia); ermitaño, m, anacoreta, mf
recognition /ˌrɛkəgˈniʃən/ n reconocimiento, m
recognizable /ˌrɛkəgˈnaizəbəl/ a que puede reconocerse; identificable
recognizance /rɪˈkɒgnəzəns, -ˈkɒnə-/ n reconocimiento, m; Law. obligación, f
recognize /ˈrɛkəgˌnaiz/ vt reconocer; confesar
recoil /n. ˈrikɔil; v. rɪˈkɔil/ n reculada, f; (of a gun) culatazo, m; (refusal) rechazo, m; (result) repercusión, f; (repugnance) aversión, repugnancia, f. vi recular; retroceder; repercutir; sentir repugnancia
recoin /riˈkɔin/ vt acuñar de nuevo
recollect /ˌrɛkəˈlɛkt/ vt acordarse de, recordar. **to r. oneself**, reponerse, recobrarse
recollection /ˌrɛkəˈlɛkʃən/ n recuerdo, m, memoria, f
recommence /ˌrikəˈmɛns/ vt and vi empezar de nuevo
recommend /ˌrɛkəˈmɛnd/ vt recomendar; aconsejar; encargar
recommendable /ˌrɛkəˈmɛndəbəl/ a recomendable
recommendation /ˌrɛkəmɛnˈdeiʃən/ n recomendación, f
recommendatory /ˌrɛkəˈmɛndəˌtɔri/ a recomendatario
recommender /ˌrɛkəˈmɛndər/ n el, m, (f, la) que recomienda
recompense /ˈrɛkəmˌpɛns/ n recompensa, f, vt recompensar
recomposition /ˌrɛkɒmpəˈziʃən/ n recomposición, f
reconcilability /ˌrɛkənˌsailəˈbiliti/ n posibilidad de reconciliación, f; compatibilidad, f
reconcilable /ˌrɛkənˈsailəbəl/ a reconciliable; compatible; conciliable
reconcile /ˈrɛkənˌsail/ vt reconciliar; (quarrels) componer, ajustar; (opposing theories, etc.) conciliar; (accounts) ajustar. **to r. oneself (to)**, aceptar; acostumbrarse (a); resignarse (a)
reconciler /ˈrɛkənˌsailər/ n reconciliador (-ra)
reconciliation /ˌrɛkənˌsiliˈeiʃən/ n reconciliación, f; (of theories, etc.) conciliación, f; (of accounts) ajuste, m
reconciliatory /ˌrɛkənˈsiliəˌtɔri/ a reconciliador
recondite /ˈrɛkənˌdait/ a recóndito
recondition /ˌrikənˈdiʃən/ vt reacondicionar
reconnaissance /rɪˈkɒnəsəns, -zəns/ n reconoci-

miento, *m*; exploración, *f*. **r. flight,** vuelo de reconocimiento, *m*. **r. plane,** avión de reconocimiento, *m*
reconnoiter /ˌrikəˈnɔitər/ *vt Mil.* reconocer; explorar. *vi Mil.* practicar un reconocimiento; correr la campaña
reconnoitering /ˌrikəˈnɔitərɪŋ/ *n* reconocimiento, *m*, *a* de reconocimiento
reconquer /riˈkɒŋkər/ *vt* reconquistar
reconquest /riˈkɒŋkwɛst/ *n* reconquista, *f*
reconsecrate /riˈkɒnsɪˌkreit/ *vt* consagrar de nuevo
reconsider /ˌrikənˈsɪdər/ *vt* considerar de nuevo, volver a considerar; volver a discutir
reconsideration /ˌrikənˌsɪdəˈreiʃən/ *n* nueva consideración, *f*; nueva discusión, *f*
reconstitute /riˈkɒnstɪˌtut/ *vt* reconstituir
reconstitution /riˌkɒnstɪˈtuʃən/ *n* reconstitución, *f*
reconstruct /ˌrikənˈstrʌkt/ *vt* reconstruir
reconstruction /ˌrikənˈstrʌkʃən/ *n* reconstrucción, *f*
reconversion /ˌrikənˈvɜrʒən/ *n* reconversión, *f*
recopy /riˈkɒpi/ *vt* copiar de nuevo
record /*v.* rɪˈkɔrd; *n.* ˈrɛkərd/ *vt* apuntar; inscribir; (recount) contar, escribir; recordar; registrar; (of thermometers, etc.) marcar, registrar; hacer un disco de gramófono de; (radio, cinema) impresionar. *n* relación, *f*; crónica, *f*; historia, *f*; (soldier's) hoja de servicios, *f*; (past) antecedentes, *m pl*; documento, *m*; inscripción, *f*; (entry) partida, *f*; testimonio, *m*; (memory) recuerdo, *m*; registro, *m*; (phonograph) disco, *m*; *Sports.* record, *m*, plusmarca, *f*; *pl* **records,** *m pl*; (notes) notas, *f pl*; (facts) datos, *m pl*; anales, *m pl*. **keeper of the records,** archivero, *m*. **off the r.,** confidencialmente. **on r.,** escrito; registrado; inscrito en los anales de la historia. **to break a r.,** supremar precedentes. **r.-holder,** plusmarquista, *mf*
recorder /rɪˈkɔrdər/ *n* registrador, *m*; archivero, *m*; *Law.* juez, *m*; (historian) historiador, *m*; *Mus.* caramillo, *m*; *Mech.* contador, indicador, *m*; (scientific) aparato registrador, *m*
recording /rɪˈkɔrdɪŋ/ *a* registrador. **r. apparatus,** (cinema, radio, record player) máquina de impresionar, *f*; (scientific) aparato registrador, *m*. **r. van,** carro de sonido, *m*
recount /rɪˈkaunt/ *vt* contar de nuevo; (tell) referir, narrar, contar
recoup /rɪˈkup/ *vt* compensar, indemnizar; recobrar; desquitarse de
recourse /ˈrikɔrs/ *n* recurso, *m*. **to have r. to,** recurrir a
recover /rɪˈkʌvər/ *vt* (regain) recobrar; *Fig.* reconquistar; (retrieve) rescatar; *Law.* reivindicar. *vi* reponerse; (in health) recuperarse, recobrar la salud, sanar, curarse; *Law.* ganar un pleito. **to r. consciousness,** volver en sí
recoverable /rɪˈkʌvərəbəl/ *a* recuperable
recovery /rɪˈkʌvəri/ *n* (regaining) recobro, *m*, recuperación, *f*; (of money) cobranza, *f*; (retrieval) rescate, *m*; *Fig.* reconquista, *f*; (from illness) mejoría, convalecencia, *f*; restablecimiento, *m*; *Law.* reivindicación, *f*
recreant /ˈrɛkriənt/ *a* traidor, falso, desleal. *n* apóstata, *mf* traidor (-ra)
recreate /ˈrɛkriˌeit/ *vt* recrear
recreation /ˌrɛkriˈeiʃən/ *n* recreación, *f*; (break in schools) recreo, *m*. **r. hall,** sala de recreo, *f*
recreative /ˈrɛkriˌeitɪv/ *a* recreativo
recriminate /rɪˈkrɪməˌneit/ *vi* recriminar
recrimination /rɪˌkrɪməˈneiʃən/ *n* recriminación, reconvención, *f*
recriminator /rɪˈkrɪməˌneitər/ *n* recriminador (-ra)
recriminatory /rɪˈkrɪmənəˌtɔri/ *a* recriminador
recross /riˈkrɔs/ *vt* volver a cruzar, cruzar de nuevo
recrudesce /ˌrikruˈdɛs/ *vi* recrudecer
recrudescence /ˌrikruˈdɛsəns/ *n* recrudescencia, *f*
recrudescent /ˌrikruˈdɛsənt/ *a* recrudescente
recruit /rɪˈkrut/ *n* recluta, *m*. *vt* reclutar; (restore) reponer
recruiting /rɪˈkrutɪŋ/ *n* reclutamiento, *m*. **r. office,** caja de reclutamiento, *f*
rectal /ˈrɛktl/ *a* rectal
rectangle /ˈrɛkˌtæŋgəl/ *n* rectángulo, *m*
rectangular /rɛkˈtæŋgyələr/ *a* rectangular

rectifiable /ˈrɛktəˌfaiəbəl/ *a* rectificable
rectification /ˌrɛktəfɪˈkeiʃən/ *n* rectificación, *f*
rectifier /ˈrɛktəˌfaiər/ *n* rectificador, *m*
rectify /ˈrɛktəˌfai/ *vt* rectificar
rectilinear /ˌrɛktlˈɪniər/ *a* rectilíneo
rectitude /ˈrɛktɪˌtud/ *n* rectitud, *f*
rector /ˈrɛktər/ *n* (of a university or school) rector, *m*; (priest) párroco, *m*
rectorship /ˈrɛktərˌʃɪp/ *n* rectorado, *m*
rectory /ˈrɛktəri/ *n* rectoral, rectoría, *f*
rectum /ˈrɛktəm/ *n* recto, *m*
recumbent /rɪˈkʌmbənt/ *a* recostado, reclinado; (of statue) yacente
recuperable /rɪˈkupərəbəl/ *a* recuperable
recuperate /rɪˈkupəˌreit/ *vt* recuperar, recobrar. *vi* restablecerse, reponerse; recuperarse
recuperation /rɪkupəˈreiʃən/ *n* recuperación, *f*
recuperative /rɪˈkupərətɪv/ *a* recuperativo
recur /rɪˈkɜr/ *vi* presentarse a la imaginación; volver (sobre); presentarse de nuevo, aparecer otra vez; repetirse; reproducirse
recurrence /rɪˈkɜrəns/ *n* reaparición, *f*; repetición, *f*
recurrent /rɪˈkɜrənt/ *a* periódico; *Med.* recurrente
recycle /riˈsaikəl/ *vt* reciclar
red /rɛd/ *a* rojo; (of wine) tinto. *n* color rojo, *m*; (in billiards) mingo, *m*, bola roja, *f*; *Polit.* rojo, *m*. **to catch red-handed,** coger con el hurto en las manos; coger con las manos en la masa, coger en el acto. **to grow red,** enrojecerse, ponerse rojo; volverse rojo. **red-berried,** con bayas rojas. **red cabbage,** lombarda, *f*. **red cedar,** cedro dulce, *m*. **red corpuscle,** glóbulo rojo, *m*. **Red Cross,** Cruz Roja, *f*. **red currant,** grosella, *f*. **red currant bush,** grosellero, *m*. **red-eyed,** con los ojos inyectados. **red fir,** pino silvestre, *m*. **red flush,** (in the sky) arrebol, *m*. **red-gold,** bermejo; (of hair, etc.) rojo. **red-haired,** pelirrojo, de pelo rojo. **red-handed,** con las manos ensangrentadas; *Fig.* en el acto. **red-head** (person) pelirrojo (-ja). **red-heat,** incandescencia, *f*. **red-hot,** candente, *m*. **red-lead,** minio, *m*. **red-letter,** de fiesta; extraordinario. **red-letter day,** día de fiesta, *m*; día extraordinario, *m*. **red mullet,** salmonete, *m*, trilla, *f*. **red ocher,** almagre, *m*. **red pepper,** pimiento, *m*; (cayenne) pimentón, *Lat. Am.* ají, *m*, **Red Sea,** mar Rojo, mar Bermejo, *m*. **red tape,** balduque, *m*; formulismo, *m*; burocracia, *f*. **red wine,** vino tinto, *m*
redbreast /ˈrɛdˌbrɛst/ *n* petirrojo, *m*
redden /ˈrɛdn/ *vt* rojear, enrojecer; pintar de rojo. *vi* enrojecerse, ponerse rojo; volverse rojo
reddish /ˈrɛdɪʃ/ *a* rojizo
redeem /rɪˈdim/ *vt* (a mortgage, bonds, etc.) amortizar; (from pawn) desempeñar; (a promise, etc.) cumplir; libertar; redimir; compensar; (a fault) expiar; (reform) reformar; (rescue) rescatar
redeemable /rɪˈdiməbəl/ *a* redimible; amortizable
redeemer /rɪˈdimər/ *n* rescatador (-ra); salvador (-ra); *Theol.* Redentor, *m*
redeeming /rɪˈdimɪŋ/ *a* redentor; compensatorio. **r. feature,** compensación, *f*; rasgo bueno, *m*. **There is no r. feature in his work,** No hay nada bueno en su obra
redemption /rɪˈdɛmpʃən/ *n* (of a mortgage, etc.) amortización, *f*; (from pawn) desempeño, *m*; (of a promise, etc.) cumplimiento, *m*; (ransom, etc.) rescate, *m*; *Theol.* redención, *f*; compensación, *f*; (of a fault) expiación, *f*; reformación, *f*
redemptive /rɪˈdɛmptɪv/ *a* redentor
redescend /ˌridiˈsɛnd/ *vi* bajar de nuevo
rediscovery /ˌridəˈskʌvəri/ *n* nuevo descubrimiento, *m*
redistribute /ˌridɪˈstrɪbyut/ *vt* distribuir de nuevo, volver a distribuir
redistribution /ˌridɪstrəˈbyuʃən/ *n* nueva distribución, *f*
redness /ˈrɛdnɪs/ *n* rojez, *f*, color rojo, *m*
redolent /ˈrɛdlənt/ *a* fragante, oloroso; *Fig.* evocador (de)
redouble /riˈdʌbəl/ *vt* redoblar. *vi* redoblarse
redoubling /riˈdʌblɪŋ/ *n* redoblamiento, *m*
redoubt /rɪˈdaut/ *n* reducto, *m*

redoubtable /rɪ'dautəbəl/ a formidable, terrible; valiente

redound /rɪ'daund/ vi redundar (en)

redress /rɪ'drɛs/ vt rectificar; reparar; remediar; hacer justicia (a); corregir

reduce /rɪ'dus/ vt reducir; disminuir; (in price) rebajar; abreviar; (exhaust, weaken) agotar; (impoverish) empobrecer; (degrade) degradar. **to r. to the ranks,** Mil. volver a las filas; degradar. **to be in reduced circumstances,** estar en la indigencia

reducible /rɪ'dusəbəl/ a reducible

reduction /rɪ'dʌkʃən/ n reducción, f; (in price) rebaja, f

redundance /rɪ'dʌndəns/ n redundancia, f

redundant /rɪ'dʌndənt/ a redundante; superfluo, excesivo

reduplicate /rɪ'duplɪˌkeit/ vt reduplicar

reduplication /rɪˌduplɪ'keiʃən/ n reduplicación, f

reecho /ri'ɛkou/ vt repetir; devolver el son de, hacer reverberar. vi repercutirse, reverberar

reed /rid/ n Bot. caña, f; (arrow) saeta, f; (pipe) caramillo, m; (in wind-instruments) lengüeta, f; Archit. junquillo, m; (in a loom) peine, m; (pastoral poetry) poesía bucólica, f. vt (thatch) bardar con cañas

reedit /ri'edɪt/ vt reeditar, volver a editar

reedy /'ridi/ a juncoso, lleno de cañas; (of the voice) silbante

reef /rif/ n arrecife, escollo, encalladero, m; Mineral. filón, m; Naut. rizo, m. vt Naut. arrizar. **to take in reefs,** Naut. hacer el rizo. **r.-knot,** nudo de marino, m

reek /rik/ n humo, m; olor, m. vi humear; oler (de); Fig. recordar, hacer pensar (en)

reeky /'riki/ a humoso

reel /ril/ n carrete, m; devanadera, f; (of a fishing rod) carrete, carretel, m; (cinema) cinta, f; (dance) baile escocés, m. vt devanar. vi tambalear, titubear; (of ships, etc.) cabecear; temblar; oscilar. **to r. about drunkenly,** (of persons) andar haciendo eses, arrimarse a las paredes. **to r. off,** recitar; enumerar; decir rápidamente

reelect /ˌrii'lɛkt/ vt reelegir

reelection /ˌrii'lɛkʃən/ n reelección, f

reeligible /ri'ɛlɪdʒəbəl/ a reelegible

reeling /'rilɪŋ/ n tambaleo, m; andar vacilante, m; (of a ship, etc.) cabeceo, m; oscilación, f

reembarcation /ˌriɛmbar'keiʃən/ n reembarque, m

reembark /ˌriɛm'bark/ vt reembarcar. vi reembarcarse

reemerge /ˌrii'mɜrdʒ/ vi reaparecer

reemergence /ˌrii'mɜrdʒəns/ n reaparición, f

reenact /ˌrii'nækt/ vt revalidar (una ley); decretar de nuevo

reenactment /ˌrii'næktmənt/ n revalidación (de una ley), f; nuevo decreto, m

reengage /ˌriin'geidʒ/ vt contratar de nuevo

reengagement /ˌriin'geidʒmənt/ n nuevo contrato, m

reenlist /ˌriin'lɪst/ vt and vi alistar(se) de nuevo

reenlistment /ˌriin'lɪstmənt/ n reenganche, m

reenter /ri'ɛntər/ vt volver a entrar (en); reingresar (en)

reentry /ri'ɛntri/ n segunda entrada, f, reingreso, m

reequip /ˌrii'kwɪp/ vt equipar de nuevo

reestablish /ˌrii'stæblɪʃ/ vt restablecer; restaurar

reestablishment /ˌrii'stæblɪʃmənt/ n restablecimiento, m; restauración, f

reexamination /ˌriigˌzæmɪ'neiʃən/ n reexaminación, f; nuevo examen, m; Law. nuevo interrogatorio, m

reexamine /ˌriig'zæmɪn/ vt reexaminar; Law. interrogar de nuevo

refashion /ri'fæʃən/ vt volver a hacer; formar de nuevo

refection /rɪ'fɛkʃən/ n refección, f

refectory /rɪ'fɛktəri/ n refectorio, m

refer /rɪ'fɜr/ vt atribuir (a); (send) enviar, remitir; (assign) referir (a), relacionar (con). vi referirse (a); aludir (a); hablar (de)

referee /ˌrɛfə'ri/ n árbitro, m; Law. juez arbitrador, m; (reference) garante, mf fiador (-ra). vi servir de árbitro

reference /'rɛfərəns/ n referencia, f; consulta, f; mención, f; alusión, f; (relation) relación, f; pl **references,** Com. referencias, f pl. **for r.,** para consulta. **in r. to,** con referencia a, respecto a, en cuanto a. **terms of r.,** puntos de consulta, m pl. **work of r.,** libro de consulta, m

reference book n libro de consulta, m

referendum /ˌrɛfə'rɛndəm/ n referéndum, m

refill /v. ri'fɪl; n. 'ri,fɪl/ vt rellenar; rehenchir; (pen) llenar de nuevo con tinta. n (for a pencil) mina de recambio, f

refine /rɪ'fain/ vt refinar; (metals) acrisolar; (fats) clarificar; Fig. perfeccionar, pulir, refinar

refined /rɪ'faind/ a refinado; fino; culto; cortés; elegante; delicado; (subtle) sutil; (affected) afectado

refinement /rɪ'fainmənt/ n refinamiento, m; finura, f; cultura, f; cortesía, f; elegancia, f; delicadeza, f; (subtlety) sutileza, f; (affectation) afectación, f

refiner /rɪ'fainər/ n refinador, m

refinery /rɪ'fainəri/ n refinería, f

refining /rɪ'fainɪŋ/ n refinación, f; Fig. refinamiento, m

refit /ri'fɪt/ vt reparar; Naut. embonar

refitting /ri'fɪtɪŋ/ n reparación, f; Naut. embonada, f

reflect /rɪ'flɛkt/ vt reflejar; reflexionar. vi reflejar; reflexionar (sobre), pensar (en), meditar (sobre). **This offer reflects credit on him,** Esta oferta le hace honor. **to r. on, upon,** reflexionar sobre; (disparage) desacreditar; (affect unfavorably) perjudicar

reflecting /rɪ'flɛktɪŋ/ a reflector

reflection /rɪ'flɛkʃən/ n Phys. reflexión, f; reflejo, m; consideración, f, pensamiento, m; (aspersion) censura, f, reproche, m. **upon mature r.,** después de pensarlo bien

reflective /rɪ'flɛktɪv/ a Phys. reflector; reflexivo, pensativo, meditabundo

reflectively /rɪ'flɛktɪvli/ adv reflexivamente

reflector /rɪ'flɛktər/ n reflector, m; (shade) pantalla, f

reflex /'riflɛks/ a reflejo. n reflejo, m; acción refleja, f. **r. action,** acción refleja, f

refloat /ri'flout/ vt (a ship) poner otra vex a flote, desvarar

reflux /'ri,flʌks/ n reflujo, m

reforestation /riˌfɔrə'steiʃən/ n nuevas plantaciones, f pl

reform /rɪ'fɔrm/ n reforma, f. a de reforma; reformista. vt reformar; formar de nuevo. vi reformarse

reformation /ˌrɛfər'meiʃən/ n reformación, f; **Reformation,** Reforma, f

reformatory /rɪ'fɔrməˌtɔri/ a reformatorio, reformador. n reformatorio, m, casa de corrección, f

reformer /rɪ'fɔrmər/ n reformador (-ra), reformista, mf

refract /rɪ'frækt/ vt refractar

refraction /rɪ'frækʃən/ n refracción, f

refractive /rɪ'fræktɪv/ a refringente

refractoriness /rɪ'fræktərinɪs/ n terquedad, obstinacia, f; rebeldía, indocilidad, f

refractory /rɪ'fræktəri/ a (of substances) refractario; recalcitrante, intratable, rebelde

refrain /rɪ'frein/ n estribillo, estrambote, m

refrain /rɪ'frein/ vi abstenerse (de), evitar

refresh /rɪ'frɛʃ/ vt refrescar

refreshing /rɪ'frɛʃɪŋ/ a refrescante; atractivo; estimulante; interesante

refreshment /rɪ'frɛʃmənt/ n (solace) solaz, m, reposo, m; recreación, f, deleite, m; (food and (or) drink) refresco, m. **r.-room,** (at a station) fonda, f. **r. stand,** Mexico fresquería, f

refrigerate /rɪ'frɪdʒəˌreit/ vt refrigerar; enfriar; refrescar

refrigeration /rɪˌfrɪdʒə'reiʃən/ n refrigeración, f; enfriamiento, m. **r. chamber,** cámara frigorífica, f

refrigerative /rɪ'frɪdʒərətɪv/ a refrigerante, frigorífico

refrigerator /rɪ'frɪdʒəˌreitər/ n refrigerador, m, nevera, f

refringent /rɪ'frɪndʒənt/ a refringente

refuel /ri'fyuəl/ vt (a furnace) cargar con carbón, etc.; (of a ship) tomar carbón; (of an airplane, motor vehicle) tomar bencina

refuge /'rɛfyudʒ/ n refugio, m; asilo, m; (resort) recurso, m; subterfugio, m; (traffic island) refugio para peatones, m. **to take r.,** refugiarse; resguardarse (de)

refugee /ˌrefyʊˈdʒi/ *a* refugiado. *n* refugiado (-da)

refulgence /rɪˈfʌldʒəns/ *n* refulgencia, *f*

refulgent /rɪˈfʌldʒənt/ *a* refulgente

refund /riˈfʌnd/ *n* reembolso, *m*; devolución, *f*. *vt* reembolsar; devolver

refurbish /riˈfɜrbɪʃ/ *vt* restaurar; renovar; (a literary work) refundir

refurnish /riˈfɜrnɪʃ/ *vt* amueblar de nuevo

refusal /rɪˈfyuzəl/ *n* negativa, *f*; (rejection) rechazo, *m*; (option) opción, *f*; preferencia, *f*

refuse /rɪˈfyuz/ *vt* negar; (reject) rechazar. *vi* negarse (a), rehusar; (of a horse) resistirse a saltar

refuse /ˈrefyus/ *n* desecho, *m*; desperdicios, *m pl*; residuo, *m*; basura, *f*. *a* de desecho. **r. dump,** muladar, *m*

refutable /rɪˈfyutəbəl/ *a* refutable

refutation /ˌrefyʊˈteɪʃən/ *n* refutación, *f*

refute /rɪˈfyut/ *vt* refutar

regain /riˈgeɪn/ *vt* recobrar, recuperar; cobrar; ganar de nuevo; *Fig.* reconquistar. **to r. one's breath,** cobrar aliento. **to r. consciousness,** volver en sí

regal /ˈrigəl/ *a* regio, real

regale /rɪˈgeɪl/ *vt* regalar, agasajar; recrear, deleitar

regalia /rɪˈgeɪliə/ *n* regalía, *f*; insignias reales, *f pl*; distintivos, *m pl*, insignias, *f pl*

regally /ˈrigəli/ *adv* regiamente

regard /rɪˈgɑrd/ *vt* mirar; observar; considerar; (respect) respetar; (concern) importar, concernir; relacionarse con. *n* mirada, *f*; atención, *f*; (esteem) aprecio, *m*, estimación, *f*; respeto, *m*; veneración, *f*; (relation) referencia, *f*; *pl* **regards,** recuerdos, saludos, *m pl.* **He has little r. for their feelings,** Le importan poco sus susceptibilidades. **With kindest regards,** Con mis saludos más afectuosos. **as regards, with r. to,** con referencia a, respecto a, en cuanto a

regardful /rɪˈgɑrdfəl/ *a* atento (a), cuidadoso (de); que se preocupa (de)

regarding /rɪˈgɑrdɪŋ/ *prep* tocante a, en cuanto a, respecto de

regardless /rɪˈgɑrdlɪs/ *a* negligente (de); indiferente (a), insensible (a); que no se interesa (en); que no se inquieta (por); sin preocuparse (de)

regatta /rɪˈgætə, -ˈgɑtə/ *n* regata, *f*

regency /ˈridʒənsi/ *n* regencia, *f*

regeneracy /rɪˈdʒenərəsi/ *n* regeneración, *f*

regenerate /rɪˈdʒenəˌreɪt/ *vt* regenerar. *a* regenerado

regeneration /rɪˌdʒenəˈreɪʃən/ *n* regeneración, *f*

regenerative /rɪˈdʒenərətɪv/ *a* regenerador

regenerator /rɪˈdʒenəˌreɪtər/ *n* regenerador (-ra)

regent /ˈridʒənt/ *n* regente, *mf*

regime /reiˈʒim/ *n* régimen, *m*

regimen /ˈredʒəmən/ *n* (*Gram. Med.*) régimen, *m*, regiment /*n.* ˈredʒəmənt; *v.* -ˌment/ *n* regimiento, *m*. *vt* regimentar. **r. of the line,** tropa de línea, *f*

regimental /ˌredʒəˈmentl/ *a* de (un) regimiento, perteneciente a un regimiento

regimentation /ˌredʒəmənˈteɪʃən/ *n* regimentación, *f*

region /ˈridʒən/ *n* región, *f*

regional /ˈridʒənl/ *a* regional

regionalism /ˈridʒənlˌɪzəm/ *n* regionalismo, *m*

regionalist /ˈridʒənlɪst/ *n* regionalista, *mf*

regionalistic /ˈridʒənlɪstɪk/ *a* regionalista

register /ˈredʒəstər/ *n* (record and *Mech. Mus. Print.*) registro, *m*; (of ships, etc.) matrícula, *f*; lista, *f*. *vt* registrar; matricular; (a ship) abanderar; inscribir; (one's child in a school) anotar (Argentina), inscribir; (of thermometers, etc.) marcar; (letters) certificar; (luggage) facturar; (in one's mind) grabar; (emotion) mostrar, manifestar. *vi* (at a hotel, etc.) registrarse; *Print.* estar en registro. **cash r.,** caja registradora, *f.* **r. of births, marriages and deaths,** registro civil, *m*

registered letter /ˈredʒəstərd/ *n* carta certificada, *f*

registrar /ˈredʒəˌstrɑr/ *n* registrador, *m*; archivero, *m*; secretario, *m*; (of a school) jefe de inscripciones, secretario general (the latter has many more duties). **r. of births, marriages and deaths,** secretario del registro civil, *m*. **registrar's office,** oficina del registro civil, *f*

registration /ˌredʒəˈstreɪʃən/ *n* registro, *m*; inscrip-

ción, *f*; (of a vehicle, etc.) matrícula, *f*; *Naut.* abanderamiento, *m*; (of a letter, etc.) certificación, *f*. **r. number,** número de matrícula, *m*

registry /ˈredʒəstri/ *n* registro, *m*; inscripción, *f*; matrícula, *f*. **r. office,** oficina civil del registro civil, *f*; (for servants) agencia doméstica, *f*

regression /rɪˈgreʃən/ *n* regresión, *f*, retroceso, *m*

regret /rɪˈgret/ *vt* sentir; lamentar, pesar; arrepentirse (de); (miss) echar de menos (a). *n* sentimiento, pesar, *m*; (remorse) remordimiento, *m*. **I r. very much that...,** Me pesa mucho que..., Siento mucho que... **to send one's regrets,** mandar sus excusas

regretful /rɪˈgretfəl/ *a* lleno de pesar; arrepentido; lamentable, deplorable. **He was most r. that...,** Lamentaba mucho que...

regretfully /rɪˈgretfəli/ *adv* con pesar

regrettable /rɪˈgretəbəl/ *a* lamentable, deplorable; doloroso; (with loss, etc.) sensible

regrettably /rɪˈgretəbli/ *adv* lamentablemente; sensiblemente

regroup /riˈgrup/ *vt* arreglar de nuevo; formar de nuevo; reorganizar

regular /ˈregyələr/ *a* regular; normal; (ordinary) corriente, común; (in order) en regla; (*Gram. Bot. Eccl. Mil. Geom.*) regular. *n Eccl.* regular, *m*; (soldier) soldado de línea, *m*; (officer) militar de carrera, *m*; (client) parroquiano habitual, *m*

regularity /ˌregyəˈlærɪti/ *n* regularidad, *m*,

regularization /ˌregyələrəˈzeɪʃən/ *n* regularización, *f*

regularize /ˈregyələˌraiz/ *vt* regularizar

regularly /ˈregyəlɑrli/ *adv* regularmente

regulate /ˈregyəˌleɪt/ *vt* regular; ajustar, arreglar; (direct) dirigir; reglamentar

regulation /ˌregyəˈleɪʃən/ *n* regulación, *f*; arreglo, *m*; (rule) reglamento, *m*, *a* de reglamento; normal

regulative /ˈregyəˌleɪtɪv/ *a* regulador

regulator /ˈregyəˌleɪtər/ *n Mech.* regulador, *m*

regurgitate /rɪˈgɜrdʒɪˌteɪt/ *vt* and *vi* regurgitar

regurgitation /rɪˌgɜrdʒɪˈteɪʃən/ *n* regurgitación, *f*

rehabilitate /ˌrihəˈbɪlɪˌteɪt/ *vt* rehabilitar

rehabilitation /ˌrihəˌbɪlɪˈteɪʃən/ *n* rehabilitación, *f*

rehash /riˈhæʃ/ *vt* (a literary work, etc.) refundir; *Inf.* hacer un refrito de

rehearing /riˈhɪərɪŋ/ *n* nueva audición, *f*, (of a case) revisión, *f*

rehearsal /rɪˈhɜrsəl/ *n Theat.* ensayo, *m*; recitación, *f*; relación, narración, *f*. **dress r.,** ensayo general, *m*

rehearse /rɪˈhɜrs/ *vt Theat.* ensayar; recitar; (narrate) narrar; enumerar

reheat /riˈhit/ *vt* recalentar

reign /rein/ *n* reinado, *m*. *vi* reinar; predominar

reigning /ˈreinɪŋ/ *a* reinante; predominante

reimburse /ˌriɪmˈbɜrs/ *vt* reembolsar

reimbursement /ˌriɪmˈbɜrsmənt/ *n* reembolso, *m*

reimport /riˈɪmpɔrt/ *vt* importar de nuevo, reimportar, *n* reimporte, *m*

reimportation /ˌriɪmpɔrˈteɪʃən/ *n* reimportación, *f*

reimpose /ˌriɪmˈpouz/ *vt* reimponer

reimposition /ˌriɪmpəˈzɪʃən/ *n* reimposición, *f*

reimprison /ˌriɪmˈprɪzən/ *vt* encarcelar de nuevo, reencarcelar

reimprisonment /ˌriɪmˈprɪzənmənt/ *n* reencarcelamiento, *m*

rein /rein/ *n* rienda, *f*. *vt* llevar las riendas (de); (hold back) refrenar. **to give r. to,** *Fig.* dar rienda suelta (a)

reincarnation /ˌriɪnkɑrˈneɪʃən/ *n* reencarnación, *f*

reincorporate /ˌriɪnˈkɔrpəˌreɪt/ *vt* reincorporar

reincorporation /ˌriɪnˌkɔrpəˈreɪʃən/ *n* reincorporación, *f*

reindeer /ˈreinˌdɪər/ *n* reno, *m*

reinforce /ˌriɪnˈfɔrs/ *vt* reforzar; (concrete) armar; fortalecer. **reinforced concrete,** *n* hormigón armado, *m*

reinforcement /ˌriɪnˈfɔrsmənt/ *n* refuerzo, *m*, (*Mil. Nav. Fig.*) refuerzo, *m*

reins *n* See **rein**

reinsert /ˌriɪnˈsɜrt/ *vt* volver a insertar

reinstall /ˌriɪnˈstɔl/ *vt* reinstalar; rehabilitar

reinstallment /ˌriɪnˈstɔlmənt/ *n* reinstalación, *f*; rehabilitación, *f*; restablecimiento, *m*

reinstate /ˌriːnˈsteit/ vt reponer, restablecer; reinstalar; rehabilitar

reinstatement /ˌriːnˈsteitmənt/ n restablecimiento, m; rehabilitación, f

reinsurance /ˌriːnʃʊrəns/ n reaseguro, m

reinsure /ˌriːnˈʃʊr, -ˈʃər/ vt reasegurar

reintegrate /riˈintəˌgreit/ vt reintegrar

reintegration /ˌriːntəˈgreiʃən/ n reintegración, f

reinter /ˌriːnˈtɜr/ vt enterrar de nuevo

reinvest /ˌriːnˈvest/ vt reinvertir

reinvestment /ˌriːnˈvestmənt/ n reinversión, f

reinvigorate /ˌriːnˈvigəˌreit/ vt reanimar, dar nuevo vigor (a)

reinvite /ˌriːnˈvait/ vt invitar de nuevo (a)

reissue /riˈiʃu/ n nueva emisión, f; (of a book, etc.) nueva edición, reimpresión, f. vt hacer una nueva emisión (de); reeditar, publicar de nuevo

reiterate /riˈitəˌreit/ vt reiterar, repetir

reiteration /riˌitəˈreiʃən/ n reiteración, f

reiterative /riˈitəˌreitiv/ a reiterativo

reject /rɪˈdʒɛkt/ vt rechazar, rehusar; repudiar; repulsar; desechar

rejection /rɪˈdʒɛkʃən/ n rechazamiento, m; repudiación, refutación, f; repulsa, f

rejoice /rɪˈdʒɔis/ vt alegrar, regocijar. vi alegrarse (de), regocijarse (de), gloriarse (en)

rejoicing /rɪˈdʒɔisiŋ/ n regocijo, júbilo, m, alegría, f; algazara, f, fiestas, f pl

rejoin /rɪˈdʒɔin/ vt and vi juntar de nuevo; volver a; reunirse con; (reply) contestar, replicar

rejoinder /rɪˈdʒɔindər/ n contestación, respuesta, f

rejuvenate /rɪˈdʒuvəˌneit/ vt rejuvenecer

rejuvenation /rɪˌdʒuvəˈneiʃən/ n rejuvenecimiento, m

rekindle /riˈkindl/ vt encender de nuevo; despertar, reavivar. vi encenderse de nuevo; reavivarse

relapse /rɪˈlæps/ n. also ˈriːlæps/ n reincidencia, recaída, f; Med. recidiva, f. vi reincidir (en); Med. recaer

relapsed /rɪˈlæpst/ a relapso

relate /rɪˈleit/ vt (recount) relatar, narrar; relacionar; unir; (of kinship) emparentar. vi ajustarse (a); referirse (a). **The first fact is not related to the second,** El primer hecho no tiene nada que ver con el segundo

related /rɪˈleitid/ a relacionado; (by kinship) emparentado. **John is well-r.,** Juan es de buena familia; Juan es de familia influyente; Juan tiene buenas relaciones

relater /rɪˈleitər/ n narrador (-ra)

relation /rɪˈleiʃən/ n (narrative) relación, narración, f; conexión, f; relación, f; (kinship) parentesco, m; (person) pariente (-ta). **in r. to,** con relación a, en cuanto a

relationship /rɪˈleiʃənˌʃip/ n parentesco, m; conexión, relación, f. Lat. Am. atingencia, f

relative /ˈrɛlətiv/ a relativo. n pariente (-ta); pl **relatives,** parientes, m pl, parentela, f

relativism /ˈrɛlətəˌvizəm/ n relativismo, m

relativity /ˌrɛləˈtiviti/ n relatividad, f

relax /rɪˈlæks/ vt relajar; aflojar; soltar; (make less severe) ablandar; (decrease) mitigar. vi relajarse; aflojar; (rest) descansar

relaxation /ˌrilækˈseiʃən/ n relajación, f; aflojamiento, m; ablandamiento, m; mitigación, f; (rest) descanso, reposo, m; (pastime) pasatiempo, m; (amusement) diversión, f

relaxing /rɪˈlæksiŋ/ a relajante; (of climate) enervante

relay /ˈriːlei/ n. ˈriːlei; v. also ˈriːlei/ n (of horses) parada, f; (shift) tanda, f; relevo, m; Elec. relais, m; Radio. redifusión, f. vt enviar por posta; Elec. reemitir; Radio. retransmitir; (lay again) colocar de nuevo. **r. race,** carrera de equipo, carrera de relevos, f

release /rɪˈlis/ vt soltar; (hurl) lanzar; (set free) poner en libertad (a); librar (de); absolver; (surrender) renunciar (a); dar al público, poner en circulación; (lease again) realquilar. n soltura, f; lanzamiento, m; liberación, f; (from pain) alivio, m; remisión, f; exoneración, f; publicación, f; (of films) representación, f; Law. soltura, f

relegate /ˈrɛliˌgeit/ vt relegar

relegation /ˌrɛliˈgeiʃən/ n relegación, f

relent /rɪˈlɛnt/ vi ablandarse, enternecerse; ceder

relenting /rɪˈlɛntiŋ/ n enternecimiento, desenojo, m

relentless /rɪˈlɛntlis/ a implacable, inexorable; despiadado

relentlessly /rɪˈlɛntlisli/ adv inexorablemente; sin piedad

relentlessness /rɪˈlɛntlisnis/ n inexorabilidad, f; falta de piedad, f

relevance /ˈrɛləvəns/ n conexión, f; pertinencia, f; aplicabilidad, f

relevant /ˈrɛləvənt/ a relativo; pertinente, a propósito, oportuno; aplicable

reliability /rɪˌlaiəˈbiliti/ n seguridad, f; formalidad, f; confianza, f; exactitud, f; veracidad, f

reliable /rɪˈlaiəbəl/ a seguro; formal; digno de crédito, de confianza, solvente digno de confianza; exacto; veraz

reliably /rɪˈlaiəbli/ adv seguramente; de una manera digna de confianza; exactamente

reliance /rɪˈlaiəns/ n confianza, f. **to place r. on,** tener confianza en

reliant /rɪˈlaiənt/ a confiado

relic /ˈrɛlik/ n vestigio, rastro, m; Eccl. reliquia, f

relief /rɪˈlif/ n (alleviation) alivio, m; desahogo, m; (help) socorro, m, ayuda, f; beneficencia, f; Mil. relevo, m; (pleasure) placer, m, satisfacción, f; (consolation) consuelo, m; Law. remisión, f; Art. relieve, m. **high r.,** alto relieve, m. **low r.,** bajo relieve, m. **r. map,** mapa en relieve, m. **r. train,** tren de socorro, m

relieve /rɪˈliv/ vt aliviar; aligerar, suavizar; mitigar; (one's feelings, etc.) desahogar; (Mil. and to take the place of) relevar; (free) librar; (dismiss) destituir; (remove) quitar; (rob) robar; (help) socorrer, remediar; (redeem) redimir; (ornament) adornar; (from a wrong) hacer justicia (a)

relieving /rɪˈliviŋ/ n alivio, m; aligeramiento, m; mitigación, f; (of the feelings) desahogo, m; Mil. relevo, m; (help) socorro, m. **r. arch,** sobrearco, m

relight /riˈlait/ vt volver a encender. vi encenderse de nuevo

religion /rɪˈlidʒən/ n religión, f

religiosity /rɪˌlidʒiˈɒsiti/ n religiosidad, f

religious /rɪˈlidʒəs/ a religioso; en religión; piadoso, crevente; devoto. n religioso (-sa). **r. orders,** órdenes religiosas, f pl. **r. toleration,** libertad de cultos, f

religiousness /rɪˈlidʒəsnis/ n religiosidad, f

relinquish /rɪˈliŋkwiʃ/ vt abandonar; (one's grip) soltar; renunciar; desistir (de), dejar (de); (a post) dimitir (de)

relinquishment /rɪˈliŋkwiʃmənt/ n abandono, m; renuncia, f; dejamiento, m; (of a post) dimisión, f

reliquary /ˈrɛliˌkwɛri/ n relicario, m

relish /ˈrɛliʃ/ n gusto, m; sabor, m; (touch, smack) dejo, m; condimento, m; apetito, m, gana, f. vt gustar de; comer con apetito; saborear, paladear; Fig. seducir, atraer, gustar. vi tener gusto de. **I do not much r. the idea,** No me seduce la idea

relishing /ˈrɛliʃiŋ/ n saboreo, m; (enjoyment) goce, m, fruición, f; consideración, f

relive /riˈliv/ vt vivir de nuevo, volver a vivir

reload / riˈloud/ vt recargar

reluctance /rɪˈlʌktəns/ n repugnancia, desgana, f. **with r.,** a regañadientes, de mala gana

reluctant /rɪˈlʌktənt/ a poco dispuesto (a), que tiene repugnancia a (hacer algo), sin gana, (forced) forzado; artificial; (hesitating) vacilante

reluctantly /rɪˈlʌktəntli/ adv de mala gana, con repugnancia, a disgusto

rely on /rɪˈlai/ vt contar con, confiar en, depender de

remain /rɪˈmein/ vi quedar; permanecer; (be left over) sobrar; continuar. **I r. yours faithfully...,** (in a letter) Queda de Vd. su att. s.s.... **It remains to be written,** Queda por escribir

remainder /rɪˈmeindər/ n (math) resto, m; restos, m pl, sobras, f pl; residuo, m. **The r. of the people went away,** Los demás se marcharon

remaining /rɪˈmeiniŋ/ pres. part and a que queda; sobrante. **r. to be paid,** Lat. Am. impago

remains /rɪˈmeinz/ n pl restos, m pl; sobras, f pl; desperdicios, m pl; ruinas, f pl

remake /ri'meik/ *vt* rehacer; reformar
remand /ri'mænd/ *vt Law.* reencarcelar. *n Law.* reencarcelamiento, *m*
remark /ri'mɑrk/ *n* observación, *f*; nota, *f*; comentario, *m. vt and vi* observar; notar. **to r. on,** comentar, hacer una observación sobre
remarkable /ri'mɑrkəbəl/ *a* notable, singular, extraordinario
remarkably /ri'mɑrkəbli/ *adv* singularmente
remarriage /'ri,mærɪdʒ/ *n* segundas nupcias, *f pl*, segundo casamiento, *m*
remarry /ri'mæri/ *vt* volver a casar (a). *vi* casarse en segundas nupcias; volver a casarse
remediable /ri'midiəbəl/ *a* remediable
remedial /ri'midiəl/ *a* remediador; curativo, terapéutico
remedy /'rɛmɪdi/ *n* remedio, *m*; recurso, *m, vt* remediar; curar
remember /ri'mɛmbər/ *vt* recordar; tener presente; acordarse de. *vi* acordarse; no olvidarse. **R. me to your mother,** Dale recuerdos míos a tu madre. **If I r. rightly...,** Si bien me acuerdo... **And r. that I shall do no more!** ¡Y no olvides que no haré más!
remembrance /ri'mɛmbrəns/ *n* recuerdo, *m*; memoria, *f*; *pl* **remembrances,** recuerdos, *m pl*
remind /ri'maind/ *vt* recordar
reminder /ri'maindər/ *n* recuerdo, *m*; (warning) advertencia, *f*. **a gentle r.,** una indirecta, una insinuación
reminisce /,rɛmə'nɪs/ *vi Inf.* recordar viejas historias
reminiscence /,rɛmə'nɪsəns/ *n* reminiscencia, *f*, recuerdo, *m*
reminiscent /,rɛmə'nɪsənt/ *a* evocador, que recuerda; de reminiscencia; que piensa en el pasado. **to be r. of,** recordar; *Inf.* oler a
reminiscently /,rɛmə'nɪsəntli/ *adv* evocadoramente, como si recordara
remiss /ri'mɪs/ *a* negligente, descuidado
remission /ri'mɪʃən/ *n* remisión, *f*
remissly /ri'mɪsli/ *adv* negligentemente
remissness /ri'mɪsnɪs/ *n* negligencia, *f*, descuido, *m*
remit /ri'mɪt/ *vt* remitir; *Com.* remesar, enviar. *vi* (pay) pagar
remittance /ri'mɪtns/ *n* remesa, *f*, envío, *m*
remitter /ri'mɪtər/ *n* remitente, *mf*
remnant /'rɛmnənt/ *n* resto, *m*; (of fabric) retal, retazo, *m*; (relic) vestigio, *m*, reliquia, *f*. **r. sale,** saldo, *m*
remodel /ri'mɒdl/ *vt* rehacer; reformar; modelar de nuevo; (a play, etc.) refundir
remodeling /ri'mɒdlɪŋ/ *n* reformación, *f*; (of a play, etc.) refundición, *f*
remonstrance /ri'mɒnstrəns/ *n* protesta, *f*; reconvención, *f*
remonstrate /ri'mɒnstreit/ *vi* protestar, objetar. **to r. with,** reprochar, reconvenir
remorse /ri'mɔrs/ *n* remordimiento, *m*
remorseful /ri'mɔrsfəl/ *a* lleno de remordimientos; penitente, arrepentido
remorsefully /ri'mɔrsfəli/ *adv* con remordimiento
remorseless /ri'mɔrslɪs/ *a* sin conciencia, sin remordimientos; despiadado, inflexible
remorselessness /ri'mɔrslɪsnɪs/ *n* inexorabilidad, crueldad, dureza, *f*
remote /ri'mout/ *a* distante, lejano; remoto; aislado; ajeno; (slight) leve, vago. **r. control,** mando a distancia, *m*; (for a television) remoto, *m*
remotely /ri'moutli/ *adv* remotamente
remoteness /ri'moutnɪs/ *n* distancia, *f*; aislamiento, *m*; alejamiento, *m*; (vagueness) vaguedad, *f*
remount /v. ri'maunt; *n.* 'ri,maunt/ *vt* subir de nuevo, montar de nuevo; *Mil.* remontar. *vi* (go back to) remontar (a), derivarse (de). *n Mil.* remonta, *f*
removable /ri'muvəbəl/ *a* que puede quitarse; (of collars, etc.) de quita y pon; transportable; (of officials, etc.) amovible
removal /ri'muvəl/ *n* acción de quitar o levantar, *f*; sacamiento, *m*; separación, *f*; eliminación, *f*; alejamiento, *m*; traslado, *m*; (from office, etc.) deposición, *f*; supresión, *f*; asesinato, *m*. **r. van,** carro de mudanzas, *m*

remove /ri'muv/ *vt* quitar; retirar; levantar; sacar; apartar; separar; eliminar; trasladar; (from office) destituir; suprimir; asesinar. *vi* trasladarse. *n* grado, *m*; distancia, *f*; (departure) partida, *f*. **to r. oneself,** quitarse de en medio. **to r. one's hat,** descubrirse.
first cousin once removed, hijo de primo carnal, primo hermano del padre, primo hermano de la madre, *m*
remunerate /ri'myunə,reit/ *vt* remunerar
remuneration /ri,myunə'reiʃən/ *n* remuneración, *f*
remunerative /ri'myunərətiv/ *a* remunerador
renaissance /'rɛnə,sans/ *n* renacimiento, *m, a* renacentista
Renaissance man /'rɛnə,sans/ *n* hombre del Renacimiento, *m*
Renaissance woman *n* mujer del Renacimiento, *f*
renal /'rinl/ *a* renal
rename /ri'neim/ *vt* poner otro nombre (a)
renascent /ri'næsənt, -'neisənt/ *a* renaciente, que renace
rend /rɛnd/ *vt* desgarrar, rasgar; *Fig.* lacerar; (split) hender; *Fig.* dividir. **to r. from,** arrancar (a). **to r. the air,** (with cries, etc.) llenar el aire
render /'rɛndər/ *vt* (return) devolver; dar; rendir; (make) hacer; (help, service) prestar; interpretar; (translate) traducir; (fat) derretir y clarificar
rendering /'rɛndərɪŋ/ *n* versión, *f*; interpretación, *f*
rendezvous /'rɑndə,vu, -dei-/ *n* cita, *f*; lugar de cita, *m*; reunión, *f. vi* reunirse
rending /'rɛndɪŋ/ *n* desgarro, *m*; hendimiento, *m*
renegade /'rɛnɪ,geid/ *a* renegado. *n* renegado (-da)
renew /ri'nu/ *vt* renovar; (resume) reanudar; (a lease, etc.) prorrogar
renewable /ri'nuəbəl/ *a* renovable
renewal /ri'nuəl/ *n* renovación, *f*; (resumption) reanudación, *f*; (of a lease, etc.) prorrogación, *f*
renewed /ri'nud/ *a* renovado; nuevo
rennet /'rɛnɪt/ *n* cuajo, *m*
renounce /ri'nauns/ *vt* renunciar; (a throne) abdicar; renegar (de), repudiar; abandonar. *vi Law.* desistir; (cards) renunciar
renouncement /ri'naunsmənt/ *n* renuncia, *f*; (of a throne) abdicación, *f*; repudiación, *f*
renovate /'rɛnə,veit/ *vt* renovar; limpiar; restaurar
renovation /,rɛnə'veiʃən/ *n* renovación, *f*; limpiadura, *f*; restauración, *f*
renovator /'rɛnə,veitər/ *n* renovador (-ra)
renown /ri'naun/ *n* renombre, *m*, fama, *f*
renowned /ri'naund/ *a* renombrado, famoso
rent /rɛnt/ *n* (tear) rasgadura, *f*; desgarro, *m*; abertura, *f*; raja hendedura, *f*; (discord) división, *f*; (hire) alquiler, *m*; arrendamiento, *m*. *vt* arrendar, alquilar. **r.-free,** sin pagar alquiler
rentable /'rɛntəbəl/ *a* alquilable, arrendable
rental /'rɛntl/ *n* See **rent**
renter /'rɛntər/ *n* arrendador (-ra)
rentier /rɑn'tyei/ *n* rentista, *mf*
renting /'rɛntɪŋ/ *n* alquiler, arrendamiento, *m*
renumber /ri'nʌmbər/ *vt* numerar de nuevo
renunciation /ri,nʌnsi'eiʃən/ *n* renunciación, renuncia, *f*
reoccupy /ri'ɒkyʊ,pai/ *vt* volver a ocupar, ocupar otra vez
reopen /ri'oupən/ *vt* abrir de nuevo, volver a abrir. *vi* abrirse nuevamente, abrirse otra vez
reopening /ri'oupənɪŋ/ *n* reapertura, *f*
reorder /ri'ɔrdər/ *vt* ordenar de nuevo, *Com.* volver a pedir. *n Com.* nuevo pedido, *m*
reorganization /,riɔrgənə'zeiʃən/ *n* reorganización, *f*
reorganize /ri'ɔrgə,naiz/ *vt* reorganizar
reorganizing /ri'ɔrgə,naizin/ *a* reorganizador
repack /ri'pæk/ *vt* reembalar; reenvasar; volver a hacer (una maleta)
repaint /ri'peint/ *vt* pintar de nuevo
repainting /ri'peintiŋ/ *n* nueva pintura, *f*
repair /ri'pɛər/ *vt* arreglar (e.g. a machine) componer; remendar; reparar; restaurar; rehacer. *vi* (with to) dirigirse a, ir a; acudir a. *n* arreglo *m*, reparación, *f*; compostura, *f*; restauración, *f*. **to keep in r.,** conservar en buen estado

repairable /rɪ'pɛərəbəl/ *a* que se puede componer

repairer /rɪ'pɛərər/ *n* componedor (-ra); restaurador (-ra)

repairing /rɪ'pɛərɪŋ/ *a* reparador

reparable /'rɛpərəbəl/ *a* reparable; remediable

reparation /ˌrɛpə'reɪʃən/ *n* reparación, *f*

repartee /ˌrɛpər'ti, -'teɪ, -ɑr-/ *n* respuestas, agudezas, *f pl*; *Inf.* dimes y diretes, *m pl*

repast /rɪ'pæst/ *n* comida, *f*; (light) colación, *f*

repatriate /ri'peɪtri,eɪt/ *vt* repatriar

repatriation /ri,peɪtri'eɪʃən/ *n* repatriación, *f*

repay /rɪ'peɪ/ *vt* reembolsar; recompensar, pagar; pagar en la misma moneda. *vi* pagar. **It well repays a visit,** Vale la pena de visitarse

repayable /rɪ'peɪəbəl/ *a* reembolsable

repayment /rɪ'peɪmənt/ *n* reembolso, *m*; pago, retorno, *m*

repeal /rɪ'pil/ *n* abrogación, revocación, *f*, *vt* abrogar, rescindir, revocar

repeat /rɪ'pit/ *vt* repetir; reiterar; (renew) renovar; duplicar. *n* repetición, *f*

repeated /rɪ'pitɪd/ *a* reiterado; redoblado

repeatedly /rɪ'pitdli/ *adv* reiteradamente, repetidamente

repeater /rɪ'pitər/ *n* repetidor (-ra); reloj de repetición, *m*; arma de repetición, *f*

repel /rɪ'pɛl/ *vt* repeler; ahuyentar; (spurn) rechazar; *Phys.* resistir; repugnar

repellent /rɪ'pɛlənt/ *a* repulsivo. *n* (insect) repelente para insectos, *m*

repent /rɪ'pɛnt/ *vt* arrepentirse de. *vi* arrepentirse

repentance /rɪ'pɛntn̩s/ *n* arrepentimiento, *m*, penitencia, *f*

repentant /rɪ'pɛntn̩t/ *a* arrepentido, penitente, contrito

repentantly /rɪ'pɛntn̩tli/ *adv* arrepentidamente, con contrición

repercuss /ˌripər'kʌs/ *vt* repercutir (en)

repercussion /ˌripər'kʌʃən/ *n* repercusión, *f*

repercussive /ˌripər'kʌsɪv/ *a* repercusivo

repertory /'rɛpər,tɔri/ *n* repertorio, *m*

repetition /ˌrɛpɪ'tɪʃən/ *n* repetición, *f*; recitación, *f*

repetitive /rɪ'pɛtɪtɪv/ *a* iterativo

repine /rɪ'paɪn/ *vi* afligirse (de); quejarse (de); padecer nostalgia

repining /rɪ'paɪnɪŋ/ *n* pesares, *m pl*; quejas, *f pl*, descontento, *m*; nostalgia, *f*

replace /rɪ'pleɪs/ *vt* (put back) reponer, colocar de nuevo; restituir, devolver; (renew) renovar; (in a post, etc.) reemplazar, substituir

replaceable /rɪ'pleɪsəbəl/ *a* restituible; renovable; reemplazable

replacement /rɪ'pleɪsmənt/ *n* reposición, *f*; restitución, devolución, *f*; renovación, *f*; reemplazo, *m*

replant /ri'plænt/ *vt* replantar

replanting /ri'plæntɪŋ/ *n* replantación, *f*

replenish /rɪ'plɛnɪʃ/ *vt* rellenar

replenishment /ri'plɛnɪʃmənt/ *n* relleno, *m*

replete /rɪ'plit/ *a* repleto

repletion /rɪ'pliʃən/ *n* repleción, *f*

replica /'rɛplɪkə/ *n* réplica, *f*

reply /rɪ'plaɪ/ *n* respuesta, contestación, *f*, *vi* responder, contestar. **Awaiting your r.,** En espera de sus noticias. **in his r.,** en su respuesta

repolish /ri'pɒlɪʃ/ *vt* repulir

repopulate /ri'pɒpyə,leɪt/ *vt* repoblar

repopulation /ri,pɒpyə'leɪʃən/ *n* repoblación, *f*

report /rɪ'pɔrt/ *n* (rumor) voz, *f*, rumor, *m*; (reputation) fama, *f*; (news) noticia, *f*; (journalistic) reportaje, *m*; (*Mil. Nav.* and from school) parte, *f*; (weather) boletín, *m*; (proceedings) actas, *f pl*; (statement) informe, *m*; relación, *f*; (of a gun, etc.) detonación, *f*, explosión, *f* *vt* dar cuenta de, relatar; informar; (measure) registrar; (*Mil. Nav.*) dar parte de; comunicar; (journalistic) hacer un reportaje de; (transcribe) transcribir; (accuse) denunciar; quejarse de. *vi* presentar informe; ser reportero; (present oneself) presentarse, comparecer. **It is reported that...,** Se informa que...

report card *n* boletín de calificaciones, *m*

reporter /rɪ'pɔrtər/ *n* reportero (-ra); *Law.* relator, *m*

reporting /rɪ'pɔrtɪŋ/ *n* reporterismo, *m*

repose /rɪ'pouz/ *n* reposo, *m*; quietud, *f*; tranquilidad, serenidad, *f*. *vt* reposar, descansar; reclinar; (place) poner. *vi* reposar; tener confianza (en); basarse (en)

repository /rɪ'pɒzɪ,tɔri/ *n* repositorio, depósito, *m*; almacén, *m*; (furniture) guardamuebles, *m*; (person) depositario (-ia)

reprehend /ˌrɛprɪ'hɛnd/ *vt* reprender, reprobar

reprehensible /ˌrɛprɪ'hɛnsəbəl/ *a* reprensible

reprehension /ˌrɛprɪ'hɛnʃən/ *n* reprensión, *f*

represent /ˌrɛprɪ'zɛnt/ *vt* representar; significar

representation /ˌrɛprɪzɛn'teɪʃən/ *n* representación, *f*

representational /ˌrɛprɪzɛn'teɪʃən̩l/ *a* *Art.* realista

representative /ˌrɛprɪ'zɛntətɪv/ *a* que representa; representativo. *n* representante, *mf*

repress /rɪ'prɛs/ *vt* reprimir

repression /rɪ'prɛʃən/ *n* represión, *f*

repressive /rɪ'prɛsɪv/ *a* represivo

reprieve /rɪ'priv/ *vt* *Law.* aplazar la ejecución (de); *Fig.* dar una tregua (a)

reprimand /'rɛprə,mænd/ *n* reprimenda, *f*, *vt* reprender

reprint /*n.* 'ri,prɪnt; *v.* ri'prɪnt/ *n* reimpresión, tirada aparte, separata, *f*, *vt* reimprimir

reprinting /'ri,prɪntɪŋ/ *n* reimpresión, *f*

reprisal /rɪ'praɪzəl/ *n* represalia, *f*. **to take reprisals,** tomar represalias

reproach /rɪ'proutʃ/ *n* reproche, *m*; censura, *f*; (shame) vergüenza, *f*. *vt* reprochar; censurar, echar en cara, afear

reproachful /rɪ'proutʃfəl/ *a* severo; lleno de reproches; de censura; (shameful) vergonzoso

reproachfully /rɪ'proutʃfəli/ *adv* con reprobación, con reprensión, severamente

reproachfulness /rɪ'proutʃfəlnɪs/ *n* severidad, *f*. **the r. of my gaze,** mi mirada llena de reproches

reprobate /'rɛprə,beit/ *n* réprobo (-ba)

reproduce /ˌriprə'dus/ *vt* reproducir. *vi* reproducirse

reproducible /ˌriprə'dusəbəl/ *a* reproducible

reproduction /ˌriprə'dʌkʃən/ *n* reproducción, *f*

reproductive /ˌriprə'dʌktɪv/ *a* reproductor; de reproducción

reproof /rɪ'pruf/ *n* reconvención, *f*

reprove /rɪ'pruv/ *vt* censurar, culpar; reprender

reprovingly /rɪ'pruvɪŋli/. See **rebukingly**

reptile /'rɛptɪl, -tail/ *a* and *n* reptil, *m*

republic /rɪ'pʌblɪk/ *n* república, *f*

republican /rɪ'pʌblɪkən/ *a* and *n* republicano (-na)

republicanism /rɪ'pʌblɪkə,nɪzəm/ *n* republicanismo, *m*

Republican Party *n* Partido Republicano, *m*

republish /rɪ'pʌblɪʃ/ *vt* publicar de nuevo; volver a editar

repudiate /rɪ'pyudi,eɪt/ *vt* repudiar; negar, rechazar

repudiation /ri,pyudi'eɪʃən/ *n* repudiación, *f*

repugnance /rɪ'pʌgnəns/ *n* repugnacia, *f*

repugnant /rɪ'pʌgnənt/ *a* repugnante; contrario; opuesto. **to be r. to,** repugnar (a)

repulse /rɪ'pʌls/ *vt* rechazar, repeler; rebatir, refutar; (refuse) rechazar, *n* repulsa, *f*; refutación, *f*; rechazo, *m*

repulsion /rɪ'pʌlʃən/ *n* *Phys.* repulsión, *f*; repugnancia, aversión, *f*

repulsive /rɪ'pʌlsɪv/ *a* repulsivo, repugnante, repelente

repulsiveness /rɪ'pʌlsɪvnɪs/ *n* carácter repulsivo, *m*; aspecto repugnante, *m*

reputable /'rɛpyətəbəl/ *a* honrado, respetable, formal

reputation /ˌrɛpyə'teɪʃən/ *n* reputación, *f*; fama, *f*, renombre, *m*. **to have the r. of,** ser reputado como, pasar por

reputed /rɪ'pyutɪd/ *a* supuesto; putativo

reputedly /rɪ'pyutɪdli/ *adv* según la opinión común, según dice la gente

request /rɪ'kwɛst/ *n* ruego, *m*, petición, *f*; instancia, *f*; solicitud, *f*; *Com.* demanda, *f*. *vt* pedir, rogar; suplicar; solicitar. **in r.,** en boga; solicitado; en demanda, **on r.,** a solicitud. **r. stop,** (for buses) parada discrecional, *f*

requiem /'rɛkwiəm/ n réquiem, m. **r. mass,** misa de difuntos, f

require /rɪ'kwaiªr/ vt exigir, requerir; necesitar; (wish) desear; invitar. vi ser necesario

required /rɪ'kwaiərd/ a necesario; obligatorio

requirement /rɪ'kwaiªrmənt/ n deseo, m; requisito, m; formalidad, f; estipulación, f; necesidad, f

requisite /'rɛkwəzɪt/ n requisito, m. a necesario, requisito, preciso. **to be r.,** ser necesario, ser menester hacer falta

requisition /,rɛkwə'zɪʃən/ n pedida, solicitud, f. vt Mil. requisar

requisitioning /,rɛkwə'zɪʃənɪŋ/ n requisa, f

requital /rɪ'kwaitl/ n recompensa, f; compensación, satisfacción, f

requite /rɪ'kwait/ vt pagar, recompensar; (affection) corresponder a

reread /ri'rid/ vt releer

resale /'ri,seil/ n reventa, f

rescind /rɪ'sɪnd/ vt rescindir

rescue /'rɛskyu/ vt salvar; librar; Mil. rescatar. n socorro, m; salvamento, m; Mil. rescate, m. **to go to the r. of,** ir al socorro de. **r. party,** expedición de salvamento, f; Mil. expedición de rescate, f

rescuer /'rɛskyuər/ n salvador (-ra)

reseal /ri'sil/ vt resellar

research /rɪ'sɜrtʃ, 'risɜrtʃ/ n investigación, f, vt investigar

researcher /rɪsɜrtʃər, 'risɜrtʃər/ n investigador (-ra)

reseda /rɪ'sidə/ n Bot. reseda, f

resell /ri'sɛl/ vt revender

resemblance /rɪ'zɛmbləns/ n parecido, m, semejanza, f. **The two sisters bear a strong r. to each other,** Las dos hermanas se parecen mucho

resemble /rɪ'zɛmbəl/ vt parecerse (a). **Mary doesn't r. her mother,** María no se parece a su madre

resent /rɪ'zɛnt/ vt resentirse de; ofenderse por, indignarse por; tomar a mal

resentful /rɪ'zɛntfəl/ a resentido; ofendido, indignado, agraviado; vengativo

resentfully /rɪ'zɛntfəli/ adv con resentimiento; con indignación

resentment /rɪ'zɛntmənt/ n resentimiento, m

reservation /,rɛzər'veiʃən/ n reservación, f; reserva, f; territorio reservado, m; santuario, m. **mental r.,** reserva mental, f

reserve /rɪ'zɜrv/ n reserva, f. vt reservar. a de reserva. **without r.,** sin reserva

reserved /rɪ'zɜrvd/ a reservado; callado, taciturno. **r. compartment,** reservado, m. **r. list,** (Mil. Nav.) sección de reserva, f

reservedly /rɪ'zɜrvɪdli/ adv con reserva

reservist /rɪ'zɜrvɪst/ n reservista, mf

reservoir /'rɛzər,vwar/ n depósito, m; cisterna, f, aljibe, tanque, m

reset /ri'sɛt/ vt montar de nuevo

resettle /ri'sɛtl/ vt repoblar; rehabilitar; (a dispute) llegar a un nuevo acuerdo sobre

resettlement /ri'sɛtlmənt/ n repoblación, f; rehabilitación, f; (of a dispute) nuevo acuerdo, m

reshape /ri'ʃeip/ vt reformar

reship /ri'ʃɪp/ vt reembarcar

reshipment /ri'ʃɪpmənt/ n reembarque, m

reshuffle /ri'ʃʌfəl/ vt volver a barajar; Fig. cambiar

reside /rɪ'zaid/ vi residir, habitar; vivir

residence /'rɛzɪdəns/ n residencia, f; permanencia, estada, f; domicilio, m

resident /'rɛzɪdənt/ a residente; (of a servant) que duerme en casa; interno. n residente, mf; (diplomacy) residente, m. **r. of the capital,** Lat. Am. capitalino (-na). **r. of Rio de Janeiro,** carioca, mf

residential /,rɛzɪ'dɛnʃəl/ a residencial

residue /'rɛzɪ,du/ n resto, m; (Law., Chem.) residuo, m

residuum /rɪ'zɪdʒuəm/ n residuo, m

resign /rɪ'zain/ vt renunciar (a); ceder; resignar. vi dimitir. **to r. oneself,** resignarse

resignation /,rɛzɪg'neiʃən/ n resignación, f; (from a post) dimisión, f. **to send in one's r.,** dimitir

resigned /rɪ'zaind/ a resignado

resignedly /rɪ'zainɪdli/ adv con resignación

resilience /rɪ'zɪlyəns/ n elasticidad, f

resilient /rɪ'zɪlyənt/ a elástico

resin /'rɛzɪn/ n resina, f, Central America, Mexico copal, m; (solid, for violin bows, etc.) colofonia, f

resinous /'rɛzənəs/ a resinoso

resist /rɪ'zɪst/ vt and vi (bear) aguantar; (impede) impedir; (repel, ward off) resistir; rechazar; hacer frente (a); oponerse (a); negarse (a)

resistance /rɪ'zɪstəns/ n resistencia, f; aguante, m, tenacidad, f; oposición, f; repugnancia, f. **passive r.,** resistencia pasiva, f. **r. coil,** Elec. resistencia, f. **r. movement,** movimiento de resistencia, m

resistant /rɪ'zɪstənt/ a resistente

resister /rɪ'zɪstər/ n el, m, (f, la) que resiste

resole /ri'soul/ vt remontar

resolute /'rɛzə,lut/ a resuelto, decidido

resolutely /,rɛzə'lutli/ adv resueltamente

resolution /,rɛzə'luʃən/ n resolución, f; (proposal placed before a legislative body, etc.) proposición, f; propósito, m

resolve /rɪ'zɒlv/ vt resolver; desarrollar, deshacer (an abbreviation, acronym, or initialism). vi resolverse. n propósito, m; (of character) resolución, firmeza, f

resonance /'rɛzənəns/ n resonancia, f; sonoridad, f

resonant /'rɛzənənt/ a resonante; reverberante, sonoro

resort /rɪ'zɔrt/ n recurso, m; punto de reunión. m; (frequentation) frecuentación, f; (gathering) concurrencia, f; reunión, f. vi acudir (a), acogerse (a); hacer uso (de); pasar (a); (frequent) frecuentar, concurrir. **health r.,** balneario, m. **holiday r.,** playa de verano, f; pueblo de veraneo, m. **in the last r.,** en último recurso

resound /rɪ'zaund/ vi resonar, retumbar, retronar; Fig. tener fama, ser celebrado. vt hacer reverberar; Fig. celebrar

resounding /rɪ'zaundɪŋ/ a retumbante, resonante

resource /'risɔrs/ n recurso, m; (of character) inventiva, f; pl **resources;** recursos, fondos, m pl

resourceful /rɪ'sɔrsfəl/ a ingenioso

resourcefulness /rɪ'sɔrsfʌlnɪs/ n ingeniosidad, f

respect /rɪ'spɛkt/ n respeto, m; consideración, f; (reference, regard) respecto, m; pl **respects,** (greetings) saludos, m pl; homenaje, m. vt respetar; honrar; (concern, regard) concernir, tocar (a). **in other respects,** por lo demás. **in r. of,** tocante a, respecto a. **in some respects,** desde algunos puntos de vista. **out of r. for,** por consideración a

respectability /rɪ,spɛktə'bɪlɪti/ n respetabilidad, f

respectable /rɪ'spɛktəbəl/ a respetable; pasable; considerable

respectably /rɪ'spɛktəbli/ adv respetablemente

respected /rɪ'spɛktɪd/ a and part respetado; apreciado, estimado; digno de respeto, honrado

respectful /rɪ'spɛktfəl/ a respetuoso

respectfully /rɪ'spɛktfəli/ adv respetuosamente

respectfulness /rɪ'spɛktfʌlnɪs/ n aire respetuoso, m; conducta respetuosa, f

respecting /rɪ'spɛktɪŋ/ prep con respecto a, en cuanto a, tocante a; a propósito de

respective /rɪ'spɛktɪv/ a respectivo; relativo

respectively /rɪ'spɛktɪvli/ adv respectivamente

respiration /,rɛspə'reiʃən/ n respiración, f

respirator /'rɛspə,reitər/ n respirador, m

respiratory /'rɛspərə,tɔri/ a respiratorio

respire /rɪ'spaiªr/ vt and vi respirar; exhalar; descansar

respite /'rɛspɪt/ n tregua, pausa, f; respiro, m; Law. espera, f. vt dar tregua (a); (postpone) aplazar; (relieve) aliviar

resplendence /rɪ'splɛndəns/ n resplandor, m, refulgencia, f, esplendor, fulgor, m

resplendent /rɪ'splɛndənt/ a resplandeciente, refulgente, relumbrante. **He was r. in a new uniform,** Lucía (or Ostentaba) un nuevo uniforme. **to be r.,** ser resplandeciente; relumbrar, refulgir

resplendently /rɪ'splɛndəntli/ adv esplendorosamente

respond /rɪ'spɒnd/ vi responder; contestar; (obey) obedecer; reaccionar

respondent /rɪ'spɒndənt/ n (in a suit) demandado (-da)

response /rɪ'spɒns/ n respuesta, f; Eccl. responso, m

responsibility /rɪ,spɒnsə'bɪlɪti/ n responsabilidad, f

responsible /rɪ'spɒnsəbəl/ a responsable

responsive /rɪ'spɒnsɪv/ a simpático; sensible, sensitivo

responsiveness /rɪ'spɒnsɪvnɪs/ n simpatía, f; sensibilidad, f

rest /rɛst/ n descanso, m; reposo, m; (the grave) última morada, f; tranquilidad, paz, f; inacción, f; (prop) soporte, apoyo, m; base, f; (for a lance) ristre, m; (for a rifle) apoyo, m; Mus. silencio, m, pausa, f; (in verse) cesura, f. **in r.**, en ristre. **the r.**, el resto; los demás, los otros. **to set at r.**, calmar, tranquilizar; (remove) quitar. **r.-cure**, cura de reposo, f. **r.-house**, hospedería, f; refugio, m. **r.-room, lounge**, sala de descanso, f; (toilet) excusado, retrete, m; (in theaters) saloncillo, m

rest /rɛst/ vi reposar, descansar; (lie down) acostarse, echarse; (stop) cesar, parar; estar en paz; apoyarse (en); descansar (sobre); posar; depender (de); (remain) quedar. vt descansar; dar un descanso (a); (lean) apoyar; basar (en). **It rests with them,** Depende de ellos. **These valuable documents now rest in the Library of Congress,** Estos valiosos documentos han parado en la Biblioteca del Congresso. **May he r. in peace!** ¡Que en paz descanse! **to r. assured,** estar seguro. **to r. on one's oars,** cesar de remar; descansar

restate /ri'steit/ vt repetir, afirmar de nuevo

restatement /ri'steitmənt/ n repetición, f

restaurant /'rɛstərənt/ n restaurante, restorán, m. **r.-car,** coche-comedor, m

restful /'rɛstfəl/ a descansado; tranquilo, sosegado

resting /'rɛstɪŋ/ n reposo, m. **last r.-place,** última morada, f. **r.-place,** descansadero, m; refugio, m

restitution /,rɛstɪ'tuʃən/ n restitución, f

restive /'rɛstɪv/ a (of a horse) repropio, ingobernable; inquieto, agitado; impaciente

restiveness /'rɛstɪvnɪs/ n inquietud, agitación, f; impaciencia, f

restless /'rɛstlɪs/ a agitado; inquieto, intranquilo; turbulento; sin reposo; (wakeful) desvelado; (ceaseless) incesante. **r. night,** noche desvelada, noche intranquila, Inf. noche toledana, f

restlessly /'rɛstlɪsli/ adv agitadamente; con inquietud; turbulentamente; incesantemente

restlessness /'rɛstlɪsnɪs/ n agitación, f; inquietud, intranquilidad, f; turbulencia, f; falta de reposo, f; (wakefulness) desvelo, m; movimiento incesante, m

restock /ri'stɔk/ vt (with goods) surtir de nuevo; proveer de nuevo; restablecer; repoblar

restoration /,rɛstə'reiʃən/ n restauración, f; renovación, f; restablecimiento, m; (returning) restitución, f

restorative /rɪ'stɔrətɪv/ a and n restaurativo m

restore /rɪ'stɔr/ vt restaurar; restituir; devolver; restablecer; reponer; (repair) reformar, reparar; reconstruir; (to former rank, etc.) rehabilitar. **He restored the book to its place,** Devolvió el libro a su sitio

restorer /rɪ'stɔrər/ n restaurador (-ra)

restrain /rɪ'strein/ vt refrenar; reprimir; (restrict) limitar, restringir; (prevent) impedir; desviar; (detain) recluir. **to r. oneself,** contenerse

restrained /rɪ'streind/ a moderado, mesurado; sobrio; (of emotion) contenido

restraining /rɪ'streinɪŋ/ a restrictivo; moderador, calmante

restraint /rɪ'streint/ n freno, m; restricción, f; limitación, f; prohibición, f; compulsión, f; (reserve) reserva, f; moderación, f

restrict /rɪ'strɪkt/ vt restringir; limitar

restriction /rɪ'strɪkʃən/ n restricción, f; limitación, f

restrictive /rɪ'strɪktɪv/ a restrictivo

result /rɪ'zʌlt/ n resultado, m; consecuencia, resulta, f; solución, f. vi resultar. **as the r. of,** de resultas de

resultant /rɪ'zʌltnt/ a resultante; consecuente. n resultado, m; Mech. resultante, f

resume /rɪ'zum/ vt reasumir; (continue) reanudar, continuar; (summarize) resumir

résumé /'rɛzʊ,mei/ n resumen, m, recapitulación, f

resummon /ri'sʌmən/ vt convocar de nuevo (a); citar de nuevo (a)

resumption /rɪ'zʌmpʃən/ n (renewal) reanudación, f; reasunción, f

resurgence /rɪ'sɜrdʒəns/ n resurgimiento, m

resurrect /,rɛzə'rɛkt/ vt Inf. desenterrar; resucitar

resurrection /,rɛzə'rɛkʃən/ n resurrección, f

resuscitate /rɪ'sʌsɪ,teit/ vt and vi resucitar

resuscitation /rɪ,sʌsɪ'teiʃən/ n resurrección, f; renovación, f; renacimiento, m

retail /'riteil/ n venta al por menor, reventa, f. adv al por menor. vt (goods) vender al por menor, revender; (tell) contar; repetir. **r. trade,** comercio al por menor, m

retailer /'riteilər/ n vendedor (-ra) al por menor; (of a story) narrador (-ra); el, m, (f, la) que cuenta algo

retain /rɪ'tein/ vt retener; guardar; conservar; (a barrister) ajustar; (hire) contratar

retainer /rɪ'teinər/ n (dependent) criado, dependiente, m; partidario, adherente, m; (fee) honorario, m; pl **retainers,** séquito, m, adherentes, m pl, gente, f

retaining wall /rɪ'teinɪŋ/ n muro de contención, m

retake /n 'riteik; v ri'teik/ n (cinema) nueva toma, f. vt volver a tomar; reconquistar

retaking /'ri,teikɪŋ/ n reconquista, f

retaliate /rɪ'tæli,eit/ vt vengarse de, desquitarse de. vi vengarse, tomar represalias

retaliation /rɪ,tæli'eiʃən/ n represalias, f pl; desquite, m, satisfacción, f. **law of r.,** talión, m,

retaliatory /rɪ'tæliə, a de represalias; de desquite

retard /rɪ'tɑrd/ vt retardar

retch /rɛtʃ/ vi tener náuseas, procurar vomitar

retching /'rɛtʃɪŋ/ n náusea, basca, f

retell /ri'tɛl/ vt repetir, volver a contar

retention /rɪ'tɛnʃən/ n retención, f; conservación, f

retentive /rɪ'tɛntɪv/ a retentivo

retentiveness /rɪ'tɛntɪvnɪs/ n poder de retención, m; (memory) retentiva, f

reticence /'rɛtəsəns/ n reticencia, reserva, f

reticent /'rɛtəsənt/ a reservado, inexpresivo, taciturno

retina /'rɛtnə, 'rɛtnə/ n retina, f

retinue /'rɛtn,u, -,yu/ n séquito, acompañamiento, m, comitiva, f

retire /rɪ'taiər/ vi retirarse; (to bed) recogerse, acostarse; (from a post) jubilarse. vt retirar; jubilar. **to r. from a post,** Mil. rendir el puesto

retired /rɪ'taiərd/ a retirado; (remote) apartado, aislado; (hidden) escondido; (former) antiguo; (from employment, etc.) jubilado; (of an officer) retirado. **to place on the r. list,** jubilar; (Mil. Nav.) dar el retiro (a)

retirement /rɪ'taiərmənt/ n retirada, f; (solitude) apartamiento, aislamiento, m; retiro, m; (superannuation) jubilación, f

retiring /rɪ'taiərɪŋ/ a que se retira; (from a post) dimitente; (with pension, etc.) de jubilación; (reserved) reservado; modesto

retort /rɪ'tɔrt/ vi replicar. vt retorcer; devolver (una acusación, etc.). n réplica, f; contestación, f; Chem. retorta, f

retouch /ri'tʌtʃ/ vt retocar

retrace /ri'treis/ vt volver a trazar; volver a andar (un camino); (one's steps) volver sobre sus pasos, volver atrás; (in memory) rememorar, recordar; buscar el origen (de); (recount) narrar, contar

retract /rɪ'trækt/ vt retractar, retirar; (draw back) retraer. vi retractarse

retraction /rɪ'trækʃən/ n retracción, f

retranslate /ri'trænsleit/ vt hacer una nueva traducción (de)

retransmission /,ritrænsm'mɪʃən/ n retransmisión, f

retread /ri'trɛd/ vt pisar de nuevo; (tires) recauchetear

retreat /rɪ'trit/ n retirada, f; (Mil. signal) retreta, f; (refuge and Eccl.) retiro, m. vi retirarse; retroceder; refugiarse

retreat house n casa de ejercicios, f

retreating /rɪ'tritɪŋ/ a que se retira; que retrocede; Mil. que se bate en retirada

retrench /rɪ'trentʃ/ vt reducir; disminuir; vi economizar, hacer economías
retrenchment /rɪ'trentʃmənt/ n disminución, reducción, f; economías, f pl
retrial /'rɪtraɪl/ n (of a person) nuevo proceso, m; (of a case) revisión, f
retribution /,retrə'byuʃən/ n retribución, f; justo castigo, m, pena merecida, f
retrievable /rɪ'trivəbəl/ a recuperable, que puede recobrarse; reparable
retrieval /rɪ'trivəl/ n recuperación, f; reparación, f; (of game) cobra, f; (of one's character) rehabilitación, f
retrieve /rɪ'triv/ vt (game, of dogs) cobrar; (regain) recobrar, recuperar; restaurar; reparar; restablecer; (one's character) rehabilitar. vi cobrar la caza
retriever /rɪ'trivər/ n (dog) perdiguero (-ra)
retroactive /,retrou'æktɪv/ a retroactivo
retrocede /,retrə'sid/ vi retroceder
retrograde /'retrə,greɪd/ a retrógrado
retrogression /,retrə'greʃən/ n retrogradación, regresión, f; Med. retroceso, m
retrogressive /,retrə'gresɪv/ a retrógrado
retrospect /'retrə,spekt/ n mirada retrospectiva, f, examen del pasado, m. **in r.,** retrospectivamente
retrospection /,retrə'spekʃən/ n retrospección, f
retrospective /,retrə'spektɪv/ a retrospectivo
retrospectively /,retrə'spektɪvli/ adv retrospectivamente
retry /ri'traɪ/ vt (a case) rever; (a person) procesar de nuevo
return /rɪ'tɜrn/ vi regresar, Lat. Am. devolverse; volver; reaparecer; presentarse de nuevo; Law. revertir; (answer) contestar, responder. vt (give back or put back) devolver; (a ball) restar; (a kindness, visit) pagar; restituir; (reciprocate) corresponder (a); recompensar; contestar (a); dar; rendir; (yield) producir; (a verdict) fallar, pronunciar; (report) dar parte de; anunciar; (exchange) cambiar; (elect) elegir. n regreso, m; vuelta, f; (giving or putting back) devolución, f; pago, m; restitución, f; correspondencia, f; recompensa, f; (reply) respuesta, f; (reappearance) reaparición, f; reinstalación, f; repetición, f; (gain) ganancia, f, provecho, m; rendimiento, m; (exchange) cambio, m; (report) parte oficial, f; informe, m; lista, f; (election) elección, f; pl **returns,** tablas estadísticas, f pl; (of an election) resultados, m pl. **Many happy returns!** ¡Feliz cumpleaños! **by return mail,** a vuelta de correo. **on my (his, etc.) r.,** a la vuelta, cuando vuelva. **to r. like for like,** pagar en la misma moneda. **r. journey, r. trip,** viaje de vuelta, m. **r. match,** partido de vuelta, m. **r. ticket,** billete de ida y vuelta, m; billete de vuelta, m
returnable /rɪ'tɜrnəbəl/ a restituible; susceptible a ser devuelto; (on adjourn) a prueba; Law. devolutivo
returning /rɪ'tɜrnɪŋ/ a que vuelve. n See **return**
"Return to Sender" «Al remitente»
reunion /ri'yunyən/ n reunión, f
reunite /,riyu'naɪt/ vt reunir. vi reunirse
revaccinate /ri'væksə,neɪt/ vt revacunar
revaccination /ri,væksə'neɪʃən/ n revacunación, f
reveal /rɪ'vil/ vt revelar; descubrir
revealer /rɪ'vilər/ n revelador (-ra)
revealing /rɪ'vilɪŋ/ a revelador. n revelación, f; descubrimiento, m
reveille /'revəli/ n Mil. diana, f, toque de la diana, m
revel /'revəl/ vi divertirse; regocijarse (en), gozarse (en); entregarse (a); (carouse) ir de parranda; emborracharse. n algazara, jarana, f; pl **revels,** fiestas, festividades, f pl
revelation /,revə'leɪʃən/ n revelación, f; descubrimiento, m; **Revelation,** (in the Bible) Apocalipsis, m
reveler /'revələr/ n convidado alegre, m; (at night) trasnochador (-ra); (drunk) borracho (-cha); (masked) máscara, mf
revelry /'revəlri/ n festividades, f pl, regocijo, m; orgías, f pl, Central America embullo, m
revenge /rɪ'vendʒ/ n venganza, f. vt vengarse de; desquitarse de
revengeful /rɪ'vendʒfəl/ a vengativo
revengefully /rɪ'vendʒfəli/ adv vengativamente

revengefulness /rɪ'vendʒfəlnɪs/ n deseo de venganza, m; carácter vengativo, m
revenger /rɪ'vendʒər/ n vengador (-ra)
revenue /'revən,yu, -ə,nu/ n rentas públicas, f pl; (treasury) fisco, m; Com. rédito, m, ingresos, m pl; beneficio, m. **Inland R.,** delegación de contribuciones, f. **r. officer,** agente fiscal, m
reverberate /rɪ'vɜrbə,reɪt/ vt and vi (of sound) retumbar, resonar; (of light, etc.) reverberar
reverberation /rɪ,vɜrbə'reɪʃən/ n (reflection) reverberación, f; (of sound) retumbo, eco, m
revere /rɪ'vɪər/ vt reverenciar, venerar, honrar
reverence /'revərəns/ n reverencia, f, vt reverenciar
reverend /'revərənd/ a reverendo
reverent /'revərənt/ a reverente
reverie /'revəri/ n ensueño, m
reversal /rɪ'vɜrsəl/ n inversión, f; (of a verdict) revocación, f
reverse /rɪ'vɜrs/ vt invertir; (a steam engine) dar contra vapor (a); (a vehicle) poner en marcha atrás; (arms) llevar a la funerala; (a judgment, etc.) revocar, derogar. vi (dancing) dar vueltas al revés. n lo contrario, lo opuesto; (back) dorso, revés, m; (change) cambio, m; (check) revés, m, vicisitud, f; (loss) pérdida, f; (defeat) derrota, f; Mech. marcha atrás, f, a inverso; contrario, opuesto. **quite the r.,** todo el contrario. **r. turn,** (of an engine) cambio de dirección, m; (in dancing) vuelta al revés, f
reversible /rɪ'vɜrsəbəl/ a reversible
reversion /rɪ'vɜrʒən, -ʃən/ n reversión, f; Biol. atavismo, m; (of offices) futura, f; (of property) reversión, f
revert /rɪ'vɜrt/ vi Law. revertir; volver (a)
review /rɪ'vyu/ n examen, análisis, m; juicio crítico, m; (journal and Mil.) revista, f; (criticism) revista, reseña, f; Law. revisión, f. vt examinar, analizar; (Mil. etc.) pasar revista (a); revisar; repasar; (a book, etc.) reseñar; Law. revisar. vi escribir revistas
review article n artículo de reseña, m
reviewer /rɪ'vyuər/ n revistero (-ra), crítico, m
revile /rɪ'vaɪl/ vt injuriar, maldecir, difamar
reviler /rɪ'vaɪlər/ n maldiciente, m, insultador (-ra)
reviling /rɪ'vaɪlɪŋ/ n insultos, m pl, injurias, f pl
revisal /rɪ'vaɪzəl/ n revisión, f
revise /rɪ'vaɪz/ vt revisar; repasar; corregir; (change) cambiar
reviser /rɪ'vaɪzər/ n revisor, m; corrector de pruebas, m
revision /rɪ'vɪʒən/ n revisión, f; repaso, m; corrección de pruebas, f
revisit /rɪ'vɪzɪt/ vt volver a visitar, visitar de nuevo
revival /rɪ'vaɪvəl/ n resurgimiento, m; renovación, f; (awakening) despertamiento, m; restablecimiento, m; resurrección, f; (of learning) renacimiento, m; Theat. reposición, f; (religious) despertar religioso, m
revive /rɪ'vaɪv/ vi reponerse; restablecerse; resucitar; renovarse; renacer; cobrar fuerzas; (recover consciousness) volver en sí. vt hacer revivir; resucitar; restablecer; renovar; restaurar; despertar; (fire, colors) avivar
reviver /rɪ'vaɪvər/ n resucitador (-ra)
revivification /rɪ,vɪvəfɪ'keɪʃən/ n revivificación, f
revivify /rɪ'vɪvə,faɪ/ vt revivificar
revocable /'revəkəbəl, rɪ'vou-/ a revocable
revocation /,revə'keɪʃən/ n revocación, f
revoke /rɪ'vouk/ vt revocar, anular, derogar; (wills) quebrantar. vi revocar, anular; (at cards) renunciar. n (cards) renuncio, m
revolt /rɪ'voult/ n rebelión, f, vi rebelarse; sublevarse. vt repugnar, indignar, dar asco (a)
revolting /rɪ'voultɪŋ/ a repugnante, asqueroso; (rebellious) rebelde
revolution /,revə'luʃən/ n revolución, f; (turn) vuelta, f, giro, m
revolutionary /,revə'luʃə,neri/ a and n revolucionario (-ia)
revolutionize /,revə'luʃə,naɪz/ vt revolucionar
revolve /rɪ'volv/ vi dar vueltas, girar; suceder periódicamente. vt hacer girar; (ponder) revolver, discurrir
revolver /rɪ'volvər/ n revólver, m
revolving /rɪ'volvɪŋ/ a giratorio; que vuelve; peri-

ódico. **r. chair,** silla giratoria, *f.* **r. door,** puerta giratoria, *f.* **r. stage,** escenario giratorio, *m*
revue /rɪ'vyu/ *n Theat.* revista, *f*
revulsion /rɪ'vʌlʃən/ *n* revulsión, *f*
revulsive /rɪ'vʌlsɪv/ *a Med.* revulsivo
rev up /rev/ *vt* (an engine) calentar
reward /rɪ'wɔrd/ *n* recompensa, *f*; retribución, *f. vt* recompensar; satisfacer, premiar
rewarding /rɪ'wɔrdɪŋ/ *a* premiador; que recompensa. *n* recompensación, *f.* **a rewarding experience,** una experiencia compensadora, *f*
rewrite /ri'rait/ *vt* escribir de nuevo; volver a escribir; redactar otra vez
rhapsody /'ræpsədi/ *n* rapsodia, *f*
rheostat /'riə,stæt/ *n* reóstato, *m*
rhetoric /'retərɪk/ *n* retórica, *f*
rhetorical /rɪ'tɔrɪkəl/ *a* retórico; declamatorio
rhetorician /,retə'rɪʃən/ *n* retórico (-ca)
rheumatic /rʊ'mætɪk/ *a* reumático. **r. fever,** reumatismo poliarticular agudo, *m*
rheumatism /'rumə,tɪzəm/ *n* reumatismo, reuma, *m*
rheumy /'rumi/ *a* catarroso; (of the eyes) legañoso
Rhine, the /rain/ el Rin, *m*
rhinestone /'rain,stoun/ circón, *m*
rhinoceros /rai'nɒsərəs/ *n* rinoceronte, *m*
Rhodes /roudz/ Rodas, *f*
rhododendron /,roudə'dɛndrən/ *n* rododendro, *m*
rhubarb /'rubɑrb/ *n* ruibarbo, *m*
rhyme /raim/ *n* rima, *f*; verso, *m. vi and vt* rimar. **without r. or reason,** sin ton ni son; a tontas y a locas
rhymer /'raimər/ *n* rimador (-ra)
rhyming /'raimɪŋ/ *a* rimador
rhythm /'rɪðəm/ *n* ritmo, *m*
rhythmic /'rɪðmɪk/ *a* rítmico
rib /rɪb/ *n* (*Anat., Bot., Aer., Naut., Archit.*) costilla, *f*; (of an umbrella or fan) varilla, *f*; (in cloth) cordoncillo, *m*, lista, *f*
ribald /'rɪbəld/ *a* escabroso, ribaldo, indecente
ribaldry /'rɪbəldri/ *n* ribaldería, escabrosidad, indecencia, *f*
ribbed /rɪbd/ *a* con costillas; (of cloth) listado, con listas
ribbon /'rɪbən/ *n* cinta, *f*; tira, *f*; (tatter) jirón, *m*. **to tear to ribbons,** hacer jirones
rice /rais/ *n* arroz, *m. a* de arroz; con arroz. **r. field,** arrozal, *m*. **r.-paper,** papel de paja de arroz, *m*. **r.-pudding,** arroz con leche, *m*
rich /rɪtʃ/ *a* rico; opulento; (happy) dichoso; (of land, etc.) fértil; abundante; (of objects) magnífico, suntuoso, hermoso; precioso; (of food) exquisito; suculento; (highly seasoned) muy sazonado; (creamy) con mucha nata; (of colors) brillante, vivo. **new r.,** ricacho (-cha). **newly-r.,** advenedizo. **to grow r.,** enriquecerse, *Lat. Am. also* fondearse
riches /'rɪtʃɪz/ *n* riqueza, *f*
richly /'rɪtʃli/ *adv* ricamente; abundantemente; magníficamente; bien
richness /'rɪtʃnɪs/ *n* riqueza, *f*; opulencia, *f*; (of land, etc.) fertilidad, *f*; abundancia, *f*; (of objects) magnificencia, suntuosidad, hermosura, *f*; preciosidad, *f*; (of food) gusto exquisito, *m*; suculencia, *f*; (piquancy) gusto picante, *m*; (of colors) viveza, *f*
rickets /'rɪkɪts/ *n* raquitismo, *m*
rickety /'rɪkɪti/ *a Med.* raquítico; destartalado, desvencijado; (unsteady) tambaleante; cojo
rickshaw /'rɪkʃɔ/ *n* riksha, *m*
ricochet /,rɪkə'ʃei/ *n* rebote, *m*, *vi* rebotar
rid /rɪd/ *vt* librar (de). **to get rid of,** librarse de; quitarse de encima (a); perder, quitarse; (dismiss) despedir. **to rid oneself of,** librarse de, deshacerse de
riddance /'rɪdns/ *n* libramiento, *m*
riddle /'rɪdl/ *n* acertijo, *m*; enigma, problema, *m*; misterio, *m*; (sieve) tamiz de alambre, *m*; *vt* (guess) adivinar; (sift) cribar; (with holes) acribillar
ride /raid/ *vi* (a horse) montar a caballo, cabalgar; pasear a caballo; (a mule, a bicycle) montar en, pasear en; (a vehicle, train) ir en; (a carriage, car) andar en, pasear en; (float) flotar; (on the wind) dejarse llevar por el viento; ser llevado por el viento; (go) ir;

(come) venir; (a distance) hacer... a caballo, en coche, etc.; *Naut.* estar al ancla; *Mech.* tener juego. *vt* (a horse, mule, bicycle) montar; ir montado sobre; manejar; (a race) hacer; (float) flotar en; (cleave, the sea, etc.) surcar. *n* paseo (a caballo, en bicicleta, en coche, etc.), *m*; viaje (en un autobús, de tren, etc.), *m*; (bridle path) camino de herradura, *m*; cabalgata, *f*, desfile a caballo, *m*; (hitch, lift) *Mexico* aventón, *m*. **a r. on horseback,** un paseo a caballo. **They gave me a r. in their car,** (e.g. to see the sights) Me llevaron a paseo en su auto, (a lift to a certain place) Me dieron un aventón. **ride at anchor,** estar fondeado. **to r. a bicycle,** montar en bicicleta. **to r. rough-shod over,** mandar a la baqueta (a), mandar a puntapiés (a). **to r. sidesaddle,** cabalgar a mujeriegas. **to r. at,** embestir con. **to r. away,** marcharse, alejarse; marcharse a caballo, etc. **to r. back,** volver; volver a caballo, en bicicleta, etc. **to r. behind,** seguir a caballo; ir inmediatamente detrás (de); (on the back seat) ocupar el asiento de atrás; (on the same animal) cabalgar en la grupa. **to r. down,** atropellar; (trample) pisotear, pasar por encima de. **to r. on,** seguir su camino. **to r. out,** salir a paseo en caballo, etc.; irse a paseo en coche, etc.; (a storm) hacer frente a, luchar con. **to r. over,** pasar por encima de; recorrer. **to r. up,** *vi* llegar, acercarse; (of a tie, etc.) subir. *vt* montar
rider /'raidər/ *n* cabalgador (-ra); jinete, *m*; persona que va en coche, etc., *f*; (on a bicycle) ciclista, *mf*; (on a motorcycle) motociclista, *mf*; (horsebreaker) domador de caballos, *m*; (clause) añadidura, *f*; corolario, *m*
ridge /rɪdʒ/ *n* cumbre, cima, *f*; (of mountains) cordillera, sierra, *f*; (of a roof, of a nose) caballete, *m*; *Agr.* lomo, caballón, *m*; (wrinkle) arruga, *f*; (on coins) cordoncillo, *m*. *vt* surcar; formar lomos (en); (wrinkle) arrugar
ridicule /'rɪdɪ,kyul/ *n* ridículo, *m*, *vt* poner en ridículo, ridiculizar; burlarse (de), mofarse (de)
ridiculous /rɪ'dɪkyələs/ *a* ridículo, absurdo
riding /'raidɪŋ/ *a* cabalgante; que va a caballo; montado (a, en, sobre); *Naut.* al ancla; (in compounds) de equitación, *f*; de montar. *n* equitación, *f*; paseo a caballo; en bicicleta, etc., *m*; acción de ir a caballo, etc., *f*; (district) comarca, *f*. **r.-boots,** botas de montar, *f pl.* **r.-habit,** traje de montar, *m*; (woman's) amazona, *f*. **r.-master,** profesor de equitación, *m*. **r.-saddle,** silla de montar, *f*. **r.-school,** escuela de equitación, *f*
rife /raif/ *a* común; corriente; frecuente; prevalente; abundante; general. **r. with,** abundante en; lleno de
riffraff /'rɪf,ræf/ *n* desperdicios, *m pl*; (rabble) gentuza, canalla, *f*
rifle /'raifəl/ *n* rifle, fusil rayado, *m. vt* robar; (a suitcase, etc.) desvalijar; (a gun) rayar. **r.-case,** *Mexico* carcaj, *m*. **r.-range,** campo de tiro, *m*. **r.-sling,** portafusil, *m*. **r.-shot,** fusilazo, *m*
rifleman /'raifəlmən/ *n* fusilero, *m*
rifler /'raiflər/ *n* saqueador (-ra)
rifling /'raiflɪŋ/ *n* (robbing) saqueo, robo, *m*; (a suitcase, etc.) desvalijamiento, *m*
rift /rɪft/ *n* hendedura, abertura, *f*; grieta, *f*
rig /rɪg/ *n Naut.* aparejo, *m*; *Inf.* atavío, *m. vt* (a ship) aparejar; equipar; (elections) falsificar. **to rig out,** proveer de; equipar con; ataviar. **to rig up,** arreglar; armar, construir
rigging /'rɪgɪŋ/ *n* (of a ship) aparejo, *m*
right /rait/ *a* recto; correcto; conveniente, debido; apropiado; exacto; (opposite of left hand) derecho; (straight) directo; en línea recta; razonable; (true) verdadero, genuino, legítimo; (just) justo; (competent) prudente; (in health) sano. **All r.!** ¡Está bien! **I feel all r.,** Me siento perfectamente bien, Estoy bien. **He is the r. man for the job,** Él es el hombre que hace falta para el puesto. **It is the r. word,** Es la palabra apropiada. **on the r.,** a la derecha. **to be r.,** (of persons) tener razón. **to make r.,** poner en orden; arreglar. **r.-angle,** ángulo recto, *m*. **r.-angled,** rectangular. **r.-angled triangle,** triángulo rectángulo, *m*. **the R. Bank (of Paris),** la Orilla derecha, la Ribera derecha, *f*. **r. hand,** *n* (mano) derecha, diestra, *f*; derecha, *f*; (person) brazo derecho, *m. a* de la mano de-

recha; de la derecha; a la derecha. **r.-handed,** derecho; diestro, hábil. **r. mind,** entero juicio, *m.* **r.-minded,** juicioso, prudente; honrado. **r.-of-way,** derecho a la vía, *m*

right /rait/ *adv* directamente; inmediatamente; derechamente; correctamente; debidamente; exactamente; bien; (quite, thoroughly) completamente; honradamente; (very) muy. **r. on,** adelante; en frente. **R. about face!** ¡Media vuelta a la derecha! **r. at the bottom,** al fondo; al final; el último (de la clase, etc.). **r. at the end of his speech,** al fin de su discurso. **r. away, r. now** en seguida, inmediatamente, *Mexico* ahorita, *elsewhere in Lat. Am.* lueguito

right /rait/ *n* razón, *f*; verdad, *f*; justicia, *f*; (good) bien, *m*; derecho, *m*; (not left side) derecha, *f*; (of political parties) derechas, *f pl.* **r. and wrong,** el bien y el mal. **"All rights reserved,"** «Derechos reservados.» **by rights,** por derecho. **It is on the r.,** Está a la derecha. **to exercise one's r.,** usar de su derecho. **r. of association,** derecho de asociación, *m.* **r. of way,** derecho de paso, *m.* **to be in the r.,** tener razón; estar en su derecho

right /rait/ *vt* enderezar; rectificar; corregir; poner en orden; *Naut.* enderezar; hacer justicia (a). **to r. wrongs,** deshacer agravios

righteous /'raitʃəs/ *a* recto, virtuoso, justo; justificado

righteously /'raitʃəsli/ *adv* virtuosamente; justamente

righteousness /'raitʃəsnis/ *n* rectitud, integridad, virtud, *f*; justicia, *f*

rightful /'raitfəl/ *a* justo; legítimo; verdadero

rightfully /'raitfəli/ *adv* justamente; legitimamente; verdaderamente

rightfulness /'raitfəlnis/ *n* justicia, *f*; legitimidad, *f*; verdad, *f*

rightly /'raitli/ *adv* justamente; debidamente; correctamente; bien. **r. or wrongly,** mal que bien

rightness /'raitnis/ *n* rectitud, *f*; derechura, *f*; justicia, *f*; exactitud, *f*

rigid /'rɪdʒɪd/ *a* rígido; inflexible; severo, riguroso

rigidity /rɪ'dʒɪdɪti/ *n* rigidez, *f*; inflexibilidad, *f*; severidad, *f*

rigmarole /'rɪgmə,roul/ *n* monserga, *f*, galimatías, *m*, jerigonza, *f*

rigor /'rɪgər/ *n* rigor, *m*

rigorous /'rɪgərəs/ *a* riguroso

rile /rail/ *vt Inf.* irritar, sacar de tino (a)

rim /rɪm/ *n* borde, *m*; orilla, *f*; (of a wheel) llanta, *f*, aro, *m*

rime /raim/ *n* escarcha, *f*, *vt* cubrir con escarcha. See also **rhyme**

rind /raind/ *n* (of fruit) cáscara, corteza, *f*; (of cheese) costra, *f*; (of bacon) piel, *f*

ring /rɪŋ/ *n* círculo, *m*; (round the eyes) ojera, *f*; (for curtains, etc.) anilla, *f*; (for the finger) anillo, *m*, sortija, *f*; (for children's games, etc.) corro, *m*; (for the ears) arete, *m*; (of smoke and for the nose) anillo, *m*; (for hitching, etc.) argolla, *f*; (for boxing) cuadrilátero, *m*; (on a racecourse) picadero, *f*; (at a circus, bull-fight) ruedo, redondel, *m*; *Fig.* arena, *f*; (group) camarilla, *f*, grupo, *m*; (metallic sound) sonido metálico, *m*; resonancia, *f*; (tinkle) tintín, *m*; (of a bell) repique, tañido, son (de la campana), *m*; (of bells) juego de campanas, *m*; (of laughter, etc.) ruido, *m*; (of truth, etc.) apariencia, *f*. **r.-bolt,** *Naut.* cáncamo, *m*. **r. finger,** dedo anular, *m*. **r.-master,** director de circo, *m*

ring /rɪŋ/ *vt* (surround) cercar, rodear; (a bull, etc.) poner un anillo (a); (sound) hacer sonar; sonar; (a door bell, etc.) tocar, apretar; (bells) echar a vuelo; (announce by pealing the bells) anunciar, proclamar; sonar, tañer. *vi* (of bells) sonar; (re-echo) resonar; (of the ears) zumbar; (tinkle) tintinar. **to r. the bell,** tocar la campana; tocar al timbre. **to r. off,** colgar el teléfono. **to r. up,** llamar por teléfono, telefonear

ringing /'rɪŋɪŋ/ *n* acción de tocar las campanas o el timbre, *f*; toque, *m*; repique, *m*; campanilleo, *m*; (in the ears) zumbido, *m. a* resonante, sonoro. **r. signal,** señal de llamada, *f*. **the r. of the bells,** el son de las campanas

ringleader /'rɪŋ,lidər/ *n* cabecilla, *m*

ringlet /'rɪŋlɪt/ *n* rizo, bucle, *m*

ringworm /'rɪŋ,wɜrm/ *n* tiña, *f*

rink /rɪŋk/ *n* pista, *f*. **skating-r.,** sala de patinar, *f*; pista de patinar, *f*

rinse /rɪns/ *n* enjuague, *m*; enjuagadura, *f*; (of clothes) aclarado, *m. vt* enjuagar; (clothes) aclarar; lavar

rinsing /'rɪnsɪŋ/ *n* See **rinse;** *pl* **rinsings,** lavazas, *f pl. a* de aclarar

Rio de Janeiro /'riou dei ʒə'nɛərou/ *n* Rio de Janeiro, *f*; a carioca, *formal* fluminense, *mf*

riot /'raiət/ *n* motín, *m*; tumulto, *m*; desorden, *m*; exceso, *m*; orgía, *f*; disipación, *f*. *vi* amotinarse; alborotarse; entregarse a la disipación (or al placer); (enjoy) gozar, disfrutar. **to run r.,** hacer excesos; perder el freno; desmandarse; *Fig.* extenderse por todas partes; crecer en abundancia, cubrir todo

rioter /'raiətər/ *n* amotinador (-ra); alborotador (-ra)

riotous /'raiətəs/ *a* sedicioso; bullicioso; disoluto; desordenado; desenfrenado

riotousness /'raiətəsnis/ *n* sedición, *f*; disolución, *f*; exceso, *m pl*, desenfreno, *m*; desorden, *m*

rip /rɪp/ *vt* rasgar; (unsew) descoser; (wood, etc.) partir; (make) hacer. *vi* rasgarse. *n* rasgón, *m*; rasgadura, *f*; desgarro, *m*; (libertine) calavera, *m*. **to rip off,** arrancar; quitar. **to rip open,** abrir; (an animal) abrir en canal

riparian /rɪ'pɛəriən/ *a* and *n* ribereño (-ña)

ripe /raip/ *a* maduro; preparado; perfecto, acabado

ripen /'raipən/ *vt* and *vi* madurar

ripeness /'raipnis/ *n* madurez, *f*

ripening /'raipənɪŋ/ *n* maduración, *f*

ripping /'rɪpɪŋ/ *n* rasgadura, *f*; (unstitching) deshiladura, *f. a Inf.* estupendo

ripple /'rɪpəl/ *n* rizo, *m*; onda, *f*; (of sound) murmullo, *m. vt* rizar. *vi* rizarse; murmurar

rippling /'rɪplɪŋ/ *n* rizado, *m*; murmullo, *m*

rise /raiz/ *vi* ascender; subir; levantarse; ponerse de pie; (of a meeting) suspenderse; (from the dead) resucitar; (grow) crecer; (swell) hincharse; (of sun, moon) salir; (of sound, gradient, price, stock exchange quotations) subir; (of river source) nacer; (in revolt) sublevarse, rebelarse; (to the mind) presentarse, surgir; (appear) aparecer; (of buildings, etc.) elevarse, alzarse; (in the world) mejorar de posición; (originate) originarse (en), proceder (de); (of mercury) alzarse; (of fish) picar. **He has risen in my estimation,** Ha ganado en mi estimación. **She rose early,** Se levantó temprano. **The color rose in her cheeks,** Se le subieron los colores a la cara. **to r. to the occasion,** estar al nivel de las circunstancias. **to r. to one's feet,** ponerse de pie. **to r. to the bait,** morder el anzuelo. **to r. again,** levantarse de nuevo; resucitar; renovarse, suscitarse otra vez. **to r. above,** alzarse por encima de; mostrarse superior a

rise /raiz/ *n* ascensión, *f*; subida, *f*; levantamiento, *m*; (in price, temperature) alza, *f*; (increase) aumento, *m*; (of the sun, moon) salida, *f*; (of a river) nacimiento, *m*; (origin) origen, *m*; (growth, development) desarrollo, crecimiento, *m*; (promotion) ascenso, *m*; (slope) cuesta, *f*; pendiente, *f*; (high ground) eminencia, altura, *f*. **to give r. to,** dar lugar a, causar. **r. and fall,** subida y baja, *f*; (of the voice) ritmo, *m*; (of music) cadencia, *f*; (of institutions) grandeza y decadencia, *f*. **r. to power,** subida al poder, *f*

riser /'raizər/ *n* el, *m*, (f, la) que se levanta; (of a step) contrahuella, *f*. **early r.,** madrugador (-ra). **late r.,** el, *m*, (f, la) que se levanta tarde

risibility /,rizə'biliti/ *n* risibilidad, *f*

risible /'rizəbəl/ *a* risible

rising /'raizɪŋ/ *n* subida, *f*; (of the source of rivers) nacimiento, *m*; (overflowing of rivers) crecimiento, *m*; (of sun, moon) salida, *f*; (from the dead) resurrección, *f*; (rebellion) sublevación, insurrección, *f* (of the tide) crecida, *f*; (of bread) levadura, *f*; (of an assembly) suspensión, *f*; (of a theater curtain) subida, *f*; (literary) renacimiento, *m, a* creciente; naciente; saliente; (promising) de porvenir; (young) joven. **the r. generation,** los jóvenes, la generación joven. **He likes r. early,** Le gusta madrugar. **On the r. of the curtain...,** Al levantarse el telón... **the r. of the**

moon, la salida de la luna, *f.* **the r. tide,** la marea creciente

risk /rɪsk/ *n* riesgo, *m*; peligro, *m. vt* arriesgar; atreverse (a), osar. **at the r. of,** al riesgo de. **to take a r.,** tomar un riesgo; correr peligro. **to r. everything on the outcome,** jugar el todo por el todo

risk capital *n* capital-riesgo, *m*

riskiness /'rɪskɪnɪs/ *n* peligro, *m*

risky /'rɪski/ *a* arriesgado, peligroso

rissole /rɪ'soul/ *n* risol, *m*, (*pl* risoles)

rite /rait/ *n* rito, *m*

rite of passage *n* rito de tránsito, *m*

ritual /'rɪtʃuəl/ *a* ritual. *n* rito, *m*, ceremonia, *f*

ritualist /'rɪtʃuəlɪst/ *n* ritualista, *mf*

ritualistic /ˌrɪtʃuə'lɪstɪk/ *a* ritualista

rival /'raivəl/ *n* rival, *mf a* competidor; rival. *vt* rivalizar con, competir con

rivalry /'raivəlri/ *n* rivalidad, *f*

river /'rɪvər/ *n* río, *m. a* del río; fluvial. **r.-basin,** cuenca de un río, *f.* **r.-bed,** lecho, cauce (de un río), *m.* **r. civilization,** civilización fluvial, *f.* **r.-god,** dios de los ríos, *m.* **r.-mouth,** ría, *f.* **r. port,** puerto fluvial, *m*

riverside /'rɪvərˌsaid/ *n* ribera, orilla de un río, *f. a* de la(s) orilla(s) de un río; situado a la orilla de un río; ribereño

rivet /'rɪvɪt/ *n* remache, roblón, *m. vt* remachar; clavar; *Fig.* fijar, concentrar; *Fig.* cautivar, absorber

riveter /'rɪvɪtər/ *n* remachador, *m*

riveting /'rɪvɪtɪŋ/ *n* remachado, remache, *m*; *Fig.* fijación, concentración, *f*; *Fig.* absorción, *f.* **r. machine,** remachadora, *f*

Riviera, the /ˌrɪvi'ɛərə/ la Riviera, *f*

rivulet /'rɪvyəlɪt/ *n* riachuelo, arroyo, *m*

road /roud/ *n* camino, *m*; carretera, *f*; ruta, *f*; *pl* **roads,** *Naut.* rada, *f.* **high r.,** camino real, *m.* **main r.,** carretera, *f.* **secondary r.,** carretera de segunda clase, *f.* **on the r. to...,** en el camino de... **to get out of the r.,** *Inf.* quitarse de en medio. **to go by r.,** ir por carretera. **"R. work ahead!"** «Carretera en reparaciones.» **r.-book,** guía de carreteras, *f.* **r. house,** albergue de carretera, *m.* **r. maker,** constructor de caminos, *m*; (navvy) peón caminero, *m.* **r. making,** construcción de caminos, *f.* **r. map,** mapa de carreteras, *m.* **r. sign,** señal de carretera, señal de tránsito, señal vial, *f*; poste indicador, *m.* **The r. to hell is paved with good intentions,** El camino del infierno está empedrado de buenas intenciones. **"R. Repairs,"** «Camino en Reparación»

roadmender /'roudˌmɛndər/ *n* peón caminero, *m*

roadside /'roudˌsaid/ *n* borde del camino, *m, a* al lado del camino

roadstead /'roudˌstɛd/ *n* rada, *f*

roadster /'roudstər/ *n* automóvil de turismo, *m*; bicicleta de carreras, *f*; caballo de aguante, *m*; buque fondeado en rada, *m*

roadway /'roudˌwei/ *n* calzada, carretera, *f*

roam /roum/ *vi* vagar, vagabundear, andar errante. *vt* errar por

roamer /'roumər/ *n* vagabundo (-da), hombre errante, *m*

roaming /'roumɪŋ/ *n* vagabundeo, *m*; excursiones, *f pl*, paseos, *m pl*; *a* errante, vagabundo; nómada

roan /roun/ *a* roano, sabino. *n* caballo roano, *m*

roar /rɔr/ *vi* rugir; (of a bull, of the wind, of a person in anger) bramar; dar voces; (of the fire) crepitar; (of cannon) retumbar; (of thunder) estallar. *vt* gritar. *n* rugido, bramido, *m*; (shout) grito, *m*; (of the fire) crepitación, *f*; (of cannon, thunder) estallido, *m*; (noise) ruido, *m.* **to r. with laughter,** reírse a carcajadas

roaring /'rɔrɪŋ/ *n* (of horses) asma de los caballos, *f*, For other meanings, see under **roar.** *a* rugiente, bramante; *Inf.* magnífico. **to do a r. trade,** hacer un buen negocio

roast /roust/ *n* asado, *m*, carne asada, *f. a* asado; tostado. *vt* asar; (coffee and to warm one's feet, etc.) tostar; (metals) calcinar; (scold) desollar vivo (a). *vi* asarse; tostarse. **r. beef,** rosbif, *m*

roaster /'roustər/ *n* asador, *m*; (for coffee or peanuts) tostador, *m*; (for chestnuts, etc.) tambor, *m*

roasting /'roustɪŋ/ *n* asación, *f*; (of coffee) tostado, *m*; (of metals) calcinación, *f.* **r. spit,** asador, *m*

rob /rɒb/ *vt* robar; quitar, privar (de). **They have robbed her of her pocketbook,** Le han robado la cartera

robber /'rɒbər/ *n* ladrón (-ona); (footpad) salteador de caminos, *m*; (brigand) bandido, *m*

robbery /'rɒbəri/ *n* robo, *m.* **It's daylight r.!** ¡Es un desuello! **to commit a r.,** cometer un robo. **r. with violence,** robo armado, *m*

robe /roub/ *n* traje talar, *m*, toga, *f*; (of a monk, nun) hábito, *m*; (of a priest, etc.) sotana, *f*; *Poet.* manto, *m*; (infant's) mantillas, *f pl*; *pl* **robes,** traje de ceremonia, *m. vt* vestir; cubrir, revestir (de). *vi* vestirse. **bath r.,** albornoz, *m*

robin /'rɒbɪn/ *n* petirrojo, *m*

robot /'roubət, -bɒt/ *n* hombre mecánico, *m*; *Aer.* piloto mecánico, *m.* **traffic r.,** señal del tráfico, *f*, aparato automático, *m.* **r. plane,** avión sin piloto, *m*

robust /rou'bʌst/ *a* robusto; fuerte, vigoroso. **to make r.,** robustecer

robustness /rou'bʌstnɪs/ *n* robustez, *f*; vigor, *m*, fuerza, *f*

rock /rɒk/ *n* roca, *f*; (in the sea) abrojo, escollo, *m*; peña, *f*, peñasco, *m.* **as firm as a r.,** como una roca. **to be on the rocks,** *Inf.* estar a la cuarta pregunta. **r. bottom,** *n* fondo, *m. a* mínimo, más bajo. **r. crystal,** cuarzo, *m.* **r.-garden,** jardincito rocoso, jardín alpestre, *m.* **r.-plant,** planta alpestre, *f.* **r.-rose,** heliantemo, *m.* **r.-salt,** sal gema, *f*

rock /rɒk/ *vt* mecer; (shake) hacer temblar, sacudir; (to sleep) arrullar. *vi* mecerse, balancearse; tambalearse; agitarse; temblar

rocker /'rɒkər/ *n* (of a chair, cradle) balancín, *m*; (chair) mecedora, *f*

rocket /'rɒkɪt/ *n* cohete, volador, *m. vi* lanzarse. **r.-launching aircraft,** caza lanzacohetes, *f*

rockiness /'rɒkinɪs/ *n* abundancia de rocas, *f*; fragosidad, escabrosidad, *f*

rocking /'rɒkɪŋ/ *n* balanceo, *m*; (staggering) tambaleo, *m*; oscilación, *f*; (of an infant) arrullo, *m.* **r.-chair,** mecedora, *f.* **r.-horse,** caballo balancín, caballo mecedor, *m*

rocky /'rɒki/ *a* rocoso; de roca; roqueño; (rough) fragoso, escabroso; (rugged) peñascoso, escarpado. **the R. Mountains,** las Montañas Rocosas, *f pl*

rococo /rə'koukou/ *n* rococó, *m*

rod /rɒd/ *n* vara, *f*; bastón de mando, *m*; (for fishing) caña, *f*; (measure) pértiga, *f*; (surveying) jalón, *m*; palo, *m*; (for punishment) vergajo, *m*; *Mech.* vástago, *m.* **connecting rod,** biela, *f.* **to fish with rod and line,** pescar con caña

rodent /'roudnt/ *a and n* roedor, *m*

roe /rou/ *n* (deer) corzo (-za); (of fish) hueva, *f.* **soft roes,** lechas, *f*

rogue /roug/ *n* bribón (-ona), pícaro (-ra), pillo (-lla), *Argentina* farabute, *mf*; *Law.* vago, *m*; (affectionate) picaruelo (-la)

roguery /'rougəri/ *n* truhanería, picardía, *f*; (knaves) pícaros, *m pl*; (mischief) travesuras, *f pl.* **novel of r.,** novela picaresca, *f*

roguish /'rougɪʃ/ *a* picaresco, bellaco; (mischievous) travieso, juguetón; malicioso

roguishly /'rougɪʃli/ *adv* como un pícaro; con malicia

roguishness /'rougɪʃnɪs/ *n* picardía, bribonería, bellaquería, *f*; (mischievousness) travesuras, *f pl*; malicia, *f*

role /roul/ *n* papel, *m*

roll /roul/ *n* (roll up); (list) rol, *m*, lista, *f*; (of bread) panecillo, *Mexico* bolillo, *m*; (of a drum) redoble, *m*; (of thunder) tronido, *m*; (of cloth) pieza, *f*; (of tobacco) rollo, *m*; (of meat, etc.) pastel, *m*; (of a ship) balanceo, *m*; *pl* **rolls,** (records) archivos, *m pl.* **He has a nautical r.,** Tiene un andar de marinero. **to call the r.,** pasar lista. **r. film,** película fotográfica, *f.* **r. of honor,** lista de honor, *f.* **r.-on corset,** faja elástica, *f*, corsé de goma, *m.* **r.-top desk,** buró de cierre enrollable, *m*

roll /roul/ *vi* rodar; dar vueltas; (wallow) revolcarse; (of a ship) balancearse, bambolearse; (in money, etc.) nadar; (flow) correr, fluir; (*Fig.* of time) pasar tranquilamente; (of vehicle) rodar; pasar rodando; (of country) ondular; (of the sea) ondear; (of drums) redoblar; (of thunder) retumbar. *vt* hacer rodar; arrollar; (a cigarette) liar; (metals) laminar; (move) mover; (the eyes) guiñar (los ojos); (the ground) apisonar; (pastry) aplanar; (of an organ) sonar; (a drum) redoblar. **Mary rolled her eyes heavenwards,** María puso los ojos en blanco. **to r. away,** alejarse; desaparecer; (of time) pasar. **to r. back,** volver, retirarse; desaparecer. **to r. by,** pasar rodando; desaparecer. **to r. down,** bajar rodando, rodar por. **to r. in,** llegar en gran cantidad (or en gran número). **to r. off,** caer de. **to r. on,** seguir su marcha; fluir sin cesar; seguir su curso; (of time) avanzar. **to r. out,** (metal) laminar; (pastry) aplanar; (bring out) sacar; desenrollar. **to r. over,** *vt* volcar; tumbar; dar la vuelta (a). *vi* dar la vuelta; volverse al otro lado. **to r. up,** arrollar; envolver; (of hedgehogs, etc.) enroscarse, hacerse un ovillo

roll-call vote /'roul,kɔl/ *n* votación nominal, *f*

roller /'roulər/ *n* rodillo, *m*; cilindro, *m*; (wheel, castor) rueda, *f*; (for flattening the ground) apisonadora, *f*; Print. rodillo, *m*; (wave) ola grande, *f*. **r.-bandage,** venda, *f*. **r. canary,** canario de raza flauta, *m*. **r.-skate,** patín de ruedas, *m*. **r.-skating,** patinaje de ruedas, *m*. **r.-towel,** toalla continua, *f*

rollicking /'rɒlɪkɪŋ/ *a* alegre, jovial; juguetón

rolling /'roulɪŋ/ *a* rodante; (of landscape) ondulante, quebrado. *n* rodadura, *f*; (wallowing) revuelco, *m*; (of metals) laminación, *f*; (of a ship) balanceo, *m*; (rolling up) enrollamiento, *m*. **r.-pin,** rollo, rodillo de pastelero, *m*. **r.-stock,** material móvil ferroviario, *m*

Roman /'roumən/ *a* romano, de los romanos; (of noses and Print.) romano. *n* romano (-na). **in R. fashion,** a la romana. **R. Catholic,** *a* católico; católico apostólico romano. *n* el católico (-ca). **R. Catholicism,** catolicismo, *m*. **R. figures,** números romanos, *m pl*. **R. nose,** nariz romana, *f*. **R. road,** vía romana, *f*. **R. type,** Print. tipo romano, *m*

Romance /'roumæns/ *a* (of languages) romance. *n* (language) romance, *m*

romance /'roumæns/ *n* novela de caballería, *f*; romance, *m*; aventura, *f*; cuento, *m*, novela, *f*; romanticismo, *m*; Mus. romanza, *f*. *vi* inventar ficciones; exagerar

romancer /rou'mænsər/ *n* romancerista, *mf*; mentiroso (-sa), embustero (-ra)

Romanesque /,roumə'nɛsk/ *a* románico; romanesco

Romania /rou'meiniə/ Romania

Romanian /rʊ'meiniən/ *a* rumano. *n* rumano (-na); (language) rumano, *m*

romantic /rou'mæntɪk/ *a* and *n* romántico (-ca)

romantically /rou'mæntɪkli/ *adv* románticamente; de un modo romántico

romanticism /rou'mæntə,sɪzəm/ *n* romanticismo, *m*

romanticist /rou'mæntəsɪst/ *n* romántico (-ca)

Rome /roum/ Roma, *f*

romp /rɒmp/ *vi* juguetear, brincar, retozar, loquear; correr rápidamente. *n* locuelo (-la), saltaparedes, *mf*; (game) retozo, *m*. **The horse romped home easily,** El caballo ganó la carrera fácilmente

romping /'rɒmpɪŋ/ *n* juegos, *m pl*, travesuras, *f pl*

rondo /'rɒndou/ *n* rondó, *m*

rood /rud/ *n* cruz, *f*; crucifijo, *m*; cuarto de acre, *m*. **By the r.!** ¡Por mi santiguada!

roof /ruf/ *n* tejado, techado, *m*; (of a motor-car, bus) tejadillo, *m*; (of coaches, etc.) imperial, *f*; cubierta, *f*; (of the mouth) paladar, *m*; (bower) enramada, *f*; (of heaven) bóveda (del cielo), *f*. *vt* techar, tejar, Lat. Am. entechar; (shelter) abrigar. **r.-garden,** azotea, *f*. **r.-gutter,** canalera, *f*

roofer /'rufər/ *n* techador, *m*; constructor de tejados, *m*

rook /rʊk/ *n* chova, *f*, grajo, *m*; (chess) torre, *f*. *vt* engañar, estafar; (overcharge) desollar vivo (a)

room /rum/ *n* (in a house) habitación, *f*, cuarto, *m*; sala, *f*; cámara, *f*; (behind a shop) trastienda, *f*; (space) sitio, espacio, *m*; lugar, *m*; (opportunity) oportunidad, *f*; (cause) motivo, *m*, causa, *f*. *vi* alojarse. **bath-r.,** cuarto de baño, *m*. **dining-r.,** comedor, *m*. **drawing-r.,** salón, *m*. **There is no r. for us in this car,** No cabemos en este coche. **There is still r. for improvement,** Se puede mejorar todavía. **There**

isn't r. for anything else, No cabe más. **to be r.,** caber, haber sitio. **to make r.,** hacer sitio

roomed /rumd/ *a* (in compounds) de... habitaciones; de... salas

roominess /'ruminɪs/ *n* espaciosidad, amplitud, amplitud de habitación, *f*; (of garments) holgura, *f*

rooming house /'rumɪd/ *n* casa de huéspedes, *f*

roommate /'rum,meit, 'rʊm-/ *n* compañero de cuarto, compañero de pieza, *m*

roomy /'rumi, 'rʊmi/ *a* espacioso, amplio; (of garments) holgado

roost /rust/ *n* percha de gallinero, *f*, Lat. Am. dormidero, *m*. *vi* dormir en una percha; recogerse. **to rule the r.,** ser el amo del cotarro

rooster /'rustər/ *n* gallo, *m*,

root /rut *or, sometimes,* rʊt/ *n* raíz, *f*; Gram. radical, *m*; Mus. base, *f*; origen, *m*; explicación, *f*. *vt* arraigar; Fig. fijar, clavar. *vi* echar raíces; Fig. arraigarse; (of pigs, etc.) hozar, escarbar; revolver. **to r. out,** arrancar de raíz; Fig. desarraigar; (destroy) extirpar. **cubed r.,** raíz cúbica, *f*. **from the r.,** (entirely) de raíz. **square r.,** raíz cuadrada, *f*. **to cut close to the r.,** cortar a raíz

rooted /'rutɪd/ *a* (in compounds) de raíces...; arraigado

rope /roup/ *n* soga, cuerda, *f*; (hawser) maroma, *f*; Naut. cabo, *m*; (tight-rope) cable, *m*, cuerda de volatinero, *f*; (string) ristra, sarta, *f*; hilo, *m*; *pl* **ropes,** (boxing) cuerdas del cuadrilátero, *f pl*. *vt* encordelar, atar con cuerdas. **to r. in,** encerrar; (a person) enganchar, coger. **to give a person plenty of r.,** dar mucha latitud (a). **to know the ropes,** conocer todos los trucos. **r.-ladder,** escala de cuerda, *f*. **r.-maker,** cordelero (-ra), soguero, *m*. **r.-making,** cordelería, soguería, *f*. **r.-trick,** truco de la cuerda, *m*. **r.-walk,** cordelería, *f*. **r.-yarn,** Naut. filástica, *f*

rosary /'rouzəri/ *n* rosario, *m*. **to pray the r.,** rezar el rosario

rose /rouz/ *n* rosa, *f*; color de rosa, *m*; (rosette) roseta, *f*; Archit. rosetón, *m*; (of watering-can) pomo, *m*, roseta, *f*. *a* de rosa, rosado. **to see the world through r.-colored glasses,** ver las cosas en color de rosa. **to turn to r.,** volverse color de rosa, rosear. **r.-bay,** Bot. rododafne, adelfa, *f*. **r.-bush,** rosal, *m*. **r.-color,** color de rosa, rosa, *m*. **r.-colored,** de color de rosa, rosado. **r.-garden,** rosalera, rosaleda, *f*. **r. grower,** cultivador (-ra) de rosas. **r. hip,** escaramujo, *m*. **r. leaf,** hoja de rosa, *f*; pétalo de rosa, *m*. **r.-like,** como una rosa. **r.-red,** de color de rosa; como una rosa. **climbing r.-tree,** rosal trepador, *m*. **dwarf r.-tree,** rosal bajo, *m*. **standard r.-tree,** rosal de tallo, *m*. **r.-water,** agua de rosas, *f*. **r.-window,** rosetón, *m*, rosa, *f*. **r.-wood,** palo de rosa, *m*

rosé /rou'zei/ *a* (of wines) rosado

rosebud /'rouz,bʌd/ *n* capullo de rosa, *m*

rosemary /'rouz,mɛəri/ *n* romero, *m*

rosin /'rɒzɪn/ *n* (solid, for violin-bows, etc.) colofonia, *f*; resina, *f*. *vt* dar con colofonia; dar con resina

rosiness /'rouzinɪs/ *n* color de rosa, *m*

roster /'rɒstər/ *n* lista, *f*; registro, *m*, matrícula, *f*

rostrum /'rɒstrəm/ *n* tribuna, *f*, podio, *m*; Zool. pico, *m*; (of a ship) espolón, *m*

rosy /'rouzi/ *a* róseo, rosado; sonrosado; Fig. de color de rosa, halagüeño; optimista. **r.-cheeked,** con (de) mejillas sonrosadas

rot /rɒt/ *n* putrefacción, podredumbre, *f*; (in trees) caries, *f*; (in sheep) comalia, *f*; (slang) patrañas, *f pl*, disparates, *m pl*, *vi* pudrirse; descomponerse; Fig. echarse a perder; (slang) decir disparates. *vt* pudrir; Fig. corromper; (slang) tomar el pelo (a)

rota /'routə/ *n* lista, *f*; orden del día, *m*

rotary /'routəri/ *a* rotativo. **r. printing press,** rotativa, *f*

rotary telephone *n* teléfono de discado, *m*

rotate /'routeit/ *vi* girar, dar vueltas; alternarse. *vt* hacer girar

rotating /'routeitɪŋ/ *a* rotativo; giratorio

rotation /rou'teifən/ *n* rotación, *f*; turno, *m*. **in r.,** por turnos. **r. of crops,** rotación de cultivos, *f*

rotatory /'routə,tɔri/ *a* rotatorio

rote, to learn by /rout/ *vt* aprender de memoria, aprender por repetición, aprender de cotorra

rotogravure /ˌroutəgrəˈvyʊr/ *n* rotograbado, *m*

rotten /ˈrɒtn/ *a* putrefacto; podrido; (of bones, teeth) cariado; dañado, echado a perder; *Fig.* corrompido; (slang) pésimo. **to smell r.,** oler a podredumbre; apestar

rottenness /ˈrɒtnɪs/ *n* putrefacción, podredumbre, *f*; *Fig.* corrupción, *f*

rotter /ˈrɒtər/ *n Slang.* perdido, *m*

rotting /ˈrɒtɪŋ/ *n* pudrición, *f, a* que se pudre

rotund /rouˈtʌnd/ *a* rotundo

rotunda /rouˈtʌndə/ *n* rotonda, *f*

rotundity /rouˈtʌndɪti/ *n* redondez, *f*; rotundidad, *f*

rouge /ruʒ/ *n* colorete, *m, vt and vi* pintar de rojo, poner(se) colorete

rough /rʌf/ *a* áspero; duro; (of country) fragoso, escabroso; (uneven) desigual; (stormy) borrascoso, tempestuoso; (of the sea) encrespado, bravo; (of movement) violento; (bristling) erizado; (of the hair) despeinado; (unpolished) tosco; basto; (unskilled, clumsy) torpe; (of sounds, tastes) áspero; (of persons) rudo, inculto; (severe) severo; (of behavior) brutal; (of manners) brusco; (rude) grosero; (approximate) aproximado. *adv* duramente, mal. *n* estado tosco, *m*; (person) matón, *m*. **in the r.,** en bruto; (roughed out) bosquejado. **to grow r.,** (of the sea) encresparse, embravecerse. **to take the r. with the smooth,** *Fig.* aceptar la realidad; tomar lo bueno con lo malo. **to r. it,** luchar contra las dificultades, pasar apuros; llevar una vida sencilla; vivir mal. **to r. out,** bosquejar. **r. and ready,** improvisado; provisional. **r. and tumble,** *n* camorra, pendencia, *f*. **r.-cast,** *vt* dar una primera capa de mezcla gruesa (a); bosquejar. **r. diamond,** diamante bruto (*en bruto*), *m*. **r.-draft,** borrador, *m*; bosquejo, *m*. **r.-haired,** (of a dog) de pelo crespo. **r.-hewn,** modelado toscamente; desbastado; *Fig.* cerril, tosco. **r.-house,** jarana, *f*. **r.-rider,** domador (de caballos), *m*. **r. sketch,** bosquejo, esbozo, *m*. **r.-spoken,** malhablado

roughen /ˈrʌfən/ *vt* poner áspero. *vi* ponerse áspero

roughly /ˈrʌfli/ *adv* rudamente, toscamente; duramente; brutalmente; bruscamente; (of tastes, sounds) ásperamente; (approximately) aproximadamente, más o menos

roughness /ˈrʌfnɪs/ *n* aspereza, *f*; dureza, *f*; tosquedad, *f*; rudeza. *f*; (of the sea, wind) braveza, *f*; violencia, *f*; (of manner) brusquedad, *f*; brutalidad, *f*; (vulgarity) grosería, *f*. **the r. of the way,** la aspereza del camino

roulette /ruˈlɛt/ *n* ruleta, *f*

round /raund/ *a* redondo; (plump) rollizo; rotundo, categórico; sonoro. **a r. sum,** una cantidad redonda; un número redondo. **to walk at a r. pace,** andar a un buen paso. **r. dance,** baile en ruedo, *m*. **r.-faced,** carrilleno, de cara redonda. **r.-house,** cuerpo de guardia, *m*; *Naut.* tumbadillo, *m*. **r.-shouldered,** cargado de espaldas, *m*; (of King Arthur) Tabla Redonda, *f*. **r. trip,** viaje redondo, viaje de ida y vuelta, *m*. **r.-up,** rodeo de ganado, *m*; arresto, *m*

round /raund/ *n* círculo, *m*; esfera, *f*; redondez, *f*; (slice) rodaja, *f*; (of a ladder) peldaño, *m*; (patrol and *Mil.*) ronda, *f*; circuito, *m*; vuelta, *f*, giro, *m*; serie, *f*, rutina, *f*; (of ammunition) andanada, descarga, *f*; (of cartridge) cartucho con bala, *m*; (of applause, etc.) salva, *f*; (of golf) partido, *m*; (in a fight) asalto, *m*; *Sports.* vuelta, *f*; (of drinks) ronda, *f*; (doctor's) visitas, *f pl*

round /raund/ *vt* redondear; (*Fig.* complete) acabar, perfeccionar; (go round, e.g. a corner) dar vuelta (a), doblar, trasponer; (encircle, cercar; (of a ship) doblar. *vi* redondearse. **to r. off,** redondear; terminar; coronar. **to r. up,** (cattle) rodear. **to r. upon,** volverse contra

round /raund/ *adv* alrededor, en derredor; por todos lados; a la redonda, en torno; en circunferencia; en conjunto (**r.** is not translated in Spanish, e.g. *I shall come r. to your house,* Vendré a tu casa). *prep* alrededor de. **all the year r.,** todo el año, el año entero. **r. about,** a la redonda de, al derredor de; (nearly) cerca de; (of time by the clock) a eso de. **The road is**

closed and we shall have to go r., El camino está cerrado y tendremos que dar una vuelta. **to come r.,** volver; dejarse persuadir; recobrar su buen humor. **to go r.,** (spin) dar vueltas; (of the wind) cambiar. **There is enough to go r.,** Hay bastante para todos

roundabout /*a*. ˈraundəˌbaut. *n*. ˈraundəˌbaut/ *a* indirecto; desviado; vago. *n* tiovivo, *m*; (traffic) redondel, *m*. **He spoke in a r. way,** Hablaba con circunloquios. **We went there by a r. way,** Fuimos dando un rodeo

roundly /ˈraundli/ *adv* en redondo; rotundamente, claramente

roundness /ˈraundnɪs/ *n* redondez, *f*; rotundidad, *f*

rouse /rauz/ *vt* despertar; animar; excitar; suscitar, provocar. **to r. oneself,** despertarse; animarse (a hacer algo)

rousing /ˈrauzɪŋ/ *a* que despierta; (moving) emocionante; (enthusiastic) entusiasta; grande, bueno

rout /raut/ *n* (rabble) chusma, *f*; (party) sarao, *m*; (defeat) derrota, *f*; (meeting) reunión, *f. vt* derrotar, poner en fuga; vencer

route /rut, raut/ *n* ruta, *f*; camino, *m*; itinerario, *m*. **r. march,** marcha de maniobras, *f*

routine /ruˈtin/ *n* rutina, *f, a* rutinario, de rutina

rove /rouv/ *vi* vagar, errar

rover /ˈrouvər/ *n* vagabundo (-da); pirata, *m*

roving /ˈrouvɪŋ/ *a* vagabundo, errante; ambulante

row /rou, rau/ *n* (line) hilera, fila, hila, *f*; (in a theater, etc.) fila, *f*; (string) ristra, *f*; (in a boat) paseo en bote, *m*; (commotion) alboroto, *m*; (noise) ruido, *m*; (altercation) gresca, camorra, *f*; (scolding) regaño, *m. vi* (a boat) remar, bogar. *vt* conducir remando; (scold) regañar. **to be a row,** (altercation) haber la de San Quintín. **to start a row,** (altercation) armar camorra.

rowboat /ˈrouˌbout/ *n* bote de remos, *m*

rowdiness /ˈraudinɪs/ *n* alboroto, *m*

rowdy /ˈraudi/ *a* alborotador. *n* trafalmejas, *mf* rufián, *m*. **rowdy party** *Lat. Am.* fandango, *m*

rower /ˈrouər/ *n* remero (-ra), bogador (-ra)

rowing /ˈrouɪŋ/ *a* que rema; de remos. *n* deporte del remo, *m*; paseo en bote, *m*. **r.-boat,** bote de remos, *m*. **r.-club,** club náutico, *m*. **r.-seat,** bancada, *f*. **r.-stroke,** bogada, *f*

royal /ˈrɔiəl/ *a* real; regio. *n Naut.* sobrejuanete, *m*. **r. academy,** real academia, *f*. **r. eagle,** águila real, *f*. **R. Highness,** Alteza Real, *f*. **r. letters patent,** cédula real, *f*. **R. Mail,** mala real, *f*. **R. Standard,** estandarte real, *m*

royalist /ˈrɔiəlɪst/ *a* and *n* realista, *mf*

royally /ˈrɔiəli/ *adv* realmente; regiamente

royalty /ˈrɔiəlti/ *n* realeza, *f*; miembro de la familia real, *m*; tanto por ciento de los ingresos, *m*; derechos de autor, *m pl*

R.R. (abbrev. of railroad) F.R. (abbrev. of *ferrocarril*)

rub /rʌb/ *vt* frotar, estregar; fregar; rozar; friccionar; (make sore) raspar. **to rub one's hands together,** frotarse las manos. **to rub the wrong way,** frotar a contrapelo. **to rub against,** rozar. **to rub along,** *Inf.* ir tirando. **to rub down,** (a horse) bruzar; limpiar; (dry) secar; (wear down) desgastar. **to rub in,** dar fricciones con; frotar con; (an idea, etc.) machacar. **to rub off,** *vt* quitar (frotando); borrar. *vi* borrarse; separarse (de). **to rub out,** *vt* borrar. *vi* borrarse. **to rub up,** (polish) limpiar; *Fig.* refrescar

rub /rʌb/ *n* frotación, *f*; roce, *m*; fricción, *f*; *Fig.* obstáculo, *m*; dificultad, *f*. **to give a rub,** frotar, etc. **rub-a-dub,** rataplán, *m*

rubber /ˈrʌbər/ *a* de caucho, de goma. *n* caucho, *m*, goma, *f*; (for erasing) goma de borrar, *f*; (masseur) masajista, *mf*; (at whist, etc.) partida, *f*; *pl* **rubbers,** zapatos de goma, chanclos, *m pl*. **synthetic r.,** caucho artificial, *m*. **r. band,** goma, banda de goma, *f*. **r. belt,** *Mech.* correa de transmisión de caucho, *f*. **r.-plant, tree,** cauchera, *f*, *Central America, Mexico* hule, *m*. **r. plantation,** cauchal, *m*. **r.-plantation worker** cauchero (-a) *mf*. **r. planter,** cauchero, *m*. **r. stamp,** estampilla, *f*

rubbing /ˈrʌbɪŋ/ *n* frotación, *f*; fricción, *f*; roce, *m*; (of floors, dishes, etc.) fregado, *m*

rubbish /ˈrʌbɪʃ/ *n* basura, *f*; desperdicios, *m pl*, desecho, *m*; (of goods) pacotilla, *f*; (nonsense) pamplinas, patrañas, *f pl*, disparates, *m pl*. **r. cart,** carro del basurero, *m*

rubbishy /'rʌbɪʃɪ/ *a* sin valor, malo; (of goods) de pacotilla, de calidad inferior

rubble /'rʌbəl/ *n* escombros, *m pl*; cascote, *m*; piedra bruta, *f*

rubicund /'rubɪˌkʌnd/ *a* rubicundo

ruble /'roublei/ *n* rublo, *m*

rubric /'rubrɪk/ *n* rúbrica, *f*

ruby /'rubi/ *n* rubí, *m*. *a* de rubíes; de rubí. **r. lips,** labios de rubí, *m pl*

rucksack /'rʌkˌsæk, 'rʊk-/ *n* mochila, *f*

rudder /'rʌdər/ *n* timón, gobernalle, *m*

ruddiness /'rʌdɪnɪs/ *n* rubicundez, *f*; rojez, *f*; frescura, *f*

ruddy /'rʌdi/ *a* rubicundo; rojo; frescote; (of animals) barcino

rude /rud/ *a* rudo; tosco; vigoroso; grosero, descortés

rudely /'rudli/ *adv* toscamente; groseramente

rudeness /'rudnɪs/ *n* rudeza, *f*; tosquedad, *f*; grosería, incivilidad, descortesía, *f*

rudiment /'rudəmənt/ *n* rudimento, *m*

rudimentary /ˌrudə'mɛntəri/ *a* rudimentario

rue /ru/ *vt* lamentar, llorar. *n Bot.* ruda, *f*

rueful /'rufəl/ *a* triste, melancólico; lamentable

ruefulness /'rufəlnɪs/ *n* tristeza, *f*

ruff /rʌf/ *n* golilla, lechuguilla, *f*; (of a bird) collarín de plumas, *m*; (of an animal) collarín de pelo, *m*

ruffian /'rʌfiən/ *n* rufián, *m*

ruffle /'rʌfəl/ *n Sew.* volante fruncido, *m*; (of a bird) collarín de plumas, *m*; (of an animal) collarín de pelo, *m*; (ripple) rizo, *m*; (annoyance) irritación, *f*. *vt* (ripple) rizar; (pleat) fruncir; (feathers) erizar; (hair) despeinar; agitar; (annoy) irritar, incomodar

ruffling /'rʌflɪŋ/ *n* (rippling) rizado, *m*; (pleating) fruncido, *m*; (of the temper) irritación, *f*

rug /rʌg/ *n* (floor) alfombra, *f*; manta de viaje, *f*. **rug strap,** portamantas, *m*

rugged /'rʌgɪd/ *a* áspero, escabroso; escarpado, abrupto; (wrinkled) arrugado; tosco; (harsh) duro, severo; inculto; rudo; mal acabado; vigoroso

ruggedness /'rʌgɪdnɪs/ *n* aspereza, escabrosidad, *f*; lo escarpado; dureza, severidad, *f*; rudeza, *f*; vigor, *m*

ruin /'ruɪn/ *n* ruina, *f*. *vt* arruinar; echar a perder, estropear por completo; (a woman) perder

ruination /ˌruə'neiʃən/ *n* ruina, perdición, *f*

ruined /'ruɪnd/ *a* arruinado; en ruinas

ruinous /'ruənəs/ *a* ruinoso; en ruinas

rule /rul/ *n* regla, *f*; gobierno, *m*; autoridad, *f*; mando, *m*; administración, *f*; (reign) reinado, *m*; (of a court, etc.) orden, *f*; (for measuring) regla, *f*; *Print.* regleta, *f*; *pl* **rules,** reglas, *f pl*; reglamento, *m*. *vt* gobernar; regentar, regir; (control) dominar; (of a chairman, etc.) disponer, decidir; (guide) guiar; (lines) reglar. *vi* gobernar; (of a monarch) reinar; (of prices) mantenerse; estar en boga, prevalecer. **as a r.,** por regla general, en general. **slide-r.,** regla de cálculo, *f*. **to make it a r.,** tener por regla; tener por costumbre; tener por máxima. **to r. out,** excluir; *Law.* no admitir. **to r. over,** (of a king, etc.) reinar sobre. **r. of the road,** reglamento del tráfico, *m*. **r. of thumb,** regla empírica, *f*; rutina, *f*

ruler /'rulər/ *n* gobernador (-ra); soberano (-na); (master) amo (ama); (for ruling lines) regla, *f*

ruling /'rulɪŋ/ *a* regente; dominante; (current) vigente. *n* gobierno, *m*; *Law.* decisión, *f*, fallo, *m*; (with lines) rayado, *m*. **r. pen,** tiralíneas, *m*

rum /rʌm/ *n* ron, *m*

rumble /'rʌmbəl/ *vi* retumbar, tronar; (of vehicles) rugir; crujir. *n* retumbo, trueno, *m*; rugido, *m*; ruido sordo, *m*; rumor, *m*; crujido, *m*

rumbling /'rʌmblɪŋ/ *a* que retumba, etc. *n* ruido sordo, *m*; retumbo, *m*; crujido, *m*; (in the bowels) rugido, *m*

ruminant /'rumənənt/ *a and n* rumiante, *mf*

ruminate /'ruməˌneit/ *vi and vt* rumiar

rumination /ˌrumə'neiʃən/ *n* rumia, *f*; meditación, reflexión, *f*

rummage /'rʌmɪdʒ/ *vt* revolver, desordenar, trastornar; explorar. **to r. out,** desenterrar

rumor /'rumər/ *n* rumor, *m*, fama, *f*. **It is rumored that...,** Hay rumores de que..., La voz corre que..., Se dice que...

rump /rʌmp/ *n* (of an animal) nalgas, ancas, *f pl*; cuarto trasero, *m*; (of a bird) rabadilla, *f*; (scornful) culo, *m*, posaderas, *f pl*. **r.-steak,** solomillo, *m*

rumple /'rʌmpəl/ *vt* arrugar; desordenar

run /rʌn/ *vi* correr; acudir; (flee) huir; (rush) precipitarse, lanzarse; (in a race) tomar parte en una carrera; competir; (pass over) deslizarse (por); (of machines) andar, marchar; (of traffic) circular; (leave, of trains, ships, etc.) salir; (ply between) hacer el trayecto entre... y...; (flow) fluir, correr; (into the sea, of rivers) desembocar (en); (spurt) chorrear, manar; (drip) gotear; (leak) dejar fugar (el agua, etc.); (of colors) correrse; caer; (of tears) correr; derramarse; (of eyes) llorar; (melt) derretirse; (of a sore) supurar; (travel or go) ir; moverse; (work) trabajar; funcionar; (of editions of a book) agotarse; (of a play) representarse; (cross) cruzar; (elapse) correr; transcurrir, pasar; (become) hacerse; (of wording) decir; (be current) correr; (for office, etc.) hacerse candidato; (navigate) navegar; (spread) extenderse; (be) estar; ser; (of thoughts) pasar; (last) durar; (tend) tender (a). *vt* (a race, a horse) correr; (drive) conducir; (a business, etc.) administrar; dirigir; (govern) gobernar, regir; (hunt) cazar; perseguir; (water, etc.) hacer correr; (pierce) clavar; introducir; (push) empujar; (one's hand, eye, etc.) pasar; (risks, etc.) correr; (possess) tener; establecer un servicio de (autobuses, etc.); (smuggle) hacer contrabando de. **The ship ran aground,** El barco encalló. **to run dry,** secarse; agotarse. **to run in the family,** estar en la familia. **to run into debt,** endeudarse, contraer deudas. **to run to seed,** granar; agotarse. **Steamers run daily between Barcelona and Mallorca,** Hay servicio diario de vapores entre Barcelona y Mallorca. **A stab of pain ran up his leg,** Sintió un dolor agudo en la pierna. **Feeling was running high,** Los ánimos estaban excitados. **My arrangements ran smoothly,** Mis planes marchaban bien. **Funds are running low,** El dinero escasea. **The tune runs in my head,** Tengo la canción metida en la cabeza. **The message runs like this,** El mensaje reza así, El mensaje dice así. **He ran his fingers through his hair,** Se mesaba los cabellos. **to run about,** andar de un lado a otro, correr por todas partes; (gad) corretear. **to run across,** cruzar corriendo; (meet) topar con, tropezar con. **to run after,** correr detrás (de); perseguir; buscar. **to run against,** (collide with) dar contra; (meet) tropezar con. **to run at,** abalanzarse hacia, precipitarse sobre; atacar. **to run away,** huir, escaparse; (slip away) escurrirse; (of a horse) dispararse, desbocarse. **to run away with,** huir con, fugarse con; (carry off) arrebatar; (steal) llevarse; (imagine) imaginarse, figurarse; (of temper, etc.) dominar, poseer. **to run back,** volver corriendo; llegar corriendo; retroceder rápidamente, correr hacia atrás. **to run backwards,** correr hacia atrás; **to run backwards and forwards,** ir y venir. **to run behind,** correr detrás (de); quedarse atrás; (be late) estar atrasado. **to run down,** *vi* bajar corriendo; descender, bajar; (of a clock) parar; (of a battery) gastarse; (of liquids) correr; fluir; (drop by drop) destilar. *vt* (capture) coger; alcanzar; (a person by a vehicle) atropellar; (a ship) echar a pique; (disparage) hablar mal de. **run-down,** (in health) agotado; (of a clock) parado. **to run for,** buscar corriendo; correr para coger (el autobús, etc.); (president, etc.) ser candidato para. **to run in,** *vi* entrar corriendo; *vt* arrestar; hacer prisionero; *Print.* encerrar. **to run into,** tropezar con; chocar con; (plunge into) meterse de cabeza en; (of sums of money, etc.) ascender a; (of streets, rivers, etc.) desembocar en. **to run off,** *vi* escaparse corriendo; marcharse corriendo. *vt* deslizarse por; (drain) vaciar; *Print.* imprimir; (compose) componer. **to run off with,** huir con. **to run on,** correr delante; continuar; (of the mind) pensar en, entregarse a; hablar sin cesar; *Print.* recorrer. **to run out,** *vi* salir corriendo; (of liquids) derramarse; salir; (end) acabarse; agotarse; (project) sobresalir. *vt* (cricket) coger al lanzador fuera de la línea de saque. **to run out of,**

no tener más de, haber terminado. **to run over,** *vi* rebosar; derramarse. *vt* (of a vehicle) atropellar, pasar por encima de, *Mexico* antellevar; (peruse) repasar; revisar. **to run pell-mell,** salir pitando, salir volando, salvarse por pies. **to run through,** correr por; pasar por; recorrer; (go directly) ir directamente (a); (pierce) traspasar, pasar de parte a parte; (squander) derrochar, malbaratar; (read) hojear, leer por encima. **to run up,** *vt* (hoist) izar; hacer de prisa; construir rápidamente; (incur) incurrir. *vi* subir corriendo; (of plants) trepar (por); (shrink) encogerse; (of expenses) aumentar. **to run up to time,** llegar a su hora. **to run up against,** tropezar con; (opposition, etc.) encontrar.

run /rʌn/ *n* carrera, corrida, *f*; (excursion) visita, excursión, *f*; (cricket) carrera, *f*; (walk) paseo, *m*; (by train or sea) viaje, *m*; (by bus, tram) trayecto, *m*; (sea crossing) travesía, *f*; (distance run) recorrido, *m*; (of events, etc.) curso, *m*; marcha, *f*; (of markets, etc.) tendencia, *f*; (rhythm) ritmo, *m*; dirección, *f*; distancia, *f*; *Mus.* serie de notas, *f*; serie, *f*; duración, *f*; *Theat.* serie de representaciones, *f*; (freedom to use) libre uso, *m*; (majority) mayoría, *f*; (on a bank) asedio, *m*; (on a book, etc.) demanda, *f*; (for sheep, etc.) terreno de pasto, *m*; (for fowls) gallinero, *m* (in a stocking) *Lat. Am.* acarraladura, *f*, *m.* **a run of bad luck,** una temporada de mala suerte. **at a run,** corriendo. **in the long run,** a la larga, al fin y al cabo. **on the run,** en fuga; ocupado. **Prices came down with a run,** Los precios bajaron de golpe. **take-off run,** *Aer.* recorrido de despegue, *m*

runaway /ˈrʌnəˌwei/ *a* fugitivo, *f*; (of a horse) desbocado

rung /rʌŋ/ *n* (of a ladder) peldaño, *m*; (of a chair) travesaño, *m*; (lath) listón, *m*

runner /ˈrʌnər/ *n* corredor (-ra); (carrier of sedan chair, etc.) silletero, *mf*; (smuggler) contrabandista, *m*; (courier) estafeta, *f*; (messenger) mensajero, *m*; (ring) anillo movible, pasador corredizo, *m*; rueda móvil, *f*; (of a sledge) patín, *m*; *Bot.* tallo rastrero, *m*. **r.-up,** el segundo

running /ˈrʌnɪŋ/ *a* corredor; (of water, bank accounts) corriente, (of a knot) corredizo; (of a sore) supurante; (continuous) continuo; (consecutive) consecutivo. *n* carrera, *f*; marcha, *f*; funcionamiento, *m*; administración, *f*; gobierno, *m*; dirección, *f*; (flowing) derrame, *m*; (of trains, buses, etc.) servicio, *m*; (smuggling) contrabando, *m*; (of a sore) supuración, *f*. **six times r.,** seis veces consecutivas. **The car is in r. order,** El auto está en buen estado. **r. away,** fuga, *f*. **r.-board,** (of a car, etc.) estribo, *m*; (of a locomotive) plataforma, *f*. **r. costs,** gastos de mantenimiento, *m pl*; (railway) gastos de tracción, *m pl*. **r. fight,** acción de retirada, *f*. **r.-knot,** lazo corredizo, *m*. **r. title,** *Print.* título de la columna, *m*

run-off match /ˈrʌnɔf/ *n* desempate, *m*

runway /ˈrʌnˌwei/ *n* (for launching a ship) grada, *f*; (of an airfield) pista de aterrizaje, *f*

rupee /ruˈpi, ˈrupi/ *n* (Indian currency) rupia, *f*

rupestrian /ruˈpestriən/ *a* rupestre

rupture /ˈrʌptʃər/ *n* rompimiento, *m*, rotura, *f*; ruptura, *f*; *Med.* hernia, *f*

ruptured /ˈrʌptʃərd/ *a* *Med.* herniado, quebrado

rupturing /ˈrʌptʃərɪŋ/ *n* ruptura, *f*

rural /ˈrʊrəl/ *a* rural, campestre, del campo; agrario

ruse /ruz/ *n* artimaña, treta, ardid, *f*

rush /rʌʃ/ *n* *Bot.* junco, *m*; acometida, *f*; ataque, *m*; (of water) torrente, *m*; (bustle) bullicio, *m*; (speed) prisa, *f*; precipitación, *f*; acceso, *m*; (crowd) tropel, *m*, masa, *f*; (struggle) lucha, *f*; furia, *f*. *vi* precipitarse, lanzarse; agolparse. *vt* llevar rápidamente (a); despachar rápidamente; precipitar; (attack) asaltar, atacar; (capture) tomar, capturar; hacer de prisa; (a bill) hacer aprobar de prisa. **to r. upon,** abalanzarse hacia; embestir. **in a r.,** en tropel, en masa; de prisa. **to r. to a conclusion,** precipitarse a una conclusión. **r.-bottomed,** con asiento de enea. **r. hour,** hora de mayor circulación, *f*, hora de aglomeración, hora-pico (Argentina), hora brava (Argentina, informal). **r. order,** pedido urgente, *m*

Russia /ˈrʌʃə/ Rusia, *f*

Russian /ˈrʌʃən/ *a* ruso. *n* ruso (-sa); (language) ruso, *m*. **R. leather,** piel de Rusia, *f*

rust /rʌst/ *n* herrumbre, *f*, orín, *m*; moho, *m*; (disease) añublo, tizón, *m*. *vt* aherrumbrar; enmohecer. *vi* aherrumbrarse; enmohecerse

rustic /ˈrʌstɪk/ *a* rústico; campesino, aldeano; (scornful) palurdo, grosero. *n* aldeano, *m*; (scornful) patán, *m*

rusticate /ˈrʌstɪˌkeit/ *vi* rusticar, vivir en el campo. *vt* enviar al campo

rustication /ˌrʌstɪˈkeiʃən/ *n* rusticación, *f*

rusticity /rʌˈstɪsɪti/ *n* rusticidad, *f*

rustiness /ˈrʌstɪnɪs/ *n* herrumbre, *f*; enmohecimiento, *m*; color rojizo, *m*; *Fig.* falta de práctica, *f*

rustle /ˈrʌsəl/ *n* susurro, *m*; murmurio, *m*; (of silk, a dress, etc.) frufrú, *m*; (of paper, etc.) crujido, *m*. *vi* susurrar; murmurar; crujir. *vt* (a paper) hacer crujir

rustless /ˈrʌstlɪs/ *a* inoxidable

rustling /ˈrʌslɪŋ/ *n* see **rustle**

rusty /ˈrʌsti/ *a* herrumbroso; enmohecido, mohoso; (red) rojizo, (worn out) usado, viejo; (out of practice) desacostumbrado; (forgotten) empolvorado, oxidado (e.g. *My Portuguese is rusty,* Mi portugués está empolvorado)

rut /rʌt/ *n* rodera, *f*, bache, surco, *m*; *Fig.* sendero trillado, *m*; *Fig.* rutina, *f*

ruthless /ˈruθlɪs/ *a* inhumano, insensible, despiadado; inexorable, inflexible

ruthlessly /ˈruθlɪsli/ *adv* inhumanamente; inflexiblemente, inexorablemente

ruthlessness /ˈruθlɪsnɪs/ *n* inhumanidad, *f*; inflexibilidad, inexorabilidad, *f*

rye /rai/ *n* centeno, *m*. **rye field,** centenar, *m*

S

s /ɛs/ *n* (letter) ese, *f*

sabbatarian /ˌsæbəˈtɛəriən/ *a* sabatario

Sabbath /ˈsæbəθ/ *n* (Jewish) sábado, *m*; (Christian) domingo, *m*

sabbatical /səˈbætɪkəl/ *a* sabático

saber /ˈseibər/ *n* sable, *m*; (soldier) jinete, *m*. *vt* dar sablazos (a), acuchillar. **s. cut, thrust,** sablazo, *m*

sable /ˈseibəl/ *n* (animal and fur) marta, *f*; *Herald.* sable, *m*. *a Herald.* sable; *Poet.* negro

sabotage /ˈsæbəˌtɑʒ/ *n* sabotaje, *m*, *vt* cometer un acto de sabotaje en

saboteur /ˌsæbəˈtɜr/ *n* saboteador, *m*

sac /sæk/ *n* *Biol.* saco, *m*

saccharin /ˈsækərɪn/ *n* sacarina, *f*

sachet /sæˈʃei/ *n* sachet, *m*; bolsa, *f*. **handkerchief s.,** bolsa para pañuelos, *f*

sack /sæk/ *n* (bag) saco, *m*; *Mil.* saqueo, saqueamiento, saco, *m*. *vt* meter en sacos; (dismiss) dar pasaporte (a), despedir; *Mil.* saquear. **to get the s.,** recibir el pasaporte. **to give the s.,** dar el pasaporte (a), poner de patitas en la calle (a). **s. coat,** saco, *m*

sackcloth /ˈsækˌklɔθ/ *n* harpillera, *f*. **to repent in s. and ashes,** ponerse cenizas en la cabeza

sacking /ˈsækɪŋ/ *n* harpillera, *f*; *Mil.* saqueo, *m*

sacrament /ˈsækrəmənt/ *n* sacramento, *m*; Eucaristía, *f*. **the Blessed S.,** el Santísimo Sacramento. **to receive the Holy S.,** comulgar. **to receive the last sacraments,** recibir los sacramentos

sacramental /ˌsækrəˈmɛntl/ *a* sacramental

sacramentalist /ˌsækrəˈmɛntlɪst/ *n* sacramentario (-ia)

sacred /ˈseikrɪd/ *a* sagrado; sacro, santo; consagrado. **Nothing is s. to them,** No hay nada sagrado para ellos, No respetan nada. **the S. Heart of Jesus,** el Sagrado Corazón (de Jesús). **S. to the memory of…**

Consagrado a la memoria de... **s. music,** música sagrada, *f*

sacredness /'seikrıdnıs/ *n* carácter sagrado, *m*; santidad, *f*; inviolabilidad, *f*

sacrifice /'sækrə,fais/ *n* sacrificio, *m*. *vt* and *vi* sacrificar. **s. of the mass,** sacrificio del altar, *m*

sacrificial /,sækrə'fıʃəl/ *a* sacrificador; del sacrificio

sacrilege /'sækrəlıdʒ/ *n* sacrilegio, *m*

sacrilegious /,sækrə'lıdʒəs/ *a* sacrílego

sacristan /'sækrıstən/ *n* sacristán, *m*

sacristy /'sækrısti/ *n* sacristía, *f*

sacrosanct /'sækrou,sæŋkt/ *a* sacrosanto

sacrum /'sækrəm, 'seikrəm/ *n* Anat. sacro, *m*

sad /sæd/ *a* triste; melancólico; (of a mistake) deplorable, funesto; *Inf.* redomado; (pensive) pensativo. **How s.!** ¡Qué lástima! ¡Qué triste! **It made me s.,** Me entristeció

sadden /'sædn/ *vt* entristecer, acongojar, afligir

saddle /'sædl/ *n* (riding) silla de montar, *Lat. Am.* albarda, *f*; (of a bicycle, etc.) sillín, *m*; *Mech.* silla, *f*; *Anat.* espalda, *f*. *vt* ensillar. **to s. with the responsibility of,** echar la responsabilidad de (a). **s. of mutton,** lomo de carnero, *m*. **s.-bag,** alforja, *Lat. Am.* buchaca, *f*. **s.-cloth,** mantilla de silla, *f*. **s.-tree,** arzón, *m*

saddler /'sædlər/ *n* sillero, guarnicionero, *m*

Sadducee /'sædʒə,si/ *n* saduceo (-ea)

sadism /'seidızəm/ *n* sadismo, *m*

sadist /'seidıst/ *n* sadista, *mf*

sadistic /sə'dıstık/ *a* sadístico

sadly /'sædli/ *adv* tristemente; (very) muy

sadness /'sædnıs/ *n* tristeza, melancolía, *f*

safe /seif/ *a* al abrigo (de); seguro; salvo; (certain) cierto; prudente; digno de confianza. *n* caja de caudales, *f*; (for food) alacena, *f*. **I stood beneath a tree s. from the rain,** Estaba de pie bajo un árbol, al abrigo de la lluvia. **to put something in a s. place,** poner algo en salvo; poner algo en un lugar seguro. **s. and sound,** sano y salvo. **s.-conduct,** salvoconducto, *m*. **s.-keeping,** lugar seguro, *m*; (of a person) buenas manos, *f pl*

safeguard /'seif,gɑrd/ *n* protección, garantía, *f*; precaución, *f*. *vt* proteger, guardar; tomar precauciones (contra)

safely /'seifli/ *adv* seguramente; sin accidente, sin novedad, sano y salvo; sin peligro. **You may s. tell him,** Puedes decírselo con toda seguridad. **to put** (something) **away s.,** poner (algo) en un lugar seguro

safety /'seifti/ *n* seguridad, *f*. *a* de seguridad; (of locks) de golpe. **a place of s.,** un lugar seguro. **in s.,** en salvo, en seguro; con seguridad. **to believe in s. first,** poner la seguridad en primer lugar. **to play for s.,** jugar seguro. **with complete s.,** con toda seguridad. **s.-belt,** (cinto) salvavidas, *m*. **s.-catch,** fiador, *m*. **s.-curtain,** telón de seguridad, telón contra incendios, *m*. **s.-fuse,** espoleta de seguridad, *f*. **s.-glass,** vidrio inastillable, *m*. **s.-island,** refugio para peatones, *m*. **s.-lamp,** lámpara de seguridad, *f*. **s.-latch,** pestillo de golpe, *m*. **s.-lock,** (of fire-arms) seguro, *m*; (of doors, etc.) cerradura de seguridad, *f*. **s.-pin,** imperdible, *m*; *Mexico* seguro, *m*. **s.-razor,** máquina de afeitar, *f*. **s.-valve,** válvula de seguridad, *f*

saffron /'sæfrən/ *n* azafrán, *m*, *a* azafranado, de color de azafrán

sag /sæg/ *vi* doblegarse, ceder; inclinarse; *Naut.* caer a sotavento; (of prices) bajar; (of spirits, etc.) flaquear

saga /'sɑgə/ *n* saga, *f*; epopeya, *f*

sagacious /sə'geiʃəs/ *a* sagaz, perspicaz; (of animals) sabio

sagacity /sə'gæsıti/ *n* sagacidad, perspicacia, *f*; (of animals) sagacidad, *f*

sage /seidʒ/ *n* sabio, *m*; *Bot.* salvia, *f*. *a* sabio; sagaz; cuerdo

Sagittarius /,sædʒı'teəriəs/ *n* Sagitario, *m*

Sahara, the /sə'hærə/ el Sáhara, *m*

said /sed/ *a* antedicho; tal dicho. **No sooner s. than done,** Dicho y hecho. **the s. Mr. Martínez,** el tal Sr. Martínez

sail /seil/ *n* (of a ship) vela, *f*; (sailing-ship) velero, *m*; (of a windmill) aspa, *f*; *Mech.* ala, *f*; (trip) paseo

en barco, *m*. *vi* navegar; ir en barco; dar un paseo en barco; (leave) salir en barco; zarpar; (of swans, etc.) deslizarse; (of clouds, etc.) flotar. *vt* (a ship) gobernar; (the sea) navegar por. **She sailed into the room,** Entró majestuosamente en la sala. **The ship sailed at eight knots,** El buque navegaba a ocho nudos. **to go for a s.,** dar un paseo en barco. **to s. around the world,** dar la vuelta al mundo. **to s. the seas,** navegar por los mares. **to set s.,** darse a la vela, zarpar. **to take in the sails,** amainar. **s.-maker,** velero, *m*. **to s. into,** entrar en. **to s. around,** (the Cape, etc.) doblar. **to s. up,** subir en barco; (of a boat) ir río arriba

sailcloth /'seil,klɔθ/ *n* lona, *f*

sailing /'seilıŋ/ *n* navegación, *f*; (departure) salida, *f*. **It's all plain s.,** Todo va viento en popa. **s.-boat,** bote de vela, *m*. **s.-ship,** buque de vela, velero, *m*

sailor /'seilər/ *n* marinero, *m*. **s.-blouse,** marinera, *f*. **s.-suit,** traje de marinero, *m*

saint /seint/ *n* santo (-ta); (before masculine names of Sts., excluding Sts. Dominic and Thomas) San; *Inf.* ángel, *m*. **All Saints' Day,** el día de Todos los Santos. **saint's day,** fiesta de un santo (or de una santa), *f*; (of a person) santo, *m*. **St. Bernard dog,** perro de San Bernardo, *m*. **St. John the Baptist,** San Juan Bautista. **St. Martin's summer,** el veranillo de San Martín. **St. Vitus's dance,** el baile de San Vito

sainthood /'seinthʊd/ *n* santidad, *f*

saintliness /'seintlınıs/ *n* santidad, *f*

saintly /'seintli/ *a* de santo; de santa; santo; *Inf.* angelical

Saint Petersburg /seint 'pitərz,bɜrg/ San Petersburgo, *m*

sake /seik/ *n* amor, *m*; causa, *f*. **for God's s.,** por el amor de Dios. **for the s. of,** para; por amor de. **to talk for talking's s.,** hablar por hablar

salable /'seiləbəl/ *a* vendible

salaciousness /sə'leiʃəsnıs/ *n* salacidad, *f*

salad /'sæləd/ *n* ensalada, *f*; (lettuce) lechuga, *f*. **fruit s.,** macedonia de frutas, *f*. **s.-bowl,** ensaladera, *f*. **s.-dressing,** aderezo, aliño, *m*, salsa para ensalada, *f*. **s.-oil,** aceite para ensaladas, *m*

salamander /'sælə,mændər/ *n* salamandra, *f*

salaried /'sælərid/ *a* a sueldo; (of posts) retribuido

salary /'sæləri/ *n* sueldo, salario, *m*

sale /seil/ *n* venta, *f*; (auction) almoneda, subasta pública, *f*. **(clearance) s.,** liquidación, *f*, saldo, *m*, *Mexico* barata, *f*. **to be on s.,** estar de venta. **"Piano for s.,"** «Se vende un piano.» **s. price,** precio de venta, *m*; precio de saldo, *m*

sales contract /seilz/ *n* contrato de compraventa, *m*

salesman /'seilzmən/ *n* dependiente de tienda, *m*; (traveller) viajante, *m*

salesmanship /'seilzmən,ʃɪp/ *n* arte de vender, *mf*

salesroom /'seilz,rum/ *n* salón de ventas, *m*

saleswoman /'seilz,wʊmən/ *n* dependiente de tienda, vendedera, *f*

salient /'seiliənt/ *a* saliente; *Fig.* prominente, conspicuo, notable, *n* saliente, *m*. **s. angle,** ángulo saliente, *m*

saline /'seilin/ *a* salino. *n* (marsh) saladar, *m*; *Med.* salino, *m*

saliva /sə'laivə/ *n* saliva, *f*

salivary /'sælə,veri/ *a* salival

salivate /'sælə,veit/ *vi* salivar

salivation /,sælə'veiʃən/ *n* salivación, *f*

sallow /'sælou/ *a* cetrino, oliváceo, lívido

sallowness /'sælounıs/ *n* amarillez, lividez, *f*; palidez, *f*

sally /'sæli/ *n* (Mil. etc.) salida, *f*; (quip) ocurrencia, salida, *f*. *vi* hacer una salida, salir. **to s. forth,** ponerse en camino

salmon /'sæmən/ *n* salmón, *m*; color de salmón, *m*. **s.-net,** salmonera, *f*. **s. trout,** trucha asalmonada, *f*

salon /sə'lɒn/ *n* salón, *m*

Salonika /sə'lɒnıkə/ Salónica, *f*

saloon /sə'lun/ *n* (bar) salón, *m*; (of a steamer) cámara, *f*, salón, *m*; (on train, for sleeping) departamento de coche cama, *m*; (on train, for dining) coche comedor, *m*; *Auto.* coche cerrado, *m*. **billiard s.,** salón de billa-

res, *m*. **dancing s.**, salón de baile, *m*. **hair-dresser's s.**, salón de peluquero, *m*. **s. bar**, bar, *m*
salsify /'sælsəfɪ/ *n Bot*. salsifí, *m*
salt /sɔlt/ *n* sal, *f*; (spice) sabor, *m*; (wit) sal, agudeza, *f*. *a* salobre, salino; salado; (of land) salitroso. *vt* (season) poner sal en; (cure) salar. **kitchen s.**, sal de cocina, *f*. **old s.**, *Inf*. lobo de mar, *m*. **rock s.**, sal gema, *f*. **sea s.**, sal marina, *f*. **to be not worth one's s.**, no merecer el pan que se come. **to take with a pinch of s.**, tomar con su grano de sal. **s.-cellar**, salero, *m*. **s. lagoon**, albufera, *f*. **s. lake**, lago salado, *m*. **s. marsh**, saladar, *m*. **s. meat**, carne salada, cecina, *f*. **s. merchant**, salinero, *m*. **s.-mine**, mina de sal, *f*. **s.-spoon**, cucharita de sal, *f*. **s. water**, agua salada, *f*; agua de mar, *f*. **s.-water fish**, pez de mar, *m*. **s.-works**, salinas, *f pl*
saltiness /'sɔltɪnɪs/ *n* sabor de sal, *m*; salobridad, *f*
salting /'sɔltɪŋ/ *n* saladura, *f*; (salt marsh) saladar, *m*
saltless /'sɔltlɪs/ *a* sin sal, soso, insípido; *Fig*. soso
saltpeter /,sɔlt'pitər/ *n* salitre, *m*. **s. bed**, salitral, *m*. **s. works**, salitrería, *f*
salty /'sɔltɪ/ *a* salado; salobre
salubrious /sə'lubrɪəs/ *a* salubre, saludable, sano
salubriousness /sə'lubrɪəsnɪs/ *n* salubridad, *f*
salutary /'sælyə,teri/ *a* saludable, beneficioso
salutation /,sælyə'teiʃən/ *n* salutación, *f*, saludo, *m*
salute /sə'lut/ *vt* and *vi* saludar. *n* saludo, *m*; (of guns) salva, *f*. **to fire a s.**, hacer salvas, saludar con... salvas. **The soldier saluted them**, El soldado les saludó. **to take the s.**, tomar el saludo. **saluting base**, puesto de mando, *m*
Salvadoran, Salvadorian /,sælvə'dɔrən; -'dɔriən/ *a* and *n* salvadoreño (-ña)
salvage /'sælvɪdʒ/ *n* salvamento, *m*, *vt* salvar
salvation /sæl'veiʃən/ *n* salvación, *f*. **to find the s. of one's soul**, salvar el alma. **the S. Army**, el Ejército de la Salvación, *m*
salve /sæv/ *n* pomada, *f*; *Fig*. bálsamo, *m*. *vt* curar; (overcome) vencer; (soothe) tranquilizar; *Naut*. salvar. **to s. one's conscience**, tranquilizar la conciencia
salver /'sælvər/ *n* salva, bandeja, *f*
salvo /'sælvou/ *n* (of guns or applause) salva, *f*; (reservation) salvedad, reservación, *f*. **s. of applause**, salva de aplausos, *f*
Samaritan /sə'mærɪtn̩/ *a* and *n* samaritano (-na)
same /seim/ *a* mismo; igual; parecido; idéntico. *adv* lo mismo; del mismo modo. **all the s.**, sin embargo; con todo, a pesar de eso. **at the s. time**, al mismo tiempo; a la vez. **just the s.**, igual; (nevertheless) sin embargo. **He bowed deeply and I did the s.**, Él hizo una profunda reverencia y yo hice lo mismo. **They do not look at things the s. as we do**, No ven las cosas del mismo modo que nosotros. **If it is the s. to her**, Si le da igual. **It's all the s.**, Es igual, Lo mismo da, Es todo uno. **Ávila, capital of the province of the s. name**, Ávila, capital de la provincia de su nombre
"Same-Day Service" /'seimdei/ «En el día» (Argentina)
sameness /'seimnɪs/ *n* identidad, *f*; semejanza, *f*, parecido, *m*; monotonía, *f*
samovar /'sæmə,vɑr/ *n* samovar, *m*
sampan /'sæmpæn/ *n* (boat) champán, *m*
sample /'sæmpəl/ *n* muestra, *f*; prueba, *f*; ejemplo, *m*. *vt* sacar una muestra de; (try) probar. **s. book**, muestrario, *m*
sampler /'sæmplər/ *n* probador, *m*; (of wines) catador, *m*; *Sew*. dechado, *m*
sanatorium /,sænə'tɔriəm/ *n* sanatorio, *m*
sanctification /,sæŋktəfɪ'keiʃən/ *n* santificación, *f*; consagración, *f*
sanctify /'sæŋktə,fai/ *vt* santificar; consagrar
sanctimonious /,sæŋktə'mouniəs/ *a* santurrón, mojigato, beato
sanctimoniousness /,sæŋktə'mouniəsnɪs/ *n* beatería, mojigatería, santurronería, *f*
sanction /'sæŋkʃən/ *n* sanción, *f*. *vt* sancionar; autorizar. **to apply sanctions**, *Polit*. aplicar sanciones
sanctity /'sæŋktɪti/ *n* santidad, *f*; lo sagrado; inviolabilidad, *f*. **odor of s.**, olor de santidad, *f*
sanctuary /'sæŋktʃu,eri/ *n* santuario, *m*; (historical)

sagrado, sagrado asilo, *m*; refugio, asilo, *m*. **to take s.**, acogerse a sagrado; refugiarse
sand /sænd/ *n* arena, *f*; (for drying writing) arenilla, *f*; granos de arena, *m pl*; *pl* **sands**, playa, *f*; (of life) horas de la vida, *f pl*. *vt* arenar. **to plow the s.**, arar en el mar. **s.-bag**, *n* saco de arena, *m*. *vt* (a building) proteger con sacos de arena; (a person) golpear con un saco de arena. **s.-bank**, banco de arena, *m*, barra, *f*. **to run on a s.-bank**, encallar. **s.-colored**, de color de arena. **s.-dune**, médano, *m*. **s.-paper**, *n* papel de lija, *m*. *vt* pulir con papel de lija, lijar. **s.-pit**, arenal, *m*. **s. shoes**, alpargatas, *f pl*
sandal /'sændl/ *n* sandalia, *f*, *Central America* caite, *m*; (rope-soled) alpargata, *f*. **s.-wood**, sándalo, *m*
sandiness /'sændɪnɪs/ *n* naturaleza arenosa, *f*; (of hair) color bermejo, *m*
sandstone /'sænd,stoun/ *n* arenisca, *f*
sandstorm /'sænd,stɔrm/ *n* tempestad de arena, *f*; simún, *m*
sandwich /'sændwɪtʃ, 'sæn-/ *n* emparedado, bocadillo, *m*. *vt* insertar. **I found myself sandwiched between two fat men**, Me encontré aplastado entre dos hombres gordos. **s.-man**, hombre sándwich, *m*
sandy /'sændi/ *a* arenoso; sabuloso; (of hair) rojo, rufo, bermejo. **a s. beach**, una playa arenosa
sane /sein/ *a* de juicio sano; razonable, prudente; sesudo. **He is a very s. person**, Es un hombre con mucho sentido común. **to be s.**, estar en su juicio; (of a policy, etc.) ser prudente, ser razonable
sangfroid /san'frwa/ *n* sangre fría, *f*; aplomo, *m*
sanguinary /'sæŋgwə,neri/ *a* sanguinario
sanguine /'sæŋgwɪn/ *a* (of complexion) rubicundo; sanguíneo; optimista, confiado. *n* (drawing) sanguina, *f*. **to be s. about the future**, ser optimista acerca del porvenir, tener confianza en el porvenir
sanhedrin /sæn'hɛdrɪn/ *n* sanedrín, *m*
sanitary /'sænɪ,teri/ *a* sanitario; higiénico, **s. inspector**, inspector de sanidad, *m*. **s. napkin, s. towel**, servilleta higiénica, toalla sanitaria, *mf*, paño higiénico, *m*
sanitation /,sænɪ'teiʃən/ *n* higiene, *f*; sanidad pública, *f*; (apparatus) instalación sanitaria, *f*
sanity /'sænɪti/ *n* juicio sano, *m*; prudencia, *f*; (common sense) sentido común, *m*, sensatez, *f*
Santa Claus /'sæntə klɔz/ *n* (Spanish equivalent) los Reyes Magos, *m pl*
São Paulo /'sau 'paulou, -lʊ/ San Pablo, *m*
sap /sæp/ *n* (*Bot*. and *Fig*.) savia, *f*; *Mil*. zapa, *f*. *vt* (undermine) debilitar, agotar; *Mil*. zapar
sapidity /sæ'pɪdɪti/ *n* sapidez, *f*
sapling /'sæplɪŋ/ *n* arbolillo, *m*
sapper /'sæpər/ *n* *Mil*. zapador, *m*
Sapphic /'sæfɪk/ *a* sáfico. **S. verse**, verso sáfico, *m*
sapphire /'sæfaiər/ *n* zafiro, *m*. *a* de zafiros; cerúleo, de zafiro
Saracen /'særəsən/ *a* and *n* sarraceno (-na)
Saragossa /,særə'gɒsə/ Zaragoza, *f*
sarcasm /'sɑrkæzəm/ *n* sarcasmo, *m*
sarcastic /sɑr'kæstɪk/ *a* sarcástico
sarcastically /sɑr'kæstɪkli/ *adv* con sarcasmo, sarcásticamente
sarcophagus /sɑr'kɒfəgəs/ *n* sarcófago, *m*
sardine /sɑr'din/ *n* sardina, *f*. **packed like sardines**, como sardinas en banasta. **s.-net**, sardinal, *m*
Sardinia /sɑr'dɪniə/ Cerdeña, *f*
Sardinian /sɑr'dɪniən/ *a* and *n* sardo (-da)
sardonic /sɑr'dɒnɪk/ *a* sardónico, *m*; sardónico
sarsaparilla /,sæspə'rɪ, ,sɑrspə-/ *n* zarzaparrilla, *f*
sash /sæʃ/ *n* (with uniform) faja, *f*; (belt) cinto, cinturón, *m*; (of a window) cerco, *m*. **s. window**, ventana de guillotina, *f*
Satan /'seitn̩/ *n* Satanás, *m*
satanic /sə'tænɪk, sei-/ *a* satánico
satchel /'sætʃəl/ *n* saquito de mano, *m*, bolsa, *f*; (school) vademécum, *m*; cartapacio, *m*, cartera, *f*
sate /seit/ *vt* saciar, hartar; satisfacer
sateen /sæ'tin/ *n* satén, *m*
satellite /'sætl̩,ait/ *n* satélite, *m*
satiable /'seiʃəbəl/ *a* saciable
satiate /*v*. 'seiʃi,eit; *a*. -ɪt, -,eit/ *vt* saciar, hartar; satisfacer. *a* harto; repleto

satiety /sə'taiiti/ n saciedad, f
satin /'sætn̩/ n raso, m. a de raso; (glossy) lustroso, terso. vt (paper) satinar
satiny /'sætn̩i/ a arrasado; lustroso, brillante
satire /'sætaiᵊr/ n sátira, f
satiric /sə'tɪrɪk/ a satírico
satirist /'sætərɪst/ n escritor (-ra) satírico (-ca)
satirize /'sætəˌraiz/ vt satirizar
satisfaction /ˌsætɪs'fækʃən/ n satisfacción, f; (contentment) contento, m, satisfacción, f; (for sin) expiación, f; (of a debt) pago, m; desquite, m; recompensa, f. **to demand s.**, pedir satisfacción. **to give** (someone) **s.**, dar contento (a), alegrar
satisfactorily /ˌsætɪs'fæktərəli/ adv satisfactoriamente
satisfactoriness /ˌsætɪs'fæktərinɪs/ n carácter satisfactorio, m, lo satisfactorio
satisfactory /ˌsætɪs'fæktəri/ a satisfactorio; (for sin) expiatorio
satisfy /'sætɪsˌfai/ vt satisfacer; (convince) convencer; (allay) tranquilizar, apaciguar. **I am satisfied with him,** Estoy satisfecho (Estoy contento) con él. **The explanation did not s. me,** La explicación no me convenció. **to s. oneself that...,** asegurarse de que... **to s. one's thirst,** apagar la sed
satisfying /'sætɪsˌfaiɪŋ/ a que satisface; satisfactorio; (of food) nutritivo
satrap /'seitræp, 'sæ-/ n sátrapa, m
saturate /'sætʃəˌreit/ vt saturar (de), empapar (de); Chem. saturar; Fig. imbuir; Fig. empapar. **to s. oneself in,** (a subject) empaparse en
saturation /ˌsætʃə'reiʃən/ n saturación, f. **s. point,** (Chem. etc.) punto de saturación, m
Saturday /'sætərˌdei/ n sábado, m
Saturn /'sætərn/ n Saturno, m
saturnine /'sætərˌnain/ a saturnino, taciturno
satyr /'seitər, 'sætər/ n sátiro, m
sauce /sɔs/ n salsa, f; (thick fruit) compota, f; Inf. insolencia, f. **s.-boat,** salsera, f
saucepan /'sɔsˌpæn/ n cazuela, cacerola, f. **double s.,** baño de María, m
saucer /'sɔsər/ n platillo, m. **flying s.,** platillo volante, m. **s.-eyed,** con ojos redondos
sauciness /'sɔsinɪs/ n impertinencia, insolencia, f
saucy /'sɔsi/ a respondón, descarado; (cheerful) alegre; (of hats, etc.) coquetón, maja
sauerkraut /'sauᵊrˌkraut/ n chucruta, f
saunter /'sɔntər/ vi pasearse, vagar, n paseo, m, vuelta, f
sausage /'sɔsɪdʒ/ n chorizo, m; salchicha, f. **s.-balloon,** globo cautivo, m. **s.-curl,** bucle, m. **s.-machine,** choricera, f. **s.-maker,** choricero (-ra)
savage /'sævɪdʒ/ a salvaje; feroz; (cruel) inhumano, cruel; (furious) furioso. n salvaje, mf
savagely /'sævɪdʒli/ adv bárbaramente, ferozmente, furiosamente
savagery /'sævɪdʒri/ n salvajismo, f; ferocidad, f; brutalidad, crueldad, f
savannah /sə'vænə/ n sabana, f. **s. dweller,** sabanero (-ra)
save /seiv/ vt salvar; (keep) guardar; conservar; reservar; (money, one's clothes, etc.) ahorrar; (time) ganar; (avoid) evitar. vi salvar, (evangelized) ser salvado (-da); hacer economías; ahorrar. **He saved my life,** Me salvó la vida. **They have saved a room for me,** Me han reservado una habitación. **to s. appearances,** guardar las apariencias. **to s. oneself trouble,** ahorrarse molestias. **to s. the situation,** estar al nivel de las circunstancias. **to s. one's soul,** salvar el alma
save /seiv/ prep salvo, excepto, menos. conjunc sino, a menos que; con la excepción de. **all s. one,** todos menos uno. **all the conspirators s. he,** todos los conspiradores con la excepción de él
saving /'seivɪŋ/ a frugal, económico; (stingy) tacaño, avaricioso; (clause) condicional. n salvación, f; (of money, time, etc.) ahorro, m, economía, f; pl **savings,** ahorros, m pl. prep salvo, excepto, fuera de. conjunc con excepción de que, fuera de que. **s. grace,** único mérito, m. **savings bank,** caja de ahorros, f. **savings fund,** montepío, m

savior /'seivyər/ n salvador (-ra). **the S.,** el Salvador, el Redentor
savor /'seivər/ n sabor, gusto, m; (aftertaste) dejo, m; (zest) salsa, f. vi saber (a), tener sabor (de); Fig. oler (a). vt saborear, paladear; (flavor) sazonar
savoriness /'seivərinɪs/ n buen sabor, m; (of a district) respetabilidad, f
savory /'seivəri/ a sabroso, apetitoso; (not sweet) no dulce; (of places) respetable; (of reputation, etc.) bueno. n entremés salado, m. **s. omelette,** tortilla, f
Savoy /sə'vɔi/ Saboya, f
saw /sɔ/ n (maxim) sentencia, f; (proverb) refrán, decir, m; (tool) sierra, f. vt aserrar, Lat. Am. aserruchar; (the air) cortar. vi usar una sierra. **two-handled saw,** tronzador, m. **saw-fish,** pez sierra, m. **saw-mill,** molino de aserrar, m. **saw-pit,** aserradero, m
sawdust /'sɔˌdʌst/ n aserrín, m
sawhorse /'sɔˌhɔrs/ n caballete de aserrar, m
sawyer /'sɔyər/ n aserrador, m
Saxon /'sæksən/ a and n sajón (-ona)
Saxony /'sæksəni/ Sajonia, f
saxophone /'sæksəˌfoun/ n saxófono, saxofón m
say /sei/ vt decir; recitar. vi decir. **Let us say that the house is worth $100,000,** Digamos que la casa vale cien mil dólares. **He has no say in the matter,** No entra ni sale en el asunto. **I have said my say,** He dicho lo que quería. **They say,** Se dice, Dicen, La gente dice. **You don't say!** ¡Calle! ¿De veras? ¡Imposible! **that is to say...,** es decir...; esto es..., a saber... **to say one's prayers,** rezar, decir sus oraciones. **to say again,** volver a decir; decir otra vez, repetir. **to say over and over again,** repetir muchas veces, decir repetidamente. **What do you say to that?** ¿Qué dices a esto?
saying /'seiɪŋ/ n decir, m; (proverb) refrán, m; (maxim) sentencia, f. **As the s. is,** Como suele decirse; Según el refrán. **It goes without s.,** Eso no tiene discusión, Huelga decir. **It's only a s.,** Es un decir, nada más
scab /skæb/ n (of a wound) costra, f; (disease) escabro, m; (blackleg) esquirol, m
scabbard /'skæbərd/ n vaina (de espada), f
scabby /'skæbi/ a costroso; (diseased) roñoso, sarnoso
scabies /'skeibiz/ n sarna, f. **s. mite,** arador de la sarna, m
scaffold /'skæfəld/ n (in building) andamio, m; (for execution) cadalso, patíbulo, m. **to go to the s.,** ir al patíbulo; acabar en el patíbulo
scaffolding /'skæfəldɪŋ/ n andamiada, f; (building, scaffold) andamio, m
scald /skɔld/ vt escaldar; quemar; (instruments) esterilizar. n quemadura, escaldadura, f. **to s. oneself,** escaldarse. **scalding hot,** hirviendo
scale /skeil/ n (of a balance) platillo, m; Zool. escama, f; Bot. bráctea, f; Bot. hojuela, f; (flake) laminita, f; (Mus., Math.) escala, f; (of charges, etc.) tarifa, f; (of salaries) escalafón, m; (of a thermometer) escala, f. vt escalar; (fish) escamar. **major s.,** escala mayor, f. **minor s.,** escala menor, f. **on a grand s.,** en gran escala. **on a small s.,** en pequeña escala. **pair of scales,** balanza, f; (for heavy weights) báscula, f. **social s.,** escala social, f. **The Scales,** Astron. Libra, f. **to draw to s.,** dibujar a escala. **to turn the scales,** pesar, f; Fig. inclinar la balanza. **to s. down,** (Art. and of charges) reducir
scaling /'skeilɪŋ/ n (of fish) escamadura, f; (of buildings) desconchadura, f; (ascent) escalamiento, m
scallop /'skɒləp, 'skæl-/ n (Ichth. and badge) venera, f; concha, f; Sew. onda, f, festón, m. vt Cul. guisar en conchas; Sew. ondear, festonear
scalp /skælp/ n Anat. pericráneo, m; cuero cabelludo, m; Fig. trofeo, m. vt escalpar. **s.-hunter,** cazador de cabelleras, m
scalpel /'skælpəl/ n escalpelo, m
scaly /'skeili/ a escamoso, conchado; (of boilers) incrustado
scamp /skæmp/ n bribón, granuja, m, vt (work) frangollar
scamper /'skæmpər/ vi retozar, brincar; correr. n ca-

rrerita, f. **to s. off,** salvarse por los pies, huir; marcharse corriendo

scan /skæn/ vt (verse) medir, escandir; (examine) escudriñar, examinar; (glance at) dar un vistazo (a)

scandal /'skændḷ/ n escándalo, m; maledicencia, f; (slander) calumnia, f. **to talk s.,** murmurar

scandalize /'skændḷ,aiz/ vt escandalizar

scandalous /'skændḷəs/ a escandaloso; infame; calumnioso

scandalously /'skændḷəsli/ adv escandalosamente

scandalousness /'skændḷəsnis/ n carácter escandaloso, m

Scandinavia /,skændə'neiviə/ Escandinavia, f

Scandinavian /,skændə'neiviən/ a escandinavo. n escandinavo (-va);

scant /skænt/ a escaso; insuficiente

scantily /'skæntḷi/ adv insuficientemente

scantiness /'skæntinis/ n escasez, f; insuficiencia, f

scanty /'skænti/ a insuficiente; escaso; (of hair) ralo; (of crops, etc.) pobre

scapegoat /'skeip,gout/ n chivo expiatorio, m, víctima propiciatoria, f; cabeza de turco, f. **to be a s. for,** pagar el pato por

scapegrace /'skeip,greis/ n bribón, m

scapula /'skæpyələ/ n Anat. escápula, f

scapulary /'skæpyə,leri// n Eccl. escapulario, m

scar /skɑr/ n cicatriz, f; Fig. señal, f. vt marcar con una cicatriz. **to s. over,** cicatrizarse

scarab /'skærəb/ n escarabajo, m; escarabajo sagrado, m

scarce /skeərs/ a escaso; insuficiente; raro. adv Poet. apenas. **to make oneself s.,** largarse, pirarse, escabullirse; ausentarse, esconderse

scarcely /'skeərsli/ adv apenas; no bien; casi; (with difficulty) a duras penas, con dificultad. **It is s. likely he said that,** No es muy probable que lo hubiese dicho. **There were s. twenty people in the building,** Había apenas veinte personas en el edificio. **S. anyone likes his pictures,** Sus cuadros no le gustan a casi nadie

scarcity /'skeərsiti/ n escasez, insuficiencia, f; (famine) carestía, f; (rarity) rareza, f

scare /skeər/ vt asustar, espantar, llenar de miedo (a), Lat. Am. also julepear; intimidar. n susto, pánico, m; alarma, f. **What a s. I got!** ¡Qué susto me ha llevado! **to s. away,** ahuyentar. **to be scared,** Lat. Am. julepearse

scarecrow /'skeər,krou/ n espantapájaros, m; Inf. estantigua, f, mamarracho, espantajo, m

scaremonger /'skeər,mʌŋgər/ n alarmista, mf

scarf /skɑrf/ n bufanda, f; (tie) corbata, f; Mil. faja, f

scarlatina /,skɑrlə'tinə/ n Med. escarlatina, f

scarlet /'skɑrlit/ n escarlata, f. a de color escarlata. **to turn s.,** (of persons) enrojecerse. **s. fever,** escarlatina, f. **s. hat,** Eccl. capelo (cardenalicio), m. **s. runner,** Bot. judía roja, f

scatheless /'skeiðlis/ a ileso, sano y salvo

scathing /'skeiðiŋ/ a mordaz, cáustico

scatter /'skætər/ vt esparcir, sembrar con; (benefits, etc.) derramar; (put to flight) derrotar; dispersar; disipar; Fig. frustrar; (squander) derrochar, desparramar. vi dispersarse. **The crowd scattered,** La muchedumbre se dispersó. **s.-brained,** de cabeza de chorlito, atolondrado

scattered /'skætərd/ a disperso, esparcido

scattered showers /'ʃauərz/ n lluvias aisladas, f pl

scattering /'skætəriŋ/ n dispersión, f; (defeat) derrota, f; esparcimiento, m; (small number) número pequeño, m

scavenge /'skævindʒ/ vt (streets) recoger la basura de, barrer

scavenger /'skævindʒər/ n (of the streets) barrendero, m; Zool. animal que se alimenta de carne muerta, m; insecto que se alimenta de estiércol, m. vt See **scavenge**

scenario /si'neəri,ou, -'nɑr-/ n escenario, m

scene /sin/ n, escena, f; teatro, lugar, m; espectáculo, m; (Theat. décor) decoración, f; (of a play) escena, f; (view) vista, perspectiva, f. **behind the scenes,** entre bastidores. **The s. is laid...,** La acción pasa... **to come**

---

on the s., entrar en escena. **to make a s.,** hacer una escena. **s.-painter,** n escenógrafo (-fa). **s.-shifter,** tramoyista, mf

scenery /'sinəri/ n Theat. decorado, m; (landscape) paisaje, m

scenic /'sinik/ a dramático; escénico; pintoresco. **s. railway,** montaña rusa, f

scenography /si'nɒgrəfi/ n escenografía, f

scent /sent/ vt perfumar; (smell) oler; (out) husmear, olfatear; (suspect) sospechar. n perfume, m; fragancia, f, aroma, m; (smell) olor, m; (of hounds) viento, m; (of game, etc.) rastro, viento, m; (Fig. of person) nariz, f; (trail) pista, f. **to lose the s.,** perder la pista. **to s. danger,** oler el peligro. **to throw off the s.,** despistar. **s.-bottle,** frasco de perfume, m. **s.-spray,** pulverizador, m

scented /'sentid/ a perfumado; (of roses, etc.) de olor, oloroso; (in compounds) de... olfato. **s. sweet pea,** guisante de olor, m

scentless /'sentlis/ a sin olor; inodoro

scepter /'septər/ n cetro, m

sceptic /'skeptik/ n escéptico (-ca)

sceptical /'skeptikəl/ a escéptico

scepticism /'skeptə,sizəm/ n escepticismo, m

schedule /'skedʒul/ n lista, m; programa, m; (of taxes) clase, f; (of trains, etc.) horario, m. vt poner en una lista; inventariar

scheme /skim/ n plan, m; proyecto, m; diagrama, esquema, m; (summary) resumen, m; (of colors, etc.) combinación, f; (plot) intriga, maquinación, f. vt proyectar. vi planear, formar planes; (intrigue) intrigar, conspirar. **color s.,** combinación de colores, f

schemer /'skimər/ n (plotter) intrigante, mf

scheming /'skimiŋ/ a intrigante; astuto. n planes, proyectos, m pl; intrigas, maquinaciones, f pl

schism /'sizəm, 'skiz-/ n cisma, mf

schismatic /siz'mætik, skiz-/ a cismático. n cismático (-ca)

scholar /'skɒlər/ n (at school) colegial (-la); (disciple) alumno (-na); (student) estudiante, mf; (learned person) erudito (-ta), hombre de letras, m; (scholarship holder) becario, m

scholarly /'skɒlərli/ a de sabio, de hombre de letras; erudito

scholarship /'skɒlərʃip/ n erudición, (research) investigación, f; saber, m; (tuition grant) beca, f. **s. holder,** becario, m

scholastic /skə'læstik/ a escolar, escolástico; pedante; (medieval) escolástico. n escolástico, m. **the s. profession,** el magisterio

school /skul/ n escuela, f; colegio, m; academia, f; Educ. departamento, m; (faculty) facultad, f; (of fish) banco, m. vt enseñar, instruir; formar; disciplinar. **in s.,** en clase. **day s.,** escuela, f, colegio, m. **the Florentine s.,** (of painting) la escuela florentina. **the lower s.,** los alumnos del preparatorio. **private s.,** colegio particular, m. **s.-bag,** vademécum, m. **s.-book,** libro escolar, m. **s.-days,** los días de escuela; los años de colegio. **in his s.-days,** cuando él iba a la escuela. **s.-fees,** gastos de la enseñanza, m pl, cuota escolar, f

schoolboy /'skul,bɔi/ n muchacho de escuela, colegial, m

school district n sector escolar, m

schoolfellow /'skul,felou/ n compañero de colegio, condiscípulo, m

schoolgirl /'skul,gɜrl/ n colegiala, f

schooling /'skuliŋ/ n educación, enseñanza, f

schoolmaster /'skul,mæstər/ n maestro de escuela, profesor, Mexico escuelante, m

schoolmistress /'skul,mistris/ n maestra de escuela, profesora, f

school of hard knocks n universidad sin tejados, f

schoolroom /'skul,rum/ n aula, sala de clase, salón de clase, m

sciatic /sai'ætik/ a ciático

sciatica /sai'ætikə/ n ciática, f

science /'saiəns/ n ciencia, f. **social s.,** las ciencias sociales, f pl

scientific /,saiən'tifik/ a científico; exacto, sistemático

scientist /'saiəntist/ n hombre de ciencia, m, científico (-ca)

scimitar /'sɪmɪtər, -,tɑr/ n cimitarra, f

scintilla /sɪn'tɪlə/ n Fig. átomo, vestigio, m

scintillate /'sɪnt̩,eit/ vi centellear, lucir, chispear; (of persons) brillar

scion /'saiən/ n (sucker) acodo, m; (shoot) vástago, renuevo, m; (human) descendiente, mf. **s. of a noble race,** vástago de una raza noble, m

scissors /'sɪzərz/ n pl tijeras, f pl, Argentina cortante, msg. **s.-sharpener,** amolador, m

sclerosis /sklɪ'rousɪs/ n Med. esclerosis, f

sclerotic /sklɪ'rɒtɪk/ n Anat. esclerótica, f

scoff /skɔf, skɒf/ n burla, mofa, f. vi burlarse. **to s. at,** burlarse de, mofarse de

scoffer /'skɔfər, 'skɒf-/ n mofador (-ra); (at religion, etc.) incrédulo (-la)

scoffing /'skɔfɪŋ, 'skɒf-/ a burlón. n mofas, burlas, f pl

scold /skould/ n virago, f, vt reñir, reprender, regañar

scolding /'skouldɪŋ/ n reprensión, increpación, f

sconce /skɒns/ n cubo de candelero, m; candelabro de pared, m; cornucopia, f

scone /skoun, skɒn/ n bollo, m

scoop /skup/ n pala de mano, f; cuchara de draga, f; (boat) achicador, m; (financial) golpe, m; (journalistic) éxito periodístico, m. vt sacar con pala (de); sacar con cuchara (de); (shares, etc.) comprar, obtener. **to s. out,** vaciar; excavar; (bail) achicar

scooter /'skutər/ n (child's) patinete, patín del diablo, m; monopatín, m

scope /skoup/ n alcance, m; esfera de acción, f; lugar, m. **to give full s. to,** dar rienda suelta a. **to have full s.,** tener plena oportunidad; tener todas las facilidades. **within the s. of,** dentro del alcance de

scorbutic /skɔr'byutɪk/ a Med. escorbútico

scorch /skɔrtʃ/ vt chamuscar; (the skin) tostar; (of the sun) abrasar, quemar; (wither) agostar. **to s. along,** ir como un relámpago. **scorching,** a abrasador, ardiente; Fig. mordaz

score /skɔr/ n (scratch) rasguño, m; señal, f; (crossing out) raya, f; (reckoning) cuenta, f, escote, m; (notch) muesca, f; Sports. tanteo, m, puntuación, Lat. Am. anotación, f; (point) punto, tanto, m; (twenty) veintena, f; (reason) motivo, m, causa, f; respecto, m; Mus. partitura, f. vt marcar; rayar; (erase) tachar, borrar; (cricket runs, etc.) hacer; (goals) marcar; (points) ganar; (reckon) apuntar. **s. a triumph,** apuntarse un triunfo; Mus. instrumentar; (for orchestra) orquestar. vi (be fortunate) llevar la ventaja. **to pay off old scores,** ajustar cuentas viejas. **to s. off someone,** ganar un punto (a), triunfar de. **on that s.,** a ese respecto; por esa causa. **On what s.?** ¿Con qué motivo? **s.-board,** marcador, m

scorer /'skɔrər/ n (of a goal, etc.) tanteador, m; (keeper of score) marcador, m

scoria /'skɔriə/ n escoria, f

scorn /skɔrn/ n desprecio, desdén, m. vt despreciar, desdeñar; reírse de. **to s. to do,** no dignarse hacer

scornful /'skɔrnfəl/ a desdeñoso, despreciativo

scornfully /'skɔrnfəli/ adv desdeñosamente, con desprecio

Scorpion /'skɔrpiən/ n Escorpión, m

scorpion /'skɔrpiən/ n escorpión, alacrán, m; Astron. Escorpión, m

Scot /skɒt/ n escocés, m

scotch /skɒtʃ/ vt (kill) matar; (thwart) frustrar; (a wheel) calzar

Scotland /'skɒtlənd/ Escocia, f

Scotswoman /'skɒts,wʊmən/ n escocesa, f

Scottish /'skɒtɪʃ/ a escocés

scoundrel /'skaundrəl/ n canalla, sinvergüenza, mf

scour /skauʳr/ vt (traverse) recorrer, batir; (pans, etc.) fregar, estregar; (free from) limpiar (de); (of water) arrastrar

scourge /skɜrdʒ/ vt azotar, flagelar; castigar, mortificar. n disciplinas, f pl; Fig. verdugo, m, plaga, f

scout /skaut/ n Mil. batidor, explorador, m. vi Mil. explorar, reconocer. vt (flout) rechazar a mano airada, rechazar con desdén. **boy s.,** muchacho explorador, m

scowl /skaul/ vi fruncir el ceño. n ceño, m. **to s. at,** mirar con ceño

scowling /'skaulɪŋ/ a amenazador

scragginess /'skrægɪnɪs/ n magrez, flaqueza, f

scraggy /'skrægi/ a flaco, magro, descarnado

scramble /'skræmbəl/ vi trepar. vt (throw) arrojar; (eggs) revolver. **scrambled eggs,** huevos revueltos, m pl. **to s. for,** andar a la rebatiña por; (for coins, etc.) luchar para. **to s. up,** escalar; subir a gatas

scrap /skræp/ n pedazo, m; fragmento, m; pizca, brizna, f; (shindy) suiza, camorra, f; (boxing) combate de boxeo, m; pl **scraps,** desperdicios, m pl; (food) restos de la comida, m pl. vt desechar; (expunge) borrar; vi (fight) armar camorra. **a few scraps of news,** algunas noticias. **Do you mind not coming? Not a s.,** ¿Te importa no venir? Ni pizca. **s.-book,** álbum de recortes, m; **s.-heap,** depósito de basura, m; Fig. olvido, m. **s. iron,** chatarra, f, hierro viejo, m

scrape /skreip/ vt raspar, rascar, raer; (one's shoes) restregar; (a musical instrument) rascar. n rasguño, m; ruido de raspar, m; (predicament) lío, apuro, m; dificultad, f. **to s. acquaintance with,** trabar amistad con. **to s. along,** Inf. ir tirando. **to s. away,** rascar; quitar. **to s. through,** (an examination) aprobar justo. **to s. together,** amontonar poco a poco

scrappy /'skræpi/ a escaso; fragmentario; (incoherent) descosido. **a s. meal,** una comida escasa

scratch /skrætʃ/ vt arañar; (the earth) escarbar; (rub) rascar; (a hole) hacer; (sketch) dibujar, trazar; (a horse) retirar de una carrera. vi arañar; rascar; escarbar; (of a pen) rasguear; (back out) retirarse. n arañazo, m; (of a pen) rasgueo, m; (in a race) línea de salida, f; (in games) cero, m. a improvisado. **The dog scratched at the door,** El perro arañó la puerta. **to come up to s.,** estar al nivel de las circunstancias. **to s. one's head,** rascarse la cabeza. **to s. a person's eyes out,** sacar los ojos con las uñas (a). **to s. the surface of,** (a subject) tratar superficialmente. **to s. out,** tachar

scrawl /skrɔl/ vi hacer garabatos. vt garabatear, garrapatear. n garabato, m

scream /skrim/ vt and vi chillar. n chillido, m. **It was a perfect s.** Era para morirse de risa. **to s. with laughter,** reírse a carcajadas, morirse de risa

screaming /'skrimɪŋ/ n chillidos, m pl. a chillador; (piercing) penetrante, agudo; (funny) divertidísimo

screech /skritʃ/ vi chillar; (of owls, etc.) ulular; graznar. n chillido, m, ululación, f; graznido, m. **s.-owl,** úlula, f

screen /skrin/ n biombo, m; (wire) tela metálica, f; (nonfolding) mampara, f; (eco) cancel, m; (cinema, television) pantalla, f; (of trees, etc., and Mil.) cortina, f; (Fig. protection) abrigo, m. vt proteger; (shelter) abrigar; (hide) esconder, ocultar; (a light) proteger con pantalla; (a film) proyectar; (sieve) cribar, cerner; (examine) investigar. **to s. from view,** ocultar la vista (de), esconder. **s.-play,** guión, m. **s. star,** estrella de la pantalla, f. **s. test,** prueba, f. **s.-writer,** guionista, mf

screw /skru/ n tornillo, m; (propeller) hélice, f; vuelta de tornillo, f; presión, f; (miser) tacaño, m; (salary) salario, m. vt atornillar; torcer; apretar, oprimir. **He has a s. loose,** Le falta un tornillo. **to s. down,** sujetar con tornillos. **to s. up,** cerrar con tornillos; Inf. meter la pata. **to s. up one's eyes,** desojarse, entornar los ojos. **s.-driver,** destornillador, Mexico desarmador, m

scribble /'skrɪbəl/ vt escribir de prisa, vi garabatear, garrapatear; escribir, ser autor. n garabato, garrapato, m; mala letra, letra ilegible, f; (note) billete, m

scribbler /'skrɪblər/ n el, m, (f, la) que tiene mala letra; (author) autor (-ra) malo (-la)

scribbling /'skrɪblɪŋ/ n garabateo, m. **s.-block,** bloque de papel, m

scribe /skraib/ n escribiente, copista, m; (Jewish history) escriba, m

scrimmage /'skrɪmɪdʒ/ n reyerta, pelea, camorra, f; (Rugby) mêlée, f

script /skrɪpt/ n letra cursiva, f; Print. plumilla, f; manuscrito, m; Law. escritura, f; examen escrito, m; (film) escenario, m; (screen-play) guión, m

scriptural /'skrɪptʃərəl/ a bíblico

Scripture /'skrɪptʃər/ n Sagrada Escritura, f.
Scriptures, Escrituras, f pl; (of non-Christian religions) los libros sagrados
scrofula /'skrɒfyələ/ n escrófula, f
scrofulous /'skrɒfyələs/ a escrofuloso
scroll /skroul/ n (of paper, etc.) rollo, m; pergamino, m; (flourish) rúbrica, f; (of an Ionic capital) voluta, f. **s. of fame,** lista de la fama, f
scrotum /'skroutəm/ n Anat. escroto, m
scrounge /skraundʒ/ vi sablear. vt dar un sablazo (a); hurtar
scrounger /'skraundʒər/ n sablista, mf, Mexico lapa, f
scrub /skrʌb/ vt fregar; limpiar; restregar. n fregado, m; limpieza, f; fricción, f; (brushwood) matorral, breñal, m, maleza, f
scrubbing /'skrʌbɪŋ/ n fregado, m. **s.-brush,** cepillo para el suelo, m
scrubby /'skrʌbi/ a (of plants) anémico; (of persons) insignificante, pobre; (of land) cubierto de maleza
scruff /skrʌf/ n nuca, f, pescuezo, m
scruple /'skrupəl/ n escrúpulo, m. vi tener escrúpulos. **to have no scruples,** no tener escrúpulos
scrupulous /'skrupyələs/ a escrupuloso; exacto, meticuloso
scrupulously /'skrupyələsli/ adv escrupulosamente; meticulosamente
scrupulousness /'skrupyələsnɪs/ n escrupulosidad, f; meticulosidad, f
scrutinize /'skrutn̩,aiz/ vt escudriñar, examinar, Lat. Am. also interiorizar; (votes) escrutar
scrutinizer /'skrutn̩,aizər/ n escudriñador (-ra); (of votes) escrutador (-ra)
scrutinizing /'skrutn̩,aizɪŋ/ a escrutador
scrutiny /'skrutn̩i/ n escrutinio, m
scud /skʌd/ vi correr; deslizarse; flotar. **to s. before the wind,** ir viento en popa
scuffle /'skʌfəl/ vi pelear, forcejear, andar a la rebatiña. n refriega, pelea, sarracina, arrebatiña, f
scull /skʌl/ n remo, m, vi remar
scullery /'skʌləri/ n fregadero, m. **s. maid,** fregona, f
sculptor /'skʌlptər/ n escultor, m, escultora, f
sculptural /'skʌlptʃərəl/ a escultural, escultórico
sculpture /'skʌlptʃər/ n escultura, f, vt esculpir
scum /skʌm/ n espuma, f; (dregs) heces, f pl. vt espumar. **s. of the earth,** las heces de la sociedad
scupper /'skʌpər/ n Naut. clava, f. vt abrir las clavas (de); (frustrate) frustrar, destruir
scurrility /skə'rɪlɪti/ n grosería, indecencia, f
scurrilous /'skərələs/ a grosero, indecente
scurry /'skəri/ vi echar a correr. n fuga precipitada, f; (of rain) chaparrón, m; (of snow) remolino, m. **to s. off,** escabullirse. **to s. through,** hacer de prisa, terminar rápidamente
scurvy /'skərvi/ a tiñoso, vil, ruin. n escorbuto, Mexico berbén, m. **a s. trick,** una mala pasada
scuttle /'skʌtl/ n (trap-door) escotillón, m; Naut. escotilla, f; (for coal) carbonera, f; (flight) huida precipitada, f. vt (a boat) echar a pique, vi (run away) escabullirse, apretar a correr
scythe /saið/ n dalle, m, guadaña, f, vt dallar, segar
sea /si/ n mar, m, or f; ola, f; multitud, f. **Black Sea,** Mar Negro. **Mediterranean Sea,** (Mar) Mediterráneo, m. **at sea,** en el mar; perplejo. **beyond the sea,** allende los mares. **by sea,** por mar. **by the sea,** a la orilla del mar. **high seas,** alta mar, f. **the seven seas,** todos los mares del mundo. **to go to sea,** hacerse marinero. **to put to sea,** hacerse a la mar, hacerse a la vela. **sea-anemone,** anémone de mar. f. **sea-bathing,** baños de mar, m pl. **sea-breeze,** brisa de mar, f. **sea captain,** capitán de mar, m. **sea chart,** carta de marear, f. **sea-coast,** litoral, m, costa marítima, f. **sea-cow,** manatí, m. **sea dog,** lobo de mar, m. **sea-fight,** combate naval, m. **sea-foam,** espuma de mar, f. **sea-girt,** rodeado por el mar. **sea-going,** de altura; navegante. **sea-going craft,** embarcación de altura mar, f. **sea-green,** verdemar, m. **sea-gull,** gaviota, f. **sea-horse,** caballo marino, m. **sea-legs,** piernas de marino, f pl. **sea-level,** nivel del mar, m. **sea-lion,** león marino, m. **sea-mist,** bruma, f. **sea-nymph,** nereida, f. **sea-power,** potencia naval, f. **sea-serpent,** serpiente de mar, f. **sea-sick,** mareado.

to be sea-sick, marearse. **sea-sickness,** mal de mar, m. **sea-trip,** viaje por mar, m. **sea-urchin,** erizo de mar, m. **sea-wall,** dique de mar, m
seafarer /'si,fɛərər/ n (traveler) viajero (-ra) por mar; (sailor) marinero, m
seafaring /'si,fɛərɪŋ/ a marinero, marino. n viajes por mar, m pl; vida del marinero, f
seal /sil/ n Zool. foca, f, lobo marino, m; piel de foca, f; sello, m; (stamp) estampillo, timbre, m; vt sellar; (stamp) estampar; (letters, etc.) cerrar; vi cazar focas. **His fate is sealed,** Su suerte está determinada. **His lips were sealed,** Sus labios estaban cerrados. **under my hand and s.,** firmado y sellado por mí. **s.-ring,** sortija de sello, f
sealing wax /'silɪŋ/ n lacre, m
sealskin /'sil,skɪn/ n piel de foca, f
seam /sim/ n Sew. costura, f; Naut. costura de los tablones, f; Anat. sutura, f; Surg. cicatriz, f; (wrinkle) arruga, f, surco, m; Geol. capa, f, yacimiento, m; Mineral. vena, f, filón, m. vt coser; juntar; (a face) surcar, arrugar
seaman /'simən/ n marinero, m; hombre de mar, m; navegante, m. **able-bodied s.,** marinero práctico, m
seamanlike /'simən,laik/ a de marinero, marino; de buen marinero
seamanship /'simən,ʃɪp/ n marinería, f; náutica, f
seamstress /'simstrɪs/ n costurera, f
seamy /'simi/ a con costuras. **the s. side of life,** el lado peor de la vida
seance /'seians/ n sesión, junta, f; sesión de espiritistas, f
seaplane /'si,plein/ n hidroavión, hidroplano, m
seaport /'si,pɔrt/ n puerto de mar, m
sear /sɪər/ a marchito. vt agostar, secar; (a wound) cauterizar; marchitar, ajar; (a conscience) endurecer
search /sərtʃ/ vt registrar; (a wound) explorar; examinar; escudriñar; investigar. vi buscar. n busca, f; (of luggage, etc.) reconocimiento, m. **in s. of,** en busca de. **to s. after, for,** buscar; ir al encuentro de. **to s. out,** ir en busca de; preguntar por. **right of s.,** (international law) derecho de visita, m. **s.-party,** pelotón de salvamento, m. **s.-warrant,** auto de reconocimiento, auto de registro domiciliario, orden de allanamiento, orden de cateo, m
searching /'sərtʃɪŋ/ a escrutador; penetrante; minucioso. **a s. look,** una mirada penetrante. **a s. wind,** un viento penetrante. **a s. question,** una pregunta perspicaz
searchlight /'sərtʃ,lait/ n reflector, proyector, m
seashore /'si,ʃɔr/ n playa, f; orilla del mar, f
seaside /'si,said/ n orilla del mar, f; playa, f. **to go to the s.,** ir al mar, ir a la playa
season /'sizən/ n estación, f; sazón, f; temporada, f; tiempo, m. vt (food) sazonar; (wood, wine) madurar; (accustom) acostumbrar, aclimatar; (with wit, etc.) salpimentar; (temper) templar, moderar. vi madurarse. **at that s.,** a la sazón. **close s.,** veda, f. **in s.,** en sazón; a su tiempo. **out of s.,** fuera de sazón; fuera de tiempo, inoportuno. **the dead s.,** la estación muerta. **the autumn s.,** (for social functions, etc.) la temporada de otoño. **s.-ticket,** billete de abono, m
seasonable /'sizənəbəl/ a de estación; tempestivo, oportuno
seasonably /'sizənəbli/ adv en sazón; oportunamente
seasonal /'sizən̩l/ a estacional; de temporada
seasonal worker n trabajador por temporada, m
seasoned /'sizənd/ a (of food) sazonado; (of wood, etc.) maduro. **highly-s.,** (of a dish) picante, con muchas especies
seasoning /'sizənɪŋ/ n Cul. condimento, m; madurez, f; aclimatación, f; Fig. salsa, sal, f
seat /sit/ n asiento, m; (bench) banco, m; (chair) silla, f; (in a cinema, etc.) localidad, f; (Theat. etc., ticket) entrada, f; (of a person) trasero, m, asentaderas, f pl; (of trousers) fondillos, m pl; (of government, etc.) sede, capital, f; (of war, etc.) teatro, m; (place) sitio, lugar, m; (house) casa solar, f. vt sentar; poner en una silla (a); proveer de asientos (a); tener... asientos; (a chair) poner asiento (a). **The hall seats a thousand,** La sala tiene mil asientos, Hay mil

asientos en la sala. **Please be seated!** ¡Haga el favor de sentarse! **to be seated,** estar sentado; sentarse. **to have a good s.,** (on a horse) caer bien a caballo. **to hold a s.** in parliament, ser diputado a Cortes. **to keep one's s.,** permanecer sentado. **to take a s.,** tomar asiento, sentarse. **s.-back,** respaldo, *m*; **s. belt,** cinturón de seguridad, *m*
seater /'sitər/ *n* de... asientos. **four-s.,** automóvil de cuatro asientos, *m*
seaweed /'si,wid/ *n* alga marina, *f*; (edible) *Lat. Am.* cochayuyo, *m*
seaworthy /'si,wɜrði/ *a* (of a ship) en buen estado; marinero
sebaceous /sɪ'beiʃəs/ *a* sebáceo
secede /sɪ'sid/ *vi* retirarse (de); separarse (de)
secessionist /sɪ'sɛʃənɪst/ *n* secesionista, *mf*; *Polit.* separatista, *mf*. *a* secesionista; *Polit.* separatista
secluded /sɪ'kludɪd/ *a* apartado, retirado; solitario
seclusion /sɪ'kluʒən/ *n* reclusión, *f*; apartamiento, retiro, *m*; soledad, *f*
second /sɪ'kɒnd/ *a* segundo; otro; igual. *adv* en segundo lugar; después. *n* segundo, *m*; (in a duel) padrino, *m*; (helper) ayudante, *m*; (boxing) segundo, *m*; (railway compartment) departamento de segunda (clase), *m*; *Mus.* segunda, *f*; (of time) segundo, *m*; (moment) instante, momento, *m*. *vt* secundar; (a motion) apoyar; *Mil.* ayudar. **the s. of May,** el dos de mayo. **James the S.,** Jaime el segundo. **on s. thoughts,** después de pensarlo bien. **every s. day,** cada dos días. **They live on the s. floor,** Viven en el primer piso (since the ground floor is not counted separately in Spanish speaking areas, the American second floor = the Spanish primer piso). **the s. largest,** el más grande menos uno. **to be s. to none,** no ser inferior a ninguno; (of persons) no ser inferior a nadie; no ceder a nadie. **to come off s.,** llegar el segundo; ser vencido. **seconds hand,** (of watch) segundero, *m*. **s.-in-command,** segundo, *m*; subjefe, *m*. **s.-best,** segundo. **My s.-best hat,** Mi sombrero número dos. **to come off s.-best,** salir mal parado, ser vencido. **s. class,** segunda clase, *f*. **s.-class,** de segunda clase; de calidad inferior; mediocre. **s. cousin,** primo (-ma) segundo (-a). **s. gear,** segunda velocidad, *f*. **s.-hand,** *a* usado; de ocasión; no nuevo. *adv* de segunda mano. **s.-hand car,** un coche de segunda mano. **s.-hand clothing,** ropa usada, *f*. **s.-hand shop,** *Lat. Am.* cambalache *m*. **s. lieutenant,** *Mil.* subteniente, segundo teniente, *m*; *Nav.* alférez de fragata, *m*. **s.-rate,** *a* inferior, mediocre. **s. sight,** doble vista, *f*
secondary /'sɛkən,dɛri/ *a* secundario; subordinado; accesorio; poco importante. **s. school** colegio, liceo. **s. education,** enseñanza secundaria, *f*
seconder /'sɛkəndər/ *n* ayudante, *m*; el, *m*, (*f*, la) que apoya una proposición
secondly /'sɛkəndli/ *adv* en segundo lugar
secrecy /'sikrəsi/ *n* secreto, *m*; reserva, *f*, silencio, *m*. **in the s. of one's own heart,** en lo más íntimo de su corazón
secret /'sikrɪt/ *a* secreto; clandestino; (of persons) reservado, taciturno; (secluded) remoto, apartado; oculto; misterioso. *n* secreto, *m*; (key) clave, *f*. **a s. code,** un código secreto. **in s.,** en secreto, secretamente. **open s.,** secreto a voces. **to keep a s.,** guardar un secreto. **to keep s.,** tener secreto, ocultar. **s. drawer,** secreto, *m*
secretarial /,sɛkrɪ'tɛəriəl/ *a* de secretario. **s. college,** academia comercial, *f*
secretariat /,sɛkrɪ'tɛəriət/ *n* secretaría, *f*
secretary /'sɛkrɪ,tɛri/ *n* secretario (-ia), *m*; (*f*, la) particular. **S. of State,** ministro, *m*; Ministro de Estado, *m*
secrete /sɪ'krit/ *vt* esconder, ocultar; *Med.* secretar
secretion /sɪ'kriʃən/ *n* escondimiento, *m*; *Med.* secreción, *f*
secretive /'sikrɪtɪv/ *a* reservado, callado
secretly /'sikrɪtli/ *adv* en secreto, secretamente; ocultamente, a escondidas
sect /sɛkt/ *n* secta, *f*
sectarian /sɛk'tɛəriən/ *a* and *n* sectario (-ia)
section /'sɛkʃən/ *n* sección, *f*; porción, *f*; subdivisión,

f; (of a law) artículo, *m*. *vt* seccionar. **conic s.,** sección cónica, *f*
sectional /'sɛkʃənḷ/ *a* en secciones. **s. bookcase,** biblioteca desmontable, *f*
sector /'sɛktər/ *n* sector, *m*
secular /'sɛkyələr/ *a* (very old) secular; (lay) seglar; laico; profano. **s. music,** música profana, *f*. **s. school,** escuela laica, *f*
secularization /,sɛkyələrə'zeiʃən/ *n* secularización, *f*
secularize /'sɛkyələ,raiz/ *vt* secularizar
secure /sɪ'kyʊr/ *a* seguro; (certain) asegurado; (safe) en seguridad; sano y salvo; (firm) firme; fijo; (confident (in)) confiado (en). *vt* asegurar; (insure) garantizar; (lock) cerrar; (confine) prender; (acquire) adquirir, obtener; lograr, conseguir
securely /sɪ'kyʊrli/ *adv* seguramente; en seguridad, sin peligro; con confianza; (firmly) firmemente
security /sɪ'kyʊrɪti/ *n* seguridad, *f*; protección, defensa, *f*; garantía, *f*; (faith) confianza, *f*; *Com.* fianza, *f*; (person) fiador, *m*; *pl* **securities,** valores, títulos, *m pl.* **government securities,** papel del Estado, *m*. **to give s.,** *Com.* dar fianza. **to stand s. for,** *Com.* salir fiador de. **S. Council (United Nations),** El Consejo de Seguridad (de las Naciones Unidas), *m*
sedan-chair /sɪ'dæn,tʃɛər/ *n* silla de manos, *f*
sedate /sɪ'deit/ *a* tranquilo, sosegado; formal, serio, grave
sedately /sɪ'deitli/ *adv* sosegadamente; seriamente
sedateness /sɪ'deitnɪs/ *n* sosiego, *m*, tranquilidad, *f*; formalidad, compostura, *f*
sedative /'sɛdətɪv/ *a* and *n* sedativo, calmante *m*
sedentary /'sɛdn̩,tɛri/ *a* sedentario
sediment /'sɛdəmənt/ *n* sedimento, *Lat. Am.* concho, *m*
sedimentation /,sɛdəmən'teiʃən/ *n* sedimentación, *f*
sedition /sɪ'dɪʃən/ *n* sedición, *f*
seditious /sɪ'dɪʃəs/ *a* sedicioso
seduce /sɪ'dus/ *vt* seducir
seducer /sɪ'dusər/ *n* seductor, *m*
seduction /sɪ'dʌkʃən/ *n* seducción, *f*
seductive /sɪ'dʌktɪv/ *a* seductivo, atractivo; persuasivo
sedulous /'sɛdʒələs/ *a* asiduo, diligente
see /si/ *n* sede, *f*. **The Holy S.,** la Santa Sede, *f*
see /si/ *vt* and *vi* ver; mirar; (understand) comprender; (visit) visitar; (attend to) atender a; ocuparse de. **He sees the matter quite differently,** Él mira el asunto de un modo completamente distinto, Su punto de vista sobre el asunto es completamente distinto. **You are not fit to be seen,** No eres nada presentable. **See you next Tuesday!** ¡Hasta el miércoles que viene! **I see!** ¡Ya! ¡Ahora comprendo! **Let's see!** ¡Vamos a ver! **Shall I see you home?** ¿Quieres que te acompañe a casa? **to go and see,** ir a ver. **to see red,** echar chispas. **to see the sights,** visitar los monumentos. **to see life,** ver mundo. **to see service,** servir (en el ejército, etc.). **to see about,** atender a; pensar en; ocuparse de. **to see after,** cuidar de; atender (a); ocuparse de. **to see again,** volver a ver. **to see into,** investigar, examinar. **to see off,** (at the station, etc.) ir a despedir; acompañar. **to see out,** (a person) acompañar a la puerta; (a play, etc.) quedarse hasta el fin (de); no dejar el puesto. **to see over,** inspeccionar. **to see through,** (a house, etc.) inspeccionar; (a person) calarle las intenciones; (a mystery) penetrar; (a person through trouble) ayudar. **to see it through,** llevarlo al cabo; quedarse hasta el fin. **to see to,** atender a; ocuparse de; encargarse de. **to see to everything,** encargarse de todo
seed /sid/ *n* semilla, *f*; simiente, *f*; (of fruit) pepita, *f*, grano, *m*; *Fig.* germen, *f*; (offspring) prole, descendencia, *f*. *vi* granar. *vt* sembrar. **s.-bed,** almáciga, *f*, semillero, *m*. **s.-pearl,** aljófar, *f*. **s.-plot,** sementera, *f*; *Fig.* semillero, *m*. **s.-time,** tiempo de sembrar, *m*
seedling /'sidlɪŋ/ *n* planta de semilla, *f*
seedsman /'sidzmən/ *n* tratante en semillas, *m*
seedy /'sidi/ *a* granado; (of clothes) raído, roto; (of persons) andrajoso, desharrapado; infeliz, desgraciado; (ill) indispuesto, malucho
seeing /'siɪŋ/ *n* vista, *f*; visión, *f*. **It is worth s.,** Vale

la pena de verse. **s. that...,** visto que, dado que, como que. **S. is believing,** Ver es creer

seek /sik/ *vt* buscar; solicitar, pretender; (demand) pedir; (investigate) investigar; (to do something) procurar, tratar de. **They are much sought after,** Son muy populares, Están en demanda. **to s. after,** buscar; perseguir. **to s. for,** buscar

seeker /'siker/ *n* el, *m*, (*f*, la) que busca; investigador (-ra)

seem /sim/ *vi* parecer. **He seemed honest,** Parecía honrado. **It seemed to me,** Me pareció a mí. **It seems that they were both at home last night,** Parece ser que ambos estaban en casa anoche

seeming /'simɪŋ/ *a* aparente; supuesto

seemingly /'simɪŋli/ *adv* aparentemente; en apariencia

seemliness /'simlinɪs/ *n* decoro, *m*

seemly /'simli/ *a* decoroso, decente

seep /sip/ *vi* filtrar; rezumarse

seer /sɪər/ *n* profeta, *m*

seesaw /'si,sɔ/ *n* columpio, *m*; vaivén, *m*. *vi* columpiarse; balancearse, oscilar. *a* de vaivén, oscilante

seethe /sið/ *vi* hervir; *Fig.* bullir

segment /'sɛgmənt/ *n* segmento, *m*

segregate /'sɛgrɪ,geit/ *vt* segregar. *vi* segregarse.

segregation /,sɛgrɪ'geifən/ *n* segregación, *f*

Seine, the /sein/ el Sena, *m*

seismic /'saizmɪk/ *a* sísmico

seismograph /'saizmə,græf/ *n* sismógrafo, *m*

seismological /,saizmə'lɒdʒɪkəl/ *a* sismológico

seismology /saiz'mɒlədʒi/ *n* sismología, *f*

seize /siz/ *vt Law.* embargar; apoderarse de; asir; (a person) prender; coger; (a meaning) comprender; (an occasion, etc.) aprovecharse de; (of emotions) dominar; (of illnesses) atacar. *vi Mech.* atascarse. **He was seized by fear,** Le dominó el miedo. **to s. the opportunity,** aprovecharse de la oportunidad. **to s. upon a pretext,** valerse de un pretexto

seizure /'siʒər/ *n* asimiento, *m*; (of property) embargo, secuestro, *m*; (of a person) captura, *f*; arresto, *m*; *Med.* ataque, *m*

seldom /'sɛldəm/ *adv* rara vez, raramente; pocas veces

select /sɪ'lɛkt/ *a* escogido, selecto; exclusivista. *vt* escoger

selection /sɪ'lɛkfən/ *n* selección, *f*. **selections from Cervantes,** trozos escogidos de Cervantes, *m pl.* **to make a s. from,** escoger entre. **s. committee,** comité de selección, *m*

selective /sɪ'lɛktɪv/ *a* selectivo

self /sɛlf/ *n* mismo (-a), propio (-a); sí mismo (-a), se; personalidad, *f*; ser, *m*. **all by one's s.,** sin ayuda de nadie; solo; *Inf.* solito. **my other s.,** mi otro yo. **my better s.,** mi mejor parte. **the s.,** el yo. **s.-abasement,** humillación de sí mismo, *f*. **s.-acting,** automático. **s.-apparent,** evidente, patente. **s.-appointed,** nombrado por uno mismo. **s.-assertion,** presunción, *f*. **s.-assertive,** presumido. **s.-assurance,** confianza en sí mismo, *f*; aplomo, *m*; (impertinence) cara dura, frescura, *f*. **s.-centered,** egocéntrico. **s.-colored,** del mismo color; de su color natural. **s.-command,** dominio de sí mismo, *m*; sangre fría, *f*. **s.-complacent,** satisfecho de sí mismo. **s.-conceit,** vanidad, arrogancia, petulancia, *f*. **s.-confidence,** confianza en sí mismo, *f*; aplomo, *m*. **s.-confident,** seguro de sí mismo, lleno de confianza en sí mismo. **s.-conscious,** turbado, confuso, apocado. **s.-consciousness,** turbación, confusión, *f*, apocamiento, azoramiento, *m*. **s.-contained,** (of a person) reservado, poco comunicativo; dueño de sí mismo; (of things) completo; (of flats, etc.) independiente; con entrada independiente. **s.-contradictory,** contradictorio. **s.-control,** dominio de sí mismo, *m*; ecuanimidad, serenidad, sangre fría, *f*. **s.-controlled,** dueño de sí mismo; ecuánime, sereno. **s.-deception,** engaño de sí mismo, *m*; ilusiones, *f pl.* **s.-defense,** defensa propia, *f*. **s.-denial,** abnegación, *f*; renunciación, *f*; frugalidad, *f*. **s.-destruction,** suicidio, *m*. **s.-determination,** libre albedrío, *m*; (of peoples) autonomía, *f*; independencia, *f*. **s.-educating,** autodidacto. **s.-esteem,** respeto para uno mismo, *m*; amor

propio, *m*. **s.-evident,** aparente, que salta a la vista. **s.-explanatory,** que se explica a sí mismo; evidente. **s.-generating,** autógeno. **s.-government,** (of a person) dominio de sí mismo, *m*; (of a state) autonomía, *f*. **s.-importance,** presunción, petulancia, *f*. **s.-important,** pagado de sí mismo. **to be s.-important,** darse importancia, darse tono. **s.-indulgence,** indulgencia con sí mismo, *f*; (of food, drink, etc.) excesos, *m pl*, falta de moderación, *f*. **s.-indulgent,** indulgente con sí mismo; dado a los placeres, sibarita. **s.-interest,** propio interés, *m*. **s.-knowledge,** conocimiento de sí mismo, *m*. **s.-love,** egolatría, *f*. **s.-made man,** hombre que ha llegado a su posición actual por sus propios esfuerzos, *m*. **self-medication,** automedicación, *f*. **s.-opinionated,** terco, obstinaz. **s.-portrait,** autorretrato, *m*. **s.-possessed,** dueño de sí mismo; reservado; de sangre fría. **s.-possession,** aplomo, *m*, sangre fría, serenidad, *f*. **s.-preservation,** protección de sí mismo, *f*. **s.-reliance,** independencia, *f*; confianza en sí mismo, *f*. **s.-reliant,** independiente; confiado en sí mismo. **s.-reproach,** remordimiento, *m*. **s.-respect,** respeto de sí mismo, *m*; amor propio, *m*, dignidad, *f*. **s.-respecting,** que se respeta; que tiene amor propio. **s.-restraint,** dominio de sí mismo, *m*; moderación, *f*. **s.-righteous,** farisaico. **s.-sacrifice,** abnegación, *f*. **s.-sacrificing,** abnegado. **s.-same,** mismo, idéntico. **s.-satisfaction,** satisfacción de sí mismo, *f*; vanidad, *f*; (of desires, etc.) satisfacción, indulgencia, *f*. **s.-satisfied,** satisfecho de sí mismo, pagado de sí mismo, *m*. **s.-seeking,** *a* egoísta, interesado. *n* egoísmo, *m*. **s.-starter,** *Mech.* arranque automático, *m*. **s.-styled,** autodenominado, autotitulado, llamado por sí mismo. **s.-sufficiency,** suficiencia, *f*; presunción, *f*. **s.-sufficient,** que basta a sí mismo; contento de sí mismo. **s.-supporting,** que vive de su propio trabajo; (of an institution, business) independiente, *m*. **s.-taught,** autodidacto. **s.-willed,** voluntarioso

selfish /'sɛlfɪf/ *a* egoísta, interesado

selfishly /'sɛlfɪfli/ *adv* interesadamente; por egoísmo

selfishness /'sɛlfɪfnɪs/ *n* egoísmo, *m*

sell /sɛl/ *vt* vender. *vi* vender; venderse. **They sold him to his enemies,** Le vendieron a sus enemigos. **House to s.,** «Se vende una casa.» **to s. at a loss,** malvender, vender con pérdida. **to s. for cash,** vender al contado. **to s. retail,** vender al por menor. **to s. wholesale,** vender al por mayor. **to s. one's life dearly,** vender cara la vida. **They sold the chair for $10,** Vendieron la silla por diez dólares. **to s. off,** (goods) liquidar, saldar. **to s. out,** vender; agotar. **The best edition is sold out,** La mejor edición está agotada. **All the nylons have been sold out,** Se han vendido todas las medias de nilón (de cristal). **to s. up,** vender

seller /'sɛlər/ *n* vendedor (-ra); comerciante (en), *m*

selling /'sɛlɪŋ/ *n* venta, *f*. **s. off,** liquidación, *f*. **s. price,** precio de venta, *m*

selvage /'sɛlvɪdʒ/ *n* (in cloth) orillo, *m*

semantic /sɪ'mæntɪk/ *a* semántico

semantics /sɪ'mæntɪks/ *n* semántica, *f*

semaphore /'sɛmə,fɔr/ *n* semáforo, *m*, *vt and vi* hacer señales semafóricas (a)

semaphoric /,sɛmə'fɔrɪk/ *a* semafórico

semblance /'sɛmbləns/ *n* apariencia, *f*. **to put on a s. of woe,** aparentar ser triste

semen /'simən/ *n* semen, *m*, esperma, *f*

semester /sɪ'mɛstər/ *n* semestre, *m*

semi- *prefix* semi; medio. **s.-conscious,** medio consciente. **s.-detached house,** casa doble, *f*

semicircle /'sɛmɪ,sɜrkəl/ *n* semicírculo, *m*

semicircular /,sɛmɪ'sɜrkyələr/ *a* semicircular

semicolon /'sɛmɪ,koulən/ *n* punto y coma, *m*

semidetached /,sɛmɪdɪ'tætʃt, ,sɛmai-/ *a* (house) apartado

semiformal /,sɛmi'fɔrməl, ,sɛmai-/ *a* de media ceremonia

seminarist /'sɛmɪnərɪst/ *n* seminarista, *mf*

seminary /'sɛmə,nɛri/ *n* seminario, *m*; (for girls) colegio interno, *m*

Semite /'sɛmait/ *n* semita, *mf*

Semitic /sə'mɪtɪk/ *a* semítico, semita

Semitism /'sɛmɪ,tɪzəm/ *n* semitismo, *m*

semolina /ˌsɛmə'linə/ n sémola, f
senate /'sɛnɪt/ n senado, m
senator /'sɛnətər/ n senador, m
senatorial /ˌsɛnə'tɔriəl/ a senatorio
send /sɛnd/ vt enviar, mandar; Com. remitir; (a ball) lanzar; (grant) conceder; permitir; (inflict) afligir (con). **I sent Jane for it,** Envié a Juana a buscarlo. **He sent us word that he could not come,** Nos mandó un recado diciéndonos que no podía venir. **to s. mad,** hacer enloquecer. **to s. packing,** mandar a paseo. **to s. again,** volver a mandar. **to s. away,** vt enviar; (dismiss) destituir; despedir; (scare off) ahuyentar, vi enviar a otra parte. **to s. back,** (goods) devolver; (persons) volver. **to s. down,** hacer bajar; (rain, etc.) mandar, derramar; (a student) suspender, expulsar. **to s. in,** mandar; (persons) hacer entrar, introducir; (food) servir; (a bill) presentar; (one's name) dar. **Please s. him in!** ¡Sírvase de invitarle a entrar! **to s. in one's resignation,** mandar su dimisión. **to s. off,** enviar, mandar; (goods) despachar; (persons) destituir; (scare) ahuyentar. **s.-off,** n despedida, f. **a good s.-off,** una despedida afectuosa. **to s. on,** (a letter) hacer seguir; (instructions) trasmitir. **to s. out,** hacer salir; mandar; (emit) despedir, dar; (new shoots, etc.) echar. **to s. round,** (the hat, etc.) hacer circular. **to s. up,** enviar arriba; mandar subir, hacer subir; mandar, enviar; (a ball) lanzar
sender /'sɛndər/ n remitente, mf; Elec. transmisor, m
sending /'sɛndɪŋ/ n envío, m
Senegal /ˌsɛnɪ'gɔl, -'gɑl/ Senegal, m
Senegalese /ˌsɛnəgə'liz/ a and n senegalés (-esa)
senile /'sinail/ a senil
senility /sɪ'nɪlɪti/ n senilidad, f
senior /'sinyər/ a mayor, de mayor edad; más antiguo. **Martinez s.,** Martínez padre. **Charles is Mary's s. by five years,** Carlos es cinco años mayor que María. **s. member,** decano, m
seniority /sin'yɔrɪti/ n ancianidad, f; antigüedad, f
senna /'sɛnə/ n Bot. sena, f
sensation /sɛn'seiʃən/ n sensación, f; sentimiento, m; impresión, f. **to create a s.,** causar una sensación
sensational /sɛn'seiʃənl/ a sensacional
sensationalism /sɛn'seiʃənlˌizəm/ n Philos. sensualismo, m; efectismo, m
sensationalist /sɛn'seiʃənlˌɪst/ n Philos. sensualista, mf; efectista, mf
sense /sɛns/ n sentido, m. vt sentir. **in a s.,** hasta cierto punto; desde un punto de vista. **in the full s. of the word,** en toda la extensión de la palabra. **common s.,** sentido común, m. **He has no s. of smell,** No tiene olfato. **the five senses,** los cinco sentidos. **to be out of one's senses,** estar fuera de sí, estar trastornado. **You must be out of your senses!** ¡Debes de haber perdido el juicio! ¡Estás loco! **to come to one's senses,** (after unconsciousness) volver en sí; (after folly) recobrar el sentido común. **to talk s.,** hablar con sentido común, hablar razonablemente. **s. organ,** órgano de los sentidos, m. **have a good s. of direction,** saber orientarse, tener buena orientación. **have no s. of smell,** ser incapaz de percibir olores. **have no s. of taste,** ser incapaz de distinguir gustos
senseless /'sɛnslɪs/ a (unconscious) sin sentido, insensible; desmayado; (silly) necio, estúpido. **to knock s.,** derribar, tumbar
senselessness /'sɛnslɪsnɪs/ n falta de sentido común, f; locura, absurdidad, f
sensibility /ˌsɛnsə'bɪlɪti/ n sensibilidad, f
sensible /'sɛnsəbəl/ a sensible; (conscious) consciente (de); sesudo. **to be s. of,** estar consciente de; estar persuadido de
sensibly /'sɛnsəbli/ adv sensiblemente; sesudamente, cuerdamente
sensitive /'sɛnsɪtɪv/ a sensitivo; susceptible (a); impresionable. **s. plant,** sensitiva, f
sensitivity /ˌsɛnsɪ'tɪvɪti/ n sensibilidad, f; susceptibilidad, f; delicadeza, f
sensitize /'sɛnsɪˌtaiz/ vt Photo. sensibilizar
sensory /'sɛnsəri/ a sensorio
sensual /'sɛnʃuəl/ a sensual; voluptuoso
sensualism /'sɛnʃuəˌlizəm/ n sensualismo, m

sensualist /'sɛnʃuəlɪst/ n sensualista, mf
sensuality /ˌsɛnʃu'ælɪti/ n sensualidad, f
sensually /'sɛnʃuəli/ adv sensualmente
sensuous /'sɛnʃuəs/ a sensorio
sensuousness /'sɛnʃuəsnɪs/ n sensualidad, f
sentence /'sɛntns/ n Law. sentencia, f; (penalty) pena, f; Gram. frase, oración, f; (maxim) máxima, sentencia, f. vt sentenciar, condenar. **to pass s.,** pronunciar sentencia, fallar. **under s. of,** bajo pena de
sententious /sɛn'tɛnʃəs/ a sentencioso
sentient /'sɛnʃənt/ a sensible
sentiment /'sɛntəmənt/ n sentimiento, m; (sentimentality) sentimentalismo, m; opinión, f
sentimental /ˌsɛntə'mɛntl/ a sentimental; (mawkish) sensiblero
sentimentalist /ˌsɛntə'mɛntlɪst/ n romántico (-ca), persona sentimental, f
sentimentality /ˌsɛntəmɛn'tælɪti/ n sentimentalismo, m, sensiblería, f
sentimentalize /ˌsɛntə'mɛntlˌaiz/ vt idealizar
sentimentally /ˌsɛntə'mɛntli/ adv sentimentalmente
sentinel /'sɛntnl/ n centinela, mf
sentry /'sɛntri/ n centinela, m. **to be on s. duty,** estar de guardia. **s.-box,** garita de centinela, f
separable /'sɛpərəbəl/ a separable
separate /a. 'sɛpərɪt; v. -ˌreit/ a separado; distinto; independiente. vt separar; dividir. vi separarse; (of husband and wife) separarse de bienes y de cuerpos
separately /'sɛpərɪtli/ adv separadamente; aparte
separation /ˌsɛpə'reiʃən/ n separación, f; Law. separación de bienes y de cuerpos, f
separatism /'sɛpərəˌtizəm/ n separatismo, m
separatist /'sɛpərətɪst/ a and n separatista mf
Sephardic /sə'fardɪk/ a Sefaradí
sepia /'sipiə/ n (color and fish) sepia, f
September /sɛp'tɛmbər/ n setiembre, septiembre, m
septic /'sɛptɪk/ a séptico
septicemia /ˌsɛptə'simiə/ n septicemia, f
septuagenarian /ˌsɛptʃuədʒə'nɛəriən/ n setentón (-ona); septuagenario (-ia)
septum /'sɛptəm/ n septo, tabique, m
sepulcher /'sɛpəlkər/ n sepulcro, m
sepulchral /sə'pʌlkrəl/ a sepulcral
sequel /'sikwəl/ n (of a story, etc.) continuación, f; consecuencia, f; resultado, m
sequence /'sikwəns/ n sucesión, f; serie, f; orden, mf; (at cards) serie, f; Gram. correspondencia, f; (Eccl. and cinema) secuencia, f. **s. of tenses,** correspondencia de los tiempos, f
sequestered /sɪ'kwɛstərd/ a aislado, remoto
sequestrate /sɪ'kwɛstreit/ vt secuestrar
sequestration /ˌsikwɛs'treiʃən/ n secuestro, m,
sequin /'sikwɪn/ n lentejuela, f
seraglio /sɪ'rælyou/ n serrallo, m
seraph /'sɛrəf/ n serafín, m
seraphic /sɪ'ræfɪk/ a seráfico
seraphim /'sɛrəfɪm/ n serafín, m
Serbia /'sɔrbiə/ Servia, f
Serbian /'sɔrbiən/ a servio. n servio (-ia); (language) servio, m
serenade /ˌsɛrə'neid/ n serenata, f, vt dar una serenata (a)
serene /sə'rin/ a sereno. **His S. Highness,** Su Alteza Serenísima
serenity /sə'rɛnɪti/ n serenidad, f; tranquilidad, f
serf /sɔrf/ n siervo (-va)
serfdom /'sɔrfdəm/ n servidumbre, f
serge /sɔrdʒ/ n estameña, f; (silk) sarga, f
sergeant /'sardʒənt/ n Mil. sargento, m; (police) sargento de policía, m. **s.-at-arms,** macero, m. **s.-major,** sargento instructor, m
serial /'sɪəriəl/ a en serie; (of a story) por entregas. n novela por entregas, f. **s. number,** número de serie, m
sericulture /'sɛrɪˌkʌltʃər/ n sericultura, f
series /'sɪəriz/ n serie, f; cadena, f; Math. serie, progresión, f. **in s.,** en serie
serious /'sɪəriəs/ a serio; sincero; verdadero; (of illness, etc.) grave; importante. **He was s.** (not laughing) **when he said it,** Lo dijo en serio. **He is very s.**

about it, Lo toma muy en serio. **to grow s.,** (of persons) ponerse serio; (of events) hacerse grave
seriously /'sɪərɪəsli/ adv seriamente; en serio; gravemente. **to take** (something) **s.,** tomar (algo) en serio.
to take oneself s., tomarse muy en serio
seriousness /'sɪərɪəsnɪs/ n seriedad, f; gravedad, f. **in all s.,** en serio, seriamente
sermon /'sɜrmən/ n sermón, m
sermonize /'sɜrmə,naiz/ vt and vi sermonear
serpent /'sɜrpənt/ n serpiente, f; Mus. serpentón, m
serpentine /'sɜrpən,tin, -,tain/ a serpentino; (of character) tortuoso. n Mineral. serpentina, f
serrated /'sereitɪd/ a serrado; dentellado
serried /'serɪd/ a apretado, apiñado
serum /'sɪərəm/ n suero, m
servant /'sɜrvənt/ n servidor (-ra); (domestic) criado (-da); (employee) empleado (-da); (slave and Fig.) siervo (-va); pl **servants,** (domestic) servidumbre, f, servicio, m. **I remain your obedient s.,** Quedo de Vd. atento y seguro servidor (att. y s.s.). **civil s.,** empleado del estado, m. **general s.,** criada para todo, f. **man s.,** criado, m. **the s. problem,** el problema del servicio. **Your s., sir,** Servidor de Vd., señor. **s.-girl,** criada, f
serve /sɜrv/ vt servir (a); ser útil (a); satisfacer; (in a shop) despachar; (an apprenticeship, etc.) hacer; (a prison sentence) cumplir; (treat) tratar; (of stallion) cubrir; (a warrant, etc.) ejecutar; (a notice) entregar; (a ball) servir; (on a jury, etc.) formar parte de; Naut. aforrar. vi servir; (Mil., Nav.) hacer el servicio. n Sports. saque, m. **It serves you right!** ¡Lo tienes merecido! **to s. at table,** servir a la mesa. **to s. as,** servir de. **to s. out,** distribuir; servir. **Serves 8,** (recipe) Da 8 porciones
server /'sɜrvər/ n Eccl. acólito, m; Sports. saque, m; (tray) bandeja, f; (for fish, etc.) pala, f
service /'sɜrvɪs/ n servicio, m; Eccl. oficio, m; servicio de mesa, m; (of a writ) entrega, f; Sports. saque, m. **coffee s.,** juego de café, m. **diplomatic s.,** cuerpo diplomático, m. **At your s.,** Para servir a Vd., A su disposición. **on active s.,** en acto de servicio; en el campo de batalla. **to go into s.,** (of servants) ir a servir. **to render s.,** prestar servicios. **s. tree,** serbal, m
serviceable /'sɜrvəsəbəl/ a (of persons) servicial; (of things) servible, utilizable; útil; práctico; (lasting) duradero
service road n vía de servicio, f
servile /'sɜrvɪl/ a servil, Lat. Am. also incondicional
servility /sər'vɪlɪti/ n servilismo, m
serving /'sɜrvɪŋ/ a sirviente; al servicio (de). **s. maid,** criada, f. **s. table,** trinchero, m
servitude /'sɜrvɪ,tud/ n servidumbre, esclavitud, f. **penal s.,** cadena perpetua, f
session /'seʃən/ n sesión, f; junta, f. **petty sessions,** tribunal de primera instancia, m
set /set/ vt poner; colocar; fijar; (seeds, etc.) plantar; (bones) reducir, componer; (gems) engastar, montar; (a clock) regular; (sails) desplegar; (the teeth of a saw) trabar, triscar; (congeal) hacer coagular; (a trap) armar; (a snare) tender; (a razor) afilar; (make ready) preparar; (type) componer; (cause) hacer; Mus. poner en música; Mus. adaptar; (order) mandar; (prescribe) dar, asignar; (estimate) estimar, evaluar; (an example, etc.) dar; (establish) establecer, crear. vi (of the sun, etc.) ponerse; (solidify) coagularse; solidificarse; (of tides) fluir; (of the wind) soplar; (of dogs) hacer punta. **The joke set him laughing,** El chiste le hizo reír. **set an example,** dar ejemplo, dar el ejemplo. **set a precedent,** sentar precedente. **to set a person's mind at rest,** tranquilizar, sosegar. **to set a trap,** armar lazo. **to set at ease,** poner a sus anchas (a), hacer cómodo (a). **to set at naught,** despreciar. **to set eyes on,** poner los ojos en. **to set fire to,** pegar fuego a, incendiar. **to set free,** poner en libertad, librar (de). **to set in motion,** poner en marcha. **to set one's teeth,** apretar los dientes. **to set people talking,** dar que hablar a la gente. **to set the fashion,** fijar la moda; poner de moda. **to set the alarm at seven o'clock,** poner el despertador a las siete. **to set the table,** poner la mesa. **to set to work,** ponerse a trabajar. **to set about,** vi (begin)

ponerse (a); empezar; (undertake) emprender. vt (a rumour, etc.) divulgar. **They set about each other,** Empezaron a golpearse, Vinieron a las manos. **to set against,** indisponer (con), enemistar (con); hacer el enemigo (de), ser hostil (a); (balance) oponer, balancear. **to set oneself against,** oponerse a; atacar, luchar contra. **to set aside,** poner a un lado; apartar; (discard) desechar; (omit) omitir, pasar por alto de; dejar aparte, excluir; (keep) reservar; (money, etc.) ahorrar; (reject) rechazar; (quash) anular. **to set back,** retrasar; hacer retroceder. **set-back,** n revés, m; contrariedad, f. **to set before,** poner ante; (facts) exponer; (introduce) presentar. **to set down,** poner en tierra; depositar; (of a bus, etc.) dejar; (in writing) poner por escrito; anotar, apuntar; narrar, contar; (attribute) atribuir; (fix) fijar, formular; (believe to be) creer. **Passengers are set down at...,** Los viajeros pueden apearse en... **to set forth,** vt (one's opinions, etc.) exponer; publicar; (display) exhibir, mostrar; (make) hacer. vi ponerse en camino. **to set going,** poner en marcha; echar a andar. **to set in,** empezar; (of the tide) fluir. **A reaction has set in,** Se ha hecho sentir una reacción. **to set off,** vt (explode) hacer estallar; (cause) hacer; (heighten) realzar; hacer resaltar; (counterbalance) contraponer. vi partir; ponerse en camino. **set-off,** n contraste, m, contraposición, f. **to set off against,** contraponer. **to set on,** vt (a dog) azuzar; (incite) instigar, incitar. vi atacar. **to set out,** vt (state) exponer, manifestar; (embellish) realzar; (display) arreglar, disponer. vi ponerse en camino, partir. **to set over,** (rule) tener autoridad sobre, gobernar. **to set to,** (begin to) ponerse a, empezar a; (work) ponerse a trabajar. **set-to,** n lucha, f; (boxing) asalto, m; (quarrel) pelea, riña, f. **to set up,** vt (a monument, etc.) erigir, levantar; (fix) fijar; (apparatus, machinery) montar; (exalt) exaltar; (found) establecer, Lat. Am. also instaurar; crear; (propound) exponer; (a howl, etc.) dar; (equip with) proveer de; instalar; (make strong) robustecer; fortificar; (type) componer; (raise) alzar. vi establecerse; dárselas de. **He sets himself up as a painter,** Se las da de pintor. **to set** (a person) **up as a model,** poner como modelo (a). **to set up house,** poner casa. **to set up a business,** establecer un comercio. **set-up,** n establecimiento, m; arreglo, m. **to set upon,** atacar
set /set/ n (of sun, etc.) puesta, f, ocaso, m; (of the head, etc.) porte, m; (of a garment) corte, m; (of the tide, etc.) dirección, f; (slant) inclinación, f; (Fig. drift) tendencia, f, movimiento, m; (of the teeth of a saw) triscamiento, m; (of men, houses, etc.) grupo, m; (of tools, golf clubs, china, etc.) juego, m; (gang) pandilla, camarilla, f; clase, f; (Dance.) tanda, f; (tennis) partido, f; Theat. decoración, f; Radio. aparato de radio, m, radio, f. **coffee set,** juego de café, m. **all-mains set,** radio de corriente eléctrica, f. **battery set,** radio de batería, f. **portable set,** radio portátil, f. **the smart set,** el mundo elegante. **to have a shampoo and set,** hacerse lavar y marcar (el pelo). **to make a set,** hacer juego. **to make a dead set at,** hacer un ataque vigoroso (a), atacar resueltamente; procurar insinuarse en el favor de. **set of teeth,** dentadura, f
set /set/ a fijo; inmóvil; (of a smile) forzado; (of a task) asignado; (of times) señalado, fijo; (prescribed) prescrito, establecido; (firm) firme; (resolved) resuelto; (well-known) consabido; (obstinate) terco, nada adaptable. **well set-up,** apuesto, bien plantado. **He is set on doing it,** Se empeña en hacerlo. **to be dead set against,** estar completamente opuesto a. **set phrase,** frase hecha, f. **set-square,** n cartabón, m
setter /'setər/ n (perro) séter, perdiguero, m. **s.-on,** instigador (-ra)
setting /'setɪŋ/ n (of the sun, etc.) puesta, f; (of mortar, etc.) fraguado, m; (of a jelly) solidificación, f; (of jewels) engaste, m, montadura, f; (of bones) aliño, m; (of teeth of saw) traba, f; (of razor) afiladura, f; (of a trap) armadura, f; (of a machine, etc.) ajuste, m; (frame) marco, m; Mus. arreglo, m; Theat. decorado, m; (emplacement) lecho, m. **the s. sun,** el sol poniente. **s. free,** liberación, f. **s. off,** partida, salida, f. **s. out,** ida, marcha, f; principio, m. **s.-up,** creación, f; institución, f, establecimiento, m; (of a machine) montaje, m; Print. composición, f

settle /'sɛtļ/ *vt* colocar; asegurar, afirmar; (a country) colonizar; (live in) establecer (en); (populate) poblar; (in a profession, etc.) dar; (install) instalar; (the imagination, etc.) sosegar, calmar; (resolve) resolver; (arrange) disponer, arreglar; (differences) componer, concertar; (an opponent, etc.) confundir; (a bill) saldar, pagar; (a claim) satisfacer; (clarify) depositar, clarificar; (end) poner fin (a). *vi* establecerse; (of weather) serenarse; (to work, etc.) empezar a, ponerse a; aplicarse a; (decide) decidirse; (alight) posarse; (of foundations, etc.) asentarse; (of a ship) zozobrar; (of sediment) depositarse; (of liquid) clarificarse. **to s. accounts with,** *Fig.* ajustar cuentas con. **to s. down,** establecerse, arraigarse; adaptarse (a); (become calm) sosegarse, calmarse; sentar el juicio; (of foundations) asentarse; (of a ship) zozobrar; (of sediment) depositarse. **to s. in,** *vt* instalar. *vi* instalarse. **to s. on,** (choose) escoger; (decide on) decidirse (a). **to s. a pension on,** señalar pensión (a). **to s. up,** (one's affairs) poner en orden; (bill) pagar, saldar. *vi* llegar a un acuerdo; pagar cuentas
settled /'sɛtļd/ *a* fijo; permanente; invariable; (of countries) colonizado; (of weather) sereno
settlement /'sɛtļmənt/ *n* (of a country) colonización, *f*; (of a dispute) arreglo, ajuste, *m*; (of a question) solución, *f*; decisión, *f*; (of a bill) saldo, pago, *m*, liquidación, *f*; (of an obligation) satisfacción, *f*; (colony) colonia, *f*; (creation) creación, institución, *f*; establecimiento, arraigo, *m*. **deed of s.,** escritura de donación, *f*. **marriage s.,** contrato matrimonial, *m*; **s. out of court,** arreglo pacífico, *m*
settler /'sɛtlər/ *n* colono, *m*; colonizador (-ra)
seven /'sɛvən/ *a* and *n* siete *m*. **It is s. o'clock,** Son las siete. **the s. deadly sins,** los siete pecados capitales
seventeen /'sɛvən'tin/ *a* diecisiete, diez y siete. *n* diecisiete, *m*. **She is just s.,** Acaba de cumplir los diez y siete años
seventeenth /'sɛvən'tinθ/ *a* décimoséptimo; (of monarchs and of the month) diez y siete. *n* décimoséptimo, *m*. **Louis the S.,** Luis diez y siete. **the s. of June,** el diez y siete de junio
seventh /'sɛvənθ/ *a* séptimo; (of the month) siete. *n* séptimo, *m*; séptima parte, *f*; *Mus.* séptima, *f*. **Edward the S.,** Eduardo séptimo. **the s. of August,** el siete de agosto
seventieth /'sɛvəntiɪθ/ *a* septuagésimo, setentavo. *n* setentavo, *m*
seventy /'sɛvənti/ *a* and *n* setenta, *m*
sever /'sɛvər/ *vt* separar; romper; dividir
several /'sɛvərəl/ *a* distinto, diferente; respectivo; varios, *m pl,* (*f pl,* varias); algunos, *m pl,* (*f pl,* algunas)
severally /'sɛvərəli/ *adv* separadamente; individualmente; independientemente
severance /'sɛvərəns/ *n* separación, *f*; (of friendship, etc.) ruptura, *f*
severe /sə'vɪər/ *a* severo; riguroso; fuerte; duro; (of style) austero; (of pain) agudo; (of illness) grave
severely /sə'vɪərli/ *adv* severamente; intensamente; gravemente
severity /sə'vɛrɪti/ *n* severidad, *f*; intensidad, *f*; (of weather) inclemencia, *f*; (of illness) gravedad, *f*
sew /sou/ *vt* and *vi* coser, *Lat. Am.* costurar, costurear. **to sew on,** coser, pegar
sewage /'suɪdʒ/ *n* aguas residuales, *f pl.* **s. system,** alcantarillado, *m*
sewer /'suər/ *n* alcantarilla, cloaca, *f*, albañal, *m*
sewing /'souɪŋ/ *n* costura, *f*. **s. bag,** costurero, *m*. **s. cotton,** hilo de coser, *m*. **s.-machine,** máquina de coser, *f*. **s. silk,** torzal, *m*
sex /sɛks/ *n* sexo, *m*. **the fair sex,** el bello sexo. **the weaker sex,** el sexo débil. **sex appeal,** atractivo, *m*
sexagenarian /ˌsɛksədʒə'nɛəriən/ *n* sexagenario (-ia)
sexless /'sɛkslɪs/ *a* neutro; frígido
sexologist /sɛk'splədʒɪst/ *n* sexólogo (-ga)
sexology /sɛk'splədʒi/ *n* sexología, *f*
sextant /'sɛkstənt/ *n* sextante, *m*
sexton /'sɛkstən/ *n* sacristán, *m*; sepulturero, *m*; (bell-ringer) campanero, *m*
sexual /'sɛkʃuəl/ *a* sexual

sexuality /ˌsɛkʃu'ælɪti/ *n* sexualidad, *f*
sh! /ʃ/ *interj* ¡Chitón! ¡Chis!
shabbily /'ʃæbəli/ *adv* (of dressing) pobremente; (of treatment) mezquinamente
shabbiness /'ʃæbinɪs/ *n* pobreza, *f*; estado andrajoso, *m*; (of behavior) mezquindad, ruindad, *f*
shabby /'ʃæbi/ *a* (of persons) desharrapado, andrajoso, *Lat. Am.* maltraído; (of garments) raído, roto; (of a neighborhood, etc.) pobre; (mean) ruin, mezquino
shack /ʃæk/ *n* choza, *f*, *Mexico* jacal, *elsewhere in Lat. Am.* bohío, *m*
shackle /'ʃækəl/ *n* traba, *f*; *pl* **shackles,** grillos, *m pl,* esposas, *f pl;* *Fig.* cadenas, *f pl.* *vt* poner esposas (a), encadenar; (a horse) apear; *Fig.* atar; (impede) estorbar
shade /ʃeid/ *n* sombra, *f*; (in a picture) toque de obscuro, *m*; (for the eyes) visera, *f*; (of a lamp) pantalla, *f*; (ghost) espectro, fantasma, *m*; (of color) matiz, *m*; (tinge) dejo, *m*. *vt* sombrear, dar sombra (a); (the face, etc.) proteger, resguardar; (a drawing) esfumar. **in the s.,** a la sombra. **80° in the s.,** ochenta grados a la sombra. **to put (a person) in the s.,** eclipsar
shadiness /'ʃeidinɪs/ *n* sombra, *f*
shading /'ʃeidɪŋ/ *n* sombra, *f*; *Art.* degradación, *f*
shadow /'ʃædou/ *n* sombra, *f*; obscuridad, *f*; (in a picture) toque de obscuro, *m*. *vt* sombrear; obscurecer; (a person) seguir to **cast a s.,** proyectar una sombra. **to s. forth,** indicar; simbolizar. **s. show,** sombras chinescas, *f pl*
shadowy /'ʃædoui/ *a* umbroso; vago, indistinto, indefinido
shady /'ʃeidi/ *a* sombreado, umbrío; sombrío; (of persons, etc.) sospechoso. **It was s. in the wood,** Hacía sombra en el bosque
shaft /ʃæft/ *n* fuste, *m*; (arrow) flecha, saeta, *f*, dardo, *m*; (of a golf club, etc.) mango, *m*; (of a cart) vara, *f*; *Mech.* árbol, eje, *m*; (of a column and a feather) cañón, *m*; (of a light) rayo, *m*; (of a mine) pozo, tiro, *m*; (air-shaft) conducto de aire, ventilador, *m*. **cam-s.,** árbol de levas, *m*. **driving s.,** árbol motor, *m*
shaggy /'ʃægi/ *a* peludo; lanudo
shah /ʃɑ, ʃɔ/ *n* cha, *m*
shake /ʃeik/ *vt* sacudir; agitar; hacer temblar; (weaken) debilitar, hacer flaquear. *vi* estremecerse; temblar; (trill) trinar. **He managed to s. himself free,** Consiguió librarse por una sacudida. **to s. hands,** darse la mano, estrecharse la mano. **to s. one's finger at,** señalar con el dedo (a). **to s. one's fist at,** amenazar con el puño (a). **to s. one's head,** mover la cabeza; negar con la cabeza. **to s. one's sides,** (with laughter) reírse a carcajadas. **to s. with fear,** temblar de miedo. **to s. down,** sacudir, hacer caer. **s.-down,** *n* cama improvisada, *f*. **to s. off,** sacudirse; librarse (de); perder; quitar de encima (a). **to s. out,** (unfurl) desplegar; sacudir. **to s. up,** agitar; sacudir, remover
shake /ʃeik/ *n* sacudida, *f*; (of the head) movimiento (de la cabeza), *m*; (of the hand) apretón (de manos), *m*; temblor, *m*; *Mus.* trino, gorjeo, *m*. **in two shakes,** *Inf.* en un periquete. **to give a person a good s.,** sacudir violentamente (a)
Shakespearean /ʃeik'spɪəriən/ *a* shakespeariano
shakiness /'ʃeikinɪs/ *n* inestabilidad, *f*; poca firmeza, *f*; temblor, *m*; lo dudoso. **the s. of his voice,** su voz trémula
shaking /'ʃeikɪŋ/ *n* sacudimiento, *m*; temblor, *m*; (of windows, etc.) zangoloteo, *m*
shaky /'ʃeiki/ *a* inestable; poco firme; (of hands, etc.) tembloroso; (of the voice) trémulo; (of gait) vacilante; dudoso
shale /ʃeil/ *n* esquisto, *m*
shall /ʃæl/ *unstressed* ʃəl/ *v aux* (expressing simple future) **1 s. arrive tomorrow,** Llegaré mañana. **S. we go to the sea next week?** ¿Iremos al mar la semana próxima?; (expressing obligation, compulsion) **You s. not go out,** No has de salir, No quiero que salgas. **He s. see her immediately,** Tiene que verla en seguida; (as a polite formula) **S. I go?** ¿Quiere Vd.

que vaya? **S. we buy the soap?** ¿Quiere Vd. que compremos el jabón? ¿Compraremos el jabón?

shallot /'ʃælət, ʃə'lɒt/ n Bot. chalote, m, ascalonia, f

shallow /'ʃælou/ a poco profundo; (of a receptacle) llano; (of persons) superficial, frívolo; (of knowledge, etc.) superficial, ligero, somero. n bajío, m

shallowness /'ʃælounɪs/ n poca profundidad, f; superficialidad, f

sham /ʃæm/ vt fingir, simular. n farsa, f; imitación, f; engaño, m; (person) farsante, m. a fingido; falso; espurio. **to s. illness,** fingirse enfermo. **to s. dead,** hacer la mortecina. **You're just a s.,** Eres un farsante

sham battle n Mil. imulacro de combate, simulacro guerrero, m

shamble /'ʃæmbəl/ vi andar arrastrándose. n andar pesado, m; pl **shambles,** matadero, m; Fig. carnicería, f

shambling /'ʃæmblɪŋ/ a pesado, lento

shame /ʃeim/ n vergüenza, f; ignominia, f; deshonra, f. vt avergonzar; deshonrar. **For s.!** ¡Qué vergüenza! **What a s.!** ¡Qué lástima! **to put to s.,** avergonzar

shamefaced /'ʃeim,feist/ a (bashful) vergonzoso, tímido; (ashamed) avergonzado

shamefacedly /ʃeim'feisɪdli/ adv vergonzosamente, tímidamente; con vergüenza

shameful /'ʃeimfəl/ a vergonzoso, escandaloso; indecente

shamefully /'ʃeimfəli/ adv escandalosamente

shameless /'ʃeimlɪs/ a desvergonzado; impúdico, indecente

shamelessly /'ʃeimlɪsli/ adv desvergonzadamente

shamelessness /'ʃeimlɪsnɪs/ n desvergüenza, poca vergüenza, f; impudicia, deshonestidad, f

shampoo /ʃæm'pu/ n champú, m. vt dar un champú (a); dar un masaje (a). **dry s.,** champú seco, m

shank /ʃæŋk/ n zanca, f; Mech. pierna, f; (handle) mango, m; (of a button) rabo, m, cola, f. **go on Shank's mare, ride on Shank's mare,** caminar en coche de San Francisco, ir en boricua de Villadiego

shanty /'ʃænti/ n choza, f

shanty town n barriada (Peru), callampa, población, f, población, callampa (Chile), f. rancho (Venezuela), m, villa-miseria (Argentina), f

shape /ʃeip/ n forma, f; bulto, m; fantasma, m; (of a garment) corte, m; (of a person) talle, m; Cul. molde, m; (of a hat) forma, f. vt formar; (a garment) cortar; (ideas) dar forma (a); adaptar; (stone, etc.) labrar; (one's life) dominar. vi (of events) desarrollarse. **to go out of s.,** perder la forma. **to take s.,** tomar forma. **to s. one's course,** dirigirse (hacia, a); Naut. dar el rumbo. **to s. well,** prometer bien

shaped /ʃeipt/ a de forma de..., que tiene figura de... **pear-s.,** piriforme

shapeless /'ʃeiplɪs/ a informe; disforme, sin forma

shapelessness /'ʃeiplɪsnɪs/ n informidad, f; deformidad, f

shapeliness /'ʃeiplɪnɪs/ n belleza de forma, f; simetría, f

shapely /'ʃeipli/ a bien formado; simétrico

share /ʃeər/ n porción, f; parte, f; cuota, f; contribución, f; (part ownership) interés, m; (in a company) acción, f. vt distribuir; compartir; dividir; tomar parte en. vi participar (de); tomar parte (en). **to fall to one's s.,** tocar, corresponder. **to go shares with,** dividir con, compartir con. **to take a s. in the conversation,** tomar parte en la conversación. **paid-up s.,** Com. acción liberada, f. **to s. out,** repartir, distribuir

sharecropper /'ʃeər,krɒpər/ Lat. Am. agregado (-da)

shareholder /'ʃeər,houldər/ n accionista, mf

sharer /'ʃeərər/ n partícipe, mf

shark /ʃɑrk/ n Ichth. tiburón, m; Inf. caimán, m

sharp /ʃɑrp/ a (of edges) afilado, cortante, Lat. Am. also filoso, filudo; (of points) punzante, puntiagudo; (of features, etc.) anguloso; (of bends, etc.) brusco; (of outlines, etc.) definido, distinto; (of pain, sound) agudo; (marked) marcado; (intense) intenso; (of winds, glance, etc.) penetrante; (of hearing) fino; (of appetite) bueno; (of showers) fuerte; (quick) rápido; (clever, etc.) vivo, listo; perspicaz; (of children) despierto, precoz; (unscrupulous) astuto, sin escrúpulos;

(of criticism, remarks) mordaz; (of rebukes, sentences, etc.) severo; (of winters, etc.) riguroso; (of fighting) encarnizado; (of taste) picante; (sour) ácido; Mus. sostenido. adv en punto; puntualmente. n Mus. sostenido, m. **at five o'clock s.,** a las cinco en punto. **Look s.!** ¡Date prisa! **s.-edged,** afilado. **s.-eyed,** con ojos de lince; de mirada penetrante. **s.-featured,** de facciones angulosas. **s.-nosed,** de nariz puntiaguda. **s.-pointed,** puntiagudo. **s. practice,** procedimientos poco honrados, m pl. **s.-tongued,** de lengua áspera. **s. turn,** curva brusca, curva cerrada, f. **s.-witted,** de inteligencia viva, listo

sharpen /'ʃɑrpən/ vt (knives) afilar, amolar; (pencils, etc.) sacar punta (a); (wits, etc.) despabilar; (appetite) abrir. **This walk has sharpened my appetite,** Este paseo me ha abierto el apetito. **to s. one's claws,** afilarse las uñas

sharper /'ʃɑrpər/ n Inf. caballero de industria, timador, m; (at cards) fullero, m

sharply /'ʃɑrpli/ adv claramente; bruscamente; severamente; ásperamente

sharpness /'ʃɑrpnɪs/ n (of cold, etc.) intensidad, f; severidad, f; (cleverness) agudeza, perspicacia, f; (of a child) precocidad, f; (sarcasm, etc.) mordacidad, f; aspereza, f; brusquedad, f

sharpshooter /'ʃɑrp,ʃutər/ n franco tirador, m

sharpsighted /'ʃɑrp,saitid/ a de vista penetrante, listo, perspicaz

shatter /'ʃætər/ vt romper, quebrantar; hacer añicos; Fig. destrozar. **You have shattered my illusions,** Has destrozado todas mis ilusiones

shave /ʃeiv/ vt afeitar, rasurar; (wood, etc.) acepillar. vi afeitarse; (of razors) afeitar. n afeitada, f. **to have a s.,** hacerse afeitar. **to have a close s.,** Inf. escapar por un pelo

shaving /'ʃeivɪŋ/ n afeitada, f; (of wood, etc.) viruta, acepilladura, f. **s.-bowl,** bacía, f. **s.-brush,** brocha de afeitar, f. **s.-glass,** espejo de afeitar, m. **s.-soap,** jabón de afeitar, m. **s.-stick,** barra de jabón de afeitar, f

shawl /ʃɔl/ n chal, mantón, rebozo, m

she /ʃi/ pers pron ella; la; (female) hembra, f; (translated by fem. ending in the case of animals, etc., e.g. she bear, osa, she cat, gata). **It is her,** Es ella. **she who is dancing,** la que baila

sheaf /ʃif/ n (of corn, etc.) gavilla, garba, f; (of arrows) haz, m; (of papers, etc.) paquete, atado, m. **to bind in sheaves,** agavillar

shear /ʃiər/ vt (sheep) esquilar, trasquilar; tonsurar; cortar; (cloth) tundir

shearer /'ʃiərər/ n (of sheep) esquilador, m

shearing /'ʃiərɪŋ/ n (of sheep) esquileo, m, tonsura, f; (of cloth) tunda, f. **s. machine,** esquiladora, f. **s. season,** esquileo, m

shears /ʃiərz/ n pl tijeras grandes, f pl, cizalla, f

sheath /ʃiθ/ n vaina, f. **s.-knife,** cuchillo de monte, m

sheathe /ʃið/ vt envainar; Naut. aforrar

shed /ʃɛd/ vt derramar; (skin, etc.) mudar; perder; (remove) quitarse, desprenderse de; (get rid of) deshacerse de. n cobertizo, sotechado, m; cabaña, f. **to s. light on,** echar luz sobre, iluminar

sheen /ʃin/ n lustre, m; brillo, m

sheep /ʃip/ n oveja, f; carnero, m; ganado lanar, m. **to cast sheep's eyes at,** lanzar miradas de carnero degollado, m. **s. breeder,** ganadero, m. **s.-dip,** desinfectante para ganado, m. **s.-dog,** perro de pastor, m. **s.-like,** ovejuno, de oveja. **s.-shearing,** esquileo, m

sheepfold /'ʃip,fould/ n aprisco, redil, m

sheepish /'ʃipiʃ/ a tímido, vergonzoso; estúpido

sheepishly /'ʃipiʃli/ adv tímidamente

sheepishness /'ʃipiʃnɪs/ n timidez, cortedad, f; estupidez, f

sheepskin /'ʃip,skɪn/ n piel de carnero, f. **s. jacket,** zamarra, f

sheer /ʃiər/ a puro; completo, absoluto; (steep) escarpado, acantilado; a pico; (of fabrics) transparente; ligero, fino. adv completamente; de un golpe; (perpendicularly) a pico. **to s. off,** desviarse; largarse, marcharse

sheet /ʃit/ n (bed) sábana, f; (shroud) mortaja, f; (of paper) hoja, f; cuartilla, f; (pamphlet) folleto, m; (news) periódico, m, hoja, f; (of metal, etc.) lámina, plancha, *f*; (of water, etc.) extensión, *f*; *Naut.* escota, *f*. *vt* poner sábanas en; envolver en sábanas; (a corpse) amortajar. **to be as white as a s.,** estar pálido como un muerto. **s. bend,** (knot) nudo de tejedor, *m*. **s. glass,** vidrio en lámina, *m*. **s. iron,** hierro en planchas, *m*

sheik /ʃik/ *n* jeque, *m*

shekel /ˈʃɛkəl/ *n* (coin) siclo, *m*; *pl* **shekels,** dinero, *m*

shelf /ʃɛlf/ *n* estante, anaquel, *m*; (reef) banco de arena, bajío, *m*; (of rock) escalón, *m*. **to be on the s.,** *Inf.* quedarse para tía, quedarse para vestir imágenes

shell /ʃɛl/ *n* (of small shellfish) concha, *f*; (of tortoise) coraza, *f*; (of insects, lobsters, etc.) caparazón, *m*; (of a nut) cáscara, *f*; (of an egg) cascarón, *m*; (of peas, beans) vaina, *f*; (*Com.* and *Mus.*) concha, *f*; (of a building) casco, *m*; (outside) exterior, *m*; (empty form) apariencia, *f*; *Mil.* granada, *f*. *vt* pelar; (nuts) descascarar; (beans, etc.) desvainar; *Mil.* bombardear. **to be under s.-fire,** sufrir un bombardeo. **s. shock,** neurosis de guerra, *f*

shellfish /ˈʃɛl.fɪʃ/ *n* crustáceo, *m*; (as food) marisco, *m*

shelling /ˈʃɛlɪŋ/ *n* *Mil.* bombardeo, *m*

shelter /ˈʃɛltər/ *n* abrigo, amparo, *m*; refugio, *m*; asilo, *m*. *vt* dar asilo (a); abrigar; (defend) amparar, proteger; (hide) esconder. *vi* refugiarse; resguardarse; esconderse

sheltered /ˈʃɛltərd/ *a* abrigado

sheltering /ˈʃɛltərɪŋ/ *a* protector

shelve /ʃɛlv/ *vt* (books) poner en un estante; (persons) destituir; (questions, etc.) aplazar, arrinconar; proveer de estantes, *vi* (slope) inclinarse, formar declive; (of sea bed) formar escalones

shelving /ˈʃɛlvɪŋ/ *a* inclinado; (of ocean bed) acantilado

shepherd /ˈʃɛpərd/ *n* pastor, *m*. *vt* guardar; guiar, conducir. **s. boy,** zagal, *m*. **shepherd's pouch,** zurrón, *m*

shepherdess /ˈʃɛpərdɪs/ *n* pastora, *f*

sherbet /ˈʃɜrbɪt/ *n* sorbete, *m*

sheriff /ˈʃɛrɪf/ *n* (in U.K.) sheriff, *m*; (U.S.A.) jefe de la policía, *m*

sherry /ˈʃɛri/ *n* (vino de) jerez, *m*. **dry s.,** jerez seco, *m*

shield /ʃild/ *n* escudo, *m*; (round) rodela, *f*; *Herald.* escudo de armas, *m*; *Fig.* defensa, *f*, amparo, *m*. *vt* proteger, amparar. **to s. a person,** proteger a una persona. **to s. one's eyes from the sun,** proteger los ojos del sol. **s.-bearer,** escudero, *m*

shift /ʃɪft/ *vt* mover; trasladar; quitar, librarse de; cambiar. *vi* moverse; (of the wind) girar; cambiar. *n* cambio, *m*; (expedient) recurso, expediente, *m*; (dodge) artificio, *m*, trampa, *f*; (of workers) tanda, *f*, turno, *m*. **to make s.,** arreglárselas (para hacer algo); procurar (hacer algo); (manage) ir tirando. **to s. for oneself,** componérselas, arreglárselas. **to s. the scenes,** *Theat.* cambiar de decoración. **to s. the helm,** *Naut.* cambiar el timón. **to work in shifts,** trabajar por turnos

shiftiness /ˈʃɪftɪnɪs/ *n* falta de honradez, informalidad, *f*; astucia, *f*

shifting /ˈʃɪftɪŋ/ *a* (of light, etc.) cambiante; (of sand, etc.) movedizo; (of wind) mudable; (of moods) voluble. **s. sand,** arena movediza, *f*

shiftless /ˈʃɪftlɪs/ *a* perezoso; sin energía, ineficaz

shiftlessness /ˈʃɪftlɪsnɪs/ *n* pereza, *f*; falta de energía, *f*

shifty /ˈʃɪfti/ *a* (tricky) tramposo, astuto; (dishonest) informal, falso; (of gaze) furtivo. **s.-eyed,** *a* de mirada furtiva

Shiite /ˈʃiait/ *a* and *n* chiita

shilling /ˈʃɪlɪŋ/ *n* chelín, *m*. **nine shillings in the £,** nueve chelines por libra. **to cut off with a s.,** desheredar

shilly shally /ˈʃɪli ˌʃæli/ *n* irresolución, vacilación, *f*, *vi* estar irresoluto, titubear, no saber qué hacer

shimmer /ˈʃɪmər/ *vi* rielar; relucir. *n* luz trémula, *f*; resplandor, *m*; viso, *m*

shin /ʃɪn/ *n* espinilla, *f*; (of beef) corvejón, *m*. **to s. up,** trepar

shine /ʃain/ *vi* brillar; resplandecer, relucir, relumbrar. *vt* (shoes) dar lustre (a). *n* brillo, *m*; lustre, *m*; (shoeshine) *Mexico* bola, *f*. **in rain or s.,** en buen o

mal tiempo. **to s. with happiness,** radiar felicidad. **to take the s. out of,** eclipsar

shingle /ˈʃɪŋɡəl/ *n* (pebbles) guijarros, *m pl*; cascajo, *m*; barda, *f*; (hair) pelo a la garçonne, *m*; *pl* **shingles,** *Med.* zona, *f*, herpe zóster, *m*. *vt* (the hair) cortar a la garçonne

shining /ˈʃainɪŋ/ *a* resplandeciente, brillante, reluciente; radiante. **s. with happiness,** radiante de felicidad. **s. example,** ejemplo notable, *m*

Shintoism /ˈʃɪntou.ɪzəm/ *n* sintoísmo, *m*

shiny /ˈʃaini/ *a* brillante; lustroso, terso; (of trousers, etc.) reluciente; (of paper) glaseado

ship /ʃɪp/ *n* buque, barco, *m*; (sailing) velero, *m*. *vt* embarcar; (oars) armar. *vi* embarcar; (as a member of crew) embarcarse. **on board s.,** a bordo. **to s. a sea,** embarcar agua. **to take s.,** embarcar. **to s. off,** mandar. **ship's boat,** lancha, *f*. **ship's boy,** grumete, *m*. **ship's carpenter,** carpintero de ribera, *m*. **ship's company,** tripulación, *f*. **s.-breaker,** desguazador, *m*. **s.-canal,** canal de navegación, *m*. **s.-load,** cargamento, *m*

shipbuilder /ˈʃɪpˌbɪldər/ *n* constructor de buques, arquitecto naval, *m*

shipbuilding /ˈʃɪpˌbɪldɪŋ/ *n* construcción naval, *f*

shipment /ˈʃɪpmənt/ *n* embarque, *m*; despacho por mar, *m*; (consignment) remesa, *f*

shipowner /ˈʃɪpˌounər/ *n* naviero, *m*

shipper /ˈʃɪpər/ *n* naviero, *m*; importador, *m*; exportador, *m*

shipping /ˈʃɪpɪŋ/ *n* embarque, *m*; buques, barcos, *m pl*; (of a country) marina, *f*. **s. agent,** consignatario de buques, *m*. **s. company,** compañía de navegación, *f*. **s. offices,** oficinas de una compañía de navegación, *f pl*

shipshape /ˈʃɪpˌʃeip/ *a* en buen orden; bien arreglado

shipwreck /ˈʃɪpˌrɛk/ *n* naufragio, *m*, *vt* hacer naufragar, echar a pique

shipwrecked person /ˈʃɪpˌrɛkt/ *n* náufrago (-ga). **to be shipwrecked,** naufragar

shipyard /ˈʃɪpˌyɑrd/ *n* astillero, varadero, *m*

shire /ʃaiᵊr/ *n* condado, *m*

shirk /ʃɜrk/ *vt* eludir, esquivar; desentenderse de. *vi* faltar al deber

shirker /ˈʃɜrkər/ *n* gandul (-la); persona que no cumple con su deber, *f*

shirt /ʃɜrt/ *n* camisa, *f*. **dress s.,** camisa de pechera dura, *f*. **hair-s.,** cilicio, *m*. **in one's s.-sleeves,** en mangas de camisa. **s.-blouse,** blusa sencilla, *f*. **s.-collar,** cuello de camisa, *m*. **s. factory** or **shop,** camisería, *f*. **shirt-front,** pechera, *f*. **s.-maker,** camisero (-ra)

shirting /ˈʃɜrtɪŋ/ *n* tela para camisas, *f*

shiver /ˈʃɪvər/ *vi* temblar, tiritar; dar diente con diente; (of a boat) zozobrar. *vt* (break) hacer añicos, romper; (sails) sacudir. *n* temblor, estremecimiento, *m*; escalofrío, *m*; (of glass, etc.) fragmento, *m*, astilla, *f*. **You give me the shivers,** Me das escalofríos

shivery /ˈʃɪvəri/ *a* tembloroso; friolero. **I feel s.,** Tengo escalofríos

shoal /ʃoul/ *n* (of fish) banco, *m*; gran cantidad, *f*; (of people) multitud, muchedumbre, *f*; (water) bajo fondo, *m*; (sand-bank) banco, bajío, *m*, a poco profundo

shock /ʃɒk/ *n* choque, *m*; *Elec.* conmoción, *f*; *Med.* shock, *m*; (*Med.* stroke) conmoción cerebral, *f*; (fright) sobresalto, susto, *m*. *vt* sacudir, dar una sacudida (a); chocar; escandalizar, horrorizar. *vi* chocar. **electric s.,** conmoción eléctrica, *f*. **She is easily shocked,** Ella se escandaliza fácilmente. **s. of hair,** mata de pelo, *f*. **s. absorber,** *Mech.* amortiguador, *m*; *Auto.* amortiguador (de los muelles), *m*. **s. troops,** tropas de asalto, *f pl*, elementos de choque, *m pl*

shocking /ˈʃɒkɪŋ/ *a* chocante; escandaloso; repugnante, horrible; espantoso. **How s.!** ¡Qué horror! **s. bad,** malísimo

shockingly /ˈʃɒkɪŋli/ *adv* horriblemente

shod /ʃɒd/ *a* calzado; (of horses) herrado

shoddy /ˈʃɒdi/ *n* pacotilla, *f*. *a* de pacotilla; espurio, falso

shoe /ʃu/ *n* zapato, *m*; (horse) herradura, *f*; (*Naut. Mech.*) zapata, *f*. *vt* (horses) herrar. **I should not like**

to be in his shoes, No me gustaría estar en su pellejo. **That is quite another pair of shoes,** Eso es harina de otro costal. **to cast a s.,** (of horses) desherrarse, perder una herradura. **to put on one's shoes,** ponerse los zapatos, calzarse. **to remove one's shoes,** quitarse los zapatos, descalzarse. **wooden shoes,** zuecos, *m pl.* **s.-buckle,** hebilla de zapato, *f.* **s.-lace,** cordón de zapato, *m.* **s.-leather,** cuero para zapatos, *m;* calzado, *m.* **s.-scraper,** limpiabarros, *m,* estregadera, *f.* **s.-shop,** zapatería, *f*

shoeblack /'ʃu‚blæk/ *n* betún, *m;* (person) limpiabotas, *m*

shoehorn /'ʃu‚hɔrn/ *n* calzador, *m*

shoemaker /'ʃu‚meikər/ *n* zapatero (-ra)

shoemaking /'ʃu‚meikɪŋ/ *n* fabricación de calzado, zapatería, *f*

shoeshine /'ʃu‚ʃain/ *n Mexico* bola, *f*

shoo! /ʃu/ *interj* ¡fuera!; ¡zape! *vt* ahuyentar

shoot /ʃut/ *vt* (throw) lanzar; precipitar; (empty) vaciar; (a rapid) salvar; (rays, etc.) echar; (an arrow, a gun, etc.) disparar; (a person, etc.) pegar un tiro (a); *Sports.* tirar; *Mil.* fusilar, pasar por las armas, *Lat. Am.* afusilar; (a film) hacer, impresionar. *vi* lanzarse, precipitarse; (of pain) latir; (sprout) brotar; disparar; tirar; (at football) tirar a gol, chutar. **s.-out,** tiroteo, *m.* **to s. a glance at,** lanzar una mirada (a). **I was shot in the foot,** Una bala me hirió en el pie. **to s. the sun,** *Naut.* tomar el sol. **to s. ahead,** tomar la delantera. **to s. at,** tirar a, *Lat. Am.* abalear. **to s. at** *Central America, Mexico* balacear. **to s. by,** pasar como una bala. **to s. down,** *Aer.* derribar; matar de un tiro. **to s. up,** (of children) espigarse; (of prices) subir mucho; (of cliffs, etc.) elevarse

shoot /ʃut/ *n* partida de caza, *f;* tiro, *m; Bot.* renuevo, retoño, *m*

shooting /'ʃutɪŋ/ *n* tiro, *m;* caza con escopeta, *f;* (of guns) tiroteo, *m;* (of an arrow) disparo, *m;* (of a film) rodaje, *m.* **to go s.,** ir a cazar con escopeta. **s.-box,** pabellón de caza, *m.* **s. butts,** tiradero, *m.* **s. dog,** perro de caza, *m.* **s.-gallery,** tiro al blanco, *m..* **s. match,** concurso de tiro, *m.* **s. pain,** punzada de dolor, *f.* **s. party,** partida de caza, *f.* **s. practice,** ejercicios de tiro, *m pl.* **s.-range,** campo de tiro, *m.* **s. star,** estrella fugaz, *f*

shop /ʃop/ *n* tienda, *f;* (workshop) taller, *m. vi* ir de compras, ir de tiendas; comprar. **to talk s.,** hablar de negocios. **s.-assistant,** dependiente (-ta). **s.-soiled,** deslucido. **s.-steward,** representante de los obreros de una fábrica o taller, *m.* **s. window,** escaparate, *Mexico* aparador, *m*

shopkeeper /'ʃɒp‚kipər/ *n* tendero (-ra), *Chile* despachero (-ra)

shoplifter /'ʃɒp‚lɪftər/ *n* ladrón (-ona) de tiendas, ratero (-ra) de las tiendas

shoplifting /'ʃɒp‚lɪftɪŋ/ *n* ratería en las tiendas, *f*

shopper /'ʃɒpər/ *n* comprador (-ra)

shopping /'ʃɒpɪŋ/ *n* compra, *f;* compras, *f pl.* **to go s.,** ir de compras. **s. basket,** cesta para compras, *f.* **s. center,** centro comercial, *m*

shopwalker /'ʃɒp‚wɔkər/ *n* jefe de recepción, *m*

shore /ʃɔr/ *n* orilla, ribera, *f;* costa, *f;* (sands) playa, *f.* **off s.,** en alta mar. **on s.,** en tierra. **to come on s.,** desembarcar. **to s. up,** apuntalar, acodalar; *Fig.* apoyar

short /ʃɔrt/ *a* corto; (of persons) bajo; breve; (of temper) vivo; insuficiente; distante (de); (brusque) seco; (of money) alcanzado. *adv* súbitamente; brevemente. *n* (vowel) vocal breve, *m;* pl **shorts,** calzones cortos, *m pl.* **for s.,** para mayor brevedad. **for a s. time,** por poco tiempo. **in a s. time,** dentro de poco. **in s.,** en breve, en resumen, en pocas palabras. **on s. notice,** con poco tiempo de aviso. **s. of,** con la excepción de, menos. **to be s.,** faltar, ser escaso. **to be s. with someone,** tratar con sequedad (a). **to fall s. of expectations,** no cumplir las esperanzas. **to go s. of,** pasarse sin. **to grow s.,** escasear. **s.-circuit,** corto circuito, *m.* **s. cut,** atajo, *Lat. Am.* desecho, *m.* **s.-haired,** pelicorto. **s.-handed,** falto de mano de obra. **s.-lived,** de vida corta; efímero, fugaz. **to be short-lived,** tener vida corta. **s.-sighted,** corto de vista. **s.-sightedness,** miopía, cortedad de vista, *f.* **s. story,** cuento, *m.* **s.-tempered,** irascible, irritable, de genio

vivo. **s.-waisted,** corto de talle. **s.-winded,** corto de resuello; asmático

shortage /'ʃɔrtɪdʒ/ *n* falta, escasez, *f;* carestía, *f.* **water s.,** carestía de agua, *f*

shortcoming /'ʃɔrt‚kʌmɪŋ/ *n* defecto, *m;* imperfección, *f*

shorten /'ʃɔrtn/ *vt* acortar; reducir, disminuir; abreviar. *vi* acortarse

shorthand /'ʃɔrt‚hænd/ *n* taquigrafía, estenografía, *f. a* taquigráfico, estenográfico

shortly /'ʃɔrtli/ *adv* dentro de poco, pronto; brevemente, en resumen, en pocas palabras; (curtly) bruscamente, secamente

shortness /'ʃɔrtnɪs/ *n* cortedad, *f;* brevedad, *f;* (of a person) pequeñez, *f;* (lack) falta, *f;* (of memory, sight) cortedad, *f;* (brusqueness) sequedad, brusquedad, *f.* **s. of breath,** falta de aliento, respiración difícil, *f*

shot /ʃɒt/ *n* perdigón, *m; Inf.* perdigones, *m pl;* bala, *f;* (firing) tiro, *m;* (person) tirador (-ra); (stroke, etc.) golpe, *m,* tirada, *f;* (cinema) fotograma, *m. a* (of silk) tornasolado. **at one s.,** de un tiro. **like a s.,** *Fig.* como una bala. **to exchange shots,** tirotearse. **to fire a s.,** disparar un tiro. **to have a s. at,** probar suerte. **s.-gun,** escopeta, *f.* **s. silk,** seda tornasolada, *f*

should /ʃʊd/ *v aux* (expressing future) **I s. like to go to the sea,** Me gustaría ir al mar; (expressing conditional) **I s. like to see them if I could,** Me gustaría verlos si pudiera; (expressing obligation) **You s. go at once,** Debes ir en seguida; (expressing probability) **They s. arrive tomorrow,** Seguramente llegarán mañana; (expressing doubt) **If the moment s. be opportune,** Si el momento fuera oportuno. **I s. just think so!** ¡Ya lo creo! ¡No lo dudo!

shoulder /'ʃouldər/ *n* hombro, *m;* (of mutton) espalda, *f;* (of a hill) falda, *f. vt* echar al hombro, echar sobre sí; (a responsibility) cargar con, hacerse responsable para; (jostle) dar codazos (a). **s. to s.,** hombro a hombro. **S. arms!** ¡Armas al hombro! **s.-blade,** omoplato, *m.* **s.-knot,** charretera, *f.* **s.-pad,** hombrera, *f.* **s.-strap,** *Mil.* dragona, *f;* (of a dress, etc.) tirante, *m;* (of a water carrier, etc.) correón, *m*

shouldered /'ʃouldərd/ *a* de hombros..., de espaldas... **round-s.,** cargado de espaldas

shout /ʃaut/ *vi* gritar, hablar a gritos. *vt* gritar. *n* grito, *m.* **shouts of applause,** aclamaciones, *f pl,* aplausos, *m pl.* **to s. from the housetops,** pregonar a los cuatro vientos. **to s. with laughter,** reírse a carcajadas. **to s. down,** silbar. **to s. out,** gritar

shouting /'ʃautɪŋ/ *n* gritos, *m pl,* vocerío, clamor, *m;* (applause) aclamaciones, *f pl*

shove /ʃʌv/ *vt* empujar; poner. *n* empujón, *m.* **to s. along,** empujar. **to s. aside,** empujar a un lado; apartar a codazos. **to s. away,** rechazar. **to s. back,** hacer retroceder. **to s. forward,** hacer avanzar, empujar hacia adelante. **to s. off,** (a boat) echar afuera. **to s. out,** empujar hacia fuera

shovel /'ʃʌvəl/ *n* pala, *f. vt* traspalar. **s. hat,** sombrero de teja, *m*

show /ʃou/ *vt* mostrar; hacer ver; (disclose) descubrir; revelar; (exhibit) exhibir; (indicate) indicar; (prove) demostrar, probar; (conduct) conducir, llevar, guiar; (explain) explicar; (oneself) presentarse. *vi* mostrarse; verse; parecer. **to s. cause,** mostrar causa. **to s. fight,** ofrecer resistencia. **s. signs of,** dar señales de. **to s. itself,** declararse, asomarse, surgir. **to s. to the door,** acompañar a la puerta. **to s. in,** (a person) hacer entrar, introducir (en). **to s. off,** *vt* exhibir; realzar; (new clothes, etc.) lucir. *vi* darse importancia; pavonearse. **to s. out,** (a person) acompañar a la puerta; (in anger) poner de patitas en la calle. **to s. through,** *vi* trasparentarse. *vt* conducir por. **to s. up,** *vt* invitar a subir; (a fraud, etc.) descubrir; (a swindler) desenmascarar; (defects) revelar. *vi* (stand out) destacarse; (be present) asomarse, asistir

show /ʃou/ *n* (exhibition) exposición, *f;* espectáculo, *m;* (sign) indicio, *m,* señal, *f;* (ostentation) pompa, *f,* aparato, *m,* ostentación, *f;* (appearance) apariencia, *f;* (affair) negocio, *m. vt* **to give the s. away,** echar los títeres a rodar. **to make a s. of,** hacer gala de. **s.-case,** escaparate, *m,* vitrina, *f.* **s. of hands,** votación por manos levantadas, *f.* **s.-room,** salón de muestras, *m*

showdown /'ʃou,daun/ n cartas boca arriba, m
shower /'ʃauər/ n chaparrón, chubasco, m; (of spray, etc.) chorro, m; (of stones, arrows, etc.) lluvia, f; (of honors) cosecha, f, (bridal) despedida de soltera, despedida de soltería, f. vt derramar; rociar; mojar; llover. vi chaparrear, llover. **shower (bath)** ducha, f, Argentina baño de China, f
shower cap n gorro de ducha, m
showery /'ʃauəri/ a lluvioso
showily /'ʃouəli/ adv aparatosamente, con ostentación
showiness /'ʃouɪnɪs/ n ostentación, f; esplendor, m, magnificencia, f
showman /'ʃoumən/ n director de un espectáculo de feria, m; titiritero, m; pregonero, m
showy /'ʃoui/ a vistoso; ostentoso, Lat. Am. also figuroso
shrapnel /'ʃræpnl/ n granada, m, granada de metralla, f
shred /ʃrɛd/ n fragmento, m; (of cloth) jirón, m; brizna, f; Fig. pizca, f. vt desmenuzar. **to tear in shreds,** hacer pedazos
shrew /ʃru/ n Zool. musaraña, f; (woman) fiera, f
shrewd /ʃrud/ a sagaz, perspicaz; prudente; (of the wind) penetrante; (pain) punzante. **to have a s. idea of,** tener una buena idea de. **a s. diplomat,** un fino diplomático
shrewdly /'ʃrudli/ adv sagazmente, con perspicacia; prudentemente
shrewdness /'ʃrudnɪs/ n sagacidad, perspicacia, f; prudencia, f
shrewish /'ʃruɪʃ/ a regañón
shrewishness /'ʃruɪʃnɪs/ n mal genio, m
shriek /ʃrik/ vi chillar, gritar. vt decir a voces, gritar. n chillido, m; grito agudo, m. **shrieks of laughter,** carcajadas, f pl
shrieking /'ʃrikɪŋ/ n gritos, chillidos, m pl
shrift /ʃrɪft/ **to give short,** enviar normala (a), enviar a paseo (a)
shrill /ʃrɪl/ a estridente, agudo
shrillness /'ʃrɪlnɪs/ n estridencia, f
shrimp /ʃrɪmp/ n camarón, m, gamba, f; (small person) Inf. renacuajo. vi pescar camarones
shrine /ʃrain/ n relicario, m; sepulcro de santo, m; templete, m, capilla, f; santuario, m
shrink /ʃrɪŋk/ vi encogerse; contraerse; disminuir, reducirse. vt encoger; reducir, disminuir; desaparecer; disiparse. **I shrank from doing it,** Me repugnaba hacerlo. **to s. away from,** retroceder ante; recular ante; huir de. **to s. back,** recular (ante)
shrinkage /'ʃrɪŋkɪdʒ/ n encogimiento, m; contracción, f; reducción, disminución, f
shrinking /'ʃrɪŋkɪŋ/ a tímido
shrive /ʃraiv/ vt confesar
shrivel /'ʃrɪvəl/ vi avellanarse; (of persons, through old age) acartonarse, apergaminarse; (wither) marchitarse; arrugarse. vt arrugar; secar, marchitar
shroud /ʃraud/ n sudario, m, mortaja, f; Naut. obenque, m. **to wrap in a s.,** amortajar
Shrove Tuesday /ʃrouv/ n martes de carnaval, m
shrub /ʃrʌb/ n arbusto, m; matajo, m
shrubbery /'ʃrʌbəri/ n arbustos, m pl, maleza, f; bosquecillo, m
shrug /ʃrʌg/ vi encogerse de hombros. n encogimiento de hombros, m
shrunken /'ʃrʌŋkən/ a contraído; acartonado, apergaminado; seco, marchito. **shrunken head,** cabeza reducida, f
shudder /'ʃʌdər/ vi estremecerse; vibrar. n estremecimiento, m; escalofrío, m; (of an engine, etc.) vibración, f
shuffle /'ʃʌfəl/ vt (the feet) arrastrar; (scrape) restregar; (cards) barajar; (papers) mezclar. vi arrastrar los pies, arrastrarse; (cards) barajar; Fig. tergiversar. n (of the cards) barajadura, f; Fig. evasiva, f; embuste, m. **to s. along,** andar arrastrando los pies
shuffling /'ʃʌflɪŋ/ n el arrastrar, m, (e.g. the shuffling of chairs, el arrastrar de sillas)
shun /ʃʌn/ vt evitar, rehuir, esquivar
shunt /ʃʌnt/ vt Rail. apartar; Elec. shuntar. vi Rail. hacer maniobras

shunting /'ʃʌntɪŋ/ n (of trains) maniobras, f pl
shut /ʃʌt/ vt and vi cerrar. **to s. again,** volver a cerrar. **to s. down,** vt cerrar; (a machine) parar. vi (of factories, etc.) cerrar. **to s. in,** encerrar; (surround) cercar, rodear. **to s. off,** (water, etc.) cortar; (isolate) aislar (de). **to s. out,** excluir; obstruir, impedir; negar la entrada (a). **to s. up,** vt cerrar; encerrar; Inf. hacer callar (a); vi Inf. callarse, cerrar la boca. **to s. oneself up,** encerrarse
shutter /'ʃʌtər/ n (window) contraventana, f, postigo, m; (of a camera) obturador, m; (of a fireplace) campana (de hogar), f. vt poner contraventanas (a); cerrar los postigos de
shuttle /'ʃʌtl/ n (weaver's, and sewing-machine) lanzadera, f, (airplane service) puente aéreo, m. **s.-cock,** volante, gallito, m
shy /ʃai/ a (of animals) tímido, salvaje; (of persons) huraño, tímido; vergonzoso. vi (of a horse) respingar; (of persons) asustarse (de). vt (a ball, etc.) lanzar. n (of a horse) respingo, m; (of a ball) lanzamiento, m; (try) prueba, tentativa, f. **to fight shy of,** procurar evitar. **to have a shy at,** probar
shyly /'ʃaili/ adv tímidamente; con vergüenza, vergonzosamente
shyness /'ʃainɪs/ n timidez, f; huraña, f; vergüenza, f
Siamese /,saiə'miz/ a siamés. n siamés (-esa) (language) siamés, m. **S. cat,** gato siamés, m
sic /sɪk/ vt atacar; abijar, azuzar (a dog); adv así (in academic prose)
Sicilian /sɪ'sɪlyən/ a and n siciliano (-na)
Sicily /'sɪsəli/ Sicilia, f
sick /sɪk/ a enfermo; mareado. **the s.,** los enfermos. **to be s.,** vomitar; estar enfermo. **to be s. of,** estar harto de. **to feel s.,** sentirse mareado. **to be on the s.-list,** estar enfermo. **s.-bed,** lecho de dolor, m. **s.-headache,** jaqueca, con náuseas, f. **s.-leave,** Mil. permiso por enfermedad, m. **s.-nurse,** enfermera, f
sicken /'sɪkən/ vi caer enfermo, enfermar; (feel sick) marearse; (recoil from) repugnar; (weary of) cansarse (de), aburrirse (de). vt marear; dar asco (a), repugnar; cansar, aburrir. **It sickens me,** Me da asco. **He is sickening for measles,** Muestra síntomas de sarampión
sickening /'sɪkənɪŋ/ a nauseabundo; repugnante; (tedious) fastidioso
sickle /'sɪkəl/ n hoz, segadera, f
sickliness /'sɪklɪnɪs/ n falta de salud, f; náusea, f; (paleness) palidez, f
sickly /'sɪkli/ a enfermizo, achacoso, malucho, Lat. Am. farruto, Central America, Mexico fifiriche; (of places, etc.) malsano; (pale) pálido; débil; (of a smell) nauseabundo; (mawkish) empalagoso
sickness /'sɪknɪs/ n enfermedad, f; mal, m; náusea, f, mareo, m
side /said/ n lado, m; (hand) mano, f; (of a river, etc.) orilla, f, margen, m; (of a person) costado, m; (of an animal) ijada, f; (of a hill) falda, pendiente, ladera, f; (of a ship) banda, f, costado, m; (aspect) aspecto, m; punto de vista, m; (party) partido, grupo, m; (team) equipo, m; (of descent) lado, m. a lateral, de lado; oblicuo. **on all sides,** por todas partes. **on both sides,** por ambos lados. **s. by s.,** lado a lado. **the other s. of the picture,** el revés de la medalla. **to change sides,** cambiar de partido. **to pick sides,** escoger el equipo. **to put on s.,** darse tono, alzar el gallo. **to split one's sides,** desternillarse de risa, reírse a carcajadas. **to s. with,** declararse por, ponerse al lado de, tomar el partido de. **wrong s. out,** al revés. **s.-car,** sidecar, asiento lateral, m. **s.-chain,** Chem. cadena lateral, f. **s.-dish,** entremés, m. **s. door,** puerta lateral, f. **s.-face,** a de perfil. n perfil, m. **s.-glance,** mirada de soslayo, f. **s.-issue,** cuestión secundaria, f. **s.-line,** negocio accesorio, m; ocupación secundaria, f; Rail. vía secundaria, f. **s.-saddle,** silla de señora, silla de montar de lado, f. **s.-show,** (at a fair) barraca, f, puesto de feria, m; exhibición secundaria, f; función secundaria, f. **s.-track,** n Rail. apartadero, m. vt desviar (de), apartar (de). **s.-view,** perfil, m. **s.-walk,** acera, f, Mexico banqueta, f, elsewhere in Lat. Am. andén m, vereda f. **s.-whiskers,** patillas, f pl

sidelight /'said,lait/ n luz lateral, f; (on a ship) ojo de buey, m; *Fig.* información incidental, f

sidelong /'said,lɔŋ/ adv de lado, lateralmente; (of glances) de soslayo. a oblicuo

side road n camino lateral, m

sideways /'said,weiz/ adv oblicuamente, de lado; (edgewise) de soslayo. a de soslayo

siding /'saidiŋ/ n Rail. apartadero, m

sidle /'saidl/ vi andar (or ir) de lado. **to s. up to,** acercarse servilmente a; arrimarse (a)

siege /sidʒ/ n asedio, sitio, cerco, m. **to lay s. to,** poner cerco (a), sitiar, asediar cercar. **to raise a s.,** levantar un sitio

sienna /si'ɛnə/ n tierra de siena natural, f. **burnt s.,** tierra de siena tostada, f

sieve /sɪv/ n cedazo, tamiz, m, criba, f, *Lat. Am.* arnero, m, vt tamizar, cerner, cribar

sift /sɪft/ vt (sieve) cerner, cribar; (sugar, etc.) salpicar (con); (a question) escudriñar, examinar minuciosamente

sifting /'sɪftɪŋ/ n cribado, m; (of a question) investigación minuciosa, f; pl **siftings,** cerniduras, f pl

sigh /sai/ vi suspirar; (of the wind) susurrar. n suspiro, m; (of the wind) susurro, m. **to s. for,** suspirar por; lamentar

sighing /'saiɪŋ/ n suspiros, m pl; (of the wind) susurro, m

sight /sait/ n vista, f; visión, f; espectáculo, m; (fright) estantigua, f. vt ver, divisar; (aim) apuntar. **front s.,** (of guns) alza, f. **short s.,** (of eyes) vista corta, f. **at first s.,** a primera vista. **in s.,** a la vista. **in s. of,** a vista de. **out of s.,** que no está a la vista; perdido de vista. **Out of s., out of mind,** Ojos que no ven, corazón que no siente. **to be lost to s.,** perderse de vista. **to lose s. of,** perder de vista (a). **to catch a s. of,** vislumbrar. **to come in s.,** aparecer, asomarse. **to know by s.,** conocer de vista (a). **s.-reading,** lectura a primera vista, f

sightly /'saitli/ a hermoso; deleitable

sightseeing /'sait,siiŋ/ n turismo, m. **to go s.,** visitar los monumentos, ver los puntos de interés

sightseer /'sait,siər/ n curioso (-sa); turista, mf

sign /sain/ n señal, f; seña, f; indicio, m; (of the zodiac and *Mus.*) signo, m; marca, f; *Eccl.* símbolo, m; (of a shop, etc.) muestra, f, rótulo, m; (symptom) síntoma, m. vt firmar; indicar; *Eccl.* persignar. **as a s. of,** en señal de. **to converse by signs,** hablar por señas. **to make the s. of the cross over,** santiguar. **to show signs (of),** dar señas (de); indicar. **s.-painter,** pintor de muestras, m

signal /'sɪgnl/ n señal, f. vt señalar; hacer señas (a). vi hacer señales. a insigne, notable. **fog-s.,** señal de niebla, f. **landing s.,** *Aer.* señal de aterrizaje, f. **to give the s. for,** dar la señal para. **s.-box,** garita de señales, f. **s. code,** *Naut.* código de señales, m

signaler /'sɪgnlər/ n señalador, m

signalize /'sɪgnl,aiz/ vt señalar, distinguir

signalman /'sɪgnl,mæn/ n Rail. guardavía, m

signatory /'sɪgnə,tɔri/ a n signatario (-ia)

signature /'sɪgnətʃər/ n firma, f; (Mus. and Print.) signatura, f

signboard /'sain,bɔrd/ n letrero, m, muestra, f

signet /'sɪgnɪt/ n sello, m. **s.-ring,** anillo de sello, m

significance /sɪg'nɪfɪkəns/ n significación, f, significado, m; importancia, f

significant /sɪg'nɪfɪkənt/ a significativo, significante; expresivo; importante

significantly /sɪg'nɪfɪkəntli/ adv significativamente; expresivamente

signify /'sɪgnə,fai/ vt significar; querer decir; importar. vi significar, tener importancia; importar

signpost /'sain,poust/ n indicador de dirección, m

silage /'sailɪdʒ/ n forraje conservado en silo, m

silence /'sailəns/ n silencio, m, interj ¡silencio! vt hacer callar, imponer silencio (a); silenciar. **to keep s.,** guardar silencio, callarse. **to pass over in s.,** pasar en silencio (por), pasar por alto de. **S. gives consent,** Quien calla otorga

silencer /'sailənsər/ n (of fire-arms) silencioso, m; *Auto.* silenciador, silencioso, m

silent /'sailənt/ a silencioso. **to become s.,** enmu

decer; callar. **to remain s.,** callarse, guardar silencio; permanecer silencioso. **s. partner,** n socio (-ia) comanditario (-ia)

silent film, silent movie n película muda, f

silently /'sailəntli/ adv silenciosamente, en silencio

silhouette /,sɪlu'ɛt/ n silueta, f. vt representar en silueta; destacar. **in s.,** en silueta. **to be silhouetted against the sky,** destacarse contra el sielo

silica /'sɪlɪkə/ n sílice, f

silk /sɪlk/ n seda, f, a de seda. **artificial s.,** seda artificial, f. **floss s.,** seda ocal, f. **sewing s.,** seda de coser, f. **twist s.,** seda cordelada, f. **as smooth as s.,** como una seda. **s. growing,** sericultura, f. **s. hat,** sombrero de copa, m. **s. merchandise,** sedería, f. **s. stocking,** media de seda, f

silken /'sɪlkən/ a de seda; sedoso

silkiness /'sɪlkinɪs/ n carácter sedoso, m; suavidad, f

silk-screen process /'sɪlk,skrin/ n imprenta por tamiz, imprenta serigráfica, imprenta tamigráfica, impresión con estarcido de seda, f, proceso tamigráfico, m; serigrafía, tamigrafía, f

silkworm /'sɪlk,wɜrm/ n gusano de seda, m

silky /'sɪlki/ a sedoso; (of wine) suave

sill /sɪl/ n (of a window) alféizar, antepecho, m; (of a door) umbral, m

silliness /'sɪlinɪs/ n tontería, estupidez, f

silly /'sɪli/ a tonto, estúpido; imbécil, *Central America also* azurumbado. n tonto (-ta)

silo /'sailou/ n silo, m

silt /sɪlt/ n aluvión, m, sedimentación, f. **to s. up,** vt cegar (or obstruir) con aluvión. vi cegarse con aluvión

silver /'sɪlvər/ n plata, f. a de plata; argénteo; (of the voice, etc.) argentino. vt platear; (mirrors) azogar; (hair) blanquear. **s. birch,** abedul, m. **s. fox,** zorro plateado, m. **s.-gray,** gris perla, m. **s.-haired,** de pelo entrecano. **s.-paper,** papel de estaño, m. **s.-plate,** n vajilla de plata, f. vt platear. **s.-tongued,** de pico de oro; de voz argentina. **s. wedding,** bodas de plata, f pl

silversmith /'sɪlvər,smɪθ/ n platero, m. **silversmith's shop,** platería, f

silvery /'sɪlvəri/ a plateado, argentado; (of sounds) argentino

simian /'sɪmiən/ a símico

similar /'sɪmələr/ a parecido (a), semejante (a); similar; *Geom.* semejante. **to be s. to,** asemejarse (a), parecerse (a)

similarity /,sɪmə'lærɪti/ n parecido, m, semejanza, f; similitud, f

similarly /'sɪmələrli/ adv de un modo parecido, asimismo

simile /'sɪməli/ n símil, m

simmer /'sɪmər/ vi hervir a fuego lento; *Fig.* estar a punto de estallar. **to s. down,** *Fig.* moderarse poco a poco. **to s. over,** *Fig.* estallar

simper /'sɪmpər/ vi sonreírse bobamente

simpering /'sɪmpərɪŋ/ n sonrisilla tonta, f

simperingly /'sɪmpərɪŋli/ adv con sonrisa necia

simple /'sɪmpəl/ a sencillo; simple; ingenuo, inocente; crédulo; (humble) humilde; (mere) mero. **s.-hearted,** inocente, cándido, sin malicia. **s.-minded,** ingenuo; crédulo. **s.-mindedness,** ingenuidad, f; credulidad, f

simpleton /'sɪmpəltən/ n primo (-ma); papanatas, m, tonto (-ta)

simplicity /sɪm'plɪsɪti/ n sencillez, f; simplicidad, candidez, f

simplifiable /,sɪmplə'faiəbəl/ a simplificable

simplification /,sɪmpləfɪ'keiʃən/ n simplificación, f

simplify /'sɪmplə,fai/ vt simplificar

simply /'sɪmpli/ adv sencillamente, simplemente, meramente; absolutamente

simulacrum /,sɪmyə'leikrəm/ n simulacro, m

simulate /'sɪmyə,leit/ vt fingir, aparentar, simular

simulation /,sɪmyə'leiʃən/ n simulación, f, fingimiento, m

simultaneous /,saiməl'teiniəs/ a simultáneo

simultaneously /,saiməl'teiniəsli/ adv simultáneamente; al mismo tiempo (que)

simultaneousness /ˌsaiməl'teiniəsnɪs/ *n* simultaneidad, *f*

sin /sɪn/ *n* pecado, *m*, *vi* pecar; faltar (a)

since /sɪns/ *adv* desde entonces, desde (que). *prep* desde. *conjunc* desde que; ya que, puesto que. **a long time s.,** hace mucho. **not long s.,** hace poco. **How long is it s....?** ¿Cuánto tiempo hace que...? **s. then,** desde entonces

sincere /sɪn'sɪər/ *a* sincero

sincerely /sɪn'sɪərli/ *adv* sinceramente. **Yours s.,** Su afectísimo...

sincerity /sɪn'sɛrɪti/ *n* sinceridad, *f*

sine /sain/ *n Math.* seno, *m*

sinecure /'saini,kyʊr/ *n* canonjía, sinecura, *f*, empleo de aviador (Mexican slang), *m*

sinew /'sɪnyu/ *n* tendón, *m*; *pl* **sinews,** nervio, *m*, fuerza, *f*

sinewy /'sɪnyui/ *a* (stringy) fibroso; musculoso, nervudo

sinful /'sɪnfəl/ *a* (of persons) pecador; (of thoughts, acts) pecaminoso

sinfulness /'sɪnfəlnɪs/ *n* pecado, *m*; culpabilidad, perversidad, maldad, *f*

sing /sɪŋ/ *vi* cantar; (of the ears) zumbar; (of wind, water) murmurar, susurrar; (of a cat) ronronear. *vt* cantar. **to s. a child to sleep,** dormir a un niño cantando. **to s. another song,** *Inf.* bajar el tono. **to s. small,** hacerse el chiquito. **to s. the praises of,** hacer las alabanzas de. **to s. out,** vocear, gritar. **s.-song,** *n* canturía, *f*; concierto improvisado, *m*. *a* monótono

Singapore /'sɪŋgə,pɔr/ Singapur, *m*

singe /sɪndʒ/ *vt* chamuscar; (a fowl) aperdigar; (hair) quemar las puntas de los cabellos

singer /'sɪŋər/ *n* cantor (-ra); (professional) cantante, *mf*; (bird) ave cantora, *f*

singing /'sɪŋɪŋ/ *n* canto, *m*; (of the ears) zumbido, *m*. *a* cantante. **s.-bird,** ave cantora, *f*. **s.-master,** maestro de cantar, *m*

single /'sɪŋgəl/ *a* único; sencillo; solo; simple; (individual) particular; individual; (unmarried) soltero. *n* (tennis) juego sencillo, individual, *m*. **in s. file,** de reata. **to s. out,** escoger; singularizar. **s. bed,** cama de monja, *f*. **s. bedroom,** habitación individual, habitación con una sola cama, *f*. **s.-breasted,** (of coats) recto. **s. combat,** combate singular, *m*. **s. entry,** *Com.* partida simple, *f*. **s.-handed,** de una mano; para una sola persona; sin ayuda, solo, en solitario. **s.-minded,** sin doblez, sincero de una sola idea. **s. ticket,** billete sencillo, *m*

singleness /'sɪŋgəlnɪs/ *n* celibato, *m*, soltería, *f*. **with s. of purpose,** con un solo objeto

single room *n Mexico* cuarto sencillo, *m*

singlet /'sɪŋglɪt/ *n* camiseta, *f*

singly /'sɪŋgli/ *adv* separadamente, uno a uno; a solas, solo; sin ayuda

singular /'sɪŋgyələr/ *a and n* singular, *m*

singularity /ˌsɪŋgyə'lærɪti/ *n* singularidad, *f*

singularly /'sɪŋgyələrli/ *adv* singularmente

sinister /'sɪnəstər/ *a* siniestro

sink /sɪŋk/ *vi* ir al fondo; bajar; hundirse; (of ships) irse a pique, naufragar; sumergirse; disminuir; caer (en); penetrar; (of persons, fires) morir; (of the sun, etc.) ponerse. *vt* (a ship) echar a pique; sumergir; hundir; dejar caer; bajar; (wells) cavar; reducir, disminuir; (invest) invertir; (one's identity, etc.) tener secreto; (differences) olvidar; (engrave) grabar. **My heart sank,** Se me cayeron las alas del corazón. **He sank to his knees,** Cayó de rodillas. **He is sinking fast,** Está en las últimas. **Their words began to s. in,** Sus palabras empezaban a tener efecto (or hacer mella). **I found her sunk in thought,** La encontré ensimismada. **to s. one's voice,** bajar la voz. **to s. down on a chair,** dejarse caer en una silla. **to s. into misery,** caer en la miseria. **to s. under,** (a responsibility, etc.) estar agobiado bajo

sink /sɪŋk/ *n* (kitchen) fregadero, *Chile, Mexico also* lavaplatos, *m*; sumidero, *m*, sentina, *f*. **s. of iniquity,** sentina, *f*

sinker /'sɪŋkər/ *n* (engraver) grabador (-ra); (of a fishing line) plomada, *f*

sinking /'sɪŋkɪŋ/ *n* hundimiento, *m*; (of the sun)

puesta, *f*; (of wells) cavadura, *f*; sumergimiento, *m*. **the s. of a boat,** el hundimiento de un buque. **with s. heart,** con la muerte en el alma. **s. fund,** fondo de amortización, *m*

sinless /'sɪnlɪs/ *a* sin pecado, inocente, puro

sinner /'sɪnər/ *n* pecador (-ra)

sinuous /'sɪnyuəs/ *a* sinuoso, tortuoso; flexible, ágil

sinus /'sainəs/ *n* (*Anat.* etc.) seno, *m*

sip /sɪp/ *vt* sorber; (wine) saborear, paladear. *n* sorbo, *m*

siphon /'saifən/ *n* sifón, *m*, *vt* sacar con sifón

sir /sər/ *n* señor, *m*; (British title) sir. **Dear s.,** Muy Señor mío

sire /saiər/ *n* (to a monarch) Señor, *m*; (father) padre, *m*; (stallion) semental, *m*. *vt* procrear, engendrar

siren /'sairən/ *n* sirena, *f*. **s. suit,** mono, *m*

sirloin /'sərlɔin/ *n* solomillo, *Mexico* diezmillo, *m*

sirocco /sə'rɒkou/ *n* siroco, *m*

sister /'sɪstər/ *n* hermana, *f*; (before nun's christian name) Sor; (hospital) hermana del hospital, *f*; enfermera, *f*. **s. language,** lengua hermana, *f*. **s. ship,** buque gemelo, *m*. **s.-in-law,** cuñada, hermana política, *f*. **S. of Mercy,** Hermana de la Caridad, *f*

sisterhood /'sɪstər,hʊd/ *n* hermandad, *f*; comunidad de monjas, *f*

sisterly /'sɪstərli/ *a* de hermana

sit /sɪt/ *vi* sentarse; estar sentado; (of birds) posarse; (of hens) empollar; (in Parliament, etc.) ser diputado; (of a committee, etc.) celebrar sesión; (on a committee, etc.) formar parte de; (function) funcionar; (of garments, food, and *Fig.*) sentar. **to sit a horse,** mantenerse a caballo; montar a caballo. **to sit oneself,** sentarse, tomar asiento. **to sit by,** (a person) sentarse (or estar sentado) al lado de. **to sit for** (a portrait) servir de modelo para; hacerse retratar. **to sit tight,** no moverse. **to sit down,** sentarse; (besiege) sitiar. **to sit on,** sentarse (en or sobre); (eggs) empollar; (a committee, etc.) formar parte de; (investigate) investigar; (snub) dejar aplastado (a). **to sit out,** quedarse hasta el fin (de). **to sit out a dance,** conversar un baile. **to sit up,** incorporarse en la cama; tenerse derecho; (at night) velar; (of dogs, etc.) pedir. **to sit up and take notice,** abrir los ojos. **to sit up in bed,** incorporarse en la cama. **to sit up late,** estar de pie hasta muy tarde

sit-down strike /'sɪt,daun/ *n* huelga de brazos caídos, huelga de sentados, *f*

site /sait/ *n* sitio, local, *m*; (for building) solar, *m*

sitting /'sɪtɪŋ/ *n* asentada, *f*; (of Parliament, etc.) sesión, *f*; (for a portrait) estadia, *f*; (of eggs) nidada, *f*. **at a s.,** de una asentada. **s.-room,** sala de estar, *f*

situated /'sɪtʃu,eitɪd/ *a* situado. **How is he s.?** ¿Cómo está situado? ¿Cuál es su situación?

situation /ˌsɪtʃu'eifən/ *n* situación, *f*; (job) empleo, *m*

six /sɪks/ *a and n* seis, *m*. **It is six o'clock,** Son las seis. **Everything is at sixes and sevens,** Todo está en desorden. **six-foot,** de seis pies. **six hundred,** seiscientos (-as)

sixfold /'sɪks,fould/ *a* séxtuplo

sixteen /'sɪks'tin/ *a and n* diez y seis, dieciséis, *m*. **John is s.,** Juan tiene dieciséis años

sixteenth /'sɪks'tinθ/ *a* décimosexto; (of the month) (el) diez y seis; (of monarch) diez y seis. *n* diecisei-savo, *m*

sixth /sɪksθ/ *a* sexto; (of the month) (el) seis; (of monarchs) sexto. *n* seisavo, *m*; sexta parte, *f*; *Mus.* sexta, *f*. **Henry the S.,** Enrique sexto. **May the s.,** el seis de mayo

sixtieth /'sɪkstiɪθ/ *a* sexagésimo. *n* sesentavo, *m*; sexagésima parte, *f*

sixty /'sɪksti/ *a and n* sesenta *m*. **John has turned s.,** Juan ha pasado los sesenta

sizable /'saizəbəl/ *a* bastante grande

size /saiz/ *n* tamaño, *m*; dimensión, *f*; (height) altura, *f*; (measurement) medida, *f*; talle, *m*; (in gloves, etc.) número, *m*; (glue) cola, *f*. *vt* clasificar por tamaños; (glaze, etc.) encolar. **to s. up,** tomar las medidas (a).

sizzle /'sɪzəl/ *vi* chisporrotear, chirriar. *n* chisporroteo, chirrido, *m*

skate /skeit/ *n* patín, *m*; *Ichth.* raya, *f*, *vi* patinar

skateboard /'skeit,bɔrd/ *n* patín, *m*

skater /'skeitər/ n patinador (-ra)
skating /'skeitŋ/ n patinaje, m. **s. rink,** sala de patinar, f; pista de hielo, pista de patinar, f, patinadero, m
skein /skein/ n madeja, f
skeleton /'skɛlɪtn̩/ n esqueleto, m; (of a building) armadura, f; (of a literary work) esquema, m. **s. key,** ganzúa, f
sketch /skɛtʃ/ n croquis, apunte, m; (for a literary work) esbozo, esquema, m; (article) cuadro, artículo, m; descripción, f; Theat. entremés, sainete, m. vt dibujar; esbozar, bosquejar; trazar; describir. **s.-book,** álbum de croquis, m
sketchily /'skɛtʃəli/ adv incompletamente
sketching /'skɛtʃɪŋ/ n arte de dibujar, mf. **He likes s.,** Le gusta dibujar
sketchy /'skɛtʃi/ a bosquejado; incompleto; escaso
skewer /'skyuər/ n broqueta, f, vt espetar
ski /ski/ n esquí, m, vi esquiar
skid /skɪd/ n (of a vehicle) patinazo, m, vi patinar
skidding /'skɪdɪŋ/ n patinaje, m
skier /'skiər/ n esquiador (-ra), mf
skiff /skɪf/ n esquife, m
skiing /'skiɪŋ/ n patinaje sobre la nieve, m, el esquiar. **to go s.,** ir a esquiar
skill /skɪl/ n habilidad, f
skilled /skɪld/ a hábil; experto
skilled worker n obrero calificado, m
skillful /'skɪlfəl/ a hábil
skim /skɪm/ vt espumar; (milk) desnatar, Lat. Am. descremar; (touch lightly) deslizarse sobre, rozar; (a book) hojear
skimp /skɪmp/ vt escatimar; escasear; (work) frangollar. vi ser parsimonioso
skimpy /'skɪmpi/ a escaso
skin /skɪn/ n tez, f, cutis, m; piel, f; (of fruit) pellejo, m, piel, f; (for wine) odre, pellejo, m; (on milk) espuma, f. vt despellejar; pelar, mondar; (graze) hacerse daño (a); Inf. desollar. **next to one's s.,** sobre la piel. **to s. over,** cicatrizarse. **to have a thin s.,** Fig. ser muy susceptible. **to save one's s.,** salvar el pellejo. **s.-deep,** superficial. **s.-tight,** escurrido, muy ajustado
skinflint /'skɪn,flɪnt/ n avaro (-ra)
skinny /'skɪni/ a flaco, descarnado, magro
skip /skɪp/ vi retozar, brincar, saltar; saltar a la comba; (bolt) largarse, escaparse. vt saltar; (a book) hojear; (omit) omitir; pasar por alto de. n brinco, pequeño salto, m
skipper /'skɪpər/ n Naut. patrón, m; (Inf. and Sports.) capitán, m
skirmish /'skɜrmɪʃ/ vi escaramuzar. n escaramuza, f
skirt /skɜrt/ n falda, f; (edge) margen, borde, m, orilla, f; (of a jacket, etc.) faldón, m. vt ladear; (hug) rodear, ceñir
skit /skɪt/ n sátira, f; parodia, f
skittish /'skɪtɪʃ/ a (of a horse) retozón; (of persons) frívolo; caprichoso
skittle /'skɪtl̩/ n bolo, m; pl **skittles,** juego de bolos, m. **s. alley,** pista de bolos, bolera, f
skulk /skʌlk/ vi estar en acecho; esconderse; rondar
skull /skʌl/ n cráneo, m; calavera, f. **s.-cap,** gorro, casquete, m; (for ecclesiastics) solideo, m
skunk /skʌŋk/ n Zool. mofeta, f, chingue, mapurite, yaguré, zorrillo, zorrino, zorro hediondo, m
sky /skai/ n cielo, m. **to praise to the skies,** poner en los cuernos de la luna. **s.-blue,** n azul celeste, m. a de color azul celeste, cerúleo. **s.-high,** hasta las nubes, hasta el cielo. **s.-line,** horizonte, m. **s.-scraper,** rascacielos, m. **s.-sign,** anuncio luminoso, m
skylight /'skai,lait/ n claraboya, f, tragaluz, m
slab /slæb/ n bloque, m; losa, f, Lat. Am. also laja, plancha, f
slack /slæk/ a lento; flojo; (lazy) perezoso; negligente, descuidado; Com. encalmado; débil. vi ser perezoso. **the s. season,** la estación muerta. **to be s. in one's work,** ser negligente en el trabajo. **to s. off,** disminuir sus esfuerzos; dejar de trabajar
slacken /'slækən/ vt and vi aflojar; disminuir, reducir. **The wind slackened,** El viento amainaba, El viento

aflojaba. **to s. one's efforts,** disminuir sus esfuerzos. **to s. speed,** disminuir la velocidad
slackening /'slækənɪŋ/ n aflojamiento, m; disminución, f
slacker /'slækər/ n gandul (-la)
slackness /'slæknɪs/ n flojedad, f; pereza, falta de energía, f; negligencia, f; Com. desanimación, f
slacks /slæks/ n pl pantalones, m pl
slake /sleik/ vt (one's thirst and lime) apagar; satisfacer
slam /slæm/ vt cerrar de golpe; golpear. n (of a door) portazo, m; golpe, m; (cards) capote, m. **He went out and slammed the door,** Salió dando un portazo
slander /'slændər/ n calumnia, f, vt calumniar
slanderer /'slændərər/ n calumniador (-ra)
slanderous /'slændərəs/ a calumnioso
slang /slæŋ/ n argot, m, jerga, f, vt poner como un trapo (a), llenar de insultos
slant /slænt/ vi estar al sesgo; inclinarse; ser oblicuo. vt inclinar. n inclinación, f; oblicuidad, f. **on the s.,** inclinado; oblicuo
slanting /'slæntɪŋ/ a al sesgo, inclinado; oblicuo
slap /slæp/ vt pegar con la mano. n bofetada, f; palmada, Lat. Am. cachetada, f. **to s. on the back,** golpear en la espalda. **s.-dash,** (of persons) irresponsable, descuidado; (of work) chapucero, sin cuidado
slash /slæʃ/ vt (gash, also sleeves, etc.) acuchillar; cortar; (with a whip) dar latigazos (a). n cuchillada, f; corte, m; latigazo, m
slashing /'slæʃɪŋ/ a mordaz, severo
slat /slæt/ n tablilla, f, vi (of sails) dar zapatazos, zapatear
slate /sleit/ n pizarra, f, esquisto, m; (for roofs and for writing) pizarra, f, vt (a roof) empizarrar; (censure) criticar severamente, censurar. **s.-colored,** apizarrado. **s. pencil,** pizarrín, m. **s. quarry,** pizarrería, f, pizarral, m
slater /'sleitər/ n pizarrero, m
slating /'sleitɪŋ/ n empizarrado, m; (criticism) crítica severa, censura, f; (scolding) peluca, f
slattern /'slætərn/ n pazpuerca, f
slatternly /'slætərnli/ a desgarbado, desaliñado
slaughter /'slɔtər/ n matanza, f; carnicería, f. vt (animals) sacrificar, matar; matar, hacer una carnicería de. **s.-house,** matadero, m
slaughterer /'slɔtərər/ n jifero, carnicero, m
Slav /slɑv, slæv/ a and n eslavo (-va)
slave /sleiv/ n esclavo (-va). vi trabajar mucho. **white s. traffic,** trata de blancas, f. **s.-bangle,** esclava, f. **s.-driver,** capataz de esclavos, m; sayón de esclavos, m. **s.-trade,** trata de esclavos, f
slaver /'sleivər/ n negrero, m
slaver /'slævər/ vi babear. n baba, f
slavering /'slævərɪŋ/ a baboso
slavery /'sleivəri/ n esclavitud, f; trabajo muy arduo, m
slavish /'sleivɪʃ/ a de esclavo; servil
slavishly /'sleivɪʃli/ adv como esclava; servilmente
Slavonic /slə'vɒnɪk/ a eslavo. n (language) eslavo, m, lengua eslava, f
slay /slei/ vt matar; asesinar
slayer /'sleiər/ n matador (-ra); asesino, mf
slaying /'sleiɪŋ/ n matanza, f; asesinato, m
sled /slɛd/ n trineo, m, rastra, f
sledge /slɛdʒ/ n trineo, m. vi ir en trineo. vt transportar por trineo. **s.-hammer,** acotillo, m
sleek /slik/ a liso, lustroso; (of general appearance) pulcro, bien aseado, elegante; (of manner) obsequioso
sleekness /'sliknɪs/ n lustre, m, lisura, f; (of an animal) gordura, f, elegancia, f
sleep /slip/ n sueño, m. vi dormir; reposar, descansar. vt dormir. **a deep s.,** un sueño pesado. **He walks in his s.,** Es un sonámbulo. **to court s.,** conciliar el sueño. **to go to s.,** dormirse; entumecerse. **My foot has gone to s.,** Se me ha dormido (or Se me ha entumecido) el pie. **to send a person to s.,** adormecer. **to s. like a top,** dormir como un lirón. **to s. oneself sober,** dormir la mona. **to s. in,** dormir tarde; dormir en casa. **to s. off,** (a cold, etc.) cu-

rarse... durmiendo; (drunkenness) dormirla. **to s. on,** *vt* (consider) dormir sobre, consultar con la almohada. *vi* seguir durmiendo. **to s. out,** dormir fuera de casa; dormir al aire libre

sleeper /'slipər/ *n* durmiente, *mf*; *Rail.* traviesa, *f*; (on a train) coche cama, *m*. **to be a bad s.,** dormir mal. **to be a good s.,** dormir bien.

sleepily /'slipəli/ *adv* soñolientamente

sleepiness /'slipinis/ *n* somnolencia, *f*; letargo, *m*

sleeping /'slipiŋ/ *a* durmiente. *n* el dormir. **between s. and waking,** entre duerme y vela. **s.-bag,** saco-cama, *m*. **s.-car,** coche camas, *m*. **s.-draft,** narcótico, *m*. **s. partner,** *n* socio (-ia) comanditario (-ia). **s. sickness,** enfermedad del sueño, *f*

sleepless /'sliplis/ *a* (of persons) insomne, desvelado; (unremitting) incansable; (of the sea, etc.) en perpetuo movimiento. **to spend a s. night,** pasar una noche en vela, pasar una noche toledana, pasar una noche sin dormir

sleeplessness /'sliplisnis/ *n* insomnio, *m*

sleepwalker /'slip,wɔkər/ *n* sonámbulo (-la)

sleepwalking /'slip,wɔkiŋ/ *n* sonambulismo, *m*

sleepy /'slipi/ *a* soñoliento; letárgico. **to be s.,** tener sueño. **s.-head,** lirón, *m*, marmota, *f*

sleet /slit/ *n* aguanieve, cellisca, nevisca, *f*, *vi* caer aguanieve, cellisquear, neviscar

sleeve /sliv/ *n* manga, *f*; (of a hose pipe, etc.) manguera, *f*; *Mech.* manguito, *m*. **to have something up one's s.,** traer algo en la manga

sleeved /slivd/ *a* con mangas...; de... manga(s)

sleeveless /'slivlis/ *a* sin manga. **s. shirt** *Lat. Am.* cusma, *f*

sleigh /slei/ *n* trineo, *m*, *vi* ir en trineo

sleight of hand /sleit/ *n* prestidigitación, *f*; juego de manos, *m*

slender /'slɛndər/ *a* delgado; esbelto; tenue; escaso; pequeño; ligero. **Their means are very s.,** Sus recursos son muy escasos. **It is a very s. hope,** Es una esperanza muy remota

slenderness /'slɛndərnis/ *n* delgadez, *f*; esbeltez, *f*; tenuidad, *f*; escasez, *f*

sleuth /sluθ/ *n* (dog) sabueso, *m*; *Inf.* detective, *m*

slice /slais/ *n* lonja, tajada, *f*; (of fruit) raja, *f*; (of bread, etc.) rebanada, *f*; (share) parte, porción, *f*; (for fish, etc.) pala, *f*. *vt* cortar en tajadas, etc.; rajar; cortar

slick /slik/ *a* hábil, listo

slide /slaid/ *vi* deslizarse, resbalar; (over a question) pasar por alto de; (into a habit, etc.) caer (en). *n* resbalón, *m*; pista de hielo, *f*; (chute) tobogán, *m*; (of a microscope) portaobjetos, *m*; (lantern) diapositiva, *f*; (for the hair) pasador, *m*; (of rock, etc.) desprendimiento, *m*; *Mech.* guía, *f*. **to let things s.,** dejar rodar la bola. **s.-rule,** regla de cálculo, *f*

sliding /'slaidiŋ/ *a* resbaladizo; corredizo; movible. **s.-door,** puerta corrediza, puerta de corradera, *f*. **s.-roof,** techo corredizo, *m*. **s.-scale,** escala graduada, *f*. **s.-seat,** asiento movible, *m*; (in a rowing-boat) bancada corrediza, *f*

slight /slait/ *a* delgado; débil, frágil; ligero; (small) pequeño; escaso; (trivial) insignificante, poco importante. *vt* desairar, despreciar; *Mexico* descolar. *n* desaire, desprecio, *m*; falta de respeto, *f*

slighting /'slaitiŋ/ *a* despreciativo, de desprecio

slightingly /'slaitiŋli/ *adv* con desprecio

slightly /'slaitli/ *adv* ligeramente; poco. **I only know her s.,** La conozco muy poco. **s. built,** de talle delgado

slightness /'slaitnis/ *n* (slimness) delgadez, *f*; ligereza, *f*; (triviality) poca importancia, insignificancia, *f*

slim /slim/ *a* delgado; escaso. *vi* adelgazarse. **He has very s. chances of success,** Tiene muy pocas posibilidades de conseguir el éxito

slime /slaim/ *n* légamo, limo, lodo, cieno, *m*; (of a snail) limazo, *m*; *Fig.* cieno, *m*

sliminess /'slaiminis/ *n* limosidad, *f*; viscosidad, *f*

slimness /'slimnis/ *n* delgadez, *f*; escasez, *f*

slimy /'slaimi/ *a* limoso, legamoso; pecinoso, viscoso; (of persons) rastrero, servil

sling /sliŋ/ *vt* arrojar, lanzar; tirar con honda; (a

sword, etc.) suspender; (lift) embragar; (a limb) poner en cabestrillo. *n* (for missiles) honda, *f*; *Naut.* balso, *m*; (for a limb) cabestrillo, *m*, charpa, *f*

slink /sliŋk/ *vi* (away, off) escurrirse, escabullirse

slip /slip/ *vi* resbalar, deslizar; (stumble) resbalar, tropezar; (fall) caer; (out of place) salirse; (become untied) desatarse; (steal away) escabullirse; (glide) deslizarse; (of years) correr, pasar; (skid) patinar. *vt* deslizar; (garments, shoes) ponerse; (dogs, cables) soltar; (an arm around, etc.) pasar; *Rail.* desacoplar; (escape) escaparse de; (free oneself of) librarse de. *n* resbalón, *m*; (skid) patinazo, *m*; (stumble) tropezón, traspié, *m*; (oversight) inadvertencia, *f*; (mistake) falta, equivocación, *f*; (moral lapse) desliz, *m*; (petticoat) combinación, *f*; (cover) funda, *f*; *Bot.* vástago, *m*; *Print.* galerada, *f*; (of paper) papeleta, *f*; *pl* **slips,** *Naut.* anguilas, *f pl*. **It slipped my memory,** Se me fue de la memoria. **There's many a s. 'twixt the cup and the lip,** Del dicho al hecho hay muy gran trecho, De la mano a la boca desaparece la sopa. **to give (someone) the slip,** escaparse de. **You ought not to let the opportunity s.,** No debes perder la oportunidad. **to let s. a secret,** revelar un secreto. **to let s. an exclamation,** soltar (dar) una exclamación. **to s. into,** colarse en, deslizarse en. **to s. into,** colarse en, deslizarse en. **to s. into one's clothes,** vestirse rápidamente. **to s. on,** (a garment) ponerse. **to s. out,** salir a hurtadillas; escaparse; (of information) divulgarse. **s. of a boy,** mozalbete, joven imberbe, *m*. **s. of the tongue,** error de lengua, *m*. **s.-knot,** nudo corredizo, *m*

slipcover /'slip,kʌvər/ *n* cubierta, cubierta para muebles, funda, funda para muebles, *f*

slipper /'slipər/ *n* babucha, chinela, *f*, pantuflo, *m*; (heelless) chancleta, *f*; (dancing) zapatilla de baile, *f*. **s.-shaped,** achinelado

slippered /'slipərd/ *a* en zapatillas

slippery /'slipəri/ *a* resbaladizo; poco firme, inestable; (of persons) informal, sin escrúpulos

slipshod /'slip,ʃɒd/ *a* descuidado, negligente; poco correcto

slit /slit/ *vt* cortar; hender, rajar; (the throat) degollar. *n* cortadura, *f*; resquicio, *f*. **to s. open,** abrir de un tajo

slither /'sliðər/ *vi* resbalar; deslizarse

sliver /'slivər/ *n* raja, *f*; (of wood) astilla, *f*; (of cloth) tira, *f*

slobber /'slɒbər/ *vi* babear; (blubber) gimotear, *n* baba, *f*

sloe /slou/ *n* (fruit) endrina, *f*; (tree) endrino, *m*. **s.-colored,** endrino. **s.-eyed,** con ojos de mora

slog /slɒg/ *vt* golpear duramente. **to s. away,** batirse el cobre, trabajar como un negro

slogan /'slougən/ *n* grito de batalla, *m*; reclamo, *m*; frase hecha, *f*; mote, *m*

slop /slɒp/ *n* charco, *m*; *pl* **slops,** agua sucia, *f*; alimentos líquidos, *m pl*. *vi* derramarse, verterse. *vt* verter, derramar

slope /sloup/ *n* inclinación, *f*; pendiente, *f*; (of a mountain, etc.) falda, ladera, cuesta, *f*; vertiente, *mf*. *vi* inclinarse; estar en declive; bajar (hacia). **to s. down,** declinar

sloping /'sloupiŋ/ *a* inclinado; en declive; (of shoulders) caídos, *m pl*

sloppy /'slɒpi/ *a* casi líquido; (muddy) lodoso, lleno de barro; (of work) chapucero; (of persons) baboso, sobón. **s. sentiment,** sensiblería, *f*

slot /slɒt/ *n* ranura, muesca, *f*. **s.-machine,** máquina expendedora, *f*, expendedor, *m*; (in amusement arcades, etc.) tragaperras, *m*

sloth /slɔθ *or, esp. for 2,* slouθ/ *n* pereza, indolencia, *f*; *Zool.* perezoso, *m*

slothful /'slɔθfəl, 'slouθ-/ *a* perezoso, indolente

slouch /slautʃ/ *n* inclinación del cuerpo, *f*. *vi* andar cabizbajo, andar arrastrando los pies. **to s. about,** vagar, golfear. **s.-hat,** sombrero gacho, *m*

slough /slʌf/ *n* (bog) cenagal, pantano, *m*, marisma, *f*; (of a snake) camisa, *f*. *vt* (a skin) mudar; (prejudices, etc.) desechar

Slovak /'slouvæk/ *n* eslovaco (-ca)

Slovakian /slou'vækiən/ *a* eslovaco

sloven /'slʌvən/ *n* puerco, *m*; (at work) chapucero, *m*
Slovene /slou'vin/ *a* and *n* esloveno (-na)
slovenliness /'slʌvənlinɪs/ *n* desaseo, desaliño, *m*; (carelessness) descuido, *m*, negligencia, *f*; (of work) chapucería, *f*
slovenly /'slʌvənli/ *a* desgarbado, desaseado, *Central America* descacharrado, *Lat. Am.* distraído; (careless) descuidado, negligente; (of work) chapucero
slow /slou/ *a* despacio; lento, *Lat. Am.* demorón; (stupid) torpe; tardo; (of clocks) atrasado; (boring) aburrido; (inactive) flojo. *adv* despacio, lentamente. **I was not s. to...,** No tardé en..., *Lat. Am.* No dilaté en... **The clock is ten minutes s.,** El reloj lleva diez minutos de atraso. **to s. down,** aflojar el paso; ir más despacio. **s.-motion,** velocidad reducida, *f.* **s. train,** tren ómnibus, *m.* **s.-witted,** lerdo tardo
"Slow Down" «Moderar Su Velocidad»
slow learner *n* alumno de lento aprendizaje, *m*
slowly /'slouli/ *adv* despacio, lentamente; poco a poco
slowness /'slounɪs/ *n* lentitud, *f*; (delay) tardanza, *f*; (stupidity) torpeza, estupidez, *f*
slug /slʌg/ *n* babosa, *f*
sluggard /'slʌgərd/ *n* gandul (-la), perezoso (-a)
sluggish /'slʌgɪʃ/ *a* perezoso; (of the market) flojo; (of temperament, etc.) calmoso, flemático; (slow) lento
sluggishness /'slʌgɪʃnɪs/ *n* pereza, *f*; (of the market) flojedad, *f*; (slowness) lentitud, *f*
sluice /slus/ *n* esclusa, *f*; canal, *m*, acequia, *f.* **to s. down,** lavar; echar agua sobre; (a person) dar una ducha (a), dar un baño (a). **s.-gate,** compuerta de esclusa, *f*; tajaderas, *f pl*, tablacho, *m*
slum /slʌm/ *nsg* (inner-city slum) barrio bajo (understood everywhere), arrabales *mpl* (Argentina, Uruguay), banda de miseria *fsg* (Argentina), barracas *fpl* (Mexico), barriada *fsg* (Peru), callampa *fsg* (Chile), cantegriles *mpl* (Spain, Uruguay), chabolas *fpl* (Spain), clandestinos *mpl* (Colombia), morenales *mpl* (Honduras), orillas *fpl* (Mexico), población *fsg* (Chile), pueblo joven *msg* (Peru), ranchos *mpl* (Venezuela), tugurios *mpl* (Colombia), villa-miseria *fsg* (Argentina), rancherío *msg*, ribera *fpl*, villorio *msg* (elsewhere in Lat. Am.); (in Brazil) favelas *fpl*; (slum on the outskirts of an urban area) suburbio *msg*
slumber /'slʌmbər/ *vi* dormir; (go to sleep) dormirse, caer dormido; (be latent) estar latente. *n* sueño, *m*
slump /slʌmp/ *n* Com. baja repentina, *f*; *Fig.* baja, racha mala, *f. vi Com.* bajar repentinamente. **the s.,** la crisis económica. **to s. into an armchair,** dejarse caer en un sillón
slur /slɜr/ *vt* (words) comerse sílabas o letras (de); (in writing) unir (las palabras); (*Mus.* of notes) ligar. **to cast a s. on,** difamar, manchar. **to s. over,** pasar por alto de, omitir, suprimir
slush /slʌʃ/ *n* lodo, *m*; agua nieve, *f*; (sentimentality) ñoñería, *f*
slushy /'slʌʃi/ *a* lodoso, fangoso
sly /slai/ *a* astuto, taimado, socarrón, *Lat. Am.* macuco; disimulado; (arch) malicioso. **on the sly,** a hurtadillas. **sly person,** *Mexico* fistol, *m*
slyness /'slainɪs/ *n* astucia, socarronería, *f*; disimulo, *m*; malicia, *f*
smack /smæk/ *n* (taste) sabor, gusto, *m*; (tinge) dejo, *m*; (blow) golpe, *m*; (with the hand) bofetada, palmada, *f*; (with a whip) latigazo, *m*; (crack of whip) restallido, chasquido, *m*; (kiss) beso sonado, *m*; (boat) lancha de pescar, *f. vi* (taste of) tener gusto de, saber a; (be tinged with) oler a. *vt* (a whip) hacer restallar; (slap) pegar con la mano. **to s. one's lips over,** chuparse los dedos
small /smɔl/ *a* pequeño; menudo; menor; poco; (petty) mezquino, vulgar. *n* parte estrecha, *f.* **a s. number,** un pequeño número. **to make a person look s.,** humillar. **to make oneself s.,** hacerse chiquito. **s.-arms,** armas portátiles, *f pl.* **s. change,** suelto, *m.* **s. craft,** embarcaciones menores, *f pl.* **s. farm,** *Lat. Am.* chacra, *Central America* labor, *f.* **s. fry,** pececillos, *m pl*; (children) gente menuda, *f*; gente sin importancia, *f.* **s. hours,** altas horas de la

noche, *f pl.* **s.-minded,** adocenado, de cortos alcances. **s.-talk,** trivialidades, *f pl*, charla frívola, *f*
small holding *n Lat. Am.* chacra, *f*
smallish /'smɔliʃ/ *a* bastante pequeño; más bien pequeño que grande
smallpox /'smɔl,pɒks/ *n* viruelas, *f pl*
smart /smɑrt/ *vi* picar; dolerse (de). *n* escozor, *m*; dolor, *m. a* severo; vivo; rápido; pronto; (competent) hábil; (clever) listo; (unscrupulous) cuco, astuto; (of personal appearance) majo; elegante, distinguido, *Lat. Am. also* fachoso; (neat) aseado; (fashionable, etc.) de moda; de buen tono. **to s. for,** ser castigado por. **to s. under,** sufrir
smarten /'smɑrtn̩/ *vt* embellecer. *vi* (up) ponerse elegante; mejorar. **I must go and s. myself up a little,** Tengo que arreglarme un poco
smartness /'smɑrtnɪs/ *n* viveza, *f*; prontitud, rapidez, *f*; (cleverness) despejo, *m*, habilidad, *f*; (wittiness) agudeza, *f*; (astuteness) cuquería, astucia, *f*; (of dress, etc.) elegancia, *f*; buen tono, *m*
smash /smæʃ/ *vt* romper, quebrar; (a ball, etc.) golpear; (annihilate) destruir; (an opponent) aplastar. *vi* romperse, quebrarse; hacerse pedazos; (collide) chocar (con, contra); estallarse (contra); (financially) hacer bancarrota. *n* rotura, *f*; quebrantamiento, *m*; estruendo, *m*; (financial) quiebra, ruina, *f*; (car, etc.) accidente, *m*; desastre, *m*, catástrofe, *f.* **to s. to atoms,** hacer trizas. **to s. up,** hacer pedazos. **s. and grab raid,** atraco a mano armada, *m*
smash hit *n* éxito arrollador, éxito rotundo, *m*
smattering /'smætərɪŋ/ *n* conocimiento superficial, *m*, tintura, *f*, barniz, *m*
smear /smɪər/ *n* mancha, *f*; *Biol.* frotis, *m. vt* embadurnar (de); manchar (con), ensuciar (con); (oneself) untarse; (blur) borrar
smell /smɛl/ *n* (sense of) olfato, *m*; (odor) olor, *m. vt* oler. *vi* oler; tener olor; (disagreeably) oler mal, tener mal olor; (stink) apestar. **How good it smells!** ¡Qué bien huele! **to s. of,** oler a. **to s. out,** husmear
smelling /'smɛlɪŋ/ *n* olfateo, *m.* **s.-bottle,** frasco de sales, *m.* **s.-salts,** sales (inglesas), *f pl*
smelt /smɛlt/ *vt* fundir. *n Ichth.* eperlano, *m*
smelter /'smɛltər/ *n* fundidor, *m*
smelting /'smɛltɪŋ/ *n* fundición, *f.* **s. furnace,** horno de fundición, *m*
smile /smail/ *vi* sonreír; reírse. *vt* expresar con una sonrisa. *n* sonrisa, *f.* **Mary smiled her thanks,** María dio las gracias con una sonrisa. **smile at adversity,** ponerse buena cara a mal tiempo. **to s. at threats,** reírse de las amenazas
smiling /'smailɪŋ/ *a* sonriente, risueño
smilingly /'smailɪŋli/ *adv* sonriendo, con una sonrisa, con cara risueña
smirch /smɜrtʃ/ *vt* manchar. *n* mancha, *f*
smirk /smɜrk/ *vi* sonreír con afectación; hacer visajes. *n* sonrisa afectada, *f*
smirking /'smɜrkɪŋ/ *a* afectado; sonriente
smite /smait/ *vt* golpear; (kill) matar; (punish) castigar; (pain) doler; (of bright light, sounds, etc.) herir; (cause remorse) remorder. **My conscience smites me,** Tengo remordimientos de conciencia. **to be smitten by,** *Inf.* estar prendado de. **I was smitten by a desire to smoke,** Me entraron deseos de fumar
smith /smɪθ/ *n* herrero, *m.* **smith's hammer,** destajador, *m*
smithereens /,smɪðə'rinz/ *n pl* añicos, *m pl*
smithy /'smɪθi, 'smɪði/ *n* herrería, *f*
smock /smɒk/ *n* blusa, *f*; (child's) delantal, *m*
smoke /smouk/ *n* humo, *m. vi* humear, echar humo; (tobacco) fumar. *vt* ahumar; ennegrecer; (tobacco) fumar. **smoked glasses,** gafas ahumadas, *f pl.* **s. helmet,** casco respiratorio, *m.* **s.-screen,** cortina de humo, *f.* **s. signal,** ahumada, *f.* **s.-stack,** chimenea, *f*
smokeless /'smouklɪs/ *a* sin humo
smoker /'smoukər/ *n* fumador (-ra)
smoking /'smoukɪŋ/ *a* humeante. *n* el fumar. **"S. Prohibited,"** «Se prohíbe fumar.» **non-s. compartment,** *Rail.* departamento de no fumadores, *m.* **s.-carriage,** *Rail.* departamento para fumadores, *m.* **s.-room,** fumadero, *m*

smoky /'smouki/ *a* humeante; lleno de humo; (black) ahumado

smooth /smuð/ *a* liso; igual; (of the skin, etc.) suave; (of water) calmo, tranquilo; (flattering, etc.) lisonjero; obsequioso; afable. *vt* allanar; (hair, etc.) alisar; (paths, etc.) igualar. **to s. down,** (a person) tranquilizar, calmar. **to s. over,** (faults) exculpar. **to s. the way for,** allanar el camino para. **s.-faced,** barbilampiño, lampiño, bien afeitado, todo afeitado; *Fig.* obsequioso, untuoso. **s.-haired,** de pelo liso. **s.-spoken,** de palabras lisonjeras; obsequioso

smoothly /'smuðli/ *adv* lisamente; (of speech) afablemente; con lisonjeras. **Everything was going s.,** Todo iba viento en popa

smoothness /'smuðnıs/ *n* igualdad, *f*; lisura, *f*; (of skin, etc.) suavidad, *f*; (of water) calma, tranquilidad, *f*; (of manner, etc.) afabilidad, *f*

smother /'smʌðər/ *vt* ahogar, sofocar; (a fire) apagar; (cover) envolver, cubrir

smoulder /'smouldər/ *vi* arder sin llama, arder lentamente; (of passions, etc.) arder; estar latente

smouldering /'smouldərıŋ/ *a* que arde lentamente; *Fig.* latente

smudge /smʌdʒ/ *vt* manchar, ensuciar; (blur) borrar. *n* mancha, *f*

smug /smʌg/ *a* satisfecho de sí mismo, pagado de sí mismo; farisaico

smuggle /'smʌgəl/ *vt* pasar de contrabando. *vi* hacer contrabando

smuggler /'smʌglər/ *n* contrabandista, *mf*

smuggling /'smʌglıŋ/ *n* contrabando, *m*

smugly /'smʌgli/ *adv* con presunción, de un aire satisfecho

smugness /'smʌgnıs/ *n* satisfacción de sí mismo, *f*; fariseísmo, *m*

smut /smʌt/ *n* copo de hollín, *m*; mancha, *f*; (disease) tizón, *m*

smutty /'smʌti/ *a* tiznado; ahumado; *Inf.* verde

snack /snæk/ *n* tentempié, piscolabis, bocado, *Lat. Am.* botana, *f*. **to take a s.,** tomar un piscolabis

snack bar *n* merendero, *m*, *Lat. Am.* lonchería, *f*

snaffle /'snæfəl/ *n* filete, *m*. *vt* (a horse) refrenar. **s.-bridle,** bridón, *f*

snag /snæg/ *n* (of a tree) tocón, *m*; (of a tooth) raigón, *m*; (problem) busilis, *m*; obstáculo inesperado, *m*

snail /sneil/ *n* caracol, *m*. **at a snail's pace,** a paso de tortuga

snake /sneik/ *n* serpiente, *f*. **s.-charmer,** encantador de serpientes, *m*

snakelike /'sneik,laik/ *a* de serpiente; serpentino

snap /snæp/ *vt* morder; (break) romper; (one's fingers) castañetear; (a whip) chasquear; (down a lid, etc.) cerrar de golpe; (beaks, etc.) cerrar ruidosamente; *Photo.* sacar una instantánea de. *vi* partirse; quebrarse; hablar bruscamente. *n* (bite) mordedura, *f*; golpe seco, *m*; chasquido, *m*; rotura, *f*; (clasp) cierre, *m*; (of weather) temporada, *f*; (spirit) vigor, brío, *m*; *Photo.* instantánea, *f*. **to s. at,** procurar morder; (an invitation, etc.) aceptar gustoso. **to s. one's fingers at,** *Fig.* burlarse de. **to s. up,** coger, agarrar; (a person) cortar la palabra (a), interrumpir. **s.-fastener,** botón de presión, *m*

snapdragon /'snæp,drægən/ *n* dragón, *m*, becerra, boca de dragón, *f*

snappily /'snæpəli/ *adv* irritablemente

snappishness /'snæpıʃnıs/ *n* irritabilidad, *f*

snappy /'snæpi/ *a* irritable; vigoroso

snapshot /'snæp,ʃɒt/ *vt* instantánea, foto, *f*

snare /snɛər/ *n* cepo, lazo, *m*, trampa, *f*; *Fig.* red, *f*. *vt* coger en el lazo; *Fig.* enredar

snarl /snɑrl/ *vi* (of dogs) regañar; (cats, etc.) gruñir. *n* regañamiento, *m*; gruñido, *m*

snarling /'snɑrlıŋ/ *n* regañamiento, *m*; gruñidos, *m pl. a* gruñidor

snatch /snætʃ/ *vt* asir; agarrar; (enjoy) disfrutar; (an opportunity) tomar, aprovecharse de. *n* asimiento, agarro, *m*; (of time) rato, *m*; instante, *m*; (of song) fragmento, *m*. **to make a s. at,** procurar agarrar; alargar la mano hacia. **to s. a hurried meal,** comer aprisa. **to s. away,** arrebatar, quitar; (carry off) robar. **to s. up,** coger rápidamente; coger en brazos

sneak /snik/ *vi* deslizarse (en), colarse (en); (lurk) rondar; (inform) acusar. *n* mandilón, *m*; (accuser) acusón (-ona). **to s. off,** escabullirse, irse a hurtadillas. **s.-thief,** *n* garduño (-ña)

sneaker /'snikər/ *n* (shoe) zapatilla de tenis, *f*

sneaking /'snikıŋ/ *a* furtivo, ruin, mezquino; secreto

sneer /snɪər/ *vi* sonreír irónicamente; burlarse, mofarse. *n* sonrisa sardónica, sonrisa de desprecio, *f*; burla, mofa, *f*. **to s. at,** mofarse de, burlarse de; hablar con desprecio de

sneering /'snɪərıŋ/ *a* mofador, burlón

sneeringly /'snɪərıŋli/ *adv* con una sonrisa sardónica, burlonamente

sneeze /sniz/ *vi* estornudar. *n* estornudo, *m*. **It's not to be sneezed at,** No es moco de pavo

sniff /snıf/ *vi* respirar fuertemente; resollar. *vt* oler, olfatear; aspirar. **to s. at,** oler. **to s. out,** *Inf.* husmear

sniffle /'snıfəl/ *n* sorbo, *m*. *vi* olfatear

snigger /'snıgər/ *vi* reírse por lo bajo, reírse disimuladamente. *n* risa disimulada, *f*

snip /snıp/ *vt* cortar con tijeras; cortar, quitar. *n* tijeretada, *f*; (of cloth, etc.) recorte, pedacito, *m*

sniper /'snaipər/ *n* *Mil.* paco, *m*

snippet /'snıpıt/ *n* pedacito, fragmento, *m*; (of prose, etc.) trocito, *m*; (of news) noticia, *f*

snivel /'snıvəl/ *vi* lloriquear, gimotear

sniveling /'snıvəlıŋ/ *n* lloriqueo, gimoteo, *m*. *a* llorón; mocoso

snob /snɒb/ *n* esnob, *mf*

snobbery /'snɒbəri/ *n* snobismo, *m*

snobbish /'snɒbıʃ/ *a* esnob

snood /snud/ *n* (for the hair) redecilla, *f*; (turkey's) moco (de pavo), *m*; (fishing) cendal, *m*

snoop /snup/ *vi* espiar; entremeterse

snooper /'snupər/ *n Lat. Am.* averigüetas, *mf*

snooze /snuz/ *vi* dormitar, echar un sueño. *n* sueñecito, *m*; (afternoon) siesta, *f*

snore /snɔr/ *vi* roncar. *n* ronquido, *m*

snoring /'snɔrıŋ/ *n* ronquidos, *m pl*

snort /snɔrt/ *vi* bufar; resoplar. *n* bufido, *m*; resoplido, *m*

snout /snaut/ *n* hocico, *m*; (of a pig) jeta, *f*

snow /snou/ *n* nieve, *f*. *vi* nevar. *vt* nevar; *Fig.* inundar. **to s. under** (with), inundar con. **to be snowed up,** estar aprisionado por la nieve. **s.-blindness,** deslumbramiento causado por la nieve, *m*. **s.-boot,** bota para la nieve, *f*. **s.-bound,** aprisionado por la nieve; bloqueado por la nieve, *m*. **s.-capped,** coronado de nieve. **s.-clad,** cubierto de nieve. **s.-drift,** acumulación de nieve, *f*. **s.-field,** ventisquero, *m*. **s.-goggles,** gafas ahumadas, *f pl.* **s.-line,** límite de las nieves perpetuas, *m*. **s.-man,** figura de nieve, *f*. **s.-plow,** quitanieve, *m*. **s.-shoe,** raqueta de nieve, *f*. **s.-white,** blanco como la nieve

snowball /'snou,bɔl/ *n* bola de nieves, *f*; *Bot.* bola de nieve, *f*

snowdrop /'snou,drɒp/ *n* campanilla de invierno, violeta de febrero, *f*

snowfall /'snou,fɔl/ *n* nevada, *f*

snowflake /'snou,fleik/ *n* copo de nieve, *m*

snowstorm /'snou,stɔrm/ *n* ventisca, *f*

snowy /'snoui/ *a* nevoso; de nieve

snub /snʌb/ *vt* repulsar; desairar, tratar con desdén, *Mexico* descolar. *n* repulsa, *f*, desaire, *m*; (nose) nariz respingona, *n*. **s.-nosed,** de nariz respingona

snuff /snʌf/ *vt* (breathe) oler, olfatear; inhalar; (a candle) atizar, despabilar. *n* (of a candle) moco, *m*, despabiladura, *f*; (tobacco) rapé, *m*. **to take s.,** tomar rapé. **to s. out,** extinguir. **s.-box,** caja de rapé, tabaquera, *f*

snuffling /'snʌflıŋ/ *a* mocoso; (of the voice) gangoso

snug /snʌg/ *a* caliente; cómodo; (hidden) escondido, *m*. **to have a s. income,** tener el riñón bien cubierto, ser acomodado

snuggle /'snʌgəl/ *vi* hacerse un ovillo; acomodarse; ponerse cómodo. **to s. up to,** arrimarse a, apretarse contra

snugly /'snʌgli/ *adv* cómodamente

snugness /'snʌgnıs/ *n* comodidad, *f*

so /sou/ *adv* así; de este modo, de esta manera; por
lo tanto; tanto; (before adjs. and advs. but not before
más, mejor, menos, peor, where **tanto** is used) tan;
(in the same way) del mismo modo, de igual modo;
(therefore) de modo que, de manera que; (also) también; (approximately) más o menos, aproximada-
mente. **Is that so?** ¿De veras? **if so...,** si así es... **He
has not yet done so,** no lo ha hecho todavía. **I told
you so!** ¡Ya te lo dije yo! **So be it!** ¡Así sea! **so far,**
hasta aquí; hasta ahora. **so forth,** etcétera. **So long!**
¡Nos vemos! **so much,** tanto. **So much the worse for
them,** Tanto peor para ellos. **so to speak...,** por decirlo así. **so as to,** a fin de, para. **so long as,** con tal
que, a condición de que. **so on,** etcétera. **so soon as,**
tan pronto como. **so that,** de suerte que, de modo
que, para que; con que. **so-and-so,** *n* fulano (-na);
mengano (-na). **so-called,** así llamado, supuesto.
so-so, así-así, regular

soak /souk/ *vt* remojar; empapar; (skins) abrevar. *vi*
estar en remojo. *n* remojo, *m*; (rain) diluvio, *m*;
(booze) borrachera, *f*. **to s. into,** filtrar en; penetrar.
to s. through, penetrar; filtrar **so-called,** así llamado,
supuesto. **so-so,** así, regular

soaked /soukt/ *a* remojado. **He is s. to the skin,** Está
calado hasta los huesos

soaking /'soukɪŋ/ *n* remojo, *m*; empapamiento, *m*,

soap /soup/ *n* jabón, *m*. *vt* jabonar; (flatter) enjabonar. **a tablet of s.,** una pastilla de jabón. **soft s.,** jabón
blando, *m*. **toilet s.,** jabón de tocador, jaboncillo, *m*. **s.-
bubble,** burbuja de jabón, *f*. **s. dish,** jabonera, *f*. **s. factory,** jabonería, *f*. **s.-flakes,** copos de jabón, *m pl*

soapbark tree /'soup,bark/ *n* quillay, palo de jabón,
m

soap box *n Lit.* caja de jabón, *f*; *Fig.* tribuna callejera, *f*

soap opera /'ɒpərə/ *n* radionovela (on radio), teleno-
vela (on television), *f*, serial lacrimógeno (derogatory), *m*

soapsuds /'soup,sʌdz/ *n pl* jabonaduras, *f pl*

soapy /'soupi/ *a* cubierto de jabón; jabonoso

soar /sɔr/ *vi* remontarse; *Fig.* elevarse; (of prices,
etc.) subir de golpe

soaring /'sɔrɪŋ/ *n* remonte, vuelo, *m*; *Fig.* aspiración,
f; (of prices, etc.) subida repentina, *f*

sob /sɒb/ *vi* sollozar. *n* sollozo, *m*. **to sob one's
heart out,** llorar a lágrima viva. **to sob out,** decir
sollozando, decir entre sollozos

s.o.b. /sɒb/ *n* (son of a bitch) hache de pe (hijo de
puta)

sobbing /'sɒbɪŋ/ *n* sollozos, *m pl*, *a* sollozante

sober /'soubər/ *a* sobrio; moderado; (of colors) obscuro. **s.-minded,** serio; reflexivo

sobriety /sə'braiiti/ *n* sobriedad, *f*; moderación, *f*; seriedad, *f*; calma, tranquilidad, *f*

sobriquet /'soubrɪ,kei, -,kɛt/ *n* apodo, *m*

soccer /'sɒkər/ *n* fútbol (Asociación), *m*

sociability /,sɒfə'bɪlɪti/ *n* sociabilidad, *f*

sociable /'soufəbəl/ *a* sociable; amistoso

sociably /'soufəbli/ *adv* sociablemente; amistosamente

social /'soufəl/ *a* social; sociable. *n* reunión, velada,
f. **s.-democrat,** *a* and *n* socialdemócrata, *mf*. **s.
event,** acontecimiento social, *m*. **s. insurance,** previsión social, *f*. **s. services,** servicios sociales, *m pl*. **s.
work,** asistencia social, *f*

socialism /'soufə,lɪzəm/ *n* socialismo, *m*

socialist /'soufəlɪst/ *a* socialista, laborista. *n* socialista, *mf*

socialization /,soufələ'zeifən/ *n* socialización, *f*

socialize /'soufə,laiz/ *vt* socializar

socially /'soufəli/ *adv* socialmente

society /sə'saiiti/ *n* sociedad, *f*; (fashionable) mundo
elegante, *m*, alta sociedad, *f*; compañía, *f*. **to go into
s.,** (of girls) ponerse de largo; entrar en el mundo elegante. **s. hostess,** dama de sociedad, *f*. **society for
the prevention of cruelty to animals,** sociedad protectora de animales, *f*. **s. news,** noticias de sociedad,
f pl

sociological /,sousiə'lɒdʒɪkəl/ *a* sociológico

sociologist /,sousi,ɒlədʒɪst/ *n* sociólogo (-ga)

sociology /,sousi'ɒlədʒi/ *n* sociología, *f*

sock /sɒk/ *n* calcetín, *m*; (for a shoe) plantilla, *f*

socket /'sɒkɪt/ *n Mech.* encaje, cubo, ojo, *m*; (of a
lamp, and *Elec.*) enchufe, *m*; (of the eye) órbita,
cuenca, *f*; (of a tooth) alvéolo, *m*; (of a joint) fosa, *f*.
His eyes started out of their sockets, Sus ojos estaban fuera de su órbita

Socratic /sə'krætɪk/ *a* socrático

sod /sɒd/ *n* césped, *m*; (cut) tepe, *m*

soda /'soudə/ *n* sosa, *f*. **caustic s.,** sosa cáustica, *f*. **s.
-ash,** carbonato sódico, *m*. **s.-fountain,** aparato de
aguas gaseosas, *m*. **s.-water,** sifón, *m*

sodden /'sɒdn/ *a* saturado, empapado

sodium /'soudiəm/ *n* sodio, *m*

Sodomite /'sɒdə,mait/ *n* sodomita, *mf*

sodomy /'sɒdəmi/ *n* sodomía, *f*

sofa /'soufə/ *n* sofá, *m*

soft /sɔft/ *a* blando; suave; muelle; (flabby) flojo; (of
disposition, etc.) dulce; (effeminate) muelle, afeminado; (lenient) indulgente; (easy) fácil; (silly)
tonto. **to have a s. spot for,** (a person) tener una debilidad para. **s. coal,** carbón bituminoso, *m*. **s. drink,**
bebida no alcohólica, *f*. **s. felt hat,** sombrero flexible,
m. **s. fruit,** fruta blanda, *f*. **s.-boiled,** (of eggs) pasado por agua; (of persons) inocente, ingenuo. **s.-
hearted,** de buen corazón; compasivo, bondadoso. **s.
-heartedness,** buen corazón, *m*, bondad, *f*. **s.-
spoken,** de voz suave; que habla con dulzura,
meloso. **s. water,** agua blanda, *f*

soften /'sɔfən/ *vt* ablandar, reblandecer) (weaken) debilitar; (mitigate) mitigar, suavizar; (the heart, etc.)
enternecer. *vi* reblandecerse; enternecerse

softening /'sɔfənɪŋ/ *n* reblandecimiento, *m*; (relenting) enternecimiento, *m*

softly /'sɔftli/ *adv* suavemente; dulcemente, tiernamente; sin ruido, silenciosamente

softness /'sɔftnɪs/ *n* blandura, *f*; suavidad, *f*; (sweetness, etc.) dulzura, *f*; (of character) debilidad de carácter, *f*; (silliness) necedad, estupidez, *f*

software /'sɔft,wɛər/ *n* programas de computo, *mpl*;
software, *m*

soggy /'sɒgi/ *a* empapado de agua; saturado

soil /sɔil/ *n* tierra, *f*; (country) país, *m*, tierra, *f*. *vt*
ensuciar; *Fig.* manchar. **my native s.,** mi tierra, mi
patria

soiled /sɔild/ *a* sucio. **s. linen,** ropa sucia, *f*

soiree /swɑ'rei/ *n* velada, *f*

sojourn /'soudʒɜrn/ *vi* morar, residir, permanecer. *n*
residencia, permanencia, *f*

sojourner /'soudʒɜrnər/ *n* morador (-ra), residente,
mf

sol /sɔl/ *n Mus.* sol, *m*. **sol-fa,** *n* solfa, *f*, solfeo, *m*. *vt*
solfear

solace /'sɒlɪs/ *n* consuelo, solaz, *m*. *vt* consolar; solazar

solar /'soulər/ *a* solar. **s. plexus,** *Anat.* plexo solar,
m. **s. system,** sistema solar, *m*

solder /'sɒdər/ *n* soldadura, *f*, *vt* soldar

soldering /'sɒdərɪŋ/ *n* soldadura, *f*

soldier /'souldʒər/ *n* soldado, *m*; militar, *m*. **He
wants to be a s.,** Quiere ser militar

soldierly /'souldʒərli/ *a* militar; marcial

soldiery /'souldʒəri/ *n* soldadesca, *f*

sole /soul/ *n* (of a foot) planta, *f*; (of a shoe) suela, *f*;
(of a plow) cepa, *f*; *Ichth.* lenguado, *m*, suela, *f*. *vt*
(shoes) solar, poner suela (a). *a* solo, único; exclusivo. **s. right,** exclusiva, *f*, derecho exclusivo, *m*

solecism /'sɒlə,sɪzəm/ *n* solecismo, *m*

solely /'soulli/ *adv* sólo; únicamente, puramente;
meramente

solemn /'sɒləm/ *a* solemne; grave; serio; (sacred) sagrado. **Why do you look so s.?** ¿Por qué estás tan
serio?

solemnity /sə'lɛmnɪti/ *n* solemnidad, *f*

solemnization /,sɒləmnə'zeifən/ *n* solemnización,
f; celebración, *f*

solemnize /'sɒləm,naiz/ *vt* solemnizar

solemnly /'sɒləmli/ *adv* solemnemente; gravemente

solicit /sə'lɪsɪt/ *vt* solicitar; implorar, rogar encarecidamente

solicitation /sə,lɪsɪ'teifən/ *n* solicitación, *f*

solicitor /sə'lɪsɪtər/ *n* abogado (-da)

solicitous /sə'lɪsɪtəs/ a ansioso (de), deseoso (de); solícito, atento; (worried) preocupado

solicitude /sə'lɪsɪ,tud/ n solicitud, f, cuidado, m; (anxiety) preocupación, f

solid /'sɒlɪd/ a sólido; macizo; (of persons) serio, formal; (unanimous) unánime. n sólido, m. **a s. meal,** una comida fuerte. **He slept for ten s. hours,** Durmió por diez horas seguidas. **solid-colored material,** tela lisa, f. **s. food,** alimentos sólidos, m pl. **s. geometry,** geometría del espacio, f. **solid gold,** oro de ley, m. **s. tire,** llanta de goma maciza, f

solidarity /,sɒlɪ'dærɪti/ n solidaridad, f

solidification /sə,lɪdəfɪ'keɪʃən/ n solidificación, f

solidify /sə'lɪdə,faɪ/ vt solidificar. vi solidificarse; congelarse

solidity /sə'lɪdɪti/ n solidez, f; unanimidad, f

solidly /'sɒlɪdli/ adv sólidamente

soliloquize /sə'lɪlə,kwaiz/ vi soliloquiar, hablar a solas

soliloquy /sə'lɪləkwi/ n soliloquio, m

solitaire /'sɒlɪ,teər/ n (diamond and game) solitario, m

solitary /'sɒlɪ,teri/ a solitario; solo, aislado, único. **He was in s. confinement for three months,** Estuvo incomunicado durante tres meses. **There is not a s. one,** No hay ni uno

solitude /'sɒlɪ,tud/ n soledad, f

solo /'soulou/ n (performance and cards) solo, m. **to sing a s.,** cantar un solo. **It was his first s. flight,** Era su primer vuelo a solas

soloist /'soulouɪst/ n solista, mf

solstice /'sɒlstɪs, 'soul-/ n solsticio, m. **summer s.,** solsticio vernal, m. **winter s.,** solsticio hiemal, m

solubility /,sɒlyə'bɪlɪti/ n solubilidad, f

soluble /'sɒlyəbəl/ a soluble

solution /sə'luʃən/ n solución, f

solvable /'sɒlvəbəl/ a que se puede resolver, soluble

solve /sɒlv/ vt resolver, hallar la solución de

solvency /'sɒlvənsi/ n solvencia, f

solvent /'sɒlvənt/ a Com. solvente; (Chem. and Fig.) disolvente. n disolvente, m

somatic /sou'mætɪk/ a somático

somber /'sɒmbər/ a sombrío

somberly /'sɒmbərli/ adv sombríamente

somberness /'sɒmbərnɪs/ n lo sombrío; sobriedad, f; melancolía, f

some /sʌm; unstressed səm/ a alguno (-a), algunos (-as); (before a masculine sing. noun) algún; unos (-as); un poco de, algo de; (as a partitive, often not translated) Give me s. wine, Dame vino); (approximately) aproximadamente, unos (-as). pron algunos (-as), unos (-as); algo, un poco. **I should like s. strawberries,** Me gustaría comer unas fresas. **s. day,** algún día. **S. say yes, others no,** Algunos dicen que sí, otros que no. **There are s. sixty people in the garden,** Hay unas sesenta personas en el jardín

somebody, someone /'sʌm,bɒdi; 'sʌm,wʌn/ n alguien, mf. **s. else,** otro (-a), otra persona, f. **S. or other said that the book is worth reading,** No sé quién dijo que el libro vale la pena de leerse. **to be s.,** Inf. ser un personaje

somehow /'sʌm,hau/ adv de un modo u otro, de alguna manera. **S. I don't like them,** No sé por qué, pero no me gustan

somersault /'sʌmər,sɔlt/ n salto mortal, m, vi dar un salto mortal

something /'sʌm,θɪŋ/ n algo, m, alguna cosa, f. adv algún tanto. **Would you like s. else?** ¿Quiere Vd. otra cosa? **He left s. like fifty thousand pounds,** Dejó algo así como cincuenta mil libras. **He has s. to live for,** Tiene para que vivir

sometime /'sʌm,taim/ adv algún día, alguna vez; en algún tiempo. a ex-. **Come and see me s. soon,** Ven a verme algún día de estos. **He will have to go abroad s. or another,** Tarde o temprano, tiene que ir al extranjero. **s. last month,** durante el mes pasado

sometimes /'sʌm,taimz/ adv algunas veces, a veces. **s. happy, s. sad,** algunas veces feliz y otras triste, feliz ora triste

somewhat /'sʌm,wʌt/ adv algo; algún tanto, un tanto; un poco. **I am s. busy,** Estoy algo ocupado. **He**

is s. of a lady-killer, Tiene sus puntos de castigador, Tiene algo de castigador

somewhere /'sʌm,weər/ adv en alguna parte. **s. about,** por ahí. **s. else,** en otra parte

somnambulism /sɒm'næmbyə,lɪzəm/ n somnambulismo, m

somnambulist /sɒm'næmbyəlɪst/ n somnámbulo (-la)

somnolence /'sɒmnələns/ n somnolencia, f

somnolent /'sɒmnələnt/ a soñoliento; soporífero

son /sʌn/ n hijo, m. **son-in-law,** yerno, hijo político, m

sonata /sə'nɑtə/ n sonata, f

song /sɒŋ/ n canto, m; canción, f; (poem) poema, verso, m. **It's nothing to make a s. about,** No es para tanto. **to break into s.,** ponerse a cantar. **to be not worth an old s.,** no valer un pito. **the S. of Songs,** Cantar de los Cantares, m. **s.-bird,** ave canora, f. **s.-book,** libro de canciones, m. **s.-writer,** compositor (-ra) de canciones

sonic /'sɒnɪk/ adj sónico. **sonic boom,** estampido sónico, m

sonnet /'sɒnɪt/ n soneto, m

sonorous /sə'nɔrəs/ a sonoro

sonorousness /sə'nɔrəsnɪs/ n sonoridad, f

soon /sun/ adv pronto; dentro de poco, luego. **as s. as,** así que, en cuanto, luego que, no bien... **as s. as possible,** lo antes posible, lo más pronto posible, con la mayor antelación posible, cuanto antes, f. **s. after,** poco después (de). **See you s.!** ¡Hasta pronto! **sooner or later,** tarde o temprano. **the sooner the better,** cuanto antes mejor. **No sooner had he left the house, when...** Apenas hubo dejado la casa, cuando... **Emily would sooner go to London,** Emilia preferiría ir a Londres (A Emilia le gustaría más ir a Londres)

soot /sʊt/ n hollín, m, vt cubrir de hollín

soothe /suð/ vt tranquilizar, calmar, (pain) aliviar, mitigar

soothing /'suðɪŋ/ a calmante, tranquilizador, sosegador; (of powders, etc.) suavizante

soothingly /'suðɪŋli/ adv con dulzura; suavemente; como un consuelo

soothsayer /'suθ,seiər/ n adivino (-na), adivinador (-ra)

soothsaying /'suθ,seiɪŋ/ n adivinanza, f

sooty /'sʊti/ a cubierto de hollín; negro como el hollín

sop /sɒp/ n sopa, f; (bribe) soborno, m

sophism /'sɒfɪzəm/ n sofisma, m

sophist /'sɒfɪst/ n Hist. sofista, m; (quibbler) sofista, mf

sophistic /sə'fɪstɪk/ a Philos. sofista; (of persons, arguments) sofístico

sophisticated /sə'fɪstɪ,keitid/ a nada ingenuo; mundano; (cultured) culto

sophistication /sə,fɪstɪ'keiʃən/ n falta de simplicidad, f; mundanería, f; cultura, f

sophistry /'sɒfəstri/ n sofistería, f

Sophoclean /,sɒfə'kliən/ a sofocleo

soporific /,sɒpə'rɪfɪk/ a soporífico

sopping /'sɒpɪŋ/ a muy mojado. **s. wet,** hecho una sopa

soprano /sə'prænou/ n (voice and part) soprano, m; (singer) soprano, tiple, mf

sorcerer /'sɔrsərər/ n encantador, mago, brujo, m

sorceress /'sɔrsərɪs/ n hechicera, bruja, f

sorcery /'sɔrsəri/ n sortilegio, m, hechicería, brujería, f; encanto, m

sordid /'sɔrdɪd/ a sórdido; (of motives, etc.) ruin, vil

sordidness /'sɔrdɪdnɪs/ n sordidez, f; (of motives, etc.) vileza, bajeza, f

sordine /'sɔrdɛn/ n Mus. sordina, f

sore /sɔr/ a doloroso, malo; (sad) triste; (annoyed) enojado; (with need, etc.) extremo. n llaga, Lat. Am. also lacra, f; (on horses, etc., caused by girths) matadura, f; Fig. herida, f; recuerdo doloroso, m. **to open an old s.,** Fig. renovar la herida. **running s.,** úlcera, f. **s. throat,** dolor de garganta, m

sorely /'sɔrli/ adv grandemente; muy; urgentemente. **He was s. tempted,** Tuvo grandes tentaciones

soreness /'sɔrnɪs/ n dolor, m; (resentment) amargura, f, resentimiento, m; (ill-feeling) rencor, m

sorrel /'sɔrəl, 'sɒr-/ a alazán. n (horse) alazán, m; Bot. acedera, f

sorrow /'sɒrou/ n pesar, m, aflicción, pesadumbre, f; tristeza, f. vi afligirse; entristecerse. **To my great s.,** Con gran pesar mío. **s.-stricken,** afligido, agobiado de pena

sorrowful /'sɒrəfəl/ a afligido, angustiado; triste

sorrowfully /'sɒrəfəli/ adv con pena, tristemente

sorrowing /'sɒrouɪŋ/ a afligido. n aflicción, f; lamentación, f

sorry, to be /'sɒri/ vi sentir. **I'm s.,** Lo siento.

sort /sɔrt/ n especie, f; clase, f; tipo, m. vt separar (de); clasificar. **a s. of hat,** una especie de sombrero. **all sorts of,** toda clase de. **He is a good s.,** Es buen chico. **He is a queer s.,** Es un tipo raro. **in some s.,** hasta cierto punto. **I am out of sorts,** Estoy destemplado. **Nothing of the s.!** ¡Nada de eso!

sorter /'sɔrtər/ n oficial de correos, m; clasificador (-ra)

sorting /'sɔrtɪŋ/ n clasificación, f

sotto voce /'sɒt'ou voutʃi/ adv a sovoz, en voz baja

soul /soul/ n alma, f; espíritu, m; (departed) ánima, f; (being) ser, m; (life) vida, f; (heart) corazón, m. **All Souls' Day,** Día de los Difuntos, m. **He is a good s.!** ¡Es un bendito! **She is a simple s.,** Ella es una alma de Dios. **without seeing a living s.,** sin ver un bicho viviente. **Upon my s.!** ¡Por mi vida! **s. in purgatory,** alma en pena, f. **s.-stirring,** emocionante

soulful /'soulfəl/ a sentimental, emocional; espiritual; romántico

soulless /'soullɪs/ a sin alma; mecánico

sound /saund/ n sonido, m; son, m; ruido, m; (strait) estrecho, m. vi sonar; hacer ruido; resonar; (seem) parecer. vt sonar; (the horn, the alarm, musical instrument) tocar; (express) expresar; proclamar; (praise) celebrar; Naut. hondear; Med. tentar; (the chest) auscultar; (try to discover) tentar, sondar; (experience) experimentar. **to the s. of,** al son de. **s.-box,** (of a gramophone) diafragma, m. **s.-detector,** fonolocalización de aviones, f. **s.-film,** película sonora, f. **s.-proof,** (of radio studios, etc.) aislado de todo sonido. **s.-track,** guía sonora, banda sonora, f. **s.-wave,** onda sonora, f

sounding /'saundɪŋ/ n Naut. sondeo, m; pl **soundings,** sondas, f pl. a sonoro. **to take soundings,** sondar, echar la plomada. **s.-board,** tabla de armonía, f

soundless /'saundlɪs/ a sin ruido, silencioso

soundly /'saundli/ adv sanamente; juiciosamente, prudentemente; bien; (deeply) profundamente

soundness /'saundnɪs/ n (of a person) perspicacia, f; (of a policy, etc.) prudencia, f; (of an argument, etc.) validez, fuerza, f; (financial) solvencia, f

soup /sup/ n sopa, f. clear s., consommé, m. **thick s.,** puré, m. **to be in the s.,** Inf. estar aviado. **s.-ladle,** cucharón, m. **s.-plate,** plato sopero, m. **s.-tureen,** sopera, f

sour /sauʳr/ a ácido, agrio; (of milk) agrio; (of persons, etc.) agrio, desabrido. vt agriar. **to go s.,** volverse agrio. **S. grapes!** ¡Están verdes!

source /sɔrs/ n (of a river, etc.) nacimiento, m; fuente, f; (of infection) foco, m. **to know from a good s.,** saber de buena tinta

sourly /'sauʳrli/ adv agriamente

sourness /'sauʳrnɪs/ n acidez, agrura, f; acrimonia, f

south /sauθ/ n sur, m; mediodía, m. a del sur. adv hacia el sur. **S. African,** a and n sudafricano (-na). **S. American,** a and n sudamericano (-na). **s.-east,** n sudeste, m. a del sudeste. adv hacia el sudeste. **s.-easter,** viento del sudeste. **s.-easterly,** a del sudeste; al sudeste. adv hacia el sudeste. **s.-eastern,** del sudeste. **s.-s.-east,** n sudsudeste, m. **s.-s.-west,** sudsudoeste, m. **s.-west,** n sudoeste, m. a del sudoeste. adv hacia el sudoeste. **s.-west wind,** viento su-

doeste, ábrego, m. **s.-westerly,** a del sudoeste. adv hacia el sudoeste. **s.-western,** a del sudoeste

South Africa /'æfrɪkə/ República Sudafricana, f

South America América del Sur, f

southerly /'sʌðərli/ a del sur; hacia el sur. **The house has a s. aspect,** La casa está orientada al sur

southern /'sʌðərn/ a del sur; del mediodía; meridional. **S. Cross,** Cruz, f, Crucero, m. **s. express,** sudexpreso, m

southerner /'sʌðərnər/ n habitante del sur, m

South Sea Mar del Sur, Mar del Pacífico, m

southward /'sauθwərd/ Naut. 'sʌðərd/ a del sur; al sur. adv hacia el sur

souvenir /,suvə'nɪər/ n recuerdo, m

sovereign /'sɒvrɪn/ a soberano. n soberano (-na); (coin) soberano, m

sovereignty /'sɒvrɪnti/ n soberanía, f

soviet /'souvi,ɛt/ n soviet, m, a soviético

Soviet Union, the la Unión Soviética, f

sow /sau/ n cerda, puerca, marrana, f; (of a wild boar) jabalina, f; (of iron) galápago, m

sow /sou/ vt sembrar; esparcir; diseminar

sower /'souər/ n sembrador (-ra)

sowing /'souɪŋ/ n sembradura, siembra, f. **s. machine,** sembradera, f. **s. time,** tiempo de la siembra, m

soya bean /'sɔiə/ n soja, f

spa /spa/ n balneario, m; (spring) manantial mineral, m, caldas, f pl

space /speis/ n espacio, m; (of time) temporada, f; intervalo, m; (Print., Mus.) espacio, m. vt espaciar. **blank s.,** blanco, m. **s.-bar,** tecla de espacios, f, espaciador, m

spacious /'speiʃəs/ a espacioso; amplio

spaciousness /'speiʃəsnɪs/ n espaciosidad, f; amplitud, f

spade /speid/ n pala, azada, f; (cards) espada, f. **to call a s. a s.,** llamar al pan pan y al vino vino, llamar a las cosas por su nombre. **s.-work,** trabajo preparatorio, m, labor de pala, f

spaghetti /spə'gɛti/ n fideos, macarrones, m pl, espagueti, m

Spain /spein/ España, f

span /spæn/ vt medir a palmos; rodear; medir; (cross) atravesar, cruzar. n palmo, m; espacio, m, duración, f; (of a bridge) vano, m; (of wing, Aer., Zool.) envergadura, f; (distance) distancia, f. **single-s. bridge,** puente de vano único. **the brief s. of human life,** la corta duración de la vida humana

spangle /'spæŋgəl/ n lentejuela, f; (tinsel) oropel, m. vt adornar con lentejuelas; sembrar (de), esparcir (de). **spangled with stars,** sembrado de estrellas

Spaniard /'spænyərd/ n español (-la). **a young S.,** un joven español

spaniel /'spænyəl/ n perro de aguas, perro sabueso español, m; (cocker) sabueso, m

Spanish /'spænɪʃ/ a español. n (language) español, castellano, m. **a S. girl,** una muchacha española. **in S. fashion,** a la española. **S. American,** a and n hispanoamericano (-na). **S. broom,** retama de olor, f. **S. fly,** cantárida, f

Spanish America Hispanoamérica, f

spank /spæŋk/ vt pegar con la mano, azotar. n azotazo, m. **to s. along,** correr rápidamente; (of a horse) galopar

spanking /'spæŋkɪŋ/ n azotamiento, vapuleo, m

spanner /'spænər/ n llave inglesa, llave de tuercas, f

spar /spar/ n Naut. mastel, m; Mineral. espato, m; (boxing) boxeo, m; (quarrel) disputa, f. vi boxear; (argue) disputar

spare /spear/ a (meager) frugal, escaso; (of persons) enjuto, flaco; (available) disponible; (extra) de repuesto. n recambio, m. **s. part,** pieza de recambio, pieza de repuesto, f. **s. room,** cuarto de amigos, m. **s. time,** ratos de ocio, m pl, tiempo disponible, m. **s. tire,** Mexico llanta de refación, f. **s. wheel,** rueda de repuesto, f

spare /spear/ vt (expense, etc.) escatimar; ahorrar; (do without) pasarse sin; (give) dar; (a life, etc.) perdonar; (avoid) evitar; dispensar de; (grant) hacer gracia de; (time) dedicar. **I cannot s. her,** No puedo estar sin ella. **They have no money to s.,** No tienen dinero de sobra. **to be sparing of,** ser avaro de

sparingly /'spɛərɪŋli/ *adv* frugalmente; escasamente. **to eat s.,** comer con frugalidad

spark /spɑrk/ *n* chispa, *f*; (gallant) pisaverde, *m. vi* chispear, echar chispas

sparking /'spɒrkɪŋ/ *a* chispeante. *n* emisión de chispas, *f*. **s.-plug,** bujía de encendido, *f*

sparkle /'spɑrkəl/ *vi* centellear, rutilar, destellar; *Fig.* brillar; (of wines) ser espumoso. *n* centelleo, destello, *m*; *Fig.* brillo, *m*

sparkling /'spɒrklɪŋ/ *a* rutilante, centelleante, reluciente; *Fig.* brillante, chispeante; (of wines) espumante

sparring match /'spɒrɪŋ/ *n* combate de boxeo amistoso, *m*

sparrow /'spærou/ *n* gorrión, *m.* **s.-hawk,** gavilán, esparaván, *m*

sparse /spɑrs/ *a* claro, ralo; esparcido

sparsely /'spɑrsli/ *adv* escasamente

Sparta /'spɑrtə/ Esparta, *f*

Spartan /'spɑrtn/ *a and n* espartano (-na)

spasm /'spæzəm/ *n* espasmo, *m*; ataque, *m*; acceso, *m*

spasmodic /spæz'mɒdɪk/ *a* espasmódico; intermitente

spasmodically /spæz'mɒdɪkli/ *adv* espasmódicamente

spat /spæt/ *n* (gaiter) polaina de tela, *f*

spate /speit/ *n* crecida, *f*; *Fig.* torrente, *m.* **in s.,** crecido

spatter /'spætər/ *vt* salpicar; (*Fig.* smirch) manchar. *vi* rociar. *n* salpicadura, *f*; rociada, *f*

spatula /'spætʃələ/ *n* espátula, *f*

spawn /spɔn/ *vt* and *vi* desovar; engendrar. *n* huevas, *f pl*, freza, *f*; (offspring) producto, *m*

speak /spik/ *vi* hablar; pronunciar un discurso; (sound) sonar. *vt* decir; (French, etc.) hablar. **She never spoke to him again,** Nunca volvió a dirigirle la palabra. **roughly speaking,** aproximadamente, más o menos. **Speaking for myself,** En cuanto a mí, Por mi parte. **without speaking,** sin decir nada, sin hablar. **to s. for,** (a person) hablar por. **to s. for itself,** hablar por sí mismo, ser evidente. **to s. one's mind,** decir lo que se piensa. **to s. of,** hablar de. **to s. out,** hablar claro; hablar alto. **to s. up for,** (a person) hablar en favor de (alguien)

speaker /'spikər/ *n* el, *m*, (*f*, la) que habla; (public) orador (-ra). **the S.,** el Presidente de la Cámara de los Comunes

speaking /'spikɪŋ/ *a* hablante; para hablar; elocuente, expresivo. *n* habla, *f*, discurso, *m*. **They are not on s. terms,** No se hablan. **within s. distance,** al habla. **s.-trumpet,** portavoz, *m.* **s.-tube,** tubo acústico, *m*

spear /spɪər/ *n* lanza, *f*; (javelin) venablo, *m*; (harpoon) arpón, *m. vt* herir con lanza, alancear; (fish) arponear. **s.-head,** punta de la lanza, *f*. **s.-thrust,** lanzada, *f*

special /'spɛʃəl/ *a* especial; particular; extraordinario. *n* (train) tren extraordinario, *m.* **s. correspondent,** corresponsal extraordinario, *m.* **s. friend,** amigo (-ga) del alma, amigo íntimo

specialist /'spɛʃəlɪst/ *n* especialista, *mf*

specialization /ˌspɛʃələ'zeiʃən/ *n* especialización, *f*

specialize /'spɛʃəˌlaiz/ *vt* especializar. *vi* especializarse

specially /'spɛʃəli/ *adv* especialmente; particularmente; sobre todo

specialty /'spɛʃəlti/ *n* particularidad, *f*; especialidad, *f*

species /'spiʃiz, -siz/ *n* especie, *f*; raza, *f*

specific /spɪ'sɪfɪk/ *a* específico; explícito. *n* específico, *m.* **s. gravity,** peso específico, *m*, densidad, *f*

specifically /spɪ'sɪfɪkli/ *adv* específicamente; explícitamente

specification /ˌspɛsəfɪ'keiʃən/ *n* especificación, *f*

specify /'spɛsəˌfai/ *vt* especificar

specimen /'spɛsəmən/ *n* espécimen, *m*; ejemplo, *m*; *Inf.* tipo, *m*

specious /'spiʃəs/ *a* especioso. **s. arguments** *Lat. Am.* abogaderas, abogaderías, *fpl*

speciousness /'spiʃəsnɪs/ *n* plausibilidad, *f*; apariencia engañosa, *f*

speck /spɛk/ *n* pequeña mancha, *f*; punto, *m*; átomo, *m*; (on fruit) maca, *f*

speckle /'spɛkəl/ *vt* motear, manchar

speckled /'spɛkəld/ *a* abigarrado; con manchas...

spectacle /'spɛktəkəl/ *n* espectáculo, *m*; escena, *f*; *pl* **spectacles,** gafas, *f pl*, anteojos, *m pl.* **s.-case,** cajita para las gafas, *f*

spectacled /'spɛktəkəld/ *a* con gafas, que lleva gafas

spectacular /spɛk'tækyələr/ *a* espectacular

spectator /'spɛkteitər/ *n* espectador (-ra)

specter /'spɛktər/ *n* espectro, fantasma, *m*

spectral /'spɛktrəl/ *a* espectral

spectrum /'spɛktrəm/ *n Phys.* espectro, *m*

speculate /'spɛkyəˌleit/ *vi* especular (sobre, acerca de); *Com.* especular (en)

speculation /ˌspɛkyə'leiʃən/ *n* especulación, *f*

speculative /'spɛkyəˌlətɪv/ *a* especulativo

speculator /'spɛkyəˌleitər/ *n* especulador (-ra)

speech /spitʃ/ *n* habla, *f*; palabra, *f*; (idiom) lenguaje, *m*; (language) idioma, *m*; *Gram.* oración, *f*; (address) discurso, *m*; disertación, *f.* **part of s.,** parte de la oración, *f.* **to make a s.,** pronunciar un discurso. **s. maker,** orador (-ra)

speechless /'spitʃlɪs/ *a* mudo; sin habla; desconcertado, turbado

speed /spid/ *n* prisa, rapidez, *f*; velocidad, *f. vt* dar la bienvenida (a); conceder éxito (a); (accelerate) acelerar. *vi* darse prisa; correr a toda prisa; (of arrows) volar. **at full s.,** a toda prisa; a toda velocidad; a todo correr. **maximum s.,** velocidad máxima, *f.* **with all s.,** a toda prisa. **s. of impact,** velocidad del choque, *f.* **s.-boat,** lancha de carrera, *f.* **s.-limit,** velocidad máxima, *f*, límite de velocidad, *m*

speedily /'spidli/ *adv* aprisa, rápidamente; prontamente

speediness /'spidɪnɪs/ *n* rapidez, prisa, celeridad, *f*; prontitud, *f*

speeding /'spidɪŋ/ *n* exceso de velocidad, *m.* **s. up,** aceleración, *f*

speedometer /spi'dɒmɪtər/ *n* cuentakilómetros, *m*

speedway /'spidˌwei/ *n* autódromo, *m*, pista de ceniza, *f*

speedy /'spidi/ *a* rápido; pronto

spell /spɛl/ *n* ensalmo, hechizo, *m*; encanto, *m*; (bout) turno, *m*; (interval) rato, *m*; temporada, *f. vt* (a word) deletrear; (a word in writing) escribir; (mean) significar; (be) ser. **a s. of good weather,** una temporada de buen tiempo. **by spells,** a ratos. **to learn to s.,** aprender la ortografía. **s.-bound,** encantado, fascinado; asombrado. **How do you spell "hinchado"?** ¿Cómo se escribe "hinchado"?

spelling /'spɛlɪŋ/ *n* deletreo, *m*; ortografía, *f.* **s.-book,** silabario, *m*; **s. mistake,** falta de ortografía, *f*

spelling bee *n* certamen de deletreo, *m*

spend /spɛnd/ *vt* gastar; (time, etc.) pasar; perder; consumir, agotar. *vi* gastar, hacer gastos. **to s. lavishly,** *Mexico* disparar. **to s. oneself,** agotarse

spendthrift /'spɛndˌθrɪft/ *n* derrochador (-ra), manirroto (-ta). *a* despilfarrado, pródigo

spent /spɛnt/ *a* agotado, rendido. **The night is far s.,** La noche está avanzada. **s. bullet,** bala fría, *f*

sperm /spɜrm/ *n Biol.* esperma, *f*; (whale) cachalote, *m*

spermaceti /ˌspɜrmə'sɛti/ *n* esperma de ballena, *f*

sphere /sfɪər/ *n* esfera, *f.* **s. of influence,** zona de influencia, *f*

spherical /'sfɛrɪkəl, 'sfɪər-/ *a* esférico

sphinx /sfɪŋks/ *n* esfinge, *f.* **s.-like,** de esfinge

spice /spais/ *n* especia, *f*; *Fig.* sabor, *m*; (trace) dejo, *m. vt* especiar. **s. cupboard,** especiero, *m*

spick and span /'spɪk ən 'spæn/ *a* limpio como una patena; (brand-new) flamante; (of persons) muy compuesto

spicy /'spaisi/ *a* especiado; aromático; *Fig.* picante

spider /'spaidər/ *n* araña, *f.* **spider's web,** telaraña, *f*

spidery /'spaidəri/ *a* de arana; lleno de arañas. **s. writing,** letra de patas de araña, *f*

spigot /'spɪgət/ *n* espiche, *m*, llave, *f*

spike /spaik/ *n* punta (de hierro, etc.), *f*; escarpia, *f*;

(for boots) clavo, *m; Bot.* espiga, *f. vt* clavetear; (a cannon) clavar

spill /spɪl/ *vt* derramar. *n* (fall) caída, *f*

spilling /'spɪlɪŋ/ *n* derramamiento, derrame, *m*

spin /spɪn/ *vt* hilar; (a cocoon) tejer; (a top) bailar; (a ball) tornear; (a coin) lanzar. *vi* hilar; girar, bailar. *n* vuelta, *f;* paseo, *m.* **to send spinning downstairs,** hacer rodar por la escalera (a). **to s. a yarn,** contar un cuento. **to s. out,** prolongar

spinach /'spɪnɪtʃ/ *n* espinaca, *f*

spinal /'spaɪnl/ *a* espinal. **s. anaesthesia,** raquianestesia, *f.* **s. column,** columna vertebral, *f*

spindle /'spɪndl/ *n* huso, *m; Mech.* eje, *m.* **s.-shaped,** ahusado

spine /spaɪn/ *n Anat.* espinazo, *m,* columna vertebral, *f; Bot.* espina, *f;* (of a porcupine, etc.) púa, *f*

spineless /'spaɪnlɪs/ *a Zool.* invertebrado; *Fig.* débil

spinet /'spɪnɪt/ *n* espineta, *f*

spinner /'spɪnər/ *n* hilandero (-ra); máquina de hilar, *f*

spinney /'spɪni/ *n* arboleda, *f;* bosquecillo, *m*

spinning /'spɪnɪŋ/ *n* hilado, *m;* hilandería, *f.* **s.-machine,** máquina de hilar, *f.* **s.-top,** trompo, *m,* peonza, *f.* **s.-wheel,** rueca, *f*

spinster /'spɪnstər/ *n* soltera, *f.* **confirmed s.,** solterona, *f*

spiny /'spaɪni/ *a* con púas; espinoso

spiral /'spaɪrəl/ *a* espiral; en espiral. *n* espiral, *f*

spirally /'spaɪrəli/ *adv* en espiral

spire /spaɪər/ *n* (of a church) aguja, *f;* espira, *f*

spirit /'spɪrɪt/ *n* espíritu, *m;* alma, *f;* (ghost) aparecido, fantasma, *m;* (outstanding person) ingenio, *m,* inteligencia, *f;* (disposition) ánimo, *m;* (courage) valor, espíritu, *m;* (for a lamp, etc.) alcohol, *m.* **the Holy S.,** El Espíritu Santo. **to be in high spirits,** no caber de contento, saltar de alegría. **to be in low spirits,** estar desalentado, estar deprimido. **to be full of spirits,** ser bullicioso, tener mucha energía. **to keep up one's spirits,** sostener el valor. **to s. away,** quitar secretamente, hacer desaparecer; (kidnap) secuestrar. **s.-level,** nivel de burbuja, *m.* **s.-stove,** cocinilla, *f*

spirited /'spɪrɪtɪd/ *a* animado, vigoroso; fogoso, animoso, brioso

spiritless /'spɪrɪtlɪs/ *a* sin espíritu, apático; flojo, débil; (depressed) abatido, desalentado; (cowardly) sin valor, cobarde

spiritual /'spɪrɪtʃuəl/ *a* espiritual

spiritualism /'spɪrɪtʃuə,lɪzəm/ *n* espiritismo, *m; Philos.* espiritualismo, *m*

spiritualist /'spɪrɪtʃuəlɪst/ *n* espiritista, *mf; Philos.* espiritualista, *mf*

spiritualistic /,spɪrɪtʃuə'lɪstɪk/ *a* espiritista; *Philos.* espiritualista. **s. séance,** sesión espiritista, *f*

spirituality /,spɪrɪtʃu'ælɪti/ *n* espiritualidad, *f*

spiritually /'spɪrɪtʃuəli/ *adv* espiritualmente

spirituous /'spɪrɪtʃuəs/ *a* espiritoso

spirt /spɜrt/ *vi, vt, n.* See **spurt**

spit /spɪt/ *n* (for roasting) espetón, asador, *m;* (sandbank) banco de arena, *m;* (of land) lengua de tierra, *f;* (spittle) saliva, *f.* **the spit of, the spit and image of, the spitting image of,** la imagen viva de, la segunda edición de, *f. vt* (skewer) espetar; (saliva, etc.) escupir; (curses, etc.) vomitar. *vi* escupir, expectorar; (of a cat) fufear, decir fu; (sputter) chisporrotear; (rain) lloviznar

spite /spaɪt/ *n* malevolencia, mala voluntad, hostilidad, *f;* rencor, *m,* ojeriza, *f. vt* contrariar, hacer daño (a). **He has a s. against them,** Les tiene rencor. **in s. of,** a pesar de; a despecho de

spiteful /'spaɪtfəl/ *a* rencoroso, malévolo

spitefully /'spaɪtfəli/ *adv* malévolamente; con rencor; por maldad; por despecho

spitefulness /'spaɪtfəlnɪs/ *n* malevolencia, *f;* rencor, *m*

spitfire /'spɪt,faɪər/ *n* cascarrabias, *mf,* furia, *f*

spittle /'spɪtl/ *n* saliva, *f*

splash /splæʃ/ *vt* salpicar (de); manchar (con). *vi* derramarse, esparcirse; chapotear, chapalear. *n* chapoteo, *m;* (of rain, etc.) chapaleteo, *m;* (stain or patch) mancha, *f.* **John was splashing about in the sea,** Juan chapoteaba en el mar. **to make a s.,** *Fig.* causar una sensación. **s.-board,** alero, *m*

spleen /splin/ *n Anat.* bazo, *m;* esplín, *m*

splendid /'splɛndɪd/ *a* espléndido; magnífico; glorioso; excelente

splendidly /'splɛndɪdli/ *adv* espléndidamente; magníficamente; excelentemente

splendor /'splɛndər/ *n* resplandor, *m;* magnificencia, *f;* (of exploits, etc.) esplendor, brillo, *m*

splice /splaɪs/ *vt* (ropes, etc.) empalmar; (marry) unir, casar. *n* empalme, *m*

splint /splɪnt/ *n Surg.* férula, *f.* **to put in a s.,** entablar

splinter /'splɪntər/ *vt* astillar, hacer astillas *vi* hacerse astillas

splintery /'splɪntəri/ *a* astilloso

split /splɪt/ *vi* henderse; resquebrajarse; (of seams) nacerse; abrirse; dividirse. *vt* hender; partir; dividir; abrir; (the atom) escindir. *n* hendedura, *f;* grieta, *f;* división, *f;* (in fabric) rasgón, *m;* (quarrel) ruptura, *f.* **to s. hairs,** andar en quisquillas, pararse en pelillos, sutilizar. **I have a splitting headache,** Tengo un dolor de cabeza que me trae loco. **to s. one's sides,** reírse a carcajadas, desternillarse de risa. **to s. on a rock,** estrellarse contra una roca. **to s. the difference,** partir la diferencia. **The blow s. his head open,** El golpe le abrió la cabeza. **to s. on,** *Inf.* delatar, denunciar

splodge /splatʃ/ *n* mancha, *f,* borrón, *m*

splutter /'splʌtər/ *vi* chisporrotear; (of a person) balbucir. *n* chisporroteo, *m.* **to s. out,** decir tartamudeando

spoil /spɔɪl/ *n* botín, despojo, *m;* (of war) trofeo, *m. vt* estropear; echar a perder; (diminish) mitigar; (a child) mimar; (injure) dañar; (destroy) arruinar, destruir. *vi* estropearse; echarse a perder. **to be spoiling for a fight,** tener ganas de pelearse. **You have spoiled my fun,** Me has aguado la fiesta. **s.-sport,** aguafiestas, *mf*

spoiled /spɔɪld/ *a* (of a child, etc.) mimado, consentido, malacostumbrado

spoke /spouk/ *n* (of a wheel) rayo, *m;* (of a ladder) travesaño, peldaño, *m; Naut.* cabilla (de la rueda del timón), *f*

spoken /'spoukən/ *a* hablado. **well-s.,** bien hablado; cortés

spokesman /'spouksmən/ *n* portavoz, *m.* **to be s.,** llevar la palabra

spoliation /,spouli'eɪʃən/ *n* expoliación, *f;* despojo, *m*

sponge /spʌndʒ/ *n* esponja, *f;* (cadger) gorrón (-ona); (cake) bizcocho, *m. vt* limpiar con esponja. **to s.,** *Inf.* vivir de gorra. **s.-holder,** esponjera, *f*

sponginess /'spʌndʒɪnɪs/ *n* esponjosidad, *f*

sponging /'spʌndʒɪŋ/ *n* esponjadura, *f; Inf.* sablazo, *m*

spongy /'spʌndʒi/ *a* esponjoso

sponsor /'spɒnsər/ *n* garante, *mf;* valedor (-ra), patron (-na); (godfather) padrino, *m;* (godmother) madrina, *f,* (radio and TV) auspiciador, patrocinador, *m*

spontaneity /,spɒntə'niti, -'neɪ-/ *n* espontaneidad, *f*

spontaneous /spɒn'teɪniəs/ *a* espontáneo. **s. combustion,** combustión espontánea, *f*

spontaneously /spɒn'teɪniəsli/ *adv* espontáneamente

spook /spuk/ *n* fantasma, espectro, *m*

spool /spul/ *n* (for thread) bobina, *f,* carrete, *m;* (in a sewing machine) canilla, *f;* (of a fishing rod) carrete, *m*

spoon /spun/ *n* cuchara, *f. vt* sacar con cuchara. *vi* (slang) besuquearse. **to s.-feed,** dar de comer con cuchara (a); tratar como un niño (a)

spoonful /'spunfʊl/ *n* cucharada, *f*

spoor /spʊr, spɔr/ *n* pista, huella de animal, *f;* rastro, *m*

sporadic /spə'rædɪk/ *a* esporádico

spore /spɔr/ *n Bot.* espora, *f; Zool.* germen, *m*

sport /spɔrt/ *n* deporte, sport, *m;* deportismo, *m;* (jest) broma, *f;* (game) juego, *m;* (plaything) juguete, *m;* (pastime) pasatiempo, *m. vi* jugar; recrearse, divertirse. *vt* llevar; ostentar, lucir. **He is a s.,** Es un buen chico. **to make s. of,** burlarse de. **sports car,** coche de deporte, *m.* **sports ground,** campo de recreo, *m.* **sports jacket,** chaqueta de sport, americana, *f.* **sports shirt,** camisa corta, *f*

sporting /'spɔrtɪŋ/ *a* deportista; caballeroso. **I think**

there is a s. chance, Me parece que hay una posibilidad de éxito

sporting goods n artículos de deporte, efectos de deportes, m pl

sportive /'spɔrtɪv/ a juguetón; bromista

sportsman /'spɔrtsmən/ n deportista, m; aficionado al sport, m; Fig. caballero, señor, m; buen chico, m

sportsmanlike /'spɔrtsmən,laik/ a de deportista; caballeroso

sportsmanship /'spɔrtsmən,ʃip/ n deportividad, f

spot /spɒt/ n mancha, f; pinta, f; (on the face, etc.) peca, f; grano, m; (place) sitio, m; lugar, m; (of liquor) trago, m; (of food) bocado, m; (of rain) gota, f. vt manchar; motear; (recognize) reconocer; (understand) darse cuenta de, comprender. a tender s., Fig. debilidad, f. on the s., en el acto. s. ball, (billiards) pinta, f. s. cash, dinero contante, m

spotless /'spɒtlɪs/ a saltando de limpio; sin mancha; inmaculado; puro; virgen

spotlight /'spɒt,lait/ n luz del proyector, f; proyector, m

spotted /'spɒtɪd/ a (stained) manchado; (of animals, etc.) con manchas; (of garments, etc.) con pintas

spotty /'spɒti/ a lleno de manchas; moteado; (pimply) con granos

spouse /spaus/ n esposo, m; esposa, f

spout /spaut/ vi chorrear; Inf. hablar incesantemente. vt arrojar; vomitar; Inf. declamar, recitar. n (of a jug, etc.) pico, m; (for water, etc.) tubo, m, cañería, f; canalón, m; (gust) ráfaga, nube, f. down s., tubo de bajada, m

spouting /'spautɪŋ/ n chorreo, m; Inf. declamación, f

sprain /sprein/ vt dislocar, torcer. n dislocación, f, esguince, m. Victoria has sprained her foot, Victoria se ha torcido el pie

sprawl /sprɔl/ vi recostarse (en); extenderse; (of plants) trepar. He went sprawling, Cayó cuan largo era

spray /sprei/ n (branch) ramo, m; (of water, etc.) rocío, m; (of the sea) espuma, f; (mechanical device) pulverizador, m. vt pulverizar; rociar; regar; (the throat) jeringar

spread /sprɛd/ vt tender; cubrir (de); poner; (stretch out) extender; (open out) desplegar; (of disease, etc.) propagar; diseminar; divulgar; difundir. vi extenderse; propagarse; difundirse; divulgarse; (become general) generalizarse. n extensión, f; expansión, f; propagación, f; divulgación, f; (Aer. and of birds) envergadura, f. Carmen s. her hands to the fire, Carmen extendió las manos al fuego. The peacock s. its tail, El pavo real hizo la rueda. The dove s. its wings, La paloma desplegó sus alas. to s. out, vt extender; desplegar; (scatter) esparcir, vi extenderse.

spread like wildfire, correr como pólvora en reguero, propagarse como un reguero de pólvora, ser un reguero de pólvora

spreading /'sprɛdɪŋ/ n (of a disease) propagación, f; (of knowledge, etc.) divulgación, f; expansión, f; extensión, f

spreadsheet /'sprɛd,ʃit/ n hoja de cálculo, f

spree /spri/ n juerga, parranda, f; excursión, f. to go on the s., ir de juerga, ir de picos pardos

sprig /sprig/ n ramita, f; (of heather, etc.) espiga, f; (scion) vástago, m

sprightliness /'spraitlinɪs/ n vivacidad, f, despejo, m; energía, f

sprightly /'spraitli/ a vivaracho, despierto; enérgico

spring /sprɪŋ/ vi saltar, brincar; (become) hacerse; (seek) buscar; (of plants, water) brotar; (of tears) arrasar, llenar; (from) originarse (en), ser causado (por); inspirarse (en). vt (a mine) volar; (a trap) soltar. to s. a surprise, dar una sorpresa. to s. a surprise on a person, coger a la imprevista (a.). to s. at a person, precipitarse sobre. to s. to one's feet, ponerse de pie de un salto. to s. back, saltar hacia atrás; recular; volver a su sitio. to s. open, abrirse súbitamente. to s. up, (of plants) brotar, crecer; (of difficulties, etc.) surgir, asomarse

spring /sprɪŋ/ n (jump) salto, brinco, m; (of water) fuente, f, manantial, m; (season) primavera, f; (of a watch, etc.) resorte, m; (of a mattress, etc.) muelle,

---

m. a primaveral. vi saltar, brincar. at one s., en un salto. to give a s., dar un salto. s.-board, trampolín, m. s.-mattress, colchón de muelles, m. s.-tide, marea viva, f

springiness /'sprɪŋinɪs/ n elasticidad, f

springlike /'sprɪŋ,laik/ a primaveral

springtime /'sprɪŋ,taim/ n primavera, f

sprinkle /'sprɪŋkəl/ vt esparcir; salpicar; rociar

sprinkling /'sprɪŋklɪŋ/ n salpicadura, f; rociadura, f; pequeño número, m. a s. of snow, una nevada ligera

sprint /sprɪnt/ vi sprintar. n sprint, m

sprite /sprait/ n trasgo, m; hada, f

sprout /spraut/ vi brotar, despuntar, retoñar, tallecer; germinar. vt salir. n brote, retoño, pimpollo, m; germen, m. Brussels sprouts, coles de Bruselas, f pl

spruce /sprus/ a peripuesto, muy aseado, pulido; elegante, n Bot. pícea, f. to s. oneself up, arreglarse, ponerse elegante

spruceness /'sprusnɪs/ n aseo, buen parecer, m, elegancia, f

spry /sprai/ a activo, ágil

spur /spɜr/ n espuela, f, aguijada, f; (of a bird) espolón, m; Bot. espuela, f; (of a mountain range) espolón, estribo, m; Fig. estímulo, m. vt espolear, picar con la espuela; calzarse las espuelas; Fig. estimular, incitar, Lat. Am. espuelar. on the s. of the moment, bajo el impulso del momento

spurious /'spyʊriəs/ a espurio; falso

spurn /spɜrn/ vt rechazar; tratar con desprecio; menospreciar

spurt /spɜrt/ vi (gush) chorrear, borbotar; brotar, surgir; (in racing, etc.) hacer un esfuerzo supremo. vt hacer chorrear; lanzar. n (jet) chorro, m; esfuerzo supremo, m

sputter /'spʌtər/ vi chisporrotear; crepitar; (of a pen) escupir; (of a person) balbucir

sputtering /'spʌtərɪŋ/ n chisporroteo, m; crepitación, f; (of a person) balbuceo, m

sputum /'spyutəm/ n esputo, m

spy /spai/ vt observar, discernir. vi espiar, ser espía. n espía, mf. to spy out the land, explorar el terreno. to spy upon, espiar; seguir los pasos (a). spy-glass, catalejo, m

spying /'spaiɪŋ/ n espionaje, m

squabble /'skwɒbəl/ n disputa, f; riña, f. vi pelearse; disputar

squabbling /'skwɒblɪŋ/ n riñas, querellas, f pl; disputas, f pl

squad /skwɒd/ n escuadra, f; pelotón, m

squadron /'skwɒdrən/ n Mil. escuadrón, m; Nav. escuadra, f; Aer. escuadrilla, f; (of persons) pelotón, m. s.-leader, comandante, m

squalid /'skwɒlɪd/ a escuálido; (of quarrels, etc.) sórdido, mezquino

squall /skwɔl/ vi berrear, chillar. n berrido, m; chillido, m; (storm) chubasco, turbión, m; (storm) chubasco, turbión, m; Fig. tormenta, tempestad, f

squalor /'skwɒlər/ n escualidez, f; sordidez, mezquindad, f

squander /'skwɒndər/ vt derrochar, tirar, desperdiciar; (time, etc.) malgastar

squanderer /'skwɒndərər/ n derrochador (-ra)

squandering /'skwɒndərɪŋ/ n derroche, desperdicio, dispendio, m; (of time, etc.) pérdida, f, desperdicio, m

square /skwɛər/ n Math. cuadrado, m; rectángulo, m; (of a chessboard) escaque, m; (of a draftboard and of graph paper) casilla, f; (in a town) plaza, f; (of troops) cuadro, m, a cuadrado; justo; igual; (honest) honrado, formal; (unambiguous) redondo, categórico; Math. cuadrado. She wore a silk s. on her head, Llevaba un pañuelo de seda en la cabeza. five s. feet, cinco pies cuadrados. nine feet s., nueve pies en cuadro. on the s., honradamente. a s. dance, contradanza, f. a s. meal, una buena comida. s. dealing, trato limpio, m. The account is s., La cuenta está justa. to get s. with, desquitarse (de), vengarse de. s. measure, medida de superficie, f. s. root, raíz cuadrada, f. s.-shouldered, de hombros cuadrados

square /skwɛər/ vt cuadrar; escuadrar; (arrange) arreglar; (bribe) sobornar; (reconcile) acomodar; Math. cuadrar. vi conformarse (con), cuadrar (con). to s.

the circle, cuadrar el círculo. **to s. one's shoulders,** enderezarse. **to s. accounts with,** saldar cuentas con.
to s. up to, (a person) avanzar belicosamente hacia
squarely /'skweǝrli/ adv en cuadro; directamente; sin ambigüedades, rotundamente; (honestly) de buena fe, honradamente
squareness /'skweǝrnıs/ n cuadratura, f; (honesty) honradez, buena fe, f
squash /skwɒʃ/ vt aplastar. vi aplastarse; apretarse. n aplastamiento, m; (of fruit, etc.) pulpa, f; (of people) agolpamiento, m; muchedumbre, f; (drink) refresco (de limón, etc.), m, (sport) frontón con raqueta, m
squashy /'skwɒʃi/ a blando y húmedo
squat /skwɒt/ vi acuclillarse, agacharse, agazaparse ponerse en cuclillas; estar en cuclillas; (on land, etc.) apropiarse sin derecho. a rechoncho
squatter /'skwɒtǝr/ n intruso (-sa); colono usurpador, m
squatter town n. See **shanty town**
squawk /skwɔk/ vi graznar; lanzar gritos agudos. n graznido, m; grito agudo, m
squeak /skwik/ vi (of carts, etc.) chirriar, rechinar; (of shoes) crujir; (of persons, mice, etc.) chillar; (slang) cantar. n chirrido, crujido, m; chillido, m. **to have a narrow s.,** escapar por un pelo
squeaking /'skwikıŋ/ n chirrido, rechinamiento, m; crujido, m; (of humans, mice, etc.) chillidos, m pl
squeal /skwil/ vi lanzar gritos agudos, chillar; (complain) quejarse; (slang) cantar. n grito agudo, chillido, m
squealing /'skwilıŋ/ n gritos agudos, chillidos, m pl
squeamish /'skwimıʃ/ a que se marea fácilmente; mareado; (nauseated) asqueado; delicado; remilgado
squeamishness /'skwimıʃnıs/ n tendencia a marearse, f; delicadeza, f; remilgos, m pl
squeeze /skwiz/ vt apretar; estrujar; (fruit) exprimir; (extort) arrancar; (money from) sangrar. n (of the hand, etc.) apretón, m; estrujón, m; (of fruit juice) algunas gotas (de). **It was a tight s. in the car,** Íbamos muy apretados en el coche. **He was in a tight s.,** Se encontraba en un aprieto. **to s. one's way through the crowd,** abrirse camino a codazos por la muchedumbre. **to s. in,** vt hacer sitio para. vi introducirse con dificultad (en)
squelch /skwɛltʃ/ vi gorgotear, chapotear. vt aplastar
squib /skwıb/ n (firework) rapapiés, buscapiés, m; (lampoon) pasquinada, f
squid /skwıd/ n calamar, m
squiggle /'skwıgǝl/ vi cimbrearse, menear
squint /skwınt/ n estrabismo, m; mirada furtiva, f; Inf. vistazo, m, mirada, f. vi ser bizco; bizcar. **to s. at,** mirar de soslayo. **s.-eyed,** bizco. **to be s.-eyed,** mirar contra el gobierno
squire /skwaiǝr/ n escudero, m; hacendado, m. vt escoltar, acompañar
squirm /skwɜrm/ vi retorcerse; (with embarrassment) no saber dónde meterse. n retorcimiento, m. **to s. along the ground,** arrastrarse por el suelo
squirrel /'skwɜrǝl// n ardilla, f
squirt /skwɜrt/ vt (liquids) lanzar. vi chorrear, salir a chorros. n chorro, m; (syringe) jeringa, f
stab /stæb/ vt apuñalar, dar de puñaladas (a); herir. n puñalada, f; herida, f; (of pain, and Fig.) pinchzo, m. **a s. in the back,** una puñalada por la espalda
stability /stǝ'bılıti/ n estabilidad, f; solidez, firmeza, f
stabilize /'steibǝ,laiz/ vt estabilizar
stable /'steibǝl/ a estable; fijo, firme. n cuadra, caballeriza, f; (for cows, etc.) establo, m. vt poner en la cuadra; alojar. **s.-boy,** mozo de cuadra, m
stack /stæk/ n (of hay) niara, f; almiar, m; (heap) montón, m; (of rifles) pabellón, m; (of a chimney) cañón, m. vt Agr. hacinar; amontonar; Mil. poner (las armas) en pabellón
stacked /stækt/ a (woman) abultada de pechera
stadium /'steidiǝm/ n estadio, m
staff /stæf/ n vara, f; (bishop's, and Fig.) báculo, m; (pilgrim's) bordón, m; (pole) palo, m; (flagstaff) asta, f; (of an office, etc.) personal, m; (editorial) redacción, f; (corps) cuerpo, m; Mil. plana mayor, f, estado mayor, m; Mus. pentagrama, m. vt proveer de

personal. **general s.,** estado mayor general, m. **s. officer,** Mil. oficial de estado mayor, m
stag /stæg/ n ciervo, m. **s.-beetle,** ciervo volante, m. **s.-hunting,** caza del ciervo, f
stage /steidʒ/ n (for workmen) andamio, m; (of a microscope) portaobjetos, m; Theat. escena, f, tablas, f pl; teatro, m; (of development, etc.) etapa, f; fase, f. vt Theat. escenificar; poner en escena; Theat. representar; (a demonstration, etc.) arreglar. **by easy stages,** poco a poco; (of a journey) a pequeñas etapas. **to come on the s.,** salir a la escena. **to go on the s.,** hacerse actor (actriz), dedicarse al teatro. **s. carpenter,** tramoyista, m. **s.-coach,** diligencia, f. **s.-craft,** arte de escribir para el teatro, f; arte escénica, f. **s.-direction,** acotación, f. **s.-door,** entrada de los artistas, f. **s.-effect,** efecto escénico, m. **s.-fright,** miedo al público, m. **s.-hand,** tramoyista, sacasillas, metesillas y sacamuertos, m. **s. manager,** director de escena, m. **s.-whisper,** aparte, m
stagger /'stægǝr/ vi tambalear; andar haciendo eses; (hesitate) titubear, vacilar. vt desconcertar. n titubeo, tambaleo, m; Aer. decalaje, m. **staggered working hours,** horas de trabajo escalonadas, f pl
staggering /'stægǝrıŋ/ a tambaleante; (surprising) asombroso, sorprendente; (dreadful) espantoso. **a s. blow,** un golpe que derriba
staging /'steidʒıŋ/ n (scaffolding) andamio, m; Theat. producción, f; representación, f; decorado, m
stagnancy /'stægnǝnsi/ n (of water) estancación, f; (inactivity) estagnación, f; paralización, f
stagnant /'stægnǝnt/ a estancado; paralizado. **to be s.,** estar estancado. **s. water,** agua estancada, f
stagnate /'stægneit/ vi estancarse; estar estancado; (of persons) vegetar
stagnation /stæg'neiʃǝn/ n (of water) estancación, f; estagnación, f; parálisis, f
staid /steid/ a serio, formal, juicioso
staidness /'steidnıs/ n seriedad, formalidad, f
stain /stein/ vt manchar; (dye) teñir. n mancha, f; colorante, m. **without a s.,** Fig. sin mancha. **stained glass,** vidrio de color, m. **s.-remover,** quitamanchas, m
stainless /'steinlıs/ a sin mancha; inmaculado, puro
stair /steǝr/ n escalón, peldaño, m; escalera, f; pl **stairs,** escalera, f. **a flight of stairs,** una escalera; un tramo de escaleras. **below stairs,** escalera abajo. **s.-carpet,** alfombra de escalera, f. **s.-rod,** varilla para alfombra de escalera, f
staircase /'steǝr,keis/ n escalera, f. **spiral s.,** escalera de caracol, f
stake /steik/ n estaca, f; (for plants) rodrigón, m; (gaming) envite, m, apuesta, f; (in an undertaking) interés, m; pl **stakes,** (prize) premio, m; (race) carrera, f. vt estacar; (plants) rodrigar; (bet) jugar. **at s.,** en juego; en peligro. **to be burnt at the s.,** morir en la hoguera. **to s. one's all,** jugarse el todo por el todo. **to s. a claim,** hacer una reclamación. **to s. out,** jalonar
stalactite /stǝ'læktait/ n estalactita, f
stalagmite /stǝ'lægmait/ n estalagmita, f
stale /steil/ a no fresco; (of bread, etc.) duro, seco; (of air) viciado; viejo; pasado de moda; (tired) cansado
stalemate /'steil,meit/ n (chess, checkers) tablas, f pl; Fig. punto muerto, m. **to reach a s.,** llegar a un punto muerto
staleness /'steilnıs/ n rancidez, f; (of bread, etc.) dureza, f; (of news, etc.) falta de novedad, f
stalk /stɔk/ n Bot. tallo, m; Bot. pedúnculo, m; (of a glass) pie, m. vi andar majestuosamente, Fig. rondar. vt (game) cazar al acecho; (a person) seguir los pasos (a)
stalking horse /'stɔkıŋ/ n boezuelo, m; Fig. pretexto, disfraz, m
stall /stɔl/ n (in a stable) puesto (individual), m; (stable) establo, m; (choir) silla de coro, f; (in a fair, etc.) barraca, f, puesto, m; Theat. butaca, f; (finger-stall) dedal, m. vt (an engine) cortar accidentalmente. vi Auto. pararse de pronto; Aer. perder velocidad; (of a cart, etc.) atascarse. **pit s.,** Theat. butaca de platea, f
stalling /'stɔlıŋ/ n Auto. parada accidental, f; Aer. pérdida de velocidad, f. **Stop s.!** ¡Déjate de rodeos!

stallion /'stælyən/ n semental, m

stalwart /'stɔlwərt/ a robusto, fornido; leal; valiente

stalwartness /'stɔlwərtnɪs/ n robustez, f; lealtad, f; valor, m

stamina /'stæmənə/ n resistencia, f

stammer /'stæmər/ vi tartamudear; (hesitate in speaking) titubear, balbucir. n tartamudez, f; titubeo, balbuceo, m

stammerer /'stæmərər/ n tartamudo (-da)

stammering /'stæmərɪŋ/ a tartamudo; balbuciente. n tartamudeo, m; balbuceo, m

stamp /stæmp/ vt estampar; imprimir; (documents) timbrar; pegar el sello de correo (a); (characterize) sellar; (Fig. engrave) grabar; (coins) acuñar; (press) apisonar; (with the foot) golpear con los pies, patear; (in dancing) zapatear. n (with the foot) patada, f, golpe con los pies, m; (mark, etc.) marca, f; (rubber, etc.) estampilla, f; matasellos, m; cuño, m; (for documents) póliza, f; timbre, m; (for letters) sello, m; Mexico timbre, m, elsewhere in Lat. Am. estampilla, f, (machine) punzón, m; mano de mortero, f; (Fig. sign) sello, m; (kind) temple, m, clase, f. **The events of that day are stamped on my memory,** Los acontecimientos de aquel día están grabados en mi memoria. **to s. out,** (a fire, etc.) extinguir, apagar; (resistance, etc.) vencer; destruir. **postage-s.,** sello de correos, m. **s.-album,** álbum de sellos, m. **s.-duty,** impuesto del timbre, m. **s.-machine,** expendedor automático de sellos de correo, m

stampede /stæm'pid/ n fuga precipitada, f; pánico, m. vi huir precipitadamente; (of animals) salir de estampía; huir en desorden. vt hacer perder la cabeza (a), sembrar el pánico entre

stamping /'stæmpɪŋ/ n selladura, f; (of documents) timbrado, m; (of fabrics, etc.) estampado, m; (with the feet) pataleo, m; (in dancing) zapateo, m

stance /stæns/ n posición de los pies, f; postura, f

stanch /stɔntʃ/ vt restañar

stand /stænd/ vi estar de pie; ponerse de pie, incorporarse; estar; hallarse; sostenerse; ser; ponerse; (halt) parar; (remain) permanecer, quedar. vt poner; (endure) resistir; tolerar; sufrir; (entertain) convidar. **S.! ¡Alto! S. up!** ¡Ponte de pie! **as things s.,** tal como están las cosas. **I cannot s. any more,** No puedo más. **I cannot s. him,** No le puedo ver. **Nothing stands between them and ruin,** No hay nada entre ellos y la ruina. **I stood him a drink,** Le convidé a un trago. **How do we s.?** ¿Cómo estamos? **It stands to reason that...,** Es lógico que... **Edward stands six feet,** Eduardo tiene seis pies de altura. **to s. accused of,** ser acusado de. **to s. godfather (or godmother) to,** sacar de pila (a). **to s. in need (of),** necesitar, tener necesidad (de). **to s. on end,** (of hair) ponerse de punta, despeluzarse. **to s. one in good stead,** ser útil, ser ventajoso. **to s. one's ground,** no ceder, tenerse fuerte. **to s. to attention,** cuadrarse, permanecer en posición de firmes. **to s. well with,** tener buenas relaciones con, ser estimado de. **to s. aside,** tenerse a un lado; apartarse; (in favor of someone) retirarse. **to s. back,** quedarse atrás; recular, retroceder. **to s. by,** estar de pie cerca de; estar al lado de; estar presente (sin intervenir); ser espectador; estar preparado; (one's friends) ayudar, proteger; (a promise, etc.) atenerse (a); ser fiel (a); (of a ship) mantenerse listo. **s.-by,** n recurso, m. **to s. for,** representar; simbolizar; (mean) significar; (Parliament, etc.) presentarse como candidato; (put up with) tolerar, sufrir. **to s. in,** colaborar. **to s. in with,** estar de acuerdo con, ser partidario de; compartir. **to s. off,** mantenerse a distancia. **to s. out,** (in relief, and Fig. of persons) destacarse; (be firm) resistir, mantenerse firme; Naut. gobernar más afuera. **S. out of the way!** ¡Quítate del medio! **to s. over,** (be postponed) quedar aplazado. **to s. up,** estar de pie; ponerse de pie, incorporarse; tenerse derecho. **to s. up against,** resistir; oponerse a. **to s. up for,** defender. **to s. up to,** hacer cara a

stand /stænd/ n puesto, m; posición, actitud, f; (for taxis, etc.) punto, m; (in a market, etc.) puesto, m; Sports. tribuna, f; (for a band) quiosco, m; (of a dish, etc.) pie, m; Mech. sostén, m; (opposition) resistencia, oposición, f. **to make a s. against,** oponerse re-

sueltamente (a); ofrecer resistencia (a). **to take one's s.,** fundarse (en), apoyarse (en). **to take up one's s. by the fire,** ponerse cerca del fuego

standard /'stændərd/ n (flag) estandarte, m, bandera, f; (for gold, weights, etc.) marco, m; norma, f; convención, regla, f; (of a lamp) pie, m; (pole) poste, m; columna, f; (level) nivel, m. a corriente; normal; típico; clásico. **It is a s. type,** Es un tipo corriente. **gold s.,** patrón de oro, m. **s. author,** autor clásico, m. **s. formula,** fórmula clásica, f. **s. of living,** nivel de vida, m. **s.-bearer,** abanderado, m. **s.-lamp,** lámpara vertical, f

standardization /,stændərdə'zeiʃən/ n (of armaments, etc.) unificación de tipos, f; (of dyestuffs, medicinals, etc.) control, m, estandardización, f

standardize /'stændər,daiz/ vt hacer uniforme; controlar

standing /'stændɪŋ/ a de pie, derecho; permanente, fijo; constante. n posición, f; reputación, f; importancia, f; antigüedad, f. **It is a quarrel of long s.,** Es una riña antigua. **s. committee,** comisión permanente, f. **s. room,** sitio para estar de pie, m. **s. water,** agua estancada, f. **standoffish,** frío, etiquetero; altanero. **stand-offishness,** frialdad, f; altanería, f. **standpoint,** punto de vista, m

standstill /'stænd,stɪl/ n parada, f; pausa, f. **at a s.,** parado; (of industry) paralizado

stanza /'stænzə/ n estrofa, estancia, f

staple /'steipəl/ n (fastener) grapa, f; (of wool, etc.) hebra, fibra, f; producto principal (de un país), m; (raw material) materia prima, f; a principal; más importante; corriente

stapler /'steiplər/ (device) cosepapeles, engrapador, m, atrochadora (Argentina), f

star /star/ n (all meanings) estrella, f; (asterisk) asterisco, m. vt estrellar, sembrar de estrellas; marcar con asterisco. vi (Theat. cinema) presentarse como estrella, ser estrella. **stars and stripes,** las barras y las estrellas. **to be born under a lucky s.,** tener estrella. **to see stars,** ver estrellas. **s.-gazing,** observación de las estrellas, f; ensimismamiento, m. **s.-spangled,** estrellado, tachonado de estrellas, sembrado de estrellas. **s.-turn,** gran atracción, f

starboard /'starbərd/ n Naut. estribor, m

starch /startʃ/ n almidón, m, las harinas, f pl, vt almidonar

starchy /'startʃi/ a almidonado; (of food) feculento; Fig. tieso, entonado, etiquetero

stare /steər/ vi mirar fijamente; abrir mucho los ojos. n mirada fija, f; stony s., mirada dura, f. **to s. at,** (a person) clavar la mirada en; mirar de hito en hito (a). **The explanation stares one in the face,** La explicación salta a la vista (or está evidente). **to s. into space,** mirar las telarañas, avergonzar con la mirada

starfish /'star,fɪʃ/ n estrella de mar, f

staring /'steərɪŋ/ a (of colors) chillón, llamativo, encendido. **s. eyes,** ojos saltones, m pl; ojos espantados, m pl

stark /stark/ a rígido; Poet. poderoso; absoluto. **s. staring mad,** loco de atar. **s.-naked,** en cueros vivos, en pelota

starless /'starlɪs/ a sin estrellas

starlight /'star,lait/ n luz de las estrellas, f, a estrellado

starry /'stari/ a estrellado, sembrado de estrellas

start /start/ vi (begin) empezar, comenzar; (upset) estremecerse, asustarse; saltar; (set out) salir; ponerse en camino; (of a train, a race) arrancar; ponerse en marcha; Aer. despegar; (of timbers) combarse. vt empezar; (a car, etc.) poner en marcha; (a race) dar la señal de partida; (a hare, etc.) levantar; (cause) provocar, causar; (a discussion, etc.) abrir; iniciar. n (fright) susto, m; (setting out) partida, salida, f; (beginning) principio, comienzo, m; (starting-point of a race) arrancadero, m; Aer. despegue, m; (advantage) ventaja, f. **at the s.,** al principio. **for a s.,** para empezar. **from s. to finish,** desde el principio hasta el fin. **She started to cry,** Se puso a llorar. **He has started his journey to Canada,** Ha empezado su viaje al Canadá. **I started up the engine,** Puse el motor en marcha. **to get a s.,** asustarse; tomar la delantera. **to give** (a person) **a s.**, asustar, dar un susto (a); dar la ventaja (a). **to give** (a person) **a s. in life,** ayudar a alguien a situarse en la vida. **to make a fresh s. (in life),** hacer vida nueva, empezar la vida de nuevo. **to s. after,** lanzarse en busca de; salir tras. **to s. back,** retroceder; emprender el viaje de regreso; marcharse. **to s. off,** salir, partir; ponerse en camino. **to s. up,** *vi* incorporarse bruscamente, ponerse de pie de un salto; (appear) surgir, aparecer. *vt* (an engine) poner en marcha

starter /'stɑrtər/ *n* iniciador (-ra); (for a race) starter, juez de salida, *m*; (competitor in a race) corredor, *m*; (of a car, etc.) arranque, *m*

starting /'stɑrtɪŋ/ *n* (setting out) salida, partida, *f*; (beginning) principio, *m*; (fear) estremecimiento, *m*; susto, *m*. **s.-gear,** palanca de arranque, *f*. **s.-handle,** manivela de arranque, *f*. **s.-point,** punto de partida, *m*; *Fig.* arrancadero, punto de arranque, *m*. **s.-post,** puesto de salida, *m*

startle /'stɑrtl/ *vt* asustar, sobresaltar, alarmar. **The news startled him out of his indifference,** Las noticias le hicieron salir de su indiferencia

startling /'stɑrtlɪŋ/ *a* alarmante; (of dress, etc.) exagerado; (of colors) chillón

starvation /stɑr'veiʃən/ *n* hambre, *f*; *Med.* inanición, *f*. **s. diet,** régimen de hambre, *m*. **s. wage,** ración de hambre, *f*

starve /stɑrv/ *vi* morir de hambre; pasar hambre, no tener bastante que comer; no comer. *vt* matar de hambre; privar de alimentos (a). **I am simply starving,** Tengo una hambre canina, Me muero de hambre. **to s. with cold,** *vi* morir de frío. *vt* matar de frío

starved /stɑrvd/ *a* muerto de hambre, hambriento. **s. of affection,** hambriento de cariño

starving /'stɑrvɪŋ/ *a* que muere de hambre, hambriento

state /steit/ *n* estado, *m*; condición, *f*; (anxiety) agitación, ansiedad, *f*; (social) rango, *m*; (pomp) magnificencia, pompa, *f*; (government, etc.) Estado, *m*; nación, *f. a* de Estado; de gala, de ceremonia. **the married s.,** el estado matrimonial. **s. of war,** estado de guerra. **in s.,** con gran pompa. **to lie in s.,** (of a body) estar expuesto. **s. apartments,** habitaciones de gala, *f pl.* **s. banquet,** comida de gala, *f.* **s. coach,** coche de gala, *m.* **s. control,** control por el Estado, *m.* **S. Department,** Departamento de Estado, *m.* **s. education,** instrucción pública, *f.* **State of the Union message,** Mensaje al Congreso, *m.* **s. papers,** documentos de Estado, *m pl*

state /steit/ *vt* decir (que), afirmar (que); declarar; (one's case, etc.) exponer; explicar; *Math.* proponer

statecraft /'steit,kræft/ *n* arte de gobernar, *m*

stated /'steitɪd/ *a* arreglado, indicado; fijo. **the s. date,** la fecha indicada. **at s. intervals,** a intervalos fijos

statehood /'steithʊd/ *n* estadidad, *f*

stateliness /'steitlinɪs/ *n* dignidad, *f*; majestad, *f*

stately /'steitli/ *a* majestuoso; imponente; noble; digno

statement /'steitmənt/ *n* afirmación, declaración, *f*; resumen, *m*; exposición, *f*; *Law.* deposición, *f*; *Com.* estado de cuenta, *m.* **to make a s.,** hacer una declaración

stateroom /'steit,rum/ *n* sala de recepción, *f*; (on a ship) camarote, *m*

statesman /'steitsmən/ *n* hombre de estado, *m*

statesmanlike /'steitsmən,laik/ *a* de hombre de estado

statesmanship /'steitsmən,ʃip/ *n* arte de gobernar, *m*

static /'stætɪk/ *a* estático

statics /'stætɪks/ *n* estática, *f*

station /'steiʃən/ *n* (place) puesto, sitio, *m*; (Rail. and Eccl.) estación, *f*; (social) posición social, *f*; *Naut.* apostadero, *m*; *Surv.* punto de marca, *m. vt* estacionar, colocar, poner. **to s. oneself,** colocarse. **Stations of the Cross,** Estaciones, *f pl.* **s.-master,** jefe de la estación, *m*

stationary /'steiʃə,nɛri/ *a* estacionario; inmóvil; *Astron.* estacional

stationer /'steiʃənər/ *n* papelero (-ra). **stationer's shop,** papelería, *f*

stationery /'steiʃə,nɛri/ *n* (shop) papelería, *f*, efectos de escritorio, *m pl*; (paper) papel de escribir, *m*

station wagon *n* pisicorre, coche camioneta, coche rural, *m*

statistical /stə'tɪstɪkəl/ *a* estadístico

statistician /,stætɪ'stɪʃən/ *n* estadista, *m*

statistics /stə'tɪstɪks/ *n* estadística, *f*

statuary /'stætʃu,ɛri/ *a* estatuario. *n* estatuaria, *f*; estatuas, *f pl*; (sculptor) estatuario, *m*

statue /'stætʃu/ *n* estatua, *f*; imagen, *f*

statuesque /,stætʃu'ɛsk/ *a* escultural

statuette /,stætʃu'ɛt/ *n* figurilla, *f*

stature /'stætʃər/ *n* estatura, *f*; (moral, etc.) valor, *m*

status /'steitəs, 'stætəs/ *n* (Law. etc.) estado, *m*; posición, *f*; rango, *m.* **What is his s. as a physicist?** ¿Cómo se le considera entre los físicos? **social s.,** posición social, *f*; rango social, *m*

statute /'stætʃut/ *n* ley, *f*; acto legislativo, *m*; estatuto, *m*; regla, *f.* **s. book,** código legal, *m*

statutory /'stætʃʊ,tɔri/ *a* establecido; reglamentario; estatutario

staunch /stɔntʃ/ *a* leal, fiel; firme, constante. *vt* restañar

staunchness /'stɔntʃnɪs/ *n* lealtad, fidelidad, *f*; firmeza, *f*

stave /steiv/ *n* (of a barrel, etc.) duela, *f*; (of a ladder) peldaño, *m*; (stanza) estrofa, *f*; *Mus.* pentagrama, *m.* **to s. in,** abrir boquete en; romper a golpes; quebrar. **to s. off,** apartar, alejar; (delay) aplazar, diferir; (avoid) evitar; (thirst, etc.) dominar

stay /stei/ *vt* detener; (a judgment, etc.) suspender. *vi* permanecer; quedarse; detenerse; (of weather, etc.) durar; (lodge) hospedarse, vivir. **to come to s.,** venir a ser permanente. **to s. a person's hand,** detenerle el brazo. **to s. at home,** quedarse en casa. **s.-at-home,** *a* casero. *n* persona casera, *f.* **to s. the course,** terminar la carrera. **S.! Say no more!** ¡Calle! ¡No diga más! **to s. away,** ausentarse. **to s. up,** no acostarse; velar. **to s. with,** quedarse con; alojarse con; quedarse en casa de, vivir con

stay /stei/ *n* estancia, permanencia, *f*; residencia, *f*; (restraint) freno, *m*; *Law.* suspensión, *f*; (endurance) aguante, *m*, resistencia, *f*; *Naut.* estay, *m*; (prop) puntal, *m*; *Fig.* apoyo, soporte, *m*; *pl* **stays,** corsé, *m*

stead /stɛd/ *n* lugar, *m.* **in the s. of,** en el lugar de, como substituto de. **It has stood me in good s.,** Me ha sido muy útil

steadfast /'stɛd,fæst/ *a* fijo; constante; firme; tenaz. **s. gaze,** mirada fija, *f*

steadfastly /'stɛd,fæstli/ *adv* fijamente; con constancia; firmemente; tenazmente

steadfastness /'stɛd,fæstnɪs/ *n* fijeza, *f*; constancia, *f*; firmeza, *f*; tenacidad, *f*

steadily /'stɛdli/ *adv* firmemente; (without stopping) sin parar; continuamente; (assiduously) diligentemente; (uniformly) uniformemente. **Prices have gone up s.,** Los precios no han dejado de subir. **He looked at it s.,** Lo miraba sin pestañear (or fijamente)

steadiness /'stɛdinɪs/ *n* estabilidad, *f*; firmeza, *f*; constancia, *f*; (of persons) seriedad, formalidad, *f*; (of workers) diligencia, asiduidad, *f*

steady /'stɛdi/ *a* firme; seguro; fijo; constante; uniforme; continuo; estacionario; (of persons) serio, formal, juicioso; (of workers) diligente, asiduo. *vt* afirmar; (persons) hacer más serio (a); (nerves, etc.) calmar, fortificar. **a s. job,** un empleo seguro. **S.!** ¡Calma!; *Naut.* ¡Seguro! **He steadied himself against the table,** Se apoyó en la mesa

steak /steik/ *n* tajada, *f*; biftec, *Argentina* bife, *m*

steal /stil/ *vt* robar, hurtar; tomar. *vi* robar, ser ladrón; (glide) deslizarse; (overwhelm) dominar, ganar insensiblemente (a). **to s. a kiss,** robar un beso. **to s. a look at,** mirar de soslayo (or de lado). **to s. away,** escurrirse, escabullirse; marcharse a hurtadillas. **to s. in,** deslizarse en, colarse en

stealthily /'stɛlθəli/ *adv* a hurtadillas; a escondidas, furtivamente

stealthiness /'stɛlθinɪs/ *n* carácter furtivo, *m*

stealthy /'stɛlθi/ *a* furtivo; cauteloso

steam /stim/ *n* vapor, *m. a* de vapor. *vi* echar vapor. *vt Cul.* cocer al vapor; (clothes) mojar; (windows,

etc.) empañar. **to have the s. up,** estar bajo presión. **The windows are steamed,** Los cristales están empañados. **s.-boiler,** caldera de vapor, f. **s.-engine,** máquina de vapor, f. **s.-hammer,** maza de fragua, f. **s.-heat,** calefacción por vapor, f. **s.-roller,** Lit. apisonadora, Fig. fuerza arrolladora, f
steamboat /'stim,bout/ n vapor, m
steamer /'stimər/ n Cul. marmita al vacío, f; Naut. buque de vapor, m
steamship /'stim,ʃɪp/ n buque de vapor, piróscafo, m
steamy /'stimi/ a lleno de vapor
steed /stid/ n corcel, m
steel /stil/ n (metal, and Poet. sword) acero, m; (for sharpening) afilón, m. a de acero; acerado. vt acerar; Fig. endurecer. **to be made of s.,** Fig. ser de bronce. **He cannot s.** himself to do it, No puede persuadirse a hacerlo. **to s.** one's heart, hacerse duro de corazón. **cold s.,** arma blanca, f. **stainless s.,** acero inoxidable, m. **s.-engraving,** grabado en acero, m
steel mill n fábrica de acero, f
steep /stip/ a acantilado, escarpado; precipitoso; (of stairs, etc.) empinado; (of price) exorbitante. vt (soak) remojar, empapar; Fig. absorber; (in a subject) empaparse (en). n remojo, m. **It's a bit s.!** Inf. ¡Es un poco demasiado!
steeping /'stipɪŋ/ n remojo, m, maceración, f
steeple /'stipəl/ n campanario, m, torre, f; aguja, f
steeplechase /'stipəl,tʃeis/ n steeplechase, m, carrera de obstáculos, f
steepness /'stipnɪs/ n carácter escarpado, m, lo precipitoso
steer /stɪər/ vt Naut. gobernar; (a car, etc.) conducir; Fig. guiar, conducir. vi Naut. timonear; Naut. navegar; Auto. conducir. n Zool. novillo, m. **to s. clear of,** evitar. **to s.** one's way through the crowd, abrirse paso entre la muchedumbre
steerage /'stɪərɪdʒ/ n gobierno, m; (stern) popa, f; (quarters) entrepuente, m. **to go s.,** viajar en tercera clase
steering /'stɪrɪŋ/ n Naut. gobierno, m; (tiller, etc.) gobernalle, timón, m; (of a vehicle) conducción, f. **s.-column,** barra de dirección, f. **s.-wheel,** Auto. volante de dirección, m; Naut. rueda del timón, f
stellar /'stɛlər/ a estelar
stem /stɛm/ n (of a tree) tronco, m; (of a plant) tallo, m; (of a glass, etc.) pie, m; (Mus. of a note) rabo, m; (of a pipe) tubo, m; (of a word) radical, m. vt (check) contener; (the tide) ir contra; (the current) vencer; (dam) estancar. **from s. to stern,** de proa a popa
stench /stɛntʃ/ n tufo, hedor, m, hediondez, Lat. Am. also fortaleza, f
stencil /'stɛnsəl/ n patrón para estarcir, m; estarcido, m. vt estarcir
stenographer /stə'nɒɡrəfər/ n estenógrafo (-fa), taquígrafo (-fa)
stenography /stə'nɒɡrəfi/ n estenografía, taquigrafía, f
stentorian /stɛn'tɔriən/ a estentóreo
step /stɛp/ n paso, m; (footprint) huella, f; (measure) medida, f; (of a stair, etc.) escalón, peldaño, m, grada, f; (of a ladder) peldaño, m; (of vehicles) estribo, m; (grade) escalón, m; Mus. intervalo, m. **at every s.,** a cada paso. **flight of steps,** escalera, f; (before a building, etc.) escalinata, f. **in steps,** en escalones. **to bend** one's steps towards, dirigirse hacia. **to keep in s.,** llevar el paso. **to take a s.,** dar un paso. **to take steps,** tomar medidas. **s. by s.,** paso a paso; poco a poco. **s.-dance,** baile típico, m. **s.-ladder,** escalera de tijera, f
step /stɛp/ vi dar un paso; pisar; andar. **Please s. in!** Sírvase de entrar. **Will you s.** this way, please? ¡Haga el favor de venir por aquí! **to s. aside,** ponerse a un lado; desviarse; Fig. retirarse (en favor de). **to s. in,** entrar; intervenir (en); (meddle) entrometerse. **He stepped into the train,** Subió al tren. **to s. on,** pisar. **to s. on board,** Naut. ir a bordo. **to s. out,** salir; (from a vehicle) bajar; (a dance) bailar. **He stepped out a moment ago,** Salió hace un instante
stepbrother /'stɛp,brʌðər/ n hermanastro, medio hermano, m

stepchild /'stɛp,tʃaild/ n hijastro (-ra)
stepdaughter /'stɛp,dɔtər/ n hijastra, f
stepfather /'stɛp,faðər/ n padrastro, m
stepmother /'stɛp,mʌðər/ n madrastra, f
steppingstone /'stɛpɪŋ,stoun/ n pasadera, f; Fig. escabel, escalón, m
stepsister /'stɛp,sɪstər/ n hermanastra, media hermana, f
stepson /'stɛp,sʌn/ n hijastro, m
stereotype /'stɛriə,taip/ n estereotipia, f, clisé, m, vt (Print. and Fig.) estereotipar
sterile /'stɛrɪl/ a estéril; árido
sterility /stə'rɪlɪti/ n esterilidad, f; aridez, f
sterilization /,stɛrələ'zeiʃən/ n esterilización, f
sterilize /'stɛrə,laiz/ vt esterilizar
sterilizer /'stɛrə,laizər/ n esterilizador, m
sterling /'stɜrlɪŋ/ a esterlina f; Fig. genuino. **pound s.,** libra esterlina, f
stern /stɜrn/ a severo, austero; duro. n Naut. popa, f
sternly /'stɜrnli/ adv con severidad, severamente, duramente
sternness /'stɜrnnɪs/ n severidad, f; dureza, f
sternum /'stɜrnəm/ n Anat. esternón, m
stethoscope /'stɛθə,skoup/ n estetoscopio, m
stevedore /'stivɪ,dɔr/ n estibador, m
stew /stu/ vt guisar a la cazuela, estofar; (mutton, etc.) hervir; (fruit) cocer. n estofado, m; Inf. agitación, f. **to be in a s.,** Inf. sudar la gota gorda. **stewed fruit,** compota de frutas, f. **s.-pot,** cazuela, olla, f, puchero, m
steward /'stuərd/ n administrador, m; mayordomo, m; (provision) despensero, m; Naut. camarero, m
stewardess /'stuərdɪs/ n Naut. camarera, f
stick /stɪk/ vt clavar (en); hundir (en); (put) poner; sacar; (stamps, etc.) pegar; fijar; (endure) resistir; tolerar. vi clavarse, hundirse; estar clavado; pegarse; (remain) quedar; (in the mud, etc.) atascarse, embarrancarse, (on a reef) encallarse; (in the throat, etc.) atravesarse; (stop) detenerse. **It sticks in my throat,** Inf. No lo puedo tragar. **Friends always s. together,** Los amigos no se abandonan. **The nickname stuck to him,** El apodo se le quedó. **to s. at,** persistir en; desistir (ante); pararse (ante); tener escrúpulos sobre. **to s. at nothing,** no tener escrúpulos. **He stuck at his work,** Siguió trabajando. **to s. down,** pegar. **to s.** one's nose into other people's business Mexico entrucharse. **to s. out,** vi proyectar; sobresalir. vt (one's chest) inflar; (one's tongue) sacar. **His ears s. out,** Tiene las orejas salientes. **to s. to,** (one's job) no dejar; (one's plans) adherirse (a); (one's principles) ser fiel (a); (one's friends) no abandonar; (one's word, etc.) cumplir; atenerse (a). **to s. up,** vi (of hair) erizarse, ponerse de punta; salirse. vt clavar; (a notice) fijar. **to s. up for,** (a person) defender
stick /stɪk/ n estaca, f; (for the fire) leña, f; (walking-s.) bastón, m; (of office) vara, f; (of sealing-wax, etc.) barra, f; palo, m; (baton) batuta, f; (of celery) tallo, m. **in a cleft s.,** entre la espada y la pared. **to give** (a person) the s., dar palo (a)
stickiness /'stɪkɪnɪs/ n viscosidad, f
sticking plaster /'stɪkɪŋ/ n esparadrapo, m
stick-in-the-mud /'stɪkɪnðə,mʌd/ n chapado a la antigua, m
stickler /'stɪklər/ n rigorista, mf. **to be a s. for etiquette,** ser etiquetero
sticky /'stɪki/ a pegajoso, viscoso; Fig. difícil
stiff /stɪf/ a rígido; inflexible; tieso; (of paste, etc.) espeso; (of manner) distante; (of a bow, etc.) frío; (of a person) almidonado, etiquetero; severo; (of examinations, etc.) difícil; (strong) fuerte; (of price, etc.) alto, exorbitante; (of a shirt front, etc.) duro. **s. with cold,** aterido de frío. **s. neck,** torticolis, m. **s.-necked,** terco, obstinaz
stiffen /'stɪfən/ vt reforzar; atiesar; (paste, etc.) hacer más espeso; (Fig. strengthen) robustecer; (make more obstinate) hacer más tenaz. vi atiesarse; endurecerse; (straighten oneself) enderezarse; (of manner) volverse menos cordial; (become firmer) robustecerse; (become more obstinate) hacerse más tenaz. **The breeze stiffened,** Refrescó el viento

stiffly /'stɪfli/ *adv* tiesamente; rígidamente; obstinadamente

stiffness /'stɪfnɪs/ *n* rigidez, *f*; tiesura, *f*; dureza, *f*; (of manner) frialdad, *f*; (obstinacy) terquedad, obstinación, *f*; (of an examination, etc.) dificultad, *f*

stifle /'staifəl/ *vt* ahogar, sofocar; apagar; suprimir

stifling /'staiflɪŋ/ *a* sofocante, bochornoso

stigma /'stɪgmə/ *n* estigma, *m*

stigmatize /'stɪgmə,taiz/ *vt* estigmatizar

stile /stail/ *n* (nearest equivalent) portilla con escalones, *f*

still /stɪl/ *a* tranquilo; inmóvil; quedo; silencioso; (of wine) no espumoso. *n* silencio, *m*. **in the s. of the night,** en el silencio de la noche. **Keep s.!** ¡Estate quieto! **to keep s.,** quedarse inmóvil, no moverse. **s.-birth,** nacimiento de un niño muerto, *m*. **s.-born,** nacido muerto. **s. life,** *Art.* bodegón, *m*, naturaleza muerta, *f*

still /stɪl/ *vt* hacer callar, acallar; calmar, tranquilizar; apaciguar; (pain) aliviar

still /stɪl/ *adv* todavía, aún; (nevertheless) sin embargo, no obstante; (always) siempre. **I think she s.** visits them every week, Me parece que sigue visitándoles cada semana. **s. and all,** con todo y eso. **s. more,** aún más. **s. to be paid,** *Lat. Am.* impago

still /stɪl/ *n* alambique, *m*. **salt water s.,** adrazo, *m*

stillness /'stɪlnɪs/ *n* quietud, tranquilidad, *f*; silencio, *m*. **in the s. of the night,** en el silencio de la noche

stilt /stɪlt/ *n* zanco, *m*

stilted /'stɪltɪd/ *a* ampuloso, campanudo, hinchado

stimulant /'stɪmyələnt/ *a and n* estimulante, *m*

stimulate /'stɪmyə,leit/ *vt* estimular; incitar (a), excitar (a)

stimulating /'stɪmyə,leitɪŋ/ *a* estimulante; (encouraging) alentador; (inspiring) sugestivo, inspirador

stimulation /,stɪmyə'leiʃən/ *n* excitación, *f*; (stimulus) estímulo, *m*

stimulus /'stɪmyələs/ *n* estímulo, *m*; *Med.* estimulante, *m*; (incentive) impulso, incentivo, *m*; acicate, aguijón, *m*

sting /stɪŋ/ *vt* picar, pinchar; (of snakes, etc.) morder; (of hot dishes) resquemar; (of hail, etc.) azotar; (pain) atormentar; (provoke) provocar (a), incitar (a). *n* (*Zool.* organ) aguijón, *m*; *Bot.* púa, *f*; (of a scorpion) uña, *f*; (of a serpent) colmillo, *m*; (pain and wound) pinchazo, *m*; (serpent's) mordedura, *f*; (stimulus) acicate, estímulo, *m*; (torment) tormento, dolor, *m*

stingily /'stɪndʒəli/ *adv* avaramente, tacañamente

stinginess /'stɪndʒɪnɪs/ *n* tacañería, avaricia, *f*

stinging /'stɪŋɪŋ/ *a* picante; *Fig.* mordaz; (of blows) que duele

stingy /'stɪndʒi/ *a* tacaño, avaro, mezquino, *Argentina* agalludo, *Chile, Peru* coñete

stink /stɪŋk/ *vi* apestar, heder, oler mal. *n* tufo, *m*, hediondez, *f*, *Lat. Am. also* fortaleza, *f*

stinking /'stɪŋkɪŋ/ *a* apestoso, hediondo, fétido, mal oliente

stint /stɪnt/ *vt* escatimar; limitar. *n* límite, *m*, restricción, *f*. **without s.,** sin límite; sin restricción.

stipend /'staipend/ *n* estipendio, salario, *m*

stipple /'stɪpəl/ *vt* *Art.* puntear. *n* punteado, *m*

stipulate /'stɪpyə,leit/ *vi* estipular, poner como condición. *vt* estipular, especificar. **They stipulated for a five-day week,** Pusieron como condición (*or* Estipularon) que trabajasen cinco días por semana

stipulation /,stɪpyə'leiʃən/ *n* estipulación, *f*; condición, *f*

stir /stɜr/ *vt* agitar; revolver; (the fire) atizar; (move) mover; (emotionally) conmover, impresionar; (the imagination) estimular. *vi* moverse. *n* movimiento, *m*; conmoción, *f*; (bustle) bullicio, *m*; sensación, *f*. **to make a s.,** causar una sensación. **to s. one's coffee,** revolver el café. **to s. up discontent,** fomentar el descontento

stirring /'stɜrɪŋ/ *a* conmovedor, emocionante, impresionante; (of times, etc.) turbulento, agitado

stirrup /'stɜrəp, 'stɪr-/ *n* estribo, *m*. **s.-cup,** última copa, *f*. **s.-pump,** bomba de mano (para líquidos), *f*

stitch /stɪtʃ/ *n* (action) puntada, *f*; (result) punto, *m*; *Surg.* punto de sutura, *m*; (pain) punzada, *f*, pinchazo, *m*. *vt* coser; *Surg.* suturar

stock /stɒk/ *n* (of a tree) tronco, *m*; (of a rifle) culata, *f*; (handle) mango, *m*; (of a horse's tail) nabo, *m*; (stem for grafting etc.) injerto, *m*; (race) raza, *f*; (lineage) linaje, *m*, estirpe, *f*; (supply) provisión, *f*; reserva, *f*; (of merchandise) surtido, *m*; *Cul.* caldo, *m*; (collar) alzacuello, *m*; *Bot.* alhelí, *m*; (government) papel del estado, *m*, valores públicos, *m pl*; (financial) valores, *m pl*, (of a company) capital, *m*; *pl* **stocks,** *Hist.* cepo, *m*; (of goods) existencias, *f pl*, stock, *m*, a corriente; del repertorio. **in s.** en existencia. **lives.,** ganado *m*. **rolling-s.,** *Rail.* materia móvil ferroviario, *m*. **s. phrase,** frase hecha, *f*. **s. size,** talla corriente, *f*. **to lay in a s. of,** hacer provisión de, almacenar. **to stand s.-still,** quedarse completamente inmóvil. **to take s.,** hacer inventario. **to take s. of,** inventariar; examinar, considerar. **s.-breeder,** ganadero, *m*. **s.-broker,** corredor de bolsa, bolsista, *m*. **s. exchange,** bolsa, *f*. **s.-in-hand,** *Com.* existencias, *f pl*. **s.-in-trade** (*Com.* etc.) capital, *m*. **s.-raising,** cría de ganados, ganadería, *f*. **s.-taking,** *Com.* inventario, *m*

stock /stɒk/ *vt* proveer (de), abastecer (de); (of shops) tener existencia de

stockade /stɒ'keid/ *n* estacada, empalizada, *f*, *vt* empalizar

stocking /'stɒkɪŋ/ *n* media, *f*. **nylon stockings,** medias de cristal (*or* de nilón), *f pl*

stocky /'stɒki/ *a* rechoncho, doblado, achaparrado

stodgy /'stɒdʒi/ *a* (of food) indigesto; (of style, etc.) pesado, amazacotado

stoic /'stouɪk/ *a and n* estoico (-ca)

stoical /'stouɪkəl/ *a* estoico

stoke /stouk/ *vt* (a furnace, etc.) cargar, alimentar; (a fire) echar carbón, etc., en. **s.-hole,** cuarto de fogoneros, *m*; *Naut.* cámara de calderas, *f*

stoker /'stoukər/ *n* fogonero, *m*; (mechanical) cargador, *m*

stole /stoul/ *n* (*Eccl.* and of fur, etc.) estola, *f*

stolid /'stɒlɪd/ *a* impasible, imperturbable

stolidly /'stɒlɪdli/ *adv* imperturbablemente

stomach /'stʌmək/ *n* estómago, vientre, *m*; apetito, estómago, *m*; (courage) corazón, valor, *m*. *vt* digerir; (tolerate) tragar, sufrir. **s.ache,** dolor de estómago, *m*

stone /stoun/ *n* piedra, *f*; (gem) piedra preciosa, *f*; (of cherries, etc.) hueso, *m*; (of grapes, etc.) pepita, *f*; *Med.* cálculo, *m. a* de piedra. *vt* apedrear; (a wall, etc.) revestir de piedra; (fruit) deshuesar. **to pave with stones,** empedrar. **to leave no s. unturned,** no dejar piedra sin remover. **within a stone's throw,** a corta distancia, a un paso. **S. Age,** edad de piedra, *f*. **s.-breaker,** cantero, picapedrero, *m*. **s.-cold,** muy frío, completamente frío. **s.-deaf,** *a* completamente sordo. **s.-fruit,** fruta de hueso, *f*. **s.-mason,** mazonero, albañil, *m*; picapedrero, *m*. **s.-quarry,** pedrera, cantera, *f*

stonily /'stounli/ *adv* fríamente; fijamente, sin pestañear

stoniness /'stounɪnɪs/ *n* lo pedregoso; (of hearts, etc.) dureza, *f*; (of stares, etc.) fijeza, inmovilidad, *f*

stoning /'stounɪŋ/ *n* apedreamiento, *m*, lapidación, *f*

stony /'stouni/ *a* pedregoso; (of hearts, etc.) duro, insensible, empedernido; (of a stare, etc.) fijo, duro

stool /stul/ *n* banquillo, taburete, *m*; (feces) excremento, *m*

stoop /stup/ *vi* inclinarse, doblarse; encorvarse; ser cargado de espaldas; andar encorvado; (demean oneself) rebajarse (a). *vt* inclinar, doblar. *n* inclinación, *f*; cargazón de espaldas, *f*

stooping /'stupɪŋ/ *a* inclinado, doblado; (of shoulders) cargado

stop /stɒp/ *vt* (a hole) obstruir, atascar; (a leak) cegar, tapar; (a tooth) empastar; (stanch) restañar; (the traffic, etc.) parar; detener; (prevent) evitar; (discontinue) cesar (de), dejarse de; (cut off) cortar; (end) poner fin (a), acabar con; (payment) suspender. *vi* parar; detenerse; cesar; terminar; (stay) quedarse, permanecer. **I stopped myself from saying what I thought,** Me abstuve de decir lo que pensaba, Me mordí la lengua. **They stopped the food-supply,** Cortaron las provisiones. **s. beating about the bush,** dejarse de historias. **to s. one's ears,** *Fig.* taparse los oídos. **to s. payments,** suspender pagos

stop /stɒp/ *n* parada, *f*; pausa, *f*; interrupción, *f*; cesación, *f*; (of an organ) registro, *m*. "Stop," (road sign) «Alto.» **full s.**, *Gram.* punto, *m*. **tram s.**, parada de tranvía, *f*. **to come to a full s.**, pararse de golpe; cesar súbitamente. **to put a s. to**, poner fin a, poner coto a, acabar con. *f pl.* **s.-watch**, cronógrafo, *m*

stopgap /'stɒp,gæp/ *n* (person) tapagujeros, *m*; substituto, *m*

stoppage /'stɒpɪdʒ/ *n* parada, *f*; cesación, *f*; suspensión, *f*; interrupción, *f*; pausa, *f*; (obstruction) impedimento, *m*; obstrucción, *f*. **s. of work**, suspensión de trabajo, *f*

stopper /'stɒpər/ *n* tapón, *m*; obturador, *m*, *vt* cerrar con tapón, taponar

stopping /'stɒpɪŋ/ *n* parada, *f*; cesación, *f*; suspensión, *f*; (of a tooth) empaste, *m*. **without s.**, sin parar. **without s. to draw breath**, de un aliento. **s.-place**, paradero, *m*; (of buses, etc.) parada, *f*. **s. train**, tren ómnibus, *m*. **s. up**, obturación, *f*

storage /'stɔrɪdʒ/ *n* almacenamiento, *m*; (charge) almacenaje, *m*; (place) depósito, *m*. **cold s.**, cámara frigorífica, *f*. **s. battery**, acumulador, *m*

store /stɔr/ *n* provisión, *f*; abundancia, *f*; reserva, *f*; (of knowledge, etc.) tesoro, *m*; (for furniture, etc.) depósito, almacén, *m*; *pl* **stores**, (shop) almacenes, *m pl*; (food) provisiones, *f pl*; (*Mil.* etc.) pertrechos, *m pl*. *vt* proveer; guardar, acumular; tener en reserva; (furniture, etc.) almacenar; (hold) caber en, tomar. **in s.**, en reserva; en depósito, en almacén. **to set s. by**, estimar en mucho; dar importancia a. **to set little s. by**, estimar en poco; conceder poca importancia a. **s.-room**, despensa, *f*

storehouse /'stɔr,haus/ *n* almacén, *m*; *Fig.* mina, *f*, tesoro, *m*

storekeeper /'stɔr,kipər/ = **shopkeeper**

storied /'stɔrid/ *a* de... pisos. **two-s.**, de dos pisos

stork /stɔrk/ *n* cigüeña, *f*

storm /stɔrm/ *n* tempestad, tormenta, *f*, temporal, *m*; *Fig.* tempestad, *f*; *Mil.* asalto, *m*. *vt Mil.* tomar por asalto, asaltar. *vi* (of persons) bramar de cólera. **to take by s.**, tomar por asalto; *Fig.* cautivar, conquistar. **s. cloud**, nubarrón, *m*. **s.-signal**, señal de temporal, *f*. **s.-tossed**, *a* sacudido por la tempestad. **s. troops**, tropas de asalto, *f pl*. **s. window**, contravidriera, *f*

stormily /'stɔrməli/ *adv* tempestuosamente; con tormenta

storming /'stɔrmɪŋ/ *n* (*Mil.* etc.) asalto, *m*; violencia, *f*. **s.-party**, pelotón de asalto, *m*

stormy /'stɔrmi/ *a* tempestuoso; de tormenta; (of life, etc.) borrascoso; (of meetings, etc.) tempestuoso

story /'stɔri/ *n* historia, *f*; cuento, *m*; anécdota, *f*; (funny) chiste, *m*; (plot) argumento, enredo, *m*; (fib) mentira, *f*; (floor) piso *m*. **It's always the same old s.**, Es siempre la misma canción (or historia). **That is quite another s.**, Eso es harina de otro costal, *Argentina, Perú* esas son otras cuarenta. **short s.**, cuento, *m*. **s. book**, libro de cuentos, *m*. **s. teller**, cuentista, *mf*; (fibber) mentiroso (-sa)

stout /staut/ *a* fuerte; (brave) intrépido, indómito; (fat) gordo, grueso; (firm) sólido, firme; (decided) resuelto; vigoroso. *n* (drink) cerveza negra, *f*. **s.-hearted**, valiente, intrépido

stove /stouv/ *n* estufa, *f*; (open, for cooking) cocina económica, *f*; (gas, etc., for cooking) cocina, *f*, fogón, *m*. **s. maker**, *Argentina* fumista, *mf*; **s. pipe**, tubo de la chimenea, *m*

stow /stou/ *vt* meter, poner; colocar; (hide) esconder; (cargo) estibar, arrimar

stowaway /'stouə,wei/ *n* polizón, llovido, *m*, *vi* embarcarse secretamente

straddle /'strædl̩/ *vi* (*Nav.* etc.) graduar el tiro. *vt* montar a horcajadas en. **s.-legged**, patiabierto

strafe /streif/ *vt* bombardear concienzudamente; castigar; reñir

straggle /'strægəl/ *vi* rezagarse; vagar en desorden; dispersarse; estar esparcido; extenderse

straggler /'stræglər/ *n* rezagado (-da)

straight /streit/ *a* derecho; recto; (of hair) lacio; directo; (tidy) en orden; (frank) franco; (honest) honrado. *adv* derecho; en línea recta, directamente. **Keep s. on!** ¡Siga Vd. derecho! **to go s. to the point,**

dejarse de rodeos, ir al grano. **to look s. in the eyes,** mirar derecho en los ojos. **s. away,** inmediatamente, en seguida. **s. out,** sin rodeos

straighten /'streitn/ *vt* enderezar; poner derecho; poner en orden; arreglar. *vi* ponerse derecho; enderezarse. **to s. one's face,** componer el semblante. **to s. the line,** *Mil.* rectificar el frente. **to s. out,** poner en orden; *Fig.* desenredar. **to s. oneself up,** erguirse

straightforward /,streit'fɔrwərd/ *a* honrado, sincero; franco; (simple) sencillo. **s. answer,** respuesta directa, *f*

straightforwardly /,streit,fɔrwərdli/ *adv* honradamente; francamente

straightforwardness /,streit'fɔrwərdnɪs/ *n* honradez, integridad, *f*; franqueza, *f*; (simplicity) sencillez, *f*

straightness /'streitnɪs/ *n* derechura, rectitud, *f*; (of persons) honradez, probidad, *f*

straightway /'streit'wei, -,wei/ *adv* al instante, inmediatamente

strain /strein/ *vt* estirar; forzar; esforzar; (one's eyes) quebrarse; (one's ears) aguzar (el oído); (a muscle, etc.) torcer; (a friendship) pedir demasiado (a), exigir demasiado (de); (a person's patience, etc.) abusar (de); (words) tergiversar; (embrace) abrazar estrechamente (a); (filter) filtrar; *Cul.* colar. *vi* hacer un gran esfuerzo, esforzarse (para). *n* tirantez, *f*; tensión, *f*; (effort) esfuerzo, *m*; (sprain) torcedura, *f*; (nervous) tensión nerviosa, *f*; *Mech.* esfuerzo, *m*; (breed) raza, *f*; *Biol.* cepa, *f*; (tendency) tendencia, *f*; (heredity) herencia, *f*; rasgo, *m*, vena, *f*; (style) estilo, *m*; *Mus.* melodía, *f*; (of mirth, etc.) son, ruido, *m*; (poetry) poesía, *f*. **to s. a point,** hacer una excepción. **to s. after effect,** buscar demasiado el efecto

strained /streind/ *a* tenso; (of muscles, etc.) torcido; (of smiles, etc.) forzado. **s. relations,** *Polit.* estado de tirantez, *m*

strainer /'streinər/ *n* filtro, *m*; coladero, *m*

strait /streit/ *n Geog.* estrecho, *m*. **to be in great straits,** estar en un apuro. **s. laced,** *Fig.* de manga estrecha

straiten /'streitn/ *vt* estrechar; limitar, **in straitened circumstances,** en la necesidad

Strait of Magellan /mə'dʒɛlən/ Estrecho de Magallanes, *m*

Straits Settlements /'streits 'sɛtl̩mənts/ Establecimientos del Estrecho, *m pl*

strand /strænd/ *n* (shore) playa, *f*; (of a river) ribera, orilla, *f*; (of rope) cabo, ramal, *m*; (of thread, etc.) hebra, *f*; (of hair) trenza, *f*. *vt* and *vi* (a ship) encallar, varar. **to be stranded,** hallarse abandonado; (by missing a train, etc.) quedarse colgado. **to leave stranded,** abandonar, dejar plantado (a)

strange /streindʒ/ *a* (unknown) desconocido; nuevo; (exotic, etc.) extraño, singular; extraordinario; raro; exótico. **I felt very s. in a s. country,** Me sentía muy solo en un país desconocido. **He is a very s. person,** Es una persona muy rara

strangely /'streindʒli/ *adv* extrañamente, singularmente; de un modo raro

strangeness /'streindʒnɪs/ *n* novedad, *f*; singularidad, *f*; rareza, *f*

stranger /'streindʒər/ *n* desconocido (-da); (from a foreign country) extranjero (-ra); (from another region, etc.) forastero (-ra).

strangle /'stræŋgəl/ *vt* estrangular; (a sob, etc.) ahogar

stranglehold /'stræŋgəl,hould/ *n* collar de fuerza, *m*. **to have a s. (on),** tener asido por la garganta; paralizar

strap /stræp/ *n* correa, *f*; tirante de botas, *m*, *vt* atar con correas

strapping /'stræpɪŋ/ *a* rozagante, robusto

stratagem /'strætədʒəm/ *n* estratagema, *f*, ardid, *m*

strategic /strə'tidʒɪk/ *a* estratégico

strategist /'strætɪdʒɪst/ *n* estratega, *m*

strategy /'strætɪdʒi/ *n* estrategia, *f*

stratification /,strætəfɪ'keiʃən/ *n* estratificación, *f*

stratosphere /'strætə,sfɪər/ *n* estratosfera, *f*

stratum /'streitəm, 'strætəm/ *n Geol.* estrato, *m*, capa, *f*; (social, etc.) estrato, *m*

straw /strɔ/ *n* paja, *f*. **I don't care a s.,** No se me da un bledo. **to be not worth a s.,** no valer un ardite. **to be the last s.,** ser el colmo. **to drink through a s.,** sorber con una paja. **s. hat,** sombrero de paja, *m.* **s.-colored,** pajizo

strawberry /'strɔ,bɛri/ *n* (plant and fruit, especially small or wild) fresa, *f*; (large cultivated) fresón, *m.* **s. bed,** fresal, *m.* **s. ice,** helado de fresa, *m*

stray /strei/ *vi* errar, vagar; perderse; (from a path, etc., also *Fig.*) descarriarse. *n* animal perdido, *m*; niño (-ña) sin hogar. *a* descarriado, perdido; errante; (sporadic) esporádico

stray bullet *n* bala perdida, *f*

streak /strik/ *n* raya, *f*; (in wood and stone) vena, *f*; (of light) rayo, *m*; (of humor, etc.) rasgo, *m. vt* rayar. **like a s.** of lightning, como un relámpago

streaky /'striki/ *a* rayado; (of bacon) entreverado

stream /strim/ *n* arroyo, riachuelo, *m*; río, *m*; (current) corriente, *f*; (of words, etc.) torrente, *m. vi* correr, fluir; manar, brotar; (float) flotar, ondear. *vt* (blood, etc.) manar, echar. **The tears streamed down Jean's cheeks,** Las lágrimas corrían por las mejillas de Juana. **s.-lined,** fuselado

streamer /'strimər/ *n* gallardete, *m*, serpentina, *f*; (on a hat, etc.) cinta colgante, *f*, siguemepollo, *m*

stream-of-consciousness /'strim əv 'kɒnʃəsnɪs/ *n* escritura automática, *f*, fluir de la conciencia, *m*, flujo de la subconciencia, monólogo interior, *m*

street /strit/ *n* calle, *f*. **the man in the s.,** el hombre medio. **at s. level,** a ras de suelo. **s. arab,** golfo, *m*. **s. cries,** gritos de vendedores ambulantes, *m pl*. **s. entertainer,** saltabanco, *m*. **s. brawl, s. fight,** algarada callejera, *f*. **s. fighting,** luchas en las calles, *f pl*. **s. musician,** músico ambulante, *m*. **s.-sweeper,** barrendero, *m*. **s.-walker,** buscona, prostituta, *f*

strength /strɛŋkθ, strɛnθ/ *n* fuerza, *f*; (of colors, etc.) intensidad, *f*; (of character) firmeza (de carácter), *f*; (of will) resolución, decisión, *f*; *Mil.* complemento, *m*. **The enemy is in s.,** El enemigo está presente en gran número. **by sheer s.,** a viva fuerza. **on the s. of,** confiando en, en razón de

strengthen /'strɛŋkθən, 'strɛn-/ *vt* fortificar; consolidar; reforzar. *vi* fortificarse; consolidarse; reforzarse

strengthening /'strɛŋkθənɪŋ, 'strɛn-/ *a* fortificante; tonificante. *n* refuerzo, *m*; fortificación, *f*; consolidación, *f*

strenuous /'strɛnyuəs/ *a* activo, enérgico; vigoroso; (arduous) arduo

strenuously /'strɛnyuəsli/ *adv* enérgicamente, vigorosamente

strenuousness /'strɛnyuəsnɪs/ *n* energía, *f*, vigor, *m*; (arduousness) arduidad, *f*

streptococcus /,strɛptə'kɒkəs/ *n Med.* estreptococo, *m*

streptomycin /,strɛptə'maisɪn/ *n Med.* estreptomicina, *f*

stress /strɛs/ *n* tensión, *f*; impulso, *m*; importancia, *f*, énfasis, *m*; *Gram.* acento (tónico), *m*; acentuación, *f*; *Mech.* esfuerzo, *m. vt* acentuar; poner énfasis en, insistir en. **under s. of circumstance,** impulsado por las circunstancias. **times of s.,** tiempos turbulentos, *m pl*. **to lay great s. on,** insistir mucho en; dar gran importancia a

stretch /strɛtʃ/ *vt* (make bigger) ensanchar; (pull) estirar; (one's hand, etc.) alargar, extender; (knock down) tumbar. *vi* ensancharse; dar de sí; ceder; extenderse. **to s. oneself,** estirarse, desperezarse. **to s. as far as,** llegar hasta, extenderse hasta. **to s. a point,** hacer una concesión. **to s. one's legs,** estirar las piernas

stretch /strɛtʃ/ *n* estirón, *m*; tensión, *f*; (of country, etc.) extensión, *f*; (scope) alcance, *m*. **by a s. of the imagination,** con un esfuerzo de imaginación. **He can sleep for hours at a s.,** Puede dormir durante horas enteras

stretcher /'strɛtʃər/ *n* (for gloves) ensanchador, *m*; dilatador, *m*; (for canvas) bastidor, *m*; (for wounded, etc.) camilla, *f*. **s.-bearer,** camillero, *m*

strew /stru/ *vt* esparcir; derramar

stricken /'strɪkən/ *a* (wounded) herido; (ill) enfermo; (with grief) afligido, agobiado de dolor. **s. in years,** entrado en años

strict /strɪkt/ *a* exacto; estricto; escrupuloso; severo

strictly /'strɪktli/ *adv* exactamente; estrictamente; severamente, con severidad. **s. speaking,** en rigor, en realidad

strictness /'strɪktnɪs/ *n* exactitud, *f*; escrupulosidad, *f*; rigor, *m*; severidad, *f*

stricture /'strɪktʃər/ *n Fig.* crítica severa, censura, *f*. **to pass strictures on,** criticar severamente

stride /straid/ *vi* andar a pasos largos, dar zancadas; cruzar a grandes trancos. *vt* cruzar de un tranco; poner una pierna en cada lado de. *n* zancada, *f*, paso largo, tranco, *m*. **to s. up and down,** dar zancadas

strident /'straidnt/ *a* estridente; (of colors) chillón

strife /straif/ *n* lucha, *f*, conflicto, *m*

strike /straik/ *vt* golpear; pegar, dar una bofetada (a); (wound) herir; (a coin) acuñar; (a light) encender; (of a snake) morder; (a blow) asestar, dar; (of ships, a rock, etc.) chocar contra; estrellarse contra; (flags) bajar, arriar; (a tent) desmontar; (camp) levantar; (come upon) llegar a; (discover) encontrar por casualidad, tropezar con; hallar, descubrir; (seem) parecer; (impress) impresionar; (of ideas) ocurrirse; (an attitude) tomar, adoptar; (of a clock) dar; (a balance) hacer; (a bargain) cerrar, llegar a; (level) nivelar; (cuttings) enraciar. *vi* golpear; (of a clock) dar la hora; (of a ship) encallar; (go) ir; (penetrate) penetrar; (of a cutting) arraigar; (sound) sonar. **He struck the table with his fist,** Golpeó la mesa con el puño. **I was very much struck by the city's beauty,** La belleza de la ciudad me impresionó mucho. **The news struck fear into their hearts,** La noticia les llenó el corazón de miedo. **The clock struck three,** El reloj dio las tres. **The hour has struck,** *Fig.* Ha llegado la hora. **How did the house s. you?** ¿Qué te pareció la casa? **to s. a bargain,** cerrar un trato. **to s. a blow,** asestar un golpe. **to s. an attitude,** tomar una actitud. **to s. home,** dar en el blanco; herir; herir en lo más vivo; hacerse sentir. **to s. at,** asestar un golpe (a); acometer, embestir; atacar. **to s. down,** derribar; (of illness) acometer. **to s. off,** (a head, etc.) cortar; (a name) borrar, tachar; (print) imprimir. **to s. out,** *vi* asestar un golpe (a); (a swimmer) nadar; echarse, lanzarse. *vt* (a word, etc.) borrar, rayar; (begin) iniciar. **to s. through,** (cross out) rayar, tachar; (of the sun's rays, etc.) penetrar. **to s. up,** *vt* tocar; empezar a cantar; (a friendship) trabar. *vi* empezar a tocar. **to s. up a march,** *Mil.* batir la marcha

strike /straik/ *n* huelga, *f*. *vi* declararse en huelga. **go-slow s.,** tortuguismo, *m*. **lock-out s.,** huelga patronal, *f*. **sit-down s.,** huelga de brazos caídos, *f*. **to go on s.,** declararse en huelga. **s.-breaker,** esquirol, *m*. **s.-pay,** subsidio de huelga, *m*

striker /'straikər/ *n* huelguista, *mf*

striking /'straikɪŋ/ *a* notable, sorprendente; (impressive) impresionante; que llama la atención; llamativo

string /strɪŋ/ *n* bramante, *m*; cuerda, *f*; (ribbon) cinta, *f*; (of beads, etc.) sarta, *f*; (of onions) ristra, *f*; (of horses, etc.) reata, *f*; hilera, *f*; (of a bridge) cable, *m*; (of oaths, lies) sarta, serie, *f*; (of beans) fibra, *f. vt* encordar; (beads, etc.) ensartar; (beans) quitar las fibras (de). **He is all strung up,** Se le crispan los nervios. **the strings,** los instrumentos de cuerda. **a s. of pearls,** un collar de perlas. **for strings,** *Mus.* para arco. **to pull strings,** *Fig.* manejar los hilos. **to s. up,** (an instrument) templar; (a person) pender, ahorcar. **s. bean,** judía verde, *f, Central America, Mexico* ejote, *m*

stringed /strɪŋd/ *a* (of musical instruments) de cuerda. **s. instrument,** instrumento de cuerda, *m*

stringent /'strɪndʒənt/ *a* estricto, severo

stringy /'strɪŋi/ *a* fibroso; filamentoso; correoso; arrugado

strip /strɪp/ *vt* desnudar; despojar (de); quitar; robar; (a cow) ordeñar hasta agotar la leche. *vi* desnudarse. *n* (tatter) jirón, *m*; tira, lista, *f*; (of wood) listón, *m*; (of earth) pedazo, *m*; (*Geog.* of land) zona, *f*. **to s. off,** *vt* quitar; (bark from a tree) descortezar; (one's clothes) despojarse de. *vi* desprenderse, separarse. **to s. the leaves from, to s. the petals from,** *Lat. Am.* deshojar

stripe /straip/ *n* raya, lista, *f*; (*Mil.* etc.) galón, *m*; (lash) azote, *m. vt* rayar. **the stripes of the tiger,** las rayas del tigre

suave

striped /straipt, 'straipɪd/ *a* listado, a rayas; con rayas. s.

trousers, pantalón de corte, *m*

stripling /'strɪplɪŋ/ *n* joven imberbe, pollo, mancebo, *m*

strive /straiv/ *vi* esforzarse (a); pugnar (por, para); trabajar (por); (fight against) luchar contra; pelear con. **He was striving to understand,** Pugnaba por (or Se esforzaba a) comprender

stroke /strouk/ *n* (blow) golpe, *m*; (of the oars) golpe del remo, *m*, remada, *f*; (at billards) tacada, *f*; (in golf) tirada, *f*; (in swimming) braza, *f*; (of a clock) campanada, *f*; (of a pen) rasgo de la pluma, *m*; (of a brush) pincelada, *f*; *Mech.* golpe de émbolo, *m*; (caress) caricia con la mano, *f*. *vt* acariciar con la mano. **on the s. of six,** al acabar de dar las seis. **to have a s.,** tener un ataque de apoplejía. **s. of genius,** rasgo de ingenio, *m*. **s. of good luck,** racha de buena suerte, *f*

stroll /stroul/ *vi* pasearse, vagar. *n* vuelta, *f*, paseo, *m*. **to go for a s.,** dar una vuelta

stroller /'stroulər/ *n* paseante, *mf*

strolling /'stroulɪŋ/ *a* errante; ambulante. **s. player,** *n* cómico (-ca) ambulante

strong /strɔŋ/ *a* fuerte; vigoroso; robusto; *Argentina* alentado; enérgico; firme; poderoso; (of colors) intenso, vivo; (of tea, coffee) cargado; *Gram.* fuerte. **The government took s. measures,** El gobierno tomó medidas enérgicas. **They gave very s. reasons,** Alegaron unas razones muy poderosas. **Grammar is not his s. point,** La gramática no es su punto fuerte. **The enemy is s. in numbers,** El enemigo es numéricamente fuerte. **The society is four thousand s.,** La sociedad tiene cuatro mil miembros. **s. box,** caja de caudales, *f*. **s. man,** hombre fuerte, *m*; (in a circus) hércules, *m*. **s.-minded,** de espíritu fuerte; independiente. **s. room,** cámara acorazada, *f*

stronghold /'strɔŋˌhould/ *n* fortaleza, *f*; refugio, *m*

strongly /'strɔŋli/ *adv* vigorosamente; fuertemente; firmemente

structural /'strʌktʃərəl/ *a* estructural

structurally /'strʌktʃərəli/ *adv* estructuralmente, desde el punto de vista de la estructura

structure /'strʌktʃər/ *n* estructura, *f*; edificio, *m*; construcción, *f*

struggle /'strʌgəl/ *vi* luchar; pelear; disputarse, *Lat. Am.* abrocharse (con...); *n* lucha, *f*; combate, *m*; conflicto, *m*. **to s. to one's feet,** luchar por levantarse. **without a s.,** sin luchar

struggling /'strʌglɪŋ/ *a* pobre, indigente, que lucha para vivir

strum /strʌm/ *vt* (a stringed instrument) rascar; tocar mal

strut /strʌt/ *vi* pavonearse. *vt* (prop) apuntalar. *n* pavonada, *f*; (prop) puntal, *m*. **to s. out,** salir de un paso majestuoso

stub /stʌb/ *n* (of a tree) tocón, *m*; (of a pencil, candle, etc.) cabo, *m*; pedazo, fragmento, *m*; (of a cigarette or cigar) colilla, *f*. **s.-book,** talonario, *m*

stubborn /'stʌbərn/ *a* inquebrantable, tenaz; persistente; (pig-headed) terco, testarudo, *Lat. Am.* empecinado

stubbornness /'stʌbərnɪs/ *n* tenacidad, *f*; terquedad, *f*, testarudez, *f*

stucco /'stʌkou/ *n* estuco, *m*, *vt* estucar

stuck /stʌk/ past part. of **stick. be stuck** (for an answer) = **be stumped**

stuck-up /'stʌk 'ʌp/ *a* = **haughty**

stud /stʌd/ *n* (of horses) caballeriza, *f*; (nail) tachón, *m*; (for collars) pasador para camisas, *m*. *vt* tachonar; sembrar. **dress s.,** botón de la pechera, *m*. **s.-farm,** potrero, *m*

student /'studnt/ *n* estudiante, *mf*. *a* estudiantil. **students** (as a body) *Lat. Am.* estudiantado, *msg.*

student body *n* *Lat. Am.* estudiantado, *m*

studied /'stʌdid/ *a* estudiado; calculado; (of style) cerebral, reflexivo; (intentional) deliberado

studio /'studiˌou/ *n* estudio, *m*. **broadcasting s.,** estudio de emisión, *m*

studious /'studiəs/ *a* estudioso, aplicado; (deliberate) intencional, deliberate; (eager) solícito, ansioso

studiously /'studiəsli/ *adv* estudiosamente; con intención, deliberadamente; solícitamente

study /'stʌdi/ *n* estudio, *m*; solicitud, *f*, cuidado, *m*; investigación, *f*; (room) gabinete, cuarto de trabajo, *m*. *vt* ocuparse de, cuidar de, atender a; considerar; estudiar; examinar; (the stars) observar; (try) procurar. *vi* estudiar. **in a brown s.,** en Babia. **to make a s. of,** hacer un estudio de, estudiar. **to s. for an examination,** prepararse para un examen

stuff /stʌf/ *n* substancia, materia, *f*; (fabric) tela, *f*, paño, *m*; (rubbish) cachivaches, *m pl*, cosas, *f pl. a* de estofa. *vt* henchir; llenar; *Cul.* rellenar; (with food) ahitar (de); (cram) atestar, apretar; (furniture) rehenchir; (an animal, bird) disecar; (put) meter, poner. **S. and nonsense!** ¡Patrañas! **to be poor s.,** ser de pacotilla; no valer para nada

stuffed animal /stʌft/ *n* animal disecado, *m*

stuffiness /'stʌfɪnɪs/ *n* mala ventilación, *f*; falta de aire, *f*; calor, *m*

stuffing /'stʌfɪŋ/ *n* (of furniture) rehenchimiento, *m*; *Cul.* relleno, *m*

stuffy /'stʌfi/ *a* mal ventilado, poco aireado, ahogado

stumble /'stʌmbəl/ *vi* tropezar; dar un traspié; (in speaking) tartamudear. *n* tropezón, *m*; traspié, *m*. **to s. through a speech,** pronunciar un discurso a tropezones. **to s. against,** tropezar contra. **to s. upon, across,** tropezar con; encontrar por casualidad

stumbling block /'stʌmblɪŋ/ *n* tropiezo, impedimento, *m*

stump /stʌmp/ *n* (of a tree) tocón, *m*; (of an arm, leg) muñón, *m*; (of a pencil, candle) cabo, *m*; (of a tooth) raigón, *m*; (of a cigar) colilla, *f*; (cricket) poste, montante, *m*; *Art.* esfumino, *m*; (leg) pata, *f*. *vt* (disconcert) desconcertar; *Art.* esfumar; recorrer. **to s. up,** *Inf.* pagar. **be stumped** (for an answer) *Mexico* atrojarse

stun /stʌn/ *vt* dejar sin sentido (a); aturdir de un golpe (a); (astound) pasmar

stunning /'stʌnɪŋ/ *a* aturdidor; que pasma; *Inf.* estupendo

stunt /stʌnt/ *vt* impedir el crecimiento de; encanijar. *n* (advertising) anuncio de reclamo, *m*; recurso (para conseguir algo), *m*; proeza, *f*

stunted /'stʌntɪd/ *a* (of trees, etc.) enano; (of children) encanijado; (of intelligence) inmaduro

stupefy /'stupəˌfai/ *vt* atontar, embrutecer; causar estupor (a), asombrar

stupendous /stu'pɛndəs/ *a* asombroso; enorme

stupid /'stupɪd/ *a* (with sleep, etc.) atontado; (silly) estúpido, tonto, *Lat. Am.* baboso, *Central America* azurumbado. *n* tonto (-ta)

stupidity /stu'pɪdɪti/ *n* estupidez, *f*; tontería, *f*

stupor /'stupər/ *n* estupor, *m*

sturdiness /'stɜrdɪnɪs/ *n* robustez, *f*, vigor, *m*; firmeza, tenacidad, *f*

sturdy /'stɜrdi/ *a* robusto, vigoroso, fuerte; firme, tenaz

sturgeon /'stɜrdʒən/ *n* *Ichth.* esturión, *m*

stutter /'stʌtər/ *vi* tartamudear. *vt* balbucir. *n* tartamudeo, *m*

stutterer /'stʌtərər/ *n* tartamudo (-da)

stuttering /'stʌtərɪŋ/ *a* tartamudo; balbuciente. *n* tartamudeo, *m*

sty /stai/ *n* (pig) pocilga, *f*; *Med.* orzuelo, *m*

style /stail/ *n* (for etching) buril, *m*; (*Lit., Art., Archit.,* etc.) estilo, *m*; (fashion) moda, *f*; (model) modelo, *m*; (behavior, etc.) tono, *m*; elegancia, *f*; (kind) especie, clase, *f*; (designation) tratamiento, *m*; *vt* llamar, nombrar. **the latest styles from Madrid,** los últimos modelos de Madrid. **He has a very individual s.,** Su estilo es muy personal. **They live in great s.,** Viven en gran lujo

stylet /'stailɪt/ *n* estilete, *m*

stylish /'stailɪʃ/ *a* elegante

stylishness /'stailɪʃnɪs/ *n* elegancia, *f*

stylist /'stailɪst/ *n* estilista, *mf*

stylize /'stailaiz/ *vt* estilizar

suasion /'sweiʒən/ *n* persuasión, *f*

suasive /'sweisɪv/ *a* suasorio, persuasivo

suave /swɑv/ *a* afable, cortés, urbano; (of wine) suave

suavity /'swɒvɪti/ n afabilidad, urbanidad, f
subaltern /sʌb'ɔltərn/ n Mil. subalterno, m, a subalterno, subordinado
subcommittee /'sʌbkə,mɪti/ n subcomisión, f
subconscious /sʌb'kɒnʃəs/ a subconsciente. **the s.,** la subconsciencia
subconsciously /sʌb'kɒnʃəsli/ adv subconscientemente
subcutaneous /,sʌbkyu'teiniəs/ a subcutáneo
subdivide /,sʌbdɪ'vaid/ vt subdividir. vi subdividirse
subdivision /'sʌbdɪ,vɪʒən/ n subdivisión, f
subdominant /sʌb'dɒmənənt/ n Mus. subdominante, f
subdue /səb'du/ vt subyugar, sojuzgar, vencer; (one's passions) dominar; (colors, voices) suavizar; (lessen) mitigar; apagar
subdued /səb'dud/ a (of colors) apagado; (of persons) sumiso; (depressed) deprimido, melancólico. **in a s. voice,** en voz baja
subheading /'sʌb,hedɪŋ/ n subtítulo, m
subhuman /sʌb'hyumən/ a subhumano
subject /n., a. 'sʌbdʒɪkt; v. səb'dʒɛkt/ a sujeto; sometido (a); expuesto (a). n (of a country) súbdito (-ta); sujeto, m; (of study) asignatura, materia, f; (theme) tema, m; (Gram., Philos.) sujeto, m. vt subyugar; someter. **It can only be done s. to his consent,** Podrá hacerse únicamente si él lo consiente. **to change the s.,** cambiar de conversación. **to s. to criticism,** criticar (a). **s.-matter,** materia, f; (of a letter) contenido, m
subjection /səb'dʒɛkʃən/ n sujeción, f; sometimiento, m. **He was in a state of complete s.,** Estaba completamente sumiso. **to bring into s.,** subyugar
subjective /səb'dʒɛktɪv/ a subjetivo
subjectiveness /səb'dʒɛktɪvnɪs/ n subjetividad, f
subjectivism /səb'dʒɛktə,vɪzəm/ n subjetivismo, m
subjoin /səb'dʒɔin/ vt añadir, adjuntar
subjugate /'sʌbdʒə,geit/ vt subyugar, someter
subjugation /,sʌbdʒə'geiʃən/ n subyugación, f
subjunctive /səb'dʒʌŋktɪv/ a and n subjuntivo m
sublet /v. sʌb'lɛt; n. 'sʌb,lɛt/ vt subarrendar. n subarriendo, m
sublimate /v. 'sʌblə,meit; n. -mɪt/ vt sublimar. n sublimado, m
sublimation /,sʌblɪ'meiʃən/ n sublimación, f
sublime /sə'blaim/ a sublime; absoluto, completo; extremo. **the s.,** lo sublime
sublimely /sə'blaimli/ adv sublimemente; completamente
submachine gun /,sʌbmə'ʃin/ n metralleta, f, subfusil ametrallador, m
submarine /,sʌbmə'rin/ a submarino. n submarino, m. **midget s.,** submarino enano, submarino de bolsillo, m. **s. chaser,** cazasubmarino, m
submerge /səb'mɜrdʒ/ vt sumergir; inundar. vi sumergirse. **The submarine submerged,** El submarino se sumergió
submergence /səb'mɜrdʒəns/ n sumergimiento, m, sumersión, f; hundimiento, m
submersible /səb'mɜrsəbəl/ a sumergible
submersion /səb'mɜrʒən/ n sumersión, f; hundimiento, m
submission /səb'mɪʃən/ n sometimiento, m; sumisión, resignación, f; docilidad, f
submissive /səb'mɪsɪv/ a sumiso, dócil, manso
submissively /səb'mɪsɪvli/ adv sumisamente, con docilidad
submissiveness /səb'mɪsɪvnɪs/ n sumisión, docilidad, f
submit /səb'mɪt/ vt someterse (a); doblarse ante; (a scheme, etc.) someter; presentar; (urge) proponer. vi someterse; resignarse; (surrender) rendirse, entregarse. **to s. to arbitration,** someter a arbitraje
subordinate /adj., n. sə'bɔrdnɪt; v. -dn,eit/ a subordinado; subalterno, inferior; secundario. n subordinado (-da). vt subordinar
subordination /sə,bɔrdn'eiʃən/ n subordinación, f
suborn /sə'bɔrn/ vt sobornar, cohechar
subplot /'sʌb,plɒt/ n intriga secundaria, trama secundaria, f
subpoena /sə'pinə/ n citación, f. vt citar

subscribe /səb'skraib/ vt and vi subscribir; (to a periodical, etc.) abonarse (a)
subscriber /səb'skraibər/ n subscriptor (-ra); abonado (-da)
subscription /səb'skrɪpʃən/ n subscripción, f; (to a periodical, series of concerts, etc.) abono, m; (to a club) cuota, f
subsection /'sʌb,sekʃən/ n subsección, f
subsequent /'sʌbsɪkwənt/ a subsiguiente, subsecuente; posterior. **s. to,** después de, posterior a. **s. upon,** de resultas de
subsequently /'sʌbsikwəntli/ adv más tarde; subsiguientemente; posteriormente
subservience /səb'sɜrviens/ n servilidad, f; utilidad, f
subservient /səb'sɜrviənt/ a servil; subordinado; útil
subside /səb'said/ vi (of water) bajar; (of ground) hundirse; (of foundations) asentarse; disminuir; calmarse; (be quiet) callarse. **to s. into a chair,** dejarse caer en un sillón
subsidence /səb'saidns/ n hundimiento, m; desplome, derrumbamiento, m; (of floods) bajada, f; (of anger, etc.) apaciguamiento, m
subsidiary /səb'sɪdi,eri/ a subsidiario
subsidize /'sʌbsɪ,daiz/ vt subvencionar
subsidy /'sʌbsɪdi/ n subvención, f, subsidio, m; prima, f
subsist /səb'sɪst/ vi subsistir
subsistence /səb'sɪstəns/ n subsistencia, f
subsoil /'sʌb,sɔil/ n subsuelo, m
substance /'sʌbstəns/ n substancia, f
substantial /səb'stænʃəl/ a substancial; sólido; importante
substantially /səb,stænʃəli/ adv substancialmente; sólidamente
substantiate /səb'stænʃi,eit/ vt establecer, verificar; justificar
substantiation /səb,stænʃi'eiʃən/ n comprobación, verificación, f; justificación, f
substantive /'sʌbstəntɪv/ a real, independiente; Gram. substantivo. n Gram. substantivo, m
substitute /'sʌbstɪ,tut/ n substituto (-ta); (material) substituto, m. vt substituir, reemplazar. **to be a s. for,** hacer las veces de
substitution /,sʌbstɪ'tuʃən/ n substitución, f, reemplazo, m
substratum /'sʌb,streitəm, -,strætəm/ n substrato, m
subterfuge /'sʌbtər,fyudʒ/ n subterfugio, m; evasiva, f
subterranean /,sʌbtə'reiniən/ a subterráneo
subtitle /'sʌb,taitl/ n subtítulo, m; (on films) guión, m
subtle /'sʌtl/ a sutil; delicado; penetrante; (crafty) astuto
subtlety /'sʌtlti/ n sutileza, f; delicadeza, f; (craftiness) astucia, f
subtly /'sʌtli/ adv sutilmente; con delicadeza
subtract /səb'trækt/ vt restar, substraer
subtraction /səb'trækʃən/ n resta, substracción, f
suburb /'sʌbɜrb/ n suburbio, m; pl **suburbs,** las afueras, f pl los arrabales, m pl
suburban /sə'bɜrbən/ a suburbano
subvention /səb'venʃən/ n subvención, f
subversion /səb'vɜrʒən/ n subversión, f
subversive /səb'vɜrsɪv/ a subversivo
subvert /səb'vɜrt/ vt subvertir
subway /'sʌb,wei/ n (passageway) pasaje subterráneo, m; (underground railway) metro (Spain, Puerto Rico), subte (Argentina), m
succeed /sək'sid/ vt seguir (a); suceder (a); heredar. vi seguir (a); suceder (a); (be successful) tener éxito. **I did not s. in doing it,** No logré hacerlo. **to s. to the throne,** subir al trono
succeeding /sək'sidɪŋ/ a subsiguiente; futuro; consecutivo; sucesivo
success /sək'ses/ n éxito, m; triunfo, m. **to be a s.,** tener éxito. **The film was a great s.,** La película tuvo mucho éxito
successful /sək'sesfəl/ a que tiene éxito; afortunado, venturoso; próspero, Lat. Am. exitoso
successfully /sək'sesfəli/ adv con éxito; prósperamente

succession /sək'sɛʃən/ n sucesión, f; (series) serie, f; (inheritance) herencia, f; (descendants) descendencia, f. **in s.,** sucesivamente
successive /sək'sɛsɪv/ a sucesivo
successor /sək'sɛsər/ n sucesor (-ra)
succinct /sək'sɪŋkt/ a sucinto, conciso
succinctly /sək'sɪŋktli/ adv sucintamente, brevemente, en pocas palabras
succor /'sʌkər/ vt socorrer, auxiliar. n socorro, m, ayuda, f
succulence /'sʌkyələns/ n suculencia, f
succulent /'sʌkyələnt/ a suculento
succumb /sə'kʌm/ vi sucumbir; someterse, ceder
such /sʌtʃ/ a tal; parecido, semejante; así; tanto; (before an adjective, adverb) tan. n el, m, (f, la) que, los, m pl, (f pl, las) que; tal. **s. men,** tales hombres. **I have never seen s. magnificence,** Nunca no he visto tanta magnificencia. **s. an important man,** un hombre tan importante. **s. pictures as these,** cuadros como estos. **S. is life!** ¡Así es la vida! **science as s.,** la ciencia como tal. **s.-and-s.,** tal y tal
suchlike /'sʌtʃ,laik/ a parecido, semejante; de esta clase
suck /sʌk/ vt chupar; (the breast) mamar; sorber; (of a vacuum cleaner, etc.) aspirar. n chupada, f; succión, f. **to s. down,** tragar. **to s. up,** aspirar; absorber
sucker /'sʌkər/ n Zool. ventosa, f; Bot. acodo, mugrón, m; (greenhorn) primo, m; (pig) lechón, m
suckle /'sʌkəl/ vt amamantar, dar el pecho (a)
suckling pig /'sʌklɪŋ/ n lechón, cochinillo, m
suction /'sʌkʃən/ n succión, f; aspiración, f. **s.-pump,** bomba aspirante, f
Sudan, the /su'dæn/ el Sudán, m
Sudanese /,sudṇ'iz/ a and n sudanés (-esa)
sudden /'sʌdṇ/ a súbito; (unexpected) inesperado, impensado; (of bends) brusco. **all of a s.,** de repente; súbitamente
suddenly /'sʌdṇli/ adv súbitamente; de pronto, de repente
suddenness /'sʌdṇnɪs/ n carácter repentino, m; (of a bend, etc.) brusquedad, f
suds /sʌdz/ n pl jabonaduras, f pl; espuma, f
sue /su/ vt Law. proceder contra, pedir en juicio; Law. demandar; litigar; (beg) suplicar. **to sue for peace,** pedir la paz
suede /sweid/ n ante, m. **s. glove,** guante de ante, m
suet /'suɪt/ n sebo, m
Suez Canal, the /su'ɛz/ el Canal de Suez, m
suffer /'sʌfər/ vt sufrir, padecer; pasar, experimentar; (tolerate) tolerar, sufrir; (allow) permitir. vi sufrir. **She suffers from her environment,** es la víctima de su medio ambiente
sufferance /'sʌfərəns/ n tolerancia, f. **on s.,** por tolerancia
sufferer /'sʌfərər/ n enfermo (-ma); víctima, f
suffering /'sʌfərɪŋ/ n sufrimiento, padecimiento, m; dolor, m. a sufriente
suffice /sə'fais/ vi ser suficiente, bastar. vt satisfacer
sufficiency /sə'fɪʃənsi/ n suficiencia, f; (of money) subsistencia, f
sufficient /sə'fɪʃənt/ a suficiente, bastante. **to be s.,** bastar, ser suficiente
sufficiently /sə'fɪʃəntli/ adv suficientemente, bastante
suffix /'sʌfɪks/ n Gram. sufijo, m
suffocate /'sʌfə,keit/ vt ahogar, sofocar, asfixiar. vi sofocarse, asfixiarse
suffocating /'sʌfə,keitɪŋ/ a sofocante, asfixiante
suffocation /,sʌfə'keiʃən/ n sofocación, asfixia, f; ahogo, m
suffrage /'sʌfrɪdʒ/ n sufragio, m; voto, m. **universal s.,** sufragio universal, m
suffragette /,sʌfrə'dʒɛt/ n sufragista, f
suffuse /sə'fyuz/ vt bañar, inundar, cubrir
sugar /'ʃʊgər/ n azúcar, m. vt azucarar. **brown s.,** azúcar moreno, m. **loaf s.,** azúcar de pilón, m. **white s.,** azúcar blanco, m. **to s. the pill,** dorar la píldora. **s.-almond,** peladilla, f. **s.-basin,** azucarera, f. **s.-beet,** remolacha, f. **s.-candy,** azúcar candi, m. **s.-cane,** caña de azúcar, f. **s.-cane syrup,** miel de caña, f. **s.-**

paste, alfeñique, m, alcorza, f. **s.-refinery,** fábrica de azúcar, f. **s.-tongs,** tenacillas para azúcar, f pl
sugary /'ʃʊgəri/ a azucarado; Fig. meloso, almibarado
suggest /səg'dʒɛst/ vt implicar; indicar, dar a entender; sugerir; (advise) aconsejar; (hint) insinuar; (evoke) evocar. **I suggested they should go to London,** Les aconsejé que fueran a Londres. **An idea suggested itself to him,** Se le ocurrió una idea
suggestion /səg'dʒɛstʃən/ n sugestión, f; insinuación, f
suggestive /səg'dʒɛstɪv/ a sugestivo; estimulante
suicidal /,suə'saidl/ a suicida. **s. tendency,** tendencia suicida, tendencia al suicidio, f
suicide /'suə,said/ n (act) suicidio, m; (person) suicida, mf. **to commit s.,** darse la muerte, quitarse la vida suicidarse
suit /sut/ n (request) petición, súplica, f; oferta de matrimonio, f; Law. pleito, m, demanda, f; (of clothes) traje, m, Colombia, Venezuela flus, m; (cards) palo, m; (of cards held) serie, f, vt convenir; sentar; ir bien (a); venir bien (a); (adapt) adaptar. **S. yourself!** ¡Haz lo que quieras! **The arrangement suits me very well,** El arreglo me viene muy bien. **The climate doesn't s. me,** El clima no me sienta bien. **The color does not s. you,** El color no te va bien. **to follow s.,** seguir el ejemplo (de); (cards) jugar el mismo palo. **s.-case,** maleta, f
suitability /,sutə'bɪlɪti/ n conveniencia, f; aptitud, f
suitable /'sutəbəl/ a conveniente; apropiado; apto; a propósito. **Not s. for children,** No apto para menores. **to make s. for,** adaptar a las necesidades de
suitably /'sutəbli/ adv convenientemente; apropiadamente
suite /swit/ n (of retainers, etc.) séquito, acompañamiento, m; (of furniture, etc.) juego, m; Mus. suite, f. **private s.,** habitaciones particulares, f pl. **s. of rooms,** apartamiento, m
suitor /'sutər/ n Law. demandante, m; pretendiente, m
sulk /sʌlk/ vi ponerse malhumorado, ser mohíno
sulkiness /'sʌlkinɪs/ n mohína, f, mal humor, m
sulky /'sʌlki/ a mohíno, malhumorado
sullen /'sʌln/ a taciturno, hosco; malhumorado, sombrío; (of a landscape, etc.) triste, sombrío
sullenly /'sʌlnli/ adv taciturnamente, hoscamente
sullenness /'sʌlnnɪs/ n taciturnidad, hosquedad, f, mal humor, m
sully /'sʌli/ vt desdorar, empañar; manchar
sulphur /'sʌlfər/ n azufre, m
sulphuric /sʌl'fyʊrɪk/ a sulfúrico
sulphurous /'sʌlfərəs/ a sulfuroso
sultan /'sʌltṇ/ n sultán, m
sultriness /'sʌltrinɪs/ n bochorno, calor sofocante, m
sultry /'sʌltri/ a bochornoso, sofocante; (seductive) seductivo
sum /sʌm/ n suma, f; total, m; cantidad, f; (in arithmetic) problema (de aritmética), m. vt sumar, calcular. **in sum,** en suma; en resumen. **to sum up,** recapitular; resumir; (a person) tomar las medidas (a)
summarily /sə'mɛərəli/ adv someramente; Law. sumariamente
summarize /'sʌmə,raiz/ vt resumir brevemente; compendiar
summary /'sʌməri/ a somero; Law. sumario. n resumen, sumario, compendio, m. **summary records,** actas resumidas, f pl
summer /'sʌmər/ n verano, estío, m. **to spend the s.,** veranear. **s.-house,** cenador, m. **s.-time,** verano, m; hora de verano, f. **s. wheat,** trigo tremesino, m
summing-up /'sʌmɪŋ ,ʌp/ n recapitulación, f
summit /'sʌmɪt/ n cima, cumbre, f; Fig. apogeo, m
summitry /'sʌmɪtri/ n diplomacia en la cumbre, f
summon /'sʌmən/ vt llamar, hacer venir; mandar, requerir; Law. citar. **to s. up one's courage,** cobrar ánimos
summons /'sʌmənz/ n llamamiento, m; Mil. intimación, f; Law. citación, f. vt Law. citar
summon /'sʌmən/ vt llamar, hacer venir; mandar, requerir; Law. citar. **to s. up one's courage,** cobrar ánimos
sump /sʌmp/ n Mineral. sumidero, m

sumptuous /'sʌmptʃuəs/ a suntuoso, lujoso, magnífico

sumptuousness /'sʌmptʃuəsnɪs/ n suntuosidad, magnificencia, f

sun /sʌn/ n sol, m. **The sun was shining,** Hacía sol, El sol brillaba. **to bask in the sun,** tomar el sol. **sunbathing,** baños de sol, m pl. **sun-blind,** toldo para el sol, m. **sun-bonnet,** capelina, f. **sun-glasses,** gafas ahumadas, f pl. **sun-helmet,** casco colonial, m. **sunspot,** Astron. mancha del sol, f; (freckle) peca, f.

sun-worship, adoración del sol, f

sunbeam /'sʌn,bim/ n rayo de sol, m

sunburn /'sʌn,bɜrn/ n quemadura del sol, f; bronceado, m

sunburned /'sʌn,bɜrnd/ a quemado por el sol; bronceado, tostado por el sol

sundae /'sʌndei/ n helado de frutas, m

Sunday /'sʌndei/ n domingo, m. **in his S. best,** en su traje dominguero, endomingado. **S. school,** escuela dominical, f

Sunday's child /'sʌndeiz/ n niño nacido de pies, niño nacido un domingo, niño mimado de la fortuna

sunder /'sʌndər/ vt dividir en dos, hender; separar

sundial /'sʌn,daiəl/ n reloj de sol, reloj solar, m

sundown /'sʌn,daun/ n puesta del sol, f

sundry /'sʌndri/ a varios (-as). n pl **sundries,** artículos diversos, m pl; Com. varios, m pl. **all and s.,** todo el mundo, todos y cada uno

sunflower /'sʌn,flauər/ n girasol, tornasol, m, trompeta de amor, f

sunken /'sʌŋkən/ a (of eyes, etc.) hundido

sunless /'sʌnlɪs/ a sin sol

sun letter n letra solar, f

sunlight /'sʌn,lait/ n luz del sol, f, rayos del sol, m pl. **artificial s.,** sol artificial, m. **in the s.,** al sol

sunny /'sʌni/ a de sol; bañado de sol; asoleado; expuesto al sol; (face) risueño; (of disposition, etc.) alegre. **to be s.,** hacer sol

sunrise /'sʌn,raiz/ n salida del sol, f. **from s. to sunset,** de sol a sol

sunset /'sʌn,set/ n puesta del sol, f. **at s.,** a la caída (or puesta) del sol

sunshade /'sʌn,ʃeid/ n parasol, quitasol, m, sombrilla, f

sunshine /'sʌn,ʃain/ n luz del sol, f. **in the s.,** al sol

sunstroke /'sʌn,strouk/ n insolación, f

sup /sʌp/ vt sorber. vi cenar. n sorbo, m

super /'supər/ n (actor) comparsa, mf; (film) superproducción, f; (of a beehive) alza, f

superabundance /,supərə'bʌndəns/ n superabundancia, sobreabundancia, f

superabundant /,supərə'bʌndənt/ a superabundante, sobreabundante. **to be s.,** sobreabundar

superannuate /,supər'ænyu,eit/ vt (retire) jubilar

superannuated /,supər'ænyu,eitɪd/ a (retired) jubilado; (out-of-date) anticuado

superannuation /,supər,ænyu'eiʃən/ n (retirement and pension) jubilación, f

superb /su'pɜrb/ a magnífico, espléndido

superbly /su'pɜrbli/ adv magníficamente

supercargo /'supər,kɑrgou/ n Naut. sobrecargo, m

supercharger /'supər,tʃɑrdʒər/ n (Auto., Aer.) compresor, m

supercilious /,supər'sɪliəs/ a altanero, altivo, orgulloso; desdeñoso

superciliousness /,supər'sɪliəsnɪs/ n altanería, altivez, f, orgullo, m; desdén, m

superficial /,supər'fɪʃəl/ a superficial

superficiality /,supər,fɪʃi'ælɪti/ n superficialidad, f

superficially /,supər'fɪʃəli/ adv superficialmente

superfine /,supər'fain/ a superfino

superfluity /,supər'fluɪti/ n superfluidad, f

superfluous /su'pɜrfluəs/ a superfluo. **to be s.,** sobrar

superfortress /'supər,fɔrtrɪs/ n Aer. superfortaleza volante, f

superhuman /,supər'hyumən/ a sobrehumano

superimpose /,supərɪm'pouz/ vt sobreponer

superintend /,supərɪn'tɛnd/ vt superentender, dirigir

superintendent /,supərɪn'tɛndənt/ n superinten-

dente, mf; director (-ra); (school) inspector; (police) subjefe de la policía, m

superior /sə'pɪəriər/ a superior; (in number) mayor; (smug) desdeñoso. n superior (-ra). **Mother S.,** (madre) superiora, f. **s. to,** superior a; encima de

superiority /sə,pɪəri'ɔrɪti/ n superioridad, f

superlative /sə'pɜrlətɪv/ a extremo, supremo; Gram. superlativo. n Gram. superlativo, m

superlatively /sə'pɜrlətɪvli/ adv en sumo grado, superlativamente

superman /'supər,mæn/ n superhombre, m

supermarket /'supər,mɑrkɪt/ n supermercado, m

supernatural /,supər'nætʃərəl/ a sobrenatural

superposition /,supərpə'zɪʃən/ n superposición, f

superscribe /'supər,skraib/ vt sobrescribir; poner el sobrescrito (a)

superscription /,supər'skrɪpʃən/ n (on letters, documents) sobrescrito, m; (heading, inscription) leyenda, f

supersede /,supər'sid/ vt reemplazar; suplantar

supersensible /,supər'sɛnsəbəl/ a suprasensible

superstition /,supər'stɪʃən/ n superstición, f

superstitious /,supər'stɪʃəs/ a supersticioso

supertax /'supər,tæks/ n impuesto suplementario, m

supervene /,supər'vin/ vi sobrevenir

supervise /'supər,vaiz/ vt superentender, vigilar; dirigir

supervision /,supər'vɪʒən/ n superintendencia, f; dirección, f

supervisor /'supər,vaizər/ n superintendente, mf; inspector (-ra); director (-ra)

supine /a. su'pain; n. 'supain/ a supino; indolente, negligente. n Gram. supino, m

supper /'sʌpər/ n cena, f. **the Last S.,** la Última Cena. **to have s.,** cenar. **s.-time,** hora de cenar, f

supplant /sə'plænt/ vt suplantar; usurpar; reemplazar

supplanter /sə'plæntər/ n suplantador (-ra)

supple /'sʌpəl/ a flexible; dócil, manso; (fawning) adulador, servil, lisonjero

supplement /'sʌpləmənt/ n suplemento, m; (of a book) apéndice, m

supplementary /,sʌplə'mɛntəri/ a suplementario; adicional

suppleness /'sʌpəlnɪs/ n flexibilidad, f; docilidad, f; servilidad, f

suppliant /'sʌpliənt/ a and n suplicante, mf

supplicate /'sʌpli,keit/ vt and vi suplicar

supplication /,sʌpli'keiʃən/ n suplicación, f; súplica, f

supply /sə'plai/ vt proveer (de); suministrar; proporcionar, dar; (a deficiency) suplir; (a post) llenar; (a post temporarily) reemplazar. n suministro, surtimiento, m; provisión, f; (of electricity, etc.) suministro, m; Com. oferta, f; (person) substituto (-ta); pl **supplies,** Com. existencias, f pl; Mil. pertrechos, m pl; víveres, m pl, provisiones, f pl. **s. and demand,** oferta y demanda, f

support /sə'pɔrt/ vt apoyar, sostener; mantener; (endure) soportar; (a cause) apoyar, defender; (corroborate) confirmar, vindicar. n apoyo, m; sostén, m; soporte, m. **to speak in s. of,** defender, abogar por. **to s. oneself,** ganarse la vida, mantenerse

supporter /sə'pɔrtər/ n apoyo, m; defensor (-ra); partidario (-ia)

suppose /sə'pouz/ vt suponer; imaginar(se); creer. **always supposing,** dado que, en el caso de que. **Supposing he had gone out?** ¿Y si hubiera salido? **I don't s. they will go to Spain,** No creo que vayan a España. **He is supposed to be clever,** Tiene fama de listo

supposed /sə'pouzd, -'pouzɪd/ a supuesto; que se llama a sí mismo

supposition /,sʌpə'zɪʃən/ n suposición, hipótesis, f

suppress /sə'prɛs/ vt reprimir; (yawns, etc.) ahogar; contener; (heresies, rebellions, books, etc.) suprimir; (dissemble) disimular, esconder; (a heckler, etc.) hacer callar

suppressed /sə'prɛst/ a reprimido; contenido; disimulado

suppression /sə'prɛʃən/ n represión, f; supresión, f; disimulación, f

suppurate /'sʌpyə,reit/ vi supurar

suppuration /ˌsʌpyəˈreiʃən/ n supuración, f
supremacy /səˈprɛməsi/ n supremacía, f
supreme /səˈprim/ a supremo; sumo. **with s. indifference**, con suma indiferencia. s. **court**, tribunal supremo, m
surcharge /ˈsɜrˌtʃɑrdʒ/ n sobrecarga, f
sure /ʃʊr/ a seguro; cierto. adv seguramente. **Be s. to...!** ¡Ten cuidado de...! ¡No dejes de...! **to be s.**, seguramente, sin duda; ¡claro!; (fancy!) ¡no me digas!; ¡qué sorpresa! **I am not so s. of that,** No diría yo tanto. **Come on Thursday for s.,** Venga el jueves sin falta. **It is s. to rain tomorrow,** Seguramente va a llover mañana. **to make s. of,** asegurarse de. **to be (or feel) s.,** estar seguro. s.-**footed,** de pie firme, seguro
surely /ˈʃʊrli/ adv seguramente; sin duda, ciertamente; por supuesto
sureness /ˈʃʊrnɛs/ n seguridad, f; certeza, f
surety /ˈʃʊriti/ n garantía, fianza, f; (person) garante, mf
surf /sɜrf/ n resaca, f; rompiente, m; oleaje, m. s.-**board,** aquaplano, m. s.-**riding,** patinaje sobre las olas, m
surface /ˈsɜrfɪs/ n superficie, f; exterior, m. a superficial. vi (of a submarine) salir a la superficie. **on the s.,** en apariencia
surface mail n correo por vía ordinaria, servicio ordinario, servicio per vía de superficie, m
surfeit /ˈsɜrfɪt/ n exceso, m, superabundancia, f; saciedad, f. vt hartar; saciar
surge /sɜrdʒ/ vi (of waves) embravecerse, hincharse; (of crowds) agitarse, bullir; (of emotions) despertarse. n (of sea, crowd, blood) oleada, f; (of anger) ola, f. **The blood surged into his face,** La sangre se le subió a las mejillas
surgeon /ˈsɜrdʒən/ n cirujano, m; (Nav., Mil.) médico, m
surgery /ˈsɜrdʒəri/ n cirugía, f; (doctor's) consultorio, m; (dispensary) dispensario, m
surgical /ˈsɜrdʒɪkəl/ a quirúrgico
surliness /ˈsɜrlɪnɪs/ n mal genio, m, taciturnidad, f; brusquedad, f
surly /ˈsɜrli/ a taciturno, huraño, malhumorado; brusco
surmise /sərˈmaiz/ n conjetura, suposición, f. vt conjeturar, adivinar; imaginar, suponer. vi hacer conjeturas
surmount /sərˈmaunt/ vt superar, vencer; coronar
surname /ˈsɜrˌneim/ n apellido, m. vt denominar, nombrar
surpass /sərˈpæs/ vt superar, exceder; aventajarse (a); eclipsar
surpassing /sərˈpæsɪŋ/ a sin par, incomparable
surplus /ˈsɜrplʌs/ n exceso, sobrante, m; (Com. of accounts) superávit, m. **sale of s. stock,** liquidación de saldos, f
surplusage /ˈsɜrplʌsɪdʒ/ n material de desecho, m
surprise /sərˈpraiz, sə-/ n sorpresa, f; asombro, m. vt sorprender; asombrar. **to s.** (someone) **in the act,** coger en el acto. **to take** (a person) **by s.,** sorprender (a). **He was surprised into admitting it,** Cogido a la imprevista, lo confesó
surprising /sərˈpraizɪŋ, sə-/ a sorprendente
surrealism /səˈriəˌlizəm/ n surrealismo, m
surrealist /səˈriəlɪst/ a and n surrealista, mf
surrender /səˈrɛndər/ vt rendir, entregar; (goods) ceder, renunciar (a). vi rendirse, entregarse; abandonarse. n rendición, capitulación, f; entrega, f; (of goods) cesión, f; (of an insurance policy) rescate, m. **to s. oneself to remorse,** abandonarse (or entregarse) al remordimiento. **to s. unconditionally,** entregarse a discreción
surreptitious /ˌsɜrəpˈtɪʃəs/ a subrepticio
surreptitiously /ˌsɜrəpˈtɪʃəsli/ adv subrepticiamente, a hurtadillas
surround /səˈraund/ vt rodear; cercar; Mil. asediar, sitiar. n borde, m. **Peter was surrounded by his friends,** Pedro estaba rodeado por sus amigos
surrounding /səˈraundɪŋ/ a (que está) alrededor de; vecino. **the s. country,** los alrededores

surroundings /səˈraundɪŋz/ n pl cercanías, f pl, alrededores, m pl; (environment) medio, m; ambiente, m
surtax /ˈsɜrˌtæks/ n impuesto suplementario, m
surveillance /sərˈveiləns/ n vigilancia, f
survey /v. sərˈvei; n. ˈsɜrvei/ vt contemplar; mirar; (events, etc.) pasar en revista; estudiar; (land, etc.) apear; (a house, etc.) inspeccionar. n vista general, f; inspección, f; (of facts, etc.) examen, m; estudio, m; (of land, etc.) apeo, m; (of literature, etc.) bosquejo, breve panorama, m
surveying /sərˈveiɪŋ/ n agrimensura, f
surveyor /sərˈveiər/ n agrimensor, m; (superintendent) inspector, m; superintendente, m
survival /sərˈvaivəl/ n supervivencia, f. s. **of the fittest,** supervivencia de los más aptos, f
survive /sərˈvaiv/ vt sobrevivir a. vi sobrevivir; (of customs) subsistir, durar
survivor /sərˈvaivər/ n sobreviviente, mf
susceptibility /səˌsɛptəˈbiliti/ n susceptibilidad, f; tendencia, f; pl **susceptibilities,** sensibilidad, f
susceptible /səˈsɛptəbəl/ a susceptible; impresionable; sensible; (to love) enamoradizo. **He is s. to bronchitis,** Es susceptible a la bronquitis
suspect /a., n. ˈsʌspɛkt; v. səˈspɛkt/ a and n sospechoso (-sa). vt sospechar; dudar; imaginar, suponer. vi tener sospechas
suspend /səˈspɛnd/ vt suspender. **suspended animation,** muerte aparente, f
suspender /səˈspɛndər/ n liga, f; pl **suspenders,** (braces) tirantes del pantalón, m pl. s.-**belt,** faja, f
suspense /səˈspɛns/ n incertidumbre, f. **to keep** (a person) **in s.,** dejar en la incertidumbre (a)
suspension /səˈspɛnʃən/ n suspensión, f. s.-**bridge,** puente colgante, m. s. **of payments,** suspensión de pagos, f,
suspicion /səˈspiʃən/ n sospecha, f; (touch) dejo, m; cantidad muy pequeña, f. **to be above s.,** estar por encima de toda sospecha. **to be under s.,** estar bajo sospecha. **I had no suspicions...,** No sospechaba...
suspicious /səˈspiʃəs/ a (by nature) suspicaz; sospechoso. **to make s.,** hacer sospechar
suspiciously /səˈspiʃəsli/ adv suspicazmente, desconfiadamente; de un modo sospechoso. **It seems s. like...,** Tiene toda la apariencia de...
suspiciousness /səˈspiʃəsnis/ n carácter sospechoso, m, lo sospechoso; suspicacia, f
sustain /səˈstein/ vt sostener; mantener; sustentar; apoyar; corroborar, confirmar; (a note) prolongar. **to s. injuries,** recibir heridas
sustenance /ˈsʌstənəns/ n mantenimiento, m; sustento, m, alimentos, m pl
suture /ˈsutʃər/ n sutura, f
svelte /svɛlt/ a esbelto, gentil
swab /swɒb/ vt Naut. lampacear; limpiar con lampazo; Surg. tamponar. n lampazo, m; Surg. torunda, f, tampón, m
swaddle /ˈswɒdl̩/ vt envolver; (infants) fajar
swaddling clothes /ˈswɒdlɪŋ/ n pl pañales, m pl. **to be still in s. clothes,** Fig. estar en mantillas, estar en pañales
swagger /ˈswægər/ vi fanfarronear, pavonearse; darse importancia. n pavoneo, m; aire importante, m; (coat) tonto, m. a majo; de última moda
swaggering /ˈswægərɪŋ/ a fanfarrón, jactancioso; importante
Swahili /swɑˈhili/ suaili; n suaili, m
swain /swein/ n zagal, m; enamorado, m; pretendiente, amante, m
swallow /ˈswɒlou/ vt tragar, engullir. n trago, m; sorbo, m; Ornith. golondrina, f. **to s. an insult** (a **story),** tragar un insulto (una historia). **to s. one's words,** retractarse. **to s. one's pride,** bajar la cerviz, humillarse. **to s. up,** tragar; absorber. s.-**tailed coat,** frac, m
swamp /swɒmp/ n pantano, m, marisma, f, Argentina fachinal, f, Central America chagüe, m. vt sumergir; (a boat) echar a pique, hundir; (inundate) inundar, dar
swampy /ˈswɒmpi/ a pantanoso
swan /swɒn/ n cisne, m. **swan's down,** plumón de cisne, m. s.-**song,** canto del cisne, m

swank /swæŋk/ n pretensiones, f pl, vi darse humos

sward /swɔrd/ n césped, m, hierba, f

swarm /swɔrm/ n enjambre, m; (of people) muchedumbre, multitud, f; tropel, m. vi (of bees) enjambrar; (of other insects) pulular; (of people) hormiguear, bullir, pulular. vt (climb) trepar. **to s. with,** estar infestado de

swarthiness /'swɔrðinɪs/ n tez morena, f; color moreno, m

swarthy /'swɔrði/ a moreno

swashbuckler /'swɒʃ,bʌklər, 'swɒʃ-/ n perdonavidas, matasiete, m

swashbuckling /'swɒʃ,bʌklɪŋ/ a de capa y espada, valentón, fanfarrón

swastika /'swɒstɪkə/ n esvástica, cruz gamada, f

swathe /swɒð/ vt envolver; fajar; (with bandages) vendar

swathing /'swɒðɪŋ/ n envoltura, f; (bandages) vendas, f pl

sway /swei/ vi balancearse; oscilar; (stagger, of persons) bambolearse; (totter, of things) tambalearse; (of carriages) cabecear; (gracefully, in walking) cimbrarse. vt balancear, mecer; oscilar; hacer tambalear; (influence) influir, inclinar; (govern) regir, gobernar. n balanceo, m; oscilación, f; vaivén, m; tambaleo, m; (influence) ascendiente, dominio, m, influencia, f; (rule) imperio, poder, m. **to hold s. over,** gobernar, regir

swear /swɛər/ vt jurar; (Law. etc.) declarar bajo juramento. vi jurar; (curse) echar pestes, blasfemar. **to s. at,** maldecir. **to s. by,** jurar por; poner fe implícita en. **to be sworn in,** prestar juramento. **to s. in,** tomar juramento (a). **to s. to,** atestiguar

sweat /swɛt/ n sudor, m; Inf. trabajo arduo, m. vi sudar. vt sudar; hacer sudar; (workers) explotar. **by the s. of one's brow,** con el sudor de la frente, con el sudor del rostro. **s.-gland,** glándula sudorípara. f

sweated /'swɛtɪd/ a (of persons) explotado; (of labor) mal retribuido

sweater /'swɛtər/ n suéter, jersey, m

sweating /'swɛtɪŋ/ n transpiración, f; (of workers) explotación, f

sweaty /'swɛti/ a sudoroso

Swede /swid/ n sueco (-ca); (vegetable) naba, f

Sweden /'swidn/ Suecia, f

sweep /swip/ vi extenderse (por); (cleave) surcar; pasar rápidamente (por); invadir; dominar; andar majestuosamente; (with a brush) barrer. vt barrer; pasar (por); (the strings of a musical instrument) rasguear; (the sea) navegar por; (mines) barrer; (the horizon, etc.) examinar; (a chimney) deshollinar; (with a brush) barrer; (remove) arrebatar; quitar; llevarse; (abolish) suprimir. **to s. along,** vt (of the current, crowds, etc.) arrastrar. vi pasar majestuosamente; correr rápidamente (por). **to s. aside,** apartar con la mano; abandonar; (a protest) desoír, no hacer caso de. **to s. away,** barrer; (remove) llevarse; destruir; suprimir. **to s. down,** vt barrer; (carry) arrastrar. vi (of cliffs, etc.) bajar; (of an enemy) abalanzarse (sobre); lanzarse (por). **to s. off,** barrer; (a person) llevarse sin perder tiempo; arrebatar con violencia (a). **to be swept off one's feet,** ser arrastrado (por); perder el balance; (of emotion) ser dominado por. **to s. on,** seguir su avance inexorable; seguir su marcha. **to s. up,** recoger, barrer

sweep /swip/ n barredura, f; (of a chimney) deshollinador, m; (of the tide) curso, m; (of a scythe, etc.) golpe, m; (range) alcance, m; (fold) pliegue, m; (curve) curva, f; (of water, etc.) extensión, f; (of wings) envergadura, f. **with a s. of the arm,** con un gesto del brazo. **to make a clean s. of,** hacer tabla rasa de

sweeping /'swipɪŋ/ a completo; comprensivo; demasiado general; radical. **a s. judgment,** un juicio demasiado general. **s. change,** cambio radicale, m pl. **s. brush,** escoba, f

sweepings /'swipɪŋz/ n pl barreduras, f pl; residuos, m pl; (of society) heces, f pl

sweepstakes /'swip,steiks/ n lotería, f

sweet /swit/ a dulce; (of scents) oloroso, fragante; (of sounds) melodioso, dulce; (charming) encantador;

amable; (pretty) bonito. n bombón, m; golosina, f; (at a meal) (plato) dulce, m; dulzura, f; (beloved) amor, m, querido (-da). **How s. it smells!** ¡Qué buen olor tiene! **the sweets of life,** las dulzuras de la vida. **s.-pea,** guisante de olor, m, haba de las Indias, f. **s.-potato,** batata, f, Lat. Am. boniato, camote, m. **s.-scented,** perfumado, fragante. **s.-tempered,** amable, de carácter dulce. **s.-toothed,** goloso. **s.-william,** Bot. clavel de la China, clavel de ramillete, clavel de San Isidro, ramillete de Constantinopla, m, minutisa, f

sweetbread /'swit,brɛd/ n lechecillas, f pl

sweeten /'switn/ vt azucarar; endulzar. **Cervantes sweetens one's bitter moments,** Cervantes endulza los momentos ásperos

sweetheart /'swit,hɑrt/ n amante, mf, amado (-da); (as address) querido (-da)

sweetish /'switɪʃ/ a algo dulce

sweetly /'switli/ adv dulcemente; (of scents) olorosamente; (of sounds) melodiosamente; (of behavior, etc.) amablemente

sweetness /'switnɪs/ n dulzura, f; (of scents) buen olor, m, fragancia, f; (of sounds) melodía, dulzura, f; (of character) bondad, amabilidad, f

sweet potato n batata, f, boniato, buniato, Mexico camote, m

sweet sixteen n (age) los dieciséis abriles, m pl; (party) quinceañera (at age fifteen) f

sweet turnip n Central America jícama, f

swell /swɛl/ vi hincharse; (of the sea) entumecerse; crecer; aumentarse. vt hinchar; aumentar. n (of the sea) oleada, f, oleaje, m; (of the ground) ondulación, f; (of sound) crescendo, m; (increase) aumento, m; (dandy) pisaverde, elegante, m; (important person) pájaro gordo, m; (at games, etc.) espada, m. a estupendo; elegantísimo; de primera, excelente. **to suffer from swelled head,** tener humos, darse importancia. **This foot is swollen,** Este pie está hinchado (or tumefacto). **The refugees have swelled the population,** Los refugiados han aumentado la población. **eyes swollen with tears,** ojos arrasados de lágrimas. **to s. with pride,** hincharse de orgullo

swelling /'swɛlɪŋ/ n hinchazón, f; Med. tumefacción, f; (bruise, etc.) chichón, m

swelter /'swɛltər/ vi abrasarse; arder. n bochorno, calor sofocante, m

swerve /swɜrv/ vi desviarse; apartarse (de); torcerse. n desvío, m

swift /swɪft/ a rápido, veloz; pronto. adv velozmente, rápidamente. n Ornith. vencejo, m. **s.-flowing,** (of rivers, etc.) de corriente rápida. **s.-footed,** de pies ligeros

swiftly /'swɪftli/ adv rápidamente, velozmente

swiftness /'swɪftnɪs/ n rapidez, velocidad, f; prontitud, f

swim /swɪm/ vi nadar; flotar; (glide) deslizarse; (fill) inundarse. vt (a horse) hacer nadar; pasar a nado; nadar. n natación, f. **eyes swimming with tears,** ojos inundados de lágrimas. **He enjoys a s.,** Le gusta nadar. **My head swims,** Se me va la cabeza. **Everything swam before my eyes,** Todo parecía bailar ante mis ojos. **to be in the s.,** formar parte (de), ser (de); (be up to date) estar al corriente. **to s. the Channel,** atravesar el canal de la Mancha a nado. **to s. with the tide,** ir con la corriente

swimmer /'swɪmər/ n nadador (-ra). **He is a bad s.,** Nada mal

swimming /'swɪmɪŋ/ n natación, f; (of the head) vértigo, m. **s.-bath,** piscina, f. **s.-pool,** piscina, Lat. Am. alberca, f

swindle /'swɪndl/ vt engañar, estafar; defraudar (de). n estafa, f, timo, m; engaño, m; impostura, f, Lat. Am. cambullón, Argentina forro, m

swindler /'swɪndlər/ n estafador (-ra), trampeador (-ra); engañador (-ra)

swine /swain/ n cerdo, puerco, m; (person) cochino (-na). **a herd of s.,** una manada de cerdos

swineherd /'swain,hɜrd/ n porquero, m

swing /swɪŋ/ vi balancearse; oscilar; (hang) colgar; pender; columpiarse; girar; dar la vuelta; (of a boat) bornear. vt balancear; (hang) colgar; (rock) mecer; (in a swing, etc.) columpiar; hacer oscilar; (raise) subir. *n* oscilación, *f*; vaivén, *m*; (rhythm) ritmo, *m*; (seat, etc.) columpio, *m*; (reach) alcance, *m*. **The door swung open,** La puerta se abrió silenciosamente. **He swung the car around,** Dio la vuelta al auto. **He swung himself into the saddle,** Montó de un salto. **to be in full s.,** estar a toda marcha. **to go with a s.,** tener mucho éxito. **s.-boat,** columpio, *m*. **s.-bridge,** puente giratorio, *m*. **s.-door,** puerta giratoria, *f*

swinging /'swɪŋɪŋ/ *a* oscilante; pendiente; rítmico. *n* balanceo, *m*; oscilación, *f*; vaivén, *m*; ritmo, *m*. **s. stride,** andar rítmico, *m*

swinish /'swaɪnɪʃ/ *a* porcuno, de cerdo; cochino, sucio

swipe /swaɪp/ *vt* golpear duro; aplastar; (steal) *Mexico* chalequear. *n* golpe fuerte, *m*

swirl /swɜrl/ *vi* arremolinarse. *n* remolino, *m*

swish /swɪʃ/ *vt* (of an animal's tail) agitar, mover, menear; (of a cane) blandir; (thrash) azotar. *vi* silbar; (of water) susurrar; (of a dress, etc.) crujir. *n* silbo, *m*; (of water) susurro, murmullo, *m*; (of a dress, etc.) crujido, *m*

Swiss /swɪs/ *a* and *n* suizo (-za)

switch /swɪtʃ/ *n* vara, *f*; (riding) látigo, *m*; (of hair) trenza, *f*; *Elec.* interruptor, *m*; *Rail.* aguja, *f*; (*Rail.* siding) desviadero, *m*. *vt* azotar; (a train) desviar; *Elec.* interrumpir; (transfer) trasladar; (of an animal, its tail) remover, mover rápidamente. **to s. off,** (*Elec.* and telephone) cortar; (*Radio.* and *Auto.*) desconectar. **to s. on,** conectar; (a light) poner (la luz); (a radio) encender

switchboard /'swɪtʃ,bɔrd/ *n* cuadro de distribución, *m*

Switzerland /'swɪtsərlənd/ Suiza, *f*

swivel /'swɪvəl/ *n* torniquete, *m*; anillo móvil, *m*; pivote, *m*. *vi* girar sobre un eje; dar una vuelta. **s.-chair,** silla giratoria, *f*. **s.-door,** puerta giratoria, *f*

swoon /swun/ *vi* desvanecerse, desmayarse. *n* desmayo, desvanecimiento, *m*

swoop /swup/ *vi* calarse, abatirse; (of robbers, etc.) abalanzarse (sobre). *n* calada, *f*. **at one fell s.,** de un solo golpe

sword /sɔrd/ *n* espada, *f*; sable, *m*. **to measure swords with,** cruzar espadas con. **to put to the s.,** pasar a cuchillo (a). **s.-arm,** brazo derecho, *m*. **s.-belt,** talabarte, *m*. **s.-cut,** sablazo, *m*. **s.-dance,** danza de espadas, *f*. **s.-fish,** pez espada, pez sierra, espadarte, *m*, jifia, *f*. **s.-play,** esgrima, *f*; manejo de la espada, *m*. **s.-stick,** bastón de estoque, *m*. **s.-thrust,** golpe de espada, *m*; estocada, *f*

swordsman /'sɔrdzmən/ *n* espadachín, *m*; esgrimidor, *m*

swordsmanship /'sɔrdzmən,ʃɪp/ *n* manejo de la espada, *m*; esgrima, *f*

sybarite /'sɪbə,raɪt/ *a* and *n* sibarita, *mf*

sybaritic /,sɪbə'rɪtɪk/ *a* sibarítico, sibarita

sycamore /'sɪkə,mɔr/ *n* sicomoro, *m*; falso plátano, *m*

sycophancy /'sɪkəfənsi/ *n* servilismo, *m*

sycophant /'sɪkəfənt/ *n* sicofanta, *m*

syllabic /sɪ'læbɪk/ *a* silábico

syllable /'sɪləbəl/ *n* sílaba, *f*

syllabus /'sɪləbəs/ *n* programa, *m*; compendio, *m*

syllogism /'sɪlə,dʒɪzəm/ *n* silogismo, *m*

sylph /sɪlf/ *n* sílfide, *f*, silfo, *m*; (woman) sílfide, *f*; (hummingbird) colibrí, *m*. **s.-like,** de sílfide; como una sílfide

sylvan /'sɪlvən/ *a* selvático, silvestre; rústico

symbiosis /,sɪmbi'ousɪs/ *n* simbiosis, *f*

symbol /'sɪmbəl/ *n* símbolo, signo, emblema, *m*; *Math.* símbolo, *m*; (of rank, etc.) insignia, *f*

symbolical /sɪm'bɒlɪkəl/ *a* simbólico

symbolism /'sɪmbə,lɪzəm/ *n* simbolismo, *m*

symbolist /'sɪmbəlɪst/ *n* simbolista, *mf*

symbolize /'sɪmbə,laɪz/ *vt* simbolizar

symmetrical /sɪ'mɛtrɪkəl/ *a* simétrico

symmetry /'sɪmɪtri/ *n* simetría, *f*

sympathetic /,sɪmpə'θɛtɪk/ *a* simpático; compasivo; (of the public, etc.) bien dispuesto. *n* *Anat.* gran simpático, *m*. **s. words,** palabras de simpatía, *f pl*. **s. ink,** tinta simpática, *f*

sympathetically /,sɪmpə'θɛtɪkli/ *adv* simpáticamente; con compasión

sympathize /'sɪmpə,θaɪz/ *vi* simpatizar (con); (understand) comprender; (condole) compadecerse (de), condolerse (de); dar el pésame

sympathizer /'sɪmpə,θaɪzər/ *n* partidario (-ia)

sympathy /'sɪmpəθi/ *n* simpatía, *f*; compasión, *f*. **Paul is in s. with their aims,** Pablo está de acuerdo con sus objetos. **Please accept my s.,** (on a bereavement) Le acompaño a Vd. en su sentimiento

symphonic /sɪm'fɒnɪk/ *a* sinfónico

symphony /'sɪmfəni/ *n* sinfonía, *f*

symposium /sɪm'pouziəm/ *n* colección de artículos, *f*

symptom /'sɪmptəm/ *n* síntoma, *m*; señal, *f*, indicio, *m*. **to show symptoms of,** dar indicios de

symptomatic /,sɪmptə'mætɪk/ *a* sintomático

synagogue /'sɪnə,gɒg/ *n* sinagoga, *f*

synchronization /,sɪŋkrənə'zeɪʃən/ *n* sincronización, *f*

synchronize /'sɪŋkrə,naɪz/ *vi* coincidir, tener lugar simultáneamente; sincronizarse. *vt* sincronizar

synchronous /'sɪŋkrənəs/ *a* sincrónico

syncopate /'sɪŋkə,peɪt/ *vt* (*Gram. Mus.*) sincopar

syncopation /,sɪŋkə'peɪʃən/ *n Mus.* síncopa, *f*

syncope /'sɪŋkə,pi/ *n* (*Med. Gram.*) síncope, *m*

syndical /'sɪndɪkəl/ *a* sindical

syndicalism /'sɪndɪkə,lɪzəm/ *n* sindicalismo, *m*

syndicalist /'sɪndɪkəlɪst/ *n* sindicalista, *mf*

syndicate /*n.* 'sɪndɪkɪt/ *v.* -,keit/ *n* sindicato, *m*, *vt* sindicar

syndication /,sɪndɪ'keɪʃən/ *n* sindicación, *f*

synod /'sɪnəd/ *n Eccl.* sínodo, *m*

synonym /'sɪnənɪm/ *n* sinónimo, *m*

synonymous /sɪ'nɒnəməs/ *a* sinónimo

synopsis /sɪ'nɒpsɪs/ *n* sinopsis, *f*

synoptic /sɪ'nɒptɪk/ *a* sinóptico

syntax /'sɪntæks/ *n* sintaxis, *f*

synthesis /'sɪnθəsɪs/ *n* síntesis, *f*

synthetic /sɪn'θɛtɪk/ *a* sintético

synthetize /'sɪnθə,taɪz/ *vt* sintetizar

syphilis /'sɪfəlɪs/ *n* sífilis, *f*

syphilitic /,sɪfə'lɪtɪk/ *a* and *n* sifilítico (-ca)

Syracuse /'sɪrə,kyus, -,kyuz/ Siracusa, *f*

syren /'saɪrən/ *n*. See **siren**

Syria /'sɪəriə/ Siria, *f*

Syrian /'sɪəriə/ *a* and *n* siríaco (-ca), sirio (-ia)

syringe /sə'rɪndʒ/ *n* jeringa, *f*, *vt* jeringar

syrup /'sɪrəp, 'sɜr-/ *n* (for coughs) jarabe, sirope, *m*; (for bottling fruit, etc.) almíbar, *m*

syrup cake *n Argentina* chancaca, *f*

syrupy /'sɪrəpi, 'sɜr-/ *a* siroposeo

system /'sɪstəm/ *n* sistema, *m*; régimen, *m*; método, *m*; (body) organismo, *m*. **He has no s. in his work,** No tiene método en su trabajo. **the nervous s.,** el sistema nervioso. **the feudal s.,** el feudalismo, el sistema feudal

systematic /,sɪstə'mætɪk/ *a* sistemático, metódico

systematically /,sɪstə'mætɪkli/ *adv* sistemáticamente, metódicamente

systematization /,sɪstəmətə'zeɪʃən/ *n* sistematización, *f*

systematize /'sɪstəmə,taɪz/ *vt* sistematizar

T

t /ti/ *n* (letter) te, *f. a* en T, en forma de T. **T band-age,** vendaje en T, *m.* **T square,** regla T, *f*
tab /tæb/ *n* oreja, *f*
tabby /'tæbi/ *n* gato romano, *m*; (female) gata, *f*; *Inf.* vieja chismosa, *f*
tabernacle /'tæbər,nækəl/ *n* tabernáculo, *m*; templo, *m*; *Archit.* templete, *m*; *Eccl.* custodia, *f*
tabes /'teibiz/ *n Med.* tabes, *f*
table /'teibəl/ *n* mesa, *f*; (food) comida, mesa, *f*; (of the law, weights, measures, contents, etc.) tabla, *f*; (of land) meseta, *f*; (of prices) lista, tarifa, *f. vt* (parliament) poner sobre la mesa; enumerar, apuntar, hacer una lista de. **to clear the t.,** alzar (or levantar) la mesa. **to lay the t.,** cubrir (or poner) la mesa. **to have a t.-d'hôte meal,** tomar el menú. **to rise from t.,** levantarse de la mesa. **to sit down to t.,** ponerse a la mesa. **The tables are turned,** Se volvió la tortilla. **side t.,** aparador, trinchero, *m.* **small t.,** mesilla, *f.* **t. of contents,** tabla de materias, *f,* índice, índice de materias, índice general, *m.* **t.-centerpiece,** centro de mesa, *m.* **t.-cloth,** mantel, *m.* **t.-companion,** comensal, *mf* **t.-knife,** cuchillo de mesa, *m.* **t.-lamp,** quinqué, *m*; lampara de mesa, *f.* **t.-land,** meseta, *f.* **t.-leg,** pata de una mesa, *f.* **t.-linen,** mantelería, *f.* **t.-napkin,** servilleta, *f.* **t.-runner,** camino de mesa, *m.* **t.-spoon,** cuchara para los legumbres, *f.* **t.-talk,** conversación de sobremesa, *f.* **t.-turning,** mesas que dan vueltas, *f pl.* **t.-ware,** artículos para la mesa, *m pl*
tableau /tæ'blou/ *n* cuadro, *m.* **tableaux vivants,** cuadros vivos, *m pl*
table d'hôte /'tɑbəl 'dout/ *n* Spain el menú, *m, Mexico* comida corrida, *f*
tablespoonful /'teibəlspun,fʊl/ *n* cucharada, *f*
tablet /'tæblɪt/ *n* tabla, *f*; (with inscription) tarjeta, losa, lápida, *f*; *Med.* comprimido, *m,* tableta, *f*; (of soap, chocolate) pastilla, *f.* **writing t.,** taco de papel, *m*
tabloid /'tæbloɪd/ *n* comprimido, *m,* pastilla, *f*
taboo /tə'bu, tæ-/ *n* tabú, *m. a* prohibido, tabú. *vt* declarar tabú, prohibir
tabor /'teibər/ *n Mus.* tamboril, tamborín, *m.* **t. player,** tamborilero, *m*
tabouret /,tæbə'rɛt/ *n* (stool) taburete, *m*; (for embroidery) tambor de bordar, *m*; *Mus.* tamborilete, *m*
tabulate /'tæbyə,leit/ *vt* resumir en tablas; hacer una lista de, catalogar
tabulation /,tæbyə'leiʃən/ *n* distribución en tablas, *f*
tacit /'tæsɪt/ *a* tácito
taciturn /'tæsɪ,tɜrn/ *a* taciturno, reservado, de pocas palabras
tack /tæk/ *n* (nail) tachuela, puntilla, *f*; *Sew.* hilván, embaste, *m*; *Naut.* amura, *f*; *Naut.* puño de amura, *m*; *Naut.* bordada, *f*; *Fig.* cambio de política, *m. vt* clavar con tachuelas; *Sew.* hilvanar, embastar; *Fig.* añadir. *vi Naut.* virar; *Fig.* cambiar de política, adoptar un nuevo plan de acción. **t. puller,** sacabrocas, *m*
tackle /'tækəl/ *n* aparejo, *m*; maniobra, *f*; *Naut.* cuadernal, *m,* jarcia, *f*; (gear) aparejos, avíos, *m pl*; (football) carga, *f. vt* agarrar, asir; *Fig.* atacar, abordar; (football) cargar; (undertake) emprender; (a problem) luchar con. **t.-block,** polea, *f*
tacky /'tæki/ *a* pegajoso, viscoso
tact /tækt/ *n* tacto, *m,* discreción, diplomacia, delicadeza, *f*
tactful /'tæktfəl/ *a* lleno de tacto, diplomático, discreto
tactfully /'tæktfəli/ *adv* discretamente, diplomáticamente
tactical /'tæktɪkəl/ *a* táctico
tactically /'tæktɪkli/ *adv* según la táctica; del punto de vista táctico
tactician /tæk'tɪʃən/ *n* táctico, *m*
tactics /'tæktɪks/ *n pl* táctica, *f*
tactile /'tæktɪl/ *a* táctil; tangible
tactless /'tæktlɪs/ *a* que no tiene tacto, sin tacto alguno, indiscreto

tactlessly /'tæktlɪsli/ *adv* impolíticamente, indiscretamente
tactlessness /'tæktlɪsnɪs/ *n* falta de tacto, *f*
tadpole /'tædpoul/ *n* renacuajo, *m*
taffeta /'tæfɪtə/ *n* tafetán, *m*
tag /tæg/ *n* herrete, *m*; (label) marbete, *m,* etiqueta, *f*; (of tail) punta del rabo, *f*; (of boot) tirador de bota, *m*; (game) marro, *m*; (rag) arrapiezo, *m*; (quotation) cita bien conocida, *f*; (of song, poem) refrán, *m.* **to play t.,** jugar al marro
Tagus /'teigəs/ el Tajo, *m*
tail /teil/ *n* cola, *f,* rabo, *m*; (plait) trenza, *f*; (wisp of hair) mechón, *m*; (of a comet) cola, cabellera, *f*; (of a note in music) rabito, *m*; (of a coat) faldon, *m*; (of a kite) cola, *f*; (of the eye), rabo, *m*; (retinue) séquito, *m,* banda, *f*; (of an airplane) cola, *f*; (end) fin, *m*; (of coin) cruz, *f*; (line) fila, cola, *f. vt* seguir de cerca, pisarle (a uno) los talones. **to t. after,** seguir de cerca. **to t. away,** disminuir; desaparecer, perderse de vista. **to t. on,** unir, juntar. **to turn t.,** volver la espalda, poner los pies en polvorosa. **with the t. between the legs,** con el rabo entre piernas. **t.-board,** (of a cart) escalera, *f.* **t.-coat,** frac, *m.* **t.-end,** extremo, *m*; fin, *m*; lo último. **t.-feather,** pena, *f.* **t.-fin,** aleta caudal, *f*; *Aer.* timón de dirección, *m.* **t.-light,** farol trasero, *m, Mexico* calavera, *f.* **t.-piece,** (of a violin, etc.) cola, *f*; *Print.* marmosete, culo de lámpara, *m.* **t. spin,** *Aer.* barrena de cola, *f.* **t. wind,** viento de cola, *m*
tailed /teild/ *a* de rabo. **big-t.,** rabudo, *de* cola grande. **long-t.,** rabilargo. **short-t.,** rabicorto
tailless /'teillɪs/ *a* sastre (-ra). rabo
tailor /'teilər/ *n* sastre (-ra). **t.-made,** *n* traje sastre, *m, a* de hechura de sastre. **tailor's shop,** sastrería, *f*
tailoring /'teilərɪŋ/ *n* sastrería, *f*; (work) corte, *m*
taint /teint/ *n* corrupción, *f*; infección, *f*; (blemish) mancha, *f*; (tinge) dejo, *m. vt* corromper, pervertir; inficionar; (meat) corromper. *vi* corromperse, inficionarse; (meat) corromperse
take /teik/ *vt* tomar; (receive) aceptar; (remove) quitar; (pick up) coger; (grab) asir, agarrar; *Math.* restar; (carry) llevar; (a person) traer, llevar; (guide) conducir, guiar; (win) ganar; (earn) cobrar, percibir; obtener; (make prisoner) hacer prisionero, prender; (a town, etc.) tomar, rendir, conquistar; (appropriate) apoderarse de, apropiarse; (steal) robar, hurtar; (ensnare) coger, cazar con trampas; (fish) pescar, coger; (a trick, in cards) hacer (una baza); (an illness) contraer, coger; (by surprise) sorprender, coger desprevenido (a); (attract) atraer; (drink) beber; (a meal) tomar; (select) escoger; (hire) alquilar; (suppose) suponer; (a journal) estar abonado a; (use) emplear, usar; (impers., require) necesitarse, hacer falta; (purchase) comprar; (assume) adoptar, asumir; (a leap) dar (un salto); (a walk) dar (un paseo); (a look) echar (un vistazo); (measures) tomar (medidas); (the chair) presidir; (understand) comprender; (a photograph) sacar (una fotografía); (believe) creer; (consider) considerar; (a note) apuntar; (jump over) saltar; (time) tomar, emplear. **I t. size three in shoes,** Calzo el número tres. **to t. to be,** (believe) suponer; (mistake) creer quivocadamente. **to t. (a thing) badly,** tomarlo (or llevarlo) a mal. **The book took me two hours to read,** Necesité dos horas para leer el libro, Leí el libro en dos horas. **And this, I t. it, is Mary?** ¿Y supongo que ésta será María? **to be taken with,** ser entusiasta de; (of persons) estar prendado de. **to t. aback,** desconcertar, coger desprevenido (a). **to t. again,** volver a tomar; llevar otra vez; (a photograph) retratar otra vez. **to t. along,** llevar; traer. **to t. a long time,** tardar, *Lat. Am.* dilatar. **to t. away,** quitar; llevarse. **to t. back,** devolver; (retract) retractar; (receive) recibir (algo) devuelto. **to t. down,** bajar; (a building) derribar; (machinery) desmontar; (hair) deshacerse (el cabello); (swallow) tragar; (in writing) apuntar; (humble) quitar los humos (a), humillar. **to t. for,** creer, imaginar; (a walk, etc.) lle-

var a; (mistake) creer erróneamente; tomar por. **Whom do you t. me for?** ¿Por quién me tomas? **to. t. for granted (assume),** dar por descontado, dar por lecho, dar por sentado, dar por supuesto; (underestimate) no hacer caso de, tratar con indiferencia. **t. the lion's share (of),** llevarse la parte del león (de), llevarse la tajada del león (de). **t. shape,** cobrar perfiles más nítidos, estructurarse con más nitidez, ir adquiriendo consistencia, tomar forma. **t. the law into one's own hands,** tomar la justicia por la mano. **to t. from,** privar, quitar de; (subtract) restar; substraer de. **to t. in,** (believe) tragar, creer; (sail) acortar las velas; (deceive) engañar; (lead in) hacer entrar; (accept) recibir, aceptar. **to t. it from somebody,** llevarse de alguien. **to t. off,** quitar; (surgically) amputar; (one's hat, etc.) quitarse (el sombrero); (eyes) sacar; (take away) llevarse; (mimic) imitar; (ridicule) ridiculizar; (unstick) despegar; (discount) descontar. **to t. on,** emprender; aceptar; (at sports) jugar. **to t. on oneself,** encargarse de, tomar por su cuenta, asumir. **to t. out,** sacar; extraer; (remove) quitar; (outside) llevar fuera; (for a walk) llevar a paseo; (obtain) obtener, sacar; (tire) agotar, rendir. **to t. over,** tomar posesión de; asumir; (show) mostrar, conducir por. **t. the bull by the horns,** ir al toro por los cuernos. **take seriously,** tomar en serio. **to t. up,** subir; (pick up) recoger; tomar; (a challenge, etc.) aceptar; (a dress, etc.) acortar; (absorb) absorber; (of space) ocupar; (of time) ocupar, hacer perder; (buy) comprar; (adopt) dedicarse a; (arrest) arrestar, prender; (criticize) censurar, criticar; (begin) empezar; (resume) continuar

take /teik/ *vi* tomar; (be successful) tener éxito; (of vaccination, etc.) prender; (a good (bad) photograph) salir bien (mal). **to t. after,** salir a, parecerse a; (of conduct) seguir el ejemplo de; **to t. off,** salir; Aer. despegar. **to t. on,** Inf. lamentarse. **to t. to,** dedicarse a; darse a; (of persons) tomar cariño a; (grow accustomed) acostumbrarse a. **to t. up with,** hacerse amigo de

take /teik/ *n* toma, *f*; cogida, *f*; *Print.* tomada, *f*; *Theat.* taquilla, *f*. **t.-in,** engaño, *m*. **t.-off,** Aer. (recorrido de) despegue, *m*; caricatura, *f*; sátira, *f*

taking /'teikɪŋ/ *n* toma, *f*; secuestro, *m*, *n pl* **takings,** ingresos, *m pl*; *Theat.* taquilla, entrada, *f. a* atractivo, encantador; simpático; (of disease) contagioso

talc /tælk/ *n Mineral.* talco, *m*

talcum powder /'tælkəm/ *n* talco, polvo de talco, *m*

tale /teil/ *n* (recital) narración, historia, *f*; relato, *m*; cuento, *m*; leyenda, historia, fábula, *f*; (number) cuenta, *f*, número, *m*; (gossip) chisme, *m*. **old wives' t.,** cuento de viejas, *m*. **to tell a t.,** contar una historia. **to tell tales,** contar cuentos; revelar secretos, chismear

talebearer /'teil,bɛərər/ *n* correveidile, *mf*; chismoso (-sa), soplón (-ona)

talebearing /'teil,bɛərɪŋ/ *n* el chismear, *m*

talent /'tælənt/ *n* (coin) talento, *m*; (ability) ingenio, *m*; habilidad, *f*. **the best t. in Spain,** la flor de la cultura española

talented /'tæləntɪd/ *a* talentoso, ingenioso

talisman /'tælɪsmən/ *n* talismán, *m*

talit /'talɪs, talit/ *n* taled, *m*

talk /tɔk/ *vi* and *vt* hablar, decir. **to t. business,** hablar de negocios. **to t. for talking's sake,** hablar por hablar. **to t. French,** hablar francés. **to t. nonsense,** decir disparates. **to t. too much,** hablar demasiado; Inf. hablar por los codos, irse (a uno) la lengua. **to t. about,** hablar de; conversar sobre. **to t. at,** decir algo a alguien para que lo entienda otro. **Are you talking at me?** ¿Lo dices por mí? **to t. away,** seguir hablando; disipar. **to t. into,** persuadir, inducir (a). **to t. of,** hablar de; charlar sobre. **to t. on,** hablar acerca de (or sobre); (continue) seguir hablando. **to t. out of,** disuadir de. **to t. out of turn,** meterse donde no le llaman, meter la pata. **to t. over,** hablar de; discutir, considerar. **to t. to,** (address) hablar a; (consult) hablar con; (scold) reprender. **to t. each other,** hablarse. **to t. up,** hablar claro

talk /tɔk/ *n* conversación, *f*; (informal lecture) charla, *f*; (empty words) palabras, *f pl*; (notoriety) escándalo, *m*; rumor, *m*. **There is t. of...,** Se dice que...; Se

habla de que. **to give a t.,** dar una charla. **to indulge in small t.,** hablar de cosas sin importancia, hablar de naderías

talkative /'tɔkətɪv/ *a* locuaz, gárrulo, hablador, decidor. **to be very t.,** ser muy locuaz; Inf. tener mucha lengua

talkativeness /'tɔkətɪvnɪs/ *n* locuacidad, garrulidad, *f*

talker /'tɔkər/ *n* hablador (-ra), conversador (-ra); (lecturer) orador (-ra); (in a derogatory sense) fanfarrón (-ona), charlatán (-ana). **to be a good t.,** hablar bien, ser buen conversacionista

talking /'tɔkɪŋ/ *a* que habla, hablante; (of birds, dolls, etc.) parlero. **to give a good t. to,** dar una peluca (a). **t.-film,** película sonora, *f*. **t.-machine,** fonógrafo, *m*

talk show *n* programa de entrevistas, *m*

tall /tɔl/ *a* alto; (of stories) exagerado. **five feet tall,** de cinco pies de altura

tallboy /'tɔl,bɔi/ *n* cómoda alta, *f*

tallness /'tɔlnɪs/ *n* altura, *f*; estatura, talla, *f*; (of stories) lo exagerado

tallow /'tælou/ *n* sebo, *m*. **t. candle,** vela de sebo, *f*. **t. chandler,** velero (-ra). **t.-faced,** con cara de color de cera

tallowy /'tæloui/ *a* seboso

tall tale *n* Peru bacho, *m*

tally /'tæli/ *n* tarja, tara, *f*; cuenta, *f*. *vt* llevar la cuenta (de). *vi* estar conforme, cuadrar

Talmud /'talmʊd/ *n* Talmud, *m*

Talmudic /tal'mʊdɪk/ *a* talmúdico

talon /'tælən/ *n* garra, *f*

tamable /'teiməbəl/ *a* domable, domesticable

tambour /'tæmbʊr, tæm'bʊr/ *n Mus.* tambor, *m*; (for embroidery) tambor (or bastidor) para bordar, *m*

tambourine /,tæmbə'rin/ *n* pandereta, *f*

tame /teim/ *a* domesticado, manso; (spiritless) sumiso; (dull) aburrido, soso. *vt* domar, domesticar; (curb) reprimir, gobernar, domar, suavizar. **to grow t.,** domesticarse

tamer /'teimər/ *n* domador (-ra)

taming /'teimɪŋ/ *n* domadura, *f*. **The T. of the Shrew,** La Fierecilla Domada

tamp /tæmp/ *vt* apisonar; (in blasting) atacar (un barreno)

tamper /'tæmpər/ *vi* (with) descomponer, estropear; (meddle with) meterse con; (witnesses) sobornar; (documents) falsificar

tampon /'tæmpɒn/ *n Surg.* tampón, tapón, *m*, *vt* taponar

tan /tæn/ *vt* curtir, adobar; (of sun) tostar, quemar; (slang) zurrar. *vi* tostarse por el sol. *n* color café claro, *m*; bronceado, cutis tostado, *m*. *a* de color café claro

tandem /'tændəm/ *n* tándem, *m*

tang /tæŋ/ *n* (of sword, etc.) espiga, *f*; (flavor) fuerte sabor, *m*; (sound) retintín, *m*

tangent /'tændʒənt/ *a* and *n* tangente *f*. **to fly off at a t.,** Fig. salir por la tangente

tangerine /,tændʒə'rin/ *a* and *n* tangerino (-na). **t. orange,** naranja mandarina, *f*

tangible /'tændʒəbəl/ *a* tangible; Fig. real

Tangier /tæn'dʒiər/ *n* Tánger, *m*

tangle /'tæŋgəl/ *n* embrollo, enredo, nudo, *m*; (of streets) laberinto, *m*; Fig. confusión, *f*. *vt* embrollar, enmarañar; (entangle) enredar; Fig. poner en confusión, complicar. *vi* enmarañarse

tank /tæŋk/ *n* tanque, depósito (de agua, etc.), *m*; cisterna, *f*; (as a reservoir) aljibe, estanque, *m*; Mil. tanque, carro de asalto, *m*. **t. up** (get drunk) Argentina acatarrarse

tankard /'tæŋkərd/ *n* pichel, bock, *m*

tanker /'tæŋkər/ *n* petrolero, *m*

tanned /tænd/ *a* bronceado, quemado por el sol, dorado por el sol

tanner /'tænər/ *n* curtidor, *m*; (slang) medio chelín, *m*. **tanner's scraper,** descarnador, *m*. **tanner's vat,** noque, *m*

tannery /'tænəri/ *n* curtiduría, *f*

tannic /wsmintænɪk/ *a Chem.* tánico. **t. acid,** ácido tánico, *m*

tannin

tannin /'tænɪn/ *n Chem.* tanino, *m*

tanning /'tænɪŋ/ *n* curtido, adobamiento, *m*

tantalize /'tæntḷ,aɪz/ *vt* tentar, atormentar, provocar

tantalizing /'tæntḷ,aɪzɪŋ/ *a* tentador, atormentador; provocativo

tantamount /'tæntə,maunt/ *a* equivalente, igual. **to be t. to,** ser equivalente a

tantrum /'tæntrəm/ *n* pataleta, rabieta, *f*, berrinche, *m*

taoism /'dauɪzəm/ *n* taoísmo, *m*

taoist /'dauɪst/ *n* taoísta, *mf*

tap /tæp/ *n* (blow) pequeño golpe, toque ligero, *m*; palmadita, *f*; (for drawing water, etc.) grifo, *m*, llave, *f*; (of a barrel) canilla, *f*; (brew of liquor) clase de vino, *f*; (tap-room) bar con mostrador, *m*; (tool) macho de terraja, *m*; (piece of leather on shoe) tapa, *f*; *pl* **taps,** *Mil.* toque de apagar las luces, *m*. *vt* (strike) golpear ligeramente, dar una palmadita a; (pierce) horadar; (a barrel) decentar; *Surg.* hacer una puntura en; (trees) sangrar; *Elec.* derivar (una corriente); (of water, current) tomar; (information) descubrir; (telephone) escuchar las conversaciones telefónicas. *vi* golpear ligeramente. **to tap at the door,** llamar suavemente a la puerta. **on tap,** en tonel. **screw-tap,** terraja, *f.* **tap-dance,** claqué, *m.* **tap-root,** raíz pivotante, *f*

tape /teip/ *n* (linen) cinta de hilo, *f*; (cotton) cinta de algodón, *f*; (telegraph machine) cinta de papel, *f*; (surveying) cinta para medir, *f.* **adhesive t.,** cinta adhesiva, *f.* **red t.,** balduque, *m*; *Fig.* burocracia, *f*; formulismo, *m.* **t.-machine,** telégrafo de cotizaciones bancarias, *m.* **t.-measure,** cinta métrica, *f*

taper /'teipər/ *n* bujía, cerilla, *f*; *Eccl.* cirio, *m. vi* ahusarse, rematar en punta. *vt* afilar

tapering /'teipərɪŋ/ *a* cónico, piramidal; (of fingers) afilado

tapestried /'tæpəstrid/ *a* cubierto de tapices, tapizado

tapestry /'tæpəstri/ *n* tapiz, *m*, **t, weaver,** tapicero, *m*

tapeworm /'teip,wɜrm/ *n* tenia, lombriz solitaria, *f*

tapioca /,tæpi'oukə/ *n* tapioca, *f*

tapir /'teipər/ *n Zool.* danta, *f*

tar /tɑr/ *n* alquitrán, *m*, brea, *f. vt* embrear, alquitranar. **to tar and feather,** emplumar. **coal t.,** alquitrán mineral, *m*

tarantella /,tærən'tɛlə/ *n* tarantela, *f*

tarantula /tə'ræntʃələ/ *n* tarántula, *f*

tardily /'tɑrdḷi/ *adv* tardíamente; lentamente

tardiness /'tɑrdɪnɪs/ *n* tardanza, lentitud, *f*

tardy /'tɑrdi/ *a* (late) tardío; (slow) lento; (reluctant) desinclinado

tare /tɛr/ *n Bot.* yero, *m*; (in the Bible) cizaña, *f*; *Com.* tara, *f*; (of a vehicle) peso en vacío, *m*

target /'tɑrgɪt/ *n* blanco (de tiro), *m*; (shield) rodela, tarja, *f.* **t. practice,** tiro al blanco, *m*

tariff /'tærɪf/ *n* tarifa, *f.* **to put a t. on,** tarifar

tarlatan /'tɑrlətṇ/ *n* tarlatana, *f*

tarmac /'tɑrmæk/ *n* alquitranado, *m*

tarn /tɑrn/ *n* lago de montaña, *m*

tarnish /'tɑrnɪʃ/ *n* deslustre, *m. vt* deslustrar, empañar; *Fig.* obscurecer, manchar. *vi* deslustrarse

tarpaulin /tɑr'pɔlɪn, 'tɑrpəlɪn/ *n* alquitranado, encerado, *m*

tarred /tard/ *a* alquitranado, embreado

tarring /'tarɪŋ/ *n* embreadura, *f*

tarry /'tɑri/ *vi* tardar, detenerse

tart /tɑrt/ *a* ácido, acerbo, agridulce; *Fig.* áspero. *n* tarta, *f*; pastelillo de fruta, *m*

tartan /'tɑrtṇ/ *n Naut.* tartana, *f*; (plaid) tartán, *m*

tartar /'tɑrtər/ *n Chem.* tártaro, *m*; (in teeth) sarro, tártaro, *m*; **cream of t.,** (cremor) tártaro, *m.* **t. emetic,** tártaro emético, *m.* **Tartar,** *a* and *n* tártaro (-ra)

tartly /'tɑrtli/ *adv* ásperamente, agriamente

tartness /'tɑrtnɪs/ *n* acidez, *f*; *Fig.* aspereza, *f*

task /tæsk/ *n* tarea, labor, *f*; empresa, *f*; misión, *f.* **to take to t.,** regañar, censurar. **t.-force,** (naval or military) contingente, *m*

taskmaster /'tæsk,mæstər/ *n* el que señala una tarea; amo, *m*

tassel /'tæsəl/ *n* borla, *f*; (of corn) panoja, espiga, *f*

taste /teist/ *n* gusto, *m*; (flavor) sabor, *m*; (speci-

men) ejemplo, *m*, idea, *f*; (small quantity) un poco, muy poco; (liking) afición, inclinación, *f*; (of drink) sorbo, trago, *m*; (tinge) dejo, *m. vt* (appraise) probar; gustar, percibir el gusto de; (experience) experimentar, conocer. *vi* tener gusto, tener sabor. **a matter of t.,** cuestión de gusto. **Each to his own t.,** Entre gustos no hay disputa. **He had not tasted a bite,** No había probado bocado. **in bad (good) t.,** de mal (buen) gusto; de mal (buen) tono. **to have a t. for,** ser aficionado a, gustar de. **to t.,** *Cul.* a gusto, a sabor. **to t. of,** tener gusto de, saber a

tasted /'teistɪd/ *a* (in compounds) de sabor...

tasteful /'teistfəl/ *a* de buen gusto

tastefully /'teistfəli/ *adv* con buen gusto

tastefulness /'teistfəlnɪs/ *n* buen gusto, *m*

tasteless /'teistlɪs/ *a* insípido, soso, insulso; de mal gusto

tastelessness /'teistlɪsnɪs/ *n* insipidez, insulsez, *f*; mal gusto, *m*

taster /'teistər/ *n* catador, *m*; (vessel) catavino, *m*

tasting /'teistɪŋ/ *n* saboreo, *m*, gustación, *f*, *a* (in compounds) de sabor...

tasty /'teisti/ *a* apetitoso, sabroso

tatter /'tætər/ *n* andrajo, harapo, *m*; jirón, *m.* **to tear in tatters,** hacer jirones

tattered /'tætərd/ *a* andrajoso, haraposo

tatting /'tætɪŋ/ *n* frivolité, *m*

tattoo /tæ'tu/ *n* tatuaje, *m*; *Mil.* retreta, *f*; (display) parada militar, *f. vt* tatuar

tattooing /tæ'tuɪŋ/ *n* tatuaje, *m*; tamboreo, *m*

taunt /tɔnt/ *n* mofa, *f*, insulto, escarnio, *m. vt* insultar, atormentar. **to t. with,** echar en cara

taunting /'tɔntɪŋ/ *a* insultante, burlón, insolente

tauntingly /'tɔntɪŋli/ *adv* burlonamente, insolentemente

Taurus /'tɔrəs/ *n* tauro, toro, *m*

taut /tɔt/ *a* tieso, tirante, tenso; en regla; *Naut.* **to make t.,** tesar

tauten /'tɔtṇ/ *vt* tesar; poner tieso

tautness /'tɔtnɪs/ *n* tensión, *f*

tautological /,tɔtḷ'ɒdʒɪkəl/ *a* tautológico

tautology /tɔ'tɒlədʒi/ *n* tautología, *f*

tavern /'tævərn/ *n* taberna, *f*; (inn) mesón, *m*, posada, *f.* **t.-keeper,** tabernero, *m*

tawdrily /'tɔdrɪli/ *adv* llamativamente, de un modo cursi

tawdriness /'tɔdrɪnɪs/ *n* charrería, *f*

tawdry /'tɔdri/ *a* chillón, charro, cursi

tawny /'tɔni/ *a* leonado

tax /tæks/ *n* contribución, gabela, imposición, *f*; *Fig.* carga, *f*; *vt* imponer contribuciones (a); *Law.* tasar; *Fig.* cargar, abrumar. **to tax with,** tachar (de), acusar (de). **direct (indirect) tax,** contribución directa (indirecta), *f.* **tax-collector,** recaudador de contribuciones, *m.* **tax-free,** libre de impuestos. **tax-rate,** tarifa de impuestos, *f*, cupo, *m.* **tax-register,** lista de contribuyentes, *f*

taxable /'tæksəbəl/ *a* imponible, sujeto a impuestos

taxation /tæk'seiʃən/ *n* imposición de contribuciones (or impuestos), *f*

tax evasion *n* evasión tributaria, *f*

taxi /'tæksi/ *n* taxi, *Mexico* libre, *m. vi* ir en un taxi; *Aer.* correr por tierra. **t. driver,** chófer de un taxi, taxista, *m.* **t. rank, taxi stand,** parada de taxis, *f*

taxidermist /'tæksɪ,dɜrmɪst/ *n* taxidermista, *mf*

taxidermy /'tæksɪ,dɜrmi/ *n* taxidermia, *f*

taximeter /'tæksi,mitər/ *n* taxímetro, *m*

taxpayer /'tæks,peiər/ *n* contribuyente, *mf*

taxpaying /'tæks,peiɪŋ/ *a* tributario, que paga contribuciones

tax reform *n* reforma impositiva, reforma tributaria, *f*

tea /ti/ *n* (liquid) té, *m*; (meal) merienda, *f.* **to have tea,** tomar el té, merendar. **tea-caddy,** bote para té, *m.* **tea-chest,** caja para té, *f.* **tea-cosy,** cubretetera, *m.* **tea-cup,** taza para té, *f.* **tea-dance,** té baile, *m.* **tea-kettle** or **tea-pot,** tetera, *f.* **tea-leaf,** hoja de té, *f.* **tea-party,** reunión para tomar el té, *f.* **tea-room,** salón de té, *m.* **tea-rose,** rosa de té, *f.* **tea-set,** juego de té, *m.* **tea-strainer,** colador de té, *m.* **tea-time,** hora de té, f. **tea-urn,** samowar, m, tetera para hacer té, f.

tea-wagon, carrito para el té, m

teach /titʃ/ vt (a person) enseñar, instruir; (a subject) enseñar; (to lecture on) ser profesor de; (a lesson) dar una lección (de). vi (be a teacher) dedicarse a la enseñanza. **to teach at...,** desempeñor una cátedra en... **to t. a person Spanish,** enseñar el castellano a alguien. **to t. how to,** enseñar a (followed by infin.)

teachability /ˌtitʃəˈbɪlɪti/ n docilidad, f

teachable /ˈtitʃəbəl/ a educable; dócil

teacher /ˈtitʃər/ n preceptor, m; profesor, maestro, m. **woman t.,** profesora, maestra, f

teaching /ˈtitʃɪŋ/ n enseñanza, f; (belief) doctrina, f, a docente. **t. profession,** magisterio, m

teaching method n método didáctico, f

teak /tik/ n Bot. teca, f; (wood) madera de teca, f

team /tim/ n (of horses) tiro, m; (of oxen, mules) par, m, pareja, yunta, f; Sports. partido, equipo, m; compañía, f, grupo, m. vt enganchar, uncir. **t.-work,** cooperación, f

teamster /ˈtimstər/ n gañán, m

tear /tεər/ vt rasgar; romper; lacerar; (in pieces) hacer pedazos, despedazar; (scratch) arañar; Fig. atormentar. **to t. asunder,** romper; desmembrar. **to t. away,** arrancar, quitar violentamente. **to t. down,** derribar, echar abajo. **to t. off,** arrancar; desgajar. **to t. oneself away,** arrancarse, desgarrarse. **to t. one's hair,** arrancarse los pelos, mesarse. **to t. open,** abrir apresuradamente. **to t. up,** hacer pedazos; (uproot) arrancar, desarraigar.

tear /tεər/ vi rasgarse; romper; correr precipitadamente. **to t. along,** correr rápidamente (por). **to t. away,** marcharse corriendo. **to t. down,** bajar corriendo. **to t. into,** entrar corriendo en. **to t. off,** irse precipitadamente, marcharse corriendo. **to t. up,** subir corriendo; llegar corriendo; atravesar rápidamente

tear /tɪər/ n lágrima, f; (drop) gota, f. **with tears in one's eyes,** con lágrimas en los ojos. **to shed tears,** llorar, lagrimear. **to wipe away one's tears,** secarse las lágrimas. **t.-drop,** lágrima, f. **t.-duct,** conductor lacrimal, m. **t.-gas,** gas lacrimante, m. **t.-stained,** mojado de lágrimas

tear /tεər/ n (rent) rasgón, m

tearful /ˈtɪərfəl/ a lloroso, lacrimoso

tearfully /ˈtɪərfəli/ adv con lágrimas en los ojos

tearing /ˈtεərɪŋ/ n rasgadura, f, desgarro, m

tearjerker /ˈtɪərˌdʒɜrkər/ n drama lacrimón, m

tease /tiz/ vt (card) cardar; (annoy) fastidiar, irritar, molestar; (chaff) tomar el pelo (a), embromar; (pester) importunar. n bromista, mf

teasel /ˈtizəl/ n Bot. cardencha, f, vt cardar

teaser /ˈtizər/ n (problem) rompecabezas, m; (person) bromista, mf

teaspoon /ˈtiˌspun/ n cucharita, f

teaspoonful /ˈtispunˌfʊl/ n cucharadita, f

teat /tit, tɪt/ n pezón, m; (of animals) teta, f

technical /ˈtεknɪkəl/ a técnico. **t. offense,** Law. cuasidelito, m. **t. school,** escuela industrial, f

technicality /ˌtεknɪˈkælɪti/ n carácter técnico, m; tecnicismo, m; detalle técnico, m

technician /tεkˈnɪʃən/ n técnico, m

technicolor /ˈtεknɪˌkʌlər/ n tecnicolor, m

technique /tεkˈnik/ n técnica, f; ejecución, f; mecanismo, m

technological /ˌtεknəˈlɒdʒɪkəl/ a tecnológico

technologist /tεkˈnɒlədʒɪst/ n tecnólogo, m

technology /tεkˈnɒlədʒi/ n tecnología, f

teddy bear /ˈtεdi/ n osito de trapo, m

tedious /ˈtidiəs/ a aburrido, tedioso, pesado

tediously /ˈtidiəsli/ adv aburridamente

tediousness /ˈtidiəsnɪs/ n aburrimiento, m, pesadez, f

tedium /ˈtidiəm/ n tedio, m, monotonía, f

tee /ti/ n Sports. meta, f; (golf) tee, m; (letter) te, f; cosa en forma de te, f. vt (golf) colocar la pelota en el tee

teem /tim/ vi rebosar (de), abundar (en); pulular, hormiguear, estar lleno (de); (with rain) diluviar

teeming /ˈtimɪŋ/ a prolífico, fecundo. **t. with,** abundante en, lleno de

teens /tinz/ n pl números y años desde trece hasta diez y nueve; edad de trece a diez y nueve años de edad. **to be still in one's t.,** no haber cumplido aún los veinte

teeter /ˈtitər/ vi balancearse, columpiarse

teethe /tið/ vi endentecer, echar los dientes

teething /ˈtiðɪŋ/ n dentición, f. **t.-ring,** chupador, m

teetotal /ˈtiˈtoutl/ a abstemio

teetotalism /ˈtiˈtoutlˌɪzəm/ n abstinencia completa de bebidas alcohólicas, f

teetotaller /ˈtiˈtoutlər/ n abstemio (-ia)

teetotum /tiˈtoutəm/ n perinola, f

telecast /ˈtεliˌkæst/ vt telefundir

telecommunication /ˌtεlikəˌmyunɪˈkeiʃən/ n telecomunicación, f

telegram /ˈtεliˌgræm/ n telegrama, m

telegraph /ˈtεliˌgræf/ n telégrafo, m. vi telegrafiar; Fig. hacer señas. vt telegrafiar, enviar por telégrafo. **t. line,** línea telegráfica, f. **t. office,** central de telégrafos, f. **t. pole,** poste telegráfico, m. **t. wire,** hilo telegráfico, m

telegraphic /ˌtεlɪˈgræfɪk/ a telegráfico

telegraphist /təˈlεgrəfɪst/ n telegrafista, mf

telegraphy /təˈlεgrəfi/ n telegrafía, f. **wireless t.,** telegrafía sin hilos, f

telemetry /təˈlεmɪtri/ n telemetría, f

teleology /ˌtεliˈɒlədʒi/ n teleología, f

telepathic /ˌtεləˈpæθɪk/ a telepático

telepathy /təˈlεpəθi/ n telepatía, f

telephone /ˈtεləˌfoun/ n teléfono, m. vi telefonear. vt telefonear, llamar por teléfono. **to be on the t.,** (speaking) estar communicando; (of subscribers) tener teléfono. **dial t.,** teléfono automático, m. **t. call,** comunicación telefónica, f; conversación telefónica, f. **t. call box,** teléfono público, m. **t. directory,** guía de teléfonos, f. **t. exchange,** central telefónica, f. **t. number,** número de teléfono, m. **t. operator,** telefonista, mf. **t. receiver,** receptor telefónico, m. **t. wire,** hilo telefónico, m

telephonic /ˌtεləˈfɒnɪk/ a telefónico

telephonist /təˈlεfənɪst/ n telefonista, mf

telephony /təˈlεfəni/ n telefonía, f. **wireless t.,** telefonía sin hilos, f

teleprinter /ˈtεləˌprɪntər/ n teletipo, m

telescope /ˈtεləˌskoup/ n telescopio, catalejo, m. vt enchufar. vi enchufarse, meterse una cosa dentro de otra

telescopic /ˌtεləˈskɒpɪk/ a telescópico; de enchufe

televise /ˈtεləˌvaiz/ vt trasmitir por televisión

television /ˈtεləˌvɪʒən/ n televisión, f. **on television,** por televisión. **I saw her on television,** La vi por televisión

television series n serie televisiva, f

tell /tεl/ vt contar, narrar; decir; revelar; expresar; (the time, of clocks) marcar; (inform) comunicar, informar; (show) indicar, manifestar; (explain) explicar; distinguir; (order) mandar; (compute) contar. vi decir; (have effect) producir efecto. **We cannot t.,** No sabemos. **Who can t.?** ¿Quién sabe? **T. that to the marines!** Cuéntaselo a tu tía! **to t. its own tale,** hacer ver por sí mismo lo que hay. **to t. again,** volver a decir; contar otra vez. **to t. off,** regañar, reñir; (on a mission) despachar, mandar. **to t. on,** delatar. **to t. upon,** afectar

teller /ˈtεlər/ n narrador (-ra); (of votes) escrutador (-ra) de votos; (payer) pagador; (bank) cajero (-ra), m

telling /ˈtεlɪŋ/ a notable, significante. n narración, f

telltale /ˈtεlˌteil/ n chismoso (-sa), soplón (-ona); (informer) acusón (-ona); Fig. indicio, m, señal, f, a revelador

temerity /təˈmεrɪti/ n temeridad, f

temper /ˈtεmpər/ n (of metals) temple, m; (nature) naturaleza, f, carácter, m; espíritu, m; (mood) humor, m; (anger) mal genio, m; (of metals) templar; moderar, mitigar; mezclar. vi templarse. **bad (good) t.,** mal (buen) humor, m. **to keep one's t.,** no enojarse, no impacientarse. **to lose one's t.,** enojarse, perder la paciencia

tempera /ˈtεmpərə/ n Art. templa, f. **in t.,** al temple, m

temperament /ˈtεmpərəmənt, -prəmənt/ n temperamento, *m*; modo de ser, natural, *m*, naturaleza, índole, *f*; *Mus.* temple, *m*

temperamental /,tɛmpərə'mɛntḷ, -prə'mɛn-/ *a* natural, innato; caprichoso

temperamentally /,tɛmpərə'mɛntḷi, -prə'mɛn-/ *adv* por naturaleza

temperance /'tɛmpərəns/ *n* moderación, templanza, *f*; sobriedad, abstinencia, *f*

temperate /'tɛmpərɪt/ *a* moderado; sobrio; (of regions) templado. **t. zone,** zona templada, *f*

temperately /'tɛmpərɪtli/ *adv* sobriamente

temperateness /'tɛmpərɪtnɪs/ *n* moderación, sobriedad, mesura, *f*; (of regions) templanza, *f*

temperature /'tɛmpərətʃər/ *n* temperatura, *f*. **to have a t.,** tener fiebre

tempered /'tɛmpərd/ *a* de humor..., de genio... **to be good (bad) t.,** ser de buen (mal) humor

tempering /'tɛmpərɪŋ/ *n* temperación, *f*

tempest /'tɛmpɪst/ *n* tempestad, borrasca, *f*, temporal, *m*; *Fig.* tormenta, *f*

tempest in a teapot /'ti,pɒt/ borrasca en un vaso de agua, *m*

tempestuous /tɛm'pɛstʃuəs/ *a* tempestuoso, borrascoso; *Fig.* impetuoso, violento

tempestuousness /tɛm'pɛstʃuəsnɪs/ *n* lo tempestuoso; *Fig.* impetuosidad, violencia, *f*

temple /'tɛmpəl/ *n* templo, *m*; *Anat.* sien, *f*

tempo /'tɛmpou/ *n Mus.* tiempo, *m*

temporal /'tɛmpərəl/ *a* temporal; (transient) transitorio, fugaz; *Anat.* temporal. *n Anat.* hueso temporal, *m*

temporality /,tɛmpə'rælɪti/ *n* temporalidad, *f*

temporarily /,tɛmpə'rɛərəli/ *adv* provisionalmente

temporariness /'tɛmpə,rɛrɪnɪs/ *n* interinidad, *f*

temporary /'tɛmpə,rɛri/ *a* provisional, interino

temporize /'tɛmpə,raiz/ *vi* ganar tiempo; contemporizar

temporizing /'tɛmpə,raizɪŋ/ *n* contemporización, *f*, *a* contemporizador

tempt /tɛmpt/ *vt* tentar; atraer, seducir

temptation /tɛmp'teiʃən/ *n* tentación, *f*; aliciente, atractivo, *m*

tempter /'tɛmptər/ *n* tentador (-ra)

tempting /'tɛmptɪŋ/ *a* tentador, atrayente; seductor

ten /tɛn/ *a* diez; (of the clock) las diez, *f pl*; (of age) diez años, *m pl*, *n* diez, *m*; (a round number) decena, *f*; **ten-millionth,** *a* and *n* diezmillonésimo *m*. **ten months old,** diezmesino. **ten syllable,** decasílabo. **ten thousand,** *a* and *n* diez mil *m*. **There are ten thousand soldiers,** Hay diez mil soldados. **ten-thousandth,** *a* and *n* diezmilésimo *m*

tenable /'tɛnəbəl/ *a* sostenible, defendible

tenacious /tə'neiʃəs/ *a* tenaz; (stubborn) porfiado, obstinaz, terco; (sticky) adhesivo. **to be t. of life,** estar muy apegado a la vida

tenaciously /tə'neiʃəsli/ *adv* tenazmente; porfiadamente

tenacity /tə'næsɪti/ *n* tenacidad, *f*; porfía, *f*; tesón, *m*

tenancy /'tɛnənsi/ *n* inquilinato, *m*; tenencia, *f*

tenant /'tɛnənt/ *n* arrendatario (-ia), inquilino (-na); habitante, *m*; morador (-ra). **t. farmer,** *Chile* inquilino (-na), *mf*

tench /tɛntʃ/ *n Ichth.* tenca, *f*

tend /tɛnd/ *vt* cuidar, atender; guardar; vigilar. *vi* tender; inclinarse (a), propender (a)

tendency /'tɛndənsi/ *n* tendencia, inclinación, propensión, *f*; proclividad, *f*

tendentious /tɛn'dɛnʃəs/ *a* tendencioso

tender /'tɛndər/ *n* guardián, *m*; *Com.* oferta, propuesta, *f*; *Naut.* falúa, *f*; (of a railway engine) ténder, *m*. **legal t.,** moneda corriente, *f*

tender /'tɛndər/ *a* tierno; delicado; (of conscience) escrupuloso; (of a subject) espinoso; compasivo, afectuoso, sensible; muelle, blando. **t.-hearted,** compasivo, tierno de corazón

tender /'tɛndər/ *vt* ofrecer; dar; presentar. *vi* hacer una oferta. **to t. condolences,** dar el pésame. **to t. one's resignation,** presentar la dimisión. **to t. thanks,** dar las gracias

tenderly /'tɛndərli/ *adv* tiernamente

tenderness /'tɛndərnɪs/ *n* ternura, *f*; sensibilidad, *f*; delicadeza, *f*; dulzura, *f*; indulgencia, *f*; compasividad, benevolencia, *f*; escrupulosidad, *f*; mimo, cariño, *m*

tendon /'tɛndən/ *n Anat.* tendón, *m*. **t. of Achilles,** tendón de Aquiles, *m*

tenement /'tɛnəmənt/ *n* casa de vecindad, *f*; vivienda, *f*, *Lat. Am.* conventillo, *m*; *Poet.* morada, *f*

Teneriffe /,tɛnə'rif/ Tenerife, *f*

tenet /'tɛnɪt/ *n* principio, dogma, *m*, doctrina, *f*

tenfold /a.'tɛn,fould/ *adv.* -'fould/ *a* décuplo. *adv* diez veces

tennis /'tɛnɪs/ *n* tenis, *m*. **to play t.,** jugar al tenis. **t. ball,** pelota de tenis, *f*. **t. court,** campo de tenis, *m*, cancha de tenis, pista de tenis, *f*. **tennis club,** club de tenis, *m*. **t. racket,** raqueta de tenis, *f*; **tennis shoe,** zapatilla de tenis, *f*

tenon /'tɛnən/ *n* espiga, *f*, *vt* espigar

tenor /'tɛnər/ *n* curso, *m*; tenor, contenido, *m*; *Mus.* tenor, *m*; *Mus.* alto, *m*; (mus. instrument) viola, *f*. *a Mus.* de tenor

tense /tɛns/ *n Gram.* tiempo, *m*. *a* tirante, estirado; tieso; tenso

tenseness /'tɛnsnɪs/ *n* tirantez, *f*; tensión, *f*

tensile /'tɛnsəl/ *a* tensor; extensible

tension /'tɛnʃən/ *n* tensión, *f*; *Elec.* voltaje, *m*, tensión, *f*; (of sewing-machine) tensahílo, *m*. **state of t.,** (diplomatic) estado de tirantez, *m*

tent /tɛnt/ *n* tienda (de campaña), *Lat. Am.* carpa, *f*; (bell) pabellón, *m*; *Surg.* tienda, *f*. **oxygen t.,** tienda oxígena, *f*. **to pitch tents,** armar las tiendas de campaña; acamparse. **to strike tents,** plegar tiendas. **t. fly,** toldo de tienda, *m*. **t. maker,** tendero, *m*. **t. peg,** clave que sujeta las cuerdas de una tienda, *f*. **t. pole,** mástil (or montante) de tienda, *m*

tentacle /'tɛntəkəl/ *n* tentáculo, *m*

tentative /'tɛntətɪv/ *a* tentativo, interino, provisional, de prueba, *n* tentativa, *f*, ensayo, *m*

tentatively /'tɛntətɪvli/ *adv* por vía de ensayo, experimentalmente

tenth /tɛnθ/ *a* décimo; (of monarchs) diez; (of the month) (el) diez. *n* décimo, *m*; (part) décima parte, *f*; *Mus.* decena, *f*

tenthly /'tɛnθli/ *adv* en décimo lugar

tenuity /tə'nuɪti/ *n* tenuidad, *f*; sutilidad, *f*; delgadez, *f*

tenuous /'tɛnyuəs/ *a* tenue; sutil; delgado; fino

tenure /'tɛnyər/ *n* tenencia, posesión, *f*; (duration) duración, *f*; (of office) administración, *f*

tepid /'tɛpɪd/ *a* tibio

tepidity /tɛ'pɪdɪti/ *n* tibieza, *f*

tercentenary /,tɜrsɛn'tɛnəri/ *n* tercer centenario, *m*

tercet /'tɜrsɪt/ *n* terceto, *m*

term /tɜrm/ *n* (limit) límite, fin, *m*; (period) plazo, tiempo, período, *m*; (schools, universities) trimestre, *m*; (*Math., Law., Logic.*) término, *m*; (word) expresión, palabra, *f pl.* **terms,** (conditions) condiciones, *f pl*; (charges) precios, *m pl*, tarifa, *f*; (words) términos, *m pl*, palabras, *f pl. vt* llamar, calificar. **for a t. of years,** por un plazo de años. **in plain terms,** en palabras claras. **on equal terms,** en condiciones iguales. **to be on bad (good) terms with,** estar en (or tener) malas (buenas) relaciones con. **to come to terms,** llegar a un acuerdo; hacer las paces. **What are your terms?** ¿Cuáles son sus condiciones? (price) ¿Cuáles son sus precios? **terms of sale,** condiciones de venta, *f pl*

termagant /'tɜrməgənt/ *n* arpía, fiera, *f*

terminable /'tɜrmənəbəl/ *a* terminable

terminal /'tɜrmənḷ/ *a* terminal, final; (of schools, universities) trimestre. *n* término, *m*; *Elec.* borne, *m*; (schools, universities) examen de fin de trimestre, *m*; (railway) estación terminal, *f*; (*Archit.* and figure) término, *m*; *Archit.* remate, *m*

terminate /'tɜrmə,neit/ *vt* limitar; terminar, concluir, poner fin (a). *vi* terminarse, concluirse (por); cesar

termination /,tɜrmə'neiʃən/ *n* terminación, conclusión, *f*; fin, *m*; *Gram.* terminación, *f*; cabo, remate, *m*

terminology /,tɜrmə'nɒlədʒi/ *n* nomenclatura, terminología, *f*

terminus /'tɜrmənəs/ *n* (railway) estación terminal, *f*;

(*Archit.* and figure) término, *m*; *Archit.* remate, *m*; *Myth.* Término

termite /'tɜrmait/ *n Ent.* termita, *m*

term paper *n* trabajo de examen, *m*

terms of trade *n* relación de los precios de intercambio, *f*

terrace /'tɛrəs/ *n* terraza, *f*, *vt* terraplenar

terraced /'tɛrəst/ *a* en terrazas; con terrazas

terracotta /ˌtɛrə'kɒtə/ *n* terracota, *f*

terrain /tə'rein/ *n* terreno, campo, *m*, región, *f*

terrapin /'tɛrəpɪn/ *n* tortuga de agua dulce, *f*

terrestrial /tə'rɛstriəl/ *a* terrestre, terrenal

terrible /'tɛrəbəl/ *a* terrible, pavoroso, espantoso; *Inf.* tremendo

terribleness /'tɛrəbəlnɪs/ *n* terribilidad, *f*, lo horrible

terrier /'tɛriər/ *n* terrier, *m*; *Inf.* soldado del ejército territorial, *m*

terrific /tə'rɪfɪk/ *a* espantoso, terrible; *Inf.* atroz, tremendo

terrify /'tɛrəˌfai/ *vt* aterrorizar, espantar, horrorizar, *Lat. Am.* also julepear. **to be terrified,** *Lat. Am.* julepearse

terrifying /'tɛrəˌfaiɪŋ/ *a* aterrador, espantoso

territorial /ˌtɛrɪ'tɔriəl/ *a* territorial. *n* soldado del ejército territorial, *m*

territoriality /ˌtɛrɪˌtɔri'ælɪti/ *n* territorialidad, *f*

territory /'tɛrɪˌtɔri/ *n* región, comarca, *f*; (state) territorio, *m*; jurisdicción, *f*. **mandated territory,** territorio bajo mandato, *m pl*

terror /'tɛrər/ *n* terror, pavor, espanto, *m*. **the Reign of T.,** el Reinado del Terror, *m*. **t.-stricken,** espantado, muerto de miedo

terrorism /'tɛrəˌrɪzəm/ *n* terrorismo, *m*

terrorist /'tɛrərɪst/ *n* terrorista, *m*

terrorization /ˌtɛrərə'zeiʃən/ *n* aterramiento, *m*

terrorize /'tɛrəˌraiz/ *vt* aterrorizar

terse /tɜrs/ *a* conciso, sucinto; seco, brusco

tersely /'tɜrsli/ *adv* concisamente; secamente

terseness /'tɜrsnɪs/ *n* concisión, *f*; brusquedad, *f*

tertiary /'tɜrʃiˌɛri, -ʃəri/ *a* tercero; *Geol.* terciario. *n Eccl.* terciario, *m*

tessera /'tɛsərə/ *n* tesela, *f*

test /tɛst/ *n* (proof) prueba, *f*; examen, *m*; investigación, *f*; (standard) criterio, *m*, piedra de toque, *f*; *Chem.* análisis, *m*; (trial) ensayo, *m*; *Zool.* concha, *f*. *vt Chem.* ensayar; probar, poner a prueba; examinar; (eyes) graduar (la vista). **to put to the t.,** poner a prueba. **to stand the t.,** soportar la prueba. **t. match,** partido internacional de cricket, *m*. **t. meal,** *Med.* comida de prueba, *f*. **t. pilot,** *Aer.* piloto de pruebas, *m*. **t. tube,** tubo de ensayo, *m*

testament /'tɛstəmənt/ *n* testamento, *m*. **the New T.,** el Nuevo Testamento, *m*. **the Old T.,** el Antiguo Testamento, *m*

testamentary /ˌtɛstə'mɛntəri/ *a* testamentario

testate /'tɛsteit/ *a* testado

testator /'tɛsteitər/ *n* testador, *m*, (**testatrix,** testadora, *f*)

testicle /'tɛstɪkəl/ *n* testículo, *m*

testification /ˌtɛstəfɪ'keiʃən/ *n* testificación, *f*

testify /'tɛstəˌfai/ *vt* and *vi* declarar, atestar; *Law.* atestiguar, testificar, dar fe

testily /'tɛstɪli/ *adv* malhumoradamente

testimonial /ˌtɛstə'mouniəl/ *n* recomendación, *f*; certificado, *m*; (tribute) homenaje, *m*

testimony /'tɛstəˌmouni/ *n* testimonio, *m*, declaración, *f*; (proof) prueba, *f*. **in t. whereof,** en fe de lo cual. **to bear t.,** atestar

testiness /'tɛstinɪs/ *n* mal humor, *m*, irritación, *f*

testing grounds /'tɛstɪŋ/ *n* campo de experimentación, campo de pruebas, *m*

testy /'tɛsti/ *a* enojadizo, irritable, irascible, quisquilloso

tetanus /'tɛtnəs/ *n* tétano, *m*

tether /'tɛðər/ *n* traba, atadura, maniota, *f*. *vt* atar con una correa. **to be at the end of one's t.,** acabarse la resistencia; acabarse la paciencia

Teutonic /tu'tɒnɪk/ *a* teutónico

text /tɛkst/ *n* texto, *m*; (subject) tema, *m*; (motto)

lema, *m*; (of a musical composition) letra, *f*. **t.-book,** libro de texto, *m*

textile /'tɛkstail/ *a* textil, de tejer. *n* textil, *m*, materia textil, *f*; tejido, *m*

textual /'tɛkstʃuəl/ *a* textual

texture /'tɛkstʃər/ *n* (material and *Biol.*) tejido, *m*; textura, *f*

Thailand /'tai,lænd/ Tailandia, *f*

thalamus /'θæləməs/ *n* (*Anat.*, *Bot.*) tálamo, *m*

Thames, the /tɛmz/ *n* el Támesis, *m*. **to set the T. on fire,** descubrir la pólvora

than /ðæn; *unstressed* ðən, ən/ *conjunc* que; (between **more, less,** or **fewer** and a number) de; (in comparisons of inequality) que, but que becomes *a del* (de la, de los, de las) que if the point of comparison is a noun in the principal clause, which has to be supplied mentally to fill up the ellipsis; (*b*) de lo que if there is no noun to act as a point of comparison, e.g. *He was older than I thought,* Era más viejo de lo que yo pensaba. *They have less than they deserve,* Tienen menos de lo que merecen. *They lose more money than* (*the money*) *they earn,* Pierden más dinero del que ganan. **He will meet with more opposition than he thought,** Va a encontrar más oposición de la que pensaba. **I have more books than you,** Tengo más libros que tú. **She has fewer than nine and more than five,** Ella tiene menos de nueve y más de cinco

thank /θæŋk/ *vt* agradecer, dar las gracias (a). **to t. for,** agradecer. **I will t. you to be more polite,** Le agradecería que fuese más cortés. **He has himself to t. for it,** Él mismo tiene la culpa de ello. **No, t. you,** No, muchas gracias. **T. goodness!** ¡Gracias a Dios!

thankful /'θæŋkfəl/ *a* agradecido. **I am t. to see,** Me alegro de ver, Me es grato ver

thankfully /'θæŋkfəli/ *adv* con gratitud, agradecido

thankfulness /'θæŋkfəlnɪs/ *n* agradecimiento, *m*; gratitud, *f*

thankless /'θæŋklɪs/ *a* ingrato; desagradecido; desagradable

thanks /θæŋks/ *n* gracias, *f pl*. **a vote of thanks,** un voto de gracias. **Many thanks!** ¡Muchas gracias! **to return thanks,** dar las gracias. **thanks to,** merced a, debido a. **a. thanks to you,** gracias a ti. **t.-offering,** ofrecimiento en acción de gracias, *m*

thanksgiving /ˌθæŋks'gɪvɪŋ/ *n* acción de gracias, *f*. **t. service,** servicio de acción de gracias, *m*. **Thanksgiving** (**Day**), *n* día de acción de dar gracias, día de gracias, *m*

that /ðæt; *unstressed* ðət/ *dem a* ese, *m*; esa, *f*; aquel, *m*; aquella, *f*, *dem. pron* ése, *m*; ésa, *f*; eso, *neut*; aquél, *m*; aquélla, *f*; aquello, *neut*; (standing for a noun) el, *m*; la, *f*; lo, *neut* All **t.** there is, Todo lo que hay. **His temperament is t. of his mother,** Su temperamento es el su madre. **We have not come to t. yet,** Todavía no hemos llegado a ese punto. **T. is what I want to know,** Eso es lo que quiero saber. **with t.,** con eso; (thereupon) en eso. **Go t. way,** Vaya Vd. por allí; Tome Vd. aquel camino. **T. is to say...,** Es decir... **What do you mean by t.?** ¿Qué quieres decir con eso? **The novel is not as bad as all t.,** La novela no es tan mala como tú piensas (*or* como dicen, etc.)

that /ðæt; *unstressed* ðət/ *pron. rel* que; el cual, *m*; la cual, *f*; lo cual, *neut*; (of persons) a quien, *mf*; a quienes, *mf pl*; (with from) de quien, *mf*; de quienes, *mf pl*; (of place) donde. **The letter t. I sent you,** la carta que te mandé. **The box t. John put them in,** la caja en la cual los puso Juan. **The last time t. I saw her,** La última vez que la vi

that /ðæt; *unstressed* ðət/ *conjunc* que; (of purpose) para que; a fin de que; (before infin.) para; (because) porque. **O t. he would come!** ¡Ojalá que viniese! **so t.,** para que; (before infin.) para; (as a result) de manera que; de modo que. **It is better t. he should not come,** Es mejor que no venga. **now t.,** ahora que

thatch /θætʃ/ *n* barda, *f*, *vt* bardar

thaw /θɔ/ *n* deshielo, *m*. *vt* deshelar; derretir. *vi* deshelarse; derretirse

the /*stressed* ði; *unstressed before a consonant* ðə, *unstressed before a vowel* ði/ *def art.* el, *m*; la, *f*; lo, *neut*; los, *m pl*; las, *f pl*; (before feminine sing. noun beginning with stressed a or ha) el; (untranslated between the name and number of a monarch, pope, ruler, e.g. *Charles the Fifth,* Carlos quinto). *adv* (before a comparative) cuanto, tanto más. **at the** or **to the,** al, *m,* (also before feminine sing. noun beginning with a or ha); a la, *f;* a lo, *neut;* a los, *m pl;* a las, *f pl.* **from the** or **of the,** del, *m,* (also before feminine sing. noun beginning with stressed a or ha); de la, *f;* de lo, *neut;* de los, *m pl;* de las, *f pl.* **the one, see one. The sooner the better,** Cuanto antes mejor. **The room will be all the warmer,** El cuarto estará tanto más caliente

theater /'θiətər/ *n* teatro, *m;* (lecture) anfiteatro, *m;* (drama) teatro, *m,* obra dramática, *f;* (scene) teatro, *m,* escena, *f.* **t. attendant,** acomodador (-ra)
theater-in-the-round /'θiətərɪnðə'raʊnd/ *n* teatro circular, teatro en círculo, *m*
Theatine /'θiətɪn/ *a* and *n Eccl.* teatino *m*
theatrical /θi'ætrɪkəl/ *a* teatral. *n pl* **theatricals,** funciones teatrales, *f pl.* **amateur theatricals,** función de aficionados, *f.* **t. company,** compañía de teatro, *f.* **t. costumier,** mascarero (-ra), alquilador (-ra) de disfraces. **t. manager,** empresario de teatro, *m*
theatricality /θi,ætrɪ'kælti/ *n* teatralidad, *f*
Theban /'θibən/ *a* and *n* tebeo (-ea), tebano (-na)
Thebes /θibz/ Tebas, *f*
thee /ði/ *pers pron* te; (after prep.) tí. **with t.,** contigo
theft /θɛft/ *n* robo, hurto, *m*
their /ðɛr; *unstressed* ðər/ *poss a* su, *mf sing;* sus, *pl;* de ellos, *m pl;* de ellas, *f pl.* **They have t. books,** Tienen sus libros. **I have t. books,** Tengo los libros de ellos
theirs /ðɛrz/ *poss pron* (el) suyo, *m;* (la) suya, *f;* (los) suyos, *m pl;* (las) suyas, *f pl;* de ellos, *m pl;* de ellas, *f pl.* **These hats are t.,** Estos sombreros son los suyos
them /ðɛm, *unstressed* ðəm, əm/ *pers pron* ellos, *m pl;* ellas, *f pl;* (as object of a verb) los, *m pl;* las, *f pl;* (to them) les
thematic /θi'mætɪk/ *a* temático
theme /θim/ *n* tema, asunto, *m;* tesis, *f; Mus.* tema, motivo, *m*
themselves /ðəm'sɛlvz, ,θɛm-/ *pers pron pl* ellos mismos, *m pl;* ellas mismas, *f pl, reflexive pron* sí; sí mismos; (with a reflexive verb) se. **They t. told me about it,** Ellos mismos me lo dijeron. **They left it for t.,** Lo dejaron para sí (mismos)
then /ðɛn/ *adv* (of future time) entonces; (of past time) a la sazón, en aquella época, entonces; (next, afterwards) luego, después, en seguida; (in that case) en este caso, entonces; (therefore) por consiguiente. *a* de entonces. *n* entonces, *m. conjunc* (moreover) además; pues. **And what t.?** ¿Y qué pasó después?; ¿Y qué pasará ahora?; ¿Y qué más? **by t.,** por entonces. **now and t.,** de vez en cuando. **now... t.,** ya... ya, ora... ora. **since t.,** desde aquel tiempo; desde entonces; desde aquella ocasión. **until t.,** hasta entonces; hasta aquella época. **well t.,** bien, pues. **t. and there,** en el acto, en seguida; allí mismo
thence /ðɛns/ *adv* desde allí, de allí; (therefore) por eso, por esa razón, por consiguiente
thenceforth /,ðɛns'fɔrθ/ *adv* de allí en adelante, desde entonces
theocracy /θi'ɒkrəsi/ *n* teocracia, *f*
theocratic /,θiə'krætɪk/ *a* teocrático
theologian /,θiə'loʊdʒən/ *n* teólogo, *m*
theological /,θiə'lɒdʒɪkəl/ *a* teológico, teolgal
theologize /θi'ɒlə,dʒaɪz/ *vi* teologizar
theology /θi'ɒlədʒi/ *n* teología, *f*
theorem /'θiərəm/ *n* teorema, *m*
theoretical /,θiə'rɛtɪkəl/ *a* teórico
theoretically /,θiə'rɛtɪkli/ *adv* teóricamente, en teoría
theorist /'θiərɪst/ *n* teórico, *m*
theorize /'θiə,raɪz/ *vi* teorizar
theory /'θiəri/ *n* teoría, *f*
theosophical /,θiə'sɒfɪkəl/ *a* teosófico
theosophist /θi'ɒsəfɪst/ *n* teósofo, *m*
theosophy /θi'ɒsəfi/ *n* teosofía, *f*
therapeutic /,θɛrə'pyutɪk/ *a* terapéutico. *n* **therapeutics,** terapéutica, *f*

therapeutist /,θɛrə'pyutɪst/ *n* terapeuta, *mf*
therapy /'θɛrəpi/ *suffix* terapia, *f*
there /ðɛr; *unstressed* ðər/ *adv* allí; ahí, allá; (at that point) en eso; (used pronominally as subject of verb) haber, e.g. *T. was once a king,* Hubo una vez un rey; *What is t. to do here?* ¿Qué hay que hacer aquí? *interj* ¡vaya!; (I told you so!) ¡ya ves! ¡ya te lo dije yo!; (in surprise) ¡toma! **about t.,** cerca de allí. **down t.,** allí abajo. **in t.,** allí dentro. **out t.,** allí fuera. **over t.,** ahí; allá a lo lejos. **up t.,** allí arriba. **T. came a time when...,** Llegó la hora cuando... **T. it is!** ¡Allí está! **t. is** or **t. are,** hay. **t. was** or **t. were,** había, hubo. **t. may be,** puede haber, quizás habrá. **t. must be,** tiene que haber. **t. will be,** habrá. **T., t.!** (to a child, etc.) ¡Vamos!
thereabouts /'ðɛrə,baʊts/ *adv* (near to a place) cerca de allí, por ahí, allí cerca; (approximately) aproximadamente, cerca de
thereafter /,ðɛr'æftər/ *adv* después, después de eso
thereby /,ðɛr'baɪ/ *adv* (near to that place) por allí cerca; (by that means) con lo cual, de este modo
therefore /'ðɛr,fɔr/ *adv* por lo tanto, por eso, así, por consiguiente, por esta razón
therein /,ðɛr'ɪn/ *adv* (inside) allí dentro; (in this, that particular) en estre, en eso, en ese particular
thereinafter /,ðɛrɪn'æftər/ *adv* posteriormente, más adelante
thereupon /'ðɛrə,pɒn/ *adv* (in consequence) por consiguiente, por lo tanto; (at that point) luego, en eso; (immediately afterwards) inmediatamente después, en seguida
thermal /'θɜrməl/ *a* termal. **t. springs,** aguas termales, termas, *f pl*
thermodynamics /,θɜrmoʊdaɪ'næmɪks/ *n* termodinámica, *f*
thermoelectric /,θɜrmoʊɪ'lɛktrɪk/ *a* termoeléctrico
thermometer /θər'mɒmɪtər/ *n* termómetro, *m*
thermos flask /'θɜrməs/ *n* termos, *m*
thermostat /'θɜrmə,stæt/ *n* termostato, *m*
thermostatic /,θɜrmə'stætɪk/ *a* termostático
thesaurus /θɪ'sɔrəs/ *n* tesoro, tesauro, *m*
these /ðiz/ *dem pron* **of this,** éstos, *m pl;* éstas, *f pl, dem* estos, *m pl;* estas, *f pl.* **Are not t. your flowers?** ¿No son éstas tus flores? **T. pictures have been sold,** Estos cuadros han se han vendito
thesis /'θisɪs/ *n* tesis, *f*
Thespian /'θɛspiən/ *a* dramático
they /ðeɪ/ *pers pron pl* ellos, *m pl;* ellas, *f pl;* (people) se (followed by sing. verb). **T. say,** Dicen, Se dice
thick /θɪk/ *a* espeso; (big) grueso, (wall) grueso, (string, cord) gordo; (vapors) denso; (muddy) turbio; (dense, close) tupido apretado; (numerous) numeroso, repetido, continuo; (full of) lleno (de); (of voice) velado, indistinto; (obtuse) estúpido, lerdo; (friendly) íntimo. *adv* densamente, continuamente, sin cesar. **three feet t.,** de tres pies de espesor. **That's a bit t.!** ¡Eso es un poco demasiado! **to be as t. as thieves,** estar unidos como los dedos de la mano. **t.-lipped,** con labios gruesos, bezudo. **t.-headed,** estúpido, lerdo. **t.-skinned,** de piel gruesa; *Zool.* paquidermo; *Fig.* sin vergüenza, insensible. **t. stroke,** (of letters) grueso, *m*
thick /θɪk/ *n* espesor, *m;* parte gruesa, *f;* lo más denso; (of a fight) lo más recio; centro, *m.* **in the t. of,** en el centro (de), en medio de
thicken /'θɪkən/ *vt* espesar; (increase) aumentar, multiplicar; *Cul.* espesar. *vi* espesarse; condensar; aumentar, multiplicarse; (of a mystery, etc.) complicarse; hacerse más denso; *Cul.* espesarse
thickening /'θɪkənɪŋ/ *n* hinchamiento, *m;* gordura, *f;* (*Cul.* and of paints) espesante, *m*
thicket /'θɪkɪt/ *n* matorral, soto, *m,* maleza, *f;* (grove) boscaje, *m*
thickly /'θɪkli/ *adv* densamente; espesamente; continuamente, sin cesar; (of speech) indistintamente
thickness /'θɪknɪs/ *n* espesor, *m;* grueso, *m;* densidad, *f;* (of liquids) consistencia, *f;* (layer) capa, *f;* (of speech) dificultad (en el hablar), *f*
thickset /'θɪk'sɛt/ *a* doblado
thief /θif/ *n* ladrón (-ona); (in a candle) moco de

vela, *m*. **Stop t.!** ¡Ladrones! **thieves' den,** *Fig.* cueva de ladrones, *f*

thieve /θiv/ *vi* hurtar, robar. *vt* robar

thievish /'θiviʃ/ *a* ladrón

thigh /θai/ *n* muslo, *m*. **t.-bone,** fémur, *m*

thimble /'θimbəl/ *n* dedal, *m*

thimbleful /'θimbəl,ful/ *n* lo que cabe en un dedal; *Fig.* dedada, *f*

thin /θin/ *a* delgado; (lean) flaco; (small) pequeño; delicado; fino; (of air, light) tenue, sutil; (clothes) ligero; (sparse) escaso; transparente; (watery) aguado; (of wine) bautizado; (not close) claro; (of arguments) flojo. *vt* adelgazar; aclarar; *Agr.* limpiar; reducir. *vi* adelgazarse; afilarse; reducirse. **somewhat t.,** (of persons) delgaducho, algo flaco. **to grow t.,** enflaquecer; afilarse. **to make t.,** hacer adelgazar volver flaco. **t.-clad,** ligero de ropa; mal vestido. **t.-faced,** de cara delgada. **t.-lipped,** de labios apretados. **t.-skinned,** de piel fina; *Fig.* sensitivo, sensible

thine. /ðain/ See **theirs.** *poss pron* (el) tuyo, *m*; (la) tuya, *f*; (los) tuyos, *m pl*; (las) tuyas, *f pl*; tu, *mf*; tus, *mf pl*; de tí. **The fault is t.,** La culpa es tuya, La culpa es de tí

thing /θiŋ/ *n* cosa, *f*; objeto, artículo, *m*; (affair) asunto, *m*; (contemptuous) sujeto, tipo, *m*; (creature) ser, *m*, criatura, *f*; *pl* **things,** (belongings) efectos, trastos, *m pl*; (luggage) equipaje, *m*; (clothes) trapitos, *m pl*; (circumstances) circunstancias, condiciones, *f pl*. **above all things,** ante todo, sobre todo. **a very pretty little t.,** (child) una pequeña muy mona. **as things are,** tal como están las cosas. **for one t.,** en primer lugar. **Her behavior is not quite the t.,** La conducta de ella no está bien vista. **It is a bad t.** that..., Lo malo es que... **It is a good t.** that..., Menos mal que...; Lo bueno es que... **No such t.!** ¡No hay tal!; ¡Nada de eso! **Poor t.!** ¡Pobrecito!; (woman) ¡Pobre mujer!; (man) ¡Pobre hombre! **to be just the t.,** venir al pelo. **with one t. and another,** entre unas cosas y otras. **I like things Spanish,** Me gusta lo español

think /θiŋk/ *vt and vi* pensar; (believe) creer; (deem) considerar, juzgar; imaginar; (suspect) sospechar; (opine) ser de opinión (que). **And to t. that...!** ¡Y pensar que...! **As you t. fit,** Como usted quiera, Como a usted le parezca bien. **He thought as much,** Se lo figuraba. **He little thought that...!** ¡Cuán lejos estaba de pensar que...! **He thinks nothing of...,** No le importa...; Desprecia, Tiene una opinión bastante mala de. **I don't t. so,** No lo creo. **I should just t. not!** ¡Claro que no! ¡Eso sí que no! **I should just t. so!** ¡Claro! ¡Ya lo creo! **It makes me t. of...,** Me hace pensar en... **One might t.,** Podría creerse... **to t. better of something,** cambiar de opinión, considerar mejor. **to t. highly (badly) of,** tener buen (mal) concepto sobre. **to t. over carefully,** pensarlo bien, considerar detenidamente. *Inf.* consultar con la almohada. **to t. proper,** creer conveniente. **to t. to oneself,** pensar para sí (or entre sí). **to t. too much of oneself,** pensar demasiado en sí; tener demasiada buena opinión de sí mismo; tener humos. **What do you t. about it?** ¿Qué te parece? **to t. about,** (of persons) pensar en; (of things) pensar de (or sobre); meditar, considerar, reflexionar sobre. **to t. for,** pensar por. **to t. of,** pensar en; pensar de (or sobre). **What do you t. of this?** ¿Qué te parece esto? **to t. out,** idear, proyectar, hacer planes para; (a problem) resolver. **to t. over,** pensar; reflexionar sobre, meditar sobre. **I shall t. it over,** Lo pensaré.

thinker /'θiŋkər/ *n* pensador, *m*

thinking /'θiŋkiŋ/ *n* pensamiento, *m*, reflexión, meditación, *f*; juicio, *m*; opinión, *f*, parecer, *m*. *a* pensador; inteligente; racional; serio. **To my way of t.,** Según pienso yo, A mi parecer. **way of t.,** modo de pensar, *m*

thinly /'θinli/ *adv* delgadamente; esparcidamente; (lightly) ligeramente; poco numeroso

thinness /'θinnis/ *n* delgadez, *f*; (leanness) flaqueza, *f*; sutileza, tenuidad, *f*; (lack) escasez, *f*; pequeño número, *m*; poca consistencia, *f*

third /θɜrd/ *a* tercero (tercer before *m*, *sing* noun); (of monarchs) tercero; (of the month) (el) tres. *n* tercio, *m*, tercera parte, *f*; *Mus.* tercera, *f*. **T. time lucky!**

¡A la tercera va la vencida! **t. class,** *n* tercera clase, *f*. *a* de tercera clase. **t. party,** tercera persona, *f*. **t.-party insurance,** seguro contra tercera persona, *m*. **t. person,** tercero (-ra); *Gram.* tercera persona, *f*. **t.-rate,** de tercera clase

thirdly /'θɜrdli/ *adv* en tercer lugar

thirst /θɜrst/ *n* sed, *f*; *Fig.* deseo, *m*, ansia, *f*; entusiasmo, *m*. **to satisfy one's t.,** apagar (or matar) la sed

thirsty /'θɜrsti/ *a* sediento. **to be t.,** tener sed. **to make t.,** dar sed.

thirteen /'θɜr'tin/ *a and n* trece *m*. **t. hundred,** *a and n* mil trescientos *m*

thirteenth /θɜr'tinθ/ *a* décimotercio; (of monarchs) trece; (of month) (el) trece, *m*, *n* décimotercio, trezavo, *m*

thirtieth /'θɜrtiəθ/ *a* trigésimo; (of month) (el) treinta, *m*. *n* treintavo, *m*

thirty /'θɜrti/ *a and n* treinta, *m*. **t.-first,** treinta y uno

this /ðis/ *dem a* este, *m*; esta, *f*, *dem pron* éste, *m*; ésta, *f*; esto, *neut* **by t. time,** a esta hora, ya. **like t.,** de este modo, así. **T. is Wednesday,** Hoy es miércoles. **What is all t.?** ¿Qué es todo esto?

thistle /'θisəl/ *n* cardo, *m*. **t.-down,** papo de cardo, vilano de cardo, *m*

thither /'θiðər, 'ðið-/ *adv* allá, hacia allá; a ese fin. *a* más remoto

thong /θɔŋ/ *n* correa, tira, *f*

thoracic /θə'ræsik/ *a* torácico

thorax /'θɔræks/ *n* tórax, *m*

thorn /θɔrn/ *n* espina, *f*; (tree) espino, *m*; *Fig.* abrojo, *m*, espina, *f*. **to be a t. in the flesh of,** ser una espina en el costado de. **t. brake,** espinar, *m*

thornless /'θɔrnlis/ *a* sin espinas

thorny /'θɔrni/ *a* espinoso; *Fig.* difícil, arduo

thorough /'θɜrou/ *a* completo; perfecto; (conscientious) concienzudo; (careful) cuidadoso. **t.-bred,** (of animals) de pura raza, de casta; (of persons) bien nacido. **t.-paced,** cabal, consumado

thoroughfare /'θɜrə,fɛər/ *n* vía pública, *f*. **"No t.,"** «Prohibido el paso», Calle cerrada

thoroughly /'θɜrəli/ *adv* completamente; (of knowing a subject) a fondo; concienzudamente

thoroughness /'θɜrənis/ *n* perfección, *f*; minuciosidad, *f*

those /ðouz/ *dem a pl* of **that,** esos, *m pl*; esas, *f pl*; aquellos, *m pl*; aquellas, *f pl*, *dem pron* ésos, *m pl*; ésas, *f pl*; aquéllos, *m pl*; aquéllas, *f pl*; (standing for a noun) los, *m pl*; las, *f pl*. **t. who,** quienes, *mf pl*; los que, *m pl*; las que, *f pl*. **t. that** or **which,** los que, *m pl*; las que, *f pl*. **Your eyes are t. of your mother,** Tus ojos son los de tu madre

thou /θau/ *pers pron* tú

though /ðou/ *conjunc* (followed by subjunc. when doubt is implied or uncertain future time) aunque, bien que; (nevertheless) sin embargo, no obstante; (in spite of) a pesar de que; (but) pero. **as t.,** como si (followed by subjunc.). **even t.,** aunque (followed by subjunc.)

thought /θɔt/ *n* pensamiento, *m*; meditación, reflexión, *f*; opinión, *f*; consideración, *f*; idea, *f*, propósito, *m*; (care) cuidado, *m*, solicitud, *f*; *Inf.* pizca, *f*. **on second thought,** después de pensarlo bien. **The t. struck him,** Se le ocurrió la idea. **to collect one's thoughts,** orientarse; informarse (de). **t.-reading,** adivinación del pensamiento, *f*. **t.-transference,** telepatía, transmisión del pensamiento, *f*

thoughtful /'θɔtfəl/ *a* pensativo, meditabundo; serio; especulativo; (provident) previsor; (kind) atento, solícito; cuidadoso; (anxious) inquieto, intranquilo

thoughtfully /'θɔtfəli/ *adv* pensativamente; seriamente; (providently) con previsión; (kindly) atentamente, solícitamente

thoughtfulness /'θɔtfəlnis/ *n* natural reflexivo, *m*, seriedad, *f*; (kindness) solicitud, atención, *f*; (fore- thought) previsión, *f*

thoughtless /'θɔtlis/ *a* irreflexivo; (careless) descuidado, negligente; (unkind) inconsiderado; (silly) necio, estúpido

thoughtlessly /'θɔtlɪsli/ adv sin pensar, irreflexivamente; negligentemente

thoughtlessness /'θɔtlɪsnɪs/ n irreflexión, f; descuido, m, negligencia, f; (unkindness) inconsideración, f; (silliness) neciedad, f

thousand /'θauzənd/ a mil. n mil, m; millar, m. **one t.,** mil, m. **one t. three hundred,** a mil trescientos, m pl; mil trescientas, f pl. n mil trescientos, m pl. **two (three) t.,** dos (tres) mil. **by thousands,** por millares; por miles. **t.-fold,** mil veces más

thousandth /'θauzəndθ/ a and n milésimo m

Thrace /θreis/ Tracia, f

thrall /θrɔl/ n esclavo (-va); esclavitud, f

thrash /θræʃ/ vt azotar, apalear Mexico festejar, Lat. Am. humear; Agr. trillar, desgranar; Inf. triunfar sobre, derrotar. vi , agr trillar el grano; arrojarse, agitarse. Fig. **to t. out,** ventilar

thrashing /'θræʃɪŋ/ n apaleamiento, m, paliza, f. Lat. Am. also azotera, f; Agr. See **threshing**

thread /θrɛd/ n hilo, m; (fiber) hebra, fibra, f, filamento, m; (of a screw) filete, m; Fig. hilo, m, a de hilo. vt (a needle) enhebrar; (beads) ensartar; (make one's way) colarse a través de, atravesar; pasar por. **to hang by a t.,** pender de un hilo. **to lose the t. of,** Fig. perder el hilo de

threadbare /'θrɛd,bɛər/ a raído; muy usado; Fig. trivial, viejo

threadlike /'θrɛd,laik/ a como un hilo, filiforme

threadworm /'θrɛd,wɜrm/ n m, lombriz intestinal, f

threat /θrɛt/ n amenaza, f

threaten /'θrɛtn/ vt and vi amenazar. **to t. with,** amenazar con

threatening /'θrɛtnɪŋ/ a amenazador. n amenazas, f pl

threateningly /'θrɛtnɪŋli/ adv con amenazas

three /θri/ a and n tres m; (of the clock) las tres, f pl; (of one's age) tres años, m pl. **t.-color process.** tricromía, f. **t.-colored,** tricolor. **t.-cornered,** triangular; (of hats) de tres picos, tricornio. **t.-cornered hat,** sombrero de tres picos, tricornio, m. **t. decker,** Naut. navío de tres puentes, m; novela larga, f. **t. deep,** en tres hileras. **t. hundred,** a and n trescientos m. **t.-hundredth,** a and n tricentésimo m. **t.-legged,** de tres patas. **t.-legged stool,** banqueta, f. **t.-per-cents,** accion al tres por ciento (3%), f. **t.-phase,** Elec. trifásico. **t.-ply,** (of yarn) triple; (of wood) de tres capas. **t.-quarter,** de tres cuartos. **t. quarters of an hour,** tres cuartos de hora, m pl. **t.-sided,** trilátero. **t. speed gear box,** cambio de marcha de tres velocidades, m. **t.-stringed,** Mus. de tres cuerdos. **t. thousand,** a tres mil, mf pl; n tres mil, m

threefold /'θri,fould/ a triple

threescore /'θri'skɔr/ a and n sesenta, m pl

threesome /'θrisəm/ n partido de tres, m

thresh /θrɛʃ/ vt trillar, desgranar. vi trillar el grano. **to t. out,** ventilar

threshing /'θrɛʃɪŋ/ n trilla, f. **t. floor,** era, f. **t. machine,** trilladora, f

threshold /'θrɛʃould/ n umbral, Lat. Am. also dintel, m; Psychol. limen, m; Fig. comienzo, principio, m; (entrance) entrada, f. **to cross the t.,** atravesar (or pisar) los umbrales

thrice /θrais/ adv tres veces

thrift /θrɪft/ n frugalidad, parsimonia, f

thriftless /'θrɪftlɪs/ a malgastador, manirroto

thrifty /'θrɪfti/ a frugal, económico

thrill /θrɪl/ n estremecimiento, m; emoción, f. vt conmover, emocionar; penetrar. vi estremecerse, emocionarse

thriller /'θrɪlər/ n libro, m, (or comedia, f) sensacional; (detective novel) novela policíaca, f

thrilling /'θrɪlɪŋ/ a sensacional, espeluznante; (moving) emocionante, conmovedor

thrive /θraiv/ vi prosperar, medrar; enriquecerse, tener éxito; (grow) desarrollarse, robustecerse; florecer; (of plants) acertar

thriving /'θraivɪŋ/ a próspero; floreciente, robusto, vigoroso

throat /θrout/ n garganta, f; orificio, m; (narrow entry) paso, m. **sore t.,** dolor de garganta, m. **to cut**

one's t., cortarse la garganta. **to take by the t.,** asir (or agarrar) por la garganta

throat cancer n cáncer de la garganta, m

throaty /'θrouti/ a indistinto, ronco

throb /θrɒb/ n latido, m; pulsación, f; vibración, f; Fig. estremecimiento, m. vi palpitar, latir; vibrar

throbbing /'θrɒbɪŋ/ n pulsación, f; vibración, f. a palpitante; vibrante. **t. pain,** dolor pungente, m

throe /θrou/ n dolor, m, agonía, angustia, f. **in the throes of,** en medio de; luchando con; en las garras de. **throes of childbirth,** dolores de parto, m pl. **throes of death,** agonía de la muerte, f

thrombosis /θrɒm'bousɪs/ n Med. trombosis, f

throne /θroun/ n trono, m; (royal power) corona, f, poder real, m. vt elevar al trono. **speech from the t.,** el discurso de la corona, m

throng /θrɔŋ/ n muchedumbre, multitud, f. vi apiñarse remolinarse, acudir. vt atestar, llenar de bote en bote

throttle /'θrɒtl/ n Mech. regulador, m; Auto. estrangulador, m; Inf. garganta, f. vt estrangular; Fig. ahogar, suprimir. **to open (close) the t.,** abrir (cerrar) el estrangulador

throttling /'θrɒtlɪŋ/ n estrangulación, f

through /θru/ prep por; al través de; de un lado a otro de; por medio de; (between) entre; por causa de; gracias a. adv al través; de un lado a otro; (whole) entero, todo; (from beginning to end) desde el principio hasta el fin; (to the end) hasta el fin. a (of passages, etc.) que va desde... hasta...; (of trains) directo. **to look t. the window,** mirar por la ventana, asomarse a la ventana. **to be wet t.,** estar calado hasta los huesos; estar muy mojado. **to carry t.,** llevar a cabo. **to fall t.,** caer por; (fail) fracasar. **to sleep the whole night t.,** dormir durante toda la noche, dormir la noche entera. **t. and t.,** completamente. **through the length and breadth of,** a lo largo y a lo ancho de, hasta los últimos rincones de. **t. traffic,** tráfico directo, m. **t. train,** tren directo, m

throughout /θru'aut/ prep por todo; durante todo. adv completamente; (from beginning to end) desde el principio hasta el fin; (everywhere) en todas partes

throw /θrou/ vt arrojar, lanzar, echar; (fire) disparar; (pottery) plasmar; (knock down) derribar; (slough) mudar (la piel); (cast off) despojarse de; (a rider) desmontar; (a glance) echar, dirigir (una mirada, etc.); (silk) torcer; (dice) echar; (light) dirigir, enfocar. **to t. oneself at the head of,** echarse a la cabeza de. **to t. open,** abrir de par en par; abrir. **to t. overboard,** Naut. echar al mar; desechar; (desert) abandonar. **to t. about,** esparcir, desparramar; derrochar. **to t. aside,** echar a un lado, desechar; abandonar, dejar. **to t. away,** tirar; desechar, Lat. Am. botar; (spend) malgastar, derrochar; (waste) sacrificar; (of opportunities) malograr, perder. **to t. back,** devolver; echar hacia atrás. **to t. down,** derribar, dar en el suelo con; (arms) rendir. **to t. down the glove,** arrojar el guante. **to t. oneself down,** tumbarse, echarse; (descend) echarse abajo. **to t. oneself down from,** arrojarse de. **to t. in,** echar dentro; (give extra) añadir; (the clutch) embragar; insertar; (a remark) hacer (una observación). **to t. off,** despojarse de; quitarse; (refuse) rechazar; sacudirse; (get rid of) despedir; (renounce) renunciar; (exhale) emitir, despedir; (verses) improvisar. **to t. on,** echar sobre; (garments) ponerse. **to t. oneself upon,** lanzarse sobre. **to t. out,** expeler; hacer salir; plantar en la calle; (utter) proferir, soltar; (one's chest) inflar; (discard) tirar, desechar, Lat. Am. botar. **to t. over,** (desert) abandonar, dejar. **to t. up,** (build) levantar; lanzar en el aire; (a post, etc.) renunciar (a), abandonar; vomitar, Central America, Mexico deponer

throw /θrou/ n echada, f; tiro, m; (at dice) lance, m; jugada, f; (wrestling) derribo, m. **within a stone's t.,** a tiro de piedra. **t.-back,** retroceso, m; Biol. atavismo, m

thrower /'θrouər/ n tirador (-ra), lanzador (-ra)

throwing /'θrouɪŋ/ n lanzamiento, m, lanzada, f. **t. the hammer,** lanzamiento del martillo, m

thrust /θrʌst/ n empujón, m; (with a sword) estocada, f; (fencing) golpe, m; (with a lance) bote, m; ataque, m; asalto, m. vt empujar; (put) meter; (insert) introducir; (pierce) atravesar; (out, through, of the head, etc.) asomar. *vi* acometer, atacar, embestir; meterse, introducirse; (intrude) entrometerse; (fencing) dar un golpe. **to t. aside,** empujar a un lado; (proposals) rechazar. **to t. back,** hacer retroceder, empujar hacia atrás; (words) tragarse; (thoughts) apartar, rechazar. **to t. down,** empujar hacia abajo; hacer bajar; *Fig.* reprimir. **to t. forward,** empujar hacia delante; hacer seguir. **to t. oneself forward,** adelantarse; *Fig.* ponerse delante de los otros, darse importancia. **to t. in,** introducir; (stick) hincar; (insert) intercalar. **to t. on,** hacer seguir; empujar sobre; (garments) ponerse rápidamente. **to t. oneself in,** introducirse; entrometerse. **to t. out,** echar fuera; hacer salir, echar; expulsar; (the tongue) sacar (la lengua); (the head, etc.) asomar. **to t. through,** atravesar; (pierce) traspasar. **to t. one's way through,** abrirse paso por. **to t. upon,** imponer, hacer aceptar

thud /θʌd/ *n* sonido sordo, *m*; golpe sordo, *m*

thug /θʌg/ *n* asesino, criminal, *m*

thumb /θʌm/ *n* pulgar, *m*. *vt* hojear; ensuciar con los dedos. **under the t. of,** *Fig.* en el poder de. **t. index,** índice pulgar, *m*. **t.-mark,** huella del dedo, *f*. **t.-screw,** tornillo de orejas, *m*, **t.-stall,** dedil, *m*. **t.-tack,** chinche, *m*

thump /θʌmp/ *n* golpe, porrazo, *m*. *vt* and *vi* golpear, aporrear; (the ground, of rabbits) zapatear

thunder /'θʌndər/ *n* trueno, *m*; (of hooves, etc.) estampido, *m*; estruendo, *m*. *vi* tronar; retumbar; *Fig.* fulminar. *vt* gritar en una voz de trueno, rugir. **to t. along,** avanzar como el trueno; galopar ruidosamente. **t.-clap,** trueno, *m*. **t.-cloud,** nube de tormenta, *f*, nubarrón, *m*. **t.-storm,** tronada, *f*. **t. struck, to be thunderstruck,** quedarse muerto, estupefacto. **to be thunderstruck,** quedarse frío

thunderbolt /'θʌndərˌboult/ *n* rayo, *m*

thunderer /'θʌndərər/ *n* fulminador, *m*. **the Thunderer,** Júpiter tonante, Júpiter tronante, *m*; el «Times» londinense, *m*

Thursday /'θɜrzdei/ *n* jueves, *m*. **Holy T.,** Jueves Santo, *m*

thus /ðʌs/ *adv* así; de este modo; en estos términos; hasta este punto. **t. far,** hasta ahora; hasta este punto; hasta aquí. **Thus it is that...,** Así es que...

thwack /θwæk/ *n* golpe, *m*; *vt* golpear

thwart /θwɔrt/ *vt* frustrar, impedir

thy /ðai/ *poss a* tu, *mf*; tus, *m pl*, and *f pl*

thyme /taim/ *n Bot.* tomillo, *m*

thymus /'θaiməs/ *n Anat.* timo, *m*

thyroid /'θairɔid/ *a* tiroideo. **t. gland,** tiroides, *f*

thyself /ðai'sɛlf/ *poss pron* tú mismo, *m*; tu misma, *f*; (with prep.) tí mismo, *m*; tí misma, *f*; (in a reflexive verb) te

tiara /ti'ærə, -'ɑrə/ *n* tiara, *f*

Tiberias /tai'biəriəs/ Tiberíades, *f*

Tibetan /tɪ'bɛtn̩/ *a* and *n* tibetano (-na); (language) tibetano, *m*

tibia /'tɪbiə/ *n Anat.* tibia, *f*

tic /tɪk/ *n* (twitch) tic nervioso, *m*

tick /tɪk/ *n Ent.* ácaro, *m*; (sound) tictac, *m*; (cover) funda de colchón, *f*; *Inf.* fiado, crédito, *m*; (mark) marca, *f* *vi* hacer tictac. *vt* poner una marca contra. **on t.,** *Inf.* al fiado. **to t. off,** poner una marca contra; *Inf.* reñir. **to t. over,** *Auto.* andar, marchar

ticket /'tɪkɪt/ *n* billete, *Lat. Am.* boleto, *m*; (for an entertainment) entrada, localidad, *f*; (label) etiqueta, *f*; (pawn) papeleta de empeño, *f*; (for luggage) talón, *m*; *Polit.* candidatura, *f*, *vt* marcar. **to take one's t.,** sacar el billete (or for entertainment) la entrada, *f*). **excursion t.,** billete de excursión, *m*. **return t.,** billete de ida y vuelta, *m*. **season t.,** billete de abono, *m*. **single t.,** billete sencillo, *m*. **t. agency,** (for travel) agencia de viajes, *f*; (for entertainments) agencia de teatros, *f*. **t. collector or inspector,** revisor, *m*. **t. holder,** tenedor de billete, *m*; abonado (-da). **t. office,** (railway) despacho de billetes, *m*; taquilla, *Lat. Am.* boletería, *f*. **t.-of-leave,** libertad condicional, *f*. **t. punch,** sacabocados, *m*; (on tramcars) clasificador de billetes, *m*

ticking /'tɪkɪŋ/ *n* (sound) tictac, *m*; (cloth) cotí, *m*

tickle /'tɪkəl/ *vt* hacer cosquillas (a), cosquillear; irri-

tar; (gratify) halagar; (amuse) divertir. *vi* tener cosquillas; hacer cosquillas; ser irritante

ticklish /'tɪklɪʃ/ *a* cosquilloso; (of persons) difícil, vidrioso; (of affairs) espinoso, delicado

tidal /'taidl̩/ *a* de marea. **t. wave,** marejada, *f*; *Fig.* ola popular, *f*

tidbit /'tɪd,bɪt/ *n* See **titbit**

tiddlywinks /'tɪdli,wɪŋks/ *n* juego de la pulga, *m*

tide /taid/ *n* marea, *f*; (season) tiempo, *m*, estación, *f*; (trend) corriente, *f*; (progress) curso, *m*; marcha, *f*. *vi* (with over) vencer, superar; aguardar la ocasión. **to go against the t.,** ir contra la corriente. **to go with the t.,** seguir la corriente. **high t.,** marea alta, *f*. **low t.,** marea baja, *f*, bajamar, *m*. **neap t.,** marea muerta, *f*. **t. mark,** lengua del agua, *f*

tidily /'taidl̩i/ *adv* aseadamente; en orden, metódicamente

tidiness /'taidnɪs/ *n* aseo, *m*; buen orden, *m*

tidings /'taidɪŋz/ *n pl* noticias, nuevas, *f pl*

tidy /'taidi/ *a* aseado; metódico, en orden; pulcro; *Inf.* considerable. *vt* poner en orden, asear; limpiar; (oneself) arreglarse

tie /tai/ *n* lazo, *m*, atadura, *f*; (knot) nudo, *m*; (for the neck) corbata, *f*; *Sports.* empate, *m*; *Mus.* ligado, *m*; *Archit.* tirante, *m*; (spiritual bond) lazo, *m*; (burden) carga, responsabilidad, *f*, **tie clasp,** pisa corbata, *mf*. **tie-pin,** alfiler de corbata, *Mexico* fistol, *m*. **tie seller,** corbatero (-ra)

tie /tai/ *vt* atar; (bind) ligar; (lace) lacear; (a knot) hacer; (with a knot) anudar; (unite) unir; (*Fig.* bind) constreñir, obligar; (limit) limitar, restringir; (occupy) ocupar, entretener; (hamper) estorbar, impedir. *vi* atarse; *Sports.* empatar. **to tie one's tie,** hacer la corbata. **to tie down,** atar a; limitar; obligar. **They tied him down to a chair,** Le ataron a una silla. **to tie together,** enlazar, ligar; atar. **to tie up,** liar, atar; (wrap) envolver; recoger; *Naut.* amarrar, atracar; (restrict) limitar, restringir; (invest) invertir

tie-breaker /'tai,breikər/ *n* desempate, *m*

tier /'tɪər/ *n* fila, hilera, *f*; (of seats, etc.) grada; (of a dress) en volantes

tiff /tɪf/ *n* riña, *m*, disgusto, *m*

tiger /'taigər/ *n* tigre, *m*. **t.-cat,** gato (-ta) atigrado (-da). **t.-lily,** tigridia, *f*

tigerish /'taigərɪʃ/ *a* atigrado, de tigre; salvaje, feroz

tight /tait/ *a* apretado; (not leaky) hermético, impermeable; (taut) tieso, tirante; (narrow) estrecho; (trim) compacto; (of clothes) muy ajustado; (shut) bien cerrado; *Naut.* estanco; (risky) peligroso, difícil; (miserly) tacaño, *Argentina* agalludo; (of money, goods) escaso; (tipsy) borracho, *Mexico* abombado. **become t.,** **get t.** (get tipsy) *Mexico* abombarse. **to be t.-fisted,** ser como un puño. **to hold t.,** agarrar fuerte. **t. corner,** *Fig.* aprieto, lance apretado, *m*. **t.-rope,** cuerda de violante, cuerda floja, *Lat. Am.* maroma, *f*. **t.-rope walker,** alambrista, equilibrista, *mf*; volatinero (-ra), bailarín de la cuerda floja, *m*, *Lat. Am.* maromero (-ra), *mf*. **t.-rope walker's pole,** balancín, *m*

tighten /'taitn̩/ *vt* estrechar, apretar, *Lat. Am.* atesar; (stretch) estirar; (of saddle girths) cinchar. *vi* estrecharse; estirarse. **t. up** *Lat. Am.* atesar

tightly /'taitli/ *adv* estrechamente

tightness /'taitnɪs/ *n* estrechez, *f*; tirantez, tensión, *f*; (feeling of constriction) opresión, *f*; (drunkenness) emborrachamiento, *m*

tights /taits/ *n pl* mallas, *f pl*

tile /tail/ *n* teja, *f*; (for flooring) baldosa, losa, *f*; (ornamental) azulejo, *m*; (hat) chistera, *f*. *vt* tejar; embaldosar. **t. floor,** enlosado, embaldosado, *m*. **t. manufacturer,** tejero, *m*. **t. works or yard,** tejar, *m*, (Colombia) galpón *m*

tiler /'tailər/ *n* solador, *m*; tejero, *m*

till /tɪl/ *n* (for money) cajón, *m*. *vt* Agr. cultivar, labrar. *prep* hasta. *conjunc* hasta que

tillable /'tɪləbəl/ *a* laborable

tiller /'tɪlər/ *n* Agr. labrador, *m*; *Bot.* mugrón, renuevo, vástago, *m*; *Naut.* caña del timón, *f*

tilling /'tɪlɪŋ/ *n* Agr. cultivo, laboreo, *m*

tilt /tɪlt/ *n* inclinación, *f*; ladeo, *f*; (fight) torneo, *m*, justa, *f*. *vt* inclinar; ladear; (a drinking vessel) empinar. *vi* inclinarse; ladearse; (fight) justar. **to t. against,** *Fig.* arremeter contra, atacar. **at full t.,** a todo correr. **t. hammer,** martinete de báscula, *m.* **t.-yard,** palestra, *f*

tilting /'tɪltɪŋ/ *n* incinación, *f;* (fighting) justas, *f pl. a* inclinado

timber /'tɪmbər/ *n* madera de construcción, *f;* (trees) árboles de monte, *m pl;* bosque, *m;* (beam) viga, *f; Naut.* cuaderna, *f. vt* enmaderar. **t. line,** límite del bosque maderable, *m.* **t. merchant,** maderero, *m.* **t. wolf,** lobo gris, *m.* **t. work,** maderaje, *m.* **t. yard,** maderería, *f,* corral de madera, *m*

timbered /'tɪmbərd/ *a* enmaderado; (with trees) arbolado

timbre /'tæmbər, 'tɪm-/ *n Mus.* timbre, *m*

timbrel /'tɪmbrəl/ *n Mus.* tamborete, tamboril, *m*

time /taɪm/ *n* (in general) tiempo, *m;* (epoch) época, edad, *f;* tiempos, *m pl;* (of the year) estación, *f;* (by the clock) hora, *f;* (lifetime) vida, *f;* (particular moment of time) momento, *m;* (occasion) sazón, ocasión, *f;* (day) día, *m;* (time allowed) plazo, *m;* (in repetition) vez, *f; Mus.* compás, *m; Mil.* paso, *m. vt* ajustar al tiempo; hacer con oportunidad; (regulate) regular; calcular el tiempo que se emplea en hacer una cosa; (a blow) calcular. **all the t.,** todo el tiempo; continuamente, sin cesar. **a long t.,** mucho tiempo. **a long t. ago,** mucho tiempo ha, hace mucho tiempo. **at a t.,** a la vez, al mismo tiempo; (of period) en una época. **at any t.,** a cualquier hora; en cualquier momento; (when you like) cuando gustes. **at no t.,** jamás, nunca. **at some t.,** alguna vez; en alguna época. **at some t. or another,** un día u otro; en una u otra ocasión; en alguna época. **at that t.,** en aquella época; en la sazón; en aquel instante. **at the one t.,** de una vez. **at the present t.,** en la actualidad, al presente. **at the proper t.,** a su debido tiempo; a la hora señalada; a la hora conveniente. **at the same t.,** al mismo tiempo. **at the same t. as.** mientras, a medida que; al mismo instante que, **at times,** a veces, en ocasiones. **behind the times,** *Fig.* atrasado de noticias; pasado de moda. **behind t.,** atrasado. **by that t.,** para entonces. **every t.,** cada vez; siempre. **for some t.,** durante algún tiempo. **for some t. past,** de algún tiempo a esta parte. **for the t. being,** de momento, por ahora, por lo pronto. **from this t.,** desde hoy; desde esta fecha. **from this t. forward,** de hoy en adelante. **from t. to t.,** de vez en cuando, de cuando en cuando, de tarde en tarde. **in a month's t.,** en un mes. **in a short t.,** en breve, dentro de poco. **in good t.,** puntualmente; temprano. **in my t.,** en mis días, en mis tiempos. **in olden times,** antiguamente, en otros tiempos. **in the course of t.,** andando el tiempo, en el transcurso de los años. **in the t. of,** en la época de. **in t.,** (promptly) a tiempo; con el tiempo. **in t. to come,** en el porvenir. **It is t. to...,** Es hora de... **many times,** frecuentemente, muchas veces. **Once upon a t.,** Érase una vez, Una vez había, Érase que érase. Érase que se era. **Since t. out of mind,** Desde tiempo inmemorial. **the last (next) t.,** la última (próxima) vez. **this t. of year,** esta estación del año. **T. hangs heavy on his hands,** El tiempo se le hace interminable. **T. flies,** El tiempo vuela. **T. will tell!** ¡El tiempo lo dirá! ¡Veremos lo que veremos! **What t. is it?** ¿Qué hora es? **The t. is...,** La hora es... **within a given t.,** dentro de un plazo dado. **to be out of t.,** estar fuera de compás. **to gain t.,** ganar tiempo. **to have a good t.,** pasarlo bien, divertirse. **to have a bad t.,** pasarlo mal; *Inf.* tener un mal cuarto de hora. **to have no t. to,** no tener tiempo para + noun or pronoun, no tener tiempo de + infinitive. **to keep t.,** guardar el compás. **to kill t.,** engañar (or entretener) el tiempo. **to mark t.,** marcar el paso; *Fig.* hacer tiempo. **to pass the t.,** pasar el rato; pasar el tiempo. **to pass the t. of day,** saludar. **to serve one's t.,** (to a trade) servir el aprendizaje; (in prison) cumplir su condena; *Mil.* hacer el servicio militar. **to take t. to,** tomar tiempo para. **to take t. by the forelock,** asir la ocasión por la melena. **to waste t.,** perder el tiempo. **t. exposure,** pose, *f.* **t. fuse,** espoleta de tiempo, espoleta graduada, *f.* **t.-honored,** tradicional, consagrado por el tiempo. **t.-keeper,** capataz, *m;* reloj, *m.* **t.-saving,** que ahorra el

tiempo. **t.-server,** lameculos, *mf* **t.-signal,** señales horarias, *f pl.* **t.-table,** horario, *m;* itinerario, programa, *m;* (railway) guía de ferrocarriles, *f.* **t. to come,** porvenir, *m,* lo venidero

timed /taɪmd/ *a* calculado; (ill-) intempestivo; (well-) oportuno

timeless /'taɪmlɪs/ *a* eterno

timeliness /'taɪmlinɪs/ *n* tempestividad, oportunidad, *f*

timely /'taɪmli/ *a* oportuno

timepiece /'taɪm,pis/ *n* reloj, *m*

time zone *n* huso esférico, huso horario, *m*

timid /'tɪmɪd/ *a* tímido, asustadizo, medroso; (shy) vergonzoso

timidity /tɪ'mɪdɪti/ *n* timidez, *f;* vergüenza, *f*

timing /'taɪmɪŋ/ *n* medida del tiempo, *f; Mech.* regulación, *f;* (timetable) horario, *m*

timorous /'tɪmərəs/ *a* timorato, apocado, asustadizo

timorousness /'tɪmərəsnɪs/ *n* encogimiento, *m,* timidez, *f*

tin /tɪn/ *n* (metal) estaño, *m;* (container) lata, *f;* (sheet) hojalata, *f;* (money) plata, *f. vt* estañar; (place in tins) envasar en lata; cubrir con hojalata, hoja de aluminio, *f.* **tin-foil,** papel de estaño, *m.* **tin hat,** casco de acero, *m.* **tin-plate,** hojalata, *f.* **tin soldier,** soldado de plomo, *m.* **tin ware,** hojalatería, *f*

tincture /'tɪŋktʃər/ *n* tintura, *f,* tinte, *m; Med.* tintura, *f;* (trace) dejo, *m;* (veneer) capa, *f. vt* teñir, tinturar

tinder /'tɪndər/ *n* yesca, *f.* **t. box,** yescas, lumbres, *f pl*

tinge /tɪndʒ/ *n* tinte, matiz, *m; Fig.* dejo, toque, *m. vt* matizar, tinturar; *Fig.* tocar

tingle /'tɪŋgəl/ *n* picazón, comezón, *f;* (thrill) estremecimiento, *m. vi* picar; (of ears) zumbar; (thrill) estremecerse (de); vibrar

tingling /'tɪŋglɪŋ/ *n* picazón, comezón, *f;* (of the ears) zumbido, *m;* (thrill) estremecimiento, *m*

tinker /'tɪŋkər/ *n* calderero remendón, *m. vt* remendar. *vi* chafallar. **to t. with,** jugar con

tinkle /'tɪŋkəl/ *n* tilín, retintín, *m;* campanilleo, *m;* cencerreo, *m. vi* tintinar. *vt* hacer tintinar

tinkling /'tɪŋklɪŋ/ *n* retintín, tintineo, *m;* campanilleo, *m*

tinned /tɪnd/ *a* (of food) en lata, en conserva

tinsel /'tɪnsəl/ *n* oropel, *m;* (cloth) lama de oro o plata, *f,* brocadillo, *m; Fig.* oropel, *m. a* de oropel; de brocadillo; *Fig.* charro. *vt* adornar con oropel

tinsmith /'tɪn,smɪθ/ *n* hojalatero, estañador, *m*

tint /tɪnt/ *n* tinta, *f,* color, *m;* matiz, *m;* tinte, *m. vt* colorar, teñir; matizar

tinting /'tɪntɪŋ/ *n* tintura, *f,* teñido, *m*

tiny /'taɪni/ *a* diminuto, minúsculo, menudo, chiquito

tip /tɪp/ *n* punta, *f;* cabo, *m,* extremidad, *f;* (of an umbrella, etc.) regatón, *m;* (of a lance) borne, *m;* (of a cigarette) boquilla, *f;* (of a shoe) puntera, *f;* (of a finger) yema, *f;* (for rubbish) depósito de basura, *m;* (gratuity) propina, *f;* (information) informe oportuno, *m;* (tap) golpecito, *m.* **to have on the tip of one's tongue,** tener en la punta de la lengua. **tip-cart,** volquete, *m.* **tip-up seat,** asiento plegable, *m*

tip /tɪp/ *vt* inclinar; volcar, voltear; (drinking vessel) empinar; dar regatón, etc. (a); *Poet.* tocar, golpear ligeramente; (reward) dar propina (a). *vi* inclinarse; (topple) tambalearse; dar propina. **to tip the wink,** guiñar el ojo (a). **to tip off,** (liquids) echar; hacer caer; (inform) decir en secreto; informar oportunamente. **to tip over,** *vt* volcar; hacer caer. *vi* volcarse; caer; (of a boat) zozobrar. **to tip up,** *vt* (a seat) levantar; (money) proporcionar (el dinero); (upset) volcar; hacer perder el equilibrio. *vi* volcarse; (lose the balance) perder el equilibrio

tippler /'tɪplər/ *n* borracho (-cha)

tipsily /'tɪpsəli/ *adv* como borracho

tipsy /'tɪpsi/ *a* achispado, algo borracho, *Lat. Am.* mamado. **to be t.,** estar entre dos luces, estar entre dos velas

tiptoe /'tɪp,tou/ (**on**) *adv* de puntillas; *Fig.* excitado, ansioso. **to stand on t.,** ponerse de puntillas, empinarse

tirade /'taɪreɪd/ *n* diatriba, *f*

tire /taiᵊr/ n (of a cart, etc.) llanta, f; *Auto.* neumático, *Lat. Am.* caucho, m; (of baby carriage, etc.) rueda de goma, f. **balloon t.**, neumático balón, m. **pneumatic t.**, neumático, m. **slack t.**, neumático desinflado, m. **solid t.**, neumático macizo, m. **spare t.**, neumático de recambio (or de repuesto), m. **t. burst**, estallido de un neumático, m. **t. valve**, válvula de cámara (del neumático), f

tire /taiᵊr/ vt cansar, fatigar; (bore) aburrir. vi cansarse, fatigarse; aburrirse. **to be tired of**, estar cansado de. **to grow tired**, empezar a cansarse. **to t. out**, rendir de cansancio

tired /taiᵊrd/ a cansado, fatigado. **to be sick and t. of**, estar hasta la coronilla (de), (of persons) con. **t. of**, cansado de; disgustado de

tiredness /'taiᵊrdnıs/ n cansancio, m, fatiga, f; aburrimiento, m

tireless /'taiᵊrlıs/ a infatigable, incansable

tiresome /'taiᵊrsəm/ a fastidioso, molesto, pesado; (dull) aburrido

tiresomeness /'taiᵊrsəmnıs/ n pesadez, f, fastidio, m; tedio, aburrimiento, m

tiring /'taiᵊrıŋ/ a fatigoso

tissue /'tıʃu/ n (cloth) tisú, m, lama, f; (paper) pañuelito m; *Biol.* tejido, m; (series) serie, sarta, f. **t. paper**, papel de seda, m

tit /tıt/ n *Ornith.* paro, m. **tit for tat**, tal para cual

Titan /'taitn̩/ n titán, m

titanic /tai'tænık/ a titánico

titbit /'tıt,bıt/ n golosina, f

tithe /taiθ/ n décima, f; fracción, pequeña parte, f, vt diezmar. **t. gatherer**, diezmero (-ra)

titillate /'tıtl̩,eit/ vt titilar, estimular

titivate /'tıtə,veit/ vi arreglarse

title /'taitl̩/ n título, m; (right) derecho, m; documento, m. **to give a t. to**, intitular; ennoblecer. **t. deed**, títulos de propiedad, m. **t. page**, portada, f. **t. role**, papel principal, m

titter /'tıtər/ vi reírse disimuladamente. n risa disimulada, f

tittle /'tıtl̩/ n adarme, tilde, ápice, m

titular /'tıtʃələr/ a titular; nominal

to /tu/ unstressed tʊ, tə/ prep a; (as far as) hasta; (in the direction of) en dirección a, hacia; (with indirect object) a; (until) hasta; (compared with) en comparación con, comparado con; (against) contra; (according to) según; (as) como; (in) en; (so that, in order to, for the purpose of) para; (indicating possession) a, de; (of time by the clock) menos; (by) por; (before verbs of motion or which imply motion) a (sometimes para); (before some other verbs) de; en; (before verbs of beginning, inviting, exhorting, obliging) a; (indicating indirect object) a; (before a subjunctive or infinitive indicating future action or obligation) que. **To** is often not translated. With most Spanish infinitives no separate translation is necessary, e.g. leer, decir, to read, to speak. Some verbs are always followed by a preposition (e.g. *to begin to speak,* empezar a hablar, etc.). adv (shut) cerrado. **to come to,** volver en sí. **to lie to,** *Naut.* ponerse a la capa. **to and from,** de un lado a otro. **face to face,** cara a cara. **He has been a good friend to them,** Ha sido un buen amigo para ellos. **That is new to me,** Eso es nuevo para mí. **He went to London,** Se fue a Londres. **to go to France (Canada),** ir a Francia (al Canadá). **the road to Madrid,** la carretera de Madrid. **She kept the secret to herself,** Guardó el secreto para sí. **to go to the dentist,** ir al dentista. **We give it to them,** Se lo damos a ellos. **It belongs to me,** Pertenece a mí. **What does it matter to you?** ¿Qué te importa a ti? **I wish to see him,** Quiero verle. **They did it to help us,** Lo hicieron para ayudarnos. **I have to go to see her,** Tengo que ir a verla. **to this day,** hasta hoy, hasta el presente. **It is a quarter to six,** Son las seis menos cuarto. **to the house of...,** a casa de, *Lat. Am. also* donde (e.g. *My wife went to her friend's house* Mi mujer fue a casa de su amiga, Mi mujer fue donde su amiga). **to the last shilling,** hasta el último chelín. **the next to me,** el que me sigue. **closed to the public,** cerrado para el público

toad /toud/ n sapo, m

toady /'toudi/ n lameculos, mf adulador (-ra). vt lamer el culo (a), adular

toast /toust/ n *Cul.* tostada, f; (drink) brindis, m. vt tostar; brindar, beber a la salud de. vi brindar. **buttered t.**, mantecada, f. **t.-rack**, portatostadas, m

toaster /'toustər/ n (device) tostador, m; (person) brindador, m

toasting /'toustıŋ/ n tostadura, f, tueste, m, a de tostar. **t.-fork**, tostadera, f

tobacco /tə'bækou/ n tabaco, m. a tabacalero. **black** or **cut t.**, picadura, f. **leaf t.**, tabaco de hoja, m. **mild t.**, tabaco flojo, m. **pipe t.**, tabaco de pipa, m. **plug t.**, tabaco para mascar, m. **strong t.**, tabaco fuerte, m. **Turkish t.**, tabaco turco, m. **Virginian t.**, tabaco rubio, m. **t.-pipe**, pipa (de tabaco), f. **t.-pipe cleaner,** escobillón para limpiar pipas, m. **t. plantation,** tabacal, m. **t. planter,** tabaquero (-ra). **t. poisoning,** tabaquismo, m. **t.-pouch** or **jar,** tabaquera, f

tobacconist /tə'bækənıst/ n tabaquero (-ra). **tobacconist's shop,** tabaquería, f, *Lat. Am.* cigarrería, f, expendio, m

toboggan /tə'bɒgən/ n tobogán, m. vi ir en tobogán. **t. run,** pista de tobogán, f

tocsin /'tɒksın/ n rebato, m

today /tə'dei/ adv hoy; ahora, actualmente, al presente, hoy día. n el día de hoy. **from t.,** desde hoy. **from t. forward,** de hoy en adelante

toddle /'tɒdl̩/ vi hacer pinos, empezar a andar; (stroll) dar una vuelta; (leave) marcharse

toddy /'tɒdi/ n ponche, m

toe /tou/ n dedo del pie, m; (cloven) pezuña, f; uña, f; (of furniture) base, f, pie, m; (of stockings, shoes) punta, f. **He stepped on my toe,** Me pisó el dedo del pie. **big toe,** dedo pulgar del pie, dedo gordo del pie, m. **little toe,** dedo pequeño del pie, m. **to toe the line,** ponerse en la raya; *Fig.* cumplir con su deber. **toe-cap,** puntera, f. **toe-dancing,** baile de puntillas, m. **toe-nail,** uña del dedo del pie, f

toffee /'tɒfi/ n caramelo, m

toga /'tougə/ n toga, f

together /tə'gɛðər/ adv junto; (uninterruptedly) sin interrupción; (in concert) simultáneamente, a la vez, al mismo tiempo; (consecutively) seguido. **t. with,** con; junto con; en compañía de; (simultaneously) a la vez que

toil /tɔil/ n labor, f, trabajo, m pl. **toils,** lazos, m pl; *Fig.* redes, f pl. vi trabajar, afanarse. **to t. along,** caminar penosamente (por); adelantar con dificultad. **to t. up,** subir penosamente

toiler /'tɔilər/ n trabajador (-ra)

toilet /'tɔilıt/ n tocado; atavío, m; vestido, m; (lavatory) retrete, excusado, m; (for ladies) tocador, m. **to make one's t.,** arreglarse. **t. case,** neceser, m. **t.-paper,** papel higiénico, m. **t.-powder,** polvos de arroz, m pl. **t. roll,** rollo de papel higiénico, m. **t.-set,** juego de tocador, m. **t. soap,** jabón de olor, jabón de tocador, m

toiling /'tɔilıŋ/ n trabajo duro, m, a laborioso, trabajador

token /'toukən/ n señal, muestra, f; prueba, f; (presage) síntoma, indicio, m; (remembrance) recuerdo, m. **as a t. of,** en señal de; como recuerdo de

Tokyo /'touki,ou/ Tokio, m

tolerable /'tɒlərəbəl/ a tolerable, soportable, llevadero; (fairly good) mediano, mediocre, regular

tolerably /'tɒlərəbli/ adv bastante

tolerance /'tɒlərəns/ n tolerancia, f; paciencia, indulgencia, f

tolerant /'tɒlərənt/ a tolerante; indulgente

tolerate /'tɒlə,reit/ vt tolerar, sufrir, soportar; permitir

toleration /,tɒlə'reiʃən/ n tolerancia, f; indulgencia, paciencia, f. **religious t.,** libertad de cultos, f

toll /toul/ n (of a bell) tañido, doble, m; (for passage) peaje, portazgo, m; (for grinding) derecho de molienda, m. vt and vi doblar, tañer. **to t. the hour,** dar la hora. **t. call,** conferencia telefónica interurbana, llamada a larga distancia, f. **t. gate,** barrera de peaje, f. **t. house,** oficina de portazgos, f

toll booth n caseta de pago, f

tolling /'toulıŋ/ n tañido, clamor (de las campanas), m

tomahawk /'tɒmə,hɔk/ n hacha de guerra de los indios, f

tomato /tə'meitou/ n tomate, jitomate (Mexico) m. **t. plant**, tomatera, f. **t. sauce**, salsa de tomate, f

tomb /tum/ n tumba, f, sepulcro, m

tombac /'tɒmbæk/ n tombac, m, tumbaga, f

tomboy /'tɒm,bɔi/ n muchachote, torbellino, m

tombstone /'tum,stoun/ n piedra mortuoria, f, monumento funerario, m

tome /toum/ n tomo, volumen, m

tomfoolery /,tɒm'fuləri/ n necedad, tontería, f; payasada, f

tomorrow /tə'mɔrou/ adv and n mañana, f. **a fortnight t.**, mañana en quince. **the day after t.**, pasado mañana. **t. afternoon (morning)**, mañana por la tarde (mañana). **T. is Friday**, Mañana es viernes

ton /tʌn/ n tonelada, f

tonality /tou'næliti/ n tonalidad, f

tone /toun/ n tono, m; (Mus., Med., Art.) tono, m; (of the voice) acento, m, entonación, f; (of musical instruments) sonido, m; (shade) matiz, m. vt entonar; Photo. virar. **to t. down**, vt (Art., Mus.) amortiguar; Fig. suavizar, modificar. vi (Art., Mus.) amortiguarse; Fig. suavizarse, modificarse. **to t. in with**, (of colors) vt armonizar con. vi armonizarse, corresponder en tono o matiz. **to t. up**, vt subir de color, intensificar el color de; Med. entonar, robustecer. **t. poem**, poema sinfónico, m

tonelessly /'tounlisli/ adv sin tono; apáticamente

tongs /tɒŋz/ n pl tenazas, f pl; tenacillas, f pl. **curling t.**, tenacillas para el pelo, f pl. **sugar t.**, tenacillas para azúcar, f pl

tongue /tʌŋ/ n Anat. lengua, f; (language) idioma, m, lengua, f; (speech) modo de hablar, m, habla, f; Mus. lengüeta, f; (of buckle) diente, m; (of shoe) oreja, f; (of land) lengua, f; (of a bell) badajo, m; (flame) lengua, f. **My t. ran away with me**, Inf. Se me fue la mula. **to give t.**, ladrar. **to hold one's t.**, cerrar el pico, tener la boca. **t. of fire**, lengua de fuego, f. **t. tied**, con impedimento en el habla; turbado, confuso; mudo. **t.-twister**, trabalenguas, m -tongued /tʌŋd/ a de voz...

tonic /'tɒnɪk/ a tónico. n Med. tónico, reconstituyente, m; Mus. tónica, f

tonight /tə'nait/ adv and n esta noche

tonnage /'tʌnɪdʒ/ n tonelaje, porte, m; (duty) derecho de tonelaje, m

tonner /'tʌnər/ n Naut. de... toneladas

tonsil /'tɒnsəl/ n amígdala, tonsila, f

tonsillitis /,tɒnsə'laitis/ n amigdalitis, f

tonsure /'tɒnʃər/ n Eccl. tonsura, f, vt tonsurar

tonsured /'tɒnʃərd/ a tonsurado

too /tu/ adv demasiado; (very) muy; también; además. **too hard**, demasiado difícil, demasiado rígido; (of persons) demasiado duro. **too much**, demasiado. **too often**, con demasiada frecuencia

tool /tul/ n herramienta, f; utensilio, m; instrumento, m; (person) criatura, f. vt labrar con herramienta; (a book) estampar en seco. **t.-bag**, capacho, m. **t. box**, caja de herramientas, f

tooling /'tulɪŋ/ n (of books) estampación en seco, f

toot /tut/ n sonido de bocina, m, vi sonar una bocina

tooth /tuθ/ n diente, m; muela, f; (of comb) púa, f; (taste) gusto, paladar, m; (cog) diente de rueda, m; (of saw) diente, m. vt dentar; mellar. vi Mech. engranar. **armed to the teeth**, armado hasta los dientes. **double t.**, muela, f. **false teeth**, dentadura postiza, f. **set of teeth**, dentadura, f. **to cut one's teeth**, echar los dientes. **to have a sweet t.**, ser muy goloso. **to show one's teeth**, enseñar los dientes. **t.-brush**, cepillo para los dientes, m. **t. drawing**, extracción de un diente, f. **t.-paste**, pasta dentífrica, f

toothache /'tuθ,eik/ n dolor de muelas, m

toothed /tuθt/ a con dientes; dentado

toothless /'tuθlis/ a desdentado, sin dientes; (of combs) sin púas

toothpick /'tuθ,pɪk/ n mondadientes, m, Mexico palillo, m

top /tɒp/ n (summit) cima, cumbre, f; (of a tree) copa, f; (of the head) coronilla, f; (of a page) cabeza, f; (crest) copete, m, cresta, f; (surface) superficie, f;

(of a wall) coronamiento, m; (tip) punta, f; (point) ápice, m; (of a tram, bus) imperial, baca, f; (of a wave) cresta, f; (acme) auge, m; (of a class) primero (de la clase), m; (highest rank) último grado, m; (of a plant) hojas, f pl; (of a piano) cima, f; Naut. cofa, f; (head of a bed, etc.) cabeza, f; (lid) tapadera, f; (toy) trompo, peón, m; (humming) trompa, f, a más alto; máximo; (chief) principal, primero. vt (cover) cubrir de; (cut off) desmochar; (come level with) llegar a la cima de; (rise above) elevarse por encima (de), coronar, dominar; (be superior to) exceder, aventajar; (golf) topear. **at the top**, a la cabeza; a la cumbre. **from top to bottom**, de arriba abajo. **on top of**, encima de; (besides) en adición a, además de. **to be top-dog**, ser un gallito. **to sleep like a top**, dormir como un lirón. **top boots**, botas de campaña, f pl. **top-dog**, vencedor, m; poderoso, m. **top-hat**, sombrero de copa, m. **top-heavy**, más pesado por arriba que por abajo

topaz /'toupæz/ n topacio, jacinto occidental, m

topcoat /'tɒp,kout/ n sobretodo, gabán, m

top floor n piso alto, m

topic /'tɒpɪk/ n asunto, tema, m

topical /'tɒpɪkəl/ a tópico; actual

topknot /'tɒp,nɒt/ n cresta, f, penacho, m; (of birds) moño, m; copete, m

topmast /'tɒp,mæst, Naut. -məst/ n mastelero, m

topmost /'tɒp,moust/ a más alto; más importante

topographer /tə'pɒgrəfər/ n topógrafo, m

topographical /,tɒpə'græfɪkəl/ a topográfico

topography /tə'pɒgrəfi/ n topografía, f

topple /'tɒpəl/ vi tambalearse, estar al punto de caer. **to t. down**, volcarse; derribarse; caer. **to t. over**, vi venirse abajo; perder el equilibrio. vt derribar, hacer caer

topsail /'tɒp,seil; Naut. -səl/ n gavia, f

topsyturvy /'tɒpsi'tɜrvi/ a desordenado. adv en desorden, patas arriba, de arriba abajo

toque /touk/ n toca, f

torch /tɔrtʃ/ n antorcha, hacha, tea, f. **electric t.**, lamparilla eléctrica, f. **t.-bearer**, hachero, m

torchlight /'tɔrtʃ,lait/ n luz de antorcha, f. **by t.**, a la luz de las antorchas

torment /v. tɔr'mɛnt, n. 'tɔrmɛnt/ n tormento, m, angustia, f; (torture) tortura, f; suplicio, m; mortificación, f; disgusto, m. vt atormentar, martirizar; (torture) torturar; molestar

tormentor /tɔr'mɛntər/ n atormentador (-ra)

tornado /tɔr'neidou/ n tornado, m

torpedo /tɔr'pidou/ n torpedo, m; Ichth. pez torpedo, m. vt torpedear. **self-propelling t.**, torpedo automóvil, m. **t.-boat**, torpedero, m. **t.-boat destroyer**, cazatorpedero, contratorpedero, m. **t. netting**, red contra torpedos, f. **t. station**, base de torpederos, f. **t. tube**, tubo lanzatorpedos, m

torpedoing /tɔr'pidouɪŋ/ n torpedeamiento, torpedeo, m

torpid /'tɔrpɪd/ a aletargado, entorpecido; (of the mind) torpe, tardo, apático

torpidity, torpor /tɔr'pɪditi, 'tɔrpər/ n letargo, m; apatía, f

torrent /'tɔrənt/ n torrente, m

torrential /tə'rɛnʃəl/ a torrencial

torrid /'tɔrɪd/ a tórrido. **t. zone**, zona tórrida, f

torsion /'tɔrʃən/ n torsión, f

torso /'tɔrsou/ n torso, m

tort /tɔrt/ n Law. tuerto, m

tortoise /'tɔrtəs/ n tortuga, f. **t.-shell**, carey, m. a de carey

tortuous /'tɔrtʃuəs/ a tortuoso

tortuousness /'tɔrtʃuəsnis/ n tortuosidad, f

torture /'tɔrtʃər/ n tortura, f, tormento, m; angustia, f. vt torturar, dar tormento (a); martirizar

torturer /'tɔrtʃərər/ n atormentador (-ra)

torturing /'tɔrtʃərɪŋ/ a torturador, atormentador; angustioso

toss /tɒs/ n sacudimiento, m, sacudida, f; (of the head) movimiento (de cabeza), m; (bull fighting) cogida, f; (from a horse) caída de caballo, f. vt echar, lanzar; agitar, sacudir; (of bulls) acornear. vi agitarse; (of plumes, etc.) ondear; (in a boat) balancearse a la merced de las olas; jugar a cara o cruz. **to t. a coin** *Mexico* echar un volado. **to t. in a blanket,** mantear, dar una manta (a). **to t. aside,** echar a un lado; abandonar. **to t. off,** beber de un trago. **to t. up,** jugar a cara o cruz

tot /tɒt/ *n* (child) nene (-na), crío (-ía); (of drink) vaso pequeño, *m*. **to tot up,** sumar

total /'toutl/ *a* total; absoluto, completo, entero. *n* total, *m*, suma, *f*. *vt* sumar. *vi* ascender (a). **t. employment,** ocupación total, *f*. **t. war,** guerra total, *f*

totalitarian /tou,tælɪ'teəriən/ *a* totalitario

totality /tou'tælɪti/ *n* totalidad, *f*

totally /'toutl̩i/ *adv* totalmente, completamente

totem /'toutəm/ *n* tótem, *m*

totemism /'toutə,mɪzəm/ *n* totemismo, *m*

totter /'tɒtər/ *vi* (of persons) bambolearse; tambalear, estar al punto de caer; *Fig.* aproximarse a su fin

tottering /'tɒtərɪŋ/ *a* vacilante; tambaleante. *n* bamboleo, *m*; tambaleo, *m*

toucan /'tukæn/ *n* *Ornith.* tucán, *m*

touch /tʌtʃ/ *vt* tocar; (brush against) rozar; (reach) alcanzar; (musical instruments) tocar; (move) emocionar, enternecer; (spur on) aguijar; (food) tomar; (affect) influir, afectar; (arouse) despertar, estimular; (equal) compararse con, igualar; (consider) tratar ligeramente (de); (money) dar un sablazo (a). *vi* tocarse; imponer las manos para curar. **I have not touched a bite,** No he probado un bocado. **This touches me nearly,** Esto me toca de cerca. **to t. at,** hacer escala en, tocar en (un puerto). **to t. off,** descargar. **to t. up,** retocar; corregir. **to t. upon,** (a subject) tratar superficialmente de, tratar ligeramente de; hablar de; considerar

touch /tʌtʃ/ *n* (sense of) tacto, *m*; (contact) toque, contacto, *m*; (brushing) roce, *m*; (tap) golpe ligero, *m*; palmadita, *f*; (of an illness) ataque ligero, *m*; *Mus.* dedeo, *m*; (little) dejo, *m*; (test) prueba, *f*, toque, *m*; *Art.* toque, *m*, pincelada, *f*. **by the t.,** a tiento. **in t. with,** en relaciones con; en comunicación con; al corriente de. **to give the finishing t.,** dar la última pincelada, dar el último toque. **t.-line,** (football) línea de toque, línea lateral, *f*. **t.-me-not,** *Inf.* erizo, *m*. **t.-stone,** piedra de toque, *f*

touched /tʌtʃt/ *a* emocionado, conmovido

touchiness /'tʌtʃɪnɪs/ *n* susceptibilidad, *f*, *Argentina* acometividad, *f*

touching /'tʌtʃɪŋ/ *a* patético, conmovedor. *prep* tocante a, acerca de. *n* tocamiento, *m*

touchy /'tʌtʃi/ *a* susceptible, quisquilloso, vidrioso

tough /tʌf/ *a* (hard) duro; vigoroso, fuerte, robusto; resistente; (of character) tenaz, firme; (of a job) difícil; espinoso. *n* chulo, *m*

toughen /'tʌfən/ *vt* endurecer. *vi* endurecerse

toughness /'tʌfnɪs/ *n* dureza, *f*; vigor, *m*, fuerza, *f*; resistencia, *f*; tenacidad, firmeza, *f*; dificultad, *f*

toupee /tu'pei/ *n* tupé, *m*

tour /tʊr/ *n* viaje, *m*, excursión, *f*. *vi* viajar. *vt* viajar por. **circular t.,** viaje redondo, *m*. **on t.,** *Theat.* en tour, de gira

touring /'tʊrɪŋ/ *a* de turismo. *n* turismo, *m*; viaje, *m*. **t. car,** coche de turismo, *m*

tourist /'tʊrɪst/ *n* turista, *mf*; viajero (-ra). **t. agency,** agencia de turismo, *f*, patronato de turismo, *m*. **t. ticket,** billete kilométrico, *m*

tournament /'tʊrnəmənt/ *n* torneo, *m*, justa, *f*; (of games) concurso, *m*

tourniquet /'tɜrnɪkɪt, 'tʊr-/ *n* torniquete, *m*

tousle /'tauzəl, -səl/ *vt* despeinar; desordenar el pelo

tout /taut/ *n* buhonero, *m*. **to t. for,** pescar, solicitar

tow /tou/ *n* remolque, *m*; (rope) estopa, *f*. *vt* (*Naut.,* *Auto.*) remolcar. **on tow,** a remolque. **tow-path,** camino de sirga, *m*. **tow rope,** cable de remolque, *m*

towage /'touɪdʒ/ *n* remolque, *m*; (fee) derechos de remolque, *m pl*

towards /tɔrdʒ/ *prep* hacia, en dirección a; (of time) sobre, cerca de; (concerning) tocante a; (with persons) para, con

towel /'tauəl/ *n* toalla, *f*. *Lat. Am. also* limpiamanos, *m*. **roller t.,** toalla continua, *f*. **t. rail,** toallero, *m*

tower /'tauər/ *n* torre, *f*; (fortress) fortaleza, *f*; (bel-

fry) campanario, *m*; (large) torreón, *m*. *vi* elevarse. **to t. above,** destacarse sobre, sobresalir; *Fig.* sobrepujar, superar

towered /'tauərd/ *a* torreado; de las... torres. **high t.,** de las altas torres

towering /'tauərɪŋ/ *a* elevado; dominante; orgulloso; *Fig.* violento, terrible

town /taun/ *n* población, *f*; pueblo, *m*; ciudad, *f*. **t. clerk,** secretario de ayuntamiento, *m*. **t. council,** concejo municipal, *m*. **t. councilor,** concejero municipal, *m*. **t. crier,** pregonero, *m*. **t. hall,** (casa de) ayuntamiento, casa consistorial, *f*. **t. house,** casa de ciudad, *f*. **t. planning,** urbanismo, *m*; reforma urbana, *f*. **t. wall,** muralla, *f*

"Town Ahead" «Poblado Próximo»

townsman /'taunzmən/ *n* ciudadano, *m*

town worthy *n* persona principal de la ciudad, *f*

toxic /'tɒksɪk/ *a* tóxico

toxicological /,tɒksɪkə'lɒdʒɪkəl/ *a* toxicológico

toxicologist /,tɒksɪ'kɒlədʒɪst/ *n* toxicólogo, *m*

toxicology /,tɒksɪ'kɒlədʒi/ *n* toxicología, *f*

toxin /'tɒksɪn/ *n* toxina, *f*

toy /tɔi/ *n* juguete, *m*. *vi* (with) jugar con; acariciar. **toy maker,** fabricante de juguetes, *m*

toyshop /'tɔi,ʃɒp/ *n* juguetería, tienda de juguetes, *f*

trace /treis/ *n* huella, pista, *f*, rastro, *m*; vestigio, *m*; indicio, *m*, evidencia, *f*; (of a harness) tirante, *m*; (touch) dejo, *m*; (of fear, etc.) sombra, *f*. *vt* trazar; (through transparent paper) calcar; seguir la pista (de); (write) escribir; (discern) distinguir; investigar; descubrir; determinar; (walk) atravesar, recorrer. **to t. back,** (of ancestry, etc.) hacer remontar (a)

traceable /'treisəbəl/ *a* que se puede trazar; atribuible

tracer /'treisər/ *n* trazador (-ra). **t. bullet,** bala luminosa, *f*

trachea /'treikiə/ *n* *Anat.* tráquea, *f*

trachoma /trə'koumə/ *n* *Med.* tracoma, *f*

tracing /'treisɪŋ/ *n* calco, *m*; trazo, *m*; seguimiento, *m*. **t.-paper,** papel de calcar, *m*

track /træk/ *n* huella, *f*, rastro, *m*; (for racing, etc.) pista, *f*; (of wheels) rodada, *f*; (railway) vía, *f*; (of a boat) estela, *f*; (path) senda, vereda, *f*; (sign) señal, evidencia, *f*; (course) ruta, *f*. *vt* rastrear, seguir la pista (de); *Naut.* sirgar. **to t. down,** seguir y capturar. **double t.,** vía doble, *f*. **off the t.,** extraviado; (of a train) descarrilado; *Fig.* por los cerros de Úbeda. **side t.,** desviadero, *m*. **to keep t. of,** *Inf.* no perder de vista (a); seguir las fortunas de

trackless /'træklɪs/ *a* sin camino; sin huella; (of trams, etc.) sin rieles; (untrodden) no pisado

tract /trækt/ *n* tracto, *m*; región, *f*; *Anat.* vía, *f*; (written) tratado, *m*

tractability /,træktəbɪliti/ *n* docilidad, *f*

tractable /'træktəbəl/ *a* dócil

traction /'trækʃən/ *n* tracción, *f*. **t.-engine,** máquina de arrastre (o de tracción), *f*

tractor /'træktər/ *n* máquina de arrastre, *f*; tractor, *m*

trade /treid/ *n* comercio, *m*; tráfico, *m*; negocio, *m*; industria, *f*; (calling) oficio, *m*, profesión, *f*; (dealers) comerciantes, *mf pl*. *vi* comerciar, traficar. *vt* cambiar. **to t. on,** explotar, aprovecharse de. **by t.,** de oficio, por profesión. **t.-mark,** marca de fábrica, *f*. **t.-name,** razón social, *f*. **t. price,** precio para el comerciante, *m*. **t. union,** sindicato, *m*. **t. unionism,** sistema de sindicatos obreros, *m*. **t.-winds,** vientos alisios, *m pl*

trader /'treidər/ *n* comerciante, traficante, *mf*; mercader, *m*; (boat) buque mercante, *m*

tradesman /'treidzmən/ *n* tendero, *m*. **tradesmen's entrance,** puerta de servicio, *f*

trading /'treidɪŋ/ *n* comercio, tráfico, *m*. *a* mercantil, comerciante, mercante. **t. ship,** buque mercante, *m*. **t. station,** factoría, *f*

tradition /trə'dɪʃən/ *n* tradición, *f*

traditional /trə'dɪʃənl/ *a* tradicional; del lugar

traditionalism /trə'dɪʃənl̩,ɪzəm/ *n* tradicionalismo, *m*

traditionalist /trə'dɪʃənl̩ɪst/ *n* tradicionalista, *mf*

traditionally /trə'dɪʃənl̩i/ *adv* según la tradición, tradicionalmente

traduce /trə'dus/ *vt* calumniar, denigrar, vituperar

traducer /trə'dusər/ n calumniador (-ra)

traffic /'træfɪk/ n comercio, negocio, tráfico, m; (in transit) transporte, m; (in movement) circulación, f. vi comerciar, traficar, negociar. **to cause a block in the t.,** interrumpir la circulación. **t. block,** obstrución del tráfico, f, atasco en la circulación, m. **t. indicator,** (on a car) indicador de dirección, m. **t. island,** refugio para peatones, salvavidas, m. **t. light,** disco, m, luz (de tráfico), f, semáforo, m. **t. roundabout,** redondel, m

trafficker /'træfɪkər/ n traficante, mf

tragedian /trə'dʒidiən/ n trágico, m

tragedy /'trædʒɪdi/ n tragedia, f

tragic /'trædʒɪk/ a trágico

tragicomedy /,trædʒɪ'kɒmɪdi/ n tragicomedia, f

tragicomic /,trædʒɪ'kɒmɪk/ a tragicómico

trail /treil/ n rastro, m, pista, huella, f; (path) sendero, m; (of a comet) cola, cabellera, f. vt rastrear, seguir el rastro de; (drag) arrastrar; (the anchor) garrar. vi arrastrar; (of plants) trepar. **on the t. of,** en busca de; siguiendo el rastro de; **put somebody on the t. of...** darle a fulano la pista de...

trailer /'treilər/ n cazador (-ra); perseguidor (-ra); Auto. remolque, m; (cinema) anuncio de próximas atracciones, m; Bot. talle rastrero, m

train /trein/ n (railway) tren, m; (of a dress) cola, f; (retinue) séquito, m; (procession) desfile, m, comitiva, f; (series) serie, sucesión, f; (of gunpowder) reguero de pólvora, m. **down t.,** tren descendente, m. **excursion t.,** tren de excursionistas, m. **express t.,** exprés, tren expreso, m. **fast t.,** rápido, m. **goods t.,** tren de mercancías, m. **mail t.,** tren correo, m. **next t.,** próximo tren, m. **passenger t.,** tren de pasajeros, m. **stopping t.,** tren ómnibus, m. **through t.,** tren directo, m. **up t.,** tren ascendente, m. **t.-bearer,** paje que lleva la cola, m; dama de honor, f; (of a cardinal, etc.) caudatario, m. **t.-ferry,** buque transbordador, m. **t.-oil,** aceite de ballena. m. **t. service,** servicio de trenes, m

train /trein/ vt educar; adiestrar; enseñar; Sports. entrenar; (firearms) apuntar; (plants) guiar; (accustom) habituar, acostumbrar; (a horse for racing) entrenar; (circus) amaestrar. vi educarse; adiestrarse; Sports. entrenarse

trainer /'treinər/ n (of men and racehorses) entrenador, m; (of performing animals) domador, m

training /'treiniŋ/ n educación, f; enseñanza, instrucción, f; Sports. entrenamiento, m. **t.-college,** escuela normal, f. **t.-ship,** buque escuela, m

trait /treit/ n rasgo, m, característica, f

traitor /'treitər/ n traidor (-ra)

trajectory /trə'dʒɛktəri/ n trayectoria, f

tram /træm/ n tranvía, m. a tranviario. **t. conductor,** cobrador de tranvía, m. **t. depot,** cochera de tranvías, f. **t. stop,** parada de tranvía, m

trammel /'træməl/ n (of a horse) traba, f; Fig. obstáculo, estorbo, m. vt travar; Fig. estorbar, impedir

tramp /træmp/ n (person) vagabundo (-da); vago (-ga); (walk) caminata, f, paseo largo, m; ruido de pasos, m; Naut. vapor volandero, m. vi ir a pie; patear; vagabundear. vt vagar por

trample /'træmpəl/ n pisoteo, m; (of feet) ruido de pasos, m. vt pisotear, pisar, hollar. vi pisar fuerte. **to t. on,** Fig. atropellar humillar

trance /træns/ n rapto, arrobamiento, m; Med. catalepsia, f

tranquil /'træŋkwɪl/ a tranquilo, apacible; sereno, sosegado

tranquillity /træŋ'kwɪlɪti/ n tranquilidad, paz, quietud, f; serenidad, f, sosiego, m; calma, f

tranquilize /'træŋkwə,laiz/ vt tranquilizar, sosegar, calmar

tranquilizer /'træŋkwə,laizər/ n calmante, m

tranquilizing /'træŋkwə,laiziŋ/ a sosegador, tranquilizador

trans- prefix tras-. **t.-Pyrenean,** a traspirenaico. **to t.-ship,** trasbordar. **t.-shipment,** trasbordo, m. **t.-Siberian,** trasiberiano

transact /træn'sækt/ vt despachar, hacer. vi despachar un negocio

transaction /træn'sækʃən/ n desempeño, m; negocio,

m; transacción, operación, f; pl **transactions** (of a society) actas, f pl

transatlantic /,trænsət'læntɪk/ a transatlántico. **t. liner,** transatlántico, m

transcend /træn'sɛnd/ vt exceder, superar, rebasar. vi trascender

transcendence /træn'sɛndəns/ n superioridad, f; trascendencia, f

transcendental /,trænsɛn'dɛntl̩/ a trascendental

transcontinental /,trænskɒntn̩'ɛntl̩/ a transcontinental

transcribe /træn'skraib/ vt transcribir, copiar; Mus. transcribir, adaptar

transcriber /træn'skraibər/ n copiador (-ra); Mus. adaptador (-ra)

transcript /'trænskrɪpt/ n traslado, trasunto, m; (student's) certificado de estudios, certificado de materias aprobadas, m, constancia de estudios, copia del expediente académico, hoja de estudios, f

transcription /træn'skrɪpʃən/ n transcripción, copia, f, trasunto, m; Mus. transcripción, adaptación, f, arreglo, m. **phonetic t.,** transcripción fonética, f

transept /'trænsɛpt/ n Archit. transepto, crucero, m

transfer /v. træns'fɜr, n. 'trænsfər/ n traslado, m; trasferencia, f, traspaso, m; Law. cesión, enajenación, f; (picture) calcomanía, f. vt trasladar; trasferir; pasar; Law. enajenar, ceder; estampar; calcografiar. vi trasbordarse. **deed of t.,** escritura de cesión, f. **t.-paper,** papel de calcar, m

transferable /træns'fɜrəbəl/ a trasferible

transferee /,trænsfə'ri/ n cesionario (-ia)

transference /træns'fɜrəns/ n traslado, m; transferencia, f; Law. cesión, enajenación, f

transferor /træns'fɜrər/ n cesionista, mf

transfiguration /,trænsfɪgyə'reiʃən/ n trasfiguración, f

transfigure /træns'fɪgyər/ vt trasfigurar, trasformar

transfix /træns'fɪks/ vt traspasar; Fig. paralizar

transfixion /træns'fɪkʃən/ n trasfixión, f

transform /træns'fɔrm/ vt trasformar; convertir, cambiar. **It is completely transformed,** Está completamente trasformado

transformation /,trænsfər'meiʃən/ n trasformación, f, conversión, f, cambio, m

transformative /træns'fɔrmətɪv/ a trasformador

transformer /træns'fɔrmər/ n Elec. trasformador, m

transfuse /træns'fyuz/ vt trasfundir

transfusion /træns'fyuʒən/ n trasfusión, f. **blood t.,** trasfusión de sangre, f

transgress /træns'grɛs/ vt exceder, sobrepasar; (violate) contravenir, violar, pecar contra. vi pecar

transgression /træns'grɛʃən/ n contravención, trasgresión, f; pecado, m

transgressor /træns'grɛsər/ n trasgresor (-ra), pecador (-ra)

transient /'trænʃənt, -ʒənt/ a transitorio, fugaz, pasajero; perecedero

transiently /'trænʃəntli, -ʒənt-/ adv pasajeramente

transistor /træn'zɪstər/ n transistor, m

transit /'trænsɪt/ n tránsito, paso, m; trasporte, m; Astron. tránsito, m. **in t.,** de tránsito

transition /træn'zɪʃən/ n transición, f; cambio, m; tránsito, paso, m

transitional /træn'zɪʃən̩l/ a de transición, transitorio

transitive /'trænsɪtɪv/ a Gram. transitivo, activo. **t. verb,** verbo transitivo, verbo activo, m

transitively /'trænsɪtɪvli/ adv transitivamente

transitorily /,trænsɪ'tɔrəli/ adv transitoriamente; provisionalmente

transitoriness /'trænsɪ,tɔrɪnɪs/ n brevedad, f, lo fugaz

transitory /'trænsɪ,tɔri/ a transitorio, fugaz, pasajero, breve

translatable /træns'leitəbəl/ a traducible

translate /træns'leit/ vt traducir; interpretar; (transfer) trasladar

translation /træns'leiʃən/ n traducción, f; versión, f; traslado, m

translator /træns'leitər/ n traductor (-ra)

translucence /træns'lusəns/ n traslucidez, f

translucent /træns'lusənt/ a traslúcido, trasparente

transmigrate /træns'maigreit/ vi trasmigrar

transmigration /ˌtrænsmaiˈgreiʃən/ n trasmigración, f
transmissibility /trænsˌmisəˈbiliti/ n trasmisibilidad, f
transmissible /trænsˈmisəbəl/ a trasmisible
transmission /trænsˈmiʃən/ n trasmisión, f
transmit /trænsˈmit/ vt trasmitir; remitir, dar
transmitter /trænsˈmitər/ n trasmisor (-ra); Radio. radiotrasmisor, m; Elec. trasmisor, m
transmutable /trænsˈmyutəbəl/ a trasmutable
transmutation /ˌtrænsmyuˈteiʃən/ n trasmutación, f
transmute /trænsˈmyut/ vt trasmutar
transoceanic /ˌtrænsouʃiˈænik/ a transoceánico
transom /ˈtrænsəm/ n travesaño, m; Naut. yugo de popa, m
transpacific /ˌtrænspəˈsifik/ a traspacífico
transparency /trænsˈpɛərənsi/ n trasparencia; diafanidad, f; (picture) trasparente, m
transparent /trænsˈpɛərənt/ a trasparente; diáfano; (of style) claro, limpio
transpire /trænˈspaiər/ vi traspirar; rezumarse; hacerse público; Inf. acontecer. vt exhalar
transplant /trænsˈplænt/ vt trasplantar
transplantation /ˌtrænsplænˈteiʃən/ n trasplante, m, trasplantación, f
transport /v. trænsˈpɔrt, n. ˈtrænspɔrt/ n trasporte, m; Naut. navío de trasporte, m; Aer. avión de trasporte, m; (fit) acceso, paroxismo, m. vt trasportar; (convicts) deportar; Fig. (joy) colmar; (rage) llenar
transportable /trænsˈpɔrtəbəl/ a trasportable
transportation /ˌtrænspərˈteiʃən/ n trasporte, m; (convicts) deportación, f
transporter /trænsˌpɔrtər/ n trasportador (-ra)
transpose /trænsˈpouz/ vt trasponer; Mus. trasportar
transposition /ˌtrænspəˈziʃən/ n trasposición, f
transversal /trænsˈvɜrsəl/ a and n trasversal, m
transverse /trænsˈvɜrs/ a trasverso, trasversal
transversely /trænsˈvɜrsli/ adv trasversalmente
transvestite /trænsˈvestait/ n travestido, m
trap /træp/ n trampa, f; cepo, m; (net) lazo, m, red, f; (for mice, rats) ratonera, f; Mech. sifón de depósito, m; pequeño carruaje de dos ruedas, m; (door) puerta caediza, f; Theat. escotillón, m; pl **traps**, trastos, m pl; equipaje, m. vt coger con trampa; hacer caer en el lazo; Fig. tender el lazo. vi armar una trampa; armar lazo. **to fall into a t.**, Fig. caer en la trampa. **to pack one's traps**, liar el hato
trapeze /træˈpiz/ n trapecio (de gimnasia), m
trapper /ˈtræpər/ n cazador de animales de piel, m
trappings /ˈtræpiŋz/ n pl arneses, jaeces, m pl; arreos, aderezos, m pl, galas, f pl
trash /træʃ/ n paja, hojarasca, f; (of sugar, etc.) bagazo, m; trastos viejos, m pl; cachivaches, m pl; (literary) paja, f
trashy /ˈtræʃi/ a de ningún valor, inútil, despreciable
traumatic /trɔˈmætik/ a Med. traumático
traumatism /ˈtrɔməˌtizəm/ n Med. traumatismo, m
travail /trəˈveil/ n dolores de parto, m pl. vi estar de parto; trabajar
travel /ˈtrævəl/ n el viajar, viajes, m pl. vi viajar; ver mundo; (of traffic) circular, pasar, ir. vt viajar por; recorrer; (with number of miles) hacer. **to t. over**, viajar por; recorrer. **t. worn**, fatigado por el viaje
travel agent n agente de viajes, mf
traveled /ˈtrævəld/ a que ha viajado, que ha visto muchas partes
traveler /ˈtrævələr/ n viajero (-ra); pasajero (-ra). **commercial t.**, viajante, mf **traveler's check**, cheque de viajeros, m. **traveler's joy**, Bot. clemátide, f
traveling /ˈtrævəliŋ/ n viajes, m pl. a viajero; para (or de) viajar; (itinerant) ambulante. **t. crane**, grúa móvil, f. **t. expenses**, gastos de viaje, m pl. **t. requisites**, objetos de viaje, m pl. **t. rug**, manta, f. **t. show**, circo ambulante, m
traversable /trəˈvɜrsəbəl/ a atravesable, transitable, practicable
traverse /n., a. ˈtrævərs; v. trəˈvɜrs/ n travesaño, m; Law. negación, f; (Mil. Archit.) través, m; (crossing) travesía, f, a transversal. vt atravesar, cruzar; Law. negar
travesty /ˈtrævəsti/ n parodia, f, vt parodiar

trawl /trɔl/ vt rastrear. vi pescar a la rastra. **t.-net**, red de arrastre, f
trawler /ˈtrɔlər/ n barco barredero, m; pescador a la rastra, m
trawling /ˈtrɔliŋ/ n pesca a la rastra, f
tray /trei/ n bandeja, f; (of a balance) platillo, m; (in a wardrobe, etc.) cajón, m; (trough) artesa, f
treacherous /ˈtretʃərəs/ a traidor, falso, pérfido, fementido; (of memory) infiel; engañoso; (of ice, etc.) peligroso
treacherously /ˈtretʃərəsli/ adv traidoramente, a traición
treachery /ˈtretʃəri/ n perfidia, traición, falsedad, f
treacle /ˈtrikəl/ n melado, m
tread /tred/ n pisada, f; paso, m; (of a stair) peldaño, m; (of tire) pastilla, f; (walk) andar, porte, m, vi pisar; (trample) pisotear; hollar; (oppress) oprimir. vt hollar; (a path) abrir; recorrer; caminar por; bailar. **to t. the grapes**, pisar las uvas. **to t. the stage**, pisar las tablas. **to t. under foot**, hollar; pisotear. **to t. on**, pisar. **to t. on one's heels**, pisarle los talones a uno; seguir de cerca. **to t. out**, (a measure) bailar
treading /ˈtrediŋ/ n pisoteo, m
treadle /ˈtredl/ n pedal, m; (of a loom) cárcola, f
treadmill /ˈtredˌmil/ n molino de rueda de escalones, m; Fig. rueda, f
treason /ˈtrizən/ n traición, f. **high t.**, alta traición, lesa majestad, f
treasonable /ˈtrizənəbəl/ a desleal, traidor
treasonably /ˈtrizənəbli/ adv traidoramente
treasure /ˈtrezər/ n tesoro, m; riqueza, f, caudal, m; Fig. perla, f. vt atesorar; acumular (or guardar) riquezas; (a memory) guardar. **t. trove**, tesoro hallado, m
treasurer /ˈtrezərər/ n tesorero (-ra)
treasury /ˈtrezəri/ n tesorería, f; (government department) Ministerio de Hacienda, m; (anthology) tesoro, m. **t. bench**, banco del Gobierno, m
treat /trit/ n (pleasure) gusto, placer, m; (present) obsequio, m; (entertainment) fiesta, f. vt tratar; Med. tratar, curar; (regale) obsequiar. vi (stand host) convidar; (of) tratar de, versar sobre; (with) negociar con
treatise /ˈtritis/ n tesis, monografía, disertación, f, tratado, m
treatment /ˈtritmənt/ n tratamiento, m; (of persons) conducta hacia, f, modo de obrar con, m; Med. tratamiento, m; (Lit., Art.) procedimiento, m, técnica, f
treaty /ˈtriti/ n tratado, pacto, m; (bargain) contrato, m
treble /ˈtrebəl/ n Mus. tiple, m; voz de tiple, f. a triple; Mus. sobreagudo. vt triplicar; vi triplicarse. **t. clef**, clave de sol, f
trebling /ˈtrebliŋ/ n triplicación, f
tree /tri/ n árbol, m; (for shoes) horma, f; (of a saddle) arzón, m. **breadfruit t.**, árbol del pan, m. **Judas t.**, árbol de amor, m. **t. of knowledge**, árbol de la ciencia, m. **t.-covered**, arbolado. **t.-frog**, rana de San Antonio, f
treeless /ˈtrilis/ a sin árboles
trefoil /ˈtrifɔil/ n trébol, trifolio, m
trek /trek/ vi caminar, andar
trellis /ˈtrelis/ n enrejado, m; (for plants) espaldera, f. vt cercar con un enrejado; construir espalderas
tremble /ˈtrembəl/ vi temblar; estremecerse; trepidar; vibrar; (sway) oscilar; (of flags) ondear; agitarse; ser tembloroso. **His fate trembled in the balance**, Su suerte estaba en la balanza. **to t. all over**, temblar de pies a cabeza
trembling /ˈtrembliŋ/ n temblor, m; estremecimiento, m; trepidación, f; vibración, f; (fear) agitación, ansiedad, f; temor, m. a tembloroso; trémulo
tremendous /triˈmendəs/ a terrible, espantoso; formidable; grande; importante; Inf. tremendo; enorme
tremendously /triˈmendəsli/ adv terriblemente; Inf. enormemente
tremor /ˈtremər/ n temblor, movimiento sísmico, m; (thrill) estremecimiento, m; vibración, f
tremulous /ˈtremyələs/ a trémulo, tembloroso; vacilante; tímido
tremulously /ˈtremyələsli/ adv trémulamente; tímidamente

tremulousness /'trɛmyələsnɪs/ n lo tembloroso; vacilación, f; timidez, f

trench /trɛntʃ/ n zanja, f, foso, m; (for irrigation) acequia, f; Mil. trinchera, f. vt hacer zanjas (en); acequiar; Mil. atrincherar. **t.-fever,** tifus exantemático, m. **t.-foot,** pie de trinchera, m. **t.-mortar,** mortero de trinchera, m

trenchant /'trɛntʃənt/ a mordaz

trencher /'trɛntʃər/ n trinchero, m

trend /trɛnd/ n curso, rumbo, m; Fig. tendencia, f; dirección, f. vi Fig. tender

trepan /trɪ'pæn/ vt Surg. trepanar

trepanning /trɪ'pænɪŋ/ n Surg. trepanación, f

trepidation /,trɛpɪ'deɪʃən/ n trepidación, f

trespass /'trɛspəs, -pæs/ n violación de propiedad, f; ofensa, f; pecado, m; (in the Lord's Prayer) deuda, f. vi (on land) entrar sin derecho, violar la propiedad; (upon) entrar sin permiso en; (with patience, etc.) abusar de; (against) pecar contra, infringir

trespasser /'trɛspəsər, -pæs-/ n violador (-ra) de la ley de propiedad. **"Trespassers will be prosecuted,"** «Entrada prohibida,» «Prohibido el paso»

tress /trɛs/ n (plait) trenza, f; rizo, bucle, m; pl **tresses,** cabellera, f

trestle /'trɛsəl/ n caballete, m; armazón, m. **trestle-table,** mesa de caballete, f

triad /'traɪæd/ n terna, trinca, f; Mus. acorde, m

trial /'traɪəl/ n prueba, f, ensayo, m; examen, m; (experiment) tentativa, f, experimento, m; (misfortune) desgracia, pena, f; (nuisance) molestia, f; Law. vista de una causa, f. **on t.,** a prueba; Law. en proceso. **to bring to t.,** procesar. **to stand one's t.,** ser procesado. **t. run,** marcha de ensayo, f. **t. trip,** Naut. viaje de ensayo, m

trial and error n tanteos, m. **by trial and error,** por tanteos.

triangle /'traɪˌæŋgəl/ n triángulo, m. **acute-angled t.,** triángulo acutángulo, m. **obtuse-angled t.,** triángulo obtusángulo, m. **right-angled t.,** triángulo rectángulo, m. **the eternal t.,** el eterno triángulo

triangular /traɪ'æŋgyələr/ a triangular, triángulo

triangulation /traɪˌæŋgyə'leɪʃən/ n (in surveying) triangulación, f

tribal /'traɪbəl/ a tribal

tribe /traɪb/ n tribu, f

tribesman /'traɪbzmən/ n miembro de una tribu, m

tribulation /,trɪbyə'leɪʃən/ n tribulación, f; pena, aflicción, desgracia, f

tribunal /traɪ'byunḷ/ n (seat) tribunal, m; (court) juzgado, m; (confessional) confesionario, m

tribunate /'trɪbyənɪt/ n tribunado, m

tribune /'trɪbyun/ n (person) tribuno, m; tribuna, f

tribunicial /,trɪbyə'nɪʃəl/ a tribúnico

tributary /'trɪbyəˌtɛri/ a and n tributario m

tribute /'trɪbyut/ n tributo, m; contribución, imposición, f

trice /traɪs/ n tris, soplo, m. **in a t.,** en un periquete, en un avemaría, en dos trancos

tricentennial /,traɪsɛn'tɛniəl/ a de trescientos años; n tercer centenario, tricentenario, m

trick /trɪk/ n (swindle) estafa, f, engaño, m; (ruse) truco, m, estratagema, ardid, f; (mischief) travesura, f; burla, f; (illusion) ilusión, f; (habit) costumbre, f; (affectation) afectación, f; (jugglery) juego de manos, m; (knack) talento, m; (at cards) baza, f. vt engañar, estafar; (with out) adornar, ataviar; (with into) inducir fraudulentamente. vi trampear. **dirty t.,** Inf. mala pasada, perrada, f. **His memory plays him tricks,** La memoria le engaña. **to play a t. on,** gastar una broma (a). **to play tricks,** hacer travesuras. **t. riding,** acrobacia ecuestre, f

trickery /'trɪkəri/ n maullería, superchería, f; fraude, engaño, m

trickle /'trɪkəl/ n chorrito, hilo (de agua, etc.) m. vi gotear. **to t. down,** deslizar por, correr por, escurrir por

trickling /'trɪklɪŋ/ n goteo, m; (sound) murmullo, m

trickster /'trɪkstər/ n embustero (-ra), trampeador (-ra). **to be a t.,** ser buena maula

tricky /'trɪki/ a informal, maullero; (of things) difícil; complicado; (clever) ingenioso; (person) = **crafty**

tricolor /'traɪˌkʌlər/ a tricolor

tricycle /'traɪsɪkəl/ n triciclo, m

tried /traɪd/ a probado

triennial /traɪ'ɛniəl/ a trienal

trifle /'traɪfəl/ n (object) baratija, fruslería, f; pequeñez, tontería, bagatela, f; cul, f; (small amount) pequeña cantidad, f, muy poco (de); (adverbially) algo. vi entretenerse, jugar. vt (away) malgastar. **to t. with,** jugar con

trifler /'traɪflər/ n persona frívola, f; (with affections) seductor (-ra)

trifling /'traɪflɪŋ/ a insignificante, sin importancia, trivial

trigger /'trɪgər/ n (of a fire-arm) gatillo, m; Mech. tirador, m

trigonometric /,trɪgənə'mɛtrɪk/ a trigonométrico

trigonometry /,trɪgə'nɒmɪtri/ n trigonometría, f

trilingual /traɪ'lɪŋgwəl/ a trilingüe

trill /trɪl/ n trino, m, vi trinar

trillion /'trɪlyən/ n trillón, m

trilogy /'trɪlədʒi/ n trilogía, f

trim /trɪm/ a aseado; bien arreglado; bien ajustado; elegante; bonito; (of sail) orientado. **She has a t. waist,** Inf. Tiene un talle juncal. n orden, m; buen estado, m; buena condición, f; (toilet) atavío, m. vt arreglar; (tidy) asear; pulir; (ornament) ornar, adornar; (adapt) ajustar, adaptar; Sew. guarnecer; (lamps) despabilar; (a fire) atizar; (hair, mustache) atusar, recortar; (trees) mondar, atusar; alisar; (sails) templar, orientar; (distribute weight in a boat) equilibrar; (of quill pens) tajar. vi (waver) nadar entre dos aguas. **to t. oneself up,** arreglarse

trimly /'trɪmli/ adv aseadamente; lindamente

trimmer /'trɪmər/ n guarnecedor (-ra); contemporizador (-ra)

trimming /'trɪmɪŋ/ n arreglo, m; guarnición, f; (on a dress) pasamanería, f; adorno, m; Agr. poda, f; adaptación, f, ajuste, m; pl **trimmings,** accesorios, m

trimness /'trɪmnɪs/ n aseo, buen orden, m; buen estado, m; elegancia, lindeza, f; (slimness) esbeltez, f

Trinidad and Tobago /'trɪnɪdæd/ təˈbeɪgoʊ/ Trinidad, f, y Tobago, m

Trinidadian /,trɪnɪ'deɪdiən/ n and a trinitario (-ria)

Trinity /'trɪnɪti/ n Trinidad, f

trinket /'trɪŋkɪt/ n joya, alhaja, f; dije, m, chuchería, baratija, f

trinomial /traɪ'noumiəl/ a Math. de tres términos. n Math. trinomio, m

trio /'triou/ n trío, m

trip /trɪp/ n excursión, f; viaje, m; (slip) traspié, tropiezo, m; (in wrestling) zancadilla, f; (mistake) desliz, m. vi (stumble) tropezar, caer; (move nimbly) andar airosamente, ir (or correr) ligeramente; (frolic) bailar, saltar; (wrestling, games) echar la zancadilla; (err) equivocarse; cometer un desliz. vt (up) hacer caer; echar la zancadilla (a); coger en una falta; hacer desdecirse; coger en un desliz; Naut. levantar (el ancla)

tripartite /traɪ'pɑrtaɪt/ a tripartito

tripartition /,traɪpɑr'tɪʃən/ n tripartición, f

tripe /traɪp/ n callos, m pl; tripas, f pl; mondongo, m

triple /'trɪpəl/ a triple. vt triplicar. vi triplicarse

triplet /'trɪplɪt/ n Poet. terceto, m; Mus. tresillo, m; cada uno (una) de tres hermanos (hermanas) gemelos (-as)

triplicate /a. 'trɪplɪkɪt, v. -,keɪt/ a triplicado, m. vt triplicar

triplication /,trɪplɪ'keɪʃən/ n triplicación, f

tripod /'traɪpɒd/ n trípode, m

Tripoli /'trɪpəli/ n Trípoli, m

tripper /'trɪpər/ n turista, excursionista, mf

tripping /'trɪpɪŋ/ a ligero, ágil

trippingly /'trɪpɪŋli/ adv ligeramente

triptych /'trɪptɪk/ n tríptico, m

trite /traɪt/ a (overused) gastado, trivial

triteness /'traɪtnɪs/ n trivialidad, vulgaridad, f

triumph /'traɪəmf/ n triunfo, m. vi triunfar; (over) triunfar de, vencer

triumphal /traɪ'ʌmfəl/ a triunfal. **t. arch,** arco de triunfo, m

triumphant /trai'ʌmfənt/ a triunfante, victorioso

triumvirate /trai'ʌmvərit/ n triunvirato, m

trivet /'trivit/ n trébedes, f pl, trípode, m

trivial /'trivial/ a trivial, frívolo; insignificante, sin importancia

triviality /ˌtrivi'æliti/ n trivialidad, frivolidad, f; insignificancia, f

trochlea /'troklia/ n Anat. tróclea, f

trodden /'trodn/ a trillado, batido

troglodyte /'troglaˌdait/ a and n troglodita, mf

Trojan /'troudʒən/ a and n troyano (-na). **the T. War,** la guerra de Troya, f

trolley /'troli/ n Elec. trole, m; (for children) carretón, m. **t.-bus,** trolebús, m. n **t. car,** tranvía, m. **t.-pole,** trole, m

trollop /'troləp/ n tarasca, ramera, f

trombone /trom'boun/ n trombón, m. **t. player,** trombón, m

troop /trup/ n banda, muchedumbre, f; Theat. compañía, f; (of cavalry) escuadrón, m; pl **troops,** Mil. tropas, f pl; ejército, m. vi ir en tropel, congregarse; (with away) marcharse en tropel, retirarse; (with out) salir en masa. **fresh troops,** tropas frescas, f pl. **storm troops,** tropas de asalto, f pl. **t.-ship,** transporte de guerra, m

trooper /'trupər/ n soldado de caballería, m

trope /troup/ n tropo, m

trophy /'troufi/ n trofeo, m

tropic /'tropik/ a and n trópico, m

tropical /'tropikəl/ a tropical, m

tropism /'troupizəm/ n tropismo, m

trot /trot/ n trote, m. vi trotar. vt hacer trotar. **to t. out,** Inf. sacar a relucir

troth /trɔθ/ n fe, f; palabra, f. **to plight one's t.,** dar palabra de matrimonio, desposarse

trotting /'trotiŋ/ a trotón. n trote, m

troubadour /'trubaˌdɔr/ n trovador, m, a trovadoresco

trouble /'trʌbəl/ n (grief) aflicción, angustia, f; (difficulty) dificultad, f; (effort) esfuerzo, m; pena, desgracia, f; (annoyance) disgusto, sinsabor, m; (unrest) confusión, f, disturbio, m; (illness) enfermedad, f; mal, m; (disagreement) desavenencia, f. **The t. is...,** Lo malo es; La dificultad está en que... **to be in t.,** estar afligido; estar en un apuro, estar entre la espada y la pared. **to be not worth the t.,** no valer la pena. **to stir up t.,** revolver el ajo; armar un lío. **to take the t. to,** tomarse la molestia de.

trouble /'trʌbəl/ vt turbar; agitar; afligir; inquietar; (badger) importunar; (annoy) molestar; (cost an effort) costar trabajo (e.g., Learning Spanish did not t. him much, No le costó mucho trabajo aprender el castellano). vi preocuparse; darse la molestia; inquietarse

troubled /'trʌbəld/ a agitado; inquieto; preocupado; (of life) accidentado, borrascoso. **to fish in t. waters,** pescar en agua turbia, pescar en río revuelto

troublemaker /'trʌbəlˌmeikər/ n Lat. Am. buscapleitos, mf

troublesome /'trʌbəlsəm/ a dificultoso; molesto; inconveniente; importuno; fastidioso

trough /trɔf/ n gamella, f; (for kneading bread) artesa, f; (of the waves) seno, m; (meteorological) mínimo, m. **drinking t.,** abrevadero, m. **stone t.,** pila, f

trounce /trauns/ vt zurrar, apalear; Fig. fustigar

troupe /trup/ n compañía, f

trousers /'trauzərz/ n pl pantalones, m pl. **plus four t.,** pantalones de golf, m pl. **striped t.,** pantalón de corte, m. **t. pocket,** bolsillo del pantalón, m. **t. press,** prensa para pantalones, f

trousseau /'trusou/ n ajuar de novia, m

trout /traut/ n trucha, f

trowel /'trauəl/ n Agr. almocafre, m; (mason's) paleta, f, palustre, m

troy weight /trɔi/ n peso de joyería, m

truant /'truənt/ n novillero, m; haragán (-ana). a haragán, perezoso. **to play t.,** (from school) hacer novillos; ausentarse

truce /trus/ n tregua, f; suspensión, cesación, f

truck /trʌk/ n camión, m; carretilla de mano, f; (railway) vagón de carga, m; (dealings) relaciones, f pl; (trash) cachivaches, m pl, cosas sin valor, f pl

truckage /'trʌkidʒ/ n camionaje, m; acarreo, m

truckle /'trʌkəl/ vi humillarse, no levantar los ojos. **t. bed,** carriola, f

truculence /'trʌkyələns/ n truculencia, agresividad, f

truculent /'trʌkyələnt/ a truculento, agresivo

trudge /trʌdʒ/ vi caminar a pie; andar con dificultad, caminar lentamente, andar trabajosamente, n caminata, f

true /tru/ a verdadero; real; leal, sincero; fiel; exacto; honesto; genuino; auténtico; alineado, a plomo. **That is t. of...** Es propio de... adv realmente; exactamente. **t.-bred,** de casta legítima. **t.-hearted,** leal, fiel, sincero

truffle /'trʌfəl/ n trufa, f. **to stuff with truffles,** trufar

truism /'truizəm/ n perogrullada, f

truly /'truli/ adv lealmente; realmente, verdaderamente; en efecto, por cierto; sinceramente, de buena fe. **Yours t.,** su seguro servidor (su s.s.)

trump /trʌmp/ n (cards) triunfo, m; son de la trompeta, m; Inf. gran persona, joya, f. vt ganar con el triunfo. **to t. up,** inventar. **t.-card,** naipe de triunfo, m

trumpery /'trʌmpəri/ a de pacotilla; ineficaz. n oropel, m

trumpet /'trʌmpit/ n trompeta, f. vt trompetear; Fig. pregonar. vi (of elephant) barritar. **ear.-t.,** trompetilla (acústica), f. **speaking t.,** portavoz, m. **t. blast,** trompetazo, m. **t. shaped,** en trompeta

trumpeter /'trʌmpitər/ n trompetero, trompeta, m

trumpeting /'trʌmpitiŋ/ n trompeteo, m; (of elephant) barrito, m

truncate /'trʌŋkeit/ a truncado. vt truncar

truncheon /'trʌntʃən/ n porra (de goma), f; bastón de mando, m. **blow with a t.,** porrazo, m

trunk /trʌŋk/ n (Anat. Bot.) tronco, m; (elephant's) trompa, f; (railway) línea principal, f; baúl, m; cofre, m; (of a car) Lat. Am. baúl m; pl **trunks,** (Elizabethan, etc.) trusas, f pl; calzoncillos cortos, m pl. **wardrobe t.,** baúl mundo, m. **t.-call,** conferencia telefónica, f. **t.-line,** tronco, m. **t.-road,** carretera de primera clase, carretera mayor, f

truss /trʌs/ n Med. braguero, m; (of straw, etc.) haz, m; (of blossom) racimo, m; (framework) armazón, f. vt atar; Cul. espetar; (a building) apuntalar

trust /trʌst/ n fe, confianza, f; deber, m; Law. fideicomiso, f; (credit) crédito, m; esperanza, expectación, f; Com. trust, m. vt tener confianza en; confiar en; esperar; creer; Com. dar crédito (a). vi confiar; Com. dar crédito. **in t.,** en confianza; en administración, en depósito. **on t.,** al fiado

trustee /trʌ'sti/ n guardián, m; Law. fideicomisario, depositario, consignatario, m

trustful /'trʌstfəl/ a confiado

trusting /'trʌstiŋ/ a Lat. Am. creído

trustingly /'trʌstiŋli/ adv confiadamente

trust release n extinción de fideicomiso, f

trustworthiness /'trʌstˌwərðinis/ n honradez, probidad, integridad, f; (of statements) exactitud, f

trustworthy /'trʌstˌwərði/ a digno de confianza, honrado; fidedigno, seguro; exacto

trusty /'trʌsti/ a leal, fiel; firme, seguro

truth /truθ/ n verdad, f; realidad, f; exactitud, f. **the plain t.,** la pura verdad. **to tell the t.,** decir la verdad

truthful /'truθfəl/ a veraz; exacto, verdadero

truthfulness /'truθfəlnis/ n veracidad, f; exactitud, f

try /trai/ vt and vi procurar, tratar de; (test) probar, ensayar; (a case, Law.) ver (el pleito); (strain) poner a prueba; (tire) cansar, fatigar; (annoy) molestar, exasperar; (afflict) hacer sufrir, afligir; (attempt) intentar; (judge) juzgar; (the weight of) tomar a pulso; (assay) refinar. n tentativa, f; (football) tiro, m. **Try as he would...,** Por más que hizo... **to try hard to,** hacer un gran esfuerzo para. **to try one's luck,** probar fortuna. **to try on,** (clothes) probarse (un vestido, etc.). **to try out,** poner a prueba, probar. **to try to,** procurar

trying /'traiiŋ/ a molesto; fatigoso; irritante; (painful) angustioso, penoso

tryst /trɪst/ *n* cita, *f*; (affair) amorío, *m*; lugar de cita, *m*. *vt* citar. *vi* citarse

tsar /zɑr, tsɑr/ *n* zar, *m*

tsarina /za'rinə, tsa-/ *n* zarina, *f*

tsetse fly /'tsɛtsi, 'titsi/ *n* mosca tsetsé, *f*

T-shirt /'ti,ʃɜrt/ *n* camiseta, *f.*, *Dominican Republic* poloché, *m*

tub /tʌb/ *n* cuba, *f*, artesón, *m*; cubeta, *f. vi* bañarse. **tub thumper,** *Inf.* gerundio, *m*

tuba /'tubə/ *n Mus.* tuba, *f*

tube /tub/ *n* tubo, *m*; *Anat.* trompa, *f.* **Eustachian t.,** *Anat.* trompa de Eustaquio, *f.* **Fallopian t.,** trompa de Falopio, *f.* **inner t.,** *Auto.* cámara de aire, *f.* **speaking t.,** tubo acústico, *m.* **test t.,** tubo de ensayo, *m*

tuber /'tubər/ *n* tubérculo, *m.* **kind of tuber resembling a sweet potato** *Central America* malanga, *f*

tubercular /tʊ'bɜrkyələr/ *a* tuberculoso

tuberculosis /tʊ,bɜrkyə'loʊsɪs/ *n* tuberculosis, *f*

tuberose /'tub,roʊz/ *n* nardo, *m*, tuberosa, *f*

tubing /'tubɪŋ/ *n* tubería, *f*

tuck /tʌk/ *n Sew.* alforzar, *f*; pliegue, *m. vt* recoger; *Sew.* alforzar. *vi* hacer alforzas. **to t. in,** (in bed) arropar; *Inf.* tragar. **to t. under,** poner debajo; doblar. **to t. up,** (in bed) arropar; (skirt) sofaldar; (sleeves) arremangar

Tuesday /'tuzdei/ *n* martes, *m.* **Shrove T.,** martes de carnaval, *m*

tuft /tʌft/ *n* (bunch) manojo, *m*; (on the head) copete, moño, *m*, cresta, *f*; (tassel) borla, *f*; mechón, *m* **tufted** /'tʌftɪd/ *a Lat. Am.* copetudo

tug /tʌg/ *n* tirón, *m*; sacudida, *f*; (boat) remolcador, *m. vt* tirar de; halar; sacudir. *vi* tirar con fuerza. **to give a tug,** dar una sacudida. **tug of war,** *Lit.* lucha de la cuerda, *f*; *Fig.* estira y afloja, *msg*

tuition /tu'ɪʃən/ *n* (teaching) instrucción, enseñanza, *f*; lecciones, *f pl*; (fee) cuota, *f*

tulip /'tulɪp/ *n* tulipán, *m.* **t. wood,** palo de rosa, *m*

tulle /tul/ *n* tul, *m*

tumble /'tʌmbəl/ *n* caída, *f*; (somersault) tumbo, *m*; voltereta, *f. vi* caer; (acrobats) voltear, dar saltos. *vt* hacer caer; desarreglar. **to t. down,** venirse abajo, caer por. **to t. down,** ruinoso, destartalado. **to t. off,** caer de. **to t. out,** *vt* hacer salir; arrojar. *vi* salir apresuradamente. **to t. over,** *vt* tropezar con. *vi* volcarse. **to t. to,** *Inf.* caer en la cuenta

tumbler /'tʌmblər/ *n* (acrobat) volteador (-ra); vaso para beber, *m*

tumefaction /,tumə'fækʃən/ *n* tumefacción, *f*

tumor /'tumər/ *n* tumor, *m*

tumult /'tumʌlt/ *n* alboroto, tumulto, *m*; conmoción, agitación, *f*; confusión, *f*

tumultuous /tu'mʌltʃuəs/ *a* tumultuoso, alborotado; ruidoso; confuso; turbulento, violento

tumulus /'tumyələs/ *n* túmulo, *m*

tun /tʌn/ *n* tonel, *m*, cuba, *f*, *vt* entonelar, embarrilar

tuna /'tunə/ *n* atún, *m*

tune /tun/ *n* melodía, *f*; son, *m*; armonía, *f*; *Fig.* tono, *m*; *Inf.* suma, *f. vt Mus.* afinar, templar; *Radio.* sintonizar; (up, an engine) ajustar (un motor). *vi* (in) sintonizar el receptor; (up, *Mus.*) templar (afinar) los instrumentos. **in t.,** *Mus.* afinado, templado; *Fig.* armonioso; (agreement) de acuerdo, conforme. **out of t.,** *Mus.* desafinado, destemplado. **to be out of t.,** desentonar, discordar; *Fig.* no armonizar, no estar en armonía. **to go out of t.,** desafinar. **to put out of t.,** destemplar. **to change one's t.,** *Inf.* bajar el tono

tuneful /'tunfəl/ *a* melodioso

tunefully /'tunfəli/ *adv* melodiosamente, armoniosamente

tunefulness /'tunfəlnɪs/ *n* melodía, *f*

tuneless /'tunlɪs/ *a* disonante, discordante

tuner /'tunər/ *n* afinador, templador, *m*; *Radio.* sintonizador, *m*

tungsten /'tʌŋstən/ *n* tungsteno, *m*

tunic /'tunɪk/ *n* túnica, *f*, *Lat. Am. also* cusma, *f*

tuning /'tunɪŋ/ *n* afinación, *f*; *Radio.* sintonización, *f.* **t. fork,** diapasón normal, *m.* **t. key,** templador, *m*

Tunis /'tunɪs/ Túnez, *m*

Tunisian /tu'niʒən/ *a* and *n* tunecino (-na)

tunnel /'tʌnl/ *n* túnel, *m. vt* hacer (or construir) un túnel por. *vi* hacer un túnel

tunneling /'tʌnlɪŋ/ *n* construcción de túneles, *f*; horadación, *f*

turban /'tɜrbən/ *n* turbante, *m*

turbid /'tɜrbɪd/ *a* turbio; *Fig.* confuso. **to make t.,** enturbiar

turbine /'tɜrbɪn, -bain/ *n* turbina, *f*

turbulence /'tɜrbyələns/ *n* turbulencia, *f*; desorden, *m*; agitación, *f*

turbulent /'tɜrbyələnt/ *a* turbulento; alborotado; (stormy) borrascoso; agitado

turf /tɜrf/ *n* césped, *m*; (fuel) turba, *f*; (racing) carreras de caballos, *f pl*

turgid /'tɜrdʒɪd/ *a* turgente, hinchado; (of style) pomposo

turgidity /tər'dʒɪdɪti/ *n* turgencia, *f*; pomposidad, *f*

Turk /tɜrk/ *n* turco (-ca). **Turk's head,** (duster) deshollinador, *m*; *Naut.* cabeza de turco, *f*

Turkey /'tɜrki/ Turquía, *f*

turkey /'tɜrki/ *n* (cock) pavo, *m*; (hen) pava, *f*; **t. red,** rojo turco, *m*

Turkish /'tɜrkɪʃ/ *a* turco. *n* (language) turco, idioma turco, *m.* **T. bath,** baño turco, *m.* **T. slipper,** babucha, *f.* **T. towel,** toalla rusa, *f*

turmeric /'tɜrmərɪk/ *n* cúrcuma, *f.* **t. paper,** papel de cúrcuma, *m*

turmoil /'tɜrmɔil/ *n* alboroto, tumulto, desorden, *m*

turn /tɜrn/ *n* torcimiento, *m*; (twist) torcimiento, *m*; (bend) recodo, *m*, vuelta, *f*; (in a river) meandro, *m*; (in a road) viraje, *m*; (revolution) vuelta, revolución, *f*; (direction) dirección, *f*; (in spiral stair) espira, *f*; *Theat.* número, *m*; (change) cambio, *m*; vicisitud, *f*; (appearance) aspecto, *m*; (service) servicio, *m*; (nature) índole, naturaleza, *f*; (of phrase) giro, *m*, expresión, *f*; (walk) vuelta, *f*, paseo, *m*; (talent) talento, *m*. **a sharp t.,** (in a road) un viraje rápido. **at every t.,** a cada instante; en todas partes. **bad t.,** flaco servicio, *m.* **by turns,** por turnos. **good t.,** servicio, favor, *m.* **in its t.,** a su vez. **in t.,** sucesivamente. **Now it's my t.,** Ahora me toca a mí. **The affair has taken a new t.,** El asunto ha cambiado de aspecto. **turn of the century,** vuelta del siglo, *f*; **turn of the millennium,** vuelta del milenio, *f.* **to a t.,** *Cul.* a la perfección. **to have a t. for,** tener talento para. **to take turns at,** alternar en. **t.-table,** (railway) plataforma, *f*; (of a record player) disco giratorio, *m.* **t. up,** barahúnda, conmoción, *f*; (of trousers) dobladillo (del pantalón), *m*

turn /tɜrn/ *vt* (on a lathe) tornear; (revolve) dar vueltas a, girar; (a key, door handle, etc.) torcer; (the leaves of a book) hojear; (the brain) trastornar; (a screw) enroscar; (the stomach) revolver (el estómago), marear; (go round) doblar, dar la vuelta a; (change) cambiar, mudar; (translate) traducir, verter; (dissuade) disuadir; (deflect) desviar; (apply) adaptar; (direct, move) volver; (concentrate) dirigir; concentrar; (turn over) volver del revés al derecho; (upside-down) volver lo de arriba abajo; (make) hacer, volver; (make sour) volver agrio; (transform) transformar convertir; *Mil.* envolver. **He has turned thirty,** Ha cumplido los treinta. **He said it without turning a hair,** Lo dijo sin pestañear. **He turned his head,** Volvió la cabeza. **They have turned the corner,** Han doblado la esquina; *Fig.* Han pasado la crisis. **"Please t. over,"** «A la vuelta (de la página).» **to t. a deaf ear to,** no dar oídos a, no hacer caso de. **to t. one's hand to,** aplicarse a. **to t. to account,** sacar ventaja (de). **to t. adrift,** dejar a la merced de las olas; echar de casa, poner en la calle; abandonar. **to t. against,** causar aversión, hacer hostil. **to t. aside,** desviar. **to t. away,** despedir; rechazar; (the head, etc.) volver; desviar. **to t. back,** hacer volver; enviar de nuevo; (raise) alzar; (fold) doblar; (the clock) retrasar. **to t. down,** (gas) bajar; (a glass, etc.) poner boca abajo; (reject) rechazar; (a suitor) dar calabazas (a). **to t. from,** alejar de, desviar de. **to t. in,** doblar hacia dentro; entregar. **to t. in one's toes,** ser patizambo. **to t. inside out,** volver al revés. **to t. into,** (enter) entrar en; (change) cambiar en, transformar en; convertir en; (translate) traducir a. **to t. off,** (dismiss) despedir; (from) desviarse de, dejar; (light) apagar; (water) cortar; *Mech.* cerrar; (disconnect) desconectar; (avoid) evitar; (refuse) rechazar. **to t. off the tap,** (water, gas) cerrar la llave (del agua, del gas). **to t. on,** (light) encender; (water, gas, etc.) abrir la llave (del agua, del gas); (steam) dar (vapor); (electric current) establecer (la corriente eléctrica); (eyes) fijar. **to t. out,** (expel) expeler, echar; (dismiss) despedir; (animals) echar al campo; (produce) producir; (dress) vestir; (equip) equipar, guarnecer; (a light) apagar. **to t. over,** (the page) volver (la hoja); (transfer) ceder, traspasar; revolver; (upset) volcar; considerar, pensar. **to t. round,** dar vuelta (a); girar; (empty) descargar. **to t. up,** levantar; apuntar; hacia arriba; (the earth) labrar, cavar; (a glass) poner boca arriba; (one's sleeves, skirt) arremangar; (fold) doblar. **to t. up one's nose at,** mirar con desprecio. **to t. upon,** atacar, volverse contra, acometer; depender de, estribar en. **to t. upside down,** volver lo de arriba abajo; revolver; revolcar

turn /tɜrn/ *vi* (in a lathe) tornear; (revolve) girar, dar vueltas; (depend) depender (de); torcer; volverse; dar la vuelta; girar sobre los talones; dirigirse (a, hacia); (move) mudar de posición; (deviate) desviarse (de); (be changed) convertirse (en); (become) hacerse, venir a ser; (begin) meterse (a); (take to) dedicarse a; (seek help) acudir; (change behavior) enmendarse, corregirse; (the stomach) revolver (el estómago); (go sour) agriarse, avinagrarse; (rebel) sublevarse. **He turned to the left,** Dio la vuelta a la izquierda; Torció hacia la izquierda. **My head turns,** (with giddiness) Se me va la cabeza. **to t. about,** voltearse, dar la vuelta. **to t. against,** coger aversión (a), disgustarse con; volverse hostil (a). **to t. aside,** desviarse; dejar el camino. **to t. away,** volver la cabeza; apartarse; alejarse. **to t. back,** volver atrás; volver de nuevo; retroceder; volver sobre sus pasos. **to t. down,** doblarse; reducirse. **to t. from,** alejarse de; apartarse de, huir de. **to t. in,** doblarse hacia dentro; (retire) acostarse. **to t. into,** transformarse en; convertirse en. **to t. off,** (depart from) desviarse (de); (fork) torcer, bifurcarse. **to t. out,** estar vuelto hacia fuera; (leave home) salir de casa; (rise) levantarse (de la cama); (arrive) llegar, presentarse; (attend) asistir, acudir; (result) resultar. **to t. over,** mudar de posición, revolverse; (upset) voltearse, volcarse. **to t. round,** girar; volverse; cambiar de frente; cambiar de dirección, dar la vuelta; (*Auto., Aer.*) virar; (change views) cambiar de opinión; (change sides) cambiar de partido. **to t. round and round,** dar vueltas, girar. **to t. to,** (apply to) acudir a; (begin) ponerse a; (become) convertirse en; (face) dirigirse hacia; (address) dirigirse a. **to t. up,** (crop up), surgir, aparecer; (arrive) llegar; (happen) acontecer; (be found again) volver a hallarse, reaparecer; (cards) venir; (of hats) levantar el ala; (of hair, etc.) doblarse. **His nose turns up,** Tiene la nariz respingona

turncoat /'tɜrnˌkout/ *n* desertor (-ra), renegado (-da). **to become a t.,** volver la casaca

turned-up /'tɜrnd 'ʌp/ *a* (of hats) con el ala levantada; (of noses) respingona

turner /'tɜrnər/ *n* (craftsman) tornero, torneador, *m*

turning /'tɜrnɪŋ/ *n* (bend) vuelta, *f*; (turnery) tornería, *f*; (of milk, etc.) agrura, *f*; *pl* **turnings,** *Sew.* ensanche, *m*. **t.-point,** punto decisivo, *m*, crisis, *f*. **t. yellow,** *Lat. Am.* amarilloso

turnip /'tɜrnɪp/ *n* nabo, *m*. **t. field,** nabar, *m*

turnover /'tɜrnˌouvər/ *n Com.* ventas, *f pl*; *Cul.* pastelillo, *m*

turnpike /'tɜrnˌpaik/ *n* barrera de portazgo, *f*

turnstile /'tɜrnˌstail/ *n* torniquete, *m*

turpentine /'tɜrpənˌtain/ *n* aguarrás, *m*, trementina, *f*

turpitude /'tɜrpɪˌtud/ *n* infamia, maldad, *f*

turquoise /'tɜrkɔiz, -kwɔiz/ *n* turquesa, *f*

turret /'tɜrɪt/ *n* torrecilla, almenilla, *f*; *Naut.* torre blindada, *f*

turreted /'tɜrɪtɪd/ *a* con torres, guarnecido de torres; en forma de torre

turtle /'tɜrtl/ *n* (dove) tórtolo (-la); (sea) tortuga de mar, *f*. **to turn t.,** voltearse patas arriba; *Naut.* zozobrar. **t. soup,** sopa de tortuga, *f*

tusk /tʌsk/ *n* colmillo, *m*

tussle /'tʌsəl/ *n* lucha, *f*; agarrada, *f*. *vi* luchar, pelear; tener una agarrada

tutelage /'tutlɪdʒ/ *n* tutela, *f*

tutelar /'tutlər/ *a* tutelar

tutor /'tutər/ *n* (private) ayo, *m*; profesor (-ra); (Roman law) tutor, *m*; (supervisor of studies) preceptor. *vt* enseñar, instruir. *vi* dar lecciones particulares, ser profesor, dar clases

tutorial /tu'tɔriəl/ *n* (university) seminario, *m*; (private) clase particular, *f*

tutoring /'tutərɪŋ/ *n* enseñanza, instrucción, *f*

twaddle /'twɒdl/ *n* disparates, *m pl*, tonterías, patrañas, *f pl*

twain /twein/ *a* and *n* dos, *m*

twang /twæŋ/ *n* punteado de una cuerda, *m*; (of a guitar) zumbido, *m*; (in speech) gangueo, *m*. *vt* puntear; (las cuerdas de un instrumento) rasguear. *vi* zumbar. **to speak with a t.,** hablar con una voz gangosa

tweak /twik/ *n* pellizco, *m*; sacudida, *f*, tirón, *m*. *vt* pellizcar; sacudir, tirar

tweed /twid/ *n* mezcla, *f*, cheviot, *m*

tweezers /'twizərz/ *n pl* pinzas, tenacillas, *f pl*

twelfth /twelfθ/ *a* duodécimo; (of the month) (el) doce; (of monarchs) doce. *n* duodécimo, *m*; (part) dozavo, *m*, duodécima parte, *f*. **T.-night,** Día de Reyes, *m*, Epifanía, *f*

twelve /twelv/ *a* and *n* doce *m*; (of age) doce años, *m pl*. **t. o'clock,** las doce; (mid-day) mediodía, *m*; (midnight) media noche, *f*, las doce de la noche. **t.-syllabled,** dodecasílabo

twentieth /'twentiɪθ/ *a* vigésimo; (of the month) (el) veinte; (of monarchs) veinte, *n* vigésimo, *m*; (part) vientavo, *m*, vigésima parte, *f*

twenty /'twenti/ *a* veinte; (of age) veinte años, *m pl*, *n* veinte, *m*; (score) veintena, *f*. **t.-first,** vigésimo primero; (of date) (el) veintiuno, *m*, (In modern Spanish the ordinals above *décimo* "tenth" are generally replaced by the cardinals, e.g. *the twenty-ninth chapter,* el capítulo veintinueve.)

twice /twais/ *adv* dos veces. **t. as many** or **as much,** el doble

twiddle /'twɪdl/ *vt* jugar con; hacer girar. *vi* girar. *n* vuelta, *f*. **to t. one's thumbs,** dar vuelta a los pulgares, estar mano sobre mano

twig /twɪg/ *n* ramita, pequeña rama, *f*

twilight /'twaiˌlait/ *n* crepúsculo, *m*; media luz, *f*. *a* crepuscular. **in the t.,** en el crepúsculo; en la media luz. **t. sleep,** parto sin dolor, *m*

twin /twɪn/ *a* gemelo, mellizo; doble. *n* gemelo (-la), mellizo (-za); (of objects) pareja, *f*, par, *m*. **t.-engined,** bimotor. **t. screw,** (*Naut. Aer.*) de dos hélices

twine /twain/ *n* bramante, cordel, *m*; guita, *f*. *vt* enroscar; (weave) tejer; (encircle) ceñir; (round, about) abrazar. *vi* (of plants) trepar; entrelazarse; (wind) serpentear

twinge /twɪndʒ/ *n* punzada, *f*, dolor agudo, *m*; *Fig.* remordimiento, tormento, *m*. *vi* causar un dolor agudo

twining /'twainɪŋ/ *a Bot.* trepante, voluble. **t. plant,** planta enredadera (or trepante), *f*

twinkle /'twɪŋkəl/ *vi* centellear, chispear, titilar; (of eyes) brillar; (of feet) moverse rápidamente, bailar. *n* (in the eye) chispa, *f*

twinkling /'twɪŋklɪŋ/ *n* centelleo, *m*; titilación, *f*; (of the eye) brillo, *m*; (glimpse) vislumbre, *m*; *Fig.* instante, momento, *m*. *a* titilante, centelleador. **in a t.,** en un dos por tres. **in the t. of an eye,** en un abrir y cerrar de ojos

twin-tailed comet /'twɪnˌteild/ *n* ceratias, *m*

twirl /twɜrl/ *n* rotación, vuelta, *f*; pirueta, *f*. *vi* hacer girar; voltear; torcer; (a stick, etc.) dar vueltas (a). *vi* girar, dar vueltas; dar piruetas

twirp /twɜrp/ *n Inf.* renacuajo, *m*

twist /twɪst/ *n* (skein) mecha, *f*; trenza, *f*; (yarn) torzal, *m* (of tobacco) rollo, *m*; (of bread) rosca de pan, *f*; (act of twisting) torcimiento, *m*, torsión, *f*; (in a road, etc.) recodo, *m*, curva, vuelta, *f*; (pull) sacudida, *f*; (contortion) regate, esguince, *m*; (winding stair) espira, *f*; (in ball games) efecto, *m*; (in a person's nature) peculiaridad, *f;* falta de franqueza, *f;* (to words) interpretación, *f. vt* torcer; enroscar; (plait) trenzar; (wring) estrujar; (weave) tejer; (encircle) ceñir; (a stick, etc.) dar vueltas a; (of hands) crispar; (distort) interpretar mal, torcer. *vi* torcerse; enroscarse; (wind) serpentear; dar vueltas; (coil) ensortijarse; (writhe) undular, retorcerse; (of a stair) dar vueltas

twisted /'twɪstɪd/ *a* torcido, *Mexico* chueco; (of persons) contrahecho

twisting /'twɪstɪŋ/ *n* torcimiento, *m;* torcedura, *f;* serpenteo, *m;* (interlacing) entrelazamiento, *m. a* sinuoso, serpenteado

twitch /twɪtʃ/ *n* sacudida, *f,* tirón, *m;* (nervous) contracción nerviosa, *f. vt* tirar bruscamente, quitar rápidamente; agarrar; (ears, etc.) mover; (hands) crispar, retorcer. *vi* crisparse; (of ears, nose) moverse

twitching /'twɪtʃɪŋ/ *n* sacudida, *f;* (contraction) crispamiento, *m,* contracción nerviosa, *f;* (pain) punzada, *f;* (of conscience) remordimiento, *m*

twitter /'twɪtər/ *n* piada, *f,* gorjeo, *m. vi* piar, gorjear

two /tu/ *a* and *n* dos, *m;* (of the clock) (las) dos, *f pl;* (of age) dos años, *m pl. a* de dos. **in two,** en dos partes. **in two's,** de dos en dos. **one or two,** uno o dos; algunos, *m pl;* algunas, *f pl.* **two against two,** dos a dos. **two by two,** de dos en dos, a pares. **Two can live as cheaply as one,** Donde come uno comen dos. **to put two and two together,** atar cabos. **two-edged,** de dos filos. **two-faced,** de dos caras; *Fig.* de dos haces. **to be two-faced,** hacer a dos caras. **two-headed,** de dos cabezas; bicéfalo. **two hundred,** *a* and *n* doscientos, *m.* **two hundredth,** *a* ducentésimo. *n* ducentésima parte, *f;* doscientos, *m.* **two-legged,** bípedo. **two-ply,** de dos hilos. **two-seater,** *a* de dos asientos. **two-speed gear box,** cambio de marcha de dos velocidades, *m.* **two-step,** paso doble, *m.* **two of a kind,** (well-matched) tal para cual. **two-way switch,** *Elec.* interruptor de dos direcciones, *m*

twofold /*a.* 'tu,fould; *adv.* -'fould/ *a* doble. *adv* doblemente, dos veces

twosome /'tusəm/ *n* partido de dos, *m*

two swords' theory *n* teoría de los dos gladios, *f*

tying /'taiɪŋ/ *n* ligadura, *f;* atadura, *f*

tympanum /'tɪmpənəm/ *n* (*Anat., Archit.*) tímpano, *m*

type /taip/ *n* tipo, *m; Print.* carácter, *m,* letra de imprenta, *f,* tipo, *m.. vt* and *vi* escribir a máquina. **t. case,** caja de imprenta, *f.* **t. founder,** fundidor de letras de imprenta, *m.* **t. foundry,** fundición de tipos, *f.* **t.-setter,** cajista, *mf* **t.-setting,** composición tipográfica, *f*

typewrite /'taip,rait/ *vt* and *vi* escribir a máquina

typewriter /'taip,raitər/ *n* máquina de escribir, *f*

typewriting /'taip,raitɪŋ/ *n* mecanografía, *f, a* mecanográfico

typewritten /'taip,rɪtn/ *a* escrito a máquina

typhoid /'taifɔid/ *n* tifoidea, fiebre tifoidea, *f*

typhoon /tai'fun/ *n* tifón, *m*

typhus /'taifəs/ *n* tifus, tabardillo pintado, *m*

typical /'tɪpɪkəl/ *a* típico, característico; simbólico. **t. Mexican dish,** (of food) antojito, *m*

typify /'tɪpə,fai/ *vt* simbolizar, representar; ser ejemplo de

typist /'taipɪst/ *n* mecanografista, *mf;* mecanógrafo (-fa)

typographer /tai'pɒgrəfər/ *n* tipógrafo, *m*

typographic /,taipə'græfɪk/ *a* tipográfico

typography /tai'pɒgrəfi/ *n* tipografía, *f*

tyrannical /tɪ'rænɪkəl/ *a* tiránico, despótico

tyrannization /,tɪrənə'zeiʃən/ *n* tiranización, *f*

tyrannize /'tɪrə,naiz/ *vi* tiranizar

tyranny /'tɪrəni/ *n* tiranía, *f,* despotismo, *m*

tyrant /'tairənt/ *n* déspota, *m,* tirano (-na)

Tyre /taiᵊr/ Tiro, *m*

tyro /'tairou/ *n* novicio (-cia), tirón (-ona), advenedizo (-za), *mf*

Tyrol, the /tɪ'roul/ el Tirol

U

U /yu/ *n* (letter) u, *f.* **U-boat,** submarino, *m.* **u-shaped,** en forma de U

ubiquitous /yu'bɪkwɪtəs/ *a* ubicuo, omnipresente

ubiquity /yu'bɪkwɪti/ *n* ubicuidad, omnipresencia, *f*

udder /'ʌdər/ *n* ubre, teta, mama, *f*

ugh /ʊx, ʌg/ *interj* ¡uf!

ugliness /'ʌglinɪs/ *n* fealdad, *f;* (moral) perversidad, *f;* (of a situation) peligro, *m,* lo difícil

ugly /'ʌgli/ *a* feo, *Lat. Am. also* feroz; (morally) repugnante, asqueroso, perverso; (of a situation) peligroso, difícil; (of a wound) grave, profundo; (of a look) amenazador; *Inf.* desagradable; (of weather) borrascoso. **to make u.,** afear, hacer feo

Ukraine /yu'krein/ Ucrania, *f*

Ukrainian /yu'kreiniən/ *a* and *n* ucranio (-ia)

ukulele /,yukə'leili/ *n Mus.* ucelele, *m*

ulcer /'ʌlsər/ *n* úlcera, *f, Lat. Am. also* lacra

ulcerate /'ʌlsə,reit/ *vt* ulcerar. *vi* ulcerarse

ulceration /,ʌlsə'reiʃən/ *n* ulceración, *f*

ulcerous /'ʌlsərəs/ *a* ulceroso

ulterior /ʌl'tɪriər/ *a* ulterior; (of place) ulterior; (of time) posterior, ulterior; (of motives) interesado, oculto; **u. motive,** segunda intención, *f*

ultimate /'ʌltəmɪt/ *a* último; fundamental, esencial

ultimately /'ʌltəmɪtli/ *adv* por fin, al final; esencialmente

ultimatum /,ʌltə'meitəm/ *n* ultimátum, *m*

ultimo /'ʌltə,mou/ *adv* del mes anterior

ultra /'ʌltrə/ *a* exagerado, extremo. *prefix* ultra-. **u-red,** ultrarrojo. **u.-violet,** ultravioleta

ultramarine /,ʌltrəmə'rin/ *a* ultramarino. *n* azul de ultramar, *m*

ultramontane /,ʌltrəmɒn'tein/ *a* ultramontano

ululation /,ʌlyə'leiʃən/ *n* ululación, *f,* ululato, *m*

umbilical /ʌm'bɪlɪkəl/ *a* umbilical

umbilicus /ʌm'bɪlɪkəs/ *n* ombligo, *m*

umbra /'ʌmbrə/ *n Astron.* cono de sombra, *m*

umbrage /'ʌmbrɪdʒ/ *n Poet.* sombra, *f;* resentimiento, enfado, *m.* **to take u.,** ofenderse, resentirse

umbrella /ʌm'brelə/ *n* paraguas, *m.* **u. maker,** paragüero (-ra). **u. shop,** paragüería, *f.* **u. stand,** paragüero, *m*

umpire /'ʌmpaiᵊr/ *n Sports.* árbitro, *m; Law.* juez arbitrador, tercero en discordia, *m. vt* arbitrar

un- *prefix* Used before adjectives, adverbs, abstract nouns, verbs and translated in Spanish by **in-, des-, nada, no, poco, sin,** as well as in other ways

unabashed /,ʌnə'bæʃt/ *a* desvergonzado, descarado, insolente; (calm) sereno, sosegado

unabashedly /,ʌnə'bæʃɪdli/ *adv* sin rubor

unabated /,ʌnə'beitɪd/ *a* no disminuido; cabal, entero

unabbreviated /,ʌnə'brivi,eitɪd/ *a* íntegro, sin abreviar

unable /ʌn'eibəl/ *a* incapaz, impotente; (physical defect) imposibilitado. **to be u. to,** no poder, serle a uno imposible. **to be u. to control,** no poder controlar

unabridged /,ʌnə'brɪdʒd/ *a.* See **unabbreviated**

unaccented /ʌn'æksɛntɪd/ *a* sin acento

unacceptability /,ʌnæk,sɛptə'bɪlɪti/ *n* lo inaceptable

unacceptable /,ʌnæk,sɛptəbəl/ *a* inaceptable

unaccepted /,ʌnæk,sɛptɪd/ *a* rechazado, no aceptado

unaccommodating /,ʌnə'kɒmə,deitɪŋ/ *a* poco complaciente, nada servicial

unaccompanied /,ʌnə'kʌmpənid/ *a* solo, sin compañía; *Mus.* sin acompañamiento

unaccomplished /,ʌnə'kɒmplɪʃt/ *a* incompleto, sin terminar, inacabado; (not clever) sin talento

unaccountability /,ʌnə,kauntə'bɪlɪti/ *n* lo inexplicable; falta de responsabilidad, irresponsabilidad, *f*

unaccountable /,ʌnə'kauntəbəl/ *a* inexplicable; irresponsable

unaccountably /ˌʌnəˈkauntəbli/ *adv* inexplicablemente, extrañamente

unaccredited /ˌʌnəˈkrɛdɪtɪd/ *a* no acreditado, extraoficial

unaccustomed /ˌʌnəˈkʌstəmd/ *a* no habituado; (unusual) desacostumbrado, insólito, inusitado

unacknowledged /ˌʌnækˈnɒlɪdʒd/ *a* no reconocido; (of letter) sin contestación, por contestar; no correspondido, sin devolver; (of crimes, etc.) inconfeso, no declarado

unacquainted /ˌʌnəˈkweintɪd/ *a* que no conoce; que desconoce, que ignora; no habituado. **to be u. with,** no conocer; ignorar; no estar acostumbrado a

unadaptable /ˌʌnəˈdæptəbəl/ *a* inadaptable (also of persons)

unadorned /ˌʌnəˈdɔrnd/ *a* sin adorno sencillo, que no tiene adornos

unadulterated /ˌʌnəˈdʌltəˌreitɪd/ *a* sin mezcla, no adulterado, natural; genuino, verdadero; puro

unadventurous /ˈʌnædˈvɛntʃərəs/ *a* nada aventurero, que no busca aventuras, tímido; tranquilo, sin incidente

unadvisability /ˌʌnædˌvaizəˈbɪlɪti/ *n* imprudencia, *f*; inoportunidad, *f*

unadvisable /ˌʌnædˌvaizəˈbəl/ *a* imprudente; inoportuno, no conveniente

unadvisedly /ˌʌnædˌvaizɪdli/ *adv* imprudentemente

unaffected /ˌʌnəˈfɛktɪd/ *a* natural, llano, sin melindres; impasible; genuino, sincero. **u. by,** no afectado por

unaffectedly /ˌʌnəˈfɛktɪdli/ *adv* sin afectación

unaffectedness /ˌʌnəˈfɛktɪdnɪs/ *n* naturalidad, sencillez, *f*; sinceridad, franqueza, *f*

unaffiliated /ˌʌnəˈfiliˌeitɪd/ *a* no afiliado

unafraid /ˌʌnəˈfreid/ *a* sin temor

unaided /ʌnˈeidɪd/ *a* sin ayuda, solo a solas

unalloyed /ˌʌnəˈlɔid/ *a* sin mezcla, puro

unalterability /ʌnˌɔltərəˈbɪlɪti/ *n* lo inalterable; constancia, *f*

unalterable /ʌnˈɔltərəbəl/ *a* inalterable; invariable, constante

unambiguous /ˌʌnæmˈbɪgyuəs/ *a* no ambiguo, nada dudoso, claro

unambitious /ˌʌnæmˈbɪʃəs/ *a* sin ambición; modesto

unamusing /ˌʌnəˈmyuzɪŋ/ *a* nada divertido

unanimity /ˌyunəˈnɪmɪti/ *n* unanimidad, *f*

unanimous /yuˈnænəməs/ *a* unánime

unanimously /yuˈnænəməsli/ *adv* unánimemente, por unanimidad. **carried a.,** adoptado por unanimidad

unanswerability /ʌnˌænsərəˈbɪlɪti/ *n* imposibilidad de negar, *f*; lo irrefutable

unanswerable /ʌnˈænsərəbəl/ *a* incontestable, incontrovertible, incontrastable, irrefutable

unanswered /ʌnˈænsərd/ *a* no contestado, sin contestar; (unrequited) no correspondido

unapparent /ˌʌnəˈpærənt/ *a* no aparente

unappealable /ˌʌnəˈpiləbəl/ *a* inapelable

unappeasable /ˌʌnəˈpizəbəl/ *a* implacable

unappeased /ˌʌnəˈpizd/ *a* no satisfecho; implacable

unappetizing /ʌnˈæpɪˌtaizɪŋ/ *a* no apetitoso; (unattractive) repugnante, feo

unappreciated /ˌʌnəˈpriʃiˌeitɪd/ *a* desestimado, no apreciado, tenido en poco; (misunderstood) mal comprendido

unapproachable /ˌʌnəˈproutʃəbəl/ *a* inaccesible

unapproachableness /ˌʌnəˈproutʃəbəlnɪs/ *n* inaccesibilidad, *f*

unappropriated /ˌʌnəˈproupriˌeitɪd/ *a* no concedido; libre

unapproved /ˌʌnəˈpruvd/ *a* sin aprobar, no aprobado

unarm /ʌnˈɑrm/ *vt* desarmar. *vi* desarmarse, quitarse las armas

unarmed /ʌnˈɑrmd/ *a* desarmado; indefenso; *Zool.*, *Bot.* inerme

unarranged /ˌʌnəˈreindʒd/ *a* no arreglado, sin clasificar; (accidental) fortuito, casual

unartistic /ˌʌnɑrˈtɪstɪk/ *a* no artístico

unascertainable /ˌʌnæsərˈteinəbəl/ *a* no verificable

unashamed /ˌʌnəˈʃeimd/ *a* sin vergüenza; tranquilo, sereno; insolente, descarado

unasked /ʌnˈæskt/ *a* sin pedir; no solicitado; espontáneo; (uninvited) no convidado

unassailable /ˌʌnəˈseiləbəl/ *a* inexpugnable; irrefutable; incontestable

unassisted /ˌʌnəˈsɪstɪd/ *a.* See **unaided**

unassuming /ˌʌnəˈsumɪŋ/ *a* modesto, sin pretensiones

unattached /ˌʌnəˈtætʃt/ *a* suelto; *Law.* no embargado; *Mil.* de reemplazo; independiente

unattainable /ˌʌnəˈteinəbəl/ *a* inasequible, irrealizable

unattainableness /ˌʌnəˈteinəbəlnɪs/ *n* imposibilidad de alcanzar (or realizar), *f*; inaccesibilidad

unattended /ˌʌnəˈtɛndɪd/ *a* solo, sin acompañamiento; (of ill person) sin tratamiento; (of entertainment, etc.) no concurrido

unattested /ˌʌnəˈtɛstɪd/ *a* sin atestación

unattractive /ˌʌnəˈtræktɪv/ *a* poco atrayente, desagradable, antipático, feo

unattractiveness /ˌʌnəˈtræktɪvnɪs/ *n* fealdad, falta de hermosura, *f*; lo desagradable

unauthentic /ˌʌnɔˈθɛntɪk/ *a* no auténtico, sin autenticidad; apócrifo

unauthorized /ʌnˈɔθəˌraizd/ *a* no autorizado

unavailable /ˌʌnəˈveiləbəl/ *a* inaprovechable

unavailing /ˌʌnəˈveilɪŋ/ *a* inútil, vano

unavenged /ˌʌnəˈvɛndʒd/ *a* no vengado, sin castigo

unavoidable /ˌʌnəˈvɔidəbəl/ *a* inevitable, preciso, necesario. **to be u.,** no poder evitarse, no tener remedio

unavoidableness /ˌʌnəˈvɔidəbəlnɪs/ *n* inevitabilidad, necesidad, *f*

unavoidably /ˌʌnəˈvɔidəbli/ *adv* irremediablemente

unaware /ˌʌnəˈwɛər/ *a* ignorante; inconsciente. **to be u. of,** ignorar, desconocer; no darse cuenta de

unawareness /ˌʌnəˈwɛərnɪs/ *n* ignorancia, *f*, desconocimiento, *m*; inconsciencia, *f*

unawares /ˌʌnəˈwɛərz/ *adv* (by mistake) sin querer, inadvertidamente; (unprepared) de sobresalto, de improviso, inopinadamente. **He caught me u.,** Me cogió desprevenido

unbalance /ʌnˈbæləns/ *vt* desequilibrar, hacer perder el equilibrio; *Fig.* trastornar

unbalanced /ʌnˈbælənst/ *a* desequilibrado; *Fig.* trastornado; *Com.* no balanceado

unbaptized /ʌnˈbæptaizd/ *a* no bautizado, sin bautizar

unbar /ʌnˈbɑr/ *vt* desatrancar; *Fig.* abrir

unbearable /ʌnˈbɛərəbəl/ *a* intolerable, insufrible, inaguantable, inllevable, insoportable

unbearably /ʌnˈbɛərəbli/ *adv* insoportablemente

unbeatable /ʌnˈbitəbəl/ *a* inmejorable

unbeaten /ʌnˈbitn/ *a* (of paths) no frecuentado, no pisado; (of armies) no derrotado, no batido; invicto

unbecoming /ˌʌnbɪˈkʌmɪŋ/ *a* impropio, inapropiado, inconveniente; indecoroso, indigno; indecente; (of clothes) que no va bien, que sienta mal

unbelief /ˌʌnbɪˈlif/ *n* incredulidad, *f*

unbelievable /ˌʌnbɪˈlivəbəl/ *a* increíble

unbelievably /ˌʌnbɪˈlivəbli/ *adv* increíblemente

unbeliever /ˌʌnbɪˈlivər/ *n* incrédulo (-la), descreído (-da)

unbeloved /ˌʌnbɪˈlʌvd/ *a* no amado

unbend /ʌnˈbɛnd/ *vt* desencorvar, enderezar; entretenerse, descansar; (*Naut.* of sails) desenvergar; (*Naut.* of cables) desamarrar. *vi* enderezarse; mostrarse afable

unbending /ʌnˈbɛndɪŋ/ *a* inflexible, rígido, tieso; *Fig.* inexorable, inflexible, duro, terco; (amiable) afable, jovial

unbiased /ʌnˈbaiəst/ *a* imparcial, ecuánime

unbidden /ʌnˈbɪdn/ *a* espontáneo; (uninvited) no convidado, no invitado

unbind /ʌnˈbaind/ *vt* desligar, desatar; (bandages) desvendar; (books) desencuadernar

unbleached /ʌnˈblitʃt/ *a* crudo, sin blanquear

unblemished /ʌnˈblɛmɪʃt/ *a* no manchado, sin mancha, inmaculado, puro

unblessed /ʌn'blest/ a no bendecido, no consagrado; (accursed) maldito; (unhappy) desdichado

unblushing /ʌn'blʌʃɪŋ/ a desvergonzado, insolente

unbolt /ʌn'boult/ vt descerrojar, desempernar

unborn /ʌn'bɔrn/ a sin nacer, no nacido todavía; venidero

unbosom /ʌn'buzəm/ vt confesar, declarar. **to u. oneself**, abrir su pecho (a) or (con)

unbought /ʌn'bɔt/ a no comprado; gratuito, libre; (not bribed) no sobornado

unbound /ʌn'baund/ a suelto, libre; (of books) en rama, no encuadernado

unbounded /ʌn'baundɪd/ a ilimitado, infinito; inmenso

unbowed /ʌn'baud/ a erguido; no encorvado; (undefeated) invicto

unbreakable /ʌn'breikəbəl/ a irrompible, inquebrantable

unbridled /ʌn'braidld/ a desenfrenado, violento; licencioso

unbroken /ʌn'broukən/ a no quebrantado, intacto, entero; continuo, incesante; no interrumpido; (of soil) virgen; (of a horse) indomado; inviolado; (of the spirit) indómito; (of a record) no batido

unbuckle /ʌn'bʌkəl/ vt deshebillar

unburden /ʌn'bɜrdn̩/ vt descargar; aliviar. **to u. oneself**, (express one's feelings) desahogarse

unburied /ʌn'bɛrid/ a insepulto

unburnt /ʌn'bɜrnt/ a no quemado; incombusto

unbusinesslike /ʌn'bɪznɪs,laik/ a informal; poco comercial, descuidado

unbutton /ʌn'bʌtn̩/ vt desabrochar, desabotonar

uncalled /ʌn'kɔld/ a no llamado, no invitado. **u.-for**, impertinente; innecesario

uncannily /ʌn'kænli/ adv misteriosamente

uncanniness /ʌn'kænɪnɪs/ n lo misterioso

uncanny /ʌn'kænɪ/ a misterioso, horroroso, pavoroso

uncared-for /ʌn'kɛərd,fɔr/ a abandonado, desatendido, desamparado

uncarpeted /ʌn'karpɪtɪd/ a sin alfombra

uncaught /ʌn'kɔt/ a no prendido, libre

unceasing /ʌn'sisɪŋ/ a continuo, incesante, sin cesar, constante

unceasingly /ʌn'sisɪŋli/ adv incesantemente, sin cesar

uncensored /ʌn'sensərd/ a no censurado

unceremonious /ˌʌnsɛrə'mouniəs/ a sin ceremonia, familiar; descortés, brusco

unceremoniousness /ˌʌnsɛrɛ'mouniəsnɪs/ n falta de ceremonia, familiaridad, f; incivilidad, descortesía, f

uncertain /ʌn'sɜrtn̩/ a incierto, dudoso; inseguro; precario; (hesitant) indeciso, vacilante, irresoluto

uncertainly /ʌn'sɜrtn̩li/ adv inciertamente

uncertainty /ʌn'sɜrtn̩ti/ n incertidumbre, duda, f; inseguridad, f; irresolución, f

uncertificated /ˌʌnsər'tɪfɪ,keitɪd/ a sin certificado (of teachers, etc.) sin título

uncertified /ʌn'sɜrtə,faid/ a sin garantía; no garantizado; (of lunatics) sin certificar

unchain /ʌn'tʃein/ vt desencadenar

unchallenged /ʌn'tʃæləndʒd/ a incontestable

unchangeable /ʌn'tʃeindʒəbəl/ a invariable, inalterable, inmutable

unchangeableness /ʌn'tʃeindʒəbəlnɪs/ n invariabilidad, inalterabilidad, f

unchanging /ʌn'tʃeindʒɪŋ/ a inmutable, invariable

uncharitable /ʌn'tʃærɪtəbəl/ a nada caritativo, duro; intolerante, intransigente

uncharitableness /ʌn'tʃærɪtəbəlnɪs/ n falta de caridad, f; intolerancia, intransigencia

uncharitably /ʌn'tʃærɪtəbli/ adv sin caridad; con intolerancia

unchaste /ʌn'tʃeist/ a incasto, incontinente; deshonesto, impuro, lascivo

unchecked /ʌn'tʃɛkt/ a desenfrenado; (unproved) no comprobado; Com. no confrontado

unchivalrous /ʌn'ʃɪvəlrəs/ a nada galante, nada caballeroso

uncircumcised /ʌn'sɜrkəm,saizd/ a incircunciso

uncircumscribed /ʌn'sɜrkəm,skraibd/ a incircunscripto

uncivil /ʌn'sɪvəl/ a descortés, incivil

uncivilizable /ʌn'sɪvə,laizəbəl/ a reacio a la civilización

uncivilized /ʌn'sɪvə,laizd/ a no civilizado, bárbaro, salvaje, inculto

uncivilly /ʌn'sɪvəli/ adv descortésmente

unclad /ʌn'klæd/ a sin vestir; desnudo

unclasp /ʌn'klæsp/ vt (jewelry) desengarzar; desabrochar; (of hands) soltar, separar

unclassifiable /ʌn'klæsə,faiəbəl/ a inclasificable

unclassified /ʌn'klæsə,faid/ a sin clasificar

uncle /'ʌŋkəl/ n tío, m; (pawnbroker) prestamista, m

unclean /ʌn'klin/ a sucio, puerco, inmundo; deseaseado; impuro, obsceno; (ritually) poluto

uncleanliness /ʌn'klɛnlɪnɪs/ n suciedad, porquería, f; desaseo, m; falta de limpieza, f

uncleanly /ʌn'klɛnli/ a sucio, puerco; desaseado

uncleanness /ʌn'klɪnnɪs/ n suciedad, f; impureza, obscenidad, inmoralidad, f

unclench /ʌn'klɛntʃ/ vt (of hands) abrir

unclouded /ʌn'klaudɪd/ a sin nubes, despejado, claro

uncoil /ʌn'kɔil/ vt desarrollar. vi desovillarse; (of snakes) desanillarse

uncollected /ˌʌnkə'lɛktɪd/ a disperso; no cobrado; (in confusion) confuso, desordenado

uncolored /ʌn'kʌlərd/ a incoloro; Fig. imparcial, objetivo, sencillo

uncombed /ʌn'koumd/ a despeinado, sin peinar

uncomfortable /ʌn'kʌmftəbəl/ a incómodo; (anxious) intranquilo, inquieto, desasosegado, preocupado; (awkward) molesto, difícil, desagradable. **to be u.**, (people) estar incómodo; (anxious) estar preocupado; (of things) ser incómodo

uncomfortableness /ʌn'kʌmfərtəbəlnɪs/ n incomodidad, f; malestar, m; intranquilidad, preocupación, f; dificultad, f; lo desagradable

uncomfortably /ʌn'kʌmfərtəbli/ adv incómodamente; intranquilamente; desagradablemente

uncomforted /ʌn'kʌmfərtɪd/ a desconsolado, sin consuelo

uncommercial /ˌʌnkə'mɜrʃəl/ a no comercial

uncommon /ʌn'kɒmən/ a poco común, extraordinario, singular, raro, extraño; infrecuente; insólito

uncommonly /ʌn'kɒmənli/ adv extraordinariamente, muy; infrecuentemente, raramente

uncommonness /ʌn'kɒmənnɪs/ n infrecuencia, rareza, f; singularidad, f

uncommunicative /ˌʌnkə'myunɪkətɪv/ a reservado, poco expresivo

uncommunicativeness /ˌʌnkə'myunɪkətɪvnɪs/ n reserva, f

uncomplaining /ˌʌnkəm'pleinɪŋ/ a resignado, que no se queja

uncomplainingly /ˌʌnkəm'pleinɪŋli/ adv con resignación

uncompliant /ˌʌnkəm'plaiant/ a sordo, inflexible

uncomplicated /ʌn'kɒmplɪ,keitɪd/ a sencillo, sin complicaciones

uncomplimentary /ˌʌnkɒmplə'mɛntəri/ a descortés, poco halagüeño, ofensivo

uncompromising /ʌn'kɒmprə,maizɪŋ/ a inflexible, estricto, intolerante; irreconciliable

unconcealed /ˌʌnkən'sild/ a no oculto; abierto

unconcern /ˌʌnkən'sɜrn/ n indiferencia, frialdad, f, desapego, m; (lack of interest) apatía, despreocupación, f; (nonchalance) desenfado, m, frescura, f

unconcerned /ˌʌnkən'sɜrnd/ a indiferente, frío, despegado; apático, despreocupado; desenfadado, fresco

unconcernedly /ˌʌnkən'sɜrnɪdli/ adv con indiferencia; sin preocuparse; con desenfado

unconditional /ˌʌnkən'dɪʃənl̩/ a incondicional, absoluto. **u. surrender**, rendición incondicional, f

unconditionally /ˌʌnkən'dɪʃənli/ adv incondicionalmente; Mil. a discreción

unconfessed /ˌʌnkən'fɛst/ a inconfeso

unconfined /ˌʌnkən'faind/ a suelto, libre; ilimitado; sin estorbo

unconfirmed /ˌʌnkənˈfɜrmd/ *a* no confirmado; (report) sin confirmar

uncongenial /ˌʌnkənˈdʒinyəl/ *a* incompatible, antipático; desagradable, repugnante

uncongeniality /ˌʌnkənˌdʒiniˈælɪti/ *n* incompatibilidad, antipatía, *f*; repugnancia, *f*; lo desagradable

unconnected /ˌʌnkəˈnɛktɪd/ *a* inconexo; *Mech.* desconectado; (relationship) sin parentesco; (confused) incoherente

unconquerable /ʌnˈkɒŋkərəbəl/ *a* invencible, indomable, inconquistable

unconquered /ʌnˈkɒŋkərd/ *a* no vencido

unconscientious /ˌʌnkɒnʃiˈɛnʃəs/ *a* poco concienzudo

unconscionable /ʌnˈkɒnʃənəbəl/ *a* excesivo, desmedido; sin conciencia

unconscious /ʌnˈkɒnʃəs/ *a* inconsciente; (senseless) insensible, sin sentido; espontáneo; (unaware) ignorante. **to be u. of,** ignorar; perder la consciencia de. **to become u.,** perder el sentido

unconsciously /ʌnˈkɒnʃəsli/ *adv* inconscientemente, involuntariamente

unconsciousness /ʌnˈkɒnʃəsnɪs/ *n* inconsciencia, *f*; (hypnosis, swoon) insensibilidad, *f*; (unawareness) ignorancia, falta de conocimiento, *f*

unconsecrated /ʌnˈkɒnsɪˌkreitɪd/ *a* no consagrado

unconsidered /ˌʌnkənˈsɪdərd/ *a* indeliberado; sin importancia, trivial

unconstitutional /ˌʌnkɒnstɪˈtuʃənl/ *a* anticonstitucional, inconstitucional

unconstitutionally /ˌʌnkɒnstɪˈtuʃənli/ *adv* inconstitucionalmente

unconstrained /ˌʌnkənˈstreind/ *a* libre; voluntario; sin freno

uncontaminated /ˌʌnkəntæmɪˈneitɪd/ *a* incontaminado; puro, sin mancha, impoluto

uncontested /ˌʌnkənˈtɛstɪd/ *a* sin oposición

uncontradicted /ˌʌnkɒntrəˈdɪktɪd/ *a* sin contradicción; incontestable

uncontrollable /ˌʌnkənˈtrouləbəl/ *a* irrefrenable, incontrolable, inmanejable; (temper) ingobernable; indomable

uncontrolled /ˌʌnkənˈtrould/ *a* libre, no controlado; desenfrenado, desgobernado

unconventional /ˌʌnkənˈvɛnʃənl/ *n* poco convencional; bohemio, excéntrico, extravagante; original

unconventionality /ˌʌnkənˌvɛnʃəˈnælɪti/ *a* excentricidad, extravagancia, independencia de ideas, *f*; (of a design) originalidad, *f*

unconversant /ˌʌnkənˈvɜrsənt/ *a* poco familiar, poco versado (en)

unconverted /ˌʌnkənˈvɜrtɪd/ *a* no convertido; sin transformar

unconvinced /ˌʌnkənˈvɪnst/ *a* no convencido

unconvincing /ˌʌnkənˈvɪnsɪŋ/ *a* no convincente, poco convincente, que no me (nos, etc.) convence; frívolo

uncooked /ʌnˈkʊkt/ *a* crudo, no cocido, sin cocer

uncork /ʌnˈkɔrk/ *vt* destapar, descorchar, quitar el corcho

uncorrected /ˌʌnkəˈrɛktɪd/ *a* sin corregir, no corregido

uncorroborated /ˌʌnkəˈrɒbəˌreitɪd/ *a* no confirmado, sin confirmar

uncorrupted /ˌʌnkəˈrʌptɪd/ *a* incorrupto; puro, no pervertido; (unbribed) no sobornado, honrado

uncorruptible /ˌʌnkəˈrʌptəbəl/ *a* incorruptible

uncountable /ʌnˈkauntəbəl/ *a* innumerable

uncounted /ʌnˈkauntɪd/ *a* no contado, sin cuenta

uncouple /ʌnˈkʌpəl/ *vt* soltar; desenganchar, desconectar

uncouth /ʌnˈkuθ/ *a* grosero, chabacano, tosco, patán

uncouthness /ʌnˈkuθnɪs/ *n* grosería, tosquedad, patanería, *f*

uncover /ʌnˈkʌvər/ *vt* descubrir; (remove lid of) destapar; (remove coverings of) desabrigar, desarropar; (leave unprotected) desamparar; (disclose) revelar, dejar al descubierto. *vi* descubrirse, quitar el sombrero

uncovered /ʌnˈkʌvərd/ *a* descubierto; desnudo; sin cubierta

uncreated /ˌʌnkriˈeitɪd/ *a* increado

uncritical /ʌnˈkrɪtɪkəl/ *a* sin sentido crítico, poco juicioso

uncross /ʌnˈkrɔs/ *vt* (of legs) descruzar

uncrossed /ʌnˈkrɔst/ *a* (of check) sin cruzar

unction /ˈʌŋkʃən/ *n* unción, *f*; untadura, *f*, untamiento, *m*; (unguent) ungüento, *m*; (zeal) fervor, *m*; (flattery) insinceridad, hipocresía, *f*; (relish) gusto, entusiasmo, *m*. **extreme u.,** extremaunción, *f*

unctuous /ˈʌŋktʃuəs/ *a* untuoso, craso; insincero, zalamero

uncultivable /ʌnˈkʌltəvəbəl/ *a* incultivable

uncultivated /ʌnˈkʌltəˌveitɪd/ *a* inculto, yermo; (barbarous) salvaje, bárbaro; (uncultured) inculto, tosco; no cultivado

uncultured /ʌnˈkʌltʃərd/ *a* inculto, iletrado

uncurbed /ʌnˈkɜrbd/ *a* sin freno; *Fig.* desenfrenado

uncurl /ʌnˈkɜrl/ *vt* desrizar *vi* desrizarse; desovillarse

uncurtained /ʌnˈkɜrtn̩d/ *a* sin cortinas; con las cortinas recogidas

uncut /ʌnˈkʌt/ *a* sin cortar, no cortado; (of gems) sin labrar

undamaged /ʌnˈdæmɪdʒd/ *a* indemne, sin daño

undated /ʌnˈdeitɪd/ *a* sin fecha

undaunted /ʌnˈdɔntɪd/ *a* intrépido, atrevido

undeceive /ˌʌndɪˈsiv/ *vt* desengañar, desilusionar

undecided /ˌʌndɪˈsaidɪd/ *a* (of question) pendiente, indeciso; dudoso; vacilante, irresoluto

undecipherable /ˌʌndɪˈsaifərəbəl/ *a* indescifrable; ilegible

undeclared /ˌʌndɪˈklɛərd/ *a* no declarado

undefended /ˌʌndɪˈfɛndɪd/ *a* indefenso

undeferable /ˌʌndɪˈfɜrəbəl/ *a* inaplazable

undefiled /ˌʌndɪˈfaild/ *a* impoluto, incontaminado; puro

undefinable /ˌʌndɪˈfainəbəl/ *a* indefinible; inefable; vago

undefined /ˌʌndɪˈfaind/ *a* indefinido; indeterminado

undelivered /ˌʌndɪˈlɪvərd/ *a* no recibido; (speech) no pronunciado; (not sent) no enviado

undemonstrative /ˌʌndəˈmɒnstrətɪv/ *a* poco expresivo, reservado

undeniable /ˌʌndɪˈnaiəbəl/ *a* incontestable, innegable, indudable; excelente; inequívoco, evidente

undeniably /ˌʌndɪˈnaiəbli/ *adv* indudablemente

undenominational /ˌʌndɪˌnɒməˈneiʃənl/ *a* sin denominación

undependable /ˌʌndɪˈpɛndəbəl/ *a* indigno de confianza

under /ˈʌndər/ *prep* debajo de; bajo; (in) en; (less than) menos de, menos que; (at the orders of) a las órdenes de, al mando de; (in less time than) en menos de; (under the weight of) bajo el peso de; (at the foot of) al abrigo de; (for less than) por menos de; (at the time of) en la época de, en tiempos de; (according to) según, conforme a, en virtud de (e.g. *under the law,* en virtud de la ley); (of monarchs) bajo (or durante) el reinado de; (of rank) inferior a; (in virtue of) en virtud dc; (of age) menor de; (with penalty, pretext, etc.) so; en; a (see below for examples); (*Agr.* of fields) plantado de, sembrado de. **u. arms,** bajo las armas. **u. contract,** bajo contrato. **u. cover,** al abrigo, bajo cubierto. **u. cover of,** bajo pretexto de, so color de. **u. fire,** bajo fuego. **u. oath,** bajo juramento. **u. pain of,** so pena de. **u. sail,** a la vela. **u. separate cover,** bajo cubierta separada, en sobre apartado, por separado. **u. steam,** al vapor. **u. way,** en camino; en marcha; en preparación. **to be u. an obligation,** deber favores; (to) tener obligacion de, estar obligado a

under /ˈʌndər/ *a* inferior; (of rank) subalterno, subordinado; bajo, bajero. *adv* debajo; abajo; más abajo; menos; (for less) para menos; (ill) mal; (insufficient) insuficiente. **to bring u.,** someter. **to keep u.,** dominar, subyugar

underact /ˌʌndərˈækt/ *vt* hacer un papel sin fogosidad

underarm /ˈʌndərˌɑrm/ *n* sobaco, *m*; a sobacal; (of bowling) de debajo del brazo. **to serve u.,** sacar por debajo

underbid /ˌʌndər'bɪd/ *vt* ofrecer menos que
underbred /ˌʌndər'brɛd/ *a* mal criado, mal educado
undercharge /ˌʌndər'tʃɑrdʒ/ *vt* cobrar menos de lo debido
underclothes /'ʌndər,klouz, -,klouðz/ *n* ropa interior, *f*, paños menores, *m pl*
undercurrent /'ʌndər,kзrənt/ *n* corriente submarina, *f*; *Fig.* tendencia oculta, *f*
undercut /'ʌndər,kʌt/ *n* (of meat) filete, *m*
underdeveloped /ˌʌndərdɪ'vɛləpt/ *a* de desarrollo atrasado; *Photo.* no revelado lo suficiente
underdog /'ʌndər,dɔg/ *n* víctima, *f*; débil, paciente, *m*. **underdogs,** los de abajo, *m pl*
underdone /'ʌndər'dʌn/ *a* (of meat) crudo, medio asado
underdress /ˌʌndər'drɛs/ *vt* and *vi* vestir(se) sin bastante elegancia
underestimate /ˌʌndər'ɛstə,meit/ *vt* tasar en menos; desestimar, menospreciar
underfeed /ˌʌndər'fid/ *vt* alimentar insuficientemente
underfoot /ˌʌndər'fʊt/ *adv* debajo de los pies, en el suelo
undergo /ˌʌndər'gou/ *vt* sufrir, padecer, pasar por. **undergo surgery,** someterse a la cirugía
undergraduate /ˌʌndər'grædʒuit/ *n* estudiante no graduado, *m*
underground /*a.*, *n.* 'ʌndər,graund; *adv.* -'graund/ *a* subterráneo; *Fig.* oculto, secreto. *adv* bajo tierra, debajo de la tierra; *Fig.* en secreto, ocultamente. *n* sótano, *m*
undergrown /'ʌndər,groun/ *a* enclenque
undergrowth /'ʌndər,grouθ/ *n* maleza, *f*
underhand /'ʌndər,hænd/ *adv* *Fig.* bajo mano, ocultamente, a escondidas. *a* *Fig.* secreto, oculto
underlie /ˌʌndər'lai/ *vt* estar debajo de; servir de base a, caracterizar
underline /'ʌndər,lain/ *vt* subrayar
underling /'ʌndərlɪŋ/ *n* subordinado (-da)
underlying /ˌʌndər'laiɪŋ/ *a* fundamental, básico, esencial
undermentioned /ˌʌndər'mɛnʃən/d *a* abajo citado
undermine /ˌʌndər'main/ *vt* socavar, excavar; minar, destruir poco a poco
undermining /'ʌndər,mainiŋ/ *n* socava, excavación, *f*; destrucción, *f*, *a* minador
underneath /ˌʌndər'niθ/ *adv* debajo. *prep* bajo, debajo de
undernourished /ˌʌndər'nзrɪʃt/ *a* mal alimentado
undernourishment /ˌʌndər'nзrɪʃmənt/ *n* desnutrición, *f*
underpaid /ˌʌndər'peid/ *a* insuficientemente retribuido, mal pagado
underpass /'ʌndər,pæs, -,pɑs/ *n* pasaje por debajo, *m*
underpay /ˌʌndər'pei/ *vt* pagar mal, remunerar (or retribuir) deficientemente
underpayment /'ʌndər,peimənt/ *n* retribución mezquina, *f*, pago insuficiente, *m*
underpin /ˌʌndər'pɪn/ *vt* apuntalar, socalzar
underpopulated /ˌʌndər'pɒpyə,leitɪd/ *a* con baja densidad de población
underprivileged /'ʌndər'prɪvəlɪdʒd/ *a* menesteroso, pobre, necesitado
underrate /ˌʌndər'reit/ *vt* tasar en menos; tener en poco, desestimar, menospreciar
underripe /'ʌndər,raip/ *a* verde
undersecretary /'ʌndər,sɛkrə,tɛri/ *n* subsecretario (-ia)
undersell /ˌʌndər'sɛl/ *vt* vender a un precio más bajo que
undershirt /'ʌndər,ʃзrt/ *n* *Spain* camiseta, *Lat. Am.* franela, *f*
underside /'ʌndər,said/ *n* revés, envés, *m*
undersigned /'ʌndər,saind/ *a* infrascrito, suscrito. **the u.,** el abajo firmado, el infrascrito
undersized /'ʌndər'saizd/ *a* muy pequeño, enclenque, enano
underskirt /'ʌndər,skзrt/ *n* enagua, *f*; refajo, *m*
understand /ˌʌndər'stænd/ *vt* comprender, entender; (know) saber; (be acquainted with) conocer; (hear) oír, tener entendido; (mean) sobrentender. *vi* com-

prender, entender; oír, tener entendido. **to u. each other,** comprenderse. **It being understood that...,** Bien entendido que...
understandable /ˌʌndər'stændəbəl/ *a* comprensible; inteligible. **It is very u. why he does not wish to come,** Se comprende muy bien por qué no quiere venir
understanding /ˌʌndər'stændɪŋ/ *n* (intelligence) entendimiento, *m*, inteligencia, *f*; (agreement) acuerdo, *m*; (knowledge) conocimiento, *m*; (wisdom) comprensión, sabiduría, *f*. *a* inteligente; sabio; (sympathetic) comprensivo, simpático. **to come to an u.,** ponerse de acuerdo
understandingly /ˌʌndərstændiŋ/ *adv* con inteligencia; con conocimiento (de); con simpatía
understate /ˌʌndər'steit/ *vt* decir menos que, rebajar, describir sin énfasis
understatement /'ʌndərsteitmənt/ *n* moderación, *f*
understudy /'ʌndər,stʌdi/ *n* sobresaliente, *mf*. *vt* sustituir
undertake /ˌʌndər'teik/ *vt* comprometerse a, encargarse de; emprender, abarcar, acometer
undertaker /'ʌndər,teikər/ *n* empresario, director de pompas fúnebres, *m*
undertaking /ˌʌndər'teikɪŋ/ *n* empresa, tarea, *f*; garantía, promesa, *f*; (funerals) funeraria, *f*
undertone /'ʌndər,toun/ *n* voz baja, *f*; *Art.* color tenue (or apagado), *m*. **in an u.,** en voz baja
undervalue /ˌʌndər'vælyu/ *vt* tasar en menos; tener en poco, despreciar
underwater /'ʌndər'wɔtər/ *a* subacuático, submarino. **u. flipper,** aleta de bucear
underweight /'ʌndər'weit/ *a* de bajo peso, que pesa menos de lo debido, flaco
underworld /'ʌndər,wзrld/ *n* (hell) infierno, averno, *m*; (slums) hampa, *f*, fondos bajos de la sociedad, *m pl*; heces de la sociedad, *f pl.* **u. slang,** *Peru* cantuja *f*
underwrite /ˌʌndər'rait/ *vt* *Com.* asegurar contra riesgos; reasegurar; obligarse a comprar todas las acciones de una compañía no subscritas por el público, mediante un pago convenido
underwriter /'ʌndər,raitər/ *n* asegurador, *m*; reasegurador, *m*
underwriting /'ʌndər,raitɪŋ/ *n* aseguro, *m*; reaseguro, *m*
undeserved /ˌʌndɪ'zзrvd/ *a* inmerecido, no merecido
undeserving /ˌʌndɪ'zзrvɪŋ/ *a* indigno, desmerecedor; que no merece
undesirable /ˌʌndɪ'zaiᵊrəbəl/ *a* no deseable; nocivo, pernicioso; (unsuitable) inconveniente
undesired /ˌʌndɪ'zaiᵊrd/ *a* no deseado; no solicitado, no buscado
undesirous /ˌʌndɪ'zaiᵊrəs/ *a* no deseoso
undestroyed /ˌʌndɪ'stroid/ *a* sin destruir, no destruido, intacto
undetected /ˌʌndɪ'tɛktɪd/ *a* no descubierto
undeveloped /ˌʌndɪ'vɛləpt/ *a* no desarrollado; rudimentario; inmaturo; (of a country) no explotado, virgen; *Photo.* no revelado; (of land) sin cultivar
undeviating /ˌʌn'divi,eitiŋ/ *a* directo; constante, persistente
undigested /ˌʌndɪ'dʒɛstɪd/ *a* no digerido, indigesto
undignified /ˌʌn'dɪgnə,faid/ *a* sin dignidad; poco serio; indecoroso
undiluted /ˌʌndɪ'lutid/ *a* sin diluir, puro
undiminished /ˌʌndɪ'mɪnɪst/ *a* no disminuido, sin disminuir, cabal, íntegro
undiplomatic /ˌʌndɪplə'mætɪk/ *a* impolítico, indiscreto
undirected /ˌʌndɪ'rɛktɪd/ *a* sin dirección; (of letters) sin señas
undiscernible /ˌʌndɪ'sзrnəbəl/ *a* imperceptible, invisible
undiscerning /ˌʌndɪ'sзrnɪŋ/ *a* sin percepción, obtuso, sin discernimiento
undisciplined /ʌn'dɪsəplɪnd/ *a* indisciplinado
undisclosed /ˌʌndɪ'sklouzd/ *a* no revelado, secreto
undiscouraged /ˌʌndɪ'skзrɪdʒd/ *a* animoso, sin flaquear, sin desaliento

undiscovered /ˌʌndɪˈskʌvərd/ a no descubierto, ignoto

undiscriminating /ˌʌndɪˈskrɪməˌneitɪŋ/ a sin distinción; sin sentido crítico

undisguised /ˌʌndɪˈskaizd/ a sin disfraz; abierto, claro

undismayed /ˌʌndɪsˈmeid/ a intrépido, impávido; sin desaliento

undisposed /ˌʌndɪˈspouzd/ a desinclinado; (of property) no enajenado, no invertido

undisputed /ˌʌndɪˈspyutɪd/ a incontestable, indisputable

undistinguishable /ˌʌndɪˈstɪŋgwɪʃəbəl/ a indistinguible

undistinguished /ˌʌndɪˈstɪŋgwɪʃt/ a (of writers) poco conocido; indistinto; sin distinción

undisturbed /ˌʌndɪˈstɜrbd/ a sin tocar; tranquilo, sereno, impasible

undivided /ˌʌndɪˈvaidɪd/ a indiviso, íntegro; junto; completo, entero

undo /ʌnˈdu/ vt anular; reparar; desatar, deshacer; desasir; abrir

undoing /ʌnˈduɪŋ/ n anulación, f; (reparation) reparación, f; (opening) abrir, m; ruina, f

undomesticated /ˌʌndəˈmɛstɪˌkeitɪd/ a salvaje, no domesticado; poco casero

undone /ʌnˈdʌn/ a and part sin hacer; deshecho; arruinado, perdido. **I am undone!** ¡Estoy perdido! **to come u.,** desatarse. **to leave u.,** dejar sin hacer

undoubted /ʌnˈdautɪd/ a indudable, evidente, incontestable

undoubtedly /ʌnˈdautɪdli/ adv sin duda

undramatic /ˌʌndrəˈmætɪk/ a no dramático

undreamed /ʌnˈdrimd/ a no soñado. **u. of,** inopinado, no imaginado

undress /ʌnˈdrɛs/ vt desnudar, desvestir, Peru calatear. vi desnudarse. n traje de casa, m; paños menores, m pl; Mil. traje de cuartel, m

undressed /ʌnˈdrɛst/ a desnudo; en paños menores; (of wounds) sin curar; Com. en rama, en bruto

undrinkable /ʌnˈdrɪŋkəbəl/ a impotable

undue /ʌnˈdu/ a excesivo, indebido; injusto; impropio; (of a bill of exchange) por vencer

undulant /ˈʌndʒələnt/ a ondulante. **u. fever,** fiebre mediterránea, fiebre de Malta, f

undulate /ˈʌndʒəˌleit/ vi ondular, ondear

undulating /ˈʌndʒəˌleitɪŋ/ a ondulante

undulation /ˌʌndʒəˈleiʃən/ n ondulación, undulación, f, ondeo, m; fluctuación, f

undulatory /ˈʌndʒələˌtɔri/ a ondulatorio, undoso

unduly /ʌnˈduli/ adv excesivamente, demasiado, indebidamente; injustamente

undutiful /ʌnˈdutəfəl/ a desobediente, irrespetuoso

undutifulness /ʌnˈdutəfəlnɪs/ n desobediencia, falta de respeto, f

undying /ʌnˈdaiɪŋ/ a inmortal, imperecedero; eterno

unearned /ʌnˈɜrnd/ a no ganado; inmerecido

unearth /ʌnˈɜrθ/ vt desenterrar; Fig. descubrir, sacar a luz

unearthing /ʌnˈɜrθɪŋ/ n desenterramiento, m; Fig descubrimiento, m, revelación, f

unearthly /ʌnˈɜrθli/ a sobrenatural; misterioso, aterrador, espantoso, Lat. Am. also extraterrenal

uneasily /ʌnˈizəli/ adv con dificultad; incómodamente; inquietamente

uneasiness /ʌnˈizɪnɪs/ n malestar, m; (discomfort) incomodidad, f; (anxiety) inquietud, intranquilidad, f, desasosiego, m

uneasy /ʌnˈizi/ a incómodo; inseguro; inquieto, intranquilo, desasosegado; aturdido, turbado. **to become u.,** inquietarse

uneaten /ʌnˈitn/ a no comido

uneconomical /ˌʌnɛkəˈnɒmɪkəl/ a poco económico, costoso, caro

unedifying /ʌnˈɛdəˌfaiɪŋ/ a poco edificante

unedited /ʌnˈɛdɪtɪd/ a inédito

uneducated /ʌnˈɛdʒəˌkeitɪd/ a ignorante; ineducado, inculto, indocto

unembarrassed /ˌʌnɛmˈbærəst/ a sereno, tranquilo, imperturbable; (financially) sin deudas, acomodado

unemotional /ˌʌnɪˈmouʃənl/ a frío, impasible

unemployable /ˌʌnɛmˈplɔiəbəl/ a sin uso, inservible; (of persons) inútil para el trabajo

unemployed /ˌʌnɛmˈplɔid/ a sin empleo; (out of work) sin trabajo, parado; desocupado, ocioso; inactivo. n paro obrero, m. **the u.,** los sin trabajo, los cesantes, los desocupados

unemployment /ˌʌnɛmˈplɔimənt/ n paro forzoso, m. **u. benefit,** subvención contra el paro obrero, f. **u. insurance,** seguro contra el paro obrero, m,

unencumbered /ˌʌnɛnˈkʌmbərd/ a libre, independiente; (of estates) libre de gravamen; (untaxable) saneado

unending /ʌnˈɛndɪŋ/ a perpetuo, eterno, sin fin; inacabable, constante, continuo, incesante

unendurable /ˌʌnɛnˈdurəbəl/ a insoportable, insufrible, intolerable

unenlightened /ˌʌnɛnˈlaitṇd/ a ignorante

unenterprising /ʌnˈɛntərˌpraizɪŋ/ a poco emprendedor, tímido

unenthusiastic /ˌʌnɛnˌθuziˈæstɪk/ a sin entusiasmo, tibio

unenviable /ʌnˈɛnviəbəl/ a no envidiable

unequal /ʌnˈikwəl/ a desigual; inferior; (out of proportion) desproporcionado; injusto; insuficiente; incapaz; (of ground) escabroso. **to be u. to the task,** ser incapaz de la tarea; no tener fuerzas para la tarea

unequalled /ʌnˈikwəld/ a sin igual, incomparable, sin par, único

unequally /ʌnˈikwəli/ adv desigualmente

unequivocal /ˌʌnɪˈkwɪvəkəl/ a inequívoco; redondo, claro, franco

unerring /ʌnˈɜrɪŋ, -ˈɛr-/ a infalible; seguro

unerringly /ʌnˈɜrɪŋli, -ˈɛr-/ adv infaliblemente; sin equivocarse

unessential /ˌʌnəˈsɛnʃəl/ a no esencial

unesthetic /ˌʌnɛsˈθɛtɪk/ a antiestético

uneven /ʌnˈivən/ a desigual; (of roads) escabroso, quebrado; (of numbers) impar; irregular

unevenly /ʌnˈivənli/ adv desigualmente

unevenness /ʌnˈivənnɪs/ n desigualdad, f; desnivel, m, irregularidad, f. **the unevenness of the terrain,** lo desigual del terreno, lo accidentado del terreno, m

uneventful /ˌʌnɪˈvɛntfəl/ a sin incidentes, sin acontecimientos notables; tranquilo

unexaggerated /ˌʌnɪgˈzædʒəˌreitɪd/ a nada exagerado

unexamined /ˌʌnɪgˈzæmɪnd/ a no examinado, sin examinar

unexampled /ˌʌnɪgˈzæmpəld/ a sin igual, sin par

unexceptionable /ˌʌnɪkˈsɛpʃənəbəl/ a intachable, irreprensible; correcto; impecable, perfecto

unexhausted /ˌʌnɪgˈzɔstid/ a no agotado; inexhausto

unexpected /ˌʌnɪkˈspɛktɪd/ a inesperado, imprevisto, inopinado, impensado; repentino, súbito

unexpectedly /ˌʌnɪkˈspɛktɪdli/ adv inesperadamente; de repente

unexpectedness /ˌʌnɪkˈspɛktɪdnɪs/ n lo inesperado

unexpired /ˌʌnɪkˈspaiᵊrd/ a (of bill of exchange) no vencido; (of lease) no caducado

unexplored /ˌʌnɪkˈsplɔrd/ a inexplorado

unexpressed /ˌʌnɪkˈsprɛst/ a no expresado; tácito, sobrentendido

unexpurgated /ˌʌnˈɛkspərˌgeitɪd/ a sin expurgar, completo

unfading /ʌnˈfeidɪŋ/ a inmarcesible, inmarchitable; eterno, inmortal

unfailing /ʌnˈfeilɪŋ/ a inagotable; inexhausto; seguro; indefectible

unfailingly /ʌnˈfeilɪŋli/ adv siempre, constantemente; sin faltar

unfair /ʌnˈfɛər/ a injusto; vil, bajo, soez; de mala fe, engañoso; (of play) sucio

unfairly /ʌnˈfɛərli/ adv injustamente; de mala fe

unfairness /ʌnˈfɛərnɪs/ n injusticia, f; mala fe, f

unfaithful /ʌnˈfeiθfəl/ a infiel; desleal; inexacto, incorrecto. **to be u. to,** ser infiel a; faltar a

unfaithfulness /ʌnˈfeiθfəlnɪs/ n infidelidad, f; deslealtad, f; inexactitud, f

unfaltering /ʌnˈfɔltərɪŋ/ a sin vacilar; resuelto, firme

unfamiliar /ˌʌnfə'mɪlyər/ a poco familiar; desconocido. **to be u. with,** ser ignorante de

unfashionable /ʌn'fæʃənəbəl/ a pasado de moda, fuera de moda; poco elegante

unfashionableness /ʌn'fæʃənəbəlnɪs/ n falta de elegancia, f

unfashionably /ʌn'fæʃənəbli/ adv contra la tendencia de la moda; sin elegancia

unfasten /ʌn'fæsən/ vt desatar; desabrochar, desenganchar; abrir; aflojar; soltar

unfathomable /ʌn'fæðəməbəl/ a insondable; impenetrable, inescrutable

unfavorable /ʌn'feivərəbəl/ a desfavorable, adverso, contrario

unfavorably /ʌn'feivərəbli/ adv desfavorablemente

unfeathered /ʌn'feðərd/ a implume, sin plumas

unfeeling /ʌn'filɪŋ/ a insensible, impasible, frío; duro, cruel

unfeigned /ʌn'feind/ a sincero, natural, verdadero

unfenced /ʌn'fenst/ a descercado, sin tapia; abierto

unfermented /ˌʌnfər'mentɪd/ a no fermentado;

unfetter /ʌn'fetər/ vt desencadenar, destrabar; poner en libertad, librar

unfilial /ʌn'fɪliəl/ a poco filial, desobediente

unfinished /ʌn'fɪnɪʃt/ a incompleto, inacabado; sin acabar, imperfecto

unfit /ʌn'fɪt/ a incapaz; incompetente, inepto; (unsuitable) impropio; (useless) inservible, inadecuado; (unworthy) indigno; (ill) enfermo, malo. vt inhabilitar, incapacitar. **u. for human consumption,** impropio para el consumo humano

unfitness /ʌn'fɪtnɪs/ n incapacidad, f; incompetencia, ineptitud, f; impropiedad, f; falta de mérito, f; falta de salud, f

unfix /ʌn'fɪks/ vt desprender, despegar, descomponer; soltar. **to come unfixed,** desprenderse

unflagging /ʌn'flægɪŋ/ a incansable, infatigable; persistente, constante

unflattering /ʌn'flætərɪŋ/ a poco halagüeño

unflinching /ʌn'flɪntʃɪŋ/ a inconmovible, resuelto, firme

unfold /ʌn'fould/ vt desplegar, desdoblar; tender; abrir; (plans) revelar, descubrir; contar, manifestar. vi abrirse

unfolding /ʌn'fouldɪŋ/ a que se abre. n despliegue, m; revelación, f; narración, f

unforced /ʌn'fɔrst/ a libre; espontáneo; fácil; natural

unforeseen /ˌʌnfɔr'sin/ a imprevisto, inesperado

unforgettable /ˌʌnfər'getəbəl/ a involvidable

unforgivable /ˌʌnfər'gɪvəbəl/ a inexcusable, imperdonable

unforgiving /ˌʌnfər'gɪvɪŋ/ a implacable, que no perdona, inexorable

unforgotten /ˌʌnfər'gɒtn̩/ a no olvidado

unformed /ʌn'fɔrmd/ a informe; rudimentario; inmaturo; (inexperienced) inexperto, sin experiencia

unfortunate /ʌn'fɔrtʃənɪt/ a desdichado, infortunado, desgraciado, desventurado. n desdichado (-da); pobre, mf; (prostitute) perdida, f

unfortunately /ʌn'fɔrtʃənɪtli/ adv por desdicha, desgraciadamente

unfounded /ʌn'faundɪd/ a infundado, inmotivado, sin fundamento, injustificado

unframed /ʌn'freimd/ a sin marco

unfrequented /ʌn'frikwəntɪd/ a poco frecuentado, solitario, retirado, aislado

unfriendliness /ʌn'frendlinɪs/ n hostilidad, falta de amistad, frialdad, f; huraña, insociabilidad, f

unfriendly /ʌn'frendli/ a hostil, enemigo; (of things, events) perjudicial; huraño, insociable

unfruitful /ʌn'frutfəl/ a estéril, infecundo; infructuoso, improductivo, vano

unfulfilled /ˌʌnfəl'fɪld/ a incumplido, sin cumplir; malogrado

unfurl /ʌn'fɜrl/ vt desplegar; Naut. izar (las velas)

unfurnished /ʌn'fɜrnɪʃt/ a desamueblado, sin muebles; desprovisto (de), sin

ungainliness /ʌn'geinlinɪs/ n falta de gracia, torpeza, f, desgarbo, m

ungainly /ʌn'geinli/ a desgarbado

ungallant /ʌn'gælənt/ a poco caballeroso, nada galante

ungenerous /ʌn'dʒɛnərəs/ a poco generoso; avaro, tacaño, mezquino; injusto

ungentlemanly /ʌn'dʒɛntl̩mənli/ a poco caballeroso, indigno de un caballero

unglazed /ʌn'gleizd/ a sin vidriar; (paper) sin satinar; deslustrado

ungloved /ʌn'glʌvd/ a sin guante(s)

unglue /ʌn'glu/ vt descolar, despegar

ungodliness /ʌn'gɒdlinɪs/ n impiedad, f

ungodly /ʌn'gɒdli/ a impío, irreligioso

ungovernable /ʌn'gʌvərnəbəl/ a ingobernable, indomable; irrefrenable

ungraceful /ʌn'greisfəl/ a desagraciado, desgarbado, sin gracia

ungracious /ʌn'greiʃəs/ a desagradable, poco cortés; desdeñoso

ungraciousness /ʌn'greiʃəsnɪs/ n descortesía, aspereza, inurbanidad, f

ungrammatical /ˌʌngrə'mætɪkəl/ a antigramatical, incorrecto

ungrateful /ʌn'greitfəl/ a ingrato, desagradecido; desagradable, odioso

ungratefulness /ʌn'greitfəlnɪs/ n ingratitud, f; lo desagradable

ungrounded /ʌn'graundɪd/ a infundado; sin motivo

ungrudging /ʌn'grʌdʒɪŋ/ a no avaro, liberal; generoso, magnánimo

ungrudgingly /ʌn'grʌdʒɪŋli/ adv de buena gana

unguarded /ʌn'gardɪd/ a indefenso, sin protección; descuidado; indiscreto, imprudente; sin reflexión

unguided /ʌn'gaidɪd/ a sin guía

unhallowed /ʌn'hæloud/ a impío, profano

unhampered /ʌn'hæmpərd/ a desembarazado, libre

unhappily /ʌn'hæpəli/ adv desafortunadamente, por desgracia

unhappiness /ʌn'hæpinɪs/ n infelicidad, desgracia, desdicha, tristeza, f

unhappy /ʌn'hæpi/ a infeliz, desgraciado, desdichado, triste; (ill-fated) aciago, funesto, malhadado; (remark) inoportuno, inapropiado

unharmed /ʌn'harmd/ a ileso, sano y salvo; (of things) indemne, sin daño

unharness /ʌn'harnɪs/ vt desaparejar; desenganchar; desarmar

unhealthiness /ʌn'hɛlθinɪs/ n falta de salud, f; (of place) insalubridad, f

unhealthy /ʌn'hɛlθi/ a enfermizo; malsano, insalubre

unheard /ʌn'hɜrd/ a no oído; sin ser escuchado; desconocido. **u.-of,** inaudito, no imaginado

unheeding /ʌn'hidɪŋ/ a distraído; desatento, sin prestar atención (a); descuidado

unhelpful /ʌn'hɛlpfəl/ a poco servicial; inútil

unhesitating /ʌn'hɛzɪˌteitɪŋ/ a resuelto, decidido; pronto, inmediato

unhesitatingly /ʌn'hɛzɪˌteitɪŋli/ adv sin vacilar

unhinge /ʌn'hɪndʒ/ vt desgoznar, desquiciar; (of the mind) trastornar

unhitch /ʌn'hɪtʃ/ vt desenganchar; descolgar

unholy /ʌn'houli/ a impío, sacrílego

unhonored /ʌn'ɒnərd/ a sin que se reconociese sus méritos; despreciado; (check) protestado

unhook /ʌn'hʊk/ vt desenganchar; desabrochar; descolgar

unhoped-for /ʌn'houpt fɔr/ a inesperado

unhurt /ʌn'hɜrt/ a ileso, incólume, sano y salvo; (of things) sin daño

unicellular /ˌyunə'sɛlyələr/ a unicelular

unicolored /'yuniˌkʌlərd/ a unicolor

unicorn /'yuniˌkɔrn/ n unicornio, m

unidentified /ˌʌnai'dɛntəˌfaid/ a no reconocido, no identificado

unification /ˌyunəfɪ'keiʃən/ n unificación, f

uniform /'yunəˌfɔrm/ a uniforme; igual, constante, invariable; homogéneo. n uniforme, m. **in full u.,** de gran uniforme. **to make u.,** uniformar, igualar, hacer uniforme

uniformity /ˌyunə'fɔrmɪti/ n uniformidad, igualdad, f

uniformly /'yunəˌfɔrmli/ adv uniformemente

unify /'yunə,fai/ *vt* unificar; unir

unilateral /,yunə'lætərəl/ *a* unilateral

unimaginable /,ʌnı'mædʒənəbəl/ *a* inimaginable, no imaginable

unimaginative /,ʌnı'mædʒənətıv/ *a* sin imaginación

unimpaired /,ʌnım'peərd/ *a* no disminuido; sin alteración; intacto, entero; sin menoscabo

unimpeachable /,ʌnım'pitʃəbəl/ *a* irreprochable, intachable

unimportance /,ʌnım'pɔrtṇs/ *n* no importancia, insignificancia, trivialidad, *f*

unimportant /,ʌnım'pɔrtṇt/ *a* sin importancia, nada importante, insignificante, trivial, *Lat. Am. also* intrascendente

unimpressive /,ʌnım'presıv/ *a* poco impresionante; nada conmovedor; (of persons) insignificante

uninflammable /,ʌnın'flæməbəl/ *a* no inflamable, incombustible

uninfluenced /,ʌnın'fluənsd/ *a* no afectado (por), libre (de)

uninformed /,ʌnın'fɔrmd/ *a* ignorante

uninhabitable /,ʌnın'hæbıtəbəl/ *a* inhabitable

uninhabited /,ʌnın'hæbıtıd/ *a* deshabitado, inhabitado, vacío, desierto

uninjured /ʌn'ındʒərd/ *a* ileso; sin daño

uninspired /,ʌnın'spaiərd/ *a* sin inspiración; pedestre, mediocre

uninstructive /,ʌnın'strʌktıv/ *a* nada instructivo

uninsured /,ʌnın'ʃʊrd/ *a* no asegurado

unintelligent /,ʌnın'telıdʒənt/ *a* nada inteligente, corto de alcances, tonto

unintelligibility /,ʌnın'telıdʒə'bılıti/ *n* incomprensibilidad, *f*, lo ininteligible

unintelligible /,ʌnın'telıdʒəbəl/ *a* ininteligible, incomprensible

unintentional /,ʌnın'tenʃənl/ *a* involuntario, inadvertido

unintentionally /,ʌnın'tenʃənli/ *adv* sin querer, involuntariamente

uninterested /ʌn'ıntərəstıd/ *a* no interesado, despreocupado

uninteresting /ʌn'ıntərəstıŋ/ *a* sin interés, poco interesante, soso

uninterrupted /,ʌnıntə'rʌptıd/ *a* ininterrum pido, sin interrupción; continuo, incesante

uninvited /,ʌnın'vaitıd/ *a* no invitado, no convidado, sin invitación; (unlooked-for) no buscado

uninviting /,ʌnın'vaitıŋ/ *a* poco atrayente; inhospitalario

union /'yunyən/ *n* unión, *f*; *Mech.* manguito de unión, *m*; conexión, *f*; (poverty) asociación, *f*; (of trade) gremio de oficios, *m*; sindicato (obrero), *m*; (workhouse) asilo, *m*; (U.S.A.) Estados Unidos de América, *m pl*

unionism /'yunyə,nızəm/ *n* unionismo, *m*

unionist /'yunyənıst/ *n Polit.* unionista, *mf*

unique /yu'nik/ *a* único, sin igual, sin par

uniqueness /yu'niknıs/ *n* unicidad, *f*; lo singular

unisexual /,yunə'sekʃuəl/ *a* unisexual

unison /'yunəsən,/ *n* unisonancia, *f*. **in u.,** al unísono

unit /'yunıt/ *n* unidad, *f*. **u. bookcase,** librería en secciones, *f*

Unitarian /,yunı'teəriən/ *a and n* unitario (-ia)

Unitarianism /,yunı'teəriə,nızəm/ *n* unitarismo, *m*

unite /yu'nait/ *vt* unir, juntar; combinar, incorporar; (of countries) unificar; (of energies, etc.) reunir. *vi* unirse, juntarse; reunirse, concertarse; convenirse

united /yu'naitıd/ *a* unido; junto. **the U. Nations,** las Naciones Unidas, *f pl*

unitedly /yu'naitıdli/ *adv* unidamente; armoniosamente, de acuerdo

United States of America los Estados Unidos de Norteamérica, *m pl*

unity /'yunıti/ *n* unidad, *f*; *Math.* la unidad; unión, *f*; conformidad, armonía, *f*. **the three unities,** las tres unidades

universal /,yunə'vɜrsəl/ *a* universal; general; común. **to make u.,** universalizar, generalizar. **u. joint,** junta universal, *f*; *Auto.* cardán, *m*

universalize /,yunə'vɜrsə,laiz/ *vt* universalizar

universe /'yunə,vɜrs/ *n* universo, *m*; creación, *f*, mundo, *m*

university /,yunə'vɜrsıti/ *n* universidad, *f. a* universitario. **u. degree,** grado universitario, *m*

unjust /ʌn'dʒʌst/ *a* injusto

unjustifiable /ʌn,dʒʌstə'faiəbəl/ *a* injustificable, indisculpable, inexcusable

unjustifiably /ʌn,dʒʌstə'faiəbli/ *adv* injustificadamente, inexcusablemente

unjustly /ʌn'dʒʌstli/ *adv* injustamente, sin razón

unkempt /ʌn'kempt/ *a* despeinado; desaseado, sucio

unkind /ʌn'kaind/ *a* nada bondadoso, nada amable; poco complaciente; duro, cruel; desfavorable, nada propicio

unkindly /ʌn'kaindli/ *adv* sin bondad; con dureza, cruelmente

unkindness /ʌn'kaindnıs/ *n* falta de bondad, *f*; severidad, crueldad, dureza, *f*, rigor, *m*; acto de crueldad, *m*

unknowable /ʌn'nouəbəl/ *a* impenetrable, incomprehensible, insondable

unknowingly /ʌn'nouıŋli/ *adv* sin querer, involuntariamente; sin saberlo; insensiblemente

unknown /ʌn'noun/ *a* ignoto, desconocido; *Math.* incógnito. *n* lo desconocido, misterio, *m*; *Math.* incógnita, *f*; (person) desconocido (-da), forastero (-ra). *Math.* **u. quantity,** incógnita, *f*

unlabeled /ʌn'leibəld/ *a* sin etiqueta

unlace /ʌn'leis/ *vt* desenlazar; desatar

unladylike /ʌn'leidi,laik/ *a* indigno (or impropio) de una dama; vulgar, ordinario, cursi

unlamented /,ʌnlə'mentıd/ *a* no llorado, no lamentado

unlatch /ʌn'lætʃ/ *vt* alzar el pestillo de, abrir

unlawful /ʌn'lɔfəl/ *a* ilegal, ilícito

unlawfulness /ʌn'lɔfəlnıs/ *n* ilegalidad, *f*

unlearn /ʌn'lɜrn/ *vt* olvidar, desaprender

unleash /ʌn'liʃ/ *vt* soltar

unleavened /ʌn'levənd/ *a* ázimo, sin levadura

unless /ʌn'les/ *conjunc* a no ser que, a menos que, como no, si no (all followed by subjunc.); salvo, excepto, con excepción de

unlicensed /ʌn'laisənst/ *a* no autorizado, sin licencia

unlike /ʌn'laik/ *a* disímil, desemejante; distinto, diferente. *prep* a distinción de, a diferencia de, al contrario de. **They are quite u.,** No se parecen nada

unlikeliness /ʌn'laiklinıs/ *n* improbabilidad, *f*

unlikely /ʌn'laikli/ *a* improbable, inverosímil; arriesgado

unlikeness /ʌn'laiknıs/ *n* desemejanza, diferencia, *f*

unlimited /ʌn'lımıtıd/ *a* ilimitado, infinito, inmenso; sin restricción; excesivo, exagerado. **unlimited telephone,** teléfono no medido (Argentina)

unlined /ʌn'laind/ *a* no forrado, sin forro; sin rayas; (of face) sin arrugas

unlit /ʌn'lıt/ *a* no iluminado, oscuro, sin luz

unload /ʌn'loud/ *vt* descargar; aligerar; *Naut.* hondear; (of shares) deshacerse de. *vi* descargar

unloading /ʌn'loudıŋ/ *n* descarga, *f*, descargue, *m*

unlock /ʌn'lɒk/ *vt* desencerrar, abrir; *Fig.* revelar, descubrir

unlooked-for /ʌn'lʊktfɔr/ *a* inopinado, inesperado

unloose /ʌn'lus/ *vt* desatar; soltar; poner en libertad

unlovable /ʌn'lʌvəbəl/ *a* indigno del querer; antipático, poco amable; repugnante

unloveliness /ʌn'lʌvlinıs/ *n* falta de hermosura, fealdad, *f*

unlovely /ʌn'lʌvli/ *a* nada hermoso, feo; desagradable

unluckily /ʌn'lʌkəli/ *adv* desafortunadamente, por desgracia

unluckiness /ʌn'lʌkınıs/ *n* mala suerte, *f*; (unsuitability) inoportunidad, *f*; lo nefasto, lo malo

unlucky /ʌn'lʌki/ *a* de mala suerte; desdichado, desgraciado, infeliz; (ill-omened) funesto, nefasto, fatal; inoportuno, inconveniente

unmanageable /ʌn'mænıdʒəbəl/ *a* indomable, indócil; ingobernable, inmanejable; (unwieldy) difícil de manejar, pesado

unmannerliness /ʌn'mænərlinɪs/ n mala crianza, descortesía, f

unmannerly /ʌn'mænərli/ a mal educado, descortés

unmarketable /ʌn'markɪtəbəl/ a invendible

unmarriageable /ʌn'mærɪdʒəbəl/ a incasable

unmarried /ʌn'mærid/ a soltero, célibe

unmask /ʌn'mæsk/ vt desenmascarar; Fig. quitar la careta (a). vi quitarse la máscara; Fig. quitarse la careta, descubrirse

unmeaning /ʌn'minɪŋ/ a sin sentido, vacío, sin significación

unmelodious /ˌʌnmə'loudiəs/ a sin melodía, discorde

unmendable /ʌn'mɛndəbəl/ a incomponible

unmentionable /ʌn'mɛnʃənəbəl/ a que no se puede mencionar; indigno de mencionarse

unmerciful /ʌn'mɜrsɪfəl/ a sin piedad, sin compasión; cruel, despiadado, duro

unmerited /ʌn'mɛrɪtɪd/ a inmerecido, desmerecido

unmethodical /ˌʌnmə'θɒdɪkəl/ a poco metódico

unmindful /ʌn'maindfəl/ a olvidadizo; desatento; negligente. **u. of,** sin pensar en, olvidando

unmistakable /ˌʌnmɪ'steikəbəl/ a inequívoco; manifiesto, evidente, indudable

unmistakably /ˌʌnmɪ'steikəbli/ adv indudablemente

unmitigated /ʌn'mɪtɪˌgeitɪd/ a no mitigado; completo, absoluto; (of rogue) redomado

unmixed /ʌn'mɪkst/ a sin mezcla; puro, sencillo; (free) limpio

unmoor /ʌn'mʊr/ vt desamarrar

unmounted /ʌn'mauntɪd/ a desmontado

unmoved /ʌn'muvd/ a fijo; (unemotional) impasible, frío; (determined) firme, inflexible, inexorable

unmuffle /ʌn'mʌfəl/ vt desembozar, descubrir

unmusical /ʌn'myuzɪkəl/ a sin afición a la música; sin oído (para la música); inarmónico

unnamable /ʌn'neiməbəl/ a que no se puede nombrar, innominable

unnatural /ʌn'nætʃərəl/ a desnaturalizado; (of vices, etc.) contra natural; innatural; (of style) rebuscado; artificial; inhumano, cruel

unnaturalness /ʌn'nætʃərəlnɪs/ n lo monstruoso; lo innatural; artificialidad, f; inhumanidad, f

unnavigable /ʌn'nævɪgəbəl/ a innavegable, no navegable

unnecessarily /ˌʌnnɛsə'sɛrəli/ adv inútilmente, innecesariamente, sin necesidad

unnecessariness /ʌn'nɛsəˌsɛrinɪs/ n inutilidad, f; superfluidad, f; lo innecesario

unnecessary /ʌn'nɛsəˌsɛri/ a innecesario, superfluo, inútil

unneighborly /ʌn'neibərli/ a de mala vecindad, impropio de vecinos, poco servicial

unnerve /ʌn'nɜrv/ vt acobardar quitar el valor, desanimar

unnoticed /ʌn'noutɪst/ a inadvertido, no observado

unobjectionable /ˌʌnəb'dʒɛkʃənəbəl/ a Lat. Am. inobjetable

unobliging /ʌnə'blaidʒɪŋ/ a nada servicial

unobservable /ˌʌnbə'zɜrvəbəl/ a inobservable

unobservant /ˌʌnəb'zɜrvənt/ a inobservante

unobserved /ˌʌnəb'zɜrvd/ a sin ser notado, desapercibido

unobstructed /ˌʌnəb'strʌktɪd/ a no obstruido; sin obstáculos; libre

unobtainable /ˌʌnəb'teinəbəl/ a inalcanzable, inasequible

unobtrusive /ˌʌnəb'trusɪv/ a discreto, modesto

unobtrusiveness /ˌʌnəb'trusɪvnɪs/ n discreción, modestia, f

unoccupied /ʌn'ɒkyəˌpaid/ a (at leisure) desocupado, ocioso, sin ocupación; vacío, vacante, libre; (untenanted) deshabitado

unofficial /ˌʌnə'fɪʃəl/ a no oficial

unopened /ʌn'oupənd/ a sin abrir, cerrado; (of exhibitions, etc.) no inaugurado

unopposed /ˌʌnə'pouzd/ a sin oposición

unorganized /ʌn'ɔrgəˌnaizd/ a inorganizado; Biol. inorgánico

unoriginal /ˌʌnə'rɪdʒənl/ a poco original

unorthodox /ʌn'ɔrθəˌdɒks/ a heterodoxo

unostentatious /ˌʌnɒstən'teiʃəs/ a sencillo, modesto, sin ostentación

unostentatiousness /ˌʌnɒstən'teiʃəsnɪs/ n sencillez, modestia, falta de ostentación, f

unpack /ʌn'pæk/ vt desempaquetar; (trunks) vaciar; (bales) desembalar. vi desempaquetar; deshacer las maletas

unpacking /ʌn'pækɪŋ/ n desembalaje, m

unpaid /ʌn'peid/ a sin pagar, no pagado, Lat. Am. also impago

unpalatable /ʌn'pælətəbəl/ a de mal sabor; desagradable

unparalleled /ʌn'pærəˌlɛld/ a sin paralelo, sin par, sin igual

unpardonable /ʌn'pardnəbəl/ a imperdonable, inexcusable, irremisible

unpatriotic /ʌnˌpeitri'ɒtɪk/ a antipatriótico

unpaved /ʌn'peivd/ a sin empedrar

unperceived /ˌʌnpər'sivd/ a inadvertido, sin ser notado

unperturbed /ˌʌnpər'tɜrbd/ a impasible, sin alterarse, sereno

unpleasant /ʌn'plɛzənt/ a desagradable, desapacible; ofensivo; (troublesome) enfadoso, molesto

unpleasantly /ʌn'plɛzəntli/ adv desagradablemente

unpleasantness /ʌn'plɛzəntnɪs/ n lo desagradable; disgusto, sinsabor, m; (disagreement) disputa, riña, f

unpleasing /ʌn'plizɪŋ/ a nada placentero; desagradable, sin atractivos

unplug /ʌn'plʌg/ vt desenchufar

unpoetic /ˌʌnpou'ɛtɪk/ a poco poético

unpolished /ʌn'pɒlɪʃt/ a sin pulir, tosco, mate; Fig. inculto, cerril. **u. diamond,** diamante en bruto, m

unpolluted /ˌʌnpə'lutɪd/ a impoluto, incontaminado; puro, sin pervertir

unpopular /ʌn'pɒpyələr/ a impopular

unpopularity /ˌʌnpɒpyə'lærɪti/ n impopularidad, f

unpractical /ʌn'præktɪkəl/ a impracticable, imposible; (of persons) sin sentido práctico

unpracticed /ʌn'præktɪst/ a no practicado; inexperto, inhábil

unpraiseworthy /ʌn'preizˌwɜrði/ a inmeritorio

unprecedented /ʌn'prɛsiˌdɛntɪd/ a sin precedente, inaudito

unprejudiced /ʌn'prɛdʒədɪst/ a sin prejuicios, imparcial

unpremeditated /ˌʌnpri'mɛdɪˌteitɪd/ a sin premeditación, indeliberado, impremeditado

unprepared /ˌʌnprɪ'pɛərd/ a sin preparación, no preparado; desprevenido; desapercibido (unready)

unpreparedness /ˌʌnprɪ'pɛərɪdnɪs/ n falta de preparación, imprevisión, f; desapercibimiento, m

unprepossessing /ˌʌnpripə'zɛsɪŋ/ a poco atrayente, antipático

unpresentable /ˌʌnprɪ'zɛntəbəl/ a impresentable

unpretentious /ˌʌnprɪ'tɛnʃəs/ a sin pretensiones, modesto

unpriced /ʌn'praist/ a sin precio

unprincipled /ʌn'prɪnsəpəld/ a sin consciencia, sin escrúpulos

unprinted /ʌn'prɪntɪd/ a sin imprimir, no impreso

unprocurable /ˌʌnprou'kyʊrəbəl/ a inalcanzable, inasequible

unproductive /ˌʌnprə'dʌktɪv/ a improductivo; infructuoso, estéril

unproductiveness /ˌʌnprə'dʌktɪvnɪs/ n infructuosidad, f; esterilidad, f

unprofessional /ˌʌnprə'fɛʃənl/ a sin profesión; contrario a la ética profesional

unprofitable /ʌn'prɒfɪtəbəl/ a improductivo, infructuoso; sin provecho; inútil; nada lucrativo

unprogressive /ˌʌnprə'grɛsɪv/ a reaccionario

unpromising /ʌn'prɒməsɪŋ/ a poco halagüeño

unpronounceable /ˌʌnprə'naunsəbəl/ a impronunciable

unpropitious /ˌʌnprə'pɪʃəs/ a desfavorable, nada propicio, nada halagüeño

unprosperous /ʌn'prɒspərəs/ a impróspero

unprotected /ˌʌnprə'tɛktɪd/ a sin protección; (of persons) indefenso, desvalido

unproved /ʌn'pruvd/ *a* no probado, sin demostrar
unprovided /ˌʌnprə'vaidɪd/ *a* desapercibido, desprovisto. **u. for,** sin provisión (para); sin medios de vida, desamparado
unprovoked /ˌʌnprə'voukt/ *a* no provocado, sin provocación; sin motivo
unpublished /ʌn'pʌblɪʃt/ *a* inédito, no publicado, sin publicar
unpunishable /ʌn'pʌnɪʃəbəl/ *a* no punible
unpunished /ʌn'pʌnɪʃt/ *a* impune, sin castigo
unpurchasable /ʌn'pɛrtʃɪsəbəl/ *a* que no puede comprarse
unqualified /ʌn'kwɒlə,faid/ *a* incapaz, incompetente; (with professions) sin título; (downright) incondicional, absoluto
unquenchable /ʌn'kwɛntʃəbəl/ *a* inextinguible, inapagable; insaciable
unquestionable /ʌn'kwɛstʃənəbəl/ *a* indiscutible, indudable, indubitable
unquestionably /ʌn'kwɛstʃənəbli/ *adv* indudablemente
unravel /ʌn'rævəl/ *vt* deshilar; destejer; (a mystery, etc.) desentrañar, desembrollar, descifrar
unraveling /ʌn'rævəlɪŋ/ *n* deshiladura, *f*; aclaración, *f*
unreadable /ʌn'ridəbəl/ *a* ilegible
unreadiness /ʌn'rɛdɪnɪs/ *n* falta de preparación, *f*, desapercibimiento, *m*; lentitud, *f*
unready /ʌn'rɛdi/ *a* desapercibido, desprevenido; lento
unreal /ʌn'riəl/ *a* irreal; falso, imaginario, ilusorio; ficticio; artificial; insincero, hipócrita; ideal; incorpóreo
unreality /ˌʌnri'ælɪti/ *n* irrealidad, *f*; falsedad, *f*; artificialidad, *f*; lo quimérico
unreasonable /ʌn'rizənəbəl/ *a* irrazonable, irracional; disparatado, extravagante; (with price, etc.) exorbitante, excesivo
unreasonableness /ʌn'rizənəbəlnɪs/ *n* irracionalidad, *f*; exorbitancia, *f*
unreasonably /ʌn'rizənəbli/ *adv* irracionalmente
unreasoning /ʌn'rizənɪŋ/ *a* irracional; sin motivo, sin causa
unreceipted /ˌʌnri'sitɪd/ *a* sin recibo
unrecognizable /ʌn'rɛkəg,naizəbəl/ *a* que no puede reconocerse; imposible de reconocer
unrecognized /ʌn'rɛkəg,naizd/ *a* no reconocido
unreconciled /ʌn'rɛkən,saild/ *a* no resignado, no reconciliado
unrectified /ʌn'rɛktə,faid/ *a* no corregido, sin rectificar
unredeemed /ˌʌnri'dimd/ *a* no redimido; no mitigado; (of pledges) sin desempeñar
unrefined /ˌʌnri'faind/ *a* no refinado, impuro; inculto, grosero
unreformed /ˌʌnri'fɔrmd/ *a* no reformado
unrefuted /ˌʌnri'fyutid/ *a* no refutado
unregenerate /ˌʌnri'dʒɛnərɪt/ *a* no regenerado
unregretted /ˌʌnri'grɛtid/ *a* no llorado, sin lamentar
unrehearsed /ˌʌnri'hɜrst/ *a* sin preparación; *Theat.* sin ensayar; (extempore) improvisado
unrelated /ˌʌnri'leitid/ *a* inconexo; (of persons) sin parentesco
unrelenting /ˌʌnri'lɛntɪŋ/ *a* implacable, inflexible, inexorable
unreliability /ˌʌnri,laiə'bɪlɪti/ *n* incertidumbre, *f*; el no poder confiar en, informalidad, inestabilidad, *f*
unreliable /ˌʌnri,laiəbəl/ *a* incierto, dudoso, indigno de confianza; (of persons) informal
unrelieved /ˌʌnri'livd/ *a* no aliviado; absoluto, completo, total
unremitting /ˌʌnri'mɪtɪŋ/ *a* incansable
unremunerative /ˌʌnri'myunərətɪv/ *a* sin remuneración, no remunerado
unrepealed /ˌʌnri'pild/ *a* vigente
unrepentant /ˌʌnri'pɛntn̩t/ *a* impenitente
unrepresentative /ˌʌnrɛpri'zɛntətɪv/ *a* poco representativo
unrepresented /ˌʌnrɛpri'zɛntid/ *a* sin representación
unrequited /ˌʌnri'kwaitid/ *a* no correspondido

unreserved /ˌʌnri'zɜrvd/ *a* no reservado; expresivo, comunicativo, expansivo, franco
unreservedly /ˌʌnri'zɜrvɪdli/ *adv* sin reserva; con toda franqueza
unresisting /ˌʌnri'zɪstɪŋ/ *a* sin oponer resistencia
unresolved /ˌʌnri'zɒlvd/ *a* sin resolverse, vacilante; incierto, dudoso, inseguro; sin solución
unresponsive /ˌʌnri'spɒnsɪv/ *a* flemático; insensible, sordo
unresponsiveness /ˌʌnri'spɒnsɪvnɪs/ *n* flema, *f*; insensibilidad, *f*
unrest /ʌn'rɛst/ *n* desasosiego, *m*, agitación, inquietud, *f*
unrestful /ʌn'rɛstfəl/ *a* agitado, inquieto, intranquilo
unrestrained /ˌʌnri'streind/ *a* desenfrenado; ilimitado, sin límites; sin reserva
unrestricted /ˌʌnri'strɪktɪd/ *a* sin restricción; ilimitado
unrevealed /ˌʌnri'vild/ *a* no revelado, por descubrir, no descubierto
unrewarded /ˌʌnri'wɔrdɪd/ *a* sin premio, no recompensado
unrighteous /ʌn'raitʃəs/ *a* injusto, malo, perverso
unrighteousness /ʌn'raitʃəsnɪs/ *n* injusticia, *f*; maldad, perversidad, *f*
unripe /ʌn'raip/ *a* verde, inmaturo
unripeness /ʌn'raipnɪs/ *n* falta de madurez, *f*
unrivaled /ʌn'raivəld/ *a* sin igual, sin par
unroll /ʌn'roul/ *vt* desarrollar. *vi* desarrollarse; (unfold) desplegarse (a la vista)
unromantic /ˌʌnrou'mæntɪk/ *a* poco (or nada) romántico
unruffled /ʌn'rʌfəld/ *a* sereno, plácido, ecuánime; no arrugado; (of hair) liso
unruliness /ʌn'rulɪnɪs/ *n* turbulencia, indisciplina, *f*; insubordinación, rebeldía, *f*
unruly /ʌn'ruli/ *a* ingobernable, revoltoso, refractario, rebelde; (of hair) indomable
unsaddle /ʌn'sædl/ *vt* desensillar; derribar (del caballo, etc.)
unsafe /ʌn'seif/ *a* inseguro; peligroso; arriesgado; (to eat) nocivo
unsafeness /ʌn'seifnɪs/ *n* inseguridad, *f*; peligro, riesgo, *m*
unsaid /ʌn'sɛd/ *a* sin decir, no dicho
unsalable /ʌn'seiləbəl/ *a* invendible
unsalaried /ʌn'sælərid/ *a* no asalariado
unsalted /ʌn'sɔltid/ *a* soso, sin sal
unsanitary /ʌn'sæni,tɛri/ *a* antihigiénico
unsatisfactoriness /ˌʌnsætɪs'fæktərɪnɪs/ *n* lo insatisfactorio
unsatisfactory /ˌʌnsætɪs'fæktəri/ *a* poco (or nada) satisfactorio; no aceptable
unsatisfied /ʌn'sætɪs,faid/ *a* no satisfecho; descontento, no convencido; (hungry) no harto; *Com.* no saldado
unsatisfying /ʌn'sætɪs,faiɪŋ/ *a* que no satisface
unsavoriness /ʌn'seivərɪnɪs/ *n* insipidez, *f*, mal sabor, *m*; lo desagradable; sordidez, suciedad, *f*
unsavory /ʌn'seivəri/ *a* insípido, de mal sabor; desagradable; sórdido, sucio
unscathed /ʌn'skeiðd/ *a* sin daño, ileso
unscented /ʌn'sɛntid/ *a* sin perfume, sin olor, no fragante
unscholarly /ʌn'skɒlərli/ *a* nada erudito; indigno de un erudito
unscientific /ˌʌnsaiən'tɪfɪk/ *a* no científico
unscrew /ʌn'skru/ *vt* destornillar, *Lat. Am.* desenroscar. *vi* destornillarse
unscrewing /ʌn'skruɪŋ/ *n* destornillamiento, *m*
unscrupulous /ʌn'skrupyələs/ *a* sin escrúpulos, poco escrupuloso, desaprensivo
unscrupulousness /ʌn'skrupyələsnɪs/ *n* falta de escrúpulos, desaprensión, *f*
unseal /ʌn'sil/ *vt* desellar, romper (or quitar) el sello (de)
unseasonable /ʌn'sizənəbəl/ *a* intempestivo, fuera de sazón; inoportuno, inconveniente. **at an u. hour,** a una hora inconveniente, a deshora

unseasonableness /ʌn'sizənəbəlnıs/ *n* lo intempestivo, inoportunidad, *f*

unseasonably /ʌn'sizənəbli/ *adv* intempestivamente; a deshora; inoportunamente

unseasoned /ʌn'sizənd/ *a Cul.* sin sazonar, soso; (wood) verde; no maduro, sin madurar

unseat /ʌn'sit/ *vt* (from horse) tirar, echar al suelo; *Polit.* desituir

unseaworthy /'ʌn'si‚wɜrði/ *a* innavegable

unseemliness /ʌn'simlınıs/ *n* falta de decoro, *f*; indecencia, *f*

unseemly /ʌn'simli/ *a* indecoroso, indigno; indecente; impropio

unseen /ʌn'sin/ *a* no visto, invisible; inadvertido; secreto, oculto. *n* versión al libro abierto, *f*. **the u.,** lo invisible

unselfish /ʌn'sɛlfıʃ/ *a* desinteresado, abnegado, nada egoísta; generoso

unselfishness /ʌn'sɛlfıʃnıs/ *n* abnegación, *f*; desinterés, *m*; generosidad, *f*

unsentimental /‚ʌnsɛntə'mɛntḷ/ *a* no sentimental

unserviceable /ʌn'sɜrvısəbəl/ *a* inservible, inútil, que no sirve para nada, sin utilidad.

unsettle /ʌn'sɛtḷ/ *vt* desarreglar; desorganizar; hacer inseguro; agitar, perturbar

unsettled /ʌn'sɛtld/ *a* inconstante, variable; *Com.* pendiente, sin pagar; incierto; sin resolver; (of estates) sin solucionar

unshackle /ʌn'ʃækəl/ *vt* desencadenar

unshakable /ʌn'ʃeikəbəl/ *a* inconmovible, firme

unshapely /ʌn'ʃeipli/ *a* desproporcionado

unshaven /ʌn'ʃeivən/ *a* sin afeitar

unsheathe /ʌn'ʃið/ *vt* desenvainar, sacar

unsheltered /ʌn'ʃɛltərd/ *a* desabrigado, desamparado; no protegido, sin protección; (of places) sin abrigo, expuesto; (from) sin defensa contra

unship /ʌn'ʃıp/ *vt* deɔembarcar; (the oarɛ) deɛarmar

unshod /ʌn'ʃɒd/ *a* descalzo; (of a horse) sin herraduras

unshrinkable /ʌn'ʃrıŋkəbəl/ *a* que no se encoge

unshrinking /ʌn'ʃrıŋkıŋ/ *a* intrépido; resoluto, sin vacilar

unsightly /ʌn'saitli/ *a* feo, horrible, repugnante, antiestético

unsinkable /ʌn'sıŋkəbəl/ *a* insumergible

unskilled /ʌn'skıld/ *a* inexperto, inhábil, imperito, torpe

unsmokable /ʌn'smoukəbəl/ *a* (of tobacco) infumable

unsociability /‚ʌnsouʃə'bılıti/ *n* insociabilidad, huraña, esquivez, *f*

unsociable /ʌn'souʃəbəl/ *a* insociable, huraño, esquivo, arisco

unsocial /ʌn'souʃəl/ *a* insocial, antisocial

unsold /ʌn'sould/ *a* no vendido, sin vender

unsolder /ʌn'sɒdər/ *vt* desoldar, desestañar

unsoldierly /ʌn'souldʒərli/ *a* indigno de un soldado; poco marcial

unsophisticated /‚ʌnsə'fıstı‚keitıd/ *a* ingenuo, inocente, cándido

unsought /ʌn'sɔt/ *a* no solicitado; no buscado

unsound /ʌn'saund/ *a* enfermo; defectuoso; (rotten) podrido; (fallacious) erróneo, poco convincente; (of persons) informal, indigno de confianza; (of religious views) heterodoxo. **of u. mind,** insano

unsoundness /ʌn'saundnıs/ *n* lo defectuoso, estado, *m*; falsedad, *f*; informalidad, *f*; heterodoxia, *f*

unsparing /ʌn'spɛərıŋ/ *a* severo, implacable; generoso, pródigo

unspeakable /ʌn'spikəbəl/ *a* indecible, inefable; que no puede mencionarse, horrible

unspecified /ʌn'spɛsə‚faid/ *a* no especificado

unspoiled /ʌn'spɔild/ *a* intacto; ileso, indemne; no corrompido; no estropeado; (of children) no mimado

unspoken /ʌn'spoukən/ *a* no pronunciado

unsportsmanlike /ʌn'spɔrtsmən‚laik/ *a* indigno de un cazador; indigno de un deportista; nada caballeroso. **to play in an u. way,** jugar sucio

unstable /ʌn'steibəl/ *a* inestable; variable; inconstante; vacilante, irresoluto

unstained /ʌn'steind/ *a* no manchado; no teñido; inmaculado, sin mancha

unstamped /ʌn'stæmpt/ *a* sin sello; no sellado

unstatesmanlike /ʌn'steitsmən‚laik/ *a* impropio (*or* indigno) de un hombre de estado

unsteadiness /ʌn'stedınıs/ *n* inestabilidad, falta de firmeza, *f*; inconstancia, *f*

unsteady /ʌn'stedi/ *a* inestable, inseguro; inconstante

unstick /ʌn'stık/ *vt* desapegar

unstitch /ʌn'stıtʃ/ *vt* desapuntar

unstressed /ʌn'strest/ *a* sin énfasis; (of syllables) sin acento

unstudied /ʌn'stʌdid/ *a* no estudiado; natural, espontáneo

unsubstantial /‚ʌnsəb'stænʃəl/ *a* insubstancial; ligero; irreal, imaginario; incorpóreo; aparente

unsuccessful /‚ʌnsək'sɛsfəl/ *a* sin éxito; infructuoso. **to be u.,** no tener éxito

unsuccessfully /‚ʌnsək'sɛsfəli/ *adv* en vano, sin éxito

unsuitability /‚ʌnsutə'bılıti/ *n* impropiedad, *f*; inconveniencia, incongruencia, *f*; incapacidad, *f*; inoportunidad, *f*

unsuitable /ʌn'sutəbəl/ *a* inapropiado; inconveniente; impropio; inservible; incapaz; inoportuno

unsung /ʌn'sʌŋ/ *a* no cantado; no celebrado en verso

unsupported /‚ʌnsə'pɔrtıd/ *a* sin apoyo; sin defensa; no favorecido

unsurpassable /‚ʌnsər'pæsəbəl/ *a* inmejorable, insuperable

unsurpassed /‚ʌnsər'pæst/ *a* sin par

unsuspecting /‚ʌnsə'spɛktıŋ/ *a* no suspicaz, confiado, no receloso

unswerving /ʌn'swɜrvıŋ/ *a* directo; sin vacilar, constante

unsymmetrical /‚ʌnsı'mɛtrıkəl/ *a* asimétrico

unsympathetic /‚ʌnsımpə'θɛtık/ *a* indiferente, incompasivo; antipático

unsystematic /‚ʌnsıstə'mætık/ *a* sin sistema, asistemático, no metódico

untalented /ʌn'tæləntıd/ *a* sin talento

untamed /ʌn'teimd/ *a* indomado, cerril, bravío, no domesticado; desenfrenado, violento. **u. horse,** *Lat. Am.* bellaco, *m*

unteach /ʌn'titʃ/ *vt* desenseñar

untenable /ʌn'tɛnəbəl/ *a* insostenible

untenanted /ʌn'tɛnəntıd/ *a* desalquilado, deshabitado; vacío, desierto

unthankful /ʌn'θæŋkfəl/ *a* ingrato, desagradecido

unthinkable /ʌn'θıŋkəbəl/ *a* inconcebible; imposible

unthinking /ʌn'θıŋkıŋ/ *a* sin reflexión; desatento; indiscreto

unthinkingly /ʌn'θıŋkıŋli/ *adv* sin pensar

unthread /ʌn'θrɛd/ *vt* deshebrar

untidily /ʌn'taidļi/ *adv* en desorden, sin aseo

untidiness /ʌn'taidınıs/ *n* desorden, *m*; desaseo, desaliño, *m*; falta de pulcritud, *f*

untidy /ʌn'taidi/ *a* desarreglado; desaseado; abandonado; en desorden, sin concierto

untie /ʌn'tai/ *vt* desatar, desanudar; (knots) deshacer

until /ʌn'tıl/ *prep* hasta. *conjunc* hasta que. (The subjunc. is required in clauses referring to future time, e.g. *No venga usted hasta que le avise yo,* Don't come until I tell you. In clauses referring to past or present time the indicative is generally used, e.g. *No la reconocí hasta que se volvió,* I didn't recognize her until she turned around)

untilled /ʌn'tıld/ *a* sin cultivar

untimeliness /ʌn'taimlınıs/ *n* inoportunidad, *f*; lo prematuro

untimely /ʌn'taimli/ *a* inoportuno, intempestivo; prematuro

untiring /ʌn'taiᵊrıŋ/ *a* incansable, infatigable

unto /'ʌntu; *unstressed* -tə/ *prep* hacia

untold /ʌn'tould/ *a* no revelado; no narrado; sin decir, no dicho; incalculable

untouchable /ʌn'tʌtʃəbəl/ *a* que no puede tocarse, intangible; (of castes) intocable

untouched /ʌn'tʌtʃt/ *a* sin tocar; intacto, incólume

untrained /ʌn'treind/ *a* indisciplinado; inexperto; no adiestrado

untranslatable /ˌʌntrænsˈleitəbəl/ *a* intraducible
untraveled /ʌnˈtrævəld/ *a* no frecuentado; (of persons) provinciano
untried /ʌnˈtraid/ *a* no experimentado. *u.* **knight,** caballero novel, *m*
untrodden /ʌnˈtrɒdṇ/ *a* no hollado, no frecuentado; inexplorado, virgen
untroubled /ʌnˈtrʌbəld/ *a* tranquilo, sosegado
untrue /ʌnˈtru/ *a* mentiroso, falso, engañoso; ficticio, imaginario; traidor, desleal; infiel
untrustworthiness /ʌnˈtrʌst,wɜrðinɪs/ *n* incertidumbre, inseguridad, *f*; (of persons) informalidad, *f*
untrustworthy /ʌnˈtrʌst,wɜrði/ *a* indigno de confianza; incierto, dudoso; desleal
untruth /ʌnˈtruθ/ *n* mentira, falsedad, *f*; ficción, *f*
untruthful /ʌnˈtruθfəl/ *a* mentiroso; falso
untruthfulness /ʌnˈtruθfəlnɪs/ *n* falsedad, *f*
untwist /ʌnˈtwɪst/ *vt* destorcer
unused /ʌnˈyuzd/ *a* no empleado; /ʌnˈyust/ desacostumbrado; inusitado; (postage stamp) sin sellar
unusual /ʌnˈyuʒuəl/ *a* fuera de lo común, desacostumbrado; extraño, raro, peregrino, extraordinario
unusually /ʌnˈyuʒuəli/ *adv* excepcionalmente; infrecuentemente
unusualness /ʌnˈyuʒuəlnɪs/ *n* lo insólito; rareza, *f*
unutterable /ʌnˈʌtərəbəl/ *a* indecible, inexpresable
unvarnished /ʌnˈvɑrnɪʃt/ *a* sin barnizar; *Fig.* sencillo
unvarying /ʌnˈveəriɪŋ/ *a* invariable, constante, uniforme
unveil /ʌnˈveil/ *vt* quitar el velo; (memorial) descubrir; *Fig.* revelar. *vi* quitarse el velo; revelarse, quitarse la careta
unventilated /ʌnˈvɛntḷeitɪd/ *a* sin ventilación; sin aire, ahogado; (of topics) no discutido
unverifiable /ʌn,vɛrəˈfaiəbəl/ *a* que no puede verificarse
unverified /ʌn,vɛrəˈfaid/ *a* sin verificar
unvisited /ʌn ˈvɪsɪtɪd/ no visitado; no frecuentado
unvoiced /ʌnˈvɔist/ *a* no expresado
unwanted /ʌnˈwɒntɪd/ *a* no deseado; superfluo, de más
unwarlike /ʌnˈwɔr,laik/ *a* nada marcial, pacífico
unwarranted /ʌnˈwɔrəntɪd/ *a* sin garantía; inexcusable, injustificable
unwashed /ʌnˈwɒʃt/ *a* sin lavar; sucio
unwatched /ʌnˈwɒtʃt/ *a* no vigilado
unwavering /ʌnˈweivərɪŋ/ *a* resuelto, firme; inexorable; (gaze) fijo
unwaveringly /ʌnˈweivərɪŋli/ *adv* sin vacilar; inexorablemente
unwearied /ʌnˈwiərid/ *a* incansable; infatigable
unwelcome /ʌnˈwɛlkəm/ *a* mal acogido; inoportuno; desagradable
unwell /ʌnˈwɛl/ *a* indispuesto
unwholesome /ʌnˈhoulsəm/ *a* malsano, nocivo, insalubre
unwholesomeness /ʌnˈhoulsəmnɪs/ *n* insalubridad, *f*
unwieldiness /ʌnˈwildinɪs/ *n* pesadez, dificultad de manejarse, *f*
unwieldy /ʌnˈwildi/ *a* pesado, abultado, difícil de manejar
unwilling /ʌnˈwɪlɪŋ/ *a* desinclinado, reluctante
unwillingly /ʌnˈwɪlɪŋli/ *adv* de mala gana
unwillingness /ʌnˈwɪlɪŋnɪs/ *n* falta de inclinación, repugnancia, *f*
unwind /ʌnˈwaind/ *vt* desenvolver; (thread) desdevanar, desovillar. *vi* desarrollarse; desdevanarse
unwise /ʌnˈwaiz/ *a* imprudente, indiscreto, incauto; (lacking wisdom) tonto
unwisely /ʌnˈwaizli/ *adv* imprudentemente, indiscretamente
unwitting /ʌnˈwɪtɪŋ/ *a* inconsciente
unwittingly /ʌnˈwɪtɪŋli/ *adv* sin darse cuenta
unwomanly /ʌnˈwumənli/ *a* poco femenino
unwonted /ʌnˈwɒntɪd/ *a* insólito, inusitado
unworkable /ʌnˈwɜrkəbəl/ *a* impráctico
unworkmanlike /ʌnˈwɜrkmən,laik/ *a* chapucero, charanguero
unworldly /ʌnˈwɜrldli/ *a* poco, mundano, espiritual
unworn /ʌnˈwɔrn/ *a* sin llevar, nuevo

unworthiness /ʌnˈwɜrðinɪs/ *n* indignidad, *f*
unworthy /ʌnˈwɜrði/ *a* indigno
unwounded /ʌnˈwundɪd/ *a* no herido, sin herida, ileso
unwrap /ʌnˈræp/ *vt* desenvolver, desempapelar
unwritten /ʌnˈrɪtṇ/ *a* no escrito. *u.* **law,** ley consuetudinaria, *f*
unyielding /ʌnˈyildɪŋ/ *a* duro, firme; (of persons) inflexible, terco, resuelto, obstinado
unyoke /ʌnˈyouk/ *vt* desuncir, quitar el yugo
up /ʌp/ *adv* (high) arriba, en alto; (higher) hacia arriba; (out of bed) levantado; (standing) de pie; (finished) concluido, terminado; (of time) llegado; (excited) agitado; (rebellious) sublevado; (of sun, etc.) salido; (come or gone up) subido; (of universities) en residencia; (for discussion) bajo consideración; (abreast of) al lado, al nivel; (incapable) incapaz, incompetente; (ill) enfermo, indispuesto. **"Up,"** (on elevators) «Para subir.» (For various idiomatic uses of **up** after verbs, see verbs themselves.) *a* (in a few expressions only) ascendente. *prep* en lo alto de; hacia arriba de; a lo largo de; (with country) en el interior de; (with current) contra. **to be up in arms,** sublevarse, rebelarse. **to be very hard up,** ser muy pobre, estar a la cuarta pregunta. **to drink up,** beberlo todo. **to go or come up,** subir. **to lay up,** acumular. **to speak up,** hablar en voz alta. **He has something up his sleeve,** Tiene algo en la manga. **It is all up,** Todo se acabó, Mi gozo en el pozo. **It is not up to much,** Vale muy poco; No es muy fuerte. **It is up to you,** Tú dirás, Tú harás lo que te parezca. **What is he up to?** ¿Qué está tramando? **What's up?** ¿Qué pasa? ¿Qué hay? **up and down,** *adv* bajando y subiendo, de arriba abajo; de un lado a otro; por todas partes. **up-and-down,** *a* fluctuante; (of roads) undulante; (of life) accidentado, borrascoso. **ups and downs,** vicisitudes, *f pl,* altibajos, *m pl.* **up-grade,** subida, *f.* **up in,** versado en, perito en. **well up in,** fuerte en. **up North,** al norte; en el norte; hacia el norte. **up there,** allí arriba, allí en lo alto. **up to,** hasta; (aware of) al corriente de, informado de. **up to date,** *adv* hasta la fecha. **up-to-date,** *a* de última moda; al día. **up to now,** hasta ahora. **up train,** tren ascendente. **Up with...!** ¡Arriba! **Up you go!** (to children) ¡Upa!
upbraid /ʌpˈbreid/ *vt* reprender, echar en cara
upbringing /ˈʌp,brɪŋɪŋ/ *n* crianza, educación, *f*
upcountry /n., *a.* ˈʌp,kʌntri; *adv.* ʌpˈkʌntri/ *n* tierra adentro, *f*; lo interior (de un país). *a* de tierra adentro, del interior. *adv* tierra adentro, hacia el interior
update /ˈʌp,deit/ *vt* actualizar, poner al día
upheaval /ʌpˈhivəl/ *n* solevantamiento, *m*; trastorno, *m*
uphill /*a, adv.* ˈʌpˈhɪl; *n.* ˈʌp,hɪl/ *a* ascendente; penoso, fatigoso, difícil. *adv* cuesta arriba, pecho arriba
uphold /ʌpˈhould/ *vt* sostener, apoyar; (help) ayudar, consolar; (protect) defender; (countenance) aprobar; *Law.* confirmar
upholder /ʌpˈhouldər/ *n* sostenedor (-ra), defensor (-ra)
upholster /ʌpˈhoulstər, əˈpoul-/ *vt* entapizar, tapizar
upholsterer /ʌpˈhoulstərər; əˈpoulẓ/ *n* tapicero, *m*
upholstery /ʌpˈhoulstəri, əˈpoulẓ/ *n* tapicería, *f*; (of car) almohadillado, *m*
upkeep /ˈʌp,kip/ *n* mantenimiento, *m*, conservación, *f*
upland /ˈʌplənd/ *n* tierra alta, *f, a* alto, elevado
uplift /*v.* ʌpˈlɪft; *n.* ˈʌp,lɪft/ *vt* elevar. *n* elevación, *f*; *Inf.* fervor, *m*
upon /əˈpɒn/ *prep.* See **on**
upper /ˈʌpər/ *a comp* superior; alto; de arriba. *n* (of shoe) pala, *f, Sports.* **u.-cut,** golpe de abajo arriba, upper-cut, *m.* **U. Egypt,** Alto Egipto, *m.* **u. hand,** dominio, *m*; superioridad, ventaja, *f.* **u. house,** cámara alta, *f*; senado, *m.* **u. ten,** los diez primeros
upper classes /ˈklæsɪz/ *a* clases altas, capas altas, *f pl*
uppermost /ˈʌpər,moust/ *a* más alto, más elevado; predominante, principal; más fuerte. *adv* en primer lugar; en lo más alto. **to be u.,** predominar
upright /ˈʌp,rait/ *a* recto, derecho; vertical; (honorable) honrado, digno, recto. *n* (stanchion) mástil, so-

porte, palo derecho, montante, *m. adv* en pie; derecho

uprightly /'ʌpˌraitli/ *adv* rectamente, honradamente

uprightness /'ʌpˌraitnɪs/ *n* rectitud, honradez, probidad, *f*

uprising /'ʌpˌraiziŋ/ *n* insurrección, sublevación, *f*

uproar /'ʌpˌrɔr/ *n* alboroto, tumulto, estrépito, *m*, conmoción, *f*

uproarious /ʌp'rɔriəs/ *a* tumultuoso, estrepitoso

uproot /ʌp'rut/ *vt* desarraigar, *Lat. Am.* destroncar; *Fig.* arrancar; (destroy) extirpar

uprooting /ʌp'rutiŋ/ *n* desarraigo, *m*; arranque, *m*; extirpación, *f*

upset /*v.* ʌp'sɛt; *n.* 'ʌpˌsɛt/ *vt* volcar; (overthrow) derribar, echar abajo; (frustrate) contrariar; desarreglar; (distress) trastornar, turbar; (of food) hacer mal. *vi* volcarse. *n* vuelco, *m*; trastorno, *m*. **u. price,** tipo de subasta, *m*

upsetting /ʌp'sɛtiŋ/ *a* turbante, inquietante

upshot /'ʌpˌʃɒt/ *n* resultado, *m*; consecuencia, *f*

upside /'ʌpˌsaid/ *n* lado superior, *m*; parte superior, *f*; (of trains) andén ascendente, *m*. **u. down,** al revés, de arriba abajo; en desorden

upstairs /'ʌp'stɛərz/ *adv* arriba, en el piso de arriba; (with go or come) al piso de arriba

upstanding /ʌp'stændiŋ/ *a* gallardo, guapo. **an u. young man (woman),** un buen mozo (una buena moza)

upstart /'ʌpˌstɑrt/ *n* arribista, *mf*; advenedizo (-za), insolente, *mf*; presuntuoso (-sa)

upstream /'ʌp'strim/ *a* and *adv* contra la corriente, agua arriba, río arriba

upturned /'ʌpˌtɜrnd/ *a* (of noses) respingada

upward /'ʌpwərd/ *a* ascendente, hacia arriba

upwards /'ʌpwərdz/ *adv* hacia arriba; en adelante. **u. of,** más de

Urals, the /'jʊrəlz/ los Urales, *m pl*

uranium /jʊ'reiniəm/ *n* Mineral. uranio, *m*

Uranus /'jʊrənəs, jʊ'rei-/ *n* Astron. Urano, *m*

urban /'ɜrbən/ *a* urbano, ciudadano

urbane /ɜr'bein/ *a* cortés, urbano, fino

urbanity /ɜr'bænɪti/ *n* urbanidad, cortesía, finura, *f*

urbanization /ˌɜrbənə'zeifən/ *n* urbanización, *f*

urbanize /'ɜrbəˌnaiz/ *vt* urbanizar

urban renewal *n* renovación urbana, renovación urbanística, *f*

urchin /'ɜrtʃɪn/ *n* galopín, granuja, pilluelo, *m*

ureter /jʊ'ritər/ *n* Anat. uréter, *m*

urethra /jʊ'riθrə/ *n* Anat. uretra, *f*

urge /ɜrdʒ/ *vt* empujar, impeler; incitar, estimular, azuzar, animar; pedir con urgencia, recomendar con ahínco, instar, insistir (en). *n* instinto, impulso, *m*; deseo, *m*; ambición, *f*

urgency /'ɜrdʒənsi/ *n* urgencia, *f*; importancia, perentoriedad, *f*

urgent /'ɜrdʒənt/ *a* urgente; importante, apremiante, perentorio. **to be u.,** urgir

urgently /'ɜrdʒəntli/ *adv* urgentemente

uric /'jʊrɪk/ *a* úrico

urinal /'jʊrənl/ *n* orinal, urinario, *m*

urinalysis /ˌjʊrə'næləsɪs/ *n* análisis de orina, urinálisis, *m*

urinary /'jʊrəˌnɛri/ *a* urinario

urinary tract *n* conducto urinario, *m*, vías urinarias, *f pl*

urinate /'jʊrəˌneit/ *vi* orinar

urine /'jʊrɪn/ *n* orín, *m*

urn /ɜrn/ *n* urna, *f*; (for coffee) cafetera, *f*; (for tea) tetera, *f*

Ursa /'ɜrsə/ *n* Astron. osa, *f*. **U. Major,** osa mayor, *f*. **U. Minor,** osa menor, *f*

urticaria /ˌɜrtɪ'kɛəriə/ *n* Med. urticaria, *f*

Uruguayan /ˌjʊrə'gweiən/ *a* and *n* uruguayo (-ya)

us /ʌs/ *pron* nos, (with prep.) nosotros. **He came toward us,** Vino hacia nosotros

usable /'juzəbəl/ *a* aprovechable, servible

usage /'jusɪdʒ/ *n* (handling) tratamiento, *m*; uso, *m*, costumbre, *f*

use /jus/ *n* uso, *m*; manejo, empleo, *m*; (custom)

costumbre práctica, *f*; (need) necesidad, *f*; (usefulness) aprovechamiento, *m*; Law. usufructo, *m*. **directions for use,** direcciones para el uso, *f pl*, **for the use of...,** para uso de... **in use,** en uso. **out of use,** anticuado; fuera de moda. **to be of no use,** no servir; ser inútil. **to have no use for,** no tener necesidad de; Inf. tener en poco. **to make use of,** servirse de, aprovechar; Law. ejercer. **to put to use,** poner en uso, poner en servicio

use /yuz/ *vt* usar; (employ) emplear; (utilize) servirse de, utilizar; (handle) manejar; hacer uso de; (consume) gastar, consumir; (treat) tratar; practicar. **to use up,** agotar, acabar con; consumir. *vi impers* acostumbrar, soler (e.g. *It used to happen that...,* Solía ocurrir que...). **(Used to** and the verb which follows are often translated simply by the imperfect tense of the following verb, e.g. *I used to see her every day,* La veía todos los días. Use of the verbs *acostumbrar* or *soler* to translate used to adds emphasis to the statement)

used /yuzd/ *a* and *past part* /yust/ acostumbrado, habituado; empleado; (clothes) usado; (postage stamp) sellado. **to become u. to,** acostumbrarse a

useful /'yusfəl/ *a* útil; provechoso; servicial

usefully /'yusfəli/ *adv* útilmente; con provecho

usefulness /'yusfəlnɪs/ *n* utilidad, *f*; valor, *m*

useless /'yuslɪs/ *a* inútil; vano, infructuoso. **to render u.,** inutilizar

uselessness /'yuslɪsnɪs/ *n* inutilidad, *f*

user /'yuzər/ *n* el, *m*, (*f*, la) que usa, comprador (-ra)

usher /'ʌʃər/ *n* ujier, *m*; (in a theater) acomodador (-ra). *vt* introducir, anunciar; acomodar

usual /'yuʒuəl/ *a* usual, acostumbrado, habitual; normal, común. **as u.,** como siempre. **in the u. form,** Com. al usado; como de costumbre. **with their u. courtesy,** con la cortesía que les es característica

usually /'yuʒuəli/ *adv* por lo general, ordinariamente. **We u. go out on Sundays,** Acostumbramos salir los domingos

usurer /'yuʒərər/ *n* usurero (-ra)

usurious /yu'ʒuriəs/ *a* usurario

usurp /yu'sɜrp/ *vt* usurpar; asumir, arrogarse

usurpation /ˌyusər'peiʃən/ *n* usurpación, *f*; arrogación, *f*

usurper /yu'sɜrpər/ *n* usurpador (-ra)

usurping /yu'sɜrpiŋ/ *a* usurpador

usury /'yuʒəri/ *n* usura, *f*. **to practice u.,** usurear, dar (or tomar) a usura

utensil /yu'tensəl/ *n* utensilio, instrumento, *m*; herramienta, *f*. **kitchen utensils,** batería de cocina, *f*

uterine /'yutərɪn/ *a* Med. uterino

uterus /'yutərəs/ *n* útero, *m*

utilitarian /yu,tɪlɪ'tɛəriən/ *a* utilitario

utilitarianism /yu,tɪlɪ'tɛəriə,nɪzəm/ *n* utilitarismo, *m*

utility /yu'tɪlɪti/ *n* utilidad, *f*; ventaja, *f*, beneficio, provecho, *m*. **u. goods,** artículos fabricados bajo la autorización del gobierno, *m pl*

utilizable /ˌyutl'aizəbəl/ *a* utilizable, aprovechable

utilization /ˌyutlə'zeiʃən/ *n* empleo, aprovechamiento, *m*

utilize /'yutlˌaiz/ *vt* utilizar, servirse de; aprovechar

utmost /'ʌtˌmoust/ *a* (innermost) extremo, íntimo; (outermost) extremo; (farthest) más remoto, más distante; (greatest) mayor, más grande. *n* lo más; todo lo posible. **to do one's u.,** hacer todo lo posible, hacer todo lo que uno pueda

utopian /yu'toupiən/ *a* utópico

utter /'ʌtər/ *a* completo, total; terminante, absoluto; sumo, extremo. **He is an u. fool,** Es un tonto de capirote

utter /'ʌtər/ *vt* pronunciar, proferir, decir, hablar; (a sigh, cry, etc.) dar; (express) manifestar, expresar, explicar; (coin) poner en circulación; (a libel) publicar; (disclose) revelar, descubrir

utterance /'ʌtərəns/ *n* expresión, manifestación, *f*; pronunciación, *f*; (style) lenguaje, *m*

utterly /'ʌtərli/ *adv* enteramente, completamente

uttermost /'ʌtər,moust/ *a.* See **utmost**

uvula /'yuvyələ/ *n* Anat. úvula, *f*

uxorious /ʌk'sɔriəs/ *a* uxorio

V

v /vi/ *n* (letter) ve, *f*; pieza en forma de V, *f*

vacancy /'veikənsi/ *n* vacío, *m*; vacancia, *f*; (mental) vacuidad, *f*; (of offices, posts) vacante, *f*; (leisure) desocupación, ociosidad, *f*; (gap, blank) vacío, *m*, laguna, *f*

vacant /'veikənt/ *a* vacío; despoblado, deshabitado; (free) libre; (of offices, etc.) vacante; (leisured) ocioso; (absent-minded) distraído; (vague) vago; (foolish) estúpido, estólido

vacantly /'veikəntli/ *adv* distraídamente; estúpidamente

vacate /'veikeit/ *vt* dejar vacío; (a post) dejar; (a throne) renunciar a; dejar vacante; *Mil.* evacuar; *Law.* anular, rescindir

vacation /vei'keiʃən/ *n* (of offices) vacante, *f*; (holiday) vacaciones, *f pl*, *f*. **the long v.**, las vacaciones de verano. **to be on a v.**, estar de vacaciones

vaccinate /'væksə,neit/ *vt* vacunar

vaccination /,væksə'neiʃən/ *n* vacunación, *f*

vaccine /væk'sin/ *n* vacuna, *f*

vacillate /'væsə,leit/ *vi* (sway) oscilar; (hesitate) vacilar, titubear, dudar

vacillating /'væsə,leitɪŋ/ *a* vacilante

vacillation /,væsə'leiʃən/ *n* vacilación, *f*

vacuity /væ'kyuiti/ *n* vacuidad, *f*

vacuous /'vækyuəs/ *a* desocupado, ocioso; estúpido, vacío

vacuum /'vækyum/ *n* vacío, *m*. **v. brake,** freno al vacío, *m*. **v. cleaner,** aspirador de polvo, *m*. **v. flask,** termos, *m*. **v. pump,** bomba neumática, *f*. **vacuum-shelf dryer,** secador al vacío, *m*

vade mecum /'vei'di mikəm, 'vɑ-/ *n* vademécum, *m*

vagabond /'vægə,bɒnd/ *n* vagabundo (-da); vago, *m*; (beggar) mendigo (-ga). *a* vagabundo, errante

vagabondage /'vægə,bɒndɪdʒ/ *n* vagabundeo, *m*, vagancia, *f*

vagary /və'gɛəri, 'veigəri/ *n* (whim) capricho, antojo, *m*, extravagancia, *f*; (of the mind) divagación, *f*

vagina /və'dʒainə/ *n* vagina, *f*

vaginal /'vædʒənl/ *a* vaginal

vagrancy /'veigrənsi/ *n* vagancia, *f*

vagrant /'veigrənt/ *n* vago, *m*, *a* vagabundo, errante

vague /veig/ *a* vago; indistinto; equívoco, ambiguo; (uncertain) incierto

vaguely /'veigli/ *adv* vagamente

vagueness /'veignɪs/ *n* vaguedad, *f*

vain /vein/ *a* vano; (fruitless) infructuoso; (useless) inútil; (unsubstantial) fútil, insubstancial; fantástico; (empty) vacío; (worthless) despreciable; (conceited) vanidoso, presumido. **in v.,** en vano, en balde, inútilmente. **v. about,** orgulloso de

vainglorious /vein'glɔriəs, -'glour-/ *a* vanaglorioso

vaingloriousness /vein'glɔriəsnɪs/ *n* vanagloria, *f*

vainly /'veinli/ *adv* vanamente; inútilmente; (conceitedly) vanidosamente, con vanidad

valance /'vælans/ *n* cenefa, *f*

vale /veil/ *n* (valley) valle, *m*. *interj* ¡adiós! *n* (goodbye) vale, *m*

valediction /,væli'dikʃən/ *n* despedida, *f*; vale, *m*

valedictory /,væli'diktəri/ *a* de despedida

Valencian /və'lɛnʃiən/ *a* and *n* valenciano (-na)

valency /'veilənsi/ *n* *Chem.* valencia, *f*

valet /'væ'lei, 'vælɪt/ *n* criado, *m*. **v. de chambre,** ayuda de cámara, *m*

valetudinarian /,væli,tudn'ɛəriən/ *a* valetudinario

Valhalla /væl'hælə, val'halə/ *n* el Valhala, *m*

valiant /'vælyənt/ *a* valiente, esforzado, animoso, bravo

valiantly /'vælyəntli/ *adv* valientemente

valid /'vælɪd/ *a* válido, valedero; (of laws in force) vigente

validate /'væli,deit/ *vt* validar

validation /,væli'deiʃən/ *n* validación, *f*

validity /və'lɪdɪti/ *n* validez, *f*

validly /'vælɪdli/ *adv* válidamente

valise /və'lis/ *n* valija, *f*, saco de viaje, *m*

valley /'væli/ *n* valle, *m*

valor /'vælər/ *n* valor, *m*, valentía, *f*

valorous /'vælərəs/ *a* valoroso, esforzado, intrépido

valuable /'vælyuəbəl/ *a* valioso; costoso; precioso; estimable; excelente. *n pl* **valuables,** objetos de valor, *m pl*

valuableness /'vælyuəbəlnɪs/ *n* valor, *m*

valuation /,vælyu'eiʃən/ *n* valuación, tasación, *f*; estimación, *f*

valuator /'vælyu,eitər/ *n* tasador, *m*

value /'vælyu/ *n* valor, *m*; precio, *m*; estimación, *f*; importancia, *f*; (*Gram. Mus.*) valor, *m*; *pl* **values,** valores morales, principios, *m pl*. *vt* tasar, valorar; estimar; apreciar; tener en mucho; hacer caso de; considerar. **to be of v.,** ser de valor

valued /'vælyud/ *a* apreciado, estimado; precioso

valueless /'vælyulɪs/ *a* sin valor; insignificante

valuer /'vælyuər/ *n* tasador, *m*

valve /vælv/ *n* (*Elec., Mech., Anat.*) válvula, *f*; (*Bot., Zool.*) valva, *f*

valved /vælvd/ *a* con válvulas; (in compounds) de... válvulas

valvular /'vælvyələr/ *a* valvular

vamp /væmp/ *n* (of a shoe) pala (de zapato), *f*; (patch) remiendo, *m*; *Mus.* acompañamiento improvisado, *m*; *Inf.* aventurera, *f*. *vt* (of shoes) poner palas (a); (patch) remendar; *Mus.* improvisar un acompañamiento; (of a woman) fascinar, engatusar

vampire /'væmpaɪ³r/ *n* vampiro, *m*

van /væn/ *n* (*Mil., Nav., Fig.*) vanguardia, *f*; camión, *m*; (for delivery) camión de reparto, *m*; (for furniture) conductora de muebles, *f*; (removal) carro de mudanzas, *m*; (mail) camión postal, *m*; (for bathing) caseta de baño, *f*; (for guard on trains) furgón de equipajes, *m*; (railroad car) vagón, *m*

vandal /'vændl/ *a* and *n* vándalo (-la); bárbaro (-ra)

vandalism /'vændl,izəm/ *n* vandalismo, *m*

vane /vein/ *n* (weathercock) veleta, *f*; (of a windmill) aspa, *f*; (of a propeller) paleta, *f*; (of a feather) barba, *f*; (of a surveying instrument) pínula, *f*

vanguard /'væn,gɑrd/ *n* vanguardia, *f*. **in the v.,** a vanguardia; *Fig.* en la vanguardia

vanilla /və'nɪlə/ *n* vainilla, *f*

vanish /'vænɪʃ/ *vi* desaparecer; desvanecerse; disiparse

vanishing /'vænɪʃɪŋ/ *n* desaparición, *f*; disipación, *f*. **v. cream,** crema desvanecedora, *f*. **v. point,** punto de la vista, *m*

vanity /'vænɪti/ *n* vanidad, *f*. **v. case,** polvera de bolsillo, *f*

vanquish /'væŋkwɪʃ/ *vt* vencer, derrotar

vanquisher /'væŋkwɪʃər/ *n* vencedor (-ra)

vantage /'væntɪdʒ, 'van-/ *n* ventaja (also in tennis), *f*. **v.-ground,** posición ventajosa, *f*, sitial de privilegio, *m*

vapid /'væpɪd/ *a* insípido, insulso; (of speeches, etc.) soso, aburrido, insípido

vapidity /væ'pɪdɪti/ *n* insipidez, sosería, *f*

vapor /'veipər/ *n* vapor, *m*; *pl* **vapors,** (hysteria) vapores, *m pl*. *vi* (boast) jactarse, baladronear; decir disparates. **v. bath,** baño de vapor, *m*

vaporizable /,veipə'raizəbəl/ *a* vaporizable

vaporization /,veipərə'zeiʃən/ *n* vaporización, *f*

vaporize /'veipə,raiz/ *vt* vaporizar. *vi* vaporizarse

vaporizer /'veipə,raizər/ *n* vaporizador, *m*

vaporous /'veipərəs/ *a* vaporoso

variability /,vɛəriə'bɪlti/ *n* variabilidad, *f*

variable /'vɛəriəbəl/ *a* variable. *n* *Math.* variable, *f*

variably /'vɛəriəbli/ *adv* variablemente

variance /'vɛəriəns/ *n* variación, *f*, cambio, *m*; desacuerdo, *m*, disensión, *f*; diferencia, contradicción, *f*. **at v.,** en desacuerdo, reñidos; hostil (a), opuesto (a); (of things) distinto (de), en contradicción (con)

variant /'vɛəriənt/ *n* variante, *f*

variation /ˌvɛəri'eiʃən/ n variación, f; cambio, m; variedad, f; diferencia, f; (*Mus.* magnetism) variación, f
varicose /'væri,kous/ a varicoso
varied success /'vɛərid/ éxito vario, m
variegate /'vɛərii,geit/ vt abigarrar, matizar, salpicar
variegated /'vɛərii,geitid/ a abigarrado; variado; mezclado
variegation /ˌvɛərii'geiʃən/ n abigarramiento, m; diversidad de colores, f
variety /və'raiti/ n variedad, f; diversidad, f; (choice) surtido, m. **v. show,** función de variedades, f
various /'vɛəriəs/ a vario, diverso; diferente
variously /'vɛəriəsli/ adv diversamente
varix /'vɛəriks/ n várice, f
varnish /'vɑrniʃ/ n barniz, m. vt barnizar; (pottery) vidriar; (conceal) disimular. **copal v.,** barniz copal, m. **japan v.,** charol japonés, m. **lacquer v.,** laca, f. **v. remover,** (for nails) quitaesmalte, m
varnishing /'vɑrniʃiŋ/ n barnizado, m; (of pottery) vidriado, m
vary /'vɛəri/ vt variar; cambiar; diversificar; modificar. vi variar; cambiar; (be different) ser distinto (de); (deviate) desviarse (de); (disagree) estar en desacuerdo, distar, estar en contradicción. **to v. directly (indirectly),** *Math.* variar en razón directa (inversa)
varying /'vɛəriiŋ/ a variante, cambiante, diverso
vascular /'væskyələr/ a vascular
vase /veis, veiz, vɑz/ n vaso, jarrón, m; urna, f
vaseline /'væsə,lin/ n vaselina, f
vassal /'væsəl/ n vasallo (-lla); esclavo (-va), siervo (-va). a tributario
vast /væst/ a vasto, extenso; enorme; grande. n vastedad, inmensidad, f
vastly /'væstli/ adv enormemente; muy; con mucho
vastness /'væstnis/ n vastedad, extensión, f; inmensidad, f; enormidad, f, gran tamaño, m; grandeza, f
vat /væt/ n cuba, tina, f; alberca, f, estanque, m. **dyeing vat,** cuba de tintorero, f. **tanning vat,** noque, m. **wine vat,** lagar, m
Vatican /'vætikən/ a and n Vaticano, m
vaticinate /və'tisə,neit/ vt and vi vaticinar, profetizar
vaticination /və,tisə'neiʃən/ n vaticinio, m, predicción, f
vaudeville /'vɔdvil/ n vodevil, m, zarzuela cómica, f
vault /vɔlt/ n *Archit.* bóveda, f; caverna, f; (for wine) bodega, cueva, f; (in a bank) cámara acorazada, f; (in a church) cripta, f; sepultura, f; (of the sky) bóveda celeste, f; (leap) salto, m; voltereta, f. vi (jump) saltar; (with a pole) saltar con pértiga; saltar por encima de; voltear. vt *Archit.* abovedar; saltar
vaulted /'vɔltid/ a abovedado
vaulter /'vɔltər/ n saltador (-ra)
vaulting /'vɔltiŋ/ n construcción de bóvedas, f; bóvedas, f pl; edificio abovedado, m; (jumping) salto, m. **v.-horse,** potro de madera, m
vaunt /vɔnt/ vi jactarse (de), hacer gala (de); triunfar (sobre). vt ostentar, sacar a relucir; (praise) alabar. n jactancia, f
veal /vil/ n ternera, f. **v.-cutlet,** chuleta de ternera, f
vector /'vɛktər/ n vector, m
Veda /'veidə/ n Veda, m
veer /vɪər/ vi (of the wind) girar; (of a ship) virar; *Fig.* cambiar (de opinión, etc.). vt virar
vegetable /'vɛdʒtəbəl/ n vegetal, m; legumbre, f; pl **vegetables,** (green and generally cooked) verduras, f pl; (raw green) hortalizas, f pl. **v. dish,** fuente de legumbres, f. **v. garden,** huerto de legumbres, m; **v. ivory,** marfil vegetal, m. **v. kingdom,** reino vegetal, m. **v. soup,** sopa de hortelano, f
vegetal /'vɛdʒitl/ a vegetal
vegetarian /ˌvɛdʒi'tɛəriən/ a and n vegetariano (-na)
vegetarianism /ˌvɛdʒi'tɛəriə,nizəm/ n vegetarianismo, m
vegetate /'vɛdʒi,teit/ vi vegetar
vegetation /ˌvɛdʒi'teiʃən/ n vegetación, f
vehemence /'viəməns/ n vehemencia, f; violencia, f; impetuosidad, f; pasión, f, ardor, m
vehement /'viəmənt/ a vehemente; violento; impetuoso; apasionado

vehemently /'viəməntli/ adv con vehemencia; violentamente; con impetuosidad; apasionadamente
vehicle /'viikəl/ n vehículo, m; (means) medio, m; instrumento, m
vehicular /vi'hikyələr/ a vehicular, de los vehículos; de los coches. **v. traffic,** circulación de los coches, f; los vehículos
veil /veil/ n velo, m; (curtain) cortina, f; (disguise) disfraz, m; (excuse) pretexto, m; (appearance) apariencia, f. vt velar; cubrir con un velo; (hide) tapar, encubrir; (dissemble) disimular; (disguise) disfrazar. **to take the v.,** tomar el velo, profesar
vein /vein/ n (*Anat.*, *Bot.*) vena, f; (*Geol.*, *Mineral.*) veta, f, filón, m; (in wood) fibra, hebra, f; (*Fig.* streak) rasgo, m; (inspiration) vena, f; (mood) humor, m
veined, veiny /veind; 'veini/ a venoso; de venas; veteado
velar /'vilər/ a velar
vellum /'vɛləm/ n vitela, f
velocity /və'lɒsiti/ n velocidad, f; rapidez, f
velodrome /'vilə,droum/ n velódromo, m
velours /və'lʊr/ n terciopelo, m
velvet /'vɛlvit/ n terciopelo, m, a hecho de terciopelo; aterciopelado
velveteen /ˌvɛlvi'tin/ n pana, f, velludillo, m
velvety /'vɛlvti/ a aterciopelado
venal /'vinl/ a venal
venality /vi'næliti/ n venalidad, f
vend /vɛnd/ vt vender
vendor /'vɛndər/ n vendedor (-ra)
veneer /və'nɪər/ vt chapear, taracear; (conceal) disimular, disfrazar. n taraceado, chapeado, m; (plate) chapa, hoja para chapear, f; (*Fig.* gloss) barniz, m, apariencia, f
venerability /ˌvɛnərə'biliti/ n venerabilidad, respetabilidad, f
venerable /'vɛnərəbəl/ a venerable
venerate /'vɛnə,reit/ vt venerar, reverenciar
veneration /ˌvɛnə'reiʃən/ n veneración, f
venerator /'vɛnə,reitər/ n venerador (-ra)
venereal /və'nɪəriəl/ a venéreo. **v. disease,** enfermedad venérea, f
Venetian /və'niʃən/ a and n veneciano (-na). **v. blinds,** persianas, celosías, f pl
Venezuelan /ˌvɛnə'zweilən/ a and n venezolano (-na)
vengeance /'vɛndʒəns/ n venganza, f
vengeful /'vɛndʒfəl/ a vengativo
venial /'viniəl/ a venial
veniality /ˌvini'æliti/ n venialidad, f
Venice /'vɛnis/ n Venecia, f
venison /'vɛnəsən/ n venado, m
venom /'vɛnəm/ n veneno, m
venomous /'vɛnəməs/ a venenoso; maligno, malicioso
venomously /'vɛnəməsli/ adv con malignidad, maliciosamente
venomousness /'vɛnəməsnis/ n venenosidad, f; malignidad, f
venous /'vinəs/ a venoso
vent /vɛnt/ n abertura, f; salida, f; (air-hole) respiradero, m; (in pipes) ventosa, f; (in fire-arms) oído, m; *Anat.* ano, m; (*Fig.* outlet) desahogo, m; expresión, f. vt dejar escapar; (pierce) agujerear; (discharge) emitir, vomitar; (relieve) desahogar; expresar, dar expresión (a), dar rienda suelta (a)
venter /'vɛntər/ n *Law.* vientre, m
ventilate /'vɛntl,eit/ vt ventilar; discutir
ventilation /ˌvɛntl'eiʃən/ n ventilación, f
ventilator /'vɛntl,eitər/ n ventilador, m
ventricle /'vɛntrikəl/ n ventrículo, m
ventriloquism /vɛn'trilə,kwizəm/ n ventriloquia, f
ventriloquist /vɛn'triləkwist/ n ventrílocuo (-ua)
venture /'vɛntʃər/ n ventura, f; riesgo, m; aventura, f; especulación, f. vt arriesgar, aventurar; (stake) jugar; (state) expresar. vi aventurarse; (dare) atreverse, osar; permitirse. **at a v.,** a la ventura. **to v. on,** arriesgarse a; probar ventura con; lanzarse a; (a remark) permitirse. **to v. out,** atreverse a salir

venturesome /'vɛntʃərsəm/ a atrevido, audaz; (dangerous) arriesgado, peligroso
venturesomeness /'vɛntʃərsəmnıs/ n atrevimiento, m, temeridad, f; (risk) riesgo, peligro, m
Venus /'vinəs/ n (planet) Venus, m; (woman) venus, f
veracious /və'reiʃəs/ a veraz, verídico; verdadero
veracity /və'ræsıti/ n veracidad, f; verdad, f
veranda /və'rændə/ n veranda, f
verb /vɜrb/ n verbo, m. **auxiliary v.,** verbo auxiliar, m. **intransitive v.,** verbo intransitivo (neutro), m. **reflexive v.,** verbo reflexivo, m. **transitive v.,** verbo transitivo, m
verbal /'vɜrbəl/ a verbal
verbally /'vɜrbali/ adv de palabra, verbalmente
verbatim /vər'beitım/ a textual. adv textualmente, palabra por palabra
verbiage /'vɜrbiidʒ/ n verbosidad, palabrería, f
verbose /vər'bous/ a verboso, prolijo
verbosity /vər'bɒsıti/ n verbosidad, f
verdancy /'vɜrdn̩si/ n verdura, f, verdor, m
verdant /'vɜrdnt/ a verde
verdict /'vɜrdıkt/ n Law. veredicto, fallo, m, sentencia, f; opinión, f, juicio, m. **to bring in a v.,** fallar sentencia.
verdigris /'vɜrdı,gris/ n cardenillo, verdin, m
verdure /'vɜrdʒər/ n verdura, f, verdor, m; Fig. lozanía, f
verge /vɜrdʒ/ n (wand) vara, f; (edge) margen, f, borde, m; (of a lake, etc.) orilla, f; (horizon) horizonte, m; Fig. víspera, f, punto, m. **on the v. of,** al margen de, a la orilla de. **to be on the v. of,** Fig. estar a punto de; estar en vísperas de
verger /'vɜrdʒər/ n macero, m; (in a church) pertiguero, m
verifiable /,vɛrə'faiəbəl/ a verificable
verification /,vɛrəfı'keiʃən/ n verificación, f
verifier /'vɛrə,faiər/ n verificador (-ra)
verify /'vɛrə,fai/ vt verificar, confirmar; probar
verily /'vɛrəli/ adv de veras, en verdad
verisimilitude /,vɛrəsı'mılı,tud/ n verosimilitud, f
veritable /'vɛrıtəbəl/ a verdadero
veritably /'vɛrıtəbli/ adv verdaderamente
verity /'vɛrıti/ n verdad, f
vermicelli /,vɜrmı'tʃɛli/ n fideos, m pl
vermilion /vər'mılyən/ n bermellón, m
vermin /'vɜrmın/ n bichos dañinos, m pl; (insects) parásitos, m pl
vermouth /vər'muθ/ n vermut, m
vernacular /vər'nækyələr/ a vernáculo; nativo; vulgar. n lengua popular, f; lenguaje vulgar, m
versatile /'vɜrsətl̩/ a Zool. versátil; inconstante, voluble; (clever) de muchos talentos; de muchos intereses; adaptable; completo, cabal
versatility /,vɜrsə'tılıti/ n (cleverness) muchos talentos, m pl; adaptabilidad, f
verse /vɜrs/ n verso, m; (stanza) estrofa, f; (in the Bible) versículo, m; (poetry) poesía, f, versos, m pl. **to make verses,** escribir versos
versed /vɜrst/ a versado, experimentado
versicle /'vɜrsıkəl/ n versículo, m
versification /,vɜrsəfı'keiʃən/ n versificación, f
versifier /'vɜrsə,faiər/ n versificador (-ra)
versify /'vɜrsə,fai/ vt and vi versificar
version /'vɜrʒən/ n versión, f; traducción, f; interpretación, f
versus /'vɜrsəs/ prep contra
vertebra /'vɜrtəbrə/ n vértebra, f
vertebral /'vɜrtəbrəl/ a vertebral
vertebrate /'vɜrtəbrıt/ n vertebrado, m
vertex /'vɜrtɛks/ n (Geom., Anat.) vértice, m; Astron. cenit, m; cumbre, f
vertical /'vɜrtıkəl/ a vertical
verticality /,vɜrtı'kælıti/ n verticalidad, f
vertiginous /vər'tıdʒənəs/ a vertiginoso
vertigo /'vɜrtı,gou/ n vértigo, m
verve /vɜrv/ n brío, m, fogosidad, f
very /'vɛri/ a mismo; (mere) mero, f; (true) verdadero; (with adjective and comparative) más grande; Inf. mismísimo; (complete) perfecto, completo. **The v. thought of it made him laugh,** Sólo con pensarlo se

rió (or La mera idea le hizo reír). **this v. minute,** este mismísimo instante. **the v. day,** el mismo día
very /'vɛri/ adv muy; mucho; demasiado; (exactly) exactamente; completamente; absolutamente. **He is v. worried,** Está muy preocupado. **He is not v. well,** (i.e. rather ill) Está bastante bien. **This cloth is the v. best,** Esta tela es la mejor que hay. **I like it v. much,** Me gusta muchísimo. **He is v. much pleased,** Está muy contento. **so v. little,** tan poco; tan pequeño. **v. well,** muy bien
vesicle /'vɛsıkəl/ n vesícula, f
vesper /'vɛspər/ n estrella vespertina, f, héspero, m; pl **vespers,** Eccl. vísperas, f pl
vessel /'vɛsəl/ n vasija, f, recipiente, m; (boat) barco, buque, m; (Anat., Bot.) vaso, m
vest /vɛst/ n camiseta, f; (waistcoat) chaleco, m. vt vestir; (with authority, etc.) revestir de; (property, etc.) hacer entrega de, ceder. vi tener validez; (dress) vestirse. **vested interests,** intereses creados, m pl. **v.-pocket,** bolsillo del chaleco, m. **v.-pocket camera,** cámara de bolsillo, f
vestal /'vɛstl̩/ a vestal; virgen, casto. n vestal, f; virgen, f
vestibule /'vɛstə,byul/ n vestíbulo, m; (anteroom) antecámara, f; (of a theatre box) antepalco, m; Anat. vestíbulo, m
vestige /'vɛstıdʒ/ n vestigio, rastro, m; sombra, f; Biol. rudimento, m
vestment /'vɛstmənt/ n hábito, m; Eccl. vestidura, f
vestry /'vɛstri/ n vestuario, m, sacristía, f
vesture /'vɛstʃər/ n traje, hábito, m, vestidura, f
Vesuvius /və'suviəs/ Vesubio, m
veteran /'vɛtərən/ a veterano; de los veteranos; aguerrido; anciano; experimentado. n veterano (-na)
veterinary /'vɛtərə,nɛri/ a veterinario. **v. science,** veterinaria, f. **v. surgeon,** veterinario, m
veto /'vitou/ n veto, m; prohibición, f. vt poner el veto; prohibir
vex /vɛks/ vt contrariar, irritar; enojar; (make impatient) impacientar; fastidiar; (afflict) afligir, acongojar; (worry) inquietar
vexation /vɛk'seiʃən/ n contrariedad, irritación, f; enojo, enfado, m; (impatience) impaciencia, f; fastidio, m; aflicción, f; inquietud, f; disgusto, m
vexatious /vɛk'seiʃəs/ a irritante; enojoso, enfadoso; fastidioso, molesto
vexatiousness /vɛk'seiʃəsnıs/ n fastidio, m, molestia, f; incomodidad, f; contrariedad, f
vexed /vɛkst/ a discutido; contencioso; (thorny) espinoso, difícil
vexing /'vɛksıŋ/ a irritante; molesto; enfadoso
via /'vaiə, 'viə/ n vía, f, prep por, por la vía de
viability /,vaiə'bılıti/ n viabilidad, f
viable /'vaiəbəl/ a viable
viaduct /'vaiə,dʌkt/ n viaducto, m
vial /'vaiəl/ n frasco, m, ampolleta, f
vibrant /'vaibrənt/ a vibrante
vibrate /'vaibreit/ vi vibrar; (of machines) trepidar; oscilar. vt hacer vibrar, vibrar
vibration /vai'breiʃən/ n vibración, f; trepidación, f; oscilación, f, Lat. Am. cimbrón, m
vibrator /'vaibreitər/ n Elec. vibrador, m; Radio. oscilador, m
vicar /'vıkər/ n vicario, m; (of a parish) cura, m. **v.-general,** vicario general, m
vicarious /vai'kɛəriəs/ a vicario; sufrido por otro; experimentado por otro
vicariously /vai'kɛəriəsli/ adv por delegación; por substitución. **I know it only v.,** Lo conozco sólo por referencia
vice /vais/ n vicio, m; defecto, m; (in a horse) vicio, resabio, m; (tool) tornillo de banco, m, prefix vice. **v.-admiral,** vicealmirante, m. **v.-chairman,** vicepresidente (-ta). **v.-chancellor,** vicecanciller, m. **v.-consul,** vice-cónsul, m. **v.-consulate,** vice-consulado, m. **v.-president,** vicepresidente (-ta)
viceroy /'vaisrɔi/ n virrey, m
vice versa /'vaisə ,vɜrsə, 'vais-/ adv viceversa
vicinity /vı'sınıti/ n vecindad, f; (nearness) cercanía,

proximidad, _f._ **to be in the v. of,** estar en la vecindad de

vicious /'vɪʃəs/ _a_ vicioso. **v. circle,** círculo vicioso, _m_

viciousness /'vɪʃəsnɪs/ _n_ viciosidad, _f;_ (in a horse) resabios, _m pl_

vicissitude /vɪ'sɪsɪ,tud/ _n_ vicisitud, _f_

vicissitudinous /vɪ,sɪsɪ'tudnəs/ _a_ accidentado, vicisitudinario

victim /'vɪktəm/ _n_ víctima, _f_

victimization /,vɪktəmə'zeiʃən/ _n_ sacrificio, _m;_ tormento, _m_

victimize /'vɪktə,maiz/ _vt_ hacer víctima (de); sacrificar; ser víctima (de), sufrir; (cheat) estafar, engañar

victor /'vɪktər/ _n_ víctor (-ora), vencedor (-ora)

victoria /vɪk'tɔriə/ _n_ victoria, _f_

Victorian /vɪk'tɔriən/ _a_ victoriano

victorious /vɪk'tɔriəs/ _a_ victorioso, triunfante. **to be v.,** triunfar, salir victorioso

victoriously /vɪk'tɔriəsli/ _adv_ victoriosamente, triunfalmente

victory /'vɪktəri/ _n_ victoria, _f_

victual /'vɪtl̩/ _n_ vitualla, vianda, _f; pl_ **victuals,** víveres, _m pl,_ provisiones, _f pl. vt_ avituallar; abastecer. _vi_ tomar provisiones

victualler /'vɪtlər/ _n_ abastecedor (-ra), proveedor (-ra)

victualling /'vɪtlɪŋ/ _n_ abastecimiento, _m_

vide /'wɪde, 'vaidi, 'videi/ _Latin imperative_ véase, véanse

videlicet /wɪ'deilɪ,kɛt, vi'dɛləsɪt/ _adv_ a saber

video /'vɪdi,ou/, _n_ vídeo, _m_

videocassette /'vɪdioukə,sɛt/ _n_ videocasete, _f_

videotape /'vɪdiou,teip/ _n_ videograbación, videocinta, _f_

vie /vai/ _vi_ (with) competir con; rivalizar con; (with a person) disputar; luchar con

Vienna /vi'ɛnə/ Viena, _f_

Viennese /,viə'niz/ _a_ and _n_ vienés (-esa)

view /vyu/ _n_ vista, _f;_ perspectiva, _f,_ panorama, _m;_ (landscape) paisaje, _m;_ escena, _f;_ inspección, _f;_ (judgment) opinión, _f,_ parecer, _m;_ consideración, _f;_ (appearance) apariencia, _f;_ aspecto, _m;_ (purpose) propósito, _m,_ intención, _f;_ (sight) alcance de la vista, _m;_ (show) exposición, _f. vt_ examinar; inspeccionar; (look at) mirar; (see) ver, contemplar; considerar. **in v. of,** en vista de. **in my v.,** en mi opinión, según creo yo. **on v.,** a la vista. **to keep in v.,** no perder de vista; _Fig._ no olvidar, tener presente. **to take a different v.,** pensar de un modo distinto. **to v. a house,** inspeccionar una casa. **with a v. to,** con el propósito de. **v.-finder,** enfocador, _m._ **v.-point,** punto de vista, _m_

viewer /'vyuər/ _n_ espectador (-ra); examinador (-ra)

viewing /'vyuɪŋ/ _n_ inspección, _f,_ examen, _m_

vigil /'vɪdʒəl/ _n_ vela, vigilia, _f; Eccl._ vigilia, _f_

vigilance /'vɪdʒələns/ _n_ vigilancia, _f,_ desvelo, _m_

vigilant /'vɪdʒələnt/ _a_ vigilante, desvelado

vigilantly /'vɪdʒələntli/ _adv_ vigilantemente

vignette /vɪn'yɛt/ _n_ viñeta, _f_

vigor /'vɪgər/ _n_ vigor, _m,_ fuerza, _f_

vigorous /'vɪgərəs/ _a_ vigoroso, enérgico, fuerte; _Argentina_ alentado

vigorously /'vɪgərəsli/ _adv_ con vigor

Viking /'vaikɪŋ/ _n_ vikingo, _m_

vile /vail/ _a_ vil; bajo; despreciable; infame; _Inf._ horrible

vilely /'vailli/ _adv_ vilmente; _Inf._ mal, horriblemente

vileness /'vailnɪs/ _n_ vileza, _f;_ bajeza, _f;_ infamia, _f_

vilification /,vɪləfɪ'keiʃən/ _n_ vilipendio, _m,_ difamación, _f_

vilifier /'vɪlə,faiər/ _n_ difamador (-ra)

vilify /'vɪlə,fai/ _vt_ vilipendiar, difamar

villa /'vɪlə/ _n_ villa, torre, casa de campo, _f;_ hotel, _m_

village /'vɪlɪdʒ/ _n_ aldea, _f,_ pueblo, _m._ **v. shop** _Lat. Am._ esquina, _f_

villager /'vɪlɪdʒər/ _n_ aldeano (-na)

villain /'vɪlən/ _n Hist._ villano, _m;_ malvado, _m_

villainous /'vɪlənəs/ _a_ malvado; infame; vil

villainously /'vɪlənəsli/ _adv_ vilmente

villainy /'vɪləni/ _n_ vileza, infamia, maldad, _f_

vindicate /'vɪndɪ,keit/ _vt_ vindicar, justificar; defender

vindication /,vɪndɪ'keiʃən/ _n_ vindicación, justificación, _f;_ defensa, _f_

vindicative /vɪn'dɪkətɪv/ _a_ vindicativo, vindicador, justificativo

vindicator /'vɪndɪ,keitər/ _n_ vindicador (-ra)

vindictive /vɪn'dɪktɪv/ _a_ vengativo; rencoroso

vindictively /vɪn'dɪktɪvli/ _adv_ vengativamente; rencorosamente

vindictiveness /vɪn'dɪktɪvnɪs/ _n_ deseo de venganza, _m;_ rencor, _m_

vine /vain/ _n_ vid, parra, _f;_ (twining plant) enredadera, _f._ **v.-arbor,** emparrado, _m._ **v.-branch,** sarmiento, _m._ **v.-clad,** cubierto de parras. **v.-grower,** vinicultor, _m._ **v.-growing,** vinicultura, _f._ **v.-leaf,** hoja de parra, _f._ **v.-pest,** filoxera, _f._ **v.-stock,** cepa, _f_

vinegar /'vɪnɪgər/ _n_ vinagre, _m._ **v.-cruet,** vinagrera, _f._ **v.-sauce,** vinagreta, _f_

vinegary /'vɪnɪgəri/ _a_ vinagroso

vineyard /'vɪnyərd/ _n_ viña, _f,_ viñedo, _m._ **v.-keeper,** viñador, _m_

vinification /,vɪnəfɪ'keiʃən/ _n_ vinificación, _f_

vinosity /vai'nɒsɪti/ _n_ vinosidad, _f_

vinous /'vainəs/ _a_ vinoso

vintage /'vɪntɪdʒ/ _n_ vendimia, _f;_ (of wine) cosecha (de vino), _f_

vintner /'vɪntnər/ _n_ vinatero, _m_

viola /vi'oulə/ _n_ (_Mus., Bot._) viola, _f._ **v. player,** viola, _mf_

violate /'vaiə,leit/ _vt_ (desecrate) profanar; (infringe) contravenir, infringir; (break) romper; (ravish) violar

violation /,vaiə'leiʃən/ _n_ profanación, _f;_ (infringement) contravención, _f;_ (rape) violación, _f_

violator /'vaiə,leitər/ _n_ violador (-ra); (ravisher) violador, _m_

violence /'vaiələns/ _n_ violencia, _f_

violent /'vaiələnt/ _a_ violento

violently /'vaiələntli/ _adv_ con violencia

violet /'vaiəlɪt/ _n_ violeta, _f. a_ violado, **v. color,** violeta, color violado, _m_

violin /,vaiə'lɪn/ _n_ violín, _m_

violinist /,vaiə'lɪnɪst/ _n_ violinista, _mf_

violoncellist /,vaiələn'tʃɛlɪst/ _n_ violoncelista, _mf_

violoncello /,vaiələn'tʃɛlou/ _n_ violoncelo, _m_

viper /'vaipər/ _n_ víbora, _f_

viperish /'vaipərɪʃ/ _a_ viperino

virago /vɪ'rɑgou/ _n_ virago, _f,_

Virgilian /vər'dʒɪliən/ _a_ virgiliano

virgin /'vɜrdʒɪn/ _n_ virgen, _f;_ (sign of the zodiac) Virgo, _m. a_ virginal; (untouched) virgen. **the V.,** la Virgen. **v. soil,** tierra virgen, _f_

virginal /'vɜrdʒənl̩/ _a_ virginal

virginity /vər'dʒɪnɪti/ _n_ virginidad, _f_

Virgo /'vɜrgou/ _n_ Virgo, _m_

virile /'vɪrəl/ _a_ viril

virility /və'rɪliti/ _n_ virilidad, _f_

virtual /'vɜrtʃuəl/ _a_ virtual

virtue /'vɜrtʃu/ _n_ virtud, _f_

virtuosity /,vɜrtʃu'ɒsɪti/ _n_ virtuosidad, _f_

virtuoso /,vɜrtʃu'ousou/ _n_ virtuoso (-sa)

virtuous /'vɜrtʃuəs/ _a_ virtuoso

virulence /'vɪryələns/ _n_ virulencia, _f_

virulent /'vɪryələnt/ _a_ virulento

virulently /'vɪryələntli/ _adv_ con virulencia

virus /'vairəs/ _n_ virus, _m_

visa /'vizə/ _n_ visado, _m_

visage /'vɪzɪdʒ/ _n_ cara, _f,_ rostro, _m;_ semblante, aspecto, _m_

viscera /'vɪsərə/ _n_ víscera, _f_

visceral /'vɪsərəl/ _a_ visceral

viscid /'vɪsɪd/ _a_ viscoso

viscosity /vɪ'skɒsɪti/ _n_ viscosidad, _f_

viscount /'vai,kaunt/ _n_ vizconde, _m_

viscountess /'vai,kauntɪs/ _n_ vizcondesa, _f_

viscous /'vɪskəs/ _a_ viscoso

visibility /,vɪzə'bɪlɪti/ _n_ visibilidad, _f._ **poor v.,** mala visibilidad, _f_

visible /'vɪzəbəl/ _a_ visible; aparente, evidente

visibly /'vɪzəbli/ _adv_ visiblemente; a ojos vistas

Visigoth /'vɪzɪ,gɒθ/ _n_ visigodo (-da)

Visigothic /ˌvɪzɪ'gɒθɪk/ a visigodo, visigótico
vision /'vɪʒən/ n visión, f; (eyesight) vista, f. **field of v.**, campo visual, m
visionary /'vɪʒəˌnɛri/ a and n visionario (-ia)
visit /'vɪzɪt/ n visita, f; (inspection) inspección, f; (doctor's) visita de médico, f. vt visitar; hacer una visita (a); ir a ver; inspeccionar; (frequent) frecuentar; (Biblical) visitar. **to be visited by an epidemic,** sufrir una epidemia. **to go visiting,** ir de visita. **to pay a v.**, hacer una visita
visitation /ˌvɪzɪ'teɪʃən/ n visita, f; Eccl. visitación, f; (inspection) inspección, f; (punishment) castigo, m
visiting /'vɪzɪtɪŋ/ a de visita. **v. card,** tarjeta de visita, f. **v. card case,** tarjetero, m. **v. hours,** horas de visita, f pl
visitor /'vɪzɪtər/ n visita, f; (official) visitador, m
visor /'vaizər/ n visera, f
vista /'vɪstə/ n vista, perspectiva, f
visual /'vɪʒuəl/ a visual. **the v. arts,** las artes visuales
visualize /'vɪʒuəˌlaiz/ vt and vi imaginarse, ver mentalmente
vital /'vait̩/ a vital; esencial; trascendental
vitalism /'vait̩ˌizəm/ n vitalismo, m
vitality /vai'tæliti/ n vitalidad, f
vitalize /'vait̩ˌaiz/ vt vitalizar, vivificar; reanimar
vitals /'vait̩z/ n pl partes vitales, f pl; Fig. entrañas, f pl
vitamin /'vaitəmɪn/ n vitamina, f
vitiate /'vɪʃiˌeit/ vt viciar; corromper, contaminar
viticultural /ˌvɪti'kʌltʃərl/ a vitícola
viticulture /'vɪtiˌkʌltʃər/ n viticultura, f
vitreous /'vɪtriəs/ a vítreo, vidrioso
vitrification /ˌvɪtrəfi'keiʃən/ n vitrificación, f
vitrify /'vɪtrəˌfai/ vt vitrificar. vi vitrificarse
vitriol /'vɪtriəl/ n vitriolo, ácido sulfúrico, m
vitriolic /ˌvɪtri'ɒlɪk/ a vitriólico
Vitruvius /vɪ'truviəs/ Vitrubio, m
vituperable /vai'tupərəbəl/ a vituperable
vituperate /vai'tupəˌreit/ vt vituperar
vituperation /vaiˌtupə'reiʃən/ n vituperio, m
vituperative /vai'tupərətɪv/ a vituperador
vivacious /vɪ'veiʃəs, vai-/ a animado, vivaracho
vivaciously /vɪ'veiʃəsli, vai-/ adv animadamente
vivacity /vɪ'væsiti, vai-/ n vivacidad, animación, f
viva voce /'vai'və vousi, 'vivə/ a oral. n examen oral, m
vivid /'vɪvɪd/ a vivo; brillante; intenso; (of descriptions, etc.) gráfico
vividly /'vɪvɪdli/ adv vivamente; brillantemente
vividness /'vɪvɪdnɪs/ n vivacidad, f; intensidad, f; (strength) fuerza, f
vivification /ˌvɪvəfɪ'keiʃən/ n vivificación, f
vivify /'vɪvəˌfai/ vt vivificar, avivar
vivifying /'vɪvəˌfaiɪŋ/ a vivificante
vivisection /ˌvɪvə'sɛkʃən/ n vivisección, f
vixen /'vɪksən/ n raposa, zorra, f; (woman) arpía, f
viz. adv a saber
vizier /vɪ'zɪər, 'vɪzyər/ n visir, m. **grand v.,** gran visir, m
vocabulary /vou'kæbyəˌlɛri/ n vocabulario, m
vocal /'voukəl/ a vocal. **v. cords,** cuerdas vocales, f pl
vocalist /'voukəlɪst/ n cantante, mf. voz, f
vocalization /ˌvoukələ'zeiʃən/ n vocalización, f
vocalize /'voukəˌlaiz/ vt vocalizar
vocation /vou'keiʃən/ n vocación, f; oficio, m; empleo, m; profesión, f
vocational /vou'keiʃənl/ a profesional; práctico. **v. guidance,** guía vocacional, orientación profesional, f. **v. training,** instrucción práctica, f; enseñanza de oficio, f
vociferate /vou'sɪfəˌreit/ vt gritar. vi vociferar, vocear
vociferation /vouˌsɪfə'reiʃən/ n vociferación, f
vociferous /vou'sɪfərəs/ a (noisy) ruidoso; vocinglero, clamoroso
vociferously /vou'sɪfərəsli/ adv ruidosamente; a gritos
vodka /'vɒdkə/ n vodca, m
vogue /voug/ n moda, f. **in v.,** en boga, de moda
voice /vɔis/ n voz, f. vt expresar, interpretar, hacerse

eco de; hablar. **in a loud v.,** en voz alta. **in a low v.,** en voz baja
voiced /vɔist/ a (in compounds) de voz...; hablado
voice mail n correo de voz, m
void /vɔid/ a (empty) vacío; (vacant) vacante; deshabitado; (lacking in) privado (de), desprovisto (de); (without) sin; Law. inválido, nulo; sin valor. n vacío, m. vt evacuar; Law. anular; invalidar
voile /vɔil/ n espumilla, f
volatile /'vɒlət̩/ a volátil; (light) ligero; (changeable) voluble, inconstante
volatility /ˌvɒlə'tɪliti/ n volatilidad, f; ligereza, f; volubilidad, f
volatilization /ˌvɒlət̩ə'zeiʃən/ n volatilización, f
volatilize /'vɒlət̩ˌaiz/ vt volatilizar. vi volatilizarse
volcanic /vɒl'kænɪk/ a volcánico
volcano /vɒl'keinou/ n volcán, m. **extinct v.,** volcán extinto, m
volition /vou'lɪʃən/ n volición, f; voluntad, f
volley /'vɒli/ n (of stones, etc.) lluvia, f; (of firearms) descarga, f; (of cannon, naval guns) andanada, f; Sports. voleo, m; (of words, etc.) torrente, m; (of applause and as a salute) salva, f. vt Sports. volear; (abuse, etc.) dirigir. vi lanzar una descarga, hacer una descarga
volt /voult/ n Elec. voltío, m; (of a horse and in fencing) vuelta, f. **v.-ampere,** voltamperio, m
voltage /'voultɪdʒ/ n voltaje, m. **v. control,** mando del voltaje, m
voltaic /vɒl'teiik/ a voltaico
Voltairian /voul'tɛəriən/ a volteriano
voltmeter /'voult̩mitər/ n voltímetro, m
volubility /ˌvɒlyə'bɪliti/ n garrulidad, locuacidad, f
voluble /'vɒlyəbəl/ a gárrulo, locuaz
volume /'vɒlyum/ n (book) tomo, m; (amount, size, space) volumen, m; (of water) caudal (de río), m; (mass) masa, f; (of smoke) humareda, f, nubes de humo, f pl
volumed /'vɒlyumd/ a (in compounds) en... volúmenes, de... tomos
volumetric /ˌvɒlyə'mɛtrɪk/ a volumétrico
voluminous /və'lumənəs/ a voluminoso
voluminousness /və'lumənəsnɪs/ n lo voluminoso
voluntarily /ˌvɒlən'tɛrəli/ adv voluntariamente
voluntariness /ˌvɒlən'tɛrinɪs/ n carácter voluntario, m
voluntary /'vɒlənˌtɛri/ a voluntario; espontáneo; libre; (charitable) benéfico; (intentional) intencional, deliberado. n solo de órgano, m
volunteer /ˌvɒlən'tɪər/ n Mil. voluntario (-ia). a de voluntarios. vt ofrecer; contribuir; expresar. vi ofrecerse para hacer algo; Mil. alistarse, ofrecerse a servir como voluntario
volunteering /ˌvɒlən'tɪərɪŋ/ n voluntariado, m
voluptuary /və'lʌptʃuˌɛri/ n voluptuoso (-sa); sibarita, mf
voluptuous /və'lʌptʃuəs/ a voluptuoso
voluptuously /və'lʌptʃuəsli/ adv voluptuosamente
voluptuousness /və'lʌptʃuəsnɪs/ n voluptuosidad, f; sensualidad, f
volute /və'lut/ n Archit. voluta, f
vomit /'vɒmɪt/ vt and vi vomitar; arrojar, devolver; Central America, Mexico deponer. n vómito, m
vomiting /'vɒmɪtɪŋ/ n vómito, m
voodoo /'vudu/ n vudú, m
voracious /vɔ'reiʃəs/ a voraz
voracity /vɔ'ræsiti/ n voracidad, f
vortex /'vɔrtɛks/ n torbellino, m, vorágine, f; Fig. vórtice, m
votary /'voutəri/ n devoto (-ta), adorante, mf; partidario (-ia)
vote /vout/ n voto, m; (voting) votación, f; (suffrage) sufragio, m; (election) elección, f. vt votar; asignar; nombrar; elegir; (consider) tener por. vi votar, dar el voto. **casting v.,** voto de calidad, m. **to put to the v.,** poner a votación. **to v. down,** desechar, rechazar. **v. of confidence,** voto de confianza, m. **v. of thanks,** voto de gracias, m
voter /'voutər/ n votante, mf, votador (-ra); elector (-ra)

voting /'voutɪŋ/ n votación, f; elección, f. a de votar; electoral. **v. paper,** papeleta de votación, f
votive /'voutɪv/ a votivo. **v. offering,** exvoto, m
vouch /vautʃ/ vi atestiguar, afirmar; garantizar; responder (de)
voucher /'vautʃər/ n (guarantor) fiador (-ra); (guarantee) garantía, f; (receipt) recibo, m; (proof) prueba, f; documento justificativo, m; vale, bono, m
vouchsafe /vautʃ'seif/ vt conceder, otorgar
vouchsafement /vautʃ'seifmənt/ n concesión, f, otorgamiento, m
vow /vau/ n voto, m; promesa solemne, f. vt hacer voto (de), hacer promesa solemne (de); jurar. **to take a vow,** hacer un voto
vowel /'vauəl/ n vocal, f
voyage /'vɔiidʒ/ n viaje (por mar), m; travesía, f. vi viajar por mar. **Good v.!** ¡Buen viaje!, Feliz viaje!
voyager /'vɔidʒər/ n viajero (-ra)
vulcanite /'vʌlkə,nait/ n ebonita, f

vulcanization /,vʌlkənə'zeifən/ n vulcanización, f
vulcanize /'vʌlkə,naiz/ vt vulcanizar
vulgar /'vʌlgər/ a vulgar; (ill-bred) ordinario, cursi; (in bad taste) de mal gusto; trivial; adocenado; (coarse) grosero. n vulgo, populacho, m. **v. fraction,** fracción común, f
vulgarism /'vʌlgə,rɪzəm/ n vulgarismo, m; vulgaridad, f
vulgarity /vʌl'gærɪti/ n vulgaridad, f; grosería, f; mal tono, m, cursilería, f
vulgarize /'vʌlgə,raiz/ vt vulgarizar; popularizar
vulgarly /'vʌlgərli/ adv vulgarmente; comúnmente; groseramente
Vulgate /'vʌlgeit/ n Vulgata, f
vulnerability /,vʌlnərə'bɪti/ n vulnerabilidad, f
vulnerable /'vʌlnərəbəl/ a vulnerable
vulpine /'vʌlpain/ a vulpino; astuto
vulture /'vʌltʃər/ n buitre, Argentina carancho, m
vulva /'vʌlvə/ n vulva, f

W

w /'dʌbəl,yu/ n doble u, doble v, f
wabble /'wɒbəl/ vi. See **wobble**
wad /wɒd/ n (of straw, etc.) atado, m; (of notes, etc.) rollo, m; (in a gun) taco, m. vt Sew. acolchar; (furniture) emborrar; (guns) atacar; (stuff) rellenar
wadding /'wɒdɪŋ/ n borra, f; (lining) entretela, f; (for guns) taco, m; (stuffing) relleno, m
waddle /'wɒdl/ n anadeo, m, vi anadear
waddling /'wɒdlɪŋ/ a patojo, que anadea
wade /weid/ vi and vt andar (en el agua, etc.); vadear; (paddle) chapotear. **to w. in,** entrar en (el agua, etc.); Fig. meterse en. **to w. through,** (a book) leer con dificultad; estudiar detenidamente; ir por
wader /'weidər/ n el, m, (f, la) que vadea; (bird) ave zancuda, f; pl **waders,** botas de vadear, f pl
wafer /'weifər/ n (host) hostia, f; (for sealing) oblea, f; (for ices) barquillo, m
waffle /'wɒfəl/ n Cul. fruta de sartén, f
waft /wɒft/ vt llevar por el aire o encima del agua; hacer flotar; (stir) mecer; (of the wind) traer. n (fragrance) ráfaga de olor, f
wag /wæg/ n (of the tail) coleada, f; movimiento, m; meneo, m; (jester) bromista, mf. vt mover ligeramente; agitar; (of the tail) menear (la cola), colear. vi menearse; moverse; oscilar; (of the world) ir. **And thus the world wags,** Y así va el mundo
wage, wages /weidʒ; 'weidʒɪz/ n salario, m; Fig. premio, galardón, m. **minimum wage,** salario mínimo, m. **wage-earner,** asalariado (-da);
wage /weidʒ/ vt emprender; sostener; hacer. **to w. war,** hacer guerra
wager /'weidʒər/ n (bet) apuesta, f; (test) prueba, f, vt (bet) apostar; (pledge) empeñar. **to lay a w.,** hacer una apuesta
wages /'weidʒɪz/ n pl. See **wage**
waggish /'wægɪʃ/ a zumbón, jocoso; cómico
waggishness /'wægɪʃnɪs/ n jocosidad, f
waggle /'wægəl/ vt menear; mover; agitar; oscilar. vi menearse; moverse; agitarse; oscilar. n meneo, movimiento, m; oscilación, f
wagon /'wægən/ n carro, m; carreta, f; (railway) vagón, m. **w.-lit,** coche cama, m. **w.-load,** carretada, f; vagón, m
wagoner /'wægənər/ n carretero, m
waif /weif/ n niño (-ña) sin hogar; animal perdido o abandonado, m; objeto extraviado, m; objeto sin dueño, m. **waifs and strays,** niños abandonados, m pl
wail /weil/ n lamento, gemido, m; (complaint) queja, f. vi lamentarse, gemir; quejarse (de). vt lamentar, deplorar
wailer /'weilər/ n lamentador (-ra)
wailing /'weilɪŋ/ n lamentaciones, f pl, gemidos, m pl, a lamentador, gemidor
wainscot /'weinskət, -skɒt/ n entablado de madera, m. vt enmaderar; poner friso de madera (a)

waist /weist/ n cintura, f; (blouse) blusa, f; (belt) cinturón, m; (bodice) corpiño, m; (narrowest portion) cuello, m, garganta, f; Naut. combés, m. **w.-band,** pretina, f. **w.-deep,** hasta la cintura. **w.-line,** cintura, f. **w. measurement,** medida de la cintura, f. **w.-coat,** chaleco, m. **w. strap,** trincha, f
wait /weit/ vi and vt esperar, aguardar; (serve) servir. **to keep waiting,** hacer esperar. **to w. at table,** servir a la mesa. **to w. on oneself,** servirse a sí mismo; cuidarse a sí mismo; hacer las cosas por sí solo. **to w. one's time,** aguardar la ocasión. **to w. for,** (until) esperar hasta que; (of persons) esperar (a), aguardar (a); (in ambush) acechar. **to w. on line,** hacer cola. **to w. upon,** (serve) servir (a); (visit) visitar; (Fig. accompany) acompañar; (follow) seguir a
wait /weit/ n espera, f; (pause) pausa, f, intervalo, m; (ambush) asechanza, f; pl **waits,** coro de nochebuena, m. **to lie in w. for,** estar en acecho para
waiter /'weitər/ n camarero, mozo, m; (tray) bandeja, f
waiting /'weitɪŋ/ n espera, f. a que espera; de espera; de servicio. **lady-in-w.,** dama de servicio, f. **w.-room,** (of a bus station, etc.) sala de espera, f; (of an office) antesala, f
waitress /'weitrɪs/ n camarera, f
waive /weiv/ vt renunciar (a); desistir (de)
wake /weik/ vi estar despierto; despertarse; (watch) velar. vt despertar; (a corpse) velar (a). n vela, f; vigilia, f; (of a corpse) velatorio, m; (holiday) fiesta, f; (of a ship) estela, f. **in the w. of,** Naut. en la estela de; después de; seguido por
wakeful /'weikfəl/ a vigilante; (awake) despierto. **to be w.,** pasar la noche en vela
wakefulness /'weikfəlnɪs/ n vigilancia, f; (sleeplessness) insomnia, f
waken /'weikən/ vi despertarse. vt despertar; (call) llamar
waking /'weikɪŋ/ a despierto; de vela. n despertar, m; (watching) vela, f
wale /weil/ n (weal) verdugo, m, huella de azote, f, vt azotar
Wales /weilz/ (País de) Gales, m
walk /wɔk/ n (pace) paso, m; (modo de) andar, m; (journey on foot) paseo, m, vuelta, f; (long) caminata, f; (promenade) paseo, m, avenida, f; (path) senda, f; (rank) clase social, f; esfera, f; profesión, f; ocupación, f. **quick w.,** paseo rápido, m; (pace) andar rápido, m. **to go for a w.,** ir de paseo. **to take a w.,** dar un paseo (or una vuelta), pasear. **to take for a w.,** llevar a paseo, sacar a paseo. **w.-out,** (strike) huelga, f. **w.-over,** triunfo, m, (or victoria, f) fácil. **w. past,** desfile, m
walk /wɔk/ vi andar; caminar; ir a pie; (take a walk) pasear, dar un paseo; (of ghosts) aparecer; (behave) conducirse. vt hacer andar; (take for a walk) sacar a

paseo; andar de una parte a otra (de), recorrer; (a specified distance) hacer a pie, andar; (a horse) llevar al paso. **to w. abroad,** dar un paseo; salir. **to w. arm in arm,** ir de bracero. **to w. past,** pasar; (in procession) desfilar. **to w. quickly,** andar de prisa. **to w. slowly,** andar despacio, andar lentamente. **to w. the hospitals,** estudiar en los hospitales. **to w. the streets,** recorrer las calles; vagar por las calles. **to w. about,** pasearse; ir y venir. **to w. after,** seguir (a), ir detrás de. **to w. along,** andar por; recorrer. **to w. away,** marcharse, irse. **to w. away with,** (win) ganar, llevarse; (steal) quitar, tomar, alzarse con. **to w. back,** volver; volver a pie, regresar a pie. **to w. down,** bajar; bajar a pie; andar por. **to w. in,** entrar en; entrar a pie en; (walk about) pasearse en. **to w. on,** seguir andando; (step on) pisar. **to w. out,** salir. **to w. over,** andar por; llevar la victoria (a); triunfar fácilmente sobre. **to w. round,** dar la vuelta a. **to w. round and round,** dar vueltas. **to w. up,** subir andando; subir. **to w. up and down,** dar vueltas, ir y venir

walker /'wɔkər/ n (pedestrian) peatón, m; andador (-ra); (promenader) paseante, mf

walking /'wɔkɪŋ/ n el andar; (excursion on foot) paseo, m. a andante; de andar; a pie; ambulante. **at a w. pace,** a un paso de andadura. **w. encyclopedia,** enciclopedia ambulante, f. **w. match,** marcha atlética, f. **w.-stick,** bastón, m. **w. tour,** excursión a pie, f

Walkyrie /wal'kɪəri/ n valquiria, f

wall /wɔl/ n muro, m; (rampart) muralla, f; (Fig. and of an organ, cavity, etc.) pared, f. **partition w.,** tabique, m. **Walls have ears,** Las paredes oyen. **w. lizard,** lagartija, f. **w. map,** mapa mural, m. **w.-painting,** pintura mural, f. **w.-paper,** papel pintado, m. **w. socket,** Elec. enchufe, m

wall /wɔl/ vt cercar con un muro; amurallar. **to w. in,** murar. **to w. up,** tapiar, tabicar

wallet /'wɔlɪt/ n cartera, f; bolsa de cuero, f

wallflower /'wɔl,flauər/ n alhelí, m

Walloon /wɒ'lun/ a and n valón (-ona)

wallop /'wɒləp/ n paliza, f; (blow) tunda, f; vt tundir, zurrar

wallow /'wɒlou/ vi revolcarse; encenagarse; (in riches, etc.) nadar (en). n revuelco, m

walnut /'wɔl,nʌt/ n (tree and wood) nogal, m; (nut) nuez de nogal, f

walrus /'wɔlrəs/ n morsa, f

waltz /wɔlts/ n vals, m. vi valsar

wan /wɑn/ a ojeroso, descolorido; (of the sky, etc.) pálido, sin color

wand /wɒnd/ n vara, f; (conductor's) batuta, f. **magic w.,** varita mágica, f

wander /'wɒndər/ vi errar, vagar; (deviate) extraviarse; (from the subject) desviarse del asunto; divagar; (be delirious) delirar. vt vagar por, errar por, recorrer

wanderer /'wɒndərər/ n vagabundo (-da); hombre, m, (f, mujer) errante; (traveler) viajero (-ra)

wandering /'wɒndərɪŋ/ a errante; vagabundo; nómada; (traveling) viajero; (delirious) delirante; (of thoughts, the mind) distraído; (of cells, kidneys, etc.) flotante. n vagancia, f; viaje, m; (delirium) delirio, m; (digression) divagación, f; (of a river, etc.) meandro, m. **the w. Jew,** el judío errante

wane /wein/ vi (of the moon, etc.) menguar; (decrease) disminuir; (Fig. decay) decaer. n (of the moon) menguante de la luna, f; mengua, f; disminución, f; decadencia, f

waning /'weinɪŋ/ a menguante

wanly /'wɑnli/ adv pálidamente; Fig. tristemente

wanness /'wɑnnɪs/ n palidez, f; Fig. tristeza, f

want /wɒnt/ vt (lack) carecer de, faltar; (need) necesitar, haber menester de; (require or wish) querer, desear; (demand) exigir; (ought) deber; (do without) pasarse sin. vi hacer falta; carecer (de); (be poor) estar necesitado. **I don't w. to,** No quiero, No me da la gana. **to be wanted,** hacer falta; (called) ser llamado. **You are wanted on the telephone,** Te llaman por teléfono

want /wɒnt/ n (lack) falta, f; escasez, carestía, f; (need) necesidad, f; (poverty) pobreza, indigencia, f; (absence) ausencia, f; (wish) deseo, m; exigencia, f.

in w. of, por falta de; en la ausencia de. **to be in w.,** estar en la necesidad, ser indigente

wanted /'wɒntɪd/ se necesita; (advertisement) demanda, f. **Estelle wants me to write a letter,** Estrella quiere que escriba una carta. **What do you w. me to do?** ¿Qué quiere Vd. que haga?; ¿En qué puedo servirle? **What does Paul w.?** ¿Qué quiere Pablo?; (require) ¿Qué necesita Pablo? **He wants (needs) a vacation,** Le hacen falta unas vacaciones, Necesita unas vacaciones

wanting /'wɒntɪŋ/ a deficiente (en); falto (de); (scarce) escaso; ausente; (in intelligence) menguado. prep (less) menos; (without) sin. **to be w.,** faltar. **to be w. in,** carecer de

wanton /'wɒntn̩/ a (playful) juguetón; (wilful) travieso; (loose) suelto, libre; (unrestrained) desenfrenado; extravagante; excesivo; caprichoso; (disheveled) en desorden; (reckless) indiscreto; (of religion) lozano; (purposeless) inútil; imperdonable; frívolo; (unchaste) disoluto; lascivo. n mujer disoluta, f; ramera, f; (child) niño (-ña) juguetón (-ona)

wantonly /'wɒntn̩li/ adv innecesariamente; sin motivo; excesivamente; lascivamente

war /wɑr/ n guerra, f. a de guerra; guerrero. vi guerrear. **at war with,** en guerra con. **cold war,** guerra tonta, f. **on a war footing,** en pie de guerra. **We are at war,** Estamos en guerra. **to be on the war-path,** Fig. Inf. buscar pendencia, tratar de armarla. **to declare war on,** declarar la guerra (a). **to make war on,** hacer la guerra (a). **war to the death,** guerra a muerte, f. **war correspondent,** corresponsal en el teatro de guerra, m. **war-cry,** alarido de guerra, grito de combate, grito de guerra m. **war-dance,** danza guerrera, f. **war horse,** caballo de batalla, m. **war loan,** empréstito de guerra, m. **war-lord,** adalid, caudillo, jefe militar, m. **war material,** pertrechos de guerra, m pl; municiones, f pl. **war memorial,** monumento a los caídos, m. **war minister,** Ministro de la Guerra, m. **war neurosis,** neurosis de guerra, f. **War Office,** Ministerio de la Guerra, m. **war plane,** avión de guerra, m. **war-ship,** barco (or buque) de guerra, m. **war-wearied,** agotado por la guerra

warble /'wɔrbəl/ vt and vi trinar; gorjear; murmurar. n trino, m; gorjeo, m; murmurio, m

ward /wɔrd/ n protección, f; (of a minor) pupilo (-la); (of locks, keys) guarda, f; (of a city) barrio, distrito, m; (of a hospital, etc.) sala, f; (of a prison) celda, f; (fencing) guardia, f. **w.-room,** cuarto de los oficiales, m. **w. sister,** hermana de una sala de hospital, f

ward /wɔrd/ vt proteger, defender. **to w. off,** desviar; evitar

warden /'wɔrdn̩/ n guardián, m; director (-ra); (of a prison) alcaide, m; (of a church) mayordomo de la iglesia, m; (of a port) capitán, m

warder /'wɔrdər/ n (jailer) guardián, m; alabardero, guardia, m

wardress /'wɔrdrɪs/ n guardiana, f

wardrobe /'wɔrdroub/ n guardarropa, ropero, m; (clothes) ropa, f; Theat. vestuario, m. **w. trunk,** baúl mundo, m

ware /wɛər/ n mercadería, f; (pottery) loza, f; pl **wares,** mercancías, f pl

war effort n esfuerzo bélico, esfuerzo de guerra, esfuerzo guerrero, m

warehouse /n. 'wɛər,haus; v. -,hauz/ n almacén, m, vt almacenar

warehouseman /'wɛər,hausmən/ n almacenero, m

warfare /'wɔr,fɛər/ n guerra, f; lucha, f; arte militar, m, or f. **chemical w.,** guerra química, f

warhead /'wɔr,hɛd/ n (of torpedo) cabeza de combate, punto de combate, f; (of missile) detonante, m

war hero n héroe de guerra, m

war heroine n heroína de guerra, f

warily /'wɛərəli/ adv con cautela, cautelosamente; prudentemente

wariness /'wɛərɪnɪs/ n cautela f; prudencia, f

warlike /'wɔr,laik/ a belicoso, guerrero; militar, de guerra; marcial. **war-spirit,** espíritu belicoso, m, marcialidad, f

warm /wɔrm/ a caliente; (lukewarm) tibio; (hot) caluroso; (affectionate) cordial, cariñoso, afectuoso;

(angry) acalorado; (enthusiastic) entusiasta, ardiente; (art) cálido; (of coats, etc.) de abrigo; (fresh) fresco, reciente; *Inf.* adinerado. *vt* calentar; *Fig.* encender; entusiasmar. *vi* calentarse; *Fig.* entusiasmarse (con). **to keep a w. at the fire,** calentarse al lado del fuego. **to be w.,** (of things) estar caliente; (of coats, etc.) ser de abrigo; (of the weather) hacer calor; (of people) tener calor. **to grow w.,** calentarse; (grow angry) excitarse, agitarse; (of a discussion) hacerse acalorado. **to keep w.,** conservar caliente; calentar. **to keep oneself w.,** estar caliente, no enfriarse. **to w. up,** calentar. **w.-blooded,** de sangre caliente; ardiente. **w.-hearted,** de buen corazón; generoso; afectuoso, cordial. **w.-heartedness,** buen corazón, *m*; generosidad, *f*; cordialidad, *f*

warming /'wɔrmɪŋ/ *n* calentamiento, *m*; calefacción, *f*. *a* calentador; para calentar. **w.-pan,** calentador, *m*

warmly /'wɔrmli/ *adv* (affectionately) cordialmente, afectuosamente; con entusiasmo; (angrily) acaloradamente. **to be w. wrapped up,** estar bien abrigado

warmonger /'wɔr,mʌŋɡər/ *n* atizador de guerra, belicista, fautor de guerra, fomentador de guerra, propagador (-ra) de guerra

warmth /wɔrmθ/ *n* calor, *m*

warn /wɔrn/ *vt* advertir; prevenir; amonestar; (inform) avisar

warning /'wɔrnɪŋ/ *n* advertencia, *f*; aviso, *m*; amonestación, *f*; (lesson) lección, *f*, escarmiento, *f*; alarma, *f*. *a* amonestador; de alarma. **to give w.,** prevenir, advertir; (dismiss) despedir. **to take w.,** escarmentar

warningly /'wɔrnɪŋli/ *adv* indicando el peligro; con alarma; con amenaza

warp /wɔrp/ *vt* torcer; combar; *Naut.* espiar; (the mind) pervertir. *vi* torcerse; combarse, bornearse; *Naut.* espiarse. *n* (in a fabric) urdimbre, *f*; (in wood) comba, *f*, torcimiento, *m*; *Naut.* espía, *f*. **w. and woof,** trama y urdimbre, *f*

warping /'wɔrpɪŋ/ *n* (of wood) combadura, *f*; (weaving) urdidura, *f*; *Naut.* espía, *f*; (of the mind) perversión, *f*. **w. frame,** urdidera, *f*

warrant /'wɔrənt, 'wɒr-/ *n* autoridad, *f*; justificación, *f*; autorización, *f*; garantía, *f*; decreto de prisión, *m*; orden, *f*; *Com.* orden de pago, *f*; *Mil.* nombramiento, *m*; motivo, *m*, razón, *f*. *vt* justificar; autorizar; garantizar, responder por; asegurar. **pay w.,** boletín de pago, *m*

warrantable /'wɔrəntəbəl/ *a* justificable

warrantor /'wɔrən,tɔr/ *n* garante, *mf*

warranty /'wɔrənti/ *n* autorización, *f*; justificación, *f*; *Law.* garantía, *f*

warren /'wɔrən/ *n* (for hunting) vedado, *m*; (rabbit) conejera, *f*; vivar, *m*, madriguera, *f*

warrior /'wɔriər/ *n* guerrero, *m*; soldado, *m*

Warsaw /'wɔrsɔ/ Varsovia, *f*

wart /wɔrt/ *n* verruga, *f*

wary /'wɛəri/ *a* cauto, cauteloso; prudente

wash /wɒʃ/ *vt* lavar; (dishes) fregar; (lave) bañar; (clean) limpiar; (furrow) surcar; (wet) regar, humedecer; (with paint) dar una capa de color o de metal. *vi* lavarse; lavar ropa. **Two of the crew were washed overboard,** El mar arrastró a dos de los tripulantes. **Will this material w.?** ¿Se puede lavar esta tela? ¿Es lavable esta tela? **to w. ashore,** echar a la playa. **w. away,** (remove by washing) quitar lavando; derrubiar; (water or waves) arrastrar, llevarse. **to w. one's hands,** lavarse las manos. **to look washed out,** estar ojeroso. **to w. down,** lavar; limpiar; (remove) llevarse; (accompany with drink) regar. **to w. off,** *vt* quitar lavando; hacer desaparecer; borrar; desteñirse. *vi* borrarse; desteñirse. **to w. up,** lavar los platos, fregar la vajilla; (cast up) desechar. **w. one's dirty laundry in public,** sacar los más sucios trapillos a la colada

wash /wɒʃ/ *n* lavadura, *f*, lavado, *m*; baño, *m*; (clothes) ropa para lavar, ropa sucia, *f*; colada, *f*; (of the waves) chapoteo, *m*; (lotion) loción, *f*; (coating) capa, *f*; (silt) aluvión, *m*. **w.-basin,** palangana, *f*; lavabo, *m*. **w.-board,** tabla de lavar, *f*. **w.-house,** lavadero, *m*. **w.-leather,** gamuza, badana, *f*. **w.-out,** fracaso, *m*. **w.-stand,** aguamanil, lavabo, *m*. **w.-tub,** cuba de lavar, *f*

washable /'wɒʃəbəl/ *a* lavable

washer /'wɒʃər/ *n* lavador (-ra); (washerwoman) lavandera, *f*; (machine) lavadora, *f*; *Mech.* arandela, *f*

washerwoman /'wɒʃər,wʊmən/ *n* lavandera, *f*

washing /'wɒʃɪŋ/ *n* lavamiento, *m*; ropa sucia, ropa para lavar, *f*; ropa limpia, *f*; ropa, *f*; (bleaching) blanqueadura, *f*; (toilet) abluciones, *f pl*; *Eccl.* lavatorio, *m*; *pl* **washings,** lavazas, *f pl*. **There is a lot of w. to be done,** Hay mucha ropa que lavar. **w.-board,** tabla de lavar, *f*. **w.-day,** día de colada, *m*. **w.-machine,** lavadora, máquina de lavar, *f*. **w.-soda,** carbonato sódico, *m*. **w.-up,** lavado de los platos, *m*. **w.-up machine,** fregador mecánico de platos, *m*

wasp /wɒsp/ *n* avispa, *f*, *Lat. Am. also* jicote, *m*. **wasp's nest,** avispero, *m*. **w.-waisted,** (of clothes) ceñido, muy ajustado

waspish /'wɒspɪʃ/ *a* enojadizo, irascible; malicioso; mordaz

waste /weist/ *vt* desperdiciar, derrochar, malgastar; (time) perder; consumir; corroer; (devastate) asolar, devastar; echar a perder; malograr; disipar; agotar. *vi* gastarse; consumirse; perderse. **to w. time,** perder el tiempo. **to w. away,** (of persons) demacrarse, consumirse

waste /weist/ *n* (wilderness) yermo, desierto, *m*; (vastness) inmensidad, vastedad, *f*; (loss) pérdida, *f*; (squandering) despilfarro, derroche, *m*; disminución, *f*; (refuse) desechos, *m pl*; (of cotton, etc.) borra, *f*; disipación, *f*. *a* (of land) sin cultivar; yermo; inútil; desechado, de desecho; superfluo. **to lay w.,** devastar. **w. land,** yermo, *m*; tierras sin cultivar, *f pl*. **w. paper,** papel usado, papel de desecho, *m*. **w.-paper basket,** cesto para papeles, *m*. **w.-pipe,** desaguadero, tubo de desagüe, *m*

wasteful /'weistfəl/ *a* pródigo, derrochador, manirroto; antieconómico; ruinoso; inútil

wastefully /'weistfəli/ *adv* pródigamente; antieconómicamente; inútilmente

wastefulness /'weistfəlnɪs/ *n* prodigalidad, *f*, despilfarro, *m*; pérdida, *f*; gasto inútil, *m*; falta de economía, *f*

waster /'weistər/ *n* gastador (-ra); disipador (-ra); (loafer) golfo, *m*

watch /wɒtʃ/ *vi* velar; mirar. *vt* mirar; observar; guardar; (await) esperar; (spy upon) espiar, acechar. **to w. for,** buscar aguardar. **to w. over,** vigilar, guardar; (care for) cuidar; proteger. **watch out!** *Mexico* ¡abusado!

watch /wɒtʃ/ *n* (at night) vela, *f*; (wakefulness) desvelo, *m*; observación, vigilancia, *f*; (*Mil. Naut.*) guardia, *f*; (sentinel) centinela, *m*; (watchman) sereno; vigilante, *m*; (guard) ronda, *f*; (timepiece) reloj de bolsillo, *m*. **to be on the w.,** estar al acecho, estar al alerta, estar a la mira. **to keep w.,** vigilar. **dog w.,** media guardia, *f*. **pocket w.,** reloj de bolsillo, *m*. **wrist w.,** reloj de pulsera, *m*. **w.-case,** caja de reloj, relojera, *f*. **w.-chain,** cadena de reloj, leontina, *f*. **w.-dog,** perro guardián, *m*. **w.-glass,** cristal de reloj, *m*. **w.-making,** relojería, *f*. **w.-night,** noche vieja, *f*. **w.-spring,** muelle de reloj, *m*, espiral, *f*

watcher /'wɒtʃər/ *n* observador (-ra); espectador (-ra); (at a sick bed) el, *m*, (*f*, la) que vela a un enfermo

watchful /'wɒtʃfəl/ *a* vigilante, alerto; observador; atento, cuidadoso

watchfully /'wɒtʃfəli/ *adv* vigilantemente; atentamente

watchfulness /'wɒtʃfəlnɪs/ *n* vigilancia, *f*; cuidado, *m*; desvelo, *m*

watching /'wɒtʃɪŋ/ *n* observación, *f*; (vigil) vela, *f*

watchmaker /'wɒtʃ,meikər/ *n* relojero (-ra). **watchmaker's shop,** relojería, *f*

watchman /'wɒtʃmən/ *n* vigilante, sereno, *m*; guardián, *m*

watchword /'wɒtʃ,wɜrd/ *n* (password) consigna, contraseña, *f*; (motto) lema, *m*

water /'wɔtər/ *n* agua, *f*; (tide) marea, *f*; (of precious stones) aguas, *f pl*; (urine) orina, *f*; (quality) calidad, clase, *f*. *a* de agua; por agua; acuático; hidráulico. **fresh w.,** (not salt) agua dulce, *f*; agua fresca, *f*. **hard w.,** agua cruda, *f*. **high w.,** marea alta, *f*. **low w.,**

marea baja, *f*. **of the first w.**, de primera clase. **running w.**, agua corriente, *f*. **soft w.**, agua blanda, *f*. **to make w.**, *Naut.* hacer agua; orinar. **to take the waters**, tomar las aguas. **under w.**, *adv* debajo del agua. *a* acuático. **w.-bird**, ave acuática, *f*. **w. blister**, ampolla, *f*. **w.-boatman**, chinche de agua, *f*. **w.-borne**, flotante. **w.-bottle**, cantimplora, *f*. **w.-brash**, acedia, *f*. **w.-butt**, barril, *m*, pipa, *f*. **w.-carrier**, aguador (-ra). **w.-cart**, carro de regar, *m*. **w.-closet**, retrete, excusado, *m*. **w.-color**, acuarela, *f*. **w.-color painting**, pintura a la acuarela, *f*. **w.-colorist**, acuarelista, *mf*. **w.-cooled**, enfriado por agua. **w.-cooler**, cantimplora, *f*. **w.-finder**, zahorí, *m*. **w. front**, (wharf) muelle, *m*; puerto, *m*; litoral, *m*. **w.-gauge**, indicador de nivel de agua, *m*, vara de aforar, *f*. **w.-glass**, vidrio soluble, silicato de sosa, *m*. **w. heater**, calentador de agua, *m*. **w.-ice**, helado, *m*. **w.-level**, nivel de las aguas, *m*. **w.-lily**, nenúfar, *m*, azucena de agua, *f*. **w.-line**, lengua de agua, *f*; (of a ship) línea de flotación, *f*. **w.-logged**, anegado en agua. **w.-main**, cañería maestra de agua, *f*. **w. man**, barquero, *m*. **w.-melon**, sandía, *f*. **w. mill**, aceña, *f*. **w.-nymph**, náyade, *f*. **w.-pipe**, cañería del agua, *f*. **w. pitcher**, jarro, *m*. **w. plant**, planta acuática, *f*. **w.-polo**, polo acuático, *m*. **w.-power**, fuerza hidráulica, *f*. **w.-rate**, cupo del consumo de agua, *m*. **w. snake**, culebra de agua, *f*. **w. softener**, generador de agua dulce, *m*; purificador de agua, *m*. **w. spaniel**, perro (-rra) de aguas. **w. sprite**, ondina, *f*. **w.-supply**, abastecimiento de agua, *m*; traída de aguas, *f*. **w. tank**, depósito para agua, *m*. **w. tower**, arca de agua, *f*. **w. wave**, ondulado al agua, *m*. **w.-way**, canal, río, *m*, o vía *f*, navegable. **w.-wheel**, rueda hidráulica, *f*, azud, *m*; (for irrigation) aceña, *f*. **w. wings**, nadaderas, *f pl*

water /'wɔtər/ *vt* (irrigate, sprinkle) regar; (moisten) mojar; (cattle, etc.) abrevar; (wine, etc.) aguar; diluir con agua; (bathe) bañar. *vi* (of animals) beber agua; (of engines, etc.) tomar agua; (of the eyes, mouth) hacerse agua. **My mouth waters**, Se me hace agua la boca

watercourse /'wɔtər,kɔrs/ *n* corriente de agua, *f*; cauce, *m*; lecho de un río, *m*

watercress /'wɔtər,krɛs/ *n* berro, mastuerzo, *m*

watered /'wɔtərd/ *a* regado, abundante en agua; (of silk) tornasolado

watered-down /'wɔtərd'daun/ *Fig.* pasado por agua

waterfall /'wɔtər,fɔl/ *n* salto de agua, *m*, cascada, catarata, *f*

wateriness /'wɔtərinɪs/ *n* humedad, *f*, acuosidad, *f*

watering /'wɔtərɪŋ/ *n* riego, *m*; irrigación, *f*; (of eyes) lagrimeo, *m*; (of cattle, etc.) el abrevar (a); *Naut.* aguada, *f*. **w.-can**, regadera, *f*. **w.-cart**, carro de regar, *m*. **w.-place**, (for animals) aguadero, *m*; (for cattle) abrevadero, *m*; (spa) balneario, *m*; (by the sea) playa de veraneo, *f*

watermark /'wɔtər,mɑrk/ *n* (in paper) filigrana, *f*; nivel del agua, *m*. *vt* filigranar

waterproof /'wɔtər,pruf/ *a* impermeable; a prueba de agua. *n* impermeable, *m*. *vt* hacer impermeable, impermeabilizar

water-repellent /'wɔtərɪ,pɛlənt/ *a* repelente al agua

watershed /'wɔtər,ʃɛd/ *n* vertiente, *f*; línea divisoria de las aguas, *f*; (river-basin) cuenca, *f*

waterspout /'wɔtər,spaut/ *n* bomba marina, manga, trompa, *f*

watertight /'wɔtər,tait/ *a* impermeable, estanco; a prueba de agua; (of arguments, etc.) irrefutable

watertightness /'wɔtər,taitnɪs/ *n* impermeabilidad, *f*

waterworks /'wɔtər,wɜrks/ *n* establecimiento para la distribución de las aguas, *f*; obras hidráulicas, *f pl*

watery /'wɔtəri/ *a* (wet) húmedo; acuoso; (of the sky) de lluvia; (of eyes) lagrimoso, lloroso; (sodden) mojado; (of soup, etc.) claro; insípido

watt /wɒt/ *n* vatio, *m*. **w. hour**, vatio hora, *m*. **w.-meter**, vatímetro, *m*

wattage /'wɒtɪdʒ/ *n* vatiaje, *m*

wattle /'wɒtl/ *n* zarzo, *m*; (of turkey) barba, *f*; (of fish) barbilla, *f*

wave /weiv/ *vi* ondear; ondular; flotar; hacer señales. *vt* (brandish) blandir; agitar; (the hair) ondular; ondear; hacer señales (de). **They waved goodby**

to him, Le hicieron adiós con la mano; Le hicieron señas de despedida; Se despidieron de él agitando el pañuelo

wave /weiv/ *n* (of the sea) ola, *f*; *Phys.* onda, *f*; (in hair or a surface) ondulación, *f*; (movement) movimiento, *m*; (of anger, etc.) ráfaga, *f*. **long w.**, onda larga, *f*. **medium w.**, onda media, *f*. **short w.**, onda corta, *f*. **sound w.**, onda sonora, *f*. **to have one's hair waved**, hacerse ondular el pelo. **w. band**, franja undosa, escala de longitudes de onda, *f*. **w. crest**, cresta de la ola, cabrilla, *f*. **w.-length**, longitud de onda, *f*

wavelet /'weivlɪt/ *n* pequeña ola, olita, *f*; (ripple) rizo (del agua), *m*

wave of immigration *n* una imigración, *f*

waver /'weivər/ *vi* ondear; oscilar; (hesitate) vacilar, titubear; (totter) tambalearse; (weaken) flaquear

waverer /'weivərər/ *n* irresoluto (-ta), vacilante, *m*

wavering /'weivərɪŋ/ *n* vacilación, irresolución, *f*. *a* oscilante; vacilante, irresoluto; flotante

waving /'weivɪŋ/ *n* ondulación, *f*; oscilación, *f*; agitación, *f*; movimiento, *m*. *a* ondulante; oscilante; que se balancea

wavy /'weivi/ *a* ondulado; flotante

wax /wæks/ *n* cera, *f*; (cobblers') cerote, *m*; (in the ear) cerilla, *f*. *a* de cera. *vt* encerar. *vi* crecer; hacerse; ponerse. **to wax enthusiastic**, entusiasmarse. **waxed paper**, papel encerado, *m*. **wax chandler**, cerero, *m*. **wax doll**, muñeca de cera, *f*. **wax modeling**, modelado en cera, *m*, ceroplástica, *f*. **wax taper**, blandón, *m*

waxen /'wæksən/ *a* de cera; como la cera; de color de cera

waxing /'wæksɪŋ/ *n* enceramiento, *m*; (of the moon) crecimiento, *m*; aumento, *m*

wax museum *n* museo de cera, *m*

waxwork /'wæks,wɜrk/ *n* figura de cera, *f*

waxy /'wæksi/ *a*. See **waxen**

way /wei/ *n* camino, *m*; senda, *f*; paso, *m*; ruta, *f*; (railway, etc.) vía, *f*; dirección, *f*; rumbo, *m*; distancia, *f*; (journey) viaje, *m*; (sea crossing) travesía, *f*; avance, progreso, *m*; (*Naut.* etc.) marcha, *f*; método, *m*; modo, *m*; (means) medio, *m*; manera, *f*; (habit) costumbre, *f*; (behavior) conducta, *f*, modo de obrar, *f*; (line of business, etc.) ramo, *m*; (state) estado, *m*, condición, *f*; (course) curso, *m*; (respect) punto de vista, *m*; (particular kind) género, *m*; (scale) escala, *f*. **a long way off**, a gran distancia, a lo lejos. **a short way off**, a poca distancia, no muy lejos. **by way of**, pasando por; por vía de; como; por medio de; a modo de. **by the way**, de paso; durante el viaje; durante la travesía; a propósito, entre paréntesis. **in a small way**, en pequeña escala. **in a way**, hasta cierto punto; desde cierto punto de vista. **in many ways**, de muchos modos; por muchas cosas. **in no way**, de ningún modo; nada. **in the way**, en el medio. **in the way of**, en cuanto a, tocante a; en materia de. **I went out of my way to**, Dejé el camino para; Me di la molestia de. **Is this the way to...?** ¿Es este el camino a...? **Is that any way to speak to your mother?** ¡Hablas así con tu madre? **Make way!** ¡Calle! **Milky Way**, vía láctea, *f*. **on the way**, en camino; al paso; durante el viaje. **out of the way**, puesto a un lado; arrinconado; apartado, alejado; (imprisoned) en prisión; fuera del camino; remoto; (unusual) original. **over the way**, en frente; al otro lado de la calle, etc.). **right of way**, derecho de paso, *m*. **The ship left on its way to...**, El barco zarpó con rumbo a... **the Way of the Cross**, vía crucis, *f*. **This way!** ¡Por aquí!; De este modo, Así. **this way and that**, en todas direcciones, por todos lados. **"This way to...,"** "Dirección a..." A... **under way**, en camino; en marcha; en preparación. **to bar the way**, cerrar el paso. **to be in the way**, estorbar. **to be out of the way of doing**, haber perdido la costumbre de hacer (algo). **to clear the way**, abrir paso, abrir calle; *Fig.* preparar el terreno. **to force one's way through**, abrirse paso por. **to find a way**, encontrar un camino; *Fig.* encontrar medios. **to find one's way**, hallar el camino; orientarse. **to get into the way of**, contraer la costumbre de. **to get under way**, *Naut.* zarpar; hacerse a la vela; ponerse en marcha. **to give way**, ceder; (break) romper. **to go a long way**, ir lejos; contribuir mucho (a). **to have one's own way**, salir con la suya. **to keep out of the way,** vt and vi esconder(se); mantener(se) alejado; mantener(se) apartado. **to lose one's way,** perder el camino; desorientarse; *Fig.* extraviarse. **to make one's way,** abrirse paso. **to make one's way down,** bajar. **to make one's way round,** dar la vuelta a. **to make one's way up,** subir. **to make way,** hacer lugar; hacer sitio; dar paso (a). **to pay one's way,** ganarse la vida; pagar lo que se debe. **to prepare one's way for,** preparar el terreno para. **to put out of the way,** poner a un lado; apartar; (kill) matar; (imprison) poner en la cárcel; hacer cautivo (a). **to see one's way,** poder ver el camino; poder orientarse; ver el modo de hacer algo; ver cómo se puede hacer algo. **ways and means,** medios y arbitrios, *m pl.* **way back,** camino de regreso, *m;* vuelta, *f.* **way down,** bajada, *f.* **way in,** entrada, *f.* **way out,** salida, *f.* **way round,** camino alrededor, *m;* solución, *f;* modo de evitar..., *m.* **way through,** paso, *m.* **way up,** subida, *f*

wayfarer /ˈweiˌfeərər/ *n* transeúnte, *mf;* viajero (-ra)
wayfaring /ˈweiˌfeərɪŋ/ *a* que va de viaje; errante, ambulante
waylay /weiˈlei/ *vt* asechar, salir al paso (de)
wayside /ˈweiˌsaid/ *n* borde del camino, *m.* *a* (of flowers) silvestre; (by the side of the road) en la carretera. **gone by the w.,** despil farrándose la vida
wayward /ˈweiwərd/ *a* caprichoso; desobediente; voluntarioso; travieso; rebelde
waywardness /ˈweiwərdnɪs/ *n* desobediencia, indocilidad, *f;* voluntariedad, *f;* travesura, *f;* rebeldía, *f*
we /wi/ *pron* nosotros, *m pl;* nosotras, *f pl,* (Usually omitted except for emphasis or for clarity.) **We are in the garden,** Estamos en el jardín. **We have come, but they are not here,** Nosotros hemos venido pero ellos no están aquí
weak /wik/ *a* débil; flojo; frágil; delicado; (insecure) inseguro; (of arguments) poco convincente; (of prices, markets, etc.) flojo, en baja; (sickly) *Lat. Am.* farruto, *Central America, Mexico* fifiriche. **w.-eyed,** de vista floja. **w.-kneed,** débil de rodillas; *Fig.* sin voluntad. **w.-minded,** sin carácter; pusilánime; **w. spot,** debilidad, *f;* flaco, *m;* lado débil, *m;* desventaja, *f*
weaken /ˈwikən/ *vt* debilitar; (diminish) disminuir. *vi* debilitarse; flaquear, desfallecer; (give way) ceder
weakening /ˈwikənɪŋ/ *n* debilitación, *f.* *a* debilitante; enervante
weaker /ˈwikər/ *a comp* más débil. **the w. sex,** el sexo débil
weakling /ˈwiklɪŋ/ *n* ser delicado, *m,* persona débil, *f;* cobarde, *m; Inf.* alfeñique, *m*
weakly /ˈwikli/ *a* enfermizo, delicado, enclenque. *adv* débilmente
weakness /ˈwiknɪs/ *n* debilidad, *f;* imperfección, *f*
weal /wil/ *n* bienestar, *m;* prosperidad, *f;* (blow) verdugo, *m*
wealth /wɛlθ/ *n* riqueza, *f;* abundancia, *f;* bienes, *m pl*
wealthy /ˈwɛlθi/ *a* rico, adinerado, acaudalado; abundante (en)
wean /win/ *vt* destetar, ablactar; separar (de); privar (de); enajenar el afecto de; (of ideas) desaferrar (de)
weaning /ˈwinɪŋ/ *n* ablactación, *f,* destete, *m*
weapon /ˈwɛpən/ *n* arma, *f; pl* **weapons,** (*Zool.,* *Bot.*) medios de defensa, *m pl.* **steel w.,** arma blanca, *f*
wear /wɛər/ *n* uso, *m;* gasto, *m;* deterioro, *m;* (fashion) moda, boga, *f.* **for hard w.,** para todo uso. **for one's own w.,** para su propio uso. **for evening w.,** para llevar de noche. **for summer w.,** para llevar en verano. **w. and tear,** uso y desgaste, *m;* deterioro natural, *m*
wear /wɛər/ *vt* llevar; llevar puesto; traer; usar; (have) tener; (exhibit) mostrar; (be clad in) vestir; (waste) gastar; deteriorar; (make) hacer; (exhaust) agotar, cansar, consumir. *vi* (last) durar; (of persons) conservar(se); (of time) correr; avanzar. **She wears well,** Está bien conservada. **to w. one's heart on one's sleeve,** tener el corazón en la mano. **to w. the trousers,** *Fig. Inf.* llevar los pantalones. **to w. well,** durar mucho. **to w. away,** *vt* gastar, roer; (rub out) borrar; consumir. *vi* (of time) pasar lentamente, transcurrir despacio. **to w. down,** gastar; consumir; reducir; agotar las fuerzas de; destruir; (tire) fatigar.

to w. off, *vt* destruir; borrar. *vi* quitarse; borrarse; *Fig.* desaparecer, pasar. **to w. on,** (of time) transcurrir, correr, pasar. **to w. out,** *vt* usar; romper con el uso; consumir, acabar con; (exhaust) agotar; (tire) rendir. *vi* usarse; romperse con el uso; consumirse
wearable /ˈwɛərəbəl/ *a* que se puede llevar
wearer /ˈwɛərər/ *n* el, *m,* (f, la) que lleva alguna cosa
weariness /ˈwɪərinɪs/ *n* cansancio, *m,* fatiga, lasitud, *f;* aburrimiento, *m;* aversión, repugnancia, *f*
wearing /ˈwɛərɪŋ/ *n* uso, *m;* desgaste, *m.* *a* (tiring) agotador; cansado. **w. apparel,** ropa, *f*
wearisome /ˈwɪərisəm/ *a* cansado; laborioso; aburrido, tedioso, pesado
wearisomeness /ˈwɪərisəmnɪs/ *n* cansancio, *m;* aburrimiento, tedio, hastío, *m*
weary /ˈwɪəri/ *a* cansado, fatigado; aburrido; hastiado; impaciente; tedioso, enfadoso. *vt* cansar, fatigar; aburrir; hastiar; molestar. *vi* cansarse, fatigarse; aburrirse. **to w. for,** anhelar, suspirar por; (miss) echar de menos (a). **to w. of,** aburrirse de; (things) impacientarse de; (people) impacientarse con
weasel /ˈwizəl/ *n* comadreja, *f*
weather /ˈwɛðər/ *n* tiempo, *m;* intemperie, *f;* (storm) tempestad, *f. a Naut.* del lado del viento; de barlovento. *vt* (of rain, etc.) desgastar; curtir; secar al aire; *Naut.* pasar a barlovento; (bear) aguantar, capear; (survive) sobrevivir a; luchar con. *vi* curtirse a la intemperie. **Andrew is a little under the w.,** Andrés está algo destemplado; (with drink) Andrés tiene una mona; (depressed) Andrés está melancólico. **to be bad (good) w.,** hacer mal (buen) tiempo. **What is the w. like?** ¿Qué tiempo hace? ¿Cómo está el tiempo? **w.-beaten,** curtido por la intemperie. **w. chart,** carta meteorológica, *f.* **w. conditions,** condiciones meteorológicas, *f pl.* **w. forecast,** pronóstico del tiempo, *m.* **w. forecaster,** meteorologista, *mf.* **w.-hardened,** endurecido a la intemperie. **w. report,** boletín meteorológico, *m.* **w.-worn,** gastado por la intemperie; curtido por la intemperie
weathercock /ˈwɛðərˌkɒk/ *n* veleta, *f*
weathering /ˈwɛðərɪŋ/ *n* desintegración por la acción atmosférica, *f*
weather-resistant /ˈwɛðərrɪˌzɪstənt/ *a* resistente a la intemperie
weave /wiv/ *vt* tejer; trenzar; entrelazar; *Fig.* tejer. *vi* tejer. *n* tejido, *m;* textura, *f*
weaver /ˈwivər/ *n* tejedor (-ra)
weaving /ˈwivɪŋ/ *n* tejido, *m;* tejeduría, *f.* **w. machine,** telar, *m*
web /wɛb/ *n* tejido, *m;* tela, *f;* (network) red, *f;* (spider's) telaraña, *f;* (of a feather) barba, *f;* (of birds, etc.) membrana interdigital, *f;* (of intrigue) red, *f;* (snarl) lazo, *m,* trampa, *f.* **web-foot,** pie palmado, *m.* **web-footed,** palmípedo.
webbed /wɛbd/ *a* (of feet) unido por una membrana
Web site *n* Sitio en la Red, *m*
wed /wɛd/ *vt* casarse con; (join in marriage, cause to marry) casar; *Fig.* unir. *vi* estar casado; casarse
wedded /ˈwɛdɪd/ *a* casado; matrimonial, conyugal; *Fig.* unido (a); aficionado (a), entusiasta (de), devoto (de); aferrado (a). **to be w. to one's own opinion,** estar aferrado a su propia opinión
wedding /ˈwɛdɪŋ/ *n* boda, *f,* casamiento, *m;* (with golden, etc.) bodas, *f pl;* (union) enlace, *m,* a de boda, nupcial, matrimonial, conyugal; de novios, de la novia. **golden w.,** bodas de oro, *f pl.* **silver w.,** bodas de plata, *f pl.* **w. bouquet,** ramo de la novia, *m.* **w.-breakfast,** banquete de bodas, *m.* **w.-cake,** torta de la boda, *f,* pan de la boda, *m.* **w.-day,** día de la boda, *m.* **w.-march,** marcha nupcial, *f.* **w.-present,** regalo de boda, regalo de la boda, *m.* **w.-ring,** anillo de la boda, *m, Lat. Am.* argolla, *f.* **w. trip,** viaje de novios, *m*
wedge /wɛdʒ/ *n* cuña, *f;* (under a wheel) calza, alzaprima, *f; Mil.* cuña, mella, *f;* (of cheese) pedazo, *m.* *vt* acuñar, meter cuñas; (a wheel) calzar; (fix) sujetar. **to drive a w.,** *Mil.* hacer mella, practicar una cuña. **to w. oneself in,** introducirse con dificultad (en). **w.-shaped,** cuneiforme
wedlock /ˈwɛdˌlɒk/ *n* matrimonio, *m*
Wednesday /ˈwɛnzdei/ *n* miércoles, *m*

wee /wi/ *a* pequeñito, chiquito. **a wee bit,** un poquito

weed /wid/ *n* mala hierba, *f*; tabaco, *m*; (cigar) cigarro, *m*; (person) madeja, *f*; (*Fig.* evil) cizaña, *f. vt* carpir, desherbar, sachar, sallar, escardar. *Lat. Am.* desmalezar; *Fig.* extirpar, arrancar. **w.-grown,** cubierto de malas hierbas. **to w. out,** extirpar; quitar

weeder /'widər/ *n* (person) escardador (-ra); (implement) sacho, *m*

weedy /'widi/ *a* lleno de malas hierbas; *Fig.* raquítico

week /wik/ *n* semana, *f.* **in a w.,** de hoy en ocho (días); en una semana; después de una semana. **once a w.,** una vez por semana. **a w. ago,** hace una semana. **a w. later** *Lat. Am.* a la semana. **Michael will come a w.** from today, Miguel llegará hoy en ocho. **w. in, w. out,** semana tras semana. **w.-day,** día de trabajo, día laborable, día de la semana que no sea el domingo. **on weekdays,** entre semana, *m.* **w.-end,** fin de semana, *m.* **w.-end case,** saco de noche, *m*

weekly /'wikli/ *a* semanal, semanario; de cada semana. *adv* semanalmente, cada semana. *n* semanario, *m*, revista semanal, *f*

weep /wip/ *vt* and *vi* llorar. **to w. for,** (a person) llorar (a); (on account of) llorar por; (with happiness, etc.) llorar de. **They wept for joy,** Lloraron de alegría

weeping /'wipɪŋ/ *n* lloro, llanto, *m*, lágrimas, *f pl. a* lloroso, que llora; (of trees) llorón. **w.-willow,** sauce llorón, *m*

weevil /'wivəl/ *n* gorgojo, *m*

weigh /wei/ *vt* pesar; (consider) considerar, ponderar, tomar en cuenta; comparar; (the anchor) levar. *vi* pesar; ser de importancia. **to w. anchor,** zarpar, levar el ancla, hacerse a la vela. **to w. down,** pesar sobre; sobrecargar; hacer inclinarse bajo; *Fig.* agobiar. **to be weighed down,** hundirse por su propio peso; *Fig.* estar agobiado. **to w. out,** pesar. **to w. with,** influir (en). **w.-bridge,** báscula, *f*

weighing /'weɪɪŋ/ *n* pesada, *f*; (weight) peso, *m*; (of the anchor) leva, *f*; (consideration) ponderación, consideración, *f.* **w.-machine,** báscula, *f*

weight /weit/ *n* peso, *m*; (heaviness) pesantez, *f*; cargo, *m*; (of a clock and as part of a system) pesa, *f*; *Fig.* peso, *m*, importancia, *f. vt* cargar; (a stick) emplomar; aumentar el peso (de); poner un peso (a). **gross w.,** peso bruto, *m.* **heavy w.,** peso pesado, *m.* **light w.,** peso ligero, *m.* **middle w.,** peso medio, *m.* **net w.,** peso neto, *m.* **to lose w.,** adelgazar. **loss of w.,** (of a person) adelgazamiento, *m.* **to put on w.,** cobrar carnes, hacerse más gordo. **to put the w.,** *Sports.* lanzar el peso. **to throw one's w. about,** *Inf.* darse importancia. **to try the w. of,** sopesar. **weights and measures,** pesas y medidas, *f pl.*

weightlifting, halterofilia, *f*

weighty /'weiti/ *a* pesado; (influential) influyente; importante, de peso; grave

weir /wɪər/ *n* presa, esclusa, *f*; (for fish) cañal, *m*

weird /wɪərd/ *a* misterioso, sobrenatural; fantástico; mágico; (queer) raro, extraño

weirdly /'wɪərdli/ *adv* misteriosamente; fantásticamente; (queerly) de un modo raro, extrañamente

weirdness /'wɪərdnɪs/ *n* misterio, *m*; cualidad fantástica, *f*; lo sobrenatural; (queerness) rareza, *f*

welcome /'wɛlkəm/ *a* bienvenido; (pleasant) grato, agradable. *n* bienvenida, *f*; buena acogida, *f*; (reception) acogida, *f. vt* dar la bienvenida (a); acoger con alegría, acoger con entusiasmo; agasajar, festejar; (receive) acoger, recibir; recibir con gusto. **W.!** ¡Bienvenido! **to bid w.,** dar la bienvenida (a). **You are w.,** Estás bienvenido. **You are w. to it,** Está a su disposición

welcoming /'wɛlkəmɪŋ/ *a* acogedor, cordial; amistoso

weld /wɛld/ *vt* soldar; combinar; unificar

welder /'wɛldər/ *n* soldador, *m*

welding /'wɛldɪŋ/ *n* soldadura, *f*; unión, fusión, *f*

welfare /'wɛl,fɛər/ *n* bienestar, bien, *m*; (health) salud, *f*; prosperidad, *f*; intereses, *m pl.* **w. state,** estado benefactor, estado de beneficencia, estado socializante, *m.* **w. work,** trabajo social, *m*

well /wɛl/ *a* bien; bien de salud; bueno; conveniente; (advantageous) provechoso; favorable; (happy) feliz; (healed) curado; (recovered) repuesto. **I am very w.,**

Estoy muy bien. **to get w.,** ponerse bien. **to make w.,** curar. **w. enough,** bastante bien

well /wɛl/ *adv* bien; (very) muy; favorablemente; convenientemente; (easily) sin dificultad. **as w.,** también. **as w. as,** tan bien como; además de. **That is all very w. but...,** Todo eso está muy bien pero... **to be w. up in,** estar versado en. **to get on w. with,** llevarse bien con. **Very w.!** ¡Está bien!; Muy bien. **w. and good,** bien está. **w. now,** ahora bien. **w. then,** conque; pues bien. **w.-advised,** bien aconsejado; prudente. **w.-aimed,** certero. **w.-appointed,** bien provisto; (furnished) bien amueblado. **w.-attended,** concurrido. **w.-balanced,** bien equilibrado. **w.-behaved,** bien educado; (of animals) manso. **w.-being,** bienestar, *m*; felicidad, *f.* **w.-born,** bien nacido, de buena familia. **w.-bred,** bien criado, bien educado; (of animals) de pura raza. **w.-chosen,** bien escogido. **w.-defined,** bien definido. **w.-deserved,** bien merecido. **w.-disposed,** bien dispuesto; favorable; bien intencionado. **w.-doing,** *n* el obrar bien; obras de caridad, *f pl,* a bondadoso, caritativo. **w.-done,** *a* bien hecho. *interj* ¡bravo! **w.-educated,** instruido, culto. **w.-favored,** guapo, de buen parecer. **w.-founded,** bien fundado. **w.-groomed,** elegante. **w.-grounded,** bien fundado; bien instruido. **w.-informed,** instruido; culto, ilustrado. **w.-intentioned,** bien intencionado. **w.-known,** bien conocido, notorio, *Lat. Am.* connotado. **w.-meaning,** bien intencionado. **w.-modulated,** armonioso. **w.-off,** acomodado, adinerado; feliz. **w.-read,** culto, instruido. **w.-shaped,** bien hecho; bien formado. **w.-shaped nose,** nariz perfilada, *f.* **w.-spent,** bien empleado. **w.-spoken,** bien hablado; bien dicho. **w.-stocked,** bien provisto. **w.-suited,** apropiado. **w.-timed,** oportuno. **w.-to-do,** acomodado, rico. **w.-wisher,** amigo (-ga). **w.-worn,** raído; (of paths) trillado

well /wɛl/ *n* pozo, *m*; (of a stair) caja, *f*; cañón de escalera, *m*; (fountain) fuente, *f*, manantial, *m*; (of a fishing boat) vivar, *m*; (of a ship) sentina, *f.* **w.-sinker,** pocero, *m*

well /wɛl/ *vi* chorrear, manar, brotar, fluir

Welsh /wɛlʃ/ *a* galés, de Gales. *n* (language) galés, *m.* **the W.,** los galeses

Welshman /'wɛlʃmən/ *n* galés, *m*

Welshwoman /'wɛlʃ,wʊmən/ *n* galesa, *f*

welt /wɛlt/ *n* (of shoe) vira, *f*, cerquillo, *m*; (in knitting) ribete, *m*; (weal) verdugo, *m*

Weltanschauung /'vɛltənˌʃaʊəŋ/ *n* cosmovisión, postura de vida, *f*

welter /'wɛltər/ *vi* revolcarse; bañarse (en), nadar (en). *n* confusión, *f*, tumulto, *m*; mezcla, *f.* **w.-weight,** peso welter, *m*

wench /wɛntʃ/ *n* mozuela, muchacha, *f*

wend /wɛnd/ *vt* dirigir, encaminar. *vi* ir. **to w. one's way,** dirigir sus pasos, seguir su camino

west /wɛst/ *n* oeste, *m*; poniente, *m*; occidente, *m. a* del oeste; occidental. *adv* hacia el oeste, a poniente; al occidente. **W. Indian,** de las Antillas, de las Indias Occidentales. **w.-north-w.,** oesnoroeste, *m.* **w.-south-w.,** oessudueste, *m.* **w. wind,** viento del oeste, poniente, *m*

westerly /'wɛstərli/ *a* del oeste; hacia el oeste; occidental

western /'wɛstərn/ *a* occidental; del oeste. *n* (novel) novela caballista, *f*; (film) película del oeste, *f*

Western Hemispheric americano

westernized /'wɛstərˌnaɪzd/ *a* influido por el occidente

westernmost /'wɛstərn,moʊst/ *a* más al oeste

West Indies /'ɪndiz/ Indias Occidentales, *f pl*

westward /'wɛstwərd/ *a* que está al oeste. *adv* hacia el oeste; hacia el occidente

wet /wɛt/ *a* mojado; húmedo; (rainy) lluvioso. *vt* mojar; humedecer. *n* (rain) lluvia, *f.* **"Mind the wet paint!"** «¡Cuidado, recién pintado!» **to be wet,** estar mojado; (of the weather) llover. **to get wet,** mojarse.

wet blanket, *Fig.* aguafiestas, *mf* **wet through,** (of persons) calado, hecho una sopa. **wet-nurse,** nodriza, *Lat. Am.* criandera, *f*

wetting /'wɛtɪŋ/ *n* mojada, *f*; humectación, *f*; (soaking) remojo, *m*

whack /wæk/ n golpe, m; (try) tentativa, f; (portion) porción, parte, f. vt golpear, aporrear, pegar

whale /weil/ n ballena, f. **sperm w.,** cachalote, m. **w.-oil,** aceite de ballena, m

whalebone /'weil,boun/ n barbas de ballena, f pl, ballena, f

whaler /'weilər/ n (man) ballenero, pescador de ballenas, m; (boat) buque ballenero, m

whaling /'weilɪŋ/ a ballenero. n pesca de ballenas, f. **w.-gun,** cañón arponero, m

wharf /wɔrf/ n muelle, embarcadero, descargadero, m, vt amarrar al muelle

what /wʌt; unstressed wət/ a pron (interrogative and exclamatory) qué; cómo; (relative) que; el que, m; la que, f; lo que, neut; los que, m pl; las que, f pl; (which, interrogative) cuál, mf; cuáles, mf pl; (how many) cuantos, m pl; cuantas, f pl; (interrogative and exclamatory) cuántos, m pl; cuántas, f pl; (how much, interrogative and exclamatory) cuánto, m; cuánta, f. **And w. not,** Y qué sé yo qué más. **Make w. changes you will,** Haz los cambios que quieras. **W. confidence he had...,** La confianza que tenía... **W. is this called?** ¿Cómo se llama esto? **W. did they go there for?** ¿Por qué fueron? **W. do you take me for?** ¿Por quién me tomas? **That was not w.** he said, No fue eso lo que dijo. **to know what's w.,** saber cuántas son cinco. **You have heard the latest news, w.?** Has oído las últimas noticias, ¿verdad? **W. a pity!** ¡Qué lástima! **W., do you really believe it?** ¿Lo crees de veras? **W. else?** ¿Qué más? **W. for?** ¿Para qué? **what's-his-name,** fulano (-na) de tal, m. **W. ho!** ¡Hola! **W. if...?** ¿Qué será si...? **W. is the matter?** ¿Qué pasa? ¿Qué hay? **w. though...,** aun cuando...; ¿Qué importa qué? **w. with one thing, w. with another,** entre una cosa y otra. **What's more,...** Es más,...

whatever /wʌt'ɛvər/ a pron cuanto; todo lo que; cualquier cosa que; cualquier. **W. sacrifice is necessary,** Cualquier sacrificio que sea necesario. **W. I have is yours,** Todo lo que tenga es vuestro. **W. happens,** Venga lo que venga. **It is of no use w.,** No sirve absolutamente para nada

wheal /wil/ n. See **weal**

wheat /wit/ n trigo, m. a. de trigo. **summer w.,** trigo tremesino, m. **whole w.,** a de trigo entero. **w.-ear,** espiga de trigo, f. **w.-field,** trigal, m. **w.-sheaf,** gavilla de trigo, f

wheedle /'widl/ vt lagotear, engatusar, Lat. Am. also engaratusar; (flatter) halagar; (with out) sacar con mimos

wheedling /'widlɪŋ/ a zalamero, mimoso; marrullero. n lagotería, f, mimos, m pl; (flattery) halagos, m pl; marrullería, f

wheel /wil/ n rueda, f; (bicycle) bicicleta, f; (for steering a ship) timón, m; rueda del timón, f; (for steering a car) volante, m; (for spinning) rueca, f; (potter's) rueda de alfarero, f; (of birds) vuelo, m; (turn) vuelta, f; Mil. conversión, f. **back w.,** rueda trasera, f. **front w.,** rueda delantera, f. **to break on the w.,** enrodar. **to go on wheels,** ir en ruedas; Fig. ir viento en popa. **to take the w.,** (in a ship) tomar el timón; tomar el volante. **w. of fortune,** rueda de la fortuna, f. **w.-chair,** silla de ruedas, f. **w.-house,** timonera, f. **w.-mark,** rodada, f

wheel /wil/ vt hacer rodar; (push) empujar; (drive) conducir; transportar; llevar; pasear; (turn) hacer girar. vi girar; dar vueltas; ir en bicicleta. **to w. about,** cambiar de frente; volverse; cambiar de rumbo

wheelbarrow /'wil,bærou/ n carretilla, f

wheeled /wild/ a de... ruedas; con ruedas. **w. chair,** silla de ruedas, f

wheeler-dealer /'wilər 'dilər/ n Lat. Am. ardilla, f

wheeling /'wilɪŋ/ n rodaje, m; Mil. conversión, f; (of birds) vuelos, m pl, vueltas, f pl. **free-w.,** rueda libre, f

wheelwright /'wil,rait/ n carpintero de carretas, ruedero, m

wheeze /wiz/ vi ser asmático; jadear, respirar fatigosamente, resollar

wheezing /'wizɪŋ/ n resuello, jadeo, m; respiración fatigada, f

whelp /wɛlp/ n cachorro (-rra). vi and vt parir

when /wɛn; unstressed wən/ adv cuando (interrogative, cuándo); (as soon as) tan pronto como, en cuanto; (meaning "and then") y luego, y entonces; (although) aunque. **I will see you w. I return,** Te veré cuando vuelva. **W. he came to see me he was already ill,** Cuando vino a verme estaba enfermo ya. **We returned a week ago, since w. I have not been out,** Volvimos hace ocho días y desde entonces no he salido. **Since w.?** ¿Desde cuándo?

whence /wɛns/ adv de donde (interrogative, de dónde); a donde (interrogative a dónde); por donde, de que; por lo que. **W. does he come?** ¿De dónde viene? **W. comes it that?** ¿Cómo es que...?

whenever /wɛn'ɛvər/ adv cuando quiera que, siempre que; cada vez que, todas las veces que; cuando

where /wɛər/ adv pron donde (interrogative, dónde); en donde; en que (interrogative, en qué); (to where with verbs of motion) a donde (interrogative, a dónde); (from where with verbs of motion) de donde (interrogative, de dónde). **W. are you going to?** ¿A dónde va Vd.? **This is w. we get out,** (of a bus, etc.) Nos apeamos aquí

whereabouts /'wɛərə,bauts/ adv (interrogative) dónde; (relative) donde. n paradero, m

whereas /wɛər'æz/ conjunc (inasmuch as) visto que, ya que; (although) mientras que

whereat /wɛər'æt/ adv por lo cual; a lo cual

whereby /wɛər'bai/ adv cómo; por qué; por el cual, con el cual

wherefore /'wɛər,fɔr/ adv (why) por qué; por lo cual. n porqué, m

wherein /wɛər'ɪn/ adv en donde (interrogative, en dónde); en que (interrogative, en qué)

whereinto /wɛər'ɪntu/ adv en donde; dentro del cual; en lo cual

whereof /wɛər'ʌv/ adv de que; (whose) cuyo

whereon /wɛər'ɒn/ adv sobre que; en qué

whereto /wɛər'tu/ adv adonde; a lo cual

whereupon /,wɛərə'pɒn/ adv dónde; sobre lo cual, con lo cual; en consecuencia de lo cual

wherever /wɛər'ɛvər/ adv dondequiera (que), en cualquier sitio; adondequiera (que). **Sit w. you like,** Siéntate donde te parezca bien

wherewith /wɛər'wɪθ, -'wɪð/ adv con que (interrogative, con qué)

wherewithal /'wɛərwɪð,ɔl, -wɪθ-/ n lo necesario; dinero necesario, m

whet /wɛt/ vt (knives, etc.) afilar, amolar, aguzar; (curiosity, etc.) excitar, estimular

whether /'wɛðər/ conjunc si; que; sea que, ya que. **W. he will or no,** Que quiera, que no quiera. **w. or not,** si o no

whetstone /'wɛt,stoun/ n afiladera, amoladera, piedra de amolar, f

whetting /'wɛtɪŋ/ n aguzadura, amoladura, f; (of curiosity, etc.) estimulación, excitación, f

whey /wei/ n suero (de la leche), m

which /wɪtʃ/ a and pron cuál, mf; cuáles, mf pl; (interrogative, qué); el cual, m; la cual, f; lo cual, neut; los cuales, m pl; las cuales, f pl; el que, m; la que, f; que, neut; los que, m pl; las que, f pl; (who) quien. **all of w.,** todo lo cual, etc. **in w.,** en donde, en que. **of w.,** del cual, la cual, etc. **W. would you like?** ¿Cuál quieres? **The documents w. I have seen,** Los documentos que he visto. **W. way have we to go?** ¿Por dónde hemos de ir?

whichever /wɪtʃ'ɛvər/ a and pron cualquiera (que), mf; cualesquiera, mf pl; el que, m; la que, f; (of persons only) quienquiera (que), mf; quienesquiera (que), mf pl **Give me w. you like,** Dame el que quieras. **I shall take w. of you would like to come,** Me llevaré a cualquiera de Vds. que guste de venir

whiff /wɪf/ n (of air) soplo, m; vaho, m; fragancia, f

while /wail/ n rato, m; momento, m; tiempo, m. **after a w.,** al cabo de algún tiempo, después de algún tiempo. **a little w. ago,** hace poco. **all this w.,** en todo este tiempo. **at whiles,** a ratos, de vez en cuando. **between whiles,** de cuando en cuando; entre tanto. **It is worth your w. to do it,** Vale la pena de hacerse. **Mary smiled the w.,** María mientras tanto se sonreía. **once in a w.**, de vez en cuando; en ocasiones

while /waıl/ *conjunc* mientras (que); al (followed by an infinitive); al mismo tiempo que; a medida que; (although) aunque; si bien. **w. I was walking down the street,** mientras andaba por la calle, al andar yo por la calle. *vt* **to w.** (away), pasar, entretener. **to w. away the time,** pasar el rato

whim /wım/ *n* capricho, antojo, *m*; manía, *f*; extravagancia, *f*; fantasía, *f*

whimper /'wımpər/ *n* quejido, sollozo, gemido, *m*, *vi* lloriquear, quejarse, sollozar, gemir

whimpering /'wımpərıŋ/ *n* lloriqueo, llanto, *m*, *a* que lloriquea

whimsical /'wımzıkəl/ *a* antojadizo, caprichoso; fantástico

whimsicality /ˌwımzı'kælıti/ *n* capricho, *m*, extravagancia, *f*; fantasía, *f*

whimsically /'wımzıkli/ *adv* caprichosamente; fantásticamente

whine /waın/ *vi* gimotear, lloriquear; quejarse

whining /'waınıŋ/ *n* gimoteo, lloriqueo, *m*; quejumbres, *f pl*. *a* que lloriquea; quejumbroso

whinny /'wıni/ *n* relincho, hin, *m*, *vi* relinchar

whip /wıp/ *vt* azotar; pegar; *Cul.* batir; *Sew.* sobrecoser; (ropes, etc.) ligar; (defeat) vencer. *vi* moverse rápidamente. **to w. down,** *vi* bajar volando, bajar corriendo. *vt* arrebatar (de). **to w. in,** entrar precipitadamente (en), penetrar apresuradamente (en). **to w. off,** cazar a latigazos, despachar a golpes; (remove) quitar rápidamente; (persons) llevar corriendo, llevar aprisa. **to w. open,** abrir rápidamente. **to w. out,** *vt* (draw) sacar rápidamente; (utter) saltar diciendo (que); proferir. *vi* escabullirse, escaparse, salir apresuradamente. **to w. round,** volverse de repente. **to w. up,** *vt* (horses, etc.) avivar con el látigo; (snatch) coger de repente agarrar; (gather) reunir. *vi* (mount) subir corriendo

whip /wıp/ *n* azote, zurriago, *Lat. Am.* chicote, *m*; (riding) látigo, *m*. **blow with a w.,** latigazo, *m*. **to have the w.-hand,** mandar, tener la sartén por el mango; tener la ventaja. **w.-cord,** tralla del látigo, *f*

whippet /'wıpıt/ *n* especie de perro (-rra) lebrero (-ra)

whipping /'wıpıŋ/ *n* paliza, *f*, vapuleo, azotamiento, *m*. **w. post,** picota, *f*. **w. top,** trompo, *m*, peonza, *f*

whirl /wɜrl/ *n* vuelta, *f*, giro, *m*; rotación, *f*; *Fig.* torbellino, *m*. *vi* girar; dar vueltas; (dance) bailar, danzar. *vt* hacer girar; dar vueltas (a); (carry) llevar rápidamente. **to w. along,** volar (por), pasar aprisa (por); dejar atrás los vientos, correr velozmente. **to w. past,** pasar volando (por); pasar como una exhalación. **to w. through,** atravesar rápidamente, cruzar volando

whirligig /'wɜrlɪˌgɪg/ *n* perinola, *f*; (merry-go-round) tiovivo, *m*

whirlpool /'wɜrlˌpul/ *n* vórtice, remolino, *m*; *Fig.* vorágine, *f*

whirlwind /'wɜrlˌwınd/ *n* torbellino, *m*, manga de viento, *f*

whirr /wɜr/ *n* zumbido, *m*; (of wings) ruido (de las alas), *m*. *vi* girar; zumbar

whirring /'wɜrıŋ/ *n* zumbido, *m*; ruido, *m*. *a* que gira; que zumba

whisk /wısk/ *n* cepillo, *m*; *Cul.* batidor, *m*; (movement) movimiento rápido, *m*. *vt Cul.* batir; (wag) menear, mover rápidamente; (with off, away) quitar rápidamente; sacudirse; arrebatar; (take away a person) llevarse (a). *vi* moverse rápidamente; andar rápidamente

whiskered /'wıskərd/ *a* bigotudo

whiskers /'wıskərz/ *n pl* mostacho, *m*, patillas, barbas, *f pl*; (of a feline) bigotes, *m pl*

whisky /'wıski/ *n* güisqui, *m*

whisper /'wıspər/ *n* cuchicheo, *m*; (rumor) voz, *f*; (of leaves, etc.) susurro, murmullo, *m*. *vi* and *vt* cuchichear, hablar al oído; (of leaves, etc.) susurrar; (of rumors) murmurar. **in a w.,** al oído, en un susurro

whisperer /'wıspərərsol *n* cuchicheador (-ra); (gossip) murmurador (-ra)

whispering /'wıspərıŋ/ *n* cuchicheo, *m*; susurro, *m*;

(gossip) murmurio, *m*. **w. gallery,** galería de los murmullos, *f*. *Inf.* sala de los secretos, *f*

whistle /'wısəl/ *n* (sound) silbido, silbo, *m*; (instrument) pito, silbato, *m*; *Inf.* gaznate, *m*. *vi* and *vt* silbar. **blast on the w.,** pitido, *m*. **to w. for,** llamar silbando; *Inf.* esperar sentado, buscar en vano

whistler /'wıslər/ *n* silbador (-ra)

whistling /'wıslıŋ/ *n* silbido, *m*, *a* silbador

whit /wıt/ *n* pizca, *f*, bledo, *m*. **not a w.,** ni pizca

white /waıt/ *a* blanco; pálido; puro. *n* color blanco, blanco, *m*; (pigment) pintura blanca, *f*; (whiteness) blancura, *f*; (of egg) clara (del huevo), *f*; (person) blanco, *m*. **Elizabeth went w.,** Isabel se puso pálida. **the w.,** (billiards) la blanca. **the w. of the eye,** lo blanco del ojo. **w. ant,** hormiga blanca, termita, *f*. **w. cabbage,** repollo, *m*. **w. caps,** (of waves) cabrillas, *f pl*; (of mountains) picos blancos, *m pl*. **w. clover,** trébol blanco, *m*. **w. corpuscle,** glóbulo blanco, *m*. **w. currant,** grosella blanca, *f*. **w. elephant,** elefante (-ta) blanco (-ca). **w. ensign,** pabellón blanco, *m*. **w.-faced,** de cara pálida. **w. fish,** pescado blanco, *m*. **w.-haired,** de pelo blanco. **w. heat,** calor blanco, *m*, candencia, *f*; ardor, *m*. **w. horses,** cabrillas, palomas, *f pl*. **w.-hot,** incandescente. **W. House, the,** la Casa Blanca, *f*. **w. lead,** albayalde, *m*. **w. lie,** mentira inocente, mentira oficiosa, mentira piadosa, la mentirilla, *f*. **w. man,** blanco, hombre de raza blanca, *m*. **the white man's burden,** la misión sagrada de la civilización blanca, *f*. **w. meat,** carne blanca, pechuga, *f*. **w. paper,** libro blanco, *m*. **w. sauce,** salsa blanca, *f*. **w. slave,** víctima de la trata de blancas, *f*. **w. slavery,** trata de blancas, *f*. **w. sugar,** azúcar blanco, azúcar de flor, *m*. **w. woman,** mujer de raza blanca, *f*

whiten /'waıtn/ *vt* blanquear. *vi* blanquearse

whiteness /'waıtnıs/ *n* blancura, *f*; palidez, *f*; pureza, *f*; *Poet.* nieve, *f*

whitening /'waıtnıŋ/ *n* blanqueo, *m*; blanco de España, *m*; blanco para los zapatos, *m*

whitewash /'waıtˌwɒʃ/ *vt* blanquear, jalbegar, encalar; (*Fig.* of faults) disculpar, justificar

whitewashing /'waıtˌwɒʃıŋ/ *n* blanqueo, *m*, encaladura, *f*

whither /'wıðər/ *adv* (interrogative) adónde; (with a clause) adonde

whithersoever /ˌwıðərsou'ɛvər/ *adv* adondequiera

whiting /'waıtıŋ/ *n* blanco de España, *m*; blanco para los zapatos, *m*; (fish) pescadilla, *f*, merlango, *m*

whitish /'waıtıʃ/ *a* blanquecino

whitlow /'wıtlou/ *n* panadizo, *m*

Whitsun /'wıtsən/ *a* de Pentecostés.

Whitsunday /'wıt'sʌndei/ *n* domingo de Pentecostés, *m*

Whitsuntide /'wıtsənˌtaid/ *n* pascua de Pentecostés, *f*

whittle /'wıtl/ *n* navaja, *f*. *vt* cercenar, cortar; (sharpen) afilar, sacar punta (a); tallar; *Fig.* reducir. **to w. away, down,** *Fig.* reducir a nada

whizz /wız/ *n* silbido, zumbido, *m*, *vi* silbar, zumbar

whizzing /'wızıŋ/ *n* silbido, *m*, *a* que zumba

who /hu/ *pron* (interrogative) quién, *mf*; quiénes, *mf pl*; (relative) quien, *mf*; quienes, *mf pl*; que; (in elliptical constructions the person that, etc.) el que, *m*; la que, *f*; los que, *m pl*; las que, *f pl*

whoa /wou/ *interj* ¡so!

whoever /hu'ɛvər/ *pron* quienquiera (que); cualquiera (que); quien. **Give it to w. you like,** Dáselo a quien te parezca bien

whole /houl/ *a* (healthy) sano; (uninjured) ileso, entero; todo. *n* todo, *m*; total, *m*; totalidad, *f*; conjunto, *m*. **on the w.,** por regla general, en general; en conjunto. **the w. week,** la semana entera, toda la semana. **w.-hearted,** sincero, genuino; entusiasta. **w.-heartedly,** de todo corazón. **w.-heartedness,** sinceridad, *f*; entusiasmo, *m*. **w. length,** *a* de cuerpo entero. **w. number,** número entero, *m*

wholemeal /'houl'mil/ *n* harina de trigo entero, *f*, *a* de trigo entero

wholeness /'houlnıs/ *n* totalidad, *f*; integridad, *f*; todo, *m*

wholesale /'houlˌseil/ *a Com.* al por mayor; en grueso; *Fig.* general; en masa. *n* venta al por mayor, *f.* **w. price,** precio al por mayor, *m.* **w. trade,** comercio al por mayor, *m*

wholesaler /'houl,seilər/ *n* comerciante al por mayor, *mf* mercader de grueso, *m*

wholesome /'houlsəm/ *a* sano; saludable; (edifying) edificante

wholesomeness /'houlsəmnıs/ *n* sanidad, *f*; lo sano; lo saludable

wholly /'houli/ *adv* completamente, enteramente, totalmente; integralmente; del todo

whom /hum/ *pron* quien; a quien, *mf*; a quienes, *mf pl*; (interrogative) a quién, *mf*; a quiénes, *mf pl*; al que, *m*; a la que, *f*; a los que, *m pl*; a las que, *f pl.* **from w.,** de quien; (interrogative) de quién. **the man w. you saw,** el hombre a quien viste

whoop /wup, wʊp/ *n* alarido, grito, *m*; estertor de la tos ferina, *m. vi* dar gritos, chillar; /hup/ (whooping-cough) toser

whooping cough /'hupıŋ/ *n* tos ferina, coqueluche, *f*

whore /hɔr/ *n* puta, ramera, *f, Lat. Am. also* araña, *f*

whorl /wɜrl, wɔrl/ *n* (of a shell) espira, *f*; *Bot.* verticilo, *m*; (of a spindle) tortera, *f*

whorled /wɜrld, wɔrld/ *a Bot.* verticilado; (of shells) en espira

whose /huz/ *pron* cuyo, *m*; cuya, *f*; cuyos, *m pl*; cuyas, *f pl*; de quien, *mf*; de quienes, *mf pl*; (interrogative) de quién, de quiénes. **W. daughter is she?** ¿De quién es ella la hija? **This is the writer w. name I always forget,** Este es el autor cuyo nombre siempre olvido

whosoever /,husou'ɛvər/ *pron.* See **whoever**

why /wai/ *adv* (interrogative) por qué; (on account of which) por el cual, *m*; por la cual, *f*; por lo cual, *neut*; por los cuales, *m pl*; por las cuales, *f pl*; (how) cómo. *n* ni porqué, *m, interj* ¡qué!; ¡cómo!; ¡toma!; si. **not to know the why or wherefore,** no saber ni el porqué ni el cómo, no saber ni el qué ni el por qué. **Why! I have just come,** ¡Si no hago más de llegar! **Why not?** ¿Por qué no? ¡Cómo no!

wick /wık/ *n* mecha, torcida, *f*

wicked /'wıkıd/ *a* malo; malvado, perverso; pecaminoso; malicioso; (mischievous) travieso

wickedly /'wıkıdli/ *adv* mal; perversamente; maliciosamente

wickedness /'wıkıdnıs/ *n* maldad, *f*; perversidad, *f*; pecado, *m*; (mischievousness) travesura, *f*

wicker /'wıkər/ *n* mimbre, *m, a* de mimbre

wicket /'wıkıt/ *n* postigo, portillo, *m*; (half-door) media puerta, *f*; (at cricket) meta, *f.* **w.-keeper,** guardameta, *m*

wide /waid/ *a* ancho; (in measurements) de ancho; vasto; extenso; grande; amplio; (loose) holgado; (distant) lejos; liberal; general, comprensivo. *adv* lejos; completamente. **far and w.,** por todas partes. **to be too w.,** ser muy ancho; estar muy ancho; (of garments) venir muy ancho. **two feet w.,** dos pies de ancho. **w.-awake,** muy despierto; despabilado; vigilante. **w.-eyed,** con los ojos muy abiertos; asombrado. **w.-open,** abierto de par en par

widely /'waidli/ *adv* extensamente; generalmente; (very) muy

widen /'waidn/ *vt* ensanchar; extender. *vi* ensancharse; extenderse

widening /'waidnıŋ/ *n* ensanche, *m*; extensión, *f*

widespread /'waid'sprɛd/ *a* universal, generalizado; extenso; esparcido. **to become w.,** generalizarse

widow /'wıdou/ *n* viuda, *f. vt* dejar viuda; dejar viudo; *Fig.* privar. **to be a grass w.,** estar viuda. **to become a w.,** enviudar, perder al esposo. **widow's pension,** viudedad, *f.* **widow's weeds,** luto de viuda, *m*

widowed /'wıdoud/ *a* viudo

widower /'wıdouər/ *n* viudo, *m.* **to become a w.,** perder a la esposa, enviudar

widowhood /'wıdou,hʊd/ *n* viudez, *f*

width /wıdθ/ *n* anchura, *f*; (of cloth) ancho, *m*; (of mind) liberalismo, *m.* **double w.,** (cloth) doble ancho, *m*

wield /wild/ *vt* (a scepter) empuñar; (power, etc.) ejercer; (a pen, sword) manejar

wife /waif/ *n* esposa, mujer, *f*; mujer, *f*; comadre, *f.* **husband and w.,** los cónyuges, los esposos. **old**

wives' tale, cuento de viejas, *m.* **The Merry Wives of Windsor,** Las alegres comadres de Windsor. **to take to w.,** contraer matrimonio con, tomar como esposa (a)

wifely /'waifli/ *a* de esposa, de mujer casada; de mujer de su casa; conyugal

wig /wıg/ *n* peluca, *f*; (hair) cabellera, *f.* **top wig,** peluquín, *m.* **wigmaker,** peluquero, *m*

wigged /wıgd/ *a* con peluca, de peluca

wigging /'wıgıŋ/ *n* (scolding) peluca, *f*

wigwam /'wıgwɒm/ *n* tienda de indios, *f*

wild /waild/ *a* (of animals, men, land) salvaje; (barren) desierto, yermo; (mountainous) riscoso, montañoso; (of plants, birds) silvestre; montés; (disarranged) en desorden, desarreglado; (complete) absoluto, completo; (dissipated) disipado; vicioso; (foolish) alocado; (of the sea) bravío; (of weather, etc.) borrascoso; (mad with delight, etc.) loco; (frantic, mad) frenético, loco; (with "talk," etc.) extravagante; insensato, desatinado; (shy) arisco; (incoherent) inconexo, incoherente; (frightened) alarmado, espantado; (willful) travieso, indomable. *n* tierra virgen, *f*; desierto, *m*; soledad, *f.* **It made me w.,** (angry) Me hizo rabiar. **to run w.,** volver al estado silvestre; (of persons) llevar una vida de salvajes; volverse loco. **to shoot w.,** errar el tiro. **to spread like w. fire,** propagarse como el fuego. **w. beast,** fiera, *f.* **w. boar,** jabalí, *m.* **w. cat,** gato montés, *Lat. Am.* lince, *m.* **w. duck,** pato silvestre, *m.* **w. goat,** cabra montesa, *f.* **w.-goose chase,** caza infructuosa, *f*; empresa quimérica, *f.* **w. oats,** avenas locas, *f pl*; *Fig.* indiscreciones de la juventud, *f pl.* **to sow one's w. oats,** andarse a la flor del berro

wilderness /'wıldərnıs/ *n* desierto, *m*; yermo, páramo, despoblado, *m*; soledad, *f*; (jungle) selva, *f*; (maze) laberinto, *m*; infinidad, *f*

wildly /'waildli/ *adv* en un estado salvaje; sin cultivo; (rashly) desatinadamente; sin reflexión, sin pensar; (incoherently) incoherentemente; (stupidly, of looking, etc.) tontamente; (in panic) con ojos espantados, con terror en los ojos, alarmado

wildness /'waildnıs/ *n* salvajez, *f*; estado silvestre, *m*; naturaleza silvestre, *f*, (ferocity) ferocidad, *f*; (of the wind, sea) braveza, *f*; (of the wind) violencia, *f*; (impetuosity) impetuosidad, *f*; (of statements, etc.) extravagancia, *f*; (incoherence) incoherencia, *f*; (disorder) desorden, *m*; (willfulness, of children) travesuras, *f pl*; (of the expression) gesto espantado, *m*

wile /wail/ *n* estratagema, *f*, engaño, *m*, ardid, *f*

wilily /'wailıli/ *adv* astutamente

wiliness /'wailınıs/ *n* astucia, *f*

will /wıl/ *n* voluntad, *f*; albedrío, *m*; (wish) deseo, *m*; (pleasure) discreción, *f*, placer, *m*; (legal document) testamento, *m.* **against my w.,** contra mi voluntad. **at w.,** a voluntad; a gusto; a discreción. **free w.,** libre albedrío, *m.* **of one's own free w.,** por su propia voluntad. **iron w.,** voluntad de hierro, *f.* **last w. and testament,** última disposición, última voluntad, *f.* **to do with a w.,** hacer con toda el alma, hacer con entusiasmo. **to make one's w.,** otorgar (hacer) su testamento. **w.-power,** fuerza de voluntad, *f*

will /wıl/ *vt* querer; disponer, ordenar; (bequeath) legar, dejar en testamento, mandar; (oblige) sugestionar (a una persona) para que haga algo; hipnotizar. *vi aux.* querer; (As a sign of the future it is not translated separately in Spanish) **I w. come tomorrow,** Vendré mañana. **John does not approve, but I w. go,** Juan no lo aprueba pero yo quiero ir. **Do what you w.,** Haga lo que a Vd. le parezca bien, Haga lo que Vd. quiera; Haga lo que haga. **Boys w. be boys,** Los niños son siempre niños. **He w. not (won't) do it,** No lo hará; No quiere hacerlo

willful /'wılfəl/ *a* rebelde, voluntarioso; (of children) travieso; (of crimes, etc.) premeditado

willfully /'wılfəli/ *adv* voluntariosamente; intencionadamente; (of committing crimes) con premeditación

willfulness /'wılfəlnıs/ *n* rebeldía, *f*; (obstinacy) terquedad, obstinación, *f*

willing /'wılıŋ/ *a* dispuesto, inclinado; (serviceable) servicial; deseoso; espontáneo; complaciente; gustoso; (willingly) de buena gana. **to be w.,** estar dispuesto (a), querer; consentir (en)

willingly /'wɪlɪŋli/ *adv* de buena gana, con gusto

willingness /'wɪlɪŋnɪs/ *n* buena voluntad, *f*; deseo de servir, *m*; complacencia, *f*; (consent) consentimiento, *m*

will-o'-the-wisp /'wɪləðə'wɪsp/ *n* fuego fatuo, *m*

willow /'wɪlou/ *n* sauce, *m*. **weeping w.,** sauce llorón, *m*. **w.-pattern china,** porcelana de estilo chino, *f*. **w. tree,** sauce, *m*

willowy /'wɪloui/ *a* lleno de sauces; (slim) cimbreño, esbelto, alto y delgado

willy nilly /'wɪli 'nɪli/ *adv* de buen o mal grado, mal que bien

wilt /wɪlt/ *vi* (of plants) marchitarse, secarse; *Fig.* languidecer; ajarse. *vt* marchitar; *Fig.* ajar; hacer languidecer

wily /'waili/ *a* astuto, chuzón

win /wɪn/ *vt* ganar; (reach) alcanzar, lograr; (a victory, etc.) llevarse; conquistar. *vi* ganar; triunfar. *n* triunfo, *m*. **to win back,** volver a ganar; recobrar

wince /wɪns/ *vi* retroceder, recular; (flinch) quejarse; (of a horse) respingar. *n* respingo, *m*. **without wincing,** sin quejarse; estoicamente

winch /wɪntʃ/ *n* cabria, *f*; (handle) manubrio, *m*

wind /wɪnd/ *n* viento, *m*; aire, *m*; (flatulence) flatulencia, *f*; (breath) respiración, *f*, aliento, *m*; (idle talk) paja, *f*. **breath of w.,** soplo de viento, *m*. **following w.,** viento en popa, *m*. **high w.,** viento alto, viento fuerte, *m*. **land w.,** viento terrenal, *m*. **It's an ill w. that blows nobody good,** No hay mal que por bien no venga. **There is something in the w.,** Hay algo en el aire, Se trama algo. **to get w. of,** husmear. **to sail before the w.,** navegar de viento en popa. **The w. stiffened,** Refrescó el viento. **You took the w. out of his sails,** Le deshinchaste las velas. **w.-instrument,** instrumento de viento, *m*. **w.-proof,** a prueba del viento. **w.-swept,** expuesto a todos los vientos. **w. storm,** ventarrón, *m*

wind /waind/ *vi* serpentear; desfilar lentamente; torcerse. *vt* (turn) dar vueltas (a); (a handle) manejar, mover; (a watch) dar cuerda (a); (wool, etc.) devanar, ovillar; (wrap) envolver; (of arms, embrace) rodear (con); (a horn) tocar. **to w. off,** devanar; desenrollar. **to w. round,** (wrap) envolver; (skirt) rodear; (embrace) ceñir con (los brazos); (pass by) pasar por; deslizarse por; (of snakes) enroscarse. **to w. up,** (a watch) dar cuerda (a); (thread) devanar; (conclude) concluir; *Com.* liquidar; (excite) agitar, emocionar

windbag /'wɪnd,bæg/ *n* pandero, *m*, sacamuelas, *mf*

winder /'waindər/ *n* (person) devanador (-ra); (machine) devanadera, *f*; (of a clock) llave, *f*

windfall /'wɪnd,fɔl/ *n* fruta caída del árbol, *f*; (good luck) breva, *f*; ganancia inesperada, lotería, *f*

windiness /'wɪndɪnɪs/ *n* tiempo ventoso, *m*; situación expuesta a todos los vientos, *f*; (of speech) pomposidad, verbosidad, *f*

winding /'waindɪŋ/ *a* tortuoso; (e.g., road) sinuoso; serpentino; en espiral. *n* tortuosidad, *f*; meandro, recoveco, *m*, vuelta, curva, *f*. **w. sheet,** mortaja, *f*, sudario, *m*. **w. stair,** escalera de caracol, *f*. **w.-up,** conclusión, *f*; *Com.* liquidación, *f*

windlass /'wɪndləs/ *n* torno, *m*

windless /'wɪndlɪs/ *a* sin viento

windmill /'wɪnd,mɪl/ *n* molino de viento, *m*

window /'wɪndou/ *n* ventana, *f*; (of a shop) escaparate, *Mexico* aparador, *m*; (in a train, car, bank, etc.) ventanilla, *f*; (booking office) taquilla, *f*; (of a church) vidriera, *f*. **casement w.,** ventana, *f*. **sash w.,** ventana de guillotina, *f*. **small w.,** ventanilla, *f*. **stained glass w.,** vidriera, *f*. **to lean out of the w.,** asomarse a la ventana. **to look out of the w.,** mirar por la ventana. **w. blind,** (Venetian) persiana, *f*; transparente, *m*; (against the sun) toldo, *m*. **w.-dresser,** decorador (-ra) de escaparates. **w. frame,** marco de ventana, *m*. **w.-pane,** cristal (de ventana), *m*. **w.-shutter,** contraventana, *f*. **w.-sill,** repisa de la ventana, *f*, alféizar, *m*

windpipe /'wɪnd,paip/ *n* tráquea, *f*

windshield /'wɪnd,ʃild/ *n* parabrisas, guardabrisa, *m*. **w.-wiper,** limpiaparabrisas, limpiavidrios, *m*

windward /'wɪndwərd/ *n* barlovento, *m*. *a* de barlovento. *adv* a barlovento

windy /'wɪndi/ *a* ventoso; expuesto al viento; (of style) hinchado, pomposo. **It is w.,** Hace viento

wine /wain/ *n* vino, *m*; zumo fermentado (de algunas frutas), *m*. *a* de vino; de vinos; para vino. **in w.,** *Cul.* en vino; (drunk) ebrio, borracho. **heavy w.,** vino fuerte, *m*. **light w.,** vino ligero, *m*. **local w.,** vino del país, *m*. **matured w.,** vino generoso, *m*. **red w.,** vino tinto, *m*. **thin w.,** vinillo, *m*. **white w.,** vino blanco, *m*. **w.-cellar,** bodega, cueva, *f*. **w.-colored,** de color de vino. **w.-cooler,** cubo para enfriar vinos, *m*. **w. country,** tierra de vino, *f*. **w. decanter,** garrafa para vino, *f*. **w.-grower,** vinicultor (-ra). **w.-growing,** *n* vinicultura, *f*. *a* vinícola. **w. lees,** zupia, *f*. **w. merchant,** comerciante en vinos, *mf*. vinatero, *m*. **w.-press,** lagar, *m*. **w.-taster,** catavinos, *m*. **w. waiter,** bodeguero, *m*

wineskin /'wain,skɪn/ *n* bota, *f*, odre, pellejo, *m*

wing /wɪŋ/ *n* (of a bird and *Zool.*, *Archit.*, *Aer.*, *Mil.*, *Bot.*) ala, *f*; (flight) vuelo, *m*; *Theat.* bastidor, *m*; *Fig.* protección, *f*. *vt* dar alas (a); llevar sobre las alas; (wound) herir en el ala; herir en el brazo; volar por. *vi* volar. **beating of wings,** batir de alas, aleteo, *m*. **in the wings,** *Theat.* entre bastidores. **on the w.,** al vuelo. **to clip a (person's) wings,** cortar (*or* quebrar) las alas (a). **under his w.,** bajo su protección. **w.-case,** élitro (de un insecto), *m*. **w. chair,** sillón con orejas, *m*. **w.-commander,** teniente coronel de aviación, *m*. **w.-span,** (*Zool.* and *Aer.*) envergadura, *f*. **w.-spread,** extensión del ala, *f*. **w.-tip,** punta del ala, *f*

winged /wɪŋd; *esp. Literary* 'wɪŋɪd/ *a* alado, con alas; (in compounds) de alas...; (swift) alado; (of style) elevado, alado

wink /wɪŋk/ *vi* (blink) pestañear; (as a signal, etc.) guiñar; (of stars, etc.) titilar, parpadear, centellear. *vt* guiñar (el ojo). *n* pestañeo, *m*; guiño, *m*. **not to sleep a w.,** no pegar los ojos. **to take forty winks,** echar una siesta. **to w. at,** guiñar el ojo (a); (ignore) hacer la vista gorda

winking /'wɪŋkɪŋ/ *n* (blinking) parpadeo, *m*; (as a signal) guiños, *m pl*; (of stars, etc.) titilación, *f*, pestañeo, *m*. *a* (of stars, etc.) titilante. **like w.,** en un abrir y cerrar de ojos

winner /'wɪnər/ *n* ganador (-ra); vencedor (-ra)

winning /'wɪnɪŋ/ *a* ganador; vencedor; (attractive) encantador. *n* ganancia, *f*. **w. number,** número galardonado, número premiado, número vencedor, *m*. **w.-post,** meta, *f*. **w. side,** *Sports.* equipo vencedor, *m*; (politics, etc.) partido vencedor, *m*

winnings /'wɪnɪŋz/ *n* ganancias, *f pl*

winnow /'wɪnou/ *vt* aventar, abalear; *Fig.* separar

winnower /'wɪnouər/ *n* aventador (-ra)

winnowing /'wɪnouɪŋ/ *n* abaleo, aventamiento, *m*; *Fig.* separación, *f*. **w. fork,** bieldo, *m*. **w. machine,** aventador mecánico, *m*

winsome /'wɪnsəm/ *a* sandunguero; dulce, encantador

winsomeness /'wɪnsəmnɪs/ *n* sandunga, *f*; encanto, *m*, dulzura, *f*

winter /'wɪntər/ *n* invierno, *m*. *a* de invierno; hiemal. *vi* pasar el invierno, invernar. *vt* (of cattle, etc.) guardar en invierno. **in w.,** en invierno, durante el invierno. **w. clothes,** ropa de invierno, *f*. **w. palace,** palacio de invierno, *m*. **w. pasture,** *Lat. Am.* invernada, *f*. **w. quarters,** invernadero, *m*. **w. season,** invierno, *m*; temporada de invierno, *f*. **w. sleep,** invernada, *f*. **w. solstice,** solsticio hiemal, *m*. **w. sports,** deportes de nieve, *m pl*. **w. wheat,** trigo de invierno, *m*

wintry /'wɪntri/ *a* de invierno; invernal; (of a smile, etc.) glacial

wipe /waip/ *vt* limpiar; (rub) frotar; (dry) secar; (remove) quitar. *n* limpión, *m*; (blow) golpe de lado, *m*. **to w. one's eyes,** enjugarse las lagrimas. **to w. off, out,** limpiar; (remove) quitar; (erase) borrar; (kill) destruir completamente, exterminar; (a military force) destrozar; (a debt) cancelar

wire /waiər/ *n* alambre, *m*; hilo metálico, *m*; telégrafo (eléctrico), *m*; *Inf.* telegrama, *m*. *vt* atar con alambre; (fence) alambrar; (snare) coger con lazo de alambre;

(of electrical equipment, etc.) instalar; (telegraph) telegrafiar; *vi* (telegraph) telegrafiar. **barbed w.,** alambre espinoso, *m.* **live w.,** alambre cargado (de electricidad), *m*; (person) fuerza viva, *f*. **w.-cutters,** cortaalambres, *m pl.* **w.-entanglement,** *Mil.* alambrada, *f.* **w. fence,** alambrera, *f*, cercado de alambre, *m.* **w. gauze,** tela metálica, *f.* **w. nail,** punta de París, *f.* **w.-netting,** malla de alambre, *f*; alambrado, *m.* **w.-pulling,** influencias secretas, *f pl*; intrigas políticas, *f pl*

wiredraw /'waiªr͵drɔ/ *vt* estirar (alambre), tirar (el hilo de hierro, plata, etc.); (arguments, etc.) sutilizar

wiredrawer /'waiªr͵drɔər/ *n* estirador, *m*

wireless /'waiªrlɪs/ *a* sin hilos; (of a message) radiotelegráfico; por radio. *n* telegrafía sin hilos, *f*; radiotelefonía, *f*; (telegram) radiocomunicación, *f*; (broadcasting) radio, *f. vt* radiotelegrafiar. **Let's listen to the w.,** Vamos a escuchar la radio. **portable w.,** radio portátil, *f.* **w. engineer,** ingeniero radiotelegrafista, *m.* **w. enthusiast,** radioaficionado (-da). **w. license,** permiso de radiorreceptor, *m.* **w. operator,** radiotelegrafista, *mf.* **w. room,** cuarto de telegrafía sin hilos, *m.* **w. set,** aparato de radio, *m.* **w. station,** estación de radiotelegrafía, *f*; (broadcasting) radioemisora, *f.* **w. telegraph,** telégrafo sin hilos, *m.* **w. telegraphy,** telegrafía sin hilos, radiotelegrafía, *f.* **w. telephony,** telefonía sin hilos, *f.* **w. transmission,** radioemisión, *f*

wiretap /'waiªr͵tæp/ *vi* poner escucha. *vt* poner escucha a

wiring /'waiªrɪŋ/ *n* instalación de alambres eléctricos, *f*

wiry /'waiªri/ *a* semejante a un alambre; (of persons) nervudo

wisdom /'wɪzdəm/ *n* sabiduría, *f*; (learning) saber, *m*; (judgment) juicio, *m.* **Book of W.,** Libro de la Sabiduría, *m.* **w.-tooth,** muela del juicio, *f*

wise /waiz/ *a* sabio; juicioso, prudente; (informed) enterado, informado. **w. man,** un sabio. **in no w.,** de ningún modo. **the W. Men of the East,** los magos. **w. guy,** *Inf.* toro corrido, *m*

wisely /'waizli/ *adv* sabiamente; prudentemente, con prudencia

wish /wɪʃ/ *n* deseo, *m.* **Best wishes for the New Year,** Los mejores deseos para el Año Nuevo. **w.-bone,** espoleta, *f*

wish /wɪʃ/ *vt* querer; desear; ansiar; (with "good morning', etc.) dar. **I w. he were here!** ¡Ojalá que estuviera aquí! **Theresa wishes us to go,** Teresa quiere que vayamos. **I w. it had happened otherwise,** Quisiera que las cosas hubiesen pasado de otra manera. **I w. you would make less noise,** Me gustaría que hicieses menos ruido. **I only w. one thing,** Solamente deseo una cosa. **I w. you good luck,** Te deseo mucha suerte. **I wished him a merry Christmas,** Le deseé unas Pascuas muy felices, Le felicité las Pascuas. **to w. a prosperous New Year,** desear un próspero Año Nuevo. **to w. good-by,** despedirse (de). **to w. good day,** dar los buenos días. **to w. for,** desear

wisher /'wɪʃər/ *n* el que, *m*, (f, la que) desea, deseador (-ra)

wishful /'wɪʃfəl/ *a* deseoso; ansioso; ávido. **w. thinking,** ilusiones, *f pl*; optimismo injustificado, optimismo exagerado, *m*

wisp /wɪsp/ *n* mechón, *m*; jirón, *m*; trozo, pedazo, *m*

wistaria /wɪ'stiəriə, -'stɛər-/ *n* vistaria, *f*

wistful /'wɪstfəl/ *a* ansioso; triste; patético; (envious) envidioso; (regretful) de pesar; (remorseful) remordimiento; (thoughtful) pensativo

wistfully /'wɪstfəli/ *adv* con ansia; tristemente; patéticamente; con envidia; con pesar; con remordimiento; pensativo

wistfulness /'wɪstfəlnɪs/ *n* ansia, *f*; tristeza, *f*; (envy) envidia, *f*; (regret) pesar, *m*; (remorse) remordimiento, *m*; (thoughtfulness) lo pensativo, lo distraído

wit, to /wɪt/ *adv* a saber

wit /wɪt/ *n* (reason) juicio, *m*; agudeza, gracia, *f*; rasgo de ingenio, *m*; ingenio, *m*; inteligencia, *f*, talento, *m*; (person) hombre de ingenio, *m*; mujer de ingenio, *f.* **my five wits,** mis cinco sentidos. **to be at one's wits' end,** no saber qué hacer. **to live by one's**

wits, ser caballero de industria. **to lose one's wits,** perder el juicio

witch /wɪtʃ/ *n* bruja, *f.* **witches' sabbath,** aquelarre, *m.* **w.-doctor,** hechizador, mago, *m.* **witch-hazel,** carpe, *m*; loción de carpe, *f*

witchcraft /'wɪtʃ͵kræft/ *n* brujería, *f*; sortilegio, encantamiento, *m*

witchery /'wɪtʃəri/ *n* brujería, *f*; *Fig.* encanto, *m*, magia, *f*

with /wɪθ, wɪð/ *prep* con; en compañia de; en casa de; (against) contra; (among) entre; en; (by) por; (towards) hacia; para con; (according to) según; (notwithstanding) a pesar de; a; (concerning) con respecto a; en el caso de. **Rose is w. Antony,** Rosa está con Antonio. **He was w. his dog,** Estaba acompañado por su perro. **He pulled at it w. both hands,** Lo tiró con las dos manos. **filled w. fear,** lleno de miedo. **to shiver w. cold,** temblarse de frío. **the girl w. golden hair,** la muchacha del pelo dorado. **They killed it w. one blow,** Lo mataron de un solo golpe. **It rests w. you to decide,** Tú tienes que decidirlo; Te toca a ti decidirlo. **to begin w.,** *adv* para empezar; *v* empezar por. **w. all speed,** a toda prisa. **to part w.,** desprenderse de; (of people) despedirse de; separarse de. **w. that...,** (at once) en esto... (disease and poverty, etc.) **are still with us,** están todavía en el mundo

withal /wɪð'ɔl, wɪθ-/ *adv* además; al mismo tiempo. *prep* con

withdraw /wɪð'drɔ, wɪθ-/ *vt* retirar; (words) retractar; (remove) quitar, privar (de); (a legal action) apartar. *vi* retirarse; retroceder; apartarse; irse

withdrawal /wɪð'drɔəl, wɪθ-/ *n* retirada, *f*; (retirement) retiro, *m*; apartamiento, *m*

withdrawn /wɪð'drɔn, wɪθ-/ *a* (abstracted) ensimismado, meditabundo

wither /'wɪðər/ *vi* marchitarse, secarse, ajarse *vt* marchitar, secar, ajar; *Fig.* hacer languidecer, matar; (snub) avergonzar

withered /'wɪðərd/ *a* marchito, mustio; muerto; (of persons) acartonado, seco

witheredness /'wɪðərdnɪs/ *n* marchitez, *f*; sequedad, *f*

withering /'wɪðərɪŋ/ *a* que marchita; (scorching) abrasador, ardiente; (scornful) despreciativo, desdeñoso; (biting) mordaz, cáustico

withers /'wɪðərz/ *n* cruz, *f*

withhold /wɪθ'hould, wɪð-/ *vt* retener; detener; (restrain) refrenar; apartar; (refuse) negar; abstenerse de; (refuse to reveal) ocultar

withholding /wɪθ'houldɪŋ, wɪð-/ *n* detención, *f*; (refusal) negación, *f*

within /wɪð'ɪn, wɪθ-/ *adv* dentro, adentro; en el interior; en casa; *Fig.* en su interior. **He stayed w.,** Se quedó dentro. **Is Mrs. González w.?** ¿Está en casa la Sra. González?

within /wɪð'ɪn, wɪθ-/ *prep* dentro de; el interior de; en; entre; (within range of) al alcance de; a la distancia de; (near) cerca de; a poco de; (of time) en el espacio de, en; dentro de; (almost) por poco, casi. **He was w. an inch of being killed,** Por poco le matan. **to be w. hearing,** estar al alcance de la voz. **seen from w.,** visto desde dentro. **twice w. a fortnight,** dos veces en quince días. **w. himself,** por sus adentros, entre sí. **w. an inch of,** *Fig.* a dos dedos de. **w. a few miles of Bogotá,** a unas millas de Bogotá. **w. a short distance,** en una corta distancia; a poca distancia

without /wɪð'aut, wɪθ-/ *prep* sin; falto de; (outside) fuera de; (beyond) más allá de. *adv* exteriormente; por fuera; hacia afuera; fuera. **It goes w. saying,** No hay que decir. **w. more ado,** sin más ni más. **w. my knowledge,** sin que yo lo supiese. **w. regard for,** sin miramientos por. **w. saying more,** sin decir más. **without batting an eyelash,** sin sobresaltos

withstand /wɪθ'stænd, wɪð-/ *vt* resistir, oponerse (a); soportar

withstanding /wɪθ'stændɪŋ, wɪð-/ *n* resistencia, oposición (a), *f*

witless /'wɪtlɪs/ *a* sin seso, tonto, necio

witness /'wɪtnɪs/ *n* (evidence) testimonio, *m*; (person) testigo, *mf*; espectador (-ra). **in w. whereof,** en

fe de lo cual. **to bear w.,** atestiguar, dar testimonio. **to bring forward witnesses,** hacer testigos. **w. my hand,** en fe de lo cual, firmo. **w.-box,** puesto de los testigos, *m*. **w. for the defense,** testigo de descargo, *mf*. **w. for the prosecution,** testigo de cargo, *mf*
witness /'wɪtnɪs/ *vt* (show) mostrar, señalar; (see) ser testigo de, ver, presenciar; *Law.* atestiguar. *vi* dar testimonio; servir de testigo
witticism /'wɪtə,sɪzəm/ *n* rasgo de ingenio, donaire, *m*, agudeza, *f*
wittily /'wɪtʃli/ *adv* ingeniosamente, donairosamente, agudamente
wittiness /'wɪtinɪs/ *n* viveza de ingenio, donosura, *f*
witty /'wɪti/ *a* salado, gracioso. **w.** sally, agudeza, *f*
wizard /'wɪzərd/ *n* mago, hechicero, *m*
wizardry /'wɪzərdri/ *n* magia, *f*
wizened /'wɪzənd/ *a* seco, arrugado; (of persons) acartonado
wobble /'wɒbəl/ *vi* tambalearse, balancearse; (quiver) temblar; oscilar; *Mech.* galopar; (stagger) titubear; *Fig.* vacilar
wobbly /'wɒbli/ *a* que se bambolea; inestable; *Fig.* vacilante
woe /wou/ *n* dolor, *m*; congoja, aflicción, *f*; mal, desastre, infortunio, *m*. **Woe is me!** ¡Ay de mí! ¡Desdichado de mí!
woebegone /'woubɪ,gɔn/ *a* angustiado
woeful /'woufəl/ *a* triste; doloroso; funesto
woefully /'woufəli/ *adv* tristemente; dolorosamente
wolf /wʊlf/ *n* lobo (-ba). **a w. in sheep's clothing,** un lobo en piel de cordero. **to cry w.,** gritar «el lobo!» **to keep the w. from the door,** ponerse a cubierto del hambre. **w.-cub,** lobezno, *m*. **w.-hound,** perro lobo, *m*. **w. pack,** manada de lobos, *f*
wolfish /'wʊlfɪʃ/ *a* lobuno, de lobo
woman /'wʊmən/ *n* mujer, *f*; hembra, *f*; (lady-in-waiting) dama de servicio, *f*. **a fine figure of a w.,** una real hembra. **w. doctor,** médica, *f*. **w.-hater,** misógino, *m*. **w. of the town,** mujer de la vida airada, *f*. **w. of the world,** mujer de mundo, *f*
womanhood /'wʊmən,hʊd/ *n* feminidad, *f*; sexo feminino, *m*
womanish /'wʊmənɪʃ/ *a* afeminado
womankind /'wʊmən,kaind/ *n* el sexo femenino, las mujeres
womanliness /'wʊmənlinɪs/ *n* feminidad, *f*; carácter femenino, *m*
womanly /'wʊmənli/ *a* femenino, de mujer
womb /wum/ *n* útero, *m*, matriz, *f*; *Fig.* seno, *m*
women's dormitory /'wɪmɪnz/ *n* residencia para señoritas, *f*
wonder /'wʌndər/ *n* maravilla, *f*; prodigio, *m*; portento, milagro, *m*; (surprise) sorpresa, *f*; admiración, *f*; asombro, *m*; (problem) enigma, *m*; misterio, *m*. *vi* admirarse, asombrarse, maravillarse; sorprenderse. *vt* (ask oneself) preguntarse; desear saber. **I wondered what the answer would be,** Me preguntaba qué sería la respuesta. **It is no w. that...,** No es mucho que..., No es sorprendente que... **It is one of the wonders of the world,** Es una de las maravillas del mundo. **to work wonders,** hacer milagros. **to w. at,** asombrarse de, maravillarse de; sorprenderse de. **w.-working,** milagroso
wonderful /'wʌndərfəl/ *a* maravilloso; magnífico; asombroso; *Inf.* estupendo
wonderfully /'wʌndərfli/ *adv* maravillosamente; admirablemente
wondering /'wʌndərɪŋ/ *a* de asombro, sorprendido; perplejo
wonderingly /'wʌndərɪŋli/ *adv* con asombro
wonderland /'wʌndər,lænd/ *n* mundo fantástico, *m*; reino de las hadas, *m*; país de las maravillas, *m*. **"Alice in W.,"** Alicia en el país de las maravillas
wonderment /'wʌndərmənt/ *n.* See **wonder**
wondrous /'wʌndrəs/ *a* maravilloso. *adv* extraordinariamente
wont /wɒnt/ *n* costumbre, *f*. *vi* soler. **as he was w.,** Como solía
won't /wount/ See **will not**
wonted /'wɒntɪd/ *a* sólito, acostumbrado
woo /wu/ *vt* galantear; hacer la corte (a), solicitar

amores a; cortejar, *Lat. Am.* afilar. *Fig.* solicitar; perseguir
wood /wʊd/ *n* bosque, *m*; madera, *f*; (for the fire, etc.) leña, *f*; (cask) barril, *m. a* de madera; (of the woods) selvático. **dead w.,** ramas muertas, *f pl*; *Fig.* paja, *f.* **w. alcohol,** alcohol metílico, *m*. **w.-anemone,** anémona de los bosques, *f.* **w.-block floor,** entarimado, *m*. **w.-borer,** xiló-fago, *m*. **w.-carver,** tallista, *mf* **w.-carving,** talla en madera, *f.* **w.-craft,** conocimiento del campo, *m*. **w.-cut,** grabado en madera, *m*. **w.-cutter,** leñador, *m*. **w.-engraver,** grabador (-ra) en madera. **w.-engraving,** grabado al boj, *m*. **w.-fibre,** fibra de madera, *f.* **w.-louse,** cochinilla, *f.* **w.-nymph,** ninfa de los bosques, *f.* **w.-pigeon,** paloma torcaz, *f.* **w.-pile,** pila de leña, leñera, *f.* **w.-pulp,** pulpa de madera, *f.* **w.-shaving,** acepilladura, *f.* **w.-splinter,** tasquil, *m*, astilla, *f.* **w.-wind,** *Mus.* madera, *f.* **w.-worm,** carcoma, *f*
wooded /'wʊdɪd/ *a* provisto de árboles, plantado de árboles, arbolado
wooden /'wʊdn/ *a* de madera; (of smiles) mecánico; (stiff) indiferente, sin emoción; (clumsy) torpe; (of character) inflexible. **He has a w. leg,** Tiene una pata de palo. **w. beam,** madero, *m*; viga de madera, *f.* **w. bridge,** pontón, *m*. **w. galley,** *Print.* galerín, *m*
woodland /*n.* 'wʊd,lænd; *a* -lənd/ *n* bosques, *m pl*. *a* de bosque; silvestre
woodpecker /'wʊd,pɛkər/ *n* pájaro carpintero, picamaderos, *m*
woodshed /'wʊd,ʃɛd/ *n* leñera, *f*
woodwork /'wʊd,wɜrk/ *n* maderaje, *m*; molduras, *f pl*; carpintería, *f*
woody /'wʊdi/ *a* leñoso; arbolado, con árboles. **w. tissue,** tejido leñoso, *m*
wooer /'wuər/ *n* pretendiente, galanteador, *m*
woof /wʊf/ *n* trama, *f*
wooing /'wuɪŋ/ *n* galanteo, *m*
wool /wʊl/ *n* lana, *f. a* de lana; lanar. **to go w.-gathering,** estar distraído. **to pull the w. over a person's eyes,** engañar como a un chino. **w.-bearing,** lanar, *m*. **w.-carding,** cardadura de lana, *f*. **w.-growing,** cría de ganado lanar, *f*. **w. merchant,** comerciante en lanas, *mf*, lanero, *m*. **w.-pack,** fardo de lana, *m*. **w. trade,** comercio de lana, *m*
woollen /'wʊlən/ *a* de lana; lanar. *n* paño de lana, *m*; género de punta de lana, *m*
woolliness /'wʊlinɪs/ *n* lanosidad, *f*
woolly /'wʊli/ *a* lanudo, lanoso; de lana; *Bot.* velloso; (of hair) lanoso, crespo. *n* género de punta de lana, *m*; (sweater) jersey, *m*
word /wɜrd/ *n* palabra, *f*; *Gram.* vocablo, *m*; *Theol.* verbo, *m*; (maxim) sentencia, *f*, dicho, *m*; (message) recado, *m*; (news) aviso, *m*, noticias, *f pl*; (*Mil.* command) voz de mando, *f*; (order) orden, *f*; (password) contraseña, *f*; (term) término, *m*. *vt* expresar; formular; (draw up) redactar; escribir. **He was as good as his w.,** Fue hombre de palabra. **I do not know how to w. this letter,** No sé cómo redactar esta carta. **in a w.,** en una palabra; en resumidas cuentas. **by w. of mouth,** de palabra. **I give you my w. for it,** Le doy mi palabra de honor. **in other words,** en otros términos; en efecto. **the W.** (of God), el Verbo (de Dios). **to have a w. with,** hablar con; conversar con; entablar conversación con. **to leave w.,** dejar recado. **to have words with,** tener palabras con. **to keep one's w.,** cumplir su palabra
word index *n* índice de vocablos, *m*
wordiness /'wɜrdinɪs/ *n* palabrería, verbosidad, *f*
wording /'wɜrdɪŋ/ *n* fraseología, *f*; expresión, *f*; estilo, *m*; (terms) términos, *m pl*; (drawing up) redacción, *f*
word processor /'prɒsɛsər/ *n* procesador de palabra, *m*
wordy /'wɜrdi/ *a* verboso, prolijo
work /wɜrk/ *n* trabajo, *m*; (sewing) labor, *f*; (literary, artistic production and theological) obra, *f*; (behavior) acción, *f*, acto, *m*; (employment) empleo, *m*; (business affairs) negocios, *m pl*; *pl* **works,** obras, fortificaciones, *f, pl*; obras públicas, *f pl*; construcciones, *f pl*; (of a machine) mecanismo, *m*; motor, *m*; (factory) fábrica, *f*, taller, *m*. **w. of art,** obra de arte. **w.**

accident, accidente del trabajo, *m.* **w.-bag,** bolsa de costura, *f*, saco de labor, *m*. **w.-box,** (on legs) costurero, *m*; (small) neceser de costura, *m*. **w.-people,** obreros (-as). **w.-room,** taller, *m*; (study) estudio, *m*; (for sewing) cuarto de costura, *m*. **w.-table,** banco de taller, *m*; (for writing) mesa de escribir, *f*

work /wɜrk/ *vi* trabajar, *Central America also* laborar; *Sew.* hacer labor de aguja, coser; (embroider) bordar; *Mech.* funcionar, marchar; (succeed) tener éxito; ser eficaz; (be busy) estar ocupado; (be employed) tener empleo; (of the face) demudarse, torcerse; (ferment) fermentar; (operate) obrar *vt* trabajar; operar, hacer funcionar; mover; (control) manejar; (a mine) explotar; (embroider) bordar; (wood) tallar; (a problem) resolver; calcular; (iron, etc.) labrar; (the soil) cultivar; (a ship) maniobrar; (do) hacer; (bring about) efectuar; traer consigo; producir; (agitate oneself) agitarse, emocionarse, excitarse. **to w. in repoussé,** repujar. **to w. loose,** desprenderse. **to w. one's passage,** trabajar por el pasaje. **to w. overtime,** trabajar horas extraordinarias. **to w. two ways,** ser espada de dos filos. **to w. at,** trabajar en; ocuparse en; dedicarse a; elaborar. **to w. in,** *vt* introducir; insinuar. *vi* combinarse. **to w. into,** penetrar en. **to w. off,** usar, emplear; (get rid of) deshacerse de, librarse de. **to w. on,** upon, influir en; obrar sobre; estar ocupado en. **to w. out,** *vt* calcular; resolver; (a mine, topic, etc.) agotar; (develop) elaborar, desarrollar; trazar, planear; (find) encontrar. *vi* llegar (a); resultar; venir a ser. **to w. up,** crear; (promote) fomentar; producir; (excite) agitar, excitar; (fashion) dar forma (a), labrar; (finish) terminar

workable /'wɜrkəbəl/ *a* laborable; factible, practicable; (of a mine) explotable

workableness /'wɜrkəbəlnɪs/ *n* practicabilidad, *f*

workaday /'wɜrkə,dei/ *a* de todos los días; prosaico

workbench /'wɜrk,bɛntʃ/ *n* banco de mecánico, *f*, banco de taller, banco de trabajo, *m*, mesa de trabajo, *f*

workday /'wɜrk,dei/ *n* día de trabajo, día laborable, *m*, jornada, *f*

worker /'wɜrkər/ *n* trabajador (-ra); (manual) obrero (-ra); (of a machine) operario (ia). **w. ant,** hormiga obrera, *f*. **w.-bee,** abeja obrera, *f*

workhouse /'wɜrk,haus/ *n* asilo, *m*

working /'wɜrkɪŋ/ *a* de trabajo; (of capital) de explotación; trabajador, que trabaja; obrero. *n* trabajo, *m*; (of a machine, organism, institution) funcionamiento, *m*; explotación, *f*; (of a mine) laboreo, *m*; (of a ship) maniobra, *f*; (of metal, stone, wood) labra, *f*; operación, *f*; (result) efecto, resultado, *m*; (calculation) cálculo, *m*. "Not w.," «No funciona.» **to be in w. order,** funcionar bien. **w.-class,** clase obrera, *f*; pueblo, *m*. **w.-clothes,** ropa de trabajo, *f*. **w.-day,** día de trabajo, *m*. **w.-hours,** horas de trabajo, horas hábiles, *f pl*. **w. hypothesis,** postulado, *m*. **w.-man,** obrero, *m*; trabajador, *m*. **w.-out,** elaboración, *f*; ensayo, *m*. **w.-plan,** plan de trabajo, *m*. **w.-woman,** obrera, *f*; trabajadora, *f*

workless /'wɜrklɪs/ *a* sin trabajo

workman /'wɜrkmən/ *n* obrero, *m*; (agricultural) labrador, *m*

workmanlike /'wɜrkmən,laik/ *a* bien hecho, bien acabado; (clever) hábil

workmanship /'wɜrkmən,ʃɪp/ *n* trabajo, *m*; manufactura, *f*; hechura, *f*; (cleverness) habilidad, *f*

workshop /'wɜrk,ʃop/ *n* taller, *m*

world /wɜrld/ *n* mundo, *m*. **For all the w. as if...,** Exactamente como si... **to see the w.,** ver mundo. **to treat the w. as one's oyster,** ponerse el mundo por montera. **w. without end,** por los siglos de los siglos. **w.-power,** potencia mundial, gran potencia, *f*. **w.-wide,** mundial, universal

world almanac *n* compendio mundial, *m*

worldliness /'wɜrldlɪnɪs/ *n* mundanería, *f*, conocimiento del mundo, *m*; frivolidad, vanidad mundana, *f*; egoísmo, *m*; prudencia, *f*

worldly /'wɜrldli/ *a* de este mundo; mundano; humano; profano; frívolo. **to be w.-wise,** tener mucho mundo

World Wide Web *n* Red Mundial, Telaraña Global, *f*

worm /wɜrm/ *n* gusano, *m*; lombriz, *f*; *Chem.* serpentín, *m*; (of a screw) tornillo sinfín, *m*; (person)

gusano, *m*; *Fig.* gusano roedor, remordimiento, *m*. **intestinal w.,** lombriz intestinal, *f*, gusano de la conciencia. **w.-eaten,** carcomido. **w.-hole,** picadura de gusano, lombriguera, *f*. **w.-powder,** polvos antihelmínticos, *m pl*. **w.-shaped,** vermiforme. **having worms, suffering from worms,** *Lat. Am.* lombriciento

worm /wɜrm/ *vt* (a dog) dar un vermífugo (a). *vi* arrastrarse como un gusano. **to w. one's way into,** deslizarse en; *Fig.* insinuarse en, introducirse en. **to w. out,** (secrets, information) sonsacar

wormwood /'wɜrm,wʊd/ *n* ajenjo, *m*

wormy /'wɜrmi/ *a* gusanoso, lleno de gusanos

worn /wɔrn/ *a* (of garments) raído; estropeado; gastado; (of paths) trillado; (of the face) arrugado, cansado. **w. out,** acabado; muy usado; (tired) rendido; (exhausted) agotado

worrier /'wɜriər/ *n* inquietador (-ra); receloso (-sa); aprensivo (-va)

worry /'wɜri/ *n* preocupación, inquietud, ansiedad, *f*; problema, cuidado, *m*. *vt* (prey) zamarrear; preocupar, inquietar; molestar; importunar. *vi* estar preocupado, estar intranquilo, inquietarse. **Don't worry,** Pierda cuidado, No pase cuidado

worrying /'wɜriɪŋ/ *a* inquietante, perturbador; molesto

worse /wɜrs/ *a comp* peor; inferior. *adv* peor; menos. *n* lo peor. **so much the w.,** tanto peor. **to be w. off,** estar peor; estar en peores circunstancias; ser menos feliz. **to be the w. for wear,** ser muy usado; estar ajado; ser ya viejo. **to grow w.,** empeorarse; (of an ill person) ponerse peor. **w. and w.,** de mal en peor, peor que peor. **w. than ever,** peor que nunca

worsen /'wɜrsən/ *vt* agravar, hacer peor; exasperar. *vi* agravarse, empeorarse; exasperarse

worsening /'wɜrsənɪŋ/ *n* agravación, *f*, empeoramiento, *m*; exasperación, *f*

worship /'wɜrʃɪp/ *n* culto, *m*; adoración, *f*; veneración, *f*. *vt* adorar; reverenciar. *vi* adorar; rezar; dar culto (a). **place of w.,** edificio de culto, *m*. **Your W.,** vuestra merced

worshipful /'wɜrʃɪpfəl/ *a* venerable, respetable

worshipper /'wɜrʃɪpər/ *n* adorador (-ra); *pl* **worshippers,** (in a church, etc.) fieles, *m pl*, congregación, *f*

worshipping /'wɜrʃɪpɪŋ/ *n* adoración, *f*, culto, *m*

worst /wɜrst/ *a* el (la, etc.) peor; más malo. *adv* el (la, etc.) peor. *n* el (la, etc.) peor; lo peor. *vt* vencer, derrotar; triunfar sobre. **If w. comes to w.,** En el peor de los casos. **The w. of it is that...,** Lo peor es que... **to have the w. of it,** salir perdiendo, llevar la peor parte

worsted /'wʊstɪd, 'wɜrstɪd/ *n* estambre, *m*, *a* de estambre

worth /wɜrθ/ *n* valor, *m*; precio, *m*; mérito, *m*, *a* (que) vale; de precio de; cuyo valor es de; equivalente a; (que) merece; digno de. **He bought six hundred pesetas w. of sweets,** Compró seiscientas pesetas de dulces. **He sang for all he was w.,** Cantó con toda su alma. **It is w. seeing,** Es digno de verse, Vale la pena de verse. **to be w.,** valer. **to be w. while,** valer la pena, merecer la pena

worthily /'wɜrðili/ *adv* dignamente

worthiness /'wɜrðinɪs/ *n* mérito, valor, *m*

worthless /'wɜrθlɪs/ *a* sin valor; sin mérito; inútil; malo; (of persons) vil, despreciable, indigno

worthlessness /'wɜrθlɪsnɪs/ *n* falta de valor, *f*; falta de mérito, *f*; inutilidad, *f*; (of persons) bajeza, vileza, *f*

worthy /'wɜrði/ *a* digno de respeto, benemérito, respetable; digno, merecedor; meritorio. *n* varón ilustre, hombre célebre, *m*; héroe, *m*; (*Inf. Ironic.*) tipo, *m*. **to be w. of,** ser digno de, merecer

would /wʊd/ *unstressed* /wəd/ *preterite* and *subjunctive* of **will.** (indicating a conditional tense) **They w. come if...,** Vendrían si...; (indicating an imperfect tense) **Often he w. sing,** Muchas veces cantaba, **Now and then a blackbird w. whistle,** De vez en cuando silbó un mirlo; (expressing wish, desire) **What w. they?** ¿Qué quieren? **The place where I w. be,** El lugar donde quisiera estar. **W. I were at home!** ¡Ojalá que estuviese en casa! **I thought that I w. tell you,** Se me ocurrió la idea de decírselo. **It w. seem that...,**

Parece ser que..., Según parece...; Se diría que... **He said that he w.** never have done it, Dijo que no lo hubiera hecho nunca. **They w.** have been killed if he had not rescued them, Habrían sido matados si él no los hubiese salvado. **He w. go,** Se empeñó en ir. **He w.** not do it, Rehusó hacerlo, Se resistió a hacerlo; No quiso hacerlo. **This w. probably be the house,** Sin duda esta sería la casa. **W. you be good enough to...,** Tenga Vd. la bondad de..., Haga el favor de...

would-be /ˈwʊdbi/ a supuesto; llamado; aspirante (a); en esperanza de (followed by infin.); (frustrated) frustrado, malogrado

wound /wund/ n herida, lesión, Lat. Am. also, lastimadura, f. vt herir; (the feelings) lastimar, lacerar. **deep w.,** herida penetrante, f. **the wounded,** los heridos.

wounding /ˈwundɪŋ/ n herida, f, a Fig. lastimador

wraith /reiθ/ n fantasma, espectro, m, sombra, f

wrangle /ˈræŋgəl/ vi discutir; altercar, disputar acaloradamente; reñir; (bargain) regatear. n argumento, m; disputa, f, altercado, m; riña, f

wrangler /ˈræŋglər/ n disputador (-ra)

wrangling /ˈræŋglɪŋ/ n disputas, f pl, altercación, f; (bargaining) regateo, m

wrap /ræp/ vt envolver; arrollar; cubrir; abrigar; (conceal) ocultar. n envoltorio, m; abrigo, m; pl **wraps,** abrigos y mantas de viaje, m pl. **W. yourself up well!** ¡Abrígate bien! **to be wrapped up in,** estar envuelto en; Fig. estar entregado a, estar absorto en; (a person) estar embelesado con

wrapper /ˈræpər/ n envoltura, f; embalaje, m; (of a newspaper) faja, f; (of a book) sobrecubierta, f; (dressing-gown) bata, f, salto de cama, m

wrapping /ˈræpɪŋ/ n envoltura, cubierta, f. **w.-paper,** papel de envolver, m

wrath /ræθ/ n ira, f

wrathful /ˈræθfəl/ a airado

wreak /rik/ vt ejecutar; (anger, etc.) descargar. **to w. one's vengeance,** vengarse

wreath /riθ/ n guirnalda, f; corona, f; trenza, f. **funeral w.,** corona funeraria, f

wreathe /rið/ vt trenzar; (entwine) entrelazar (de); (garland) coronar (de), enguirnaldar (con); (encircle) ceñir, rodear; (a face in smiles) iluminar

wreck /rek/ n naufragio, m; buque naufragado, m; destrucción, f; Fig. ruina, f; (remains) restos, m pl; (person) sombra, f. vt hacer naufragar; destruir; Fig. arruinar; hacer fracasar. **I am a complete w.,** Inf. Estoy hecho una ruina. **to be wrecked,** irse a pique, naufragar; Fig. arruinarse; frustrarse

wreckage /ˈrekɪdʒ/ n naufragio, m; restos de naufragio, m pl; ruinas, f pl; (of a car, plane, etc.) restos, m pl; accidente, m

wrecked /rekt/ a naufragado

wrecker /ˈrekər/ n destructor (-ra); (of ships) raquero, m

wrench /rentʃ/ n (jerk) arranque, m; (pull) tirón, m; (sprain) torcedura, f; (tool) llave, f; (pain) dolor, m. vt arrancar; forzar; torcer, dislocar. **He has wrenched his arm,** Se ha torcido el brazo

wrest /rest/ vt arrebatar, arrancar

wrestle /ˈresəl/ vi luchar. n lucha grecorromana, f; Fig. lucha, f. **to w. with,** Fig. luchar con; luchar contra, Lat. Am. abrocharse (con...)

wrestler /ˈreslər/ n luchador, m

wrestling /ˈreslɪŋ/ n lucha grecorromana, f. **all-in-w.,** lucha libre, f. **w.-match,** lucha, f

wretch /retʃ/ n infeliz, mf; (ruffian) infame, m; (playful) picaruelo (-la). **a poor w.,** un pobre diablo

wretched /ˈretʃɪd/ a (unhappy) infeliz, desdichado; miserable; pobre; (ill) enfermo; horrible; malo; mezquino; despreciable; lamentable

wretchedly /ˈretʃɪdli/ adv tristemente; pobremente; muy mal; ruinmente

wretchedness /ˈretʃɪdnɪs/ n infelicidad, desdicha, f; miseria, pobreza, f; escualidez, f; ruindad, f

wriggle /ˈrɪgəl/ vi retorcerse; moverse; menearse; serpear, culebrear; retorcerse. n See under **wriggling. to w. into,** insinuarse en, deslizarse dentro (de). **to w. out,** escaparse. **to w. out of a difficulty,** extricarse de una dificultad

wriggling /ˈrɪglɪŋ/ n meneo, m; retorcimiento, m; serpenteo, culebreo, m

wring /rɪŋ/ vt torcer; estrujar; exprimir; arrancar; (force) forzar. **to w. one's hands,** restregarse las manos. **to w. the neck of,** torcer el pescuezo (a). **to w. out,** exprimir; estrujar

wringer /ˈrɪŋər/ n torcedor (-ra); (for clothes) exprimidor de ropa, m

wringing /ˈrɪŋɪŋ/ n torsión, f. **w.-machine,** exprimidor de ropa, m

wrinkle /ˈrɪŋkəl/ n arruga, f; pliegue, m; Inf. noción, f. vt arrugar. vi arrugarse. **to w. one's brow,** (frown) fruncir el ceño; (in perplexity) arrugar la frente

wrinkling /ˈrɪŋklɪŋ/ n arrugamiento, m

wrinkly /ˈrɪŋkli/ a arrugado

wrist /rɪst/ n muñeca, f. **w.-band,** tira del puño de la camisa, f. **w. bandage,** pulsera, f

wristlet /ˈrɪstlɪt/ n pulsera, f; manguito elástico, m. **w. watch,** reloj de pulsera, m

writ /rɪt/ n escritura, f; Law. decreto judicial, mandamiento, m; orden, f; título ejecutorio, m; hábeas corpus, m. **Holy W.,** la Sagrada Escritura. **to issue a w.,** dar orden. **to serve a w.,** notificar una orden. **w. of privilege,** auto de excarcelación, m

write /rait/ vt and vi escribir; Fig. mostrar. **He writes a good hand,** Tiene buena letra. **I shall w. to them for a list,** Les escribiré pidiendo una lista. **to w. back,** contestar por escrito; contestar a una carta. **to w. down,** poner por escrito; anotar, apuntar; describir. **to w. for,** escribir para; escribir para pedir algo; escribir algo en vez de otra persona. **to w. off,** escribir; escribir rápidamente; cancelar. **to w. on,** seguir escribiendo; escribir sobre. **to w. out,** copiar; redactar. **to w. over again,** escribir de nuevo, escribir otra vez, volver a escribir. **to w. up,** redactar; Com. poner al día; (praise) escribir alabando

writer /ˈraitər/ n escritor (-ra); autor (-ra). **the present w.,** el que, m, (f, la que) esto escribe. **writer's cramp,** calambre del escribiente, m

writhe /raið/ vi retorcerse

writhing /ˈraiðɪŋ/ n retorsión, f

writing /ˈraitɪŋ/ n escritura, f; (work) escrito, m; inscripción, f; documento, m; (style) estilo, m; (hand) letra, f; el arte de escribir; trabajo literario, m. **in one's own w.,** de su propia letra. **in w.,** por escrito. **w.-case,** escribanía, f. **w.-desk,** escritorio, m. **w.-pad,** taco de papel, m. **w.-paper,** papel de escribir, m. **w.-table,** mesa de escribir, f

written /ˈrɪtn/ a escrito

wrong /rɔŋ/ a injusto; mal; equivocado, erróneo; inexacto; falso; incorrecto; desacertado; inoportuno. **It is the w. one,** No es el que hacía falta; No es el que quería. **to be in the w. place,** estar mal situado; estar mal colocado. **to be w.,** estar mal; no tener razón; (mistaken) estar equivocado; (of deeds or things) estar mal hecho; (be unjust) ser injusto; (of clocks) andar mal. **to do w.,** hacer mal; obrar mal. **to get out of bed on the w. side,** levantarse del izquierdo. **to go w.,** (of persons) descarriarse; (of affairs) ir mal; salir mal; frustrarse; (of apparatus) estropearse, no funcionar. **We have taken the w. road,** Nos hemos equivocado de camino. **You were very w. to...,** Has hecho muy mal en... **w.-headed,** terco, obstinado; disparatado. **w.-headedness,** terquedad, obstinación, f. **w. number,** (telephone) número errado, m. **w. side,** revés, m; lado malo, m. **w. side out,** al envés; al revés

wrong /rɔŋ/ adv mal; injustamente; sin razón; incorrectamente; equivocadamente; (inside out) al revés. **to get it w.,** (a sum) calcular mal; (misunderstand) comprender mal

wrong /rɔŋ/ n mal, m; injusticia, f; perjuicio, m; ofensa, f; agravio, m; culpa, f; error, m. **to be in the w.,** no tener razón; haber hecho mal. **to put one in the w.,** echar la culpa a, hacer responsable (de)

wrong /rɔŋ/ vt hacer mal (a); perjudicar; ser injusto con; ofender

wrongdoer /ˈrɔŋˌduər/ n malhechor (-ra); pecador (-ra); perverso (-sa)

wrongdoing /'rɔŋ,duɪŋ/ *n* maldad, maleficencia, *f;* pecado, *m;* injusticia, *f*

wrongful /'rɔŋfəl/ *a* injusto; perjudicial; falso

wrongfully /'rɔŋfəli/ *adv* injustamente; falsamente

wrongly /'rɔŋli/ *adv* injustamente; erróneamente, equivocadamente; perversamente; mal

wrongness /'rɔŋnɪs/ *n* mal, *m;* injusticia, *f;* falsedad, *f;* inexactitud, *f,* error, *m*

wrought /rɔt/ *a* forjado; labrado; (hammered) batido; trabajado. **w. iron,** hierro dulce, hierro forjado, *m.* **w. up,** muy excitado, muy agitado, muy nervioso

wry /rai/ *a* torcido; tuerto; triste; pesimista; desilusionado; irónico. **wry face,** mueca *f,* de desengaño, de ironía, de disgusto, etc. **make a wry face,** torcer el gesto, *Mexico* engestarse. **wry neck,** *Ornith.* torcecuello, *m*

wryly /'raili/ *adv* tristemente; irónicamente

wye /wai/ *n* (letter) ye, i griega, *f;* horquilla, cosa en forma de Y, *f*

X Y Z

x /ɛks/ *n* equis, *f*

x-ray /'ɛks,rei/ *vt* tomar una radiografía (de). **x-ray,** rayo x, *m pl.* **x-ray examination,** examen con rayos x, *m.* **x-ray photograph,** radiografía, *f*

xylophone /'zailə,foun/ *n* xilófono, *m*

y /wai/ *n* (letter) i griega, ye, *f*

yacht /yɒt/ *n* yate, *m.* **y. club,** club marítimo, *m.* **y. race,** regata de yates, *f*

yachting /'yɒtɪŋ/ *n* navegación en yate, *f,* paseo en yate, *m*

yachtsman /'yɒtsmən/ *n* deportista náutico, balandrista, balandrismo, *m*

yam /yæm/ *n* batata, *f, Lat. Am.* boniato, camote, *m*

yank /yæŋk/ *n* tirón, *m,* sacudida, *f. vt* dar un tirón (a); sacar de un tirón

Yankee /'yæŋki/ *a* and *n* yanqui, *mf*

yap /yæp/ *vi* ladrar. *n* ladrido, *m*

yapper /'yæpər/ *n* (yapping dog) gozque, gozquejo, *m*

yapping /'yæpɪŋ/ *n* ladridos, *m pl, a* que ladra

yard /yard/ *n* (measure) yarda, *f; Naut.* verga, *f;* corral, *m;* (courtyard) patio, *m. vt* acorralar. **goods y.,** estación de mercancías, *f.* **y.-arm,** penol (de la verga), *m.* **y.-stick,** vara de medir de una yarda, *f*

yarn /yarn/ *n* hilaza, *f;* hilo, *m;* (story) historia, *f,* cuento, *m.* **to spin a y.,** contar una historia

yaw /yɔ/ *vi Naut.* guiñar; *Aer.* serpentear. *n Naut.* guiñada, *f; Aer.* serpenteo, *m*

yawn /yɔn/ *vi* bostezar; quedarse con la boca abierta; (of chasms, etc.) abrirse. *n* bostezo, *m.* **to stifle a y.,** ahogar un bostezo

yawning /'yɔnɪŋ/ *a* abierto. *n* bostezos, *m pl*

yea /yei/ *adv* en verdad, ciertamente; y aun... no sólo... sino. *n* si, *m*

year /yɪər/ *n* año, *m; pl* **years,** años, *m pl,* edad, *f.* **We are getting on in years,** Nos vamos haciendo viejos. **He is five years old,** Tiene cinco años. **all the y. round,** todo el año, el año entero. **by the y.,** al año. **every other y.,** cada dos años, un año sí y otro no. **in after years,** en años posteriores. **last y.,** el año pasado. **next y.,** el año próximo. el año que viene. **y. after y.,** año tras año. **New Y.,** Año Nuevo, *m.* **to see the New Y. in,** ver empezar el Año Nuevo. **New Year's Day,** día de Año Nuevo, *m.* **(A) Happy New Y.!** ¡Feliz Año Nuevo! **y.-book,** anuario, *m.* **a y. later,** *Lat. Am.* al año

yearling calf /'yɪərlɪŋ/ *n* becerra *f*

yearly /'yɪərli/ *a* anual. *adv* anualmente, cada año; una vez al año

yearn /yɜrn/ *vi* anhelar, suspirar (por); desear vivamente

yearning /'yɜrnɪŋ/ *n* sed, ansia, *f;* anhelo, deseo vehemente, *m. a* ansioso; anhelante; (tender) tierno

yeast /yist/ *n* levadura, *f*

yell /yɛl/ *vi* and *vt* chillar; gritar. *n* chillido, *m;* grito, *m*

yelling /'yɛlɪŋ/ *n* chillidos, *m pl;* gritos, *m pl,* gritería, *f*

yellow /'yɛlou/ *a* amarillo; (of hair) rubio; (cowardly) cobarde; (newspaper) amarillista, sensacionalista. **to turn y.,** *vi* ponerse amarillo; amarillear. *vt* volver amarillo. **y. fever,** fiebre amarilla, *f.* **y.-hammer,** *Ornith.* emberizo, *m*

yellowing /'yɛlouɪŋ/ *n* amarilleo, *m*

yellowish /'yɛlouɪʃ/ *a* amarillento, *Lat. Am.* amarilloso

yellowness /'yɛlounɪs/ *n* amarillez, *f*

yellow pages /'peidʒɪz/ *n* páginas amarillas, páginas doradas, *f pl*

yelp /yɛlp/ *vi* gañir. *n* gañido, *m*

yelping /'yɛlpɪŋ/ *n* gañidos, *m pl*

yen /yɛn/ *n* (currency) yen, *m;* (desire) deseo vivo, *m*

yeoman /'youmən/ *n* pequeño propietario rural, *m;* soldado de caballería, *m.* **Y. of the Guard,** alabardero de la Casa Real, *m*

yes /yɛs/ *adv* sí. **Yes?** ¿De verdad? ¿Y qué pasó después? ¿Y entonces? **to say yes,** decir que sí; dar el sí. **yes-man,** amenista, sacristán de amén, *m*

yesterday /'yɛstər,dei/ *adv* ayer. *n* ayer, *m.* **the day before y.,** anteayer

yet /yɛt/ *adv* aún, todavía. **as yet,** hasta ahora; todavía. **He has not come yet,** No ha venido todavía. **yet again,** otra vez

yet /yɛt/ *conjunc* sin embargo, no obstante, con todo; pero. **The book is well written and yet I do not like it,** El libro está bien escrito, y sin embargo no me gusta

yew /yu/ *n* tejo, *m;* madera de tejo, *m*

Yiddish /'yɪdɪʃ/ *n* yídis, yídish, yídico, *m; a* yídico

yield /yild/ *vt* producir; dar; (grant) otorgar; (afford) ofrecer; (surrender) ceder. *vi* producir; (submit) rendirse, someterse; (of disease) responder; (give way) flaquear, doblegarse; dar de sí; (consent) consentir (en); (to circumstances, etc.) ceder (a), sucumbir (a). *n* producción, *f,* producto, *m; Com.* rédito, *m;* (crop) cosecha, *f.* **to y. to temptation,** ceder a la tentación. **to y. up,** entregar; devolver

yielding /'yildɪŋ/ *a* flexible; (soft) blando; dócil; sumiso; fácil; condescendiente

yogurt /'yougərt/ *n* yogur, *m*

yoke /youk/ *n* yugo, *m;* (of oxen) yunta, *f;* (for pails) balancín, *m;* (of a garment) canesú, *m; Fig.* férula, *f,* yugo, *m. vt* uncir, acoplar. **to throw off the y.,** sacudir el yugo

yokel /'youkəl/ *n* patán, rústico, *m*

yolk /youk/ *n* (of an egg) yema, *f*

yonder /'yɒndər/ *a* aquel, *m;* aquella, *f;* aquellos, *m pl;* aquellas, *f pl.* *adv* allí, allá a lo lejos

yore /yɔr/ *n* **in days of y.,** antaño; en otro tiempo

you /yu; *unstressed* yʊ, yə/ *pers pron nominative* (polite form) usted (Vd.), *mf;* ustedes (Vds.), *mf pl;* (familiar form) *sing* tu, *mf;* (plural) vosotros, *m pl;* vosotras, *f pl;* (one) uno, *m;* una, *f;* se (followed by 3rd pers. sing. of verb). *pers pron accusative* (polite form) le, *m;* la, *f;* les, *m pl;* las, *f pl;* a usted, a ustedes; (informal form) te, *mf,* os, *mf pl;* (after most prepositions) ti, *mf;* vosotros, *m pl;* vosotras, *f pl.* **Are you there?** (telephone) ¡Oiga! **I gave the parcel to you,** Te (os) di el paquete a usted (a ustedes). **I shall wait for you in the garden,** Te (os) esperaré en el jardín; Esperaré a Vds. (a Vd.) en el jardín. **This present is for you,** Este regalo es para tí (para vosotros, para Vd. (Vds.)). **Away with you!** ¡Vete! ¡Marchaos! **Between you and me,** Entre tú y yo. **You can't have your cake and eat it too,** no hay rosa sin espinas. **You never can tell,** No se sabe nunca, Uno no sabe nunca

young /yʌŋ/ *a* joven; nuevo, reciente; inexperto; poco avanzado. *n* cría, *f,* hijuelos, *m pl.* **y. blood,** *Inf.* sangre nueva, *f.* **y. girl,** jovencita, *f.* **y. man,** joven, *m.* **y. people,** jóvenes, *m pl.* **in his y. days,** en su juventud. **The night is y.,** La noche está poca avan-

zada. **to grow y. again,** rejuvenecer. **with y.,** (of animals) preñada *f*
younger /'yʌŋgər/ *a* más joven; menor. **Peter is his y. brother,** Pedro es su hermano menor. **to look y.,** parecer más joven
youngish /'yʌŋgɪʃ/ *a* bastante joven
youngster /'yʌŋstər/ *n* jovencito, chico, muchacho, *m*; niño, *m*
your /yʊr, yɔr; *unstressed* yər/ *a poss* (polite form) su (*pl* sus), de usted (Vd.), (*pl* de ustedes (Vds.)); (familiar form) tu (*pl* vuestro). **I have y. papers,** Tengo tus (vuestros) papeles; Tengo los papeles de Vd. (*or* de Vds.). **How is y. mother?** ¿Cómo está su (tu) madre? **It is y. turn,** Te toca a ti, Le toca a Vd.
yours /yʊrz, yɔrz/ *pron poss* (polite form) (el) suyo, *m*; (la) suya, *f*; (los) suyos, *m pl*; (las) suyas, *f pl*; el, *m*; la, *f*; lo, *neut*; los, *m pl*; las, *f pl*; de usted (Vd.), *mf sing* or de ustedes (Vds.), *mf pl*; (familiar form) (el) tuyo, *m*; (la) tuya, *f*; (los) tuyos, *m pl*; (las) tuyas, *f pl*; (el) vuestro, *m*; (la) vuestra, *f*; (los) vuestros, *m pl*; (las) vuestras, *f pl*. **This is a picture of y.,** (addressing one person), Este es uno de los cuadros de usted (Vd.), Este es uno de tus cuadros. **This hat is mine, it is not y.,** Este sombrero es el mío, no es el tuyo. **The horse is y.,** El caballo es tuyo (de Vd.). **Y. affectionately,** Un abrazo de tu amigo... **Y. faithfully,** Queda de Vd. su att. (atentísimo) s.s. (seguro servidor). **Y. sincerely,** Queda de Vd. su aff. (afectuoso)
yourself /yʊr'sɛlf, yɔr- yər-/ *pron pers* (familiar form *sing*) tú mismo, *m*; tú misma, *f*; (after a preposition) tí, *mf*; (polite form) usted (Vd.) mismo, *m*; usted misma, *f*; *pl* **yourselves,** (familiar form) vosotros mismos, *m pl*; vosotras mismas, *f pl*; (polite form) ustedes (Vds.) mismos, *m pl*; ustedes mismas, *f pl.* **This is for y.,** Esto es para ti; Esto es para Vd.
youth /yuθ/ *n* juventud, *f*; (man) joven, chico, mozalbete, *m*; (collectively) jóvenes, *m pl*, juventud, *f*
youthful /'yuθfəl/ *a* joven, juvenil; de la juventud
yowl /yaul/ *n* gañido, aullido, *m. vi* gañir, aullar
Yucatan /,yukə'tæn/ *a* yucateco
yucca /'yʌkə/ *n Bot.* yuca, *f*
Yugoslav /'yugou,slɑv/ *n* yugoeslavo (-va). *a* yugoeslavo

Yugoslavia /,yugou'slaviə/ Yugoeslavia, *f*
Yukon, the /'yukɒn/ el Yukón, *m*
Yule /yul/ *n* Navidad, *f.* **y.-log,** leño de Navidad, *m.* **y-tide,** Navidades, *f pl*
z /zi/ *n* (letter) zeda, zeta, *f*
zeal /zil/ *n* celo, entusiasmo, *m*; ardor, fervor, *m*
zealot /'zɛlət/ *n* fanático (-ca)
zealous /'zɛləs/ *a* celoso, entusiasta
zealously /'zɛləsli/ *adv* con entusiasmo
zebra /'zibrə/ *n* cebra, *f*
zenith /'zinɪθ/ *n* cenit, *m*; *Fig.* apogeo, punto culminante, *m*
zephyr /'zɛfər/ *n* céfiro, *m*, brisa, *f*
zero /'zɪərou/ *n* cero, *m.* **below z.,** bajo cero. **z. hour,** hora cero, *f*
zest /zɛst/ *n* sabor, gusto, *m*; entusiasmo, *m.* **to eat with z.,** comer con buen apetito. **to enter on with z.,** emprender con entusiasmo
zigzag /'zɪg,zæg/ *n* zigzag, *m. a* and *adv* en zigzag. *vi* zigzaguear, hacer zigzags, serpentear; (of persons) andar haciendo eses
Zimbabwe /zɪm'bɑbwei/ Zimbabue
zinc /zɪŋk/ *n* cinc, *m.* **z. oxide,** óxido de cinc, *m*
Zion /'zaiən/ *n* Sión, *m*
Zionism /'zaiə,nɪzəm/ *n* sionismo, *m*
Zionist /'zaiənɪst/ *n* and *a* sionista
zip /zɪp/ *n* (of a bullet) silbido, *m*; *Inf.* energía, *f*
zip code *n* código postal, *m*
zipper /'zɪpər/ *n* cremallera, *f*, cierre relámpago, *m*, cierre, cerrador, *m*
zircon /'zɜrkɒn/ *n* circón, *m*
zither /'zɪθər/ *n* cítara, *f*
zodiac /'zoudi,æk/ *n* zodiaco, *m*
zone /zoun/ *n* zona, *f*; faja, *f*
zoo /zu/ *n* jardín zoológico, *m*
zoological /,zouə'lɒdʒɪkəl/ *a* zoológico. **z. garden,** jardín zoológico, *m*
zoologist /zou'ɒlədʒɪst/ *n* zoólogo, *m*
zoology /zou'ɒlədʒi/ *n* zoología, *f*
zoom /zum/ *n* zumbido, *m*; (photography) lente zoom. *vi* zumbar; *Aer.* empinarse
Zulu /'zulu/ *a* and *n* zulú *mf*

Spanish Irregular Verbs

Infinitive	Present	Future	Preterit	Past Part.
andar	ando	andaré	anduve	andado
caber	quepo	cabré	cupe	cabido
caer	caigo	caeré	caí	caído
conducir	conduzco	conduciré	conduje	conducido
dar	doy	daré	di	dado
decir	digo	diré	dije	dicho
estar	estoy	estaré	estuve	estado
haber	he	habré	hube	habido
hacer	hago	haré	hice	hecho
ir	voy	iré	fui	ido
jugar	juego	jugaré	jugué	jugado
morir	muero	moriré	morí	muerto
oir	oigo	oiré	oí	oído
poder	puedo	podré	pude	podido
poner	pongo	pondré	puse	puesto
querer	quiero	querré	quise	querido
saber	sé	sabré	supe	sabido
salir	salgo	saldré	salí	salido
ser	soy	seré	fui	sido
tener	tengo	tendré	tuve	tenido
traer	traigo	traeré	traje	traído
valer	valgo	valdré	valí	valido
venir	vengo	vendré	vine	venido
ver	veo	veré	vi	visto

Las formas del verbo inglés

1. Se forma la 3ª persona singular del tiempo presente exactamente al igual que el plural de los sustantivos, añadiendo **-es** o **-s** a la forma sencilla según las mismas reglas, así:

(1)	teach	pass	wish	fix	buzz		
	teaches	passes	wishes	fixes	buzzes		

(2)	place	change	judge	please	freeze		
	places	changes	judges	pleases	freezes		

(3a)	find	sell	clean	hear	love	buy	know
	finds	sells	cleans	hears	loves	buys	knows

(3b)	think	like	laugh	stop	hope	meet	want
	thinks	likes	laughs	stops	hopes	meets	wants

(4)	cry	try	dry	carry	deny		
	cries	tries	dries	carries	denies		

Cinco verbos muy comunes tienen 3ª persona singular irregular:

(5)	go	do	say	have	be
	goes	does	says	has	is

2. Se forman el tiempo pasado y el participio de modo igual, añadiendo a la forma sencilla la terminación -**ed** o -**d** según las reglas que siguen:

(1)   Si la forma sencilla termina en -**d** o -**t,** se le pone -**ed** como sílaba aparte:

end	fold	need	load	want	feast	wait	light
ended	folded	needed	loaded	wanted	feasted	waited	lighted

(2)   Si la forma sencilla termina en cualquier otra consonante, se añade también -**ed** pero sin hacer sílaba aparte:

(2a)
bang	sail	seem	harm	earn	weigh
banged	sailed	seemed	harmed	earned	weighed

(2b)
lunch	work	look	laugh	help	pass
lunched	worked	looked	laughed	helped	passed

(3)   Si la forma sencilla termina en -**e,** se le pone sólo -**d:**

(3a)
hate	taste	waste	guide	fade	trade
hated	tasted	wasted	guided	faded	traded

(3b)
free	judge	rule	name	dine	scare
freed	judged	ruled	named	dined	scared

(3c)
place	force	knife	like	hope	base
placed	forced	knifed	liked	hoped	based

(4)   Una -**y** final que sigue a cualquier consonante se cambia en -**ie** al añadir la -**d** del pasado/participio:

cry	try	dry	carry	deny
cried	tried	dried	carried	denied

3. Varios verbos muy comunes forman el tiempo pasado y el participio de manera irregular. Pertenecen a tres grupos.

(1) Los que tienen una sola forma irregular para tiempo pasado y participio, como los siguientes:

bend	bleed	bring	build	buy	catch	creep	deal
bent	bled	brought	built	bought	caught	crept	dealt

dig	feed	feel	fight	find	flee	get	hang
dug	fed	felt	fought	found	fled	got	hung

have	hear	hold	keep	lead	leave	lend	lose
had	heard	held	kept	led	left	lent	lost

make	mean	meet	say	seek	sell	send	shine
made	meant	met	said	sought	sold	sent	shone

shoot	sit	sleep	spend	stand	strike	sweep	teach
shot	sat	slept	spent	stood	struck	swept	taught

(2) Los que tienen una forma irregular para el tiempo pasado y otra forma irregular para el participio, como los siguientes:

be	beat	become	begin	bite
was	beat	became	began	bit
been	beaten	become	begun	bitten

blow	break	choose	come	do
blew	broke	chose	came	did
blown	broken	chosen	come	done

draw	drink	drive	eat	fall
drew	drank	drove	ate	fell
drawn	drunk	driven	eaten	fallen

fly	forget	freeze	give	go
flew	forgot	froze	gave	went
flown	forgotten	frozen	given	gone

grow	hide	know	ride	ring
grew	hid	knew	rode	rang
grown	hidden	known	ridden	rung

rise	run	see	shake	shrink
rose	ran	saw	shook	shrank
risen	run	seen	shaken	shrunk

sing	sink	speak	steal	swear
sang	sank	spoke	stole	swore
sung	sunk	spoken	stolen	sworn

swim	tear	throw	wear	write
swam	tore	threw	wore	wrote
swum	torn	thrown	worn	written

(3) Los que no varían del todo, la forma sencilla funcionando también como
pasado/participio; entre éstos son de mayor frecuencia:

bet	burst	cast	cost	cut
hit	hurt	let	put	quit
read	set	shed	shut	slit
spit	split	spread	thrust	wet

Numbers/Números

Cardinal/Cardinales

one	1	uno, una
two	2	dos
three	3	tres
four	4	cuatro
five	5	cinco
six	6	seis
seven	7	siete
eight	8	ocho
nine	9	nueve
ten	10	diez
eleven	11	once
twelve	12	doce
thirteen	13	trece
fourteen	14	catorce
fifteen	15	quince
sixteen	16	dieciséis
seventeen	17	diecisiete
eighteen	18	dieciocho
nineteen	19	diecinueve
twenty	20	veinte
twenty-one	21	veinte y uno (or veintiuno)
twenty-two	22	veinte y dos (or veintidós)
thirty	30	treinta
thirty-one	31	treinta y uno
thirty-two	32	treinta y dos
forty	40	cuarenta
fifty	50	cincuenta
sixty	60	sesenta
seventy	70	setenta
eighty	80	ochenta
ninety	90	noventa

one hundred	100	cien
one hundred one	101	ciento uno
one hundred two	102	ciento dos
two hundred	200	doscientos, -as
three hundred	300	trescientos, -as
four hundred	400	cuatrocientos, -as
five hundred	500	quinientos, -as
six hundred	600	seiscientos, -as
seven hundred	700	setecientos, -as
eight hundred	800	ochocientos, -as
nine hundred	900	novecientos, -as
one thousand	1,000	mil
two thousand	2,000	dos mil
one hundred thousand	100,000	cien mil
one million	1,000,000	un millón
two million	2,000,000	dos millones

Ordinal/Ordinales

first	1st / 1°	primero
second	2nd / 2°	segundo
third	3rd / 3°	tercero
fourth	4th / 4°	cuarto
fifth	5th / 5°	quinto
sixth	6th / 6°	sexto
seventh	7th / 7°	séptimo
eighth	8th / 8°	octavo
ninth	9th / 9°	noveno
tenth	10th / 10°	décimo

Days of the Week/Días de la Semana

Sunday	domingo	Thursday	jueves
Monday	lunes	Friday	viernes
Tuesday	martes	Saturday	sábado
Wednesday	miércoles		

Months/Meses

January	enero	July	julio
February	febrero	August	agosto
March	marzo	September	septiembre
April	abril	October	octubre
May	mayo	November	noviembre
June	junio	December	diciembre

Useful Phrases/Locuciones Útiles

Good day, Good morning. Buenos días.
Good afternoon. Buenas tardes.
Good night, Good evening. Buenas noches.
Hello. ¡Hola!
Welcome! ¡Bienvenido!
See you later. Hasta luego.
Goodbye. ¡Adiós!
How are you? ¿Cómo está usted?
I'm fine, thank you. Estoy bien, gracias.
I'm pleased to meet you. Mucho gusto en conocerle.
May I introduce . . . Quisiera presentar . . .
Thank you very much. Muchas gracias.
You're welcome. De nada or No hay de qué.
Please. Por favor.
Excuse me. Con permiso.
Good luck. ¡Buena suerte!
To your health. ¡Salud!

Please help me. Ayúdeme, por favor.
I don't know. No sé.
I don't understand. No entiendo.
Do you understand? ¿Entiende usted?
I don't speak Spanish. No hablo español.
Do you speak English? ¿Habla usted inglés?
How do you say . . . in Spanish? ¿Cómo se dice . . . en español?
What do you call this? ¿Cómo se llama esto?
Speak slowly, please. Hable despacio, por favor.
Please repeat. Repita, por favor.
I don't like it. No me gusta.
I am lost. Ando perdido; Me he extraviado.

What is your name? ¿Cómo se llama usted?
My name is . . . Me llamo . . .
I am an American. Soy norteamericano.
Where are you from? ¿De dónde es usted?
I'm from . . . Soy de . . .
How is the weather? ¿Qué tiempo hace?
It's cold (hot) today. Hace frío (calor) hoy.
What time is it? ¿Qué hora es?

How much is it? ¿Cuánto es?
It is too much. Es demasiado.

What do you wish? ¿Qué desea usted?
I want to buy . . . Quiero comprar . . .
May I see something better? ¿Podría ver algo mejor?
May I see something cheaper? ¿Podría ver algo menos caro?
It is not exactly what I want. No es exactamente lo que quiero.

I'm hungry. Tengo hambre.
I'm thirsty. Tengo sed.
Where is there a restaurant? ¿Dónde hay un restaurante?
I have a reservation. Tengo una reservación.
I would like . . . Quisiera . . .; Me gustaría . . .
Please give me . . . Por favor, déme usted . . .
Please bring me . . . Por favor, tráigame usted . . .
May I see the menu? ¿Podría ver el menú?
The bill, please. La cuenta, por favor.
Is service included in the bill? ¿El servicio está incluido en la cuenta?
Where is there a hotel? ¿Dónde hay un hotel?
Where is the post office? ¿Dónde está el correo?
Is there any mail for me? ¿Hay correo para mí?
Where can I mail this letter? ¿Dónde puedo echar esta carta al correo?

Take me to . . . Lléveme a . . .
I believe I am ill. Creo que estoy enfermo.
Please call a doctor. Por favor, llame al médico.
Please call the police. Por favor, llame a la policía.
I want to send a telegram. Quiero poner un telegrama.
As soon as possible. Cuanto antes.

Round trip. Ida y vuelta.
Please help me with my luggage. Por favor, ayúdeme con mi equipaje.
Where can I get a taxi? ¿Dónde puedo coger un taxi?
What is the fare to . . . ¿Cuánto es el pasaje hasta . . . ?
Please take me to this address. Por

favor, lléveme a esta dirección.

Where can I change my money? ¿Dónde puedo cambiar mi dinero?

Where is the nearest bank? ¿Dónde está el banco más cercano?

Can you accept my check? ¿Puede aceptar usted mi cheque?

Do you accept traveler's checks? ¿Aceptan cheques de viaje?

What is the postage? ¿Cuánto es el franqueo?

Where is the nearest drugstore? ¿Dónde está la farmacia más cercana?

Where is the men's (women's) room? ¿Dónde está el servicio de caballeros (de señoras)?

Please let me off at. . . Por favor, déjeme bajar en . . .

Right away. ¡Pronto!

Help. ¡Socorro!

Who is it? ¿Quién es?

Just a minute! ¡Un momento no más!

Come in. ¡Pase usted!

Pardon me. Disculpe usted.

Stop. ¡Pare!

Look out. ¡Cuidado!

Hurry. ¡De prisa! *or* ¡Dése prisa!

Go on. ¡Siga!

To (on, at) the right. A la derecha.

To (on, at) the left. A la izquierda.

Straight ahead. Adelante.